shuf·fle 1. *v/t Ka...*
umordnen, hier...
shuffle one's f...
fen; *Karten* mi...
schlurfender Ga...

in *italics*

evening class·es Abendkurs *m*, Abendunterricht *m*
evening dress Gesellschaftsanzug *m*;
Frack *m*, Smoking *m*; Abendkleid *n*

Compounds

kultivieren [kʊltiˈviːrən] *v/t (no -ge-, h)* cultivate
Künstler [ˈkʏnstlɐ] *m (-s; -)*, **Künstlerin**
[ˈkʏnstlərɪn] *f (-; -nen)* artist, MUS, THEA
a. performer

Grammatical information

shy 1. scheu; schüchtern; 2. scheuen (*at*
vor *dat*); **shy away from** *fig* zurückschrecken vor (*dat*)

Entries divided into
grammatical categories

Kumpel [ˈkʊmpəl] *m (-s; -)* miner; F mate,
buddy, pal

Register labels

Abschlusszeugnis *n Am* diploma, *Br*
school-leaving certificate

American and British variants

A B C D E F G H I J K L M N O P Q R S T U V W X Y Z

Langenscheidt
Pocket Dictionary

German

German – English
English – German

Langenscheidt

Activity section by Jessie McGuire

1. Auflage 2015 (1,03 - 2023)
© PONS Langenscheidt GmbH,
Stöckachstraße 11, 70190 Stuttgart 2015
All Rights Reserved.

www.langenscheidt.com

Print: Druckerei C. H. Beck Nördlingen
Printed in Germany

ISBN 978-3-12-514028-8

Preface

This new dictionary of English and German is a tool with more than 55,000 references for learners of the German language at beginner's or intermediate level.

Thousands of colloquial and idiomatic expressions have been included and the new German spelling has been used. The user-friendly layout with all head-words in blue allows the user to have quick access to all the words, expressions and their translations.

Clarity of presentation has been a major objective. Is the *mouse* you need for your computer, for example, the same in German as the *mouse* you don't want in the house? This dictionary is rich in sense distinctions like this – and in translation options tied to specific, identified senses.

Vocabulary needs grammar to back it up. In this dictionary you will find extra grammar information on German declension and conjugation as well as on German irregular verb forms.

Another feature is the special quick-reference section listing the States of Germany and Austria and the Cantons of Switzerland, German weights and measures etc.

The additional activity section provides the user with an opportunity to develop language skills with a selection of engaging word puzzles. The games are designed specifically to improve vocabulary, spelling, grammar and comprehension in an enjoyable style.

Designed for a wide variety of uses, this dictionary will be of great value to those who wish to learn German and have fun at the same time.

Contents

Guide for the User

This dictionary endeavors to do everything it can to help you find the words and translations you are looking for as quickly and easily as possible.

To enable you to get the most out of your dictionary, you will be shown exactly where and how to find the information that will help you choose the right translation in every situation – whether at school or at home, when writing letters, or in everyday conversation.

1. German and English headwords

1.1 When you are looking for a particular word it is important to know that the dictionary entries are arranged in strict **alphabetical order**:

> Aal – ab
> beugen – biegen
> hay – haze

In the German-English section the umlauts *ä ö ü* are treated as *a o u*. *ß* is treated as *ss*.

1.2 Besides the headwords and their derivatives and compounds, the past tense and past participle of irregular German verbs are also given as individual entries in alphabetical order in the German-English section, e.g. **ging, gegangen**.

1.3 Many German and English proper names and abbreviations are included in the vocabulary.

1.4 How then do you go about finding a particular word? Take a look at the words in bold print at the top of each page. These are the so-called **running heads** and they serve as a guide to tracing your word as quickly as possible. The running head on the top left gives you the first headword on the left-hand page, while the one on the top right gives you the last word on the right-hand page, e.g.

Gesundheit – Glanz

1.5 What about entries comprising hyphenated expressions or two or more words, such as **D-Zug, left-handed** or **mass media**? Expressions of this kind are treated in the same way as single words and thus appear in strict alphabetical order. Should you be unable to find a compound in the dictionary, just break it down into its components and look these up separately. In this way the meaning of many compound expressions can be derived indirectly.

6

2. Spelling

2.1 Where American and British spelling of a word differs, the American spelling is given first as in

> center, *Br* centre
> center (*Br* centre) forward
> dialog, *Br* dialogue

or in the English-German section as a separate headword, e.g. **theater, defense** etc.

A 'u' or an 'l' in parentheses in a word also indicates variant spellings:

> colo(u)red means: *American* colored, *British* coloured
> travel(l)er means: *American* traveler, *British* traveller

2.2 Word division in a German word is possible after each syllable, e.g.

> ein-hül-len, Zu-cker, ba-cken, tes-ten

In the English-German section the centered dots within a headword indicate syllabification breaks.

3. The different typefaces and their functions

3.1 **Bold type** is used for the German and English headwords and for Arabic numerals separating different parts of speech (nouns, transitive and intransitive verbs, adjectives and adverbs etc.) and different grammatical forms of a word:

> **bieten 1.** *v/t* ... **2.** *v/i* ...
> **hängen 1.** *v/i* (*irr, ge-, h*) hang (*an dat* on...);
> **2.** *v/t* (*ge-, h*) hang (*an acc* on)
> **feed 1.** Futter *n*; ... **2.** *v/t* füttern

3.2 *Italics* are used for

a) grammatical and other abbreviations: *v/t, v/i, adj, adv, appr, fig* etc.
b) gender labels (masculine, feminine and neuter): *m, f, n*
c) grammatical references in brackets in the German-English section
d) any additional information preceding or following a translation (including dative or accusative objects):

> **knacken** *v/t and v/i* ... *twig:* snap; *fire, radio:* crackle
> **Etikett** *n* ... label (*a. fig*)
> **Gedanke** *m* (*-n; -n*) ...
> **geben** (*irr, ge-, h*) ...

befolgen … follow, take (*advice*); observe
 (*rule etc*)
file … *Briefe etc* ablegen
labored schwerfällig (*style etc*); mühsam
 (*breathing etc*)

3.3 *Boldface italics* are used for phraseology etc., notes on German grammar and prepositions taken by the headword:

Lage *f* … *in der Lage sein zu inf* be able to
 inf
BLZ … ABBR *of Bankleitzahl*
abheben (*irr*, **heben**, *sep*, *-ge-*, *h*)
abfahren … (*irr*, **fahren**, *sep*, *-ge-*, *sein*)
 leave, depart (*both*: *nach* for)
line … *hold the line* TEL bleiben Sie am Apparat
agree … sich einigen (*on* über *acc*)

3.4 Normal type is used for translations of the headwords.

4. Pronunciation

When you have found the headword you are looking for in the German-English section, you will notice that very often this word is followed by certain symbols enclosed in square brackets. This is the phonetic transcription of the word, which tells you how it is pronounced. And one phonetic alphabet has come to be used internationally, namely that of the International Phonetic Association. This phonetic system is known by the abbreviation **IPA**. The symbols used in this dictionary are listed in the following tables on page 8 and 9.

4.1 The length of vowels is indicated by [ː] following the vowel symbol.

4.1.1 Stress is indicated by ['] or [ˌ] preceding the stressed syllable. ['] stands for strong stress, [ˌ] for weak stress:

Kabel [ˈkaːbəl] - **Kabine** [kaˈbiːnə]
'nachsehen – **Be'sitz** – **be'sprechen**
Jus'tizminisˌterium – **Miˈnisterpräsiˌdent**

4.1.2 The glottal stop [ʔ] is the forced stop between one word or syllable and a following one beginning with a vowel, as in

Analphabet [anʔalfaˈbeːt]
beeindrucken [bəˈʔaindrʊkən]

4.2 No transcription of compounds is given if the parts appear as separate entries. Each individual part should be looked up, as with

'Blumenbeet (= Blume and Beet)

4.2.1 If only part of the pronunciation changes or if a compound word consists of a new component, only the pronunciation of the changed or new part is given:

Demonstrant [demɔn'strant]
Demonstration [-stra'tsjoːn]
'Kinderhort [-hɔrt]

4.3 Guide to pronunciation for the German-English section

A. Vowels

[a] as in French *carte*: **Mann** [man]

[aː] as in *father*: **Wagen** ['vaːgən]

[e] as in *bed*: **Tenor** [te'noːɐ]

[eː] resembles the first sound in English [eɪ]: **Weg** [veːk]

[ə] unstressed e as in *ago*: **Bitte** ['bɪtə]

[ɛ] as in *fair*: **männlich** ['mɛnlɪç], **Geld** [gɛlt]

[ɛː] same sound but long: **zählen** ['tsɛːlən]

[ɪ] as in *it*: **Wind** [vɪnt]

[i] short, otherwise like [iː]: **Kapital** [kapi'taːl]

[iː] long, as in *meet*: **Vieh** [fiː]

[ɔ] as in *long*: **Ort** [ɔrt]

[o] as in *molest*: **Moral** [mo'raːl]

[oː] resembles the English sound in *go* [gəʊ] but without the [ʊ]: **Boot** [boːt]

[øː] as in French *feu*. The sound may be acquired by saying [e] through closely rounded lips: **schön** [ʃøːn]

[ø] same sound but short: **ökumenisch** [øku'meːnɪʃ]

[œ] as in French *neuf*. The sound resembles the English vowel in *her*. Lips, however, must be well rounded as for [ɒ]: **öffnen** ['œfnən]

[ʊ] as in *book*: **Mutter** ['mʊtɐ]

[u] short, otherwise like [uː]: **Musik** [mu'ziːk]

[uː] long, as in *boot*: **Uhr** [uːɐ]

[ʏ] short, opener than [yː]: **Hütte** ['hʏtə]

[y] almost like the French u as in *sur*. It may be acquired by saying [ɪ] through fairly closely rounded lips: **Büro** [by'roː]

[yː] same sound but long: **führen** ['fyːrən]

B. Diphthongs

[aɪ] as in *like*: **Mai** [maɪ]

[aʊ] as in *mouse*: **Maus** [maʊs]

[ɔʏ] as in *boy*: **Beute** ['bɔʏtə], **Läufer** ['lɔʏfɐ]

C. Consonants

[b] as in *better*: **besser** ['bɛsɐ]

[d] as in *dance*: **du** [duː]

[f] as in *find*: **finden** ['fɪndən], **Vater** ['faːtɐ], **Philosoph** [filo'zoːf]

[g] as in *gold*: **Gold** [gɔlt]

[ʒ] as in *measure*: **Genie** [ʒe'niː]

[h] as in *house* but not aspirated: **Haus** [haʊs]

[ç] an approximation to this sound may be acquired by assuming the mouth-configuration for [ɪ] and emitting a strong current of breath: **Licht** [lɪçt], **Mönch** [mœnç], **lustig** ['lʊstɪç]

[x] as in Scottish *loch*. Whereas [ç] is pronounced at the front of the mouth, [x] is pronounced in the throat: **Loch** [lɔx]

[j] as in *year*: **ja** [jaː]

[k] as in *kick*: **keck** [kɛk], **Tag** [taːk], **Chronik** ['kroːnɪk], **Café** [ka'feː]

[l] as in *lump*. Pronounced like English initial „clear l": **lassen** ['lasən]

[m] as in *mouse*: **Maus** [maʊs]

[n] as in *not*: **nein** [naɪn]

[ŋ] as in *sing*, *drink*: **singen** ['zɪŋən], **trinken** ['trɪŋkən]

[p] as in *pass*: **Pass** [pas], **Trieb** [triːp], **obgleich** [ɔp'glaɪç]

[r] as in *rot*. There are two pronunciations: the frontal or lingual r: **rot** [roːt] and the uvular r [ʁ] (unknown in the English language): **Mauer** ['maʊɐ]

[s] as in *miss*. Unvoiced when final, doubled, or next a voiceless consonant: **Glas** [glaːs], **Masse** ['masə], **Mast** [mast], **nass** [nas]

[z] as in *zero*. S voiced when initial in a word or syllable: **Sohn** [zoːn], **Rose** ['roːzə]

[ʃ] as in *ship*: **Schiff** [ʃɪf], **Charme** [ʃarm], **Spiel** [ʃpiːl], **Stein** [ʃtaɪn]

[t] as in *tea*: **Tee** [teː], **Thron** [troːn], **Stadt** [ʃtat], **Bad** [baːt], **Findling** ['fɪntlɪŋ], **Wind** [vɪnt]

[v] as in *vast*: **Vase** ['vaːzə], **Winter** ['vɪntɐ]

[ã, ɛ̃, õ] are nasalized vowels. Examples: **Ensemble** [ã'sãːbəl], **Terrain** [tɛ'rɛ̃ː], **Bonbon** [bõ'bõː]

4.3.1 Phonetic changes in plurals

singular		plural		example
-g	[-k]	-ge	[-gə]	Flug – Flüge
-d	[-t]	-de	[-də]	Grund – Gründe, Abend – Abende
-b	[-p]	-be	[-bə]	Stab – Stäbe
-s	[-s]	-se	[-zə]	Los – Lose
-ch	[-x]	-che	[-çə]	Bach – Bäche
-iv	[-iːf]	-ive	[-iːvə]	Stativ – Stative

4.3.2 The German alphabet

a [aː], b [beː], c [tseː], d [deː], e [eː], f [ɛf], g [geː], h [haː], i [iː], j [jɔt], k [kaː], l [ɛl], m [ɛm], n [ɛn], o [oː], p [peː], q [kuː], r [ɛr], s [ɛs], t [teː], u [uː], v [fau], w [veː], x [ɪks], y ['ʏpsilɔn], z [tsɛt]

4.3.3 List of suffixes

The German suffixes are not transcribed unless they are parts of headwords.

-bar	[-baːɐ]	-isch	[-ɪʃ]
-chen	[-çən]	-ist	[-ɪst]
-d	[-t]	-keit	[-kaɪt]
-de	[-də]	-lich	[-lɪç]
-ei	[-aɪ]	-ling	[-lɪŋ]
-en	[-ən]	-losigkeit	[-loːzɪçkaɪt]
-end	[-ənt]	-nis	[-nɪs]
-er	[-ɐ]	-sal	[-zaːl]
-haft	[-haft]	-sam	[-zaːm]
-heit	[-haɪt]	-schaft	[-ʃaft]
-icht	[-ɪçt]	-sieren	[-ziːrən]
-ie	[-iː]	-ste	[-stə]
-ieren	[-iːrən]	-tät	[-tɛːt]
-ig	[-ɪç]	-tum	[-tuːm]
-ik	[-ɪk]	-ung	[-ʊŋ]
-in	[-ɪn]	-ungs-	[-ʊŋs-]
		-wärts	[-vɛrts]

5. Abbreviations of grammatical terms and subject areas are designed to help the user choose the appropriate headword or translation of a word.

In the dictionary words which are predominantly used in British English are marked by the abbreviation *Br*.

> **Bürgersteig** *m* sidewalk, *Br* pavement
> **girl guide** *Br* Pfadfinderin *f*

List of abbreviations

a.	*also*, auch	*cj*	*conjunction*, Konjunktion
ABBR	*abbreviation*, Abkürzung	*coll*	*collectively*, als Sammelwort
acc	*accusative (case)*, Akkusativ	*comp*	*comparative*, Komparativ
adj	*adjective*, Adjektiv	*contp*	*contemptuously*, verächtlich
adv	*adverb*, Adverb	*cpds*	*compounds*, Zusammensetzungen
AGR	*agriculture*, Landwirtschaft		
Am	*American English*, amerikanisches Englisch	*dat*	*dative (case)*, Dativ
ANAT	*anatomy*, Anatomie	ECON	*economy*, Wirtschaft
appr	*approximately*, etwa	EDP	*electronic data processing*, Elektronische Datenverarbeitung
ARCH	*architecture*, Architektur		
art	*article*, Artikel	*e-e*	*a(n)*, eine
ASTR	*astrology*, Astrologie; *astronomy*, Astronomie	*e.g.*	*for example*, zum Beispiel
		ELECTR	*electrical engineering*, Elektrotechnik
attr	*attributively*, attributiv		
AVIAT	*aviation*, Luftfahrt	*e-m*	*einem, to a(n)*
		e-n	*einen, a(n)*
BIOL	*biology*, Biologie	*e-r*	*einer, of a(n), to a(n)*
BOT	*botany*, Botanik	*e-s*	*eines, of a(n)*
Br	*British English*, britisches Englisch	*esp.*	*especially*, besonders
		et., et.	etwas, *something*
CHEM	*chemistry*, Chemie	*etc*	*et cetera, and so on*, usw., und so weiter

F	*colloquial*, umgangssprachlich	PHYS	*physics*, Physik
f	*feminine*, weiblich	pl	*plural*, Plural
fig	*figuratively*, übertragen	POET	*poetry*, Dichtung
		POL	*politics*, Politik
GASTR	*gastronomy*, Kochkunst	POSS	*possessive*, besitzanzeigend
gen	*genitive (case)*, Genitiv	POST	*post and telecommunications*,
GEOGR	*geography*, Geografie		Postwesen
GEOL	*geology*, Geologie	pp	*past participle*, Partizip Perfekt
ger	*gerund*, Gerundium	pred	*predicative*, prädikativ
GR	*grammar*, Grammatik	pres	*present*, Präsens
		pres p	*present participle*, Partizip Präsens
h	*haben*, have	pret	*preterit(e)*, Präteritum
HIST	*history*, Geschichte	PRINT	*printing*, Druckwesen
HUMOR	*humorous*, humorvoll	pron	*pronoun*, Pronomen
		prp	*preposition*, Präposition
impers	*impersonal*, unpersönlich	PSYCH	*psychology*, Psychologie
indef	*indefinite*, unbestimmt		
inf	*infinitive (mood)*, Infinitiv	RAIL	*railroad, railway*, Eisenbahn
int	*interjection*, Interjektion	refl	*reflexive*, reflexiv
interr	*interrogative*, fragend	REL	*religion*, Religion
irr	*irregular*, unregelmäßig	RHET	*rhetoric*, Rhetorik
j-m	*jemandem*, to someone	s-e	*seine*, his, one's
j-n	*jemanden*, someone	sep	*separable*, abtrennbar
j-s	*jemandes*, someone's	sg	*singular*, Singular
JUR	*jurisprudence*, Recht	sl	*slang*, Slang
		s-m	*seinem*, to his, to one's
LING	*linguistics*, Sprachwissenschaft	s-n	*seinen*, his, one's
LIT	*literary*, nur in der Schrift-sprache vorkommend	s.o., *s.o.*	*someone*, jemand(en)
		SPORT	*sports*, Sport
m	*masculine*, männlich	s-r	*seiner*, of his, of one's, to his, to one's
MAR	*maritime term*, Schifffahrt		
MATH	*mathematics*, Mathematik	s-s	*seines*, of his, of one's
m-e	*my*, meine	s.th., *s.th.*	*something*, etwas
MED	*medicine*, Medizin	su	*substantive*, Substantiv
METEOR	*meteorology*, Meteorologie	subj	*subjunctive (mood)*, Konjunktiv
MIL	*military term*, militärisch	sup	*superlative*, Superlativ
MOT	*motoring*, Kraftfahrwesen		
m-r	*meiner*, of my, to my	TECH	*technology*, Technik
mst	*mostly , usually*, meistens	TEL	*telegraphy*, Telegrafie; *telephony*, Fernsprechwesen
MUS	*music*, Musik		
		THEA	*theater*, Theater
n	*neuter*, sächlich	TV	*television*, Fernsehen
neg!	*negative, usually considered offensive*, kann als beleidigend empfunden werden	u., *u.*	*und*, and
		UNIV	*university*, Hochschulwesen, Studentensprache
nom	*nominative (case)*, Nominativ		
num	*numeral*, Zahlwort	v	*vulgar*, vulgär, unanständig
		v/aux	*auxiliary verb*, Hilfsverb
OPT	*optics*, Optik	vb	*verb*, Verb
o.s., *o.s.*	*oneself*, sich	VET	*veterinary medicine*, Veterinär-medizin, Tiermedizin
		v/i	*intransitive verb*, intransitives Verb
PAINT	*painting*, Malerei		
PARL	*parliamentary term*, parlamen-tarischer Ausdruck	v/refl	*reflexive verb*, reflexives Verb
		v/t	*transitive verb*, transitives Verb
pass	*passive voice*, Passiv		
PED	*pedagogy*, Schulwesen	ZO	*zoology*, Zoologie
pers	*personal*, persönlich	→	*see, refer to*, siehe
PHARM	*pharmacy*, Pharmazie		
PHIL	*philosophy*, Philosophie	®	*registered trademark*, eingetra-gene Marke
PHOT	*photography*, Fotografie		

6. Translations and phraseology

After the boldface headword in the German-English section, the phonetic transcription of this word, its part of speech label, and its grammar, we finally come to the most important part of the entry: **the translation(s).**

6.1 It is quite rare for a headword to be given just one translation. Usually a word will have several related translations, which are separated by a **comma**.

6.2 Different senses of a word are indicated by

a) **semicolons:**

> **Fest** ... celebration; party; REL festival
> **balance** ... Waage *f*; Gleichgewicht *n*

b) italics for **definitions:**

> **Läufer** ... runner (*a . carpet*); *chess*: bishop
> **call** ... Berufung *f* (**to** in *ein Amt*; auf *einen Lehrstuhl*)
> **cake** ... Tafel *f Schokolade*, Stück *n Seife*

c) **abbreviations** of subject areas:

> **Bug** *m* ... MAR bow; AVIAT nose
> **Gespräch** *n* talk (*a.* POL); ... TEL call
> **daisy** BOT Gänseblümchen *n*
> **duck** ... ZO Ente *f*

6.2.1 Where a word has fundamentally different meanings, it very often appears as two or more separate entries distinguished by **exponents** or raised figures:

> **betreten**[1] *v/t* ... step on; enter
> **betreten**[2] *adj* embarrassed
> **Bauer**[1] *m* ... farmer
> **Bauer**[2] *n, m* ... (bird)cage
> **chap**[1] ... Riss *m*
> **chap**[2] ... *Br* F Bursche *m*

This does not apply to senses which have directly evolved from the primary meaning of the word.

6.3 When a headword can be several different parts of speech, these are distinguished by boldface **Arabic numerals** (see also the section on p.6, paragraph 3.1 concerning the different typefaces):

> **geräuschlos** **1.** *adj* noiseless (*adjective*)
> **2.** without a sound (*adverb*)
>
> **work** **1.** Arbeit *f* (*noun*)
> **2.** *v/i* arbeiten (*verb*)
>
> **green** **1.** grün (*adjective*)
> **2.** Grün *n* (*noun*)

6.3.1 In the German-English section boldface Arabic numerals are also used to distinguish between transitive, intransitive and reflexive verbs (if this affects their translation) and to show that where there is a change of meaning a verb may be differently conjugated:

> **fahren** (*irr, ge-*) **1.** *v/i* (*sein*) go; *bus etc*: run;
> ... **2.** *v/t* (*h*) drive (*car etc*) ...

If grammatical indications come before the subdivision they refer to all translations that follow:

> **bauen** (*ge-, h*) **1.** *v/t* build ...; **2.** *fig v/i*:
> **bauen auf** ...

6.3.2 Boldface Arabic numerals are also used to indicate the different meanings of nouns which can occur in more than one gender and to show that where there is a change of meaning a noun may be differently inflected:

> **Halfter 1.** *m, n* (*-s; -*) halter; **2.** *n* (*-s; -*), *f* (*-;
> -n*) holster

6.4 Illustrative phrases in boldface italics are generally given within the respective categories of the dictionary article:

> **baden 1.** *v/i* ... **baden gehen** go swimming;
> **2.** *v/t* ...
> **good 1.** ... **real good** F echt gut (= *adjec-
> tive*); **2.** ... **for good** für immer (= *noun*)

7. Grammatical references

Knowing what to do with the grammatical information available in the dictionary will enable the user to get the most out of this dictionary.

7.1 Verbs (see the list of irregular German verbs on page 662).

Verbs have been treated in the following ways:

a) **bändigen** *v/t* (*ge-, h*)

The past participle of this word is formed by means of the prefix *ge-* and the auxiliary verb *haben*: **er hat gebändigt.**

b) **abfassen** *v/t* (*sep, -ge-, h*)

In conjugation the prefix *ab* must be separated from the primary verb *fassen*: **sie fasst ab; sie hat abgefasst.**

c) **finden** *v/t* (*irr, ge-, h*)

irr following a verb means that it is an irregular verb. The principal parts of this particular word can be found as an individual headword in the main part of the German-English section and in the list of irregular German verbs on page 662: **sie fand; sie hat gefunden.**

d) **abfallen** *v/i* (*irr, fallen, sep, -ge-, sein*)

A reference such as *irr, fallen* indicates that the compound word **abfallen** is conjugated in exactly the same way as the primary verb **fallen** as given in the list of irregular German verbs on page 662: **er fiel ab; er ist abgefallen.**

e) **senden** *v/t* ([*irr.*] ge-, h)

The square brackets indicate that **senden** can be treated as a regular or an irregular verb: *sie sandte* or *sie sendete*; *sie hat gesandt* or *sie hat gesendet.*

7.2 Nouns

The inflectional forms (*genitive singular; nominative plural*) follow immediately after the indication of gender. No forms are given for compounds if the parts appear as separate headwords.

The horizontal stroke replaces the part of the word which remains unchanged in the inflection:

Affäre *f* (-; -n)
Keks *m, n* (-es; -e)
Bau *m* (-[e]s; *Bauten*)
Blatt *n* (-[e]s; *Blätter* ['blɛtɐ])

The inflectional forms of German nouns ending in **-in** are given in the following ways:

Ärztin *f* (-; -nen)
Chemiker(in) (-s; -/-; -nen) = **Chemiker** *m*
(-s; -) and **Chemikerin** *f* (-; -nen)

7.3 Prepositions

If, for instance, a headword (verb, adjective or noun) is governed by certain prepositions, these are given in boldface italics and in brackets together with their English or German translations and placed next to the appropriate translation. If the German or English preposition is same for all or several translations, it is given only once before or after the first translation and then also applies to the translations which follow it:

abrücken ... **1.** *v/t* (*h*) move away (**von**
from)
befestigen *v/t* (*no* -ge-, *h*) fasten (**an** *dat* to),
fix (to), attach (to)
dissent ... **2.** anderer Meinung sein (**from**
als)
dissimilar (**to**) unähnlich (*dat*); verschieden
(**von**)

With German prepositions which can take the dative or the accusative, the case is given in brackets:

fürchten ... **sich fürchten** ... be afraid (**vor**
dat of)
bauen ... **bauen auf** (*acc*) rely *or* count on

We hope that this somewhat lengthy introduction has shown you that this dictionary contains a great deal more than simple one-to-one translations, and that you are now well-equipped to make the most of all it has to offer.

A

à [a] *prp* **5 Karten à Euro 20** 5 tickets at 20 euros each *or* a piece

Aal [a:l] *m* (-[*e*]s; -e) *zo* eel

aalen [a:lən] *v/refl* (*ge-*, *h*) **sich in der Sonne aalen** bask in the sun

'aal'glatt *fig adj* (as) slippery as an eel

Aas [a:s] *n* (-[*e*]s) a) *no pl* carrion, b) F *contp pl* **Äser** beast, *sl* bastard

'Aasgeier *m* zo vulture (*a. fig*)

ab [ap] *prp and adv:* **München ab 13.55** departure from Munich (at) 1.55; **ab 7 Uhr** from 7 o'clock (on); **ab morgen (1. März)** starting tomorrow (March 1st); **von jetzt ab** from now on; **ab und zu** now and then; **ein Film ab 18** an X(-rated) film; **ein Knopf ist ab** a button has come off

'abarbeiten *v/t* (*sep*, *-ge-*, *h*) work out *or* off (*debts*); **sich abarbeiten** wear o.s. out

Abart ['ap²art] *f* (-; -en) variety

abartig ['ap²artıç] *adj* abnormal

Abb. ABBR *of* **Abbildung** fig., illustration

'Abbau *m* (-[*e*]s; *no pl*) mining; TECH dismantling; *fig* overcoming (*of prejudices etc*); reduction (*of expenditure, staff etc*)

'abbauen *v/t* (*sep*, *-ge-*, *h*) mine; TECH dismantle; *fig* overcome (*prejudices etc*); reduce (*expenditure, staff etc*); **sich abbauen** BIOL break down

'abbeißen *v/t* (*irr*, *beißen*, *sep*, *-ge-*, *h*) bite off

'abbeizen *v/t* (*sep*, *-ge-*, *h*) remove *old paint etc* with corrosives

'abbekommen *v/t* (*irr*, *kommen*, *sep*, *no -ge-*, *h*) get off; **s-n Teil** *or* **et. abbekommen** get one's share; **et. abbekommen** *fig* get hurt, get damaged

'abberufen *v/t* (*irr*, *rufen*, *sep*, *no -ge-*, *h*), **'Abberufung** *f* recall

'abbestellen *v/t* (*sep*, *no -ge-*, *h*) cancel one's subscription (*or* order) for

'Abbestellung *f* cancellation

'abbiegen *v/i* (*irr*, *biegen*, *sep*, *-ge-*, *sein*) turn (off); **nach rechts (links) abbiegen** turn right (left)

'abbilden *v/t* (*sep*, *-ge-*, *h*) show, depict

'Abbildung *f* (-; -en) picture, illustration

'Abbitte *f* apology; **j-m Abbitte leisten wegen** apologize to s.o. for

'abblasen F *v/t* (*irr*, *blasen*, *sep*, *-ge-*, *h*) call off, cancel

'abblättern *v/i* (*sep*, *-ge-*, *sein*) paint etc: flake off

'abblenden 1. *v/t* (*sep*, *-ge-*, *h*) dim; **2.** *v/i*

MOT dim (*Br* dip) the headlights

'Abblendlicht *n* MOT dimmed (*Br* dipped) headlights *pl*, low beam

'abbrechen *v/t* (*irr*, *brechen*, *sep*, *-ge-*) **1.** *v/t* (*h*) break off (*a. fig*); pull down, demolish (*building etc*); strike (*camp, tent*); **2.** *v/i* a) (*sein*) break off, b) (*h*) *fig* stop

'abbremsen *v/t* (*sep*, *-ge-*, *h*) slow down

'abbrennen *v/t* (*irr*, *brennen*, *sep*, *-ge-*) **1.** *v/i* (*sein*) burn down; **2.** *v/t* (*h*) burn down (*building etc*); let *or* set off (*fireworks*)

'abbringen *v/t* (*irr*, *bringen*, *sep*, *-ge-*, *h*) **j-n von e-r Sache abbringen** talk s.o. out of (doing) s.th.; **j-n vom Thema abbringen** get s.o. off a subject

'Abbruch *m* (-[*e*]s; *no pl*) breaking off; demolition

'abbruchreif *adj* derelict, due for demolition

'abbuchen *v/t* (*sep*, *-ge-*, *h*) debit (**von** to)

'Abbuchung *f* debit

'abbürsten *v/t* (*sep*, *-ge-*, *h*) brush off (*dust etc*); brush (*coat etc*)

Abc [a:be:'tse:] *n* (-; *no pl*) ABC, alphabet

ABC-Waffen *pl* MIL nuclear, biological and chemical weapons

'abdanken *v/i* (*sep*, *-ge-*, *h*) resign; *king etc:* abdicate

'Abdankung *f* (-; -en) resignation; abdication

'abdecken *v/t* (*sep*, *-ge-*, *h*) uncover; untile (*roof*); unroof (*house*); clear (*the table*); ECON cover (up)

'abdichten *v/t* (*sep*, *-ge-*, *h*) TECH seal

'abdrängen *v/t* (*sep*, *-ge-*, *h*) push aside

'abdrehen 1. *v/t* (*sep*, *-ge-*, *h*) turn *or* switch off (*light, water etc*); **2.** *v/i* (*a. sein*) *ship, plane:* change one's course

'Abdruck *m* print, mark

'abdrucken *v/t* (*sep*, *-ge-*, *h*) print

'abdrücken (*sep*, *-ge-*, *h*) **1.** *v/t* fire (*gun*); **2.** *v/i* pull the trigger

Abend ['a:bənt] *m* (-s; -e) evening; **am Abend** in the evening, at night; **heute Abend** tonight; **morgen (gestern) Abend** tomorrow (last) night; → **bunt**, **essen**

Abendbrot *n* (-[*e*]s; *no pl*), **Abendessen** *n* supper, dinner, *Br a.* high tea

Abendkasse *f* THEA *etc* box office

Abendkleid *n* evening dress *or* gown

Abendkurs *m* evening classes *pl*

'Abendland *n* (-[*e*]s; *no pl*) West, Occident

'abendländisch [-lɛndɪʃ] adj Western, Occidental

'Abendmahl n (-[e]s; no pl) the (Holy) Communion, the Lord's Supper; **das Abendmahl empfangen** receive Communion

abends ['a:bənts] adv in the evening, at night; **dienstags abends** (on) Tuesday evenings

'Abendschule f evening classes pl, night school

Abenteuer ['a:bəntɔyɐ] n (-s; -) adventure (a. in cpds ...ferien, ...spielplatz)

'abenteuerlich adj adventurous; fig risky; fantastic

Abenteurer ['a:bəntɔyɐ] m (-s; -) adventurer

'Abenteurerin [-rərm] f (-; -nen) adventuress

aber ['a:bɐ] cj and adv but; **oder aber** or else; **aber, aber!** now then!; **aber nein!** not at all!

'Aberglaube m superstition

abergläubisch ['a:bɐglɔybɪʃ] adj superstitious

'aberkennen v/t (irr, kennen, sep, no -ge-, h) **j-m et. aberkennen** deprive s.o. of s.th. (a. JUR)

'Aberkennung f (-; -en) deprivation (a. JUR)

abermalig ['a:bɐma:lɪç] adj repeated

abermals ['a:bɐma:ls] adv once more or again

'aber'tausend adj: **tausende und abertausende** thousands upon thousands

'abfahren (irr, fahren, sep, -ge-) **1.** v/i (sein) leave, depart (both: **nach** for); F (**voll**) **abfahren auf** (acc) really go for; **2.** v/t (h) carry or cart away

'Abfahrt f departure (**nach** for), start (for); skiing: descent

'Abfahrtslauf m downhill skiing (or race)

'Abfahrtszeit f (time of) departure

'Abfall m waste, refuse, garbage, trash, Br a. rubbish

'Abfallbeseitigung f waste disposal

'Abfalleimer m → Mülleimer

'abfallen v/i (irr, fallen, sep, -ge-, sein) fall (off); terrain: slope (down); fig fall away (**von** from); esp POL secede (from); **vom Glauben abfallen** renounce one's faith; **abfallen gegen** compare badly with

'abfällig **1.** adj derogatory; **2.** adv: **abfällig von j-m sprechen** run s.o. down

'Abfallprodukt n waste product

'abfälschen v/t (sep, -ge-, h) SPORT deflect

'abfangen v/t (irr, fangen, sep, -ge-, h) catch, intercept; MOT, AVIAT right

'abfärben v/i (sep, -ge-, h) color etc: run, material: a. bleed; fig **abfärben auf** (acc) rub off on

'abfassen v/t (sep, -ge-, h) compose, word, write

'abfertigen v/t (sep, -ge-, h) dispatch; customs: clear; serve (customers); check in (passengers etc); **j-n kurz abfertigen** be short with s.o.

'Abfertigung f dispatch; clearance; check-in

'abfeuern v/t (sep, -ge-, h) fire (off); launch (rocket)

'abfinden v/t (irr, finden, sep, -ge-, h) ECON pay off (creditor); buy out (partner); compensate; **sich mit e-r Sache abfinden** put up with s.th.

'Abfindung f (-; -en) ECON satisfaction; compensation

'abflachen v/t and v/refl (sep, -ge-, h) flatten

'abflauen v/i (sep, -ge-, h) wind etc: drop (a. fig)

'abfliegen v/i (irr, fliegen, sep, -ge-, sein) AVIAT leave, depart

'abfließen v/i (irr, fließen, sep, -ge-, sein) flow off, drain (off or away)

'Abflug m AVIAT departure

'Abfluss m (-es; Abflüsse) a) no pl flowing off, b) TECH drain

'Abflussrohr n wastepipe, drain(pipe)

'abfragen v/t (sep, -ge-, h) quiz or question s.o. (**über** acc about), test s.o. orally

'Abfuhr ['apfu:ɐ] f (-; -en) removal; **j-m e-e Abfuhr erteilen** rebuff (F SPORT lick) s.o.

'abführen (sep, -ge-, h) **1.** v/t lead or take away; ECON pay (over) (**an** acc to); **2.** v/i MED move one's bowels; act as a laxative

'abführend adj, 'Abführmittel n MED laxative

'abfüllen v/t (sep, -ge-, h) bottle; can

'Abgabe f (-; -n) a) no pl handing in, b) SPORT pass, c) ECON rate; duty

'abgabenfrei adj tax-free

'abgabenpflichtig adj dutiable

'Abgang m (-[e]s; Abgänge) a) no pl departure; Am graduation; Br school-leaving; THEA exit (a. fig), b) SPORT dismount

Abgänger ['apgɛŋɐ] m (-s; -) Am graduate, Br school-leaver

'Abgas n waste gas; pl emission(s pl); MOT exhaust fumes pl

'abgasfrei adj emission-free

'Abgasuntersuchung f MOT Am emissions test, Br exhaust emission test

'abgearbeitet adj worn out

'abgeben v/t (irr, geben, sep, -ge-, h) leave (**bei** with); hand in; deposit (one's baggage etc), hand over (ticket etc) (**an** *acc* to); cast (*vote*); pass (*ball*); *give off,* emit (*heat etc*); make (*offer, statement etc*); **j-m et. abgeben von** share s.th. with s.o.; **sich abgeben mit** concern o.s. with *s.th.*, associate with *s.o.*

'abgebrannt *adj* burnt down; F *fig* broke

abgebrüht *fig adj* hard-boiled

abgedroschen *adj* hackneyed

abgefahren *adj tires:* worn out

abgegriffen *adj* worn

abgehackt *fig adj* disjointed

abgehangen *adj:* **gut abgehangenes Fleisch** well-hung meat

abgehärtet *adj* hardened (**gegen** to)

'abgehen *v/i (irr, gehen, sep, -ge-, sein) train etc:* leave; *mail, goods:* get off; THEA go off (stage); *button etc:* come off; *path etc:* branch off; **von der Schule abgehen** leave school; **abgehen von** drop (*plan etc*); **von s-r Meinung abgehen** change one's mind *or* opinion; **ihm geht … ab** he lacks …; **gut abgehen** end well, pass off well

'abgehetzt, abgekämpft *adj* exhausted, worn out

abgekartet ['apgəkartət] F *adj:* **abgekartete Sache** put-up job

abgelegen *adj* remote, distant

abgemacht *adj* fixed; **abgemacht!** it's a deal!

abgemagert *adj* emaciated

abgeneigt *adj:* **e-r Sache abgeneigt sein** be averse to s.th.; **ich wäre nicht abgeneigt, et. zu tun** I wouldn't mind doing s.th.

abgenutzt *adj* worn out

Abgeordnete ['apgə^ʔɔrdnətə] *m, f (-n; -n) Am* representative, congressman (-woman), *Br* Member of Parliament (ABBR MP)

'Abgeordnetenhaus *n Am* House of Representatives, *Br* House of Commons

'abgepackt *adj* prepack(ag)ed

abgeschieden *adj* secluded

'Abgeschiedenheit *f (-; no pl)* seclusion

'abgeschlossen *adj* completed; **abgeschlossene Wohnung** self-contained apartment (*Br* flat)

abgesehen *adj:* **abgesehen von** aside (*Br a.* apart) from; **ganz abgesehen von** not to mention, let alone

abgespannt *adj* exhausted, weary

abgestanden *adj* stale

abgestorben *adj* dead (*tree etc*); numb (*leg etc*)

abgestumpft *adj* insensitive, indifferent (**gegen** to)

abgetragen, abgewetzt *adj* worn out; threadbare, shabby

abgewöhnen *v/t (sep, -ge-, h)* **j-m et. abgewöhnen** make s.o. give up s.th.; **sich** (*dat*) **das Rauchen abgewöhnen** stop *or* give up smoking

'Abgott *m* idol (*a. fig*)

abgöttisch ['apgœtɪʃ] *adv:* **j-n abgöttisch lieben** idolize s.o.

'abgrasen *v/t (sep, -ge-, h)* graze; *fig* scour

'abgrenzen *v/t (sep, -ge-, h)* mark off; delimit (**gegen** from)

'Abgrund *m* abyss, chasm, gulf (*all a. fig*); **am Rande des Abgrunds** *fig* on the brink of disaster

abgrund'tief *adj* abysmal

'abgucken F *v/t (sep, -ge-, h)* **j-m et. abgucken** learn s.th. from (watching) s.o.; → **abschreiben**

'Abguss *m* cast

'abhaben F *v/t (irr, haben, sep, -ge-, h)* **willst du et. abhaben?** do you want some (of it)? 'abhacken *v/t (sep, -ge-, h)* chop *or* cut off

'abhaken *v/t (sep, -ge-, h)* check (*Br* tick) off; F forget

'abhalten *v/t (irr, halten, sep, -ge-, h)* hold (*meeting etc*); **j-n von der Arbeit abhalten** keep s.o. from his work; **j-n davon abhalten, et. zu tun** keep s.o. from doing s.th.

'abhandeln *v/t (sep, -ge-, h)* treat (*subject etc*); **j-m et. abhandeln** make a deal with s.o. for s.th.

'Abhandlung *f* treatise (**über** *acc* on)

'Abhang *m* slope

'abhängen¹ *v/t (sep, -ge-, h)* take down (*picture etc*); RAIL *etc* uncouple; F shake *s.o.* off

'abhängen² *v/i (irr, hängen, sep, -ge-, h)* **abhängen von** depend on; **das hängt davon ab** that depends

abhängig ['aphɛŋɪç] *adj:* **abhängig von** dependent on; *a.* addicted to *drugs etc*

'Abhängigkeit *f (-; -en)* dependence (**von** on); addiction (to)

'abhärten *v/t (sep, -ge-, h)* **sich abhärten** harden o.s. (**gegen** to)

'abhauen *(irr, hauen, sep, -ge-)* **1.** *v/t (h)* cut *or* chop off; **2.** F *v/i (sein)* make off (*mit* with), run away (with); **hau ab!** beat it!, scram!

'abheben *(irr, heben, sep, -ge-, h)* **1.** *v/t* lift *or* take off; pick up (*receiver*); (with)-draw (*money*); cut (*cards*); **sich abheben** stand out (*von* among, from), *fig a.* contrast with; **2.** *v/i* cut the cards; answer the phone; *plane:* take (*esp rocket:* lift) off

'abheften *v/t (sep, -ge-, h)* file

'abheilen *v/i (sep, -ge-, sein)* heal (up)

'abhetzen *v/refl (sep, -ge-, h)* wear o.s. out

'**Abhilfe** f remedy; **Abhilfe schaffen** take remedial measures
'**Abholdienst** m pickup service
'**abholen** v/t (sep, -ge-, h) pick up, collect; **j-n von der Bahn abholen** meet s.o. at the station
'**abholzen** v/t (sep, -ge-, h) fell, cut down (trees); deforest (area)
'**abhorchen** v/t (sep, -ge-, h) MED auscultate, sound
'**abhören** v/t (sep, -ge-, h) listen in on, tap (telephone conversation), F bug; → **abfragen**
'**Abhörgerät** n bugging device, F bug
'**Abitur** [abi'tuːɐ] n (-s; -e) school-leaving examination (qualifying for university entrance)
'**abjagen** v/t (sep, -ge-, h) **j-m et. abjagen** recover s.th. from s.o.
'**abkanzeln** F v/t (sep, -ge-, h) tell s.o. off
'**abkaufen** v/t (sep, -ge-, h) **j-m et. abkaufen** buy s.th. from s.o.
'**Abkehr** ['apkeːɐ] f (-; no pl) break (von with)
'**abkehren** v/refl (sep, -ge-, h) **sich abkehren von** turn away from
'**abklingen** v/i (irr, **klingen**, sep, -ge-, sein) fade away; pain etc: ease off
'**abklopfen** v/t (sep, -ge-, h) MED sound
'**abknallen** F v/t (sep, -ge-, h) pick off
'**abknicken** v/t (sep, -ge-, h) snap or break off; bend
'**abkochen** v/t (sep, -ge-, h) boil
'**abkommandieren** v/t (sep, no -ge-, h) MIL detach (**zu** for)
'**abkommen** v/i (irr, **kommen**, sep, -ge-, sein) **abkommen von** get off; drop (plan etc); **vom Thema abkommen** stray from the point; → **Weg**
'**Abkommen** n (-s; -) agreement, treaty; **ein Abkommen schließen** make an agreement
'**Abkömmling** ['apkœmlɪŋ] m (-s; -e) descendant
'**abkoppeln** v/t (sep, -ge-, h) uncouple (**von** from); undock (spacecraft)
'**abkratzen** (sep, -ge-, h) **1.** v/t (h) scrape off; **2.** F v/i (sein) kick the bucket
'**abkühlen** v/t and v/refl (sep, -ge-, h) cool down (a. fig)
'**Abkühlung** f cooling
'**abkürzen** v/t (sep, -ge-, h) shorten; abbreviate; **den Weg abkürzen** take a short cut
'**Abkürzung** f abbreviation; short cut
'**abladen** v/t (irr, **laden**, sep, -ge-, h) unload; dump (waste etc)
'**Ablage** f (-; -n) a) no pl filing, b) filing tray, c) Swiss → **Zweigstelle**

'**ablagern** (sep, -ge-, h) **1.** v/t season (wood); let wine age; GEOL etc deposit; **sich ablagern** settle, be deposited; **2.** v/i (a. sein) season; age
'**Ablagerung** f (-; -en) CHEM, GEOL deposit, sediment
'**ablassen** (irr, **lassen**, sep, -ge-, h) **1.** v/t drain off (liquid); let off (steam); drain (pond etc); **2.** v/i: **von et. (j-m) ablassen** stop doing s.th. (leave s.o. alone)
'**Ablauf** m (-[e]s; Abläufe) a) course; process; order of events, b) no pl expiration, Br expiry, c) → **Abfluss**
'**ablaufen** (irr, **laufen**, sep, -ge-, h) **1.** v/i (sein) water etc: run off; performance etc: go, proceed; come to an end; period, passport etc: expire; time, record, tape: run out; clock: run down; **gut ablaufen** turn out well; **2.** v/t (h) wear down
'**ablecken** v/t (sep, -ge-, h) lick (off)
'**ablegen** (sep, -ge-, h) **1.** v/t take off (clothes); file (letters etc); give up (habit etc); take (examination, oath); **abgelegte Kleider** cast-offs pl; **2.** v/i take off one's (hat and) coat; MAR put out, sail
'**Ableger** m (-s; -) BOT layer; offshoot (a. fig)
'**ablehnen** v/t (sep, -ge-, h) refuse; turn down (application etc); PARL reject; object to; condemn
ablehnend adj negative
'**Ablehnung** f (-; -en) refusal; rejection; objection (gen to)
'**ableiten** v/t (sep, -ge-, h) divert; LING, MATH derive (**aus** dat, **von** from) (a. fig)
'**Ableitung** f diversion; LING, MATH derivation (a. fig)
'**ablenken** v/t (sep, -ge-, h) divert (**von** from); soccer: turn away (ball); deflect (rays etc); **j-n von der Arbeit ablenken** distract s.o. from his work; **er lässt sich leicht ablenken** he is easily diverted
'**Ablenkung** f diversion
'**ablesen** v/t (irr, **lesen**, sep, -ge-, h) read
'**abliefern** v/t (sep, -ge-, h) deliver (**bei** at); hand over (to)
'**ablösbar** adj detachable
'**ablösen** v/t (sep, -ge-, h) detach; take off; take s.o.'s place, take over from s.o.; esp MIL relieve; replace; **sich ablösen** take turns (driving etc)
'**Ablösesumme** f SPORT transfer fee
'**Ablösung** f relief
'**abmachen** v/t (sep, -ge-, h) remove, take off; settle, arrange
'**Abmachung** f (-; -en) arrangement, agreement, deal
'**abmagern** v/i (sep, -ge-, sein) get thin
'**Abmagerung** f (-; -en) emaciation

'**Abmagerungskur** f slimming diet

'**abmähen** v/t (sep, -ge-, h) mow

'**abmalen** v/t (sep, -ge-, h) copy

'**Abmarsch** m (-[e]s; no pl) start; MIL marching off

'**abmar,schieren** v/i (sep, no -ge-, sein) start; MIL march off

'**abmelden** v/t (sep, -ge-, h) cancel the registration of (car etc); cancel s.o.'s membership (in a club etc); give notice of s.o.'s withdrawal (from school); **sich abmelden** give notice of change of address; report off duty

'**Abmeldung** f notice of withdrawal; notice of change of address

'**abmessen** v/t (irr, **messen**, sep, -ge-, h) measure

'**Abmessung** f measurement; pl dimensions

'**abmon,tieren** v/t (sep, no -ge-, h) take off; take down; TECH dismantle

'**abmühen** v/refl (sep, -ge-, h) work very hard; try hard (to do s.th.); struggle (**mit** with)

'**abnagen** v/t (sep, -ge-, h) gnaw (at)

'**Abnahme** f ['apna:mə] f (-; -n) reduction, decrease; loss (a. of weight); ECON purchase; TECH acceptance

'**abnehmbar** adj removable

'**abnehmen** (irr, **nehmen**, sep, -ge-, h) **1.** v/t take off (a. MED), remove; pick up (receiver); TECH accept; ECON buy; **j-m et. abnehmen** take s.th. (away) from s.o.; **2.** v/i decrease, diminish; lose weight; answer the phone; moon: wane

'**Abnehmer** m (-s; -) buyer; customer

'**Abneigung** f (**gegen**) dislike (of, for); aversion (to)

abnorm [ap'nɔrm] adj abnormal; exceptional, unusual

Abnormität [apnɔrmi'tɛ:t] f (-; -en) abnormality

'**abnutzen**, '**abnützen** v/t and v/refl (sep, -ge-, h) wear out

'**Abnutzung**, '**Abnützung** f (-; no pl) wear (and tear) (a. fig)

Abonnement [abɔnə'mã:] n (-s; -s) subscription (**auf** acc to)

Abonnent [abɔ'nɛnt] m (-en; -en) subscriber; THEA season-ticket holder

abonnieren [abɔ'ni:rən] v/t (no -ge-, h) subscribe to

'**Abordnung** f (-; -en) delegation

Abort [a'bɔrt] m (-[e]s; -e) lavatory, toilet

'**abpassen** v/t (sep, -ge-, h) watch or wait for (s.o., s.th.); waylay s.o. (a. fig)

'**abpfeifen** v/t and v/i (irr, **pfeifen**, sep, -ge-, h) SPORT blow the final whistle; stop the game

'**abplagen** v/refl (sep, -ge-, h) struggle (**mit** with)

'**abprallen** v/i (sep, -ge-, sein) rebound, bounce (off); bullet: ricochet

'**abputzen** v/t (sep, -ge-, h) wipe off; clean

'**abraten** v/i (irr, **raten**, sep, -ge-, h) **j-m ab-raten von** advise or warn s.o. against

'**abräumen** v/t (sep, -ge-, h) clear away; clear (the table)

'**abrea,gieren** v/t (sep, no -ge-, h) work off (one's anger etc) (**an** dat on); **sich abrea-gieren** F let off steam

'**abrechnen** (sep, -ge-, h) **1.** v/t deduct, subtract; claim (expenses); **2.** v/i: **mit j-m abrechnen** settle accounts (fig a. get even) with s.o.

'**Abrechnung** f settlement; F fig showdown

'**abreiben** v/t (irr, **reiben**, sep, -ge-, h) rub off; rub down (body); polish

'**Abreise** f departure (**nach** for)

'**abreisen** v/i (sep, -ge-, sein) depart, leave, start, set out (all: **nach** for)

'**abreißen** (sep, -ge-) **1.** v/t (h) tear or pull off; pull down (building); **2.** v/i (sein) break; button etc: come off

'**Abreißka,lender** m tear-off calendar

'**abrichten** v/t (sep, -ge-, h) train (animal), a. break a horse in

'**abriegeln** v/t (sep, -ge-, h) block off, cordon off

'**Abriss** m (-es; -e) a) (no pl) demolition, b) outline, summary

'**abrollen** v/i (sep, -ge-, sein) and v/t (h) unroll (a. fig)

'**abrücken** (sep, -ge-) **1.** v/t (h) move away (**von** from); **2.** v/i (sein) draw away (**von** from); MIL march off

'**Abruf** m: **auf Abruf** ECON on call

'**abrufen** v/t (irr, **rufen**, sep, -ge-, h) call away; EDP recall, fetch, retrieve

'**abrunden** v/t (sep, -ge-, h) round (off)

'**abrupfen** v/t (sep, -ge-, h) pluck (off)

abrupt [ap'rʊpt] adj abrupt

'**abrüsten** v/i (sep, -ge-, h) MIL disarm

'**Abrüstung** f (-; no pl) MIL disarmament

'**abrutschen** v/i (sep, -ge-, sein) slide down; slip (off) (**von** from)

ABS [a:be:'ɛs] → **Antiblockiersystem**

'**Absage** ['apza:gə] f (-; -n) refusal; cancellation

'**absagen** (sep, -ge-, h) **1.** v/t call off, cancel (event etc); **2.** v/i call off; **j-m absagen** a. cancel one's appointment with s.o.; decline (the invitation)

'**absägen** v/t (sep, -ge-, h) saw off; F fig oust, sack s.o.

'**absahnen** F v/i (sep, -ge-, h) cash in

'**Absatz** m paragraph; ECON sales pl; shoe:

heel; *stairs*: landing

'**abschaben** v/t (*sep*, *-ge-*, *h*) scrape off

'**abschaffen** v/t (*sep*, *-ge-*, *h*) do away with, abolish; repeal (*law*); put an end to (*a-buses etc*)

'**Abschaffung** f (-; *no pl*) abolition; repeal

'**abschalten** (*sep*, *-ge-*, *h*) **1.** v/t switch or turn off; **2.** F v/i relax, switch off

'**abschätzen** v/t (*sep*, *-ge-*, *h*) estimate; assess; size up

abschätzig ['apʃɛtsɪç] *adj* contemptuous; derogatory

Abschaum m (-s; *no pl*) scum (*a. fig*)

'**Abscheu** m (-s; *no pl*) disgust (**vor, gegen** at, for); **e-n Abscheu haben vor** abhor, detest; **Abscheu erregend → abscheuerregend**

'**abscheuerregend** *adj* revolting, repulsive

ab'**scheulich** *adj* abominable, despicable (*a. person*), *a.* atrocious (*crime*)

'**abschicken** v/t (*sep*, *-ge-*, *h*) **→ absenden**

'**abschieben** *fig* v/t (*irr*, **schieben**, *sep*, *-ge-*, *h*) push away; get rid of; deport; **et. auf j-n abschieben** shove s.th. off on (to) s.o.

Abschied ['apʃiːt] m (-[e]s; *-e*) parting, farewell; **Abschied nehmen (von)** say goodbye (to), take leave (of); **s-n Abschied nehmen** resign, retire

'**Abschiedsfeier** f farewell party

'**Abschiedskuss** m goodbye kiss

'**abschießen** v/t (*irr*, **schießen**, *sep*, *-ge-*, *h*) shoot off (AVIAT down); launch (*rocket*); shoot, kill (*deer*); F pick s.o. off; oust; get rid of s.o.

'**abschirmen** v/t (*sep*, *-ge-*, *h*) shield (**gegen** from); *fig* protect (**gegen** against, from)

'**Abschirmung** f (-; *-en*) shield, screen; *fig* protection

'**abschlachten** v/t (*sep*, *-ge-*, *h*) slaughter (*a. fig*)

'**Abschlag** m SPORT kickout; ECON down payment

'**abschlagen** v/t (*irr*, **schlagen**, *sep*, *-ge-*, *h*) knock off; cut off (*head*); cut down (*tree*); refuse (*request etc*), turn s.th. down

'**abschleifen** v/t (*irr*, **schleifen**, *sep*, *-ge-*, *h*) grind off; sand(paper), smooth

'**Abschleppdienst** m MOT emergency road (*Br* breakdown) service

'**abschleppen** v/t (*sep*, *-ge-*, *h*) MOT (give s.o. a) tow; *police:* tow away

'**Abschleppseil** n towrope

Abschleppwagen m *Am* tow truck, *Br* breakdown lorry

'**abschließen** (*irr*, **schließen**, *sep*, *-ge-*, *h*) **1.** v/t lock (up); close, finish; complete;

take out (*insurance*); conclude (*research etc*); **e-n Handel abschließen** strike a bargain; **sich abschließen** shut o.s. off; **→ Wette**; **2.** v/i close, finish

abschließend 1. *adj* concluding; final; **2.** *adv:* **abschließend sagte er** he concluded by saying

'**Abschluss** m conclusion, close

Abschlussprüfung f final examination, finals *pl*, *esp Am* a. graduation; **s-e Abschlussprüfung machen** graduate (**an** *dat* from)

Abschlusszeugnis n *Am* diploma, *Br* school-leaving certificate

'**abschmecken** v/t (*sep*, *-ge-*, *h*) season

'**abschmieren** v/t (*sep*, *-ge-*, *h*) TECH lubricate, grease

'**abschminken** v/t (*sep*, *-ge-*, *h*) **sich abschminken** remove one's make-up

'**abschnallen** v/t (*sep*, *-ge-*, *h*) undo; take off (*skis*); **sich abschnallen** MOT, AVIAT unfasten one's seat belt

'**abschneiden** (*irr*, **schneiden**, *sep*, *-ge-*, *h*) **1.** v/t cut (off) (*a. fig*); **j-m das Wort abschneiden** cut s.o. short; **2.** v/i: **gut abschneiden** come off well

'**Abschnitt** m passage, section (*of book etc*); paragraph; MATH, BIOL segment; period (*of time*), stage (*of journey*), phase (*of development*); coupon, slip, stub (*of check etc*)

'**abschnittweise** *adv* section by section

'**abschrauben** v/t (*sep*, *-ge-*, *h*) unscrew

'**abschrecken** v/t (*sep*, *-ge-*, *h*) deter (**von** from); GASTR douse *eggs etc* with cold water

abschreckend *adj* deterrent; **abschreckendes Beispiel** warning example

'**Abschreckung** f (-; *-en*) deterrence

'**abschreiben** v/t (*irr*, **schreiben**, *sep*, *-ge-*, *h*) copy; PED crib; ECON write off (*a.* F *fig*)

'**Abschrift** f copy, duplicate

'**abschürfen** v/t (*sep*, *-ge-*, *h*) graze

'**Abschürfung** f (-; *-en*) abrasion

Abschuss m launch(ing) (*of rocket*); AVIAT shooting down, downing; kill

Abschussbasis f MIL launching base

abschüssig ['apʃʏsɪç] *adj* sloping; steep

'**Abschussliste** f: **auf der Abschussliste stehen** be on the hit list

'**Abschussrampe** f MIL launching pad

'**abschütteln** v/t (*sep*, *-ge-*, *h*) shake off

'**abschwächen** v/t (*sep*, *-ge-*, *h*) lessen, diminish

'**abschweifen** *fig* v/i (*sep*, *-ge-*, *sein*) digress (**von** from)

'**Abschweifung** f (-; *-en*) digression

absehbar ['apzeːbaːɐ] *adj* foreseeable; **in absehbarer (auf absehbare) Zeit** in the

(for the) foreseeable future
'**absehen** v/t (*irr*, **sehen**, *sep*, *-ge-*, *h*) foresee; **es ist kein Ende abzusehen** there is no end in sight; **es abgesehen haben auf** (*acc*) be after; **absehen von** refrain from
'**abseilen** v/refl (*sep*, *-ge-*, *h*) descend by a rope, *Br a.* abseil; F make a getaway
abseits ['apzaɪts] *adv and prp* away *or* remote from
'**Abseitsfalle** f soccer: offside trap
abseitsstehen v/i (*irr*, **stehen**, *sep*, *-ge-*, *h*) soccer: be offside; *fig* be left out
'**absenden** v/t (*sep*, **senden**.] *sep*, *-ge-*, *h*) send (off), dispatch; mail, *esp Br* post (*letter etc*)
'**Absender** m (*-s*; *-*) sender
absetzbar ['apzɛtsbaːɐ] *adj*: **steuerlich absetzbar** deductible from tax
'**absetzen** (*sep*, *-ge-*, *h*) **1.** v/t take off (*hat, glasses etc*); set *or* put down (*bag etc*); drop (*passenger*); dismiss (*employee*); THEA, *film*: take off; deduct (*from tax*); depose (*king etc*); ECON sell; **sich absetzen** CHEM, GEOL settle, be deposited; **2.** v/i: **ohne abzusetzen** without stopping
'**Absetzung** f (*-*; *-en*) dismissal; deposition; THEA, *film*: withdrawal
'**Absicht** f (*-*; *-en*) intention; **mit Absicht** on purpose
'**absichtlich** **1.** *adj* intentional; **2.** *adv* on purpose
'**absitzen** (*irr*, **sitzen**, *sep*, *-ge-*) **1.** v/i (*sein*) dismount (*von* from); **2.** v/t (*h*) serve (*sentence*); F sit out (*play etc*)
absolut [apzo'luːt] *adj* absolute
Absolvent [apzɔl'vɛnt] m (*-en*; *-en*), **Absol'ventin** f (*-*; *-nen*) graduate
absolvieren [apzɔl'viːrən] v/t (*no -ge-*, *h*) attend (*school*); complete (*studies*); graduate from (*college etc*)
'**absondern** v/t (*sep*, *-ge-*, *h*) separate; MED, BIOL secrete; **sich absondern** cut o.s. off (*von* from)
'**Absonderung** f (*-*; *-en*) separation; MED, BIOL secretion
absorbieren [apzɔr'biːrən] v/t (*no -ge-*, *h*) absorb (*a. fig*)
'**abspeichern** v/t (*sep*, *-ge-*, *h*) EDP store, save
abspenstig ['apʃpɛnstɪç] *adj*: **j-m die Freundin abspenstig machen** steal s.o.'s girlfriend
'**absperren** v/t (*sep*, *-ge-*, *h*) lock; turn off (*water, gas etc*); block off (*road*); cordon off
'**Absperrung** f (*-*; *-en*) barrier; cordon
'**abspielen** v/t (*sep*, *-ge-*, *h*) play (*record etc*); SPORT pass (*the ball*); **sich abspielen**

happen, take place
'**Absprache** f agreement
'**absprechen** v/t (*irr*, **sprechen**, *sep*, *-ge-*, *h*) agree upon; arrange; **j-m die Fähigkeit etc absprechen** dispute s.o.'s ability *etc*
'**abspringen** v/i (*irr*, **springen**, *sep*, *-ge-*, *sein*) jump off, AVIAT jump, bail out; *fig* back out (*von* of)
'**Absprung** m jump; SPORT take-off; *fig* **den Absprung schaffen** make it
'**abspülen** v/t (*sep*, *-ge-*, *h*) rinse; wash up
'**abstammen** v/i (*sep*, *no past participle*) be descended (*von* from); CHEM, LING derive
'**Abstammung** f (*-*; *no pl*) descent; derivation
'**Abstammungslehre** f theory of the origin of species
'**Abstand** m distance (*a. fig*); interval; **Abstand halten** keep one's distance; *fig* **mit Abstand** by far
abstatten ['apʃtatən] v/t (*sep*, *-ge-*, *h*) **j-m e-n Besuch abstatten** pay a visit to s.o.
'**abstauben** v/t (*sep*, *-ge-*, *h*) dust; F *fig* sponge; swipe
'**Abstauber** F m (*-s*; *-*), '**Abstaubertor** n SPORT opportunist goal
'**abstechen** (*irr*, **stechen**, *sep*, *-ge-*, *h*) **1.** v/t stick (*pig etc*); **2.** v/i contrast (*von* with)
'**Abstecher** m (*-s*; *-*) side-trip, excursion (*a. fig*)
'**abstecken** v/t (*sep*, *-ge-*, *h*) mark out
'**abstehen** v/i (*irr*, **stehen**, *sep*, *-ge-*, *h*) stick out, protrude; → **abgestanden**
'**absteigen** v/i (*irr*, **steigen**, *sep*, *-ge-*, *sein*) get off (*a horse etc*); climb down; stay (*in dat* at); SPORT *Am* be moved down to a lower division, *Br* be relegated
'**Absteiger** m (*-s*; *-*) SPORT *Br* relegated club
'**abstellen** v/t (*sep*, *-ge-*, *h*) put down; leave (*s.th. with s.o.*); turn off (*gas etc*); park (*car*); *fig* put an end to s.th.
'**Abstellgleis** n RAIL siding; **j-n aufs Abstellgleis schieben** F push s.o. aside
'**Abstellraum** m storeroom
'**abstempeln** v/t (*sep*, *-ge-*, *h*) stamp
'**absterben** v/i (*irr*, **sterben**, *sep*, *-ge-*, *sein*) die off; *limb*: go numb
'**Abstieg** ['apʃtiːk] m (*-[e]s*; *-e*) descent; *fig* decline; SPORT *Br* relegation
'**abstimmen** v/i (*sep*, *-ge-*, *h*) vote (*über acc* on)
'**Abstimmung** f vote; *radio*: tuning
Abstinenzler [apsti'nɛntslɐ] m (*-s*; *-*) teetotal(l)er
'**Abstoß** m SPORT goal-kick
'**abstoßen** v/t (*irr*, **stoßen**, *sep*, *-ge-*, *h*) re-

pel; MED reject; push off (*boat*); F get rid of *s.th.*

abstoßend *fig adj* repulsive

abstrakt [ap'strakt] *adj* abstract

'**abstreiten** *v/t* (*irr*, **streiten**, *sep*, -*ge*-, *h*) deny

'**Abstrich** *m* MED smear; *pl* ECON cuts; *fig* reservations

'**abstufen** *v/t* (*sep*, -*ge*-, *h*) graduate; gradate (*colors*)

'**abstumpfen** (*sep*, -*ge*-) **1.** *v/t* (*h*) blunt, dull (*a. fig*); **2.** *fig v/i* (*sein*) become unfeeling

'**Absturz** *m*, '**abstürzen** *v/i* (*sep*, -*ge*-, *sein*) fall; AVIAT, EDP crash

'**absuchen** *v/t* (*sep*, -*ge*-, *h*) search (**nach** for)

absurd [ap'zʊrt] *adj* absurd, preposterous

Abszess [aps'tsɛs] *m* (-*es*; -*e*) MED abscess

Abt [apt] *m* (-[*e*]*s*; *Äbte* ['ɛptə]) REL abbot

'**abtasten** *v/t* (*sep*, -*ge*-, *h*) feel (for); MED palpate; frisk; TECH, EDP scan

'**abtauen** *v/t* (*sep*, -*ge*-, *h*) defrost

Abtei [ap'tai] *f* (-; -*en*) REL abbey

Abteil [ap'tail] *n* (-[*e*]*s*; -*e*) RAIL compartment

'**abteilen** *v/t* (*sep*, -*ge*-, *h*) divide; ARCH partition off

Ab'teilung *f* (-; -*en*) department (*a.* ECON); ward (*of hospital*); MIL detachment

Ab'teilungsleiter *m* head of (a) department; *Am* floorwalker, *Br* shopwalker

Äbtissin [ɛp'tɪsɪn] *f* (-; -*nen*) REL abbess

'**abtöten** *v/t* (*sep*, -*ge*-, *h*) kill (*bacteria etc*); *fig* deaden (*feelings etc*)

'**abtragen** *v/t* (*irr*, **tragen**, *sep*, -*ge*-, *h*) wear out (*clothes*); clear away (*dishes etc*); pay off (*debt*)

'**Abtrans,port** *m* transportation

'**abtreiben** (*irr*, **treiben**, *sep*, -*ge*-) **1.** *v/i* MED (*h*) have an abortion; MAR, AVIAT (*sein*) be blown off course; **2.** *v/t* (*h*) MED abort

'**Abtreibung** *f* (-; -*en*) abortion; *e-e* **Ab'treibung vornehmen** perform an abortion

'**abtrennen** *v/t* (*sep*, -*ge*-, *h*) detach; separate; MED sever

'**abtreten** (*irr*, **treten**, *sep*, -*ge*-) **1.** *v/t* (*h*) wear down (*heels*); wipe (*one's feet*); *fig* give up (**an** *acc* to); **2.** *v/i* (*sein*) resign; THEA; exit

'**Abtreter** *m* (-*s*; -) doormat

'**abtrocknen** (*sep*, -*ge*-, *h*) **1.** *v/t* dry; *sich* **abtrocknen** dry o.s. off; **2.** *v/i* dry the dishes, *Br a.* dry up

abtrünnig ['aptrʏnɪç] *adj* unfaithful, disloyal

'**Abtrünnige** [-nɪgə] *m*, *f* (-*n*; -*n*) renegade,

turncoat

abtun *v/t* (*irr*, **tun**, *sep*, -*ge*-, *h*) dismiss (**als** as), brush *s.o.*, *s.th.* aside

abwägen ['apvɛːgən] *v/t* (*irr*, **wägen**, *sep*, -*ge*-, *h*) weigh (**gegen** against)

'**abwählen** *v/t* (*sep*, -*ge*-, *h*) vote out

'**abwälzen** *v/t* (*sep*, -*ge*-, *h*) **et. auf j-n abwälzen** shove s.th. off on (to) s.o.

'**abwandeln** *v/t* (*sep*, -*ge*-, *h*) vary, modify

'**abwandern** *v/i* (*sep*, -*ge*-, *sein*) migrate (**von** from; **nach** to)

'**Abwanderung** *f* migration

'**Abwandlung** *f* modification, variation

'**Abwärme** *f* TECH waste heat

Abwart ['apvart] *m* (-*s*; -*e*) Swiss → **Hausmeister**

'**abwarten** (*sep*, -*ge*-, *h*) **1.** *v/t* wait for, await; **2.** *v/i* wait; **warten wir ab!** let's wait and see!; **wart nur ab!** just wait!

abwärts ['apvɛrts] *adv* down, down-ward(s)

Abwasch ['apvaʃ] *m* (-[*e*]*s*; *no pl*) **den Abwasch machen** do the washing-up

'**abwaschbar** *adj* washable

'**abwaschen** (*irr*, **waschen**, *sep*, -*ge*-, *h*) **1.** *v/t* wash off; **2.** *v/i* do the dishes, *Br a.* wash up

'**Abwaschwasser** *n* dishwater

'**Abwasser** *n* TECH waste water, sewage

Abwasseraufbereitung *f* TECH sewage treatment

'**abwechseln** *v/i* (*sep*, -*ge*-, *h*) alternate; *sich mit j-m abwechseln* take turns (**bei et.** at [doing] s.th.)

'**abwechselnd** *adv* by turns

'**Abwechslung** *f* (-; -*en*) change; *zur Ab'wechslung* for a change

'**abwechslungsreich** *adj* varied; colo(u)rful

'**Abweg** *m*: *auf Abwege geraten* go astray

abwegig ['apveːgɪç] *adj* absurd, unrealistic

'**Abwehr** *f* (-; *no pl*) defen|se, *Br* -ce (*a.* SPORT); warding off (*of blow etc*); save (*of ball*)

'**abwehren** *v/t* (*sep*, -*ge*-, *h*) ward off (*blow etc*); beat off; SPORT block

'**Abwehrfehler** *m* SPORT defensive error

'**Abwehrkräfte** *pl* MED resistance

'**Abwehrspieler** *m* SPORT defender

'**Abwehrstoffe** *pl* MED antibodies

'**abweichen** *v/i* (*irr*, **weichen**, *sep*, -*ge*-, *sein*) deviate (**von** from); digress

'**Abweichung** *f* (-; -*en*) deviation

'**abweisen** *v/t* (*irr*, **weisen**, *sep*, -*ge*-, *h*) turn away; rebuff; decline, turn down (*request etc*)

'**abweisend** *adj* unfriendly

'**abwenden** *v/t* ([*irr*, **wenden**,] *sep*, -*ge*-, *h*) turn away (*a. **sich abwenden***) (**von** from); avert (*tragedy etc*)

'**abwerfen** *v/t* (*irr,* **werfen**, *sep,* -ge-, *h*) throw off; AVIAT drop; BOT shed (*leaves*); ECON yield (*profit*)

'**abwerten** *v/t* (*sep,* -ge-, *h*) ECON devalue

'**abwertend** *fig adj* disparaging

'**Abwertung** *f* ECON devaluation

'**abwesend** *adj* absent

'**Abwesenheit** *f* (-; *no pl*) absence

'**abwickeln** *v/t* (*sep,* -ge-, *h*) unwind; ECON handle; transact (*business*)

'**abwiegen** *v/t* (*irr,* **wiegen**, *sep,* -ge-, *h*) weigh (out)

'**abwischen** *v/t* (*sep,* -ge-, *h*) wipe (off)

'**Abwurf** *m* dropping; *soccer:* throw-out

'**abwürgen** F *v/t* (*sep,* -ge-, *h*) MOT stall; *fig* stifle

'**abzahlen** *v/t* (*sep,* -ge-, *h*) make *monthly etc* payments for; pay off

'**abzählen** *v/t* (*sep,* -ge-, *h*) count

'**Abzahlung** *f: et. auf Abzahlung kaufen* *Am* buy s.th. on the instalment plan (*Br* on hire purchase)

'**abzapfen** *v/t* (*sep,* -ge-, *h*) tap, draw off

'**Abzeichen** *n* badge; medal

'**abzeichnen** *v/t* (*sep,* -ge-, *h*) copy, draw; sign, initial; *sich abzeichnen* (begin to) show; stand out (*gegen* against)

'**Abziehbild** *n Am* decal, *Br* transfer

'**abziehen** (*irr,* **ziehen**, *sep,* -ge-, *h*) **1.** *v/t* (*h*) take off, remove; MATH subtract; strip (*bed*); take out (*key*); *das Fell abziehen* skin; **2.** *v/i* (*sein*) go away; MIL withdraw; *smoke:* escape; *storm, clouds:* move off

'**Abzug** *m* ECON deduction; discount; MIL withdrawal; PRINT copy; PHOT print; *gun:* trigger; TECH vent, outlet; cooker hood

abzüglich ['aptsy:kliç] *prp* less, minus

'**abzweigen** (*sep,* -ge-) **1.** *v/t* (*h*) divert (*resources etc*) (*für* to); **2.** *v/i* (*sein*) *path etc:* branch off

'**Abzweigung** *f* (-; -en) junction

ach [ax] *int* oh!; *ach je!* oh dear!; *ach so!* I see; *ach was!* *surprised:* really?, *annoyed:* of course not!, nonsense!

Achse ['aksə] *f* (-; -n) TECH axle; MATH *etc* axis; F *auf Achse sein* be on the move

Achsel ['aksəl] *f* (-; -n) ANAT shoulder; *die Achseln zucken* shrug one's shoulders

'**Achselhöhle** *f* ANAT armpit

acht [axt] *adj* eight; *heute in acht Tagen* a week from today, *esp Br* today week; (*heute*) *vor acht Tagen* a week ago (today)

Acht *f: Acht geben →* **achtgeben***; außer Acht lassen* disregard; *sich in Acht nehmen* be careful, look *or* watch out (*vor dat* for)

achtgeben *v/i* (*irr,* **geben**, *sep,* -ge-, *h*) be careful; pay attention (*auf acc* to); take care (*auf acc* of); *gib acht!* look *or* watch out!, be careful!

achte ['axtə] *adj* eighth

'**achteckig** *adj* octagonal

Achtel ['axtəl] *n* (-s; -) eighth (part)

achten (-ge-, *h*) **1.** *v/t* respect; **2.** *v/i:* **achten auf** (*acc*) pay attention to; keep an eye on; watch; be careful with; *darauf achten, dass* see to it that

ächten ['ɛçtən] *v/t* (*sep,* -ge-, *h*) ban; *esp* HIST outlaw

Achter ['axtə] *m* (-s; -) *rowing:* eight

'**Achterbahn** *f* roller coaster

'**achtfach** *adj and adv* eightfold

'**achtlos** *adj* careless, heedless

'**Achtung** *f* (-; *no pl*) respect (*vor dat* for); *Achtung!* look out!; MIL attention!; *Achtung! Achtung!* attention please!; *Achtung! Fertig! Los!* On your marks! Get set! Go!; *Achtung Stufe!* Am caution: step!, *Br* mind the step!

'**achtzehn** *adj* eighteen

'**achtzehnte** *adj* eighteenth

achtzig ['axtsɪç] *adj* eighty; *die achtziger Jahre* the eighties

'**achtzigste** *adj* eightieth

ächzen ['ɛçtsən] *v/i* (*sep,* -ge-, *h*) groan (*vor dat* with)

Acker ['akɐ] *m* (-s; *Äcker* ['ɛkɐ]) field

Ackerbau *m* (-[e]s; *no pl*) agriculture; farming; *Ackerbau und Viehzucht* crop and stock farming

Ackerland *n* (-[e]s; *no pl*) farmland

'**ackern** F *v/i* (*sep,* -ge-, *h*) slog (away)

Adapter [a'daptɐ] *m* (-s; -) TECH adapter

addieren [a'di:rən] *v/t* (*no* -ge-, *h*) add (up)

Addition [adi'tsio:n] *f* (-; -en) addition, adding up

Adel ['a:dəl] *m* (-s; *no pl*) aristocracy

adeln *v/t* (*sep,* -ge-, *h*) ennoble (*a. fig*); *Br* knight

Ader ['a:dɐ] *f* (-; -n) ANAT blood vessel, vein

Adjektiv ['atjɛkti:f] *n* (-s; -e) LING adjective

Adler ['a:dlɐ] *m* (-s; -) ZO eagle

adlig ['a:dlɪç] *adj* noble

Adlige ['a:dligə] *m, f* (-n; -n) noble|man (-woman)

Admiral [atmi'ra:l] *m* (-s; -e) MAR admiral

adoptieren [adɔp'ti:rən] *v/t* (*no* -ge-, *h*) adopt

Adoptivkind [adɔp'ti:f-] *n* adopted child

Adressbuch [a'drɛs-] *n* directory

Adresse [a'drɛsə] *f* (-; -n) address

adressieren [adrɛ'si:rən] *v/t* (*no* -ge-, *h*)

address (*an* acc to)
Advent [at'vɛnt] *m* (-[e]s; *no pl*) REL Advent; Advent Sunday
Ad'ventszeit *f* Christmas season
Adverb [at'vɛrp] *n* (-s; *Adverbien* [at'vɛr-biən]) LING adverb
Aerobic [ɛ'roːbɪk] *n* (-s; *no pl*) aerobics
Affäre [a'fɛːrə] *f* (-; -n) affair
Affe ['afə] *m* (-n; -n) ZO monkey; ape
Affekt [a'fɛkt] *m* (-[e]s; -e) *im Affekt* in the heat of passion (*a.* JUR)
affektiert [afɛk'tiːɐt] *adj* affected
Afrika ['aːfrika] Africa
Afrikaner(in) [afri'kaːnɐ] *m* (-s; -), **Afri'kanerin** [-nərin] *f* (-; -nen), **afri'kanisch** *adj* African
After ['aftɐ] *m* (-s; -) ANAT anus
AG ABBR *of* **Aktiengesellschaft** *Am* (stock) corporation, *Br* PLC, public limited company
Agent [a'gɛnt] *m* (-en; -en), **A'gentin** *f* (-; -nen) agent; POL (secret) agent
Agentur [agɛn'tuːɐ] *f* (-; -en) agency
Aggression [agrɛ'sioːn] *f* (-; -en) aggression
aggressiv [agrɛ'siːf] *adj* aggressive
Aggressivität [agrɛsivi'tɛːt] *f* (-; *no pl*) aggressiveness
Agitator [agi'taːtoːɐ] *m* (-s; -en [-ta-'toːrən]) agitator
ah [aː] *int* ah!
äh [ɛː] *int* er; *disgusted:* ugh!
aha [a'ha] *int* I see!, oh!
A'ha-Erlebnis *n* aha-experience
Ahn [aːn] *m* (-[e]s; -en; -en) ancestor, *pl a.* forefathers
ähneln ['ɛːnəln] *v/i* (*ge-*, *h*) resemble, look like
ahnen ['aːnən] *v/t* (*ge-*, *h*) suspect; foresee, know
ähnlich ['ɛːnlɪç] *adj* similar (*dat* to); *j-m ähnlich sehen* look like s.o.
'Ähnlichkeit *f* (-; -en) likeness, resemblance, similarity (*mit* to)
'Ahnung *f* (-; -en) presentiment, *a.* foreboding; notion, idea; *ich habe keine Ahnung* I have no idea
'ahnungslos *adj* unsuspecting, innocent
Ahorn ['aːhɔrn] *m* (-s; -e) BOT maple
Ähre ['ɛːrə] *f* (-; -n) BOT ear; spike
Aids [eɪdz] *n* (-; *no pl*) MED AIDS
'Aids-Kranke *m*, *f* MED AIDS victim *or* sufferer
Aidstest *m* MED AIDS test
Airbag ['ɛːbæg] *m* (-s; -s) MOT airbag
Akademie [akade'miː] *f* (-; -n) academy, college
Akademiker(in) [aka'deːmikɐ (-kərin)] (-s; -/-; -nen) university graduate

akademisch [-'deːmɪʃ] *adj* academic
akklimatisieren [aklimati'ziːrən] *v/refl* (*no -ge-*, *h*) acclimatize (*an* acc to)
Akkord [a'kɔrt] *m* (-[e]s; -e) MUS chord; *im Akkord* ECON by the piece *or* job
Akkordarbeit *f* ECON piecework
Akkordarbeiter(in) *m* ECON pieceworker
Akkordeon [a'kɔrdeɔn] *n* (-s; -s) MUS accordion
Ak'kordlohn *m* ECON piece wages
Akku ['aku] F *m* (-s; -s), **Akkumulator** [akumu'laːtoːɐ] *m* (-s; -en [-la'toːrən]) TECH (storage) battery, *Br a.* accumulator
Akkusativ ['akuzatiːf] *m* (-s; -e) LING accusative (case)
Akne ['aknə] *f* (-; -n) MED acne
Akrobat [akro'baːt] *m* (-en; -en), **Akro'batin** *f* (-; -nen) acrobat
akro'batisch *adj* acrobatic
Akt [akt] *m* (-[e]s; -e) act(ion); THEA act; PAINT, PHOT nude
Akte ['aktə] *f* (-; -n) file; *pl.* files, records; *zu den Akten legen* file
'Aktendeckel *m* folder
Aktenkoffer *m* attaché case
Aktenordner *m* file
Aktentasche *f* briefcase
Aktenzeichen *n* reference (number)
Aktie ['aktsiə] *f* (-; -n) ECON share, *esp Am* stock
'Aktiengesellschaft *f Am* corporation, *Br* joint-stock company
Aktion [ak'tsioːn] *f* (-; -en) campaign, drive; MIL *ect* operation; *in Aktion* in action
Aktionär [aktsio'nɛːɐ] *m* (-s; -e), **Aktio-'närin** *f* (-; -nen) ECON shareholder, *esp Am* stockholder
aktiv [ak'tiːf] *adj* active
Aktiv ['aktiːf] *n* (-s; *no pl*) LING active voice
Aktivist [akti'vist] *m* (-en; -en) *esp* POL activist
Ak'tivurlaub *m* activity vacation
aktualisieren [aktuäli'ziːrən] *v/t* (*no -ge-*, *h*) update
aktuell [aktu'ɛl] *adj* topical; current; up-to-date; TV, *radio*: *e-e aktuelle Sendung* a current affairs *or* news feature
Akupunktur [akupʊŋk'tuːɐ] *f* (-; -en) MED acupuncture
Akustik [a'kʊstɪk] *f* (-; *no pl*) acoustics
a'kustisch *adj* acoustic
akut [a'kuːt] *adj* urgent (*problem etc*); *a.* MED acute
Akzent [ak'tsɛnt] *m* (-[e]s; -e) accent; stress (*a. fig*)
akzeptabel [aktsɛp'taːbəl] *adj* acceptable; reasonable (*price etc*)

akzeptieren [aktsɛp'tiːrən] *v/t* (*no -ge-*, *h*) accept

Alarm [a'larm] *m* (*-[e]s*; *-e*) alarm; *Alarm schlagen* sound the alarm

Alarmanlage *f* alarm system

Alarmbereitschaft *f*: *in Alarmbereitschaft* on standby, on the alert

alarmieren [alar'miːrən] *v/t* (*no -ge-*, *h*) call; alert

alarmierend *adj* alarming

albern ['albən] *adj* silly, foolish

Album ['albʊm] *n* (*-s*; *Alben* ['albən]) album (*a. record*)

Algen ['algən] *pl* BOT algae

Algenpest *f* plague of algae, algal bloom

Algebra ['algəbra] *f* (*-*; *no pl*) MATH algebra

Alibi ['aːlibi] *n* (*-s*; *-s*) JUR alibi

Alimente [ali'mɛntə] *pl* JUR alimony

Alkohol ['alkohoːl] *m* (*-s*; *no pl*) alcohol

'alkoholfrei *adj* nonalcoholic, soft

Alkoholiker(in) [alko'hoːlikɐ (-kərɪn)] (*-s*; *-/-*; *-nen*) alcoholic

alko'holisch *adj* alcoholic

Alkoholismus [alkoho'lɪsmʊs] *m* (*-*; *no pl*) alcoholism

alkoholsüchtig *adj* addicted to alcohol

Alkoholtest *m* MOT breath test

all [al] *indef pron and adj* all; *alles* everything; *alles (Beliebige)* anything; *alle (Leute)* everybody; anybody; *alle beide* both of them; *wir alle* all of us; *alles in allem* all in all; *auf alle Fälle* in any case; *alle drei Tage* every three days; → *Art*, *Gute*, *vor*

All *n* (*-s*; *no pl*) universe; (outer) space

alle ['alə] F *adj*: *alle sein* be all gone; *mein Geld ist alle* I'm out of money

Allee [a'leː] *f* (*-*; *-n*) avenue

allein [a'lain] *adj and adv* alone; lonely; by o.s.; *ganz allein* all alone; *er hat es ganz allein gemacht* he did it all by himself; *allein stehend* → *alleinstehend*

Al'leinerziehende *m*, *f* (*-n*; *-n*) single parent

Alleingang *m*: *im Alleingang* single-handedly, solo

alleinig [a'lainɪç] *adj* sole

Al'leinsein *n* (*-s*; *no pl*) loneliness

alleinstehend *adj* single

Allerbeste ['alɐ'bɛstə]: *der (die, das) Allerbeste* the best of all, the very best

allerdings ['alɐ'dɪŋs] *adv* however, though; *allerdings!* certainly!, *esp Am* F sure!

'aller'erste *adj* very first

Allergie [alɛr'giː] *f* (*-*; *-n*) MED allergy (*gegen* to)

allergisch [a'lɛrgɪʃ] *adj* allergic (*gegen* to)

'aller'hand F *adj* a good deal (of); *das ist ja allerhand!* that's a bit much!

'Aller'heiligen *n* REL All Saints' Day

allerlei ['alɐ'lai] *adj* all kinds *or* sorts of

'aller'letzte *adj* last of all, very last

aller'liebst 1. *adj* (most) lovely; **2.** *adv*: *am allerliebsten mögen* like best of all

aller'meiste *adj* (by far the) most

aller'nächste *adj* very next; *in allernächster Zeit* in the very near future

aller'neu(e)ste *adj* very latest

'Aller'seelen *n* REL All Souls' Day

allerseits ['alɐ'zaits] *adv* F: *Tag allerseits!* hi, everybody!

'aller'wenigst *adv*: *am allerwenigsten* least of all

allesamt ['aləˈzamt] *adv* all together

'allge'mein 1. *adj* general; common; universal; **2.** *adv*: *im Allgemeinen* in general, generally; *allgemein verständlich* intelligible (to all), popular

'Allge'meinbildung *f* general education

'Allge'meinheit *f* (*-*; *no pl*) (general) public

allgemeinver'ständlich *adj* → *allgemein*

All'heilmittel *n* cure-all (*a. fig*)

Allianz [a'ljants] *f* (*-*; *-en*) alliance

Alligator [ali'gaːtoːɐ] *m* (*-s*; *-en*) alligator

Alliierte [ali'iːɐtə]: *die Alliierten* *pl* POL the Allies

'all'jährlich *adv* every year; *alljährlich stattfindend* annual

all'mächtig *adj* omnipotent; *Almighty (God)*

allmählich [al'mɛːlɪç] **1.** *adj* gradual; **2.** *adv* gradually

'Allradantrieb *m* MOT four-wheel drive

allseitig ['alzaitɪç] *adv*: *allseitig interessiert sein* have all-round interests

'Alltag *m* everyday life

'all'täglich *adj* everyday; *fig a.* ordinary

all'wissend *adj* omniscient

'allzu *adv* (all) too; *allzu viel* too much

Alm [alm] *f* (*-*; *-en*) alpine pasture, mountain pasture

Almosen ['almoːzən] *n* (*-s*; *-*) alms

'Alpdruck *m* (*-[e]s*; *no pl*) nightmare (*a. fig*)

Alphabet [alfa'beːt] *n* (*-[e]s*; *-e*) alphabet

alpha'betisch *adj* alphabetical

alpin [al'piːn] *adj* alpine

'Alptraum *m* nightmare (*a. fig*)

als [als] *cj time*: when; while; *after comp*: than; *als ich ankam* when I arrived; *als Kind (Geschenk)* as a child (present); *älter als* older than; *als ob* as if, as though; *nichts als* nothing but

also ['alzo] *cj* so, therefore; F well, you

know; *also gut!* very well (then)!, all right (then)!; *also doch* so ... after all; *du willst also gehen etc?* so you want to go to *etc?*

alt [alt] *adj* old; HIST ancient; classical (*language*); *ein 12 Jahre alter Junge* a twelve-year-old boy

Alt *m* (-s; *no pl*) MUS alto

Altar [al'taːɐ] *m* (-s; *Altäre* [al'tɛːrə]) REL altar

'**Alte** *m*, *f* (-n; -n) *der Alte* the old man (*a. fig*); the boss; *die Alte* the old woman (*a. fig*); *die Alten pl* the old

'**Altenheim** *n* → *Altersheim*

'**Altenpfleger(in)** geriatric nurse

Alter ['altɐ] *n* (-s; *no pl*) age; old age; *im Alter von ...* at the age of ...; *er ist in deinem Alter* he's your age

älter ['ɛltɐ] *adj* older; *mein älterer Bruder* my elder brother; *ein älterer Herr* an elderly gentleman

'**altern** *v/i* (ge-, sein) grow old, age

alternativ [altɛrna'tiːf] *adj* alternative; POL ecological, green; *a.* counter-culture (*movement etc*)

Alternative¹ [altɛrna'tiːvə] *f* (-; -n) alternative; option, choice

Alterna'tive² *m*, *f* (-n; -n) ecologist, member of the counterculture movement

'**Altersgrenze** *f* age limit; retirement age

'**Altersheim** *n* old people's home

'**Altersrente** *f* old-age pension

'**Altersschwäche** *f* (-; *no pl*) infirmity; *an Altersschwäche sterben* die of old age

'**Altersversorgung** *f* old age pension (scheme)

'**Altertum** *n* (-s; *no pl*) antiquity

'**Altglascon,tainer** *m Am* glass recycling bin, *Br* bottle bank

'**altklug** *adj* precocious

'**Altlasten** *pl* residual pollution

'**Alt me,tall** *n* scrap (metal)

'**altmodisch** *adj* old-fashioned

'**Altöl** *n* waste oil

'**Altpa,pier** *n* waste paper

'**altsprachlich** *adj*: *altsprachliches Gymnasium appr* classical secondary school

'**Altstadt** *f* old town

Altstadtsa,nierung *f* town-cent|er (*Br* -re) rehabilitation

'**Altwarenhändler** *m* second-hand dealer

Alt'weibersommer *m* Indian summer; gossamer

Aluminium [alu'miːnjʊm] *n* (-s; *no pl*) alumin(i)um

am [am] *prp* at the (*window etc*); time: in the (*morning etc*); at the (*weekend etc*); on (*Sunday etc*); *am 1. Mai* on May 1st; *am Tage* during the day; *am Himmel*

in the sky; *am meisten* most; *am Leben* alive

Amateur [ama'tøːɐ] *m* (-s; -e) amateur

Amateurfunker *m* radio amateur, F radio ham

Amboss ['ambɔs] *m* (-es; -e) anvil

ambulant [ambu'lant] *adv*: *ambulant behandelt werden* MED get outpatient treatment

Ambulanz [ambu'lants] *f* (-; -en) MED outpatients' department; MOT ambulance

Ameise ['aːmaizə] *f* (-; -n) zo ant

'**Ameisenhaufen** *m* zo anthill

Amerika [a'meːrika] America

Amerikaner [ameri'kaːnɐ] *m* (-s; -), **Ameri'kanerin** [-nərin] *f* (-; -nen), **ameri'kanisch** *adj* American

Amnestie [amnɛs'tiː] *f* (-; -n), **amnes'tieren** *v/t* (*no* -ge-, *h*) JUR amnesty

Amok ['aːmɔk] *m*: *Amok laufen* run amok

Ampel ['ampəl] *f* (-; -n) traffic light(s)

Amphibie [am'fiːbjə] *f* (-; -n) zo amphibian

Ampulle [am'pʊlə] *f* (-; -n) ampoule

Amputation [amputa'tsjoːn] *f* (-; -en) MED amputation

amputieren [ampu'tiːrən] *v/t* (*no* -ge-, *h*) MED amputate

Amsel ['amzəl] *f* (-; -n) zo blackbird

Amt [amt] *n* (-[e]s; *Ämter* ['ɛmtɐ]) office, department, *esp Am* bureau; position; duty, function; TEL exchange

'**amtlich** *adj* official

'**Amtsarzt** *m* medical examiner (*Br* officer)

'**Amtseinführung** *f* inauguration

'**Amtsgeheimnis** *n* official secret

'**Amtsgeschäfte** *pl* official duties

'**Amtszeichen** *n* TEL dial (*Br* dialling) tone

'**Amtszeit** *f* term (of office)

Amulett [amu'lɛt] *n* (-[e]s; -e) amulet, (lucky) charm

amüsant [amy'zant] *adj* amusing, entertaining

amüsieren [amy'ziːrən] *v/t* (*no* -ge-, *h*) amuse; *sich amüsieren* enjoy o.s., have a good time; *sich amüsieren über* (*acc*) laugh at

an [an] **1.** *prp*: *an der Themse* (*Küste, Wand*) on the Thames (coast, wall); *an s-m Schreibtisch* at his desk; *an der Hand* by the hand; *an der Arbeit* at work; *an den Hausaufgaben* sitzen sit over one's homework; *et. schicken an* (*acc*) send s.th. to; *sich lehnen an* (*acc*) lean against; *an die Tür etc klopfen* knock at the door *etc*; *an e-m Sonntagmorgen* on a Sunday morning; *an dem*

Tag, ... on the day ...; *an Weihnachten etc* at Christmas *etc*; → *Mangel, Stelle, sterben*; **2.** *adv so* (*a. light etc*); *von jetzt* (*da, heute*) *an* from now (that time, today) on; *München an 16.45* arrival Munich 4.45 p.m.

Anabolikum [ana'boːlikʊm] *n* (*-s; -ka*) PHARM anabolic steroid

analog [ana'loːk] *adj* analogous

Ana'log... *in cpds* analog(ue) (*computer etc*)

Analphabet [anʔalfa'beːt] *m* (*-en; -en*), **Analpha'betin** *f* (*-; -nen*) illiterate (person)

Analyse [ana'lyːzə] *f* (*-; -n*) analysis

analysieren [analy'ziːrən] *v/t* (*no -ge-, h*) analy|ze, *Br* -se

Ananas ['ananas] *f* (*-; -, -se*) BOT pineapple

Anarchie [anar'çiː] *f* (*-; -n*) anarchy

Anatomie [anato'miː] *f* (*-; -n*) anatomy

anatomisch [ana'toːmɪʃ] *adj* anatomical

'anbahnen *v/t* (*sep, -ge-, h*) pave the way for; *sich anbahnen* be developing; be impending

'Anbau *m* (*-[e]s; -ten*) a) AGR (*no pl*) cultivation, b) ARCH annex, extension

'anbauen *v/t* (*sep, -ge-, h*) AGR cultivate, grow; ARCH add (*an acc* to), build on

'anbehalten *v/t* (*irr, halten, sep, no -ge-, h*) keep on

an'bei *adv* ECON enclosed

'anbeißen (*irr, beißen, sep, -ge-, h*) **1.** *v/t* take a bite of; **2.** *v/i fish*: bite; *fig* take the bait

'anbellen *v/t* (*sep, -ge-, h*) bark at

'anbeten *v/t* (*sep, -ge-, h*) adore, worship (*a. fig*)

'Anbetracht *m*: *in Anbetracht* (*dessen, dass*) considering (that)

'anbetteln *v/t* (*sep, -ge-, h*) *j-n um et. anbetteln* beg s.o. for s.th.

'anbiedern [-biːdɐn] *v/refl* (*sep, -ge-, h*) curry favo(u)r (*bei* with)

'anbieten *v/t* (*irr, bieten, sep, -ge-, h*) offer

'anbinden *v/t* (*irr, binden, sep, -ge-, h*) tie up; *anbinden an* (*acc or dat*) tie to

'Anblick *m* sight

'anblicken *v/t* (*sep, -ge-, h*) look at; glance at

'anbohren *v/t* (*sep, -ge-, h*) tap

'anbrechen (*irr, brechen, sep, -ge-*) **1.** *v/t* (*h*) break into (*supplies*); open; **2.** *v/i* (*sein*) begin; *day*: break; *night*: fall

'anbrennen *v/i* (*irr, brennen, sep, -ge-, sein*) burn (*a. anbrennen lassen*)

'anbringen *v/t* (*irr, bringen, sep, -ge-, h*) fix (*an dat* to)

'Anbruch *m* (*-[e]s; no pl*) beginning; *bei Anbruch der Nacht* at nightfall

'anbrüllen *v/t* (*sep, -ge-, h*) roar at

Andacht ['andaxt] *f* (*-; -en*) REL a) (*no pl*) devotion, b) service; prayers

andächtig ['andɛçtɪç] *adj* REL devout

'andauern *v/i* (*sep, -ge-, h*) continue, go on, last

andauernd *adj and adv* → *dauernd*

'Andenken *n* (*-s; -*) keepsake; souvenir (*both*: *an acc* of); *zum Andenken an* (*acc*) in memory of

andere ['andərə] *adj and indef pron* other, different; *mit anderen Worten* in other words; *am anderen Morgen* the next morning; *et.* (*nichts*) *anderes* s.th. (nothing) else; *nichts anderes als* nothing but; *die anderen* the others; *alle anderen* everybody else

andererseits ['andərə'zaits] *adv* on the other hand

ändern ['ɛndɐn] *v/t* (*ge-, h*) change; alter (*clothes*); *ich kann es nicht ändern* I can't help it; *sich ändern* change

'andern'falls *adv* otherwise

anders ['andɐs] *adv* different(ly); *jemand anders* somebody else; *anders werden* change; *anders sein* (*als*) be different (from); *es geht nicht anders* there is no other way

andersherum 1. *adv* the other way round; **2.** F *adj* queer

anderswo(hin) *adv* elsewhere

anderthalb ['andɐt'halp] *adj* one and a half

'Änderung *f* (*-; -en*) change; alteration

'andeuten *v/t* (*sep, -ge-, h*) hint (at), suggest; indicate; *j-m andeuten, dass* give s.o. a hint that

'Andeutung *f* (*-; -en*) hint, suggestion

'Andrang *m* (*-[e]s; no pl*) crush; ECON rush (*nach* for), run (*zu, nach* on)

'andrehen *v/t* (*sep, -ge-, h*) turn on; F *j-m et. andrehen* fob sth. off on s.o.

'androhen *v/t* (*sep, -ge-, h*) *j-m et. androhen* threaten s.o. with s.th.

'aneignen *v/refl* (*sep, -ge-, h*) acquire; *esp* JUR appropriate

anei'nander *adv* tie *etc* together; *aneinander denken* think of each other; *aneinandergeraten* *v/t* (*irr, geraten, sein*) clash (*mit* with)

Anekdote [anɛk'doːtə] *f* (*-; -n*) anecdote

anekeln *v/t* (*sep, -ge-, h*) disgust, sicken; *es ekelt mich an* it makes me sick

anerkannt *adj* acknowledged, recognized

'anerkennen *v/t* (*irr, kennen, sep, no -ge-, h*) acknowledge, recognize; appreciate

anerkennend *adj* appreciative

'Anerkennung *f* (*-; -en*) acknowledge(e)-ment, recognition; appreciation '**anfahren** (*irr*, **fahren**, *sep*, *-ge-*) **1.** *v/i* (*sein*) start; **2.** *v/t* (*h*) deliver; MOT *etc* hit, *car etc*: *a.* run into; *fig* **j-n anfahren** jump on s.o.

'**Anfahrt** *f* journey, ride

'**Anfall** *m* MED fit, attack

'**anfallen** *v/t* (*irr*, **fallen**, *sep*, *-ge-*, *h*) attack, assault; *dog*: go for

'**anfällig** *adj* delicate; **anfällig für** susceptible to

'**Anfang** *m* beginning, start; **am Anfang** at the beginning; **Anfang Mai** early in May; **Anfang nächsten Jahres** early next year; **Anfang der neunziger Jahre** in the early nineties; **er ist Anfang 20** he is in his early twenties; **von Anfang an** from the beginning *or* start

'**anfangen** *v/t and v/i* (*irr*, **fangen**, *sep*, *-ge-*, *h*) begin, start; do

'**Anfänger** *m* (*-s*; *-*), '**Anfängerin** *f* (*-*; *-nen*) beginner

'**anfangs** *adv* at first

'**Anfangsbuchstabe** *m* initial (letter); **großer Anfangsbuchstabe** capital (letter)

Anfangsstadium *n*: **im Anfangsstadium** at an early stage

'**anfassen** *v/t* (*sep*, *-ge-*, *h*) touch; take (hold of); **sich anfassen** take each other by the hands; F **zum Anfassen** everyman's

'**anfechtbar** *adj* contestable

'**anfechten** *v/t* (*irr*, **fechten**, *sep*, *-ge-*, *h*) contest

'**Anfechtung** *f* (*-*; *-en*) contesting

'**anfertigen** *v/t* (*sep*, *-ge-*, *h*) make, manufacture

'**anfeuchten** *v/t* (*sep*, *-ge-*, *h*) moisten

'**anfeuern** *fig v/t* (*sep*, *-ge-*, *h*) cheer

'**anflehen** *v/t* (*sep*, *-ge-*, *h*) implore

'**anfliegen** *v/t* (*irr*, **fliegen**, *sep*, *-ge-*, *h*) AVIAT approach; fly (regularly) to

'**Anflug** *m* AVIAT approach; *fig* touch

'**anfordern** *v/t* (*sep*, *-ge-*, *h*) demand; request

'**Anforderung** *f* (*-*; *-en*) demand; request; *pl* requirements, qualifications

'**Anfrage** *f* (*-*; *-n*) inquiry

'**anfragen** *v/i* (*sep*, *-ge-*, *h*) inquire (**bei j-m nach et.** of s.o. about s.th.)

'**anfreunden** *v/refl* (*sep*, *-ge-*, *h*) make friends (**mit** with)

'**anfühlen** *v/refl* (*sep*, *-ge-*, *h*) feel; **es fühlt sich weich an** it feels soft

'**anführen** *v/t* (*sep*, *-ge-*, *h*) lead; state; F fool

'**Anführer(in)** leader

'**Anführungszeichen** *pl* quotation marks, inverted commas

'**Angabe** *f* (*-*; *-n*) statement; indication; F big talk; *tennis*: service; *pl* information, data; TECH specifications

'**angeben** (*irr*, **geben**, *sep*, *-ge-*, *h*) **1.** *v/t* give, state; *customs*: declare; indicate; quote (*price*); **2.** *v/i* F *fig* brag, show off; *tennis*: serve

'**Angeber** F *m* (*-s*; *-*) braggart, show-off

Angeberei [angeːbəˈraɪ] F *f* (*-*; *no pl*) bragging, showing off

angeblich [ˈangəplɪç] *adj* alleged

angeblich ist er … he is said to be …

'**angeboren** *adj* innate, inborn; MED congenital

'**Angebot** *n* (*-[e]s*, *-e*) offer (*a.* ECON); **Angebot und Nachfrage** supply and demand

'**angebracht** *adj* appropriate

angebunden *adj*: **kurz angebunden** curt

angegossen F *adj*: **wie angegossen sitzen** fit like a glove

angeheitert *adj* tipsy, *Br a.* (slightly) merry

'**angehen** (*irr*, **gehen**, *sep*, *-ge-*, *sein*) **1.** *v/i light etc*: go on; **2.** *v/t* concern; **das geht dich nichts an** that is none of your business

angehend *adj* future; **angehender Arzt** doctor-to-be

'**angehören** *v/i* (*sep*, *no -ge-*, *h*) belong to

'**Angehörige** *m*, *f* (*-n*; *-n*) relative; member; **die nächsten Angehörigen** the next of kin

'**Angeklagte** *m*, *f* (*-n*; *-n*) JUR defendant

Angel [ˈaŋəl] *f* (*-*; *-n*) fishing tackle; TECH hinge

'**Angelegenheit** *f* (*-*; *-en*) matter, affair

angelehnt *adj door etc*: ajar

'**angelernt** *adj* semi-skilled (*worker*)

'**Angelhaken** *m* fishhook

'**angeln** (*ge-*, *h*) **1.** *v/i* (*nach* for) fish, angle (*both a. fig*); **2.** *v/t* catch, hook

'**Angelrute** *f* fishing rod

'**Angelsachse** [-zaksə] *m* (*-n*; *-n*), '**angelsächsisch** [-zɛksɪʃ] *adj* Anglo-Saxon

'**Angelschein** *m* fishing permit

'**Angelschnur** *f* fishing line

angemessen *adj* proper, suitable; just (*punishment*); reasonable (*price*)

'**angenehm** *adj* pleasant, agreeable; **angenehm!** pleased to meet you

'**angenommen** *cj* (let's) suppose, supposing

angeregt *adj* animated; lively

angeschrieben *adj*: **bei j-m gut** (**schlecht**) **angeschrieben sein** be in s.o.'s good (bad) books

angesehen *adj* respected

'**angesichts** *prp* (*gen*) in view of

'**Angestellte** m, f (-n; -n) employee (**bei** with), pl the staff

'**angetan** adj: **ganz angetan sein von** be taken with

angetrunken adj (slightly) drunk; **in angetrunkenem Zustand** under the influence of alcohol

angewandt adj applied

angewiesen adj: **angewiesen auf** (acc) dependent (up)on

'**angewöhnen** v/t (sep, no -ge-, h) **sich** (j-m) **angewöhnen, et. zu tun** get (s.o.) used to doing s.th.; **sich das Rauchen angewöhnen** take to smoking

'**Angewohnheit** f habit

Angina [an'gi:na] f (-; -nen) MED tonsillitis

'**angleichen** v/t (irr, **gleichen**, sep, -ge-, h) adjust (**an** acc to)

'**Angler** ['aŋlɐ] m (-s; -) angler

Anglist [aŋ'glɪst] m (-en; -en), **An'glistin** f (-; -nen) student of (or graduate in) English

'**angreifen** v/t (irr, **greifen**, sep, -ge-, h) attack (a. SPORT and fig); affect (health etc); touch (supplies)

'**Angreifer** m (-s; -) attacker, SPORT a. offensive player; esp POL aggressor

'**angrenzend** adj adjacent (**an** acc to)

'**Angriff** m attack (a. SPORT and fig); MIL assault, charge; **in Angriff nehmen** set about

'**angriffslustig** adj aggressive

Angst [aŋst] f (-; Ängste ['ɛŋstə]) fear (**vor** dat of); **Angst haben** (**vor** dat) be afraid or scared (of); **j-m Angst einjagen** frighten or scare s.o.; (**hab**) **keine Angst!** don't be afraid!

Angsthase F m chicken

'**ängstigen** ['ɛŋstɪgən] v/t (ge-, h) frighten, scare; **sich ängstigen** be afraid (**vor** dat of); be worried (**um** about)

'**ängstlich** ['ɛŋstlɪç] adj timid, fearful; anxious

'**anhaben** F v/t (irr, **haben**, sep, -ge-, h) have on (a. light etc), a. wear, be wearing (dress etc)

'**anhalten** (irr, **halten**, sep, -ge-, h) **1.** v/t stop; **den Atem anhalten** hold one's breath; **2.** v/i stop; continue

anhaltend adj continual

'**Anhalter** m (-s; -) hitchhiker; F **per Anhalter fahren** hitchhike

'**Anhaltspunkt** m clue

an'hand prp (gen) by means of

'**Anhang** m a) appendix, b) (no pl) relations

'**anhängen** v/t (sep, -ge-, h) add; hang up; RAIL, MOT couple (**an** acc to)

'**Anhänger** m (-s; -) follower, supporter (a.

SPORT); pendant; label, tag; MOT trailer

'**anhänglich** adj affectionate; contp clinging

'**anhäufen** v/t and v/refl (sep, -ge-, h) heap up, accumulate

'**Anhäufung** f (-; -en) accumulation

'**anheben** v/t (irr, **heben**, sep, -ge-, h) lift, raise (a. price); MOT jack up

'**anheften** v/t (sep, -ge-, h) attach, tack (both: **an** acc to)

Anhieb m: **auf Anhieb** on the first try

'**anhimmeln** F v/t (sep, -ge-, h) idolize, worship

'**Anhöhe** f rise, hill, elevation

'**anhören** v/t (sep, -ge-, h) listen to; **mit anhören** overhear; **es hört sich ... an** it sounds ...

'**Anhörung** f (-; -en) hearing

animieren [ani'mi:rən] v/t (no -ge-, h) encourage; stimulate

'**ankämpfen** v/i (sep, -ge-, h) **ankämpfen gegen** fight s.th.

'**Ankauf** m purchase

Anker ['aŋkɐ] m (-s; -) MAR anchor; **vor Anker gehen** drop anchor

'**ankern** v/i (ge-, h) MAR anchor

'**anketten** v/t (sep, -ge-, h) chain up

'**Anklage** f (-; no pl) JUR accusation, charge (a. fig)

'**anklagen** v/t (sep, -ge-, h) JUR accuse (**wegen** of), charge (with) (both a. fig)

'**anklammern** v/t (sep, -ge-, h) clip s.th. on; **sich anklammern** (**an** acc) cling (to)

Anklang m: **Anklang finden** meet with approval

'**ankleben** v/t (sep, -ge-, h) stick on (**an** dat or acc to)

'**anklicken** v/t (sep, -ge-, h) EDP click

'**anklopfen** v/i (sep, -ge-, h) knock (**an** dat or acc at)

'**anknipsen** v/t (sep, -ge-, h) switch on

'**anknüpfen** v/t (sep, -ge-, h) tie (**an** acc to); fig begin; **Beziehungen anknüpfen** (**zu**) establish contacts (with)

'**ankommen** v/i (irr, **kommen**, sep, -ge-, sein) arrive; **nicht gegen j-n ankommen** be no match for s.o.; **es kommt** (**ganz**) **darauf an** it (all) depends; **es kommt darauf an, dass** what matters is; **darauf kommt es nicht an** that doesn't matter; **es darauf ankommen lassen** take a chance; **gut ankommen** (**bei**) fig go down well (with)

'**ankündigen** v/t (sep, -ge-, h) announce; advertise

'**Ankündigung** f announcement; advertisement

Ankunft ['ankunft] f (-; no pl) arrival

'**anlächeln**, '**anlachen** v/t (sep, -ge-, h)

smile at

'Anlage f arrangement; facility; plant; TECH system; (stereo etc) set; ECON investment; enclosure; fig gift; pl park, gardens; **sanitäre Anlagen** sanitary facilities

Anlass ['anlas] m (-es; Anlässe ['anlɛsə]) occasion; cause

'anlassen v/t (irr, **lassen**, sep, -ge-, h) MOT start; F keep on, leave on (a. light etc)

'Anlasser m (-s; -) MOT starter

anlässlich ['anlɛslɪç] prp (gen) on the occasion of

'Anlauf m SPORT run-up; fig start

'anlaufen (irr, **laufen**, sep, -ge-) **1.** v/i (sein) run up; fig start; metal: tarnish; glasses etc: steam up; **2.** v/t (h) MAR call or touch at

'anlegen (sep, -ge-, h) **1.** v/t put on (dress etc); lay out (garden etc); build (road etc); invest (money); found (town etc); MED apply (dressing etc); lay in (supplies); **sich mit j-m anlegen** pick a quarrel with s.o.; MAR land; moor; **es anlegen auf** (acc) aim at

'Anleger m (-s; -) ECON investor; MAR landing stage

'anlehnen v/t (sep, -ge-, h) lean (**an** acc against); leave door etc ajar; **sich anlehnen an** (acc) lean against, fig lean on s.o.

Anleihe ['anlaiə] f (-; -n) ECON loan

'Anleitung f (-; -en) guidance, instruction; written instructions

'Anliegen n (-s; -) request; message (of a film etc)

'Anlieger ['anli:gɐ] m (-s; -) resident

'anlocken v/t (sep, -ge-, h) attract, lure

'anmachen v/t (sep, -ge-, h) light (fire etc); turn on (light etc); dress (salad); F chat s.o. up; turn s.o. on

'anmalen v/t (sep, -ge-, h) paint

'Anmarsch m: **im Anmarsch** on the way

anmaßen v/t (sep, -ge-, h) **sich anmaßen** assume; claim (right); **sich anmaßen, et. zu tun** presume to do s.th.

anmaßend adj arrogant

'anmelden v/t (sep, -ge-, h) announce (visitor); register (birth etc); customs: declare; **sich anmelden** enrol(l) (for classes etc); register (at a hotel); **sich anmelden bei** make an appointment with (doctor etc)

'Anmeldung f announcement; registration, enrol(l)ment

'anmerken v/t (sep, -ge-, h) **j-m et. anmerken** notice s.th. in s.o.; **sich et. (nichts) anmerken lassen** (not) let it show

'Anmerkung f (-; -en) note; annotation, footnote

Anmut ['anmu:t] f (-; no pl) grace

'anmutig adj graceful

'annähen v/t (sep, -ge-, h) sew on (**an** acc to)

'annähernd adv approximately

'Annäherung f (-; -en) approach (**an** acc to)

'Annäherungsversuche pl advances, F pass

Annahme ['anna:mə] f (-; -n) a) (no pl) acceptance (a. fig), b) assumption

annehmbar adj acceptable; reasonable (price etc)

'annehmen v/t (irr, **nehmen**, sep, -ge-, h) accept; suppose; adopt (child, name); take (ball); take on (color, look etc); **sich e-r Sache** or **j-s annehmen** take care of s.th. or s.o.

'Annehmlichkeiten pl comforts, amenities

Annonce [a'nõ:sə] f (-; -n) advertisement

annullieren [anʊ'li:rən] v/t (no -ge-, h) annul; ECON cancel

anöden ['an'ø:dən] F v/t (sep, -ge-, h) bore s.o. to death

anonym [ano'ny:m] adj anonymous

Anonymität [anonymi'tɛ:t] f (-; no pl) anonymity

Anorak ['anorak] m (-s; -s) anorak

'anordnen v/t (sep, -ge-, h) arrange; give order(s), order

'Anordnung f (-; -en) arrangement; direction, order

anorganisch adj CHEM inorganic

'anpacken F fig (sep, -ge-, h) **1.** v/t tackle; **2.** v/i: **mit anpacken** lend a hand

'anpassen v/t (sep, -ge-, h) adapt, adjust (both a. **sich anpassen**) (dat, **an** acc to)

'Anpassung f (-; -en) adaptation, adjustment

anpassungsfähig adj adaptable

'Anpassungsfähigkeit f adaptability

'Anpfiff m SPORT starting whistle; F fig dressing-down

'anpflanzen v/t (sep, -ge-, h) cultivate, plant

'Anpflanzung f cultivation

'anpöbeln v/t (sep, -ge-, h) accost; shout abuse at

anprangern ['anpraŋɐn] v/t (sep, -ge-, h) denounce

'anpreisen v/t (irr, **preisen**, sep, -ge-, h) push; plug

'anpro,bieren v/t (no -ge-, h) try on

'anpumpen F v/t (sep, -ge-, h) touch s.o. (**um** for)

'anraten v/t (irr, **raten**, sep, -ge-, h) advise

'anrechnen v/t (sep, -ge-, h) charge; allow

'Anrecht n: **ein Anrecht haben auf** (acc)

'be entitled to
'**Anrede** f address
'**anreden** v/t (sep, -ge-, h) address (**mit Namen** by name)
'**anregen** v/t (sep, -ge-, h) stimulate; suggest
'**anregend** adj stimulating
'**Anregung** f stimulation; suggestion
'**Anregungsmittel** n PHARM stimulant
'**Anreiz** m incentive
'**anrichten** v/t (sep, -ge-, h) GASTR prepare, dress; cause, do (damage etc)
'**anrüchig** ['anrʏçɪç] adj disreputable
'**Anruf** m call (a. TEL)
'**Anrufbeantworter** m TEL answering machine
'**anrufen** v/t (irr, rufen, sep, -ge-, h) TEL call or ring up, phone
'**anrühren** v/t (sep, -ge-, h) touch; mix
'**Ansage** f announcement
'**ansagen** v/t (sep, -ge-, h) announce
'**Ansager** ['anzaːɡɐ] m (-s; -), '**Ansagerin** [-gərɪn] f (-; -nen) announcer
'**ansammeln** v/t and v/refl (sep, -ge-, h) accumulate
'**Ansammlung** f collection, accumulation; crowd
'**Ansatz** m start (**zu** of); attempt (**zu** at); approach; TECH attachment; MATH set--up; pl first signs
'**anschaffen** v/t (sep, -ge-, h) get; **sich et. anschaffen** buy or get (o.s.) s.th.
'**Anschaffung** f (-; -en) purchase, buy
'**anschauen** v/t (sep, -ge-, h) → **ansehen**
'**anschaulich** adj graphic (account etc)
'**Anschauung** f (-; -en) (**von**) view (of), opinion (about, of)
'**Anschauungsmateri**al n PED visual aids
'**Anschein** m (-[e]s; no pl) appearance; **allem Anschein nach** to all appearances; **den Anschein erwecken, als (ob)** give the impression of …
'**anscheinend** adv apparently
'**anschieben** v/t (irr, schieben, sep, -ge-, h) give a push (a. MOT)
'**Anschlag** m attack; poster; bill, notice; typewriter: stroke; MUS, swimming: touch; **e-n Anschlag auf j-n verüben** make an attempt on s.o.'s life
'**Anschlagbrett** n bulletin (esp Br notice) board
'**anschlagen** (irr, schlagen, sep, -ge-, h) **1.** v/t post; MUS strike; chip (cup etc); **2.** v/i dog: bark; take (effect) (a. MED); swimming: touch the wall
'**anschließen** v/t (irr, schließen, sep, -ge-, h) ELECTR, TECH connect; **sich anschließen** follow; agree with; **sich j-m or e-r Sache anschließen** join s.o. or s.th.

'**anschließend 1.** adj following; **2.** adv then, afterwards
'**Anschluss** m connection; **im Anschluss an** (acc) following; **Anschluss finden** (**bei**) make contact or friends (with); **Anschluss bekommen** TEL get through
'**anschmiegen** v/refl (sep, -ge-, h) snuggle up (**an** acc to)
'**anschmiegsam** adj affectionate
'**anschnallen** v/t (sep, -ge-, h) strap on, put on (a. ski); **sich anschnallen** AVIAT, MOT fasten one's seat belt
'**anschnauzen** F v/t (sep, -ge-, h) tell s.o. off, Am a. bawl s.o. out
'**anschneiden** v/t (irr, schneiden, sep, -ge-, h) cut; fig bring up
'**anschrauben** v/t (sep, -ge-, h) screw on (**an** acc to)
'**anschreiben** v/t (irr, schreiben, sep, -ge-, h) write on the (black)board; **j-n anschreiben** write to s.o.; (**et.**) **anschreiben lassen** buy (s.th.) on credit; → **angeschrieben**
'**anschreien** v/t (irr, schreien, sep, -ge-, h) shout at
'**Anschrift** f address
'**Anschuldigung** f (-; -en) accusation
'**anschwellen** v/i (irr, schwellen, sep, -ge-, en) swell (a. fig)
'**anschwemmen** v/t (sep, -ge-, h) wash ashore
'**ansehen** v/t (irr, sehen, sep, -ge-, h) look at, have or take a look at; watch; see (all a. **sich** [dat] **ansehen**); observe; **et. mit ansehen** watch or witness s.th.; **man sieht ihm an, dass** … one can see that …
'**Ansehen** n (-s; no pl) reputation
'**ansehnlich** ['anzeːnlɪç] adj considerable
'**anseilen** v/t and v/refl (sep, -ge-, h) rope
'**ansetzen** (sep, -ge-, h) **1.** v/t put (**an** acc to); put on, add; fix, set (date etc); **Fett** etc ansetzen put on weight etc; **2.** v/i: **ansetzen zu** prepare for (landing etc)
'**Ansicht** f (-; -en) view, a. opinion, a. sight; **der Ansicht sein, dass …** be of the opinion that …; **meiner Ansicht nach** in my opinion; **zur Ansicht** ECON on approval
'**Ansichtskarte** f picture postcard
'**Ansichtssache** f matter of opinion
'**anspannen** v/t (sep, -ge-, h) strain
'**Anspannung** f (-; -en) strain, exertion
'**anspielen** v/i (sep, -ge-, h) soccer: kick off; **anspielen auf** (acc) allude to, hint at
'**Anspielung** f (-; -en) allusion, hint
'**anspitzen** v/t (sep, -ge-, h) sharpen
'**Ansporn** m (-[e]s; no pl) incentive
'**anspornen** v/t (sep, -ge-, h) encourage,

spur *s.o.* on

'Ansprache *f* address, speech; *e-e Ansprache halten* deliver an address

'ansprechen *v/t* (*irr*, *sprechen*, *sep*, *-ge-*, *h*) address, speak to; *fig* appeal to

ansprechend *adj* attractive

'Ansprechpartner *m* s.o. to talk to, contact

'anspringen (*irr*, *springen*, *sep*, *-ge-*) **1.** *v/i* (*sein*) *engine:* start; **2.** *v/t* (*h*) jump (up)on

'anspritzen *v/t* (*sep*, *-ge-*, *h*) spatter

'Anspruch *m* claim (*auf acc* to) (*a.* JUR); *Anspruch haben auf* (*acc*) be entitled to; *Anspruch erheben auf* (*acc*) claim; *Zeit in Anspruch nehmen* take up time

'anspruchslos *adj* modest; light, undemanding (*reading etc*); *contp* trivial

'anspruchsvoll *adj* demanding; sophisticated, refined (*tastes etc*)

Anstalt ['anʃtalt] *f* (*-*; *-en*) establishment, institution; mental hospital; *Anstalten machen zu* get ready for

'Anstand *m* (*-[e]s*; *no pl*) decency; manners

'anständig *adj* decent (*a. fig*)

'anstandslos *adv* unhesitatingly; without difficulty

'anstarren *v/t* (*sep*, *-ge-*, *h*) stare at

an'statt *prp* (*gen*) *and cj* instead of

'anstechen *v/t* (*irr*, *stechen*, *sep*, *-ge-*, *h*) tap (*barrel*)

'anstecken *v/t* (*sep*, *-ge-*, *h*) stick on; put on (*ring*); light; set fire to; MED infect; *sich bei j-m anstecken* MED catch s.th. from s.o.

ansteckend *adj* MED infectious, contagious, catching (*all a. fig*)

'Anstecknadel *f* pin, button

'Ansteckung *f* (*-*; *no pl*) MED infection, contagion

'anstehen *v/i* (*irr*, *stehen*, *sep*, *-ge-*, *h* (*nach* for) stand in line, *Br* queue up

'ansteigen *v/i* (*irr*, *steigen*, *sep*, *-ge-*, *sein*) rise

'anstellen *v/t* (*sep*, *-ge-*, *h*) engage, employ; TV *etc:* turn on; MOT start; F be up to (*s.th. illegal etc*); make (*inquiries etc*); *sich anstellen* line up (*nach* for), *Br* queue up (for); F (make a) fuss

'Anstellung *f* job, position; *e-e Anstellung finden* find employment

Anstieg ['anʃtiːk] *m* (*-[e]s*; *no pl*) rise, increase

'anstiften *v/t* (*sep*, *-ge-*, *h*) incite

'Anstifter *m* instigator

'Anstiftung *f* incitement

'anstimmen *v/t* (*sep*, *-ge-*, *h*) MUS strike up

'Anstoß *m* soccer: kickoff; *fig* initiative,

impulse; offen|se, *Br* -ce; *Anstoß erregen* give offense (*bei* to); *Anstoß nehmen an* take offense at; *den Anstoß zu et. geben* start s.th., initiate s.th.

'anstoßen (*irr*, *stoßen*, *sep*, *-ge-*) **1.** *v/t* (*h*) nudge *s.o.*; **2.** *v/i a*) (*sein*) knock, bump, b) (*h*) clink glasses; *anstoßen auf* (*acc*) drink to *s.o. or s.th.*

anstößig ['anʃtøːsɪç] *adj* offensive

'anstrahlen *v/t* (*sep*, *-ge-*, *h*) illuminate; beam at *s.o.*

'anstreichen *v/t* (*irr*, *streichen*, *sep*, *-ge-*, *h*) paint; PED mark (*mistakes etc*)

'Anstreicher *m* (house)painter

'anstrengen *v/refl* (*sep*, *-ge-*, *h*) try (hard), make an effort

anstrengend *adj* strenuous, hard

'Anstrengung *f* (*-*; *-en*) exertion, strain; effort

Ansturm *fig m* (*-[e]s*; *no pl*) rush (*auf acc* for)

Anteil *m* share (*a.* ECON), portion; *Anteil nehmen an* (*dat*) take an interest in; sympathize with

Anteilnahme [-naːmə] *f* (*-*; *no pl*) sympathy; interest

Antenne [an'tɛnə] *f* (*-*; *-n*) antenna, *Br* aerial

Anti-..., anti... *in cpds* anti...

Antialko'holiker *m* teetotal(l)er

Anti'babypille F *f* birth control pill, F the pill

Anti'biotikum *n* MED antibiotic

Antiblo'ckiersys,tem *n* MOT anti-lock braking system

antik [an'tiːk] *adj* antique, HIST *a.* ancient

An'tike *f* (*-*; *no pl*) ancient world

'Antikörper *m* MED antibody

Antilope [anti'loːpə] *f* (*-*; *-n*) zo antelope

Antipathie [antipa'tiː] *f* (*-*; *-n*) antipathy

Antiquariat [antikva'rjaːt] *n* (*-[e]s*; *-e*) second-hand bookshop

antiquarisch [anti'kvaːrɪʃ] *adj and adv* second-hand

Antiquitäten [antikvi'tɛːtən] *pl* antiques

Antiquitätenladen *m* antique shop

Antisemit [-ze'miːt] *m* (*-en*; *-en*) anti--Semite

antise'mitisch *adj* anti-Semitic

Antisemitismus [-zemi'tɪsmʊs] *m* (*-*; *no pl*) anti-Semitism

Antrag ['antraːk] *m* (*-[e]s*; *Anträge* ['antrɛːgə]) application; PARL motion; proposal; *Antrag stellen auf* (*acc*) make an application for; PARL move for

Antragsteller(in)[-ʃtɛlɐ(-lərɪn)] *m* (*-s*; *-/-*; *-nen*) applicant; PARL mover

'antreiben (*irr*, *treiben*, *sep*, *-ge-*) **1.** *v/t* (*h*) TECH drive; urge *s.o.* (on); **2.** *v/i* (*sein*) float ashore

'**antreten** (*irr*, **treten**, *sep*, *-ge-*) **1.** *v/t* (*h*) enter upon (*office etc*); take up (*position*); set out on (*journey*); **2.** *v/i* (*sein*) take one's place; MIL line up

'**Antrieb** *m* TECH drive (*a. fig*), propulsion; *fig* motive, impulse; **aus eigenem Antrieb** of one's own accord

'**antun** *v/t* (*irr*, **tun**, *sep*, *-ge-*, *h*) **j-m et. antun** do s.th. to s.o.; **sich et. antun** lay hands on o.s.

'**Antwort** ['antvɔrt] *f* (*-*; *-en*) answer (**auf** *acc*), reply (to)

'**antworten** *v/i* (*ge-*, *h*) answer (**j-m** s.o., **auf** s.th.), reply (to s.o. *or* s.th.)

'**anvertrauen** *v/t* (*sep*, *no -ge-*, *h*) **j-m et. anvertrauen** (*en*)trust s.o. with s.th.; confide s.th. to s.o.

'**anwachsen** *v/i* (*irr*, **wachsen**, *sep*, *-ge-*, *sein*) BOT take root; *fig* increase

Anwalt ['anvalt] *m* (*-[e]s*; *Anwälte* ['anvɛltə]) → **Rechtsanwalt**

'**Anwärter** *m* candidate (**auf** *acc* for)

'**anweisen** *v/t* (*irr*, **weisen**, *sep*, *-ge-*, *h*) instruct; direct, order

'**Anweisung** *f* instruction; order

'**anwenden** *v/t* ([*irr*, **wenden**,] *sep*, *-ge-*, *h*) use; apply (**auf** *acc* to)

'**Anwendung** *f* use; application

'**anwerben** *v/t* (*irr*, **werben**, *sep*, *-ge-*, *h*) recruit (*a. fig*)

'**Anwesen** *n* (*-s*; *-*) estate; property

'**anwesend** *adj* present

'**Anwesenheit** *f* (*-*; *no pl*) presence; PED attendance; **die Anwesenheit feststellen** call the roll

'**Anwesenheitsliste** *f* attendance record (*Br* list)

anwidern ['anvi:dɐn] *v/t* (*sep*, *-ge-*, *h*) make *s.o.* sick

'**Anzahl** *f* (*-*; *no pl*) number, quantity

'**anzahlen** *v/t* (*sep*, *-ge-*, *h*) pay on account

'**Anzahlung** *f* down payment

'**anzapfen** *v/t* (*sep*, *-ge-*, *h*) tap

'**Anzeichen** *n* symptom (*a.* MED), sign

Anzeige ['antsaigə] *f* (*-*; *-n*) advertisement; announcement; JUR information; EDP display; TECH reading

'**anzeigen** *v/t* (*sep*, *-ge-*, *h*) announce; report to the police; TECH indicate, show

'**anziehen** *v/t* (*irr*, **ziehen**, *sep*, *-ge-*, *h*) put on (*dress etc*); dress *s.o.*; *fig* attract, draw; tighten (*screw*); pull (*lever etc*); **sich anziehen** get dressed; dress

anziehend *adj* attractive

'**Anziehung** *f* (*-*; *no pl*), '**Anziehungskraft** *f* (*-*; *no pl*) PHYS attraction, *fig a.* appeal

'**Anzug** *m* suit

anzüglich ['antsy:klıç] *adj* suggestive (*joke*); personal, offensive (*remark etc*)

'**anzünden** *v/t* (*sep*, *-ge-*, *h*) light; set on fire

apart [a'part] *adj* striking

Apartment [a'partmənt] *n* (*-s*; *-s*) studio (apartment *or Br* flat)

apathisch [a'pa:tıʃ] *adj* apathetic

Apfel ['apfəl] *m* (*-s*; *Äpfel* ['ɛpfəl]) BOT apple

Apfelmus *n* GASTR apple sauce

Apfelsine [apfəl'zi:nə] *f* (*-*; *-n*) BOT orange

'**Apfelwein** *m* cider

Apostel [a'pɔstəl] *m* (*-s*; *-*) REL apostle

Apostroph [apo'stro:f] *m* (*-s*; *-e*) apostrophe

Apotheke [apo'te:kə] *f* (*-*; *-n*) pharmacy, drugstore, *Br* chemist's

Apotheker [apo'te:kɐ] *m* (*-s*; *-*), **Apo'thekerin** *f* (*-*; *-nen*) pharmacist, druggist, *Br* chemist

App. ABBR *of* **Apparat** TEL ext., extension

Apparat [apa'ra:t] *m* (*-[e]s*; *-e*) apparatus; device; (tele)phone; radio; TV set; camera; POL *etc* machine(ry); **am Apparat!** TEL speaking!; **am Apparat bleiben** TEL hold the line

Appell [a'pɛl] *m* (*-s*; *-e*) appeal (**an** *acc* to); MIL roll call

appellieren [apɛ'li:rən] *v/i* (*no -ge-*, *h*) (make an) appeal (**an** *acc* to)

Appetit [ape'ti:t] *m* (*-[e]s*; *no pl*) appetite (**auf** *acc* for); **Appetit auf et. haben** feel like s.th.; **guten Appetit!** enjoy your meal!

appe'titanregend *adj* appetizing

Appe'tithappen *m* GASTR appetizer

appe'titlich *adj* appetizing, savo(u)ry, *fig a.* inviting

applaudieren [aplau'di:rən] *v/i* (*no -ge-*, *h*) applaud

Applaus [a'plaus] *m* (*-es*; *no pl*) applause

Aprikose [apri'ko:zə] *f* (*-*; *-n*) BOT apricot

April [a'prıl] *m* (*-[s]*; *no pl*) April; **April!** April fool!

Aquaplaning [akva'pla:nıŋ] *n* (*-[s]*; *no pl*) MOT hydroplaning, *Br* aquaplaning

Aquarell [akva'rɛl] *n* (*-s*; *-e*) watercolo(u)r

Aquarium [a'kva:rjʊm] *n* (*-s*; *-ien*) aquarium

Äquator [ɛ'kva:to:ɐ] *m* (*-s*; *no pl*) equator

Ära ['ɛ:ra] *f* (*-*; *no pl*) era

Araber ['arabɐ] *m* (*-s*; *-*), **Araberin** [-bə-rın] *f* (*-*; *-nen*) Arab

arabisch [a'ra:bıʃ] *adj* Arabian; Arabic

Arbeit ['arbait] *f* (*-*; *-en*) work, ECON, POL *a.* labo(u)r; employment, job; PED test; *scientific etc* paper; workmanship; **bei der Arbeit** at work; **zur Arbeit gehen**

or fahren go to work; *gute Arbeit leisten* make a good job of it; *sich an die Arbeit machen* set to work

'arbeiten *v/i* (*ge-*, *h*) work (*an dat* at, on)

'Arbeiter *m* (*-s*; *-*), 'Arbeiterin *f* (*-*; *-nen*) worker

'Arbeitgeber *m* (*-s*; *-*) employer

'Arbeitnehmer *m* (*-s*; *-*) employee

'Arbeitsamt *n Am* labor office, *Br* job centre

Arbeitsblatt *n* PED worksheet

Arbeitserlaubnis *f* green card, *Br* work permit

'arbeitsfähig *adj* fit for work

'Arbeitsgang *m* TECH operation

Arbeitsgemeinschaft *f* work *or* study group

Arbeitsgericht *n* JUR labor court, *Br* industrial tribunal

Arbeitshose *f* overalls

Arbeitskleidung *f* working clothes

Arbeitskräfte *pl* workers, labo(u)r

'arbeitslos *adj* unemployed, out of work

'Arbeitslose *m*, *f* (*-n*; *-n*) *die Arbeitslosen pl* the unemployed

'Arbeitslosengeld *n* unemployment compensation (*Br* benefit); *Arbeitslosengeld beziehen* F be on the dole

'Arbeitslosigkeit *f* (*-*; *no pl*) unemployment

'Arbeitsmarkt *m* labo(u)r market

Arbeitsmi,nister *m Am* Secretary of Labor; *Br* Minister of Labour

Arbeitsniederlegung *f* strike, walkout

Arbeitspause *f* break, intermission

Arbeitsplatz *m* workplace; job

'arbeitsscheu *adj* work-shy

'Arbeitsspeicher *m* EDP main memory

Arbeitssuche *f*: *er ist auf Arbeitssuche* he is looking for a job

Arbeitssüchtige *m*, *f* workaholic

Arbeitstag *m* workday

'arbeitsunfähig *adj* unfit for work; *permanently* disabled

'Arbeitsweise *f* method (of working)

Arbeitszeit *f* (*gleitende* flexible) working hours

Arbeitszeitverkürzung *f* fewer working hours

Arbeitszimmer *n* study

Archäologe [arçɛoˈloːgə] *m* (*-n*; *-n*) arch(a)eologist

Archäologie [arçɛoloˈgiː] *f* (*-*; *no pl*) arch(a)eology

Archäo'login *f* (*-*; *-nen*) arch(a)eologist

Arche [ˈarçə] *f* (*-*; *-n*) ark; *die Arche Noah* Noah's ark

Architekt [arçiˈtɛkt] *m* (*-en*; *-en*), Archi-'tektin *f* (*-*; *-nen*) architect

architektonisch [-tɛkˈtoːnɪʃ] *adj* architectural

Architektur [-tɛkˈtuːɐ] *f* (*-*; *-en*) architecture

Archiv [arˈçiːf] *n* (*-s*; *-e*) archives; record office

Arena [aˈreːna] *f* (*-*; *-nen*) ring

Ärger [ˈɛrgɐ] *m* (*-s*; *no pl*) anger (*über acc* at); trouble; F *j-m Ärger machen* cause s.o. trouble

'ärgerlich *adj* angry (*über*, *auf acc* at s.th.; with s.o.); annoying

'ärgern *v/t* (*ge-*, *h*) annoy; *sich ärgern* be annoyed (*über acc* at, about s.th., with s.o.)

'Ärgernis *n* (*-ses*; *-se*) nuisance

arglos [ˈarkloːs] *adj* innocent

Argwohn [ˈarkvoːn] *m* (*-[e]s*; *no pl*) suspicion (*gegen* of)

'argwöhnisch [-vøːnɪʃ] *adj* suspicious

Arie [ˈaːrjə] *f* (*-*; *-n*) MUS aria

Aristokratie [aristokraˈtiː] *f* (*-*; *-n*) aristocracy

arm [arm] *adj* poor; *die Armen* the poor

Arm *m* (*-[e]s*; *-e*) ANAT arm; GEOGR branch; F *j-n auf den Arm nehmen* pull s.o.'s leg

Armaturen [armaˈtuːrən] *pl* TECH instruments; (plumbing) fixtures

Armaturenbrett *n* MOT dashboard

'Armband *n* bracelet

'Armbanduhr *f* wrist-watch

Armee [arˈmeː] *f* (*-*; *-n*) MIL armed forces; army

Ärmel [ˈɛrməl] *m* (*-s*; *-*) sleeve

ärmlich [ˈɛrmlɪç] *adj* poor (*a. fig*); shabby

'Armreif(en) *m* bangle

'armselig *adj* wretched, miserable

Armut [ˈarmuːt] *f* (*-*; *no pl*) poverty; *Armut an* (*dat*) lack of

Aroma [aˈroːma] *n* (*-s*; *-men*) flavo(u)r; aroma

Arrest [aˈrɛst] *m* (*-[e]s*; *-e*) PED detention; *Arrest bekommen* be kept in

arrogant [aroˈgant] *adj* arrogant, conceited

Arsch [arʃ] V *m* (*-es*; *Ärsche* [ˈɛrʃə]) ass, *Br* arse

Arschloch V *n* asshole, *Br* arsehole

Art [art] *f* (*-*; *-en*) way, manner; kind, sort; BIOL species; *auf diese Art* (in) this way; *e-e Art …* a sort of …; *Geräte aller Art* all kinds *or* sorts of tools

'Artenschutz *m* protection of endangered species

Arterie [arˈteːrjə] *f* (*-*; *-n*) ANAT artery

Ar'terienverkalkung *f* MED arteriosclerosis

Arthritis [arˈtriːtɪs] *f* (*-*; *-tiden*) MED arthritis

artig ['artıç] *adj* good, well-behaved; *sei artig!* be good!, be a good boy (*or* girl)!

Artikel [ar'ti:kəl] *m* (-s; -) article

Artillerie [artılə'ri:] *f* (-; *no pl*) MIL artillery

Artist [ar'tıst] *m* (-en; -en), **Ar'tistin** *f* (-; -nen) acrobat, (circus) performer

Arznei [a:rts'nai] *f* (-; -en), **Arzneimittel** *n* medicine, drug

Arzt [a:rtst] *m* (-es; *Ärzte* ['ɛ:rtstə]) doctor, physician

Ärztin ['ɛ:rtstın] *f* (-; -nen) (lady) doctor *or* physician

'ärztlich *adj* medical; *sich ärztlich behandeln lassen* undergo treatment

As [as] *n* (-; -) MUS A flat

Asbest [as'bɛst] *m* (-[e]s; -e) asbestos

Asche ['aʃə] *f* (-; -n) ash(es)

'Aschenbahn *f* SPORT cinder-track, MOT dirt track

Aschenbecher *m* ashtray

Ascher'mittwoch *m* Ash Wednesday

äsen ['ɛ:zən] *v/i* (ge-, h) HUNT feed, browse

Asiat [a'zja:t] *m* (-en; -en), **Asi'atin** *f* (-; -nen) Asian

asi'atisch *adj* Asian, Asiatic

Asien ['a:zjən] *n* (-s; *no pl*) Asia

Asket [as'ke:t] *m* (-en; -en), **as'ketisch** *adj* ascetic

'asozial *adj* antisocial

Asphalt [as'falt] *m* (-s; -e) asphalt

asphaltieren [asfal'ti:rən] *v/t* (*no* -ge-, h) (cover with) asphalt

Ass [as] *n* (-es; -e) ace (*a.* tennis and *fig*)

aß [a:s] *pret of* **essen**

Assistent [asıs'tɛnt] *m* (-en; -en), **Assis'tentin** *f* (-; -nen) assistant

Assis'tenzarzt *m* Am intern, Br houseman

Ast [ast] *m* (-es; *Äste* ['ɛstə]) BOT branch

Astronaut [astro'naut] *m* (-en; -en), **Astro'nautin** *f* (-; -nen) astronaut

Astronom [astro'no:m] *m* (-en; -en) astronomer

Astronomie [-no'mi:] *f* (-; *no pl*) astronomy

ASU ['a:zu] *ABBR of* **Abgas-Sonder-Untersuchung** MOT *Am* emissions test, *Br* exhaust emission test

Asyl [a'zy:l] *n* (-s; -e) asylum

Asylant [azy'lant] *m* (-en; -en), **Asy'lantin** *f* (-; -nen) asylum seeker, (political) refugee

A'sylbewerber(in) asylum seeker

Asylrecht *n* right of (political) asylum

Atelier [ate'lje:] *n* (-s; -s) studio

Atem ['a:təm] *m* (-s; *no pl*) breath; *außer Atem* out of breath; *(tief) Atem holen*

take a (deep) breath

'atemberaubend *adj* breathtaking

'Atemgerät *n* MED respirator

'atemlos *adj* breathless

'Atempause *f* F breather

'Atemzug *m* breath

Äther ['ɛ:tər] *m* (-s; *no pl*) CHEM ether; *radio etc:* air

Athlet [at'le:t] *m* (-en; -en), **Ath'letin** *f* (-; -nen) SPORT athlete

ath'letisch *adj* athletic

Atlas ['atlas] *m* (-ses; -se, *Atlanten*) atlas

atmen ['a:tmən] *v/i and v/t* (ge-, h) breathe

Atmosphäre [atmo'sfɛ:rə] *f* (-; -n) atmosphere

'Atmung *f* (-; *no pl*) breathing, respiration

Atoll [a'tɔl] *n* (-s; -e) atoll

Atom [a'to:m] *n* (-s; -e) atom

A'tom... *in cpds* -energie, -forschung, -kraft, -krieg, -müll, -rakete, -reaktor, -waffen *etc* nuclear ...

atomar [ato'ma:r] *adj* atomic, nuclear

A'tombombe *f* MIL atom(ic) bomb

A'tomkern *m* PHYS (atomic) nucleus

a'tomwaffenfrei *adj* nuclear-free

Attentat ['atənta:t] *n* (-[e]s; -e) assassination attempt, attempt on *s.o.*'s life; *Opfer e-s Attentats werden* be assassinated

'Attentäter *m* (-s; -) assassin

Attest [a'tɛst] *n* (-[e]s; -e) (doctor's) certificate

Attraktion [atrak'tsjo:n] *f* (-; -en) attraction

attraktiv [-'ti:f] *adj* attractive

Attrappe [a'trapə] *f* (-; -n) dummy

Attribut [atri'bu:t] *n* (-[e]s; -e) LING attribute (*a. fig*)

ätzend ['ɛtsənt] *adj* corrosive, caustic (*a. fig*); F gross; *das ist echt ätzend* it's the pits

au [au] *int* ouch!; *au fein!* oh, good!

Aubergine [ober'ʒi:nə] *f* (-; -n) BOT eggplant, *Br* aubergine

auch [aux] *cj* also, too, as well; *ich auch* so am (*or* do) I, F me too; *auch nicht* not ... either; *wenn auch* even if; *wo auch (immer)* wherever; *ist es auch wahr?* is it really true?

Audienz [au'djɛnts] *f* (-; -en) audience (*bei* with)

auf [auf] *prp* (*dat and acc*) *and adv* on; in; at; open; up; *auf Seite 20* on page 20; *auf der Straße* on (*Br* in) the street; on the road; *auf der Welt* in the world; *auf See* at sea; *auf dem Lande* in the country; *auf dem Bahnhof etc* at the station *etc*; *auf Urlaub* on vacation; *die Uhr stellen auf* (*acc*) set the watch to; *auf* *deutsch* in German; *auf deinen Wunsch* at your request; *auf die Sekunde genau* to the second; *auf und ab* up and down

'aufarbeiten *v/t* (*sep*, *-ge-*, *h*) catch up on (*backlog*); refurbish

aufatmen *v/i* (*sep*, *-ge-*, *h*) heave a sigh of relief

'Aufbau *m* (*-[e]s*; *no pl*) building (up); structure

'aufbauen *v/t* (*sep*, *-ge-*, *h*) build (up) (*a. fig*); set up; construct

'aufbauschen *v/t* (*sep*, *-ge-*, *h*) exaggerate

aufbekommen *v/t* (*irr*, *kommen*, *sep*, *no -ge-*, *h*) get *door etc* open; be given (*a task etc*)

aufbereiten *v/t* (*sep*, *no -ge-*, *h*) process, clean, treat

aufbessern *v/t* (*sep*, *-ge-*, *h*) raise (*salary etc*)

aufbewahren *v/t* (*sep*, *no -ge-*, *h*) keep

aufbieten *v/t* (*irr*, *bieten*, *sep*, *-ge-*, *h*) muster

aufblasen *v/t* (*irr*, *blasen*, *sep*, *-ge-*, *h*) blow up

aufbleiben *v/i* (*irr*, *bleiben*, *sep*, *-ge-*, *sein*) stay up; *door etc*: remain open

aufblenden *v/i* (*sep*, *-ge-*, *h*) MOT turn the headlights up

aufblicken *v/i* (*sep*, *-ge-*, *h*) look up (*zu* at) (*a. fig*)

aufblitzen *v/i* (*sep*, *-ge-*, *h*, *sein*) flash (*a. fig*)

'aufbrausen *v/i* (*sep*, *-ge-*, *sein*) fly into a temper

aufbrausend *adj* irascible

'aufbrechen (*irr*, *brechen*, *sep*, *-ge-*) **1.** *v/t* (*h*) break *or* force open; **2.** *v/i* (*sein*) burst open; *fig* leave (**nach** for)

'aufbringen *v/t* (*irr*, *bringen*, *sep*, *-ge-*, *h*) raise (*money*); muster (*courage etc*); start (*fashion etc*); → *aufgebracht*

'Aufbruch *m* (*-[e]s*; *no pl*) departure, start

'aufbrühen *v/t* (*sep*, *-ge-*, *h*) make

aufbürden *v/t* (*sep*, *-ge-*, *h*) *j-m et. aufbürden* burden s.o. with s.th.

aufdecken *v/t* (*sep*, *-ge-*, *h*) uncover

aufdrängen *v/t* (*sep*, *-ge-*, *h*) *j-m et. aufdrängen* force s.th. on s.o.; *sich j-m aufdrängen* impose on s.o.; *sich aufdrängen fig* suggest itself

aufdrehen *v/t* (*sep*, *-ge-*, *h*) **1.** *v/t* turn on; **2.** *v/i* MOT step on the gas

'aufdringlich *adj* obtrusive

'Aufdruck *m* imprint; *on stamps*: overprint, surcharge

aufei'nander *adv* on top of each other; one after another; *aufeinanderfolgend adj* successive

---

Aufenthalt ['aufɛnthalt] *m* (*-[e]s*; *-e*) stay; RAIL stop

'Aufenthaltsgenehmigung *f* residence permit

Aufenthaltsraum *m* lounge, recreation room

'auferstehen *v/i* (*irr*, *stehen*, *sep*, *no -ge-*, *sein*) rise (from the dead)

'Auferstehung *f* (*-*; *-en*) REL resurrection

'aufessen *v/t* (*irr*, *essen*, *sep*, *-ge-*, *h*) eat up

'auffahren *v/i* (*irr*, *fahren*, *sep*, *-ge-*, *sein*) crash (*auf acc* into); *fig* start up

'Auffahrt *f* approach; driveway, *Br* drive

'Auffahrunfall *m* MOT rear-end collision; pileup

'auffallen *v/i* (*irr*, *fallen*, *sep*, *-ge-*, *sein*) attract attention; *j-m auffallen* strike s.o.

'auffallend, 'auffällig *adj* striking; conspicuous; flashy (*clothes*)

'auffangen *v/t* (*irr*, *fangen*, *sep*, *-ge-*, *h*) catch (*a. fig*)

'auffassen *v/t* (*sep*, *-ge-*, *h*) understand (*als* as)

'Auffassung *f* view; interpretation

'auffinden *v/t* (*irr*, *finden*, *sep*, *-ge-*, *h*) find, discover

'auffordern *v/t* (*sep*, *-ge-*, *h*) *j-n auffordern, et. zu tun* ask (*or* tell) s.o. to do s.th.

'Aufforderung *f* request; demand

'auffrischen *v/t* (*sep*, *-ge-*, *h*) freshen up; brush up

'aufführen *v/t* (*sep*, *-ge-*, *h*) THEA *etc* perform, present; state; *sich aufführen* behave

'Aufführung *f* THEA *etc* performance; *film*: showing

'Aufgabe *f* task, job; duty; PED task, assignment; MATH problem; *fig* surrender; *es sich zur Aufgabe machen* make it one's business

'Aufgang *m* staircase; AST rising

aufgeben (*irr*, *geben*, *sep*, *-ge-*, *h*) **1.** *v/t* give up; mail, send, *Br* post; check (*baggage*); PED set, give, assign (*homework etc*); ECON place (*order etc*); **2.** *v/i* give up *or* in

'aufgebracht *adj* furious

aufgedreht F *adj* excited

aufgedunsen ['aufgədʊnzən] *adj* puffed(-up)

'aufgehen *v/i* (*irr*, *gehen*, *sep*, *-ge-*, *sein*) open; *sun*, *dough etc*: rise; MATH come out even; *in Flammen aufgehen* go up in flames

'aufgehoben *fig adj*: *gut aufgehoben sein bei* be in good hands with

aufgelegt *adj*: *zu et. aufgelegt sein* feel

like (doing) s.th.; *gut* (*schlecht*) *aufgelegt* in a good (bad) mood

aufgeregt *adj* excited; nervous

aufgeschlossen *fig adj* open-minded; *aufgeschlossen für* open to

aufgeweckt *fig adj* bright

'**aufgreifen** *v/t* (*irr*, *greifen*, *sep*, *-ge-*, *h*) pick up

auf'grund (*gen*) because of

'**aufhaben** F *v/t* (*irr*, *haben*, *sep*, *-ge-*, *h*) have on, wear; PED have *homework etc* to do

aufhalten *v/t* (*irr*, *halten*, *sep*, *-ge-*, *h*) stop, hold up (*a. traffic*, *thief etc*); keep open; *sich aufhalten* (*bei j-m*) stay (with s.o.)

aufhängen *v/t* (*sep*, *-ge-*, *h*) hang (up); *j-n aufhängen* hang s.o.

aufheben *v/t* (*irr*, *heben*, *sep*, *-ge-*, *h*) pick up; keep; abolish (*law etc*); break up (*meeting etc*); *sich gegenseitig aufheben* neutralize each other; → *aufgehoben*

'**Aufheben** *n* (*-s*; *no pl*) *viel Aufhebens machen* make a fuss (*von* about)

'**aufheitern** *v/t* (*sep*, *-ge-*, *h*) cheer up; *sich aufheitern* weather: clear up

aufhelfen *v/i* (*irr*, *helfen*, *sep*, *-ge-*, *h*) help s.o. up

aufhellen *v/t and v/refl* (*sep*, *-ge-*, *h*) brighten

aufhetzen *v/t* (*sep*, *-ge-*, *h*) *j-n aufhetzen gegen* set s.o. against

aufholen (*sep*, *-ge-*, *h*) **1.** *v/t* make up for; **2.** *v/i* catch up (*gegen* with)

'**aufhorchen** *v/i* (*sep*, *-ge-*, *h*) prick (up) one's ears; *aufhorchen lassen* make s.o. sit up

aufhören *v/i* (*sep*, *-ge-*, *h*) stop, end, finish, quit; *mit et. aufhören* stop (doing) s.th.; *hör(t) auf!* stop it!

aufkaufen *v/t* (*sep*, *-ge-*, *h*) buy up

'**aufklären** *v/t* (*sep*, *-ge-*, *h*) clear up, *a.* solve (*crime*); *j-n aufklären über* (*acc*) inform s.o. about; *j-n* (*sexuell*) *aufklären* F tell s.o. the facts of life

'**Aufklärung** *f* (*-*; *no pl*) clearing up, solution; information; sex education; PHILOS Enlightenment; MIL reconnaissance

'**aufkleben** *v/t* (*sep*, *-ge-*, *h*) paste *or* stick on

'**Aufkleber** *m* (*-s*; *-*) sticker

'**aufknöpfen** *v/t* (*sep*, *-ge-*, *h*) unbutton

'**aufkommen** *v/i* (*irr*, *kommen*, *sep*, *-ge-*, *sein*) come up; come into fashion *or* use; *rumo*(*u*)*r etc*: arise; *aufkommen für* sg (for)

'**aufladen** *v/t* (*irr*, *laden*, *sep*, *-ge-*, *h*) load; ELECTR charge

'**Auflage** *f* edition; circulation

'**auflassen** F *v/t* (*irr*, *lassen*, *sep*, *-ge-*, *h*) leave *door etc* open; keep *one's hat etc* on

auflauern *v/i* (*sep*, *-ge-*, *h*) *j-m auflauern* waylay s.o.

'**Auflauf** *m* crowd; GASTR soufflé, pudding

'**auflaufen** *v/i* (*irr*, *laufen*, *sep*, *-ge-*, *sein*) MAR run aground

aufleben *v/i* (*sep*, *-ge-*, *sein*) *a.* (*wieder*) *aufleben lassen* revive

auflegen (*sep*, *-ge-*, *h*) **1.** *v/t* put on, lay on; **2.** *v/i* TEL hang up

auflehnen *v/t and v/refl* (*sep*, *-ge-*, *h*) lean (*auf acc* on); *sich auflehnen* rebel, revolt (*gegen* against)

'**Auflehnung** *f* (*-*; *-en*) rebellion, revolt

auflesen *v/t* (*irr*, *lesen*, *sep*, *-ge-*, *h*) pick up (*a. fig*)

aufleuchten *v/i* (*sep*, *-ge-*, *h*) flash (up)

'**auflisten** *v/t* (*sep*, *-ge-*, *h*) list (*a.* EDP)

auflockern *v/t* (*sep*, *-ge-*, *h*) loosen up; *fig* liven up

'**auflösen** *v/t* (*sep*, *-ge-*, *h*) dissolve; solve (*a.* MATH); disintegrate

'**Auflösung** *f* (dis)solution; disintegration

'**aufmachen** F *v/t* (*sep*, *-ge-*, *h*) open; *sich aufmachen* set out

'**Aufmachung** *f* (*-*; *-en*) get-up

'**aufmerksam** *adj* attentive (*auf acc* to); thoughtful; *j-n aufmerksam machen auf* (*acc*) call s.o.'s attention to

'**Aufmerksamkeit** *f* (*-*; *-en*) *a*) (*no pl*) attention, b) small present

'**aufmuntern** *v/t* (*sep*, *-ge-*, *h*) encourage; cheer up

Aufnahme ['aufnaːmə] *f* (*-*; *-n*) taking up; reception (*a.* MED *etc*); admission; photo (-graph); recording; *film*: shooting

'**aufnahmefähig** *adj* receptive (*für* of)

'**Aufnahmegebühr** *f* admission fee

Aufnahmeprüfung *f* entrance exam(ination)

'**aufnehmen** *v/t* (*irr*, *nehmen*, *sep*, *-ge-*, *h*) take up (*a. post etc*); pick up; put *s.o.* up; hold; take *s.th.* in; receive; PED *etc* admit; PHOT take a picture of; record; take (*the ball*); *es aufnehmen mit* be a match for

'**aufpassen** *v/i* (*sep*, *-ge-*, *h*) pay attention; take care; *aufpassen auf* (*acc*) take care of, look after; keep an eye on; *pass auf!* look out!

Aufprall *m* (*-*[*e*]*s*; *no pl*) impact

'**aufprallen** *v/i* (*sep*, *-ge-*, *sein*) *aufprallen auf* (*dat or acc*) hit

aufpumpen *v/t* (*sep*, *-ge-*, *h*) pump up

'**aufputschen** *v/t* (*sep*, *-ge-*, *h*) pep up

'**Aufputschmittel** *n* PHARM stimulant, pep pill

'**aufraffen** *v/refl* (*sep*, *-ge-*, *h*) *sich aufraffen zu* bring o.s. to *do s.th.*

aufräumen v/t (sep, -ge-, h) tidy up; clear
'**aufrecht** adj and adv upright (a. fig)
aufrechterhalten v/t (irr, **halten**, sep, no -ge-, h) maintain, keep up
'**aufregen** v/t (sep, -ge-, h) excite, upset; **sich aufregen** get excited or upset (**über** acc about)
aufregend adj exciting
'**Aufregung** f excitement; fuss
'**aufreiben** fig v/t (irr, **reiben**, sep, -ge-, h) wear down
aufreibend adj stressful
'**aufreißen** v/t (irr, **reißen**, sep, -ge-, h) tear open; fling door etc open; open one's eyes wide; F pick s.o. up
'**aufreizend** adj provocative
'**aufrichten** v/t (sep, -ge-, h) put up, raise; **sich aufrichten** straighten up; sit up
'**aufrichtig** adj sincere; frank
'**Aufrichtigkeit** f (-; no pl) sincerity; frankness
'**Aufriss** m (-es; -e) ARCH elevation
'**aufrollen** v/t and v/refl (sep, -ge-, h) roll up
'**Aufruf** m call; appeal (**zu** for)
'**aufrufen** v/t (irr, **rufen**, sep, -ge-, h) call on
'**Aufruhr** ['aufru:ɐ] m (-s; no pl) revolt; riot; turmoil
'**Aufrührer** m (-s; -) rebel; rioter
aufrührerisch ['aufry:rərɪʃ] adj rebellious
'**aufrunden** v/t (sep, -ge-, h) round off
'**aufrüsten** v/t and v/i (sep, -ge-, h) (re)arm
'**Aufrüstung** f (re)armament
'**aufrütteln** fig v/t (sep, -ge-, h) shake up, rouse
aufsagen v/t (sep, -ge-, h) say; a. recite (poem)
aufsässig ['aufzɛsɪç] adj rebellious
'**Aufsatz** m PED essay, Am a. theme; (newspaper etc) article; TECH top
'**aufsaugen** v/t (sep, -ge-, h) absorb (a. fig)
aufscheuern v/t (sep, -ge-, h) chafe
aufschichten v/t (sep, -ge-, h) pile up
aufschieben fig v/t (irr, **schieben**, sep, -ge-, h) put off, postpone; delay
'**Aufschlag** m impact; ECON extra charge; lapel; cuff; (tent); tennis: service
'**aufschlagen** (irr, **schlagen**, sep, -ge-, h) **1.** v/t open (book, eyes etc); pitch (tent); cut (one's knee etc); **Seite 3 aufschlagen** open at page 3; **2.** v/i tennis: serve; **auf dem Boden aufschlagen** hit the ground
'**aufschließen** v/t (irr, **schließen**, sep, -ge-, h) unlock, open
'**aufschlitzen** v/t (sep, -ge-, h) slit or rip open
'**Aufschluss** m information (**über** acc on)

'**aufschnappen** F fig v/t (sep, -ge-, h) pick up
'**aufschneiden** (irr, **schneiden**, sep, -ge-, h) **1.** v/t cut open; GASTR cut up; **2.** F fig v/i brag, boast, talk big
'**Aufschnitt** m (-[e]s; no pl) GASTR cold cuts, Br (slices of) cold meat
'**aufschnüren** v/t (sep, -ge-, h) untie; unlace
aufschrauben v/t (sep, -ge-, h) unscrew
aufschrecken (sep, -ge-) **1.** v/t (h) startle; **2.** v/i (sein) start (up)
'**Aufschrei** m yell; scream, outcry (a. fig)
'**aufschreiben** v/t (irr, **schreiben**, sep, -ge-, h) write down
aufschreien v/i (irr, **schreien**, sep, -ge-, h) cry out, scream
'**Aufschrift** f inscription
'**Aufschub** m postponement; delay; adjournment; respite
'**Aufschwung** m SPORT swing-up; esp ECON recovery, upswing; boom
'**Aufsehen** n (-s; no pl) **Aufsehen erregen** attract attention; cause a sensation; **Aufsehen erregend → aufsehenerregend**
'**aufsehenerregend** adj sensational
'**Aufseher** m (-s; -), '**Aufseherin** f (-; -nen) guard
'**aufsetzen** (sep, -ge-, h) **1.** v/t put on; draw up (letter etc); **sich aufsetzen** sit up; **2.** v/i AVIAT touch down
'**Aufsetzer** m (-s; -) SPORT awkward bouncing ball
'**Aufsicht** f (-; no pl) supervision, control; **Aufsicht führen** PED etc be on (break) duty; proctor, Br invigilate
'**Aufsichtsbehörde** f supervisory board
Aufsichtsrat m ECON board of directors; supervisory board
'**aufsitzen** v/i (irr, **sitzen**, sep, -ge-, sein) mount
aufspannen v/t (sep, -ge-, h) stretch; put up (umbrella); spread
aufsparen v/t (sep, -ge-, h) save
aufsperren v/t (sep, -ge-, h) unlock; F open wide
aufspielen v/refl (sep, -ge-, h) show off; **sich aufspielen als** play
aufspießen v/t (sep, -ge-, h) spear, skewer; animal: gore
aufspringen v/i (irr, **springen**, sep, -ge-, sein) jump up; door etc: fly open; lips etc: chap
aufspüren v/t (sep, -ge-, h) track down
aufstacheln v/t (sep, -ge-, h) goad (s.o. into doing s.th.)
aufstampfen v/i (sep, -ge-, h) stamp (one's foot)

'Aufstand *m* revolt, rebellion

'aufständische *m, f (-n; -n)* rebel

'aufstapeln *v/t (sep, -ge-, h)* pile up

aufstechen *v/t (irr, **stechen**, sep, -ge-, h)* puncture, prick open; MED lance

aufstecken *v/t (sep, -ge-, h)* put up *(hair)*; F *fig* give up

aufstehen *v/i (irr, **stehen**, sep, -ge-, sein)* get up, rise

aufsteigen *v/i (irr, **steigen**, sep, -ge-, sein)* rise *(a. fig)*; get on *(horse, bicycle)*; be promoted; SPORT *Am a.* be moved up to a higher division

'aufstellen *v/t (sep, -ge-, h)* set up, put up; post *(guard)*; set *(trap, record etc)*; nominate *s.o.*; draw up *(table, list etc)*

'Aufstellung *f* putting up; nomination; list; SPORT line-up

Aufstieg ['auf∫tiːk] *m (-[e]s; -e)* ascent, *fig a.* rise

'aufstöbern *fig v/t (sep, -ge-, h)* ferret out

aufstoßen *(irr, **stoßen**, sep, -ge-, h)* **1.** *v/t* push open; **2.** *v/i* belch

aufstützen *v/refl (sep, -ge-, h)* lean *(**auf** acc or dat on)*

aufsuchen *v/t (sep, -ge-, h)* visit; see

'Auftakt *m* MUS upbeat; *fig* prelude

'auftanken *v/t (sep, -ge-, h)* fill up; MOT, AVIAT refuel

auftauchen *v/i (sep, -ge-, sein)* appear; MAR surface

auftauen *v/t (sep, -ge-, h)* thaw; GASTR defrost

aufteilen *v/t (sep, -ge-, h)* divide (up)

Auftrag ['auftraːk] *m (-[e]s; Aufträge* ['auftrɛːgə]) instructions, order *(a.* ECON); MIL mission; *im Auftrag von* on behalf of

auftragen *v/t (irr, **tragen**, sep, -ge-, h)* serve (up) *(food)*; apply *(paint)*; *j-m et. auftragen* ask *(or* tell) *s.o.* to do *s.th;* F *dick auftragen* exaggerate

'Auftraggeber *m (-s; -)* principal; customer

'auftreffen *v/i (irr, **treffen**, sep, -ge-, sein)* strike, hit

auftreiben F *v/t (irr, **treiben**, sep, -ge-, h)* get hold of; raise *(money)*

auftrennen *v/t (sep, -ge-, h)* undo *(seam)*, cut open

auftreten *v/i (irr, **treten**, sep, -ge-, sein)* THEA *etc* appear *(**als** as)*; behave, act; occur

'Auftreten *n (-s; no pl)* appearance; behavio(u)r; occurrence

'Auftrieb *m (-[e]s; no pl)* PHYS buoyancy *(a. fig)*, AVIAT lift; *fig* impetus

'Auftritt *m* THEA entrance

auftun *v/refl (irr, **tun**, sep, -ge-, h)* open *(a.* *fig); abyss:* yawn

auftürmen *v/t (sep, -ge-, h)* pile *or* heap up; *sich auftürmen* pile up

aufwachen *v/i (sep, -ge-, sein)* wake up

aufwachsen *v/i (irr, **wachsen**, sep, -ge-, sein)* grow up

Aufwand ['aufvant] *m (-[e]s; no pl)* expenditure *(**an** dat of), a.* expense; pomp

aufwändig ['aufvɛndɪç] *adj* costly; extravagant *(lifestyle)*

'aufwärmen *v/t (sep, -ge-, h)* warm up; F *fig contp* bring up

aufwärts ['aufvɛrts] *adv* upward(s); *aufwärtsgehen* *v/i (irr, **gehen**, sep, -ge-, sein) fig* improve

'aufwecken *v/t (sep, -ge-, h)* wake (up)

aufweichen *v/t (sep, -ge-, h)* soften; soak

aufweisen *v/t (irr, **weisen**, sep, -ge-, h)* show, have

aufwenden *v/t ([irr, **wenden**,] sep, -ge-, h)* spend *(**für** on); Mühe aufwenden* take pains

aufwendig → **aufwändig**

'aufwerfen *v/t (irr, **werfen**, sep, -ge-, h)* raise *(question etc)*

'aufwerten *v/t (sep, -ge-, h)* ECON revalue; *fig* increase the value of

'Aufwertung *f* revaluation

'aufwickeln *v/t and v/refl (sep, -ge-, h)* wind up, roll up; put *hair* in curlers

aufwiegeln ['aufviːgəln] *v/t (sep, -ge-, h)* stir up, incite, instigate

'aufwiegen *v/t (irr, **wiegen**, sep, -ge-, h)* make up for

Aufwiegler ['aufviːglə] *m (-s; -)* agitator; instigator

'Aufwind *m* upwind; *im Aufwind fig* on the upswing

'aufwirbeln *v/t (sep, -ge-, h)* whirl up; *fig (viel) Staub aufwirbeln* make (quite) a stir

aufwischen *v/t (sep, -ge-, h)* wipe up

aufwühlen *fig v/t (sep, -ge-, h)* stir, move

'aufzählen *v/t (sep, -ge-, h)* name (one by one), list

'Aufzählung *f* enumeration, list

'aufzeichnen *v/t (sep, -ge-, h)* TV, *radio etc:* record, tape; draw

'Aufzeichnung *f* recording; *pl* notes

'aufzeigen *v/t (sep, -ge-, h)* show; demonstrate; point out *(mistake etc)*

'aufziehen *(irr, **ziehen**, sep, -ge-)* **1.** *v/t (h)* draw *or* pull up; (pull) open; bring up *(child)*; wind up *(clock)*; mount *(photo etc)*; *j-n aufziehen* tease *s.o.*; **2.** *v/i (sein)* come up

'Aufzug *m* elevator, *Br* lift; THEA act; F *contp* get-up

'aufzwingen *v/t (irr, **zwingen**, sep, -ge-, h)*

j-m et. aufzwingen force s.th. upon s.o.

Augapfel ['auk-] *m* ANAT eyeball

Auge ['auɡə] *n* (-s; -n) ANAT eye; *ein blaues Auge* a black eye; *mit bloßem Auge* with the naked eye; *mit verbundenen Augen* blindfold; *in meinen Augen* in my view; *mit anderen Augen* in a different light; *aus den Augen verlieren* lose sight of; *ein Auge zudrücken* turn a blind eye; *unter vier Augen* in private; F *ins Auge gehen* go wrong

Augenarzt *m* eye specialist

Augenblick *m* moment, instant

augenblicklich 1. *adj* present; immediate; momentary; **2.** *adv* at present, at the moment; immediately

Augenbraue *f* eyebrow

Augenlicht *n* (-[e]s; *no pl*) eyesight

Augenlid *n* eyelid

Augenmaß *n*: *ein gutes Augenmaß* a sure eye; *nach dem Augenmaß* by the eye

Augenmerk *n*: *sein Augenmerk richten auf* (*acc*) turn one's attention to, *fig a.* have in view

Augenschein *m* (-s; *no pl*) appearance; *in Augenschein nehmen* examine, inspect

Augenzeuge *m* eyewitness

August [au'ɡust] *m* (-; *no pl*) August

Auktion [auk'tsjoːn] *f* (-; -en) auction

Auktionator [auktsjoˈnaːtoːɐ] *m* (-s; -en [-naˈtoːrən]) auctioneer

Aula ['aula] *f* (-; -s, *Aulen*) auditorium, *Br* (assembly) hall

aus [aus] *prp* (*dat*) *and adv mst* out of, from; of (*silk etc*); out of (*spite etc*); *light etc*: out, off; *play etc*: over, finished; *aus dem Fenster etc* out of the window *etc*; *aus München* from Munich; *aus Holz* (made) of wood; *aus Mitleid* out of pity; *aus Spaß* for fun; *aus Versehen* by mistake; *aus diesem Grunde* for this reason; *von hier aus* from here; F *von mir aus!* I don't care!; *aus der Mode* out of fashion; F *aus sein* be over; be out; *aus sein auf* (*acc*) be out for; be after (*s.o.'s money etc*); *die Schule (das Spiel) ist aus* school (the game) is over; *einlaus* TECH on / off

Aus *n*: *im Aus* *ball*: out of play

ausarbeiten *v/t* (*sep*, -ge-, h) work out; prepare

ausarten *v/i* (*sep*, -ge-, sein) get out of hand

ausatmen *v/t and v/i* (*sep*, -ge-, h) breathe out

ausbaden F *v/t* (*sep*, -ge-, h) *et. ausbaden müssen* take the rap for s.th.

Ausbau *m* (-[e]s; *no pl*) extension; com-

pletion; removal

ausbauen *v/t* (*sep*, -ge-, h) extend; complete; remove; improve

ausbaufähig *adj*: *et. ist ausbaufähig* there is potential for growth *or* development

ausbessern *v/t* (*sep*, -ge-, h) mend, repair, F *a.* fix

Ausbesserung *f* (-; -en) repair(ing)

Ausbeute *f* (-; *no pl*) gain, profit; yield

ausbeuten *v/t* (*sep*, -ge-, h) exploit (*a. contp*)

Ausbeutung *f* (-; *no pl*) exploitation

ausbilden *v/t* (*sep*, -ge-, h) train, instruct; *j-n ausbilden zu* train s.o. to be

Ausbilder *m* (-s; -) instructor

Ausbildung *f* (-; -en) training, instruction

ausbleiben *v/i* (*irr*, **bleiben**, *sep*, -ge-, sein) stay out; fail to come; *es konnte nicht ausbleiben* it was inevitable

Ausblick *m* view (*auf acc* of); *fig* outlook (*for*)

ausbrechen *v/i* (*irr*, **brechen**, *sep*, -ge-, sein) break out (*a. fig*); *in Tränen ausbrechen* burst into tears

Ausbrecher *m* (-s; -) escaped prisoner

ausbreiten *v/t* (*sep*, -ge-, h) spread (out); *sich ausbreiten* spread

Ausbreitung *f* (-; *no pl*) spreading

ausbrennen *v/i* (*irr*, **brennen**, *sep*, -ge-, sein) burn out

Ausbruch *m* escape, breakout; outbreak (*of fire etc*); eruption (*of volcano*); (out)-burst (*of resentment etc*)

ausbrüten *v/t* (*sep*, -ge-, h) hatch (*a. fig*)

Ausdauer *f* perseverance, stamina, *esp* SPORT *a.* staying power

ausdauernd *adj* persevering; SPORT tireless

ausdehnen *v/t and v/refl* (*sep*, -ge-, h) stretch; *fig* expand, extend

Ausdehnung *f* expansion; extension

ausdenken *v/t* (*irr*, **denken**, *sep*, -ge-, h) think *s.th.* up; invent (*a. fig*)

Ausdruck *m* expression, term; EDP print-out

ausdrucken *v/t* (*sep*, -ge-, h) EDP print out

ausdrücken *v/t* (*sep*, -ge-, h) stub out (*cigarette etc*); *fig* express

ausdrücklich ['ausdrʏklɪç] *adj* express, explicit

ausdruckslos *adj* expressionless, blank

ausdrucksvoll *adj* expressive

Ausdrucksweise *f* language, style

Ausdünstung *f* (-; -en) exhalation; perspiration; odo(u)r

auseinander [ausˈʔaiˈnandɐ] *adv* apart; separate(d); *auseinanderbringen* *v/t* (*irr*, **bringen**, *sep*, -ge-, h) separate, *aus-*

einandergehen *v/i* (*irr, gehen, sep, -ge-, sein*) part; *meeting etc*: break up; *opinions etc*: differ; *married couple*: separate; **auseinanderhalten** *v/t* (*irr, halten, sep, -ge-, h*) tell apart; **auseinandernehmen** *v/t* (*irr, nehmen, sep, -ge-, h*) take apart (*a. fig*); **auseinandersetzen** *v/t* (*sep, -ge-, h*) explain; **sich auseinander setzen mit** *v/refl* deal with; argue with *s.o.*

Ausei'nandersetzung *f* (-; *-en*) argument

'auserlesen *adj* choice, exquisite

'ausfahren (*irr, fahren, sep, -ge-*) **1.** *v/i* (*sein*) go for a drive *or* ride; **2.** *v/t* (*h*) take *s.o.* out; AVIAT extend (*landing gear*)

'Ausfahrt *f* drive, ride; MOT exit

'Ausfall *m* TECH, MOT, SPORT failure; loss

'ausfallen *v/i* (*irr, fallen, sep, -ge-, sein*) fall out; not take place, be cancelled; TECH, MOT break down, fail; **gut etc ausfallen** turn out well etc; **ausfallen lassen** cancel; **die Schule fällt aus** there is no school

'ausfallend, 'ausfällig *adj* insulting

'ausfertigen *v/t* (*sep, -ge-, h*) draw up (*contract etc*); make out (*check etc*)

'Ausfertigung *f* drawing up; copy; **in doppelter Ausfertigung** in duplicate

'ausfindig machen find

ausflippen ['ausflɪpən] F *v/i* (*sep, -ge-, sein*) freak out

Ausflüchte ['ausflʏçtə] *pl* excuses

'Ausflug *m* trip, excursion, outing

Ausflügler ['ausflyːklɐ] *m* (-*s*; -) daytripper

'Ausfluss *m* TECH outlet; MED discharge

'ausfragen *v/t* (*sep, -ge-, h*) question (**über** *acc* about); sound out

ausfransen *v/i* (*sep, -ge-, sein*) fray

ausfressen F *v/t* (*irr, fressen, sep, -ge-, h*) **et. ausfressen** be up to no good

Ausfuhr ['ausfuːɐ̯] *f* (-; *-en*) ECON export(ation)

'ausführbar *adj* practicable

'ausführen *v/t* (*sep, -ge-, h*) take *s.o.* out; carry out (*task etc*); ECON export; explain

ausführlich ['ausfyːɐ̯lɪç] **1.** *adj* detailed; comprehensive; **2.** *adv* in detail

'Ausführlichkeit *f*: **in aller Ausführlichkeit** in great detail

'Ausführung *f* execution, performance; type, model, design

'ausfüllen *v/t* (*sep, -ge-, h*) fill out (*Br in*) (*form*)

'Ausgabe *f* distribution; edition; expense; issue; EDP output

'Ausgang *m* exit, way out; end; result, outcome; TECH, ELECTR output, outlet

'Ausgangspunkt *m* starting point

'Ausgangssperre *f* POL curfew

'ausgeben *v/t* (*irr, geben, sep, -ge-, h*) give out; spend; F **j-m e-n ausgeben** buy s.o. a drink; **sich ausgeben als** pass o.s. off as

'ausgebeult *adj* baggy

'ausgebildet *adj* trained, skilled

'ausgebucht *adj* booked up

'ausgedehnt *adj* extensive

ausgedient *adj*: **ausgedient haben** fig have had its day

'ausgefallen *adj* odd, unusual

'ausgeglichen *adj* (well-)balanced

'ausgehen *v/i* (*irr, gehen, sep, -ge-, sein*) go out; end; *hair*: fall out; *money, supplies*: run out; **leer ausgehen** get nothing; **ausgehen von** start from *or* at; come from; **davon ausgehen, dass** assume that; **ihm ging das Geld aus** he ran out of money

'ausgekocht *fig adj* cunning; out-and-out (*villain etc*)

'ausgelassen *fig adj* cheerful; hilarious; **ausgelassen sein** be in high spirits

'ausgemacht *adj* agreed(-on); downright (*nonsense*)

'ausgeprägt *adj* marked, pronounced

'ausgerechnet *adv*: **ausgerechnet er** he of all people; **ausgerechnet heute** today of all days

'ausgeschlossen *adj* out of the question

'ausgestorben *adj* extinct

'ausgesucht *adj* select, choice

'ausgewachsen *adj* fullgrown

'ausgewogen *adj* (well-)balanced

'ausgezeichnet *adj* excellent

ausgiebig ['ausgiːbɪç] *adj* extensive, thorough; substantial (*meal*)

'ausgießen *v/t* (*irr, gießen, sep, -ge-, h*) pour out

'Ausgleich *m* (-[*e*]*s*; *no pl*) compensation; SPORT even score, *Br* equalization; *tennis*: deuce

'ausgleichen *v/t and v/i* (*irr, gleichen, sep, -ge-, h*) compensate; equalize (*Br a. SPORT*); ECON balance; SPORT make the score even

'Ausgleichssport *m* remedial exercises

Ausgleichstor *n*, **Ausgleichstreffer** *m* SPORT tying point, *Br* equalizer

'ausgraben *v/t* (*irr, graben, sep, -ge-, h*) dig out *or* up (*a. fig*)

'Ausgrabungen *f/pl* excavations

'ausgrenzen *v/t* (*sep, -ge-, h*) isolate

'Ausguss *m* (kitchen) sink

'aushalten *v/t* (*irr, halten, sep, -ge-, h*) **1.** *v/t* bear, stand; keep (*mistress etc*); **nicht auszuhalten sein** be unbearable; **2.** *v/i* hold out

'aushändigen ['aushɛndɪgən] v/t (sep, -ge-, h) hand over

'Aushang m notice; bulletin

'aushängen v/t (sep, -ge-, h) hang out, put up; unhinge (door)

'ausheben v/t (irr, **heben**, sep, -ge-, h) dig (trench); raid (place etc)

'aushelfen v/i (irr, **helfen**, sep, -ge-, h) help out

'Aushilfe f (temporary) help

'Aushilfs... in cpds -kellner etc: temporary

'ausholen v/i (sep, -ge-, h) **zum Schlag ausholen** swing (to strike); fig **weit ausholen** go far back

aus'horchen v/t (sep, -ge-, h) sound (**über** acc on)

'aushungern v/t (sep, -ge-, h) starve out

'auskennen v/i/refl (irr, **kennen**, sep, -ge-, h) **sich auskennen** (**in** dat) know one's way (about); fig know a lot (about)

'ausklingen v/i (irr, **klingen**, sep, -ge-, sein) draw to a close

'ausklopfen v/t (sep, -ge-, h) knock out

'auskommen v/i (irr, **kommen**, sep, -ge-, sein) get by; **auskommen mit** manage with s.th.; get along with s.o.

Auskunft ['auskʊnft] f (-; Auskünfte ['auskʏnftə]) a) information, b) (no pl) information desk; TEL inquiries

'auslachen v/t (sep, -ge-, h) laugh at (**wegen** for)

'ausladen v/t (irr, **laden**, sep, -ge-, h) unload

'Auslage f window display; pl expenses

'Ausland n (-[e]s; no pl) **das Ausland** foreign countries; **ins Ausland, im Ausland** abroad

Ausländer ['auslɛndɐ] m (-s; -) foreigner

Ausländerfeindlichkeit f hostility to foreigners, xenophobia

Ausländerin ['auslɛndərɪn] f (-; -nen) foreigner

'ausländisch [-lɛndɪʃ] adj foreign

'Auslandsgespräch n international call

Auslandskorrespondent(in) foreign correspondent

'auslassen v/t (irr, **lassen**, sep, -ge-, h) leave out; melt (butter etc); let out (seam); **s-n Zorn an j-m auslassen** take it out on s.o.; **sich auslassen über** (acc) express o.s. on

'Auslassung f (-; -en) omission

'Auslassungszeichen n LING apostrophe

'Auslauf m room to move about; dog: exercise

'auslaufen v/i (irr, **laufen**, sep, -ge-, sein) MAR leave port; pot etc: leak; liquid etc: run out

'Ausläufer m METEOR ridge, trough; pl GEOGR foothills

'Auslaufmo,dell n ECON close-out (Br phase-out) model

'auslegen v/t (sep, -ge-, h) lay out; carpet; line (with paper etc); display (goods); interpret (text etc); advance (money)

'Auslegung f (-; -en) interpretation

'ausleihen v/t (irr, **leihen**, sep, -ge-, h) lend (out), loan; **sich** (dat) **et. ausleihen** borrow s.th.

'Auslese f choice, selection; fig pick

'auslesen v/t (irr, **lesen**, sep, -ge-, h) pick out, select; finish (book etc)

'ausliefern v/t (sep, -ge-, h) hand or turn over, deliver (up); POL extradite

'Auslieferung f delivery; extradition

'ausliegen v/i (irr, **liegen**, sep, -ge-, h) be laid out

'auslöschen v/t (sep, -ge-, h) put out; fig wipe out

'auslosen v/t (sep, -ge-, h) draw (lots) for

'auslösen v/t (sep, -ge-, h) TECH release; ransom, redeem; cause, start, trigger s.th. off

'Auslöser m (PHOT shutter) release; trigger

'ausmachen v/t (sep, -ge-, h) put out (fire); turn off (light etc); arrange (date etc); agree on (price etc); make up; amount to; settle (dispute); sight, spot; **macht es Ihnen et. aus (, wenn...)?** do you mind (if ...)?; **es macht mir nichts aus** I don't mind; **das macht (gar) nichts aus** that doesn't matter (at all)

'ausmalen v/t (sep, -ge-, h) paint; **sich et. ausmalen** imagine s.th.

'Ausmaß n extent; pl proportions

ausmerzen ['ausmɛrtsən] v/t (sep, -ge-, h) eliminate

'ausmessen v/t (irr, **messen**, sep, -ge-, h) measure

Ausnahme ['ausnaːmə] f (-; -n) exception

Ausnahmezustand m POL state of emergency

'ausnahmslos adv without exception

'ausnahmsweise adv by way of exception; just this once

'ausnehmen v/t (irr, **nehmen**, sep, -ge-, h) clean (chicken etc); except; F contp fleece s.o.

ausnehmend adv exceptionally

'ausnutzen v/t (sep, -ge-, h) use; take advantage of (a. contp); exploit

auspacken (sep, -ge-, h) **1.** v/t unpack; **2.** F

v/i talk

'auspfeifen *v/t* (*irr*, **pfeifen**, *sep*, -*ge*-, *h*) boo, hiss

'ausplaudern *v/t* (*sep*, -*ge*-, *h*) blab out

'ausplündern *v/t* (*sep*, -*ge*-, *h*) plunder, rob

'auspro,bieren *v/t* (*sep*, *no* -*ge*-, *h*) try (out), test

'Auspuff *m* MOT exhaust

'Auspuffgase *pl* MOT exhaust fumes

'Auspuffrohr *n* MOT exhaust pipe

'Auspufftopf *m* MOT muffler, *Br* silencer

'ausquar,tieren *v/t* (*sep*, *no* -*ge*-, *h*) move out

'ausra,dieren *v/t* (*sep*, *no* -*ge*-, *h*) erase; *fig* wipe out

'ausran,gieren *v/t* (*sep*, *no* -*ge*-, *h*) discard

'ausrauben *v/t* (*sep*, -*ge*-, *h*) rob

'ausräumen *v/t* (*sep*, -*ge*-, *h*) empty; clear out (*room etc*); *fig* clear up (*doubt etc*)

'ausrechnen *v/t* (*sep*, -*ge*-, *h*) work out

'Ausrede *f* excuse

'ausreden (*sep*, -*ge*-, *h*) **1.** *v/i* finish speaking; *j-n ausreden lassen* hear s.o. out; **2.** *v/t*: *j-m et. ausreden* talk s.o. out of s.th.

'ausreichen *v/t* (*sep*, -*ge*-, *h*) be enough

'ausreichend *adj* sufficient, enough; *grade*: (barely) passing, only average, weak, D

'Ausreise *f* departure

'ausreisen *v/i* (*sep*, -*ge*-, *sein*) leave (a *or* one's country)

'Ausreisevisum *n* exit visa

'ausreißen (*irr*, **reißen**, *sep*, -*ge*-) **1.** *v/t* (*h*) pull *or* tear out; **2.** F *v/i* (*sein*) run away

'Ausreißer *m* (-*s*; -) runaway

'ausrenken *v/t* (*sep*, -*ge*-, *h*) MED dislocate

'ausrichten *v/t* (*sep*, -*ge*-, *h*) tell *s.o. s.th.*; deliver (*message*); accomplish; arrange (*party etc*); *richte ihr e-n Gruß von mir aus!* give her my regards!; *kann ich et. ausrichten?* can I take a message

'ausrotten *v/t* (*sep*, -*ge*-, *h*) exterminate

'Ausrottung *f* (-; -*en*) extermination

'ausrücken *v/i* (*sep*, -*ge*-, *sein*) F run away; MIL march out

'Ausruf *m* cry, shout

'ausrufen *v/t* (*irr*, **rufen**, *sep*, -*ge*-, *h*) cry, shout, exclaim; call out (*name*); POL proclaim

'Ausrufung *f* (-; -*en*) POL proclamation

'Ausrufungszeichen *n* LING exclamation mark

'ausruhen *v/i*, *v/t and v/refl* (*sep*, -*ge*-, *h*) rest

'ausrüsten *v/t* (*sep*, -*ge*-, *h*) equip

'Ausrüstung *f* equipment

'ausrutschen *v/i* (*sep*, -*ge*-, *sein*) slip

'Aussage *f* statement; JUR evidence

'aussagen *v/t* (*sep*, -*ge*-, *h*) state, declare;

JUR testify

'ausschalten *v/t* (*sep*, -*ge*-, *h*) switch off; *fig* eliminate

'Ausschau *f*: *Ausschau halten nach* → 'ausschauen *v/i* (*sep*, -*ge*-, *h*) *Ausschau nach* look out for, watch out for

'ausscheiden (*irr*, **scheiden**, *sep*, -*ge*-) **1.** *v/i* (*sein*) be ruled out; SPORT *etc* drop out (*aus dat* of); retire (*aus dat* from *office etc*); *ausscheiden aus* (*dat*) leave (a *firm etc*); **2.** *v/t* (*h*) eliminate; MED *etc* secrete, exude

'Ausscheidung *f* elimination (a. SPORT); MED secretion

'Ausscheidungs... *in cpds* ...*spiel etc*: SPORT qualifying ...

'ausschlachten *fig v/t* (*sep*, -*ge*-, *h*) salvage, *Br a.* cannibalize; *contp* exploit

'ausschlafen (*irr*, **schlafen**, *sep*, -*ge*-) **1.** *v/i* sleep in; **2.** *v/t* sleep off

'Ausschlag *m* MED rash; TECH deflection; *den Ausschlag geben* decide it

'ausschlagen (*irr*, **schlagen**, *sep*, -*ge*-, *h*) **1.** *v/t* knock out (*tooth etc*); *fig* refuse, decline (*offer etc*); **2.** *v/i* *horse*: kick; BOT bud; TECH deflect

'ausschlaggebend *adj* decisive

'ausschließen *v/t* (*irr*, **schließen**, *sep*, -*ge*-, *h*) lock out (*tooth etc*); *fig* exclude; expel; SPORT disqualify

'ausschließlich *adj* exclusive

'Ausschluss *m* exclusion; expulsion; SPORT disqualification; *unter Ausschluss der Öffentlichkeit* in closed session

'ausschmücken *v/t* (*sep*, -*ge*-, *h*) decorate; *fig* embellish

'ausschneiden *v/t* (*irr*, **schneiden**, *sep*, -*ge*-, *h*) cut out

'Ausschnitt *m clothing*: neck; (*press*) clipping (*Br* cutting); *fig* part; extract; *mit tiefem Ausschnitt* low-necked

'ausschreiben *v/t* (*irr*, **schreiben**, *sep*, -*ge*-, *h*) write out (a. *check etc*); advertise (*post etc*)

'Ausschreibung *f* advertisement

'Ausschreitungen *pl* violence, riots

'Ausschuss *m* committee, board; TECH (*no pl*) refuse, waste, rejects

'ausschütteln *v/t* (*sep*, -*ge*-, *h*) shake out

'ausschütten *v/t* (*sep*, -*ge*-, *h*) pour out (a. *fig*); spill; ECON pay; *sich vor Lachen ausschütten* split one's sides

'ausschweifend *adj* dissolute

'Ausschweifung *f* (-; -*en*) debauchery, excess

'aussehen *v/i* (*irr*, **sehen**, *sep*, -*ge*-, *h*) look; *krank* (*traurig*) *aussehen* look ill (sad); *aussehen wie ...* look like ...;

wie sieht er aus? what does he look like? **'Aussehen** n (-s; no pl) look(s), appearance

außen ['ausən] adv outside; **nach außen** (*hin*) outward(s); fig outwardly

'Außenbordmotor m outboard motor

aussenden v/t ([irr, **senden**,] sep, -ge-, h) send out

'Außendienst m field service

Außenhandel m foreign trade

Außenmi,nister m Am Secretary of State, Br Foreign Secretary

Außenminis,terium n Am State Department, Br Foreign Office

Außenpoli,tik f foreign affairs; foreign policy

'außenpo,litisch adj foreign-policy

'Außenseite f outside

'Außenseiter [-zaitə] m (-s; -) outsider

'Außenspiegel m MOT outside rearview mirror

Außenstände pl ECON receivables

Außenstelle f branch

Außenstürmer m SPORT winger

Außenwelt f outside world

außer ['ausɐ] **1.** prp (dat) out of; aside from, Br beside(s); except; **außer sich sein** be beside o.s. (**vor Freude** with joy); **alle außer e-m** all but one; → **Betrieb, Gefahr; 2.** cj: **außer dass** except that; **außer wenn** unless

'außerdem cj besides, moreover

äußere ['ɔysərə] adj exterior, outer, outward

'Äußere n (-n; no pl) exterior, outside; (outward) appearance

'außergewöhnlich adj unusual

'außerhalb prp (gen) and adv outside; out of; beyond

'außerirdisch adj extraterrestrial

'äußerlich adj external, outward

'Äußerlichkeit f (-; -en) formality; minor detail

äußern ['ɔysɐn] v/t (sep, -, h) utter, express; **sich äußern** say s.th.; **sich äußern zu** or **über** (acc) express o.s. on

'außer'ordentlich adj extraordinary

'außerplanmäßig adj unscheduled

äußerst ['ɔysɐst] **1.** adj outermost; fig extreme; **im äußersten Fall** at (the) worst; at (the) most **2.** adv extremely

außer'stande adj: **außerstande sein** be unable

'Äußerung f (-; -en) utterance, remark

'aussetzen (sep, -ge-, h) **1.** v/t abandon; expose (dat to); **et. auszusetzen haben an** (dat) find fault with; **2.** v/i stop, break off; MOT, TECH fail

'Aussicht f view (**auf** acc of); fig prospect

(of), chance (**auf Erfolg** of success)

'aussichtslos adj hopeless, desperate

'Aussichtspunkt m vantage point

'aussichtsreich adj promising

'Aussichtsturm m lookout tower

'Aussiedler m resettler, evacuee

'aussitzen v/t (irr, **sitzen**, sep, -ge-, h) sit s.th. out

aussöhnen ['auszø:nən] v/refl (sep, -ge-, h) **sich aussöhnen** (**mit**) become reconciled (with), F make it up (with)

'Aussöhnung f (-; -en) reconciliation

'aussor,tieren v/t (sep, no -ge-, h) sort out

ausspannen (sep, -ge-, h) **1.** v/t unharness; **2.** fig v/i (take a) rest, relax

'aussperren v/t (sep, -ge-, h) lock out (a. ECON)

'Aussperrung f (-; -en) ECON lock-out

'ausspielen (sep, -ge-, h) **1.** v/t play; **j-n gegen j-n ausspielen** play s.o. off against s.o.; **2.** v/i card game: lead; **er hat ausgespielt** fig he is done for

'ausspio,nieren v/t (sep, no -ge-, h) spy out

'Aussprache f pronunciation; discussion; private heart-to-heart (talk)

'aussprechen v/t (irr, **sprechen**, sep, -ge-, h) pronounce; express; **sich aussprechen für** (**gegen**) speak for (against); **sich mit j-m gründlich aussprechen** have a heart-to-heart talk with s.o.

'Ausspruch m saying; remark

'ausspucken v/i and v/t (sep, -ge-, h) spit out

ausspülen v/t (sep, -ge-, h) rinse

'Ausstand m strike, F walkout

'ausstatten v/t (sep, -ge-, h) fit out, equip, furnish

'Ausstattung f (-; -en) equipment, furnishings; design

'ausstechen v/t (irr, **stechen**, sep, -ge-, h) GASTR cut out (a. fig); put out (eyes)

ausstehen (irr, **stehen**, sep, -ge-, h) **1.** v/t stand, endure; F **ich kann ihn** (**es**) **nicht ausstehen** I can't stand him (it); **2.** v/i: (**noch**) **ausstehen** be outstanding or overdue

'aussteigen v/i (irr, **steigen**, sep, -ge-, sien) get out (**aus** dat of); (a. **aussteigen aus** dat) get off a bus, train; F fig drop out

'Aussteiger F m (-s; -) drop-out

'ausstellen v/t (sep, -ge-, h) exhibit, display, show; make out (check etc); issue (passport)

'Aussteller m (-s; -) exhibitor; issuer; drawer (of check)

'Ausstellung f exhibition, show

'aussterben v/i (irr, **sterben**, sep, -ge-, sein) die out, become extinct (both a. fig)

'Aussteuer f trousseau; dowry

'aussteuern v/t (sep, -ge-, h) ELECTR modulate

'Aussteuerung f ELECTR modulation; level control

Ausstieg ['ausʃtiːk] m (-[e]s; -e) exit; fig withdrawal (**aus** dat from)

'ausstopfen v/t (sep, -ge-, h) stuff; pad

'Ausstoß m TECH, PHYS discharge, ejection; ECON output

'ausstoßen v/t (irr, **stoßen**, sep, -ge-, h) TECH, PHYS give off, eject, emit; ECON turn out; give (cry, sigh); expel

'ausstrahlen v/t (sep, -ge-, h) radiate (happiness etc); TV, radio: broadcast, transmit

'Ausstrahlung f radiation; broadcast; fig magnetism, charisma

'ausstrecken v/t (sep, -ge-, h) stretch (out)

ausstreichen v/t (irr, **streichen**, sep, -ge-, h) strike out

ausströmen v/i (sep, -ge-, sein) escape (**aus** dat from)

aussuchen v/t (sep, -ge-, h) choose, pick

'Austausch m (-[e]s; no pl) exchange

'austauschbar adj exchangeable

'austauschen v/t (sep, -ge-, h) exchange (**gegen** for)

'Austauschschüler(in) exchange student

'austeilen v/t (sep, -ge-, h) distribute, hand out; deal (out) (cards, blows)

Auster ['austɐ] f (-; -n) zo oyster

'austragen v/t (irr, **tragen**, sep, -ge-, h) deliver (mail); settle (dispute etc); hold (contest etc); **das Kind austragen** have the baby

'Austragungsort m SPORT venue

Australien [aus'traːljən] Australia

Australier [aus'traːljɐ] m (-s; -), **Aust'ralierin** [-ljərɪn] f (-; -nen), **aust'ralisch** adj Australian

'austreiben v/t (irr, **treiben**, sep, -ge-, h) exorcise; F **j-m et. austreiben** cure s.o. of s.th.

austreten (irr, **treten**, sep, -ge-) **1.** v/t (h) tread or stamp out (fire); wear out (shoes); **2.** v/i (sein) escape (**aus** dat from); F go to the bathroom (Br toilet); **austreten aus** (dat) leave (a club etc); resign from

austrinken v/t (irr, **trinken**, sep, -ge-, h) drink up; empty

'Austritt m leaving; resignation; escape

'austrocknen v/t (sep, -ge-, h) and v/i (sein) dry up

'ausüben v/t (sep, -ge-, h) practi|ce, Br -se; hold (office); exercise (power etc); exert (pressure etc)

'Ausübung f (-; no pl) practice; exercise

'Ausverkauf m ECON (clearance) sale

'ausverkauft adj ECON, THEA sold out; **vor ausverkauftem Haus spielen** play to a full house

'Auswahl f choice, selection (both a. ECON); SPORT representative team

'auswählen v/t (sep, -ge-, h) choose, select

'Auswanderer m emigrant

'auswandern v/i (sep, -ge-, sein) emigrate

'Auswanderung f emigration

auswärtig ['ausvɛrtɪç] adj out-of-town; POL foreign

'auswärts adv out of town

'Auswärtssieg m SPORT away victory

Auswärtsspiel n SPORT away game

'auswechseln v/t (sep, -ge-, h) exchange (**gegen** for); change (tire); replace; **A gegen B auswechseln** SPORT substitute B for A; **wie ausgewechselt** (like) a different person

'Auswechselspieler m SPORT substitute

'Ausweg m way out

'ausweglos adj hopeless

'Ausweglosigkeit f (-; no pl) hopelessness

'ausweichen v/i (irr, **weichen**, sep, -ge-, sein) make way (dat for); fig avoid s.o.; evade (question)

'ausweichend adj evasive

'ausweinen v/refl (sep, -ge-, h) have a good cry

Ausweis ['ausvais] m (-es; -e) identification (card); card

'ausweisen v/t (irr, **weisen**, sep, -ge-, h) expel; **sich ausweisen** identify o.s.

'Ausweispa,piere pl documents

'Ausweisung f (-; -en) expulsion

'ausweiten fig v/t (sep, -ge-, h) expand

'auswendig adv by heart; **et. auswendig können** know s.th. by heart; **auswendig lernen** memorize; learn by heart

'auswerfen v/t (irr, **werfen**, sep, -ge-, h) throw out; cast (anchor); TECH eject

'auswerten v/t (sep, -ge-, h) evaluate, analyze, interpret; utilize, exploit

'Auswertung f evaluation; utilization

'auswickeln v/t (sep, -ge-, h) unwrap

'auswirken v/refl (sep, -ge-, h) **sich auswirken auf** (acc) affect; **sich positiv auswirken** have a favo(u)rable effect

'Auswirkung f effect

'auswischen v/t (sep, -ge-, h) wipe out

'auswringen v/t (irr, **wringen**, sep, -ge-, h) wring out

'Auswuchs m (-es; Auswüchse ['ausvyːksə]) excrescence; fig pl excesses

'auswuchten v/t (sep, -ge-, h) TECH balance: **auszahlen** v/t (sep, -ge-, h) pay (out); pay s.o. off; **sich auswuchten** pay

auszählen v/t (sep, -ge-, h) count; boxing:

count out
'**Auszahlung** f payment; paying off
'**auszeichnen** v/t (sep, -ge-, h) price, mark (out) (goods); **sich auszeichnen** distinguish o.s.; **j-n mit et. auszeichnen** award s.th. to s.o.
'**Auszeichnung** f marking; fig distinction, hono(u)r; award; decoration
'**ausziehen** (irr, ziehen, sep, -ge-) **1.** v/t (h) take off (coat etc); pull out (table etc); **sich ausziehen** undress; **2.** v/i (sein) move out
'**Auszubildende** m, f (-n; -n) apprentice, trainee
'**Auszug** m move, removal; extract, excerpt; statement (of account)
authentisch [au'tɛntɪʃ] adj authentic, genuine
Autismus [au'tɪsmus] m PSYCH autism
autistisch [au'tɪstɪʃ] adj PSYCH autistic
Auto ['auto] n (-s; -s) car, auto(mobile); (mit dem) **Auto fahren** drive, go by car
'**Autobahn** f Am expressway, Br motorway
Autobahndreieck n interchange
Autobahngebühr f toll
Autobahnkreuz n interchange
Autobiogra'phie f autobiography
'**Autobombe** f car bomb
Autobus m → **Bus**
Autofähre f car ferry
Autofahrer(in) motorist, driver
Autofahrt f drive

Autofriedhof F m car dump, auto junkyard
Autogramm [auto'gram] n autograph
Autogrammjäger m autograph hunter
'**Autokarte** f road map
Autokino n drive-in theater (Br cinema)
Automat [auto'maːt] m (-en; -en) vending (Br a. slot) machine; TECH robot; → **Spielautomat**
Automatik [auto'maːtɪk] f (-; no pl) automatic (system or control); MOT automatic transmission; automatic
Automation [automa'tsjoːn] f (-; no pl) automation
auto'matisch adj automatic
'**Autome,chaniker** m car mechanic
autonom [auto'noːm] adj autonomous
'**Autonummer** f license (Br licence) number
Autor ['autoːɐ] m (-s; -en [au'toːrən]) author
'**Autorepara,turwerkstatt** f garage, car repair shop
Autorin [au'toːrɪn] f (-; -nen) author(ess)
autorisieren [autori'ziːrən] v/t (no -ge-, h) authorize
autoritär [autori'tɛːɐ] adj authoritarian
Autorität [autori'tɛːt] f (-; -en) authority
'**Autotele,fon** n car phone
Autovermietung f car rental (Br hire) service
Autowaschanlage f car wash
Axt [akst] f (-; Äxte ['ɛkstə]) ax(e)

B

Bach [bax] m (-[e]s; Bäche ['bɛçə]) brook, stream, Am a. creek
'**Backblech** n baking sheet
'**Backbord** n (-s; no pl) MAR port
Backe ['bakə] f (-; -n) ANAT cheek
backen v/t and v/i ([irr, backen,] -ge-, h) bake
'**Backenzahn** m ANAT molar (tooth)
Bäcker ['bɛkɐ] m (-s; -) baker; **beim Bäcker** at the baker's
Bäckerei [bɛkə'rai] f (-; -en) bakery, baker's (shop)
'**Backform** f baking tin
Backhendl ['bakhɛndl] Austrian n (-s; -n) fried chicken
Backobst n dried fruit

Backofen m oven
Backpflaume f prune
Backpulver n baking powder
Backstein m brick
backte ['baktə] pret of **backen**
'**Backwaren** pl breads and pastries
Bad [baːt] n (-[e]; Bäder ['bɛːdɐ]) bath; swim; bathroom; → **Badeort**; **ein Bad nehmen** → **baden 1**
'**Badeanstalt** f swimming pool, public baths
Badeanzug m swimsuit
Badehose f bathing trunks
Badekappe f bathing cap
Bademantel m bathrobe
Bademeister m pool or bath attendant

baden ['baːdən] (ge-, h) **1.** v/i bathe, take or have a bath; swim; **baden gehen** go swimming; **2.** v/t bathe (a. MED); Br a. bath

'**Badeort** m seaside (or health) resort

'**Badetuch** n bath towel

'**Badewanne** f bathtub

'**Badezimmer** n bathroom

baff [baf] adj: F **baff sein** be flabbergasted

Bagatelle [baga'tɛlə] f (-; -n) trifle

Baga'tellschaden m superficial damage

Bagger ['bagɐ] m (-s; -) TECH excavator; dredge(r)

'**baggern** v/i (ge-, h) TECH excavate; dredge

Bahn [baːn] f (-; -en) railroad, Br railway; train; way, path, course; SPORT track; **mit der Bahn** by train; **Bahn frei!** make way!; cpds → a. **Eisenbahn**

'**bahnbrechend** adj epoch-making

'**Bahndamm** m railroad (Br railway) embankment

'**bahnen** v/t (ge-, h) **den Weg bahnen** clear the way (dat for s.o. or s.th.); **sich e-n Weg bahnen** force or work one's way

'**Bahnhof** m (railroad, Br railway) station

'**Bahnlinie** f railroad (Br railway) line

'**Bahnsteig** [-ʃtaik] m (-[e]s; -e) platform

'**Bahnübergang** m grade (Br level) crossing

Bahre ['baːrə] f (-; -n) stretcher; bier

Baisse ['bɛːsə] f (-; -n) ECON fall, slump

Bakterien [bak'teːrjən] pl MED bacteria, germs

balancieren [balã'siːrən] v/t and v/i (no -ge-, h) balance

bald [balt] adv soon; F almost, nearly; **so bald wie möglich** as soon as possible

baldig ['baldɪç] adj speedy; **baldige Antwort** ECON early reply; **auf(ein) baldiges Wiedersehen!** see you again soon!

balgen ['balgən] v/refl (ge-, h) scuffle (**um** for)

Balken ['balkən] m (-s; -) beam

Balkon [bal'kɔn] m (-s; -s, -e [-'koːnə]) balcony

Balkontür f French window

Ball [bal] m (-[e]s; Bälle ['bɛlə]) ball; dance; **am Ball sein** SPORT have the ball; **am Ball bleiben** fig stick to it

Ballade [ba'laːdə] f (-; -n) ballad

Ballast ['balast] m (-[e]s; no pl) ballast, fig a. burden

Ballaststoffe pl MED roughage, bulk

ballen ['balən] v/t (ge-, h) clench (fist)

'**Ballen** m (-s; -) bale; ANAT ball

Ballett [ba'lɛt] n (-[e]s; -e) ballet

Ballon [ba'lɔn] m (-s; -s) balloon

'**Ballungsraum** m, **Ballungszentrum** n congested area, conurbation

Balsam ['balzaːm] m (-s; no pl) balm

Bambus ['bambus] m (-ses, -; -se) BOT bamboo

Bambusrohr n BOT bamboo (cane)

banal [ba'naːl] adj banal, trite

Banane [ba'naːnə] f (-; -n) BOT banana

Banause [ba'nauzə] m (-n; -n) philistine

band [bant] pret of **binden**

Band¹ n (-[e]s; Bänder ['bɛndɐ]) ribbon; tape; (hat) band; ANAT ligament; fig tie, link; **auf Band aufnehmen** tape; **am laufenden Band** fig continuously

Band² m (-[e]s; Bände ['bɛndə]) volume

Bandage [ban'daːʒə] f (-; -n) bandage

bandagieren [banda'ʒiːrən] v/t (no -ge-, h) bandage (up)

'**Bandbreite** f ELECTR bandwidth; fig range

Bande ['bandə] f (-; -n) gang; billiards: cushions; ice hockey: boards; bowling: gutter

'**Bänderriss** m MED torn ligament

bändigen ['bɛndɪgən] v/t (ge-, h) tame (a. fig); restrain, control (children etc)

Bandit [ban'diːt] m (-en; -en) bandit, outlaw

'**Bandmaß** n tape measure

Bandscheibe f ANAT (intervertebral) disk (Br disc)

Bandscheibenschaden m, **Bandscheibenvorfall** m MED slipped disk

Bandwurm m ZO tapeworm

bange ['baŋə] adj afraid; anxious

'**Bange** f: **j-m Bange machen** frighten or scare s.o.; **keine Bange!** (have) no fear!

'**bangen** v/i (ge-, h) be anxious or worried (**um** about)

Bank¹ [baŋk] f (-; Bänke ['bɛŋkə]) bench; F **durch die Bank** without exception; **die lange Bank schieben** put off

Bank² f (-; -en) bank; **auf der Bank** in the bank

'**Bankangestellte** m, f bank clerk or employee

'**Bankauto,mat** m → **Geldautomat**

Bankett [baŋ'kɛt] n (-[e]s; -e) banquet

'**Bankgeschäfte** pl banking transactions

'**Bankier** [baŋ'kjeː] m (-s; -s) banker

'**Bankkonto** n bank(ing) account

Bankleitzahl f A.B.A. number, Br bank (sorting) code

Banknote f bill, Br (bank) note

Bankraub m bank robbery

bankrott [baŋ'krɔt] adj ECON bankrupt

Bank'rott m (-[e]s; -e) ECON bankruptcy; **Bankrott machen** go bankrupt

'Bankverbindung f account(s), account details

Bann [ban] m (-[e]s; *no pl*) ban; spell

'bannen v/t (ge-, h) ward off; **(wie) gebannt** spellbound

Banner ['banɐ] n (-s; -) banner (*a. fig*)

bar [baːr] *adj* (in) cash; **gegen bar** for cash

Bar f (-; -s) bar; nightclub

Bär [bɛːɐ] m (-en; -en) zo bear

Baracke [baˈrakə] f (-; -n) hut; *contp* shack

Barbar [barˈbaːɐ] m (-en; -en) barbarian

barbarisch [barˈbaːrɪʃ] *adj* barbarous, *a.* atrocious (*crime etc*)

'Bardame f barmaid

'barfuß *adj and adv* barefoot

barg [bark] *pret of* **bergen**

'Bargeld n cash

'bargeldlos *adj* noncash

'Barhocker m bar stool

Bariton ['baːritɔn] m (-s; -e [-toːnə]) MUS baritone

Barkasse [barˈkasə] f (-; -n) MAR launch

barm'herzig *adj* merciful; charitable

Barm'herzigkeit f (-; *no pl*) mercy; charity

'Barmixer m barman

Barometer [baroˈmeːtɐ] n (-s; -) barometer

Baron [baˈroːn] m (-s; -e) baron

Ba'ronin f (-; *-nen*) baroness

Barren ['barən] m (-s; -) bar, ingot, *a.* gold, silver bullion; SPORT parallel bars

Barriere [baˈrjeːrə] f (-; -n) barrier

Barrikade [bariˈkaːdə] f (-; -n) barricade

barsch [barʃ] *adj* rough, gruff, brusque

Barsch m (-[e]s; -e) zo perch

'Barscheck m (negotiable) check, *Br* open cheque

barst [barst] *pret of* **bersten**

Bart [baːɐt] m (-[e]s; Bärte ['bɛːɐtə]) beard; TECH bit; **sich e-n Bart wachsen lassen** grow a beard

bärtig ['bɛːɐtɪç] *adj* bearded

'Barzahlung f cash payment

Basar [baˈzaːɐ] m (-s; -e) bazaar

Base ['baːzə] f (-; -n) cousin; CHEM base

basieren [baˈziːrən] v/i (*no ge-*, h) **basieren auf** (*dat*) be based on

Basis ['baːzɪs] f (-; *Basen*) basis; MIL, ARCH base

Baskenmütze ['baskən-] f beret

Bass [bas] m (-es; Bässe ['bɛsə]) MUS bass

Bassin [baˈsɛ̃ː] n (-s; -s) basin; (swimming) pool

Bassist [baˈsɪst] m (-en; -en) MUS bass singer *or* player

Bast [bast] m (-[e]s; -e) bast; HUNT velvet

Bastard ['bastart] m (-s; -e) BIOL hybrid; mongrel; V bastard

basteln ['bastəln] (*ge-*, h) **1.** v/i make *or* repair things o.s.; **2.** v/t build, make

Bastler ['bastlɐ] m (-s; -) home handyman, do-it-yourselfer

bat [baːt] *pret of* **bitten**

Batik ['baːtɪk] m (-s; -en), f (-; -en) batik

Batist [baˈtɪst] m (-[e]s; -e) cambric

Batterie [batəˈriː] f (-; -n) ELECTR, MIL battery

Bau [bau] m (-[e]s; Bauten) a) (*no pl*) building, construction; build, frame, b) building, c) zo (*pl Baue*) hole, den; **im Bau** under construction

Bauarbeiten *pl* construction work; road works

Bauarbeiter m construction worker

Bauart f style (of construction); type, model

Bauch [baux] m (-[e]s; Bäuche ['bɔyçə]) belly (*a. fig*), ANAT abdomen; F tummy

'bauchig *adj* bulgy

'Bauchlandung f AVIAT belly landing

Bauchredner m ventriloquist

Bauchschmerzen *pl* stomachache

Bauchtanz m belly dancing

bauen ['bauən] (*ge-*, h) **1.** v/t build, construct, *a.* make (*furniture etc*); **2.** fig v/i: **bauen auf** (*acc*) rely *or* count on

Bauer¹ ['bauɐ] m (-n; -n) farmer; *chess:* pawn

'Bauer² n, m (-s; -) (bird)cage

Bäuerin ['bɔyərɪn] f (-; *-nen*) farmer's wife; farmer

bäuerlich ['bɔyɐlɪç] *adj* rural; rustic

'Bauernfänger *contp* m trickster, conman

Bauernhaus n farmhouse

Bauernhof m farm

Bauernmöbel *pl* rustic furniture

'baufällig *adj* dilapidated

'Baufirma f builders and contractors

Baugenehmigung f building permit

Baugerüst n scaffold(ing)

Bauherr m owner

Bauholz n lumber, *Br a.* timber

Bauinge,nieur m civil engineer

Baujahr n year of construction; **Baujahr 1995** 1995 model

Baukasten m box of building blocks (*Br* bricks); TECH construction set; kit

Bauleiter m building supervisor

'baulich *adj* structural

Baum [baum] m (-[e]s; Bäume ['bɔymə]) BOT tree

'Baumarkt m do-it-yourself superstore

baumeln ['bauməln] v/i (*ge-*, h) dangle, swing; **mit den Beinen baumeln** dangle one's legs

'**Baumschule** f nursery
Baumstamm m trunk; log
Baumwolle f cotton
'**Bauplan** m architectural drawing; blueprints
Bauplatz m building site
Bausch [bauʃ] m (-[e]s; -e) wad, ball; *in Bausch und Bogen* lock, stock and barrel
'**Bausparkasse** f building and loan association, Br building society
'**Baustein** m brick; (building) block; fig element
Baustelle f building site; MOT construction zone, Br roadworks
Baustil m (architectural) style
Baustoff m building material
Bautechniker m engineer
Bauteil n component (part), unit, module
Bauunternehmer m building contractor
Bauvorschriften pl building regulations
Bauwerk n building
Bauzaun m hoarding
Bauzeichner m draftsman, Br draughtsman
Bayern ['baiən] Bavaria
Bayer ['baiɐ] m (-n; -n), **Bayerin** ['baiərɪn] f (-; -nen), **bay(e)risch** ['bai(ə)rɪʃ] adj Bavarian
Bazillus [ba'tsɪlʊs] m (-; -len) MED bacillus, germ
beabsichtigen [bə'ʔapzɪçtɪɡən] v/t (no -ge-, h) intend, plan; *es war beabsichtigt* it was intentional
be'**achten** v/t (no -ge-, h) pay attention to; observe, follow (rule etc); *beachten Sie, dass ...* note that ...; *nicht beachten* take no notice of; disregard
be'**achtlich** adj remarkable; considerable
Be'**achtung** f (-; no pl) attention; consideration; observance
Beamte [bə'ʔamtə] m (-n; -n), **Beamtin** f (-; -nen) official; (police etc) officer; civil servant
be'**ängstigend** adj alarming
beanspruchen [bə'ʔanʃprʊxən] v/t (no -ge-, h) claim; take up (time etc); TECH stress
Be'**anspruchung** f (-; -en) claim; TECH stress, strain (a. fig)
beanstanden [bə'ʔanʃtandən] v/t (no -ge-, h) complain about; object to
beantragen [bə'ʔantra:ɡən] v/t (no -ge-, h) apply for; JUR, PARL move (for); propose
be'**antworten** v/t (no -ge-, h) answer, reply to
be'**arbeiten** v/t (no -ge-, h) work; AGR till; hew (stone); process; be in charge of (a

case etc); treat (subject); revise; THEA adapt (*nach* from); esp MUS arrange; F *j-n bearbeiten* work on s.o.
Be'**arbeitung** f (-; -en) working; revision; THEA adaptation; esp MUS arrangement; TECH processing, treatment
be'**atmen** v/t (no -ge-, h) MED give artificial respiration to s.o.
beaufsichtigen [bə'ʔaufzɪçtɪɡən] v/t (no -ge-, h) supervise; look after
Be'**aufsichtigung** f (-; -en) supervision; looking after
be'**auftragen** v/t (no -ge-, h) commission; instruct; *beauftragen mit* put s.o. in charge of
Be'**auftragte** [-tra:ktə] m, f (-n; -n) agent; representative; commissioner
be'**bauen** v/t (no -ge-, h) build on; AGR cultivate
beben ['be:bən] v/i (ge-, h) shake, tremble; shiver (all: *vor* with); earth: quake
bebildern [bə'bɪldɐn] v/t (no -ge-, h) illustrate
Becher ['bɛçɐ] m (-s; -) cup, mug
Becken ['bɛkən] n (-s; -) basin, bowl; pool; ANAT pelvis; MUS cymbal(s)
bedacht [bə'daxt] adj: *darauf bedacht sein zu* inf be anxious to inf
bedächtig [bə'dɛçtɪç] adj deliberate; measured
bedang [bə'daŋ] pret of **bedingen**
be'**danken** v/refl (no -ge-, h) *sich bei j-m für et. bedanken* thank s.o. for s.th.
Bedarf [bə'darf] m (-[e]s; no pl) need (an dat of), want (of); ECON demand (for); *bei Bedarf* if necessary
Be'**darfshaltestelle** f request stop
bedauerlich [bə'dauɐlɪç] adj regrettable
be'**dauerlicher'weise** adv unfortunately
be'**dauern** v/t (no -ge-, h) feel or be sorry for s.o., pity s.o.; regret s.th.
Be'**dauern** n (-s; no pl) regret (*über* acc at)
be'**dauernswert** adj pitiable, deplorable
be'**decken** v/t (no -ge-, h) cover
be'**deckt** adj METEOR overcast
be'**denken** v/t (irr, **denken**, no -ge-, h) consider, think s.th. over
Be'**denken** pl doubts; scruples; objections
be'**denkenlos** adv unhesitatingly; without scruples
be'**denklich** adj doubtful; serious, critical; alarming
Be'**denkzeit** f: *e-e Stunde Bedenkzeit* one hour to think it over
be'**deuten** v/t (no -ge-, h) mean
bedeutend adj important; considerable; distinguished
Be'**deutung** f (-; -en) meaning; impor-

tance

be'deutungslos *adj* insignificant; meaningless

be'deutungsvoll *adj* significant; meaningful

be'dienen [*no* -ge-, h] **1.** *v/t* serve, wait on *s.o.*; TECH operate, work; *sich bedienen* help o.s.; *bedienen Sie sich!* help yourself! **2.** *v/i* serve; wait (at table); *card games*: follow suit

Be'dienung *f* (-; -en) a) (*no pl*) service, b) waiter, waitress; shop assistant, clerk, c) TECH operation, control

Be'dienungsanleitung *f* operating instructions

bedingen [bə'dɪŋən] *v/t* ([*irr.*] *no* -ge-, h) require; cause; imply, involve

be'dingt *adj*: *bedingt durch* caused by, due to

Be'dingung *f* (-; -en) condition; *pl* ECON terms; requirements; conditions; *unter einer Bedingung* on one condition

be'dingungslos *adj* unconditional

be'drängen [*no* -ge-, h] press (hard)

be'drohen *v/t* [*no* -ge-, h] threaten, menace

be'drohlich *adj* threatening

Be'drohung *f* threat, menace (*gen* to)

be'drücken *v/t* [*no* -ge-, h] depress, sadden

bedungen [bə'dʊŋən] *pp of* **bedingen**

Bedürfnis [bə'dyrfnɪs] *n* (-ses; -se) need, necessity (*für, nach* for)

Bedürfnisanstalt *f* comfort station, *Br* public convenience (*or* toilets)

be'dürftig *adj* needy, poor

be'eilen *v/refl* [*no* -ge-, h] hurry (up)

beeindrucken [bə'ʔaindrʊkən] *v/t* [*no* -ge-, h] impress

beeinflussen [bə'ʔainflʊsən] *v/t* [*no* -ge-, h] influence; affect

beeinträchtigen [bə'ʔaintrɛçtɪgən] *v/t* [*no* -ge-, h] affect, impair

be'end(ig)en *v/t* [*no* -ge-, h] (bring to an) end, finish, conclude, close

beengen [bə'ɛŋən] *v/t* [*no* -ge-, h] make *s.o.* (feel) uncomfortable

be'engt *adj*: *beengt wohnen* live in cramped quarters

be'erben *v/t* [*no* -ge-, h] *j-n beerben* be *s.o.*'s heir

beerdigen [bə'ʔeːɐdɪgən] *v/t* [*no* -ge-, h] bury

Be'erdigung *f* (-; -en) burial, funeral

Beere ['beːrə] *f* (-; -n) BOT berry; grape

Beet [beːt] *n* (-[e]s; -e) bed, patch

befähigen [bə'fɛːɪgən] *v/t* [*no* -ge-, h] enable; qualify (*für, zu* for)

be'fähigt *adj* (cap)able; *zu et. befähigt* fit

or qualified for s.th.

Be'fähigung *f* (-; *no pl*) qualification(s), (cap)ability

befahl [bə'faːl] *pret of* **befehlen**

be'fahrbar *adj* passable, practicable; MAR navigable

be'fahren *v/t* (*irr*, **fahren**, *no* -ge-, h) drive *or* travel on; MAR navigate

be'fallen *v/t* (*irr*, **fallen**, *no* -ge-, h) attack, seize (*a. fig*)

be'fangen *adj* self-conscious; prejudiced, JUR *a.* bias(s)ed

Be'fangenheit *f* (-; *no pl*) self-consciousness; bias, prejudice

be'fassen *v/refl* [*no* -ge-, h] *sich befassen mit* engage *or* occupy o.s. with; work on *s.th.*; deal with *s.o.*, *s.th.*

Befehl [bə'feːl] *m* (-[e]s; -e) order; command (*über acc* of)

be'fehlen *v/t* (*irr*, *no* -ge-, h) order; command

Be'fehlshaber *m* (-s; -) MIL commander

be'festigen *v/t* [*no* -ge-, h] fasten (*an dat* to), fix (to), attach (to); MIL fortify

Be'festigung *f* (-; -en) fixing, fastening; MIL fortification

be'feuchten *v/t* [*no* -ge-, h] moisten, damp

be'finden *v/refl* (*irr*, **finden**, *no* -ge-, h) be (situated)

Be'finden *n* (-s; *no pl*) (state of) health

be'flecken *v/t* [*no* -ge-, h] stain; *fig a.* sully

befohlen [bə'foːlən] *pp of* **befehlen**

be'folgen *v/t* [*no* -ge-, h] follow, take (*advice*); observe (*rule etc*); REL keep

Be'folgung *f* (-; *no pl*) following; observance

be'fördern *v/t* [*no* -ge-, h] carry, transport; haul, ship; promote (*zu* to)

Be'förderung *f* (-; -en) a) (*no pl*) transport(ation); shipment, b) promotion

be'fragen *v/t* [*no* -ge-, h] question, interview

be'freien *v/t* [*no* -ge-, h] free, liberate; rescue; exempt (*von* from)

Be'freiung *f* (-; *no pl*) liberation; exemption

Befremden [bə'frɛmdən] *n* (-s; *no pl*) irritation, displeasure

be'fremdet *adj* irritated, displeased

befreunden [bə'frɔyndən] *v/refl* [*no* -ge-, h] *sich befreunden mit* make friends with; *fig* warm to

be'freundet *adj* friendly; *befreundet sein* be friends

befriedigen [bə'friːdɪgən] *v/t* [*no* -ge-, h] satisfy; *sich selbst befriedigen* masturbate

befriedigend *adj* satisfactory; *grade*: fair

befriedigt [bə'fri:dɪçt] *adj* satisfied, pleased

Be'friedigung *f* (-; *no pl*) satisfaction

be'fristet *adj* limited (**auf** *acc* to); temporary

be'fruchten *v/t* (*no -ge-, h*) BIOL fertilize, inseminate

Be'fruchtung *f* (-; *-en*) BIOL fertilization, insemination

Befugnis [bə'fu:knɪs] *f* (-; *-se*) authority; *esp* JUR competence

befugt [bə'fu:kt] *adj* authorized; competent

be'fühlen *v/t* (*no -ge-, h*) feel, touch

Be'fund *m* finding(s) (*a.* MED, JUR)

be'fürchten *v/t* (*no -ge-, h*) fear, be afraid of; suspect

Be'fürchtung *f* (-; *-en*) fear, suspicion

befürworten [bə'fy:ɐvɔrtən] *v/t* (*no -ge-, h*) advocate, speak *or* plead for

Be'fürworter *m* (*-s; -*) advocate

begabt [bə'ga:pt] *adj* gifted, talented

Be'gabung *f* (-; *-en*) gift, talent(s)

begann [bə'gan] *pret of* beginnen

be'geben *v/refl* (*irr, geben, no -ge-, h*) **sich in Gefahr begeben** expose o.s. to danger

Be'gebenheit *f* (-; *-en*) incident, event

begegnen [bə'ge:gnən] *v/i* (*no -ge-, sein*) meet (*a. fig mit* with); **sich begegnen** meet

Be'gegnung *f* (-; *-en*) meeting, encounter (*a.* SPORT)

be'gehen *v/t* (*irr, gehen, no -ge-, h*) walk (on); celebrate (*birthday etc*); commit (*crime*); make (*mistake*); **ein Unrecht begehen** do wrong

begehren [bə'ge:rən] *v/t* (*no -ge-, h*) desire

be'gehrenswert *adj* desirable

be'gehrlich *adj* desirous, covetous

begehrt [bə'ge:ɐt] *adj* (very) popular, (much) in demand

begeistern [bə'gaistɐn] *v/t* (*no -ge-, h*) fill with enthusiasm; carry away (*audience*); **sich begeistern für** be enthusiastic about

be'geistert *adj* enthusiastic

Be'geisterung *f* (-; *no pl*) enthusiasm

Begierde [bə'gi:ɐdə] *f* (-; *-n*) desire (**nach** for), appetite (for)

be'gierig *adj* greedy; eager (**nach**, **auf** *acc* for; **zu** *inf* to inf)

be'gießen *v/t* (*irr, gießen, no -ge-, h*) water; GASTR baste; F *fig* celebrate *s.th.* (with a drink)

Beginn [bə'gɪn] *m* (-[*e*]*s; no pl*) beginning, start; **zu Beginn** at the beginning

be'ginnen *v/t and v/i* (*irr, no -ge-, h*) begin, start

beglaubigen [bə'glaubɪgən] *v/t* (*no -ge-, h*) attest, certify

Be'glaubigung *f* (-; *-en*) attestation, certification

be'gleichen *v/t* (*irr, gleichen, no -ge-, h*) pay, settle

be'gleiten *v/t* (*no -ge-, h*) accompany (*a.* MUS **auf** *dat* on); **j-n nach Hause begleiten** see s.o. home

Be'gleiter(in) (*-s; -/-; -nen*) companion; MUS accompanist

Be'gleiterscheinung *f* concomitant; MED side effect

Be'gleitschreiben *n* covering letter

Be'gleitung *f* (-; *-en*) company; *esp* MIL escort; MUS accompaniment

be'glückwünschen *v/t* (*no -ge-, h*) congratulate (**zu** on)

begnadigen [bə'gna:dɪgən] *v/t* (*no -ge-, h*), **Be'gnadigung** *f* (-; *-en*) JUR pardon; amnesty

begnügen [bə'gny:gən] *v/refl* (*no -ge-, h*) **sich begnügen mit** be satisfied with; make do with

begonnen [bə'gɔnən] *pp of* beginnen

be'graben *v/t* (*irr, graben, no -ge-, h*) bury (*a. fig*)

Begräbnis [bə'grɛ:pnɪs] *n* (*-ses; -se*) burial; funeral

begradigen [bə'gra:dɪgən] *v/t* (*no -ge-, h*) straighten

be'greifen *v/t* (*irr, greifen, no -ge-, h*) comprehend, understand

be'greiflich *adj* understandable

be'grenzen *v/t* (*no -ge-, h*) limit, restrict (**auf** *acc* to)

be'grenzt *adj* limited

Be'griff *m* (*-[e]s; -e*) idea, notion; term (*a.* MATH); **im Begriff sein zu** *inf* be about to *inf*

be'griffsstutzig *contp adj* F slow on the uptake

be'gründen *v/t* (*no -ge-, h*) give reasons for

be'gründet *adj* well-founded, justified

Be'gründung *f* (-; *-en*) reasons, arguments

be'grünen *v/t* (*no -ge-, h*) landscape

be'grüßen *v/t* (*no -ge-, h*) greet, welcome (*a. fig*)

Be'grüßung *f* (-; *-en*) greeting, welcome

begünstigen [bə'gynstɪgən] *v/t* (*no -ge-, h*) favo(u)r

be'gutachten *v/t* (*no -ge-, h*) give an (expert's) opinion on; examine; **begutachten lassen** obtain expert opinion on

begütert [bə'gy:tɐt] *adj* wealthy

be'haart *adj* hairy

behäbig [bəˈhɛːbɪç] adj slow; portly

be'haftet adj: **mit Fehlern behaftet** flawed

behagen [bəˈhaːgən] v/i (no -ge-, h) **j-m behagen** please or suit s.o.

Be'hagen n (-s; no pl) pleasure, enjoyment

behaglich [bəˈhaːklɪç] adj comfortable; cozy, snug

be'halten v/t (irr, halten, no -ge-, h) keep (fig **für sich** to o.s.); remember

Behälter [bəˈhɛltɐ] m (-s; -) container, receptacle

be'handeln v/t (no -ge-, h) handle; treat (a. MED); **sich (ärztlich) behandeln lassen** undergo (medical) treatment

Be'handlung f (-; -en) handling; a. MED treatment

beharren [bəˈharən] v/i (no -ge-, h) insist (**auf** dat on)

be'harrlich adj persistent

behaupten [bəˈhauptən] v/t (no -ge-, h) claim; pretend

Be'hauptung f (-; -en) statement, claim

be'heben v/t (irr, heben, no -ge-, h) repair (damage etc)

be'heizen v/t (no -ge-, h) heat

be'helfen v/refl (irr, helfen, no -ge-, h) **sich behelfen mit** make do with; **sich behelfen ohne** do without

Be'helfs… in cpds mst temporary

beherbergen [bəˈhɛrbɛrgən] v/t (no -ge-, h) accommodate

be'herrschen v/t (no -ge-, h) rule (over), govern; ECON dominate, control; have a (good) command of (language); **sich beherrschen** control o.s.

Be'herrschung f (-; no pl) command, control

beherzigen [bəˈhɛrtsɪgən] v/t (no -ge-, h) take to heart, mind

be'hilflich adj: **j-m behilflich sein** help s.o. (**bei** with, in)

be'hindern v/t (no -ge-, h) hinder; obstruct (a. SPORT)

be'hindert adj MED handicapped; disabled

Be'hinderung f (-; -en) obstruction; MED handicap

Behörde [bəˈhøːdə] f (-; -n) authority, mst the authorities; board

be'hüten v/t (no -ge-, h) guard (**vor** dat from)

behutsam [bəˈhuːtzaːm] adj careful; gentle

bei [bai] prp (dat) near; at; with; by; time: during; at; **bei München** near Munich; **wohnen bei** stay (or live) with; **bei mir (ihr)** at my (her) place; **bei uns (zu Hau-**

se) at home; **arbeiten bei** work for; **e-e Stelle bei** a job with; **bei der Marine** in the navy; **bei Familie Müller** at the Müllers'; **bei Müller** c/o Müller; **ich habe kein Geld bei mir** I have no money with or on me; **bei e-r Tasse Tee** over a cup of tea; **wir haben Englisch bei Herrn X** we have Mr X for English; **bei Licht** by light; **bei Tag** during the day; **bei Nacht (Sonnenaufgang)** at night (sunrise); **bei s-r Geburt** at his birth; **bei Regen (Gefahr)** in case of rain (danger); **bei 100 Grad** at a hundred degrees; → **Arbeit, beim, weit**

'beibehalten v/t (irr, halten, sep, no -ge-, h) keep up, retain

'beibringen v/t (irr, bringen, sep, no -ge-, h) teach; tell; inflict (dat on)

Beichte [ˈbaiçtə] f (-; -n) REL confession

'beichten v/t and v/i (ge-, h) REL confess (a. fig)

Beichtstuhl m REL confessional

beide [ˈbaidə] adj and pron both; **m-e beiden Brüder** my two brothers; **wir beiden** the two of us; both of us; **keiner von beiden** neither of them; **30 beide** tennis: 30 all

beiei'nander adv together

Beifahrer m front(-seat) passenger

Beifall m (-[e]s; no pl) applause; fig approval

Beifallssturm m (standing) ovation

'beifügen v/t (sep, -ge-, h) enclose (dat with)

beige [beːʃ] adj beige

'beigeben (irr, geben, sep, -ge-, h) **1.** v/t add; **2.** F v/i: **klein beigeben** knuckle under

Beigeschmack m smack (**von** of) (a. fig)

Beihilfe f aid, allowance; JUR aiding and abetting

Beil [bail] n (-[e]s; -e) hatchet; ax(e)

Beilage f supplement; GASTR side dish; vegetables

'beiläufig adj casual

'beilegen v/t (sep, -ge-, h) add (dat to); enclose (with); settle (dispute)

Beilegung f (-; -en) settlement

Beileid n (-[e]s; no pl) condolence; **herzliches Beileid** my deepest sympathy

'beiliegen v/i (irr, liegen, sep, -ge-, h) be enclosed (dat with)

beim [baim] prp: **beim Bäcker** at the baker's; **beim Sprechen** etc while speaking etc; **beim Spielen** at play; → a. **bei**

'beimessen v/t (irr, messen, sep, -ge-, h) attach importance etc (dat to)

Bein [bain] n (-[e]s; -e) ANAT leg; bone

beinah(e) [ˈbainaː(ə)] adv almost, nearly

'**Beinbruch** m MED fracture of the leg
'**beipflichten** v/i (sep, -ge-, h) agree (dat with)
be'irren v/t (no -ge-, h) confuse
beisammen [bai'zamən] adv together
Bei'sammensein n: **geselliges Beisammensein** get-together
'**Beischlaf** m JUR sexual intercourse
bei'seite adv aside; **beiseiteschaffen** v/t (sep, -ge-, h) remove; liquidate s.o.
'**beisetzen** v/t (sep, -ge-, h) bury
'**Beisetzung** f (-; -en) funeral
'**Beispiel** n [-[e]s; -e] example; **zum Beispiel** for example, for instance; **sich an j-m ein Beispiel nehmen** follow s.o.'s example
'**beispielhaft** adj exemplary
'**beispiellos** adj unprecedented, unparalleled
'**beispielsweise** adv such as
beißen ['baisən] v/t and v/i (irr, -ge-, h) bite (a. fig); **sich beißen** colors: clash
beißend adj biting, pungent (both a. fig)
'**Beistand** m [-[e]s; no pl] assistance
'**beistehen** v/i (irr, **stehen**, sep, -ge-, h) **j-m beistehen** assist or help s.o.
'**beisteuern** v/t (sep, -ge-, h) contribute (**zu** to)
Beitrag ['baitra:k] m [-[e]s; Beiträge ['bai-tre:gə]) contribution; dues, Br subscription
'**beitragen** v/t (irr, **tragen**, sep, -ge-, h) contribute (**zu** to)
'**beitreten** v/i (irr, **treten**, sep, -ge-, sein) join
'**Beitritt** m [-[e]s; -e] joining
'**Beiwagen** m MOT sidecar
bei'zeiten adv early, in good time
beizen ['baitsən] v/t (ge-, h) stain (wood); pickle (meat)
bejahen [bə'ja:ən] v/t (no -ge-, h) answer in the affirmative, affirm
bejahend adj affirmative
be'kämpfen v/t (no -ge-, h) fight (against)
bekannt [bə'kant] adj (well-)known; familiar; **et. bekannt geben** announce s.th.; **j-n mit j-m bekannt machen** introduce s.o. to s.o.
Be'kannte m, f (-n; -n) acquaintance, mst friend
be'kanntgeben v/t (irr, **geben**, sep, -ge-, h) →**bekannt**
be'kanntlich adv as you know
be'kanntmachen v/t (sep, -ge-, h) → **bekannt**; **Be'kanntmachung** f (-; -en) announcement
Be'kanntschaft f (-; -en) acquaintance
be'kehren v/t (no -ge-, h) convert
be'kennen v/t (irr, **kennen**, no -ge-, h)

confess (a. REL); admit; **sich schuldig bekennen** JUR plead guilty; **sich bekennen zu** profess s.th.; claim responsibility for
Be'kennerbrief m letter claiming responsibility
Be'kenntnis n (-ses; -se) confession, REL a. denomination
be'klagen v/t (no -ge-, h) deplore; **sich beklagen** complain (**über** acc about)
be'klagenswert adj deplorable
be'kleben v/t (no -ge-, h) stick (or paste) on s.th.; **mit Etiketten bekleben** label s.th.
be'kleckern F v/t (no -ge-, h) stain; **sich bekleckern mit** spill s.th. over o.s.
Be'kleidung f (-; -en) clothing, clothes
be'kommen (irr, **kommen**, no -ge-) **1.** v/t (h) get, receive; MED catch; be having (baby); **2.** v/i (sein) **j-m (gut) bekommen** agree with s.o.
bekömmlich [bə'kœmlɪç] adj wholesome
be'kräftigen v/t (no -ge-, h) confirm
be'kreuzigen v/refl (no -ge-, h) cross o.s.
bekümmert [bə'kʏmɐt] adj worried
be'laden v/t (irr, **laden**, no -ge-, h) load, fig a. burden
Belag [bə'la:k] m [-[e]s; Beläge [bə'lɛ:gə]) covering; TECH coat(ing); MOT lining; (road) surface; MED fur; plaque; GASTR topping; spread; (sandwich) filling
be'lagern v/t (no -ge-, h) MIL besiege (a. fig)
Be'lagerung f (-; -en) MIL siege
be'lassen v/t (irr, **lassen**, no -ge-, h) leave; **es dabei belassen** leave it at that
be'langlos adj irrelevant
be'lastbar adj resistant to strain or stress; TECH loadable
be'lasten v/t (no -ge-, h) load; fig burden; JUR incriminate; pollute; damage; **j-s Konto belasten mit** charge s.th. to s.o.'s account
belästigen [bə'lɛstɪgən] v/t (no -ge-, h) molest; annoy; disturb, bother
Be'lästigung f (-; -en) molestation; annoyance; disturbance
Be'lastung f (-; -en) load (a. TECH); fig burden; strain; stress; JUR incrimination; pollution, contamination
Be'lastungszeuge m JUR witness for the prosecution
be'laufen v/refl (irr, **laufen**, no -ge-, h) **sich belaufen auf** (acc) amount to
be'lauschen v/t (no -ge-, h) eavesdrop on
be'leben fig v/t (no -ge-, h) stimulate
belebend adj stimulating
belebt [bə'le:pt] adj busy, crowded
Beleg [bə'le:k] m [-[e]s; -e] proof; receipt;

document

be'legen v/t (no -ge-, h) cover; reserve (seat); prove; enrol(l) for, take (classes) GASTR put s.th. on; **den ersten** etc **Platz belegen** SPORT take first etc place

Be'legschaft f (-; -en) staff

be'legt adj taken, occupied; hotel etc: full; TEL busy, Br engaged; MED coated; **belegtes Brot** sandwich

be'lehren v/t (no -ge-, h) teach, instruct, inform; **sich belehren lassen** take advice

beleidigen [bə'laidɪɡən] v/t (no -ge-, h) offend (a. fig); insult

beleidigend adj offensive, insulting

Be'leidigung f (-; -en) offense, Br offence, insult

be'lesen adj well-read

be'leuchten v/t (no -ge-, h) light (up), illuminate (a. fig); fig throw light on

Be'leuchtung f (-; -en) light(ing); illumination

Belgien ['bɛlɡjən] Belgium

Belgier ['bɛlɡjə] m (-s; -), 'Belgierin [-ɡjərɪn] f (-; -nen), 'belgisch adj Belgian

be'lichten v/t (no -ge-, h) PHOT expose

Be'lichtungsmesser m PHOT exposure meter

Be'lieben n: **nach Belieben** at will

beliebig [bə'li:bɪç] adj any; optional; **jeder beliebige** anyone

beliebt [bə'li:pt] adj popular (**bei** with)

Be'liebtheit f (-; no pl) popularity

be'liefern v/t (no -ge-, h) supply, furnish (**mit** with)

Be'lieferung f supply

bellen ['bɛlən] v/i (ge-, h) bark (a. fig)

be'lohnen v/t (no -ge-, h) reward

Be'lohnung f (-; -en) reward; **zur Belohnung** as a reward

be'lügen v/t (irr, lügen, no -ge-, h) **j-n belügen** lie to s.o.

belustigen [bə'lʊstɪɡən] v/t (no -ge-, h) amuse

be'lustigt adj amused

Be'lustigung f (-; -en) amusement

bemächtigen [bə'mɛçtɪɡən] v/refl (no -ge-, h) get hold of, seize

be'malen v/t (no -ge-, h) paint

bemängeln [bə'mɛŋəln] v/t (no -ge-, h) find fault with

bemannt [bə'mant] adj manned

be'merkbar adj noticeable; **sich bemerkbar machen** draw attention to o.s.; begin to show

be'merken v/t (no -ge-, h) notice; remark

be'merkenswert adj remarkable

Be'merkung f (-; -en) remark (**über** acc about)

be'mitleiden v/t (no -ge-, h) pity, feel sorry for

be'mitleidenswert adj pitiable

be'mühen v/refl (no -ge-, h) try (hard); **sich bemühen um** try to get s.th.; try to help s.o.; **bitte bemühen Sie sich nicht!** please don't bother

Be'mühung f (-; -en) effort; **danke für Ihre Bemühungen!** thank you for your trouble

be'muttern v/t (no -ge-, h) mother s.o.

be'nachbart adj neighbo(u)ring

benachrichtigen [bə'na:xrɪçtɪɡən] v/t (no -ge-, h) inform, notify

Be'nachrichtigung f (-; -en) information, notification

benachteiligen [bə'na:xtailɪɡən] v/t (no -ge-, h) place s.o. at a disadvantage; discriminate against s.o.

benachteiligt [bə'na:xtailɪçt] adj disadvantaged; **die Benachteiligten** the underprivileged

Be'nachteiligung f (-; -en) disadvantage; discrimination

be'nehmen v/refl (irr, nehmen, no -ge-, h) behave (o.s.)

Be'nehmen n (-s; no pl) behavio(u)r; manners

be'neiden v/t (no -ge-, h) **j-n um et. beneiden** envy s.o. s.th.

be'neidenswert adj enviable

BENELUX ['be:nelʊks] ABBR of **Belgien, Niederlande, Luxemburg** Belgium, the Netherlands and Luxembourg

be'nennen v/t (irr, nennen, no -ge-, h) name

Bengel ['bɛŋəl] m (-s; -) (little) rascal, urchin

benommen [bə'nɔmən] adj dazed, F dopey

be'noten v/t (no -ge-, h) grade, Br mark

be'nötigen v/t (no -ge-, h) need, want, require

be'nutzen v/t (no -ge-, h) use

Be'nutzer m (-s; -) user

be'nutzerfreundlich adj user-friendly

Be'nutzeroberfläche f EDP user interface

Be'nutzung f use

Benzin [bɛn'tsi:n] n (-s; -e) gasoline, F gas, Br petrol

beobachten [bə'ʔo:baxtən] v/t (no -ge-, h) watch; observe

Be'obachter m (-s; -) observer

Be'obachtung f (-; -en) observation

be'pflanzen v/t (no -ge-, h) plant (**mit** with)

bequem [bə'kve:m] adj comfortable; easy; lazy

be'quemen v/refl (no -ge-, h) **sich beque-**

men zu inf bring o.s. to *inf*
Be'quemlichkeit f (-; *-en*) a) comfort; *alle Bequemlichkeiten* all conveniences, b) (*no pl*) laziness
be'raten v/t (*irr*, **raten**, *no -ge-*, *h*) advise s.o.; debate, discuss s.th.; *sich beraten* confer (*mit j-m* with s.o.; *über et.* on s.th.)
Be'rater m (-s; -) adviser, consultant
Be'ratung f (-; *-en*) advice (*a.* MED); debate; consultation, conference
Be'ratungsstelle f counsel(l)ing center (*Br* centre)
be'rauben v/t (*no -ge-*, *h*) rob
be'rauschend *adj* intoxicating; F *fig nicht gerade berauschend!* not so hot!
be'rauscht *fig adj*: **berauscht von** drunk with
be'rechnen v/t (*no -ge-*, *h*) calculate; ECON charge (*zu* at)
be'rechnend *adj* calculating
Be'rechnung f calculation (*a. fig*)
berechtigen [bə'rɛçtɪɡən] v/t: *j-n berechtigen zu* entitle (*or* authorize) s.o. to
be'rechtigt [-tɪçt] *adj* entitled (*zu* to); authorized (to); legitimate
Be'rechtigung f (-; *no pl*) right (*zu* to); authority
Beredsamkeit [bə'reːtzaːmkaɪt] f (-; *no pl*) eloquence
beredt [bə'reːt] *adj* eloquent (*a. fig*)
Be'reich m (-[e]s; *-e*) area; range; field
bereichern [bə'raɪçərn] v/t (*no -ge-*, *h*) enrich; *sich bereichern* get rich (*an dat* on)
Be'reicherung [bə'raɪçərʊŋ] f (-; *no pl*) enrichment
Be'reifung f (-; *-en*) (set of) tires (*Br* tyres)
be'reinigen v/t (*no -ge-*, *h*) settle
be'reisen v/t (*no -ge-*, *h*) tour; cover
bereit [bə'raɪt] *adj* ready, prepared; willing
be'reiten v/t (*no -ge-*, *h*) prepare; cause
be'reithalten v/t (*irr*, **halten**, *sep*, *-ge-*, *h*) have s.th. ready; *sich bereithalten* stand by
be'reits *adv* already
Be'reitschaft f (-; *no pl*) readiness; *in Bereitschaft* on standby
Be'reitschaftsdienst m: *Bereitschaftsdienst haben* doctor etc: be on call
be'reitstellen v/t (*sep*, *-ge-*, *h*) provide
be'reitwillig *adj* ready, willing
be'reuen v/t (*no -ge-*, *h*) repent (of); regret
Berg [bɛrk] m (-[e]s; *-e*) mountain; *Berge von* F loads of; *die Haare standen ihm zu Berge* his hair stood on end
berg'ab *adv* downhill (*a. fig*)
'Bergarbeiter m miner
berg'auf *adv* uphill

'Bergbahn f mountain railroad (*Br* railway)
Bergbau m (-[e]s; *no pl*) mining
bergen ['bɛrɡən] v/t (*irr*, *ge-*, *h*) rescue, save s.o.; salvage s.th.; recover (*body*)
'Bergführer m mountain guide
bergig ['bɛrɡɪç] *adj* mountainous
'Bergkette f mountain range
Bergmann m (-[e]s; *-leute*) miner
'Bergrutsch m landslide
'Bergschuhe *pl* mountain(eering) boots
'Bergspitze f (mountain) peak
'Bergsteigen n mountaineering, (mountain) climbing
'Bergsteiger m (-s; -) mountaineer, (mountain) climber
'Bergung f (-; *-en*) recovery; rescue
'Bergungsarbeiten *pl* rescue work; salvage operations
'Bergwacht f alpine rescue service
'Bergwerk n mine
Bericht [bə'rɪçt] m (-[e]s; *-e*) report (*über acc* on), account (of)
be'richten v/t and v/i (*no -ge-*, *h*) report (*über acc* on); *j-m et. berichten* inform s.o. of s.th.; tell s.o. about s.th.
Be'richterstatter m (-s; -) reporter; correspondent
Be'richterstattung f (-; *-en*) report(ing)
berichtigen [bə'rɪçtɪɡən] v/t (*no -ge-*, *h*) correct
Be'richtigung f (-; *-en*) correction
be'rieseln v/t (*no -ge-*, *h*) sprinkle
Bernstein ['bɛrnʃtaɪn] m (-[e]s; *no pl*) amber
bersten ['bɛrstən] v/i (*irr*, *-ge-*, *sein*) burst (*fig vor dat* with)
berüchtigt [bə'rʏçtɪçt] *adj* notorious (*wegen* for)
berücksichtigen [bə'rʏkzɪçtɪɡən] v/t (*no -ge-*, *h*) take into consideration; *nicht berücksichtigen* disregard
Be'rücksichtigung f: *unter Berücksichtigung* (*gen*) in consideration of
Be'ruf m (-[e]s; *-e*) job, occupation; trade; profession
be'rufen v/t (*irr*, **rufen**, *no -ge-*, *h*) appoint (*zu* [as] s.o.; to s.th.); *sich berufen auf* (*acc*) refer to
be'ruflich *adj* professional; *beruflich unterwegs* away on business
Be'rufs... *in cpds ...sportler etc*: professional ...
Berufsausbildung f vocational (*or* professional) training
Berufsberater m careers advisor
Berufsberatung f careers guidance
Berufsbezeichnung f job designation *or* title
Berufskleidung f work clothes

Berufskrankheit f occupational disease

Berufsschule f vocational school

be'**rufstätig** adj: **berufstätig sein** (go to) work, have a job

Be'**rufstätige** m, f (-n; -n) working person, pl working people

Be'**rufsverkehr** m rush-hour traffic

Be'**rufung** f (-; -en) appointment (**zu** to); JUR appeal (**bei** to); **unter Berufung auf** (acc) with reference to; on the grounds of

be'**ruhen** v/i (no -ge-, h) **beruhen auf** (dat) be based on; **et. auf sich beruhen lassen** let s.th. rest

be**ruhigen** [bə'ruːɪɡən] v/t (no -ge-, h) quiet(en), calm, soothe; reassure s.o.; **sich beruhigen** calm down

be**ruhigend** adj reassuring; MED sedative

Be'**ruhigung** f (-; -en) calming (down); soothing; relief

Be'**ruhigungsmittel** n MED sedative; tranquil(l)izer

be**rühmt** [bə'ryːmt] adj famous (**wegen** for)

Be'**rühmtheit** f (-; -en) a) (no pl) fame, b) celebrity, star

be'**rühren** v/t (no -ge-, h) touch (a. fig); concern

Be'**rührung** f (-; -en) touch; **in Berührung kommen** come into contact

Be'**rührungsangst** f fear of contact

Be**rührungspunkt** m point of contact

be**sänftigen** [bə'zɛnftɪɡən] v/t (no -ge-, h) appease, calm, soothe

Be'**satzung** f (-; -en) AVIAT, MAR crew; MIL occupying forces

Be'**satzungsmacht** f MIL occupying power

Be'**satzungstruppen** pl MIL occupying forces

be'**saufen** F v/refl (irr, **saufen**, no -ge-, h) get drunk, get bombed

be'**schädigen** v/t (no -ge-, h) damage

Be'**schädigung** f (-; -en) damage

be'**schaffen** v/t (no -ge-, h) provide, get; raise (money)

Be'**schaffenheit** f (-; no pl) state, condition

be**schäftigen** [bə'ʃɛftɪɡən] v/t (no -ge-, h) employ; keep s.o. busy; **sich beschäftigen** occupy o.s.

be'**schäftigt** [-tɪçt] adj busy, occupied

Be'**schäftigte** m, f (-n; -n) employed person, pl employed people

Be'**schäftigung** f (-; -en) employment; occupation

be'**schämen** v/t (no -ge-, h) shame s.o., make s.o. feel ashamed

be**schämend** adj shameful; humiliating

be'**schämt** adj ashamed (**über** acc of)

be'**schatten** fig v/t (no -ge-, h) shadow, F tail

Bescheid [bə'ʃaɪt] m (-[e]s; -e) answer; JUR decision; information (**über** acc on, about); **sagen Sie mir Bescheid** let me know; (**gut**) **Bescheid wissen über** (acc) know all about

be'**scheiden** adj modest (a. fig); humble

Be'**scheidenheit** f (-; no pl) modesty

be**scheinigen** [bə'ʃaɪnɪɡən] v/t (no -ge-, h) certify

Be'**scheinigung** f (-; -en) a) (no pl) certification, b) certificate

be'**scheißen** V v/t (irr, **scheißen**, no -ge-, h) cheat; **j-n bescheißen um** do s.o. out of

be'**schenken** v/t (no -ge-, h) **j-n (reich) beschenken** give s.o. (shower s.o. with) presents

Be'**scherung** f (-; -en) distribution of (Christmas) presents; F fig mess

be'**schichten** v/t (no -ge-, h) TECH coat

Be'**schichtung** f (-; -en) TECH coat

be'**schießen** v/t (irr, **schießen**, no -ge-, h) MIL fire or shoot at; bombard (a. PHYS), shell

be'**schimpfen** v/t (no -ge-, h) abuse, insult; swear at

Be'**schimpfung** f (-; -en) abuse, insult

be'**schissen** V adj lousy, rotten

Be'**schlag** m TECH metal fitting(s); **in Beschlag nehmen** fig monopolize s.o.; bag; occupy

be'**schlagen** (irr, **schlagen**, no -ge-) **1.** v/t (h) cover; TECH fit, mount; shoe (horse); **2.** v/i (sein) window etc: steam up; **3.** adj steamed-up; fig well-versed (**auf**, **in** in)

Be'**schlagnahme** [bə'ʃlaːknaːmə] f (-; -n) confiscation

be'**schlagnahmen** v/t (no -ge-, h) confiscate

be**schleunigen** [bə'ʃlɔɪnɪɡən] v/t and v/i (no -ge-, h) accelerate, speed up

Be'**schleunigung** f (-; -en) acceleration

be'**schließen** v/t (irr, **schließen**, no -ge-, h) decide (on); pass (law); conclude

Be'**schluss** m decision

be'**schmieren** v/t (no -ge-, h) smear, soil; scrawl all over; cover wall etc with graffiti; spread (toast etc)

be'**schmutzen** v/t (no -ge-, h) soil (a. fig), dirty

be'**schneiden** v/t (irr, **schneiden**, no -ge-, h) clip, cut (a. fig); prune; MED circumcise

be'**schönigen** [bə'ʃøːnɪɡən] v/t (no -ge-, h) gloss over

be**schränken** [bə'ʃrɛŋkən] v/t (no -ge-, h) confine, limit, restrict; **sich beschrän-**

ken auf (*acc*) confine o.s. to

be'schränkt *adj* limited; *contp* dense; narrow-minded

Be'schränkung *f* (-; -en) limitation, restriction

be'schreiben *v/t* (*irr, schreiben, no -ge-, h*) describe; write on

Be'schreibung *f* (-; -en) description

be'schriften *v/t* (*no -ge-, h*) inscribe; mark (*goods*)

Be'schriftung *f* (-; -en) inscription

beschuldigen [bə'ʃʊldɪɡən] *v/t* (*no -ge-, h*) blame; *j-n e-r Sache beschuldigen* accuse s.o. of s.th. (*a. JUR*)

Be'schuldigung *f* (-; -en) accusation

be'schummeln F *v/t* (*no -ge-, h*) cheat

Be'schuss *m*: *unter Beschuss* MIL under fire

be'schützen *v/t* (*no -ge-, h*) protect, shelter, guard (*vor dat* from)

Be'schützer *m* (-s; -) protector

Beschwerde [bə'ʃveːɐdə] *f* (-; -n) complaint (*über acc* about; *bei* to); *pl* MED complaints, trouble

beschweren [bə'ʃveːrən] *v/t* (*no -ge-, h*) weight *s.th.*; *sich beschweren* complain (*über acc* about; *bei* to)

be'schwerlich *adj* hard, arduous

beschwichtigen [bə'ʃvɪçtɪɡən] *v/t* (*no -ge-, h*) appease (*a. POL*), calm

be'schwindeln *v/t* (*no -ge-, h*) tell a fib *or* lie; cheat

beschwingt [bə'ʃvɪŋt] *adj* buoyant; MUS lively, swinging

beschwipst [bə'ʃvɪpst] F *adj* tipsy

be'schwören *v/t* (*irr, schwören, no -ge-, h*) swear to; implore; conjure up

beseitigen [bə'zaɪtɪɡən] *v/t* (*no -ge-, h*) remove (*a. s.o.*), *a.* dispose of (*waste etc*); eliminate; POL liquidate

Be'seitigung *f* (-; *no pl*) removal; disposal; elimination

Besen [ˈbeːzən] *m* (-s; -) broom

'Besenstiel *m* broomstick

besessen [bə'zɛsən] *adj* obsessed (*von* by, with); *wie besessen* like mad

be'setzen *v/t* (*no -ge-, h*) occupy (*a. MIL*); fill (*post etc*); THEA cast; trim; squat in

be'setzt *adj* occupied; *seat*: taken; *bus etc*: full up; TEL busy, *Br* engaged

Be'setztzeichen *n* TEL busy signal, *Br* engaged tone

Be'setzung *f* (-; -en) THEA cast; MIL occupation

besichtigen [bə'zɪçtɪɡən] *v/t* (*no -ge-, h*) visit, see the sights of; inspect

Be'sichtigung *f* (-; -en) sightseeing; visit (*gen* to); inspection (of)

be'siedeln *v/t* (*no -ge-, h*) settle; colonize; populate

be'siedelt *adj*: *dicht* (*dünn*) *besiedelt* densely (sparsely) populated

Be'siedlung *f* (-; -en) settlement; colonization; population

be'siegeln *v/t* (*no -ge-, h*) seal

be'siegen *v/t* (*no -ge-, h*) defeat, beat; conquer (*a. fig*)

besinnen *v/refl* (*irr, sinnen, no -ge-, h*) remember; think (*auf acc* about); *sich anders besinnen* change one's mind

be'sinnlich *adj* contemplative

Be'sinnung *f* (-; *no pl*) MED consciousness; (*wieder*) *zur Besinnung kommen* MED come round; *fig* come to one's senses

be'sinnungslos *adj* MED unconscious

Be'sitz *m* (-es; *no pl*) possession; property; *Besitz ergreifen von* take possession of

be'sitzanzeigend *adj* LING possessive

be'sitzen *v/t* (*irr, sitzen, no -ge-, h*) possess, own

Be'sitzer *m* (-s; -) possessor, owner; *den Besitzer wechseln* change hands

Be'soldung *f* (-; -en) pay; salary

besondere [bə'zɔndərə] *adj* special, particular; peculiar

Be'sonderheit *f* (-; -en) peculiarity

be'sonders *adv* especially, particularly; chiefly, mainly

be'sonnen *adj* prudent, level-headed

be'sorgen *v/t* (*no -ge-, h*) get, buy; → *erledigen*

Be'sorgnis [bə'zɔrknɪs] *f* (-; -se) concern, alarm, anxiety (*über acc* about, at); *Besorgnis erregend* → *besorgniserregend*

be'sorgniserregend *adj* alarming

besorgt [bə'zɔrkt] *adj* worried, concerned

Be'sorgung *f* (-; -en) *Besorgungen machen* go shopping

be'spielen *v/t* (*no -ge-, h*) make a recording on

be'spitzeln *v/t* (*no -ge-, h*) spy on *s.o.*

be'sprechen *v/t* (*irr, sprechen, no -ge-, h*) discuss, talk *s.th.* over; review (*book etc*)

Be'sprechung *f* (-; -en) discussion, talk(s); meeting, conference; review

be'spritzen *v/t* (*no -ge-, h*) spatter

besser [ˈbɛsɐ] *adj und adv* better; *es ist besser, wir fragen ihn* we had better ask him; *immer besser* better and better; *es geht ihm besser* he is better; *oder bes-*

ser gesagt or rather; **es besser wissen** know better; **es besser machen als** do better than; **besser ist besser** just to be on the safe side

'**bessern** v/refl (ge-, h) improve, get better

'**Besserung** f (-; no pl) improvement; **auf dem Wege der Besserung** on the way to recovery; **gute Besserung!** get better soon

'**Besserwisser** [-vɪsə] m (-s; -) F smart aleck

Be'**stand** m a) (no pl) (continued) existence, b) stock; **Bestand haben** last, be lasting

be'**ständig** adj constant, steady (a. character); settled; **...beständig** in cpds ...-resistant, ...proof

Be'**standsaufnahme** f ECON stocktaking (a. fig); **Bestandsaufnahme machen** take stock (a. fig)

Be'**standteil** m part, component

be'**stärken** v/t (no -ge-, h) confirm, strengthen, encourage (**in** dat in)

be'**stätigen** [bə'ʃtɛːtɪɡən] v/t (no -ge-, h) confirm; certify; acknowledge (receipt); **sich bestätigen** prove (to be) true; come true; **sich bestätigt fühlen** feel affirmed

Be'**stätigung** f (-; -en) confirmation; certificate; acknowledg(e-)ment; letter of confirmation

be'**statten** [bə'ʃtatən] v/t (no -ge-, h) bury

Be'**stattungsinsti,tut** n funeral home, Br undertakers

be'**stäuben** v/t (no -ge-, h) dust; BOT pollinate

'**beste** [bɛstə] adj and adv best; **am besten** best; **welches gefällt dir am besten?** which one do you like best?; **am besten nehmen Sie den Bus** it would be best to take a bus

'**Beste** m, f (-n; -n), n (-n; no pl) the best; **das Beste geben** do one's best; **das Beste machen aus** make the best of; **(nur) zu deinem Besten** for your own good

be'**stechen** v/t (irr, **stechen**, no -ge-, h) bribe; fascinate (**durch** by)

be'**stechlich** adj corrupt

Be'**stechung** f (-; -en) bribery, corruption

Be'**stechungsgeld** n bribe

Be'**steck** [bə'ʃtɛk] n (-[e]s; -e) (set of) knife, fork and spoon; cutlery

be'**stehen** (irr, **stehen**, no -ge-, h) **1.** v/t pass (examination etc); **2.** v/i be, exist; **bestehen auf** (dat) insist on; **bestehen aus** (**in**) (**in**) consist of (in); **bestehen bleiben** last, survive

Be'**stehen** n (-s; no pl) existence

be'**stehlen** v/t (irr, **stehlen**, no -ge-, h) **j-n**

be'**stehlen** steal s.o.'s money etc

be'**steigen** v/t (irr, **steigen**, no -ge-, h) climb; get on a bus etc; ascend (the throne)

be'**stellen** v/t (no -ge-, h) order; book (room etc); reserve (seat etc); call (taxi); give, send (message etc); AGR cultivate; **kann ich et. bestellen?** can I take a message?; **bestellen Sie ihm bitte, ...** please tell him ...

Be'**stellschein** m ECON order form

Be'**stellung** f (-; -en) booking; reservation; ECON order; **auf Bestellung** to order

'**bestenfalls** adv at best

'**bestens** adv very well

bestialisch [bɛs'tjaːlɪʃ] adj fig bestial

Bestie ['bɛstjə] f (-; -n) beast, fig a. brute

be'**stimmen** v/t (no -ge-, h) determine, decide; define; choose, pick; **zu bestimmen haben** be in charge, F be the boss; **bestimmt für** meant for

be'**stimmt 1.** adj determined, firm; LING definite (article); **bestimmte Dinge** certain things; **2.** adv certainly; **ganz bestimmt** definitely; **er ist bestimmt ...** he must be ...

Be'**stimmung** f (-; -en) regulation; destiny

Be'**stimmungsort** m destination

'**Bestleistung** f SPORT (personal) record

be'**strafen** v/t (no -ge-, h) punish

Be'**strafung** f (-; -en) punishment

be'**strahlen** v/t (no -ge-, h) irradiate (a. MED)

Be'**strahlung** f (-; -en) irradiation; MED ray treatment, radiotherapy

be'**streichen** v/t (irr, **streichen**, no -ge-, h) spread

be'**streiten** v/t (irr, **streiten**, no -ge-, h) challenge; deny; pay for, finance

be'**streuen** v/t (no -ge-, h) sprinkle (**mit** with)

be'**stürmen** v/t (no -ge-, h) urge; bombard

be'**stürzt** adj dismayed (**über** acc at)

Be'**stürzung** f (-; no pl) consternation, dismay

Besuch [bə'zuːx] m (-[e]s; -e) visit (gen, **bei,** in dat to); call (**bei** on; **in** dat at); attendance (gen at); **Besuch haben** have company or guests

be'**suchen** v/t (no -ge-, h) visit; call on, (go to) see; look s.o. up; attend (meeting etc); go to (pub etc)

Be'**sucher(in)** (-s; -/-; -nen) visitor, guest

Be'**suchszeit** f visiting hours

be'**sucht** adj: **gut (schlecht) besucht** well (poorly) attended; much (little) frequented

betagt [bə'taːkt] adj aged

be'tasten *v/t* (*no -ge-, h*) touch, feel

be'tätigen *v/t* (*no -ge-, h*) TECH operate; apply (*brake*); **sich betätigen** be active

Be'tätigung *f* (*-; -en*) activity

betäuben [bə'tɔybən] *v/t* (*no -ge-, h*) stun (*a. fig*), daze; MED an(a)esthetize

Be'täubung *f* (*-; -en*) MED an(a)esthetization; an(a)esthesia; *fig* daze, stupor

Be'täubungsmittel *n* MED an(a)esthetic; narcotic

Bete ['be:tə] *f* (*-; -n*) **rote Bete** BOT beet, *Br* beetroot

beteiligen [bə'tailɪgən] *v/t* (*no -ge-, h*) **j-n beteiligen** give s.o. a share (*an dat* in); **sich beteiligen** take part (*an dat, bei* in), participate (in) (*a. JUR*)

beteiligt [bə'tailɪçt] *adj* concerned; **beteiligt sein an** (*dat*) be involved in; ECON have a share in

Be'teiligung *f* (*-; -en*) participation (*a. JUR, ECON*); involvement; share (*a. ECON*)

beten ['be:tən] *v/i* (*ge-, h*) pray (**um** for), say one's prayers; say grace

beteuern [bə'tɔyən] *v/t* (*no -ge-, h*) protest (*one's innocence etc*)

Beton [be'tɔŋ] *m* (*-s*) [be'tɔːnə] concrete

betonen [be'toːnən] *v/t* (*no -ge-, h*) stress, *fig a.* emphasize

betonieren [beto'niːrən] *v/t* (*no -ge-, h*) (cover with) concrete

Be'tonung *f* (*-; -en*) stress; *fig* emphasis

betören [bə'tøːrən] *v/t* (*no -ge-, h*) infatuate, bewitch

Betr. ABBR *of* betrifft re

Betracht [bə'traxt] *m*: **in Betracht ziehen** take into account; **nicht in Betracht kommen** be out of the question

be'trachten *v/t* (*no -ge-, h*) look at, *fig a.* view; **betrachten als** look upon *or* regard as, consider

Be'trachter *m* (*-s; -*) viewer

beträchtlich [bə'trɛçtlıç] *adj* considerable

Be'trachtung *f* (*-; -en*) view; **bei näherer Betrachtung** on closer inspection

Betrag [bə'traːk] *m* (*-[e]s; Beträge* [bə-'trɛːgə]) amount, sum

be'tragen (*irr, tragen, no -ge-, h*) **1.** *v/t* amount to; **2.** *v/refl* behave (o.s.)

Be'tragen *n* (*-s; no pl*) behavio(u)r, conduct

be'trauen *v/t* (*no -ge-, h*) entrust (**mit** with)

be'treffen *v/t* (*irr, treffen, no -ge-, h*) concern; refer to; **was ... betrifft** as for ..., as to ...; **betrifft** (ABBR **Betr.**) re

betreffend *adj* concerning; **die betreffenden Personen** *etc* the people *etc* con-

cerned

be'treiben *v/t* (*irr, treiben, no -ge-, h*) operate, run; go in for (*sport etc*)

be'treten¹ *v/t* (*irr, treten, no -ge-, h*) step on; enter; **Betreten** (**des Rasens**) **verboten!** keep out! (keep off the grass!)

be'treten² *adj* embarrassed

betreuen [bə'trɔyən] *v/t* (*no -ge-, h*) look after, take care of

Be'treuung *f* (*-; no pl*) care (*gen* of, for)

Betrieb [bə'triːp] *m* (*-[e]s; -e*) a) business, firm, company, b) (*no pl*) operation, running, c) (*no pl*) rush; **in Betrieb sein** (**setzen**) be in (put into) operation; **außer Betrieb** out of order; **im Geschäft war viel Betrieb** the shop was very busy

Be'triebsanleitung *f* operating instructions

Betriebsberater *m* business consultant

Betriebsferien *pl* company (*Br a.* works) holiday

Betriebsfest *n* annual company fête

Betriebskapi,tal *n* working capital

Betriebsklima *n* working atmosphere

Betriebskosten *pl* operating costs

Betriebsleitung *f* management

Betriebsrat *m* works council

be'triebssicher *adj* safe to operate

Be'triebsstörung *f* TECH breakdown

Betriebssys,tem *n* EDP operating system

Betriebsunfall *m* industrial accident

Betriebswirtschaft *f* business administration

be'trinken *v/refl* (*irr, trinken, no -ge-, h*) get drunk

betroffen [bə'trɔfən] *adj* affected, concerned; dismayed, shocked

Be'troffenheit *f* (*-; no pl*) dismay, shock

betrübt [bə'tryːpt] *adj* sad, grieved (**über** *acc* at)

Betrug [bə'truːk] *m* (*-[e]s; no pl*) cheat; JUR fraud; deceit

be'trügen *v/t* (*irr, trügen, no -ge-, h*) deceive; cheat (**beim Kartenspiel** at cards); swindle, trick (**um** *et.* out of s.th.); be unfaithful to

Be'trüger(in) (*-s; -/-; -nen*) swindler, trickster

betrunken [bə'trʊŋkən] *adj* drunken; **betrunken sein** be drunk

Be'trunkene *m, f* (*-n; -n*) drunk

Bett [bɛt] *n* (*-[e]s; -en*) bed; **am Bett** at the bedside; **ins Bett gehen** (**bringen**) go (put) to bed

Bettbezug *m* comforter case, *Br* duvet cover

Bettdecke *f* blanket; quilt

betteln ['bɛtəln] *v/i* (*ge-, h*) beg (**um** for)

'Bettgestell *n* bedstead

'bettlägerig [-lɛːgəriç] *adj* bedridden
'Bettlaken *n* sheet
Bettler ['bɛtlɐ] *m* (-s; -) beggar
'Bettnässer [-nɛsɐ] *m* (-s; -) MED bed wetter
Bettruhe *f* bed rest; *j-m Bettruhe verordnen* tell s.o. to stay in bed
Bettvorleger *m* bedside rug
Bettwäsche *f* bed linen
Bettzeug *n* bedding, bedclothes
beugen ['bɔygən] *v/t* (ge-, h) bend; LING inflect; *sich beugen (vor* dat) bend, bow
Beule ['bɔylə] *f* (-; -n) MED bump; MOT dent
beunruhigen [bə'ʔunruːɪgən] *v/t* (no -ge-, h) alarm, worry
beurlauben [bə'ʔuːɐlaubən] *v/t* give s.o. leave *or* time off; suspend; *sich beurlauben lassen* ask for leave
be'urlaubt [-laupt] *adj* on leave
be'urteilen *v/t* (no -ge-, h) judge (*nach* by); rate
Be'urteilung *f* (-; -en) judg(e)ment; evaluation
Beute ['bɔytə] *f* (-; no pl) booty, loot; zo prey (*a. fig*); HUNT bag; *fig a.* victim
Beutel ['bɔytəl] *m* (-s; -) bag; pouch
bevölkern [bə'fœlkɐn] *v/t* (no -ge-, h) populate
be'völkert *adj* → *besiedelt*
Be'völkerung *f* (-; -en) population
bevollmächtigen [bə'fɔlmɛçtɪgən] *v/t* (no -ge-, h) authorize
be'vor *cj* before
bevormunden [bə'foːɐmundən] *v/t* (no -ge-, h) patronize
bevorstehen *v/i* (irr, *stehen*, sep, -ge-, h) be approaching; lie ahead; be imminent; *j-m bevorstehen* be in store for s.o., await s.o.
be'vorzugen [-tsuːgən] *v/t* (no -ge-, h) prefer; favo(u)r
Be'vorzugung *f* (-; -en) preferential treatment
be'wachen *v/t* (no -ge-, h) guard, watch over
Be'wacher *m* (-s; -) guard; SPORT marker
Be'wachung *f* (-; -en) a) (no pl) guarding; SPORT marking, b) guard
bewaffnen [bə'vafnən] *v/t* (no -ge-, h) arm (*a. fig*)
Be'waffnung *f* (-; -en) armament; arms
be'wahren *v/t* (no -ge-, h) keep; *bewahren vor* (dat) keep or save from
be'währen *v/refl* (no -ge-, h) prove successful; *sich bewähren als* prove to be
be'währt [bə'vɛːɐt] *adj* (well-)tried, reliable; experienced
Be'währung *f* (-; -en) JUR probation

Be'währungsfrist *f* JUR (period of) probation
Bewährungshelfer *m* JUR probation officer
Bewährungsprobe *f* (acid) test
bewaldet [bə'valdət] *adj* wooded, woody
bewältigen [bə'vɛltɪgən] *v/t* (no -ge-, h) manage, cope with; cover (*distance*)
be'wandert *adj* (well-)versed (*in* dat in)
be'wässern *v/t* (no -ge-, h) irrigate
Be'wässerung *f* (-; -en) irrigation
bewegen [bə'veːgən] *v/t and v/refl* (no -ge-, h) move (*a. fig*); *nicht bewegen!* don't move!; (irr) *j-n zu et. bewegen* get s.o. to do s.th.
be'weggrund *m* motive
beweglich [bə'veːklɪç] *adj* movable; agile; flexible; TECH moving (*parts*)
Be'weglichkeit *f* (-; no pl) mobility; agility
be'wegt *adj* rough (*sea*); choked (*voice*); eventful (*life*); *fig* moved, touched
Be'wegung *f* (-; -en) movement (*a. POL*); motion (*a. PHYS*); exercise; *fig* emotion; *in Bewegung setzen* set in motion
Be'wegungsfreiheit *f* (-; no pl) freedom of movement (*fig a.* of action)
be'wegungslos *adj* motionless
Be'weis [bə'vais] *m* (-es; -e) proof (*für* of); *Beweis(e)* evidence (*esp* JUR)
be'weisen *v/t* (irr, *weisen*, no -ge-, h) prove; show
Be'weismittel *n* JUR (piece of) evidence
Be'weisstück *n* (piece of) evidence, JUR exhibit
be'wenden *v/i: es dabei bewenden lassen* leave it at that
be'werben *v/refl* (irr, *werben*, no -ge-, h) *sich bewerben um* apply for
Be'wer-ber(in) (-s; -/-; -nen) applicant
Be'werbung *f* (-; -en) application
Be'werbungsschreiben *n* (letter of) application
be'werten *v/t* (no -ge-, h) assess; judge
Be'wertung *f* (-; -en) assessment
bewilligen [bə'vɪlɪgən] *v/t* (no -ge-, h) grant, allow
be'wirken *v/t* (no -ge-, h) cause
bewirten [bə'vɪrtən] *v/t* (no -ge-, h) entertain
be'wirtschaften *v/t* (no -ge-, h) run; AGR farm
be'wirtschaftet *adj* open (to the public)
Be'wirtung *f* (-; -en) catering; service; hospitality
bewog [bə'voːk] *pret of* **bewegen**
bewogen [bə'voːgən] *pp of* **bewegen**
be'wohnen *v/t* (no -ge-, h) live in; inhabit
Be'wohner(in) (-s; -/-; -nen) inhabitant;

occupant

be'wohnt adj inhabited; occupied

bewölken [bə'vœlkən] v/refl (no -ge-, h) METEOR cloud over (a. fig)

be'wölkt adj METEOR cloudy, overcast

Be'wölkung f (-; no pl) METEOR clouds

Bewunderer [bə'vʊndərə] m (-s; -) admirer

be'wundern v/t (no -ge-, h) admire (**wegen** for)

be'wundernswert adj admirable

Be'wunderung f (-; no pl) admiration

bewusst [bə'vʊst] adj conscious; intentional; **sich e-r Sache bewusst sein** be conscious or aware of s.th., realize s.th.; **j-m et. bewusst machen** make s.o. realize s.th.

be'wusstlos adj MED unconscious

be'wusstmachen v/t → **bewusst**

Be'wusstsein n (-s; no pl) MED consciousness; **bei Bewusstsein** consciousness

be'zahlen v/t (no -ge-, h) pay; pay for (a. fig)

be'zahlt adj: **bezahlter Urlaub** paid leave; **es macht sich bezahlt** it pays

Be'zahlung f (-; no pl) payment; pay

be'zaubern v/t (no -ge-, h) charm

bezaubernd adj charming, F sweet, darling

be'zeichnen v/t (no -ge-, h) **bezeichnen als** call, describe as

bezeichnend adj characteristic, typical (**für** of)

Be'zeichnung f (-; -en) name, term

be'zeugen v/t (no -ge-, h) JUR testify to

be'ziehen v/t (irr, ziehen, no -ge-, h) cover; put clean sheets on (bed); move into; receive; subscribe to (paper etc); **beziehen auf** (acc) relate to; **sich beziehen** cloud over; **sich beziehen auf** (acc) refer to

Be'ziehung f (-; -en) relation (**zu** to s.th.; with s.o.); connection (**zu** to s.th.); relationship; respect; **Beziehungen haben** have connections

be'ziehungsweise cj respectively; or; or rather

Bezirk [bə'tsɪrk] m (-[e]s; -e) precinct, Br a. district

Bezug [bə'tsuːk] m (-[e]s; Bezüge [bə'tsyːgə]) a) cover(ing); case, slip, b) (no pl) ECON purchase; subscription (gen to), c) pl earnings; **Bezug nehmen auf** (acc) refer to; **in Bezug auf** (acc) → **bezüglich**

bezüglich [bə'tsyːklɪç] prp (gen) regarding, concerning

Be'zugsper,son f PSYCH person to relate to, role model

Bezugspunkt m reference point

Bezugsquelle f source (of supply)

be'zwecken v/t (no -ge-, h) aim at, intend

be'zweifeln v/t (no -ge-, h) doubt, question

be'zwingen v/t (irr, zwingen, no -ge-, h) conquer, defeat

Bibel ['biːbəl] f (-; -n) Bible

Biber ['biːbɐ] m (-s; -) ZO beaver

Bibliothek [biblio'teːk] f (-; -en) library

Bibliothekar [bibliote'kaːɐ] m (-s; -e), **Bibliothe'karin** f (-; -nen) librarian

biblisch ['biːblɪʃ] adj biblical

bieder ['biːdɐ] adj honest; square

biegen ['biːgən] v/t (irr, ge-, h) and v/i (sein) bend (a. sich biegen), road: a. turn; **um die Ecke biegen** turn (round) the corner

biegsam ['biːkzaːm] adj flexible

'Biegung f (-; -en) curve

Biene ['biːnə] f (-; -n) ZO bee

'Bienenkönigin f ZO queen (bee)

Bienenkorb m, **Bienenstock** m (bee)hive

Bienenwachs n beeswax

Bier [biːɐ] n (-[e]s; -e) beer; **Bier vom Faß** draft (Br draught) beer

Bierdeckel m coaster, beer mat

Bierkrug m beer mug, stein

Biest [biːst] F fig n (-[e]s; -er) beast; (kleines) **Biest** brat, little devil, stinker

bieten ['biːtən] v/t (irr, ge-, h) **1.** v/t offer; **sich bieten** present itself; **2.** v/i auction: (make a) bid

Bigamie [biga'miː] f (-; -n) bigamy

Bikini [bi'kiːni] m (-s; -s) bikini

Bilanz [bi'lants] f (-; -en) ECON balance; fig result; **Bilanz ziehen aus** (dat) fig take stock of

Bild [bɪlt] n (-[e]s; -er ['bɪldɐ]) picture; image; **sich ein Bild machen von** get an idea of

Bildausfall m TV blackout

Bildbericht m photo(graphic) essay (Br report)

bilden ['bɪldən] v/t (ge-, h) form (a. sich bilden); shape; fig educate (sich o.s.); be, constitute

'Bilderbuch n picture book

'Bildfläche f: F **auf der Bildfläche erscheinen (von der Bildfläche verschwinden)** appear on (disappear from) the scene

'Bildhauer m (-s; -), **'Bildhauerin** f (-; -nen) sculptor

'bildlich adj graphic; figurative

'Bildnis n (-ses; -se) portrait

'Bildplatte f videodisk (Br -disc)

'Bildröhre f picture tube

'Bildschirm m TV screen, EDP a. display,

monitor
Bildschirmarbeitsplatz *m* workstation
Bildschirmgerät *n* visual display unit, VDU
Bildschirmschoner *m* (-*s*; -) screen saver
Bildschirmtext *m* videotext, *Br* viewdata
'**bild schön** *adj* most beautiful
'**Bildung** *f* (-; -*en*) a) (*no pl*) education, b) formation
'**Bildungs...** in *cpds* ...*chancen*, ...*reform*, ...*urlaub etc*: educational ...
Bildungslücke *f* gap in one's knowledge
'**Bildunterschrift** *f* caption
Billard ['bɪljart] *n* (-*s*; -*e*) billiards, pool
Billardkugel *f* billiard ball
Billardstock *m* cue
Billett [bɪl'jɛt] *n* (-[*e*]*s*; -*e*) *Swiss* ticket
billig ['bɪlɪç] *adj* cheap (*a. contp*), inexpensive
billigen ['bɪlɪgən] *v/t* (*ge*-, *h*) approve of
'**Billigung** *f* (-; *no pl*) approval
Billion [bɪ'ljoːn] *f* (-; -*en*) trillion
bimmeln ['bɪməln] *F v/i* (*ge*-, *h*) jingle; TEL ring
binär [bi'nɛːɐ] *adj* MATH, PHYS *etc* binary
Binde ['bɪndə] *f* (-; -*n*) bandage; sling; → *Damenbinde*
Bindegewebe *n* ANAT connective tissue
Bindeglied ['bɪnt-] *n* (connecting) link
'**Bindehaut** *f* ANAT conjunctiva
Bindehautentzündung *f* MED conjunctivitis
binden (*irr*, *ge*-, *h*) **1.** *v/t* bind (*a. book*), tie (*an acc* to); make (*wreath etc*); knot (*tie*); *sich binden* bind *or* commit o.s.; **2.** *v/i* bind
'**Bindestrich** *m* LING hyphen
'**Bindewort** *n* LING conjunction
Bindfaden ['bɪnt-] *m* string
'**Bindung** *f* (-; -*en*) tie, link, bond; *skiing*: binding
Binnenhafen ['bɪnən-] *m* inland port
Binnenhandel *m* domestic trade
Binnenmarkt *m*: *Europäischer Binnenmarkt* European single market
Binnenschifffahrt *f* inland navigation
Binnenverkehr *m* inland traffic *or* transport
Binse ['bɪnzə] *f* (-; -*n*) BOT rush
'**Binsenweisheit** *f* (-; -*en*) truism
Bio..., **bio...** [bio-] in *cpds* ...*chemie*, ...*dynamisch*, ...*sphäre etc*: bio...
Biografie, Biographie [biogra'fiː] *f* (-; -*n*) biography
bio'grafisch, bio'graphisch *adj* biographic(al)
Bioladen ['biːo-] *m* health food shop *or* store
Biologe [bio'loːgə] *m* (-*n*; -*n*) biologist

Biologie [biolo'giː] *f* (-; *no pl*) biology
Bio'login *f* (-; -*nen*) biologist
biologisch [bio'loːgɪʃ] *adj* biological; AGR organic; *biologisch abbaubar* biodegradable
'**Biorhythmus** *m* biorhythm
'**Biotechnik** *f* (-; *no pl*) biotechnology
Biotop [bio'toːp] *n* (-*s*; -*e*) biotope
Birke ['bɪrkə] *f* (-; -*n*) BOT birch (tree)
Birne ['bɪrnə] *f* (-; -*n*) BOT pear; ELECTR (light) bulb
bis [bɪs] *prp* (*acc*) *and adv and cj time*: till, until, (up) to; *space*: (up) to, as far as; *von ... bis ...* from ... to ...; *bis auf* (*acc*) except; *bis zu* up to; *bis später!* see you later!; *bis jetzt* up to now, so far; *bis Montag* by Monday; *zwei bis drei* two or three; *wie weit ist es bis ...?* how far is it to ...?
Bischof ['bɪʃɔf] *m* (-*s*; *Bischöfe* ['bɪʃœfə]) REL bishop
bisexuell [bizɛ'ksuɛl] *adj* bisexual
bis'her *adv* up to now, so far; *wie bisher* as before
bisherig [bɪs'heːrɪç] *adj* previous
Biskuit [bɪs'kviːt] *n* (-[*e*]*s*; -*e*) sponge cake (mix)
biss [bɪs] *pret of* **beißen**
Biss *m* (-*es*; -*e*) bite (*a. fig*)
bisschen ['bɪsçən] *adj and adv*: *ein bisschen* a little, a (little) bit (of); *nicht ein bisschen* not in the least
Bissen ['bɪsən] *m* (-*s*; -) bite; *keinen Bissen* not a thing
bissig ['bɪsɪç] *adj fig* cutting; *ein bissiger Hund* a dog that bites; *Vorsicht!, bissiger Hund!* beware of the dog!
Bistum ['bɪstuːm] *n* (-*s*; *Bistümer* ['bɪstyːmɐ]) REL bishopric, diocese
bis'weilen *adv* at times, now and then
Bit [bɪt] *n* (-[*s*]; -[*s*]) EDP bit
bitte ['bɪtə] *adv* please; *bitte nicht!* please don't!; *bitte (schön)!* that's all right, not at all, you're welcome; here you are; (*wie*) *bitte?* pardon?; *bitte sehr?* can I help you?
'**Bitte** *f* (-; -*n*) request (*um* for); *ich habe e-e Bitte (an dich)* I have a favo(u)r to ask of you
'**bitten** *v/t* (*irr*, *ge*-, *h*) *j-n um et. bitten* ask s.o. for s.th.; *darf ich bitten?* may I have (the pleasure of) this dance?; → *Erlaubnis*
bitter ['bɪtɐ] *adj* bitter (*a. fig*), *a.* biting (*cold*)
bitter'kalt *adj* bitterly cold
blähen ['blɛːən] *v/refl* (*ge*-, *h*) swell
'**Blähungen** *pl* MED flatulence, *Br a.* wind
blamabel [bla'maːbəl] *adj* embarrassing

Blamage [bla'ma:ʒə] f (-; -n) disgrace, shame

blamieren [bla'mi:rən] v/t (no -ge-, h) j-n **blamieren** make s.o. look like a fool; **sich blamieren** make a fool of o.s.

blank [blaŋk] adj shining, shiny, bright; polished; F broke

Blanko... ['blaŋko] in cpds ECON blank

Bläschen ['blɛːsçən] n (-s; -) MED vesicle, small blister

Blase ['bla:zə] f (-; -n) bubble; ANAT bladder; MED blister

'**Blasebalg** m (pair of) bellows

'**blasen** v/t (irr, ge-, h) blow (a. MUS)

'**Blasinstru,ment** n MUS wind instrument

'**Blaska,pelle** f brass band

'**Blasrohr** n blowpipe

blass [blas] adj pale (**vor** with); **blass werden** turn pale

Blässe ['blɛsə] f (-; no pl) paleness, pallor

Blatt [blat] n (-[e]s; Blätter ['blɛtɐ]) BOT leaf; piece, sheet (a. MUS); (news)paper; card games: hand

blättern ['blɛtɐn] v/i (ge-, h) **blättern in** (dat) leaf through

'**Blätterteig** m puff pastry

blau [blau] adj blue; F loaded, stoned; **blaues Auge** black eye; **blauer Fleck** bruise; **Fahrt ins Blaue** mystery tour

'**blauäugig** [-ɔʏɡɪç] adj blue-eyed; fig starry-eyed

'**Blaubeere** f BOT blueberry, Br bilberry

'**blaugrau** adj bluish-gray (Br -grey)

bläulich ['blɔʏlɪç] adj bluish

'**Blaulicht** n (-[e]s; -er) flashing light(s)

'**Blauhelme** pl MIL UN soldiers

'**blaumachen** F v/i (sep, -ge-, h) stay away from work or school

'**Blausäure** f CHEM prussic acid

Blech [blɛç] n (-[e]s; -e) sheet metal; in cpds ...dach, ...löffel etc: tin ...; ...instrument: MUS brass ...

'**blechen** F v/t and v/i (ge-, h) shell out

'**Blechbüchse, Blechdose** f can, Br a. tin

'**Blechschaden** m MOT bodywork damage

Blei [blai] n (-[e]s; -e) lead; **aus Blei** leaden

Bleibe ['blaibə] f (-; -n) place to stay

'**bleiben** v/i (irr, ge-, sein) stay, remain; **bleiben bei** stick to; F **et. bleiben lassen** not do s.th.; **lass das bleiben!** stop that!; **das wirst du schön bleiben lassen!** you'll do nothing of the sort!; → **Appa-rat, ruhig**

bleibend adj lasting, permanent

'**bleibenlassen** v/i → **bleiben**

bleich [blaiç] adj pale (**vor** dat with)

'**bleichen** v/t ([irr], ge-, h) bleach

bleiern ['blaiɐn] adj lead(en fig)

'**bleifrei** adj MOT unleaded

'**Bleistift** m pencil

Bleistiftspitzer m pencil sharpener

Blende ['blɛndə] f (-; -n) blind; PHOT aperture; (**bei) Blende 8** (at) f-8

'**blenden** v/t (ge-, h) blind, dazzle (both a. fig)

blendend adj dazzling (a. fig); brilliant; **blendend aussehen** look great

'**blendfrei** adj OPT antiglare

blich [blɪç] pret of **bleichen**

Blick [blɪk] m (-[e]s; -e) look (**auf** acc at); view (of); **flüchtiger Blick** glance; **auf den ersten Blick** at first sight

'**blicken** v/i (ge-, h) look, glance (both: **auf** acc, **nach** at)

'**Blickfang** m eye-catcher

'**Blickfeld** n field of vision

blieb [bli:p] pret of **bleiben**

blies [bli:s] pret of **blasen**

blind [blɪnt] adj blind (a. fig **gegen, für** to; **vor** dat with); dull (mirror etc); **blinder Alarm** false alarm; **blinder Passagier** stowaway; **auf e-m Auge blind** blind in one eye; **ein Blinder** a blind man; **e-e Blinde** a blind woman; **die Blinden** the blind

'**Blinddarm** m ANAT appendix

Blinddarmentzündung f MED appendicitis

Blinddarmoperati,on f MED appendectomy

Blindenhund ['blɪndən-] m seeing eye (Br guide) dog

Blindenschrift f braille

'**Blindgänger** [-ɡɛŋɐ] m (-s; -) MIL dud

'**Blindheit** f (-; no pl) blindness

blindlings ['blɪntlɪŋs] adv blindly

'**Blindschleiche** f ZO blindworm

blinken ['blɪŋkən] v/i (ge-, h) sparkle, shine; twinkle; flash (a signal); MOT indicate

Blinker ['blɪŋkɐ] m (-s; -) MOT turn signal, Br indicator

blinzeln ['blɪntsəln] v/i (ge-, h) blink (one's eyes)

Blitz [blɪts] m (-es; -e) (flash of) lightning; PHOT flash

'**Blitzableiter** m (-s; -) lightning conductor

'**blitzen** v/i (ge-, h) flash; **es blitzt** it's lightening

'**Blitzgerät** n PHOT (electronic) flash

'**Blitzlampe** f PHOT flashbulb; flash cube

'**Blitzlicht** n (-[e]s; -er) PHOT flash(light)

'**Blitzschlag** m lightning stroke

'**blitz'schnell** adj and adv like a flash; attr split-second

Block [blɔk] m (-[e]s; Blöcke ['blœkə]) block; POL, ECON bloc; (writing) pad

Blockade [blɔˈkaːdə] f (-; -n) MAR, MIL blockade

'**Blockflöte** f recorder

'**Blockhaus** n log cabin

blockieren [blɔˈkiːrən] v/t and v/i (no -ge-, h) block; MOT lock

'**Blockschrift** f block letters

blöde [ˈbløːdə] F adj silly, stupid

'**blödeln** v/i (ge-, h) fool or clown around

'**Blödheit** [ˈbløːthait] f (-; no pl) stupidity

'**Blödsinn** F m (-[e]s; no pl) rubbish, nonsense

'**blödsinnig** F adj stupid, idiotic

blöken [ˈbløːkən] v/i (ge-, h) zo bleat

blond [blɔnt] adj blond, fair

Blondine [blɔnˈdiːnə] f (-; -n) blonde

bloß [bloːs] **1.** adj bare; naked (eye); mere; **bloß legen** v/t (sep, -ge-, h) lay bare, expose; **2.** adv only, just, merely

Blöße [ˈbløːsə] f (-; -n) nakedness; **sich e-e Blöße geben** lay o.s. open to attack or criticism

'**bloßlegen** v/t → **bloß**

'**bloßstellen** v/t (sep, -ge-, h) expose, compromise, unmask; **sich bloßstellen** compromise o.s.

blühen [ˈblyːən] v/i (ge-, h) (be in) bloom; (be in) blossom; fig flourish

Blume [ˈbluːmə] f (-; -n) flower; GASTR bouquet; head, froth

'**Blumenbeet** n flowerbed

'**Blumenhändler** m florist

Blumenkohl m BOT cauliflower

'**Blumenladen** m flower shop, florist's

'**Blumenstrauß** m bunch of flowers; bouquet

'**Blumentopf** m flowerpot

'**Blumenvase** f vase

Bluse [ˈbluːzə] f (-; -n) blouse

Blut [bluːt] n (-[e]s; no pl) blood

'**blutarm** adj MED an(a)emic (a. fig)

'**Blutarmut** f MED an(a)emia

Blutbad n massacre

'**Blutbahn** f ANAT bloodstream

'**Blutbank** f (-; -en) MED blood bank

'**blutbefleckt** adj bloodstained

'**Blutbild** n MED blood count

'**Blutblase** f MED blood blister

'**Blutdruck** m MED blood pressure

Blüte [ˈblyːtə] f (-; -n) flower; bloom (a. fig); blossom; fig height, heyday; **in (voller) Blüte** in (full) bloom

'**Blutegel** m zo leech

'**bluten** v/i (ge-, h) bleed (**aus** dat from)

'**Blütenblatt** n petal

'**Blütenstaub** m pollen

Bluter [ˈbluːtɐ] m (-s; -) MED h(a)emophiliac

'**Bluterguss** m bruise; MED h(a)ematoma

Blutgefäß n ANAT blood vessel

'**Blutgerinnsel** n MED blood clot

'**Blutgruppe** f MED blood group

Bluthund m zo bloodhound

'**blutig** adj bloody; **blutiger Anfänger** rank beginner, F greenhorn

'**Blutkörperchen** n MED blood corpuscle

'**Blutkreislauf** m MED (blood) circulation

'**Blutlache** f pool of blood

'**blutleer** adj bloodless

'**Blutprobe** f MED blood test

'**blutrünstig** [-rynstɪç] adj bloodthirsty, gory

'**Blutschande** f JUR incest

'**Blutspender** m blood donor

'**Blutsverwandte** m, f blood relation

'**Blutübertragung** f MED blood transfusion

'**Blutung** f (-; -en) MED bleeding, h(a)emorrhage

'**blutunterlaufen** adj bloodshot

'**Blutvergießen** n (-s; no pl) bloodshed

Blutvergiftung f MED blood poisoning

Blutwurst f black sausage (Br pudding)

BLZ [beːˈɛlˈtsɛt] ABBR of **Bankleitzahl** A.B.A. number, Br bank (sorting) code

Bö [bøː] f (-; -en) gust, squall

Bob [bɔp] m (-s; -s) bob(sled)

Bobbahn f bob run

Bobfahrer m bobber

Bock [bɔk] m (-[e]s; Böcke [ˈbœkə]) zo buck; he-goat, billy-goat; ram; SPORT buck; F **e-n Bock schießen** (make a) blunder; F **keinen** (or **null**) **Bock auf et. haben** have zero interest in s.th.

'**bocken** v/i (ge-, h) buck; sulk

'**bockig** adj obstinate; sulky

'**Bockspringen** n leapfrog

Boden [ˈboːdən] m (-s; Böden [ˈbøːdən]) ground; AGR soil; bottom; floor; attic

'**Bodenperso,nal** n AVIAT ground crew

'**Bodenre,form** f land reform

'**Bodenschätze** pl mineral resources

Bodenstati,on f AVIAT ground control

'**Bodenturnen** n floor exercises

Body [ˈbɔdi] m (-s; -s) bodysuit

bog [boːk] pret of **biegen**

Bogen [ˈboːgən] m (-s; Bögen [ˈbøːgən]) bend, curve; MATH arc; ARCH arch; skiing: turn; bow; sheet

'**Bogenschießen** n archery

'**Bogenschütze** m archer

Bohle [ˈboːlə] f (-; -n) plank

Bohne [ˈboːnə] f (-; -n) BOT bean; **grüne Bohnen** green (Br a. French) beans

'**Bohnenstange** f beanpole (a. F)

bohnern [ˈboːnɐn] v/t (ge-, h) polish, wax

'**Bohnerwachs** n floor polish

bohren [ˈboːrən] v/t (ge-, h) bore, drill (a.

dentist)

bohrend *fig adj* piercing (*look*); insistent (*questions etc*)

Bohrer ['boːrɐ] *m* (-s; -) TECH drill

'**Bohrinsel** *f* oil rig

Bohrloch *n* borehole, well(head)

Bohrma,schine *f* (electric) drill

Bohrturm *m* derrick

'**Bohrung** *f* (-; -en) drilling; bore

Boje ['boːjə] *f* (-; -n) MAR buoy

Bolzen ['bɔltsən] *m* (-s; -) TECH bolt

bombardieren [bɔmbar'diːrən] *v/t* (*no -ge-, h*) bomb; *fig* bombard

Bombe ['bɔmbə] *f* (-; -n) bomb; *fig* bombshell

'**Bombenangriff** *m* air raid

Bombenanschlag *m* bomb attack

Bombenerfolg F *m* roaring success; THEA *etc* smash hit

Bombengeschäft F *n* super deal

'**Bombenleger** *m* (-s; -) bomber

'**bombensicher** *adj* bombproof

Bomber ['bɔmbɐ] F *m* (-s; -) MIL bomber (*a.* SPORT)

Bon [bɔŋ] *m* (-s; -s) coupon, voucher

Bonbon [bɔŋ'bɔŋ] *m, n* (-s; -s) candy, *Br* sweet

Boot [boːt] *n* (-[e]s; -e) boat

'**Bootsmann** *m* (-[e]s; -leute) boatswain

Bord[1] [bɔrt] *n* (-[e]s; -e) shelf

Bord[2] *m*: *an Bord* AVIAT, MAR on board; *über Bord* MAR overboard; *von Bord gehen* MAR disembark

Bordell [bɔr'dɛl] *n* (-s; -e) brothel, F whorehouse

'**Bordkarte** *f* AVIAT boarding pass

'**Bordstein** *m* curb, *Br* kerb

borgen ['bɔrgən] *v/t* (*ge-, h*) borrow; *sich et. von j-m borgen* borrow s.th. from s.o.; *j-m et. borgen* lend s.th. to s.o.

Borke ['bɔrkə] *f* (-; -n) BOT bark

borniert [bɔr'niːrt] *adj* narrow-minded

Börse ['bœrzə] *f* (-; -n) ECON stock exchange

'**Börsenbericht** *m* market report

Börsenkurs *m* quotation

Börsenmakler *m* stockbroker

Börsenspeku,lant *m* stock-jobber

Borste ['bɔrstə] *f* (-; -n) bristle

'**borstig** *adj* bristly

Borte ['bɔrtə] *f* (-; -n) border; braid, lace

bösartig ['bøːs-] *adj* vicious; MED malignant

Böschung ['bœʃʊŋ] *f* (-; -en) slope, bank; RAIL embankment

böse ['bøːzə] *adj* bad, evil, wicked; angry (*über acc* about; *auf j-n* with s.o.), mad (*auf acc* at); *er meint es nicht böse* he means no harm

'**Böse** *n* (-n; *no pl*) (the) evil

'**Bösewicht** *m* (-[e]s; -er) villain

boshaft ['boːshaft] *adj* malicious

Bosheit ['boːshaɪt] *f* (-; *no pl*) malice

'**böswillig** *adj* malicious; JUR *a.* wil(l)ful

bot [boːt] *pret of* **bieten**

Botanik [bo'taːnɪk] *f* (-; *no pl*) botany

Bo'taniker *m* (-s; -) botanist

bo'tanisch *adj* botanical

Bote ['boːtə] *m* (-n; -n) messenger

'**Botengang** *m* errand; *Botengänge machen* run errands

Botschaft ['boːtʃaft] *f* (-; -en) message; POL embassy

'**Botschafter** *m* (-s; -) POL ambassador (*in dat* to)

'**Botschafterin** *f* (-; -nen) POL ambassadress (*in dat* to)

Bottich ['bɔtɪç] *m* (-s; -e) tub, vat

Bouillon [bʊl'jɔŋ] *f* (-; -s) consommé, bouillon, broth

Boulevardblatt [bulə'vaːɐ-] *n*, **Boulevardzeitung** *f* tabloid

Bowle ['boːlə] *f* (-; -n) (cold) punch; bowl

boxen ['bɔksən] (*ge-, h*) **1.** *v/i* box; **2.** *v/t* punch

'**Boxen** *n* (-s; *no pl*) boxing

Boxer ['bɔksɐ] *m* (-s; -) boxer

'**Boxhandschuh** *m* boxing glove

Boxkampf *m* boxing match, fight

Boxsport *m* boxing

Boykott [bɔy'kɔt] *m* (-[e]s; -e), **boykottieren** [bɔykɔ'tiːrən] *v/t* (*no -ge-, h*) boycott

brach [braːx] *pret of* **brechen**

brachliegend *adj* AGR fallow

brachte ['braxtə] *pret of* **bringen**

Branche ['brãːʃə] *f* (-; -n) ECON line (of business)

'**Branchenverzeichnis** *n* TEL yellow pages

Brand [brant] *m* (-[e]s; *Brände* ['brɛndə]) fire; *in Brand geraten* catch fire; *in Brand stecken* set fire to

Brandblase *f* MED blister

branden ['brandən] *v/i* (*ge-, sein*) surge (*gegen* against)

'**Brandfleck** *m* burn

Brandmal *n* brand

'**brandmarken** *fig v/t* (*ge-, h*) brand, stigmatize

'**Brandmauer** *f* fire wall

Brandstätte *f*, **Brandstelle** *f* scene of fire

Brandstifter *m* arsonist

Brandstiftung *f* arson

'**Brandung** *f* (-; *no pl*) surf, surge, breakers

'**Brandwunde** *f* MED burn; scald

brannte ['brantə] *pret of* **brennen**

'**Branntwein** *m* brandy, spirits

B

braten ['bra:tən] v/t (irr, ge-, h) roast; grill; broil; fry; *am Spieß braten* roast on a spit, barbecue

'**Braten** m (-s; -) roast (meat); joint

'**Bratenfett** n dripping

'**Bratensoße** f gravy

'**Bratfisch** m fried fish

'**Brathuhn** n roast chicken

'**Bratkar,toffeln** pl fried potatoes

'**Bratofen** m oven

'**Bratpfanne** f frying pan

'**Bratsche** ['bra:tʃə] f (-; -n) MUS viola

'**Bratwurst** f grilled sausage

Brauch [braux] m (-[e]s; *Bräuche* ['brɔy-çə]) custom; habit, practice

'**brauchbar** adj useful

'**brauchen** v/t (ge-, h) need; require; take (time); use; *wie lange wird er brauchen?* how long will it take him?; *du brauchst es nur zu sagen* just say the word; *ihr braucht es nicht zu tun* you don't have to do it; *er hätte nicht zu kommen brauchen* he need not have come

brauen ['brauən] v/t (ge-, h) brew

Brauerei [brauə'rai] f (-; -en) brewery

braun [braun] adj brown; (sun)tanned; *braun werden* (get a) tan

Bräune ['brɔynə] f (no pl) (sun)tan

'**bräunen** (ge-, h) 1. v/t brown, tan; 2. v/i (get a) tan

'**Braunkohle** f brown coal, lignite

'**bräunlich** adj brownish

Brause [brauzə] f (-; -n) shower; → *Limonade*

'**brausen** v/i a) (ge-, h) roar, b) (sein) rush, c) (h) → *duschen*

Braut [braut] f (-; *Bräute* ['brɔytə]) bride; fiancée

Bräutigam ['brɔytɪgam] m (-s; -e) (bride)-groom; fiancé

'**Brautjungfer** f bridesmaid

'**Brautkleid** n wedding-dress

'**Brautpaar** n bride and (bride)groom; engaged couple

brav [bra:f] adj good; honest; *sei(d) brav!* be good!

BRD [be:'er'de:] ABBR of *Bundesrepublik Deutschland* FRG, Federal Republic of Germany

brechen ['brɛçən] (irr, ge-) 1. v/t (h) break (a. fig); MED vomit; *sich brechen* OPT be refracted; *sich den Arm brechen* break one's arm; 2. v/i a) (h) MED vomit, F throw up, Br a. be sick; *mit j-m brechen* break with s.o.; *brechend voll* crammed, packed; b) (sein) break, get broken, fracture

'**Brechreiz** m MED nausea

'**Brechstange** f crowbar

'**Brechung** f (-; -en) OPT refraction

Brei [brai] m (-[e]s; -e) pulp, mash; pap; porridge; pudding

'**breiig** adj pulpy, mushy

breit [brait] adj wide; broad (a. fig)

'**breitbeinig** adj with legs (wide) apart

Breite ['braitə] f (-; -n) width, breadth; ASTR, GEOGR latitude

'**breiten** v/t (ge-, h) spread

'**Breitengrad** m degree of latitude

'**Breitenkreis** m parallel (of latitude)

breitmachen v/refl (sep, -ge-, h): *sich breitmachenmachen* F spread o.s., take up room

'**Breitwand** f film: wide screen

Bremsbelag ['brɛms-] m brake lining

Bremse ['brɛmzə] f (-; -n) TECH brake; ZO gadfly

'**bremsen** (ge-, h) 1. v/i MOT brake, put on the brake(s); slow down; 2. v/t MOT brake; fig curb

'**Bremslicht** n (-[e]s; -er) MOT stop light

Bremspe,dal n MOT brake pedal

'**Bremsspur** f MOT skid marks

'**Bremsweg** m MOT stopping distance

'**brennbar** adj combustible; (in)flammable

brennen ['brɛnən] (irr, ge-, h) 1. v/t burn; distil(l) (whisky etc); bake (bricks); 2. v/i burn; be on fire; wound, eyes: smart, burn; F *darauf brennen zu* inf be dying to inf; *es brennt!* fire!

Brenner ['brɛnə] m (-s; -) burner

'**Brennholz** n firewood

'**Brennmateri,al** n fuel

'**Brennnessel** f BOT (stinging) nettle

'**Brennpunkt** m focus, focal point

'**Brennspiritus** m methylated spirit

'**Brennstab** m TECH fuel rod

'**Brennstoff** m fuel

brenzlig ['brɛntslɪç] adj burnt; fig hot

Bresche ['brɛʃə] f (-; -n) breach (a. fig), gap

Brett [brɛt] n (-[e]s; -er) board

'**Bretterzaun** m wooden fence

'**Brettspiel** n board game

Brezel ['bre:tsəl] f (-; -n) pretzel

Brief [bri:f] m (-[e]s; -e) letter

'**Briefbeschwerer** m (-s; -) paperweight

'**Briefbogen** m sheet of (note)paper

'**Brieffreund(in)** pen pal (Br friend)

'**Briefkasten** m mailbox, Br letterbox

'**brieflich** adj and adv by letter

'**Briefmarke** f (postage) stamp

'**Briefmarkensammlung** f stamp collection

Brieföffner m letter opener, Br paper knife

Briefpa,pier n stationery
Brieftasche f wallet
Brieftaube f zo carrier pigeon
Briefträger(in) (-s; -/-; -nen) mailman (mailwoman), Br postman (postwoman)
Briefumschlag m envelope
Briefwahl f postal vote
Briefwechsel m correspondence
briet [bri:t] pret of **braten**
Brikett [bri'kɛt] n (-s; -s) briquet(te)
brillant [brɪl'jant] adj brilliant
Bril'lant m (-en; -en) (cut) diamond
Bril'lantring m diamond ring
Brille ['brɪlə] f (-; -n) (pair of) glasses, spectacles; goggles; toilet seat
'Brillenetui n eyeglass case (Br spectacle) case
Brillenträger(in) (-s; -/-; -nen) **Brillenträger sein** wear glasses
bringen ['brɪŋən] v/t (irr, ge-, h) bring; take; cause; make (sacrifice); yield (profit); **j-n nach Hause bringen** see (or take) s.o. home; **in Ordnung bringen** put in order; **das bringt mich auf e-e Idee** that gives me an idea; **j-n dazu bringen, et. zu tun** get s.o. to do s.th.; **et. mit sich bringen** involve s.th.; **j-n um et. bringen** deprive s.o. of s.th.; **j-n zum Lachen bringen** make s.o. laugh; **j-n wieder zu sich bringen** bring s.o. round; **es zu et. (nichts) bringen** go far (get nowhere); F **es bringen** make it; **das bringt nichts** it's no use
Brise ['bri:zə] f (-; -n) breeze
Brite ['brɪtə] m (-n; -n), **'Britin** f (-; -nen) Briton; **die Briten** pl the British
'britisch adj British
bröckeln ['brœkəln] v/i (ge-, h, sein) crumble
Brocken ['brɔkən] m (-s; -) piece; lump; rock; GASTR chunk; morsel; **ein paar Brocken Englisch** a few scraps of English; **ein harter Brocken** a hard nut to crack
Brombeere ['brɔm-] f BOT blackberry
Bronchitis [brɔn'çi:tɪs] f (-; -tiden [brɔn-çi'ti:dən]) MED bronchitis
Bronze ['brõ:sə] f (-; -n) bronze
Bronzezeit f (-; no pl) HIST Bronze Age
Brosche ['brɔʃə] f (-; -n) brooch, pin
broschiert [brɔ'ʃi:ɐt] adj paperback
Broschüre [brɔ'ʃy:rə] f (-; -n) pamphlet, brochure
Brot [bro:t] n (-[e]s; -e) bread; sandwich; **ein (Laib) Brot** a loaf (of bread); **e-e Scheibe Brot** a slice of bread; **sein Brot verdienen** earn one's living
Brötchen ['brø:tçən] n (-s; -) roll
'Brotrinde f crust
Brot(schneide)ma,schine f bread cutter
Bruch [brʊx] m (-[e]s; Brüche ['bryçə])

break; MED fracture; hernia; MATH fraction; GEOL fault; fig breach (of promise etc); JUR violation; **zu Bruch gehen** be wrecked
Bruchbude F f dump, hovel
brüchig ['bryçɪç] adj brittle
'Bruchlandung f AVIAT crash landing
Bruchrechnung f MATH fractional arithmetic, F fractions
'bruchsicher adj breakproof
'Bruchstrich m MATH fraction bar
Bruchstück n fragment
Bruchteil m fraction; **im Bruchteil e-r Sekunde** in a split second
Bruchzahl f MATH fraction(al) number
Brücke ['brykə] f (-; -n) bridge (a. SPORT); rug
'Brückenpfeiler m pier
Bruder ['bru:dɐ] m (-s; Brüder ['bry:dɐ]) brother (a. REL)
Bruderkrieg m civil war
brüderlich ['bry:dəlɪç] **1.** adj brotherly; **2.** adv: **brüderlich teilen** share and share alike
'Brüderlichkeit f (-; no pl) brotherhood
'Bruderschaft f: **Bruderschaft trinken** agree to use the familiar 'du' form of address
Brühe ['bry:ə] f (-; -n) broth; stock; F dishwater; slops; F filthy water, bilge
'Brühwürfel m beef cube
brüllen ['brylən] v/i (ge-, h) roar (**vor Lachen** with laughter); zo bellow; F bawl; **brüllendes Gelächter** roars of laughter
brummen ['brʊmən] v/i (ge-, h) growl; zo hum, buzz (a. engine etc); head: be buzzing
'brummig adj grumpy
brünett [bry'nɛt] adj brunette, dark--haired
Brunnen ['brʊnən] m (-s; -) well, spring, fountain
Brunstzeit ['brʊnst-] f zo rutting season
Brust [brʊst] f (-; Brüste ['brystə]) ANAT a) (no pl) chest, b) breast(s), bosom
Brustbein n ANAT breastbone
Brustbeutel m neck pouch, Br money bag
brüsten ['brystən] v/refl (ge-, h) boast, brag (**mit** of)
'Brustkasten m, **Brustkorb** m ANAT chest, thorax
Brustschwimmen n breaststroke
'Brüstung f (-; -en) parapet
'Brustwarze f ANAT nipple
Brut [bru:t] f (-; -en) zo brooding; brood (a. F), hatch; fry
brutal [bru'ta:l] adj brutal
Brutalität [brutali'tɛ:t] f (-; -en) brutality
'Brutappa,rat m zo incubator

brüten ['bry:tən] v/i (ge-, h) zo brood, sit (on eggs); **brüten über** (dat) fig brood over

'Brutkasten m MED incubator

brutto ['bruto] adv ECON gross

'Bruttoeinkommen n ECON gross earnings

Bruttosozi,alpro,dukt n ECON gross national product

Bube ['bu:bə] m (-n; -n) boy, lad; card game: knave, jack

Buch [bu:x] n (-[e]s; Bücher ['by:çɐ]) book

Buchbinder m (-s; -) (book)binder

Buchdrucker m printer

Buchdruckerei f print shop, Br printing office

Buche ['bu:xə] f (-; -n) BOT beech

'buchen v/t (ge-, h) book; ECON enter

Bücherbord ['by:çɐ-] n bookshelf

Bücherei [by:çə'rai] f (-; -en) library

'Bücherre,gal n bookshelf

'Bücherschrank m bookcase

'Buchfink m ZO chaffinch

Buchhalter(in) bookkeeper

Buchhaltung f (-; no pl) bookkeeping

Buchhändler(in) bookseller

Buchhandlung f bookstore, Br bookshop

Buchmacher m bookmaker

Büchse ['bʏksə] f (-; -n) can, Br tin; box; rifle

'Büchsenfleisch n canned (Br tinned) meat

Büchsenöffner m can (Br tin) opener

Buchstabe ['bu:xʃta:bə] m (-n; -n) letter; großer (kleiner) Buchstabe capital (small) letter

buchstabieren [bu:xʃta'bi:rən] v/t (no -ge-, h) spell

buchstäblich ['bu:xʃtɛ:plɪç] adv literally

'Buchstütze f bookend

Bucht [bʊxt] f (-; -en) bay; creek, inlet

'Buchung f (-; -en) booking; ECON entry

Buckel ['bʊkəl] m (-s; -) hump; hunch; e-n Buckel machen hump or hunch one's back

bücken ['bʏkən] v/refl (ge-, h) bend (down), stoop

bucklig ['bʊklɪç] adj hunchbacked

Bucklige ['bʊklɪɡə] m, f (-n; -n) hunchback

Bückling ['bʏklɪŋ] m (-s; -e) smoked herring, Br kipper

Buddhismus [bʊ'dɪsmʊs] m (-; no pl) Buddhism

Buddhist [bʊ'dɪst] m (-en; -en), bud'dhistisch adj Buddhist

Bude ['bu:də] f (-n; -n) stall, booth; hut; F pad, Br digs; contp shack, dump, hole

Budget [by'dʒe:] n (-s; -s) budget

Büfett [by'fɛt] n (-[e]s; -s, -e) counter, bar, buffet; sideboard, cupboard; kaltes Büfett GASTR cold buffet (meal)

Büffel ['byfəl] m (-s; -) zo buffalo

'büffeln F v/i (ge-, h) grind, cram, swot

Bug [bu:k] m (-[e]s; -e) MAR bow; AVIAT nose; ZO, GASTR shoulder

Bügel ['by:ɡəl] m (-s; -) hanger; bow

Bügelbrett n ironing board

Bügeleisen n iron

Bügelfalte f crease

'bügelfrei adj no(n)-iron

'bügeln v/t (ge-, h) iron, press

buh [bu:] int boo!

buhen ['bu:ən] v/i (ge-, h) boo

Bühne ['by:nə] f (-; -n) stage, fig a. scene

'Bühnenbild n (stage) set(ting)

'Bühnenbildner(in) (-s; -/-; -nen) stage designer

'Buhrufe pl boos

Bullauge ['bʊl-] n MAR porthole

'Bulldogge f zo bulldog

Bulle ['bʊlə] m (-n; -n) zo bull (a. fig); F contp cop, pl the fuzz

Bummel ['bʊməl] F m (-s; -) stroll

Bummelei [bʊmə'lai] f (-; no pl) F contp dawdling; slackness

'bummeln F v/i a) (ge-, sein) stroll, saunter, b) (ge-, h) contp dawdle; ECON go slow

'Bummelstreik m ECON slowdown, Br go-slow (strike)

Bummler ['bʊmlɐ] F m (-s; -) stroller; contp dawdler, slowpoke, Br slowcoach

bumsen ['bʊmzən] v/i and v/t (ge-, h) F → krachen; V screw

Bund[1] [bʊnt] m (-[e]s; Bünde ['bʏndə]) union, federation, alliance; association; (waist)band; der Bund POL the Federal Government; F → Bundeswehr

Bund[2] n (-[e]s; -e) bundle; bunch

Bündel ['bʏndəl] n (-s; -) bundle

'bündeln v/t (ge-, h) bundle (up)

Bundes... ['bʊndəs-] in cpds Federal ...; German ...

Bundesbahn f Federal Railroad(s)

Bundesgenosse m ally

Bundeskanzler(in) Federal Chancellor

Bundesland n appr (federal) state, Land

Bundesliga f SPORT First Division

Bundespost f Federal Postal Administration

Bundespräsi,dent m Federal President

Bundesrat m Bundesrat, Upper House of German Parliament

Bundesrepu,blik f Federal Republic

Bundesstaat m federal state; confederation

Bundesstraße f Federal Highway

Bundestag m (-[e]s; no pl) Bundestag, Lower House of German Parliament
Bundestrainer m coach of the (German) national team
Bundesverfassungsgericht n Federal Constitutional Court, Am appr Supreme Court
Bundeswehr f (-; no pl) MIL (German Federal) Armed Forces
bündig['bʏndɪç] adj TECH flush; **kurz und bündig** terse(ly); point-blank
Bündnis ['bʏntnɪs] n (-ses; -se) alliance
Bunker ['bʊŋkɐ] m (-s; -) air-raid shelter, bunker
bunt [bʊnt] adj colo(u)red; multicolo(u)red; colo(u)rful (a. fig); varied; **bunter Abend** evening of entertainment; F **mir wird's zu bunt** that's all I can take
'**Buntstift** m colo(u)red pencil, crayon
Bürde ['bʏrdə] f (-; -n) burden (**für j-n** to s.o.)
Burg [bʊrk] f (-; -en) castle
Bürge['bʏrgə] m (-n; -n) JUR guarantor (a. fig)
'**bürgen** v/i (ge-, h) **für j-n bürgen** JUR stand surety for s.o.; **für et. bürgen** guarantee s.th.
Bürger ['bʏrgɐ] m (-s; -), '**Bürgerin** f (-; -nen) citizen
Bürgerinitia,tive f (citizen's or local) action group
Bürgerkrieg m civil war
'**bürgerlich** adj civil; middle-class; esp contp bourgeois; **bürgerliche Küche** home cooking
'**Bürgerliche,r** m, f (-n; -n) commoner
'**Bürgermeister** m mayor
Bürgerrechte pl civil rights
Bürgersteig[-ʃtaik] m (-[e]s; -e) sidewalk, Br pavement
'**Bürgschaft** f (-; -en) JUR surety; bail
Büro [by'roː] n (-s; -s) office
Büroangestellte m, f (-n; -n) clerk, office worker
Büroklammer f (paper) clip
Bürokrat[byro'kraːt] m (-en; -en) bureaucrat
Bürokratie [byrokra'tiː] f (-; -n) bureaucracy; contp red tape
Bü'rostunden pl office hours
Bursche ['bʊrʃə] m (-n; -n) fellow, guy
burschikos [bʊrʃi'koːs] adj (tom)boyish, pert
Bürste ['bʏrstə] f (-; -n) brush
'**bürsten** v/t (ge-, h) brush
'**Bürstenschnitt** m crew cut
Bus [bʊs] m (-ses; -se) bus; coach
Busch [bʊʃ] m (-[e]s; Büsche ['bʏʃə]) BOT bush, shrub
Büschel ['bʏʃəl] n (-s; -) bunch; tuft
buschig adj bushy
Busen ['buːzən] m (-s; -) ANAT bosom, breast(s)
'**Busfahrer** m bus driver
'**Bushaltestelle** f bus stop
Bussard ['bʊsart] m (-s; -e) ZO buzzard
Buße ['buːsə] f (-; -n) REL penance; repentance; **Buße tun** do penanc
büßen ['byːsən] v/t (ge-, h) pay or suffer for s.th.; REL repent
'**Bußgeld** n fine, penalty
'**Bußtag** m REL day of repentance
Büste ['byːstə] f (-; -n) bust
'**Büstenhalter** m bra
Butter ['bʊtɐ] f (-; no pl) butter
Butterblume f BOT buttercup
Butterbrot n (slice or piece of) bread and butter; F **für ein Butterbrot** for a song
Butterbrotpa,pier n greaseproof paper
Butterdose f butter dish
Buttermilch f buttermilk
b.w. ABBR of **bitte wenden** PTO, please turn over
bzw. ABBR of **beziehungsweise** resp., respectively

C

C ABBR of **Celsius** C, Celsius, centigrade
ca. ABBR of **circa** approx., approximately
Café [ka'feː] n (-s; -s) café, coffee house
campen ['kɛmpən] v/i (ge-, h) camp
Camper ['kɛmpɐ] m (-s; -) camper
Camping... ['kɛmpɪŋ-] in cpds ...bett, ...tisch etc camp ...
Campingbus m camper (van Br)
Campingplatz m campground, Br campsite
Catcher ['kɛtʃɐ] m (-s; -) wrestler
Casino [ka'ziːno] n → **Kasino**

CD [tse:'de:] f (-; -s) CD, compact disk (Br disc)

C'D-ROM f CD-ROM

C'D-Spieler m CD player

Cellist [tʃe'lɪst] m (-en; -en), **Cel'listin** f (-; -nen) MUS cellist

Cello ['tʃelo] n (-s; -s, Celli) MUS Cello

Celsius ['tsɛlzjʊs] 5 Grad Celsius (ABBR 5° C) five degrees centigrade or Celsius

Cembalo ['tʃɛmbalo] n (-s; -s, -li) MUS harpsichord

Champagner [ʃam'panjɐ] m (-s; -) champagne

Champignon ['ʃampɪnjɔŋ] m (-s; -s) BOT mushroom

Chance ['ʃã:sə] f f (-; -n) chance; **die Chancen stehen gleich (3 zu 1)** the odds are even (three to one)

'Chancengleichheit f equal opportunities

Chaos ['ka:ɔs] n (-; no pl) chaos

Chaot [ka'o:t] m (-en; -en) chaotic person; POL anarchist, pl a. lunatic fringe

cha'otisch adj chaotic

Charakter [ka'raktɐ] m (-s; -e [-'te:rə]) character, nature

charakterisieren [-teri'zi:rən] v/t (no -ge-, h) characterize, describe (**als** as)

charakteristisch [-te'rɪstɪʃ] adj characteristic, typical (**für** of)

Cha'rakterzug m trait

charmant [ʃar'mant] adj charming

Charme [ʃarm] m (-s; no pl) charm

Chassis [ʃa'si:] n (-; -) TECH chassis

Chauffeur [ʃɔ'fø:ɐ] m (-s; -e) chauffeur, driver

Chauvi ['ʃo:vi] m (-s; -s) F male chauvinist (pig)

Chauvinismus [ʃovi'nɪsmʊs] m (-; no pl) chauvinism, POL a. jingoism

Chef [ʃɛf] m (-s; -s) head, chief, F boss

Chefarzt m medical director, Br senior consultant

Chefsekre'tärin f executive secretary

Chemie [çe'mi:] f (-; no pl) chemistry

Chemiefaser f synthetic fiber (Br fibre)

Chemikalien [çemi'ka:ljən] pl chemicals

Chemiker(in) ['çe:mikɐ (-kərɪn)] (-s; -/-; -nen) (analytical) chemist

chemisch ['çe:mɪʃ] adj chemical; **chemische Reinigung** dry cleaning

Chemothera'pie [çemo-] f MED chemotherapy

Chiffre ['ʃɪfrə] f (-; -n) code, cipher; box (number)

chiffrieren [ʃɪ'fri:rən] v/t (no -ge-, h) (en)-code

China ['çi:na] China

Chinese [çi'ne:zə] m (-n; -n), **Chi'nesin** f (-; -nen), **chi'nesisch** adj Chinese

Chinin [çi'ni:n] n (-s; no pl) PHARM quinine

Chip [tʃɪp] m (-s; -s) a. EDP chip; GASTR pl chips, Br crisps

Chirurg [çi'rʊrk] m (-en; -en) surgeon

Chirurgie [çirʊr'gi:] f (-; -n) surgery

Chirurgin [çi'rʊrgɪn] f (-; no pl) surgeon

chirurgisch [çi'rʊrgɪʃ] adj surgical

Chlor [klo:ɐ] n (-s; no pl) CHEM chlorine

chloren ['klo:rən] v/t (ge-, h) chlorinate

Cholera ['ko:lera] f (-; no pl) MED cholera

cholerisch [ko'le:rɪʃ] adj choleric

Cholesterin [çoleste'ri:n] n (-s; no pl) MED cholesterol

Chor [ko:ɐ] m (-[e]s; Chöre ['kø:rə]) MUS choir (a. ARCH); **im Chor** in chorus

Choral [ko'ra:l] m (-s; Choräle [ko'rɛ:lə]) MUS, REL chorale, hymn

Christ [krɪst] m (-en; -en) REL Christian

Christbaum m Christmas tree

'Christenheit: die Christenheit REL Christendom

'Christentum n (-s; no pl) REL Christianity

Christin ['krɪstɪn] f (-; -nen) REL Christian

'Christkind n Infant Jesus; Father Christmas, Santa Claus

'christlich adj REL Christian

Christus ['krɪstʊs] REL Christ; **vor Christus** B.C.; **nach Christus** A.D.

Chrom [kro:m] n (-s; no pl) chrome, CHEM a. chromium

Chromosom [kromo'zo:m] n (-s; -en) BIOL chromosome

Chronik ['kro:nɪk] f (-; -en) chronicle

chronisch ['kro:nɪʃ] adj MED chronic

chronologisch [krono'lo:gɪʃ] adj chronological

circa → zirka

City ['sɪti] f (-; -s) downtown, (city) center, Br centre

Clique ['klɪkə] f (-; -n) F group, set; contp clique

Clou [klu:] m (-s; -s) highlight, climax; **der Clou daran** the whole point of it

Compact Disc, Compact Disk ['kɔmpæktdɪsk] f (-; -s) compact disk (Br disc)

Computer [kɔm'pju:tɐ] m (-s; -) computer

Computerausdruck m computer printout

com'putergesteuert adj computer-controlled

computergestützt adj computer-aided

Com'putergrafik f computer graphics

computerisieren [kɔmpjutəri'zi:rən] v/t (no -ge-, h) computerize

Com'puterspiel n computer game

Computervirus m EDP computer virus

Conférencier [kõferãˈsjeː] *m* (*-s*; *-s*) master of ceremonies, F emcee, MC, *Br* compère
Cord *etc* → **Kord** *etc*
Couch [kautʃ] *f* (*-*; *-s*) couch
Coupé [kuˈpeː] *n* (*-s*; *-s*) MOT coupé

Coupon → **Kupon**
Cousin [kuˈzɛː] *m* (*-s*; *-s*), **Cousine** [kuˈziːnə] *f* (*-*; *-n*) cousin
Creme [kreːm] *f* (*-*; *-s*) cream (*a. fig*)
Curry [ˈkari] *m* (*-s*; *-s*) curry powder
Cursor [ˈkɔːsə] *m* (*-s*; *-s*) EDP cursor

D

D

da [daː] **1.** *adv space*: there; here; *time*: then, at that time; **da drüben** (**draußen, hinten**) over (out, back) there; **von da aus** from there; **das … da** that … (over there); **da kommt er** here he comes; **da bin ich** here I am; **da sein** be there; exist; **ist noch … da?** is any … left?; **noch nie da gewesen** unprecedented; **er ist gleich wieder da** he'll be right back; **von da an** or **ab** from then on; **2.** *cj* as, since, because
'dabehalten *v/t* (*irr*, **halten**, *sep*, *no -ge-*, *h*) keep; **j-n dabehalten** keep s.o. in
dabei [daˈbai] *adv* there, present; near or close by; at the same time; included with it; **dabei sein** be there; take part; be in on it; **ich bin dabei!** count me in!; **er ist gerade dabei zu gehen** he's just leaving; **es ist nichts dabei** there's nothing to it; there's no harm in it; **was ist schon dabei?** (so) what of it?; **lassen wir es dabei!** let's leave it at that!
dabeibleiben *v/i* (*irr*, **bleiben**, *sep*, *-ge-*, *sein*) stick to it
dabeihaben F *v/t* (*irr*, **haben**, *sep*, *-ge-*, *h*) have with (or on) one
'dableiben *v/i* (*irr*, **bleiben**, *sep*, *-ge-*, *sein*) stay
Dach [dax] *n* (*-[e]s*; *Dächer* [ˈdɛçɐ]) roof
'Dachboden *m* attic
Dachdecker [-dɛkɐ] *m* (*-s*; *-*) roofer
Dachfenster *n* dormer window
Dachgepäckträger *m* MOT roof-rack
'Dachgeschoss *n*, **'Dachgeschoß** *Austrian n* attic
Dachgeschosswohnung *f* loft apartment, *Br* attic flat
'Dachkammer *f* garret
Dachluke *f* skylight
Dachpappe *f* roofing felt
Dachrinne *f* gutter
Dachs [daks] *m* (*-es*; *-e*) ZO badger
'Dachstuhl *m* roof framework

dachte [ˈdaxtə] *pret of* **denken**
'Dachter,rasse *f* roof terrace
'Dachverband *m* ECON *etc* umbrella organization
Dackel [ˈdakəl] *m* (*-s*; *-*) ZO dachshund
'dadurch *adv and cj* this *or* that way; for this reason, so; **dadurch, dass** due to the fact that
dafür [daˈfyːɐ] *adv* for it, for that; instead; in return, in exchange; **dafür sein** be in favo(u)r of it; **er kann nichts dafür** it is not his fault; **dafür sorgen, dass** see to it that
da'gegen *adv and cj* against it; however, on the other hand; **dagegen sein** be against (or opposed to) it; **haben Sie et. dagegen, dass ich …?** do you mind if I …?; **wenn Sie nichts dagegen haben** if you don't mind; **… ist nichts dagegen** … can't compare
da'heim *adv* at home
'daher *adv and cj* from there; that's why
da'hin *adv* there, to that place; gone, past; **bis dahin** till then; up to there
da'hinten *adv* back there
da'hinter *adv* behind it; **es steckt nichts dahinter** there is nothing to it; F **dahinter kommen** find out (about it)
'dalassen F *v/t* (*irr*, **lassen**, *sep*, *-ge-*, *h*) leave behind
damalig [ˈdaːmaːlɪç] *adj* then
damals [ˈdaːmaːls] *adv* then, at that time
Dame [ˈdaːmə] *f* (*-*; *-n*) lady; partner; *cards, chess*: queen; checkers, *Br* draughts
'Damen… *in cpds* ladies' …; SPORT women's …
Damenbinde *f* sanitary napkin (*Br* towel)
'damenhaft *adj* ladylike
'Damentoi,lette *f* ladies' room (*Br* toilet), *the* ladies
Damenwahl *f* ladies' choice
damit 1. [ˈdaːmɪt] *adv* with it *or* that; by it,

with it; *was will er damit sagen?* what's he trying to say?; *wie steht es damit?* how about it?; *damit einverstanden sein* have no objections; [da'mɪt] *cj* so that; in order to *inf*; *damit nicht* so as not to *inf*

Damm [dam] *m* (-[e]s; *Dämme* ['dɛmə]) dam; embankment

'**dämmerig** ['dɛmərɪç] *adj* dim

'**Dämmerlicht** *n* (-[e]s; *no pl*) twilight

'**dämmern** ['dɛmən] *v/i* (ge-, h) dawn (a. F *j-m* s.o.); get dark *or* dusky

'**Dämmerung** *f* (-; -en) dusk; dawn

Dämon ['dɛːmɔn] *m* (-s; -en [dɛ'moːnən]) demon

dämonisch [dɛ'moːnɪʃ] *adj* demoniac(al)

Dampf [dampf] *m* (-[e]s; *Dämpfe* ['dɛmpfə]) steam; PHYS vapo(u)r

'**dampfen** *v/i* (ge-, h *and* sein) steam

'**dämpfen** ['dɛmpfən] *v/t* (ge-, h) deaden; muffle (*voice*); soften (*light, sound, blow*); GASTR steam, stew; steam-iron; *fig* put a damper on; curb (*a.* ECON)

'**Dampfer** ['dampfɐ] *m* (-s; -) steamer, steamship

'**Dampfkochtopf** *m* pressure cooker

Dampfma,schine *f* steam engine

Dampfschiff *n* steamer, steamship

da'nach after it *or* that; afterwards; for it; according to it; *ich fragte ihn danach* I asked him about it; F *mir ist nicht danach* I don't feel like it

Däne ['dɛːnə] *m* (-n; -n) Dane

da'neben *adv* next to it, beside it; besides, as well, at the same time; beside the mark

danebenbenehmen F *v/refl* (*irr*, **nehmen**, *sep*, *no* -ge-, h) step out of line

danebengehen F *v/i* (*irr*, **gehen**, *sep*, -ge-, sien) miss (the target); F misfire

'**Dänemark** Denmark

Dänin ['dɛːnɪn] *f* (-; -nen) Danish woman *or* girl

'**dänisch** *adj* Danish

dank [daŋk] *prp* (*gen*) thanks to

Dank *m* (-[e]s; *no pl*) thanks; *Gott sei Dank!* thank God!; *vielen Dank!* many thanks!

'**dankbar** *adj* grateful (*j-m* to s.o.); rewarding (*task etc*)

'**Dankbarkeit** *f* (-; *no pl*) gratitude

'**danken** *v/i* (ge-, h) thank (*j-m für et.* s.o. for s.th.); *danke (schön)* thank you (very much); (*nein*), *danke* no, thank you; *nichts zu danken* not at all

dann [dan] *adv* then; *dann und wann* (every) now and then

daran [da'ran] *adv* on it; *die, think etc* of it; *believe etc* in it; *suffer etc* from it; →

liegen

darauf [da'rauf] *adv* on (top of) it; after (that); *listen, drink etc* to it; *proud etc* of it; *wait etc* for it; *am Tage darauf* the day after; *zwei Jahre darauf* two years later; *darauf kommt es an* that's what matters

darauf'hin *adv* after that; as a result

daraus [da'raus] *adv* from (*or* out of) it; *was ist daraus geworden?* what has become of it?; *daraus wird nichts!* F nothing doing!

Darbietung ['daːɐbiːtʊŋ] *f* (-; -en) presentation; performance

darin [da'rɪn] *adv* in it; ['daːrɪn] in that

darlegen ['daːɐ-] *v/t* (sep, -ge-, h) explain, set out

Darlehen ['daːɐleːən] *n* (-s; -) loan; *ein Darlehen geben* grant a loan

Darm [darm] *m* (-[e]s; *Därme* ['dɛrmə]) ANAT bowel(s), intestine(s); GASTR skin

Darmgrippe *f* MED intestinal flu

darstellen ['daːɐ-] *v/t* (sep, -ge-, h) represent, show, depict; describe; THEA play, do; trace, graph

'**Darsteller(in)** ['daːɐ-] *m* (-s; -/-; -nen) THEA performer, actor (actress)

'**Darstellung** *f* (-; -en) representation; description; account; portrayal

darüber [da'ryːbɐ] *adv* over *or* above it; across it; in the meantime; *write, talk etc* about it; *... und darüber ...* and more; *darüber werden Jahre vergehen* that will take years

darum [da'rum] *adv and cj* (a)round it; because of it, that's why; *darum bitten* ask for it; → *gehen*

darunter [da'runtɐ] *adv* under *or* below it, underneath; among them; including; *... und darunter ...* and less; *was verstehst du darunter?* what do you understand by it?

das [das] → *der*

'**Dasein** *n* (-s; *no pl*) life, existence

dass [das] *cj* that; so (that); *es sei denn, dass* unless; *nicht dass ich wüsste* not that I know of

'**dastehen** *v/i* (*irr*, **stehen**, *sep*, -ge-, h) stand (there)

Datei [da'tai] *f* (-; -en) EDP file

Dateiverwaltung *f* EDP file management

Daten ['daːtən] *pl* data (*a.* EDP); facts; particulars

Datenbank *f* (-; -en) EDP database, data bank

Datenschutz *m* JUR data protection

Datenspeicher *m* data memory *or* storage

Datenträger *m* data medium *or* carrier

Datenübertragung *f* data transfer

Datenverarbeitung *f* data processing

datieren [da'tiːrən] *v/t and v/i* (*no -ge-, h*) date

Dativ ['daːtiːf] *m* (*-s; -e*) dative (case)

Dattel ['datəl] *f* (*-; -n*) BOT date

Datum ['daːtʊm] *n* (*-s; Daten* ['daːtən]) date; *welches Datum haben wir heute?* what's the date today?

Dauer ['daʊɐ] *f* (*-; no pl*) duration; continuance; *auf die Dauer* in the long run; *für die Dauer von* for a period *or* term of; *von Dauer sein* last

Dauerarbeitslosigkeit *f* long-term unemployment

Dauerauftrag *m* ECON standing order

Dauergeschwindigkeit *f* MOT etc cruising speed

'**dauerhaft** *adj* lasting; durable

'**Dauerkarte** *f* season ticket

'**Dauerlauf** *m* SPORT jogging; *im Dauerlauf* at a jog

Dauerlutscher *m* lollipop

dauern ['daʊɐn] (*ge-, h*) last, take; → *lange*

'**Dauerwelle** *f* permanent, *Br* perm

Daumen ['daʊmən] *m* (*-s; -*) ANAT thumb; F *j-m den Daumen halten* keep one's fingers crossed (for s.o.); *am Daumen lutschen* suck one's thumb

Daunen ['daʊnən] *pl* down

'**Daunendecke** *f* eiderdown

da'von *adv* (away) from it; by it; about it; away; of it *or* them; *et. davon haben* get s.th. out of it; *das kommt davon!* there you are!, that will teach you!

davonkommen *v/i* (*irr, kommen, sep, -ge-, sein*) escape, get away

davonlaufen *v/i* (*irr, laufen, sep, -ge-, sein*) run away

da'vor *adv* before it; in front of it; *be afraid, warn* s.o. etc of it

da'zu *adv* for it, for that purpose; in addition; *noch dazu* into the bargain; *dazu ist es da* that's what it's there for; *Salat dazu?* a salad with it?; → *kommen, Lust*

dazugehören *v/i* (*sep, no -ge-, h*) belong to it, be part of it

dazugehörig *adj* belonging to it

dazukommen *v/i* (*irr, kommen, sep, -ge-, sein*) join s.o.; be added

da'zwischen *adv* between (them); in between; among them

dazwischenkommen *v/i* (*irr, kommen, sep, -ge-, sein*) intervene, happen; *wenn nichts dazwischenkommt* if all goes well

DB [deː'beː] *ABBR of Deutsche Bahn* German Rail

dealen ['diːlən] *v/i* (*ge-, h*) F push drugs

Dealer ['diːlɐ] *m* (*-s; -*) drug dealer, F pusher

Debatte [de'batə] *f* (*-; -n*) debate

debattieren [deba'tiːrən] *v/i* (*no -ge-, h*) debate (*über acc* on)

Debüt [de'byː] *n* (*-s; -s*) debut; *sein Debüt geben* make your debut

dechiffrieren [deʃɪ'friːrən] *v/t* (*no -ge-, h*) decipher, decode

Deck [dɛk] *n* (*-[e]s; -s*) MAR deck

Decke ['dɛkə] *f* (*-; -n*) blanket; quilt; ARCH ceiling

Deckel ['dɛkəl] *m* (*-s; -*) lid, cover, top

'**decken** *v/t and v/i* (*ge-, h*) cover (*a. zo*), SPORT *a.* mark; *sich decken* (*mit*) coincide (with); → *Tisch*

'**Deckung** *f* (*-; no pl*) cover; *boxing*: guard; *in Deckung gehen* take cover

defekt [de'fɛkt] *adj* defective, faulty; TECH out of order

De'fekt *m* (*-[e]s; -e*) defect, fault

defensiv [defɛn'siːf] *adj*, **Defensive** [-'ziːvə] *f* (*-; no pl*) defensive

definieren [defi'niːrən] *v/t* (*no -ge-, h*) define

Definition [defini'tsjoːn] *f* (*-; -en*) definition

Defizit ['deːfitsɪt] *n* (*-s; -e*) deficit; deficiency

Degen ['deːgən] *m* (*-s; -*) sword; *fencing*: épée

degradieren [degra'diːrən] *v/t* (*no -ge-, h*) degrade (*a. fig*)

dehnbar ['deːnbaːɐ] *adj* flexible, elastic (*a. fig*)

dehnen ['deːnən] *v/t* (*ge-, h*) stretch (*a. fig*)

Deich [daɪç] *m* (*-[e]s; -e*) dike

Deichsel ['daɪksəl] *f* (*-; -n*) pole, shaft

dein [daɪn] *poss pron* your; *deiner, deine, dein(e)s* yours

deinerseits ['daɪnɐ'zaɪts] *adv* on your part

deines'gleichen ['daɪnəs-] *pron contp* the likes of you

deinetwegen ['daɪnət'veːgən] *adv* for your sake; because of you

Dekan [de'kaːn] *m* (*-s; -e*), **De'kanin** *f* (*-; -nen*) REL, UNIV dean

Deklination [deklina'tsjoːn] *f* (*-; -en*) LING declension

deklinieren [dekli'niːrən] *v/t* (*no -ge-, h*) decline

Dekolleté [dekɔl'teː] *n* (*-s; -s*) low neckline

Dekorateur [dekora'tøːɐ] *m* (*-s; -e*), **Dekora'teurin** *f* (*-; -nen*) decorator; window dresser

Dekoration [-'tsjoːn] *f* (*-; -en*) decoration;

(window) display; THEA scenery
dekorativ [-'ti:f] *adj* decorative
dekorieren [deko'ri:rən] *v/t* (*no -ge-, h*) decorate; dress
Delfin → **Delphin**
delikat [deli'ka:t] *adj* delicious, exquisite; *fig* delicate, ticklish
Delikatesse [delika'tɛsə] *f* (-; -n) delicacy
Delika'tessenladen *m* delicatessen, F deli
Delphin [dɛl'fi:n] *m* (-s; -e) zo dolphin
Dementi [de'mɛnti] *n* (-s; -s) (official) denial
dementieren [demɛn'ti:rən] *v/t* (*no -ge-, h*) deny (officially)
dementsprechend, demgemäß ['de:m-] *adv* accordingly
'**demnach** *adv* according to that
'**demnächst** *adv* shortly, before long
Demo ['de:mo] F *f* (-; -s) demo
Demokrat [demo'kra:t] *m* (-en; -en) democrat
Demokratie [demokra'ti:] *f* (-; -n) democracy
Demo'kratin *f* (-; -nen) democrat
demo'kratisch *adj* democratic
demolieren [demo'li:rən] *v/t* (*no -ge-, h*) demolish, wreck
Demonstrant [demɔn'strant] *m* (-en; -en),
Demon'strantin *f* (-; -nen) demonstrator
Demonstration [-stra'tsjo:n] *f* (-; -en) demonstration
demonstrieren [-'stri:rən] *v/t and v/i* (*no -ge-, h*) demonstrate
demontieren [demɔn'ti:rən] *v/t* (*no -ge-, h*) dismantle
demoralisieren [demorali'zi:rən] *v/t* (*no -ge-, h*) demoralize
Demoskopie [demosko'pi:] *f* (-; -n) public opinion research
Demut ['de:mu:t] *f* (-; *no pl*) humility, humbleness
demütig ['de:my:tɪç] *adj* humble
demütigen ['de:my:tɪgən] *v/t* (*ge-, h*) humiliate
'**Demütigung** *f* (-; -en) humiliation
denkbar ['dɛŋkba:ɐ̯] **1.** *adj* conceivable; **2.** *adv*: **denkbar einfach** most simple
denken ['dɛŋkən] *v/t and v/i* (*irr, ge-, h*) think (**an** *acc*, **über** *acc* of, about); **daran denken (zu** *inf*) remember (to *inf*)
'**Denkfa,brik** *f* think tank
'**Denkmal** *n* monument; memorial
'**denkwürdig** *adj* memorable
denn [dɛn] *cj and adv* for, because; **es sei denn, dass** unless; **mehr denn je** more than ever
dennoch ['dɛnnɔx] *cj* yet, still, nevertheless
Denunziant [denun'tsjant] *m* (-en; -en)

informer
denunzieren [-'tsi:rən] *v/t* (*no -ge-, h*) inform on *or* against
Deodorant [de'?odo'rant] *n* (-s; -e, -s) deodorant
Deponie [depo'ni:] *f* (-; -n) dump, waste disposal site
deponieren [depo'ni:rən] *v/t* (*no -ge-, h*) deposit, leave
Depot [de'po:] *n* (-s; -s) depot (*a.* MIL); *Swiss:* deposit
Depression [deprɛ'sjo:n] *f* (-; -en) depression (*a.* ECON)
depressiv [deprɛ'si:f] *adj* depressive
deprimieren [depri'mi:rən] *v/t* (*no -ge-, h*) depress
deprimierend *adj* depressing
deprimiert [depri'mi:ɐ̯t] *adj* depressed
der [de:ɐ̯], **die** [di:], **das** [das] **1.** *art* the; **2.** *dem pron* that, this; he, she, it; **die** *pl* these, those, they; **3.** *rel pron* who, which, that
'**derartig 1.** *adv* so (much); like that; **2.** *adj* such (as this)
derb [dɛrp] *adj* coarse; tough, sturdy
'**der'gleichen** *dem pron*: **nichts dergleichen** nothing of the kind
'**der-**, '**die-**, '**dasjenige** [-je:nɪgə] *dem pron* the one; **diejenigen** *pl* the ones, those
dermaßen ['de:ɐ̯ma:sən] *adv* so (much), like that
Dermatologe [dɛrmato'lo:gə] *m* (-n; -n), **Dermato'login** *f* (-; -nen) dermatologist
der-, die-, dasselbe [-'zɛlbə] *dem pron* the same
Deserteur [dezɛr'tø:ɐ̯] *m* (-s; -e) MIL deserter
desertieren [dezɛr'ti:rən] *v/i* (*no -ge-, sein*) MIL desert
deshalb ['dɛs'halp] *cj and adv* therefore, for that reason, that is why, so
Desinfektionsmittel [dɛs?ɪnfɛk'tsjo:ns-] *n* MED disinfectant
desinfizieren [dɛs?ɪnfi'tsi:rən] *v/t* (*no -ge-, h*) MED disinfect
'**Desinteresse** *n* (-s; *no pl*) indifference
'**desinteres,siert** *adj* uninterested, indifferent
destillieren [dɛstɪ'li:rən] *v/t* (*no -ge-, h*) distil(l)
desto ['dɛsto] *cj and adv* → **je**
'**des'wegen** *cj and adv* → **deshalb**
Detail [de'tai] *n* (-s; -s) detail
detailliert [deta'ji:ɐ̯t] *adj* detailed
Detektiv [detɛk'ti:f] *m* (-s; -e) detective
deuten ['dɔytən] (*ge-, h*) **1.** *v/t* interpret; **2.** *v/i*: **deuten auf** (*acc*) point at
'**deutlich** *adj* clear, distinct, plain

deutsch [dɔʏtʃ] *adj* German; *auf Deutsch* in German

'**Deutsche** *m*, *f* (-*n*; -*n*) German

'**Deutschland** Germany

Devise [deˈviːzə] *f* (-; -*n*) motto

De'visen *pl* ECON foreign currency

Dezember [deˈtsɛmbɐ] *m* (-[*s*]; -) December

dezent [deˈtsɛnt] *adj* discreet, unobtrusive; conservative (*clothes etc*); soft (*music etc*)

Dezimal... [detsiˈmaːl-] MATH *in cpds* ...*bruch*, ...*system etc*: decimal ...

Dezimalstelle *f* MATH decimal (place)

DGB [deːɡeːˈbeː] *ABBR of Deutscher Gewerkschaftsbund* Federation of German Trade Unions

d. h. *ABBR of das heißt* i. e., that is

Dia [ˈdiːa] *n* (-*s*; -*s*) PHOT slide

Diagnose [diaˈɡnoːzə] *f* (-; -*n*) diagnosis

diagonal [diaɡoˈnaːl] *adj*, **Diago'nale** *f* (-; -*n*) diagonal

Dialekt [diaˈlɛkt] *m* (-[*e*]*s*; -*e*) dialect

Dialog [diaˈloːk] *m* (-[*e*]*s*; -*e*) dialog, *Br* dialogue

Diamant [diaˈmant] *m* (-*en*; -*en*) diamond

'**Diaprojektor** *m* slide projector

Diät [diˈɛːt] *f* (-; -*en*) diet; *e-e Diät machen* (*Diät leben*) be on (keep to) a diet

Di'äten *pl* PARL allowance

dich [dɪç] *pers pron* you; *dich* (*selbst*) yourself

dicht [dɪçt] **1.** *adj* dense, *a.* thick (*fog*); heavy (*traffic*); F closed, shut; **2.** *adv*: *dicht an* (*dat*) or *bei* close to

'**dichten** *v/t and v/i* (*ge-*, *h*) write (poetry)

Dichter(in) [ˈdɪçtɐ (-tərɪn)] (-*s*; -/-; -*nen*) poet; writer

dichterisch [ˈdɪçtərɪʃ] *adj* poetic; *dichterische Freiheit* poetic licen|se, *Br* -ce

'**dichthalten** F *v/i* (*irr*, *halten*, *sep*, *ge-*, *h*) keep mum

'**Dichtung**[1] *f* (-; -*en*) TECH seal(ing)

'**Dichtung**[2] *f* (-; -*en*) poetry

dick [dɪk] *adj* thick; fat; *es macht dick* it's fattening

'**Dicke** *f* (-; -*n*) thickness; fatness

'**dickfellig** F *adj* thick-skinned

'**dickflüssig** *adj* thick; TECH viscous

Dickicht [ˈdɪkɪçt] *n* (-[*e*]*s*; -*e*) thicket

'**Dickkopf** *m* stubborn *or* pig-headed person

Dickmilch *f* soured milk

Dieb [diːp] *m* (-[*e*]*s*; -*e* [ˈdiːbə]), **Diebin** [ˈdiːbɪn] *f* (-; -*nen*) thief

diebisch [ˈdiːbɪʃ] *adj* thievish; *fig* malicious (*glee etc*)

Diebstahl [ˈdiːpʃtaːl] *m* (-[*e*]*s*; -*stähle* [-ʃtɛːlə]) theft; JUR *mst* larceny

Diele [ˈdiːlə] *f* (-; -*n*) board, plank; hallway, *Br a.* hall

dienen [ˈdiːnən] *v/i* (*ge-*, *h*) serve (*j-m* s.o.; *als* as)

Diener [ˈdiːnɐ] *m* (-*s*; -) servant; *fig* bow (*vor dat* to)

Dienst [diːnst] *m* (-[*e*]*s*; -*e*) service; work; *Dienst haben* be on duty; *im* (*außer*) *Dienst* on (off) duty; *Dienst tuend* on duty

Dienst... *in cpds* ...*wagen*, ...*wohnung etc*: official ..., company ..., business ...

'**Dienstag** *m* (-[*e*]*s*; -*e*) Tuesday

'**Dienstalter** *n* seniority, length of service

'**dienstbereit** *adj* on duty

'**diensteifrig** *adj* (*contp* over-)eager

'**Dienstgrad** *m* grade, rank (*a.* MIL)

'**Dienstleistung** *f* service

'**dienstlich** *adj* official

'**Dienstreise** *f* business trip

'**Dienststunden** *pl* office hours

'**Dienstweg** *m* official channels

dies [diːs], **dieser** [ˈdiːzɐ], **diese** [ˈdiːzə], **dieses** [ˈdiːzəs] *dem pron* this; this one; *diese pl* these

'**diesig** [ˈdiːzɪç] *adj* hazy, misty

'**diesjährig** [-jɛːrɪç] *adj* this year's

'**diesmal** *adv* this time

'**diesseits** [-zaits] *prp* (*gen*) on this side of

'**Diesseits** *n* (-; *no pl*) this life *or* world

Dietrich [ˈdiːtrɪç] *m* (-*s*; -*e*) TECH picklock, skeleton key

Differenz [dɪfəˈrɛnts] *f* (-; -*en*) difference; disagreement

differenzieren [dɪfərɛnˈtsiːrən] *v/i* (*no* -*ge*-, *h*) distinguish

Digital... [diɡiˈtaːl] *in cpds* ...*anzeige*, ...*uhr etc*: digital ...

Diktat [dɪkˈtaːt] *n* (-[*e*]*s*; -*e*) dictation

Diktator [dɪkˈtaːtoːɐ] *m* (-*s*; -*en*) [dɪktaˈtoːrən]) dictator

diktatorisch [dɪktaˈtoːrɪʃ] *adj* dictatorial

Diktatur [dɪktaˈtuːɐ] *f* (-; -*en*) dictatorship

diktieren [dɪkˈtiːrən] *v/t and v/i* (*no* -*ge*-, *h*) dictate

Dik'tiergerät *n* Dictaphone®

Dilettant [dileˈtant] *m* (-*en*; -*en*) amateur

dilet'tantisch *adj* amateurish

DIN [diːn] *ABBR of Deutsches Institut für Normung* German Institute for Standardization

Ding [dɪŋ] *n* (-[*e*]*s*; -*e*) thing; *vor allen Dingen* above all; F *ein Ding drehen* pull a job

'**Dings(bums)** *m*, *f*, *n*, **Dingsda** *m*, *f*, *n* F thingamajig, whatchamacallit

Dinosaurier [dinoˈzaʊrjɐ] *m* (-*s*; -) ZO dinosaur

Dioxid [diˈʔɔksyːt] *n* (-*s*; -*e*) CHEM dioxide

Dioxin [diɔˈksiːn] n (-s; -e) CHEM dioxin

Diphtherie [dɪfteˈriː] f (-; -n) MED diphtheria

Diplom [diˈploːm] n (-s; -e) diploma, degree

Diplom... in cpds ...ingenieur etc: qualified ..., graduate ...

Diplomat [diplo'maːt] m (-en; -en) diplomat

Diplomatie [diploma'tiː] f (-; no pl) diplomacy

Diplo'matin f (-; -nen) diplomat

diplo'matisch adj diplomatic (a. fig)

dir [diːɐ] pers pron (to) you; **dir (selbst)** yourself

direkt [diˈrɛkt] **1.** adj direct; fig directly, right; TV live; **direkt gegenüber (von)** right across

Direktion [dirɛkˈtsjoːn] f (-; -en) management

Direktor [diˈrɛktoːɐ] m (-s; -en [dirɛkˈtoːrən]) director, manager; PED principal, Br headmaster

Direktorin [dirɛkˈtoːrɪn] (-; -nen) director, manager; PED principal, Br headmistress

Di'rektübertragung f TV live transmission or broadcast

Dirigent [diriˈgɛnt] m (-en; -en) conductor

dirigieren [diriˈgiːrən] v/t and v/i (no -ge-, h) MUS conduct; fig direct

Dirne [ˈdɪrnə] f (-; -n) prostitute, whore

Disharmo'nie [dɪs-] f MUS dissonance (a. fig)

dishar'monisch adj MUS discordant

Diskette [dɪsˈkɛtə] f (-; -n) EDP diskette, floppy (disk)

Dis'kettenlaufwerk n EDP disk drive

Disko [ˈdɪsko] f (-; -s) disco

Diskont [dɪsˈkɔnt] m (-s; -e) ECON discount

Diskothek [dɪskoˈteːk] f (-; -en) disco, discotheque

diskret [dɪsˈkreːt] adj discreet

Diskretion [dɪskreˈtsjoːn] f (-; no pl) discretion

diskriminieren [dɪskrimiˈniːrən] v/t (no -ge-, h) discriminate against

Diskrimi'nierung f (-; -en) discrimination (**von** against)

Diskussion [dɪskuˈsjoːn] f (-; -en) discussion, debate

Diskussi'onsleiter m (panel) chairman

Diskussionsrunde f, **Diskussionsteilnehmer** pl panel

Diskuswerfen [ˈdɪskus-] n (-s; no pl) SPORT discus throwing

diskutieren [dɪskuˈtiːrən] v/t and v/i (no -ge-, h) discuss

Disqualifikati'on f SPORT disqualification

(**wegen** for)

disqualifi'zieren v/t (no -ge-, h) SPORT disqualify

Dissident [dɪsiˈdɛnt] m (-en; -en), **Dissi'dentin** f (-; -nen) POL dissident

Distanz [dɪsˈtants] f (-; -en) distance

distanzieren [dɪstanˈtsiːrən] v/refl (no -ge-, h) distance o.s. (**von** from)

Distel [ˈdɪstəl] f (-; -n) BOT thistle

Distrikt [dɪsˈtrɪkt] m (-[e]s; -e) district

Disziplin [dɪstsiˈpliːn] f (-; -en) a) (no pl) discipline, b) SPORT event

diszipliniert [dɪstsipliˈniːɐt] adj disciplined

divers [diˈvɛrs] adj various; several

Dividende [diviˈdɛndə] f (-; -n) ECON dividend

dividieren [diviˈdiːrən] v/t (no -ge-, h) MATH divide (**durch** by)

Division [diviˈzjoːn] f (-; -en) MATH, MIL division

DJH [deːjɔtˈhaː] ABBR of **Deutsches Jugendherbergswerk** German Youth Hostel Association

DM [deːˈɛm] ABBR of **Deutsche Mark** German mark(s)

doch [dɔx] cj and adv but, however, yet; **kommst du nicht (mit)? - doch!** aren't you coming? - (oh) yes, I am!; **ich war es nicht- doch!** I didn't do it - yes, you did!; **er kam also doch?** so he did come after all?; **du kommst doch?** you're coming, aren't you?; **kommen Sie doch herein!** do come in!; **wenn doch ...!** if only ...!

Docht [dɔxt] m (-[e]s; -e) wick

Dock [dɔk] n (-s; -s) MAR dock

Dogge [ˈdɔgə] f (-; -n) ZO mastiff; Great Dane

Dogma [ˈdɔgma] n (-s; Dogmen [ˈdɔgmən]) dogma

dogmatisch [dɔgˈmaːtɪʃ] adj dogmatic

Dohle [ˈdoːlə] f (-; -n) ZO (jack)daw

Doktor [ˈdɔktoːɐ] m (-s; -en [dɔkˈtoːrən]) doctor; UNIV doctor's degree

Doktorarbeit f UNIV (doctoral or PhD) thesis

Dokument [dokuˈmɛnt] n (-[e]s; -e) document

Dokumentar... [dokumɛnˈtaːɐ-] in cpds ...spiel etc: documentary ...

Dokumentarfilm m documentary (film)

Dolch [dɔlç] m (-[e]s; -e) dagger

Dollar [ˈdɔlar] m (-[s]; -s) dollar

dolmetschen [ˈdɔlmɛtʃən] v/i (ge-, h) interpret

'Dolmetscher(in) (-s; -/-; -nen) interpreter

Dom [doːm] m (-[e]s; -e) cathedral

dominierend [domiˈniːrənt] adj (pre-)

drei

dominant

Dompteur ['dɔmp'tøːɐ] m (-s; -e), **Dompteuse** [dɔmp'tøːzə] f (-; -n) animal tamer or trainer

Donner ['dɔnɐ] m (-s; no pl) thunder

'**donnern** v/i (ge-, h) thunder (a. fig)

'**Donnerstag** m (-[e]s; -e) Thursday

'**Donnerwetter** F n (-s; -) dressing-down; **Donnerwetter!** wow!

doof [doːf] F adj stupid, dumb

Doppel ['dɔpəl] n (-s; -) duplicate; tennis etc: doubles

Doppel... in cpds ...bett, ...zimmer etc: double ...

'**Doppeldecker** [-dɛkɐ] m (-s; -) AVIAT biplane; MOT double-decker (bus)

'**Doppelgänger** [-gɛŋɐ] m (-s; -) double, look-alike

'**Doppelhaus** n duplex, Br pair of semis

Doppelhaushälfte f semidetached (house)

'**Doppelpass** m soccer: wall pass

Doppelpunkt m LING colon

Doppelstecker m ELECTR two-way adapter

doppelt adj double; **doppelt so viel (wie)** twice as much (as)

'**Doppelverdiener** pl two-income family

Dorf [dɔrf] n (-[e]s; Dörfer ['dœrfɐ]) village

Dorfbewohner m villager

Dorn [dɔrn] m (-[e]s; -en) BOT thorn (a. fig); TECH tongue; spike

'**dornig** adj thorny (a. fig)

Dorsch [dɔrʃ] m (-[e]s; -e) ZO cod(fish)

dort [dɔrt] adv there

'**dorther** adv from there

'**dorthin** adv there

Dose ['doːzə] f (-; -n) can, Br a. tin

'**Dosen...** in cpds canned, Br a. tinned

dösen ['døːzən] F v/i (ge-, h) doze

'**Dosenöffner** m can (Br tin) opener

Dosis ['doːzɪs] f (-; Dosen) MED dose

Dotter ['dɔtɐ] m, n (-s; -) yolk

Double ['duːbəl] n (-s; -s) film: stunt man (or woman)

Dozent [do'tsɛnt] m (-en; -en), **Do'zentin** f (-; -nen) (university) lecturer, assistant professor

Dr. ABBR of **Doktor** Dr., Doctor

Drache ['draxə] m (-n; -n) dragon

'**Drachen** m (-s; -) kite; SPORT hang glider; **e-n Drachen steigen lassen** fly a kite

Drachenfliegen n SPORT hang gliding

Draht [draːt] m (-[e]s; Drähte ['drɛːtə]) wire; F **auf Draht sein** be on the ball

drahtig ['draːtɪç] fig adj wiry

'**drahtlos** adj wireless

'**Drahtseil** n TECH cable; circus: tightrope

Drahtseilbahn f cable railway

'**Drahtzieher** fig m (-s; -) wirepuller

drall [dral] adj buxom, strapping

Drall m (-[e]s; no pl) twist, spin

Drama ['draːma] n (-s; Dramen) drama

Dramatiker [dra'maːtikɐ] m (-s; -) dramatist, playwright

dra'matisch adj dramatic

dran [dran] F adv → **daran**; **du bist dran** it's your turn; fig you're in for it

drang [draŋ] pret of **dringen**

Drang m (-[e]s; no pl) urge, drive (**nach** for)

drängeln ['drɛŋəln] F v/t and v/i (ge-, h) push, shove

drängen ['drɛŋən] v/t and v/i (ge-, h) push, shove; **j-n zu et. drängen** press or urge s.o. to do s.th.; **sich drängen** press; force one's way

drängend adj pressing

'**drankommen** F v/i (irr, **kommen**, sep, -ge-, sein) have one's turn; **als erster drankommen** be first

drastisch ['drastɪʃ] adj drastic

drauf [drauf] F adv → **darauf**; **drauf und dran sein, et. zu tun** be just about to do s.th.

'**Draufgänger** [-gɛŋɐ] m (-s; -) daredevil

draus [draus] F adv → **daraus**

draußen ['drausən] adv outside; outdoors; **da draußen** out there; **bleib(t) draußen!** keep out!

drechseln ['drɛksəln] v/t (ge-, h) turn (on a lathe)

Drechsler ['drɛkslɐ] m (-s; -) turner

Dreck [drɛk] F m (-[e]s; no pl) dirt; filth (a. fig); mud; fig trash

dreckig ['drɛkɪç] F adj dirty; filthy (both a. fig)

Dreharbeiten ['dreː-] pl film: shooting

Drehbank f (-; -bänke) TECH lathe

'**drehbar** adj revolving, rotating

'**Drehbuch** n film: script

drehen ['dreːən] v/t (ge-, h) turn; film: shoot; roll; **sich drehen** turn, rotate; spin; **sich drehen um** fig be about; → **Ding**

Dreher ['dreːɐ] m (-s; -) TECH turner

'**Drehkreuz** n turnstile

Drehorgel f barrel-organ

Drehort m film: location

Drehstrom m ELECTR three-phase current

Drehstuhl m swivel chair

Drehtür f revolving door

'**Drehung** f (-; -en) turn; rotation

'**Drehzahl** f TECH (number of) revolutions

Drehzahlmesser m MOT rev(olution) counter

drei [drai] adj three

Drei f (-; -en) three; *grade*: fair, C
'**dreibeinig** adj three-legged
dreidimensio'nal adj three-dimensional
'**Dreieck** n (-[e]s; -e) triangle
'**dreieckig** adj triangular
dreierlei ['draiɐ'lai] adj three kinds of
'**dreifach** adj threefold, triple
'**Dreigang...** TECH *in cpds* three-speed ...
Dreikampf m SPORT triathlon
Dreirad n tricycle
Dreisatz m (-es; no pl) MATH rule of three
Dreisprung m (-[e]s; no pl) SPORT triple jump
dreißig ['draisiç] adj thirty
'**dreißigste** adj thirtieth
dreist [draist] adj brazen, impertinent
'**dreistufig** [-ʃtuːfiç] adj three-stage
'**dreizehn(te)** adj thirteen(th)
Dresche ['drɛʃə] F f (-; no pl) thrashing
'**dreschen** v/t and v/i (irr, ge-, h) AGR thresh; thrash
'**Dreschma,schine** f AGR threshing machine
dressieren [drɛ'siːrən] v/t (no -ge-, h) train
Dressman ['drɛsmən] m (-s; -men) male model
Dressur [drɛ'suːɐ] f (-; -en) training; act
Dressurreiten n dressage
dribbeln ['dribəln] v/i (ge-, h), **Dribbling** n (-s; -s) SPORT dribble
drillen ['drilən] v/t (ge-, h) MIL drill (a. fig)
Drillinge ['driliŋə] pl triplets
drin [drin] F adv → **darin**; **das ist nicht drin!** no way!
dringen ['driŋən] v/i (irr, ge-, h) **dringen auf** (acc) insist on; **dringen aus** come from; **dringen durch** force one's way through, penetrate, pierce; **dringen in** (acc) penetrate into; **darauf dringen, dass** urge that
dringend adj urgent, pressing; strong (suspicion etc)
drinnen ['drinən] F adv inside; indoors
dritte ['dritə] adj third; **wir sind zu dritt** there are three of us; **die Dritte Welt** the Third World
'**Drittel** n (-s; -) third
'**drittens** adv thirdly
'**Dritte-Welt-Laden** m third world shop
Droge ['droːgə] f (-; -n) drug
'**drogenabhängig** adj addicted to drugs; **drogenabhängig sein** be a drug addict
'**Drogenabhängige** m, f (-n; -n) drug addict
Drogenmissbrauch m drug abuse
'**drogensüchtig** → **drogenabhängig**
'**Drogentote** m, f drug victim
Drogerie [droɡə'riː] f (-; -n) drugstore, Br

chemist's (shop)
Drogist [dro'gist] m (-en; -en), **Dro'gistin** f (-; -nen) chemist
drohen ['droːən] v/i (ge-, h) threaten, menace
dröhnen ['drøːnən] v/i (ge-, h) roar
'**Drohung** f (-; -en) threat (**gegen** to)
drollig ['drɔliç] adj funny, droll
Dromedar [dromə'daːɐ] n (-s; -e) ZO dromedary
drosch [drɔʃ] pret of **dreschen**
Drossel ['drɔsəl] f (-; -n) ZO thrush
'**drosseln** v/t (ge-, h) TECH throttle
drüben ['dryːbən] adv over there (a. fig)
drüber ['dryːbɐ] F adv → **darüber, drunter**
Druck [druk] m (-[e]s; -e) pressure; printing; print
'**Druckbuchstabe** m block letter
Drückeberger ['drykəbɛrgɐ] F m (-s; -) shirker
'**drucken** v/t (ge-, h) print; **et. drucken lassen** have s.th. printed or published
drücken ['drykən] (ge-, h) **1.** v/t press; push; fig force down; **j-m die Hand drücken** shake hands with s.o.; **2.** v/i pinch; **3.** F v/refl: **sich vor et. drücken** shirk (doing) s.th.
drückend adj heavy, oppressive
Drucker ['drukɐ] m (-s; -) printer (a. EDP)
Drücker ['drykɐ] m (-s; -) latch; trigger; F hawker
Druckerei [drukə'rai] f (-; -en) printers
'**Druckfehler** m misprint
Druckkammer f pressurized cabin
Druckknopf m snap fastener, Br press stud; TECH (push) button
Druckluft f TECH compressed air
Drucksache f printed (or second-class) matter
Druckschrift f block letters
Drucktaste f TECH push button
drunter ['druntɐ] F adv → **darunter**; **es ging drunter und drüber** it was absolutely chaotic
Drüse ['dryːzə] f (-; -n) ANAT gland
Dschungel ['dʒuŋəl] m (-s; -) jungle (a. fig)
Dschunke ['dʒuŋkə] f (-; -n) MAR junk
du [duː] pers pron you
Dübel ['dyːbəl] m (-s; -), '**dübeln** v/t (ge-, h) TECH dowel
ducken ['dukən] v/refl (ge-, h) duck; fig cringe (**vor** dat before); crouch
Duckmäuser ['dukmɔyzɐ] m (-s; -) coward; yes-man
Dudelsack ['duːdəlzak] m MUS bagpipes
Duell [du'ɛl] n (-s; -e) duel
duellieren [duɛ'liːrən] v/refl (no -ge-, h) fight a duel

Duett [du'ɛt] n (-[e]s; -e) MUS duet

Duft [dʊft] m (-[e]s; Düfte ['dʏftə]) scent, fragrance, smell (**nach** of)

'duften v/i (ge-, h) smell (**nach** of)

'duftend adj fragrant

'duftig adj dainty

dulden ['dʊldən] v/t (ge-, h) tolerate, put up with; suffer

'duldsam ['dʊltza:m] adj tolerant

dumm [dʊm] adj stupid, F dumb

'Dummheit f (-; -en) a) (no pl) stupidity, ignorance; b) stupid or foolish thing

'Dummkopf m contp fool, blockhead

dumpf [dʊmpf] adj dull; fig vague

Düne ['dy:nə] f (-; -n) (sand) dune

Dung [dʊŋ] m (-s; no pl) dung, manure

düngen ['dʏŋən] v/t (ge-, h) fertilize; manure

Dünger ['dʏŋɐ] m (-s; -) fertilizer; manure

dunkel ['dʊŋkəl] adj dark (a. fig)

'Dunkelheit f (-; no pl) dark(ness)

'Dunkelkammer f PHOT darkroom

'Dunkelziffer f number of unreported cases

dünn [dʏn] adj thin; weak (coffee etc)

Dunst [dʊnst] m (-[e]s; Dünste ['dʏnstə]) haze, mist; CHEM vapo(u)r

dünsten ['dʏnstən] v/t (ge-, h) GASTR stew, braise

'dunstig adj hazy, misty

Duplikat [dupli'ka:t] n (-[e]s; -e) duplicate; copy

Dur [du:ɐ] n (-; no pl) MUS major (key)

durch [dʊrç] prp (acc) and adv through; across; MATH divided by; GASTR (well) done; **durch j-n (et.)** by s.o. (s.th.); **durch und durch** through and through

'durcharbeiten (sep, -ge-, h) 1. v/t study thoroughly; **sich durcharbeiten durch** work (one's way) through a text etc; 2. v/i work without a break

durch'aus adv absolutely, quite; **durchaus nicht** by no means

'durchblättern v/t (sep, -ge-, h) leaf or thumb through

'Durchblick fig m grasp of s.th.

'durchblicken v/i (sep, -ge-, h) look through; **durchblicken lassen** give to understand; **ich blicke (da) nicht durch** I don't get it

durch'bohren v/t (no -ge-, h) pierce; perforate

'durchbraten v/t (irr, braten, sep, -ge-, h) roast thoroughly

'durchbrechen[1] (irr, brechen, sep, -ge-) 1. v/t (h) break (in two); 2. v/i (sein) break through or apart

durch'brechen[2] v/t (irr, brechen, no -ge-, h) break through

'durchbrennen v/i (irr, **brennen**, sep, -ge-, sein) ELECTR blow; reactor: melt down; F run away

'durchbringen v/t (irr, **bringen**, sep, -ge-, h) get (MED pull) s.o. through; go through one's money; support (family)

'Durchbruch m breakthrough (a. fig)

durch'dacht adj (well) thought-out

'durchdrehen (sep, -ge-, h) 1. v/i wheels: spin; F fig crack up, flip; 2. v/t GASTR grind, Br mince

'durchdringend adj piercing

durchei'nander adv confused; (in) a mess

Durchei'nander n (-s; no pl) confusion, mess; **Durcheinanderbringen** v/t (irr, **bringen**, sep, -ge-, h confuse, mix up; mess up

durch'fahren[1] v/t (irr, **fahren**, no -ge-, h) go (or pass, drive) through

'durchfahren[2] v/i (irr, **fahren**, sep, -ge-, sein) go (or pass, drive) through

'Durchfahrt f passage; **Durchfahrt verboten** no thoroughfare

'Durchfall m MED diarrh(o)ea

'durchfallen v/i (irr, **fallen**, sep, -ge-, sein) fall through; fail, F flunk (test etc); F be a flop; **j-n durchfallen lassen** fail (F flunk) s.o.

durchfragen v/refl (sep, -ge-, h) ask one's way (**nach, zu** to)

'durchführbar adj practicable, feasible

'durchführen v/t (sep, -ge-, h) carry out, do

'Durchgang m passage

'Durchgangs... in cpds ...verkehr etc: through ...; ...lager etc: transit ...

'durchgebraten adj well done

'durchgehen (irr, **gehen**, sep, -ge-, sein) 1. v/i go through (a. RAIL and PARL); fig run away (**mit** with); horse: bolt; 2. v/t go or look through; **durchgehen lassen** tolerate

durchgehend adj continuous; **durchgehender Zug** through train; **durchgehend geöffnet** open all day

'durchgreifen fig v/i (irr, **greifen**, sep, -ge-, h) take drastic measures

durchgreifend adj drastic; radical

'durchhalten v/t (irr, **halten**, sep, -ge-, h) 1. v/t keep up; 2. v/i hold out

'durchhängen v/i (irr, **hängen**, sep, -ge-, h) sag; F have a low

'durchkämpfen v/t (sep, -ge-, h) fight out; **sich durchkämpfen** fight one's way through

'durchkommen v/i (irr, **kommen**, sep, -ge-, sein) come through (a. MED); get through; get along; get away (**mit e-r Lüge** etc with a lie etc) durch'kreuzen v/t (no -ge-, h) cross, thwart

'durchlassen v/t (irr, lassen, sep, -ge-, h) let pass, let through

'durchlässig adj permeable (für to)

'durchlaufen[1] (irr, laufen, sep, -ge-) 1. v/i (sein) run through; 2. v/t (h) wear through

durch'laufen[2] v/t (irr, laufen, no -ge-, h) pass through

'Durchlauferhitzer m (-s; -) (instant) water heater, Br a. geyser

'durchlesen v/t (irr, lesen, sep, -ge-, h) read through

durch'leuchten v/t (no -ge-, h) MED X-ray; fig screen

durchlöchern [-'lœçɐn] v/t (no -ge-, h) perforate, make holes in

'durchmachen F (sep, -ge-, h) go through; viel durchmachen suffer a lot; die Nacht durchmachen make a night of it

'Durchmesser m (-s; -) diameter

durch'nässen v/t (no -ge-, h) soak

'durchnehmen v/t (irr, nehmen, sep, -ge-, h) PED do, deal with

'durchpausen v/t (sep, -ge-, h) trace

durch'queren v/t (no -ge-, h) cross

'Durchreiche f (-; -n) hatch

'Durchreise f: ich bin nur auf der Durchreise I'm only passing through

'durchreisen v/i (sep, -ge-, sein) travel through

'Durchreisevisum n transit visa

'durchreißen (irr, reißen, sep, -ge-) 1. v/t (h) tear (in two); 2. v/i (sein) tear, break

durchringen v/refl (irr, ringen, sep, -ge-, h) sich durchringen, et. zu tun bring o.s. to do s.th.

'Durchsage f announcement

durch'schauen v/t (no -ge-, h) see through s.o. or s.th.

'durchscheinen v/i (irr, scheinen, sep, -ge-, h) shine through

durchscheinend adj transparent

'durchscheuern v/t (sep, -ge-, h) chafe; wear through

'durchschlafen v/i (irr, schlafen, sep, -ge-, h) sleep through

'Durchschlag m (carbon) copy

durch'schlagen[1] v/t (irr, schlagen, no -ge-, h) cut in two; bullet etc: go through, pierce

'durchschlagen[2] (irr, schlagen, sep, -ge-) 1. v/refl (h): sich durchschlagen nach make one's way to; 2. v/i (sein) come through (a. fig)

durchschlagend adj sweeping; effective

'Durchschlagpa,pier n carbon paper

'Durchschlagskraft fig f force, impact

'durchschneiden v/t (irr, schneiden, sep, -ge-, h) cut (through)

'Durchschnitt m average; im (über, unter dem) Durchschnitt on an (above, below) average; im Durchschnitt betragen (verdienen etc) average

'durchschnittlich 1. adj average; ordinary; 2. adv on an average

'Durchschnitts... in cpds average ...

'Durchschrift f (carbon) copy

'durchsehen v/t (irr, sehen, sep, -ge-, h) look or go through; check

durchsetzen v/t (sep, -ge-, h) put (or push) s.th. through; s-n Kopf durchsetzen have one's way; sich durchsetzen get one's way; be successful; sich durchsetzen können have authority (bei over)

durch'setzt adj: durchsetzt mit interspersed with

'durchsichtig adj transparent (a. fig); clear; see-through

'durchsickern v/i (sep, -ge-, sein) seep through; fig leak out

'durchstarten v/i (sep, -ge-, sein) AVIAT climb and reaccelerate

durch'stechen v/t (irr, stechen, no -ge-, h) pierce

'durchstecken v/t (sep, -ge-, h) stick through

durchstehen v/t (irr, stehen, sep, -ge-, h) go through

durch'stoßen v/t (irr, stoßen, no -ge-, h) break through

'durchstreichen v/t (irr, streichen, sep, -ge-, h) cross out

durch'suchen v/t (no -ge-, h) search, F frisk

Durch'suchung f (-; -en) search

Durch'suchungsbefehl m search warrant

durchtrieben [-'triːbən] adj cunning, sly

durch'wachsen adj GASTR streaky

'Durchwahl f (-; no pl) TEL direct dial-(l)ing

'durchwählen v/i (sep, -ge-, h) TEL dial direct

'durchweg [-vɛk] adv without exception

durch'weicht adj soaked, drenched

durch'wühlen v/t (no -ge-, h) rummage through

'durchzählen v/t (sep, -ge-, h) count off (Br up)

durchziehen (irr, ziehen, sep, -ge-) 1. v/i (sein) pass through; 2. v/t (h) pull s.th. through; fig carry s.th. through (to the end)

durch'zucken v/t (no -ge-, h) flash through

'**Durchzug** m (-[e]s; no pl) draft, Br draught

dürfen ['dʏrfən] **1.** v/aux (irr, no -ge-, h) be allowed or permitted to inf; **darf ich gehen?** may I go?; **ja**, **du darfst**) yes, you may; **du darfst nicht** you must not, you aren't allowed to; **dürfte ich …?** could I …?; **das dürfte genügen** that should be enough; **2.** v/i (irr, ge-, h) **er darf (nicht)** he is (not) allowed to inf

durfte ['dʊrftə] pret of **dürfen**

dürftig ['dʏrftɪç] adj poor; scanty

dürr [dʏr] adj dry; barren, arid; skinny

Dürre ['dʏrə] f (-; -n) a) a drought, b) (no pl) barrenness

Durst [dʊrst] m (-[e]s; no pl) thirst (**auf** acc for); **Durst haben** be thirsty

'**durstig** adj thirsty

Dusche ['duʃə] f (-; -n) shower

'**duschen** v/refl and v/i (ge-, h) have or take a shower

Düse ['dy:zə] f (-; -n) TECH nozzle; jet

'**düsen** F v/i (ge-, sein) jet

'**Düsenantrieb** m jet propulsion; **mit Düsenantrieb** jet-propelled

Düsenflugzeug n jet (plane)

Düsenjäger m MIL jet fighter

Düsentriebwerk n jet engine

düster ['dy:stɐ] adj dark, gloomy (both a. fig); dim (light); fig dismal

Dutzend ['dʊtsənt] n (-s; -e) dozen

'**dutzendweise** adv by the dozen

duzen ['du:tsən] v/t (ge-, h) use the familiar 'du' with s.o.; **sich duzen** be on 'du' terms

Dynamik [dy'na:mɪk] f (-; no pl) PHYS dynamics; fig dynamism

dy'namisch adj dynamic

Dynamit [dyna'mi:t] n (-s; no pl) dynamite

Dynamo [dy'an:mo] m (-s; -s) ELECTR dynamo, generator

D-Zug ['de:-] m express train

E

Ebbe ['ɛbə] f (-; -n) ebb, low tide

eben ['e:bən] **1.** adj even; flat; MATH plane; **zu ebener Erde** on the first (Br ground) floor; **2.** adv just; **an eben dem Tag** on that very day; **so ist es eben** that's the way it is; **gerade eben so** or **noch** just barely

'**Ebenbild** n image

'**ebenbürtig** [-bʏrtɪç] adj: **j-m ebenbürtig sein** be a match for s.o., be s.o.'s equal

Ebene ['e:bənə] f (-; -n) GEOGR plain; MATH plane; fig level

'**ebenerdig** adj and adv at street level; on the first (Br ground) floor

'**ebenfalls** adv as well, too

'**Ebenholz** n ebony

'**Ebenmaß** n (-es; no pl) symmetry; harmony; regularity

'**ebenmäßig** adj symmetrical; harmonious; regular

'**ebenso** adv and cj just as; as well; **ebenso wie** in the same way as; **ebenso gern**, **ebenso gut** just as well; **ebenso sehr**, **ebenso viel** just as much; **ebenso wenig** just as little or few

Eber ['e:bɐ] m (-s; -) ZO boar

ebnen ['e:bnən] v/t (ge-, h) even, level; fig smooth

Echo ['ɛço] n (-s; -s) echo; fig response

echt [ɛçt] adj genuine (a. fig), real; true; pure; fast (color); authentic; F **echt gut** real good

'**Echtheit** f (-; no pl) genuineness; authenticity

'**Eckball** ['ɛk-] m SPORT corner (kick)

Ecke ['ɛkə] f (-; -n) corner; edge; SPORT **lange (kurze) Ecke** far (near) corner; → **Eckball**

eckig ['ɛkɪç] adj square, angular; fig awkward

'**Eckzahn** m canine tooth

edel ['e:dəl] adj noble; MIN precious

'**Edelmetall** n precious metal

'**Edelstahl** m stainless steel

'**Edelstein** m precious stone; gem

EDV [e:de:'fau] ABBR of **Elektronische Datenverarbeitung** EDP, electronic data processing

Efeu ['e:fɔy] m (-s; no pl) BOT ivy

Effekt [ɛ'fɛkt] m (-[e]s; -e) effect

effektiv [ɛfɛk'ti:f] **1.** adj effective; **2.** adv actually

Effektivität [ɛfɛktivi'tɛ:t] f (-; no pl) effectiveness

ef'fektvoll adj effective, striking

Effet [ɛ'feː] m (-s; -s) SPORT spin

EG [eː'geː] HIST ABBR of **Europäische Gemeinschaft** EC, European Community

egal [e'gaːl] F adj: **egal ob (warum, wer** etc) no matter if (why, who, etc); **das ist egal** it doesn't matter; **das ist mir egal** I don't care, it's all the same to me

Egge ['ɛɡə] f (-; -n), **eggen** v/t (ge-, h) AGR harrow

Egoismus [ego'ɪsmʊs] m (-; no pl) ego(t)ism

Egoist(in) [ego'ɪst(ɪn)] (-en; -en/-; -nen) ego(t)ist

ego'istisch adj selfish, ego(t)istic(al)

ehe ['eːə] cj before; **nicht ehe** not until

Ehe ['eːə] f (-; -n) marriage (**mit** to)

'Eheberatung f marriage counseling (Br guidance)

'Ehebrecher m (-s; -) adulterer

'Ehebrecherin f (-; -nen) adulteress

'ehebrecherisch adj adulterous

'Ehebruch m adultery

'Ehefrau f wife

'Eheleute pl married couple

'ehelich adj conjugal; JUR legitimate

'ehemalig ['eːəmaːlɪç] adj former, ex-...

ehemals ['eːəmaːls] adv formerly

'Ehemann m husband

'Ehepaar n (married) couple

eher ['eːɐ] adv earlier, sooner; **je eher, desto lieber** the sooner the better; **nicht eher als** not until or before

'Ehering m wedding ring

ehrbar ['eːɐbaːɐ] adj respectable

Ehre ['eːrə] f (-; -n) hono(u)r; **zu Ehren (von)** in hono(u)r of

'ehren v/t (ge-, h) hono(u)r; respect

'ehrenamtlich adj honorary

'Ehrenbürger m honorary citizen

'Ehrendoktor m UNIV honorary doctor

'Ehrengast m guest of hono(u)r

'Ehrenkodex m code of hono(u)r

'Ehrenmann m man of hono(u)r

'Ehrenmitglied n honorary member

'Ehrenplatz m place of hono(u)r

'Ehrenrechte pl civil rights

'Ehrenrettung f rehabilitation

'ehrenrührig adj defamatory

'Ehrenrunde f esp SPORT lap of hono(u)r

'Ehrensache f point of hono(u)r

Ehrentor n, 'Ehrentreffer m SPORT consolation goal

'ehrenwert adj hono(u)rable

'Ehrenwort n (-[e]s; -e) word of hono(u)r; F **Ehrenwort!** cross my heart!

ehrerbietig ['eːɐʔɛɐbiːtɪç] adj respectful

'Ehrfurcht ['eːɐ-] f (-; no pl) respect (**vor** dat for); awe (of); **Ehrfurcht gebietend** awe-inspiring, awesome

'ehrfürchtig [-fʏrçtɪç] adj respectful

'Ehrgefühl n (-[e]s; no pl) sense of hono(u)r

'Ehrgeiz m ambition

'ehrgeizig adj ambitious

'ehrlich adj honest; frank; fair

'Ehrlichkeit f (-; no pl) honesty; fairness

'Ehrung f (-; -en) hono(u)r(ing)

'ehrwürdig adj venerable

Ei [ai] n (-[e]s; Eier ['aiɐ]) egg; V pl balls

Eiche ['aiçə] f (-; -n) oak(-tree)

Eichel ['aiçəl] f (-; -n) BOT acorn; card games: club(s); ANAT glans (penis)

eichen ['aiçən] v/t (ge-, h) ga(u)ge

'Eichhörnchen ['aiçhœrnçən] n (-s; -) ZO squirrel

Eid [ait] m (-[e]s; -e) oath; **e-n Eid ablegen** take an oath

'Eidechse ['aidɛksə] f (-; -n) ZO lizard

'eidesstattlich ['aidəs-] adj: **eidesstattliche Erklärung** JUR statutory declaration

'Eidotter m, n (egg) yolk

'Eierbecher m eggcup

'Eierkuchen m pancake

Eierli,kör m eggnog

'Eierschale f eggshell

'Eierstock m ANAT ovary

Eieruhr f egg timer

Eifer ['aifɐ] m (-s; no pl) zeal, eagerness; **glühender Eifer** ardo(u)r

'Eifersucht f (-; no pl) jealousy

'eifersüchtig adj jealous (**auf** acc of)

eifrig adj eager, zealous; ardent

'Eigelb n (-[e]s; -e) (egg) yolk

eigen ['aigən] adj own, of one's own; peculiar; particular, F fussy

...eigen in cpds staatseigen etc: ...-owned

'Eigenart f peculiarity

'eigenartig adj peculiar; strange

'Eigenbedarf m personal needs

'Eigengewicht n dead weight

'eigenhändig [-hɛndɪç] **1.** adj personal; **2.** adv personally, with one's own hands

'Eigenheim n home of (one's own)

'Eigenliebe f self-love

'Eigenlob n self-praise

'eigenmächtig adj arbitrary

'Eigenname m proper noun

'Eigennutz m (-es; no pl) self-interest

'eigennützig [-nʏtsɪç] adj selfish

'eigens adv (e)specially, expressly

'Eigenschaft f (-; -en) quality; TECH, PHYS, CHEM property; **in s-r Eigenschaft als** in his capacity as

'Eigenschaftswort n (-[e]s; -wörter) LING adjective

'Eigensinn m (-[e]s; no pl) stubbornness

'eigensinnig adj stubborn, obstinate

eigentlich ['aigəntlıç] **1.** *adj* actual, true, real; exact; **2.** *adv* actually, really; originally

'**Eigentor** *n* SPORT own goal (*a. fig*)

'**Eigentum** *n* (-[e]s; *no pl*) property

'**Eigentümer** ['aigəntyːmɐ] *m* (-s; -), '**Eigentümerin** *f* (-; -nen) owner, proprietor (proprietress)

'**eigentümlich** [-tyːmlıç] *adj* peculiar; strange, odd

'**Eigentümlichkeit** *f* (-; -en) peculiarity

'**Eigentumswohnung** *f* condominium, F condo, *Br* owner-occupied flat

'**eigenwillig** *adj* wil(l)ful; individual, original (*style etc*)

eignen ['aignən] *v/refl* (ge-, h) **sich eignen für** be suited or fit for

'**Eignung** *f* (-; *no pl*) suitability; aptitude, qualification

'**Eignungsprüfung** *f*, '**Eignungstest** *m* aptitude test

'**Eilbote** ['ail-] *m*: **durch Eilboten** by special delivery

'**Eilbrief** *m* special delivery (*Br* express) letter

Eile ['ailə] *f* (-; *no pl*) haste, hurry

eilen *v/i* a) (ge-, *sein*) hurry, hasten, rush, b) (ge-, h) be urgent

'**eilig** *adj* hurried, hasty; urgent; **es eilig haben** be in a hurry

Eimer ['aimɐ] *m* (-s; -) bucket, pail

ein [ain] **1.** *adj* one; **2.** *indef art* a, an; **3.** *adv*: "**einlaus**" "on / off"; **ein und aus gehen** come and go; **nicht mehr ein noch aus wissen** be at one's wits' end

einander [ai'nandɐ] *pron* each other, one another

'**einarbeiten** *v/t* (sep, -ge-, h) train, acquaint *s.o.* with his work, F break *s.o.* in; **sich einarbeiten** work o.s. in

'**einarmig** [-armıç] *adj* one-armed

einäschern ['ain'ɛʃɐn] *v/t* (sep, -ge-, h) cremate

Einäscherung ['ain'ɛʃərʊŋ] *f* (-; -en) cremation

'**einatmen** *v/t* (sep, -ge-, h) inhale, breathe

'**einäugig** [-ɔygıç] *adj* one-eyed

'**Einbahnstraße** *f* one-way street

einbalsamieren ['ainbalzami:rən] *v/t* (*no -ge-, h*) embalm

'**Einband** *m* (-[e]s; -bände) binding, cover

'**Einbau** *m* (-[e]s; -bauten) installation, fitting; **Einbau...** *in cpds* ...möbel *etc*: built-in ...

'**einbauen** *v/t* (sep, -ge-, h) build in, install(l), fit

'**einberufen** *v/t* (irr, *rufen*, sep, no -ge-, h) MIL draft, *Br* call up; call (*meeting etc*)

'**Einberufung** *f* (-; -en) MIL draft, *Br* call-up

'**einbeziehen** *v/t* (irr, *ziehen*, sep, no -ge-, h) include

einbiegen *v/i* (irr, *biegen*, sep, -ge-, *sein*) turn (**in** *acc* into)

'**einbilden** *v/refl* (sep, -ge-, h) imagine; **sich et. einbilden auf** (acc) be conceited about

'**Einbildung** *f* (-; *no pl*) imagination, fancy; conceit

'**einblenden** *v/t* (sep, -ge-, h) TV fade in

'**Einblick** *m* insight (**in** *acc* into)

'**einbrechen** *v/i* (irr, *brechen*, sep, -ge-, *sein*) collapse; *winter*: set in; **einbrechen in** (acc) break into, burgle; fall through (the ice)

'**Einbrecher** *m* (-s; -) burglar

'**einbringen** *v/t* (irr, *bringen*, sep, -ge-, h) bring in; yield (*profit etc*)

'**Einbruch** *m* burglary; **bei Einbruch der Nacht** at nightfall

'**einbürgern** [-byrgɐn] *v/t* (sep, -ge-, h) naturalize; **sich einbürgern** *fig* come into use

'**Einbürgerung** *f* (-; -en) naturalization

'**Einbuße** *f* (-; -n) loss

'**einbüßen** *v/t* (sep, -ge-, h) lose

'**eindämmen** [-dɛmən] *v/t* (sep, -ge-, h) dam (up), *fig a.* get under control

'**eindecken** *fig v/t* (sep, -ge-, h) provide (**mit** with)

'**eindeutig** [-dɔytıç] *adj* clear

'**eindrehen** *v/t* (sep, -ge-, h) put *hair* in curlers

'**eindringen** *v/i* (irr, *dringen*, sep, -ge-, *sein*) **eindringen in** (acc) enter (*a. fig*); force one's way into; MIL invade

'**eindringlich** *adj* urgent

'**Eindringling** *m* (-s; -e) intruder; MIL invader

'**Eindruck** *m* impression

'**eindrücken** *v/t* (sep, -ge-, h) break or push in

'**eindrucksvoll** *adj* impressive

'**eineiig** ['ain'aiıç] *adj* identical (*twins*)

'**eineinhalb** *adj* one and a half

'**einengen** ['ain'ɛŋən] *v/t* (sep, -ge-, h) confine, restrict

einer ['ainɐ], **eine** ['ainə], **ein(e)s** ['ain(-ə)s] *indef pron* one

'**Einer** *m* (-s; -) MATH unit; *rowing*: single sculls

einerlei ['ainɐ'lai] *adj*: **ganz einerlei** all the same; **einerlei ob** no matter if

'**Einer'lei** *n*: **das tägliche Einerlei** the daily grind or rut

'**einer'seits** *adv* on the one hand

'**einfach** *adj* simple; easy; plain; one-way (*Br* single) (*ticket*)

'**Einfachheit** f (-; no pl) simplicity
'**einfädeln** [-fɛ:dəln] v/t (sep, -ge-, h)
thread; F start, set afoot; MOT merge
'**einfahren** (irr, fahren, sep, -ge-) **1.** v/t (h)
MOT run in; bring in (harvest); **2.** v/i (sein)
come in, RAIL a. pull in
'**Einfahrt** f entrance, way in
'**Einfall** m idea; MIL invasion
'**einfallen** v/i (irr, fallen, sep, -ge-, sein) fall
in; collapse; MUS join in; **einfallen in**
(acc) MIL invade; **ihm fiel ein, dass** it
came to his mind that; **mir fällt nichts
ein** I have no ideas; **es fällt mir nicht
ein** I can't think of it; **dabei fällt mir
ein** that reminds me; **was fällt dir ein?**
what's the idea?
'**einfältig** ['ainfɛltɪç] adj simple-minded;
stupid
'**Einfa'milienhaus** n detached house
'**einfarbig** adj solid-colored, Br self-col-
oured
'**einfassen** v/t (sep, -ge-, h) border
'**einfetten** v/t (sep, -ge-, h) grease
'**einfinden** v/refl (irr, finden, sep, -ge-, h)
appear, arrive
'**einflechten** fig v/t (irr, flechten, sep, -ge-,
h) work in
'**einfliegen** v/t (irr, fliegen, sep, -ge-, h) fly
in
'**einfließen** v/i (irr, fließen, sep, -ge-, sein)
fig **et. einfließen lassen** slip s.th. in
'**einflößen** v/t (sep, -ge-, h) pour (j-m into
s.o.'s mouth); fig fill with (awe etc)
'**Einfluss** m influence
'**einflussreich** adj influential
'**einförmig** [-fœrmɪç] adj uniform
'**einfrieren** (irr, frieren, sep, -ge-) **1.** v/i
(sein) freeze (in); **2.** v/t (h) freeze (a. fig)
'**einfügen** v/t (sep, -ge-, h) put in; fig insert; **sich einfügen** fit in; adjust (o.s.)
(in acc to)
'**Einfügetaste** f EDP insert key
'**einfühlsam** ['ainfy:lza:m] adj sympathetic
'**Einfühlungsvermögen** n (-s; no pl) em-
pathy
'**Einfuhr** ['ainfu:ɐ] f (-; -en) ECON a) (no pl)
importation, b) import
'**einführen** v/t (sep, -ge-, h) introduce; in-
stal(l) s.o.; insert; ECON import
'**Einfuhrstopp** m ECON import ban
'**Einführung** f (-; -en) introduction
'**Einführungs...** in cpds ...kurs, ...preis
etc: introductory ...
'**Eingabe** f petition; EDP input
'**Eingabetaste** f EDP enter or return key
'**Eingang** m entrance; ECON arrival; receipt
'**eingängig** adj catchy (tune etc)

'**eingangs** adv at the beginning
'**eingeben** v/t (irr, geben, sep, -ge-, h) MED
administer (dat to); EDP feed, enter
'**eingebildet** adj imaginary; conceited
(auf acc of)
'**Eingeborene** m, f (-n; -n) native
'**Eingebung** f (-; -en) inspiration; impulse
'**eingefallen** adj sunken, hollow
'**eingefleischt** adj confirmed
'**eingehen** (irr, gehen, sep, -ge-, sein) **1.** v/i
ECON come in, arrive; BOT, ZO die; fabric:
shrink; **eingehen auf** (acc) agree to; go
into (detail); listen to s.o.; **2.** v/t enter into
(a contract etc); make (a bet); take (a risk
etc)
'**eingehend** adj thorough; detailed
'**eingemacht** adj preserved
'**eingemeinden** ['aingəmaindən] v/t (sep,
no -ge-, h) incorporate (in acc into)
'**eingenommen** adj partial (für to); prejudiced (gegen against); **von sich eingenommen** full of o.s.
'**eingeschlossen** adj locked in; trapped;
ECON included
'**eingeschnappt** F adj in a huff
'**eingeschrieben** adj registered
'**eingespielt** adj: (gut) aufeinander eingespielt sein work well together, be a
good team
'**eingestellt** adj: **eingestellt auf** (acc) prepared for; **eingestellt gegen** opposed to
'**Eingeweide** ['aingəvaidə] pl ANAT intes-
tines, guts
'**Eingeweihte** m, f (-n; -n) insider
'**eingewöhnen** v/refl (sep, no -ge-, h) **sich
eingewöhnen in** (acc) get used to, settle
in
'**eingießen** v/t (irr, gießen, sep, -ge-, h)
pour
'**eingleisig** [-glaizɪç] adj single-track
'**eingliedern** v/t (sep, -ge-, h) integrate
'**Eingliederung** f integration
'**eingraben** v/t (irr, graben, sep, -ge-, h)
bury
'**eingra,vieren** v/t (sep, no -ge-, h) engrave
'**eingreifen** v/i (irr, greifen, sep, -ge-, h)
step in, interfere
'**Eingriff** m intervention, interference;
MED operation
'**einhaken** v/t (sep, -ge-, h) hook in; **sich
einhaken** link arms, take s.o.'s arm
'**Einhalt** m: **Einhalt gebieten** put a stop
(dat to)
'**einhalten** v/t (irr, halten, sep, -ge-, h)
keep
'**einhängen** (sep, -ge-, h) **1.** v/t hang in; TEL
hang up (receiver); **sich einhängen →
einhaken; 2.** v/i TEL hang up
'**einheimisch** adj native, local; ECON

home, domestic

'**Einheimische** m, f (-n; -n) local, native

'**Einheit** f (-; -en) unit; POL unity

'**einheitlich** adj uniform; homogeneous

'**Einheits...** in cpds ...preis etc: standard

einhellig ['ainhɛlıç] adj unanimous

'**einholen** v/t (sep, -ge-, h) catch up with (a. fig); make up for lost time; make (inquiries) (**über** acc about); seek (advice) (**bei** from); ask for permission etc; strike (sail); **einholen gehen** go shopping

'**Einhorn** n MYTH unicorn

'**einhüllen** v/t (sep, -ge-, h) wrap (up); fig shroud

einig ['ainıç] adj: **sich einig sein** agree; **sich nicht einig sein** disagree, differ

einige ['ainıgə] indef pron some, a few, several

einigen ['ainıgən] v/t (ge-, h) **sich einigen über** (acc) agree on

einigermaßen ['ainıgɐ'maːsən] adv quite, fairly; not too bad

'**einiges** indef pron some, something; quite a lot

'**Einigkeit** f (-; no pl) unity; agreement

'**Einigung** f (-; -en) agreement, settlement; POL unification

'**einjagen** v/t (sep, -ge-, h) **j-m e-n Schrecken einjagen** give s.o. a fright, frighten or scare s.o.

'**einjährig** [-jɛːrıç] adj one-year-old; **einjährige Pflanze** annual

'**einkalku,lieren** v/t (no -ge-, h) take into account, allow for

'**Einkauf** m purchase; **Einkäufe machen** → einkaufen 1

'**einkaufen** (sep, -ge-, h) **1.** v/t buy, ECON a. purchase; **2.** v/i go shopping

'**Einkaufs...** in cpds shopping ...

Einkaufsbummel m shopping spree

Einkaufspreis m ECON purchase price

Einkaufswagen m grocery or shopping cart, Br (supermarket) trolley

Einkaufszentrum n (shopping) mall, Br shopping centre

'**einkehren** v/i (sep, -ge-, sein) stop (**in** dat at)

'**einklammern** v/t (sep, -ge-, h) put in brackets

'**Einklang** m (-[e]s; no pl) MUS unison; fig harmony

'**einkleiden** v/t (sep, -ge-, h) clothe (a. fig)

'**einklemmen** v/t (sep, -ge-, h) squeeze, jam; **eingeklemmt sein** be stuck, be jammed

'**einkochen** (sep, -ge-) **1.** v/t (h) preserve; **2.** v/i (sein) boil down

'**Einkommen** n (-s; -) income

Einkommensteuererklärung f income-

-tax return

'**einkreisen** v/t (sep, -ge-, h) encircle, surround

Einkünfte ['ainkʏnftə] pl income

'**einladen** v/t (irr, laden, sep, -ge-, h) invite; load

einladend adj inviting

'**Einladung** f (-; -en) invitation

'**Einlage** f (-; -n) ECON investment; MED arch support; THEA, MUS interlude

Einlass ['ainlas] m (-es; no pl) admission, admittance

'**einlassen** v/t (irr, lassen, sep, -ge-, h) let in; run (a bath); **sich einlassen auf** (acc) get involved in; let o.s. in for; agree to; **sich mit j-m einlassen** get involved with s.o.

'**Einlauf** m SPORT finish; MED enema

'**einlaufen** (irr, laufen, sep, -ge-) **1.** v/i (sein) come in (a. SPORT); water: run in; MAR enter port; fabric: shrink; **2.** v/t (h) break new shoes in; **sich einlaufen** warm up

'**einleben** v/refl (sep, -ge-, h) settle in

'**einlegen** v/t (sep, -ge-, h) put in; set (hair); GASTR pickle; MOT change into

'**Einlegesohle** f insole

'**einleiten** v/t (sep, -ge-, h) start; introduce; MED induce; TECH dump, discharge (sewage)

einleitend adj introductory

'**Einleitung** f introduction

'**einlenken** v/i (sep, -ge-, h) come round

'**einleuchten** v/i (sep, -ge-, h) be evident, be obvious; **das leuchtet mir (nicht) ein** that makes (doesn't make) sense to me

'**einliefern** v/t (sep, -ge-, h) take (**ins Gefängnis** to) prison; **in die Klinik** to [the] hospital)

'**einlösen** v/t (sep, -ge-, h) redeem; cash (check)

'**einmachen** v/t (sep, -ge-, h) preserve

'**einmal** adv once; some or one day, sometime; **auf einmal** suddenly; at the same time, at once; **noch einmal** once more or again; **noch einmal so ... (wie)** twice as ... (as); **es war einmal** once (upon a time) there was; **haben Sie schon einmal ...?** have you ever ...?; **schon einmal dort gewesen sein** have been there before; **nicht einmal** not even

'**Einmal...** in cpds disposable ...

Einmal'eins n (-; no pl) multiplication table

einmalig ['ainmaːlıç] adj single; fig unique; F fabulous

'**Einmann...** in cpds one-man ...

'**Einmarsch** m entry; MIL invasion

'einmar,schieren v/i (no -ge-, sein) march in; einmarschieren in (acc) MIL invade
'einmischen v/refl (sep, -ge-, h) meddle (in acc in, with), interfere (with)
'Einmündung f junction
'einmütig [-my:tɪç] adj unanimous
'Einmütigkeit f (-; no pl) unanimity
Einnahmen ['aɪnnaːmən] pl takings, receipts
'einnehmen v/t (irr, nehmen, sep, -ge-, h) take (a. MIL); earn, make
'einnehmend adj engaging
'einnicken v/i (sep, -ge-, sein) doze off
'einnisten v/refl (sep, -ge-, h) sich bei j-m einnisten park o.s. on s.o.
'Einöde f (-; -n) desert, wilderness
'einordnen v/t (sep, -ge-, h) put in its proper place; file; sich einordnen MOT get in lane
einpacken v/t (sep, -ge-, h) pack (up); wrap up
einparken v/t and v/i (sep, -ge-, h) park (between two cars)
einpferchen v/t (sep, -ge-, h) pen in; coop up
einpflanzen v/t (sep, -ge-, h) plant; fig implant (a. MED)
einplanen v/t (sep, -ge-, h) allow for
einprägen v/t (sep, -ge-, h) impress; sich et. einprägen keep s.th. in mind; memorize s.th.
einquartieren F v/t (no -ge-, h) put s.o. up (bei j-m at s.o.'s place); sich einquartieren bei (dat) move in with
einrahmen v/t (sep, -ge-, h) frame
einräumen v/t (sep, -ge-, h) put away; furnish; fig grant, concede
einreden (sep, -ge-, h) 1. v/t: j-m et. einreden talk s.o. into (believing) s.th.; 2. v/i: auf j-n einreden keep on at s.o.
einreiben v/t (irr, reiben, sep, -ge-, h) rub in
einreichen v/t (sep, -ge-, h) hand or send in
einreihen v/t (sep, -ge-, h) place (among); sich einreihen take one's place
'einreihig [-raɪç] adj single-breasted
'Einreise f entry (a. in cpds)
'einreisen v/i (sep, -ge-, sein) enter (in ein Land a country)
'einreißen (irr, reißen, sep, -ge-) 1. v/t (h) tear; pull down; 2. v/i (sein) tear; fig spread
einrenken v/t (sep, -ge-, h) MED set; fig straighten out
'einrichten v/t (sep, -ge-, h) furnish; establish; arrange; sich einrichten furnish one's home; sich einrichten auf (acc) prepare for
'Einrichtung f (-; -en) furnishings; fittings;

TECH installation(s), facilities; institution, facility
'einrücken (sep, -ge-) 1. v/i (sein) MIL join the forces; march in; 2. v/t (h) PRINT indent
eins [aɪns] pron and adj one; one thing; es ist alles eins it's all the same (thing)
Eins f (-; -en) one; grade: excellent, A
einsam ['aɪnzaːm] adj lonely, lonesome; solitary
'Einsamkeit f (-; no pl) loneliness; solitude
'einsammeln v/t (sep, -ge-, h) collect
'Einsatz m TECH inset, insert; stake(s) (a. fig); MUS entry; fig effort(s), zeal; use, employment; MIL action, mission; deployment; im Einsatz in action; unter Einsatz des Lebens at the risk of one's life
'einsatzbereit adj ready for action
einsatzfreudig adj dynamic, zealous
'einschalten v/t (sep, -ge-, h) ELECTR switch or turn on; call s.o. in; sich einschalten step in
'Einschaltquote f TV rating
'einschärfen v/t (sep, -ge-, h) urge (j-m et. s.o. to do s.th.)
einschätzen v/t (sep, -ge-, h) estimate; judge, rate; falsch einschätzen misjudge
einschenken v/t (sep, -ge-, h) pour (out)
einschicken v/t (sep, -ge-, h) send in
einschieben v/t (irr, schieben, sep, -ge-, h) slip in; insert
einschlafen v/i (irr, schlafen, sep, -ge-, sein) fall asleep, go to sleep
einschläfern [-ʃlɛːfərn] v/t (sep, -ge-, h) put to sleep
einschl. ABBR of einschließlich incl., including
'Einschlag m strike, impact; fig touch
'einschlagen (irr, schlagen, sep, -ge-, h) 1. v/t knock in (or out); break (in), smash; wrap up; take (road etc); turn (wheels); → Laufbahn; 2. v/i lightning etc: strike; fig be a success
'einschlägig [-ʃlɛːgɪç] adj relevant
'einschleusen fig v/t (sep, -ge-, h) infiltrate (in acc into)
einschließen v/t (irr, schließen, sep, -ge-, h) lock in or up; enclose; MIL surround, encircle; fig include
einschließlich prp (gen) including, ... included
einschmeicheln v/refl (sep, -ge-, h) sich einschmeicheln bei ingratiate o.s. with
einschnappen v/i (sep, -ge-, sein) snap shut; fig go into a huff; → eingeschnappt

'**einschneidend** *fig adj* drastic; farreaching

'**Einschnitt** *m* cut; notch; *fig* break

'**einschränken** *v/t* (*sep*, *-ge-*, *h*) restrict, reduce (*both*: *auf acc* to); cut down on; *sich einschränken* economize

'**Einschränkung** *f* (*-*; *-en*) restriction, reduction, cut; *ohne Einschränkung* without reservation

'**Einschreibebrief** *m* registered letter

'**einschreiben** *v/t* (*irr*, *schreiben*, *sep*, *-ge-*, *h*) enter; book; enrol(l) (*a.* MIL.); (*sich*) *einschreiben lassen* (*für*) enrol(l) (o.s.) (for)

'**einschreiten** *fig v/i* (*irr*, *schreiten*, *sep*, *-ge-*, *sein*) step in, intervene; *einschreiten* (*gegen*) take (legal) measures (against)

'**einschüchtern** *v/t* (*sep*, *-ge-*, *h*) intimidate; bully

'**Einschüchterung** *f* (*-*; *-en*) intimidation

'**einschulen** *v/t* (*sep*, *-ge-*, *h*) *eingeschult werden* start school

'**Einschuss** *m* bullet hole

'**einschweißen** *v/t* (*sep*, *-ge-*, *h*) shrink-wrap

'**einsegnen** *v/t* (*sep*, *-ge-*, *h*) REL consecrate; confirm

'**Einsegnung** *f* (*-*; *-en*) REL consecration; confirmation

'**einsehen** *v/t* (*irr*, *sehen*, *sep*, *-ge-*, *h*) see, realize; *das sehe ich nicht ein!* I don't see why!

'**Einsehen** *n*: *ein Einsehen haben* show some understanding

'**einseifen** *v/t* (*sep*, *-ge-*, *h*) soap; lather; F *fig j-n einseifen* take s.o. for a ride

'**einseitig** [-zaitɪç] *adj* one-sided; MED, POL, JUR unilateral

'**einsenden** *v/t* (*irr*, *senden*,] *sep*, *-ge-*, *h*) send in

'**Einsendeschluss** *m* closing date (for entries)

'**einsetzen** (*sep*, *-ge-*, *h*) **1.** *v/t* put in, insert; appoint; use, employ; TECH put into service; ECON invest, stake; bet; risk; *sich einsetzen* try hard, make an effort; *sich einsetzen für* stand up for; **2.** *v/i* set in, start

'**Einsicht** *f* (*-*; *-en*) a) insight, b) (*no pl*) understanding; *zur Einsicht kommen* listen to reason; *Einsicht nehmen in* (*acc*) take a look at

'**einsichtig** *adj* understanding; reasonable

'**Einsiedler** *m* (*-s*; *-*) hermit

'**einsilbig** [-zɪlbɪç] *adj* monosyllabic; *fig* taciturn

'**einspannen** *v/t* (*sep*, *-ge-*, *h*) harness; TECH clamp, fix; F rope *s.o.* in

'**einsparen** *v/t* (*sep*, *-ge-*, *h*) save, economize on

'**einsperren** *v/t* (*sep*, *-ge-*, *h*) lock *or* shut up

'**einspielen** warm up; *fig* get going; → *eingespielt*

'**Einspielergebnisse** *pl film*: box-office returns

'**einspringen** *v/i* (*irr*, *springen*, *sep*, *-ge-*, *sein*) *für j-n einspringen* take s.o.'s place

'**Einspritz...** *in cpds* MOT fuel-injection

'**Einspruch** *m* objection (*a.* JUR), protest; POL veto; appeal

'**einspurig** [-ʃpuːrɪç] *adj* RAIL single-track; MOT single-lane

'**einst** [ainst] *adv* once, at one time

'**Einstand** *m* start; *tennis*: deuce

'**einstecken** *v/t* (*sep*, *-ge-*, *h*) pocket (*a. fig*); ELECTR plug in; mail, post; *fig* take

'**einstehen** *v/i* (*irr*, *stehen*, *sep*, *-ge-*, *h*) *einstehen für* stand up for

'**einsteigen** *v/i* (*irr*, *steigen*, *sep*, *-ge-*, *sein*) get in; get on (*bus etc*); *alles einsteigen!* RAIL all aboard!

'**einstellen** *v/t* (*sep*, *-ge-*, *h*) engage, employ, hire; give up; stop; SPORT equal; TECH adjust (*auf acc* to); *radio*: tune in (to); OPT, PHOT focus (on); *die Arbeit einstellen* (go on) strike, walk out; *das Feuer einstellen* MIL cease fire; *sich einstellen auf* (*acc*) adjust to; be prepared for

'**Einstellung** *f* attitude (*zu* towards); employment; cessation; TECH adjustment; OPT, PHOT focus(s)ing; *film*: take

'**Einstellungsgespräch** *n* interview

'**Einstieg** ['ainʃtiːk] *m* (*-[e]s*; *-e*) entrance, entry (*a.* POL, ECON)

'**Einstiegsdroge** *f* gateway drug

'**einstig** ['ainstɪç] *adj* former, one-time

'**einstimmen** *v/i* (*sep*, *-ge-*, *h*) MUS join in

'**einstimmig** [-ʃtɪmɪç] *adj* unanimous

'**einstöckig** [-ʃtœkɪç] *adj* one-storied, Br one-storey(ed)

'**einstu'dieren** *v/t* (*no -ge-*, *h*) THEA rehearse

'**einstufen** *v/t* (*sep*, *-ge-*, *h*) grade, rate

'**Einstufungsprüfung** *f* placement test

'**einstufig** [-ʃtuːfɪç] *adj* single-stage

'**Einsturz** *m*, '**einstürzen** *v/i* (*sep*, *-ge-*, *sein*) collapse

'**einst'weilen** *adv* for the present

'**einstweilig** [-vailɪç] *adj* temporary

'**eintauschen** *v/t* (*sep*, *-ge-*, *h*) exchange (*gegen* for)

'**einteilen** *v/t* (*sep*, *-ge-*, *h*) divide (*in acc* into); organize

'**einteilig** [-tailɪç] *adj* one-piece

'**Einteilung** *f* (*-*; *-en*) division; organization; arrangement

'eintönig [-tø:nɪç] *adj* monotonous
'Eintönigkeit *f* (-; *no pl*) monotony
'Eintopf *m* GASTR stew
'Eintracht *f* (-; *no pl*) harmony, unity
'einträchtig *adj* harmonious, peaceful
Eintrag ['aintra:k] *m* (-[e]s; *Einträge* ['aintrɛ:gə]) entry (*a.* ECON), registration
eintragen *v/t* (*irr, tragen, sep, -ge-, h*) enter (*in acc* in); register (*bei* with); enrol(l) (with); *fig* earn; *sich eintragen* register, *hotel: a.* check in
einträglich ['aintrɛ:klɪç] *adj* profitable
'eintreffen *v/i* (*irr, treffen, sep, -ge-, sein*) arrive; happen; come true
eintreiben *fig v/t* (*irr, treiben, sep, -ge-, h*) collect
eintreten (*irr, treten, sep, -ge-*) 1. *v/i* (*sein*) enter; happen, take place; *eintreten für* stand up for, support; *eintreten in* (*acc*) join (*club etc*); 2. *v/t* (*h*) kick in (*door etc*); *sich et. eintreten* run s.th. into one's foot
'Eintritt *m* entry; admission; *Eintritt frei!* admission free!; *Eintritt verboten!* keep out!
'Eintrittsgeld *n* entrance *or* admission (fee)
Eintrittskarte *f* (admission) ticket
'einüben *v/t* (*sep, -ge-, h*) practise; rehearse
'einverstanden *adj*: *einverstanden sein* agree (*mit* to); *einverstanden!* agreed!
'Einverständnis *n* (-ses; *no pl*) agreement
Einwand ['ainvant] *m* (-[e]s; *Einwände* ['ainvɛndə]) objection (*gegen* to)
'Einwanderer *m*, 'Einwanderin *f* immigrant
'einwandern *v/t* (*sep, -ge-, sein*) immigrate
'Einwanderung *f* immigration
'einwandfrei *adj* perfect, faultless
einwärts ['ainvɛrts] *adv* inward(s)
'Einweg... ...rasierer, ...spritze *etc*: disposable
Einwegflasche *f* non-returnable bottle
Einwegpackung *f* throwaway pack
'einweichen *v/t* (*sep, -ge-, h*) soak
'einweihen *v/t* (*sep, -ge-, h*) dedicate, *Br* inaugurate; *j-n einweihen in* (*acc*) F let s.o. in on
'Einweihung *f* (-; -en) dedication, *Br* inauguration
'einweisen *v/t* (*irr, weisen, sep, -ge-, h*) *j-n einweisen in* (*acc*) send (*esp JUR* commit) s.o. to; instruct s.o. in, brief s.o. in
'einwenden *v/t* (*[irr, wenden,] sep, -ge-, h*) object (*gegen* to)
'Einwendung *f* (-; -en) objection
'einwerfen *v/t* (*irr, werfen, sep, -ge-, h*) throw in (*a. fig*, SPORT *a. v/i*); break (*window*); mail, *Br* post; insert (*coin*)
'einwickeln *v/t* (*sep, -ge-, h*) wrap (up); F take *s.o.* in
'Einwickelpa,pier *n* wrapping-paper
einwilligen ['ainvɪlɪgən] *v/i* (*sep, -ge-, h*) consent (*in acc* to), agree (to)
'Einwilligung *f* (-; -en) consent (*in acc* to), agreement
'einwirken *v/i* (*sep, -ge-, h*) *einwirken auf* (*acc*) act (up)on; *fig* work on *s.o.*
'Einwirkung *f* effect, influence
Einwohner ['ainvo:nɐ] *m* (-s; -), 'Einwohnerin *f* (-; -nen) inhabitant
'Einwohnermeldeamt *n* registration office
'Einwurf *m* slot; SPORT throw-in
'Einzahl *f* (-; *no pl*) LING singular
'einzahlen *v/t* (*sep, -ge-, h*) pay in
'Einzahlung *f* payment, deposit
einzäunen ['aintsɔynən] *v/t* (*sep, -ge-, h*) fence in
Einzel ['aintsəl] *n* (-s; -) tennis: singles
'Einzel... *in cpds* ...bett, ...zimmer *etc*: single ...
Einzelfall *m* special case
Einzelgänger [-gɛŋɐ] *m* (-s; -) F loner
Einzelhaft *f* solitary confinement
Einzelhandel *m* retail trade
Einzelhändler *m* retailer
Einzelhaus *n* detached house
'Einzelheit *f* (-; -en) detail
'einzeln *adj* single; odd (*shoe etc*); *Einzelne pl* several, some; *der Einzelne* the individual; *einzeln eintreten* enter one at a time; *einzeln angeben* specify; *im Einzelnen* in detail; *jeder Einzelne* each and every one
'einziehen (*irr, ziehen, sep, -ge-*) 1. *v/t* (*h*) draw in; *esp* TECH retract; duck; strike (*sail etc*); MIL draft, *Br* call up; confiscate; withdraw (*license etc*); make (*inquiries*); 2. *v/i* (*sein*) move in; march in; soak in
einzig ['aintsɪç] *adj* only; single; *kein Einziger ...* not a single ...; *das Einzige* the only thing; *der (die) Einzige* the only one
einzigartig *adj* unique, singular
'Einzug *m* moving in; entry
Eis [ais] *n* (-es; *no pl*) ice; GASTR ice cream; *Eis am Stiel* ice lolly
Eisbahn *f* skating rink
Eisbär *m* ZO polar bear
Eisbecher *m* sundae
Eisbein *n* GASTR (pickled) pork knuckles
Eisberg *m* iceberg
Eisbrecher *m* (-s; -) MAR icebreaker
Eisdiele *f* ice-cream parlo(u)r
Eisen ['aizən] *n* (-s; -) iron

'**Eisenbahn** f railroad, Br railway; train set

'**Eisenbahner** [-ba:nɐ] m (-s; -) railroadman, Br railwayman

'**Eisenbahnwagen** m (railroad) car, Br coach, railway carriage

'**Eisenerz** n iron ore

'**Eisengießerei** f iron foundry

'**Eisenhütte** f TECH ironworks

'**Eisenwaren** pl hardware, ironware

Eisenwarenhandlung f hardware store, Br ironmonger's

eisern ['aizɐn] adj iron (a. fig), of iron

'**eisgekühlt** adj iced

'**Eishockey** n hockey, Br ice hockey

eisig ['aizɪç] adj icy (a. fig)

'**eis kalt** adj ice-cold

'**Eiskunstlauf** m (-[e]s; no pl) figure skating

Eiskunstläufer(in) figure skater

'**Eismeer** n polar sea

Eisre vue f ice show

'**Eisschnelllauf** m speed skating

Eisscholle f ice floe

'**Eisverkäufer** m iceman

'**Eiswürfel** m ice cube

Eiszapfen m icicle

Eiszeit f (-; no pl) GEOL ice age

eitel ['aitəl] adj vain

'**Eitelkeit** f (-; no pl) vanity

Eiter ['aitɐ] m (-s; no pl) MED pus

'**Eiterbeule** f MED abscess, boil

'**eitern** v/i (ge-, h) MED fester

eitrig ['aitrɪç] adj MED purulent, festering

'**Eiweiß** n (-es; no pl) white of egg; BIOL protein

'**eiweißarm** adj low in protein, low-protein

eiweißreich adj rich in protein, high-protein

'**Eizelle** f BIOL egg cell, ovum

Ekel ['e:kəl] **1.** m (-s; no pl) disgust (vor dat at), loathing (for); **Ekel erregend** → **ekelhaft**; **2.** F n (-s; -) beast

ekelerregend adj → **ekelhaft**

'**ekelhaft**, '**ek(e)lig** adj sickening, disgusting, repulsive

'**ekeln** v/refl and v/impers (ge-, h) **ich ekle mich davor** it makes me sick

Ekstase [ɛk'sta:zə] f (-; -n) ecstasy

Elan [e'la:n] m (-s; no pl) vigo(u)r

elastisch [e'lastɪʃ] adj elastic, flexible

Elch [ɛlç] m (-[e]s; -e) ZO elk; moose

Elefant [ele'fant] m (-en; -en) ZO elephant

Ele fantenhochzeit F f ECON jumbo merger

elegant [ele'gant] adj elegant

Eleganz [ele'gants] f (-; no pl) elegance

Elektriker [e'lɛktrɪkɐ] m (-s; -) electrician

elektrisch [e'lɛktrɪʃ] adj electrical; electric

elektrisieren [elɛktri'zi:rən] v/t (no -ge-, h) electrify

Elektrizität [elɛktritsi'tɛ:t] f (-; no pl) electricity

Elektrizi tätswerk n (electric) power station

Elektrogerät [e'lɛktro-] n electric appliance

Elektronik [elɛk'tro:nɪk] f electronics; electronic system

elektronisch [elɛk'tro:nɪʃ] adj electronic

E'lektrora sierer m (-; -) electric razor

Elektro technik f electrical engineering

Elektro techniker m electrical engineer

Element [ele'mɛnt] n (-[e]s; -e) element

elementar [elemɛn'ta:ɐ] adj elementary

elend ['e:lɛnt] adj miserable

Elend n (-s; no pl) misery

Elendsviertel n slums

elf [ɛlf] adj eleven

Elf f (-; -en) eleven; soccer: team

Elfe ['ɛlfə] f (-; -n) elf, fairy

'**Elfenbein** n ivory

Elf meter m (-s; -) soccer: penalty

Elfmeterpunkt m penalty spot

Elfmeterschießen n penalty shoot-out

'**elfte** adj eleventh

Elite [e'li:tə] f (-; -n) elite

Ellbogen ['ɛl-] m ANAT elbow

Elster ['ɛlstɐ] f (-; -n) ZO magpie

elterlich ['ɛltɐlɪç] adj parental

Eltern ['ɛltɐn] pl parents

'**Elternhaus** n (one's parents') home

'**elternlos** adj orphan(ed)

'**Elternteil** m parent

Elternvertretung f appr Parent-Teacher Association

Email [e'mai] n (-s; -s), **Emaille** [e'maljə] f (-; -n) enamel

Emanze [e'mantsə] F f (-; -n) women's libber

Emanzipation [emantsipa'tsjo:n] f (-; -en) emancipation; women's lib(eration)

emanzipieren [emantsi'pi:rən] v/refl (no -ge-, h) become emancipated

Embargo [ɛm'bargo] n (-s; -s) ECON embargo

Embolie [ɛmbo'li:] f (-; -n) MED embolism

Embryo ['ɛmbryo] m (-s; -en [ɛmbry'o:nən]) BIOL embryo

Emigrant [emi'grant] m (-en; -en), **Emi grantin** f (-; -nen) emigrant, esp POL refugee

Emigration [emigra'tsjo:n] f (-; -en) emigration; **in der Emigration** in exile

emigrieren [emi'gri:rən] v/i (no -ge-, sein) emigrate

Emission [emi'sjoːn] f (-; -en) PHYS emission; ECON issue

empfahl [ɛmˈpfaːl] pret of **empfehlen**

Empfang [ɛmˈpfaŋ] m (-[e]s; Empfänge [ɛmˈpfɛŋə]) reception (a. radio, hotel), welcome; receipt (**nach, bei** on)

emp'fangen v/t (irr, **fangen**, no -ge-, h) receive; welcome

Emp'fänger(in) (-s; -/-; -nen) receiver (m a. radio); addressee

emp'fänglich adj susceptible (**für** to)

Empfängnis [ɛmˈpfɛŋnɪs] f (-; no pl) MED conception

Empfängnisverhütung f MED contraception, birth control

Emp'fangsbescheinigung f receipt

Empfangsdame f receptionist

empfehlen [ɛmˈpfeːlən] v/t (irr, no -ge-, h) recommend

emp'fehlenswert adj advisable

Emp'fehlung f (-; -en) recommendation

empfinden [ɛmˈpfɪndən] v/t (irr, **finden**, no -ge-, h) feel (**als** ... to be ...)

empfindlich [ɛmˈpfɪntlɪç] adj sensitive (**für, gegen** to) (a. PHOT, CHEM); tender, delicate; touchy; irritable (a. MED); severe (punishment etc); **empfindliche Stelle** sore spot

Emp'findlichkeit f (-; -en) sensitivity; PHOT speed; delicacy; touchiness

empfindsam [ɛmˈpfɪntzaːm] adj sensitive

Emp'findung f (-; -en) sensation; perception; feeling, emotion

empfohlen [ɛmˈpfoːlən] pp of **empfehlen**

empor [ɛmˈpoːr] adv up, upward(s)

empören [ɛmˈpøːrən] v/t (no -ge-, h) outrage; shock; **sich empören** (**über** acc) be outraged or shocked (at)

empörend adj shocking, outrageous

Em'porkömmling [-kœmlɪŋ] contp m (-s; -e) upstart

empört [ɛmˈpøːrt] adj indignant (**über** acc at), shocked (at)

Em'pörung f (-; no pl) indignation

emsig [ˈɛmzɪç] adj busy

'Emsigkeit f (-; no pl) activity

Ende [ˈɛndə] n (-s; no pl) end; film: ending; **am Ende** at the end; in the end, finally; **zu Ende** over; time: up; **zu Ende gehen** come to an end; **zu Ende lesen** finish reading; **er ist Ende zwanzig** he is in his late twenties; **Ende Mai** at the end of May; **Ende der achtziger Jahre** in the late eighties; radio: **Ende!** over!

'enden v/i (ge-, h) (come to an) end; stop, finish; F **enden als** end up as

'Endergebnis n final result

'endgültig adj final, definitive

Endlagerung [ˈɛnt-] f final disposal (of radioactive waste)

'endlich adv finally, at last

'endlos adj endless

'Endrunde f, **Endspiel** n SPORT final(s)

Endspurt m SPORT final spurt (a. fig)

Endstati,on f RAIL terminus, terminal

Endsumme f (sum) total

'Endung f (-; -en) LING ending

Energie [enerˈgiː] f (-; -n) energy; TECH, ELECTR power; **Energiesparen** n energy saving, conservation of energy

ener'giebewusst adj energy-conscious

Ener'giekrise f energy crisis

ener'gielos adj lacking in energy

Ener'giequelle f source of energy

Energieversorgung f power supply

energisch [eˈnɛrgɪʃ] adj energetic, vigorous

eng [ɛŋ] adj narrow; tight; cramped; fig close; **eng beieinander** close(ly) together

Engagement [ãɡaʒəˈmãː] n (-s; -s) THEA etc engagement; POL commitment

engagieren [ãɡaˈʒiːrən] v/t (no -ge-, h) engage; **sich engagieren für** be very involved in

engagiert [ãɡaˈʒiːrt] adj involved, committed

Enge [ˈɛŋə] f (-; no pl) narrowness; cramped conditions; **in die Enge treiben** drive into a corner

Engel [ˈɛŋəl] m (-s; -) angel

'England England

Engländer [ˈɛŋlɛndə] m (-s; -) Englishman; **die Engländer** pl the English

Engländerin [ˈɛŋlɛndərɪn] f (-; -nen) Englishwoman

'englisch adj English; **auf Englisch** in English

'Englischunterricht m English lesson(s) or class(es); teaching of English

'Engpass m bottleneck (a. fig)

'engstirnig [-ʃtɪrnɪç] adj narrow-minded

Enkel [ˈɛŋkəl] m (-s; -) grandchild; grandson

'Enkelin f (-; -nen) granddaughter

enorm [eˈnɔrm] adj enormous; F terrific

Ensemble [ãˈsãːbl] n (-s; -s) THEA company; cast

entarten [ɛntʔˈaːrtən] v/i (no -ge-, sein), **ent'artet** adj degenerate

Ent'artung f (-; -en) degeneration

entbehren [ɛntˈbeːrən] v/t (no -ge-, h) do without; spare; miss

entbehrlich [ɛntˈbeːrlɪç] adj dispensable; superfluous

Ent'behrung f (-; -en) want, privation

ent'binden (irr, **binden**, no -ge-, h) **1.** v/i MED have the baby; **2.** v/t: **j-n entbinden**

von fig relieve s.o. of; *entbunden werden von* MED give birth to

Ent'bindung f (-; -en) MED delivery

Ent'bindungsstati,on f MED maternity ward

entblößen [ɛntˈbløːsən] v/t (no -ge-, h) bare, uncover

ent'decken v/t (no -ge-, h) discover

Ent'decker m (-s; -), **Ent'deckerin** f (-; -nen) discoverer

Ent'deckung f (-; -en) discovery

Ente [ˈɛntə] f (-; -n) zo duck; F fig hoax

ent'ehren v/t (no -ge-, h) dishono(u)r

enteignen [ɛntˈʔaɪɡnən] v/t (no -ge-, h) expropriate; dispossess *s.o.*

Ent'eignung f (-; -en) expropriation; dispossession

ent'erben v/t (no -ge-, h) disinherit

entern [ˈɛntɐn] v/t (ge-) MAR board

entfachen [ɛntˈfaxən] v/t (no -ge-, h) kindle, fig a. rouse

entfallen v/i (irr, fallen, no -ge-, sein) be cancelled; *entfallen auf* (acc) fall to s.o. ('s share); *es ist mir entfallen* it has slipped my memory

entfalten v/t (no -ge-, h) unfold; fig develop; *sich entfalten* unfold; fig develop (*zu* into)

entfernen [ɛntˈfɛrnən] v/t (no -ge-, h) remove (a. fig); *sich entfernen* leave

ent'fernt adj distant (a. fig); *weit* (*zehn Meilen*) *entfernt* far (10 miles) away

Ent'fernung f (-; -en) distance; removal

Ent'fernungsmesser m (-s; -) PHOT range finder

ent'flammbar adj (in)flammable

entfremden [ɛntˈfrɛmdən] v/t (no -ge-, h) estrange (*dat* from)

Ent'fremdung f (-; -en) estrangement, alienation

ent'führen v/t (no -ge-, h) kidnap; AVIAT hijack

Ent'führer m (-s; -) kidnapper; AVIAT hijacker

Ent'führung f (-; -en) kidnapping; AVIAT hijacking

ent'gegen prp (dat) and adv contrary to; toward(s)

entgegengehen v/i (irr, gehen, sep, -ge-, sein) go to meet

entgegengesetzt adj opposite

entgegenkommen v/i (irr, kommen, sep, -ge-, sein) come to meet; *j-m entgegenkommen* meet s.o. halfway

entgegenkommend fig adj obliging

entgegennehmen v/t (irr, nehmen, sep, -ge-, h) accept; receive

entgegensehen v/i (irr, sehen, sep, -ge-, h) await; look forward to s.th.

entgegensetzen v/t (sep, -ge-, h) *j-m Widerstand entgegensetzen* put up resistance to s.o.

entgegentreten v/i (irr, treten, sep, -ge-, sein) walk towards; oppose; face

entgegnen [ɛntˈɡeːɡnən] v/i (no -ge-, h) reply, answer; retort

Ent'gegnung f (-; -en) reply; retort

ent'gehen v/i (irr, gehen, no -ge-, sein) escape; miss

entgeistert [ɛntˈɡaɪstɐt] adj aghast

Entgelt [ɛntˈɡɛlt] n (-[e]s; -e) remuneration; fee

entgiften [ɛntˈɡɪftən] v/t (no -ge-, h) decontaminate

entgleisen [ɛntˈɡlaɪzən] v/i (no -ge-, sein) RAIL be derailed; fig blunder

ent'gleiten fig v/i (irr, gleiten, no -ge-, sein) get out of control

entgräten [ɛntˈɡrɛːtən] v/t (no -ge-, h) bone, fil(l)et

ent'halten v/t (irr, halten, no -ge-, h) contain, hold; include; *sich enthalten* (gen) abstain or refrain from

ent'haltsam adj abstinent; moderate

Ent'haltsamkeit f (-; no pl) abstinence; moderation

Ent'haltung f (-; -en) abstention

ent'härten v/t (no -ge-, h) soften

enthaupten [ɛntˈhaʊptən] v/t (no -ge-, h) behead, decapitate

ent'hüllen v/t (no -ge-, h) uncover; unveil; fig reveal, disclose

Ent'hüllung f (-; -en) unveiling; fig revelation, disclosure

Enthusiasmus [ɛntuˈzjasmʊs] m (-; no pl) enthusiasm

Enthusiast(in) [-ˈzjast(-ɪn)] (-en, -en/-; -nen) enthusiast; film, SPORT F fan

enthusi'astisch adj enthusiastic

ent'kleiden v/t and v/refl (no -ge-, h) undress, strip

ent'kommen v/i (irr, kommen, no -ge-, sein) escape (dat from)

ent'korken v/t (no -ge-, h) uncork

entkräften [ɛntˈkrɛftən] v/t (no -ge-, h) weaken (a. fig)

Ent'kräftung f (-; -en) weakening, exhaustion

ent'laden v/t (irr, laden, no -ge-, h) unload; esp ELECTR discharge; *sich entladen* esp ELECTR discharge; fig explode

Ent'ladung f (-; -en) unloading; esp ELECTR discharge; fig explosion

ent'lang prp (dat) and adv along; *hier entlang, bitte!* this way, please!; *die Straße etc entlang* along the street etc

entlarven [ɛntˈlarfən] v/t (no -ge-, h) unmask, expose

ent'lassen v/t (irr, **lassen**, no -ge-, h) dismiss, F fire, give s.o. the sack; MED discharge; JUR release

Ent'lassung f (-; -en) dismissal; MED discharge; JUR release

ent'lasten v/t (no -ge-, h) relieve s.o. of some of his work; JUR exonerate, clear s.o. of a charge; **den Verkehr entlasten** relieve the traffic congestion

Ent'lastung f (-; -en) relief; JUR exoneration

Ent'lastungszeuge m JUR witness for the defense (Br defence)

ent'laufen v/i (irr, **laufen**, no -ge-, sein) run away (dat from)

ent'legen adj remote, distant

ent'locken v/t (no -ge-, h) draw, elicit (dat from)

ent'lohnen v/t (no -ge-, h) pay (off)

ent'lüften v/t (no -ge-, h) ventilate

entmachten [ɛntˈmaxtən] v/t (no -ge-, h) deprive s.o. of his power

entmilitarisieren [ɛntmilitariˈziːrən] v/t (no -ge-, h) demilitarize

entmündigen [ɛntˈmʏndɪgən] v/t (no -ge-, h) JUR place under disability

entmutigen [ɛntˈmuːtɪgən] v/t (no -ge-, h) discourage

ent'nehmen v/t (irr, **nehmen**, no -ge-, h) take (dat from); **entnehmen aus** (with-)-draw from; fig gather or learn from

ent'puppen v/refl (no -ge-, h) **sich entpuppen als** turn out to be

ent'rahmen v/t (no -ge-, h) skim

ent'reißen v/t (irr, **reißen**, no -ge-, h) snatch (away) (dat from)

ent'rinnen v/i (irr, **rinnen**, no -ge-, sein) escape (dat from)

ent'rollen v/t (no -ge-, h) unroll

ent'rüsten v/t (no -ge-, h) fill with indignation; **sich entrüsten** become indignant (**über** acc at s.th., with s.o.)

ent'rüstet adj indignant (**über** acc at s.th., with s.o.;) Ent'rüstung f (-; -en) indignation

Entsafter [ɛntˈzaftɐ] m (-s; -) juice extractor

ent'salzen v/t (no -ge-, h) desalinize

ent'schädigen v/t (no -ge-, h) compensate

Ent'schädigung f (-; -en) compensation

ent'schärfen v/t (no -ge-, h) defuse (a. fig)

ent'scheiden v/t and v/i and v/refl (irr, **scheiden**, no -ge-, h) decide (**für** on, in favo[u]r of; **gegen** against); settle; **er kann sich nicht entscheiden** he can't make up his mind

entscheidend adj decisive; crucial

Ent'scheidung f (-; -en) decision

entschieden [ɛntˈʃiːdən] adj decided, determined, resolute; **entschieden dafür** strongly in favo(u)r of it

Ent'schiedenheit f (-; no pl) determination

ent'schließen v/refl (irr, **schließen**, no -ge-, h) decide, determine, make up one's mind

Ent'schließung f (-; -en) POL resolution

entschlossen [ɛntˈʃlɔsən] adj determined, resolute

Ent'schlossenheit f (-; no pl) determination, resoluteness

Ent'schluss m decision, resolution

entschlüsseln [ɛntˈʃlʏsəln] v/t (no -ge-, h) decipher, decode

entschuldigen [ɛntˈʃʊldɪgən] v/t (no -ge-, h) excuse; **sich entschuldigen** apologize (**bei** to; **für** for); excuse o.s.; **entschuldigen Sie!** (I'm) sorry!; excuse me!

Ent'schuldigung f (-; -en) excuse; apology; **um Entschuldigung bitten** apologize; **Entschuldigung!** (I'm) sorry!; excuse me!

ent'setzen v/t (no -ge-, h) shock; horrify

Ent'setzen n (-s; no pl) horror, terror

ent'setzlich adj horrible, dreadful, terrible; atrocious

ent'setzt adj shocked; horrified

ent'sichern v/t (no -ge-, h) release the safety catch of

ent'sinnen v/refl (irr, **sinnen**, no -ge-, h) remember, recall

ent'sorgen v/t (no -ge-, h) dispose of

Ent'sorgung f (-; -en) (waste) disposal

ent'spannen v/t and v/refl (no -ge-, h) relax; **sich entspannen** a. take it easy; fig ease (up)

ent'spannt adj relaxed

Ent'spannung f (-; -en) relaxation; POL détente

ent'spiegelt adj OPT non-glare

ent'sprechen v/i (irr, **sprechen**, no -ge-, h) correspond to; answer to a description; meet (requirements etc)

entsprechend adj corresponding (dat to); appropriate

Ent'sprechung f (-; -en) equivalent

ent'springen v/i (irr, **springen**, no -ge-, sein) river: rise

ent'stehen v/i (irr, **stehen**, no -ge-, sein) come into being; arise; emerge, develop; **entstehen aus** originate from

Ent'stehung f (-; -en) origin

ent'stellen v/t (no -ge-, h) disfigure, deform; fig distort

Ent'stellung f (-; -en) disfigurement, deformation, distortion (a. fig)

entstört [ɛntˈʃtøːɐt] adj ELECTR interference-free

ent'**täuschen** v/t (no -ge-, h) disappoint

Ent'**täuschung** f (-; -en) disappointment

entwaffnen [ɛnt'vafnən] v/t (no -ge-, h) disarm

Ent'**warnung** f all clear (signal)

ent'**wässern** v/t (no -ge-, h) drain

Ent'**wässerung** f (-; -en) drainage; CHEM dehydration

'**entweder** cj: **entweder ... oder** either ... or

ent'**weichen** v/i (irr, **weichen**, no -ge-, sein) escape (**aus** from)

ent'**weihen** v/t (no -ge-, h) desecrate

ent'**wenden** v/t (no -ge-, h) pilfer, steal

ent'**werfen** v/t (irr, **werfen**, no -ge-, h) design; draw up

ent'**werten** v/t (no -ge-, h) lower the value of (a. fig); cancel

Ent'**wertung** f (-; -en) devaluation; cancellation

ent'**wickeln** v/t and v/refl (no -ge-, h) develop (a. PHOT) (**zu** into)

Ent'**wicklung** f (-; -en) development, BIOL a. evolution; adolescence, age of puberty

Ent'**wicklungshelfer** m, Entwicklungshelferin f POL, ECON development aid volunteer; Peace Corps volunteer, Br VSO worker

Entwicklungshilfe f development aid

Entwicklungsland n POL developing country

entwirren [ɛnt'vɪrən] v/t (no -ge-, h) disentangle (a. fig)

ent'**wischen** v/i (no -ge-, sein) get away

ent'**würdigend** adj degrading

Ent'**wurf** m outline, (rough) draft, plan; design; sketch

ent'**wurzeln** v/t (no -ge-, h) uproot

ent'**ziehen** v/t (irr, **ziehen**, no -ge-, h) take away (dat from); revoke (license etc); deprive of rights etc; CHEM extract; **sich j-m (e-r Sache) entziehen** evade s.o. (s.th.)

Ent'**ziehungsanstalt** f substance (Br drug) abuse clinic

Entziehungskur f detoxi(fi)cation (treatment), a. F drying out

entziffern [ɛnt'tsɪfən] v/t (no -ge-, h) decipher, make out

ent'**zücken** v/t (no -ge-, h) charm, delight

Ent'**zücken** n (-s; no pl) delight

ent'**zückend** adj delightful, charming, F sweet

ent'**zückt** adj delighted (**über** acc, **von** at, with)

Ent'**zug** m withdrawal; revocation

Ent'**zugserscheinung** f MED withdrawal symptom

entzündbar [ɛnt'tsʏntbaːɐ] adj (in-)

flammable

ent'**zünden** v/refl (no -ge-, h) catch fire; MED become inflamed

Ent'**zündung** f (-; -en) MED inflammation

ent'**zwei** adv in two, to pieces

Enzyklopädie [ɛntsyklopɛ'diː] f (-; -n) encyclop(a)edia

Epidemie [epide'miː] f (-; -n) MED epidemic (disease)

Epilog [epi'loːk] m (-[e]s; -e [epi'loːɡə]) epilog, Br epilogue

episch ['eːpɪʃ] adj epic

Episode [epi'zoːdə] f (-; -n) episode

Epoche [e'pɔxə] f (-; -n) epoch, period, era

Epos ['eːpɔs] n (-; Epen ['eːpən]) epic (poem)

er [eːɐ] pers pron he; it

Er'**achten** n: **meines Erachtens** in my opinion

Erbanlage ['ɛrp-] f BIOL genes, genetic code

erbarmen [ɛɐ'barmən] v/refl (no -ge-, h) **sich j-s erbarmen** take pity on s.o.

erbärmlich [ɛɐ'bɛrmlɪç] adj pitiful, pitiable; miserable; mean

er'**barmungslos** adj pitiless, merciless

er'**bauen** v/t (no -ge-, h) build, construct

Er'**bauer** m (-s; -) builder, constructor

er'**baulich** adj edifying

Er'**bauung** fig f (-; -en) edification, uplift

Erbe ['ɛrbə] **1.** m (-n; -n) heir; **2.** n (-s; no pl) inheritance, heritage

erben ['ɛrbən] v/t (ge-, h) inherit

erbeuten [ɛɐ'bɔʏtən] v/t (no -ge-, h) MIL capture; thief: get away with

'**Erbfaktor** m BIOL gene

Erbin ['ɛrbɪn] f (-; -nen) heir, heiress

er'**bitten** v/t (irr, **bitten**, no -ge-, h) ask for, request

erbittert [ɛɐ'bɪtɐt] adj fierce, furious

'**Erbkrankheit** f MED hereditary disease

erblich ['ɛrplɪç] adj hereditary

er'**blicken** v/t (no -ge-, h) see, catch sight of

erblinden [ɛɐ'blɪndən] v/i (no -ge-, sein) go blind

er'**brechen** v/t and v/refl (irr, **brechen**, no -ge-, h) MED vomit

Erbschaft ['ɛrpʃaft] f (-; -en) inheritance, heritage

Erbse ['ɛrpsə] f (-; -n) BOT pea; (**grüne**) **Erbsen** green peas

'**Erbstück** n heirloom

Erdapfel ['eːɐt-] Austrian m potato

Erdball m (-[e]s; no pl) globe

Erdbeben n (-s; -) earthquake

Erdbeere f BOT strawberry

Erdboden m earth, ground

Erde ['eːrdə] *f* (-; -n) a) (*no pl*) earth, b) ground, soil; → **eben**

'**erden** *v/t* (ge-, h) ELECTR earth, ground

erdenklich [ɛɐ'dɛŋklɪç] *adj* imaginable

Erdgas ['eːrt-] *n* natural gas

Erdgeschoss *n*, **Erdgeschoß** *Austrian n* first (*Br* ground) floor

er'**dichten** *v/t* (*no -ge-, h*) invent, make up

er'**dichtet** *adj* invented, made-up

erdig ['eːrdɪç] *adj* earthy

'**Erdklumpen** *m* clod, lump of earth

Erdkruste *f* earth's crust

Erdkugel *f* globe

Erdkunde *f* (-; *no pl*) geography

Erdleitung *f* ELECTR ground (*Br* earth) connection; underground pipe(line)

Erdnuss *f* BOT peanut

Erdöl *n* (mineral) oil, petroleum

Erdreich *n* ground, soil

erdreisten [ɛɐ'draistən] *v/refl* (*no -ge-, h*) F have the nerve

er'**drosseln** *v/t* (*no -ge-, h*) throttle

er'**drücken** *v/t* (*no -ge-, h*) crush (to death)

erdrückend *fig adj* overwhelming

'**Erdrutsch** *m* (-[e]s; -e) landslide (*a.* POL)

Erdteil *m* GEOGR continent

'**Erdumlaufbahn** *f* earth orbit

'**Erdung** *f* (-; -en) ELECTR grounding, *Br* earthing

'**Erdwärme** *f* GEOL geothermal energy

er'**eifern** *v/refl* (*no -ge-, h*) get excited

ereignen [ɛɐ'?aignən] *v/refl* (*no -ge-, h*) happen, occur

Ereignis [ɛɐ'?aignɪs] *n* (-ses; -se) event, occurrence

er'**eignisreich** *adj* eventful

Erektion [erɛk'tsjoːn] *f* (-; -en) erection

Eremit [ere'miːt] *m* (-en; -en) hermit, anchorite

er'**fahren**[1] *v/t* (*irr*, **fahren**, *no -ge-, h*) hear; learn; experience

er'**fahren**[2] *adj* experienced

Er'fahrung *f* (-; -en) (work) experience

Er'fahrungsaustausch *m* exchange of experience

er'**fahrungsgemäß** *adv* as experience shows

er'**fassen** *v/t* (*no -ge-, h*) grasp; record, register; cover, include; EDP collect

er'**finden** *v/t* (*irr*, **finden**, *no -ge-, h*) invent

Er'finder(in) (-s; -/-; -nen) inventor

erfinderisch [ɛɐ'fɪndərɪʃ] *adj* inventive

Er'findung *f* (-; -en) invention

Er'findungskraft *f* (-; *no pl*) inventiveness

Erfolg [ɛɐ'fɔlk] *m* (-[e]s; -e) success; result; **viel Erfolg!** good luck!; **Erfolg versprechend** promising

er'**folgen** *v/i* (*no -ge-, sein*) happen, take place

er'**folglos** *adj* unsuccessful; futile

Er'folglosigkeit *f* (-; *no pl*) lack of success

er'**folgreich** *adj* successful

Er'folgserlebnis *n* sense of achievement

erforderlich [ɛɐ'fɔrdəlɪç] *adj* necessary, required

er'**fordern** *v/t* (*no -ge-, h*) require, demand

Erfordernis [ɛɐ'fɔrdənɪs] *n* (-ses; -se) requirement, demand

er'**forschen** *v/t* (*no -ge-, h*) explore; investigate, study

Er'forscher *m* explorer

Er'forschung *f* exploration

er'**freuen** *v/t* (*no -ge-, h*) please

erfreulich [ɛɐ'frɔylɪç] *adj* pleasing, pleasant; gratifying

er'**freut** *adj* pleased (**über** *acc* at, about); **sehr erfreut!** pleased to meet you

er'**frieren** *v/i* (*irr*, **frieren**, *no -ge-, sein*) freeze to death

Er'frierung *f* (-; -en) MED frostbite

er'**frischen** *v/t and v/refl* (*no -ge-, h*) refresh (o.s.)

erfrischend *adj* refreshing

Er'frischung *f* (-; -en) refreshment

erfroren [ɛɐ'froːrən] *adj* frostbitten; BOT killed by frost

er'**füllen** *fig v/t* (*no -ge-, h*) fulfil(l); keep (*promise etc*); serve (*purpose etc*); meet (*requirements etc*); **erfüllen mit** fill with; **sich erfüllen** be fulfilled, come true

Er'füllung *f* (-; -en) fulfil(l)ment; **in Erfüllung gehen** come true

ergänzen [ɛɐ'gɛntsən] *v/t* (*no -ge-, h*) complement (**einander** each other); supplement, add

ergänzend *adj* complementary, supplementary

Er'gänzung *f* (-; -en) completion; supplement, addition

ergattern [ɛɐ'gatən] F *v/t* (*no -ge-, h*) (manage to) get hold of

er'**geben** (*irr*, **geben**, *no -ge-, h*) **1.** *v/t* amount *or* come to; **2.** *v/refl* surrender; *fig* arise; **sich ergeben aus** result from; **sich ergeben in** (*acc*) resign o.s. to

Er'gebenheit *f* (-; *no pl*) devotion

Ergebnis [ɛɐ'geːpnɪs] *n* (-ses; -se) result, SPORT *a.* score; outcome

er'**gebnislos** *adj* without result

er'**gehen** *v/i* (*irr*, **gehen**, *no -ge-, sein*) order *etc*: be issued (**an** *acc* to); **wie ist es dir ergangen?** how did things go with you?; *et.* **über sich ergehen lassen** (patiently) endure s.th.

ergiebig [ɛɐ'giːbɪç] *adj* productive, rich

Er'giebigkeit *f* (-; *no pl*) (high) yield; productiveness

er'gießen v/refl (irr, *gießen*, no -ge-, h)
sich ergießen über (acc) pour down on
er'grauen v/i (no -ge-, sein) turn gray (Br
grey)
er'greifen v/t (irr, *greifen*, no -ge-, h)
seize, grasp, take hold of; take (*measures
etc*); take up; *fig* move, touch
ergriffen v/t (irr, *greifen*, no -ge-, h) moved
Er'griffenheit f (-; no pl) emotion
er'gründen v/t (no -ge-, h) find out, fath-
om
er'haben adj raised, elevated; *fig* sublime;
erhaben sein über (acc) be above
er'halten¹ v/t (irr, *halten*, no -ge-, h) get,
receive; keep, preserve; protect; support, maintain (*family etc*)
er'halten² adj: *gut erhalten* in good condition
erhältlich [ɛɐ'hɛltlɪç] adj obtainable,
available
Er'haltung f (-; no pl) preservation; up-
keep
er'hängen v/t (no -ge-, h) hang (*sich* o.s.)
er'heben v/t (irr, *heben*, no -ge-, h) raise
(a. voice), lift; *sich erheben* rise up (*gegen* against)
erheblich [ɛɐ'heːplɪç] adj considerable
Er'hebung f (-; -en) survey; revolt
erheitern [ɛɐ'haitɐn] v/t (no -ge-, h) cheer
up, amuse
erhellen [ɛɐ'hɛlən] v/t (no -ge-, h) light up;
fig throw light upon
erhitzen [ɛɐ'hɪtsən] v/t (no -ge-, h) heat;
sich erhitzen get hot
er'hoffen v/t (no -ge-, h) hope for
erhöhen [ɛɐ'høːən] v/t (no -ge-, h) raise;
increase
Er'höhung f (-; -en) increase
er'holen v/refl (no -ge-, h) recover; relax,
rest
erholsam [ɛɐ'hoːlzaːm] adj restful, relax-
ing
Er'holung f (-; no pl) recovery; relaxation
Er'holungsheim n rest home
erinnern [ɛɐ'?ɪnɐn] v/t (no -ge-, h) *j-n erinnern an* (acc) remind s.o. of; *sich erinnern an* (acc) remember, recall
Erinnerung [ɛɐ'ɪnərʊŋ] f (-; -en) memory
(*an* acc of); remembrance, souvenir;
keepsake; *zur Erinnerung an* (acc) in
memory of
erkalten [ɛɐ'kaltən] v/i (no -ge-, sein) cool
down (a. fig)
erkälten [ɛɐ'kɛltən] v/refl (no -ge-, h) *sich
erkälten* catch (a) cold; (*stark*) *erkältet
sein* have a (bad) cold
Er'kältung f (-; -en) cold
erkennbar [ɛɐ'kɛnbaːɐ] adj recognizable
er'kennen v/t (irr, *kennen*, no -ge-, h) rec-

ognize (*an* dat by), know (by); see, realize
er'kenntlich adj: *sich (j-m) erkenntlich
zeigen* show (s.o.) one's gratitude
Er'kenntnis f (-; -se) realization; discovery; *pl* findings
Er'kennungsdienst m (police) records
department
Erkennungsmelo,die f signature tune
Erkennungszeichen n badge; AVIAT
markings
Erker ['ɛrkɐ] m (-s; -) ARCH bay
Erkerfenster n ARCH bay window
er'klären v/t (no -ge-, h) explain (*j-m* to
s.o.); declare; *j-n (offiziell) für ... erklären* pronounce s.o. ...
erklärend adj explanatory
erklärlich [ɛɐ'klɛːɐlɪç] adj explainable
er'klärt adj declared
Er'klärung f (-; -en) explanation; declaration; definition; *e-e Erklärung abgeben*
make a statement
er'klingen v/i (irr, *klingen*, no -ge-, sein)
(re)sound, ring (out)
erkranken [ɛɐ'kraŋkən] v/i (no -ge-, sein)
fall ill, get sick; *erkranken an* (dat) get
Er'krankung f (-; -en) illness, sickness
erkunden [ɛɐ'kʊndən] v/t (no -ge-, h) explore
erkundigen [ɛɐ'kʊndɪgən] v/refl (no -ge-,
h) inquire (*nach* about s.th.; *after* s.o.);
make inquiries (about); *sich (bei j-m)
nach dem Weg erkundigen* ask (s.o.)
the way
Er'kundigung f (-; -en) inquiry
Er'kundung f (-; -en) exploration; MIL reconnaissance
Erlagschein [ɛɐ'laːk-] Austrian m mon-
ey-order form
er'lahmen v/i (no -ge-, sein) flag
Erlass [ɛɐ'las] m (-es; -e) decree; JUR re-
mission
er'lassen v/t (irr, *lassen*, no -ge-, h) issue;
enact (*bill etc*); *j-m et. erlassen* release
s.o. from s.th.
erlauben [ɛɐ'laubən] v/t (no -ge-, h) allow,
permit; *sich et. erlauben* permit o.s. (or
dare) to do s.th.; treat s.th. to s.th.
Erlaubnis [ɛɐ'laupnɪs] f (-; no pl) permission; authority; *um Erlaubnis bitten* ask
s.o.'s permission
Erlaubnisschein m permit
erläutern [ɛɐ'lɔytɐn] v/t (no -ge-, h) explain, illustrate
Er'läuterung f (-; -en) explanation; annotation
Erle ['ɛrlə] f (-; -n) BOT alder
er'leben v/t (no -ge-, h) experience; go
through; see; have; *das werden wir*

nicht mehr erleben we won't live to see that

Erlebnis [ɛɐˈleːpnɪs] *n* (*-ses*; *-se*) experience; adventure

er'lebnisreich *adj* eventful

erledigen [ɛɐˈleːdɪɡən] *v/t* (*no -ge-, h*) take care of, do, handle; settle; F finish *s.o.* (*a.* SPORT); do *s.o.* in

erledigt [ɛɐˈleːdɪçt] *adj* finished, settled; F worn out; F *der ist erledigt!* he is done for

Er'ledigung *f* (*-*; *-en*) a) (*no pl*) settlement, b) *pl* things to do, shopping

er'legen *v/t* (*no -ge-, h*) HUNT shoot

erleichtern [ɛɐˈlaɪçtɐn] *v/t* (*no -ge-, h*) ease, relieve

er'leichtert *adj* relieved

Er'leichterung [-təruŋ] *f* (*-*; *no pl*) relief (*über acc* at)

er'leiden *v/t* (*irr, leiden, no -ge-, h*) suffer

er'lesen *adj* choice, select

er'leuchten *v/t* (*no -ge-, h*) illuminate

er'liegen *v/i* (*irr, liegen, no -ge-, sein*) succumb to

Er'liegen *n*: *zum Erliegen kommen* (*bringen*) come (bring) to a standstill

erlogen [ɛɐˈloːɡən] *adj* false; *erlogen sein* be a lie

Erlös [ɛɐˈløːs] *m* (*-es*; *-e*) proceeds; profit(s)

erlosch [ɛɐˈlɔʃ] *pret of* **erlöschen**

erloschen [ɛɐˈlɔʃən] **1.** *pp of* **erlöschen**; **2.** *adj* extinct (*volcano*)

er'löschen *v/i* (*irr, no -ge-, sein*) go out; die; JUR lapse, expire

er'lösen *v/t* (*no -ge-, h*) deliver, free (*both: von* from)

Erlöser [ɛɐˈløːzɐ] *m* (*-s*; *no pl*) REL Savio(u)r

Er'lösung *f* (*-*; *no pl*) REL salvation; relief

ermächtigen [ɛɐˈmɛçtɪɡən] *v/t* (*no -ge-, h*) authorize

Er'mächtigung *f* (*-*; *-en*) authorization; authority

er'mahnen *v/t* (*no -ge-, h*) admonish; reprove, warn (*a.* SPORT)

Er'mahnung *f* (*-*; *-en*) admonition; warning; *esp* SPORT (first) caution

Er'mangelung *f*: *in Ermangelung* (*gen*) for want of

ermäßigt [ɛɐˈmɛːsɪçt] *adj* reduced, cut

Er'mäßigung *f* (*-*; *-en*) reduction, cut

er'messen *v/t* (*irr, messen, no -ge-, h*) assess; judge

Er'messen *n* (*-s*; *no pl*) discretion; *nach eigenem Ermessen* at one's own discretion

er'mitteln (*no -ge-, h*) **1.** *v/t* find out; determine; **2.** *v/i esp* JUR investigate

Er'mittlung *f* (*-*; *-en*) finding; JUR investigation

er'möglichen *v/t* (*no -ge-, h*) make possible

er'morden *v/t* (*no -ge-, h*) murder; *esp* POL assassinate

Er'mordung *f* (*-*; *-en*) murder; *esp* POL assassination

ermüden [ɛɐˈmyːdən] (*no -ge-*) **1.** *v/t* (*h*) tire, fatigue; **2.** *v/i* (*sein*) tire, get tired, fatigue (*a.* TECH)

Er'müdung *f* (*-*; *no pl*) fatigue, tiredness

er'muntern [ɛɐˈmʊntɐn] *v/t* (*no -ge-, h*) encourage; stimulate

Er'munterung *f* (*-*; *-en*) encouragement; incentive

er'mutigen [ɛɐˈmuːtɪɡən] *v/t* (*no -ge-, h*) encourage

ermutigend *adj* encouraging

Er'mutigung *f* (*-*; *-en*) encouragement

er'nähren *v/t* (*no -ge-, h*) feed; support (*family etc*); *sich ernähren von* live on

Er'nährer *m* (*-s*; *-*) breadwinner, supporter

Er'nährung *f* (*-*; *no pl*) nutrition, food, diet

er'nennen *v/t* (*irr, nennen, no -ge-, h*) *j-n ernennen zu* appoint s.o. (to be)

Er'nennung *f* (*-*; *-en*) appointment

erneuern [ɛɐˈnɔʏɐn] *v/t* (*no -ge-, h*) renew

Er'neuerung *f* (*-*; *-en*) renewal

er'neut **1.** *adj* renewed **2.** *adv* once more

erniedrigen [ɛɐˈniːdrɪɡən] *v/t* (*no -ge-, h*) humiliate; *sich erniedrigen* degrade o.s.

Er'niedrigung *f* (*-*; *-en*) humiliation

ernst [ɛrnst] *adj* serious, earnest; *ernst nehmen* take s.o. or s.th. seriously

Ernst *m* (*-es*; *no pl*) seriousness, earnest; *im Ernst*(?) seriously(?); *ist das dein Ernst?* are you serious?

'ernsthaft, 'ernstlich *adj* serious

Ernte ['ɛrntə] *f* (*-*; *-n*) harvest; crop(s)

'Erntedankfest *n* Thanksgiving (Day), *Br* harvest festival

'ernten *v/t* (*ge-, h*) harvest, reap (*a. fig*)

er'nüchtern *v/t* (*no -ge-, h*) sober, *fig a.* disillusion

Er'nüchterung *f* (*-*; *-en*) sobering up; *fig* disillusionment

Eroberer [ɛɐˈʔoːbərɐ] *m* (*-s*; *-*) conqueror

erobern [ɛɐˈʔoːbɐn] *v/t* (*no -ge-, h*) conquer

Er'oberung *f* (*-*; *-en*) conquest (*a. fig*)

er'öffnen *v/t* (*no -ge-, h*) open; inaugurate; disclose *s.th.* (*j-m* to s.o.)

Er'öffnung *f* (*-*; *-en*) opening; inauguration; disclosure

erörtern [ɛɐˈʔœrtɐn] *v/t* (*no -ge-, h*) discuss

Er'örterung f (-; -en) discussion

Erotik [e'ro:tɪk] f (-; no pl) eroticism

erotisch [e'ro:tɪʃ] adj erotic

er'pressen v/t (no -ge-, h) blackmail; extort

Er'presser(in) (-s; -/-; -nen) blackmailer

Er'pressung f (-; -en) blackmail(ing); extortion

er'proben v/t (no -ge-, h) try, test

er'raten v/t (irr, raten, no -ge-, h) guess

er'rechnen v/t (no -ge-, h) calculate, work s.th. out

erregbar [ɛɐ're:kbaːɐ] adj excitable; irritable

er'regen v/t (no -ge-, h) excite, sexually: a. arouse; fig rouse; cause; **sich erregen** get excited

erregend adj exciting, thrilling

Er'reger m (-s; -) MED germ, virus

Er'regung f (-; -en) excitement

erreichbar [ɛɐ'raiçbaːɐ] adj within reach (a. fig); available; **leicht erreichbar** within easy reach; **nicht erreichbar** out of reach; not available

er'reichen v/t (no -ge-, h) reach; catch (train etc); **es erreichen, dass ...** succeed in doing s.th.; **et. erreichen** get somewhere; **telefonisch zu erreichen sein** have a (Br be on the) phone

er'richten v/t (no -ge-, h) put up, erect; fig found, esp ECON set up

Er'richtung f (-; -en) erection; fig establishment

er'ringen v/t (irr, ringen, no -ge-, h) win, gain; achieve

er'röten v/i (no -ge-, sein) blush

Errungenschaft [ɛɐ'ruŋənʃaft] f (-; -en) achievement; **m-e neueste Errungenschaft** my latest acquisition

Ersatz [ɛɐ'zats] m (-es; no pl) replacement; substitute; surrogate; compensation; damages; **als Ersatz für** in exchange for

Ersatzdienst m → **Zivildienst**

Ersatzmann m (-[e]s; -leute) substitute (a. SPORT)

Ersatzmine f refill

Ersatzreifen m MOT spare tire (Br tyre)

Ersatzspieler m SPORT substitute

Ersatzteil n TECH spare part

er'schaffen v/t (irr, schaffen, no -ge-, h) create

er'schallen v/i ([irr, schallen,] no -ge-, sein) (re)sound, ring (out)

er'scheinen v/i (irr, scheinen, no -ge-, sein) appear, F turn up; be published

Er'scheinen n (-s; no pl) appearance; publication

Er'scheinung f (-; -en) appearance; apparition; phenomenon

er'schießen v/t (irr, schießen, no -ge-, h) shoot (dead)

erschlaffen [ɛɐ'ʃlafən] v/i (no -ge-, sein) go limp; fig weaken

er'schlagen v/t (irr, schlagen, no -ge-, h) kill

er'schließen v/t (irr, schließen, no -ge-, h) open up; develop

erschollen [ɛɐ'ʃɔlən] pp of **erschallen**

er'schöpfen v/t (no -ge-, h) exhaust

er'schöpft adj exhausted

Er'schöpfung f (-; no pl) exhaustion

erschrak [ɛɐ'ʃraːk] pret of **erschrecken** 2

er'schrecken 1. v/t (no -ge-, h) frighten, scare; **2.** v/i (no -ge-, sein) be frightened (**über** acc at)

erschreckend adj alarming; terrible

erschrocken [ɛɐ'ʃrɔkən] pp of **erschrecken** 2

erschüttern [ɛɐ'ʃʏtɐn] v/t (no -ge-, h) shake; fig a. shock; fig move

Er'schütterung f (-; -en) shock (a. fig); TECH vibration

erschweren [ɛɐ'ʃve:rən] v/t (no -ge-, h) make more difficult; aggravate

er'schwindeln v/t (no -ge-, h) obtain s.th. by fraud; (**sich**) **et. von j-m erschwindeln** swindle s.o. out of s.th.

er'schwingen v/t (irr, schwingen, no -ge-, h) afford

er'schwinglich adj within one's means, affordable; reasonable (price)

er'sehen v/t (irr, sehen, no -ge-, h) see, learn, gather (all: **aus** from)

ersetzbar [ɛɐ'zɛtsbaːɐ] adj replaceable; reparable

er'setzen v/t (no -ge-, h) replace (**durch** by); compensate for; **j-m et. ersetzen** reimburse s.o. for s.th.

er'sichtlich adj evident, obvious

er'sparen v/t (no -ge-, h) save; **j-m et. ersparen** spare s.o. s.th.

Ersparnisse [ɛɐ'ʃpaːɐnɪsə] pl savings

erst [e:ɐst] adv first; at first; **erst jetzt** (**gestern**) only now (yesterday); **erst nächste Woche** not before or until next week; **es ist erst neun Uhr** it's only nine o'clock; **eben erst** just (now); **erst recht** all the more; **erst recht nicht** even less; → **einmal**

er'starren v/i (no -ge-, sein) stiffen; fig freeze

er'starrt adj stiff; numb

erstatten [ɛɐ'ʃtatən] v/t (no -ge-, h) refund, reimburse (**j-m et.** s.o. for s.th.); **Bericht erstatten** (give a) report (**über** acc on); **Anzeige erstatten** report to the police

'Erstaufführung f THEA first night or performance, premiere, film: a. first run

er'staunen v/t (no -ge-, h) surprise, astonish

Er'staunen n (-s; no pl) surprise, astonishment; **in Erstaunen (ver)setzen** astonish

er'staunlich adj surprising, astonishing

er'staunt adj astonished

'Erstausgabe f first edition

'erst'beste adj first; any old

'erste adj first; **auf den ersten Blick** at first sight; **fürs Erste** for the time being; **als Erste(r)** first; **zum ersten Mal(e)** for the first time; **am Ersten** on the first

er'stechen v/t (irr, stechen, no -ge-, h) stab

'erstens adv first(ly), in the first place

'Erstere: **der (die, das) Erstere** the former

er'sticken v/t (no -ge-, h) and v/i (sein) choke, suffocate

Er'stickung f (-; no pl) suffocation

'erstklassig [-klasıç] adj first-class, F a. super

erstmalig [-ma:lıç] adj first

erstmals [-ma:ls] adv for the first time

er'streben v/t (no -ge-, h) strive after

er'strebenswert adj desirable

er'strecken v/refl (no -ge-, h) extend, stretch (**bis, auf** acc to; **über** acc over); **sich erstrecken über** (acc) a. cover

'Erstschlag m MIL first strike

er'suchen v/t (no -ge-, h) request

er'tappen v/t (no -ge-, h) catch; → **Tat**

er'tönen v/i (no -ge-, sein) (re)sound

Ertrag [ɛɐ'traːk] m (-[e]s; Erträge [ɛɐ'trɛː-gə]) AGR yield, produce, TECH a. output; ECON proceeds, returns

er'tragen v/t (irr, tragen, no -ge-, h) bear, endure; stand

erträglich [ɛɐ'trɛːklıç] adj bearable, tolerable

er'tränken v/t (no -ge-, h) drown

er'trinken v/i (irr, trinken, no -ge-, sein) drown

erübrigen [ɛɐ'ʔyːbrıgən] v/t (no -ge-, h) spare; **sich erübrigen** be unnecessary

er'wachen v/i (no -ge-, sein) wake (up); esp fig awake, awaken

Erw. ABBR of **Erwachsene(r)** adult(s)

er'wachsen¹ v/i (irr, wachsen, no -ge-, sein) arise (**aus** from)

er'wachsen² adj grown-up, adult

Er'wachsene m, f (-n; -n) adult; **nur für Erwachsene!** adults only!

Er'wachsenenbildung f adult education

erwägen [ɛɐ'vɛːgən] v/t (irr, wägen, no -ge-, h) consider, think s.th. over

Er'wägung f (-; -en) consideration; **in Erwägung ziehen** take into consideration

erwähnen [ɛɐ'vɛːnən] v/t (no -ge-, h) mention

Er'wähnung f (-; -en) mention(ing)

er'wärmen v/t and v/refl (no -ge-, h) warm (up); fig **sich erwärmen für** warm to

Er'wärmung f (-; -en) warming up; **Erwärmung der Erdatmosphäre** global warming

er'warten v/t (no -ge-, h) expect; wait for, await

Er'wartung f (-; -en) expectation, anticipation

er'wartungsvoll adj and adv full of expectation, expectant(ly)

er'wecken fig v/t (no -ge-, h) awaken; arouse; → **Anschein**

er'weisen v/t (irr, weisen, no -ge-, h) do (service etc); show (respect etc); **sich erweisen als** prove to be

erweitern [ɛɐ'vaitən] v/t and v/refl (no -ge-, h) extend, enlarge; esp ECON expand

Er'weiterung f (-; -en) extension, enlargement, expansion

Erwerb [ɛɐ'vɛrp] m (-[e]s; -e) acquisition; purchase; income

er'werben v/t (irr, werben, no -ge-, h) acquire (a. fig); purchase

er'werbslos adj unemployed

erwerbstätig adj (gainfully) employed, working

erwerbsunfähig adj unable to work

Er'werbung f (-; -en) acquisition; purchase

erwidern [ɛɐ'viːdən] v/t (no -ge-, h) reply, answer; return (visit etc)

Er'widerung f (-; -en) reply, answer; return

er'wischen v/t (no -ge-, h) catch, get; **ihn hat's erwischt** he's had it

er'wünscht adj desired; desirable; welcome

er'würgen v/t (no -ge-, h) strangle

Erz [eːɐts] n (-es; -e) ore

er'zählen v/t (no -ge-, h) tell; narrate; **man hat mir erzählt** I was told

Er'zähler m (-s; -), Er'zählerin f (-; -nen) narrator

Er'zählung f (-; -en) (short) story, tale

'Erzbischof m REL archbishop

'Erzbistum n REL archbishopric

'Erzengel m REL archangel

er'zeugen v/t (no -ge-, h) ECON produce (a. fig); TECH make, manufacture; ELECTR generate; fig cause, create

Er'zeuger m (-s; -) ECON producer

Er'zeugnis n (-ses; -se) ECON product (a. fig)

Er'zeugung f (-; -en) ECON production

er'ziehen v/t (irr, **ziehen**, no -ge-, h) bring up, raise; educate; *j-n zu et. erziehen* teach s.o. to be *or* to do s.th.

Erzieher [ɛɐˈtsiːɐ] m (-s; -), **Erzieherin** [ɛɐˈtsiːərɪn] f (-; -nen) educator; teacher; (qualified) kindergarten teacher

er'zieherisch adj educational, pedagogic(al)

Er'ziehung f (-; no pl) upbringing; education

Er'ziehungsanstalt f reform (Br approved) school

Erziehungsberechtigte m, f (-n; -n) parent or guardian

Erziehungswesen n (-s; no pl) educational system

er'zielen v/t (no -ge-, h) achieve; SPORT score

erzogen [ɛɐˈtsoːɡən] adj: *gut erzogen sein* be well-bred; *schlecht erzogen sein* be ill-bred

er'zwingen v/t (irr, **zwingen**, no -ge-, h) (en)force

es [ɛs] pers pron it; he; she; *es gibt* there is, there are; *ich bin es* it's me; *ich hoffe es* I hope so; *ich kann es* I can (do it)

Esche [ˈɛʃə] f (-; -n) BOT ash (tree)

Esel [ˈeːzəl] m (-s; -) zo donkey, ass (a. F)

'Eselsbrücke f mnemonic

'Eselsohr fig n dog-ear

Eskorte [ɛsˈkɔrtə] f (-; -n) MIL escort, MAR a. convoy

essbar [ˈɛsbaːɐ] adj eatable; edible

essen [ˈɛsən] v/t and v/i (irr, ge-, h) eat; *zu Mittag essen* (have) lunch; *zu Abend essen* have supper (or dinner); *essen gehen* eat or dine out

'Essen n (-s; -) food; meal; dish; dinner

'Essenmarke f meal ticket

Essenszeit f lunchtime; dinner or supper time

Essig [ˈɛsɪç] m (-s; -e) vinegar

'Essiggurke f pickled gherkin, pickle

Esslöffel m tablespoon

Essstäbchen pl chopsticks

Esstisch m dining table

Esszimmer n dining room

Estrich [ˈɛstrɪç] m (-s; -e) ARCH flooring, subfloor; Swiss: loft, attic, garret

etablieren [etaˈbliːrən] v/refl (no -ge-, h) establish o.s.

Etage [eˈtaːʒə] f (-; -n) floor, stor(e)y; *auf der ersten Etage* on the second (Br first) floor

E'tagenbett n bunk bed

Etappe [eˈtapə] f (-; -n) stage, SPORT a. leg

Etat [eˈtaː] m (-s; -s) budget

Ethik [ˈeːtɪk] f (-; no pl) ethics

ethisch [ˈeːtɪʃ] adj ethical

ethnisch [ˈɛtnɪʃ] adj ethnic

Etikett [etiˈkɛt] n (-[e]s; -e[n]) label (a. fig); (price) tag

Eti'kette f (-; -n) etiquette

etikettieren [etikɛˈtiːrən] v/t (no -ge-, h) label

etliche [ˈɛtlɪçə] indef pron several, quite a few

Etui [ɛtˈviː] n (-s; -s) case

etwa [ˈɛtva] adv about, around; perhaps, by any chance; *nicht etwa, dass* not that

etwaig [ˈɛtvaɪç] adj any

etwas [ˈɛtvas] **1.** indef pron something; anything; **2.** adj some; any; **3.** adv a little, somewhat

EU [eːˈuː] ABBR of *Europäische Union* EU, European Union

euch [ɔyç] pers pron you; *euch (selbst)* yourselves

euer [ˈɔyɐ] poss pron your; *der (die, das) Eu(e)re* yours

Eule [ˈɔylə] f (-; -n) zo owl; *Eulen nach Athen tragen* carry coals to Newcastle

euresgleichen [ˈɔyrəsˈɡlaɪçən] pron people like you, F contp the likes of you

Euro... [ˈɔyro] in cpds ...cheque etc: Euro...

Europa [ɔyˈroːpa] Europe; *Europa... in cpds* European

Europäer [ɔyroˈpɛːɐ] m (-s; -), **Europäerin** [-ˈpɛːərɪn] f (-; -nen), **euro'päisch** adj European; *Europäische Gemeinschaft* European Community

Euter [ˈɔytɐ] n (-s; -) udder

ev. ABBR of *evangelisch* Prot., Protestant

evakuieren [evakuˈiːrən] v/t (no -ge-, h) evacuate

evangelisch [evaŋˈɡeːlɪʃ] adj REL Protestant; *evangelisch-lutherisch* Lutheran

Evangelium [evaŋˈɡeːljʊm] n (-s; -lien) Gospel

eventuell [eventuˈɛl] **1.** adj possible; **2.** adv possibly, perhaps

evtl. ABBR of *eventuell* poss., possibly

ewig [ˈeːvɪç] adj eternal; F constant, endless; *auf ewig* for ever

'Ewigkeit f (-; no pl) eternity; F *eine Ewigkeit* (for) ages

exakt [ɛˈksakt] adj exact, precise

Ex'aktheit f (-; no pl) exactness, precision

Examen [ɛˈksaːmən] n (-s; Examina [ɛˈksaːmina]) exam, examination

Exekutive [ɛksekuˈtiːvə] f (-; -n) POL executive (power)

Exemplar [ɛksɛmˈplaːɐ] n (-s; -e) specimen; copy

exerzieren [ɛksɛrˈtsiːrən] v/i (no -ge-, h) MIL drill

Exil [ɛ'ksiːl] *n* (*-s; -e*) exile
Existenz [ɛksɪs'tɛnts] *f* (*-; -en*) existence; living, livelihood
Existenzkampf *m* struggle for survival
Existenzminimum *n* subsistence level
existieren [ɛksɪs'tiːrən] *v/i* (*no -ge-, h*) exist; live (**von** on)
exklusiv [ɛksklu'ziːf] *adj* exclusive, select
exotisch [ɛ'ksoːtɪʃ] *adj* exotic
Expansion [ɛkspan'zjoːn] *f* (*-; -en*) expansion
Expedition [ɛkspedi'tsjoːn] *f* (*-; -en*) expedition
Experiment [ɛksperi'mɛnt] *n* (*-[e]s; -e*), **experimentieren** [ɛksperimɛn'tiːrən] *v/i* (*no -ge-, h*) experiment
Experte [ɛks'pɛrtə] *m* (*-n; -n*), **Ex'pertin** *f* (*-; -nen*) expert (**für** on)
explodieren [ɛksplo'diːrən] *v/i* (*no -ge-, sein*) explode (*a. fig*), burst
Explosion [ɛksplo'zjoːn] *f* (*-; -en*) explosion (*a. fig*)
explosiv [-'ziːf] *adj* explosive

Export [ɛks'pɔrt] *m* (*-[e]s; -e*) a) (*no pl*) export(ation), b) exports
exportieren [ɛkspɔr'tiːrən] *v/t* (*no -ge-, h*) export
Express [ɛks'prɛs] *m* (*-es; no pl*) RAIL express; *per Express* by special delivery, *Br* express
extra ['ɛkstra] *adv* extra; separately; F on purpose; *extra für dich* especially for you
Extra *n* (*-s; -s*), **Extrablatt** *n* extra
Extrakt [ɛks'trakt] *m* (*-[e]s; -e*) extract
extravagant [ɛkstrava'gant] *adj* flamboyant
extrem [ɛks'treːm] *adj*, **Ex'trem** *n* (*-s; -e*) extreme
Extremist(in) [ɛkstre-'mɪst(ɪn)] (*-en/-; -nen*), **extre'mistisch** *adj* extremist, ultra
Exzellenz [ɛkstsɛ'lɛnts] *f* (*-; -en*) Excellency
exzentrisch [ɛks'tsɛntrɪʃ] *adj* eccentric
Exzess [ɛks'tsɛs] *m* (*-ses; -se*) excess

F

Fa. ABBR of *Firma* firm; Messrs.
Fabel ['faːbəl] *f* (*-; -n*) fable (*a. fig*) **'fabelhaft** *adj* fantastic, wonderful
Fabrik [fa'briːk] *f* (*-; -en*) factory, works, shop
Fabrikant [fabri'kant] *m* (*-en; -en*) factory owner; manufacturer
Fa'brikarbeiter *m* factory worker
Fabrikat [fabri'kaːt] *n* (*-[e]s; -e*) make, brand; product
Fabrikation [fabrika'tsjoːn] *f* (*-; -en*) manufacturing, production
Fabrikati'onsfehler *m* flaw
Fa'brikbesitzer *m* factory owner
Fabrikware *f* manufactured product(s)
Fach [fax] *n* (*-[e]s; Fächer* ['fɛçɐ]) compartment; pigeonhole; shelf; PED, UNIV subject; → **Fachgebiet**
Facharbeiter *m* skilled worker
Facharzt *m*, **Fachärztin** *f* specialist (**für** in)
Fachausbildung *f* professional training
Fachausdruck *m* technical term
Fachbuch *n* specialist book
Fächer ['fɛçɐ] *m* (*-s; -*) fan
'Fachfrau *f* expert

Fachgebiet *n* line, field; trade, business
Fachgeschäft *n* dealer (specializing in …)
Fachhochschule *f appr* (technial) college, *esp Br* polytechnic
Fachkenntnisse *pl* specialized knowledge
'fachkundig *adj* competent, expert
'fachlich *adj* professional, specialized
'Fachlitera,tur *f* specialized literature
Fachmann *m* (*-[e]s; -leute*) expert
'fachmännisch [-mɛnɪʃ] *adj* expert
'Fachschule *f* technical school *or* college
fachsimpeln ['faxzɪmpəln] *v/i* (*ge-, h*) talk shop
'Fachwerk *n* framework
Fachwerkhaus *n* half-timbered house
Fachzeitschrift *f* (professional *or* specialist) journal
Fackel ['fakəl] *f* (*-; -n*) torch
Fackelzug *m* torchlight procession
fade ['faːdə] *adj* GASTR tasteless, flat; stale; *fig* dull, boring
Faden ['faːdən] *m* (*-s; Fäden* ['fɛːdən]) thread (*a. fig*)
'fadenscheinig *adj* threadbare; *fig* flimsy

(excuse etc)

fähig ['fɛːɪç] *adj* capable (**zu** of [*doing*] *s.th.*), able (*to do s.th.*)

'Fähigkeit *f* (-; -*en*) (cap)ability; talent, gift

fahl [faːl] *adj* pale; ashen (*face*)

fahnden ['faːndən] *v/i* (*ge-, h*) search (**nach** for)

'Fahndung *f* (-; -*en*) search

'Fahndungsliste *f* wanted list

Fahne ['faːnə] *f* (-; -*n*) flag; *mst fig* banner; **F** *e-e* **Fahne haben** reek of alcohol

'Fahnenflucht *f* (-; *no pl*) MIL desertion

Fahnenstange *f* flagpole, flagstaff

Fahrbahn ['faːr-] *f* road(way), pavement; MOT lane

'fahrbar *adj* mobile

Fähre ['fɛːrə] *f* (-; -*n*) ferry(boat)

fahren ['faːrən] (*irr, ge-*) **1.** *v/i* (*sein*) go; *bus etc*: run; leave; MOT drive; ride; **mit dem Auto** (*Zug, Bus etc*) **fahren** go by car (train, bus *etc*); **über** *e-e* **Brücke** *etc* **fahren** cross a bridge *etc*; **mit der Hand über et. fahren** run one's hand over s.th.; **was ist denn in dich gefahren?** what's got into you?; **2.** *v/t* (*h*) drive (*car etc*); ride (*bicycle etc*); carry

Fahrer ['faːrə] *m* (-*s*; -) driver

Fahrerflucht *f* hit-and-run offense (*Br* offence)

'Fahrerin *f* (-; -*nen*) driver

Fahrgast ['faːr-] *m* passenger

Fahrgeld *n* fare

Fahrgelegenheit *f* means of transport(ation)

Fahrgemeinschaft *f* car pool

Fahrgestell *n* MOT chassis; AVIAT → **Fahrwerk**

Fahrkarte *f* ticket

'Fahrkartenauto,mat *m* ticket machine

Fahrkartenentwerter *m* (-*s*; -) ticket-cancel(l)ing machine

Fahrkartenschalter *m* ticket window

'fahrlässig *adj* careless, reckless (*a.* JUR); **grob fahrlässig** grossly negligent

'Fahrlehrer *m* driving instructor

'Fahrplan *m* timetable, schedule

'fahrplanmäßig 1. *adj* scheduled; **2.** *adv* according to schedule; on time

'Fahrpreis *m* fare

Fahrprüfung *f* driving test

Fahrrad *n* bicycle, F bike

Fahrschein *m* ticket

Fahrschule *f* driving school

Fahrschüler *m* MOT student driver, *Br* learner (driver); PED non-local student

Fahrstuhl *m* elevator, *Br* lift

Fahrstunde *f* driving lesson

Fahrt [faːrt] *f* (-; -*en*) ride, MOT drive; trip, journey, MAR voyage; cruise; speed (*a.* MOT); **in voller Fahrt** at full speed

Fährte ['fɛːrtə] *f* (-; -*n*) track (*a. fig*)

'Fahrtenschreiber *m* MOT tachograph

'Fahrwasser *n* MAR fairway

'Fahrwerk *n* AVIAT landing gear

Fahrzeug *n* (-[*e*]*s*; -*e*) vehicle

Fairness ['fɛːrnɪs] *f* (-; *no pl*) fair play

Faktor ['faktoːr] *m* (-*s*; -*en* [fak'toːrən]) factor

Fakultät [fakul'tɛːt] *f* (-; -*en*) UNIV faculty, department

Falke ['falkə] *m* (-*n*; -*n*) ZO hawk, falcon

Fall [fal] *m* (-[*e*]*s*; *Fälle* ['fɛlə]) fall; LING, JUR, MED case; **auf jeden Fall** in any case; **auf keinen Fall** on no account; **für den Fall, dass …** in case …; **gesetzt den Fall, dass** suppose (that); **zu Fall bringen** *fig* defeat

Falle ['falə] *f* (-; -*n*) trap (*a. fig*)

fallen ['falən] *v/i* (*irr, ge-, sein*) fall (*a. rain etc*), drop; **fallen lassen** drop (*a. fig*); MIL be killed (in action); **ein Tor fiel** SPORT a goal was scored

fällen ['fɛlən] *v/t* (*ge-, h*) fell, cut down (*tree*); JUR pass (*sentence*); make (*a decision etc*)

fällig ['fɛlɪç] *adj* due; payable

'fallenlassen ['faləlasən] *v/i* (*irr, fallen, no ge-, h*) *fig* drop

'Fallobst *n* windfall

Fallrückzieher *m* soccer: overhead kick

falls [fals] *cj* if, in case; **falls nicht** unless

Fallschirm *m* parachute

Fallschirmjäger *m* MIL paratrooper

Fallschirmspringen *n* MIL parachuting; SPORT skydiving

Fallschirmspringer *m* MIL parachutist; SPORT skydiver

Falltür *f* trapdoor

falsch [falʃ] *adj and adv* wrong; false (*a. fig*); forged; **falsch gehen** *watch*: be wrong; **et. falsch aussprechen** (**schreiben, verstehen** *etc*) mispronounce (misspell, misunderstand *etc*) s.th.; **falsch verbunden!** TEL sorry, wrong number

fälschen ['fɛlʃən] *v/t* (*ge-, h*) forge, fake; counterfeit

'Fälscher *m* (-*s*; -) forger

'Falschgeld *n* counterfeit *or* false money

Falschmünzer [-myntsə] *m* (-*s*; -) counterfeiter

Falschspieler *m* cheat

'Fälschung *f* (-; -*en*) forgery; counterfeit

'fälschungssicher *adj* forgery-proof

Falt… ['falt-] *in cpds* …*bett*, …*boot etc*: folding …

Falte ['faltə] *f* (-; -*n*) fold; wrinkle; pleat; crease

'**falten** v/t (ge-, h) fold
'**Faltenrock** m pleated skirt
Falter ['faltɐ] m (-s; -) zo butterfly
faltig ['faltɪç] adj wrinkled
familiär [fami'ljɛːɐ] adj personal; informal; **familiäre Probleme** family problems
Familie [fa'miːljə] f (-; -n) family (a. zo, BOT)
Fa'milienangelegenheit f family affair
Familienanschluss m: **Familienanschluss haben** live as one of the family
Familienname m family (or last) name, surname
Familienpackung f family size (package)
Familienplanung f family planning
Familienstand m marital status
Familienvater m family man
Fanatiker [fa'naːtikɐ] m (-s; -), **Fa'natikerin** f (-; -nen), **fa'natisch** adj fanatic
Fanatismus [fana'tɪsmʊs] m (-; no pl) fanaticism
fand [fant] pret of **finden**
Fang [faŋ] m (-[e]s; Fänge ['fɛŋə]) catch (a. fig)
'**fangen** v/t (irr, ge-, h) catch (a. fig); **sich wieder fangen** get a grip on o.s. again; **Fangen spielen** play tag (Br catch)
'**Fangzahn** m zo fang
Fantasie [fanta'ziː] f (-; -n) imagination; fantasy
fanta'sielos adj unimaginative
fanta'sieren v/i (no -ge-, h) daydream; MED be delirious; F talk nonsense
fanta'sievoll adj imaginative
Fantast [fan'tast] m (-en; -en) dreamer
fan'tastisch adj fantastic, F a. great, terrific
Farbband ['farp-] n (typewriter) ribbon
Farbe ['farbə] f (-; -n) colo(u)r; paint; complexion; tan; card games: suit
'**farbecht** adj colo(u)r-fast
färben ['fɛrbən] v/t (ge-, h) dye; esp fig colo(u)r; **sich rot färben** turn red; → **abfärben**
'**farbenblind** adj colo(u)r-blind
farbenfroh, farbenprächtig adj colo(u)rful
'**Farbfernsehen** n colo(u)r television
Farbfernseher m colo(u)r TV set
Farbfilm m colo(u)r film
Farbfoto n colo(u)r photo
farbig ['farbɪç] adj colo(u)red; stained (glass); fig colo(u)rful
Farbige ['farbɪgə] m, f (-n; -n) → **Schwarze**
'**Farbkasten** m paintbox
'**farblos** adj colo(u)rless (a. fig)
'**Farbstift** m colo(u)red pencil, crayon

'**Farbstoff** m dye; GASTR colo(u)ring
'**Farbton** m shade, tint
'**Färbung** f (-; -en) colo(u)ring; hue
Farnkraut ['farn-] n BOT fern
Fasan [fa'zaːn] m (-[e]s; -e[n]) zo pheasant
Faschismus [fa'ʃɪsmʊs] m (-; no pl) POL fascism
Faschist [fa'ʃɪst] m (-en; -en), **fa'schistisch** adj POL fascist
faseln ['faːzəln] F v/i (ge-, h) drivel
Faser ['faːzɐ] f (-; -n) fiber, Br fibre; grain
faserig ['faːzərɪç] adj fibrous
'**fasern** v/i (ge-, h) fray
Fass [fas] n (-es; Fässer ['fɛsɐ]) cask, barrel; **vom Fass** on tap
Fassade [fa'saːdə] f (-; -n) ARCH facade, front (a. fig)
'**Fassbier** n draft (Br draught) beer
fassen ['fasən] (ge-, h) 1. v/t take hold of, grasp; seize; catch (criminal); hold, take; set (jewels); fig grasp, understand; pluck up (courage); make (a decision); **sich fassen** compose o.s.; **sich kurz fassen** be brief; **es ist nicht zu fassen** that's incredible 2. v/i: **fassen nach** reach for
'**Fassung** f (-; -en) a) setting; frame (of glasses); ELECTR socket; draft(ing); wording, version, b) (no pl) composure; **die Fassung verlieren** lose one's composure; **j-n aus der Fassung bringen** put s.o. out
'**fassungslos** adj stunned; speechless
'**Fassungsvermögen** n capacity
fast [fast] adv almost, nearly; **fast nie (nichts)** hardly ever (anything)
fasten ['fastən] v/i (ge-, h) fast
'**Fastenzeit** f REL Lent
'**Fastnacht** f → **Karneval**
fatal [fa'taːl] adj unfortunate; awkward; disastrous
fauchen ['fauxən] v/i (ge-, h) zo hiss
faul [faul] adj rotten, bad, GASTR a. spoiled; fig lazy; F fishy; **faule Ausrede** lame excuse
faulen v/i (ge-, h, sein) rot, go bad; decay
faulenzen ['faulɛntsən] v/i (ge-, h) laze, loaf (about)
'**Faulenzer(in)** [-tsɐ (-tsə-rɪn)] (-s; -/-; -nen) lazybones; contp loafer
'**Faulheit** f (-; no pl) laziness
faulig ['faulɪç] adj rotten
Fäulnis ['fɔylnɪs] f (-; no pl) rottenness, decay (a. fig)
Faulpelz F m → **Faulenzer**
Faultier n zo sloth
Faust [faust] f (-; Fäuste ['fɔystə]) fist; **auf eigene Faust** on one's own initiative
Fausthandschuh m mitten

Faustregel f (**als Faustregel** as a) rule of thumb

Faustschlag m punch

Favorit [favoˈriːt] m (-en; -en), **Favoˈritin** f (-; -nen) favo(u)rite

Fax [faks] n (-; -[e]) fax; fax machine

faxen [ˈfaksən] v/i and v/t (ge-, h) fax, send a fax (to)

'**Faxgerät** n fax machine

FCKW [ɛftseːkaːˈveː] ABBR of **Fluorchlorkohlenwasserstoff** chlorofluorocarbon, CFC

Feber [ˈfeːbɐ] Austrian m (-s; -), **Februar** [ˈfeːbruaːɐ] m (-s; -e) February

fechten [ˈfɛçtn] v/i (irr, ge-, h) SPORT fence; fig fight

'**Fechten** n (-s; no pl) SPORT fencing

Fechter(in) [ˈfɛçtɐ (-tərɪn)] (-s; -/-; -nen) SPORT fencer

Feder [ˈfeːdɐ] f (-; -n) feather; plume; nib; TECH spring

'**Federball** m SPORT badminton; shuttlecock

'**Federbett** n comforter, Br duvet

'**Federgewicht** n SPORT featherweight

'**Federhalter** m penholder

'**feder'leicht** adj (as) light as a feather

'**Federmäppchen** [-mɛpçən] n (-s; -) pencil case

'**federn** (ge-, h) **1.** v/i be springy; **2.** v/t TECH spring

federnd adj springy, elastic

'**Federstrich** m stroke of the pen

'**Federung** [ˈfeːdərʊŋ] f (-; -en) springs; MOT suspension; **e-e gute Federung haben** be well sprung

'**Federzeichnung** f pen-and-ink drawing

Fee [feː] f (-; -n) fairy

fegen [ˈfeːgən] v/t (ge-, h) and fig v/i (sein) sweep

fehl [feːl] adj: **fehl am Platze** out of place

'**Fehlbetrag** m deficit

'**fehlen** v/i (ge-, h) be missing; be absent; **ihm fehlt (es an)** ... he is lacking ...; **du fehlst uns** we miss you; **was dir fehlt, ist** ... what you need is ...; **was fehlt Ihnen?** what's wrong with you?

Fehler [ˈfeːlɐ] m (-s; -) mistake; fault; TECH a. defect, flaw; EDP error

'**fehlerfrei** adj faultless, flawless

'**fehlerhaft** adj faulty; full of mistakes; TECH defective

'**Fehlermeldung** f EDP error message

'**Fehlernährung** f malnutrition

'**Fehlgeburt** f MED miscarriage

'**Fehlgriff** m mistake; wrong choice

'**Fehlschlag** m failure

'**fehlschlagen** v/i (irr, **schlagen**, sep, -ge-, sein) fail

'**Fehlstart** m false start

'**Fehltritt** m slip; fig lapse

'**Fehlzündung** f MOT backfire (a. **Fehlzündung haben**)

Feier [ˈfaiɐ] f (-; -n) celebration; party

'**Feierabend** m end of a day's work; closing time; evening (at home); **Feierabend machen** finish (work), F knock off; **nach Feierabend** after work

'**feierlich** adj solemn; festive

'**Feierlichkeit** f (-; -en) a) (no pl) solemnity, b) ceremony

'**feiern** v/t and v/i (ge-, h) celebrate; have a party

'**Feiertag** m holiday; **gesetzlicher Feiertag** public (or legal, Br a. bank) holiday

feig [faik], **feige** [ˈfaigə] adj cowardly; **feig sein** be a coward

Feige [ˈfaigə] f (-; -n) fig

'**Feigheit** f (-; no pl) cowardice

'**Feigling** m (-s; -e) coward

Feile [ˈfailə] f (-; -n), **feilen** v/t and v/i (ge-, h) file

feilschen [ˈfailʃn] v/i (ge-, h) haggle (**um** about, over)

fein [fain] adj fine; choice; excellent; keen (ear); delicate; distinguished, F posh; **fein!** good!, okay!

Feind [faint] m (-[e]s; -e) enemy (a. fig)

'**Feindbild** n enemy image

Feindin [ˈfaindɪn] f (-; -nen) enemy

'**feindlich** adj hostile; MIL enemy

'**Feindschaft** f (-; no pl) hostility

'**feindselig** adj hostile (**gegen** to)

'**Feindseligkeit** f (-; no pl) hostility

'**feinfühlig** [ˈfainfyːlɪç] adj sensitive

'**Feingefühl** n (-[e]s; no pl) sensitiveness

'**Feinheit** f (-; -en) a) (no pl) fineness; keenness; delicacy, b) pl niceties

'**Feinkostgeschäft** n delicatessen

Feinme,chaniker m precision mechanic

'**Feinschmecker** m (-s; -) gourmet

feist [faist] adj fat, stout

Feld [fɛlt] n (-[e]s; -er [ˈfɛldɐ]) field (a. fig); chess; square

'**Feldarbeit** f AGR work in the fields; fieldwork

'**Feldbett** n cot, Br camp bed

'**Feldflasche** f water bottle, canteen

'**Feldlerche** f ZO skylark

'**Feldmarschall** m MIL field marshal

'**Feldstecher** [-ʃtɛçɐ] m (-s; -) field glasses

'**Feldwebel** [-veːbəl] m (-s; -) MIL sergeant

'**Feldzug** m MIL campaign (a. fig)

Felge [ˈfɛlgə] f (-; -n) rim; SPORT circle

Fell [fɛl] n (-[e]s; -e) ZO coat; skin, fur

Fels [fɛls] m (-en; -en) rock

'**Felsbrocken** m boulder

Felsen ['fɛlzən] *m* (-s; -) rock

felsig ['fɛlzɪç] *adj* rocky

'**Felsspalte** *f* crevice

'**Felsvorsprung** *m* ledge

feminin [femi'ni:n] *adj* feminine (*a.* LING); *contp* effeminate

Feminismus [femi'nɪsmʊs] *m* (-; *no pl*) feminism

Feministin [femi'nɪstɪn] *f* (-; -nen), femi-'**nistisch** *adj* feminist

Fenchel ['fɛnçəl] *m* (-s; *no pl*) BOT fennel

Fenster ['fɛnstɐ] *n* (-s; -) window

'**Fensterbank** *f* (-; -*bänke*), '**Fensterbrett** *n* windowsill

'**Fensterflügel** *m* casement

'**Fensterladen** *m* shutter

'**Fensterrahmen** *m* window frame

'**Fensterscheibe** *f* (window)pane

Ferien ['fe:riən] *pl* vacation, *esp Br* holiday(s *pl*); **Ferien haben** be on vacation

'**Ferienhaus** *n* vacation home, cottage

'**Ferienlager** *n* summer camp

'**Ferienwohnung** *f* vacation rental, *Br* holiday apartment

Ferkel ['fɛrkəl] *n* (-s; -) ZO piglet; F pig

fern [fɛrn] *adj and adv* far(away), far-off, distant; **von fern** from a distance

'**Fernamt** *n* telephone exchange

'**Fernbedienung** *f* remote control

'**fernbleiben** *v/i* (*irr*, **bleiben**, *sep*, *-ge-*, *sein*) stay away (*dat* from)

Ferne ['fɛrnə] *f* (-; *no pl*) distance; **aus der Ferne** from a distance

ferner ['fɛrnɐ] *adv* further(more); in addition, also

'**Fernfahrer** *m* long-haul truck driver, *Br* trucker, *Br* long-distance lorry driver

Ferngespräch *n* TEL long-distance call

'**ferngesteuert** *adj* remote-controlled; MIL guided (*missile etc*)

'**Fernglas** *n* binoculars

'**fernhalten** *v/t* (*irr*, **halten**, *sep*, *-ge-*, *h*) keep away (**von** from)

Fernheizung *f* district heating

Fernko,pierer *m* fax machine

Fernkurs *m* correspondence course

Fernlaster F *m* (-s; -) MOT longhaul truck, *Br* long-distance lorry

Fernlenkung *f* remote control

Fernlicht *n* MOT full (*or* high) beam

'**fernliegen** *v/i* (*irr*, **liegen**, *sep*, *-ge-*, *h*): **es liegt mir fernliegen zu** far be it from me to

'**Fernmeldesatel,lit** *m* communications satellite

Fernmeldetechnik *f*, **Fernmeldewesen** *n* (-s; *no pl*) telecommunications

'**Fernrohr** *n* telescope

Fernschreiben *n*, **Fernschreiber** *m* telex

'**fernsehen** *v/i* (*irr*, **sehen**, *sep*, *-ge-*, *h*) watch television

'**Fernsehen** *n* (-s; *no pl*) television (**im** on)

'**Fernseher** F *m* (-s; -) TV (set); TV viewer

'**Fernsehschirm** *m* (TV) screen

Fernsehsendung *f* TV program(me)

Fernsprechamt *n* telephone exchange

'**Fernsteuerung** *f* remote control

'**Fernverkehr** *m* long-distance traffic

Ferse ['fɛrzə] *f* (-; -*n*) ANAT heel (*a. fig*)

fertig ['fɛrtɪç] *adj* ready; finished; **fertig bringen** manage; *iro* be capable of; **fertig machen** finish (*a.* F *s.o.*); get *s.th.* ready; F give *s.o.* hell, do *s.o.* in; **sich fertig machen** get ready; (**mit et.**) **fertig sein** have finished (s.th.); **mit et. fertig werden** cope with *a problem etc*; F **völlig fertig** dead beat

'**fertigbringen** *v/t* (*irr*, **bringen**, *sep*, *-ge-*, *h*) → **fertig**

'**Fertiggericht** *n* ready(-to-serve) meal

Fertighaus *n* prefabricated house, F prefab

'**Fertigkeit** *f* (-; -*en*) skill

'**fertigmachen** *v/t* (*irr*, **bringen**, *sep*, *-ge-*, *h*) → **fertig**

'**Fertigstellung** *f* (-; *no pl*) completion

'**fertigwerden** *v/i* (*irr*, **bringen**, *sep*, *-ge-*, *sein*) → **fertig**

fesch [fɛʃ] *Austrian adj* smart, chic

Fessel ['fɛsəl] *f* (-; -*n*) shackle (*a. fig*); ANAT ankle

'**fesseln** *v/t* (*ge-*, *h*) bind, tie (up); *fig* fascinate

fest [fɛst] *adj* firm (*a. fig*); solid; fast; *fig* fixed (*date etc*); sound (*sleep*); steady (*girlfriend etc*); **fest schlafen** be fast asleep

Fest *n* (-[*e*]*s*; -*e*) celebration; party; REL festival, feast; → **froh**

'**festbinden** *v/t* (*irr*, **binden**, *sep*, *-ge-*, *h*) fasten, tie (**an** *dat* to)

'**Festessen** *n* banquet, feast

'**festfahren** *v/refl* (*irr*, **fahren**, *sep*, *-ge-*, *h*) get stuck

Festhalle *f* (festival) hall

'**festhalten** (*irr*, **halten**, *sep*, *-ge-*, *h*) **1.** *v/i*: **festhalten an** (*dat*) stick to; **2.** *v/t* hold on to; hold *s.o. or s.th.* tight; **sich festhalten an** (*dat*) hold on to

festigen ['fɛstɪɡən] *v/t* (*ge-*, *h*) strengthen; **sich festigen** grow firm *or* strong

Festigkeit ['fɛstɪçkaɪt] *f* (-; *no pl*) firmness; strength

'**Festland** *n* mainland; *the* Continent

'**festlegen** *v/t* (*sep*, *-ge-*, *h*) fix, set; **sich festlegen auf** (*acc*) commit o.s. to *s.th.*

'**festlich** *adj* festive

'**festmachen** *v/t* (*sep*, *-ge-*, *h*) fasten, fix

(*an dat* to); MAR moor; ECON fix

'**Festnahme** [-naːmə] *f* (-; -*n*), '**festnehmen** *v/t* (*irr*, *nehmen*, *sep*, -*ge*-, *h*) arrest

'**Festplatte** *f* EDP hard disk

festschrauben *v/t* (*sep*, -*ge*-, *h*) screw (on) tight

festsetzen *v/t* (*sep*, -*ge*-, *h*) fix

festsitzen *v/i* (*irr*, *sitzen*, *sep*, -*ge*-, *h*) be stuck; be (left) stranded

'**Festspiele** *pl* festival

'**feststehen** *v/i* (*irr*, *stehen*, *sep*, -*ge*-, *h*) be certain; *date etc*: be fixed

feststehend *adj* established (*fact etc*); set (*phrase etc*)

'**feststellen** *v/t* (*sep*, -*ge*-, *h*) find (out); establish; see, notice; state; TECH lock, arrest

'**Feststellung** *f* (-; -*en*) finding(s); realization; statement

'**Festtag** *m* holiday; REL religious holiday; F red-letter day

'**Festung** *f* (-; -*en*) fortress

'**Festwertspeicher** *m* EDP read-only memory, ROM

'**Festzug** *m* procession

fett [fɛt] *adj* fat (*a. fig*); PRINT bold; *fett gedruckt* boldface, in bold type (*or* print)

Fett *n* (-[*e*]*s*; -*e*) fat; dripping; shortening; TECH grease

'**fettarm** *adj* low-fat, *pred* low in fat

'**Fettfleck** *m* grease spot

fettig ['fɛtɪç] *adj* greasy

'**Fettnäpfchen** *n*: *ins Fettnäpfchen treten* put one's foot in it

Fetzen ['fɛtsən] *m* (-*s*; -) shred; rag; scrap (*of paper etc*)

feucht [fɔʏçt] *adj* moist, damp; humid

Feuchtigkeit ['fɔʏçtɪçkaɪt] *f* (-; *no pl*) moisture; dampness; humidity

feudal [fɔʏ'daːl] *adj* POL feudal; F posh, *Br* swish

Feuer ['fɔʏɐ] *n* (-*s*; -) fire (*a. fig*); *j-m Feuer geben* give s.o. a light; *Feuer fangen* catch fire; *fig* fall for s.o.

Feuera‚larm *m* fire alarm

Feuerbestattung *f* cremation

Feuereifer *m* ardo(u)r

'**feuerfest** *adj* fireproof, fire-resistant

'**Feuergefahr** *f* danger of fire

'**feuergefährlich** *adj* inflammable

'**Feuerleiter** *f* fire escape

Feuerlöscher [-lœʃɐ] *m* (-*s*; -) fire extinguisher

Feuermelder [-mɛldɐ] *m* (-*s*; -) fire alarm

feuern ['fɔʏɐn] *v/i* and *v/t* (*ge*-, *h*) fire (*a.* F *s.o.*)

'**feuer‚rot** *adj* blazing red; crimson

'**Feuerschiff** *n* lightship

Feuerstein *m* flint

Feuerwache *f* fire station

Feuerwaffe *f* firearm, gun

Feuerwehr *f* (-; -*en*) fire brigade (*or* department); fire truck (*Br* engine)

Feuerwehrmann *m* (-[*e*]*s*, -*männer*, -*leute*) fireman, fire fighter

Feuerwerk *n* fireworks

Feuerwerkskörper *m* firework, firecracker

Feuerzeug *n* (cigarette) lighter

feurig ['fɔʏrɪç] *adj* fiery, ardent

Fiasko [fɪ'fjasko] *n* (-*s*; -*s*) fiasco, (complete) failure

Fibel ['fiːbəl] *f* (-; -*n*) primer, first reader

Fiber ['fiːbɐ] *f* fiber, *Br* fibre

Fiberglas *n* fiberglass, *Br* fibreglass

Fichte ['fɪçtə] *f* (-; -*n*) BOT spruce, F *mst* pine *or* fir (tree)

ficken ['fɪkən] V *v/i* and *v/t* (*ge*-, *h*) fuck

Fieber ['fiːbɐ] *n* (-*s*; *no pl*) MED temperature, fever (*a. fig*); *Fieber haben* (*messen*) have a (take s.o.'s) temperature; *Fieber senkend* MED antipyretic

'**fieberhaft** *adj* MED feverish (*a. fig*)

'**fiebern** *v/i* (*ge*-, *h*) MED have *or* run a temperature; *fiebern nach* fig crave for

'**Fieberthermo‚meter** *n* fever (*Br* clinical) thermometer

fiel [fiːl] *pret of* **fallen**

fies [fiːs] F *adj* mean, nasty

Figur [fi'guːɐ] *f* (-; -*en*) figure

Filet [fi'leː] *n* (-*s*; -*s*) GASTR fil(l)et

Filiale [fi'ljaːlə] *f* (-; -*n*) branch

Film [fɪlm] *m* (-[*e*]*s*; -*e*) film; movie, *esp Br* (motion) picture; *the movies*, *Br the cinema*; *e-n Film einlegen* PHOT load a camera

Filmaufnahme *f* filming, shooting; take, shot

filmen ['fɪlmən] (*ge*-, *h*) **1.** *v/t* film, shoot; **2.** *v/i* make a film

'**Filmgesellschaft** *f* motion-picture (*Br* film) company

Filmkamera *f* motion-picture (*Br* film) camera

Filmkas‚sette *f* film magazine, cartridge

Filmpro‚jektor *m* film (*or* movie) projector

Filmregis‚seur *m* film director

Filmschauspieler(in) film (*or* screen, movie) actor (actress)

Filmstudio *n* film studio(s)

Filmthe‚ater *n* → *Kino*

Filmverleih *m* film distributors

Filmvorführer *m* (-*s*; -) projectionist

Filter ['fɪltɐ] *m*, *esp* TECH *n* (-*s*; -) filter

'**Filterkaffee** *m* filter coffee

'**filtern** *v/t* (*ge*-, *h*) filter

'**Filterziga‚rette** *f* filter(-tipped) cigarette,

filter tip

Filz [fɪlts] m (-es; -e) felt; F POL corruption, sleaze

'filzen F v/t (ge-, h) frisk

'Filzschreiber [-ʃraibə] m (-s; -), **Filzstift** m felt(-tipped) pen

Finale [fi'naːlə] n (-s; -) finale; SPORT final(s)

Finanzamt [fi'nants-] n tax office; Internal (Br Inland) Revenue

Finanzbeamte m tax officer

Finanzen [fi'nantsən] pl finances

finanziell [finan'tsjɛl] adj financial

finanzieren [finan'tsiːrən] v/t (no -ge-, h) finance

Fi'nanzmi,nister m minister of finance; Secretary of the Treasury, Br Chancellor of the Exchequer

Finanzminis,terium n ministry of finance; Treasury Department, Br Treasury

Finanzwesen n (-s; no pl) finance

Findelkind ['fɪndəl-] n JUR foundling

finden v/t (irr, ge-, h) find; think, believe; **ich finde ihn nett** I think he's nice; **wie finden Sie ...?** how do you like ...?; **finden Sie (nicht)?** do (don't) you think so?; **das wird sich finden** we'll see

Finder ['fɪndɐ] m (-s; -) finder

'Finderlohn m finder's reward

findig ['fɪndɪç] adj clever

fing [fɪŋ] pret of **fangen**

Finger ['fɪŋɐ] m (-s; -) ANAT finger

Fingerabdruck m fingerprint

Fingerfertigkeit f (-; no pl) manual skill

Fingerhut m thimble; BOT foxglove

Fingernagel m ANAT fingernail

Fingerspitze f fingertip

Fingerspitzengefühl n (-[e]s; no pl) sure instinct; tact

fingiert [fɪn'giːɐt] adj faked; fictitious

Fink [fɪŋk] m (-en; -en) ZO finch

Finne ['fɪnə] m (-n; -n), **Finnin** ['fɪnɪn] f (-; -nen) Finn

'finnisch adj Finnish

Finnland ['fɪn-] Finland

finster ['fɪnstɐ] adj dark, gloomy; fig grim; shady

'Finsternis f (-; -se) darkness, gloom

Finte ['fɪntə] f (-; -n) trick; SPORT feint

Firma ['fɪrma] f (-; -men) firm, company

firmen ['fɪrmən] v/t (ge-, h) REL confirm

'Firmung f (-; -en) REL confirmation

First [fɪrst] m (-[e]s; -e) ARCH ridge

Fisch [fɪʃ] m (-[e]s; -e) ZO fish; pl ASTR Pisces; **er ist (ein) Fisch** he's (a) Pisces

'Fischdampfer m trawler

fischen ['fɪʃən] v/t and v/i (ge-, h) fish

Fischer ['fɪʃɐ] m (-s; -) fisherman; **Fi-**

scher... in cpds ...boot, ...dorf etc: fishing ...

Fischerei [fɪʃə'rai] f (-; no pl) fishing

'Fischfang m (-[e]s; no pl) fishing

Fischgräte f fishbone

Fischgrätenmuster n herring-bone (pattern)

Fischgründe pl fishing grounds

Fischhändler m fish dealer, esp Br fishmonger

Fischkutter m smack

Fischlaich m spawn

Fischstäbchen n GASTR fish stick (Br finger)

Fischzucht f fish farming

Fischzug m catch, haul (both a. fig)

Fisole [fi'zoːlə] Austrian f (-; -n) BOT string bean

Fistel ['fɪstəl] f (-; -n) MED fistula

'Fistelstimme f falsetto

fit [fɪt] adj fit; **sich fit halten** keep fit

'Fitness f (-; no pl) fitness

Fitnesscenter n health club, fitness center, gym

fix [fɪks] adj ECON fixed; F quick; F smart, bright; F **fix und fertig sein** be dead beat; be a nervous wreck; **fixe Idee** PSYCH obsession

fixen ['fɪksən] F v/i (ge-, h) shoot, fix; be a junkie

Fixer ['fɪksɐ] F m (-s; -) junkie, mainliner

fixieren [fɪ'ksiːrən] v/t (no -ge-, h) fix (a. PHOT); stare at s.o.

'Fixstern m ASTR fixed star

FKK [ɛfka:'ka:] ABBR of **Freikörperkultur** nudism

FK'K-Strand m nudist beach

flach [flax] adj flat; level, even, plane; fig shallow

Fläche ['flɛçə] f (-; -n) surface (a. MATH); area (a. MATH); expanse, space

'flächendeckend adj exhaustive

Flächeninhalt m MATH (surface) area

Flächenmaß n square or surface measure

Flachland n (-[e]s; no pl) lowland, plain

Flachs [flaks] m (-es; no pl) BOT flax

flackern ['flakɐn] v/i (ge-, h) flicker

Fladenbrot ['flaːdən-] n round flat bread (or loaf)

Flagge ['flagə] f (-; -n) flag

'flaggen v/i (ge-, h) fly a flag or flags

Flak [flak] f (-; -) MIL anti-aircraft gun

Flamme ['flamə] f (-; -n) flame (a. fig)

Flanell [fla'nɛl] m (-s; -e) flannel

Flanke ['flaŋkə] f (-; -n) flank, side; soccer: cross; SPORT flank vault

flankieren [flaŋ'kiːrən] v/t (no -ge-, h) flank

Flasche ['flaʃə] f (-; -n) bottle; baby's bottle; F *contp* dead loss

'Flaschenbier *n* bottled beer

Flaschenhals *m* neck of a bottle

Flaschenöffner *m* bottle opener

Flaschenpfand *n* (bottle) deposit

Flaschenzug *m* TECH block and tackle, pulley

flatterhaft ['flatəhaft] *adj* fickle, flighty

flattern ['flatən] *v/i* (*ge-, sein*) flutter; TECH (*h*) wobble

flau [flau] *adj* queasy; *fig* flat; ECON slack

Flaum [flaum] *m* (-[e]s; *no pl*) down, fluff, fuzz

Flausch [flauʃ] *m* (-es; -e) fleece

flauschig ['flauʃɪç] *adj* fleecy, fluffy

Flausen ['flauzən] F *pl* (funny) ideas

Flaute ['flautə] *f* (-; -n) MAR calm; ECON slack period

Flechte ['flɛçtə] *f* (-; -n) plait, braid; BOT, MED lichen

'**flechten** [flauʃtən] *v/t* (*irr, ge-, h*) plait, braid (*hair*); weave (*basket*)

Fleck [flɛk] *m* (-[e]s; -e) stain, mark; speck; dot; blot(ch); *fig* place, spot; patch; *blauer Fleck* bruise; *vom Fleck weg* on the spot; *nicht vom Fleck kommen* not get anywhere

'**Flecken** *m* → *Fleck*

'**Fleckenentferner** *m* stain remover

'**fleckenlos** *adj* spotless (*a. fig*)

fleckig ['flɛkɪç] *adj* spotted; stained

Fledermaus ['fle:dɐ-] *f* ZO bat

Flegel ['fle:gəl] *m* (-s; -) lout, boor

'**flegelhaft** *adj* loutish

'**Flegeljahre** *pl* awkward age

'**flegeln** F *contp v/refl* (*ge-, h*) lounge

flehen ['fle:ən] *v/i* (*ge-, h*) beg; pray (*um* for)

flehentlich ['fle:əntlɪç] *adj* imploring, entreating

Fleisch [flaiʃ] *n* (-[e]s; *no pl*) flesh (*a. fig*); GASTR meat; *Fleisch fressend →* *fleischfressend*

Fleischbrühe *f* (meat) broth, consommé

Fleischer ['flaiʃɐ] *m* (-s; -) butcher

Fleischerei [flaiʃə'rai] *f* (-; -en) butcher's (shop)

'**fleischfressend** *adj* BOT, ZO carnivorous

'**Fleischhauer** [-hauə] *Austrian m* (-s; -) butcher

fleischig ['flaiʃɪç] *adj* fleshy

'**Fleischklößchen** *n* (-s; -) meatball

Fleischkon,serven *pl* canned (*Br* tinned) meat

'**fleischlos** *adj* meatless

'**Fleischwolf** *m* meat grinder, *Br* mincer

Fleiß [flais] *m* (-es; *no pl*) diligence, hard work

fleißig ['flaisɪç] *adj* diligent, hard-work-

ing; *fleißig sein* work hard

fletschen ['flɛtʃən] *v/t* (*ge-, h*) bare

flexibel [flɛ'ksi:bəl] *adj* flexible

Flexibilität [flɛksibili'tɛ:t] *f* (-; *no pl*) flexibility

flicken ['flɪkən] *v/t* (*ge-, h*) mend, repair, *a. fig* patch (up)

'**Flicken** *m* (-s; -) patch

'**Flickwerk** *n* patchwork (*a. fig*)

'**Flickzeug** *n* TECH repair kit

Flieder ['fli:dɐ] *m* (-s; -) BOT lilac

Fliege ['fli:gə] *f* (-; -n) ZO fly; bow tie

'**fliegen** *v/i* (*irr, ge-, sein*) *and v/t* (*h*) fly (*a. fliegen lassen*); F fall; F be fired, F get the sack; be kicked out *of school*; F *fliegen auf* (*acc*) really go for; F *in die Luft fliegen* blow up

'**Fliegen** *n* (-s; *no pl*) flying; aviation

'**Fliegenfänger** *m* flypaper

'**Fliegenfenster** *n* flyscreen

'**Fliegengewicht** *n* SPORT flyweight

'**Fliegengitter** *n* wire mesh (screen)

'**Fliegenklatsche** *f* flyswatter

'**Fliegenpilz** *m* BOT fly agaric

Flieger ['fli:gɐ] *m* (-s; -) MIL airman; F plane; *cycling:* sprinter

Fliegeralarm *m* air-raid warning

fliehen ['fli:ən] *v/i* (*irr, ge-, sein*) flee, run away (*both:* **vor** *dat* from)

'**Fliehkraft** *f* PHYS centrifugal force

Fliese ['fli:zə] *f* (-; -n), '**fliesen** *v/t* (*ge-, h*) tile

'**Fliesenleger** *m* (-s; -) tiler

Fließband ['fli:s-] *n* (-[e]s; *-bänder*) TECH assembly line; conveyor belt

fließen ['fli:sən] *v/i* (*irr, ge-, sein*) flow (*a. fig*); run

fließend 1. *adj* flowing; running; LING fluent; **2.** *adv:* *er spricht fließend Englisch* he speaks English fluently *or* fluent English

'**Fließheck** *n* MOT fastback

flimmern ['flɪmɐn] *v/i* (*ge-, h*) shimmer; *film:* flicker

flink [flɪŋk] *adj* quick, nimble

Flinte ['flɪntə] *f* (-; -n) shotgun; F gun

Flipper ['flɪpɐ] F *m* (-s; -) pinball machine

'**flippern** *v/i* (*ge-, h*) play pinball

Flirt [flœrt] *m* (-s; -s) flirtation

flirten ['flœrtən] *v/i* (*ge-, h*) flirt

Flittchen ['flɪtçən] F *n* (-s; -) floozie

Flitter ['flɪtɐ] *m* (-s; -) tinsel (*a. fig*), spangles

'**Flitterwochen** *pl* honeymoon

flitzen ['flɪtsən] F *v/i* (*ge-, sein*) flit, whizz, shoot

flocht [flɔxt] *pret of* **flechten**

Flocke ['flɔkə] *f* (-; -n) flake

flockig ['flɔkɪç] *adj* fluffy, flaky

flog [floːk] *pret of* **fliegen**

floh [floː] *pret of* **fliehen**

Floh *m* (-[e]s; *Flöhe* ['fløːə]) zo flea

'**Flohmarkt** *m* flea market

Florett [floˈrɛt] *n* (-[e]s; -e) foil

florieren [floˈriːrən] *v/i* (*no* -ge-; h) flourish, prosper

Floskel ['flɔskəl] *f* (-; -n) empty *or* cliché(d) phrase

floss [flɔs] *pret of* **fließen**

Floß [floːs] *n* (-es; *Flöße* ['fløːsə]) raft, float

Flosse ['flɔsə] *f* (-; -n) zo fin, a. SPORT flipper

Flöte ['fløːtə] *f* (-; -n) MUS flute; recorder

flott [flɔt] *adj* brisk (*pace*); F smart, chic; MAR afloat

Flotte ['flɔtə] *f* (-; -n) MAR fleet; navy

'**Flottenstützpunkt** *m* MIL naval base

Fluch [fluːx] *m* (-[e]s; *Flüche* ['flyːçə]) curse; swear word

fluchen ['fluːxən] *v/i* (ge-; h) swear, curse

Flucht [fluxt] *f* (-; -en) flight (**vor** *dat* from); escape, getaway (**aus** *dat* from)

'**fluchtartig** *adv* hastily

'**Fluchtauto** *n* getaway car

flüchten ['flʏçtən] *v/i* (ge-; sein) flee (**nach, zu** to), run away; escape, get away

flüchtig ['flʏçtɪç] *adj* quick; superficial; careless; fugitive, *criminal etc*: on the run, at large; **flüchtiger Blick** glance; **flüchtiger Eindruck** glimpse

'**Flüchtigkeitsfehler** *m* slip

Flüchtling ['flʏçtlɪŋ] *m* fugitive; POL refugee

'**Flüchtlingslager** *n* refugee camp

Flug [fluːk] *m* (-[e]s; *Flüge* ['flyːgə]) flight; **im Flug(e)** rapidly, quickly

Flugabwehrra,kete *f* MIL anti-aircraft missile

'**Flugbahn** *f* trajectory

'**Flugball** *m* *tennis*: volley

Flugbegleiter(in) flight attendant

'**Flugblatt** *n* handbill, leaflet

'**Flugdienst** *m* air service

Flügel ['flyːgəl] *m* (-s; -) zo wing (*a.* SPORT); TECH blade; *windmill*: sail; MUS grand piano

'**Flügelmutter** *f* TECH wing nut

'**Flügelschraube** *f* TECH thumb screw

'**Flügelstürmer** *m* SPORT wing forward

'**Flügeltür** *f* folding door

'**Fluggast** *m* (air) passenger

flügge ['flʏgə] *adj* full-fledged

'**Fluggesellschaft** *f* airline

Flughafen *m* airport

Fluglinie *f* air route; → *Fluggesellschaft*

Fluglotse *m* air traffic controller

Flugplan *m* air schedule

Flugplatz *m* airfield, airport

Flugschein *m* (flight) ticket

'**Flugschreiber** *m* (-s; -) flight recorder, black box

Flugsicherung *f* air traffic control

Flugverkehr *m* air traffic

'**Flugzeug** *n* (-[e]s; -e) (air)plane, aircraft, *Br a.* aeroplane; **mit dem Flugzeug** by air *or* plane

Flugzeugabsturz *m* air *or* plane crash

Flugzeugentführung *f* hijacking, skyjacking

Flugzeughalle *f* hangar

Flugzeugträger *m* MAR MIL aircraft carrier

Flunder ['flʊndɐ] *f* (-; -n) zo flounder

flunkern ['flʊŋkɐn] *v/i* (ge-; h) fib; brag

Fluor ['fluːoːɐ] *n* (-s; *no pl*) CHEM fluorine; fluoride

'**Fluorchlorkohlenwasserstoff** *m* CHEM chlorofluorocarbon, CFC

Flur [fluːɐ] *m* (-[e]s; -e) hall; corridor

Fluss [flʊs] *m* (-es; *Flüsse* ['flʏsə]) river; stream; **im Fluss** *fig* in (a state of) flux

fluss'abwärts *adv* downstream

fluss'aufwärts *adv* upstream

'**Flussbett** *n* river bed

flüssig ['flʏsɪç] *adj* liquid; melted; *fig* fluent; ECON available

'**Flüssigkeit** *f* (-; -en) a) liquid, b) (*no pl*) liquidity; *fig* fluency

'**Flüssigkris,tallanzeige** *f* liquid crystal display, LCD

'**Flusslauf** *m* course of a river

Flusspferd *n* zo hippopotamus, F hippo

Flussufer *n* riverbank, riverside

flüstern ['flʏstɐn] *v/i and v/t* (ge-; h) whisper

Flut [fluːt] *f* (-; -en) flood (*a. fig*); high tide; **es ist Flut** the tide is in

Flutlicht *n* floodlights

Flutwelle *f* tidal wave

focht [fɔxt] *pret of* **fechten**

Fohlen ['foːlən] *n* (-s; -) zo foal; colt; filly

Föhn[1] [føːn] *m* (-[e]s; -e) hairdrier

Föhn[2] *m* (-[e]s; -e) METEOR foehn, föhn

föhnen ['føːnən] *v/t* (ge-; h) blow-dry

Folge ['fɔlgə] *f* (-; -n) result, consequence; effect; succession; order; series; TV *etc*: sequel, episode; aftermath; MED aftereffect

folgen ['fɔlgən] *v/i* (ge-; sein) follow; obey; **hieraus folgt, dass** from this it follows that; **wie folgt** as follows

folgend *adj* following, subsequent

folgendermaßen ['fɔlgəndɐ'maːsən] *adv* as follows

'**folgenschwer** *adj* momentous

'**folgerichtig** *adj* logical; consistent

folgern ['fɔlgɐn] *v/t* (ge-; h) conclude (**aus**

dat from)

Folgerung ['fɔlgərʊŋ] *f* (-; -en) conclusion

folglich ['fɔlklɪç] *cj* consequently, thus, therefore

folgsam ['fɔlkza:m] *adj* obedient

Folie ['fo:ljə] *f* (-; -n) foil; transparency

Folter ['fɔltə] *f* (-; -n) torture; **auf die Folter spannen** tantalize

'**foltern** *v/t* (ge-, h) torture, *fig a.* torment

Fön® *m* → **Föhn¹**

Fonds [fõ:] *m* (-; -) ECON fund

fönen *v/t* → **föhnen**

Fontäne [fɔn'tɛ:nə] *f* (-; -n) jet, spout; gush

Förderband ['fœrdə-] *n* TECH conveyor belt

Förderkorb *m* mining: cage

fordern ['fɔrdɐn] *v/t* (ge-, h) demand, *esp* JUR *a.* claim; ECON ask, charge

fördern ['fœrdɐn] *v/t* (ge-, h) promote; support (*a.* UNIV); sponsor; PED tutor, provide remedial classes for; TECH mine

Forderung ['fɔrdərʊŋ] *f* (-; -en) demand; claim (*a.* JUR); ECON charge

Förderung ['fœrdərʊŋ] *f* (-; -en) promotion, advancement; support, sponsorship; UNIV etc: grant; PED tutoring, remedial classes; TECH mining

Forelle [fo'rɛlə] *f* (-; -n) ZO trout

Form [fɔrm] *f* (-; -en) form, shape, SPORT *a.* condition; TECH mo(u)ld; **gut in Form** in great form

formal [fɔr'ma:l] *adj* formal

Formalität [fɔrmali'tɛ:t] *f* (-; -en) formality

Format [fɔr'ma:t] *n* (-[e]s; -e) size; format; *fig* caliber, *Br* calibre

formatieren [fɔrma'ti:rən] *v/t* (no -ge-, h) EDP format

Forma'tierung *f* (-; -en) EDP formatting

Formel ['fɔrməl] *f* (-; -n) formula

formell [fɔr'mɛl] *adj* formal

formen ['fɔrmən] *v/t* (ge-, h) shape, form; *fig* mo(u)ld

'**Formfehler** *m* irregularity

formieren [fɔr'mi:rən] *v/t and v/refl* (no -ge-, h) form (up)

förmlich ['fœrmlɪç] **1.** *adj* formal; *fig* regular; **2.** *adv* formally; *fig* literally

'**formlos** *adj* shapeless; *fig* informal

'**formschön** *adj* well-designed

Formular [fɔrmu'la:ə] *n* (-s; -e) form, blank

formulieren [fɔrmu'li:rən] *v/t* (no -ge-, h) word, phrase; formulate; express

Formu'lierung *f* (-; -en) wording, phrasing; formulation; expression, phrase

forsch [fɔrʃ] *adj* dashing

forschen ['fɔrʃən] *v/i* (ge-, h) research, do

research; **forschen nach** search for

Forscher ['fɔrʃɐ] *m* (-s; -), '**Forscherin** *f* (-; -nen) explorer; (research) scientist

Forschung ['fɔrʃʊŋ] *f* (-; -en) research (work)

Forst [fɔrst] *m* (-[e]s; -e[n]) forest

Förster ['fœrstɐ] *m* (-s; -) forester; forest ranger

'**Forstwirtschaft** *f* (-; *no pl*) forestry

fort [fɔrt] *adv* off, away; gone; missing

Fort [fo:r] *n* (-s; -s) MIL fort

'**fortbestehen** *v/i* (*irr*, **stehen**, *sep*, *no -ge-*, h) continue

'**fortbewegen** *v/refl* (*sep*, *no -ge-*, h) move

'**Fortbewegung** *f* moving; (loco)motion

'**Fortbildung** *f* (-, *no pl*) further education *or* training

'**fortfahren** *v/i* (*irr*, **fahren**, *sep*, *-ge-*) a) (*sein*) leave, go away, MOT *a.* drive off, b) (*h*) continue, go *or* keep on (**et. zu tun** doing s.th.)

fortführen *v/t* (*sep*, *-ge-*, h) continue, carry on

'**fortgehen** *v/i* (*irr*, **gehen**, *sep*, *-ge-*, *sein*) go away, leave

'**fortgeschritten** *adj* advanced

'**fortlaufend** *adj* consecutive, successive

'**fortpflanzen** *v/refl* (*sep*, *-ge-*, h) BIOL reproduce; *fig* spread

'**Fortpflanzung** *f* BIOL reproduction

'**fortschreiten** *v/i* (*irr*, **schreiten**, *sep*, *-ge-*, *sein*) advance, proceed, progress

fortschreitend *adj* progressive

'**Fortschritt** *m* progress

'**fortschrittlich** *adj* progressive

'**fortsetzen** *v/t* (*sep*, *-ge-*, h) continue, go on with

'**Fortsetzung** *f* (-; -en) continuation; *film etc*: sequel; **Fortsetzung folgt** to be continued

'**Fortsetzungsro,man** *m* serialized novel

'**fortwährend** *adj* continual, constant

fossil [fɔ'si:l] *adj*, **Fos'sil** *n* (-s; -ien) GEOL fossil (*a. fig* F)

Foto ['fo:to] *n* (-s; -s) photo(graph); **ein Foto machen (von)** take a photo (of)

'**Fotoalbum** *n* photo album

'**Fotoappa,rat** *m* camera

Fotograf [foto'gra:f] *m* (-en; -en) photographer

Fotografie [fotogra'fi:] *f* (-; -n) a) (*no pl*) photography, b) photograph, picture

fotografieren [fotogra'fi:rən] *v/t and v/i* (no -ge-, h) take a photo(graph) *or* picture (of); **sich fotografieren lassen** have one's picture taken

Foto'grafin *f* (-; -nen) photographer

'**Fotohandy** *n* camera phone

Fotoko'pie *f* photocopy

fotoko'pieren v/t (no -ge-, h) (photo)copy

'**Fotomo,dell** n model

'**Fotozelle** f photoelectric cell

Fotze ['fɔtsə] V f (-; -n) cunt

Foul [faul] n (-s; -s) SPORT foul

foulen ['faulən] v/t and v/i (ge-, h) SPORT foul

Foyer [foa'je:] n (-s; -s) foyer, lobby, lounge

Fr. ABBR of *Frau* Mrs, Ms

Fracht [fraxt] f (-; -en) freight, load, MAR, AVIAT a. cargo; ECON freight, Br carriage

Frachtbrief m RAIL bill of lading (a. MAR), Br consignment note

Frachter ['fraxtɐ] m (-s; -) MAR freighter

Frack [frak] m (-[e]s; Fräcke ['frɛkə]) tails, tailcoat

Frage ['fra:gə] f (-; -n) question; *e-e Frage stellen* ask a question; → *infrage*

'**Fragebogen** m question(n)aire

'**fragen** v/t and v/i (ge-, h) ask (**nach** for; **wegen** about); *nach dem Weg (der Zeit) fragen* ask the way (time); *sich fragen* wonder

'**Fragewort** n LING interrogative

'**Fragezeichen** n LING question mark

fraglich ['fra:klɪç] adj doubtful, uncertain; ... in question

fraglos ['fra:klo:s] adv undoubtedly, unquestionably

Fragment [fra'gmɛnt] n (-[e]s; -e) fragment

fragwürdig ['fra:k-] adj dubious, F shady

Fraktion [frak'tsjoːn] f (-; -en) (parliamentary) group or party

Frakti'onsführer m PARL floor leader, Br chief whip

Franc [frãː] m (-; -s), **Franken** ['fraŋkən] m (-; -) franc

frankieren [fraŋ'kiːrən] v/t (no -ge-, h) stamp; frank

Frankreich ['fraŋkraiç] France

Franse ['franzə] f (-; -n) fringe

fransig ['franziç] adj frayed

Franzose [fran'tso:zə] m (-n; -n) Frenchman; *die Franzosen pl* the French

Französin [fran'tsø:zɪn] f (-; -nen) Frenchwoman

französisch [fran'tsø:zɪʃ] adj French

fraß [fra:s] pret of *fressen*

Fraß F contp m (-es; no pl) muck

Fratze ['fratsə] f (-; -n) grimace

Frau [frau] f (-; -en) woman; wife; *Frau X* Mrs (or Ms) X

Frauchen ['frauçən] n mistress (of dog)

'**Frauenarzt** m, **Frauenärztin** f gyn(a)e-cologist

Frauenbewegung f: *die Frauenbewegung* POL women's lib(eration)

'**frauenfeindlich** adj sexist

'**Frauenhaus** n women's shelter (Br refuge)

Frauenklinik f gyn(a)ecological hospital

Frauenrechtlerin [-rɛçtlərɪn] f (-; -nen) feminist

Fräulein ['frɔylain] n (-s; -) Miss

'**fraulich** adj womanly, feminine

frech [frɛç] adj sassy, Br cheeky

'**Frechheit** f (-; no pl) F Br cheek

frei [frai] adj free (**von** from, of); independent; freelance; vacant; candid, frank; SPORT unmarked; *ein freier Tag* a day off; *morgen haben wir frei* there is no school tomorrow; *im Freien* outdoors; → *Fuß*; *sich frei machen* undress; *sich frei machen von* free o.s. from; → *a.* **freibekommen, freigeben, freihaben;** *frei halten* keep clear (exit), → *freihalten*

'**Freibad** n open-air swimming-pool

'**freibekommen** v/t (irr, kommen, sep, no -ge-, h) get a day etc off

'**freiberuflich** adj freelance, self-employed

'**Freiexem,plar** n free copy

'**Freigabe** f (-; no pl) release

'**freigeben** (irr, geben, sep, -ge-, h) **1.** v/t release; *e-n Tag etc freigeben* give a day etc off; **2.** v/i: *j-m freigeben* give s.o. time off

'**freigebig** [-ge:bɪç] adj generous

'**Freigepäck** n AVIAT baggage allowance

'**freihaben** F v/i (irr, haben, sep, -ge-, h) have a day off (Br a. a holiday)

'**Freihafen** m free port

'**freihalten** v/t (irr, halten, sep, -ge-, h) keep, save (seat etc); treat (s.o.)

'**Freihandel** m free trade

Freihandelszone f free trade area

'**freihändig** [-hɛndɪç] adv with no hands

'**Freiheit** f (-; -en) freedom, liberty; *sich Freiheiten herausnehmen gegen* take liberties with

'**Freiheitsstrafe** f JUR prison sentence

'**Freikarte** f free ticket

'**freikaufen** v/t (irr, halten, sep, -ge-, h) ransom

'**Freikörperkul,tur** f (-; no pl) nudism

'**freilassen** v/t (irr, lassen, sep, -ge-, h) release, set free

'**Freilassung** f (-; -en) release

'**Freilauf** m freewheel (a. *im Freilauf fahren*)

'**freilich** adv indeed, of course

'**Freilicht...** in cpds open-air ...

'**freimachen** v/t (sep, -ge-, h) post: stamp; *sich freimachen* undress; *sich freimachen von* free o.s. from; → *frei;* → *Oberkörper*

'**Freimaurer** m freemason

'freimütig [-my:tɪç] *adj* candid, frank
'freischaffend *adj* freelance
'freischwimmen *v/refl* (*irr*, **schwimmen**, *sep*, *-ge-*, *h*) pass a 15-minute swimming test
'freisprechen *v/t* (*irr*, **sprechen**, *sep*, *-ge-*, *h*) *esp* REL absolve (**von** from); JUR acquit (of)
'Freispruch *m* JUR acquittal
'Freistaat *m* POL free state
'freistehen *v/i* (*irr*, **stehen**, *sep*, *-ge-*, *h*) be unoccupied; SPORT be unmarked; **es steht dir frei zu** *inf* you are free to *inf*
freistellen *v/t* (*sep*, *-ge-*, *h*) **j-n freistellen** exempt s.o. (**von** from) (*a*. MIL); **j-m et. freistellen** leave s.th. (up) to s.o.
'Freistil *m* freestyle
Freistoß *m soccer*: free kick
Freistunde *f* PED free period
Freitag *m* Friday
Freitod *m* suicide
Freitreppe *f* outdoor stairs
Freiübungen *pl* exercises
Freiwild *fig n* fair game
'freiwillig *adj* voluntary; **sich freiwillig melden** volunteer (**zu** for)
Freiwillige(r) [ˈfraivɪlɪɡə] *m*, *f* (-*n*; -*n*) volunteer
'Freizeit *f* free *or* leisure time
Freizeitgestaltung *f* leisure-time activities
Freizeitkleidung *f* leisurewear
Freizeitpark *m* amusement park
Freizeitzentrum *n* leisure center (*Br* centre)
'freizügig *adj* permissive; *film etc*: explicit
fremd [frɛmt] *adj* strange; foreign; unknown; **ich bin auch fremd hier** I'm a stranger here myself
'fremdartig *adj* strange, exotic
Fremde(r) [ˈfrɛmdə] *m*, *f* (-*n*; -*n*) stranger; foreigner
Fremdenführer *m*, **Fremdenführerin** *f* (-; -*nen*) (tourist) guide
Fremdenhass *m* xenophobia
Fremdenlegi,on *f* Foreign Legion
Fremdenverkehr *m* tourism
Fremdenverkehrsbü,ro *n* tourist office
Fremdenzimmer *n* guest room; **Fremdenzimmer** (**zu vermieten**) rooms to let
'fremdgehen F *v/i* (*irr*, **gehen**, *sep*, *-ge-*, *sein*) be unfaithful (to one's wife *or* husband), play around
'Fremdkörper *m* MED foreign body; *fig* alien element
Fremdsprache *f* foreign language
Fremdsprachensekre,tärin *f* bilingual secretary
'fremdsprachig, fremdsprachlich *adj*

foreign-language
'Fremdwort *n* (-[*e*]*s*; -*wörter*) foreign word
Frequenz [freˈkvɛnts] *f* (-; -*en*) PHYS frequency
Fresse [ˈfrɛsə] V *f* (-; -*n*) big (fat) mouth
'fressen *v/t* (*irr*, *ge-*, *h*) ZO eat, feed on; F gobble (up); *fig* devour
Freude [ˈfrɔydə] *f* (-; -*n*) joy, delight; pleasure; **Freude haben an** (*dat*) take pleasure in
'Freudengeschrei *n* shouts of joy, cheers
Freudenhaus F *n* brothel
Freudentag *m* red-letter day
Freudentränen *pl* tears of joy
'freudestrahlend *adj* radiant (with joy)
freudig [ˈfrɔydɪç] *adj* joyful, cheerful; happy (*event etc*)
freudlos [ˈfrɔyt-] *adj* joyless, cheerless
freuen [ˈfrɔyən] *v/t* (*ge-*, *h*) **es freut mich, dass** I'm glad *or* pleased (that); **sich freuen über** (*acc*) be pleased *or* glad about; **sich freuen auf** (*acc*) look forward to
Freund [frɔynt] *m* (-[*e*]*s*; -*e* [ˈfrɔyndə]) friend; boyfriend
Freundin [ˈfrɔyndɪn] *f* (-; -*nen*) friend; girlfriend
'freundlich *adj* friendly, kind, nice; *fig* cheerful (*room etc*)
'Freundlichkeit *f* (-; *no pl*) friendliness, kindness
Freundschaft *f* (-; -*en*) friendship; **Freundschaft schließen** make friends
'freundschaftlich *adj* friendly
'Freundschaftsspiel *n* SPORT friendly (game)
Frevel [ˈfreːfəl] *m* (-*s*; -) outrage (**an** *dat*, **gegen** on)
Frieden [ˈfriːdən] *m* (-*s*; *no pl*) peace; **im Frieden** in peacetime; **lass mich in Frieden!** leave me alone!
Friedensbewegung *f* peace movement
Friedensforschung *f* peace studies
Friedensverhandlungen *pl* peace negotiations *or* talks
Friedensvertrag *m* peace treaty
friedfertig [ˈfriːt-] *adj* peaceable
Friedhof *m* cemetery, graveyard
'friedlich *adj* peaceful
'friedliebend *adj* peace-loving
frieren [ˈfriːrən] *v/i* (*irr*, *ge-*, *h*) freeze; **ich friere** I am *or* feel cold; I'm freezing
Fries [friːs] *m* (-*es*; -*e*) ARCH frieze
Frikadelle [frikaˈdɛlə] *f* (-; -*n*) meatball
frisch [frɪʃ] *adj* fresh; clean (*shirt etc*); **frisch gestrichen!** wet (*or* fresh) paint!
Frische [ˈfrɪʃə] *f* (-; *no pl*) freshness
'Frischhaltebeutel *m* polythene bag
Frischhaltefolie *f* plastic wrap, *Br* cling

film

Friseur [fri'zø:ɐ] m (-s; -e) hairdresser; barber

Friseursa,lon m hairdresser's (shop), barber's shop

Friseuse [fri'zø:zə] f (-; -n) hairdresser

frisieren [fri'zi:rən] v/t (no -ge-, h) do s.o.'s hair; F MOT soup up

Frisör etc → **Friseur** etc

Frist [frist] f (-; -en) (fixed) period of time; deadline; extension (a. ECON)

fristen ['fristən] v/t (ge-, h) **sein Dasein fristen** scrape a living

fristlos adj without notice

Frisur [fri'zu:ɐ] f (-; -en) hairstyle, hairdo

Fritten ['fritən] F pl fries, Br chips

frittieren [fri'ti:rən] v/t (no -ge-, h) deep-fry

frivol [fri'vo:l] adj frivolous; suggestive

froh [fro:] adj glad (**über** acc about); cheerful; happy; **frohes Fest!** happy holiday!; Merry Christmas!

fröhlich ['frø:lɪç] adj cheerful, happy; merry

Fröhlichkeit f (-; no pl) cheerfulness, merriment

fromm [frɔm] adj pious, devout; meek; steady (horse); **frommer Wunsch** pious hope

Frömmigkeit ['frœmɪçkait] f (-; no pl) religiousness, piety

Fronleichnam ['fro:n-] m (-[e]s; no pl) REL Corpus Christi

Front [frɔnt] f (-; -en) front (a. fig), ARCH a. face, MIL a. line; **in Front liegen** SPORT be ahead

frontal [frɔn'ta:l] adj MOT head-on

Fron'talzusammenstoß m MOT head-on collision

Frontantrieb m MOT front-wheel drive

fror [fro:ɐ] pret of **frieren**

Frosch [frɔʃ] m (-[e]s; Frösche ['frœʃə]) zo frog

Froschmann m frogman

Froschperspek,tive f worm's-eye view

Froschschenkel pl GASTR frog's legs

Frost [frɔst] m (-[e]s; Fröste ['frœstə]) frost

Frostbeule f chilblain

frösteln ['frœstəln] v/i (ge-, h) feel chilly, shiver (a. fig)

frostig adj frosty, fig a. chilly

Frostschutzmittel n MOT antifreeze

Frottee [frɔ'te:] n, m (-[s]; -s) terry(-cloth)

frottieren [frɔ'ti:rən] v/t (no -ge-, h) rub down

Frucht [fruxt] f (-; Früchte ['fryçtə]) BOT fruit (a. fig)

fruchtbar adj BIOL fertile, esp fig a. fruit-ful

Fruchtbarkeit f (-; no pl) fertility; fig fruitfulness

fruchtlos adj fruitless, futile

Fruchtsaft m fruit juice

früh [fry:] adj and adv early; **zu früh kommen** be early; **früh genug** soon enough; **heute (morgen) früh** this (tomorrow) morning

Frühaufsteher m (-s; -) early riser (F bird)

Frühe ['fry:ə] f: **in aller Frühe** (very) early in the morning

früher ['fry:ɐ] 1. adj former; previous; 2. adv in former times, at one time; **früher oder später** sooner or later; **ich habe früher (einmal)** ... I used to ...

frühestens adv at the earliest

Frühgeburt f MED premature birth; premature baby

Frühjahr n spring

Frühjahrsputz m spring cleaning

früh'morgens adv early in the morning

frühreif adj precocious

Frühstück n breakfast (**zum** for)

frühstücken v/i (ge-, h) (have) breakfast

Frust [frust] F m (-[e]s; no pl) frustration

Frustration [frustra'tsjo:n] f (-; -en) frustration

frustrieren [frus'tri:rən] v/t (no -ge-, h) frustrate

frz. ABBR of **französisch** Fr., French

Fuchs [fuks] m (-es; Füchse ['fyksə]) zo fox (a. fig); sorrel

Fuchsjagd f foxhunt(ing)

Fuchsschwanz m TECH handsaw

'fuchs'teufels'wild F adj hopping mad

fuchteln ['fuxtəln] v/i (ge-, h) **fuchteln mit** wave s.th. around

Fuge ['fu:gə] f (-; -n) TECH joint; MUS fugue

fügen ['fy:gən] v/t/refl (ge-, h) submit (**in** acc, dat to s.th.)

fühlbar ['fy:l-] fig adj noticeable; considerable

fühlen ['fy:lən] v/t and v/i and v/refl (ge-, h) feel, fig a. sense; **sich wohl fühlen** → **wohlfühlen**

Fühler ['fy:lɐ] m (-s; -) zo feeler (a. fig)

fuhr [fu:ɐ] pret of **fahren**

führen ['fy:rən] (ge-, h) 1. v/t lead; guide; take; run; manage; ECON sell, deal in; keep (account, books etc); have (a talk etc); bear (name etc); MIL command; **j-n führen durch** show s.o. round; **sich führen** conduct o.s.; 2. v/i lead (**zu** to, a. fig), SPORT a. be leading, be ahead

führend adj leading

Führer ['fy:rɐ] m (-s; -) leader (a. POL);

guide; head, chief; guide(book)
'**Führerschein** *m* MOT driver's license, *Br* driving licence
'**Führung** *f* (-; -*en*) a) (*no pl*) leadership, control; ECON management, b) (guided) tour; *gute Führung* good conduct; *in Führung gehen* (*sein*) SPORT take (be in) the lead
'**Führungszeugnis** *n* certificate of (good) conduct
'**Fuhrunternehmen** ['fu:ɐ-] *n* trucking company, *Br* haulage contractors
'**Fuhrwerk** *n* horse-drawn vehicle
Fülle ['fʏlə] *f* (-; *no pl*) crush; *fig* wealth, abundance; GASTR body
'**füllen** *v/t* and *v/refl* (*ge*-, *h*) fill (*a.* MED), stuff (*a.* GASTR)
Füller ['fʏlɐ] *m* (-*s*; -), '**Füllfederhalter** *m* fountain pen
füllig ['fʏlɪç] *adj* stout, portly
'**Füllung** *f* (-; -*en*) filling (*a.* MED), stuffing (*a.* GASTR)
fummeln ['fʊməln] F *v/i* (*ge*-, *h*) fiddle, tinker (*both*: *an dat* with); F grope
Fund [fʊnt] *m* (-[*e*]*s*; -*e* ['fʊndə]) discovery; find
Fundament [fʊnda'mɛnt] *n* (-[*e*]*s*; -*e*) ARCH foundation(s), *fig a.* basis
Fundamentalist [fʊndamɛnta'lɪst] *m* (-*en*; -*en*) fundamentalist
'**Fundbü,ro** *n* lost and found (office), *Br* lost-property office
'**Fundgrube** *fig f* treasure trove
Fundi ['fʊndi] F *m* (-*s*; -*s*) POL radical Green
fundiert [fʊn'di:ɐt] *adj* well-founded (*argument etc*); sound (*knowledge*)
fünf [fʏnf] *adj* five; *grade*: F, N, *Br* fail, poor, E
'**Fünfeck** *n* (-[*e*]*s*; -*e*) pentagon
'**fünffach** *adj* fivefold
'**Fünfkampf** *m* SPORT pentathlon
'**Fünflinge** *pl* quintuplets
'**fünfte** *adj* fifth
'**Fünftel** *n* (-*s*; -) fifth
'**fünftens** *adv* fifth(ly), in the fifth place
'**fünfzehn(te)** *adj* fifteen(th)
fünfzig ['fʏnftsɪç] *adj* fifty
'**fünfzigste** *adj* fiftieth
fungieren [fʊŋ'gi:rən] *v/i* (*no -ge-, h*) *fungieren als* act as, function as
Funk [fʊŋk] *m* (-*s*; *no pl*) radio; *über or durch Funk* by radio
'**Funkama,teur** *m* radio ham
Funke ['fʊŋkə] *m* (-*n*; -*n*) spark; *fig a.* glimmer
funkeln ['fʊŋkəln] *v/i* (*ge*-, *h*) sparkle, glitter; twinkle
'**funken** *v/t* (*ge*-, *h*) radio, transmit

Funker ['fʊŋkɐ] *m* (-*s*; -) radio operator
'**Funkgerät** *n* radio set
'**Funkhaus** *n* broadcasting center (*Br* centre)
Funksig,nal *n* radio signal
'**Funkspruch** *m* radio message
Funkstati,on *f* radio station
'**Funkstreife** *f* (radio) patrol car
Funktele,fon *n* cellular phone
Funktion [fʊŋk'tsjo:n] *f* (-; -*en*) function
Funktionär [fʊŋktsjo'nɛːɐ] *m* (-*s*; -*e*) functionary, official (*a.* SPORT)
funktionieren [fʊŋktsjo'ni:rən] *v/i* (*no -ge-, h*) work
'**Funkturm** *m* radio tower
'**Funkverkehr** *m* radio communication
für [fyːɐ] *prp* (*acc*) for; in favo(u)r of; on behalf of; *für immer* forever; *Tag für Tag* day by day; *Wort für Wort* word by word; *jeder für sich* everyone by himself; *was für ...?* what (*kind or* sort of) ...?; *das Für und Wider* the pros and cons
Furche ['fʊrçə] *f* (-; -*n*) furrow; rut
Furcht [fʊrçt] *f* (-; *no pl*) fear, dread (*both*: *vor dat* of); *aus Furcht*(*, dass*) for fear (that); *Furcht erregend → furchterregend*
'**furchtbar** *adj* terrible, awful
fürchten ['fʏrçtən] *v/t* and *v/i* (*ge*-, *h*) fear, be afraid of; dread; *fürchten um* fear for; *sich fürchten* be scared; be afraid (*vor dat* of); *ich fürchte, ...* I'm afraid ...
fürchterlich ['fʏrçtəlɪç] *→ furchtbar*
'**furchterregend** *adj* frightening
furchtlos *adj* fearless
furchtsam *adj* timid
füreinander *adv* for each other
Furnier [fʊr'niːɐ] *n* (-[*e*]*s*; -*e*), **furnieren** [fʊr'niːrən] *v/t* (*no -ge-, h*) veneer
'**Fürsorge** *f* (-; *no pl*) care; *öffentliche Fürsorge* (public) welfare (work)
Fürsorgeempfänger *m* social security beneficiary
'**fürsorglich** [-zɔrklɪç] *adj* considerate
'**Fürsprache** *f* intercession (*für* for; *bei* with)
'**Fürsprech** *m* (-[*e*]*s*; -*e*) *Swiss*: lawyer
Fürsprecher(in) advocate (*a. fig*)
Fürst [fʏrst] *m* (-*en*; -*en*) prince
'**Fürstentum** *n* (-*s*; -*tümer* [-ty:mɐ]) principality
'**Fürstin** *f* (-; -*nen*) princess
'**fürstlich** *adj* princely (*a. fig*)
Furt [fʊrt] *f* (-; -*en*) ford
Furunkel [fu'rʊŋkəl] *m* (-*s*; -) MED boil, furuncle
'**Fürwort** *n* (-[*e*]*s*; -*wörter*) LING pronoun
Furz [fʊrts] *m* (-*es*; -*e*), '**furzen** *v/i* (*ge*-, *h*) fart

Fusion [fu'zjo:n] f (-; -en) ECON merger, amalgamation

fusionieren [fuzjo'ni:rən] v/i (no -ge-, h) ECON merge, amalgamate

Fuß [fu:s] m (-es; Füße ['fy:sə] ANAT foot; stand; stem; **zu Fuß** on foot; **zu Fuß gehen** walk; **gut zu Fuß sein** be a good walker; **Fuß fassen** become established; **auf freiem Fuß** at large

'Fußball m a) (no pl) soccer, Br football, b) soccer ball, Br football

'Fußballer [-balə] m (-s; -) footballer

'Fußballfeld n football field

Fußballrowdy m (football) hooligan

Fußballspiel n soccer or football match

Fußballspieler(in) football player, footballer

Fußballtoto n football pools

'Fußboden m floor; flooring

Fußbodenheizung f underfloor heating

'Fußbremse f MOT footbrake

Fussel ['fusəl] f (-; -n), m (-s; -[n]) piece of lint (Br fluff); pl lint, Br fluff

'fusselrowdy m (football) hooligan

'fusselig ['fusəliç] adj linty, Br covered in fluff

'fusseln v/i (ge-, h) shed a lot of lint (Br fluff), F mo(u)lt

'Fußgänger [-gɛŋɐ] m (-s; -), 'Fußgängerin f (-; -nen) pedestrian

'Fußgängerzone f (pedestrian or shopping) mall, Br pedestrian precinct

'Fußgeher Austrian m → Fußgänger

'Fußgelenk n ANAT ankle

Fußmatte f doormat

Fußnote f footnote

Fußpflege f pedicure; MED podiatry, Br. chiropody

Fußpfleger(in) podiatrist, Br chiropodist

Fußpilz m MED athlete's foot

Fußsohle f ANAT sole (of the foot)

Fußspur f footprint; track

Fußstapfen pl: **in j-s Fußstapfen treten** follow in s.o.'s footsteps

Fußtritt m kick

Fußweg m foothpath; **e-e Stunde Fußweg** an hour's walk

Futter[1] ['fute] n (-s; no pl) AGR feed, fodder, food

'Futter[2] n (-s; -) lining

Futteral [futə'ra:l] n (-s; -e) case; cover

füttern[1] ['fytɛn] v/t (ge-, h) AGR feed

'füttern[2] v/t (ge-, h) in j-s line

'Futternapf m (feeding) bowl

Fütterung ['fytəruŋ] f (-; -en) feeding (time)

Futur [fu'tu:ɐ] n (-s; -e) future (a. LING)

G

gab [ga:p] pret of **geben**

Gabe ['ga:bə] f (-; -n) gift, present; MED dose; fig talent, gift; **milde Gabe** alms

Gabel ['ga:bəl] f (-; -n) fork; TEL cradle

'gabeln v/refl (ge-, h) fork, branch

'Gabelstapler [-ʃta:plə] m (-s; -) TECH fork-lift (truck)

Gabelung ['ga:bəluŋ] f (-; -en) fork(ing)

gackern ['gakɛn] v/i (ge-, h) cluck, cackle (a. fig)

gaffen ['gafən] v/i (ge-, h) gawk, gawp, F rubberneck

Gaffer ['gafɐ] m (-s; -) F rubberneck(er), Br nosy parker

Gage ['ga:ʒə] f (-; -n) fee

gähnen ['gɛ:nən] v/i (ge-, h) yawn

Gala ['ga:la] f (-; -s) gala

galant [ga'lant] adj gallant, courteous

Galeere [ga'le:rə] f (-; -n) MAR galley

Galerie [galə'ri:] f (-; -n) gallery

Galgen ['galgən] m (-s; -) gallows

Galgenfrist f reprieve

Galgenhumor m gallows humo(u)r

Galgenvogel F m crook

Galle ['galə] f (-; -n) ANAT gall; bile

'Gallenblase f ANAT gall bladder

Gallenstein m MED gallstone

Gallert ['galɐt] n (-[es]; -e), Gallerte [ga-'lɛrtə] f (-; -n) jelly

Galopp [ga'lɔp] m (-s; -s, -e) gallop

galoppieren [galɔ'pi:rən] v/i (no -ge-, sein) gallop

galt [galt] pret of **gelten**

gammeln ['gaməln] F v/i (ge-, h) loaf (about), bum around

Gammler(in) ['gamlɐ (-lɐrin)] F (-s; -/-; -nen) loafer, bum

Gämse ['gɛmzə] f (-; -n) ZO chamois

gang [gaŋ] adj: **gang und gäbe** nothing unusual, (quite) usual

Gang [gaŋ] m (-[e]s; Gänge ['gɛŋə]) walk, gait, way s.o. walks; ARCH passage, a. AVIAT *etc* aisle; corridor; MOT gear; GASTR course; *et. in Gang bringen* get s.th. going, start s.th.; *in Gang kommen* get started; *im Gang(e) sein* be (going) on, be in progress; *in vollem Gang(e)* in full swing

gängeln ['gɛŋəln] *v/t* (*ge-, h*) lead *s.o.* by the nose

gängig ['gɛŋɪç] *adj* current; ECON sal(e)-able

'**Gangschaltung** *f* MOT gears

Ganove [ga'noːvə] F *m* (*-n; -n*) crook

Gans [gans] *f* (*-; Gänse* ['gɛnzə]) ZO goose

Gänseblümchen ['gɛnzə-] *n* BOT daisy

Gänsebraten *m* roast goose

Gänsehaut *f* (*-; no pl*) gooseflesh; *dabei kriege ich e-e Gänsehaut* F it gives me the creeps

Gänsemarsch *m* (*-[e]s; no pl*) single *or* Indian file

Gänserich ['gɛnzərɪç] *m* (*-s; -e*) ZO gander

ganz [gants] **1.** *adj* whole, entire, total; F undamaged; full (*hour etc*); *den ganzen Tag* all day; *die ganze Zeit* all the time; *auf der ganzen Welt* all over the world; *sein ganzes Geld* all his money; **2.** *adv* completely, totally; very; quite, rather, fairly; *ganz allein* all by oneself; *ganz aus Holz etc* all wood *etc*; *ganz und gar* completely, totally; *ganz und gar nicht* not at all, by no means; *ganz wie du willst* just as you like; *nicht ganz* not quite; → *voll*

Ganze ['gantsə] *n* (*-n; no pl*) whole; *das Ganze* the whole thing; *im Ganzen* in all, altogether; *im großen Ganzen* on the whole; *aufs Ganze gehen* go all out

gänzlich ['gɛntslɪç] *adv* completely, entirely

'**Ganztagsbeschäftigung** *f* full-time job

'**Ganztagsschule** *f* all-day school(ing)

gar [gaːr] **1.** *adj* GASTR done; **2.** *adv:* *gar nicht* not at all; *gar nichts* nothing at all; *gar zu ...* (a bit) too ...

Garage [ga'raːʒə] *f* (*-; -n*) garage

Garantie [garan'tiː] *f* (*-; -n*) guarantee, *esp* ECON warranty

garantieren [garan'tiːrən] *v/t* and *v/i* (*no -ge-, h*) guarantee (*für et.* s.th.)

Garbe ['garbə] *f* (*-; -n*) AGR sheaf

Garde ['gardə] *f* (*-; -n*) guard; MIL (the) Guards

Garderobe [gardə'roːbə] *f* (*-; -n*) a (*no pl*) wardrobe, clothes; b) checkroom, *Br* cloakroom; THEA dressing room

Garde'robenfrau *f* checkroom (*Br* cloakroom) attendant

Garderobenmarke *f* coatcheck (*Br* cloakroom) ticket

Garderobenständer *m* coat stand *or* rack

Gardine [gar'diːnə] *f* (*-; -n*) curtain

Gar'dinenstange *f* curtain rod

gären ['gɛːrən] *v/i* ([*irr,*] *ge-, h, sein*) ferment, work

Garn [garn] *n* (*-[e]s; -e*) yarn; thread; cotton

Garnele [gar'neːlə] *f* (*-; -n*) ZO shrimp; prawn

garnieren [gar'niːrən] *v/t* (*no -ge-, h*) garnish (*a. fig*)

Garnison [garni'zoːn] *f* (*-; -en*) MIL garrison, post

Garnitur [garni'tuːr] *f* (*-; -en*) set; suite

Garten ['gartən] *m* (*-s; Gärten* ['gɛrtən]) garden

Gartenarbeit *f* gardening

Gartenbau *m* (*-[e]s; no pl*) horticulture

Gartenerde *f* (garden) mo(u)ld

Gartenfest *n* garden party

Gartengeräte *pl* gardening tools

Gartenhaus *n* summerhouse

Gartenlo,kal *n* beer garden; outdoor restaurant

Gartenschere *f* pruning shears

Gartenstadt *f* garden city

Gartenzwerg *m* (garden) gnome

Gärtner ['gɛrtnə] *m* (*-s; -*) gardener

Gärtnerei [gɛrtnə'raɪ] *f* (*-; -en*) truck farm, *Br* market garden

'**Gärtnerin** *f* (*-; -nen*) gardener

Gärung ['gɛːrʊŋ] *f* (*-; -en*) fermentation

Gas [gaːs] *n* (*-es; -e* ['gaːzə]) gas; *Gas geben* MOT accelerate, F step on the gas

'**gasförmig** [-fœrmɪç] *adj* gaseous

'**Gashahn** *m* gas valve (*or* cock, *Br* tap)

'**Gasheizung** *f* gas heating

'**Gasherd** *m* gas cooker *or* stove

'**Gaskammer** *f* gas chamber

Gasla,terne *f* gas (street) lamp

'**Gasleitung** *f* gas main

'**Gasmaske** *f* gas mask

'**Gasofen** *m* gas stove

Gaspe,dal *n* MOT gas pedal, *Br* accelerator (pedal)

Gasse ['gasə] *f* (*-; -n*) lane, alley

Gast [gast] *m* (*-[e]s; Gäste* ['gɛstə]) guest; visitor; customer

'**Gastarbeiter** *m*, '**Gastarbeiterin** *f* foreign worker

Gästebuch ['gɛstə-] *n* visitors' book

Gästezimmer *n* guest (*or* spare) room

'**gastfreundlich** *adj* hospitable

'**Gastfreundschaft** *f* hospitality

'**Gastgeber** [-geːbə] *m* (*-s; -*) host

'**Gastgeberin** [-geːbərɪn] *f* (*-; -nen*) hostess

'**Gasthaus** *n*, **Gasthof** *m* restaurant, inn

gastieren [gas'tiːrən] *v/i* (*no -ge-, h*) give

performances; THEA guest, give a guest performance

'gastlich adj hospitable

'Gastmannschaft f SPORT visiting team

Gastspiel n THEA guest performance

Gaststätte f restaurant

Gaststube f taproom; restaurant

Gastwirt m landlord

Gastwirtschaft f restaurant, inn

'Gaswerk n TECH gasworks

'Gaszähler m TECH gas meter

Gatte ['gatə] m (-n; -n) husband

Gatter ['gatə] n (-s; -) fence; gate

Gattin ['gatɪn] f (-; -nen) wife

Gattung ['gatʊŋ] f (-; -en) type, class, sort; BIOL genus; species

GAU [gau] (ABBR of größter anzunehmender Unfall) m (-[s]; no pl) worst case scenario, Br maximum credible accident, MCA

Gaul [gaul] m (-[e]s; Gäule ['gɔylə]) nag

Gaumen ['gaumən] m (-s; -) ANAT palate

Gauner ['gaunə] m (-s; -), 'Gaunerin f (-; -nen) F crook

Gaze ['ga:zə] f (-; -n) gauze

Gazelle [ga'tsɛlə] f (-; -n) ZO gazelle

geb. ABBR of geboren b., born

Gebäck [gə'bɛk] n (-[e]s; -e) pastry; cookies, Br biscuits

ge'backen pp of backen

Gebälk [gə'bɛlk] n (-[e]s; -e) timberwork, beams

gebar [gə'ba:ɐ] pret of gebären

Gebärde [gə'bɛːɐdə] f (-; -n) gesture

ge'bärden v/refl (no -ge-, h) behave, act (wie like)

gebären [gə'bɛːrən] v/t (irr, no -ge-, h) give birth to

Gebärmutter [gə'bɛːɐ-] f ANAT uterus, womb

Gebäude [gə'bɔydə] n (-s; -) building, structure

Ge'beine pl bones, mortal remains

geben ['ge:bən] v/t (irr, ge-, h) give (j-m et. s.o. sth.); hand, pass; deal (cards); make; sich geben pass; get better; von sich geben utter, let out; j-m die Schuld geben blame s.o.; es gibt there is, there are; was gibt es? what's up?; what's for lunch etc?; TV etc what's on?; das gibt's nicht! that can't be true; that's out

Gebet [gə'be:t] n (-[e]s; -e) prayer

ge'beten pp of bitten

Gebiet [gə'bi:t] n (-[e]s; -e) region, area; esp POL territory; fig field

ge'bieterisch adj imperious

ge'bietsweise adv regionally; gebietsweise Regen local showers

Gebilde [gə'bɪldə] n (-s; -) thing, object

gebildet [gə'bɪldət] adj educated

Gebirge [gə'bɪrgə] n (-s; -) mountains

gebirgig [gə'bɪrgɪç] adj mountainous

Ge'birgsbewohner m mountain-dweller

Gebirgszug m mountain range

Ge'biss n (-es; -e) (set of) teeth; (set of) false teeth, denture(s)

ge'bissen pp of beißen

Gebläse [gə'blɛːzə] n (-s; -) TECH blower, (MOT air) fan

ge'blasen pp of blasen

geblichen [gə'blɪçən] pp of bleichen

geblieben [gə'bli:bən] pp of bleiben

geblümt [gə'bly:mt] adj floral

gebogen [gə'bo:gən] 1. pp of biegen; 2. adj bent, curved

geboren [gə'bo:rən] 1. pp of gebären; 2. adj born; ein geborener Deutscher German by birth; geborene Smith née Smith; ich bin am ... geboren I was born on the ...

geborgen [gə'bɔrgən] 1. pp of bergen; 2. adj safe, secure

Ge'borgenheit f (-; no pl) safety, security

geborsten [gə'bɔrstən] pp of bersten

Gebot [gə'bo:t] n (-[e]s; -e) REL commandment; fig rule; necessity; auction etc: bid

geboten [gə'bo:tən] pp of bieten

gebracht [gə'braxt] pp of bringen

gebrannt [gə'brant] pp of brennen

ge'braten pp of braten

Ge'brauch m (-[e]s; no pl) use; application

ge'brauchen v/t (no -ge-, h) use; employ; gut (nicht) zu gebrauchen sein be useful (useless); ich könnte ... gebrauchen I could do with ...

gebräuchlich [gə'brɔyçlɪç] adj in use; common, usual; current

Ge'brauchsanweisung f directions or instructions for use

ge'brauchsfertig adj ready for use; instant (coffee etc)

Ge'brauchsgrafiker m commercial artist

ge'braucht adj used, ECON a. second-hand

Ge'brauchtwagen m MOT used or second-hand car

Gebrauchtwagenhändler m used car dealer

Ge'brechen n (-s; -) defect, handicap

gebrechlich [gə'brɛçlɪç] adj frail; infirm

Ge'brechlichkeit f (-; no pl) frailty; infirmity

gebrochen [gə'brɔxən] pp of brechen

Ge'brüder pl brothers

Gebrüll [gə'brʏl] n (-[e]s; no pl) roar(-ing)

Gebühr [gə'by:ɐ] f (-; -en) charge (a. TEL), fee; postage; due

ge'bührend [gə'byːrənt] *adj* due; proper
ge'bührenfrei *adj* free of charge; TEL toll-free, *Br* nonchargeable
gebührenpflichtig *adj* chargeable; **ge-bührenpflichtige Straße** toll road; **ge-bührenpflichtige Verwarnung** fine
gebunden [gə'bʊndən] **1.** *pp of* **binden**; **2.** *adj* bound, *fig a.* tied
Geburt [gə'buːrt] *f* (-; -en) birth; **Deutscher von Geburt** German by birth
Ge'burtenkon,trolle *f*, **Geburtenregelung** *f* birth control
ge'burtenschwach *adj* low-birthrate
geburtenstark *adj*: **geburtenstarke Jahrgänge** baby boom
Ge'burtenziffer *f* birthrate
gebürtig [gə'byrtɪç] *adj* by birth
Ge'burtsanzeige *f* birth announcement
Geburtsdatum *n* date of birth
Geburtsfehler *m* congenital defect
Geburtshelfer(in) obstetrician
Geburtsjahr *n* year of birth
Geburtsland *n* native country
Geburtsort *m* birthplace
Geburtstag *m* birthday
Geburtstagsfeier *f* birthday party
Geburtstagskind *n* birthday boy (*or* girl)
Geburtsurkunde *f* birth certificate
Gebüsch [gə'byʃ] *n* (-[e]s; -e) bushes, shrubbery
gedacht [gə'daxt] *pp of* **denken**
Gedächtnis [gə'dɛçtnɪs] *n* (-ses; -se) memory; **aus dem Gedächtnis** from memory; **zum Gedächtnis an** (*acc*) in memory (*or* commemoration) of; **im Gedächtnis behalten** keep in mind, remember
Gedächtnislücke *f* memory lapse
Gedächtnisschwund *m* MED amnesia; blackout
Gedächtnisstütze *f* memory aid
Gedanke [gə'daŋkə] *m* (-n; -n) thought; idea; **was für ein Gedanke!** what an idea!; **in Gedanken** absorbed in thought; absent-minded; **sich Gedanken machen über** (*acc*) think about; be worried *or* concerned about; **j-s Gedanken lesen** read s.o.'s mind
Ge'dankenaustausch *m* exchange of ideas
Gedankengang *m* train of thought
ge'dankenlos *adj* thoughtless
Ge'dankenstrich *m* dash
Gedankenübertragung *f* telepathy
Gedeck [gə'dɛk] *n* (-[e]s; -e) cover; **ein Gedeck auflegen** set a place
gedeihen [gə'daɪən] *v/i* (*irr, no -ge-, sein*) thrive, prosper; grow; flourish
ge'denken *v/i* (*irr, denken, no -ge-, h*)

(*gen*) think of; commemorate; mention
Gedenkfeier [gə'dɛŋk-] *f* commemoration
Gedenkmi,nute *f*: **e-e Gedenkminute** a moment's (*Br* minute's) silence
Gedenkstätte *f*, **Gedenkstein** *m* memorial
Gedenktafel *f* plaque
Gedicht [gə'dɪçt] *n* (-[e]s; -e) poem
gediegen [gə'diːɡən] *adj* solid; tasteful
gedieh [gə'diː] *pret of* **gedeihen**
gediehen [gə'diːən] *pp of* **gedeihen**
Gedränge [gə'drɛŋə] *n* (-s; -) crowd, crush
ge'drängt *fig adj* concise
gedroschen [gə'drɔʃən] *pp of* **dreschen**
ge'drückt *fig adj* depressed
gedrungen [gə'drʊŋən] **1.** *pp of* **dringen**; **2.** *adj* squat, stocky; thickset
Geduld [gə'dʊlt] *f* (-; *no pl*) patience
ge'dulden *v/refl* (*no -ge-, h*) wait (patiently)
geduldig [gə'dʊldɪç] *adj* patient
Ge'duldspiel *n* puzzle (*a. fig*)
gedurft [gə'dʊrft] *pp of* **dürfen**
geehrt [gə'ʔeːrt] *adj* hono(u)red; **Sehr geehrter Herr N.** Dear Mr N.
geeignet [gə'ʔaɪɡnət] *adj* suitable; suited, qualified; right
Gefahr [gə'faːr] *f* (-; -en) danger; threat; risk; **auf eigene Gefahr** at one's own risk; **außer Gefahr** out of danger, safe
gefährden [gə'fɛːrdən] *v/t* (*no -ge-, h*) endanger; risk, jeopardize
ge'fahren *pp of* **fahren**
gefährlich [gə'fɛːrlɪç] *adj* dangerous; risky
ge'fahrlos *adj* without risk, safe
Gefährte [gə'fɛːrtə] *m* (-n; -n), **Ge'fährtin** *f* (-; -nen) companion
Gefälle [gə'fɛlə] *n* (-s; -) fall, slope, descent; gradient (*a.* PHYS)
ge'fallen 1. *pp of* **fallen**; **2.** *v/i* (*irr, fallen, no -ge-, h*) please; **es gefällt mir** (*nicht*) I (don't) like it; **wie gefällt dir …?** how do you like …?; **sich et. gefallen lassen** put up with s.th.
Ge'fallen¹ *m* (-s; -) favo(u)r; **j-n um e-n Gefallen bitten** ask a favo(u)r of s.o.
Ge'fallen² *n*: **Gefallen finden an** (*dat*) enjoy, like
ge'fällig *adj* pleasant; agreeable; obliging; kind; **j-m gefällig sein** do s.o. a favo(u)r
Ge'fälligkeit *f* (-; -en) a) (*no pl*) kindness, b) favo(u)r
ge'fangen 1. *pp of* **fangen**; **2.** *adj* captive; imprisoned; **gefangen halten** keep s.o. prisoner; **gefangen nehmen** take s.o. prisoner; *fig* captivate

G

Ge'fangene m, f (-n; -n) prisoner; convict

Ge'fangennahme f (-; no pl) capture

Ge'fangenschaft f (-; no pl) captivity, imprisonment; *in Gefangenschaft sein* be a prisoner of war

Gefängnis [gə'fɛŋnıs] n (-ses; -se) prison, jail, Br a. gaol; *ins Gefängnis kommen* go to jail or prison

Gefängnisdi,rektor m governor, warden

Gefängnisstrafe f (sentence or term of) imprisonment

Gefängniswärter m prison guard

Gefäß [gə'fɛːs] n (-es; -e) vessel (a. ANAT), container

gefasst [gə'fast] adj composed; *gefasst auf* (acc) prepared for

Gefecht [gə'fɛçt] n (-[e]s; -e) MIL combat, action

gefedert [gə'feːdərt] adj: *gut gefedert sein* MOT have good suspension

gefeit [gə'fait] adj: *gefeit gegen* immune to

Gefieder [gə'fiːdə] n (-s; -) ZO plumage, feathers

geflochten [gə'flɔxtən] pp of **flechten**

geflogen [gə'floːgən] pp of **fliegen**

geflohen [gə'floːən] pp of **fliehen**

geflossen [gə'flɔsən] pp of **fließen**

Ge'flügel n (-s; no pl) poultry

ge'flügelt adj: *geflügeltes Wort* saying

gefochten [gə'fɔxtən] pp of **fechten**

Ge'folge n (-s; -) entourage, retinue, train

Gefolgschaft [gə'fɔlkʃaft] f (-; -en) followers

gefragt [gə'fraːkt] adj in demand, popular

gefräßig [gə'frɛːsıç] adj greedy, voracious

Gefreite [gə'fraitə] m (-n; -n) MIL private first class, Br lance corporal

ge'fressen pp of **fressen**

ge'frieren v/i (irr, frieren, no -ge-, sein) freeze

Gefrierfach [gə'friːɐ-] n freezer, freezing compartment

Gefrierfleisch n frozen meat

ge'friergetrocknet adj freeze-dried

Ge'frierpunkt m freezing point

Gefriertruhe f freezer, deep-freeze

gefroren [gə'froːrən] pp of **frieren**

Ge'frorene Austrian n (-n; no pl) ice cream

Gefüge [gə'fyːgə] n (-s; -) structure, texture

gefügig [gə'fyːgıç] adj pliant

Ge'fügigkeit f (-; no pl) pliancy

Gefühl [gə'fyːl] n (-[e]s; -e) feeling; sense; sensation; emotion

ge'fühllos adj insensible, numb; unfeeling, heartless

ge'fühlsbetont adj (highly) emotional

ge'fühlvoll adj (full of) feeling; tender; sentimental

gefunden [gə'fʊndən] pp of **finden**

gegangen [gə'gaŋən] pp of **gehen**

gegeben [gə'geːbən] pp of **geben**

gegen ['geːgən] prp (acc) against, JUR, SPORT a. versus; about, around; (in return) for; MED etc for; compared with

'Gegen... in cpds ...aktion, ...angriff, ...argument, ...frage etc: counter-...

Gegenbesuch m return visit

Gegend ['geːgənt] f (-; -en) region, area; countryside; neighbo(u)rhood

gegenei'nander adv against one another or each other

'Gegenfahrbahn f MOT opposite or oncoming lane

Gegengewicht n counterweight; *ein Gegengewicht bilden zu et.* counterbalance s.th.

Gegenkandi,dat m rival candidate

Gegenleistung f quid pro quo; *als Gegenleistung* in return

Gegenlicht n (-[e]s; no pl) PHOT back light; *im or bei Gegenlicht* against the light

Gegenmaßnahme f countermeasure

Gegenmittel n MED antidote (a. fig)

Gegenpar,tei f other side; POL opposition; SPORT opposite side

Gegenrichtung f opposite direction

'Gegensatz m contrast; opposite; *im Gegensatz zu* in contrast to or with

'gegensätzlich [-zɛtslıç] adj contrary, opposite

'Gegenseite f opposite side

'gegenseitig [-zaitıç] adj mutual

'Gegenseitigkeit f: *auf Gegenseitigkeit beruhen* be mutual

'Gegenspieler m, **Gegenspielerin** f SPORT opponent (a. fig)

Gegensprechanlage f intercom (system)

'Gegenstand m object (a. fig); fig subject

'gegenständlich [-ʃtɛntlıç] adj art: representational

'gegenstandslos adj invalid; irrelevant; art: abstract, nonrepresentational

'Gegenstimme f PARL vote against, no; *nur drei Gegenstimmen* only three noes

Gegenstück n counterpart

'Gegenteil n opposite; *im Gegenteil* on the contrary

'gegenteilig adj contrary, opposite

gegen'über adv and prp (dat) opposite; fig to, toward(s); compared with

Gegen'über n (-s; -) person opposite; neighbo(u)r across the street gegen'überstehen *v/i* (*irr*, **stehen**, *sep*, *-ge-*, *h*) face, be faced with

Gegen'überstellung *f* confrontation

'**Gegenverkehr** *m* oncoming traffic

'**Gegenwart** [-vart] *f* (-; *no pl*) present (time); presence; LING present (tense)

'**gegenwärtig** [-vertɪç] **1.** *adj* present, current; **2.** *adv* at present

'**Gegenwehr** [-veːɐ] *f* (-; *no pl*) resistance

Gegenwert *m* equivalent (value)

Gegenwind *m* head wind

'**gegenzeichnen** *v/t* (*sep*, *-ge-*, *h*) countersign

'**Gegenzug** *m* countermove; RAIL train coming from the opposite direction

gegessen [gə'gɛsən] *pp of* **essen**

geglichen [gə'glɪçən] *pp of* **gleichen**

geglitten [gə'glɪtən] *pp of* **gleiten**

geglommen [gə'glɔmən] *pp of* **glimmen**

Gegner ['geːgnɐ] *m* (-s; -), '**Gegnerin** *f* (-; *-nen*) opponent (*a.* SPORT), adversary; MIL enemy

'**gegnerisch** *adj* opposing; MIL (of the) enemy, hostile

'**Gegnerschaft** *f* (-; *-en*) opposition

gegolten [gə'gɔltən] *pp of* **gelten**

gegoren [gə'goːrən] *pp of* **gären**

gegossen [gə'gɔsən] *pp of* **gießen**

ge'graben *pp of* **graben**

gegriffen [gə'grɪfən] *pp of* **greifen**

gehabt [gə'haːpt] *pp of* **haben**

Gehackte [gə'haktə] *n* → **Hackfleisch**

Gehalt [gə'halt] **1.** *m* (-[e]s; -e) content; **2.** *n* (-[e]s; *Gehälter* [gə'hɛltɐ]) salary

ge'halten *pp of* **halten**

Ge'haltsempfänger *m* salaried employee

Gehaltserhöhung *f* raise, *Br* increase or rise in salary

ge'haltvoll *adj* substantial; nutritious

gehangen [gə'haŋən] *pp of* **hängen** 1

gehässig [gə'hɛsɪç] *adj* malicious, spiteful

Ge'hässigkeit *f* (-; *no pl*) malice, spite (-fulness)

ge'hauen *pp of* **hauen**

Gehäuse [gə'hɔyzə] *n* (-s; -) case, box; TECH casing; ZO shell; BOT core

Gehege [gə'heːgə] *n* (-s; -) enclosure

geheim [gə'haim] *adj* secret; **et. geheim halten** keep s.th. (a) secret

Ge'heima,gent *m* secret agent

Geheimdienst *m* secret service

Geheimnis [gə'haimnɪs] *n* (*-ses; -se*) secret; mystery

ge'heimnisvoll *adj* mysterious

Ge'heimnummer *f* TEL unlisted (*Br* ex-directory) number

Geheimpoli,zei *f* secret police

Geheimschrift *f* code, cipher

ge'heißen *pp of* **heißen**

gehemmt [gə'hɛmt] *adj* inhibited, self--conscious

gehen ['geːən] *v/i* (*irr*, *ge-*, *sein*) go; walk; leave; TECH work (*a. fig*); ECON sell; *fig* last; **einkaufen (schwimmen) gehen** go shopping (swimming); **gehen wir!** let's go!; **wie geht es dir (Ihnen)?** how are you?; **es geht mir gut (schlecht)** I'm fine (not feeling well); **gehen in** (*acc*) go into

gehen nach *road etc*: lead to; *window etc*: face; *fig* go or judge by; **das geht nicht** that's impossible; **das geht schon** that's o.k.; **es geht nichts über** (*acc*) ... there is nothing like ...; **worum geht es?** what is it about?; **darum geht es (nicht)** that's (not) the point; **sich gehen nach lassen** let s.o. go

'**gehenlassen** *v/refl* (*irr*, **lassen**, *sep*, *no -ge-*, *h*) → **gehen**

geheuer [gə'hɔyɐ] *adj*: **nicht (ganz) geheuer** eerie, creepy, F fishy

Geheul [gə'hɔyl] *n* (-[e]s; *no pl*) howling

Ge'hirn *n* (-[e]s; *-e*) ANAT brain(s)

Gehirnerschütterung *f* MED concussion (of the brain)

Gehirnschlag *m* MED (cerebral) apoplexy

Gehirnwäsche *f* brainwashing

gehoben [gə'hoːbən] **1.** *pp of* **heben**; **2.** *adj* elevated; high(er); **gehobene Stimmung** high spirits

Gehöft [gə'hœft] *n* (-[e]s; *-e*) farm(stead)

geholfen [gə'hɔlfən] *pp of* **helfen**

Gehölz [gə'hœlts] *n* (-es; *-e*) wood, copse, copse

Gehör [gə'hoːɐ] *n* (-[e]s; *-e*) (sense of) hearing; ear; **nach dem Gehör** by ear; **sich Gehör verschaffen** make o.s. heard

ge'horchen *v/i* (*no -ge-*, *h*) obey; **nicht gehorchen** disobey

ge'hören *v/i* (*no -ge-*, *h*) belong (*dat or zu* to); **gehört dir das?** is this yours?; **es gehört sich (nicht)** it is proper or right (not done); **das gehört nicht hierher** that's not to the point

ge'hörig **1.** *adj* due, proper; necessary; decent; **zu et. gehörig** belonging to s.th.; **2.** *adv* properly, thoroughly

ge'hörlos *adj* deaf; **die Gehörlosen** the deaf

gehorsam [gə'hoːɐzaːm] *adj* obedient

Ge'horsam *m* (-s; *no pl*) obedience

'**Gehsteig** *m*, '**Gehweg** *m* sidewalk, *Br* pavement

Geier ['gaiɐ] *m* (-s; -) ZO vulture, buzzard

Geige ['gaigə] *f* (-; *-n*) MUS violin, F fiddle; (**auf der**) **Geige spielen** play (on) the violin

'**Geigenbogen** *m* MUS (violin) bow

Geigenkasten *m* MUS violin case

'**Geiger** ['gaigɐ] *m* (-s; -), **Geigerin** ['gai-gərin] *f* (-; -nen) MUS violinist

'**Geigerzähler** *m* PHYS Geiger counter

geil [gail] *adj* V hot, horny; *contp* lecherous, lewd; BOT rank; F awesome; *Br* brill, ace

Geisel ['gaizəl] *f* (-; -n) hostage

Geiselnehmer [-ne:mɐ] *m* (-s; -) kidnap-(p)er

Geißel ['gaisəl] *fig f* (-; -n) scourge

Geist [gaist] *m* (-[e]s; -er) a) (no pl) spirit; soul; mind; intellect; wit, b) ghost; *der Heilige Geist* REL the Holy Ghost or Spirit

Geisterbahn ['gaistɐ-] *f* tunnel of horror, *Br* ghost train

Geisterfahrer F *m* MOT wrong-way driver

'**geisterhaft** *adj* ghostly

'**geistesabwesend** *adj* absent-minded

'**Geistesarbeiter** *m* brainworker

'**Geistesblitz** *m* brainstorm, *Br* brainwave

'**Geistesgegenwart** *f* presence of mind

'**geistesgegenwärtig** *adj* alert; quick-witted

'**geistesgestört** *adj* mentally disturbed, deranged

'**geisteskrank** *adj* mentally ill

'**Geisteskrankheit** *f* mental illness

'**geistesschwach** *adj* feeble-minded

'**Geisteswissenschaften** *pl* the arts, the humanities

'**Geisteszustand** *m* mental state

geistig ['gaistiç] *adj* mental; intellectual; spiritual; *geistig behindert* mentally handicapped; *geistige Getränke* spirits

'**geistlich** *adj* religious; spiritual; ecclesiastical; clerical

'**Geistliche** (-n; -n) clergyman; priest; minister; *die Geistlichen* the clergy

'**geistlos** *adj* trivial, inane, silly

'**geistreich, 'geistvoll** *adj* witty, clever

Geiz [gaits] *m* (-es; no pl) stinginess

'**Geizhals** *m* miser, niggard

geizig ['gaitsiç] *adj* stingy, miserly

Ge'jammer F *n* (-s; no pl) wailing, complaining

gekannt [gə'kant] *pp of* **kennen**

Ge'kläff F *n* (-[e]s; no pl) yapping

Ge'klapper [gə'klapɐ] F *n* (-s; no pl) clatter(ing)

Ge'klimper F *n* (-s; no pl) tinkling

geklungen [gə'kluŋən] *pp of* **klingen**

gekniffen [gə'knifən] *pp of* **kneifen**

ge'kommen *pp of* **kommen**

gekonnt [gə'kɔnt] **1.** *pp of* **können**; **2.** *adj* masterly

gekränkt [gə'krɛŋkt] *adj* hurt, offended

Gekritzel [gə'kritsəl] *contp n* (-s; no pl) scrawl, scribble

gekrochen [gə'krɔxən] *pp of* **kriechen**

gekünstelt [gə'kynstəlt] *adj* affected; artificial

Gelächter [gə'lɛçtɐ] *n* (-s; no pl) laughter

ge'laden *pp of* **laden**

Ge'lage *n* (-s; -) feast; carouse

Gelände [gə'lɛndə] *n* (-s; -) area, country, ground; site; *auf dem Gelände* on the premises; *Gelände... in cpds ...lauf, ...ritt, ...wagen etc*: cross-country ...

Geländer [gə'lɛndɐ] *n* (-s; -) banisters; handrail, rail(ing); parapet

ge'lang *pret of* **gelingen**

ge'langen *v/i* (no -ge-, sein) **gelangen an** (acc) or **nach** reach, arrive at, get or come to; **gelangen in** (acc) get or come into; *fig* **zu et. gelangen** gain or win or achieve s.th.

ge'lassen 1. *pp of* **lassen**; **2.** *adj* calm, composed, cool

Gelatine [ʒela'ti:nə] *f* (-; no pl) gelatin(e)

ge'laufen *pp of* **laufen**

ge'läufig *adj* common, current; familiar

gelaunt [gə'launt] *adj*: **schlecht** (**gut**) **gelaunt sein** be in a bad (good) mood

gelb [gɛlp] *adj* yellow

'**gelblich** *adj* yellowish

'**Gelbsucht** *f* (-; no pl) MED jaundice

Geld [gɛlt] *n* (-[e]s; -er ['gɛldɐ]) money; *zu Geld machen* turn into cash

'**Geldangelegenheiten** *pl* money or financial matters or affairs

'**Geldanlage** *f* investment

'**Geldausgabe** *f* expense

'**Geldauto,mat** *m* automatic teller machine, ATM, autoteller, *Br* cash dispenser

'**Geldbeutel** *m*, **Geldbörse** *f* purse

'**Geldbuße** *f* fine, penalty

Geldgeber(in) [-ge:bɐ (-bərin)] (-s; -/-; -nen) financial backer; investor

'**geldgierig** *adj* greedy for money

'**Geldknappheit** *f*, **Geldmangel** *m* lack of money; ECON (financial) stringency

'**Geldmittel** *pl* funds, means, resources

Geldschein *m* bill, *Br* (bank)note

'**Geldschrank** *m* safe

'**Geldsendung** *f* remittance

'**Geldstrafe** *f* fine

'**Geldstück** *n* coin

'**Geldverlegenheit** *f* financial embarrassment

'**Geldverschwendung** *f* waste of money

'**Geldwaschanlage** *f* money laundering scheme

'**Geldwechsel** *m* exchange of money

Geldwechsler [-vɛkslə] *m* (-s; -) change machine

Gelee [ʒeˈleː] *n*, *m* (-s; -s) jelly; gel

ge'legen 1. *pp of* **liegen**; **2.** *adj* situated, located; *fig* convenient, opportune

Ge'legenheit *f* (-; -en) occasion; opportunity, chance; *bei Gelegenheit* on occasion

Ge'legenheitsarbeit *f* casual *or* odd job

Gelegenheitsarbeiter *m* casual labo(u)rer, odd-job man

Gelegenheitskauf *m* bargain

gelegentlich [gəˈleːgəntlɪç] *adv* occasionally

gelehrig [gəˈleːrɪç] *adj* docile

Gelehrsamkeit [gəˈleːɐzaːmkait] *f* (-; no *pl*) learning

gelehrt [gəˈleːɐt] *adj* learned

Ge'lehrte *m*, *f* (-n; -n) scholar, learned man *or* woman

Geleise [gəˈlaizə] *n* → **Gleis**

Geleit [gəˈlait] *n* (-[e]s; -e) escort

ge'leiten *v/t* (*no* -ge-, h) accompany, conduct, escort

Ge'leitzug *m* MAR, MIL convoy

Gelenk [gəˈlɛŋk] *n* (-[e]s; -e) ANAT, TECH joint

ge'lenkig *adj* flexible (*a.* TECH); lithe, supple

gelernt [gəˈlɛrnt] *adj* skilled, trained

ge'lesen *pp of* **lesen**

geliebt [gəˈliːpt] *adj* (be)loved, dear

Ge'liebte 1. *m* (-n; -n) lover; **2.** *f* (-n; -n) mistress

geliehen [gəˈliːən] *pp of* **leihen**

gelingen [gəˈlɪŋən] *v/i* (*irr*, *no* -ge-, sein) succeed, manage; turn out well; *es gelang mir, et. zu tun* I succeeded in doing (I managed to do) s.th.

Ge'lingen *n* (-s; no *pl*) success; *gutes Gelingen!* good luck!

gelitten [gəˈlɪtən] *pp of* **leiden**

gelogen [gəˈloːgən] *pp of* **lügen**

gelten [ˈgɛltən] *v/i and v/t* (*irr*, -ge-, h) be worth; *fig* count for; be valid; SPORT count; ECON be effective; *gelten für* apply to; *gelten als* be regarded *or* looked upon as, be considered *or* supposed to be; *gelten lassen* accept (*als* as)

geltend *adj* accepted; *geltend machen* assert; *s-n Einfluss (bei j-m) geltend machen* bring one's influence to bear (on s.o.)

'Geltung *f* (-; no *pl*) prestige; weight; *zur Geltung kommen* show to advantage

'Geltungsbedürfnis *n* (-ses; no *pl*) need for recognition

Gelübde [gəˈlypdə] *n* (-s; -) vow

gelungen [gəˈlʊŋən] **1.** *pp of* **gelingen**; **2.**

adj successful, a success

gemächlich [gəˈmɛːçlɪç] *adj* leisurely

ge'mahlen *pp of* **mahlen**

Gemälde [gəˈmɛːldə] *n* (-s; -) painting, picture

Gemäldegale,rie *f* art (*or* picture) gallery

gemäß [gəˈmɛːs] *prp* (*dat*) according to

gemäßigt [gəˈmɛːsɪçt] *adj* moderate; temperate (*climate etc*)

gemein [gəˈmain] *adj* mean; dirty, filthy (*joke etc*); BOT, ZO common

Gemeinde [gəˈmaində] *f* (-; -n) POL municipality; local government; REL parish; congregation

Gemeinderat *m* (member of the) city (*Br* local) council

Gemeinderätin [-rɛːtɪn] *f* (-; -nen) member of the city (*Br* local) council

Gemeindesteuern *pl* local taxes, *Br* (local) rates

ge'meingefährlich *adj:* **gemeingefährlicher Mensch** public enemy

Ge'meinheit *f* (-; -en) a) (no *pl*) meanness, b) mean thing (to do *or* say), F dirty trick

ge'meinnützig [-nʏtsɪç] *adj* non-profit, *Br* non-profitmaking

Ge'meinplatz *m* commonplace

ge'meinsam 1. *adj* common, joint; mutual; **2.** *adv* together

Ge'meinschaft *f* (-; -en) community

Ge'meinschaftsarbeit *f* teamwork

Gemeinschaftskunde *f* (-; no *pl*) PED social studies

Gemeinschaftsproduktion *f* coproduction

Gemeinschaftsraum *m* recreation room, lounge

Ge'meinsinn *m* (-[e]s; no *pl*) public spirit; (sense of) solidarity

ge'meinverständlich *adj* popular

Ge'meinwohl *n* public welfare

ge'messen 1. *pp of* **messen**; **2.** *adj* measured; formal; grave

Gemetzel [gəˈmɛtsəl] *n* (-s; -) slaughter, massacre

gemieden [gəˈmiːdən] *pp of* **meiden**

Gemisch [gəˈmɪʃ] *n* (-[e]s; -e) mixture (*a.* CHEM)

gemocht [gəˈmɔxt] *pp of* **mögen**

gemolken [gəˈmɔlkən] *pp of* **melken**

Gemse → **Gämse**

Gemurmel [gəˈmʊrməl] *n* (-s; no *pl*) murmur, mutter

Gemüse [gəˈmyːzə] *n* (-s; -) vegetable(s); greens

Gemüsehändler *m* greengrocer('s)

gemusst [gəˈmʊst] *pp of* **müssen**

Gemüt [gəˈmyːt] *n* (-[e]s; -er) mind, soul; heart; nature, mentality ge'mütlich *adj* comfortable, snug, cozy, *Br* cosy; peaceful, pleasant, relaxed; **mach es dir gemütlich** make yourself at home

Ge'mütlichkeit *f (-; no pl)* snugness, coziness, *Br* cosiness; cozy (*Br* cosy) *or* relaxed atmosphere

Ge'mütsbewegung *f* emotion

ge'mütskrank *adj* emotionally disturbed

Ge'mütszustand *m* state of mind

Gen [ge:n] *n (-s; -e)* BIOL gene

genannt [gə'nant] *pp of* **nennen**

genas [gə'naːs] *pret of* **genesen** 1

genau [gə'nau] **1.** *adj* exact, precise, accurate; careful, close; strict; **Genaueres** further details; **2.** *adv*: **genau um 10 Uhr** at 10 o'clock sharp; **genau der ...** that very ...; **genau zuhören** listen closely; **es genau nehmen (mit et.)** be particular (about s.th.)

Ge'nauigkeit *f (-; no pl)* accuracy, precision, exactness

ge'nauso *adv* → **ebenso**

genehmigen [gə'ne:mɪɡən] *v/t (no -ge-, h)* permit, allow; approve

Ge'nehmigung *f (-; -en)* permission; approval; permit; licen|se, *Br* -ce

geneigt [gə'naikt] *adj* inclined (**zu** to)

General [genə'ra:l] *m (-s; Generäle* [genə're:lə]) MIL general

Generaldi,rektor *m* ECON president, *Br* chairman

Generalkonsul *m* consul general

Generalkonsu,lat *n* consulate general

Generalprobe *f* THEA dress rehearsal

Generalsekre,tär *m* secretary-general

Generalstab *m* MIL general staff

Generalstreik *m* general strike

Generalversammlung *f* general meeting

Generalvertreter *m* ECON sole agent

Generation [genəra'tsjo:n] *f (-; -en)* generation

Generati'onenkon,flikt *m* generation gap

Generator [genə'ra:to:ɐ] *m (-s; -en* [-ra'to:rən]) ELECTR generator

generell [genə'rɛl] *adj* general, universal

genesen [gə'ne:zən] **1.** *v/i (irr, no -ge-, sein)* recover (**von** from), get well; **2.** *pp of* **genesen** 1

Ge'nesung *f (-; no pl)* recovery

Genetik [ge'ne:tɪk] *f (-; no pl)* BIOL genetics

ge'netisch *adj* BIOL genetic; **genetischer Fingerabdruck** genetic fingerprint

genial [ge'nja:l] *adj* brilliant, of genius

Genialität [genjali'tɛ:t] *f (-; no pl)* genius

Genick [gə'nɪk] *n (-[e]s; -e)* ANAT (back or nape of) neck

Genie [ʒe'ni:] *n (-s; -s)* genius

genieren [ʒe'ni:rən] *v/refl (no -ge-, h)* be embarrassed

genießen [gə'ni:sən] *v/t (irr, no -ge-, h)* enjoy

Genießer [gə'ni:sɐ] *m (-s; -)* gourmet

Genitiv ['ge:niti:f] *m (-s; -e)* LING genitive *or* possessive (case)

genommen [gə'nɔmən] *pp of* **nehmen**

genormt [gə'nɔrmt] *adj* standardized

genoss [gə'nɔs] *pret of* **genießen**

Genosse [gə'nɔsə] *m (-n; -n)* POL comrade; F pal, buddy, *Br* mate

genossen [gə'nɔsən] *pp of* **genießen**

Ge'nossenschaft *f (-; -en)* cooperative

Ge'nossin *f (-; -nen)* POL comrade

'Gentechnik *f,* 'Gentechnolo,gie *f* genetic engineering

genug [gə'nu:k] *adj* enough, sufficient

Genüge [gə'ny:gə] *f*: **zur Genüge** (well) enough, sufficiently

ge'nügen *v/i (no -ge-, h)* be enough, be sufficient; **das genügt** that will do

genügend *adj* enough, sufficient; plenty of

genügsam [gə'ny:kza:m] *adj* easily satisfied; frugal; modest

Ge'nügsamkeit *f (-; no pl)* modesty; frugality

Ge'nugtuung *f (-; no pl)* satisfaction

Genus ['ge:nʊs] *n (-; Genera* ['ge:nera]) LING gender

Genuss [gə'nʊs] *m (-es; Genüsse* [gə'nʏsə]) a) pleasure, b) (*no pl*) consumption; **ein Genuss** a real treat; *food:* a. delicious

Genussmittel *n* excise item, *Br* (semi-) luxury

Geografie, Geographie [geogra'fi:] *f (-; no pl)* geography

geografisch, geographisch [geo'gra:fɪʃ] *adj* geographic(al)

Geologe [geolo'ɡə] *m (-n; -n)* geologist

Geologie [geolo'gi:] *f (-; no pl)* geology

Geo'login *f (-; -nen)* geologist

geologisch [geo'lo:gɪʃ] *adj* geologic(al)

Geometrie [geome'tri:] *f (-; no pl)* geometry

geometrisch [geo'me:trɪʃ] *adj* geometric(al)

Gepäck [gə'pɛk] *n (-[e]s; no pl)* baggage, luggage

Gepäckablage *f* baggage (or luggage) rack

Gepäckaufbewahrung *f* baggage room, *Br* left-luggage office

Gepäckkon,trolle *f* baggage check, *Br* luggage inspection

Gepäckschalter *m* baggage (or luggage) counter

Gepäckschein *m* baggage check, *Br* luggage ticket

Gepäckträger *m* porter; *bicycle:* carrier

gepanzert [gə'pantsɐt] *adj* MOT armo(u)red

Gepard [ge'part] *m* (-s, -e) ZO cheetah

gepfiffen [gə'pfɪfən] *pp of* **pfeifen**

gepflegt [gə'pfleːkt] *adj* well-groomed, neat; *fig* cultivated

Gepflogenheit [gə'pfloːɡənhaɪt] *f* (-; -en) habit, custom

Geplapper [gə'plapɐ] F *n* (-s; *no pl*) babbling, chatter(ing)

Geplauder [gə'plaudɐ] *n* (-s; *no pl*) chat (-ting)

Gepolter [gə'pɔltɐ] *n* (-s; *no pl*) rumble

gepriesen [gə'priːzən] *pp of* **preisen**

Gequassel [gə'kvasəl] F *n* (-s; *no pl*), **Gequatsche** [gə'kvatʃə] F *n* (-s; *no pl*) blather, blabber

gequollen [gə'kvɔlən] *pp of* **quellen**

gerade [gə'raːdə] **1.** *adj* straight (*a. fig*); even (*number*); direct; upright, erect (*posture*); **2.** *adv* just; *nicht gerade* not exactly; *das ist es ja gerade!* that's just it!; *gerade deshalb* that's just why; *gerade rechtzeitig* just in time; *warum gerade ich?* why me of all people?; *da wir gerade von ... sprechen* speaking of ...

Ge'rade *f* (-n; -n) MATH (straight) line; SPORT straight; *linke* (*rechte*) *Gerade* boxing: straight left (right)

gerade'aus *adv* straight on *or* ahead

gerade'raus *adj* straightforward, frank

ge'radestehen *v/i* (*irr,* **stehen,** *sep, -ge-,* h) stand straight; *geradestehen für* answer for

ge'radewegs *adv* straight, directly

ge'radezu *adv* simply

gerannt [gə'rant] *pp of* **rennen**

Gerät [gə'rɛːt] *n* (-[e]s; -e) device; F gadget; appliance; (kitchen) utensil; *radio,* TV set; *coll, a.* STEREO *etc* equipment; SPORT apparatus; TECH tool; instrument

ge'raten 1. *pp of* **raten; 2.** *v/i* (*irr,* **raten,** *no -ge-, sein*) turn out (*gut* well); *geraten an* (*acc*) come across; *geraten in* (*acc*) get into; *in Brand geraten* catch fire

Ge'räteturnen *n* apparatus gymnastics

Ge'ratewohl *n:* **aufs Geratewohl** at random

geräumig [gə'rɔʏmɪç] *adj* spacious, roomy

Geräusch [gə'rɔʏʃ] *n* (-[e]s; -e) sound, noise

ge'räuschlos 1. *adj* noiseless (*a.* TECH); **2.** *adv* without a sound

ge'räuschvoll *adj* noisy

gerben ['ɡɛrbən] *v/t* (*ge-,* h) tan

Gerberei [ɡɛrbə'raɪ] *f* (-; -en) tannery

ge'recht *adj* just, fair; (*j-m, e-r Sache*) *gerecht werden* do justice to; meet (*demands etc*)

Ge'rechtigkeit *f* (-; *no pl*) justice

Ge'rede F *n* (-s; *no pl*) talk; gossip

gereizt [gə'raɪtst] *adj* irritable

Ge'reiztheit *f* (-; *no pl*) irritability

Gericht¹ [gə'rɪçt] *n* (-[e]s; -e) GASTR dish

Ge'richt² *n* (-[e]s; -e) JUR court; *vor Gericht stehen* (*stellen*) stand (bring) to trial; *vor Gericht gehen* go to court

ge'richtlich *adj* JUR judicial, legal

Ge'richtsbarkeit *f* (-; *no pl*) JUR jurisdiction

Ge'richtsgebäude *n* JUR law court(s), courthouse

Gerichtshof *m* JUR law court

Gerichtsmedi,zin *f* JUR forensic medicine

Gerichtssaal *m* JUR courtroom

Gerichtsverfahren *n* JUR lawsuit

Gerichtsverhandlung *f* JUR hearing; trial

Gerichtsvollzieher [-fɔltsiːɐ] *m* (-s; -) JUR marshal, *Br* bailiff

gerieben [gə'riːbən] *pp of* **reiben**

gering [gə'rɪŋ] *adj* little, small; slight, minor; low; *gering schätzen* think little of

ge'ringfügig *adj* slight, minor; petty

ge'ringschätzen *v/t* (*sep, -ge-,* h) → **geringschätzen**

geringschätzig [-ʃɛtsɪç] *adj* contemptuous

ge'ringst *adj* least; *nicht im Geringsten* not in the least

ge'rinnen *v/i* (*irr,* **rinnen,** *no -ge-, sein*) coagulate; curdle; clot

Ge'rippe *n* (-s; -) skeleton (*a. fig*); TECH framework

gerissen [gə'rɪsən] **1.** *pp of* **reißen; 2.** F *adj* cunning, smart

geritten [gə'rɪtən] *pp of* **reiten**

germanisch [ɡɛr'maːnɪʃ] *adj* Germanic

Germanist(in) [ɡɛrma'nɪst(ɪn)] (-en; -en/-; -nen) student of (*or* graduate in) German

gern [ɡɛrn] *adv* willingly, gladly; *et.* (*sehr*) *gern tun* like (love) to do s.th. *or* doing s.th.; *ich möchte gern* I'd like (to); *gern geschehen!* not at all, (you're) welcome

gernhaben *v/t* (*irr,* **haben,** *sep, -ge-,* h) like, be fond of;

gerochen [gə'rɔxən] *pp of* **riechen**

Geröll [gə'rœl] *n* (-[e]s; -e) scree; boulders

geronnen [gə'rɔnən] *pp of* **rinnen**

Gerste ['ɡɛrstə] *f* (-; -n) BOT barley

'Gerstenkorn *n* MED sty(e)

Gerte ['ɡɛrtə] *f* (-; -n) switch, rod, twig

Geruch [gə'rʊx] *m* (-[e]s; *Gerüche* [gə-'ryçə]) smell; odo(u)r; scent

ge'ruchlos adj odo(u)rless
Ge'ruchssinn m (sense of) smell
Gerücht [gə'rɣçt] n (-[e]s; -e) rumo(u)r
ge'rufen pp of **rufen**
gerührt [gə'ryːɐt] adj touched, moved
Gerümpel [gə'rɣmpəl] n (-s; no pl) lumber, junk
Gerundium [ge'rʊndiʊm] n (-s; -ien) LING gerund
gerungen [gə'rʊŋən] pp of **ringen**
Gerüst [gə'rɣst] n (-[e]s; -e) frame(-work); scaffold(ing); stage
ge'salzen pp of **salzen**
gesamt [gə'zamt] adj whole, entire, total, all
Ge'samt... in cpds ...ergebnis etc: mst total ...
Gesamtausgabe f complete edition
Gesamtschule f comprehensive school
gesandt [gə'zant] pp of **senden**
Gesandte [gə'zantə] m, f (-n; -n) POL envoy
Ge'sandtschaft f (-; -en) legation, mission
Gesang [gə'zaŋ] m (-[e]s; Gesänge [gə-'zɛŋə]) singing; song; voice
Gesangbuch n REL hymn book
Gesang(s)lehrer(in) singing teacher
Gesangverein m choral society, glee club
Gesäß [gə'zɛːs] n (-es; -e) ANAT buttocks, bottom
ge'schaffen pp of **schaffen¹**
Geschäft [gə'ʃɛft] n (-[e]s; -e) business; store, Br shop; bargain
ge'schäftig adj busy, active
Ge'schäftigkeit f (-; no pl) activity
ge'schäftlich 1. adj business ...; commercial; 2. adv on business
Ge'schäftsbrief m business letter
Geschäftsfrau f businesswoman
Geschäftsfreund m business friend
Geschäftsführer m manager
Geschäftsführung f management
Geschäftsinhaber m proprietor
Geschäftsmann m businessman
ge'schäftsmäßig adj businesslike
Ge'schäftsordnung f PARL standing orders; rules (of procedure)
Geschäftspartner m (business) partner
Geschäftsräume pl (business) premises
Geschäftsreise f business trip
Geschäftsschluss m closing time; nach Geschäftsschluss a. after business hours
Geschäftsstelle f office
Geschäftsstraße f shopping street
Geschäftsträger m POL chargé d'affaires
'**ge'schäftstüchtig** adj efficient, smart
Ge'schäftsverbindung f business connection

Geschäftsviertel n commercial district; downtown
Geschäftszeit f office or business hours
Geschäftszweig m branch or line (of business)
geschah [gə'ʃaː] pret of **geschehen** 1
geschehen [gə'ʃeːən] 1. v/i (irr, no -ge-, sein) happen, occur, take place; be done; **es geschieht ihm recht** it serves him right; 2. pp of **geschehen** 1
gescheit [gə'ʃait] adj clever, bright, F brainy
Geschenk [gə'ʃɛŋk] n (-[e]s; -e) present, gift
Geschenkpackung f gift box
Geschichte [gə'ʃɪçtə] f (-; -n) a) story, b) (no pl) history, c) F business, thing
ge'schichtlich adj historical
Ge'schichtsschreiber m (-s; -), Geschichtswissenschaftler m historian
Geschick [gə'ʃɪk] n (-[e]s; -e) fate, destiny; → **Ge'schicklichkeit** f (-; no pl) skill; dexterity
ge'schickt adj skil(l)ful, skilled; dext(e)rous; clever
geschieden [gə'ʃiːdən] 1. pp of **scheiden**; 2. adj divorced, marriage: dissolved
geschienen [gə'ʃiːnən] pp of **scheinen**
Geschirr [gə'ʃɪr] n (-[e]s; -e) a) dishes, china, b) (no pl) kitchen utensils, pots and pans, crockery, c) harness; **Geschirr spülen** wash or do the dishes
Ge'schirrspüler m (-s; -) dishwasher
geschissen [gə'ʃɪsən] pp of **scheißen**
ge'schlafen pp of **schlafen**
ge'schlagen pp of **schlagen**
Geschlecht [gə'ʃlɛçt] n (-[e]s; -er) a) (no pl) sex, b) kind, species, c) family, line (-age); generation, d) LING gender
Ge'schlechtskrankheit f MED venereal disease
Geschlechtsreife f puberty
Geschlechtsteile pl genitals
Geschlechtstrieb m sexual instinct or urge
Geschlechtsverkehr m (sexual) intercourse
Geschlechtswort n LING article
geschlichen [gə'ʃlɪçən] pp of **schleichen**
geschliffen [gə'ʃlɪfən] 1. pp of **schleifen²**; 2. adj cut; fig polished
geschlossen [gə'ʃlɔsən] 1. pp of **schließen**; 2. adj closed
geschlungen [gə'ʃlʊŋən] pp of **schlingen**
Geschmack [gə'ʃmak] m (-[e]s; Geschmäcke [gə'ʃmɛkə]) taste (a. fig); flavo(u)r; **Geschmack finden an** (dat) de-

velop a taste for

Ge'schmacklos *adj a. fig* tasteless

Ge'schmacklosigkeit *f (-; no pl)* tastelessness; **das war e-e Geschmacklosigkeit** that was in bad taste

Ge'schmack(s-)sache *f* matter of taste

ge'schmackvoll *adj* tasteful, in good taste

geschmeidig [gə'ʃmaidɪç] *adj* supple, pliant

geschmissen [gə'ʃmɪsən] *pp of* **schmeißen**

geschmolzen [gə'ʃmɔltsən] *pp of* **schmelzen**

geschnitten [gə'ʃnɪtən] *pp of* **schneiden**

geschoben [gə'ʃoːbən] *pp of* **schieben**

Geschöpf [gə'ʃœpf] *n (-[e]s; -e)* creature

geschoren [gə'ʃoːrən] *pp of* **scheren**

Geschoss [gə'ʃɔs] *n (-es; -e)*, Geschoß [gə'ʃoːs] *Austrian n (-es; -e)* projectile, missile; stor(e)y, floor

ge'schossen *pp of* **schießen**

Ge'schrei F *n (-s; no pl)* shouting, yelling; screams; crying; *fig* fuss

geschrieben [gə'ʃriːbən] *pp of* **schreiben**

geschrie(e)n [gə'ʃriː(ə)n] *pp of* **schreien**

geschritten [gə'ʃrɪtən] *pp of* **schreiten**

geschunden [gə'ʃʊndən] *pp of* **schinden**

Geschütz [gə'ʃʏts] *n (-es; -e)* MIL gun, cannon

Geschwader [gə'ʃvaːdɐ] *n (-s; -)* MIL MAR squadron; AVIAT group, *Br* wing

Geschwätz [gə'ʃvɛts] F *n (-es; no pl)* chatter, babble; gossip; *fig* nonsense

ge'schwätzig *adj* talkative; gossipy

geschweige [gə'ʃvaigə] *cj:* **geschweige (denn)** let alone

geschwiegen [gə'ʃviːgən] *pp of* **schweigen**

geschwind [gə'ʃvɪnt] *adj* quick, swift

Geschwindigkeit [gə'ʃvɪndɪçkait] *f (-; -en)* speed; fastness, quickness; PHYS velocity; **mit e-r Geschwindigkeit von ...** at a speed *or* rate of ...

Ge'schwindigkeitsbegrenzung *f* speed limit

Geschwindigkeitsüberschreitung *f* MOT speeding

Geschwister [gə'ʃvɪstɐ] *pl* brother(s) and sister(s); JUR siblings

geschwollen [gə'ʃvɔlən] **1.** *pp of* **schwellen**; **2.** *adj* MED swollen; *fig* bombastic, pretentious, pompous

geschwommen [gə'ʃvɔmən] *pp of* **schwimmen**

geschworen [gə'ʃvoːrən] *pp of* **schwören**

Ge'schworene *m, f (-n; -n)* member of a

jury; **die Geschworenen** the jury

Geschwulst [gə'ʃvʊlst] *f (-; Geschwülste* [gə'ʃvʏlstə])* MED growth, tumo(u)r

geschwunden [gə'ʃvʊndən] *pp of* **schwinden**

geschwungen [gə'ʃvʊŋən] *pp of* **schwingen**

Geschwür [gə'ʃvyːɐ] *n (-s; -e)* MED abscess, ulcer

ge'sehen *pp of* **sehen**

Geselchte [gə'zɛlçtə] *Austrian n (-n; no pl)* GASTR smoked meat

Geselle [gə'zɛlə] *m (-n; -n)* journeyman

ge'sellen *v/refl (no -ge-, h)* **sich zu j-m gesellen** join s.o.

ge'sellig *adj* sociable; ZO *etc* social; **geselliges Beisammensein** get-together

Ge'sellin *f (-; -nen)* trained woman *hairdresser etc*, journeywoman

Gesellschaft [gə'zɛlʃaft] *f (-; -en)* society; company; party; ECON company, corporation; **j-m Gesellschaft leisten** keep s.o. company

ge'sellschaftlich *adj* social

Ge'sellschafts... in *cpds* ...kritik, ...ordnung *etc*: social ...

Gesellschaftsreise *f* group tour

Gesellschaftsspiel *n* parlo(u)r game

Gesellschaftstanz *m* ballroom dance

gesessen [gə'zɛsən] *pp of* **sitzen**

Gesetz [gə'zɛts] *n (-es; -e)* JUR law; act

Gesetzbuch *n* JUR code (of law)

Gesetzentwurf *m* PARL bill

ge'setzgebend *adj* JUR legislative

Ge'setzgeber *m (-s; -)* JUR legislator

Ge'setzgebung *f (-; -en)* JUR legislation

ge'setzlich **1.** *adj* legal; lawful; **2.** *adv:* **gesetzlich geschützt** JUR patented, registered

ge'setzlos *adj* lawless

ge'setzmäßig *adj* legal, lawful

gesetzt [gə'zɛtst] **1.** *adj* staid, dignified; mature *(age)*; **2.** *cj:* **gesetzt den Fall(, dass) ...** supposing (that)

ge'setzwidrig *adj* illegal, unlawful

Gesicht [gə'zɪçt] *n (-[e]s; -er)* face; **zu Gesicht bekommen** catch sight of

Ge'sichtsausdruck *m* look, expression

Gesichtfarbe *f* complexion

Gesichtpunkt *m* point of view, aspect, angle

Gesichtzug *m* feature

Gesindel [gə'zɪndəl] *n (-s; no pl)* trash, the riff-raff

gesinnt [gə'zɪnt] *adj* minded; **j-m feindlich gesinnt sein** be ill-disposed towards s.o.

Ge'sinnung *f (-; -en)* mind; attitude; POL conviction(s)

ge'sinnungslos *adj* unprincipled
ge'sinnungstreu *adj* loyal
Ge'sinnungswechsel *m* about-face, *Br* about-turn
gesittet [gə'zɪtət] *adj* civilized, well-mannered
gesoffen [gə'zɔfən] *pp of* **saufen**
gesogen [gə'zo:gən] *pp of* **saugen**
gesotten [gə'zɔtən] *pp of* **sieden**
gespalten [gə'ʃpaltən] *pp of* **spalten**
Gespann [gə'ʃpan] *n* (-[e]s; -e) team (*a. fig*)
gespannt [gə'ʃpant] *adj* tense (*a. fig*); **gespannt sein auf** (acc) be anxious to see; **ich bin gespannt, ob** (**wie**) I wonder if (how)
Gespenst [gə'ʃpɛnst] *n* (-[e]s; -er) ghost, apparition, *esp fig* specter, *Br* spectre
ge'spenstisch *adj* ghostly, F spooky
gespie(e)n [gə'ʃpi:(ə)n] *pp of* **speien**
Gespinst [gə'ʃpɪnst] *n* (-[e]s; -e) web, tissue (*both a. fig*)
gesponnen [gə'ʃpɔnən] *pp of* **spinnen**
Gespött [gə'ʃpœt] *n* (-[e]s; *no pl*) mockery, ridicule; **j-n zum Gespött machen** make a laughingstock of s.o.
Gespräch [gə'ʃprɛ:ç] *n* (-[e]s; -e) talk (*a.* POL), conversation; TEL call
ge'sprächig *adj* talkative
gesprochen [gə'ʃprɔxən] *pp of* **sprechen**
gesprossen [gə'ʃprɔsən] *pp of* **sprießen**
gesprungen [gə'ʃpruŋən] *pp of* **springen**
Gespür [gə'ʃpy:r] *n* (-s; *no pl*) flair, nose
Gestalt [gə'ʃtalt] *f* (-; -en) shape, form; figure
ge'stalten *v/t* (*no -ge-, h*) arrange; design
Ge'staltung *f* (-; -en) arrangement; design; decoration
gestanden [gə'ʃtandən] *pp of* **stehen**
ge'ständig *adj*: **geständig sein** confess; have confessed
Geständnis [gə'ʃtɛntnɪs] *n* (-ses; -se) confession (*a. fig*)
Gestank [gə'ʃtaŋk] *m* (-[e]s; *no pl*) stench, stink
gestatten [gə'ʃtatən] *v/t* (*no -ge-, h*) allow, permit
Geste ['gɛstə] *f* (-; -n) gesture (*a. fig*)
ge'stehen *v/t and v/i* (*irr,* **stehen**, *no -ge-, h*) confess
Ge'stein *n* (-[e]s; -e) rock, stone
Gestell [gə'ʃtɛl] *n* (-[e]s; -e) stand, base, pedestal; shelves; frame
gestern ['gɛstən] *adv* yesterday; **gestern Abend** last night
gestiegen [gə'ʃti:gən] *pp of* **steigen**
gestochen [gə'ʃtɔxən] *pp of* **stechen**
gestohlen [gə'ʃto:lən] *pp of* **stehlen**

gestorben [gə'ʃtɔrbən] *pp of* **sterben**
ge'stoßen *pp of* **stoßen**
gestreift [gə'ʃtraift] *adj* striped
gestrichen [gə'ʃtrɪçən] *pp of* **streichen**
gestrig ['gɛstrɪç] *adj* yesterday's, of yesterday
gestritten [gə'ʃtrɪtən] *pp of* **streiten**
Gestrüpp [gə'ʃtryp] *n* (-[e]s; -e) brushwood, undergrowth; *fig* jungle, maze
gestunken [gə'ʃtuŋkən] *pp of* **stinken**
Gestüt [gə'ʃty:t] *n* (-[e]s; -e) stud
Gesuch [gə'zu:x] *n* (-[e]s; -e) application, request
gesund [gə'zunt] *adj* healthy; healthful, *fig a.* sound; **gesunder Menschenverstand** common sense; (**wieder**) **gesund werden** get well (again), recover
Ge'sundheit *f* (-; *no pl*) health; **auf j-s Gesundheit trinken** drink to s.o.'s health; **Gesundheit!** bless you!
ge'sundheitlich **1.** *adj*: **gesundheitlicher Zustand** state of health; **aus gesundheitlichen Gründen** for health reasons; **2.** *adv*: **gesundheitlich geht es ihm gut** he is in good health
Ge'sundheitsamt *n* Public Health Department (*Br* Office)
ge'sundheitsschädlich *adj* bad for one's health
Ge'sundheitszeugnis *n* health certificate
Gesundheitszustand *m* state of health
gesungen [gə'zuŋən] *pp of* **singen**
gesunken [gə'zuŋkən] *pp of* **sinken**
getan [gə'ta:n] *pp of* **tun**
Getöse [gə'tø:zə] *n* (-s; *no pl*) din, (deafening) noise
ge'tragen *pp of* **tragen**
Getränk [gə'trɛŋk] *n* (-[e]s; -e) drink, beverage
Ge'tränkeauto,mat *m* drinks machine
Getreide [gə'traidə] *n* (-s; -) cereals, grain, *Br a.* corn
Getreideernte *f* grain harvest (*or* crop)
ge'treten *pp of* **treten**
Getriebe [gə'tri:bə] *n* (-s; -) MOT transmission
ge'trieben [gə'tri:bən] *pp of* **treiben**
getroffen [gə'trɔfən] *pp of* **treffen**
getrogen [gə'tro:gən] *pp of* **trügen**
getrost [gə'tro:st] *adv* safely
getrunken [gə'truŋkən] *pp of* **trinken**
Getue [gə'tu:ə] F *n* (-s; *no pl*) fuss
Getümmel [gə'tyml] *n* (-s; -) turmoil
Gewächs [gə'vɛks] *n* (-es; -e) plant; MED growth
ge'wachsen **1.** *pp of* **wachsen**[1]; **2.** *fig adj*: **j-m gewachsen sein** be a match for s.o.; **e-r Sache gewachsen sein** be equal to s.th., be able to cope with s.th.

Ge'wächshaus *n* greenhouse, hothouse

gewagt [gə'va:kt] *adj* daring; *fig* risqué

gewählt [gə've:lt] *adj* refined

Gewähr [gə've:ɐ] *f*: *Gewähr übernehmen (für)* guarantee

ge'währen *v/t (no -ge-, h)* grant, allow

ge'währleisten *v/t (no -ge-, h)* guarantee

Gewahrsam [gə'va:ɐza:m] *m*: *et. (j-n) in Gewahrsam nehmen* take s.th. in safekeeping (s.o. into custody)

Gewalt [gə'valt] *f* (-; -en) a) *(no pl)* force, violence, b) power; *mit Gewalt* by force; *höhere Gewalt* act of God; *häusliche Gewalt* domestic violence; *in s-e Gewalt bringen* seize by force; *die Gewalt verlieren über* (acc) lose control over

Gewaltherrschaft *f* tyranny

ge'waltig *adj* powerful, mighty; enormous

ge'waltlos *adj* nonviolent

Ge'waltlosigkeit *f* (-; *no pl*) nonviolence

ge'waltsam 1. *adj* violent; **2.** *adv* by force; *gewaltsam öffnen* force open

ge'walttätig *adj* violent

Ge'walttätigkeit *f* (-; -en) a) *(no pl)* violence, b) act of violence

Ge'waltverbrechen *n* crime of violence

Gewand [gə'vant] *n* (-[e]s; *Gewänder* [gə'vɛndɐ]) robe, gown; REL vestment

gewandt [gə'vant] **1.** *pp of* **wenden** *(v/refl)*; **2.** *adj* nimble; skil(l)ful; clever

Ge'wandtheit *f* (-; *no pl*) nimbleness; skill; ease

gewann [gə'van] *pret of* **gewinnen**

ge'waschen *pp of* **waschen**

Gewässer [gə'vɛsɐ] *n* (-s; -) body of water; *pl* waters

Gewebe [gə've:bə] *n* (-s; -) fabric; BIOL tissue

Gewehr [gə've:ɐ] *n* (-[e]s; -e) gun; rifle; shotgun

Gewehrkolben *m* (rifle) butt

Gewehrlauf *m* (rifle *or* gun) barrel

Geweih [gə'vai] *n* (-[e]s; -e) ZO antlers, horns

Gewerbe [gə'vɛrbə] *n* (-s; -) trade, business

Gewerbeschein *m* trade licen|se, *Br* -ce

Gewerbeschule *f* vocational *or* trade school

gewerblich [gə'vɛrplɪç] *adj* commercial, industrial

gewerbsmäßig [gə'vɛrps-] *adj* professional

Gewerkschaft [gə'vɛrkʃaft] *f* (-; -en) labor union, *Br* (trade) union

Ge'werkschaft(l)er *m* (-s; -), **Ge'werkschaft(l)erin** *f* (-; -nen) labor (*Br* trade) unionist

ge'werkschaftlich *adj*, **Ge'werkschafts...** *in cpds* labor (*Br* trade) union ...

ge'wesen *pp of* **sein**[1]

gewichen [gə'vɪçən] *pp of* **weichen**

Gewicht [gə'vɪçt] *n* (-[e]s; -e) weight; importance; *Gewicht legen auf* (acc) stress

gewiesen [gə'vi:zən] *pp of* **weisen**

gewillt [gə'vɪlt] *adj* willing, ready

Gewimmel [gə'vɪməl] *n* (-s; *no pl*) throng

Gewinde [gə'vɪndə] *n* (-s; -) TECH thread; *ein Gewinde bohren in* (acc) tap

Gewinn [gə'vɪn] *m* (-[e]s; -e) ECON profit (*a. fig*); gain(s); prize; winnings; *Gewinn bringend → gewinnbringend*

ge'winnbringend *adj* profitable

ge'winnen *v/t and v/i (irr, no -ge-, h)* win; gain

gewinnend *fig adj* winning, engaging

Gewinner [gə'vɪnɐ] *m* (-s; -), **Ge'winnerin** *f* (-; -nen) winner

Ge'winnzahl *f* winning number

Gewirr [gə'vɪr] *n* (-[e]s; *no pl*) tangle; maze

gewiss [gə'vɪs] **1.** *adj* certain; **2.** *adv* certainly

Ge'wissen *n* (-s; -) conscience

ge'wissenhaft *adj* conscientious

ge'wissenlos *adj* unscrupulous

Ge'wissensbisse *pl* pricks *or* pangs of conscience

Gewissensfrage *f* question of conscience

Gewissensgründe *pl*: *aus Gewissensgründen* for reasons of conscience

Ge'wissheit *f* (-; *no pl*) certainty; *mit Gewissheit* know etc for certain *or* sure

Gewitter [gə'vɪtɐ] *n* (-s; -) thunderstorm

Gewitterregen *m* thundershower

Gewitterwolke *f* thundercloud

gewoben [gə'vo:bən] *pp of* **weben**

gewogen [gə'vo:gən] *pp of* **wiegen**[1] *and* **wägen**

ge'wöhnen [gə'vø:nən] *v/t and v/refl (no -ge-, h) sich (j-n) gewöhnen an* (acc) get (s.o.) used to

Gewohnheit [gə'vo:nhait] *f* (-; -en) habit (*et. zu tun* of doing s.th.)

ge'wohnheitsmäßig *adj* habitual

gewöhnlich [gə'vø:nlɪç] *adj* common, ordinary, usual; vulgar, F common

gewohnt [gə'vo:nt] *adj* usual; *et. (zu tun) gewohnt sein* be used *or* accustomed to (doing) s.th.

Gewölbe [gə'vœlbə] *n* (-s; -) vault

gewölbt [gə'vœlpt] *adj* arched

gewonnen [gə'vɔnən] *pp of* **gewinnen**

geworben [gə'vɔrbən] *pp of* **werben**

geworden [gə'vɔrdən] *pp of* **werden**

geworfen [gə'vɔrfən] *pp of* **werfen**

gewrungen [gə'vruŋən] *pp of* **wringen**

Gewühl [gə'vy:l] *n* (-[e]s; *no pl*) crowd, crush

gewunden [gə'vʊndən] **1.** *pp of* **winden**; **2.** *adj* winding

Gewürz [gə'vʏrts] *n* (-es; -e) spice

Gewürzgurke *f* pickle(d gherkin)

gewusst [gə'vʊst] *pp of* **wissen**

gezackt [gə'tsakt] *adj* jagged, serrated

Ge'zeiten *pl* tide(s)

Gezeter [gə'tse:tɐ] *contp n* (-s; *no pl*) (shrill) clamo(u)r; nagging

geziert [gə'tsi:ɐt] *adj* affected

gezogen [gə'tso:gən] *pp of* **ziehen**

Gezwitscher [gə'tsvɪtʃɐ] *n* (-s; *no pl*) chirp(ing), twitter(ing)

gezwungen [gə'tsvʊŋən] **1.** *pp of* **zwingen**; **2.** *adj* forced, unnatural

Gicht [gɪçt] *f* (-; *no pl*) MED gout

Giebel [ˈgiːbəl] *m* (-s; -) gable

Gier [giːɐ] *f* (-; *no pl*) greed(iness) (**nach** for)

gierig [ˈgiːrɪç] *adj* greedy (**nach, auf** *acc* for, after)

gießen [ˈgiːsən] *v/t and v/i* (irr, ge-, h) pour; TECH cast; water

Gieße'rei *f* (-; -en) TECH foundry

'Gießkanne *f* watering pot (*Br* can)

Gift [gɪft] *n* (-[e]s; -e) poison, zo *a.* venom (*a. fig*)

'giftig *adj* poisonous; venomous (*a. fig*); poisoned; MED toxic

'Giftmüll *m* toxic waste

Giftmülldepo,nie *f* toxic waste dump

'Giftschlange *f* zo poisonous *or* venomous snake

'Giftstoff *m* poisonous *or* toxic substance; pollutant

'Giftzahn *m* zo poison fang

Gigant [gi'gant] *m* (-en; -en) giant

gi'gantisch *adj* gigantic

ging [gɪŋ] *pret of* **gehen**

Gipfel [ˈgɪpfəl] *m* (-s; -) top, peak, summit, *fig a.* height

Gipfelkonfe,renz *f* POL summit (meeting *or* conference)

'gipfeln *v/i* (ge-, h) culminate (**in** *dat* in)

Gips [gɪps] *m* (-es; -e) plaster (of Paris); **in Gips** MED in (a) plaster (cast)

Gipsabdruck *m*, Gipsabguss *m* plaster cast

'gipsen *v/t* (ge-, h) plaster (*a.* F MED)

'Gipsverband *m* MED plaster cast

Giraffe [gi'rafə] *f* (-; -n) zo giraffe

Girlande [gɪr'landə] *f* (-; -n) garland, festoon

Girokonto [ˈʒiːro-] *n* checking (*or* current) account; postal check (*Br* giro) account

Gischt [gɪʃt] *m* (-[e]s; -e), *f* (-; -en) (sea) spray, spindrift

Gitarre [gi'tarə] *f* (-; -n) MUS guitar

Gitarrist [gita'rɪst] *m* (-en; -en) guitarist

Gitter [ˈgɪtɐ] *n* (-s; -) lattice; grating; F **hinter Gittern** (**sitzen**) (be) behind bars

'Gitterbett *n* crib, *Br* cot

'Gitterfenster *n* lattice (window)

Glanz [glants] *m* (-es; *no pl*) shine, gloss (*a.* TECH), luster, brilliance (*a. fig*); *fig* splendo(u)r, glamo(u)r

glänzen [ˈglɛntsən] *v/i* (ge-, h) shine, gleam; glitter, glisten

glänzend *adj* shining, shiny, bright; PHOT glossy; *fig* brilliant, excellent

'Glanzleistung *f* brilliant achievement

Glanzzeit *f* heyday

Glas [glaːs] *n* (-es; Gläser [ˈglɛːzɐ]) glass

Glaser [ˈglaːzɐ] *m* (-s; -) glazier

gläsern [ˈglɛːzərn] *adj* (of) glass

'Glasfaser *f*, Glasfiber *f* glass fiber (*Br* fibre)

Glashütte *f* TECH glassworks

glasieren [gla'ziːrən] *v/t* (*no* -ge-, h) glaze; GASTR ice, frost

glasig [ˈglaːzɪç] *adj* glassy

'glasklar *adj* crystal-clear (*a. fig*)

'Glasscheibe *f* (glass) pane

Glasur [gla'zuːɐ] *f* (-; -en) glaze; GASTR icing

glatt [glat] *adj* smooth (*a. fig*); slippery; *fig* clear

Glätte [ˈglɛtə] *f* (-; *no pl*) smoothness (*a. fig*); slipperiness

'Glatteis *n* (glare, *Br* black) ice; **es herrscht Glatteis** the roads are icy; F **j-n aufs Glatteis führen** mislead s.o.

glätten [ˈglɛtən] *v/t* (ge-, h) smooth; *Swiss:* → **bügeln**

'glattgehen *v/i* (irr, sep, -ge-, sein) F work (out well), go (off) well

Glatze [ˈglatsə] *f* (-; -n) bald head; **e-e Glatze haben** be bald

Glaube [ˈglaubə] *m* (-ns; *no pl*) belief, *esp* REL faith (*both:* **an** *acc* in)

'glauben *v/t and v/i* (ge-, h) believe; think, guess; **glauben an** (*acc*) believe in (*a.* REL)

'Glaubensbekenntnis *n* REL creed, profession *or* confession of faith

Glaubenslehre *f*, Glaubenssatz *m* dogma, doctrine

glaubhaft [ˈglauphaft] *adj* credible, plausible

gläubig [ˈglɔybɪç] *adj* religious; devout; **die Gläubigen** the faithful

Gläubiger [ˈglɔybɪgɐ] *m* (-s; -), 'Gläubigerin *f* (-; -nen) ECON creditor

'glaubwürdig *adj* credible; reliable

gleich [glaiç] **1.** *adj* same; equal (*right etc*);

auf die gleiche Art (in) the same way; *zur gleichen Zeit* at the same time; *das ist mir gleich* it's all the same to me; *ganz gleich, wann etc* no matter when *etc*; *das Gleiche* the same; (*ist*) *gleich ...* MATH equals ..., is ...; *gleich bleibend* → *gleichbleibend*; *gleich gesinnt* like-minded; *gleich lautend* → *gleichlautend*; **2.** *adv* equally, alike; at once, right away; in a moment *or* minute; *gleich groß* (*alt*) of the same size (age); *gleich nach* (*neben*) right after (next to); *gleich gegenüber* just opposite *or* across the street; *es ist gleich 5 Uhr* it's almost 5 o'clock; *gleich aussehen* (*gekleidet sein*) look (be dressed) alike; *bis gleich!* see you soon *or* later!

gleichaltrig ['glaɪç'ʔaltrɪç] *adj* (of) the same age

'**gleichberechtigt** *adj* equal, having equal rights

'**Gleichberechtigung** *f* (-; *no pl*) equal rights

'**gleichbleibend** *adj* constant, steady

'**gleichen** *v/i* (*irr, ge-, h*) (*dat*) be *or* look like

'**gleichfalls** *adv* also, likewise; *danke, gleichfalls!* (thanks,) the same to you

'**gleichförmig** [-fœrmɪç] *adj* uniform

'**Gleichgewicht** *n* (-[e]s; *no pl*) balance (*a. fig*)

'**gleichgültig** *adj* indifferent (*gegen* to); careless; *das* (*er*) *ist mir gleichgültig* I don't care (for him)

'**Gleichgültigkeit** *f* (-; *no pl*) indifference

'**Gleichheit** *f* (-; *no pl*) equality

'**gleichkommen** *v/i* (*irr, kommen, sep, -ge-, sein*) *e-r Sache gleichkommen* amount to s.th.; *j-m gleichkommen* equal s.o. (*an dat* in)

'**gleichlautend** *adj* identical

'**gleichmäßig** *adj* regular; constant; even

'**gleichnamig** [-na:mɪç] *adj* of the same name

'**Gleichnis** *n* (-ses; -se) parable

'**gleichsam** *adv* as it were, so to speak

'**gleichseitig** [-zaɪtɪç] *adj* MATH equilateral

'**gleichsetzen, gleichstellen** *v/t* (*sep, -ge-, h*) equate (*dat* to, with); put *s.o.* on an equal footing (with)

'**Gleichstrom** *m* ELECTR direct current

'**Gleichung** *f* (-; -en) MATH equation

'**gleichwertig** *adj* equally good; *j-m gleichwertig sein* be a match for s.o. (*a. SPORT*)

'**gleichzeitig** *adj* simultaneous; *beide gleichzeitig* both at the same time

Gleis [glaɪs] *n* (-es; -e) RAIL rail(s), track(s), line; platform, gate

gleiten ['glaɪtən] *v/i* (*irr, ge-, sein*) glide, slide

gleitend *adj*: *gleitende Arbeitszeit* flexible working hours, flextime, *Br a.* flexi-time

'**Gleitflug** *m* glide

'**Gleitschirmfliegen** *n* paragliding

'**Gleitschirmflieger** *m* paraglider

Gletscher ['glɛtʃɐ] *m* (-s; -) glacier

Gletscherspalte *f* crevasse

glich [glɪç] *pret of* **gleichen**

Glied [gli:t] *n* (-[e]s; *Glieder* ['gli:dɐ]) ANAT limb; penis; TECH link

gliedern ['gli:dɐn] *v/t* (*ge-, h*) structure; divide (*in acc* into)

Gliederung *f* (-; -en) structure, arrangement; outline

Gliedmaßen *pl* ANAT limbs, extremities

glimmen ['glɪmən] *v/i* ([*irr,*] *ge-, h*) glow; smo(u)lder

'**Glimmstängel** F *m* (-s; -) cigarette, *Br sl* fag

glimpflich ['glɪmpflɪç] **1.** *adj* lenient, mild; **2.** *adv*: *glimpflich davonkommen* get off lightly

glitschig ['glɪtʃɪç] *adj* slippery

glitt [glɪt] *pret of* **gleiten**

glitzern ['glɪtsɐn] *v/i* (*ge-, h*) glitter, sparkle, glint

global [glo'ba:l] *adj* global

Globus ['glo:bʊs] *m* (-[*ses*]; -se) globe

Glocke ['glɔkə] *f* (-; -n) bell

Glockenblume *f* bluebell

Glockenspiel *n* chimes

Glockenturm *m* bell tower, belfry

glomm [glɔm] *pret of* **glimmen**

glorreich ['glo:raɪç] *adj* glorious

Glotze ['glɔtsə] F *f* (-; -n) TV *the* tube, *Br* goggle box

'**glotzen** F *v/i* (*ge-, h*) goggle, gape, stare

Glück [glʏk] *n* (-[e]s; *no pl*) (good) luck, fortune; happiness; *Glück haben* be lucky; *zum Glück* fortunately; *viel Glück!* good luck!

Glucke ['glʊkə] *f* (-; -n) ZO sitting hen; *fig* hen

gluckern ['glʊkɐn] *v/i* (*ge-, h*) gurgle

'**glücklich** *adj* happy; *glücklicher Zufall* lucky chance

'**glücklicherweise** *adv* fortunately

'**Glücksbringer** *m* (-s; -) lucky charm

Glücksfall *m* lucky chance

Glückspfennig *m* lucky penny

Glückspilz *m* lucky fellow

Glücksspiel *n* game of chance; *coll* gambling

Glücksspieler *m* gambler

Glückstag *m* lucky day

'**glückstrahlend** *adj* radiant

'Glückwunsch *m* congratulations; *herzlichen Glückwunsch!* congratulations!; happy birthday!

Glühbirne ['gly:-] *f* ELECTR light bulb

glühen ['gly:ən] *v/i* (*ge-, h*) glow (*a. fig*)

glühend ['gly:ənt] *adj* glowing; red-hot (*iron*); *fig* burning; *glühend heiß* blazing hot

'Glühwein *m* mulled wine

Glut [glu:t] *f* (-; *-en*) (glowing) fire; embers; live coals; *fig* ardo(u)r

'Gluthitze *f* blazing heat

GmbH [ge:ʔɛmbe:'ha:] ABBR *of Gesellschaft mit beschränkter Haftung* private limited liability company

Gnade ['gna:də] *f* (-; *-n*) mercy, *esp* REL *a.* grace; favo(u)r

'Gnadenfrist *f* reprieve

Gnadengesuch *n* JUR petition for mercy

'gnadenlos *adj* merciless

gnädig ['gnɛ:dɪç] *adj* gracious; *esp* REL merciful

Gold [gɔlt] *n* (-[*e*]*s*; *no pl*) gold

Goldbarren *m* gold bar *or* ingot; *coll* bullion

golden ['gɔldən] *adj* gold; *fig* golden

'Goldfisch *m* ZO goldfish

'goldgelb *adj* golden (yellow)

'Goldgräber [-grɛ:bə] *m* (-*s*; -) gold digger

Goldgrube *fig* f goldmine, bonanza

goldig ['gɔldɪç] F *adj* sweet, lovely, cute

'Goldmine f goldmine

Goldmünze f gold coin

Goldschmied *m* goldsmith

Goldstück *n* gold coin

Golf[1] [gɔlf] *m* (-[*e*]*s*; *-e*) GEOGR gulf

Golf[2] *n* (-*s*; *no pl*) SPORT golf

Golfplatz *m* golf course

Golfschläger *m* golf club

Golfspieler *m* golfer

Gondel ['gɔndəl] *f* (-; *-n*) gondola; cabin

Gong ['gɔŋ-] *m* (-*s*; -*s*) gong

gönnen ['gœnən] *v/t* (*ge-, h*) *j-m et. gönnen* not (be)grudge s.o. s.th.; *j-m et. nicht gönnen* (be)grudge s.o. s.th.; *sich et. gönnen* allow o.s. s.th., treat o.s. to s.th.

gönnerhaft ['gœnɐhaft] *adj* patronizing

gor [go:ɐ] *pret of gären*

Gorilla [go'rɪla] *m* (-*s*; -*s*) ZO gorilla

goss [gɔs] *pret of gießen*

Gosse ['gɔsə] *f* (-; *-n*) gutter (*a. fig*)

Gotik ['go:tɪk] *f* (-; *no pl*) ARCH Gothic style *or* period

'gotisch *adj* Gothic

Gott [gɔt] *m* (-[*e*]*s*; *Götter* ['gœtɐ]) REL God, Lord; MYTH god; *Gott sei Dank*(!) thank God(!); *um Gottes Willen!* for heaven's sake!

'gottergeben *adj* resigned (to the will of God)

'Gottesdienst *m* REL (divine) service

'gottesfürchtig [-fʏrçtɪç] *adj* god-fearing

'Gotteslästerer [-lɛstərɐ] *m* (-*s*; -) blasphemer

'Gotteslästerung *f* (-; *-en*) blasphemy

'Gottheit *f* (-; *-en*) deity, divinity

Göttin ['gœtɪn] *f* (-; *-nen*) goddess

göttlich ['gœtlɪç] *adj* divine

gott'lob *int* thank God *or* goodness!

'gottlos *adj* godless, wicked

'gottverlassen F *adj* godforsaken

'Gottvertrauen *n* trust in God

Götze ['gœtsə] *m* (-*n*; -*n*), **'Götzenbild** *n* idol

Gouverneur [guvɛr'nø:ɐ] *m* (-*s*; -*e*) governor

Grab [gra:p] *n* (-[*e*]*s*; *Gräber* ['grɛ:bɐ]) grave; tomb

graben ['gra:bən] *v/t and v/i* (*irr, ge-, h*) dig, ZO *a.* burrow

'Graben *m* (-*s*; *Gräben* ['grɛ:bən]) ditch; MIL trench

'Grabmal *n* monument; tomb

Grabrede *f* funeral address

Grabschrift *f* epitaph

Grabstätte *f* burial place; grave, tomb

Grabstein *m* tombstone, gravestone

Grad [gra:t] *m* (-[*e*]*s*; *-e*) degree; MIL *etc* rank, grade; *15 Grad Kälte* 15 degrees below zero

Gradeinteilung *f* graduation

graduell [gra'duɛl] *adj* in degree

Graf [gra:f] *m* (-*en*; *-en*) count, *Br* earl

Graffiti [gra'fi:ti] *pl* graffiti

Grafik ['gra:fɪk] *f* (-; *-en*) a) (*no pl*) graphic arts, b) print, c) MATH, TECH graph, diagram, d) (*no pl*) art(work), illustrations, e) (*no pl*) EDP graphics

'Grafiker *m* (-*s*; -), **'Grafikerin** *f* (-; *-nen*) graphic artist

Gräfin ['grɛ:fɪn] *f* (-; *-nen*) countess

grafisch ['gra:fɪʃ] *adj* graphic

Grafologie *f → Graphologie*

'Grafschaft *f* (-; *-en*) county

Gramm [gram] *n* (-*s*; *-e*) gram

Grammatik [gra'matɪk] *f* (-; *-en*) grammar

gram'matisch *adj* grammatical

Granat [gra'na:t] *m* (-[*e*]*s*; *-e*) MIN garnet

Gra'nate *f* (-; *-n*) MIL shell

Gra'natsplitter *m* MIL shell splinter

Granatwerfer *m* MIL mortar

grandios [gran'djo:s] *adj* magnificent, grand

Granit [gra'ni:t] *m* (-*s*; *-e*) granite

Graphik *f etc → Grafik etc*

Graphologie [grafolo'gi:] *f* (-; *no pl*) graphology

Gras [gra:s] *n* (-*es*; *Gräser* ['grɛ:zɐ]) grass

grasen ['gra:zən] *v/i* (*ge-*, *h*) graze

'**Grashalm** *m* blade of grass

grassieren [gra'si:rən] *v/i* (*no -ge-*, *h*) rage, be rife

grässlich ['grɛslɪç] *adj* hideous, atrocious

Gräte ['grɛ:tə] *f* (-; -*n*) (fish)bone

Gratifikation [gratifika'tsjo:n] *f* (-; -*en*) gratuity, bonus

gratis ['gra:tɪs] *adv* free (of charge)

'**Grätsche** ['grɛ:tʃə] *f* (-; -*n*), '**grätschen** *v/i* (*ge-*, *h*) straddle; *soccer*: stride tackle

Gratulant [gratu'lant] *m* (-*en*; -*en*), **Gratu'lantin** *f* (-; -*nen*) congratulator

Gratulation [-la'tsjo:n] *f* (-; -*en*) congratulation

gratulieren [-'li:rən] *v/i* (*no -ge-*, *h*) congratulate (*j-m zu et.* s.o. on s.th.); *j-m zum Geburtstag gratulieren* wish s.o. many happy returns (of the day)

grau [grau] *adj* gray, *Br* grey

'**Graubrot** *n* rye bread

Gräuel ['grɔʏəl] *m* (-*s*; -) horror

'**Gräueltat** *f* atrocity

'**grauen** *v/i* (*ge-*, *h*) *mir graut es vor* (*dat*) I dread (the thought of)

'**Grauen** *n* (-*s*; -) horror

'**grauenhaft**, '**grauenvoll** *adj* horrible, horrifying

Graupel ['graupəl] *f* (-; -*n*) sleet, soft hail

grausam ['grauza:m] *adj* cruel

'**Grausamkeit** *f* (-; -*en*) cruelty

grausig ['grauzɪç] *adj* → **grauenhaft**

Grauzone *f* fig gray (*Br* grey) area

gravieren [gra'vi:rən] *v/t* (*no -ge-*, *h*) engrave

gravierend *adj* serious

Gravur [gra'vu:ɐ] *f* (-; -*en*) engraving

Grazie ['gra:tsjə] *f* (-; *no pl*) grace

graziös [gra'tsjø:s] *adj* graceful

greifen ['graifən] (*irr, ge-*, *h*) **1.** *v/t* seize, grasp, grab, take *or* catch hold of; **2.** *v/i fig* take effect; *greifen nach* reach for; grasp at

Greis [grais] *m* (-*es*; -*e*) (very) old man

greisenhaft ['graizənhaft] *adj* senile (*a.* MED)

Greisin ['graizɪn] *f* (-; -*nen*) (very) old woman

grell [grɛl] *adj* glaring; shrill

Grenze ['grɛntsə] *f* (-; -*n*) border; boundary; *fig* limits

'**grenzen** *v/i* (*ge-*, *h*) *grenzen an* (*acc*) border on

'**grenzenlos** *adj* boundless

'**Grenzfall** *m* borderline case

Grenzland *n* borderland, frontier

Grenzlinie *f* borderline, POL demarcation line

Grenzstein *m* boundary stone

Grenzübergang *m* frontier crossing (point), checkpoint

Greuel *m* → **Gräuel**

Grieche ['gri:çə] *m* (-*n*; -*n*) Greek

'**Griechenland** Greece

'**Griechin** *f* (-; -*nen*), '**griechisch** *adj* Greek

Grieß [gri:s] *m* (-*es*; -*e*) semolina

griff [grɪf] *pret of* **greifen**

Griff *m* (-[*e*]*s*; -*e*) grip, grasp; handle

'**griffbereit** *adj* at hand, handy

Grill [grɪl] *m* (-*s*; -*s*) grill

Grille ['grɪlə] *f* (-; -*n*) zo cricket

'**grillen** *v/t* (*ge-*, *h*) grill, barbecue

Grimasse [grɪ'masə] *f* (-; -*n*) grimace; *Grimassen schneiden* pull faces

grimmig ['grɪmɪç] *adj* grim

grinsen ['grɪnzən] *v/i* (*ge-*, *h*) grin (*über acc* at); *höhnisch or spöttisch grinsen* (*über acc*) sneer (at)

'**Grinsen** *n* (-*s*; *no pl*) grin; *höhnisches or spöttisches Grinsen* sneer

Grippe ['grɪpə] *f* (-; -*n*) MED influenza, F flu

Grips [grɪps] *m* (-*es*; *no pl*) brains

grob [gro:p] **1.** *adj* coarse (*a. fig*); *fig* gross; crude; rude; rough; **2.** *adv*: *grob geschätzt* at a rough estimate

'**Grobheit** *f* (-; *no pl*) coarseness; roughness; rudeness

grölen ['grø:lən] F *v/t and v/i* (*ge-*, *h*) bawl

Groll [grɔl] *m* (-[*e*]*s*; *no pl*) grudge, ill will

'**grollen** *v/i* (*ge-*, *h*) *j-m grollen* bear s.o. a grudge

Groschen ['grɔʃən] *m* (-*s*; -) *Austrian* groschen; F ten-pfennig piece, ten pfennigs

groß [gro:s] *adj* big; large (*a. family*); tall; grown-up; F big (*brother etc*); *fig* great (*a. fun, trouble, pain etc*); capital (*letter*); *großes Geld* bills, *Br* notes; *große Ferien* summer vacation, *Br* summer holiday(s); *Groß und Klein* young and old; *im Großen und Ganzen* on the whole; F *groß in et. sein* be great at (doing) s.th.; *wie groß ist es?* what size is it?; *wie groß bist du?* how tall are you?

'**großartig** *adj* great, F *a.* terrific

'**Großaufnahme** *f* film: close-up

Größe ['grø:sə] *f* (-; -*n*) size; height; *esp* MATH quantity; *fig* greatness; celebrity

'**Großeltern** *pl* grandparents

'**größenteils** *adv* to a large *or* great extent, largely

'**Größenwahn** *m* megalomania (*a. fig*)

'**Großfa,milie** *f* extended family

Großhandel *m* ECON wholesale (trade)

Großhändler *m* ECON wholesale dealer, wholesaler

Großhandlung f ECON wholesale business
Großindus,**trie** f big industry; big business
Großindustri,**elle** m big industrialist, F tycoon
Großmacht f POL great power
Großmarkt m ECON hypermarket; wholesale market
Großmaul F n braggart
Großmutter f grandmother
Großraum m conurbation, metropolitan area; *der Großraum München* Greater Munich, the Greater Munich area
Großraumflugzeug n wide-bodied jet
'**großschreiben** v/t (irr, *schreiben*, sep, -ge-, h) capitalize
'**Großschreibung** f (use of) capitalization
'**großsprecherisch** [-ʃpreçərɪʃ] adj boastful
'**großspurig** [-ʃpuːrɪç] adj arrogant
'**Großstadt** f big city
'**großstädtisch** adj of or in a big city, urban
'**größten**'**teils** adv mostly, mainly
'**großtun** v/i (irr, *tun*, sep, -ge-, h) show off; *sich mit et. großtun* brag about s.th.
'**Großvater** m grandfather
'**Großverdiener** m (-s; -) big earner
'**Großwild** n big game
'**großziehen** v/t (irr, *ziehen*, sep, -ge-, h) raise, rear; bring up
'**großzügig** adj generous, liberal; ... on a large scale; spacious
'**Großzügigkeit** f (-; no pl) generosity, liberality; spaciousness
grotesk [gro'tɛsk] adj grotesque
Grotte ['grɔtə] f (-; -n) grotto
grub [gruːp] pret of *graben*
Grübchen ['gryːpçən] n (-s; -) dimple
Grube ['gruːbə] f (-; -n) pit; mine
Grübelei [gryːbə'laɪ] f (-; -en) pondering, musing
grübeln ['gryːbəln] v/i (ge-, h) ponder, muse (*über acc* on, over)
Gruft [gruft] f (-; *Grüfte* ['gryftə]) tomb, vault
grün [gryːn] adj green
Grün n (-s; -) green; *im Grünen* in the country
'**Grünanlage** f park
Grund [grunt] m (-[e]s; *Gründe* ['gryndə]) reason; cause; ground, AGR a. soil; bottom; *Grund und Boden* property, land; *aus diesem Grund(e)* for this reason; *von Grund auf* entirely; *im Grunde (genommen)* actually, basically; → *aufgrund*; → *zugrunde*
'**Grund-** ... in cpds ...bedeutung, ...bedingung, ...regel, ...prinzip, ...wortschatz

etc: *mst* basic ...
Grundbegriffe pl basics, fundamentals
Grundbesitz m property, land
Grundbesitzer m landowner
gründen ['grʏndən] v/t (ge-, h) found (*a. family*), set up, establish; *sich gründen auf* (dat) be based or founded on
Gründer ['grʏndɐ] m (-s; -), '**Gründerin** f (-; -nen) founder
'**grund**'**falsch** adj absolutely wrong
'**Grundfläche** f MATH base; ARCH area
'**Grundgedanke** m basic idea
'**Grundgeschwindigkeit** f AVIAT ground speed
'**Grundgesetz** n POL Basic (Constitutional) Law (for the Federal Republic of Germany)
'**Grundlage** f foundation, *fig a.* basis; pl (basic) elements
'**grundlegend** adj fundamental, basic
gründlich ['grʏntlɪç] adj thorough
'**Grundlinie** f tennis etc: base line
'**grundlos** adj groundless, unfounded
'**Grundmauer** f foundation
Grün'**donnerstag** m REL Maundy or Holy Thursday
'**Grundrechnungsart** f MATH basic arithmetical operation
'**Grundriss** m ARCH ground plan
'**Grundsatz** m principle
grundsätzlich ['grʊntzɛtslɪç] **1.** adj fundamental; **2.** adv: *ich bin grundsätzlich dagegen* I am against it on principle
'**Grundschule** f elementary (or grade) school, Br primary (or junior) school
'**Grundstein** m ARCH foundation stone; *fig* foundations
'**Grundstück** n plot (of land), lot; (building) site; premises
'**Grundstücksmakler** m realtor, Br real estate agent
'**Gründung** f (-; -en) foundation, establishment, setting up
'**grund**'**ver**'**schieden** adj totally different
'**Grundwasser** n ground water
'**Grundzahl** f cardinal number
'**Grundzug** m main feature, characteristic
Grüne ['gryːnə] m, f (-n; -n) POL Green
'**Grünfläche** f green space
'**grünlich** adj greenish
'**Grünspan** m (-[e]s; no pl) verdigris
grunzen ['grʊntsən] v/i and v/t (ge-, h) grunt
Gruppe ['grʊpə] f (-; -n) group
'**Gruppenreise** f group tour
gruppieren [grʊ'piːrən] v/t (no -ge-, h) group, arrange in groups; *sich gruppieren* form groups
Grusel... ['gruːzəl-] in cpds ...film etc:

horror …

'**gruselig** adj eerie, creepy; spine-chilling

'**gruseln** v/t and v/refl (ge-, h) **es gruselt mich** F it gives me the creeps

Gruß [gru:s] m (-es; Grüße ['gry:sə]) greeting(s); MIL salute; **viele Grüße an** (acc) or my regards (or love) to …; **mit freundlichen Grüßen** yours sincerely; **herzliche Grüße** best wishes; love

grüßen ['gry:sən] v/t (ge-, h) greet, F say hello to; MIL salute; **grüßen Sie ihn von mir** give my regards (or love) to him

gucken ['gʊkən] v/i (ge-, h) look

'**Guckloch** n peephole

Güggeli ['gʏgəli] n (-s; -) Swiss chicken

gültig ['gʏltɪç] adj valid; current

'**Gültigkeit** f (-; no pl) validity; **s-e Gültigkeit verlieren** expire

Gummi ['gʊmi] m, n (-s; -[s]) rubber

Gummiband n (-[e]s; -bänder) rubber (esp Br a. elastic) band

Gummibärchen pl gummy bears

Gummibaum m BOT rubber tree; rubber plant

Gummibon,bon m, n gumdrop

gummieren [gʊ'mi:rən] v/t (no -ge-, h) gum

'**Gummiknüppel** m truncheon

Gummistiefel m rubber boot, esp Br wellington (boot)

Gummizug m elastic

Gunst [gʊnst] f (-; no pl) favo(u)r, goodwill; → **zugunsten**

günstig ['gʏnstɪç] adj favo(u)rable (**für** to); convenient; **im günstigsten Fall** at best; **günstige Gelegenheit** chance

Gurgel ['gʊrgəl] f (-; -n) throat; **j-m an die Gurgel springen** fly at s.o.'s throat

'**gurgeln** v/i (ge-, h) MED gargle

Gurke ['gʊrkə] f (-; -n) BOT cucumber

gurren ['gʊrən] v/i (ge-, h) zo coo

Gurt [gʊrt] m (-[e]s; -e) belt (a. MOT and AVIAT); strap

Gürtel ['gʏrtəl] m (-s; -) belt

Gürtelreifen m MOT radial (tire, Br tyre)

GUS [gʊs, ge:ʔuː'?es] ABBR of **Gemeinschaft Unabhängiger Staaten** CIS, Commonwealth of Independent States

Guss [gʊs] m (-es; Güsse ['gʏsə]) downpour; TECH casting; GASTR icing; fig **aus e-m Guss** of a piece

'**Gusseisen** n cast iron

'**gusseisern** adj cast-iron

gut [gu:t] **1.** adj good; fine; **ganz gut** not bad; **also gut!** all right (then)!; **schon gut!** never mind!; **(wieder) gut werden** come right (again), be all right; **gute Reise!** have a nice trip!; **sei bitte so gut und …** would you be so good as to or good

enough to …; **in et. gut sein** be good at (doing) s.th.; **2.** adv well; look, taste etc good; **du hast es gut** you are lucky; **es ist gut möglich** it may well be; **es gefällt mir gut** I (do) like it; **gut gebaut** well-built; **gut gelaunt** in a good mood; **gut gemacht!** well done!; **mach's gut!** take care (of yourself)!; **gut gehen** go (off) well, work out well or all right; **wenn alles gut geht** if nothing goes wrong; **mir geht es gut** I'm (doing) well

Gut n (-[e]s; Güter ['gy:tɐ]) estate; pl goods

'**Gutachten** n (-s; -) (expert) opinion; certificate

Gutachter ['gu:t?axtɐ] m (-s; -) expert

'**gutartig** adj good-natured; MED benign

Gutdünken ['gu:tdʏŋkən] n: **nach Gutdünken** at one's discretion

Gute ['gu:tə] n (-n; no pl) good; **Gutes tun** do good; **alles Gute!** all the best!, good luck!

Güte ['gy:tə] f (-; no pl) goodness, kindness; ECON quality; F **meine Güte!** good gracious!

Güterbahnhof ['gy:tɐ-] m freight depot, Br goods station

Gütergemeinschaft f JUR community of property

Gütertrennung f JUR separation of property

Güterverkehr m freight (Br goods) traffic

Güterwagen m freight car, Br goods wag(g)on

Güterzug m freight (Br goods) train

'**gutgläubig** adj credulous

'**Guthaben** n (-s; -) ECON credit (balance)

'**gutheißen** v/t (irr, heißen, sep, -ge-, h) approve (of)

'**gutherzig** adj kind(-hearted)

gütig ['gy:tɪç] adj good, kind(ly)

gütlich ['gy:tlɪç] adv: **sich gütlich einigen** come to an amicable settlement

'**gutmachen** v/t (sep, -ge-, h) make up for, repay

'**gutmütig** [-my:tɪç] adj good-natured

Gutmütigkeit f (-; no pl) good nature

'**Gutsbesitzer** m, '**Gutsbesitzerin** f (-; -nen) estate owner

Gutschein m coupon, esp Br voucher

'**gutschreiben** v/t (irr, schreiben, sep, -ge-, h) **j-m et. gutschreiben** credit s.th. to s.o.'s account

Gutschrift f credit

'**Gutshaus** n manor (house)

'**Gutshof** m estate, manor

'**gutstehen** v/refl (irr, stehen, sep, -ge-, h): **sich gutstehen** be well off; F **sich gut mit j-m stehen** → **stehen**

'**Gutsverwalter** *m* steward, manager
'**gutwillig** *adj* willing
Gymnasium [gʏmˈnaːzjʊm] *n* (-*s*; -*ien*) high school, *Br appr* grammar school
Gymnastik [gʏmˈnastɪk] *f* (-; *no pl*) exercises, gymnastics

gym'nastisch *adj*: *gymnastische Übungen* physical exercises
Gynäkologe [gʏnɛkoˈloːgə] *m* (-*n*; -*n*),
Gynäko'login *f* (-; -*nen*) MED gyn(a)ecologist

H

Haar [haːɐ] *n* (-[*e*]*s*; -*e* [ˈhaːrə]) hair; *sich die Haare kämmen (schneiden lassen)* comb one's hair (have one's hair cut); *sich aufs Haar gleichen* look absolutely identical; *um ein Haar* by a hair's breadth
'**Haarausfall** *m* loss of hair
'**Haarbürste** *f* hairbrush
haaren [ˈhaːrən] *v/i and v/refl* (*ge-*, *h*) *zo* lose its hair; *fur:* shed hairs
'**Haaresbreite** *f*: *um Haaresbreite* by a hair's breadth
'**haarfein** *adj* (as) fine as a hair
'**Haarfestiger** *m* (-*s*; -) setting lotion
'**Haargefäß** *n* ANAT capillary (vessel)
'**haargenau** *F adv* precisely; (*stimmt*) *haargenau!* dead right!
haarig [ˈhaːrɪç] *adj* hairy
'**haarklein** *F adv* to the last detail
'**Haarklemme** *f* bobby pin, *Br* hair clip
Haarnadel *f* hairpin
Haarnadelkurve *f* hairpin bend
Haarnetz *n* hair-net
'**haarscharf** *F adv* by a hair's breadth
'**Haarschnitt** *m* haircut
Haarspalterei *f* (-; *no pl*) hair-splitting
Haarspange *f* barrette, *Br* (hair) slide
Haarspray *m*, *n* hairspray
'**haarsträubend** *adj* hair-raising
Haarteil *n* hairpiece
Haartrockner *m* hair dryer
Haarwäsche *f*, **Haarwaschmittel** *n* shampoo
Haarwasser *n* hair tonic
Haarwuchs *m*: *starken Haarwuchs haben* have a lot of hair
Haarwuchsmittel *n* hair restorer
haben [ˈhaːbən] *v/t* (*irr*, *ge-*, *h*) have (got); *Hunger haben* be hungry; *Durst haben* be thirsty; *Ferien (Urlaub) haben* be on vacation (*Br* holiday); *er hat Geburtstag* it's his birthday; *welche Farbe hat …?* what colo(u)r is …?; *zu haben sein* be

available; *F sich haben* make a fuss; *F was hast du?* what's the matter with you?; *F da haben wir's!* there we are!; → *Datum*
'**Haben** *n* (-*s*; *no pl*) ECON credit
Habgier [ˈhaːp-] *f* greed(iness)
'**habgierig** *adj* greedy
Habicht [ˈhaːbɪçt] *m* (-*s*; -*e*) zo hawk
'**Habseligkeiten** *pl* belongings
Hacke [ˈhakə] *f* (-; -*n*) AGR hoe; (pick-)axe; ANAT heel
'**hacken** *v/t* (*ge-*, *h*) chop; AGR hoe; zo peck
'**Hackentrick** *m soccer*: backheeler
Hacker [ˈhakɐ] *m* (-*s*; -) EDP hacker
'**Hackfleisch** *n* ground (*Br* minced) meat
'**Hackordnung** *f* zo pecking order
Hafen [ˈhaːfən] *m* (-*s*; *Häfen* [ˈhɛːfən]) harbo(u)r, port
Hafenarbeiter *m* docker, longshoreman
Hafenstadt *f* (sea)port
Hafer [ˈhaːfɐ] *m* (-*s*; -) BOT oats
Haferbrei *m* oatmeal, *Br* porridge
Haferflocken *pl* (rolled) oats
Haferschleim *m* gruel
Haft [haft] *f* (-; *no pl*) JUR confinement, imprisonment; *in Haft* under arrest
'**haftbar** *adj* responsible, JUR liable
'**Haftbefehl** *m* JUR warrant of arrest
'**haften** *v/i* (*ge-*, *h*) stick, adhere (*an dat* to); *haften für* JUR answer for, be liable for
Häftling [ˈhɛftlɪŋ] *m* (-*s*; -*e*) prisoner, convict
'**Haftpflicht** *f* JUR liability
Haftpflichtversicherung *f* liability insurance; MOT third party insurance
'**Haftung** *f* (-; -*en*) responsibility, JUR liability; *mit beschränkter Haftung* limited
Hagel [ˈhaːgəl] *m* (-*s*; *no pl*) hail, *fig a.* shower, volley
'**Hagelkorn** *n* hailstone

hageln v/i (ge-, h) hail (a. fig)

Hagelschauer m hail shower

hager ['ha:gɐ] adj lean, gaunt, haggard

Hahn [ha:n] m (-[e]s; Hähne ['hɛ:nə]) zo cock, rooster; TECH (water) tap, faucet

Hähnchen ['hɛ:nçən] n (-s; -) zo chicken

Hahnenkamm m zo cockscomb

Hai [hai] m (-[e]s; -e), **Haifisch** m zo shark

häkeln ['hɛ:kəln] v/t and v/i (ge-, h) crochet

Haken ['ha:kən] m (-s; -) hook (a. boxing), peg; check, Br tick; F snag, catch

Hakenkreuz n swastika

halb [halp] adj and adv half; **e-e halbe Stunde** half an hour; **ein halbes Pfund** half a pound; **zum halben Preis** at half-price; **auf halbem Wege (entgegen-kommen)** (meet) halfway; **halb so viel** half as much; F **(mit j-m) halbe-halbe machen** go halves or fifty-fifty (with s.o.); **halb gar** GASTR underdone

Halbbruder m half-brother

Halbdunkel n semi-darkness

Halbe ['halbə] f (-n; -n) pint (of beer)

halbfett adj GASTR medium-fat; PRINT semi-bold

Halbfi,nale n SPORT semifinal

Halbgott m demigod

halbherzig adj half-hearted

halbieren [hal'bi:rən] v/t (no -ge-, h) halve; MATH bisect

Halbinsel f peninsula

Halbjahr n six months

halbjährig [-jɛ:rɪç] adj six-month

halbjährlich 1. adj half-yearly; **2.** adv half-yearly, twice a year

Halbkreis m semicircle

Halbkugel f hemisphere

halblaut 1. adj low, subdued; **2.** adv in an undertone

Halbleiter m ELECTR semiconductor

halbmast adv (at) half-mast

Halbmond m half-moon, crescent

Halbpensi,on f (-; no pl) esp Br half board

Halbschlaf m doze

Halbschuh m (low) shoe

Halbschwester f half-sister

halbtags adv: **halbtags arbeiten** work part-time

Halbtagsarbeit f (-; no pl) part-time job

Halbtagskraft f part-time worker, F part-timer

halbwegs [-ve:ks] adv reasonably

Halbwüchsige [-vy:ksɪgə] m, f (-n; -n) adolescent

Halbzeit f SPORT half (time)

Halbzeitstand m SPORT half-time score

Halde ['haldə] f (-; -n) slope; dump

half [half] pret of **helfen**

Hälfte ['hɛlftə] f (-; -n) half; **die Hälfte von** half of

Halfter ['halftɐ] **1.** m, n (-s; -) halter; **2.** n (-s; -), f (-; -n) holster

Halle ['halə] f (-; -n) hall; lounge; **in der Halle** SPORT etc indoors

hallen v/i (ge-, h) resound, reverberate

Hallenbad n indoor swimming pool

Hallensport m indoor sports

Halm [halm] m (-[e]s; -e) BOT blade; ha(u)lm, stalk; straw

Hals [hals] m (-es; Hälse ['hɛlzə]) ANAT neck; throat; **Hals über Kopf** helter-skelter; F **sich vom Hals schaffen** get rid of; F **es hängt mir zum Hals(e) (he)raus** I'm fed up with it; fig **bis zum Hals** up to one's neck

Halsband n (-[e]s; -bänder) necklace; collar

Halsentzündung f MED sore throat

Halskette f necklace

Halsschmerzen pl: **Halsschmerzen haben** have a sore throat

halsstarrig [-ʃtarɪç] adj stubborn, obstinate

Halstuch n neckerchief; scarf

Halt m (-[e]s; -e, -s) a) (no pl) hold; support (a. fig); fig stability, b) stop

halt [halt] int stop!, MIL halt!

haltbar adj durable; GASTR not perishable; fig tenable; **haltbar bis ...** best before ...

Haltbarkeitsdatum n best-by (or best-before) date

halten ['haltən] (irr, ge-, h) **1.** v/t hold; keep (animal, promise etc); make (speech); give (lecture); take (Br a. in) a paper etc; SPORT save; **halten für** regard as; (mis)take for; **viel (wenig) halten von** think highly (little) of; **sich halten** last; GASTR keep; **sich gut halten** do well; **sich halten an** (acc) keep to; **2.** v/i hold, last; stop, halt; ice: bear; rope etc: hold; **halten zu** stand by, F stick to

Halter(in) ['hal-tɐ(-tərɪn)] (-s; -/-; -nen) owner; TECH holder

Haltestelle f stop, RAIL a. station

Halteverbot n MOT no stopping (area)

haltlos adj unsteady; fig baseless

haltmachen v/i (sep, -ge-, h) stop; fig **vor nichts haltmachen** stop at nothing

Haltung f (-; -en) posture; fig attitude (**zu** towards)

hämisch ['hɛ:mɪʃ] adj malicious, sneering

Hammel ['haməl] m (-s; -) zo wether

Hammelfleisch n GASTR mutton

Hammer ['hamɐ] m (-s; Hämmer ['hɛmɐ]) hammer (a. SPORT)

hämmern ['hɛmɐn] v/t and v/i (ge-, h)

hammer

Hämorrhoiden, Hämorriden [hemɔroˈiːdən] pl MED h(a)emorrhoids, F Br piles

Hampelmann [ˈhampəl-] m jumping jack

Hamster [ˈhamstɐ] m (-s; -) zo hamster

ˈhamstern v/t and v/i (ge-, h) hoard

Hand [hant] f (-; Hände [ˈhɛndə]) hand; von Hand, mit der Hand by hand; an Hand von (or gen) by means of; zur Hand at hand; aus erster (zweiter) Hand first-hand (second-hand); an die Hand nehmen take by the hand; sich die Hand geben shake hands; aus der Hand legen lay aside; Hand breit → handbreit; Hand voll → handvoll; Hände hoch (weg)! hands up (off)!

Handarbeit f a) (no pl) manual labo(u)r, b) needlework; es ist Handarbeit it is handmade

Handball m SPORT (European) handball

Handbetrieb m TECH manual operation

Handbreit f (-; -) hand's breadth

Handbremse f MOT handbrake

Handbuch n manual, handbook

Händedruck [ˈhɛndə-] m (-[e]s; -drücke) handshake

Handel [ˈhandəl] m (-s; no pl) commerce, business; trade; market; transaction, deal, bargain; Handel treiben ECON trade (mit with s.o.)

ˈhandeln v/i (ge-, h) act, take action; bargain (um for), haggle (over); mit j-m handeln ECON trade with s.o.; handeln mit deal in; handeln von deal with, be about; es handelt sich um it concerns, it is about; it is a matter of

ˈHandelsabkommen n trade agreement

Handelsbank f (-; -banken) commercial bank

Handelsbi,lanz f balance of trade

ˈhandelseinig adj: handelseinig werden come to terms

ˈHandelsgesellschaft f (trading) company

Handelskammer f chamber of commerce

Handelsschiff n merchant ship

Handelsschule f commercial school

Handelsvertreter m (traveling) salesman, Br sales representative

Handelsware f commodity, merchandise

ˈHandfeger [-feːgə] m (-s; -) handbrush

Handfertigkeit f manual skill

ˈhandfest adj solid

ˈHandfläche f ANAT palm

ˈhandgearbeitet adj handmade

ˈHandgelenk n ANAT wrist

Handgepäck n hand baggage (Br luggage)

Handgra,nate f MIL hand grenade

ˈhandgreiflich [-graiflɪç] adj: handgreiflich werden turn violent, get tough

ˈhandhaben v/t (ge-, h) handle, manage; TECH operate

Händler [ˈhɛndlɐ] m (-s; -), ˈHändlerin f (-; -nen) dealer, trader

ˈhandlich adj handy, manageable

Handlung [ˈhandlʊŋ] f (-; -en) act, action; film etc: story, plot

ˈHandlungsreisende m sales representative, travel(l)ing salesman

Handlungsweise f conduct, behavio(u)r

ˈHandrücken m ANAT back of the hand

Handschellen pl handcuffs; j-m Handschellen anlegen handcuff s.o.

Handschlag m handshake

Handschrift f hand(writing)

ˈhandschriftlich adj handwritten

ˈHandschuh m glove

Handspiel n soccer: hand ball

Handstand m handstand

Handtasche f handbag, purse

Handtuch n towel

Handvoll f handful

Handwagen m handcart

Handwerk n craft, trade

ˈHandwerker [-vɛrkə] m (-s; -) craftsman; workman

ˈHandwerkszeug n (kit of) tools

ˈHandwurzel f ANAT wrist

Handy [ˈhɛndi] n (-s; -s) mobile (phone), cellular phone

Hanf [hanf] m (-es; no pl) BOT hemp; cannabis

Hang [haŋ] m (-[e]s; Hänge [ˈhɛŋə]) a) slope, b) (no pl) fig inclination (zu for), tendency (towards)

Hängebrücke [ˈhɛŋə-] f suspension bridge

Hängelampe f hanging lamp

Hängematte f hammock

hängen [ˈhɛŋən] 1. v/i (irr, ge-, h) hang (an dat on the wall etc; from the ceiling etc); hängen bleiben get stuck (a. fig); hängen bleiben an (dat) get caught on; hängen an (dat) be fond of; be devoted to; alles, woran ich hänge everything that is dear to me; 2. v/t (ge-, h) hang (an acc on)

hängenbleiben v/i (irr, bleiben, sep, -ge-, sein) fig get stuck; → hängen

hänseln [ˈhɛnzəln] v/t (ge-, h) tease (wegen about)

Hanswurst [hansˈvʊrst] m (-[e]s; -e) fool, clown

Hantel [ˈhantəl] f (-; -n) dumbbell

hantieren [hanˈtiːrən] v/i (no -ge-, h) hantieren mit handle; hantieren an (dat) fiddle about with

Happen ['hapən] *m* (-*s*; -) morsel, bite; snack

Hardware ['hɑːdwɛə] *f* (-; -*s*) EDP hardware

Harfe ['harfə] *f* (-; -*n*) MUS harp

Harfenist [harfə'nɪst] *m* (-*en*; -*en*), **Harfe'nistin** *f* (-; -*nen*) MUS harpist

Harke ['harkə] *f* (-; -*n*), **'harken** *v/t* (*ge*-, *h*) rake

harmlos ['harmloːs] *adj* harmless

Harmonie [harmo'niː] *f* (-; -*n*) harmony (*a.* MUS)

harmo'nieren *v/i* (*no -ge-, h*) harmonize (*mit* with)

harmonisch [har'moːnɪʃ] *adj* harmonious

Harn [harn] *m* (-[*e*]*s*; -*e*) MED urine

'Harnblase *f* ANAT (urinary) bladder

'Harnröhre *f* ANAT urethra

Harpune [har'puːnə] *f* (-; -*n*) harpoon

harpunieren [harpu'niːrən] *v/t* (*no -ge-, h*) harpoon

hart [hart] **1.** *adj* hard, F *a.* tough; SPORT rough; severe; **hart gekocht** hard-boiled; **2.** *adv* hard

Härte ['hɛrtə] *f* (-; -*n*) hardness; toughness; roughness; severity; *esp* JUR hardship

'Härtefall *m* case of hardship

'härten *v/t* (*ge*-, *h*) harden

'Hartfaserplatte *f* hardboard

'Hartgeld *n* coin(s)

'hartgesotten [-gəzɔtən] *adj* hard-boiled

'hartherzig *adj* hard-hearted

'hartnäckig [-nɛkɪç] *adj* stubborn, obstinate; persistent

Harz [haːɐts] *n* (-*es*; -*e*) resin; rosin

'harzig *adj* resinous

Hasch [haʃ] F *n* (-*s*; *no pl*) hash

'haschen F *v/i* (*ge*-, *h*) smoke hash

Haschisch ['haʃɪʃ] *n* (-[*s*]; *no pl*) hashish

Hase ['haːzə] *m* (-*n*; -*n*) ZO hare

Haselmaus ['haːzəl-] *f* ZO dormouse

'Haselnuss *f* BOT hazelnut

'Hasenscharte *f* MED harelip

Hass [has] *m* (-*es*; *no pl*) hatred, hate (**auf** *acc*, **gegen** of, for)

hassen ['hasən] *v/t* (*ge*-, *h*) hate

hässlich ['hɛslɪç] *adj* ugly, *fig a.* nasty

Hast [hast] *f* (-; *no pl*) hurry, haste; rush

hasten ['hastən] *v/i* (*ge*-, *sein*) hurry, hasten, rush

'hastig *adj* hasty, hurried

hätscheln ['hɛːtʃəln] *v/t* (*ge*-, *h*) fondle; *contp* pamper

hatte ['hatə] *pret of* **haben**

Haube ['haubə] *f* (-; -*n*) bonnet (*a.* Br MOT); cap; ZO crest; MOT hood

Hauch [haux] *m* (-[*e*]*s*; -*e*) breath; whiff; *fig* touch, trace

hauchen ['hauxən] *v/t* (*ge*-, *h*) breathe

hauen F *v/t* ([*irr,*] *ge*-, *h*) hit, beat, thrash; TECH hew; **sich hauen** (have a) fight

Haufen ['haufən] *m* (-*s*; -) heap, pile (*both a.* F); F crowd

häufen ['hɔyfən] *v/t* (*ge*-, *h*) heap (up), pile (up); **sich häufen** *fig* become more frequent, be on the increase

häufig ['hɔyfɪç] **1.** *adj* frequent; **2.** *adv* frequently, often

Haupt [haupt] *n* (-[*e*]*s*; *Häupter* ['hɔyptɐ]) head, *fig a.* leader

Hauptbahnhof *m* main or central station

Hauptbeschäftigung *f* chief occupation

Hauptbestandteil *m* chief ingredient

Hauptdarsteller(in) leading actor (actress), lead

Häuptelsa,lat ['hɔyptəl-] *Austrian m* BOT lettuce

'Hauptfach *n* UNIV major, Br main subject

Hauptfilm *m* feature (film)

Hauptgericht *n* GASTR main course

Hauptgewinn *m* first prize

Hauptgrund *m* main reason

Hauptleitung *f* TECH main

Häuptling ['hɔyptlɪŋ] *m* (-*s*; -*e*) chief

'Hauptmann *m* (-[*e*]*s*; -*leute*) MIL captain

Hauptme,nü *n* EDP main menu

Hauptmerkmal *n* chief characteristic

Hauptper,son F *f* center (Br centre) of attention

Hauptquar,tier *n* headquarters

Hauptrolle *f* THEA *etc* lead(ing part)

'Hauptsache *f* main thing or point

'hauptsächlich *adj* main, chief, principal

'Hauptsatz *m* LING main clause

Hauptsendezeit *f* TV prime time, Br peak time (*or* viewing hours)

Hauptspeicher *m* EDP main memory

Hauptstadt *f* capital

Hauptstraße *f* main street; main road

Hauptverkehrsstraße *f* arterial road

Hauptverkehrszeit *f* rush or peak hour(s)

Hauptversammlung *f* general meeting

Hauptwohnsitz *m* main place of residence

Hauptwort *n* (-[*e*]*s*; -*wörter*) LING noun

Haus [haus] *n* (-*es*; *Häuser* ['hɔyzɐ]) house; building; **zu Hause** at home, in; **nach Hause kommen** (**bringen**) come *or* get (take) home

Hausangestellte *m, f* domestic (servant)

Hausapo,theke *f* medicine cabinet

Hausarbeit *f* housework

Hausarzt *m*, **Hausärztin** *f* family doctor

Hausaufgaben *pl* PED homework, assignment; **s-e Hausaufgabenn machen** *a. fig* do one's homework

Hausbar *f* cocktail cabinet

Hausbesetzer *m* (-*s*; -) squatter

Hausbesetzung f squatting
Hausbesitzer m house owner
Hauseinweihung f house-warming (party)
hausen ['hauzən] v/i (ge-, h) live; fig play havoc
'**Hausflur** m (entrance) hall, hallway
'**Hausfrau** f housewife
'**Hausfriedensbruch** m JUR trespass
'**hausgemacht** adj homemade
'**Haushalt** m (-[e]s; -e) household; PARL budget; **(j-m) den Haushalt führen** keep house for s.o.)
'**Haushälterin** [-hɛltərɪn] f (-; -nen) housekeeper
'**Haushaltsgeld** n housekeeping money
Haushaltsplan m PARL budget
Haushaltswaren pl household articles
'**Hausherr** m head of the household; host
Hausherrin f lady of the house; hostess
'**haushoch** adj huge; crushing (defeat etc)
hausieren [hau'zi:rən] v/i (no -ge-, h) peddle, hawk (**mit et.** s.th.) (a. fig)
Hau'sierer m (-s; -) pedlar, hawker
häuslich ['hɔyslɪç] adj domestic; home-loving
'**Hausmädchen** n (house)maid
Hausmann m house husband
Hausmannskost f plain fare
Hausmeister m caretaker, janitor
Hausmittel n household remedy
Hausordnung f house rules
Hausrat m (-[e]s; no pl) household effects
Hausschlüssel m front-door key
Hausschuh m slipper
Hausse ['ho:s(ə)] f (-; -n) ECON rise, boom
'**Haussuchung** f (-; -en) house search
Haustier n domestic animal
Haustür f front door
Hausverwaltung f property management
Hauswirt m landlord
Hauswirtin f landlady
Hauswirtschaft f (-; no pl) housekeeping
Hauswirtschaftslehre f domestic science, home economics
Hauswirtschaftsschule f domestic science (or home economics) school
Haut [haut] f (-; Häute ['hɔytə]) skin; complexion; **bis auf die Haut durchnässt** soaked to the skin
Hautabschürfung f MED abrasion
Hautarzt m, **Hautärztin** f dermatologist
Hautausschlag m MED rash
'**hauteng** adj skin-tight
'**Hautfarbe** f colo(u)r of the skin; complexion
Hautkrankheit f skin disease
Hautpflege f skin care
Hautschere f cuticle scissors

Hbf. ABBR of **Hauptbahnhof** cent. sta., central station
H-Bombe ['ha:bɔmbə] f MIL H-bomb
Hebamme ['he:pʔamə] f (-; -n) midwife
Hebebühne ['he:bə-] f MOT car hoist
Hebel ['he:bəl] m (-s; -) TECH lever
heben ['he:bən] v/t (irr, ge-, h) lift, raise (a. fig); heave; hoist; fig a. improve; **sich heben** rise, go up
Hecht [hɛçt] m (-[e]s; -e) ZO pike
'**hechten** v/i (ge-, sein) dive (**nach** for); SPORT do a long-fly
Heck [hɛk] n (-[e]s; -e) MAR stern; AVIAT tail; MOT rear
Hecke ['hɛkə] f (-; -n) BOT hedge
'**Heckenrose** f BOT dogrose
'**Heckenschütze** m MIL sniper
'**Heckscheibe** f MOT rear window
Heer [he:ɐ] n (-[e]s; -e) MIL army, fig a. host
Hefe ['he:fə] f (-; -n) yeast
Heft [hɛft] n (-[e]s; -e) notebook; exercise book; booklet; issue, number
heften ['hɛftən] v/t (ge-, h) fix, fasten, attach (**an** acc to); pin (to); tack, baste; stitch
Hefter ['hɛftɐ] m (-s; -) stapler; file
heftig ['hɛftɪç] adj violent, fierce; heavy
'**Heftklammer** f staple
'**Heftpflaster** n bandage, Band Aid®, Br (adhesive or sticking) plaster
Hehl [he:l] n: **kein Hehl aus et. machen** make no secret of s.th.
Hehler ['he:lɐ] m (-s; -) JUR receiver of stolen goods, sl fence
Hehlerei [he:lə'rai] f (-; -en) JUR receiving stolen goods
Heide[1] ['haidə] m (-n; -n) REL heathen
Heide[2] f (-; -n) heath(land)
'**Heidekraut** n (-[e]s; no pl) BOT heather, heath
'**Heidenangst** F f: **e-e Heidenangst haben** be scared stiff
Heidengeld F n: **ein Heidengeld** a fortune
Heidenlärm F m: **ein Heidenlärm** a hell of a noise
Heidenspaß F m: **e-n Heidenspaß haben** have a ball
'**Heidentum** n (-s; no pl) REL heathenism
Heidin ['haidɪn] f (-; -nen), '**heidnisch** ['haidnɪʃ] adj REL heathen
heikel ['haikəl] adj delicate, tricky; tender; F fussy
heil [hail] adj safe, unhurt; undamaged, whole, intact
Heil n (-s; no pl) REL grace; **sein Heil versuchen** try one's luck
Heiland ['hailant] m (-[e]s; no pl) REL Sav-

io(u)r, Redeemer

'**Heilanstalt** f sanatorium, sanitarium; mental home

'**Heilbad** n health resort, spa

'**heilbar** adj curable

heilen ['hailən] **1.** v/t (ge-, h) cure; **2.** v/i (ge-, sein) heal (up)

'**Heilgym,nastik** f physiotherapy

heilig ['hailɪç] adj REL holy; sacred (a. fig)

'**Heilig,abend** m Christmas Eve

Heilige ['hailɪgə] m, f (-n; -n) REL saint

heiligen ['hailɪgən] v/t (ge-, h) REL sanctify (a. fig), hallow

'**heiligsprechen** v/t (irr, **sprechen**, sep, -ge-, -sein) canonize

'**Heiligtum** n (-s; -tümer [-ty:mɐ]) REL sanctuary, shrine

'**Heilkraft** f healing or curative power

'**heilkräftig** adj curative

'**Heilkraut** n BOT medicinal herb

'**heillos** fig adj utter, hopeless

'**Heilmittel** n remedy, cure (both a. fig)

Heilpraktiker(in) [-praktikɐ (-kərɪn)] (-s; -/-; -nen) nonmedical practitioner

'**Heilquelle** f (medicinal) mineral spring

'**heilsam** fig adj salutary

'**Heilsar,mee** f Salvation Army

'**Heilung** f (-; -en) cure; healing

heim [haim] adv home

Heim n (-[e]s; -e) a) (no pl) home, b) hostel

Heim... in cpds ...computer, ...mannschaft, ...sieg, ...spiel etc: home

Heimat ['haima:t] f (-; no pl) home; home country; home town; **in der (meiner) Heimat** at home

'**heimatlos** adj homeless

'**Heimatstadt** f home town

'**Heimatvertriebene** m, f expellee

heimisch ['haimɪʃ] adj home, domestic; BOT, ZO etc native; fig homelike, hom(e)y; **sich heimisch fühlen** feel at home

'**Heimkehr** [-ke:ɐ] f (-; no pl) return (home)

'**heimkehren** v/i (sep, -ge-, sein) return home, come back

'**heimlich** adj secret

'**Heimlichkeit** f (-; -en) a) (no pl) secrecy, b) pl secrets

'**Heimreise** f journey home

'**heimsuchen** v/t (sep, -ge-, h) strike

'**heimtückisch** adj insidious (a. MED); treacherous

'**heimwärts** [-vɛrts] adv homeward(s)

'**Heimweg** m way home

'**Heimweh** n (-s; no pl) homesickness; **Heimweh haben** be homesick

'**Heimwerker** [-vɛrkɐ] m (-s; -) do-it-yourselfer

Heirat ['haira:t] f (-; -en) marriage

heiraten ['haira:tən] v/t and v/i (ge-, h) marry, get married (to)

'**Heiratsantrag** m proposal (of marriage); **j-m e-n Heiratsantrag machen** propose to s.o.

Heiratsschwindler m marriage impostor

Heiratsvermittler(in) (-s; -/-; -nen) marriage broker

Heiratsvermittlung f marriage bureau

heiser ['haizɐ] adj hoarse, husky

'**Heiserkeit** f (-; no pl) hoarseness, huskiness

heiß [hais] adj hot, fig a. passionate, ardent; **mir ist heiß** I am or feel hot

heißen ['haisən] v/i (irr, ge-, h) be called; mean; **wie heißen Sie?** what's your name?; **wie heißt das?** what do you call this?; **was heißt ... auf Englisch?** what is ... in English?; **es heißt im Text** it says in the text; **das heißt** that is (ABBR **d. h.** i. e.)

heiter ['haitɐ] adj cheerful; humorous (film etc); METEOR fair; fig **aus heiterem Himmel** out of the blue

'**Heiterkeit** f (-; no pl) cheerfulness; amusement

heizbar ['haitsba:ɐ] adj heated

heizen ['haitsən] v/t and v/i (ge-, h) heat; **mit Kohlen heizen** burn coal

Heizer ['haitsɐ] m (-s; -) MAR, RAIL stoker

'**Heizkessel** m boiler

'**Heizkissen** n electric cushion

'**Heizkörper** m radiator

'**Heizkraftwerk** n thermal power-station

'**Heizmateri,al** n fuel

'**Heizöl** n fuel oil

'**Heizung** f (-; -en) heating

Held [hɛlt] m (-en; -en [hɛldən]) hero

heldenhaft ['hɛldənhaft] adj heroic

'**Heldentat** f heroic deed

'**Heldentum** n (-s; no pl) heroism

Heldin ['hɛldɪn] f (-; -nen) heroine

helfen ['hɛlfən] v/i (irr, ge-, h) help, aid; assist; **j-m bei et. helfen** help s.o. with or in (doing) s.th.; **helfen gegen** MED etc be good for; **er weiß sich zu helfen** he can manage; **es hilft nichts** it's no use

Helfer ['hɛlfɐ] m (-s; -), **Helferin** f (-; -nen) helper, assistant

'**Helfershelfer** contp m accomplice

hell [hɛl] adj bright (light, flame etc); light (color etc); light-colo(u)red (dress etc); clear (voice etc); pale (beer); fig bright, clever; **es wird schon hell** it's getting light already

'**hellblau** adj light blue

'**hellblond** adj very fair

hellhörig adj quick of hearing; ARCH poorly soundproofed; **hellhörig werden**

prick up one's ears

'**Hellseher** m (-s; -), '**Hellseherin** f (-; -nen) clairvoyant

Helm [hɛlm] m (-[e]s; -e) helmet

Hemd [hɛmt] n (-[e]s; -en ['hɛmdən]) shirt; vest

Hemdbluse f shirt

Hemdblusenkleid n shirtwaist, Br shirt-waister

Hemisphäre [hemi'sfɛːrə] f (-; -n) hemisphere

hemmen ['hɛmən] v/t (ge-, h) check, stop; hamper

'**Hemmung** f (-; -en) PSYCH inhibition; scruple

'**hemmungslos** adj unrestrained; unscrupulous

Hengst [hɛŋst] m (-[e]s; -e) zo stallion

Henkel ['hɛŋkəl] m (-s; -) handle

Henker ['hɛŋkɐ] m (-s; -) hangman, executioner

Henne ['hɛnə] f (-; -n) zo hen

her [heːɐ] adv here; **das ist lange her** that was a long time ago

herab [hɛ'rap] adv down

herablassen fig v/refl (irr, **lassen**, sep, -ge-, h) condescend

herablassend adj condescending

herabsehen fig v/i (irr, **sehen**, sep, -ge-, h) **herabsehen auf** (acc) look down upon

herabsetzen v/t (sep, -ge-, h) reduce; fig disparage

heran [hɛ'ran] adv close, near; **heran an** (acc) up or near to

herangehen v/i (irr, **gehen**, sep, -ge-, sein) **herangehen an** (acc) walk up to; fig set about a task etc

herankommen v/i (irr, **kommen**, sep, -ge-, sein) come near (a. fig)

heranwachsen v/i (irr, **wachsen**, sep, -ge-, sein) grow (up) (**zu** into)

He'ranwachsende m, f (-n; -n) adolescent

he'ranwinken v/t (sep, -ge-, h) hail (taxi etc)

herauf [hɛ'rauf] adv up (here); upstairs

heraufbeschwören v/t (irr, **schwören**, sep, no -ge-, h) call up; bring on, provoke

heraus [hɛ'raus] adv out; fig **aus** (dat) ... **heraus** out of ...; **zum Fenster heraus** out of the window; **heraus mit der Sprache!** speak out!, out with it!

herausbekommen v/t (irr, **kommen**, sep, no -ge-, h) get; get back (change); fig find out

herausbringen v/t (irr, **bringen**, sep, -ge-, h) bring out; PRINT publish; THEA stage; fig find out

herausfinden (irr, **finden**, sep, -ge-, h) **1.** v/t find; fig find out, discover; **2.** v/i find one's way out

He'rausforderer m (-s; -) challenger

he'rausfordern v/t (sep, -ge-, h) challenge; provoke; F ask for it

He'rausforderung f challenge; provocation

he'rausgeben v/t (irr, **geben**, sep, -ge-, h) give back; give up; PRINT publish; issue; give change (**auf** acc for)

He'rausgeber(in) [-geːbɐ (-bərin)] (-s; -/-; -nen) publisher

he'rauskommen v/i (irr, **kommen**, sep, -ge-, sein) come out; book: be published; stamps: be issued; **herauskommen aus** get out of; F **groß herauskommen** be a great success

herausnehmen v/t (irr, **nehmen**, sep, -ge-, h) take out; SPORT take s.o. off the team; fig **sich et. herausnehmen** take liberties, go too far

herausputzen v/t and v/refl (sep, -ge-, h) spruce (o.s.) up

herausreden v/refl (sep, -ge-, h) make excuses; talk one's way out

herausstellen v/t (sep, -ge-, h) put out; fig emphasize; **sich herausstellen als** turn out or prove to be

herausstrecken v/t (sep, -ge-, h) stick out

heraussuchen v/t (sep, -ge-, h) pick out; **j-m et. heraussuchen** find s.o. s.th.

herb [hɛrp] adj tart; dry (wine etc); fig harsh; bitter

her'bei adv up, over, here

herbeieilen v/i (sep, -ge-, sein) come running up

herbeiführen fig v/t (sep, -ge-, h) cause, bring about

Herberge ['hɛrbergə] f (-; -n) inn; lodging; hostel

Herbst [hɛrpst] m (-[e]s; -e) fall, autumn

Herd [heːɐt] m (-[e]s; -e) ['heːɐdə]) cooker, stove; fig center, Br centre; MED focus, seat

Herde ['heːɐdə] f (-; -n) zo herd (a. fig contp); flock (of sheep, geese etc)

herein [hɛ'rain] adv in (here); **herein!** come in!

hereinbrechen v/i (irr, **brechen**, sep, -ge-, sein) night: fall; **hereinbrechen über** (acc) befall s.o.

hereinfallen F v/i (irr, **fallen**, sep, -ge-, sein) be taken in (**auf** acc by)

hereinlegen F v/t (sep, -ge-, h) take s.o. in

'**herfallen** v/i (irr, **fallen**, sep, -ge-, sein) **herfallen über** (acc) attack (a. fig)

'**Hergang** m: **j-m den Hergang schildern** tell s.o. what happened '**hergeben** v/t (irr, **geben**, sep, -ge-, h) give up, part with; **sich hergeben zu** lend o.s. to

Hering ['heːrɪŋ] m (-s; -e) zo herring

'**herkommen** v/i (irr, **kommen**, sep, -ge-, sein) come (here); **herkommen von** come from, fig a. be caused by

'**herkömmlich** [-kœmlɪç] adj conventional (a. MIL)

'**Herkunft** [-kʊnft] f (-; no pl) origin; birth, descent

heroisch [heˈroːɪʃ] adj heroic

Herr [hɛr] m (-n; -en) gentleman; master; REL the Lord; **Herr Brown** Mr Brown; **Herr der Lage** master of the situation

'**Herrenbekleidung** f menswear

Herrendoppel n tennis: men's doubles

Herreneinzel n tennis: men's singles

'**herrenlos** adj abandoned; stray (dog)

'**Herrentoi,lette** f men's restroom (Br toilet or lavatory)

'**herrichten** v/t (sep, -ge-, h) get ready, F fix

herrisch ['hɛrɪʃ] adj imperious

herrlich ['hɛrlɪç] adj marvel(l)ous, wonderful, F fantastic

'**Herrlichkeit** f (-; -en) glory

'**Herrschaft** f (-; no pl) rule, power, control (a. fig) (**über** acc over); **die Herrschaft verlieren über** (acc) lose control of

herrschen ['hɛrʃən] v/i (ge-, h) rule; **es herrschte ...** there was ...

Herrscher(in) ['hɛrʃɐ (-ʃərɪn)] (-s; -/-; -nen) ruler; sovereign, monarch

'**herrschsüchtig** adj domineering, F bossy

'**herrühren** v/i (sep, -ge-, h) **herrühren von** come from, be due to

'**herstellen** v/t (sep, -ge-, h) make, produce; fig establish

'**Herstellung** f (-; no pl) production; fig establishment

'**Herstellungskosten** pl production cost(s)

herüber [hɛ'ryːbɐ] adv over (here), across

herum [hɛ'rʊm] adv (a)round; F **anders herum** the other way round

herumführen v/t (sep, -ge-, h) **j-n (in der Stadt** etc) **herumführen** show s.o. (a)round (the town etc)

herumkommen F v/i (irr, **kommen**, sep, -ge-, sein) (**weit** or **viel**) **herumkommen** get around; **um et. herumkommen** fig get (a)round s.th.

herumkriegen F v/t (sep, -ge-, h) **j-n zu et. herumkriegen** get s.o. round to (doing) s.th.

herumlungern F v/i (sep, -ge-, h) loaf or hang around

herumreichen v/t (sep, -ge-, h) pass or hand round

herumsprechen v/refl (irr, **sprechen**, sep, -ge-, h) get around

herumtreiben F v/refl (irr, **treiben**, sep, -ge-, h) gad or knock about

He'rumtreiber F m (-s; -), **He'rumtreiberin** F f (-; -nen) tramp, loafer

herunter [hɛ'rʊntɐ] adv down; downstairs

heruntergekommen adj run-down; seedy, shabby

herunterhauen F v/t (sep, -ge-, h) **j-m e-e herunterhauen** smack or slap s.o. ('s face)

heruntermachen F v/t (sep, -ge-, h) run s.o. or s.th. down

herunterspielen F v/t (sep, -ge-, h) play s.th. down

hervor [hɛɐ'foːɐ] adv out of or from, forth

hervorbringen v/t (irr, **bringen**, sep, -ge-, h) bring out, produce (a. fig); yield; utter

hervorgehen v/i (irr, **gehen**, sep, -ge-, sein) **hervorgehen aus** (dat) follow from; **als Sieger hervorgehen** come off victorious

hervorheben v/t (irr, **heben**, sep, -ge-, h) stress, emphasize

hervorragend adj outstanding, excellent, superior; prominent, eminent

hervorrufen v/t (irr, **rufen**, sep, -ge-, h) cause, bring about; create

hervorstechend adj striking

hervortretend adj prominent; protruding, bulging

hervortun v/refl (irr, **tun**, sep, -ge-, h) distinguish o.s. (**als** as)

Herz [hɛrts] n (-ens; -en) ANAT heart (a. fig); cards: heart(s); **j-m das Herz brechen** break s.o.'s heart; **sich ein Herz fassen** take heart; **mit ganzem Herzen** whole-heartedly; **schweren Herzens** with a heavy heart; **sich et. zu Herzen nehmen** take s.th. to heart; **es nicht übers Herz bringen zu** inf not have the heart to inf; **et. auf dem Herzen haben** have s.th. on one's mind; **ins Herz schließen** take to one's heart

Herzanfall m heart attack

'**Herzenslust** f: **nach Herzenslust** to one's heart's content

Herzenswunsch m heart's desire, dearest wish

'**Herzfehler** m cardiac defect

'**herzhaft** adj hearty; savo(u)ry

'**herzig** adj sweet, lovely, cute

Herzin,farkt m MED cardiac infarct(-ion), F mst heart attack, coronary

Herzklopfen n (-s; no pl) palpitation; **er hatte Herzklopfen (vor** dat) his heart was throbbing (with)

'**herzkrank** *adj* suffering from (a) heart disease
'**herzlich 1.** *adj* cordial, hearty; warm, friendly; **2.** *adv:* **herzlich gern** with pleasure
'**herzlos** *adj* heartless
Herzog ['hɛrtsoːk] *m* (-s; *Herzöge* ['hɛrt-søːɡə]) duke
Herzogin ['hɛrtsoːɡɪn] *f* (-; -*nen*) duchess
'**Herzschlag** *m* heartbeat; MED heart failure
Herzschrittmacher *m* MED (cardiac) pacemaker
Herztransplantati,on *f* MED heart transplant
'**herzzerreißend** *adj* heart-rending
Hetze ['hɛtsə] *f* (-; *no pl*) hurry, rush; *etc* agitation, campaign(ing) (**gegen** against)
'**hetzen 1.** *v/t* (*ge*-, h) rush; *zo* hunt, chase; **e-n Hund auf j-n hetzen** set a dog on s.o.; **2.** *v/i* a) (*ge*-, *sein*) hurry, rush, b) (*ge*-, h) POL *etc* agitate (**gegen** against)
'**hetzerisch** *adj* inflammatory
'**Hetzjagd** *f* hunt(ing), chase (*a. fig*); *fig* rush
'**Hetzkam,pagne** *f* POL smear campaign
Heu [hɔy] *n* (-[e]s; *no pl*) hay
'**Heuboden** *m* hayloft
Heuchelei [hɔyçə'lai] *f* (-; -*en*) hypocrisy; cant
heucheln ['hɔyçəln] *v/i* and *v/t* (*ge*-, h) feign, simulate
Heuchler(in) ['hɔyçlɐ (-lərɪn)] (-s; -/-; -*nen*) hypocrite
'**heuchlerisch** ['hɔyçlərɪʃ] *adj* hypocritical
heuer ['hɔyɐ] *Austrian adv* this year
Heuer ['hɔyɐ] *f* (-; -*n*) MAR pay
'**heuern** *v/t* (*ge*-, h) hire, MAR a. sign on
heulen ['hɔylən] *v/i* (*ge*-, h) howl; F *contp* bawl; MOT roar; *siren:* whine
'**Heuschnupfen** *m* MED hay fever
'**Heuschrecke** *f* (-; -*n*) zo grasshopper; locust
heute ['hɔytə] *adv* today; **heute Abend** this evening, tonight; **heute früh**, **heute Morgen** this morning; **heute in acht Tagen** a week from now; **heute vor acht Tagen** a week ago today
heutig ['hɔytɪç] *adj* today's; of today, present(-day)
'**heutzutage** *adv* nowadays, these days
Hexe ['hɛksə] *f* (-; -*n*) witch (*a. fig*); **alte Hexe** (old) hag
'**hexen** *v/i* (*ge*-, h) practice witchcraft; F work miracles
'**Hexenkessel** *m* inferno
Hexenschuss *m* (-*es*; *no pl*) MED lumbago
hieb [hiːp] *pret of* **hauen**

Hieb [hiːp] *m* (-[e]*s*; -*e* ['hiːbə]) blow, stroke; punch; lash, cut; *pl* beating; thrashing
hielt [hiːlt] *pret of* **halten**
hier [hiːɐ] *adv* here, in this place; present; **hier entlang!** this way!
hieran ['hiːran] *adv* from *or* in this
hierauf ['hiːrauf] *adv* on it *or* this; after this, then
hieraus ['hiːraus] *adv* from *or* out of this
'**hier bei** *adv* here, in this case; on this occasion
'**hier durch** *adv* by this, hereby, this way
'**hier für** *adv* for this
'**hier her** *adv* (over) here, this way; **bis hierher** so far
hierin ['hiːrɪn] *adv* in this
'**hier mit** *adv* with this
'**hier nach** *adv* after this; according to this
hierüber ['hiː'ryːbɐ] *adv* about this (subject)
hierunter ['hiː'rʊntɐ] *adv* under this; among these; *understand etc* by this *or* that
'**hier von** *adv* of *or* from this
'**hier zu** *adv* for this; to this
hiesig ['hiːzɪç] *adj* local; **ein Hiesiger** one of the locals
hieß [hiːs] *pret of* **heißen**
Hilfe ['hɪlfə] *f* (-; -*n*) help; aid (*a. ECON*, assistance (*a. MED*), relief (**für** to); **Erste Hilfe** first aid; **um Hilfe rufen** cry for help; **Hilfe!** help!; → **mithilfe**
Hilfeme,nü *n* EDP help menu
Hilferuf *m* call (*or* cry) for help
Hilfestellung *f* support (*a. fig*)
'**hilflos** *adj* helpless
'**hilfreich** *adj* helpful
'**Hilfsakti,on** *f* relief action
'**Hilfsarbeiter** *m*, '**Hilfsarbeiterin** *f* unskilled worker
'**hilfsbedürftig** *adj* needy
'**hilfsbereit** *adj* helpful, ready to help
'**Hilfsbereitschaft** *f* (-; *no pl*) readiness to help, helpfulness
Hilfsmittel *n* aid, TECH *a.* device
Hilfsorganisati,on *f* relief organization
Hilfsverb *n* LING auxiliary (verb)
Himbeere ['hɪmbeːrə] *f* BOT raspberry
Himmel ['hɪməl] *m* (-s; -*s*) sky; REL heaven (*a. fig*); **um Himmels willen** for Heaven's sake; → **heiter**
'**Himmelfahrt** REL Ascension (Day)
'**Himmelskörper** *m* AST celestial body
Himmelsrichtung *f* direction; cardinal point
himmlisch ['hɪmlɪʃ] *adj* heavenly, *fig a.* marvel(l)ous
hin [hɪn] **1.** *adv* there; **bis hin zu** as far as;

noch lange hin still a long way off; *auf s-e Bitte (s-n Rat) hin* at his request (advice); *hin und her* to and fro, back and forth; *hin und wieder* now and then; *hin und zurück* there and back; RAIL round trip, round-trip ticket, *esp Br* return (ticket); **2.** F *pred adj* ruined; done for; gone

hi'nab *adv → hinunter*

'**hinarbeiten** *v/i (sep, -ge-, h)* **hinarbeiten auf** *(acc)* work towards

hi'nauf *adv* up (there); upstairs; *die Straße etc hinauf* up the street *etc*

hinaufgehen *v/i (irr, gehen, sep, -ge-, sein)* go up, *fig a.* rise

hi'naus *adv* out; *aus ... hinaus* out of ...; *in (acc) ... hinaus* out into ...; *hinaus (mit dir)!* (get) out!, out you go!

hinausgehen *v/i (irr, gehen, sep, -ge-, sein)* go out(side); *hinausgehen über (acc)* go beyond; *hinausgehen auf (acc)* window etc: look out onto

hinauslaufen *v/i (irr, laufen, sep, -ge-, sein)* run out(side); *hinauslaufen auf (acc)* come or amount to

hinausschieben *v/t (irr, schieben, sep, -ge-, h)* put off, postpone

hinausstellen *v/t (sep, -ge-, h)* SPORT send *s.o.* off (the field)

hinauswerfen *v/t (irr, werfen, sep, -ge-, h)* throw out (*a. fig*), *fig a.* kick out; (give) *s.o.* the) sack, fire

hinauswollen *v/i (sep, -ge-, h)* **hinauswollen auf** *(acc)* aim (or drive or get) at; *hoch hinauswollen* aim high

'**Hinblick** *m*: *im Hinblick auf (acc)* in view of, with regard to

'**hinbringen** *v/t (irr, bringen, sep, -ge-, h)* take there

hinderlich ['hɪndəlɪç] *adj* hindering, impeding; *j-m hinderlich sein* be in s.o.'s way

hindern ['hɪndɐn] *v/t (ge-, h)* hinder, hamper; *hindern an (dat)* prevent from

Hindernis ['hɪndɐnɪs] *n (-ses; -se)* obstacle *(a. fig)*

Hindernisrennen *n* steeplechase

Hindu ['hɪndu] *m (-[s]; -[s])* Hindu

Hinduismus [hɪndu'ɪsmʊs] *m (-; no pl)* hinduism

hin'durch *adv* through; *das ganze Jahr etc hindurch* throughout the year *etc*

hi'nein *adv* in; *hinein mit dir!* in you go!

hineingehen *v/i (irr, gehen, sep, -ge-, sein)* go in; *hineingehen in (acc)* go into

'**hinfallen** *v/i (irr, fallen, sep, -ge-, sein)* fall (down)

'**hinfällig** *adj* frail, infirm; invalid

hing [hɪŋ] *pret of hängen 1*

'**Hingabe** *f (-; no pl)* devotion (*an acc* to)

'**hingeben** *v/t (irr, geben, sep, -ge-, h)* give (up); *sich hingeben (dat)* give o.s. to; devote o.s. to

'**hinhalten** *v/t (irr, halten, sep, -ge-, h)* hold out; *j-n hinhalten* put s.o. off

hinken ['hɪŋkən] *v/i (h)* (walk with a) limp, b) *(ge-, sein)* limp

'**hinkommen** *v/i (irr, kommen, sep, -ge-, sein)* get there

hinkriegen F *v/t (sep, -ge-, h)* manage

'**hinlänglich** *adj* sufficient

'**hinlegen** *v/t (sep, -ge-, h)* lay or put down; *sich hinlegen* lie down

'**hinnehmen** *v/t (irr, nehmen, sep, -ge-, h)* put up with

'**hinreißen** *v/t (irr, reißen, sep, -ge-, h)* carry away

hinreißend *adj* entrancing; breathtaking

'**hinrichten** *v/t (sep, -ge-, h)* execute

'**Hinrichtung** *f (-; -en)* execution

'**hinsetzen** *v/t (sep, -ge-, h)* set or put down; *sich hinsetzen* sit down

'**Hinsicht** *f (-; no pl)* respect; *in gewisser Hinsicht* in a way

'**hinsichtlich** *prp (gen)* with respect or regard to

'**Hinspiel** *n* SPORT first leg

'**hinstellen** *v/t (sep, -ge-, h)* put (down); *hinstellen als* make *s.o. or s.th.* appear to be

hinten ['hɪntən] *adv* at the back; MOT in the back; *von hinten* from behind

hinter ['hɪntɐ] *prp (dat)* behind

'**Hinter...** *in cpds* ...achse, ...eingang, ...rad etc: rear ...

Hinterbein *n* hind leg

Hinterbliebenen [-'bliːbənən] *pl the* bereaved; *esp* JUR surviving dependents

hinterei'nander *adv* one after the other; *dreimal hintereinander* three times in a row

'**Hintergedanke** *m* ulterior motive

hinter'gehen *v/t (irr, gehen, no -ge-, h)* deceive

'**Hintergrund** *m* background *(a. fig)*

'**Hinterhalt** *m* ambush

'**hinterhältig** [-hɛltɪç] *adj* insidious, underhand(ed)

'**Hinterhaus** *n* rear building

hinter'her *adv* behind, after; afterwards

'**Hinterhof** *m* backyard

'**Hinterkopf** *m* back of the head

hinter'lassen *v/t (irr, lassen, no -ge-, h)* leave (behind)

Hinter'lassenschaft *f (-; -en)* property (left), estate

hinter'legen *v/t (no -ge-, h)* deposit (*bei* with)

'Hinterlist f deceit(fulness); (underhanded) trick

'hinterlistig adj deceitful; underhand(ed)

'Hintermann m person (car etc) behind (one); fig mst pl person behind the scenes, brain(s), mastermind

'Hintern F m (-s; -) bottom, backside, behind, Br bum

'hinterrücks [-ryks] adv from behind

'Hinterseite f back

Hinterteil F n → Hintern

'Hintertreppe f back stairs

'Hintertür f back door

hinter'ziehen v/t (irr, ziehen, no -ge-, h) evade (taxes)

'Hinterzimmer n back room

hi'nüber adv over, across; hinüber sein F be ruined; GASTR be spoilt

hi'nunter adv down; downstairs; die Straße hinunter down the road

Hinweg ['hɪnveːk] m way there

hinweg [hɪn'vɛk] adv: über (acc) ... hinweg over ...

hinweg'kommen v/i (irr, kommen sep, -ge-, sein) hinwegkommen über (acc) get over

hinweg'sehen v/i (irr, sehen, sep, -ge-, h) hinwegsehen über (acc) ignore

hinweg'setzen v/refl (sep, -ge-, h) sich hinwegsetzen über (acc) ignore, disregard

Hinweis ['hɪnvaɪs] m (-es; -e) reference (auf acc to); hint, tip (as to, regarding); indication (of), clue (as to)

'hinweisen (irr, weisen, sep, -ge-, h) 1. v/t: j-n hinweisen auf (acc) draw or call s.o.'s attention to; 2. v/i: hinweisen auf (acc) point at or to, indicate; fig point out, indicate; hint at

'Hinweisschild n, Hinweistafel f sign, notice

'hinwerfen v/t (irr, werfen, sep, -ge-, h) throw down

hin'zielen v/refl (irr, ziehen, sep, -ge-, h) extend (bis zu to), stretch (to); drag on

hin'zufügen v/t (sep, -ge-, h) add (zu to) (a. fig)

hinzu'kommen v/i (irr, kommen, sep, -ge-, sein) be added; hinzu kommt, dass add to this ..., and what is more, ...

hinzu'ziehen v/t (irr, ziehen, sep, -ge-, h) call in, consult

Hirn [hɪrn] n (-[e]s; -e) ANAT brain; fig brain(s), mind

'Hirngespinst n fantasy

Hirsch [hɪrʃ] m (-[e]s; -e) ZO stag

'Hirschgeweih n ZO antlers

'Hirschkuh f ZO hind

Hirse ['hɪrzə] f (-; -n) BOT millet

Hirte ['hɪrtə] m (-n; -n) herdsman; shepherd (a. fig)

hissen ['hɪsən] v/t (ge-, h) hoist

Historiker [hɪs'toːrikɐ] m (-s; -), His'torikerin f (-; -nen) historian

his'torisch adj historical; historic (event etc)

Hitliste ['hɪtlɪstə] f top 40 etc, charts

Hitze ['hɪtsə] f (-; no pl) heat

'Hitzewelle f heat wave

'hitzig adj hot-tempered, peppery; heated (debate etc)

'Hitzkopf m hothead

'Hitzschlag m MED heatstroke

HIV-negativ [haːʔiːˈfaʊ] adj MED HIV negative

HIV-positiv adj MED HIV positive

HIV-Positive m, f (-n; -n) MED HIV carrier

H-Milch ['haː-] f Br long-life milk

hob [hoːp] pret of heben

Hobby ['hɔbi] n (-s; -s) hobby

'Hobby... in cpds amateur ...

Hobel ['hoːbəl] m (-s; -) TECH plane

'Hobelbank f (-; -bänke) TECH carpenter's bench

'hobeln v/t (ge-, h) TECH plane

hoch [hoːx] adj and adv high; tall; heavy (fine etc); distinguished (guest); great, old (age); deep (snow); 10 hoch 4 MATH 10 to the power of 4; 3000 Meter hoch fly etc at an altitude of 3,000 meters; in hohem Maße highly, greatly; hoch verschuldet heavily in debt; F das ist mir zu hoch that's above me

Hoch n (-s; -s) METEOR high (a. fig)

'Hochachtung f (deep) respect (vor dat for)

'hochachtungsvoll adv Yours sincerely

'Hochbau m (-[e]s; no pl) Hoch- und Tiefbau structural and civil engineering

Hochbetrieb F m (-[e]s; no pl) rush

'hochdeutsch adj High or standard German

'Hochdruck m high pressure (a. fig)

'Hochebene f plateau, tableland

'Hochform f: in Hochform in top form or shape

Hochfre,quenz f ELECTR high frequency

'Hochgebirge n high mountains

'Hochgenuss m real treat

'hochgezüchtet adj ZO, TECH highbred, TECH a. sophisticated; MOT tuned up, F souped up

'hochhackig [-hakɪç] adj high-heeled

'Hochhaus n high rise, tower block

Hochkonjunk,tur f ECON boom

'Hochland n highlands

Hochleistungs... in cpds ...sport etc: high-performance ...

'Hochmut *m* arrogance
'hochmütig [-my:tɪç] *adj* arrogant
'Hochofen *m* TECH blast furnace
'hochpro,zentig *adj* high-proof
'Hochrechnung *f* projection; POL computer prediction
Hochsai,son *f* peak (*or* height of the) season
Hochschulabschluss *m* degree
Hochschulausbildung *f* higher education
Hochschule *f* university; college; academy
Hochseefischerei *f* deep-sea fishing
Hochsommer *m* midsummer
Hochspannung *f* ELECTR high tension (*a. fig*) *or* voltage
Hochsprung *m* SPORT high jump
höchst [høːçst] **1.** *adj* highest, *fig a.* supreme; extreme; **2.** *adv* highly, most, extremely
'Höchst... *in cpds mst* maximum ..., top ...
'Hochstapler [-ʃtaːplɐ] *m* (-s; -), 'Hochstaplerin *f* (-; -nen) impostor, swindler
'höchstens *adv* at (the) most, at best
'Höchstform *f* SPORT top form *or* shape
Höchstgeschwindigkeit *f* top speed (**mit** at); speed limit
Höchstleistung *f* SPORT record (performance); TECH maximum output
Höchstmaß *n* maximum (**an** at of)
'höchstwahr'scheinlich *adv* most likely *or* probably
'Hochtechnolo,gie *f* high technology, hi tech
'hochtrabend *adj* pompous
'Hochverrat *m* high treason
'Hochwasser *n* high tide; flood
'hochwertig [-veːɐtɪç] *adj* high-grade, high-quality
Hochzeit *f* ['hɔxtsait] *f* (-; -en) wedding
'Hochzeits... *in cpds* ...geschenk, ...kleid, ...tag *etc*: wedding ...
Hochzeitsreise *f* honeymoon
Hocke ['hɔkə] *f* (-; -n) crouch, squat
'hocken *v/i* (ge-, h) squat, crouch; F sit
Hocker ['hɔkɐ] *m* (-s; -) stool
Höcker ['hœkɐ] *m* (-s; -) ZO hump
Hockey ['hɔki] *n* (-s; *no pl*) SPORT field hockey, Br field hockey
Hoden ['hoːdən] *m* (-s; -) ANAT testicle
Hof [hoːf] *m* (-[e]s; Höfe ['høːfə]) yard; AGR farm; court(yard); court
Hofdame *f* lady-in-waiting
hoffen ['hɔfən] *v/i* and *v/t* (ge-, h) hope (**auf** acc for); trust (in); **das Beste hoffen** hope for the best; **ich hoffe es** I hope so; **ich hoffe nicht, ich will es nicht hoffen**

I hope not
'hoffentlich *adv* I hope, let's hope, hopefully
'Hoffnung *f* (-; -en) hope (**auf** acc of); **sich Hoffnungen machen** have hopes; **die Hoffnung aufgeben** lose hope
'hoffnungslos *adj* hopeless
'hoffnungsvoll *adj* hopeful; promising
höflich ['høːflɪç] *adj* polite, courteous (**zu** to)
'Höflichkeit *f* (-; *no pl*) politeness, courtesy
Höhe ['høːə] *f* (-; -n) height; AVIAT, MATH, ASTR, GEOGR altitude; peak (*a. fig*); *fig* amount; level; extent (*of damage etc*); MUS pitch; **auf gleicher Höhe mit** on a level with; **in die Höhe** up; F **ich bin nicht ganz auf der Höhe** I'm not feeling up to the mark
Hoheit ['hoːhait] *f* (-; *no pl*) POL sovereignty; Highness
'Hoheitsgebiet *n* territory
Hoheitsgewässer *pl* territorial waters
Hoheitszeichen *n* national emblem
'Höhenluft *f* mountain air
Höhenmesser *m* altimeter
Höhenruder *n* AVIAT elevator
Höhensonne *f* MED ultraviolet lamp, sunlamp
Höhenzug *m* mountain chain
'Höhepunkt *m* climax, culmination, height, peak; highlight
hohl [hoːl] *adj* hollow (*a. fig*)
Höhle ['høːlə] *f* (-; -n) cave, cavern; ZO hole, burrow; den, lair
Hohlmaß *n* measure of capacity
Hohlraum *m* hollow, cavity
Hohlspiegel *m* concave mirror
Hohn [hoːn] *m* (-[e]s; *no pl*) derision, scorn
'Hohngelächter *n* jeers, jeering laughter
höhnisch ['høːnɪʃ] *adj* derisive, scornful; **höhnisches Lächeln** sneer
holen ['hoːlən] *v/t* (ge-, h) (go and) get, fetch, go for; draw (*breath*); call (*s.o., the police etc*); **holen lassen** send for; **sich holen** catch, get (*a cold etc*); seek (*advice*)
Holland ['hɔlant] Holland, *the* Netherlands
Holländer ['hɔlɛndɐ] *m* (-s; -) Dutchman
'Hol'länderin [-dərɪn] *f* (-; -nen) Dutchwoman
'holländisch *adj* Dutch
Hölle ['hœlə] *f* (-; *no pl*) hell
'Höllenlärm *m* F a hell of a noise
Holler ['hɔlɐ] *Austrian m* (-s; -) BOT elder
höllisch ['hœlɪʃ] *adj* infernal, F hellish
holperig ['hɔlpərɪç] *adj* bumpy (*a. fig*),

rough, uneven; *fig* clumsy (*style etc*)
holpern ['hɔlpɐn] *v/i* (*ge-*, *sein*) jolt, bump; *fig* be bumpy
Holunder [ho'lundɐ] *m* (*-s*; *-*) BOT elder
Holz [hɔlts] *n* (*-es*; *Hölzer* ['hœltsɐ]) wood; lumber, *Br a.* timber; *aus Holz* (made) of wood, wooden; *Holz hacken* chop wood
Holzblasinstru,ment *n* MUS woodwind (instrument)
hölzern ['hœltsɐn] *adj* wooden, *fig a.* clumsy
'**Holzfäller** [-fɛlɐ] *m* (*-s*; *-*) woodcutter, lumberjack
Holzhammer *m* mallet; *fig* sledgehammer
holzig ['hɔltsɪç] *adj* woody; stringy
'**Holzkohle** *f* charcoal
Holzschnitt *m* woodcut
Holzschnitzer *m* wood carver
Holzschuh *m* clog
Holzweg *fig m*: *auf dem Holzweg sein* be barking up the wrong tree
Holzwolle *f* wood shavings, excelsior
Holzwurm *m* zo woodworm
homöopathisch [homøo'pa:tɪʃ] *adj* hom(o)eopathic
homosexuell [homozɛ'ksuɛl] *adj*, **Homosexu'elle** *m*, *f* (*-n*; *-n*) homosexual
Honig ['ho:nɪç] *m* (*-s*; *-e*) honey
'**Honigwabe** *f* honeycomb
Honorar [hono'ra:ɐ] *n* (*-s*; *-e*) fee
honorieren [hono'ri:rən] *v/t* (*no -ge-*, *h*) pay (a fee to); *fig* appreciate, reward
Hopfen ['hɔpfən] *m* (*-s*; *-*) BOT hop; *brewing*: hops
hoppla ['hɔpla] *int* (wh)oops!
hopsen ['hɔpsən] F *v/i* (*ge-*, *sein*) hop, jump
Hörappa,rat ['hø:ɐ-] *m* hearing aid
hörbar ['hø:ɐba:ɐ] *adj* audible
horchen ['hɔrçən] *v/i* (*ge-*, *h*) listen (*auf acc* to); eavesdrop
Horcher ['hɔrçɐ] *m* (*-s*; *-*) eavesdropper
Horde ['hɔrdə] *f* (*-*; *-n*) horde (*a.* zo), *contp a.* mob, gang
hören ['hø:rən] *v/i and v/t* (*ge-*, *h*) hear; listen to; obey, listen; *hören auf* (*acc*) listen to; *von j-m hören* hear from (or of, about) s.o.; *er hört schwer* his hearing is bad; *hör(t) mal!* listen!; look (here)!; *nun* or *also hör(t) mal!* wait a minute!; now look or listen here!
Hörer ['hø:rɐ] *m* (*-s*; *-*) listener; TEL receiver
'**Hörerin** [-rərɪn] *f* (*-*; *-nen*) listener
Hörfehler ['hø:ɐ-] *m* MED hearing defect
Hörgerät *n* hearing aid
hörig ['hø:rɪç] *adj*: *j-m hörig sein* be s.o.'s

slave
Horizont [hori'tsɔnt] *m* (*-[e]s*; *-e*) horizon (*a. fig*); *s-n Horizont erweitern* broaden one's mind; *das geht über meinen Horizont* that's beyond me
horizontal [horitsɔn'ta:l] *adj* horizontal
Hormon [hɔr'mo:n] *n* (*-s*; *-e*) hormone
Horn [hɔrn] *n* (*-[e]s*; *Hörner* ['hœrnɐ]) horn
Hornhaut *f* horny skin, callus(es); ANAT cornea
Hornisse [hɔr'nɪsə] *f* (*-*; *-n*) zo hornet
Horoskop [horo'sko:p] *n* (*-s*; *-e*) horoscope
Hörrohr ['hø:ɐ-] *n* MED stethoscope
Hörsaal *m* lecture hall, auditorium
Hörspiel *n* radio play
Hörweite *f*: *in* (*außer*) *Hörweite* within (out of) earshot
Höschen ['hø:sçən] *n* (*-s*; *-*) panties
Hose ['ho:zə] *f* (*-*; *-n*) (*e-e Hose* a pair of) pants, *Br* trousers; slacks; shorts
'**Hosenanzug** *m* pants (*Br* trouser) suit
Hosenrock *m* (*ein Hosenrock* a pair of) culottes
Hosenschlitz *m* fly
Hosentasche *f* trouser pocket
Hosenträger *pl* (a pair of) suspenders or *Br* braces
Hospital [hɔspi'ta:l] *n* (*-s*; *-täler* [-'tɛ:lɐ]) hospital
Hostie ['hɔstjə] *f* (*-*; *-n*) REL host
Hotel [ho'tɛl] *n* (*-s*; *-s*) hotel
Hoteldi,rektor *m* hotel manager
Hotelfach *n* (*-[e]s*; *no pl*) hotel business
Hotelzimmer *n* hotel room
HP ABBR of *Halbpension* half-board
Hr(n). ABBR of *Herrn* Mr
Hubraum ['hu:p-] *m* MOT cubic capacity
hübsch [hypʃ] *adj* pretty, nice(-looking), cute; *fig* nice, lovely
Hubschrauber ['hu:pʃraubɐ] *m* (*-s*; *-*) helicopter
Hubschrauberlandeplatz *m* heliport
Huf [hu:f] *m* (*-[e]s*; *-e*) zo hoof
'**Hufeisen** *n* horseshoe
Hüfte ['hyftə] *f* (*-*; *-n*) ANAT hip
'**Hüftgelenk** *n* ANAT hip joint
'**Hüftgürtel** *m* girdle
Hügel ['hy:gəl] *m* (*-s*; *-*) hill
'**hügelig** *adj* hilly
'**Hügelland** *n* downs
Huhn [hu:n] *n* (*-[e]s*; *Hühner* ['hy:nɐ]) zo chicken; hen
Hühnchen ['hy:nçən] *n* (*-s*; *-*) chicken; F *mit j-m ein Hühnchen zu rupfen haben* have a bone to pick with s.o.
'**Hühnerauge** *n* MED corn
Hühnerbrühe *f* chicken broth

Hühnerei n hen's egg
Hühnerfarm f poultry or chicken farm
Hühnerhof m poultry or chicken yard
Hühnerleiter f chicken ladder
Hühnerstall m henhouse
huldigen ['huldɪgən] v/i (ge-, h) pay homage to; fig indulge in
Hülle ['hʏlə] f (-; -n) cover(ing), wrap (-ping); jacket, Br sleeve; sheath; *in Hülle und Fülle* in abundance
'hüllen v/t (ge-, h) *hüllen in* (acc) wrap (-up) in, cover in
Hülse ['hʏlzə] f (-; -n) BOT pod; husk; TECH case
'Hülsenfrüchte pl pulse
human [hu'maːn] adj humane
humanitär [humani'tɛːr] adj humanitarian
Humanität [humani'tɛːt] f (-; no pl) humanity
Hummel ['huməl] f (-; -n) zo bumblebee
Hummer ['humɐ] m (-s; -) zo lobster
Humor [hu'moːɐ] m (-s; no pl) humo(u)r; *(keinen) Humor haben* have a (no) sense of humo(u)r
Humorist [humo'rɪst] m (-en; -en) humorist
humo'ristisch, hu'morvoll adj humorous
humpeln ['humpəln] v/i a) (ge-, h) hobble, b) (ge-, sein) limp
Hund [hunt] m (-[e]s; -e) zo dog
Hundehütte ['hundə-] f doghouse, Br kennel
Hundekuchen m dog biscuit
Hundeleine f lead, leash
'hunde'müde adj dog-tired
hundert ['hundɐt] adj a or one hundred; *zu hunderten* by the hundreds
'hundertfach adj hundredfold
Hundert'jahrfeier f centenary, centennial
'hundertjährig [-jɛːrɪç] adj a hundred years old; a hundred years of
'hundertste adj hundredth
Hündin ['hʏndɪn] f (-; -nen) zo bitch
hündisch ['hʏndɪʃ] adj doglike, slavish
Hüne ['hyːnə] m (-n; -n) giant
'Hünengrab n dolmen
Hunger ['huŋɐ] m (-s; no pl) hunger; *Hunger bekommen* get hungry; *Hunger haben* be hungry; *vor Hunger sterben* die of starvation, starve to death
'Hungerlohn m starvation wages
'hungern v/i (ge-, h) go hungry, starve
'Hungersnot f famine
'Hungerstreik m hunger strike
'Hungertod m (death from) starvation
hungrig ['huŋrɪç] adj hungry *(nach, auf* acc for)
Hupe ['huːpə] f (-; -n) MOT horn

'hupen v/i (ge-, h) MOT sound one's horn, hoot, honk
hüpfen ['hʏpfən] v/i (ge, sein) hop, skip; *ball etc:* bounce
Hürde ['hʏrdə] f (-; -n) hurdle, fig a. obstacle; zo fold, pen
'Hürdenlauf m SPORT hurdles
'Hürdenläufer m, **'Hürdenläuferin** f SPORT hurdler
Hure ['huːrə] f (-; -n) whore, prostitute
huschen ['huʃən] v/i (ge-, sein) flit, dart
hüsteln ['hyːstəln] v/i (ge-, h) cough slightly; *iro* hem
husten ['huːstən] v/i (ge-, h), **'Husten** m (-s; no pl) cough
'Hustenbon,bon m, n cough drop
Hustensaft m PHARM cough syrup
Hut[1] [huːt] m (-[e]s; Hüte ['hyːtə]) hat; *den Hut aufsetzen (abnehmen)* put on (take off) one's hat
Hut[2] f: *auf der Hut sein* be on one's guard *(vor* dat against)
hüten ['hyːtən] v/t (ge-, h) guard, protect, watch over; zo herd, mind; look after; *das Bett hüten* be confined to (one's) bed; *sich hüten vor* (dat) beware of; *sich hüten, et. zu tun* be careful not to do s.th.
'Hutkrempe f (hat) brim
hutschen ['hutʃən] Austrian v/t and v/i → **schaukeln**
Hütte ['hʏtə] f (-; -n) hut; contp shack; cottage, cabin; mountain hut; TECH ironworks
Hyäne ['hyɛːnə] f (-; -n) zo hy(a)ena
Hyazinthe [hya'tsɪntə] f (-; -n) BOT hyacinth
Hydrant [hy'drant] m (-en; -en) hydrant
hydraulisch [hy'draulɪʃ] adj hydraulic
Hydrokultur ['hyːdro-] f hydroponics
Hygiene [hy'gjeːnə] f (-; no pl) hygiene
hygienisch [hy'gjeːnɪʃ] adj hygienic
Hypnose [hyp'noːzə] f (-; -n) hypnosis
Hypnotiseur [hypnoti'zøːɐ] m (-s; -e) hypnotist
hypnotisieren [hypnoti-'ziːrən] v/t (no -ge-, h) hypnotize
Hypotenuse [hypote'nuːzə] f (-; -n) MATH hypotenuse
Hypothek [hypo'teːk] f (-; -en) ECON mortgage; *e-e Hypothek aufnehmen* take out a mortgage
Hypothese [hypo'teːzə] f (-; -n) hypothesis, supposition
hypothetisch [hypo'teːtɪʃ] adj hypothetical
Hysterie [hyste'riː] f (-; -n) hysteria
hysterisch [hys'teːrɪʃ] adj hysterical

I

i. A. ABBR of **im Auftrag** p. p., per procuration

ICE [iːtseːˈ'ʔeː] ABBR of *Intercityexpresszug* intercity express (train)

ich [ɪç] *pers pron* I; *ich selbst* (I) myself; *ich bin's* it's me

ideal [ideˈaːl] *adj*, **Ide'al** n (-s; -e) ideal

Idealismus [ideaˈlɪsmʊs] m (-; no pl) idealism

Idea'list(in) (-en; -en/-; -nen) idealist

Idee [iˈdeː] f (-; -n) idea

identifizieren [identifiˈtsiːrən] v/t (no -ge-, h) identify; *sich identifizieren mit* identify with

identisch [iˈdɛntɪʃ] *adj* identical

Identitätskarte [identiˈtɛːts-] *Austrian* f identity card

Ideologe [ideoˈloːgə] m (-n; -n) ideologist

Ideologie [ideoloˈɡiː] f (-; -n) ideology

ideo'logisch *adj* ideological

idiomatisch [idioˈmaːtɪʃ] *adj* LING idiomatic; *idiomatischer Ausdruck* idiom

Idiot [iˈdjoːt] m (-en; -en) idiot

Idi'otenhügel F m *skiing:* nursery slope

idi'otisch *adj* idiotic

Idol [iˈdoːl] n (-s; -e) idol

Idyll [iˈdyl] n (-s; -e), **I'dylle** f (-; -n) idyl(l)

i'dyllisch *adj* idyllic

Igel [ˈiːgəl] m (-s; -) zo hedgehog

Iglu [ˈiːglu] m (-s; -s) igloo

ignorieren [ɪgnoˈriːrən] v/t (no -ge-, h) ignore, disregard

i. H. ABBR of *im Hause* on the premises

ihr [iːɐ] *poss pron* her; pl their; **Ihr** your

ihrerseits [ˈiːɐzaits] *adv* on her (pl their) part

ihresgleichen [ˈiːrəs-] *indef pron* her (pl their) equals, people like herself (pl themselves)

ihretwegen [ˈiːrət-] *adv* for her (pl their) sake

Ikone [iˈkoːnə] f (-; -n) icon (a. EDP)

illegal [ˈɪlegaːl] *adj* JUR illegal

illegitim [ˈɪlegiˈtiːm] *adj* JUR illegitimate

Illusion [ɪluˈzjoːn] f (-; -en) illusion

illusorisch [ɪluˈzoːrɪʃ] *adj* illusory

Illustration [ɪlustraˈtsjoːn] f (-; -en) illustration

illustrieren [ɪlusˈtriːrən] v/t (no -ge-, h) illustrate

Illustrierte [ɪlusˈtriːtə] f (-n; -n) magazine

im [ɪm] *prep* in the; *im Bett* in bed; *im Kino etc* at the cinema *etc*; *im Erdge-

schoss* on the first (Br ground) floor; *im Mai* in May; *im Jahre 1997* in (the year) 1997; *im Stehen* (while) standing up; → *in*

imaginär [imagiˈnɛːɐ] *adj* imaginary

Imbiss [ˈɪmbɪs] m (-es; -e) snack

'Imbissstube f snack bar

imitieren [imiˈtiːrən] v/t (no -ge-, h) imitate

Imker [ˈɪmkɐ] m (-s; -) beekeeper

immatrikulieren [ɪmatrikuˈliːrən] v/t and v/refl (no -ge-, h) UNIV enrol(l), register

immer [ˈɪmɐ] *adv* always, all the time; *immer mehr* more and more; *immer wieder* again and again; *für immer* for ever, for good

'immergrün n BOT evergreen

'immer'hin *adv* after all

'immer'zu *adv* all the time, constantly

Immigrant [ɪmiˈgrant] m (-en; -en), **Immi'grantin** f (-; -nen) immigrant

Immissionen [ɪmɪˈsjoːnən] pl (harmful effects of) noise, pollutants *etc*

Immobilie [ɪmoˈbiːljən] pl real estate

Immobilienmakler m realtor, real estate agent

immun [ɪˈmuːn] *adj* immune (*gegen* to, against, from); *immun machen* → **immunisieren** [ɪmuniˈziːrən] v/t (no -ge-, h) immunize

Immunität [ɪmuniˈtɛːt] f (-; no pl) immunity

Im'munschwäche f (-; -n) *Erworbene Immunschwäche* MED AIDS

Imperativ [ˈɪmperatiːf] m (-s; -e) LING imperative (mood)

Imperfekt [ˈɪmpɛrfɛkt] n (-s; -e) LING past (tense)

Imperialismus [ɪmperjaˈlɪsmʊs] m (-; no pl) imperialism

Imperialist [ɪmperjaˈlɪst] m (-en; -en), **imperia'listisch** *adj* imperialist

impfen [ˈɪmpfən] v/t (ge-, h) MED vaccinate

'Impfpass m MED vaccination card

'Impfschein m MED vaccination certificate

'Impfstoff m MED vaccine, serum

'Impfung f (-; -en) MED vaccination

imponieren [ɪmpoˈniːrən] v/i (no -ge-, h) *j-m imponieren* impress s.o.

Import [ɪmˈpɔrt] m (-[e]s; -e) ECON import(ation)

Importeur [ɪmpɔrˈtøːɐ] m (-s; -e) ECON importer

importieren [-'ti:rən] *v/t (no -ge-, h)* ECON import

imposant [ɪmpo'zant] *adj* impressive, imposing

imprägnieren [ɪmprɛ'gni:rən] *v/t (no -ge-, h)*, **imprägniert** [ɪmprɛ'gni:ɛt] *adj* waterproof

improvisieren [ɪmprovi'zi:rən] *v/t and v/i (no -ge-, h)* improvise

Impuls [ɪm'pʊls] *m (-es; -e)* impulse; stimulus

impulsiv [ɪmpʊl'zi:f] *adj* impulsive

imstande [ɪm'ʃtandə] *adj*: **imstande sein zu** *inf* be capable of *ger*

in [ɪn] *prp (dat and acc)* **1.** in, at; within, inside; into, in; **überall in** all over; **in der Stadt** in town; **in der Schule** at school; **in die Schule** to school; **ins Kino** to the cinema; **ins Bett** to bed; **warst du schon mal in …?** have you ever been to …?; → **im**; **2.** in, at, during; **in dieser (der nächsten) Woche** this (next) week; **in diesem Alter (Augenblick)** at this age (moment); **in der Nacht** at night; **heute in acht Tagen** a week from now; **heute in e-m Jahr** this time next year; → **im**; **3.** in, at; **gut sein in** (*dat*) be good at; **in Eile** in a hurry; **in Behandlung (Reparatur)** under treatment (repair); **in Deutsche** into German; → **im**; **4.** F **in sein** be in

'Inbegriff *m* epitome

'inbegriffen *adj* ECON included

in'dem *cj* while, as; by *doing s.th.*

Inder ['ɪndɐ] *m (-s; -)*, **Inderin** ['ɪndərɪn] *f (-; -nen)* Indian

Indian ['ɪndja:n] *Austrian m (-s; -e)* ZO turkey (cock)

Indianer [ɪn'dja:nɐ] *m (-s; -)*, **Indianerin** [ɪn'dja:nərɪn] *f (-; -nen)* Native American, (American) Indian

Indien ['ɪndjən] India

Indikativ ['ɪndikati:f] *m (-s; -e)* LING indicative (mood)

indirekt ['ɪndirɛkt] *adj* indirect, LING *a.* reported

indisch ['ɪndɪʃ] *adj* Indian

indiskret ['ɪndɪskre:t] *adj* indiscreet

Indiskretion [ɪndɪskre'tsjo:n] *f (-; -en)* indiscretion

indiskutabel [ɪndɪsku'ta:bəl] *adj* out of the question

individuell [ɪndivi'duɛl] *adj*, **Individuum** [ɪndi'vi:duʊm] *n (-s; -en)* individual

Indiz [ɪn'di:ts] *n (-es; -ien)* indication, sign; *pl* JUR circumstantial evidence

industrialisieren [ɪndʊstriali'zi:rən] *v/t (no -ge-, h)* industrialize

Industriali'sierung *f (-; no pl)* industrialization

Industrie [ɪndʊs'tri:] *f (-; -n)* industry

Indus'triegebiet *n* industrial area

industriell [ɪndʊstri'ɛl] *adj* industrial

Industri'elle *m (-n; -n)* industrialist

inei'nander *adv* into one another; **ineinander verliebt** in love with each other; **ineinandergreifen** *v/t (irr, greifen, sep, -ge-, h)* TECH interlock (*a. fig*)

Infanterie ['ɪnfantəri:] *f (-; -n)* MIL infantry

Infanterist ['ɪnfantərɪst] *m (-en; -en)* MIL infantryman

Infektion [ɪnfɛk'tsjo:n] *f (-; -en)* MED infection

Infekti'onskrankheit *f* infectious disease

Infinitiv ['ɪnfiniti:f] *m (-s; -e)* LING infinitive (mood)

infizieren [ɪnfi'tsi:rən] *v/t (no -ge-, h)* MED infect

Inflation [ɪnfla'tsjo:n] *f (-; -en)* inflation

in'folge *prp (gen)* owing to, due to

infolge'dessen *adv* consequently

Informatik [ɪnfɔr'ma:tɪk] *f (-; no pl)* computer science

Infor'matiker(in) [ɪnfɔr'ma:tikɐ (-kərɪn)] (*-s; -/-; -nen*) computer scientist

Information [ɪnfɔrma'tsjo:n] *f (-; -en)* information; **die neuesten Informationen** the latest information

informieren [ɪnfɔr'mi:rən] *v/t (no -ge-, h)* inform; **falsch informieren** misinform

in'frage *f*: **infrage stellen** question; put in jeopardy; **infrage kommen** be possible (*person*: eligible); **nicht infrage kommen** be out of the question

infrarot ['ɪnfra-] *adj* PHYS infrared

'Infrastruk,tur *f* infrastructure

Ing. ABBR of **Ingenieur** eng., engineer

Ingenieur [ɪnʒe'njø:ɐ] *m (-s; -e)*, **Inge'nieurin** *f (-; -nen)* engineer

Ingwer ['ɪŋvɐ] *m (-s; no pl)* ginger

Inhaber ['ɪnha:bɐ] *m (-s; -)*, **'Inhaberin** *f (-; -nen)* owner, proprietor (proprietress); holder

Inhalt ['ɪnhalt] *m (-[e]s; -e)* contents; volume, capacity; *fig* meaning

'Inhaltsangabe *f* summary

'Inhaltsverzeichnis *n* table of contents

Initiative [initsja'ti:və] *f (-; -n)* initiative; **die Initiative ergreifen** take the initiative

inklusive [ɪnklu'zi:və] *prp* ECON including

inkonsequent ['ɪnkɔnzekvɛnt] *adj* inconsistent

In-'Kraft-Treten *n (-s; no pl)* coming into force, taking effect

'Inland *n (-[e]s; no pl)* home (country)

Inlandflug *m* domestic (*or* internal) flight

inländisch ['ɪnlɛndɪʃ] *adj* domestic, home, inland

Inlett ['ɪnlet] n (-[e]s; -e) ticking

in'mitten prp (gen) in the middle of

innen ['ɪnən] adv inside; **nach innen** inwards

'**Innenarchi,tekt** m, **Innenarchi,tektin** f interior designer

'**Innenarchitek,tur** f interior design

'**Innenmi,nister(in)** minister of the interior; Secretary of the Interior, Br Home Secretary

'**Innenminis,terium** n ministry of the interior; Department of the Interior, Br Home Office

'**Innenpoli,tik** f domestic politics

'**innenpo,litisch** adj domestic, internal

'**Innenseite** f: **auf der Innenseite** (on the) inside

'**Innenstadt** f downtown, (city or town) center or Br centre

inner ['ɪnɐ] adj inside; fig inner; MED, POL internal

Innere ['ɪnərə] n (-n; no pl) interior, inside

Innereien [ɪnə'raɪən] pl GASTR offal

'**innerhalb** prp (gen) within

'**innerlich** adj internal (a. MED)

innert ['ɪnɐt] Swiss prp (gen or dat) with in

innig ['ɪnɪç] adj tender, affectionate

Innung ['ɪnʊŋ] f (-; -en) guild

'**inoffiziell** adj unofficial

ins [ɪns] → **in**

Insasse ['ɪnzasə] m (-n; -n) inmate; MOT passenger

'**Insassenversicherung** f MOT passenger insurance

'**Insassin** f (-; -nen) inmate; MOT passenger

insbe'sondere adv (e)specially

'**Inschrift** f inscription, legend

Insekt [ɪn'zɛkt] n (-s; -en) ZO insect, bug

In'sektenstich m insect bite

Insel ['ɪnzəl] f (-; -n) island

'**Inselbewohner** m islander

Inserat [ɪnze'raːt] n (-[e]s; -e) advertisement, F ad

inserieren [ɪnze'riːrən] v/t and v/i (no -ge-, h) advertise

insge'heim adv secretly

insge'samt adv altogether, in all

inso'fern 1. adv as far as that goes; **2.** cj: **insofern als** in so far as

Inspektion [ɪnspɛk'tsjoːn] f (-; -en) inspection; MOT service

Inspektor [ɪn'spɛktoːɐ] m (-s; -en [ɪnspɛk'toːrən]), **Inspek'torin** f (-; -nen) inspector

inspizieren [ɪnspi'tsiːrən] v/t (no -ge-, h) inspect

Installateur [ɪnstala'tøːɐ] m (-s; -e) plumber; (gas or electrical) fitter

installieren [ɪnsta'liːrən] v/t (no -ge-, h) put in, fit, install(l)

instand [ɪn'ʃtant] adv: **instand halten** keep in good condition or repair; TECH maintain; **instand setzen** repair

In'standhaltung f (-; no pl) maintenance

'**inständig** adv: **j-n inständig bitten** implore s.o.

In'standsetzung f (-; -en) repair

Instanz [ɪn'stants] f (-; -en) authority; JUR instance

Instinkt [ɪn'stɪŋkt] m (-[e]s; -e) instinct

instinktiv [ɪnstɪŋk'tiːf] adv instinctively

Institut [ɪnsti'tuːt] n (-[e]s; -e) institute

Institution [ɪnstitu'tsjoːn] f (-; -en) institution

Instrument [ɪnstru'mɛnt] n (-[e]s; -e) instrument

inszenieren [ɪnstse'niːrən] v/t (no -ge-, h) (put on) stage; film: direct; fig stage

Inszenierung f (-; -en) production

intellektuell [ɪntɛlɛk'tuɛl] adj, **Intellektu'elle** m, f (-n; -n) intellectual, F highbrow

intelligent [ɪntɛli'gɛnt] adj intelligent

Intelligenz [ɪntɛli'gɛnts] f (-; -en) intelligence

Intelligenzquoti,ent m I.Q.

Intendant [ɪntɛn'dant] m (-en; -en), **Inten'dantin** f (-; -nen) THEA etc director

intensiv [ɪntɛn'ziːf] adj intensive; intense

Inten'sivkurs m crash course

interessant [ɪntərɛ'sant] adj interesting

Interesse [ɪntə'rɛsə] n (-s; -n) interest (**an** dat, **für** in)

Inte'ressengebiet n field of interest

Interessent [ɪntərɛ'sɛnt] m (-en; -en), **Interes'sentin** f (-; -nen) interested person; ECON prospect, Br prospective buyer

interessieren [ɪntərɛ'siːrən] v/t (no -ge-, h) interest (**für** in); **sich interessieren für** take an interest in; be interested in

intern [ɪn'tɛrn] adj internal

Internat [ɪntɛ'naːt] n (-[e]s; -e) boarding school

internatio'nal [ɪntɐ-] adj international

Internet ['ɪntɛnɛt] n (-[s]; no pl) Internet

Internist [ɪntɛ'nɪst] m (-en; -en), **Inter'nistin** f (-; -nen) MED internist

Interpretation [ɪntɛprɛta'tsjoːn] f (-; -en) interpretation; analysis

interpretieren [ɪntɛprɛ'tiːrən] v/t (no -ge-, h) interpret, ana,lyze, Br -lyse

Interpunktion [ɪntɛpʊŋk'tsjoːn] f (-; no pl) punctuation

Intervall [ɪntɛ'val] n (-[e]s; -e) interval

intervenieren [ɪntɛve'niːrən] v/i (no -ge-, h) intervene

Interview ['ɪntɛvjuː] n (-s; -s), **interview-**

en [ɪntɐ'vjuːən] v/t (no -ge-, h) interview

intim [ɪn'tiːm] adj intimate (**mit** with) (a. sexually)

Intimität [ɪntimi'tɛːt] f (-; no pl) intimacy

In'timsphäre f privacy

intolerant ['ɪntolerant] adj intolerant (**gegen** of)

Intoleranz ['ɪntolerants] f (-; no pl) intolerance

intransitiv ['ɪntranzitiːf] adj LING intransitive

Intrige [ɪn'triːgə] f (-; -n) intrigue, scheme, plot

intrigieren [ɪntri'giːrən] v/i (no -ge-, h) (plot and) scheme

Invalide [ɪnva'liːdə] m (-n; -n) invalid

Inva'lidenrente f disability pension

Invalidität [ɪnvalidi'tɛːt] f (-; no pl) disablement, disability

Inventar [ɪnvɛn'taːɐ] n (-s; -e) inventory, stock

Inventur [ɪnvɛn'tuːɐ] f (-; -en) ECON stocktaking; **Inventur machen** take stock

investieren [ɪnvɛs'tiːrən] v/t (no -ge-, h) ECON invest (a. fig)

Investition [ɪnvɛsti'tsjoːn] f (-; -en) ECON investment

inwiefern [ɪnvi'fɛrn] cj and adv in what respect or way

inwie'weit cj and adv to what extent

'Inzucht f inbreeding

in'zwischen adv meanwhile, in the meantime; by now

irdisch ['ɪrdɪʃ] adj earthly, worldly

Ire ['iːrə] m (-n; -n) Irishman; pl the Irish

irgend ['ɪrgənt] adv in cpds: some...; **wenn irgend möglich** if at all possible; **wenn du irgend kannst** if you possibly can; F **irgend so ein ...** some ...

irgend'ein(e) indef pron some(one); any (-one)

irgend'ein(e)s indef pron some; any

irgendetwas something; anything

irgendjemand someone, somebody; anyone, anybody

irgend'wann adv sometime (or other); (at) any time

irgend'wie adv somehow (or other)

irgend'wo adv somewhere; anywhere

Irin ['iːrɪn] f (-; -nen) Irishwoman

irisch ['iːrɪʃ] adj Irish

Irland ['ɪrlant] Ireland

Ironie [iro'niː] f (-; no pl) irony

ironisch [i'roːnɪʃ] adj ironic(al)

irre ['ɪrə] adj mad, crazy, insane; confused; F super, terrific

'Irre m, f (-n; -n) madman (madwoman), lunatic; **wie ein Irrer** like mad or a madman

'irreführen v/t (sep, -ge-, h) mislead, lead astray

irreführend adj misleading

'irregehen v/i (irr, gehen, sep, -ge-, sein) go astray, fig a. be wrong

irremachen v/t (sep, -ge-, h) confuse

irren ['ɪrən] **1.** v/refl (ge-, h) be wrong, be mistaken; **sich irren** be wrong; **sich in et. irren** get s.th. wrong; **2.** v/i (ge-, sein) wander, stray, err

irritieren [ɪri'tiːrən] v/t (no -ge-, h) irritate; F confuse

'Irrlicht n (-[e]s; -er) will-o'-the-wisp

'Irrsinn m (-[e]s; no pl) madness

'irrsinnig adj insane, mad; F terrific

Irrtum ['ɪrtuːm] m (-s; Irrtümer ['ɪrtyːmɐ]) error, mistake; **im Irrtum sein** be mistaken

'irrtümlich adv by mistake

Ischias ['ɪʃjas] m, n, f (-; no pl) MED sciatica

Islam [ɪs'laːm] m (-[s]; no pl) Islam

Island ['iːslant] Iceland

Isländer [ɪs'lɛndɐ] m (-s; -), **'Isländerin** [-dərɪn] f (-; -nen) Icelander

'isländisch adj Icelandic

Isolierband [izo'liːɐ-] n (-[e]s; -bänder) insulating tape

isolieren [izo'liːrən] v/t (no -ge-, h) isolate; ELECTR, TECH insulate

Iso'lierstation f MED isolation ward

Iso'lierung f (-; -en) isolation; ELECTR, TECH insulation

Israel ['ɪsraeːl] Israel

Israeli [ɪsra'eːli] m (-[s]; -[s]), f (-; -[s]), **israelisch** [ɪsra'eːlɪʃ] adj Israeli

Italien [i'taːljən] Italy

Italiener [ita'ljeːnɐ] m (-s; -), **Itali'enerin** [-nərɪn] f (-; -nen), **itali'enisch** adj Italian

J

ja [ja:] adv yes, F a. yeah; PARL yea, aye; **wenn ja** it's so; **da ist er ja!** well, there he is!; **ich sagte es Ihnen ja** I told you so; **ich bin ja** (schließlich) ... after all, I am ...; **tut es 'ja nicht!** don't you dare do it!; **sei 'ja vorsichtig!** do be careful!; **vergessen Sie es 'ja nicht!** be sure not to forget it!; **ja, weißt du nicht?** why, don't you know?; **du kommst doch, ja?** you're coming, aren't you?
Jacht [jaxt] f (-; -en) MAR yacht
Jacke ['jakə] f (-; -n) jacket; coat
Jackett [ʒa'kɛt] n (-s; -s) jacket, coat
Jagd [ja:kt] f (-; -en) hunt(ing) (a. fig); shoot(ing); fig chase; → **Jagdrevier**; **auf (die) Jagd gehen** go hunting or shooting; **Jagd machen auf** (acc) hunt (for); a. chase s.o.
Jagdaufseher m gamekeeper
Jagdflugzeug n MIL fighter (plane)
Jagdhund m ZO hound
Jagdhütte f (hunting) lodge
Jagdre'vier n hunting ground
Jagdschein m hunting or shooting licen|se, Br -ce
jagen ['ja:gən] v/t and v/i (ge-, h) hunt; shoot; fig race, dash; hunt, chase; **j-n aus dem Haus etc jagen** drive or chase s.o. out of the house etc
Jäger ['jɛ:gɐ] m (-s; -) hunter, huntsman
Jaguar ['ja:gua:ɐ] m (-s; -e) ZO jaguar
jäh [jɛ:] adj sudden; steep
Jahr [ja:ɐ] n (-[e]s; -e ['ja:rə]) year; **ein drei viertel Jahr** nine months; **einmal im Jahr** once a year; **im Jahre 1995** in (the year) 1995; **ein 10 Jahre altes Auto** a ten-year-old car; **mit 18 Jahren, im Alter von 18 Jahren** at (the age of) eighteen; **heute vor e-m Jahr** a year ago today; **die 80er-Jahre** the eighties
jahr'aus adv: **jahraus, jahrein** year in, year out; year after year
'Jahrbuch n yearbook, annual
jahrelang ['ja:rəlaŋ] **1.** adj longstanding, (many) years of; **2.** adv for (many) years
Jahres- ['ja:rəs-] in cpds ...bericht, ...bilanz, ...einkommen etc: annual ...
Jahresanfang m beginning of the year
Jahresende n end of the year
Jahrestag m anniversary
Jahreswechsel m turn of the year
Jahreszahl f date, year
Jahreszeit f season, time of (the) year
'Jahrgang m age group; PED year, class

(**1995** of '95); GASTR vintage
Jahr'hundert n (-s; -e) century
Jahrhundertwende f turn of the century
jährlich ['jɛ:rliç] **1.** adj annual, yearly; **2.** adv every year, yearly, once a year
'Jahrmarkt m fair
Jahr'tausend n (-s; -e) millennium
Jahr'zehnt n (-[e]s; -e) decade
'Jähzorn m violent (fit of) temper
'jähzornig adj hot-tempered
Jalousie [ʒalu'zi:] f (-; -n) (venetian) blind
Jammer ['jamɐ] m (-s; no pl) misery; **es ist ein Jammer** it is a pity
jämmerlich ['jɛmɐliç] adj miserable, wretched; pitiful, sorry; **jämmerlich versagen** fail miserably
'jammern v/i (ge-, h) moan, lament (**über** acc over, about); complain (of, about)
jammer'schade adj: **es ist jammerschade, dass** it's a crying shame that
Janker ['jaŋkɐ] Austrian m (-s; -) jacket
Jänner ['jɛnɐ] Austrian m (-s; -), **Januar** ['janua:ɐ] m (-[s]; -e) January
Japan ['ja:pan] Japan
Japaner [ja'pa:nɐ] m (-s; -), **Ja'panerin** [-nərın] f (-; -nen), **ja'panisch** adj Japanese
Jargon [ʒar'gõ:] m (-s; -s) jargon; slang
'Jastimme f PARL aye, yea
jäten ['jɛ:tən] v/t (ge-, h) weed
Jauche ['jauxə] f (-; -n) liquid manure
jauchzen ['jauxtsən] v/i (ge-, h) shout for or with joy; exult, rejoice
Jause ['jauzə] Austrian f (-; -n) snack
ja'wohl adv (that's) right, (yes,) indeed
je [je:] adv and cj ever; each; per; **der beste Film, den ich je gesehen habe** the best film I have ever seen; **je zwei** (**Pfund**) two (pounds) each; **drei Mark je Kilo** three marks per kilo; **je nach Größe** (**Geschmack**) according to size (taste); **je nachdem**(, **wie**) it depends (on how); **je ..., desto ...** the ... the ...
Jeans [dʒi:nz] pl, a. f (-; -) (**e-e Jeans** a pair of) jeans
Jeansjacke f denim jacket
jede ['je:də], **jeder** ['je:dɐ], **jedes** ['je:dəs] indef pron every; any; each; either; **jeder weiß** (**das**) everybody knows; **du kannst jeden fragen** (you can) ask anyone; **jeder von uns** (**euch**) each of us (you); **jeder, der** whoever; **jeden zweiten Tag** every other day; **jeden Augenblick** any moment now; **jedes Mal** every

time; *jedes Mal wenn* whenever

'jeden'falls *adv* in any case, anyhow

'jedermann *indef pron* everyone, everybody

'jeder'zeit *adv* any time, always

je'doch *cj* however

je'her *adv: von jeher* always

jemals ['je:ma:ls] *adv* ever

jemand ['je:mant] *indef pron* someone, somebody; anyone, anybody

jene ['je:nə], jener ['je:nɐ], jenes ['je:nəs] *dem pron* that (one); *pl* those; *dies und jenes* this and that

jenseitig ['je:nzaitɪç] *adj* opposite

jenseits ['je:nzaits] *adv and prp* (*gen*) on the other side (of), beyond (*a. fig*)

'Jenseits *n* (-; *no pl*) next world, hereafter

jetzig ['jetsɪç] *adj* present; existing

jetzt [jetst] *adv* now, at present; *bis jetzt* up to now, so far; *erst jetzt* only now; *jetzt gleich* right now or away; *für jetzt* for the present; *von jetzt an* from now on

jeweilig ['je:'vailɪç] *adj* respective

jeweils ['je:'vails] *adv* each; at a time

Jh. ABBR of *Jahrhundert* cent., century

Jochbein ['jɔx-] *n* ANAT cheekbone

Jockei ['dʒɔke] *m* (-s; -s) jockey

Jod [jo:t] *n* (-[e]s; *no pl*) CHEM iodine

jodeln ['jo:dəln] *v/i* (ge-, h) yodel

Joga → *Yoga*

joggen ['dʒɔgən] *v/i* (ge-, h) jog

Jogger ['dʒɔgɐ] *m* (-s; -) jogger

Jogging ['dʒɔgɪŋ] *n* (-s; *no pl*) jogging

Jogginganzug *m* tracksuit

Jogginghose *f* tracksuit trousers

Joghurt ['jo:gʊrt] *m, n* (-[s]; -[s]) yog(h)urt, yoghourt

Johannisbeere [jo'hanɪs-] *f: rote Johannisbeere* redcurrant; *schwarze Johannisbeere* blackcurrant

johlen ['jo:lən] *v/i* (ge-, h) howl, yell

Jolle ['jɔlə] *f* (-; -n) MAR dinghy

Jongleur [ʒõ'gløːɐ] *m* (-s; -e) juggler

jonglieren [ʒõ'gliːrən] *v/t and v/i* (no -ge-, h) juggle

Joule [dʒu:l] *n* (-[s]; -) PHYS joule

Journalismus [ʒʊrna'lɪsmʊs] *m* (-; *no pl*) journalism

Journalist(in) [ʒʊrna-'lɪst(ɪn)] (-en; -en/-; -nen) journalist

jr. → *jun.*

Jubel ['ju:bəl] *m* (-s; *no pl*) cheering, cheers; rejoicing

'jubeln *v/i* (ge-, h) cheer, shout for joy; rejoice

Jubiläum [jubi'lɛːʊm] *n* (-s; -läen) anniversary; *50-jähriges Jubiläum* fiftieth anniversary, (golden) jubilee

jucken ['jʊkən] *v/t and v/i* (ge-, h) itch; *es*

juckt mich am … my … itches

Jude ['ju:də] *m* (-n; -n) Jewish person; *er ist Jude* he is Jewish

Jüdin ['jy:dɪn] *f* (-; -nen) Jewish woman or girl; *sie ist Jüdin* she is Jewish

jüdisch ['jy:dɪʃ] *adj* Jewish

Judo ['ju:do] *n* (-[s]; *no pl*) SPORT judo

Jugend ['ju:gənt] *f* (-; *no pl*) youth; *die Jugend* young people

Jugendamt *n* youth welfare office

Jugendarbeitslosigkeit *f* youth unemployment

'jugendfrei *adj: jugendfreier Film* G(-rated) (*Br* U[-rated]) film; *nicht jugendfrei* X-rated

'Jugendfürsorge *f* youth welfare

Jugendgericht *n* JUR juvenile court

Jugendherberge *f* youth hostel

Jugendklub *m* youth club

Jugendkriminali,tät *f* juvenile delinquency

'jugendlich *adj* youthful, young

'Jugendliche *m, f* (-n; -n) young person, *m a.* youth, *f* juvenile

'Jugendstil *m* (-s; *no pl*) Art Nouveau

Jugendstrafanstalt *f* detention center (*Br* centre), reformatory

Jugendverbot *n* for adults only; → *jugendfrei*

Jugendzentrum *n* youth center (*Br* centre)

Juli ['ju:li] *m* (-[s]; -s) July

Jumbojet ['jumbo-] *m* jumbo (jet)

jun. ABBR of *junior* Jun., jun., Jnr., Jr., junior

jung [jʊŋ] *adj* young

Junge¹ ['jʊŋə] *m* (-n; -n) boy; lad; *cards:* jack, knave

'Junge² *n* (-n; -n) ZO young; puppy; kitten; cub; *Junge bekommen* or *werfen* have young

'jungenhaft *adj* boyish

'Jungenstreich *m* boyish prank

jünger ['jʏŋɐ] *adj* younger

'Jünger *m* (-s; -) REL disciple (*a. fig*)

Jungfer ['jʊŋfɐ] *f* (-; -n) *alte Jungfer* old maid

'Jungfernfahrt *f* MAR maiden voyage

Jungfernflug *m* AVIAT maiden flight

'Jungfrau *f* virgin; ASTR Virgo; *er ist Jungfrau* he's (a) Virgo

Junggeselle *m* bachelor, single (man)

Junggesellin *f* bachelor girl, single (woman); *esp* JUR spinster

jüngste ['jʏŋstə] *adj* youngest; *fig* latest; *in jüngster Zeit* lately, recently; *das Jüngste Gericht* the Last Judg(e)ment; *der Jüngste Tag* Doomsday

Juni ['ju:ni] *m* (-[s]; -s) June

junior ['ju:njoːɐ] *adj*, **'Junior** *m* (-s; -en [ju'njoːrən]), **Juni'orin** *f* (-; -nen) junior (*a.* SPORT)
Jupe [ʒyːp] *Swiss m* (-s; -s) skirt
Jura ['juːra]: *Jura studieren* study (the) law
juridisch [ju'riːdɪʃ] *Austrian* → **juristisch**
Jurist(in) [ju'rɪst(ɪn)] (-en; -en/-; -nen) lawyer; law student
ju'ristisch *adj* legal
Jurorenkomitee [ju'roːrən-] *Austrian n* → **Jury**
Jury [ʒy'riː] *f* (-; -s) jury
justieren [jʊs'tiːrən] *v/t* (*no* -ge-, *h*) TECH adjust, set
Justiz [jʊs'tiːts] *f* (-; *no pl*) (administration of) justice, (the) law
Justizbeamte *m* judicial officer
Justizirrtum *m* error of justice
Justizmi,nister *m* minister of justice; Attorney General, *Br* Lord Chancellor
Justizminis,terium *n* ministry of justice; Department of Justice
Jute ['juːtə] *f* (-; *no pl*) jute
Juwel [ju've:l] *m*, *n* (-s; -en) jewel, gem (*both a. fig*); *pl* jewel(le)ry
Juwelier [juve'liːɐ] *m* (-s; -e) jewel(l)er

K

Kabarett [kaba'rɛt] *n* (-s; -s) (political) revue
Kabel ['kaːbəl] *n* (-s; -) cable
'Kabelfernsehen *n* cable TV
Kabeljau ['kaːbəljau] *m* (-s; -e, -s) ZO cod(fish)
Kabine [ka'biːnə] *f* (-; -n) cabin; cubicle; SPORT dressing room; TECH car; TEL etc booth
Ka'binenbahn *f* cable railway
Kabinett [kabi'nɛt] *n* (-s; -e) POL cabinet
Kabis ['kaːbɪs] *Swiss m* (-; *no pl*) green cabbage
Kabriolett [kabrio'lɛt] *n* (-s; -s) MOT convertible
Kachel ['kaxəl] *f* (-; -n), **'kacheln** *v/t* (*ge-*, *h*) tile
'Kachelofen *m* tiled stove
Kadaver [ka'daːvɐ] *m* (-s; -) carcass
Kadett [ka'dɛt] *m* (-en; -en) MIL cadet
Käfer ['kɛːfɐ] *m* (-s; -) ZO beetle, bug
Kaffee ['kafe] *m* (-s; -s) coffee; *Kaffee kochen* make coffee; *Kaffee mit Milch* white coffee
Kaffeeauto,mat *m* coffee machine
Kaffeebohne *f* coffee bean
Kaffeehaus [ka'fe:-] *Austrian n* café, coffee house
Kaffeekanne *f* coffee pot
Kaffeema,schine *f* coffeemaker
Kaffeemühle *f* coffee grinder
Käfig ['kɛːfɪç] *m* (-s; -e) cage (*a. fig*)
kahl [kaːl] *adj* bald; *fig* bare (*rock, wall etc*); barren, bleak (*landscape*)
Kahn [kaːn] *m* (-[e]s; *Kähne* ['kɛːnə])

boat; barge
Kai [kai] *m* (-s; -s) quay, wharf
Kaiser ['kaizɐ] *m* (-s; -) emperor
Kaiserin ['kaizərɪn] *f* (-; -nen) empress
'Kaiserreich *n* empire
Kajüte [ka'jyːtə] *f* (-; -n) MAR cabin
Kakao [ka'kau] *m* (-s; -s) cocoa; (hot) chocolate; chocolate milk
Kaktee [kak'teː] *f* (-; -n), **Kaktus** ['kaktʊs] *m* (-; *Kakteen*) BOT cactus
Kalb [kalp] *n* (-[e]s; *Kälber* ['kɛlbɐ]) ZO calf
kalben ['kalbən] *v/i* (*ge-*, *h*) calve
'Kalbfleisch *n* veal
'Kalbsbraten *m* roast veal
Kalbsschnitzel *n* veal cutlet; escalope (of veal)
Kaldaunen [kal'daunən] *pl* GASTR tripe
Kalender [ka'lɛndɐ] *m* (-s; -) calendar
Kalenderjahr *n* calendar year
Kali ['kaːli] *n* (-s; *no pl*) CHEM potash
Kaliber [ka'liːbɐ] *n* (-s; -) caliber, *Br* calibre (*a. fig*)
Kalk [kalk] *m* (-[e]s; -e) lime; GEOL limestone, chalk; MED calcium
'kalken *v/t* (*ge-*, *h*) whitewash; AGR lime
'kalkig *adj* limy
'Kalkstein *m* limestone
Kalorie [kalo'riː] *f* (-; -n) calorie
kalo'rienarm *adj*, **kalorienredu,ziert** *adj* low-calorie, low in calories
kalorienreich *adj* high-calorie, high *or* rich in calories
kalt [kalt] *adj* cold; *mir ist kalt* I'm cold; *es (mir) wird kalt* it's (I'm) getting cold;

kalt bleiben *fig* keep (one's) cool; *das lässt mich kalt* that leaves me cold
'**kaltblütig** [-bly:tɪç] **1.** *adj* cold-blooded (*a. fig*); **2.** *adv* in cold blood
Kälte ['kɛltə] *f (-; no pl)* cold; *fig* coldness; *vor Kälte zittern* shiver with cold; *fünf Grad Kälte* five degrees below zero
Kälteeinbruch *m* cold snap
Kältegrad *m* degree below zero
Kälteperi,ode *f* cold spell
'**kaltmachen** F *v/t (sep, -ge-, h)* bump off
kam [ka:m] *pret of* **kommen**
Kamee [ka'me:ə] *f (-; -n)* cameo
Kamel [ka'me:l] *n (-s; -e)* zo camel
Ka'melhaar *n (-[e]s; no pl)* camelhair
Kamera ['kaməra] *f (-; -s)* camera
Kamerad [kamə'ra:t] *m (-en; -en* [-'ra:-dən]) companion, F mate, pal, buddy
Kameradin [-'ra:dɪn] *f (-; -nen)* companion
Kame'radschaft *f (-; no pl)* comradeship
'**Kameramann** *m* cameraman
'**Kamera,korder** *m (-s; -)* camcorder
Kamille [ka'mɪlə] *f (-; -n)* BOT camomile
Kamin [ka'mi:n] *m (-s; -e)* fireplace; chimney (*a.* MOUNT); *am Kamin* by the fire (-side)
Kaminkehrer [-ke:rɐ] *m (-s; -)* chimney sweep
Kaminsims *m, n* mantelpiece
Kamm [kam] *m (-[e]s; Kämme* ['kɛmə]) comb, zo *a.* crest (*a. fig*)
kämmen ['kɛmən] *v/t (ge-, h)* comb; *sich (die Haare) kämmen* comb one's hair
Kammer ['kamɐ] *f (-; -n)* (small) room, storeroom, closet; garret; POL, ECON chamber; JUR division
'**Kammermu,sik** *f* chamber music
'**Kammgarn** *n* worsted (yarn)
Kampagne [kam'panjə] *f (-; -n)* campaign
Kampf [kampf] *m (-[e]s; Kämpfe* ['kɛmp-fə]) fight (*a. fig*), struggle (*a. fig*), *esp* MIL combat, battle (*a. fig*); SPORT contest, match; *boxing:* fight, bout; *fig* conflict
'**kampfbereit** *adj* ready for battle (MIL combat)
kämpfen ['kɛmpfən] *v/i (ge-, h)* fight (*gegen* against; *mit* with; *um* for) (*a. fig*); struggle (*a. fig*); *fig* contend, wrestle
Kampfer ['kampfɐ] *m (-s; no pl)* CHEM camphor
Kämpfer ['kɛmpfɐ] *m (-s; -)*, '**Kämpferin** *f (-; -nen)* fighter (*a. fig*)
kämpferisch ['kɛmpfərɪʃ] *adj* fighting, aggressive
'**Kampfflugzeug** *n* MIL combat aircraft
Kampfkraft *f (-; no pl)* fighting strength
Kampfrichter *m* SPORT judge
Kampfsportarten *pl* martial arts

Kanada ['kanada] Canada
Kanadier [ka'na:djɐ] *m (-s; -)*, **Ka'nadierin** [-djərɪn] *f (-; -nen)*, **ka'nadisch** *adj* Canadian
Kanal [ka'na:l] *m (-s; Kanäle* [ka'nɛ:lə]) canal; channel (*a.* TV, TECH, *fig*); sewer, drain; *der Kanal* the (English) Channel
Kanalisation [kanaliza'tsjo:n] *f (-; -en)* sewerage (system); canalization
kanalisieren [kanali'zi:rən] *v/t (no -ge-, h)* sewer; canalize; *fig* channel
Ka'naltunnel *m* Channel Tunnel, F Chunnel
Kanarienvogel [ka'na:rjən-] *m* canary
Kandidat [kandi'da:t] *m (-en; -en)*, **Kandi'datin** *f (-; -nen)* candidate
Kandidatur [kandida'tu:ɐ] *f (-; -en)* candidacy, *Br a.* candidature
kandidieren [kandi'di:rən] *v/i (no -ge-, h)* stand *or* run for election; *kandidieren für ...* run for the office of ...
Känguru, Känguruh ['kɛnguru] *n (-s; -s)* zo kangaroo
Kaninchen [ka'ni:nçən] *n (-s; -)* zo rabbit
Kanister [ka'nɪstɐ] *m (-s; -)* (fuel) can
Kanne ['kanə] *f (-; -n)* pot; can
Kannibale [kani'ba:lə] *m (-n; -n)* cannibal
kannte ['kantə] *pret of* **kennen**
Kanon ['ka:nɔn] *m (-s; -s)* MUS canon
Kanone [ka'no:nə] *f (-; -n)* MIL gun; cannon; F ace, *esp* SPORT *a.* crack
Kante ['kantə] *f (-; -n)* edge
'**kanten** *v/t (ge-, h)* set on edge; tilt; edge (*skis*)
'**Kanten** *m (-s; -)* crust
kantig ['kantıç] *adj* angular, square(d)
Kantine [kan'ti:nə] *f (-; -n)* canteen
Kanton [kan'to:n] *m (-s; -e)* POL canton
Kanu ['ka:nu] *n (-s; -s)* canoe
Kanüle [ka'ny:lə] *f (-; -n)* MED cannula, (drain) tube
Kanzel ['kantsəl] *f (-; -n)* REL pulpit; AVIAT cockpit
Kanzlei [kants'lai] *f (-; -en)* office
Kanzler ['kantslɐ] *m (-s; -)* chancellor
Kanzlerin ['kantslərɪn] *f (-; -nen)* chancellor
Kap [kap] *n (-s; -s)* cape, headland
Kapazität [kapatsi'tɛ:t] *f (-; -en)* capacity; *fig* authority
Kapelle [ka'pɛlə] *f (-; -n)* REL chapel; MUS band
Ka'pellmeister *m* MUS conductor
kapern ['ka:pɐn] *v/t (ge-, h)* MAR capture, seize
kapieren [ka'pi:rən] F *v/t (no -ge-, h)* get; *kapiert?* got it?
Kapital [kapi'ta:l] *n (-s; -e, -ien)* ECON capital, funds

Kapitalanlage f investment

Kapitalismus [kapita'lɪsmʊs] m (-; no pl) capitalism

Kapita'list m (-en; -en), **kapita'listisch** adj capitalist

Kapi'talverbrechen n capital crime, JUR felony

Kapitän [kapi'tɛːn] m (-s; -e) captain (a. SPORT)

Kapitel [ka'pɪtəl] n (-s; -) chapter (a. fig); F fig story

Kapitulation [kapitula'tsjoːn] f (-; -en) capitulation, surrender (a. fig)

kapitulieren [kapitu'liːrən] v/i (no -ge-, h) capitulate, surrender (a. fig)

Kaplan [ka'plaːn] m (-s; Kapläne [ka-'plɛːnə]) REL curate

Kappe ['kapə] f (-; -n) cap, TECH a. top, hood

'kappen v/t (ge-, h) cut (rope); lop, top (tree)

Kapsel ['kapsəl] f (-; -n) capsule

kaputt [ka'pʊt] F adj broken (a. fig); TECH out of order; fig dead beat; ruined; **kaputt machen** F v/t (sep, -ge-, h) break, wreck (a. fig), ruin; fig → **kaputtmachen**; **kaputtgehen** F v/i (irr, gehen, sep, -ge-, sein) break; MOT etc break down; fig break up

kaputtmachen v/t (sep, -ge-, h) F fig wreck, ruin

Kapuze [ka'puːtsə] f (-; -n) hood; cowl

Karabiner [kara'biːne] m (-s; -) carbine

Karabinerhaken m karabiner, snaplink

Karaffe [ka'rafə] f (-; -n) decanter

Karambolage [karambo'laːʒə] f (-; -n) collision, crash

Karat [ka'raːt] n (-[e]s; -e) carat

Karate [ka'raːtə] n (-[s]; no pl) SPORT karate

Karawane [kara'vaːnə] f (-; -n) caravan

Kardinal [kardi'naːl] m (-s; Kardinäle [kardi'nɛːlə]) REL cardinal

Karfiol [kar'fjoːl] m Austrian (-s; no pl) BOT cauliflower

Kar'freitag [kaːɐ-] m REL Good Friday

karg [kark], **kärglich** ['kɛrklɪç] adj meagre, Br -re, scanty; frugal; poor

kariert [ka'riːɐt] adj checked, checkered, Br chequered; squared

Karies ['kaːrjes] f (-; no pl) MED (dental) caries

Karikatur [karika'tuːɐ] f (-; -en) mst cartoon, esp fig caricature

Karikaturist [karikatu'rɪst] m (-en; -en) cartoonist

karikieren [kari'kiːrən] v/t (no -ge-, h) caricature

Karneval ['karnəval] m (-s; -e, -s) carnival

Karo ['kaːro] n (-s; -s) square, check; cards: diamonds

Karosserie [karɔsə'riː] f (-; -n) MOT body

Karotte [ka'rɔtə] f (-; -n) BOT carrot

Karpfen ['karpfən] m (-s; -) ZO carp

Karre ['karə] f (-; -n), **'Karren** m (-s; -) cart; wheelbarrow; F MOT jalopy

Karriere [ka'rjeːrə] f (-; -n) career; **Karriere machen** work one's way up, get to the top

Karte ['kartə] f (-; -n) card; ticket; GEOGR map; chart; GASTR menu; **gute (schlechte) Karten** a good (bad) hand

Kartei [kar'tai] f (-; -en) card index

Karteikarte f index or file card

'Kartenhaus n house of cards (a. fig); MAR chartroom

Kartenspiel n card game; deck (Br pack) of cards

Kartentele,fon n cardphone

Kartenvorverkauf m advance booking; box office

Kartoffel [kar'tɔfəl] f (-; -n) BOT potato

Kartoffelbrei m mashed potatoes

Kartoffelchips pl (potato) chips, Br crisps

Kartoffelkloß m, **Kartoffelknödel** m potato dumpling

Kartoffelpuffer m potato fritter

Kartoffelschalen pl potato peelings

Kartoffelschäler m potato peeler

Karton [kar'tɔŋ] m (-s; -s) cardboard; pasteboard; cardboard box

Karussell [karu'sɛl] n (-s; -s) roundabout, car(r)ousel, merry-go-round

Karwoche ['kaːɐ-] f REL Holy Week

Kaschmir ['kaʃmiːɐ] m (-s; -e) cashmere

Käse ['kɛːzə] m (-s; -) cheese

Kaserne [ka'zɛrnə] f (-; -n) barracks

Ka'sernenhof m barrack square

käsig ['kɛːzɪç] adj cheesy; pasty

Kasino [ka'ziːno] n (-s; -s) casino; MIL (officers') mess

Kasperle ['kaspələ] n, m (-s; -) Punch

Kasperlethe,ater n Punch and Judy show

Kassa ['kasa] Austrian f (-; Kassen), **Kasse** ['kasə] f (-; -n) till; cash register; checkout (counter); cash desk; cashier's counter; THEA etc box office; F **gut (knapp) bei Kasse sein** be flush (be a bit hard up)

'Kassenbeleg m, **Kassenbon** m sales slip, Br receipt

Kassenerfolg m THEA etc box-office success

Kassenpati,ent m MED health plan (Am medicaid, Br NHS) patient

Kassenschlager F m blockbuster

Kassenwart [-vart] m (-[e]s; -e) treasurer

Kassette [ka'setə] f (-; -n) box, case; MUS,

TV, PHOT *etc* cassette; casket

Kas'setten... *in cpds* **...rekorder** *etc:* cassette ...

kassieren [ka'si:rən] *v/t and v/i* (*no -ge-, h*) collect, take (the money)

Kassierer [ka'si:rɐ] *m* (*-s; -*), **Kas'siererin** *f* (*-; -nen*) cashier; teller; collector

Kastanie [kas'ta:njə] *f* (*-; -n*) BOT chestnut

Kasten ['kastən] *m* (*-s; Kästen* ['kɛstən]) box (*a.* F TV, SPORT *etc*); case; chest

kastrieren [kas'tri:rən] *v/t* (*no -ge-, h*) MED, VET castrate

Kasus ['ka:zʊs] *m* (*-; -*) LING case

Katalog [kata'lo:k] *m* (*-[e]s; -e*) catalog(ue *Br*)

Katalysator [kataly'za:tɔ:ɐ] *m* (*-s; -en* [-za'to:rən]) CHEM catalyst; MOT catalytic converter

Katapult [kata'pʊlt] *m, n* (*-[e]s; -e*), **katapultieren** [katapʊl'ti:rən] *v/t* (*no -ge-, h*) catapult

katastrophal [katastro'fa:l] *adj* disastrous (*a. fig*)

Katastrophe [katas'tro:fə] *f* (*-; -n*) catastrophe, disaster (*a. fig*)

Kata'strophengebiet *n* disaster area

Katastrophenschutz *m* disaster control

Katechismus [katɛ'çɪsmʊs] *m* (*-; -men*) REL catechism

Kategorie [katego'ri:] *f* (*-; -n*) category

Kater ['ka:tɐ] *m* (*-s; -*) ZO male cat, tomcat; F hangover

kath. ABBR *of* **katholisch** Cath., Catholic

Kathedrale [kate'dra:lə] *f* (*-; -n*) cathedral

Katholik [kato'li:k] *m* (*-en; -en*), **Katholikin** *f* (*-; -nen*), **katholisch** [ka'to:lɪʃ] *adj* (Roman) Catholic

Kätzchen ['kɛtsçən] *n* (*-s; -*) ZO kitten, pussy (*a.* BOT)

Katze ['katsə] *f* (*-; -n*) ZO cat; kitten

Kauderwelsch ['kaudɐvɛlʃ] *n* (*-[s]; no pl*) gibberish

kauen ['kauən] *v/t and v/i* (*ge-, h*) chew

kauern ['kauɐn] *v/i and v/refl* (*ge-, h*) crouch, squat

Kauf [kauf] *m* (*-[e]s; Käufe* ['kɔʏfə]) purchase (*a.* ECON, F buy; purchasing, buying; *ein guter Kauf* a bargain, F a good buy; *zum Kauf anbieten* offer for sale

kaufen *v/t* (*ge-, h*) buy (*a. fig*), purchase

Käufer ['kɔʏfɐ] *m* (*-s; -*), **Käuferin** *f* (*-; -nen*) buyer; customer

'Kauffrau *f* (*-; -en*) businesswoman

'Kaufhaus *n* department store

Kaufkraft *f* (*-; no pl*) ECON purchasing power

käuflich ['kɔʏflɪç] *adj* for sale; *fig* venal

'Kaufmann *m* (*-[e]s; -leute*) businessman; dealer, trader, merchant; storekeeper, *Br*

mst shopkeeper; grocer

'kaufmännisch [-mɛnɪʃ] *adj* commercial, business; *kaufmännischer Angestellter* clerk

'Kaufvertrag *m* contract of sale

'Kaugummi *m* (*-s; -s*) chewing gum

kaum [kaum] *adv* hardly; *kaum zu glauben* hard to believe

Kaution [kau'tsjo:n] *f* (*-; -en*) security; JUR bail

Kautschuk ['kautʃʊk] *m* (*-s; -e*) (india) rubber

Kavalier [kava'li:ɐ] *m* (*-s; -e*) gentleman

Kaviar ['ka:vjar] *m* (*-s; -e*) caviar(e)

keck [kɛk] *adj* cheeky, saucy, pert

Kegel ['ke:gəl] *m* (*-s; -*) skittle, pin; MATH, TECH cone

Kegelbahn *f* bowling (*esp Br* skittle) alley

'kegelförmig [-fœrmɪç] *adj* conical

'Kegelkugel *f* bowling (*esp Br* skittle) ball

'kegeln *v/i* (*ge-, h*) bowl, go bowling, *esp Br* play (at) skittles *or* ninepins

Kehle ['ke:lə] *f* (*-; -n*) ANAT throat

'Kehlkopf *m* ANAT larynx

Kehre ['ke:rə] *f* (*-; -n*) (sharp) bend

'kehren *v/t* (*ge-, h*) sweep; *j-m den Rücken kehren* turn one's back on s.o.

Kehricht ['ke:rɪçt] *m* (*-s; no pl*) sweepings

Kehrichtschaufel *f* dustpan

kehrtmachen ['ke:ɐt-] *v/i* (*sep, -ge-, h*) turn back

keifen ['kaifən] *v/i* (*ge-, h*) nag, bitch

Keil [kail] *m* (*-[e]s; -e*) wedge; gusset

Keiler ['kailɐ] *m* (*-s; -*) ZO wild boar

'Keilriemen *m* MOT fan belt

Keim [kaim] *m* (*-[e]s; -e*) BIOL, MED germ; BOT bud, sprout; *fig* seed(s)

'keimen *v/i* (*ge-, h*) BOT germinate, sprout; *fig* form, grow; stir

'keimfrei *adj* MED sterile

'keimtötend *adj* MED germicidal

Keimzelle *f* BIOL germ cell

kein [kain] *indef pron* **1.** *adj:* *kein(e)* no, not any; *kein anderer* no one else; *kein(e) ... mehr* not any more ...; *kein Geld (keine Zeit) mehr* no money (time) left; *kein Kind mehr* no longer a child; **2.** *su:* *keiner, keine, kein(e)s* none, no one, nobody; *keiner von beiden* neither (of the two); *keiner von uns* none of us

'keines'falls *adv* by no means, under no circumstances

'keineswegs [-'ve:ks] *adv* by no means, not in the least

'keinmal *adv* not once, not a single time

Keks [ke:ks] *m, n* (*-es, -e*) cookie, *Br* biscuit

Kelch [kɛlç] *m* (*-[e]s; -e*) cup (*a.* BOT); REL chalice

             K

Kelle

Kelle ['kɛlə] f (-; -n) GASTR ladle, scoop; TECH trowel; signaling disk

Keller ['kɛlɐ] m (-s; -) cellar; → **Kellergeschoss** n, **Kellergeschoß** Austrian n basement

Kellerwohnung f basement (apartment, esp Br flat)

Kellner ['kɛlnɐ] m (-s; -) waiter

Kellnerin ['kɛlnərɪn] f (-; -nen) waitress

keltern ['kɛltɐn] v/t (ge-, h) press

kennen ['kɛnən] v/t (irr, ge-, h) know, be acquainted with; **kennen lernen →** **kennenlernen**

kennenlernen (sep, -ge-, -ge-, h) get to know, become acquainted with; meet s.o.; **als ich ihn kennenlernte** when I first met him

Kenner ['kɛnɐ] m (-s; -), **Kennerin** f (-; -nen) expert

kenntlich ['kɛntlɪç] adj recognizable (**an** dat by)

Kenntnis f (-; -se) knowledge; **gute** **Kenntnisse in** (dat) a good knowledge of

Kennwort n password

Kennzeichen n mark, sign; (distinguishing) feature, characteristic; MOT license (Br registration) number

kennzeichnen v/t (ge-, h) mark; fig characterize

kentern ['kɛntɐn] v/i (ge-, sein) MAR capsize

Keramik [ke'ra:mɪk] f (-; -en) ceramics

Kerbe ['kɛrbə] f (-; -n) notch

Kerker ['kɛrkɐ] m (-s; -) dungeon

Kerl [kɛrl] F m (-s; -e) fellow, guy; **armer** **Kerl** poor devil; **ein anständiger Kerl** a decent sort

Kern [kɛrn] m (-[e]s; -e) BOT pip, seed, stone, kernel; TECH core (a. fig); PHYS nucleus

Kern... in cpds ...energie, ...forschung, ...physik, ...reaktor, ...technik etc: nuclear ...

Kernfach n PED basic subject

Kernfa‚milie f nuclear family

Kerngehäuse n BOT core

kernge'sund adj F (as) sound as a bell

kernig ['kɛrnɪç] adj full of seeds (Br pips), fig robust; pithy

Kernkraft f PHYS nuclear power

Kernkraftgegner m anti-nuclear activist

Kernkraftwerk n nuclear power station or plant

kernlos adj BOT seedless

Kernspaltung f PHYS nuclear fission

Kernwaffen pl MIL nuclear weapons

kernwaffenfrei adj: **kernwaffenfreie Zone** MIL nuclear-free zone

Kernwaffenversuch m MIL nuclear test

Kernzeit f ECON core time

Kerze ['kɛrtsə] f (-; -n) candle; SPORT shoulder stand

kess [kɛs] F adj cheeky, saucy, pert

Kessel ['kɛsəl] m (-s; -) kettle; TECH boiler; tank

Kette ['kɛtə] f (-; -n) chain (a. fig); necklace; **e-e Kette bilden** form a line

Ketten... in cpds ...antrieb, ...laden, ...rauchen, ...raucher, ...reaktion etc: chain ...

ketten v/t (ge-, h) chain (**an** acc to)

Kettenfahrzeug n tracked vehicle

Ketzer ['kɛtsɐ] m (-s; -) heretic

Ketzerei [kɛtsə'raɪ] f (-; -en) heresy

keuchen ['kɔʏçən] v/i (ge-, h) pant, gasp

Keuchhusten m MED whooping cough

Keule ['kɔʏlə] f (-; -n) club; GASTR leg

keusch [kɔʏʃ] adj chaste

Keuschheit f (-; no pl) chastity

Kfz [ka:?ɛf'tsɛt] ABBR of **Kraftfahrzeug** motor vehicle

Kfz-Brief m, **Kfz-Schein** m vehicle registration document

Kfz-Steuer f road or automobile tax

Kfz-Werkstatt f garage

KG [ka:'ge:] ABBR of **Kommanditgesellschaft** ECON limited partnership

kichern ['kɪçɐn] v/i (ge-, h) giggle

Kiebitz ['ki:bɪts] m (-es; -e) ZO peewit, lapwing; F kibitzer

Kiefer¹ ['ki:fɐ] m (-s; -) ANAT jaw(bone)

Kiefer² f (-; -n) BOT pine(tree)

Kiel [ki:l] m (-[e]s; -e) MAR keel

Kielflosse f AVIAT tail fin

Kielraum m MAR bilge

Kielwasser n (-s; -) MAR wake (a. fig)

Kieme ['ki:mə] f (-n; -n) ZO gill

Kies [ki:s] m (-es; -e) gravel (a. mit Kies bestreuen); F dough

Kiesel ['ki:zəl] m (-s; -) pebble

Kilo ['ki:lo] n (-s; -) → **Kilogramm**

Kilo‚gramm [kilo-] n kilogram(me)

Kilohertz [-'hɛrts] n (-; -) kilohertz

Kilo‚meter m kilometer, Br kilometre

Kilo‚watt n ELECTR kilowatt

Kind [kɪnt] n (-[e]s; -er ['kɪndɐ]) child; **ein** **Kind erwarten** be expecting a baby

Kinderarzt m, **Kinderärztin** f p(a)ediatrician

Kindergarten m kindergarten, nursery school

Kindergärtnerin [-gɛrtnərɪn] f (-; -nen) nursery-school or kindergarten teacher

Kindergeld n child benefit

Kinderhort [-hɔrt] m (-[e]s; -e), **Kinderkrippe** f day nursery

Kinderlähmung f MED polio(-myelitis)

'kinderlieb *adj* fond of children

'kinderlos *adj* childless

'Kindermädchen *n* nurse(maid), nanny

Kinderspiel *fig n:* ***ein Kinderspiel sein*** be child's play

Kinderstube *fig f* manners, upbringing

Kinderwagen *m* baby carriage, buggy, *Br* pram

Kinderzimmer *n* children's room

Kindesalter ['kındəs-] *n* childhood; infancy

Kindesentführung *f* kidnap(p)ing

Kindesmisshandlung *f* child abuse

'Kindheit *f (-; no pl)* (***von Kindheit an*** from) childhood

kindisch ['kındıʃ] *adj* childish

'kindlich *adj* childlike

Kinn [kın] *n (-[e]s; -e)* ANAT chin

Kinnbacke *f*, **'Kinnbacken** *m (-s; -)* ANAT jaw(-bone)

Kinnhaken *m boxing:* hook (to the chin), uppercut

Kino ['kiːno] *n (-s; -s)* a) *(no pl)* motion pictures, *esp Br* cinema, F the movies, b) movie theater, *esp Br* cinema

'Kinobesucher *m*, **'Kinogänger** [-gɛŋə] *m (-s; -)* moviegoer, *Br* cinemagoer

Kippe ['kıpə] *f (-; -n)* F butt, *esp Br* stub; SPORT upstart

'kippen *1. v/i (ge-, sein)* tip or topple (over); *2. v/t (ge-, h)* tilt, tip over or up

Kirche ['kırçə] *f (-; -n)* church; *in die Kirche gehen* go to church

'Kirchenbuch *n* parish register

'Kirchendiener *m* sexton

'Kirchengemeinde *f* parish

'Kirchenjahr *n* Church or ecclesiastical year

'Kirchenlied *n* hymn

'Kirchenmu,sik *f* sacred or church music

'Kirchenschiff *n* ARCH nave

'Kirchensteuer *f* church tax

'Kirchenstuhl *m* pew

'Kirchentag *m* church congress

'Kirchgang *m* churchgoing

'Kirchgänger [-gɛŋə] *m (-s; -)* churchgoer

'kirchlich *adj* church, ecclesiastical

'Kirchturm *m* steeple; spire; church tower

Kirsche ['kırʃə] *f (-; -n)* BOT cherry

Kissen ['kısən] *n (-s; -)* pillow; cushion

Kissenbezug *m*, **Kissenhülle** *f* pillowcase, pillowslip

Kiste ['kıstə] *f (-; -n)* box, chest; crate

Kitsch [kıtʃ] *m (-[e]s; no pl)* kitsch; trash; F slush

'kitschig *adj* kitschy; trashy; slushy

Kitt [kıt] *m (-[e]s; -e)* cement; putty

Kittel ['kıtəl] *m (-s; -)* smock; overall; MED (white) coat

'kitten *v/t (ge-, h)* cement; putty

Kitzel ['kıtsəl] *m (-s; -)* tickle, *fig a.* thrill, kick

'kitzeln *v/i and v/t (ge-, h)* tickle

Kitzler ['kıtslə] *m (-s; -)* ANAT clitoris

kitzlig ['kıtslıç] *adj* ticklish (*a. fig*)

kläffen ['klɛfən] *v/i (ge-, h)* yap, yelp

klaffend ['klafənt] *adj* gaping; yawning

Klage ['klaːgə] *f (-; -n)* complaint; lament; JUR action, (law)suit

'klagen *v/i (ge-, h)* complain (***über*** *acc* of, about; ***bei*** to); lament; JUR go to court; ***gegen j-n klagen*** JUR sue s.o.

Kläger ['klɛːgə] *m (-s; -)*, **'Klägerin** *f (-; -nen)* JUR plaintiff

kläglich ['klɛːklıç] → *jämmerlich*

Klamauk [kla'mauk] *m (-s; no pl)* racket; THEA *etc* slapstick

klamm [klam] *adj* numb; clammy

Klammer ['klamə] *f (-; -n)* TECH cramp, clamp; clip; clothespin, *Br* (clothes) peg; MED brace; MATH, PRINT bracket(s)

'klammern *v/t (ge-, h)* fasten or clip together; ***sich klammern an*** *(acc)* cling to

klang [klaŋ] *pret of* **klingen**

Klang *m (-[e]s; Klänge* ['klɛŋə]*)* sound; tone; clink; ringing

'klangvoll *adj* sonorous; *fig* illustrious

Klappe ['klapə] *f (-; -n)* flap; hinged lid; MOT tailgate, *Br* tailboard; TECH, BOT, ANAT valve; F trap

'klappen *(ge-, h)* **1.** *v/t:* ***nach oben klappen*** lift up, raise; put or fold up; ***nach unten klappen*** lower, put down; ***es lässt sich (nach hinten) klappen*** it folds (backward); **2.** *v/i* clap, clack; F work, work out (well)

Klapper ['klapə] *f (-; -n)* rattle

'klappern *v/i (ge-, h)* clatter, rattle (***mit et.*** s.th.)

'Klapperschlange *f* zo rattlesnake

Klappfahrrad ['klap-] *n* folding bicycle

Klappfenster *n* top-hung window

Klappmesser *n* jack knife, clasp knife

klapprig ['klaprıç] *adj* MOT rattly, ramshackle; F shaky

'Klappsitz *m* folding or tip-up seat

'Klappstuhl *m* folding chair

'Klapptisch *m* folding table

Klaps [klaps] *m (-es; -e)* slap, pat; smack

klar [klaːr] *adj* clear (*a. fig*); *ist dir klar, dass ...?* do you realize that ...?; *das ist mir (nicht ganz) klar* I (don't quite) understand; *(na) klar!* of course!; *alles klar?* everything okay?

'Kläranlage ['klɛːr-] *f* sewage works

klären ['klɛːrən] *v/t (ge-, h)* TECH purify; treat; *fig* clear up; settle; SPORT clear

'Klarheit *f (-; no pl)* clearness, *fig a.* clarity

K

Klarinette [klari'netə] f (-; -n) MUS clarinet
'**Klarsicht...** in cpds transparent
Klasse ['klasə] f (-; -n) class (a. POL), PED a. grade, Br form; classroom; F **klasse sein** be super, be fantastic
'**Klassenarbeit** f (classroom) test
Klassenbuch n classbook, Br (class) register
Klassenkame,rad m classmate
'**Klassenlehrer(in)** homeroom teacher, Br form teacher, a. form master (mistress)
Klassensprecher m class representative
Klassenzimmer n classroom
klassifizieren [klasifi'tsi:rən] v/t (no -ge-, h) classify
'**Klassifi,zierung** f (-; -en) classification
Klassiker ['klasikɐ] m (-s; -) classic
klassisch ['klasıʃ] adj classic(al)
Klatsch [klatʃ] F m (-es; no pl) gossip
'**Klatschbase** f gossip
'**klatschen** v/i and v/t (ge-, h) clap, applaud; F slap, bang; splash; F gossip; **in die Hände klatschen** clap one's hands
'**klatschhaft** adj gossipy
'**Klatschmaul** F n (old) gossip
'**klatsch'nass** F adj soaking wet
klauben ['klaubən] Austrian v/t (ge-, h) pick; gather
Klaue ['klauə] f (-; -n) ZO claw; pl fig clutches
klauen ['klauən] F v/t (ge-, h) pinch
Klausel ['klauzəl] f (-; -n) JUR clause; condition
Klausur [klau'zu:ɐ] f (-; -en) test (paper), exam(ination)
Klavier [kla'vi:ɐ] n (-s; -e) MUS piano; **Klavier spielen** play the piano
Klavierkon,zert n MUS piano concerto; piano recital
Klebeband ['kle:bə-] n (-[e]s; -bänder) adhesive tape
kleben ['kle:bən] (ge-, h) **1.** v/t glue, paste; stick; **2.** v/i stick, cling (**an** dat to) (a. fig)
klebrig ['kle:brıç] adj sticky
Klebstoff ['kle:p-] m adhesive; glue
Klebstreifen m adhesive tape
kleckern ['klɛkɐn] F (ge-, h) **1.** v/i make a mess; **2.** v/t spill
Klecks [klɛks] F m (-es; -e) (ink)blot; blob
klecksen ['klɛksən] F v/i (ge-, h) blot, make blots
Klee [kle:] m (-s; no pl) BOT clover
'**Kleeblatt** n cloverleaf
Kleid [klait] n (-[e]s; -er ['klaidɐ]) dress; pl clothes
kleiden ['klaidən] v/t (ge-, h) dress, clothe; **j-n gut kleiden** suit s.o.; **sich gut** etc **kleiden** dress well etc
Kleiderbügel ['klaidɐ-] m (coat) hanger

Kleiderbürste f clothes brush
Kleiderhaken m coat hook
Kleiderschrank m wardrobe
Kleiderständer m coat stand
Kleiderstoff m dress material
'**kleidsam** adj becoming
Kleidung f (-; no pl) clothes, clothing
'**Kleidungsstück** n article of clothing
Kleie ['klaiə] f (-; -n) AGR bran
klein [klain] adj small, esp F little (a. finger, brother); short; **von klein auf** from an early age; **ein klein wenig** a little bit; **Groß und Klein** young and old; **die Kleinen** the little ones; **klein schneiden** cut up (into small pieces)
'**Kleinanzeige** f want ad, Br small ad
Kleinbildkamera f 35 mm camera
Kleinfa,milie f nuclear family
Kleingeld n (small) change
Kleinholz n matchwood
Kleinigkeit ['klainıçkait] f (-; -en) little thing, trifle; little something; **e-e Kleinigkeit sein** be nothing, be child's play
Kleinkind n baby, infant
'**Kleinkram** F m odds and ends
'**kleinlaut** adj subdued
'**kleinlich** adj small-minded, petty; mean; pedantic, fussy
'**kleinschneiden** v/t (irr, **schneiden**, sep, -ge-, h) → **klein**
'**Kleinstadt** f small town
'**kleinstädtisch** adj small-town, provincial
'**Kleintrans,port** m MOT pick-up
'**Kleinwagen** m MOT small or compact car, F runabout
Kleister ['klaistɐ] m (-s; -) paste
Klemme ['klɛmə] f (-; -n) TECH clamp; (hair) clip; F **in der Klemme sitzen** be in a fix or tight spot
'**klemmen** v/i and v/t (ge-, h) jam; stick; be stuck, be jammed; **sich klemmen** jam one's finger or hand
Klempner ['klɛmpnɐ] m (-s; -) plumber
Klepper ['klɛpɐ] m (-s; -) ZO nag
Klerus ['kle:rus] m (-; no pl) REL clergy
Klette ['klɛtə] f (-; -n) BOT bur(r); fig leech
klettern ['klɛtɐn] v/i (ge-, sein) climb; **auf e-n Baum klettern** climb (up) a tree
'**Kletterpflanze** f BOT climber
Klient [kli'ent] m (-en; -en), **Kli'entin** f (-; -nen) client
Klima ['kli:ma] n (-s; -s) climate, fig a. atmosphere
'**Klimaanlage** f air-conditioning
klimatisch [kli'ma:tıʃ] adj climatic
klimpern ['klımpɐn] v/i (ge-, h) jingle, chink (**mit** et. s.th.); F MUS strum (away) (**auf** dat on)
Klinge ['klıŋə] f (-; -n) blade

Klingel ['klɪŋəl] f (-; -n) bell
Klingelknopf m bell (push)
'**klingeln** v/i (ge-, h) ring (the bell); **es klingelt** the (door)bell is ringing
'**klingen** v/i (irr, ge-, h) sound; bell, metal etc: ring; glasses etc: clink
Klinik ['kli:nɪk] f (-; -en) hospital; clinic
klinisch ['kli:nɪʃ] adj clinical
Klinke ['klɪŋkə] f (-; -n) (door) handle
Klippe ['klɪpə] f (-; -n) cliff, rock(s); fig obstacle
klirren ['klɪrən] v/i (ge-, h) window: rattle; glasses etc: clink; broken glass: tinkle; swords: clash; keys, coins: jingle
Klischee [kli'ʃeː] n (-s; -s) cliché
klobig ['kloːbɪç] adj bulky, clumsy
klopfen ['klɔpfən] (ge-, h) **1.** v/i heart etc: beat, throb; knock (**an** acc at, on); tap; pat; **es klopft** there's a knock at the door; **2.** v/t beat; knock; drive (nail etc)
Klosett [klo'zɛt] n (-s; -s) lavatory, toilet
Klosettbrille f toilet seat
Klosettpapier n toilet paper
Kloß [kloːs] m (-es; Klöße ['kløːsə]) clod, lump (a. fig); GASTR dumpling
Kloster ['kloːstə] n (-s; Klöster ['kløːstə]) REL monastery; convent
Klotz [klɔts] m (-es; Klötze ['klœtsə]) block; log
Klub [klub] m (-s; -s) club
'**Klubsessel** m lounge chair
Kluft [klʊft] f (-; Klüfte ['klʏftə]) gap (a. fig); abyss
klug [kluːk] adj intelligent, clever, F bright, smart; wise; **daraus (aus ihm) werde ich nicht klug** I don't know what to make of it (him)
'**Klugheit** f (-; no pl) intelligence, cleverness, F brains; good sense; knowledge
Klumpen ['klʊmpən] m (-s; -) lump; clod; nugget
'**Klumpfuß** m MED club foot
'**klumpig** adj lumpy; cloddish
knabbern ['knabən] v/t and v/i (ge-, h) nibble, gnaw
Knabe ['knaːbə] m (-n; -n) boy
'**knabenhaft** adj boyish
Knäckebrot ['knɛkə-] n crispbread
knacken ['knakən] v/t and v/i (ge-, h) crack; twig: snap; fire, radio: crackle
Knacks F m (-es; -e) crack; fig defect
Knall [knal] m (-[e]s; -e) bang; crack, report; pop; F crash (gegen into); F **j-m e-e knallen** slap s.o.('s face)
'**Knallbon,bon** m, n cracker
'**knallen** v/i and v/t (ge-, h) bang; slam; crack; pop; F crash (**gegen** into); F **j-m e-e knallen** slap s.o.('s face)
'**knallig** F adj flashy, loud
'**Knallkörper** m firecracker

knapp [knap] adj scarce; scanty, meager, F meagre (food, pay etc); bare (a. majority etc); limited (time etc); narrow (escape etc); tight (dress etc); brief; **knapp an Geld (Zeit etc)** short of money (time etc); **mit knapper Not** only just, barely
Knappe ['knapə] m (-n; -n) miner
'**knapphalten** v/t (irr, halten, sep, -ge-, h): **j-n knapphalten** keep s.o. short
'**Knappheit** f (-; no pl) shortage
Knarre ['knarə] f (-; -n) rattle; F gun
'**knarren** v/i (ge-, h) creak
Knast [knast] F m (-[e]s; Knäste ['knɛstə]) sl clink
'**Knastbruder** F m jailbird
knattern ['knatən] v/i (ge-, h) crackle; MOT roar
Knäuel ['knɔyəl] m, n (-s; -) ball; tangle
Knauf [knauf] m (-[e]s; Knäufe ['knɔyfə]) knob; pommel
knau(e)rig ['knauz(ə)rɪç] F adj stingy
knautschen ['knautʃən] v/t and v/i (ge-, h) crumple
'**Knautschzone** f MOT crumple zone
Knebel ['kneːbəl] m (-s; -), '**knebeln** v/t (ge-, h) gag (a. fig)
Knecht [knɛçt] m (-[e]s; -e) farmhand; fig slave
'**Knechtschaft** fig f (-; no pl) slavery
kneifen ['knaifən] v/t and v/i (irr, ge-, h) pinch (**j-m in den Arm** s.o.'s arm); F chicken out
'**Kneifzange** f pincers
Kneipe ['knaipə] F f (-; -n) saloon, bar, esp Br pub
kneten ['kneːtən] v/t (ge-, h) knead; mo(u)ld
'**Knetmasse** f Plasticine®, Play-Doh®
Knick [knɪk] m (-[e]s; -e, -s) fold, crease; bend
'**knicken** v/t (ge-, h) fold, crease; bend; break; **nicht knicken!** do not bend!
Knicks [knɪks] m (-es; -e) curts(e)y; **e-n Knicks machen** → 'knicksen v/i (ge-, h) curts(e)y (**vor** dat to)
Knie [kniː] n (-s; - ['kniːə, kniː]) ANAT knee
'**Kniebeuge** f SPORT knee bend
'**Kniekehle** f ANAT hollow of the knee
knien [kniːn] v/i (ge-, h) kneel, be on one's knees (**vor** dat before)
'**Kniescheibe** f ANAT kneecap
'**Kniestrumpf** m knee(-length) sock
kniff [knɪf] pret of **kneifen**
Kniff m (-[e]s; -e) crease, fold; pinch; trick, knack
kniff(e)lig ['knɪf(ə)lɪç] adj tricky
knipsen ['knɪpsən] v/t and v/i (ge-, h) F PHOT take a picture (of); punch, clip
Knirps [knɪrps] m (-es; -e) little guy

knirschen ['knɪrʃən] *v/i* (ge-, h) crunch; *mit den Zähnen knirschen* grind *or* gnash one's teeth

knistern ['knɪstən] *v/i* (ge-, h) crackle; rustle

knittern ['knɪtən] *v/t and v/i* (ge-, h) crumple, crease, wrinkle

Knoblauch ['kno:plaux] *m* (-[e]s; *no pl*) BOT garlic

Knöchel ['knœçəl] *m* (-s; -) ANAT ankle; knuckle

Knochen ['knɔxən] *m* (-s; -) ANAT bone

'**Knochenbruch** *m* MED fracture

knochig ['knɔxɪç] *adj* bony

Knödel ['knø:dəl] *m* (-s; -) dumpling

Knolle ['knɔlə] *f* (-; -n) BOT tuber; bulb

Knopf [knɔpf] *m* (-es; *Knöpfe* ['knœpfə]), **knöpfen** ['knœpfən] *v/t* (ge-, h) button

'**Knopfloch** *n* buttonhole

Knorpel ['knɔrpəl] *m* (-s; -) GASTR gristle; ANAT cartilage

knorrig ['knɔrɪç] *adj* gnarled, knotted

Knospe ['knɔspə] *f* (-; -n), '**knospen** *v/i* (ge-, h) BOT bud

knoten [kno:tən] *v/t* (ge-, h) knot, make a knot in

'**Knoten** *m* (-s; -) knot (*a. fig*)

'**Knotenpunkt** *m* center, *Br* centre; RAIL junction

knüllen ['knʏlən] *v/t and v/i* (ge-, h) crumple

Knüller ['knʏlɐ] F *m* (-s; -) smash (hit); scoop

knüpfen ['knʏpfən] *v/t* (ge-, h) tie; weave

Knüppel ['knʏpəl] *m* (-s; -) stick, cudgel; truncheon

'**Knüppelschaltung** *f* floor shift

knurren ['knʊrən] *v/i* (ge-, h) growl, snarl; *fig* grumble (*über acc* at); *stomach*: rumble

knusp(e)rig ['knʊsp(ə)rɪç] *adj* crisp, crunchy

knutschen ['knu:tʃən] F *v/i* (ge-, h) pet, neck, smooch

k.o. [ka:'ʔo:] *adj* knocked out; *fig* beat

Koalition [koali'tsjo:n] *f* (-; -en) *esp* POL coalition

große Koalition grand coalition

Kobold ['ko:bɔlt] *m* (-[e]s; -e) (hob)goblin, imp (*a. fig*)

Koch [kɔx] *m* (-[e]s; *Köche* ['kœçə]) cook; chef

Kochbuch *n* cookbook, *Br* cookery book

'**kochen** [kɔxən] *v/t* (ge-, h) **1.** *v/t* cook; boil (*eggs etc*); make (*coffee etc*); **2.** *v/i* cook, do the cooking; boil (*a. fig*); **gut kochen** be a good cook; F *vor Wut kochen* boil with rage; *kochend heiß* boiling hot

Kocher ['kɔxɐ] *m* (-s; -) ELECTR cooker

Köchin ['kœçɪn] *f* (-; -nen) cook; chef

'**Kochlöffel** *m* (wooden) spoon

Kochnische *f* kitchenette

Kochplatte *f* hotplate

Kochsalz *n* common salt

Kochtopf *m* saucepan, pot

Köder ['kø:dɐ] *m* (-s; -) bait, decoy (*both a. fig*), lure

'**ködern** *v/t* (ge-, h) bait, decoy (*both a. fig*)

Kodex ['ko:dɛks] *m* (-es; -, -e) code

kodieren [ko'di:rən] *v/t* (*no ge-*, h) (en-)-code

Ko'dierung *f* (-; -en) (en-) coding

Koffein [kɔfe'i:n] *n* (-s; *no pl*) caffeine

Koffer ['kɔfɐ] *m* (-s; -) (suit)case; trunk

Kofferradio *n* portable (radio)

Kofferraum *m* MOT trunk, *Br* boot

Kognak ['kɔnjak] *m* (-s; -s) (French) brandy, cognac

Kohl [ko:l] *m* (-[e]s; -e) BOT cabbage

Kohle ['ko:lə] *f* (-; -n) coal; ELECTR carbon; F dough

'**Kohlehy,drat** *n* carbohydrate

'**Kohlen...** *in cpds* ...dioxid *etc:* CHEM carbon ...

Kohlenbergwerk *n* coalmine, colliery

Kohlenofen *m* coal-burning stove

'**Kohlensäure** *f* CHEM carbonic acid; GASTR F fizz

'**kohlensäurehaltig** *adj* carbonated, F fizzy

'**Kohlenstoff** *m* CHEM carbon

Kohlenwasserstoff *m* CHEM hydrocarbon

'**Kohlepa,pier** *n* carbon paper

Kohlezeichnung *f* charcoal drawing

Kohlrabi ['ra:bi] *m* (-s; -s) BOT kohlrabi

Koje ['ko:jə] *f* (-; -n) MAR berth, bunk

Kokain [koka'i:n] *n* (-s; *no pl*) cocaine

kokettieren [koke'ti:rən] *v/i* (*no ge-*, h) flirt; *fig* **kokettieren mit** toy with

Kokosnuss ['ko:kɔs-] *f* (-; Kokosnüsse) BOT coconut

Koks [ko:ks] *m* (-es; *no pl*) coke; F dough; *sl* coke, snow

Kolben ['kɔlbən] *m* (-s; -) butt; TECH piston

Kolbenstange *f* TECH piston rod

Kolibri ['ko:libri] *m* (-s; -s) ZO humming bird

Kolleg [kɔ'le:k] *n* (-s; -s) UNIV course (of lectures)

Kollege [kɔ'le:gə] *m* (-n; -n), **Kol'legin** *f* (-; -nen) colleague

Kollegium [kɔ'le:gjʊm] *n* (-s; -ien) UNIV faculty, *Br* teaching staff

Kollekte [kɔ'lɛktə] *f* (-; -n) REL collection

Kollektion [kɔlɛk'tsjo:n] *f* (-; -en) ECON collection; range

kollektiv [kɔlɛk'ti:f] *adj*, **Kollek'tiv** *n* (-s; -e) collective (*a. in cpds*)

Koller ['kɔlɐ] F m (-s; -) fit; rage

kollidieren [kɔli'diːrən] v/i (no -ge-, sein) collide

Kollision [kɔli'zjoːn] f (-; -en) collision, fig a. clash, conflict

Kölnischwasser ['kœlnɪʃ-] n (-s; -) (eau de) cologne

Kolonie [kolo'niː] f (-; -n) colony

kolonisieren [koloni'ziːrən] v/t (no -ge-, h) colonize

Koloni'sierung f (-; -en) colonization

Kolonne [ko'lɔnə] f (-; -n) column; MIL convoy; gang, crew

Koloss [ko'lɔs] m (-es; -e) colossus, fig a. giant (of a man)

kolossal [kolo'saːl] adj gigantic

Kombi ['kɔmbi] m (-[s]; -s) MOT station wagon, Br estate (car)

Kombination [kɔmbina'tsjoːn] f (-; -en) combination; set; coveralls, Br overalls; flying suit; soccer: combined move

kombinieren [kɔmbi'niːrən] (no -ge-, h) **1.** v/t combine; **2.** v/i reason

Kombüse [kɔm'byːzə] f (-; -n) MAR galley

Komet [ko'meːt] m (-en; -en) ASTR comet

Komfort [kɔm'foːɐ] m (-s; no pl) (modern) conveniences; luxury

komfortabel [kɔmfɔr'taːbəl] adj comfortable; well-appointed; luxurious

Komik ['koːmɪk] f (-; no pl) humo(u)r; comic effect

Komiker ['koːmikɐ] m (-s; -) comedian

komisch ['koːmɪʃ] adj comic(al), funny; strange, odd

Komitee [komi'teː] n (-s; -s) committee

Komma ['kɔma] n (-s; -s, -ta) comma; **sechs Komma vier** six point four

Kommandant [kɔman'dant] m (-en; -en), **Kommandeur** [kɔman'døːɐ] m (-s; -e) MIL commander, commanding officer

kommandieren [kɔman'diːrən] v/i and v/t (no -ge-, h) command, be in command of

Kommando [kɔ'mando] n (-s; -s) command; order; MIL commando

Komm'mandobrücke f MAR (navigating) bridge

kommen ['kɔmən] v/i (irr, ge-, sein) come; arrive; get; reach; **zu spät kommen** be late; **weit kommen** get far; **zur Schule kommen** start school; **ins Gefängnis kommen** go to jail; **kommen lassen** send for s.o., call s.o.; order s.th.; **kommen auf** (acc) think of, hit upon; remember; **hinter et. kommen** find s.th. out; **um et. kommen** lose s.th.; miss s.th.; **zu et. kommen** come by s.th.; **wieder zu sich kommen** come round or to; **wohin kommt ...?** where does ... go?; **daher kommt es, dass** that's why; **woher**

kommt es, dass ...? why is it that ...?, F how come ...?

'kommenlassen v/t (irr, **lassen**, sep, no -ge-, h) → **kommen**

Kommentar [kɔmɛn'taːɐ] m (-s; -e) commentary; **kein Kommentar!** no comment

Kommentator [kɔmɛn'taːtoːɐ] m (-s; -en [-ta'toːrən]), **Kommentatorin** [-ta-'toːrɪn] f (-; -nen) commentator

kommentieren [kɔmɛn'tiːrən] v/t (no -ge-, h) comment (on)

kommerzialisieren [kɔmɛrtsjali'ziːrən] v/t (no -ge-, h) commercialize

Kommissar [kɔmɪ'saːɐ] m (-s; -e) commissioner; superintendent

Kommission [kɔmɪ'sjoːn] f (-; -en) commission; committee

Kommode [kɔ'moːdə] f (-; -n) bureau, Br chest (of drawers)

Kommunal... [kɔmu'naːl-] in cpds ...politik etc: local ...

Kommune [kɔ'muːnə] f (-; -n) commune

Kommunikation [kɔmunika'tsjoːn] f (-; no pl) communication

Kommunion [kɔmu'njoːn] f (-; -en) REL (Holy) Communion

Kommunismus [kɔmu'nɪsmʊs] m (-; no pl) POL communism

Kommunist [kɔmu'nɪst] m (-en; -en), **Kommu'nistin** f (-; -nen), **kommu'nistisch** adj POL communist

Komödie [ko'møːdjə] f (-; -n) comedy; **Komödie spielen** put on an act, play-act

kompakt [kɔm'pakt] adj compact

Kom'paktanlage f stereo system, music center (Br centre)

Kompanie [kɔmpa'niː] f (-; -n) MIL company

Kompass ['kɔmpas] m (-es; -e) compass

kompatibel [kɔmpa'tiːbəl] adj compatible (a. EDP)

komplett [kɔm'plɛt] adj complete

Komplex [kɔm'plɛks] m (-es; -e) complex (a. PSYCH)

Kompliment [kɔmpli'mɛnt] n (-[e]s; -e) compliment; **j-m ein Kompliment machen** pay s.o. a compliment

Komplize [kɔm'pliːtsə] m (-n; -n) accomplice

komplizieren [kɔmpli'tsiːrən] v/t (no -ge-, h) complicate

kompliziert [kɔmpli'tsiːɐt] adj complicated, complex

Kom'plizin f (-; -nen) accomplice

Komplott [kɔm'plɔt] n (-[e]s; -e) plot, conspiracy

komponieren [kɔmpo'niːrən] v/t and v/i (no -ge-, h) MUS compose; write

K

Komponist [kɔmpo'nɪst] m (-en; -en) MUS composer

Komposition [kɔmpozi'tsjoːn] f (-; -en) MUS composition

Kompott [kɔm'pɔt] n (-[e]s; -e) GASTR compot(e), stewed fruit

Kompresse [kɔm'prɛsə] f (-; -n) MED compress

komprimieren [kɔmpri'miːrən] v/t (no -ge-, h) compress

Kompromiss [kɔmpro'mɪs] m (-es; -e) compromise

kompro'misslos adj uncompromising

kompromittieren [kɔmprɔmɪ'tiːrən] v/t (no -ge-, h) compromise (**sich** o.s.)

kompromittierend adj compromising

Kondensator [kɔndɛn'zaːtoːr] m (-en; [-za'toːrən]) ELECTR capacitor; TECH condenser

kondensieren [kɔndɛn'ziːrən] v/t (no -ge-, h) condense

Kondensmilch [kɔn'dɛns-] f condensed milk

Kondition [kɔndi'tsjoːn] f (-; -en) a) condition, b) (no pl) SPORT condition, shape, form; **gute Kondition** (great) stamina

konditional [kɔnditsjoˈnaːl] adj LING conditional

Kondi'tionstraining n fitness training

Konditor [kɔn'diːtoːr] m (-s; -en [-di'toːrən]) confectioner, pastrycook

Konditorei [kɔndito'rai] f (-; -en) cake shop; café, tearoom

Konditoreiwaren pl confectionery

Kondom [kɔn'doːm] n, m (-s; -e) condom

Kondukteur [kɔndʊk'tøːr] Swiss m (-s; -e) → **Schaffner**

Konfekt [kɔn'fɛkt] n (-[e]s; -e) sweets, chocolates

Konfektion [kɔnfɛk'tsjoːn] f (-; no pl) ready-made clothing

Konfekti'ons... in cpds ready-made ..., off-the-peg ...

Konferenz [kɔnfe'rɛnts] f (-; -en) conference

Konfession [kɔnfɛ'sjoːn] f (-; -en) religion, denomination

konfessionell [kɔnfɛsjoˈnɛl] adj confessional, denominational

Konfessi'onsschule f denominational school

Konfirmand [kɔnfɪr'mant] m (-en; -en), **Konfir'mandin** f (-; -nen) REL confirmand

Konfirmation [kɔnfɪrma'tsjoːn] f (-; -en) REL confirmation

konfirmieren [kɔnfɪr'miːrən] v/t (no -ge-, h) confirm

konfiszieren [kɔnfɪs'tsiːrən] v/t (no -ge-,

h) JUR confiscate

Konfitüre [kɔnfi'tyːrə] f (-; -n) jam

Konflikt [kɔn'flɪkt] m (-[e]s; -e) conflict

konfrontieren [kɔnfrɔn'tiːrən] v/t (no -ge-, h) confront

konfus [kɔn'fuːs] adj confused, mixed-up

Kongress [kɔn'grɛs] m (-es; -e) convention, Br congress

König ['køːnɪç] m (-s; -e) king

Königin ['køːnɪgɪn] f (-; -nen) queen

königlich ['køːnɪklɪç] adj royal

Königreich ['køːnɪk-] n kingdom

Konjugation [kɔnjuga'tsjoːn] f (-; -en) LING conjugation

konjugieren [kɔnju'giːrən] v/t (no -ge-, h) LING conjugate

Konjunktiv ['kɔnjʊŋktiːf] m (-s; -e) LING subjunctive (mood)

Konjunktur [kɔnjʊŋk'tuːr] f (-; -en) economic situation

konkret [kɔn'kreːt] adj concrete

Konkurrent [kɔnku'rɛnt] m (-en; -en), **Konkur'rentin** f (-; -nen) competitor, rival

Konkurrenz [kɔnku'rɛnts] f (-; no pl) competition; **die Konkurrenz** one's competitors; **außer Konkurrenz** not competing; → **konkurrenzlos**

konkur'renzfähig adj competitive

Konkur'renzkampf m competition

konkur'renzlos adj without competition, unrival(l)ed

konkurrieren [kɔnku'riːrən] v/i (no -ge-, h) compete

Konkurs [kɔn'kʊrs] m (-es; -e) ECON, JUR bankruptcy; **in Konkurs gehen** go bankrupt

Konkursmasse f JUR bankrupt's estate

können ['kœnən] v/t and v/i (irr, ge-, h), v/aux (irr, no -ge-, h) can, be able to; may, be allowed to; **kann ich gehen etc?** can or may I go etc?; **du kannst nicht** you cannot or can't; **ich kann nicht mehr** I can't go on; I can't manage or eat any more; **es kann sein** it may be; **ich kann nichts dafür** it's not my fault; **e-e Sprache können** know or speak a language

'Können n (-s; no pl) ability, skill

Könner ['kœnər] m (-s; -), **'Könnerin** f (-; -nen) master, expert; esp SPORT ace, crack

konnte ['kɔntə] pret of **können**

konsequent [kɔnze'kvɛnt] adj consistent

Konsequenz [kɔnze'kvɛnts] f (-; -en) a) (no pl) consistency; b) consequence

konservativ [kɔnzerva'tiːf] adj conservative

Konserven [kɔn'zɛrvən] pl canned (Br tinned) foods

Konservenbüchse *f*, **Konservendose** *f* can, *Br a.* tin

Konservenfa,brik *f* cannery

konservieren [kɔnzɛr'viːrən] *v/t (no -ge-, h)* preserve

Konser'vierungsmittel *n* preservative

Konsonant [kɔnzo'nant] *m (-en; -en)* LING consonant

konstruieren [kɔnstru'iːrən] *v/t (no -ge-, h)* construct; design

Konstrukteur [kɔnstrʊk'tøːɐ] *m (-s; -e)* TECH designer

Konstruktion [kɔnstrʊk'tsjoːn] *f (-; -en)* construction

Konsul ['kɔnzʊl] *m (-s; -n)* consul

Konsulat [kɔnzu'laːt] *n (-[e]s; -e)* consulate

konsultieren [kɔnzʊl'tiːrən] *v/t (no -ge-, h)* consult

Konsum¹ [kɔn'zuːm] *m (-s; no pl)* consumption

Konsum² ['kɔnzuːm] *m (-s; -s)* cooperative (society *or* store), F co-op

Konsument [kɔnzu'mɛnt] *m (-en; -en)*, **Konsu'mentin** *f (-; -nen)* consumer

Kon'sumgesellschaft *f* consumer society

konsumieren [kɔnzu'miːrən] *v/t (no -ge-, h)* consume

Kontakt [kɔn'takt] *m (-[e]s; -e)* contact *(a.* ELECTR*)*; **Kontakt aufnehmen** get in touch; **Kontakt haben** *or* **in Kontakt stehen mit** be in contact *or* touch with; **den Kontakt verlieren** lose touch

kon'taktfreudig *adj* sociable

Kon'taktlinsen *pl* OPT contact lenses

Konter ['kɔntɐ] *m (-s; -)*, **'kontern** *v/i (ge-, h)* counter *(a. fig)*

Kontinent [kɔnti'nɛnt] *m (-[e]s; -e)* continent

Konto ['kɔnto] *n (-s; Konten)* account

'Kontoauszug *m* (bank) statement

Kontrast [kɔn'trast] *m (-[e]s; -e)* contrast *(a.* PHOT, TV *etc)*

Kontrolle [kɔn'trɔlə] *f (-; -n)* control; supervision; check(up)

Kontrolleur [kɔntrɔ'løːɐ] *m (-s; -e)*, **Kontrol'leurin** *f (-; -nen)* inspector, RAIL *a.* conductor

kontrollieren [kɔntrɔ'liːrən] *v/t (no -ge-, h)* check; check up on *s.o.*; control

Kon'trollpunkt *m* checkpoint

Kontroverse [kɔntro'vɛrzə] *f (-; -n)* controversy

konventionell [kɔnvɛntsjo'nɛl] *adj* conventional

Konversation [kɔnvɛrza'tsjoːn] *f (-; -en)* conversation

Konversati'onslexikon *n* encyclop(a)edia

Konzentration [kɔntsɛntra'tsjoːn] *f (-; -en)* concentration

Konzentrati'onslager *n* concentration camp

konzentrieren [kɔntsɛn'triːrən] *v/t and v/refl (no -ge-, h)* concentrate; **sich auf et. konzentrieren** concentrate on

Konzept [kɔn'tsɛpt] *n (-[e]s; -e)* (rough) draft; conception; **j-n aus dem Konzept bringen** put s.o. out

Konzern [kɔn'tsɛrn] *m (-[e]s; -e)* ECON combine, group

Konzert [kɔn'tsɛrt] *n (-[e]s; -e)* MUS concert; concerto

Konzerthalle *f*, **Konzertsaal** *m* concert hall, auditorium

Konzession [kɔntsɛ'sjoːn] *f (-; -en)* concession; license, *Br* licence

Kopf [kɔpf] *m (-[e]s; Köpfe)* head *(a. fig)*; top; *fig a.* brains, mind; **Kopf hoch!** chin up!; **j-m über den Kopf wachsen** outgrow s.o.; *fig* be too much for s.o.; **sich den Kopf zerbrechen** *(über acc)* rack one's brains (over); **sich et. aus dem Kopf schlagen** put s.th. out of one's mind; **Kopf an Kopf** neck and neck

Kopfball *m* SPORT header; headed goal

Kopfbedeckung *f* headgear; **ohne Kopfbedeckung** bareheaded

köpfen ['kœpfən] *v/t (ge-, h)* behead, decapitate; SPORT head *(ins Tor* home)

'Kopfende *n* head

Kopfhörer *pl* headphones

Kopfjäger *m* headhunter

Kopfkissen *n* pillow

'kopflos *adj* headless; *fig* panicky

'Kopfrechnen *n* mental arithmetic

Kopfsa,lat *m* BOT lettuce

Kopfschmerzen *pl* headache

Kopfsprung *m* SPORT header

Kopfstand *m* SPORT headstand

Kopftuch *n* scarf, (head)kerchief

kopf'über *adv* headfirst *(a. fig)*

'Kopfweh *n →* **Kopfschmerzen**

'Kopfzerbrechen *n: j-m Kopfzerbrechen machen** give s.o. a headache

Kopie [ko'piː] *f (-; -n)*, **ko'pieren** *v/t (no -ge-, h)* copy

Kopiergerät [ko'piːɐ-] *n* copier

Ko'pierstift *m* indelible pencil

Koppel¹ ['kɔpəl] *f (-; -n)* paddock

'Koppel² *n (-s; -)* MIL belt

'koppeln *v/t (ge-, h)* couple; dock

Koralle [ko'ralə] *f (-; -n)* ZO coral

Korb [kɔrp] *m (-[e]s; Körbe* ['kœrbə]*)* basket

Korbmöbel *pl* wicker furniture

Kord [kɔrt] *m (-[e]s; -e)* corduroy

Kordel 166

Kordel ['kɔrdəl] f (-; -n) cord
'Kordhose f corduroys
Korinthe [ko'rɪntə] f (-; -n) currant
Kork [kɔrk] m (-[e]s; -e) BOT cork
'Korkeiche f BOT cork oak
Korken ['kɔrkən] m (-s; -) cork
Korkenzieher [-tsiːɐ] m (-s; -) corkscrew
Korn¹ [kɔrn] n (-[e]s; Körner ['kœrnɐ]) BOT a) grain; seed, b) (no pl) grain, Br a. corn, c) (pl -e) TECH front sight
Korn² F m (-[e]s; -e) (grain) schnapps
körnig ['kœrnɪç] adj grainy
Körper ['kœrpɐ] m (-s; -) body (a. PHYS, CHEM), MATH a. solid, Körperbau m (-[e]s; no pl) build, physique
'körperbehindert adj (physically) disabled or handicapped
'Körpergeruch m body odo(u)r, BO
Körpergröße f height
Körperkraft f physical strength
'körperlich adj physical
'Körperpflege f personal hygiene
Körperschaft f (-; -en) corporation, (corporate) body
'Körperteil m part of the body
Körperverletzung f JUR bodily injury
korrekt [kɔ'rɛkt] adj correct
Korrektur [kɔrɛk'tuːɐ] f (-; -en) correction; PED etc grading, Br marking
Korrespondent [kɔrɛspɔn'dɛnt] m (-en; -en), Korrespon'dentin f (-; -nen) correspondent
Korrespondenz [-'dɛnts] f (-; -en) correspondence
korrespondieren [-'diːrən] v/i (no -ge-, h) correspond (mit with)
Korridor ['kɔridoːɐ] m (-s; -e) corridor; hall
korrigieren [kɔri'giːrən] v/t (no -ge-, h) correct; PED etc grade, Br mark
korrupt [kɔ'rʊpt] adj corrupt(ed)
Korruption [kɔrʊp'tsjoːn] f (-; -en) corruption
Korsett [kɔr'zɛt] n (-s; -s) corset (a. fig)
Kosename ['koːzə-] m pet name
Kosmetik [kɔs'meːtɪk] f (-; no pl) beauty culture; cosmetics, toiletries
Kosmetikerin [kɔs'meːtikərin] f (-; -nen) beautician, cosmetician
Kost [kɔst] f (-; no pl) food, diet; board
'kostbar adj precious, valuable; costly
'Kostbarkeit f (-; -en) precious object, treasure (a. fig)
kosten¹ ['kɔstən] v/t (ge-, h) cost, be; fig take (time etc); was or wie viel kostet ...? how much is it ...?
'kosten² v/t (ge-, h) taste, try
'Kosten pl cost(s); price; expenses; charges; auf j-s Kosten at s.o.'s expense

'kostenlos 1. adj free; 2. adv free of charge
köstlich ['kœstlɪç] adj delicious; fig priceless; sich köstlich amüsieren have great fun, F have a ball
'Kostprobe f taste, sample (a. fig)
'kostspielig adj expensive, costly
Kostüm [kɔs'tyːm] n (-s; -e) costume; dress; suit
Kostümfest n fancy-dress ball
Kot [koːt] m (-[e]s; no pl) excrement, zo a. droppings
Kotelett [kotə'lɛt] n (-s; -s) chop, cutlet
Koteletten [kotə'letən] pl sideburns
'Kotflügel m MOT fender, Br wing
kotzen ['kɔtsən] V v/i (ge-, h) puke
Krabbe ['krabə] f (-; -n) zo shrimp; prawn
krabbeln ['krabəln] v/i (ge-, sein) crawl
Krach [krax] m (-[e]s; Kräche ['krɛçə]) a) crash, bang, b) (no pl) noise, c) F quarrel, fight
'krachen v/i (ge-, h) crack, bang, crash
Kracher ['kraxɐ] m (-s; -) (fire)cracker
krächzen ['krɛçtsən] v/t and v/i (ge-, h) croak
Kraft [kraft] f (-; Kräfte ['krɛftə]) strength, force (a. POL), power (a. ELECTR, TECH, POL); in Kraft sein (setzen, treten) JUR etc be in (put in, come into) force
'Kraftbrühe f GASTR consommé, clear soup
Kraftfahrer(in) driver, motorist
Kraftfahrzeug n motor vehicle
kräftig ['krɛftɪç] adj strong (a. fig), powerful; substantial (food); good
'kraftlos adj weak, feeble
'Kraftprobe f test of strength
Kraftstoff m MOT fuel
Kraftverschwendung f waste of energy
Kraftwerk n power station
Kragen ['kraːgən] m (-s; -) collar
Krähe ['krɛːə] f (-; -n) zo crow
krähen ['krɛːən] v/i (ge-, h) crow
Krake ['kraːkə] m (-n; -n) zo octopus
Kralle ['kralə] f (-; -n) zo claw (a. fig)
'krallen v/refl (ge-, h) cling (an acc on), clutch (at)
Kram [kraːm] F m (-[e]s; no pl) stuff, (one's) things
Krampf [krampf] m (-[e]s; Krämpfe ['krɛmpfə]) MED cramp; spasm, convulsion
Krampfader f MED varicose vein
'krampfhaft fig adj forced (smile etc); desperate (attempt etc)
Kran [kraːn] m (-[e]s; Kräne ['krɛːnə]) TECH crane
Kranich ['kraːnɪç] m (-s; -e) zo crane
krank [kraŋk] adj ill, sick; krank werden get sick, Br fall ill

'**Kranke** *m, f (-n; -n)* sick person, patient; **die Kranken** the sick

kränken ['krɛŋkən] *v/t (ge-, h)* hurt (*s.o.'s* feelings), offend

'**Krankenbett** *n* sickbed

Krankengeld *n* sickness benefit

Krankengym,nastik *f* physiotherapy

Krankenhaus *n* hospital

Krankenkasse *f* health insurance scheme; **in e-r Krankenkasse sein** be a member of a health insurance scheme *or* plan

Krankenpflege *f* nursing

Krankenpfleger *m* male nurse

Krankenschein *m* health insurance certificate

Krankenschwester *f* nurse

Krankenversicherung *f* health insurance

Krankenwagen *m* ambulance

Krankenzimmer *n* sickroom

'**krankhaft** *adj* morbid (*a. fig*)

'**Krankheit** *f (-; -en)* illness, sickness, disease

'**Krankheitserreger** *m* germ

kränklich ['krɛŋklɪç] *adj* sickly, ailing

'**Kränkung** ['krɛŋkʊŋ] *f (-; -en)* insult, offense, Br offence

Kranz [krants] *m (-es; Kränze* ['krɛntsə]*)* wreath; *fig* ring, circle

krass [kras] *adj* crass, gross; blunt

Krater ['kraːtɐ] *m (-s; -)* crater

kratzen ['kratsən] *v/t and v/refl (ge-, h)* scratch (o.s.); scrape (**von** off)

Kratzer ['kratsɐ] *m (-s; -)* scratch (*a.* MED)

kraulen ['kraulən] **1.** *v/t (ge-, h)* stroke; run one's fingers through; **2.** *v/i (ge-, sein)* SPORT do the crawl

kraus [kraus] *adj* curly (*hair*); wrinkled

Krause ['krauzə] *f (-; -n)* ruff; friz(z)

kräuseln ['krɔyzəln] *v/t and v/refl (ge-, h)* curl, friz(z); *water:* ripple

Kraut [kraut] *n (-[e]s; Kräuter* ['krɔytɐ]*)* BOT herb; tops, leaves; cabbage

Krawall [kra'val] *m (-s; -e)* riot; F row, racket

Krawatte [kra'vatə] *f (-; -n)* tie

kreativ [krea'tiːf] *adj* creative

Kreativität [kreativi'tɛːt] *f (-; no pl)* creativity

Kreatur [krea'tuːɐ] *f (-; -en)* creature

Krebs [kreːps] *m (-es; -e)* ZO crayfish; MED cancer; AST Cancer; **sie ist (ein) Krebs** she's (a) Cancer; **Krebs erregend → krebserregend**

Krebs... MED cancerous

krebserregend *adj* MED carcinogenic

Krebsgeschwulst *f* MED carcinoma

Krebskranke *m, f* cancer patient

Kredit [kre'diːt] *m (-[e]s; -e)* ECON credit; loan

Kredithai *m* loan shark

Kreditkarte *f* credit card, *pl coll* F plastic money

Kreide ['kraidə] *f (-; -n)* chalk; crayon

Kreis [krais] *m (-es; -e)* circle (*a. fig*); POL district, county

Kreisbahn *f* AST orbit

kreischen ['kraiʃən] *v/i (ge-, h)* screech; squeal

Kreisel ['kraizəl] *m (-s; -)* (spinning) top; PHYS gyro(scope)

'**kreiseln** *v/i (ge-, h, sein)* spin around

kreisen ['kraizən] *v/i (ge-, h, sein)* (move in a) circle, revolve, rotate; circulate

'**kreisförmig** [-fœrmɪç] *adj* circular

'**Kreislauf** *m* MED, ECON circulation; BIOL cycle (*a. fig*), TECH, ELECTR *a.* circuit

Kreislaufstörungen *pl* MED circulatory trouble

'**Kreissäge** *f* circular saw

Kreisverkehr *m* traffic circle, Br roundabout

Krempe ['krɛmpə] *f (-; -n)* brim

Kren [kreːn] *Austrian m (-[e]s; no pl)* GASTR horseradish

Krepp [krɛp] *m (-s; -s)* crepe

Kreuz [krɔyts] *n (-es; -e)* cross (*a. fig*); ANAT (small of the) back; *cards:* clubs; MUS sharp; **über Kreuz** crosswise; F **j-n aufs Kreuz legen** take s.o. in

kreuzen ['krɔytsən] **1.** *v/t and v/refl (ge-, h)* cross; clash; **2.** *v/i (ge-, sein)* MAR cruise

Kreuzer ['krɔytsɐ] *m (-s; -)* MAR cruiser

'**Kreuzfahrer** *m* HIST crusader

'**Kreuzfahrt** *f* MAR cruise

kreuzigen ['krɔytsɪɡən] *v/t (ge-, h)* crucify

'**Kreuzigung** *f (-; -en)* crucifixion

'**Kreuzotter** *f* ZO adder

'**Kreuzschmerzen** *pl* backache

'**Kreuzung** *f (-; -en)* RAIL, MOT crossing, junction; intersection, crossroads; BIOL cross(breed)ing; cross(breed); *fig* cross

'**Kreuzverhör** *n* JUR cross-examination; **ins Kreuzverhör nehmen** cross-examine

'**kreuzweise** *adv* crosswise, crossways

'**Kreuzworträtsel** *n* crossword (puzzle)

Kreuzzug *m* HIST crusade

kriechen ['kriːçən] *v/i (irr, ge-, sein)* creep, crawl; *fig* **vor j-m kriechen** toady to s.o.

Kriecher ['kriːçɐ] *contp m (-s; -)* toady

'**Kriechspur** *f* MOT slow lane

Krieg [kriːk] *m (-[e]s; -e* ['kriːɡə]*)* war; **Krieg führen gegen** be at war with

kriegen ['kriːɡən] F *v/t (ge-, h)* get; catch

Krieger ['kriːɡɐ] *m (-s; -)* warrior

'**Kriegerdenkmal** *n* war memorial

kriegerisch ['kriːɡərɪʃ] *adj* warlike, martial

'Kriegführung f (-; no pl) warfare

'Kriegsbeil fig n: **das Kriegsbeil begraben** bury the hatchet

Kriegsdienstverweigerer m (-s; -) conscientious objector

Kriegserklärung f declaration of war

Kriegsgefangene m prisoner of war,
P.O.W.

Kriegsgefangenschaft f captivity

Kriegsrecht n JUR martial law

Kriegsschauplatz m theater (Br theatre)
of war

Kriegsschiff n warship

Kriegsteilnehmer m (war) veteran, Br ex-
-serviceman

'Kriegstreiber [-traibɐ] m (-s; -) POL war-
monger

Kriegsverbrechen n war crime

Kriegsverbrecher m war criminal

Krimi ['kri:mi] F m (-s; -s) (crime) thriller,
detective novel

Kriminalbeamte [krimi'na:l-] m detective, plain-clothesman

Kriminalpolizei f criminal investigation
department

Kriminalroman m → **Krimi**

kriminell [krimi'nɛl] adj, Krimi'nelle m, f
(-n; -n) criminal

Krippe ['krɪpə] f (-; -n) crib, manger (a.
REL); REL crèche, Br crib

Krise ['kri:zə] f (-; -n) crisis

'Krisenherd m esp POL. trouble spot

Kristall[1] ['krɪs'tal] m (-s; -e) crystal

Kris'tall[2] n (s; no pl), Kristallglas n crystal

kristallisieren [krɪstali'zi:rən] v/i and
v/refl (no -ge-, h) crystallize

Kriterium [kri'te:rjʊm] n (-s; -ien) criteri-
on (**für** for)

Kritik [kri'ti:k] f (-; -en) criticism; THEA,
MUS etc review, critique; **gute Kritiken**
a good press; **Kritik üben an** (dat) criticize

Kritiker(in) ['kri:tikɐ (-kərın)] (-s; -/-;
-nen) critic

kri'tiklos adj uncritical

kritisch ['kri:tɪʃ] adj critical (a. fig) (**gegenüber** of)

kritisieren [kriti'zi:rən] v/t (no -ge-, h)
criticize

kritzeln ['krɪtsəln] v/t and v/i (ge-, h)
scrawl, scribble

kroch [krɔx] pret of **kriechen**

Krokodil [kroko'di:l] n (-s; -e) ZO croco-
dile

Krone ['kro:nə] f (-; -n) crown; coronet

krönen ['krø:nən] v/t (ge-, h) crown; **j-n
zum König krönen** crown s.o. king

'Kronleuchter m chandelier

'Kronprinz m crown prince

'Kronprin,zessin f crown princess

'Krönung f (-; -en) coronation; fig crown-
ing event, climax, high point

Kropf [krɔpf] m (-[e]s; Kröpfe ['krœpfə])
MED goiter, Br goitre; ZO crop

Kröte ['krø:tə] f (-; -n) ZO toad

Krücke ['krykə] f (-; -n) crutch

Krug [kru:k] m (-[e]s; Krüge ['kry:gə])
jug, pitcher; mug, stein; tankard

Krümel ['kry:məl] m (-s; -) crumb

krümelig ['kry:məlɪç] adj crumbly

'krümeln v/t and v/i (ge-, h) crumble

krumm [krum] adj crooked (a. fig), bent

'krummbeinig [-bainɪç] adj bow-legged

krümmen ['krymən] v/t (ge-, h) bend (a.
TECH), crook; **sich krümmen** bend;
writhe (with pain)

'Krümmung f (-; -en) bend, curve; GEOGR,
MATH, MED curvature

Krüppel ['krypəl] m (-s; -) cripple

Kruste ['krʊstə] f (-; -n) crust

Kto. ABBR of **Konto** a/c, account

Kübel ['ky:bəl] m (-s; -) bucket, pail; tub

Kubikmeter [ku'bi:k-] n, m cubic meter
(Br metre)

Kubikwurzel f MATH cube root

Küche ['kyçə] f (-; -n) kitchen; GASTR
cooking, cuisine; **kalte (warme) Küche**
cold (hot) meals

Kuchen ['ku:xən] m (-s; -) cake; tart, pie

'Küchengeräte pl kitchen utensils (or ap-
pliances)

Küchengeschirr n kitchen crockery,
kitchenware

Küchenherd m cooker

Küchenschrank m (kitchen) cupboard

Kuckuck ['kukuk] m (-s; -s) ZO cuckoo

Kufe ['ku:fə] f (-; -n) runner; AVIAT skid

Kugel ['ku:gəl] f (-; -n) ball; bullet; MATH,
GEOGR sphere; SPORT shot

'kugelförmig [-fœrmɪç] adj ballshaped,
esp ASTR, MATH spheric(al)

'Kugelgelenk n TECH, ANAT ball (and socket) joint

Kugellager n TECH ball bearing

'kugeln v/i (ge-, sein) and v/t (h) roll

Kugelschreiber [-ʃraibɐ] m (-s; -) ballpoint (pen)

'kugelsicher adj bulletproof

'Kugelstoßen n (-s; no pl) SPORT shot
put(ting)

'Kugelstoßer [-ʃto:sɐ] m (-s; -), Kugel-
stoßerin [-ʃto:sərın] f (-; -nen) SPORT
shot-putter

Kuh [ku:] f (-; Kühe ['ky:ə]) ZO cow

kühl [ky:l] adj cool (a. fig)

'Kühle f (-; no pl) cool(ness)

'kühlen v/t (ge-, h) cool; chill; refrigerate; refresh

Kühler ['ky:lɐ] m (-s; -) MOT radiator

'Kühlerhaube f MOT hood, Br bonnet

'Kühlmittel n coolant

'Kühlraum m cold-storage room

'Kühlschrank m fridge, refrigerator

'Kühltruhe f deep-freeze, freezer

'Kühlwasser n MOT cooling water

kühn [ky:n] adj bold

'Kühnheit f (-; no pl) boldness

'Kuhstall m cowshed

Küken ['ky:kən] n (-s; -) ZO chick (a. fig)

Kukuruz ['kʊkʊrʊts] Austrian m → Mais

Kuli ['ku:li] F m (-s; -s) ballpoint

Kulissen [ku'lɪsən] pl THEA wings; scenery; **hinter den Kulissen** backstage, esp fig behind the scenes

Kult [kʊlt] m (-[e]s; -e) cult; rite, ritual (act)

kultivieren [kʊlti'vi:rən] v/t (no -ge-, h) cultivate

Kultur [kʊl'tu:ɐ] f (-; -en) culture (a. BIOL), civilization; AGR cultivation

Kul'turbeutel m toilet bag

kulturell [kʊltu'rɛl] adj cultural

Kul'turgeschichte f history of civilization

Kulturvolk n civilized people

Kulturzentrum n cultural center (Br centre)

Kultusmi,nister ['kʊltʊs-] m minister of education and cultural affairs

Kummer ['kʊmɐ] m (-s; no pl) grief, sorrow; trouble, worry; **Kummer haben mit** have trouble or problems with

kümmerlich ['kʏmɐlɪç] adj miserable; poor, scanty

kümmern ['kʏmɐn] v/refl and v/t (ge-, h) **sich kümmern um** look after, take care of, mind; care or worry about, be interested in

Kumpel ['kʊmpəl] m (-s; -) miner; F mate, buddy, pal

Kunde ['kʊndə] m (-n; -n) customer, client

'Kundendienst m after-sales service; (customer) service; service department; TECH servicing

Kundgebung ['kʊntge:bʊŋ] f (-; -en) meeting, rally, demonstration

kündigen ['kʏndɪgən] v/i and v/t (ge-, h) cancel; **j-m kündigen** give s.o. his / her / one's notice; dismiss s.o., F sack or fire s.o.

'Kündigung f (-; -en) cancellation; (period of) notice

Kundin ['kʊndɪn] f (-; -nen) customer, client

Kundschaft ['kʊntʃaft] f (-; -en) customers, clients

Kunst [kʊnst] f (-; Künste ['kʏnstə]) art; skill

Kunst... in cpds ...herz, ...leder, ...licht etc: artificial ...

Kunstaka,demie f academy of arts

Kunstausstellung f art exhibition

Kunstdünger m AGR artificial fertilizer

Kunsterziehung f PED art (education)

Kunstfaser f man-made or synthetic fiber (Br fibre)

Kunstfehler m professional blunder

Kunstfliegen n stunt flying, aerobatics

Kunstgeschichte f history of art

Kunstgewerbe n, Kunsthandwerk n arts and crafts

Künstler ['kʏnstlɐ] m (-s; -), Künstlerin ['kʏnstlərɪn] f (-; -nen) artist, MUS, THEA a. performer

künstlerisch ['kʏnstlərɪʃ] adj artistic

künstlich ['kʏnstlɪç] adj artificial; false; synthetic; man-made

'Kunstschwimmen n water ballet

Kunstseide f rayon

Kunstspringen n springboard diving

Kunststoff m plastic

Kunststück n trick, stunt, esp fig feat

Kunstturnen n gymnastics

Kunstturner m gymnast

'kunstvoll adj artistic; elaborate

'Kunstwerk n work of art

Kupfer ['kʊpfɐ] n (-s; no pl) copper (**aus** of)

Kupferstich m copperplate (engraving)

Kupon [ku'põ:] m (-s; -s) coupon

Kuppe ['kʊpə] f (-; -n) (rounded) hilltop; ANAT head

Kuppel ['kʊpəl] f (-; -n) ARCH dome; cupola

Kuppelei [kʊpə'lai] f (-; -en) JUR procuring

'kuppeln v/i (ge-, h) MOT put the clutch in or out

Kupplung ['kʊplʊŋ] f (-; -en) MOT clutch

Kur [ku:ɐ] f (-; -en) course of treatment; cure

Kür [ky:ɐ] f (-; -en) SPORT free skating; free exercises

Kurbel ['kʊrbəl] f (-; -n) crank, handle

'kurbeln v/t (ge-, h) crank; wind (up etc)

'Kurbelwelle f TECH crankshaft

Kürbis ['kʏrbɪs] m (-ses; -se) BOT pumpkin, gourd, squash

'Kurgast m visitor

kurieren [ku'ri:rən] v/t (no -ge-, h) cure (**von** of)

kurios [ku'rjo:s] adj curious, odd, strange

'Kürlauf m SPORT free skating

'Kurort m health resort, spa

Kurpfuscher ['ku:ɐpfʊʃɐ] m (-s; -) quack (doctor)

K

Kurs [kʊrs] *m* (*-es*; *-e*) AVIAT, MAR course (*a. fig*); PED *etc* class(es); ECON (exchange) rate; (stock) price

Kursbuch *n* railroad (*Br* railway) guide

Kürschner ['kʏrʃnɐ] *m* (*-s*; -) furrier

kursieren [kʊr'ziːrən] *v/i* (*no -ge-, h*) circulate (*a. fig*)

Kurve ['kʊrvə] *f* (-; *-n*) curve (*a.* MATH *and fig*); bend, turn

'**kurvenreich** *adj* winding, full of bends; F curvaceous

kurz [kʊrts] *adj* short; brief; **kurze Hose** shorts; (**bis**) **vor kurzem** (until) recently; (**erst**) **seit kurzem** (only) for a short time; **kurz vorher** (**darauf**) shortly before (after[wards]); **kurz vor uns** just ahead of us; **kurz nacheinander** in quick succession; **kurz fortgehen** *etc* go away for a short time *or* a moment; **kurz gesagt** in short; **zu kurz kommen** go short; **kurz angebunden** curt

'**Kurzarbeit** *f* ECON short time

'**kurzarbeiten** *v/i* (*sep, ge-, h*) ECON work short time

'**kurzatmig** [-ʔaːtmɪç] *adj* short of breath

Kürze ['kʏrtsə] *f* (-; *no pl*) shortness; brevity; **in Kürze** soon, shortly, before long

'**kürzen** *v/t* (*ge-, h*) shorten (**um** by); abridge; cut, reduce (*a.* MATH)

kurzerhand ['kʊrtsɐ'hant] *adv* without hesitation, on the spot

'**kurzfassen** *v/refl* (*sep, -ge-, h*): **sich kurzfassen** be brief, put it briefly

'**kurzfristig 1.** *adj* short-term; **2.** *adv* at short notice

'**Kurzgeschichte** *f* short story

'**kurzlebig** [-leːbɪç] *adj* short-lived

kürzlich ['kʏrtslɪç] *adv* recently, not long ago

'**Kurznachrichten** *pl* news summary

Kurzschluss *m* ELECTR short circuit, F short

Kurzschrift *f* shorthand

'**kurzsichtig** *adj* nearsighted, *Br* short-sighted

'**Kurzstrecke** *f* short distance

'**Kürzung** *f* (-; *-en*) cut, reduction (*a.* MATH)

'**Kurzwaren** *pl* notions, *Br* haberdashery

'**kurzweilig** [-vaɪlɪç] *adj* entertaining

'**Kurzwelle** *f* PHYS, *radio*: short wave

kuscheln ['kʊʃəlɪç] F *adj* cozy, *Br* cosy, snug

kuscheln ['kʊʃəln] *v/refl* (*ge-, h*) snuggle, cuddle (**an** *acc* up to; **in** *acc* in)

Kusine *f* → **Cousine**

Kuss [kʊs] *m* (*-es*; *Küsse* ['kʏsə]) kiss

'**kusssecht** *adj* kiss-proof

küssen ['kʏsən] *v/t* (*ge-, h*) kiss

Küste ['kʏstə] *f* (-; *-n*) coast, shore; **an der Küste** on the coast; **an die Küste** ashore

'**Küstengewässer** *pl* coastal waters

Küstenschifffahrt *f* coastal shipping

Küstenschutz *m*, **Küstenwache** *f* coast guard

Küster ['kʏstɐ] *m* (*-s*; -) REL verger, sexton

Kutsche ['kʊtʃə] *f* (-; *-n*) carriage, coach

Kutscher ['kʊtʃɐ] *m* (*-s*; -) coachman

Kutte ['kʊtə] *f* (-; *-n*) (monk's) habit

Kutteln ['kʊtəln] *pl* GASTR tripe

Kutter ['kʊtɐ] *m* (*-s*; -) MAR cutter

Kuvert [ku'veːɐ] *n* (*-s*; *-s*) envelope

Kybernetik [kybɐ'neːtɪk] *f* (-; *no pl*) cybernetics

L

labil [la'biːl] *adj* unstable

Labor [la'boːɐ] *n* (*-s*; *-e*) laboratory, F lab

Laborant(in) [labo'rant(ɪn)] (*-en*; *-en/-*; *-nen*) laboratory assistant

Labyrinth [laby'rɪnt] *n* (*-[e]s*; *-e*) labyrinth, maze (*both a. fig*)

Lache ['laxə] *f* (-; *-n*) pool, puddle

lächeln ['lɛçəln] *v/i* (*ge-, h*), '**Lächeln** *n* (*-s*; *no pl*) smile

lachen ['laxən] *v/i* (*ge-, h*) laugh (**über** *acc* at)

'**Lachen** *n* (*-s*; *no pl*) laugh(-ter); **j-n zum Lachen bringen** make s.o. laugh

lächerlich ['lɛçɐlɪç] *adj* ridiculous; **lächerlich machen** ridicule, make fun of; **sich lächerlich machen** make a fool of o.s.

Lachs [laks] *m* (*-es*; *-e*) ZO salmon

Lack [lak] *m* (*-[e]s*; *-e*) varnish; lacquer; MOT paint(work)

lackieren [la'kiːrən] *v/t* (*no -ge-, h*) varnish; lacquer; paint (*a.* MOT)

'**Lackschuhe** *pl* patent-leather shoes

Ladefläche ['laːdə-] *f* loading space

'Ladegerät n ELECTR battery charger

'Ladehemmung f MIL jam

laden ['la:dn] v/t (irr, ge-, h) load; ELECTR charge; EDP boot (up); fig **et. auf sich laden** burden o.s. with s.th.

'Laden m (-s; Läden ['lɛ:dn]) store, Br shop; shutter

Ladendieb m shoplifter

Ladendiebstahl m shoplifting

Ladeninhaber m storekeeper, Br shopkeeper

Ladenkasse f till

Ladenschluss m closing time; **nach Ladenschluss** after hours

Ladentisch m counter

'Laderampe f loading platform or ramp

'Laderaum m loading space; MAR hold

'Ladung f (-; -en) load, freight; AVIAT, MAR cargo; ELECTR, MIL charge; **e-e Ladung ...** a load of ...

lag [la:k] pret of **liegen**

Lage ['la:gə] f (-; -n) situation, position (both a. fig); location; layer; round (of beer etc); **in schöner (ruhiger) Lage** beautifully (peacefully) situated; **in der Lage sein zu** inf be able to inf, be in a position to inf

Lager ['la:gɐ] n (-s; -) bed; camp (a. fig); ECON stock, store; GEOL deposit; TECH bearing; **et. auf Lager haben** have s.th. in store (a. fig for s.o.)

Lagerfeuer n campfire

Lagerhaus n warehouse

'lagern (ge-, h) **1.** v/i camp; ECON be stored; **2.** v/t store, keep; MED lay, rest; **kühl lagern** keep in a cool place

'Lagerraum m storeroom

Lagerung ['la:gərʊŋ] f (-; no pl) storage

Lagune [la'gu:nə] f (-; -n) lagoon

lahm [la:m] adj lame

lahmen ['la:mən] v/i (ge-, h) be lame (**auf** dat in)

'lahmlegen v/t (sep, -ge-, h) → **lähmen**

lähmen ['lɛ:mən] v/t (ge-, h) paralyze, Br paralyse; bring traffic etc to a standstill

'Lähmung f (-; -en) MED paralysis

Laib [laɪp] m (-[e]s; -e ['laɪbə]) loaf

Laich [laɪç] m (-[e]s; -e), **laichen** ['laɪçən] v/i (ge-, h) spawn

Laie ['laɪə] m (-n; -n) layman; amateur

'laienhaft adj amateurish

'Laienspiel n amateur play

Laken ['la:kn] n (-s; -) sheet; bath towel

Lakritze [la'krɪtsə] f (-; -n) liquorice

lallen ['lalən] v/i and v/t (ge-, h) speak drunkenly; baby: babble

Lamm [lam] n (-[e]s; Lämmer ['lɛmɐ]) ZO lamb

Lammfell n lambskin

Lampe ['lampə] f (-; -n) lamp, light; bulb

'Lampenfieber n stage fright

'Lampenschirm m lampshade

Lampion [lam'pjõː] m (-s; -s) Chinese lantern

Land [lant] n (-[e]s; Länder ['lɛndɐ]) land; country; place; AGR ground, soil; ECON land, property; **an Land gehen** MAR go ashore; **auf dem Lande** in the country; **aufs Land fahren** go into the country; **außer Landes gehen** go abroad

Landarbeiter m farmhand

Landbevölkerung f country or rural population

Landebahn ['landə-] f AVIAT runway

land'einwärts adv up-country, inland

landen ['landən] v/i (ge-, sein) land; fig **landen in** (dat) end up in

'Landenge f neck of land, isthmus

'Landeplatz m AVIAT landing field

Länderspiel ['lɛndɐ-] n SPORT international match

'Landesgrenze f national border

Landesinnere n interior

Landesre'gierung f Land (Austrian Provincial) government

Landessprache f national language

'landesüblich adj customary

'Landesverrat m treason

Landesverräter m traitor (to one's country)

Landesverteidigung f national defen|se, Br -ce

Landflucht f rural exodus

Landfriedensbruch m JUR breach of the public peace

Landgericht n JUR appr regional superior court

Landgewinnung f reclamation of land

Landhaus n country house, cottage

Landkarte f map

Landkreis m district

'landläufig adj customary, current, common

ländlich ['lɛntlɪç] adj rural; rustic

Landrat m, **Landrätin** [-rɛ:tɪn] f (-; -nen) appr District Administrator

Landratte F f MAR landlubber

Landschaft f (-; -en) countryside; scenery; esp PAINT landscape

'landschaftlich adj scenic

Landsmann m (-[e]s; -leute) (fellow) countryman

'Landsmännin [-mɛnɪn] f (-; -nen) fellow countrywoman

Landstraße f country (or ordinary) road

Landstreicher(in) tramp

Landstreitkräfte pl MIL land forces

Landtag m Land parliament

'Landung f (-; -en) landing, AVIAT a. touch-down

'Landungssteg m MAR gangway

'Landvermesser [-fɛɛmesɐ] m (-s; -) land surveyor

Landvermessung f (-; -en) land surveying

Landweg m: **auf dem Landwege** by land

'Landwirt(in) farmer

'Landwirtschaft f (-; no pl) agriculture, farming

'landwirtschaftlich adj agricultural

'Landzunge f GEOGR promontory, spit

lang [laŋ] adj and adv long; F tall; **drei Jahre (einige Zeit)** lang for three years (some time); **den ganzen Tag lang** all day long; **seit langem** for a long time; **vor langer Zeit** (a) long (time) ago; **über kurz oder lang** sooner or later; **lang ersehnt** long-hoped-for; **lang erwartet** long-awaited; **gleich lang** the same length

'langatmig [-ˀaːtmɪç] adj long-winded

lange ['laŋə] adv (for a) long (time); **es ist schon lange her(, seit)** it has been a long time (since); **(noch) nicht lange her** not long ago; **noch lange hin** still a long way off; **es dauert nicht lange** it won't take long; **ich bleibe nicht lange fort** I won't be long; **wie lange noch?** how much longer?

Länge ['lɛŋə] f (-; -n) length; GEOGR longitude; **der Länge nach** (at) full length; **(sich) in die Länge ziehen** stretch (a. fig)

langen ['laŋən] F v/i (ge-, h) reach (**nach** for); be enough; **mir langt es** I've had enough, fig a. I'm sick of it

'Längengrad m GEOGR degree of longitude

Längenmaß n linear measure

Langeweile f (-; no pl) boredom; **Langeweile haben** be bored; **aus Langeweile** to pass the time

langfristig adj long-term

langjährig [-jɛːrɪç] adj longstanding; **langjährige Erfahrung** many years of experience

Langlauf m (-[e]s; no pl) SPORT cross-country (skiing)

langlebig [-leːbɪç] adj long-lived

länglich ['lɛŋlɪç] adj longish, oblong

längs [lɛŋs] **1.** prp (gen) along(side); **2.** adv lengthwise

langsam adj slow; **langsamer werden** or **fahren** slow down

'Langschläfer [-ʃleːfɐ] m (-s; -), **Langschläferin** [-fərɪn] f (-; -nen) late riser

Langspielplatte f long-playing record, mst LP

längst [lɛŋst] adv long ago or before; **längst vorbei** long past; **ich weiß es längst** I have known it for a long time

längstens ['lɛŋstəns] adv at (the) most

'Langstrecken... in cpds long-distance ...; AVIAT, MIL long-range ...

langweilen v/t (ge-, h) bore; **sich langweilen** be bored

langweilig [-vailɪç] adj boring, dull; **langweilige Person** bore

'Langwelle f PHYS, radio: long wave

langwierig [-viːrɪç] adj lengthy, protracted (a. MED)

Lanze ['lantsə] f (-; -n) lance

Lappalie [la'paːljə] f (-; -n) trifle

Lappen ['lapən] m (-s; -) (piece of) cloth; rag (a. fig)

läppisch ['lɛpɪʃ] adj silly; ridiculous

Lärche ['lɛrçə] f (-; -n) BOT larch

Lärm [lɛrm] m (-s; no pl) noise

lärmen ['lɛrmən] v/i (ge-, h) be noisy

lärmend adj noisy

Larve ['larfə] f (-; -n) mask; ZO larva

las [laːs] pret of **lesen**

lasch [laʃ] F adj slack, lax

Lasche ['laʃə] f (-; -n) flap; tongue

Laser ['leːzɐ] m (-s; -) PHYS laser

Laserdrucker m EDP laser printer

Laserstrahl m PHYS laser beam

Lasertechnik f laser technology

lassen ['lasən] v/t (irr, ge-, h) and v/aux (irr, no -ge-, h) let, leave; (j-n et. tun lassen) let s.o. do s.th.; allow s.o. to do s.th.; make s.o. do s.th.; **j-n (et.) zu Hause lassen** leave s.o. (s.th.) at home; **j-n allein (in Ruhe) lassen** leave s.o. alone; **sich die Haare schneiden lassen** have or get one's hair cut; **sein Leben lassen (für)** lose (give) one's life (for); **rufen lassen** send for, call in; **es lässt sich machen** it can be done; **lass alles so, wie (wo) es ist** leave everything as (where) it is; **er kann das Rauchen etc nicht lassen** he can't stop smoking etc; **lass das!** stop it! → **grüßen, kommen**

lässig ['lɛsɪç] adj casual; careless

Last [last] f (-; -en) load, burden, weight (all a. fig); **j-m zur Last fallen** be a burden to s.o.; **j-m et. zur Last legen** charge s.o. with s.th.

Lastenaufzug m freight elevator, Br goods lift

Laster¹ ['lastɐ] m (-s; -) → **Lastwagen**

Laster² n (-s; -) vice

lästern ['lɛstɐn] v/i (ge-, h) **lästern über** (acc) run down

lästig ['lɛstɪç] adj troublesome, annoying;

(j-m) lästig sein be a nuisance (to s.o.)

'Lastkahn *m* barge

Lasttier *n* pack animal

Lastwagen *m* MOT truck, *Br a.* lorry

Lastwagenfahrer *m* MOT truck (*Br a.* lorry) driver, trucker

Latein [la'taɪn] *n* (-s; *no pl*) Latin

La'teina,merika Latin America

La'teinameri,kaner(in), la'teinameri,kanisch *adj* Latin American

la'teinisch *adj* Latin

Laterne [la'tɛrnə] *f* (-; -n) lantern; streetlight

La'ternenpfahl *m* lamppost

Latte ['latə] *f* (-; -n) lath; pale; SPORT bar

'Lattenzaun *m* paling, picket fence

Lätzchen ['lɛtsçən] *n* (-s; -) bib

Laub [laup] *n* (-[e]s; *no pl*) foliage, leaves

'Laubbaum *m* deciduous tree

Laube ['laubə] *f* (-; -n) arbo(u)r

'Laubfrosch *m* ZO tree frog

'Laubsäge *f* fretsaw

Lauch [laux] *m* (-[e]s; -e) BOT leek

Lauer ['lauɐ] *f*: *auf der Lauer liegen* or *sein* lie in wait

'lauern *v/i* (ge-, h) lurk; *lauern auf* (*acc*) lie in wait for

Lauf [lauf] *m* (-[e]s; *Läufe* ['lɔyfə]) run; course; *gun*: barrel; *im Lauf(e) der Zeit* in the course of time

'Laufbahn *f* career

Laufdiszi,plin *f* SPORT track event

laufen ['laufən] *v/i and v/t* (*irr, ge-, sein*) run (*a.* TECH, MOT, ECON); walk; *fig* work, run; *j-n laufen lassen* let s.o. go; let s.o. off

laufend 1. *fig adj* present, current (*a.* ECON); continual; *auf dem Laufenden sein* be up to date; 2. *adv* continuously; regularly; always

'laufenlassen *v/t* (*irr, lassen, sep, no* -ge-, *h* → *laufen*

Läufer ['lɔyfɐ] *m* (-s; -) runner (*a.* carpet); *chess*: bishop

'Läuferin *f* (-; -nen) runner

'Laufgitter *n* playpen

Laufmasche *f* run, *Br* ladder

Laufschritt *m*: *im Laufschritt* on the double

Laufschuhe *pl* walking shoes; SPORT trainers

Laufsteg *m* footbridge; TECH, *fashion*: catwalk; MAR gangway

Lauge ['laugə] *f* (-; -n) suds; CHEM lye

Laune ['launə] *f* (-; -n) mood, temper; *gute (schlechte) Laune haben* be in a good (bad) mood or temper

launenhaft, 'launisch *adj* moody; bad-tempered

Laus [laus] *f* (-; *Läuse* ['lɔyzə]) ZO louse

Lauschangriff ['lauʃ-] *m* bugging operation

lauschen ['lauʃən] *v/i* (ge-, h) listen (*dat* to); eavesdrop

lauschig ['lauʃɪç] *adj* snug, cozy, *Br* cosy

laut[1] [laut] 1. *adj* loud; noisy; 2. *adv* loud(ly); *laut vorlesen* read (out) aloud; *(sprich) lauter, bitte!* speak up, please!

laut[2] *prp* (*gen or dat*) according to

Laut *m* (-[e]s; -e) sound, noise

lauten ['lautən] *v/i* (ge-, h) read; be

läuten ['lɔytən] *v/i and v/t* (ge-, h) ring; *es läutet (an der Tür)* the (door)bell is ringing

lauter ['lautɐ] *adv* sheer (*nonsense etc*); nothing but; (so) many

'lautlos *adj* silent, soundless; hushed

'Lautschrift *f* phonetic transcription

'Lautsprecher *m* TECH (loud)speaker

'Lautstärke *f* loudness, ELECTR *a.* (sound) volume; *mit voller Lautstärke* (at) full blast

Lautstärkeregler *m* volume control

lauwarm ['lau-] *adj* lukewarm (*a. fig*)

Lava ['laːva] *f* (-; *Laven*) GEOL lava

Lavabo [la'vaːbo] *Swiss n* → *Waschbecken*

Lavendel [la'vɛndəl] *m* (-s; -) BOT lavender

Lawine [la'viːnə] *f* (-; -n) avalanche

Lazarett [latsa'rɛt] *n* (-[e]s; -e) (military) hospital

leben ['leːbən] (ge-, h) 1. *v/i* live; be alive; *von et. leben* live on s.th.; 2. *v/t* live

'Leben *n* (-s; -) life; *am Leben bleiben* stay alive; survive; *am Leben sein* be alive; *ums Leben bringen* kill; *sich das Leben nehmen* take one's (own) life, commit suicide; *ums Leben kommen* lose one's life, be killed; *um sein Leben laufen (kämpfen)* run (fight) for one's life; *das tägliche Leben* everyday life; *mein Leben lang* all my life

'lebend *adj* living

lebendig [le'bɛndɪç] *adj* living, alive; *fig* lively

'Lebensabend *m* old age, the last years of one's life

Lebensbedingungen *pl* living conditions

Lebensdauer *f* life-span; TECH (service) life

'Lebenserfahrung *f* experience of life

Lebenserwartung *f* life expectancy

'lebensfähig *adj* MED viable (*a. fig*)

'Lebensgefahr *f* mortal danger; *in (unter) Lebensgefahr* in danger (at the risk) of one's life

'lebensgefährlich *adj* dangerous (to life),

L

perilous

'lebensgroß *adj* life-size(d)

'Lebensgröße *f:* **e-e Statue in Lebensgröße** a life-size(d) statue

Lebenshaltungskosten *pl* cost of living

'lebenslänglich 1. *adj* lifelong; **lebenslängliche Freiheitsstrafe** JUR life sentence; **2.** *adv* for life

'Lebenslauf *m* personal record, curriculum vitae

'lebenslustig *adj* fond of life

'Lebensmittel *pl* food(stuffs); groceries

Lebensmittelgeschäft *n* grocery, supermarket

'lebensmüde *adj* tired of life

'Lebensnotwendigkeit *f* vital necessity

Lebensretter(in) lifesaver, rescuer

Lebensstandard *m* standard of living

Lebensunterhalt *m* livelihood; **s-n Lebensunterhalt verdienen** earn one's living (**als** as; **mit** out of, by)

Lebensversicherung *f* life insurance

Lebensweise *f* way of life

'lebenswichtig *adj* vital, essential

'Lebenszeichen *n* sign of life

'Lebenszeit *f* lifetime; **auf Lebenszeit** for life

Leber ['le:bɐ] *f* (-; -n) ANAT liver

Leberfleck *m* mole

Lebertran *m* cod-liver oil

Lebewesen *n* living being, creature

lebhaft ['le:phaft] *adj* lively; heavy (*traffic etc*)

Lebkuchen *m* gingerbread

'leblos *adj* lifeless (*a. fig*)

Lebzeiten *pl:* **zu s-n Lebzeiten** in his lifetime

lechzen ['lɛçtsən] *v/i* (ge-, h) **lechzen nach** thirst for

leck [lɛk] *adj* leaking, leaky

Leck *n* (-[e]s; -s) leak

lecken¹ ['lɛkən] *v/t and v/i* (ge-, h). **lecken an** (*dat*) lick

lecken² *v/i* (ge-, h) leak

lecker ['lɛkɐ] *adj* delicious, tasty, F yummy

'Leckerbissen *m* delicacy, treat (*a. fig*)

Leder ['le:dɐ] *n* (-s; -) leather

ledern *adj* leather(n)

'Lederwaren *pl* leather goods

ledig ['le:dɪç] *adj* single, unmarried

lediglich ['le:dɪklɪç] *adv* only, merely

Lee [le:] *f* (-; *no pl*) MAR lee; **nach Lee** leeward

leer [le:ɐ] **1.** *adj* empty (*a. fig*); vacant (*house etc*); blank (*page etc*), ELECTR dead, Br flat; **leer stehend** unoccupied, vacant; **2.** *adv:* **leer laufen** TECH idle

Leere ['le:rə] *f* (-; *no pl*) emptiness (*a. fig*)

'leeren *v/t and v/refl* (ge-, h) empty

'Leergut *n* empties

'Leerlauf *m* TECH idling; neutral (gear); *fig* running on the spot

'Leertaste *f* space bar

'Leerung *f* (-; -en) post collection

legal [le'ga:l] *adj* legal, lawful

legalisieren [legali'zi:rən] *v/t* (*no -ge-, h*) legalize

Legali'sierung *f* (-; -en) legalization

Legasthenie [legaste'ni:] *f* (-; -n) PSYCH dyslexia, F word blindness

Legastheniker [legas'te:nikɐ] *m* (-s; -), **Legas'thenikerin** *f* (-; -nen) PSYCH dyslexic

legen ['le:gən] *v/t and v/i* (ge-, h) lay (*a. eggs*); place, put; set (*hair*); **sich legen** lie down; *fig* calm down; *pain:* wear off

Legende [le'gɛndə] *f* (-; -n) legend

leger [le'ʒeːɐ] *adj* casual, informal

Legislative [legisla'ti:və] *f* (-; -n) legislative power

legitim [legi'ti:m] *adj* legitimate

Lehm [le:m] *m* (-[e]s; -e) loam; clay

lehmig ['le:mɪç] *adj* loamy, F muddy

Lehne ['le:nə] *f* (-; -n) back(rest); arm (-rest)

lehnen *v/t and v/i* lean (*a. sich lehnen*) rest (**an** *acc*, **gegen** against; **auf** *acc* on); **sich aus dem Fenster lehnen** lean out of the window

'Lehnsessel *m*, **'Lehnstuhl** *m* armchair, easy chair

Lehrbuch ['le:ɐ-] *n* textbook

Lehre ['le:rə] *f* (-; -n) science; theory; REL, POL teachings, doctrine; moral; ECON apprenticeship; **in der Lehre sein** be apprenticed (**bei** to); **das wird ihm e-e Lehre sein** that will teach him a lesson

'lehren *v/t* (ge-, h) teach, instruct; show

Lehrer ['le:rɐ] *m* (-s; -) teacher, instructor, Br a. master

Lehrerausbildung *f* teacher training

Lehrerin ['le:rərɪn] *f* (-; -nen) (lady) teacher, Br a. mistress

'Lehrerkol,legium *n* (teaching) staff

Lehrerzimmer *n* staff *or* teachers' room

'Lehrgang *m* course (of instruction *or* study); training course

Lehrherr *m* master

Lehrjahr *n* year (of apprenticeship)

Lehrling ['le:ɐlɪŋ] *m* (-s; -e) apprentice, trainee

'Lehrmeister *m*, **Lehrmeisterin** *f* master; *fig* teacher

Lehrmittel *pl* teaching aids

Lehrplan *m* curriculum, syllabus

Lehrprobe *f* demonstration lesson

'lehrreich *adj* informative, instructive

Lehrstelle *f* apprenticeship; vacancy for an apprentice
Lehrstuhl *m* professorship
Lehrtochter *Swiss f* apprentice
Lehrvertrag *m* indenture(s)
Lehrzeit *f* apprenticeship
Leib [laip] *m* (-[e]s; *Leiber* ['laibɐ]) body; belly, ANAT abdomen; stomach; *bei lebendigem Leibe* alive; *mit Leib und Seele* (with) heart and soul
Leibeserziehung ['laibəs-] *f* PED physical education, ABBR PE
Leibeskräfte *pl*: *aus Leibeskräften* with all one's might
'**Leibgericht** *n* GASTR favo(u)rite dish
leibhaftig [laip'haftiç] *adj*: *der leibhaftige Teufel* the devil incarnate; *leibhaftiges Ebenbild* living image; *ich sehe ihn noch leibhaftig vor mir* I can see him (before me) now
'**leiblich** *adj* physical
'**Leibrente** *f* life annuity
Leibwache *f*, **Leibwächter** *m* bodyguard
Leibwäsche *f* underwear
Leiche ['laiçə] *f* (-; -n) (dead) body, corpse
'**leichen'blass** *adj* deadly pale
Leichenhalle *f* mortuary
Leichenschauhaus *n* morgue
Leichenverbrennung *f* cremation
Leichenwagen *m* hearse
leicht [laiçt] *adj/adv* 1. (a. *fig*); easy, simple; slight, minor; TECH light(weight); *leicht möglich* quite possible; *leicht gekränkt* easily offended; *es fällt mir (nicht) leicht (zu inf)* I find it easy (difficult) (to *inf*); *das ist leicht gesagt* it's not as easy as that; *es geht leicht kaputt* it breaks easily; *leicht verständlich* easy to understand
'**Leichtath,let** *m* SPORT (track-and-field) athlete
Leichtath,letik *f* SPORT track and field (events), athletics
Leichtath,letin *f* SPORT (track-and-field) athlete
Leichtgewicht *n* SPORT lightweight
'**leichtgläubig** *adj* credulous
Leichtigkeit ['laiçtiçkait] *f*: *mit Leichtigkeit* easily, with ease
'**leichtlebig** [-le:bɪç] *adj* happy-go-lucky
'**Leichtme,tall** *n* light metal
'**leichtnehmen** *v/t* (*irr*, *nehmen*, *sep*, -*ge*-, *h*): *et. leichtnehmen* not worry about s.th.; make light of s.th.; *nimm's leichtnehmen!* never mind!, don't worry about it!
'**Leichtsinn** *m* (-[e]s; *no pl*) carelessness; recklessness
'**leichtsinnig** *adj* careless; reckless

'**leichtverständlich** *adj* → **leicht**
Leid [lait] *n* (-[e]s; *no pl*) sorrow, grief; pain; *es tut mir Leid* I'm sorry (*um* for; *wegen* about; *dass ich zu spät komme* for being late)
leiden ['laidən] *v/t and v/i* (*irr*, *ge*-, *h*) suffer (*an dat*, *unter dat* from); *j-n gut leiden können* like s.o.; *ich kann ... nicht leiden* I don't like ...; I can't stand ...
'**Leiden** *n* (-*s*; -) suffering(s); MED disease
'**Leidenschaft** *f* (-; -*en*) passion
'**leidenschaftlich** *adj* passionate; vehement
'**Leidensgenosse** *m*, '**Leidensgenossin** *f* fellow sufferer
leider ['laidɐ] *adv* unfortunately; *leider ja* (*nein*) I'm afraid so (not)
'**leidlich** *adj* passable, F so-so
'**Leidtragende** *m*, *f* (-*n*; -*n*) mourner; *er ist der Leidtragende dabei* he is the one who suffers for it
'**Leidwesen** *n*: *zu m-m Leidwesen* to my regret
Leierkasten ['laiɐ-] *m* barrel organ
Leierkastenmann *m* organ grinder
leiern ['laiɐn] *v/i and v/t* (*ge*-, *h*) crank (up); *fig* drone
Leihbücherei ['lai-] *f* public library
leihen ['laiən] *v/t* (*irr*, *ge*-, *h*) lend; rent (*Br* hire) out; borrow (*von* from); rent, hire
'**Leihgebühr** *f* rental, lending fee
Leihhaus *n* pawnshop, pawnbroker's (shop)
Leihmutter F *f* surrogate mother
Leihwagen *m* MOT rented (*Br* hire) car
'**leihweise** *adv* on loan
Leim [laim] *m* (-[e]s; -e), **leimen** ['laimən] *v/t* (*ge*-, *h*) glue
Leine ['lainə] *f* (-; -n) line; lead, leash
Leinen ['lainən] *n* (-*s*; -) linen; canvas; *in Leinen gebunden* clothbound
'**Leinenschuh** *m* canvas shoe
'**Leinsamen** *m* BOT linseed
Leintuch *n* (linen) sheet
Leinwand *f* linen; PAINT canvas; screen
leise ['laizə] *adj* quiet, *a.* low, soft (*voice*, *a. music etc*); *fig* slight, faint; *leiser stellen* turn (the volume) down
Leiste ['laistə] *f* (-; -n) ledge; ANAT groin
leisten *v/t* (*ge*-, *h*) do, work; achieve, accomplish; render (*service etc*); take (*oath*); *gute Arbeit leisten* do a good job; *sich et. leisten* treat o.s. to s.th.; *ich kann es mir (nicht) leisten* I can('t) afford it
'**Leistung** *f* (-; -*en*) performance; achievement, PED *a.* (piece of) work, result, TECH *a.* output; service; benefit
'**Leistungsdruck** *m* (-[e]s; *no pl*) pressure,

stress

'**leistungsfähig** *adj* efficient; (physically) fit

'**Leistungsfähigkeit** *f* (-; *no pl*) efficiency (*a.* TECH, ECON); fitness

'**Leistungskon,trolle** *f* (achievement *or* proficiency) test

Leistungskurs *m* PED *appr* special subject

Leistungssport *m* competitive sport(s)

Leitar,tikel ['laɪt-] *m* editorial, *esp Br* leader, leading article

leiten ['laɪtən] *v/t* (*ge-, h*) lead, guide (*a. fig*), conduct (*a.* PHYS, MUS); run (*a.* PED), be in charge of, manage; TV *etc* direct; host

leitend *adj* leading; PHYS conductive; *leitende Stellung* key position; *leitender Angestellter* executive

Leiter¹ ['laɪtɐ] *f* (-; -n) ladder

'**Leiter²** *m* (-s; -) leader; conductor (*a.* PHYS, MUS); ECON *etc* head, manager; chairman; → *Schulleiter*

Leiterin ['laɪtərɪn] *f* (-; -nen) leader; head; chairwoman

'**Leitfaden** *m* manual, guide

Leitplanke *f* MOT guardrail, *Br* crash barrier

Leitspruch *m* motto

'**Leitung** *f* (-; -en) ECON management; head office; administration; chairmanship; organization; THEA *etc* direction; TECH main, pipe(s); ELECTR, TEL line; *die Leitung haben* be in charge; *unter der Leitung von* MUS conducted by

'**Leitungsrohr** *n* pipe

'**Leitungswasser** *n* tap water

Lektion [lɛkˈtsjoːn] *f* (-; -en) lesson

Lektüre [lɛkˈtyːrə] *f* (-; -n) reading (matter); PED reader

Lende ['lɛndə] *f* (-; -n) ANAT loin; GASTR sirloin

lenken ['lɛŋkən] *v/t* (*ge-, h*) steer, drive; *fig* guide *s.o.*; direct (*traffic etc*)

Lenker ['lɛŋkɐ] *m* (-s; -) handlebar

'**Lenkrad** *n* MOT steering wheel

'**Lenkung** *f* (-; -en) MOT steering (system)

Leopard [leoˈpart] *m* (-en; -en) ZO leopard

Lerche ['lɛrçə] *f* (-; -n) ZO lark

lernen ['lɛrnən] *v/t and v/i* (*ge-, h*) learn; study; *er lernt leicht* he is a quick learner; *lesen lernen* learn (how) to read

'**Lernmittelfreiheit** *f* free books *etc*

lesbar ['leːsbaːɐ] *adj* readable

Lesbierin ['lɛsbjərɪn] *f* (-; -nen), **lesbisch** ['lɛsbɪʃ] *adj* lesbian

Lesebuch ['leːzə-] *n* reader

'**Leselampe** *f* reading lamp

lesen ['leːzən] *v/i and v/t* (*irr, ge-, h*) read; AGR harvest

'**lesenswert** *adj* worth reading

Leser ['leːzɐ] *m* (-s; -) reader

'**Leseratte** F *f* bookworm

'**Leserbrief** *m* letter to the editor

Leserin *f* (-; -nen) reader

'**leserlich** *adj* legible

'**Lesestoff** *m* reading matter

'**Lesezeichen** *n* bookmark

Lesung *f* (-; -en) reading (*a.* PARL)

Letzt [lɛtst] *f*: *zu guter Letzt* in the end

letzte ['lɛtstə] *adj* last; latest; *zum letzten Mal(e)* for the last time; *in letzter Zeit* recently; *als Letzter ankommen etc* arrive *etc* last; *Letzter sein* be last (*a.* SPORT); *das ist das Letzte!* that's the limit!

'**letztens** *adv* finally; *erst letztens* just recently

letztere ['lɛtstərə] *adj* latter; *der (die, das) Letztere* the latter

Leuchtanzeige ['lɔʏçt-] *f* luminous *or* LED display light

leuchten ['lɔʏçtən] *v/i* (*ge-, h*) shine; glow

'**Leuchten** *n* (-s; *no pl*) shining; glow

'**leuchtend** *adj* shining (*a. fig*); bright

Leuchter ['lɔʏçtɐ] *m* (-s; -) candlestick

'**Leuchtfarbe** *f* luminous paint

Leuchtre,klame *f* neon sign(s)

Leucht(stoff)röhre *f* ELECTR fluorescent lamp

Leuchtturm *m* lighthouse

Leuchtziffer *f* luminous figure

leugnen ['lɔʏgnən] *v/t and v/i* (*ge-, h*) deny (*et. getan zu haben* having done s.th.)

Leute ['lɔʏtə] *pl* people, F folks

Leutnant ['lɔʏtnant] *m* (-s; -s) MIL second lieutenant

Lexikon ['lɛksikɔn] *n* (-s; -ka, -ken) encyclop(a)edia; dictionary

Libelle [liˈbɛlə] *f* (-; -n) ZO dragonfly

liberal [libeˈraːl] *adj* liberal

Libero [ˈliːbero] *m* (-s; -s) soccer: sweeper

licht ['lɪçt] *adj* bright; *fig* lucid

Licht *n* (-[e]s; -er ['lɪçtɐ]) a) light, b) (*no pl*) brightness; *Licht machen* switch *or* turn on the light(s)

'**Lichtbild** *n* photo(graph); slide

Lichtbildervortrag *m* slide lecture

'**Lichtblick** *m* ray of hope; bright moment

'**lichtempfindlich** *adj* sensitive to light; PHOT sensitive

'**Lichtempfindlichkeit** *f* (light) sensitivity; PHOT speed

lichten ['lɪçtən] *v/t* (*ge-, h*) clear; *den Anker lichten* MAR weigh anchor; *sich lichten* get thin(ner); *fig* be thinning (out)

'**Lichtgeschwindigkeit** *f* speed of light

Lichtgriffel *m* light pen

Lichthupe *f* MOT (headlight) flash(er); *die Lichthupe betätigen* flash one's lights

Lichtjahr n light year
Lichtma,schine f MOT generator
Lichtorgel f colo(u)r organ
Lichtpause f blueprint
Lichtschacht m well
Lichtschalter m (light) switch
'**lichtscheu** fig adj shady
'**Lichtschutzfaktor** m sun protection factor, SPF
Lichtstrahl m ray or beam of light (a. fig)
'**Lichtung** f (-; -en) clearing
Lid [liːt] n (-[e]s; Lider ['liːdɐ]) ANAT (eye)-lid
Lidschatten m eye shadow
lieb [liːp] adj dear; sweet; nice, kind; good; **lieb gewinnen** get fond of; **lieb haben** love, be fond of
Liebe ['liːbə] f (-; no pl) love (zu of, for); **aus Liebe zu** out of love for; **Liebe auf den ersten Blick** love at first sight
'**lieben** v/t (ge-, h) love, a. be in love with s.o.; make love to
liebenswert adj lovable, charming, sweet
'**liebenswürdig** adj kind
'**Liebenswürdigkeit** f (-; no pl) kindness
lieber ['liːbɐ] adv rather, sooner; **lieber haben** prefer, like better; **ich möchte lieber (nicht)** ... I'd rather (not) ...; **du solltest lieber (nicht)** ... you had better (not) ...
'**Liebesbrief** m love letter
Liebeserklärung f: **j-m e-e Liebeserklärung machen** declare one's love to s.o.
Liebeskummer m: **Liebeskummer haben** be lovesick
Liebespaar n lovers
'**liebevoll** adj loving, affectionate
'**liebgewinnen** v/t (irr, gewinnen, sep, h) → lieb
'**liebhaben** v/t (irr, haben, sep, -ge-, h) → lieb
Liebhaber ['liːphaːbɐ] m (-s; -) lover (a. fig); **Liebhaber...** in cpds ...preis, ...stück etc: collector's ...
Liebhaberei [liːphaːbəˈrai] f (-; -en) hobby
Liebkosung [liːpˈkoːzʊŋ] f (-; -en) caress
'**lieblich** adj lovely, charming, sweet (a. wine)
'**Liebling** m (-s; -e) darling; favo(u)rite
'**Lieblings...** in cpds mst favo(u)rite
'**lieblos** adj unloving, cold; unkind (words etc); fig careless
Lied [liːt] n (-[e]s; -er ['liːdɐ]) song; tune
liederlich ['liːdɐlɪç] adj slovenly, sloppy
Liedermacher ['liːdɐ-] m (-s; -) singer-songwriter
lief [liːf] pret of laufen
Lieferant [lifəˈrant] m (-en; -en) ECON sup-

plier
lieferbar ['liːfɐbaːɐ] adj ECON available
'**Lieferfrist** f ECON term of delivery
liefern ['liːfɐn] v/t (ge-, h) ECON deliver; **j-m et. liefern** supply s.o. with s.th.
Lieferung ['liːfərʊŋ] f (-; -en) ECON delivery; supply
'**Lieferwagen** m MOT (delivery) van
Liege ['liːɡə] f (-; -n) couch
liegen ['liːɡən] v/i (irr, ge-, h) lie, a. be (situated); (krank) **im Bett liegen** be (ill) in bed; **nach Osten (der Straße) liegen** face east (the street); **daran liegt es(, dass)** that's (the reason) why; **es (er) liegt mir nicht** F it (he) is not my cup of tea; **mir liegt viel (wenig) daran** it means a lot (doesn't mean much) to me; **liegen bleiben** stay in bed; be left behind; **liegen lassen** leave (behind); F **j-n links liegen lassen** ignore s.o., give s.o. the cold shoulder
'**liegenbleiben** v/i (irr, bleiben, sep, sein) → liegen
'**liegenlassen** v/i (irr, lassen, sep, no -ge-, h) → liegen
'**Liegesitz** m reclining seat
Liegestuhl m deckchair
Liegestütz m (-es; -e) SPORT push-up, Br press-up
Liegewagen m RAIL couchette
lieh [liː] pret of leihen
ließ [liːs] pret of lassen
Lift [lɪft] m (-[e]s; -e, -s) elevator, Br lift; ski lift
Liga ['liːɡa] f (-; Ligen) league, SPORT a. division
Likör [liˈkøːɐ] m (-s; -e) liqueur
lila ['liːla] adj purple, violet
Lilie ['liːljə] f (-; -n) BOT lily
Liliputaner [lilipuˈtaːnɐ] m (-s; -) dwarf, midget
Limonade [limoˈnaːdə] f (-; -n) pop; lemon soda, Br lemonade
Limousine [limuˈziːnə] f (-; -n) MOT sedan, Br saloon car; limousine
Linde ['lɪndə] f (-; -n) BOT lime (tree), linden
lindern ['lɪndɐn] v/t (ge-, h) relieve, ease, alleviate
Linderung ['lɪndərʊŋ] f (-; no pl) relief, alleviation
Lineal [lineˈaːl] n (-s; -e) ruler
Linie ['liːnjə] f (-; -n) line; **auf s-e Linie achten** watch one's weight
'**Linienflug** m AVIAT scheduled flight
Linienrichter m SPORT linesman
'**linientreu** adj POL: **linientreu sein** follow the party line
linieren [liˈniːrən], **liniieren** [liniˈiːrən] v/t

(*no -ge-, h*) rule, line

linke ['lɪŋkə] *adj* left (*a.* POL); **auf der lin-ken Seite** on the left(-hand side)

'**Linke** *m, f (-n; -n)* POL leftist, left-winger

linkisch ['lɪŋkɪʃ] *adj* awkward, clumsy

links [lɪŋks] *adv* on the left (*a.* POL); on the wrong side; **nach links** (to the) left; **links von** to the left of

Links... *in cpds ...verkehr etc:* left-hand

Links'außen *m (-; -)* SPORT outside left, left wing

'**Linkshänder** [-hɛndɐ] *m (-s; -)*, '**Links-händerin** *f (-; -nen)* left-hander

'**Linksradi,kale** *m, f (-n; -n)* POL left-wing extremist

Linse ['lɪnzə] *f (-; -n)* BOT lentil; OPT lens

Lippe ['lɪpə] *f (-; -n)* ANAT lip

'**Lippenstift** *m* lipstick

liquidieren [likvɪ'diːrən] *v/t (no -ge-, h)* ECON liquidate (*a.* POL)

lispeln ['lɪspəln] *v/i (ge-, h)* (have a) lisp

List [lɪst] *f (-; -en)* a) trick, b) (*no pl*) cunning

Liste ['lɪstə] *f (-; -n)* list; roll

listig ['lɪstɪç] *adj* cunning, tricky, sly

Liter ['liːtɐ] *n, m (-s; -)* liter, *Br* litre

literarisch [lɪtə'raːrɪʃ] *adj* literary

Literatur [lɪtəra'tuːɐ] *f (-; -en)* literature

Literatur... *in cpds ...kritik etc: mst* literary

Litfaßsäule ['lɪtfas-] *f* advertising pillar

litt [lɪt] *pret of* **leiden**

Lizenz [li'tsɛnts] *f (-; -en)* license, *Br* licence

Lkw, LKW ['ɛlkaveː] *m (-[s]; -)* ABBR of **Lastkraftwagen** truck, *Br a.* lorry

Lob [loːp] *n (-[e]s; no pl)*, **loben** ['loːbən] *v/t (ge-, h)* praise

'**lobenswert** *adj* praiseworthy, laudable

Loch [lɔx] *n (-[e]s; Löcher ['lœçɐ])* hole (*a. fig*); puncture

lochen ['lɔxən] *v/t (ge-, h)* punch (*a.* TECH)

Locher ['lɔxɐ] *m (-s; -)* punch

Locke ['lɔkə] *f (-; -n)* curl; lock

locken[1] ['lɔkən] *v/t and v/refl (ge-, h)* curl

locken[2] *v/t (ge-, h)* lure, entice, *fig a.* attract, tempt

'**Lockenkopf** *m* curly head

Lockenwickler [-vɪklɐ] *m (-s; -)* curler, roller

locker ['lɔkɐ] *adj* loose, slack; *fig* relaxed

'**lockern** *v/t (ge-, h)* loosen, slacken; relax (*a. fig*); **sich lockern** loosen, (be)come loose; SPORT limber up; *fig* relax

lockig ['lɔkɪç] *adj* curly, curled

'**Lockvogel** *m* decoy (*a. fig*)

lodern ['loːdɐn] *v/i (ge-, h)* blaze, flare

Löffel ['lœfəl] *m (-s; -)* spoon; ladle

'**löffeln** *v/t (ge-, h)* spoon up

---

log [loːk] *pret of* **lügen**

Logbuch ['lɔk-] *n* MAR log

Loge ['loːʒə] *f (-; -n)* THEA box; lodge

Logik ['loːgɪk] *f (-; no pl)* logic

logisch ['loːgɪʃ] *adj* logical

'**logischer'weise** *adv* obviously

Lohn [loːn] *m (-[e]s; Löhne ['løːnə])* ECON wages, pay(ment); *fig* reward

Lohnempfänger *m* wageworker, *Br* wage earner

lohnen ['loːnən] *v/refl (ge-, h)* be worth (-while), pay; **es (die Mühe) lohnt sich** it's worth it (the trouble); **das Buch (der Film) lohnt sich** the book (film) is worth reading (seeing)

lohnend *adj* paying; *fig* rewarding

'**Lohnerhöhung** *f* raise, *Br* increase in wages, rise

Lohnsteuer *f* income tax

Lohnstopp *m* wage freeze

Lohntüte *f* pay packet

Loipe ['lɔYpə] *f (-; -n)* (cross-country) course

Lokal [lo'kaːl] *n (-s; -e)* restaurant; bar, saloon, *esp Br* pub

Lo'kal... *in cpds mst* local

Lok [lɔk] *f (-; -s)* → **Lokomotive**

Lokführer *m* RAIL engineer, *Br* train driver

Lokomotive [lokomo'tiːvə] *f (-; -n)* RAIL engine

Lorbeer ['lɔrbeːɐ] *m (-s; -en)* BOT laurel; GASTR bay leaf

Lore ['loːrə] *f (-; -n)* TECH tipcart

los [loːs] *adj and adv* off; *dog etc:* loose; **los sein** be rid of; **was ist los?** what's the matter?, F what's up?; what's going on (here)?; **hier ist nicht viel los** there's nothing much going on here; F **da ist was los!** that's where the action is!; F **also los!** okay, let's go!

Los [loːs] *n (-es; -e* ['loːzə]*)* lot, *fig a.* fate; (lottery) ticket; number

'**losbinden** *v/t (irr, binden, sep, -ge-, h)* untie

Löschblatt ['lœʃ-] *n* blotting paper

löschen ['lœʃən] *v/t (ge-, h)* extinguish, put out; quench (*thirst*); blot (*ink*); wipe off the blackboard; erase, EDP *a.* delete; slake (*lime*); MAR unload

'**Löschpa,pier** *n* blotting paper

lose ['loːzə] *adj* loose

Lösegeld ['løːzə-] *n* ransom

losen ['loːzən] *v/i (ge-, h)* draw lots (**um** for)

lösen ['løːzən] *v/t (ge-, h)* undo (*knot etc*); loosen, relax; TECH release; take off; solve (*problem etc*); settle (*conflict etc*); buy, get (*ticket etc*); dissolve (*a.* CHEM);

sich lösen come loose *or* undone; *fig* free o.s. (**von** from)

'losfahren *v/i* (*irr, fahren, sep, -ge-, sein*) leave; drive off

losgehen *v/i* (*irr, gehen, sep, -ge-, sein*) leave; start, begin; *shot etc:* go off; *auf j-n losgehen* go for s.o.; *ich gehe jetzt los* I'm off now

losketten *v/t* (*sep, -ge-, h*) unchain

loskommen *v/i* (*irr, kommen, sep, -ge-, sein*) get away (**von** from)

loslassen *v/t* (*irr, lassen, sep, -ge-, h*) let go; *den Hund loslassen auf* (*acc*) set the dog on

loslegen F *v/i* (*sep, -ge-, h*) get cracking

löslich ['løːslɪç] *adj* CHEM soluble

'losmachen *v/t* (*sep, -ge-, h*) → **lösen**

losreißen *v/t* (*irr, reißen, sep, -ge-, h*) tear off; *sich losreißen* break away; *esp fig* tear o.s. away (*both:* **von** from)

lossagen *v/refl* (*sep, -ge-, h*) *sich lossagen von* break with

losschlagen *v/i* (*irr, schlagen, sep, -ge-, h*) strike (*auf j-n* out at s.o.)

losschnallen *v/t* (*sep, -ge-, h*) unbuckle; *sich losschnallen* MOT, AVIAT unfasten one's seatbelt

losstürzen *v/i* (*irr, sep, -ge-, sein*) *losstürzen auf* (*acc*) rush at

Losung ['loːzʊŋ] *f* (-; -en) MIL password; *fig* slogan

Lösung ['løːzʊŋ] *f* (-; -en) solution (*a. fig*); settlement

'Lösungsmittel *n* solvent

'loswerden *v/t* (*irr, werden, sep, -ge-, sein*) get rid of; lose (*money*)

'losziehen *v/i* (*irr, ziehen, sep, -ge-, sein*) set out, take off, march away

Lot [loːt] *n* (-[e]s; -e) plumbline

löten ['løːtən] *v/t* (*ge-, h*) TECH solder

Lotion [lo'tsjoːn] *f* (-; -en) lotion

Lotse ['loːtsə] *m* (-n; -n), 'lotsen *v/t* (*ge-, h*) MAR pilot

Lotterie [lɔtə'riː] *f* (-; -n) lottery

Lotteriegewinn *m* prize

Lotterielos *n* lottery ticket

Lotto ['lɔto] *n* (-s; -s) lotto, bingo; *Br* national lottery; *in Germany:* Lotto; (*im*) *Lotto spielen* do Lotto

Lottoschein *m* Lotto coupon

Lottoziehung *f* Lotto draw

Löwe ['løːvə] *m*(-n; -n) ZO lion; AST Leo; *er ist (ein) Löwe* he's (a) Leo

'Löwenzahn *m* BOT dandelion

Löwin ['løːvɪn] *f* (-; -nen) ZO lioness

loyal [loa'jaːl] *adj* loyal, faithful

Luchs [lʊks] *m* (-es; -e) ZO lynx

Lücke ['lʏkə] *f* (-; -n) gap (*a. fig*)

'Lückenbüßer *m* stopgap

'lückenhaft *adj* full of gaps; *fig* incomplete

'lückenlos *adj* without a gap; *fig* complete

'Lückentest *m* PSYCH completion *or* fill-in test

lud [luːt] *pret of* **laden**

Luft [lʊft] *f* (-; no pl) air; *an der frischen Luft* (out) in the fresh air; (*frische*) *Luft schöpfen* get a breath of fresh air; *die Luft anhalten* catch (*esp fig a.* hold) one's breath; *tief Luft holen* take a deep breath; *in die Luft sprengen* (F *fliegen*) blow up

'Luftangriff *m* air raid

Luftballon *m* balloon

Luftbild *n* aerial photograph *or* view

Luftblase *f* air bubble

Luftbrücke *f* airlift

'luftdicht *adj* airtight

'Luftdruck *m* (-[e]s; no pl) PHYS, TECH air pressure

lüften ['lʏftən] *v/t and v/i* (*ge-, h*) air, ventilate; *fig* reveal

'Luftfahrt *f* (-; no pl) aviation, aeronautics

Luftfeuchtigkeit *f* (atmospheric) humidity

'Luftgewehr *n* airgun

'luftig *adj* airy; breezy; light (*dress etc*)

'Luftkissen *n* air cushion

Luftkissenfahrzeug *n* hovercraft

Luftkrankheit *f* air-sickness

Luftkrieg *m* air warfare

Luftkurort *m* (climatic) health resort

'luftleer *adj: luftleerer Raum* vacuum

'Luftlinie *f: 50 km Luftlinie* 50 km as the crow flies

Luftpost *f* air mail

Luftpumpe *f* air pump; bicycle pump

Luftröhre *f* ANAT windpipe, trachea

Luftschlange *f* streamer

Luftschloss *n* castle in the air

Luftsprünge *pl: Luftsprünge machen vor Freude* jump for joy

'Lüftung *f* (-; -en) airing; TECH ventilation

'Luftveränderung *f* change of air

Luftverkehr *m* air traffic

Luftverschmutzung *f* air pollution

Luftwaffe *f* MIL air force

Luftweg *m: auf dem Luftweg* by air

Luftzug *m* draft, *Br* draught

Lüge ['lyːgə] *f* (-; -n) lie

'lügen *v/i* (*irr, ge-, h*) lie, tell a lie *or* lies; *das ist gelogen* that's a lie

Lügner(in) ['lyːgnɐ (-nərɪn)] (*-s; -/-; -nen*) liar

'lügnerisch [-nərɪʃ] *adj* false

Luke ['luːkə] *f* (-; -n) hatch; skylight

Lümmel ['lʏməl] F *m* (-s; -) rascal

lumpen ['lʊmpən] F *v/t: sich nicht lum-*

pen lassen be generous
'Lumpen *m* (-s; -) rag; **in Lumpen** in rags
Lumpenpack F *n sl* bastards
lumpig ['lʊmpɪç] *adj:* **für lumpige zwei Mark** for a paltry two marks
Lunge ['lʊŋə] *f* (-; -n) ANAT lungs; *(auf)* **Lunge rauchen** inhale
Lungenflügel *m* ANAT lung
Lungenentzündung *f* MED pneumonia
Lungenzug *m:* **e-n Lungenzug machen** inhale
Lupe ['luːpə] *f* (-; -n) magnifying glass; **unter die Lupe nehmen** scrutinize (closely)
Lust [lʊst] *f* (-; Lüste ['lystə]) a) *(no pl)* desire, interest; pleasure, delight, b) lust; **Lust haben auf et. (et. zu tun)** feel like (doing) s.th.; **hättest du Lust auszugehen?** would you like to go out?, how about going out?; **ich habe keine Lust** I don't feel like it, I'm not in the mood for it; **die Lust an et. verlieren (j-m die Lust an et. nehmen)** (make s.o.) lose

all interest in s.th.
lüstern ['lystɐn] *adj* greedy *(nach* for)
lustig ['lʊstɪç] *adj* funny; cheerful; **er ist sehr lustig** he is full of fun; **es war sehr lustig** it was great fun; **sich lustig machen über** *(acc)* make fun of
lustlos *adj* listless, indifferent
Lustmord *m* sex murder
Lustspiel *n* THEA comedy
lutschen ['lʊtʃən] *v/i and v/t* (ge-, h) suck
Luv [luːf] *f* (-; *no pl*) MAR windward, weather side
luxuriös [lʊksuˈrjøːs] *adj* luxurious
Luxus ['lʊksʊs] *m* (-; *no pl*) luxury
Luxusar,tikel *m* luxury (article)
Luxusausführung *f* deluxe version
Luxusho,tel *n* five-star (*or* luxury) hotel
Lymphdrüse ['lʏmf-] *f* ANAT lymph gland
lynchen ['lʏnçən] *v/t* (ge-, h) lynch
Lyrik ['lyːrɪk] *f* (-; *no pl*) poetry
Lyriker ['lyːrikɐ] *m* (-s; -), **'Lyrikerin** *f* (-; -nen) (lyric) poet
lyrisch ['lyːrɪʃ] *adj* lyrical *(a. fig)*

M

machbar ['maxbaːɐ] *adj* feasible
machen ['maxən] *v/t* (ge-, h) do; make; GASTR make, prepare; fix *(a. fig)*; be, come to, amount to; take, pass *(test etc)*; make, go on *(a trip etc)*; **Hausaufgaben machen** do one's homework; **da (-gegen) kann man nichts machen** it can't be helped!; **mach, was du willst!** do as you please!; **(nun) mach mal or schon!** hurry up!, come on *or* along now!; **mach's gut!** take care (of yourself)!, good luck!; **(das) macht nichts** it doesn't matter; **mach dir nichts d(a)raus!** never mind!, don't worry!; **das macht mir nichts aus** I don't mind *or* care; **was or wie viel macht das?** how much is it?; **sich et. (nichts) machen aus** (not) care about; (not) care for
Machenschaften *pl* machinations; **unsaubere Machenschaften** sleaze *(esp* POL)
Macher ['maxɐ] *m* (-s; -) man of action, doer
Macho ['matʃo] *m* (-s; -s) macho
Macht [maxt] *f* (-; Mächte ['mɛçtə]) power *(über acc* of); **an der Macht** in power;

mit aller Macht with all one's might
Machthaber [-haːbɐ] *m* (-s; -) POL ruler
mächtig ['mɛçtɪç] *adj* powerful, mighty *(a. F)*; enormous, huge
Machtkampf *m* struggle for power
machtlos *adj* powerless
Machtmissbrauch *m* abuse of power
Machtpoli,tik *f* power politics
Machtübernahme *f* takeover
Machtwechsel *m* transition of power
Mädchen ['mɛːtçən] *n* (-s; -) girl; maid
mädchenhaft *adj* girlish
Mädchenname *m* girl's name; maiden name
Mädchenschule *f* girls' school
Made ['maːdə] *f* (-; -n) ZO maggot; worm
Mädel ['mɛːdəl] *n* (-s; -s) girl
madig *adj* maggoty, worm-eaten; F **'madigmachen** *v/t (sep, -ge-, h):* F **j-m et. madig** spoil s.th. for s.o.
Magazin [magaˈtsiːn] *n* (-s; -e) magazine *(a. MIL, PHOT, TV)*; store(room), warehouse
Magd [maːkt] *f* (-; Mägde ['mɛːktə]) (female) farmhand
Magen ['maːgən] *m* (-s; Mägen ['mɛːgən])

ANAT stomach

Magenbeschwerden pl MED stomach trouble

Magengeschwür n MED (stomach) ulcer

Magenschmerzen pl stomachache

mager ['ma:gɐ] adj lean, thin, skinny; GASTR low-fat (*cheese*), lean (*meat*), skim (*milk*); fig meager, Br meagre

Magie [ma'gi:] f (-; no pl) magic

magisch ['ma:gɪʃ] adj magic(al)

Magister [ma'gɪstɐ] m (-s; -) UNIV Master of Arts or Science; Austrian → **Apotheker**

Magistrat [magɪs'tra:t] m (-[e]s; -e) municipal council

Magnet [ma'gne:t] m (-[e]s, -en; -e[n]) magnet (a. fig)

Magnet... in cpds ...band, ...feld, ...nadel etc: magnetic ...

mag'netisch adj magnetic (a. fig)

magnetisieren [magneti'zi:rən] v/t (no -ge-, h) magnetize

Mahagoni [maha'go:ni] n (-s; no pl) mahogany

mähen ['mɛ:ən] v/t (ge-, h) mow; cut; AGR reap

Mähdrescher [-drɛʃɐ] m (-s; -) AGR combine (harvester)

mahlen ['ma:lən] v/t (irr, ge-, h) grind; mill

Mahlzeit f (-; -en) meal; feed(ing)

Mähne ['mɛ:nə] f (-; -n) ZO mane (a. F)

mahnen ['ma:nən] v/t (ge-, h) remind; ECON send s.o. a reminder

Mahngebühr f reminder fee

Mahnmal n memorial

Mahnung f (-; -en) reminder

Mai [mai] m (-[e]s; -e) May; *der Erste Mai* May Day

Maibaum m maypole

Maiglöckchen n BOT lily of the valley

Maikäfer m ZO cockchafer

Mais [mais] m (-es; -e) BOT corn, Br maize

Majestät [majes'tɛ:t] f: *Seine* (*Ihre, Eure*) *Majestät* His (Her, Your) Majesty

majes'tätisch adj majestic

Majonäse f → **Mayonnaise**

Major [ma'jo:ɐ] m (-s; -e) MIL major

makaber [ma'ka:bɐ] adj macabre

Makel ['ma:kəl] m (-s; -) blemish (a. fig)

mäkelig ['mɛ:kəlɪç] F adj picky, esp Br choos(e)y

'makellos adj immaculate (a. fig)

mäkeln ['mɛ:kəln] F v/i (ge-, h) carp, pick, nag (*an dat* at)

Makler ['ma:klɐ] m (-s; -) ECON real estate agent; broker

Maklergebühr f fee, commission

'Maklerin f (-; -nen) ECON → **Makler**

mal [ma:l] adv MATH times, multiplied by;

by; F → *einmal*; *12 mal 5 ist* (*gleich*) *60* 12 times or multiplied by 5 is or equals 60; *ein 7 mal 4 Meter großes Zimmer* a room 7 meters by 4

Mal¹ n (-[e]s; -e) time; *zum ersten* (*letzten*) *Mal*(*e*) for the first (last) time; *mit e-m Mal*(*e*) all of a sudden; *ein für alle Mal*(*e*) once and for all

Mal² n mark

malen ['ma:lən] v/t (ge-, h) paint

Maler ['ma:lɐ] m (-s; -) painter

Malerei [ma:lə'rai] f (-; -en) painting

Malerin ['ma:lərɪn] f (-; -nen) (woman) painter

'malerisch fig adj picturesque

'Malkasten m paintbox

'malnehmen → *multiplizieren*

Malz [malts] n (-es; no pl) malt

'Malzbier n malt beer

Mama ['mama] F f (-; -s) mom(my), Br mum(my)

Mammut ['mamut] n (-s; -e, -s) ZO mammoth

man [man] indef pron you, one; they, people; *wie schreibt man das?* how do you spell it?; *man sagt, dass* they or people say (that); *man hat mir gesagt* I was told

Manager ['mɛnidʒɐ] m (-s; -), **'Managerin** f (-; -nen) ECON executive; SPORT manager

manch [manç], **mancher** ['mançɐ], **manche** ['mançə], **manches** ['mançəs] indef pron (mst pl) some; quite a few, many

'manchmal adv sometimes, occasionally

Mandant [man'dant] m (-en; -en), **Man'dantin** f (-; -nen) JUR client

Mandarine [manda'ri:nə] f (-; -n) BOT tangerine

Mandat [man'da:t] n (-[e]s; -e) POL mandate; seat

Mandatar [manda'ta:ɐ] Austrian m → **Abgeordnete**

Mandel ['mandəl] f (-; -n) BOT almond; ANAT tonsil

Mandelentzündung f MED tonsillitis

Manege [ma'ne:ʒə] f (-; -n) (circus) ring

Mangel¹ ['maŋəl] m (-s; Mängel ['mɛŋəl]) a) (no pl) lack (*an dat* of), shortage, b) TECH defect, fault; shortcoming; *aus Mangel an* (dat) for lack of

'Mangel² f (-; -n) mangle

'mangelhaft adj poor (*quality etc*); defective (*goods etc*); PED unsatisfactory, failing

'mangeln v/t (ge-, h) mangle

'mangels prp (gen) for lack or want of

'Mangelware f: *Mangelware sein* be scarce

Manie [ma'ni:] f (-; -n) mania (a. fig)

Manieren [ma'ni:rən] pl manners

manierlich [ma'niːɐlıç] adv: **sich manierlich betragen** behave (decently)
Manifest [mani'fɛst] n (-[e]s; -e) manifes-
to
manipulieren [manipu'liːrən] v/t (no -ge-,
h) manipulate
Mann [man] m (-[e]s; Männer ['mɛnɐ])
man; husband
Männchen ['mɛnçən] n (-s; -) zo male
'Manndeckung f SPORT man-to-man
marking
Mannequin [manəkɛ:] n (-s; -s) model
mannigfach ['manıçfax], 'mannigfaltig
adj many and various
männlich ['mɛnlıç] adj BIOL male; masculine (a. LING)
'Mannschaft f (-; -en) SPORT team; MAR,
AVIAT crew
Manöver [ma'nøːvɐ] n (-s; -), manövrieren [manø'vriːrən] v/i (no -ge-, h) maneuver, Br manoeuvre
Mansarde [man'zardə] f (-; -n) room or
apartment in the attic
Manschette [man'ʃɛtə] f (-; -n) cuff; TECH
gasket
Man'schettenknopf m cuff-link
Mantel ['mantəl], pl Mäntel ['mɛntəl])
coat; tire: casing, bicycle: tire (Br tyre)
cover; TECH jacket, shell
Manuskript [manu'skrıpt] n (-[e]s; -e)
manuscript; copy
Mappe ['mapə] f (-; -n) briefcase; school
bag, satchel; folder
Märchen ['mɛ:ɐçən] n (-s; -) fairytale (a.
fig)
Märchenland n (-[e]s; no pl) fairyland
Marder ['mardɐ] m (-s; -) zo marten
Margarine [marga'riːnə] f (-; no pl) mar-
garine
Margerite [margə'riːtə] f (-; -n) BOT mar-
guerite
Marienkäfer [ma'riːən-] m zo lady bug, Br
ladybird
Marihuana [mari'hua:na] n (-s; no pl)
marijuana, sl grass
Marihuanaziga,rette f sl joint
Marille [ma'rılə] Austrian f (-; -n) BOT apri-
cot
Marine [ma'riːnə] f (-; -n) MIL navy
ma'rineblau adj navy blue
Marionette [marjo'nɛtə] f (-; -n) puppet
(a. fig)
Mario'nettenthe,ater n puppet show
Mark[1] [mark] f (-; -) mark
Mark[2] n (-[e]s; no pl) marrow; BOT pulp
Marke ['markə] f (-; -n) ECON brand; TECH
make; trademark; stamp; badge, tag;
mark
markieren [mar'kiːrən] v/t (no -ge-, h)

mark (a. SPORT); F fig act
Mar'kierung f (-; -en) mark
Markise [mar'kiːzə] f (-; -n) awning, sun
blind
Markt [markt] m (-[e]s; Märkte ['mɛrktə])
ECON market; **auf den Markt bringen** put
on the market
Marktplatz m market place
Marktwirtschaft f market economy
Marmelade [marmə'la:də] f (-; -n) jam
Marmor ['marmo:ɐ] m (-s; -e) marble
Marsch[1] [marʃ] m (-[e]s; Märsche
['mɛrʃə]) march (a. MUS)
Marsch[2] f (-; -en) GEOGR marsh, fen
Marschall ['marʃal] m (-s; Marschälle
['marʃɛlə]) MIL marshal
'Marschbefehl m MIL marching orders
marschieren [mar'ʃiːrən] v/i (no -ge-,
sein) march
Marsmensch ['mars-] m Martian
Marter ['martɐ] f (-; -n) torture
'martern v/t (ge-, h) torture
'Marterpfahl m stake
Martinshorn ['martiːns-] n (police etc) si-
ren
Märtyrer ['mɛrtyrɐ] m (-s; -), 'Märtyrerin f
(-; -nen) martyr (a. fig)
Marxismus [mar'ksısmʊs] m (-; no pl)
POL Marxism
Marxist [mar'ksıst] m (-en; -en), mar'xis-
tisch adj POL Marxist
März [mɛrts] m (-[es]; -e) March
Marzipan [martsi'pa:n] n (-s; -e) marzipan
Masche ['maʃə] f (-; -n) stitch; mesh; F
trick
'Maschendraht m wire netting
Maschine [ma'ʃiːnə] f (-; -n) machine;
MOT engine; AVIAT plane; motorcycle; **Ma-
schine schreiben** type
Ma'schinenbau m (-[e]s; no pl) mechan-
ical engineering
Maschinengewehr n MIL machinegun
ma'schinenlesbar adj EDP machine-read-
able
Ma'schinenöl n engine oil
Maschinenpis,tole f MIL submachine
gun, machine pistol
Maschinenschaden m engine trouble or
failure
Maschinenschlosser m (engine) fitter
Masern ['ma:zən] pl MED measles
Maserung ['ma:zərʊŋ] f (-; -en) grain
Maske ['maskə] f (-; -n) mask (a. EDP)
'Maskenball m fancy-dress ball
'Maskenbildner [-bıldnɐ] m (-s; -), 'Mas-
kenbildnerin f (-; -nen) THEA etc make-
-up artist
maskieren [mas'kiːrən] v/t (no -ge-, h)
mask; **sich maskieren** put on a mask

maskulin [masku'li:n] *adj* masculine (*a.* LING)

maß [ma:s] *pret of* **messen**

Maß[1] *n* (*-es*; *-e*) measure (**für** of); dimensions, measurements, size; *fig* extent, degree; *Maße und Gewichte* weights and measures; *nach Maß* (*gemacht*) made to measure; *in gewissem* (*hohem*) *Maße* to a certain (high) degree; *in zunehmendem Maße* increasingly; *Maß halten* → *maßhalten*

Maß[2] *f* (*-*; *-[e]*) liter (*Br* litre) of beer

Massage [ma'sa:ʒə] *f* (*-*; *-n*) massage

Massaker [ma'sa:kɐ] *n* (*-s*; *-*) massacre

Masse ['masə] *f* (*-*; *-n*) mass; substance; bulk; F *e-e Masse Geld etc* loads or heaps of; *die* (*breite*) *Masse*, POL *die Massen pl* the masses

Maßeinheit *f* unit of measure(ment)

Massen... *in cpds* ...*medien*, ...*mörder etc*: mass ...

Massenandrang *m* crush

'**massenhaft** F *adv* masses or loads of

'**Massenkarambo,lage** *f* MOT pileup

'**Massenprodukti,on** *f* ECON mass production

Masseur [ma'sø:ɐ] *m* (*-s*; *-e*) masseur

Masseurin [ma'sø:rɪn] *f* (*-*; *-nen*), **Masseuse** [ma'sø:zə] *f* (*-*; *-n*) masseuse

'**maßgebend**, '**maßgeblich** [-ge:plɪç] *adj* authoritative

'**maßhalten** *v/i* (*irr*, *halten*, *sep*, *-ge-*, *h*) be moderate (**in** *dat* in)

massieren [ma'si:rən] *v/t* (*no -ge-*, *h*) massage

massig ['masɪç] *adj* massive, bulky

mäßig ['mɛ:sɪç] *adj* moderate; poor

mäßigen ['mɛ:sɪgən] *v/t and v/refl* (*ge-*, *h*) moderate

'**Mäßigung** *f* (*-*; *no pl*) moderation; restraint

massiv [ma'si:f] *adj* solid

Mas'siv *n* (*-s*; *-e*) GEOL massif

'**Maßkrug** *m* beer mug, stein

'**maßlos** *adj* immoderate; gross (*exaggeration*)

'**Maßnahme** [-na:mə] *f* (*-*; *-n*) measure, step

'**Maßregel** *f* rule

'**maßregeln** *v/t* (*ge-*, *h*) reprimand; discipline

'**Maßstab** *m* scale; *fig* standard; *im Maßstab 1:10* on the scale of 1:10

'**maßstabgetreu** *adj* true to scale

'**maßvoll** *adj* moderate

Mast[1] [mast] *m* (*-[e]s*; *-en*) MAR, TECH mast

Mast[2] *f* (*-*; *-en*) AGR fattening

'**Mastdarm** *m* ANAT rectum

mästen ['mɛstən] *v/t* (*ge-*, *h*) AGR fatten; F

stuff *s.o.*

masturbieren [mastur'bi:rən] *v/i* (*no -ge-*, *h*) masturbate

Match [mɛtʃ] *n* (*-[e]s*; *-s*, *-e*) game, *Br* match

Matchball *m tennis*: match point

Material [mate'rja:l] *n* (*-s*; *-ien*) material (*a. fig*); TECH materials

Materialismus [materja'lɪsmus] *m* (*-*; *no pl*) materialism

Materialist [-'lɪst] *m* (*-en*; *-en*) materialist

materia'listisch *adj* materialistic

Materie [ma'te:rjə] *f* (*-*; *-n*) matter (*a. fig*); *fig* subject (matter)

materiell [mate'rjɛl] *adj* material

Mathematik [matema'ti:k] *f* (*-*; *no pl*) mathematics

Mathematiker [mate'ma:tikɐ] *m* (*-s*; *-*) mathematician

mathe'matisch *adj* mathematical

Matinee [mati'ne:] *f* (*-*; *-n*) THEA *etc* morning performance

Matratze [ma'tratsə] *f* (*-*; *-n*) mattress

Matrize [ma'tri:tsə] *f* (*-*; *-n*) stencil

Matrose [ma'tro:zə] *m* (*-n*; *-n*) MAR sailor, seaman

Matsch [matʃ] F *m* (*-[e]s*; *no pl*) mud, slush

'**matschig** *adj* muddy, slushy

matt [mat] *adj* weak; exhausted, worn out; dull, pale (*color*); PHOT mat(t); frosted (*glass*); *chess*: checkmate

Matte ['matə] *f* (*-*; *-n*) mat

Mattigkeit ['matɪçkait] *f* (*-*; *no pl*) exhaustion, weakness

'**Mattscheibe** *f* screen; PHOT focus(s)ing screen; F (boob) tube, *Br* telly, box

Matura [ma'tu:ra] *Austrian, Swiss f* → **Abitur**

Mauer ['mauɐ] *f* (*-*; *-n*) wall

Mauerblümchen *fig n* wallflower

Mauerwerk *n* (*-[e]s*; *no pl*) masonry, brickwork

'**mauern** *v/i* (*ge-*, *h*) lay bricks

Maul [maul] *n* (*-[e]s*; *Mäuler* ['mɔylɐ]) ZO mouth; *sl halt's Maul!* shut up!

maulen ['maulən] F *v/i* (*ge-*, *h*) grumble, sulk, pout

'**Maulkorb** *m* muzzle (*a. fig*)

Maultier *n* mule

Maulwurf *m* ZO mole

Maulwurfshaufen *m*, **Maulwurfshügel** *m* molehill

Maurer ['mauɐ] *m* (*-s*; *-*) bricklayer

Maurerkelle *f* trowel

Maurermeister *m* master bricklayer

Maurerpo,lier *m* foreman bricklayer

Maus [maus] *f* (*-*; *Mäuse* ['mɔyzə]) ZO mouse (*a.* EDP)

'**Mausefalle** ['mauzə-] f mousetrap

Mauser ['mauzə] f (-; *no pl*) zo mo(u)lt (-ing); *in der Mauser sein* be mo(u)lting

Maut [maut] *Austrian* f (-; -en) toll

Mautstraße f turnpike, toll road

maximal [maksi'maːl] **1.** *adj* maximum; **2.** *adv* at (the) most

Maximum ['maksimʊm] n (-s; -ma) maximum

Mayonnaise [majo'nɛːzə] f (-; -n) GASTR mayonnaise

Mäzen [mɛ'tseːn] m (-s; -e) patron; SPORT sponsor

Mechanik [me'çaːnɪk] f (-; -en) a) (*no pl*) PHYS mechanics, b) TECH mechanism

Mechaniker [me'çaːnɪkɐ] m (-s; -) mechanic

mechanisch [me'çaːnɪʃ] *adj* TECH mechanical

mechanisieren [meçani'ziːrən] v/t (*no -ge-*, h) mechanize

Mechanisierung f (-; -en) mechanization

Mechanismus [meça'nɪsmʊs] m (-; -men) TECH mechanism; works

meckern ['mɛkɐn] v/i (ge-, h) zo bleat; F grumble, bitch (*über acc* at, about)

Medaille [me'daljə] f (-; -n) medal

Me'daillengewinner m medal(l)ist

Medaillon [medal'jõː] n (-s; -s) locket

Medien ['meːdjən] pl mass media; teaching aids; audio-visual aids

Medikament [medika'mɛnt] n (-[e]s; -e) drug; medicine

meditieren [medi'tiːrən] v/i (*no -ge-*, h) meditate (*über acc* on)

Medizin [medi'tsiːn] f (-; -en) a) (*no pl*) (science of) medicine, b) medicine, remedy (*gegen* for)

Mediziner [medi'tsiːnɐ] m (-s; -), **Medi'zinerin** f (-; -nen) (medical) doctor; UNIV medical student

medizinisch [medi'tsiːnɪʃ] *adj* medical

Meer [meːɐ] n (-[e]s; -e ['meːrə]) sea (*a. fig*), ocean

Meerenge f GEOGR straits

Meeresboden ['meːrəs-] m seabed

Meeresfrüchte pl GASTR seafood

Meeresspiegel m sea level

'**Meerjungfrau** f MYTH mermaid

'**Meerrettich** m (-s; -e) horseradish

'**Meerschweinchen** [-ʃvaiçən] n (-s; -) zo guinea pig

Megabyte [mega'bait] n EDP megabyte

Mehl [meːl] n (-[e]s; -e) flour; meal

mehlig ['meːlɪç] *adj* mealy

'**Mehlspeise** *Austrian* f sweet (dish)

mehr [meːɐ] *indef pron* and *adv* more; *immer mehr* more and more; *nicht mehr* no longer, not any longer (*or* more);

noch mehr even more; *es ist kein ... mehr da* there isn't any ... left

'**mehrdeutig** [-dɔytɪç] *adj* ambiguous

mehrere ['meːrərə] *adj and indef pron* several

'**Mehrheit** f (-; -en) majority

'**Mehrkosten** pl extra costs

'**mehrmals** *adv* several times

'**Mehrwegflasche** f returnable (*or* deposit) bottle

Mehrwertsteuer f ECON value-added tax (ABBR VAT)

Mehrzahl f (-; *no pl*) majority; LING plural (form)

'**Mehrzweck...** *in cpds* ...*fahrzeug etc*: multi-purpose ...

meiden ['maidən] v/t (*irr, ge-, h*) avoid

Meile ['mailə] f (-; -n) mile

'**meilenweit** *adv* (for) miles

mein [main] *poss pron and adj* my; *das ist meiner (meine, mein[e]s)* that's mine

'**Meineid** m JUR perjury

meinen ['mainən] v/t (ge-, h) think, believe; mean; say; *meinen Sie wirklich?* do you (really) think so?; *wie meinen Sie das?* what do you mean by that?; *sie meinen es gut* they mean well; *ich habe es nicht so gemeint* I didn't mean it; *wie meinen Sie?* (I beg your) pardon?

meinet'wegen ['mainət-] *adv* for my sake; because of me; F I don't mind *or* care!

'**Meinung** f (-; -en) opinion (*über acc*, *von* about, of); *meiner Meinung nach* in my opinion; *der Meinung sein, dass* be of the opinion that, feel *or* believe that; *s-e Meinung äußern* express one's opinion; *s-e Meinung ändern* change one's mind; *ich bin Ihrer (anderer) Meinung* I (don't) agree with you; *j-m die Meinung sagen* give s.o. a piece of one's mind

'**Meinungsaustausch** m exchange of views (*über acc* on)

Meinungsforscher m pollster

Meinungsfreiheit f (-; *no pl*) freedom of speech *or* opinion

Meinungsumfrage f opinion poll

Meinungsverschiedenheit f disagreement (*über acc* about)

Meise ['maizə] f (-; -n) zo titmouse

Meißel ['maisəl] m (-s; -) chisel

'**meißeln** v/t and v/i (ge-, h) chisel, carve

meist [maist] **1.** *adj* most; *das meiste (davon)* most of it; *die meisten (von ihnen)* most of them; *die meisten Leute* most people; *die meiste Zeit* most of the time; **2.** *adv* → *meistens*; *am meisten* (the)

meistens ['maɪstəns] adv usually; most of the time

Meister ['maɪstɐ] m (-s; -) master (a. fig); SPORT champion, F champ

'meisterhaft 1. adj masterly; 2. adv in a masterly manner or way

'Meisterin f (-; -nen) master (a. fig); SPORT champion

'meistern ['maɪstɐn] v/t (ge-, h) master

'Meisterschaft f (-; -en) a) (no pl) mastery, b) SPORT championship, cup; title

'Meisterstück n, 'Meisterwerk n masterpiece

Melancholie [melaŋkoˈliː] f (-; -n) melancholy

melancholisch [melaŋˈkoːlɪʃ] adj melancholy; melancholisch sein feel depressed, F have the blues

Melange [meˈlãːʒə] Austrian f (-; -n) coffee with milk

melden ['mɛldən] (ge-, h) 1. v/t report s.th. or s.o. (bei to); radio etc: announce, report; j-m et. melden notify s.o. of s.th.; 2. v/refl: sich melden report (bei to, für, zu for); register (bei with); PED etc: put up one's hand; TEL answer the phone; SPORT enter (für, zu for); volunteer (für, zu for)

'Meldung f (-; -en) report, news, announcement; information, notice; notification; registration (bei with); SPORT entry (für, zu for)

melken ['mɛlkən] v/t ([irr,] ge-, h) milk

Melodie [meloˈdiː] f (-; -n) MUS melody, tune

melodisch [meˈloːdɪʃ] adj MUS melodious, melodic

Melone [meˈloːnə] f (-; -n) BOT melon; F derby, Br bowler (hat)

Memoiren [meˈmoaːrən] pl memoirs

Menge ['mɛŋə] f (-; -n) amount, quantity; MATH set; F e-e Menge Geld plenty (or lots) of money; → Menschenmenge

'Mengenlehre f (-; no pl) MATH set theory; PED new math(ematics)

Mensa ['mɛnza] f (-; -s, Mensen) cafeteria, Br refectory, canteen

Mensch [mɛnʃ] m (-en; -en) human being; man; person, individual; pl people; mankind; kein Mensch nobody; Mensch! wow!

Menschenaffe m ZO ape

Menschenfresser m cannibal

Menschenfreund m philanthropist

Menschenhandel m slave trade

Menschenkenntnis f: Menschenkenntnis haben know human nature

Menschenleben n human life

'menschenleer adj deserted

'Menschenmenge f crowd

Menschenrechte pl human rights

Menschenseele f: keine Menschenseele not a (living) soul

'menschenunwürdig adj degrading; housing etc: unfit for human beings

'Menschenverstand m: gesunder Menschenverstand common sense

Menschenwürde f human dignity

Menschheit: die Menschheit mankind, the human race

'menschlich adj human; humane

'Menschlichkeit f (-; no pl) humanity

Menstruation [mɛnstrua'tsjoːn] f (-; -en) MED menstruation

Mentalität [mɛntaliˈtɛːt] f (-; -en) mentality

Menü [meˈnyː] n (-s; -s) set meal (or lunch); EDP menu

Meridian [meriˈdjaːn] m (-s; -e) GEOGR, ASTR meridian

merkbar ['mɛrkbaːɐ] adj marked, distinct; noticeable

Merkblatt n leaflet

merken ['mɛrkən] v/t (ge-, h) notice; feel; find (out), discover; sich et. merken remember s.th., keep or bear s.th. in mind

'merklich adj → merkbar

'Merkmal n sign; feature, trait

'merkwürdig adj strange, odd, curious

'merkwürdiger'weise adv strangely enough

messbar ['mɛsbaːɐ] adj measurable

'Messbecher m measuring cup

Messe ['mɛsə] f (-; -n) ECON fair; REL mass; MIL, MAR mess

messen ['mɛsən] v/t (irr, ge-, h) measure; take (temperature etc); sich nicht mit j-m messen können be no match for s.o.; gemessen an (dat) compared with

Messer ['mɛsɐ] n (-s; -) knife; bis aufs Messer to the knife; auf des Messers Schneide stehen be on a razor edge, be touch and go (ob whether)

Messerstecherei [-ʃteçəˈraɪ] f (-; -en) knife fight

'Messerstich m stab (with a knife)

Messing ['mɛsɪŋ] n (-s; -e) brass

'Messinstru,ment n measuring instrument

'Messung f (-; -en) measuring; reading

Metall [meˈtal] n (-s; -e) metal

metallen [meˈtalən], me'tallisch adj metallic

Me'tallwaren pl hardware

Metamorphose [metamɔrˈfoːzə] f (-; -n) metamorphosis

Metastase [metaˈstaːzə] f (-; -n) MED metastasis

Meteor [mete'o:ɐ] *m* (-s; -e) ASTR meteor

Meteorit [meteo'ri:t] *m* (-en; -e[n]) ASTR meteorite

Meteorologe [meteoro'lo:gə] *m* (-n; -n) meteorologist

Meteorologie [meteorolo'gi:] *f* (-; no pl) meteorology

Meteo'rologin *f* (-; -nen) meteorologist

Meter ['me:tɐ] *n*, *m* (-s; -) meter, *Br* metre

Metermaß *n* tape measure

Methode [me'to:də] *f* (-; -n) method, TECH *a.* technique

methodisch [me'to:dɪʃ] *adj* methodical

metrisch ['me:trɪʃ] *adj* metric; *metrisches Maßsystem* metric system

Metropole [metro'po:lə] *f* (-; -n) metropolis

Metzger ['mɛtsgɐ] *m* (-s; -) butcher

Metzgerei [mɛtsgə'rai] *f* (-; -en) butcher's (shop)

Meute ['mɔytə] *f* (-; -n) pack (of hounds); *fig* mob, pack

Meuterei [mɔytə'rai] *f* (-; -en) mutiny

Meuterer ['mɔytərɐ] *m* (-s; -) mutineer

meutern ['mɔytɐn] *v/i* (ge-, h) mutiny (**gegen** against)

MEZ *ABBR of* **Mitteleuropäische Zeit** CET, Central European Time

miau [mi'au] *int* ZO meow, *Br* miaow

miauen [mi'auən] *v/i* (no -ge-, h) ZO meow, *Br* miaow

mich [mɪç] *pers pron* me; *mich (selbst)* myself

mied [mi:t] *pret of* **meiden**

Mieder ['mi:dɐ] *n* (-s; -) corset(s); bodice

Miederhöschen *n* pantie girdle

Miederwaren *pl* foundation garments

Miene ['mi:nə] *f* (-; -n) expression, look, air; *gute Miene zum bösen Spiel machen* grin and bear it

mies [mi:s] F *adj* rotten, lousy

Miete ['mi:tə] *f* (-; -n) rent; hire charge; *zur Miete wohnen* be a tenant; lodge (*bei* with)

'mieten *v/t* (ge-, h) rent; (take on) lease; AVIAT, MAR charter; *ein Auto etc mieten* rent (*Br* hire) a car *etc*

Mieter(in) ['mi:tɐ (-tərɪn)] (-s; -/-; -nen) tenant, lodger

'Mietshaus *n* apartment building or house, *Br* block of flats, tenement

'Mietvertrag *m* lease (contract)

'Mietwohnung *f* apartment, *Br* (rented) flat

Migräne [mi'grɛ:nə] *f* (-; -n) MED migraine

Mikro ['mi:kro] F *n* (-s; -s) mike

Mikro... ['mi:kro-] *in cpds* ...chip, ...computer, ...elektronik, ...film, ...prozessor

etc: micro...

Mikrofon [mikro'fo:n] *n* (-s; -e) microphone

Mikroskop [mikro'sko:p] *n* (-s; -e) microscope

mikro'skopisch *adj* microscopic(al)

Mikrowelle ['mi:kro-] F *f*, **'Mikrowellenherd** *m* microwave oven

Milbe ['mɪlbə] *f* (-; -n) ZO mite

Milch [mɪlç] *f* (-; no pl) milk

Milchgeschäft *n* dairy, creamery

Milchglas *n* frosted glass

milchig ['mɪlçɪç] *adj* milky

'Milchkaffee *m* white coffee

Milchkännchen *n* (milk) jug

Milchkanne *f* milk can

Milchmann F *m* milkman

Milchmixgetränk *n* milk shake

Milchpro,dukte *pl* dairy products

Milchpulver *n* powdered milk

Milchreis *m* rice pudding

Milchstraße *f* ASTR Milky Way, Galaxy

Milchtüte *f* milk carton

Milchwirtschaft *f* dairy farming

Milchzahn *m* milk tooth

mild [mɪlt] *adj* mild, soft; gentle

milde ['mɪldə] *adv* mildly; *milde ausgedrückt* to put it mildly

'Milde *f* (-; no pl) mildness, gentleness; leniency, mercy

mildern ['mɪldɐn] *v/t* (ge-, h) lessen, soften

mildernd *adj*: *mildernde Umstände* JUR mitigating circumstances

'mildtätig *adj* charitable

Milieu [mi'ljø:] *n* (-s; -s) environment; social background

Militär [mili'tɛ:ɐ] *n* (-s; no pl) the military, armed forces; army

Militärdienst *m* (-[e]s; no pl) military service

Militärdikta,tur *f* military dictatorship

Militärgericht *n* court martial

militärisch [mili'tɛ:rɪʃ] *adj* military

Militarismus [milita'rɪsmʊs] *m* (-; no pl) militarism

Militarist [milita'rɪst] *m* (-en; -en) militarist

milita'ristisch *adj* militaristic

Mili'tärre,gierung *f* military government

Milliarde [mɪ'ljardə] *f* (-; -n) billion, *Br old use a.* a thousand million(s)

Millimeter ['mɪlime:tɐ] *n*, *m* (-s; -) millimet|er, *Br* -re

Millimeterpa,pier *n* graph paper

Million [mɪ'ljo:n] *f* (-; -en) million

Millionär [mɪljo'nɛ:ɐ] *m* (-s; -e), **Millio'närin** *f* (-; -nen) millionaire

Milz [mɪlts] *f* (-; no pl) ANAT spleen

Mimik ['mi:mɪk] *f* (-; *no pl*) facial expression

minder ['mɪndɐ] **1.** *adj* → **geringer**, **weniger**; **2.** *adv* less; **nicht minder** no less

Minderheit *f* (-; -en) minority

'**minderjährig** [-jɛ:rɪç] *adj*: **minderjährig sein** be under age, be a minor

'**Minderjährige** [-jɛ:rɪgə] *m*, *f* (-n; -n) minor

'**Minderjährigkeit** *f* (-; *no pl*) minority

'**minderwertig** *adj* inferior, of inferior quality

'**Minderwertigkeit** *f* (-; *no pl*) inferiority, ECON inferior quality

'**Minderwertigkeits,kom,plex** *m* PSYCH inferiority complex

mindest ['mɪndəst] *adj* least; **das Mindeste** the (very) least; **nicht im Mindesten** not the least, not at all

'**Mindest...** *in cpds* ...alter, ...einkommen, ...lohn *etc*: minimum ...

mindestens ['mɪndəstəns] *adv* at least

'**Mindesthaltbarkeitsdatum** *n* pull date, *Br* best-before (*or* best-by, sell-by) date

Mindestmaß *n* minimum; **auf ein Mindestmaß herabsetzen** reduce to a minimum

Mine ['mi:nə] *f* (-; -n) mine (*a.* MAR, MIL); lead; cartridge; refill

Mineral [minə'ra:l] *n* (-s; -e, -ien) mineral

Mineralogie [mineralo'gi:] *f* (-; *no pl*) mineralogy

Mine'ralöl *n* mineral oil

Mine'ralwasser *n* mineral water

Miniatur [minja'tu:ɐ] *f* (-; -en) miniature

Minigolf ['mɪni-] *n* miniature (*Br* crazy) golf

minimal [mini'ma:l] *adj*, *adv* minimal; minimum; at least

Minimum ['mi:nimʊm] *n* (-s; -ma) minimum

Minirock ['mɪni-] *m* miniskirt

Minister [mi'nɪstɐ] *m* (-s; -), **Mi'nisterin** *f* (-; -nen) minister, secretary, *Br a.* secretary of state

Ministerium [minɪs'te:riʊm] *n* (-s; -ien) ministry, department, *Br a.* office

Mi'nisterpräsi,dent *m*, **Mi'nisterpräsi,dentin** *f* prime minister

minus ['mi:nʊs] *adv* MATH minus; **bei 10 Grad minus** at 10 degrees below zero

Minute [mi'nu:tə] *f* (-; -n) minute

Mi'nutenzeiger *m* minute hand

Mio ABBR *of* **Million(en)** m, million

mir [mi:ɐ] *pers pron* (to) me

Mischbatte,rie ['mɪʃ-] *f* mixing faucet, *Br* mixer tap

'**Mischbrot** *n* wheat and rye bread

mischen ['mɪʃən] *v/t* (ge-, h) mix; blend

(*tea etc*); shuffle (*cards*); **sich mischen** mingle *or* mix (**unter** with)

'**Mischling** *m* (-s; -e) *esp contp* half-caste; BOT, ZO hybrid; mongrel

'**Mischmasch** F *m* (-[e]s; -e) hotchpotch, jumble

'**Mischma,schine** *f* TECH mixer

Mischpult *n* radio, TV: mixer, mixing console

'**Mischung** *f* (-; -en) mixture; blend; assortment

'**Mischwald** *m* mixed forest

miserabel [mizə'ra:bəl] F *adj* lousy, rotten

miss'achten [mɪs-] *v/t* (*no -ge-, h*) disregard, ignore; despise

Miss'achtung *f* disregard; contempt; neglect (*all*: *gen* of)

'**Missbildung** *f* (-; -en) deformity, malformation

miss'billigen *v/t* (*no -ge-, h*) disapprove of

'**Missbrauch** *m* abuse (*a.* JUR); misuse

miss'brauchen *v/t* (*no -ge-, h*) abuse; misuse

miss'deuten *v/t* (*no -ge-, h*) misinterpret

'**Misserfolg** *m* failure; F flop

'**Missernte** *f* bad harvest, crop failure

miss'fallen *v/i* (*irr*, **fallen**, *no -ge-, h*) **j-m missfallen** displease s.o.

Miss'fallen *n* (-s; *no pl*) displeasure, dislike

'**missgebildet** *adj* deformed, malformed

'**Missgeburt** *f* deformed child *or* animal; freak

'**Missgeschick** *n* (-[e]s; -e) mishap

miss'glücken *v/i* (*no -ge-, sein*) fail

miss'gönnen *v/t* (*no -ge-, h*) **j-m et. missgönnen** envy s.o. s.th.

'**Missgriff** *m* mistake

miss'handeln *v/t* (*no -ge-, h*) ill-treat, maltreat (*a. fig*); beat

Miss'handlung *f* ill-treatment, maltreatment, *esp* JUR assault and battery

Mission [mɪ'sjo:n] *f* (-; -en) mission (*a.* POL *and fig*)

Missionar(in) [mɪsjo'na:ɐ (-'na:rɪn)] (-s; -e/-; -nen) missionary

'**Missklang** *m* dissonance, discord (*both a. fig*)

'**Misskre,dit** *m* discredit

misslang [mɪs'laŋ] *pret of* **misslingen**

misslingen [mɪs'lɪŋən] *v/i* (*irr*, *no -ge-, sein*) fail

misslungen [mɪs'lʊŋən] *pp of* **misslingen**; **das ist mir misslungen** I've bungled it

'**missmutig** *adj* bad-tempered, grumpy, glum

miss'raten 1. *v/i* (*irr*, **raten**, *no -ge-, sein*)

fail; turn out badly; **2.** *adj* wayward
'**miss'trauen** *v/i* (*no -ge-, h*) distrust
'**Misstrauen** *n* (*-s; no pl*) distrust, suspicion (*both*: **gegenüber** of)
'**Misstrauensantrag** *m* PARL motion of no confidence
'**Misstrauensvotum** *n* PARL vote of no confidence
misstrauisch ['mɪstrauɪʃ] *adj* distrustful, suspicious
'**Missverhältnis** *n* disproportion
'**Missverständnis** *n* (*-ses; -se*) misunderstanding
'**missverstehen** *v/t* (*irr*, **stehen**, *no -ge-, h*) misunderstand
'**Misswahl** *f* beauty contest *or* competition
Mist [mɪst] *m* (*-[e]s; no pl*) AGR dung, manure; F trash, rubbish
'**Mistbeet** *n* AGR hotbed
Mistel ['mɪstəl] *f* (*-; -n*) BOT mistletoe
'**Mistgabel** *f* AGR dung fork
'**Misthaufen** *m* AGR manure heap
mit [mɪt] *prp* (*dat*) *and adv* with; **mit Gewalt** by force; **mit Absicht** on purpose; **mit dem Auto** (**der Bahn** *etc*) by car (train *etc*); **mit 20 Jahren** at (the age of) 20; **mit 100 Stundenkilometern** at 100 kilometers per hour; **mit einem Mal(e)** all of a sudden; (all) at the same time; **mit lauter Stimme** in a loud voice; **mit anderen Worten** in other words; **ein Mann mit dem Namen ...** a man by the name of ...; **j-n mit Namen kennen** know s.o. by name; **mit der Grund dafür, dass** one of the reasons why; **mit der Beste** one of the best
'**Mitarbeit** *f* cooperation; assistance; PED activity, class participation
'**Mitarbeiter** *m*, '**Mitarbeiterin** *f* colleague; employee; assistant; **freie(r) Mitarbeiter(in)** freelance
'**mitbekommen** F *v/t* (*irr*, **kommen**, *sep*, *no -ge-, h*) get; catch
mitbenutzen *v/t* (*sep*, *no -ge-, h*) share
'**Mitbestimmungsrecht** *n* (right of) codetermination, worker participation
Mitbewerber(in) (rival) competitor; fellow applicant
Mitbewohner(in) roommate, *Br* flatmate
'**mitbringen** *v/t* (*irr*, **bringen**, *sep*, *-ge-, h*) bring s.th. *or* s.o. with one; **j-m et. mitbringen** bring s.o. s.th.
'**Mitbringsel** ['mɪtbrɪŋzəl] F *n* (*-s; -*) little present; souvenir
'**Mitbürger** *m*, '**Mitbürgerin** *f* fellow citizen
mitei'nander *adv* with each other, with one another; together, jointly

'**miterleben** *v/t* (*sep*, *no -ge-, h*) live to see
'**Mitesser** *m* MED blackhead
'**mitfahren** *v/i* (*irr*, **fahren**, *sep*, *-ge-, sein*) **mit j-m mitfahren** drive *or* go with s.o.; **j-n mitfahren lassen** give s.o. a lift
'**Mitfahrgelegenheit** *f* lift
Mitfahren,trale *f* car pool(ing) service
'**mitfühlend** *adj* sympathetic
'**mitgeben** *v/t* (*irr*, **geben**, *sep*, *-ge-, h*) **j-m et. mitgeben** give s.o. s.th. (to take along)
'**Mitgefühl** *n* (*-[e]s; no pl*) sympathy
'**mitgehen** *v/i* (*irr*, **gehen**, *sep*, *-ge-, sein*) **mit j-m mitgehen** go *or* come along with s.o.; F **et. mitgehen lassen** walk off with s.th.
'**Mitgift** *f* (*-; -en*) dowry
'**Mitglied** *n* member (**bei** of)
'**Mitgliedsbeitrag** *m* subscription
'**Mitgliedschaft** *f* (*-; -en*) membership
'**mithaben** *v/t* (*irr*, **haben**, *sep*, *-ge-, h*) **ich habe kein Geld mit** I haven't got any money with me *or* on me
'**Mithilfe** *f* (*-; no pl*) assistance, help, cooperation (**bei** in; **von** of)
mit'hilfe *prp*: **mithilfe von** (*or gen*) with the help of, *fig a.* by means of
'**mithören** *v/t* (*sep*, *-ge-, h*) listen in to; overhear
'**Mitinhaber** *m*, '**Mitinhaberin** *f* joint owner
'**mitkommen** *v/i* (*irr*, **kommen**, *sep*, *-ge-, sein*) come along (**mit** with); *fig* keep pace (**mit** with), follow; PED get on, keep up (with the class)
'**Mitlaut** *m* LING consonant
'**Mitleid** *n* (*-[e]s; no pl*) pity (**mit** for); **aus Mitleid** out of pity; **Mitleid haben mit** feel sorry for
'**mitleidig** ['mɪtlaidɪç] *adj* compassionate, sympathetic
'**mitleidslos** *adj* pitiless
'**mitmachen** (*sep*, *-ge-, h*) **1.** *v/i* join in; **2.** *v/t* take part in; follow (*a fashion etc*); F go through
'**Mitmenschen**: **die Mitmenschen** one's fellow human beings; people
'**mitnehmen** *v/t* (*irr*, **nehmen**, *sep*, *-ge-, h*) take *s.th. or s.o.* with one; **j-n (im Auto) mitnehmen** give s.o. a lift
'**mitreden** *v/t* (*sep*, *-ge-, h*) **et. mitzureden haben** (**bei**) have a say (in)
'**mitreißen** *v/t* (*irr*, **reißen**, *sep*, *-ge-, h*) drag along; *fig* carry away (*mst passive*)
mitreißend *fig adj* electrifying (*speech etc*)
'**mitschneiden** *v/t* (*irr*, **schneiden**, *sep*, *-ge-, h*) radio, TV record, tape(-record)
'**mitschreiben** (*irr*, **schreiben**, *sep*, *-ge-, h*) **1.** *v/t* take down; take, do (*a test*); **2.**

v/i take notes

'**Mitschuld** *f* (-; *no pl*) partial responsibility

'**mitschuldig** *adj*: **mitschuldig sein** be partly to blame (**an** *dat* for)

'**Mitschüler** *m*, '**Mitschülerin** *f* classmate; schoolmate, fellow student

'**mitspielen** *v/i* (*sep*, *-ge-*, *h*) SPORT, MUS play; join in a *game etc*; **in e-m Film** *etc* **mitspielen** be or appear in a film *etc*

'**Mitspieler** *m*, '**Mitspielerin** *f* partner, SPORT *a.* team-mate

Mittag ['mɪtaːk] *m* (-s; -e) noon, midday; **heute Mittag** at noon today; **zu Mittag essen** (have) lunch

Mittagessen *n* lunch; **was gibt es zum Mittagessen?** what's for lunch?

'**mittags** *adv* at noon; **12 Uhr mittags** 12 o'clock noon

'**Mittagspause** *f* lunch break

'**Mittagsruhe** *f* midday rest

'**Mittagsschlaf** *m* after-dinner nap

'**Mittagszeit** *f* lunchtime

Mitte ['mɪtə] *f* (-; *no pl*) middle; center, *Br* centre (*a.* POL); **Mitte Juli** in the middle of July; **Mitte dreißig** in one's mid thirties

'**mitteilen** *v/t* (*sep*, *-ge-*, *h*) **j-m et. mitteilen** inform s.o. of s.th.

'**mitteilsam** *adj* communicative

'**Mitteilung** *f* (-; *-en*) report, information, message

Mittel ['mɪtəl] *n* (-s; -) means, way; measure; PHARM remedy (**gegen** for) (*a.* *fig*); average; MATH mean; PHYS medium; *pl* means, money

'**Mittelalter** *n* (-s; *no pl*) Middle Ages

'**mittelalterlich** *adj* medi(a)eval

'**Mittelding** *n* cross (**zwischen** between)

'**Mittelfeld** *n* SPORT midfield

'**Mittelfeldspieler(in)** midfield player, midfielder

'**Mittelfinger** *m* ANAT middle finger

'**mittelfristig** *adj* medium-term

'**Mittelgewicht** *n* (-[e]s; *no pl*) SPORT middleweight (class)

'**mittelgroß** *adj* of medium height; medium-sized

'**Mittelklasse** *f* middle class (*a.* MOT)

'**Mittellinie** *f* SPORT halfway line

'**mittellos** *adj* without means

'**mittelmäßig** *adj* average

'**Mittelpunkt** *m* center, *Br* centre (*a.* *fig*)

'**mittels** *prp* (*gen*) by (means of), through

'**Mittelschule** *f* → **Realschule**

'**Mittelstrecke** *f* SPORT middle distance

Mittelstreckenra,kete *f* MIL medium-range missile

'**Mittelstreifen** *m* MOT median strip, *Br* central reservation

'**Mittelstufe** *f* PED junior highschool, *Br* middle school

'**Mittelstürmer(in)** SPORT center (*Br* centre) forward

'**Mittelweg** *m* middle course

'**Mittelwelle** *f* radio: medium wave (ABBR AM)

'**Mittelwort** *n* (-[e]s; *-wörter*) LING participle

mitten ['mɪtən] *adv*: **mitten in** (**auf, unter** *dat*) in the midst or middle of

mitten'drin F *adv* right in the middle

mitten'durch F *adv* right through (the middle); right in two

Mitternacht ['mɪtɐ-] *f* midnight

mittlere ['mɪtlərə] *adj* middle, central; average, medium

mittlerweile ['mɪtlɐ'vailə] *adv* meanwhile, (in the) meantime

Mittwoch ['mɪtvɔx] *m* (-[s]; -e) Wednesday

mit'unter *adv* now and then

'**Mitverantwortung** *f* share of the responsibility

'**mitwirken** *v/i* (*sep*, *-ge-*, *h*) take part (**bei** in)

'**Mitwirkende** *m*, *f* (*-n*; *-n*) THEA, MUS performer; *pl* THEA the cast

'**Mitwirkung** *f* (-; *no pl*) participation

mixen ['mɪksən] *v/t* (*ge-*, *h*) mix

'**Mixbecher** *m* shaker

Mixer ['mɪksɐ] *m* (-s; -) mixer

'**Mixgetränk** *n* mixed drink, cocktail, shake

Möbel ['møːbəl] *pl* furniture

'**Möbelspediti,on** *f* removal firm

'**Möbelstück** *n* piece of furniture

'**Möbelwagen** *m* moving (*Br* furniture) van

mobil [mo'biːl] *adj* mobile; **mobil machen** MIL mobilize

Mobiliar [mobi'ljaːɐ] *n* (-s; *no pl*) furniture

Mo'biltele,fon *n* mobile phone

möblieren [mø'bliːrən] *v/t* (*no -ge-*, *h*) furnish

mochte ['mɔxtə] *pret of* **mögen**

Mode ['moːdə] *f* (-; *-n*) fashion; **in Mode** in fashion; **Mode sein** be in fashion, F be in; **die neueste Mode** the latest fashion; **mit der Mode gehen** follow the fashion; **in (aus der) Mode kommen** come into (go out of) fashion

Modell [mo'dɛl] *n* (-s; -e) model; **j-m Modell stehen** or **sitzen** pose or sit for s.o.

'**Modellbau** *m* model construction

'**Modellbaukasten** *m* model construction kit

'**Modelleisenbahn** *f* model railway

modellieren [mode'li:rən] *v/t (no -ge-, h)* model

Modem ['mo:dɛm] *m, n (-s; -s)* EDP modem

'**Modenschau** *f* fashion show

Moderator [mode'ra:to:ɐ] *m (-s; -en* [modera'to:rən]), **Modera'torin** *f (-; -nen)* TV etc presenter, host, anchorman (anchorwoman)

moderieren [mode'ri:rən] *v/t (no -ge-, h)* TV etc present, host

moderig ['mo:dərɪç] *adj* musty, mo(u)ldy

modern[1] ['mo:dɐn] *v/i (ge-, h, sein)* mo(u)ld, rot, decay

modern[2] [mo'dɛrn] *adj* modern; fashionable

modernisieren [modɛrni'zi:rən] *v/t (no -ge-, h)* modernize, bring up to date

'**Modeschmuck** *m* costume jewel(le)ry

Modeschöpfer(in) fashion designer

Modewaren *pl* fashionwear

Modewort *n (-[e]s; -wörter)* vogue word, F in word

Modezeichner(in) fashion designer

Modezeitschrift *f* fashion magazine

modisch ['mo:dɪʃ] *adj* fashionable, stylish

Modul[1] [mo'du:l] *n (-s; -e)* EDP module

Modul[2] ['mo:dʊl] *m (-s;-n)* MATH, TECH module

Mofa ['mo:fa] *n (-s; -s)* (small) moped, motorized bicycle

mogeln ['mo:gəln] F *v/i (ge-, h)* cheat; crib

mögen ['mø:gən] *v/t (irr, ge-, h)* and *v/aux (irr, no -ge-, h)* like; **er mag sie (nicht)** he likes (doesn't like) her; **lieber mögen** like better, prefer; **nicht mögen** dislike; **was möchten Sie?** what would you like?; **ich möchte, dass du es weißt** I'd like you to know (it); **ich möchte lieber bleiben** I'd rather stay; **es mag sein** (, **dass**) it may be (that)

möglich ['mø:klɪç] **1.** *adj* possible; **alle möglichen** all sorts of; **sein Möglichstes tun** do what one can; do one's utmost; **nicht möglich!** you don't say (so)!; **so bald (schnell, oft) wie möglich** as soon (quickly, often) as possible; **2.** *adv*: **möglichst bald** *etc* as soon *etc* as possible

'**möglicher'weise** *adv* possibly

'**Möglichkeit** *f (-; -en)* possibility; opportunity; chance; **nach Möglichkeit** if possible

Mohammedaner [mohame'da:nɐ] *m (-s; -), **mohamme'danisch** *adj* Muslim

Mohn [mo:n] *m (-[e]s; -e)* BOT poppy

Möhre ['mø:rə] *f (-; -n)*, **Mohrrübe** ['mo:ʁə-] *f* BOT carrot

Molch [mɔlç] *m (-[e]s; -e)* ZO salamander

Mole ['mo:lə] *f (-; -n)* MAR mole, jetty

Molekül [mole'ky:l] *n (-s; -e)* CHEM molecule

molk [mɔlk] *pret of* **melken**

Molkerei [mɔlkə'rai] *f (-; -en)* dairy

Moll [mɔl] *n (-; no pl)* MUS minor (key); **a-Moll** A minor

mollig ['mɔlɪç] F *adj* snug, cozy, Br cosy; plump, chubby

Moment [mo'mɛnt] *m (-[e]s; -e)* moment; **(e-n) Moment bitte!** just a moment please!; **im Moment** at the moment

Monarch [mo'narç] *m (-en; -en)* monarch

Monarchie [monar'çi:] *f (-; -n)* monarchy

Monarchin [mo'narçɪn] *f (-; -nen)* monarch

Monarchist [monar'çɪst] *m (-en; -en)* monarchist

Monat ['mo:nat] *m (-[e]s; -e)* month; **zweimal im** *or* **pro Monat** twice a month

'**monatelang** *adv* for months

'**monatlich** *adj* and *adv* monthly

'**Monatsbinde** *f* sanitary napkin (Br towel)

Monatskarte *f* commuter ticket, Br (monthly) season ticket

Mönch [mœnç] *m (-[e]s; -e)* monk; friar

Mond [mo:nt] *m (-[e]s; -e* ['mo:ndə]) moon

Mondfinsternis *f* lunar eclipse

'**mondhell** *adj* moonlit

'**Mondlandefähre** *f* lunar module

Mondlandung *f* moon landing

Mondoberfläche *f* moon surface, lunar soil

Mondschein *m (-[e]s; no pl)* moonlight

Mondsichel *f* crescent

Mondumkreisung *f*, **Mondumlaufbahn** *f* lunar orbit

Monitor ['mo:nito:ɐ] *m (-s; -en* [moni'to:rən]) TV etc monitor

Monolog [mono'lo:k] *m (-[e]s; -e)* monolog(ue Br)

Monopol [mono'po:l] *n (-s; -e)* ECON monopoly

monoton [mono'to:n] *adj* monotonous

Monotonie [monoto'ni:] *f (-; -n)* monotony

Monoxid ['mo:nɔksi:t] *n* CHEM monoxide

Monster ['mɔnstɐ] *n (-s; -)* monster

Montag ['mo:nta:k] *m (-[e]s; -e)* Monday

Montage [mɔn'ta:ʒə] *f (-; -n)* TECH assembly; installation; **auf Montage sein** be away on a field job

Montageband *n (-[e]s; -bänder)* TECH assembly line

Montagehalle *f* TECH assembly shop

Monteur [mɔn'tøːɐ] *m* (-s; -e) TECH fitter; *esp* MOT, AVIAT mechanic

montieren [mɔn'tiːrən] *v/t* (*no* -ge-, h) TECH assemble; fit, attach; install(l)

Moor [moːɐ] *n* (-[e]s; -e) bog, moor(-land)

moorig ['moːrɪç] *adj* boggy

Moos [moːs] *n* (-es; -e) BOT moss

moosig ['moːzɪç] *adj* mossy

Moped ['moːpɛt] *n* (-s; -s) moped

Mops [mɔps] *m* (-es; *Möpse* ['mœpsə]) ZO pug(dog)

Moral [mo'raːl] *f* (-; *no pl*) morals, moral standards; MIL *etc* morale

mo'ralisch *adj* moral

moralisieren [morali'ziːrən] *v/i* (*no* -ge-, h) moralize

Morast [mo'rast] *m* (-[e]s; -e) morass, mire, mud

Mord [mɔrt] *m* (-[e]s; -e ['mɔrdə]) murder (*an dat* of); *e-n Mord begehen* commit murder

Mordanschlag *m esp* POL assassination attempt

Mörder ['mœrdɐ] *m* (-s; -), **'Mörderin** *f* (-; -nen) murderer; (hired) killer; *esp* POL assassin

'Mordkommissi,on *f* homicide division, *Br* murder squad

Mordpro,zess *m* JUR murder trial

'Mordsangst F *f*: *e-e Mordsangst haben* be scared stiff

Mordsglück F *n* stupendous luck

Mordskerl F *m* devil of a fellow

Mordswut F *f*: *e-e Mordswut haben* be in a hell of a rage

'Mordverdacht *m* suspicion of murder

Mordversuch *m* attempted murder

morgen ['mɔrgən] *adv* tomorrow; *morgen Abend* (*früh*) tomorrow night (morning); *morgen Mittag* at noon tomorrow; *morgen in e-r Woche* a week from tomorrow; *morgen um diese Zeit* this time tomorrow; *... von morgen* tomorrow's ...; ..., of tomorrow

'Morgen *m* (-s; -) morning; AGR acre; *heute Morgen* this morning; *am* (*frühen*) *Morgen* (early) in the morning; *am nächsten Morgen* the next morning

Morgenessen *Swiss n* breakfast

Morgengrauen *n* dawn; *im* or *bei Morgengrauen* at dawn

Morgenland *n* (-[e]s; *no pl*) Orient

Morgenmantel *m*, **Morgenrock** *m* dressing gown

'morgens *adv* in the morning; *von morgens bis abends* from morning till night

morgig ['mɔrgɪç] *adj* tomorrow's ...

Morphium ['mɔrfjʊm] *n* (-s; *no pl*) PHARM morphine

morsch [mɔrʃ] *adj* rotten; *morsch werden* rot

Morsealpha,bet ['mɔrzə-] *n* Morse code

Mörser ['mœrzə] *m* (-s; -) mortar (*a.* MIL)

'Morsezeichen *n* Morse signal

Mörtel ['mœrtəl] *m* (-s; -) mortar

Mosaik [moza'iːk] *n* (-s; -en) mosaic

Mosa'ikstein *m* piece

Moschee [mɔ'ʃeː] *f* (-; -n) mosque

Moskito [mɔs'kiːto] *m* (-s; -s) ZO mosquito

Moslem ['mɔslɛm] *m* (-s; -s), **moslemisch** [mɔs'leːmɪʃ] *adj*, **Moslime** [mɔs'leːmɪʃ] *f* (-; -n) Muslim

Most [mɔst] *m* (-[e]s; -e) grape juice; cider

Motiv [mo'tiːf] *n* (-s; -e) motive; PAINT, MUS motif

Motivation [motiva'tsjoːn] *f* (-; -en) motivation

motivieren [moti'viːrən] *v/t* (*no* -ge-, h) motivate

Motor ['moːtoːɐ, mo'toːɐ] *m* (-s; -en [mo'toːrən]) motor, engine

Motorboot *n* motor boat

Motorhaube *f* hood, *Br* bonnet

motorisieren [motori'ziːrən] *v/t* (*no* -ge-, h) motorize

'Motorleistung *f* (engine) performance

Motorrad *n* motorcycle, F motorbike; *Motorrad fahren* ride a motorcycle

Motorradfahrer(in) motorcyclist, biker

Motorroller *m* (motor) scooter

Motorsäge *f* power saw

Motorschaden *m* engine trouble (*or* failure)

Motte ['mɔtə] *f* (-; -n) ZO moth

Mottenkugel *f* mothball

mottenzerfressen *adj* moth-eaten

Motto ['mɔto] *n* (-s; -s) motto

Möwe ['møːvə] *f* (-; -n) ZO (sea)gull

Mücke ['mʏkə] *f* (-; -n) ZO gnat, midge, mosquito; *aus e-r Mücke e-n Elefanten machen* make a mountain out of a molehill

'Mückenstich *m* gnat bite

müde ['myːdə] *adj* tired; weary; sleepy; *müde sein* (*werden*) be (get) tired (*fig e-r Sache* of s.th.)

'Müdigkeit *f* (-; *no pl*) tiredness

Muff [mʊf] *m* (-[e]s; -e) muff

Muffe ['mʊfə] *f* (-; -n) TECH sleeve, socket

Muffel ['mʊfəl] F *m* (-s; -) sourpuss

muff(e)lig ['mʊf(ə)lɪç], **muffig** ['mʊfɪç] F *adj* musty; *contp* sulky, sullen

Mühe ['myːə] *f* (-; -n) trouble; effort; difficulty (*mit* s.th.); (*nicht*) *der Mühe wert* (not) worth the trouble; *j-m Mühe machen* give s.o. trouble; *sich Mühe geben* try hard; *sich die Mühe sparen* save o.s. the trouble; *mit Mühe und Not*

(just) barely
'**mühelos** *adv* without difficulty
mühen ['my:ən] *v/refl* (ge-, h) struggle, work hard
'**mühevoll** *adj* laborious
Mühle ['my:lə] *f* (-; -n) mill; morris
Mühsal ['my:za:l] *f* (-; -e) toil
mühsam ['my:za:m], '**mühselig 1.** *adj* laborious; **2.** *adv* with difficulty
Mulatte [mu'latə] *m* (-n; -n), **Mu'lattin** *f* (-; -nen) mulatto
Mulde ['muldə] *f* (-; -n) hollow
Mull [mul] *m* (-[e]s; -e) muslin; *esp Br* gauze
Müll [myl] *m* (-s; *no pl*) garbage, trash, *Br* refuse, rubbish
Müllabfuhr *f* garbage (*Br* refuse) collection
Müllbeseitigung *f* waste disposal
Müllbeutel *m* garbage bag, *Br* dustbin liner
'**Mullbinde** *f* MED gauze bandage
'**Müllcon,tainer** *m* garbage (*Br* rubbish) skip
Mülldepo,nie *f* dump
Mülleimer *m* garbage can, *Br* dustbin
Müllfahrer *m* garbage man, *Br* dustman
Müllhalde *f* dump
Müllhaufen *m* garbage (*Br* rubbish) heap
Müllkippe *f* dump
Müllschlucker *m* garbage (*Br* refuse) chute
Mülltonne *f* garbage can, *Br* dustbin
Müllverbrennungsanlage *f* (waste) incineration plant
Müllwagen *m* garbage truck, *Br* dustcart
Multiplikation [multiplika'tsjo:n] *f* (-; -en) MATH multiplication
multiplizieren [multipli'tsi:rən] *v/t* (*no -ge-, h*) MATH multiply (*mit* by)
Mumie ['mu:mjə] *f* (-; -n) mummy
Mumps [mumps] *m*, *f* (-; *no pl*) MED mumps
Mund [munt] *m* (-[e]s; *Münder* ['myndɐ]) mouth; F **den Mund vollnehmen** talk big; **halt den Mund!** shut up!
Mundart *f* dialect
münden ['myndən] *v/i* (ge-, h, sein) **münden in** (*acc*) *river etc:* flow into; *road etc:* lead into
'**Mundgeruch** *m* bad breath
'**Mundhar,monika** *f* MUS mouth organ, harmonica
mündig ['myndıç] *adj* emancipated; **mündig** (**werden**) JUR (come) of age
mündlich ['myntlıç] *adj* oral; verbal
'**Mundstück** *n* mouthpiece; tip
'**Mündung** *f* (-; -en) *river:* mouth; *gun:* muzzle

'**Mundwasser** *n* mouthwash
Mundwerk F *n:* **ein gutes Mundwerk haben** have the gift of the gab; **ein loses Mundwerk** a loose tongue
Mundwinkel *m* corner of the mouth
'**Mund-zu-'Mund-Beatmung** *f* (-; -en) MED mouth-to-mouth resuscitation, F kiss of life
Munition [muni'tsjo:n] *f* (-; -en) ammunition
munkeln ['muŋkəln] F *v/t* (ge-, h) **man munkelt, dass** rumo(u)r has it that
Münster ['mynstɐ] *n* (-s; -) cathedral, minster
munter ['muntɐ] *adj* awake; lively; merry
Münze ['myntsə] *f* (-; -n) coin; medal
Münzeinwurf *m* (coin) slot
Münzfernsprecher *m* pay phone
Münztank (**auto,mat**) *m* coin-operated (gas, *Br* petrol) pump
Münzwechsler *m* (-s; -) change machine
mürbe ['myrbə] *adj* tender; brittle; GASTR crisp
'**Mürbeteig** *m* short pastry; shortcake
Murmel ['murməl] *f* (-; -n) marble
'**murmeln** *v/t and v/i* (ge-, h) murmur
'**Murmeltier** *n* ZO marmot
murren ['murən] *v/i* (ge-, h) complain (*über* acc about)
mürrisch ['myrıʃ] *adj* sullen; grumpy
Mus [mu:s] *n* (-es; -e) mush; stewed fruit
Muschel ['muʃəl] *f* (-; -n) ZO mussel; shell
Museum [mu'ze:um] *n* (-s; *Museen*) museum
Musik [mu'zi:k] *f* (-; *no pl*) music
musikalisch [muzi'ka:lıʃ] *adj* musical
Mu'sikanlage *f* hi-fi or stereo set
Musikauto,mat *m*, **Musikbox** *f* juke box
Musiker ['mu:zikɐ] *m* (-s; -), '**Musikerin** *f* (-; -nen) musician
Mu'sikinstru,ment *n* musical instrument
Musikka,pelle *f* band
Musikkas,sette *f* music cassette
Musiklehrer(in) music teacher
Musikstunde *f* music lesson
musisch ['mu:zıʃ] *adv:* **musisch interessiert** (**begabt**) fond of (gifted for) fine arts and music
musizieren [muzi'tsi:rən] *v/i* (*no -ge-, h*) make music
Muskat [mus'ka:t] *m* (-[e]s; -e), **Muskatnuss** *f* BOT nutmeg
Muskel ['muskəl] *m* (-s; -n) ANAT muscle
Muskelkater F *m* aching muscles
Muskelzerrung *f* MED pulled muscle
muskulös [musku'lø:s] *adj* muscular, brawny
Müsli ['my:sli] *n* (-s; -) GASTR granola, *Br* muesli

Muss *n* (-; *no pl*) necessity; *es ist ein Muss* it is a must

Muße ['muːsə] *f* (-; *no pl*) leisure; spare time

müssen ['mysən] *v/i* (*irr, ge-*) *and v/aux* (*irr, no -ge-, h*) must, have (got) to; *du musst den Film sehen!* you must see the film!; *ich muss jetzt (m-e) Hausaufgaben machen* I have (got) to do my homework now; *sie muss krank sein* she must be ill; *du musst es nicht tun* you need not do it; *das müsstest du (doch) wissen* you ought to know (that); *sie müsste zu Hause sein* she should (ought to be) be (at) home; *das müsste schön sein!* that would be nice!; *du hättest ihm helfen müssen* you ought to have helped him

müßig ['myːsɪç] *adj* idle; useless

musste ['mʊstə] *pret of* **müssen**

Muster ['mʊstɐ] *n* (-s; -) pattern; sample; model

'**mustergültig, musterhaft** *adj* exemplary; *sich mustergültig benehmen* behave perfectly

'**Musterhaus** *n* showhouse

'**mustern** *v/t* (*ge-, h*) eye *s.o.*; size *s.o.* up; MIL *gemustert werden* F have one's medical

Musterung ['mʊstərʊŋ] *f* (-; *-en*) MIL medical (examination for military service)

Mut [muːt] *m* (-[e]s; *no pl*) courage; *j-m Mut machen* encourage *s.o.*; *den Mut verlieren* lose courage; → *zumute*

mutig ['muːtɪç] *adj* courageous, brave

'**mutlos** *adj* discouraged

'**mutmaßen** *v/t* (*ge-, h*) speculate

'**mutmaßlich** *adj* probable; presumed

'**Mutprobe** *f* test of courage

Mutter ['mʊtɐ] *f* (-; *Mütter* ['mytɐ]) mother; TECH nut

Mutterboden *m*, **Muttererde** *f* AGR topsoil

mütterlich ['mytɐlɪç] *adj* motherly

'**mütterlicherseits** *adv*: *Onkel etc mütterlicherseits* maternal uncle *etc*

'**Mutterliebe** *f* motherly love

'**mutterlos** *adj* motherless

'**Muttermal** *n* birthmark, mole

Muttermilch *f* mother's milk

Mutterschaftsurlaub *m* maternity leave

Mutterschutz *m* JUR legal protection of expectant and nursing mothers

Muttersöhnchen *contp n* sissy

Muttersprache *f* mother tongue

Muttersprachler [-ʃpraːxlɐ] *m* (-s; -) native speaker

Muttertag *m* Mother's Day

Mutti ['mʊti] F *f* (-; *-s*) mom(my), *esp Br* mum(my)

'**mutwillig** *adj* wanton

Mütze ['mytsə] *f* (-; *-n*) cap

MwSt ABBR *of* **Mehrwertsteuer** VAT, value-added tax

mysteriös [mysteˈrjøːs] *adj* mysterious

mystisch ['mystɪʃ] *adj* mystic(al)

mythisch ['myːtɪʃ] *adj* mythical

Mythologie [mytoloˈgiː] *f* (-; *-n*) mythology

Mythos ['myːtɔs] *m* (-; *Mythen*) myth

N

N ABBR *of* **Nord(en)** N, north

na [na] *int* well; *na und?* so what?; *na gut!* all right then; *na ja* (oh) well; *na(, na)!* come on!, come now!; *na so (et)was!* what do you know!, *Br* I say!; *na, dann nicht!* oh, forget it!; *na also!* there you are!; *na, warte!* just you wait!

Nabe ['naːbə] *f* (-; *-n*) TECH hub

Nabel ['naːbəl] *m* (-s; -) ANAT navel

'**Nabelschnur** *f* ANAT umbilical chord

nach [naːx] *prp* (*dat*) *and adv* to, toward(s), for; after; *time*: after, past; according to, by; *nach Hause* home; *abfahren nach* leave for; *nach rechts (Süden)* to the right (south); *nach oben* up (-stairs); *nach unten* down(stairs); *nach vorn (hinten)* to the front (back); *der Reihe nach* one after the other; *s-e Uhr nach dem Radio stellen* set one's watch by the radio; *nach m-r Uhr* by my watch; *suchen (fragen) nach* look (ask) for; *nach Gewicht (Zeit)* by weight (the hour); *riechen (schmecken) nach* smell (taste) of; *nach und nach* gradually; *nach wie vor* as before, still

'**nachahmen** [-aːmən] *v/t* (*sep, -ge-, h*) imitate, copy; take off

'**Nachahmung** *f* (-; *-en*) imitation

Nachbar ['naxbaːɐ] m (-n; -n), **'Nachbarin** f (-; -nen) neighbo(u)r

'Nachbarschaft f (-; no pl) neighbo(u)rhood, vicinity

'Nachbau m (-[e]s; -ten) TECH reproduction

'nachbauen v/t (sep, -ge-, h) copy, reproduce

'Nachbildung f (-; -en) copy, imitation; replica; dummy

'nachblicken v/i (sep, -ge-, h) look after

nach'dem cj after, when; **je nachdem wie** depending on how

'nachdenken v/i (irr, **denken**, sep, -ge-, h) think; **nachdenken über** (acc) think about, think s.th. over

'nachdenklich adj thoughtful; **es macht e-n nachdenklich** it makes you think

'Nachdruck[1] m (-[e]s; no pl) emphasis, stress

'Nachdruck[2] (-[e]s; -e) reprint

'nachdrucken v/t (sep, -ge-, h) reprint

'nachdrücklich [-dryklıç] adj emphatic; forceful; **nachdrücklich raten** (**empfehlen**) advise (recommend) strongly

'nacheifern v/i (sep, -ge-, h) **j-m nacheifern** emulate s.o.

nachei'nander adv one after the other, in (or by) turns

'nacherzählen v/t (sep, no -ge-, h) retell

'Nacherzählung f (-; -en) PED reproduction

'Nachfolge f (-; no pl) succession; **j-s Nachfolge antreten** succeed s.o.

'nachfolgen v/i (sep, -ge-, sein) (dat) succeed s.o.

'Nachfolger(in) [-fɔlgɐ (-gərɪn)] (-s; -/-; -nen) successor

'nachforschen v/i (sep, -ge-, h) investigate

'Nachforschung f (-; -en) investigation, inquiry

'Nachfrage f (-; -n) inquiry; ECON demand

'nachfragen v/i (sep, -ge-, h) inquire, ask

'nachfühlen v/t (sep, -ge-, h) **j-m et. nachfühlen** understand how s.o. feels

'nachfüllen v/t (sep, -ge-, h) refill

'nachgeben v/i (irr, **geben**, sep, -ge-, h) give (way); fig give in

'Nachgebühr f (-; -en) post surcharge

'nachgehen v/i (irr, **gehen**, sep, -ge-, sein) follow (a. fig); watch: be slow; **e-r Sache nachgehen** investigate s.th.; **s-r Arbeit nachgehen** go about one's work

'Nachgeschmack m (-[e]s; no pl) aftertaste (a. fig)

'nachgiebig [-giːbıç] adj yielding, soft (both a. fig)

'Nachgiebigkeit f (-; no pl) yieldingness, softness (both a. fig)

'nachhaltig [-haltıç] adj lasting, enduring

nach'hause → **Haus**

nach'her adv afterwards; **bis nachher!** see you later!, so long!

'Nachhilfe f help, assistance; PED → **Nachhilfestunden** pl, **Nachhilfeunterricht** m PED private lesson(s), coaching

'nachholen v/t (sep, -ge-, h) make up for, catch up on

'Nachkomme m (-n; -n) descendant, pl esp JUR issue

'nachkommen v/i (irr, **kommen**, sep, -ge-, sein) follow, come later; (dat) comply with

'Nachkriegs... in cpds postwar ...

Nachlass ['naːxlas] m (-es; -lässe [-lɛsə]) ECON reduction, discount; JUR estate

'nachlassen v/i (irr, **lassen**, sep, -ge-, h) decrease, diminish, go down; effect etc: wear off; student etc: slacken one's effort; interest etc: flag; health etc: fail, deteriorate

'nachlässig adj careless, negligent

'nachlaufen v/i (irr, **laufen**, sep, -ge-, sein) run after

'nachlesen v/t (irr, **lesen**, sep, -ge-, h) look up

'nachmachen v/t (sep, -ge-, h) imitate, copy; counterfeit, forge

'Nachmittag m afternoon; **heute Nachmittag** this afternoon

'nachmittags adv in the afternoon

Nachnahme ['naːxnaːmə] f (-; -n) ECON cash on delivery; **per Nachnahme schicken** send C.O.D.

'Nachname m surname, last (or family) name

Nachporto n surcharge

'nachprüfen v/t (sep, -ge-, h) check (up), make sure (of)

'nachrechnen v/t (sep, -ge-, h) check

'Nachrede f: **üble Nachrede** malicious gossip; JUR defamation (of character), slander

Nachricht ['naːxrɪçt] f (-; -en) news; message; report; information, notice; pl news (report), newscast; **e-e gute (schlechte) Nachricht** good (bad) news; **Sie hören Nachrichten** here is the news

'Nachrichtendienst m news service; MIL intelligence service

Nachrichtensatel,lit m communications satellite

Nachrichtensprecher(in) newscaster, esp Br newsreader

Nachrichtentechnik f telecommunications

'Nachruf m obituary

'nachrüsten v/i (sep, -ge-, h) POL, MIL close

the armament gap

nachsagen *v/t* (*sep*, *-ge-*, *h*) *j-m Schlechtes nachsagen* speak badly of s.o.; *man sagt ihm nach, dass er …* he is said to *inf*

'**Nachsai,son** *f* off-peak season; *in der Nachsaison* out of season

nachschlagen (*irr*, *schlagen*, *sep*, *-ge-*, *h*) **1.** *v/t* look up; **2.** *v/i*: *nachschlagen in* (*dat*) consult

'**Nachschlagewerk** *n* reference book

'**Nachschlüssel** *m* duplicate (*or* skeleton) key

Nachschrift *f* postscript; dictation

Nachschub *m esp* MIL supplies

'**nachsehen** (*irr*, *sehen*, *sep*, *-ge-*, *h*) **1.** *v/t* follow with one's eyes; (have a) look; *nachsehen ob* (go and) see whether; **2.** *v/t* look *or* go over *or* through; correct, mark; check (*a.* TECH)

nachsenden *v/t* ([*irr*, *senden*,] *sep*, *-ge-*, *h*) send on, forward; *bitte nachsenden!* *post* please forward!

'**Nachsilbe** *f* LING suffix

'**nachsitzen** *v/i* (*irr*, *sitzen*, *sep*, *-ge-*, *h*) stay in (after school), be kept in; *nachsitzen lassen* keep in, detain

'**Nachspann** *m* (*-[e]s; -e*) film: credits *pl*

'**Nachspiel** *n* sequel, consequences

'**nachspielen** *v/i* (*sep*, *-ge-*, *h*) SPORT *5 Minuten nachspielen lassen* allow 5 minutes for injury time

'**Nachspielzeit** *f esp* soccer: injury time

'**nachspio,nieren** *v/i* (*no -ge-*, *h*) spy (up-)on

nachsprechen *v/t* (*irr*, *sprechen*, *sep*, *-ge-*, *h*) *j-m et. nachsprechen* say *or* repeat s.th. after s.o.

nächst'beste ['nɛːçst-] *adj* first, F any old; next-best, second-best

nächste ['nɛːçstə] *adj* next; nearest (*a. relative*); *in den nächsten Tagen* (*Jahren*) in the next few days (years); *in nächster Zeit* in the near future; *was kommt als Nächstes?* what comes next?; *der Nächste, bitte!* next please!

'**nachstehen** *v/i* (*irr*, *stehen*, *sep*, *-ge-*, *h*) *j-m in nichts nachstehen* be in no way inferior to s.o.

'**nachstellen** (*sep*, *-ge-*, *h*) **1.** *v/t* put back (*watch*); TECH (re)adjust; **2.** *v/i*: *j-m nachstellen* be after s.o.

'**Nachstellung** *f* (*-; -en*) persecution

'**Nächstenliebe** *f* charity

Nacht [naxt] *f* (*-; Nächte* ['nɛçtə]) night; *Tag und Nacht* night and day; *die ganze Nacht* all night (long); *heute Nacht* tonight; last night

'**Nachtdienst** *m* night duty; *Nachtdienst*

haben PHARM be open all night

'**Nachteil** *m* disadvantage, drawback; *im Nachteil sein* be at a disadvantage (*gegenüber* compared with)

'**nachteilig** [-tailiç] *adj* disadvantageous

'**Nachtessen** *Swiss n → Abendbrot*

Nachtfalter *m* ZO moth

Nachthemd *n* nightgown, nightdress, F nightie; nightshirt

Nachtigall ['naxtigal] *f* (*-; -en*) ZO nightingale

'**Nachtisch** *m* (*-[e]s; no pl*) dessert; sweet

nächtlich ['nɛçtliç] *adj* nightly; at *or* by night

'**Nachtlo,kal** *n* nightclub

Nachtrag ['naːxtraːk] *m* (*-[e]s; -träge* [-trɛːɡə]) supplement

nachtragen *fig v/t* (*irr*, *tragen*, *sep*, *-ge-*, *h*) *j-m et. nachtragen* bear s.o. a grudge

'**nachtragend** *adj* unforgiving

'**nachträglich** [-trɛːkliç] *adj* additional; later; belated

nachts *adv* at night, in the night(time)

'**Nachtschicht** *f* night shift; *Nachtschicht haben* be on night shift

'**nachtschlafend** *adj*: *zu nachtschlafender Zeit* in the middle of the night

'**Nachttisch** *m* bedside table

'**Nachttopf** *m* chamber pot

'**Nachtwächter** *m* night watchman

'**nachwachsen** *v/i* (*irr*, *wachsen*, *sep*, *-ge-*, *sein*) grow again

'**Nachwahl** *f* PARL special election, *Br* by-election

Nachweis ['naːxvais] *m* (*-es; -e*) proof, evidence

'**nachweisbar** *adj* demonstrable; *esp* CHEM *etc* detectable

'**nachweisen** *v/t* (*irr*, *weisen*, *sep*, *-ge-*, *h*) prove; *esp* CHEM *etc* detect

'**nachweislich** *adv* as can be proved

'**Nachwelt** *f* (*-; no pl*) posterity

Nachwirkung *f* aftereffect(s), *pl a.* aftermath

Nachwort *n* (*-[e]s; -worte*) epilog(ue)

'**Nachwuchs** *m* (*-es; no pl*) young talent, F new blood

Nachwuchs… *in cpds …autor, …schauspieler etc*: talented *or* promising young …, up-and-coming …

'**nachzahlen** *v/t* (*sep*, *-ge-*, *h*) pay extra

'**nachzählen** *v/t* (*sep*, *-ge-*, *h*) count over (again), check

'**Nachzahlung** *f* additional *or* extra payment

'**Nachzügler** ['naːxtsyːklɐ] *m* (*-s; -*) straggler, latecomer

Nacken ['nakən] *m* (*-s; -*) ANAT (back *or* nape of the) neck

Nackenstütze f headrest
nackt [nakt] adj naked; *esp* PAINT, PHOT nude; bare (a. fig); fig plain; **völlig nackt** stark naked; **sich nackt ausziehen** strip; **nackt baden** swim in the nude; **j-n nackt malen** paint s.o. in the nude
Nadel ['naːdəl] f (-; -n) needle; pin; brooch
Nadelbaum m BOT conifer(ous tree)
Nadelöhr n eye of a needle
Nadelstich m pinprick (a. fig)
Nagel ['naːɡəl] m (-s; Nägel ['nɛːɡəl]) nail; **an den Nägeln kauen** bite one's nails
Nagellack m nail varnish or polish
'nageln v/t (ge-, h) nail (**an** acc, **auf** acc to)
'nagelneu F adj brand-new
Nagelpflege f manicure
nagen ['naːɡən] (ge-, h) **1.** v/i gnaw (**an** dat at); **an e-m Knochen nagen** pick a bone; **2.** v/t gnaw
Nagetier n ZO rodent
Nahaufnahme f PHOT etc close-up
nahe [naːə] adj near, close (**bei** to); nearby; **nahe kommen** (dat) come close to; fig →**nahekommen**; →**nahelegen**; →**nahelegen**; →**naheliegend**
Nähe ['nɛːə] f (-; no pl) nearness; neighbo(u)rhood, vicinity; **in der Nähe des Bahnhofs** near the station; **ganz in der Nähe** quite near, close by; **in deiner Nähe** near you
nahegehen v/i (irr, gehen, sep, -ge-, sein): **j-m nahegehen** affect s.o. deeply
'nahekommen v/i (irr, kommen, sep, -ge-, sein) fig come close to
'nahelegen v/t (sep, -ge-, h) suggest
'naheliegen v/i (irr, liegen, sep, -ge-, h) seem likely
'naheliegend adj likely, obvious
nahen ['naːən] v/i (ge-, sein) approach
nähen ['nɛːən] v/t and v/i (ge-, h) sew; make
Nähere ['nɛːərə] n (-n; no pl) details, particulars
nähern ['nɛːɛn] v/refl (ge-, h) approach, get near(er) or close(r) (dat to)
'nahezu adv nearly, almost
'Nähgarn n (sewing) cotton
'Nahkampf m MIL close combat
nahm [naːm] pret of **nehmen**
'Nähmaschine f sewing machine
'Nähnadel f (sewing) needle
nähren ['nɛːrən] v/t (ge-, h) feed; fig nurture
nahrhaft ['naːɐhaft] adj nutritious, nourishing
Nährstoff ['nɛːɐ-] m nutrient
Nahrung ['naːrʊŋ] f (-; no pl) food, nourishment; AGR feed; diet

'Nahrungsmittel pl food(stuffs)
Nährwert ['nɛːɐ-] m nutritional value
Naht [naːt] f (-; Nähte ['nɛːtə]) seam; MED suture
'Nahverkehr m local traffic
'Nahverkehrszug m local or commuter train
'Nähzeug n sewing kit
naiv [naˈiːf] adj naive
Naivität [naiviˈtɛːt] f (-; no pl) naivety
Name ['naːmə] m (-ns; -n) name; **im Namen von** on behalf of; **nur dem Namen nach** in name only
'namenlos adj nameless, fig a. unspeakable
'namens adv by (the) name of, named, called
'Namenstag m name day
Namensvetter m namesake
Namenszug m signature
namentlich ['naːməntlɪç] adj and adv by name
nämlich ['nɛːmlɪç] adv that is (to say), namely; you see or know
nannte ['nantə] pret of **nennen**
Napf [napf] m (-[e]s; Näpfe ['nɛpfə]) bowl, basin
Narbe ['narbə] f (-; -n) scar
narbig ['narbɪç] adj scarred
Narkose [narˈkoːzə] f (-; -n) MED an(a)esthesia; **in Narkose** under an an(a)esthetic
Narr [nar] m (-en; -en) fool; **j-n zum Narren halten** fool s.o.
'narrensicher adj foolproof
närrisch ['nɛrɪʃ] adj foolish; **närrisch vor** (dat) mad with
Narzisse [narˈtsɪsə] f (-; -n) BOT daffodil
nasal [naˈzaːl] adj nasal
naschen ['naʃən] v/i and v/t (ge-, h) nibble (**an** dat at); **gern naschen** have a sweet tooth
Nascherei [naʃəˈraiən] pl dainties, goodies, sweets
'naschhaft adj sweet-toothed
Nase ['naːzə] f (-; -n) ANAT nose (a. fig); **sich die Nase putzen** blow one's nose; **in der Nase bohren** pick one's nose; F **die Nase voll haben (von)** be fed up (with)
'Nasenbluten n MED nosebleed
Nasenloch n nostril
Nasenspitze f tip of the nose
Nashorn n ZO rhinoceros, F rhino
nass [nas] adj wet; **triefend nass** soaking (wet)
Nässe ['nɛsə] f (-; no pl) wet(-ness)
'nässen (ge-, h) **1.** v/t wet; **2.** v/i MED weep
'nasskalt adj damp and cold, raw

Nation [naˈtsjoːn] *f* (-; *-en*) nation
national [natsjoˈnaːl] *adj* national
Natio'nalhymne *f* national anthem
Nationalismus [natsjonaˈlɪsmʊs] *m* (-; *no pl*) nationalism
Nationalität [natsjonaliˈtɛːt] *f* (-; *-en*) nationality
Natio'nalmannschaft *f* SPORT national team
Nationalpark *m* national park
Natio'nalsozia,lismus *m* HIST National Socialism, *contp* Nazism
Natio'nalsozia,list *m*, **natio'nalsozia,listisch** *adj* HIST National Socialist, *contp* Nazi
Natter [ˈnatɐ] *f* (-; *-n*) ZO adder, viper (*a. fig*)
Natur [naˈtuːɐ] *f* (-; *-en*) nature; ***von Natur (aus)*** by nature
Naturalismus [naturaˈlɪsmʊs] *m* (-; *no pl*) naturalism
Na'turereignis *n*, **Naturerscheinung** *f* natural phenomenon
Naturforscher *m* naturalist
Naturgeschichte *f* natural history
Naturgesetz *n* law of nature
na'turgetreu *adj* true to life; lifelike
Na'turkata,strophe *f* (natural) catastrophe *or* disaster, act of God
natürlich [naˈtyːɐlɪç] **1.** *adj* natural; **2.** *adv* naturally, of course
Na'turschätze *pl* natural resources
Naturschutz *m* nature conservation; ***unter Naturschutz*** protected
Naturschützer [-ʃʏtsɐ] *m* (-s; -) conservationist
Naturschutzgebiet *n* nature reserve; national park
Naturvolk *n* primitive race
Naturwissenschaft *f* (natural) science
n. Chr. ABBR *of* **nach Christus** AD, Anno Domini
Nebel [ˈneːbəl] *m* (-s; -) fog; mist; haze; smoke
Nebelhorn *n* foghorn
Nebelleuchte *f* MOT fog light
neben [ˈneːbən] *prp* (*dat and acc*) beside, next to; besides, apart from; compared with; ***neben anderem*** among other things; ***setz dich neben mich*** sit by me *or* by my side
neben'an *adv* next door
neben'bei *adv* in addition, at the same time; ***nebenbei (gesagt)*** by the way
'Nebenberuf *m* second job, sideline
'nebenberuflich *adv* as a sideline
'Nebenbuhler [-buːlɐ] *m* (-s; -), **'Nebenbuhlerin** *f* (-; *-nen*) rival
'nebenei'nander *adv* side by side; next

(door) to each other; **nebeneinander bestehen** coexist
'Nebeneinkünfte *pl*, **Nebeneinnahmen** *pl* extra money
Nebenfach *n* PED *etc* minor (subject), *Br* subsidiary subject
Nebenfluss *m* tributary
Nebengebäude *n* next-door *or* adjoining building; annex(e)
Nebenhaus *n* house next door
Nebenkosten *pl* extras
Nebenmann *m*: ***dein Nebenmann*** the person next to you
Nebenpro,dukt *n* by-product
Nebenrolle *f* THEA supporting role, minor part (*a. fig*); cameo (role)
Nebensache *f* minor matter; ***das ist Nebensache*** that's of little *or* no importance
'nebensächlich *adj* unimportant
'Nebensatz *m* LING subordinate clause
Nebenstelle *f* TEL extension
Nebenstraße *f* side street; minor road
Nebenstrecke *f* RAIL branch line
Nebentisch *m* next table
Nebenverdienst *m* extra earnings
Nebenwirkung *f* side effect
Nebenzimmer *n* adjoining room
neblig [ˈneːblɪç] *adj* foggy; misty; hazy
necken [ˈnɛkən] *v/t* (*ge-, h*) tease
Neckerei [nɛkəˈrai] *f* (-; *-en*) teasing
'neckisch *adj* playful, teasing
Neffe [ˈnɛfə] *m* (-n; -n) nephew
negativ [neˈgatiːf] *adj* negative
'Negativ *n* (-s; *-e*) PHOT negative
Neger [ˈneːgɐ] *m* (-s; -), **Negerin** [ˈneːgə-rɪn] *f* (-; *-nen*) *neg!* → **Schwarze**
nehmen [ˈneːmən] *v/t* (*irr, ge-, h*) take (*a. sich nehmen*); ***j-m et. nehmen*** take s.th. (away) from s.o. (*a. fig*); ***sich e-n Tag frei nehmen*** take a day off; ***j-n an die Hand nehmen*** take s.o. by the hand
Neid [nait] *m* (-es; *no pl*) envy; ***reiner Neid*** sheer envy; **neidisch** [ˈnaidɪʃ] *adj* envious (***auf*** *acc* of)
Neige [ˈnaigə] *f*: ***zur Neige gehen*** draw to its close; run out
'neigen (*ge-, h*) **1.** *v/t and refl* bend, incline; **2.** *v/i*: ***zu et. neigen*** tend to (do) s.th.
'Neigung *f* (-; *-en*) inclination (*a. fig*), slope, incline; *fig* tendency
nein [nain] *adv* no
Nektar [ˈnɛktaːɐ] *m* (-s; *-e*) BOT nectar
Nelke [ˈnɛlkə] *f* (-; *-n*) BOT carnation; GASTR clove
nennen [ˈnɛnən] *v/t* (*irr, ge-, h*) name, call; mention; ***sich nennen*** call o.s., be called; ***man nennt ihn ...*** he is called ...;

das nenne ich ...! that's what I call ...!

'nennenswert adj worth mentioning

Nenner ['nɛnɐ] m (-s; -) MATH denominator

'Nennwert m ECON nominal or face value; ***zum Nennwert*** at par

Neo..., **neo...** [neo-] in cpds ...faschist etc: neo-...

Neon ['ne:ɔn] n (-s; no pl) CHEM neon

'Neonröhre f neon tube

Nepp [nɛp] F m (-s; no pl) rip-off

neppen ['nɛpən] F v/t (ge-, h) fleece, rip s.o. off

Nerv [nɛrf] m (-s; -en) ANAT nerve; ***j-m auf die Nerven fallen*** or ***gehen*** get on s.o.'s nerves; ***die Nerven behalten*** (***verlieren***) keep (lose) one's head

nerven ['nɛrfən] F v/t and v/i (ge-, h) be a pain in the neck (***j-n*** to s.o.)

'Nervenarzt m, **'Nervenärztin** f neurologist

'nervenaufreibend adj nerve-racking

'Nervenbelastung f nervous strain

'Nervenkitzel m thrill, F kick(s)

'nervenkrank adj mentally ill

'Nervensäge F f pain in the neck

Nervensys,tem n nervous system

Nervenzusammenbruch m nervous breakdown

nervös [nɛr'vøːs] adj nervous

Nervosität [nɛrvozi'tɛːt] f (-; no pl) nervousness

Nerz [nɛrts] m (-es; -e) ZO mink

Nessel ['nɛsəl] f (-; -n) BOT nettle

Nest [nɛst] n (-[e]s; -er ['nɛstɐ]) ZO nest; F contp one-horse town

nett [nɛt] adj nice; kind; ***so nett sein und et.*** (or ***et. zu***) ***tun*** be so kind as to do s.th.

netto ['nɛto] adv ECON net

Netz [nɛts] n (-es; -e) net; RAIL, TEL, EDP network; ELECTR mains; ***am Netz sein*** EDP be in the network

Netzhaut f ANAT retina

Netzkarte f RAIL area season ticket

neu [nɔy] adj new; fresh; fig modern; ***neuere Sprachen*** modern languages; ***neueste Nachrichten*** (***Mode***) latest news (fashion); ***von neuem*** anew, afresh; ***seit neu(st)em*** since (very) recently; ***viel Neues*** a lot of new things; ***was gibt es Neues?*** what's the news?, what's new?

'neuartig adj novel

'Neubau m (-[e]s; -ten) new building

Neubaugebiet n new housing estate

neuerdings ['nɔyɐ'dɪŋs] adv lately, recently

Neuerer ['nɔyərɐ] m (-s; -) innovator

'Neuerung f (-; -en) innovation

'Neugestaltung f reorganization, reformation

'Neugier f, **Neugierde** ['nɔygiːɐdə] f (-; no pl) curiosity

'neugierig adj curious (***auf*** acc about); F contp nos(e)y; ***ich bin neugierig, ob*** I wonder if

'Neugierige [-giːrigə] contp pl rubbernecks

'Neuheit f (-; -en) novelty

Neuigkeit ['nɔyɪçkaɪt] f (-; -en) (piece of) news

'Neujahr n New Year('s Day); ***Prost Neujahr!*** Happy New Year!

'neulich adv the other day

Neuling ['nɔylɪŋ] m (-s; -e) newcomer, F greenhorn

'neumodisch contp adj newfangled

'Neumond m new moon

neun [nɔyn] adj nine

'neunte adj ninth

'Neuntel n (-s; -) ninth (part)

'neuntens adv ninthly

'neunzehn adj nineteen

'neunzehnte adj nineteenth

'neunzig adj ninety

'neunzigste adj ninetieth

Neurose [nɔy'roːzə] f (-; -n) MED neurosis

neurotisch [nɔy'roːtɪʃ] adj MED neurotic

'neusprachlich adj modern-language

neutral [nɔy'traːl] adj neutral

Neutralität [nɔytrali'tɛːt] f (-; no pl) neutrality

Neutronen... [nɔy'troːnən-] PHYS in cpds ...bombe etc: neutron ...

Neutrum ['nɔytrʊm] n (-s; -tra) LING neuter

'Neuverfilmung f remake

'neuwertig adj as good as new

'Neuzeit f (-; no pl) modern times

nicht [nɪçt] adv not; ***überhaupt nicht*** not at all; ***nicht*** (***ein***)***mal***, ***gar nicht erst*** not even; ***nicht mehr*** not any more or longer; ***sie ist nett*** (***wohnt hier***), ***nicht*** (***wahr***)***?*** she's nice (lives here), isn't (doesn't) she?; ***nicht so ... wie*** not as ... as; ***noch nicht*** not yet; ***nicht besser*** (***als***) no (or not any) better (than); ***ich*** (***auch***) ***nicht*** I don't or I'm not (either); (***bitte***) ***nicht!*** (please) don't!

'Nicht... in cpds ...mitglied, ...schwimmer etc: mst non-...

Nichtbeachtung f disregard; non-observance

Nichte ['nɪçtə] f (-; -n) niece

nichtig ['nɪçtɪç] adj trivial; JUR void, invalid

'Nichtraucher m, **'Nichtraucherin** f nonsmoker

nichts *indef pron* nothing, not anything; **nichts** (**anderes**) **als** nothing but; **gar nichts** nothing at all; F **das ist nichts** that's no good; **nichts sagend** meaningless

Nichts *n* (-s; *no pl*) nothing(ness); **aus dem Nichts** appear *etc* from nowhere; build *etc* from nothing

nichtsdesto'weniger *adv* nevertheless

'nichtsnutzig [-nʊtsɪç] *adj* good-for--nothing, worthless

'nichtssagend *adj* meaningless

'Nichtstuer [-tu:ɐ] *m* (-s; -) do-nothing, F bum

nicken ['nɪkən] *v/i* (ge-, h) nod (one's head)

nie [ni:] *adv* never, at no time; **fast nie** hardly ever; **nie und nimmer** never ever

nieder ['ni:dɐ] **1.** *adj* low; **2.** *adv* down

'Niedergang *m* (-[e]s; *no pl*) decline

'niedergeschlagen *adj* depressed, (feeling) down

'Niederlage *f* defeat, F beating

'niederlassen *v/refl* (*irr*, *lassen*, *sep*, -ge-, h) settle (down); ECON set up (**als** as)

'Niederlassung *f* (-; -en) ECON establishment; branch

'niederlegen *v/t* (*sep*, -ge-, h) lay down (*a. office etc*); **die Arbeit niederlegen** (go on) strike, down tools, F walk out; **sich niederlegen** lie down; go to bed

niedermetzeln *v/t* (*sep*, -ge-, h) massacre

'Niederschlag *m* METEOR rain(fall); PHYS fallout; CHEM precipitate; boxing: knock-down

'niederschlagen *v/t* (*irr*, *schlagen*, *sep*, -ge-, h) knock down; cast down (*eyes*); fig put down (*revolt etc*); JUR quash; **sich niederschlagen** CHEM precipitate

'niederschmettern fig *v/t* (*sep*, -ge-, h) shatter, crush

'niederträchtig *adj* base, mean

Niederung ['ni:dərʊŋ] *f* (-; -en) lowland(s)

niedlich ['ni:tlɪç] *adj* pretty, sweet, cute

niedrig ['ni:drɪç] *adj* low (*a. fig*); fig light (*sentence etc*); **niedrig fliegen** fly low

niemals ['ni:ma:ls] → **nie**

niemand ['ni:mant] *indef pron* nobody, no one, not anybody; **niemand von ihnen** none of them

'Niemandsland *n* (-[e]s; *no pl*) no-man's-land

Niere ['ni:rə] *f* (-; -n) ANAT kidney

nieseln ['ni:zəln] *v/i* (ge-, h) drizzle

'Nieselregen *m* drizzle

niesen ['ni:zən] *v/i* (ge-, h) sneeze

Niete[1] ['ni:tə] *f* (-; -n) TECH rivet

'Niete[2] *f* (-; -n) blank; F failure

Nikolaustag ['nɪkolaus-] *m* St. Nicholas' Day

Nikotin [niko'ti:n] *n* (-s; *no pl*) CHEM nicotine

Nilpferd ['ni:l-] *n* ZO hippopotamus, F hippo

Nippel ['nɪpəl] *m* (-s; -) TECH nipple

nippen ['nɪpən] *v/i* (ge-, h) sip (**an** *dat* at)

nirgends ['nɪrgənts] *adv* nowhere

Nische ['ni:ʃə] *f* (-; -n) niche, recess

nisten ['nɪstən] *v/i* (ge-, h) ZO nest

'Nistplatz *m* ZO nesting place

Niveau [ni'vo:] *n* (-s; -s) level, fig *a.* standard

Nixe ['nɪksə] *f* (-; -n) water nymph, mermaid

noch [nɔx] *adv* still; **noch nicht** not yet; **noch nie** never before; **er hat nur noch 5 Mark** (**Minuten**) he has only 5 marks (minutes) left; (*sonst*) **noch et.?** anything else?; **ich möchte noch et.** (**Tee**) I'd like some more (tea); **noch ein**(**e**, **-n**)**...**, **bitte** another ..., please; **noch einmal** once more *or* again; **noch zwei Stunden** another two hours, two hours to go; **noch besser** (**schlimmer**) even better (worse); **noch gestern** only yesterday; **und wenn es noch so ... ist** however (*or* no matter how) ... it may be

'nochmalig [-ma:lɪç] *adj* new, renewed

'nochmals *adv* once more *or* again

Nockerl ['nɔkəl] *Austrian n* (-s; -n) GASTR small dumpling

Nomade [no'ma:də] *m* (-n; -n), **No'madin** *f* (-; -nen) nomad

Nominativ ['no:minati:f] *m* (-s; -e) LING nominative (case)

nominieren [nomi'ni:rən] *v/t* (*no* -ge-, h) nominate

Nonne ['nɔnə] *f* (-; -n) REL nun

'Nonnenkloster *n* REL convent

Norden ['nɔrdən] *m* (-s; *no pl*) north; **nach Norden** north(wards)

nordisch ['nɔrdɪʃ] *adj* northern; SPORT **nordische Kombination** Nordic Combined

nördlich ['nœrtlɪç] **1.** *adj* north(ern); northerly; **2.** *adv*: **nördlich von** north of

Nordlicht ['nɔrt-] *n* (-[e]s; -er) ASTR northern lights

Nord'osten *m* northeast

nord'östlich *adj* northeast(ern); northeasterly

Nordpol *m* North Pole

Nord'westen *m* northwest

nord'westlich *adj* northwest(ern); northwesterly

Nordwind *m* north wind

nörgeln ['nœrgəln] *v/i* (ge-, h) nag (**an** *dat*

N

at)

Nörgler ['nœrglɐ] m (-s; -), 'Nörglerin f (-; -nen) nagger

Norm [nɔrm] f (-; -en) standard, norm

normal [nɔr'maːl] adj normal; F **nicht ganz normal** not quite right in the head

Nor'mal... esp TECH in cpds ...maß, ...zeit etc: standard ...

Normalben‚zin n regular (gas, Br petrol)

normalerweise [nɔr'maːlɐ'vaizə] adv normally, usually

normalisieren [nɔrmali'ziːrən] v/refl (no -ge-, h) return to normal

normen ['nɔrmən] v/t (ge-, h) standardize

Norwegen ['nɔrveːgən] Norway

Norweger ['nɔrveːgɐ] m (-s; -), 'Norwegerin [-gərin] f (-; -nen), 'norwegisch adj Norwegian

Not [noːt] f (-; Nöte ['nøːtə]) need; want; poverty; hardship; misery; difficulty; emergency; distress; **Not leidend** needy; **in Not sein** be in trouble; **zur Not** if need be, if necessary

Notar [no'taːɐ] m (-s; -e), No'tarin f (-; -nen) JUR notary (public)

'Notaufnahme f MED emergency room, Br casualty

'Notausgang m emergency exit

Notbehelf m (-[e]s; -e) makeshift, expedient

'Notbremse f emergency brake

'Notdienst m emergency duty

'notdürftig adj scanty; temporary

Note ['noːtə] f (-; -n) note (a. MUS and POL); ECON bill, esp Br (bank)note; PED grade, Br mark; pl MUS (sheet) music; **Noten lesen** read music

Notebook ['noutbʊk] n (-s; -s) EDP notebook

'Notendurchschnitt m PED etc average

'Notenständer m music stand

'Notfall m emergency

'notfalls adv if necessary

'notgedrungen adv: **et. notgedrungen tun** be forced to do s.th.

notieren [no'tiːrən] v/t (no -ge-, h) make a note of, note (down); ECON quote

nötig ['nøːtɪç] adj necessary; **nötig haben** need; **nötig brauchen** need badly; **das Nötigste** the (bare) necessities or essentials

nötigen ['nøːtɪgən] v/t (ge-, h) force, compel; press, urge

'Nötigung f (-; -en) coercion; JUR intimidation

Notiz [no'tiːts] f (-; -en) note; **keine Notiz nehmen von** take no notice of, ignore; **sich Notizen machen** take notes

Notizblock m memo pad, Br notepad

Notizbuch n notebook

'Notlage f awkward (or difficult) situation; difficulties; emergency

'notlanden v/i (-ge-, sein) AVIAT make an emergency landing

'Notlandung f AVIAT emergency landing

'Notlösung f expedient

'Notlüge f white lie

notorisch [no'toːrɪʃ] adj notorious

'Notruf m TEL emergency call

'Notrufsäule f TEL emergency phone

Notsig‚nal n emergency or distress signal

Notstand m state of (national) emergency

Notstandsgebiet n disaster area; ECON depressed area

Notstandsgesetze pl POL emergency laws

Notverband m MED emergency dressing

'Notwehr f (-; no pl) JUR self-defense, Br self-defence

'notwendig adj necessary

Notwendigkeit f (-; -en) necessity

Notzucht f (-; no pl) JUR rape

Novelle [no'vɛlə] f (-; -n) novella; PARL amendment

November [no'vɛmbɐ] m (-[s]; -) November

Nr. ABBR of **Nummer** No., no., number

Nu [nuː] m: **im Nu** in no time

Nuance ['nyãːsə] f shade

nüchtern ['nʏçtɐn] adj sober (a. fig); matter-of-fact; **auf nüchternen Magen** on an empty stomach; **nüchtern werden (machen)** sober up

'Nüchternheit f (-; no pl) sobriety

Nudel ['nuːdəl] f (-; -n) noodle

nuklear [nukle'aːɐ] adj nuclear

null [nʊl] adj zero, F nought; TEL 0; SPORT nil, nothing; tennis: love; **null Grad** zero degrees; **null Fehler** no mistakes; **gleich Null sein** be nil

'Nulldi‚ät f low-calorie (or F starvation) diet

Nullpunkt m zero (point or fig level)

Nullta‚rif m free fare(s); **zum Nulltarif** free (of charge)

Numerus clausus ['nuːmerus 'klauzus] m (-; no pl) UNIV restricted admission(s)

Nummer ['nʊmɐ] f (-; -n) number; issue; size

nummerieren [nʊmə'riːrən] v/t (no -ge-, h) number

'Nummernschild n MOT license plate, Br numberplate

nun [nuːn] adv now; well

nur [nuːɐ] adv only, just; merely; nothing but; **er tut nur so** he's just pretending; **nur so (zum Spaß)** just for fun; **warte nur!** just you wait!; **mach nur!, nur zu!** go ahead!; → **Erwachsene**

Nuss [nʊs] f (-; *Nüsse* ['nʏsə]) ʙοτ nut
Nussbaum m walnut (tree)
Nussknacker m nutcracker
Nussschale f nutshell
Nüstern ['nʏstɐn] pl ᴢο nostrils
Nutte ['nʊtə] F f (-; -n) hooker, sl tart
Nutzanwendung ['nʊts-] f practical application

'**nutzbar** adj usable; *nutzbar machen* utilize; exploit; harness
'**nutzbringend** adj profitable, useful
nütze ['nʏtsə] adj useful; *zu nichts nütze sein* be (of) no use; be good for nothing
Nutzen ['nʊtsən] m (-s; -) profit, gain; advantage; *Nutzen ziehen aus* (dat)

benefit or profit from or by; *zum Nutzen von* (or gen) for the benefit of
'**nutzen, 'nützen** (ge-; h) **1.** v/i: *j-m nutzen* be of use to s.o.; *es nützt nichts (es zu tun)* it's no use (doing it); **2.** v/t use, make use of; take advantage of
nützlich ['nʏtslɪç] adj useful, helpful; advantageous; *sich nützlich machen* make o.s. useful
'**nutzlos** adj useless, (of) no use
'**Nutzung** f (-; -en) use, utilization
Nylon® ['naɪlɔn] n (-s; no pl) nylon
Nylonstrümpfe pl nylon stockings
Nymphe ['nʏmfə] f (-; -n) nymph

O

O ᴀʙʙʀ of *Osten* E, east
o int oh!; *o weh!* oh dear!
o. Ä. ᴀʙʙʀ of *oder Ähnliche(s)* or the like
Oase [o'a:zə] f (-; -n) oasis (a. fig)
ob [ɔp] cj whether, if; *als ob* as if, as though; *und ob!* and how!, you bet!
Obacht ['o:baxt] f: *Obacht geben auf* (acc) pay attention to; *(gib) Obacht!* watch out!
Obdach ['ɔpdax] n (-[e]s; no pl) shelter
'**obdachlos** adj homeless, without shelter
'**Obdachlose** m, f (-n; -n) homeless person
'**Obdachlosen,syl** n shelter for the homeless
Obduktion [ɔpdʊk'tsjo:n] f (-; -en) ᴍᴇᴅ autopsy
obduzieren [ɔpdu'tsi:rən] v/t (no -ge-, h) ᴍᴇᴅ perform an autopsy on
oben ['o:bən] adv above; up; on (the) top; at the top (a. fig); on the surface; upstairs; *da oben* up there; *von oben bis unten* from top to bottom (or toe); *links oben* (at the) top left; *siehe oben* see above; F *oben ohne* topless; *von oben herab* fig patronizing(ly), condescending(ly); *oben erwähnt* or *genannt* above-mentioned
oben'an adv at the top
oben'auf adv on the top; on the surface; F feeling great
oben'drein adv besides, into the bargain, at that
oben'hin adv superficially

Ober ['o:bɐ] m (-s; -) waiter
'**Oberarm** m ᴀɴᴀᴛ upper arm
Oberarzt m, **Oberärztin** f assistant medical director
Oberbefehl m ᴍɪʟ supreme command
Oberbegriff n generic term
Oberbürgermeister m mayor, Br Lord Mayor
obere ['o:bərə] adj upper, top, fig a. superior
'**Oberfläche** f surface (a. fig) (*an dat* on)
'**oberflächlich** adj superficial
'**oberhalb** prp (gen) above
'**Oberhand** f: *die Oberhand gewinnen* (*über* acc) get the upper hand (of)
Oberhaupt n head, chief
Oberhaus n (-es; no pl) Br ᴘᴀʀʟ House of Lords
Oberhemd n shirt
'**Oberherrschaft** f (-; no pl) supremacy
Oberin ['o:bərɪn] f (-; -nen) ʀᴇʟ Mother Superior
'**oberirdisch** adj above ground; ᴇʟᴇᴄᴛʀ overhead
'**Oberkellner** m head waiter
Oberkiefer m ᴀɴᴀᴛ upper jaw
Oberkörper m upper part of the body; *den Oberkörper frei machen* strip to the waist
Oberleder n uppers
'**Oberleitung** f chief management; ᴇʟᴇᴄᴛʀ overhead contact line
Oberlippe f ᴀɴᴀᴛ upper lip
Obers ['o:bɐs] *Austrian* n (-; no pl) ɢᴀsᴛʀ

cream

'Oberschenkel *m* ANAT thigh

'Oberschule *f appr* highschool, *Br* grammar school

Oberst ['o:bəst] *m* (-en; -en) MIL colonel

oberste ['o:bəstə] *adj* up(per)most, top (-most); highest; *fig* chief, first

'Oberstufe *f appr* senior highschool, *Br appr* senior classes

Oberteil *n* top

ob'gleich *cj* (al)though

Obhut ['ɔphu:t] *f* (-; *no pl*) care, charge; **in s-e Obhut nehmen** take care *or* charge of

obig ['o:bɪç] *adj* above(-mentioned)

Objekt [ɔp'jɛkt] *n* (-[e]s; -e) object (*a.* LING); ECON property

objektiv [ɔpjɛk'ti:f] *adj* objective; impartial, unbias(s)ed

Objek'tiv *n* (-s; -e) PHOT (object) lens

Objektivität [ɔpjɛktivi'tɛ:t] *f* (-; *no pl*) objectivity; impartiality

Oblate [o'bla:tə] *f* (-; -n) wafer; REL host

obligatorisch [obliga'to:rɪʃ] *adj* compulsory

Oboe [o'bo:ə] *f* (-; -n) MUS oboe

Oboist [obo'ɪst] *m* (-en; -en) MUS oboist

Observatorium [ɔpzɛrva'to:rjum] *n* (-s; -ien) ASTR observatory

Obst [o:pst] *n* (-[e]s; *no pl*) fruit

Obstgarten *m* orchard

Obstkon,serven *pl* canned fruit

Obstladen *m* fruit store, *esp Br* fruiterer's (shop)

Obsttorte *f* fruit pie (*Br* flan)

obszön [ɔps'tsø:n] *adj* obscene, filthy

ob'wohl *cj* (al)though

Occasion [ɔka'zjo:n] *Swiss f* (-; -en) bargain, good buy

Ochse ['ɔksə] *m* (-n; -n) ZO ox, bullock; F blockhead

od. ABBR of **oder** or

öde ['ø:də] *adj* deserted, desolate; waste; *fig* dull, dreary, tedious

oder ['o:də] *cj* or; **oder aber** or else, otherwise; **oder vielmehr** or rather; **oder so** or so; **er kommt doch, oder?** he's coming, isn't he?; **du kennst ihn ja nicht, oder doch?** you don't know him, or do you?

Ofen ['o:fən] *m* (-s; Öfen ['ø:fən]) stove; oven; TECH furnace

Ofenheizung *f* stove heating

Ofenrohr *n* stovepipe

offen ['ɔfən] **1.** *adj* open (*a. fig*); vacant (*post*); *fig* frank; **2.** *adv*: **offen gesagt** frankly (speaking); **offen s-e Meinung sagen** speak one's mind (freely); **offen stehen** be open; ECON be outstanding

'offenbar *adj* obvious, evident; apparent

offenbaren [-'ba:rən] *v/t* (*ge-, h*) reveal, disclose, show

Offen'barung *f* (-; -en) revelation

'Offenheit *f* (-; *no pl*) openness, frankness

'offenherzig *adj* open-hearted, frank, candid; *fig* revealing (*dress*)

'offensichtlich *adj* → **offenbar**

offensiv [ɔfɛn'zi:f] *adj*, Offensive [ɔfɛn'zi:və] *f* (-; -n) offensive

'offenstehen *v/i* (*irr, stehen, sep, -ge-, h*): **j-m offenstehen** *fig* be open to s.o.

öffentlich ['œfəntlɪç] *adj* public; **öffentliche Verkehrsmittel** *pl* public transport; **öffentliche Schulen** *pl* public (*Br* state) schools; **öffentlich auftreten** appear in public

'Öffentlichkeit *f* (-; *no pl*) the public; **in aller Öffentlichkeit** in public, openly; **an die Öffentlichkeit bringen** make public

offiziell [ɔfi'tsjɛl] *adj* official

Offizier [ɔfi'tsi:ɐ] *m* (-s; -e) MIL (commissioned) officer

öffnen ['œfnən] *v/t and v/refl* (*ge-, h*) open

Öffner ['œfnɐ] *m* (-s; -) opener

'Öffnung *f* (-; -en) opening

'Öffnungszeiten *pl* business *or* office hours

oft [ɔft] *adv* often, frequently

oh [o:] *int* o(h)!

ohne ['o:nə] *prp* (*acc*) and *cj* without; **ohne mich!** count me out!; **ohne ein Wort (zu sagen)** without (saying) a word

ohne'gleichen *adv* unequal(l)ed, unparalleled

ohne'hin *adv* anyhow, anyway

Ohnmacht ['o:nmaxt] *f* (-; -en) MED unconsciousness; *fig* helplessness; **in Ohnmacht fallen** faint, pass out

'ohnmächtig *adj* MED unconscious; *fig* helpless; **ohnmächtig werden** faint, pass out

Ohr [o:ɐ] *n* (-[e]s; -en ['o:rən]) ANAT ear; F **j-n übers Ohr hauen** cheat s.o.; **bis über die Ohren verliebt (verschuldet)** head over heels in love (over your head in debt)

Öhr [ø:ɐ] *n* (-[e]s; -e ['ø:rə]) eye

Ohrenarzt ['o:rən-] *m* ear specialist

'ohrenbetäubend *adj* deafening

'Ohrenschmerzen *pl* earache

Ohrenschützer *pl* earmuffs

Ohrenzeuge *m* earwitness

'Ohrfeige *f* slap in the face (*a. fig*)

'ohrfeigen [-faɪɡən] *v/t* (*ge-, h*) **j-n ohrfeigen** slap s.o.'s face

'Ohrläppchen [-lɛpçən] *n* (-s; -) ANAT earlobe

Ohrring *m* earring

oje [o'jeː] *int* oh dear!, dear me!

Ökologe [øko'loːgə] *m* (*-n; -n*) ecologist

Ökologie [økolo'giː] *f* (*-; no pl*) ecology

ökologisch [øko'loːgɪʃ] *adj* ecological

Ökonomie [økono'miː] *f* (*-; no pl*) economy; ECON economics

ökonomisch [øko'noːmɪʃ] *adj* economical; ECON economic

Ökosys, tem ['øːko-] *n* ecosystem

Oktave [ɔk'taːvə] *f* (*-; -n*) MUS octave

Oktober [ɔk'toːbɐ] *m* (*-[s]; -*) October

ökumenisch [øku'meːnɪʃ] *adj* REL ecumenical

Öl [øːl] *n* (*-[e]s; Öle*) oil; petroleum; **nach Öl bohren** drill for oil; **auf Öl stoßen** strike oil

'Ölbaum *m* BOT olive (tree)

Oldtimer ['ouldtaimɐ] *m* (*-s; -*) MOT veteran car

ölen ['øːlən] *v/t* (*ge-, h*) oil, TECH *a.* lubricate

'Ölfarbe *f* oil (paint)

Ölfeld *n* oilfield

'Ölförderland *n* oil-producing country

'Ölförderung *f* oil production

Ölgemälde *n* oil painting

Ölheizung *f* oil heating

ölig ['øːlɪç] *adj* oily, greasy (*both a. fig*)

oliv [o'liːf] *adj* olive

Olive [o'liːvə] *f* (*-; -n*) BOT olive

'Ölleitung *f* (oil) pipeline

Ölmessstab *m* MOT dipstick

Ölpest *f* oil pollution

Ölquelle *f* oil well

Ölsar, dine *f* canned (*Br a.* tinned) sardine

Öltanker *m* MAR oil tanker

Ölteppich *m* oil slick

Ölstand *m* oil level

'Ölung *f* (*-; no pl*) oiling, TECH *a.* lubrication; **Letzte Ölung** REL extreme unction

'Ölwanne *f* MOT oil pan, *Br* sump

Ölwechsel *m* MOT oil change

Ölzeug *n* oilskins

Olympia... [o'lʏmpja-] *in cpds ...mannschaft, ...medaille etc:* Olympic ...

Olympiade [olʏm'pjaːdə] *f* (*-; -n*) SPORT Olympic Games, Olympics

Oma ['oːma] *f* (*-; -s*) grandma

Omi ['oːmi] *f* (*-; -s*) granny

Omnibus ['ɔmnibʊs] *m* → **Bus**

onanieren [ona'niːrən] *v/i* (*no -ge-, h*) masturbate

Onkel ['ɔŋkəl] *m* (*-s; -*) uncle

Online... ['ɔnlain-] EDP online ...

Opa ['oːpa] *m* (*-s; -s*) grandpa

Oper ['oːpɐ] *f* (*-; -n*) MUS opera, opera (house)

Operation [opəra'tsjoːn] *f* (*-; -en*) MED op-

eration; **e-e Operation vornehmen** perform an operation

Operati'onssaal *m* MED operating room (*Br* theatre)

Operette [opə'rɛtə] *f* (*-; -n*) MUS operetta

operieren [opə'riːrən] (*no -ge-, h*) **1.** *v/t* MED **j-n operieren** operate on s.o. (**wegen** for); **operiert werden** be operated on, have an operation; **sich operieren lassen** undergo an operation; **2.** *v/i* MED, MIL operate; proceed

Opernsänger(in) *(m)* opera singer

Opfer ['ɔpfɐ] *n* (*-s; -*) sacrifice; offering; victim; **ein Opfer bringen** make a sacrifice; (*dat*) **zum Opfer fallen** fall victim to

'opfern *v/t and v/i* (*ge-, h*) sacrifice

Opium ['oːpjʊm] *n* (*-s; no pl*) opium

Opposition [ɔpozi'tsjoːn] *f* (*-; -en*) opposition (*a.* PARL)

Optik ['ɔptik] *f* (*-; no pl*) optics; PHOT optical system

Optiker ['ɔptikɐ] *m* (*-s; -*), **'Optikerin** *f* (*-; -nen*) optician

optimal [ɔpti'maːl] *adj* optimum, best

Optimismus [ɔpti'mɪsmʊs] *m* (*-; no pl*) optimism

Optimist(in) [ɔpti'mɪst(ɪn)] (*-en; -en/-; -nen*) optimist

opti'mistisch *adj* optimistic

Option [ɔp'tsjoːn] *f* (*-; -en*) option

optisch ['ɔptiʃ] *adj* optical

Orange [o'rãːʒə] *f* (*-; -n*) BOT orange

Orchester [ɔr'kɛstɐ] *n* (*-s; -*) MUS orchestra

Orchidee [ɔrçi'deː] *f* (*-; -n*) bot orchid

Orden ['ɔrdən] *m* (*-s; -*) medal, decoration; *esp* REL order

'Ordensschwester *f* REL sister, nun

ordentlich ['ɔrdəntlɪç] **1.** *adj* tidy, neat, orderly; proper; thorough; decent (*a.* F); respectable; full (*member etc*); JUR ordinary; reasonable (*performance etc*); F good, sound; **2.** *adv:* **s-e Sache ordentlich machen** do a good job; **sich ordentlich benehmen (anziehen)** behave (dress) properly *or* decently

ordinär [ɔrdi'nɛːɐ] *adj* vulgar; common

ordnen ['ɔrdnən] *v/t* (*ge-, h*) put in order; arrange, sort (out); file; settle

Ordner ['ɔrdnɐ] *m* (*-s; -*) file; folder; attendant, guard

'Ordnung *f* (*-; no pl*) order; orderliness, tidiness; arrangement; system, set-up; class; **in Ordnung** all right; TECH *etc* in (good) order; **in Ordnung bringen** put right (*a. fig*); tidy up; repair, fix (*a. fig*); (**in**) **Ordnung halten** keep (in) order; **et. ist nicht in Ordnung (mit)** there is s.th. wrong (with)

O

'**ordnungsgemäß 1.** *adj* correct, regular; **2.** *adv* duly, properly

'**Ordnungsstrafe** *f* JUR fine, penalty

Ordnungszahl *f* MATH ordinal number

Organ [ɔrˈgaːn] *n* (-*s*; -*e*) organ

Organempfänger *m* MED organ recipient

Organhandel *m* sale of (transplant) organs

Organisation [ɔrganizaˈtsjoːn] *f* (-; -*en*) organization

Organisator [ɔrganiˈzaːtoːɐ] *m* (-*s*; -*en* [-zaˈtoːrən]) organizer

Organisa'torin *f* (-; -*nen*) organizer

organisatorisch [-zaˈtoːrɪʃ] *adj* organizational

organisch [ɔrˈgaːnɪʃ] *adj* organic

organisieren [ɔrganiˈziːrən] *v/t* organize; F get (hold of); ***sich organisieren*** organize; ECON unionize

organisiert [ɔrganiˈziːɐt] *adj* organized; ECON unionized

Organismus [ɔrgaˈnɪsmʊs] *m* (-; -*men*) BIOL organism

Organist [ɔrgaˈnɪst] *m* (-*en*; -*en*), **Organistin** *f* (-; -*nen*) MUS organist

Or'ganspender *m* MED (organ) donor

Orgasmus [ɔrˈgasmʊs] *m* (-; -*men*) orgasm

Orgel [ˈɔrgəl] *f* (-; -*n*) MUS organ

'**Orgelpfeife** *f* MUS organ pipe

Orgie [ˈɔrgjə] *f* (-; -*n*) orgy

Orientale [orjɛnˈtaːlə] *m* (-*n*; -*n*), **Orien'talin** *f* (-; -*nen*), **orien'talisch** *adj* oriental

orientieren [orjɛnˈtiːrən] *v/t* (*no -ge-, h*) inform (*über acc* about), brief (on); ***sich orientieren*** orient(ate) o.s. (*a. fig*) (*nach* by); inform o.s.

Orien'tierung *f* (-; *no pl*) orientation, *fig a.* information; ***die Orientierung verlieren*** lose one's bearings

Orien'tierungssinn *m* [-*[e]s*; *no pl*] sense of direction

original [origiˈnaːl] *adj* original; real, genuine; TV live

Origi'nal *n* (-*s*; -*e*) original; *fig* real (*or* quite a) character

Origi'nal... *in cpds* ...aufnahme, ...ausgabe *etc*: original ...

Originalübertragung *f* live broadcast *or* program(me)

originell [origiˈnɛl] *adj* original; ingenious; witty

Orkan [ɔrˈkaːn] *m* (-*[e]s*; -*e*) hurricane

or'kanartig *adj* violent; *fig* thunderous

Ort [ɔrt] *m* (-*[e]s*; -*e*) place; village, (small) town; spot, point; scene; ***vor Ort*** mining; at the (pit) face; *fig* in the field, on the spot

orten [ˈɔrtən] *v/t* (*ge-, h*) locate, spot

orthodox [ɔrtoˈdɔks] *adj* orthodox

Orthographie [ɔrtograˈfiː] *f* (-; -*n*) orthography

Orthopäde [ɔrtoˈpɛːdə] *m* (-*n*; -*n*), **Ortho'pädin** *f* (-; -*nen*) MED orthop(a)edic specialist

örtlich [ˈœrtlɪç] *adj* local

'**Ortsbestimmung** *f* AVIAT, MAR location; LING adverb of place

'**Ortschaft** *f* → **Ort**

'**Ortsgespräch** *n* TEL local call

'**Ortskenntnis** *f*: ***Ortskenntnis besitzen*** know a place

'**Ortsnetz** *n* TEL local exchange

'**Ortszeit** *f* local time

Öse [ˈøːzə] *f* (-; -*n*) eye; eyelet

Ostblock [ˈɔst-] *m* (-*[e]s*; *no pl*) HIST POL East(ern) Bloc

Osten [ˈɔstən] *m* (-*s*; *no pl*) east; POL *the* East; ***nach Osten*** east(wards)

Osterei [ˈoːstɐ-] *n* Easter egg

Osterhase *m* Easter bunny *or* rabbit

Ostern [ˈoːstɐn] *n* (-; -) Easter (***zu, an** at*); ***frohe Ostern!*** Happy Easter!

Österreicher [ˈøːstəraɪçɐ] *m* (-*s*; -), **Österreicherin** [-raɪçərɪn] *f* (-; -*nen*), **österreichisch** *adj* Austrian

östlich [ˈœstlɪç] **1.** *adj* east(ern); easterly; **2.** *adv*: ***östlich von*** (to the) east of

ostwärts [ˈɔstvɛrts] *adv* east(wards)

'**Ostwind** *m* east wind

Otter [ˈɔtɐ] zo **1.** *m* (-*s*; -) otter; **2.** *f* (-; -*n*) adder, viper

outen [ˈaʊtən] *v/t* (*ge-, h*) out

Ouvertüre [uvɛrˈtyːrə] *f* (-; -*n*) MUS overture

oval [oˈvaːl] *adj*, **O'val** *n* (-*s*; -*e*) oval

Oxid [ɔˈksiːt] *n* (-*[e]s*; -*e* [ɔˈksiːdə]) CHEM oxide

oxidieren [ɔksiˈdiːrən] *v/t* (*no -ge-, h*) *and v/i* (*h, sein*) CHEM oxidize

Oxyd *n* → **Oxid**

Ozean [ˈoːtseaːn] *m* (-*s*; -*e*) ocean, sea

Ozon [oˈtsoːn] *n* (-*s*; *no pl*) CHEM ozone

o'zonfreundlich *adj* ozone-friendly

O'zonloch *n* ozone hole

Ozonschicht *f* ozone layer

Ozonschild *m* ozone shield

Ozonwerte *pl* ozone levels

P

paar [paːɐ] *indef pron:* **ein paar** a few, some, F a couple of; **ein paar Mal** a few times

Paar *n* (-[e]s; -e) pair; couple; **ein Paar (neue) Schuhe** a (new) pair of shoes

paaren [ˈpaːrən] *v/t and v/refl* (ge-, h) zo mate; *fig* combine

'Paarlauf *m* SPORT pair skating

'Paarung *f* (-; -en) zo mating, copulation; SPORT matching

'paarweise *adv* in pairs, in twos

Pacht [paxt] *f* (-; -en) lease; rent

'pachten *v/t* (ge-, h) (take on) lease

Pächter [ˈpɛçtɐ] *m* (-s; -), **'Pächterin** *f* (-; -nen) leaseholder; AGR tenant

'Pachtvertrag *m* lease

Pachtzins *m* rent

Pack[1] [pak] *m* → **Packen**

Pack[2] *contp n* (-[e]s; *no pl*) rabble

Päckchen [ˈpɛkçən] *n* (-s; -) pack, *Br* packet; small parcel

packen [ˈpakən] *v/t and v/i* (ge-, h) pack; make up (*parcel etc*); grab, seize (**an** *dat* by); *fig* grip

'Packen *m* (-s; -) pack, pile (*a. fig*)

Packer [ˈpakɐ] *m* (-s; -) packer; removal man

'Packpapier *n* packing *or* brown paper

'Packung *f* (-; -en) package, box; pack, *Br* packet

Pädagoge [pɛdaˈgoːgə] *m* (-n; -n), **Pädagogin** *f* (-; -nen) teacher; education(al)ist

päda'gogisch *adj* pedagogic, educational; **pädagogische Hochschule** college of education

Paddel [ˈpadəl] *n* (-s; -) paddle

'Paddelboot *n* canoe

'paddeln *v/i* (ge-, h, sein) paddle, canoe

Page [ˈpaːʒə] *m* (-n; -n) page(boy)

Paket [paˈkeːt] *n* (-[e]s; -e) package; parcel

Paketkarte *f* parcel post slip, *Br* parcel mailing form

Paketpost *f* parcel post

Paketschalter *m* parcel counter

Paketzustellung *f* parcel delivery

Pakt [pakt] *m* (-[e]s; -e) POL pact

Palast [paˈlast] *m* (-[e]s; *Paläste* [paˈlɛstə]) palace

Palme [ˈpalmə] *f* (-; -n) BOT palm (tree)

Palm'sonntag *m* REL Palm Sunday

Pampelmuse [ˈpampəlmuːzə] *f* (-; -n) BOT grapefruit

paniert [paˈniːɐt] *adj* GASTR breaded

Panik [ˈpaːnɪk] *f* (-; -en) panic; **in Panik geraten (versetzen)** panic; **in Panik** panic-stricken, F panicky

panisch [ˈpaːnɪʃ] *adj:* **panische Angst** mortal terror

Panne [ˈpanə] *f* (-; -n) breakdown, MOT *a.* engine trouble; *fig* mishap

'Pannenhilfe *f* MOT breakdown service

Panter, Panther [ˈpantɐ] *m* (-s; -) zo panther

Pantoffel [panˈtɔfəl] *m* (-s; -n) slipper

Pantoffelheld F *m* henpecked husband

Pantomime [pantoˈmiːmə] THEA **1.** *f* (-; -n) mime, dumb show; **2.** *m* (-n; -n) mime (artist)

panto'mimisch *adv:* **pantomimisch darstellen** mime

Panzer [ˈpantsɐ] *m* (-s; -) armo(u)r (*a. fig*), MIL tank; zo shell

Panzerglas *n* bulletproof glass

'panzern *v/t* (ge-, h) armo(u)r; → **gepanzert**

'Panzerschrank *m* safe

Panzerung [ˈpantsərʊŋ] *f* (-; -en) armo(u)r plating

Papa [paˈpaː] F *m* (-s; -s) dad(dy), pa

Papagei [papaˈɡai] *m* (-[e]n; -en) zo parrot

Papeterie [papetəˈriː] *Swiss f* (-; -n) stationer('s shop)

Papier [paˈpiːɐ] *n* (-s; -e) paper; *pl* papers, documents; identification (paper)

Pa'pier... *in cpds* **...geld, ...handtuch, ...serviette, ...tüte etc:** *mst* paper ...

Papiergeschäft *n* stationer('s store, *Br* shop)

Papierkorb *m* wastepaper basket

Papierkrieg F *m* red tape

Papierschnitzel *pl* scraps of paper

Papierwaren *pl* stationery

Pappe [ˈpapə] *f* (-; -n) cardboard, pasteboard

Pappel [ˈpapəl] *f* (-; -n) BOT poplar

'Pappkarton *m* cardboard box, carton

Pappteller *m* paper plate

Paprika [ˈpaprika] *m* (-s; -[s]) a) BOT sweet pepper, b) (*no pl*) GASTR paprika

Papst [paːpst] *m* (-[e]s; *Päpste* [ˈpɛːpstə]) pope

'päpstlich *adj* papal

Parade [paˈraːdə] *f* (-; -n) parade; *soccer etc:* save; *boxing, fencing:* parry

Paradeiser [paraˈdaizɐ] *Austrian m* (-s; -) BOT tomato

Paradies [paraˈdiːs] *n* (-es; -e) paradise

paradiesisch [para'di:zɪʃ] *fig adj* heavenly, delightful

paradox [para'dɔks] *adj* paradoxical

Paragraph [para'graːf] *m* (-en; -en) JUR article, section; paragraph

parallel [para'leːl] *adj*. **Paral'lele** *f* (-; -n) parallel

Parasit [para'ziːt] *m* (-en; -en) parasite

Parfüm [par'fyːm] *n* (-s; -s) perfume, *Br a.* scent

Parfümerie [parfymə'riː] *f* (-; -n) perfumery

parfümieren [parfy'miːrən] *v/t* (*no -ge-, h*) perfume, scent; **sich parfümieren** put on perfume

parieren [pa'riːrən] *v/t and v/i* (*no -ge-, h*) SPORT parry, *fig a.* counter (**mit** with); pull up (*horse*); obey

Park [park] *m* (-s; -s) park

parken ['parkən] *v/i and v/t* (*ge-, h*) MOT park; **Parken verboten!** no parking!

Parkett [par'kɛt] *n* (-[e]s; -e, -s) parquet (floor); THEA orchestra, *Br* stalls; dance floor

'**Parkgebühr** *f* parking fee

Park(hoch-)haus *n* parking garage, *Br* multi-storey car park

parkieren [par'kiːrən] *Swiss v/t and v/i* → **parken**

'**Parkkralle** *f* wheel clamp

'**Parklücke** *f* parking space

Parkplatz *m* parking lot, *Br* car park; → **Parklücke**; **e-n Parkplatz suchen (finden)** look for (find) somewhere to park the car

Parkscheibe *f* parking disk (*Br* disc)

Parksünder *m* parking offender

Parkuhr *f* MOT parking meter

Parkwächter *m* park keeper; MOT parking lot (*Br* car park) attendant

Parlament [parla'mɛnt] *n* (-[e]s; -e) parliament

parlamentarisch [parlamɛn'taːrɪʃ] *adj* parliamentary

Parodie [paro'diː] *f* (-; -n), **paro'dieren** *v/t* (*no -ge-, h*) parody

Parole [pa'roːlə] *f* (-; -n) MIL password; *fig* watchword; POL *a.* slogan

Partei [par'taɪ] *f* (-; -en) party (*a.* POL); *j-s Partei ergreifen* take sides with s.o., side with s.o.

par'teiisch *adj* partial (**für** to); prejudiced (**gegen** against)

par'teilos *adj* POL independent

Par'teimitglied *n* POL party member

Parteiprogramm *n* POL platform

Parteitag *m* POL convention

Parteizugehörigkeit *f* POL party membership

Parterre [par'tɛrə] *n* (-s; -s) first (*Br* ground) floor

Partie [par'tiː] *f* (-; -n) game, SPORT *a.* match; part, passage (*a.* MUS); **e-e gute etc Partie sein** be a good *etc* match

Partisan [parti'zaːn] *m* (-s; -en, -en), **Parti'sanin** *f* (-; -nen) MIL partisan, guerilla

Partitur [parti'tuːɐ] *f* (-; -en) MUS score

Partizip [parti'tsiːp] *n* (-s; -ien) LING participle

Partner ['partnɐ] *m* (-s; -), '**Partnerin** *f* (-; -nen) partner

'**Partnerschaft** *f* (-; -en) partnership

'**Partnerstadt** *f* twin town

paschen ['paʃən] *Austrian v/t and v/i* (*ge-, h*) smuggle

Pascher ['paʃɐ] *Austrian m* (-s; -) smuggler

Pass [pas] *m* (-es; *Pässe* ['pɛsə]) passport; SPORT, GEOGR pass; **langer Pass** SPORT long ball

Passage [pa'saːʒə] *f* (-; -n) passage

Passagier [pasa'ʒiːɐ] *m* (-s; -e) passenger

Passagierflugzeug *n* passenger plane; airliner

Passa'gierin *f* (-; -nen) passenger

Passah ['pasa] *n* (-s; *no pl*), '**Passahfest** *n* REL Passover

Passant [pa'sant] *m* (-en; -en), **Pas'santin** *f* (-; -nen) passerby

'**Passbild** *n* passport photo(graph)

passen ['pasən] **1.** *v/i* (*ge-, h*) fit (*j-m* s.o.; **auf** *or* **für** *or* **zu** et. s.th.); suit (*j-m* s.o.) be convenient; *cards, sport* pass; **passen zu** go with, match; *sie passen gut zueinander* they are well suited to each other; *passt es Ihnen morgen?* would tomorrow suit you *or* be all right (with you)?; *das (es) passt mir gar nicht* I don't like that (him) at all; *das passt (nicht) zu ihm* that's just like him (not like him, not his style)

passend *adj* fitting; matching; suitable, right

passierbar [pa'siːɐbaːɐ] *adj* passable

passieren [pa'siːrən] (*no -ge-*) **1.** *v/i* (*sein*) happen; **2.** *v/t* (*h*) pass (through)

Pas'sierschein *m* pass, permit

Passion [pa'sjoːn] *f* (-; -en) passion; REL Passion

passiv ['pasiːf] *adj* passive

'**Passiv** *n* (-s; *no pl*) LING passive (voice)

Paste ['pastə] *f* (-; -n) paste

Pastell [pas'tɛl] *n* (-[e]s; -e) PAINT pastel

Pastete [pas'teːtə] *f* (-; -n) GASTR pie

Pate ['paːtə] *m* (-n; -n) godfather

'**Patenkind** *n* godchild

'**Patenschaft** *f* (-; -en) sponsorship

Patent [pa'tɛnt] *n* (-[e]s; -e) patent; MIL

commission

Patentamt *n* patent office

Patentanwalt *m* JUR patent agent

patentieren [patɛnˈtiːrən] *v/t (no -ge-, h)* patent; **(sich) et. patentieren lassen** take out a patent for s.th.

Paˈtentinhaber *m* patentee

pathetisch [paˈteːtɪʃ] *adj* pompous

Patient [paˈtsjɛnt] *m (-en; -en)*, **Paˈtientin** *f (-; -nen)* MED patient

Patin [ˈpaːtɪn] *f (-; -nen)* godmother

Patriot [patriˈoːt] *m (-en; -en)* patriot

patriˈotisch *adj* patriotic

Patrone [paˈtroːnə] *f (-; -n)* cartridge

Patrouille [paˈtruljə] *f (-; -n)* MIL patrol

patrouillieren [patrulˈjiːrən] *v/i (no -ge-, h)* MIL patrol

Patsche [ˈpatʃə] F *f: in der Patsche sitzen* be in a fix or jam

patschen F *v/i (ge-, h)* (s)plash

ˈpatschˈnass *adj* soaking wet

patzen [ˈpatsən] F *v/i (ge-, h)*, **Patzer** [ˈpatsə] F *m (-s; -)* blunder

Pauke [ˈpaukə] *f (-; -n)* MUS bass drum; kettledrum

ˈpauken F *v/i and v/t (ge-, h)* cram

Pauschale [pauˈʃaːlə] *f (-; -n)* lump sum

Pauˈschalgebühr *f* flat rate

Pauschalreise *f* package tour

Pauschalurteil *n* sweeping judg(e)ment

Pause¹ [ˈpauzə] *f (-; -n)* recess, *Br* break, *esp* THEA, SPORT intermission, *Br* interval; pause; rest (*a.* MUS)

ˈPause² *f (-; -n)* TECH tracing

ˈpausen *v/t (ge-, h)* TECH trace

ˈpausenlos *adj* uninterrupted, nonstop

ˈPausenzeichen *n* radio: interval signal; PED bell

pausieren [pauˈziːrən] *v/i (no -ge-, h)* pause, rest

Pavian [ˈpaːvjaːn] *m (-s; -e)* zo baboon

Pavillon [ˈpavɪljɔŋ] *m (-s; -s)* pavilion

Pazifist [patsiˈfɪst] *m (-en; -en)*, **Paziˈfistin** *f (-; -nen)*, **paziˈfistisch** *adj* pacifist

PC [peːˈtseː] *m (-[s]; -[s])* ABBR of **personal computer** PC

Pech [pɛç] *n (-s; no pl)* pitch; F bad luck

Pechsträhne F *f* run of bad luck

Pechvogel F *m* unlucky fellow

pedantisch [peˈdantɪʃ] *adj* pedantic, fussy

Pegel [ˈpeːgəl] *m (-s; -)* level (*a. fig*)

peilen [ˈpailən] *v/t (ge-, h)* sound

peinigen [ˈpainɪgən] *v/t (ge-, h)* torment

Peiniger [ˈpainɪgə] *m (-s; -)* tormentor

peinlich [ˈpainlɪç] *adj* embarrassing; **peinlich genau** meticulous (**bei, in** *dat* in); **es war mir peinlich** I was or felt embarrassed

Peitsche [ˈpaitʃə] *f (-; -n)*, **ˈpeitschen** *v/t (ge-, h)* whip

ˈPeitschenhieb *m* lash

Pelle [ˈpɛlə] *f (-; -n)* skin; peel

ˈpellen *v/t (ge-, h)* peel

ˈPellkarˌtoffeln *pl* potatoes (boiled) in their jackets

Pelz [pɛlts] *m (-es; -e)* fur; skin

ˈpelzgefüttert *adj* fur-lined

ˈPelzgeschäft *n* fur(rier's) store (*Br* shop)

pelzig [ˈpɛltsɪç] *adj* furry; MED furred

ˈPelzmantel *m* fur coat

ˈPelztiere *pl* furred animals, furs

Pendel [ˈpɛndəl] *n (-s; -)* pendulum

ˈpendeln *v/i (ge-, h)* swing; RAIL *etc* shuttle; commute

ˈPendeltür *f* swing door

ˈPendelverkehr *m* RAIL *etc* shuttle service; commuter traffic

Pendler(in) [ˈpɛndlə (-lərɪn)] *(-s; -/-; -nen)* RAIL *etc* commuter

Penis [ˈpeːnɪs] *m (-; -se)* ANAT penis

Penner [ˈpɛnə] F *m (-s; -)* tramp, bum

Pension [pãˈsjoːn] *f (-; -en)* pension; boarding-house, private hotel; *in Pension sein* be retired

Pensionär(in) [pãsjoˈnɛːɐ (-ˈnɛːrɪn)] *(-s; -e/-; -nen)* (old age) pensioner; boarder

Pensionat [pãsjoˈnaːt] *n (-[e]s; -e)* boarding school

pensionieren [pãsjoˈniːrən] *v/t (no -ge-, h)* pension (off); **sich pensionieren lassen** retire

Pensioˈnierung *f (-; -en)* retirement

Pensionist [pãsjoˈnɪst] *Austrian, Swiss m (-en; -en)* (old age) pensioner

Pensiˈonsgast *m* boarder

Pensum [ˈpɛnzʊm] *n (-s; Pensen, Pensa)* (work) quota, stint

per [pɛr] *prp (acc)* per; by

perfekt [pɛrˈfɛkt] *adj* perfect; **perfekt machen** settle

Perfekt *n (-s; -e)* LING present perfect

Pergament [pɛrgaˈmɛnt] *n (-[e]s; -e)* parchment

Periode [peˈrjoːdə] *f (-; -n)* period, MED *a.* menstruation

periodisch [peˈrjoːdɪʃ] *adj* periodic(al)

Peripherie [perifeˈriː] *f (-; -n)* periphery, outskirts

Peripheriegeräte *pl* EDP peripheral equipment

Perle [ˈpɛrlə] *f (-; -n)* pearl; bead

ˈperlen *v/i (ge-, h)* sparkle, bubble

ˈPerlenkette *f* pearl necklace

ˈPerlmuschel *f* zo pearl oyster

Perlmutt [ˈpɛrlmʊt] *n (-s; no pl)* mother-of-pearl

Perron [pɛˈrõː] *m (-s; -s)* Swiss platform

Perser ['pɛrzɐ] m (-s; -) Persian; Persian carpet

Perserin ['pɛrzərɪn] f (-; -nen) Persian (woman)

Persien ['pɛrzjən] Persia

persisch ['pɛrzɪʃ] adj Persian

Person [pɛr'zoːn] f (-; -en) person, THEA etc a. character; *ein Tisch für drei Personen* a table for three

Personal [pɛrzo'naːl] n (-s; no pl) staff, personnel; *zu wenig Personal haben* be understaffed

Personalabbau m staff reduction

Personalabteilung f personnel department

Personalausweis m identity card

Personalchef m staff manager

Personalien [pɛrzo'naːljən] pl particulars, personal data

Perso'nalpro,nomen n LING personal pronoun

Per'sonen(kraft)wagen (ABBR **PKW**) m (Br a. motor)car, auto(mobile)

Personenzug m passenger train; local or commuter train

personifizieren [pɛrzonifi'tsiːrən] v/t (no -ge-, h) personify

persönlich [pɛr'zøːnlɪç] adj personal

Per'sönlichkeit f (-; -en) personality

Perücke [pe'rykə] f (-; -n) wig

pervers [pɛr'vɛrs] adj perverted; *perverser Mensch* pervert

Pessimismus [pɛsi'mɪsmʊs] m (-; no pl) pessimism

Pessimist(in) [pɛsi'mɪst(ɪn)] (-en; -en/-; -nen) pessimist

pessi'mistisch adj pessimistic

Pest [pɛst] f (-; no pl) MED plague

Pestizid [pɛsti'tsiːt] n (-s; -e) pesticide

Petersilie [pe:tɐ'ziːljə] f (-; -n) BOT parsley

Petroleum [pe'troːleʊm] n (-s; no pl) kerosene, Br paraffin

Petroleumlampe f kerosene (Br paraffin) lamp

petzen ['pɛtsən] F v/i (ge-, h) tell tales, Br a. sneak

Pfad [pfaːt] m (-[e]s; -e ['pfaːdə]) path, track

Pfadfinder m boy scout

Pfadfinderin [-fɪndərɪn] f (-; -nen) girl scout, Br girl guide

Pfahl [pfaːl] m (-[e]s; Pfähle ['pfɛːlə]) stake; post; pole

Pfand [pfant] n (-[e]s; Pfänder ['pfɛndɐ]) security; pawn, pledge; deposit; forfeit

Pfandbrief m ECON mortgage bond

pfänden ['pfɛndən] v/t (ge-, h) seize

Pfandhaus n → **Leihhaus**

Pfandleiher [-laiɐ] m (-s; -) pawnbroker

Pfandschein m pawn ticket

Pfändung f (-; -en) JUR seizure

Pfanne ['pfanə] f (-; -n) pan, skillet

Pfannkuchen m pancake

Pfarrbezirk ['pfar-] m parish

Pfarrer ['pfarɐ] m (-s; -) vicar; pastor; (parish) priest

Pfarrgemeinde f parish

Pfarrhaus n parsonage; rectory, vicarage

Pfarrkirche f parish church

Pfau [pfau] m (-[e]s; -en) ZO peacock

Pfeffer ['pfɛfɐ] m (-s; -) pepper

Pfefferkuchen m gingerbread

Pfefferminze [-mɪntsə] f (-; no pl) BOT peppermint

pfeffern v/t (ge-, h) pepper

Pfefferstreuer m (-s; -) pepper caster

pfeffrig ['pfɛfrɪç] adj peppery

Pfeife ['pfaifə] f (-; -n) whistle; pipe (a. MUS)

pfeifen v/i and v/t (irr, ge-, h) whistle (*j-m* to s.o.); F *pfeifen auf* (acc) not give a damn about

Pfeil [pfail] m (-[e]s; -e) arrow

Pfeiler ['pfailɐ] m (-s; -) pillar; pier

Pfennig ['pfɛnɪç] m (-s; -e) pfennig; fig penny

Pferch [pfɛrç] m (-[e]s; -e) fold, pen

pferchen v/t (ge-, h) cram (*in* acc into)

Pferd [pfeːɐt] n (-[e]s; -e) ZO horse (a. SPORT); *zu Pferde* on horseback

Pferdegeschirr ['pfeːɐdə-] n harness

Pferdekoppel f paddock

Pferderennen n horserace

Pferdestall m stable

Pferdestärke f TECH horsepower

Pferdewagen m (horse-drawn) carriage

pfiff [pfɪf] pret of **pfeifen**

Pfiff m (-[e]s; -e) whistle

pfiffig ['pfɪfɪç] adj smart

Pfingsten ['pfɪŋstən] n (-; -) REL Pentecost, Br Whitsun (*zu, an* at)

Pfingst'montag m REL Whit Monday

Pfingstrose f BOT peony

Pfingst'sonntag m REL Pentecost, Br Whit Sunday

Pfirsich ['pfɪrzɪç] m (-s; -e) BOT peach

Pflanze ['pflantsə] f (-; -n) plant; *Pflanzen fressend* zo herbivorous

pflanzen v/t (ge-, h) plant

Pflanzenfett n vegetable fat

pflanzlich adj vegetable

Pflanzung f (-; -en) plantation

Pflaster ['pflastɐ] n (-s; -) pavement; MED Band-Aid®, Br plaster

pflastern v/t (ge-, h) pave

Pflasterstein m paving stone

Pflaume ['pflaumə] f (-; -n) BOT plum

Pflege ['pfleːgə] f (-; no pl) care; MED

nursing; *fig* cultivation; TECH maintenance; *j-n in Pflege nehmen* take s.o. into one's care; *Pflege...* in cpds *...eltern, ...kind, ...sohn etc*: foster ...; *...heim, ...kosten, ...personal etc*: nursing ...

'pflegebedürftig *adj* needing care

'Pflegefall *m* constant-care patient

'pflegeleicht *adj* wash-and-wear, easy-care

'pflegen *v/t* (*ge-*, *h*) care for, look after, *esp* MED *a.* nurse; TECH maintain; *fig* cultivate; keep up (*custom etc*); *sie pflegte zu sagen* she used to *or* would say

Pfleger ['pfle:ɡɐ] *m* (*-s*; *-*) male nurse

Pflegerin ['pfle:ɡərɪn] *f* (*-*; *-nen*) nurse

'Pflegestelle *f* nursing place

Pflicht [pflɪçt] *f* (*-*; *-en*) duty (*gegen* to); SPORT compulsory events

'pflichtbewusst *adj* conscientious

'Pflichtbewusstsein *n* sense of duty

Pflichterfüllung *f* performance of one's duty

Pflichtfach *n* PED compulsory subject

'pflichtgemäß, pflichtgetreu *adj* dutiful

pflichtvergessen *adv*: *pflichtvergessen handeln* neglect one's duty

'Pflichtversicherung *f* compulsory insurance

Pflock ['pflɔk] *m* (*-[e]s*; *Pflöcke* ['pflœkə]) peg, pin; plug

pflücken ['pflʏkən] *v/t* (*ge-*, *h*) pick, gather

Pflug [pflu:k] *m* (*-[e]s*; *Pflüge* ['pfly:ɡə]) plow, *Br* plough

pflügen ['pfly:ɡən] *v/t and v/i* (*ge-*, *h*) plow, *Br* plough

Pforte ['pfɔrtə] *f* (*-*; *-n*) gate, door, entrance

Pförtner ['pfœrtnɐ] *m* (*-s*; *-*) doorman, doorkeeper, porter

Pfosten ['pfɔstən] *m* (*-s*; *-*) post

Pfote ['pfo:tə] *f* (*-*; *-n*) ZO paw (*a.* F)

pfropfen ['pfrɔpfən] *v/t* (*ge-*, *h*) stopper; cork; plug; AGR graft; F cram, stuff

'Pfropfen *m* (*-s*; *-*) stopper; cork; plug; MED clot

pfui [pfui] *int* ugh!; *audience*: boo!

Pfund [pfʊnt] *n* (*-[e]s*; *-e* ['pfʊndə]) pound (*453,59 g*); pound (sterling); *10 Pfund* ten pounds

'pfundweise *adv* by the pound

pfuschen ['pfuʃən] F *v/i* (*ge-*, *h*), **Pfuscherei** [pfuʃə'rai] F *f* (*-*; *-en*) bungle, botch

Pfütze ['pfʏtsə] *f* (*-*; *-n*) puddle, pool

Phänomen [feno'me:n] *n* (*-s*; *-e*) phenomenon

phänomenal [fenome'na:l] *adj* phenomenal

Phantasie *etc* → *Fantasie etc*

pharmazeutisch [farma'tsɔytɪʃ] *adj* pharmaceutic(al)

Phase ['fa:zə] *f* (*-*; *-n*) phase (*a.* ELECTR), stage

Philosoph [filo'zo:f] *m* (*-en*; *-en*) philosopher

Philosophie [filozo'fi:] *f* (*-*; *-n*) philosophy

philosophieren [filozo'fi:rən] *v/i* (*no -ge-*, *h*) philosophize (*über acc* on)

Philo'sophin *f* (*-*; *-nen*) (woman) philosopher

philosophisch [filo'zo:fɪʃ] *adj* philosophical

phlegmatisch [fle'gma:tɪʃ] *adj* phlegmatic

Phonetik [fo'ne:tɪk] *f* (*-*; *no pl*) phonetics

pho'netisch *adj* phonetic

Phosphor ['fɔsfo:ɐ] *m* (*-s*; *-e*) CHEM phosphorus

Photo... → *Foto...*

Phrase ['fra:zə] *contp f* (*-*; *-n*) cliché (phrase)

Physik [fy'zi:k] *f* (*-*; *no pl*) physics

physikalisch [fyzi'ka:lɪʃ] *adj* physical

Physiker ['fy:zikɐ] *m* (*-s*; *-*), **'Physikerin** *f* (*-*; *-nen*) physicist

physisch ['fy:zɪʃ] *adj* physical

Pianist [pja'nɪst] *m* (*-en*; *-en*), **Pia'nistin** *f* (*-*; *-nen*) MUS pianist

Piano ['pja:no] *n* (*-s*; *-s*) MUS piano

Picke ['pɪkə] *f* (*-*; *-n*) TECH pick(axe)

Pickel[1] ['pɪkəl] *m* (*-s*; *-*) TECH pick(axe)

Pickel[2] *m* (*-s*; *-*) MED pimple

pickelig ['pɪkəlɪç] *adj* MED pimpled, pimply

picken ['pɪkən] *v/i and v/t* (*ge-*, *h*) ZO peck, pick

Picknick ['pɪknɪk] *n* (*-s*; *-e*, *-s*) picnic

'picknicken *v/i* (*ge-*, *h*) (have) a picnic

piekfein ['pi:k-] F *adj* posh

piep(s)en ['pi:p(s)ən] *v/i* (*ge-*, *h*) chirp, cheep; ELECTR bleep

Pietät [pje'tɛ:t] *f* (*-*; *no pl*) reverence; piety

pie'tätlos *adj* irreverent

pie'tätvoll *adj* reverent

Pik [pi:k] *n* (*-[s]*; *-[s]*) *cards*: spade(s)

pikant [pi'kant] *adj* piquant, spicy (*both a. fig*)

Pilger ['pɪlɡɐ] *m* (*-s*; *-*) pilgrim

Pilgerfahrt *f* pilgrimage

'Pilgerin *f* (*-*; *-nen*) pilgrim

'pilgern *v/i* (*ge-*, *sein*) (go on a) pilgrimage

Pille ['pɪlə] *f* (*-*; *-n*) pill; F *die Pille nehmen* be on the pill

Pilot [pi'lo:t] *m* (*-en*; *-en*), **Pi'lotin** *f* (*-*; *-nen*) pilot

Pilz [pɪlts] *m* (*-es*; *-e*) BOT mushroom (*a.*

fig); toadstool; MED fungus; **Pilze suchen** (*gehen*) go mushrooming

Pinguin ['pɪŋguiːn] *m* (-s; -e) ZO penguin

pinkeln ['pɪŋkəln] F *v/i* (ge-, h) (have a) pee, piddle

Pinsel ['pɪnzəl] *m* (-s; -) (paint)brush

'**Pinselstrich** *m* brushstroke

Pinzette [pɪn'tsɛtə] *f* (-; -n) tweezers

Pionier [pjo'niːɐ] *m* (-s; -e) pioneer, MIL *a.* engineer

Pirat [pi'raːt] *m* (-en; -en) pirate

Pisse ['pɪsə] V *f* (-; *no pl*), '**pissen** V *v/i* (ge-, h) piss

Piste ['pɪstə] *f* (-; -n) course; AVIAT runway

Pistole [pɪs'toːlə] *f* (-; -n) pistol, gun

Pkw, PKW ['peːkaːveː] ABBR *of* **Personenkraftwagen** (Br *a.* motor)car, automobile

Plache [plaxə] *Austrian f* (-; -n) awning, tarpaulin

placieren *etc* → **platzieren** *etc*

plädieren [plɛ'diːrən] *v/i* (no -ge-, h) JUR plead (**für** for)

Plädoyer [plɛdoa'jeː] *n* (-s; -s) JUR final speech, pleading

Plage ['plaːgə] *f* (-; -n) trouble, misery; plague; nuisance, F pest

'**plagen** *v/t* (ge-, h) trouble; bother; pester; **sich plagen** toil, drudge

Plakat [pla'kaːt] *n* (-[e]s; -e) poster, placard, bill

Plakette [pla'kɛtə] *f* (-; -n) plaque, badge

Plan [plaːn] *m* (-[e]s; *Pläne* ['plɛːnə]) plan; intention

Plane ['plaːnə] *f* (-; -n) awning, tarpaulin

'**planen** *v/t* (ge-, h) plan, make plans for

Planet [pla'neːt] *m* (-en; -en) ASTR planet

planieren [pla'niːrən] *v/t* (no -ge-, h) TECH level, plane, grade

Planke ['plaŋkə] *f* (-; -n) plank, (thick) board

plänkeln ['plɛŋkəln] *v/i* (ge-, h) skirmish

'**planlos** *adj* without plan; aimless

'**planmäßig 1.** *adj* scheduled (*arrival etc*); **2.** *adv* according to plan

Plan(t)schbecken ['planʃ-] *n* paddling pool

plan(t)schen ['planʃən] *v/i* (ge-, h) splash

Plantage [plan'taːʒə] *f* (-; -n) plantation

Plappermaul ['plapə-] F *n* chatterbox

plappern ['plapən] F *v/i* (ge-, h) chatter, prattle, babble, jabber

plärren ['plɛrən] F *v/i* and *v/t* (ge-, h) blubber; bawl; *radio:* blare

Plastik¹ ['plastɪk] *f* (-; -en) sculpture

'**Plastik²** *n* (-s; *no pl*) plastic; **Plastik...** in *cpds* ...besteck *etc:* plastic ...

plastisch ['plastɪʃ] *adj* plastic; three-dimensional; *fig* graphic

Platin ['plaːtiːn] *n* (-s; *no pl*) platinum

plätschern ['plɛtʃən] *v/i* (ge-, h) ripple (*a. fig*), splash

platt [plat] *adj* flat, level, even; *fig* trite; F flabbergasted

Platte ['platə] *f* (-; -n) sheet, plate; slab; board; panel; MUS record, disk, Br disc; EDP disk; GASTR dish; F bald pate; **kalte Platte** GASTR plate of cold cuts (Br meats)

plätten ['plɛtən] *v/t* (ge-, h) iron, press

'**Plattenspieler** *m* record player

'**Plattenteller** *m* turntable

'**Plattform** *f* platform

'**Plattfuß** *m* MED flat foot

'**Plattheit** *fig f* (-; -en) triviality; platitude

Plättli ['plɛtli] *Swiss n* (-s; -s) tile

Platz [plats] *m* (-es; *Plätze* ['plɛtsə]) place, spot; site; room, space; square; circus; seat; **es ist** (**nicht**) **genug Platz** there's (there isn't) enough room; **Platz machen für** make room for; make way for; **Platz nehmen** take a seat, sit down; **ist dieser Platz noch frei?** is this seat taken?; **j-n vom Platz stellen** SPORT send s.o. off; **auf eigenem Platz** SPORT at home; **auf die Plätze, fertig, los!** SPORT on your marks, get set, go!

'**Platzanweiser** *m* (-s; -) usher

Platzanweiserin *f* (-; -nen) usherette

Plätzchen ['plɛtsçən] *n* (-s; -) (little) place, spot; GASTR cookie, Br biscuit

platzen ['platsən] *v/i* (ge-, sein) burst (*a. fig*); crack, split; explode (*a. fig* w*ith*), blow up; F come to grief *or* nothing, fall through, blow up, *sl* go phut; break up

platzieren [pla'tsiːrən] *v/t* (no -ge-, h) place; **sich platzieren** SPORT be placed

Plat'zierung *f* (-; -en) place, placing

'**Platzkarte** *f* reservation (ticket)

Plätzli ['plɛtsli] *Swiss n* (-s; -) cutlet

'**Platzpa,trone** *f* blank (cartridge)

Platzregen *m* cloudburst, downpour

Platzreser,vierung *f* seat reservation

Platzverweis *m:* **e-n Platzverweis erhalten** SPORT be sent off

Platzwart *m* (-s; -e) SPORT groundkeeper, Br groundsman

Platzwunde *f* MED cut, laceration

Plauderei [plaudə'rai] *f* (-; -en) chat

plaudern ['plaudən] *v/i* (ge-, h) (have a) chat

plauschen ['plauʃən] *Austrian v/i* (have a) chat

pleite ['plaitə] F *adj* broke

'**Pleite** F *f* (-; -n) bankruptcy; *fig* flop

pleitegehen go broke

Plombe ['plɔmbə] *f* (-; -n) TECH seal; MED

filling
plombieren [plɔm'biːrən] *v/t* (*no -ge-, h*)
TECH seal; MED fill
plötzlich ['plœtslɪç] **1.** *adj* sudden; **2.** *adv*
suddenly, all of a sudden
plump [plʊmp] *adj* clumsy
plumps *int* thud, plop
plumpsen ['plʊmpsən] *v/i* (*ge-, sein*) thud,
plop, flop
Plunder ['plʊndɐ] F *m* (*-s; no pl*) trash,
junk
Plünderer ['plʏndərɐ] *m* (*-s; -*) looter,
plunderer
plündern ['plʏndɐn] *v/i and v/t* (*ge-, h*)
plunder, loot
Plural ['pluːraːl] *m* (*-s; -e*) LING plural
plus [plʊs] *adv* plus
Plusquamperfekt ['pluskvamperfɛkt] *n*
(*-s; -e*) LING past perfect
Pneu [pnɔy] *Swiss m* (*-s; -s*) tire, *Br* tyre
Po [poː] F *m* (*-s; -s*) bottom, behind
Pöbel ['pøːbəl] *m* (*-s; no pl*) mob, rabble
pochen ['pɔxən] *v/i* (*ge-, h*) knock, rap
(*both:* **an** *acc* at)
Pocke ['pɔkə] *f* (*-; -n*) MED pock
'**Pocken** *pl* MED smallpox
Pockenimpfung *f* MED smallpox vaccina-
tion
Podest [po'dɛst] *n, m* (*-[e]s; -e*) platform;
fig pedestal
Podium ['poːdjʊm] *n* (*-s; -ien*) podium,
platform
'**Podiumsdiskussi̱on** *f* panel discussion
Poesie [poe'ziː] *f* (*-; -n*) poetry
Poet [po'eːt] *m* (*-en; -en*), **Po'etin** *f* (*-;
-nen*) poet
poetisch [po'eːtɪʃ] *adj* poetic(al)
Pointe ['poɛ̃tə] *f* (*-; -n*) point, punch line
Pokal [po'kaːl] *m* (*-s; -e*) goblet; SPORT cup
'**Pokalendspiel** *n* SPORT cup final
'**Pokalsieger** *m* SPORT cup winner
'**Pokalspiel** *n* SPORT cup tie
pökeln ['pøːkəln] *v/t* (*ge-, h*) salt
Pol [poːl] *m* (*-s; -e*) GEOGR pole
polar [po'laːɐ] *adj* polar
Pole ['poːlə] *m* (*-n; -n*) Pole
'**Polen** Poland
Polemik [po'leːmɪk] *f* (*-; -en*) polemic(s)
po'lemisch *adj* polemic(al)
polemisieren [polemi'ziːrən] *v/i* (*no -ge-,
h*) polemize
Police [po'liːsə] *f* (*-; -n*) policy
Polier [po'liːɐ] *m* (*-s; -e*) TECH foreman
polieren [po'liːrən] *v/t* (*no -ge-, h*) polish
Polin ['poːlɪn] *f* (*-; -nen*) Pole, Polish wom-
an
Politik [poli'tiːk] *f* (*-; no pl*) politics; pol-
icy (*a. fig*)
Politiker(in) [po'liːtikɐ (-kərɪn)] (*-s; -/-;*

-nen) politician
politisch [po'liːtɪʃ] *adj* political
politisieren [politi'ziːrən] *v/i* (*no -ge-, h*)
talk politics
Polizei [poli'tsai] *f* (*-; no pl*) police
Polizeiauto *n* police car
Polizeibeamte *m*, **-in** *f* police officer
poli'zeilich *adj* (of or by the) police
Poli'zeiprä̱sidium *n* police headquarters
Polizeire̱vier *n* police station; precinct,
Br district
Polizeischutz *m*: *unter Polizeischutz*
under police guard
Polizeistreife *f* police patrol
Polizeistunde *f* closing time
Polizeiwache *f* police station
Polizist [poli'tsɪst] *m* (*-en; -en*) policeman
Poli'zistin *f* (*-; -nen*) policewoman
polnisch ['pɔlnɪʃ] *adj* Polish
Polster ['pɔlstɐ] *n* (*-s; -*) upholstery; cush-
ion; pad(ding); *fig* bolster
Polstergarni̱tur *f* three-piece suite
'**Polstermöbel** *pl* upholstered furniture
'**polstern** *v/t* (*ge-, h*) upholster; pad
'**Polstersessel** *m* easy chair, armchair
'**Polsterstuhl** *m* upholstered chair
Polsterung ['pɔlstərʊŋ] *f* (*-; -en*) uphol-
stery; padding
poltern ['pɔltɐn] *v/i* (*ge-, h*) rumble; *fig*
bluster
Pommes frites [pɔm'frɪt] *pl* French fries,
French fried potatoes, *Br* chips
Pomp [pɔmp] *m* (*-[e]s; no pl*) pomp
pompös [pɔm'pøːs] *adj* showy
Pony[1] ['pɔni] *n* (*-s; -s*) ZO pony
'**Pony**[2] *m* (*-s; -s*) fringe, bangs
Popgruppe ['pɔp-] *f* MUS pop group
'**Popmu̱sik** *f* pop music
populär [popu'lɛːɐ] *adj* popular
Popularität [populari'tɛːt] *f* (*-; no pl*) pop-
ularity
Pore ['poːrə] *f* (*-; -n*) pore
Porno ['pɔrno] F *m* (*-s; -s*), **Pornofilm** *m*
porn (film), blue movie
Pornoheft *n* porn magazine
porös [po'røːs] *adj* porous
Portemonnaie [pɔrtmɔ'neː] *n* (*-s; -s*)
purse
Portier [pɔr'tjeː] *m* (*-s; -s*) doorman, por-
ter
Portion [pɔr'tsjoːn] *f* (*-; -en*) portion,
share; helping, serving
Portmonee *n* → **Portemonnaie**
Porto ['pɔrto] *n* (*-s; -s, -ti*) postage
Porträt [pɔr'trɛː] *n* (*-s; -s*) portrait
porträtieren [pɔrtrɛ'tiːrən] *v/t* (*no -ge-, h*)
portray
Portugal ['pɔrtugal] Portugal
Portugiese [pɔrtu'giːzə] *m* (*-n; -n*), **Por-**

tu'giesin f (-; -nen), portu'giesisch adj Portuguese

Porzellan [pɔrtsɛ'laːn] n (-s; -e) china, porcelain

Posaune [po'zaunə] f (-; -n) MUS trombone; fig trumpet

Pose ['poːzə] f (-; -n) pose, attitude

Position [pozi'tsjoːn] f (-; -en) position (a. fig)

positiv ['poːzitiːf] adj positive

possessiv [pɔsɛ'siːf] adj LING possessive

Posses'sivpro,nomen n LING possessive pronoun

Post [pɔst] f (-; no pl) mail, esp Br post; letters; **mit der Post** by post or mail

Postamt n post office

Postanweisung f money order

Postbeamte m, **-in** f post office clerk

Postbote m mailman, Br postman

Posten ['pɔstən] m (-s; -) post; job, position; MIL sentry; ECON item; lot, parcel

'Postfach n (PO) box

postieren [pɔs'tiːrən] v/t (no -ge-, h) post, station, place; **sich postieren** station o.s.

'Postkarte f postcard

'Postkutsche f stagecoach

'postlagernd adj (in care of) general delivery, Br poste restante

'Postleitzahl f zip code, Br post(al) code

Postmi,nister m Postmaster General

Postscheck m postal check (Br cheque)

Postsparbuch n post-office savings book

Poststempel m postmark

'postwendend adv by return mail, Br by return of post

'Postwertzeichen n (postage) stamp

Postzustellung f postal or mail delivery

Potenz [po'tɛnts] f (-; -en) a) (no pl) MED potency, b) MATH power

Pracht [praxt] f (-; no pl) splendo(u)r, magnificence

prächtig ['prɛçtiç] adj splendid, magnificent, fig a. great, super

Prädikat [prɛdi'kaːt] n (-[e]s; -e) LING predicate

prägen ['prɛːgən] v/t (ge-, h) stamp, coin (a. fig)

prahlen ['praːlən] v/i (ge-, h) brag, boast (both: **mit** of), talk big, show off

Prahler [pra:le] m (-s; -) boaster, braggart

Prahlerei [praːləˈrai] f (-; -en) boasting, bragging

'prahlerisch adj boastful; showy

Praktikant [prakti'kant] m (-en; -en), **Prakti'kantin** f (-; -nen) trainee

Praktiken ['praktikən] pl practices

'Praktikum n (-s; -ka) practical training

'praktisch 1. adj practical; useful, handy; **praktischer Arzt** general practitioner; **2.** adv practically; virtually

praktizieren [prakti'tsiːrən] v/t (no -ge-, h) practice (Br practise) medicine or law

Prälat [prɛ'laːt] m (-en; -en) REL prelate

Praline [pra'liːnə] f (-; -n) chocolate

prall [pral] adj tight; well-rounded; bulging; blazing (sun)

prallen ['pralən] v/i (ge-, sein) **prallen gegen** (or **auf** acc) crash or bump into

Prämie ['prɛːmjə] f (-; -n) premium; prize; bonus

prämieren [prɛ'miːrən], **prämieren** [prɛmi'iːrən] v/t (no -ge-, h) award a prize to

Pranke ['praŋkə] f (-; -n) zo paw (a. F)

Präparat [prɛpa'raːt] n (-[e]s; -e) preparation

präparieren [prɛpa'riːrən] v/t (no -ge-, h) prepare; MED, BOT, ZO dissect

Präposition [prɛpozi'tsjoːn] f (-; -en) LING preposition

Prärie [prɛ'riː] f (-; -n) prairie

Präsens ['prɛːzɛns] n (-; -sentia [prɛ'zɛntsja]) LING present (tense)

präsentieren [prɛzɛn'tiːrən] v/t (no -ge-, h) present; offer

Präsident [prɛzi'dɛnt] m (-en; -en), **Präsi'dentin** f (-; -nen) president; chairman (chairwoman)

präsidieren [prɛzi'diːrən] v/i preside (**in** dat over)

Präsidium [prɛ'ziːdjum] n (-s; -ien) presidency

prasseln ['prasəln] v/i (ge-, h) rain etc: patter; fire: crackle

Präteritum [prɛ'teːritum] n (-s; -ta) LING past (tense)

Praxis ['praksis] f (-; Praxen) a) (no pl) practice (a. MED, JUR), b) MED doctor's office, Br surgery

Präzedenzfall [prɛtse'dɛnts-] m precedent

präzis [prɛ'tsiːs], **präzise** [prɛ'tsiːzə] adj precise

Präzision [prɛtsi'zjoːn] f (-; no pl) precision

predigen ['preːdigən] v/i and v/t (ge-, h) preach

Prediger ['preːdigɐ] m (-s; -), **'Predigerin** f (-; -nen) preacher

Predigt ['preːdiçt] f (-; -en) sermon

Preis [prais] m (-es; -e) price (a. fig); prize; film etc: award; reward; **um jeden Preis** at all costs

'Preisausschreiben n competition

Preiselbeere ['praizəl-] f BOT cranberry

preisen ['praizən] v/t (irr, ge-, h) praise

'Preiserhöhung f rise or increase in

price(s)

'preisgeben v/t (irr, **geben**, sep, -ge-, h) abandon; reveal, give away

'preisgekrönt adj prize-winning; film etc: award-winning

'Preisgericht n jury

Preislage f price range

Preisliste f price list

Preisnachlass m discount

Preisrätsel n competition

Preisrichter(in) judge

Preisschild n price tag

Preisstopp m price freeze

Preisträger(in) prizewinner

'preiswert adj cheap

prellen ['prɛlən] v/t (ge-, h) fig cheat (**um** out of); **sich et. prellen** MED bruise s.th.

'Prellung f (-; -en) MED contusion, bruise

Premiere [prə'mjeːrə] f (-; -n) THEA etc first night, première

Premiermi,nister [prə'mjeː-] m, **Pre'miermi,nisterin** f prime minister

Presse ['prɛsə] f (-; -n a) (no pl) press, b) squeezer

Presse... in cpds ...agentur, ...konferenz, ...fotograf etc: press ...

Pressefreiheit f freedom of the press

Pressemeldung f news item

'pressen v/t (ge-, h) press; squeeze

'Pressetri,büne f press box

Pressevertreter m reporter

'Pressluft f compressed air

Pressluft... in cpds ...bohrer, ...hammer etc: pneumatic ...

Prestige [prɛs'tiːʒə] n (-s; no pl) prestige

Prestigeverlust m loss of prestige or face

Preuße ['prɔysə] m (-n; -n), **'Preußin** f (-; -nen), **'preußisch** adj Prussian

prickeln ['prɪkəln] v/i (ge-, h) prickle; tingle

pries [priːs] pret of **preisen**

Priester ['priːstə] m (-s; -) priest

Priesterin ['priːstərɪn] f (-; -nen) priestess

'priesterlich adj priestly

prima ['priːma] F adj great, super

primär [pri'mɛːɐ] adj primary

Primararzt [pri'maːɐ-] Austrian m → **Oberarzt**

Primarschule Swiss f → **Grundschule**

Primel ['priːməl] f (-; -n) BOT primrose

primitiv [primi'tiːf] adj primitive

Prinz [prɪnts] m (-en; -en) prince

Prinzessin [prɪn'tsɛsɪn] f (-; -nen) princess

'Prinzgemahl m prince consort

Prinzip [prɪn'tsiːp] n (-s; -ien) principle (**aus** on; **im** in)

prinzipiell [prɪntsi'pjɛl] adv as a matter of principle

Prise ['priːzə] f (-; -n) **e-e Prise Salz** etc a pinch of salt etc

Prisma ['prɪsma] n (-s; -men) prism

Pritsche ['prɪtʃə] f (-; -n) plank bed; MOT platform

privat [pri'vaːt] adj private; personal

Pri'vat... in cpds ...leben, ...schule, ...detektiv etc: private ...

Privatangelegenheit f personal or private matter or affair; **das ist m-e Privatangelegenheit** that's my own business

Privileg [privi'leːk] n (-[e]s; -gien [privi-'leːgjən]) privilege

pro [proː] prp (acc) per; **2 Mark pro Stück** two marks each

Pro n: **das Pro und Kontra** the pros and cons

Probe ['proːbə] f (-; -n) trial, test; sample; THEA rehearsal; MATH proof; **auf Probe** on probation; **auf die Probe stellen** put to the test

Probealarm m test alarm, fire drill

Probeaufnahmen pl film: screen test

Probefahrt f test drive

Probeflug m test flight

'proben v/i and v/t (ge-, h) THEA etc rehearse

'probeweise adv on trial; on probation

'Probezeit f (time of) probation

probieren [pro'biːrən] v/t (no -ge-, h) try; taste

Problem [pro'bleːm] n (-s; -e) problem

problematisch [proble'maːtɪʃ] adj problematic(al)

Produkt [pro'dʊkt] n (-[e]s; -e) product (a. MATH); result

Produktion [prodʊk'tsjoːn] f (-; -en) production; output

produktiv [prodʊk'tiːf] adj productive

Produktivität [prodʊktivi'tɛːt] f (-; no pl) productivity

Produzent [produ'tsɛnt] m (-en; -en), **Produ'zentin** f (-; -nen) producer

produzieren [produ'tsiːrən] v/t (no -ge-, h) produce

professionell [profesjo'nɛl] adj professional

Professor [pro'fɛsoːɐ] m (-s; -en [profɛ-'soːrən]), **Profes'sorin** f (-; -nen) professor

Professur [profɛ'suːɐ] f (-; -en) professorship, chair (**für** of)

Profi ['proːfi] m (-s; -s) pro

Profi... in cpds ...boxer, ...fußballer etc: professional

Profil [pro'fiːl] n (-s; -e) profile; MOT tread

profilieren [profi'liːrən] v/refl (no -ge-, h) distinguish o.s.

Profit [pro'fiːt] m (-[e]s; -e) profit

profitieren [profi'ti:rən] v/i (no -ge-, h) profit (**von** or **bei et.** from or by s.th.)

Prognose [pro'gno:zə] f (-; -n) prediction; METEOR forecast; MED prognosis

Programm [pro'gram] n (-s; -e) program(me Br), TV a. channel; EDP program

Programmfehler m EDP program error, bug

programmieren [progra'mi:rən] v/t (no -ge-, h) program (a. EDP)

Programmierer [progra'mi:rɐ] m (-s; -), **Program'miererin** f (-; -nen) EDP programmer

Projekt [pro'jɛkt] n (-[e]s; -e) project

Projektion [projɛk'tsjo:n] f (-; -en) projection

Projektor [pro'jɛkto:ɐ] m (-s; -en [projɛk'to:rən]) projector

proklamieren [prokla'mi:rən] v/t (no -ge-, h) proclaim

Prokurist [proku'rɪst] m (-en; -en), **Proku'ristin** f (-; -nen) authorized signatory

Proletarier [prole'ta:rjɐ] m (-s; -), **proletarisch** [-'ta:rɪʃ] adj proletarian

Prolog [pro'lo:k] m (-[e]s; -e) prologue

Promillegrenze [pro'milə-] f (blood) alcohol limit

prominent [promi'nɛnt] adj prominent

Prominenz [promi'nɛnts] f (-; no pl) notables; high society

Promotion [promo'tsjo:n] f (-; -en) UNIV doctorate

promovieren [promo'vi:rən] v/i (no -ge-, h) do one's doctorate

prompt [prɔmpt] adj prompt; quick

Pronomen [pro'no:mən] n (-s; -mina) LING pronoun

Propeller [pro'pɛlɐ] m (-s; -) propeller

Prophet [pro'fe:t] m (-en; -en) prophet

pro'phetisch adj prophetic

prophezeien [profe'tsaiən] v/t (no -ge-, h) prophesy, predict

Prophe'zeiung f (-; -en) prophecy, prediction

Proportion [propɔr'tsjo:n] f (-; -en) proportion

Proporz [pro'pɔrts] m (-es; -e) POL proportional representation

Prosa ['pro:za] f (-; no pl) prose

Prospekt [pro'spɛkt] m (-[e]s; -e) prospectus; brochure, pamphlet

prost [pro:st] int cheers!

Prostituierte [prostitu'i:rtə] f (-n; -n) prostitute

Protest [pro'tɛst] m (-[e]s; -e) protest; **aus Protest** in (or as a) protest

Protestant [protɛs'tant] m (-en; -en), **Protes'tantin** f (-; -nen), **protes'tantisch** adj REL Protestant

protestieren [protɛs'ti:rən] v/i (no -ge-, h) protest

Prothese [pro'te:zə] f (-; -n) MED artificial limb; denture

Protokoll [proto'kɔl] n (-s; -e) record, minutes; protocol; (**das**) **Protokoll führen** take or keep the minutes; **zu Protokoll nehmen** JUR record

Protokollführer m keeper of the minutes

protokollieren [protokɔ'li:rən] v/t and v/i (no -ge-, h) take the minutes (of); JUR record

protzen ['prɔtsən] F v/i (ge-, h) show off (**mit et.** s.th.)

protzig ['prɔtsɪç] adj showy, flashy

Proviant [pro'vjant] m (-s; no pl) provisions, food

Provinz [pro'vɪnts] f (-; -en) province; fig country

provinziell [provɪn'tsjɛl] adj provincial (a. contp)

Provision [provi'zjo:n] f (-; -en) ECON commission

provisorisch [provi'zo:rɪʃ] adj provisional, temporary

provozieren [provo'tsi:rən] v/t (no -ge-, h) provoke

Prozent [pro'tsɛnt] n (-[e]s; -e) per cent; F pl discount

Prozentsatz m percentage

prozentual [protsɛn'tua:l] adj proportional; **prozentualer Anteil** percentage

Prozess [pro'tsɛs] m (-es; -e) process (a. TECH, CHEM etc); JUR action; lawsuit, case; trial; **j-m den Prozess machen** take s.o. to court; **e-n Prozess gewinnen (verlieren)** win (lose) a case

prozessieren [protsɛ'si:rən] v/i (no -ge-, h) JUR go to court; **gegen j-n prozessieren** bring an action against s.o., take s.o. to court

Prozession [protsɛ'sjo:n] f (-; -en) procession

Prozessor [pro'tsɛso:ɐ] m (-s; -en [protsɛ'so:rən]) EDP processor

prüde ['pry:də] adj prudish; **prüde sein** be a prude

prüfen ['pry:fən] v/t (ge-, h) PED etc examine, test (a. TECH); check; inspect (a. TECH); fig consider

prüfend adj searching

Prüfer ['pry:fɐ] m (-s; -), **'Prüferin** f (-; -nen) PED etc examiner; esp TECH tester

Prüfling ['pry:flɪŋ] m (-s; -e) candidate

'Prüfstein m touchstone (**für** of)

'Prüfung f (-; -en) examination, F exam; test; check(ing), inspection; **e-e Prüfung machen (bestehen, nicht bestehen)** take (pass, fail) an exam(ination)

'**Prüfungsarbeit** f examination or test paper

Prügel ['pry:gəl] F pl (**e-e Tracht**) **Prügel bekommen** get a (good) beating or hiding or thrashing

Prüge'lei F f (-; -en) fight

'**prügeln** v/t (ge-, h) beat, flog; **sich prügeln** (have a) fight

'**Prügelstrafe** f corporal punishment

Prunk [pruŋk] m (-[e]s; no pl) splendo(u)r, pomp

'**prunkvoll** adj splendid, magnificent

PS [pe:'ʔɛs] ABBR of **Pferdestärke** horsepower, HP

Psalm [psalm] m (-s; -en) REL psalm

Pseudonym [psɔydo'ny:m] n (-s; -e) pseudonym

pst [pst] int sh!, ssh!; psst!

Psyche ['psy:çə] f (-; -n) mind, psyche

Psychiater [psy'çja:tɐ] m (-s; -), **Psy'chiaterin** f (-; -nen) psychiatrist

psychiatrisch [psy'çja:trɪʃ] adj psychiatric

psychisch ['psy:çɪʃ] adj mental, MED a. psychic

Psychoana'lyse [psyço-] f psychoanalysis

Psychologe [psyço'lo:gə] m (-n; -n) psychologist (a. fig)

Psychologie [psyçolo'gi:] f (-; no pl) psychology

psycho'login f (-; -nen) psychologist

psycho'logisch adj psychological

Psychose [psy'ço:zə] f (-; -n) MED psychosis

psychosomatisch [psyçozo'ma:tɪʃ] adj MED psychosomatic

Pubertät [pubɛr'tɛ:t] f (-; no pl) puberty

Publikum ['pu:blikum] n (-s; no pl) audience, TV a. viewers, radio: a. listeners; SPORT crowd, spectators; ECON customers; public

publizieren [publi'tsi:rən] v/t (no -ge-, h) publish

Pudding ['pudɪŋ] m (-s; -e, -s) pudding, esp Br blancmange

Pudel ['pu:dəl] m (-s; -) ZO poodle

Puder ['pu:dɐ] m (-s; -) powder

'**Puderdose** f powder compact

'**pudern** v/t (ge-, h) powder; **sich pudern** powder one's face

'**Puderzucker** m confectioner's (Br icing) sugar

Puff[1] [puf] F m (-s; -s) brothel

Puff[2] m (-[e]s; Püffe ['pyfə]) hump; poke

Puffer ['pufɐ] m (-s; -) RAIL buffer (a. fig)

'**Puffmais** m popcorn

Pulli ['puli] F m (-s; -s) (light) sweater

Pullover [pu'lo:vɐ] m (-s; -) sweater, pullover

Puls [puls] m (-es; -e) MED pulse; pulse rate

Pulsader f ANAT artery

pulsieren [pul'zi:rən] v/i (no -ge-, h) MED pulsate (a. fig)

Pult [pult] n (-[e]s; -e) desk

Pulver ['pulvɐ] n (-s; -) powder; F cash, sl dough

pulv(e)rig ['pulv(ə)rɪç] adj powdery

pulverisieren [pulveri'zi:rən] v/t (no -ge-, h) pulverize

'**Pulverkaffee** m instant coffee

'**Pulverschnee** m powder snow

pumm(e)lig ['pum(ə)lɪç] F adj chubby, plump, tubby

Pumpe ['pumpə] f (-; -n) TECH pump

'**pumpen** v/i and v/t TECH pump; F lend; borrow

Punker ['paŋkɐ] F m (-s; -), '**Punkerin** f (-; -nen) punk

Punkt [puŋkt] m (-[e]s; -e) point (a. fig); dot; full stop, period; fig spot; place; **um Punkt zehn** (Uhr) at ten (o'clock) sharp; **nach Punkten gewinnen** etc SPORT win etc on points

punktieren [puŋk'ti:rən] v/t (no -ge-, h) dot; MED puncture

pünktlich ['pyŋktlɪç] adj punctual; **pünktlich sein** be on time

'**Pünktlichkeit** f (-; no pl) punctuality

'**Punktsieger** m SPORT winner on points

Punktspiel n SPORT league game

Pupille [pu'pilə] f (-; -n) ANAT pupil

Puppe ['pupə] f (-; -n) doll, F a. chick; THEA puppet (a. fig); MOT dummy; ZO chrysalis, pupa

'**Puppenspiel** n puppet show

'**Puppenstube** f doll's house

Puppenwagen m doll carriage, Br doll's pram

pur [pu:ɐ] adj pure (a. fig); whisky etc: straight, Br neat

Purpur ['purpur] m (-s; no pl) crimson

'**purpurrot** adj crimson

Purzelbaum ['purtsəl-] m somersault; **e-n Purzelbaum schlagen** turn a somersault

purzeln ['purtsəln] v/i (ge-, sein) tumble

Pute ['pu:tə] f (-; -n) ZO turkey (hen)

Puter ['pu:tɐ] m (-s; -) ZO turkey (cock)

Putsch [putʃ] m (-[e]s; -e) putsch, coup (d'état)

'**putschen** v/i (ge-, h) revolt, make a putsch

Putz [puts] m (-es; no pl) ARCH plaster (-ing); **unter Putz** ELECTR concealed

putzen ['putsən] (ge-, h) **1.** v/t clean; polish; wipe; **sich die Nase putzen** blow

one's nose; **sich die Zähne putzen** brush one's teeth; **2.** v/i do the cleaning; **putzen** (**gehen**) work as a cleaner
'**Putzfrau** f cleaner, cleaning woman or lady
putzig ['pʊtsɪç] adj funny, cute

'**Putzlappen** m cleaning rag
'**Putzmittel** n clean(s)er; polish
Puzzle ['pazəl] n (-s; -s) jigsaw (puzzle)
Pyjama [py'dʒa:ma] m (-s; -s) pajamas, Br pyjamas
Pyramide [pyra'mi:də] f (-; -n) pyramid

Q

Quacksalber ['kvakzalbɐ] m (-s; -) quack (doctor)
Quadrat [kva'dra:t] n (-[e]s; -e) square; **ins Quadrat erheben** MATH square; **Quadrat...** in cpds ...meile, ...meter, ...wurzel, ...zahl etc: square ...
qua'dratisch adj square; MATH quadratic
quaken ['kva:kən] v/i (ge-, h) duck: quack; frog: croak
quäken ['kvɛ:kən] v/i (ge-, h) squeak
Qual [kva:l] f (-; -en) pain, torment, agony; anguish
quälen ['kvɛ:lən] v/t (ge-, h) torment (a. fig); torture; fig pester, plague
Qualifikation [kvalifika'tsjo:n] f (-; -en) qualification
Qualifikati'ons... in cpds ...spiel etc: qualifying ...
qualifizieren [kvalifi'tsi:rən] v/t and v/refl (no -ge-, h) qualify
Qualität [kvali'tɛ:t] f (-; -en) quality
qualitativ [kvalita'ti:f] adj and adv in quality
Quali'täts... in cpds ...arbeit, ...waren etc: high-quality ...
Qualm [kvalm] m (-[e]s; no pl) (thick) smoke
qualmen ['kvalmən] v/i (ge-, h) smoke; F be a heavy smoker
'**qualvoll** adj very painful; agonizing
Quantität [kvanti'tɛ:t] f (-; -en) quantity
quantitativ [kvantita'ti:f] adj and adv in quantity
Quantum ['kvantʊm] n (-s; Quanten) amount, fig a. share
Quarantäne [karan'tɛ:nə] f (-; -n) (**unter Quarantäne stellen** put in) quarantine
Quark [kvark] m (-s; no pl) curd, cottage cheese
Quartal [kvar'ta:l] n (-s; -e) quarter (of a year)
Quartett [kvar'tɛt] n (-[e]s; -e) MUS quartet(te)

Quartier [kvar'ti:ɐ] n (-s; -e) accommodation; Swiss: quarter
Quarz [kva:ɐts] m (-es; -e) MIN quartz
Quatsch [kvatʃ] F m (-[e]s; no pl) nonsense, rubbish, sl rot, crap, bullshit; **Quatsch machen** fool around; joke, F kid
quatschen ['kvatʃən] F v/i (ge-, h) talk rubbish; chat
Quecksilber ['kvɛkzɪlbɐ] n (-s; no pl) mercury, quicksilver
Quelle ['kvɛlə] f (-; -n) spring, source (a. fig), well, fig a. origin
'**quellen** v/i (irr, ge-, sein) pour (**aus** from)
'**Quellenangabe** f reference
quengeln ['kvɛŋəln] F v/i (ge-, h) whine
quer [kveːɐ] adv across; crosswise; **kreuz und quer** all over the place; **kreuz und quer durch Deutschland fahren** travel all over Germany
Quere ['kveːrə] f: F **j-m in die Quere kommen** get in s.o.'s way
Querfeld'einlauf m SPORT cross-country race
'**Querlatte** f SPORT crossbar
'**Querschläger** m MIL ricochet
'**Querschnitt** m cross-section (a. fig)
'**querschnitt(s)gelähmt** adj MED paraplegic
'**Querstraße** f intersecting road; **zweite Querstraße rechts** second turning on the right
Querulant [kveru'lant] m (-en; -en), **Queru'lantin** f (-; -nen) querulous person
quetschen ['kvɛtʃən] v/t and v/refl (ge-, h) squeeze; MED bruise (o.s.)
'**Quetschung** f (-; -en) MED bruise
quiek(s)en ['kvi:k(s)ən] v/i (ge-, h) squeak, squeal
quietschen ['kvi:tʃən] v/i (ge-, h) squeal; screech; squeak, creak
quitt [kvɪt] adj: **mit j-m quitt sein** be quits

or even with s.o. (*a. fig*)
quittieren [kvɪ'tiːrən] *v/t* (*no -ge-, h*) ECON give a receipt for
'**Quittung** *f* (-; *-en*) receipt; *fig* answer
quoll [kvɔl] *pret of* **quellen**

Quote ['kvoːtə] *f* (-; *-n*) quota; share; rate
'**Quotenregelung** *f* quota system
Quotient [kvo'tsjɛnt] *m* (*-en*; *-en*) MATH quotient

R

Rabatt [ra'bat] *m* (-[*e*]*s*; *-e*) ECON discount, rebate
Rabe ['raːbə] *m* (*-n*; *-n*) ZO raven
rabiat [ra'bjaːt] *adj* rough, tough
Rache ['raxə] *f* (-; *no pl*) revenge; *aus Rache für* in revenge for
Rachen ['raxən] *m* (*-s*; -) ANAT throat
rächen ['rɛçən] *v/t* (*ge-, h*) avenge *s.th.*; revenge *s.o.*; *sich an j-m für et. rächen* revenge o.s. *or* take revenge on s.o. for s.th.
Rächer ['rɛçɐ] *m* (*-s*; -) avenger
rachsüchtig ['rax-] *adj* revengeful, vindictive
Rad [raːt] *n* (-[*e*]*s*; *Räder* ['rɛːdɐ]) wheel; bicycle, F bike; *Rad fahren* cycle, ride a bicycle, F bike; *ein Rad schlagen* peacock: spread its tail; SPORT turn a (cart)-wheel
Radar [ra'daːɐ] *m*, *n* (*-s*; *-e*) radar
Radarfalle *f* MOT speed trap
Radarkon,trolle *f* MOT radar speed check
Radarschirm *m* radar screen
Radarstati,on *f* radar station
radeln ['raːdəln] F *v/i* (*ge-, sein*) bike
Rädelsführer ['rɛːdəls-] *m* ringleader
Räderwerk ['rɛːdɐ-] *n* TECH gearing
'**Radfahrer** *m* (*-s*; -), '**Radfahrerin** *f* (-; *-nen*) cyclist
radieren [ra'diːrən] *v/t* (*no -ge-, h*) erase, rub out; *art:* etch
Radiergummi [ra'diːɐ-] *m* eraser, *Br a.* rubber
Ra'dierung *f* (-; *-en*) *art:* etching
Radieschen [ra'diːsçən] *n* (*-s*; -) BOT (red) radish
radikal [radi'kaːl] *adj*, **Radi'kale** *m, f* (*-n*; *-n*) radical
Radikalismus [radika'lɪsmʊs] *m* (-; *no pl*) radicalism
Radio ['raːdjo] *n* (*-s*; *-s*) radio; *im Radio* on the radio; *Radio hören* listen to the radio
radioak'tiv [radjo-] *adj* PHYS radioactive; *radioaktiver Niederschlag* fall-out

Radioaktivi'tät *f* (-; *no pl*) radioactivity
'**Radiowecker** *m* clock radio
Radius ['raːdjʊs] *m* (*-s*; *Radien*) radius
'**Radkappe** *f* hubcap
Radrennbahn *f* cycling track
Radrennen *n* cycle race
Radsport *m* cycling
Radsportler *m* cyclist
Radweg *m* cycle track *or* path, bikeway
raffen ['rafən] *v/t* (*ge-, h*) gather up; *an sich raffen* grab
Raffinerie [rafinə'riː] *f* (-; *-n*) CHEM refinery
Raffinesse [rafi'nɛsə] *f* (-; *-n*) a) (*no pl*) shrewdness, b) refinement
raffiniert [rafi'niːɐt] *adj* refined (*a. fig*); *fig* shrewd, clever
ragen ['raːgən] *v/i* (*ge-, h*) tower (up), rise (high)
Rahe ['raːə] *f* (-; *-n*) MAR yard
Rahm [raːm] *m* (-[*e*]*s*; *no pl*) cream
rahmen ['raːmən] *v/t* (*ge-, h*) frame; PHOT mount
'**Rahmen** *m* (*-s*; -) frame; *fig* framework; setting; scope; *aus dem Rahmen fallen* be out of the ordinary
Rakete [ra'keːtə] *f* (-; *-n*) rocket, MIL *a.* missile; *ferngelenkte Rakete* guided missile; *e-e Rakete abfeuern (starten)* launch a rocket *or* missile
Ra'ketenantrieb *m* rocket propulsion; *mit Raketenantrieb* rocket-propelled
Raketenbasis *f* MIL rocket *or* missile base *or* site
rammen ['ramən] *v/t* (*ge-, h*) ram; MOT *etc* hit, collide with
Rampe ['rampə] *f* (-; *-n*) (loading) ramp
'**Rampenlicht** *n* (-[*e*]*s*; *no pl*) THEA footlights; *fig* limelight
Ramsch [ramʃ] F *m* (*-es*; *no pl*) junk
Rand [rant] *m* (-[*e*]*s*; *Ränder* ['rɛndɐ]) edge, border; brink (*a. fig*); rim; brim; margin; *am Rand(e) des Ruins etc* on the brink of ruin *etc*

randalieren [randa'li:rən] *v/i (no -ge-, h)* kick up a racket

Randalierer [randa'li:rə] *m (-s; -)* rowdy, hooligan

'**Randbemerkung** *f* marginal note; *fig* comment

Randgruppe *f* fringe group

'**randlos** *adj* rimless

'**Randstreifen** *m* MOT shoulder

rang [raŋ] *pret of* **ringen**

Rang *m (-[e]s; Ränge* ['reŋə]*)* position, rank (*a.* MIL); THEA balcony, *Br* circle; *pl* SPORT terraces

rangieren [raŋ'ʒi:rən] *(no -ge-, h)* **1.** *v/t* RAIL switch, *Br* shunt; **2.** *fig v/i* rank (**vor j-m** before s.o.)

'**Rangordnung** *f* hierarchy

Ranke ['raŋkə] *f (-; -n)* BOT tendril

'**ranken** *v/refl (ge-, h)* BOT creep, climb

rann [ran] *pret of* **rinnen**

rannte ['rantə] *pret of* **rennen**

Ranzen ['rantsən] *m (-s; -)* knapsack; satchel

ranzig ['rantsɪç] *adj* rancid, rank

Rappe ['rapə] *m (-n; -n)* ZO black horse

rar [ra:ɐ] *adj* rare, scarce

Rarität [rari'tɛ:t] *f (-; -en)* a) curiosity, b) *(no pl)* rarity

rasch [raʃ] *adj* quick, swift; prompt

rascheln ['raʃəln] *v/i (ge-, h)* rustle

rasen ['ra:zən] *v/i* a) *(ge-, sein)* F MOT race, tear, speed, b) *(ge-, h)* rage; **rasen vor Begeisterung** roar with enthusiasm

'**Rasen** *m (-s; -)* lawn, grass

'**rasend** *adj* breakneck; raging; agonizing; splitting; thunderous

'**Rasenmäher** *m* lawn mower

Rasenplatz *m* lawn; *tennis:* grass court

Raserei [ra:zə'raɪ] *f (-; -en)* a) *(no pl)* frenzied rage; frenzy, madness, b) *f* MOT reckless driving

Rasierappa,rat [ra'zi:ɐ-] *m* (safety) razor; *esp* **elektrischer Rasierapparat** shaver

Rasiercreme *f* shaving cream

rasieren [ra'zi:rən] *v/t and v/refl (no -ge-, h)* shave

Ra'sierklinge *f* razor blade

Rasiermesser *n* (straight) razor

Rasierpinsel *m* shaving brush

Rasierseife *f* shaving soap

Rasierwasser *n* aftershave (lotion)

Rasse ['rasə] *f (-; -n)* race; zo breed

'**Rassehund** *m* ZO pedigree dog

Rassel ['rasəl] *f (-; -n)*, '**rasseln** *v/i (ge-, h)* rattle

'**Rassen...** *in cpds* ...diskriminierung, ...konflikt, ...probleme *etc: mst* racial ...

Rassentrennung *f* POL (racial) segregation; HIST apartheid

Rassenunruhen *pl* race riots

rassig ['rasɪç] *adj* classy

rassisch ['rasɪʃ] *adj* racial

Rassismus [ra'sɪsmʊs] *m (-; no pl)* POL racism

Ras'sist(in) *(-en; -en/-; -nen)*, **ras'sistisch** *adj* POL racist

Rast [rast] *f (-; -en)* rest, stop; break

rasten ['rastən] *v/i (ge-, h)* rest, stop, take a break

'**rastlos** *adj* restless

'**Rastplatz** *m* resting place; MOT rest area, *Br* lay-by

'**Raststätte** *f* MOT service area

Rasur [ra'zu:ɐ] *f (-; -en)* shave

Rat [ra:t] *m (-[e]s; Räte* ['rɛ:tə]*)* a) *(no pl)* (piece of) advice, b) council; **j-n um Rat fragen** ask s.o.'s advice; **j-s Rat befolgen** take s.o.'s advice

Rate ['ra:tə] *f (-; -en)* rate; ECON instal(l)-ment; **auf Raten** by instal(l)ments

raten ['ra:tən] *v/t and v/i (irr, ge-, h)* advise; guess; solve; **j-m zu et. raten** advise s.o. to do s.th.; **rate mal!** (have a) guess!

'**Ratenzahlung** *f →* **Abzahlung**

'**Rateteam** *n* TV *etc* panel

Ratgeber [-ge:bɐ] *m (-s; -)*, '**Ratgeberin** *f (-; -nen)* adviser, counsel(l)or; *m* guide (**über** *acc* to)

'**Rathaus** *n* city (*Br* town) hall

ratifizieren [ratifi'tsi:rən] *v/t (no -ge-, h)* ratify

Ration [ra'tsjo:n] *f (-; -en)* ration

rational [ratsjo'na:l] *adj* rational

rationell [ratsjo'nɛl] *adj* efficient; economical

rationieren [ratsjo'ni:rən] *v/t (no -ge-, h)* ration

'**ratlos** *adj* at a loss

'**ratsam** *adj* advisable, wise

'**Ratschlag** *m* piece of advice; **ein paar gute Ratschläge** some good advice

Rätsel ['rɛ:tsəl] *n (-s; -)* puzzle; riddle (*both a. fig*); mystery

'**rätselhaft** *adj* puzzling; mysterious

Ratte ['ratə] *f (-; -n)* ZO rat (*a. contp*)

rattern ['ratən] *v/i (ge-, h, sein)* rattle, clatter

rau [rau] *adj* rough, rugged (*both a. fig*); harsh; chapped; sore

Raub [raup] *m (-[e]s; no pl)* robbery; loot, booty; prey

Raubbau *m (-[e]s; no pl)* overexploitation (*an dat* of); **Raubbau mit s-r Gesundheit treiben** ruin one's health

rauben ['raubən] *v/t (ge-, h)* rob, steal; kidnap; **j-m et. rauben** rob s.o. of s.th. (*a. fig*)

Räuber ['rɔybɐ] *m (-s; -)* robber

'Raubfisch *m* predatory fish

Raubmord *m* murder with robbery

Raubmörder *m* murderer and robber

Raubtier *n* beast of prey

Raubüberfall *m* holdup, (armed) robbery; mugging

Raubvogel *m* bird of prey

Raubzug *m* raid

Rauch [raux] *m* (-[e]s; *no pl*) smoke; CHEM *etc* fume

rauchen ['rauxən] *v/i and v/t* (*ge-*, *h*) smoke; CHEM *etc* fume; ***Rauchen verboten!*** no smoking; ***Pfeife rauchen*** smoke a pipe

Raucher(in) ['rauxɐ (-xərin)] (*-s; -/-t; -nen*) smoker (*m a.* RAIL)

Räucher... ['rɔʏçɐ-] *in cpds* ...*aal*, ...*speck etc*: smoked ...

'räuchern *v/t* (*ge-*, *h*) smoke

'Räucherstäbchen *n* joss stick

'Rauchfahne *f* trail of smoke

rauchig ['rauxɪç] *adj* smoky

'Rauchwaren *pl* tobacco products; furs

Rauchzeichen *n* smoke signal

Räude ['rɔʏdə] *f* (-; -n) VET mange

'räudig *adj* VET mangy

raufen ['raufən] (*ge-*, *h*) **1.** *v/t*: ***sich die Haare raufen*** tear one's hair; **2.** *v/i* fight, scuffle

Rauferei [raufə'rai] *f* (-; -en) fight, scuffle

Raum [raum] *m* (-[e]s; *Räume* ['rɔʏmə]) room; space; area; (outer) space

Raumanzug *m* spacesuit

Raumdeckung *f* SPORT zone marking

räumen ['rɔʏmən] *v/t* (*ge-*, *h*) leave, move out of; check out of; clear (*von* of); evacuate (*a.* MIL); ***s-e Sachen in ...*** (*acc*) ***räumen*** put one's things (away) in ...

'Raumfahrer F *m* spaceman

Raumfahrt *f* (-; *no pl*) space travel *or* flight; astronautics

Raumfahrt... *in cpds* ...*technik*, ...*zentrum etc*: space ...

Raumfähre *f* space shuttle

Raumflug *m* space flight

Rauminhalt *m* volume

Raumkapsel *f* space capsule

Raumla,bor *n* space lab

räumlich ['rɔʏmlɪç] *adj* three-dimensional

'Raumschiff *n* spacecraft; spaceship

Raumsonde *f* space probe

Raumstati,on *f* space station

'Räumung *f* (-; -en) clearance; evacuation (*a.* MIL); JUR eviction

'Räumungsverkauf *m* ECON clearance sale

raunen ['raunən] *v/i* (*ge-*, *h*) whisper, murmur

Raupe ['raupə] *f* (-; -n) ZO caterpillar, TECH *a.* track

'Raupenschlepper *m* MOT caterpillar tractor

'Raureif *m* hoarfrost

raus [raus] F *int* get out (of here)!

Rausch [rauʃ] *m* (-es; *Räusche* ['rɔʏʃə]) drunkenness, intoxication; F high; *fig* ecstasy; ***e-n Rausch haben*** be drunk; ***s-n Rausch ausschlafen*** sleep it off

rauschen ['rauʃən] *v/i* a) (*ge-*, *h*) water *etc*: rush; *brook*: murmur; *storm*: roar, b) (*ge-*, *sein*) sweep

rauschend *adj* thunderous (*applause*); ***rauschendes Fest*** lavish celebration

'Rauschgift *n* drug(s), narcotic(s)

Rauschgiftdezer,nat *n* narcotics *or* drugs squad

Rauschgifthandel *m* drug traffic(king)

Rauschgifthändler *m* drug trafficker, F pusher

räuspern ['rɔʏspɐn] *v/refl* (*ge-*, *h*) clear one's throat

Razzia ['ratsja] *f* (-; -ien) raid, roundup

Reagenzglas [rea'gɛnts-] *n* CHEM test tube

reagieren [rea'giːrən] *v/i* (*no -ge-*, *h*) CHEM, MED react (*auf acc* to), *fig a.* respond (to)

Reaktion [reak'tsjoːn] *f* (-; -en) CHEM, MED, PHYS, POL reaction (*auf acc* to), *fig a.* response (to)

Reaktor [re'aktoːɐ] *m* (-s; -en [reak'toːrən]) PHYS (nuclear *or* atomic) reactor

real [re'aːl] *adj* real; concrete

realisieren [reali'ziːrən] *v/t* (*no -ge-*, *h*) realize

Realismus [rea'lɪsmʊs] *m* (-; *no pl*) realism

rea'listisch *adj* realistic

Realität [reali'tɛːt] *f* (-; *no pl*) reality

Re'alschule *f appr* (junior) highschool, *Br* secondary (modern) school

Rebe ['reːbə] *f* (-; -n) BOT vine

Rebell [re'bɛl] *m* (-en; -en) rebel

rebellieren [rebɛ'liːrən] *v/i* (*no -ge-*, *h*) rebel, revolt, rise (*all*: ***gegen*** against)

Re'bellin *f* (-; -nen) rebel

re'bellisch *adj* rebellious

Rebhuhn ['reːp-] *n* ZO partridge

'Rebstock *m* BOT vine

Rechen ['rɛçən] *m* (-s; -), **'rechen** *v/t* (*ge-*, *h*) rake

'Rechenaufgabe *f* MATH (arithmetical) problem

Rechenfehler *m* MATH arithmetical error, miscalculation

Rechenma,schine *f* calculator; computer

'Rechenschaft *f*: ***Rechenschaft ablegen***

R

über (*acc*) account for; *zur Rechenschaft ziehen* call to account (*wegen* for)

'Rechenschieber *m* MATH slide rule
Rechenwerk *n* EDP arithmetic unit
Rechenzentrum *n* computer center (*Br* centre)
rechnen ['rɛçnən] *v/i and v/t* (*ge-, h*) calculate, reckon; work out, do sums; count; *rechnen mit fig* expect; count on; *mit mir kannst du nicht rechnen!* count me out!
'Rechnen *n* (*-s; no pl*) arithmetic
Rechner ['rɛçnɐ] *m* (*-s; -*) calculator; computer
'rechnerabhängig *adj* EDP online
rechnerisch ['rɛçnərɪʃ] *adj* arithmetical
'rechnerunabhängig *adj* EDP offline
'Rechnung *f* (*-; -en*) MATH calculation; problem, sum; ECON invoice, bill, check; *die Rechnung, bitte!* can I have the check, please?; *das geht auf m-e Rechnung* that's on me
recht [rɛçt] **1.** *adj* right; correct; POL right-wing; *auf der rechten Seite* on the right(-hand side); *mir ist es recht* I don't mind; **2.** *adv* right(ly), correctly; rather, quite; *ich weiß nicht recht* I don't really know; *es geschieht ihm recht* it serves him right; *erst recht* all the more; *erst recht nicht* even less; *du kommst gerade recht (zu)* you're just in time (for); *j-m recht geben* agree with s.o.; *recht haben* be right
Recht *n* (*-[e]s; -e*) a right, claim (*both: auf acc* to), b) (*no pl*) JUR law; justice; *gleiches Recht* equal rights; *Recht haben* → *recht*; *j-m Recht geben* → *recht*; *im Recht sein* be in the right; *er hat es mit (vollem) Recht getan* he was (perfectly) right to do so; *ein Recht auf et. haben* be entitled to s.th.
'Rechteck *n* (*-[e]s; -e*) rectangle
'rechteckig *adj* rectangular
'rechtfertigen *v/t* (*ge-, h*) justify
'Rechtfertigung *f* (*-; -en*) justification
'rechtlich *adj* JUR legal
'rechtlos *adj* without rights; outcast
'rechtmäßig *adj* JUR lawful; legitimate; legal
'Rechtmäßigkeit *f* (*-; no pl*) JUR lawfulness, legitimacy
rechts [rɛçts] *adv* on the right(-hand side); *nach rechts* to the right
Rechts... *in cpds* POL right-wing ...
Rechtsanspruch *m* legal claim (*auf acc* to)
Rechtsanwalt *m*, Rechtsanwältin [-anvɛltɪn] *f* (*-; -nen*) lawyer

Rechts'außen *m* (*-; -*) *soccer*: outside right
'rechtschaffen *adj* honest
'Rechtschreibfehler *m* spelling mistake
Rechtschreibung *f* (*-; no pl*) spelling, orthography
'rechtsextre,mistisch *adj* POL extreme right
'Rechtsfall *m* JUR (law) case
'Rechtshänder [-hɛndɐ] *m* (*-s; -*), 'Rechtshänderin *f* (*-; -nen*) right-handed person; *sie ist Rechtshänderin* she is right-handed
'Rechtsprechung *f* (*-; no pl*) jurisdiction
'rechtsradi,kal *adj* POL extreme right-wing
'Rechtsschutz *m* legal protection; legal costs insurance
'rechtswidrig *adj* JUR illegal, unlawful
'rechtwink(e)lig *adj* rectangular
'rechtzeitig **1.** *adj* punctual; **2.** *adv* in time (*zu* for)
Reck [rɛk] *n* (*-[e]s; -e*) horizontal bar
recken ['rɛkən] *v/t* (*ge-, h*) stretch; *sich recken* stretch o.s.
recyceln [ri'saikəln] *v/t* (*no -ge-, h*) recycle
Recyclingpa,pier [ri'saiklɪŋ-] *n* recycled paper
Redakteur [redak'tø:ɐ] *m* (*-s; -e*), Redak'teurin *f* (*-; -nen*) editor
Redaktion [redak'tsjo:n] *f* (*-; -en*) a) (*no pl*) editing, b) editorial staff, editors, c) editorial office *or* department
redaktionell [redaktsjo'nel] *adj* editorial
Rede ['re:də] *f* (*-; -n*) speech, address; talk (*von* of); *e-e Rede halten* make a speech; *direkte (indirekte) Rede* LING direct (reported *or* indirect) speech; *j-n zur Rede stellen* take s.o. to task; *nicht der Rede wert* not worth mentioning
'redegewandt *adj* eloquent
reden ['re:dən] *v/i and v/t* (*ge-, h*) talk, speak (*both: mit* to; *über acc* about, of); *ich möchte mit dir reden* I'd like to talk to you; *die Leute reden* people talk; *j-n zum Reden bringen* make s.o. talk
'Redensart *f* saying, phrase
redlich ['re:tlɪç] *adj* upright, honest; *sich redlich(e) Mühe geben* do one's best
Redner ['re:dnɐ] *m* (*-s; -*), 'Rednerin *f* (*-; -nen*) speaker
'Rednerpult *n* speaker's desk
redselig ['re:tze:lɪç] *adj* talkative
reduzieren [redu'tsi:rən] *v/t* (*no -ge-, h*) reduce (*auf acc* to)
Reeder ['re:dɐ] *m* (*-s; -*) shipowner
Reederei [re:də'rai] *f* (*-; -en*) shipping

company

reell [re'ɛl] *adj* reasonable, fair (*price*); real (*chance*); solid (*firm*)

Referat [refe'ra:t] *n* (-[e]s; -e) paper; report; lecture; *ein Referat halten* read a paper

Referendar [referɛn'da:ɐ] *m* (-s; -e), **Referen'darin** *f* (-; -nen) *appr* trainee teacher

Referent [refe'rɛnt] *m* (-en; -en), **Refe'rentin** *f* (-; -nen) speaker

Referenz [refe'rɛnts] *f* (-; -en) reference

referieren [refe'ri:rən] *v/i* (*no* -ge-, h) (give a) report *or* lecture (*über acc on*)

reflektieren [reflɛk'ti:rən] *v/t and v/i* (*no* -ge-, h) reflect (*fig über acc* [up]on)

Reflex [re'flɛks] *m* (-es; -e) reflex

reflexiv [reflɛ'ksi:f] *adj* LING reflexive

Reform [re'fɔrm] *f* (-; -en) reform

Reformator [refɔr'ma:to:ɐ] *m* (-s; -en [-ma'to:rən]), **Reformer(in)** [re'fɔrmɐ (-mərin)] (-s; -/-; -nen) reformer

Re'formhaus *n* health food store (*Br* shop)

reformieren [refɔr'mi:rən] *v/t* (*no* -ge-, h) reform

Refrain [rə'frɛ̃] *m* (-s; -s) refrain, chorus

Regal [re'ga:l] *n* (-s; -e) shelf (unit), shelves

rege ['re:gə] *adj* lively; busy; active

Regel ['re:gəl] *f* (-; -n) rule; MED period, menstruation; *in der Regel* as a rule

regelmäßig *adj* regular

regeln ['re:gəln] *v/t* (*ge-*, h) regulate, TECH *a.* adjust; ECON settle

'regelrecht *adj* regular (*a.* F)

'Regeltechnik *f* control engineering

'Regelung *f* (-; -en) regulation; adjustment; ECON settlement; TECH control

'regelwidrig *adj* against the rule(s); SPORT unfair; *regelwidriges Spiel* foul play

regen ['re:gən] *v/t and v/refl* (*ge-*, h) move, stir

'Regen *m* (-s; -) rain; *starker Regen* heavy rain(fall)

Regenbogen *m* rainbow

Regenbogenhaut *f* ANAT iris

Regenguss *m* (heavy) shower, downpour

Regenmantel *m* raincoat

Regenschauer *m* shower

Regenschirm *m* umbrella

Regentag *m* rainy day

Regentropfen *m* raindrop

Regenwald *m* rain forest

Regenwasser *n* rainwater

Regenwetter *n* rainy weather

Regenwurm *m* ZO earthworm

Regenzeit *f* rainy season, the rains

Regie [re'ʒi:] *f* (-; *no pl*) THEA, *film etc*: di-

rection; *unter der Regie von* directed by

Re'gieanweisung *f* stage direction

regieren [re'gi:rən] (*no* -ge-, h) **1.** *v/i* reign; **2.** *v/t* govern (*a.* LING), rule

Re'gierung *f* (-; -en) government, administration; reign

Re'gierungsbezirk *m* administrative district

Regierungschef *m* head of government

Regierungswechsel *m* change of government

Regime [re'ʒi:m] *n* (-s; -) POL regime

Re'gimekritiker *m* POL dissident

Regiment [regi'mɛnt] *n* (-[e]s; -er) a) (*no pl*) rule (*a. fig*), b) MIL regiment

Regisseur [reʒɪ'sø:ɐ] *m* (-s; -e), **Regis'seurin** *f* (-; -nen) THEA, *film etc*: director, THEA *Br a.* producer

Register [re'gɪstɐ] *n* (-s; -) register (*a.* MUS), record; index

registrieren [regɪs'tri:rən] *v/t* (*no* -ge-, h) register, record; *fig* note

Registrierkasse [regɪs'tri:ɐ-] *f* cash register

Reglement [reglə'mã:] *n* (-s; -s) regulation, order, rule

Regler ['re:glɐ] *m* (-s; -) TECH control

regnen ['re:gnən] *v/i* (*ge-*, h) rain (*a. fig*); *es regnet in Strömen* it's pouring with rain

'regnerisch *adj* rainy

regulär [regu'lɛ:ɐ] *adj* regular; normal

regulierbar [regu'li:ɐba:ɐ] *adj* adjustable; controllable

regulieren [regu'li:rən] *v/t* (*no* -ge-, h) regulate, adjust; control

'Regung *f* (-; -en) movement, motion; emotion; impulse

'regungslos *adj* motionless

Reh [re:] *n* (-[e]s; -e) ZO deer, roe; doe; GASTR venison

rehabilitieren [rehabili'ti:rən] *v/t* (*no* -ge-, h) rehabilitate

'Rehbock *m* ZO (roe)buck

Rehkeule *f* GASTR leg of venison

Rehkitz *n* ZO fawn

Reibe ['raibə] *f* (-; -n), **Reibeisen** ['raip-] *n* (-s; -) grater, rasp

reiben ['raibən] *v/i and v/t* (*irr*, ge-, h) rub; grate, grind; *sich die Augen (Hände) reiben* rub one's eyes (hands)

'Reibung *f* (-; -en) TECH etc friction

'reibungslos *adj* TECH etc frictionless; *fig* smooth

reich [raiç] *adj* rich (*an dat* in), wealthy; abundant

Reich *n* (-[e]s; -e) empire, kingdom (*a.* REL, BOT, ZO); *fig* world

reichen ['raiçən] (*ge-*, h) **1.** *v/t* reach;

R

hand, pass; give, hold out (*one's hand*); **2.** *v/i* last, do; **reichen bis** reach *or* come up to; **das reicht** that will do; F **mir reicht's!** I've had enough

'**reichhaltig** *adj* rich

'**reichlich 1.** *adj* rich, plentiful; plenty of; **2.** *adv* rather; generously

'**Reichtum** *m* (-*s*; *no pl*) wealth (**an** *dat of*) (*a. fig*)

'**Reichweite** *f* reach, AVIAT, MIL *etc* range; **in (außer) (j-s) Reichweite** within (out of) (s.o.'s) reach

reif [raif] *adj* ripe, *esp fig* mature

Reif *m* (-*[e]s*; *no pl*) white frost, hoarfrost

Reife ['raifə] *f* (-; *no pl*) ripeness, *esp fig* maturity

'**reifen** *v/i* (*ge-, sein*) ripen, mature (*both a. fig*)

Reifen ['raifən] *m* (-*s*; -) hoop; MOT *etc* tire, Br tyre

Reifenpanne *f* MOT flat tire (Br tyre), puncture, F flat

'**Reifeprüfung** *f* → **Abitur**

'**reiflich** *adj* careful

Reihe ['raiə] *f* (-; -*n*) line, row; number; series; **der Reihe nach** in turn; **ich bin an der Reihe** it's my turn

'**Reihenfolge** *f* order

'**Reihenhaus** *n* row (Br terraced) house

'**reihenweise** *adv* in rows; F *fig* by the dozen

Reiher ['raiɐ] *m* (-*s*; -) ZO heron

Reim [raim] *m* (-*[e]s*; -*e*) rhyme

reimen ['raimən] *v/t and v/refl* (*ge-, h*) rhyme (**auf** *acc* with)

rein [rain] *adj* pure (*a. fig*); clean; *fig* clear (*conscience*); plain (*truth*); mere, sheer, nothing but

Reinfall F *m* flop; let-down

'**Reingewinn** *m* ECON net profit

'**reinhauen** F *v/i* (*sep, -ge-, h*) tuck in

'**Reinheit** *f* (-; *no pl*) purity (*a. fig*); cleanness

reinigen ['rainɪgən] *v/t* (*ge-, h*) clean; cleanse (*a. MED*); dry-clean; *fig* purify

'**Reinigung** *f* (-; -*en*) clean(s)ing; *fig* purification; (dry) cleaners; **chemische Reinigung** dry cleaning; dry cleaner's

'**Reinigungsmittel** *n* cleaning agent, cleaner, detergent

'**reinlich** *adj* clean; cleanly

'**reinrassig** *adj* ZO purebred, pedigree; thoroughbred

'**Reinschrift** *f* fair copy

Reis [rais] *m* (-*es*; -*e*) BOT rice

Reise ['raizə] *f* (-; -*n*) trip; journey; tour; MAR voyage; **auf Reisen sein** be travel(l)ing; **e-e Reise machen** take a trip; **gute Reise!** have a nice trip!

Reiseandenken *n* souvenir

Reisebü,ro *n* travel agency *or* bureau

Reiseführer *m* guide(book)

Reisegesellschaft *f* tourist party; tour operator

Reisekosten *pl* travel(l)ing expenses

Reisekrankheit *f* travel sickness

Reiseleiter(in) tour guide *or* manager, Br courier

'**reisen** *v/i* (*ge-, sein*) travel; **durch Frankreich reisen** tour France; **ins Ausland reisen** go abroad

'**Reisende** *m, f* (-*n*; -*n*) travel(l)er; tourist; passenger

'**Reisepass** *m* passport

'**Reisescheck** *m* travel(l)er's check (Br cheque)

'**Reisetasche** *f* travel(l)ing bag, holdall

Reisig ['raizɪç] *n* (-*s*; *no pl*) brushwood

'**Reißbrett** ['rais-] *n* drawing board

reißen ['raisən] (*irr, ge-*) **1.** *v/t* (*h*) tear (**in Stücke** to pieces); rip; pull, drag; zo kill; F crack (*jokes*); SPORT knock down; **an sich reißen** seize, snatch, grab; **2.** *v/i* (*sein*) break, burst; **sich um et. reißen** scramble for (*or* to get) s.th.

'**reißend** *adj* torrential

'**Reißer** ['raisɐ] F *m* (-*s*; -) thriller; hit

'**reißerisch** ['raisərɪʃ] *adj* sensational, loud

'**Reißverschluss** *m* zipper; **den Reißverschluss an et. öffnen (schließen)** unzip (zip up) s.th.

'**Reißzwecke** *f* thumbtack, Br drawing pin

reiten ['raitən] (*irr, ge-*) **1.** *v/i* (*sein*) ride, go on horseback; **2.** *v/t* (*h*) ride

'**Reiten** *n* (-*s*; *no pl*) horseback riding

Reiter ['raitɐ] *m* (-*s*; -) rider, horseman

Reiterin ['raitərɪn] *f* (-; -*nen*) rider, horsewoman

'**Reitpferd** *n* saddle *or* riding horse

Reiz [raits] *m* (-*es*; -*e*) charm, attraction, appeal; thrill; MED, PSYCH stimulus; (**für j-n**) **den Reiz verlieren** lose one's appeal (for s.o.)

'**reizbar** *adj* irritable, excitable

reizen ['raitsən] (*ge-, h*) **1.** *v/t* irritate (*a. MED*), annoy; zo bait; provoke; appeal to, attract; tempt; challenge; **2.** *v/i cards*: bid

'**reizend** *adj* charming, delightful; lovely, sweet, cute

'**reizlos** *adj* unattractive

'**Reizung** *f* (-; -*en*) irritation (*a. MED*)

'**reizvoll** *adj* attractive; challenging

'**Reizwort** *n* (-*[e]s*; -*wörter*) emotive word

rekeln ['re:kəln] F *v/refl* (*ge-, h*) loll

Reklamation [reklama'tsjo:n] *f* (-; -*en*) complaint

Reklame [re'kla:mə] *f* (-; -*n*) advertising,

publicity; advertisement, F ad; **Reklame machen für** advertise, promote

reklamieren [rekla'mi:rən] v/i (no -ge-, h) complain (**wegen** about), protest (against)

Rekord [re'kɔrt] m (-[e]s; -e) record; **e-n Rekord aufstellen** set or establish a record

Rekrut [re'kru:t] m (-en; -en) MIL recruit

rekrutieren [rekru'ti:rən] v/t (no -ge-, h) recruit

Rektor ['rɛkto:ɐ] m (-s; -en [rɛk'to:rən]) principal, Br headmaster; UNIV president, Br rector

Rektorin [rɛk'to:rɪn] f (-; -nen) principal, Br headmistress; UNIV president, Br rector

relativ [rela'ti:f] adj relative

Relief [re'ljɛf] n (-s; -s) relief

Religion [reli'gjo:n] f (-; -en) religion

religiös [reli'gjø:s] adj religious

Reling ['re:lɪŋ] f (-; -s) MAR rail

Reliquie [re'li:kvjə] f (-; -n) relic

Rempelei [rɛmpə'lai] F f (-; -en), **rempeln** ['rɛmpəln] F v/t (ge-, h) jostle

Rennbahn ['rɛn-] f racecourse, racetrack; cycling track

'**Rennboot** n racing boat; speedboat

rennen ['rɛnən] v/i and v/t (irr, ge-, sein) run

'**Rennen** n (-s; -) race (a. fig); heat

'**Rennfahrer** m, **Rennfahrerin** f racing driver; racing cyclist

Rennläufer m ski racer

Rennpferd n racehorse, racer

Rennrad n racing bicycle, racer

Rennsport m racing

Rennstall m racing stable

Rennwagen m race (Br racing) car, racer

renommiert [reno'mi:ɐt] adj renowned

renovieren [reno'vi:rən] v/t (no -ge-, h) renovate, F do up; redecorate

rentabel [rɛn'ta:bəl] adj ECON profitable, paying

Rente ['rɛntə] f (-; -n) (old age) pension; **in Rente gehen** retire

'**Rentenalter** n retirement age

Rentenversicherung f pension scheme

Rentier ['rɛnti:ɐ] n (-s; -e) ZO reindeer

rentieren [rɛn'ti:rən] v/refl (no -ge-, h) ECON pay; fig be worth it

Rentner ['rɛntnɐ] m (-s; -), '**Rentnerin** [-nərɪn] f (-; -nen) (old age) pensioner

Reparatur [repara'tu:ɐ] f (-; -en) repair

Reparaturwerkstatt f repair shop; MOT garage

reparieren [repa'ri:rən] v/t (no -ge-, h) repair, mend, F fix

Reportage [repɔr'ta:ʒə] f (-; -n) report

Reporter [re'pɔrtɐ] m (-s; -), **Re'porterin** f (-; -nen) reporter

Repräsentant [reprezɛn'tant] m (-en; -en) representative

Repräsentantenhaus n PARL House of Representatives

Repräsen'tantin f (-; -nen) representative

repräsentieren [reprezɛn'ti:rən] v/t (no -ge-, h) represent

Repressalie [reprɛ'sa:ljə] f (-; -n) reprisal

Reproduktion [reprodok'tsjo:n] f (-; -en) reproduction, print

reproduzieren [reprodu'tsi:rən] v/t (no -ge-, h) reproduce

Reptil [rɛp'ti:l] n (-s; -ien) ZO reptile

Republik [repu'bli:k] f (-; -en) republic

Republikaner [republi'ka:nɐ] m (-s; -), **Republi'kanerin** f (-; -nen), **republi'kanisch** adj POL republican

Reservat [rezɛr'va:t] n (-[e]s; -e) (p)reserve; reservation

Reserve [re'zɛrvə] f (-; -n) reserve (a. MIL)

Reserve... in cpds ...kanister, ...rad etc; spare ...

reservieren [rezɛr'vi:rən] v/t (no -ge-, h) reserve (a. **reservieren lassen**); **j-m e-n Platz reservieren** keep or save a seat for s.o.

reserviert [rezɛr'vi:ɐt] adj reserved (a. fig); aloof

Reser'viertheit f (-; no pl) aloofness

Residenz [rezi'dɛnts] f (-; -en) residence

Resignation [rezɪgna'tsjo:n] f (-; no pl) resignation

resignieren [rezɪ'gni:rən] v/i (no -ge-, h) give up

resigniert [rezɪ'gni:ɐt] adj resigned

Resoziali'sierung f (-; -en) rehabilitation

Respekt [re'spɛkt] m (-[e]s; no pl) respect (**vor** dat for)

respektieren [respɛk'ti:rən] v/t (no -ge-, h) respect

re'spektlos adj irreverent, disrespectful

re'spektvoll adj respectful

Ressort [rɛ'so:ɐ] n (-s; -s) department, province

Rest [rɛst] m (-[e]s; -e) rest; pl remains, remnants; GASTR leftovers; F **das gab ihm den Rest** that finished him (off)

Restaurant [rɛsto'rã:] n (-s; -s) restaurant

restaurieren [rɛsto'ri:rən] v/t (no -ge-, h) restore

'**Restbetrag** m remainder

'**restlich** adj remaining

'**restlos** adv completely

Resultat [rezol'ta:t] n (-[e]s; -e) result (a. SPORT), outcome

Retorte [re'tɔrtə] f (-; -n) CHEM retort

Re'tortenbaby F n test-tube baby

R

retten ['rɛtən] v/t (ge-, h) save, rescue (*both*: **aus** *dat*, **vor** *dat* from)

Retter ['rɛtɐ] m (-s; -), **'Retterin** f (-; -nen) rescuer

Rettich ['rɛtɪç] m (-s; -e) BOT radish

'Rettung f (-; -en) rescue (**aus** *dat*, **vor** *dat* from); **das war s-e Rettung** that saved him

'Rettungsboot n lifeboat

Rettungsmannschaft f rescue party

Rettungsring m life belt, life buoy

Rettungsschwimmer m lifeguard

Reue ['rɔʏə] f (-; *no pl*) remorse, repentance (*both*: **über** *acc* for)

reumütig ['rɔʏmyːtɪç] adj repentant

Revanche [re'vãːʃ(ə)] f (-; -n) revenge

revanchieren [revã'ʃiːrən] v/refl (*no -ge-*, h) have one's revenge (**bei**, **an** *dat* on); make it up (**bei j-m** to s.o.)

Revers [re'veːɐ] n, m (-; -) lapel

revidieren [revi'diːrən] v/t (*no -ge-*, h) revise; ECON audit

Revier [re'viːɐ] n (-s; -e) district; ZO territory (*a. fig*); → **Polizeirevier**

Revision [revi'zjoːn] f (-; -en) revision; ECON audit; JUR appeal

Revolte [re'vɔltə] f (-; -n), **revoltieren** [revɔl'tiːrən] v/i (*no -ge-*, h) revolt

Revolution [revolu'tsjoːn] f (-; -en) revolution

revolutionär [revolutsjo'nɛːɐ] adj, **Revolutio'när(in)** (-s; -e/-; -nen) revolutionary

Revolver [re'vɔlvɐ] m (-s; -) revolver, F gun

Revue [re'vyː] f (-; -n) THEA (musical) show

Rezept [re'tsɛpt] n (-[e]s; -e) MED prescription; GASTR recipe (*a. fig*)

Rezession [retse'sjoːn] f (-; -en) ECON recession

Rhabarber [ra'barbɐ] m (-s; *no pl*) BOT rhubarb

rhetorisch [re'toːrɪʃ] adj rhetorical

Rheuma ['rɔʏma] n (-s; *no pl*) MED rheumatism

rhythmisch ['rʏtmɪʃ] adj rhythmic(al)

Rhythmus ['rʏtmʊs] m (-; -men) rhythm

Ribisel ['riːbiːzəl] *Austrian* f (-; -[n]) → **Johannisbeere**

richten ['rɪçtən] v/t (ge-, h) fix; get *s.th.* ready, prepare; do (*room, one's hair*); (**sich**) **richten an** (*acc*) address (o.s. to); put a question to; **richten auf** (*acc*) direct or turn to; point or aim *camera, gun etc* at; **richten gegen** direct against; **sich richten nach** go by, act according to; follow (*fashion etc*); depend on; **ich richte mich ganz nach dir** I leave it to you

Richter ['rɪçtɐ] m (-s; -), **'Richterin** f (-;
-nen) judge

'richterlich adj judicial

'Richtgeschwindigkeit f MOT recommended speed

richtig ['rɪçtɪç] **1.** adj right; correct, proper; true; real; **2.** adv: **richtig nett** (**böse**) really nice (angry); **et. richtig machen** do s.th. right; **m-e Uhr geht richtig** my watch is right

'Richtigkeit f (-; *no pl*) correctness

richtigstellen v/t (sep, -ge-, h) fig put or set right

'Richtlinien pl guidelines

Richtpreis m ECON recommended price

'Richtung f (-; -en) direction; POL leaning; PAINT *etc* style

'richtungslos adj aimless, disorient(at)ed

'richtungweisend adj pioneering

rieb [riːp] pret of **reiben**

riechen ['riːçən] v/i and v/t (irr, ge-, h) smell (**nach** of; **an** dat at)

rief [riːf] pret of **rufen**

Riegel ['riːgəl] m (-s; -) bolt, bar

Riemen ['riːmən] m (-s; -) strap; TECH belt; MAR oar

Riese ['riːzə] m (-n; -n) giant (*a. fig*)

rieseln ['riːzəln] v/i (ge-, sein) trickle; *rain*: drizzle; *snow*: fall gently

'Riesen... *in cpds mst* giant ..., gigantic ..., enormous ...

Riesenerfolg m huge success, *film etc*: smash hit

'riesengroß, **'riesenhaft** → **riesig**

'Riesenrad n Ferris wheel

riesig ['riːzɪç] adj enormous, gigantic, giant

Riesin f (-; -nen) giantess (*a. fig*)

riet [riːt] pret of **raten**

Riff [rɪf] n (-[e]s; -e) GEOGR reef

Rille ['rɪlə] f (-; -n) groove

Rind [rɪnt] n (-[e]s; -er ['rɪndɐ]) ZO cow, pl cattle; GASTR beef

Rinde ['rɪndə] f (-; -n) BOT bark; GASTR rind; crust

Rinderbraten ['rɪndɐ-] m roast beef

Rinderherde f herd of cattle

'Rindfleisch n GASTR beef

Rind(s)leder n cowhide

Rindvieh n ZO cattle

Ring [rɪŋ] m (-[e]s; -e) ring (*a. fig*); MOT ring road; *subway etc*: circle (line)

'Ringbuch n loose-leaf or ring binder

ringeln ['rɪŋəln] v/refl (ge-, h) curl, coil (*a. zo*)

'Ringelnatter f ZO grass snake

'Ringelspiel *Austrian* n → **Karussell**

ringen ['rɪŋən] v/i (irr, ge-, h) **1.** v/i SPORT wrestle (**mit** with), *fig a.* struggle (against, with; **um** for); **nach Atem rin-**

gen gasp (for breath); **2.** *v/t* wring

'**Ringen** *n* (*-s; no pl*) SPORT wrestling

Ringer ['rɪŋɐ] *m* (*-s; -*) SPORT wrestler

'**ringförmig** [-fœrmɪç] *adj* circular

'**Ringkampf** *m* SPORT wrestling match

'**Ringrichter** *m* SPORT referee

rings *adv*: **rings um** around

'**ringshe'rum**, '**rings'um**, '**ringsum'her** *adv* all around; everywhere

Rinne ['rɪnə] *f* (*-; -n*) groove, channel; gutter

'**rinnen** *v/i* (*irr, ge-, sein*) run; flow, stream

Rinnsal ['rɪnzaːl] *n* (*-s; -e*) trickle

'**Rinnstein** *m* gutter

Rippe ['rɪpə] *f* (*-; -n*) ANAT rib

'**Rippenfell** *n* ANAT pleura

'**Rippenfellentzündung** *f* MED pleurisy

'**Rippenstoß** *m* nudge in the ribs

Risiko ['riːziko] *n* (*-s; -s, -ken*) risk; **ein (kein) Risiko eingehen** take a risk (no risks); **auf eigenes Risiko** at one's own risk

riskant [rɪs'kant] *adj* risky

riskieren [rɪs'kiːrən] *v/t* (*no ge-, h*) risk

riss [rɪs] *pret of* **reißen**

Riss *m* (*-es; -e*) tear, rip, split (*a. fig*); crack; MED chap, laceration

rissig ['rɪsɪç] *adj* chapped; cracky, cracked

Rist [rɪst] *m* (*-es; -e*) ANAT instep

ritt [rɪt] *pret of* **reiten**

Ritt *m* (*-[e]s; -e*) ride (on horseback)

Ritter ['rɪtɐ] *m* (*-s; -*) knight; **j-n zum Ritter schlagen** knight s.o.

'**ritterlich** *fig adj* chivalrous

Ritz [rɪts] *m* (*-es; -e*), **Ritze** ['rɪtsə] *f* (*-; -n*) crack, chink; gap

Rivale [ri'vaːlə] *m* (*-n; -n*), **Ri'valin** *f* (*-; -nen*) rival

rivalisieren [rivali'ziːrən] *v/i* (*no ge-, h*) compete

Rivalität [rivali'tɛːt] *f* (*-; -en*) rivalry

rk., r.-k. ABBR *of* **römisch-katholisch** RC, Roman Catholic

Robbe ['rɔbə] *f* (*-; -n*) ZO seal

Robe ['roːbə] *f* (*-; -n*) robe, gown

Roboter ['rɔbɔtɐ] *m* (*-s; -*) robot

robust [ro'bust] *adj* robust, strong, tough

roch [rɔx] *pret of* **riechen**

röcheln ['rœçəln] (*ge-, h*) **1.** *v/i* moan; **2.** *v/t* gasp

Rock [rɔk] *m* (*-[e]s; Röcke* ['rœkə]) skirt

Rodelbahn ['roːdəl-] *f* toboggan run

rodeln ['roːdəln] *v/i* (*ge-, sein*) sled(ge), coast; SPORT toboggan

'**Rodelschlitten** *m* sled(ge); toboggan

roden ['roːdən] *v/t* (*ge-, h*) clear; stub

Rogen ['roːgən] *m* (*-s; -*) (hard) roe

Roggen ['rɔgən] *m* (*-s; -*) BOT rye

roh [roː] *adj* raw; rough; *fig* brutal; **mit roher Gewalt** with brute force

'**Rohbau** *m* (*-[e]s; -ten*) carcass

'**Rohkost** *f* raw vegetables and fruit

Rohling *m* (*-s; -e*) TECH blank; *fig* brute

'**Rohmateri,al** *n* raw material

Rohöl *n* crude (oil)

Rohr [roːɐ] *n* (*-[e]s; -e* ['roːrə]) TECH pipe, tube; duct; BOT reed; cane

Röhre ['røːrə] *f* (*-; -n*) pipe, tube (*a.* TV), TV *etc* valve

'**Rohrleitung** *f* duct, pipe(s); plumbing; pipeline

'**Rohrstock** *m* cane

'**Rohrzucker** *m* cane sugar

'**Rohstoff** *m* raw material

Rollbahn ['rɔl-] *f* AVIAT runway

Rolle ['rɔlə] *f* (*-; -n*) roll (*a.* SPORT), TECH *a.* roller; cost; caster, castor; THEA part, role (*both a.* fig); **e-e Rolle Garn** a spool of thread, *Br* a reel of cotton; **das spielt keine Rolle** that doesn't matter, that makes no difference; **Geld spielt k-e Rolle** money is no object

'**rollen** *v/i* (*ge-, sein*) *and v/t* (*ge-, h*) roll

Roller ['rɔlɐ] *m* (*-s; -*) (motor) scooter

'**Rollfilm** *m* PHOT roll film

'**Rollkragen** *m* turtleneck, *esp Br* polo neck

Rollladen *m* rolling shutter

Rollo ['rɔlo] *n* (*-s; -s*) shades, *Br* (roller) blind

'**Rollschuh** *m* roller skate; **Rollschuh laufen** roller-skate

'**Rollschuhbahn** *f* roller-skating rink

'**Rollschuhläufer** *m* roller skater

'**Rollstuhl** *m* wheelchair

'**Rolltreppe** *f* escalator

Roman [ro'maːn] *m* (*-s; -e*) novel

Romanik [ro'maːnɪk] *f* (*-; no pl*) ARCH Romanesque (style *or* period)

romanisch [ro'maːnɪʃ] *adj* LING Romance; ARCH Romanesque

Romanist [roma'nɪst] *m* (*-en; -en*), **Roma'nistin** *f* (*-; -nen*) student of Romance languages

Ro'manschriftsteller *m*, **Ro'manschriftstellerin** *f* novelist

Romantik [ro'mantɪk] *f* (*-; no pl*) romance; HIST Romanticism

romantisch [ro'mantɪʃ] *adj* romantic

Römer ['røːmɐ] *m* (*-s; -*), **Römerin** *f* (*-; -nen*), **römisch** ['røːmɪʃ] *adj* Roman

röntgen ['rœntgən] *v/t* (*ge-, h*) MED X-ray

'**Röntgenappa,rat** *m* MED X-ray apparatus

Röntgenaufnahme *f*, **Röntgenbild** *n* MED X-ray

R

Röntgenstrahlen pl PHYS X-rays

Röntgenuntersuchung f MED X-ray

rosa ['roːza] adj pink; fig rose-colo(u)red

Rose ['roːzə] f (-; -n) BOT rose

'**Rosenkohl** m BOT Brussels sprouts

'**Rosenkranz** m REL rosary

rosig ['roːzɪç] adj rosy (a. fig)

Rosine [ro'ziːnə] f (-; -n) raisin

'**Rosshaar** n (-[e]s; no pl) horsehair

Rost [rɔst] m (-[e]s; -e) a) (no pl) CHEM rust, b) TECH grate; GASTR grid(iron), grill

rosten ['rɔstən] v/i (ge-, sein) rust

rösten ['rœstən] v/t (ge-, h) roast (a. fig); toast; fry

'**Rostfleck** m rust stain

'**rostfrei** adj rustproof, stainless

'**rostig** adj rusty

rot [roːt] adj red (a. POL); **rot glühend** red-hot; **rot werden** blush; **in den roten Zahlen** ECON in the red

Rot n (-s; -) red; **die Ampel steht auf Rot** the lights are red; **bei Rot** at red

'**rotblond** adj sandy(-haired)

Röte ['røːtə] f (-; no pl) redness, red (colo[u]r); fig blush

Röteln ['røːtəln] pl MED German measles

röten ['røːtən] v/i/refl (ge-, h) redden; flush

'**rothaarig** adj red-haired

'**Rothaarige** m, f (-n; -n) redhead

rotieren [ro'tiːrən] v/i (no -ge-, h) rotate

'**Rotkehlchen** n (-s; -) ZO robin

'**Rotkohl** m BOT red cabbage

rötlich ['røːtlɪç] adj reddish

'**Rotstift** m red crayon or pencil

Rotwein m red wine

Rotwild n ZO (red) deer

Rotznase [rɔts-] F f snotty nose

Route ['ruːtə] f (-; -n) route

Routine [ru'tiːnə] f (-; no pl) routine; experience

Routinesache f routine (matter)

routiniert [ruti'niːɐt] adj experienced

Rübe ['ryːbə] f (-; -n) BOT turnip; (sugar) beet

Rubin [ru'biːn] m (-s; -e) MIN ruby

Rübli ['ryːpli] Swiss n (-s; -) carrot

Rubrik [ru'briːk] f (-; -en) heading; column

Ruck [rʊk] m (-[e]s; -e) jerk, jolt, start; fig POL swing

Rückantwortschein ['rʏk-] m reply coupon

'**ruckartig** adj jerky, abrupt

'**rückbezüglich** adj LING reflexive

'**Rückblende** f flashback (**auf** acc to)

'**Rückblick** m review (**auf** acc of); **im Rückblick** in retrospect

rücken ['rʏkən] **1.** v/t (ge-, h) move, shift, push; **2.** v/i (ge-, sein) move; move over;

näher rücken approach

'**Rücken** m (-s; -) ANAT back (a. fig)

Rückendeckung fig f backing, support

Rückenlehne f back(rest)

Rückenmark n ANAT spinal cord

Rückenschmerzen pl backache

Rückenschwimmen n backstroke

Rückenwind m following wind, tailwind

Rückenwirbel m ANAT dorsal vertebra

'**Rückerstattung** f (-; -en) refund

Rückfahrkarte f round-trip ticket, Br a. return (ticket)

Rückfahrt f return trip; **auf der Rückfahrt** on the way back

Rückfall m relapse

'**rückfällig** adj: **rückfällig werden** relapse

'**Rückflug** m return flight

'**Rückgabe** f (-; no pl) return

'**Rückgang** m drop, fall; ECON recession

'**rückgängig** adj: **rückgängig machen** cancel

'**Rückgewinnung** f (-; no pl) recovery

Rückgrat n ANAT spine, backbone (both a. fig)

Rückhalt m (-[e]s; no pl) support

Rückhand f, **Rückhandschlag** m tennis: backhand

Rückkauf m ECON repurchase

Rückkehr ['rʏkkeːɐ] f (-; no pl) return; **nach s-r Rückkehr aus** ... on his return from ...

'**Rückkopplung** f ELECTR feedback (a. fig)

Rücklage f (-; -n) reserve(s); savings

Rücklauf m TECH rewind

'**rückläufig** adj falling, downward

'**Rücklicht** n (-[e]s; -er) MOT rear light, taillight

rücklings ['rʏklɪŋs] adv backward(s); from behind

'**Rückporto** n return postage

'**Rückreise** f → **Rückfahrt**

Rucksack ['rʊkzak] m rucksack, backpack

Rucksacktou,rismus m backpacking

Rucksacktou,rist m backpacker

'**Rückschlag** m SPORT return; fig setback

'**Rückschluss** m conclusion

Rückschritt m fig step back(ward)

Rückseite f back; reverse; flip side

Rücksendung f return

'**Rücksicht** f (-; -en) consideration, regard; **aus (ohne) Rücksicht auf** (acc) out of (without any) consideration or regard for; **Rücksicht nehmen auf** (acc) show consideration for

'**rücksichtslos** adj inconsiderate (**gegen** of), thoughtless (of); ruthless; reckless

'**rücksichtsvoll** adj considerate (**gegen** of), thoughtful

'**Rücksitz** *m* MOT back seat

Rückspiegel *m* MOT rear-view mirror

'**Rückspiel** *n* SPORT return match

Rückstand *m* CHEM residue; *mit der Arbeit (e-m Tor) im Rückstand sein* be behind with one's work (down by one goal)

'**rückständig** *adj* backward; underdeveloped; *rückständige Miete* arrears of rent

'**Rückstau** *m* MOT tailback

Rückstelltaste *f* backspace key

Rücktritt *m* resignation; withdrawal; TECH → **Rücktrittbremse** *f* coaster (*Br* back-pedal) brake

rückwärts ['rykverts] *adv* backward(s); *rückwärts aus (dat) ... fahren* back out of ...; *rückwärts in (acc) ... fahren* back into ...

'**Rückwärtsgang** *m* MOT reverse (gear)

'**Rückweg** *m* way back

'**ruckweise** *adv* jerkily, in jerks

'**rückwirkend** *adj* retroactive

'**Rückwirkung** *f* reaction (*auf acc* upon)

Rückzahlung *f* repayment

Rückzieher *m* (*-s; -*) soccer: overhead kick; F *e-n Rückzieher machen* back (*or* chicken) out (*von* of)

Rückzug *m* retreat

Rüde ['ry:də] *m* (*-n; -n*) ZO male (dog *ect*)

Rudel ['ru:dəl] *n* (*-s; -*) ZO pack; herd

Ruder ['ru:də] *n* (*-s; -*) AVIAT, MAR rudder; SPORT oar; *am Ruder* at the helm (*a. fig*)

Ruderboot *n* rowing boat, rowboat

Ruderer ['ru:dərə] *m* (*-s; -*) rower, oarsman

'**Ruderin** *f* (*-; -nen*) rower, oarswoman

'**rudern** *v/i and v/t* (*ge-, h*) row

'**Ruderre,gatta** *f* (rowing) regatta, boat race

Rudersport *m* rowing

Ruf [ru:f] *m* (*-[e]s; -e*) call (*a. fig*); cry, shout; *fig* reputation

'**rufen** *v/i and v/t* (*irr, ge-, h*) call (*a. doctor etc*); cry, shout; *rufen nach* call for (*a. fig*); *rufen lassen* send for (*um Hilfe rufen* call *or* cry for help

'**Rufnummer** *f* telephone number

'**Rufweite** *f*: *in (außer) Rufweite* within (out of) call(ing distance)

Rüge ['ry:gə] *f* (*-; -n*) reproof, reproach (*both*: *wegen* for)

'**rügen** *v/t* (*ge-, h*) reprove, reproach

Ruhe ['ru:ə] *f* (*-; no pl*) quiet, calm; silence; rest; peace; calm(ness); *zur Ruhe kommen* come to rest; *j-n in Ruhe lassen* leave s.o. in peace; *lass mich in Ruhe!* leave me alone!; *et. in Ruhe tun* take one's time (doing s.th.); *die Ruhe behalten* F keep (one's) cool, play it cool; *sich*

zur Ruhe setzen retire; *Ruhe, bitte!* (be) quiet please!

'**ruhelos** *adj* restless

'**ruhen** *v/i* (*ge-, h*) rest (*auf dat* on)

'**Ruhepause** *f* break

Ruhestand *m* (*-[e]s; no pl*) retirement

Ruhestörer *m* (*-s; -*) *esp* JUR disturber of the peace

Ruhetag *m* a day's rest; *Montag Ruhetag* closed on Mondays

ruhig ['ru:iç] *adj* quiet; silent; calm; cool; TECH smooth; *ruhig bleiben* F keep (one's) cool, play it cool

Ruhm [ru:m] *m* (*-[e]s; no pl*) fame, *esp* POL, MIL *etc* glory

rühmen ['ry:mən] *v/t* (*ge-, h*) praise (*wegen* for); *sich e-r Sache rühmen* boast of s.th.

rühmlich ['ry:mliç] *adj* laudable, praiseworthy

'**ruhmlos** *adj* inglorious

'**ruhmreich** *adj* glorious

Ruhr [ru:ɐ] *f* (*-; no pl*) MED dysentery

Rührei ['ry:ɐʔaie] *pl* scrambled eggs

rühren ['ry:rən] *v/t* (*ge-, h*) stir; move (*a. fig*); *fig* touch, affect; *das rührt mich gar nicht* that leaves me cold; *rührt euch!* MIL (stand) at ease!

rührend *fig adj* touching, moving; very kind

rührig ['ry:rıç] *adj* active, busy

rührselig ['ry:ɐ-] *adj* sentimental

'**Rührung** *f* (*-; no pl*) emotion

Ruin [ru'i:n] *m* (*-s; no pl*) ruin

Ruine [ru'i:nə] *f* (*-; -n*) ruin

ruinieren [rui'ni:rən] *v/t* (*no -ge-, h*) ruin

rülpsen ['rylpsən] *v/i* (*ge-, h*), **Rülpser** ['rylpsɐ] *m* (*-s; -*) belch

Rumäne [ru'mɛ:nə] *m* (*-n; -n*) Romanian

Rumänien Romania

Ru'mänin *f* (*-; -nen*), **ru'mänisch** *adj* Romanian

Rummel ['roməl] F *m* (*-s; no pl*) (hustle and) bustle; F ballyhoo

Rummelplatz F *m* amusement park, fairground

rumoren [ru'mo:rən] *v/i* (*no -ge-, h*) rumble

Rumpelkammer ['rompəl-] F *f* lumber room

rumpeln ['rompəln] F *v/i* (*ge-, h, sein*) rumble

Rumpf [rompf] *m* (*-es; Rümpfe* ['rympfə]) ANAT trunk; MAR hull; AVIAT fuselage

rümpfen ['rympfən] *v/t* (*ge-, h*) *die Nase rümpfen* turn up one's nose (*über acc* at), sneer (at)

rund [ront] **1.** *adj* round (*a. fig*); **2.** *adv* about; *rund um* (a)round

R

'Rundblick m panorama

Runde ['rundə] f (-; -n) round (a. fig and SPORT); racing: lap; **s-e Runde machen in** (dat) patrol; **die Runde machen** go the round(s)

'Rundfahrt f tour (**durch** round)

'Rundfunk m (-s; no pl) radio; broadcasting corporation; **im Rundfunk** on the radio; **im Rundfunk übertragen** or **senden** broadcast

Rundfunkhörer(in) listener, pl a. (radio) audience

Rundfunksender m broadcasting or radio station

'Rundgang m tour (**durch** of)

'rundhe'raus adv frankly, plainly

'rundhe'rum adv all around

'rundlich adj plump, chubby

'Rundreise f tour (**durch** of)

Rundschau f review

Rundschreiben n circular (letter)

Rundspruch Swiss m → **Rundfunk**

'Rundung f (-; -en) curve

'rundweg [-'vɛk] adv flatly, plainly

runter ['rʊntɐ] F adv → **herunter**

Runzel ['rʊntsəl] f (-; -n) wrinkle

runz(e)lig ['rʊnts(ə)lıç] adj wrinkled

'runzeln v/t (ge-, h) **die Stirn runzeln** frown (**über** acc at)

Rüpel ['ry:pəl] m (-s; -) lout

rupfen ['rʊpfən] v/t (ge-, h) pluck

Rüsche ['ry:ʃə] f (-; -n) frill, ruffle

Ruß ['ru:s] m (-es; no pl) soot

Russe ['rʊsə] m (-n; -n) Russian

Rüssel ['rʏsəl] m (-s; -) zo trunk; snout

rußen ['ru:sən] v/i (ge-, h) smoke

rußig ['ru:sıç] adj sooty

Russin ['rʊsın] f (-; -nen), russisch ['rʊsıʃ] adj Russian

'Russland Russia

rüsten ['rʏstən] (ge-, h) 1. v/i MIL arm; 2. v/refl get ready, prepare (**zu, für** for); arm o.s. (**gegen** for)

rüstig ['rʏstıç] adj vigorous, sprightly

rustikal [rʊstiˈkaːl] adj rustic

'Rüstung f (-; -en) MIL armament; armo(u)r

'Rüstungsindus,trie f armament industry

Rüstungswettlauf m arms race

'Rüstzeug n equipment

Rute ['ru:tə] f (-; -n) rod (a. fig), switch

Rutschbahn ['rʊtʃ-] f, Rutsche ['rʊtʃə] f (-; -n) slide, chute

'rutschen v/i (ge-, sein) slide, slip; glide; MOT etc skid

rutschig ['rʊtʃıç] adj slippery

'rutschsicher adj MOT etc non-skid

rütteln ['rʏtəln] (ge-, h) 1. v/t shake; 2. v/i jolt; **an der Tür rütteln** rattle at the door

S

S ABBR of **Süd(en)** S, south

S. ABBR of **Seite** p., page

s. ABBR of **siehe** see

Saal [za:l] m (-[e]s; Säle ['zɛ:lə]) hall

Saat [za:t] f (-; -en) a) (no pl) sowing, b) seed(s) (a. fig); crop(s)

Sabbat ['zabat] m (-s; -e) sabbath (day)

sabbern ['zabɐn] F v/i (ge-, h) slobber, slaver

Säbel ['zɛ:bəl] m (-s; -) saber, Br sabre (a. SPORT), sword

'säbeln F v/t (ge-, h) cut, hack

Sabotage [zaboˈta:ʒə] f (-; -n) sabotage

Saboteur [zaboˈtø:ɐ] m (-s; -e) saboteur

sabotieren [zaboˈti:rən] v/t (no -ge-, h) sabotage

Sachbearbeiter ['zax-] m, Sachbearbeiterin f official in charge

Sachbeschädigung f damage to property

Sachbuch n specialized book, pl coll nonfiction

'sachdienlich adj: **sachdienliche Hinweise** relevant information

Sache ['zaxə] f (-; -n) thing; matter; business; issue, problem, question; cause; JUR matter, case; pl things, clothes; **zur Sache kommen (bei der Sache bleiben)** come (keep) to the point; **nicht zur Sache gehören** be irrelevant

'sachgerecht adj proper

'Sachkenntnis f expert knowledge

'sachkundig adj expert

'sachlich adj matter-of-fact, businesslike; unbias(s)ed, objective; practical, technical; **sachlich richtig** factually correct

sächlich ['zɛçlıç] adj LING neuter

'Sachre,gister n (subject) index

'**Sachschaden** *m* damage to property

sacht [zaxt] *adj* soft, gentle; slow

'**Sachverhalt** *m* (-[e]s; -e) facts (of the case)

Sachverstand *m* know-how

Sachverständige *m, f* (-n; -n) expert; JUR expert witness

Sachwert *m* (-[e]s; *no pl*) real value

Sachzwänge *pl* inherent necessities

Sack [zak] *m* (-[e]s; *Säcke* ['zɛkə]) sack, bag; V balls

sacken ['zakən] F *v/i* (*ge-, sein*) sink

'**Sackgasse** *f* blind alley (*a. fig*), dead end (*a. fig*); *fig* impasse

Sadismus [za'dɪsmʊs] *m* (-; *no pl*) sadism

Sadist [za'dɪst] *m* (-en; -en) sadist

sa'distisch *adj* sadistic

säen ['zɛːən] *v/t and v/i* (*ge-, h*) sow (*a. fig*)

Safari [za'faːri] *f* (-; -s) safari

Safaripark *m* wildlife reserve, safari park

Saft [zaft] *m* (-[e]s; *Säfte* ['zɛftə]) juice; BOT sap (*both a. fig*)

saftig ['zaftɪç] *adj* juicy (*a. fig*); lush; F fancy (*prices etc*)

Sage ['zaːɡə] *f* (-; -n) legend, myth

Säge ['zɛːɡə] *f* (-; -n) saw

'**Sägemehl** *n* sawdust

sagen ['zaːɡən] *v/i and v/t* (*ge-, h*) say; *j-m et. sagen* tell s.o. s.th.; *die Wahrheit sagen* tell the truth; *er lässt dir sagen* he asked me to tell you; *sagen wir ...* (let's) say ...; *man sagt, er sei reich* he is said to be rich; *er lässt sich nichts sagen* he will not listen to reason; *das hat nichts zu sagen* it doesn't matter; *et. (nichts) zu sagen haben (bei)* have a say (no say) (in); *sagen wollen mit* mean by; *das sagt mir nichts* it doesn't mean anything to me; *unter uns gesagt* between you and me

sägen ['zɛːɡən] *v/t and v/i* (*ge-, h*) saw

'**sagenhaft** *adj* legendary; F fabulous, incredible, fantastic

'**Sägespäne** *pl* sawdust

'**Sägewerk** *n* sawmill

sah [zaː] *pret of* **sehen**

Sahne ['zaːnə] *f* (-; *no pl*) cream

Saison [zɛ'zõ:] *f* (-; -s) season; *in der Saison* in season

sai'sonbedingt *adj* seasonal

Saite ['zaitə] *f* (-; -n) MUS string, chord (*a. fig*)

'**Saiteninstru,ment** *n* MUS string(ed) instrument

Sakko ['zako] *m, n* (-s; -s) (sports) jacket, sport(s) coat

Sakristei [zakrɪs'tai] *f* (-; -en) REL vestry, sacristy

Salat [za'laːt] *m* (-[e]s; -e) BOT lettuce; GASTR salad

Salatsauce *f* salad dressing

Salbe ['zalbə] *f* (-; -n) ointment

'**Salbung** *f* (-; -en) unction

'**salbungsvoll** *adj* unctuous

Saldo ['zaldo] *m* (-s; -s, -di) ECON balance

Salon [za'lõ:] *m* (-s; -s) salon; MAR saloon; drawing room

salopp [za'lɔp] *adj* casual; *contp* sloppy

Salpeter [zal'peːtɐ] *m* (-s; *no pl*) CHEM salt|peter (*Br* -petre), niter, *Br* nitre

Salto ['zalto] *m* (-s; -s, -ti) somersault

Salut [za'luːt] *m* (-[e]s; -e) MIL salute; *Salut schießen* fire a salute

salutieren [zalu'tiːrən] *v/i* (*no -ge-, h*) MIL (give a) salute

Salve ['zalvə] *f* (-; -n) MIL volley (*a. fig*); salute

Salz [zalts] *n* (-es; -e) salt

'**Salzbergwerk** *n* salt mine

salzen ['zaltsən] *v/t* ([*irr,*] *ge-, h*) salt

salzfrei ['zaltsfrai] *adj* salt-free, no-salt diet

salzig ['zaltsɪç] *adj* salty

'**Salzkar,toffeln** *pl* boiled potatoes

Salzsäure *f* (-; *no pl*) CHEM hydrochloric acid

Salzstange *f* pretzel (*Br* salt) stick

Salzstreuer *m* (-s; -) salt shaker, *Br* salt cellar

Salzwasser *n* salt water

Same ['zaːmə] *m* (-n; -n), **Samen** (-s -) BOT seed (*a. fig*); BIOL sperm, semen

'**Samenbank** *f* (-; -en) MED, VET sperm bank

Samenerguss *m* ejaculation

Samenkorn *n* BOT seedcorn

Sammel... ['zaməl-] *in cpds* ...begriff, ...bestellung, ...konto *etc*: collective ...

Sammelbüchse *f* collecting box

'**sammeln** *v/t* (*ge-, h*) collect; gather, pick; accumulate; *sich sammeln* assemble; *fig* compose o.s.

Sammler ['zamlɐ] *m* (-s; -), '**Sammlerin** *f* (-; -nen) collector

'**Sammlung** *f* (-; -en) collection

Samstag ['zamstaːk] *m* (-[e]s; -e) Saturday

samt [zamt] *prp* (*dat*) together *or* along with

Samt *m* (-[e]s; -e) velvet

sämtlich ['zɛmtlɪç] *adj*: *sämtliche pl* all the; the complete *works etc*

Sanatorium [zana'toːrjʊm] *n* (-s; -ien) sanatorium, sanitarium

Sand [zant] *m* (-[e]s; -e) sand

Sandale [zan'daːlə] *f* (-; -n) sandal

Sandalette [zanda'lɛtə] *f* (-; -n) high-heeled sandal

'Sandbahn f SPORT dirt track
Sandbank f (-; -bänke) sandbank
Sandboden m sandy soil
Sandburg f sandcastle
sandig ['zandɪç] adj sandy
'Sandmann m, Sandmännchen n sand-man
Sandpa,pier n sandpaper
Sandsack m sand bag
Sandstein m sandstone
Sandstrand m sandy beach
sandte ['zantə] pret of senden
'Sanduhr f hourglass
sanft [zanft] adj gentle, soft; mild; easy (death)
'sanftmütig [-my:tɪç] adj gentle, mild
sang [zaŋ] pret of singen
Sänger ['zɛŋɐ] m (-s; -), Sängerin ['zɛŋə-rɪn] f (-; -nen) singer
sanieren [za'ni:rən] v/t (no -ge-, h) redevelop (a. ECON), rehabilitate (a. ARCH)
Sa'nierung f (-; -en) redevelopment, rehabilitation
Sa'nierungsgebiet n redevelopment area
sanität [zani'tɛ:t] adj sanitary
Sanitäter [zani'tɛ:tɐ] m (-s; -) paramedic; MIL medic, Br medical orderly
sank [zaŋk] pret of sinken
Sankt [zaŋkt] Saint, ABBR St
Sardelle [zar'dɛlə] f (-; -n) ZO anchovy
Sardine [zar'di:nə] f (-; -n) ZO sardine
Sarg [zark] m (-[e]s; Särge ['zɛrgə]) cas-ket, esp Br coffin
Sarkasmus [zar'kasmʊs] m (-; no pl) sar-casm
sar'kastisch adj sarcastic
saß [za:s] pret of sitzen
Satan ['za:tan] m (-s; -e) Satan; fig devil
Satellit [zatɛ'li:t] m (-en; -en) satellite (a. fig); über Satellit by or via satellite
Satel'liten... in cpds ...bild, ...staat, ...stadt, ...-TV: satellite ...
Satin [za'tɛ̃] m (-s; -s) satin; sateen
Satire [za'ti:rə] f (-; -n) satire (auf acc on)
Satiriker [za'ti:rikɐ] m (-s; -) satirist
sa'tirisch adj satiric(al)
satt [zat] adj F full (up); ich bin satt I've had enough, F I'm full (up); sich satt es-sen eat one's fill (an dat of)
Sattel ['zatəl] m (-s; Sättel ['zɛtəl]) saddle
'satteln v/t (ge-, h) saddle
'Sattelschlepper m MOT semi-trailer truck, Br articulated lorry
'satthaben v/t (irr, haben, sep, -ge-, h) F be tired or F sick of, be fed up with
sättigen ['zɛtɪgən] (ge-, h) 1. v/t satisfy; feed; CHEM, PHYS saturate; 2. v/i be sub-stantial, be filling

'Sättigung f (-; -en) satiety; CHEM, ECON saturation (a. fig)
Sattler ['zatlɐ] m (-s; -) saddler
Sattlerei [zatlə'rai] f (-; -en) saddlery
Satz [zats] m (-es; Sätze ['zɛtsə]) leap; LING sentence; tennis etc: set; ECON rate; MUS movement
'Satzaussage f LING predicate
Satzbau m (-[e]s; no pl) LING syntax; con-struction
Satzgegenstand m LING subject
Satzung f ['zatsʊŋ] f (-; -en) statute
'Satzzeichen n LING punctuation mark
Sau [zau] f (-; Säue ['zɔʏə]) ZO sow; HUNT wild sow; F swine, pig
sauber ['zaubɐ] adj clean (a. F fig); pure; neat (a. fig), tidy; decent; iro fine, nice; sauber halten keep clean (sich o.s.); sauber machen clean (up)
'Sauberkeit f (-; no pl) clean(li)ness; tidi-ness, neatness; purity; decency
'saubermachen v/t and v/i (sep, -ge-, h) → sauber
säubern ['zɔʏbɐn] v/t (ge-, h) clean (up); cleanse (a. MED); säubern von clear (POL a. purge) of
'Säuberung(sakti,on) f POL purge
sauer ['zauɐ] adj sour (a. fig), acid (a. CHEM); GASTR pickled; F mad (auf acc at), cross (with); sauer werden turn sour; F get mad; saurer Regen acid rain
säuerlich ['zɔʏɐlɪç] adj sharp; F wry
'Sauerstoff m (-[e]s; no pl) CHEM oxygen
Sauerstoffgerät n MED oxygen apparatus
Sauerstoffzelt n MED oxygen tent
'Sauerteig m leaven
saufen ['zaufən] v/t and v/i (irr, ge-, h) drink; F booze
Säufer(in) ['zɔʏfɐ (-fərɪn)] F (-s; -/-; -nen) drunkard, F boozer
saugen ['zaugən] v/i and v/t ([irr,] ge-, h) suck (an et. [at] s.th.)
säugen ['zɔʏgən] v/t (ge-, h) suckle (a. ZO), nurse, breastfeed
'Säugetier n mammal
saugfähig ['zauk-] adj absorbent
Säugling ['zɔʏklɪŋ] m (-s; -e) baby, infant
'Säuglingsheim n (baby) nursery
Säuglingspflege f infant care
Säuglingsschwester f baby nurse
Säuglingsstati,on f neonatal care unit
Säuglingssterblichkeit f infant mortality
Säule ['zɔʏlə] f (-; -n) column; pillar (a. fig)
'Säulengang m colonnade
Saum [zaum] m (-[e]s; Säume ['zɔʏmə]) hem(line); seam
säumen ['zɔʏmən] v/t (ge-, h) hem; bor-der, edge; line

Sauna ['zauna] *f* (-; -s, *Saunen*) sauna

Säure ['zɔyrə] *f* (-; -n) CHEM acid

'säurehaltig [-haltɪç] *adj* acid

sausen ['zauzən] *v/i* a) (*ge-, sein*) F rush, dash, b) (*ge-, h*) ears: buzz; wind: howl

'Saustall *m* pigsty (*a.* F *contp*)

Saxophon [zakso'foːn] *n* (-s; -e) MUS saxophone, F sax

S-Bahn ['ɛsbaːn] *f* rapid transit, *Br* suburban train

Schabe ['ʃaːbə] *f* (-; -n) ZO cockroach

'schaben *v/t* (*ge-, h*) scrape (*von* from)

schäbig ['ʃɛːbɪç] *adj* shabby, *fig a.* mean

Schablone [ʃa'bloːnə] *f* (-; -n) stencil; *fig* stereotype

Schach [ʃax] *n* (-s; *no pl*) chess; *Schach!* check!; *j-n Schach und matt!* checkmate!; *j-n in Schach halten* keep s.o. in check

Schachbrett *n* chessboard

Schachfeld *n* square

Schachfi‚gur *f* chessman, piece

schach'matt *adj: j-n schachmatt setzen* checkmate s.o.

'Schachspiel *n* (game of) chess; chessboard and men

Schacht [ʃaxt] *m* (-[e]s; *Schächte* ['ʃɛçtə]) shaft, *mining: a.* pit

Schachtel ['ʃaxtəl] *f* (-; -n) box; carton; *e-e Schachtel Zigaretten* a pack (*esp Br* packet) of cigarettes

'Schachzug *m* move (*a. fig*)

schade ['ʃaːdə] *pred adj: es ist schade* it's a pity; *wie schade!* what a pity *or* shame!; *zu schade sein für* be too good for

Schädel ['ʃɛːdəl] *m* (-s; -) ANAT skull

Schädelbruch *n* MED fracture of the skull

schaden ['ʃaːdən] *v/i* (*ge-, h*) damage, do damage to, harm; hurt; *der Gesundheit schaden* be bad for one's health; *das schadet nichts* it doesn't matter; *es könnte ihm nicht schaden* it wouldn't hurt him

'Schaden *m* (-s; *Schäden* ['ʃɛːdən]) damage (*an dat* to); *esp* TECH trouble, defect (*a.* MED); *fig* disadvantage; ECON loss; *j-m Schaden zufügen* do s.o. harm

Schadenersatz *m* damages; *Schadenersatz leisten* pay damages

Schadenfreude *f: Schadenfreude empfinden über* (*acc*) gloat over

'schadenfroh *adv* gloatingly

schadhaft ['ʃaːthaft] *adj* damaged; defective, faulty; leaking (*pipes*)

schädigen ['ʃɛːdɪɡən] *v/t* (*ge-, h*) damage, harm

schädlich ['ʃɛːtlɪç] *adj* harmful, injurious; bad (for your health)

Schädling ['ʃɛːtlɪŋ] *m* (-s; -e) BIOL pest

'Schädlingsbekämpfung *f* pest control

Schädlingsbekämpfungsmittel *n* pesticide

Schadstoff ['ʃaːt-] *m* harmful substance; pollutant

'schadstoffarm *adj* MOT low-emission

Schaf [ʃaːf] *n* (-[e]s; -e) ZO sheep

'Schafbock *m* ZO ram

Schäfer ['ʃɛːfɐ] *m* (-s; -) shepherd

Schäferhund *m* sheepdog; *Deutscher Schäferhund* German shepherd, *esp Br* Alsatian

'Schaffell *n* sheepskin; ZO fleece

schaffen¹ ['ʃafən] *v/t* (*irr, ge-, h*) create

'schaffen² (*ge-, h*) **1.** *v/t* cause, bring about; manage, get *s.th.* done; take; *es schaffen* make it, *a.* succeed; *2. v/i* work; *j-m zu schaffen machen* cause s.o. trouble; *sich zu schaffen machen an* (*dat*) tamper with

Schaffner ['ʃafnɐ] *m* (-s; -), **'Schaffnerin** *f* (-; -nen) conductor; *Br* RAIL guard

Schafott [ʃa'fɔt] *n* (-[e]s; -e) scaffold

Schaft [ʃaft] *m* (-[e]s; *Schäfte* ['ʃɛftə]) shaft; stock; shank; leg

'Schafwolle *f* sheep's wool

'Schafzucht *f* sheep breeding

schäkern ['ʃɛːkɐn] *v/i* (*ge-, h*) joke; flirt

schal [ʃaːl] *adj* stale, flat, *fig a.* empty

Schal *m* (-s; -s) scarf

Schale ['ʃaːlə] *f* (-; -n) bowl, dish; GASTR shell; peel, skin

schälen ['ʃɛːlən] *v/t* (*ge-, h*) peel, pare; *sich schälen skin:* peel (off)

Schall [ʃal] *m* (-[e]s; -e) sound

Schalldämpfer *m* silencer (*a. Br* MOT), MOT muffler

'schalldicht *adj* soundproof

schallen ['ʃalən] *v/i* (*irr*[?] *ge-, h*) sound; ring (out); *schallendes Gelächter* roars of laughter

'Schallgeschwindigkeit *f* speed of sound

Schallmauer *f* sound barrier

Schallplatte *f* record, disk, *Br* disc

Schallwelle *f* PHYS sound wave

schalten ['ʃaltən] *v/i* and *v/t* (*ge-, h*) switch, turn; MOT shift (*esp Br* change) gear; F get it; react

Schalter ['ʃaltɐ] *m* (-s; -) counter; RAIL ticket window; AVIAT desk; ELECTR switch

'Schalthebel *m* MOT gear lever; TECH, AVIAT control lever; ELECTR switch lever

Schaltjahr *n* leap year

Schalttafel *f* ELECTR switchboard, control panel

Schaltuhr *f* time switch

'Schaltung *f* (-; -en) MOT gearshift; ELECTR circuit

Scham [ʃaːm] *f* (-; *no pl*) shame; *vor*

S

Scham with shame
schämen ['ʃɛːmən] v/refl (ge-, h) be or feel ashamed (*gen*, *wegen* of); *du solltest dich (was) schämen!* you ought to be ashamed of yourself!
'Schamgefühl n (-[e]s; no pl) sense of shame
Schamhaare pl pubic hair
'schamhaft adj bashful
'schamlos adj shameless; indecent
Schande ['ʃandə] f (-; no pl) shame, disgrace
schänden ['ʃɛndən] v/t (ge-, h) disgrace; desecrate; rape
Schandfleck ['ʃant-] m eyesore
schändlich ['ʃɛntlɪç] adj disgraceful
'Schandtat f atrocity
Schanze ['ʃantsə] f (-; -n) SPORT ski jump
Schar [ʃaːr] f (-; -en ['ʃaːrən]) troop, band; F horde; crowd; ZO flock
'scharen v/refl (ge-, h) *sich scharen um* gather round
scharf [ʃarf] adj sharp (a. fig), PHOT a. in focus; clear; savage, fierce (*dog*); live (*ammunition*), armed (*bomb etc*); GASTR hot; F hot, sexy; F *scharf sein auf* (*acc*) be keen on; *scharf (ein)stellen* PHOT focus; F *scharfe Sachen* hard liquor
Schärfe ['ʃɛrfə] f (-; -n) sharpness (a. PHOT); fig severity, fierceness
'schärfen v/t (ge-, h) sharpen
'Scharfrichter m executioner
'Scharfschütze m sharpshooter; sniper
'scharfsichtig adj sharp-sighted; fig clear-sighted
'Scharfsinn m (-[e]s; no pl) acumen
'scharfsinnig adj sharp-witted, shrewd
'scharfstellen v/t (sep, -ge-, h) → *scharf*
Scharlach ['ʃarlax] m (-s; no pl) scarlet; MED scarlet fever
'scharlachrot adj scarlet
Scharlatan ['ʃarlatan] m (-s; -e) charlatan, fraud
Scharnier [ʃar'niːɐ] n (-s; -e) TECH hinge
Schärpe ['ʃɛrpə] f (-; -n) sash
scharren ['ʃarən] v/i (ge-, h) scrape, scratch
schartig ['ʃartɪç] adj jagged, notchy
Schaschlik ['ʃaʃlɪk] m, n (-s; -s) GASTR shish kebab
Schatten ['ʃatən] m (-s; -) shadow (a. fig); shade; *im Schatten* in the shade
'schattenhaft adj shadowy
Schattierung [ʃa'tiːruŋ] f (-; -en) shade; fig colo(u)r
schattig ['ʃatɪç] adj shady
Schatz [ʃats] m (-es; Schätze ['ʃɛtsə]) treasure; fig darling

Schatzamt n POL Treasury Department, Br Treasury
schätzen ['ʃɛtsən] v/t (ge-, h) estimate, value (*both*: *auf* acc at); appreciate; think highly of; F reckon, guess
'Schatzkammer f treasury (a. fig)
Schatzkanzler m Chancellor of the Exchequer
Schatzmeister(in) treasurer
'Schätzung f (-; -en) estimate; valuation
Schau [ʃau] f (-; -en) show, exhibition; *zur Schau stellen* exhibit, display
Schauder ['ʃaudɐ] m (-s; -) shudder
'schauderhaft adj horrible, dreadful
'schaudern v/i (ge-, h) shudder, shiver (*both*: *vor* dat with)
schauen ['ʃauən] v/i (ge-, h) look (*auf* acc at)
Schauer ['ʃauɐ] m (-s; -) METEOR shower; shudder, shiver
Schauergeschichte f horror story (a. fig)
'schauerlich adj dreadful, horrible
Schaufel ['ʃaufəl] f (-; -n) shovel; dustpan
'schaufeln v/t (ge-, h) shovel; dig
'Schaufenster n shop window
Schaufensterauslage f window display
Schaufensterbummel m: *e-n Schaufensterbummel machen* go window-shopping
Schaufensterdekoration f window dressing
Schaukel ['ʃaukəl] f (-; -n) swing
'schaukeln (ge-, h) 1. v/i swing; *boat etc*: rock; 2. v/t rock
Schaukelpferd n rocking horse
Schaukelstuhl m rocking chair, rocker
Schaulustige [-lʊstɪgə] pl (curious) onlookers, F rubbernecks
Schaum [ʃaum] m (-[e]s; Schäume ['ʃɔymə]) foam; GASTR froth, head; lather; spray
schäumen ['ʃɔymən] v/i (ge-, h) foam (a. fig), froth; lather; spray
'Schaumgummi m foam rubber
schaumig ['ʃaumɪç] adj foamy, frothy
'Schaumlöscher m foam extinguisher
'Schauplatz m scene
'Schauprozess m JUR show trial
schaurig ['ʃaurɪç] adj creepy; horrible
'Schauspiel n THEA play; fig spectacle
'Schauspieler(in) actor (actress)
'Schauspielschule f drama school
'Schausteller [-ʃtɛlɐ] m (-s; -) showman
Scheck [ʃɛk] m (-s; -s) ECON check, Br cheque
Scheckheft n checkbook, Br chequebook
scheckig ['ʃɛkɪç] adj spotty
'Scheckkarte f check cashing (Br cheque) card

scheffeln ['ʃɛfəln] F v/t (ge-, h) rake in

Scheibe ['ʃaibə] f (-; -n) disk, Br disc; slice; pane; target

ˈScheibenbremse f MOT disk (Br disc) brake

Scheibenwischer m MOT windshield (Br windscreen) wiper

Scheide ['ʃaidə] f (-; -n) sheath; scabbard; ANAT vagina

ˈscheiden (irr, ge-) **1.** v/t (h) separate, part (both: **von** from); divorce; **sich scheiden lassen** get a divorce, **von j-m**: divorce s.o.; **2.** v/i (sein) part; **scheiden aus** (dat) retire from

ˈScheideweg m crossroads

ˈScheidung f (-; -en) divorce

ˈScheidungsklage f JUR divorce suit

Schein[1] [ʃain] m (-[e]s; -e) certificate; blank, Br form; bill, Br note

Schein[2] m (-[e]s; no pl) light; fig appearance; **et. (nur) zum Schein tun** (only) pretend to do s.th.

ˈscheinbar adj seeming, apparent

scheinen ['ʃainən] v/i (irr, ge-, h) shine; fig seem, appear, look

ˈscheinheilig adj hypocritical

ˈScheinwerfer m searchlight; MOT headlight; THEA spotlight

Scheiß... [ʃais-] V in cpds damn ..., fucking ..., esp Br bloody ...

ˈScheiße ['ʃaisə] V f (-; no pl) shit, crap; **ˈscheißen** V v/i (irr, ge-, h) shit, crap

Scheit [ʃait] n (-[e]s; -e) piece of wood

Scheitel ['ʃaitəl] m (-s; -) parting

ˈscheiteln v/t (ge-, h) part

Scheiterhaufen ['ʃaitɐ-] m pyre; HIST stake

scheitern ['ʃaitɐn] v/i (ge-, sein) fail, go wrong

Schelle ['ʃɛlə] f (-; -n) (little) bell; TECH clamp, clip

Schellfisch ['ʃɛl-] m ZO haddock

Schelm [ʃɛlm] m (-[e]s; -e) rascal

schelmisch ['ʃɛlmɪʃ] adj impish

Schema ['ʃeːma] n (-s; -s, -ta) pattern, system

schematisch [ʃeˈmaːtɪʃ] adj schematic; mechanical

Schemel ['ʃeːməl] m (-s; -) stool

schemenhaft ['ʃeːmən-] adj shadowy

Schenkel ['ʃɛŋkəl] m (-s; -) ANAT thigh; shank; MATH leg

schenken ['ʃɛŋkən] v/t (ge-, h) give (as a present) (**zu** for)

ˈSchenkung f (-; -en) JUR donation

Scherbe ['ʃɛrbə] f (-; -n), **ˈScherben** m (-s; -) (broken) piece, fragment

Schere ['ʃeːrə] f (-; -n) scissors; ZO claw

scheren[1] ['ʃeːrən] v/t (irr, ge-, h) ZO shear;

BOT clip; cut

ˈscheren[2] v/i/refl (ge-, h) **sich scheren um** bother about

Schererein [ʃeːrəˈraiən] pl trouble, bother

Schermaus ['ʃeːrɐ-] Austrian f ZO mole

Scherz [ʃɛrts] m (-es; -e) joke; **im (zum) Scherz** for fun

scherzen ['ʃɛrtsən] v/i (ge-, h) joke (**über** acc at)

ˈscherzhaft adj joking; **scherzhaft gemeint** meant as a joke

scheu [ʃɔy] adj shy (a. ZO); bashful; **scheu machen** frighten

Scheu f (-; no pl) shyness; awe

scheuen ['ʃɔyən] (ge-, h) **1.** v/i shy (**vor** dat at), take fright (at); **2.** v/t shun, avoid; fear; **sich scheuen, et. zu tun** be afraid of doing s.th.

scheuern ['ʃɔyɐn] v/t and v/i (ge-, h) scrub, scour; chafe

ˈScheuertuch n floor cloth

ˈScheuklappen pl blinders, Br blinkers (both a. fig)

ˈscheumachen v/t (sep, -ge-, h) → **scheu**

Scheune ['ʃɔynə] f (-; -n) barn

Scheusal ['ʃɔyzaːl] n (-s; -e) monster (a. fig); fig beast

scheußlich ['ʃɔyslɪç] adj horrible (a. F), atrocious

Schicht [ʃɪçt] f (-; -en) layer; coat; film; ECON shift; class

schichten ['ʃɪçtən] v/t (ge-, h) arrange in layers, pile up

ˈschichtweise adv in layers

schick [ʃɪk] adj smart, chic, stylish

schicken ['ʃɪkən] v/t (ge-, h) send (**nach**, **zu** to); **das schickt sich nicht** that isn't done

Schickeria [ʃɪkəˈriːa] F f (-; no pl) smart set, beautiful people, trendies

Schickimicki [ʃɪkiˈmɪki] F contp m (-s; -s) trendy

Schicksal ['ʃɪkzaːl] n (-s; -e) fate, destiny; lot

Schiebedach ['ʃiːbə-] n MOT sliding roof, sunroof

Schiebefenster n sliding window; sash window

schieben ['ʃiːbən] v/t (irr, ge-, h) push

Schieber ['ʃiːbɐ] m (-s; -) TECH slide; bolt; F profiteer

ˈSchiebetür f sliding door

ˈSchiebung f (-; -en) swindle, fix (a. SPORT)

schied [ʃiːt] pret of **scheiden**

Schiedsrichter ['ʃiːts-] m, **ˈSchiedsrichterin** f soccer: referee; tennis: umpire; judge, esp pl a. jury

schief [ʃiːf] adj crooked, not straight; sloping, oblique (a. MATH); leaning; fig false

Schiefer [ˈʃiːfɐ] m (-s; -) GEOL slate

'Schiefertafel f slate

'schiefgehen v/i (irr, **gehen**, sep, -ge-, sein) F go wrong

schielen [ˈʃiːlən] v/i (ge-, h) squint, be cross-eyed

schien [ʃiːn] pret of **scheinen**

Schienbein [ˈʃiːn-] n ANAT shin(bone)

Schiene [ˈʃiːnə] f (-; -n) TECH etc rail; MED splint

'schienen v/t (ge-, h) MED splint

Schießbude [ˈʃiːs-] f shooting gallery

schießen [ˈʃiːsən] v/i and v/t (irr, ge-, h) shoot, fire (both: **auf** acc at); SPORT score

Schießerei [ʃiːsəˈrai] f (-; -en) shooting, gunfight

'Schießpulver n gunpowder

Schießscharte f MIL loophole, embrasure

Schießscheibe f target

Schießstand m shooting range

Schiff [ʃɪf] n (-[e]s; -e) ship, boat; ARCH nave; **mit dem Schiff** by boat

Schiffahrt f → **Schifffahrt**

'schiffbar adj navigable

Schiffbau m (-[e]s; no pl) shipbuilding

'Schiffbruch m shipwreck (a. fig); **Schiffbruch erleiden** be shipwrecked

Schiffer [ˈʃɪfɐ] m (-s; -) sailor; skipper

'Schifffahrt f (-; no pl) shipping, navigation

'Schiffsjunge m ship's boy

Schiffsladung f shipload; cargo

Schiffsschraube f (ship's) propeller

Schiffswerft f shipyard

Schikane [ʃiˈkaːnə] f (-; -n) a. pl harassment; **aus reiner Schikane** out of sheer spite; F **mit allen Schikanen** with all the trimmings

schikanieren [ʃikaˈniːrən] v/t (no -ge-, h) harass; bully

Schild[1] [ʃɪlt] n (-[e]s; -er [ˈʃɪldɐ]) sign, plate

Schild[2] m (-[e]s; -e) shield

'Schilddrüse f ANAT thyroid (gland)

schildern [ˈʃɪldɐn] v/t (ge-, h) describe; depict; portray

Schilderung [ˈʃɪldərʊŋ] f (-; -en) description, portrayal; account

'Schildkröte f zo tortoise; turtle

Schilf [ʃɪlf] n (-[e]s; no pl) BOT reed(s)

schillern [ˈʃɪlɐn] v/i (ge-, h) be iridescent

schillernd adj iridescent; fig dubious

Schimmel [ˈʃɪməl] m zo white horse; BOT mo(u)ld

schimm(e)lig [ˈʃɪm(ə)lɪç] adj mo(u)ldy, musty

'schimmeln v/i (ge-, h, sein) go mo(u)ldy

Schimmer [ˈʃɪmɐ] m (-s; -) glimmer (a. fig), gleam, fig a. trace, touch

'schimmern v/i (ge-, h) shimmer, glimmer, gleam

Schimpanse [ʃɪmˈpanzə] m (-n; -n) zo chimpanzee

schimpfen [ˈʃɪmpfən] v/i and v/t (ge-, h) scold (**mit j-m** s.o.); F tell s.o. off, bawl s.o. out; **schimpfen über** (acc) complain about

'Schimpfwort n swearword

Schindel [ˈʃɪndəl] f (-; -n) shingle

schinden [ˈʃɪndən] v/t (irr, ge-, h) maltreat; slave-drive; **sich schinden** drudge, slave away

Schinder [ˈʃɪndɐ] m (-s; -) slave driver

Schinderei [ʃɪndəˈrai] f (-; -en) slavery, drudgery

Schinken [ˈʃɪŋkən] m (-s; -) ham

Schippe [ˈʃɪpə] f (-; -n), 'schippen v/t (ge-, h) shovel

Schirm [ʃɪrm] m (-[e]s; -e) umbrella; sunshade; TV, EDP etc: screen; shade; peak, visor

Schirmherr(in) patron, sponsor

Schirmherrschaft f patronage, sponsorship; **unter der Schirmherrschaft von** under the auspices of

Schirmmütze f peaked cap

Schirmständer m umbrella stand

schiss [ʃɪs] pret of **scheißen**

Schlacht [ʃlaxt] f (-; -en) battle (**bei** at)

'schlachten v/t (ge-, h) slaughter, kill, butcher

Schlachter [ˈʃlaxtɐ] m (-s; -) butcher

'Schlachtfeld n MIL battlefield, battleground

Schlachthaus n, Schlachthof m slaughterhouse

Schlachtplan m MIL plan of action (a. fig)

Schlachtschiff n MIL battleship

Schlacke [ˈʃlakə] f (-; -n) cinders; GEOL, METALL slag

Schlaf [ʃlaːf] m (-[e]s; no pl) sleep; **e-n leichten** (**festen**) **Schlaf haben** be a light (sound) sleeper; F fig **im Schlaf** blindfold

'Schlafanzug m pajamas, Br pyjamas

Schläfe [ˈʃlɛːfə] f (-; -n) ANAT temple

schlafen [ˈʃlaːfən] v/i (irr, ge-, h) sleep (a. fig); **schlafen gehen, sich schlafen legen** go to bed; **fest schlafen** be fast asleep; **j-n schlafen legen** put s.o. to bed or to sleep

schlaff [ʃlaf] adj slack (a. fig); flabby; limp

'Schlafgelegenheit f sleeping accommodation

Schlafkrankheit *f* MED sleeping sickness

Schlaflied *n* lullaby

'schlaflos *adj* sleepless

'Schlaflosigkeit *f* (*-; no pl*) sleeplessness, MED insomnia

'Schlafmittel *n* MED sleeping pill(s)

'Schlafmütze *fig f* sleepyhead; slowpoke, *Br* slowcoach

schläfrig ['ʃlɛːfrɪç] *adj* sleepy, drowsy

'Schlafsaal *m* dormitory

Schlafsack *m* sleeping bag

Schlafta,blette *f* sleeping pill

'schlaftrunken *adj* (very) drowsy

'Schlafwagen *m* RAIL sleeping car, sleeper

Schlafwandler(in) [-vandlɐ (-lərɪn)] (*-s; -/-; -nen*) sleepwalker, somnambulist

Schlafzimmer *n* bedroom

Schlag [ʃlaːk] *m* (*-[e]s; Schläge* ['ʃlɛːgə]) blow (*a. fig*); slap; punch; pat, tap; *a. tennis*: stroke; ELECTR shock (*a. fig*); MED beat; *pl* beating; → *Schlaganfall*

Schlagader *f* ANAT artery

Schlaganfall *m* MED (apoplectic) stroke

'schlagartig 1. *adj* sudden, abrupt; **2.** *adv* all of a sudden, abruptly

'Schlagbaum *m* barrier

'Schlagbohrer *m* TECH percussion drill

schlagen ['ʃlaːgən] (*irr, ge-, h*) **1.** *v/t* hit, beat (*a. GASTR*), strike, knock; fell, cut (down); *sich schlagen* fight (*um* over); *sich geschlagen geben* admit defeat; **2.** *v/i* hit, beat (*a. heart etc*), strike (*a. clock*), knock; *an or gegen et. schlagen* hit s.th., bump or crash into s.th.

Schlager ['ʃlaːgɐ] *m* (*-s; -*) MUS hit (*a. fig*), (pop) song

Schläger ['ʃlɛːgɐ] *m* (*-s; -*) *tennis etc*: racket; *table tennis, cricket, baseball*: bat; *golf*: club; *hockey*: stick; *contp* thug

Schlägerei [ʃlɛːgəˈrai] *f* (*-; -en*) fight, brawl

'schlagfertig *adj* quick-witted; *schlagfertige Antwort* (witty) repartee

'Schlaginstru,ment *n* MUS percussion instrument

Schlagkraft *f* (*-; no pl*) striking power (*a. MIL*)

Schlagloch *n* pot-hole

Schlagobers *Austrian n*, **Schlagsahne** *f* whipped cream

Schlagseite *f* MAR list; *Schlagseite haben* be listing

Schlagstock *m* baton, truncheon

Schlagwort *n* catchword, slogan

Schlagzeile *f* headline

'Schlagzeug *n* MUS drums

'Schlagzeuger [-tsɔygɐ] *m* (*-s; -*) MUS drummer

schlaksig ['ʃlaːksɪç] *adj* lanky, gangling

Schlamm [ʃlam] *m* (*-[e]s; -e*) mud

schlammig ['ʃlamɪç] *adj* muddy

Schlampe ['ʃlampə] F *f* (*-; -n*) slut

schlampig ['ʃlampɪç] F *adj* sloppy

schlang [ʃlaŋ] *pret of schlingen*

Schlange ['ʃlaŋə] *f* (*-; -n*) zo snake, serpent (*a. fig*); *fig* line, *esp Br* queue; *Schlange stehen* line up, stand in line, *esp Br* queue (up) (*nach* for)

schlängeln ['ʃlɛŋəln] *v/refl* (*ge-, h*) wind or weave (one's way), *person*: worm one's way

'Schlangenlinie *f* serpentine line; *in Schlangenlinien fahren* weave

schlank [ʃlaŋk] *adj* slim, slender; *j-n schlank machen* make s.o. look slim; *schlanke Unternehmensstruktur* ECON lean management

'Schlankheitskur *f*: *e-e Schlankheitskur machen* be slimming

'schlankmachen *v/t* (*sep, -ge-, h*): *j-n schlankmachen → schlank*

schlapp [ʃlap] F *adj* worn out; weak

Schlappe ['ʃlapə] F *f* (*-; -n*) setback, beating

'schlappmachen F *v/i* (*sep, -ge-, h*) flake out

'Schlappschwanz F *m* weakling, wimp

schlau [ʃlau] *adj* clever, smart, bright; sly, cunning, crafty

Schlauch [ʃlaux] *m* (*-[e]s; Schläuche* ['ʃlɔyçə]) tube; hose

Schlauchboot *n* (inflatable or rubber) dinghy

Schlaufe ['ʃlaufə] *f* (*-; -n*) loop

schlecht [ʃlɛçt] *adj* bad; poor; *mir ist (wird) schlecht* I feel (I'm getting) sick to my stomach; *schlecht aussehen* look ill; *sich schlecht fühlen* feel bad; *schlecht werden* GASTR go bad; *es geht ihm sehr schlecht* he is in a bad way; *schlecht gelaunt* in a bad temper or mood, bad-tempered; F *j-n schlecht machen* run s.o. down, backbite s.o.

'schlechtmachen *v/t* (*sep, -ge-, h*): F *j-n schlechtmachen* run s.o. down, backbite s.o.

schleichen ['ʃlaiçən] *v/i* (*irr, ge-, sein*) creep (*a. fig*), sneak

'Schleichweg *m* secret path

Schleichwerbung *f* plugging; *für et. Schleichwerbung machen* plug s.th.

Schleier ['ʃlaiɐ] *m* (*-s; -*) veil (*a. fig*); haze

'schleierhaft *adj*: F *es ist mir schleierhaft* it's a mystery to me

Schleife ['ʃlaifə] *f* (*-; -n*) bow; ribbon; AVIAT, EDP, ELECTR, GEOGR loop

schleifen[1] ['ʃlaifən] *v/t and v/i* (*ge-, h*)

S

drag (along); rub

'**schleifen**² v/t (irr, ge-, h) grind (a. TECH), sharpen; sand(paper); cut; F drill s.o. hard

Schleifer ['ʃlaifɐ] m (-s; -), '**Schleifmaschine** f TECH grinder

'**Schleifpapier** n sandpaper

'**Schleifstein** m grindstone; whetstone

Schleim [ʃlaim] m (-[e]s; -e) slime; MED mucus

'**Schleimhaut** f ANAT mucous membrane

schleimig ['ʃlaimɪç] adj slimy (a. fig); MED mucous

schlemmen ['ʃlɛmən] v/i (ge-, h) feast

schlendern ['ʃlɛndɐn] v/i (ge-, sein) stroll, saunter, amble

schlenkern ['ʃlɛŋkɐn] v/i and v/t (ge-, h) dangle, swing (**mit den Armen** one's arms)

schleppen ['ʃlɛpən] v/t (ge-, h) drag (a. fig); MOT, MAR tow; **sich schleppen** drag (on)

schleppend adj dragging; fig drawling

Schlepper ['ʃlɛpɐ] m (-s; -) MAR tug; MOT tractor

'**Schlepplift** m T-bar (lift), drag lift, ski tow

Schlepptau n tow-rope; **im (ins) Schlepptau** in tow (a. fig)

Schleuder ['ʃlɔydɐ] f (-; -n) catapult, slingshot; TECH spin drier

'**schleudern** (ge-, h) **1.** v/t fling, hurl (both a. fig); spin-dry; **2.** v/i MOT skid

'**Schleudersitz** m AVIAT ejection (esp Br ejector) seat

schleunigst ['ʃlɔynɪçst] adv immediately

Schleuse ['ʃlɔyzə] f (-; -n) sluice; lock

schlich [ʃlɪç] pret of **schleichen**

schlicht [ʃlɪçt] adj plain, simple

schlichten ['ʃlɪçtən] v/t (ge-, h) settle

'**Schlichtung** f (-; -en) settlement

'**schlief** [ʃliːf] pret of **schlafen**

schließen ['ʃliːsən] v/t and v/i (irr, ge-, h) shut, close (down); fig close, finish; **schließen aus** (dat) conclude from; **nach ... zu schließen** judging by ...

Schließfach ['ʃliːs-] n safe-deposit box; RAIL etc: (left luggage) locker

schließlich ['ʃliːslɪç] adv finally; eventually, in the end; after all

schliff [ʃlɪf] pret of **schleifen**²

Schliff m (-[e]s; -e) cut; polish (a. fig)

schlimm [ʃlɪm] adj bad; awful; **das ist nicht or halb so schlimm** it's not as bad as that; **das Schlimme daran** the bad thing about it

'**schlimmsten'falls** adv at (the) worst

Schlinge ['ʃlɪŋə] f (-; -n) loop; noose; HUNT snare (a. fig); MED sling

Schlingel ['ʃlɪŋəl] m (-s; -) rascal

schlingen ['ʃlɪŋən] v/t (irr, ge-, h) wind, twist; tie; wrap (**um** [a]round); gobble; **sich um et. schlingen** wind (a)round s.th.

schlingern ['ʃlɪŋɐn] v/i (ge-, h) MAR roll

'**Schlingpflanze** f BOT creeper, climber

Schlips [ʃlɪps] m (-es; -e) necktie, esp Br tie

schlitteln ['ʃlɪtəln] Swiss v/i (ge-, sein) go sledging, go tobogganing

Schlitten ['ʃlɪtən] m (-s; -) sled, Br sledge; sleigh; SPORT toboggan; **Schlitten fahren** go sledging, go tobogganing

'**Schlittschuh** ['ʃlɪt-] m ice-skate (a. **Schlittschuh laufen**)

'**Schlittschuhläufer**(in) ice-skater

Schlitz [ʃlɪts] m (-es; -e) slit; slot

schlitzen ['ʃlɪtsən] v/t (ge-, h) slit, slash

schloss [ʃlɔs] pret of **schließen**

Schloss n (-es; Schlösser ['ʃlœsə]) TECH lock; ARCH castle, palace; **ins Schloss fallen** door: slam shut; **hinter Schloss und Riegel** locked up, under lock and key

Schlosser ['ʃlɔsɐ] m (-s; -) metalworker; locksmith

Schlosserei [ʃlɔsə'rai] f (-; -en) metalwork shop

schlottern ['ʃlɔtɐn] v/i (ge-, h) shake, tremble (both: **vor** dat with); bag

Schlucht [ʃlʊxt] f (-; -en) canyon, gorge, ravine

schluchzen ['ʃlʊxtsən] v/i (ge-, h), **Schluchzer** ['ʃlʊxtsɐ] m (-s; -) sob

Schluck [ʃlʊk] m (-[e]s; -e) draught, swallow; sip; gulp

'**Schluckauf** m (-s; no pl) hiccups; (**e-n**) **Schluckauf haben** have (the) hiccups

schlucken ['ʃlʊkən] v/t and v/i (ge-, h) swallow (a. fig)

'**Schluckimpfung** f MED oral vaccination

schlug [ʃluːk] pret of **schlagen**

Schlummer ['ʃlʊmɐ] m (-s; no pl) slumber

'**schlummern** v/i (ge-, h) lie asleep; fig slumber

schlüpfen ['ʃlʏpfən] v/i (ge-, sein) slip, slide; zo hatch (out)

Schlüpfer ['ʃlʏpfɐ] m (-s; -) briefs, panties

schlüpfrig ['ʃlʏpfrɪç] adj slippery; contp risqué, off-colo(u)r

'**Schlupfwinkel** ['ʃlʊpf-] m hiding place

schlurfen ['ʃlʊrfən] v/i (ge-, sein) shuffle (along)

schlürfen ['ʃlʏrfən] v/t and v/i (ge-, h) slurp

Schluss [ʃlʊs] m (-es; no pl) end; conclusion; ending; **Schluss machen** finish; break up; **Schluss machen mit** stop s.th., put an end to s.th.; **zum Schluss** finally; **(ganz) bis zum Schluss** to the (very) end; **Schluss für heute!** that's all for today!

Schlüssel [ˈʃlʏsəl] m (-s; -) key (**für, zu** to)

Schlüsselbein n ANAT collarbone

Schlüsselblume f BOT cowslip, primrose

Schlüsselbund m, n bunch of keys

Schlüsselkind F n latchkey child

Schlüsselloch n keyhole

Schlüsselwort n keyword, EDP a. password

Schlussfolgerung f conclusion

schlüssig [ˈʃlʏsɪç] adj conclusive; **sich schlüssig werden** make up one's mind (**über** acc about)

Schlusslicht n MOT etc: tail-light

Schlusspfiff m SPORT final whistle

Schlussphase f final stage(s)

Schlussverkauf m ECON (end-of-season) sale

schmächtig [ˈʃmɛçtɪç] adj slight, thin, frail

schmackhaft [ˈʃmakhaft] adj tasty

schmal [ʃmaːl] adj narrow; thin, slender (a. fig)

schmälern [ˈʃmɛːlɐn] v/t (ge-, h) detract from

Schmalfilm m cinefilm

Schmalspur f RAIL narrow ga(u)ge

Schmalspur... fig in cpds small-time ...

Schmalz [ʃmalts] n (-es; -e) grease; lard

schmalzig [ˈʃmaltsɪç] F adj schmaltzy, mushy, Br soapy

schmarotzen [ʃmaˈrɔtsən] F v/i (no -ge-, h) sponge (**bei** on)

Schmarotzer [ʃmaˈrɔtsɐ] m (-s; -) BOT, ZO parasite, fig a. sponger

schmatzen [ˈʃmatsən] v/i smack (one's lips), eat noisily

schmecken [ˈʃmɛkən] v/i and v/t (ge-, h) taste (**nach** of); **gut (schlecht) schmecken** taste good (bad); **(wie) schmeckt dir ...?** (how) do you like ...? (a. fig); **es schmeckt süß (nach nichts)** it has a sweet (no) taste

Schmeichelei [ʃmaɪçəˈlaɪ] f (-; -en) flattery

schmeichelhaft adj flattering

schmeicheln v/i (ge-, h) flatter (**j-m** s.o.)

Schmeichler(in) [ˈʃmaɪçlɐ (-lərɪn)] (-s; -/-; -nen) flatterer

schmeichlerisch [ˈʃmaɪçlərɪʃ] adj flattering

schmeißen [ˈʃmaɪsən] F v/t and v/i (irr, ge-, h) throw, chuck; slam; **mit Geld um sich schmeißen** throw one's money about

Schmeißfliege f ZO blowfly, bluebottle

schmelzen [ˈʃmɛltsən] v/i (irr, ge-, sein) and v/t (h) melt; thaw; TECH smelt

Schmelzofen m (s)melting furnace

Schmelztiegel m melting pot (a. fig)

Schmerz [ʃmɛrts] m (-es; -en) pain (a. fig), ache; fig grief, sorrow

schmerzen [ˈʃmɛrtsən] v/i and v/t (ge-, h) hurt (a. fig), ache; esp fig pain

schmerzfrei adj without pain

schmerzhaft adj painful

schmerzlich adj painful, sad

schmerzlos adj painless

Schmerzmittel n PHARM painkiller

schmerzstillend adj painkilling

Schmetterling [ˈʃmɛtɐlɪŋ] m (-s; -e) ZO butterfly

schmettern [ˈʃmɛtɐn] (ge-, h) **1.** v/t smash (a. tennis); F MUS belt out; **2.** v/i a) (sein) crash, slam, b) MUS blare

Schmied [ʃmiːt] m (-[e]s; -e) (black-)-smith

Schmiede [ˈʃmiːdə] f (-; -n) forge, smithy

Schmiedeeisen n wrought iron

schmieden v/t (ge-, h) forge; fig make (plans etc)

schmiegen [ˈʃmiːgən] v/refl (ge-, h) **sich schmiegen an** (acc) snuggle up to; dress etc: cling to

Schmiere [ˈʃmiːrə] f (-; -n) grease

schmieren v/t (ge-, h) TECH grease, oil, lubricate; spread (butter etc); contp scribble, scrawl

Schmiererei [ʃmiːrəˈraɪ] f (-; -en) scrawl; graffiti

schmierig [ˈʃmiːrɪç] adj greasy; dirty; filthy; contp slimy

Schmiermittel [ˈʃmiːɐ-] n TECH lubricant

Schminke [ˈʃmɪŋkə] f (-; -n) make-up (a. THEA)

schminken v/t (ge-, h) make s.o. up; **sich schminken** make o.s. or one's face up

Schmirgelpa,pier [ˈʃmɪrgəl-] n emery paper

schmiss [ʃmɪs] pret of **schmeißen**

schmollen [ˈʃmɔlən] v/i (ge-, h) sulk, be sulky, pout

schmolz [ʃmɔlts] pret of **schmelzen**

schmoren [ˈʃmoːrən] v/t and v/i (ge-, h) GASTR braise, stew (a. fig)

Schmuck [ʃmʊk] m (-[e]s; no pl) jewel-(le)ry, jewels; decoration(s), ornament(s)

schmücken [ˈʃmʏkən] v/t (ge-, h) decorate

schmucklos adj unadorned; plain

Schmuckstück n piece of jewel(le)ry; fig gem

Schmuggel [ˈʃmʊgəl] m (-; no pl), **Schmuggelei** [ʃmʊgəˈlaɪ] f (-; -en) smuggling

'schmuggeln v/t and v/i (ge-, h) smuggle

'Schmuggelware f smuggled goods

Schmuggler ['ʃmʊglɐ] m (-s; -) smuggler

schmunzeln ['ʃmʊntsəln] v/i (ge-, h) smile to o.s.

schmusen ['ʃmuːzən] F v/i (ge-, h) (kiss and) cuddle, smooch

Schmutz [ʃmʊts] m (-es; no pl) dirt, filth, fig a. smut

Schmutzfleck m smudge

schmutzig ['ʃmʊtsɪç] adj dirty, filthy (both a. fig); **schmutzig werden, sich schmutzig machen** get dirty

Schnabel ['ʃnaːbəl] m (-s; Schnäbel ['ʃnɛːbəl]) zo bill, beak

Schnalle ['ʃnalə] f (-; -n) buckle

'schnallen v/t (ge-, h) buckle; **et. schnallen an** (acc) strap s.th. to

schnalzen ['ʃnaltsən] v/i (ge-, h) snap one's fingers; click one's tongue

schnappen ['ʃnapən] (ge-, h) **1.** v/i snap, snatch (both: **nach** at); F **nach Luft schnappen** gasp for breath; **2.** F v/t catch

'Schnappschuss m PHOT snapshot

Schnaps [ʃnaps] m (-es; Schnäpse ['ʃnɛpsə]) spirits, schnapps, F booze

schnarchen ['ʃnarçən] v/i (ge-, h) snore

schnarren ['ʃnarən] v/i (ge-, h) rattle; voice: rasp

schnattern ['ʃnatɐn] v/i (ge-, h) zo cackle; chatter (a. F)

schnauben ['ʃnaʊbən] v/i and v/t (ge-, h) snort; **sich die Nase schnauben** blow one's nose

schnaufen ['ʃnaʊfən] v/i (ge-, h) breathe hard, pant, puff

Schnauze ['ʃnaʊtsə] f (-; -n) zo snout, mouth, muzzle; F AVIAT, MOT nose; TECH spout; V trap, kisser; V **die Schnauze halten** keep one's trap shut

Schnecke ['ʃnɛkə] f (-; -n) zo snail; slug

'Schneckenhaus n zo snail shell

Schneckentempo n: **im Schneckentempo** at a snail's pace

Schnee [ʃneː] m (-s; no pl) snow (a. sl); **Schnee räumen** remove snow

Schneeball m snowball

Schneeballschlacht f snowball fight

'schneebedeckt adj snow-capped

'Schneefall m snowfall

Schneeflocke f snowflake

Schneegestöber [-gəʃtøːbɐ] n (-s; -) snow flurry

Schneeglöckchen n BOT snowdrop

Schneegrenze f snow line

Schneemann m snowman

Schneematsch m slush

Schnee,bil n snowmobile

Schneepflug m snowplow, Br snow-plough

Schneeregen m sleet

Schneesturm m snowstorm, blizzard

Schneeverwehung f snowdrift

'schnee'weiß adj snow-white

Schneewittchen [ʃneː'vɪtçən] n (-s; no pl) Snow White

Schneid [ʃnaɪt] F m (-[e]s) grit, guts

Schneidbrenner m TECH cutting torch

Schneide ['ʃnaɪdə] f (-; -n) edge

'schneiden v/t and v/i (irr, ge-, h) cut (a. fig), film etc: a. edit; GASTR carve

Schneider ['ʃnaɪdɐ] m (-s; -) tailor

Schneiderei [ʃnaɪdə'raɪ] f (-; -en) a) (no pl) tailoring, dressmaking, b) tailor's or dressmaker's shop

'Schneiderin f (-; -nen) dressmaker; seamstress

'schneidern v/i and v/t (ge-, h) do dressmaking; make, sew

'Schneidezahn m incisor

schneidig ['ʃnaɪdɪç] adj dashing; smart

schneien ['ʃnaɪən] v/i (ge-, h) snow

schnell [ʃnɛl] adj fast, quick; prompt; rapid; **es geht schnell** it won't take long; **(mach[t]) schnell!** hurry up!

'Schnell... in cpds ...dienst, ...paket, ...zug etc: MST express ...

schnellen ['ʃnɛlən] v/t (ge-, h) and v/i (ge-, sein) shoot, spring

'Schnellhefter m folder

Schnelligkeit ['ʃnɛlɪçkaɪt] f (-; no pl) speed; quickness, rapidity

'Schnellimbiss m snack bar

Schnellstraße f expressway, thruway, Br motorway

schnetzeln ['ʃnɛtsəln] esp Swiss v/t (ge-, h) GASTR chop up

Schnippchen ['ʃnɪpçən] n: F **j-m ein Schnippchen schlagen** outwit s.o.

schnippisch ['ʃnɪpɪʃ] adj sassy, pert

schnipsen ['ʃnɪpsən] v/i (ge-, h) snap one's fingers

schnitt [ʃnɪt] pret of schneiden

Schnitt m (-[e]s; -e) cut (a. fig); average

'Schnittblumen pl cut flowers

Schnitte ['ʃnɪtə] f (-; -n) slice; open sandwich

schnittig ['ʃnɪtɪç] adj stylish; MOT sleek

Schnittlauch m BOT chives

Schnittmuster n pattern

Schnittpunkt m (point of) intersection

Schnittstelle f film etc: cut; EDP interface

Schnittwunde f MED incise

Schnitzel[1] ['ʃnɪtsəl] n (-s; -) GASTR cutlet; **Wiener Schnitzel** schnitzel

'Schnitzel[2] n, m (-s; -) chip; scrap

schnitzen ['ʃnɪtsən] v/t (ge-, h) carve, cut

(in wood)

Schnitzer ['ʃnɪtsɐ] *m* (-s; -) (wood) carver

Schnitzerei [ʃnɪtsə'rai] *f* (-; -en) (wood) carving

Schnorchel ['ʃnɔrçəl] *m* (-s; -), **'schnorcheln** *v/i* (*ge-,* h) snorkel

Schnörkel ['ʃnœrkəl] *m* (-s; -) flourish, ARCH scroll

schnorren ['ʃnɔrən] F *v/t* (*ge-,* h) mooch, *Br* cadge

schnüffeln ['ʃnyfəln] *v/i* (*ge-,* h) sniff (*an dat* at); F snoop (about *or* around)

Schnuller ['ʃnʊlɐ] *m* (-s; -) pacifier, *Br* dummy

Schnulze ['ʃnʊltsə] F *f* (-; -n) tearjerker; schmal(t)zy song

'Schnulzensänger F *m*, **'Schnulzensängerin** *f* crooner

schnulzig ['ʃnʊltsɪç] F *adj* schmal(t)zy

Schnupfen ['ʃnʊpfən] *m* (-s; -) MED cold; **e-n Schnupfen haben** (**bekommen**) have a (catch [a]) cold

'Schnupftabak *m* snuff

schnuppern ['ʃnʊpɐn] *v/i* (*ge-,* h) sniff (*an et.* [at] s.th.)

Schnur [ʃnuːɐ] *f* (-; *Schnüre* ['ʃnyːrə]) string, cord; ELECTR flex

Schnürchen ['ʃnyːrçən] *n*: **wie am Schnürchen** like clockwork

schnüren ['ʃnyːrən] *v/t* (*ge-,* h) lace (up); tie up

'schnurgerade *adv* dead straight

'schnurlos *adj*: **schnurloses Telefon** cordless phone

Schnürlsamt ['ʃny:ɐl-] *Austrian m* corduroy

Schnurrbart ['ʃnur-] *m* m(o)ustache

schnurren ['ʃnʊrən] *v/i* (*ge-,* h) purr

Schnürschuh ['ʃny:ɐ-] *m* laced shoe

Schnürsenkel [-zɛŋkəl] *m* (-s; -) shoestring, *Br* shoelace

schnurstracks ['ʃnu:ɐ'ʃtraks] *adv* direct(ly), straight; straight away

schob [ʃoːp] *pret of* **schieben**

Schober ['ʃoːbɐ] *m* (-s; -) haystack; hayrick; barn

Schock [ʃɔk] *m* (-[e]s; -s) MED shock; **unter Schock stehen** be in a (state of) shock

schocken ['ʃɔkən] F *v/t* (*ge-,* h) shock

schockieren [ʃɔ'ki:rən] *v/t* (*no -ge-,* h) shock

Schokolade [ʃoko'la:də] *f* (-; -n) chocolate; **e-e Tafel Schokolade** a bar of chocolate

scholl [ʃɔl] *pret of* **schallen**

Scholle ['ʃɔlə] *f* (-; -n) clod; (ice)floe; zo flounder, *Br* plaice

schon [ʃoːn] *adv* already; ever; even; **schon damals** even then; **schon 1968** as early as 1968; **schon der Gedanke** the very idea; **ist sie schon da (zurück)?** has she come (is she back) yet?; **habt ihr schon gegessen?** have you eaten yet?; **bist du schon einmal dort gewesen?** have you ever been there?; **ich wohne hier schon seit zwei Jahren** I've been living here for two years now; **ich kenne ihn schon, aber** I do know him, but; **er macht das schon** he'll do it all right; **schon gut!** never mind!, all right!

schön [ʃøːn] **1.** *adj* beautiful, lovely; METEOR *a.* fine, fair; nice (*a.* F *iro*); (**na,**) **schön** all right; **2.** *adv*: **schön warm** (**kühl**) nice and warm (cool); **ganz schön teuer** (**schnell**) pretty expensive (fast); **j-n ganz schön erschrecken** (**überraschen**) give s.o. quite a start (surprise)

schonen ['ʃoːnən] *v/t* (*ge-,* h) take care of, go easy on (*a.* TECH); spare; **sich schonen** take it easy; save o.s. *or* one's strength

schonend 1. *adj* gentle; mild; **2.** *adv*: **schonend umgehen mit** take (good) care of; handle with care; go easy on

'Schönheit *f* (-; -en) beauty

'Schönheitspflege *f* beauty care

'Schonung *f* (-; -en) a) (*no pl*) (good) care; rest; preservation, b) tree nursery

'schonungslos *adj* relentless, brutal

schöpfen ['ʃœpfən] *v/t* (*ge-,* h) scoop, ladle; draw (water); → **Luft**, **Verdacht**

Schöpfer ['ʃœpfɐ] *m* (-s; -), **'Schöpferin** *f* (-; -nen) creator

schöpferisch ['ʃœpfərɪʃ] *adj* creative

'Schöpfung *f* (-; -en) creation

schor [ʃoːɐ] *pret of* **scheren**

Schorf [ʃɔrf] *m* (-[e]s; -e) MED scab

Schornstein ['ʃɔrnʃtain] *m* chimney; MAR, RAIL funnel

'Schornsteinfeger *m* chimneysweep

schoss [ʃɔs] *pret of* **schießen**

Schoß [ʃoːs] *m* (-es; *Schöße* ['ʃøːsə]) lap; womb

Schote ['ʃoːtə] *f* (-; -n) BOT pod, husk

Schotte ['ʃɔtə] *m* (-n; -n) Scot(sman); *pl* the Scots, the Scottish (people)

Schotter ['ʃɔtɐ] *m* (-s; -) gravel, road metal

Schottin ['ʃɔtɪn] *f* (-; -nen) Scotswoman

'schottisch *adj* Scots, Scottish; Scotch

'Schottland Scotland

schräg [ʃrɛːk] **1.** *adj* slanting, sloping, oblique; diagonal; **2.** *adv*: **schräg gegenüber** diagonally opposite

Schramme ['ʃramə] *f* (-; -n), **'schrammen**

S

v/t and v/i (*ge-, h*) scratch (*a.* MED)

Schrank [ʃraŋk] *m* (-[e]s; *Schränke* ['ʃrɛŋ-kə]) cupboard; closet; wardrobe

Schranke ['ʃraŋkə] *f* (-; -*n*) barrier (*a. fig*), RAIL *a.* gate; JUR bar; *pl* limits, bounds

'**schrankenlos** *fig adj* boundless

'**Schrankenwärter** *m* RAIL gatekeeper

'**Schrankwand** *f* wall units

Schraube ['ʃraʊbə] *f* (-; -*n*), '**schrauben** *v/t* (*ge-, h*) TECH screw

'**Schraubenschlüssel** *m* TECH spanner, wrench

Schraubenzieher *m* TECH screwdriver

Schraubstock ['ʃraʊp-] *m* vise, *Br* vice

Schreck [ʃrɛk] *m* (-[e]s; -*e*) fright, shock; *j-m e-n Schreck einjagen* give s.o. a fright, scare s.o.

Schrecken ['ʃrɛkən] *m* (-*s*; -) terror, fright; horror(*s*)

'**Schreckensnachricht** *f* dreadful news

'**schreckhaft** *adj* jumpy; skittish

'**schrecklich** *adj* awful, terrible; horrible, dreadful, atrocious

Schrei [ʃraɪ] *m* (-[e]s; -*e*) cry, shout, yell, scream (*all:* **um, nach** for)

schreiben ['ʃraɪbən] *v/t and v/i* (*irr, ge-, h*) write (*an* to s.o.; *über acc* about); type; spell; *falsch schreiben* misspell; *wie schreibt man ...?* how do you spell ...?

'**Schreiben** (-*s*; -) letter

'**Schreibfehler** *m* spelling mistake

'**Schreibheft** *n* exercise book

'**Schreibkraft** *f* typist

'**Schreibmaschine** *f* typewriter

'**Schreibmateri,al** *n* writing materials, stationery

'**Schreibschutz** *m* EDP write *or* file protection

'**Schreibtisch** *m* desk

'**Schreibung** *f* (-; -*en*) spelling

'**Schreibwaren** *pl* stationery

'**Schreibwarengeschäft** *n* stationer's, stationery shop

'**Schreib,zentrale** *f* typing pool

schreien ['ʃraɪən] *v/i and v/t* (*irr, ge-, h*) cry, shout, yell, scream (*all:* **um, nach** [out] for); *schreien vor Schmerz (Angst)* cry out with pain (in terror); *es war zum Schreien* it was a scream

schreiend *fig adj* loud (*colors*); flagrant (*abuse etc*), glaring (*injustices etc*)

Schreiner ['ʃraɪnɐ] *m* (-*s*; -) → *Tischler*

schreiten ['ʃraɪtən] *v/i* (*irr, ge-, sein*) stride

schrie [ʃriː] *pret of* **schreien**

schrieb [ʃriːp] *pret of* **schreiben**

Schrift [ʃrɪft] *f* (-; -*en*) (hand)writing, hand; PRINT type; character, letter; *pl* works, writings; *die Heilige Schrift* REL the Scriptures

Schriftart *f* script; PRINT typeface

Schriftdeutsch *n* standard German

'**schriftlich** *adj* written; *schriftlich übersetzen* translate in writing

'**Schriftsteller** [-ʃtɛlɐ] *m* (-*s*; -), '**Schriftstellerin** *f* (-; -*nen*) author, writer

'**Schriftverkehr** *m*, **Schriftwechsel** *m* correspondence

Schriftzeichen *n* character, letter

schrill [ʃrɪl] *adj* shrill (*a. fig*), piercing

schritt [ʃrɪt] *pret of* **schreiten**

Schritt *m* (-[e]s; -*e*) step (*a. fig*); pace; *fig* **Schritte unternehmen** take steps; **Schritt fahren!** MOT dead slow

Schrittmacher *m* SPORT pacemaker (*a.* MED), pacesetter

'**schrittweise** *adv* step by step, gradually

schroff [ʃrɔf] *adj* steep; jagged; *fig* gruff

Schrot [ʃroːt] *m, n* (-[e]s; -*e*) *a)* (*no pl*) coarse meal, *b)* HUNT (small) shot; pellet

Schrotflinte *f* shotgun

Schrott [ʃrɔt] *m* (-[e]s; -*e*) scrap (metal)

'**Schrotthaufen** *m* scrap heap

'**Schrottplatz** *m* scrapyard

schrubben ['ʃrʊbən] *v/t* (*ge-, h*) scrub, scour

schrumpfen ['ʃrʊmpfən] *v/i* (*ge-, sein*) shrink

Schub [ʃuːp] *m* (-[e]s; *Schübe* ['ʃyːbə]) → *Schubkraft*

'**Schubfach** *n* drawer

'**Schubkarren** *m* wheelbarrow

'**Schubkasten** *m* drawer

'**Schubkraft** *f* PHYS, TECH thrust

'**Schublade** *f* drawer

Schubs [ʃups] F *m* (-*es*; -*e*), **schubsen** ['ʃupsən] F *v/t* (*ge-, h*) push

schüchtern ['ʃʏçtɐn] *adj* shy, bashful

'**Schüchternheit** *f* (-; *no pl*) shyness, bashfulness

schuf [ʃuːf] *pret of* **schaffen**[1]

Schuft [ʃuft] *m* (-[e]s; -*e*) contp bastard

schuften ['ʃuftən] F *v/i* (*ge-, h*) slave away, drudge

Schuh [ʃuː] *m* (-[e]s; -*e*) shoe; *j-m et. in die Schuhe schieben* put the blame for s.th. on s.o.

Schuhanzieher *m* shoehorn

Schuhcreme *f* shoe polish

Schuhgeschäft *n* shoe store (*Br* shop)

Schuhlöffel *m* shoehorn

Schuhmacher *m* shoemaker

Schuhputzer [-putsɐ] *m* (-*s*; -) shoeshine boy

'**Schulabbrecher** *m* (-*s*; -) dropout

Schulabgänger [-apɡɛŋɐ] *m* (-*s*; -) school leaver

Schulamt *n* school board, *Br* education authority

Schularbeit f schoolwork; pl homework

Schulbesuch m (school) attendance

Schulbildung f education

Schulbuch n textbook

Schuld [ʃʊlt] f (-; -en [ˈʃʊldən]) a) (no pl) JUR guilt, esp REL sin, b) mst pl debt; **j-m die Schuld (an et.) geben** blame s.o. (for s.th.); **es ist (nicht) deine Schuld** it is(n't) your fault; **Schulden haben (machen)** be in (run into) debt; → **sich schulden**

schuldbewusst adj: **schuldbewusste Miene** guilty look

schulden [ˈʃʊldən] v/t (ge-, h) **j-m et. schulden** owe s.o. s.th.

schuldig [ˈʃʊldɪç] adj esp JUR guilty (**an** dat of); responsible or to blame (for); **j-m et. schuldig sein** owe s.o. s.th.

Schuldige [ˈʃʊldɪgə] m, f (-n; -n) culprit; JUR guilty person, offender

'schuldlos adj innocent

Schuldner [ˈʃʊldnɐ] m (-s; -)

'Schuldnerin f (-; -nen) debtor

'Schuldschein m ECON promissory note, IOU (= I owe you)

Schule [ˈʃuːlə] f (-; -n) school (a. fig); **höhere Schule** appr (senior) high school, Br secondary school; **auf or in der Schule** at school; **in die or zur Schule gehen (kommen)** go to (start) school

'schulen v/t (ge-, h) train, school

Schüler [ˈʃyːlɐ] m (-s; -) student, schoolboy, esp Br a. pupil

Schüleraustausch m student exchange (program[me])

Schülerin [ˈʃyːlərɪn] f (-; -nen) student, schoolgirl, esp Br a. pupil

'Schülervertretung f appr student government (Br council)

Schulferien pl vacation, Br holidays

Schulfernsehen n educational TV

Schulfunk m schools programmes

Schulgebäude n school (building)

Schulgeld n school fee(s); tuition

Schulheft n exercise book

Schulhof m school yard, playground

Schulkame,rad m schoolfellow

Schulleiter m principal, Br headmaster, head teacher

Schulleiterin f principal, Br headmistress

Schulmappe f schoolbag; satchel

Schulordnung f school regulations

'schulpflichtig adj: **schulpflichtiges Kind** school-age child

'Schulschiff n training ship

Schulschluss m end of school (or term); **nach Schulschluss** after school

Schulschwänzer [-ʃvɛntsɐ] m (-s; -) truant

Schulstunde f lesson, class, period

Schultasche f schoolbag

Schulter [ˈʃʊltɐ] f (-; -n) ANAT shoulder

Schulterblatt n ANAT shoulder-blade

'schulterfrei adj strapless

'schultern v/t (ge-, h) shoulder

'Schultertasche f shoulder bag

'Schulwesen n (-s; no pl) education(al system)

schummeln [ˈʃʊməln] F v/i (ge-, h) cheat

Schund [ʃʊnt] m (-[e]s; no pl) trash, rubbish, junk

schund [ʃʊnt] pret of **schinden**

Schuppe [ˈʃʊpə] f (-; -n) ZO scale; pl MED dandruff

'Schuppen m (-s; -) shed, esp F contp shack

schuppig [ˈʃʊpɪç] adj ZO scaly

schüren [ˈʃyːrən] v/t (ge-, h) stir up (a. fig)

schürfen [ˈʃʏrfən] v/i (ge-, h) prospect (**nach** for)

'Schürfwunde f MED graze, abrasion

Schurke [ˈʃʊrkə] m (-n; -n) esp THEA etc villain

Schurwolle f (-; -) virgin wool

Schürze [ˈʃʏrtsə] f (-; -n) apron

Schuss [ʃʊs] m (-es; Schüsse [ˈʃʏsə]) shot; GASTR dash; SPORT shot, soccer: a. strike; skiing: schuss (a. **Schuss fahren**); sl shot, fix; F **gut in Schuss sein** be in good shape

Schüssel [ˈʃʏsəl] f (-; -n) bowl, dish; basin

'Schusswaffe f firearm

Schusswunde f MED gunshot or bullet wound

Schuster [ˈʃuːstɐ] m (-s; -) shoemaker

Schutt [ʃʊt] m (-[e]s; no pl) rubble, debris

'Schüttelfrost m MED shivering fit, the shivers

schütteln [ˈʃʏtəln] v/t (ge-, h) shake

schütten [ˈʃʏtən] v/t (ge-, h) pour; throw

Schutz [ʃʊts] m (-es; no pl) protection (**gegen, vor** dat against), defense, Br defence (against, from); shelter (from); safeguard (against); cover

Schutzblech n fender, Br mudguard

Schutzbrille f goggles

Schütze [ˈʃʏtsə] m (-n; -n) MIL rifleman; hunter; SPORT scorer; ASTR Sagittarius; **er ist (ein) Schütze** he's (a) Sagittarius; **ein guter Schütze** a good shot

schützen [ˈʃʏtsən] v/t (ge-, h) protect (**gegen, vor** dat against, from), defend (against, from), guard (against, from); shelter (from); safeguard

'Schutzengel m guardian angel

'Schützengraben m MIL trench

'Schutzgeld n protection money

Schutzgelderpressung f protection

racket

'Schutzhaft f JUR protective custody

'Schutzheilige m, f patron (saint)

Schutzimpfung f MED protective inoculation; vaccination

'Schutzkleidung f protective clothing

Schützling ['ʃʏtslɪŋ] m (-s; -e) protégé(e)

'schutzlos adj unprotected; defenseless, Br defenceless

'Schutzmaßnahme f safety measure

Schutzpa·tron m REL patron (saint)

Schutzumschlag m dust cover

Schutzzoll m ECON protective duty (or tariff)

schwach [ʃvax] adj weak (a. fig); poor; faint; delicate, frail; **schwächer werden** grow weak; decline; fail; fade

Schwäche ['ʃvɛçə] f weakness (a. fig), MED infirmity; fig drawback, shortcoming; **e-e Schwäche haben für** be partial to

'schwächen v/t (ge-, h) weaken (a. fig); lessen

'schwächlich adj weakly, feeble; delicate, frail

'Schwächling m (-s; -e) weakling (a. fig), softy, sissy

'schwachsinnig adj feeble-minded; F stupid, idiotic

'Schwachstrom m ELECTR low-voltage current

Schwager ['ʃvaːgɐ] m (-s; Schwäger ['ʃvɛːgɐ]) brother-in-law

Schwägerin ['ʃvɛːgərɪn] f (-; -nen) sister-in-law

Schwalbe ['ʃvalbə] f (-; -n) ZO swallow; soccer: dive

Schwall [ʃval] m (-[e]s; -e) gush, esp fig a. torrent

schwamm [ʃvam] pret of **schwimmen**

Schwamm m (-[e]s; Schwämme ['ʃvɛmə]) sponge; BOT fungus; F dry rot

Schwammerl ['ʃvaməl] Austrian m (-s; -[n]) → **Pilz**

schwammig ['ʃvamɪç] adj spongy; puffy; fig woolly

Schwan [ʃvaːn] m (-[e]s; Schwäne ['ʃvɛːnə]) ZO swan

schwand [ʃvant] pret of **schwinden**

schwang [ʃvaŋ] pret of **schwingen**

schwanger ['ʃvaŋɐ] adj pregnant

'Schwangerschaft f (-; -en) pregnancy

'Schwangerschaftsabbruch m abortion

schwanken ['ʃvaŋkən] v/i (ge-, h) sway, roll (a. MAR); stagger; fig **schwanken zwischen ... und ...** waver between ... and ...; prices: range from ... to ...

'Schwankung f (-; -en) change, variation (a. ECON)

Schwanz [ʃvants] m (-es; Schwänze ['ʃvɛntsə]) ZO tail (a. AVIAT, ASTR); V cock

schwänzen ['ʃvɛntsən] v/i and v/t (ge-, h) **(die Schule) schwänzen** play truant (F hooky)

Schwarm [ʃvarm] m (-[e]s; Schwärme ['ʃvɛrmə]) swarm; crowd, F bunch; zo shoal, school; F dream; idol

schwärmen ['ʃvɛrmən] v/i a. (ge-, sein) zo swarm, b) (ge-, h) **schwärmen für** be mad about; dream of; have a crush on s.o.; **schwärmen von** rave about

Schwarte ['ʃvartə] f (-; -n) rind; F contp (old) tome

schwarz [ʃvarts] adj black (a. fig); **Schwarzes Brett** bulletin board, Br notice board; **schwarz auf weiß** in black and white

'Schwarzarbeit f (-; no pl) illicit work

'Schwarzbrot n rye bread

Schwarze ['ʃvartsə] m, f (-n; -n) black (man or woman); pl the Blacks

schwärzen ['ʃvɛrtsən] v/t (ge-, h) blacken

'Schwarzfahrer m fare dodger

'Schwarzhändler m black marketeer

'Schwarzmarkt m black market

'Schwarzseher m pessimist; (TV) license (Br licence) dodger

Schwarz'weiß... in cpds ...film, ...fernseher etc: black-and-white ...

schwatzen ['ʃvatsən], schwätzen ['ʃvɛtsən] v/i (ge-, h) chat(ter); PED talk

Schwätzer ['ʃvɛtsə] contp m (-s; -), 'Schwätzerin f (-; -nen) loudmouth

schwatzhaft ['ʃvatshaft] adj chatty

Schwebebahn ['ʃveːbə-] f cableway, ropeway

Schwebebalken m SPORT beam

schweben ['ʃveːbən] v/i (ge-, h) be suspended; zo, AVIAT hover (a. fig); glide; esp JUR be pending; **in Gefahr schweben** be in danger

Schwede ['ʃveːdə] m (-n; -n) Swede

Schweden ['ʃveːdən] Sweden

Schwedin ['ʃveːdɪn] f (-; -nen) Swede

'schwedisch adj Swedish

Schwefel ['ʃveːfəl] m (-s; no pl) CHEM sulfur, Br sulphur

Schwefelsäure f CHEM sulfuric (Br sulphuric) acid

Schweif [ʃvaif] m (-[e]s; -e) ZO tail (a. ASTR)

schweifen ['ʃvaifən] v/i (ge-, sein) wander (a. fig), roam

schweigen ['ʃvaigən] v/i (irr, ge-, h) be silent

'Schweigen n (-s; no pl) silence

'schweigend adj silent

schweigsam ['ʃvaikzaːm] adj quiet, taciturn, reticent

Schwein [ʃvain] n (-[e]s; -e) zo pig, hog; F contp (filthy) pig; swine, bastard; F **Schwein haben** be lucky

'**Schweinebraten** m roast pork

'**Schweinefleisch** n pork

Schweinerei [ʃvainəˈrai] F f (-; -en) mess; fig dirty trick; dirty or crying shame; filth(y story or joke)

'**Schweinestall** m pigsty (a. fig)

schweinisch F adj filthy, obscene

'**Schweinsleder** n pigskin

Schweiß [ʃvais] m (-es; no pl) sweat, perspiration

schweißen v/t (ge-, h) TECH weld

Schweißer m (-s; -) TECH welder

'**schweißgebadet** adj soaked in sweat

'**Schweißgeruch** m body odo(u)r, BO

Schweiz [ʃvaits] Switzerland

Schweizer ['ʃvaitsɐ] m (-s; -), adj Swiss

Schweizerin ['ʃvaitsərɪn] f (-; -nen) Swiss woman or girl

schweizerisch ['ʃvaitsərɪʃ] adj Swiss

schwelen ['ʃveːlən] v/i (ge-, h) smo(u)lder (a. fig)

schwelgen ['ʃvɛlɡən] v/i (ge-, h) **schwelgen in** (dat) revel in

Schwelle ['ʃvɛlə] f (-; -n) threshold (a. fig); RAIL tie, Br sleeper

'**schwellen 1.** v/i (irr, ge-, sein) swell; **2.** v/t (ge-, h) swell

'**Schwellung** f (-; -en) MED swelling

Schwemme ['ʃvɛmə] f (-; -n) ECON glut, oversupply

'**schwemmen** v/t (ge-, h) **an Land schwemmen** wash ashore

Schwengel ['ʃvɛŋəl] m (-s; -) clapper; handle

schwenken ['ʃvɛŋkən] v/t (ge-, h) and v/i (ge-, sein) swing, wave

schwer [ʃveːɐ] **1.** adj heavy; fig difficult, hard; GASTR strong, rich; MED etc serious, severe; heavy, violent (storm etc); **schwere Zeiten** hard times; **es schwer haben** have a bad time; **100 Pfund schwer sein** weigh a hundred pounds; **2.** adv: **schwer arbeiten** work hard; → **schwerfallen**; → **hören**; **schwer beschädigt** → **schwerbeschädigt**; **schwer verdaulich** indigestible, heavy (both a. fig); **schwer verständlich** difficult or hard to understand; **schwer verwundet** seriously wounded

'**schwerbeschädigt** adj seriously disabled

Schwere ['ʃveːrə] f (-; no pl) weight (a. fig); fig seriousness

'**schwerfallen** v/i (irr, **fallen**, sep, -ge-, sein): **j-m schwerfallen** be difficult for

s.o.; **es fällt ihm schwer zu …** he finds it difficult to …

'**schwerfällig** adj awkward, clumsy

'**Schwergewicht** n (-[e]s; no pl) heavyweight; fig (main) emphasis

'**schwerhörig** adj hard of hearing

'**Schwerindustrie** f heavy industry

Schwerkraft f (-; no pl) PHYS gravity

Schwerme,tall n heavy metal

'**schwermütig** [-myːtɪç] adj melancholy; **schwermütig sein** have the blues

'**Schwerpunkt** m center (Br centre) of gravity; fig (main) emphasis

Schwert [ʃveːɐt] n (-[e]s; -er) sword

'**Schwerverbrecher** m dangerous criminal, JUR felon

'**schwerverdaulich** adj → **schwer**

schwerverständlich adj → **schwer**

schwerver,wundet adj → **schwer**

'**schwerwiegend** fig adj weighty, serious

Schwester ['ʃvɛstɐ] f (-; -n) sister, REL a. nun; MED nurse

schwieg [ʃviːk] pret of **schweigen**

Schwieger... ['ʃviːɡɐ-] in cpds ...eltern, ...mutter, ...sohn etc: ...-in-law

Schwiele ['ʃviːlə] f (-; -n) MED callus

schwielig ['ʃviːlɪç] adj horny

schwierig ['ʃviːrɪç] adj difficult, hard

'**Schwierigkeit** f (-; -en) difficulty, trouble; **in Schwierigkeiten geraten** get or run into trouble; **Schwierigkeiten haben, et. zu tun** have difficulty in doing s.th.

Schwimmbad [-ʃvɪm-] n (indoor) swimming pool

schwimmen ['ʃvɪmən] v/i (irr, ge-, sein) swim; float; **schwimmen gehen** go swimming

'**Schwimmflosse** f swimfin, Br flipper

'**Schwimmgürtel** m swimming belt

Schwimmhaut f zo web

Schwimmlehrer m swimming instructor

Schwimmweste f life jacket

Schwindel ['ʃvɪndəl] m (-s; no pl) MED giddiness, dizziness; F swindle, fraud; **Schwindel erregend** dizzy

'**schwindeler,regend** adj dizzy

'**schwindeln** v/i (ge-, h) fib, tell fibs

schwinden ['ʃvɪndən] v/i (irr, ge-, sein) dwindle, decline

Schwindler ['ʃvɪndlɐ] F m (-s; -), '**Schwindlerin** f (-; -nen) swindler, crook; liar

schwindlig ['ʃvɪndlɪç] adj MED dizzy, giddy; **mir ist schwindlig** I feel dizzy

Schwinge ['ʃvɪŋə] f (-; -n) zo wing

schwingen ['ʃvɪŋən] v/i and v/t (irr, ge-, h) swing; wave; PHYS oscillate; vibrate

'**Schwingung** f (-; -en) PHYS oscillation;

vibration
Schwips [ʃvɪps] F m: **e-n Schwips haben** be tipsy
schwirren ['ʃvɪrən] v/i a) (ge-, sein) whirr, whizz, esp zo buzz (a. fig), b) (ge-, h) **mir schwirrt der Kopf** my head is buzzing
schwitzen ['ʃvɪtsən] v/i (ge-, h) sweat, perspire
schwoll [ʃvɔl] pret of **schwellen** 1
schwor [ʃvoːɐ] pret of **schwören**
schwören ['ʃvøːrən] v/t and v/i (irr, ge-, h) swear; JUR take an or the oath; fig **schwören auf** (acc) swear by
schwul [ʃvuːl] F adj gay; contp queer
schwül [ʃvyːl] adj sultry (a. fig), close
schwülstig ['ʃvʏlstɪç] adj bombastic, pompous
Schwung [ʃvʊŋ] m (-[e]s; Schwünge ['ʃvʏŋə]) swing; fig verve, pep, drive; **in Schwung kommen** get going; **et. in Schwung bringen** get s.th. going
'**schwungvoll** adj full of energy or verve; MUS swinging
Schwur [ʃvuːɐ] m (-[e]s; Schwüre ['ʃvyːrə]) oath
Schwurgericht n JUR jury court
sechs [zɛks] adj six; grade: F, Br a. poor
'**Sechseck** n (-[e]s; -e) hexagon
'**sechseckig** adj hexagonal
'**sechsfach** adj sixfold
'**sechsmal** adv six times
Sechs'tagerennen n SPORT six-day race
'**sechstägig** [-tɛːgɪç] adj lasting or of six days
'**sechste** adj sixth
Sechstel ['zɛkstəl] n (-s; -) sixth (part)
'**sechstens** adv sixthly, in the sixth place
sechzehn(te) ['zɛçtseːn(tə)] adj sixteen(th)
sechzig ['zɛçtsɪç] adj sixty
'**sechzigste** adj sixtieth
See¹ [zeː] m (-s; -n) lake
See² f (-; no pl) sea, ocean; **auf See** at sea; **auf hoher See** on the high seas; **an der See** at the seaside; **zur See gehen (fahren)** go to sea (be a sailor); **in See stechen** put to sea
Seebad n seaside resort
Seefahrt f navigation
Seegang m (-[e]s; no pl): **hoher Seegang** heavy sea
Seehafen m seaport
Seehund m zo seal
Seekarte f nautical chart
'**seekrank** adj seasick
'**Seekrankheit** f seasickness
Seele ['zeːlə] f (-; -n) soul (a. fig)
'**seelenlos** adj soulless
'**Seelenruhe** f peace of mind; **in aller**

Seelenruhe as cool as you please
seelisch ['zeːlɪʃ] adj mental
'**Seelsorge** f (-; no pl) pastoral care
'**Seelsorger** [-zɔrgɐ] m (-s; -), '**Seelsorgerin** f (-; -nen) pastor
'**Seemacht** f sea power
Seemann m (-[e]s; -leute) seaman, sailor
Seemeile f nautical mile
Seenot f (-; no pl) distress (at sea)
Seenotkreuzer m MAR rescue cruiser
Seeräuber m pirate
Seereise f voyage, cruise
Seerose f BOT water lily
Seesack m kit bag
Seeschlacht f MIL naval battle
Seestreitkräfte pl MIL naval forces, navy
'**seetüchtig** adj seaworthy
'**Seewarte** f naval observatory
Seeweg m sea route; **auf dem Seeweg** by sea
Seezeichen n seamark
Seezunge f zo sole
Segel ['zeːgəl] n (-s; -) sail
Segelboot n sailboat, Br sailing boat
Segelfliegen n gliding
Segelflugzeug n glider
'**segeln** v/i (ge-, sein) sail, SPORT a. yacht
'**Segelschiff** n sailing ship; sailing vessel
Segelsport m sailing, yachting
Segeltuch n canvas, sailcloth
Segen ['zeːgən] m (-s; -) blessing (a. fig)
Segler ['zeːglɐ] m (-s; -) yachtsman
Seglerin ['zeːglərɪn] f (-; -nen) yachtswoman
segnen ['zeːgnən] v/t (ge-, h) bless
'**Segnung** f (-; -nen) blessing
Sehbeteiligung f (-; -en) (TV) ratings
sehen ['zeːən] v/i and v/t (irr, ge-, h) see; watch; notice; **sehen nach** look after; look for; **sich sehen lassen** show up; **das sieht man (kaum)** it (hardly) shows; **siehst du** (you) see; I told you; **siehe oben (unten, Seite ...)** see above (below, page ...)
'**sehenlassen** v/refl (irr, lassen, sep, no -ge-, h) → **sehen**
'**sehenswert** adj worth seeing
'**Sehenswürdigkeit** f (-; -en) place etc worth seeing, sight, pl sights
Sehkraft f (-; no pl) eyesight, vision
Sehne ['zeːnə] f (-; -n) ANAT sinew; string
sehnen ['zeːnən] v/refl (ge-, h) long (**nach** for), yearn (for); **sich danach sehnen zu** inf be longing to inf
'**Sehnerv** m ANAT optic nerve
sehnig ['zeːnɪç] adj sinewy, GASTR a. stringy
sehnlichst ['zeːnlɪçst] adj dearest
'**Sehnsucht** f, '**sehnsüchtig** adj longing,

yearning

sehr [zeːɐ] adv before adj and adv: very; with verbs: very much, greatly

Sehtest m sight test

seicht [zaiçt] adj shallow (a. fig)

Seide ['zaidə] f (-; -n), '**seiden** adj silk

'**Seidenpa,pier** n tissue paper

'**Seidenraupe** f zo silkworm

seidig ['zaidɪç] adj silky

Seife ['zaifə] f (-; -n) soap

'**Seifenblase** f soap bubble

Seifenlauge f (soap)suds

'**Seifenoper** f TV soap opera

'**Seifenschale** f soap dish

'**Seifenschaum** m lather

seifig ['zaifɪç] adj soapy

Seil [zail] n (-[e]s; -e) rope

'**Seilbahn** f cable railway

'**seilspringen** v/i (only inf) skip

sein[1] [zain] v/i (irr, ge-, sein) be; exist; **et. sein lassen** stop or quit (doing) s.th.

sein[2] poss pron his, her, its; **seiner, seine, sein(e)s** his, hers

Sein n (-s; no pl) being; existence

seinerseits ['zainɐzaits] adv for his part

seiner'zeit adv then, in those days

seines'gleichen ['zainəs-] pron his equals

seinet'wegen ['zainət-] → **meinetwegen**

'**seinlassen** v/t (irr, sep, -ge-, h): **et. seinlassen** → **sein**

seit [zait] prp and cj since; **seit 1982** since 1982; **seit drei Jahren** for three years (now); **seit langem (kurzem)** for a long (short) time

seit'dem 1. adv since then, since that time, ever since; **2.** cj since

Seite ['zaitə] f (-; -n) side (a. fig); page; **auf der linken Seite** on the left(-hand side); fig **auf der e-n (anderen) Seite** on the one (other) hand

Seitenansicht f side view, profile

Seitenblick m sidelong glance

Seitenhieb m sideswipe

Seitenlinie f esp soccer: touchline

seitens ['zaitəns] prp (gen) on the part of, by

'**Seitensprung** F m: **e-n Seitensprung machen** cheat (on one's wife or husband)

'**Seitenstechen** n (-s; no pl) MED a stitch (in the side)

'**seitlich** adj side ..., at the side(s)

'**seitwärts** [-vɛrts] adv sideways, to the side

Sekretär [zekre'tɛːɐ] m (-s; -e) secretary; bureau

Sekretariat [-ta'rjaːt] n (-[e]s; -e) (secretary's) office

Sekretärin [-'tɛːrɪn] f (-; -nen) secretary

Sekt [zekt] m (-[e]s; -e) sparkling wine, champagne

Sekte ['zɛktə] f (-; -n) sect

Sektion [zɛk'tsjoːn] f (-; -en) section; MED autopsy

Sektor ['zɛktoːɐ] m (-s; -en [zɛk'toːrən]) sector; fig field

Sekunde [ze'kʊndə] f (-; -n) second; **auf die Sekunde** to the second

Se'kundenzeiger m second(s) hand

selbe ['zɛlbə] adj same

selber ['zɛlbɐ] pron → **selbst** 1

selbst [zɛlbst] **1.** pron: **ich (du etc) selbst** I (you etc) myself (yourself etc); **mach es selbst** do it yourself; **et. selbst tun** do s.th. by oneself; **von selbst** by itself; **selbst gemacht** homemade; **2.** adv even

'**Selbstachtung** f self-respect

'**selbständig** etc → **selbstständig** etc

'**Selbstbedienung(sladen** m) f self-service (store, Br shop)

Selbstbefriedigung f masturbation

Selbstbeherrschung f self-control

Selbstbestimmung f self-determination

'**selbstbewusst** adj self-confident, self--assured

'**Selbstbewusstsein** n self-confidence

'**Selbstbildnis** n self-portrait

Selbsterhaltungstrieb m survival instinct

Selbsterkenntnis f (-; no pl) self-knowledge

'**selbstgerecht** adj self-righteous

'**Selbsthilfe** f self-help

'**Selbsthilfegruppe** f self-help group

Selbstkostenpreis m: **zum Selbstkostenpreis** ECON at cost (price)

'**selbstkritisch** adj self-critical

'**Selbstlaut** m LING vowel

'**selbstlos** adj unselfish

'**Selbstmord** m, **Selbstmörder(in)** suicide

'**selbstmörderisch** adj suicidal

'**selbstsicher** adj self-confident, self-assured

'**selbstständig** adj independent, self-reliant; self-employed

'**Selbstständigkeit** f (-; no pl) independence

'**Selbststudium** n (-s; no pl) self-study

'**selbstsüchtig** adj selfish, ego(t)istic(al)

'**selbsttätig** adj automatic

'**Selbsttäuschung** f self-deception

'**selbstverständlich 1.** adj natural; **das ist selbstverständlich** that's a matter of course; **2.** adv of course, naturally; **selbstverständlich!** a. by all means!

'**Selbstverständlichkeit** f (-; -en) matter

S

of course

'Selbstverteidigung f self-defense, Br self-defence

Selbstvertrauen n self-confidence, self--reliance

Selbstverwaltung f self-government, autonomy

Selbstwähldienst m TEL automatic long--distance dial(l)ing service

'selbstzufrieden adj self-satisfied

selchen ['zɛlçən] Austrian → **räuchern**

selig ['ze:lɪç] adj REL blessed; late; fig overjoyed

Sellerie ['zɛləri] m (-s; -[s]), f (-; -) BOT celeriac; celery

selten ['zɛltən] **1.** adj rare; **selten sein** be rare, be scarce; **2.** adv rarely, seldom

'Seltenheit f (-; no pl) rarity

seltsam ['zɛltza:m] adj strange, odd

Semester [ze'mɛstɐ] n (-s; -) UNIV semester, esp Br term

Semikolon [zemi'ko:lɔn] n (-s; -s) LING semicolon

Seminar [zemi'na:ɐ̯] n (-s; -e) UNIV department; seminar; REL seminary; teacher training college

sen. ABBR of **senior** sen., Sen., Sr, Snr, senior

Senat [ze'na:t] m (-[e]s; -e) senate

Senator [ze'na:to:ɐ̯] m (-s; -en [zena'to:rən]), **Sena'torin** f (-; -nen) senator

Sendemast m ELECTR mast

senden ['zɛndən] v/t (irr, ge-), h) send (**mit der Post** by mail, Br by post); ELECTR broadcast, transmit, a. televise

Sender ['zɛndɐ] m (-s; -) radio or television station; ELECTR transmitter

'Sendereihe f TV or radio series

Sendeschluss n close-down, F sign-off

Sendezeichen n call letters (Br sign)

Sendezeit f air time

'Sendung f (-; -en) broadcast, program(-me), a. telecast; ECON consignment, shipment; **auf Sendung sein** be on the air

Senf [zɛnf] m (-[e]s; -e) mustard (a. BOT)

senil [ze'ni:l] adj senile

Senilität [zenili'tɛ:t] f (-; no pl) senility

Senior ['ze:njoːɐ̯] **1.** m (-s; -en [ze'njoːrən]) senior (a. SPORT); senior citizen; **2.** adj senior

Seni'orenheim n old people's home

Seni'orin f (-; -nen) senior citizen

Senke ['zɛŋkə] f (-; -n) GEOGR depression, hollow

'senken v/t (ge-, h) lower (a. one's voice), a. bow (one's head); ECON a. reduce, cut; **sich senken** drop, a. give or come down

'senkrecht adj vertical

Sensation [zɛnza'tsjoːn] f (-; -en) sensation

sensationell [zɛnzatsjo'nɛl] adj, **Sensati'ons...** in cpds ...blatt etc: sensational (...)

Sense ['zɛnzə] f (-; -n) AGR scythe

sensibel [zɛn'zi:bəl] adj sensitive

sensibilisieren [zɛnzibili'zi:rən] v/t (no -ge-, h) sensitize (**für** to)

sentimental [zɛntimɛn'taːl] adj sentimental

Sentimentalität [zɛntimɛntali'tɛːt] f (-; -en) sentimentality

September [zɛp'tɛmbɐ] m (-[s]; -) September

Serenade [zere'naːdə] f (-; -n) MUS serenade

Serie ['zeːrjə] f (-; -n) series, TV etc a. serial; set; **in Serie** produce etc in series

'serienmäßig adj series(-produced); standard

'Seriennummer f serial number

Serienwagen m MOT standard-type car

seriös [ze'rjøːs] adj respectable; honest; serious

Serum ['zeːrʊm] n (-s; -ren, -ra) serum

Service¹ [zɛr'viːs] n (-; -[s]; -) set; service

Service² ['zøːɐ̯vɪs] m, n (-; -s) service

servieren [zɛr'viːrən] v/t (no -ge-, h) serve

Serviererin [zɛr'viːrərɪn] f (-; -nen) waitress

Serviertochter [zɛr'viːɐ̯-] Swiss f waitress

Serviette [zɛr'vjɛtə] f (-; -n) napkin, esp Br serviette

Servobremse ['zɛrvo-] f MOT servo or power brake

Servolenkung f MOT servo(-assisted) or power steering

Sessel ['zɛsəl] m (-s; -) armchair, easy chair

Sessellift m chair lift

sesshaft ['zɛshaft] adj: **sesshaft werden** settle (down)

Set [zɛt] n, m (-s; -s) place mat

setzen ['zɛtsən] v/t and v/i (ge-, h) put, set (a. PRINT, AGR, MAR), AGR a. plant; place; seat s.o.; **setzen über** (acc) jump over; cross (river); **setzen auf** (acc) bet on, back; **sich setzen** sit down; CHEM etc settle; **sich setzen auf** (acc) get on, mount; **sich setzen in** (acc) get into; **sich zu j-m setzen** sit beside or with s.o.; **setzen Sie sich bitte!** take or have a seat!

Setzer ['zɛtsɐ] m (-s; -) PRINT compositor, typesetter

Setzerei [zɛtsə'rai] f (-; -en) PRINT composing room

Seuche ['zɔyçə] f (-; -n) epidemic (disease)

S

seufzen ['zɔyftsən] v/i (ge-, h), **Seufzer** ['zɔyftsə] m (-s; -) sigh

Sexismus [zɛ'ksɪsmʊs] m (-; no pl) sexism

Sexist [zɛ'ksɪst] m (-en; -en), **se'xistisch** adj sexist

Sexual... [zɛ'ksuaːl-] in cpds ...erziehung, ...leben, ...trieb etc: sex(ual) ...

Sexualverbrechen n sex crime

sexuell [zɛ'ksuɛl] adj sexual; **sexuelle Belästigung** (sexual) harassment

sexy ['zɛksi] adj sexy

sezieren [ze'tsiːrən] v/t (no -ge-, h) MED dissect (a. fig); perform an autopsy on

Showgeschäft ['ʃou-] n (-[e]s; no pl) show business

sich [zɪç] refl pron oneself; himself; herself, itself; pl themselves; yourself, pl yourselves; **sich ansehen** look at oneself; look at each other

Sichel ['zɪçəl] f (-; -n) AGR sickle; ASTR crescent

sicher ['zɪçə] **1.** adj safe (**vor** dat from), secure (from); esp TECH proof (**gegen** against); fig certain, sure; reliable; (**sich**) **sicher sein** be sure (**e-r Sache** of s.th.; **dass** that); **2.** adv safely; **sicher!** of course, sure(ly); certainly; probably; **du hast** (**bist**) **sicher ...** you must have (be) ...

'**Sicherheit** f (-; -en) a) (no pl) security (a. MIL, POL, ECON); safety (a. TECH); (certainty; skill; (**sich**) **in Sicherheit bringen** get to safety, b) ECON cover

'**Sicherheits...** esp TECH in cpds ...glas, ...nadel, ...schloss etc: safety ...

Sicherheitsgurt m seat belt, safety belt

Sicherheitsmaßnahme f safety (POL security) measure

'**sicherlich** adv → **sicher** 2

'**sichern** v/t (ge-, h) protect, safeguard; secure (a. MIL, TECH); EDP save; **sich sichern** secure o.s. (**gegen, vor** dat against, from)

'**sicherstellen** v/t (sep, -ge-, h) secure; guarantee

Sicherung ['zɪçərʊŋ] f (-; -en) securing; safeguard(-ing); TECH safety device; ELECTR fuse

'**Sicherungskasten** m ELECTR fuse box

Sicherungsko.pie f EDP backup; **e-e Sicherungskopie machen** (**von**) back up

Sicht [zɪçt] f (-; no pl) visibility; view; **in Sicht kommen** come into sight or view; **auf lange Sicht** in the long run

'**sichtbar** adj visible

sichten ['zɪçtən] v/t (ge-, h) sight; fig sort (through or out)

'**Sichtkarte** f season ticket

'**sichtlich** adv visibly

'**Sichtweite** f visibility; **in** (**außer**) **Sichtweite** within (out of) sight

sickern ['zɪkən] v/i (ge-, sein) trickle, ooze, seep

sie [ziː] pers pron she; it; pl they; **Sie** you

Sieb [ziːp] n (-[e]s; -e) sieve; strainer

sieben[1] ['ziːbən] v/t (ge-, h) sieve, sift

'**sieben**[2] adj seven

Sieben'meter m SPORT penalty shot or throw

siebte ['ziːptə] adj, '**Siebtel** n (-s; -) seventh

siebzehn(te) ['ziːp-] adj seventeen(th)

siebzig ['ziːptsɪç] adj seventy

'**siebzigste** adj seventieth

siedeln ['ziːdəln] v/i (ge-, h) settle

sieden ['ziːdən] v/t and v/i ([irr,] ge-, h) boil, simmer

'**Siedepunkt** m boiling point (a. fig)

'**Siedler** ['ziːdlə] m (-s; -) settler

Siedlung ['ziːdlʊŋ] f (-; -en) settlement; housing development

Sieg [ziːk] m (-[e]s; -e) victory, SPORT a. win

Siegel ['ziːgəl] n (-s; -) seal, signet

'**Siegellack** m sealing wax

'**siegeln** v/t (ge-, h) seal

siegen ['ziːgən] v/i (ge-, h) win

Sieger ['ziːgə] m (-s; -), **Siegerin** ['ziːgərɪn] f (-; -nen) winner

'**siegreich** adj winning; victorious

Signal [zɪ'gnaːl] n (-s; -e), **signalisieren** [zɪgnali'ziːrən] v/t (no -ge-, h) signal

signieren [zɪ'gniːrən] v/t (no -ge-, h) sign

Silbe ['zɪlbə] f (-; -n) syllable

'**Silbentrennung** f LING syllabification

Silber ['zɪlbə] n (-s; no pl) silver; silverware

'**silbergrau** adj silver-gray (Br -grey)

'**Silberhochzeit** f silver wedding

'**silbern** adj silver

Silhouette [zi'luɛtə] f (-; -n) silhouette; skyline

Silikon [zili'koːn] n (-s; -e) CHEM silicone

Silizium [zi'liːtsjʊm] n (-s; no pl) CHEM silicon

Silvester [zɪl'vɛstə] n (-s; -) New Year's Eve

Sims [zɪms] m, n (-es; -e) ledge; windowsill

simulieren [zimu'liːrən] v/t and v/i TECH etc simulate; sham

simultan [zimʊl'taːn] adj simultaneous

Sinfonie [zɪnfoˈniː] f (-; -n) MUS symphony

singen ['zɪŋən] v/t and v/i (irr, ge-, h) sing (**richtig** [**falsch**] in [out of] tune)

Singular ['zɪŋgulaːɐ] m (-s; -e) LING singular

Singvogel

Singvogel ['zɪŋ-] *m* ZO songbird

sinken ['zɪŋkən] *v/i* (*irr, ge-, sein*) sink (*a. fig*), go down (*a.* ECON, ASTR *a.* set; *prices etc*: fall, drop

Sinn [zɪn] *m* (*-[e]s; -e*) sense (**für** of); mind; meaning; point, idea; **im Sinn haben** have in mind; **es hat keinen Sinn (zu warten** *etc*) it's no use *or* good (waiting *etc*)

'**Sinnbild** *n* symbol

'**sinnentstellend** *adj* distorting

Sinnesorgan ['zɪnəs-] *n* sense organ

Sinnestäuschung *f* hallucination

Sinneswandel *m* change of mind

'**sinnlich** *adj* sensuous; sensory; sensual

'**Sinnlichkeit** *f* (*-; no pl*) sensuality

'**sinnlos** *adj* senseless; useless

'**sinnverwandt** *adj* synonymous

'**sinnvoll** *adj* meaningful; useful; wise, sensible

Sintflut ['zɪnt-] *f the* Flood

Sippe ['zɪpə] *f* (*-; -n*) (extended) family, clan

Sirene [zi're:nə] *f* (*-; -n*) siren

Sirup ['zi:rʊp] *m* (*-s; -e*) sirup, *Br* syrup; treacle, molasses

Sitte ['zɪtə] *f* (*-; -n*) custom, tradition; *pl* morals; manners

'**Sittenlosigkeit** *f* (*-; no pl*) immorality

'**Sittenpoli,zei** *f* vice squad

'**sittenwidrig** *adj* immoral

'**Sittlichkeitsverbrechen** *n* sex crime

Situation [zitua'tsjo:n] *f* (*-; -en*) situation; position

Sitz [zɪts] *m* (*-es; -e*) seat; fit

Sitzblo,ckade *f* sit-down demonstration

sitzen ['zɪtsən] *v/i* (*irr, ge-, h*) sit (**an** *dat* at; **auf** *dat* on); be; fit; F do time; **sitzen bleiben** keep one's seat; PED have to repeat a year; F **sitzen bleiben auf** (*dat*) be left with; F **j-n sitzen lassen** leave s.o. in the lurch, let s.o. down

'**sitzenbleiben** *v/i* (*irr, bleiben, sep, -ge-, sein*) → **sitzen**

sitzenlassen *v/i* (*irr, lassen, sep, no -ge-, sein*) *a. fig* → **sitzen**

'**Sitzplatz** *m* seat

'**Sitzstreik** *m* sit-down strike

'**Sitzung** *f* (*-; -en*) session (*a.* PARL), meeting, conference

Skala ['ska:la] *f* (*-; -en*) scale, *fig a.* range

Skalp [skalp] *m* (*-s; -e*) scalp

skalpieren [skal'pi:rən] *v/t* (*no -ge-, h*) scalp

Skandal [skan'da:l] *m* (*-s; -e*) scandal; **ein Skandal sein** be scandalous

skandalös [skanda'lø:s] *adj* scandalous, shocking

Skelett [ske'lɛt] *n* (*-[e]s; -e*) skeleton

Skepsis ['skɛpsɪs] *f* (*-; no pl*) skepticism,

Br scepticism

Skeptiker ['skɛptikɐ] *m* (*-s; -*) skeptic, *Br* sceptic

skeptisch ['skɛptɪʃ] *adj* skeptical, *Br* sceptical

Ski [ʃiː] *m* (*-s; -er* ['ʃiːɐ]) ski; **Ski laufen** or **fahren** ski

Skifahrer(in) skier

Skifliegen *n* ski flying

Skilift *m* ski lift

Skipiste *f* ski run

Skischuh *m* ski boot

Skisport *m* skiing

Skispringen *n* ski jumping

Skizze ['skɪtsə] *f* (*-; -n*), **skizzieren** [skɪ-'tsiːrən] *v/t* (*no -ge-, h*) sketch

Sklave ['skla:və] *m* (*-n; -n*) slave (*a. fig*)

Sklaverei [skla:və'rai] *f* (*-; no pl*) slavery

Sklavin *f* (*-; -nen*) slave (*a. fig*)

'**sklavisch** *adj* slavish (*a. fig*)

Skonto ['skɔnto] *m, n* (*-s; -s*) ECON (cash) discount

Skorpion [skɔr'pjo:n] *m* (*-s; -e*) ZO scorpion; ASTR Scorpio; **er ist (ein) Skorpion** he's (a) Scorpio

Skrupel ['skru:pəl] *m* (*-s; -*) scruple, qualm

'**skrupellos** *adj* unscrupulous

Skulptur ['skʊlp'tuːɐ] *f* (*-; -en*) sculpture

Slalom ['sla:lɔm] *m* (*-s; -s*) slalom

Slawe ['sla:və] *m* (*-n; -n*), **Slawin** *f* (*-; -nen*) Slav

'**slawisch** *adj* Slav(ic)

Slip [slɪp] *m* (*-s; -s*) briefs, panties

'**Slipeinlage** *f* panty liner

Slipper ['slɪpɐ] *m* (*-s; -*) loafer, *esp Br* slip-on (shoe)

Slowake [slo'va:kə] *m* (*-n; -n*) Slovak

Slowakei [slova'kai] *f* Slovakia

Slo'wakin *f* (*-; -nen*), **slo'wakisch** *adj* Slovak

Smaragd [sma'rakt] *m* (*-[e]s; -e*) MIN, **sma'ragdgrün** *adj* emerald

Smoking ['smo:kɪŋ] *m* (*-s; -s*) tuxedo, *Br* dinner jacket

Snob [snɔp] *m* (*-s; -s*) snob

Snobismus [sno'bɪsmʊs] *m* (*-; no pl*) snobbery

sno'bistisch *adj* snobbish

so [zoː] **1.** *adv* so; like this *or* that, this *or* that way; thus; such; (*nicht*) **so groß wie** (not) as big as; **so ein(e)** such a; **so sehr** so (F that) much; **und so weiter** and so on; **oder so** or s.th. like that; **oder so** or so; **so, fangen wir an!** well *or* all right, let's begin!; F **so weit sein** be ready; **es ist so weit** it's time; **so genannt** so-called; **doppelt so viel** twice as much; **so viel wie möglich** as much as possible; **2.** *cj* so, therefore; **so dass** so that; **3.** *int*: **so!** all right!, o.k.!; that's it!; **ach so!** I see

s.o. ABBR of **siehe oben** see above

so'bald [zo-] *cj* as soon as

Socke ['zɔkə] *f* (-; -*n*) sock

Sockel ['zɔkəl] *m* (-*s*; -) base; pedestal

Sodbrennen ['zoːt-] *n* (-*s*; *no pl*) MED heartburn

soeben [zo'eːbən] *adv* just (now)

Sofa ['zoːfa] *n* (-*s*; -*s*) sofa, settee, davenport

sofern [zo'fɛrn] *cj* if, provided that; **sofern nicht** unless

soff [zɔf] *pret of* **saufen**

sofort [zo'fɔrt] *adv* at once, immediately, right away

So'fortbildkamera *f* PHOT instant camera

Software ['zɔftwɛːɐ] *f* EDP software

Softwarepaket *n* software package

sog [zoːk] *pret of* **saugen**

Sog *m* (-[*e*]*s*; -*e*) suction, MAR *a.* wake

sogar [zo'gaːɐ] *adv* even

Sohle ['zoːlə] *f* (-; -*n*) sole; *mining:* floor

Sohn [zoːn] *m* (-[*e*]*s*; *Söhne* ['zøːnə]) son

Sojabohne ['zoːjaː-] *f* BOT soybean

so'lange [zo-] *cj* as long as

Solar... [zo'laːɐ-] *in cpds* ...*energie etc*: solar ...

solch [zɔlç] *dem pron* such, like this *or* that

Sold [zɔlt] *m* (-[*e*]*s*; -*e*) MIL pay

Soldat [zɔl'daːt] *m* (-*en*; -*en*), **Sol'datin** *f* (-; -*nen*) soldier

Söldner ['zœldnɐ] *m* (-*s*; -) MIL mercenary

Sole ['zoːlə] *f* (-; -*n*) brine, salt water

solidarisch [zoli'daːrɪʃ] *adj*: **sich solidarisch erklären mit** declare one's solidarity with

solide [zo'liːdə] *adj* solid, *fig a.* sound; reasonable (*prices*); steady (*person*)

Solist [zo'lɪst] *m* (-*en*; -*en*), **So'listin** *f* (-; -*nen*) soloist

Soll [zɔl] *n* (-[*s*]; -[*s*]) ECON debit; target, quota; **Soll und Haben** debit and credit

sollen ['zɔlən] *v/i* (*ge-*, *h*) *and v/aux* (*irr, no -ge-, h*) be to; be supposed to; **(was) soll ich ...?** (what) shall I ...?; **du solltest (nicht) ...** you shouldn't ...; **was soll das?** what's the idea?

Solo ['zoːlo] *n* (-*s*, -*s*, *Soli*) *esp* MUS solo; SPORT solo attempt *etc*

so'mit [zo-] *cj* thus, so, consequently

Sommer ['zɔmɐ] *m* (-*s*; -) summer (time); **im Sommer** in (the) summer

Sommerferien *pl* summer vacation (*Br* holidays)

Sommerfrische *f* summer resort

'sommerlich *adj* summery

'Sommersprosse *f* freckle

'sommersprossig *adj* freckled

'Sommerzeit *f* summertime; daylight saving (*Br* summer) time

Sonate [zo'naːtə] *f* (-; -*n*) MUS sonata

Sonde ['zɔndə] *f* (-; -*n*) probe (*a.* MED)

Sonder... ['zɔndɐ-] *in cpds* ...*angebot*, ...*ausgabe*, ...*flug*, ...*preis*, ...*wunsch*, ...*zug etc*: special ...

'sonderbar *adj* strange, F funny

'Sonderling *m* (-*s*; -*e*) eccentric

'Sondermüll *m* hazardous (*or* special toxic) waste

Sondermülldepo,nie *f* special waste dump

sondern ['zɔndɐn] *cj* but; **nicht nur ..., sondern auch ...** not only ... but also ...

'Sonderschule *f* special school (for the handicapped *etc*)

Sonnabend ['zɔn-] *m* Saturday

Sonne ['zɔnə] *f* (-; -*n*) sun

sonnen ['zɔnən] *v/refl* (*ge-*, *h*) sunbathe

Sonnenaufgang *m* (**bei Sonnenaufgang** at) sunrise

'Sonnenbad *n*: **ein Sonnenbad nehmen** sunbathe

Sonnenbank *f* (-; -*bänke*) sunbed

Sonnenblume *f* BOT sunflower

Sonnenbrand *m* sunburn

Sonnenbräune *f* suntan

Sonnenbrille *f* sunglasses

Sonnencreme *f* suntan lotion, *Br* sun cream

Sonnenener,gie *f* solar energy

Sonnenfinsternis *f* solar eclipse

'sonnen'klar F *adj* (as) clear as daylight

'Sonnenkol,lektor *m* solar panel

Sonnenlicht *n* (-[*e*]*s*; *no pl*) sunlight

Sonnenöl *n* suntan oil

Sonnenschein *m* sunshine

Sonnenschirm *m* sunshade

Sonnenschutz *m* suntan lotion

Sonnenseite *f* sunny side (*a. fig*)

Sonnenstich *m* sunstroke

Sonnenstrahl *m* sunbeam

Sonnensys,tem *n* solar system

Sonnenuhr *f* sundial

Sonnenuntergang *m* sunset

sonnig ['zɔnɪç] *adj* sunny (*a. fig*)

Sonntag ['zɔn-] *m* Sunday; (**am**) **Sonntag** on Sunday

'sonntags *adv* on Sundays

'Sonntagsfahrer *contp m* MOT Sunday driver

sonst [zɔnst] *adv* else; otherwise, or (else); normally, usually; **sonst noch et. (jemand)?** anything (anyone) else?; **sonst noch Fragen?** any other questions?; **sonst nichts** nothing else; **alles wie sonst** everything as usual; **nichts ist wie sonst** nothing is as it used to be

'**sonstig** adj other

Sopran [zo'praːn] m (-s; -e) MUS, **Sopranistin** [zopra'nɪstɪn] f (-; -nen) MUS soprano

Sorge ['zɔrgə] f (-; -n) worry; sorrow; trouble; care; **sich Sorgen machen (um)** worry or be worried (about); **keine Sorge!** don't worry!

sorgen ['zɔrgən] (ge-; h) **1.** v/i: **sorgen für** care for, take care of; **dafür sorgen, dass** see (to it) that; **2.** v/refl: **sich sorgen um** worry or be worried about

'**Sorgenkind** n problem child

Sorgfalt ['zɔrkfalt] f (-; no pl) care

sorgfältig ['zɔrkfɛltɪç] adj careful

sorglos ['zɔrk-] adj carefree; careless

Sorte ['zɔrtə] f (-; -n) sort, kind, type

sortieren [zɔr'tiːrən] v/t (no -ge-; h) sort; arrange

Sortiment [zɔrti'mɛnt] n (-[e]s; -e) ECON assortment

Soße ['zoːsə] f (-; -n) sauce; gravy

sott [zɔt] pret of **sieden**

Souffleur [zu'fløːɐ] m (-s; -e), **Souffleuse** [zu'fløːzə] f (-; -n) THEA prompter

soufflieren [zu'fliːrən] v/i (no -ge-; h) THEA prompt (**j-m** s.o.)

souverän [zuvə'rɛːn] adj POL sovereign

Souveränität [zuvərenι'tɛːt] f (-; no pl) POL sovereignty

so'**viel** [zo-] cj as far as; → **so**

so'**weit** cj as far as; → **so**

so'**wie** cj as well as, and ... as well; as soon as

sowie'**so** adv anyway, anyhow, in any case

Sowjet [zo'vjɛt] m (-s; -s), **sow**'**jetisch** adj HIST Soviet

so'**wohl** [zo-] cj: **sowohl Lehrer als (auch) Schüler** both teachers and students

sozial [zo'tsjaːl] adj social

Sozi'**al...** in cpds ...arbeiter, ...demokrat, ...versicherung etc: social ...

Sozialhilfe f welfare; Br social security; **Sozialhilfe beziehen** be on welfare (Br social security)

Sozialismus [zotsja'lɪsmʊs] m (-; no pl) socialism

Sozialist(in) [-en/-; -en/ -nen), **sozia**'**listisch** adj socialist

Sozi'**alkunde** f PED social studies

Sozi'**alstaat** m welfare state

Soziologe [zotsjo'loːgə] m (-n; -n) sociologist

Soziologie [zotsjolo'giː] f (-; no pl) sociology

Sozio'**login** f (-; -nen) sociologist

soziologisch [zotsjo'loːgɪʃ] adj sociological

sozu'**sagen** adv so to speak

Spagat [ʃpa'gaːt] m: **Spagat machen** do the splits

Spalier [ʃpa'liːɐ] n (-s; -e) BOT espalier; MIL etc lane

Spalt [ʃpalt] m (-[e]s; -e) crack, gap

Spalte ['ʃpaltə] f (-; -n) → **Spalt**; PRINT column

'**spalten** v/t ([irr,] ge-, h) split (a. fig); POL divide; **sich spalten** split (up)

'**Spaltung** f (-; -en) split(ting); PHYS fission; fig split; POL division

Span [ʃpaːn] m (-[e]s; Späne ['ʃpɛːnə]) chip; pl TECH shavings

Spange ['ʃpaŋə] f (-; -n) clasp

Spaniel ['ʃpaːnjəl] m (-s; -s) ZO spaniel

Spanien ['ʃpaːnjən] Spain

Spanier ['ʃpaːnjɐ] m (-s; -), **Spanierin** ['ʃpaːnjərɪn] f (-; -nen) Spaniard

spanisch ['ʃpaːnɪʃ] adj Spanish

spann [ʃpan] pret of **spinnen**

Spann m (-[e]s; -e) ANAT instep

Spanne ['ʃpanə] f (-; -n) span

'**spannen** (ge-; h) **1.** v/t stretch, tighten; put up (line); cock (gun); draw, bend (bow); **2.** v/i be (too) tight

'**spannend** adj exciting, thrilling, gripping

'**Spannung** f (-; -en) tension (a. TECH, POL, PSYCH); ELECTR voltage; fig suspense, excitement

'**Spannweite** f span, fig a. range

Sparbuch ['ʃpaːɐ-] n savings book

Sparbüchse f esp Br money box

sparen ['ʃpaːrən] v/i and v/t (ge-, h) save; economize; **sparen für** or **auf** (acc) save up for

Sparer(in) ['ʃpaːrə (-rərɪn)] (-s; -/-; -nen) saver

'**Sparschwein(chen)** n piggy bank

Spargel ['ʃpargəl] m (-s; -) BOT asparagus

'**Sparkasse** f savings bank

'**Sparkonto** n savings account

spärlich ['ʃpɛːrlɪç] adj sparse; scant; scanty; poor (attendance)

sparsam ['ʃpaːrzaːm] adj economical (**mit** of); **sparsam leben** lead a frugal life; **sparsam umgehen mit** use sparingly; go easy on

'**Sparsamkeit** f (-; no pl) economy

Spaß [ʃpaːs] m (-es; Späße ['ʃpɛːsə]), Austrian a. **Spass** fun; joke; **aus (nur zum) Spaß** (just) for fun; **es macht viel (keinen) Spaß** it's great (no) fun; **j-m den Spaß verderben** spoil s.o.'s fun; **er macht nur Spaß** he is only joking (F kidding); **keinen Spaß verstehen** have no sense of humo(u)r**spaßen** ['ʃpɑːsən] v/i (ge-, h) joke

spaßig ['ʃpɑːsɪç] adj funny

'**Spaßvogel** m joker

spät [ʃpɛːt] adj and adv late; **am späten Nachmittag** late in the afternoon; **wie spät ist es?** what time is it?; **von früh bis spät** from morning till night; **(fünf Minuten) zu spät kommen** be (five minutes) late; **bis später!** see you (later)!; → **früher**

Spaten ['ʃpɑːtən] m (-s; -) spade

spätestens adv at the latest

Spatz [ʃpats] m (-en; -en) ZO sparrow

spazieren [ʃpaˈtsiːrən]: **spazieren fahren** go (take s.o.) for a drive; take s.o. out; **spazieren gehen** go for a walk

Spazierfahrt [ʃpaˈtsiːɐ-] f drive, ride

Spa'ziergang m walk; **e-n Spaziergang machen** go for a walk

Spa'ziergänger(in) [-gɛŋɐ (-ŋərɪn)] (-s; -/-nen) walker

Specht [ʃpɛçt] m (-[e]s; -e) ZO woodpecker

Speck [ʃpɛk] m (-[e]s; -e) bacon

speckig ['ʃpɛkɪç] fig adj greasy

Spediteur [ʃpediˈtøːɐ] m (-s; -e) shipping agent; remover

Spedition [ʃpediˈtsjoːn] f (-; -en) shipping agency; moving (Br removal) firm

Speer [ʃpeːɐ] m (-[e]s; -e) spear; SPORT javelin

Speiche ['ʃpaɪçə] f (-; -n) spoke

Speichel ['ʃpaɪçəl] m (-s; no pl) saliva, spit

Speicher ['ʃpaɪçɐ] m (-s; -) storehouse; tank, reservoir; ARCH attic; EDP memory, store

Speicherdichte f EDP bit density

Speicherkapazi,tät f EDP memory capacity

speichern v/t (ge-, h) store (up)

Speicherung ['ʃpaɪçərʊŋ] f (-; -en) storage

speien ['ʃpaɪən] v/t (irr, ge-, h) spit; spout; volcano etc: belch

Speise ['ʃpaɪzə] f (-; -n) food; dish

Speiseeis n ice cream

Speisekammer f larder, pantry

Speisekarte f menu

speisen (ge-, h) **1.** v/i dine; **2.** v/t feed (a. ELECTR etc)

Speiseröhre f ANAT gullet

Speisesaal m dining hall

Speisewagen m RAIL diner, esp Br dining car

Spekulant [ʃpekuˈlant] m (-en; -en) ECON speculator

Spekulation [ʃpekulaˈtsjoːn] f (-; -en) speculation, ECON a. venture

spekulieren [ʃpekuˈliːrən] v/i (no -ge-, h) ECON speculate (**auf** acc on; **mit** in)

Spende ['ʃpɛndə] f (-; -n) gift; contribution; donation

'**spenden** v/t (ge-, h) give (a. fig); donate (a. MED)

Spender ['ʃpɛndɐ] m (-s; -) giver; donor (a. MED), **Spenderin** f (-; -nen) donor (a. MED)

spendieren [ʃpɛnˈdiːrən] v/t (no -ge-, h) **j-m et. spendieren** treat s.o. to s.th.

Spengler ['ʃpɛŋlɐ] Austrian m → **Klempner**

Sperling ['ʃpɛrlɪŋ] m (-s; -e) ZO sparrow

Sperre ['ʃpɛrə] f (-; -n) barrier, RAIL a. gate; fig stop; TECH lock(ing device); barricade; SPORT suspension; PSYCH mental block; ECON embargo

'**sperren** v/t (ge-, h) close; ECON embargo; cut off; stop (check); SPORT suspend; obstruct; **sperren in** (acc) lock (up) in

'**Sperrholz** n plywood

Sperrmüllabfuhr f removal of bulky refuse

'**Sperrung** f (-; -en) closing

Spesen ['ʃpeːzən] pl expenses

Spezi ['ʃpeːtsi] F m (-s; -[s]) buddy, pal

Spezialausbildung [ʃpeˈtsjaːl-] f special training

Spezialgebiet n special field, special(i)ty

Spezialgeschäft n specialized shop or store

spezialisieren [ʃpetsjaliˈziːrən] v/refl (no -ge-, h) specialize (**auf** acc in)

Spezialist(in) [ʃpetsjaˈlɪst(ɪn)] (-en; -en/-; -nen) specialist

Spezialität [ʃpetsjaliˈtɛːt] f (-; -en) special(i)ty

speziell [ʃpeˈtsjɛl] adj specific, particular

spezifisch [ʃpeˈtsiːfɪʃ] adj specific; **spezifisches Gewicht** specific gravity

Sphäre ['sfɛːrə] f (-; -n) sphere (a. fig)

spicken ['ʃpɪkən] (ge-, h) **1.** v/t GASTR lard (a. fig); **2.** F v/i PED crib

spie [ʃpiː] pret of **speien**

Spiegel ['ʃpiːɡəl] m (-s; -) mirror (a. fig)

'**Spiegelbild** n reflection (a. fig)

'**Spiegelei** n GASTR fried egg

'**spiegel'glatt** adj glassy; icy

'**spiegeln** v/i and v/t (ge-, h) reflect (a. fig); shine; **sich spiegeln** be reflected (a. fig)

'**Spiegelung** f (-; -en) reflection

Spiel [ʃpiːl] n (-[e]s; -e) game (a. fig); match; play (a. THEA etc); gambling; fig gamble; **auf dem Spiel stehen** be at stake; **aufs Spiel setzen** risk

spielen ['ʃpiːlən] v/i and v/t (ge-, h) play (a. fig) (**um** for); THEA act; perform; gam-

ble; do (*the pools etc*); **Klavier** *etc* **spie-
len** play the piano *etc*
'spielend *fig adv* easily
Spieler ['ʃpiːlɐ] *m* (-s; -), Spielerin ['ʃpiː-
lərɪn] *f* (-; *-nen*) player; gambler
'Spielfeld *n* (playing) field, pitch
Spielca,sino *n* casino
Spielfilm *m* feature film
Spielhalle *f* amusement arcade, game
room
Spielkame,rad(in) playmate
Spielkarte *f* playing card
Spielka,sino *n* casino
Spielmarke *f* counter, chip
Spielplan *m* THEA, SPORT *etc* program(me)
Spielplatz *m* playground
Spielraum *fig m* play, scope
Spielregel *f* rule (of the game)
Spielsachen *pl* toys
Spielstand *m* score
Spieluhr *f* music (*Br* musical) box
Spielverderber(in) (-s; -/-; *-nen*) spoil-
sport
Spielwaren *pl* toys
Spielzeit *f* THEA, SPORT season; playing
(*film*: running) time
'Spielzeug *n* toy(s); **Spielzeug...** *in cpds*
...pistole *etc*: toy ...
Spieß [ʃpiːs] *m* (-es; -e) MIL spear; GASTR
spit; skewer
spießen ['ʃpiːsən] *v/t* (*ge-, h*) skewer
Spießer ['ʃpiːsɐ] F *contp m* (-s; -), 'spie-
ßig F *contp adj* philistine
Spinat [ʃpi'naːt] *m* (-[e]s; -e) BOT spinach
Spind [ʃpɪnt] *n, m* (-[e]s; -e) locker
Spindel ['ʃpɪndəl] *f* (-; *-n*) spindle
Spinne ['ʃpɪnə] *f* (-; *-n*) ZO spider
'spinnen (*irr, ge-, h*) **1.** *v/t* spin (*a. fig*); **2.** F
contp v/i be nuts; talk nonsense
Spinner ['ʃpɪnɐ] *m* (-s; -), 'Spinnerin (-;
-nen) spinner; F *contp* nut, crackpot
'Spinnrad *n* spinning wheel
'Spinnwebe *f* (-; *-n*) cobweb
Spion [ʃpi'oːn] *m* (-s; -e) spy
Spionage [ʃpio'naːʒə] *f* (-; *no pl*) espio-
nage
spionieren [ʃpio'niːrən] *v/i* (*no -ge-, h*)
spy; F snoop
Spi'onin *f* (-; *-nen*) spy
Spirale [ʃpi'raːlə] *f* (-; *-n*), spi'ralförmig
[-fœrmɪç] *adj* spiral
Spirituosen [ʃpiri'tuoːzən] *pl* spirits
Spiritus ['ʃpiːrɪtus] *m* spirit
Spital [ʃpi'taːl] *Austrian, Swiss n* (-s; *Spi-
täler* [ʃpi'tɛːlə]) hospital
spitz [ʃpɪts] *adj* pointed (*a. fig*); MATH
acute; **spitze Zunge** sharp tongue
'Spitzbogen *m* ARCH pointed arch
Spitze ['ʃpɪtsə] *f* (-; *-n*) point; tip; ARCH

spire; BOT, GEOGR top; head (*a. fig*); lace;
F MOT top speed; **spitze sein** F be super,
be (the) tops; **an der Spitze** at the top (*a.
fig*)
Spitzel ['ʃpɪtsəl] *m* (-s; -) informer, F
stoolpigeon
spitzen ['ʃpɪtsən] *v/t* (*ge-, h*) point, sharp-
en; purse; ZO prick up (*its ears*)
'Spitzen... *in cpds* top ...; hi-tech ...
Spitzentechnolo,gie *f* high technology,
hi tech
'spitzfindig *adj* quibbling
'Spitzfindigkeit *f* (-; *-en*) subtlety
'Spitzhacke *f* pickax(e), pick
'Spitzname *m* nickname
Splitter ['ʃplɪtɐ] *m* (-s; -), 'splittern *v/i*
(*ge-, h, sein*) splinter
'splitter'nackt F *adj* stark naked
sponsern ['ʃpɔnzɐn] *v/t* (*ge-, h*) sponsor
Sponsor ['ʃpɔnzɐ] *m* (-s; *-en* [ʃpɔn'zoː-
rən]) sponsor
spontan [ʃpɔn'taːn] *adj* spontaneous
Sporen ['ʃpoːrən] *pl* spurs (*a. zo*); BIOL
spores
Sport [ʃpɔrt] *m* (-[e]s; *no pl*) sport(s); PED
physical education; **Sport treiben** do
sports
'Sport... *in cpds* ...ereignis, ...geschäft,
...heim, ...verein, ...zentrum *etc*: *mst*
sports ...
Sportkleidung *f* sportswear
Sportler ['ʃpɔrtlɐ] *m* (-s; -), Sportlerin
['ʃpɔrtlərɪn] *f* (-; *-nen*) athlete
'sportlich *adj* athletic; casual, sporty
'Sportnachrichten *pl* sports news
'Sportplatz *m* sports grounds
Sporttauchen *n* scuba diving
Sportwagen *m* stroller, *Br* pushchair; MOT
sports car
Spott [ʃpɔt] *m* (-[e]s; *no pl*) mockery; derision
'spott'billig F *adj* dirt cheap
spotten ['ʃpɔtən] *v/i* (*ge-, h*) mock (**über**
acc at), scoff (at); make fun (of)
Spötter ['ʃpœtɐ] *m* (-s; -) mocker, scoffer
'spöttisch *adj* mocking, derisive
'Spottpreis *m*: **für e-n Spottpreis** dirt
cheap
sprach [ʃpraːx] *pret of* **sprechen**
Sprache ['ʃpraːxə] *f* (-; *-n*) language (*a.
fig*); speech; **zur Sprache kommen**
(**bringen**) come up (bring *s.th.* up)
'Sprachfehler *m* speech defect
'Sprachgebrauch *m* usage
'Sprachla,bor *n* language laboratory
'Sprachlehre *f* grammar
'Sprachlehrer(in) language teacher
'sprachlich **1.** *adj* language ...; **2.** *adv*:
sprachlich richtig grammatically cor-

rect

'sprachlos *adj* speechless

'Sprachrohr *fig n* mouthpiece

Sprachunterricht *m* language teaching

Sprachwissenschaft *f* linguistics

sprang [ʃpraŋ] *pret of* **springen**

Spraydose ['ʃpreː-] *f* spray can, aerosol (can)

Sprechanlage ['ʃpreç-] *f* intercom

sprechen ['ʃpreçən] *v/t and v/i* (*irr*, *ge-*, *h*) speak (*-j-n, mit j-m* to s.o.); talk (to) (*both*: *über acc, von* about, of); *nicht zu sprechen sein* be busy

Sprecher(in) ['ʃpreçɐ (-çərɪn)] (*-s*; */-*; *-nen*) speaker; announcer; spokesman (spokeswoman)

'Sprechstunde *f* office hours; MED office (*Br* consulting) hours, *Br* surgery

'Sprechzimmer *n* office, *Br a.* consulting room

spreizen ['ʃpraɪtsən] *v/t* (*ge-*, *h*) spread

sprengen ['ʃprɛŋən] *v/t* (*ge-*, *h*) blow up; blast; sprinkle; water; *fig* break up

'Sprengkopf *m* MIL warhead

'Sprengstoff *m* MIL explosive

Sprengung *f* (*-*; *-en*) blasting; blowing up

sprenkeln ['ʃprɛŋkəln] *v/t* (*ge-*, *h*) speck (-le), spot, dot

Spreu [ʃprɔy] *f* (*-*; *no pl*) chaff (*a. fig*)

Sprichwort ['ʃprɪç-] *n* proverb, saying

'sprichwörtlich *adj* proverbial (*a. fig*)

sprießen ['ʃpriːsən] *v/i* (*irr*, *ge-*, *sein*) BOT sprout

'Springbrunnen *m* fountain

springen ['ʃprɪŋən] *v/i* (*irr*, *ge-*, *sein*) jump; leap; *ball etc:* bounce; SPORT dive; *glass etc:* crack; break; burst; *in die Höhe (zur Seite) springen* jump up (aside)

Springer ['ʃprɪŋɐ] *m* (*-s*; *-*) jumper; diver; *chess:* knight

'Springflut *f* spring tide

'Springreiten *n* show jumping

Spritze ['ʃprɪtsə] *f* (*-*; *-n*) MED injection, F shot; syringe

spritzen 1. *v/i and v/t* (*ge-*, *h*) splash; spray (*a.* TECH, AGR); MED inject; give s.o. an injection of; **2.** *v/i* (*ge-*, *sein*) spatter; gush (*aus* from)

Spritzer ['ʃprɪtsɐ] *m* (*-s*; *-*) splash; dash

'Spritzpis,tole *f* TECH spray gun

'Spritztour F *f* MOT spin

spröde ['ʃprøːdə] *adj* brittle (*a. fig*); rough

spross [ʃprɔs] *pret of* **sprießen**

Sprosse ['ʃprɔsə] *f* (*-*; *-n*) rung

Spruch [ʃprʊx] *m* (*-[e]s*; *Sprüche* ['ʃpryːçə]) saying; decision

'Spruchband *n* banner

Sprudel ['ʃpruːdəl] *m* (*-s*; *-*) mineral water

'sprudeln *v/i* (*ge-*, *sein*) bubble

Sprühdose ['ʃpryː-] *f* spray can, aerosol (can)

sprühen ['ʃpryːən] *v/t and v/i* (*ge-*, *h*) spray; throw out (*sparks*)

'Sprühregen *m* drizzle

Sprung [ʃprʊŋ] *m* (*-[e]s*; *Sprünge* ['ʃpryŋə]) jump, leap; SPORT dive; crack, fissure

Sprungbrett *n* SPORT diving board; springboard; *fig* stepping stone

Sprungschanze *f* ski jump

Spucke ['ʃpʊkə] *f* (*-*; *no pl*) spit

'spucken *v/i and v/t* (*ge-*, *h*) spit; F throw up

Spuk [ʃpuːk] *m* (*-[e]s*; *-e*) apparition, ghost

spuken ['ʃpuːkən] *v/i* (*ge-*, *h*) **spuken in** (*dat*) haunt; *hier spukt es* this place is haunted

Spule ['ʃpuːlə] *f* (*-*; *-n*) spool, reel; bobbin; ELECTR coil

'spulen *v/t* (*ge-*, *h*) spool, wind, reel

spülen ['ʃpyːlən] *v/t and v/i* (*ge-*, *h*) wash up, do the dishes; rinse; flush the toilet

'Spülma,schine *f* dishwasher

Spur [ʃpuːɐ] *f* (*-*; *-en*) track(s); trail; print; lane; trace (*a. fig*); *j-m auf der Spur sein* be on s.o.'s trail

spüren ['ʃpyːrən] *v/t* (*ge-*, *h*) feel, sense; notice

'spurlos *adv* without leaving a trace

'Spurweite *f* RAIL ga(u)ge; MOT track

St. ABBR *of* **Sankt** St, Saint

Staat [ʃtaːt] *m* (*-[e]s*; *-en*) state; POL government

Staatenbund *m* confederacy, confederation

staatenlos *adj* stateless

'staatlich 1. *adj* state ...; public, national; **2.** *adv:* **staatlich geprüft** qualified, registered

'Staatsangehörige *m*, *f* national, citizen, subject

Staatsangehörigkeit *f* (*-*; *no pl*) nationality

Staatsanwalt *m* JUR district attorney, *Br* (public) prosecutor

Staatsbesuch *m* official *or* state visit

Staatsbürger *m* citizen

Staatschef *m* head of state

Staatsdienst *n* civil (*or* public) service

'staatseigen *adj* state-owned

'Staatsfeind *m* public enemy

'staatsfeindlich *adj* subversive

'Staatshaushalt *m* budget

Staatskasse *f* treasury

Staatsmann *m* statesman

Staatsoberhaupt *n* head of (the) state

Staatssekre,tär(in) undersecretary of

S

state

Staatsstreich m coup d'état

Staatsvertrag m treaty

Staatswissenschaft f political science

Stab [ʃtaːp] m (-[e]s; Stäbe ['ʃtɛːbə]) staff (a. fig); bar; SPORT, MUS baton; SPORT pole

Stäbchen ['ʃtɛːpçən] n chopstick

'**Stabhochsprung** m SPORT pole vault

stabil [ʃtaˈbiːl] adj stable (a. ECON, POL); solid, strong; sound

stabilisieren [ʃtabiliˈziːrən] v/t (no -ge-, h) stabilize

Stabilität [-ˈtɛːt] f (-; no pl) stability

stach [ʃtax] pret of **stechen**

Stachel ['ʃtaxəl] m (-s; -n) BOT spine, prick; ZO sting

Stachelbeere f BOT gooseberry

Stacheldraht m barbed wire

stachelig ['ʃtaxəlɪç] adj prickly

'**Stachelschwein** n ZO porcupine

Stadel ['ʃtaːdəl] Austrian m (-s; -[n]) barn

Stadion ['ʃtaːdjɔn] n (-s; -ien) stadium

Stadium ['ʃtaːdjʊm] n (-s; -ien) stage, phase

Stadt [ʃtat] f (-; Städte ['ʃtɛːtə]) town; city; **die Stadt Berlin** the city of Berlin; **in die Stadt fahren** go downtown, esp Br go (in)to town

Stadtbahn f urban railway

Städter ['ʃtɛːtɐ] m (-s; -), '**Städterin** f (-; -nen) city dweller, F townie, often contp city slicker

'**Stadtgebiet** n urban area

Stadtgespräch fig n talk of the town

städtisch ['ʃeːtɪʃ] adj urban; POL municipal

'**Stadtplan** m city map

Stadtrand m outskirts

Stadtrat m town council; city councilman, Br town council(l)or

Stadtrundfahrt f sightseeing tour

Stadtstreicher(in) m city vagrant

Stadtteil m, **Stadtviertel** n quarter

Staffel ['ʃtafəl] f (-; -n) SPORT relay race or team; MIL, AVIAT squadron

Staffelei [ʃtafəˈlaɪ] f (-; -en) PAINT easel

'**staffeln** v/t (ge-, h) grade, scale

stahl [ʃtaːl] pret of **stehlen**

Stahl [ʃtaːl] m (-[e]s; Stähle ['ʃtɛːlə]) steel

'**Stahlwerk** n steelworks

stak [ʃtaːk] pret of **stecken** 2

Stall [ʃtal] m (-[e]s; Ställe ['ʃtɛlə]) stable

'**Stallknecht** m stableman

Stamm [ʃtam] m (-[e]s; Stämme ['ʃtɛmə]) BOT stem (a. LING), trunk; tribe; stock; fig regulars; **Stamm...** in cpds ...gast, ...kunde, ...spieler etc: regular ...

Stammbaum m family tree; ZO pedigree

stammeln ['ʃtaməln] v/t (ge-, h) stammer

stammen ['ʃtamən] v/i (ge-, h) **stammen aus (von)** come from; be from; **stammen von** work of art etc: be by

'**Stammformen** pl LING principal parts, mst tenses

stämmig ['ʃtɛmɪç] adj sturdy; stout

'**Stammkneipe** F f Br local

stampfen ['ʃtampfən] (ge-, h) **1.** v/t mash; **2.** v/i stamp (**mit dem Fuß** one's foot)

stand [ʃtant] pret of **stehen**

Stand [ʃtant] m (-[e]s; Stände ['ʃtɛndə]) a) (no pl) stand(ing), standing or upright position; footing, foothold; ASTR position; TECH: height, level (a. fig); reading; SPORT score; racing: standings; fig state; social standing, status, b) stand, stall, c) class; profession; **auf den neuesten Stand bringen** bring up to date; **e-n schweren Stand haben** have a hard time (of it); → **außerstande**; → **imstande**; → **instand**; → **zustande**

Standard ['ʃtandart] m (-s; -s) standard

'**Standbild** n statue

Ständchen ['ʃtɛntçən] n (-s; -) MUS serenade

Ständer ['ʃtɛndɐ] m (-s; -) stand; rack

Standesamt ['ʃtandəs-] n marriage license bureau, Br registry office

'**standesamtlich** adj: **standesamtliche Trauung** civil marriage

'**Standesbeamte** m, -**in** f civil magistrate, Br registrar

'**Standfoto** n still

'**standhaft** adj steadfast, firm; **standhaft bleiben** resist temptation

'**standhalten** v/i (irr, halten, sep, -ge-, h) withstand, resist

ständig ['ʃtɛndɪç] adj constant; permanent (address)

'**Standlicht** n (-[e]s; no pl) MOT parking light

Standort m position; location; MIL post, garrison

Standpauke F f: **j-m e-e Standpauke halten** give s.o. a talking-to

Standplatz m stand

Standpunkt m (point of) view, standpoint

Standrecht n (-[e]s; no pl) MIL martial law

Standspur f MOT (Br hard) shoulder

Standuhr f grandfather clock

Stange ['ʃtaŋə] f (-; -n) pole; staff; rod, bar; carton (of cigarettes)

Stängel ['ʃtɛŋəl] m (-s; -) BOT stalk, stem

stank [ʃtaŋk] pret of **stinken**

Stanniol [ʃtaˈnjoːl] n (-s; -e) tin foil

Stanze ['ʃtantsə] f (-; -n), '**stanzen** v/t (ge-, h) TECH punch

Stapel ['ʃtaːpəl] m (-s; -) pile, stack; heap; **vom Stapel lassen** MAR launch (a. fig);

vom Stapel laufen MAR be launched
Stapellauf *m* MAR launch
stapeln *v/t* (ge-, h) pile (up), stack
stapfen ['ʃtapfən] *v/i* (ge-, sein) trudge
Star[1] [ʃtaːɐ] *m* (-s; -e) ZO starling; MED cataract
Star[2] *m* (-s; -s) THEA *etc*: star
starb [ʃtarp] *pret of* **sterben**
stark [ʃtark] **1.** *adj* strong (*a.* GASTR); powerful; *fig* heavy; F super, great; **2.** *adv*: **stark beeindruckt** greatly impressed; **stark beschädigt** badly damaged
Stärke ['ʃtɛrkə] *f* (-; -n) a) (*no pl*) strength, power; intensity, b) degree, c) CHEM starch
stärken *v/t* (ge-, h) strengthen (*a. fig*); starch; **sich stärken** take some refreshment
Starkstrom *m* ELECTR high-voltage (*or* heavy) current
Stärkung *f* (-; -en) strengthening; refreshment
Stärkungsmittel *n* MED tonic
starr [ʃtar] *adj* stiff; rigid (*a.* TECH); frozen (*face*); **starrer Blick** (fixed) stare; **starr vor Kälte** (**Entsetzen**) frozen (scared) stiff
starren *v/i* (ge-, h) stare (**auf** *acc* at)
starrköpfig [-kœpfɪç] *adj* stubborn, obstinate
Starrsinn *m* (-[e]s; *no pl*) stubbornness, obstinacy
Start [ʃtart] *m* (-[e]s; -s) start (*a. fig*); AVIAT take-off; *rocket*: lift-off
Startbahn *f* AVIAT runway
startbereit *adj* ready to start; AVIAT ready for take-off
starten ['ʃtartən] *v/i* (ge-, sein) and *v/t* (ge-, h) start (*a.* F); AVIAT take off; lift off; launch (*a. fig*)
Station [ʃtaˈtsjoːn] *f* (-; -en) station; MED ward
stationär [ʃtatsjoˈnɛːɐ] *adj*: **stationärer Patient** MED in-patient
stationieren [ʃtatsjoˈniːrən] *v/t* (*no* -ge-, h) MIL station; deploy
Stationsvorsteher *m* RAIL stationmaster
Statist [ʃtaˈtɪst] *m* (-en; -en) THEA extra
Statistik [ʃtaˈtɪstɪk] *f* (-; -en) statistics
Sta'tistiker [-tikə] *m* (-s; -) statistician
sta'tistisch *adj* statistical
Stativ [ʃtaˈtiːf] *n* (-s; -e) PHOT tripod
statt [ʃtat] *prp* instead of; **statt et. zu tun** instead of doing s.th.
statt'dessen instead
Stätte ['ʃtɛtə] *f* (-; -n) place; scene
stattfinden *v/i* (irr, **finden**, sep, -ge-, h) take place; happen
stattlich *adj* imposing; handsome

Statue ['ʃtaːtuə] *f* (-; -n) statue
Statur [ʃtaˈtuːɐ] *f* (-; -en) build
Status ['ʃtaːtʊs] *m* (-; -) state; status
Statussym,bol *n* status symbol
Statuszeile *f* EDP status line
Stau [ʃtau] *m* (-[e]s; -s, -e) MOT traffic jam *or* congestion
Staub [ʃtaup] *m* (-[e]s; TECH -e, **Stäube** ['ʃtɔybə]) dust (*a.* **Staub wischen**)
Staubecken *n* reservoir
stauben ['ʃtaubən] *v/i* (ge-, h) give off *or* make dust
staubig ['ʃtaubɪç] *adj* dusty
staubsaugen *v/i and v/t* (ge-, h) vacuum, F Br hoover
Staubsauger *m* vacuum cleaner, F Br hoover
Staubtuch *n* duster
Staudamm *m* dam
Staude ['ʃtaudə] *f* (-; -n) BOT herbacious plant
stauen ['ʃtauən] *v/t* (ge-, h) dam up; **sich stauen** MOT *etc* be stacked up
staunen ['ʃtaunən] *v/i* (ge-, h) be astonished *or* surprised (**über** *acc* at)
Staunen *n* (-s; *no pl*) astonishment, amazement
Staupe ['ʃtaupə] *f* (-; -n) VET distemper
Stausee *m* reservoir
stechen ['ʃteçən] *v/i and v/t* (*irr*, ge-, h) prick; ZO sting, bite; stab; pierce; **mit et. stechen in** (*acc*) stick s.th. in(to); **sich stechen** prick o.s.
stechend *fig adj* piercing (*look*); stabbing (*pain*)
Stechuhr *f* time clock
Steckbrief ['ʃtɛk-] *m* JUR „wanted“ poster
steckbrieflich *adv*: **er wird steckbrieflich gesucht** JUR a warrant is out against him
Steckdose *f* ELECTR (wall) socket
stecken ['ʃtɛkən] (ge-, h) **1.** *v/t* stick; put; *esp* TECH insert (**in** *acc* into); pin (**an** *acc* to, on); AGR set, plant; **2.** *v/i* ([*irr*]) stick, be stuck; **stecken bleiben** get stuck
steckenbleiben *v/i* (*irr*, **bleiben**, sep, -ge-, sein) *fig* get stuck
Steckenpferd *n* hobby horse; *fig* hobby
Stecker ['ʃtɛkə] *m* (-s; -) ELECTR plug
Steckkon,takt *m* ELECTR plug (connection)
Stecknadel *f* pin
Steckplatz *m* EDP slot
Steg [ʃteːk] *m* (-[e]s; -e) footbridge
Stegreif ['ʃteːkraif] *m*: **aus dem Stegreif** extempore, ad-lib; **aus dem Stegreif sprechen** *or* **spielen** *etc* extemporize, ad-lib

S

stehen ['ʃteːən] *v/i* (*irr, ge-, h*) stand; be; stand up; *es steht ihr* it suits (*or* looks well *on*) her; *wie steht es* (*or das Spiel*)? what's the score?; *hier steht, dass* it says here that; *wo steht das?* where does it say so *or* that?; *sich schlecht stehen* be badly off; F *sich gut mit j-m stehen* get along well with s.o.; *wie steht es mit …?* what about …?; F *darauf stehe ich* it turns me on; *stehen bleiben* stop; *esp* TECH come to a standstill (*a. fig*); *stehen lassen* leave (untouched); leave behind; *alles stehen und liegen lassen* drop everything; *sich e-n Bart stehen lassen* grow a beard

'**stehenbleiben** *v/i* (*irr, bleiben, sep, -ge-, sein*) → **stehen**

stehenlassen *v/t* (*irr, lassen, sep, no -ge-, h*) → **stehen**

'**Stehkragen** *m* stand-up collar

Stehlampe *f* floor (*Br* standard) lamp

Stehleiter *f* step ladder

stehlen ['ʃteːlən] *v/t and v/i* (*irr, ge-, h*) steal (*a. fig* **stehlen**)

'**Stehplatz** *m* standing ticket; *pl* standing room

steif [ʃtaif] *adj* stiff (*vor dat* with)

Steigbügel ['ʃtaik-] *m* stirrup

steigen ['ʃtaigən] *v/i* (*irr, ge-, sein*) go, step; climb (*a.* AVIAT); *fig* rise, go up; *steigen in* (*auf*) (*acc*) get on (*bus, bike etc*); *steigen aus* (*von*) get off (*bus, horse etc*); *aus dem Bett steigen* get out of bed

steigern ['ʃtaigən] *v/t* (*ge-, h*) raise, increase; heighten; improve; LING compare; *sich steigern* improve, get better

Steigerung ['ʃtaigərʊŋ] *f* (*-; -en*) rise, increase; heightening; improvement; LING comparison

'**Steigung** *f* (*-; -en*) gradient; slope

steil [ʃtail] *adj* steep (*a. fig*)

Stein [ʃtain] *m* (*-[e]s; -e*) stone (*a.* BOT, MED), rock

Steinbock *m* ZO rock goat; ASTR Capricorn; *er ist* (*ein*) *Steinbock* he's a(n) Capricorn

Steinbruch *m* quarry

steinern ['ʃtainən] *adj* (of) stone; *fig* stony

'**Steingut** *n* (*-[e]s; -e*) earthenware

steinig ['ʃtainɪç] *adj* stony

steinigen ['ʃtainɪgən] *v/t* (*ge-, h*) stone

'**Steinkohle** *f* (hard) coal

Steinmetz [-mɛts] *m* (*-en; -en*) stonemason

Steinzeit *f* (*-; no pl*) Stone Age

Stellage [ʃtɛˈlaːʒə] *Austrian f* (*-; -n*) stand, rack, shelf

Stelle ['ʃtɛlə] *f* (*-; -n*) place; spot; point;

job; authority; MATH figure; *freie Stelle* vacancy, opening; *auf der* (*zur*) *Stelle* on the spot; *an erster Stelle stehen* (*kommen*) be (come) first; *an j-s Stelle* in s.o.'s place; *ich an deiner Stelle* if I were you

'**stellen** *v/t* (*ge-, h*) put; set (*trap, clock, task etc*); turn (*up, down, off etc*); ask (*question*); provide; corner, hunt down (*criminal etc*); *sich stellen* give o.s. up, turn o.s. in; *sich gegen* (*hinter*) *j-n stellen* *fig* oppose (back) s.o.; *sich schlafend etc stellen* pretend to be asleep *etc*; *stell dich dorthin!* (go and) stand over there!

'**Stellenangebot** *n* vacancy; *ich habe ein Stellenangebot* I was offered a job

Stellenanzeige *f* job ad(vertisement), employment ad

Stellengesuch *n* application for a job

'**stellenweise** *adv* partly, in places

'**Stellung** *f* (*-; -en*) position; post, job; *Stellung nehmen zu* comment on, give one's opinion of

Stellungnahme [-naːmə] *f* (*-; -n*) comment, opinion (*both: zu* on)

'**stellungslos** *adj* unemployed, jobless

'**stellvertretend** *adj* acting, deputy, vice-…

'**Stellvertreter(in)** (*-s; -/-; -nen*) representative; deputy

Stelze ['ʃtɛltsə] *f* (*-; -n*) stilt

'**stelzen** *v/i* (*ge-, sein*) stalk

stemmen ['ʃtɛmən] *v/t* (*ge-, h*) lift (*weight*); *sich stemmen gegen* press o.s. against; *fig* resist *or* oppose s.th.

Stempel ['ʃtɛmpəl] *m* (*-s; -*) stamp; postmark; hallmark; BOT pistil

'**Stempelkissen** *n* ink pad

'**stempeln** (*ge-, h*) **1.** *v/t* stamp; cancel; hallmark; **2.** F *v/i: stempeln gehen* be on the dole

Stengel → **Stängel**

Stenografie [ʃtenograˈfiː] *f* (*-; -n*) shorthand

stenogra'fieren *v/t* (*no -ge-, h*) take down in shorthand

Stenogramm [ʃtenoˈgram] *n* (*-[e]s; -e*) shorthand notes

Stenotypistin [-tyˈpɪstɪn] *f* (*-; -nen*) shorthand typist

Steppdecke ['ʃtɛp-] *f* quilt

steppen ['ʃtɛpən] (*ge-, h*) **1.** *v/t* quilt; stitch; **2.** *v/i* tap dance

'**Stepptanz** *m* tap dancing

Sterbebett ['ʃtɛrbə-] *n* deathbed

'**Sterbeklinik** *f* MED hospice

sterben ['ʃtɛrbən] *v/i* (*irr, ge-, sein*) die (*an dat*) (*a. fig*); *im Sterben liegen* be dying sterblich ['ʃtɛrplɪç] adj mortal

'Sterblichkeit f (-; no pl) mortality

Stereo ['ʃteːreo] n (-s; -s) stereo

steril [ʃteˈriːl] adj sterile

Sterilisation [ʃteriliza'tsjoːn] f (-; -en) sterilization

sterilisieren [ʃteriliˈziːrən] v/t (no -ge-, h) sterilize

Stern [ʃtɛrn] m (-[e]s; -e) star (a. fig)

'Sternbild n ASTR constellation; sign of the zodiac

'Sternchen n (-s; -) PRINT asterisk

'Sternenbanner n Star-Spangled Banner, Stars and Stripes

'Sternenhimmel m starry sky

'sternklar adj starry

'Sternkunde f (-; no pl) astronomy

'Sternschnuppe f (-; -n) shooting or falling star

'Sternwarte f (-; -n) observatory

stetig ['ʃteːtɪç] adj continual, constant; steady

stets [ʃteːts] adv always

'Steuer¹ ['ʃtɔyɐ] n (-s; -) MOT (steering) wheel; MAR helm, rudder

'Steuer² f (-; -n) tax (auf acc on)

'Steuerbeamte m revenue officer

'Steuerberater m tax adviser

'Steuerbord n MAR starboard

'Steuererklärung f tax return

'Steuerermäßigung f tax allowance

'steuerfrei adj tax-free

'Steuerhinterziehung f tax evasion

'Steuerknüppel m AVIAT control column or stick

'Steuermann m MAR helmsman; rowing: cox, coxswain

'steuern v/t and v/i (ge-, h) steer, AVIAT, MAR a. navigate, pilot, MOT a. drive; TECH control (a. fig); fig direct

'steuerpflichtig adj taxable

'Steuerrad n MOT steering wheel

'Steuerruder n MAR helm, rudder

'Steuersenkung f tax reduction

'Steuerung ['ʃtɔyərʊŋ] f (-; -en) steering (system); ELECTR, TECH control (a. fig)

'Steuerzahler m, 'Steuerzahlerin f taxpayer

Stich [ʃtɪç] m (-[e]s; -e) prick; zo sting, bite; stab; cards: trick; engraving; im Stich lassen desert or abandon s.o., s.th., leave s.o. in the lurch, let s.o. down

Stichelei [ʃtɪçə'lai] F f (-; -en) dig, gibe

sticheln ['ʃɪçəln] F v/i (ge-, h) make digs, gibe (gegen at)

'Stichflamme f jet of flame

'stichhaltig adj valid, sound; watertight; nicht stichhaltig sein F not hold water

'Stichprobe f spot check

Stichtag m cutoff date; deadline

'Stichwahl f POL run-off

Stichwort n a) (-[e]s; -e) headword b) (-[e]s; -wörter) headword; THEA cue, b) Stichworte pl notes; das Wichtigste in Stichworten an outline of the main points

'Stichwortverzeichnis n index

'Stichwunde f MED stab

sticken ['ʃtɪkən] v/t and v/i (ge-, h) embroider

Stickerei [ʃtɪkə'rai] f (-; -en) embroidery

stickig ['ʃtɪkɪç] adj stuffy

'Stickstoff m (-[e]s; no pl) CHEM nitrogen

Stief... [ʃtiːf-] in cpds ...mutter etc: step...

Stiefel ['ʃtiːfəl] m (-s; -) boot

'Stiefmütterchen [-mʏtçən] n (-s; -) BOT pansy

stieg [ʃtiːk] pret of steigen

Stiege ['ʃtiːgə] Austrian f (-; -n) → Treppe

Stiel [ʃtiːl] m (-[e]s; -e) handle; stick; stem; BOT stalk

Stier [ʃtiːɐ] m (-[e]s; -e) zo bull; ASTR Taurus; er ist (ein) Stier he's a) Taurus

'Stierkampf m bullfight

stieß [ʃtiːs] pret of stoßen

Stift [ʃtɪft] m (-[e]s; -e) pen; pencil; crayon; TECH pin; peg

stiften ['ʃtɪftən] v/t (ge-, h) donate; fig cause

'Stiftung f (-; -en) donation

Stil [ʃtiːl] m (-[e]s; -e) style (a. fig); in großem Stil in (grand) style; fig on a large scale

stilistisch [ʃtiˈlɪstɪʃ] adj stylistic

still [ʃtɪl] adj quiet, silent; still; sei(d) still! be quiet!; halt still! keep still!; sich still verhalten keep quiet (or still)

Stille ['ʃtɪlə] f (-; no pl) silence, quiet (-ness); in aller Stille quietly; secretly

Stilleben n → Stillleben

stillen ['ʃtɪlən] v/t (ge-, h) nurse, breast-feed; fig relieve (pain); satisfy (curiosity etc); quench (one's thirst)

'stillhalten v/i (irr, halten, sep, -ge-, h) keep still

'Stillleben n PAINT still life

'stilllegen v/t (sep, -ge-, h) close down

'stillos adj lacking style, tasteless

'stillschweigend adj tacit

'Stillstand m (-[e]s; no pl) standstill, stop, fig a. stagnation (a. ECON); deadlock

'stillstehen v/i (irr, stehen, sep, -ge-, h) (have) stop(ped), (have) come to a standstill

'Stilmöbel pl period furniture

'stilvoll adj stylish; stilvoll sein have style

'Stimmband n ANAT vocal cord

'stimmberechtigt adj entitled to vote

Stimme ['ʃtɪmə] f (-; -n) voice; POL vote;

S

sich der Stimme enthalten abstain

'stimmen (*ge-*, *h*) **1.** *v/i* be right, be true, be correct; POL vote (*für* for; *gegen* against); *es stimmt et. nicht* (*damit* or *mit ihm*) there's s.th. wrong (with it or him); **2.** *v/t* MUS tune; *j-n traurig etc stimmen* make s.o. sad *etc*

'Stimmenthaltung *f* abstention

'Stimmrecht *n* right to vote

'Stimmung *f* (-; *-en*) mood; atmosphere; feeling

'stimmungsvoll *adj* atmospheric

'Stimmzettel *m* ballot (paper)

stinken ['ʃtɪŋkən] *v/i* (*irr*, *ge-*, *h*) stink (*a. fig*) (*nach* of)

Stipendium [ʃtiˈpɛndjʊm] *n* (-*s*; *-ien*) UNIV scholarship, grant

stippen ['ʃtɪpən] *v/t* (*ge-*, *h*) dip

'Stippvi‚site F *f* flying visit

Stirn [ʃtɪrn] *f* (-; *-en*) ANAT forehead; *die Stirn runzeln* frown

stöbern ['ʃtøːbən] F *v/i* (*ge-*, *h*) rummage (about)

stochern ['ʃtɔxən] *v/i* (*ge-*, *h*) *im Feuer stochern* poke the fire; *im Essen stochern* pick at one's food; *in den Zähnen stochern* pick one's teeth

Stock [ʃtɔk] *m* (-[*e*]*s*; *Stöcke* ['ʃtœkə]) stick; cane; ARCH stor(e)y, floor; *im ersten Stock* on the second (*Br* first) floor

'stock'dunkel F *adj* pitch-dark

stocken ['ʃtɔkən] *v/i* (*ge-*, *h*) stop (short); falter; *traffic*: be jammed

'stockend **1.** *adj* halting; **2.** *adv*: *stockend lesen* stumble through a text; *stockend sprechen* speak haltingly

'Stockfleck *m* mo(u)ld stain

'Stockung *f* (-; *-en*) holdup, delay

'Stockwerk *n* stor(e)y, floor

Stoff [ʃtɔf] *m* (-[*e*]*s*; *-e*) material, stuff (*a. F*); fabric, textile; cloth; CHEM, PHYS *etc* substance; *fig* subject (matter)

'stofflich *adj* material

'Stofftier *n* soft toy animal

'Stoffwechsel *m* BIOL metabolism

stöhnen ['ʃtøːnən] *v/i* (*ge-*, *h*) groan, moan (*a. fig*)

Stollen ['ʃtɔlən] *m* (-*s*; *-*) tunnel, gallery

stolpern ['ʃtɔlpən] *v/i* (*ge-*, *sein*) stumble (*über* acc over), trip (over) (*both a. fig*)

stolz [ʃtɔlts] *adj* proud (*auf* acc of)

Stolz *m* (-*es*; *no pl*) pride (*auf* acc in)

stolzieren [ʃtɔlˈtsiːrən] *v/i* (*no -ge-*, *sein*) strut, stalk

stopfen ['ʃtɔpfən] *v/t* (*ge-*, *h*) darn, mend; stuff, fill (*a. pipe*)

Stoppel ['ʃtɔpəl] *f* (-; *-n*) stubble

'Stoppelbart F *m* stubbly beard

'stoppelig *adj* stubbly, bristly

'Stoppelzieher *Austrian m* corkscrew

stoppen ['ʃtɔpən] *v/i* and *v/t* (*ge-*, *h*) stop (*a. fig*); *esp* SPORT time

'Stopplicht *n* (-[*e*]*s*; *-er*) MOT stop light

'Stoppschild *n* stop sign

'Stoppuhr *f* stopwatch

Stöpsel ['ʃtœpsəl] *m* (-*s*; *-*) stopper; plug

Storch [ʃtɔrç] *m* (-[*e*]*s*; *Störche* ['ʃtœrçəl]) ZO stork

stören ['ʃtøːrən] *v/t* and *v/i* (*ge-*, *h*) disturb; trouble; bother, annoy; be in the way; *lassen Sie sich nicht stören!* don't let me disturb you!; *darf ich Sie kurz stören?* may I trouble you for a minute?; *es (er) stört mich nicht* it (he) doesn't bother me, I don't mind (him); *stört es Sie(‚ wenn ich rauche)?* do you mind (my smoking or if I smoke)?

'Störenfried [-friːt] *m* (-[*e*]*s*; *-e*) troublemaker; intruder

'Störfall ['ʃtøːɐ̯-] *m* TECH accident

störrisch ['ʃtœrɪʃ] *adj* stubborn, obstinate

'Störung *f* (-; *-en*) disturbance; trouble (*a. TECH*); TECH breakdown; TV, *radio*: interference

Stoß [ʃtoːs] *m* (-*es*; *Stöße* ['ʃtøːsə]) push, shove; thrust; kick; butt; blow, knock; shock; MOT jolt; bump, esp TECH, PHYS impact; pile, stack

'Stoßdämpfer *m* MOT shock absorber

stoßen ['ʃtoːsən] *v/t* (*irr*, *ge-*, *h*) and *v/i* (*sein*) push, shove; thrust; kick; butt; knock, strike; pound; *stoßen gegen* or *an* (*acc*) bump or run into or against; *sich den Kopf stoßen* (*an dat*) knock one's head (against); *stoßen auf* (*acc*) strike (*oil etc*); *fig* come across; meet with

'stoßgesichert *adj* shockproof, shock-resistant

'Stoßstange *f* MOT bumper

'Stoßzahn *m* ZO tusk

'Stoßzeit *f* rush hour, peak hours

stottern ['ʃtɔtən] *v/i* and *v/t* (*ge-*, *h*) stutter

Str. ABBR of *Straße* St, Street; Rd, Road

'Strafanstalt *f* prison, penitentiary

'strafbar *adj* punishable, penal; *sich strafbar machen* commit an offense (*Br* offence)

Strafe ['ʃtraːfə] *f* (-; *-n*) punishment; JUR, ECON, SPORT penalty (*a. fig*); fine; *20 Mark Strafe zahlen müssen* be fined 20 marks; *zur Strafe* as a punishment

'strafen *v/t* (*ge-*, *h*) punish

straff [ʃtraf] *adj* tight; *fig* strict

'straffrei *adj*: *straffrei ausgehen* go unpunished

'Strafgefangene *m*, *f* prisoner, convict

Strafgesetz *n* criminal law

S

sträflich ['ʃtrɛːflɪç] **1.** adj inexcusable; **2.** adv: **sträflich vernachlässigen** neglect badly

Strafmi‚nute f SPORT penalty minute

Strafpro‚zess m JUR criminal action, trial

Strafraum m SPORT penalty area (F box)

Strafstoß m SPORT penalty kick

Straftat f JUR criminal offense (Br offence); crime

Strafzettel m ticket

Strahl [ʃtraːl] m -[e]s, -en ray (a. fig); beam; flash; jet

strahlen ['ʃtraːlən] v/i (ge-, h) radiate; shine (brightly); fig beam (**vor** with)

'Strahlen... in cpds PHYS \133schutz etc: radiation ...

'Strahlung f (-; -en) PHYS radiation

Strähne ['ʃtrɛːnə] f (-; -n) strand; streak

stramm [ʃtram] adj tight

strammstehen MIL stand to attention

strampeln ['ʃtrampəln] v/i (ge-, h) kick

Strand [ʃtrant] m -[e]s; Strände ['ʃtrɛndə] beach; **am Strand** on the beach

stranden ['ʃtrandən] v/i (ge-, sein) MAR strand; fig fail

'Strandgut n flotsam and jetsam (a. fig)

Strandkorb m roofed wicker beach chair

Strang [ʃtraŋ] m -[e]s; Stränge ['ʃtrɛŋə] rope; esp ANAT cord

Strapaze [ʃtra'paːtsə] f (-; -n) strain, exertion, hardship

strapazieren [ʃtrapa'tsiːrən] v/t (no -ge-, h) wear s.o. or s.th. out; be hard on F

strapazierfähig adj longwearing, Br hardwearing

strapaziös [ʃtrapa'tsjøːs] adj strenuous

Straße ['ʃtraːsə] f (-; -n) road; street; GEOGR strait; **auf der Straße** on the road; on (Br a. in) the street

'Straßenarbeiten pl roadworks

Straßenbahn f streetcar, Br tram

Straßenca‚fé n sidewalk (Br pavement) café

Straßenkarte f road map

Straßenkehrer [-keːrɐ] m (-s; -) street sweeper

Straßenkreuzung f crossroads; intersection

Straßenlage f MOT roadholding

Straßenrand m roadside; **am Straßenrand** at or by the roadside

Straßensperre f road block

strategisch [ʃtra'teːgɪʃ] adj strategic

sträuben ['ʃtrɔʏbən] v/t and v/refl (ge-, h) ruffle (up); bristle (up); **sich sträuben gegen** struggle against

Strauch [ʃtraʊx] m (-[e]s; Sträucher ['ʃtrɔʏçɐ] BOT shrub, bush

straucheln ['ʃtraʊxəln] v/i (ge-, sein) stumble

Strauß¹ [ʃtraʊs] m (-es; -e) ZO ostrich

Strauß² m (-es; Sträuße ['ʃtrɔʏsə]) bunch, bouquet

Strebe ['ʃtreːbə] f (-; -n) prop, stay (a. AVIAT, MAR)

'streben v/i (ge-, h) strive (**nach** for, after)

Streber(in) ['ʃtreːbɐ] m (-s; -) pusher; PED etc grind, Br swot

strebsam ['ʃtreːp-] adj ambitious

Strecke ['ʃtrɛkə] f (-; -n) distance (a. SPORT, MATH), way; route; RAIL line; SPORT course; stretch; **zur Strecke bringen** kill; esp fig hunt down

'strecken v/t (ge-, h) stretch (out), extend

Streich [ʃtraɪç] m (-[e]s; -e) trick, prank, practical joke; **j-m e-n Streich spielen** play a trick or joke on s.o.

streicheln ['ʃtraɪçəln] v/t (ge-, h) stroke, caress

streichen ['ʃtraɪçən] v/t and v/i (irr, ge-, h) paint; spread; cross out; cancel; MAR strike; MUS bow; **mit der Hand streichen über** (acc) run one's hand over; **streichen durch** roam (acc)

Streicher(in) ['ʃtraɪçɐ (-çərɪn]) (-s; -/-; -nen) MUS string player, pl the strings

'Streichholz n match

'Streichinstru‚ment n MUS string instrument

Streichor‚chester n MUS string orchestra

'Streichung f (-; -en) cancellation; cut

Streife ['ʃtraɪfə] f (-; -n) patrol; **auf Streife gehen** go on patrol; **auf Streife sein** in (dat) patrol

'streifen v/t and v/i (ge-, h) touch, brush (against); MOT scrape against; graze; slip (**von** off); fig touch on; **streifen durch** roam (acc), wander through

'Streifen m (-s; -) stripe; strip

'Streifenwagen m squad (Br patrol) car

'Streifschuss m MED graze

'Streifzug m tour (**durch** of)

Streik [ʃtraɪk] m (-[e]s; -s) strike, walkout; **wilder Streik** wildcat strike

'Streikbrecher m strikebreaker, Br blackleg, contp scab

streiken ['ʃtraɪkən] v/i (ge-, h) (go or be on) strike; F fig refuse (to work etc)

'Streikende m, f (-n; -n) striker

'Streikposten m picket

Streit [ʃtraɪt] m (-[e]s; -e) quarrel; argument; fight; POL etc dispute; **Streit anfangen** pick a fight or quarrel; **Streit suchen** be looking for trouble

streiten ['ʃtraɪtən] v/i and v/refl (irr, ge-, h) quarrel, argue, fight (all: **wegen, über** acc about, over); **sich streiten um** fight for

'Streitfrage f (point at) issue
streitig ['ʃtraitɪç] adj: **j-m et. streitig machen** dispute s.o.'s right to s.th.
'Streitkräfte pl MIL (armed) forces
'streitsüchtig adj quarrelsome
streng [ʃtrɛŋ] adj strict; severe; harsh; rigid; **streng genommen** strictly speaking
Strenge ['ʃtrɛŋə] f (-; no pl) strictness; severity; harshness; rigidity
'strenggläubig adj REL orthodox
Stress [ʃtrɛs] m (-es; no pl) stress; **im Stress** under stress
Streu [ʃtrɔy] f (-; -en) AGR litter
'streuen v/t and v/i (ge-, h) scatter (a. PHYS); spread; sprinkle; grit
streunen ['ʃtrɔynən] v/i (ge-, sein), streunend adj stray
strich [ʃtrɪç] pret of streichen
Strich m (-[e]s; -e) line; stroke; F redlight district; F **auf den Strich gehen** walk the streets
Strichkode m bar code
Strichjunge F m male prostitute
'strichweise adv in parts; **strichweise Regen** scattered showers
Strick [ʃtrɪk] m (-[e]s; -e) cord; rope
stricken ['ʃtrɪkən] v/t and v/i (ge-, h) knit
'Strickjacke f cardigan
'Strickleiter f rope ladder
'Stricknadel f knitting needle
'Strickwaren pl knitwear
'Strickzeug n knitting (things)
Striemen ['ʃtriːmən] m (-s; -) welt, weal
stritt [ʃtrɪt] pret of streiten
strittig ['ʃtrɪtɪç] adj controversial; **strittiger Punkt** point at issue
Stroh [ʃtroː] n (-[e]s; no pl) straw; thatch
'Strohdach n thatch(ed) roof
'Strohhalm m straw
'Strohhut m straw hat
'Strohwitwe F f grass widow
'Strohwitwer F m grass widower
Strom [ʃtroːm] m (-[e]s; Ströme ['ʃtrøːmə]) (large) river; current (a. ELECTR); **ein Strom von** a stream of (a. fig); **es gießt in Strömen** it's pouring (with rain)
strom'ab(wärts) adv downstream
strom'auf(wärts) adv upstream
'Stromausfall m ELECTR power failure, blackout
strömen ['ʃtrøːmən] v/i (ge-, sein) stream (a. fig), flow, run; pour (a. fig)
'Stromkreis m ELECTR circuit
'stromlinienförmig adj streamlined
'Stromschnelle f (-; -n) GEOGR rapid
'Stromstärke f ELECTR amperage
'Strömung f (-; -en) current, fig a. trend
Strophe ['ʃtroːfə] f (-; -n) stanza, verse

strotzen ['ʃtrɔtsən] v/i (ge-, h) **strotzen von** be full of, abound with; **strotzen vor** (dat) be bursting with
Strudel ['ʃtruːdəl] m (-s; -) whirlpool (a. fig), eddy
Struktur [ʃtrʊkˈtuːɐ] f (-; -en) structure, pattern
Strumpf [ʃtrʊmpf] m (-[e]s; Strümpfe ['ʃtrʏmpfə]) stocking
'Strumpfhose f pantyhose, Br tights
struppig ['ʃtrʊpɪç] adj shaggy
Stück [ʃtyk] n (-[e]s; -e) piece; part; lump; AGR head (a. pl); THEA play; **2 Mark das Stück** 2 marks each; **im** or **am Stück** in one piece; **in Stücke schlagen (reißen)** smash (tear) to pieces
'stückweise adv bit by bit (a. fig); ECON by the piece
Student [ʃtuˈdɛnt] m (-en; -en), Stu'dentin f (-; -nen) student
Studie ['ʃtuːdjə] f (-; -n) study (**über** acc of)
'Studienplatz m university or college place
studieren [ʃtuˈdiːrən] v/t and v/i (no -ge-, h) study, be a student (of) (an dat at)
Studium ['ʃtuːdjʊm] n (-s; -ien) studies; **das Studium der Medizin** etc the study of medicine etc
Stufe ['ʃtuːfə] f (-; -n) step; level; stage
'Stufenbarren m SPORT uneven parallel bars
Stuhl [ʃtuːl] m (-[e]s; Stühle ['ʃtyːlə]) chair; MED stool
'Stuhlgang m (-[e]s; no pl) MED (bowel) movement
'Stuhllehne f back of a chair
stülpen ['ʃtʏlpən] v/t (ge-, h) put (auf acc, über acc over, on)
stumm [ʃtʊm] adj dumb, mute; fig silent
Stummel ['ʃtʊməl] m (-s; -) stub, stump, butt
'Stummfilm m silent film
Stümper ['ʃtʏmpɐ] F m (-s; -) bungler
stumpf [ʃtʊmpf] adj blunt, dull (a. fig)
Stumpf m (-[e]s; Stümpfe ['ʃtʏmpfə]) stump, stub
'stumpfsinnig adj dull; monotonous
Stunde ['ʃtʊndə] f (-; -n) hour; PED class, lesson; period
'Stundenkilo,meter m kilometer (Br kilometre) per hour
'stundenlang 1. adj: **nach stundenlangem Warten** after hours of waiting; 2. adv for hours (and hours)
'Stundenlohn m hourly wage
'Stundenplan m schedule, Br timetable
'stundenweise adv by the hour
'Stundenzeiger m hour hand

stündlich ['ʃtʏntlɪç] **1.** *adj* hourly; **2.** *adv* hourly, every hour

Stupsnase ['ʃtʊps-] F *f* snub nose

stur [ʃtuːɐ] F *adj* pigheaded

Sturm [ʃtʊrm] *m* (-[e]s; *Stürme* ['ʃtʏrmə]) storm (*a. fig*)

stürmen ['ʃtʏrmən] *v/t* (*ge-, h*) *and v/i* (*ge-, sein*) storm; SPORT attack; rush

Stürmer(in) ['ʃtʏrmɐ (-[mərɪn]) (-s; -/-; -nen) SPORT forward; *esp* soccer: striker

stürmisch ['ʃtʏrmɪʃ] *adj* stormy; *fig* wild, vehement

Sturz [ʃtʊrts] *m* (-es; *Stürze* ['ʃtʏrtsə]) fall (*a. fig*); POL etc: overthrow

stürzen ['ʃtʏrtsən] **1.** *v/i* (*ge-, sein*) fall; crash; rush, dash; *schwer stürzen* have a bad fall; **2.** *v/t* (*ge-, h*) throw; POL etc: overthrow; *j-n ins Unglück stürzen* ruin s.o.; *sich stürzen aus* throw o.s. out of; *sich stürzen auf* (*acc*) throw o.s. at

Sturzflug *m* AVIAT nosedive

Sturzhelm *m* crash helmet

Stute ['ʃtuːtə] *f* (-; -n) ZO mare

Stütze ['ʃtʏtsə] *f* (-; -n) support, prop; *fig a.* aid

stutzen ['ʃtʊtsən] (*ge-, h*) **1.** *v/t* trim, clip; **2.** *v/i* stop short; (begin to) wonder

stützen ['ʃtʏtsən] *v/t* (*ge-, h*) support (*a. fig*); *sich stützen auf* (*acc*) lean on; *fig* be based on

Stützpfeiler *m* ARCH supporting column

Stützpunkt *m* MIL base (*a. fig*)

Styropor® [ʃtyro'poːɐ] *n* (-s; *no pl*) Styrofoam®, *Br* polystyrene

s. u. ABBR *of* *siehe unten* see below

Subjekt [zʊp'jɛkt] *n* (-[e]s; -e) LING subject; *contp* character

subjektiv [zʊpjɛk'tiːf] *adj* subjective

Substantiv ['zʊpstantiːf] *n* (-s; -e) LING noun

Substanz [zʊp'stants] *f* (-; -en) substance (*a. fig*)

subtrahieren [zʊptra'hiːrən] *v/t* (*no ge-, h*) MATH subtract

Subtraktion [zʊptrak'tsjoːn] *f* (-; -en) MATH subtraction

subventionieren [zʊpvɛntsjo'niːrən] *v/t* (*no ge-, h*) subsidize

Suche ['zuːxə] *f* (-; *no pl*) search (*nach* for); *auf der Suche nach* in search of

suchen *v/t and v/i* (*ge-, h*) look for; search for; *gesucht: ...* wanted ...; *was hat er hier zu suchen?* what's he doing here?; *er hat hier nichts zu suchen* he has no business to be here

Sucher [zu:xɐ] *m* (-s; -) PHOT viewfinder

Sucht [zʊxt] *f* (-; *Süchte* ['zʏçtə]) addiction (*nach* to); mania (*for*)

süchtig ['zʏçtiç] *adj*: *süchtig sein* be ad-

dicted to *drugs* etc, be a *drug* etc addict

Süchtige ['zʏçtigə] *m*, *f* (-n; -n) addict

Süden ['zyːdən] *m* (-s; *no pl*) south; *nach Süden* south(wards)

Südfrüchte ['zyːt-] *pl* tropical *or* southern fruits

'**südlich 1.** *adj* south(ern); southerly; **2.** *adv*: *südlich von* (to the) south of

Süd|osten *m* southeast

süd|östlich *adj* southeast(ern); southeasterly

'**Südpol** *m* South Pole

'**südwärts** [-vɛrts] *adv* southward(s)

'**Südwesten** *m* southwest

süd|westlich *adj* southwest(ern); southwesterly

'**Südwind** *m* south wind

Sülze ['zʏltsə] *f* (-; -n) GASTR jellied meat

Summe ['zʊmə] *f* (-; -n) sum (*a. fig*); amount; (sum) total

summen ['zʊmən] *v/i and v/t* (*ge-, h*) buzz, hum

summieren [zʊ'miːrən] *v/refl* (*no ge-, h*) add up (*auf acc* to)

Sumpf [zʊmpf] *m* (-es; *Sümpfe* ['zʏmpfə]) swamp, bog

'**sumpfig** *adj* swampy, marshy

Sünde ['zʏndə] *f* (-; -n) sin (*a. fig*)

Sündenbock F *m* scapegoat

Sünder ['zʏndɐ] *m* (-s; -), **Sünderin** *f* (-; -nen) sinner

sündig ['zʏndɪç] *adj* sinful

sündigen ['zʏndɪgən] *v/i* (*ge-, h*) (commit a) sin

Super... ['zuːpɐ-] *in cpds ...macht etc: mst* super...

'**Super** *n* (-s; *no pl*) soup

Supermarkt *m* supermarket

Suppe ['zʊpə] *f* (-; -n) soup

'**Suppen...** *in cpds ...löffel, ...teller, ...küche etc:* soup ...

Surfbrett ['zœːɐf-] *n* sail board; surfboard

surfen *v/i* (*ge-, h*) go surfing

surren ['zʊrən] *v/i* (*ge-, h*) whirr; buzz

süß [zyːs] *adj* sweet, sugary (*both a. fig*)

Süße ['zyːsə] *f* (-; *no pl*) sweetness

'**süßen** *v/t* (*ge-, h*) sweeten

Süßigkeiten ['zyːsɪçkaitən] *pl* sweets, candy

'**süßlich** *adj* sweetish; *contp* mawkish, sugary

'**süß|sauer** *adj* GASTR sweet-and-sour

'**Süßstoff** *m* sweetener

'**Süßwasser** *n* fresh water

Symbol [zʏm'boːl] *n* (-s; -e) symbol

S

Symbolik [zym'bo:lɪk] *f* (-; *no pl*) symbolism

sym'bolisch *adj* symbolic(al)

Symmetrie [zyme'tri:] *f* (-; *-n*) symmetry

symmetrisch [zy'me:trɪʃ] *adj* symmetric(al)

Sympathie [zympa'ti:] *f* (-; *-n*) liking (**für** for); sympathy

Sympathisant(in) [zympati'zant(ɪn)] (*-en; -en/-; -nen*) sympathizer

sympathisch [zym'pa:tɪʃ] *adj* nice, likable; *er ist mir sympathisch* I like him

Symphonie [zymfo'ni:] *f* (-; *-n*) *etc* → *Sinfonie*

Symptom [zymp'to:m] *n* (-s; *-e*) symptom

Synagoge [zyna'go:gə] *f* (-; *-n*) synagogue

synchron [zyn'kro:n] *adj* TECH synchronous

synchronisieren [zynkroni'zi:rən] *v/t* (*no -ge-, h*) synchronize; *film etc:* dub

synonym [zyno'ny:m] *adj* synonymous

Syno'nym *n* (-s; *-e*) synonym

Synthese [zyn'te:zə] *f* (-; *-n*) synthesis

synthetisch [zyn'te:tɪʃ] *adj* synthetic

System [zys'te:m] *n* (-s; *-e*) system

systematisch [zyste'ma:tɪʃ] *adj* systematic, methodical

Sys'temfehler *m* EDP system error

Szene ['stse:nə] *f* (-; *-n*) scene (*a. fig*)

Szenerie [stsenə'ri:] *f* (-; *-n*) scenery; setting

T

Tabak ['ta:bak] *m* (-s; *-e*) tobacco

Tabakgeschäft *n* SPORT tobacconist's

Tabakwaren *pl* tobacco products

Tabelle [ta'bɛlə] *f* (-; *-n*) table (*a.* MATH, SPORT)

Ta'bellenkalkulati,on *f* EDP spreadsheet

Tabellenplatz *m* SPORT position

Tablett [ta'blɛt] *n* (-[*e*]*s; -s*) tray

Tablette [ta'blɛtə] *f* (-; *-n*) tablet

tabu [ta'bu:] *adj*, **Ta'bu** *n* (-s; *-s*) taboo

Tabulator [tabu'la:tor] *m* (-s; *-en* [-la'to:rən]) tabulator

Tachometer [taxo'me:tɐ] *m, n* (-s; -) MOT speedometer

Tadel ['ta:dəl] *m* (-s; -) blame; censure, reproof, rebuke

'tadellos *adj* faultless; blameless; excellent; perfect

'tadeln *v/t* (*ge-, h*) criticize, blame; censure, reprove, rebuke (*all:* **wegen** for)

Tafel ['ta:fəl] *f* PED *etc* blackboard; (bulletin, *esp Br* notice) board; sign; tablet, plaque; GASTR bar (*of chocolate*)

'täfeln ['tɛ:fəln] *v/t* (*ge-, h*) panel

'Täfelung *f* (-; *-en*) panel(l)ing

Taft [taft] *m* (-[*e*]*s; -e*) taffeta

Tag [ta:k] *m* (-[*e*]*s; -e* ['ta:gə]) day; daylight; *welchen Tag haben wir heute?* what day is it today?; *heute* (*morgen*) *in 14 Tagen* two weeks from today (tomorrow); *e-s Tages* one day; *den ganzen Tag* all day; *am Tage* during the day; *Tag und Nacht* night and day; *am*

helllichten Tag in broad daylight; *ein freier Tag* a day off; *guten Tag!* hello!, hi!; how do you do?; (*j-m*) *guten Tag sagen* say hello (to s.o.); F *sie hat ihre Tage* she has her period; *unter Tage* underground; → *zutage*

Tagebau ['ta:gə-] *m* (-[*e*]*s; -e*) opencast mining

Tagebuch *n* diary; *Tagebuch führen* keep a diary

'tagelang *adv* for days

'tagen *v/i* (*ge-, h*) meet, hold a meeting; JUR be in session

'Tagesanbruch *m*: *bei Tagesanbruch* at daybreak, at dawn

Tagesgespräch *n* talk of the day

Tageskarte *f* day ticket; GASTR menu for the day

Tageslicht *n* (-[*e*]*s; no pl*) daylight

Tagesmutter *f* childminder

Tagesordnung *f* agenda

Tagesstätte *f* day care center (*Br* centre)

Tagestour *f* day trip

Tageszeit *f* time of day; *zu jeder Tageszeit* at any hour

Tageszeitung *f* daily (paper)

'tageweise *adv* by the day

täglich ['tɛ:klɪç] *adj and adv* daily

'Tagschicht *f* ECON day shift

'tagsüber *adv* during the day

'Tagung *f* (-; *-en*) conference

Taille ['taljə] *f* (-; *-n*) waist; waistline

tailliert [ta'ji:ɐt] *adj* waisted, tapered

Takelage [takə'la:ʒə] *f* (-; -n) MAR rigging

Takt [takt] *m* (-[e]s; -e) a) (*no pl*) MUS time, measure, beat, b) MUS bar, c) MOT stroke, d) (*no pl*) tact; **den Takt halten** MUS keep time

Taktik ['taktik] *f* (-; -en) MIL tactics (*a. fig*)

'**taktisch** *adj* tactical

'**taktlos** *adj* tactless

'**Taktstock** *m* MUS baton

'**Taktstrich** *m* MUS bar

'**taktvoll** *adj* tactful

Tal [ta:l] *n* (-[e]s; Täler ['tɛ:lɐ]) valley

Talar [ta'la:ɐ] *m* (-s; -e) robe, gown

Talent [ta'lɛnt] *n* (-[e]s; -e) talent (*a. person*), gift

talentiert [talɛn'ti:ɐt] *adj* talented, gifted

Talg [talk] *m* (-[e]s; -e) tallow; GASTR suet

Talisman ['ta:lɪsman] *m* (-s; -e) talisman, charm

Talkmaster ['tɔ:k-] *m* (-s; -) TV talk (*Br* chat) show host

Talkshow [-ʃoʊ] *f* (-; -s) TV talk (*Br* chat) show

'**Talsperre** *f* dam, barrage

Tampon ['tampɔn] *m* (-s; -s) tampon

Tandler ['tandlɐ] *Austrian m* (-s; -) second-hand dealer

Tang [taŋ] *m* (-[e]s; -e) BOT seaweed

Tank [taŋk] *m* (-s; -s) tank

tanken ['taŋkən] *v/t* (ge-, h) get some gasoline (*Br* petrol), fill up

Tanker ['taŋkɐ] *m* (-s; -) MAR tanker

'**Tankstelle** *f* filling (*or* gas, *Br* petrol) station

'**Tankwart** *m* (-[e]s; -e) gas station (*Br* petrol pump) attendant

Tanne ['tanə] *f* (-; -n) BOT fir (tree)

'**Tannenbaum** *m* Christmas tree

'**Tannenzapfen** *m* BOT fir cone

Tante ['tantə] *f* (-; -n) aunt; **Tante Lindy** Aunt Lindy

Tante-Emma-Laden F *m* mom-and-pop store, *Br* corner shop

Tantiemen [tɑ̃'tjeːmən] *pl* royalties

Tanz [tants] *m* (-es; Tänze ['tɛntsə]), **tanzen** ['tantsən] *v/i* (ge-, h, sein) *and v/t* (ge-, h) dance

Tänzer ['tɛntsɐ] *m* (-s; -), **Tänzerin** ['tɛntsərɪn] *f* (-; -nen) dancer

'**Tanzfläche** *f* dance floor

'**Tanzkurs** *m* dancing lessons

'**Tanzmu,sik** *f* dance music

'**Tanzschule** *f* dancing school

Tapete [ta'peːtə] *f* (-; -n), **tapezieren** [tape'tsiːrən] *v/t* (*no* -ge-, h) wallpaper

tapfer ['tapfɐ] *adj* brave; courageous

'**Tapferkeit** *f* (-; *no pl*) bravery; courage

Tarif [ta'riːf] *m* (-[e]s; -e) rate(s), tariff; (wage) scale

Tariflohn *m* standard wage(s)

Tarifverhandlungen *pl* wage negotiations, collective bargaining

tarnen ['tarnən] *v/t* (ge-, h) camouflage; *fig* disguise

'**Tarnung** *f* (-; -en) camouflage

Tasche ['taʃə] *f* (-; -n) bag; pocket

'**Taschenbuch** *n* paperback

'**Taschendieb** *m* pickpocket

'**Taschengeld** *n* allowance, *Br* pocket money

'**Taschenlampe** *f* flashlight, *Br* torch

'**Taschenmesser** *n* penknife, pocketknife

'**Taschenrechner** *m* pocket calculator

'**Taschenschirm** *m* telescopic umbrella

'**Taschentuch** *n* handkerchief, F hankie

'**Taschenuhr** *f* pocket watch

Tasse ['tasə] *f* (-; -n) cup; **e-e Tasse Tee** *etc* a cup of tea *etc*

Tastatur [tasta'tuːɐ] *f* (-; -en) keyboard, keys

Taste ['tastə] *f* (-; -n) key

tasten ['tastən] *v/i* (ge-, h) **1.** *v/i* grope (**nach** for), feel (for); fumble (for); **2.** *v/t* touch, feel; **sich tasten** feel *or* grope (*a. fig*) one's way

'**Tastentele,fon** *n* push-button phone

'**Tastsinn** *m* (-[e]s; *no pl*) sense of touch

tat [ta:t] *pret of* **tun**

Tat *f* (-; -en) act, deed; action; JUR offense, *Br* offence; **j-n auf frischer Tat ertappen** catch s.o. in the act

'**tatenlos** *adj* inactive, passive

Täter ['tɛːtɐ] *m* (-s; -), **Täterin** *f* (-; -nen) culprit; JUR offender

tätig ['tɛːtɪç] *adj* active; busy; **tätig sein bei** be employed with; **tätig werden** act, take action

'**Tätigkeit** *f* (-; -en) activity; work; occupation, job; **in Tätigkeit** in action

'**Tatkraft** *f* (-; *no pl*) energy

'**tatkräftig** *adj* energetic, active

tätlich ['tɛːtlɪç] *adj* violent; **tätlich werden gegen** assault

'**Tätlichkeiten** *pl* (acts of) violence; JUR assault (and battery)

Tatort *m* JUR scene of the crime

tätowieren [tɛto'viːrən] *v/t* (*no* -ge-, h), **Täto'wierung** *f* (-; -en) tattoo

'**Tatsache** *f* fact

'**tatsächlich 1.** *adj* actual, real; **2.** *adv* actually, in fact; really

tätscheln ['tɛːtʃəln] *v/t* (ge-, h) pat, pet

Tatze ['tatsə] *f* (-; -n) ZO paw (*a. fig*)

Tau[1] [tau] *n* (-[e]s; -e) rope

Tau[2] *m* (-[e]s; *no pl*) dew

taub [taup] *adj* deaf (*fig* **gegen** to); numb, benumbed

Taube ['taubə] *f* (-; -n) ZO pigeon; *esp fig*

dove

'Taubenschlag *m* pigeonhouse

'Taubheit *f* (-; *no pl*) deafness; numbness

'taubstumm *adj* deaf-and-dumb

'Taubstumme *m, f* (-n; -n) deaf mute

tauchen ['tauxən] **1.** *v/i* (ge-, *h, sein*) dive (**nach** for); SPORT skin-dive; *submarine:* a. submerge; stay underwater; **2.** *v/t* (*h*) dip (**in** *acc* into); duck

Taucher ['tauxɐ] *m* (-s; -) (SPORT skin) diver

'Tauchsport *m* skin diving

tauen ['tauən] *v/i* (ge-, *sein*) and *v/t* (ge-, *h*) thaw, melt

Taufe ['taufə] *f* (-; -n) baptism, christening

'taufen *v/t* (ge-, *h*) baptize, christen

'Taufpate *m* godfather

'Taufpatin *f* godmother

'Taufschein *m* certificate of baptism

taugen ['taugən] *v/i* (ge-, *h*) be good *or* fit *or* of use *or* suited (*all:* **zu, für** for); **nichts taugen** be no good; F **taugt es was?** is it any good?

tauglich ['taukliç] *adj* MIL fit (for service)

Taumel ['tauməl] *m* (-s; *no pl*) dizziness; rapture, ecstasy

'taumelig *adj* dizzy

'taumeln *v/i* (ge-, *sein*) stagger, reel

Tausch [tauʃ] *m* (-[e]s; -e) exchange, F swap

tauschen ['tauʃən] *v/t* (ge-, *h*) exchange, F swap (*both:* **gegen** for); switch; change; **ich möchte nicht mit ihm tauschen** I wouldn't like to be in his shoes

täuschen ['tɔyʃən] *v/t* (ge-, *h*) deceive, fool; delude; cheat; *a.* SPORT feint; **sich täuschen** deceive o.s.; be mistaken; **sich täuschen lassen von** be taken in by; **täuschende Ähnlichkeit** striking similarity

'Täuschung *f* (-; -en) deception; delusion; JUR deceit; *a.* PED cheating

tausend ['tauzənt] *adj* a thousand

'tausendst *adj* thousandth

'Tausendstel *n* (-s; -) thousandth (part)

'Tautropfen *m* dewdrop

'Tauwetter *n* thaw

'Tauziehen *n* (-s; *no pl*) SPORT tug-of-war (*a. fig*)

Taxi ['taksi] *n* (-s; -s) taxi(cab), cab

taxieren [ta'ksiːrən] *v/t* (*no* -ge-, *h*) rate, estimate (**auf** *acc* at)

'Taxistand *m* cabstand, *esp Br* taxi rank

Technik ['tɛçnɪk] *f* (-; -en) a) (*no pl*) technology, engineering, b) technique (*a.* SPORT *etc*), MUS execution

Techniker ['tɛçnɪkɐ] *m* (-s; -), 'Technikerin *f* (-; -nen) engineer; technician (*a.* SPORT *etc*)

technisch ['tɛçnɪʃ] *adj* technical; technological; **technische Hochschule** school *etc* of technology

Technologie [tɛçnolo'giː] *f* (-; -n) technology

technologisch [tɛçno'loːgɪʃ] *adj* technological

Tee [teː] *m* (-s; -s) tea; (**e-n**) **Tee trinken** have some tea; (**e-n**) **Tee machen** or **ko-chen** make some tea

'Teebeutel *m* teabag

'Teekanne *f* teapot

'Teelöffel *m* teaspoon

Teer [teːɐ] *m* (-[e]s; -e), teeren ['teːrən] *v/t* (ge-, *h*) tar

'Teesieb *n* tea strainer

'Teetasse *f* teacup

Teich [taiç] *m* (-[e]s; -e) pool, pond

Teig [taik] *m* (-[e]s; -e) dough, paste

teigig ['taigiç] *adj* doughy, pasty

'Teigwaren *pl* pasta

Teil [tail] *m, n* (-[e]s; -e) part; portion, share; component; **zum Teil** partly, in part

Teil... *in cpds* ...**erfolg** *etc:* partial ...

'teilbar *adj* divisible

'Teilchen *n* (-s; -) particle

teilen ['tailən] *v/t* (ge-, *h*) divide; share

'teilhaben *v/i* (*irr,* **haben**, *sep, -ge-, h*) **teilhaben an** (*dat*) have a share in

'Teilhaber(in) [-haːbɐ (-bərɪn)] (-s; -/-; -nen) ECON partner

'Teilnahme [-naːmə] *f* (-; *no pl*) participation (**an** *dat* in); *fig* interest (in); sympathy (for)

'teilnahmslos *adj* indifferent; *esp* MED apathetic

'Teilnahmslosigkeit *f* (-; *no pl*) indifference; apathy

'teilnehmen *v/i* (*irr,* **nehmen**, *sep, -ge-, h*) **teilnehmen an** (*dat*) take part *or* participate in; share (in)

'Teilnehmer(in) [-neːmɐ (-mərɪn)] (-s; -/-; -nen) participant; UNIV student; SPORT competitor

teils *adv* partly

'Teilstrecke *f* stage, leg

'Teilung *f* (-; -en) division

'teilweise *adv* partly, in part

'Teilzahlung *f* → **Abzahlung, Rate**

Teint [tɛ̃ː] *m* (-s; -s) complexion

Tel. *ABBR of* Telefon tel., telephone

Telefon [tele'foːn] *n* (-s; -e) telephone, phone; **am Telefon** on the (tele)phone; **Telefon haben** have a (*Br* be on the) (tel-e)phone; **ans Telefon gehen** answer the (tele)phone

Telefonanruf *m* (tele)phone call

Telefonanschluss *m* telephone connection

Telefonapparat *m* telephone, phone

Telefonat [telefoˈnaːt] *n* (-[e]s; -e) → **Telefongespräch**

Tele'fonbuch *n* telephone directory, phone book

Telefongebühr *f* telephone charge

Telefongespräch *n* (tele)phone call

telefonieren [telefoˈniːrən] *v/i* (no -ge-, h) (tele)phone; be on the phone; **mit j-m telefonieren** talk to s.o. on the phone

telefonisch [teleˈfoːnɪʃ] **1.** *adj* telephonic, telephone ...; **2.** *adv* by (tele)phone, over the (tele)phone

Telefonist [telefoˈnɪst] *m* (-en; -en), **Telefo'nistin** *f* (-; -nen) (telephone) operator

Tele'fonkarte *f* phonecard

Telefonleitung *f* telephone line

Telefonnetz *n* telephone network

Telefonnummer *f* (tele)phone number

Telefonzelle *f* (tele)phone booth, *esp Br* (tele)phone box, *Br* call box

Telefonzen,trale *f* switchboard

telegrafieren [telegraˈfiːrən] *v/t and v/i* (no -ge-, h) telegraph, wire; cable

telegrafisch [teleˈgraːfɪʃ] *adj and adv* by telegraph, by wire, by cable

Telegramm [teleˈgram] *n* (-s; -e) telegram, wire, cable(gram)

Teleobjektiv [ˈteːlə-] *n* telephoto lens

Telephon *n* → **Telefon**

Teletext [ˈteːlə-] *m* teletext

Teller [ˈtɛlə] *m* (-s; -) plate

Tellerwäscher [-vɛʃə] *m* (-s; -) dishwasher

Tempel [ˈtɛmpəl] *m* (-s; -) temple

Temperament [tɛmpəraˈmɛnt] *n* (-[e]s; -e) temper(ament); life, F pep

tempera'mentlos *adj* lifeless, dull

temperamentvoll *adj* full of life *or* F pep

Temperatur [tɛmpəraˈtuːɐ] *f* (-; -en) temperature; **j-s Temperatur messen** take s.o.'s temperature

Tempo [ˈtɛmpo] *n* (-s; -s, -pi) speed; *MUS* time; **mit Tempo ...** at a speed of ... an hour

Tendenz [tɛnˈdɛnts] *f* (-; -en) tendency, trend; leaning

tendenziös [tɛndɛnˈtsjøːs] *adj* tendentious

tendieren [tɛnˈdiːrən] *v/i* (no -ge-, h) tend (**zu** towards; **dazu, et. zu tun** to do s.th.)

Tennis [ˈtɛnɪs] *n* (-; no pl) tennis

Tennisplatz *m* tennis court

Tennisschläger *m* tennis racket

Tennisspieler(in) *m* tennis player

Tenor [teˈnoːɐ] *m* (-s; Tenöre [teˈnøːrə]) *MUS* tenor

Teppich [ˈtɛpɪç] *m* (-s; -e) carpet

'**Teppichboden** *m* fitted carpet, wall-to--wall carpeting

Termin [tɛrˈmiːn] *m* (-s; -e) date; deadline; engagement; **e-n Termin vereinbaren (einhalten, absagen)** make (keep, cancel) an appointment

Terminal [ˈtøːəminal] a) *m, n* (-s; -s) AVIAT terminal, b) *n* (-s; -s) EDP terminal

Terrasse [tɛˈrasə] *f* (-; -n) terrace

ter'rassenförmig [-fœrmɪç] *adj* terraced, in terraces

Terrine [tɛˈriːnə] *f* (-; -n) tureen

Territorium [tɛriˈtoːrjum] *n* (-s; -ien) territory

Terror [ˈtɛroːɐ] *m* (-s; no pl) terror

terrorisieren [tɛroriˈziːrən] *v/t* (no -ge-, h) terrorize

Terrorismus [tɛroˈrɪsmus] *m* (-; no pl) terrorism

Terrorist(in) [-ˈrɪst(ɪn)] (-en; -en/-; -nen), **terro'ristisch** *adj* terrorist

Testament [tɛstaˈmɛnt] *n* (-[e]s; -e) (last) will; JUR last will and testament

testamentarisch [tɛstamɛnˈtaːrɪʃ] *adv* by will

Testa'mentsvollstrecker *m* executor

Testbild [ˈtɛst-] *n* TV test card

testen [ˈtɛstən] *v/t* (no -ge-, h) test

'**Testpi,lot** *m* test pilot

Tetanus [ˈteːtanus] *m* (-; no pl) MED tetanus

teuer [ˈtɔYɐ] *adj* expensive; **wie teuer ist es?** how much is it?

Teufel [ˈtɔYfəl] *m* (-s; -) devil (*a. fig*): **wer (wo, was) zum Teufel ...?** who (where, what) the hell ...?

'**Teufelskerl** F *m* devil of a fellow

'**Teufelskreis** *m* vicious circle

teuflisch [ˈtɔYflɪʃ] *adj* devilish, diabolic(al)

Text [tɛkst] *m* (-[e]s; -e) text; MUS words, lyrics

Texter [ˈtɛkstɐ] *m* (-s; -), '**Texterin** *f* (-; -nen) MUS songwriter

Textil... [tɛksˈtiːl-] *in cpds* textile ...

Textilien [tɛksˈtiːljən] *pl* textiles

'**Textverarbeitung** *f* EDP word processing

'**Textverarbeitungsgerät** *n* EDP word processor

Theater [teˈaːtɐ] *n* (-s; -) theater, *Br* theatre; F **Theater machen (um)** make a fuss (about)

Theaterbesucher *m* theatergoer, *Br* theatregoer

Theaterkarte *f* theater (*Br* theatre) ticket

Theaterkasse *f* box office

Theaterstück *n* play

Thema [ˈteːma] *n* (-s; Themen) subject, topic; MUS theme; **das Thema wechseln**

change the subject

Theologe [teo'lo:gə] *m* (*-n*; *-n*) theologian

Theologie [teolo'gi:] *f* (*-*; *-n*) theology

Theo'login *f* (*-*; *-nen*) theologian

theo'logisch *adj* theological

Theoretiker [teo're:tikɐ] *m* (*-s*; *-*) theorist

theo'retisch *adj* theoretical

Theorie [teo'ri:] *f* (*-*; *-n*) theory

Therapeut [tera'pɔyt] *m* (*-en*; *-en*), **Therapeutin** *f* (*-*; *-nen*) therapist

Therapie [-'pi:] *f* (*-*; *-n*) therapy

Thermometer [tɛrmo'me:tɐ] *n* (*-s*; *-*) thermometer

Thermosflasche ['tɛrmɔs-] *f* thermos®

These ['te:zə] *f* (*-*; *-n*) thesis

Thon [to:n] *Swiss m* (*-s*; *-s*) tuna (fish)

Thrombose [trɔm'bo:zə] *f* (*-*; *-n*) MED thrombosis

Thron [tro:n] *m* (*-[e]s*; *-e*) throne

'Thronfolger [-fɔlgɐ] *m* (*-s*; *-*), **'Thronfolgerin** [-fɔlgərin] *f* (*-*; *-nen*) successor to the throne

Thunfisch ['tu:n-] *m* tuna (fish)

Tick [tik] F *m* (*-[e]s*; *-s*) quirk

ticken ['tikən] *v/i* (*ge-*, *h*) tick

Tiebreak, Tie-Break ['taibreik] *m*, *in tennis:* tiebreak(er)

tief [ti:f] *adj* deep (*a. fig*); low

Tief *n* (*-s*; *-s*) METEOR depression (*a. PSYCH, ECON*), low (*a. fig*)

Tiefe ['ti:fə] *f* (*-*; *-n*) depth (*a. fig*)

'Tiefebene *f* lowland(s)

Tiefflieger *m* low-flying air plane

Tiefgang *m* MAR draft, *Br* draught; *fig* depth

Tiefga,rage *f* parking *or* underground garage, *Br* underground car park

'tiefgekühlt *adj* deep-frozen

'Tiefkühlfach *n* freezing compartment

Tiefkühlschrank *m*, **Tiefkühltruhe** *f* freezer, deep-freeze

Tiefkühlkost *f* frozen foods

Tier [ti:ɐ] *n* (*-[e]s*; *-e*) animal; F *hohes Tier* bigwig, big shot

Tierarzt *m*, **-ärztin** *f* veterinarian, *Br* veterinary surgeon, F vet

Tierfreund *m* animal lover

Tiergarten *m* → *Zoo*

Tierheim *n* animal shelter

tierisch ['ti:riʃ] *adj* animal; *fig* bestial, brutish

'Tierkreis *m* ASTR zodiac

Tierkreiszeichen *n* sign of the zodiac

'Tiermedi,zin *f* veterinary medicine

Tierquäle'rei *f* cruelty to animals

'Tierreich *n* animal kingdom

Tierschutz *m* protection of animals

Tierschutzverein *m* society for the prevention of cruelty to animals

Tierversuch *m* MED experiment with animals

Tiger ['ti:gɐ] *m* (*-s*; *-*) ZO tiger

Tigerin ['ti:gərin] *f* (*-*; *-nen*) ZO tigress

tilgen ['tilgən] *v/t* (*ge-*, *h*) ECON pay off

Tinte ['tintə] *f* (*-*; *-n*) ink

'Tintenfisch *m* ZO squid

Tipp [tip] *m* (*-s*; *-s*) hint, tip; tip-off; *j-m e-n Tipp geben* tip s.o. off

tippen ['tipən] *v/i and v/t* (*ge-*, *h*) tap; type; F guess; do *lotto etc*

Tisch [tiʃ] *m* (*-es*; *-e*) table; *am Tisch sitzen* sit at the table; *bei Tisch* at table; *den Tisch decken* (*abräumen*) lay (clear) the table

Tischdecke *f* tablecloth

Tischgebet *n* REL grace; *das Tischgebet sprechen* say grace

Tischler ['tiʃlɐ] *m* (*-s*; *-*) joiner; cabinet-marker

'Tischplatte *f* tabletop

Tischrechner *m* desktop computer

Tischtennis *n* table tennis

Tischtuch *n* tablecloth

Titel ['ti:tl] *m* (*-s*; *-*) title

Titelbild *n* cover picture

Titelblatt *n*, **Titelseite** *f* title page; cover, front page

Toast [to:st] *m* (*-[e]s*; *-s*), **toasten** ['to:stən] *v/t* (*ge-*, *h*) toast

toben ['to:bən] *v/i* (*ge-*, *h*) rage (*a. fig*); romp

tobsüchtig ['to:p-] *adj* raving mad

'Tobsuchtsanfall *m* tantrum

Tochter ['tɔxtɐ] *f* (*-*; *Töchter*) [ˈtœçtɐ] daughter

Tochtergesellschaft *f* ECON subsidiary (company)

Tod [to:t] *m* (*-[e]s*; *no pl*) death (*a. fig*) (*durch* from)

tod... *in cpds* *...ernst*, *...müde*, *...sicher*: dead ...

Todesängste ['to:dəs-] *pl*: *Todesängste ausstehen* be scared to death

Todesanzeige *f* obituary (notice)

Todesfall *m* (case of) death

Todeskampf *m* agony

Todesopfer *n* casualty

Todesstrafe *f* JUR capital punishment; death penalty

Todesursache *f* cause of death

Todesurteil *n* JUR death sentence

'Todfeind *m* deadly enemy

'tod'krank *adj* mortally ill

tödlich ['to:tliç] *adj* fatal; deadly; *esp fig* mortal

'Todsünde *f* mortal *or* deadly sin

Toilette [toa'lɛtə] *f* (*-*; *-n*) bathroom, *Br* toilet, lavatory; *pl* rest rooms, *Br* ladies'

or men's rooms

Toi'letten... in cpds ...papier, ...seife etc: toilet ...

Toilettentisch m dressing table

tolerant [tole'rant] adj tolerant (**gegen** of, towards)

Toleranz [tole'rants] f (-; -en) tolerance (a. TECH)

tolerieren [tole'riːrən] v/t (no -ge-, h) tolerate

toll [tɔl] adj wild; F great, fantastic

'tollkühn adj daredevil

'Tollwut f VET rabies

'tollwütig [-vyːtɪç] adj VET rabid

Tomate [to'maːtə] f (-; -n) BOT tomato

Ton¹ [toːn] m (-[e]s; -e) clay

Ton² m (-[e]s; Töne ['tøːnə]) tone (a. MUS, PAINT), PAINT a. shade; sound (a. TV, film); note; stress; **kein Ton** not a word

Tonabnehmer m ELECTR pickup

Tonart f MUS key

Tonband n (-[e]s; -bänder) (recording) tape

Tonbandgerät n tape recorder

tönen ['tøːnən] (ge-, h) **1.** v/i sound, ring; **2.** v/t tinge, tint, shade

Tonfall m tone (of voice); accent

Tonfilm m sound film

Tonkopf m ELECTR (magnetic) head

Tonlage f MUS pitch

Tonleiter f MUS scale

Tonne ['tɔnə] f (-; -n) barrel; (metric) ton

'Tontechniker m sound engineer

Tönung f (-; -en) tint, tinge, shade

Topf [tɔpf] m (-[e]s; Töpfe ['tœpfə]) pot; saucepan

Topfen ['tɔpfən] Austrian m (-s; no pl) GASTR curd(s)

Töpfer ['tœpfɐ] m (-s; -) potter

Töpferei [tœpfə'raɪ] f (-; -en) pottery

'Töpferin f (-; -nen) potter

'Töpferscheibe f potter's wheel

'Töpferware f pottery, earthenware

Tor [toːɐ] n (-[e]s; -e) gate; soccer etc: goal; **ein Tor schießen** score (a goal); **im Tor stehen** keep goal

Torf [tɔrf] m (-[e]s; -e) peat

'Torfmull m peat dust

'Torhüter [-hyːtɐ] m → **Torwart**

torkeln ['tɔrkəln] F v/i (ge-, h, sein) reel, stagger

Torlatte f SPORT crossbar

Torlinie f SPORT goal line

torpedieren [tɔrpe'diːrən] v/t (no -ge-, h) MIL torpedo (a. fig)

'Torpfosten m SPORT goalpost

Torraum m SPORT goalmouth

Torschuss m SPORT shot at goal

Torschütze m SPORT scorer

Torte ['tɔrtə] f (-; -n) pie, esp Br flan; cream cake, gateau

'Torwart [-vart] m (-[e]s; -e) SPORT goalkeeper, F goalie

tosen ['toːzən] v/i roar; thunder

tosend adj thunderous (applause)

tot [toːt] adj dead (a. fig); late; **tot geboren** MED stillborn; **tot umfallen** drop dead

total [to'taːl] adj total, complete

totalitär [totali'tɛːɐ] adj POL totalitarian

Tote m, f (-n; -n) dead man or woman; (dead) body, corpse; mst pl casualty; pl the dead

töten ['tøːtən] v/t (ge-, h) kill

Totenbett n deathbed

'toten'blass adj deadly pale

'Totengräber [-grɛːbɐ] m (-s; -) gravedigger

Totenkopf m skull; skull and crossbones

Totenmaske f death mask

Totenmesse f REL mass for the dead, requiem (a. MUS)

Totenschädel m skull

Totenschein m death certificate

'toten'still adj deathly still

'totlachen F v/refl (sep, -ge-, h) kill o.s. laughing

Toto ['toːto] m, F n (-s; -s) football pools

Totschlag m (-[e]s; no pl) JUR manslaughter

'totschlagen v/t (irr, **schlagen**, sep, -ge-, h) kill; **j-n totschlagen** beat s.o. to death; **die Zeit totschlagen** kill time

'totschweigen v/t (irr, **schweigen**, sep, -ge-, h) hush up

Toupet [tu'peː] n (-s; -s) toupee

toupieren [tu'piːrən] v/t (no -ge-, h) Br backcomb

Tour [tuːɐ] f (-; -en) tour (**durch** of), trip; excursion; TECH turn, revolution; **auf Touren kommen** MOT pick up speed; F **krumme Touren** underhand methods

Touren... ['tuːrən-] in cpds ...rad etc: touring ...

Tourismus [tu'rɪsmʊs] m (-; no pl) tourism

Tourismusgeschäft n tourist industry

Tourist [tu'rɪst] m (-en; -en), **Tou'ristin** f (-; -nen) tourist

tou'ristisch adj touristic

Tournee [tʊr'neː] f (-; -s, -n) tour; **auf Tournee gehen** go on tour

Trab [traːp] m (-[e]s; no pl) trot

Trabant [tra'bant] m (-en; -en) ASTR satellite

Tra'bantenstadt f satellite town

traben ['traːbən] v/i (ge-, sein) trot

Traber ['traːbɐ] m (-s; -) ZO trotter

'Trabrennen *n* trotting race

Tracht [traxt] *f* (-; -en) costume; uniform; dress; F *e-e Tracht Prügel* a thrashing

trächtig ['trɛçtɪç] *adj* zo with young, pregnant

Tradition [tradi'tsjoːn] *f* (-; -en) tradition

traditionell [traditsjo'nɛl] *adj* traditional

traf [traːf] *pret of* **treffen**

Trafik [tra'fɪk] *Austrian f* (-; -en) → *Tabakgeschäft*

Trafikant [trafi'kant] *Austrian m* (-en; -en) tobacconist

Tragbahre ['traːk-] *f* stretcher

'tragbar *adj* portable; wearable; *fig* bearable; *person:* acceptable

Trage ['traːgə] *f* (-; -n) stretcher

träge ['trɛːgə] *adj* lazy, indolent; PHYS inert (*a. fig*)

tragen [traːgən] (*irr, ge-, h*) **1.** *v/t* carry; wear; *fig* bear; *sich gut tragen* wear well; **2.** *v/i* BOT bear fruit; *fig* hold

tragend *adj* ARCH supporting; THEA leading

Träger ['trɛːgɐ] *m* (-s; -) carrier; porter; (shoulder) strap; TECH support; ARCH girder; *fig* bearer

'trägerlos *adj* strapless

'Tragetasche *f* carrier bag; carrycot

'tragfähig *adj* load-bearing; *fig* sound

'Tragfläche *f* AVIAT wing

Trägheit ['trɛːkhait] *f* (-; *no pl*) laziness, indolence; PHYS inertia (*a. fig*)

Tragik ['traːgɪk] *f* (-; *no pl*) tragedy

tragisch ['traːgɪʃ] *adj* tragic

Tragödie [tra'gøːdjə] *f* (-; -n) tragedy

'Tragriemen *m* strap; sling

'Tragweite *f* range; *fig* significance

Trainer ['trɛːnɐ] *m* (-s; -), 'Trainerin *f* (-; -nen) SPORT trainer, coach

trainieren [trɛ'niːrən] *v/i and v/t* (*no -ge-, h*) SPORT train, coach

'Training *n* (-s; -s) training

'Trainingsanzug *m* track suit

Traktor ['traktoːɐ] *m* (-s; -en [trak'toːrən]) MOT tractor

trällern ['trɛlɐn] *v/t and v/i* (*ge-, h*) warble, trill

Tram [tram] *Austrian f* (-; -s), *Swiss n* (-s; -s) streetcar, *Br* tram

trampeln ['trampəln] *v/i* (*ge-, h*) trample, stamp

'Trampelpfad *m* beaten track

trampen ['trɛmpən] *v/i* (*ge-, sein*) hitchhike

Tramper(in) ['trɛmpɐ (-pərɪn)] (-s; -/-; -nen) hitchhiker

Träne ['trɛːnə] *f* (-; -n) tear; *in Tränen ausbrechen* burst into tears

'tränen *v/i* (*ge-, h*) water

'Tränengas *n* tear gas

trank [traŋk] *pret of* **trinken**

Tränke ['trɛŋkə] *f* (-; -n) watering place

'tränken *v/t* (*ge-, h*) zo water; soak, drench

Transfer [trans'feːɐ] *m* (-s; -s) transfer (*a. SPORT*)

Transformator [transfɔr'maːtoːɐ] *m* (-s; -en [-ma'toːrən]) ELECTR transformer

Transfusion [transfu'zjoːn] *f* (-; -en) MED transfusion

Transistor [tran'zɪstoːɐ] *m* (-s; -en [-zɪs'toːrən]) ELECTR transistor

Transit [tran'ziːt] *m* (-s; -e) transit

transitiv ['tranzitiːf] *adj* LING transitive

transparent [transpa'rɛnt] *adj* transparent

Transpa'rent *n* (-[e]s; -e) banner

Transplantation [transplanta'tsjoːn] *f* (-; -en), transplantieren [-'tiːrən] *v/t* (*no -ge-, h*) MED transplant

Transport [trans'pɔrt] *m* (-[e]s; -e) transport; shipment

transportabel [transpɔr'taːbəl], trans'portfähig *adj* transportable

transportieren [transpɔr'tiːrən] *v/t* (*no -ge-, h*) transport, ship, carry, MOT *a.* haul

Trans'portmittel *n* (means of) transport(ation)

Transportunternehmen *n* hauler, *Br* haulier

Trapez [tra'peːts] *n* (-es; -e) MATH trapezoid, *Br* trapezium; SPORT trapeze

trappeln ['trapəln] *v/i* (*ge-, sein*) clatter; patter

trat [traːt] *pret of* **treten**

Traube ['traubə] *f* (-; -n) BOT bunch of grapes; grape; *pl* grapes; *fig* cluster

'Traubensaft *m* grape juice

'Traubenzucker *m* glucose

trauen ['trauən] (*ge-, h*) **1.** *v/t* marry; **2.** *v/i* trust (*j-m* s.o.); *sich trauen, et. zu tun* dare (to) do s.th.; *ich traute meinen Augen nicht* I couldn't believe my eyes

Trauer ['trauɐ] *f* (-; *no pl*) grief, sorrow; mourning; *in Trauer* in mourning

'Trauerfall *m* death

'Trauerfeier *f* funeral service

'Trauermarsch *m* MUS funeral march

'trauern *v/i* (*ge-, h*) mourn (*um* for)

'Trauerrede *f* funeral oration

'Trauerzug *m* funeral procession

träufeln ['trɔyfəln] *v/t* (*ge-, h*) drip, trickle

Traum [traum] *m* (-[e]s; Träume ['trɔymə]) dream (*a. fig*)

Traum... *in cpds* ...beruf, ...mann *etc*: dream ..., ... of one's dreams

träumen ['trɔymən] *v/i and v/t* (*ge-, h*) dream (*a. fig*) (*von* about, of); *schlecht*

träumen have bad dreams

Träumer ['trɔʏmɐ] *m* (*-s*; *-*) dreamer (*a. fig*)

Träumerei [trɔʏmə'raɪ] *fig f* (day)dream(s), reverie (*a.* MUS)

träumerisch ['trɔʏmərɪʃ] *adj* dreamy

traurig ['traʊrɪç] *adj* sad (*über acc*, *wegen* about)

'Traurigkeit *f* (*-*; *no pl*) sadness

Trauring ['traʊ-] *m* wedding ring

'Trauschein *m* marriage certificate

'Trauung *f* (*-*; *-en*) marriage, wedding

'Trauzeuge *m*, **'Trauzeugin** *f* witness to a marriage

Trecker ['trɛkɐ] *m* (*-s*; *-*) MOT tractor

Treff [trɛf] F *m* (*-s*; *-s*) meeting place

treffen ['trɛfən] *v/t and v/i* (*irr, ge-, h*) hit (*a. fig*); hurt; meet *s.o.*; take (*measures etc*); **nicht treffen** miss; **sich treffen** (*mit j-m*) meet (s.o.); **gut treffen** PHOT *etc*: capture well

'Treffen *n* (*-s*; *-*) meeting

'treffend 1. *adj* apt (*remark etc*); **2.** *adv*: **treffend gesagt** well put

Treffer ['trɛfɐ] *m* (*-s*; *-*) hit (*a. fig*); SPORT goal; win

'Treffpunkt *m* meeting place

Treibeis ['traɪp-] *n* drift ice

treiben ['traɪbən] (*irr, ge-*) **1.** *v/t* (*h*) drive (*a.* TECH *and fig*); SPORT *etc*: do; push, press *s.o.*; BOT put forth; F do, be up to; **2.** *v/i* (*sein*) drift (*a. fig*), float; BOT shoot (up); **sich treiben lassen** drift along (*a. fig*); **treibende Kraft** driving force

'Treiben *n* (*-s*; *no pl*) doings, goingson; **geschäftiges Treiben** bustle

'treibenlassen *v/refl* (*irr, lassen, sep, no -ge-, h*) → **treiben**

'Treibhaus *n* hothouse

'Treibhausef,fekt *m* greenhouse effect

Treibholz *n* driftwood

'Treibriemen *m* TECH driving belt

'Treibsand *m* quicksand

'Treibstoff *m* fuel

trennen ['trɛnən] *v/t* (*ge-, h*) separate; sever; part; divide (*a.* LING, POL); segregate; TEL disconnect; **sich trennen** separate (*von* from), part (*a. fig*); **sich trennen von** part with *s.th.*; leave *s.o.*

'Trennung *f* (*-*; *-en*) separation; division; segregation

'Trennwand *f* partition

Treppe ['trɛpə] *f* (*-*; *-n*) staircase, stairs

'Treppenabsatz *m* landing

Treppengeländer *n* banisters

'Treppenhaus *n* staircase; hall

Tresor [tre'zoːɐ] *m* (*-s*; *-e*) safe; strongroom, vault

treten ['treːtən] *v/i and v/t* (*irr, ge-, h*) kick;

step (*aus* out of; *in acc* into; *auf acc* on[-to]); pedal (away)

treu [trɔʏ] *adj* faithful (*a. fig*); loyal; devoted

Treue ['trɔʏə] *f* (*-*; *no pl*) fidelity, faithfulness, loyalty

'Treuhänder [-hɛndɐ] *m* (*-s*; *-*) JUR trustee

'treulos *adj* faithless, disloyal, unfaithful (*all*: **gegen** to)

Tribüne [tri'byːnə] *f* (*-*; *-n*) platform; stand

Trichter ['trɪçtɐ] *m* (*-s*; *-*) funnel; crater

Trick [trɪk] *m* (*-s*; *-s*) trick

Trickaufnahme *f* trick shot

Trickbetrüger(in) confidence trickster

trieb [triːp] *pret of* **treiben**

Trieb *m* (*-[e]s*; *-e* ['triːbə]) BOT (young) shoot, sprout; *fig* impulse, drive; sex drive

Triebfeder *f* mainspring (*a. fig*)

triefen ['triːfən] *v/i* (*ge-, h*) drip, be dripping (*von* with)

triftig ['trɪftɪç] *adj* weighty; good

Trikot [tri'koː] *n* (*-s*; *-s*) SPORT shirt, jersey; leotard

Triller ['trɪlɐ] *m* (*-s*; *-*) MUS trill

'trillern *v/i and v/t* (*ge-, h*) trill; ZO warble

trimmen ['trɪmən] *v/refl* (*ge-, h*) keep fit

'Trimmpfad *m* fitness trail

trinkbar ['trɪŋkbaːə] *adj* drinkable

trinken ['trɪŋkən] *v/t and v/i* (*irr, ge-, h*) drink (*auf acc* to); have; **et. zu trinken** a drink

Trinker(in) ['trɪŋkɐ (-kərɪn)] (*-s*; *-/-*; *-nen*) drinker, alcoholic

'Trinkgeld *n* tip; **j-m** (*e-e Mark*) **Trinkgeld geben** tip *s.o.* (one mark)

'Trinkspruch *m* toast

Trinkwasser *n* drinking water

Trio ['triːo] *n* (*-s*; *-s*) MUS trio (*a. fig*)

trippeln ['trɪpəln] *v/i* (*ge-, sein*) mince

Tripper ['trɪpɐ] *m* (*-s*; *-*) MED gonorrh(o)ea

Tritt [trɪt] *m* (*-[e]s*; *-e*) kick; step

'Trittbrett *n* step; MOT running board

Trittleiter *f* stepladder

Triumph [tri'ʊmf] *m* (*-[e]s*; *-e*) triumph

triumphal [triʊm'faːl] *adj* triumphant

triumphieren [triʊm'fiːrən] *v/i* (*no -ge-, h*) triumph (*über acc* over)

trocken ['trɔkən] *adj* dry (*a. fig*)

'Trocken... *in cpds* dried ...; drying ...

'Trockenhaube *f* hairdryer

'Trockenheit *f* (*-*; *no pl*) dryness; AGR drought

'trockenlegen *v/t* (*sep, -ge-, h*) drain; change (*a baby*)

trocknen ['trɔknən] *v/t* (*ge-, h*) *and v/i* (*sein*) dry

Trockner ['trɔknɐ] *m* (*-s*; *-*) dryer

Troddel ['trɔdəl] *f* (*-*; *-n*) tassel

Trödel ['trø:dəl] *m* (-s; *no pl*) junk

trödeln ['trø:dəln] *v/i* (*ge-*, *h*) dawdle

Trödler ['trø:dlɐ] *m* (-s; -) junk dealer; dawdler

trog [tro:k] *pret of* **trügen**

Trog *m* (-[e]s; *Tröge* ['trø:gə]) trough

Trommel ['trɔməl] *f* (-; -n) MUS drum (*a.* TECH)

Trommelfell *n* ANAT eardrum

'**trommeln** *v/i and v/t* (*ge-*, *h*) drum

Trommler ['trɔmlɐ] *m* (-s; -) drummer

Trompete [trɔm'pe:tə] *f* (-; -n) MUS trumpet

trom'peten *v/i and v/t* (*no -ge-*, *h*) trumpet (*a.* ZO)

Trompeter [trɔm'pe:tɐ] *m* (-s; -) trumpeter

Tropen ['tro:pən] *pl* **die Tropen** *pl* the tropics

'**Tropen...** *in cpds* tropical ...

Tropf [trɔpf] *m* (-[e]s; *Tröpfe* ['trœpfə]) MED drip

Tröpfchen ['trœpfçən] *n* (-s; -) droplet

tröpfeln ['trœpfəln] *v/i and v/t* (*ge-*, *h*) drip; **es tröpfelt** it's spitting

tropfen ['trɔpfən] *v/i and v/t* (*ge-*, *h*) drip, drop

'**Tropfen** *m* (-s; -) drop (*a. fig*); **ein Tropfen auf den heißen Stein** a drop in the bucket

'**tropfenweise** *adv* in drops, drop by drop

Trophäe [tro'fɛ:ə] *f* (-; -n) trophy (*a. fig*)

tropisch ['tro:pɪʃ] *adj* tropical

Trosse ['trɔsə] *f* (-; -n) cable

Trost [tro:st] *m* (-[e]s; *no pl*) comfort, consolation; **ein schwacher Trost** cold comfort

trösten ['trø:stən] *v/t* (*ge-*, *h*) comfort, console; **sich trösten** console o.s. (**mit** with)

tröstlich ['trø:stlɪç] *adj* comforting

'**trostlos** *adj* miserable; desolate

Trott [trɔt] *m* (-[e]s; -e) trot; F **der alte Trott** the old routine

Trottel ['trɔtəl] F *m* (-s; -) dope

trottelig ['trɔtəlɪç] F *adj* dopey

trotten ['trɔtən] *v/i* (*ge-*, *sein*) trot

Trottinett ['trɔtinet] *Swiss n* (-s; -e) scooter

Trottoir [trɔ'toa:ɐ] *Swiss n* (-s; -e, -s) sidewalk, *Br* pavement

trotz [trɔts] *prp* (*gen*) in spite of, despite

Trotz *m* (-es; *no pl*) defiance; **j-m zum Trotz** to spite s.o.

'**trotzdem** *adv* in spite of it, nevertheless, F anyhow, anyway

trotzen ['trɔtsən] *v/i* (*ge-*, *h*) defy (*dat s.o.* or *s.th.*); sulk

trotzig ['trɔtsɪç] *adj* defiant; sulky

trüb [try:p], **trübe** ['try:bə] *adj* cloudy;

muddy; dim; dull, *fig a.* gloomy

Trubel ['tru:bəl] *m* (-s; *no pl*) (hustle and) bustle

trüben ['try:bən] *v/t* (*ge-*, *h*) cloud; *fig* spoil, mar

Trübsal ['try:pza:l] *f*: **Trübsal blasen** mope

'**trübselig** *adj* sad, gloomy; dreary

'**Trübsinn** *m* (-[e]s; *no pl*) melancholy, gloom, low spirits

'**trübsinnig** *adj* melancholy, gloomy

trug [tru:k] *pret of* **tragen**

trügen ['try:gən] (*irr, ge-*, *h*) **1.** *v/t* deceive; **2.** *v/i* be deceptive

trügerisch ['try:gərɪʃ] *adj* deceptive

'**Trugschluss** *m* fallacy

Truhe ['tru:ə] *f* (-; -n) chest

Trümmer ['trymɐ] *pl* ruins; debris; pieces, bits

Trumpf [trʊmpf] *m* (-[e]s; *Trümpfe* ['trympfə]) trump (card) (*a. fig*); **Trumpf sein** be trumps; *fig* **s-n Trumpf ausspielen** play one's trump card

Trunkenheit ['trʊŋkənhaɪt] *f* (-; *no pl*) *esp* JUR; **Trunkenheit am Steuer** drunk (*Br* drink) driving

'**Trunksucht** *f* (-; *no pl*) alcoholism

Trupp [trʊp] *m* (-s; -s) band, party; group

Truppe ['trʊpə] *f* (-; -n) MIL troop, *pl* troops, forces; THEA company, troupe

'**Truppengattung** *f* MIL branch (of service)

'**Truppenübungsplatz** *m* training area

Truthahn ['tru:t-] *m* ZO turkey

Tscheche ['tʃɛçə] *m* (-n; -n) Czech

Tschechien ['tʃɛçjən] Czech Republic

'**Tschechin** *f* (-; -nen) Czech

'**tschechisch** *adj* Czech; **Tschechische Republik** Czech Republic

Tube ['tu:bə] *f* (-; -n) tube

Tuberkulose [tubɛrku'lo:zə] *f* (-; -n) MED tuberculosis

Tuch [tu:x] *n* (-[e]s) a) (*pl -e*) cloth, b) (*pl Tücher* ['ty:çɐ]) scarf

'**Tuchfühlung** *f*: **auf Tuchfühlung** in close contact

tüchtig ['tʏçtɪç] *adj* (cap)able, competent; skil(l)ful; efficient; F *fig* good

'**Tüchtigkeit** *f* (-; *no pl*) (cap)ability, qualities; skill; efficiency

tückisch ['tʏkɪʃ] *adj* malicious; MED insidious; treacherous

tüfteln ['tʏftəln] F *v/i* (*ge-*, *h*) puzzle (**an** *dat* over)

Tugend ['tu:gənt] *f* (-; -en) virtue (*a. fig*)

Tulpe ['tʊlpə] *f* (-; -n) BOT tulip

Tumor ['tu:mo:ɐ] *m* (-s; -en [tu'mo:rən]) MED tumo(u)r

Tümpel ['tʏmpəl] *m* (-s; -) pool

Tumult [tu'mʊlt] *m* (-[e]s; -e) tumult, uproar

tun [tu:n] *v/t and v/i* (*irr, ge-, h*) do; take (*a step etc*); F put; **zu tun haben** have work to do; be busy; *ich weiß* (**nicht**), *was ich tun soll* or *muss* I (don't) know what to do; **so tun, als ob** pretend to *inf*

Tünche ['tʏnçə] *f* (*-; -n*), **'tünchen** *v/t* (*ge-, h*) whitewash

Tunfisch *m* → **Thunfisch**

Tunke ['tʊŋkə] *f* (*-; -n*) sauce

Tunnel ['tʊnəl] *m* (*-s; -) tunnel

Tüpfelchen ['tʏpfəlçən] *n*: *das Tüpfelchen auf dem i* the icing on the cake

tupfen ['tʊpfən] *v/t* (*ge-, h*) dab

'Tupfen *m* (*-s; -) dot, spot

Tupfer ['tʊpfɐ] *m* (*-s; -) MED swab

Tür [ty:ɐ] *f* (*-; -en* ['ty:rən]) door (*a. fig*); *die Tür(en) knallen* slam the door(s); F *j-n vor die Tür setzen* throw s.o. out; *Tag der offenen Tür* open house (*Br day*)

Turban ['tʊrba:n] *m* (*-s; -e*) turban

Turbine [tʊr'bi:nə] *f* (*-; -n*) TECH turbine

Turbolader ['tʊrbolaːdɐ] *m* (*-s; -) MOT turbo(charger)

Türke ['tʏrkə] *m* (*-n; -n*) Turk

Türkei [tʏr'kai] *f* Turkey

Türkin ['tʏrkɪn] *f* (*-; -nen*) Turk(ish woman)

'türkisch *adj* Turkish

'Türklingel *f* doorbell

'Türklinke *f* door handle

'Türknauf *m* doorknob

Turm [tʊrm] *m* (*-[e]s; Türme* ['tʏrmə]) tower; steeple; *chess*: castle, rook

türmen ['tʏrmən] *v/t* (*ge-, h*) pile up (*a. sich türmen*)

'Turmspitze *f* spire

'Turmspringen *n* SPORT platform diving

turnen ['tʊrnən] *v/i* (*ge-, h*) SPORT do gym-

nastics

'Turnen *n* (*-s; no pl*) SPORT gymnastics; PED physical education (ABBR PE)

Turner ['tʊrnɐ] *m* (*-s; -), **Turnerin** ['tʊrnərɪn] *f* (*-; -nen*) SPORT gymnast

'Turnhalle *f* gymnasium, F gym

'Turnhemd *n* gym shirt

'Turnhose *f* gym shorts

Turnier [tʊr'ni:ɐ] *n* (*-s; -e*) tournament

Tur'niertanz *m* ballroom dancing

'Turnlehrer(in) gym(nastics) or PE teacher

Turnschuh *m* sneaker, *Br* trainer

Turnverein *m* gymnastics club

'Türpfosten *m* doorpost

'Türrahmen *m* doorframe

Türschild *n* doorplate

Türsprechanlage *f* entryphone

Tusche ['tʊʃə] *f* (*-; -n*) Indian ink; water-colo(u)r

'Tuschkasten *m* paintbox

Tüte ['ty:tə] *f* (*-; -n*) (paper *or* plastic) bag; *e-e Tüte ...* a bag of ...

TÜV [tʏf] ABBR *of Technischer Überwachungs-Verein Br appr* MOT (test), compulsory car inspection; (*nicht*) *durch den TÜV kommen* pass (fail) its *or* one's MOT

Typ [ty:p] *m* (*-s; -en*) type; model; F fellow, guy

Type ['ty:pə] *f* (*-; -n*) TECH type; F character

Typhus ['ty:fʊs] *m* (*-; no pl*) MED typhoid (fever)

typisch ['ty:pɪʃ] *adj* typical (*für* of)

Tyrann [ty'ran] *m* (*-en; -en*) tyrant

Tyrannei [tyra'nai] *f* (*-; -en*) tyranny

tyrannisch [ty'ranɪʃ] *adj* tyrannical

tyrannisieren [tyrani'zi:rən] *v/t* (*no -ge-, h*) tyrannize, bully

U

u. a. ABBR *of unter anderem* among other things; *und andere* and others

U-Bahn ['u:ba:n] *f* underground, subway, *in London*: tube

übel ['y:bəl] *adj* bad; *mir ist übel* I feel sick; *et. übel nehmen* be offended by s.th.; *übel riechend* foul-smelling, foul

'Übel *n* (*-s; -) evil

'Übelkeit *f* (*-; -en*) nausea

'übelnehmen *v/t* (*irr, nehmen, sep, -ge-,*

h) → **übel**

'Übeltäter *m*, **'Übeltäterin** *f* *esp iro* culprit

üben ['y:bən] *v/t and v/i* (*ge-, h*) practice, *Br* practise; *Klavier etc* **üben** practice the piano *etc*

über ['y:bɐ] *prp* (*dat or acc*) over; above (*a. fig*); more than; across; *fig* about, of, *lecture etc a.* on; *sprechen* (*nachdenken etc*) *über* (*acc*) talk (think *etc*) about; *über Nacht bleiben* stay overnight; *über*

München nach Rom to Rome via Munich

über'all *adv* everywhere; **überall in ...** (*dat*) *a.* throughout ..., all over ...

über'anstrengen *v/t and v/refl* (*no -ge-, h*) overstrain (o.s.)

über'arbeiten *v/t* (*no -ge-, h*) revise; **sich überarbeiten** overwork o.s.

'überaus *adv* most, extremely

'überbelichten *v/t* (*no -ge-, h*) PHOT overexpose

über'bieten *v/t* (*irr, bieten, no -ge-, h*) at *auction*: outbid (**um** by); *fig* beat, *a.* outdo *s.o.*

'Überblick *m* view; *fig* overview (**über** *acc* of); general idea, outline

über'blicken *v/t* (*no -ge-, h*) overlook; *fig* be able to calculate

über'bringen *v/t* (*irr, bringen, no -ge-, h*) deliver

Über'bringer(in) (*-s; -/-; -nen*) ECON bearer

über'brücken *v/t* (*no -ge-, h*) bridge (*a. fig*)

überdacht [-'daxt] *adj* roofed, covered

über'dauern *v/t* (*no -ge-, h*) outlast, survive

über'denken *v/t* (*irr, denken, no -ge-, h*) think *s.th.* over

'überdimensio,nal *adj* oversized

'Überdosis *f* MED overdose

überdrüssig [-drysɪç] *adj*: **überdrüssig sein** be weary *or* sick (*gen* of)

'überdurchschnittlich *adj* above--average

übereifrig *adj* overzealous

über'eilen *v/t* (*no -ge-, h*) rush; **nichts übereilen!** don't rush things!

über'eilt *adj* rash, hasty

überei'nander *adv* on top of each other; *talk etc* about one another

übereinanderschlagen *v/t* (*irr, schlagen, sep, -ge-, h*): **die Beine übereinanderschlagen** cross one's legs

über'einkommen *v/i* (*irr, kommen, sep, -ge-, sein*) agree

Über'einkommen *n* (*-s; -*), Über'einkunft *f* (*-; -künfte*) agreement

über'einstimmen *v/i* (*sep, -ge-, h*) tally, correspond (with); **mit j-m übereinstimmen** agree with s.o. (*in dat* on)

über'einstimmung *f* (*-; -en*) agreement; correspondence; **in Übereinstimmung mit** in accordance with

über'fahren *v/t* (*irr, fahren, no -ge-, h*) run *s.o.* over, knock *s.o.* down

'Überfahrt *f* MAR crossing

'Überfall *m* assault (**auf** *acc* on); hold-up (on, of); mugging (of); MIL raid (on); invasion (of)

über'fallen *v/t* (*irr, fallen, no -ge-, h*) attack; assault; hold up; mug; MIL raid; invade

'überfällig *adj* overdue

über'fliegen *v/t* (*irr, fliegen, no -ge-, h*) fly over *or* across; *fig* glance over, skim (through)

über'fließen *v/i* (*irr, fließen, sep, -ge-, sein*) overflow

'Überfluss *m* (*-es; no pl*) abundance (**an** *dat* of); affluence; **im Überfluss haben** abound in

über'flüssig *adj* superfluous

über'fluten *v/t* (*no -ge-, h*) flood (*a. fig*)

über'fordern *v/t* (*no -ge-, h*) overtax

überfragt [-'fra:kt] *adj*: F **da bin ich überfragt** you've got me there

über'führen *v/t* (*no -ge-, h*) transport; JUR convict (**e-r Tat** of a crime)

Über'führung *f* (*-; -en*) transfer; JUR conviction; MOT overpass, Br flyover; footbridge

über'füllt *adj* overcrowded, packed

über'füttern *v/t* (*no -ge-, h*) overfeed

'Übergang *m* crossing; *fig* transition

über'geben *v/t* (*irr, geben, no -ge-, h*) hand over; MIL surrender; **sich übergeben** vomit

über'gehen[1] *v/t* (*irr, gehen, no -ge-, h*) pass over, ignore

'übergehen[2] *v/i* (*irr, gehen, sep, -ge-, sein*) pass (**zu** on to); **übergehen in** (*acc*) change *or* turn (in)to

'übergeschnappt F *adj* cracked

'Übergewicht *n* (**Übergewicht haben** be) overweight; *fig* predominance

'übergewichtig *adj* overweight

'überglücklich *adj* overjoyed

über'greifen *v/i* (*irr, greifen, sep, -ge-, h*) **übergreifen auf** (*acc*) spread to

'Übergriff *m* infringement (**auf** *acc* of); (act of) violence

'Übergröße *f* outsize; **in Übergrößen** outsized, oversize(d)

über'handnehmen *v/i* (*irr, nehmen, sep, -ge-, h*) become rampant

über'häufen *v/t* (*no -ge-, h*) swamp; shower

über'haupt *adv* ... at all; anyway; **überhaupt nicht** (**nichts**) not (nothing) at all

überheblich [-'he:plɪç] *adj* arrogant

Über'heblichkeit *f* (*-; no pl*) arrogance

über'hitzen *v/t* (*no -ge-, h*) overheat (*a. fig*)

überhöht [-'hø:t] *adj* excessive

über'holen *v/t* (*no -ge-, h*) pass, overtake (*a. SPORT*); TECH overhaul, service

über'holt *adj* outdated, antiquated

über'hören v/t (no -ge-, h) miss, not catch or get; ignore

'überirdisch adj supernatural

über'kleben v/t (no -ge-, h) paste up, cover

'überkochen v/i (sep, -ge-, sein) boil over

über'kommen v/t (irr, kommen, no -ge-, h) ... überkam ihn he was seized with or overcome by ...

über'laden v/t (irr, laden, no -ge-, h) overload (a. ELECTR.); fig clutter

über'lassen v/t (irr, lassen, no -ge-, h) j-m et. überlassen let s.o. have s.th., leave s.th. to s.o. (a. fig); j-n sich selbst überlassen leave s.o. to himself; j-n s-m Schicksal überlassen leave s.o. to his fate

über'lasten v/t (no -ge-, h) overload (a. ELECTR.); fig overburden

'überlaufen¹ v/i (irr, laufen, sep, -ge-, sein) run or flow over; MIL desert

über'laufen² v/t (irr, laufen, no -ge-, h) es überlief mich heiß und kalt I went hot and cold

über'laufen³ adj overcrowded

'Überläufer m MIL deserter; POL defector

über'leben v/t and v/i (no -ge-, h) survive (a. fig); live through s.th.

Über'lebende m, f (-n; -n) survivor

'überlebensgroß adj larger than life

über'legen¹ v/t and v/i (no -ge-, h) think about s.th., think s.th. over; consider; lassen Sie mich überlegen let me think; ich habe es mir (anders) überlegt I've made up (changed) my mind

über'legen² adj superior (j-m to s.o.)

Über'legenheit f (-; no pl) superiority

über'legt adj deliberate; prudent

Über'legung f (-; -en) consideration, reflection

'überleiten v/i (sep, -ge-, h) überleiten zu lead up or over to

über'liefern v/t (no -ge-, h) hand down, pass on

Über'lieferung f (-; -en) tradition

über'listen v/t (no -ge-, h) outwit

'Übermacht f (-; no pl) superiority; esp MIL superior forces; in der Übermacht sein be superior in numbers

'übermächtig adj superior; fig overpowering

'Übermaß n (-es; no pl) excess (an dat of)

'übermäßig adj excessive

'übermenschlich adj superhuman

über'mitteln v/t (no -ge-, h) convey

'übermorgen the day after tomorrow

über'müdet adj overtired

'übermütig [-my:tıç] adj high-spirited

'übernächst adj the next but one; über-

nächste Woche the week after next

über'nachten [-'naxtən] v/i (no -ge-, h) stay overnight (bei j-m at s.o.'s [house], with s.o.), spend the night (at, with)

Über'nachtung f (-; -en) night; Übernachtung und Frühstück bed and breakfast

Über'nahme ['y:bɐnaːmə] f (-; -n) taking (over); adoption

'überna,türlich adj supernatural

über'nehmen v/t (irr, nehmen, no -ge-, h) take over; adopt; take (responsibility etc); undertake to do

über'prüfen v/t (no -ge-, h) check, examine; verify; esp POL screen

Über'prüfung f check, examination; verification; screening

über'queren v/t (no -ge-, h) cross

über'ragen v/t (no -ge-, h) tower above (a. fig)

über'ragend adj outstanding

überraschen [y:bɐ'raʃən] v/t (no -ge-, h) surprise; j-n bei et. überraschen a. catch s.o. doing s.th.

Über'raschung f (-; -en) surprise

über'reden v/t (no -ge-, h) persuade (et. zu tun to do s.th.); j-n zu et. überreden talk s.o. into (doing) s.th.

Über'redung f (-; no pl) persuasion

'überregio,nal adj national

über'reichen v/t (no -ge-, h) present, hand s.th. over (dat to)

über'reizen v/t (no -ge-, h) overexcite

über'reizt adj overwrought, F on edge

'Überrest m remains; pl relics; GASTR leftovers

über'rumpeln v/t (no -ge-, h) (take s.o. by) surprise

über'runden v/t (no -ge-, h) SPORT lap

übersät [-'zɛːt] adj: übersät mit strewn with garbage; studded with stars

übersättigt [-'zɛtıçt] adj sated, surfeited

'Überschall... in cpds supersonic ...

über'schatten v/t (no -ge-, h) overshadow (a. fig)

über'schätzen v/t (no -ge-, h) overrate, overestimate

'Überschlag m AVIAT loop; SPORT somersault; ECON rough estimate

'überschlagen¹ (irr, schlagen, sep, -ge-) 1. v/t (h) cross (one's legs); 2. v/i (sein) fig überschlagen in (acc) turn into

über'schlagen² (no -ge-, h) 1. v/t skip; 2. ECON make a rough estimate of; 2. v/refl turn (right) over; go head over heels; voice: break

'überschnappen F v/i (no -ge-, sein) crack up

über'schneiden v/refl (irr, schneiden, no

-ge-, h) overlap (a. fig); intersect

über'schreiben v/t (irr, **schreiben**, no -ge-, h) make s.th. over (dat to)

über'schreiten v/t (irr, **schreiten**, no -ge-, h) cross; fig go beyond; pass; break (the speed limit etc)

'Überschrift f heading, title; headline; caption

'Überschuss m, 'überschüssig [-ʃʏsɪç] adj surplus

über'schütten v/t (no -ge-, h) **überschütten mit** cover with; shower with; heap s.th. on

'überschwänglich [-ʃvɛŋlɪç] adj effusive

über'schwemmen v/t (no -ge-, h), **Über'-schwemmung** f (-; -en) flood

'überschwenglich → überschwänglich

'Übersee: **in (nach) Übersee** oversea

über'sehen v/t (irr, **sehen**, no -ge-, h) overlook; ignore

über'setzen[1] v/t (no -ge-, h) translate (**in** acc into)

'übersetzen[2] (sep, -ge-) **1.** v/i (h, sein) cross (**über e-n Fluss** a river); **2.** v/t (h) take over

Über'setzer [-'zɛtsɐ] m (-s; -), **Über'setze-rin** f (-; -nen) translator

Über'setzung f (-; -en) translation (**aus** dat from; **in** acc into)

'Übersicht f (-; -en) overview (**über** acc of); outline, summary

'übersichtlich adj clear(ly arranged)

'übersiedeln v/i (sep, -ge-, sein) move (**nach** to)

'Übersied(e)lung f move

über'spannen v/t (no -ge-, h) span

über'spannt fig adj eccentric; extravagant

über'spielen v/t (no -ge-, h) record; tape; fig cover up

über'spitzt adj exaggerated

über'springen v/t (irr, **springen**, no -ge-, h) jump (over), esp SPORT a. clear; fig skip

über'stehen[1] v/t (irr, **stehen**, no -ge-, h) get over; survive (a. fig), live through

'überstehen[2] v/i (irr, **stehen**, sep, -ge-, h) jut out

über'steigen fig v/t (irr, **steigen**, no -ge-, h) exceed

über'stimmen v/t (no -ge-, h) outvote

'überstreifen v/t (sep, -ge-, h) slip s.th. on

über'strömen v/i (sep, -ge-, sein) overflow (**vor** dat with)

'Überstunden pl overtime; **Überstunden machen** work overtime

über'stürzen v/t (no -ge-, h) et. **überstürzen** rush things; **sich überstürzen** events: follow in rapid succession

über'stürzt adj (over)hasty; rash

über'teuert adj overpriced

über'tönen v/t (no -ge-, h) drown (out)

über'tragbar adj transferable; MED contagious

über'tragen[1] adj figurative

über'tragen[2] v/t (irr, **tragen**, no -ge-, h) broadcast, a. televise; translate; MED, TECH transmit; MED transfuse (blood); JUR, ECON transfer

Über'tragung f (-; -en) radio, TV broadcast; transmission; translation; MED transfusion; JUR, ECON transfer

über'treffen v/t (irr, **treffen**, no -ge-, h) outstrip, outdo, surpass, beat

über'treiben v/i and v/t (irr, **treiben**, no -ge-, h) exaggerate; overdo

Über'treibung f (-; -en) exaggeration

'übertreten[1] v/i (irr, **treten**, sep, -ge-, sein) **übertreten zu** go over to, REL convert to

über'treten[2] v/t (irr, **treten**, no -ge-, h) **1.** break, violate; **2.** v/i SPORT foul (a jump or throw)

Über'tretung f (-; -en) violation, JUR a. of-fen|se, Br -ce

'Übertritt m change (**zu** to); REL, POL conversion (to)

über'völkert [-'fœlkɐt] adj overpopulated

über'wachen v/t (no -ge-, h) supervise, oversee; control; observe

Über'wachung f (-; -en) supervision, control; observance; surveillance

über'wältigen v/t (irr, no -ge-, h) overwhelm, overpower, fig a. overcome

über'wältigend adj overwhelming, overpowering

über'weisen v/t (irr, **weisen**, no -ge-, h) ECON transfer (**an j-n** to s.o.'s account); remit; MED refer (**an** acc to)

Über'weisung f (-; -en) ECON transfer; remittance; MED referral

'überwerfen[1] v/t (irr, **werfen**, sep, -ge-, h) slip s.th. on

über'werfen[2] v/refl (irr, **werfen**, no -ge-, h) **sich überwerfen (mit j-m)** fall out with each other (with s.o.)

über'wiegen v/i (irr, **wiegen**, no -ge-, h) predominate

über'wiegend adj predominant; vast (majority)

über'winden v/t (irr, **winden**, no -ge-, h) overcome (a. fig); defeat; **sich überwinden zu** inf bring o.s. to inf

über'wintern [-'vɪntɐn] v/i (no -ge-, h) spend the winter (**in** dat in)

über'wuchern v/t (no -ge-, h) overgrow

'Überzahl f (-; no pl) majority; **in der Überzahl sein** outnumber s.o.

über'zeugen v/t (no -ge-, h) convince (**von** of), persuade; **sich überzeugen, dass** make sure that; **sich selbst über-**

zeugen (go and) see for o.s.

überzeugt [-'tsɔykt] *adj* convinced; *überzeugt sein a.* be *or* feel (quite) sure

Über'zeugung *f* (-; -en) conviction

'überziehen¹ *v/t* (*irr, ziehen, sep, -ge-, h*) put *s.th.* on

über'ziehen² *v/t* (*irr, ziehen, no, -ge-, h*) TECH *etc* cover; ECON overdraw

Über'ziehungskre,dit *m* ECON overdraft (facility)

'Überzug *m* cover; coat(ing)

üblich ['y:plɪç] *adj* usual, normal; *es ist üblich* it's the custom; *wie üblich* as usual

'U-Boot *n* submarine

übrig ['y:brɪç] *adj* remaining; *die Übrigen pl* the others, the rest; *übrig sein* (*haben*) be (have) left; *übrig bleiben* be left, remain; *es bleibt mir nichts anderes übrig* (*als zu inf*) there is nothing else I can do (but *inf*); *übrig lassen* leave

übrigens ['y:brɪɡəns] *adv* by the way

'übriglassen *v/i* (*irr, lassen, sep, -ge-, sein*) (*a. fig*) → *übrig*

Übung ['y:bʊŋ] *f* (-; -en) exercise; practice; *in* (*aus der*) *Übung* in (out of) practice

Ufer ['u:fɐ] *n* (-s; -) shore; bank; *ans Ufer* ashore

Uhr [u:ɐ] *f* (-; -en ['u:rən]) clock; watch; *um vier Uhr* at four o'clock

'Uhrarmband *n* watchstrap

Uhrmacher *m* (-s; -) watchmaker

Uhrwerk *n* clockwork

Uhrzeiger *m* hand

Uhrzeigersinn *m*: *im Uhrzeigersinn* clockwise; *entgegen dem Uhrzeigersinn* counterclockwise, *Br* anticlockwise

Uhu ['u:hu] *m* (-s; -s) ZO eagle owl

UKW [u:ka:'ve:] *ABBR of Ultrakurzwelle* VHF, very high frequency

Ulk [ʊlk] *m* (-s; -e) joke; hoax

ulkig ['ʊlkɪç] *adj* funny

Ulme ['ʊlmə] *f* (-; -n) BOT elm

Ultimatum [ʊlti'ma:tʊm] *n* (-s; -ten) ultimatum; *j-m ein Ultimatum stellen* deliver an ultimatum to s.o.

um [ʊm] *prp* (*acc*) *and cj* (a)round; at; about, around; *um Geld* for money; *um e-e Stunde* (*10 cm*) by an hour (10 cm); *um ... willen* for the sake of ...; *um zu inf* (in order) to *inf*; *um sein* F be over; *die Zeit ist um* time's up; → *umso*

umarmen [ʊm'ʔarmən] *v/t* (*no -ge-, h*) (*a. sich umarmen*) embrace, hug

Um'armung *f* (-; -en) embrace, hug

'Umbau *m* (-[e]s; -e, -ten) rebuilding, re-construction

'umbauen *v/t* (*sep, -ge-, h*) rebuild, reconstruct

'umbinden *v/t* (*irr, binden, sep, -ge-, h*) put *s.th.* on

umblättern *v/i* (*sep, -ge-, h*) turn (over) the page

umbringen *v/t* (*irr, bringen, sep, -ge-, h*) kill; *sich umbringen* kill o.s.

umbuchen *v/t* (*sep, -ge-, h*) change; ECON transfer (*auf acc* to)

umdenken *v/i* (*irr, denken, sep, -ge-, h*) change one's way of thinking

umdispo,nieren *v/i* (*sep, no -ge-, h*) change one's plans

umdrehen *v/t* (*sep, -ge-, h*) turn (round); *sich umdrehen* turn round

Um'drehung *f* (-; -en) turn; PHYS, TECH rotation, revolution

umei'nander *adv* care *etc* about *or* for each other

'umfahren¹ *v/t* (*irr, fahren, sep, -ge-, h*) run down

um'fahren² *v/t* (*irr, fahren, no -ge-, h*) drive (MAR sail) round

'umfallen *v/i* (*irr, fallen, sep, -ge-, sein*) fall down *or* over; collapse; *tot umfallen* drop dead

'Umfang *m* circumference; size; extent; *in großem Umfang* on a large scale

'umfangreich *adj* extensive; voluminous

um'fassen *fig v/t* (*no -ge-, h*) cover; include

umfassend *adj* comprehensive; complete

'umformen *v/t* (*sep, -ge-, h*) turn, change; ELECTR, LING, MATH *a.* transform, convert (*all: in acc* [in]to)

'Umformer *m* (-s; -) ELECTR converter

'Umfrage *f* opinion poll

'Umgang *m* (-[e]s; *no pl*) company; *Umgang haben mit* associate with; *beim Umgang mit* when dealing with

'umgänglich [-gɛnlɪç] *adj* sociable

'Umgangsformen *pl* manners

Umgangssprache *f* colloquial speech; *die englische Umgangssprache* colloquial English

um'geben *v/t* (*irr, geben, no -ge-, h*) surround (*mit* with)

Um'gebung *f* (-; -en) surroundings; environment

'umgehen¹ *v/i* (*irr, gehen, sep, -ge-, sein*) *umgehen mit* deal with, handle; *umgehen können mit* have a way with, be good with

um'gehen² *v/t* (*irr, gehen, no -ge-, h*) avoid; bypass

'umgehend *adv* immediately

Um'gehungsstraße *f* bypass; beltway, *Br*

U

ring road

umgekehrt ['ʊmgəke:ɐt] **1.** *adj* reverse; opposite; **(genau) umgekehrt** (just) the other way round; **2.** *adv* the other way round; **und umgekehrt** and vice versa

'**umgraben** v/t (*irr*, **graben**, *sep*, *-ge-*, *h*) dig (up), break up

'**Umhang** *m* cape

'**umhängen** v/t (*sep*, *-ge-*, *h*) put around or over s.o.'s shoulders *etc*; rehang

'**umhauen** v/t (*irr*, **hauen**, *sep*, *-ge-*, *h*) fell, cut down; F knock *s.o.* out

um'her *adv* (a)round, about

um'herstreifen v/i (*sep*, *-ge-*, *sein*) roam or wander around

'**umkehren** (*sep*, *-ge-*) **1.** v/i (*sein*) turn back; **2.** v/t (*h*) reverse

'**Umkehrung** *f* (*-; -en*) reversal (*a. fig*)

'**umkippen** (*sep*, *-ge-*) **1.** v/t (*h*) tip over, upset; **2.** v/i (*sein*) fall down *or* over, overturn

um'klammern v/t (*no -ge-*, *h*), **Um'klammerung** *f* (*-; -en*) clasp, clutch, clench

'**Umkleidekabine** *f* changing cubicle

Umkleideraum *m esp* SPORT changing *or* locker room; THEA dressing room

'**umkommen** v/i (*irr*, **kommen**, *sep*, *-ge-*, *sein*) be killed (**bei**) in), die (in); F **umkommen vor** (*dat*) be dying with

'**Umkreis** *m*: **im Umkreis von** within a radius of

um'kreisen v/t (*no -ge-*, *h*) circle; ASTR revolve around; *satellite etc*: orbit

'**umkrempeln** v/t (*sep*, *-ge-*, *h*) roll up

'**Umlauf** *m* circulation; PHYS, TECH rotation; ECON circular; **im (in) Umlauf sein (bringen)** be in (put into) circulation, circulate

Umlaufbahn *f* ASTR orbit

'**umlaufen** v/i (*irr*, **laufen**, *sep*, *-ge-*, *sein*) circulate

'**umlegen** v/t (*sep*, *-ge-*, *h*) put on; move; share (*expenses etc*); TECH pull; F do *s.o.* in, bump *s.o.* off

'**umleiten** v/t (*sep*, *-ge-*, *h*) divert

'**Umleitung** *f* (*-; -en*) detour, *Br* diversion

'**umliegend** *adj* surrounding

'**umpacken** v/t (*sep*, *-ge-*, *h*) repack

'**umpflanzen** v/t (*sep*, *-ge-*, *h*) repot

umranden [ʊm'randən] v/t (*no -ge-*, *h*), **Um'randung** *f* (*-; -en*) edge, border

um'räumen v/t (*sep*, *-ge-*, *h*) rearrange

'**umrechnen** v/t (*sep*, *-ge-*, *h*) convert (**in** *acc* into)

'**Umrechnung** *f* (*-; -en*) conversion

'**Umrechnungskurs** *m* exchange rate

'**umreißen** v/t (*irr*, **reißen**, *sep*, *-ge-*, *h*) knock *s.o.* down

um'ringen v/t (*no -ge-*, *h*) surround

'**Umriss** *m* outline (*a. fig*), contour

'**umrühren** v/t (*sep*, *-ge-*, *h*) stir

umrüsten v/t (*sep*, *-ge-*, *h*) TECH convert (**auf** *acc* to)

umsatteln F v/i (*sep*, *-ge-*, *h*) **umsatteln von ... auf** (*acc*) ... switch from ... to ...

'**Umsatz** *m* ECON sales

'**umschalten** v/t and v/i (*sep*, *-ge-*, *h*) switch (over) (**auf** *acc* to) (*a. fig*)

'**Umschlag** *m* envelope; cover, wrapper; jacket; cuff, *Br* turn-up; MED compress; ECON handling

'**umschlagen** (*irr*, **schlagen**, *sep*, *-ge-*) **1.** v/t (*h*) cut down, fell; turn up; turn down; ECON handle; **2.** v/i (*sein*) turn over; *fig* change (suddenly)

'**Umschlagplatz** *m* trading center (*Br* centre)

'**umschnallen** v/t (*sep*, *-ge-*, *h*) buckle on

'**umschreiben**[1] v/t (*irr*, **schreiben**, *sep*, *-ge-*, *h*) rewrite

um'schreiben[2] v/t (*irr*, **schreiben**, *no -ge-*, *h*) paraphrase

Um'schreibung *f* (*-; -en*) paraphrase

'**Umschrift** *f* transcription

'**umschulen** v/t (*sep*, *-ge-*, *h*) retrain; transfer to another school

umschwärmt [ʊm'ʃvɛrmt] *adj* idolized

'**Umschwung** *m* (drastic) change, *esp* POL *a.* swing

um'segeln v/t (*no -ge-*, *h*) sail round; circumnavigate

'**umsehen** v/refl (*irr*, **sehen**, *sep*, *-ge-*, *h*) look around (**in e-m Laden** a shop; **nach** for); look back (**nach** at); **sich umsehen nach** be looking for

umsetzen v/t (*sep*, *-ge-*, *h*) move (*a.* PED); ECON sell; **umsetzen in** (*acc*) convert (into; **in die Tat umsetzen** put into action; **sich umsetzen** change places

'**umsiedeln** v/i (*sep*, *-ge-*, *sein*) and v/t (*h*) resettle; → **umziehen**

'**Umsied(e)lung** *f* (*-; -en*) resettlement

'**Umsiedler** *m* (*-s; -*) resettler

'**umso 1. je später** *etc*, **umso schlechter** *etc* the later *etc*, the worse *etc*; **2. umso besser** so much the better

um'sonst *adv* free (of charge), for nothing; F for free; *fig* in vain

um'spannen v/t (*no -ge-*, *h*) span (*a. fig*)

'**umspringen** v/i (*irr*, **springen**, *sep*, *-ge-*, *sein*) shift, change (suddenly) (*a. fig*); **umspringen mit** treat (badly)

'**Umstand** *m* circumstance; fact; detail; **unter diesen (keinen) Umständen** under the (no) circumstances; **unter Umständen** possibly; **keine Umstände machen** not cause *s.o.* any trouble; not go to any trouble; no put o.s. out; *in anderen Umständen sein* be expecting

umständlich ['ʊmʃtɛntlɪç] *adj* awkward; complicated; long-winded; *das ist (mir) viel zu umständlich* that's far too much trouble (for me)

'Umstandskleid *n* maternity dress

Umstandswort *n* (-[e]s; -wörter) LING adverb

'Umstehende: die Umstehenden *pl* the bystanders

'umsteigen *v/i* (*irr, steigen, sep, -ge-, sein*) change (**nach** for), RAIL *a.* change trains (for)

'umstellen *v/t* (*sep, -ge-, h*) change (**auf** *acc* to), make a change *or* changes in, *esp* TECH *a.* switch (over) (to), convert (to); adjust (to); rearrange (*a. furniture*), reorganize; reset (*watch*); *sich umstellen auf* (*acc*) change *or* switch (over) to; adjust (to.s.); get used to

'Umstellung *f* (-; -en) change; switch, conversion; adjustment; rearrangement, reorganization

'umstimmen *v/t* (*sep, -ge-, h*) *j-n umstimmen* change s.o.'s mind

'umstoßen *v/t* (*irr, stoßen, sep, -ge-, h*) knock over, upset (*a. fig*)

umstritten [ʊmˈʃtrɪtən] *adj* controversial

'Umsturz *m* overthrow

'umstürzen *v/i* (*sep, -ge-, sein*) overturn, fall over

Umtausch *m*, **'umtauschen** *v/t* (*sep, -ge-, h*) exchange (**gegen** for)

'umwälzend *adj* revolutionary

'Umwälzung *f* (-; -en) radical change

'umwandeln *v/t* (*sep, -ge-, h*) turn (**in** *acc* into), transform (into), *esp* CHEM, ELECTR, PHYS *a.* convert ([in]to)

'Umwandlung *f* (-; -en) transformation, conversion

'Umweg *m* roundabout route *or* way (*a. fig*), *esp* MOT *a.* detour; *ein Umweg von 10 Minuten* ten minutes out of the way; *fig auf Umwegen* in a roundabout way

'Umwelt *f* (-; *no pl*) environment

'Umwelt... *in cpds mst* environmental ...

Umweltforschung *f* ecology

'umweltfreundlich *adj* environment-friendly, non-polluting

umweltschädlich *adj* harmful, noxious, polluting

'Umweltschutz *m* conservation, environmental protection, pollution control

Umweltschützer *m* environmentalist, conservationist

Umweltschutzpa,pier *n* recycled paper

Umweltsünder *m* (environmental) polluter

Umweltverschmutzer *m* (-s; -) polluter

Umweltverschmutzung *f* (environmental) pollution

Umweltzerstörung *f* ecocide

'umziehen (*irr, ziehen, sep -ge-*) **1.** *v/i* (*sein*) move (**nach** to); **2.** *v/refl* (*h*) change (one's clothes)

umzingeln [ʊmˈtsɪŋəln] *v/t* (*no -ge-, h*) surround, encircle

'Umzug *m* move (**nach** to), removal (to); parade

unabhängig ['ʊn-] *adj* independent (**von** of); *unabhängig davon, ob* (**was**) regardless of whether (what)

'Unabhängigkeit *f* (-; *no pl*) independence (**von** from)

'unabsichtlich *adj* unintentional; *et. unabsichtlich tun* do s.th. by mistake

unab'wendbar *adj* inevitable

'unachtsam *adj* careless, negligent

'Unachtsamkeit *f* (-; *no pl*) carelessness, negligence

unan'fechtbar *adj* incontestable

'unangebracht *adj* inappropriate; *unangebracht sein* be out of place

unangemessen *adj* unreasonable; inadequate

unangenehm *adj* unpleasant; embarrassing

unan'nehmbar *adj* unacceptable

Unannehmlichkeiten ['ʊnˀanneːmlɪçkaɪtən] *pl* trouble, difficulties

'unansehnlich *adj* unsightly

'unanständig *adj* indecent, obscene

unan'tastbar *adj* inviolable

'unappetitlich *adj* unappetizing

Unart ['ʊnˀart] *f* (-; -en) bad habit

'unartig *adj* naughty, bad

'unaufdringlich *adj* unobtrusive

'unauffällig *adj* inconspicuous, unobtrusive

unauf'findbar *adj* not to be found, untraceable

'unaufgefordert *adv* without being asked, of one's own accord

unaufhörlich [ʊnˀaufˈhøːrlɪç] *adj* continuous

'unaufmerksam *adj* inattentive

'Unaufmerksamkeit *f* (-; *no pl*) inattention, inattentiveness

'unaufrichtig *adj* insincere

unauslöschlich [ʊnˀausˈlœʃlɪç] *adj* indelible

unausstehlich [-ˈʃteːlɪç] *adj* unbearable

unbarmherzig *adj* merciless

'unbeabsichtigt *adj* unintentional

unbeachtet *adj* unnoticed

unbeaufsichtigt *adj* unattended

unbebaut adj undeveloped
unbedacht [-bədaxt] adj thoughtless
unbedenklich 1. adj safe; **2.** adv without hesitation
unbedeutend adj insignificant; minor
unbedingt 1. adj unconditional, absolute; **2.** adv by all means, absolutely; *need etc* badly
unbefahrbar adj impassable
unbefangen adj unprejudiced, unbias(s)ed; unembarrassed
unbefriedigend adj unsatisfactory
unbefriedigt adj dissatisfied
unbegabt adj untalented
unbegreiflich adj inconceivable, incomprehensible
unbegrenzt adj unlimited, boundless
unbegründet adj unfounded
'Unbehagen n (-s; no pl) uneasiness, discomfort
'unbehaglich adj uneasy, uncomfortable
unbehelligt [unbə'hɛlıçt] adj unmolested
'unbeherrscht adj uncontrolled, lacking self-control
unbeholfen [-bəhɔlfən] adj clumsy, awkward
unbeirrt adj unwavering
unbekannt adj unknown
'Unbekannte f (-; -n) MATH unknown quantity
'unbekümmert adj light-hearted, cheerful
unbelehrbar adj: **er ist unbelehrbar** he'll never learn
unbeliebt adj unpopular; **er ist überall unbeliebt** nobody likes him
unbemannt adj unmanned
unbemerkt adj unnoticed
unbenutzt adj unused
unbequem adj uncomfortable; inconvenient
unberechenbar adj unpredictable
unberechtigt adj unauthorized; unjustified
unbeschädigt adj undamaged
unbescheiden adj immodest
unbe'schränkt adj unlimited; absolute (*power*)
unbeschreiblich [-bə'fraiplıç] adj indescribable
unbe'sehen adv unseen
unbesiegbar [-bə'zi:kba:ɐ] adj invincible
'unbesonnen adj thoughtless, imprudent; rash
unbe'spielbar adj SPORT unplayable
unbeständig adj unstable; METEOR changeable, unsettled
unbestätigt adj unconfirmed
unbe'stechlich adj incorruptible

'unbestimmt adj indefinite (*a.* LING); uncertain; vague
unbe'streitbar adj indisputable
unbestritten [-bə'ʃtrıtən] adj undisputed
'unbeteiligt adj not involved; indifferent
unbetont adj unstressed
unbeugsam [un'bɔykza:m] adj inflexible
'unbewacht adj unwatched, unguarded (*a. fig*)
unbewaffnet adj unarmed
unbeweglich adj immovable; motionless
unbe'wohnbar adj uninhabitable
'unbewohnt adj uninhabited; unoccupied, vacant
'unbewusst adj unconscious
unbe'zahlbar fig adj invaluable, priceless
'unbezahlt adj unpaid
'unblutig 1. adj bloodless; **2.** adv without bloodshed
'unbrauchbar adj useless
und [unt] cj and; F **na und?** so what?
'undankbar adj ungrateful (**gegen** to); thankless
'Undankbarkeit f (-; no pl) ingratitude, ungratefulness
undefi'nierbar adj undefinable
un'denkbar adj unthinkable
'undeutlich adj indistinct; inarticulate; *fig* vague
'undicht adj leaky
'unduldsam adj intolerant
'Unduldsamkeit f (-; no pl) intolerance
undurch'dringlich adj impenetrable
undurch'führbar adj impracticable
'undurchlässig adj impervious, impermeable
undurchsichtig adj opaque; *fig* mysterious
'uneben adj uneven
'Unebenheit f a) (-; no pl) unevenness, b) (-; -en) bump
'unecht adj false; artificial; imitation ...; F contp fake, phon(e)y
'unehelich adj illegitimate
'unehrenhaft adj dishono(u)rable
'unehrlich adj dishonest
'uneigennützig adj unselfish
'uneinig adj: (**sich**) **uneinig sein** disagree (**über** acc on)
'Uneinigkeit f (-; no pl) disagreement; dissension
unein'nehmbar adj impregnable
'unempfänglich adj insusceptible (**für** to)
'unempfindlich adj insensitive (**gegen** to)
un'endlich adj infinite; endless, never-ending
Un'endlichkeit f (-; no pl) infinity (*a. fig*)
unentbehrlich [un'ʔɛnt'be:ɐlıç] adj indispensable

unentgeltlich [-'gɛltlɪç] *adj and adv* free (of charge)

'**unentschieden** *adj* undecided; *unent-schieden enden* SPORT end in a draw or tie; *es steht unentschieden* the score is even

'**Unentschieden** *n* (*-s; -*) SPORT draw, tie

'**unentschlossen** *adj* irresolute

unent'schuldbar *adj* inexcusable

unentwegt [ʊn'ʔɛnt'veːkt] *adv* untiringly; continuously

'**unerfahren** *adj* inexperienced

'**unerfreulich** *adj* unpleasant

'**unerfüllt** *adj* unfulfilled

'**unergiebig** *adj* unproductive

'**unerheblich** *adj* irrelevant (*für* to); insignificant

unerhört [ʊn'ʔɛːɐ'høːɐt] *adj* outrageous

'**unerkannt** *adj* unrecognized

uner'klärlich *adj* inexplicable

unerlässlich *adj* essential, indispensable

'**unerlaubt** *adj* unallowed; unauthorized

'**unerledigt** *adj* unsettled (*a.* ECON)

uner'messlich *adj* immeasurable

unermüdlich [ʊn'ʔɛɐ'myːtlɪç] *adj* indefatigable; untiring

uner'reichbar *adj* inaccessible; *esp fig* unattainable

uner'reicht *adj* unequal(l)ed

unersättlich [ʊn'ʔɛɐ'zɛtlɪç] *adj* insatiable

'**unerschlossen** *adj* undeveloped

unerschöpflich [ʊn'ʔɛɐ'ʃœpflɪç] *adj* inexhaustible

unerschütterlich [-'ʃʏtɐlɪç] *adj* imperturbable

unerschwinglich [-'ʃvɪŋlɪç] *adj* exorbitant; *für j-n unerschwinglich sein* be beyond s.o.'s means

unersetzlich [-'zɛtslɪç] *adj* irreplaceable

unerträglich [-'trɛːklɪç] *adj* unbearable

'**unerwartet** *adj* unexpected

'**unerwünscht** *adj* unwanted

'**unfähig** *adj* incompetent; incapable (*zu tun* of doing), unable (to *inf*)

'**Unfähigkeit** *f* (*-; no pl*) incompetence; incapacity, inability

'**Unfall** *m* accident; crash

'**Unfallstelle** *f* scene of the accident

un'**fehlbar** *adj* infallible (*a.* REL); unfailing

unförmig [ʊnˈfœrmɪç] *adj* shapeless; misshapen; monstrous

'**unfrankiert** *adj* unstamped

'**unfrei** *adj* not free; *post* unpaid

'**unfreiwillig** *adj* involuntary; unconscious (*humor*)

'**unfreundlich** *adj* unfriendly (*zu* to), unkind (to); *fig* cheerless

'**Unfrieden** *m* (*-s; no pl*) discord; *Unfrieden stiften* make mischief

'**unfruchtbar** *adj* infertile

'**Unfruchtbarkeit** *f* (*-; no pl*) infertility

Unfug ['ʊnfuːk] *m* (*-[e]s; no pl*) nonsense; *Unfug treiben* be up to mischief, fool around

Ungar ['ʊŋɡar] *m* (*-n; -n*), '**Ungarin** *f* (*-; -nen*), '**ungarisch** *adj* Hungarian

'**Ungarn** Hungary

'**ungastlich** *adj* inhospitable

'**ungeachtet** *prp* (*gen*) regardless of; despite

ungeahnt *adj* unthought-of

ungebeten *adj* uninvited, unasked

ungebildet *adj* uneducated

ungeboren *adj* unborn

ungebräuchlich *adj* uncommon, unusual

ungebührlich [-ɡəbyːɐlɪç] *adj* unseemly

ungebunden *fig adj* free, independent; *frei und ungebunden* footloose and fancy-free

ungedeckt *adj* ECON uncovered; SPORT unmarked

'**Ungeduld** *f* (*-; no pl*) impatience

'**ungeduldig** *adj* impatient

'**ungeeignet** *adj* unfit; unqualified; inappropriate

ungefähr ['ʊnɡəfɛːɐ] **1.** *adj* approximate; rough; **2.** *adv* approximately, roughly, about, around, ... or so; *so ungefähr* something like that

'**ungefährlich** *adj* harmless; safe

'**ungeheuer** *adj* enormous (*a. fig*), huge, vast

'**Ungeheuer** *n* (*-s; -*) monster (*a. fig*)

unge'heuerlich *adj* monstrous

'**ungehindert** *adj and adv* unhindered

'**ungehobelt** *fig adj* uncouth, rough

'**ungehörig** *adj* improper, unseemly

'**ungehorsam** *adj* disobedient

Ungehorsam *m* (*-s; no pl*) disobedience

'**ungekocht** *adj* uncooked

ungekünstelt *adj* unaffected

ungekürzt *adj* unabridged

ungelegen *adj* inconvenient; *j-m ungelegen kommen* be inconvenient for s.o.

ungelenk ['ʊnɡəlɛŋk] *adj* awkward, clumsy

'**ungelernt** *adj* unskilled

'**ungemütlich** *adj* uncomfortable; F *ungemütlich werden* get nasty

ungenau *adj* inaccurate; *fig* vague

'**Ungenauigkeit** *f* (*-; -en*) inaccuracy

ungeniert ['ʊnʒeniːɐt] *adj* uninhibited

'**ungenießbar** *adj* uneatable; undrinkable; F unbearable

ungenügend *adj* insufficient; PED poor, unsatisfactory; *grade*: *a.* F

ungepflegt *adj* neglected; untidy, unkempt

U

ungerade *adj* uneven; odd

ungerecht *adj* unfair, unjust

'**Ungerechtigkeit** *f* (-; *no pl*) injustice, unfairness

'**ungern** *adv* unwillingly; *et. ungern tun* hate *or* not like to do s.th.

'**ungeschehen** *adj*: *ungeschehen machen* undo

ungeschickt *adj* awkward, clumsy

ungeschliffen *adj* uncut (*diamond etc*); unpolished (*a. fig*)

ungeschminkt *adj* without make-up; *fig* unvarnished, plain (*truth*)

ungesetzlich *adj* illegal, unlawful

ungestört *adj* undisturbed

ungestraft *adj*: *ungestraft davonkommen* get off unpunished (F scot-free)

ungesund *adj* unhealthy (*a. fig*)

ungeteilt *adj* undivided (*a. fig*)

Ungetüm ['ʊŋgətyːm] *n* (-s; -e) monster, *fig a.* monstrosity

'**ungewiss** *adj* uncertain; *j-n im Ungewissen lassen* keep s.o. in the dark (*über acc* about)

'**Ungewissheit** *f* (-; *no pl*) uncertainty

'**ungewöhnlich** *adj* unusual

'**ungewohnt** *adj* strange, unfamiliar;

Ungeziefer ['ʊŋgətsiːfɐ] *n* (-s; *no pl*) vermin

'**ungezogen** *adj* naughty, bad; spoilt

'**ungezwungen** *adj* relaxed, informal; easygoing

'**ungläubig** *adj* incredulous, unbelieving (*a.* REL)

unglaublich [ʊn'glauplɪç] *adj* incredible, unbelievable

'**unglaubwürdig** *adj* implausible; unreliable (*witness etc*)

'**ungleich** *adj* unequal, different; unlike

ungleichmäßig *adj* uneven; irregular

'**Unglück** *n* (-[e]s; -e) a) (*no pl*) bad luck, misfortune; misery, b) accident; disaster

'**unglücklich** *adj* unhappy, miserable; unfortunate

'**unglücklicher'weise** *adv* unfortunately

'**ungültig** *adj* invalid; *für ungültig erklären* JUR invalidate

'**Ungunst** *f*: *zu Ungunsten → zuungunsten*

'**ungünstig** *adj* unfavo(u)rable; disadvantageous

'**ungut** *adj*: *ungutes Gefühl* misgivings (*bei et.* about s.th.); *nichts für ungut!* no offense (*Br* offence) meant!

'**unhaltbar** *adj* untenable; intolerable; SPORT unstoppable

'**unhandlich** *adj* unwieldy

'**unhar,monisch** *adj* MUS discordant

'**Unheil** *n* (-s; *no pl*) mischief; evil; disaster

'**unheilbar** *adj* MED incurable

'**unheilvoll** *adj* disastrous; sinister

'**unheimlich** *adj* creepy, spooky, eerie; F tremendous; F *unheimlich gut* terrific, fantastic

'**unhöflich** *adj* impolite; rude

'**Unhöflichkeit** *f* (-; *no pl*) impoliteness; rudeness

un'**hörbar** *adj* inaudible

'**unhygienisch** *adj* insanitary

Uniform [uni'fɔrm] *f* (-; -en) uniform

'**uninteressant** *adj* uninteresting

uninteressiert ['ʊn'ɪntəresiːɐt] *adj* uninterested (*an dat* in)

Union [u'njoːn] *f* (-; -en) union

Universität [univerzi'tɛːt] *f* (-; -en) university

Universum [uni'vɛrzʊm] *n* (-s; *no pl*) universe

Unke ['ʊŋkə] *f* (-; -n) ZO toad

'**unkenntlich** *adj* unrecognizable

'**Unkenntnis** *f* (-; *no pl*) ignorance

'**unklar** *adj* unclear; uncertain; confused, muddled; *im Unklaren sein* (*lassen*) be (leave *s.o.*) in the dark

'**unklug** *adj* imprudent, unwise

'**Unkosten** *pl* expenses, costs

'**Unkraut** *n* (-[e]s; *no pl*) weed(s); *Unkraut jäten* weed (the garden)

unkündbar ['ʊnkʏntbaːɐ] *adj* permanent (*post*)

'**unlängst** *adv* lately, recently

'**unleserlich** *adj* illegible

'**unlogisch** *adj* illogical

un'**lösbar** *adj* insoluble

'**unmännlich** *adj* unmanly, effeminate

'**unmäßig** *adj* excessive

'**Unmenge** *f* vast quantity *or* number(s) (*von* of), F loads (of), tons (of)

'**Unmensch** *m* monster, brute

'**unmenschlich** *adj* inhuman, cruel

'**Unmenschlichkeit** *f* (-; -en) a) (*no pl*) inhumanity, b) cruelty

un'**merklich** *adj* imperceptible

'**unmissverständlich** *adj* unmistakable

'**unmittelbar 1.** *adj* immediate, direct; **2.** *adv*: *unmittelbar nach* (*hinter*) right after (behind)

'**unmöbliert** *adj* unfurnished

'**unmodern** *adj* out of fashion *or* style

'**unmöglich 1.** *adj* impossible; **2.** *adv*: *ich kann es unmöglich tun* I can't possibly do it

'**unmoralisch** *adj* immoral

'**unmündig** *adj* JUR under age

'**unmusikalisch** *adj* unmusical

'**unnachahmlich** *adj* inimitable

'**unnachgiebig** *adj* unyielding

'**unnachsichtig** *adj* strict, severe

unnahbar [ʊnˈnaːbaːɐ] *adj* standoffish, cold

'unnatürlich *adj* unnatural (*a. fig*); affected

'unnötig *adj* unnecessary, needless

unnütz ['ʊnnʏts] *adj* useless

'unordentlich *adj* untidy; *unordentlich sein* room etc: be (in) a mess

'Unordnung *f* (-; *no pl*) disorder, mess

'unparteiisch *adj* impartial, unbias(s)ed

'Unparteiische *m, f* (-n; -n) SPORT referee

'unpassend *adj* unsuitable; improper; inappropriate

'unpassierbar *adj* impassable

unpässlich ['ʊnpɛslɪç] *adj* indisposed

'unpersönlich *adj* impersonal (*a.* LING)

'unpolitisch *adj* unpolitical

'unpraktisch *adj* impractical

'unpünktlich *adj* unpunctual

'unrecht *adj* wrong; *unrecht haben* be wrong; *j-m unrecht tun* do s.o. wrong

'Unrecht *n* (-[e]s; *no pl*) injustice, wrong; *zu Unrecht* wrong(ful)ly; *Unrecht haben → unrecht; unrecht tun → unrecht*

'unrechtmäßig *adj* unlawful

'unregelmäßig *adj* irregular (*a.* LING)

'Unregelmäßigkeit *f* (-; -en) irregularity

'unreif *adj* unripe; *fig* immature

'Unreife *fig f* immaturity

'unrein *adj* unclean; impure (*a.* REL)

'Unreinheit *f* (-; -en) impurity

'unrichtig *adj* incorrect, wrong

'Unruhe *f* (-; -n) a) (*no pl*) restlessness, unrest (*a.* POL); anxiety, alarm, b) *pl* disturbances, riots

'unruhig *adj* restless; uneasy; worried, alarmed; MAR rough

uns [ʊns] *pers pron* (to) us; each other; *uns (selbst)* (to) ourselves; *ein Freund von uns* a friend of ours

'unsachgemäß *adj* improper

unsachlich *adj* unobjective

unsanft *adj* rude, rough

unsauber *adj* unclean, *esp fig a.* impure; SPORT unfair; *fig* underhand

unschädlich *adj* harmless

unscharf *adj* PHOT blurred, out of focus

un'schätzbar *adj* inestimable, invaluable

'unscheinbar *adj* inconspicuous; plain

unschicklich *adj* indecent

unschlüssig *adj* irresolute; undecided

unschön *adj* unsightly; *fig* unpleasant

'Unschuld *f* (-; *no pl*) innocence; *fig* virginity

unschuldig *adj* innocent (*an dat* of)

'unselbstständig *adj* dependent on others

'Unselbstständigkeit *f* lack of independence, dependence on others

unser ['ʊnzɐ] *poss pron* our; *unserer, unsere, unseres* ours

'unsicher *adj* unsafe, insecure; self-conscious; uncertain

'Unsicherheit *f* (-; -en) a) (*no pl*) insecurity, unsafeness; self-consciousness, b) uncertainty

'unsichtbar *adj* invisible

'Unsinn *m* (-[e]s; *no pl*) nonsense

'unsinnig *adj* nonsensical, stupid; absurd

'Unsitte *f* bad habit; abuse

'unsittlich *adj* immoral, indecent

'unsozial *adj* unsocial

'unsportlich *adj* unathletic; *fig* unfair

'unsterblich 1. *adj* immortal (*a. fig*); 2. *adv: unsterblich verliebt* madly in love (*in acc* with)

'Unsterblichkeit *f* immortality

'Unstimmigkeit *f* (-; -en) discrepancy; *pl* disagreements

'unsympathisch *adj* disagreeable; *er (es) ist mir unsympathisch* I don't like him (it)

'untätig *adj* inactive; idle

'Untätigkeit *f* (-; *no pl*) inactivity

'untauglich *adj* unfit (*a.* MIL); incompetent

un'teilbar *adj* indivisible

unten ['ʊntən] *adv* (down) below, down (*a. nach unten*); downstairs; *unten auf* (*dat*) at the bottom of *the page etc*; *siehe unten* see below; *von oben bis unten* from top to bottom

unter ['ʊntɐ] *prp* under; below (*a. fig*); among; *fig* less than; *unter anderem* among other things; *unter uns (gesagt)* between you and me; *unter Wasser* underwater

'Unterarm *m* ANAT forearm

'unterbelichtet *adj* PHOT underexposed

unterbesetzt *adj* understaffed

'Unterbewusstsein *n* subconscious; *im Unterbewusstsein* subconsciously

unter'bieten *v/t* (*irr, bieten, no -ge-, h*) underbid; undercut; beat (*record*)

unter'binden *fig v/t* (*irr, binden, no -ge-, h*) put a stop to; prevent

unter'brechen *v/t* (*irr, brechen, no -ge-, h*) interrupt

Unter'brechung *f* (-; -en) interruption

'unterbringen *v/t* (*irr, bringen, sep, -ge-, h*) accommodate, put *s.o.* up; find a place for, put (*in acc* into)

'Unterbringung *f* (-; -en) accommodation

unter'dessen *adv* in the meantime, meanwhile

unter'drücken *v/t* (*no -ge-, h*) oppress; suppress

Unter'drücker *m* (-s; -) oppressor

U

Unter'drückung f (-; -en) oppression; suppression

untere ['ʊntərə] adj lower (a. fig)

'unterentwickelt adj underdeveloped

'unterernährt adj undernourished, underfed

'Unterernährung f (-; no pl) undernourishment, malnutrition

Unter'führung f (-; -en) underpass, Br a. subway

'Untergang m ASTR setting; MAR sinking; fig downfall; decline; fall

'untergehen v/i (irr, gehen, sep, -ge-, sein) go down (a. fig), ASTR a. set, MAR a. sink

'untergeordnet adj subordinate, inferior; secondary

'Untergewicht n (-[e]s; no pl), **'untergewichtig** adj underweight

unter'graben fig v/t (irr, graben, no -ge-, h) undermine

'Untergrund m subsoil; POL underground; **in den Untergrund gehen** go underground

Untergrundbahn f → **U-Bahn**

'unterhalb prp (gen) below, under

'Unterhalt m (-[e]s; no pl) support, maintenance (a. JUR)

unter'halten v/t (irr, halten, no -ge-, h) entertain; support; **sich unterhalten (mit)** talk (to, with); **sich (gut) unterhalten** enjoy o.s., have a good time

unter'haltsam adj entertaining

Unter'haltung f (-; -en) talk, conversation; entertainment

Unter'haltungsindus,trie f show business

'Unterhändler m negotiator

'Unterhaus n (-es; no pl) Br PARL House of Commons

'Unterhemd n undershirt, Br vest

'Unterholz n (-es; no pl) undergrowth

'Unterhose f shorts, esp Br underpants, panties, Br pants; **e-e lange Unterhose, lange Unterhosen** (a pair of) long johns

'unterirdisch adj underground

'Unterkiefer m ANAT lower jaw

'Unterkleid n slip

'unterkommen v/i (irr, kommen, sep, -ge-, sein) find accommodation; find work or a job (**bei** with)

Unterkunft ['ʊntəkʊnft] f (-; -künfte [-kʏnftə]) accommodation, lodging(s); MIL quarters; **Unterkunft und Verpflegung** board and lodging

'Unterlage f TECH base; pl documents; data

unter'lassen v/t (irr, lassen, no -ge-, h) omit, fail to do s.th.; stop or quit doing s.th.

Unter'lassung f (-; -en) omission (a. JUR)

'unterlegen¹ v/t (sep, -ge-, h) underlay

unter'legen² adj inferior (dat to)

Unter'legenheit f (-; no pl) inferiority

'Unterleib m ANAT abdomen, belly

unter'liegen v/i (irr, liegen, no -ge-, sein) be defeated (j-m by s.o.), lose (to s.o.); fig be subject to

'Unterlippe f ANAT lower lip

'Untermieter m, **'Untermieterin** f roomer, Br lodger

unter'nehmen v/t (irr, nehmen, no -ge-, h) make, take, go on a trip etc; **et. unternehmen** do s.th. (**gegen** about s.th.), take action (against s.o.)

Unter'nehmen n (-s; -) firm, business; venture; undertaking; enterprise; MIL operation

Unter'nehmensberater(in) management consultant

Unter'nehmer m (-s; -) businessman, entrepreneur; employer

Unter'nehmerin f (-; -nen) businesswoman

unter'nehmungslustig adj active, dynamic; adventurous

'Unteroffizier m MIL non-commissioned officer

unter'ordnen v/t and v/refl (sep, -ge-, h) subordinate (o.s.) (dat to)

Unter'redung f (-; -en) talk(s)

Unterricht ['ʊntəʀɪçt] m (-[e]s; no pl) instruction, teaching; PED school, classes, lessons

unter'richten v/i and v/t (no -ge-, h) teach; give lessons; inform (**über** acc of)

'Unterrichtsstunde f lesson, PED a. class, period

'Unterrock m slip

unter'sagen v/t (no -ge-, h) prohibit

unter'schätzen v/t (no -ge-, h) underestimate; underrate

unter'scheiden v/t and v/i (irr, scheiden, no -ge-, h) distinguish (**zwischen** between; **von** from); tell apart; **sich unterscheiden** differ (**von** from; **in** dat in; **durch** by)

Unter'scheidung f (-; -en) distinction

Unterschied ['ʊntəʃiːt] m (-[e]s; -e) difference; **im Unterschied zu** unlike, as opposed to

'unterschiedlich adj different; varying

unter'schlagen v/t (irr, schlagen, no -ge-, h) embezzle

Unter'schlagung f (-; -en) embezzlement

Unterschlupf ['ʊntəʃlʊpf] m (-[e]s; no pl) hiding place

unter'schreiben v/t and v/i (irr, schreiben, no -ge-, h) sign

'Unterschrift f signature; caption

'**Unterseeboot** n → **U-Boot**
Untersetzer ['ʊntɐzɛtsɐ] m (-s; -) coaster; saucer
unter'setzt adj thickset, stocky
'**Unterstand** m shelter, MIL a. dugout
unter'stehen (irr, **stehen**, no -ge-, h) **1.** v/i (dat) be under (the control of); **2.** v/refl dare; **unterstehen Sie sich** (**et. zu tun**)! don't you dare ([to] do s.th.)!
'**unterstellen**[1] v/t (sep, -ge-, h) put s.th. in; store; **sich unterstellen** take shelter
unter'stellen[2] v/t (no -ge-, h) assume; **j-m unterstellen, dass er ...** insinuate that s.o. ...
Unter'stellung f (-; -en) insinuation
unter'streichen v/t (irr, **streichen**, no -ge-, h) underline (a. fig)
unter'stützen v/t (no -ge-, h) support; back (up)
Unter'stützung f (-; -en) support; aid; welfare (payments)
unter'suchen v/t (no -ge-, h) examine (a. MED), investigate (a. JUR); search; CHEM analyze
Unter'suchung f (-; -en) examination (a. MED), investigation (a. JUR), a. (medical) checkup; CHEM analysis
Unter'suchungsgefangene m, f JUR prisoner on remand
Untersuchungsgefängnis n JUR remand prison
Untersuchungshaft f: **in Untersuchungshaft sein** JUR be on remand
Untersuchungsrichter m JUR examining magistrate
Untertan ['ʊntɐtaːn] m (-s; -en) subject
'**Untertasse** f saucer
'**untertauchen** (sep, -ge-) **1.** v/i (sein) dive, submerge; fig disappear; esp POL go underground; **2.** v/t (h) duck
'**Unterteil** n, m lower part, bottom
unter'teilen v/t (no -ge-, h) subdivide
Unter'teilung f (-; -en) subdivision
'**Untertitel** m subtitle, film: a. caption
'**Unterton** m undertone
Unter'treibung f (-; -en) understatement
'**untervermieten** v/t (no -ge-, h) sublet
unter'wandern v/t (no -ge-, h) infiltrate
'**Unterwäsche** f underwear
'**Unterwasser-** in cpds underwater ...
unterwegs [ʊntɐ'veːks] adv on the or one's way (**nach** to)
unter'weisen v/t (irr, **weisen**, no -ge-, h) instruct
Unter'weisung f (-; -en) instruction
'**Unterwelt** f (-; no pl) underworld
unter'werfen v/t (irr, **werfen**, no -ge-, h) subject (dat to); subjugate; **sich unterwerfen** submit (to)

Unter'werfung f (-; -en) subjection; submission (**unter** acc to)
unterwürfig [ʊntɐ'vʏrfɪç] adj servile
unter'zeichnen v/t (no -ge-, h) sign
Unter'zeichnete m, f (-n; -n) the undersigned
Unter'zeichnung f (-; -en) signing
'**unterziehen**[1] v/t (irr, **ziehen**, sep, -ge-, h) put s.th. on underneath
unter'ziehen[2] v/t (irr, **ziehen**, no -ge-, h) **sich** e-r Behandlung, Prüfung etc **unterziehen** undergo (treatment etc), take (an examination etc)
'**Untiefe** f shallow, shoal
un'tragbar adj unbearable, intolerable
un'trennbar adj inseparable
'**untreu** adj unfaithful (dat to)
un'tröstlich adj inconsolable
untrüglich [ʊn'tryːklɪç] adj unmistakable
'**Untugend** f vice, bad habit
'**unüberlegt** adj thoughtless
unübersichtlich adj blind (bend etc)
unübertrefflich [ʊnʔyːbɐ'trɛflɪç] adj unsurpassable, matchless
unübertroffen [-'trɔfən] adj unequal(l)ed
unüberwindlich [-'vɪntlɪç] adj insuperable, invincible
unumgänglich [ʊnʔʊm'gɛŋlɪç] adj inevitable
unumschränkt [-'ʃrɛŋkt] adj unlimited; POL absolute
unumstritten [-'ʃtrɪtən] adj undisputed
unumwunden [-'vʊndən] adv straight out, frankly
ununterbrochen ['ʊnʔʊntɐbrɔxən] adj uninterrupted; continuous
unver'änderlich adj unchanging
unver'antwortlich adj irresponsible
'**unver'besserlich** adj incorrigible
unver'bindlich adj noncommittal, ECON not binding
unver'daulich adj indigestible (a. fig)
'**unverdient** adj undeserved
'**unverdünnt** adj undiluted; straight
unver'einbar adj incompatible
unver'fälscht adj unadulterated
unver'fänglich adj harmless
unver'froren adj brazen, impertinent
unver'gänglich adj immortal, eternal
unver'geßlich adj unforgettable
unver'gleichlich adj incomparable
unver'hältnismäßig adv disproportionately; **unverhältnismäßig hoch** excessive
unverheiratet adj unmarried, single
unverhofft ['ʊnfɐɛhɔft] adj unhoped-for; unexpected
unverhohlen ['ʊnfɐɛhoːlən] adj undisguised, open

U

'unver'käuflich *adj* not for sale; unsal(e)-able

unver'kennbar *adj* unmistakable

'unverletzt *adj* unhurt

unver'meidlich [ʊnfɛɐˈmaitlɪç] *adj* inevitable

'unvermindert *adj* undiminished

'unvermittelt *adj* abrupt, sudden

'Unvermögen *n* (-s; *no pl*) inability, incapacity

'unvermutet *adj* unexpected

'unvernünftig *adj* unreasonable; foolish

unver'schämt *adj* rude, impertinent; outrageous (*price etc*)

Unver'schämtheit *f* (-; -en) impertinence; *die Unverschämtheit haben zu inf* have the nerve to *inf*

'unverschuldet *adj* through no fault of one's own

unversehens ['ʊnfɛɐˌzeːəns] *adv* unexpectedly, all of a sudden

'unversehrt *adj* unhurt; undamaged

unver'söhnlich *adj* irreconcilable (*a. fig*), implacable

'unversorgt *adj* unprovided for

unver'ständlich *adj* unintelligible; *es ist mir unverständlich* I can't see how *or* why, F it beats me

unver'sucht *adj*: *nichts unversucht lassen* leave nothing undone

unver'wundbar *adj* invulnerable

unver'wüstlich [ʊnfɛɐˈvyːstlɪç] *adj* indestructible

unver'zeihlich [-'tsailɪç] *adj* inexcusable

unver'züglich [-'tsyːklɪç] **1.** *adj* immediate, prompt; **2.** *adv* immediately, without delay

'unvollendet *adj* unfinished

'unvollkommen *adj* imperfect

'unvollständig *adj* incomplete

'unvorbereitet *adj* unprepared

'unvoreingenommen *adj* unprejudiced, unbias(s)ed

'unvorhergesehen *adj* unforeseen

'unvorhersehbar *adj* unforeseeable

'unvorsichtig *adj* careless

'Unvorsichtigkeit *f* (-; *no pl*) carelessness

unvor'stellbar *adj* unthinkable

'unvorteilhaft *adj* unbecoming

'unwahr *adj* untrue

'Unwahrheit *f* untruth

'unwahrscheinlich *adj* improbable, unlikely; F fantastic

unwegsam ['ʊnveːkzaːm] *adj* difficult, rough (*terrain*)

unweigerlich [ʊnˈvaigɐlɪç] *adv* inevitably

'unweit *prp* (*gen*) not far from

'Unwetter *n* (-s; -) disastrous (thunder)storm

'unwichtig *adj* unimportant

unwiderlegbar [ʊnviːdɐˈleːkbaːɐ] *adj* irrefutable

unwiderruflich [-ˈruːflɪç] *adj* irrevocable

unwiderstehlich [-ˈʃteːlɪç] *adj* irresistible

'Unwille(n) *m* indignation (*über acc* at)

'unwillig *adj* indignant (*über acc* at); unwilling, reluctant

'unwillkürlich *adj* involuntary

'unwirklich *adj* unreal

'unwirksam *adj* ineffective

unwirsch ['ʊnvɪrʃ] *adj* surly, gruff

unwirtlich ['ʊnvɪrtlɪç] *adj* inhospitable

'unwirtschaftlich *adj* uneconomic(al)

'unwissend *adj* ignorant

'Unwissenheit *f* (-; *no pl*) ignorance

'unwohl *adj* unwell; uneasy

'unwürdig *adj* unworthy (*gen* of)

'unzählig [ʊnˈtsɛːlɪç] *adj* innumerable, countless

unzer'brechlich *adj* unbreakable

unzer'reißbar *adj* untearable

unzer'störbar *adj* indestructible

unzer'trennlich *adj* inseparable

'Unzucht *f* (-; *no pl*) sexual offense (*Br* offence)

'unzüchtig *adj* indecent; obscene

'unzufrieden *adj* discontent(ed) (*mit* with), dissatisfied (with)

'Unzufriedenheit *f* discontent, dissatisfaction

'unzugänglich *adj* inaccessible

'unzulänglich *adj* inadequate

'unzulässig *adj* inadmissible

unzu'mutbar *adj* unacceptable; unreasonable

'unzurechnungsfähig *adj* JUR irresponsible

'Unzurechnungsfähigkeit *f* (-; *no pl*) JUR irresponsibility

'unzureichend *adj* insufficient

'unzusammenhängend *adj* incoherent

'unzuverlässig *adj* unreliable, untrustworthy; uncertain

üppig ['ʏpɪç] *adj* luxuriant, lush (*both a. fig*); voluptuous, luscious; opulent; rich

uralt ['uːɐʔalt] *adj* ancient (*a. iro*)

Uran [uˈraːn] *n* (-s; *no pl*) uranium

'Uraufführung *f* première, first performance (*film: showing*)

urbar ['uːɐbaːɐ] *adj* arable; *urbar machen* cultivate; reclaim

'Urbevölkerung *f*, 'Ureinwohner *pl* aboriginal inhabitants; *in Australia:* Aborigines

Urenkel *m* great-grandson

Urenkelin *f* great-granddaughter

'Urgroß... *in cpds* ...eltern, ...mutter, ...vater: great-grand...

Urheberrechte ['u:ɐhe:bɐ-] *pl* copyright (**an** *dat* on, for)

Urin [u'ri:n] *m* (*-s*; *-e*) urine

urinieren [uri'ni:rən] *v/i* (*no -ge-*, h) urinate

Urkunde ['u:ɐkʊndə] *f* (*-*; *-n*) document; diploma

'**Urkundenfälschung** *f* forgery of documents

Urlaub ['u:ɐlaup] *m* (*-[e]s*; *-e*) vacation, *Br* holiday(s); MIL leave; **in** *or* **im Urlaub sein** (**auf Urlaub gehen**) be (go) on vacation (*Br* holiday); **e-n Tag** (**ein paar Tage**) **Urlaub nehmen** take a day (a few days) off

Urlauber(in) ['u:ɐlaubɐ (-bərɪn)] (*-s*; *-/-*; *-nen*) vacationist, vacationer, *Br* holidaymaker

Urne ['ʊrnə] *f* (*-*; *-n*) urn; ballot box

'**Ursache** *f* (*-*; *-n*) cause; reason; **keine Ursache!** not at all, you're welcome

'**Ursprung** *m* origin

ursprünglich ['u:ɐʃprʏŋlɪç] *adj* original; natural, unspoilt

Urteil ['urtail] *n* (*-[e]s*; *-e*) judg(e)ment; JUR sentence; **sich ein Urteil bilden** form a judg(e)ment (**über** *acc* about)

'**urteilen** *v/i* (*ge-*, h) judge (**über j-n, et.** s.o., s.th.; **nach** by)

'**Urwald** *m* primeval forest; jungle

urwüchsig ['u:ɐvy:ksɪç] *adj* coarse, earthy

'**Urzeit** *f* prehistoric times

usw. ABBR *of* **und so weiter** etc., and so on

Utensilien [utɛn'si:ljən] *pl* utensils

Utopie [uto'pi:] *f* (*-*; *-n*) illusion

utopisch [u'to:pɪʃ] *adj* utopian; fantastic

V

Vagabund [vaga'bʊnt] *m* (*-en*; *-en*) vagabond, tramp, F bum

vage ['va:gə] *adj* vague

Vakuum ['va:kuʊm] *n* (*-s*; *-kua*, *-kuen*) vacuum

Vampir ['vampi:ɐ] *m* (*-s*; *-e*) ZO vampire (*a. fig*)

Vanille [va'nɪljə] *f* (*-*; *no pl*) vanilla

variabel [va'rja:bəl] *adj* variable

Variante [va'rjantə] *f* (*-*; *-n*) variant

Variation [varja'tsio:n] *f* (*-*; *-en*) variation

Varieté, *a.* **Varieté** [varje'te:] *n* (*-s*; *-s*) vaudeville, *Br* variety theatre, music hall

variieren [vari'i:rən] *v/i and v/t* (*no -ge-*, h) vary

Vase ['va:zə] *f* (*-*; *-n*) vase

Vater ['fa:tɐ] *m* (*-s*; *Väter* ['fɛ:tɐ]) father

'**Vaterland** *n* native country

'**Vaterlandsliebe** *f* patriotism

väterlich ['fɛ:təlɪç] *adj* fatherly, paternal

'**Vaterschaft** *f* (*-*; *-en*) JUR paternity

'**Vater'unser** *n* (*-s*; *-*) REL Lord's Prayer

v. Chr. ABBR *of* **vor Christus** BC, before Christ

V-Ausschnitt ['fau-] *m* V-neck

Vegetarier [vege'ta:rjɐ] *m* (*-s*; *-*), **Vegeta'rierin** *f* (*-*; *-nen*), **vegetarisch** [vege'ta:rɪʃ] *adj* vegetarian

Vegetation [vegeta'tsio:n] *f* (*-*; *-en*) vegetation

vegetieren [vege'ti:rən] *v/i* (*no -ge-*, h) vegetate

Veilchen ['failçən] *n* (*-s*; *-*) BOT violet

Velo ['ve:lo] *Swiss n* (*-s*; *-s*) bicycle, F bike

Ventil [vɛn'ti:l] *n* (*-s*; *-e*) TECH valve; *fig* vent, outlet

Ventilation [vɛntila'tsio:n] *f* (*-*; *-en*) ventilation

Ventilator [vɛnti'la:to:ɐ] *m* (*-s*; *-en* [-la'to:rən]) fan

verabreden [fɛɐ'ˀap-] *v/t* (*no -ge-*, h) agree (up)on, arrange; appoint, fix; **sich verabreden** make a date (*or* an appointment) (**mit** with)

Ver'abredung *f* (*-*; *-en*) appointment; date

ver'abreichen *v/t* (*no -ge-*, h) give; MED administer

verabscheuen *v/t* (*no -ge-*, h) loathe, detest

verabschieden [fɛɐ'ˀapʃi:dən] *v/t* (*no -ge-*, h) say goodbye to (*a.* **sich verabschieden von**); dismiss; JUR pass

Ver'abschiedung *f* (*-*; *-en*) dismissal; JUR passing

ver'achten *v/t* (*no -ge-*, h) despise

verächtlich [fɛɐ'ˀɛçtlɪç] *adj* contemptuous

Ver'achtung *f* (*-*; *no pl*) contempt

verallgemeinern [fɛɐ'ˀalgə'mainɐn] *v/t* (*no -ge-*, h) generalize

ver'altet *adj* antiquated, out of date

Veranda [ve'randa] *f* (-; *-den*) porch, *Br* veranda(h)

veränderlich [fɛɐ'ʔɛndɐlɪç] *adj* changeable (*a.* METEOR), variable (*a.* MATH, LING)

ver'ändern *v/t and v/refl* (*no -ge-, h*), **Ver'änderung** *f* change

verängstigt [fɛɐ'ʔɛŋstɪçt] *adj* frightened, scared

ver'anlagen *v/t* (*no -ge-, h*) ECON assess

veranlagt [fɛɐ'ʔanla:kt] *adj* inclined (**zu**, **für** to); **künstlerisch** (**musikalisch**) **veranlagt sein** have a gift *or* bent for art (music)

Ver'anlagung *f* (-; *-en*) (pre)disposition (*a.* MED); talent, gift; ECON assessment

ver'anlassen *v/t* (*no -ge-, h*) make arrangements (*or* arrange) for *s.th.*; **j-n zu et. veranlassen** make s.o. do s.th.

Ver'anlassung *f* (-; *-en*) cause (**zu** for)

ver'anschaulichen *v/t* (*no -ge-, h*) illustrate

ver'anschlagen *v/t* (*no -ge-, h*) estimate (**auf** *acc* at)

ver'anstalten *v/t* (*no -ge-, h*) arrange, organize; hold, give (*concert, party etc*)

Ver'anstaltung *f* (-; *-en*) event, SPORT *a.* meet, *Br* meeting

ver'antworten *v/t* (*no -ge-, h*) take the responsibility for

ver'antwortlich *adj* responsible; **j-n verantwortlich machen für** hold s.o. responsible for

Ver'antwortung *f* (-; *no pl*) responsibility; **auf eigene Verantwortung** at one's own risk; **j-n zur Verantwortung ziehen** call s.o. to account

Ver'antwortungsgefühl *n* (-[e]s; *no pl*) sense of responsibility

ver'antwortungslos *adj* irresponsible

ver'arbeiten *v/t* (*no -ge-, h*) process; *fig* digest; **et. verarbeiten zu** manufacture (*or* make) s.th. into

ver'ärgern *v/t* (*no -ge-, h*) make s.o. angry, annoy

ver'armt *adj* impoverished

ver'arschen *v/t* (*no -ge-, h*) **j-n verarschen** take the piss out of s.o.

Verb [vɛrp] *n* (-s; *-en* ['vɛrbən]) LING verb

Verband [fɛɐ'bant] *m* (-es; *Verbände* [fɛɐ-'bɛndə]) MED dressing, bandage; ECON association; MIL formation, unit

Verband(s)kasten *m* MED first-aid kit *or* box

Verband(s)zeug *n* MED dressing material

ver'bannen *v/t* (*no -ge-, h*) banish (*a. fig*), exile

Ver'bannung *f* (-; *-en*) banishment, exile

verbarrika'dieren *v/t* (*no -ge-, h*) barri-

cade; block

ver'bergen *v/t* (*irr*, **bergen**, *no -ge-, h*) hide (*a.* **sich verbergen**), conceal

ver'bessern *v/t* (*no -ge-, h*) improve; correct

Ver'besserung *f* (-; *-en*) improvement; correction

ver'beugen *v/refl* (*no -ge-, h*), **Ver'beugung** *f* (-; *-en*) bow (**vor** to)

ver'biegen *v/t* (*irr*, **biegen**, *no -ge-, h*) twist

ver'bieten *v/t* (*irr*, **bieten**, *no -ge-, h*) forbid; prohibit; → **verboten**

ver'billigen *v/t* (*no -ge-, h*) reduce in price

verbilligt [-'bɪlɪçt] *adj* reduced, at reduced prices

verbinden *v/t* (*irr*, **binden**, *no -ge-, h*) MED dress, bandage; bandage *s.o.* up; *a.* TECH connect, join, link (up); TEL put s.o. through (**mit** to); combine (*a.* CHEM **sich verbinden**); *fig* unite; associate; **j-m die Augen verbinden** blindfold s.o.; **damit sind beträchtliche Kosten verbunden** that involves considerable cost(s *pl*); **falsch verbunden!** wrong number!

verbindlich [fɛɐ'bɪntlɪç] *adj* obligatory, compulsory (*a.* PED); obliging

Ver'bindlichkeit *f* (-; *-en*) a) (*no pl*) obligingness, b) *pl* ECON liabilities

Ver'bindung *f* (-; *-en*) connection; combination; CHEM compound; UNIV fraternity, *Br* society; **sich in Verbindung setzen mit** get in touch with; **in Verbindung stehen** (**bleiben**) be (keep) in touch

verbissen [fɛɐ'bɪsən] *adj* dogged

ver'bittert *adj* bitter, embittered

verblassen [fɛɐ'blasən] *v/i* (*no -ge-, sein*) fade (*a. fig*)

Verbleib [fɛɐ'blaip] *m* (-[e]s; *no pl*) whereabouts

ver'bleiben *v/i* (*irr*, **bleiben**, *no -ge-, sein*) remain

verbleit [fɛɐ'blait] *adj* leaded

ver'blendet *fig adj* blind

Ver'blendung *fig f* (-; *-en*) blindness

verblichen [fɛɐ'blɪçən] *adj* faded

verblüffen [fɛɐ'blʏfən] *v/t* (*no -ge-, h*) amaze, F flabbergast

Ver'blüffung *f* (-; *-en*) amazement

ver'blühen *v/i* (*no -ge-, sein*) fade, wither (*both a. fig*)

ver'bluten *v/i* (*no -ge-, sein*) MED bleed to death

verborgen [fɛɐ'bɔrgən] *adj* hidden, concealed; **im Verborgenen** in secret

Verbot [fɛɐ'bo:t] *n* (-[e]s; *-e*) prohibition, ban (**on** *s.th.*)

ver'boten *adj*: **Rauchen verboten** no smoking

Ver'brauch *m* (-[e]s; *no pl*) consumption (**an** *dat* of)

Ver'brauchen *v/t* (*no -ge-, h*) consume, use up

Verbraucher [fɛɐ'brauxə] *m* (-s; -), Ver-'braucherin *f* (-; *-nen*) consumer

Verbraucherschutz *m* consumer protection

Ver'brechen *n* (-s; -) crime; **ein Verbrechen begehen** commit a crime

Ver'brecher(in) (-s; -/-; *-nen*), ver'brecherisch *adj* criminal

ver'breiten *v/t and v/refl* (*no -ge-, h*) spread (**in** *dat*, **über** *acc* over, through); circulate

verbreitern [fɛɐ'braitən] *v/t and v/refl* (*no -ge-, h*) widen, broaden

Ver'breitung *f* (-; *no pl*) spread(ing); circulation

ver'brennen *v/i* (*irr*, **brennen**, *no -ge-, sein*) and *v/t* (*h*) burn (up); cremate

Ver'brennung *f* (-; *-en*) burning; cremation; TECH combustion; MED burn

ver'bringen *v/t* (*irr*, **bringen**, *no -ge-, h*) spend, pass

verbrüdern [fɛɐ'bry:dən] *v/refl* (*no -ge-, h*) fraternize

Verbrüderung [fɛɐ'bry:dərʊŋ] *f* (-; *-en*) fraternization

ver'brühen *v/t* (*no -ge-, h*) scald

ver'buchen *v/t* (*no -ge-, h*) book

verbünden [fɛɐ'byndən] *v/refl* (*no -ge-, h*) ally o.s. (**mit** to, with)

Ver'bündete *m, f* (-*n*; -*n*) ally (*a. fig*)

ver'bürgen *v/refl* (*no -ge-, h*) **sich verbürgen für** vouch for, guarantee

ver'büßen *v/t* (*no -ge-, h*) serve a sentence, serve time

verchromt [fɛɐ'daxt] *m* (-[e]s; *-e*) chromium-plated

Ver'dacht [fɛɐ'daxt] *m* (-[e]s; *-e*) suspicion; **Verdacht schöpfen** become suspicious

verdächtig [fɛɐ'dɛçtɪç] *adj* suspicious, suspect

Verdächtige [fɛɐ'dɛçtɪgə] *m, f* (-*n*; -*n*) suspect

ver'dächtigen *v/t* (*no -ge-, h*) suspect (*j-n e-r Tat* s.o. of [doing] s.th.)

Ver'dächtigung *f* (-; *-en*) suspicion

verdammen [fɛɐ'damən] *v/t* (*no -ge-, h*) condemn (**zu** to), damn (*a.* REL)

Ver'dammnis *f* (-; *no pl*) REL damnation

ver'dammt **1.** *adj* damned, F *a.* damn, darn(ed), *Br sl a.* bloody; F **verdammt (noch mal)!** damn (it)!; **2.** *adv:* **verdammt gut** *etc* damn (*Br sl a.* bloody) good *etc*

Ver'dammung *f* (-; *-en*) condemnation; REL damnation

ver'dampfen *v/t* (*no -ge-, h*) and *v/i* (*sein*) evaporate

ver'danken *v/t* (*no -ge-, h*) **j-m (e-m Umstand) et. verdanken** owe s.th. to s.o. (s.th.)

verdarb [fɛɐ'darp] *pret of* verderben

verdauen [fɛɐ'dauən] *v/t* (*no -ge-, h*) digest (*a. fig*)

ver'daulich *adj* digestible; **leicht (schwer) verdaulich** easy (hard) to digest

Ver'dauung *f* (-; *no pl*) digestion

Ver'deck *n* (-[e]s; *-e*) top

ver'decken *v/t* (*no -ge-, h*) cover (up) (*a. fig*)

ver'denken *v/t* (*irr*, **denken**, *no -ge-, h*) **ich kann es ihm nicht verdenken(, dass er ...)** I can't blame him (for *doing*)

verderben [fɛɐ'dɛrbən] (*irr*, *no -ge-*) **1.** *v/i* (*sein*) spoil (*a. fig*); GASTR go bad; **2.** *v/t* (*h*) spoil (*a. fig*), ruin; **sich den Magen verderben** upset one's stomach

Ver'derben *n* (-s; *no pl*) ruin

ver'derblich [fɛɐ'dɛrplɪç] *adj* perishable; **leicht verderbliche Lebensmittel** perishables

ver'dichten *v/t* (*no -ge-, h*) compress, condense

ver'dienen *v/t* (*no -ge-, h*) earn, make; *fig* deserve

Ver'dienst[1] *m* (-[e]s; *-e*) earnings; salary; wages; gain, profit

Ver'dienst[2] *n* (-[e]s; *-e*) merit; **es ist sein Verdienst, dass** it is thanks to him that

ver'dient *adj* (well-)deserved

ver'doppeln *v/t and v/refl* (*no -ge-, h*) double

verdorben [fɛɐ'dɔrbən] **1.** *pp of* verderben; **2.** *adj* GASTR spoilt, bad (*both a. fig*); MED upset

verdorren [fɛɐ'dɔrən] *v/i* (*no -ge-, sein*) wither, dry up

ver'drängen *v/t* (*no -ge-, h*) supplant, supersede; replace; PHYS displace; PSYCH repress, suppress

ver'drehen *v/t* (*no -ge-, h*) twist, *fig a.* distort; **die Augen verdrehen** roll one's eyes; **j-m den Kopf verdrehen** turn s.o.'s head

ver'dreht F *fig adj* mixed up

ver'dreifachen *v/t and v/refl* (*no -ge-, h*) treble, triple

verdrießen [fɛɐ'dri:sən] *v/t* (*irr*, *no -ge-, h*) annoy

verdrießlich [fɛɐ'dri:slɪç] *adj* glum, morose, sullen

verdross [fɛɐ'drɔs] *pret of* verdrießen

verdrossen [fɛɐ'drɔsən] **1.** *pp of* verdrießen; **2.** *adj* grumpy, sullen

V

Verdruss [fɛɐˈdrʊs] m (-es; -e) annoyance

ver'dummen (no -ge-) **1.** v/t (h) make stupid, stultify; **2.** v/i (sein) become stultified

ver'dunkeln v/t and v/refl (no -ge-, h) darken; black out; fig obscure

Ver'dunk(e)lung f (-; -en) darkening; blackout; JUR collusion

ver'dünnen v/t (no -ge-, h) dilute

ver'dunsten v/i (no -ge-, sein) evaporate

ver'dursten v/i (no -ge-, sein) die of thirst

verdutzt [fɛɐˈdʊtst] adj puzzled

ver'edeln v/t (no -ge-, h) BOT graft; TECH process, refine

Ver'ed(e)lung f (-; -en) BOT grafting; TECH processing, refinement

ver'ehren v/t (no -ge-, h) admire; adore, worship (both a. fig), esp REL a. revere, venerate

Ver'ehrer(in) (-s; -/-; -nen) admirer, esp film etc a. fan

Ver'ehrung f (-; no pl) admiration; adoration, worship; esp REL reverence, veneration

vereidigen [fɛɐˈʔaidɪɡən] v/t (no -ge-, h) swear s.o. in; JUR put s.o. under an oath

Verein [fɛɐˈʔain] m (-[e]s; -e) club (a. SPORT); society, association

vereinbar [fɛɐˈʔainbaːɐ] adj compatible (**mit** with)

vereinbaren [fɛɐˈʔainbaːrən] v/t (no -ge-, h) agree (up)on, arrange

Ver'einbarung f (-; -en) agreement, arrangement

ver'einen → vereinigen

ver'einfachen v/t (no -ge-, h) simplify

Ver'einfachung f (-; -en) simplification

ver'einheitlichen v/t (no -ge-, h) standardize

ver'einigen v/t and v/refl (no -ge-, h) unite (**zu** into); combine, join

Ver'einigung f (-; -en) union; combination; alliance

ver'einsamen v/i (no -ge-, sein) become lonely or isolated

vereinzelt [fɛɐˈʔaintsəlt] adj occasional, odd; **vereinzelt Regen** scattered showers

ver'eiteln v/t (no -ge-, h) prevent; frustrate

ver'enden v/i (no -ge-, sein) esp ZO die, perish

ver'engen v/t and v/refl (no -ge-, h) narrow

ver'erben v/t (no -ge-, h) **j-m et. vererben** leave (BIOL transmit) s.th. to s.o.; **sich vererben (auf** acc) be passed on or down (to) (a. BIOL and fig)

Ver'erbung f (-; no pl) BIOL heredity

Ver'erbungslehre f BIOL genetics

verewigen [fɛɐˈʔeːvɪɡn] v/t (no -ge-, h) immortalize

ver'fahren (irr, fahren, no -ge-) **1.** v/i (sein) proceed; **verfahren mit** deal with; **2.** v/refl (h) MOT get lost

Ver'fahren n (-s; -) procedure, method, esp TECH a. technique, way; JUR (legal) proceedings (**gegen** against)

Ver'fall m (-[e]s; no pl) decay (a. fig); dilapidation; fig decline; ECON etc expiry

ver'fallen (irr, fallen, no -ge-, sein) **1.** v/i decay (a. fig), dilapidate; esp fig decline; ECON expire; MED waste away; become addicted to; (**wieder**) **verfallen in** (acc) fall (back) into; **verfallen auf** (acc) hit (up)on; **2.** adj decayed; dilapidated; **j-m verfallen sein** be s.o.'s slave

Ver'fallsdatum n expiry date; GASTR pull date, Br best-before (or best-by) date; PHARM sell-by date

ver'fälschen v/t (no -ge-, h) falsify; distort; GASTR adulterate

verfänglich [fɛɐˈfɛŋlɪç] adj delicate, tricky; embarrassing, compromising

ver'färben v/refl (no -ge-, h) discolo(u)r

ver'fassen v/t (no -ge-, h) write

Verfasser [fɛɐˈfasə] m (-s; -), **Ver'fasserin** f (-; -nen) author

Ver'fassung f (-; -en) state (of health or of mind), condition; POL constitution

ver'fassungsmäßig adj POL constitutional

verfassungswidrig adj POL unconstitutional

ver'faulen v/i (no -ge-, sein) rot, decay

ver'fechten v/t (irr, fechten, no -ge-, h), **Ver'fechter(in)** (-s; -/-; -nen) advocate

ver'fehlen v/t (no -ge-, h) miss (**sich each** other)

Ver'fehlung f (-; -en) offense, Br offence

verfeinden [fɛɐˈfaindən] v/refl (no -ge-, h) become enemies

ver'feindet adj hostile; **verfeindet sein** be enemies

ver'feinern v/t and v/refl (no -ge-, h) refine

ver'filmen v/t (no -ge-, h) film

Ver'filmung f (-; -en) filming; film version

ver'flechten v/t (irr, flechten, no -ge-, h) intertwine (a. **sich verflechten**)

ver'fluchen v/t (no -ge-, h) curse

ver'flucht → verdammt

ver'folgen v/t (no -ge-, h) pursue (a. fig); chase, hunt (both a. fig), POL, REL persecute; follow (track etc); fear etc: haunt s.o.; **j-n gerichtlich verfolgen** prosecute s.o.

Verfolger [fɛɐˈfɔlɡɐ] m (-s; -) pursuer; persecutor

Ver'folgung f (-; -en) pursuit (a. cycling); chase, hunt; persecution; **gerichtliche Verfolgung** prosecution

ver'frachten v/t (no -ge-, h) freight, ship; F bundle s.o., s.th. (**in** acc into)

verfremden [fɛɐ'frɛmdən] v/t (no -ge-, h) esp art: alienate

ver'früht adj premature

verfügbar [fɛɐ'fyːkbaːɐ] adj available

ver'fügen (no -ge-, h) **1.** v/t decree, order; **2.** v/i: **verfügen über** (acc) have at one's disposal

Ver'fügung f (-; -en) a) decree, order, b) (no pl) disposal; **j-m zur Verfügung stehen** (**stellen**) be (place) at s.o. 's disposal

ver'führen v/t (no -ge-, h) seduce (**et. zu tun** into doing s.th.)

Ver'führer m (-s; -) seducer

Ver'führerin f (-; -nen) seductress

ver'führerisch adj seductive; tempting

Ver'führung f (-; -en) seduction

vergangen [fɛɐ'gaŋən] adj gone, past; **im vergangenen Jahr** last year

Ver'gangenheit f (-; no pl) past; LING past tense

vergänglich [fɛɐ'gɛŋlɪç] adj transitory, transient

vergasen [fɛɐ'gaːzən] v/t (no -ge-, h) gas; CHEM gasify

Vergaser [fɛɐ'gaːzɐ] m (-s; -) MOT carbu-ret(t)or

vergaß [fɛɐ'gaːs] pret of **vergessen**

ver'geben v/t (irr, **geben**, no -ge-, h) give away (a. fig); award (prize etc); forgive

ver'gebens adv in vain

vergeblich [fɛɐ'geːplɪç] **1.** adj futile; **2.** adv in vain

Ver'gebung f (-; -en) forgiveness, pardon

ver'gehen (irr, **gehen**, no -ge-, sein) **1.** v/i time etc: go by, pass; pain, effect etc: wear off; **vergehen vor** (dat) be dying with; **wie die Zeit vergeht!** how time flies!; **2.** v/refl **sich vergehen an** (dat) violate; rape

Vergehen n (-s; -) JUR offen|se, Br -ce

ver'gelten v/t (irr, **gelten**, no -ge-, h) re-pay; reward

Ver'geltung f (-; -en) retaliation (a. MIL)

vergessen [fɛɐ'gɛsən] **1.** v/t (irr, **gessen**, h) forget; leave; **2.** pp of **vergessen** 1

Ver'gessenheit f: **in Vergessenheit gera-ten** fall into oblivion

vergesslich [fɛɐ'gɛslɪç] adj forgetful

vergeuden [fɛɐ'gɔydən] v/t (no -ge-, h), **Ver'geudung** f (-; -en) waste

vergewaltigen [fɛɐgə'valtɪgən] v/t (no -ge-, h) rape, violate (a. fig)

Verge'waltigung f (-; -en) rape, violation (a. fig)

vergewissern [fɛɐgə'vɪsən] v/refl (no -ge-, h) make sure (**e-r Sache** of s.th.; **ob** whether; **dass** that)

ver'gießen v/t (irr, **gießen**, no -ge-, h) shed (blood, tears); spill

ver'giften v/t (no -ge-, h) poison (a. fig); contaminate

Ver'giftung f (-; -en) poisoning (a. fig); contamination

ver'gittert adj barred (window etc)

Ver'gleich m (-[e]s; -e) comparison; JUR compromise

ver'gleichbar adj comparable (**mit** to, with)

ver'gleichen v/t (irr, **gleichen**, no -ge-, h) compare (**mit** with or to); **... ist nicht zu vergleichen mit** ... cannot be compared to; ... cannot compare with; **verglichen mit** compared to or with

ver'gleichsweise adv comparatively, rel-atively

ver'glühen v/i (no -ge-, sein) burn out (or up)

vergnügen [fɛɐ'gnyːgən] v/refl (no -ge-, h) enjoy o.s. (**mit et.** doing s.th.)

Ver'gnügen n (-s; -) pleasure, enjoyment, fun; **mit Vergnügen** with pleasure; **viel Vergnügen!** have fun!, have a good time!

vergnügt [fɛɐ'gnyːkt] adj cheerful

Ver'gnügung f (-; -en) pleasure, amuse-ment, entertainment

Ver'gnügungspark m amusement park

ver'gnügungssüchtig adj pleasure-seek-ing

Ver'gnügungsviertel n nightlife district

ver'golden v/t (no -ge-, h) gild

vergöttern [fɛɐ'gœtɐn] v/t (no -ge-, h) idolize, adore

ver'graben v/t (irr, **graben**, no -ge-, h) bury (a. fig)

ver'greifen v/refl (irr, **greifen**, no -ge-, h) **sich vergreifen an** (dat) lay hands on

vergriffen [fɛɐ'grɪfən] adj out of print

ver'größern [fɛɐ'grøːsən] v/t (no -ge-, h) enlarge (a. PHOT); increase; OPT magnify; **sich vergrößern** increase, grow, expand

Ver'größerung f (-; -en) increase; PHOT en-largement; OPT magnification

Ver'größerungsglas n OPT magnifying glass

Vergünstigung [fɛɐ'gʏnstɪgʊŋ] f (-; -en) privilege

vergüten [fɛɐ'gyːtən] v/t (no -ge-, h) re-imburse, pay (for)

Ver'gütung f (-; -en) reimbursement

ver'haften v/t (no -ge-, h), **Ver'haftung** f (-; -en) arrest

ver'halten[1] v/refl (irr, **halten**, no -ge-, h) behave, conduct o.s., act; **sich ruhig ver-**

V

halten keep quiet

ver'halten² *adj* restrained; subdued

Ver'halten *n* (-s; *no pl*) behavio(u)r, conduct

Ver'haltensforschung *f* behavio(u)ral science

ver'haltensgestört *adj* disturbed, maladjusted

Verhältnis [fɛɐ'hɛltnɪs] *n* (-ses; -se) relationship, relations; attitude; proportion, relation, *esp* MATH ratio; F affair; *pl* circumstances, conditions; *über j-s Verhältnisse* beyond s.o.'s means

ver'hältnismäßig *adv* comparatively, relatively

Ver'hältniswort *n* (-[e]s; -wörter) LING preposition

ver'handeln *no* (-ge-, h) **1.** *v/i* negotiate; **2.** *v/t* argue

Ver'handlung *f* (-; -en) negotiation, talk; JUR hearing; trial

Ver'handlungsbasis *f* ECON asking price

ver'hängen *v/t* (*no* -ge-, h) cover (*mit* with); impose (*über acc* on)

Verhängnis [fɛɐ'hɛŋnɪs] *n* (-ses; -se) fate; disaster

ver'hängnisvoll *adj* fatal, disastrous

verharmlosen [fɛɐ'harmloːzən] *v/t* (*no* -ge-, h) play s.th. down

verhärmt [fɛɐ'hɛrmt] *adj* careworn

ver'hasst *adj* hated; hateful

ver'hätscheln *v/t* (*no* -ge-, h) coddle, pamper, spoil

ver'hauen F *v/t* (*no* -ge-, h) spank

verheerend [fɛɐ'heːrənt] *adj* disastrous

ver'heilen *v/i* (*no* -ge-, *sein*) heal (up)

verheimlichen [fɛɐ'haɪmlɪçən] *v/t* (*no* -ge-, h) hide, conceal

ver'heiraten *v/t* (*no* -ge-, h) marry (*s.o.* off) (*mit* to); *sich verheiraten* get married

ver'heiratet *adj* married (*mit* to)

ver'heißungsvoll *adj* promising

ver'helfen *v/i* (*irr*, **helfen**, *no* -ge-, h) *j-m zu et. verhelfen* help s.o. to get s.th.

ver'herrlichen *v/t* (*no* -ge-, h) glorify, *contr a.* idolize

Ver'herrlichung *f* (-; -en) glorification

ver'hexen *v/t* (*no* -ge-, h) bewitch

ver'hindern *v/t* (*no* -ge-, h) prevent (*dass j. et. tut* s.o. from doing s.th.)

ver'hindert *adj* unable to come; F *ein verhinderter ...* a would-be ...

ver'hinderung *f* (-; -en) prevention

ver'höhnen *v/t* (*no* -ge-, h) deride, mock (at), jeer (at)

Verhör [fɛɐ'høːɐ] *n* (-[e]s; -e) JUR interrogation

ver'hören (*no* -ge-, h) **1.** *v/t* interrogate,

question; **2.** *v/refl* get it wrong

ver'hüllen *v/t* (*no* -ge-, h) cover, veil

ver'hungern *v/i* (*no* -ge-, *sein*) die of hunger, starve (to death)

Ver'hungern *n* (-s; *no pl*) starvation

ver'hüten *v/t* (*no* -ge-, h) prevent

Ver'hütung *f* (-; -en) prevention

Ver'hütungsmittel *n* MED contraceptive

ver'irren *v/refl* (*no* -ge-, h) get lost, lose one's way, go astray (*a. fig*)

Ver'irrung *f* (-; -en) aberration

ver'jagen *v/t* (*no* -ge-, h) chase *or* drive away

verjähren [fɛɐ'jɛːrən] *v/i* (*no* -ge-, *sein*) JUR come under the statute of limitations

ver'jährt *adj* JUR statute-barred

verjüngen [fɛɐ'jʏŋən] *v/t* (*no* -ge-, h) make *s.o.* (look) younger, rejuvenate; *sich verjüngen* ARCH, TECH taper (off)

ver'kabeln *v/t* (*no* -ge-, h) ELECTR cable

Ver'kauf *m* sale

ver'kaufen *v/t* (*no* -ge-, h) sell; *zu verkaufen* for sale; *sich gut verkaufen* sell well

Ver'käufer *m* (-s; -) (sales)clerk, salesman, *Br* shop assistant; ECON seller

Ver'käuferin *f* (-; -nen) (sales)clerk, saleslady, *Br* shop assistant

ver'käuflich *adj* for sale; *schwer verkäuflich* hard to sell

Verkehr [fɛɐ'keːɐ] *m* (-s; *no pl*) traffic; transportation; *Br* transport; *fig* contact, dealings; intercourse; circulation; *starker (schwacher) Verkehr* heavy (light) traffic

ver'kehren (*no* -ge-, h) **1.** *v/i* bus etc: run; *verkehren in (dat)* frequent; *verkehren mit* associate *or* mix with; have intercourse with; **2.** *v/t* turn (*in acc* into); *ins Gegenteil verkehren* reverse

Ver'kehrsader *f* arterial road

Verkehrsampel *f* traffic light(s)

Verkehrsbehinderung *f* hold-up, delay; JUR obstruction of traffic

Ver'kehrsde,likt *n* traffic offense (*Br* offence)

Verkehrsflugzeug *n* airliner

Verkehrsfunk *m* traffic bulletin

Verkehrsinsel *f* traffic island

Verkehrsmeldung *f* traffic announcement, flash

Verkehrsmi,nister *m* minister of transportation

Verkehrsminis,terium *n* ministry of transportation

Verkehrsmittel *n* means of transportation; *öffentliche Verkehrsmittel* public transportation

Verkehrsopfer *n* road casualty

Verkehrspoli,zei *f* traffic police

Verkehrsrowdy *m* F road hog
ver'kehrssicher *adj* MOT roadworthy
Ver'kehrssicherheit *f* MOT road safety; roadworthiness
Verkehrsstau *m* traffic jam
Verkehrssünder(in) F traffic offender
Verkehrsteilnehmer(in) road user
Verkehrsunfall *m* traffic accident; (car) crash
Verkehrsunterricht *m* traffic instruction
Verkehrszeichen *n* traffic sign
ver'kehrt *adj and adv* wrong; upside down; inside out
ver'kennen *v/t* (*irr*, *kennen*, *no -ge-, h*) mistake, misjudge
ver'klagen *v/t* (*no -ge-, h*) JUR sue (**auf** *acc*, **wegen** for)
ver'klappen *v/t* (*no -ge-, h*) dump (into the sea)
ver'kleben *v/t* (*no -ge-, h*) glue (together)
ver'kleiden *v/t* (*no -ge-, h*) disguise (**als** as), dress *s.o.* up (as); TECH cover, (en-)case; panel; **sich verkleiden** disguise o.s., dress (o.s.) up
Ver'kleidung *f* (-; *-en*) disguise; TECH cover, encasement; panel(l)ing; MOT fairing
ver'kleinern [fɛɐ'klaɪnɐn] *v/t* (*no -ge-, h*) make smaller, reduce, diminish
Ver'kleinerung [fɛɐ'klaɪnəruŋ] *f* (-; *-en*) reduction
ver'klingen *v/i* (*irr*, *klingen*, *no -ge-, sein*) die away
ver'knallt F *adj*: **verknallt sein in** (*acc*) be madly in love with, have a crush on
ver'knoten *v/t* (*no -ge-, h*) knot
ver'knüpfen *v/t* (*no -ge-, h*) knot together; *fig* connect, combine
ver'kohlen *v/t* (*no -ge-, sein*) char
ver'kommen **1.** *v/i* (*irr*, *kommen*, *no -ge-, sein*) become run-down *or* dilapidated; go to seed; GASTR go bad; **2.** *adj* run-down, dilapidated; neglected; depraved, rotten (to the core)
ver'korken *v/t* (*no -ge-, h*) cork (up)
ver'körpern *v/t* (*no -ge-, h*) personify; embody; *esp* THEA impersonate
ver'kriechen *v/refl* (*irr*, *kriechen*, *no -ge-, h*) hide
ver'krümmt *adj* crooked, curved (*a.* MED)
ver'krüppelt *adj* crippled
ver'kümmern *v/i* (*no -ge-, sein*) BIOL become stunted
ver'kümmert *adj* BIOL stunted
ver'künden [fɛɐ'kʏndən] *v/t* (*no -ge-, h*) announce; proclaim; JUR pronounce; REL preach
Ver'kündung *f* (-; *-en*) announcement; proclamation; JUR pronouncement; REL preaching

ver'kürzen *v/t* (*no -ge-, h*) shorten; reduce
ver'laden *v/t* (*irr*, *laden*, *no -ge-, h*) load (**auf** *acc* onto; **in** *acc* into)
Verlag [fɛɐ'laːk] *m* (-[*e*]*s*, -*e* [-'laːgə]) publishing house *or* company, publisher(s)
ver'lagern *v/t and v/refl* (*no -ge-, h*) shift (**auf** *acc* to)
ver'langen *v/t* (*no -ge-, h*) ask for; demand; claim; charge; take, call for
Ver'langen *n* (-*s*; -) desire (**nach** for); longing (for), yearning (for); **auf Verlangen** by request; ECON on demand
ver'längern [fɛɐ'lɛŋɐn] *v/t* (*no -ge-, h*) lengthen, make longer; prolong, extend (*a.* ECON)
Ver'längerung [fɛɐ'lɛŋərʊŋ] *f* (-; *-en*) lengthening; prolongation, extension; SPORT overtime, *Br* extra time
ver'langsamen *v/t and v/refl* (*no -ge-, h*) slacken, slow down (*both a. fig*)
ver'lassen 1. *v/t* (*irr*, *lassen*, *no -ge-, h*) leave; abandon, desert; **2.** *v/refl*: **sich verlassen auf** (*acc*) rely *or* depend on
verlässlich [fɛɐ'lɛslɪç] *adj* reliable, dependable
Ver'lauf *m* course
ver'laufen (*irr*, *laufen*, *no -ge-*) **1.** *v/i* (*sein*) run; go; end (up); **2.** *v/refl* (*h*) get lost, lose one's way
ver'leben *v/t* (*no -ge-, h*) spend; have
ver'legen[1] *v/t* (*no -ge-, h*) move; mislay; TECH lay; put off, postpone; publish
ver'legen[2] *adj* embarrassed
Ver'legenheit *f* (-; *-en*) a) (*no pl*) embarrassment, b) embarrassing situation
Verleger [fɛɐ'leːgɐ] *m* (-*s*; -), **Ver'legerin** *f* (-; *-nen*) publisher
Verleih [fɛɐ'laɪ] *m* (-[*e*]*s*, -*e*) a) (*no pl*) hire, rental, b) *film*: distributor(s)
ver'leihen *v/t* (*irr*, *leihen*, *no -ge-, h*) lend, loan; MOT *etc* rent (*Br* hire) out; award (*prize etc*); grant (*privilege etc*)
Ver'leihung *f* (-; *-en*) award(ing), presentation; grant(ing)
ver'leiten *v/t* (*no -ge-, h*) **j-n zu et. verleiten** make s.o. do s.th., lead s.o. to do s.th.
ver'lernen *v/t* (*no -ge-, h*) forget
ver'lesen *v/t* (*irr*, *lesen*, *no -ge-, h*) **1.** *v/t* read (*or* call) out; **2.** *v/refl* make a slip (in reading); misread *s.th.*
verletzen [fɛɐ'lɛtsən] *v/t* (*no -ge-, h*) hurt, injure, *fig a.* offend; **sich verletzen** hurt o.s., get hurt
verletzend *adj* offensive
Ver'letzte *m*, *f* (-*n*; -*n*) injured person; *pl* *the* injured
Ver'letzung *f* (-; *-en*) injury, *esp pl a.* hurt; JUR violation
ver'leugnen *v/t* (*no -ge-, h*) deny; re-

V

nounce

verleumden [fɛɐ'lɔʏmdən] v/t (no -ge-, h) defame; JUR slander, libel
ver'leumderisch adj JUR slanderous, libel(l)ous
Ver'leumdung f (-; -en) JUR slander; libel
ver'lieben v/refl (no -ge-, h) fall in love (**in** acc with)
verliebt [fɛɐ'liːpt] adj in love (**in** acc with); amorous (look etc)
Ver'liebte m, f (-n; -n) lover
verlieren [fɛɐ'liːrən] v/t and v/i (irr, no -ge-, h) lose
Ver'lierer(in) (-s; -/-; -nen) loser
ver'loben v/refl (no -ge-, h) get engaged (**mit** to)
Verlobte [fɛɐ'loːptə] 1. m (-n; -n) fiancé; 2. f (-n; -n) fiancée
Ver'lobung f (-; -en) engagement
ver'locken v/t (no -ge-, h) tempt
verlockend adj tempting
Ver'lockung f (-; -en) temptation
verlogen [fɛɐ'loːgən] adj untruthful, lying
verlor [fɛɐ'loːɐ] pret of **verlieren**
verloren [fɛɐ'loːrən] 1. pp of **verlieren**; 2. adj lost; wasted; **verloren gehen** be or get lost
ver'lorengehen v/i (irr, **gehen**, sep, -ge-, sein) → **verloren**
ver'losen v/t (no -ge-, h) raffle (off)
Ver'losung f (-; -en) raffle
Verlust [fɛɐ'lʊst] m (-[e]s; -e) loss (a. fig); pl esp MIL casualties
ver'machen v/t (no -ge-, h) leave, will
Vermächtnis [fɛɐ'mɛçtnɪs] n (-ses; -se) legacy (a. fig)
ver'markten v/t (no -ge-, h) market, merchandize
Ver'marktung f (-; -en) marketing, merchandizing
ver'mehren v/t and v/refl increase (**um** by), multiply (by) (a. BIOL); BIOL reproduce, esp ZO a. breed
Ver'mehrung f (-; -en) increase; BIOL reproduction
vermeidbar [fɛɐ'maitbaːɐ] adj avoidable
ver'meiden v/t (irr, **meiden**, no -ge-, h) avoid
vermeintlich [fɛɐ'maintlɪç] adj supposed, alleged
ver'mengen v/t (no -ge-, h) mix, mingle, blend
Vermerk [fɛɐ'mɛrk] m (-[e]s; -e) note
ver'merken v/t (no -ge-, h) make a note of
ver'messen¹ v/t (irr, **messen**, no -ge-, h) measure; survey
ver'messen² adj presumptuous
Ver'messung f (-; -en) measuring; survey(ing)

ver'mieten v/t (no -ge-, h) let, rent, lease (out); rent (Br hire) out (cars etc); **zu vermieten** for rent, Br to let, for hire
Ver'mieter n (-s; -) landlord
Ver'mieterin f (-; -nen) landlady
Ver'mietung f (-; -en) letting, renting
ver'mischen v/t and v/refl (no -ge-, h) mix, mingle, blend (**mit** with)
ver'mischt adj mixed; miscellaneous
vermissen [fɛɐ'mɪsən] v/t (no -ge-, h) miss
ver'misst adj missing; **die Vermissten** pl the missing
ver'mitteln (no -ge-, h) 1. v/t arrange; give, convey (impression etc); **j-m et. vermitteln** get or find s.o. s.th.; 2. v/i mediate (**zwischen** between)
Ver'mittler m (-s; -) mediator, go-between; ECON agent, broker
Ver'mittlung f (-; -en) mediation; arrangement; agency; office; (telephone) exchange; operator
ver'modern v/i (no -ge-, sein) rot, mo(u)lder
Ver'mögen n (-s; -) fortune, property, possessions; ECON assets
ver'mögend adj well-to-do, well-off
vermummen [fɛɐ'mʊmən] v/refl (no -ge-, h) mask o.s., disguise o.s.
vermuten [fɛɐ'muːtən] v/t (no -ge-, h) suppose, expect, think, guess
ver'mutlich adv probably
Ver'mutung f (-; -en) supposition; speculation
vernachlässigen [fɛɐ'naːxlɛsɪgən] v/t (no -ge-, h), **Ver'nachlässigung** f (-; -en) neglect
ver'narben v/i (no -ge-, sein) scar over; fig heal
ver'narrt adj: **vernarrt in** (acc) mad or crazy about
ver'nehmen v/t (irr, **nehmen**, no -ge-, h) JUR question, interrogate
ver'nehmlich adj clear, distinct
Ver'nehmung f (-; -en) JUR interrogation, examination
ver'neigen v/refl (no -ge-, h), **Ver'neigung** f (-; -en) bow (**vor** dat to) (a. fig)
ver'neinen (no -ge-, h) 1. v/t deny; 2. v/i say no, answer in the negative
verneinend adj negative
Ver'neinung f (-; -en) denial, negative (a. LING)
ver'nichten v/t (no -ge-, h) destroy
vernichtend adj devastating (a. fig); crushing
Ver'nichtung f (-; -en) destruction; extermination

V

Vernunft [fɛɐˈnʊnft] f (-; no pl) reason; *Vernunft annehmen* listen to reason; *j-n zur Vernunft bringen* bring s.o. to reason

vernünftig [fɛɐˈnynftɪç] adj sensible, reasonable (a. ECON); F decent

ver'öden v/i (no -ge-, sein) become deserted

ver'öffentlichen v/t (no -ge-, h) publish

Ver'öffentlichung f (-; -en) publication

ver'ordnen v/t (no -ge-, h) order, MED a. prescribe (*gegen* for)

Ver'ordnung f (-; -en) order; MED prescription

ver'pachten v/t (no -ge-, h) lease

Ver'pächter m lessor

ver'packen v/t (no -ge-, h) pack (up); TECH package; wrap up

Ver'packung f (-; -en) pack(ag)ing; wrapping

Ver'packungsmüll m superfluous packaging

ver'passen v/t (no -ge-, h) miss

ver'patzen F v/t (no -ge-, h) mess up, spoil

verpesten [fɛɐˈpɛstən] v/t (no -ge-, h) pollute, foul, contaminate; stink up (*Br* out)

ver'petzen F v/t (no -ge-, h) *j-n verpetzen* tell on s.o. (*bei* to)

ver'pfänden v/t (no -ge-, h) pawn; fig pledge

ver'pflanzen v/t (no -ge-, h), **Ver'pflanzung** f (-; -en) transplant (a. MED)

ver'pflegen v/t (no -ge-, h) feed

Ver'pflegung f (-; -en) food

ver'pflichten v/t (no -ge-, h) oblige; engage; *sich verpflichten, et. zu tun* undertake (ECON agree) to do s.th.

ver'pflichtet adj: *verpflichtet sein* (*sich verpflichtet fühlen*) *et. zu tun* be (feel) obliged to do s.th.

Ver'pflichtung f (-; -en) obligation; duty; ECON, JUR liability; engagement, commitment

ver'pfuschen F v/t (no -ge-, h) bungle, botch

ver'plappern v/refl (no -ge-, h) blab

verpönt [fɛɐˈpøːnt] adj taboo

ver'prügeln F v/t (no -ge-, h) beat s.o. up

Ver'putz m (-es; no pl), **ver'putzen** v/t (no -ge-, h) ARCH plaster

verquollen [fɛɐˈkvɔlən] adj face etc: puffy, swollen; *wood*: warped

Verrat [fɛɐˈraːt] m (-[e]s; no pl) betrayal (*an* dat of); treachery (to); JUR treason (to)

ver'raten v/t (irr, **raten**, no -ge-, h) betray, give away (*both a.* fig); *sich verraten* betray o.s., give o.s. away

Verräter [fɛɐˈrɛːtɐ] m (-s; -), **Ver'räterin** f

(-; -nen) traitor

verräterisch [fɛɐˈrɛːtərɪʃ] adj treacherous; fig telltale

ver'rechnen (no -ge-, h) **1.** v/t offset (*mit* against); **2.** v/refl miscalculate, make a mistake (a. fig); *sich um e-e Mark verrechnen* be one mark out

Ver'rechnungsscheck m ECON voucher check, *Br* crossed cheque

ver'regnet adj rainy

ver'reisen v/i (no -ge-, sein) go away (*geschäftlich* on business)

ver'reist adj away (*geschäftlich* on business)

verrenken [fɛɐˈrɛŋkən] v/t (no -ge-, h) MED dislocate, luxate; *sich et. verrenken* MED dislocate s.th.; *sich den Hals verrenken* crane one's neck

Ver'renkung f (-; -en) MED dislocation, luxation

ver'richten v/t (no -ge-, h) do, perform, carry out

ver'riegeln v/t (no -ge-, h) bolt, bar

verringern [fɛɐˈrɪŋɐn] v/t (no -ge-, h) decrease, lessen (*both a.* *sich verringern*), reduce, cut down

Ver'ringerung f (-; -en) reduction, decrease

ver'rosten v/i (no -ge-, sein) rust, get rusty (a. fig)

verrotten [fɛɐˈrɔtən] v/i (no -ge-, sein) rot

ver'rottet adj rotten

ver'rücken v/t (no -ge-, h) move, shift

ver'rückt adj mad, crazy (*both a.* fig *nach* about); *wie verrückt* like mad; *verrückt werden* go mad, go crazy; *j-n verrückt machen* drive s.o. mad

Ver'rückte m, f (-n; -n) madman (madwoman), lunatic, maniac (*all a.* F)

Ver'rücktheit f (-; -en) a) (no pl) madness, craziness, b) crazy thing

Ver'ruf m: *in Verruf bringen* bring discredit (up)on; *in Verruf kommen* get into discredit

ver'rufen adj disreputable, notorious

ver'rutschen v/i (no -ge-, sein) slip, get out of place

Vers [fɛrs] m (-es; -e [ˈfɛrzə]) verse; line

ver'sagen (no -ge-, h) **1.** v/i fail (a. MED), MOT etc a. break down; *gun etc:* misfire; **2.** v/t deny, refuse

Ver'sagen n (-s; no pl) failure

Ver'sager m (-s; -) failure

ver'salzen v/t (no -ge-, h) oversalt

ver'sammeln v/t (no -ge-, h) gather, assemble; *sich versammeln* v. meet

Ver'sammlung f (-; -en) assembly, meeting

Versand [fɛɐˈzant] m (-[e]s; no pl) dis-

patch, shipment; **Versand...** in cpds
...haus, ...katalog etc: mail-order ...
ver'**säumen** v/t (no -ge-, h) miss; **versäumen et. zu tun** fail to do s.th.
Versäumnis [fɛɐˈzɔʏmnɪs] n (-ses; -se)
omission
ver'**schaffen** v/t (no -ge-, h) get, find; **sich verschaffen** a. obtain
ver'**schämt** adj bashful
ver'**schanzen** v/refl (no -ge-, h) entrench
o.s. (a. fig **hinter** behind)
ver'**schärfen** v/t (no -ge-, h) aggravate;
tighten up; increase; **sich verschärfen**
get worse
ver'**schenken** v/t (no -ge-, h) give away (a.
fig)
ver'**scherzen** v/t (no -ge-, h) forfeit
ver'**scheuchen** v/t (no -ge-, h) chase away
(a. fig)
ver'**schicken** v/t (no -ge-, h) send off, esp
ECON dispatch
ver'**schieben** v/t (irr, **schieben**, no -ge-,
h) move, shift (a. **sich verschieben**);
postpone, put off
Ver'schiebung f (-; -en) shift(ing); postponement
ver'**schieden** [fɛɐˈʃiːdən] adj different
(**von** from); **verschiedene ...** pl various
..., several...
verschiedenartig adj different; various
Ver'schiedenheit f (-; -en) difference
ver'**schiedentlich** adv repeatedly
ver'**schiffen** v/t (no -ge-, h) ship
Ver'schiffung f (-; -en) shipment
ver'**schimmeln** v/i (no -ge-, sein) get
mo(u)ldy
ver'**schlafen** (irr, **schlafen**, no -ge-, h) **1.**
v/i oversleep; **2.** v/t sleep through; **3.** adj
sleepy (a. fig)
Ver'schlag m shed
ver'**schlagen**[1] v/t (irr, **schlagen**, no -ge-,
h) **j-m den Atem verschlagen** take s.o.'s
breath away; **j-m die Sprache verschlagen** leave s.o. speechless; **es hat ihn
nach X verschlagen** he ended up in X
ver'**schlagen**[2] adj sly, cunning
verschlechtern [fɛɐˈʃlɛçtən] v/t and
v/refl (no -ge-, h) make (refl get) worse,
worsen, deteriorate
Ver'schlechterung f (-; -en) deterioration; change for the worse
ver'**schleiern** v/t (no -ge-, h) veil (a. fig)
Verschleiß [fɛɐˈʃlaɪs] m (-es; no pl) wear
(and tear)
ver'**schleißen** v/t (irr, no -ge-, h) wear out
ver'**schleppen** v/t (no -ge-, h) carry off;
POL displace; draw out, delay; MED neglect
ver'**schleudern** v/t (no -ge-, h) waste;

ECON sell dirt cheap
ver'**schließen** v/t (irr, **schließen**, no -ge-,
h) close (a. fig one's eyes); lock (up)
ver'**schlingen** v/t (irr, **schlingen**, no -ge-,
h) devour (a. fig); gulp (down)
verschliss [fɛɐˈʃlɪs] pret of **verschleißen**
verschlissen [fɛɐˈʃlɪsən] pp of ver-**schleißen**
ver'**schlossen** [fɛɐˈʃlɔsən] adj closed; fig
aloof, reserved
Ver'schlossenheit f (-; no pl) aloofness
ver'**schlucken** (no -ge-, h) **1.** v/t swallow
(fig up); **2.** v/refl choke; **ich habe mich
verschluckt** it went down the wrong way
Ver'schluss m fastener; clasp; catch; lock;
cover, lid; cap, top; PHOT shutter; **unter
Verschluss** under lock and key
ver'**schlüsseln** v/t (no -ge-, h) (en)code,
(en)cipher
verschmähen [fɛɐˈʃmɛːən] v/t (no -ge-, h)
disdain, scorn
ver'**schmelzen** v/i (irr, **schmelzen**, no
-ge-, sein) and v/t (h) merge, fuse (both
a. ECON, POL etc), melt
Ver'schmelzung f (-; -en) fusion (a. fig)
ver'**schmerzen** v/t (no -ge-, h) get over
s.th.
ver'**schmieren** v/t (no -ge-, h) smear,
smudge
verschmitzt [fɛɐˈʃmɪtst] adj mischievous
ver'**schmutzen** (no -ge-) **1.** v/t (h) soil,
dirty; pollute; **2.** v/i (sein) get dirty; get
polluted
ver'**schnaufen** F v/i and v/refl (no -ge-, h)
stop for breath
ver'**schneit** adj snow-covered, snowy
Ver'schnitt m blend; waste
verschnupft [fɛɐˈʃnʊpft] adj: **verschnupft sein** MED have a cold; F be
in a huff
ver'**schnüren** v/t (no -ge-, h) tie up
verschollen [fɛɐˈʃɔlən] adj missing; JUR
presumed dead
ver'**schonen** v/t (no -ge-, h) spare; **j-n mit
et. verschonen** spare s.o. s.th.
verschönern [fɛɐˈʃøːnən] v/t (no -ge-, h)
embellish
Verschönerung [fɛɐˈʃøːnərʊŋ] f (-; -en)
embellishment
verschossen [fɛɐˈʃɔsən] adj faded; F **verschossen sein in** (acc) have a crush on
verschränken [fɛɐˈʃrɛŋkən] v/t (no -ge-,
h) fold; cross (one's legs)
ver'**schreiben** (irr, **schreiben**, no -ge-, h)
1. v/t MED prescribe (**gegen** for); **2.** v/refl
make a slip of the pen
ver'**schreibungspflichtig** adj PHARM
available on prescription only
verschroben [fɛɐˈʃroːbən] adj eccentric,

odd

ver'schrotten v/t (no -ge-, h) scrap

ver'schüchtert adj intimidated

ver'schulden v/t (no -ge-, h) be responsible for, cause, be the cause of; **sich verschulden** get into debt

ver'schuldet adj in debt

ver'schütten v/t (no -ge-, h) spill; bury s.o. (alive)

verschwägert [fɛɐ'ʃvɛːgɐt] adj related by marriage

ver'schweigen v/t (irr, **schweigen**, no -ge-, h) keep s.th. a secret, hide

verschwenden [fɛɐ'ʃvɛndən] v/t (no -ge-, h) waste

Verschwender [fɛɐ'ʃvɛndɐ] m (-s; -) spendthrift

verschwenderisch [fɛɐ'ʃvɛndərɪʃ] adj wasteful, extravagant; lavish

Verschwendung f (-; -en) waste

verschwiegen [fɛɐ'ʃviːgən] adj discreet; hidden, secret

Ver'schwiegenheit f (-; no pl) secrecy, discretion

ver'schwimmen v/i (irr, **schwimmen**, no -ge-, sein) become blurred

ver'schwinden v/i (irr, **schwinden**, no -ge-, sein) disappear, vanish; F **verschwinde!** beat it!

Ver'schwinden n (-s; no pl) disappearance

verschwommen [fɛɐ'ʃvɔmən] adj blurred (a. PHOT), fig a. vague, hazy

ver'schwören v/refl (irr, **schwören**, no -ge-, h) conspire, plot

Verschwörer [fɛɐ'ʃvøːrɐ] m (-s; -) conspirator

Ver'schwörung f (-; -en) conspiracy, plot

verschwunden [fɛɐ'ʃvʊndən] adj missing

ver'sehen (irr, **sehen**, no -ge-, h) 1. v/t hold (an office etc); **versehen mit** provide with; 2. v/refl make a mistake

Ver'sehen n (-s; -) mistake, error; **aus Versehen** → versehentlich [fɛɐ'zeːəntlɪç] adv by mistake, unintentionally

Versehrte [fɛɐ'zeːɐtə] m, f (-n; -n) disabled person

ver'sengen v/t (no -ge-, h) singe, scorch

ver'senken v/t (no -ge-, h) sink; **sich versenken in** (acc) become absorbed in

versessen [fɛɐ'zɛsən] adj: **versessen auf** (acc) keen on, mad or crazy about

ver'setzen v/t (no -ge-, h) move, shift; transfer; PED promote, Br move s.o. up; give (s.o. a kick etc); pawn; AGR transplant; F **j-n versetzen** stand s.o. up; **j-n in die Lage versetzen zu** inf to be in a position to inf, enable s.o. to inf; **sich in j-s Lage versetzen** put o.s. in

s.o.'s place

Ver'setzung f (-; -en) transfer; PED promotion

ver'seuchen v/t (no -ge-, h) contaminate

Ver'seuchung f (-; -en) contamination

ver'sichern v/t (no -ge-, h) ECON insure (**bei** with); assure (j-m et. s.o. of s.th.), assert; **sich versichern** insure o.s.; make sure (**dass** that)

Ver'sicherte m, f (-n; -n) the insured

Ver'sicherung f (-; -en) insurance; assurance, assertion

Ver'sicherungsgesellschaft f insurance company

Versicherungspo,lice f, Versicherungsschein m insurance policy

ver'sickern v/i (no -ge-, sein) trickle away

ver'siegeln v/t (no -ge-, h) seal

ver'siegen v/i (no -ge-, sein) dry up, run dry

ver'silbern v/t (no -ge-, h) silver-plate; F turn s.th. into cash

ver'sinken v/i (irr, **sinken**, no -ge-, sein) sink; → **versunken**

Version [vɛr'zjoːn] f (-; -en) version

'Versmaß n meter, Br metre

versöhnen [fɛɐ'zøːnən] v/t (no -ge-, h) reconcile; **sich (wieder) versöhnen** make it up (**mit** with)

ver'söhnlich adj conciliatory

Ver'söhnung f (-; -en) reconciliation; esp POL appeasement

ver'sorgen v/t (no -ge-, h) provide (**mit** with), supply (with); support; take care of, look after

Ver'sorgung f (-; no pl) supply (**mit** with); support; care

ver'späten v/refl (no -ge-, h) be late

ver'spätet adj belated, late, RAIL etc a. delayed

Ver'spätung f (-; -en) being or coming late, RAIL etc delay; **20 Minuten Verspätung haben** be 20 minutes late

ver'speisen v/t (no -ge-, h) eat (up)

ver'sperren v/t (no -ge-, h) bar, block (up), obstruct (a. view); lock

ver'spielen v/t (no -ge-, h) lose

ver'spielt adj playful

ver'spotten v/t (no -ge-, h) make fun of, ridicule

ver'sprechen (irr, **sprechen**, no -ge-, h) 1. v/t promise (a. fig); **sich zu viel versprechen (von)** expect too much (of); 2. v/refl make a mistake or slip

Ver'sprechen n (-s; -) promise; **ein Versprechen geben (halten, brechen)** make (keep, break) a promise

Ver'sprecher F m (-s; -) slip (of the tongue)

V

ver'staatlichen v/t (no -ge-, h) ECON nationalize

Ver'staatlichung f (-; -en) ECON nationalization

Verstädterung [fɛɐ'ʃtɛːtərʊŋ] f (-; -en) urbanization

Verstand [fɛɐ'ʃtant] m (-[e]s; no pl) mind, intellect; reason, (common) sense; intelligence, brains; **nicht bei Verstand** out of one's mind, not in one's right mind; **den Verstand verlieren** go out of one's mind

verstandesmäßig [fɛɐ'ʃtandəsmɛːsɪç] adj rational

ver'ständig adj reasonable, sensible

verständigen [fɛɐ'ʃtɛndɪgən] v/t (no -ge-, h) inform (**von** of), notify (of); call (doctor, police etc); **sich verständigen** communicate; come to an agreement (**über** acc on)

Ver'ständigung f (-; no pl) communication (a. TEL); agreement

verständlich [fɛɐ'ʃtɛntlɪç] adj audible; intelligible; comprehensible; understandable; **schwer (leicht) verständlich** difficult (easy) to understand; **j-m et. verständlich machen** make s.th. clear to s.o.; **sich verständlich machen** make o.s. understood

Verständnis [fɛɐ'ʃtɛntnɪs] n (-ses; no pl) comprehension, understanding; sympathy; (**viel**) **Verständnis haben** be (very) understanding; **Verständnis haben für** understand; appreciate

ver'ständnislos adj uncomprehending; blank (look etc)

ver'ständnisvoll adj understanding, sympathetic; knowing (look etc)

ver'stärken v/t (no -ge-, h) reinforce (a. TECH, MIL); strengthen (a. TECH); radio, PHYS amplify; intensify

Ver'stärker m (-s; -) amplifier

Ver'stärkung f (-; -en) strengthening; reinforcement(s MIL); amplification; intensification

ver'stauben v/i (no -ge-, sein) get dusty

verstauchen [fɛɐ'ʃtauxən] v/t (no -ge-, h), Ver'stauchung f (-; -en) MED sprain

ver'stauen v/t (no -ge-, h) stow away

Versteck [fɛɐ'ʃtɛk] n (-[e]s; -e) hiding place, hideout, hideaway

ver'stecken v/t and v/refl (no -ge-, h) hide (a. fig); **Verstecken spielen** play (at) hide-and-seek

ver'stehen v/t (irr, stehen, no -ge-, h) understand, F get; catch; see; realize; know; **es verstehen zu** inf know how to inf; **zu verstehen geben** give s.o. to understand, suggest; **ich verstehe!** I see!;

falsch verstehen misunderstand; **wa• verstehen Sie unter …?** what do you mean or understand by …?; **sich (gut• verstehen** get along (well) (**mit** with) **es versteht sich von selbst** it goes with out saying

ver'steifen (no -ge-, h) **1.** v/t stiffen (a sich versteifen); TECH strut, brace; **2** v/refl: **sich auf et. versteifen** insist on (doing) s.th.

ver'steigern v/t (no -ge-, h) auction off

Ver'steigerung f (-; -en) auction (sale)

ver'steinern v/i (no -ge-, sein) petrify (a fig)

ver'stellbar adj adjustable

ver'stellen v/t (no -ge-, h) block; move; se• s.th. wrong or the wrong way; TECH ad just, regulate; disguise (one's voice etc) **sich verstellen** pretend

Ver'stellung f (-; no pl) disguise, make--believe, (false) show

ver'steuern v/t (no -ge-, h) pay duty or tax on

verstiegen [fɛɐ'ʃtiːgən] adj high-flown

ver'stimmen v/t (no -ge-, h) MUS put out of tune; fig annoy

ver'stimmt adj annoyed; MUS out of tune MED upset

Ver'stimmung f (-; -en) annoyance

verstockt [fɛɐ'ʃtɔkt] adj stubborn, obstinate

verstohlen [fɛɐ'ʃtoːlən] adj furtive stealthy

ver'stopfen v/t (no -ge-, h) plug (up) block, jam; MED constipate

ver'stopft adj MED constipated

Ver'stopfung f (-; -en) block(age); MED constipation

verstorben [fɛɐ'ʃtɔrbən] adj late, deceased

Ver'storbene m, f (-n; -n) the deceased **die Verstorbenen** the deceased

verstört [fɛɐ'ʃtøːɐt] adj upset; distracted wild (look etc)

Ver'stoß m offense, Br offence (**gegen** against), violation (of)

ver'stoßen (irr, stoßen, no -ge-, h) **1.** v/• expel (**aus** from); disown; **2.** v/i: **versto• ßen gegen** offend against, violate

ver'strahlt adj (radioactively) contaminated

ver'streichen (irr, streichen, no -ge-) **1** v/i (sein) time: pass, go by; date: expire **2.** v/t (h) spread

ver'streuen v/t (no -ge-, h) scatter

verstümmeln [fɛɐ'ʃtʏməln] v/t (no -ge-, h) mutilate (a. fig)

Ver'stümmelung f (-; -en) mutilation (a. fig)

ver'stummen v/i (no -ge-, sein) grow silent; stop; die down

Versuch [fɛɐˈzuːx] m (-[e]s; -e) attempt, try; trial, test; PHYS experiment; **mit et. (j-m) e-n Versuch machen** give s.th. (s.o.) a try (at it)

ver'suchen v/t (no -ge-, h) try, attempt; taste; REL tempt; **es versuchen** have a try (at it)

Ver'suchs... in cpds ...bohrung etc: test ..., trial ...

Versuchska,ninchen n guinea pig

Versuchsstadium n experimental stage

Versuchstier n laboratory or test animal

ver'suchsweise adv by way of trial

Ver'suchung f (-; -en) temptation; **j-n in Versuchung führen** tempt s.o.

versunken [fɛɐˈzʊŋkən] fig adj: **versunken in** (acc) absorbed or lost in

ver'süßen v/t (no -ge-, h) sweeten

ver'tagen v/t and v/refl (no -ge-, h) adjourn

Ver'tagung f (-; -en) adjournment

ver'tauschen v/t (no -ge-, h) exchange (**mit** for)

verteidigen [fɛɐˈtaidɪɡən] v/t (no -ge-, h) defend (**sich** o.s.)

Verteidiger(in) [fɛɐˈtaidɪɡɐ (-ɡərɪn)] (-s; -/-; -nen) defender, SPORT a. back; fig advocate

Ver'teidigung f (-; -en) defense, Br defence

Ver'teidigungs... in cpds ...politik etc: mst defense ..., Br defence ...

Verteidigungsmi,nister m Secretary of Defense, Br Minister of Defence

Verteidigungsminis,terium n Department of Defense, Br Ministry of Defence

ver'teilen v/t (no -ge-, h) distribute; hand out

Ver'teiler m (-s; -) distributor

Ver'teilung f (-; -en) distribution

ver'tiefen v/t and v/refl (no -ge-, h) deepen (a. fig); **sich vertiefen in** (acc) become absorbed in

Ver'tiefung f (-; -en) hollow, depression, dent; fig deepening

vertikal [vɛrtiˈkaːl] adj, Verti'kale f (-; -n) vertical

ver'tilgen v/t (no -ge-, h) exterminate; F consume

Ver'tilgung f (-; no pl) extermination

vertonen [fɛɐˈtoːnən] v/t (no -ge-, h) set to music

Vertrag [fɛɐˈtraːk] m (-[e]s; Verträge [fɛɐˈtrɛːɡə]) contract; POL treaty

ver'tragen v/t (irr, tragen, no -ge-, h) endure, bear, stand; **ich kann ... nicht vertragen** ... doesn't agree with me; I can't

stand ...; **er kann viel vertragen** he can take a lot; he can hold his drink; F **ich (es) könnte ... vertragen** I (it) could do with ...; **sich (gut) vertragen** get along (well) (**mit** with); **sich wieder vertragen** make it up

ver'träglich adv by contract

verträglich [fɛɐˈtrɛːklɪç] adj easy to get on with; GASTR (easily) digestible

ver'trauen v/i (no -ge-, h) trust (**auf** acc in)

Ver'trauen n (-s; no pl) confidence, trust, faith; **im Vertrauen (gesagt)** between you and me; **wenig Vertrauen erweckend aussehen** inspire little confidence

Ver'trauensfrage f: **die Vertrauensfrage stellen** PARL ask for a vote of confidence

Vertrauenssache f: **das ist Vertrauenssache** that is a matter of confidence

Vertrauensstellung f position of trust

ver'trauensvoll adj trustful, trusting

Ver'trauensvotum n PARL vote of confidence

ver'trauenswürdig adj trustworthy

ver'traulich adj confidential; familiar

ver'traut adj familiar; close

Ver'traute m, f (-n; -n) confidant(e f)

Ver'trautheit f (-; no pl) familiarity

ver'treiben v/t (irr, treiben, no -ge-, h) drive or chase away (a. fig); pass (the time); ECON sell; **vertreiben aus** drive out of

Ver'treibung f (-; -en) expulsion (**aus** from)

ver'treten v/t (irr, treten, no -ge-, h) substitute for, replace, stand in for; POL, ECON represent, PARL a. sit for; JUR act for s.o.; **j-s Sache vertreten** JUR plead s.o.'s cause; **die Ansicht vertreten, dass** argue that; **sich den Fuß vertreten** sprain one's ankle; F **sich die Beine vertreten** stretch one's legs

Ver'treter m (-s; -), Ver'treterin f (-; -nen) substitute, deputy; POL, ECON representative, ECON a. agent; MED locum

Ver'tretung f (-; -en) substitution, replacement; substitute, stand-in, a. supply teacher; ECON, POL representation

Vertrieb [fɛɐˈtriːp] m (-[e]s; no pl) ECON sale, distribution

Vertriebene [fɛɐˈtriːbənə] m, f (-n; -n) POL expellee, refugee

ver'trocknen v/i (no -ge-, sein) dry up

ver'trödeln F v/t (no -ge-, h) dawdle away, waste

ver'trösten v/t (no -ge-, h) put s.o. off

ver'tuschen F v/t (no -ge-, h) cover up

ver'übeln v/t (no -ge-, h) take amiss; **ich kann es ihr nicht verübeln** I can't blame her for it

ver'üben v/t (no -ge-, h) commit

verunglücken [fɛɐˈ'ʔʊnglʏkən] v/i (no -ge-, sein) have an accident; fig go wrong; **tödlich verunglücken** die in an accident

ver'ursachen v/t (no -ge-, h) cause

ver'urteilen v/t (no -ge-, h) condemn (**zu** to) (a. fig), sentence (to), convict (**wegen** of)

Ver'urteilung f (-; -en) condemnation (a. fig)

ver'vielfachen v/t (no -ge-, h) multiply

vervielfältigen [fɛɐˈfiːlfɛltɪgən] v/t (no -ge-, h) copy, duplicate

Ver'vielfältigung f (-; -en) duplication; copy

ver'vollkommnen v/t (no -ge-, h) perfect; improve

vervollständigen [fɛɐˈfɔlʃtɛndɪgən] v/t (no -ge-, h) complete

ver'wachsen adj MED deformed, crippled; fig **verwachsen mit** deeply rooted in, bound up with

ver'wackelt F adj PHOT blurred

ver'wahren v/t (no -ge-, h) keep (in a safe place); **sich verwahren gegen** protest against

verwahrlost [fɛɐˈvaːɐloːst] adj uncared-for, neglected

ver'walten v/t (no -ge-, h) manage, esp POL a. administer

Ver'walter m (-s; -) manager; administrator

Ver'waltung f (-; -en) administration, management

Ver'waltungs... in cpds ...gericht, ...kosten etc: administrative ...

ver'wandeln v/t (no -ge-, h) change, turn (both a. **sich verwandeln**), esp PHYS, CHEM a. transform, convert (all: **in** acc into)

Ver'wandlung f (-; -en) change, transformation; conversion

verwandt [fɛɐˈvant] adj related (**mit** to)

Ver'wandte m, f (-n; -n) relative; (**alle**) **m-e Verwandten** (all) my relatives or relations; **der nächste Verwandte** the next of kin

Ver'wandtschaft f (-; -en) a) relationship, b) (no pl) relations

ver'warnen v/t (no -ge-, h) Br caution; SPORT book

Ver'warnung f (-; -en) Br caution; SPORT booking

ver'waschen adj washed-out

ver'wässern v/t (no -ge-, h) water down (a. fig)

ver'wechseln v/t (no -ge-, h) confuse (**mit** with), mix up (with), mistake (for)

Ver'wechs(e)lung f (-; -en) mistake, F mix-up

ver'wegen adj daring, bold

Ver'wegenheit f (-; no pl) boldness, daring

ver'weichlicht adj soft

ver'weigern v/t (no -ge-, h) refuse; disobey

Ver'weigerung f (-; -en) denial, refusal

ver'weilen v/i (no -ge-, h) stay; fig rest

Verweis [fɛɐˈvais] m (-es; -e) reprimand, reproof; reference (**auf** acc to)

ver'weisen v/t (irr, **weisen**, no -ge-, h) refer (**auf** acc, **an** acc to); expel (gen from)

ver'welken v/i (no -ge-, sein) wither, fig a. fade

ver'wenden v/t (no -ge-, h) use; spend (time etc) (**auf** acc on)

Ver'wendung f (-; -en) use; **keine Verwendung haben für** have no use for

ver'werfen v/t (irr, **werfen**, no -ge-, h) drop, give up; reject

ver'werten v/t (no -ge-, h) use, make use of

verwesen [fɛɐˈveːzən] v/i (no -ge-, sein), Ver'wesung f (-; no pl) decay

ver'wickeln fig v/t (no -ge-, h) involve; **sich verwickeln in** (acc) get caught in

ver'wickelt fig adj complicated; **verwickelt sein** (**werden**) **in** (acc) be (get) involved in

Ver'wicklung fig f (-; -en) involvement; complication

ver'wildern v/i (no -ge-, sein) grow (or run) wild

ver'wildert adj wild (a. fig), overgrown

ver'winden v/t (irr, **winden**, no -ge-, h) get over s.th.

ver'wirklichen v/t (no -ge-, h) realize; **sich verwirklichen** come true; **sich selbst verwirklichen** fulfil(l) o.s.

Ver'wirklichung f (-; -en) realization

ver'wirren v/t (no -ge-, h) tangle (up); fig confuse

Ver'wirrung fig f (-; -en) confusion

ver'wirrt fig adj confused

ver'wischen v/t (no -ge-, h) blur (a. fig); cover (track etc)

verwittern [fɛɐˈvitən] v/i (no -ge-, sein) GEOL weather

ver'witwet adj widowed

verwöhnen [fɛɐˈvøːnən] v/t (no -ge-, h) spoil

ver'wöhnt adj spoilt

verworren [fɛɐˈvɔrən] adj confused, muddled; complicated

verwundbar [fɛɐˈvʊntbaːɐ] adj vulnerable (a. fig)

ver'wunden v/t (no -ge-, h) wound

ver'wunderlich *adj* surprising

Ver'wunderung [fɛɐ'vʊndərʊŋ] *f* (-; *no pl*) (*zu m-r etc* **Verwunderung** to my *etc*) surprise

ver'wundete m, *f* (-n; -n) wounded (person), casualty

Ver'wundung *f* (-; -en) wound, injury

ver'wünschen *v/t* (*no -ge-, h*), Ver'wünschung *f* (-; -en) curse

ver'wüsten *v/t* (*no -ge-, h*) lay waste, devastate, ravage

Ver'wüstung *f* (-; -en) devastation, ravage

ver'zählen *v/refl* (*no -ge-, h*) count wrong

verzärteln [fɛɐ'tsɛrtəln] *v/t* (*no -ge-, h*) coddle, pamper

ver'zaubern *v/t* (*no -ge-, h*) enchant, *fig a.* charm; **verzaubern in** (*acc*) turn into

ver'zehren *v/t* (*no -ge-, h*) consume (*a. fig*)

ver'zeichnen *v/t* (*no -ge-, h*) record, keep a record of, list; *fig* achieve; suffer

Ver'zeichnis *n* (-ses; -se) list, catalog(ue); record, register; index

verzeihen [fɛɐ'tsaiən] *v/t and v/i* (*irr, no -ge-, h*) forgive *s.o.*; pardon, excuse *s.th.*

ver'zeihlich *adj* pardonable

Ver'zeihung *f* (-; *no pl*) pardon; (*j-n*) **um Verzeihung bitten** apologize (to s.o.); **Verzeihung!** (I'm) sorry!; excuse me!

ver'zerren *v/t* (*no -ge-, h*) distort (*a. fig*); **sich verzerren** become distorted

Ver'zerrung *f* (-; -en) distortion

Verzicht [fɛɐ'tsɪçt] *m* (-[e]s; -e) renunciation (**auf** *acc* of); *mst* giving up, doing without *etc*

ver'zichten *v/i* (*no -ge-, h*) **verzichten auf** (*acc*) do without; give up; renounce (*a. JUR*)

verzieh [fɛɐ'tsiː] *pret of* **verzeihen**

ver'ziehen (*irr, ziehen, no -ge-*) **1.** *v/i* (*sein*) move (**nach** to); **2.** *v/t* (*h*) spoil; **das Gesicht verziehen** make a face; **sich verziehen** wood: warp; *storm etc:* pass (over); F disappear; **3.** *pp of* **verziehen**

ver'zieren *v/t* (*no -ge-, h*) decorate

Ver'zierung *f* (-; -en) decoration, ornament

ver'zinsen *v/t* (*no -ge-, h*) pay interest on; **sich verzinsen** yield interest

Ver'zinsung *f* (-; -en) interest

ver'zögern *v/t* (*no -ge-, h*) delay; **sich verzögern** be delayed

Ver'zögerung *f* (-; -en) delay

ver'zollen *v/t* (*no -ge-, h*) pay duty on; **et. (nichts) zu verzollen haben** have s.th. (nothing) to declare

verzückt [fɛɐ'tsʏkt] *adj* ecstatic

Ver'zückung *f* (-; -en) ecstasy; **in Verzückung geraten** go into ecstasies *or* rap-

tures (**wegen, über** *acc* over)

Verzug [fɛɐ'tsuːk] *m* (-[e]s; *no pl*) delay; ECON default

ver'zweifeln *v/i* (*no -ge-, h*) despair (**an** *dat* of)

ver'zweifelt *adj* desperate, despairing

Ver'zweiflung *f* (-; *no pl*) despair; **j-n zur Verzweiflung bringen** drive s.o. to despair

verzweigen [fɛɐ'tsvaigən] *v/refl* (*no -ge-, h*) branch

verzwickt [fɛɐ'tsvɪkt] F *adj* tricky

Veteran [vete'raːn] *m* (-en; -en) MIL veteran (*a. fig*)

Veterinär [veteri'nɛːɐ] *m* (-s; -e), Veteri'närin *f* (-; -nen) veterinarian, *Br* veterinary surgeon, F vet

Veto ['veːto] *n* (-s; -s) veto; (**s)ein Veto einlegen gegen** veto

Vetter ['fɛtɐ] *m* (-s; -n) cousin

'Vetternwirtschaft *f* (-; *no pl*) nepotism

vgl. ABBR *of* **vergleiche** cf., confer

VHS ABBR *of* **Volkshochschule** adult education program(me); adult evening classes

Vibration [vibra'tsjoːn] *f* (-; -en) vibration

vibrieren [vi'briːrən] *v/i* (*no -ge-, h*) vibrate

Video ['viːdeo] *n* (-s; -s) video (*a. in cpds* ...aufnahme, ...clip, ...kamera, ...kassette, ...recorder etc*); **auf Video aufnehmen** video(tape), tape

Videoband *n* videotape

Videotext *m* teletext

Videothek [video'teːk] *f* (-; -en) video (-tape) library; video store (*Br* shop)

Vieh [fiː] *n* (-[e]s; *no pl*) cattle; **20 Stück Vieh** 20 head of cattle

Viehbestand *m* livestock

Viehhändler *m* cattle dealer

'viehisch *contp adj* bestial, brutal

'Viehmarkt *m* cattle market

Viehzucht *f* cattle breeding, stockbreeding

Viehzüchter *m* cattle breeder, stockbreeder

viel [fiːl] *adj and adv* a lot (of), plenty (of), F lots of; **viele** many; **nicht viel** not much; **nicht viele** not many; **sehr viel** a great deal (of); **sehr viele** very many, a lot (of); **das viele Geld** all that money; **ziemlich viel** quite a lot (of); **ziemlich viele** quite a few; **viel besser** much better; **viel teurer** much more expensive; **e-r zu viel** one too many; **viel zu viel** far too much; **viel zu wenig** not nearly enough; **viel lieber** much rather; **wie viel** how much (*pl* many); **viel beschäftigt** very busy; **viel sagend** meaningful; **viel**

ver'sprechend promising
'**vieldeutig** [-dɔytɪç] *adj* ambiguous
vielerlei ['fiːlɐlai] *adj* all kinds *or* sorts of
'**vielfach 1.** *adj* multiple; **2.** *adv* in many
cases, (very) often
'**Vielfalt** *f* (-; *no pl*) (great) variety (*gen* of)
'**vielfarbig** *adj* multicolo(u)red
vielleicht [fi'laiçt] *adv* perhaps, maybe;
vielleicht ist er … he may *or* might be …
'**vielmals** *adv*: (*ich*) *danke* (*Ihnen*) *vielmals* thank you very much; *entschuldi-
gen Sie vielmals* I'm very sorry, I do
apologize
viel'mehr *cj* rather
'**vielsagend** *adj* meaningful
vielversprechend *adj* promising
'**vielseitig** [-zaitɪç] *adj* versatile
'**Vielseitigkeit** *f* (-; *no pl*) versatility
vier [fiːɐ] *adj* four; *zu viert sein* be four;
auf allen vieren on all fours; *unter vier
Augen* in private, privately
'**Vierbeiner** [-bainɐ] *m* (-s; -) ZO quadru-
ped, four-legged animal
'**vierbeinig** *adj* four-legged
'**Viereck** *n* quadrangle, quadrilateral
'**viereckig** *adj* quadrangular, square
Vierer ['fiːrɐ] *m* (-s; -) *rowing*: four
'**vierfach** *adj* fourfold; *vierfache Ausfertigung* four copies
'**vierfüßig** [-fyːsɪç] *adj* four-footed
'**Vierfüßler** [-fyːslɐ] *m* (-s; -) ZO quadru-
ped
'**vierhändig** [-hɛndɪç] *adj* MUS four-hand-
ed
'**vierjährig** [-jɛːrɪç] *adj* four-year-old, *or*
four
Vierlinge ['fiːrlɪŋə] *pl* quadruplets, quads
'**viermal** *adv* four times
'**Vierradantrieb** *m* MOT four-wheel drive
'**vierseitig** [-zaitɪç] *adj* MATH quadrilateral
'**vierspurig** [-ʃpuːrɪç] *adj* MOT four-lane
'**vierstöckig** [-ʃtœkɪç] *adj* four-storied, *Br*
four-storey …
'**Viertaktmotor** *m* four-stroke engine
vierte ['fiːrtə] *adj* fourth
Viertel ['fɪrtəl] *n* (-s; -) fourth (part); quarter; (*ein*) *Viertel vor* (*nach*) (a) quarter
to (past)
Viertelfi,nale *n* SPORT quarter finals
Viertel'jahr *n* three months
'**vierteljährlich 1.** *adj* quarterly; **2.** *adv* every three months, quarterly
vierteln ['fɪrtəln] *v/t* (*ge-, h*) quarter
'**Viertelnote** *f* MUS quarter note, *Br* crotch-
et
Viertelpfund *n* quarter of a pound
Viertel'stunde *f* quarter of an hour
'**viertens** ['fiːrtəns] *adv* fourthly
vierzehn ['fɪrtseːn] *adj* fourteen; *vier-*

zehn Tage two weeks, *esp Br a.* a fort-
night
'**vierzehnte** *adj* fourteenth
vierzig ['fɪrtsɪç] *adj* forty
'**vierzigste** *adj* fortieth
Villa ['vɪla] *f* (-; *Villen*) villa
violett [vio'let] *adj* violet, purple
Violine [vio'liːnə] *f* (-; -n) MUS violin
Virtuelle Realität [vɪr'tuɛlə] *f* EDP virtual
reality, Cyberspace
virtuos [vɪr'tuoːs] *adj* virtuoso …, master-
ly
Vir'tuose [vɪr'tuoːzə] *m* (-n; -n) virtuoso
Virtuosität [vɪrtuoziˈtɛːt] *f* (-; *no pl*) vir-
tuosity
Virus ['viːrʊs] *n*, *m* (-; *Viren*) MED virus
Visier [vi'ziːɐ] *n* (-s; -e) sights; visor
Vision [vi'zjoːn] *f* (-; -en) vision
Visite [vi'ziːtə] *f* (-; -n) MED round
Vi'sitenkarte *f* (visiting) card
Visum ['viːzʊm] *n* (-s; *Visa*) visa
vital [vi'taːl] *adj* vigorous
Vitalität [vitaliˈtɛːt] *f* (-; *no pl*) vigo(u)r
Vitamin [vita'miːn] *n* (-s; -e) vitamin
Vitrine [vi'triːnə] *f* (-; -n) (glass) cabinet;
showcase
Vize… ['fiːtsə-] *in cpds* vice(-)…
Vogel ['foːgəl] *m* (-s; *Vögel* ['føːgəl]) ZO
bird; F *den Vogel abschießen* take
the cake
'**Vogelbauer** *n* birdcage
'**vogelfrei** *adj* outlawed
'**Vogelfutter** *n* birdseed
'**Vogelgrippe** *f* bird flu, avian flu
Vogelkunde *f* ornithology
Vogelkäfig *m* birdcage
vögeln ['føːgəln] V *v/t* and *v/i* (*ge-, h*)
screw
'**Vogelnest** *n* bird's nest
Vogelperspektive *f* bird's-eye view
Vogelscheuche *f* scarecrow (*a. fig*)
Vogelschutzgebiet *n* bird sanctuary
Vogelwarte *f* ornithological station
Vogelzug *m* bird migration
Vokabel [vo'kaːbəl] *f* (-; -n) word; *pl* → *Vo-
kabular* [vokabu'laːɐ] *n* (-s; -e) vocabu-
lary
Vokal [vo'kaːl] *m* (-s; -e) LING vowel
Volant [vo'lãː] *Austrian m* → *Lenkrad*
Volk [fɔlk] *n* (-[e]s; *Völker* ['fœlkɐ]) peo-
ple, nation; *the* people; ZO swarm; *ein
Mann aus dem Volke* a man of the peo-
ple
Völkerkunde ['fœlkɐ-] *f* ethnology
Völkermord *m* genocide
Völkerrecht *n* (-[e]s; *no pl*) international
law
Völkerwanderung *f* migration of peoples;
F mass exodus

Volksabstimmung f POL referendum

Volksfest n funfair

Volkshochschule f adult evening classes

Volkslied n folk song

Volksmund m: **im Volksmund** in the vernacular

Volksmu,sik f folk music

Volksrepu,blik f people's republic

Volksschule HIST f → **Grundschule**

Volkssport m popular sport

Volkssprache f vernacular

Volksstamm m tribe, race

Volkstanz m folk dance

Volkstracht f national costume

volkstümlich [-ty:mlɪç] adj popular, folk …; traditional

Volksversammlung f public meeting

Volkswirt m economist

Volkswirtschaft f (national) economy; → **Volkswirtschaftslehre** f economics

Volkszählung f census

voll [fɔl] **1.** adj full (a. fig); full up (a. F); F plastered; thick, rich (hair); **voller** full of, filled with, a. covered with dirt etc; **2.** adv fully; completely, totally, wholly; pay etc in full, the full price; hit etc full, straight, right; **voll entwickelt** fully developed; **(nicht) für voll nehmen** (not) take seriously

vollauf adv perfectly, quite

vollauto,matisch adj fully automatic

Vollbart m (full) beard

Vollbeschäftigung f full employment

Vollblut… in cpds full-blooded (a. fig)

Vollblüter [-bly:tɐ] m (-s; -) zo thoroughbred

voll'bringen v/t (irr, bringen, no -ge-, h) accomplish, achieve; perform

Volldampf m full steam; F **mit Volldampf** (at) full blast

voll'enden v/t (no -ge-, h) finish, complete

voll'endet adj completed; fig perfect

vollends ['fɔlɛnts] adv completely

Voll'endung f (-; no pl) finishing, completion; fig perfection

voll'führen v/t (no -ge-, h) perform

voll'füllen v/t (sep, -ge-, h) (gießen) fill (up)

Vollgas n (-es; no pl) MOT full throttle; **Vollgas geben** F step on it

völlig ['fœlɪç] **1.** adj complete, absolute, total; **2.** adv completely, **völlig unmöglich** absolutely impossible

volljährig [-jɛːrɪç] adj JUR **volljährig sein (werden)** be (come) of age; **noch nicht volljährig** under age

Volljährigkeit f (-; no pl) JUR majority

voll'kommen adj perfect; → **völlig**

Voll'kommenheit f (-; no pl) perfection

Vollkornbrot n wholemeal bread

voll'machen v/t (sep, -ge-, h) fill (up); F soil, dirty; **um das Unglück voll zu machen** to crown it all

Vollmacht f (-; -en) full power(s), authority; JUR power of attorney; **Vollmacht haben** be authorized

Vollmilch f full-cream milk

Vollmond m full moon

voll'packen v/t (sep, -ge-, h) load (**mit** with) (a. fig)

Vollpensi,on f full board

voll'schlank adj plump

vollständig adj complete; → **völlig**

voll'stopfen v/t (sep, -ge-, h) stuff, fig a. cram, pack (all: **mit** with)

voll'strecken v/t (no -ge-, h) JUR execute

Voll'streckung f (-; -en) JUR execution

voll'tanken v/t (sep, -ge-, h): **bitte volltanken!** MOT fill her up, please!

Volltreffer m direct hit; bull's eye (a. fig)

Vollversammlung f plenary session

vollwertig adj full

Vollwertkost f wholefoods

vollzählig ['fɔltsɛ:lɪç] adj complete

voll'ziehen v/t (irr, ziehen, no -ge-, h) execute; perform; **sich vollziehen** take place

Voll'ziehung f (-; no pl), **Voll'zug** m (-[e]s; no pl) execution

Volontär [volɔn'tɛ:ɐ] m (-s; -e), **Volon'tärin** f (-; -nen) unpaid trainee

Volt [vɔlt] n (-; -) ELECTR volt

Volumen [vo'lu:mən] n (-s; -, -mina) volume; size

von [fɔn] prp from; instead of gen: of; passive: by; about s.o. or s.th.; **südlich von** south of; **weit von** far from; **von Hamburg** from Hamburg; **von nun an** from now on; **ein Freund von mir** a friend of mine; **die Freunde von Alice** Alice's friends; **ein Brief (Geschenk) von Tom** a letter (gift) from Tom; **ein Bild (Bild) von Orwell (Picasso)** a book (painting) by Orwell (Picasso); **der König (Bürgermeister etc) von …** the King (Mayor etc) of …; **ein Kind von 10 Jahren** a child of ten; **müde von der Arbeit** tired from work; **es war nett (gemein) von dir** it was nice (mean) of you; **reden (hören) von** talk (hear) about or of; **von Beruf (Geburt)** by profession (birth); **von selbst** by itself; **von mir aus!** I don't mind or care

von'stattengehen v/i (irr, gehen, sep, -ge-, sein) go, come off

vor [fo:ɐ] prp (dat and acc) in front of; outside; before; … ago; with, for; **vor der Klasse** in front of the class; **vor**

der Schule in front of *or* outside the school; before school; **vor kurzem (e-r Stunde)** a short time (an hour) ago; **5 Minuten vor 12** five (minutes) to twelve; **vor j-m liegen** be *or* lie ahead of s.o. (*a. fig and* SPORT); **vor sich hin** smile *etc* to o.s.; **sicher vor** safe from; **vor Kälte** with cold; **vor Angst** for fear; **vor allem** above all; **vor sich gehen** go on, happen

'Vorabend *m* eve (*a. fig*)

'Vorahnung *f* presentiment, foreboding

voran [fo'ran] *adv* at the head (*dat* of), in front (of), before; **Kopf voran** head first

voran|gehen *v/i* (*irr, gehen, sep, -ge-, sein*) go in front *or* first; *fig* lead the way

voran|kommen *v/i* (*irr, kommen, sep, -ge-, sein*) get on *or* along (*a. fig*), make headway

'Voranzeige *f* preannouncement; *film:* trailer

'vorarbeiten *v/i* (*sep, -ge-, h*) work in advance; *fig* pave the way

'Vorarbeiter *m* foreman

voraus [fo'raus] *adv* ahead (*dat* of); **im Voraus** in advance, beforehand

vo'rausgehen *v/i* (*irr, gehen, sep, -ge-, sein*) precede; → **vorangehen**

vo'rausgesetzt *cj:* **vorausgesetzt, dass** provided that

Vo'raussage *f* (*-; -n*) prediction; METEOR forecast

vo'raussagen *v/t* (*sep, -ge-, h*) predict; forecast

vo'rausschicken *v/t* (*sep, -ge-, h*) send on ahead

voraussehen *v/t* (*irr, sehen, sep, -ge-, h*) foresee, see *s.th.* coming

vo'raussetzen *v/t* (*sep, -ge-, h*) assume; take *s.th.* for granted

Vo'raussetzung *f* (*-; -en*) condition, prerequisite; assumption; **die Voraussetzungen erfüllen** meet the requirements

Vo'raussicht *f* (*-; no pl*) foresight; **aller Voraussicht nach** in all probability

vo'raussichtlich *adv* probably; **er kommt voraussichtlich morgen** he is expected to arrive tomorrow

Vo'rauszahlung *f* advance payment

'Vorbedeutung *f* omen

'Vorbedingung *f* prerequisite

Vorbehalt ['fo:ɐbəhalt] *m* (*-[e]s; -e*) reservation

'vorbehalten **1.** *v/t* (*irr, halten, sep, no -ge-, h*) **sich (das Recht) vorbehalten zu** *inf* reserve the right to *inf*; **2.** *adj* sie reserved

'vorbehaltlos **1.** *adj* unconditional; **2.** *adv* without reservation

vor'bei *adv time:* over, past; finished; gone; *space:* past, by; **jetzt ist alles vorbei** it's all over now; **vorbei!** missed!

vorbei|fahren *v/i* (*irr, fahren, sep, -ge-, sein*) go (*or* drive) past (**an** *dat s.o. or s.th.*), pass (*s.o. or s.th.*)

vorbei|gehen *v/i* (*irr, gehen, sep, -ge-, sein*) walk past; *a. fig* go by, pass; *shot etc:* miss

vorbei kommen *v/i* (*irr, kommen, sep, -ge-, sein*) pass (**an** *dat s.th.*); get past (**an** *obstacle etc*); F drop in (**bei j-m** on s.o.); *fig* avoid

vorbei|lassen *v/t* (*irr, lassen, sep, -ge-, h*) let *s.o.* pass

'Vorbemerkung *f* preliminary remark

'vorbereiten *v/t and v/refl* (*sep, no -ge-, h*) prepare (**auf** *acc* for)

'Vorbereitung *f* (*-; -en*) preparation (**auf** *acc* for)

'vorbestellen *v/t* (*sep, no -ge-, h*) book (*or* order) in advance; reserve (*room, seat etc*)

'Vorbestellung *f* (*-; -en*) advance booking; reservation

'vorbestraft *adj:* **vorbestraft sein** have a police record

'vorbeugen (*sep, -ge-, h*) **1.** *v/i* prevent (**e-r Sache** s.th.); **2.** *v/refl* bend forward

'vorbeugend *adj* preventive, MED *a.* prophylactic

'Vorbeugung *f* (*-; -en*) prevention

'Vorbild *n* model, pattern; (**j-m**) **ein Vorbild sein** set an example (to s.o.); **sich j-n zum Vorbild nehmen** follow s.o.'s example

'vorbildlich *adj* exemplary

'Vorbildung *f* education(al background)

'vorbringen *v/t* (*irr, bringen, sep, -ge-, h*) bring forward; say, state

vorda'tieren *v/t* (*no -ge-, h*) antedate; postdate

Vorder... ['fɔrdɐ-] *in cpds* ...achse, ...rad, ...sitz, ...tür, ...zahn *etc*: front ...

vordere ['fɔrdərə] *adj* front

'Vordergrund *m* foreground (*a. fig*)

Vordermann *m:* **mein Vordermann** the man *or* boy in front of me

'Vorderseite *f* front (side); head

'vordräng(e)ln *v/refl* (*sep, -ge-, h*) cut into line, Br jump the queue

vordringen *v/i* (*irr, dringen, sep, -ge-, sein*) advance; **vordringen (bis) zu** work one's way through to (*a. fig*)

'vordringlich **1.** *adj* (most) urgent; **2.** *adv:* **et. vordringlich behandeln** give s.th. priority

'Vordruck *m* (*-[e]s; -e*) form, blank

'voreilig *adj* hasty, rash, precipitate; **vor-**

eilige Schlüsse ziehen jump to conclusions

voreingenommen *adj* prejudiced, bias(s)ed

Voreingenommenheit *f* (-; *no pl*) prejudice, bias

vorenthalten *v/t* (*irr*, **halten**, *sep*, *no* -ge-, h) keep back, withhold (*both:* **j-m et.** s.th. from s.o.)

Vorentscheidung *f* preliminary decision

vorerst *adv* for the present, for the time being

Vorfahr ['foːɐfaːɐ] *m* (-en; -en) ancestor

vorfahren *v/i* (*irr*, **fahren**, *sep*, -ge-, *sein*) drive up (*or* on)

Vorfahrt *f* (-; *no pl*) right of way, priority

Vorfall *m* incident, occurrence, event

vorfallen *v/i* (*irr*, **fallen**, *sep*, -ge-, *sein*) happen, occur

vorfinden *v/t* (*irr*, **finden**, *sep*, -ge-, h) find

Vorfreude *f* anticipation

vorführen *v/t* (*sep*, -ge-, h) show, present; perform (*trick etc*); demonstrate; JUR bring (*j-m* before s.o.)

Vorführer *m* demonstrator

Vorführung *f* presentation, show(ing); performance; demonstration; JUR production

Vorführwagen *m* MOT demonstrator, *Br* demonstration car

Vorgabe *f* handicap

Vorgang *m* event, occurrence, happening; file, record(s); BIOL, TECH process; *e-n Vorgang schildern* give an account of what happened

Vorgänger(in) ['foːɐgɛŋɐ (-ŋərɪn)] (-s; -/-; -nen) predecessor

Vorgarten *m* front yard (*Br* garden)

vorgeben *v/t* (*irr*, **geben**, *sep*, -ge-, h, SPORT give; *fig* use *s.th.* as a pretext

Vorgebirge *n* foothills

vorgefasst *adj* preconceived

vorgefertigt *adj* prefabricated

Vorgefühl *n* presentiment

vorgehen *v/i* (*irr*, **gehen**, *sep*, -ge-, *sein*) go on; (*come*) first; act; JUR sue (*gegen j-n* s.o.); proceed; *watch*: be fast

Vorgehen *n* (-s; *no pl*) procedure

vorgeschichtlich *adj* prehistoric

Vorgeschmack *m* foretaste (*auf acc* of)

Vorgesetzte(r) *m*, *f* (-n; -n) superior, F boss

vorgestern *adv* the day before yesterday

vorgreifen *v/i* (*irr*, **greifen**, *sep*, -ge-, h) anticipate *s.o. or s.th.*

vorhaben *v/t* (*irr*, **haben**, *sep*, -ge-, h) plan, intend; *haben Sie heute Abend et. vor?* have you anything on tonight?; *was hat er jetzt wieder vor?* what is he up to now?

Vorhaben *n* (-s; -) plan(s), intention; TECH, ECON *a*. project

Vorhalle *f* (entrance) hall, lobby

vorhalten (*irr*, **halten**, *sep*, -ge-, h) **1.** *v/t*: *j-m et. vorhalten* hold s.th. in front of s.o.; *fig* blame s.o. for (doing) s.th.; **2.** *v/i* last

Vorhaltungen *pl* reproaches; *j-m Vorhaltungen machen (für et.)* reproach s.o. (with s.th., for being …)

Vorhand *f* (-; *no pl*) *tennis*: forehand

vorhanden [foːɐ'handən] *adj* available; in existence; *vorhanden sein* exist; *es ist nichts mehr vorhanden* there's nothing left

Vor'handensein *n* (-s; *no pl*) existence

Vorhang *m* curtain

Vorhängeschloss *n* padlock

vor'her *adv* before, earlier; in advance, beforehand

vor'herbestimmen *v/t* (*sep*, *no* -ge-, h) predetermine

vorherig [foːɐ'heːrɪç] *adj* previous

Vor'herrschaft *f* (-; *no pl*) predominance

vor'herrschen *v/i* (*sep*, -ge-, h) predominate, prevail

vor'herrschend *adj* predominant, prevailing

vor'hersehbar *adj* foreseeable

vor'hersehen *v/t* (*irr*, **sehen**, *sep*, -ge-, h) foresee

vor'hin *adv* a (little) while ago

Vorhut *f* (-; -en) MIL vanguard

vorig ['foːrɪç] *adj* last; former, previous

vorjährig ['foːrjɛːrɪç] *adj* of last year, last year' …

Vorkämpfer *m*, **Vorkämpferin** *f* champion, pioneer

Vorkehrungen ['foːrkeːruŋən] *pl*: *Vorkehrungen treffen* take precautions

Vorkenntnisse *pl* previous knowledge *or* experience (*in dat* of)

vorkommen *v/i* (*irr*, **kommen**, *sep*, -ge-, *sein*) be found; happen; *es kommt mir … vor* it seems … to me

Vorkommen *n* (-s; -) MIN deposit(s)

Vorkommnis ['foːrkɔmnɪs] *n* (-ses; -se) occurrence, incident, event

Vorkriegs… *in cpds* prewar …

vorladen *v/t* (*irr*, **laden**, *sep*, -ge-, h) JUR summon

Vorladung *f* (-; -en) JUR summons

Vorlage *f* model; pattern; copy; presentation; PARL bill; *soccer etc*: pass

vorlassen *v/t* (*irr*, **lassen**, *sep*, -ge-, h) let *s.o.* go first; let *s.o.* pass; *vorgelassen werden* be admitted (*bei* to)

Vorlauf *m* recorder: fast-forward; SPORT (preliminary) heat

V

'Vorläufer *m* forerunner, precursor

'vorläufig **1.** *adj* provisional, temporary; **2.** *adv* for the present, for the time being

'vorlaut *adj* pert, cheeky

'Vorleben *n* (-*s*; *no pl*) former life, past

'vorlegen *v/t* (*sep*, *-ge-*, *h*) present; produce; show

'Vorleger *m* (-*s*; -) rug; mat

'vorlesen *v/t* (*irr*, **lesen**, *sep*, *-ge-*, *h*) read out (aloud); ***j-m et. vorlesen*** read s.th. to s.o.

'Vorlesung *f* (-; -*en*) lecture (***über*** *acc* on; ***vor*** *dat* to); ***e-e Vorlesung halten*** (give a) lecture

'vorletzte *adj* last but one; ***vorletzte Nacht (Woche)*** the night (week) before last

'vorliebnehmen *v/i* (*irr*, **nehmen**, *sep*, *-ge-*, *h*) **mit** make do with

'Vorliebe *f* (-; -*n*) preference, special liking

'vorliegen *v/i* (*irr*, **liegen**, *sep*, *-ge-*, *h*) **es liegen (keine) ... vor** there are (no) ...; **was liegt gegen ihn vor?** what is he charged with?

vorliegend *adj* present, in question

'vorlügen *v/t* (*irr*, **lügen**, *sep*, *-ge-*, *h*) **j-m et. vorlügen** tell s.o. lies

'vormachen *v/t* (*sep*, *-ge-*, *h*) **j-m et. vormachen** show s.th. to s.o., show s.o. how to do s.th.; *fig* fool s.o.

'Vormachtstellung *f* supremacy

'Vormarsch *m* MIL advance (*a.* fig)

'vormerken *v/t* (*sep*, *-ge-*, *h*) **j-n vormerken** put s.o.'s name down

'Vormittag *m* morning; **heute Vormittag** this morning

'vormittags *adv* in the morning; **sonntags vormittags** on Sunday mornings

'Vormund *m* (-[e]*s*; -*e*) JUR guardian

Vormundschaft *f* (-; -*en*) JUR guardianship

vorn [fɔrn] *adv* in front; **nach vorn** forward; **von vorn** from the front; from the beginning; **j-n von vorn(e) sehen** see s.o.'s face; **noch einmal von vorn(e) (anfangen)** (start) all over again

'Vorname *m* first *or* Christian name, forename

vornehm ['foːrneːm] *adj* distinguished; noble; fashionable, exclusive, F smart, posh; **die vornehme Gesellschaft** (high) society; **vornehm tun** put on airs

'vornehmen *v/t* (*irr*, **nehmen**, *sep*, *-ge-*, *h*) carry out, do; make (*changes etc*); **sich et. vornehmen** decide *or* resolve to do s.th.; make plans for s.th.; **sich fest vorgenommen haben zu** *inf* have the firm intention to *inf*, be determined to *inf*

'vornherein *adv*: **von vornherein** from the start *or* beginning

'Vorort *m* suburb

Vorort(s)zug *m* suburban *or* local *or* commuter train

'Vorposten *m* outpost (*a.* MIL)

'vorprogram,mieren *v/t* (*sep*, *no* *-ge-*, *sein*) (pre)program(me); *fig* **das war vorprogrammiert** that was bound to happen

'Vorrang *m* (-[e]*s*; *no pl*) precedence (**vor** *dat* over), priority (over)

'Vorrat *m* (-[e]*s*; *-räte*) store, stock, supply (*all*: **an** *dat* of); GASTR provisions; ECON resources, reserves; **e-n Vorrat anlegen** *an* (*dat*) stockpile

'vorrätig ['foːrɛːtɪç] *adj* available; ECON in stock

'Vorrecht *n* privilege

'Vorredner *m* previous speaker

'Vorrichtung *f* TECH device

'vorrücken (*sep*, *-ge-*) **1.** *v/t* (*h*) move forward; **2.** *v/i* (*sein*) advance

'Vorrunde *f* SPORT preliminary round

'vorsagen *v/i* (*sep*, *-ge-*, *h*) **j-m vorsagen** prompt s.o.

'Vorsai,son *f* off-peak season

'Vorsatz *m* resolution; intention; JUR intent

vor'sätzlich ['foːrzɛtslɪç] *adj* intentional; *esp* JUR wil(l)ful

'Vorschau *f* preview (**auf** *acc* of), *film*, TV *a.* trailer

'Vorschein *m*: **zum Vorschein bringen** produce; *fig* bring out; **zum Vorschein kommen** appear; *fig* come to light

'vorschieben *v/t* (*irr*, **schieben**, *sep*, *-ge-*, *h*) push forward; slip (*bolt*); *fig* use as a pretext

vor'schießen *v/t* (*irr*, **schießen**, *sep*, *-ge-*, *h*) advance (*money*)

'Vorschlag *m* suggestion, proposal (*a.* PARL *etc*); **den Vorschlag machen** → 'vorschlagen *v/t* (*irr*, **schlagen**, *sep*, *-ge-*, *h*) suggest, propose

'Vorschlussrunde *f* SPORT semifinal

'vorschnell *adj* hasty, rash

'vorschreiben *fig v/t* (*irr*, **schreiben**, *sep*, *-ge-*, *h*) prescribe; tell; **ich lasse mir nichts vorschreiben** I won't be dictated to

'Vorschrift *f* rule, regulation; instruction, direction; **Dienst nach Vorschrift machen** work to rule

'vorschriftsmäßig *adj* correct, proper

vorschriftswidrig *adj and adv* contrary to regulations

'Vorschub *m*: **Vorschub leisten** (*dat*) encourage; JUR aid and abet

'Vorschul... *in cpds* pre-school ...

'Vorschule *f* preschool

Vorschuss *m* advance

vorschützen *v/t* (*sep, -ge-, h*) use *s.th.* as a pretext

vorsehen (*irr, sehen, sep, -ge-, h*) **1.** *v/t* plan; JUR provide; **vorsehen für** intend (*or* designate) for; **2.** *v/refl* be careful, take care, watch out (**vor** *dat* for)

Vorsehung *f* (-; *no pl*) providence

vorsetzen *v/t* (*sep, -ge-, h*) **j-m et. vorsetzen** put *s.th.* before *s.o.*; offer *s.o.* *s.th.*

Vorsicht *f* (-; *no pl*) caution, care; **Vorsicht!** look *or* watch out!, (be) careful!; **Vorsicht, Stufe!** mind the step!

vorsichtig *adj* careful, cautious

vorsichtshalber[-halbɐ] *adv* to be on the safe side

Vorsichtsmaßnahme *f* precaution, precautionary measure; **Vorsichtsmaßnahmen treffen** take precautions

Vorsilbe *f* LING prefix

vorsingen *v/t and v/i* (*irr, singen, sep, -ge-, h*) **j-m et. vorsingen** sing *s.th.* to *s.o.*; (have an) audition

Vorsitz *m* chair(manship), presidency; **den Vorsitz haben (übernehmen)** be in (take) the chair, preside (**bei** over, at)

Vorsitzende *m, f* (-*n; -n*) chairman (chairwoman), president

Vorsorge *f* (-; *no pl*) precaution; **Vorsorge treffen** take precautions

Vorsorgeuntersuchung *f* MED preventive checkup

vorsorglich 1. *adj* precautionary; **2.** *adv* as a precaution

Vorspann *m* (-[*e*]*s; -e*) film *etc*: credits

Vorspeise *f* hors d'œuvre, *Br* starter

Vorspiel *n* MUS prelude (*a. fig*); foreplay

vorspielen *v/t* (*sep, -ge-, h*) **j-m et. vorspielen** *v/t* to *s.o.*

vorsprechen (*irr, sprechen, sep, -ge-, h*) **1.** *v/t* pronounce (**j-m** for *s.o.*); **2.** *v/i* call (**bei** at); THEA (have an) audition

vorspringen *fig v/i* (*irr, springen, sep, -ge-, sein*) project, protrude (*both a.* ARCH)

Vorsprung *m* ARCH projection; SPORT lead; **e-n Vorsprung haben** be leading (**von** by); *esp fig* **e-n Vorsprung von zwei Jahren haben** be two years ahead

Vorstadt *f* suburb

Vorstand *m* ECON board (of directors); managing committee (*of a club etc*)

vorstehen *v/i* (*irr, stehen, sep, -ge-, h*) project, protrude

vorstellen *v/t* (*sep, -ge-, h*) introduce (**sich** o.s.; **j-n j-m** s.o. to s.o.); put *watch* forward (**um** by); *fig* mean; **sich et. (j-n als …) vorstellen** imagine s.th. (s.o. as …); **so stelle ich mir … vor** that's my

idea of …; **sich vorstellen bei** have an interview with *a firm etc*

Vorstellung *f* (-; *-en*) introduction; interview; THEA performance, film *etc*: a. show; idea; expectation

Vorstellungskraft *f* (-; *no pl*), **Vorstellungsvermögen** *n* (-*s; no pl*) imagination

Vorstopper ['foːɐʃtɔpɐ] *m* (-*s; -*) SPORT center (*Br* centre) back

Vorstoß *m* MIL advance; *fig* attempt

Vorstrafe *f* previous conviction

vorstrecken *v/t* (*sep, -ge-, h*) advance (*money*)

Vorstufe *f* preliminary stage

vortäuschen *v/t* (*sep, -ge-, h*) feign, fake

Vorteil *m* advantage (*a.* SPORT); benefit, profit; **die Vorteile und Nachteile** the pros and cons

vorteilhaft *adj* advantageous, profitable

Vorteilsregel *f* SPORT advantage rule

Vortrag ['foːɐtraːk] *m* (-[*e*]*s; Vorträge* ['foːɐtrɛːgə]) talk, *esp* UNIV lecture; MUS *etc* recital; **e-n Vortrag halten** give a talk *or* lecture (**vor** *dat* to; **über** *acc* on)

vortragen *v/t* (*irr, tragen, sep, -ge-, h*) express, state; MUS *etc* perform, play; recite (*poem etc*)

vortreten *v/i* (*irr, treten, sep, -ge-, sein*) step forward; *fig* protrude, stick out

Vortritt *m* (-[*e*]*s; no pl*) precedence; **j-m den Vortritt lassen** let s.o. go first

vorüber [foˈryːbɐ] *adv*: **vorüber sein** be over

vorübergehen *v/i* (*irr, gehen, sep, -ge-, sein*) pass, go by

vorübergehend *adj* temporary

Vorübung *f* preparatory exercise

Voruntersuchung *f* JUR, MED preliminary examination

Vorurteil *n* prejudice

vorurteilslos *adj* unprejudiced, unbias(s)ed

Vorverkauf *m* THEA advance booking

vorverlegen *v/t* (*sep, no -ge-, h*) advance

Vorwahl *f* TEL area (*Br* STD *or* dialling) code; POL primary, *Br* preliminary election

Vorwand *m* pretext, excuse

vorwärts ['foːɐvɛrts] *adv* forward, on (-ward), ahead; **vorwärts!** come on!, let's go!

vorwärtskommen *v/i* (*irr, kommen, sep, -ge-, sein*) make headway (*a. fig*)

vorweg [foːɐˈvɛk] *adv* beforehand

vorwegnehmen *v/t* (*irr, nehmen, sep, -ge-, h*) anticipate

vorweisen *v/t* (*irr, weisen, sep, -ge-, h*) produce, show; **et. vorweisen können**

V

boast s.th.
vorwerfen fig v/t (irr, **werfen**, sep, -ge-, h)
  j-m et. vorwerfen reproach s.o. with s.th.
'**vorwiegend** adv predominantly, chiefly,
  mainly, mostly
'**vorwitzig** adj cheeky, pert
'**Vorwort** n (-[e]s; -e) foreword; preface
'**Vorwurf** m reproach; **j-m Vorwürfe machen (wegen)** reproach s.o. (for)
'**vorwurfsvoll** adj reproachful
'**Vorzeichen** n omen, sign (a. MATH)
'**vorzeigen** v/t (sep, -ge-, h) show; produce
'**vorzeitig** adj premature, early
'**vorziehen** v/t (irr, **ziehen**, sep, -ge-, h)

draw; fig prefer
'**Vorzimmer** n anteroom; outer office;
  Austrian → **Hausflur**
'**Vorzug** m advantage; merit
vorzüglich [foːˈtsyːklɪç] adj excellent,
  exquisite
'**vorzugsweise** adv preferably
Votum ['voːtum] n (-s; -ta, -ten) vote
VP ABBR of **Vollpension** full board; (full)
  board and lodging
vulgär [vulˈgɛːɐ] adj vulgar
Vulkan [vulˈkaːn] m (-s; -e) volcano
Vulkanausbruch m volcanic eruption
vulˈkanisch adj volcanic

W

W ABBR of **West(en)** W, west; **Watt** W,
  watt(s)
Waage ['vaːgə] f (-; -n) scale(s Br); balance; ASTR Libra; **sich die Waage halten**
  balance each other; **er ist (e-e) Waage**
  he's a (a) Libra
'**waagerecht** adj horizontal
Waagschale ['vaːk-] f scale
Wabe ['vaːbə] f (-; -n) honeycomb
wach [vax] adj awake; **wach rütteln**
  rouse; fig → **wachrütteln**; **wach werden**
  wake (up), esp fig → **wachwerden**
Wache ['vaxə] f (-; -n) guard (a. MIL); sentry; MAR, MED etc watch; police station;
  Wache haben be on guard (MAR watch);
  Wache halten keep watch
'**wachen** v/i (ge-, h) (keep) watch (**über**
  acc over)
'**Wachhund** m watchdog
'**Wachmann** m (-[e]s; -männer, -leute)
  watchman; Austrian → **Polizist**
Wacholder [va'xɔldɐ] m (-s; -) BOT juniper
'**wachrufen** v/t (irr, **rufen**, sep, -ge-, h) call
  up, evoke
wachrütteln v/t (sep, -ge-, h) fig rouse (a.
  fig)
Wachs [vaks] n (-es; -e) wax
wachsam ['vaxzaːm] adj watchful, on
  one's guard, vigilant
'**Wachsamkeit** f (-; no pl) watchfulness,
  vigilance
wachsen[1] ['vaksən] v/i (irr, ge-, sein) grow
  (a. **sich wachsen lassen**), fig a. increase
'**wachsen**[2] v/t (ge-, h) wax
'**Wachsfi,gurenkabi,nett** n waxworks

Wachstuch n oilcloth
'**Wachstum** n (-s; no pl) growth, fig a. increase
Wachtel ['vaxtəl] f (-; -n) zo quail
Wächter ['vɛçtɐ] m (-s; -) guard
'**Wachtmeister** m (-s; no pl) patrolman,
  Br (police) constable
'**Wach(t)turm** m watchtower
'**wachwerden** v/i (irr, **werden**, sep, -ge-,
  sein) fig awake; → **wach**
wackelig ['vakəlɪç] adj shaky (a. fig);
  loose (tooth)
'**wackeln** v/i (ge-, h) shake; table etc: wobble; tooth: be loose; PHOT move; **wackeln
  mit** waggle
Wade ['vaːdə] f (-; -n) ANAT calf
Waffe ['vafə] f (-; -n) weapon (a. fig), pl a.
  arms
Waffel ['vafəl] f (-; -n) waffle; wafer
'**Waffengewalt** f: **mit Waffengewalt** by
  force of arms
'**Waffenschein** m gun license (Br licence)
'**Waffenstillstand** m armistice (a. fig);
  truce
wagen ['vaːgən] v/t (ge-, h) dare; risk;
  sich wagen venture
Wagen m (-s; -) MOT car; RAIL car, Br carriage
wägen ['vɛːgən] lit v/t (irr, ge-, h) weigh
  (one's words etc)
'**Wagenheber** m TECH jack
Wagenladung f cartload
Waggon [va'gõː] m (-s, -s) (railroad) car,
  Br (railway) carriage; freight car, Br
  goods waggon

Vagnis ['va:knɪs] *n* (*-ses*; *-se*) venture, risk

Vagon *m* → **Waggon**

Vahl [va:l] *f* (*-*; *-en*) choice; alternative; selection; POL election; voting, poll; vote; *die Wahl haben* (*s-e Wahl treffen*) have the (make one's) choice; *keine* (*andere*) *Wahl haben* have no choice *or* alternative

wahlberechtigt *adj* POL entitled to vote

Wahlbeteiligung *f* POL poll, (voter) turnout; *hohe* (*niedrige*) *Wahlbeteiligung* heavy (light) poll

Wahlbezirk *m* → **Wahlkreis**

wählen ['vɛːlən] *v/t and v/i* (*ge-*, *h*) choose, pick, select; POL vote (for); elect; TEL dial

Wähler *m* (*-s*; *-*) voter

Wahlergebnis *n* election result

wählerisch ['vɛːlərɪʃ] *adj* F picky (*in dat* about), *esp Br* choos(e)y

Wählerschaft *f* (*-*; *-en*) electorate, voters

Wahlfach *n* PED *etc* elective, optional subject

Wahlka,bine *f* voting (*esp Br* polling) booth

Wahlkampf *m* election campaign

Wahlkreis *m* electoral district, *Br* constituency

Wahllo,kal *n* polling place (*Br* station)

wahllos *adj* indiscriminate

Wahlpro,gramm *n* election platform

Wahlrecht *n* (*-[e]s*; *no pl*) (right to) vote, suffrage, franchise

Wahlrede *f* election speech

Wählscheibe *f* TEL dial

Wahlsieg *m* election victory

Wahlsieger *m* election winner

Wahlspruch *m* motto

Wahlurne *f* ballot box

Wahlversammlung *f* election rally

Wahnsinn *m* (*-[e]s*; *no pl*) madness (*a.* F), insanity

wahnsinnig 1. *adj* mad (*a.* F), insane, F *a.* crazy; F awful, terrible; **2.** F *adv* terribly, awfully; madly (*in love*)

Wahnsinnige *m*, *f* (*-n*; *-n*) madman (madwoman), lunatic, maniac (*all a.* F)

Wahnvorstellung *f* delusion, hallucination

wahr [va:ɐ] *adj* true; real; genuine

wahren ['va:rən] *v/t* (*ge-*, *h*) protect; *den Schein wahren* keep up appearances

während ['vɛːrənt] **1.** *prp* (*gen*) during; **2.** *cj* while; whereas

wahrhaft, **wahr'haftig** *adv* really, truly

Wahrheit *f* (*-*; *-en*) truth

wahrheitsgemäß, **wahrheitsgetreu** *adj* true, truthful

wahrheitsliebend *adj* truthful

wahrnehmbar ['va:ɐnɛːmba:ɐ] *adj* noticeable, perceptible

'wahrnehmen *v/t* (*irr*, *nehmen*, *sep*, *-ge-*, *h*) perceive, notice, seize, take (*chance etc*); look after (*s.o.'s interests etc*)

'Wahrnehmung *f* (*-*; *-en*) perception

'wahrsagen *v/i* (*sep*, *-ge-*, *h*) *j-m wahrsagen* tell s.o. his fortune; *sich wahrsagen lassen* have one's fortune told

'Wahrsager [-za:gɐ] *m* (*-s*; *-*), **'Wahrsagerin** [-za:gərɪn] *f* (*-*; *-nen*) fortune-teller

wahr'scheinlich 1. *adj* probable, likely; **2.** *adv* probably, (very *or* most) likely; *wahrscheinlich gewinnt er* (*nicht*) he is (not) likely to win

Wahr'scheinlichkeit *f* (*-*; *-en*) probability, likelihood

Währung ['vɛːrʊŋ] *f* (*-*; *-en*) currency

'Währungs... *in cpds* ...politik, ...reform *etc*: monetary ...

'Wahrzeichen *n* landmark

Waise ['vaizə] *f* (*-*; *-n*) orphan; *Waise werden* be orphaned

'Waisenhaus *n* orphanage

Wal [va:l] *m* (*-[e]s*; *-e*) ZO whale

Wald [valt] *m* (*-[e]s*; *Wälder* ['vɛldɐ]) wood(s), forest

Waldbrand *m* forest fire

'waldreich *adj* wooded

'Waldsterben *n* dying of forests

Walfang *m* whaling

Walfänger *m* whaler

Walkman® *m* (*-s*; *-men*) personal stereo, Walkman®

Wall [val] *m* (*-[e]s*; *Wälle* ['vɛlə]) mound; MIL rampart

Wallach ['valax] *m* (*-[e]s*; *-e*) ZO gelding

wallen ['valən] *v/i* (*ge-*, *sein*) flow

Wallfahrer *m*, **'Wallfahrerin** *f* pilgrim

'Wallfahrt *f* pilgrimage

'Walnuss *f* BOT walnut

Walross *n* ZO walrus

Walze ['valtsə] *f* (*-*; *-n*) roller; cylinder; TECH, MUS barrel

'walzen *v/t* (*ge-*, *h*) roll (*a.* TECH)

wälzen ['vɛltsən] *v/t* (*ge-*, *h*) roll (*a. sich wälzen*); *fig* turn *s.th.* over in one's mind

Walzer ['valtsɐ] *m* (*-s*; *-*) MUS waltz (*a. Walzer tanzen*)

wand [vant] *pret of* **winden**

Wand *f* (*-*; *Wände* ['vɛndə]) wall, *fig a.* barrier

Wandale [van'da:lə] *m* (*-n*; *-n*) vandal

Wandalismus [vanda'lɪsmʊs] *m* (*-*; *no pl*) vandalism

Wandel ['vandəl] *m* (*-s*; *no pl*), **'wandeln** *v/t and v/refl* (*ge-*, *h*) change

Wanderer ['vandərɐ] *m* (*-s*; *-*), **'Wanderin**

W

f (-; -nen) hiker

wandern ['vandən] v/i (ge-, sein) hike; ramble (about); eyes etc: roam, wander

'**Wanderpo,kal** m challenge cup

'**Wanderpreis** m challenge trophy

'**Wanderschuhe** pl walking shoes

'**Wandertag** m (school) outing or excursion

'**Wanderung** f (-; -en) walking tour, hike; zo etc migration

'**Wandgemälde** n mural

'**Wandka,lender** m wall calendar

'**Wandkarte** f wallchart

'**Wandlung** ['vandluŋ] f (-; -en) change

'**Wandschrank** m closet, Br built-in cupboard

'**Wandtafel** f blackboard

wandte ['vantə] pret of **wenden**

'**Wandteppich** m tapestry

Wange ['vaŋə] f (-; -n) ANAT cheek

Wankelmotor ['vaŋkəl-] m rotary piston or Wankel engine

wankelmütig ['vaŋkəlmy:tɪç] adj fickle

wanken ['vaŋkən] v/i (ge-, sein) stagger, reel; fig rock

wann [van] interr adv when, (at) what time; **seit wann?** since when?

Wanne ['vanə] f (-; -n) tub (a. F); bath(tub)

Wanze ['vantsə] f (-; -n) zo bug (a. F)

Wapitihirsch ['va:pi:ti-] m zo elk

Wappen ['vapən] n (-s; -) (coat of) arms

'**Wappenkunde** f heraldry

wappnen ['vapnən] fig v/refl (ge-, h) arm o.s.

war [va:ɐ] pret of **sein**[1]

warb [varp] pret of **werben**

Ware ['va:rə] f (-; -n) coll mst goods; article; product

'**Warenhaus** n department store

'**Warenlager** n stock

'**Warenprobe** f sample

'**Warenzeichen** n trademark

warf [varf] pret of **werfen**

warm [varm] adj warm (a. fig); GASTR hot; **schön warm** nice and warm; **warm halten** keep warm; **warm machen** warm (up)

Wärme ['vɛrmə] f (-; no pl) warmth; PHYS heat

'**Wärmeiso,lierung** f heat insulation

'**wärmen** v/t (ge-, h) warm

'**Wärmflasche** f hot-water bottle

'**warmherzig** adj warm-hearted

'**warmmachen** v/t (sep, -ge-, h) → **warm**

Warm'**wasserbereiter** m (-s; -) water heater

Warmwasserversorgung f hot-water supply

'**Warnblinkanlage** f MOT warning flasher

Warndreieck n MOT warning triangle

warnen ['varnən] v/t (ge-, h) warn (**vor** dat of, against); **j-n davor warnen, et. zu tun** warn s.o. not to do s.th.

'**Warnschild** n danger sign

'**Warnsig,nal** n warning signal

'**Warnstreik** m token strike

'**Warnung** f (-; -en) warning

warten[1] ['vartən] v/i (ge-, h) wait (**auf** acc for); **j-n warten lassen** keep s.o. waiting

'**warten**[2] v/t (ge-, h) TECH service, maintain

Wärter ['vɛrtə] m (-s; -), '**Wärterin** f (-; -nen) attendant; zo keeper

'**Warteliste** f waiting list

Wartesaal m, **Wartezimmer** n waiting room

'**Wartung** f (-; -en) TECH maintenance

warum [va'rum] interr adv why

Warze ['vartsə] f (-; -n) MED wart

was [vas] **1.** interr pron what; **was gibt's?** what is it?, F what's up?; what's for lunch etc?; **was soll's?** so what?; **was machen Sie?** what are you doing?; what do you do?; **was kostet ...?** how much is ...?; **was für ...?** what kind or sort of ...?; **was für e-e Farbe (Größe)?** what colo(u)r (size)?; **was für ein Unsinn** what nonsense!; **was für e-e gute Idee!** what a good idea!; **2.** rel pron what; **was (auch) immer** whatever; **alles, was ich habe (brauche)** all I have (need); **ich weiß nicht, was ich tun (sagen) soll** I don't know what to do (say); **..., was mich ärgerte ...**, which made me angry; **3.** F indef pron → **etwas**

waschbar ['vaʃba:ɐ] adj washable

'**Waschbecken** n washbowl, Br washbasin

Wäsche ['vɛʃə] f (-; -n) a washing, b) (no pl) laundry; linen; underwear; **in der Wäsche** in the wash; **schmutzige Wäsche waschen** wash one's dirty linen in public

'**waschecht** adj washable; fast (color); fig trueborn, genuine

'**Wäscheklammer** f clothespin, Br clothes peg

Wäscheleine f clothesline

waschen ['vaʃən] v/t and v/refl (irr, ge-, h) wash; **sich die Haare (Hände) waschen** wash one's hair (hands)

Wäscherei [vɛʃə'rai] f (-; -en) laundry

'**Waschlappen** m washcloth, Br flannel, facecloth

Waschma,schine f washing machine, F washer

'**waschma,schinenfest** adj machine-washable

Waschmittel n, **Waschpulver** n washing powder

Waschraum m lavatory, washroom

Waschsa|**lon** m laundromat, Br launderette

Waschstraße f MOT car wash

Wasser ['vasɐ] n (-s; -) water

Wasserball m beach ball; SPORT water polo

Wasserbett n water bed

Wasserdampf m steam

'wasserdicht adj waterproof; esp MAR watertight (a. fig)

'Wasserfall m waterfall; falls

Wasserfarbe f water colo(u)r

Wasserflugzeug n seaplane

Wassergraben m SPORT water jump

Wasserhahn m tap, faucet

wässerig ['vɛsərɪç] adj watery; **j-m den Mund wässerig machen** make s.o.'s mouth water

'Wasserkessel m kettle

Wasserklo, **sett** n water closet, W.C.

Wasserkraft f (-; no pl) water power

Wasserkraftwerk n hydroelectric power station or plant

Wasserlauf m watercourse

Wasserleitung f waterpipe(s)

Wassermangel m (-s; no pl) water shortage

Wassermann m (-[e]s; no pl) ASTR Aquarius; **er ist (ein) Wassermann** he's (an) Aquarius

wassern v/i (ge-, h) AVIAT touch down on water; spacecraft: splash down

wässern ['vɛsɐn] v/t (ge-, h) water; AGR irrigate; GASTR soak; PHOT rinse

Wasserpflanze f BOT aquatic plant

Wasserrohr n TECH water pipe

'Wasserscheide f GEOGR watershed

wasserscheu adj afraid of water

Wasserski 1. m water ski; **2.** n (-s; no pl) water skiing; **Wasserski fahren** water-ski

Wasserspiegel m water level

Wassersport m water or aquatic sports, aquatics

Wasserspülung f TECH flushing cistern; **Toilette mit Wasserspülung** (flush) toilet, W.C.

Wasserstand m water level

Wasserstoff m (-[e]s; no pl) CHEM hydrogen

Wasserstoffbombe f MIL hydrogen bomb, H-bomb

Wasserstrahl m jet of water

Wasserstraße f waterway

Wassertier n aquatic animal

Wasserverschmutzung f water pollution

Wasserversorgung f water supply

Wasserwaage f (Br spirit) level

Wasserweg m waterway; **auf dem Wasserweg** by water

Wasserwelle f water wave

Wasserwerk(e pl) n waterworks

Wasserzeichen n watermark

waten ['va:tən] v/i (ge-, sein) wade

watscheln ['va:tʃəln] v/i (ge-, sein) waddle

Watt¹ [vat] n (-s; -) ELECTR watt

Watt² n (-[e]s; -en) GEOGR mud flats

Watte ['vatə] f (-; -n) cotton wool

wattiert [va'ti:ɐt] adj padded; quilted

weben ['ve:bən] v/t and v/i ([irr,] ge-, h) weave

Weber ['ve:bɐ] m (-s; -) weaver

Weberei [ve:bə'raɪ] f (-; -en) weaving mill

Weberin f (-; -nen) weaver

Webstuhl ['ve:p-] m loom

Wechsel ['vɛksəl] m (-s; -) change; exchange; ECON bill of exchange; allowance

'Wechselgeld n (small) change

wechselhaft adj changeable

'Wechseljahre pl MED menopause

'Wechselkurs m ECON exchange rate

'wechseln v/t and v/i (ge-, h) change; exchange; vary

wechselnd adj varying

'wechselseitig [-zaɪtɪç] adj mutual, reciprocal

'Wechselstrom m ELECTR alternating current

Wechselstube f ECON exchange office

Wechselwirkung f interaction

wecken ['vɛkən] v/t (ge-, h) wake (up), call; fig awaken (memories etc); rouse (s.o.'s curiosity etc)

Wecker ['vɛkɐ] m (-s; -) alarm (clock)

wedeln ['ve:dəln] v/i (ge-, h) wave (mit et. s.th.); skiing: wedel; **mit dem Schwanz wedeln** wag its tail

weder ['ve:dɐ] cj: **weder ... noch ...** neither ... nor ...

Weg [ve:k] m (- [e]s; -e ['ve:gə]) way (a. fig); road (a. fig); path; route; walk; **auf friedlichem (legalem) Wege** by peaceful (legal) means; **j-m aus dem Weg gehen** get (fig keep) out of s.o.'s way; **j-n aus dem Weg räumen** put s.o. out of the way; **vom Weg abkommen** lose one's way; → **halb**

weg [vɛk] adv away; gone; off; F in raptures (von over, about); **Finger weg!** (keep your) hands off!; **nichts wie weg!** let's get out of here!; F **weg sein** be out

wegbleiben F v/i (irr, **bleiben**, sep, -ge-,

sein) stay away; be left out

wegbringen F *v/t* (*irr, **bringen**, sep, -ge-, h*) take away; ***wegbringen von*** get *s.o.* away from

wegen ['ve:gən] *prp* (*gen*) because of; for the sake of; due *or* owing to; JUR for

wegfahren ['vɛk-] (*irr, **fahren**, sep, -ge-*) **1.** *v/i* (*sein*) leave; **2.** *v/t* (*h*) take away, remove

'**wegfallen** *v/i* (*irr, **fallen**, sep, -ge-, sein*) be dropped; stop, be stopped

Weggang ['vɛk-] *m* (*-[e]s; no pl*) leaving

'**weggehen** *v/i* (*irr, **gehen**, sep, -ge-, sein*) go away (*a. fig*), leave; *stain etc*: come off; ECON sell

wegjagen ['vɛk-] *v/t* (*sep, -ge-, h*) drive *or* chase away

wegkommen F *v/i* (*irr, **kommen**, sep, -ge-, sein*) get away; get lost; ***gut wegkommen*** come off well; ***mach, dass du wegkommst!*** get out of here!, *sl* get lost!

weglassen *v/t* (*irr, **lassen**, sep, -ge-, h*) let *s.o.* go; leave *s.th.* out

weglaufen *v/i* (*irr, **laufen**, sep, -ge-, h*) run away ([*vor*] *j-m* from s.o.) (*a. fig*)

weglegen *v/t* (*sep, -ge-, h*) put away

wegnehmen *v/t* (*irr, **nehmen**, sep, -ge-, h*) take away (***von*** from); take up (*room, time*); take (*a. s.o.'s girlfriend etc*); ***j-m et. wegnehmen*** take s.th. (away) from s.o.

wegräumen *v/t* (*sep, -ge-, h*) clear away, remove

wegschaffen *v/t* (*sep, -ge-, h*) remove

wegschicken *v/t* (*sep, -ge-, h*) send away *or* off

wegsehen *v/i* (*irr, **sehen**, sep, -ge-, h*) look away

wegsetzen *v/t* (*sep, -ge-, h*) move

Wegweiser ['ve:kvaizɐ] *m* (*-s; -*) signpost; *fig* guide

Wegwerf... ['vɛkvɛrf-] *in cpds* ...*geschirr*, ...*besteck*, ...*rasierer etc*: throwaway ..., disposable ...; ...*flasche etc*: non-returnable ...

'**wegwerfen** *v/t* (*irr, **werfen**, sep, -ge-, h*) throw away

'**wegwischen** ['vɛk-] *v/t* (*sep, -ge-, h*) wipe off

wegziehen (*irr, **ziehen**, sep, -ge-*) **1.** *v/i* (*sein*) move away; **2.** *v/t* (*h*) pull away

weh [ve:] *adv: **weh tun** → **wehtun***

wehen ['ve:ən] *v/i* (*ge-, h*) blow; wave

'**Wehen** *pl* MED labo(u)r

wehmütig ['ve:my:tɪç] *adj* melancholy; wistful

Wehr¹ [ve:ɐ] *n* (*-[e]s; -e* ['ve:rə]) weir

Wehr² *f: **sich zur Wehr setzen** → **wehren***

'**Wehrdienst** *m* (*-[e]s; no pl*) military service

Wehrdienstverweigerer *m* (*-s; -*) conscientious objector

wehren ['ve:rən] *v/refl* (*ge-, h*) defend o.s. (***gegen*** against), fight (*a. fig **gegen et.** s.th.*)

'**wehrlos** *adj* defenseless, *Br* defenceless; *fig* helpless

'**Wehrpflicht** *f* (*-; no pl*) compulsory military service

'**wehrpflichtig** *adj* liable to military service

'**Wehrpflichtige** *m* (*-n; -n*) draftee, *Br* conscript

'**wehtun** hurt (***j-m*** s.o.; *fig* s.o.'s feelings); be aching; ***sich (am Finger) wehtun*** hurt o.s. (hurt one's finger)

Weib [vaip] *n* (*-[e]s; -er* ['vaibɐ]) *contp* woman; bitch

'**Weibchen** *n* (*-s; -*) ZO female

weibisch ['vaibɪʃ] *adj* effeminate, F sissy

'**weiblich** *adj* female; feminine (*a. LING*)

weich [vaiç] *adj* soft (*a. fig*), tender; GASTR done; soft-boiled (*egg*); ***weich werden*** soften; *fig* give in

Weiche ['vaiçə] *f* (*-; -n*) RAIL switch, points

weichen ['vaiçən] *v/i* (*irr, ge-, sein*) give way (*dat* to), yield (to); go away

'**weichlich** *adj* soft, effeminate, F sissy

'**Weichling** *m* (*-s; -e*) weakling, F softy, sissy

'**weichmachen** *v/t* (*sep, -ge-, h*): F ***j-n weichmachen*** soften s.o. up

'**Weichspüler** *m* (*-s; -*) fabric softener

'**Weichtier** *n* ZO mollusk, *Br* mollusc

Weide¹ ['vaidə] *f* (*-; -n*) BOT willow

Weide² *f* (*-; -n*) AGR pasture; ***auf die (der) Weide*** to (at) pasture

'**Weideland** *n* pasture(land), range

'**weiden** *v/t and v/i* (*ge-, h*) graze; pasture; *fig **sich weiden an*** (*dat*) feast on; *contp* gloat over

weigern ['vaigɐn] *v/refl* (*ge-, h*) refuse

Weigerung ['vaigərʊŋ] *f* (*-; -en*) refusal

Weihe ['vaiə] *f* (*-; -n*) REL consecration; ordination

'**weihen** *v/t* (*ge-, h*) consecrate; ***zum Priester weihen*** ordain s.o. priest

Weiher ['vaiɐ] *m* (*-s; -*) pond

Weihnachten ['vainaxtən] *n* (*-; -*) Christmas, F Xmas

'**Weihnachtsabend** *m* Christmas Eve

'**Weihnachtsbaum** *m* Christmas tree

'**Weihnachtseinkäufe** *pl* Christmas shopping

'**Weihnachtsgeschenk** *n* Christmas present

'**Weihnachtslied** *n* (Christmas) carol

'**Weihnachtsmann** *m* Father Christmas,

Santa Claus
Weihnachtsmarkt *m* Christmas fair
Weihnachtstag *m* Christmas Day; *zweiter Weihnachtstag* day after Christmas, *esp Br* Boxing Day
Weihnachtszeit *f* Christmas season
Weihrauch *m* REL incense
Weihwasser *n* (-*s; no pl*) REL holy water
weil [vaɪl] *cj* because; since, as
Weilchen *n: ein Weilchen* a little while
Weile ['vaɪlə] *f: e-e Weile* a while
Wein [vaɪn] *m* (-[*e*]*s; -e*) wine; BOT vine
Wein(an)bau *m* (-[*e*]*s; no pl*) wine growing
Weinbeere *f* grape
Weinberg *m* vineyard
Weinbrand *m* brandy
weinen ['vaɪnən] *v/i* (*ge-, h*) cry (*vor dat* with; *nach* for; *wegen* about, over); weep (*um* for, over; *über acc* at; *vor dat* for with)
weinerlich ['vaɪnəlɪç] *adj* tearful; whining
Weinfass *n* wine cask *or* barrel
Weinflasche *f* wine bottle
Weinhändler *m* wine merchant
Weinhauer *Austrian m* → *Winzer*
Weinkarte *f* wine list
Weinkeller *m* wine cellar *or* vault, vaults
Weinkellerei *f* winery
Weinkenner *m* wine connoisseur
Weinlese *f* vintage
Weinpresse *f* wine press
Weinprobe *f* wine tasting
Weinrebe *f* BOT vine
weinrot *adj* claret
Weinstock *m* BOT vine
Weintraube *f* → *Traube*
weise ['vaɪzə] *adj* wise
Weise *f* (-; -*n*) way; MUS tune; *auf diese (die gleiche) Weise* this (the same) way; *auf m-e (s-e) Weise* my (his) way
weisen ['vaɪzən] *v/t and v/i* (*irr, ge-, h*) show; *j-n von der Schule weisen* expel s.o. from school; *weisen auf* (*acc*) point to *or* at; *von sich weisen* reject; repudiate
Weisheit ['vaɪshaɪt] *f* (-; -*en*) wisdom; *mit s-r Weisheit am Ende sein* be at one's wit's end
Weisheitszahn *m* wisdom tooth
weismachen ['vaɪs-] F *v/t: j-m weismachen, dass* make s.o. believe that; *du kannst mir nichts weismachen* you can't fool me
weiß [vaɪs] *adj* white; *weiß werden or machen* whiten
Weißbrot *n* white bread
Weiße *m, f* (-*n; -n*) white, white man (woman), *pl die Weißen* the whites

weißen *v/t* (*ge-, h*) whitewash
Weißkohl *m*, **Weißkraut** *n* BOT (green, *Br* white) cabbage
weißlich *adj* whitish
weißmachen *v/t* (*sep, -ge-, h*) → *weiß*
Weißwein *m* white wine
Weisung ['vaɪzʊŋ] *f* (-; -*en*) instruction, directive
weit [vaɪt] **1.** *adj* wide, *clothes: a.* big; long (*way, trip etc*); **2.** *adv* far, a long way (*a. time and fig*); *weit weg* far away (*von* from); *von weitem* from a distance; *weit und breit* far and wide; *bei weitem* by far; *bei weitem nicht so ...* not nearly as ...; *weit über* (*acc*) well over; *weit besser* far *or* much better; *zu weit gehen* go too far; *es weit bringen* go far; *wir haben es weit gebracht* we have come a long way; *weit blickend* far-sighted; *weit reichend* far-reaching; *weit verbreitet* widespread
weit'ab *adv* far away (*von* from)
weit'aus *adv* (by) far, much
Weite ['vaɪtə] *f* (-; -*n*) width; vastness, expanse; *esp* SPORT distance
weiten *v/t and v/refl* (*ge-, h*) widen
weiter ['vaɪtə] *adv* on, further; (*mach*) *weiter!* go on!; (*geh*) *weiter!* move on!; *und so weiter* and so on *or* forth, et cetera; *nichts weiter* nothing else
weiterarbeiten *v/i* (*sep, -ge-, h*) go on working
weiterbilden *v/refl* (*sep, -ge-, h*) improve one's knowledge; continue one's education *or* training
Weiterbildung *f* (-; *no pl*) further education *or* training
weitere ['vaɪtərə] *adj* further, additional; *alles Weitere* the rest; *bis auf weiteres* until further notice; *ohne weiteres* easily; *Weiteres* more, (further) details
weitergeben *v/t* (*irr, geben, sep, -ge-, h*) pass (*dat, an acc* to) (*a. fig*)
weitergehen *v/i* (*irr, gehen, sep, -ge-, sein*) move on; *fig* continue, go on
weiter'hin *adv* further(more); *et. weiterhin tun* go on doing s.th., continue to do s.th.
weiterkommen *v/i* (*irr, kommen, sep, -ge-, sein*) get on (*fig in* life)
weiterleben *v/i* (*sep, -ge-, h*) live on, *fig* survive
weitermachen *v/t and v/i* (*sep, -ge-, h*) go *or* carry on, continue
Weiterverkauf *m* resale
weitgehend 1. *adj* considerable; **2.** *adv* largely
weitläufig *adj* spacious; distant (*relative*)
weitsichtig *adj* MED farsighted (*a. fig*), *Br*

W

longsighted

'**Weitsprung** *m* broad (*Br* long) jump

'**Weitwinkelobjek,tiv** *n* PHOT wide-angle lens

Weizen ['vaitsən] *m* ⟨-s; -⟩ BOT wheat

welche ['vɛlçə], **welcher** ['vɛlçɐ], **welches** ['vɛlçəs] **1.** *interr pron* what, which; **welcher?** which one?; **welcher von beiden?** which of the two?; **2.** *rel pron* who, that; which, that; **3.** F **welche** *indef pron* some, any

welk [vɛlk] *adj* faded, withered; flabby

welken ['vɛlkən] *v/i* ⟨ge-, sein⟩ fade, wither

'**Wellblech** ['vɛl-] *n* corrugated iron

Welle ['vɛlə] *f* ⟨-; -n⟩ wave (*a.* PHYS *and fig*); TECH shaft

'**wellen** *v/t and v/refl* ⟨ge-, h⟩ wave

'**Wellenlänge** *f* ELECTR wavelength

'**Wellensittich** [-zɪtɪç] *m* ⟨-s; -e⟩ ZO budgerigar, F budgie

wellig ['vɛlɪç] *adj* wavy

Welt [vɛlt] *f* ⟨-; -en⟩ world; **die ganze Welt** the whole world; **auf der ganzen Welt** all over *or* throughout the world; **das beste** *etc* ... **der Welt** the best *etc* ... in the world, the world's best *etc* ...; **zur Welt kommen** be born; **zur Welt bringen** give birth to

'**Weltall** *n* universe

'**weltberühmt** *adj* world-famous

'**Weltergewicht** ['vɛltɐ-] *n* ⟨-[e]s; *no pl*⟩,
'**Weltergewichtler** *m* ⟨-s; -⟩ SPORT welterweight

'**weltfremd** *adj* naive, unrealistic

'**Weltfriede(n)** *m* world peace

'**Weltgeschichte** *f* world history

'**weltklug** *adj* worldlywise

'**Weltkrieg** *m* war; **der Zweite Weltkrieg** World War II

'**Weltkugel** *f* globe

'**weltlich** *adj* worldly

'**Weltlitera,tur** *f* world literature

'**Weltmacht** *f* POL world power

'**Weltmarkt** *m* ECON world market

'**Weltmeer** *n* ocean

'**Weltmeister(in)** world champion

'**Weltmeisterschaft** *f* world championship; *esp soccer*: World Cup

'**Weltraum** *m* ⟨-[e]s; *no pl*⟩ (outer) space

'**Weltreich** *n* empire

'**Weltreise** *f* world trip

'**Weltre,kord** *m* world record

'**Weltruf** *m* (**von Weltruf** of) worldwide reputation

'**Weltstadt** *f* metropolis

'**Weltuntergang** *m* end of the world

'**weltweit** *adj* worldwide

'**Weltwirtschaft** *f* world economy

'**Weltwirtschaftskrise** *f* worldwide economic crisis

'**Weltwunder** *n* wonder of the world

Wende ['vɛndə] *f* ⟨-; -n⟩ turn (*a.* swimming); change

Wendekreis *m* ASTR, GEOGR tropic; MOT turning circle

Wendeltreppe ['vɛndəl-] *f* spiral staircase

wenden *v/t and v/i* ⟨ge-, h⟩ *and v/refl* ⟨[*irr*], ge-, h⟩ turn (**nach** to; **gegen** against); MOT turn (round); GASTR turn over; **sich an j-n um Hilfe wenden** to s.o. for help; **bitte wenden** please turn over, pto

'**Wendepunkt** *m* turning point

wendig ['vɛndɪç] *adj* MOT, MAR maneuverable, *Br* manoeuvrable; *fig* nimble

'**Wendung** *f* ⟨-; -en⟩ turn, *fig a.* change; expression, phrase

wenig ['ve:nɪç] *indef pron and adv* little; **wenig(e)** *pl* few; **nur wenige** only few; only a few; **(in) weniger als** (in) less than; **am wenigsten** least of all; **er spricht wenig** he doesn't talk much; **(nur) ein (klein) wenig** (just) a little (bit)

'**wenigstens** *adv* at least

wenn [vɛn] *cj* when; if; **wenn ... nicht** if ... not, unless; **wenn auch** (al)though, even though; **wie** *or* **als wenn** as though, as if; **wenn ich nur ... wäre!** if only I were ...!; **wenn auch noch so ...** no matter how ...; **und wenn nun ...?** what if ...?

wer [ve:ɐ] **1.** *interr pron* who, which; **wer von euch?** which of you?; **2.** *rel pron* who; **wer auch (immer)** who(so)ever; **3.** F *indef pron* somebody, anybody

Werbeabteilung ['vɛrbə-] *f* publicity department

Werbeagen,tur *f* advertising agency

Werbefeldzug *m* advertising campaign

Werbefernsehen *n* commercial television

Werbefilm *m* promotion(al) film

Werbefunk *m* radio commercials

werben ['vɛrbən] ⟨*irr*, ge-, h⟩ **1.** *v/i* advertise (**für et.** s.th.), promote (s.th.), give s.th. *or* s.o. publicity; *esp* POL make propaganda (**für** for), canvass (for); **werben um** court (*a. fig*); **2.** *v/t* recruit; canvass, solicit

'**Werbesendung** *f*, '**Werbespot** [-ʃpɔt] *m* ⟨-s; -s⟩ (TV) commercial

'**Werbung** *f* ⟨-; *no pl*⟩ advertising, (sales) promotion; *a.* POL *etc* publicity, propaganda; recruitment; **Werbung machen für et.** advertise s.th.

Werdegang ['ve:ɐdəgaŋ] *m* career

werden ['ve:ɐdən] *v/i* ⟨*irr*, ge-, sein⟩ *and v/aux* become; get; turn, go; grow; turn out; *wir werden* we will (*or* shall), we are going to; *geliebt werden* be loved (*von* by); *was willst du werden?* what do you want to be?; *mir wird schlecht* I'm going to be sick; F *es wird schon wieder* (*werden*) it'll be all right

verfen ['vɛrfən] *v/i and v/t* (*irr, ge-, h*) throw (*a.* zo) ([*mit*] *et. nach* s.th. at); drop (*bombs*); cast (*shadow*)

Verft [vɛrft] *f* (*-; -en*) MAR shipyard, dockyard

Verk [vɛrk] *n* (*-[e]s; -e*) work, deed; TECH mechanism; ECON works, factory; *ans Werk gehen* set *or* go to work

Verkbank *f* (*-; -bänke*) TECH workbench

Verkmeister *m* TECH foreman

Werkstatt *f* (*-; -stätten*) workshop; MOT garage

Werktag *m* workday

werktags *adv* on workdays

werktätig *adj* working

Werkzeug *n* tool (*a. fig*); *coll* tools; instrument

Verkzeugmacher *m* toolmaker

vert [veːrt] *adj* worth; *die Mühe* (*e-n Versuch*) *wert* worth the trouble (a try); *fig nichts wert* no good

Vert *m* (*-[e]s; -e*) value, *esp fig a.* worth; *pl* data, figures; *... im Wert(e) von 20 Dollar* 20 dollars' worth of ...; *großen Wert legen auf* (*acc*) set great store by

werten ['veːrtən] *v/t* (*ge-, h*) value; *a.* SPORT rate, judge

Wertgegenstand *m* article of value

wertlos *adj* worthless

Wertpa,piere *pl* securities

Wertsachen *pl* valuables

Wertung *f* (*-; -en*) valuation; *a.* SPORT rating, judging; score, points

wertvoll *adj* valuable

Wesen ['veːzən] *n* (*-s; -*) being, creature; *fig* essence; nature, character; *viel Wesens machen um* make a fuss about

wesentlich *adj* essential; considerable; *im Wesentlichen* on the whole

veshalb [vɛsˈhalp] *interr adv* → *warum*

Vespe ['vɛspə] *f* (*-; -n*) zo wasp

Veste ['vɛstə] *f* (*-; -n*) vest, Br waistcoat

Vesten ['vɛstən] *m* (*-s; no pl*) west; POL West

Vestern ['vɛstən] *m* (*-s; -*) western

westlich 1. *adj* western; westerly; POL West(ern); **2.** *adv*: *westlich von* (to the) west of

Vestwind *m* west(erly) wind

Vettbewerb ['vɛtbəvɛrp] *m* (*-[e]s; -e*) competition (*a.* ECON), contest

Wettbü,ro *n* betting office

Wette ['vɛtə] *f* (*-; -n*) bet; *e-e Wette ab-*

schließen make a bet; *um die Wette laufen etc* race (*mit j-m* s.o.)

'wetteifern *v/i* (*ge-, h*) compete (*mit* with; *um* for)

'wetten *v/i and v/t* (*ge-, h*) bet; *mit j-m um 10 Dollar wetten* bet s.o. ten dollars; *wetten auf* (*acc*) bet on, back

Wetter ['vɛtə] *n* (*-s; -*) weather

'Wetterbericht *m* weather report

'Wetterfahne *f* weather vane

'wetterfest *adj* weatherproof

'Wetterkarte *f* weather chart

'Wetterlage *f* weather situation

'Wetterleuchten *n* sheet lightning

'Wettervorhersage *f* weather forecast

'Wetterwarte *f* weather station

'Wettkampf *m* competition, contest

'Wettkämpfer(in) contestant, competitor

'Wettlauf *m* race (*a. fig* **mit** against)

'Wettläufer(in) runner

'wettmachen *v/t* (*sep, -ge-, h*) make up for

'Wettrennen *n* race

'Wettrüsten *n* (*-s; no pl*) arms race

'Wettstreit *m* contest, competition

wetzen ['vɛtsən] *v/t* (*ge-, h*) whet, sharpen

wich [vɪç] *pret of weichen*

wichtig ['vɪçtɪç] *adj* important

'Wichtigkeit *f* (*-; no pl*) importance

wickeln *v/t* (*ge-, h*) change (*baby*); *wickeln in* (*acc*) wrap in; *wickeln um* wrap (a)round

Widder ['vɪdɐ] *m* (*-s; -*) zo ram; ASTR Aries; *er ist* (*ein*) *Widder* he's (an) Aries

wider ['viːdɐ] *prp* (*acc*) *wider Willen* against one's will; *wider Erwarten* contrary to expectations

'Widerhaken *m* barb

'widerhallen *v/i* (*sep, -ge-, h*) resound (*von* with)

wider'legen *v/t* (*no -ge-, h*) refute, disprove

'widerlich *adj* sickening, disgusting

'widerrechtlich *adj* illegal, unlawful

'Widerruf *m* JUR revocation; withdrawal

wider'rufen *v/t* (*irr, rufen, no -ge-, h*) revoke; withdraw

Widersacher ['viːdɐzaxɐ] *m* (*-s; -*) adversary, rival

'Widerschein *m* reflection

wider'setzen *v/refl* (*no -ge-, h*) (*dat*) oppose, resist

'widersinnig *adj* absurd

widerspenstig ['viːdɐʃpɛnstɪç] *adj* unruly, stubborn

'widerspiegeln *v/t* (*sep, -ge-, h*) reflect (*a. fig*); *sich widerspiegeln in* (*dat*) be reflected in

wider'sprechen *v/i* (*irr, sprechen, no -ge-, h*) (*dat*) contradict

W

'Widerspruch *m* contradiction
widersprüchlich ['viːdɐʃpryçlɪç] *adj* contradictory
'widerspruchslos *adv* without contradiction
'Widerstand *m* resistance (*a.* ELECTR), opposition; **Widerstand leisten** offer resistance (*dat* to)
'widerstandsfähig *adj* resistant (*a.* TECH)
wider'stehen *v/i* (*irr*, **stehen**, *no -ge-, h*) (*dat*) resist
wider'streben *v/i* (*no -ge-, h*) **es widerstrebt mir, dies zu tun** I hate doing *or* to do that
widerstrebend *adv* reluctantly
widerwärtig ['viːdɐvɛrtɪç] *adj* disgusting
'Widerwille *m* aversion (**gegen** to), dislike (of, for); disgust (at)
'widerwillig *adj* reluctant, unwilling
widmen ['vɪtmən] *v/t* (*ge-, h*) dedicate
'Widmung *f* (*-; -en*) dedication
wie [viː] **1.** *interr adv* how; **wie geht es Gordon?** how is Gordon?; **wie ist er?** what's he like?; **wie ist das Wetter?** what's the weather like?; **wie heißen Sie?** what's your name?; **wie nennt man ...?** what do you call ...?; **wie wäre (ist, steht) es mit ...?** what *or* how about ...?; **wie viele ...?** how many ...?; **2.** *cj* like; as; **wie neu (verrückt)** like new (mad); **doppelt so ... wie** twice as ... as; **wie (zum Beispiel)** such as, like; **wie üblich** as usual; **wie er sagte** as he said; **ich zeige (sage) dir, wie (...)** I'll show (tell) you how (...)
wieder ['viːdɐ] *adv* again; *in cpds often* re...; **immer wieder** again and again; **wieder aufbauen** reconstruct; **wieder aufnehmen** resume; **wieder beleben** MED resuscitate, revive (*a. fig*); **wieder erkennen** recognize (*an dat* by); **wieder finden** find (what one has lost); *fig* regain; **wieder gutmachen** make up for; **wieder herstellen** restore; **wieder sehen** see *or* meet again; **wieder verwendbar** reusable; **wieder verwerten** TECH recycle
Wieder'aufbau *m* (*-[e]s; no pl*) reconstruction, rebuilding
Wieder'aufbereitung *f* TECH recycling, reprocessing (*a.* NUCL)
Wieder'aufbereitungsanlage *f* TECH reprocessing plant
Wieder'aufleben *n* (*-s; no pl*) revival
Wieder'aufnahme *f* (*-; no pl*) resumption
'wiederbekommen *v/t* (*irr*, **kommen**, *sep*, *no -ge-, h*) get back
'Wiederbelebung *f* (*-; -en*) MED resuscitation

Wiederbelebungsversuch *m* MED attempt at resuscitation
'wiederbringen *v/t* (*irr*, **bringen**, *sep*, *-ge-, h*) bring back; return
Wieder'einführung *f* reintroduction
'Wiederentdeckung *f* rediscovery
'Wiedergabe *f* TECH reproduction, playback
'wiedergeben *v/t* (*irr*, **geben**, *sep*, *-ge-, h*) give back, return; *fig* describe; TECH play back, reproduce
Wieder'gutmachung *f* (*-; -en*) reparation
'wiederholen[1] *v/t* (*sep*, *-ge-, h*) (go and) get *s.o. or s.th.* back
wieder'holen[2] *v/t* (*no -ge-, h*) repeat; PED revise, review; TECH replay; **sich wiederholen** repeat o.s. (*a. fig*)
wieder'holt *adv* repeatedly, several times
Wieder'holung *f* (*-; -en*) repetition; PED review; TV *etc* rerun; SPORT replay
Wiederkehr ['viːdɐkeːɐ] *f* (*-; no pl*) return; recurrence
'wiederkehren *v/i* (*sep*, *-ge-, sein*) return; recur
'wiederkommen *v/i* (*irr*, **kommen**, *sep*, *-ge-, sein*) come back, return
'Wiedersehen *n* (*-s*; *-*) seeing *s.o.* again; reunion; **auf Wiedersehen!** goodbye!
wiederum ['viːdərʊm] *adv* again; on the other hand
'Wiedervereinigung *f* reunion, *esp* POL *a.* reunification
Wiederverkauf *m* resale
Wiederverwendung *f* reuse
Wiederverwertung *f* (*-; -en*) TECH recycling
Wiederwahl *f* POL re-election
Wiege ['viːɡə] *f* (*-; -n*) cradle
wiegen[1] ['viːɡən] *v/t and v/i* (*irr*, *ge-, h*) weigh
'wiegen[2] *v/t* (*ge-, h*) rock (**in den Schlaf** to sleep)
'Wiegenlied *n* lullaby
wiehern ['viːɐn] *v/i* (*ge-, h*) ZO neigh
wies [viːs] *pret of* **weisen**
Wiese ['viːzə] *f* (*-; -n*) meadow
Wiesel ['viːzəl] *n* (*-s*; *-*) ZO weasel
wieso [vi'zoː] *interr adv* → **warum**
wievielt ['viˈfiːlt] *adj*: **zum wievielten Male?** how many times?
wild [vɪlt] *adj* wild (*a. fig*) (F **auf acc** about); violent; **wilder Streik** wildcat strike
Wild *n* (*-[e]s; no pl*) HUNT game; GASTR *ms* venison
Wildbach *m* torrent
Wilde ['vɪldə] *m, f* (*-n; -n*) savage; F **wie ein Wilder** like mad
Wilderer ['vɪldərɐ] *m* (*-s*; *-*) poacher

ildern v/i (ge-, h) poach
Vildhüter m gamekeeper
Vildkatze f zo wild cat
Vildleder n suede
Vildnis f (-; -se) wilderness
Vildpark m, **Wildreser**,**vat** n game park or reserve
Vildschwein n zo wild boar
ille ['vɪlə] m (-ns; -n) will; intention; *s-n Willen durchsetzen* have or get one's own way; *j-m s-n Willen lassen* let s.o. have his (own) way
villenlos adj weak(-willed)
Villenskraft f (-; no pl) willpower; *durch Willenskraft erzwingen* will
villensstark adj strong-willed
illig ['vɪlɪç] adj willing
ill'kommen adj welcome (a. *willkommen heißen*) (*in* dat to)
illkürlich ['vɪlkyːrlɪç] adj arbitrary; random
immeln ['vɪməln] v/i (ge-, h) **wimmeln von** be teeming with
immern ['vɪmɐn] v/i (ge-, h) whimper
impel ['vɪmpəl] m (-s; -) pennant
imper ['vɪmpɐ] f (-; -n) eyelash; *ohne mit der Wimper zu zucken* without turning a hair
Wimperntusche f mascara
ind [vɪnt] m (-[e]s; -e ['vɪndə]) wind
inde ['vɪndə] f (-; -n) winch, windlass, hoist
indel ['vɪndəl] f (-; -n) diaper, Br nappy
inden ['vɪndən] v/t (irr, ge-, h) wind, TECH a. hoist; *sich winden* wind (one's way); writhe (*with* pain etc)
Windhund m zo greyhound
indig ['vɪndɪç] adj windy
Windmühle f windmill
Windpocken pl MED chickenpox
indrichtung f direction of the wind
indschutzscheibe f MOT windshield, Br windscreen
indstärke f wind force
indstill adj, '**Windstille** f calm
Windstoß m gust
Windsurfen n windsurfing
Windung f (-; -en) bend, turn (a. TECH)
ink [vɪŋk] m (-[e]s; -e) sign; fig hint
inkel ['vɪŋkəl] m (-s; -) corner; MATH angle
winkelig adj angular; crooked
inken ['vɪŋkən] v/i (ge-, h) wave (one's hand etc), signal; beckon
inseln ['vɪnzəln] v/i (ge-, h) whimper, whine
inter ['vɪntɐ] m (-s; -) winter
winterlich adj wintry
Winterreifen m MOT snow tire (Br tyre)

Winterschlaf m zo hibernation
Winterspiele pl: *Olympische Winterspiele* SPORT Winter Olympics
Wintersport m winter sports
Winzer ['vɪntsɐ] m (-s; -) winegrower
winzig ['vɪntsɪç] adj tiny, diminutive
Wipfel ['vɪpfəl] m (-s; -) (tree)top
Wippe ['vɪpə] f (-; -n), '**wippen** v/i (ge-, h) seesaw
wir [viːr] pers pron we; *wir drei* the three of us; F *wir sind's!* it's us!
Wirbel ['vɪrbəl] m (-s; -) whirl (a. fig); ANAT vertebra
'wirbeln v/i (ge-, sein) whirl
Wirbelsäule f ANAT spinal column, spine
Wirbelsturm m cyclone, tornado
Wirbeltier n vertebrate
Wirbelwind m whirlwind
wirken ['vɪrkən] (ge-, h) **1.** v/i work; be effective (*gegen* against); look; *anregend etc wirken* have a stimulating etc effect (*auf* acc [up]on); *wirken als* act as; **2.** v/t weave; fig work (*miracles etc*)
wirklich ['vɪrklɪç] adj real, actual; true, genuine
'Wirklichkeit f (-; -en) reality; *in Wirklichkeit* in reality, actually
wirksam ['vɪrkzaːm] adj effective
'Wirkung f (-; -en) effect
'wirkungslos adj ineffective
'wirkungsvoll adj effective
wirr [vɪr] adj confused, mixed-up; *hair*: tousled
Wirren ['vɪrən] pl disorder, confusion
Wirrwarr ['vɪrvar] m (-s; no pl) confusion, mess, welter
Wirt [vɪrt] m (-[e]s; -e) landlord
'Wirtin f (-; -nen) landlady
Wirtschaft f (-; -en) ECON, POL economy; business; → *Gastwirtschaft*
'wirtschaften v/i (ge-, h) keep house; manage one's money or affairs or business; economize; *gut (schlecht) wirtschaften* be a good (bad) manager
Wirtschafterin f (-; -nen) housekeeper
'wirtschaftlich adj economic; economical
'Wirtschafts... ECON in cpds ...gemeinschaft, ...gipfel, ...krise, ...system, ...wunder etc: economic ...
'Wirtshaus n → *Gastwirtschaft*
wischen ['vɪʃən] v/t (ge-, h) wipe; *Staub wischen* dust
wispern ['vɪspɐn] v/t and v/i (ge-, h) whisper
wissbegierig ['vɪs-] adj curious
wissen ['vɪsən] v/t and v/i (irr, ge-, h) know; *ich möchte wissen* I'd like to know, I wonder; *soviel ich weiß* as far as I know; *weißt du* you know; *weißt*

du noch? (do you) remember?; **woher weißt du das?** how do you know?; **man kann nie wissen** you never know; **ich will davon (von ihm) nichts wissen** I don't want anything to do with it (him)

'Wissen *n* (-s; *no pl*) knowledge; know-how; *m-s Wissens* as far as I know

'Wissenschaft *f* (-; -en) science

'Wissenschaftler *m* (-s; -), 'Wissenschaftlerin *f* (-; -nen) scientist

'wissenschaftlich *adj* scientific

'wissenswert *adj* worth knowing; **Wissenswertes** useful facts; **alles Wissenswerte (über** *acc*) all you need to know (about)

wittern ['vɪtɐn] *v/t* (ge-, h) scent, smell (*both a. fig*)

Witwe ['vɪtvə] *f* (-; -n) widow

Witwer ['vɪtvɐ] *m* (-s; -) widower

Witz [vɪts] *m* (-es; -e) joke; **Witze reißen** crack jokes

witzig ['vɪtsɪç] *adj* funny; witty

wo [voː] *adv* where; **wo ... doch** when, although

wob [voːp] *pret of* **weben**

wobei [voˈbaɪ] *adv*: **wobei bist du?** what are you at?; **wobei mir einfällt** which reminds me

Woche ['vɔxə] *f* (-; -n) week

'Wochen... *in cpds* ...lohn, ...markt, ...zeitung *etc*: weekly ...

Wochenende *n* weekend; **am Wochenende** on (*Br* at) the weekend

'wochenlang 1. *adj*: **wochenlanges Warten** (many) weeks of waiting; 2. *adv* for weeks

'Wochenschau *f* film: newsreel

'Wochentag *m* weekday

wöchentlich ['vœçəntlɪç] 1. *adj* weekly; 2. *adv* weekly, every week; **einmal wöchentlich** once a week

wodurch [voˈdʊrç] *adv* how; through which

wofür [voˈfyːɐ] *adv* for which; **wofür?** what (...) for?

wog [voːk] *pret of* **wiegen¹** and **wägen**

Woge ['voːgə] *f* (-; -n) wave, *esp fig a.* surge; breaker

'wogen *v/i* (ge-, h) surge, heave (*both a. fig*)

woher [voˈheːɐ] *adv* where ... from; **woher weißt du (das)?** how do you know?

wohin [voˈhɪn] *adv* where (... to)

wohl [voːl] *adv and cj* well; probably; I suppose; **sich wohl fühlen → wohlfühlen**; **wohl oder übel** willy-nilly, whether you *etc* like it or not; **wohl kaum** hardly

Wohl *n* (-[e]s; *no pl*) well-being; **auf j-s Wohl trinken** drink to s.o.('s health);

zum Wohl! to your health!; F cheers!

'wohlbehalten *adv* safely

'Wohlfahrtsstaat *m* welfare state

'wohlgemerkt *adv* mind you

'wohlgenährt *adj* well-fed

wohlgesinnt *adj*: **j-m wohlgesinnt sein** be well-disposed towards s.o.

wohlhabend *adj* well-off, well-to-do

'wohlfühlen *v/refl* (*sep*, -ge-, h): **sich wohlfühlen** feel well, be well; feel good; feel at home (*Br* with); **ich fühle mich nicht wohl** I don't feel well

wohlig ['voːlɪç] *adj* snug, cozy, *Br* cosy

'Wohlstand *m* (-[e]s; *no pl*) prosperity, affluence

Wohlstandsgesellschaft *f* affluent society

'Wohltat *f* (-; *no pl*) pleasure; relief; blessing

'Wohltäter(in) benefactor (benefactress)

'wohltätig *adj* charitable; **für wohltätige Zwecke** for charity

'Wohltätigkeits... *in cpds* ...ball, ...konzert *etc*: charity ...

'wohltun *v/i* (*irr*, **tun**, *sep*, -ge-, h): **j-m wohltun** do s.o. good

'wohlverdient *adj* well-deserved

'wohlwollend *adj* benevolent

wohnen ['voːnən] *v/i* (ge-, h) live (**in** *dat* in; **bei j-m** with s.o.); stay (**in** *dat* at; **bei** with)

'Wohngebiet *n* residential area

'Wohngemeinschaft *f*: (**mit j-m**) **in e-r Wohngemeinschaft leben** share an apartment (*Br* a flat) *or* a house (with s.o.)

wohnlich ['voːnlɪç] *adj* comfortable, snug, cozy, *Br* cosy

'Wohnmobil *n* (-s; -e) camper, motor home (*Br* caravan)

'Wohnsiedlung *f* housing development (*Br* estate)

Wohnsitz *m* residence; **ohne festen Wohnsitz** of no fixed abode

'Wohnung *f* (-; -en) apartment, *Br* flat; **m-e** *etc* **Wohnung** my *etc* place

'Wohnungsamt *n* housing office

Wohnungsbau *m* (-[e]s; *no pl*) house building

Wohnungsnot *f* housing shortage

'Wohnwagen *m* trailer, *Br* caravan; mobile home

'Wohnzimmer *n* sitting *or* living room

wölben ['vœlbən] *v/refl* (ge-, h), 'Wölbung *f* (-; -en) vault, arch

Wolf [vɔlf] *m* (-[e]s; Wölfe ['vœlfə]) zo wolf

Wolke ['vɔlkə] *f* (-; -n) cloud

'Wolkenbruch *m* cloudburst

Wolkenkratzer m (-s; -) skyscraper

wolkenlos adj cloudless

wolkig ['vɔlkɪç] adj cloudy, clouded

Woll... [vɔl-] in cpds ...schal, ...socken etc: wool(l)en ...

Volldecke f blanket

Volle ['vɔlə] f (-; -n) wool

vollen ['vɔlən] v/t and v/i (ge-, h) and v/aux (no -ge-, h) want (to); **lieber wollen** prefer; **wollen wir (gehen** etc)? shall we (go etc)?; **wollen Sie bitte ...** will or would you please ...; **wie (was, wann) du willst** as (whatever, whenever) you like; **sie will, dass ich komme** she wants me to come; **ich wollte, ich wäre (hätte) ...** I wish I were (had) ...

vomit [vo'mɪt] adv with which; **womit** what ... with?

Vonne ['vɔnə] f (-; -n) joy, delight

woran [vo'ran] adv: **woran denkst du?** what are you thinking of?; **woran liegt es, dass ...?** how is it that ...?; **woran sieht man, welche (ob) ...?** how can you tell which (if) ...?

vorauf [vo'rauf] adv after which; on which; **worauf?** what ... on?; **worauf wartest du?** what are you waiting for?

voraus [vo'raus] adv from which; **woraus ist es?** what's it made of?

worin [vo'rɪn] adv in which; **worin?** where?

Wort [vɔrt] n (-[e]s; -e, Wörter ['vœrtə]) word; **mit anderen Worten** in other words; **sein Wort geben (halten, brechen)** give (keep, break) one's word; **j-n beim Wort nehmen** take s.o. at his word; **ein gutes Wort einlegen für** put in a good word for; **j-m ins Wort fallen** cut s.o. short

Wortart f LING part of speech

Wörterbuch n (-[e]s; -bücher-] n dictionary

Wörterverzeichnis n vocabulary, list of words

Wortführer m spokesman

Wortführerin f spokeswoman

wortkarg adj taciturn

vörtlich ['vœrtlɪç] adj literal; **wörtliche Rede** LING direct speech

Wortschatz m vocabulary

Wortspiel n pun

Wortstellung f LING word order

worüber [vo'ry:bə] adv about which; **worüber lachen Sie?** what are you laughing at or about?

worum [vo'rʊm] adv about which; **worum handelt es sich?** what is it about?

worunter [vo'rʊntə] adv among which; **worunter?** what ... under?

vovon [vo'fɔn] adv about which; **wovon**

redest du? what are you talking about?

wovor [vo'fo:ɐ] adv of which; **wovor hast du Angst?** what are you afraid of?

wozu [vo'tsu:] adv: **wozu er mir rät** what he advised me to do; **wozu?** what (...) for?; why?

Wrack [vrak] n (-[e]s; -s) MAR wreck (a. fig)

wrang [vraŋ] pret of **wringen**

wringen ['vrɪŋən] v/t (irr, ge-, h) wring

Wucher ['vu:xə] m (-s; no pl) usury

Wucherer ['vu:xərə] m (-s; -) usurer

wuchern v/i (ge-, h) grow (fig be) rampant

Wucherung ['vu:xərʊŋ] f (-; -en) MED growth

Wuchs [vu:ks] m (-es; no pl) growth; build

wuchs [vu:ks] pret of **wachsen¹**

Wucht [vʊxt] f (-; no pl) force; impact

wuchtig ['vʊxtɪç] adj massive; powerful

wühlen ['vy:lən] v/i (ge-, h) dig; zo root; rummage (in dat in, through)

Wulst [vʊlst] m (-es; Wülste ['vYlstə]), f (-; Wülste) bulge; roll (of fat)

wulstig ['vʊlstɪç] adj bulging; thick

wund [vʊnt] adj MED sore; **wunde Stelle** MED sore; **wunder Punkt** fig sore point

Wunde ['vʊndə] f (-; -n) MED wound

Wunder ['vʊndə] n (-s; -) miracle, fig a. wonder; **Wunder wirken** work wonders; **(es ist) kein Wunder, dass du müde bist** no wonder you are tired

'wunderbar adj wonderful, marvel(l)ous

'Wunderkind n infant prodigy

'wunderlich adj funny, odd; senile

'wundern v/refl (ge-, h) be surprised or astonished (über acc at)

'wundervoll adj wonderful

'Wundstarrkrampf m (-es; no pl) MED tetanus

Wunsch [vʊnʃ] m (-[e]s; Wünsche ['vYnʃə]) wish; request; **auf j-s Wunsch** at s.o.'s request; **auf eigenen Wunsch** at one's own request; **(je) nach Wunsch** as desired

wünschen ['vYnʃən] v/t (ge-, h) wish; **sich et. (zu Weihnachten** etc) **wünschen** want s.th. (for Christmas etc); **das habe ich mir (schon immer) gewünscht** that's what I (always) wanted; **alles, was man sich nur wünschen kann** everything one could wish for; **ich wünschte, ich wäre (hätte) ...** I wish I were (had) ...

'wünschenswert adj desirable

wurde ['vʊrdə] pret of **werden**

Würde ['vYrdə] f (-; -n) dignity

'würdelos adj undignified

'Würdenträger m dignitary

W

'**würdevoll** *adj* dignified
würdig ['vʏrdɪç] *adj* worthy (*gen* of); dignified
würdigen ['vʏrdɪgən] *v/t* (*ge-*, h) appreciate; *j-n keines Blickes würdigen* ignore s.o. completely
'**Würdigung** *f* (-; *-en*) appreciation
Wurf [vʊrf] *m* (*-[e]s*; *Würfe* ['vʏrfə]) throw; zo litter
Würfel ['vʏrfəl] *m* (-s; -) cube (*a.* MATH); dice
'**würfeln** *v/i* (*ge-*, h) throw dice (*um* for); play dice; GASTR dice; *e-e Sechs würfeln* throw a six
'**Würfelzucker** *m* lump sugar
'**Wurfgeschoss** *n* missile
würgen ['vʏrgən] *v/i and v/t* (*ge-*, h) choke; throttle *s.o.*
Wurm [vʊrm] *m* (*-[e]s*; *Würmer* ['vʏrmɐ]) zo worm
wurmen ['vʊrmən] F *v/t* (*ge-*, h) gall *s.o.*
'**wurmstichig** ['vʊrmʃtɪçɪç] *adj* worm-eaten
Wurst [vʊrst] *f* (-; *Würste* ['vʏrstə]) sausage

Würstchen ['vʏrstçən] *n* (-s; -) small sausage, frankfurter, wiener; hot dog
Würze [vʏrtsə] *f* (-; *-n*) spice (*a. fig*)
Wurzel ['vʊrtsəl] *f* (-; *-n*) root (*a.* MATH); *Wurzeln schlagen* take root (*a. fig*)
'**wurzeln** *v/i* (*ge-*, h) **wurzeln in** (*dat*) be rooted in (*a. fig*)
'**würzen** *v/t* (*ge-*, h) spice, season, flavo(u)r
würzig ['vʏrtsɪç] *adj* spicy, well-seasoned
wusch [vʊʃ] *pret of* **waschen**
wusste ['vʊstə] *pret of* **wissen**
Wust [vuːst] F *m* (*-[e]s*; *no pl*) tangled mass
wüst [vyːst] *adj* waste; confused; wild, dissolute
Wüste ['vyːstə] *f* (-; *-n*) desert
Wut [vuːt] *f* (-; *no pl*) rage, fury; *e-e Wut haben* be furious (*auf acc* with)
'**Wutanfall** *m* fit of rage
wüten ['vyːtən] *v/i* (*ge-*, h) rage (*a. fig*)
'**wütend** *adj* furious (*auf acc* with; *über acc* at), F mad (at)
'**wutschnaubend** *adj* fuming

X, Y

X-Beine ['ɪksbaɪnə] *pl* knock-knees; *sie hat X-Beine* she's knock-kneed
x-beinig ['ɪksbaɪnɪç] *adj* knock-kneed
x-be'liebig *adj*: *jede(r, -s) x-Beliebige ...* any ... you like, F any old ...
'**x-mal** F *adv* umpteen times

x-te ['ɪkstə] *adj*: *zum x-ten Male* for the umpteenth time
Xylophon [ksylo'foːn] *n* (-s; *-e*) MUS xylophone
Yacht [jaxt] *f* (-; *-en*) MAR yacht
Yoga ['joːga] *m, n* (*-[s]*; *no pl*) yoga

Z

Zacke ['tsakə] *f* (-; *-n*), '**Zacken** *m* (-s; -) (sharp) point; tooth
zackig ['tsakɪç] *adj* serrated; jagged; *fig* smart
zaghaft ['tsaːkhaft] *adj* timid
zäh [tsɛː] *adj* tough (*a. fig*)
zähflüssig *adj* thick, viscous; *fig* slow-moving (*traffic*)

Zähigkeit ['tsɛːɪçkaɪt] *f* (-; *no pl*) toughness, *fig a.* stamina
Zahl [tsaːl] *f* (-; *-en*) number; figure
'**zahlbar** *adj* payable (*an acc* to; *bei* at)
zählbar ['tsɛːlbaːɐ] *adj* countable
zahlen ['tsaːlən] *v/i and v/t* (*ge-*, h) pay; *zahlen, bitte!* the check (*Br* bill), please!
zählen ['tsɛːlən] *v/t and v/i* (*ge-*, h) count

(*bis* up to; *fig* **auf** acc on); **zählen zu** rank with *the best etc*

ahlenmäßig 1. *adj* numerical; **2.** *adv*: **j-m zahlenmäßig überlegen sein** outnumber s.o.

ähler ['tse:lɐ] *m* (-s; -) counter (*a.* TECH); MATH numerator; ELECTR *etc* meter

ahlkarte *f post* deposit (*Br* paying-in) slip

ahllos *adj* countless

ahlmeister *m* MIL paymaster; MAR purser

ahlreich 1. *adj* numerous; **2.** *adv* in great number

ahltag *m* payday

ahlung *f* (-; -en) payment

ahlung *f* (-; -en) count; POL census

ahlungsaufforderung *f* request for payment

ahlungsbedingungen *pl* terms of payment

ahlungsbefehl *m* order to pay

ahlungsfähig *adj* solvent

ahlungsfrist *f* term of payment

ahlungsmittel *n* currency; **gesetzliches Zahlungsmittel** legal tender

ahlungsschwierigkeiten *pl* financial difficulties

ahlungster,min *m* date of payment

ahlungsunfähig *adj* insolvent

ählwerk *n* TECH counter

ahlwort *n* LING numeral

ahm [tsa:m] *adj* tame (*a. fig*)

ähmen ['tsɛ:mən] *v/t* (*ge-*, *h*) tame (*a. fig*)

ähmung *f* (-; *no pl*) taming

ahn [tsa:n] *m* (-[e]s; *Zähne* ['tsɛ:nə]) tooth, TECH *a.* cog

ahnarzt *m*, **Zahnärztin** *f* dentist, dental surgeon

ahnbürste *f* toothbrush

ahncreme *f* toothpaste

ahnen ['tsa:nən] *v/i* (*ge-*, *h*) cut one's teeth, teethe

ahnfleisch *n* gums

ahnlos *adj* toothless

ahnlücke *f* gap between the teeth

ahnmedi,zin *f* dentistry

ahnpasta, **Zahnpaste** *f* toothpaste

ahnradbahn *f* rack railroad

ahnschmerzen *pl* toothache

ahnspange *f* MED brace

ahnstein *m* tartar

ahnstocher *m* (-s; -) toothpick

ange ['tsaŋə] *f* (-; -n) TECH pliers; pincers; tongs; MED forceps; ZO pincer

anken ['tsaŋkən] *v/i/refl* (*ge-*, *h*) quarrel (**wegen** about; **um** over), fight, argue (about; over)

---

zänkisch ['tsɛŋkɪʃ] *adj* quarrelsome

Zäpfchen ['tsɛpfçən] *n* (-s; -) ANAT uvula; PHARM suppository

zapfen ['tsapfən] *v/t* (*ge-*, *h*) tap

Zapfen *m* (-s; -) faucet, *Br* tap; TECH peg, pin; bung; tenon; pivot; BOT cone

Zapfenstreich *m* MIL tattoo, taps

'**Zapfhahn** *m* faucet, *Br* tap; MOT nozzle

Zapfsäule *f* MOT gasoline (*Br* petrol) pump

zappelig ['tsapəlɪç] *adj* fidgety

zappeln ['tsapəln] *v/i* (*ge-*, *h*) fidget, wriggle

zappen ['zɛpən] F *v/i* (*ge-*, *h*) TV zap

zart [tsa:ɐt] *adj* tender; gentle; **zart fühlend** sensitive

'**Zartgefühl** *n* (-[e]s; *no pl*) delicacy (of feeling), sensitivity, tact

zärtlich ['tsɛ:ɐtlɪç] *adj* tender, affectionate (**zu** with)

'**Zärtlichkeit** *f* (-; -en) a) (*no pl*) tenderness, affection, b) caress

Zauber ['tsaubɐ] *m* (-s; -) magic, spell, charm (*all a. fig*), *fig* enchantment

Zauberei [tsaubə'rai] *f* (-; -en) magic, witchcraft

Zauberer ['tsaubərɐ] *m* (-s; -) magician, sorcerer, wizard (*a. fig*)

'**zauberhaft** *fig adj* enchanting, charming

Zauberin ['tsaubərɪn] *f* (-; -nen) sorceress

'**Zauberkraft** *f* magic power

Zauberkünstler *m* magician, conjurer

Zauberkunststück *n* conjuring trick

'**zaubern** (*ge-*, *h*) **1.** *v/i* practise magic; do conjuring tricks; **2.** *v/t* conjure (up)

'**Zauberspruch** *m* spell

zaudern ['tsaudɐn] *v/i* (*ge-*, *h*) hesitate

Zaum [tsaum] *m* (-[e]s; *Zäume* ['tsɔymə]) bridle; **im Zaum halten** control (**sich** o.s.), keep in check

zäumen ['tsɔymən] *v/t* (*ge-*, *h*) bridle

'**Zaumzeug** *n* (-[e]s; -e) bridle

Zaun [tsaun] *m* (-[e]s; *Zäune* ['tsɔynə]) fence

Zaungast *m* onlooker

Zaunpfahl *m* pale

z. B. ABBR *of* **zum Beispiel** e.g., for example, for instance

Zebra ['tse:bra] *n* (-s; -s) ZO zebra

'**Zebrastreifen** *m* MOT zebra crossing

Zeche ['tsɛçə] *f* (-; -n) check, *Br* bill; (coal) mine, pit; **die Zeche bezahlen müssen** F have to foot the bill

Zeh [tse:] *m* (-s; -en), **Zehe** ['tse:ə] *f* (-; -n) ANAT toe; **große** (**kleine**) **Zeh** big (little) toe

'**Zehennagel** *m* ANAT toenail

'**Zehenspitze** *f* tip of the toe; **auf Zehenspitzen gehen** (walk on) tiptoe

Z

zehn [tseːn] adj ten
'zehnfach adj tenfold
'zehnjährig [-jɛːrɪç] adj ten-year-old (boy etc); ten-year anniversary etc; absence etc of ten years
Zehnkampf m SPORT decathlon
'zehnmal adv ten times
'zehnte adj tenth
'Zehntel n (-s; -) tenth
'zehntens adv tenthly
Zeichen n ['tsaiçən] n (-s; -) sign; mark; signal; zum Zeichen gen as a token of
Zeichenblock m sketch pad
Zeichenbrett n drawing board
Zeichendreieck n MATH set square
Zeichenfolge f EDP string
Zeichenlehrer(in) art teacher
Zeichensetzung f (-; no pl) LING punctuation
Zeichensprache f sign language
Zeichentrickfilm m (animated) cartoon
zeichnen ['tsaiçnən] v/i and v/t (ge-, h) draw; mark (a. fig); sign; fig leave its mark on s.o.
'Zeichnen n (-s; no pl) drawing; PED art
'Zeichner ['tsaiçnɐ] m (-s; -) mst graphic artist; draftsman; Br draughtsman
'Zeichnung f (-; -en) drawing; diagram; ZO marking
Zeigefinger ['tsaigə-] m ANAT forefinger, index finger
zeigen ['tsaigən] (ge-, h) 1. v/t show (a. sich zeigen); 2. v/i: zeigen nach point to; (mit dem Finger) zeigen auf (acc) point (one's finger) at
Zeiger ['tsaigɐ] m (-s; -) hand; TECH pointer, needle
'Zeigestock m pointer
Zeile ['tsailə] f (-; -n) line (a. TV); j-m ein paar Zeilen schreiben drop s.o. a line
Zeit [tsait] f (-; -en) time; age, era; LING tense; vor einiger Zeit some time ago, a while ago; in letzter Zeit lately, recently; in der (or zur) Zeit gen in the days of; ... aller Zeiten ... of all time; die Zeit ist um time's up; e-e Zeit lang for some time, for a while; sich Zeit lassen take one's time; es wird Zeit, dass ... it's time to inf; das waren noch Zeiten those were the days; Zeit raubend → zeitraubend; → zurzeit
'Zeitabschnitt m period (of time)
Zeitalter n age
Zeitbombe f time bomb (a. fig)
Zeitdruck m: unter Zeitdruck stehen be pressed for time
Zeitfahren n (-s; no pl) cycling: time trials
'zeitgemäß adj modern, up-to-date
'Zeitgenosse m, 'Zeitgenossin f, 'zeit-

genössisch [-gənœsɪʃ] adj contemporary
'Zeitgeschichte f (-; no pl) contemporary history
Zeitgewinn m (-[e]s; no pl) gain of time
Zeitkarte f season ticket
'Zeitlang f → Zeit
zeit'lebens adv all one's life
'zeitlich 1. adj time ...; 2. adv: et. zeitlich planen or abstimmen time s.th.
'zeitlos adj timeless; classic
Zeitlupe f: in Zeitlupe in slow motion
Zeitnot f: in Zeitnot sein be pressed for time
Zeitpunkt m moment
Zeitraffer m: im Zeitraffer in quick motion
'zeitraubend adj time-consuming
'Zeitraum m period (of time)
'Zeitschrift f magazine
Zeitung ['tsaitʊŋ] f (-; -en) (news)paper
'Zeitungsabonne,ment n subscription to a paper
Zeitungsar,tikel m newspaper article
Zeitungsausschnitt m (newspaper) clipping (Br cutting)
Zeitungsjunge m paper boy
Zeitungskiosk m newspaper kiosk
Zeitungsno,tiz f press item
Zeitungspa,pier n newspaper
Zeitungsstand m newsstand
Zeitungsverkäufer(in) newsdealer, Br news vendor
'Zeitverlust m (-[e]s; no pl) loss of time
'Zeitverschiebung f AVIAT time lag
'Zeitverschwendung f waste of time
'Zeitvertreib [-fɛrtraip] m (-[e]s; -e) pastime; zum Zeitvertreib to pass the time
zeitweilig ['tsaitvailɪç] adj temporary
'zeitweise adv at times, occasionally
'Zeitwort n (-[e]s; -wörter) LING verb
Zeitzeichen n radio: time signal
Zeitzünder m MIL time fuse
Zelle ['tsɛlə] f (-; -n) cell
Zellstoff ['tsɛl-] m, Zellulose [tsɛlu'loːzə] f (-; -n) TECH cellulose
Zelt [tsɛlt] n (-[e]s; -e) tent
zelten ['tsɛltən] v/i (ge-, h) camp
'Zeltlager n camp
'Zeltplatz m campsite
Zement [tse'mɛnt] m (-[e]s; -e), zementieren [tsemɛn'tiːrən] v/t (no -ge-, h) cement
Zenit [tse'niːt] m (-[e]s; no pl) zenith
zensieren [tsɛn'ziːrən] v/t (no -ge-, h) censor; PED mark, grade
Zensor ['tsɛnzoːɐ] m (-s; -en [tsɛn'zoːrən]) censor
Zensur [tsɛn'zuːɐ] f (-; -en [tsɛn'zuːrən])

a) (no pl) censorship, b) PED mark, grade

Zentimeter [tsɛnti'meːtɐ] n, m (-s; -) centimeter, Br centimetre

Zentner ['tsɛntnɐ] m (-s; -) 50 kilograms, metric hundredweight

zentral [tsɛn'traːl] adj central

Zentrale [tsɛn'traːlə] f (-; -n) head office; headquarters; TEL switchboard; TECH control room

Zen'tralheizung f central heating

Zentralverriegelung f MOT central locking

Zentrum ['tsɛntrʊm] n (-s; Zentren) center, Br centre

Zepter ['tsɛptɐ] n (-s; -) scepter, Br sceptre

zer'brechen v/i (irr, **brechen**, no -ge-, sein) and v/t (h) break; → **Kopf**

zer'brechlich adj fragile

zer'bröckeln v/t (no -ge-, h) and v/i (sein) crumble

zer'drücken v/t (no -ge-, h) crush

Zeremonie [tseremo'niː] f (-; -n) ceremony

zeremoniell [tseremo'njɛl] adj, **Zeremoni'ell** n (-s; -e) ceremonial

Zer'fall m (-[e]s; no pl) disintegration, decay

zer'fallen v/i (irr, **fallen**, no -ge-, sein) disintegrate, decay; **zerfallen in** (acc) break up into

zer'fetzen v/t (no -ge-, h) tear to pieces

zer'fressen v/t (irr, **fressen**, no -ge-, h) eat (holes in); CHEM corrode

zer'gehen v/i (irr, **gehen**, no -ge-, sein) melt, dissolve

zer'hacken v/t (no -ge-, h) chop (a. ELECTR)

zerknirscht [tsɛɐ'knɪrʃt] adj remorseful

zer'knittern v/t (no -ge-, h) (c)rumple, crease

zer'knüllen v/t (no -ge-, h) crumple up

zer'kratzen v/t (no -ge-, h) scratch

zer'krümeln v/t (no -ge-, h) crumble

zer'lassen v/t (irr, **lassen**, no -ge-, h) melt

zer'legen v/t (no -ge-, h) take apart or to pieces; TECH dismantle; GASTR carve; CHEM, LING, fig analyze; Br analyse

zer'lumpt adj ragged, tattered

zer'mahlen v/t (no -ge-, h) grind

zer'mürben v/t (no -ge-, h) wear down

zer'quetschen v/t (no -ge-, h) crush

Zerrbild ['tsɛɐ-] n caricature

zer'reiben v/t (irr, **reiben**, no -ge-, h) rub to powder, pulverize

zer'reißen v/t (irr, **reißen**, no -ge-) **1.** v/t (h) tear up or to pieces; **sich die Hose zerreißen** tear one's trousers; **2.** v/i (sein) tear; break

zerren ['tsɛrən] (ge-, h) **1.** v/t tug, drag, pull (a. MED); **2.** v/i: **zerren an** (dat) tug (or strain) at

Zerrung f (-; -en) MED pulled muscle

zer'rütten [tsɛɐ'rʏtən] v/t (no -ge-, h) ruin

zer'rüttet adj: **zerrüttete Ehe** (**Verhältnisse**) broken marriage (home)

zer'sägen v/t (no -ge-, h) saw up

zerschellen [-'ʃɛlən] v/i (no -ge-, sein) be smashed, AVIAT a. crash

zer'schlagen 1. v/t (irr, **schlagen**, no -ge-, h) smash (to pieces); fig smash; **sich zerschlagen** come to nothing; **2.** adj: **sich zerschlagen fühlen** be (all) worn out, F be dead beat

zer'schmettern v/t (no -ge-, h) smash (to pieces), shatter (a. fig)

zer'schneiden v/t (irr, **schneiden**, no -ge-, h) cut (up)

zer'setzen v/t (no -ge-, h) CHEM decompose (a. **sich zersetzen**); fig corrupt, undermine

zer'splittern v/t (no -ge-, h) and v/i (sein) split (up), splinter; shatter

zer'springen v/i (irr, **springen**, no -ge-, sein) crack; shatter

zer'stampfen v/t (no -ge-, h) pound; GASTR mash

zer'stäuben v/t (no -ge-, h) spray

Zerstäuber [tsɛɐ'ʃtɔybɐ] m (-s; -) atomizer, sprayer

zer'stören v/t (no -ge-, h) destroy, ruin (both a. fig)

Zer'störer m (-s; -) destroyer (a. MAR)

zer'störerisch adj destructive

Zer'störung f (-; -en) destruction

zer'streuen v/t and v/refl (no -ge-, h) scatter, disperse; break up (crowd etc); fig take s.o.'s (refl one's) mind off things

zer'streut fig adj absent-minded

Zer'streutheit f (-; no pl) absent-mindedness

Zer'streuung fig f (-; -en) diversion, distraction

zer'stückeln v/t (no -ge-, h) cut up or (into-) to pieces; dismember (body)

Zertifikat [tsɛrtifi'kaːt] n (-[e]s; -e) certificate

zer'treten v/t (irr, **treten**, no -ge-, h) crush (a. fig)

zer'trümmern v/t (no -ge-, h) smash

zerzaust [tsɛɐ'tsaust] adj tousled, dishevel(l)ed

Zettel ['tsɛtəl] m (-s; -) slip (of paper); note; label, sticker

Zeug [tsɔyk] n (-[e]s; -e) stuff (a. F); things; **er hat das Zeug dazu** he's got what it takes; **dummes Zeug** nonsense

Zeuge ['tsɔygə] m (-n; -n) witness

Z

'zeugen¹ v/i (ge-, h) JUR give evidence (**für** for); **fig zeugen von** testify to

'zeugen² v/t (ge-, h) BIOL procreate; father

Zeugenaussage f JUR testimony, evidence

Zeugenbank f (-; -bänke) JUR witness stand (Br box)

'Zeugin f (-; -nen) JUR (female) witness

Zeugnis ['tsɔʏknɪs] n (-ses; -se) report card, Br (school) report; certificate, diploma; reference; pl credentials

'Zeugung f (-; -en) BIOL procreation

z. H(d). ABBR of **zu Händen** attn, attention

Zickzack ['tsɪktsak] m (-[e]s; -e) (a. im **Zickzack fahren**) zigzag

Ziege ['tsiːgə] f (-; -n) ZO (nanny) goat; F contp (**blöde**) **Ziege** (silly old) cow

Ziegel ['tsiːgəl] m (-s; -) brick; tile

'Ziegeldach n tiled roof

Ziegelei [tsiːgəˈlaɪ] f (-; -en) brickyard

'Ziegelstein m brick

'Ziegenbock m ZO billy goat

Ziegenleder n kid (leather)

Ziegenpeter [-peːtɐ] m (-s; -) MED mumps

ziehen ['tsiːən] (irr, ge-) **1.** v/t (h) pull, draw; take off one's hat (**vor** dat to) (a. fig); AGR grow; pull or take out (**aus** of); **j-n ziehen an** (dat) pull s.o. by; **auf sich ziehen** attract (attention etc); **sich ziehen** run; stretch; → **Länge, Erwägung**; **2.** v/i a) (h) pull (**an** dat at), b) (sein) move; ZO etc migrate; go; travel; wander, roam; **es zieht** there's a draft (Br draught)

Ziehharmonika [ˈtsiːharmoˌnikaː] f (-; -s) MUS accordion

'Ziehung f (-; -en) draw

Ziel [tsiːl] n (-[e]s; -e) aim, target, mark (all a. fig), fig a. goal, objective; destination; SPORT finish; **sich ein Ziel setzen** set o.s. a goal; **sein Ziel erreichen** reach one's goal; **sich zum Ziel gesetzt haben, et. zu tun** aim to do or at doing s.th.

'Zielband n (-[e]s; -bänder) SPORT tape

zielen ['tsiːlən] v/i (ge-, h) (take) aim (**auf** acc at)

'Ziellinie f SPORT finishing line

'ziellos adj aimless

'Zielscheibe f target, fig a. object

zielstrebig ['tsiːlʃtreːbɪç] adj purposeful, determined

ziemlich ['tsiːmlɪç] **1.** adj quite a; **2.** adv rather, fairly, quite, F pretty; **ziemlich viele** quite a few

Zierde ['tsiːɐdə] f (-; -n) (**zur** as a) decoration

zieren ['tsiːrən] v/t (ge-, h) decorate; **sich zieren** be coy; make a fuss

zierlich ['tsiːɐlɪç] adj dainty; petite

Zierpflanze ['tsiːɐ-] f ornamental plant

Ziffer ['tsɪfɐ] f (-; -n) figure

'Zifferblatt n dial, face

Zigarette [tsigaˈrɛtə] f (-; -n) cigarette

Ziga'rettenauto,mat m cigarette machine

Ziga'rettenstummel m cigarette end, stub, butt

Zigarre [tsiˈgarə] f (-; -n) cigar

Zigeuner [tsiˈgɔʏnɐ] m (-s; -), Zi'geunerin [-nərɪn] f (-; -nen) gypsy, Br gipsy

Zimmer ['tsɪmɐ] n (-s; -) room; apartment

Zimmereinrichtung f furniture

Zimmermädchen n (chamber)maid

Zimmermann m carpenter

'zimmern v/t (ge-, h) build, make

'Zimmerpflanze f indoor plant

Zimmerservice m room service

Zimmersuche f: **auf Zimmersuche sein** be looking (or hunting) for a room

Zimmervermittlung f accommodation office

zimperlich ['tsɪmpɐlɪç] adj prudish; soft, F sissy

Zimt [tsɪmt] m (-[e]s; -e) cinnamon

Zink [tsɪŋk] n (-[e]s; no pl) CHEM zinc

Zinke ['tsɪŋkə] f (-; -n) tooth; prong

Zinn [tsɪn] n (-[e]s; no pl) CHEM tin; pewter

Zins [tsɪns] m (-es; -en) ECON interest (a. pl); **3% Zinsen bringen** bear interest at 3%

'zinslos adj ECON interest-free

'Zinssatz m ECON interest rate

Zipfel ['tsɪpfəl] m (-s; -) corner; point; tail; GASTR end

Zipfelmütze f pointed cap

zirka ['tsɪrka] adv about, approximately

Zirkel ['tsɪrkəl] m (-s; -) circle (a. fig), MATH compasses, dividers

zirkulieren [tsɪrkuˈliːrən] v/i (no ge-, h) circulate

Zirkus ['tsɪrkʊs] m (-; -se) circus

zirpen ['tsɪrpən] v/i (ge-, h) chirp

zischen ['tsɪʃən] v/i and v/t (ge-, h) hiss; fat etc: sizzle; fig whiz(z)

ziselieren [tsizəˈliːrən] v/t (no ge-, h) TECH chase

Zitat [tsiˈtaːt] n (-[e]s; -e) quotation, F quote

zitieren [tsiˈtiːrən] v/t (no ge-, h) quote, cite (a. JUR), JUR summon

Zitrone [tsiˈtroːnə] f (-; -n) BOT lemon

Zi'tronenlimo,nade f lemon soda or pop, Br (fizzy) lemonade

Zitronensaft m lemon juice

Zitronenschale f lemon peel

zitterig ['tsɪtərɪç] adj shaky

zittern ['tsɪtɐn] v/i (ge-, h) tremble, shake (both: **vor** dat with)

zivil [tsiˈviːl] adj civil, civilian

Z

'Zi|vil n (-s; no pl) civilian clothes; *Polizist in Zivil* plainclothes policeman

Zi'vildienst m MIL alternative service (*in lieu of military service*)

Zivilisation [tsiviliza'tsjo:n] f (-; -en) civilization

zivilisieren [tsivili'zi:rən] v/t (no -ge-, h) civilize

Zivilist [tsivi'lɪst] m (-en; -en) civilian

Zi'vilrecht n (-[e]s; no pl) JUR civil law

Zi'vilschutz m civil defen|se, Br -ce

Znüni ['tsny:ni] Swiss m, n (-s; -) mid-morning snack, tea (or coffee) break

zog [tso:k] pret of *ziehen*

zögern ['tsø:gən] v/i (ge-, h) hesitate

'Zögern n (-s; no pl) hesitation

Zoll¹ [tsɔl] m (-[e]s; -) inch

Zoll² m (-[e]s; Zölle ['tsœlə]) a) (no pl) customs, b) duty

'Zollabfertigung f customs clearance

'Zollbeamte m customs officer

'Zollerklärung f customs declaration

'zollfrei adj duty-free

'Zollkon,trolle f customs examination

'zollpflichtig adj liable to duty

'Zollstock m (folding) rule

Zone ['tso:nə] f (-; -n) zone

Zoo [tso:] m (-s; -s) zoo

'Zoohandlung f pet shop

Zoologe [tsoo'lo:gə] m (-n; -n) zoologist

Zoologie [tsoolo'gi:] f (-; no pl) zoology

zoo'login f (-; -nen) zoologist

zoo'logisch adj zoological

Zopf [tsɔpf] m (-[e]s; Zöpfe ['tsœpfə]) plait; pigtail

Zorn [tsɔrn] m (-[e]s; no pl) anger

zornig ['tsɔrnɪç] adj angry

Zote ['tso:tə] f (-; -n) filthy joke, obscenity

zottelig ['tsɔtəlɪç] adj shaggy

z. T. ABBR of *zum Teil* partly

zu [tsu:] **1.** *prp* (dat) to, toward(s); at; *purpose:* for; *zu Fuß* (*Pferd*) on foot (horseback); *zu Hause* (*Ostern etc*) at home (Easter *etc*); *zu Weihnachten* give *etc* for Christmas; *Tür* (*Schlüssel*) *zu ...* door (key) to ...; *zu m-r Überraschung* to my surprise; *wir sind zu dritt* there are three of us; *zu zweien* two by two; *zu e-r Mark* at *or* for one mark; SPORT **1 zu 1** one all; **2 zu 1 gewinnen** win two one, win by two goals *etc* to one; *zu auch* F closed, shut; *ein zu großes Risiko* too much of a risk; *zu viel* too much, too many; *zu wenig* too little, too few; **b)** *to; es ist zu erwarten* it is to be expected; **2.** *adv closed, shut; ein zu großes Risiko* too much of a risk; *zu viel* too much, too many; *zu wenig* too little, too few; **3.** *cj* to

Zubehör ['tsu:bəhø:ɐ] n (-[e]s; -e) accessories

'zubereiten v/t (sep, no -ge-, h) prepare

'Zubereitung f (-; -en) preparation

'zubinden v/t (irr, binden, sep, -ge-, h) tie (up)

'zubleiben v/i (irr, bleiben, sep, -ge-, sein) stay shut

'zublinzeln v/i (sep, -ge-, h) (dat) wink at

'Zubringer m (-s; -), Zubringerstraße f MOT feeder (road), access road

Zucht [tsʊxt] f (-; -en) breed; zo breeding; BOT cultivation

züchten ['tsyçtən] v/t (ge-, h) zo breed; BOT grow, cultivate

Züchter(in) ['tsyçtɐ (-tərɪn)] m (-s; -/-; -nen) zo breeder; BOT grower

'Zuchtperle f culture(d) pearl

zucken ['tsʊkən] v/i (ge-, h) jerk; twitch (*mit et.* s.th.); wince; *lightning:* flash

zücken ['tsʏkən] v/t (ge-, h) draw (*weapon*); F pull out (*one's wallet etc*)

Zucker ['tsʊkɐ] m (-s; -) sugar

'Zuckerdose f sugar bowl

'Zuckerguss m icing, frosting

'zuckerkrank adj, 'Zuckerkranke m, f (-n; -n) MED diabetic

'Zuckerkrankheit f MED diabetes

'Zuckermais m sweet corn

'zuckern v/t (ge-, h) sugar

'Zuckerrohr n BOT sugarcane

'Zuckerrübe f BOT sugar beet

'Zuckerwatte f candy floss

'Zuckerzange f sugar tongs

'Zuckung f (-; -en) twitch(ing); tic; convulsion, spasm

'zudecken v/t (sep, -ge-, h) cover (up)

zudem [tsu'de:m] adv besides, moreover

'zudrehen v/t (sep, -ge-, h) turn off; *j-m den Rücken zudrehen* turn one's back on s.o.

'zudringlich adj: *zudringlich werden* F get fresh (*j-m gegenüber* with s.o.)

'zudrücken v/t (sep, -ge-, h) close, push s.th. shut; → *Auge*

zuerst [tsu'ʔe:ɐst] adv first; at first; first (of all), to begin with

'Zufahrt f approach; drive(way)

'Zufahrtsstraße f access road

'Zufall m chance; *durch Zufall* by chance, by accident

'zufallen v/i (irr, fallen, sep, -ge-, sein) door etc: slam (shut); fig fall to s.o.; *mir fallen die Augen zu* I can't keep my eyes open

'zufällig **1.** adj accidental, chance ...; **2.** adv by accident, by chance; *zufällig tun* happen to do

'Zuflucht f: *Zuflucht suchen* (*finden*) look for (find) refuge *or* shelter (*vor dat* from; *bei* with); (*s-e*) *Zuflucht nehmen zu* resort to

zufrieden [tsu'fri:dən] adj content(ed),

satisfied; **zufrieden stellen** satisfy; **zufrieden stellend** satisfactory

Zu'friedenheit f (-; no pl) contentment, satisfaction

zu'friedengeben v/refl (irr, **geben**, sep, -ge-, h): **sich zufriedengeben mit** content o.s. with

zufriedenlassen v/t (irr, **lassen**, sep, -ge-, h) leave s.o. alone

zufriedenstellen v/t (sep,-ge-, h) satisfy

zufriedenstellend adj satisfactory

'zufrieren v/i (irr, **frieren**, sep, -ge-, sein) freeze up or over

'zufügen v/t (sep, -ge-, h) do, cause; **j-m Schaden zufügen** a. harm s.o.

Zufuhr ['tsu:fu:ɐ] f (-; -en) supply

Zug [tsu:k] m (-[e]s; Züge ['tsy:gə]) RAIL train; procession, line; parade; fig feature; trait; tendency; chess etc: move (a. fig); swimming: stroke; pull (a. TECH), PHYS a. tension; smoking: puff; draft, Br draught; PED stream; fig gen in the course of; **in e-m Zug** at one go; **Zug um Zug** step by step; **in groben Zügen** in broad outlines

'Zugabe f addition; THEA encore

'Zugang m access (a. fig)

'zugänglich [-gɛŋlɪç] adj accessible (**für** to) (a. fig)

'Zugbrücke f drawbridge

'zugeben v/t (irr, **geben**, sep, -ge-, h) add; fig admit

'zugehen v/i (irr, **gehen**, sep, -ge-, sein) F door etc: close, shut; **zugehen auf** (acc) walk up to, approach (a. fig); **es geht auf 8 Uhr zu** it's getting on for 8; **es ging lustig zu** we had a lot of fun

'Zugehörigkeit f (-; no pl) membership

'Zügel ['tsy:gəl] m (-s; -) rein (a. fig)

'Zugeständnis n concession

'zugestehen v/t (irr, **stehen**, sep, no -ge-, h) concede, grant

'zugetan adj attached (dat to)

'Zugführer m RAIL conductor, Br guard

zugig ['tsu:gɪç] adj drafty, Br draughty

'Zugkraft f a) TECH traction, b) (no pl) attraction, draw, appeal

'zugkräftig adj: **zugkräftig sein** be a draw

zu'gleich [tsu-] adv at the same time

'Zugluft f (-; no pl) draft, Br draught

'Zugma,schine f MOT tractor

'zugreifen v/i (irr, **greifen**, sep, -ge-, h) grab (at) it; fig grab the opportunity; **greifen Sie zu!** help yourself!; **mit zugreifen** lend a hand

'Zugriffscode m EDP access code

'Zugriffszeit f EDP access time

zugrunde [tsu'grʊndə] adv: **zugrunde gehen** (an dat) perish (of); **e-r Sache et. zugrunde legen** base s.th. on s.th.; **zugrunde richten** ruin

zugunsten [tsu'gʊnstən] prp (gen) in favo(u)r of

zu'gute [tsu-] adv: **zugute halten** → **zugutehalten**; **zugute kommen** → **zugutekommen**; **zugutehalten** v/t (irr, **halten**, sep, -ge-, h): **j-m et. zugute** give s.o. credit for s.th.; make allwances for s.o.'s ...

zugutekommen v/i (irr, **kommen**, sep, -ge-, sein): **j-m zugutekommen** be for the benefit of s.o. 'Zugvogel m zo bird of passage

'zuhalten v/t (irr, **halten**, sep, -ge-, h) keep shut; **sich die Ohren (Augen) zuhalten** cover one's ears (eyes) with one's hands; **sich die Nase zuhalten** hold one's nose

Zuhälter ['tsu:hɛltɐ] m (-s; -) pimp

Zuhause [tsu'hauzə] n (-s; no pl) home

zu'hause adv → **Haus**

'zuhören v/i (sep, -ge-, h) listen (dat to)

'Zuhörer m, **'Zuhörerin** f listener, pl a. the audience

'zujubeln v/i (sep, -ge-, h) cheer

'zukleben v/t (sep, -ge-, h) seal

'zuknöpfen v/t (sep, -ge-, h) button (up)

'zukommen v/i (irr, **kommen**, sep, -ge-, sein) **zukommen auf** (acc) come up to; fig be ahead of; **die Dinge auf sich zukommen lassen** wait and see

Zukunft ['tsu:kʊnft] f (-; no pl) future (a. LING)

'zukünftig 1. adj future; **2.** adv in future

'zulächeln v/i (sep, -ge-, h) smile at

'Zulage f bonus

'zulangen F v/i (sep, -ge-, h) tuck in

'zulassen v/t (irr, **lassen**, sep, -ge-, h) F keep s.th. closed; fig allow; MOT etc license, register; **j-n zu et. zulassen** admit s.o. to s.th.

zulässig adj admissible (a. JUR); **zulässig sein** be allowed

'Zulassung f (-; -en) admission; MOT etc license, Br licence

'zulegen v/t (sep, -ge-, h) add; F **sich ... zulegen** get o.s. s.th.; adopt (name)

zu'letzt [tsu-] adv in the end; come etc last; finally; **wann hast du ihn zuletzt gesehen?** when did you last see him?

zu'liebe [tsu-] adv: **j-m zuliebe** for s.o.'s sake

zum [tsʊm] prp **zu dem** → **zu**; **zum ersten Mal** for the first time; **et. zum Kaffee** s.th. with one's coffee; **zum Schwimmen etc gehen** go swimming etc

'zumachen F (sep, -ge-, h) **1.** v/t close,

shut; button (up); **2.** v/i close (down)

'zumauern v/t (*sep*, *-ge-*, *h*) brick *or* wall up

zumutbar ['tsu:muːtbaːɐ] *adj* reasonable

zu'mute [tsu-] *adv*: **mir ist ... zumute** I feel ...

'zumuten v/t (*sep*, *-ge-*, *h*) **j-m et. zumuten** expect s.th. of s.o.; **sich zu viel zumuten** overtax o.s.

'Zumutung f: **das ist e-e Zumutung** that's asking *or* expecting a bit much

zu'nächst [tsu-] *adv* → **zuerst**

'zunageln v/t (*sep*, *-ge-*, *h*) nail up

'zunähen v/t (*sep*, *-ge-*, *h*) sew up

Zunahme ['tsu:naːmə] f (-; *-n*) increase

'Zuname *m* surname

zünden ['tsyndən] v/i (*ge-*, *h*) kindle; ELECTR, MOT ignite, fire

zündend *fig adj* stirring

Zünder ['tsyndɐ] *m* (*-s; -*) MIL fuse; *pl Austrian* matches

Zündholz ['tsynt-] *n* match

Zündkerze f MOT spark plug

Zündschlüssel *m* MOT ignition key

Zündschnur f fuse

'Zündung f (-; *-en*) MOT ignition

'zunehmen v/i (*irr*, *nehmen*, *sep*, *-ge-*, *h*) increase (**an** *dat* in); put on weight; *moon*: wax; *days*: grow longer

'Zuneigung f (-; *-en*) affection

Zunft [tsunft] f (-; *Zünfte* ['tsynftə]) guild

Zunge [tsuŋə] f (-; *-n*) ANAT tongue; **es liegt mir auf der Zunge** it's on the tip of my tongue

züngeln ['tsyŋəln] v/i (*ge-*, *h*) *flames*: lick, flicker

'Zungenspitze f tip of the tongue

'zunicken v/i (*sep*, *-ge-*, *h*) (*dat*) nod at

zunutze [tsu'nʊtsə] *adv*: **sich et. zunutze machen** make (good) use of s.th.; take advantage of s.th.

zupfen [tsʊpfən] v/t *and* v/i (*ge-*, *h*) pull (**an** *dat* at); pick, pluck (*at*) (*a.* MUS)

zur [tsuːɐ] *prp zu der* → **zu**; **zur Schule (Kirche) gehen** go to school (church); **zur Hälfte** half (of it *or* them); **zur Belohnung** *etc* as a reward *etc*

'zurechnungsfähig *adj* JUR responsible

'Zurechnungsfähigkeit f (-; *no pl*) JUR responsibility

zu'rechtfinden v/refl (*irr*, *finden*, *sep*, *-ge-*, *h*) find one's way; *fig* cope, manage

zurechtkommen v/i (*irr*, *kommen*, *sep*, *-ge-*, *sein*) get along (**mit** with); cope (with)

zurechtlegen v/t (*sep*, *-ge-*, *h*) arrange; *fig* **sich et. zurechtlegen** think s.th. out

zurechtmachen F v/t (*sep*, *-ge-*, *h*) get

ready, prepare, fix; **sich zurechtmachen** do o.s. up

zurechtrücken v/t (*sep*, *-ge-*, *h*) put *s.th.* straight (*a. fig*)

zu'rechtweisen v/t (*irr*, *weisen*, *sep*, *-ge-*, *h*), Zu'rechtweisung f reprimand

'zureden v/i (*sep*, *-ge-*, *h*) **j-m zureden** encourage s.o.

zureiten v/t (*irr*, *reiten*, *sep*, *-ge-*, *h*) break in

zurichten F *fig* v/t (*sep*, *-ge-*, *h*) **übel zurichten** batter, *a.* beat s.o. badly, *a.* make a mess of s.th., ruin

zurück [tsu'rʏk] *adv* back; behind (*a. fig*)

zurückbehalten v/t (*irr*, *halten*, *sep*, *no -ge-*, *h*) keep back, retain

zurückbekommen v/t (*irr*, *kommen*, *sep*, *no -ge-*, *h*) get back

zurückbleiben v/i (*irr*, *bleiben*, *sep*, *-ge-*, *sein*) stay behind, be left behind; fall behind (*a. PED etc*)

zurückblicken v/i (*sep*, *-ge-*, *h*) look back (**auf** *acc* at, *fig* on)

zurückbringen v/t (*irr*, *bringen*, *sep*, *-ge-*, *h*) bring *or* take back, return

zurückda,tieren v/t (*sep*, *no -ge-*, *h*) backdate (**auf** *acc* to)

zurückfallen *fig* v/i (*irr*, *fallen*, *sep*, *-ge-*, *sein*) fall behind, SPORT *a.* drop back

zurückfinden v/i (*irr*, *finden*, *sep*, *-ge-*, *h*) find one's way back (**nach**, **zu** to); *fig* return (to)

zurückfordern v/t (*sep*, *-ge-*, *h*) reclaim

zurückführen v/t (*sep*, *-ge-*, *h*) lead back; **zurückführen auf** (*acc*) attribute to

zurückgeben v/t (*irr*, *geben*, *sep*, *-ge-*, *h*) give back, return

zurückgeblieben *fig adj* backward; retarded

zurückgehen v/i (*irr*, *gehen*, *sep*, *-ge-*, *sein*) go back, return; *fig* decrease; go down, drop

zurückgezogen *fig adj* secluded

zurückgreifen v/i (*irr*, *greifen*, *sep*, *-ge-*, *h*) **zurückgreifen auf** (*acc*) fall back (up)on

zu'rückhalten (*irr*, *halten*, *sep*, *-ge-*, *h*) **1.** v/t hold back; **2.** v/refl control o.s.; be careful

zurückhaltend *adj* reserved

Zu'rückhaltung f (-; *no pl*) reserve

zu'rückkehren v/i (*sep*, *-ge-*, *sein*) return

zurückkommen v/i (*irr*, *kommen*, *sep*, *-ge-*, *sein*) come back, return (*both fig* **auf** *acc* to)

zurücklassen v/t (*irr*, *lassen*, *sep*, *-ge-*, *h*) leave (behind)

zurücklegen v/t (*sep*, *-ge-*, *h*) put back; put aside, save (*money*); cover, do (*miles*) zurücknehmen v/t (irr, **nehmen**, sep, -ge-, h) take back (a. fig)

zurückrufen (irr, **rufen**, sep, -ge-, h) **1.** v/t call back (a. TEL); ECON recall; **ins Gedächtnis zurückrufen** recall; **2.** v/i TEL call back

zurückschlagen (irr, **schlagen**, sep, -ge-, h) **1.** v/t beat off; tennis: return; fold back; **2.** v/i hit back; MIL retaliate (a. fig)

zurückschrecken v/i (sep, -ge-, sein) **zurückschrecken vor** (dat) shrink from; **vor nichts zurückschrecken** stop at nothing

zurücksetzen v/t (sep, -ge-, h) MOT back (up); fig neglect s.o.

zurückstehen v/i (irr, **stehen**, sep, -ge-, h) stand aside

zurückstellen v/t (sep, -ge-, h) put back (a. watch); put aside; MIL defer

zurückstrahlen v/t (sep, -ge-, h) reflect

zurücktreten v/i (irr, **treten**, sep, -ge-, sein) step or stand back; resign (**von e-m Amt** [**Posten**]) one's office [post]); ECON, JUR withdraw (**von** from)

zurückweichen v/i (irr, **weichen**, sep, -ge-, sein) fall back (a. MIL)

zurückweisen v/t (irr, **weisen**, sep, -ge-, h) turn down; JUR dismiss

zurückzahlen v/t (sep, -ge-, h) pay back (a. fig)

zurückziehen v/t (irr, **ziehen**, sep, -ge-, h) draw back; fig withdraw; **sich zurückziehen** retire, withdraw, MIL a. retreat

'Zuruf m shout

'zurufen v/t (irr, **rufen**, sep, -ge-, h) **j-m et. zurufen** shout s.th. to s.o.

zur'zeit adv at the moment, at present

'Zusage f promise; assent

'zusagen v/i and v/t (sep, -ge-, h) accept (an invitation); (dat) suit, appeal to; **s-e Hilfe zusagen** promise to help

zusammen [tsu'zamən] adv together; **alles zusammen** (all) in all; **das macht zusammen ...** that makes ... altogether

Zu'sammenarbeit f (-; no pl) cooperation; **in Zusammenarbeit mit** in collaboration with

zu'sammenarbeiten v/i (sep, -ge-, h) cooperate, collaborate

zu'sammenbeißen v/t (irr, **beißen**, sep, -ge-, h) **die Zähne zusammenbeißen** clench one's teeth

zu'sammenbrechen v/i (irr, **brechen**, sep, -ge-, sein) break down, collapse (both a. fig)

Zu'sammenbruch m breakdown, collapse

zu'sammenfallen v/i (irr, **fallen**, sep, -ge-, sein) coincide

zusammenfalten v/t (sep, -ge-, h) fold up

zu'sammenfassen v/t (sep, -ge-, h) summarize, sum up

Zu'sammenfassung f (-; -en) summary

zu'sammenfügen v/t (sep, -ge-, h) join (together)

zusammengesetzt adj compound

zusammenhalten v/i and v/t (irr, **halten**, sep, -ge-, h) hold together (a. fig); F stick together

Zu'sammenhang m (-[e]s; -hänge) connection; context; **im Zusammenhang stehen** (**mit**) be connected (with)

zu'sammenhängen v/i (irr, **hängen**, sep, -ge-, h) be connected

zusammenhängend adj coherent

zu'sammenhang(s)los adj incoherent, disconnected

zu'sammenklappen v/i (sep, -ge-, sein) and v/t (h) TECH fold up; F break down

zusammenkommen v/i (irr, **kommen**, sep, -ge-, sein) meet

Zu'sammenkunft [-kʊnft] f (-; -künfte [-kʏnftə]) meeting

zu'sammenlegen (sep, -ge-, h) **1.** v/t combine; fold up; **2.** v/i club together

zusammennehmen v/t (irr, **nehmen**, sep, -ge-, h) muster (up); **sich zusammennehmen** pull o.s. together

zusammenpacken v/t (sep, -ge-, h) pack up

zusammenpassen v/i (sep, -ge-, h) harmonize; match

zusammenrechnen v/t (sep, -ge-, h) add up

zusammenreißen F v/refl (irr, **reißen**, sep, -ge-, h) pull o.s. together

zusammenrollen v/t (sep, -ge-, h) roll up; **sich zusammenrollen** coil up

zusammenrotten [-rɔtən] v/refl (sep, -ge-, h) band together

zusammenrücken (sep, -ge-) **1.** v/t (h) move closer together; **2.** v/i (sein) move up

zusammenschlagen v/t (irr, **schlagen**, sep, -ge-, h) clap (hands); click (one's heels); beat s.o. up; smash (up)

zu'sammenschließen v/refl (irr, **schließen**, sep, -ge-, h) join, unite

Zu'sammenschluss m union

zu'sammenschreiben v/t (irr, **schreiben**, sep, -ge-, h) write in one word

zusammenschrumpfen v/i (sep, -ge-, sein) shrink

zu'sammensetzen v/t (sep, -ge-, h) put together; TECH assemble; **sich zusammensetzen aus** (dat) consist of, be composed of

Zu'sammensetzung f (-; -en) composition; CHEM, LING compound; TECH assembly

zu'sammenstellen v/t (sep, -ge-, h) put together; arrange

Zu'sammenstoß m collision (a. fig), crash; impact; fig clash

zu'sammenstoßen v/i (irr, **stoßen**, sep, -ge-, sein) collide (a. fig); fig clash; **zusammenstoßen mit** run or bump into; fig have a clash with

zu'sammentreffen v/i (irr, **treffen**, sep, -ge-, sein) meet, encounter; coincide (**mit** with)

Zu'sammentreffen n (-s; -) meeting; coincidence; encounter

zu'sammentreten v/i (irr, **treten**, sep, -ge-, sein) meet

zusammentun v/refl (irr, **tun**, sep, -ge-, h) join (forces), F team up

zusammenwirken v/i (sep, -ge-, h) combine

zusammenzählen v/t (sep, -ge-, h) add up

zusammenziehen (irr, **ziehen**, sep, -ge-) **1.** v/t and v/refl (h) contract; **2.** v/i (sein) move in (**mit** with)

zusammenzucken v/i (sep, -ge-, sein) wince, flinch

'Zusatz m addition; chemical etc additive; **Zusatz...** in cpds mst additional ..., supplementary ...; auxiliary ...

zusätzlich ['tsu:zɛtslɪç] adj additional, extra

'zuschauen v/i (sep, -ge-, h) look on (**bei et.** at s.th.); **j-m zuschauen** watch s.o. (**bei et.** doing s.th.)

Zuschauer ['tsu:ʃauɐ] m (-s; -), 'Zuschauerin f (-; -nen) spectator; TV viewer, pl a. the audience

'Zuschauerraum m auditorium

'Zuschlag m extra charge; RAIL etc excess fare; bonus; auction: knocking down

'zuschlagen v/t (irr, **schlagen**, sep, -ge-, sein) and v/t (h) door etc: slam or bang shut; boxing etc: hit, strike (a blow); fig act; **j-m et. zuschlagen** auction: knock s.th. down to s.o.

'zuschließen v/t (irr, **schließen**, sep, -ge-, h) lock (up)

'zuschnallen v/t (sep, -ge-, h) buckle (up)

'zuschnappen v/i (sep, -ge-) a) (h) dog: snap, b) (sein) door etc: snap shut

'zuschneiden v/t (irr, **schneiden**, sep, -ge-, h) cut out; cut (to size)

'zuschnüren v/t (sep, -ge-, h) tie (or lace) up

'zuschrauben v/t (sep, -ge-, h) screw shut

'zuschreiben v/t (irr, **schreiben**, sep, -ge-, h) ascribe or attribute (dat to)

'Zuschrift f letter

zuschulden [tsu'ʃʊldən] adv: **sich et. (nichts) zuschulden kommen lassen** do s.th. (nothing) wrong

'Zuschuss m allowance; subsidy

'zuschütten v/t (sep, -ge-, h) fill up

'zusehen → **zuschauen**

zusehends ['tsu:ze:ənts] adv noticeably; rapidly

'zusetzen (sep, -ge-, h) **1.** v/t add; lose (money); **2.** v/i lose money; **j-m zusetzen** press s.o. (hard)

'zuspielen v/t (sep, -ge-, h) SPORT pass

'zuspitzen v/t (sep, -ge-, h) point; **sich zuspitzen** become critical

'Zuspruch m (-[e]s; no pl) encouragement; words of comfort

'Zustand m condition, state, F shape

zustande [tsu'ʃtandə] adv: **zustande bringen** bring about, manage (to do); **zustande kommen** come about; **es kam nicht zustande** it didn't come off

'zuständig adj responsible (**für** for), in charge (of)

'zustehen v/i (irr, **stehen**, sep, -ge-) **j-m steht et. (zu tun) zu** s.o. is entitled to (do) s.th.

'zustellen v/t (sep, -ge-, h) post: deliver

'Zustellung f post: delivery

'zustimmen v/i (sep, -ge-, h) agree (dat to s.th.; with s.o.)

'Zustimmung f approval, consent; (**j-s) Zustimmung finden** meet with (s.o.'s) approval

'zustoßen v/i (irr, **stoßen**, sep, -ge-, sein) **j-m zustoßen** happen to s.o.

zutage [tsu'ta:gə] adv: **zutage bringen (kommen)** bring (come) to light

'Zutaten pl ingredients

'zuteilen v/t (sep, -ge-, h) assign, allot

'Zuteilung f (-; -en) allotment; ration

'zutragen v/refl (irr, **tragen**, sep, -ge-, h) happen

'zutrauen v/t (sep, -ge-, h) **j-m et. zutrauen** credit s.o. with s.th.; **sich zu viel zutrauen** overrate o.s.

zutraulich ['tsu:traulɪç] adj trusting; zo friendly

'zutreffen v/i (irr, **treffen**, sep, -ge-, h) be true; **zutreffen auf** (acc) apply to, go for

zutreffend adj true, correct

'zutrinken v/i (irr, **trinken**, sep, -ge-, h) **j-m zutrinken** drink to s.o.

'Zutritt m (-[e]s; no pl) admission; access; **Zutritt verboten!** no admittance!

zu'ungunsten adv to s.o.'s disadvantage

zuverlässig ['tsu:fɛɐlɛsɪç] adj reliable, dependable; safe

'Zuverlässigkeit f (-; no pl) reliability, dependability

Z

Zuversicht ['tsuːfɛɐzɪçt] f (-; no pl) confidence

'zuversichtlich adj confident, optimistic

zuviel → zu

zu'vor [tsu-] adv before, previously; first

zu'vorkommen v/i (irr, kommen, sep, -ge-, sein) anticipate; prevent; j-m zuvorkommen a. F beat s.o. to it

zuvorkommend adj obliging; polite

Zuwachs ['tsuːvaks] m (-es; no pl) increase, growth

'zuwachsen v/i (irr, wachsen, sep, -ge-, sein) become overgrown; MED close

zu'weilen [tsu-] adv occasionally, now and then

'zuweisen v/t (irr, weisen, sep, -ge-, h) assign

'zuwenden v/t and v/refl ([irr, wenden], sep, -ge-, h) turn to (a. fig)

'Zuwendung f (-; -en) a) payment, b) (no pl) attention; (loving) care, love, affection

zuwenig → zu

'zuwerfen v/t (irr, werfen, sep, -ge-, h) slam (shut); j-m et. zuwerfen throw s.o. s.th.; j-m e-n Blick zuwerfen cast a glance at s.o.

zu'wider [tsu-] adj: ... ist mir zuwider I hate or detest ...

zuwiderhandeln v/i (sep, -ge-, h) (dat) act contrary to; violate

'zuwinken v/i (sep, -ge-, h) wave to; signal to

zuzahlen v/t (sep, -ge-, h) pay extra

zuziehen (irr, ziehen, sep, -ge-) 1. v/t (h) draw (curtains etc); pull tight; fig consult; sich zuziehen MED catch; 2. v/i (sein) move in

zuzüglich ['tsuːtsyːklɪç] prp (gen) plus

Zvieri ['tsfiːri] Swiss m, n (-s; -s) afternoon snack, tea or coffee break

zwang [tsvaŋ] pret of zwingen

Zwang m (-[e]s; Zwänge ['tsvɛŋə]) compulsion, constraint; restraint; coercion; force; Zwang sein be compulsory

zwängen ['tsvɛŋən] v/t (ge-, h) press, squeeze, force

'zwanglos adj informal; casual

'Zwanglosigkeit f (-; no pl) informality

'Zwangsarbeit f JUR hard labo(u)r

Zwangsherrschaft f (-; no pl) despotism, tyranny

Zwangslage f predicament

'zwangsläufig adv inevitably

'Zwangsmaßnahme f sanction

Zwangsvollstreckung f JUR compulsory execution

Zwangsvorstellung f PSYCH obsession

'zwangsweise adv by force

zwanzig ['tsvantsɪç] adj twenty

'zwanzigste adj twentieth

zwar [tsvaːɐ] adv: ich kenne ihn zwar, aber ... I do know him, but ..., I know him all right, but ...; und zwar that is (to say), namely

Zweck [tsvɛk] m (-[e]s; -e) purpose, aim; s-n Zweck erfüllen serve its purpose; es hat keinen Zweck (zu warten etc) it's no use (waiting etc)

'zwecklos adj useless

'zweckmäßig adj practical; wise; TECH, ARCH functional

'Zweckmäßigkeit f (-; no pl) practicality, functionality

zwecks prp (gen) for the purpose of

zwei [tsvai] adj two

'zweibeinig [-bainɪç] adj two-legged

'Zweibettzimmer n twin-bedded room

'zweideutig [-dɔytɪç] adj ambiguous; off--colo(u)r

Zweier ['tsvaiɐ] m (-s; -) rowing: pair

zweierlei ['tsvaiɐlai] adj two kinds of

'zweifach adj double, twofold

Zweifa'milienhaus n duplex, Br two-family house

Zweifel ['tsvaifəl] m (-s; -) doubt

'zweifelhaft adj doubtful, dubious

'zweifellos adv undoubtedly, no or without doubt

'zweifeln v/i (ge-, h) zweifeln an (dat) doubt s.th., have one's doubts about

Zweig [tsvaik] m (-[e]s; -e) BOT branch (a. fig); twig

Zweiggeschäft n, Zweigniederlassung f, Zweigstelle f branch

'zweijährig [-jɛːrɪç] adj two-year-old, of two (years)

Zweikampf m duel

'zweimal adv twice

'zweimalig adj (twice) repeated

'zweimotorig [-motoːrɪç] adj twin-engined

zweireihig [-raiɪç] adj double-breasted (suit)

'zweischneidig adj double-edged, two--edged (both a. fig)

'zweiseitig [-zaitɪç] adj two-sided; reversible; POL bilateral; EDP double-sided

'Zweisitzer [-zɪtsɐ] m (-s; -) esp MOT two--seater

'zweisprachig [-ʃpraːxɪç] adj bilingual

'zweistimmig [-ʃtimɪç] adj MUS ... for two voices

'zweistöckig [-ʃtœkɪç] adj two-storied, Br two-storey ...

zweit [tsvait] adj second; ein zweiter ... another ...; jede(r, -s) zweite ... every other ...; aus zweiter Hand second-hand; *wir sind zu zweit* there are two of us

'zweitbeste *adj* second-best

'zweiteilig *adj* two-piece (*suit etc*)

zweitens ['tsvaitəns] *adv* secondly

'zweitklassig [-klasɪç] adj, 'zweitrangig [-raŋɪç] *adj* second-class *or* -rate

Zwerchfell ['tsvɛrç-] *n* ANAT diaphragm

Zwerg [tsvɛrk] *m* (-[e]s; -e ['tsvɛrgə]) dwarf; gnome; *fig* midget; *Zwerg... in cpds* BOT dwarf ...; ZO pygmy ...

Zwetsch(g)e ['tsvɛtʃ(g)ə] *f* (-; -n) BOT plum

zwicken ['tsvikən] *v/t and v/i* (*ge-, h*) pinch, nip

Zwieback ['tsvi:bak] *m* (-[e]s; -e, -bäcke [-bɛkə]) rusk, zwieback

Zwiebel ['tsvi:bəl] *f* (-; -n) GASTR onion; BOT bulb

Zwiegespräch ['tsvi:-] *n* dialog(ue)

'Zwielicht *n* (-[e]s; *no pl*) twilight

'Zwiespalt *m* (-[e]s; -e) conflict

'zwiespältig [-ʃpɛltɪç] *adj* conflicting

'Zwietracht *f* (-; *no pl*) discord

Zwilling ['tsvilɪŋ] *m* (-s; -e) twin; *pl* ASTR Gemini; *er ist (ein) Zwilling* he's a (a) Gemini

'Zwillingsbruder *m* twin brother

Zwillingsschwester *f* twin sister

Zwinge ['tsviŋə] *f* (-; -n) TECH clamp

zwingen ['tsviŋən] *v/t* (*irr, ge-, h*) force, compel

zwingend *adj* compelling; cogent

Zwinger ['tsviŋɐ] *m* (-s; -) kennels

zwinkern ['tsviŋkɐn] *v/i* (*ge-, h*) wink, blink

Zwirn [tsvirn] *m* (-[e]s; -e) thread, yarn, twist

zwischen ['tsviʃən] *prp* (*dat and acc*) between; among

'zwischen'durch F *adv* in between

'Zwischenergebnis *n* intermediate result

Zwischenfall *m* incident

Zwischenhändler *m* ECON middleman

Zwischenlandung *f* AVIAT stopover; *ohne Zwischenlandung* nonstop

'Zwischenraum *m* space, interval

Zwischenruf *m* (loud) interruption; *pl* heckling

Zwischenrufer *m* (-s; -) heckler

'Zwischenspiel *n* interlude

Zwischenstati,on *f* stop(over); *Zwischenstation machen* (*in dat*) stop over (in)

Zwischenwand *f* partition (wall)

'Zwischenzeit *f*: *in der Zwischenzeit* in the meantime, meanwhile

Zwist [tsvist] *m* (-[e]s; -e) discord

zwitschern ['tsvitʃɐn] *v/i* (*ge-, h*) twitter, chirp

Zwitter ['tsvitɐ] *m* (-s; -) BIOL hermaphrodite

zwölf [tsvœlf] *adj* twelve; *um zwölf (Uhr)* at twelve (o'clock); at noon; at midnight

'zwölfte *adj* twelfth

Zyankali [tsya:n'ka:li] *n* (-s; *no pl*) CHEM potassium cyanide

Zyklus ['tsy:klʊs] *m* (-; -klen) cycle; series, course

Zylinder [tsi'lindɐ] *m* (-s; -) top hat; MATH, TECH cylinder

zylindrisch [tsi'lindrɪʃ] *adj* cylindrical

Zyniker ['tsy:nikɐ] *m* (-s; -) cynic

zynisch ['tsy:nɪʃ] *adj* cynical

Zynismus [tsy'nismʊs] *m* (-; *-men*) cynicism

Zypresse [tsy'presə] *f* (-; -n) BOT cypress

Zyste ['tsystə] *f* (-; -n) MED cyst

z.Z(t). ABBR *of zur Zeit* at the moment, at present

Activity & Reference Section

The following section contains three parts, each of which will help you in your learning:

Games and puzzles to help you learn to use this dictionary and practice your German-language skills. You'll learn about the different features of this dictionary and how to look something up effectively.

Basic words and expressions to reinforce your learning and help you master the basics.

A short grammar reference to help you use the language correctly.

Using Your Dictionary

Using a bilingual dictionary is important if you want to speak, read or write in a foreign language. Unfortunately, if you don't understand the symbols in your dictionary or the structure of the entries, you'll make mistakes.

What kind of mistakes? Think of some of the words you know in English that sound or look alike. For example, think about the word *ring*. How many meanings can you think of for the word *ring*? Try to list at least three:

a. _____

b. _____

c. _____

Now look up *ring* in the English side of the dictionary. There are more than ten German words that correspond to the single English word *ring*. Some of these German words are listed below in scrambled form.

Unscramble the jumbled German words, then draw a line connecting each German word with the appropriate English meaning or context.

German jumble

1. LKGENNLI

2. NGRI

3. EGAEMN

4. FEANRNU

5. GRNIBXO

6. EIKRS

English meanings

a. a circle around something

b. the action a bell or telephone does (to ring)

c. jewelry worn on the finger

d. the boxing venue

e. one of the venues at a circus

f. the action of calling someone

With so many German words to choose from, each meaning something different, you must be careful to choose the right one to fit the context of your translation. Using the wrong word can make it hard for people to understand you. Imagine the confusing sentences you would make if you never looked beyond the first translation.

For example:

The boxer wearily entered the circle.

She always wore the circle left to her by her grandmother.

I was waiting for the phone to circle when there was a knock at the door.

If you choose the wrong meaning, you simply won't be understood. Mistakes like these are easy to avoid once you know what to look for when using your dictionary. The following pages will review the structure of your dictionary and show you how to pick the right word for your context. Read the tips and guidelines, then complete the puzzles and exercises to practice what you have learned.

Identifying Headwords

If you are looking for a single word in the dictionary, you simply look for that word's location in alphabetical order. However, if you are looking for a phrase, or an object that is described by several words, you will have to decide which word to look up.

Two-word terms are listed by their first word. If you are looking for the German equivalent of *shooting star*, you will find it under *shooting*.

So-called phrasal verbs, verbs used in combination with other words, are found in a block under the main verb. The phrasal verbs *go ahead*, *go at*, *go for*, *go on*, *go out*, and *go up* are all found in a block after *go*.

Idiomatic expressions are found under the key word in the expression. The phrase *give someone a ring*, meaning to call someone, is found in the entry for *ring*.

Headwords referring specifically to males or females with the same profession or nationality are listed together in alphabetical order. In German, a male dancer is called a **Tänzer** and a female dancer is a **Tänzerin**. Both of the words are found in alphabetical order under the masculine form, **Tänzer**.

Find the following words and phrases in your bilingual dictionary. Identify the headword that each is found under. Then, try to find all of the headwords in the word-search puzzle on the next page.

1. get the message
2. be in shock
3. give someone a break
4. make a dash for
5. with no strings attached
6. be mixed up with
7. minor key
8. get away with
9. it's going to rain
10. take advantage of
11. charakterisieren
12. 20 Minuten Verspätung haben
13. Hund
14. sich wahrsagen lassen
15. Apotheke

V	X	R	T	R	G	F	Z	N	A	M	D	N	V	W
K	E	V	V	N	E	P	R	C	D	I	D	Y	I	M
A	O	R	I	V	D	K	H	C	V	N	A	E	M	Y
G	K	R	S	A	C	A	E	G	A	O	I	O	E	U
Z	T	N	S	P	R	W	M	H	N	R	G	B	G	Q
S	F	H	K	A	Ä	X	D	W	T	E	O	Y	A	N
E	D	R	K	X	G	T	M	X	A	O	O	B	S	V
W	U	T	I	M	I	P	U	P	G	B	P	C	S	M
Z	E	D	N	U	H	M	A	N	E	Z	Z	A	E	P
R	H	K	J	B	O	Z	N	Q	G	I	E	N	M	T
N	E	G	A	S	R	H	A	W	S	H	O	C	K	E
C	Z	E	A	M	K	E	Q	Z	W	Q	U	Z	Q	G
M	Z	K	N	P	S	A	A	J	D	G	M	I	J	D
F	G	W	K	N	Z	O	P	K	F	N	O	G	X	W
N	P	E	K	C	O	O	P	V	Z	A	P	V	W	N

Alphabetization

The entries in a bilingual dictionary are in alphabetical order. If words begin with the same letter or letters, they are alphabetized from A to Z using the first unique letter in each word.

Umlauts ä, ö, and ü are treated the same as a, o, and u. If they are in a list together, the non-umlauted form goes before the umlauted one (schon, schön). The "eszet" (ß) is alphabetized as if it were ss.

Rewrite the following words in alphabetical order. Next to each word also write the number associated with it. Then follow that order to connect the dots on the next page. Not all of the dots will be used, only those whose numbers appear in the word list.

zu	1	langsam	54
anrufen	4	jährlich	56
zusammen	8	Regenmantel	64
schön	11	Gasthaus	65
Jacke	16	schon	68
Gast	22	Mechanikerin	72
Tante	28	Museum	73
interessant	33	Flughafen	76
hin und zurück	34	Bäckerei	78
Badehose	35	können	47
Öl	37	Computer	84
Weißwein	38	Elefant	87
Regenschirm	40	danke	90
trinken	46	wissen	93
kommen	82	Bad	98
fahren	49	Volkswagen	99
Ohrring	53		

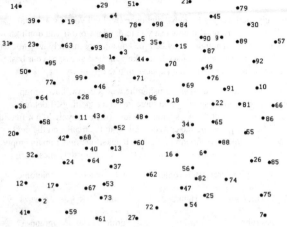

Welches Land sehen Sie?

__ __ __ __ __ __ __ __ __ __ __

Spelling

Like any dictionary, a bilingual dictionary will tell you if you have
spelled a word right. But how can you look up a word if you don't know
how to spell it? Though it may be time consuming, the only way to check
your spelling with a dictionary is to take your best guess, or your best
guesses, and look to see which appears in the dictionary.

Practice checking your spelling using the words below. Each group
includes one correct spelling and three incorrect spellings. Look up the
words and cross out the misspelled versions (the ones you do not find in
the dictionary). Rewrite the correct spelling in the blanks on the next
page. When you have filled in all of the blanks (one may remain empty
in some words), use the circled letters to reveal a mystery message.

1. telephonieren	televonieren	telewonieren	telefonieren
2. Hout	Haut	Häut	Howt
3. gruhn	gruin	grün	greun
4. Universität	Universitat	Universitaat	Universiteet
5. Addrese	Addresse	Adrässe	Adresse
6. Meßer	Mezser	Mezzer	Messer
7. Räzel	Retsel	Rätsel	Reezel
8. Hilfe	Hülfe	Hilpe	Helfe
9. Esszimmer	Ässzimmer	Eßzimmer	Eszimmer
10. Tish	Tisch	Tich	Tichs
11. Shild	Schildt	Schild	Schilt

1. _ _ _ _ _ ◯ _ _ _ _ _ _ _ _ _

2. _ ◯ _ _ _

3. _ _ _ ◯ _ _

4. _ _ _ _ _ _ _ ◯ _ _ _

5. ◯ _ _ _ _ _ _ _

6. _ _ ◯ _ _ _ _

7. _ _ ◯ _ _ _

8. _ ◯ _ _ _

9. _ _ ◯ _ _ _ _ _

10. _ _ _ ◯ _ _

11. _ _ ◯ _ _ _ _

_ _ _ _ _ _ _ _ _ _ _ !
1 2 3 4 5 6 7 8 9 10 11

Entries in Context

In addition to the literal translation of each headword in the dictionary, entries sometimes include compound words or phrases using that word.

Solve the crossword puzzle below using the correct word in context.

Hint: Each clue contains key words that will help you find the answer. Look up the key words in each clue. You'll find the answers in expressions within each entry.

ACROSS

3. You need to stay away from him. You must **von ihm** _____.

4. _____ (nowadays), many women have careers. This may not have been the case with previous generations.

6. Needing a light for her candle, she asked the man: "Haben Sie _____?"

10. The woman chased after the pickpocket, yelling "Halt! _____!"

12. I'm sorry. **Es tut mir** _____.

13. To answer the telephone is **ans Telefon** _____.

14. The sign indicating a one-way street reads _____.

15. She was so sad. She went home with a heavy heart, _____ **Herzens**.

DOWN

1. Last but not least! "Nicht _____ , nicht zu vergessen."

2. Those bright ornaments catch my eye. They **fallen ins** _____.

3. I had heard that my friend had been ill, so I asked how he was. I said: "_____ _____?" (4 words)

5. I'd prefer to eat on the open-air patio, **im** _____.

7. When the Germans fall in love, they _____ **sich**.

8. In order to reach my ideal weight, I must **25 Pfund** _____.

9. What a pity! Wie _____!

11. I wondered what time it was; I asked a friend, "Wie _____ ist es?"

Word Families

Some English words have several related meanings that are represented by different words in German. These related meanings belong to the same word family and are grouped together under a single English headword. Other words, while they look the same, do not belong to the same word family. These words are written under a separate headword.

Think back to our first example, *ring*. The translations **Ring**, **Boxring**, **Manege** and **Kreis** all refer to related meanings of *ring* in English. They are all circular things, though in different contexts. **Klingeln** and **anrufen**, however, refer to a totally different meaning of *ring* in English: the sound a bell or phone makes.

The word family for circles, with all of its nuanced German translations, is grouped together under *ring¹*. The word family for sounds is grouped together under *ring²*.

Study the lists of words below. Each group includes three German translations belonging to one word family, and one German translation of an identical-looking but unrelated English word. Eliminate the translation that is not in the same word family as the others. Then rewrite the misfit word in the corresponding blanks. When you have filled in all of the blanks, use the circled letters to reveal a bonus message.

Hint: Look up the German words to find out what they mean. Then look up those translations in the English-German side of your dictionary to find the word family that contains the German words.

1. klingeln	Manege	Ring	Kreis
2. leicht	unbedeutend	beleidigen	gering
3. stampfen	Briefmarke	trampeln	stempeln
4. Pause	ausruhen	rasten	Rest
5. Menge	Messe	Masse	Mehrzahl
6. stecken	Stock	Schläger	Zweig

1. (◯) __ __ __ __ __ __ __

2. __ __ (◯) __ __ __ __ __ __ __

3. __ __ __ __ __ (◯) __ __ __

4. __ __ (◯) __

5. __ __ __ (◯) __

6. __ __ (◯) __ __ __ __ __

__ __ __ __ __ __ !
 1   2   3   4   5   6

Running Heads

Running heads are the words printed in blue at the top of each page. The running head on the left tells you the first headword on the left-hand page. The running head on the right tells you the last headword on the right-hand page. All the words that fall in alphabetical order between the two running heads appear on those two dictionary pages.

Look up the running head on the page where each headword appears, and write it in the space provided. Then unscramble the jumbled running heads and match them with what you wrote.

Headword	Running head	Jumbled running head
1. Bart	BANKVERBINDUNG	UFRATZPU
2. Dunkelheit		IUJN
3. Gesundheit		DORK
4. Jugend		MENRUDCHKMO
5. Kartoffel		TRAUSSIMNE
6. konventionell		RADIESCHISPA
7. mitbringen		STSON
8. Nachmittag		BEUTANSCHGAL
9. Pass		SINNUNGELOSS
10. quatschen		VERGNUDNIBBNAK
11. Software		BRACHAN
12. Taxistand		PITAKALLANAEG

Pronunciation

Though German has more vowel sounds than English, pronunciation in the two languages is similar. Refer to the pronunciation guide in this dictionary to see equivalent sounds across the two languages. Study the guide to familiarize yourself with the symbols used to give pronunciations in this dictionary.

Practice recognizing pronunciations as they are written in the dictionary. Look at each of the pronunciations below, then connect it to its correct English or German spelling.

1. frend		A. Imbiss	
2. 'evri		B. language	
3. æpl		C. Bad	
4. naïf		D. every	
5. 'lægwidʒ		E. selig	
6. baːt		F. friend	
7. 'ımbıs		G. Fang	
8. 'zeˑlıç		H. knife	
9. faŋ		I. gekränkt	
10. gə'krɛŋkt		J. apple	

Parts of Speech

In German and English, words are categorized into different ***parts of speech***. These labels tell us what function a word performs in a sentence. In this dictionary, the part of speech is given before a word's definition.

Nouns are people, places or things. ***Verbs*** describe actions. ***Adjectives*** describe nouns in sentences. For example, the adjective *pretty* tells you about the noun *girl* in the phrase *a pretty girl*. ***Adverbs*** also describe, but they modify verbs, adjectives, and other adverbs. The adverb *quickly* tells you more about how the action is carried out in the phrase *ran quickly*. Adjectives usually take endings when used in a German sentence. Adverbs do not. Most adjectives are also used as adverbs. *The fast (adj) runners ran fast (adv) to the finish line.* The only way to identify whether a particular word is an adjective or adverb is to observe its use in the sentence.

Prepositions specify relationships in time and space. They are words such as *in*, *on*, *before*, or *with*. ***Articles*** are words that accompany nouns. Words like *the* and *a* or *an* modify the noun, marking it as specific or general, and known or unknown.

Conjunctions are words like *and*, *but*, and *if* that join phrases and sentences together. ***Pronouns*** take the place of nouns in a sentence.

The following activity uses words from the dictionary in a Sudoku-style puzzle. In Sudoku puzzles, the numbers 1 to 9 are used to fill in grids. All digits 1 to 9 must appear, but cannot be repeated, in each square, row, and column.

In the following puzzles, you are given a set of words for each part of the grid. Look up each word to find out its part of speech. Then arrange the words within the square so that, in the whole puzzle, you do not repeat any part of speech within a column or row.

Hint: If one of the words given in the puzzle is a noun, then you know that no other nouns can be put in that row or column of the grid. Use the process of elimination to figure out where the other parts of speech can go.

Let's try a small puzzle first. Use the categories noun *n*, verb *v*, adjective/adverb *adj/adv*, and preposition *prep* to solve this puzzle. Each section corresponds to one quarter of the puzzle.

Section 1

denken, Hund, schwarz, mit

Section 2

Euro, auf, machen, toll

Section 3

ehrlich, vor, Bilder, spielen

Section 4

Lotterie, staatlich, schaden, nach

denken (v)			**Euro** (n)
		schaden (v)	
ehrlich (adj/adv)			

Now try a larger puzzle. For this puzzle, use the categories noun *n*, verb *v*, adjective/adverb *adj/adv*, preposition *prep*, article *art*, and pronoun *pro*. The sections are numbered from top left to bottom right.

Section 1

Aufzug, attraktiv, **steigen**, wir, ein, über

Section 2

andere, ehe, **sortieren**, Bilder, das, sie

Section 3

mit, Käse, **planen**, mild, er, eine

Section 4

schreiben, **exklusiv**, du, die, **Lampen**, ohne

Section 5

nach, diskret, Etappe, wohnen, ich, der

Section 6

Familie, **ihm**, zwischen, gut, kaufen, einen

wir (pron)		steigen (v)	Bilder (n)		
Aufzug (n)					sortieren (v)
	planen (v)			Lampen (n)	
eine (art)	er (pron)			exklusiv (adj/adv)	
nach (prep)		der (art)			ihm (pron)
		ich (pron)	zwischen (prep)		

Pluralization of Nouns

There are sixteen different patterns used to pluralize German nouns. You can familiarize yourself with them in the appendix of this dictionary. The plural form is indicated in parentheses after the gender of the noun in its dictionary entry. First you see an –s, -(e)s or –es. That indicates the genitive form of the noun (the form that says *of the…*). Following that is the abbreviated indicator of the plural form. The symbol –e means that the word adds an –e to become plural. Many feminine nouns add –en in the plural. Many masculine and neuter nouns add an umlaut on the stem vowel and then an –e.

Write the plurals of the nouns in the list and then check your spelling by finding them in the following word search.

Singular	Plural
1. Kind	_____
2. Mutter	_____
3. Hund	_____
4. Bruder	_____
5. Auto	_____
6. Frau	_____
7. Haus	_____
8. Gericht	_____
9. Arbeiter	_____
10. Lehrerin	_____

A	F	A	A	E	S	M	J	Z	M	O	D	R	Q	T
D	R	L	B	U	T	O	H	K	C	C	G	E	Z	G
F	A	I	V	X	E	H	T	E	M	O	K	T	H	A
P	U	E	D	N	U	H	C	U	W	K	E	I	Y	T
U	E	I	Z	Q	M	H	A	I	A	S	O	E	H	Q
K	N	L	I	M	U	T	T	E	R	V	F	B	X	H
X	H	I	N	B	Q	B	F	Q	D	E	D	R	N	J
J	I	M	Z	Z	F	S	A	G	B	S	G	A	R	H
W	Q	V	W	F	B	K	R	V	M	R	A	O	A	O
N	E	N	N	I	R	E	R	H	E	L	Ü	U	T	B
B	E	U	T	A	D	S	J	L	S	L	S	D	Y	T
B	B	J	W	N	V	M	Z	N	N	E	R	A	E	X
D	T	D	I	W	P	L	E	Q	R	Z	S	J	H	R
K	P	K	Q	B	V	K	A	K	J	E	T	P	T	B
D	P	Y	O	X	T	C	J	Y	L	V	Y	Y	I	R

Gender

German nouns are easily recognizable. They are always capitalized, even in the middle of a sentence. They all belong to one of three groups: masculine, feminine, or neuter. A noun's gender is indicated in an entry after the headword or pronunciation with m for masculine, f for feminine, and n for neuter.

Look up the words listed below and mark the gender of each word. Then use the genders to lead you through the puzzle: if a word is masculine, go left; if a word is feminine, go right; if a word is neuter, go up.

	m (go left)	*f* (go right)	*n* (go up)
1. Gericht			
2. Katze			
3. Mond			
4. Sonne			
5. Wagen			
6. Kuchen			
7. Großmutter			
8. Freundschaft			
9. Aufzug			
10. Frühstück			
11. Person			
12. Professor			
13. Bestellung			
14. Reis			

Start

352

Adjectives

In German, adjectives take different endings in order to agree in gender and number with the noun they modify. In most cases, an –e is added to the adjective for the feminine form, and an –n is added for the plural form. A table of adjective endings can be found in the appendix of this dictionary.

Use the dictionary to determine whether the nouns in the following phrases are masculine or feminine, singular or plural. Then write in the correct form of the adjective to complete the phrase. We have added the correct endings for you. Check your answers against the word search. The correct forms will be found in the puzzle with their endings.

1. a friendly smile = ein _____es Lächeln

2. a blonde woman = eine _____e Frau

3. an important message = eine _____e Nachricht

4. public school = _____e Schule

5. the green car = der _____e Wagen

6. an unforgettable picnic = ein _____es Picknick

7. a pretty girl = ein _____es Mädchen

8. in a good book = in einem _____en Buch

9. an interesting speaker = ein _____er Redner

10. a German piano player = ein _____er Klavierspieler

11. a heavy backback = ein _____er Rucksack

U	E	T	R	Y	G	M	I	E	S	X	O	V	J	X
K	N	H	O	E	A	C	N	F	C	V	H	L	Z	M
S	H	V	M	D	N	N	T	R	H	D	V	V	C	D
F	L	X	E	X	O	U	E	Y	W	G	R	G	Z	E
W	W	Q	F	R	Y	P	R	X	E	F	Q	S	G	H
L	I	M	T	N	G	S	E	G	R	N	M	V	O	C
W	L	C	M	N	C	E	S	R	E	E	G	N	B	I
F	M	N	H	H	K	I	S	S	R	T	R	F	J	L
Q	B	W	Ö	T	B	X	A	S	L	U	J	D	L	T
Z	C	N	Q	H	I	H	N	F	L	G	Y	S	E	N
Q	E	X	Q	J	F	G	T	W	O	I	E	K	T	E
S	E	D	N	O	L	B	E	V	Z	I	C	F	C	F
N	D	U	R	F	U	S	R	M	B	T	O	H	X	F
S	E	H	C	I	L	D	N	U	E	R	F	I	E	Ö
D	E	U	T	S	C	H	E	R	K	L	E	B	C	S

Verbs

Verbs are listed in the dictionary in their infinitive form. To use the verb in a sentence, you must conjugate it and use the form that agrees with the sentence's subject.

Most verbs are regular and conjugate like the chart in the appendix of this dictionary. A few are irregular and require a vowel change in the present tense. A list of all irregular verbs can also be found in the appendix.

For this puzzle, conjugate the given verbs in the present tense. Use the context and the subject pronoun to determine the person and number of the form you need. The correct answer fits in the crossword spaces provided.

ACROSS

2. Am Samstag _____ es auch einen Gemüsemarkt in der Marburger Straße. **geben**

4. Das Kind _____ mit seinen Freunden ins Kino. **gehen**

6. Zur gleichen Zeit _____ ich in die Stadt einkaufen. **fahren**

7. Der Film _____ den Kindern gut. Sie wollen ihn ein zweites Mal sehen. **gefallen**

9. Die Nachbarin _____ dem Ehepaar zum Hochzeitstag. **gratulieren**

12. Was _____ ich meinen Eltern zum Hochzeitstag? Zwei Schiffskarten für eine Kreuzfahrt im Mittelmeer. **schenken**

13. Wir _____ drei Dutzend Eier, da wir backen wollen. **kaufen**

14. Mein Vater _____ seine neue Digitalkamera auf die Reise mit. **nehmen**

17. Die Suppe _____ der Familie sehr gut und ist sehr gesund. **schmecken**

18. Die Feier war so toll, dass alle Gäste nächstes Jahr wieder kommen _____ . **wollen**

DOWN

1. Die Kinder _____ den Film "Superman" am Samstag an. **sehen**

3. Der Supermarkt _____ Eier zum halben Preis an. **bieten**

5. Mein Mann _____ den Kindern immer bei den Hausaufgaben. Er ist Lehrer. **helfen**

6. Die Großeltern _____ am Sonntag ihren fünfzigsten Hochzeitstag. **feiern**

8. Meine Nachbarn _____ den Brokkoli vom Leoni-Markt. **mögen**

10. Bevor sie wegfahren, _____ sie uns immer an und verabschieden sich. **rufen**

11. Katarina _____ früh nach Hause gehen und ihre Hausaufgaben für Montag machen. **müssen**

12. Morgen _____ die ganze Familie nach Ulm zu den Großeltern. **fahren**

16. Meine 10-jährige Tochter _____ jeden Abend in ihr Tagebuch. **schreiben**

17. Seine Bilder _____ sehr gut geworden. **sein**

19. Mein Babysitter muss heute schon früh gehen, also _____ ich nur 15 Minuten auf der Fete. **bleiben**

When you are reading German, you face a different challenge. You see a conjugated verb in context and need to determine what its infinitive is in order to understand its meaning.

Often you will see a preposition at the end of the sentence with no object. That's called a separable prefix and is considered part of the verb. **Ich rufe meine Mutter jetzt an.** The verb is **anrufen**. The prefix **an** is separated from the verb in the sentence, but must be added back onto the infinitive in order to insure that you find the correct meaning.

For the next puzzle, you will see conjugated verbs in the sentences. Figure out which verb the conjugated form represents, and write the infinitive (the headword form) in the puzzle.

ACROSS

2. Das Kind **versteckte** seinen Teddybär unter seinem Kopfkissen.

3. Machst du eine Diät? Du **siehst** gut **aus**.

6. Das brave Kind **gehorcht** seinen Eltern immer.

8. Gerd und Gerlinde **kamen** drei Stunden zu spät **an**.

10. Matthias **weiß**, wie wir hinkommen.

11. Wir **rufen** unsere Tante um sechs Uhr **an**.

13. Sie **steht** jeden Morgen um 7.30 **auf**.

16. Der Film **gefällt** den Kindern.

17. Sie **isst** jeden Abend zusammen mit ihrer Familie.

18. Das Telefon **klingelt** sehr laut.

DOWN

1. Carsten **bestellt** ein Käsebrot mit einem Glas Bier.

4. Die Katze **schläft** in der Sonne.

5. Ich **verstehe** nicht, was der Lehrer sagt.

7. Der König **heiratet** seine Prinzessin am Dienstag in der Schlosskapelle.

9. **Kannst** du mir helfen?

12. Du **hast verloren**!

14. Ich **sehe** dich hinter der Couch!

15. Die Schauspielerinnen **sind** sehr hübsch.

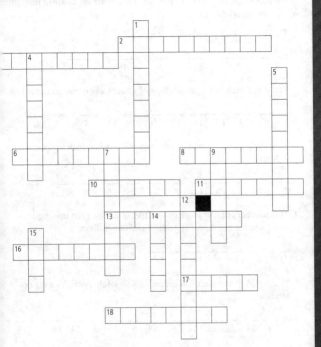

Riddles

Solve the following riddles in English. Then write the German translation of the answer on the lines.

1. This cold season is followed by spring.

___ ___ ___ ___ ___ ___
6   9   12   5   18   10

2. You don't want to forget this type of glasses when you go to the beach.

___ ___ ___ ___ ___ ___ ___ ___ ___ ___ ___ ___
3 17 12 12 18 12 11 10 9 1 1 18

3. This thing protects you from the rain, but it's bad luck to open it indoors!

___ ___ ___ ___ ___ ___ ___ ___ ___ ___ ___
10 18 23 18 12 3 24 25 9 10 21

4. This number comes before the number one. You need this digit to write out the numbers ten, twenty, and one million.

___ ___ ___ ___
12 14 1 1

5. You fasten this around you to remain safe while riding in a car or airplane.

___ ___ ___ ___ ___ ___ ___ ___ ___ ___ ___ ___ ___ ___ ___
3 9 24 25 18 10 25 18 9 5 3 23 14 10 5

6. If you are injured or very ill, you should go to this place.

___ ___ ___ ___ ___ ___ ___ ___ ___ ___ ___
7 10 15 12 7 18 12 25 15 14 3

7. This mode of transportation has only two wheels. It is also good exercise!

___ ___ ___ ___ ___ ___ ___
13 15 25 10 10 15 2

8. This large mammal lives in the ocean.

___ ___ ___
6   15   1

9. This person is your mother's mother.

___ ___ ___ ___ ___ ___ ___ ___ ___ ___
23   10   17   27   21   14   5   5   18   10

10. There are twelve of these in a year.

___ ___ ___ ___ ___ ___
21   17   12   15   5   18

11. Snow White bit into this red fruit and fell into a long slumber.

___ ___ ___ ___ ___
15   4   13   18   1

12. This professional brings letters and packages to your door.

___ ___ ___ ___ ___ ___ ___ ___ ___ ___ ___
11   10   9   18   13   5   10   8   23   18   10

13. This midday meal falls between breakfast and dinner.

___ ___ ___ ___ ___ ___ ___ ___ ___ ___ ___
21   9   5   5   15   23   18   3   3   18   12

14. A very young cat is referred to as this.

___ ___ ___ ___ ___ ___ ___ ___
7   8   5   16   24   25   28   12

15. An archer uses a bow and this.

___ ___ ___ ___ ___
4   13   18   9   1

16. My mother was married to this relative of mine when she was twenty-three.

___ ___ ___ ___ ___
19   15   5   18   10

Cryptogram

Write the letter that corresponds to each number in the spaces. When you are done, read the German message. It's a quote from a famous German author and expresses our wish that you look forward to your German language experience.

21	15	12		21	14	3	3		9	21	21
18	10		18	5	6	15	3		25	15	11
18	12		6	17	10	15	14	13		21	15
12		3	9	24	25		13	10	18	14	5
	16	9	5	15	5		19	17	12		18
2	14	15	10	2		21	Ö	10	9	7	18

"___ ___ ___   ___ ___ ___ ___ ___   ___ ___ ___ ___ ___ ___ ___ ___

___ ___ ___ ___ ___ ___   ___ ___ ___ ___ ___ ___ ,

___ ___ ___ ___ ___ ___ ___ ___ ___ ___ ___ ___ ___ ___ ___ ___ ___ ___ ___

___ ___ ___ ___ ___ ___ ___ , " ___ ___ ___ ___ ___ ___ ___

___ ___ ___

___ ___ ___ ___ ___ ___ ___ ___   ___ ___ ___ ___ ___ ___

Answer Key

Using Your Dictionary

a–c. Answers will vary

1. klingeln, b
2. Ring, c
3. Manege, e

4. anrufen, f
5. Boxring, d
6. Kreis, a

Identifying Headwords

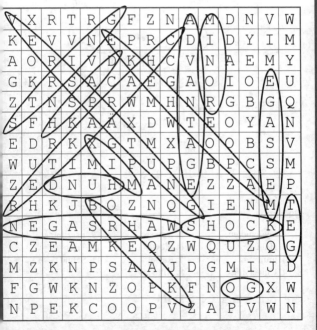

Alphabetization

anrufen, Bäckerei, Bad, Badehose, Computer, danke, Elefant, fahren,
Flughafen, Gast, Gasthaus, hin und zurück, interessant, Jacke,
jährlich, kommen, können, langsam, Mechanikerin, Museum,
Ohrring, Öl, Regenmantel, Regenschirm, schon, schön, Tante, trinken,
Volkswagen, Weißwein, wissen, zu, zusammen

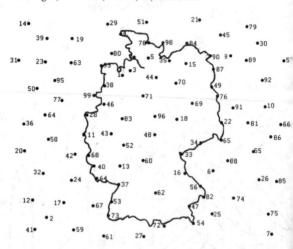

D E U T S C H L A N D

Spelling

1. telefonieren   5. Adresse   9. Esszimmer
2. Haut   6. Messer   10. Tisch
3. grün   7. Rätsel   11. Schild
4. Universität   8. Hilfe

F A N T A S T I S C H !

Entries in Context

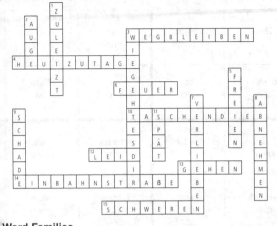

Word Families

1. klingeln
2. beleidigen
3. Briefmarke

4. Rest
5. Messe
6. stecken

K L A S S E!

Pronunciation

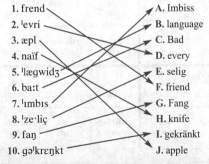

1. frend
2. ˈevri
3. æpl
4. naïf
5. ˈlægwidʒ
6. baɪt
7. ˈɪmbɪs
8. ˈzeˑliç
9. faŋ
10. gəˈkreŋkt

A. Imbiss
B. language
C. Bad
D. every
E. selig
F. friend
G. Fang
H. knife
I. gekränkt
J. apple

Parts of Speech

Hund (n)	schwarz (adj/adv)	auf (prep)	machen (v)
denken (v)	mit (prep)	toll (adj/adv)	**Euro** (n)
vor (prep)	Bilder (n)	**schaden** (v)	staatlich (adj/adv)
ehrlich (adj/adv)	spielen (v)	Lotterie (n)	nach (prep)

wir (pron)	**ein** (art)	**steigen** (v)	**Bilder** (n)	ehe (prep)	andere (adj/adv)
Aufzug (n)	**über** (prep)	attraktiv (adj/adv)	das (art)	sie (pron)	**sotieren** (v)
mild (adj/adv)	**planen** (v)	mit (prep)	du (pron)	**Lampen** (n)	sie (art)
eine (art)	**er** (pron)	Käse (n)	schreiben (v)	**exklusiv** (adj/adv)	ohne (prep)
nach (prep)	Etappe (n)	**der** (art)	gut (adj/adv)	kaufen (v)	**ihm** (pron)
wohnen (v)	diskret (adj/adv)	**ich** (pron)	**zwischen** (prep)	einen (art)	Familie (n)

Pluralization of Nouns

A	F	A	A	E	S	M	J	Z	M	O	D	R	Q	T
D	R	L	B	U	T	O	H	K	C	C	G	E	Z	G
F	A	I	V	X	E	H	T	E	M	O	K	T	H	A
P	U	E	D	N	U	H	C	U	W	K	E	I	Y	T
U	E	I	Z	Q	M	H	A	I	A	S	O	E	H	Q
K	N	L	I	M	Ü	T	T	E	R	V	F	B	X	H
X	H	I	N	B	Q	B	F	Q	D	E	D	R	N	J
J	I	M	Z	Z	F	S	A	G	B	S	A	R	H
W	Q	V	W	F	B	K	R	V	M	R	A	O	A	O
N	E	N	N	I	R	E	R	H	E	L	U	U	T	B
B	E	U	T	A	D	S	J	L	S	I	S	D	Y	T
B	B	J	W	N	V	M	Z	N	N	E	R	A	E	X
D	T	D	I	W	P	L	E	Q	R	Z	S	J	H	R
K	P	K	Q	B	V	K	A	K	J	E	T	P	T	B
D	P	Y	O	X	T	C	J	Y	L	V	Y	Y	I	R

Kinder, Mütter, Hunde, Brüder, Autos, Frauen, Häuser, Gerichte, Arbeiter, Lehrerinnen

Gender

1. Gericht *n* 2. Katze *f* 3. Kind *n* 4. Sonne *f* 5. Auto *n*
6. Kuchen *m* 7. Holz *n* 8. Freundschaft *f* 9. Bett *n*
10. Person *f* 11. Brot *n* 12. Bestellung *f* 13. Pferd *n*

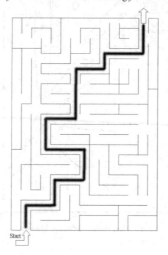

Running Heads

Headword	Running head	*Jumbled running head*
1. Bart	BANKVERBINDUNG	UFRATZPU
2. Dunkelheit	DURCHKOMMEN	IUJN
3. Gesundheit	GESINNUNGSLOS	DORK
4. Jugend	JUNI	MENRUDCHKMO
5. Kartoffel	KAPITALANLAGE	TRAUSSIMNE
6. konventionell	KORD	RADIESCHISPA
7. mitbringen	MISSTRAUEN	STSON
8. Nachmittag	NACHBAR	BEUTANSCHGAL
9. Pass	PARADIESISCH	SINNUNGELOSS
10. quatschen	PUTZFRAU	VERGNUDNIBBNAK
11. Software	SONST	BRACHAN
12. Taxistand	TAUBENSCHLAG	PITAKALLANAEG

Adjectives

1. ein freundliches Lächeln
2. eine blonde Frau
3. eine wichtige Nachricht
4. öffentliche Schule
5. der grüne Wagen
6. ein unvergessliches Picknick
7. ein schönes Mädchen
8. in einem guten Buch
9. ein interessanter Redner
10. ein deutscher Klavierspieler
11. ein schwerer Rucksack

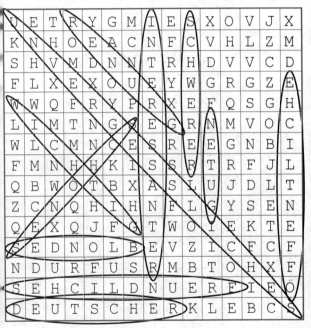

Verbs

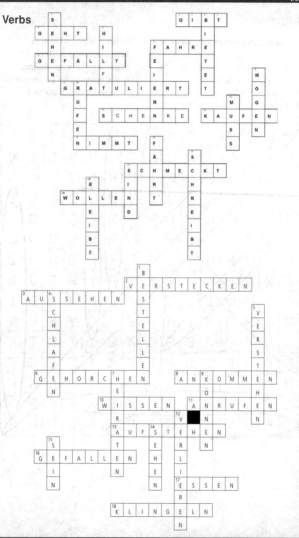

Riddles

1. Winter	9. Großmutter
2. Sonnenbrille	10. Monate
3. Regenschirm	11. Apfel
4. null	12. Briefträger
5. Sicherheitsgurt	13. Mittagessen
6. Krankenhaus	14. Kätzchen
7. Fahrrad	15. Pfeil
8. Wal	16. Vater

Cryptogram

21	15	12		21	14	3	3		9	21	21
M	A	N		M	U	S	S		I	M	M
18	10		18	5	6	15	3		25	15	11
E	R		E	T	W	A	S		H	A	B
18	12		6	17	10	15	14	13		21	15
E	N		W	O	R	A	U	F		M	A
12		3	9	24	25		13	10	18	14	5
N		S	I	C	H		F	R	E	U	T
	16	9	5	15	5		19	17	12		18
	Z	I	T	A	T		V	O	N		E
2	14	15	10	2		21		10	9	7	18
D	U	A	R	D		M	Ö	R	I	K	E

„Man muss immer etwas haben, worauf man sich freut." Zitat von Eduard Mörike.

Eduard Mörike was a German lyrical poet who lived from 1805–1875 and wrote that, "One must always have something to look forward to." We hope that you look forward to learning German and to working with this dictionary.

BASIC GERMAN PHRASES & GRAMMAR

Pronunciation

In this section we have used a simplified phonetic system to represent the sounds of German. Simply read the pronunciation as if it were English.

Stress

Generally, as in English, the first syllable is stressed in German, except when short prefixes are added to the beginning of the word. Then the second syllable is stressed (e.g. **bewegen** *to move*, **gesehen** *seen*).

BASIC PHRASES

Essential

Good afternoon!	**Guten Tag!**	goo-ten tahk
Good evening!	**Guten Abend!**	goo-ten ah-bent
Goodbye!	**Auf Wiedersehen!**	owf vee-duh-zay-en
…, please!	**…, bitte!**	bit-tuh
Thank you!	**Danke!**	dahn-kuh
Yes.	**Ja.**	yah
No.	**Nein.**	nine
Sorry!	**Entschuldigung!**	ent-shool-dee-goong
Where are the restrooms?	**Wo ist die Toilette?**	vo ist dee toi-let-tuh
When?	**Wann?**	vahn
What?	**Was?**	vahs
Where?	**Wo?**	vo
Here.	**Hier.**	here
There.	**Dort.**	dawt
On the right.	**Rechts.**	rekhts
On the left.	**Links.**	linx
Do you have …?	**Haben Sie …?**	hah-ben zee
I'd like …	**Ich möchte …**	ikh merkh-tuh
How much is that?	**Was kostet das?**	vahs kaws-tet dahs
Where is …?	**Wo ist …?**	vo ist
Where can I get …?	**Wo gibt es …?**	vo gheept es

Communication Difficulties

Do you speak English?	**Sprechen Sie Englisch?**	shpre-khen zee ayng-lish
Does anyone here speak English?	**Spricht hier jemand Englisch?**	shprikht here yay-mahnt ayng-lish
Did you understand that?	**Haben Sie das verstanden?**	hah-ben zee dahs fair-stahn-den
I understand.	**Ich habe verstanden.**	ikh hah-beh fair-shtahnd-den
I didn't understand that.	**Ich habe das nicht verstanden.**	ikh hah-beh dahs nikht fair-shtahn-den
Could you speak a bit more slowly, please?	**Könnten Sie bitte etwas langsamer sprechen?**	kern-ten zee bit-tuh et-vahs lahng-zah-mer shpre-khen
Could you please repeat that?	**Könnten Sie das bitte wiederholen?**	kern-ten zee dahs bit-tuh veeder-ho-len
What's that in German?	**Wie heißt das auf Deutsch?**	vee highst dahs owf doitch
What does … mean?	**Was bedeutet …?**	vahs buh-doi-tet
Could you write it down for me, please?	**Könnten Sie es mir bitte aufschreiben?**	kern-ten zee es meer bit-tuh owf-shry-ben

Greetings

Good morning!	**Guten Morgen!**	goo-ten maw-ghen
Good afternoon!	**Guten Tag!**	goo-ten tahk
Good evening!	**Guten Abend!**	goo-ten ah-bent
Goodnight!	**Gute Nacht!**	goo-tuh nakht
Hello!	**Hallo!**	hah-lo
How are you?	**Wie geht es Ihnen / dir?**	vee gate es ee-nen / deer
Fine, thanks. And you?	**Danke, gut. Und Ihnen / dir?**	dahn-kuh goot oont eenen / deer
I'm afraid I have to go.	**Es tut mir Leid, aber ich muss gehen.**	es toot meer lite ah-buh ikh moos gain
Goodbye!	**Auf Wiedersehen!**	owf vee-duh-zay-en
See you soon / tomorrow!	**Bis bald / morgen!**	bis bahlt / maw-ghen
Bye!	**Tschüs!**	chews

| It was nice meeting you. | **Schön, Sie / dich kennen gelernt zu haben.** | shern zee / dikh ken-nen guh-lairnt tsoo hah-ben |
| Have a good trip! | **Gute Reise!** | goo-tuh reye-suh |

Meeting People

What's your name?	**Wie heißen Sie / heißt du?**	vee high-sen zee / highst doo
My name is …	**Ich heiße …**	ikh high-suh
May I introduce …	**Darf ich bekannt machen? Das ist …**	dahf ikh buh-kahnt mah-khen dahs ist
– my husband.	**mein Mann.**	mighn mahn
– my wife.	**meine Frau.**	migh-nuh frow
– my boyfriend.	**mein Freund.**	mighn froint
– my girlfriend.	**meine Freundin.**	migh-nuh froin-din
Where are you from?	**Woher sind Sie?**	vo-hair zind zee
I'm from …	**Ich komme aus …**	ikh kom-uh ows
– the US.	**den USA.**	dane oo-es-ah
– Canada.	**Kanada.**	kah-nah-dah
– the UK.	**Großbritannien.**	gross-brit-tahn-ee-en

Expressing Likes and Dislikes

Very good!	**Sehr gut!**	zair goot
I'm very happy.	**Ich bin sehr zufrieden!**	ikh bin zair tsoo-free-den
I like that.	**Das gefällt mir.**	dahs guh-felt meer
What a shame!	**Wie schade!**	vee shah-duh
I'd rather …	**Ich würde lieber …**	ikh vewr-duh lee-buh …
I don't like it.	**Das gefällt mir nicht.**	dahs guh-felt meer nikht
I'd rather not.	**Das möchte ich lieber nicht.**	dahs merkh-tuh ikh lee-buh nisht
Certainly not.	**Auf keinen Fall.**	owf keye-nen fahl

373

Expressing Requests and Thanks

English	German	Pronunciation
Thank you very much.	Vielen Dank.	fee-len dahnk
Thanks, you too.	Danke, gleichfalls.	dahn-kuh gleyekh-fahls
May I?	Darf ich?	dahf ikh
Please, …	Bitte, …	bit-tuh
No, thank you.	Nein, danke.	nine dahn-kuh
Could you help me, please?	Könnten Sie mir bitte helfen?	kern-ten zee meer bit-tuh hel-fen
Thank you, that's very nice of you.	Vielen Dank, das ist sehr nett von Ihnen.	fee-len dahnk dahs ist zair net fun ee-nen
Thank you very much for all your trouble / help.	Vielen Dank für Ihre Mühe / Hilfe.	fee-len dahnk fewr ee-ruh mew-uh / hil-fuh
You're welcome.	Gern geschehen.	gehrn guh-shay-en
Sorry!	Entschuldigung!	ent-shool-dee-goong
Excuse me!	Entschuldigen Sie!	ent-shool-dee-ghen zee
I'm sorry about that.	Das tut mir Leid.	dahs toot meer lite
Don't worry about it!	Macht nichts!	makht nikhts
How embarrassing!	Das ist mir sehr unangenehm.	dahs ist meer zair oon-ahn-guh-name
It was a misunderstanding.	Das war ein Missverständnis.	dahs vah eye-n miss-fair-shtent-niss

GRAMMAR

Regular Verbs and Their Tenses

The past is often expressed by using *to have* haben + past participle. The future is formed with werden + infinitive.

Infinitive:	kaufen *to buy*	arbeiten *to work*
Past Participle:	gekauft *bought*	gearbeitet *worked*

	Present	*Past*	*Future*
ich *I*	kaufe	habe gekauft	werde kaufen
du *you inform.*	kaufst	hast gekauft	wirst kaufen
Sie *you form.*	kaufen	haben gekauft	werden kaufen
er/sie/es *he/she/it*	kauft	hat gekauft	wird kaufen
wir *we*	kaufen	haben gekauft	werden kaufen
ihr *you pl. inform.*	kauft	habt gekauft	werdet kaufen
Sie *you pl. form.*	kaufen	haben gekauft	werden kaufen
sie *they*	kaufen	haben gekauft	werden kaufen

Irregular verbs have to be memorized. Verbs that indicate movement are conjugated with *to be* sein, e.g. *to go* gehen:

	Present	*Past*	*Future*
ich *I*	gehe	bin gegangen	werde gehen
du *you inform.*	gehst	bist gegangen	wirst gehen
Sie *you form.*	gehen	sind gegangen	werden gehen
er/sie/es *he/she/it*	geht	ist gegangen	wird gehen
wir *we*	gehen	sind gegangen	werden gehen
ihr *you pl. inform.*	geht	seid gegangen	werdet gehen
Sie *you pl. form.*	gehen	sind gegangen	werden gehen
sie *they*	gehen	sind gegangen	werden gehen

To express future, usually the present tense is used together with a time adverb: *I'll work tomorrow.* **Ich arbeite morgen.**

Nouns and Articles

All nouns are written with a capital letter. Their definite articles indicate their gender: **der** (masculine = m), **die** (feminine = f), **das** (neuter = n). The plural article is always **die**, regardless of gender.

Examples:	*Singular*	*Plural*
	der Mann *the man*	die Männer *the men*
	die Frau *the woman*	die Frauen *the women*
	das Kind *the child*	die Kinder *the children*

The indefinite article also indicates the gender of the noun: ein (m, n), eine (f). There is no indefinite article in the plural.

Examples:	*Singular*	*Plural*
	ein Zug *a train*	Züge *trains*
	eine Karte *a map*	Karten *maps*

Possessives also relate to the gender of the noun that follows.

Nominative (m, n/f)	Accusative (n/f/m)	Dative (m, n/f)
mein/e *my*	mein/e/en *my*	meinem / meiner *my*
dein/e *your inform.*	dein/e/en *your*	deinem / deiner *your*
Ihr/e *your form.*	Ihr/e/en *your*	Ihrem / Ihrer *your*
sein/e *his*	sein/e/en *his*	seinem / seiner *his*
ihr/e *her*	ihr/e/en *her*	ihrem / ihrer *her*
sein/e *its*	sein/e/en *its*	seinem / seiner *its*
unser/e *our*	unser/e/en *our*	unserem / unserer *our*
euer/e *your pl. inform.*	euer/e/en *your*	eurem / eurer *your*
Ihr/e *your pl. form.*	Ihr/e/en *your*	Ihrem / Ihrer *your*
ihr/e *their*	ihr/e/en *their*	ihrem / ihrer *their*

Examples:	Wo ist meine Fahrkarte?	*Where is my ticket?*
	Ihr Taxi ist hier.	*Your taxi is here.*
	Hier ist euer Pass.	*Here is your passport.*

Word Order

The conjugated verb comes after the subject and before the object. When a sentence doesn't begin with a subject, the word order changes.

Examples:	Er ist in Berlin.	*He is in Berlin.*
	Heute ist er in Berlin.	*Today he is in Berlin.*
	Wir sind in Berlin gewesen.	*We were in Berlin.*

Questions are formed by reversing the order of subject and verb.

Examples:	Haben Sie Bücher?	*Do you have books?*
	Wie ist das Wetter?	*How is the weather?*
	Seid ihr in Köln gewesen?	*Have you been to Cologne?*

Negations

Negative sentences are formed by adding **nicht** (*not*) to that part of the sentence which is to be negated.

Examples:	Wir rauchen nicht.	We don't smoke.
	Der Bus fährt nicht ab.	The bus doesn't leave.
	Warum schreibst du nicht?	Why don't you write?

If a noun is used, the negation is made by adding **kein**. Its ending is defined by the noun's gender.

Examples:	Ich trinke kein Bier.	*I don't drink beer.*
	Wir haben keine Einzelzimmer.	*We don't have any single rooms.*
	Gibt es keinen Zimmerservice?	*Is there no room service?*

Imperatives (Command Form)

du *you sing. inform.*	Geh! *Go!*	Sei still! *Be quiet!*
ihr *you pl. inform.*	Geht! *Go!*	Seid still! *Be quiet!*
Sie *you sing./pl. form.*	Gehen Sie! *Go!*	Seien Sie still! *Be quiet!*
wir *we*	Gehen wir! *Let's go!*	Seien wir still! *Let's be quiet!*

| *Examples:* | Hört mal alle zu! | *Listen everybody!* |
| | Seid nicht so laut! | *Don't be so noisy!* |

Pronouns

Pronouns serve as substitutes for nouns and relate to their gender.

Nominative	*Accusative*	*Dative*
ich *I*	mich *me*	mir *me*
du *you inform.*	dich *you*	dir *you*
Sie *you form.*	Sie *you*	Ihnen *you*

er *he*	ihn *him*	ihm *him*
sie *she*	sie *her*	ihr *her*
es *it*	es *it*	ihm *him*
wir *we*	uns *us*	uns *us*
ihr *you pl. inform.*	euch *you*	euch *you*
Sie *you pl. form.*	Sie *you*	Ihnen *you*
sie *they*	sie *them*	ihnen *them*

Examples: Ich sehe sie. — *I see them.*
Hören Sie mich? — *Do you hear me?*

Adjectives

Adjectives describe nouns. Their endings depend on the case.

Examples: Wir haben ein altes Auto. — *We have an old car.*
Wo ist mein neuer Koffer? — *Where is my new suitcase?*
Gute Arbeit, Richard! — *Good work, Richard!*

Adverbs and Adverbial Expressions

In German, adverbs are usually identical with adjectives. They describe verbs but, unlike adjectives, their endings don't change.

Examples: Linda fährt sehr langsam. — *Linda drives very slowly.*
Robert ist sehr nett. — *Robert is very nice.*
Sie sprechen gut Deutsch. — *You speak German well.*

Some common adverbial time expressions:

zurzeit	*presently*
bald	*soon*
immer noch	*still*
nicht mehr	*not anymore*

Comparisons and Superlatives

Most German adjectives add –er for their comparative and –(e)st for their superlative. The following list contains only a small selection to illustrate formation and irregularities.

Adjective	Comparative	Superlative
klein *small, little*	kleiner *smaller*	am kleinsten *the smallest*
billig *cheap*	billiger *cheaper*	am billigsten *the cheapest*
neu *new*	neuer *newer*	am neusten *the newest*
schlecht *bad*	schlechter *worse*	am schlechtesten *the worst*
groß *big, large*	größer *bigger*	am größten *the biggest*
alt *old*	älter *older*	am ältesten *the oldest*
lang *long*	länger *longer*	am längsten *the longest*
kurz *short*	kürzer *shorter*	am kürzesten *the shortest*
gut *good*	besser *better*	am besten *the best*
teuer *expensive*	teurer *more expensive*	am teuersten *the most expensive*
Examples:	Diese Postkarten sind billiger.	*These postcards are cheaper.*
	Wo ist der beste Buchladen?	*Where is the best bookstore?*

A

A, a A, a n; **from A to Z** von A bis Z

A grade Eins

a before vowel: **an** indef art ein(e); per, pro, je; **not a(n)** kein(e); **all of a size** alle gleich groß; **100 dollars a year** 100 Dollar im Jahr; **twice a week** zweimal die or in der Woche

a·back: taken aback überrascht, verblüfft; bestürzt

a·ban·don aufgeben, preisgeben; verlassen; überlassen; **be found abandoned** MOT etc verlassen aufgefunden werden

a·base erniedrigen, demütigen

a·base·ment Erniedrigung f, Demütigung f

a·bashed verlegen

ab·at·toir Br Schlachthof m

ab·bess REL Äbtissin f

ab·bey REL Kloster n; Abtei f

ab·bot REL Abt m

ab·bre·vi·ate (ab)kürzen

ab·bre·vi·a·tion Abkürzung f, Kurzform f

ABC Abc n, Alphabet n

ab·di·cate Amt, Recht etc aufgeben, verzichten auf (acc); **abdicate (from) the throne** abdanken

ab·di·ca·tion Verzicht m; Abdankung f

ab·do·men ANAT Unterleib m

ab·dom·i·nal ANAT Unterleibs...

ab·er·ra·tion Verirrung f

a·bet → **aid** l

ab·hor verabscheuen

ab·hor·rence Abscheu m (**of** vor dat)

ab·hor·rent zuwider (**to** dat); abstoßend

a·bide v/i: **abide by the law** etc sich an das Gesetz etc halten; v/t: **he can't abide him** er kann ihn nicht ausstehen

a·bil·i·ty Fähigkeit f

ab·ject verächtlich, erbärmlich; **in abject poverty** in äußerster Armut

ab·jure abschwören; entsagen (dat)

a·blaze in Flammen; fig glänzend, funkelnd (**with** or dat)

a·ble fähig; geschickt; **be able to** inf in der Lage sein zu inf, können

a·ble-bod·ied kräftig

ab·nor·mal abnorm, ungewöhnlich; anomal

a·board an Bord; **all aboard!** MAR alle Mann or Reisenden an Bord!; RAIL alles einsteigen!; **aboard a bus** in e-m Bus; **go aboard a train** in e-n Zug einsteigen

a·bode a. **place of abode** Aufenthaltsort m, Wohnsitz m; **of or with no fixed abode** ohne festen Wohnsitz

a·bol·ish abschaffen, aufheben

ab·o·li·tion Abschaffung f, Aufhebung f

A-bomb → **atom(ic) bomb**

a·bom·i·na·ble abscheulich, scheußlich

a·bom·i·nate verabscheuen

a·bom·i·na·tion Abscheu m

ab·o·rig·i·nal 1. eingeboren, Ur...; **2.** Ureinwohner m

ab·o·rig·i·ne Ureinwohner m

a·bort v/t MED Schwanger(schaft); MED Kind abtreiben; v/i fehlschlagen, scheitern; MED e-e Fehlgeburt haben

a·bor·tion MED Fehlgeburt f; Schwangerschaftsabbruch m, Abtreibung f; **have an abortion** abtreiben (lassen)

a·bor·tive misslungen, erfolglos

a·bound reichlich vorhanden sein; Überfluss haben, reich sein (**in** an dat); voll sein (**with** von)

a·bout 1. prp um (... herum); bei (dat); (irgendwo) herum in (dat); um, gegen, etwa; im Begriff, dabei; über (acc); **I had no money about me** ich hatte kein Geld bei mir; **2.** adv herum, umher; in der Nähe; etwa, ungefähr

a·bove 1. prp über (dat or acc); oberhalb (gen); fig über, erhaben über (acc); **above all** vor allem; **2.** adv oben; darüber; **3.** adj obig, oben erwähnt

a·breast nebeneinander; **keep abreast of, be abreast of** fig Schritt halten mit

a·bridge (ab-, ver)kürzen

a·bridg(e)·ment Kürzung f; Kurzfassung f

a·broad im or ins Ausland; überall(hin); **the news soon spread abroad** die Nachricht verbreitete sich rasch

a·brupt abrupt; jäh; schroff

ab·scess MED Abszess m

ab·sence Abwesenheit f; Mangel m

ab·sent 1. abwesend; fehlend; nicht vorhanden; **be absent** fehlen (**from school** in der Schule; **from work** am Arbeitsplatz); **2.** absent o.s. **from** fernbleiben (dat) or von

ab·sent-mind·ed zerstreut, geistesabwesend

ab·so·lute absolut; unumschränkt; vollkommen; unbedingt; CHEM rein, unvermischt

ab·so·lu·tion REL Absolution f

ab·solve freisprechen, lossprechen
ab·sorb absorbieren, aufsaugen, einsaugen; *fig* ganz in Anspruch nehmen
ab·sorb·ing *fig* fesselnd, packend
ab·stain sich enthalten (*from gen*)
ab·ste·mi·ous enthaltsam; mäßig
ab·sten·tion Enthaltung *f*; POL Stimmenthaltung *f*
ab·sti·nence Abstinenz *f*, Enthaltsamkeit *f*
ab·sti·nent abstinent, enthaltsam
ab·stract 1. abstrakt; 2. *das* Abstrakte; Auszug *m*; 3. abstrahieren; entwenden
ab·stract·ed *fig* zerstreut
ab·strac·tion Abstraktion *f*; abstrakter Begriff
ab·surd absurd; lächerlich
a·bun·dance Überfluss *m*; Fülle *f*; Überschwang *m*
a·bun·dant reich, reichlich
a·buse 1. Missbrauch *m*; Beschimpfung(en *pl*) *f*; *abuse of drugs* Drogenmissbrauch *m*; *abuse of power* Machtmissbrauch *m*; 2. missbrauchen; beschimpfen
a·bu·sive beleidigend, Schimpf...
a·but (an)grenzen (*on* an *acc*)
a·byss Abgrund *m* (*a. fig*)
ac·a·dem·ic 1. Hochschullehrer *m*; 2. akademisch
a·cad·e·mi·cian Akademiemitglied *n*
a·cad·e·my Akademie *f*; *academy of music* Musikhochschule *f*
ac·cede *accede to* zustimmen (*dat*); Amt antreten; Thron besteigen
ac·cel·e·rate *v/t* beschleunigen; *v/i* schneller werden, MOT *a.* beschleunigen, Gas geben
ac·cel·e·ra·tion Beschleunigung *f*
ac·cel·e·ra·tor MOT Gaspedal *n*
ac·cent 1. Akzent *m* (*a.* LING); 2. → ac·cen·tu·ate akzentuieren, betonen
ac·cept annehmen; akzeptieren; hinnehmen
ac·cept·a·ble annehmbar; *person:* tragbar
ac·cept·ance Annahme *f*; Aufnahme *f*
ac·cess Zugang *m* (*to* zu); *fig* Zutritt *m* (*to* bei, zu); EDP Zugriff *m* (*to* auf *acc*); *easy of access* zugänglich (*person*)
ac·ces·sa·ry → accessory
ac·cess code EDP Zugriffskode *m*
ac·ces·si·ble (leicht) zugänglich
ac·ces·sion (Neu)Anschaffung *f* (*to* für); Zustimmung *f* (*to* zu); Antritt *m* (*e-s Amtes*); *accession to power* Machtübernahme *f*; *accession to the throne* Thronbesteigung *f*
ac·ces·so·ry JUR Komplize *m*, Komplizin *f*, Mitschuldige *m*, *f*; *mst pl* Zubehör *n*,

fashion: a. Accessoires *pl*, TECH *a.* Zubehörteile *pl*
access time EDP Zugriffszeit *f*
ac·ci·dent Unfall *m*, Unglück *n*, Unglücksfall *m*; NUCL Störfall *m*; *by accident* zufällig
ac·ci·den·tal zufällig; versehentlich
ac·claim feiern (*as* als)
ac·cla·ma·tion lauter Beifall; Lob *n*
ac·cli·ma·tize (sich) akklimatisieren *or* eingewöhnen
ac·com·mo·date unterbringen; Platz haben für, fassen; anpassen (*to dat* or an *acc*)
ac·com·mo·da·tion Unterkunft *f*, Unterbringung *f*
accommodation of·fice Zimmervermittlung *f*
ac·com·pa·ni·ment MUS Begleitung *f*
ac·com·pa·ny begleiten (*a.* MUS)
ac·com·plice JUR Komplize *m*, Komplizin *f*, Helfershelfer(in)
ac·com·plish erreichen; leisten
ac·com·plished fähig, tüchtig
ac·com·plish·ment Fähigkeit *f*, Talent *n*
ac·cord 1. Übereinstimmung *f*; *of one's own accord* von selbst; *with one accord* einstimmig; 2. übereinstimmen (*with* mit)
ac·cord·ance *in accordance with* entsprechend (*dat*)
ac·cord·ing *according to* laut; nach
ac·cord·ing·ly folglich, also; (dem)entsprechend
ac·cost *j-n* ansprechen
ac·count 1. ECON Rechnung *f*, Berechnung *f*; Konto *n*; Rechenschaft *f*; Bericht *m*; *by all accounts* nach allem, was man so hört; *of no account* ohne Bedeutung; *on no account* auf keinen Fall; *on account of* wegen; *take into account, take account of* in Betracht or Erwägung ziehen, berücksichtigen; *turn s.th. to* (*good*) *account* et. (gut) ausnutzen; *keep accounts* die Bücher führen; *call to account* zur Rechenschaft ziehen; *give* (*an*) *account of* Rechenschaft ablegen über (*acc*); *give an account of* Bericht erstatten über (*acc*); 2. *v/i: account for* Rechenschaft über et. ablegen, (sich) erklären
ac·count·a·ble verantwortlich; erklärlich
ac·coun·tant ECON Buchhalter(in)
ac·count·ing ECON Buchführung *f*
acct ABBR *of* Konto *n*
ac·cu·mu·late (sich) (an)häufen *or* ansammeln

ac·cu·mu·la·tion Ansammlung *f*

ac·cu·mu·la·tor ELECTR Akkumulator *m*

ac·cu·ra·cy Genauigkeit *f*

ac·cu·rate genau

ac·cu·sa·tion Anklage *f*; Anschuldigung *f*, Beschuldigung *f*

ac·cu·sa·tive *a.* **accusative case** LING Akkusativ *m*

ac·cuse JUR anklagen; beschuldigen (*of* gen); **the accused** der *or* die Angeklagte, die Angeklagten *pl*

ac·cus·er JUR Ankläger(in)

ac·cus·ing anklagend, vorwurfsvoll

ac·cus·tom gewöhnen (*to* an *acc*)

ac·cus·tomed gewohnt, üblich; gewöhnt (*to* an *acc*, zu *inf*)

ace Ass *n* (*a. fig*); **have an ace in the hole** (*Br* **up one's sleeve**) *fig* (noch) e-n Trumpf in der Hand haben; **within an ace** um ein Haar

ache 1. schmerzen, wehtun; **2.** *anhaltender* Schmerz

a·chieve zustande bringen; *Ziel* erreichen

a·chieve·ment Zustandebringen *n*, Leistung *f*, Ausführung *f*

ac·id 1. sauer; *fig* beißend, bissig; **2.** CHEM Säure *f*

a·cid·i·ty Säure *f*

acid rain saurer Regen

ac·knowl·edge anerkennen; zugeben; *Empfang* bestätigen

ac·knowl·edg(e)·ment Anerkennung *f*; (*Empfangs*)Bestätigung *f*; Eingeständnis *n*

a·corn BOT Eichel *f*

a·cous·tics Akustik *f*

ac·quaint bekannt machen; **acquaint s.o. with s.th.** j-m et. mitteilen; **be acquainted with** kennen

ac·quaint·ance Bekanntschaft *f*; Bekannte *m*, *f*

ac·quire erwerben; sich aneignen

ac·qui·si·tion Erwerb *m*; Anschaffung *f*, Errungenschaft *f*

ac·quit JUR freisprechen (*of* von); **acquit o.s. well** s-e Sache gut machen

ac·quit·tal JUR Freispruch *m*

a·cre Acre *m* (*4047 qm*)

ac·rid scharf, beißend

ac·ro·bat Akrobat(in)

ac·ro·bat·ic akrobatisch

a·cross 1. *adv* hinüber, herüber; (quer) durch; drüben, auf der anderen Seite; über Kreuz; **2.** *prp* über (*acc*); (quer) durch; auf der anderen Seite von (*or* gen), jenseits (gen); über (*dat*); **come across, run across** *fig* stoßen auf (*acc*)

act 1. *v/i* handeln; sich verhalten *or* beneh-

men; (ein)wirken; funktionieren; (Theater) spielen; *v/t* THEA spielen (*a. fig*), *Stück* aufführen; **act as** fungieren als; **2.** Handlung *f*, Tat *f*; JUR Gesetz *n*; THEA Akt *m*

act·ing THEA Spiel(en) *n*

ac·tion Handlung *f* (*a.* THEA), Tat *f*; *film etc*: Action *f*; Funktionieren *n*; (Ein-)Wirkung *f*; JUR Klage *f*, Prozess *m*; MIL Gefecht *n*, Einsatz *m*; **take action** handeln

ac·tive aktiv; tätig, rührig; lebhaft (*a.* ECON), rege; wirksam

ac·tiv·ist *esp* POL Aktivist(in)

ac·tiv·i·ty Tätigkeit *f*; Aktivität *f*; Betriebsamkeit *f*; *esp* ECON Lebhaftigkeit *f*

activity va·ca·tion Aktivurlaub *m*

ac·tor Schauspieler *m*

ac·tress Schauspielerin *f*

ac·tu·al wirklich, tatsächlich, eigentlich

ac·u·men Scharfsinn *m*

ac·u·punc·ture MED Akupunktur *f*

ad F → **advertisement**

ad·a·mant unerbittlich

a·dapt anpassen (*to* dat *or* an *acc*); *Text* bearbeiten (*from* nach); TECH umstellen (*to* auf *acc*); umbauen (*to* für)

a·dapt·a·ble anpassungsfähig

ad·ap·ta·tion Anpassung *f*; Bearbeitung *f*

a·dapt·er, a·dapt·or ELECTR Adapter *m*

add *v/t* hinzufügen; **add up** zusammenzählen, addieren; *v/i*: **add to** vermehren, beitragen zu, hinzukommen zu; **add up** MATH ergeben; F sich summieren; *fig* e-n Sinn ergeben; **add up to** *fig* hinauslaufen auf (*acc*)

ad·der ZO Natter *f*

ad·dict Süchtige *m*, *f*; **alcohol** (**drug**) **addict** Alkoholsüchtige (Drogen- *or* Rauschgiftsüchtige); (*Fußball- etc*) Fanatiker(in); (*Film- etc*)Narr *m*

ad·dict·ed süchtig, abhängig (**to** von); **be addicted to alcohol** (**drugs**) alkoholsüchtig (drogenabhängig *or* -süchtig) sein

ad·dic·tion Sucht *f*, Süchtigkeit *f*

ad·di·tion Hinzufügen *n*; Zusatz *m*; Zuwachs *m*; ARCH Anbau *m*; MATH Addition *f*; **in addition** außerdem; **in addition to** außer (*dat*)

ad·di·tion·al zusätzlich

ad·dress 1. *Worte* richten (**to** an *acc*), j-n anreden *or* ansprechen; **2.** Adresse *f*, Anschrift *f*; Rede *f*, Ansprache *f*

ad·dress·ee Empfänger(in)

ad·ept erfahren, geschickt (**at, in** in *dat*)

ad·e·qua·cy Angemessenheit *f*
ad·e·quate angemessen
ad·here (to) kleben, haften (an *dat*); *fig* festhalten (an *dat*)
ad·her·ence Anhaften *n*; *fig* Festhalten *n*
ad·her·ent Anhänger(in)
ad·he·sive 1. klebend; **2.** Klebstoff *m*
adhesive plas·ter MED Heftpflaster *n*
adhesive tape Klebeband *n*, Klebstreifen *m*; MED Heftpflaster *n*
ad·ja·cent angrenzend, anstoßend (**to** an *acc*); benachbart
ad·jec·tive LING Adjektiv *n*, Eigenschaftswort *n*
ad·join (an)grenzen an (*acc*)
ad·journ *v/t* verschieben, (*v/i* sich) vertagen
ad·journ·ment Vertagung *f*, Verschiebung *f*
ad·just anpassen; TECH einstellen, regulieren
ad·just·a·ble TECH verstellbar, regulierbar
ad·just·ment Anpassung *f*; TECH Einstellung *f*
ad-lib aus dem Stegreif (sprechen *or* spielen)
ad·min·is·ter verwalten; PHARM geben, verabreichen; **administer justice** Recht sprechen
ad·min·is·tra·tion Verwaltung *f*; POL Regierung *f*; Amtsperiode *f*
ad·min·is·tra·tive Verwaltungs…
ad·min·is·tra·tor Verwaltungsbeamte *m*
ad·mi·ra·ble bewundernswert; großartig
ad·mi·ral MAR Admiral *m*
ad·mi·ra·tion Bewunderung *f*
ad·mire bewundern; verehren
ad·mir·er Verehrer *m*
ad·mis·si·ble zulässig
ad·mis·sion Eintritt *m*, Zutritt *m*; Aufnahme *f*; Eintrittsgeld *n*; Eingeständnis *n*; **admission free** Eintritt frei
ad·mit *v/t* zugeben; (her)einlassen (**to, into** in *acc*), eintreten lassen; zulassen (**to** zu)
ad·mit·tance Einlass *m*, Eintritt *m*, Zutritt *m*; **no admittance** Zutritt verboten
ad·mon·ish ermahnen; warnen (**of, against** vor *dat*)
a·do Getue *n*, Lärm *m*; **without more or further ado** ohne weitere Umstände
ad·o·les·cence Jugend *f*, Adoleszenz *f*
ad·o·les·cent 1. jugendlich, heranwachsend; **2.** Jugendliche *m, f*
a·dopt adoptieren; übernehmen; **adopted child** Adoptivkind *n*
a·dop·tion Adoption *f*
a·dop·tive par·ents Adoptiveltern *pl*
a·dor·a·ble F bezaubernd, entzückend

ad·o·ra·tion Anbetung *f*, Verehrung *f*
a·dore anbeten, verehren
a·dorn schmücken, zieren
a·dorn·ment Schmuck *m*, Verzierung *f*
a·droit geschickt
ad·ult 1. erwachsen; **2.** Erwachsene *m, f*; **adults only** nur für Erwachsene!
adult ed·u·ca·tion Erwachsenenbildung *f*
a·dul·ter·ate verfälschen, *Wein* panschen
a·dul·ter·er Ehebrecher *m*
a·dul·ter·ess Ehebrecherin *f*
a·dul·ter·ous ehebrecherisch
a·dul·ter·y Ehebruch *m*
ad·vance 1. *v/i* vordringen, vorrücken (*a. time*); Fortschritte machen; *v/t* vorrücken; *Termin etc* vorverlegen; *Argument etc* vorbringen; *Geld* vorstrecken, F vorschießen; (be)fördern; *Preis* erhöhen; *Wachstum etc* beschleunigen; **2.** Vorrücken *n*, Vorstoß *m* (*a. fig*); Fortschritt *m*; ECON Vorschuss *m*; Erhöhung *f*; **in advance** im Voraus
ad·vanced fortgeschritten; **advanced for one's years** weit *or* reif für sein Alter
ad·vance·ment Fortschritt *m*, Verbesserung *f*
ad·van·tage Vorteil *m* (*a. SPORT*); **advantage rule** SPORT Vorteilsregel *f*; **take advantage of** ausnutzen
ad·van·ta·geous vorteilhaft
ad·ven·ture Abenteuer *n*, Wagnis *n*
ad·ven·tur·er Abenteurer *m*
ad·ven·tur·ess Abenteu(r)erin *f*
ad·ven·tur·ous abenteuerlich; verwegen, kühn
ad·verb LING Adverb *n*, Umstandswort *n*
ad·ver·sa·ry Gegner(in)
ad·ver·tise ankündigen, bekannt machen; inserieren; Reklame machen (für)
ad·ver·tise·ment Anzeige *f*, Inserat *n*
ad·ver·tis·ing 1. Reklame *f*, Werbung *f*; **2.** Reklame…, Werbe…
advertising a·gen·cy Werbeagentur *f*
advertising cam·paign Werbefeldzug *m*
ad·vice Rat(schlag) *m*; ECON Benachrichtigung *f*; **take medical advice** e-n Arzt zu Rate ziehen; **take my advice** hör auf mich
ad·vice cen·ter, *Br* **advice cen·tre** Beratungsstelle *f*
ad·vis·a·ble ratsam
ad·vise *v/t j-n* beraten; *j-m* raten; *esp* ECON benachrichtigen, avisieren; *v/i* sich beraten
ad·vis·er *esp Br*, **ad·vis·or** Berater *m*
ad·vi·so·ry beratend
ad·vo·cate 1. befürworten, verfechten; **2.** Befürworter(in), Verfechter(in)
aer·i·al 1. luftig; Luft…; **2.** Antenne *f*

aer·i·al pho·to·graph, aerial view Luftaufnahme *f*, Luftbild *n*

aer·o... Aero..., Luft...

aer·o·bics SPORT Aerobic *n*

aer·o·drome *esp Br* Flugplatz *m*

aer·o·dy·nam·ic aerodynamisch

aer·o·dy·nam·ics Aerodynamik *f*

aer·o·nau·tics Luftfahrt *f*

aer·o·plane *Br* Flugzeug *n*

aer·o·sol Spraydose *f*, Sprühdose *f*

aes·thet·ic *etc* → **esthetic** *etc*

a·far: from afar von weit her

af·fair Angelegenheit *f*, Sache *f*; F Ding *n*, Sache *f*; Affäre *f*

af·fect beeinflussen; MED angreifen, befallen; bewegen, rühren; e-e Vorliebe haben für; vortäuschen

af·fec·tion Liebe *f*, Zuneigung *f*

af·fec·tion·ate liebevoll, herzlich

af·fil·i·ate *als Mitglied* aufnehmen; angliedern

af·fin·i·ty Affinität *f*; (geistige) Verwandtschaft; Neigung *f* (**for, to** zu)

af·firm versichern; beteuern; bestätigen

af·fir·ma·tion Versicherung *f*, Beteuerung *f*; Bestätigung *f*

af·fir·ma·tive 1. bejahend; **2. answer in the affirmative** bejahen

af·fix (**to**) anheften, ankleben (an *acc*), befestigen (an *dat*); beifügen, hinzufügen (*dat*)

af·flict heimsuchen, plagen; **afflicted with** geplagt von, leidend an (*dat*)

af·flic·tion Gebrechen *n*; Elend *n*, Not *f*

af·flu·ence Überfluss *m*; Wohlstand *m*

af·flu·ent reich, reichlich

affluent so·ci·e·ty Wohlstandsgesellschaft *f*

af·ford sich leisten; gewähren, bieten; **I can afford it** ich kann es mir leisten

af·front 1. beleidigen; **2.** Beleidigung *f*

a·float MAR flott, schwimmend; **set afloat** MAR flottmachen; *fig* Gerücht etc in Umlauf setzen

a·fraid: be afraid of sich fürchten *or* Angst haben vor (*dat*); **I'm afraid she won't come** ich fürchte, sie wird nicht kommen; **I'm afraid I must go now** leider muss ich jetzt gehen

a·fresh von neuem

Af·ri·ca Afrika *n*

Af·ri·can 1. afrikanisch; **2.** Afrikaner(in)

af·ter 1. *adv* hinterher, nachher, danach; **2.** *prp* nach; hinter (*dat*) (... her); **after all** schließlich (doch); **3.** *cj* nachdem; **4.** *adj* später; Nach...

after ef·fect MED Nachwirkung *f* (*a. fig*)

af·ter·glow Abendrot *n*

af·ter·math Nachwirkungen *pl*, Folgen *pl*

af·ter·noon Nachmittag *m*; **this afternoon** heute Nachmittag; **good afternoon!** guten Tag!

af·ter·taste Nachgeschmack *m*

af·ter·thought nachträglicher Einfall

af·ter·ward, *Br* **af·ter·wards** nachher, später

a·gain wieder; wiederum; ferner; **again and again, time and again** immer wieder; **as much again** noch einmal so viel

a·gainst gegen; an (*dat or acc*); **as against** verglichen mit; **he was against it** er war dagegen

age 1. (Lebens)Alter *n*; Zeit(alter *n*) *f*; Menschenalter *n*; (**old**) **age** (hohes) Alter; **at the age of** im Alter von; *s.o.* **your age** in deinem *or* Ihrem Alter; (**come**) **of age** mündig *or* volljährig (werden); **be over age** die Altersgrenze überschritten haben; **under age** minderjährig; unmündig; **wait for ages** F e-e Ewigkeit warten; **2.** alt werden *or* machen

a·ged¹ alt, betagt

a·ged²: aged twenty 20 Jahre alt

age·less zeitlos; ewig jung

a·gen·cy Agentur *f*; Geschäftsstelle *f*, Büro *n*

a·gen·da Tagesordnung *f*

a·gent Agent *m* (*a.* POL), Vertreter *m*; (*Grundstücks- etc*)Makler *m*; CHEM Wirkstoff *m*, Mittel *n*

ag·glom·er·ate (sich) zusammenballen; (sich) (an)häufen

ag·gra·vate erschweren, verschlimmern; F ärgern

ag·gre·gate 1. sich belaufen auf (*acc*); **2.** gesamt; **3.** Gesamtmenge *f*, Summe *f*; TECH Aggregat *n*

ag·gres·sion Angriff *m*

ag·gres·sive aggressiv, Angriffs...; *fig* energisch

ag·gres·sor Angreifer *m*

ag·grieved verletzt, gekränkt

a·ghast entgeistert, entsetzt

ag·ile flink, behend

a·gil·i·ty Flinkheit *f*, Behendigkeit *f*

ag·i·tate *v/t fig* aufregen, aufwühlen; *Flüssigkeit* schütteln; *v/i* POL agitieren, hetzen (**against** gegen)

ag·i·ta·tion Aufregung *f*; POL Agitation *f*

ag·i·ta·tor POL Agitator *m*

a·glow: be aglow strahlen (**with** vor)

a·go: a year ago vor e-m Jahr

ag·o·ny Qual *f*; Todeskampf *m*

a·gree *v/i* übereinstimmen; sich vertragen; einig werden, sich einigen (**on** über *acc*); übereinkommen; **agree to** zustimmen (*dat*), einverstanden sein mit

a·gree·a·ble (**to**) angenehm (für); übereinstimmend (mit)

a·gree·ment Übereinstimmung *f*; Vereinbarung *f*; Abkommen *n*

ag·ri·cul·tur·al landwirtschaftlich

ag·ri·cul·ture Landwirtschaft *f*

a·ground MAR gestrandet; *run aground* stranden, auf Grund laufen

a·head vorwärts, voraus; vorn; *go ahead!* nur zu!, mach nur!; *straight ahead* geradeaus

aid 1. unterstützen, *j-m* helfen (*in* bei); fördern; *he was accused of aiding and abetting* JUR er wurde wegen Beihilfe angeklagt; 2. Hilfe *f*, Unterstützung *f*

AIDS, Aids MED Aids *n*; *person with AIDS* Aids-Kranke *m*, *f*

ail kränklich sein

ail·ment Leiden *n*

aim 1. *v/i* zielen (*at* auf *acc*, nach); *aim at* *fig* beabsichtigen; *be aiming to do s.th.* vorhaben, et. zu tun; *v/t*: *aim at* Waffe *etc* richten *auf or* gegen (*acc*); 2. Ziel *n* (*a. fig*); Absicht *f*; *take aim at* zielen auf (*acc*) *or* nach

aim·less ziellos

air[1] 1. Luft *f*; Luftzug *m*; Miene *f*, Aussehen *n*; *by air* auf dem Luftwege; *in the open air* im Freien; *on the air* im Rundfunk *or* Fernsehen; *be on the air* senden; in Betrieb sein; *go off the air* die Sendung beenden (*person*); sein Programm beenden (*station*); *give o.s. airs, put on airs* vornehm tun; 2. (aus)lüften; *fig* an die Öffentlichkeit bringen; erörtern

air[2] MUS Arie *f*, Weise *f*, Melodie *f*

air·bag MOT Airbag *m*

air·base MIL Luftstützpunkt *m*

air·bed Luftmatratze *f*

air·borne AVIAT in der Luft; MIL Luftlande...

air·brake TECH Druckluftbremse *f*

air·bus AVIAT Airbus *m*, Großraumflugzeug *n*

air-con·di·tioned mit Klimaanlage

air-con·di·tion·ing Klimaanlage *f*

air·craft car·ri·er MAR, MIL Flugzeugträger *m*

air·field Flugplatz *m*

air force MIL Luftwaffe *f*

air host·ess AVIAT Stewardess *f*

air jack·et Schwimmweste *f*

air·lift AVIAT Luftbrücke *f*

air·line AVIAT Fluggesellschaft *f*

air·lin·er AVIAT Verkehrsflugzeug *n*

air·mail Luftpost *f*; *by airmail* mit Luftpost

air·man MIL Flieger *m*

air·plane Flugzeug *n*

air·pock·et AVIAT Luftloch *n*

air pol·lu·tion Luftverschmutzung *f*

air·port Flughafen *m*

air raid MIL Luftangriff *m*

air-raid pre·cau·tions MIL Luftschutz *m*

air-raid shel·ter MIL Luftschutzraum *m*

air route AVIAT Flugroute *f*

air·sick luftkrank

air·space Luftraum *m*

air·strip (behelfsmäßige) Start- und Landebahn *f*

air ter·mi·nal Flughafenabfertigungsgebäude *n*

air·tight luftdicht

air time Sendezeit *f*

air traf·fic AVIAT Flugverkehr *m*

air-traf·fic con·trol AVIAT Flugsicherung *f*

air-traffic con·trol·ler AVIAT Fluglotse *m*

air·way AVIAT Fluggesellschaft *f*

air·wor·thy AVIAT flugtüchtig

air·y luftig

aisle ARCH Seitenschiff *n*; Gang *m*

a·jar halb offen, angelehnt

a·kin verwandt (*to* mit)

a·lac·ri·ty Bereitwilligkeit *f*

a·larm 1. Alarm(zeichen *n*) *m*; Wecker *m*; Angst *f*; 2. alarmieren; beunruhigen

alarm clock Wecker *m*

al·bum Album *f* (*a. record*)

al·bu·mi·nous BIOL eiweißhaltig

al·co·hol Alkohol *m*

al·co·hol·ic 1. alkoholisch; 2. Alkoholiker(in)

al·co·hol·ism Alkoholismus *m*, Trunksucht *f*

a·lert 1. wachsam; munter; 2. Alarm *m*; Alarmbereitschaft *f*; *on the alert* auf der Hut; in Alarmbereitschaft; 3. warnen (*to* vor *dat*), alarmieren

al·ga BOT Alge *f*

al·ge·bra MATH Algebra *f*

al·i·bi JUR Alibi *n*

a·li·en 1. ausländisch; fremd; 2. Ausländer(in); Außerirdische *m*, *f*

a·li·en·ate veräußern; entfremden; *esp art*: verfremden

a·li·en·a·tion Entfremdung *f*; *esp art*: Verfremdung *f*

a·light 1. in Flammen; 2. aussteigen; absteigen, absitzen; ZO sich niederlassen; AVIAT landen

a·lign (sich) ausrichten (*with* nach)

a·like 1. *adj* gleich; 2. *adv* gleich, ebenso

al·i·men·ta·ry nahrhaft

alimentary ca·nal ANAT Verdauungskanal *m*

al·i·mo·ny JUR Unterhalt *m*

a·live lebendig; (noch) am Leben; lebhaft; *alive and kicking* gesund und munter; *be alive with* wimmeln von

all 1. *adj* all; ganz; jede(r, -s); **2.** *pron* alles; alle *pl*; **3.** *adv* ganz, völlig; ***all at once*** auf einmal; ***all the better*** desto besser; ***all but*** beinahe, fast; ***all in*** F fertig, ganz erledigt; ***all right*** in Ordnung; ***for all that*** dessen ungeachtet, trotzdem; ***for all I know*** soviel ich weiß; ***at all*** überhaupt; ***not at all*** überhaupt nicht; ***the score was two all*** das Spiel stand zwei zu zwei

all-A·mer·i·can typisch amerikanisch; die ganzen USA vertretend

al·lay beruhigen; lindern

al·le·ga·tion *unerwiesene* Behauptung

al·lege behaupten

al·leged angeblich, vermeintlich

al·le·giance Treue *f*

al·li·ance Bündnis *n*

al·li·ga·tor ZO Alligator *m*

al·lo·cate zuteilen, anweisen

al·lo·ca·tion Zuteilung *f*

al·lot zuteilen, an-, zuweisen

al·lot·ment Zuteilung *f*; Parzelle *f*

al·low erlauben, bewilligen, gewähren; zugeben; ab-, anrechnen, vergüten; ***al·low for*** einplanen, berücksichtigen (*acc*)

al·low·a·ble erlaubt, zulässig

al·low·ance Erlaubnis *f*; Bewilligung *f*; Taschengeld *n*, Zuschuss *m*; Vergütung *f*; *fig* Nachsicht *f*; ***make allowance(s) for s.th.*** et. berücksichtigen

al·loy TECH **1.** Legierung *f*; **2.** legieren

all-round vielseitig

all-round·er Alleskönner *m*; Allround-sportler *m*, -spieler *m*

al·lude anspielen (***to*** auf *acc*)

al·lure locken, an-, verlocken

al·lure·ment Verlockung *f*

al·lu·sion Anspielung *f*

all-wheel drive MOT Allradantrieb *m*

al·ly 1. (sich) vereinigen, verbünden (***to***, ***with*** mit); **2.** Verbündete *m*, *f*, Bundesgenosse *m*, Bundesgenossin *f*; ***the Allies*** MIL die Alliierten *pl*

al·might·y allmächtig; ***the Almighty*** REL der Allmächtige

al·mond BOT Mandel *f*

al·most fast, beinah(e)

alms Almosen *n*

a·loft (hoch) (dr)oben

a·lone allein; ***let alone***, ***leave alone*** in Ruhe lassen, bleiben lassen; ***let alone ...*** geschweige denn ...

a·long 1. *adv* weiter, vorwärts; da; dahin; ***all along*** die ganze Zeit; ***along with*** (zu-

sammen) mit; ***come along*** mitkommen, mitgehen; ***get along*** vorwärtskommen, weiterkommen; auskommen, sich vertragen (***with s.o.*** mit j-m); ***take along*** mitnehmen; **2.** *prp* entlang (*dat*), längs (*gen*)

a·long·side Seite an Seite; neben

a·loof abseits; reserviert, zurückhaltend, verschlossen

a·loof·ness Reserviertheit *f*; Verschlossenheit *f*

a·loud laut

al·pha·bet Alphabet *n*

al·pine (Hoch)Gebirgs..., alpin

al·read·y bereits, schon

al·right → *all right*

Al·sa·tian *esp Br* ZO Deutscher Schäferhund

al·so auch, ferner

al·tar REL Altar *m*

al·ter ändern, sich (ver)ändern; ab-, umändern

al·ter·a·tion Änderung *f* (***to*** an *dat*), Veränderung *f*

al·ter·nate 1. abwechseln (lassen); **2.** abwechselnd

al·ter·nat·ing cur·rent ELECTR Wechselstrom *m*

al·ter·na·tion Abwechslung *f*; Wechsel *m*

al·ter·na·tive 1. alternativ, wahlweise; **2.** Alternative *f*, Wahl *f*, Möglichkeit *f*

al·though obwohl, obgleich

al·ti·tude Höhe *f*; ***at an altitude of*** in e-r Höhe von

al·to·geth·er im Ganzen, insgesamt; ganz (und gar), völlig

al·u·min·i·um *Br*, **a·lu·mi·num** Aluminium *n*

al·ways immer, stets

am, AM ABBR *of before noon* (*Latin* ante meridiem) morgens, vorm., vormittags

a·mal·gam·ate (sich) zusammenschließen, ECON a. fusionieren

am·a·teur Amateur(in); Dilettant(in); Hobby...

a·maze in Erstaunen setzen, verblüffen

a·maze·ment Staunen *n*, Verblüffung *f*

a·maz·ing erstaunlich

am·bas·sa·dor POL Botschafter *m* (***to*** in *e-m Land*)

am·bas·sa·dress POL Botschafterin *f* (***to*** in *e-m Land*)

am·ber Bernstein *m*

am·bi·gu·i·ty Zwei-, Mehrdeutigkeit *f*

am·big·u·ous zwei-, mehr-, vieldeutig

am·bi·tion Ehrgeiz *m*

am·bi·tious ehrgeizig, strebsam

am·ble 1. Passgang *m*; **2.** im Passgang gehen *or* reiten; schlendern

am·bu·lance Krankenwagen *m*

am·bush 1. Hinterhalt *m*; *be or lie in am·bush for s.o.* j-m auflauern; **2.** auflauern (*dat*); überfallen

a·men *int* REL amen

a·mend verbessern, berichtigen; PARL abändern, ergänzen

a·mend·ment Bess(e)rung *f*; Verbesserung *f*; PARL Abänderungsantrag *m*, Ergänzungsantrag *m*; Zusatzartikel *m* zur Verfassung

a·mends (Schaden)Ersatz *m*; *make amends* Schadenersatz leisten, es wieder gutmachen; *make amends to s.o. for s.th.* j-n für et. entschädigen

a·men·i·ty *often pl* Annehmlichkeiten *pl*

A·mer·i·ca Amerika *n*

A·mer·i·can 1. amerikanisch; **2.** Amerikaner(in)

A·mer·i·can·is·m LING Amerikanismus *m*

A·mer·i·can·ize (sich) amerikanisieren

A·mer·i·can plan Vollpension *f*

a·mi·a·ble liebenswürdig, freundlich

am·i·ca·ble freundschaftlich, *a.* JUR gütlich

a·mid(st) inmitten (*gen*), (mitten) in *or* unter

a·miss verkehrt, falsch, übel; *take s.th. amiss* et. übel nehmen, et. verübeln

am·mo·ni·a CHEM Ammoniak *n*

am·mu·ni·tion Munition *f*

am·nes·ty JUR **1.** Amnestie *f*; **2.** begnadigen

a·mok: *run amok* Amok laufen

a·mong(st) (mitten) unter, zwischen

am·o·rous verliebt

a·mount 1. (*to*) sich belaufen (auf *acc*); hinauslaufen (auf *acc*); **2.** Betrag *m*, (Gesamt)Summe *f*; Menge *f*

am·per·age ELECTR Stromstärke *f*

am·ple weit, groß, geräumig; reich, reichlich, beträchtlich

am·pli·fi·ca·tion Erweiterung *f*; PHYS Verstärkung *f*

am·pli·fi·er ELECTR Verstärker *m*

am·pli·fy erweitern; ELECTR verstärken

am·pli·tude Umfang *m*, Weite *f*, Fülle *f*; ELECTR, PHYS Amplitude *f*

am·pu·tate MED amputieren

a·muck → *amok*

a·muse (*o.s.* sich) amüsieren, unterhalten, belustigen

a·muse·ment Unterhaltung *f*, Vergnügen *n*, Zeitvertreib *m*

amusement park Vergnügungspark *m*, Freizeitpark *m*

a·mus·ing amüsant, unterhaltend

an → *a*

an·a·bol·ic ster·oid PHARM Anabolikum *n*

a·nae·mi·a *Br* → **anemia**

an·aes·thet·ic *Br* → **anesthetic**

a·nal ANAT anal, Anal...

a·nal·o·gous analog, entsprechend

a·nal·o·gy Analogie *f*, Entsprechung *f*

an·a·lyse *esp Br*, **an·a·lyze** analysieren; zerlegen

a·nal·y·sis Analyse *f*

an·arch·y Anarchie *f*, Gesetzlosigkeit *f*; Chaos *n*

a·nat·o·mize MED zerlegen; zergliedern

a·nat·o·my MED Anatomie *f*; Zergliederung *f*, Analyse *f*

an·ces·tor Vorfahr *m*, Ahn *m*

an·ces·tress Vorfahrin *f*, Ahnfrau *f*

an·chor MAR **1.** Anker *m*; *at anchor* vor Anker; **2.** verankern

an·chor·man TV Moderator *m*

an·chor·wom·an TV Moderatorin *f*

an·cho·vy ZO Anschovis *f*, Sardelle *f*

an·cient 1. alt, antik; uralt; **2.** *the ancients* HIST die Alten, die antiken Klassiker

and und

an·ec·dote Anekdote *f*

a·ne·mi·a MED Blutarmut *f*, Anämie *f*

an·es·thet·ic MED **1.** betäubend, Narkose...; **2.** Betäubungsmittel *n*

an·gel Engel *m*

an·ger 1. Zorn *m*, Ärger *m* (*at* über *acc*); **2.** erzürnen, (ver)ärgern

an·gle[1] Winkel *m* (*a.* MATH)

an·gle[2] angeln (*for* nach)

an·gler Angler(in)

An·gli·can REL **1.** anglikanisch; **2.** Anglikaner(in)

An·glo-Sax·on 1. angelsächsisch; **2.** Angelsachse *m*

an·gry zornig, verärgert, böse (*at, with* über *acc*, mit *dat*)

an·guish Qual *f*, Schmerz *m*

an·gu·lar winkelig; knochig

an·i·mal 1. Tier *n*; **2.** tierisch

animal lov·er Tierfreund *m*

animal shel·ter Tierheim *n*

an·i·mate beleben; aufmuntern, anregen

an·i·mat·ed lebendig; lebhaft, angeregt

animated car·toon Zeichentrickfilm *m*

an·i·ma·tion Lebhaftigkeit *f*; Animation *f*, Herstellung *f* von (Zeichen-)Trickfilmen; EDP bewegtes Bild

an·i·mos·i·ty Animosität *f*, Feindseligkeit *f*

an·kle ANAT (Fuß)Knöchel *m*

an·nals Jahrbücher *pl*

an·nex 1. anhängen; annektieren; **2.** Anhang *m*; ARCH Anbau *m*

an·ni·ver·sa·ry Jahrestag *m*; Jahresfeier *f*

an·no·tate mit Anmerkungen versehen;

kommentieren

an·nounce ankündigen; bekannt geben; *radio*, TV ansagen; durchsagen

an·nounce·ment Ankündigung *f*; Bekanntgabe *f*; *radio*, TV Ansage *f*; Durchsage *f*

an·nounc·er *radio*, TV Ansager(in), Sprecher(in)

an·noy ärgern; belästigen

an·noy·ance Störung *f*, Belästigung *f*; Ärgernis *n*

an·noy·ing ärgerlich, lästig

an·nu·al 1. jährlich, Jahres...; **2.** einjährige Pflanze; Jahrbuch *n*

an·nu·i·ty (Jahres)Rente *f*

an·nul für ungültig erklären, annullieren

an·nul·ment Annullierung *f*, Aufhebung *f*

an·o·dyne MED **1.** schmerzstillend; **2.** schmerzstillendes Mittel

a·noint REL salben

a·nom·a·lous anomal

a·non·y·mous anonym

an·o·rak Anorak *m*

an·oth·er ein anderer; ein Zweiter; noch eine(r, -s)

an·swer 1. *v/t et.* beantworten; *j-m* antworten; entsprechen (*dat*); Zweck erfüllen; TECH *dem Steuer* gehorchen; JUR *e-r Vorladung* Folge leisten; *e-r Beschreibung* entsprechen; *answer the bell or door* (die Tür) aufmachen; *answer the telephone* ans Telefon gehen; *v/i* antworten (*to* auf *acc*); entsprechen (*to dat*); *answer s.o. back* freche Antworten geben; widersprechen; *answer for* einstehen für; **2.** Antwort *f* (*to* auf *acc*)

an·swer·a·ble verantwortlich

an·swer·ing ma·chine TEL Anrufbeantworter *m*

ant ZO Ameise *f*

an·tag·o·nism Feindschaft *f*

an·tag·o·nist Gegner(in)

an·tag·o·nize bekämpfen; sich *j-n* zum Feind machen

Ant·arc·tic antarktisch

an·te·ced·ent vorhergehend, früher (*to* als)

an·te·lope ZO Antilope *f*

an·ten·na¹ ZO Fühler *m*

an·ten·na² ELECTR Antenne *f*

an·te·ri·or vorhergehend, früher (*to* als); vorder

an·them MUS Hymne *f*

an·ti... Gegen..., gegen ... eingestellt, Anti..., anti...

an·ti·air·craft MIL Fliegerabwehr..., Flugabwehr...

an·ti·bi·ot·ic MED Antibiotikum *n*

an·ti·bod·y BIOL Antikörper *m*, Abwehrstoff *m*

an·tic·i·pate voraussehen, ahnen; erwarten; zuvorkommen; vorwegnehmen

an·tic·i·pa·tion (Vor)Ahnung *f*; Erwartung *f*; Vorwegnahme *f*; Vorfreude *f*; *in anticipation* im Voraus

an·ti·clock·wise *Br* entgegen dem Uhrzeigersinn

an·tics Mätzchen *pl*

an·ti·dote Gegengift *n*, Gegenmittel *n*

an·ti·for·eign·er vi·o·lence Gewalt *f* gegen Ausländer

an·ti·freeze Frostschutzmittel *n*

an·ti·lock brak·ing sys·tem MOT Antiblockiersystem *n* (ABBR *ABS*)

an·ti·mis·sile MIL Raketenabwehr...

an·ti·nu·cle·ar ac·tiv·ist Kernkraftgegner(in)

an·tip·a·thy Abneigung *f*

an·ti·quat·ed veraltet

an·tique 1. antik, alt; **2.** Antiquität *f*

an·tique deal·er Antiquitätenhändler(in)

antique shop *esp Br*, **antique store** Antiquitätenladen *m*

an·tiq·ui·ty Altertum *n*, Vorzeit *f*

an·ti·sep·tic MED **1.** antiseptisch; **2.** antiseptisches Mittel

ant·lers ZO Geweih *n*

a·nus ANAT After *m*

an·vil Amboss *m*

anx·i·e·ty Angst *f*, Sorge *f*

anx·ious besorgt, beunruhigt (*about* wegen); begierig, gespannt (*for* auf *acc*); bestrebt (*to do* zu tun)

an·y 1. *adj and pron* (irgend)eine(r, -s), (irgend)welche(r, -s); (irgend)etwas; jede(r, -s) (beliebige); einige *pl*, welche *pl*; *not any* keiner; **2.** *adv* irgend(wie) ein wenig, (noch) etwas

an·y·bod·y (irgend)jemand; jeder

an·y·how irgendwie; trotzdem, jedenfalls; wie dem auch sei

an·y·one → anybody

an·y·thing (irgend)etwas; alles; *anything but* alles andere als; *anything else?* sonst noch etwas?; *not anything* nichts

an·y·way → anyhow

an·y·where irgendwo(hin); überall

a·part einzeln, für sich; beiseite; *apart from* abgesehen von

a·part·heid POL Apartheid *f*, Politik *f* der Rassentrennung

a·part·ment Wohnung *f*

apartment build·ing, apartment house Mietshaus *n*

ap·a·thet·ic apathisch, teilnahmslos, gleichgültig

ap·a·thy Apathie *f*, Teilnahmslosigkeit *f*

ape ZO (Menschen)Affe *m*

ap·er·ture Öffnung *f*

a·pi·a·ry Bienenhaus *n*

a·piece für jedes Stück, pro Stück, je

a·pol·o·gize sich entschuldigen (*for* für; *to* bei)

a·pol·o·gy Entschuldigung *f*; Rechtfertigung *f*; *make an apology* (*for s.th.*) sich (für et.) entschuldigen

ap·o·plex·y MED Schlaganfall *m*, F Schlag *m*

a·pos·tle REL Apostel *m*

a·pos·tro·phe LING Apostroph *m*

ap·pal(l) erschrecken, entsetzen

ap·pal·ling erschreckend, entsetzlich

ap·pa·ra·tus Apparat *m*, Vorrichtung *f*, Gerät *n*

ap·par·ent offenbar; anscheinend; scheinbar

ap·pa·ri·tion Erscheinung *f*, Gespenst *n*

ap·peal 1. JUR Berufung *or* Revision einlegen, Einspruch erheben, Beschwerde einlegen; appellieren, sich wenden (*to* an *acc*); *appeal to* gefallen (*dat*), zusagen (*dat*), wirken auf (*acc*); j-n dringend bitten (*for* um); 2. JUR Revision *f*, Berufung *f*; Beschwerde *f*; Einspruch *m*; Appell *m* (*to* an *acc*), Aufruf *m*; Wirkung *f*, Reiz *m*; Bitte *f* (*to* an *acc*; *for* um); *appeal for mercy* JUR Gnadengesuch *n*

ap·peal·ing flehend; ansprechend

ap·pear (er)scheinen; sich zeigen; öffentlich auftreten; sich ergeben *or* herausstellen

ap·pear·ance Erscheinen *n*; Auftreten *n*; Äußere *n*, Erscheinung *f*, Aussehen *n*; Anschein *m*, äußerer Schein *f*; *keep up appearances* den Schein wahren; *to or by all appearances* allem Anschein nach

ap·pease besänftigen, beschwichtigen; *Durst etc* stillen; *Neugier* befriedigen

ap·pend an-, hinzu-, beifügen

ap·pend·age Anhang *m*; Anhängsel *n*

ap·pen·di·ci·tis MED Blinddarmentzündung *f*

ap·pen·dix Anhang *m*; *a.* *vermiform appendix* ANAT Wurmfortsatz *m*, Blinddarm *m*

ap·pe·tite (*for*) Appetit *m* (auf *acc*); *fig* Verlangen *n* (nach)

ap·pe·tiz·er Appetithappen *m*, appetitanregendes Gericht *or* Getränk

ap·pe·tiz·ing appetitanregend

ap·plaud applaudieren, Beifall spenden; loben

ap·plause Applaus *m*, Beifall *m*

ap·ple BOT Apfel *m*

ap·ple cart: *upset s.o.'s apple cart* F j-s

Pläne über den Haufen werfen

ap·ple pie (*warmer*) gedeckter Apfelkuchen

ap·ple·pie or·der: F *in applepie order* in schönster Ordnung

ap·ple sauce Apfelmus *n*; *sl* Schmus *m*, Quatsch *m*

ap·pli·ance Vorrichtung *f*; Gerät *n*; Mittel *n*

ap·plic·a·ble anwendbar (*to* auf *acc*)

ap·pli·cant Antragsteller(in), Bewerber(in) (*for* um)

ap·pli·ca·tion Anwendung *f* (*to* auf *acc*); Bedeutung *f* (*to* für); Gesuch *n* (*for* um); Bewerbung *f* (*for* um)

ap·ply *v/t* (*to*) (auf)legen, auftragen (auf *acc*); anwenden (auf *acc*); verwenden (für); *apply o.s. to* sich widmen (*dat*); *v/i* (*to*) passen, zutreffen, sich anwenden lassen (auf *acc*); gelten (für); sich wenden (an *acc*); *apply for* sich bewerben um, *et.* beantragen

ap·point bestimmen, festsetzen; verabreden; ernennen (*s.o. governor* j-n zum ...); berufen (*to* auf *e-n Posten*)

ap·point·ment Bestimmung *f*; Verabredung *f*; Termin *m*; Ernennung *f*, Berufung *f*; Stelle *f*

appointment book Terminkalender *m*

ap·por·tion verteilen, zuteilen

ap·prais·al (Ab)Schätzung *f*

ap·praise (ab)schätzen, taxieren

ap·pre·ci·a·ble nennenswert, spürbar

ap·pre·ci·ate *v/t* schätzen; würdigen; dankbar sein für; *v/i* im Wert steigen

ap·pre·ci·a·tion Würdigung *f*; Dankbarkeit *f*; (richtige) Beurteilung *f*; ECON Wertsteigerung *f*

ap·pre·hend ergreifen, fassen; begreifen; befürchten

ap·pre·hen·sion Ergreifung *f*, Festnahme *f*; Besorgnis *f*

ap·pre·hen·sive ängstlich, besorgt (*for* um; *that* dass)

ap·pren·tice 1. Auszubildende *m*, *f*, Lehrling *m*, *Swiss* Lehrtochter *f*; 2. in die Lehre geben

ap·pren·tice·ship Lehrzeit *f*, Lehre *f*, Ausbildung *f*

ap·proach 1. *v/i* näher kommen, sich nähern; *v/t* sich nähern (*dat*); herangehen *or* herantreten an (*acc*); 2. (Heran)Nahen *n*; Einfahrt *f*, Zufahrt *f*, Auffahrt *f*; Annäherung *f*; Methode *f*

ap·pro·ba·tion Billigung *f*, Beifall *m*

ap·pro·pri·ate 1. sich aneignen; verwenden; PARL bewilligen; 2. (*for, to*) angemessen (*dat*), passend (für, zu)

ap·prov·al Billigung *f*; Anerkennung *f*,

Beifall *m*

ap·prove billigen, anerkennen

ap·proved bewährt

ap·prox·i·mate annähernd, ungefähr

a·pri·cot BOT Aprikose *f*

A·pril (ABBR **Apr**) April *m*

a·pron Schürze *f*

apron strings: *be tied to one's mother's* *apron strings* an Mutters Schürzenzipfel hängen

apt geeignet, passend; treffend; begabt; *apt to* geneigt zu

ap·ti·tude (*for*) Begabung *f* (für), Befähigung *f* (für), Talent *n* (zu)

ap·ti·tude test Eignungsprüfung *f*

aq·ua·plan·ing *Br* MOT Aquaplaning *n*

a·quar·i·um Aquarium *n*

A·quar·i·us ASTR Wassermann *m*; *he* (*she*) *is* (*an*) *Aquarius* er (sie) ist (ein) Wassermann

a·quat·ic Wasser...

a·quat·ic plant Wasserpflanze *f*

a·quat·ics, a·quat·ic sports Wassersport *m*

aq·ue·duct Aquädukt *m*

Ar·ab Araber(in)

A·ra·bi·a Arabien *n*

Ar·a·bi·c **1.** arabisch; **2.** LING Arabisch *n*

ar·a·ble AGR anbaufähig; Acker...

ar·bi·tra·ry willkürlich, eigenmächtig

ar·bi·trate entscheiden, schlichten

ar·bi·tra·tion Schlichtung *f*

ar·bi·tra·tor Schiedsrichter *m*; Schlichter *m*

ar·bo(u)r Laube *f*

arc Bogen *m*; ELECTR Lichtbogen *m*

ar·cade Arkade *f*; Lauben-, Bogengang *m*; Durchgang *m*, Passage *f*

arch[1] **1.** Bogen *m*; Gewölbe *n*; **2.** (sich) wölben; krümmen

arch[2] erste(r, -s), oberste(r, -s), Haupt..., Erz...

arch[3] schelmisch

ar·cha·ic veraltet

arch·an·gel Erzengel *m*

arch·bish·op REL Erzbischof *m*

ar·cher Bogenschütze *m*

ar·cher·y Bogenschießen *n*

ar·chi·tect Architekt(in)

ar·chi·tec·ture Architektur *f*

ar·chives Archiv *n*

arch·way (Bogen)Gang *m*

arc·tic arktisch, nördlich, Polar...

ar·dent feurig, glühend; *fig* leidenschaftlich, heftig; eifrig

ar·do(u)r Leidenschaft *f*, Glut *f*, Feuer *n*; Eifer *m*

are *du* bist, *wir or sie or Sie* sind, *ihr* seid

ar·e·a (Boden)Fläche *f*; Gegend *f*, Gebiet

n; Bereich *m*

ar·e·a code TEL Vorwahl(nummer) *f*

Ar·gen·ti·na Argentinien *n*

Ar·gen·tine **1.** argentinisch; **2.** Argentinier(in)

a·re·na Arena *f*

ar·gue argumentieren; streiten; diskutieren

ar·gu·ment Argument *n*; Wortwechsel *m*, Auseinandersetzung *f*

ar·id dürr, trocken (*a. fig*)

Ar·ies ASTR Widder *m*; *he* (*she*) *is* (*an*) *Aries* er (sie) ist (ein) Widder

a·rise entstehen; auftauchen, auftreten

ar·is·toc·ra·cy Aristokratie *f*, Adel *m*

ar·is·to·crat Aristokrat(in), Adlige *m*, *f*

ar·is·to·crat·ic aristokratisch, adlig

a·rith·me·tic[1] Rechnen *n*

ar·ith·met·ic[2] arithmetisch, Rechen...

ar·ith·met·ic u·nit EDP Rechenwerk *n*

ark Arche *f*; *Noah's ark* die Arche Noah

arm[1] ANAT Arm *m*; Armlehne *f*; *keep s.o.* *at arm's length* sich j-n vom Leibe halten

arm[2] MIL (sich) bewaffnen; (auf)rüsten

ar·ma·ment MIL Bewaffnung *f*; Aufrüstung *f*

arm·chair Lehnstuhl *m*, Sessel *m*

ar·mi·stice MIL Waffenstillstand *m*

ar·mo(u)r **1.** MIL Rüstung *f*, Panzer *m* (*a. fig, zo*); **2.** panzern

ar·mo(u)red car gepanzertes Fahrzeug

arm·pit ANAT Achselhöhle *f*

arms Waffen *pl*; Waffengattung *f*

arms con·trol Rüstungskontrolle *f*

arms race Wettrüsten *n*, Rüstungswettlauf *m*

ar·my MIL Armee *f*, Heer *n*

a·ro·ma Aroma *n*, Duft *m*

ar·o·mat·ic aromatisch, würzig

a·round **1.** *adv* (rings)herum, (rund-) herum, ringsumher, überall; umher, herum; in der Nähe; da; **2.** *prp* um, um... herum, rund um; in (*dat*) ... herum; ungefähr, etwa

a·rouse (auf)wecken; *fig* aufrütteln, erregen

ar·range (an)ordnen; festlegen, festsetzen; arrangieren (*a.* MUS); vereinbaren; MUS, THEA bearbeiten

ar·range·ment Anordnung *f*; Vereinbarung *f*; Vorkehrung *f*; MUS Arrangement *n*, Bearbeitung *f* (*a.* THEA)

ar·rears Rückstand *m*, Rückstände *pl*

ar·rest JUR **1.** Verhaftung *f*, Festnahme *f*; **2.** verhaften, festnehmen

ar·riv·al Ankunft *f*; Erscheinen *n*; Ankömmling *m*; *arrivals* AVIAT, RAIL *etc* 'Ankunft' (*timetable*)

ar·rive (an)kommen, eintreffen, erscheinen; *arrive at* fig erreichen (*acc*), kommen zu

ar·ro·gance Arroganz f, Überheblichkeit f

ar·ro·gant arrogant, überheblich

ar·row Pfeil m

ar·row·head Pfeilspitze f

ar·se·nic CHEM Arsen n

ar·son JUR Brandstiftung f

art 1. Kunst f; 2. Kunst...; *art exhibition* Kunstausstellung f; → *arts*

ar·te·ri·al ANAT Schlagader...

ar·te·ri·al road Hauptverkehrsstraße f, Verkehrsader f

ar·te·ri·o·scle·ro·sis MED Arteriosklerose f, Arterienverkalkung f

ar·te·ry ANAT Arterie f, Schlagader f; (Haupt)Verkehrsader f

art·ful schlau, verschmitzt

art gal·le·ry Gemäldegalerie f

ar·thri·tis MED Arthritis f, Gelenkentzündung f

ar·ti·choke BOT Artischocke f

ar·ti·cle Artikel m (a. LING)

ar·tic·u·late 1. deutlich (aus)sprechen; 2. deutlich ausgesprochen; gegliedert

ar·tic·u·lat·ed Gelenk...; *articulated lorry* Br MOT Sattelschlepper m

ar·tic·u·la·tion (deutliche) Aussprache; TECH Gelenk n

ar·ti·fi·cial künstlich, Kunst...; *artificial person* juristische Person

ar·til·le·ry MIL Artillerie f

ar·ti·san Handwerker m

art·ist Künstler(in)

ar·tis·tic künstlerisch, Kunst...

art·less schlicht; naiv

arts Geisteswissenschaften pl; *Arts Department*, Br *Faculty of Arts* philosophische Fakultät

as 1. *adv* so, ebenso; wie; als; 2. *cj* (gerade) wie, so wie; ebenso wie; als, während; obwohl, obgleich; da, weil; *as ... as* (eben)so ... wie; *as for, as to* was ... (an-)betrifft; *as from* von e-m Zeitpunkt an, ab; *as it were* sozusagen; *as Hamlet* THEA als Hamlet

as·bes·tos Asbest m

as·cend (auf)steigen; ansteigen; besteigen

as·cen·dan·cy, as·cen·den·cy Überlegenheit f; Einfluss m

as·cen·sion Aufsteigen n (esp ASTR); Aufstieg m

As·cen·sion (Day) REL Himmelfahrt(stag m) f

as·cent Aufstieg m; Besteigung f; Steigung f

as·cet·ic asketisch

a·sep·tic MED 1. aseptisch, keimfrei; 2. aseptisches Mittel

ash[1] BOT Esche f; Eschenholz n

ash[2] a. *ashes* Asche f

a·shamed beschämt; *be ashamed of* sich schämen für (*or gen*)

ash·en Aschen...; aschfahl, aschgrau

a·shore am *or* ans Ufer *or* Land

ash·tray Asch(en)becher m

Ash Wednes·day Aschermittwoch m

A·sia Asien n

A·sian, A·si·at·ic 1. asiatisch; 2. Asiat(in)

a·side beiseite (a. THEA), seitwärts; *aside from* abgesehen von

ask *v/t* fragen (*s.th.* nach et.); verlangen (*of, from s.o.* von j-m); bitten (*s.o.* [*for*] *s.th.* j-n um et.; *that* darum, dass); erbitten; *ask (s.o.) a question* (j-m) e-e Frage stellen; *v/i ask for* bitten um; fragen nach; *he asked for it or for trouble* er wollte es ja so haben; *to be had for the asking* umsonst zu haben sein

a·skance: *look askance at s.o.* j-n schief *or* misstrauisch ansehen

a·skew schief

a·sleep schlafend; *be (fast, sound) asleep* (fest) schlafen; *fall asleep* einschlafen

as·par·a·gus BOT Spargel m

as·pect Lage f; Aspekt m, Seite f, Gesichtspunkt m

as·phalt 1. Asphalt m; 2. asphaltieren

as·pic GASTR Aspik m, Gelee n

as·pi·rant Bewerber(in)

as·pi·ra·tion Ambition f, Bestrebung f

as·pire streben (*to, after*) nach

ass ZO Esel m

as·sail angreifen; *be assailed with doubts* von Zweifeln befallen werden

as·sail·ant Angreifer(in)

as·sas·sin (esp politischer) Mörder, Attentäter m

as·sas·sin·ate esp POL ermorden; *be assassinated* e-m Attentat *or* Mordanschlag zum Opfer fallen

as·sas·sin·a·tion (of) (esp politischer) Mord (an *dat*), Ermordung f (*gen*), Attentat n (auf *acc*)

as·sault 1. Angriff m, Überfall m; 2. angreifen, überfallen

as·sem·blage Ansammlung f; TECH Montage f

as·sem·ble (sich) versammeln; TECH montieren

as·sem·bly Versammlung f, Gesellschaft f; TECH Montage f

assembly line TECH Fließband n

as·sent 1. Zustimmung f; 2. (*to*) zustimmen (*dat*); billigen (*acc*)

as·sert behaupten; geltend machen; *assert o.s.* sich behaupten, sich durchsetzen

as·ser·tion Behauptung *f*; Erklärung *f*; Geltendmachung *f*

as·sess *Kosten etc* festsetzen; *Einkommen etc* (zur Steuer) veranlagen (*at* mit); *fig* abschätzen, beurteilen

as·sess·ment Festsetzung *f*; (Steuer-) Veranlagung *f*; *fig* Einschätzung *f*

as·set ECON Aktivposten *m*; *fig* Plus *n*, Gewinn *m*; *pl* ECON Aktiva *pl*; JUR Vermögen(smasse *f*) *n*; Konkursmasse *f*

as·sid·u·ous emsig, fleißig

as·sign an-, zuweisen; bestimmen; zuschreiben

as·sign·ment An-, Zuweisung *f*; Aufgabe *f*; Auftrag *m*; JUR Abtretung *f*; Übertragung *f*

as·sim·i·late (sich) angleichen *or* anpassen (*to, with dat*)

as·sim·i·la·tion Assimilation *f*, Angleichung *f*, Anpassung *f* (*all*: *to* an *acc*)

as·sist *j-m* beistehen, helfen; *j-n* unterstützen

as·sist·ance Beistand *m*, Hilfe *f*

as·sist·ant 1. stellvertretend, Hilfs...; **2.** Assistent(in), Mitarbeiter(in); (*shop*) *assistant Br* Verkäufer(in)

as·so·ci·ate 1. vereinigen, verbinden, zusammenschließen; assoziieren; *associate with* verkehren mit; **2.** Teilhaber(in)

as·so·ci·a·tion Vereinigung *f*, Verbindung *f*; Verein *m*

as·sort sortieren, aussuchen, zusammenstellen

as·sort·ment ECON (*of*) Sortiment *n* (von), Auswahl *f* (an *dat*)

as·sume annehmen, voraussetzen; übernehmen

as·sump·tion Annahme *f*, Voraussetzung *f*; Übernahme *f*; *the Assumption* REL Mariä Himmelfahrt *f*

as·sur·ance Zusicherung *f*, Versicherung *f*; *esp Br* (Lebens)Versicherung *f*; Sicherheit *f*, Gewissheit *f*; Selbstsicherheit *f*

as·sure *j-m* versichern; *esp Br* *j-s* Leben versichern

as·sured 1. sicher; **2.** *esp Br* Versicherte *m*, *f*

as·sur·ed·ly ganz gewiss

as·te·risk PRINT Sternchen *n*

asth·ma MED Asthma *n*

as·ton·ish in Erstaunen setzen; *be astonished* erstaunt sein (*at* über *acc*)

as·ton·ish·ing erstaunlich

as·ton·ish·ment (Er)Staunen *n*, Verwunderung *f*

as·tound verblüffen

a·stray: *go astray* vom Weg abkommen; *fig* auf Abwege geraten; irregehen; *lead astray fig* irreführen; verleiten

a·stride rittlings (*of* auf *dat*)

as·trin·gent MED **1.** adstringierend; **2.** Adstringens *n*

as·trol·o·gy Astrologie *f*

as·tro·naut Astronaut *m*, (Welt)Raumfahrer *m*

as·tron·o·my Astronomie *f*

as·tute scharfsinnig; schlau

a·sun·der auseinander, entzwei

a·sy·lum Asyl *n*; *right of asylum* Asylrecht *n*

a·sy·lum seek·er Asylant(in), Asylbewerber(in)

at *prp place*: in, an, bei, auf; *direction*: auf, nach, gegen, zu; *occupation*: bei, beschäftigt mit, in; *manner, state*: in, bei, zu, unter; *price etc*: für, um; *time, age*: um, bei; *at the baker's* beim Bäcker; *at the door* an der Tür; *at school* in der Schule; *at 10 dollars* für 10 Dollar; *at 18* mit 18 (Jahren); *at the age of* im Alter von; *at 8 o'clock* um 8 Uhr

a·the·ism Atheismus *m*

ath·lete SPORT (Leicht)Athlet(in)

ath·let·ic SPORT athletisch

ath·let·ics SPORT (Leicht)Athletik *f*

At·lan·tic 1. *a.* *Atlantic Ocean* der Atlantik; **2.** atlantisch

at·mo·sphere Atmosphäre *f* (*a. fig*)

at·mo·spher·ic atmosphärisch

at·oll Atoll *n*

at·om Atom *n*

atom bomb Atombombe *f*

a·tom·ic atomar, Atom...

atomic age Atomzeitalter *n*

atomic bomb Atombombe *f*

atomic en·er·gy Atomenergie *f*

atomic pile Atomreaktor *m*

atomic pow·er Atomkraft *f*

atomic-pow·ered atomgetrieben

atomic waste Atommüll *m*

atomic weight CHEM Atomgewicht *n*

at·om·ize atomisieren; *Flüssigkeit* zerstäuben

at·om·iz·er Zerstäuber *m*

a·tone: *atone for* büßen für, *et.* sühnen

a·tone·ment Buße *f*, Sühne *f*

a·tro·cious grässlich; grausam

a·troc·i·ty Scheußlichkeit *f*; Greueltat *f*

at sign EDP at-Zeichen *n*

at·tach *v/t* (*to*) anheften, ankleben (an *acc*), befestigen, anbringen (an *dat*); *Wert, Wichtigkeit etc* beimessen (*dat*); *be attached to fig* hängen an

at·tach·ment Befestigung *f*; Bindung *f* (*to*

an *acc*); Anhänglichkeit *f* (**to** an *acc*)
at·tack 1. angreifen; **2.** Angriff *m*; MED Anfall *m*
at·tempt 1. versuchen; **2.** Versuch *m*; *an attempt on s.o.'s life* ein Mordanschlag *or* Attentat auf j-n
at·tend *v/t* (ärztlich) behandeln; *Kranke* pflegen; teilnehmen an (*dat*), *Schule, Vorlesung etc* besuchen; *fig* begleiten; *v/i* anwesend sein; erscheinen; *attend to* j-n (*im Laden*) bedienen; *are you being attended to?* werden Sie schon bedient?; *attend to s.th.* etwas erledigen
at·tend·ance Dienst *m*, Bereitschaft *f*; Pflege *f*; Anwesenheit *f*, Erscheinen *n*; Besucher *pl*, Teilnehmer *pl*; Besuch(erzahl *f*) *m*, Beteiligung *f*
at·tend·ant Begleiter(in); Aufseher(in); (*Tank-*)Wart *m*
at·ten·tion Aufmerksamkeit *f* (*a. fig*); *pay attention* aufpassen
at·ten·tive aufmerksam
at·tic Dachboden *m*; Dachkammer *f*
at·ti·tude (Ein)Stellung *f*; Haltung *f*
at·tor·ney Bevollmächtigte *m, f*; JUR (Rechts)Anwalt *m*, (Rechts)Anwältin *f*; *power of attorney* Vollmacht *f*
At·tor·ney Gen·er·al JUR Justizminister; *Br* erster Kronanwalt
at·tract anlocken; *Aufmerksamkeit* erregen; *fig* reizen
at·trac·tion Anziehung *f*, Anziehungskraft *f*, Reiz *m*; Attraktion *f*, THEA *etc* Zugnummer *f*, Zugstück *n*
at·trac·tive anziehend; attraktiv; reizvoll
at·trib·ute¹ zuschreiben (**to** *dat*); zurückführen (**to** auf *acc*)
at·tri·bute² Attribut *n* (*a.* LING), Eigenschaft *f*, Merkmal *n*
at·tune: *attune to fig* einstellen auf (*acc*)
au·ber·gine BOT Aubergine *f*
au·burn kastanienbraun
auc·tion 1. Auktion *f*, Versteigerung *f*; **2.** *mst auction off* versteigern
auc·tion·eer Auktionator *m*
au·da·cious unverfroren, dreist
au·dac·i·ty Unverfrorenheit *f*, Dreistigkeit *f*
au·di·ble hörbar
au·di·ence Publikum *n*, Zuhörer *pl*, Zuschauer *pl*, Besucher *pl*, Leser(kreis *m*) *pl*; Audienz *f*
au·di·o·vis·u·al aids audiovisuelle Unterrichtsmittel *pl*
au·dit ECON **1.** Buchprüfung *f*; **2.** prüfen
au·di·tion MUS Vorsingen *n*; THEA Vorsprechen *n*; *have an audition* vorsingen, THEA vorsprechen
au·di·tor ECON Buchprüfer *m*; UNIV Gast-

hörer(in)
au·di·to·ri·um Zuhörer-, Zuschauerraum *m*; Vortrags-, Konzertsaal *m*
au·ger TECH großer Bohrer
Au·gust (ABBR *Aug*) August *m*
aunt Tante *f*
au pair (girl) Au-pair-Mädchen *n*
aus·pic·es: *under the auspices of* unter der Schirmherrschaft (*gen*)
aus·tere streng; enthaltsam; dürftig; einfach, schmucklos
Aus·tra·li·a Australien
Aus·tra·li·an 1. australisch; **2.** Australier(in)
Aus·tri·a Österreich *n*
Aus·tri·an 1. österreichisch; **2.** Österreicher(in)
au·then·tic authentisch; zuverlässig; echt
au·thor Urheber(in); Autor(in), Verfasser(in), Schriftsteller(in)
au·thor·ess Autorin *f*, Verfasserin *f*, Schriftstellerin *f*
au·thor·i·ta·tive gebieterisch, herrisch; maßgebend
au·thor·i·ty Autorität *f*; Nachdruck *m*, Gewicht *n*; Vollmacht *f*; Einfluss *m* (**over** auf *acc*); Ansehen *n*; Quelle *f*; Autorität *f*, Kapazität *f*; *mst pl* Behörde *f*
au·thor·ize j-n autorisieren, ermächtigen, bevollmächtigen
au·thor·ship Urheberschaft *f*
au·to... Auto *n*
au·to... auto..., selbst..., Auto..., Selbst...
au·to·bi·og·ra·phy Autobiografie *f*
au·to·graph Autogramm *n*
au·to·mat Automatenrestaurant *n*
au·to·mate automatisieren
au·to·mat·ic 1. automatisch; **2.** Selbstladepistole *f*, -gewehr *n*; Auto *n* mit Automatik
automatic tel·ler ma·chine (ABBR *ATM*) Geld-, Bankautomat *m*
au·to·ma·tion TECH Automation *f*
au·tom·a·ton Roboter *m*
au·to·mo·bile Auto *n*, Automobil *n*
au·ton·o·my POL Autonomie *f*
au·top·sy MED Autopsie *f*
au·to·tel·ler Geld-, Bankautomat *m*
au·tumn Herbst *m*
au·tum·nal herbstlich, Herbst...
aux·il·i·a·ry helfend, Hilfs...
a·vail: *to no avail* vergeblich
a·vail·a·ble verfügbar, vorhanden; erreichbar; ECON lieferbar, vorrätig, erhältlich
av·a·lanche Lawine *f*
av·a·rice Habsucht *f*

a·va·ri·cious habgierig

a·venge rächen

a·veng·er Rächer(in)

av·e·nue Allee f; Boulevard m, Prachtstraße f

av·e·rage **1.** Durchschnitt m; **2.** durchschnittlich, Durchschnitts...

a·verse abgeneigt (**to** dat)

a·ver·sion Widerwille m, Abneigung f

a·vert abwenden (a. fig)

avian flu Vogelgrippe f

a·vi·a·ry Vogelhaus n, Voliere f

a·vi·a·tion Luftfahrt f

a·vi·a·tor Flieger m

av·id gierig (**for** nach); begeistert

av·o·ca·do BOT Avocado f

a·void (ver)meiden; ausweichen

a·void·ance Vermeidung f

a·vow·al Bekenntnis n, (Ein)Geständnis n

a·wait erwarten, warten auf (acc)

a·wake **1.** wach, munter; **2.** a. a·wak·en v/t (auf)wecken; v/i aufwachen, erwachen;

a·wak·en·ing Erwachen n

a·ward **1.** Belohnung f; Preis m, Auszeichnung f; **2.** zuerkennen, Preis etc verleihen

a·ware: **be aware of s.th.** von etwas wissen, sich e-r Sache bewusst sein; **become aware of s.th.** etwas merken

a·way weg, fort; (weit) entfernt; immer weiter, d(a)rauflos; SPORT Auswärts...; **away match** SPORT Auswärtsspiel n

awe **1.** Furcht f, Scheu f; **2.** j-m (Ehr)Furcht or großen Respekt einflößen

aw·ful furchtbar, schrecklich

awk·ward ungeschickt, linkisch; unangenehm; unhandlich, sperrig; ungünstig, ungelegen

awl Ahle f, Pfriem m

aw·ning Plane f; Markise f

a·wry schief

ax(e) Axt f, Beil n

ax·is MATH etc Achse f

ax·le TECH (Rad)Achse f, Welle f

ay(e) PARL Jastimme f

A-Z Br appr Stadtplan m

az·ure azurblau, himmelblau

B

B, b B, b n

b ABBR of **born** geb., geboren

bab·ble **1.** stammeln; plappern, schwatzen; plätschern; **2.** Geplapper n, Geschwätz n

babe kleines Kind, Baby n; F Puppe f

ba·boon ZO Pavian m

ba·by **1.** Baby n, Säugling m, kleines Kind; F Puppe f; **2.** Baby..., Kinder...; klein

baby bug·gy, baby car·riage Kinderwagen m

ba·by·hood Säuglingsalter n

ba·by·ish contp kindisch

ba·by·mind·er Br Tagesmutter f

ba·by·sit babysitten

ba·by·sit·ter Babysitter(in)

bach·e·lor Junggeselle m

back **1.** Rücken m; Rückseite f; (Rück)Lehne f; hinterer or rückwärtiger Teil; SPORT Verteidiger m; **2.** adj Hinter..., Rück..., hintere(r, -s), rückwärtig; ECON rückständig; alt, zurückliegend; **3.** adv zurück, rückwärts; **4.** v/t mit e-m Rücken versehen; wetten or setzen auf (acc); a. **back up** unterstützen; zurückbewegen; MOT zurückstoßen mit; **back up** EDP

e-e Sicherungskopie machen von; v/i often **back up** sich rückwärts bewegen, zurückgehen or -fahren, MOT a. zurückstoßen; **back in(to a parking space)** MOT rückwärts einparken; **back up** EDP e-e Sicherungskopie machen

back·ache Rückenschmerzen pl

back·bite verleumden, schlechtmachen

back·bone ANAT Rückgrat n (a. fig)

back·break·ing erschöpfend, mörderisch

back·chat Br freche Antwort(en pl)

back·comb Br toupieren

back door Hintertür f; fig Hintertürchen n

back·er Unterstützer m, Geldgeber m

back·fire MOT Früh- or Fehlzündung haben; fig fehlschlagen

back·ground Hintergrund m

back·hand SPORT Rückhand f, Rückhandschlag m

back·heel·er soccer: Hackentrick m

back·ing Unterstützung f

back num·ber alte Nummer

back·pack großer Rucksack

back·pack·er Rucksacktourist(in)

back·pack·ing Rucksacktourismus m

back-ped·al brake *Br* Rücktritt *m*, Rücktrittbremse *f*

back seat MOT Rücksitz *m*

back·side Gesäß *n*, F Hintern *m*, Po *m*

back·space (key) EDP Rücktaste *f*

back stairs Hintertreppe *f*

back street Seitenstraße *f*

back·stroke Rückenschwimmen *n*

back talk freche Antwort(en *pl*)

back·track *fig* e-n Rückzieher machen

back·up Unterstützung *f*; TECH Ersatzgerät *n*; EDP Backup *n*, Sicherungskopie *f*; MOT Rückstau *m*

back·ward 1. *adj* Rück..., Rückwärts...; zurückgeblieben; rückständig; *a backward glance* ein Blick zurück; **2.** *adv* *a.* **backwards** rückwärts, zurück

back·yard Garten *m* hinter dem Haus; *Br* Hinterhof *m*

ba·con Speck *m*

bac·te·ri·a BIOL Bakterien *pl*

bad schlecht, böse, schlimm; *go bad* schlecht werden, verderben; *he is in a bad way* es geht ihm schlecht; *he is badly off* es geht ihm finanziell schlecht; *badly wounded* schwer verwundet; *want badly* dringend brauchen

badge Abzeichen *n*; Dienstmarke *f*

bad·ger 1. ZO Dachs *m*; **2.** *j-n* plagen, *j-m* zusetzen

bad·min·ton Federball(spiel *n*) *m*, SPORT Badminton *n*

bad-tempered schlecht gelaunt

bag 1. Beutel *m*, Sack *m*; Tüte *f*; Tasche *f*; *bag and baggage* (mit) Sack und Pack; **2.** in e-n Beutel *etc* tun; in Beutel verpacken *or* abfüllen; HUNT zur Strecke bringen; schlottern; *a. bag out* sich bauschen

bag·gage (Reise)Gepäck *n*

baggage car RAIL Gepäckwagen *m*

baggage check Gepäckschein *m*

baggage claim AVIAT Gepäckausgabe *f*

baggage room RAIL Gepäckaufbewahrung *f*

bag·gy bauschig; ausgebeult

bag·pipes MUS Dudelsack *m*

bail 1. Bürge *m*; JUR Kaution *f*; *be out on bail* gegen Kaution auf freiem Fuß sein; *go or stand bail for s.o.* für *j-n* Kaution stellen; **2.** *bail out* JUR *j-n* gegen Kaution freibekommen; AVIAT (mit dem Fallschirm) abspringen

bai·liff (Guts)Verwalter *m*; *Br* JUR Gerichtsvollzieher *m*

bait 1. Köder *m* (*a. fig*); **2.** mit e-m Köder versehen; *fig* ködern

bake backen, im (Back)Ofen braten; TECH brennen; dörren

bak·er Bäcker *m*

bak·er·y Bäckerei *f*

bak·ing pow·der Backpulver *n*

bal·ance 1. Waage *f*; Gleichgewicht *n* (*a. fig*); ECON Bilanz *f*; Saldo *m*, Kontostand *m*, Guthaben *n*; Restbetrag *m*; *keep one's balance* das Gleichgewicht halten; *lose one's balance* das Gleichgewicht verlieren; *fig* die Fassung verlieren; *balance of payments* ECON Zahlungsbilanz *f*; *balance of power* POL Kräftegleichgewicht *n*; *balance of trade* ECON Handelsbilanz *f*; **2.** *v/t* abwägen; im Gleichgewicht halten, balancieren; ECON ausgleichen; *v/i* balancieren; ECON sich ausgleichen; *balance each other* sich die Waage halten

bal·ance sheet ECON Bilanz *f*

bal·co·ny Balkon *m* (*a.* THEA)

bald kahl

bale¹ ECON Ballen *m*

bale²: *bale out* *Br* AVIAT (mit dem Fallschirm) abspringen

bale·ful hasserfüllt

balk 1. Balken *m*; **2.** stutzen; scheuen

ball¹ 1. Ball *m*; Kugel *f*; ANAT (Hand-, Fuß)Ballen *m*; Knäuel *m, n*; Kloß *m*; *start the ball rolling* den Stein ins Rollen bringen; *play ball* F mitmachen; *long ball* SPORT langer Pass; **2.** ballen; sich zusammenballen

ball² Ball *m*, Tanzveranstaltung *f*

bal·lad Ballade *f*

bal·last 1. Ballast *m*; **2.** mit Ballast beladen

ball bear·ing TECH Kugellager *n*

bal·let Ballett *n*

bal·lis·tics MIL Ballistik *f*

bal·loon 1. Ballon *m*; Sprech-, Denkblase *f*; **2.** sich (auf)blähen

bal·lot 1. Stimmzettel *m*; (geheime) Wahl; **2.** (*for*) stimmen (für), (in geheimer Wahl) wählen (*acc*)

ballot box Wahlurne *f*

ballot pa·per Stimmzettel *m*

ball·point (pen) Kugelschreiber *m*, F Kuli *m*

ball·room Ballsaal *m*, Tanzsaal *m*

balls V Eier *pl*

balm Balsam *m* (*a. fig*)

balm·y lind, mild

ba·lo·ney F Quatsch *m*

bal·us·trade Balustrade *f*, Brüstung *f*, Geländer *n*

bam·boo BOT Bambus(rohr *n*) *m*

bam·boo·zle F betrügen, *j-n* übers Ohr hauen

ban 1. (amtliches) Verbot, Sperre *f*; REL Bann *m*; **2.** verbieten

ba·nal banal, abgedroschen

ba·na·na BOT Banane *f*

band 1. Band *n*; Streifen *m*; Schar *f*, Gruppe *f*; *contp* Bande *f*; (Musik)Kapelle *f*, (Tanz-, Unterhaltungs)Orchester *n*, (Jazz-, Rock)Band *f*; **2. band together** sich zusammentun *or* -rotten

ban·dage MED **1.** Bandage *f*; Binde *f*; Verband *m*; (Heft)Pflaster *n*; **2.** bandagieren; verbinden

'Band-Aid® MED (Heft)Pflaster *n*

b & b, B & B ABBR *of* **bed and breakfast** Übernachtung *f* mit Frühstück

ban·dit Bandit *m*

band·lead·er MUS Bandleader *m*

band·mas·ter MUS Kapellmeister *m*

ban·dy-legged säbelbeinig, o-beinig

bang 1. heftiger Schlag; Knall *m*; *mst pl* Pony *m*; **2.** dröhnend (zu)schlagen

ban·gle Armreif *m*, Fußreif *m*

ban·ish verbannen

ban·ish·ment Verbannung *f*

ban·is·ter *a. pl* Treppengeländer *n*

ban·jo MUS Banjo *n*

bank¹ ECON **1.** Bank *f* (*a.* MED.); **2.** *v/t* bei e-r Bank einzahlen; *v/i* ein Bankkonto haben (**with** bei)

bank² (Erd)Wall *m*; Böschung *f*; (Fluss- *etc*)Ufer *n*; (Sand-, Wolken)Bank *f*

bank ac·count Bankkonto *n*

bank bill Banknote *f*, Geldschein *m*

bank·book Sparbuch *n*

bank code ECON Bankleitzahl *f*

bank·er Bankier *m*, Banker *m*; **banker's card** Scheckkarte *f*

bank hol·i·day *Br* gesetzlicher Feiertag *m*

bank·ing ECON **1.** Bankgeschäft *n*, Bankwesen *n*; **2.** Bank...

bank note *Br* → **bank bill**

bank rate ECON Diskontsatz *m*

bank·rupt JUR **1.** Konkursschuldner *m*; **2.** bankrott; *go bankrupt* in Konkurs gehen, Bankrott machen; **3.** *j-n*, *Unternehmen* Bankrott machen

bank·rupt·cy JUR Bankrott *m*, Konkurs *m*

bank sort·ing code → **bank code**

ban·ner Transparent *n*

banns Aufgebot *n*

ban·quet Bankett *n*

ban·ter necken

bap·tism REL Taufe *f*

bap·tize REL taufen

bar 1. Stange *f*, Stab *m*; SPORT (Tor-, Quer-, Sprung)Latte *f*; Riegel *m*; Schranke *f*, Sperre *f*; *fig* Hindernis *n*; (Gold- *etc*)Barren *m*; MUS Taktstrich *m*; *ein* Takt *m*; dicker Strich; *a.* JUR (Gerichts)Schranke *f*; JUR Anwaltschaft *f*; Bar *f*, Lokal *n*, Imbissstube *f*; *pl* Gitter *n*; *a bar of choco-*

late ein Riegel *or* e-e Tafel Schokolade; *a bar of soap* ein Stück Seife; **2.** zuriegeln, verriegeln; versperren; einsperren; (ver)hindern); ausschließen

barb Widerhaken *m*

bar·bar·i·an 1. barbarisch; **2.** Barbar(in)

bar·be·cue 1. Bratrost *m*, Grill *m*; Barbecue *n*; **2.** auf dem Rost *or* am Spieß braten, grillen

barbed wire Stacheldraht *m*

bar·ber (Herren)Friseur *m*, (-)Frisör *m*

bar code Strichkode *m*

bare 1. nackt, bloß; kahl; leer; **2.** entblößen

bare·faced unverschämt, schamlos

bare·foot, bare·foot·ed barfuß

bare·head·ed barhäuptig

bare·ly kaum

bar·gain 1. Geschäft *n*, Handel *m*; vorteilhaftes Geschäft, Gelegenheitskauf *m*; *a (dead) bargain* spottbillig; *it's a bargain!* abgemacht!; *into the bargain* obendrein; **2.** (ver)handeln

bargain sale Verkauf *m* zu herabgesetzten Preisen; Ausverkauf *m*

barge 1. Lastkahn *m*; **2.** *barge in* F hereinplatzen (**on** bei)

bark¹ BOT Borke *f*, Rinde *f*

bark² 1. bellen; *bark up the wrong tree* F auf dem Holzweg sein; an der falschen Adresse sein; **2.** Bellen *n*

bar·ley BOT Gerste *f*; Graupe *f*

barn Scheune *f*; (Vieh)Stall *m*

ba·rom·e·ter Barometer *n*

bar·on Baron *m*; Freiherr *m*

bar·on·ess Baronin *f*; Freifrau *f*

bar·racks MIL Kaserne *f*; *contp* Mietskaserne *f*

bar·rage Staudamm *m*; MIL Sperrfeuer *n*; *fig* (Wort- *etc*)Schwall *m*

bar·rel Fass *n*, Tonne *f*; (Gewehr)Lauf *m*; TECH Trommel *f*, Walze *f*

bar·rel or·gan MUS Drehorgel *f*

bar·ren unfruchtbar; trocken

bar·rette Haarspange *f*

bar·ri·cade 1. Barrikade *f*; **2.** verbarrikadieren; sperren

bar·ri·er Schranke *f* (*a. fig*), Barriere *f*, Sperre *f*; Hindernis *n*

bar·ris·ter *Br* JUR Barrister *m*

bar·row Karre *f*

bar·ter 1. Tausch(handel) *m*; **2.** tauschen (*for* gegen)

base¹ gemein

base² 1. Basis *f*; Grundlage *f*; Fundament *n*; Fuß *m*; MIL Standort *m*; MIL Stützpunkt *m*; **2.** gründen, stützen (**on** auf *acc*)

base³ CHEM Base *f*

base·ball SPORT Baseball(spiel *n*) *m*

base·board Scheuerleiste f
base·less grundlos
base·line *tennis etc*: Grundlinie f
base·ment ARCH Fundament n; Kellergeschoss n
bash·ful scheu, schüchtern
ba·sic[1] 1. Grund..., grundlegend; 2. *pl* Grundlagen *pl*
ba·sic[2] CHEM basisch
ba·sic·al·ly im Grunde
ba·sin Becken n, Schale f, Schüssel f; Tal-, Wasser-, Hafenbecken n
ba·sis Basis f; Grundlage f
bask sich sonnen (*a. fig*)
bas·ket Korb m
bas·ket·ball SPORT Basketball(spiel n) m
bass[1] MUS Bass m
bass[2] ZO (Fluss-, See)Barsch m
bas·tard Bastard m
baste[1] GASTR mit Fett begießen
baste[2] (an)heften
bat[1] ZO Fledermaus f; *as blind as a bat* stockblind
bat[2] *baseball, cricket* 1. Schlagholz n, Schläger m; F *right off the bat* sofort; 2. am Schlagen sein
batch Stapel m, Stoß m
batch pro·cess·ing EDP Stapelverarbeitung f
bate: *with bated breath* mit angehaltenem Atem
bath 1. (Wannen)Bad n; *pl* Bad n, Badeanstalt f; Badeort m; *have a bath Br, take a bath* (*Br* im Bad nehmen; 2. *Br* v/t j-n baden; v/i baden, ein Bad nehmen
bathe v/t baden (*a. MED*); v/i baden, ein Bad nehmen; schwimmen
bath·ing 1. Baden n; 2. Bade...
bath·ing suit → *swimsuit*
bath·robe Bademantel m; Morgenrock m, Schlafrock m
bath·room Badezimmer n; Toilette f
bath·tub Badewanne f
bat·on Stab m; MUS Taktstock m; Schlagstock m, Gummiknüppel m
bat·tal·i·on MIL Bataillon n
bat·ten Latte f
bat·ter[1] heftig schlagen; misshandeln; verbeulen; *batter down, batter in* einschlagen
bat·ter[2] GASTR Rührteig m
bat·ter[3] *baseball, cricket*: Schläger m, Schlagmann m
bat·ter·y ELECTR Batterie f; JUR Tätlichkeit f, Körperverletzung f; *assault and battery* JUR tätliche Beleidigung
bat·ter·y charg·er ELECTR Ladegerät n
bat·ter·y-op·er·at·ed ELECTR batteriebetrieben

bat·tle 1. MIL Schlacht f (*of* bei); *fig* Kampf m (*for* um); 2. kämpfen
bat·tle·field, bat·tle·ground MIL Schlachtfeld n
bat·tle·ments ARCH Zinnen *pl*
bat·tle·ship MIL Schlachtschiff n
baulk → *balk*
Ba·va·ri·a Bayern n
Ba·va·ri·an 1. bay(e)risch; 2. Bayer(in)
bawd·y obszön
bawl brüllen, schreien; *bawl s.o. out* mit j-m schimpfen
bay[1] GEOGR Bai f, Bucht f; ARCH Erker m
bay[2] *a. bay tree* BOT Lorbeer(baum) m
bay[3] 1. ZO bellen, Laut geben; 2. *hold or keep at bay* j-n in Schach halten; et. von sich fernhalten
bay[4] 1. rotbraun; 2. ZO Braune m
bay·o·net MIL Bajonett n
bay·ou GEOGR sumpfiger Flussarm
bay win·dow ARCH Erkerfenster n
ba·zaar Basar m
BC ABBR *of before Christ* v. Chr., vor Christus
be sein; *to form the passive*: werden; stattfinden; *he wants to be a doctor etc* er möchte Arzt *etc* werden; *how much are the shoes?* was kosten die Schuhe?; *that's five dollars* das macht *or* kostet fünf Dollar; *she is reading* sie liest gerade; *there is, there are* es gibt
beach Strand m
beach ball Wasserball m
beach bug·gy MOT Strandbuggy m
beach·wear Strandkleidung f
bea·con Leucht-, Signalfeuer n
bead (Glas-, Schweiß- *etc*)Perle f; *pl* REL Rosenkranz m
bead·y klein, rund und glänzend
beak ZO Schnabel m; TECH Tülle f
beam 1. Balken m; (Licht)Strahl m; AVIAT *etc* Peil-, Leit-, Richtstrahl m; 2. ausstrahlen; strahlen (*a. fig with* vor *dat*)
bean BOT Bohne f; *be full of beans* F aufgekratzt sein; → *spill 1*
bear[1] ZO Bär m
bear[2] tragen; zur Welt bringen, gebären; ertragen, aushalten; *I can't bear him* (*it*) ich kann ihn (es) nicht ausstehen *or* leiden; *bear out* bestätigen
bear·a·ble erträglich
beard Bart m; BOT Grannen *pl*
beard·ed bärtig
bear·er Träger(in); ECON Überbringer(in), Inhaber(in)
bear·ing Ertragen n; Betragen n; (Körper)Haltung f; *fig* Beziehung f; Lage f, Richtung f, Orientierung f; *take one's bearings* sich orientieren; *lose one's*

bearings die Orientierung verlieren
beast (*a. wildes*) Tier; Bestie *f*
beast·ly scheußlich
beast of prey zo Raubtier *n*
beat 1. schlagen; (ver)prügeln; besiegen; übertreffen; F **beat s.o. to it** j-m zuvorkommen; **beat it!** F hau ab!; **that beats all!** das ist doch der Gipfel *or* die Höhe!; **that beats me** F das ist mir zu hoch; **beat about the bush** wie die Katze um den heißen Brei herumschleichen; **beat down** ECON drücken, herunterhandeln; **beat s.o. up** j-n zusammenschlagen; **2.** Schlag *m*; MUS Takt(schlag) *m*; *jazz*: Beat *m*; Pulsschlag *m*; Runde *f*, Revier *n*; **3.** **(dead) beat** F wie erschlagen, fix und fertig
beat·en track Trampelpfad *m*; **off the beaten track** ungewohnt, ungewöhnlich
beat·ing (Tracht *f*) Prügel *pl*
beau·ti·cian Kosmetikerin *f*
beau·ti·ful schön
beaut·y Schönheit *f*; **Sleeping Beauty** Dornröschen *n*
beauty care Schönheitspflege *f*
beauty par·lo(u)r, beauty sal·on Schönheitssalon *m*
bea·ver zo Biber *m*; Biberpelz *m*
be·cause weil; **because of** wegen (*gen*)
beck·on (zu)winken (*dat*)
be·come *v/i* werden (**of** aus); *v/t* sich schicken für; j-m stehen, j-n kleiden
be·com·ing passend; schicklich; kleidsam
bed 1. Bett *n*; zo Lager *n*; AGR Beet *n*; Unterlage *f*; **bed and breakfast** Zimmer *n* mit Frühstück; **2. bed down** sein Nachtlager aufschlagen
bed·clothes Bettwäsche *f*
bed·ding Bettzeug *n*; AGR Streu *f*
bed·lam Tollhaus *n*
bed·rid·den bettlägerig
bed·room Schlafzimmer *n*
bed·side: at the bedside am (*a. Kranken*)Bett
bed·side lamp Nachttischlampe *f*
bed·sit F, **bed·sit·ter, bed·sit·ting room** *Br* möbliertes Zimmer; Einzimmerappartement *n*
bed·spread Tagesdecke *f*
bed·stead Bettgestell *n*
bed·time Schlafenszeit *f*
bee zo Biene *f*; **have a bee in one's bonnet** F e-n Fimmel *or* Tick haben
beech BOT Buche *f*
beech·nut BOT Buchecker *f*
beef GASTR Rindfleisch *n*
beef·bur·ger GASTR *Br* Hamburger *m*
beef tea GASTR (Rind)Fleischbrühe *f*

beef·y F bullig
bee·hive Bienenkorb *m*, Bienenstock *m*
bee·keep·er Imker *m*
bee·line: make a beeline for F schnurstracks losgehen auf (*acc*)
beep·er TECH Piepser *m*
beer Bier *n*
beet BOT Runkelrübe *f*, Rote Bete, Rübe
bee·tle zo Käfer *m*
beet·root BOT *Br* Rote Bete, Rote Rübe
be·fore 1. *adv space:* vorn, voran; *time:* vorher, früher, schon (früher); **2.** *cj* bevor, ehe, bis; **3.** *prp* vor
be·fore·hand zuvor, im Voraus, vorweg
be·friend sich *j*-s annehmen
beg *v/t et.* erbitten (**of s.o.** von j-m); betteln um; *j*-n bitten; *v/i* betteln; (dringend) bitten
be·get (er)zeugen
beg·gar 1. Bettler(in); F Kerl *m*; **2. it beggars all description** es spottet jeder Beschreibung
be·gin beginnen, anfangen
be·gin·ner Anfänger(in)
be·gin·ning Beginn *m*, Anfang *m*
be·grudge missgönnen
be·guile täuschen; betrügen (**of, out of** um); sich die Zeit vertreiben
be·half: in (*Br* **on**) **behalf of** im Namen von (*or* gen)
be·have sich (gut) benehmen
be·hav·io(u)r Benehmen *n*, Betragen *n*, Verhalten *n*
be·hav·io(u)r·al sci·ence PSYCH Verhaltensforschung *f*
be·head enthaupten
be·hind 1. *adv* hinten, dahinter; zurück; **2.** *prp* hinter (*dat or acc*); **3.** F Hinterteil *n*, Hintern *m*
beige beige
be·ing Sein *n*, Dasein *n*, Existenz *f*; (Lebe)Wesen *n*, Geschöpf *n*; *j*-s Wesen *n*, Natur *f*
be·lat·ed verspätet
belch 1. aufstoßen, rülpsen; *a.* **belch out** speien, ausstoßen; **2.** Rülpser *m*
bel·fry Glockenturm *m*, -stuhl *m*
Bel·gium Belgien *n*
Bel·gian 1. belgisch; **2.** Belgier(in)
be·lief Glaube *m* (**in** an *acc*)
be·liev·a·ble glaubhaft
be·lieve glauben (**in** an *acc*); **I couldn't believe my ears (eyes)** ich traute m-n Ohren (Augen) nicht
be·liev·er REL Gläubige *m*, *f*
be·lit·tle *fig* herabsetzen
bell Glocke *f*; Klingel *f*
bell·boy *Br*, **bell·hop** (Hotel)Page *m*

bel·lig·er·ent kriegerisch; streitlustig, aggressiv; Krieg führend
bel·low 1. brüllen; **2.** Gebrüll n
bel·lows Blasebalg m
bel·ly 1. Bauch m; Magen m; **2. belly out** (an)schwellen lassen; bauschen
bel·ly·ache F Bauchweh n
be·long gehören; **belong to** gehören dat or zu
be·long·ings Habseligkeiten pl, Habe f
be·loved 1. (innig) geliebt; **2.** Geliebte m, f
be·low 1. adv unten; **2.** prp unter (dat or acc)
belt 1. Gürtel m; Gurt m; GEOGR Zone f, Gebiet n; TECH (Treib)Riemen m; **2. belt out** MUS schmettern; a. **belt up** den Gürtel (gen) zumachen; **belt up** MOT sich anschnallen
belt·ed mit e-m Gürtel
belt·way Umgehungsstraße f; Ringstraße f
be·moan betrauern, beklagen
bench Sitzbank f, Bank f (a. SPORT); TECH Werkbank f; JUR Richterbank f; Richter m or pl
bend 1. Biegung f, Kurve f; **drive s.o. round the bend** F j-n noch wahnsinnig machen; **2.** (sich) biegen or krümmen; neigen; beugen; fig richten (**to, on** auf acc)
be·neath → **below**
ben·e·dic·tion REL Segen m
ben·e·fac·tor Wohltäter m
ben·e·fi·cent wohltätig
ben·e·fi·cial wohltuend, zuträglich, nützlich
ben·e·fit 1. Nutzen m, Vorteil m; Wohltätigkeitsveranstaltung f; (Sozial-, Versicherungs- etc)Leistung f; (Arbeitslosen- etc)Unterstützung f; (Kranken- etc)Geld n; **2.** nützen; **benefit by, benefit from** Vorteil haben von or durch, Nutzen ziehen aus
be·nev·o·lence Wohlwollen n
be·nev·o·lent wohltätig; wohlwollend
be·nign MED gutartig
bent 1. bent on doing entschlossen zu tun; **2.** Hang m, Neigung f; Veranlagung f
ben·zene CHEM Benzol n
ben·zine CHEM Leichtbenzin n
be·queath JUR vermachen
be·quest JUR Vermächtnis n
be·reave berauben
be·ret Baskenmütze f
ber·ry BOT Beere f
berth 1. MAR Liege-, Ankerplatz m; Koje f; RAIL (Schlafwagen)Bett n; **2.** MAR festma-

chen, anlegen
be·seech (inständig) bitten (um); anflehen
be·set heimsuchen; **beset with difficulties** mit vielen Schwierigkeiten verbunden
be·side prp neben (dat or acc); **beside o.s.** außer sich (**with** vor); **beside the point, beside the question** nicht zur Sache gehörig
be·sides 1. adv außerdem; **2.** prp abgesehen von, außer (dat)
be·siege belagern
be·smear beschmieren
be·spat·ter bespritzen
best 1. adj beste(r, -s) höchste(r, -s), größte(r, -s), meiste; **best before** GASTR haltbar bis; **2.** adv am besten; **3.** der, die, das Beste; **all the best!** alles Gute!, viel Glück!; **to the best of ...** nach bestem ...; **make the best of** das Beste machen aus (dat); **at best** bestenfalls; **be at one's best** in Hoch- or Höchstform sein
be·stow geben, verleihen (**on** dat)
best·sell·er Bestseller m
bet 1. Wette f; **make a bet** e-e Wette abschließen; **2.** wetten; **bet s.o. ten dollars** mit j-m um zehn Dollar wetten; **you bet** F und ob!
be·tray verraten (a. fig); verleiten
be·tray·al Verrat m
be·tray·er Verräter(in)
bet·ter 1. adj besser; **he is better** es geht ihm besser; **better and better** immer besser; **2.** das Bessere; **get the better of** die Oberhand gewinnen über (acc); et. überwinden; **3.** adv besser; mehr; **do better than** es besser machen als; **know better** es besser wissen; **so much the better** desto besser; **you had better go** Br, F **you better go** es wäre besser, wenn du gingest; **better off** (finanziell) besser gestellt; **he is better off than I am** es geht ihm besser als mir; **4.** v/t verbessern; v/i sich bessern
be·tween 1. adv dazwischen; **in between** zwischendurch; F **few and far between** (ganz) vereinzelt; **2.** prp zwischen (dat or acc); unter (dat); **between you and me** unter uns or im Vertrauen (gesagt)
bev·el TECH abkanten, abschrägen
bev·er·age Getränk n
bev·y ZO Schwarm m, Schar f
be·ware (of) sich in Acht nehmen (vor dat), sich hüten (vor dat); **beware of the dog!** Vorsicht, bissiger Hund!

be·wil·der verwirren

be·wil·der·ment Verwirrung *f*

be·witch bezaubern, verhexen

be·yond 1. *adv* darüber hinaus; **2.** *prp* jenseits (*gen*); über … (*acc*) hinaus

bi... zwei, zweifach, zweimal

bi·as Neigung *f*; Vorurteil *n*

bi·as(s)ed voreingenommen; JUR befangen

bi·ath·lete SPORT Biathlet *m*

bi·ath·lon SPORT Biathlon *n*

bib (Sabber)Lätzchen *n*

Bi·ble Bibel *f*

bib·li·cal biblisch, Bibel...

bib·li·og·ra·phy Bibliografie *f*

bi·car·bon·ate *a.* ***bicarbonate of soda*** CHEM doppeltkohlensaures Natron

bi·ceps ANAT Bizeps *m*

bick·er sich zanken *or* streiten

bi·cy·cle Fahrrad *n*

bid 1. *auction*: bieten; **2.** ECON Gebot *n*, Angebot *n*

bi·en·ni·al zweijährlich; BOT zweijährig

bi·en·ni·al·ly alle zwei Jahre

bier (Toten)Bahre *f*

big groß; dick, stark; ***talk big*** F den Mund voll nehmen

big·a·my Bigamie *f*

big busi·ness Großunternehmertum *n*

big·head F Angeber *m*

big shot, big·wig F hohes Tier

bike F **1.** (Fahr)Rad *n*; **2.** Rad fahren

bik·er Motorradfahrer(in); Radfahrer(in), Radler(in)

bi·lat·er·al bilateral

bile Galle *f* (*a. fig*)

bi·lin·gual zweisprachig

bill[1] ZO Schnabel *m*

bill[2] ECON Rechnung *f*; POL (Gesetzes-)Vorlage *f*; JUR (An)Klageschrift *f*; Plakat *n*; Banknote *f*, (Geld)Schein *m*

bill·board Reklametafel *f*

bill·fold Brieftasche *f*

bil·li·ards Billard(spiel) *n*

bil·li·on Milliarde *f*

bill of de·liv·er·y ECON Lieferschein *m*

bill of ex·change ECON Wechsel *m*

bill of sale JUR Verkaufsurkunde *f*

bil·low 1. Woge *f*; (*Rauch- etc*) Schwaden *m*; **2.** *a.* ***billow out*** sich bauschen *or* blähen

bil·ly goat ZO Ziegenbock *m*

bin (großer) Behälter

bi·na·ry MATH, PHYS *etc* binär, Binär...

bi·na·ry code EDP Binärcode *m*

bi·na·ry num·ber MATH Binärzahl *f*

bind *v/t* (an-, ein-, um-, auf-, fest-, ver-)

binden; *a.* vertraglich binden, verpflichten; einfassen; *v/i* binden

bind·er (*esp Buch*)Binder(in); Einband *m*; Aktendeckel *m*

bind·ing 1. bindend, verbindlich; **2.** Einband *m*; Einfassung *f*, Borte *f*

bin·go Bingo *n*

bi·noc·u·lars Fern-, Opernglas *n*

bi·o·chem·is·try Biochemie *f*

bi·o·de·gra·da·ble biologisch abbaubar, umweltfreundlich

bi·og·ra·pher Biograf *m*

bi·og·ra·phy Biografie *f*

bi·o·log·i·cal biologisch

bi·ol·o·gist Biologe *m*, Biologin *f*

bi·ol·o·gy Biologie *f*

bi·o·rhythms Biorhythmus *m*

bi·o·tope Biotop *n*

bi·ped ZO Zweifüßer *m*

birch BOT Birke *f*

bird ZO Vogel *m*

bird·cage Vogelkäfig *m*

bird flu Vogelgrippe *f*

bird of pas·sage ZO Zugvogel *m*

bird of prey ZO Raubvogel *m*

bird sanc·tu·a·ry Vogelschutzgebiet *n*

bird·seed Vogelfutter *n*

bird's-eye view Vogelperspektive *f*

bi·ro® Kugelschreiber *m*

birth Geburt *f*; Herkunft *f*; ***give birth to*** gebären, zur Welt bringen

birth cer·tif·i·cate Geburtsurkunde *f*

birth con·trol Geburtenregelung *f*

birth control pill MED Antibabypille *f*

birth·day Geburtstag *m*; ***happy birthday!*** alles Gute *or* herzlichen Glückwunsch zum Geburtstag!

birth·mark Muttermal *n*

birth·place Geburtsort *m*

birth·rate Geburtenziffer *f*

bis·cuit *Br* Keks *m*, *n*, Plätzchen *n*

bi·sex·u·al bisexuell

bish·op REL Bischof *m*; *chess*: Läufer *m*

bish·op·ric REL Bistum *n*

bi·son ZO Bison *m*; Wisent *m*

bit Bisschen *n*, Stück(chen) *n*; Gebiss *n* (*am Zaum*); (Schlüssel)Bart *m*; EDP Bit *n*; ***a (little) bit*** ein (kleines) bisschen

bitch ZO Hündin *f*; F *contp* Miststück *n*, Schlampe *f*

bit den·si·ty EDP Speicherdichte *f*

bite 1. Beißen *n*; Biss *m*; Bissen *m*, Happen *m*; TECH Fassen *n*, Greifen *n*; **2.** (an-)beißen; ZO stechen; GASTR brennen; *fig* schneiden (*cold etc*); beißen (*smoke etc*); TECH fassen, greifen

bit·ter bitter; *fig* verbittert

bit·ters GASTR Magenbitter *m*

biz F → *business*

black 1. schwarz; dunkel; finster; *have s.th. in black and white* et. schwarz auf weiß haben *or* besitzen; *be black and blue* blaue Flecken haben; *beat s.o. black and blue* j-n grün und blau schlagen; **2.** schwärzen; *black out* verdunkeln; **3.** Schwarz *n*; Schwärze *f*; Schwarze *m*, *f*

black·ber·ry BOT Brombeere *f*

black·bird ZO Amsel *f*

black·board (Schul-, Wand)Tafel *f*

black box AVIAT Flugschreiber *m*

black cur·rant BOT schwarze Johannisbeere

black·en *v/t* schwärzen; *fig* anschwärzen; *v/i* schwarz werden

black eye blaues Auge, Veilchen *n*

black·head MED Mitesser *m*

black ice Glatteis *n*

black·ing schwarze Schuhwichse

black·leg *Br* Streikbrecher *m*

black·mail 1. Erpressung *f*; **2.** j-n erpressen

black·mail·er Erpresser(in)

black mar·ket Schwarzmarkt *m*

black·ness Schwärze *f*

black·out Verdunkelung *f*; Black-out *n*, *m*; ELECTR Stromausfall *m*; Ohnmacht *f*

black pud·ding GASTR Blutwurst *f*

black sheep *fig* schwarzes Schaf

black·smith Schmied *m*

blad·der ANAT Blase *f*

blade TECH Blatt *n*, Schaufel *f*; Klinge *f*; Schneide *f*; BOT Halm *m*

blame 1. Tadel *m*; Schuld *f*; **2.** tadeln; *be to blame for* schuld sein an (*dat*)

blame·less untadelig

blanch *v/t* bleichen; GASTR blanchieren; *v/i* erbleichen, bleich werden

blank 1. leer; unausgefüllt, unbeschrieben; ECON Blanko...; verdutzt; **2.** Leere *f*; leerer Raum, Lücke *f*; unbeschriebenes Blatt, Formular *n*; *lottery*: Niete *f*

blank car·tridge Platzpatrone *f*

blank check (*Br* **cheque**) ECON Blankoscheck *m*

blan·ket 1. (Woll)Decke *f*; **2.** zudecken

blare brüllen, plärren (*radio etc*), schmettern (*trumpet*)

blas·pheme lästern

blas·phe·my Gotteslästerung *f*

blast 1. Windstoß *m*; MUS Ton *m*; TECH Explosion *f*; Druckwelle *f*; Sprengung *f*; **2.** sprengen; zunichtemachen; *blast off (into space)* in den Weltraum schießen; *blast off* abheben, starten (*rocket*); *blast!* verdammt!; *blast you!* der Teufel soll dich holen!; *blasted* verdammt, ver-

flucht

blast fur·nace TECH Hochofen *m*

blast-off Start *m* (*of a rocket*)

bla·tant offenkundig, eklatant

blaze 1. Flamme(n *pl*) *f*, Feuer *n*; heller Schein; *fig* Ausbruch *m*; **2.** brennen, lodern; leuchten

blaz·er Blazer *m*

bla·zon Wappen *n*

bleach bleichen

bleak öde, kahl; rau; *fig* trüb, freudlos, finster

blear·y trübe, verschwommen

bleat ZO **1.** Blöken *n*; **2.** blöken

bleed *v/i* bluten; *v/t* MED zur Ader lassen; F schröpfen

bleed·ing MED Blutung *f*; Aderlass *m*

bleep 1. Piepton *m*; **2.** j-n anpiepsen

bleep·er *Br* F Piepser *m*

blem·ish 1. (*a.* Schönheits)Fehler *m*; Makel *m*; **2.** entstellen

blend 1. (sich) (ver)mischen; GASTR verschneiden; **2.** Mischung *f*; GASTR Verschnitt *m*

blend·er Mixer *m*, Mixgerät *n*

bless segnen; preisen; *be blessed with* gesegnet sein mit; (*God*) *bless you!* alles Gute!; Gesundheit!; *bless me!*, *bless my heart!*, *bless my soul!* F du meine Güte!

bless·ed selig, gesegnet; F verflixt

bless·ing Segen *m*

blight BOT Mehltau *m*

blind 1. blind (*fig to* gegen[über]); unübersichtlich; **2.** Rouleau *n*, Rollo *n*; *the blind* die Blinden *pl*; **3.** blenden; *fig* blind machen (*to* für, gegen)

blind al·ley Sackgasse *f*

blind·ers Scheuklappen *pl*

blind·fold 1. blindlings; **2.** j-m die Augen verbinden; **3.** Augenbinde *f*

blind·ly *fig* blindlings

blind·ness Blindheit *f*; Verblendung *f*

blind·worm ZO Blindschleiche *f*

blink 1. Blinzeln *n*; **2.** blinzeln, zwinkern; blinken

blink·ers *Br* Scheuklappen *pl*

bliss Seligkeit *f*, Wonne *f*

blis·ter MED, TECH **1.** Blase *f*; **2.** Blasen hervorrufen auf (*dat*); Blasen ziehen *or* TECH werfen

blitz MIL **1.** heftiger Luftangriff; **2.** schwer bombardieren

bliz·zard Blizzard *m*, Schneesturm *m*

bloat·ed (an)geschwollen, (auf)gedunsen; *fig* aufgeblasen

bloat·er GASTR Bückling *m*

blob Klecks *m*

block 1. Block *m*, Klotz *m*; Baustein *m*,

(Bau)Klötzchen n; (Schreib-, Notiz-) Block m; (Häuser)Block m; fig geistige etc Sperre; **block (of flats)** Br Wohn-, Mietshaus n; **2.** a. **block up** (ab-, ver)sperren, blockieren, verstopfen

block·ade 1. Blockade f; **2.** blockieren

block·bust·er F Kassenmagnet m, Kassenschlager m

block·head F Dummkopf m

block let·ters Blockschrift f

blond 1. Blonde m; **2.** blond; hell (skin)

blonde 1. blond; **2.** Blondine f

blood Blut n; **in cold blood** kaltblütig

blood bank MED Blutbank f

blood clot MED Blutgerinnsel n

blood cor·pus·cle MED Blutkörperchen n

blood·cur·dling grauenhaft

blood do·nor MED Blutspender(in)

blood group MED Blutgruppe f

blood·hound ZO Bluthund m

blood pres·sure MED Blutdruck m

blood·shed Blutvergießen n

blood·shot blutunterlaufen

blood·thirst·y blutdürstig

blood ves·sel ANAT Blutgefäß n

blood test MED Blutprobe f

blood·y blutig; Br F verdammt, verflucht

bloom 1. Blume f, Blüte f; fig Blüte(zeit) f; **2.** blühen; fig (er)strahlen

blos·som 1. Blüte f; **2.** blühen; fig **blossom into** erblühen zu

blot 1. Klecks m; fig Makel m; **2.** beklecksen

blotch Klecks m; Hautfleck m

blotch·y fleckig

blot·ter (Tinten)Löscher m

blot·ting pa·per Löschpapier n

blouse Bluse f

blow¹ Schlag m (a. fig), Stoß m

blow² v/i blasen, wehen; keuchen, schnaufen; explodieren; platzen (tire); ELECTR durchbrennen; **blow up** in die Luft fliegen; explodieren; v/t: **blow one's nose** sich die Nase putzen; **blow one's top** F an die Decke gehen (vor Wut); **blow out** ausblasen; **blow up** sprengen; PHOT vergrößern

blow-dry föhnen

blow·fly ZO Schmeißfliege f

blow·pipe Blasrohr n

blow-up PHOT Vergrößerung f

blud·geon Knüppel m

blue 1. blau; F melancholisch, traurig, schwermütig; **2.** Blau n; **out of the blue** fig aus heiterem Himmel

blue·ber·ry BOT Blau-, Heidelbeere f

blue·bot·tle ZO Schmeißfliege f

blue-col·lar work·er Arbeiter(in)

blues MUS Blues m; F Melancholie f; **have the blues** F den Moralischen haben

bluff¹ Steilufer n

bluff² **1.** Bluff m; **2.** bluffen

blu·ish bläulich

blun·der 1. Fehler m, F Schnitzer m; **2.** e-n (groben) Fehler machen; verpfuschen, F verpatzen

blunt stumpf; fig offen

blunt·ly freiheraus

blur [blɜː] **1.** v/t verwischen; verschmieren; PHOT, TV verwackeln, verzerren; fig trüben; **2.** v/i verschwimmen (a. fig)

blurt: **blurt out** herausplatzen mit

blush 1. Erröten n, Schamröte f; **2.** erröten, rot werden

blus·ter brausen (wind); fig poltern, toben

BMX ABBR of **bicycle motocross** Querfeldeinrennen n

BMX bike BMX-Rad n

BO ABBR → **body odo(ur)**

boar ZO Eber m; Keiler m

board 1. Brett n; (Anschlag)Brett n; Konferenztisch m; Ausschuss m, Kommission f; Behörde f; Verpflegung f; Pappe f, Karton m; SPORT (Surf)Board m; **on board a train** in e-m Zug; **2.** v/t dielen, verschalen; beköstigen; an Bord gehen; MAR entern; RAIL etc einsteigen in; v/i in Kost sein, wohnen

board·er Kostgänger(in); Pensionsgast m; Internatsschüler(in)

board game Brettspiel n

board·ing card AVIAT Bordkarte f

boarding house Pension f, Fremdenheim n

boarding school Internat n

board of di·rec·tors ECON Aufsichtsrat m

Board of Trade Handelskammer f; Br Handelsministerium n

board·walk Strandpromenade f

boast 1. Prahlerei f; **2.** (of, about) sich rühmen (gen), prahlen (mit)

boat Boot n; Schiff n

bob 1. Knicks m; kurzer Haarschnitt; Br HIST F Schilling m; **2.** v/t Haar kurz schneiden; v/i sich auf und ab bewegen; knicksen

bob·bin Spule f (a. ELECTR)

bob·sleigh SPORT Bob m

bod·ice Mieder n; Oberteil n

bod·i·ly körperlich

bod·y Körper m, Leib m; Leiche f; JUR Körperschaft f; Hauptteil m; MOT Karosserie f; MIL Truppenkörper m

bod·y·guard Leibwache f; Leibwächter m

bod·y o·do(ur) (ABBR **BO**) Körpergeruch

m

body stock·ing Body *m*
bod·y·work MOT Karosserie *f*
Boer 1. Bure *m*; **2.** Buren...
bog Sumpf *m*, Morast *m*
bo·gus falsch; Schwindel...
boil¹ MED Geschwür *n*, Furunkel *m, n*
boil² **1.** kochen, sieden; **2.** Kochen *n*, Sieden *n*
boil·er (Dampf)Kessel *m*; Boiler *m*
boil·er suit Overall *m*
boil·ing point Siedepunkt *m* (*a. fig*)
bois·ter·ous ungestüm; heftig, laut; lärmend
bold kühn, verwegen; keck, dreist, unverschämt; steil; PRINT fett; *as bold as brass* F frech wie Oskar; *words in bold print* fett gedruckt
bold·ness Kühnheit *f*, Verwegenheit *f*; Dreistigkeit *f*
bol·ster 1. Keilkissen *n*; **2.** *bolster up fig* (unter)stützen, *j-m* Mut machen
bolt 1. Bolzen *m*; Riegel *m*; Blitz(strahl) *m*; plötzlicher Satz, Fluchtversuch *m*; **2.** *adv*: *bolt upright* kerzengerade; **3.** *v/t* verriegeln; F hinunterschlingen; *v/i* davonlaufen, ausreißen; zo scheuen, durchgehen
bomb 1. Bombe *f*; *the bomb* die Atombombe; **2.** bombardieren
bom·bard bombardieren
bomb·er AVIAT Bomber *m*; Bombenleger *m*
bomb·proof bombensicher
bomb·shell Bombe *f* (*a. fig*)
bo·nan·za *fig* Goldgrube *f*
bond Bund *m*, Verbindung *f*; ECON Schuldverschreibung *f*, Obligation *f*; *in bond* ECON unter Zollverschluss
bond·age Hörigkeit *f*
bonds *fig* Bande *pl*
bone 1. ANAT Knochen *m, pl a.* Gebeine *pl*; zo Gräte *f*; *bone of contention* Zankapfel *m*; *have a bone to pick with s.o.* mit *j-m* ein Hühnchen zu rupfen haben; *make no bones about* nicht lange fackeln mit; **2.** die Knochen auslösen (aus); entgräten
bon·fire Feuer *n* im Freien; Freudenfeuer *n*
bon·net Haube *f*; *Br* Motorhaube *f*
bo·nus ECON Bonus *m*, Prämie *f*; Gratifikation *f*
bon·y knöchern; knochig
boo *int* buh!; THEA *boo off the stage*, *soccer*: *boo off the park* auspfeifen
boobs *sl* Titten *pl*
boo·by F Trottel *m*
book 1. Buch *n*; Heft *n*; Liste *f*; Block *m*;

2. buchen; eintragen; SPORT verwarnen; *Fahrkarte etc* lösen; *Platz etc* (vor)bestellen, reservieren lassen; *Gepäck* aufgeben; *book in esp Br* sich (*im Hotel*) eintragen; *book in* at absteigen in (*dat*); *booked up* ausgebucht, ausverkauft, belegt
book·case Bücherschrank *m*
book·ing Buchen *n*, (Vor)Bestellung *f*; SPORT Verwarnung *f*
booking clerk Schalterbeamte *m*, -beamtin *f*
booking of·fice Fahrkartenausgabe *f*, -schalter *m*; THEA Kasse *f*
book·keep·er ECON Buchhalter(in)
book·keep·ing ECON Buchhaltung *f*, Buchführung *f*
book·let Büchlein *n*, Broschüre *f*
book·mak·er Buchmacher *m*
book·mark(·er) Lesezeichen *n*
book·sell·er Buchhändler(in)
book·shelf Bücherregal *n*
book·shop *esp Br*, **book·store** Buchhandlung *f*
book·worm *fig* Bücherwurm *m*
boom¹ ECON **1.** Boom *m*, Aufschwung *m*, Hochkonjunktur *f*, Hausse *f*; **2.** e-n Boom erleben
boom² MAR Baum *m*, Spiere *f*; TECH (Kran)Ausleger *m*; *film*, TV (Mikrofon)Galgen *m*
boom³ dröhnen, donnern
boor·ish ungehobelt
boost 1. hochschieben; ECON in die Höhe treiben; ankurbeln; ELECTR verstärken; TECH erhöhen; *fig* stärken, Auftrieb geben (*dat*); **2.** Erhöhung *f*; Auftrieb *m*; ELECTR Verstärkung *f*
boot¹ Stiefel *m*; *Br* MOT Kofferraum *m*
boot²: *boot (up)* EDP laden
boot³: *to boot* obendrein
boot·ee (*Damen*)Halbstiefel *m*
booth (Markt- *etc*)Bude *f*; (Messe-) Stand *m*; (Wahl- *etc*)Kabine *f*; (Telefon)Zelle *f*
boot·lace Schnürsenkel *m*
boot·y Beute *f*
booze F **1.** saufen; **2.** Zeug *n*; Sauferei *f*
bor·der 1. Rand *m*, Saum *m*, Einfassung *f*; Rabatte *f*; Grenze *f*; **2.** einfassen; (um)säumen; grenzen (*on* an *acc*)
bore¹ **1.** Bohrloch *n*; TECH Kaliber *n*; **2.** bohren
bore² **1.** Langweiler *m*; langweilige *or* lästige Sache *f*; **2.** *j-n* langweilen; *be bored* sich langweilen
bore·dom Lang(e)weile *f*
bor·ing langweilig
bo·rough Stadtteil *m*; Stadtgemeinde *f*; Stadtbezirk *m*

bor·row (sich) *et.* borgen *or* (aus)leihen

bos·om Busen *m*; *fig* Schoß *m*

boss F **1.** Boss *m*, Chef *m*; **2.** *a. boss about, boss around* herumkommandieren

boss·y F herrisch

bo·tan·i·cal botanisch

bot·a·ny Botanik *f*

botch 1. Pfusch *m*; **2.** verpfuschen

both beide(s); *both ... and ...* sowohl ... als (auch) ...

both·er 1. Belästigung *f*, Störung *f*, Plage *f*, Mühe *f*; **2.** belästigen, stören, plagen; *don't bother!* bemühen Sie sich nicht!

bot·tle 1. Flasche *f*; **2.** in Flaschen abfüllen

bottle bank *Br* Altglascontainer *m*

bot·tle·neck *fig* Engpass *m*

bot·tle o·pen·er Flaschenöffner *m*

bot·tom unterster Teil, Boden *m*, Fuß *m*, Unterseite *f*; Grund *m*; F Hintern *m*, Popo *m*; *be at the bottom of s.th.* hinter e-r Sache stecken; *get to the bottom of s.th.* e-r Sache auf den Grund gehen

bough Ast *m*, Zweig *m*

boul·der Geröllblock *m*, Findling *m*

bounce 1. aufprallen *or* aufspringen (lassen); springen, hüpfen, stürmen; ECON F platzen (*check*); **2.** Sprung *m*, Satz *m*; F Schwung *m*

bounc·ing kräftig, stramm

bound¹ unterwegs (*for* nach)

bound² *mst pl* Grenze *f*, *fig a.* Schranke *f*

bound³ 1. Sprung *m*, Satz *m*; **2.** springen, hüpfen; auf-, abprallen

bound·a·ry Grenze *f*

bound·less grenzenlos

boun·te·ous, boun·ti·ful freigebig, reichlich

boun·ty Freigebigkeit *f*; großzügige Spende *f*; Prämie *f*

bou·quet Bukett *n* (*a.* GASTR), Strauß *m*; GASTR Blume *f*

bout SPORT (*Box-, Ring*)Kampf *m*; MED Anfall *m*

bou·tique Boutique *f*

bow¹ 1. Verbeugung *f*; **2.** *v/i* sich verbeugen *or* verneigen (*to vor dat*); *fig* sich beugen *or* unterwerfen (*to dat*); *v/t* biegen; beugen, neigen

bow² MAR Bug *m*

bow³ Bogen *m*; Schleife *f*

bow·els ANAT Darm *m*; Eingeweide *pl*

bowl¹ Schale *f*, Schüssel *f*, Napf *m*; (*Zucker-*)Dose *f*; Becken *n*; (*Pfeifen-*) Kopf *m*

bowl² 1. (*Bowling-, Kegel- etc*)Kugel *f*; **2.** kegeln; rollen (*bowling ball*); *cricket*: werfen

bow-leg·ged o-beinig

bowl·er¹ Bowlingspieler(in); Kegler(in)

bowl·er², *a.* **bowler hat** *esp Br* Bowler *m*, F Melone *f*

bowl·ing Bowling *n*; Kegeln *n*; *go bowling* kegeln

bowling al·ley Kegelbahn *f*

bowling ball Kegelkugel *f*

box¹ Kasten *m*, Kiste *f*; Büchse *f*, Dose *f*, Kästchen *n*; Schachtel *f*; Behälter *m*; TECH Gehäuse *n*; Postfach *m*; *Br* (Telefon)Zelle *f*; JUR Zeugenstand *m*; THEA Loge *f*; MOT, ZO Box *f*

box² 1. SPORT boxen; F *box s.o.'s ears* j-n ohrfeigen; **2.** *a box on the ear* e-e Ohrfeige

box³ [bɒks] BOT Buchsbaum *m*

box·er Boxer *m*

box·ing Boxen *n*, Boxsport *m*

Box·ing Day *Br* der zweite Weihnachtsfeiertag

box num·ber Chiffre(nummer) *f*

box of·fice Theaterkasse *f*

boy Junge *m*, Knabe *m*, Bursche *m*

boy·cott 1. boykottieren; **2.** Boykott *m*

boy·friend Freund *m*

boy·hood Knabenjahre *pl*, Jugend(-zeit) *f*

boy·ish jungenhaft

boy scout Pfadfinder *m*

bra BH *m* (*Büstenhalter*)

brace 1. TECH Strebe *f*, Stützbalken *m*; (*Zahn*)Klammer *f*, (-)Spange *f*; **2.** TECH verstreben, versteifen, stützen

brace·let Armband *n*

brac·es *Br* Hosenträger *pl*

brack·et TECH Träger *m*, Halter *m*, Stütze *f*; PRINT Klammer *f*; (*esp Alters-, Steuer*)-Klasse *f*; *lower income bracket* niedrige Einkommensgruppe

brack·ish brackig, salzig

brag prahlen (*about* mit)

brag·gart Prahler *m*, F Angeber *m*

braid 1. Zopf *m*, Borte *f*, Tresse *f*; **2.** flechten; mit Borte besetzen

brain ANAT Gehirn *n*, *often pl fig a.* Verstand *m*, Intelligenz *f*, Kopf *m*

brain·storm Geistesblitz *m*

brain·wash j-n e-r Gehirnwäsche unterziehen

brain·wash·ing Gehirnwäsche *f*

brain·wave *Br* Geistesblitz *m*

brain·y F gescheit

braise GASTR schmoren

brake TECH **1.** Bremse *f*; **2.** bremsen

brake·light MOT Bremslicht *n*

bram·ble BOT Brombeerstrauch *m*

bran AGR Kleie *f*

branch 1. Ast *m*, Zweig *m*; *fig* Fach *n*; Linie *f* (*des Stammbaumes*); ECON Zweigstelle f, Filiale f; **2.** sich verzweigen; abzweigen

brand 1. ECON (Schutz-, Handels)Marke f, Warenzeichen n; Markenname m; Sorte f, Klasse f; Brandmal n; **2.** einbrennen; brandmarken

bran·dish schwingen

brand name ECON Markenname m

brand-new nagelneu

bran·dy Kognak m, Weinbrand m

brass Messing n; F Unverschämtheit f

brass band MUS Blaskapelle f

bras·sière Büstenhalter m

brat contp Balg m, n, Gör n

brave 1. tapfer, mutig, unerschrocken; **2.** trotzen; mutig begegnen (dat)

brav·er·y Tapferkeit f

brawl 1. Krawall m; Rauferei f; **2.** Krawall machen; raufen

brawn·y muskulös

bray 1. ZO Eselsschrei m; **2.** ZO schreien; fig wiehern

bra·zen unverschämt, unverfroren, frech

Bra·zil Brasilien n

Bra·zil·ian 1. brasilianisch; **2.** Brasilianer(in)

breach 1. Bruch m; fig Verletzung f; MIL Bresche f; **2.** e-e Bresche schlagen in (acc)

bread Brot n; **brown bread** Schwarzbrot n; **know which side one's bread is buttered** F s-n Vorteil (er)kennen

breadth Breite f

break 1. Bruch m; Lücke f; Pause f (Br a. PED), Unterbrechung f; (plötzlicher) Wechsel, Umschwung m; (Tages)Anbruch m; **bad break** F Pech n; **lucky break** F Dusel m, Schwein n; **give s.o. a break** F j-m e-e Chance geben; **take a break** e-e Pause machen; **without a break** ununterbrochen; **2.** v/t (ab-, auf-, durch-, zer)brechen; zerschlagen, kaputt machen; ZO a. **break in** zähmen, abrichten, zureiten; Gesetz, Vertrag etc brechen; Kode etc knacken; schlechte Nachricht (schonend) beibringen; v/i brechen (a. fig); (zer-)brechen, (zer)reißen, kaputtgehen; anbrechen (Tag), METEOR umschlagen; fig ausbrechen (**into** in Tränen etc); **break away** ab-, losbrechen; sich losmachen or losreißen; **break down** ein-, niederreißen, abbrechen; zusammenbrechen (a. fig); versagen, MOT e-e Panne haben; fig scheitern; **break in** einbrechen, eindringen; **break into** einbrechen in (ein Haus etc); **break off** abbrechen, fig a. Schluss machen mit; **break out** ausbrechen; **break through** durchbrechen; fig den Durchbruch

schaffen; **break up** abbrechen, beenden, schließen; (sich) auflösen; fig zerbrechen, auseinandergehen

break·a·ble zerbrechlich

break·age Bruch m

break·a·way 1. Trennung f; **2.** Splitter...

break·down Zusammenbruch m (a. fig); TECH Maschinenschaden m; MOT Panne f; **nervous breakdown** MED Nervenzusammenbruch m

breakdown lor·ry Br MOT Abschleppwagen m

breakdown ser·vice Br MOT Pannendienst m, Pannenhilfe f

breakdown truck Br MOT Abschleppwagen m

break·fast Frühstück n; **have breakfast** → **2.** frühstücken

break·through fig Durchbruch m

break-up Aufhebung f; Auflösung f

breast ANAT Brust f; Busen m; fig Herz n; **make a clean breast of s.th.** et. offen (ein)gestehen

breast·stroke Brustschwimmen n

breath Atem(zug) m; Hauch m; **be out of breath** außer Atem sein; **waste one's breath** in den Wind reden

breath·a·lyse Br, **breath·a·lyze** F (ins Röhrchen) blasen or pusten lassen

breath·a·lys·er Br, **breath·alyz·er®** Alkoholtestgerät n, F Röhrchen n

breathe atmen

breath·less atemlos

breath-tak·ing atemberaubend

breech·es Kniebund-, Reithosen pl

breed 1. ZO Rasse f, Zucht f; **2.** v/t BOT, ZO züchten; v/i BIOL sich fortpflanzen

breed·er Züchter(in); Zuchttier n; PHYS Brüter m

breed·ing BIOL Fortpflanzung f; (Tier-) Zucht f; fig Erziehung f; (gutes) Benehmen

breeze Brise f

breth·ren esp REL Brüder pl

brew brauen; Tee zubereiten, aufbrühen

brew·er (Bier)Brauer m

brew·er·y Brauerei f

bri·ar → **brier**

bribe 1. Bestechungsgeld n, -geschenk n; Bestechung f; **2.** bestechen

brib·er·y Bestechung f

brick 1. Ziegel(stein) m, Backstein m; Br Baustein m, (Bau)Klötzchen n

brick·lay·er Maurer m

brick·yard Ziegelei f

brid·al Braut...

bride Braut f

bride·groom Bräutigam m

brides·maid Brautjungfer f

bridge 1. Brücke f; 2. e-e Brücke schlagen über (acc); fig überbrücken

bri·dle 1. Zaum m; Zügel m; 2. (auf)zäumen; zügeln

bridle path Reitweg m

brief 1. kurz, bündig; 2. instruieren, genaue Anweisungen geben (dat)

brief·case Aktenmappe f

briefs Slip m

bri·er BOT Dornstrauch m; Wilde Rose

bri·gade MIL Brigade f

bright hell, glänzend; klar; heiter; lebhaft; gescheit

bright·en v/t a. **brighten up** heller machen, aufhellen, erhellen; aufheitern; v/i a. **brighten up** sich aufhellen

bright·ness Helligkeit f; Glanz m; Heiterkeit f; Gescheitheit f

brill Br F super, toll

bril·liance, bril·lian·cy Glanz m; fig Brillanz f

bril·liant 1. glänzend; hervorragend, brillant; 2. Brillant m

brim 1. Rand m; Krempe f; 2. bis zum Rande füllen or voll sein

brim·ful(l) randvoll

brine Sole f; Lake f

bring bringen, mitbringen, herbringen; j-n dazu bringen (**to do** zu tun); **bring about** zustande bringen; bewirken; **bring forth** hervorbringen; **bring off** et. fertigbringen, schaffen; **bring on** verursachen; **bring out** herausbringen; **bring round** Ohnmächtigen wieder zu sich bringen; Kranken wieder auf die Beine bringen; **bring up** auf-, großziehen; erziehen; zur Sprache bringen

brink Rand m (a. fig)

brisk flott; lebhaft; frisch

bris·tle 1. Borste f; (Bart)Stoppel f; 2. a. **bristle up** sich sträuben; zornig werden; strotzen, wimmeln (**with** von)

bris·tly stoppelig, Stoppel...

Brit F Brite m, Britin f

Brit·ain Britannien f

Brit·ish britisch; **the British** die Briten pl

Brit·on Brite m, Britin f

brit·tle spröde, zerbrechlich

broach Thema anschneiden

broad breit; weit; hell; deutlich (hint etc); derb (humor etc); stark (accent); allgemein; weitherzig; liberal

broad·cast 1. im Rundfunk or Fernsehen bringen, ausstrahlen, übertragen; senden; 2. radio, TV Sendung f

broad·cast·er Rundfunk-, Fernsehsprecher(in)

broad·en verbreitern, erweitern

broad jump SPORT Weitsprung m

broad·mind·ed liberal

bro·cade Brokat m

bro·chure Broschüre f, Prospekt m

brogue fester Straßenschuh

broil grillen

broke F pleite, abgebrannt

bro·ken zerbrochen, kaputt; gebrochen (a. fig); zerrüttet

brok·en-heart·ed verzweifelt, untröstlich

bro·ker ECON Makler m

bron·chi·tis MED Bronchitis f

bronze 1. Bronze f; 2. bronzefarben; Bronze...

brooch Brosche f

brood ZO 1. Brut f; 2. Brut...; 3. brüten (a. fig)

brook Bach m

broom Besen m

broth GASTR Fleischbrühe f

broth·el Bordell n

broth·er Bruder m; **brother(s) and sister(s)** Geschwister pl

broth·er-in-law Schwager m

broth·er·hood REL Bruderschaft f

broth·er·ly brüderlich

brow ANAT (Augen)Braue f; Stirn f; GEOGR Rand m

brow·beat einschüchtern

brown 1. braun; 2. Braun n; 3. bräunen; braun werden

browse grasen, weiden; fig schmökern

bruise 1. MED Quetschung f, blauer Fleck; 2. quetschen; anstoßen; MED e-e Quetschung or e-n blauen Fleck bekommen

brunch Brunch m

brush 1. Bürste f; Pinsel m; ZO (Fuchs)Rute f; Scharmützel n; Unterholz n; 2. bürsten; fegen; streifen; **brush against s.o.** j-n streifen; **brush away, brush off** wegbürsten, abwischen; **brush aside, brush away** et. abtun; **brush up (on)** fig aufpolieren, auffrischen

brush·wood Gestrüpp n, Unterholz n

brusque brüsk, barsch

Brus·sels sprouts BOT Rosenkohl m

bru·tal brutal, roh

bru·tal·i·ty Brutalität f

brute 1. brutal; **with brute force** mit roher Gewalt; 2. Vieh n; F Untier n, Scheusal n; Rohling m

brut·ish fig tierisch

bub·ble 1. Blase f; 2. sprudeln

buck[1] 1. ZO Bock m; 2. bocken

buck[2] F Dollar m

buck·et Eimer m, Kübel m

buck·le 1. Schnalle f, Spange f; 2. a. **buckle up** zu-, festschnallen; **buckle on** anschnallen

buck·skin Wildleder n

bud 1. BOT Knospe *f*; *fig* Keim *m*; **2.** knospen, keimen

bud·dy F Kamerad *m*; Kumpel *m*, Spezi *m*

budge *v/i* sich (von der Stelle) rühren; *v/t* (vom Fleck) bewegen

bud·ger·i·gar ZO Wellensittich *m*

bud·get Budget *n*, Etat *m*; PARL Haushaltsplan *m*

bud·gie F → *budgerigar*

buf·fa·lo ZO Büffel *m*

buff·er TECH Puffer *m*

buf·fet¹ schlagen; *buffet about* durchrütteln, durchschütteln

buf·fet² Büfett *n*, Anrichte *f*

buf·fet³ *(Frühstücks- etc)* Büfett *n*; Theke *f*

bug 1. ZO Wanze *f* (*a. F fig*); Insekt *n*; EDP Programmfehler *m*; **2.** F Wanzen anbringen in (*dat*); F ärgern

bug·ging de·vice Abhörgerät *n*

bug·ging op·e·ra·tion Lauschangriff *m*

bug·gy Kinderwagen *m*; MOT Buggy *m*

bu·gle MUS Wald-, Signalhorn *n*

build 1. (er)bauen, errichten; **2.** Körperbau *m*, Figur *f*, Statur *f*

build·er Erbauer *m*; Bauunternehmer *m*

build·ing 1. (Er)Bauen *n*; Bau *m*, Gebäude *n*; **2.** Bau...

building site Baustelle *f*

built-in eingebaut, Einbau...

built-up: *built-up area* bebautes Gelände *or* Gebiet; geschlossene Ortschaft

bulb BOT Zwiebel *f*, Knolle *f*; ELECTR (Glüh)Birne *f*

bulge 1. (Aus)Bauchung *f*, Ausbuchtung *f*; **2.** sich (aus)bauchen; hervorquellen

bulk Umfang *m*, Größe *f*, Masse *f*; Großteil *m*; *in bulk* ECON lose, unverpackt; en gros

bulk·y sperrig

bull ZO Bulle *m*, Stier *m*

bull·dog ZO Bulldogge *f*

bull·doze planieren; F einschüchtern

bull·doz·er TECH Bulldozer *m*, Planierraupe *f*

bul·let Kugel *f*

bul·le·tin Bulletin *n*, Tagesbericht *m*

bul·le·tin board Schwarzes Brett

bul·let·proof kugelsicher

bull·fight Stierkampf *m*

bul·lion Gold-, Silberbarren *m*

bul·lock ZO Ochse *m*

bull's-eye: *hit the bull's-eye* ins Schwarze treffen (*a. fig*)

bul·ly 1. tyrannische Person, Tyrann *m*; **2.** einschüchtern, tyrannisieren

bul·wark Bollwerk *n* (*a. fig*)

bum F 1. Gammler *m*; Tippelbruder *m*, Vagabund *m*; Nichtstuer *m*; **2.** *v/t* schnorren; *bum around* herumgammeln

bum·ble·bee ZO Hummel *f*

bump 1. heftiger Schlag *or* Stoß; Beule *f*; Unebenheit *f*; **2.** stoßen; rammen, auf *ein Auto* auffahren; zusammenstoßen; holpern; *bump into fig* j-n zufällig treffen; F *bump s.o. off* j-n umlegen

bump·er MOT Stoßstange *f*

bump·y holp(e)rig

bun süßes Brötchen; (Haar)Knoten *m*

bunch Bund *n*, Bündel *n*; F Verein *m*, Haufen *m*; *bunch of flowers* Blumenstrauß *m*; *bunch of grapes* Weintraube *f*; *bunch of keys* Schlüsselbund *m*, *n*

bun·dle 1. Bündel *n* (*a. fig*), Bund *n*; **2.** *v/t bundle up* bündeln

bun·ga·low Bungalow *m*

bun·gee elastisches Seil

bun·gee jump·ing Bungeespringen *n*

bunk 1. Pfusch *m*; **2.** (ver)pfuschen

bunk Koje *f*; → *bunk bed* Etagenbett *n*

bun·ny Häschen *n*

buoy 1. MAR Boje *f*; **2.** *buoy up fig* Auftrieb geben (*dat*)

bur·den 1. Last *f*; Bürde *f*; **2.** belasten

bu·reau *Br* Schreibtisch *m*; (Spiegel-) Kommode *f*; Büro *n*

bu·reauc·ra·cy Bürokratie *f*

burg·er GASTR Hamburger *m*

bur·glar Einbrecher *m*

bur·glar·ize einbrechen in (*acc*)

bur·glar·y Einbruch *m*

bur·gle *Br* → *burglarize*

bur·i·al Begräbnis *n*

bur·ly stämmig, kräftig

burn 1. MED Verbrennung *f*, Brandwunde *f*; verbrannte Stelle; **2.** (ver-, an-)brennen; *burn down* ab-, niederbrennen; *burn out* ausbrennen; *burn up* auflodern; verbrennen; verglühen (*rocket etc*)

burn·ing brennend (*a. fig*)

burp F rülpsen, aufstoßen; ein Bäuerchen machen (lassen)

bur·row 1. ZO Bau *m*; **2.** graben; sich eingraben *or* vergraben

burst 1. Bersten *n*; Riss *m*; *fig* Ausbruch *m*; **2.** *v/i* bersten, (zer)platzen; zerspringen; explodieren; *burst from* sich losreißen von; *burst in on or upon s.o.* bei j-m hereinplatzen; *burst into tears* in Tränen ausbrechen; *burst out* herausplatzen; *v/t* (auf)sprengen

bur·y begraben, vergraben; beerdigen

bus Omnibus *m*, Bus *m*

bus driv·er Busfahrer *m*

bush Busch *m*; Gebüsch *n*

bush·el Bushel *m*, Scheffel *m* (*Am 35,24 l*, *Br 36,37 l*)

bush·y buschig

busi·ness Geschäft *n*; Arbeit *f*, Beschäftigung *f*, Beruf *m*, Tätigkeit *f*; Angelegenheit *f*; Sache *f*, Aufgabe *f*; *business of the day* Tagesordnung *f*; *on business* geschäftlich, beruflich; *you have no business doing* (*or* *to do*) *that* Sie haben kein recht, das zu tun; *that's none of your business* das geht Sie nichts an; → *mind 2*

busi·ness hours Geschäftszeit *f*
busi·ness·like geschäftsmäßig, sachlich
busi·ness·man Geschäftsmann *m*
busi·ness trip Geschäftsreise *f*
busi·ness·wom·an Geschäftsfrau *f*
bus stop Bushaltestelle *f*
bust[1] Büste *f*
bust[2]: *go bust* F pleitegehen
bus·tle 1. geschäftiges Treiben; **2.** *bustle about* geschäftig hin und her eilen
bus·y 1. beschäftigt; geschäftig; fleißig (*at* bei, an *dat*); belebt (*street*); arbeitsreich (*dat*); TEL besetzt; **2.** (*mst busy o.s.*) sich beschäftigen (*with* mit)
bus·y·bod·y aufdringlicher Mensch, Gschaftlhuber *m*
bus·y sig·nal TEL Besetztzeichen *n*
but 1. *cj* aber, jedoch; sondern; außer, als; ohne dass; dennoch; *but then* and(e)rerseits; *he could not but laugh* er musste einfach lachen; **2.** *prp* außer (*dat*); *all but him* alle außer ihm; *the last but one* der Vorletzte; *the next but one* der Übernächste; *nothing but* nichts als; *but for* wenn nicht ... gewesen wäre, ohne; **3.** der (die *or* das) nicht; *there is no one but knows* es gibt niemand, der es nicht weiß; **4.** *adv* nur; erst, gerade; *all but* fast, beinahe
butch·er 1. Fleischer *m*, Metzger *m*; **2.** (*fig* ab)schlachten
but·ler Butler *m*
butt[1] **1.** (*Gewehr*)Kolben *m*; (*Zigarren etc*)Stummel *m*, (*Zigaretten*)Kippe *f*; (*Kopf*)Stoß *m*; **2.** (mit dem Kopf) stoßen; *butt in* F sich einmischen (*on* in *acc*)
butt[2] Wein-, Bierfaß *m*; Regentonne *f*
but·ter 1. Butter *f*; **2.** mit Butter bestreichen
but·ter·cup BOT Butterblume *f*
but·ter·fly ZO Schmetterling *m*, Falter *m*
but·tocks ANAT Gesäß *n*, F *or* ZO Hinter-

teil *n*
but·ton 1. Knopf *m*; Button *m*, (Ansteck)-Plakette *f*, Abzeichen *n*; **2.** *mst* *button up* zuknöpfen
but·ton·hole Knopfloch *n*
but·tress Strebepfeiler *m*
bux·om drall, stramm
buy 1. F Kauf *m*; **2.** (an-, ein)kaufen (*of, from* von; *at* bei); *Fahrkarte* lösen; *buy out* j-n abfinden, auszahlen; *Firma* aufkaufen; *buy up* aufkaufen
buy·er Käufer(in); ECON Einkäufer(in)
buzz 1. Summen *n*, Surren *n*; Stimmengewirr *n*; **2.** *v/i* summen, surren; *buzz off!* F schwirr ab!, hau ab!
buz·zard ZO Bussard *m*
buzz·er ELECTR Summer *m*
by 1. *prp* (nahe *or* dicht) bei *or* an, neben (*side by side* Seite an Seite); vorbei *or* vorüber an; *time:* bis um, bis spätestens (*be back by 9.30* sei um 9 Uhr 30 zurück); während, bei (*by day* bei Tage); per, mit (*by bus* mit dem Bus; *by rail* per Bahn); nach, ...weise (*by the dozen* dutzendweise); nach, gemäß (*by my watch* nach *or* auf m-r Uhr); von (*by nature* von Natur aus); von, durch (*a play by ...* ein Stück von ...; *by o.s.* allein); um (*by an inch* um e-n Zoll); MATH mal (*2 by 4*); geteilt durch (*6 by 3*); **2.** *adv* vorbei, vorüber (*go by* vorbeigehen, -fahren; *time:* vergehen); beiseite (*put by* beiseitelegen, zurücklegen); *by and large* im Großen und Ganzen
by... Neben...; Seiten...
bye, bye-bye *int* F Wiedersehen!, tschüs(s)!
by-e·lec·tion PARL Nachwahl *f*
by·gone 1. vergangen; **2.** *let bygones be bygones* lass(t) das Vergangene ruhen
by·pass 1. Umgehungsstraße *f*; MED Bypass *m*; **2.** umgehen; vermeiden
by-prod·uct Nebenprodukt *n*
by·road Nebenstraße *f*
by·stand·er Zuschauer(in), *pl* die Umstehenden *pl*
byte EDP Byte *n*
by·way Nebenstraße *f*
by·word Inbegriff *m*; *be a byword for* stehen für

C

C, c C, c *n*
C ABBR *of Celsius* C, Celsius; *centigrade* hundertgradig
c ABBR *of cent(s)* Cent *m or pl*; *century* Jh., Jahrhundert *n*; *circa* ca., zirca, ungefähr; *cubic* Kubik…
cab Droschke *f*, Taxi *n*; RAIL Führerstand *m*; MOT Fahrerhaus *n*, *a.* TECH Führerhaus *n*
cab·a·ret Varieteedarbietung(en *pl*) *f*
cab·bage BOT Kohl *m*
cab·in Hütte *f*; MAR Kabine *f*, Kajüte *f*; AVIAT Kanzel *f*
cab·i·net Schrank *m*, Vitrine *f*; POL Kabinett *n*
cab·i·net-mak·er Kunsttischler *m*
cab·i·net meet·ing POL Kabinettssitzung *f*
ca·ble 1. Kabel *n*; (Draht)Seil *n*; **2.** telegrafieren; *j-m Geld* telegrafisch anweisen; TV verkabeln
ca·ble car Kabine *f*; Wagen *m*
ca·ble·gram (Übersee)Telegramm *n*
ca·ble rail·way Drahtseil-, Kabinenbahn *f*
cable tel·e·vi·sion, cable TV Kabelfernsehen *n*
cab rank, cab·stand Taxi-, Droschkenstand *m*
cack·la ZO **1.** Gegacker *n*, Geschnatter *n*; **2.** gackern, schnattern
cac·tus BOT Kaktus *m*
ca·dence MUS Kadenz *f*; (Sprech-) Rhythmus *m*
ca·det MIL Kadett *m*
cadge *Br* F schnorren
café, ca·fe Café *n*
caf·e·te·ri·a Cafeteria *f*, Selbstbedienungsrestaurant *n*, *a.* Kantine *f*, UNIV Mensa *f*
cage Käfig *m*; *mining*: Förderkorb *m*; **2.** einsperren
cake 1. Kuchen *m*, Torte *f*; Tafel *f* Schokolade, Stück *n* Seife; F *take the cake* den Vogel abschießen; **2.** *caked with mud* schmutzverkrustet
ca·lam·i·ty großes Unglück, Katastrophe *f*
cal·cu·late *v/t* kalkulieren; be-, aus-, errechnen; F vermuten; *v/i: calculate on* rechnen mit *or* auf (*acc*), zählen auf (*acc*)
cal·cu·la·tion Berechnung *f (a. fig)*; ECON Kalkulation *f*; *fig* Überlegung *f*
cal·cu·la·tor (Taschen)Rechner *m*
cal·en·dar Kalender *m*
calf[1] ANAT Wade *f*

calf[2] ZO Kalb *n*
calf-skin Kalb(s)fell *n*
cal·i·ber, *esp Br* **cal·i·bre** Kaliber *n*
call 1. Ruf *m*; TEL Anruf *m*, Gespräch *n*; Ruf *m*, Berufung *f* (*to in ein Amt*; auf *e-n Lehrstuhl*); Aufruf *m*, Aufforderung *f*; Signal *n*; (kurzer) Besuch; *on call* nur Abruf; *be on call* MED Bereitschaftsdienst haben; *make a call* telefonieren; **2.** *v/t* (herbei)rufen; (ein)berufen; TEL *j-n* anrufen; *j-n* berufen, ernennen (*to* zu); nennen; *Aufmerksamkeit* lenken (*to* auf *acc*); *be called* heißen; *call s.o. names* *j-n* beschimpfen, *j-n* beleidigen; *v/i* rufen; TEL anrufen; e-n (kurzen) Besuch machen (*on s.o., at s.o.'s [house]* bei *j-m*); *call at a port* im Hafen anlaufen; *call for* rufen nach; *et.* anfordern; *et.* abholen; *to be called for* postlagernd; *call on* sich an *j-n* wenden (*for wegen*); appellieren an (*acc*) (*to do* zu tun); *call on s.o.* *j-n* besuchen
call box *Br* Telefonzelle *f*
call·er Besucher(in); TEL Anrufer(in)
call girl Callgirl *n*
call-in → *phone-in*
call·ing Berufung *f*; Beruf *m*
cal·lous schwielig; *fig* gefühllos
cal·lus Schwiele *f*
calm 1. still, ruhig; **2.** (Wind)Stille *f*, Ruhe *f*; **3.** *often calm down* besänftigen, (sich) beruhigen
cal·o·rie Kalorie *f*; *high or rich in calories* kalorienreich; *low in calories* kalorienarm, kalorienreduziert
cal·o·rie-con·scious kalorienbewusst
calve *zo* kalben
cam·cor·der Camcorder *m*, Kamerarekorder *m*
cam·el ZO Kamel *n*
cam·e·o Kamee *f*; THEA, *film*: kleine Nebenrolle, kurze Szene
cam·e·ra Kamera *f*, Fotoapparat *m*
cam·o·mile BOT Kamille *f*
cam·ou·flage 1. Tarnung *f*; **2.** tarnen
camp 1. (*Zelt- etc*)Lager *n*; **2.** lagern; *camp out* zelten, campen
cam·paign 1. MIL Feldzug *m* (*a. fig*); *fig* Kampagne *f*, Aktion *f*; POL Wahlkampf *m*; **2.** *fig* kämpfen (*for* für; *against* gegen)
camp bed *Br*, **camp cot** Feldbett *n*
camp·er (van) Campingbus *m*, Wohnmobil *n*

camp·ground, **camp·site** Lagerplatz *m*; Zeltplatz *m*, Campingplatz *m*

cam·pus Campus *m*, Universitätsgelände *n*

can[1] *v/aux ich* kann, *du* kannst *etc*; dürfen, können

can[2] **1.** Kanne *f*; (Blech-, Konserven-) Dose *f*, (-)Büchse *f*; **2.** einmachen, eindosen

Can·a·da Kanada *n*

Ca·na·di·an 1. kanadisch; **2.** Kanadier(in)

ca·nal Kanal *m* (*a.* ANAT)

ca·nar·y ZO Kanarienvogel *m*

can·cel (durch-, aus)streichen; entwerten; rückgängig machen; absagen; *be can·cel(l)ed* ausfallen

Can·cer ASTR Krebs *m*; *he* (*she*) *is* (*a*) *Cancer* er (sie) ist (ein) Krebs

can·cer MED Krebs *m*

can·cer·ous MED Krebs..., krebsbefallen

can·cer pa·tient MED Krebskranke *m*, *f*

can·did aufrichtig, offen

can·di·date Kandidat(in) (*for* für), Bewerber(in) (*for* um)

can·died kandiert

can·dle Kerze *f*; Licht *n*; *burn the candle at both ends* mit s-r Gesundheit Raubbau treiben

can·dle·stick Kerzenleuchter *m*, Kerzenständer *m*

can·do(u)r Aufrichtigkeit *f*, Offenheit *f*

can·dy **1.** Kandis(zucker) *m*; Süßigkeiten *pl*; **2.** kandieren

candy floss Zuckerwatte *f*

candy store Süßwarengeschäft *n*

cane Rohr *n*; (Rohr)Stock *m*

ca·nine Hunde...

canned Dosen..., Büchsen...; *canned fruit* Obstkonserven *pl*

can·ne·ry Konservenfabrik *f*

can·ni·bal Kannibale *m*

can·non MIL Kanone *f*

can·ny schlau

ca·noe 1. Kanu *n*, Paddelboot *n*; **2.** Kanu fahren, paddeln

can·on Kanon *m*; Regel *f*

can o·pen·er Dosen-, Büchsenöffner *m*

can·o·py Baldachin *m*

cant Jargon *m*; Phrase(n *pl*) *f*

can·tan·ker·ous F zänkisch, mürrisch

can·teen *esp Br* Kantine *f*; MIL Feldflasche *f*; Besteck(kasten *m*) *n*

can·ter 1. Kanter *m*; **2.** kantern

can·vas Segeltuch *n*; Zelt-, Packleinwand *f*; Segel *pl*; PAINT Leinwand *f*; Gemälde *n*

can·vass 1. POL Wahlfeldzug *m*; ECON Werbefeldzug *m*; **2.** *v/t* eingehend untersuchen *or* erörtern *or* prüfen; POL werben um (*Stimmen*); *v/i* POL e-n Wahlfeldzug

veranstalten

can·yon GEOGR Cañon *m*, Schlucht *f*

cap 1. Kappe *f*; Mütze *f*; Haube *f*; Zündkapsel *f*; **2.** (mit e-r Kappe *etc*) bedecken; *fig* krönen; übertreffen

ca·pa·bil·i·ty Fähigkeit *f*

ca·pa·ble fähig (*of* zu)

ca·pac·i·ty (Raum)Inhalt *m*; Fassungsvermögen *n*; Kapazität *f*; Aufnahmefähigkeit *f*; (TECH Leistungs)Fähigkeit *f* (*for* *ger zu inf*); *in my capacity as* in meiner Eigenschaft als

cape[1] GEOGR Kap *n*, Vorgebirge *n*

cape[2] Cape *n*, Umhang *m*

ca·per 1. Kapriole *f*, Luftsprung *m*; *cut capers* → **2.** Freuden- *or* Luftsprünge machen

ca·pil·la·ry ANAT Haar-, Kapillargefäß *n*

cap·i·tal 1. ECON Kapital *n*; Hauptstadt *f*; Großbuchstabe *m*; **2.** Kapital...; Tod(es)...; Haupt...; großartig, prima

capital crime JUR Kapitalverbrechen *n*

cap·i·tal·ism ECON Kapitalismus *m*

cap·i·tal·ist ECON Kapitalist *m*

cap·i·tal·ize großschreiben; ECON kapitalisieren

capital let·ter Großbuchstabe *m*

capital pun·ish·ment JUR Todesstrafe *f*

ca·pit·u·late kapitulieren (*to* vor *dat*)

ca·pri·cious launisch

Cap·ri·corn ASTR Steinbock *m*; *he* (*she*) *is* (*a*) *Capricorn* er (sie) ist (ein) Steinbock

cap·size MAR *v/i* kentern; *v/t* zum Kentern bringen

cap·sule Kapsel *f*

cap·tain (An)Führer *m*; MAR, ECON Kapitän *m*; AVIAT Flugkapitän *m*; MIL Hauptmann *m*; SPORT (Mannschafts-) Kapitän *m*, Spielführer *m*

cap·tion Überschrift *f*, Titel *m*; Bilduntershrift *f*; *film:* Untertitel *m*

cap·ti·vate *fig* gefangen nehmen, fesseln

cap·tive 1. gefangen; gefesselt; *hold captive* gefangen halten; **2.** Gefangene *m*, *f*

cap·tiv·i·ty Gefangenschaft *f*

cap·ture 1. Eroberung *f*; Gefangennahme *f*; **2.** fangen, gefangen nehmen; erobern; erbeuten; MAR kapern

car Auto *n*, Wagen *m*; (Eisenbahn-, Straßenbahn)Wagen *m*; Gondel *f* (*of a balloon etc*); Kabine *f*; *by car* mit dem Auto, im Auto

car·a·mel Karamell *m*; Karamelle *f*

car·a·van Karawane *f*; *Br* Wohnwagen *m*

caravan site Campingplatz *m* für Wohnwagen

car·a·way BOT Kümmel *m*

car·bine MIL Karabiner *m*

car·bo·hy·drate CHEM Kohle(n)hydrat *n*

car bomb Autobombe f

car·bon CHEM Kohlenstoff m; → **carbon copy, carbon paper**

car·bon cop·y Durchschlag m

car·bon pa·per Kohlepapier n

car·bu·ret(t)or MOT Vergaser m

car·case Br, **car·cass** Kadaver m, Aas n; GASTR Rumpf m

car·cin·o·gen·ic MED karzinogen, krebserregend

car·ci·no·ma MED Krebsgeschwulst f

card Karte f; **play cards** Karten spielen; **have a card up one's sleeve** fig (noch) e-n Trumpf in der Hand haben

card·board Pappe f

cardboard box Pappschachtel f, Pappkarton m

car·di·ac MED Herz...

cardiac pace·mak·er MED Herzschrittmacher m

car·di·gan Strickjacke f

car·di·nal 1. Grund..., Haupt..., Kardinal...; scharlachrot; 2. REL Kardinal m

car·di·nal num·ber MATH Kardinalzahl f, Grundzahl f

card in·dex Kartei f

card phone Kartentelefon n

card·sharp·er Falschspieler m

car dump Autofriedhof m

care 1. Sorge f; Sorgfalt f; Vorsicht f; Obhut f, Pflege f; **needing care** MED pflegebedürftig; **medical care** ärztliche Behandlung; **take care of** aufpassen auf (acc); versorgen; **with care!** Vorsicht!; 2. Lust haben (**to** inf zu inf); **care about** sich kümmern um; **care for** sorgen für, sich kümmern um; sich etwas machen aus; **I don't care!** F meinetwegen!; **I couldn't care less** F es ist mir völlig egal

ca·reer 1. Karriere f, Laufbahn f; Beruf(s...); Karriere...; 3. rasen

ca·reers ad·vice Berufsberatung f

careers ad·vi·sor Berufsberater m

careers guidance Berufsberatung f

careers of·fice Berufsberatungsstelle f

careers of·fi·cer Berufsberater m

care·free sorgenfrei, sorglos

care·ful vorsichtig; sorgsam bedacht (**of** auf acc); sorgfältig; **be careful!** pass auf!

care·less nachlässig, unachtsam; leichtsinnig, unvorsichtig; sorglos

care·less·ness Nachlässigkeit f, Unachtsamkeit f; Leichtsinn m; Sorglosigkeit f

ca·ress 1. Liebkosung f; Zärtlichkeit f; 2. liebkosen, streicheln

care·tak·er Hausmeister m; (Haus- etc) Verwalter m

care·worn abgehärmt, verhärmt

car fer·ry Autofähre f

car·go Ladung f

car hire Br Autovermietung f

car·i·ca·ture 1. Karikatur f, Zerrbild n; 2. karikieren

car·i·ca·tur·ist Karikaturist m

car·ies, a. **dental caries** MED Karies f

car me·chan·ic Automechaniker m

car·mine Karmin(rot) n

car·na·tion BOT Nelke f

car·nap·per F Autoentführer m

car·ni·val Karneval m

car·niv·o·rous ZO fleischfressend

car·ol Weihnachtslied n

carp[1] ZO Karpfen m

carp[2] nörgeln

car park esp Br Parkplatz m; Parkhaus n

car·pen·ter Zimmermann m

car·pet 1. Teppich m; **fitted carpet** Teppichboden m; **sweep s.th. under the carpet** fig et. unter den Teppich kehren; 2. mit Teppich(boden) auslegen

car phone Autotelefon n

car pool Fahrgemeinschaft f

car pool(·ing) ser·vice Mitfahrzentrale f

car·port MOT überdachter Abstellplatz

car rent·al Autovermietung f

car re·pair shop Autoreparaturwerkstatt f

car·riage Beförderung f, Transport m; Transportkosten pl; Kutsche f; Br RAIL (Personen)Wagen m; (Körper-)Haltung f

car·riage·way Fahrbahn f

car·ri·er Spediteur m; Gepäckträger m (on a bicycle); MIL Flugzeugträger m

car·ri·er bag Br Trag(e)tasche f, -tüte f

car·ri·on 1. Aas n; 2. Aas...

car·rot BOT Karotte f, Mohrrübe f

car·ry v/t bringen, führen, tragen (a. v/i), fahren, befördern; (bei sich) haben or tragen; Ansicht durchsetzen; Gewinn, Preis davontragen; Ernte, Zinsen tragen; (weiter)führen, Mauer ziehen; Antrag durchbringen; **be carried** PARL etc angenommen werden; **carry the day** den Sieg davontragen; **carry s.th. too far** et. übertreiben, et. zu weit treiben; **get carried away** fig die Kontrolle über sich verlieren; sich hinreißen lassen; **carry forward, carry over** ECON übertragen; **carry on** fortsetzen, weiterführen; betreiben; **carry out, carry through** aus-, durchführen

car·ry·cot Br (Baby)Trag(e)tasche f

car·ry·ing **put the cart before the horse** fig das Pferd beim Schwanz aufzäumen; 2. karren

cart·i·lage ANAT Knorpel m

cart·load Wagenladung f

car·ton Karton *m*; *a carton of cigarettes* e-e Stange Zigaretten

car·toon Cartoon *m, n*; Karikatur *f*; Zeichentrickfilm *m*

car·toon·ist Karikaturist *m*

car·tridge Patrone *f* (*a.* MIL); (Film-) Patrone *f*, (Film)Kassette *f*; Tonabnehmer *m*

cart·wheel: *turn cartwheels* Rad schlagen

carve GASTR vorschneiden, zerlegen; TECH schnitzen; meißeln

carv·er (Holz)Schnitzer *m*; Bildhauer *m*; GASTR Tranchierer *m*; Tranchiermesser *n*

carv·ing Schnitzerei *f*

car wash Autowäsche *f*; (Auto)Waschanlage *f*, Waschstraße *f*

cas·cade Wasserfall *m*

case¹ 1. Behälter *m*; Kiste *f*, Kasten *m*; Etui *n*; Gehäuse *n*; Schachtel *f*; (*Glas-*) Schrank *m*; (*Kissen*)Bezug *m*; TECH Verkleidung *f*; **2.** in ein Gehäuse *or* Etui stecken; TECH verkleiden

case² Fall *m* (*a.* JUR), LING *a.* Kasus *m*; MED (Krankheits)Fall *m*, Patient(in); Sache *f*, Angelegenheit *f*

case·ment Fensterflügel *m*; → *casement window* Flügelfenster *n*

cash 1. Bargeld *n*; Barzahlung *f*; *cash down* gegen bar; *cash on delivery* Lieferung *f* gegen bar; (per) Nachnahme *f*; **2.** einlösen

cash·book ECON Kassenbuch *n*

cash desk Kasse *f*

cash dis·pens·er *esp Br* Geld-, Bankautomat *m*

cash·ier Kassierer(in)

cash·less bargeldlos

cash ma·chine Geld-, Bankautomat *m*

cash·mere Kaschmir *m*

cash·point *Br* → *cash machine*

cash reg·is·ter Registrierkasse *f*

cas·ing (Schutz)Hülle *f*; Verschalung *f*, Verkleidung *f*, Gehäuse *n*

cask Fass *n*

cas·ket Kästchen *n*; Sarg *m*

cas·sette (*Film-, Band-, Musik*)Kassette *f*

cassette deck Kassettendeck *n*

cassette player Kassettenrekorder *m*

cassette ra·di·o Radiorekorder *m*

cassette re·cord·er Kassettenrekorder *m*

cas·sock REL Soutane *f*

cast 1. Wurf *m*; TECH Guss(form *f*) *m*; Abguss *m*, Abdruck *m*; Schattierung *f*, Anflug *m*; Form *f*, Art *f*; Auswerfen *n* (*of a fishing line etc*); THEA Besetzung *f*; **2.** (ab-, aus-, hin-, um-, weg)werfen; ZO abwerfen (*skin*); verlieren (*teeth*); verwerfen; gestalten; TECH gießen; *a. cast up* ausrechnen, zusammenzählen; THEA

Stück besetzen; *Rollen* verteilen (**to** an *acc*); *cast lots* losen (**for** um); *cast away* wegwerfen; *be cast down* niedergeschlagen sein; *cast off Kleidung* ausrangieren; MAR losmachen; *Freund etc* fallen lassen; *knitting*: abketten; *v/i: cast about for, cast around for* suchen (nach), *fig a.* sich umsehen nach

cas·ta·net Kastagnette *f*

cast·a·way Schiffbrüchige *m, f*

caste Kaste *f* (*a. fig*)

cast·er Laufrolle *f*; *Br* (*Salz-, Zucker-etc*)Streuer *m*

cast i·ron Gusseisen *n*

cast-i·ron gusseisern

cas·tle Burg *f*, Schloss *n*; *chess*: Turm *m*

cast·or → *caster*

cast·or oil PHARM Rizinusöl *n*

cas·trate kastrieren

cas·u·al zufällig; gelegentlich; flüchtig; lässig

cas·u·al·ty Unfall *m*; Verunglückte *m, f*, Opfer *n*; MIL Verwundete *m*; Gefallene *m*; *casualties* Opfer *pl*, MIL *mst* Verluste *pl*

casualty (de·part·ment) MED Notaufnahme *f*

casualty ward MED Unfallstation *f*

cas·u·al wear Freizeitkleidung *f*

cat ZO Katze *f*

cat·a·log, *esp Br* **cat·a·logue 1.** Katalog *m*; Verzeichnis *n*, Liste *f*; **2.** katalogisieren

cat·a·lyt·ic con·vert·er MOT Katalysator *m*

cat·a·pult *Br* Schleuder *f*; Katapult *n*, *m*

cat·a·ract Wasserfall *m*; Stromschnelle *f*; MED grauer Star

ca·tarrh(**h**) *m*

ca·tas·tro·phe Katastrophe *f*

catch 1. Fangen *n*; Fang *m*, Beute *f*; Halt *m*, Griff *m*; TECH Haken *m* (*a. fig*); (Tür-) Klinke *f*; Verschluss *m*; **2.** *v/t* (auf-, ein)fangen; packen, fassen, ergreifen; überraschen, ertappen; *Blick etc* auffangen; F *Zug etc* (noch) kriegen, erwischen; *et.* erfassen, verstehen; *Atmosphäre etc* einfangen; sich *e-e Krankheit* holen; *catch* (*a*) *cold* sich erkälten; *catch the eye* ins Auge fallen; *catch s.o.'s eye* j-s Aufmerksamkeit auf sich lenken; *catch s.o. up* j-n einholen; *be caught up in* verwickelt sein in (*acc*); *v/i* sich verfangen, hängen bleiben; fassen, greifen; TECH ineinandergreifen; klemmen; einschnappen; *catch up with* einholen

catch·er Fänger *m*

catch·ing packend; MED ansteckend (*a. fig*)

catch·word Schlagwort *n*; Stichwort *n*

catch·y MUS eingängig

cat·e·chis·m REL Katechismus *m*

cat·e·go·ry Kategorie *f*

ca·ter: *cater for* Speisen und Getränke liefern für; *fig* sorgen für

cat·er·pil·lar ZO Raupe *f*

Cat·er·pil·lar® MOT Raupenfahrzeug *n*

Caterpillar trac·tor® MOT Raupenschlepper *m*

cat·gut MUS Darmsaite *f*

ca·the·dral Dom *m*, Kathedrale *f*

Cath·o·lic REL **1.** katholisch; **2.** Katholik(in)

cat·kin BOT Kätzchen *n*

cat·tle Vieh *n*

cattle breed·er Viehzüchter *m*

cattle breed·ing Viehzucht *f*

cattle dealer Viehhändler *m*

cattle mar·ket Viehmarkt *m*

ca(u)l·dron großer Kessel

cau·li·flow·er BOT Blumenkohl *m*

cause 1. Ursache *f*; Grund *m*; Sache *f*; **2.** verursachen; veranlassen

cause·less grundlos

cau·tion 1. Vorsicht *f*; Warnung *f*; Verwarnung *f*; **2.** warnen; verwarnen; JUR belehren

cau·tious behutsam, vorsichtig

cav·al·ry HIST MIL Kavallerie *f*

cave 1. Höhle *f*; **2.** *v/i*: *cave in* einstürzen

cav·ern (große) Höhle

cav·i·ty Höhle *f*; MED Loch *n*

caw ZO **1.** krächzen; **2.** Krächzen *n*

CD ABBR of *compact disk* CD *f*

CD play·er CD-Spieler *m*

CD-ROM ABBR of *compact disk read-only memory* CD-ROM

CD vid·e·o CD-Video *n*

cease aufhören; beenden

cease-fire MIL Feuereinstellung *f*; Waffenruhe *f*

cease·less unaufhörlich

cei·ling (Zimmer)Decke *f*; ECON Höchstgrenze *f*, oberste Preisgrenze

cel·e·brate feiern

cel·e·brat·ed gefeiert, berühmt (*for* für, wegen)

cel·e·bra·tion Feier *f*

ce·leb·ri·ty Berühmtheit *f*

cel·e·ry BOT Sellerie *m*, *f*

ce·les·ti·al himmlisch

cel·i·ba·cy Ehelosigkeit *f*

cell BIOL Zelle *f*, ELECTR *a.* Element *n*

cel·lar Keller *m*

cel·list MUS Cellist(in)

cel·lo MUS (Violon)Cello *n*

cel·lo·phane® Cellophan® *n*

cel·lu·lar BIOL Zell(en)...

cel·lu·lar phone Handy *n*

Cel·tic keltisch

ce·ment 1. Zement *m*; Kitt *m*; **2.** zementieren; (ver)kitten

cem·e·tery Friedhof *m*

cen·sor 1. Zensor *m*; **2.** zensieren

cen·sor·ship Zensur *f*

cen·sure 1. Tadel *m*, Verweis *m*; **2.** tadeln

cen·sus Volkszählung *f*

cent Hundert *m*; Cent *m* (*1/100 Dollar*); *per cent* Prozent *n*

cen·te·na·ry Hundertjahrfeier *f*, hundertjähriges Jubiläum

cen·ten·ni·al 1. hundertjährig; **2.** → *centenary*

cen·ter 1. Zentrum *n*, Mittelpunkt *m*; *soccer:* Flanke *f*; **2.** (sich) konzentrieren; zentrieren

center back *soccer:* Vorstopper *m*

center for·ward SPORT Mittelstürmer(in)

center of grav·i·ty PHYS Schwerpunkt *m*

cen·ti·grade: *10 degrees centigrade* 10 Grad Celsius

cen·ti·me·ter, *Br* **cen·ti·me·tre** Zentimeter *m*, *n*

cen·ti·pede ZO Tausendfüß(l)er *m*

cen·tral zentral; Haupt..., Zentral...; Mittel...

central heat·ing Zentralheizung *f*

cen·tral·ize zentralisieren

cen·tral lock·ing MOT Zentralverriegelung *f*

central res·er·va·tion *Br* MOT Mittelstreifen *m*

cen·tre *Br* → *center*

cen·tu·ry Jahrhundert *n*

ce·ram·ics Keramik *f*, keramische Erzeugnisse *pl*

ce·re·al 1. Getreide...; **2.** BOT Getreide *n*; Getreidepflanze *f*; GASTR Getreideflocken *pl*, Frühstückskost *f*

cer·e·bral ANAT Gehirn...

cer·e·mo·ni·al 1. zeremoniell; **2.** Zeremoniell *n*

cer·e·mo·ni·ous zeremoniell; förmlich

cer·e·mo·ny Zeremonie *f*; Feier *f*, Feierlichkeit *f*; Förmlichkeit(en *pl*) *f*

cer·tain sicher, gewiss; zuverlässig; bestimmt; gewisse(r, -s)

cer·tain·ly sicher, gewiss; *int* sicherlich, bestimmt, natürlich

cer·tain·ty Sicherheit *f*, Bestimmtheit *f*, Gewissheit *f*

cer·tif·i·cate Zeugnis *n*; Bescheinigung *f*; *certificate of (good) conduct* Führungszeugnis *n*; *General Certificate of Education advanced level* (*A level*) *Br* PED *appr* Abitur(zeugnis) *n*; *General Certificate of Education ordinary level*

(*O level*) *Br* PED *appr* mittlere Reife; *medical certificate* ärztliches Attest

cer·ti·fy *et.* bescheinigen; beglaubigen

cer·ti·tude Sicherheit *f*, Bestimmtheit *f*, Gewissheit *f*

CET ABBR *of* **Central European Time** MEZ, mitteleuropäische Zeit

cf (*Latin* **confer**) ABBR *of* **compare** vgl., vergleiche

CFC ABBR *of* **chlorofluorocarbon** FCKW, Fluorchlorkohlenwasserstoff *m*

chafe *v/t* warm reiben; aufreiben, wund reiben; *v/i* sich (durch)reiben, scheuern

chaff AGR Spreu *f*; Häcksel *n*

chaf·finch ZO Buchfink *m*

cha·grin **1.** Ärger *m*; **2.** ärgern

chain 1. Kette *f*; *fig* Fessel *f*; **2.** (an)ketten; fesseln

chain re·ac·tion Kettenreaktion *f*

chain-smoke F Kette rauchen

chain-smok·er Kettenraucher(in)

chain-smok·ing Kettenrauchen *n*

chain store Kettenladen *m*

chair Stuhl *m*; UNIV Lehrstuhl *m*; ECON *etc* Vorsitz *m*; *be in the chair* den Vorsitz führen

chair lift Sessellift *m*

chair·man Vorsitzende *m*, Präsident *m*; Diskussionsleiter *m*; ECON *Br* Generaldirektor *m*

chair·man·ship Vorsitz *m*

chair·wom·an Vorsitzende *f*, Präsidentin *f*; Diskussionsleiterin *f*

chal·ice REL Kelch *m*

chalk 1. Kreide *f*; **2.** mit Kreide schreiben *or* zeichnen

chal·lenge 1. Herausforderung *f*; **2.** herausfordern

chal·len·ger Herausforderer *m*

cham·ber TECH, PARL *etc* Kammer *f*

cham·ber·maid Zimmermädchen *n*

cham·ber of com·merce ECON Handelskammer *f*

cham·ois ZO Gämse *f*

cham·ois (**leath·er**) Fensterleder *n*

champ F SPORT → **champion**

cham·pagne Champagner *m*

cham·pi·on 1. Verfechter(in), Fürsprecher(in); SPORT Meister(in); **2.** verfechten, eintreten für

cham·pi·on·ship SPORT Meisterschaft *f*

chance 1. Zufall *m*; Chance *f*, (günstige) Gelegenheit; Aussicht *f* (*of* auf *acc*); Möglichkeit *f*; Risiko *n*; *by chance* zufällig; *take a chance* es darauf ankommen lassen; *take no chances* nichts riskieren (wollen); **2.** zufällig; **3.** F riskieren

chan·cel·lor Kanzler(in)

chan·de·lier Kronleuchter *m*

change 1. Veränderung *f*, Wechsel *m*; Abwechslung *f*; Wechselgeld *n*; Kleingeld *n*; *for a change* zur Abwechslung; *change for the better* (*worse*) Bess(e)rung *f* (Verschlechterung *f*); **2.** *v/t* (ver)ändern, umändern; (aus)wechseln; (aus-, ver-) tauschen (*for* gegen); umbuchen; MOT, TECH schalten; *change over* umschalten; umstellen; *change trains* umsteigen; *v/i* sich (ver)ändern, wechseln; sich umziehen

change·a·ble veränderlich

change ma·chine Münzwechsler *m*

change-o·ver Umstellung *f* (*to* auf *acc*)

chang·ing room *esp* SPORT Umkleidekabine *f*, Umkleideraum *m*

chan·nel 1. Kanal *m* (*a. fig*); (*Fernseh-etc*)Kanal *m*, (*Fernseh-etc*)Programm *n*; *fig* Weg *m*; **2.** *fig* lenken

Chan·nel Tun·nel Kanaltunnel *m*, Eurotunnel *m*

chant 1. (Kirchen)Gesang *m*; Singsang *m*; **2.** in Sprechchören rufen

cha·os Chaos *n*

chap¹ 1. Riss *m*; **2.** rissig machen *or* werden; aufspringen

chap² *Br* F Bursche *m*, Kerl *m*

chap·el ARCH Kapelle *f*; REL Gottesdienst *m*

chap·lain REL Kaplan *m*

chap·ter Kapitel *n*

char verkohlen

char·ac·ter Charakter *m*; Ruf *m*, Leumund *m*; Schriftzeichen *n*, Buchstabe *m*; *novel etc*: Figur *f*, Gestalt *f*; THEA Rolle *f*

char·ac·ter·is·tic 1. charakteristisch (*of* für); **2.** Kennzeichen *n*

char·ac·ter·ize charakterisieren

char·coal Holzkohle *f*

charge 1. *v/t* ELECTR (auf)laden; *Gewehr etc* laden; *j-n* beauftragen (**with** mit); *j-n* beschuldigen *or* anklagen (**with** *e-r Sache*) (*a.* JUR); ECON berechnen, verlangen, fordern (**for** für); MIL angreifen; stürmen; *charge s.o. with s.th.* ECON *j-m* et. in Rechnung stellen; *v/i*: *charge at s.o.* auf *j-n* losgehen; **2.** Ladung *f* (*a.* ELECTR *etc*); (Spreng)Ladung *f*; Beschuldigung *f*, *a.* JUR Anklage(-punkt *m*) *f*; ECON Preis *m*; Forderung *f*; Gebühr *f*; *a. pl* Unkosten *pl*, Spesen *pl*; Verantwortung *f*; Schützling *m*, Mündel *n*, *m*; *free of charge* kostenlos, gebührenfrei; *be in charge of* verantwortlich sein für; *take charge of* die Leitung etc übernehmen, die Sache in die Hand nehmen

char·i·ot HIST Streit-, Triumphwagen *m*

cha·ris·ma Charisma *n*, Ausstrahlung *f*,

Ausstrahlungskraft f

char·i·ta·ble wohltätig

char·i·ty Nächstenliebe f; Wohltätigkeit f; Güte f, Nachsicht f; milde Gabe

char·la·tan Scharlatan m; Quacksalber m, Kurpfuscher m

charm 1. Zauber m; Charme m, Reiz m; Talisman m, Amulett n; **2.** bezaubern, entzücken

charm·ing charmant, bezaubernd

chart (See-, Himmels-, Wetter)Karte f; Diagramm n, Schaubild n; pl MUS Charts pl, Hitliste(n pl) f

char·ter 1. Urkunde f; Charta f; Chartern n; **2.** chartern, mieten

char·ter flight Charterflug m

char·wom·an Putzfrau f, Raumpflegerin f

chase 1. Jagd f; Verfolgung f; **2.** v/t jagen, hetzen; Jagd machen auf (acc); TECH ziselieren; v/i rasen, rennen

chasm Kluft f, Abgrund m

chaste keusch; schlicht

chas·tise züchtigen

chas·ti·ty Keuschheit f

chat 1. Geplauder n, Schwätzchen n, Plauderei f; **2.** plaudern

chat show Br TV Talkshow f

chat show host Br TV Talkmaster m

chat·ter 1. plappern; schnattern; klappern; **2.** Geplapper n; Klappern n

chat·ter·box F Plappermaul n

chat·ty gesprächig

chauf·feur Chauffeur m

chau·vi F Chauvi m

chau·vin·ist Chauvinist m; F **male chauvinist pig** Chauvi m; contp Chauvischwein n

cheap billig; fig schäbig, gemein

cheap·en (sich) verbilligen; fig herabsetzen

cheat 1. Betrug m, Schwindel m; Betrüger(in); **2.** betrügen; F schummeln

check 1. Schach(stellung f) n; Hemmnis n, Hindernis n (**on** für); Einhalt m; Kontrolle f (**on** gen); Kontrollabschnitt m, -schein m; Gepäckschein m; Garderobenmarke f; ECON Scheck m (**for** über); Häkchen n (**on** a list etc); ECON Kassenzettel m, Rechnung f; karierter Stoff; **2.** v/i (plötzlich) innehalten; **check in** sich (in e-m Hotel) anmelden; einstempeln; AVIAT einchecken; **check out** (aus e-m Hotel) abreisen; ausstempeln; **check up (on)** F (e-e Sache) nachprüfen, (e-e Sache, j-n) überprüfen; v/t hemmen, hindern, aufhalten; zurückhalten; checken, kontrollieren, überprüfen; auf e-r Liste abhaken; Mantel etc in der Garderobe abgeben; Gepäck aufgeben

check card ECON Scheckkarte f

checked kariert

check·ers Damespiel n

check-in Anmeldung f; Einstempeln n; AVIAT Einchecken n

check-in coun·ter, check-in desk AVIAT Abfertigungsschalter m

check·ing ac·count ECON Girokonto n

check·list Check-, Kontrollliste f

check·mate 1. (Schach)Matt n; **2.** (schach)matt setzen

check-out Abreise f; Ausstempeln n

check-out coun·ter Kasse f

check·point Kontrollpunkt m

check·room Garderobe f; Gepäckaufbewahrung f

check-up Überprüfung f; MED Check-up m, Vorsorgeuntersuchung f

cheek ANAT Backe f, Wange f; Br Unverschämtheit f

cheek·y Br frech

cheer 1. Stimmung f, Fröhlichkeit f; Hoch n, Hochruf m, Beifall m, Beifallsruf m; pl SPORT Anfeuerungsrufe pl; **three cheers!** dreimal hoch!; **cheers!** prost!; **2.** v/t mit Beifall begrüßen; a. **cheer on** anspornen; a. **cheer up** aufheitern; v/i hoch rufen, jubeln; a. **cheer up** Mut fassen; **cheer up!** Kopf hoch!

cheer·ful vergnügt

cheer·i·o int Br F tschüs(s)!

cheer·lead·er SPORT Einpeitscher m, Cheerleader m

cheer·less freudlos; unfreundlich

cheer·y vergnügt

cheese Käse m

chee·tah ZO Gepard m

chef Küchenchef m; Koch m

chem·i·cal 1. chemisch; **2.** Chemikalie f

chem·ist Chemiker(in); Apotheker(in); Drogist(in)

chem·is·try Chemie f

chem·ist's shop Apotheke f; Drogerie f

chem·o·ther·a·py MED Chemotherapie f

cheque Br ECON Scheck m; **crossed cheque** Verrechnungsscheck m

cheque ac·count Br Girokonto n

cheque card Br Scheckkarte f

cher·ry BOT Kirsche f

chess Schach(spiel) n; **a game of chess** e-e Partie Schach

chess·board Schachbrett n

chess·man, chess·piece Schachfigur f

chest Kiste f; Truhe f; ANAT Brust f, Brustkasten m; **get s.th. off one's chest** F sich et. von der Seele reden

chest·nut 1. BOT Kastanie f; **2.** kastanienbraun

chest of drawers Kommode f

chew (zer)kauen

chew·ing gum Kaugummi *m*

chic schick, *Austrian* fesch

chick zo Küken *n*, junger Vogel; F Biene *f*, Puppe *f* (*girl*)

chick·en zo Huhn *n*; Küken *n*; GASTR (*Brat*)Hähnchen *n*, (*Brat*)Hühnchen *n*

chick·en-heart·ed furchtsam, feige

chick·en pox MED Windpocken *pl*

chic·o·ry BOT Chicorée *m*, *f*

chief 1. oberste(r, -s) Ober..., Haupt..., Chef...; wichtigste(r, -s) 2. Chef *m*; Häuptling *m*

chief·ly hauptsächlich

chil·blain MED Frostbeule *f*

child Kind *n*; *from a child* von Kindheit an; *with child* schwanger

child a·buse JUR Kindesmisshandlung *f*

child ben·e·fit *Br* Kindergeld *n*

child·birth Geburt *f*, Niederkunft *f*

child·hood Kindheit *f*; *from childhood* von Kindheit an

child·ish kindlich; kindisch

child·like kindlich

child·mind·er Tagesmutter *f*

chill 1. kalt, frostig, kühl (*a. fig*) 2. Frösteln *n*; Kälte *f*, Kühle *f* (*a. fig*) MED Erkältung *f*; 3. abkühlen; *j-n* frösteln lassen; kühlen

chill·y kalt, frostig, kühl (*a. fig*)

chime 1. Glockenspiel *n*; Geläut *n*; 2. läuten; schlagen (*clock*)

chim·ney Schornstein *m*

chim·ney sweep Schornsteinfeger *m*

chimp F, chim·pan·zee zo Schimpanse *m*

chin ANAT Kinn *m*; *chin up!* Kopf hoch!, halt die Ohren steif!

chi·na Porzellan *n*

Chi·na China *n*

Chi·nese 1. chinesisch; 2. Chinese *m*, Chinesin *f*; LING Chinesisch *n*; *the Chinese* die Chinesen *pl*

chink Ritz *m*, Spalt *m*

chip 1. Splitter *m*, Span *m*, Schnitzel *n*, *m*; dünne Scheibe; Spielmarke *f*; EDP Chip *m*; 2. *v/t* schnitzeln; anschlagen, abschlagen; *v/i* abbröckeln

chips (Kartoffel)Chips *pl*; *Br* Pommes frites *pl*, F Fritten *pl*

chi·ro·po·dist Fußpfleger(in), Pediküre *f*

chirp zo zirpen, zwitschern, piepsen

chis·el 1. Meißel *m*; 2. meißeln

chit-chat Plauderei *f*

chiv·al·rous ritterlich

chive(s) BOT Schnittlauch *m*

chlo·ri·nate *Wasser etc* chloren

chlo·rine CHEM Chlor *n*

chlo·ro·fluo·ro·car·bon (ABBR *CFC*) CHEM Fluorchlorkohlenwasserstoff *m*

(ABBR *FCKW*)

chlor·o·form MED 1. Chloroform *n*; 2. chloroformieren

choc·o·late Schokolade *f*; Praline *f*; *pl* Pralinen *pl*, Konfekt *n*

choice 1. Wahl *f*; Auswahl *f*; 2. auserlesen, ausgesucht, vorzüglich

choir ARCH, MUS Chor *m*

choke 1. *v/t* (er)würgen; (*a. v/i*) ersticken; *choke back* Ärger etc unterdrücken, Tränen zurückhalten; *choke down* hinunterwürgen; *a. choke up* verstopfen; 2. MOT Choke *m*, Luftklappe *f*

cho·les·te·rol MED Cholesterin *n*

choose (aus)wählen, aussuchen

choos·(e)y *esp Br* wählerisch

chop 1. Hieb *m*, (Handkanten)Schlag *m*; GASTR Kotelett *n*; 2. *v/t* (zer)hacken, hauen; *chop down* fällen; *v/i* hacken

chop·per Hackmesser *n*, Hackbeil *n*; F Hubschrauber *m*

chop·py unruhig (*sea*)

chop·stick Essstäbchen *n*

cho·ral MUS Chor...

cho·rale MUS Choral *m*

chord MUS Saite *f*; Akkord *m*

chore schwierige *or* unangenehme Aufgabe; *pl* Hausarbeit *f*

cho·rus MUS Chor *m*; Kehrreim *m*, Refrain *m*; Tanzgruppe *f*

Christ REL Christus *m*

chris·ten REL taufen

chris·ten·ing REL 1. Taufe *f*; 2. Tauf...

Chris·tian REL 1. christlich; 2. Christ(in)

Chris·ti·an·i·ty REL Christentum *n*

Chris·tian name Vorname *m*

Christ·mas Weihnachten *n and pl*; *at Christmas* zu Weihnachten

Christmas Day erster Weihnachtsfeiertag

Christmas Eve Heiliger Abend

chrome Chrom *n*

chro·mi·um CHEM Chrom *n*

chron·ic chronisch; ständig, (an)dauernd

chron·i·cle Chronik *f*

chron·o·log·i·cal chronologisch

chro·nol·o·gy Zeitrechnung *f*; Zeitfolge *f*

chub·by F rundlich, pumm(e)lig; pausbäckig

chuck F werfen, schmeißen; *chuck out j-n* rausschmeißen; *et.* wegschmeißen; *chuck up Job etc* hinschmeißen

chuck·le 1. *chuckle (to o.s.)* (stillvergnügt) in sich hineinlachen; 2. leises Lachen

chum F Kamerad *m*, Kumpel *m*

chum·my F dick befreundet

chump Holzklotz *m*; F Trottel *m*

chunk Klotz *m*, Klumpen *m*

Chun·nel F → *Channel Tunnel*

church 1. Kirche *f*; 2. Kirch..., Kirchen...
church ser·vice REL Gottesdienst *m*
church·yard Kirchhof *m*
churl·ish grob, flegelhaft
churn 1. Butterfass *n*; 2. buttern; *Wellen* aufwühlen, peitschen
chute Stromschnelle *f*; Rutsche *f*, Rutschbahn *f*; F Fallschirm *m*
ci·der *a.* **hard cider** Apfelwein *m*; (*sweet*) *cider* Apfelmost *m*, Apfelsaft *m*
ci·gar Zigarre *f*
cig·a·rette Zigarette *f*
cinch F todsichere Sache
cin·der Schlacke *f*; *pl* Asche *f*
Cin·de·rel·la Aschenbrödel *n*, Aschenputtel *n*
cin·der track SPORT Aschenbahn *f*
cin·e·cam·e·ra (Schmal)Filmkamera *f*
cin·e·film Schmalfilm *m*
cin·e·ma *Br* Kino *n*; Film *m*
cin·na·mon Zimt *m*
ci·pher Geheimschrift *f*, Chiffre *f*; Null *f* (*a. fig*)
cir·cle 1. Kreis *m*; THEA Rang *m*; *fig* Kreislauf *m*; 2. (um)kreisen
cir·cuit Kreislauf *m*; ELECTR Stromkreis *m*; Rundreise *f*; SPORT Zirkus *m*; *short circuit* ELECTR Kurzschluss *m*
cir·cu·i·tous gewunden; weitschweifig; *circuitous route* Umweg *m*
cir·cu·lar 1. kreisförmig; Kreis...; 2. Rundschreiben *n*; Umlauf *m*; (Post-)Wurfsendung *f*
cir·cu·late *v/i* zirkulieren, im Umlauf sein; *v/t* in Umlauf setzen
cir·cu·lat·ing li·bra·ry Leihbücherei *f*
cir·cu·la·tion (*a.* Blut)Kreislauf *m*, Zirkulation *f*; ECON Umlauf *m*; *newspaper etc:* Auflage *f*
cir·cum·fer·ence (Kreis)Umfang *m*
cir·cum·nav·i·gate umschiffen, umsegeln
cir·cum·scribe MATH umschreiben; *fig* begrenzen
cir·cum·spect umsichtig, vorsichtig
cir·cum·stance Umstand *m*; *pl* (Sach-)Lage *f*, Umstände *pl*; Verhältnisse *pl*; *in or under no circumstances* unter keinen Umständen, auf keinen Fall; *in or under the circumstances* unter diesen Umständen
cir·cum·stan·tial ausführlich; umständlich
circumstantial ev·i·dence JUR Indizien *pl*, Indizienbeweis *m*
cir·cus Zirkus *m*
CIS ABBR *of* **Commonwealth of Independent States** die GUS, die Gemeinschaft unabhängiger Staaten
cis·tern Wasserbehälter *m*; Spülkasten *m*

ci·ta·tion Zitat *n*; JUR Vorladung *f*
cite zitieren; JUR vorladen
cit·i·zen Bürger(in); Städter(in); Staatsangehörige *m*, *f*
cit·i·zen·ship Staatsangehörigkeit *f*
cit·y 1. (Groß)Stadt *f*; *the City* die (Londoner) City; 2. städtisch, Stadt...
city cen·tre *Br* Innenstadt *f*, City *f*
city coun·cil·(l)or Stadtrat *m*, Stadträtin *f*
city hall Rathaus *n*; Stadtverwaltung *f*
city slick·er *often contp* Städter(in), Stadtmensch *m*
city va·grant Stadtstreicher(in), Nichtsesshafte *m*, *f*
civ·ic städtisch, Stadt...
civ·ics PED Staatsbürgerkunde *f*
civ·il staatlich, Staats...; (staats)bürgerlich, Bürger...; zivil, Zivil...; JUR zivilrechtlich; höflich
ci·vil·ian Zivilist *m*
ci·vil·i·ty Höflichkeit *f*
civ·i·li·za·tion Zivilisation *f*, Kultur *f*
civ·i·lize zivilisieren
civ·il rights (Staats)Bürgerrechte *pl*
civil rights ac·tiv·ist Bürgerrechtler(in)
civil rights move·ment Bürgerrechtsbewegung *f*
civ·il ser·vant Staatsbeamte *m*, -beamtin *f*
civil ser·vice Staatsdienst *m*
civil war Bürgerkrieg *m*
clad gekleidet
claim 1. Anspruch *m*; Anrecht *n* (*to* auf *acc*); Forderung *f*; Behauptung *f*; Claim *m*; 2. beanspruchen; fordern; behaupten
clair·voy·ant 1. hellseherisch; 2. Hellseher(in)
clam·ber (mühsam) klettern
clam·my feuchtkalt, klamm
clam·o(u)r 1. Geschrei *n*, Lärm *m*; 2. lautstark verlangen (*for* nach)
clamp TECH Zwinge *f*
clan Clan *m*, Sippe *f*
clan·des·tine heimlich
clang klingen, klirren; erklingen lassen
clank 1. Gerassel *n*, Geklirr *n*; 2. rasseln or klirren (mit)
clap 1. Klatschen *n*; Schlag *m*, Klaps *m*; 2. schlagen or klatschen (mit)
clar·et roter Bordeaux(wein); Rotwein *m*
clar·i·fy *v/t* (auf)klären, klarstellen; *v/i* sich (auf)klären, klar werden
clar·i·net MUS Klarinette *f*
clar·i·ty Klarheit *f*
clash 1. Zusammenstoß *m*; Konflikt *m*; 2. zusammenstoßen; *fig* nicht zusammenpassen or harmonieren
clasp 1. Haken *m*, Schnalle *f*; Schloss *n*, (Schnapp)Verschluss *m*; Umklamme-

rung *f*; **2.** einhaken, zuhaken; ergreifen, umklammern

lasp knife Taschenmesser *n*

lass 1. Klasse *f*; (Bevölkerungs-) Schicht *f*; (Schul)Klasse *f*; (Unterrichts)Stunde *f*; Kurs *m*; Jahrgang *m*; **2.** (in Klassen) einteilen, einordnen, einstufen

las·sic 1. Klassiker *m*; **2.** klassisch

las·si·cal klassisch

las·sic car Klassiker *m*

las·si·fi·ca·tion Klassifizierung *f*, Einteilung *f*

las·si·fied ad Kleinanzeige *f*

lassified klassifiziert; MIL, POL geheim

las·si·fy klassifizieren, einstufen

lass·mate Mitschüler(in)

lass·room Klassenzimmer *n*

lat·ter 1. Geklapper *n*; **2.** klappern (mit)

lause JUR Klausel *f*, Bestimmung *f*; LING Satz(teil *n*) *m*

law 1. ZO Klaue *f*, Kralle *f*; (*Krebs*-) Schere *f*; **2.** (zer)kratzen; umkrallen, packen

clay Ton *m*, Lehm *m*

lean 1. *adj* rein; sauber, glatt, eben; *sl* clean; **2.** *adv* völlig, ganz und gar; **3.** reinigen, säubern, putzen; *clean out* reinigen; *clean up* gründlich reinigen; aufräumen

clean·er Rein(e)machefrau *f*, (*Fenster-etc*)Putzer *m*; Reinigungsmittel *n*, Reiniger *m*; *take to the cleaners* et. zur Reinigung bringen; F *j-n* ausnehmen

clean·ing: *do the cleaning* sauber machen, putzen

cleaning la·dy, cleaning wom·an Putzfrau *f*

clean·li·ness Reinlichkeit *f*

clean·ly 1. *adv* sauber; **2.** *adj* reinlich

cleanse reinigen, säubern

cleans·er Putzmittel *n*, Reinigungsmittel *n*, Reiniger *m*

clear 1. klar; hell; rein; deutlich; frei (*of* von); ECON Netto…, Rein…; **2.** *v/t* reinigen, säubern; *Wald* lichten, roden; wegräumen (*a. clear away*); räumen, leeren; *Hindernis* nehmen; SPORT klären; ECON verzollen; JUR freisprechen; EDP löschen; *v/i* klar *or* hell werden; METEOR aufklaren; sich verziehen (*fog*); *clear out* aufräumen; ausräumen, entfernen; F abhauen; *clear up* aufräumen; *Verbrechen etc* aufklären; METEOR aufklaren

clear·ance Räumung *f*; TECH lichter Abstand; Freigabe *f*

clearance sale ECON Räumungsverkauf *m*, Ausverkauf *m*

clear·ing Lichtung *f*

cleave spalten

cleav·er Hackmesser *n*

clef MUS Schlüssel *m*

cleft Spalt *m*, Spalte *f*

clem·en·cy Milde *f*, Nachsicht *f*

clem·ent mild (*a.* METEOR)

clench *Lippen etc* (fest) zusammenpressen; *Zähne* zusammenbeißen; *Faust* ballen

cler·gy REL Klerus *m*, die Geistlichen *pl*

cler·gy·man REL Geistliche *m*

clerk Verkäufer(in); (Büro-*etc*)Angestellte *m*, *f*, (Bank-, Post)Beamte *m*, (-)Beamtin *f*

clev·er klug, gescheit; geschickt

click 1. Klicken *n*; **2.** *v/i* klicken; zu-, einschnappen; *mit der Zunge* schnalzen; *v/t* klicken *or* einschnappen lassen; mit *der Zunge* schnalzen; *click on* EDP anklicken

cli·ent JUR Klient(in), Mandant(in); Kunde *m*, Kundin *f*, Auftraggeber(in)

cliff Klippe *f*, Felsen *m*

cli·mate Klima *n*

cli·max Höhepunkt *m*; Orgasmus *m*

climb klettern; (er-, be)steigen; *climb (up) a tree* auf e-n Baum klettern

climb·er Kletterer *m*, Bergsteiger(in); BOT Kletterpflanze *f*

clinch 1. TECH sicher befestigen; (ver-)nieten; *boxing:* umklammern (*v/i* clinchen); *fig* entscheiden; *that clinched it* damit war die Sache entschieden; **2.** *boxing:* Clinch *m*

cling (to) festhalten (an *dat*), sich klammern (an *acc*); sich (an)schmiegen (an *acc*)

cling·film® *esp Br* Frischhaltefolie *f*

clin·ic Klinik *f*

clin·i·cal klinisch

clink 1. Klirren *n*, Klingen *n*; *sl* Knast *m*; **2.** klingen *or* klirren (lassen); klimpern mit

clip¹ 1. ausschneiden; *Schafe etc* scheren; **2.** Schnitt *m*; Schur *f*; (*Film-etc*) Ausschnitt *m*; (*Video*)Clip *m*

clip² 1. (Heft-, Büro-*etc*)Klammer *f*; (*Ohr*)Klipp *m*; **2.** *a. clip on* anklammern

clip·per: (*a pair of*) *clippers* (e-e) (*Nagel-etc*)Schere *f*, Haarschneidemaschine *f*

clip·pings Abfälle *pl*, Schnitzel *pl*; (*Zeitungs- etc*)Ausschnitte *pl*

clit·o·ris ANAT Klitoris *f*

cloak 1. Umhang *m*; **2.** *fig* verhüllen

cloak·room *Br* Garderobe *f*; Toilette *f*

clock 1. (*Wand-, Stand-, Turm*)Uhr *f*; *9 o'clock* 9 Uhr; **2.** SPORT Zeit stoppen; *clock in, clock on* einstempeln; *clock out, clock off* ausstempeln

clock ra·di·o Radiowecker *m*

clock·wise im Uhrzeigersinn

clock·work Uhrwerk n; *like clockwork* wie am Schnürchen

clod (Erd)Klumpen m

clog 1. (Holz)Klotz m; Holzschuh m; 2. a. *clog up* verstopfen

clois·ter ARCH Kreuzgang m; REL Kloster n

close 1. adj geschlossen; knapp (*result etc*); genau, gründlich (*inspection etc*); eng (anliegend); stickig, schwül; eng (*friend*), nah (*relative*); *keep a close watch on* scharf im Auge behalten (*acc*); 2. adv eng, nahe, dicht; *close by* ganz in der Nähe, nahe or dicht bei; 3. Ende n, (Ab)Schluss m; *come or draw to a close* sich dem Ende nähern; Einfriedung f; 4. v/t (ab-, ver-, zu)schließen, zumachen; ECON schließen; Straße (ab)sperren; v/i sich schließen; schließen, zumachen; enden, zu Ende gehen; *close down* Geschäft etc schließen, Betrieb stilllegen; radio, TV das Programm beenden, Sendeschluss haben; *close in* bedrohlich nahe kommen; hereinbrechen (*night*); *close up* (ab-, ver-, zu)schließen; aufschließen, aufrücken

closed geschlossen; R pred zu

clos·et (Wand)Schrank m

close-up PHOT, FILM: Großaufnahme f

clos·ing date Einsendeschluss m

clos·ing time Laden-, Geschäftsschluss m; Polizeistunde f (*of a pub*)

clot 1. Klumpen m, Klümpchen n; *clot of blood* MED Blutgerinnsel n; 2. gerinnen; Klumpen bilden

cloth Stoff m, Tuch n; Lappen m

cloth·bound in Leinen gebunden

clothe (an-, be)kleiden; einkleiden

clothes Kleider pl, Kleidung f; Wäsche f

clothes bas·ket Wäschekorb m

clothes·horse Wäscheständer m

clothes·line Wäscheleine f

clothes peg Br, clothes·pin Wäscheklammer f

cloth·ing (Be)Kleidung f

cloud 1. Wolke f; fig Schatten m; 2. (sich) bewölken, (sich) trüben

cloud·burst Wolkenbruch m

cloud·less wolkenlos

cloud·y bewölkt; trüb; fig unklar

clout Stoff m; fig Einfluss m

clove¹ GASTR (Gewürz)Nelke f; *clove of garlic* Knoblauchzehe f

clo·ven hoof ZO der Huf m der Paarzeher

clo·ver BOT Klee m

clown Clown m, Hanswurst m

club 1. Keule f; Knüppel m; SPORT Schlagholz n; (Golf)Schläger m; Klub m; pl card game: Kreuz n; 2. einknüppeln

auf (*acc*), niederknüppeln

club·foot MED Klumpfuß m

cluck ZO 1. gackern; glucken; 2. Gacker n; Glucken n

clue Anhaltspunkt m, Fingerzeig m, Spur f

clump 1. Klumpen m; (*Baum- etc -*) Gruppe f; 2. trampeln

clum·sy unbeholfen, ungeschickt, plump

clus·ter 1. BOT Traube f, Büschel n; Haufen m; 2. sich drängen

clutch 1. Griff m; TECH Kupplung f; fig Klaue f; 2. (er)greifen; umklammern

clut·ter fig überladen

c/o ABBR of *care of* c/o, (wohnhaft) bei

Co ABBR of *company* ECON Gesellschaft f

coach 1. Reisebus m; Br RAIL (Personen) Wagen m; Kutsche f; SPORT Trainer(in f) m; PED Nachhilfelehrer(in); 2. SPORT trainieren; PED j-m Nachhilfeunterricht geben

coach·man Kutscher m

co·ag·u·late gerinnen (lassen)

coal (Stein)Kohle f; *carry coals to New castle* F Br Eulen nach Athen tragen

co·a·li·tion POL Koalition f; Bündnis n, Zusammenschluss m

coal·mine, coal·pit Kohlengrube f

coarse grob; rau; derb; ungeschliffen; gemein

coast 1. Küste f; 2. MAR die Küste entlang fahren; im Leerlauf (*car*) or im Freilauf (*bicycle*) fahren; rodeln

coast·er brake Rücktritt(bremse f) m

coast·guard (Angehörige m der) Küstenwache f

coast·line Küstenlinie f, -strich m

coat 1. Mantel m; ZO Pelz m, Fell n; (*Farbe etc*)Überzug m, Anstrich m, Schicht f; 2 (an)streichen, überziehen, beschichten

coat hang·er Kleiderbügel m

coat·ing (*Farb- etc*)Überzug m, Anstrich m; Schicht f; Mantelstoff m

coat of arms Wappen(schild m, n) n

coax überreden, beschwatzen

cob Maiskolben m

cob·bled: *cobbled street* Straße f mit Kopfsteinpflaster

cob·bler (Flick)Schuster m

cob·web Spinn(en)gewebe n

co·caine Kokain n

cock 1. ZO Hahn m; V Schwanz m; 2. aufrichten; *cock one's ears* die Ohren spitzen

cock·a·too ZO Kakadu m

cock·chaf·er ZO Maikäfer m

cock·eyed F schielend; (krumm und) schief

Cock·ney Cockney m, waschechter Londoner

** cock·pit** AVIAT Cockpit *n*
cock·roach zo Schabe *f*
cock·sure F übertrieben selbstsicher
cock·tail Cocktail *m*
cock·y großspurig, anmaßend
co·co BOT Kokospalme *f*
co·coa Kakao *m*
co·co·nut BOT Kokosnuss *f*
co·coon (Seiden)Kokon *m*
cod zo Kabeljau *m*, Dorsch *m*
COD ABBR of **collect** (Br **cash**) **on delivery** per Nachnahme
cod·dle verhätscheln, verzärteln
code 1. Kode *m*; **2.** verschlüsseln, chiffrieren; kodieren
cod·fish → **cod**
cod·ing Kodierung *f*
cod-liv·er oil Lebertran *m*
co·ed·u·ca·tion PED Gemeinschaftserziehung *f*
co·ex·ist gleichzeitig *or* nebeneinander bestehen *or* leben
co·ex·ist·ence Koexistenz *f*
cof·fee Kaffee *m*; **black** (**white**) **coffee** Kaffee ohne (mit) Milch
coffee bar Br Café *n*; Imbissstube *f*
coffee bean Kaffeebohne *f*
coffee grind·er Kaffeemühle *f*
coffee machine Kaffeeautomat *m*
cof·fee·mak·er Kaffeemaschine *f*
cof·fee pot Kaffeekanne *f*
coffee shop Café *n*; Imbissstube *f*
coffee ta·ble Couchtisch *m*
cof·fin Sarg *m*
cog TECH (Rad)Zahn *m*; → **cog·wheel** TECH Zahnrad *n*
co·her·ence, **co·her·en·cy** Zusammenhang *m*
co·her·ent zusammenhängend
co·he·sion Zusammenhalt *m*
co·he·sive (fest) zusammenhaltend
coif·fure Frisur *f*
coil 1. *a.* **coil up** aufrollen, (auf)wickeln; sich zusammenrollen; **2.** Spirale *f* (*a.* TECH, MED); Rolle *f*, Spule *f*
coin 1. Münze *f*; **2.** prägen
co·in·cide zusammentreffen; übereinstimmen
co·in·ci·dence (zufälliges) Zusammentreffen; Zufall *m*
coin-op·e·rat·ed: coin-operated (**gas**, Br **petrol**) **pump** Münztank(automat) *m*
coke Koks *m* (*a.* F **cocaine**)
Coke® F Coke *n*, Cola *n*, *f*, Coca *n*, *f*
cold 1. kalt; **2.** Kälte *f*; MED Erkältung *f*; **catch** (**a**) **cold** sich erkälten; **have a cold** erkältet sein
cold-blood·ed kaltblütig
cold cuts GASTR Aufschnitt *m*

cold-heart·ed kaltherzig
cold·ness Kälte *f*
cold sweat Angstschweiß *m*; **he broke out in a cold sweat** ihm brach der Angstschweiß aus
cold war POL kalter Krieg
cold wave METEOR Kältewelle *f*
cole·slaw Krautsalat *m*
col·ic MED Kolik *f*
col·lab·o·rate zusammenarbeiten
col·lab·o·ra·tion Zusammenarbeit *f*; **in collaboration with** gemeinsam mit
col·lapse 1. zusammenbrechen (*a.* fig), einstürzen; umfallen; *fig* scheitern; **2.** Einsturz *m*; *fig* Zusammenbruch *m*
col·lap·si·ble Klapp..., zusammenklappbar
col·lar 1. Kragen *m*; (Hunde- *etc*)Halsband *n*; **2.** beim Kragen packen; *j-n* festnehmen, F schnappen
col·lar·bone ANAT Schlüsselbein *n*
col·league Kollege *m*, Kollegin *f*, Mitarbeiter(in)
col·lect *v/t* (ein)sammeln; *Daten* erfassen; *Geld* kassieren; *j-n* or *et.* abholen; *Gedanken etc* sammeln; *v/i* sich (ver-)sammeln
col·lect·ed *fig* gefasst
col·lect·ing box Sammelbüchse *f*
col·lec·tion Sammlung *f*; ECON Eintreibung *f*; REL Kollekte *f*; Abholung *f*
col·lec·tive gesammelt; Sammel...; **collective bargaining** ECON Tarifverhandlungen
col·lec·tive·ly insgesamt; zusammen
col·lec·tor Sammler(in); Steuereinnehmer *m*; ELECTR Stromabnehmer *m*
col·lege College *n*; Hochschule *f*; höhere Lehranstalt
col·lide zusammenstoßen, kollidieren (*a.* fig)
col·lie·ry Kohlengrube *f*
col·li·sion Zusammenstoß *m*, Kollision *f* (*a.* fig)
col·lo·qui·al umgangssprachlich
co·lon LING Doppelpunkt *m*
colo·nel MIL Oberst *m*
co·lo·ni·al·ism POL Kolonialismus *m*
col·o·nize kolonisieren, besiedeln
col·o·ny Kolonie *f*
col·o(u)r 1. Farbe *f*; *pl* MIL Fahne *f*; MAR Flagge *f*; **what colo(u)r is ...?** welche Farbe hat ...?; **2.** *v/t* färben; anmalen, bemalen, anstreichen; *fig* beschönigen; *v/i* sich (ver)färben; erröten
col·o(u)r bar Rassenschranke *f*
col·o(u)r-blind farbenblind
col·o(u)red bunt; farbig
col·o(u)r·fast farbecht

col·o(u)r film PHOT Farbfilm *m*
col·o(u)r·ful farbenprächtig; *fig* farbig, bunt
col·o(u)r·ing Färbung *f*; Farbstoff *m*; Gesichtsfarbe *f*
col·o(u)r·less farblos
col·o(u)r line Rassenschranke *f*
col·o(u)r set Farbfernseher *m*
colo(u)r tel·e·vi·sion Farbfernsehen *n*
colt ZO (Hengst)Fohlen *n*
col·umn Säule *f*; PRINT Spalte *f*; MIL Kolonne *f*
col·umn·ist Kolumnist(in)

comb 1. Kamm *m*; **2.** kämmen; striegeln
com·bat 1. Kampf *m*; *single combat* Zweikampf *m*; **2.** kämpfen gegen, bekämpfen
com·ba·tant MIL Kämpfer *m*
com·bi·na·tion Verbindung *f*, Kombination *f*
com·bine 1. (sich) verbinden; **2.** ECON Konzern *m*; AGR a. *combine harvester* Mähdrescher *m*
com·bus·ti·ble 1. brennbar; **2.** Brennstoff *m*, Brennmaterial *n*
com·bus·tion Verbrennung *f*
come kommen; *to come* künftig, kommend; *come and go* kommen und gehen; *come to see* besuchen; *come about* geschehen, passieren; *come across* auf j-n or et. stoßen; *come along* mitkommen, mitgehen; *come apart* auseinanderfallen; *come away* sich lösen, ab-, losgehen (*button etc*); *come back* zurückkommen; *come by s.th.* zu et. kommen; *come down* herunterkommen (*a. fig*); einstürzen; sinken (*prices*); überliefert werden; *come down with* F erkranken an (*dat*); *come for* abholen kommen, kommen wegen; *come forward* sich melden; *come from* kommen aus; kommen von; *come home* nach Hause (*Austrian, Swiss a.* nachhause) kommen; *come in* hereinkommen; eintreffen (*news*); einlaufen (*train*); *come in!* herein!; *come loose* sich ablösen, abgehen; *come off* ab-, losgehen (*button etc*); *come on!* los!, vorwärts!, komm!; *come out* herauskommen; *come over* vorbeikommen (*visitor*); *come round* vorbeikommen (*visitor*); wieder zu sich kommen; *come through* durchkommen; *Krankheit etc* überstehen, überleben; *come to* sich belaufen auf (*acc*); wieder zu sich kommen; *come up to* entsprechen (*dat*), heranreichen an (*acc*)
come·back Come-back *n*
co·me·di·an Komiker *m*
com·e·dy Komödie *f*, Lustspiel *n*

come·ly attraktiv, gut aussehend
com·fort 1. Komfort *m*, Bequemlichkeit *f*, Trost *m*; *cold comfort* schwacher Trost; **2.** trösten
com·for·ta·ble komfortabel, behaglich, bequem; tröstlich
com·fort·er Tröster *m*; *esp Br* Schnuller *m*; Steppdecke *f*
com·fort·less unbequem; trostlos
com·fort sta·tion Bedürfnisanstalt *f*
com·ic komisch; Komödien..., Lustspiel...
com·i·cal komisch, spaßig
com·ics Comics *pl*, Comic-Hefte *pl*
com·ma LING Komma *n*
com·mand 1. Befehl *m*; Beherrschung *f*, MIL Kommando *n*; **2.** befehlen; MIL kommandieren; verfügen über (*acc*); beherrschen
com·mand·er MIL Kommandeur *m*, Befehlshaber *m*
commander in chief MIL Oberbefehlshaber *m*
com·mand·ment REL Gebot *n*
com·mand mod·ule Kommandokapsel *f*
com·man·do MIL Kommando *n*
com·mem·o·rate gedenken (*gen*)
com·mem·o·ra·tion: *in commemoration of* zum Gedenken or Gedächtnis an (*acc*)
com·mem·o·ra·tive Gedenk..., Erinnerungs...
com·ment 1. (*on*) Kommentar *m* (zu); Bemerkung *f* (zu); Anmerkung *f* (zu); *no comment!* kein Kommentar!; **2.** *v/i comment on* e-n Kommentar abgeben zu; sich äußern über (*acc*); *v/t* bemerken (*that* dass)
com·men·ta·ry Kommentar *m* (*on* zu)
com·men·ta·tor Kommentator *m*, *radio*, TV *a.* Reporter *m*
com·merce ECON Handel *m*
com·mer·cial 1. ECON Handels..., Geschäfts...; kommerziell, finanziell; **2.** *radio*, TV Werbespot *m*, Werbesendung *f*
commercial art Gebrauchsgrafik *f*
commercial art·ist Gebrauchsgrafiker(in)
com·mer·cial·ize kommerzialisieren
com·mer·cial tel·e·vi·sion Werbefernsehen *n*; kommerzielles Fernsehen
com·mis·e·rate: *commiserate with* Mitleid empfinden mit
com·mis·e·ra·tion Mitleid *n* (*for* mit)
com·mis·sion 1. Auftrag *m*; Kommission *f*, Ausschuss *m*; ECON Kommission *f*; Provision *f*; Begehung *f* (*of a crime*); **2.** beauftragen; *et.* in Auftrag geben
com·mis·sion·er Beauftragte *m*, *f*; Kommissar(in)

om·mit anvertrauen, übergeben (*to dat*); JUR *j-n* einweisen (*to* in *acc*); *Verbrechen* begehen; *j-n* verpflichten (*to* zu), *j-n* festlegen (*to* auf *acc*)

om·mit·ment Verpflichtung *f*; Engagement *n*

om·mit·tal JUR Einweisung *f*

om·mit·tee Komitee *n*, Ausschuss *m*

om·mod·i·ty ECON Ware *f*, Artikel *m*

com·mon 1. gemeinsam, gemeinschaftlich; allgemein; alltäglich; gewöhnlich; einfach; **2.** Gemeindeland *n*; *in common* gemeinsam (*with* mit)

om·mon·er Bürgerliche *m*, *f*

com·mon law (ungeschriebenes englisches) Gewohnheitsrecht

Com·mon Mar·ket ECON, POL HIST Gemeinsamer Markt

om·mon·place 1. Gemeinplatz *m*; **2.** alltäglich; abgedroschen

Com·mons: *the Commons, the House of Commons* Br PARL das Unterhaus

com·mon sense gesunder Menschenverstand

Com·mon·wealth: *the Commonwealth (of Nations)* das Commonwealth

om·mo·tion Aufregung *f*; Aufruhr *m*, Tumult *m*

om·mu·nal Gemeinde...; Gemeinschafts...

om·mune Kommune *f*

om·mu·ni·cate *v/t* mitteilen; *v/i* sich besprechen; sich in Verbindung setzen (*with s.o.* mit *j-m*); (durch e-e Tür) verbunden sein

om·mu·ni·ca·tion Mitteilung *f*; Verständigung *f*, Kommunikation *f*; Verbindung *f*; *pl* Kommunikationsmittel *pl*; Verkehrswege *pl*

om·mu·ni·ca·tions sat·el·lite Nachrichtensatellit *m*

om·mu·ni·ca·tive mitteilsam, gesprächig

Com·mu·nion *a.* **Holy Communion** REL (heilige) Kommunion, Abendmahl *n*

om·mu·nis·m POL Kommunismus *m*

om·mu·nist POL **1.** Kommunist(in); **2.** kommunistisch

om·mu·ni·ty Gemeinschaft *f*; Gemeinde *f*

om·mute JUR Strafe *mildernd* umwandeln; RAIL *etc* pendeln

om·mut·er Pendler(in)

commuter train Pendlerzug *m*, Nahverkehrszug *m*

om·pact 1. Puderdose *f*; MOT Kleinwagen *m*; **2.** *adj* kompakt; eng, klein; knapp (*style*)

compact car MOT Kleinwagen *m*

compact disk (ABBR **CD**) Compact Disc *f*, CD *f*

compact disk play·er CD-Player *m*, CD--Spieler *m*

com·pan·ion Begleiter(in); Gefährte *m*, Gefährtin *f*; Gesellschafter(in); Handbuch *n*, Leitfaden *m*

com·pan·ion·ship Gesellschaft *f*

com·pa·ny Gesellschaft *f*, ECON *a.* Firma *f*; MIL Kompanie *f*; THEA Truppe *f*; *keep s.o. company* *j-m* Gesellschaft leisten

com·pa·ra·ble vergleichbar

com·par·a·tive 1. vergleichend; verhältnismäßig; **2.** *a.* **comparative degree** LING Komparativ *m*

com·par·a·tive·ly vergleichsweise; verhältnismäßig

com·pare 1. *v/t* vergleichen; *compared with* im Vergleich zu; *v/i* sich vergleichen lassen; **2.** *beyond compare, without compare* unvergleichlich

com·par·i·son Vergleich *m*

com·part·ment Fach *n*; RAIL Abteil *n*

com·pass Kompass *m*; *pair of compasses* Zirkel *m*

com·pas·sion Mitleid *n*

com·pas·sion·ate mitleidig

com·pat·i·ble vereinbar; *be compatible (with)* passen (zu), zusammenpassen; EDP *etc* kompatibel sein (mit)

com·pat·ri·ot Landsmann *m*, Landsmännin *f*

com·pel (er)zwingen

com·pel·ling bezwingend

com·pen·sate *j-n* entschädigen; *et.* ersetzen; ausgleichen

com·pen·sa·tion Ersatz *m*; Ausgleich *m*; Schadenersatz *m*, Entschädigung *f*; Bezahlung *f*, Gehalt *n*

com·pere Br Conférencier *m*

com·pete sich (mit)bewerben (*for* um); konkurrieren; SPORT (am Wettkampf) teilnehmen

com·pe·tence Können *n*, Fähigkeit *f*

com·pe·tent fähig, tüchtig; fachkundig, sachkundig

com·pe·ti·tion Wettbewerb *m*; Konkurrenz *f*

com·pet·i·tive konkurrierend

com·pet·i·tor Mitbewerber(in), Konkurrent(in); SPORT (Wettbewerbs-)Teilnehmer(in)

com·pile kompilieren, zusammentragen, zusammenstellen

com·pla·cence, com·pla·cen·cy Selbstzufriedenheit *f*, Selbstgefälligkeit *f*

com·pla·cent selbstzufrieden, selbstgefällig

com·plain sich beklagen *or* beschweren

C

(*about* über *acc*; *to* bei); klagen (*of* über *acc*)

com·plaint Klage *f*, Beschwerde *f*; MED Leiden *n*, *pl* MED *a*. Beschwerden *pl*

com·ple·ment 1. Ergänzung *f*; **2.** ergänzen

com·ple·men·ta·ry (sich) ergänzend

com·plete 1. vollständig; vollzählig; **2.** vervollständigen; beenden, abschließen

com·ple·tion Vervollständigung *f*; Abschluss *m*

completion test PSYCH Lückentext *m*

com·plex 1. zusammengesetzt; komplex, vielschichtig; **2.** Komplex *m* (*a.* PSYCH)

com·plex·ion Gesichtsfarbe *f*, Teint *m*

com·plex·i·ty Komplexität *f*, Vielschichtigkeit *f*

com·pli·ance Einwilligung *f*; Befolgung *f*; *in compliance with* gemäß (*dat*)

com·pli·ant willfährig

com·pli·cate komplizieren

com·pli·cat·ed kompliziert

com·pli·ca·tion Komplikation *f* (*a.* MED)

com·plic·i·ty JUR Mitschuld *f*, Mittäterschaft *f* (*in* an *dat*)

com·pli·ment 1. Kompliment *n*; Empfehlung *f*; Gruß *m*; **2.** *v/t j-m* ein Kompliment *or* Komplimente machen (*on* über *acc*)

com·ply (*with*) einwilligen (in *acc*); (*e-e Abmachung etc*) befolgen

com·po·nent Bestandteil *m*; TECH, ELECTR Bauelement *n*

com·pose zusammensetzen, -stellen; MUS komponieren; verfassen; *be composed of* bestehen *or* sich zusammensetzen aus; *compose o.s.* sich beruhigen

com·posed ruhig, gelassen

com·pos·er MUS Komponist(in)

com·po·si·tion Zusammensetzung *f*; MUS Komposition *f*; PED Aufsatz *m*

com·po·sure Fassung *f*, (Gemüts)Ruhe *f*

com·pound¹ Lager *n*; Gefängnishof *m*; (Tier)Gehege *n*

com·pound² 1. Zusammensetzung *f*; Verbindung *f*; LING zusammengesetztes Wort; **2.** zusammengesetzt; *compound interest* ECON Zinseszinsen *pl*; **3.** *v/t* zusammensetzen; steigern, *esp* verschlimmern

com·pre·hend begreifen, verstehen

com·pre·hen·si·ble verständlich

com·pre·hen·sion Verständnis *n*; Begriffsvermögen *n*, Verstand *m*; *past comprehension* unfassbar, unfasslich

com·pre·hen·sive 1. umfassend; **2.** *a. comprehensive school* Br Gesamtschule *f*

com·press zusammendrücken, -pressen;

compressed air Druckluft *f*

com·pres·sion PHYS Verdichtung *f*; TECH Druck *m*

com·prise einschließen, umfassen; bestehen aus

com·pro·mise 1. Kompromiss *m*; **2.** *v* bloßstellen, kompromittieren; *v/i* e-n Kompromiss schließen

com·pro·mis·ing kompromittierend; verfänglich

com·pul·sion Zwang *m*

com·pul·sive zwingend, Zwangs..., PSYCH zwanghaft

com·pul·so·ry obligatorisch; Pflicht..., Zwangs...

com·punc·tion Gewissensbisse *pl*; Reue *f*; Bedenken *pl*

com·pute berechnen; schätzen

com·put·er Computer *m*, Rechner *m*

com·put·er-aid·ed computergestützt

computer-con·trolled computergesteuert

com·put·er game Computerspiel *n*

computer graph·ics Computergrafik *f*

com·put·er·ize (sich) auf Computer umstellen; computerisieren; mit Hilfe e-s Computers errechnen *or* zusammenstellen

com·put·er pre·dic·tion Hochrechnung *f*

computer sci·ence Informatik *f*

computer sci·en·tist Informatiker *m*

computer vi·rus EDP Computervirus *m*

com·rade Kamerad *m*; (Partei)Genosse *m*

con¹ → *contra*

con² F reinlegen, betrügen

con·ceal verbergen; verheimlichen

con·cede zugestehen, einräumen

con·ceit Einbildung *f*, Dünkel *m*

con·ceit·ed eingebildet (*of* auf *acc*)

con·cei·va·ble denkbar, begreiflich

con·ceive *v/i* schwanger werden; *v/t* Kind empfangen; sich *et.* vorstellen *or* denken

con·cen·trate (sich) konzentrieren

con·cept Begriff *m*; Gedanke *m*

con·cep·tion Vorstellung *f*, Begriff *m*; BIOL Empfängnis *f*

con·cern 1. Angelegenheit *f*; Sorge *f*; ECON Geschäft *n*, Unternehmen *n*; **2.** betreffen, angehen; beunruhigen

con·cerned besorgt; beteiligt (*in* an *dat*)

con·cern·ing *prp* betreffend, hinsichtlich (*gen*), was ... (*acc*) (an)betrifft

con·cert MUS Konzert *n*

con·cert hall Konzerthalle *f*, -saal *m*

con·ces·sion Zugeständnis *n*; Konzession *f*

con·cil·i·a·to·ry versöhnlich, vermittelnd

con·cise kurz, knapp

con·cise·ness Kürze f
con·clude schließen, beenden; *Vertrag etc* abschließen; *et.* folgern, schließen (**from** aus); *to be concluded* Schluss folgt
con·clu·sion (Ab)Schluss m, Ende n; Abschluss m (*of a contract etc*); (Schluss)Folgerung f; → *jump*
con·clu·sive schlüssig
con·coct (zusammen)brauen; *fig* aushecken, ausbrüten
con·coc·tion Gebräu n; *fig* Erfindung f
con·crete¹ konkret
con·crete² 1. Beton m; 2. Beton...; 3. betonieren
con·cur übereinstimmen
con·cur·rence Zusammentreffen n; Übereinstimmung f
con·cus·sion MED Gehirnerschütterung f
con·demn verurteilen (a. JUR); verdammen; für unbrauchbar or unbewohnbar etc erklären; *condemn to death* JUR zum Tode verurteilen
con·dem·na·tion Verurteilung f (a. JUR); Verdammung f
con·den·sa·tion Kondensation f; Zusammenfassung f
con·dense kondensieren; zusammenfassen
con·densed milk Kondensmilch f
con·dens·er TECH Kondensator m
con·de·scend sich herablassen
con·de·scend·ing herablassend, gönnerhaft
con·di·ment Gewürz n, Würze f
con·di·tion 1. Zustand m; (*körperlicher or Gesundheits*)Zustand m; SPORT Kondition f, Form f; Bedingung f; pl Verhältnisse pl, Umstände pl; *on condition that* unter der Bedingung, dass; *out of condition* in schlechter Verfassung, in schlechtem Zustand; 2. bedingen; in Form bringen
con·di·tion·al 1. (*on*) bedingt (durch), abhängig (von); 2. a. *conditional clause* LING Bedingungs-, Konditionalsatz m; a. *conditional mood* LING Konditional m
con·do → *condominium*
con·dole kondolieren (**with** dat)
con·do·lence Beileid n
con·dom Kondom n, m
con·do·min·i·um Eigentumswohnanlage f; Eigentumswohnung f
con·done verzeihen, vergeben
con·du·cive dienlich, förderlich (**to** dat)
con·duct 1. Führung f; Verhalten n, Betragen n; 2. führen; PHYS leiten; MUS dirigieren; *conducted tour* Führung f (*of* durch)

con·duc·tor Führer m, Leiter m; (*Bus-, Straßenbahn*)Schaffner m; RAIL Zugbegleiter m; MUS Dirigent m; PHYS Leiter m; ELECTR Blitzableiter m
cone Kegel m; GASTR Eistüte f; BOT Zapfen m
con·fec·tion Konfekt n
con·fec·tion·er Konditor m
con·fec·tion·e·ry Süßigkeiten pl, Süß-, Konditoreiwaren pl; Konfekt n; Konditorei f; Süßwarengeschäft n
con·fed·e·ra·cy (Staaten)Bund m; **the Confederacy** HIST die Konföderation
con·fed·er·ate 1. verbündet; 2. Verbündete m, Bundesgenosse m; 3. (sich) verbünden
con·fed·er·a·tion Bund m, Bündnis n; (Staaten)Bund m
con·fer v/t *Titel etc* verleihen (**on** dat); v/i sich beraten
con·fe·rence Konferenz f
con·fess gestehen; beichten
con·fes·sion Geständnis n; REL Beichte f
con·fes·sion·al REL Beichtstuhl m
con·fes·sor REL Beichtvater m
con·fi·dant(e) Vertraute m (f)
con·fide: confide s.th. to s.o. j-m et. anvertrauen; *confide in s.o.* sich j-m anvertrauen
con·fi·dence Vertrauen n; Selbstvertrauen n
confidence man → *conman*
confidence trickster Trickbetrüger m
con·fi·dent überzeugt, zuversichtlich
con·fi·den·tial vertraulich
con·fine begrenzen, beschränken; einsperren; *be confined of* entbunden werden von
con·fine·ment Haft f; Beschränkung f; MED Entbindung f
con·firm bestätigen; bekräftigen; REL konfirmieren, firmen
con·fir·ma·tion Bestätigung f; REL Konfirmation f, Firmung f
con·fis·cate beschlagnahmen
con·fis·ca·tion Beschlagnahme f
con·flict 1. Konflikt m, Zwiespalt m; 2. im Widerspruch stehen (**with** zu)
con·flict·ing widersprüchlich, zwiespältig
con·form (sich) anpassen (**to** dat, an acc)
con·found verwirren, durcheinanderbringen
con·front gegenübertreten, -stehen (dat); sich stellen (dat); konfrontieren
con·fron·ta·tion Konfrontation f
con·fuse verwechseln; verwirren
con·fused verwirrt; verlegen; verworren
con·fu·sion Verwirrung f; Verlegenheit f; Verwechslung f

con·geal erstarren (lassen); gerinnen (lassen)

con·gest·ed überfüllt; verstopft

con·ges·tion MED Blutandrang m; a. **traffic congestion** Verkehrsstockung f, Verkehrsstörung f, Verkehrsstau m

con·grat·u·late beglückwünschen, j-m gratulieren

con·grat·u·la·tion Glückwunsch m; **congratulations!** ich gratuliere!, herzlichen Glückwunsch!

con·gre·gate (sich) versammeln

con·gre·ga·tion REL Gemeinde f

con·gress Kongress m; **Congress** PARL der Kongress

Con·gress·man PARL Kongressabgeordnete m

Con·gress·wom·an PARL Kongressabgeordnete f

con·ic, con·i·cal esp TECH konisch, kegelförmig

co·ni·fer BOT Nadelbaum m

con·jec·ture 1. Vermutung f; 2. vermuten

con·ju·gal ehelich

con·ju·gate LING konjugieren, beugen

con·ju·ga·tion LING Konjugation f, Beugung f

con·junc·tion Verbindung f; LING Konjunktion f, Bindewort n

con·junc·ti·vi·tis MED Bindehautentzündung f

con·jure zaubern; *Teufel etc* beschwören; **conjure up** heraufbeschwören (a. fig)

con·jur·er esp Br → **conjuror**

con·jur·ing trick Zauberkunststück n

con·jur·or Zauberer m, Zauberin f, Zauberkünstler(in)

con·man Betrüger m; Hochstapler m

con·nect verbinden; ELECTR anschließen, zuschalten; RAIL, AVIAT etc Anschluss haben (**with** an acc)

con·nect·ed verbunden; (logisch) zusammenhängend (speech etc); **be well connected** gute Beziehungen haben

con·nec·tion, Br **con·nex·ion** Verbindung f, Anschluss m (a. ELECTR, RAIL, AVIAT, TEL); Zusammenhang m; mst pl Beziehungen pl, Verbindungen pl; Verwandte pl

con·quer erobern; (be)siegen

con·quer·or Eroberer m

con·quest Eroberung f (a. fig); erobertes Gebiet

con·science Gewissen n

con·sci·en·tious gewissenhaft; Gewissens…

con·sci·en·tious·ness Gewissenhaftigkeit f

con·sci·en·tious ob·jec·tor MIL Wehr-dienstverweigerer m

con·scious MED bei Bewusstsein; bewusst; **be conscious of** sich bewusst sein (gen)

con·scious·ness Bewusstsein n (a. MED)

con·script MIL 1. einberufen; 2. Wehrpflichtige m

con·scrip·tion MIL Einberufung f; Wehrpflicht f

con·se·crate REL weihen; widmen

con·se·cra·tion REL Weihe f

con·sec·u·tive aufeinanderfolgend; fortlaufend

con·sent 1. Zustimmung f; 2. einwilligen, zustimmen

con·se·quence Folge f, Konsequenz f; Bedeutung f

con·se·quent·ly folglich, daher

con·ser·va·tion Erhaltung f; Naturschutz m; Umweltschutz m; **conservation area** (Natur)Schutzgebiet n

con·ser·va·tion·ist Naturschützer(in), Umweltschützer(in)

con·ser·va·tive 1. erhaltend; konservativ, vorsichtig; 2. **Conservative** POL Konservative m, f

con·ser·va·to·ry Treibhaus n, Gewächshaus n; Wintergarten m

con·serve erhalten

con·sid·er v/t nachdenken über (acc); betrachten als, halten für; sich überlegen, erwägen; in Betracht ziehen, berücksichtigen; v/i nachdenken, überlegen

con·sid·e·ra·ble ansehnlich, beträchtlich

con·sid·e·ra·bly bedeutend, ziemlich (sehr) viel

con·sid·er·ate rücksichtsvoll

con·sid·e·ra·tion Erwägung f, Überlegung f; Berücksichtigung f; Rücksicht (-nahme) f; **take into consideration** in Erwägung or in Betracht ziehen

con·sid·er·ing in Anbetracht (der Tatsache, dass)

con·sign ECON Waren zusenden

con·sign·ment ECON (Waren)Sendung f, Zusendung f

con·sist: consist in bestehen in (dat); **consist of** bestehen aus

con·sis·tence, con·sis·ten·cy Konsistenz f, Beschaffenheit f; Übereinstimmung f; Konsequenz f

con·sis·tent übereinstimmend, vereinbar (**with** mit); konsequent; SPORT etc: beständig

con·so·la·tion Trost m

con·sole trösten

con·sol·i·date festigen; fig zusammenschließen, -legen

con·so·nant LING Konsonant m, Mitlaut

C

m

on·spic·u·ous deutlich sichtbar; auffallend

on·spi·ra·cy Verschwörung *f*

on·spi·ra·tor Verschwörer *m*

on·spire sich verschwören

on·sta·ble *Br* Polizist *m*

on·stant konstant, gleichbleibend; (be)-ständig, (an)dauernd

on·stant-care pa·tient MED Pflegefall *m*

on·ster·na·tion Bestürzung *f*

on·sti·pat·ed MED verstopft

on·sti·pa·tion MED Verstopfung *f*

on·stit·u·en·cy POL *Br* Wählerschaft *f*; Wahlkreis *m*

on·stit·u·ent (wesentlicher) Bestandteil; POL Wähler(in)

on·sti·tute ernennen, einsetzen, bilden, ausmachen

on·sti·tu·tion POL Verfassung *f*; Konstitution *f*, körperliche Verfassung

on·sti·tu·tion·al konstitutionell; POL verfassungsmäßig

on·strained gezwungen, unnatürlich

on·strict zusammenziehen

on·stric·tion Zusammenziehung *f*

on·struct bauen, errichten, konstruieren

on·struc·tion Konstruktion *f*; Bau *m*, Bauwerk *n*; **under construction** im Bau (befindlich)

construction site Baustelle *f*

on·struc·tive konstruktiv

on·struc·tor Erbauer *m*, Konstrukteur *m*

on·sul Konsul *m*

on·su·late Konsulat *n*

onsulate gen·e·ral Generalkonsulat *n*

on·sul gen·e·ral Generalkonsul *m*

on·sult *v/t* konsultieren, um Rat fragen; in *e-m Buch* nachschlagen; *v/i* (sich) beraten

on·sul·tant (fachmännischer) Berater; *Br* Facharzt *m*

on·sul·ta·tion Konsultation *f*, Beratung *f*, Rücksprache *f*

on·sult·ing beratend

consulting hours *Br* MED Sprechstunde *f*

consulting room *Br* MED Sprechzimmer *n*

on·sume *v/t* Essen *etc* zu sich nehmen, verzehren (*a. fig*); verbrauchen, konsumieren; zerstören, vernichten

on·sum·er ECON Verbraucher(in)

consumer so·ci·e·ty Konsumgesellschaft *f*

on·sum·mate 1. vollendet; **2.** vollenden; *Ehe* vollziehen

con·sump·tion Verbrauch *m*

cont ABBR *of* **continued** Forts., Fortsetzung *f*; fortgesetzt

con·tact 1. Berührung *f*; Kontakt *m*; Ansprechpartner(in), Kontaktperson *f* (*a.* MED); **make contacts** Verbindungen anknüpfen *or* herstellen; **2.** sich in Verbindung setzen mit, Kontakt aufnehmen mit

contact lens MED Kontaktlinse *f*, -schale *f*, Haftschale *f*

con·ta·gious MED ansteckend (*a. fig*)

con·tain enthalten; *fig* zügeln, zurückten

con·tain·er Behälter *m*; ECON Container *m*

con·tain·er·ize ECON auf Containerbetrieb umstellen; in Containern transportieren

con·tam·i·nate verunreinigen; infizieren, vergiften; (*a.* radioaktiv) verseuchen; **radioactively contaminated** verstrahlt; **contaminated soil** Altlasten *pl*

con·tam·i·na·tion Verunreinigung *f*; Vergiftung *f*; (*a.* radioaktive) Verseuchung *f*

contd ABBR *of* **continued** (→ **cont**)

con·tem·plate (nachdenklich) betrachten; nachdenken über (*acc*); erwägen, beabsichtigen

con·tem·pla·tion (nachdenkliche) Betrachtung; Nachdenken *n*

con·tem·pla·tive nachdenklich

con·tem·po·ra·ry 1. zeitgenössisch; **2.** Zeitgenosse *m*, Zeitgenossin *f*

con·tempt Verachtung *f*

con·temp·ti·ble verachtenswert

con·temp·tu·ous geringschätzig, verächtlich

con·tend kämpfen, ringen (**for** um; **with** mit)

con·tend·er *esp* SPORT Wettkämpfer(in)

con·tent[1] Gehalt *m*, Aussage *f*, *pl* Inhalt *m*; **(table of) contents** Inhaltsverzeichnis *n*

con·tent[2] **1.** zufrieden; **2.** befriedigen; **content o.s.** sich begnügen

con·tent·ed zufrieden

con·tent·ment Zufriedenheit *f*

con·test 1. (Wett)Kampf *m*; Wettbewerb *m*; **2.** sich bewerben um; bestreiten, *a.* JUR anfechten

con·tes·tant Wettkämpfer(in), (Wettkampf)Teilnehmer(in)

con·text Zusammenhang *m*

con·ti·nent Kontinent *m*, Erdteil *m*; **the Continent** *Br* das (europäische) Festland

con·ti·nen·tal kontinental, Kontinental...

con·tin·gen·cy Möglichkeit *f*, Eventualität *f*; **contingency plan** Notplan *m*

con·tin·gent 1. be contingent on abhängen von; **2.** Kontingent *n* (*a.* MIL)

con·tin·u·al fortwährend, unaufhörlich

con·tin·u·a·tion Fortsetzung f; Fortbestand m, Fortdauer f

con·tin·ue v/t fortsetzen, fortfahren mit; beibehalten; **to be continued** Fortsetzung folgt; v/i fortdauern; andauern, anhalten; fortfahren, weitermachen

con·ti·nu·i·ty Kontinuität f

con·tin·u·ous ununterbrochen

continuous form LING Verlaufsform f

con·tort verdrehen; verzerren

con·tor·tion Verdrehung f; Verzerrung f

con·tour Umriss m

con·tra wider, gegen

con·tra·band ECON Schmuggelware f

con·tra·cep·tion MED Empfängnisverhütung f

con·tra·cep·tive MED 1. empfängnisverhütend; 2. Verhütungsmittel n

con·tract 1. Vertrag m; 2. (sich) zusammenziehen; sich *e-e Krankheit* zuziehen; e-n Vertrag abschließen; sich vertraglich verpflichten

con·trac·tion Zusammenziehung f

con·trac·tor a. **building contractor** Bauunternehmer m

con·tra·dict widersprechen (dat)

con·tra·dic·tion Widerspruch m

con·tra·dic·to·ry (sich) widersprechend

con·tra·ry 1. entgegengesetzt (**to** dat); gegensätzlich; **contrary to expectations** wider Erwarten; 2. Gegenteil n; **on the contrary** im Gegenteil

con·trast 1. Gegensatz m; Kontrast m; 2. v/t gegenüberstellen, vergleichen; v/i sich abheben (**with** von, gegen); im Gegensatz stehen (**with** zu)

con·trib·ute beitragen, beisteuern, spenden (**to** für)

con·tri·bu·tion Beitrag m; Spende f

con·trib·u·tor Beitragende m, f; Mitarbeiter(in)

con·trib·u·to·ry beitragend

con·trite zerknirscht

con·trive zustande bringen; es fertig bringen

con·trol 1. Kontrolle f, Herrschaft f, Macht f, Gewalt f, Beherrschung f; Aufsicht f; TECH Steuerung f; *mst pl* TECH Steuervorrichtung f; **get (have, keep) under control** unter Kontrolle bringen (haben, halten); **get out of control** außer Kontrolle geraten; **lose control of** die Herrschaft or Gewalt or Kontrolle verlieren über; 2. beherrschen, die Kontrolle haben über (acc); *e-r Sache* Herr werden, (erfolgreich) bekämpfen; kontrollieren, überwachen; ECON (staatlich) lenken, *Preise* binden; ELECTR, TECH steuern, regeln, regulieren

control desk ELECTR Schalt-, Steuerpult

control pan·el ELECTR Schalttafel f

control tow·er AVIAT Kontrollturm m, Tower m

con·tro·ver·sial umstritten

con·tro·ver·sy Kontroverse f, Streit m

con·tuse MED sich et. prellen or quetsche

con·tu·sion MED Prellung f, Quetschung

con·va·lesce gesund werden, genesen

con·va·les·cence Rekonvaleszenz f, Genesung f

con·va·les·cent 1. genesend; 2. Rekonvaleszent(in), Genesende m, f

con·vene (sich) versammeln; zusammenkommen; *Versammlung* einberufen

con·ve·ni·ence Annehmlichkeit f, Bequemlichkeit f; Br Toilette f; **all (mod ern) conveniences** aller Komfort; **a your earliest convenience** möglichs bald

con·ve·ni·ent bequem; günstig, passend

con·vent REL (Nonnen)Kloster n

con·ven·tion Zusammenkunft f, Tagun f, Versammlung f; Abkommen n; Konvention f, Sitte f

con·ven·tion·al herkömmlich, konventionell

con·verge konvergieren; zusammenlau fen, -strömen

con·ver·sa·tion Gespräch n, Unterhal tung f

con·ver·sa·tion·al Unterhaltungs…; **conversational English** Umgangseng lisch n

con·verse sich unterhalten

con·ver·sion Umwandlung f, Verwand lung f; Umbau m; Umstellung f (**to** au acc); REL Bekehrung f, Übertritt m; MATH Umrechnung f

conversion ta·ble Umrechnungstabelle

con·vert (sich) umwandeln or verwan deln; umbauen (**into** zu); umstellen (**to** auf acc); REL etc (sich) bekehren; MATH umrechnen

con·vert·er ELECTR Umformer m

con·vert·i·ble 1. umwandelbar, verwan delbar; ECON konvertierbar; 2. MOT Kabrio(lett) n

con·vey befördern, transportieren, bringen; überbringen, übermitteln; *Ideen etc* mitteilen, vermitteln

con·vey·ance Beförderung f, Transport m; Übermittlung f; Verkehrsmittel n

con·vey·or belt TECH Förderband n

con·vict 1. Verurteilte m, f; Strafgefange ne m, f; 2. JUR **(of)** überführen (gen); ver urteilen (wegen)

con·vic·tion Überzeugung f; JUR Verurteilung f

con·vince überzeugen

con·voy 1. MAR Geleitzug *m*, Konvoi *m*; MOT (Wagen)Kolonne *f*; (Geleit-) Schutz *m*; **2.** Geleitschutz geben (*dat*), eskortieren

con·vul·sion MED Zuckung *f*, Krampf *m*

con·vul·sive krampfhaft, krampfartig, konvulsiv

coo zo gurren (*a. fig*)

cook 1. Koch *m*; Köchin *f*; **2.** kochen; *F Bericht etc* frisieren; **cook up** F sich ausdenken, erfinden

cook·book Kochbuch *n*

cook·er *Br* Ofen *m*, Herd *m*

cook·e·ry Kochen *n*; Kochkunst *f*

cook·e·ry book *Br* Kochbuch *n*

cook·ie (süßer) Keks, Plätzchen *n*

cook·ing GASTR Küche *f*

cook·y → **cookie**

cool 1. kühl; *fig* kalt(blütig), gelassen; abweisend; gleichgültig; F klasse, prima, cool; **2.** Kühle *f*; F (Selbst)Beherrschung *f*; **3.** (sich) abkühlen; **cool down, cool off** sich beruhigen

coon F zo Waschbär *m*

coop 1. Hühnerstall *m*; **2.** **coop up, coop in** einsperren, einpferchen

co-op F Co-op *m*

co·op·e·rate zusammenarbeiten; mitwirken, helfen

co·op·e·ra·tion Zusammenarbeit *f*; Mitwirkung *f*, Hilfe *f*

co·op·e·ra·tive 1. zusammenarbeitend; kooperativ, hilfsbereit; Genossenschafts..., Gemeinschafts...; **2.** *a.* **cooperative society** Genossenschaft *f*; Co-op *m*, Konsumverein *m*; *a.* **cooperative store** Co-op *m*, Konsumladen *m*

co·or·di·nate 1. koordinieren, aufeinander abstimmen; **2.** koordiniert, gleichgeordnet

co·or·di·na·tion Koordinierung *f*, Koordination *f*; harmonisches Zusammenspiel

cop F Bulle *m*

cope: cope with gewachsen sein (*dat*), fertigwerden mit

cop·i·er Kopiergerät *n*, Kopierer *m*

co·pi·ous reich(lich); weitschweifig

cop·per 1. MIN Kupfer *n*; Kupfermünze *f*; **2.** kupfern, Kupfer...

cop·pice, copse Gehölz *n*

cop·y 1. Kopie *f*; Abschrift *f*; Nachbildung *f*; Durchschlag *m*; Exemplar *n*; (*Zeitungs*)Nummer *f*; PRINT Satzvorlage *f*; **fair copy** Reinschrift *f*; **2.** kopieren, abschreiben, e-e Kopie anfertigen von; EDP *Daten* übertragen; nachbilden; nachahmen

cop·y·book Schreibheft *n*

cop·y·ing Kopier...

cop·y·right Urheberrecht *n*, Copyright *n*

cor·al zo Koralle *f*

cord 1. Schnur *f* (*a.* ELECTR), Strick *m*; Kordsamt *m*; **2.** ver-, zuschnüren

cor·di·al[1] Fruchtsaftkonzentrat *n*; MED Stärkungsmittel *n*

cor·di·al[2] herzlich

cor·di·al·i·ty Herzlichkeit *f*

cord·less schnurlos

cord·less phone schnurloses Telefon

cor·don 1. Kordon *m*, Postenkette *f*; **2.** **cordon off** abriegeln, absperren

cor·du·roy Kord *m*; (**a pair of**) **corduroys** (e-e) Kordhose

core 1. Kerngehäuse *n*; Kern *m*, *fig a.* das Innerste; **2.** entkernen

core time ECON Kernzeit *f*

cork 1. Kork(en) *m*; **2.** *a.* **cork up** zu-, verkorken

cork·screw Korkenzieher *m*

corn[1] **1.** Korn *n*, Getreide *n*; *a.* **Indian corn** Mais *m*; **2.** pökeln

corn[2] MED Hühnerauge *n*

cor·ner 1. Ecke *f*; Winkel *m*; *soccer:* Eckve *f*; *soccer:* Eckball *m*, Ecke *f*; *fig* schwierige Lage, Klemme *f*; **2.** Eck...; **3.** in die Ecke (*fig* Enge) treiben

corner kick *soccer:* Eckball *m*, Eckstoß *m*

corner shop *Br* Tante-Emma-Laden *m*

cor·net MUS Kornett *n*; *Br* GASTR Eistüte *f*

cor·nice ARCH Gesims *n*, Sims *m*

corn·flakes Cornflakes *pl*

cor·o·na·ry 1. ANAT Koronar...; **2.** F MED Herzinfarkt *m*

cor·o·na·tion Krönung *f*

cor·o·net Adelskrone *f*

cor·po·ral MIL Unteroffizier *m*

cor·po·ral pun·ish·ment körperliche Züchtigung

cor·po·rate gemeinsam; Firmen...

cor·po·ra·tion JUR Körperschaft *f*; Stadtverwaltung *f*; ECON (Aktien)Gesellschaft *f*

corpse Leichnam *m*, Leiche *f*

cor·pu·lent beleibt

cor·ral 1. Korral *m*, Hürde *f*, Pferch *m*; **2.** *Vieh* in e-n Pferch treiben

cor·rect 1. korrekt, richtig, *a.* genau (*time*); **2.** korrigieren, verbessern, berichtigen

cor·rec·tion Korrektur *f*, Verbess(e)rung *f*; Bestrafung *f*

cor·rect·ness Richtigkeit *f*

cor·re·spond (with, to) entsprechen (*dat*), übereinstimmen (mit); korrespondieren (**with** mit)

cor·re·spon·dence Übereinstimmung *f*;

Korrespondenz f, Briefwechsel m

cor·re·spon·dence course Fernkurs m

cor·re·spon·dent 1. entsprechend; **2.** Briefpartner(in); Korrespondent(in)

cor·re·spon·ding entsprechend

cor·ri·dor Korridor m, Gang m

cor·rob·o·rate bekräftigen, bestätigen

cor·rode zerfressen; CHEM korrodieren; rosten

cor·ro·sion CHEM Korrosion f; Rost m

cor·ro·sive CHEM ätzend; *fig* nagend, zersetzend

cor·ru·gat·ed i·ron Wellblech n

cor·rupt 1. korrupt, bestechlich, käuflich; *moralisch* verdorben; **2.** bestechen; *moralisch* verderben

cor·rupt·i·ble korrupt, bestechlich, käuflich

cor·rup·tion Verdorbenheit f; Unredlichkeit f; Korruption f; Bestechlichkeit f; Bestechung f

cor·set Korsett n

cos·met·ic 1. kosmetisch, Schönheits...; **2.** kosmetisches Mittel, Schönheitsmittel n

cos·me·ti·cian Kosmetiker(in)

cos·mo·naut Kosmonaut m, (Welt-)Raumfahrer m

cos·mo·pol·i·tan 1. kosmopolitisch; **2.** Weltbürger(in)

cost 1. Preis m; Kosten pl; Schaden m; **2.** kosten

cost·ly kostspielig; teuer erkauft

cost of living Lebenshaltungskosten pl

cos·tume Kostüm n, Kleidung f, Tracht f

costume jew·el·(le)ry Modeschmuck m

co·sy Br → **cozy**

cot Feldbett n; Br Kinderbett n

cot·tage Cottage n, (kleines) Landhaus; Ferienhaus n, Ferienhäuschen n

cot·ton 1. Baumwolle f; Baumwollstoff m; (Baumwoll-)Garn n, (Baumwoll-) Zwirn m; (Verband)Watte f; **2.** baumwollen, Baumwoll...

cot·ton·wood BOT e-e amer. Pappel

cot·ton wool Br (Verband)Watte f

couch Couch f, Sofa n; Liege f

cou·chette RAIL Liegewagenplatz m; a. **couchette coach** Liegewagen m

cou·gar ZO Puma m

cough 1. Husten m; **2.** husten

coun·cil Rat m, Ratsversammlung f

council house Br gemeindeeigenes Wohnhaus

coun·cil·(l)or Ratsmitglied n, Stadtrat m, Stadträtin f

coun·sel 1. Beratung f; Rat(schlag) m; JUR (Rechts)Anwalt m; **counsel for the defense** (Br **defence**) Verteidiger m;

counsel for the prosecution Anklagevertreter m; **2.** j-m raten; zu et. raten

counseling center (Br **counseling centre**) Beratungsstelle f

coun·sel·(l)or (Berufs- etc)Berater(in); JUR (Rechts)Anwalt m

count¹ Graf m

count² 1. Zählung f; JUR Anklagepunkt m; **2.** v/t (ab-, auf-, aus-, nach-, zusammen)zählen; aus-, berechnen; *fig* halten für, betrachten als; v/i zählen; gelten; **count ten** bis zehn zählen; **count down** *Geld* hinzählen; den Count-down durchführen für, letzte (Start)Vorbereitungen treffen für; **count on** zählen auf (acc) sich verlassen auf (acc), sicher rechnen mit

count·down Count-down m, n, letzte (Start)Vorbereitungen f

coun·te·nance Gesichtsausdruck m; Fassung f, Haltung f

count·er¹ TECH Zähler m; Br Spielmarke f

coun·ter² Ladentisch m; Theke f; (Bankpost)Schalter m

coun·ter³ 1. (ent)gegen, Gegen...; **2.** entgegentreten (dat), entgegnen (dat), bekämpfen; abwehren

coun·ter·act entgegenwirken (dat); neutralisieren

coun·ter·bal·ance 1. Gegengewicht n; **2.** ein Gegengewicht bilden zu; ausgleichen

coun·ter·clock·wise entgegen dem Uhrzeigersinn

coun·ter·es·pi·o·nage Spionageabwehr f

coun·ter·feit 1. falsch, gefälscht; **2.** Fälschung f; **3.** Geld, Unterschrift etc fälschen

counterfeit mon·ey Falschgeld n

coun·ter·foil Kontrollabschnitt m

coun·ter·mand Befehl etc widerrufen; Ware abbestellen

coun·ter·pane Tagesdecke f

coun·ter·part Gegenstück n; genaue Entsprechung f

coun·ter·sign gegenzeichnen

coun·tess Gräfin f

count·less zahllos

coun·try 1. Land n, Staat m; Gegend f Landschaft f; **in the country** auf dem Lande; **2.** Land..., ländlich

coun·try·man Landbewohner m; Bauer m; a. **fellow countryman** Landsmann m

coun·try road Landstraße f

coun·try·side (ländliche) Gegend; Landschaft f

coun·try·wom·an Landbewohnerin f; Bäuerin f; a. **fellow countrywoman** Landsmännin f

coun·ty (Land)Kreis m; Br Grafschaft f

county seat Kreis(haupt)stadt *f*

county town *Br* Grafschaftshauptstadt *f*

coup Coup *m*; Putsch *m*

cou·ple 1. Paar *n*; *a couple of* F ein paar; **2.** (zusammen)koppeln; TECH kuppeln; ZO (sich) paaren

cou·pon Gutschein *m*; Kupon *m*, Bestellzettel *m*

cour·age Mut *m*

cou·ra·geous mutig, beherzt

cou·ri·er Kurier *m*, Eilbote *m*; Reiseleiter *m*

course AVIAT, MAR Kurs *m* (*a. fig*); SPORT (*Renn*)Bahn *f*, (*Renn*)Strecke *f*; (*Golf-*)Platz *m*; Verlauf *m*; GASTR Gang *m*; Reihe *f*, Zyklus *m*; Kurs *m*, Lehrgang *m*; *of course* natürlich, selbstverständlich; *the course of events* der Gang der Ereignisse, der Lauf der Dinge

court 1. Hof *m*; kleiner Platz; SPORT Platz *m*, (Spiel)Feld *n*; JUR Gericht *n*, Gerichtshof *m*; *go to court* JUR prozessieren; *take s.o. to court* JUR gegen j-n prozessieren; j-m den Prozess machen; **2.** *j-m* den Hof machen; werben um

cour·te·ous höflich

cour·te·sy Höflichkeit *f*; *by courtesy of* mit freundlicher Genehmigung von (*or gen*)

court·house Gerichtsgebäude *n*

court·ier Höfling *m*

court·ly höfisch; höflich

court mar·tial MIL Kriegsgericht *n*

court-mar·tial MIL vor ein Kriegsgericht stellen

court·room Gerichtssaal *m*

court·ship Werben *n*

court·yard Hof *m*

cous·in Cousin *m*, Vetter *m*; Cousine *f*, Kusine *f*

cove kleine Bucht

cov·er 1. Decke *f*; Deckel *m*; (Buch-)Deckel *m*, Einband *m*; Umschlag *m*; Titelseite *f*; Hülle *f*; Überzug *m*, Bezug *m*; Schutzhaube *f*, Schutzplatte *f*; Abdeckhaube *f*; Briefumschlag *m*; GASTR Gedeck *n*; Deckung *f*; Schutz *m*; fig Tarnung *f*; *take cover* in Deckung gehen; *under plain cover* in neutralem Umschlag; *under separate cover* mit getrennter Post; **2.** (be-, zu)decken; einschlagen, einwickeln; verbergen; decken, schützen; ECON (ab)decken; versichern; *Thema* erschöpfend behandeln; *radio, TV* berichten über (*acc*); sich über *e-e Fläche etc* erstrecken; *Strecke* zurücklegen; SPORT *Gegenspieler* decken; *j-n* beschatten; *cover up* ab-, zudecken; *fig* verheimlichen, vertuschen; *cover up for*

s.o. j-n decken

cov·er·age Berichterstattung *f* (*of* über *acc*)

cov·er girl Covergirl *n*, Titelblattmädchen *n*

cov·er·ing Decke *f*; Überzug *m*; Hülle *f*; (*Fußboden*)Belag *m*

cov·er sto·ry Titelgeschichte *f*

cow¹ ZO Kuh *f*

cow² einschüchtern

cow·ard 1. feig(e); **2.** Feigling *m*

cow·ard·ice Feigheit *f*

cow·ard·ly feig(e)

cow·boy Cowboy *m*

cow·er kauern; sich ducken

cow·herd Kuhhirt *m*

cow·hide Rind(s)leder *n*

cow·house Kuhstall *m*

cowl Mönchskutte *f*; Kapuze *f*; TECH Schornsteinkappe *f*

cow·shed Kuhstall *m*

cow·slip BOT Schlüsselblume *f*; Sumpfdotterblume *f*

cox, cox·swain Bootsführer *m*; *rowing*: Steuermann *m*

coy schüchtern, scheu

coy·ote ZO Kojote *m*, Präriewolf *m*

co·zy 1. behaglich, gemütlich; **2.** → *egg cosy, tea cosy*

CPU ABBR *of central processing unit* EDP Zentraleinheit *f*

crab ZO Krabbe *f*, Taschenkrebs *m*

crack 1. Knall *m*; Sprung *m*, Riss *m*; Spalt(e *f*) *m*, Ritze *f*; (heftiger) Schlag; **2.** erstklassig; **3.** *v/i* krachen, knallen, knacken; (zer)springen; überschnappen (*voice*); *a. crack up* zusammenbrechen; F *crack up* überschnappen; *get cracking* F loslegen; *v/t* knallen mit (*Peitsche*), knacken mit (*Fingern*); zerbrechen; *Nuss*, F *Kode*, *Safe etc* knacken; *crack a joke* e-n Witz reißen

crack·er GASTR Cracker *m*, Kräcker *m*; Schwär·mer *m*, Knallfrosch *m*, Knallbonbon *m*, *n*

crack·le knattern, knistern, prasseln

cra·dle 1. Wiege *f*; **2.** wiegen; betten

craft¹ Boot(e *pl*) *n*; Schiff(e *pl*) *n*; Flugzeug(e *pl*) *n*; (Welt)Raumfahrzeug(e *pl*) *n*

craft² Handwerk *n*, Gewerbe *n*; Schlauheit *f*, List *f*

crafts·man (Kunst)Handwerker *m*

craft·y gerissen, listig, schlau

crag Klippe *f*, Felsenspitze *f*

cram *v/t* (voll)stopfen; nudeln, mästen; mit *j-m* pauken; *v/i* pauken, büffeln (*for* für)

cramp 1. MED Krampf *m*; TECH Klammer

f; *fig* Fessel f; **2.** einengen, hemmen

cran·ber·ry BOT Preiselbeere f

crane¹ TECH Kran m

crane² **1.** ZO Kranich m; **2.** den Hals recken; **crane one's neck** sich den Hals verrenken (**for** nach)

crank **1.** TECH Kurbel f; TECH Schwengel m; F Spinner m, komischer Kauz; **2.** (an-)kurbeln

crank·shaft TECH Kurbelwelle f

crank·y wack(e)lig; verschroben; schlecht gelaunt

cran·ny Riss m, Ritze f

crape Krepp m, Flor m

crash **1.** Krach m, Krachen n; MOT Unfall m, Zusammenstoß m; AVIAT Absturz m; ECON Zusammenbruch m, (Börsen-)Krach m; **2.** v/t zertrümmern; e-n Unfall haben mit; AVIAT abstürzen mit; v/i krachend einstürzen, zusammenkrachen; *esp* ECON zusammenbrechen; krachen (**against, into** gegen); MOT zusammenstoßen, verunglücken; AVIAT abstürzen; **3.** Schnell..., Sofort...

crash bar·ri·er MOT Leitplanke f

crash course Schnell-, Intensivkurs m

crash di·et radikale Schlankheitskur

crash hel·met Sturzhelm m

crash-land·ing AVIAT e-e Bruchlandung machen (mit)

crash land·ing AVIAT Bruchlandung f

crate (Latten)Kiste f

cra·ter Krater m; Trichter m

crave sich sehnen (**for, after** nach)

crav·ing heftiges Verlangen

craw·fish → **crayfish**

crawl **1.** Kriechen n; **2.** kriechen; krabbeln; kribbeln; wimmeln (**with** von); *swimming*: kraulen; **it makes my skin crawl** F mir läuft e-e Gänsehaut über den Rücken

cray·fish ZO Flusskrebs m

cray·on Zeichen-, Buntstift m

craze Verrücktheit f, F Fimmel m; **be the craze** Mode sein

cra·zy verrückt (**about** nach)

creak knarren, quietschen

cream **1.** GASTR Rahm m, Sahne f; Creme f; *fig* Auslese f, Elite f; **2.** creme(farben)

cream·y sahnig; weich

crease **1.** (Bügel)Falte f; **2.** (zer)knittern

cre·ate (er)schaffen; hervorrufen; verursachen

cre·a·tion Schöpfung f

cre·a·tive schöpferisch

cre·a·tor Schöpfer m

crea·ture Geschöpf n; Kreatur f

crèche (Kinder)Krippe f; (Weihnachts-)Krippe f

cre·den·tials Beglaubigungsschreiben n Referenzen pl; Zeugnis n; Ausweis m Ausweispapiere pl

cred·i·ble glaubwürdig

cred·it **1.** Glaube(n) m; Ruf m, Ansehen n Verdienst n; ECON Kredit m; Guthaben m **credit (side)** Kredit(seite f) n, Haben m **on credit** auf Kredit; **2.** *j-m* glauben; *j-m* trauen; ECON gutschreiben; **credit s.o with s.th.** j-m et. zutrauen; j-m et. zu schreiben

cred·i·ta·ble achtbar, ehrenvoll (**to** für)

cred·i·tor ECON Gläubiger m

cred·its *film*: Vorspann m, Nachspann m

cred·it·wor·thy ECON kreditwürdig

cred·u·lous leichtgläubig

creed REL Glaubensbekenntnis n

creek Bach m; *Br* kleine Bucht

creep kriechen; schleichen (*a. fig*); **creep in** (sich) hinein- or hereinschleichen; sich einschleichen (*mistake etc*); **it makes my flesh creep** mir läuft e-e Gänsehaut über den Rücken

creep·er BOT Kriech-, Kletterpflanze f

creep·y unheimlich

cre·mate verbrennen, einäschern

cres·cent Halbmond m

cress BOT Kresse f

crest ZO Haube f, Büschel n; (Hahnen-) Kamm m; Bergrücken m, Kamm m (Wellen)Kamm m; Federbusch m; **family crest** Familienwappen n

crest·fal·len niedergeschlagen

cre·vasse GEOL (Gletscher)Spalte f

crev·ice GEOL Riss m, Spalte f

crew crowd, MAR Besatzung f, Crew f, MAR Mannschaft f

crib **1.** (Futter)Krippe f; Kinderbettchen n; *esp Br* (Weihnachts)Krippe f; F PED Spickzettel m; **2.** F abschreiben, spicken

crick: **a crick in one's back** (**neck**) ein steifer Rücken (Hals)

crick·et¹ ZO Grille f

crick·et² SPORT Kricket n

crime JUR Verbrechen n; *coll* Verbrechen pl

crime nov·el Kriminalroman m

crim·i·nal **1.** kriminell; Kriminal... Straf...; **2.** Verbrecher(in), Kriminelle m, f

crimp kräuseln

crim·son karmesinrot; puterrot

cringe sich ducken

crin·kle **1.** Falte f, Fältchen n; **2.** (sich) kräuseln; knittern

crip·ple **1.** Krüppel m; **2.** zum Krüppel machen; *fig* lähmen

cri·sis Krise f

crisp knusp(e)rig, mürbe; frisch, knackig (*vegetable*); scharf, frisch (*air*); kraus (*hair*)

crisp·bread Knäckebrot *n*

crisps *a.* **potato crisps** *Br* (Kartoffel)-Chips *pl*

criss-cross 1. Netz *n* sich schneidender Linien; **2.** kreuz und quer ziehen durch; kreuz und quer (ver)laufen

cri·te·ri·on Kriterium *n*

crit·ic Kritiker(in)

crit·i·cal kritisch; bedenklich

crit·i·cis·m Kritik *f* (**of** an *dat*)

crit·i·cize kritisieren; kritisch beurteilen; tadeln

cri·tique Kritik *f*, Besprechung *f*, Rezension *f*

croak zo krächzen; quaken (*both a. fig*)

cro·chet 1. Häkelei *f*; Häkelarbeit *f*; **2.** häkeln

crock·e·ry Geschirr *n*

croc·o·dile zo Krokodil *n*

cro·ny F alter Freund

crook 1. Krümmung *f*; Hirtenstab *m*; F Gauner *m*; **2.** (sich) krümmen *or* biegen

crook·ed gekrümmt krumm; F unehrlich, betrügerisch

croon schmachtend singen; summen

croon·er Schnulzensänger(in)

crop 1. AGR (Feld)Frucht *f*; Ernte *f*; zo Kropf *m*; kurzer Haarschnitt; kurz geschnittenes Haar; **2.** zo abfressen, abweiden; *Haar* kurz schneiden; **crop up** fig plötzlich auftauchen

cross 1. Kreuz *n* (*a. fig*); BIOL Kreuzung *f*; *soccer:* Flanke *f*; **2.** böse, ärgerlich; **3.** (sich) kreuzen; *Straße* überqueren; *Plan etc* durchkreuzen; BIOL kreuzen; **cross off, cross out** ausstreichen, durchstreichen; **cross o.s.** sich bekreuzigen; **cross one's arms** die Arme verschränken; **cross one's legs** die Beine übereinanderschlagen; **keep one's fingers crossed** den Daumen drücken

cross-bar SPORT Tor-, Querlatte *f*

cross-breed Mischling *m*, Kreuzung *f*

cross-coun·try Querfeldein…, Gelände…; **cross-country skiing** Skilanglauf *m*

cross-ex·am·i·na·tion JUR Kreuzverhör *n*

cross-ex·am·ine JUR ins Kreuzverhör nehmen

cross-eyed: be cross-eyed schielen

cross·ing (Straßen- *etc*)Kreuzung *f*; Straßenübergang *m*; *Br* Fußgängerübergang *m*; MAR Überfahrt *f*

cross·road Querstraße *f*

cross·roads (Straßen)Kreuzung *f*; *fig* Scheideweg *m*

cross-sec·tion Querschnitt *m*

cross-walk Fußgängerüberweg *m*

cross-wise kreuzweise

cross·word (puz·zle) Kreuzworträtsel *n*

crotch ANAT Schritt *m*

crotch·et MUS *Br* Viertelnote *f*

crouch 1. sich ducken; **2.** Hockstellung *f*

crow 1. zo Krähe *f*; Krähen *n*; **2.** krähen

crow-bar TECH Brecheisen *n*

crowd 1. (Menschen)Menge *f*; Masse *f*; Haufen *m*; **2.** sich drängen; *Straßen etc* bevölkern; vollstopfen

crowd·ed überfüllt, voll

crown 1. Krone *f*; **2.** krönen; *Zahn* überkronen; **to crown it all** zu allem Überfluss

cru·cial entscheidend, kritisch

cru·ci·fix REL Kruzifix *n*

cru·ci·fix·ion REL Kreuzigung *f*

cru·ci·fy REL kreuzigen

crude roh, unbearbeitet; *fig* roh, grob

crude (oil) Rohöl *n*

cru·el grausam; roh, gefühllos

cru·el·ty Grausamkeit *f*; **cruelty to animals** Tierquälerei *f*; **society for the prevention of cruelty to animals** Tierschutzverein *m*; **cruelty to children** Kindesmisshandlung *f*

cru·et Essig-, Ölfläschchen *n*

cruise 1. Kreuzfahrt *f*, Seereise *f*; **2.** kreuzen, e-e Kreuzfahrt *or* Seereise machen; AVIAT, MOT mit Reisegeschwindigkeit fliegen *or* fahren

cruise mis·sile MIL Marschflugkörper *m*

cruis·er Kreuzfahrtschiff *n*; MIL MAR Kreuzer *m*; (Funk)Streifenwagen *m*

crumb Krume *f*, Krümel *m*

crum·ble zerkrümeln, zerbröckeln

crum·ple *v/t* zerknittern; *v/i* knittern; zusammengedrückt werden

crumple zone MOT Knautschzone *f*

crunch geräuschvoll (zer)kauen; knirschen

cru·sade HIST Kreuzzug *m* (*a. fig*)

crush 1. Gedränge *n*; **have a crush on s.o.** für j-n schwärmen, F in j-n verknallt sein; **2.** *v/t* zerquetschen, zermalmen, zerdrücken; TECH zerkleinern, zermahlen; *auspressen*; *fig* nieder-, zerschmettern, vernichten; *v/i* sich drängen

crush bar·ri·er Barriere *f*, Absperrung *f*

crust (Brot)Kruste *f*, (Brot)Rinde *f*

crus·ta·cean zo Krebs-, Krusten-, Schalentier *n*

crust·y krustig

crutch Krücke *f*

cry 1. Schrei *m*, Ruf *m*; Geschrei *n*; Weinen *n*; **2.** schreien, rufen (**for** nach); weinen; heulen, jammern crypt Gruft f, Krypta f

crys·tal Kristall m; Uhrglas n

crys·tal·line kristallen

crys·tal·lize kristallisieren

cub zo Junge n

cube Würfel m (a. MATH); PHOT Blitzwürfel m; MATH Kubikzahl f

cube root MATH Kubikwurzel f

cu·bic, cu·bi·cal würfelförmig; kubisch; Kubik...

cu·bi·cle Kabine f

cuck·oo zo Kuckuck m

cu·cum·ber BOT Gurke f; (as) *cool as a cucumber* f eiskalt, kühl und gelassen

cud AGR wiedergekäutes Futter; *chew the cud* wiederkäuen; fig überlegen

cud·dle v/t an sich drücken; schmusen mit; v/i: *cuddle up* sich kuscheln or schmiegen (*to* an acc)

cud·gel 1. Knüppel m; 2. prügeln

cue[1] THEA etc Stichwort n (a. fig); fig Wink m

cue[2] billiards: Queue n

cuff[1] Manschette f; (Hosen-, Br Ärmel-) Aufschlag m

cuff[2] 1. Klaps m; 2. j-m e-n Klaps geben

cuff link Manschettenknopf m

cui·sine GASTR Küche f

cul·mi·nate gipfeln (*in* in dat)

cu·lottes (*a pair of*) ein) Hosenrock m

cul·prit Schuldige m, f, Täter(in)

cul·ti·vate AGR anbauen, bebauen; kultivieren; *Freundschaft etc* pflegen

cul·ti·vat·ed AGR bebaut; fig gebildet, kultiviert

cul·ti·va·tion AGR Kultivierung f, Anbau m; fig Pflege f

cul·tu·ral kulturell; Kultur...

cul·ture Kultur f (a. BIOL.); zo Zucht f

cul·tured kultiviert; gezüchtet, Zucht...

cum·ber·some lästig, hinderlich; klobig

cu·mu·la·tive sich (an)häufend, anwachsend; Zusatz...

cun·ning 1. schlau, listig; 2. List f, Schlauheit f

cup 1. Tasse f; Becher m; Schale f; Kelch m; SPORT Cup m, Pokal m; 2. *die Hand* hohl machen; *she cupped her chin in her hand* sie stützte das Kinn in die Hand

cup·board (Geschirr-, Speise-, Br a. Wäsche-, Kleider)Schrank m

cup·board bed Schrankbett n

cup fi·nal SPORT Pokalendspiel n

cu·po·la ARCH Kuppel f

cup tie SPORT Pokalspiel n

cup win·ner SPORT Pokalsieger m

cur Köter m; Schurke m

cu·ra·ble MED heilbar

cu·rate REL Hilfsgeistliche m

cu·ra·tive heilkräftig; *curative powe[* Heilkraft f

curb 1. Kandare f (a. fig); Bordstein m; 2[an die Kandare legen (a. fig); fig zügel[

curd a. pl Dickmilch f, Quark m

cur·dle v/t Milch gerinnen lassen; v/i ge[rinnen, dick werden; *the sight mad[my blood curdle* bei dem Anblick er starrte mir das Blut in den Adern

cure 1. MED Kur f; (Heil)Mittel n; Heilun[f; 2. MED heilen; GASTR pökeln; räuchern trocknen

cur·few MIL Ausgangsverbot n, -sperre f

cu·ri·o Rarität f

cu·ri·os·i·ty Neugier f; Rarität f

cu·ri·ous neugierig; wissbegierig; selt sam, merkwürdig

curl 1. Locke f; 2. (sich) kräuseln or locker

curl·er Lockenwickler m

curl·y gekräuselt; gelockt, lockig

cur·rant BOT Johannisbeere f; GASTR Ko rinthe f

cur·ren·cy ECON Währung f; *foreign cur rency* Devisen pl

cur·rent 1. laufend; gegenwärtig, aktuell üblich, gebräuchlich; *current events* Ta gesereignisse pl; 2. Strömung f, Strom m (*both a. fig*); ELECTR Strom m

current ac·count Br ECON Girokonto m

cur·ric·u·lum Lehr-, Stundenplan m

cur·ric·u·lum vi·tae Lebenslauf m

cur·ry[1] GASTR Curry m, n

cur·ry[2] *Pferd* striegeln

curse 1. Fluch m, Verwünschung f; 2[(ver)fluchen, verwünschen

curs·ed verflucht

cur·sor EDP Cursor m

cur·so·ry flüchtig, oberflächlich

curt knapp; barsch, schroff

cur·tail *Ausgaben etc* kürzen; *Rechte* be schneiden

cur·tain 1. Vorhang m, Gardine f; *draw the curtains* die Vorhänge auf- or zuzie hen; 2. *curtain off* mit Vorhängen abtei len

curt·s(e)y 1. Knicks m; 2. knicksen (*to* vo[dat)

cur·va·ture Krümmung f

curve 1. Kurve f; Krümmung f, Biegung f 2. (sich) krümmen or biegen

cush·ion 1. Kissen n, Polster n; 2. pols tern; *Stoß etc* dämpfen

cuss 1. Fluch m; 2. (ver)fluchen

cus·tard Eiercreme f, Vanillesoße f

cus·to·dy JUR Haft f; Sorgerecht n

cus·tom Brauch m, Gewohnheit f; ECON Kundschaft f

cus·tom·a·ry üblich

us·tom-built nach Kundenangaben gefertigt

us·tom·er Kunde *m*, Kundin *f*, Auftraggeber(in)

us·tom house Zollamt *n*

us·tom-made maßgefertigt, Maß...

us·toms Zoll *m*

ustoms clear·ance Zollabfertigung *f*

ustoms of·fi·cer, customs of·fi·cial Zollbeamte *m*

ut 1. Schnitt *m*; MED Schnittwunde *f*; GASTR Schnitte *f*, Stück *n*; (Zu)Schnitt *m* (*clothes*); TECH Schnitt *m*, Schliff *m*; Haarschnitt *m*; *fig* Kürzung *f*, Senkung *f*; *cards*: Abheben *n*; **2.** schneiden; ab-, an-, auf-, aus-, be-, durch-, zer-, zuschneiden; *Edelstein etc* schleifen; *Gras* mähen, *Bäume* fällen, *Holz* hacken; MOT *Kurve* schneiden; *Löhne etc* kürzen; *Preise* herabsetzen, senken; *Karten* abheben; **cut one's teeth** Zähne bekommen, zahnen; **cut s.o. (dead)** *fig* F j-n schneiden; **cut s.o. or s.th. short** j-n *or* et. unterbrechen; j-m ins Wort fallen; **cut across** quer durch ... gehen; **cut back** *Pflanze* beschneiden, stutzen; einschränken; **cut down** *Bäume* fällen; verringern, einschränken, reduzieren; **cut in** F sich einmischen, unterbrechen; **cut in on s.o.** MOT j-n schneiden; **cut off** abschneiden; unterbrechen, trennen; *Strom etc* sperren; **cut out** (her)ausschneiden; *Kleid etc* zuschneiden; **be cut out for** wie geschaffen sein für; **cut up** zerschneiden

cut·back Kürzung *f*

cute F schlau; niedlich, süß

cu·ti·cle Nagelhaut *f*

cut·le·ry (Ess)Besteck *n*

cut·let GASTR Kotelett *n*; (*Kalbs-, Schweine*)Schnitzel *n*; Hacksteak *n*

cut-off date Stichtag *m*

cut-price, cut-rate ECON herabgesetzt, ermäßigt; Billig...

cut·ter Zuschneider *m*; (*Glas-, Diamant*)-Schleifer *m*; Schneidemaschine *f*, -werkzeug *n*; *film*: Cutter(in); MAR Kutter *m*

cut·throat 1. Mörder *m*; Killer *m*; **2.** mörderisch

cut·ting 1. schneidend; scharf; TECH Schneid(e)..., Fräs...; **2.** Schneiden *n*; BOT Steckling *m*; *esp Br* Ausschnitt *m*

cut·tings Schnipsel *pl*; Späne *pl*

cut·ting torch TECH Schneidbrenner *m*

Cy·ber·space → virtual reality

cy·cle[1] Zyklus *m*; Kreis(lauf) *m*

cy·cle[2] **1.** Fahrrad *n*; **2.** Rad fahren

cy·cle path, cycle track (Fahr)Radweg *m*

cy·cling Radfahren *n*

cy·clist Radfahrer(in); Motorradfahrer(in)

cy·clone Wirbelsturm *m*

cyl·in·der Zylinder *m*, TECH *a.* Walze *f*, Trommel *f*

cyn·ic Zyniker(in)

cyn·i·cal zynisch

cyn·i·cism Zynismus *m*

cy·press BOT Zypresse *f*

cyst MED Zyste *f*

czar → tsar

Czech 1. tschechisch; *Czech Republic* Tschechien *n*, Tschechische Republik; **2.** Tscheche *m*, Tschechin *f*; LING Tschechisch *n*

D

D, d D, d *n*

d ABBR *of* **died** gest., gestorben

dab 1. Klecks *m*, Spritzer *m*; **2.** betupfen, abtupfen

dab·ble bespritzen; *dabble at, dabble in* sich oberflächlich *or contp* in dilettantischer Weise beschäftigen mit

dachs·hund zo Dackel *m*

dad F, **dad·dy** F Papa *m*, Vati *m*

dad·dy long·legs zo Schnake *f*; Weberknecht *m*

daf·fo·dil BOT gelbe Narzisse

dag·ger Dolch *m*; *be at daggers drawn* *fig* auf Kriegsfuß stehen (*with* mit)

dai·ly 1. täglich; *the daily grind or rut* das tägliche Einerlei; **2.** Tageszeitung *f*; Putzfrau *f*

dain·ty 1. zierlich, reizend; wählerisch; **2.** Leckerbissen *m*

dair·y Molkerei *f*; Milchwirtschaft *f*; Milchgeschäft *n*

dai·sy BOT Gänseblümchen *n*

dal·ly: *dally about* herumtrödeln

dam 1. (Stau)Damm *m*; **2.** *a.* *dam up* stauen, eindämmen

dam·age 1. Schaden *m*, (Be)Schädigung *f*; *pl* JUR Schadenersatz *m*; **2.** (be)schädigen

dam·ask Damast *m*

damn 1. verdammen; verurteilen; *damn (it)!* F verflucht!, verdammt!; **2.** *adj* and *adv* F → *damned*; **3.** *I don't care a damn* F das ist mir völlig gleich(gültig) *or* egal

dam·na·tion Verdammung *f*; REL Verdammnis *f*

damned F verdammt

damn·ing vernichtend, belastend

damp 1. feucht, klamm; **2.** Feuchtigkeit *f*; **3.** *a.* damp en an-, befeuchten; dämpfen

damp·ness Feuchtigkeit *f*

dance 1. Tanz *m*; Tanzveranstaltung *f*; **2.** tanzen

danc·er Tänzer(in)

danc·ing 1. Tanzen *n*; **2.** Tanz...

dan·de·li·on BOT Löwenzahn *m*

dan·druff (Kopf)Schuppen *pl*

Dane Däne *m*, Dänin *f*

dan·ger Gefahr *f*; *be out of danger* außer Lebensgefahr sein

danger ar·e·a Gefahrenzone *f*, Gefahrenbereich *m*

dan·ger·ous gefährlich

dan·ger zone → *danger area*

dan·gle baumeln (lassen)

Da·nish 1. dänisch; **2.** LING Dänisch *n*

dank feucht, nass(kalt)

dare *v/i* es wagen, sich (ge)trauen; *I dare say* ich glaube wohl; allerdings; *how dare you!* was fällt dir ein!; untersteh dich!; *v/t et.* wagen

dare·dev·il Draufgänger *m*

dar·ing 1. kühn, verwegen, waghalsig; **2.** Mut *m*, Kühnheit *f*, Verwegenheit *f*

dark 1. dunkel; finster; *fig* düster, trüb(e); geheim(nisvoll); *before* (*at, after*) *dark* vor (bei, nach) Einbruch der Dunkelheit; *keep s.o. in the dark about s.th.* j-n über et. im Ungewissen lassen

Dark Ag·es *das* frühe Mittelalter

dark·en (sich) verdunkeln *or* verfinstern

dark·ness Dunkelheit *f*, Finsternis *f*

dark·room PHOT Dunkelkammer *f*

dar·ling 1. Liebling *m*; **2.** lieb; F goldig

darn stopfen, ausbessern

dart 1. Wurfpfeil *m*; Sprung *m*, Satz *m*; *darts* Darts *n*; **2.** *v/t* werfen, schleudern; *v/i* schießen, stürzen

dart·board Dartsscheibe *f*

dash 1. Schlag *m*; Klatschen *n*; GASTR Prise *f* (*of salt*), Schuss *m* (*of rum etc*), Spritzer *m* (*of lemon etc*); Gedankenstrich *m*; SPORT Sprint *m*; *fig* Anflug *m*; *a dash of*

blue ein Stich ins Blaue; *make a dash for* losstürzen auf (*acc*); **2.** *v/t* schleudern; schmettern; *Hoffnung etc* zerstören, zunichtemachen; *v/i* stürmen; *dash off* davonstürzen

dash·board MOT Armaturenbrett *n*

dash·ing schneidig, forsch

da·ta Daten *pl* (*a*. EDP), Angaben *pl*

data bank, data·base EDP Datenbank *f*

data cap·ture Datenerfassung *f*

data car·ri·er Datenträger *m*

data in·put Dateneingabe *f*

data me·di·um Datenträger *m*

data mem·o·ry Datenspeicher *m*

data output Datenausgabe *f*

data pro·cess·ing Datenverarbeitung *f*

data pro·tec·tion JUR Datenschutz *m*

data stor·age Datenspeicher *m*

data trans·fer Datenübertragung *f*

date[1] BOT Dattel *f*

date[2] Datum *n*; Zeit *f*, Zeitpunkt *m*; Termin *m*; Verabredung *f*; F (Verabredungs)Partner(in); *out of date* veraltet, unmodern; *up to date* zeitgemäß, modern; auf dem Laufenden; **1.** datieren; F sich verabreden mit, (aus)gehen mit

dat·ed veraltet, überholt

da·tive *a. dative case* LING Dativ *m*, dritter Fall

daub (be)schmieren

daugh·ter Tochter *f*

daugh·ter-in-law Schwiegertochter *f*

daunt entmutigen

dav·en·port Sofa *n*

daw ZO Dohle *f*

daw·dle F (herum)trödeln

dawn 1. (Morgen)Dämmerung *f*; *at dawn* bei Tagesanbruch; **2.** dämmern; *dawn on* *fig* j-m dämmern

day Tag *m*; *often pl* (Lebens)Zeit *f*; *any day* jederzeit; *these days* heutzutage; *the other day* neulich; *the day after tomorrow* übermorgen; *the day before yesterday* vorgestern; *open all day* durchgehend geöffnet; *let's call it a day!* machen wir Schluss für heute!, Feierabend!

day·break Tagesanbruch *m*

day care cen·ter (*Br* care cen·tre) → *day nursery*

day·dream 1. Tag-, Wachtraum *m*; **2.** (mit offenen Augen) träumen

day·dream·er Träumer(in)

day·light Tageslicht *n*; *in broad daylight* am helllichten Tag

day nur·se·ry (Kinder)Tagesstätte *f*

day off freier Tag

day re·turn *Br* Tagesrückfahrkarte *f*

day·time: *in the daytime* am Tag, bei Tage

aze 1. blenden; betäuben; **2. *in a daze*** benommen, betäubt

ead 1. tot; unempfindlich (***to*** für); matt; blind (*window etc*); erloschen; ECON flau; tot (*capital etc*); völlig, total; ***dead stop*** völliger Stillstand; ***drop dead*** tot umfallen; **2.** *adv* völlig, total; plötzlich, abrupt; genau, direkt; ***dead slow*** MOT Schritt fahren!; ***dead slow*** tödmüde; **3.** *the dead* die Toten *pl*; *in the dead of winter* im tiefsten Winter; *in the dead of night* mitten in der Nacht

ead·en abstumpfen; (ab)schwächen; dämpfen

ead end Sackgasse *f* (*a. fig*)

ead heat SPORT totes Rennen

ead·line letzter (Ablieferungs)Termin; Stichtag *m*

ead·lock *fig* toter Punkt

ead·locked *fig* festgefahren

ead loss Totalverlust *m*; F *he's a dead loss* er ist e-e e-e Niete

eaf 1. taub; **2.** *the deaf* die Tauben *pl*

eaf-and-dumb taubstumm

eaf·en taub machen; betäuben

eaf-mute Taubstumme *m, f*

eal 1. F Geschäft *n*, Handel *m*; Menge *f*; *it's a deal!* abgemacht!; *a good deal* ziemlich viel; *a great deal* sehr viel; **2.** *v/t* (aus-, ver-, zu)teilen; *j-m Karten* geben; *j-m e-n Schlag* versetzen; *v/i* handeln (*in* mit *e-r Ware*); *sl* dealen; *cards*: geben; ***deal with*** sich befassen mit, behandeln; ECON Handel treiben mit, Geschäfte machen mit

eal·er ECON Händler(in); *cards*: Geber(in); *sl* Dealer *m*

eal·ing *mst pl* Umgang *m*, Beziehungen *pl*

ean REL, UNIV Dekan *m*

ear 1. teuer; lieb; *Dear Sir* Sehr geehrter Herr ...; **2.** Liebste *m, f*, Schatz *m*; *my dear* m-e Liebe, mein Lieber; **3.** *int* *(oh) dear!*, *dear, dear!*, *dear me!* F du liebe Zeit!, ach herrje!

ear·est sehnlichst

ear·ly innig, von ganzem Herzen; ECON teuer

eath Tod *m*; Todesfall *m*

eath·bed Sterbebett *n*

eath cer·tif·i·cate Totenschein *m*

eath·ly tödlich; *deathly still* totenstill

eath war·rant JUR Hinrichtungsbefehl *m*; *fig* Todesurteil *n*

e·bar: *debar s.o. from* j-n ausschließen aus

e·base erniedrigen; mindern

de·ba·ta·ble umstritten

de·bate 1. Debatte *f*, Diskussion *f*; **2.** debattieren, diskutieren

deb·it ECON **1.** Soll *n*; (Konto)Belastung *f*; ***debit and credit*** Soll und Haben *n*; **2.** *j-n, ein Konto* belasten

deb·ris Trümmer *pl*, Schutt *m*

debt Schuld *f*; *be in debt* Schulden haben, verschuldet sein; *be out of debt* schuldenfrei sein; *get into debt* sich verschulden, Schulden machen

debt·or Schuldner(in)

de·bug TECH, EDP Fehler beseitigen

de·but Debüt *n*

Dec ABBR *of December* Dez., Dezember *m*

dec·ade Jahrzehnt *n*

dec·a·dent dekadent

de·caf·fein·at·ed koffeinfrei

de·camp F verschwinden

de·cant abgießen; umfüllen

de·cant·er Karaffe *f*

de·cath·lete SPORT Zehnkämpfer *m*

de·cath·lon SPORT Zehnkampf *m*

de·cay 1. zerfallen; verfaulen; kariös *or* schlecht werden (*tooth*); **2.** Zerfall *m*; Verfaulen *n*

de·cease *esp* JUR Tod *m*, Ableben *n*

de·ceased *esp* JUR **1.** *the deceased* der *or* die Verstorbene; die Verstorbenen *pl*; **2.** verstorben

de·ceit Betrug *m*; Täuschung *f*

de·ceit·ful betrügerisch

de·ceive betrügen; täuschen

de·ceiv·er Betrüger(in)

De·cem·ber (ABBR *Dec*) Dezember *m*

de·cen·cy Anstand *m*

de·cent anständig; F annehmbar, (ganz) anständig; F nett

de·cep·tion Täuschung *f*

de·cep·tive trügerisch; *be deceptive* täuschen, trügen

de·cide (sich) entscheiden; bestimmen; beschließen, sich entschließen

de·cid·ed entschieden; bestimmt; entschlossen

dec·i·mal MATH **1.** *a.* *decimal fraction* Dezimalbruch *m*; **2.** Dezimal...

de·ci·pher entziffern

de·ci·sion Entscheidung *f*; Entschluss *m*; Entschlossenheit *f*; *make a decision* e-e Entscheidung treffen; *reach or come to a decision* zu e-m Entschluss kommen

de·ci·sive entscheidend; ausschlaggebend; entschieden

deck 1. MAR Deck *n*; Spiel *n*, Pack *m* (Spiel)Karten; **2.** *deck out* schmücken

deck-chair Liegestuhl *m*

dec·la·ra·tion Erklärung *f*; Zollerklärung

f

de·clare erklären; deklarieren, verzollen

de·clen·sion LING Deklination *f*

de·cline 1. abnehmen, zurückgehen; fallen; verfallen; (höflich) ablehnen; LING deklinieren; **2.** Abnahme *f*, Rückgang *m*, Verfall *m*

de·cliv·i·ty (Ab)Hang *m*

de·clutch MOT auskuppeln

de·code entschlüsseln

de·com·pose zerlegen; (sich) zersetzen; verwesen

de·con·tam·i·nate entgasen, entgiften, entseuchen, entstrahlen

de·con·tam·i·na·tion Entseuchung *f*

dec·o·rate verzieren, schmücken; tapezieren; (an)streichen; dekorieren

dec·o·ra·tion Verzierung *f*, Schmuck *m*, Dekoration *f*; Orden *m*

dec·o·ra·tive dekorativ; Zier…

dec·o·ra·tor Dekorateur *m*; Maler *m* und Tapezierer *m*

dec·o·rous anständig

de·co·rum Anstand *m*

de·coy 1. Lockvogel *m* (*a. fig*); Köder *m* (*a. fig*); **2.** ködern; locken (*into* in *acc*); verleiten (*into* zu)

de·crease 1. Abnahme *f*; **2.** abnehmen; (sich) vermindern

de·cree 1. Dekret *n*, Erlass *m*, Verfügung *f*; *esp* JUR Entscheid *m*, Urteil *n*; **2.** verfügen

ded·i·cate widmen

ded·i·cat·ed engagiert

ded·i·ca·tion Widmung *f*; Hingabe *f*

de·duce ableiten; folgern

de·duct *Betrag* abziehen (*from* von)

de·duct·i·ble: *tax-deductible* steuerlich absetzbar

de·duc·tion Abzug *m*; (Schluss-)Folgerung *f*, Schluss *m*

deed Tat *f*; Heldentat *f*; JUR (Übertragungs)Urkunde *f*

deep 1. tief (*a. fig*); **2.** Tiefe *f*

deep·en (sich) vertiefen, *fig a.* (sich) verstärken

deep freeze 1. tiefkühlen, einfrieren; **2.** Tiefkühl-, Gefriertruhe *f*

deep-fro·zen tiefgefroren

deep fry frittieren

deep·ness Tiefe *f*

deer zo Hirsch *m*; Reh *n*

de·face entstellen; unleserlich machen; ausstreichen

def·a·ma·tion Verleumdung *f*

de·fault 1. JUR Nichterscheinen *n* vor Gericht; SPORT Nichtantreten *n*; ECON Verzug *m*; **2.** s-n Verpflichtungen nicht nachkommen, ECON *a.* im Verzug sein; JUR

nicht vor Gericht erscheinen; SPORT nich antreten

de·feat 1. Niederlage *f*; **2.** besiegen, schla gen; vereiteln, zunichtemachen

de·fect Defekt *m*, Fehler *m*; Mangel *m*

de·fec·tive mangelhaft; schadhaft, defek

de·fence *Br* → *defense*

de·fence·less *Br* → *defenseless*

de·fend (*from, against*) verteidigen (ge gen), schützen (vor *dat*, gegen)

de·fen·dant Angeklagte *m, f*; Beklagt *m, f*

de·fend·er Verteidiger(in); SPORT Ab wehrspieler(in)

de·fense Verteidigung *f* (*a.* MIL, JUR SPORT), Schutz *m*; SPORT Abwehr *f*; *wi* *ness for the defense* Entlastungszeug *m*

de·fense·less schutzlos, wehrlos

de·fen·sive 1. Defensive *f*, Verteidigung *f* Abwehr *f*; **2.** defensiv; Verteidigungs… Abwehr…

de·fer aufschieben, verschieben

de·fi·ance Herausforderung *f*; Trotz *m*

de·fi·ant herausfordernd; trotzig

de·fi·cien·cy Unzulänglichkeit *f*; Mange *m*

de·fi·cient mangelhaft, unzureichend

def·i·cit ECON Defizit *n*, Fehlbetrag *m*

de·file beschmutzen

de·fine definieren; erklären; bestimmen

def·i·nite bestimmt; endgültig, definitiv

def·i·ni·tion Definition *f*, Bestimmung *f* Erklärung *f*

de·fin·i·tive endgültig, definitiv

de·flect *v/t* ablenken; *Ball* abfälschen; *v/* abweichen

de·form entstellen, verunstalten

de·formed deformiert, verunstaltet; ver wachsen

de·for·mi·ty Missbildung *f*

de·fraud betrügen (*of* um)

de·frost *v/t Windschutzscheibe etc* ent frosten; *Kühlschrank etc* abtauen, *Tief kühlkost etc* auftauen; *v/i* ab-, auftauen

deft geschickt, gewandt

de·fy herausfordern; trotzen (*dat*)

de·gen·e·rate 1. entarten; **2.** entartet

deg·ra·da·tion Erniedrigung *f*

de·grade erniedrigen, demütigen

de·gree Grad *m*; Stufe *f*; (akademischer Grad; *by degrees* allmählich; *take one's degree* e-n akademischen Grad erwerben, promovieren

de·hy·drate austrocknen, TECH das Was ser entziehen (*dat*)

de·i·fy vergöttern; vergöttlichen

deign sich herablassen

de·i·ty Gottheit *f*

de·jec·ted niedergeschlagen, mutlos, deprimiert

de·jec·tion Niedergeschlagenheit *f*

de·lay 1. Aufschub *m*; Verzögerung *f*; RAIL *etc* Verspätung *f*; **2.** ver-, aufschieben; verzögern; aufhalten; *be delayed* sich verzögern; RAIL *etc* Verspätung haben

del·e·gate 1. abordnen, delegieren; *Vollmachten etc* übertragen; **2.** Delegierte *m*, *f*, bevollmächtigter Vertreter

del·e·ga·tion Übertragung *f*; Abordnung *f*, Delegation *f*

de·lete (aus)streichen; EDP löschen

de·lib·e·rate absichtlich, vorsätzlich; bedächtig, besonnen

de·lib·e·ra·tion Überlegung *f*; Beratung *f*; Bedächtigkeit *f*

del·i·ca·cy Delikatesse *f*, Leckerbissen *m*; Zartheit *f*; Feingefühl *n*, Takt *m*

del·i·cate delikat (*a. fig*), schmackhaft; zart; fein; zierlich; zerbrechlich; heikel; empfindlich

del·i·ca·tes·sen Delikatessen *pl*, Feinkost *f*; Feinkostgeschäft *n*

de·li·cious köstlich

de·light 1. Vergnügen *n*, Entzücken *n*; **2.** entzücken, erfreuen; *delight in* (große) Freude haben an (*dat*)

de·light·ful entzückend

de·lin·quen·cy Kriminalität *f*

de·lin·quent 1. straffällig; **2.** Straffällige *m*, *f*; → *juvenile 1*

de·lir·i·ous MED im Delirium, fantasierend

de·lir·i·um MED Delirium *n*

de·liv·er ausliefern, (ab)liefern; *Briefe* zustellen; *Rede etc* halten; befreien, erlösen; *be delivered of* MED entbunden werden von

de·liv·er·ance Befreiung *f*

de·liv·er·er Befreier(in)

de·liv·er·y (Ab-, Aus)Lieferung *f*; *post* Zustellung *f*; Halten *n* (*e-r Rede*); Vortrag(sweise *f*) *m*; MED Entbindung *f*

de·liv·er·y van *Br* MOT Lieferwagen *m*

dell kleines Tal

de·lude täuschen

del·uge Überschwemmung *f*; *fig* Flut *f*

de·lu·sion Täuschung *f*; Wahn(vorstellung *f*) *m*

de·mand 1. Forderung *f* (*for* nach); Anforderung *f* (*on* an *acc*); Nachfrage *f* (*for* nach), Bedarf *m* (*for* an *dat*); *on demand* auf Verlangen; **2.** verlangen, fordern; (*fordernd*) fragen nach; erfordern

de·mand·ing anspruchsvoll

de·ment·ed wahnsinnig

dem·i... Halb..., halb...

de·mil·i·ta·rize entmilitarisieren

dem·o F Demo *f*

de·mo·bi·lize demobilisieren

de·moc·ra·cy Demokratie *f*

dem·o·crat Demokrat(in)

dem·o·crat·ic demokratisch

de·mol·ish demolieren; ab-, ein-, niederreißen; zerstören

de·mo·li·tion Demolierung *f*; Niederreißen *n*, Abbruch *m*

de·mon Dämon *m*; Teufel *m*

dem·on·strate demonstrieren; beweisen; zeigen; vorführen

dem·on·stra·tion Demonstration *f*, *a.* Kundgebung *f*, *a.* Vorführung *f*

demonstration car *Br* Vorführwagen *m*

de·mon·stra·tive: *be demonstrative* s-e Gefühle (offen) zeigen

dem·on·stra·tor Demonstrant(in); Vorführer(in); MOT Vorführwagen *m*

de·mor·al·ize demoralisieren

de·mote degradieren

de·mure ernst, zurückhaltend

den ZO Höhle *f* (*a. fig*); F Bude *f*

de·ni·al Ablehnung *f*; Leugnen *n*; Verweigerung *f*; *official denial* Dementi *n*

den·ims Jeans *pl*

Den·mark Dänemark *n*

de·nom·i·na·tion REL Konfession *f*; ECON Nennwert *m*

de·note bezeichnen; bedeuten

de·nounce (öffentlich) anprangern

dense dicht; *fig* beschränkt, begriffsstutzig

den·si·ty Dichte *f*

dent 1. Beule *f*, Delle *f*; **2.** ver-, einbeulen

den·tal Zahn...

dental plaque Zahnbelag *m*

dental plate (Zahn)Prothese *f*

dental surgeon Zahnarzt *m*, Zahnärztin *f*

den·tist Zahnarzt *m*, Zahnärztin *f*

den·tures (Zahn)Prothese *f*, (künstliches) Gebiss

de·nun·ci·a·tion Denunziation *f*

de·nun·ci·a·tor Denunziant(in)

de·ny abstreiten, bestreiten, dementieren; (ab)leugnen; *j-m et.* verweigern, abschlagen

de·o·do·rant De(s)odorant *n*, Deo *n*

de·part abreisen; abfahren, abfliegen; abweichen (*from* von)

de·part·ment Abteilung *f*, UNIV *a.* Fachbereich *m*; POL Ministerium *n*

De·part·ment of De·fense Verteidigungsministerium *n*

Department of the En·vi·ron·ment *Br* Umweltministerium *n*

Department of the In·te·ri·or Innenministerium *n*

Department of State *a.* **State Depart-**

D

ment Außenministerium *n*
de·part·ment store Kaufhaus *n*, Warenhaus *n*
de·par·ture Abreise *f*; RAIL *etc* Abfahrt *f*; AVIAT Abflug *m*; *fig* Abweichung *f*; *departures* 'Abfahrt'
departure gate AVIAT Flugsteig *m*
departure lounge AVIAT Abflughalle *f*
de·pend: depend on sich verlassen auf (*acc*); abhängen von; angewiesen sein auf (*acc*); *that depends* das kommt darauf an
de·pend·a·ble zuverlässig
de·pend·a·bil·i·ty Zuverlässigkeit *f*
de·pend·ant Angehörige *m*, *f*
de·pen·dence Abhängigkeit *f*; Vertrauen *n*
de·pen·dent 1. (*on*) abhängig (von); angewiesen (auf *acc*); **2.** → *dependant*
de·plor·a·ble bedauerlich, beklagenswert
de·plore beklagen, bedauern
de·pop·u·late entvölkern
de·port ausweisen, *Ausländer a.* abschieben; deportieren
de·pose *j-n* absetzen; JUR unter Eid erklären
de·pos·it 1. absetzen, abstellen; CHEM, GEOL (sich) ablagern *or* absetzen; deponieren, hinterlegen; ECON *Betrag* anzahlen; **2.** CHEM Ablagerung *f*, GEOL *a.* (*Erz- etc*)Lager *n*; Deponierung *f*, Hinterlegung *f*; ECON Anzahlung *f*; *make a deposit* e-e Anzahlung leisten (*on* für)
dep·ot Depot *n*; Bahnhof *m*
de·prave *moralisch* verderben
de·pre·ci·ate an Wert verlieren
de·press (nieder)drücken; deprimieren, bedrücken
de·pressed deprimiert, niedergeschlagen; ECON flau (*market*); Not leidend (*industry*)
depressed ar·e·a ECON Notstandsgebiet *n*
de·press·ing deprimierend, bedrückend
de·pres·sion Depression *f*, Niedergeschlagenheit *f*; ECON Depression *f*, Flaute *f*; Senke *f*, Vertiefung *f*; METEOR Tief *n* (-druckgebiet) *f*
de·prive: deprive s.o. of s.th. j-m et. entziehen *or* nehmen
de·prived benachteiligt
dept, Dept ABBR *of* **department** Abt., Abteilung *f*
depth 1. Tiefe *f*; **2.** Tiefen…
dep·u·ta·tion Abordnung *f*
dep·u·tize: deputize for s.o. j-n vertreten
dep·u·ty (Stell)Vertreter(in); PARL Abgeordnete *m*, *f*; *a.* **deputy sheriff** Hilfssheriff *m*
de·rail: be derailed entgleisen

de·ranged geistesgestört
der·by F Melone *f*
der·e·lict heruntergekommen, baufällig
de·ride verhöhnen, verspotten
de·ri·sion Hohn *m*, Spott *m*
de·ri·sive höhnisch, spöttisch
de·rive herleiten (**from** von); (sich) ableiten (**from** von); abstammen (**from** von); *derive pleasure from* Freude finden *or* haben an (*dat*)
der·ma·tol·o·gist Dermatologe *m*, Hautarzt *m*
de·rog·a·to·ry abfällig, geringschätzig
der·rick TECH Derrickkran *m*; MAR Ladebaum *m*; TECH Bohrturm *m*
de·scend herab-, hinabsteigen, herunter-hinuntersteigen, -gehen, -kommen; AVIAT niedergehen; abstammen, herkommen (**from** von); *descend on* herfallen über (*acc*); überfallen (*acc*) (*visitor etc*)
de·scen·dant Nachkomme *m*
de·scent Herab-, Hinuntersteigen *n*, -gehen *n*; AVIAT Niedergehen *n*; Gefälle *n*; Abstammung *f*, Herkunft *f*
de·scribe beschreiben
de·scrip·tion Beschreibung *f*, Schilderung *f*; Art *f*, Sorte *f*
de·scrip·tive beschreibend; anschaulich
des·e·crate entweihen
de·seg·re·gate die Rassentrennung aufheben in (*dat*)
de·seg·re·ga·tion Aufhebung *f* der Rassentrennung
des·ert¹ 1. Wüste *f*; **2.** Wüsten…
de·sert² *v/t* verlassen, im Stich lassen; *v/i* MIL desertieren
de·sert·er MIL Deserteur *m*
de·ser·tion (JUR *a.* böswilliges) Verlassen; MIL Fahnenflucht *f*
de·serve verdienen
de·serv·ed·ly verdientermaßen
de·serv·ing verdienstvoll
de·sign 1. Design *n*, Entwurf *m*, (TECH Konstruktions)Zeichnung *f*; Design *n*, Muster *n*; (*a.* böse)Absicht *f*; **2.** entwerfen, TECH konstruieren; gestalten; ausdenken; bestimmen, vorsehen (**for** für)
des·ig·nate *et. or j-n* bestimmen
de·sign·er Designer(in); TECH Konstrukteur *m*; (*Mode*)Schöpfer(in)
de·sir·a·ble erwünscht, wünschenswert; begehrenswert
de·sire 1. Wunsch *m*, Verlangen *n*, Begierde *f* (**for** nach); **2.** wünschen; begehren
de·sist Abstand nehmen (**from** von)
desk Schreibtisch *m*; Pult *n*; Empfang *m*, Rezeption *f*; Schalter *m*
desk·top com·put·er Desktop-Computer *m*, Tischcomputer *m*, Tischrechner *m*

diagonal

desktop pub·lish·ing (ABBR **DTP**) EDP Desktop-Publishing n

des·o·late einsam, verlassen; trostlos

de·spair 1. Verzweiflung f; **drive s.o. to despair** j-n zur Verzweiflung bringen; **2.** verzweifeln (**of** an dat)

de·spair·ing verzweifelt

de·spatch → dispatch

des·per·ate verzweifelt; F hoffnungslos, schrecklich

des·per·a·tion Verzweiflung f

des·pic·a·ble verachtenswert, verabscheuungswürdig

de·spise verachten

de·spite trotz (gen)

de·spon·dent mutlos, verzagt

des·pot Despot m, Tyrann m

des·sert Nachtisch m, Dessert n

des·ti·na·tion Bestimmung f; Bestimmungsort m

des·tined bestimmt; MAR etc unterwegs (**for** nach)

des·ti·ny Schicksal n

des·ti·tute mittellos

de·stroy zerstören, vernichten; Tier töten, einschläfern

de·stroy·er Zerstörer(in); MAR MIL Zerstörer m

de·struc·tion Zerstörung f, Vernichtung f

de·struc·tive zerstörend, vernichtend; zerstörerisch

de·tach (ab-, los)trennen, (los)lösen

de·tached einzeln, frei or allein stehend; unvoreingenommen, distanziert; **de·tached house** Einzelhaus n

de·tach·ment (Los)Lösung f, (Ab-) Trennung f; MIL (Sonder)Kommando n

de·tail 1. Detail n, Einzelheit f; MIL (Sonder)Kommando n; **in detail** ausführlich; **2.** genau schildern; MIL abkommandieren

de·tailed detailliert, ausführlich

de·tain aufhalten; JUR in (Untersuchungs)Haft behalten

de·tect entdecken, (heraus)finden

de·tec·tion Entdeckung f

de·tec·tive Kriminalbeamte m, Detektiv m

detective nov·el, detective sto·ry Kriminalroman m

de·ten·tion JUR Haft f; PED Nachsitzen n

de·ter abschrecken (**from** von)

de·ter·gent Reinigungs-, Wasch-, Geschirrspülmittel n

de·te·ri·o·rate (sich) verschlechtern, nachlassen; verderben

de·ter·mi·na·tion Entschlossenheit f, Bestimmtheit f; Entschluss m; Feststellung f, Ermittlung f

de·ter·mine et. beschließen, bestimmen; feststellen, ermitteln; (sich) entscheiden; sich entschließen

de·ter·mined entschlossen

de·ter·rence Abschreckung f

de·ter·rent 1. abschreckend; **2.** Abschreckungsmittel n

de·test verabscheuen

de·throne entthronen

de·to·nate v/t zünden; v/i detonieren, explodieren

de·tour Umweg m; Umleitung f

de·tract: detract from ablenken von; schmälern (acc)

de·tri·ment Nachteil m, Schaden m

deuce cards etc: Zwei f; tennis: Einstand m

de·val·u·a·tion Abwertung f

de·val·ue abwerten

dev·a·state verwüsten

dev·a·stat·ing verheerend, vernichtend; F umwerfend, toll

de·vel·op (sich) entwickeln; Naturschätze, Bauland erschließen, Altstadt etc sanieren

de·vel·op·er PHOT Entwickler m; (Stadt-) Planer m

de·vel·op·ing Entwicklungs…

developing coun·try, developing nation Entwicklungsland n

de·vel·op·ment Entwicklung f; Erschließung f, Sanierung f

de·vi·ate abweichen (**from** von)

de·vi·a·tion Abweichung f

de·vice Vorrichtung f, Gerät n; Plan m, Trick m; **leave s.o. to his own devices** j-n sich selbst überlassen

dev·il Teufel m (a. fig)

dev·il·ish teuflisch

de·vi·ous abwegig; gewunden; unaufrichtig; **devious route** Umweg m

de·vise (sich) ausdenken

de·void: devoid of ohne (acc)

de·vote widmen (**to** dat)

de·vot·ed ergeben; hingebungsvoll; eifrig, begeistert

dev·o·tee begeisterter Anhänger

de·vo·tion Ergebenheit f; Hingabe f; Frömmigkeit f, Andacht f

de·vour verschlingen

de·vout fromm; sehnlichst, innig

dew Tau m

dew·y taufeucht, taufrisch

dex·ter·i·ty Gewandtheit f

dex·ter·ous, dex·trous gewandt

di·a·bol·i·cal teuflisch

di·ag·nose diagnostizieren

di·ag·no·sis Diagnose f

di·ag·o·nal 1. diagonal; **2.** Diagonale f

diagram 440

di·a·gram Diagramm n, grafische Darstellung

di·al 1. Zifferblatt n; TEL Wählscheibe f; TECH Skala f; **2.** TEL wählen; *dial direct* durchwählen (*to* nach); *direct dial(l)ing* Durchwahl f

di·a·lect Dialekt m, Mundart f

di·al·ling code Br TEL Vorwahl(nummer) f

di·a·log, Br **di·a·logue** Dialog m, (Zwie-) Gespräch n

di·am·e·ter Durchmesser m; *in diameter* im Durchmesser

di·a·mond Diamant m; Raute f, Rhombus m; *cards:* Karo n

di·a·per Windel f

di·a·phragm ANAT Zwerchfell n; OPT Blende f; TEL Membran(e) f

di·ar·rh(o)e·a MED Durchfall m

di·a·ry Tagebuch n

dice 1. Würfel m; **2.** GASTR in Würfel schneiden; würfeln

dic·tate diktieren; *fig* vorschreiben

dic·ta·tion Diktat n

dic·ta·tor Diktator m

dic·ta·tor·ship Diktatur f

dic·tion Ausdrucksweise f, Stil m

dic·tion·a·ry Wörterbuch n

die¹ sterben; ZO eingehen, verenden; *die of hunger* verhungern; *die of thirst* verdursten; *die away* sich legen (*wind*); verklingen (*sound*); *die down* nachlassen; herunterbrennen; schwächer werden; *die out* aussterben (*a. fig*)

die² Würfel m

di·et 1. Diät f; Nahrung f, Kost f; *be on a diet* Diät leben; *put s.o. on a diet* j-m e-e Diät verordnen; **2.** Diät leben

di·e·ti·cian Diätassistent(in)

dif·fer sich unterscheiden; anderer Meinung sein (*with, from* als); abweichen

dif·fe·rence Unterschied m; Differenz f; Meinungsverschiedenheit f

dif·fe·rent verschieden; andere(r, -s); anders (*from* als)

dif·fe·ren·ti·ate (sich) unterscheiden

dif·fi·cult schwierig

dif·fi·cul·ty Schwierigkeit f, pl Unannehmlichkeiten pl

dif·fi·dence Schüchternheit f

dif·fi·dent schüchtern

dif·fuse verbreiten; **2.** diffus; *esp* PHYS zerstreut; weitschweifig

dif·fu·sion CHEM, PHYS (Zer)Streuung f

dig 1. graben; *dig (up)* umgraben; *dig (up or out)* ausgraben (*a. fig*); *dig s.o. in the ribs* j-m e-n Rippenstoß geben; **2.** F Puff m, Stoß m; Seitenhieb m (*at* auf acc)

di·gest 1. verdauen; *digest well* leicht

verdaulich sein; **2.** Abriss m; Auslese f, Auswahl f

di·gest·i·ble verdaulich

di·ges·tion Verdauung f

di·ges·tive verdauungsfördernd; Verdauungs…

dig·ger (*esp* Gold)Gräber m

di·git Ziffer f; *three-digit number* dreistellige Zahl

di·gi·tal digital, Digital…

dig·i·tal clock, digital watch Digitaluhr

dig·ni·fied würdevoll, würdig

dig·ni·ta·ry Würdenträger(in)

dig·ni·ty Würde f

di·gress abschweifen

dike¹ 1. Deich m, Damm m; Graben m; **2.** eindeichen, eindämmen

dike² sl Lesbe f

di·lap·i·dat·ed verfallen, baufällig, klapp(e)rig

di·late (sich) ausdehnen or (aus)weiten; *Augen* weit öffnen

di·la·to·ry verzögernd, hinhaltend; langsam

dil·i·gence Fleiß m

dil·i·gent fleißig, emsig

di·lute 1. verdünnen; *fig* verwässern; **2.** verdünnt; *fig* verwässert

dim 1. (halb)dunkel, düster; undeutlich verschwommen; schwach, trüb(e) (*light*) **2.** (sich) verdunkeln or verdüstern; (sich) trüben; undeutlich werden; *dim one's headlights* MOT abblenden

dime Zehncentstück n

di·men·sion Dimension f, Maß n, Abmessung f; pl a. Ausmaß n

di·min·ish (sich) vermindern or verringern

di·min·u·tive klein, winzig

dim·ple Grübchen n

din Getöse n, Lärm m

dine essen, speisen; *dine in* zu Hause essen; *dine out* auswärts essen, essen gehen

din·er Speisende m, f; Gast m; Speiselokal n; RAIL Speisewagen m

din·ghy MAR Jolle f; Dingi n; Beiboot n Schlauchboot n

din·gy schmutzig, schmudd(e)lig

din·ing car RAIL Speisewagen m

din·ing room Ess-, Speisezimmer n

din·ner (Mittag-, Abend)Essen n; Diner n, Festessen n

dinner jack·et Smoking m

dinner par·ty Dinnerparty f, Abendgesellschaft f

dinner ser·vice, dinner set Speiseservice n, Tafelgeschirr n

din·ner·time Essens-, Tischzeit f

D

i·no F → **dinosaur**

i·no·saur ZO Dinosaurier *m*

ip 1. *v/t* (ein)tauchen; senken; schöpfen; *dip one's headlights* Br MOT abblenden; *v/i* (unter)tauchen; sinken; sich neigen, sich senken; **2.** (Ein-, Unter-)Tauchen *n*; F kurzes Bad; Senkung *f*, Neigung *f*, Gefälle *n*; GASTR Dip *m*

iph·ther·i·a MED Diphtherie *f*

i·plo·ma Diplom *n*

i·plo·ma·cy Diplomatie *f*

ip·lo·mat Diplomat *m*

ip·lo·mat·ic diplomatisch

ip·per Schöpfkelle *f*

ire schrecklich; höchste(r, -s), äußerste(r, -s)

i·rect 1. *adj* direkt; gerade; unmittelbar; offen, aufrichtig; **2.** *adv* direkt, unmittelbar; **3.** richten; lenken, steuern; leiten; anordnen; *j-n* anweisen; *j-m* den Weg zeigen; *Brief* adressieren; Regie führen bei

direct cur·rent ELECTR Gleichstrom *m*

direct train durchgehender Zug

di·rec·tion Richtung *f*; Leitung *f*, Führung *f*; *film etc*: Regie *f*; *mst pl* Anweisung *f*, Anleitung *f*; *directions for use* Gebrauchsanweisung *f*; *sense of direction* Ortssinn *m*

direction in·di·ca·tor MOT Fahrtrichtungsanzeiger *m*, Blinker *m*

di·rec·tive Anweisung *f*

di·rect·ly 1. *adv* sofort; **2.** *cj* F sobald, sowie

di·rec·tor Direktor *m*; *film etc*: Regisseur(in)

di·rec·to·ry Adressbuch *n*

direct speech LING wörtliche Rede

dirt Schmutz *m*; (lockere) Erde

dirt cheap F spottbillig

dirt·y 1. schmutzig (*a. fig*); **2.** *v/t* beschmutzen; *v/i* schmutzig werden, schmutzen

dis·a·bil·i·ty Unfähigkeit *f*

dis·a·bled 1. arbeitsunfähig, erwerbsunfähig, invalid(e); MIL kriegsversehrt; *körperlich or geistig behindert*; **2.** *the disabled* die Behinderten *pl*

dis·ad·van·tage Nachteil *m*; Schaden *m*

dis·ad·van·ta·geous nachteilig, ungünstig

dis·a·gree nicht übereinstimmen; uneinig sein; nicht bekommen (*with s.o.* j-m)

dis·a·gree·a·ble unangenehm

dis·a·gree·ment Verschiedenheit *f*, Unstimmigkeit *f*, Uneinigkeit *f*; Meinungsverschiedenheit *f*

dis·ap·pear verschwinden

dis·ap·pear·ance Verschwinden *n*

dis·ap·point *j-n* enttäuschen; *Hoffnun-*

gen etc zunichtemachen

dis·ap·point·ing enttäuschend

dis·ap·point·ment Enttäuschung *f*

dis·ap·prov·al Missbilligung *f*

dis·ap·prove missbilligen; dagegen sein

dis·arm *v/t* entwaffnen (*a. fig*); *v/i* MIL, POL abrüsten

dis·ar·ma·ment Entwaffnung *f*; MIL, POL Abrüstung *f*

dis·ar·range in Unordnung bringen

dis·ar·ray Unordnung *f*

di·sas·ter Unglück *n*, Unglücksfall *m*, Katastrophe *f*

disaster ar·e·a Katastrophen-, Notstandsgebiet *n*

disaster con·trol Katastrophenschutz *m*

di·sas·trous katastrophal, verheerend

dis·be·lief Unglaube *m*; Zweifel *m* (*in an dat*)

dis·be·lieve *et.* bezweifeln, nicht glauben

disc Br → **disk**

dis·card *Karten* ablegen, *Kleidung etc a.* ausrangieren; *Freund etc* fallen lassen

di·scern wahrnehmen, erkennen

di·scern·ing kritisch, scharfsichtig

di·scern·ment Scharfblick *m*

dis·charge 1. *v/t* entladen, ausladen; *j-n* befreien, entbinden; *j-n* entlassen; *Gewehr etc* abfeuern; von sich geben, ausströmen, -senden, -stoßen; MED absondern; *Pflicht etc* erfüllen; *Zorn etc* auslassen (*on* an *dat*); *v/i* ELECTR sich entladen; sich ergießen, münden (*river*); MED eitern; **2.** MAR Entladung *f*; MIL Abfeuern *n*; Ausströmen *n*; MED Absonderung *f*, Ausfluss *m*; Ausstoßen *n*; ELECTR Entladung *f*; Entlassung *f*; Erfüllung *f* (*e-r Pflicht*)

di·sci·ple Schüler *m*; Jünger *m*

dis·ci·pline 1. Disziplin *f*; **2.** disziplinieren; *well disciplined* diszipliniert; *badly disciplined* disziplinlos, undiszipliniert

dis·claim abstreiten, bestreiten; *Verantwortung* ablehnen; JUR verzichten auf (*acc*)

dis·close bekannt geben *or* machen; enthüllen, aufdecken

dis·clo·sure Enthüllung *f*

dis·co Disko *f*

dis·col·o(u)r (sich) verfärben

dis·com·fort 1. Unbehagen *n*; Unannehmlichkeit *f*; **2.** *j-m* Unbehagen verursachen

dis·con·cert aus der Fassung bringen

dis·con·nect trennen (*a. ELECTR*); TECH auskuppeln; ELECTR *Gerät* abschalten; *Gas, Strom, Telefon* abstellen; TEL *Gespräch* unterbrechen

dis·con·nect·ed zusammenhang(s)los

disconsolate   44.

dis·con·so·late untröstlich
dis·con·tent Unzufriedenheit f
dis·con·tent·ed unzufrieden
dis·con·tin·ue aufgeben, aufhören mit; unterbrechen
dis·cord Uneinigkeit f, Zwietracht f, Zwist m; MUS Missklang m
dis·cord·ant nicht übereinstimmend; MUS unharmonisch, misstönend
dis·co·theque Diskothek f
dis·count ECON Diskont m; Preisnachlass m, Rabatt m, Skonto m, n
dis·cour·age entmutigen; abschrecken, abhalten, j-m abraten (from von)
dis·cour·age·ment Entmutigung f; Abschreckung f
dis·course 1. Unterhaltung f, Gespräch n; Vortrag m; 2. e-n Vortrag halten (on über acc)
dis·cour·te·ous unhöflich
dis·cour·te·sy Unhöflichkeit f
dis·cov·er entdecken; ausfindig machen, (heraus)finden
dis·cov·e·ry Entdeckung f
dis·cred·it 1. Zweifel m; Misskredit m, schlechter Ruf; bring discredit (up)on in Verruf bringen; 2. nicht glauben; in Misskredit bringen
dis·creet besonnen, vorsichtig; diskret, verschwiegen
dis·crep·an·cy Diskrepanz f, Widerspruch m
dis·cre·tion Ermessen n, Gutdünken n; Diskretion f, Verschwiegenheit f
dis·crim·i·nate unterscheiden; discriminate against benachteiligen, diskriminieren
dis·crim·i·nat·ing kritisch, urteilsfähig
dis·crim·i·na·tion unterschiedliche (esp nachteilige) Behandlung; Diskriminierung f, Benachteiligung f; Urteilsfähigkeit f
dis·cus SPORT Diskus m
dis·cuss diskutieren, erörtern, besprechen
dis·cus·sion Diskussion f, Besprechung f
dis·cus throw SPORT Diskuswerfen n
dis·cus throw·er SPORT Diskuswerfer(in)
dis·ease Krankheit f
dis·eased krank
dis·em·bark von Bord gehen (lassen); MAR Waren ausladen
dis·en·chant·ed: be disenchanted with sich keine Illusionen mehr machen über (acc)
dis·en·gage (sich) frei machen; losmachen; TECH auskuppeln, loskuppeln
dis·en·tan·gle entwirren; (sich) befreien
dis·fa·vo(u)r Missfallen n; Ungnade f

dis·fig·ure entstellen
dis·grace 1. Schande f; Ungnade f; 2 Schande bringen über (acc), j-m Schand bereiten
dis·grace·ful schändlich; skandalös
dis·guise 1. verkleiden (as als); Stimm etc verstellen; et. verbergen, verschlei ern; 2. Verkleidung f; Verstellung f; Ve schleierung f; in disguise maskiert, ve kleidet; fig verkappt; in the disguise o verkleidet als
dis·gust 1. Ekel m, Abscheu m; 2. (an) ekeln; empören, entrüsten
dis·gust·ing ekelhaft
dish 1. flache Schüssel; (Servier)Platte f GASTR Gericht n, Speise f; the dishes da Geschirr; wash or do the dishes abspü len, abwaschen; 2. dish out F austeilen often dish up Speisen anrichten, auftra gen; F Geschichte etc auftischen
dish·cloth Geschirrtuch n
dis·heart·en entmutigen
di·shev·el(l)ed zerzaust
dis·hon·est unehrlich, unredlich
dis·hon·es·ty Unehrlichkeit f; Unred lichkeit f
dis·hon·o(u)r 1. Schande f; 2. Schande bringen über (acc); ECON Wechsel nich honorieren or einlösen
dis·hon·o(u)·ra·ble schändlich, unehren haft
dish·wash·er Tellerwäscher m, Spü ler(in); TECH Geschirrspülmaschine f Geschirrspüler m
dish·wa·ter Spülwasser n
dis·il·lu·sion 1. Ernüchterung f, Desillusi on f; 2. ernüchtern, desillusionieren; be disillusioned with sich keine Illusionen mehr machen über (acc)
dis·in·clined abgeneigt
dis·in·fect MED desinfizieren
dis·in·fec·tant Desinfektionsmittel n
dis·in·her·it JUR enterben
dis·in·te·grate (sich) auflösen; verfallen, zerfallen
dis·in·terest·ed uneigennützig, selbstlos; objektiv, unvoreingenommen
disk Scheibe f; (Schall)Platte f; Park scheibe f; EDP Diskette f; Anat Band scheibe f; slipped disk MED Bandschei benvorfall m
disk drive EDP Diskettenlaufwerk n
disk·ette EDP Floppy f, Diskette f
disk jock·ey Diskjockey m
disk park·ing MOT Parken n mit Park scheibe
dis·like 1. Abneigung f, Widerwille m (of, for gegen); take a dislike to s.o. gegen j-n e-e Abneigung fassen; 2. nicht leiden

43 dissipate

können, nicht mögen

dis·lo·cate MED sich *den Arm etc* verrenken *or* ausrenken

dis·loy·al treulos, untreu

dis·mal trüb(e), trostlos, elend

dis·man·tle TECH demontieren

dis·may 1. Schreck(en) *m*, Bestürzung *f*; *in dismay, with dismay* bestürzt; *to my dismay* zu m-r Bestürzung; **2.** *v/t* erschrecken, bestürzen

dis·miss *v/t* entlassen; wegschicken; ablehnen; *Thema etc* fallen lassen; JUR abweisen

dis·miss·al Entlassung *f*; Aufgabe *f*, JUR Abweisung *f*

dis·mount *v/i* absteigen, absitzen (*from* von); *v/t* demontieren; TECH auseinandernehmen

dis·o·be·di·ence Ungehorsam *m*

dis·o·be·di·ent ungehorsam

dis·o·bey nicht gehorchen, ungehorsam sein (*gegen*)

dis·or·der Unordnung *f*; Aufruhr *m*; MED Störung *f*

dis·or·der·ly unordentlich; ordnungswidrig; unruhig; aufrührerisch

dis·or·gan·ize durcheinanderbringen; desorganisieren

dis·own nicht anerkennen; *Kind* verstoßen; ablehnen

dis·par·age verächtlich machen, herabsetzen; gering schätzen

dis·par·i·ty Ungleichheit *f*; *disparity of or in age* Altersunterschied *m*

dis·pas·sion·ate leidenschaftslos; objektiv

dis·patch 1. schnelle Erledigung; (Ab-)Sendung *f*; Abfertigung *f*; Eile *f*; (Eil-)Botschaft *f*; Bericht *m*; **2.** schnell erledigen; absenden, abschicken, *Telegramm* aufgeben, abfertigen

dis·pel *Menge etc* zerstreuen (*a. fig*), *Nebel* zerteilen

dis·pen·sa·ble entbehrlich

dis·pen·sa·ry Werks-, Krankenhaus-, Schul-, MIL Lazarettapotheke *f*

dis·pen·sa·tion Austeilung *f*; Befreiung *f*; Dispens *m*; göttliche Fügung

dis·pense austeilen; *Recht* sprechen; *Arzneien* zubereiten und abgeben; *dispense with* auskommen ohne; überflüssig machen

dis·pens·er Spender *m*, *a.* Abroller *m* (*for adhesive tape etc*), (*Briefmarken-etc*)Automat *m*

dis·perse verstreuen; (sich) zerstreuen

dis·pir·it·ed entmutigt

dis·place verschieben; ablösen, entlassen; *j-n* verschleppen; ersetzen; verdrängen

dis·play 1. Entfaltung *f*; (Her)Zeigen *n*; (protzige) Zurschaustellung; EDP Display *n*, Bildschirm *m*, Datenanzeige *f*; ECON Display *n*, Auslage *f*; *be on display* ausgestellt sein; **2.** entfalten; zur Schau stellen; zeigen

dis·please *j-m* missfallen

dis·pleased ungehalten

dis·pleas·ure Missfallen *n*

dis·pos·a·ble Einweg...; Wegwerf...

dis·pos·al Beseitigung *f*, Entsorgung *f*; Endlagerung *f*; Verfügung(srecht *n*) *f*; *be (put) at s.o.'s disposal* j-m zur Verfügung stehen (stellen)

dis·pose *v/t* (an)ordnen, einrichten; geneigt machen, bewegen; *v/i*: *dispose of* verfügen über (*acc*); erledigen; loswerden; wegschaffen, beseitigen; *Abfall, a. Atommüll etc* entsorgen

dis·posed geneigt; ...gesinnt

dis·po·si·tion Veranlagung *f*

dis·pos·sess enteignen, vertreiben; berauben (*of* gen)

dis·pro·por·tion·ate(·ly) unverhältnismäßig

dis·prove widerlegen

di·spute 1. Disput *m*, Kontroverse *f*; Streit *m*; Auseinandersetzung *f*; **2.** streiten (über *acc*); bezweifeln

dis·qual·i·fy unfähig *or* untauglich machen; für untauglich erklären; SPORT disqualifizieren

dis·re·gard 1. Nichtbeachtung *f*; Missachtung *f*; **2.** nicht beachten

dis·rep·u·ta·ble übel; verrufen

dis·re·pute schlechter Ruf

dis·re·spect Respektlosigkeit *f*; Unhöflichkeit *f*

dis·re·spect·ful respektlos; unhöflich

dis·rupt unterbrechen

dis·sat·is·fac·tion Unzufriedenheit *f*

dis·sat·is·fied unzufrieden (*with* mit)

dis·sect MED sezieren, zerlegen, zergliedern (*a. fig*)

dis·sen·sion Meinungsverschiedenheit(en *pl*) *f*, Differenz(en *pl*) *f*; Uneinigkeit *f*

dis·sent 1. abweichende Meinung; **2.** anderer Meinung sein (*from* als)

dis·sent·er Andersdenkende *m, f*

dis·si·dent Andersdenkende *m, f*, POL Dissident(in), Regime-, Systemkritiker(-in)

dis·sim·i·lar (to) unähnlich (*dat*); verschieden (von)

dis·sim·u·la·tion Verstellung *f*

dis·si·pate (sich) zerstreuen; verschwenden

dis·si·pat·ed ausschweifend, zügellos

dis·so·ci·ate trennen; **dissociate o.s.** sich distanzieren (**from** von)

dis·so·lute → **dissipated**

dis·so·lu·tion Auflösung f

dis·solve (sich) auflösen

dis·suade j-m abraten (**from** von)

dis·tance 1. Abstand m; Entfernung f; Ferne f; Strecke f; fig Distanz f, Zurückhaltung f; **at a distance** von weitem; in einiger Entfernung; **keep s.o. at a distance** j-m gegenüber reserviert sein; **2.** hinter sich lassen

distance race SPORT Langstreckenlauf m

distance run·ner SPORT Langstreckenläufer(in), Langstreckler(in)

dis·tant entfernt; fern, Fern…; distanziert

dis·taste Widerwille m, Abneigung f

dis·taste·ful ekelerregend; unangenehm; **be distasteful to s.o.** j-m zuwider sein

dis·tem·per VET Staupe f

dis·tend (sich) (aus)dehnen; (auf)blähen; sich weiten

dis·til(l) destillieren

dis·tinct verschieden; deutlich, klar

dis·tinc·tion Unterscheidung f; Unterschied m; Auszeichnung f; Rang m

dis·tinc·tive unterscheidend; kennzeichnend, bezeichnend

dis·tin·guish unterscheiden; auszeichnen; **distinguish o.s.** sich auszeichnen

dis·tin·guished berühmt; ausgezeichnet; vornehm

dis·tort verdrehen; verzerren

dis·tract ablenken

dis·tract·ed beunruhigt, besorgt; (**by, with** vor dat) außer sich, wahnsinnig

dis·trac·tion Ablenkung f; Zerstreuung f; Wahnsinn m; **drive s.o. to distraction** j-n wahnsinnig machen

dis·traught → **distracted**

dis·tress 1. Leid n, Kummer m, Sorge f; Not(lage) f; **2.** beunruhigen, mit Sorge erfüllen

dis·tressed Not leidend

distressed ar·e·a Notstandsgebiet n

dis·tress·ing besorgniserregend

dis·trib·ute ver-, aus-, zuteilen; ECON Waren vertreiben, absetzen; Filme verleihen

dis·tri·bu·tion Ver-, Aus-, Zuteilung f; ECON Vertrieb m, Absatz m; film: Verleih m

dis·trict Bezirk m; Gegend f

dis·trust 1. Misstrauen n; **2.** misstrauen (dat)

dis·trust·ful misstrauisch

dis·turb stören; beunruhigen

dis·turb·ance Störung f; Unruhe f; **disturbance of the peace** JUR Störung f der öffentlichen Sicherheit und Ordnung; **cause a disturbance** für Unruhe sorgen; ruhestörenden Lärm machen

dis·turbed geistig gestört; verhaltensgestört

dis·used nicht mehr benutzt (machinery etc), stillgelegt (colliery etc)

ditch Graben m

di·van Diwan m

divan bed Bettcouch f

dive 1. (unter)tauchen; vom Sprungbrett springen; e-n Hecht- or Kopfsprung machen; hechten (**for** nach); e-n Sturzflug machen; **2.** swimming: Springen n; Kopfsprung m, Hechtsprung m; soccer: Schwalbe f; AVIAT Sturzflug m; F Spelunke f

div·er Taucher(in); SPORT Wasserspringer(in)

di·verge auseinanderlaufen; abweichen

di·ver·gence Abweichung f

di·ver·gent abweichend

di·verse verschieden; mannigfaltig

di·ver·si·fy verschieden(artig) or abwechslungsreich gestalten

di·ver·sion Ablenkung f; Zeitvertreib m; Br MOT Umleitung f

di·ver·si·ty Verschiedenheit f; Mannigfaltigkeit f

di·vert ablenken; j-n zerstreuen, unterhalten; Br Verkehr umleiten

di·vide 1. v/t teilen; ver-, aus-, aufteilen; trennen; MATH dividieren, teilen (**by** durch); v/i sich teilen; sich aufteilen; MATH sich dividieren or teilen lassen (**by** durch); **2.** GEOGR Wasserscheide f

di·vid·ed geteilt; **divided highway** Schnellstraße f

div·i·dend ECON Dividende f

di·vid·ers (**a pair of dividers**) ein) Stechzirkel m

di·vine göttlich

di·vine ser·vice REL Gottesdienst m

div·ing 1. Tauchen n; SPORT Wasserspringen n; **2.** Taucher…

div·ing·board Sprungbrett n

div·ing·suit Taucheranzug m

di·vin·i·ty Gottheit f; Göttlichkeit f; Theologie f

di·vis·i·ble teilbar

di·vi·sion Teilung f; Trennung f; Abteilung f; MIL, MATH Division f

di·vorce 1. (Ehe)Scheidung f; **get a divorce** sich scheiden lassen (**from** von); **2.** JUR j-n, Ehe scheiden; **get divorced** sich scheiden lassen

di·vor·cee Geschiedene m, f

DIY ABBR → **do-it-yourself**

DIY store Baumarkt m

diz·zy schwind(e)lig

do v/t tun, machen; (zu)bereiten; *Zimmer* aufräumen; *Geschirr* abwaschen; *Wegstrecke* zurücklegen, schaffen; **do you know him? no, I don't** kennst du ihn? nein; **what can I do for you?** was kann ich für Sie tun?, womit kann ich (Ihnen) dienen?; **do London** F London besichtigen; **have s.o.'s hair done** sich die Haare machen *or* frisieren lassen; **have done reading** fertig sein mit Lesen; v/i tun, handeln; sich befinden; genügen; **that will do** das genügt; **how do you do?** guten Tag!; **do be quick** beeil dich doch; **do you like New York? I do** gefällt Ihnen New York? ja; **she works hard, doesn't she?** sie arbeitet viel, nicht wahr?; **do well** s-e Sache gut machen; gute Geschäfte machen; **do away with** beseitigen, weg-, abschaffen; **do s.o. in** F j-n umlegen; **I'm done in** F ich bin geschafft; **do up** *Kleid etc* zumachen; *Haus etc* instand setzen; *Päckchen* zurechtmachen; **do o.s. up** sich zurechtmachen; **I could do with ...** ich könnte ... brauchen *or* vertragen; **do without** auskommen *or* sich behelfen ohne

doc F → **doctor**

do·cile gelehrig; fügsam

dock¹ stutzen, kupieren

dock² **1.** MAR Dock n; Kai m, Pier m; JUR Anklagebank f; **2.** v/t MAR (ein)docken; *Raumschiff* koppeln; v/i MAR anlegen; andocken, ankoppeln (*Raumschiff*)

dock·er Dock-, Hafenarbeiter m

dock·ing Docking n, Ankopp(e)lung f

dock·yard MAR Werft f

doc·tor Doktor m (a. UNIV), Arzt m, Ärztin f

doc·tor·al: *doctoral thesis* UNIV Doktorarbeit f

doc·trine Doktrin f, Lehre f

doc·u·ment 1. Urkunde f; **2.** (urkundlich) belegen

doc·u·men·ta·ry 1. urkundlich; *film etc:* Dokumentar...; **2.** Dokumentarfilm m

dodge (rasch) zur Seite springen, ausweichen; F sich drücken (vor *dat*)

dodg·er Drückeberger m

doe ZO (Reh)Geiß f, Ricke f

dog 1. ZO Hund m; **2.** j-n beharrlich verfolgen

dog-eared mit Eselsohren (*book*)

dog·ged verbissen, hartnäckig

dog·ma Dogma n; Glaubenssatz m

dog·mat·ic dogmatisch

do-it-your·self 1. Heimwerken f. Heimwerker...

do-it-your·self·er Heimwerker m

dole 1. milde Gabe; *Br* F Stempelgeld n; **go** *or* **be on the dole** *Br* F stempeln gehen; **2. dole out** sparsam ver- *or* austeilen

dole·ful traurig, trübselig

doll Puppe f

dol·lar Dollar m

dol·phin ZO Delphin m

dome Kuppel f

do·mes·tic 1. häuslich; inländisch, einheimisch; zahm; **2.** Hausangestellte m, f

do·mes·tic an·i·mal Haustier n

do·mes·tic flight AVIAT Inlandsflug m

domestic mar·ket ECON Binnenmarkt m

domestic trade ECON Binnenhandel m

domestic vi·o·lence häusliche Gewalt

dom·i·cile Wohnsitz m

dom·i·nant dominierend, (vor)herrschend

dom·i·nate beherrschen; dominieren

dom·i·na·tion (Vor)Herrschaft f

dom·i·neer·ing herrisch, tyrannisch

do·nate schenken; stiften; spenden (a. MED)

do·na·tion Schenkung f

done getan; erledigt; fertig; GASTR gar

don·key ZO Esel m

do·nor Spender(in) (a. MED)

do-noth·ing F Nichtstuer m

doom 1. Schicksal n, Verhängnis n; **2.** verurteilen, verdammen

Dooms·day der Jüngste Tag

door Tür f; Tor n; **next door** nebenan

door·bell Türklingel f

door han·dle Türklinke f

door·keep·er Pförtner m

door·knob Türknauf m

door·mat (Fuß)Abtreter m

door·step Türstufe f

door·way Türöffnung f

dope 1. F Stoff m (*Rauschgift*); Betäubungsmittel n; SPORT Dopingmittel n; sl Trottel m; **2.** F j-m Stoff geben; SPORT dopen

dope test SPORT Dopingkontrolle f

dor·mant schlafend, ruhend; untätig

dor·mi·to·ry Schlafsaal m; Studentenwohnheim n

dor·mo·bile® Campingbus m, Wohnmobil n

dor·mouse ZO Haselmaus f

dose 1. Dosis f; **2.** j-m e-e Medizin geben

dot 1. Punkt m; Fleck m; **on the dot** F auf die Sekunde pünktlich; **2.** punktieren; tüpfeln; *fig* sprenkeln; *dotted line* punktierte Linie

dote: dote on vernarrt sein in (*acc*)

dot·ing vernarrt

doub·le 1. doppelt; Doppel...; zweifach; **2.** Doppelte *n*; Doppelgänger(in); *film*, TV Double *n*; **3.** (sich) verdoppeln; *film*, TV *j*-n doubeln; *a.* **double up** falten; *Decke* zusammenlegen; **double back** kehrtmachen; **double up with** sich krümmen vor (*dat*)

dou·ble-breast·ed zweireihig

dou·ble-check genau nachprüfen

dou·ble chin Doppelkinn *n*

dou·ble-cross ein doppeltes *or* falsches Spiel treiben mit

dou·ble-deal·ing 1. betrügerisch; **2.** Betrug *m*

dou·ble-deck·er Doppeldecker *m*

dou·ble-edged zweischneidig (*a. fig*); zweideutig

dou·ble fea·ture *film*: Doppelprogramm *n*

dou·ble-park MOT in zweiter Reihe parken

dou·bles *esp tennis*: Doppel *n*; **men's doubles** Herrendoppel *n*; **women's doubles** Damendoppel *n*

dou·ble-sid·ed EDP zweiseitig

doubt 1. *v/i* zweifeln; *v/t* bezweifeln; misstrauen (*dat*); **2.** Zweifel *m*; **be in doubt about** Zweifel haben an (*dat*); **no doubt** ohne Zweifel

doubt·ful zweifelhaft

doubt·less ohne Zweifel

douche 1. Spülung *f* (*a.* MED); Spülapparat *m*; **2.** spülen (*a.* MED)

dough Teig *m*

dough·nut *appr* Krapfen *m*, Berliner Pfannkuchen, Schmalzkringel *m*

dove ZO Taube *f*

dow·dy unelegant; unmodern

dow·el TECH Dübel *m*

down¹ Daunen *pl*; Flaum *m*

down² 1. *adv* nach unten, herunter, hinunter, herab, hinab, abwärts; unten; **2.** *prp* herab, hinab, herunter, hinunter; **down the river** flussabwärts; **3.** *adj* nach unten gerichtet; deprimiert, niedergeschlagen; **down platform** Abfahrtsbahnsteig *m* (*in* London); **down train** Zug *m* (von London fort); **4.** *v/t* niederschlagen; *Flugzeug* abschießen; F *Getränk* runterkippen; **down tools** die Arbeit niederlegen, in den Streik treten

down·cast niedergeschlagen

down·fall Platzregen *m*; *fig* Sturz *m*

down·heart·ed niedergeschlagen

down·hill 1. *adv* bergab; **2.** *adj* abschüssig; *skiing*: Abfahrts...; **3.** Abhang *m*; *skiing*: Abfahrt *f*

down pay·ment ECON Anzahlung *f*

down·pour Regenguss *m*, Platzregen *m*

down·right 1. *adv* völlig, ganz und gar, ausgesprochen; **2.** *adj* glatt (*lie etc*); ausgesprochen

downs Hügelland *n*

down·stairs die Treppe herunter *or* hinunter; (nach) unten

down·stream stromabwärts

down-to-earth realistisch

down·town 1. *adv* im *or* ins Geschäftsviertel; **2.** *adj* im Geschäftsviertel (gelegen *or* tätig); **3.** Geschäftsviertel *n*, Innenstadt *f*, City *f*

down·ward(s) abwärts, nach unten

down·y flaumig

dow·ry Mitgift *f*

doze 1. dösen, ein Nickerchen machen; **2.** Nickerchen *n*

doz·en Dutzend *n*

drab trist; düster; eintönig

draft 1. Entwurf *m*; (Luft)Zug *m*; Zugluft *f*; Zug *m*, Schluck *m*; MAR Tiefgang *m*; ECON Tratte *f*, Wechsel *m*; MIL Einberufung *f*; **beer on draft, draft beer** Bier *n* vom Fass, Fassbier *n*; **2.** entwerfen; *Brief etc* aufsetzen; MIL einberufen

draft·ee MIL Wehr(dienst)pflichtige *m*

drafts·man TECH Zeichner *m*

drafts·wom·an TECH Zeichnerin *f*

draft·y zugig

drag 1. Schleppen *n*, Zerren *n*; *fig* Hemmschuh *m*; F *et.* Langweiliges; **2.** schleppen, zerren, ziehen, schleifen; *a.* **drag behind** zurückbleiben, nachhinken; **drag on** weiterschleppen; *fig* sich dahinschleppen; *fig* sich in die Länge ziehen

drag lift Schlepplift *m*

drag·on MYTH Drache *m*

drag·on·fly ZO Libelle *f*

drain 1. Abfluss(kanal) *m*, Abflussrohr *n*; Entwässerungsgraben *m*; **2.** *v/t* abfließen lassen; entwässern; austrinken, leeren; *v/i*: **drain off, drain away** abfließen, ablaufen

drain·age Abfließen *n*, Ablaufen *n*, Entwässerung *f*; Entwässerungsanlage *f*, -system *n*

drain·pipe Abflussrohr *n*

drake ZO Enterich *m*, Erpel *m*

dram Schluck *m*

dra·ma Drama *n*

dra·mat·ic dramatisch

dram·a·tist Dramatiker *m*

dram·a·tize dramatisieren

drape 1. drapieren; in Falten legen; **2.** *mst* **drapes** Vorhänge *pl*

drap·er·y Br Textilien *pl*

dras·tic drastisch, durchgreifend

draught Br → **draft**

draughts Br Damespiel *n*

draughts·man etc → draftsman etc

draugh·ty Br → drafty

draw 1. v/t ziehen; *Vorhänge* auf-, zuziehen; *Atem* holen; *Tee* ziehen lassen; *fig Menge* anziehen; *Interesse* auf sich ziehen; zeichnen; *Geld* abheben; *Scheck* ausstellen; v/i ziehen; SPORT unentschieden spielen; **draw back** zurückweichen; **draw near** sich nähern; **draw out** *Geld* abheben; *fig* in die Länge ziehen; **draw up** *Schriftstück* aufsetzen; MOT (an)halten; vorfahren; 2. Ziehen *n*; *lottery*: Ziehung *f*; SPORT Unentschieden *n*; Attraktion *f*, Zugnummer *f*

draw·back Nachteil *m*, Hindernis *n*

draw·bridge Zugbrücke *f*

draw·er[1] Schublade *f*, Schubfach *n*

draw·er[2] Zeichner(in); ECON Aussteller(-in)

draw·ing Zeichnen *n*; Zeichnung *f*

drawing board Reißbrett *n*

drawing pin *Br* Reißzwecke *f*, Reißnagel *m*, Heftzwecke *f*

drawing room → *living room*; Salon *m*

drawl gedehnt sprechen

drawn abgespannt; SPORT unentschieden

dread 1. (große) Angst, Furcht *f*; 2. (sich) fürchten

dread·ful schrecklich, furchtbar

dream 1. Traum *m*; 2. träumen

dream·er Träumer(in)

dream·y träumerisch, verträumt

dredge 1. (Schwimm)Bagger *m*; 2. (aus)baggern

dredg·er (Schwimm)Bagger *m*

dregs Bodensatz *m*; *fig* Abschaum *m*

drench durchnässen

dress 1. Kleidung *f*; Kleid *n*; 2. (sich) ankleiden *or* anziehen; schmücken, dekorieren; zurechtmachen; GASTR zubereiten, *Salat* anmachen; MED *Wunde* verbinden; *Haare* frisieren; **get dressed** sich anziehen; **dress s.o. down** F j-m e-e Standpauke halten; **dress up** (sich) fein machen; sich kostümieren *or* verkleiden

dress cir·cle THEA erster Rang

dress de·sign·er Modezeichner(in)

dress·er Anrichte *f*; Toilettentisch *m*

dress·ing An-, Zurichten *n*; Ankleiden *n*; MED Verband *m*; GASTR Dressing *n*, Füllung *f*

dressing-down F Standpauke *f*

dress·ing gown *esp Br* Morgenrock *m*, -mantel *m*; SPORT Bademantel *m*

dressing room THEA *etc* (Künstler)Garderobe *f*; SPORT (Umkleide)Kabine *f*

dressing ta·ble Toilettentisch *m*

dress·mak·er (Damen)Schneider(in)

dress re·hears·al THEA *etc* Generalprobe *f*

drib·ble tröpfeln (lassen); sabbern, geifern; *soccer*: dribbeln

dried getrocknet, Dörr...

dri·er → *dryer*

drift 1. (Dahin)Treiben *n*; (Schnee)Verwehung *f*; Schnee-, Sandwehe *f*; *fig* Tendenz *f*; 2. (dahin)treiben; wehen; sich häufen

drill 1. TECH Bohrer *m*; MIL Drill *m* (*a. fig*), Exerzieren *n*; 2. bohren; MIL drillen (*a. fig*)

drill·ing site TECH Bohrgelände *n*, Bohrstelle *f*

drink 1. Getränk *n*; 2. trinken; **drink to s.o.** j-m zuprosten *or* zutrinken

drink-driv·ing *Br* Trunkenheit *f* am Steuer

drink·er Trinker(in)

drinks ma·chine Getränkeautomat *m*

drip 1. Tröpfeln *n*; MED Tropf *m*; 2. tropfen *or* tröpfeln (lassen); triefen

drip-dry bügelfrei

drip·ping Bratenfett *n*

drive 1. Fahrt *f*; Aus-, Spazierfahrt *f*; Zufahrt(sstraße) *f*; (private) Auffahrt; TECH Antrieb *m*; EDP Laufwerk *n*; MOT (*Links-etc*)Steuerung *f*; PSYCH Trieb *m*; *fig* Kampagne *f*; *fig* Schwung *m*, Elan *m*, Dynamik *f*; 2. v/t treiben; *Auto etc* fahren, lenken, steuern; (im *Auto etc*) fahren; TECH (an)treiben; *a.* **drive off** vertreiben; v/i treiben; (*Auto*) fahren; **drive off** wegfahren; **what are you driving at?** F worauf wollen Sie hinaus?

drive-in 1. Auto...; **drive-in cinema** *Br*, **drive-in motion-picture theater** Autokino *n*; 2. Autokino *n*; Drive-in-Restaurant *n*; Autoschalter *m*, Drive-in-Schalter *m*

driv·el 1. faseln; 2. Geschwätz *n*, Gefasel *n*

driv·er MOT Fahrer(in); (*Lokomotiv*-)Führer *m*

driv·er's li·cense Führerschein *m*

driv·ing (an)treibend; TECH Antriebs..., Treib..., Trieb...; MOT Fahr...

driv·ing force *fig* Triebkraft *f*

driv·ing li·cence *Br* Führerschein *m*

driv·ing test Fahrprüfung *f*

driz·zle 1. Sprühregen *m*; 2. sprühen, nieseln

drone 1. ZO Drohne *f* (*a. fig*); 2. summen; dröhnen

droop (schlaff) herabhängen

drop 1. Tropfen *m*; Fallen *n*, Fall *m*; *fig* Fall *m*, Sturz *m*; Bonbon *m*, *n*; **fruit drops** Drops *pl*; 2. v/t tropfen (lassen); fallen lassen(*a. fig*); *Brief* einwerfen;

Fahrgast absetzen; senken; **drop s.o. a few lines** j-m ein paar Zeilen schreiben; *v/i* tropfen; herab-, herunterfallen; umsinken, fallen; **drop in** (kurz) hereinschauen; **drop off** abfallen; zurückgehen, nachlassen; F einnicken; **drop out** heraus fallen; aussteigen (*of* aus); *a.* **drop out of school** (**university**) die Schule (das Studium) abbrechen

drop·out Drop-out *m*, Aussteiger *m*; (Schul-, Studien)Abbrecher *m*

drought Trockenheit *f*, Dürre *f*

drown *v/t* ertränken; überschwemmen; *fig* übertönen; *v/i* ertrinken

drow·sy schläfrig; einschläfernd

drudge sich (ab)placken, schuften, sich schinden

drudg·e·ry (stumpfsinnige) Plackerei *or* Schinderei *or* Schufterei

drug 1. Arzneimittel *n*, Medikament *n*; Droge *f*, Rauschgift *n*; **be on drugs** drogenabhängig *or* drogensüchtig sein; **be off drugs** clean sein; **2.** j-m Medikamente geben; *j-n* unter Drogen setzen; ein Betäubungsmittel beimischen (*dat*); betäuben (*a. fig*)

drug a·buse Drogenmissbrauch *m*; Medikamentenmissbrauch *m*

drug ad·dict Drogenabhängige *m*, *f*, Drogensüchtige *m*, *f*; **be a drug addict** drogenabhängig *or* drogensüchtig sein

drug·gist Apotheker(in); Inhaber(in) e-s Drugstores

drug·store Apotheke *f*; Drugstore *m*

drug vic·tim Drogentote *m*, *f*

drum 1. MUS Trommel *f*; ANAT Trommelfell *n*; *pl* MUS Schlagzeug *n*; **2.** trommeln

drum·mer MUS Trommler *m*; Schlagzeuger *m*

drunk 1. *adj* betrunken; **get drunk** sich betrinken; **2.** Betrunkene *m*, *f*; → **drunkard**

drunk·ard Trinker(in), Säufer(in)

drunk driv·ing Trunkenheit *f* am Steuer

drunk·en betrunken

drunken driv·ing *Br* Trunkenheit *f* am Steuer

dry 1. trocken, GASTR *a.* herb; F durstig; **2.** trocknen; dörren; **dry out** trocknen; e-e Entziehungskur machen; F trocken werden; **dry up** austrocknen; versiegen

dry-clean chemisch reinigen

dry clean·er's chemische Reinigung

dry·er TECH Trockner *m*

dry goods Textilien *pl*

du·al doppelt, Doppel...

dual car·riageway *Br* Schnellstraße *f*

dub *Film* synchronisieren

du·bi·ous zweifelhaft

duch·ess Herzogin *f*

duck 1. ZO Ente *f*; Ducken *n*; F Schatz *m*; **2.** (unter)tauchen; (sich) ducken

duck·ling ZO Entchen *n*

due 1. zustehend; gebührend; angemessen; ECON fällig; **due to** wegen (*gen*) **be due to** zurückzuführen sein au (*acc*); **2.** *adv* direkt, genau (*nach Oster etc*)

du·el Duell *n*

dues Gebühren *pl*; Beitrag *m*

du·et MUS Duett *n*

duke Herzog *m*

dull 1. dumm; träge, schwerfällig; stumpf matt (*eyes etc*); schwach (*hearing*); langweilig; abgestumpft, teilnahmslos dumpf; trüb(e); ECON flau; **2.** stumpf machen *or* werden; (sich) trüben; mildern dämpfen; *Schmerz* betäuben; *fig* abstumpfen

du·ly ordnungsgemäß; gebührend; rechtzeitig

dumb stumm; sprachlos; F doof, dumm blöd

dum(b)·found·ed verblüfft, sprachlos

dum·my Attrappe *f*; Kleider-, Schaufensterpuppe *f*; MOT Dummy *m*, Puppe *f*; *Br* Schnuller *m*

dump 1. *v/t* (hin)plumpsen *or* (hin)fallen lassen; auskippen; *Schutt etc* abladen: *Schadstoffe* in e-n *Fluss etc* einleiten *im Meer* verklappen (**into** in); ECON *Waren* zu Dumpingpreisen verkaufen; **2.** Plumps *m*; Schuttabladeplatz *m*, Müllkippe *f*, Müllhalde *f*, (Müll)Deponie *f*

dump·ing ECON Dumping *n*, Ausfuhr *f* zu Schleuderpreisen

dune Düne *f*

dung AGR **1.** Dung *m*; **2.** düngen

dun·geon (Burg)Verlies *n*

dupe betrügen, täuschen

du·plex 1. doppelt, Doppel...; **2.** *a.* **duplex apartment** Maisonette *f*, Maisonettewohnung *f*; *a.* **duplex house** Doppel-, Zweifamilienhaus *n*

du·pli·cate 1. doppelt; **duplicate key** Zweit-, Nachschlüssel *m*; **2.** Duplikat *n*; Zweit-, Nachschlüssel *m*; **3.** doppelt ausfertigen; kopieren, vervielfältigen

du·plic·i·ty Doppelzüngigkeit *f*

du·ra·ble haltbar; dauerhaft

du·ra·tion Dauer *f*

du·ress Zwang *m*

dur·ing während

dusk (Abend)Dämmerung *f*

dusk·y dämmerig, düster (*a. fig*); schwärzlich

dust 1. Staub *m*; **2.** *v/t* abstauben; (be)streuen; *v/i* Staub wischen, abstauben

dust·bin *Br* Abfall-, Mülleimer *m*; Ab-

fall-, **Mülltonne** f
dustbin lin·er Br Müllbeutel m
dust-cart Br Müllwagen m
dust·er Staubtuch n
dust cov·er, dust jack·et Schutzumschlag m
dust·man Br Müllmann m
dust·pan Kehrichtschaufel f
dust·y staubig
Dutch 1. adj holländisch, niederländisch; **2.** adv: **go Dutch** getrennte Kasse machen; **3.** LING Holländisch n, Niederländisch n; **the Dutch** die Holländer pl, die Niederländer pl
Dutch·man Holländer m, Niederländer m
Dutch·wom·an Holländerin f, Niederländerin f
du·ti·a·ble ECON zollpflichtig
du·ty Pflicht f; Ehrerbietung f; ECON Abgabe f; Zoll m; Dienst m; **on duty** dienst-

habend; **be on duty** Dienst haben; **be off duty** dienstfrei haben
du·ty-free zollfrei
dwarf 1. Zwerg(in); **2.** verkleinern, klein erscheinen lassen
dwell wohnen; fig verweilen (**on** bei)
dwell·ing Wohnung f
dwin·dle (dahin)schwinden, abnehmen
dye 1. Farbe f; **of the deepest dye** fig von der übelsten Sorte; **2.** färben
dy·ing 1. sterbend; Sterbe…; **2.** Sterben n; **dying of forests** Waldsterben n
dyke → **dike**[1, 2]
dy·nam·ic dynamisch, kraftgeladen
dy·nam·ics Dynamik f
dy·na·mite 1. Dynamit n; **2.** (mit Dynamit) sprengen
dys·en·te·ry MED Ruhr f
dys·pep·si·a MED Verdauungsstörung f

E

E, e E, e n
each jede(r, -s); **each other** einander, sich; je, pro Person, pro Stück
ea·ger begierig; eifrig
ea·ger·ness Begierde f; Eifer m
ea·gle ZO Adler m; HIST Zehndollarstück n
ea·gle-eyed scharfsichtig
ear BOT Ähre f; ANAT Ohr n; Öhr n; Henkel m; **keep an ear to the ground** die Ohren offen halten
ear·ache Ohrenschmerzen pl
ear·drum ANAT Trommelfell n
earl englischer Graf
ear·lobe ANAT Ohrläppchen n
ear·ly früh; Früh…; Anfangs…, erste(r, -s); bald(ig); **as early as May** schon im Mai; **as early as possible** so bald wie möglich; **early on** schon früh, frühzeitig
ear·ly bird Frühaufsteher(in)
ear·ly warn·ing sys·tem MIL Frühwarnsystem n
ear·mark 1. Kennzeichen n; Merkmal n; **2.** kennzeichnen; zurücklegen (**for** für)
earn verdienen; einbringen
ear·nest 1. ernst, ernstlich; ernsthaft; ernst gemeint; **2.** Ernst m; **in earnest** im Ernst; ernsthaft
earn·ings Einkommen n

ear·phones Ohrhörer pl; Kopfhörer pl
ear·piece TEL Hörmuschel f
ear·ring Ohrring m
ear·shot: within (out of) earshot in (außer) Hörweite
earth 1. Erde f; Land n; **2.** v/t ELECTR erden
earth·en irden
earth·en·ware Steingut(geschirr) n
earth·ly irdisch, weltlich; F denkbar
earth·quake Erdbeben n
earth·worm ZO Regenwurm m
ease 1. Bequemlichkeit f; (Gemüts)Ruhe f; Sorglosigkeit f; Leichtigkeit f; **at (one's) ease** ruhig, entspannt; unbefangen; **be or feel ill at ease** sich (in s-r Haut) nicht wohlfühlen; **2.** v/t erleichtern; beruhigen; Schmerzen lindern; v/i mst **ease off, ease up** nachlassen; sich entspannen (situation etc)
ea·sel Staffelei f
east 1. Ost m; Osten m; **2.** adj östlich, Ost…; **3.** adv nach Osten, ostwärts
Eas·ter Ostern n; Oster…
Easter bun·ny Osterhase m
Easter egg Osterei n
eas·ter·ly östlich, Ost…
east·ern östlich, Ost…
east·ward(s) östlich, nach Osten
eas·y leicht; einfach; bequem; gemäch-

lich, gemütlich; ungezwungen; *go easy on* schonen, sparsam umgehen mit; *go easy, take it easy* sich Zeit lassen; *take it easy!* immer mit der Ruhe!

eas·y chair Sessel *m*

eas·y·go·ing gelassen; ungezwungen

eat essen; (zer)fressen; *eat out* essen gehen; *eat up* aufessen

eat·a·ble essbar, genießbar

eat·er Esser(in)

eaves Dachrinne *f*, Traufe *f*

eaves·drop (heimlich) lauschen *or* horchen; *eavesdrop on* belauschen

ebb 1. Ebbe *f*; **2.** zurückgehen; *ebb away* abnehmen

ebb tide Ebbe *f*

eb·o·ny Ebenholz *n*

ec ABBR *of* **Eurocheque** *Br* Eurocheque *m*

ec·cen·tric 1. exzentrisch; **2.** Exzentriker *m*, Sonderling *m*

ec·cle·si·as·tic, ec·cle·si·as·ti·cal geistlich, kirchlich

ech·o 1. Echo *n*; **2.** widerhallen; *fig* echoen, nachsprechen

e·clipse ASTR (*Sonnen-, Mond*)Finsternis *f*; *fig* Niedergang *m*

e·co·cide Umweltzerstörung *f*

e·co·lo·gi·cal ökologisch, Umwelt…

e·col·o·gist Ökologe *m*

e·col·o·gy Ökologie *f*

ec·o·nom·ic Wirtschafts…, wirtschaftlich; *economic growth* Wirtschaftswachstum *n*

ec·o·nom·i·cal wirtschaftlich, sparsam

ec·o·nom·ics Volkswirtschaft(slehre) *f*

e·con·o·mist Volkswirt *m*

e·con·o·mize sparsam wirtschaften (mit)

e·con·o·my 1. Wirtschaft *f*; Wirtschaftlichkeit *f*, Sparsamkeit *f*; Einsparung *f*; **2.** Spar…

e·co·sys·tem Ökosystem *n*

ec·sta·sy Ekstase *f*, Verzückung *f*

ec·stat·ic verzückt

ed·dy 1. Wirbel *m*; **2.** wirbeln

edge 1. Schneide *f*; Rand *m*; Kante *f*; Schärfe *f*; *be on edge* nervös *or* gereizt sein; **2.** schärfen; (um)säumen; (sich) drängen

edge·ways, edge·wise seitlich, von der Seite

edg·ing Einfassung *f*; Rand *m*

edg·y scharf(kantig); F nervös; F gereizt

ed·i·ble essbar, genießbar

e·dict Edikt *n*

ed·i·fice Gebäude *n*

ed·it *Text* herausgeben, redigieren; EDP editieren; *Zeitung* als Herausgeber leiten

e·di·tion (*Buch*)Ausgabe *f*; Auflage *f*

ed·i·tor Herausgeber(in); Redakteur(in)

ed·i·to·ri·al 1. Leitartikel *m*; **2.** Redaktions…

EDP ABBR *of* **electronic data processing** EDV, elektronische Datenverarbeitung

ed·u·cate erziehen; unterrichten

ed·u·cat·ed gebildet

ed·u·ca·tion Erziehung *f*; (Aus)Bildung *f*; Bildungs-, Schulwesen *n*; *Ministry of Education* appr Unterrichtsministerium

ed·u·ca·tion·al erzieherisch, pädagogisch, Erziehungs…; Bildungs…

ed·u·ca·tion·(al·)ist Pädagoge *m*

eel ZO Aal *m*

ef·fect (Aus)Wirkung *f*; Effekt *m*, Eindruck *m*; *pl* ECON Effekten *pl*; *be in effect* in Kraft sein; *in effect* in Wirklichkeit; *take effect* in Kraft treten

ef·fec·tive wirksam; eindrucksvoll; tatsächlich

ef·fem·i·nate verweichlicht; weibisch

ef·fer·vesce brausen, sprudeln

ef·fer·ves·cent sprudelnd, schäumend

ef·fi·cien·cy Leistung *f*; Leistungsfähigkeit *f*; *efficiency measure* ECON Rationalisierungsmaßnahme *f*

ef·fi·cient wirksam; leistungsfähig, tüchtig

ef·flu·ent Abwasser *n*, Abwässer *pl*

ef·fort Anstrengung *f*, Bemühung *f* (*at* um); Mühe *f*; *without effort → ef·fort·less* mühelos, ohne Anstrengung

ef·fron·te·ry Frechheit *f*

ef·fu·sive überschwänglich

egg¹ Ei *n*; *put all one's eggs in one basket* alles auf eine Karte setzen

egg² *egg on* anstacheln

egg co·sy *Br* Eierwärmer *m*

egg·cup Eierbecher *m*

egg·head F Eierkopf *m*

egg·plant BOT Aubergine *f*

egg·shell Eierschale *f*

egg tim·er Eieruhr *f*

e·go·is·m Egoismus *m*, Selbstsucht *f*

e·go·ist Egoist(in)

E·gypt Ägypten *n*

E·gyp·tian 1. ägyptisch; **2.** Ägypter(in)

ei·der·down Eiderdaunen *pl*; Daunendecke *f*

eight 1. acht; **2.** Acht *f*

eigh·teen 1. achtzehn; **2.** Achtzehn *f*

eigh·teenth achtzehnte(r, -s)

eight·fold achtfach

eighth 1. achte(r, -s); **2.** Achtel *n*

eighth·ly achtens

eigh·ti·eth achtzigste(r, -s)

eigh·ty 1. achtzig; *the eighties* die Achtzigerjahre; **2.** Achtzig *f*

ei·ther jede(r, -s) (*von zweien*): eine(r, -s)

(von zweien); beides; *either ... or* entweder ... oder; *not either* auch nicht
e·jac·u·late v/t Samen ausstoßen; v/i eja-
kulieren, e-n Samenerguss haben
e·jac·u·la·tion Samenerguss *m*
e·ject *j-n* hinauswerfen; TECH ausstoßen,
auswerfen
eke: *eke out Vorräte etc* strecken; *Einkommen* aufbessern; *eke out a living*
sich (mühsam) durchschlagen
e·lab·o·rate 1. sorgfältig (aus)gearbeitet;
kompliziert; **2.** sorgfältig ausarbeiten
e·lapse verfließen, verstreichen
e·las·tic 1. elastisch, dehnbar; *elastic
band Br* → **2.** Gummiring *m*, Gummiband *n*
e·las·ti·ci·ty Elastizität *f*
e·lat·ed begeistert (*at, by* von)
el·bow 1. Ellbogen *m*; (scharfe) Biegung;
TECH Knie *n*; *at one's elbow* bei der
Hand; **2.** mit dem Ellbogen (weg)stoßen;
elbow one's way through sich (mit den
Ellbogen) e-n Weg bahnen durch
el·der¹ 1. ältere(r, -s); **2.** der, die Ältere;
(Kirchen)Älteste(r) *m*
el·der² BOT Holunder *m*
el·der·ly ältlich, ältere(r, -s)
el·dest älteste(r, -s)
e·lect 1. gewählt; **2.** (aus-, er)wählen
e·lec·tion Wahl *f*
election vic·to·ry POL Wahlsieg *m*
election win·ner POL Wahlsieger *m*
e·lec·tor Wähler(in); POL Wahlmann *m*;
HIST Kurfürst *m*
e·lec·to·ral Wähler..., Wahl...; *electoral
college* POL Wahlmänner *pl*; *electoral
district* POL Wahlkreis *m*
elec·to·rate POL Wähler(schaft *f*) *pl*
e·lec·tric elektrisch, Elektro...
e·lec·tri·cal elektrisch; Elektro...
electrical en·gi·neer Elektroingenieur *m*,
Elektrotechniker *m*
electrical en·gi·neer·ing Eletrotechnik *f*
e·lec·tric chair elektrischer Stuhl
e·lec·tri·cian Elektriker *m*
e·lec·tri·ci·ty Elektrizität *f*
e·lec·tric ra·zor Elektrorasierer *m*
e·lec·tri·fy elektrifizieren; elektrisieren
(a. fig)
e·lec·tro·cute auf dem elektrischen Stuhl
hinrichten; durch elektrischen Strom töten
e·lec·tron Elektron *n*
e·lec·tron·ic elektronisch, Elektronen...
electronic da·ta pro·cess·ing elektronische Datenverarbeitung
e·lec·tron·ics Elektronik *f*
el·e·gance Eleganz *f*
el·egant elegant; geschmackvoll; erst-

klassig
el·e·ment CHEM Element *n*; Urstoff *m*;
(Grund)Bestandteil *m*; *pl* Anfangsgründe *pl*, Grundlage(n *pl*) *f*; Elemente *pl*,
Naturkräfte *pl*
el·e·men·tal elementar; wesentlich
el·e·men·ta·ry elementar; Anfangs...
elementary school Grundschule *f*
el·e·phant ZO Elefant *m*
el·e·vate erhöhen; *fig* erheben
el·e·vat·ed erhöht; *fig* gehoben, erhaben
el·e·va·tion Erhebung *f*; Erhöhung *f*; Höhe *f*; Erhabenheit *f*
el·e·va·tor TECH Lift *m*, Fahrstuhl *m*, Aufzug *m*
e·lev·en 1. elf; **2.** Elf *f*
e·lev·enth 1. elfte(r, -s); **2.** Elftel *n*
elf Elf *m*, Elfe *f*; Kobold *m*
e·li·cit *et.* entlocken (*from dat*); ans (Tages)Licht bringen
el·i·gi·ble infrage kommend, geeignet;
annehmbar, akzeptabel
e·lim·i·nate entfernen, beseitigen; ausscheiden
e·lim·i·na·tion Entfernung *f*, Beseitigung
f; Ausscheidung *f*
é·lite Elite *f*; Auslese *f*
elk ZO Elch *m*; Wapitihirsch *m*
el·lipse MATH Ellipse *f*
elm BOT Ulme *f*
e·lon·gate verlängern
e·lope (mit s-m *or* s-r Geliebten) ausreißen *or* durchbrennen
el·o·quent redegewandt, beredt
else sonst, weiter; andere(r, -s)
else·where anderswo(hin)
e·lude geschickt entgehen, ausweichen,
sich entziehen (*all: dat*); *fig* nicht einfallen (*dat*)
e·lu·sive schwer fassbar
e·ma·ci·ated abgezehrt; ausgemergelt
em·a·nate ausströmen; ausgehen (*from*
von)
em·a·na·tion Ausströmen *n*; *fig* Ausstrahlung *f*
e·man·ci·pate emanzipieren
e·man·ci·pa·tion Emanzipation *f*
em·balm (ein)balsamieren
em·bank·ment (Bahn-, Straßen-) Damm
m; (Erd)Damm *m*; Uferstraße *f*
em·bar·go ECON Embargo *n*, (Hafen-,
Handels)Sperre *f*
em·bark AVIAT, MAR an Bord nehmen *or* gehen, MAR *a.* (sich) einschiffen; *Waren* ver-
laden; *embark on et.* anfangen, *et.* beginnen
em·bar·rass in Verlegenheit bringen, verlegen machen, in e-e peinliche Lage
bringen

em·bar·rass·ing unangenehm, peinlich; verfänglich

em·bar·rass·ment Verlegenheit f

em·bas·sy POL Botschaft f

em·bed (ein)betten, (ein)lagern

em·bel·lish verschönern; fig ausschmücken, beschönigen

em·bers Glut f

em·bez·zle unterschlagen

em·bez·zle·ment Unterschlagung f

em·bit·ter verbittern

em·blem Sinnbild n; Wahrzeichen n

em·bod·y verkörpern; enthalten

em·bo·lis·m MED Embolie f

em·brace 1. (sich) umarmen; einschließen; 2. Umarmung f

em·broi·der (be)sticken; fig ausschmücken

em·broi·der·y Stickerei f; fig Ausschmückung f

em·broil verwickeln (in in acc)

e·mend Texte verbessern, korrigieren

em·e·rald 1. Smaragd m; 2. smaragdgrün

e·merge auftauchen; sich herausstellen or ergeben

e·mer·gen·cy 1. Not f, Notlage f, Notfall m, Notstand m; state of emergency POL Ausnahmezustand m; 2. Not...

emergency brake Notbremse f

emergency call Notruf m

emergency ex·it Notausgang m

emergency land·ing AVIAT Notlandung f

emergency num·ber Notruf(nummer f) m

emergency room MED Notaufnahme f

em·i·grant Auswanderer m, esp POL Emigrant(in)

em·i·grate auswandern, esp POL emigrieren

em·i·gra·tion Auswanderung f, esp POL Emigration f

em·i·nence Berühmtheit f, Bedeutung f; Eminence REL Eminenz f

em·i·nent hervorragend, berühmt; bedeutend

eminently ganz besonders, äußerst

e·mis·sion Ausstoß m, Ausstrahlung f, Ausströmen n

emission-free abgasfrei

e·mit aussenden, ausstoßen, ausstrahlen, ausströmen; von sich geben

e·mo·tion (Gemüts)Bewegung f, Gefühl n, Gefühlsregung f; Rührung f

e·mo·tion·al emotional; gefühlsmäßig; gefühlsbetont

e·mo·tion·al·ly emotional, gefühlsmäßig; emotionally disturbed seelisch gestört

e·mo·tion·less gefühllos

e·mo·tive word PSYCH Reizwort n

em·pe·ror Kaiser m

em·pha·sis Gewicht n; Nachdruck m

em·pha·size nachdrücklich betonen

em·phat·ic nachdrücklich; deutlich; bestimmt

em·pire Reich n, Imperium n; Kaiserreich n

em·pir·i·cal erfahrungsgemäß

em·ploy 1. beschäftigen, anstellen; anverwenden, gebrauchen; 2. Beschäftigung f; in the employ of angestellt bei;

em·ploy·ee Angestellte m, f, Arbeitnehmer(in)

em·ploy·er Arbeitgeber(in)

em·ploy·ment Beschäftigung f, Arbeit f

employment ad Stellenanzeige f

employment of·fice Arbeitsamt n

em·pow·er ermächtigen; befähigen

em·press Kaiserin f

emp·ti·ness Leere f (a. fig)

emp·ty 1. leer (a. fig); 2. leeren, ausleeren, entleeren; sich leeren

em·u·late wetteifern mit; nacheifern (dat); es gleichtun (dat)

e·mul·sion Emulsion f

en·a·ble befähigen, es j-m ermöglichen; ermächtigen

en·act Gesetz erlassen; verfügen

e·nam·el 1. Email n, Emaille f; ANAT (Zahn)Schmelz m; Glasur f, Lack m; Nagellack m; 2. emaillieren; glasieren; lackieren

en·am·o·u(u)red: enamo(u)red of verliebt in (acc)

en·camp·ment esp MIL (Feld)Lager n

en·cased: encased in gehüllt in (acc)

en·chant bezaubern

en·chant·ing bezaubernd

en·chant·ment Bezauberung f; Zauber m

en·cir·cle einkreisen, umzingeln; umfassen, umschließen

en·close einschließen, umgeben; beilegen, beifügen

en·clo·sure Einzäunung f; Anlage f

en·code verschlüsseln, chiffrieren; kodieren

en·com·pass umgeben

en·coun·ter 1. Begegnung f; Gefecht n; 2. begegnen (dat); auf Schwierigkeiten etc stoßen; mit j-m feindlich zusammenstoßen

en·cour·age ermutigen; fördern

en·cour·age·ment Ermutigung f; Anfeuerung f; Unterstützung f

en·cour·ag·ing ermutigend

en·croach (on) eingreifen (in j-s Recht etc), eindringen (in acc); über Gebühr in Anspruch nehmen (acc)

en·croach·ment Ein-, Übergriff m

en·cum·ber belasten; (be)hindern

en·cum·brance Belastung *f*

en·cy·clo·p(a)e·di·a Enzyklopädie *f*

end 1. Ende *n*; Ziel *n*, Zweck *m*; *no end of* unendlich viel(e), unzählige; *at the end of May* Ende Mai; *in the end* am Ende, schließlich; *on end* aufrecht; *stand on end* zu Berge stehen (*hair*); *to no end* vergebens; *go off the deep end* F fig in die Luft gehen; *make (both) ends meet* durchkommen, finanziell über die Runden kommen; **2.** enden; beend(-ig)en

en·dan·ger gefährden

en·dear beliebt machen (*to s.o.* bei j-m)

en·dear·ing gewinnend; liebenswert

en·dear·ment: *words of endearment, endearments* zärtliche Worte *pl*

en·deav·o(u)r 1. Bestreben *n*, Bemühung *f*; **2.** sich bemühen

end·ing Ende *n*; Schluss *m*; LING Endung *f*

en·dive BOT Endivie *f*

end·less endlos, unendlich; TECH ohne Ende

en·dorse ECON *Scheck etc* indossieren; *et.* vermerken (*on* auf der Rückseite); billigen

en·dorse·ment Vermerk *m*; ECON Indossament *n*, Giro *n*

en·dow fig ausstatten; *endow s.o. with s.th.* j-m et. stiften

en·dow·ment Stiftung *f*; *mst pl* Begabung *f*, Talent *n*

en·dur·ance Ausdauer *f*; *beyond endurance, past endurance* unerträglich

en·dure ertragen

end us·er Endverbraucher *m*

en·e·my 1. Feind *m*; **2.** feindlich

en·er·get·ic energisch; tatkräftig

en·er·gy Energie *f*

en·er·gy cri·sis Energiekrise *f*

en·er·gy-sav·ing energiesparend

en·er·gy sup·ply Energieversorgung *f*

en·fold einhüllen; umfassen

en·force (mit Nachdruck, *a.* gerichtlich) geltend machen; *Gesetz etc* durchführen; durchsetzen, erzwingen

en·force·ment ECON, JUR Geltendmachung *f*; Durchsetzung *f*; Erzwingung *f*

en·fran·chise j-m das Wahlrecht verleihen

en·gage *v/t* j-s *Aufmerksamkeit* auf sich ziehen; TECH einrasten lassen; MOT *e-n Gang* einlegen; j-n einstellen, anstellen, *Künstler* engagieren; *v/i* TECH einrasten, greifen; *engage in* sich einlassen auf (*acc*) or in (*acc*); sich beschäftigen mit

en·gaged verlobt (*to* mit); beschäftigt (*in, on* mit); besetzt (*a. Br* TEL); *engaged*

tone or signal Br TEL Besetztzeichen *n*

en·gage·ment Verlobung *f*; Verabredung *f*; MIL Gefecht *n*

en·gag·ing einnehmend; gewinnend

en·gine Maschine *f*; Motor *m*; RAIL Lokomotive *f*

engine driv·er *Br* RAIL Lokomotivführer *m*

en·gi·neer 1. Ingenieur *m*, Techniker *m*, Mechaniker *m*; RAIL Lokomotivführer *m*; MIL Pionier *m*; **2.** bauen; *fig* (geschickt) in die Wege leiten

en·gi·neer·ing Technik *f*, Ingenieurwesen *n*, Maschinen- und Gerätebau *m*

En·gland England *n*

En·glish 1. englisch; **2.** LING Englisch *n*; *the English* die Engländer *pl*; *in plain English fig* unverblümt

Eng·lish·man Engländer *m*

Eng·lish·wom·an Engländerin *f*

en·grave (ein)gravieren, (ein)meißeln, (ein)schnitzen; *fig* einprägen

en·grav·er Graveur *m*

en·grav·ing (Kupfer-, Stahl)Stich *m*; Holzschnitt *m*

en·grossed: *engrossed in* (voll) in Anspruch genommen von, vertieft *or* versunken in (*acc*)

en·hance erhöhen, verstärken, steigern

e·nig·ma Rätsel *n*

en·ig·mat·ic rätselhaft

en·joy sich erfreuen an (*dat*); genießen; *did you enjoy it?* hat es Ihnen gefallen?; *enjoy o.s.* sich amüsieren, sich gut unterhalten; *enjoy yourself!* viel Spaß!; *I enjoy my dinner* es schmeckt mir

en·joy·a·ble angenehm, erfreulich

en·joy·ment Vergnügen *n*, Freude *f*; Genuss *m*

en·large (sich) vergrößern *or* erweitern, ausdehnen; PHOT vergrößern; sich verbreiten *or* auslassen (*on* über *acc*)

en·large·ment Erweiterung *f*; Vergrößerung *f* (*a.* PHOT)

en·light·en aufklären, belehren

en·light·en·ment Aufklärung *f*

en·list MIL *v/t* anwerben; *v/i* sich freiwillig melden; *enlisted men* Unteroffiziere *pl* und Mannschaften *pl*

en·liv·en beleben

en·mi·ty Feindschaft *f*

en·no·ble adeln; veredeln

e·nor·mi·ty Ungeheuerlichkeit *f*

e·nor·mous ungeheuer

e·nough genug

en·quire, en·qui·ry → inquire, inquiry

en·rage wütend machen

en·raged wütend (*at* über *acc*)

en·rap·ture entzücken, hinreißen

en·rap·tured entzückt, hingerissen

en·rich bereichern; anreichern

en·rol(l) (sich) einschreiben or eintragen; UNIV (sich) immatrikulieren

en·sign MAR *esp* (National)Flagge *f*; MIL Leutnant *m* zur See

en·sue (darauf-, nach)folgen

en·sure sichern

en·tail mit sich bringen, zur Folge haben

en·tan·gle verwickeln

en·ter *v/t* hinein-, hereingehen, -kommen, -treten in (*acc*), eintreten, einsteigen in (*acc*), betreten; einreisen in (*acc*); MAR, RAIL einlaufen, einfahren in (*acc*); eindringen in (*acc*); *Namen etc* eintragen, einschreiben; SPORT melden, nennen (*for* für); *fig* eintreten in (*acc*), beitreten (*dat*); EDP eingeben; *v/i* eintreten, herein-, hineinkommen, herein-, hineingehen; THEA auftreten; sich eintragen or einschreiben or anmelden (*for* für); SPORT melden, nennen (*for* für)

en·ter key EDP Eingabetaste *f*

en·ter·prise Unternehmen *n* (*a.* ECON); ECON Unternehmertum *n*; Unternehmungsgeist *m*

en·ter·pris·ing unternehmungslustig; wagemutig; kühn

en·ter·tain unterhalten; bewirten

en·ter·tain·er Entertainer(in), Unterhaltungskünstler(in)

en·ter·tain·ment Unterhaltung *f*; Entertainment *n*; Bewirtung *f*

en·thral(l) fesseln, bezaubern

en·throne inthronisieren

en·thu·si·asm Begeisterung *f*, Enthusiasmus *m*

en·thu·si·ast Enthusiast(in)

en·thu·si·as·tic begeistert, enthusiastisch

en·tice (ver)locken

en·tice·ment Verlockung *f*, Reiz *m*

en·tire ganz, vollständig; ungeteilt

en·tire·ly völlig; ausschließlich

en·ti·tle berechtigen (*to* zu)

en·ti·ty Einheit *f*

en·trails ANAT Eingeweide *pl*

en·trance Eintreten *n*, Eintritt *m*; Eingang *m*, Zugang *m*; Zufahrt *f*; Einlass *m*, Eintritt *m*, Zutritt *m*

en·trance ex·am(·**i·na·tion**) Aufnahmeprüfung *f*

entrance fee Eintritt *m*, Eintrittsgeld *n*; Aufnahmegebühr *f*

en·treat inständig bitten, anflehen

en·trea·ty dringende or inständige Bitte

en·trench MIL verschanzen (*a. fig*)

en·tre·pre·neur ECON Unternehmer(in)

en·tre·pre·neu·ri·al ECON unternehmerisch

en·trust anvertrauen (*s.th. to s.o.* j-m et.); *j-n* betrauen (*with* mit)

en·try Eintreten *n*, Eintritt *m*; Einreise *f*; Beitritt *m* (*into* zu); Einlass *m*, Zutritt *m*; Zugang *m*, Eingang *m*, Einfahrt *f*; Eintrag(ung *f*) *m*; Stichwort *n*; SPORT Nennung *f*, Meldung *f*; *no entry!* Zutritt verboten!, MOT keine Einfahrt!

en·try per·mit Einreiseerlaubnis *f*, -genehmigung *f*

en·try·phone Türsprechanlage *f*

en·try vi·sa Einreisevisum *n*

en·twine ineinander schlingen

e·nu·me·rate aufzählen

en·vel·op (ein)hüllen, einwickeln

en·ve·lope Briefumschlag *m*

en·vi·a·ble beneidenswert

en·vi·ous neidisch

en·vi·ron·ment Umgebung *f*, *a.* Milieu *n*; Umwelt *f*

en·vi·ron·men·tal Milieu...; Umwelt...

en·vi·ron·men·tal·ist Umweltschützer(in)

en·vi·ron·men·tal law Umweltschutzgesetz *n*

environmental pol·lu·tion Umweltverschmutzung *f*

en·vi·ron·ment friend·ly umweltfreundlich

en·vi·rons Umgebung *f*

en·vis·age sich *et.* vorstellen

en·voy Gesandte *m*, Gesandtin *f*

en·vy 1. Neid *m*; **2.** beneiden

ep·ic 1. episch; **2.** Epos *n*

ep·i·dem·ic MED **1.** seuchenartig; **epidemic disease** → **2.** Epidemie *f*, Seuche *f*

ep·i·der·mis ANAT Oberhaut *f*

ep·i·lep·sy MED Epilepsie *f*

ep·i·log, *Br* **ep·i·logue** Epilog *m*, Nachwort *n*

e·pis·co·pal REL bischöflich

ep·i·sode Episode *f*

ep·i·taph Grabinschrift *f*

e·poch Epoche *f*, Zeitalter *n*

equa·ble ausgeglichen (*a.* METEOR)

e·qual 1. gleich; gleichmäßig; **equal to** *fig* gewachsen (*dat*); **equal opportunities** Chancengleichheit *f*; **equal rights for women** Gleichberechtigung *f* der Frau; **2.** Gleiche *m*, *f*; **3.** gleichen (*dat*)

e·qual·i·ty Gleichheit *f*

e·qual·i·za·tion Gleichstellung *f*; Ausgleich *m*

e·qual·ize gleichmachen, gleichstellen, angleichen; SPORT ausgleichen

e·qual·iz·er SPORT Ausgleich *m*, Ausgleichstor *n*, -treffer *m*

eq·ua·nim·i·ty Gleichmut *m*

e·qua·tion MATH Gleichung *f*

e·qua·tor Äquator *m*

e·qui·lib·ri·um Gleichgewicht n

e·quip ausrüsten

e·quip·ment Ausrüstung f, Ausstattung f; TECH Einrichtung f; fig Rüstzeug n

e·quiv·a·lent 1. gleichwertig, äquivalent; gleichbedeutend (**to** mit); **2.** Äquivalent n, Gegenwert m

e·ra Zeitrechnung f; Zeitalter n

e·rad·i·cate ausrotten

e·rase ausradieren, ausstreichen, löschen (a. EDP); fig auslöschen

e·ras·er Radiergummi m

e·rect 1. aufrecht; **2.** aufrichten; Denkmal etc errichten; aufstellen

e·rec·tion Errichtung f; MED Erektion f

er·mine ZO Hermelin n

e·rode GEOL erodieren

e·ro·sion GEOL Erosion f

e·rot·ic erotisch

err (sich) irren

er·rand Botengang m, Besorgung f; **go on an errand, run an errand** e-e Besorgung machen

errand boy Laufbursche m

er·rat·ic sprunghaft, unstet, unberechenbar

er·ro·ne·ous irrig

er·ror Irrtum m, Fehler m (a. EDP); **in error** irrtümlicherweise; **error of judg(e)·ment** Fehleinschätzung f; **errors excepted** ECON Irrtümer vorbehalten

error mes·sage EDP Fehlermeldung f

e·rupt ausbrechen (volcano etc); durchbrechen (teeth)

e·rup·tion (Vulkan-) Ausbruch m; MED Ausschlag m

ESA ABBR of **European Space Agency** Europäische Weltraumbehörde

es·ca·late eskalieren; ECON steigen, in die Höhe gehen

es·ca·la·tion Eskalation f

es·ca·la·tor Rolltreppe f

es·ca·lope GASTR (esp Wiener) Schnitzel n

es·cape 1. entgehen (dat); entkommen, entrinnen (both dat); entweichen; j-m entfallen; **2.** Entrinnen n; Entweichen n, Flucht f; **have a narrow escape** mit knapper Not davonkommen

es·cape chute AVIAT Notrutsche f

es·cape key EDP Escape-Taste f

es·cort 1. MIL Eskorte f; Geleit(schutz) m; **2.** MIL eskortieren; AVIAT, MAR Geleit (-schutz) geben; geleiten

es·cutch·eon Wappenschild m, n

es·pe·cial besondere(r, -s)

es·pe·cial·ly besonders

es·pi·o·nage Spionage f

es·pla·nade (esp Strand)Promenade f

es·say Aufsatz m, kurze Abhandlung, Es-

say m, n

es·sence Wesen n; Essenz f; Extrakt m

es·sen·tial 1. wesentlich; unentbehrlich; **2.** mst pl das Wesentliche

es·sen·tial·ly im Wesentlichen, in der Hauptsache

es·tab·lish einrichten, errichten; **establish o.s.** sich etablieren or niederlassen; beweisen, nachweisen

es·tab·lish·ment Einrichtung f, Errichtung f; ECON Unternehmen n, Firma f; **the Establishment** das Establishment, die etablierte Macht, die herrschende Schicht

es·tate (großes) Grundstück, Landsitz m, Gut n; JUR Besitz m, (Erb)Masse f, Nachlass m; **housing estate** (Wohn)Siedlung f; **industrial estate** Industriegebiet n; **real estate** Liegenschaften pl

estate a·gent Br Grundstücks-, Immobilienmakler m

estate car Br MOT Kombiwagen m

es·teem 1. Achtung f, Ansehen n (**with** bei); **2.** achten, (hoch) schätzen

es·thet·ic ästhetisch

es·thet·ics Ästhetik f

es·ti·mate 1. (ab-, ein)schätzen; veranschlagen; **2.** Schätzung f; (Kosten)Voranschlag m

es·ti·ma·tion Meinung f; Achtung f, Wertschätzung f

es·tranged entfremdet

es·trange·ment Entfremdung f

es·tu·a·ry weite Flussmündung

etch ätzen; radieren

etch·ing Radierung f; Kupferstich m

e·ter·nal ewig

e·ter·ni·ty Ewigkeit f

e·ther Äther m

e·the·re·al ätherisch (a. fig)

eth·i·cal sittlich, ethisch

eth·ics Sittenlehre f, Ethik f

eu·ro Euro m

Eu·ro·cheque Br Eurocheque m

Eu·rope Europa n

Eu·ro·pe·an 1. europäisch; **2.** Europäer(in)

European Com·mu·ni·ty (ABBR **EC**) Europäische Gemeinschaft (ABBR EG)

e·vac·u·ate entleeren; evakuieren; Haus etc räumen

e·vade (geschickt) ausweichen (dat); umgehen

e·val·u·ate schätzen; abschätzen, bewerten, beurteilen

e·vap·o·rate verdunsten, verdampfen (lassen)

evaporated milk Kondensmilch f

e·vap·o·ra·tion Verdunstung f, Verdampfung f

e·va·sion Umgehung f, Vermeidung f; (Steuer)Hinterziehung f; Ausflucht f

e·va·sive ausweichend; *be evasive* ausweichen

eve Vorabend m; Vortag m; *on the eve of* unmittelbar vor (dat), am Vorabend (gen)

e·ven 1. adj eben, gleich; gleichmäßig; ausgeglichen; glatt; gerade (Zahl); *get even with s.o.* es j-m heimzahlen; **2.** adv selbst, sogar, auch; *not even* nicht einmal; *even though, even if* wenn auch; **3.** *even out* sich einpendeln; sich ausgleichen

eve·ning Abend m; *in the evening* am Abend, abends

evening class·es Abendkurs m, Abendunterricht m

evening dress Gesellschaftsanzug m; Frack m, Smoking m; Abendkleid n

e·ven·song REL Abendgottesdienst m

e·vent Ereignis n; Fall m; SPORT Disziplin f; SPORT Wettbewerb m; *at all events* auf alle Fälle; *in the event of* im Falle (gen)

e·vent·ful ereignisreich

e·ven·tu·al(·ly) schließlich

ev·er immer (wieder); je(mals); *ever after, ever since* seitdem; *ever so* F sehr, noch so; *for ever* für immer, auf ewig; *Yours ever, ..., Ever yours, ...* Viele Grüße, dein(e) or Ihr(e), ...; *have you ever been to Boston?* bist du schon einmal in Boston gewesen?

ev·er·green 1. immergrün; unverwüstlich, esp immer wieder gern gehört; **2.** immergrüne Pflanze; MUS Evergreen m, n

ev·er·last·ing ewig

ev·er·more (for) evermore für immer

ev·ery jede(r, -s); alle(r, -s); *every now and then* von Zeit zu Zeit, dann und wann; *every one of them* jeder von ihnen; *every other day* jeden zweiten Tag, alle zwei Tage

ev·ery·bod·y jeder(mann)

ev·ery·day Alltags...

ev·ery·one jeder(mann)

ev·ery·thing alles

ev·ery·where überall(hin)

e·vict JUR zur Räumung zwingen; j-n gewaltsam vertreiben

ev·i·dence Beweis(material n) m, Beweise pl; (Zeugen)Aussage f; *give evidence* (als Zeuge) aussagen

ev·i·dent augenscheinlich, offensichtlich

e·vil 1. übel, schlimm, böse; **2.** Übel n; das Böse

e·vil-mind·ed bösartig

e·voke (herauf)beschwören; Erinnerun-

gen wachrufen

ev·o·lu·tion Entwicklung f; BIOL Evolution f

e·volve (sich) entwickeln

ewe ZO Mutterschaf n

ex prp ECON ab; *ex works* ab Werk

ex... Ex..., ehemalig

ex·act 1. exakt, genau; **2.** fordern, verlangen

ex·act·ing streng, genau; aufreibend, anstrengend

ex·act·ly exakt, genau; *exactly!* ganz recht!, genau!

ex·act·ness Genauigkeit f

ex·ag·ge·rate übertreiben

ex·ag·ge·ra·tion Übertreibung f

ex·am F Examen n

ex·am·i·na·tion Examen n, Prüfung f; Untersuchung f; JUR Vernehmung f, Verhör n

ex·am·ine untersuchen; JUR vernehmen, verhören; PED etc prüfen (in in dat; on über acc)

ex·am·ple Beispiel n; Vorbild n, Muster n; *for example* zum Beispiel

ex·as·pe·rate wütend machen

ex·as·pe·rat·ing ärgerlich

ex·ca·vate ausgraben, ausheben, ausschachten

ex·ceed überschreiten; übertreffen

ex·ceed·ing übermäßig

ex·ceed·ing·ly außerordentlich, überaus

ex·cel v/t übertreffen; v/i sich auszeichnen

ex·cel·lence ausgezeichnete Qualität

Ex·cel·len·cy Exzellenz f

ex·cel·lent ausgezeichnet, hervorragend

ex·cept 1. ausnehmen, ausschließen; **2.** prp ausgenommen, außer; *except for* abgesehen von, bis auf (acc)

ex·cept·ing prp ausgenommen

ex·cep·tion Ausnahme f; Einwand m (to gegen); *make an exception* e-e Ausnahme machen; *take exception to* Anstoß nehmen an (dat); *without exception* ohne Ausnahme, ausnahmslos

ex·cep·tion·al außergewöhnlich

ex·cep·tion·al·ly ungewöhnlich, außergewöhnlich

ex·cerpt Auszug m

ex·cess 1. Übermaß n; Überschuss m; Ausschweifung f; **2.** Mehr...

excess baggage AVIAT Übergepäck n

excess fare (Fahrpreis)Zuschlag m

ex·ces·sive übermäßig, übertrieben

excess lug·gage → excess baggage

excess post·age Nachgebühr f

ex·change 1. (aus-, ein-, um)tauschen (for gegen); wechseln; **2.** (Aus-, Um-) Tausch m; (esp Geld)Wechsel m; ECON a. *bill of*

exchange Wechsel *m*; Börse *f*; Wechselstube *f*; TEL Fernsprechamt *n*; ECON **for-eign exchange(s)** Devisen *pl*; **rate of ex-change → exchange rate**

exchange of·fice Wechselstube *f*

exchange rate Wechselkurs *m*

exchange student Austauschschüler(in), Austauschstudent(in)

Ex·cheq·uer: Chancellor of the Exche-quer *Br* Finanzminister *m*

ex·cise Verbrauchssteuer *f*

ex·ci·ta·ble reizbar, (leicht) erregbar

ex·cite erregen, anregen; reizen

ex·cit·ed erregt, aufgeregt

ex·cite·ment Aufregung *f*, Erregung *f*

ex·cit·ing erregend, aufregend, spannend

ex·claim (aus)rufen

ex·cla·ma·tion Ausruf *m*, (Auf)Schrei *m*; **exclamation point** Ausrufe-, Ausrufungszeichen *n*

ex·clude ausschließen

ex·clu·sion Ausschließung *f*, Ausschluss *m*

ex·clu·sive ausschließlich; exklusiv; Exklusiv…; **exclusive of** abgesehen von, ohne

ex·com·mu·ni·cate REL exkommunizieren

ex·com·mu·ni·ca·tion REL Exkommunikation *f*

ex·cre·ment Kot *m*

ex·crete MED ausscheiden

ex·cur·sion Ausflug *m*

ex·cu·sa·ble entschuldbar

ex·cuse entschuldigen; **excuse me** entschuldige(n Sie); **2.** Entschuldigung *f*

ex·di·rec·to·ry num·ber *Br* TEL Geheimnummer *f*

ex·e·cute ausführen; vollziehen; MUS vortragen; hinrichten; JUR *Testament* vollstrecken

ex·e·cu·tion Ausführung *f*; Vollziehung *f*; JUR (Zwangs-) Vollstreckung *f*; Hinrichtung *f*; MUS Vortrag *m*; **put or carry a plan into execution** e-n Plan ausführen *or* verwirklichen

ex·e·cu·tion·er JUR Henker *m*, Scharfrichter *m*

ex·ec·u·tive 1. vollziehend, ausübend, POL Exekutiv…; ECON leitend; **2.** POL Exekutive *f*, vollziehende Gewalt; ECON *der, die* leitende Angestellte

ex·em·pla·ry vorbildlich

ex·em·pli·fy veranschaulichen

ex·empt 1. befreit, frei; **2.** ausnehmen, befreien

ex·er·cise 1. Übung *f*; Ausübung *f*; PED Übung(sarbeit) *f*, Schulaufgabe *f*; MIL Manöver *n*; (körperliche) Bewegung; **do one's exercises** Gymnastik machen; **take exercise** sich Bewegung machen; **2.** üben; ausüben; (sich) bewegen; sich Bewegung machen; MIL exerzieren

ex·er·cise book Schul-, Schreibheft *n*

ex·ert *Einfluss etc* ausüben; **exert o.s.** sich anstrengen *or* bemühen

ex·er·tion Ausübung *f*; Anstrengung *f*, Strapaze *f*

ex·hale ausatmen; *Gas, Geruch etc* verströmen; *Rauch* ausstoßen

ex·haust 1. erschöpfen; *Vorräte* ver-, aufbrauchen; **2.** TECH Auspuff *m*; *a.* **exhaust fumes** TECH Auspuff-, Abgase *pl*

ex·haust·ed erschöpft, aufgebraucht (*supplies*), vergriffen (*book*)

ex·haus·tion Erschöpfung *f*

ex·haus·tive erschöpfend

ex·haust pipe TECH Auspuffrohr *n*

ex·hib·it 1. ausstellen; vorzeigen; *fig* zeigen, zur Schau stellen; **2.** Ausstellungsstück *n*; JUR Beweisstück *n*

ex·hi·bi·tion Ausstellung *f*; Zurschaustellung *f*

ex·hil·a·rat·ing erregend, berauschend

ex·hort ermahnen

ex·ile 1. Exil *n*; im Exil Lebende *m*, *f*; **2.** ins Exil schicken

ex·ist existieren; vorhanden sein; leben; bestehen

ex·ist·ence Existenz *f*; Vorhandensein *n*, Vorkommen *n*; Leben *n*, Dasein *n*

ex·ist·ent vorhanden

ex·it 1. Abgang *m*; Ausgang *m*; (Autobahn)Ausfahrt *f*; Ausreise *f*; **2.** *v/i* verlassen; EDP (das Programm) beenden; **exit Macbeth** THEA Macbeth (geht) ab

ex·o·dus Auszug *m*; Abwanderung *f*; **general exodus** allgemeiner Aufbruch

ex·on·e·rate entlasten, entbinden, befreien

ex·or·bi·tant übertrieben, maßlos; unverschämt (*price etc*)

ex·or·cize *böse Geister* beschwören, austreiben (**from** aus); befreien (**of** von)

ex·ot·ic exotisch; fremd(artig)

ex·pand ausbreiten; (sich) ausdehnen *or* erweitern; ECON *a.* expandieren

ex·panse weite Fläche, Weite *f*

ex·pan·sion Ausbreitung *f*; Ausdehnung *f*, Erweiterung *f*

ex·pan·sive mitteilsam

ex·pat·ri·ate *j-n* ausbürgern, *j-m* die Staatsangehörigkeit aberkennen

ex·pect erwarten; F annehmen; **be ex-pecting** in anderen Umständen sein

ex·pec·tant erwartungsvoll; **expectant mother** werdende Mutter

ex·pec·ta·tion Erwartung *f*; Hoffnung *f*,

Aussicht *f*
ex·pe·di·ent 1. zweckdienlich, zweckmäßig; ratsam; **2.** (Hilfs)Mittel *n*, (Not)Be-
helf *m*
ex·pe·di·tion Expedition *f*, (Forschungs)-
Reise *f*
ex·pe·di·tious schnell
ex·pel (*from*) vertreiben (aus); ausweisen
(aus); ausschließen (von, aus)
ex·pen·di·ture Ausgaben *pl*, (Kosten-)
Aufwand *m*
ex·pense Ausgaben *pl*; *pl* ECON Unkosten
pl, Spesen *pl*, Auslagen *pl*; *at the expense of* auf Kosten (*gen*)
ex·pen·sive kostspielig, teuer
ex·pe·ri·ence 1. Erfahrung *f*; (Le·bens)-
Praxis *f*; Erlebnis *n*; **2.** erfahren, erleben
ex·pe·ri·enced erfahren
ex·per·i·ment 1. Versuch *m*; *experiment
with animals* MED Tierversuch *m*; **2.** experimentieren
ex·per·i·men·tal Versuchs...
ex·pert 1. erfahren, geschickt; fachmännisch; **2.** Fachmann *m*; Sachverständige
m, *f*
ex·pi·ra·tion Ablauf *m*, Ende *n*; Verfall *m*
ex·pire ablaufen, erlöschen; verfallen
ex·plain erklären
ex·pla·na·tion Erklärung *f*
ex·plic·it ausdrücklich; ausführlich; offen, deutlich; (*sexually*) *explicit* freizügig (*film etc*)
ex·plode *v/t* zur Explosion bringen; *v/i* explodieren; *fig* ausbrechen (*with* in *acc*),
platzen (*with* vor); *fig* sprunghaft ansteigen
ex·ploit 1. (Helden)Tat *f*; **2.** ausbeuten; *fig*
ausnutzen
ex·ploi·ta·tion Ausbeutung *f*, Auswertung *f*, Verwertung *f*, Abbau *m*
ex·plo·ra·tion Erforschung *f*
ex·plore erforschen
ex·plor·er Forscher(in); Forschungsrei-
sende *m*, *f*
ex·plo·sion Explosion *f*; *fig* Ausbruch *m*;
fig sprunghafter Anstieg
ex·plo·sive 1. explosiv; *fig* aufbrausend;
fig sprunghaft ansteigend; **2.** Sprengstoff
m
ex·po·nent MATH Exponent *m*, Hochzahl
f; Vertreter(in), Verfechter(in)
ex·port ECON **1.** exportieren, ausführen; **2.**
Export *m*, Ausfuhr *f*; *mst pl* Export-,
Ausfuhrartikel *m*
ex·por·ta·tion ECON Ausfuhr *f*
ex·port·er ECON Exporteur *m*
ex·pose aussetzen; PHOT belichten; *Waren*
ausstellen; *j-n* entlarven, bloßstellen, *et.*
aufdecken

ex·po·si·tion Ausstellung *f*
ex·po·sure Aussetzen *n*, Ausgesetztsein *n*
(*to dat*); *fig* Bloßstellung *f*, Aufdeckung
f, Enthüllung *f*, Entlarvung *f*; PHOT Be-
lichtung *f*; PHOT Aufnahme *f*; *die of exposure* an Unterkühlung sterben
exposure me·ter PHOT Belichtungsmes-
ser *m*
ex·press 1. ausdrücklich, deutlich; Express..., Eil...; **2.** Eilbote *m*; Schnellzug
m; *by express* → **3.** *adv* durch Eilboten;
als Eilgut; **4.** äußern, ausdrücken
ex·pres·sion Ausdruck *m*
ex·pres·sion·less ausdruckslos
ex·pres·sive ausdrucksvoll; *be expressive of et.* ausdrücken
ex·press let·ter *Br* Eilbrief *m*
ex·press·ly ausdrücklich, eigens
ex·press train Schnellzug *m*
ex·press·way Schnellstraße *f*
ex·pro·pri·ate JUR enteignen
ex·pul·sion (*from*) Vertreibung *f* (aus);
Ausweisung *f* (aus)
ex·pur·gate reinigen
ex·qui·site erlesen; fein
ex·tant noch vorhanden
ex·tem·po·re aus dem Stegreif
ex·tem·po·rize aus dem Stegreif sprechen
or spielen
ex·tend (aus)dehnen, (aus)weiten; *Hand
etc* ausstrecken; *Betrieb etc* vergrößern,
ausbauen; *Frist, Pass etc* verlängern; sich
ausdehnen *or* erstrecken
ex·tend·ed fam·i·ly Großfamilie *f*
ex·ten·sion Ausdehnung *f*; Vergrößerung
f, Erweiterung *f*; (Frist)Verlängerung *f*;
ARCH Erweiterung *f*, Anbau *m*; TEL Ne-
benanschluss *m*, (-)Apparat *m*; *a. extension cord* (*Br lead*) ELECTR Verlänge-
rungskabel *n*, -schnur *f*
ex·ten·sive ausgedehnt, umfassend
ex·tent Ausdehnung *f*; Umfang *m*, (Aus-)
Maß *n*, Grad *m*; *to some extent, to a
certain extent* bis zu e-m gewissen Grade; *to such an extent that* so sehr, dass
ex·ten·u·ate abschwächen, mildern; beschönigen; *extenuating circumstances*
JUR mildernde Umstände *pl*
ex·te·ri·or 1. äußerlich, äußere(r, -s), Außen...; **2.** *das* Äußere; Außenseite *f*; äußere Erscheinung
ex·ter·mi·nate ausrotten (*a. fig*), vernichten, *Ungeziefer, Unkraut a.* vertilgen
ex·ter·nal äußere(r, -s), äußerlich; Außen...
ex·tinct erloschen; ausgestorben
ex·tinc·tion Erlöschen *n*; Aussterben *n*,
Untergang *m*; Vernichtung *f*, Zerstörung
f

ex·tin·guish (aus)löschen; vernichten
ex·tin·guish·er (*Feuer*)Löscher *m*
ex·tort erpressen (**from** von)
ex·tra 1. *adj* zusätzlich, Extra..., Sonder...; *be extra* gesondert berechnet werden; **2.** *adv* extra, besonders; *charge extra for et.* gesondert berechnen; **3.** Sonderleistung *f; esp* MOT Extra *n*; Zuschlag *m*; Extrablatt *n*; THEA, *film*: Statist(in)
ex·tract 1. Auszug *m;* **2.** (heraus)ziehen; herauslocken; ableiten, herleiten
ex·trac·tion (Heraus)Ziehen *n*; Herkunft *f*
ex·tra·dite ausliefern; *j-s* Auslieferung erwirken;
ex·tra·di·tion Auslieferung *f*
extra·or·di·na·ry außerordentlich; ungewöhnlich; Sonder...
ex·tra pay Zulage *f*
ex·tra·ter·res·tri·al außerirdisch
ex·tra time SPORT (Spiel)Verlängerung *f*
ex·trav·a·gance Übertriebenheit *f*; Verschwendung *f*; Extravaganz *f*
ex·trav·a·gant übertrieben, überspannt; verschwenderisch; extravagant
ex·treme 1. äußerste(r, -s), größte(r, -s), höchste(r, -s); außergewöhnlich; *extreme right* POL rechtsextrem(istisch); *extreme right wing* POL rechtsradikal; **2.** *das* Äußerste; Extrem *n*; höchster Grad
ex·treme·ly äußerst, höchst
ex·trem·ism POL Extremismus *m*
ex·trem·ist POL Extremist(in)
ex·trem·i·ties Gliedmaßen *pl*, Extremitä-ten *pl*
ex·trem·i·ty *das* Äußerste; höchste Not; äußerste Maßnahme
ex·tri·cate herauswinden, herausziehen; befreien
ex·tro·vert Extrovertierte *m, f*
ex·u·be·rance Fülle *f*; Überschwang *m*
ex·u·be·rant reichlich, üppig; überschwänglich; ausgelassen
ex·ult frohlocken, jubeln
eye 1. ANAT Auge *n*; Blick *m*; Öhr *n*; Öse *f*; *see eye to eye with s.o.* mit j-m völlig übereinstimmen; *be up to the eyes in work* bis über die Ohren in Arbeit stecken; *with an eye to s.th.* im Hinblick auf et.; **2.** ansehen; mustern
eye·ball ANAT Augapfel *m*
eye·brow ANAT Augenbraue *f*
eye-catch·ing ins Auge fallend, auffallend
eye doc·tor F Augenarzt *m*, -ärztin *f*
eye·glass·es *a.* **pair of eyeglasses** Brille *f*
eye·lash ANAT Augenwimper *f*
eye·lid ANAT Augenlid *n*
eye·lin·er Eyeliner *m*
eye-o·pen·er: *that was an eye-opener to me* das hat mir die Augen geöffnet
eye shad·ow Lidschatten *m*
eye·sight Augen(licht *n*) *pl*, Sehkraft *f*
eye·sore F Schandfleck *m*
eye spe·cial·ist Augenarzt *m*, -ärztin *f*
eye·strain Ermüdung *f or* Überanstrengung *f der* Augen
eye·wit·ness Augenzeuge *m*, -zeugin *f*

F

F, f F, f *n*
fa·ble Fabel *f*; Sage *f*
fab·ric Gewebe *n*, Stoff *m*; Struktur *f*
fab·ri·cate fabrizieren (*mst fig*)
fab·u·lous sagenhaft, der Sage angehörend; fabelhaft
fa·cade, fa·çade ARCH Fassade *f*
face 1. Gesicht *n*; Gesichtsausdruck *m*, Miene *f*; (Ober)Fläche *f*; Vorderseite *f*; Zifferblatt *n; face to face with* Auge in Auge mit; *save (lose) one's face* das Gesicht wahren (verlieren); *on the face of it* auf den ersten Blick; *pull a long face* ein langes Gesicht machen; *have the face to do s.th.* die Stirn haben, et. zu tun; **2.** *v/t* ansehen; gegenüberstehen (*dat*); (hinaus)gehen auf (*acc*); die Stirn bieten (*dat*); einfassen; ARCH bekleiden; *v/i:* **face about** sich umdrehen
face-cloth, *Br* **face flan·nel** Waschlappen *m*
face-lift Facelifting *n*, Gesichtsstraffung *f*; *fig* Renovierung *f*, Verschönerung *f*
fa·ce·tious witzig
fa·cial 1. Gesichts...; **2.** Gesichtsbehand-

lung f

fa·cile leicht; oberflächlich

fa·cil·i·tate erleichtern

fa·cil·i·ty Leichtigkeit f; Oberflächlichkeit f; *mst pl* Erleichterung(en *pl*) f; Einrichtung(en *pl*) f, Anlage(n *pl*) f

fac·ing TECH Verkleidung f; *pl* Besatz m

fact Tatsache f, Wirklichkeit f, Wahrheit f; Tat f; *pl* Daten; *in fact* in der Tat, tatsächlich

fac·tion *esp* POL Splittergruppe f; Zwietracht f

fac·ti·tious künstlich

fac·tor Faktor m

fac·to·ry Fabrik f

fac·ul·ty Fähigkeit f; Kraft f; *fig* Gabe f; UNIV Fakultät f; Lehrkörper m

fad Mode f, Modeerscheinung f, -torheit f; (vorübergehende) Laune

fade (ver)welken (lassen); verschießen, verblassen (*color*); schwinden; immer schwächer werden (*person*); *film, radio,* TV *fade in* auf- *or* eingeblendet werden; auf- *or* einblenden; *fade out* aus- *or* abgeblendet werden; aus- *or* abblenden; *faded jeans* ausgewaschene Jeans *pl*

fail *v/i* versagen; misslingen, fehlschlagen; versiegen; nachlassen; durchfallen (*candidate*); *v/t* im Stich lassen; *j-n* in *e-r* Prüfung durchfallen lassen; **2.** *without fail* mit Sicherheit, ganz bestimmt

fail·ure Versagen n; Fehlschlag m, Misserfolg m; Versäumnis n; Versager m, F Niete f

faint 1. schwach, matt; **2.** ohnmächtig werden, in Ohnmacht fallen (*with* vor); **3.** Ohnmacht f

faint-heart·ed verzagt

fair[1] gerecht, ehrlich, anständig, fair; recht gut, ansehnlich; schön (*weather*); klar (*sky*); blond (*hair*); hell (*skin*); play *fair* fair spielen; *fig* sich an die Spielregeln halten

fair[2] (Jahr)Markt m; Volksfest n; Ausstellung f, Messe f

fair game *fig* Freiwild n

fair·ground Rummelplatz m

fair·ly gerecht; ziemlich

fair·ness Gerechtigkeit f, Fairness f

fair play SPORT *and fig* Fair Play n, Fairness f

fai·ry Fee f; Zauberin f; Elf m, Elfe f

fai·ry·land Feen-, Märchenland n

fai·ry sto·ry, fairy tale Märchen n (*a. fig*)

faith Glaube m; Vertrauen n

faith·ful treu (*to dat*); *Yours faithfully* Hochachtungsvoll (*letter*)

faith·less treulos

fake 1. Schwindel m; Fälschung f;

Schwindler m; **2.** fälschen; imitieren, nachmachen; vortäuschen, simulieren; **3.** gefälscht; fingiert

fal·con ZO Falke m

fall 1. Fallen n, Fall m; Sturz m; Verfall m; Einsturz m; Herbst m; ECON Sinken n (*of prices etc*); Gefälle n; *mst pl* Wasserfall m; **2.** fallen, stürzen; ab-, einfallen; sinken; sich legen (*wind*); *in e-n Zustand* verfallen; *fall ill, fall sick* krank werden; *fall in love with* sich verlieben in (*acc*); *fall short of* den Erwartungen *etc* nicht entsprechen; *fall back* zurückweichen; *fall back on fig* zurückgreifen auf (*acc*); *fall for* hereinfallen auf (*acc*); F sich in *j-n* verknallen; *fall off* zurückgehen (*business, demand etc*), nachlassen; *fall on* herfallen über (*acc*); *fall out* sich streiten (*with* mit); *fall through* durchfallen (*a. fig*); *fall to* reinhauen, tüchtig zugreifen

fal·la·cious trügerisch

fal·la·cy Trugschluss m

fall guy F der Lackierte, der Dumme

fal·li·ble fehlbar

fall·ing star Sternschnuppe f

fall·out Fall-out m, radioaktiver Niederschlag

fal·low ZO falb; AGR brach(liegend)

false falsch

false·hood, false·ness Falschheit f; Unwahrheit f

false start Fehlstart m

fal·si·fi·ca·tion (Ver)Fälschung f

fal·si·fy (ver)fälschen

fal·si·ty Falschheit f, Unwahrheit f

fal·ter schwanken; stocken (*voice*); stammeln; *fig* zaudern

fame Ruf m, Ruhm m

famed berühmt (*for* wegen)

fa·mil·i·ar 1. vertraut; gewohnt; familiär; **2.** Vertraute m, f

fa·mil·i·ar·i·ty Vertrautheit f; (plumpe) Vertraulichkeit f

fa·mil·i·ar·ize vertraut machen

fam·i·ly 1. Familie f; **2.** Familien..., Haus...; *be in the family way* F in anderen Umständen sein

family al·low·ance → *child benefit*

family doc·tor Hausarzt m

family name Familien-, Nachname m

family plan·ning Familienplanung f

family tree Stammbaum m

fam·ine Hungersnot f; Knappheit f (*of an dat*)

fam·ished verhungert; *be famished* F am Verhungern sein

fa·mous berühmt

fan[1] 1. Fächer m; Ventilator m; **2.** (zu-)fächeln; anfachen; *fig* entfachen

fan² (*Sport- etc*)Fan *m*

fa·nat·ic Fanatiker(in)

fa·nat·i·cal fanatisch

fan belt TECH Keilriemen *m*

fan·ci·er BOT, ZO Liebhaber(in), Züchter(in)

fan·ci·ful fantastisch

fan club Fanklub *m*

fan·cy 1. Fantasie *f*; Einbildung *f*; plötzlicher Einfall, Idee *f*; Laune *f*; Vorliebe *f*, Neigung *f*; **2.** ausgefallen; Fantasie…; **3.** sich vorstellen; sich einbilden; ***fancy that!*** stell dir vor!, denk nur!; sieh mal einer an!

fan·cy ball Kostümfest *n*, Maskenball *m*

fancy dress (Masken)Kostüm *n*

fan·cy-free → *footloose*

fan·cy goods Modeartikel *pl*, -waren *pl*

fan·cy·work Stickerei *f*

fang ZO Reiß-, Fangzahn *m*; Hauer *m*; Giftzahn *m*

fan mail Fanpost *f*, Verehrerpost *f*

fan·tas·tic fantastisch

fan·ta·sy Fantasie *f*

far 1. *adj* fern, entfernt, weit; **2.** *adv* fern; weit; (sehr) viel; ***as far as*** bis; ***in so far as*** insofern als

far·a·way weit entfernt

fare 1. Fahrgeld *n*; Fahrgast *m*; Verpflegung *f*, Kost *f*; **2.** *gut* leben; ***he fared well*** es (er)ging ihm gut

fare dodg·er Schwarzfahrer(in)

fare·well 1. *int* lebe(n Sie) wohl!; **2.** Abschied *m*, Lebewohl *n*

far·fetched *fig* weit hergeholt, gesucht

farm 1. Bauernhof *m*, Gut *n*, Gehöft *n*, Farm *f*; **2.** *Land, Hof* bewirtschaften

farm·er Bauer *m*, Landwirt *m*, Farmer *m*

farm·house Bauernhaus *n*

farm·ing 1. Acker…, landwirtschaftlich; **2.** Landwirtschaft *f*

farm·stead Bauernhof *m*, Gehöft *n*

farm·yard Wirtschaftshof *m*

far-off entfernt, fern

far right POL rechtsgerichtet

far·sight·ed weitsichtig, *fig a.* weitblickend

fas·ci·nate faszinieren

fas·ci·nat·ing faszinierend

fas·ci·na·tion Zauber *m*, Reiz *m*, Faszination *f*

fas·cism POL Faschismus *m*

fas·cist POL **1.** Faschist *m*; **2.** faschistisch

fash·ion Mode *f*; Art *f* und Weise *f*; ***be in fashion*** in Mode sein; ***out of fashion*** unmodern; **1.** formen, gestalten

fash·ion·a·ble modisch, elegant; in Mode

fash·ion pa·rade, fashion show Mode(n)-schau *f*

fast¹ 1. Fasten *n*; **2.** fasten

fast² 1. schnell; fest; treu; echt, beständig (*color*); flott; ***be fast*** vorgehen (*watch*)

fast·back MOT (Wagen *m* mit) Fließheck *n*

fast breed·er (**re·ac·tor**) PHYS Schneller Brüter

fas·ten befestigen, festmachen, anheften, anschnallen, anbinden, zuknöpfen, zu-, verschnüren; *Blick etc* richten (**on** auf *acc*); sich festmachen *or* schließen lassen

fast food Schnellgericht(e *pl*) *n*

fas·ten·er Verschluss *m*

fast-food res·tau·rant Schnellimbiss *m*, Schnellgaststätte *f*

fas·tid·i·ous anspruchsvoll, heikel, wählerisch, verwöhnt

fast lane MOT Überholspur *f*

fat 1. fett; dick; fettig, fetthaltig; **2.** Fett *n*; ***be low in fat*** fettarm sein

fa·tal tödlich; verhängnisvoll, fatal (**to** für)

fa·tal·i·ty Verhängnis *n*; tödlicher Unfall; (Todes)Opfer *n*

fate Schicksal *n*; Verhängnis *n*

fa·ther Vater *m*

Fa·ther Christ·mas *esp Br* der Weihnachtsmann, der Nikolaus

fa·ther·hood Vaterschaft *f*

fa·ther-in-law Schwiegervater *m*

fa·ther·less vaterlos

fa·ther·ly väterlich

fath·om 1. MAR Faden *m*; **2.** MAR loten; *fig* ergründen

fath·om·less unergründlich

fa·tigue 1. Ermüdung *f*; Strapaze *f*; **2.** ermüden

fat·ten dick *or contp* fett machen *or* werden; mästen

fat·ty fett; fettig

fau·cet TECH (Wasser)Hahn *m*

fault Fehler *m*; Defekt *m*; Schuld *f*; ***find fault with*** et. auszusetzen haben an (*dat*); ***be at fault*** Schuld haben

fault·less fehlerfrei, fehlerlos

fault·y fehlerhaft, TECH *a.* defekt

fa·vo(u)r 1. Gunst *f*; Gefallen *m*; Begünstigung *f*; ***in favo(u)r of*** zu Gunsten von (*or gen*); ***do s.o. a favo(u)r*** j-m e-n Gefallen tun; **2.** begünstigen; bevorzugen, vorziehen; wohlwollend gegenüberstehen; SPORT favorisieren

fa·vo(u)r·a·ble günstig

fa·vo(u)r·ite 1. Liebling *m*; SPORT Favorit *m*; **2.** Lieblings…

fawn 1. ZO (Reh)Kitz *n*; Rehbraun *n*; **2.** rehbraun

fax 1. Fax *n*; **2.** faxen; ***fax s.th. (through)***

to s.o. j-m et. faxen
fax (ma·chine) Faxgerät *n*
fear 1. Furcht *f* (*of* vor *dat*); Befürchtung *f*; Angst *f*; 2. (be)fürchten; sich fürchten vor (*dat*)
fear·ful furchtsam; furchtbar
fear·less furchtlos
fea·si·ble durchführbar
feast 1. REL Fest *n*, Feiertag *m*; Festessen *n*; *fig* Fest *n*, (Hoch)Genuss *m*; 2. *v/t* festlich bewirten; *v/i* sich gütlich tun (*on* an *dat*), schlemmen
feat große Leistung; (Helden)Tat *f*
fea·ther 1. Feder *f*; *a. pl* Gefieder *n*; *birds of a feather* Leute vom gleichen Schlag; *birds of a feather flock together* Gleich und Gleich gesellt sich gern; *that is a feather in his cap* darauf kann er stolz sein; 2. mit Federn polstern *or* schmücken; *Pfeil* fiedern
feath·er·bed verhätscheln
feath·er·brained F hohlköpfig
feath·ered ZO gefiedert
feath·er·weight SPORT Federgewicht *n*, Federgewichtler *m*; Leichtgewicht *n* (*person*)
feath·er·y gefiedert; federleicht
fea·ture 1. (Gesichts)Zug *m*; (charakteristisches) Merkmal; *radio*, TV etc Feature *n*; Haupt-, Spielfilm *m*; 2. groß herausbringen; *film*: in der Hauptrolle zeigen
feature film Haupt-, Spielfilm *m*
Feb ABBR *of* February Febr., Februar *m*
Feb·ru·a·ry (ABBR *Feb*) Februar *m*
fed·er·al POL Bundes-
Fed·er·al Re·pub·lic of Ger·man·y *die* Bundesrepublik Deutschland (ABBR *BRD*)
fed·er·a·tion POL Bundesstaat *m*; Föderation *f*, Staatenbund *m*; ECON, SPORT etc (Dach)Verband *m*
fee Gebühr *f*; Honorar *n*; (Mitglieds-)Beitrag *m*; Eintrittsgeld *n*
fee·ble schwach
feed 1. Futter *n*; Nahrung *f*; Fütterung *f*; TECH Zuführung *f*, Speisung *f*; 2. *v/t* füttern; ernähren; TECH *Maschine* speisen; EDP eingeben; AGR weiden lassen; *be fed up with s.th.* (*s.th.*) j-n (et.) satthaben; *well fed* wohlgenährt; *v/i* (fr)essen; sich ernähren; weiden
feed·back ELECTR Feed-back *n*, Rückkoppelung *f*; *radio*, TV Reaktion *f*
feed·er Esser *m*
feed·er road Zubringer(straße *f*) *m*
feed·ing bot·tle (Saug)Flasche *f*
feel 1. (sich) fühlen; berühren; empfinden; sich anfühlen; *feel sorry for s.o.* j-n bedauern *or* bemitleiden; 2. Gefühl *n*;

Empfindung *f*
feel·er ZO Fühler *m*
feel·ing Gefühl *n*
feign *Interesse etc* vortäuschen, *Krankheit a.* simulieren
feint Finte *f*
fell niederschlagen; fällen
fel·low 1. Gefährte *m*, Gefährtin *f*, Kamerad(in); Gegenstück *n*; F Kerl *m*; *old fellow* F alter Knabe; *the fellow of a glove* der andere Handschuh; 2. Mit...
fellow be·ing Mitmensch *m*
fellow cit·i·zen Mitbürger *m*
fellow coun·try·man Landsmann *m*
fel·low·ship Gemeinschaft *f*; Kameradschaft *f*
fel·low trav·el·(l)er Mitreisende *m*, *f*, Reisegefährte *m*, -gefährtin *f*; POL Mitläufer(in)
fel·on JUR Schwerverbrecher *m*
fel·o·ny JUR (schweres) Verbrechen, Kapitalverbrechen *n*
felt Filz *m*
felt pen, felt tip, felt-tip(ped) pen Filzstift *m*, Filzschreiber *m*
fe·male 1. weiblich; 2. *contp* Weib *n*, Weibsbild *n*; ZO Weibchen *n*
fem·i·nine weiblich, Frauen...; feminin
fem·i·nism Feminismus *m*
fem·i·nist 1. Feminist(in); 2. feministisch
fen Fenn *n*, Sumpf-, Marschland *n*
fence 1. Zaun *m*; *sl* Hehler *m*; 2. *v/t: fence in* einzäunen, umzäunen; einsperren; *fence off* abzäunen; *v/i* SPORT fechten
fenc·er SPORT Fechter *m*
fenc·ing 1. Einfriedung *f*; SPORT Fechten *n*; 2. Fecht...
fend: *fend off* abwehren; *fend for o.s.* für sich selbst sorgen
fend·er Schutzvorrichtung *f*; Schutzblech *n*; MOT Kotflügel *m*; Kamingitter *n*, Kaminvorsetzer *m*
fen·nel BOT Fenchel *m*
fer·ment 1. Ferment *n*; Gärung *f*; 2. gären (lassen)
fer·men·ta·tion Gärung *f*
fern BOT Farn(kraut *n*) *m*
fe·ro·cious wild; grausam
fe·ro·ci·ty Wildheit *f*
fer·ret 1. ZO Frettchen *n*; *fig* Spürhund *m*; 2. herumstöbern; *ferret out* aufspüren, aufstöbern
fer·ry 1. Fähre *f*; 2. übersetzen
fer·ry·boat Fährboot *n*, Fähre *f*
fer·ry·man Fährmann *m*
fer·tile fruchtbar; reich (*of, in* an *dat*)
fer·til·i·ty Fruchtbarkeit *f* (*a. fig*)
fer·ti·lize fruchtbar machen; befruchten; AGR düngen

463   **fill**

fer·ti·liz·er AGR (*esp* Kunst)Dünger *m*, Düngemittel *n*
fer·vent glühend, leidenschaftlich
fer·vo(u)r Glut *f*; Inbrunst *f*
fes·ter MED eitern
fes·ti·val Fest *n*; Festival *n*, Festspiele *pl*
fes·tive festlich
fes·tiv·i·ty Festlichkeit *f*
fes·toon Girlande *f*
fetch holen; *Preis* erzielen; *Seufzer* ausstoßen
fetch·ing F reizend
fete, fête 1. Fest *n*; *village fete* Dorffest *n*; **2.** feiern
fet·id stinkend
fet·ter 1. Fessel *f*; **2.** fesseln
feud Fehde *f*
feud·al Feudal..., Lehns...
feu·dal·ism Feudalismus *m*, Feudal-, Lehnssystem *n*
fe·ver·ish MED Fieber *n*
fe·ver·ish MED fieb(e)rig, fieberhaft (*a. fig*)
few wenige; *a few* ein paar, einige; *no fewer than* nicht weniger als; *quite a few, a good few* e-e ganze Menge
fi·an·cé Verlobte *m*
fi·an·cée Verlobte *f*
fi·as·co Fiasko *n*
fib F 1. Flunkerei *f*, Schwindelei *f*; 2. schwindeln, flunkern
fi·ber, *Br* **fi·bre** Faser *f*
fi·ber·glass TECH Fiberglas *n*, Glasfaser *f*
fi·brous faserig
fick·le wankelmütig; unbeständig
fic·tion Erfindung *f*; Prosaliteratur *f*, Belletristik *f*; Romane *pl*
fic·tion·al erdichtet; Roman...
fic·ti·tious erfunden, fiktiv
fid·dle 1. Fiedel *f*, Geige *f*; *play first (second)* fiddle *esp fig* die erste (zweite) Geige spielen; (*as*) *fit as a fiddle* kerngesund; **2.** MUS fiedeln; *a. fiddle about* or *around* (*with*) herumfingern (an *dat*), spielen (mit)
fid·dler Geiger(in)
fi·del·i·ty Treue *f*; Genauigkeit *f*
fid·get F nervös machen; (herum)zappeln
fid·get·y zapp(e)lig, nervös
field Feld *n*; SPORT Spielfeld *n*; Arbeitsfeld *n*; Gebiet *n*; Bereich *m*; *field of vision* OPT Gesichtsfeld *n*
field e·vents SPORT Sprung- und Wurfdisziplinen *pl*
field glass·es *a.* **pair of field glasses** Feldstecher *m*, Fernglas *n*
field mar·shal MIL Feldmarschall *m*
field·work praktische (wissenschaftliche) Arbeit, *a.* Arbeit *f* im Gelände; ECON

Feldarbeit *f*
fiend Satan *m*, Teufel *m*; F (*Frischluft-etc*)Fanatiker(in)
fiend·ish teuflisch, boshaft
fierce wild; scharf; heftig
fierce·ness Wildheit *f*, Schärfe *f*; Heftigkeit *f*
fi·er·y feurig; hitzig
fif·teen 1. fünfzehn; **2.** Fünfzehn *f*
fif·teenth fünfzehnte(r, -s)
fifth 1. fünfte(r, -s); **2.** Fünftel *n*
fifth·ly fünftens
fif·ti·eth fünfzigste(r, -s)
fif·ty 1. fünfzig; **2.** Fünfzig *f*
fif·ty-fif·ty F halbe-halbe
fig BOT Feige *f*
fight 1. Kampf *m*; MIL Gefecht *n*; Schlägerei *f*; *boxing*: Kampf *m*, Fight *m*; **2.** *v/t* bekämpfen; kämpfen gegen *or* mit, SPORT *a.* boxen gegen; *v/i* kämpfen, sich schlagen; SPORT boxen
fight·er Kämpfer *m*; SPORT Boxer *m*, Fighter *m*; *a.* **fighter plane** MIL Jagdflugzeug *n*
fight·ing Kampf *m*
fig·u·ra·tive bildlich
fig·ure 1. Figur *f*; Gestalt *f*; Zahl *f*, Ziffer *f*; Preis *m*; *be good at figures* ein guter Rechner sein; **2.** *v/t* abbilden, darstellen; F meinen, glauben; sich *et.* vorstellen; *figure out Problem* lösen, F rauskriegen; verstehen; *figure up* zusammenzählen; *v/i* erscheinen, vorkommen; *figure on* rechnen mit
figure skat·er Eiskunstläufer(in)
figure skat·ing Eiskunstlauf *m*
fil·a·ment ELECTR Glühfaden *m*
filch F klauen, stibitzen
file¹ 1. Ordner *m*; Karteikasten *m*; Akte *f*, Akten *pl*; Ablage *f*; EDP Datei *f*; Reihe *f*; MIL Rotte *f*; *on file* bei den Akten; **2.** *v/t Briefe etc* ablegen, zu den Akten nehmen, einordnen; *Antrag* einreichen, *Berufung* einlegen; *v/i* hintereinander marschieren
file² TECH 1. Feile *f*; **2.** feilen
file man·age·ment EDP Dateiverwaltung *f*
file pro·tec·tion EDP Schreibschutz *m*
fil·et GASTR Filet *n*
fil·i·al kindlich, Kindes...
fil·ing Ablegen *n*
fil·ing cab·i·net Aktenschrank *m*
fill 1. (sich) füllen; an-, aus-, erfüllen, vollfüllen; *Pfeife* stopfen; *Zahn* füllen, plombieren; *fill in* einsetzen; *fill out* (*Br in*) *Formular* ausfüllen; *fill up* vollfüllen; sich füllen; *fill her up!* F MOT volltanken, bitte!; **2.** Füllung *f*; *eat one's fill* sich satt essen

fil·let → *filet*

fill·ing Füllung f; MED (Zahn)Füllung f, Plombe f

filling sta·tion Tankstelle f

fil·ly ZO Stutenfohlen n

film 1. Häutchen n; Membran(e) f; Film m (a. PHOT); *take or shoot a film* e-n Film drehen; **2.** (ver)filmen; sich verfilmen lassen

film star *esp Br* Filmstar m

fil·ter 1. Filter m; **2.** filtern

fil·ter tip Filter m; Filterzigarette f

fil·ter-tipped: *filtertipped cigarette* Filterzigarette f

filth Schmutz m

filth·y schmutzig; *fig* unflätig

fin ZO Flosse f; SPORT Schwimmflosse f

fi·nal 1. letzte(r, -s); End…, Schluss…; endgültig; **2.** SPORT Finale n; *mst pl* Schlussexamen n, -prüfung f

fi·nal dis·pos·al Endlagerung f

fi·nal·ist SPORT Finalist(in)

fi·nal·ly endlich, schließlich; endgültig

fi·nal whis·tle SPORT Schlusspfiff m, Abpfiff m

fi·nance 1. Finanzwesen n; *pl* Finanzen *pl*; **2.** finanzieren

fi·nan·cial finanziell

fi·nan·cier Finanzier m

finch ZO Fink m

find 1. finden; (an)treffen; herausfinden; JUR *j-n* für (*nicht*) *schuldig* erklären; beschaffen, besorgen; *find out v/t et.* herausfinden; *v/i* es herausfinden; **2.** Fund m, Entdeckung f

find·ings Befund m; JUR Feststellung f, Spruch m

fine¹ 1. *adj* fein; schön; ausgezeichnet; großartig; *I'm fine* mir geht es gut; **2.** *adv* F sehr gut, bestens

fine² 1. Geldstrafe f, Bußgeld n; **2.** zu e-r Geldstrafe verurteilen

fin·ger 1. ANAT Finger m; → *cross 3*; **2.** betasten, (herum)fingern an (*dat*)

fin·ger·nail ANAT Fingernagel m

fin·ger·print Fingerabdruck m

fin·ger·tip Fingerspitze f

fin·i·cky pedantisch; wählerisch

fin·ish 1. (be)enden, aufhören (mit); *a. finish off* vollenden, zu Ende führen, erledigen, *Buch etc* auslesen; *a. finish off, finish up* aufessen, austrinken; **2.** Ende n, Schluss m; SPORT Endspurt m, Finish n; Ziel n; Vollendung f, letzter Schliff m

fin·ish·ing line SPORT Ziellinie f

Fin·land Finnland n

Finn Finne m, Finnin f

Finn·ish 1. finnisch; **2.** LING Finnisch n

fir a. **fir tree** BOT Tanne f

fir cone BOT Tannenzapfen m

fire 1. Feuer n; *be on fire* in Flammen stehen, brennen; *catch fire* Feuer fangen, in Brand geraten; *set on fire, set fire to* anzünden; **2.** *v/t* anzünden, entzünden; *fig* anfeuern; abfeuern; *Ziegel etc* brennen; F *j-n* rausschmeißen; heizen; *v/i* Feuer fangen (*a. fig*); feuern

fire a·larm Feueralarm m; Feuermelder m

fire·arms Schusswaffen *pl*

fire bri·gade *Br* Feuerwehr f

fire·bug F Feuerteufel m

fire·crack·er Knallfrosch m; Knallbonbon m, n

fire de·part·ment Feuerwehr f

fire en·gine *Br* Löschfahrzeug n

fire es·cape Feuerleiter f, -treppe f

fire ex·tin·guish·er Feuerlöscher m

fire fight·er Feuerwehrmann m

fire·guard *Br* Kamingitter n

fire hy·drant *Br* Hydrant m

fire·man Feuerwehrmann m; Heizer m

fire·place (offener) Kamin

fire·plug Hydrant m

fire·proof feuerfest

fire-rais·ing *Br* Brandstiftung f

fire·screen Kamingitter n

fire ser·vice *Br* Feuerwehr f

fire·side (offener) Kamin

fire sta·tion Feuerwache f

fire truck Löschfahrzeug n

fire·wood Brennholz n

fire·works Feuerwerk n

fir·ing squad MIL Exekutionskommando n

firm¹ fest; hart; standhaft

firm² Firma f

first 1. *adj* erste(r, -s); beste(r, -s); **2.** *adv* erstens; zuerst; *first of all* an erster Stelle; zu allererst; **3.** Erste(r, -s); *at first* zuerst, anfangs; *from the first* von Anfang an

first aid MED Erste Hilfe

first aid box, first aid kit Verband(s)kasten m

first-born erstgeborene(r, -s), älteste(r, -s)

first class RAIL *etc* 1. Klasse

first-class erstklassig

first floor Erdgeschoss n, *Br* erster Stock; → *second floor*

first-hand aus erster Hand

first leg SPORT Hinspiel n

first·ly erstens

first name Vorname m

first-rate erstklassig

firth Förde f, Meeresarm m

fish 1. ZO Fisch m; **2.** fischen, angeln

fish·bone Gräte f

fish·er·man Fischer m

fish·e·ry Fischerei f
fish fin·ger Br GASTR Fischstäbchen n
fish-hook Angelhaken m
fish·ing Fischen n, Angeln n
fishing line Angelschnur f
fishing rod Angelrute f
fishing tack·le Angelgerät n
fish-mon·ger esp Br Fischhändler m
fish stick GASTR Fischstäbchen n
fish·y Fisch...; F verdächtig
fis·sion PHYS Spaltung f
fis·sure GEOL Spalt m, Riss m
fist Faust f
fit¹ 1. geeignet, passend; tauglich; SPORT
fit, (gut) in Form; **keep fit** sich fit halten;
2. v/t passend machen (**for** für), anpassen; TECH einbauen, einbauen; anbringen; **fit in** j-m e-n Termin geben, j-n, et.
einschieben; a. **fit on** anprobieren; a.
fit out ausrüsten, ausstatten, einrichten
(**with** mit); a. **fit up** einrichten (**with**
mit); montieren, installieren; v/i passen,
sitzen (dress etc); **3.** Sitz m
fit² MED Anfall m; **give s.o. a fit** F j-n auf
die Palme bringen; j-m e-n Schock versetzen
fit·ful unruhig (sleep etc)
fit·ness Tauglichkeit f; esp SPORT Fitness f,
(gute) Form
fitness cen·ter (Br **cen·tre**) Fitnesscenter
n
fit·ted zugeschnitten; **fitted carpet**
Spannteppich m, Teppichboden m; **fitted
kitchen** Einbauküche f
fit·ter Monteur m; Installateur m
fit·ting 1. passend; schicklich; **2.** Montage
f, Installation f; pl Ausstattung f; Armaturen pl
five 1. fünf; **2.** Fünf f
fix 1. befestigen, anbringen (**to** an dat);
Preis festsetzen; fixieren; Blick etc richten (**on** auf acc); Aufmerksamkeit etc fesseln; reparieren, in Ordnung bringen (a.
fig); Essen zubereiten; **2.** F Klemme f; sl
Fix m
fixed fest; starr
fix·ings GASTR Beilagen pl
fix·ture Inventarstück n; **lighting fixture**
Beleuchtungskörper m
fizz zischen, sprudeln
flab·ber·gast F verblüffen; **be flabbergasted** F platt sein
flab·by schlaff
flac·cid schlaff, schlapp
flag¹ 1. Fahne f, Flagge f; **2.** beflaggen
flag² 1. (Stein)Platte f, Fliese f; **2.** mit
(Stein)Platten or Fliesen belegen, fliesen
flag³ nachlassen, erlahmen
flag·pole, flag·staff Fahnenstange f

flag·stone (Stein)Platte f, Fliese f
flake 1. Flocke f; Schuppe f; **2.** mst **flake
off** abblättern; F **flake out** schlappmachen
flak·y flockig; blätt(e)rig
flak·y pas·try GASTR Blätterteig m
flame 1. Flamme f (a. fig); **be in flames** in
Flammen stehen; **2.** flammen, lodern
flam·ma·ble TECH brennbar, leicht entzündlich, feuergefährlich
flan GASTR Obst-, Käsekuchen m
flank 1. Flanke f; **2.** flankieren
flan·nel Flanell m; Br Waschlappen m; pl
Br Flanellhose f
flap 1. Flattern n, (Flügel)Schlag m; Klappe f; **2.** mit den Flügeln etc schlagen; flattern
flare 1. flackern; sich weiten; **flare up** auf-
flammen; fig aufbrausen; **2.** Lichtsignal
n
flash 1. Aufblitzen n, Aufleuchten n, Blitz
m; radio etc: Kurzmeldung f; PHOT F Blitz
m; F Taschenlampe f; **like a flash** wie der
Blitz; **in a flash** im Nu; **a flash of lightning** ein Blitz; **2.** (auf)blitzen or aufleuchten (lassen); zucken; rasen, flitzen
flash·back film: Rückblende f
flash freeze GASTR schnell einfrieren
flash·light PHOT Blitzlicht n; Taschenlampe f
flash·y protzig; auffallend
flask Taschenflasche f
flat¹ 1. flach, eben, platt; schal; ECON flau;
MOT platt (tire); **2.** adv **fall flat** danebengehen; **sing flat** zu tief singen; **3.** Fläche
f, Ebene f; flache Seite; Flachland n,
Niederung f; MOT Reifenpanne f
flat² Br Wohnung f
flat-foot·ed plattfüßig
flat·mate Br Mitbewohner(in)
flat·ten (ein)ebnen; abflachen; a. **flatten
out** flach(er) werden
flat·ter schmeicheln (dat)
flat·ter·er Schmeichler(in)
flat·ter·y Schmeichelei f
fla·vo(u)r 1. Geschmack m; Aroma n; Blume f; fig Beigeschmack m; Würze f; **2.**
würzen
fla·vo(u)r·ing Würze f, Aroma n
flaw Fehler m, TECH a. Defekt m
flaw·less einwandfrei, tadellos
flax BOT Flachs m
flea ZO Floh m
flea mar·ket Flohmarkt m
fleck Fleck(en) m; Tupfen m
fledged ZO flügge
fledg(e)·ling ZO Jungvogel m; fig Grün-
schnabel m
flee fliehen; meiden

fleece 1. Vlies *n, esp* Schafsfell *n*; **2.** F *j-n* neppen

fleet MAR Flotte *f*

flesh Fleisch *n*

flesh·y fleischig; dick

flex¹ *esp* ANAT biegen

flex² *esp Br* ELECTR (Anschluss-, Verlängerungs)Kabel *n*, (-)Schnur *f*

flex·i·ble flexibel, biegsam; *fig* anpassungsfähig; ***flexible working hours*** Gleitzeit *f*

flex·i·time *Br,* **flex·time** Gleitzeit *f*

flick schnippen; schnellen

flick·er 1. flackern; TV flimmern; **2.** Flackern *n*; TV Flimmern *n*

fli·er AVIAT Flieger *m*; Reklamezettel *m*

flight Flucht *f*; Flug *m* (*a. fig*); zo Schwarm *m*; *a.* ***flight of stairs*** Treppe *f*; ***put to flight*** in die Flucht schlagen; ***take (to) flight*** die Flucht ergreifen

flight at·tend·ant AVIAT Flugbegleiter(in)

flight·less zo flugunfähig

flight re·cord·er AVIAT Flugschreiber *m*

flight·y flatterhaft

flim·sy dünn; zart; *fig* fadenscheinig

flinch (zurück)zucken, zusammenfahren; zurückschrecken (***from*** vor *dat*)

fling 1. werfen, schleudern; ***fling o.s.*** sich stürzen; ***fling open (to)*** *Tür etc* aufreißen (zuschlagen); **2.** ***have a fling*** sich ausbeben; ***have a fling at*** es versuchen *or* probieren mit

flint Feuerstein *m*

flip schnippen, schnipsen; *Münze* hochwerfen

flip·pant respektlos, F schnodd(e)rig

flip·per zo Flosse *f*; Schwimmflosse *f*

flirt 1. flirten; **2.** ***be a flirt*** gern flirten

flir·ta·tion Flirt *m*

flit flitzen, huschen

float 1. *v/i* (auf dem Wasser) schwimmen, (im Wasser) treiben; schweben; *a.* ECON in Umlauf sein; *v/t* schwimmen *or* treiben lassen; MAR flottmachen; ECON *Wertpapiere etc* in Umlauf bringen; *Währung* floaten, den Wechselkurs (*gen*) freigeben; **2.** Festwagen *m*

float·ing 1. schwimmend, treibend; ECON umlaufend; frei (*exchange rate*); frei konvertierbar (*currency*); **2.** ECON Floating *n*

float·ing vot·er POL Wechselwähler(in)

flock 1. zo Herde *f* (*a.* REL); Menge *f*, Schar *f*; **2.** *fig* strömen

floe (treibende) Eisscholle

flog prügeln, schlagen

flog·ging Tracht *f* Prügel

flood 1. *a.* ***flood tide*** Flut *f*; Überschwemmung *f*; **2.** überfluten, überschwemmen

flood·gate Schleusentor *n*

flood·lights ELECTR Flutlicht *n*

floor 1. (Fuß)Boden *m*; Stock *m*, Stockwerk *n*, Etage *f*; Tanzfläche *f*; → ***first floor***, ***second floor***; ***take the floor*** das Wort ergreifen; **2.** e-n (Fuß)Boden legen in; zu Boden schlagen; *fig* F *j-n* umhauen

floor·board (Fußboden)Diele *f*

floor cloth Putzlappen *m*

floor·ing (Fuß)Bodenbelag *m*

floor lamp Stehlampe *f*

floor lead·er PARL Fraktionsführer *m*

floor-length bodenlang

floor show Nachtklubvorstellung *f*

floor·walk·er Aufsicht *f*

flop 1. sich (hin)plumpsen lassen; F durchfallen, danebengehen, ein Reinfall sein; **2.** Plumps *m*; F Flop *m*, Reinfall *m*, Pleite *f*; Versager *m*

flop·py (disk) EDP Floppy Disk *f*, Diskette *f*

flor·id rot, gerötet

flor·ist Blumenhändler(in)

floun·der¹ zo Flunder *f*

floun·der² zappeln; strampeln; *fig* sich verhaspeln

flour (feines) Mehl

flour·ish 1. Schnörkel *m*; MUS Tusch *m*; **2.** *v/i* blühen, gedeihen; *v/t* schwenken

flow 1. fließen, strömen; wallen; **2.** Fluß *m*, Strom *m* (*both a. fig*)

flow·er 1. Blume *f*; Blüte *f* (*a. fig*); **2.** blühen

flow·er·bed Blumenbeet *n*

flow·er·pot Blumentopf *m*

fluc·tu·ate schwanken

fluc·tu·a·tion Schwankung *f*

flu F MED Grippe *f*

flue Rauchfang *m*, Esse *f*

flu·en·cy Flüssigkeit *f*; (Rede)Gewandtheit *f*

flu·ent flüssig; gewandt; ***speak fluent French*** fließend Französisch sprechen

fluff 1. Flaum *m*; Staubflocke *f*; **2.** zo aufplustern

fluff·y flaumig

flu·id 1. flüssig; **2.** Flüssigkeit *f*

flunk F durchfallen (lassen)

flu·o·res·cent fluoreszierend

flu·o·ride CHEM Fluor *n*

flu·o·rine CHEM Fluor *n*

flur·ry Windstoß *m*; (Regen-, Schnee-) Schauer *m*; *fig* Aufregung *f*, Unruhe *f*

flush 1. (Wasser)Spülung *f*; Erröten *n*; Röte *f*; **2.** *v/t a.* ***flush out*** (aus)spülen; ***flush down*** hinunterspülen; ***flush the toilet*** spülen; *v/i* erröten, rot werden; spülen; **3.** ***be flush*** F gut bei Kasse sein

flus·ter 1. nervös machen *or* werden; **2.** Nervosität *f*

flute MUS 1. Flöte f; 2. (auf der) Flöte spielen

flut·ter 1. flattern; 2. Flattern n; fig Erregung f

flux fig Fluss m

fly¹ zo Fliege f

fly² Hosenschlitz m; Zeltklappe f

fly³ fliegen (lassen); stürmen, stürzen; flattern, wehen; (ver)fliegen (time); Drachen steigen lassen; **fly at s.o.** auf j-n losgehen; **fly into a passion** or **rage** in Wut geraten

fly·er → flier

fly·ing fliegend; Flug...

flying sau·cer fliegende Untertasse

flying squad Überfallkommando n

flying vis·it F Stippvisite f

fly·o·ver Br (Straßen-, Eisenbahn-) Überführung f

fly·screen Fliegenfenster n

fly·weight boxing: Fliegengewicht n, Fliegengewichtler m

fly·wheel TECH Schwungrad n

foal zo Fohlen n

foam 1. Schaum m; 2. schäumen

foam ex·tin·guish·er Schaumlöscher m, -löschgerät n

foam rub·ber Schaumgummi m

foam·y schaumig

fo·cus 1. Brennpunkt m, fig a. Mittelpunkt m; OPT, PHOT Scharfeinstellung f; 2. OPT, PHOT scharf einstellen; fig konzentrieren (**on** akk auf akk)

fod·der AGR (Trocken)Futter n

foe POET Feind m, Gegner m

fog (dichter) Nebel

fog·gy neb(e)lig; fig nebelhaft

foi·ble (kleine) Schwäche

foil¹ Folie f; fig Hintergrund m

foil² vereiteln

foil³ fencing: Florett n

fold¹ 1. Falte f; Falz m; 2. ...fach, ...fältig; 3. (sich) falten; falzen; Arme verschränken; einwickeln; often **fold up** zusammenfalten, -legen, -klappen

fold² AGR Schafhürde f, Pferch m; REL Herde f

fold·er Aktendeckel m; Schnellhefter m; Faltprospekt m, -blatt n, Broschüre f

fold·ing zusammenlegbar; Klapp...

folding bed Klappbett n

folding bi·cy·cle Klapprad n

folding boat Faltboot n

folding chair Klappstuhl m

folding door(s) Falttür f

fo·li·age BOT Laub n, Laubwerk n

folk 1. Leute pl; pl F m-e etc Leute pl; 2. Volks...

folk·lore Volkskunde f; Volkssagen pl; Folklore f

folk mu·sic Volksmusik f

folk song Volkslied n; Folksong m

fol·low folgen (dat); folgen auf (akk); befolgen; verfolgen; s-m Beruf etc nachgehen; **follow through** Plan etc bis zum Ende durchführen; **follow up** e-r Sache nachgehen; e-e Sache weiterverfolgen; **as follows** wie folgt

fol·low·er Nachfolger(in); Verfolger(in); Anhänger(in)

fol·low·ing 1. Anhängerschaft f, Anhänger pl; Gefolge n; **the following** das Folgende; die Folgenden pl; 2. folgende(r, -s); 3. im Anschluss an (akk)

fol·ly Torheit f

fond zärtlich; vernarrt (**of** in akk); **be fond of** gernhaben, lieben

fon·dle liebkosen; streicheln; (ver)hätscheln

fond·ness Zärtlichkeit f; Vorliebe f

font REL Taufstein m, Taufbecken n

food Nahrung f, Essen n; Nahrungs-, Lebensmittel pl; AGR Futter n

fool 1. Narr m, Närrin f, Dummkopf m; **make a fool of s.o.** j-n zum Narren halten; **make a fool of o.s.** sich lächerlich machen; 2. zum Narren halten; betrügen (**out of** um); **fool about, fool around** herumtrödeln; Unsinn machen, herumalbern

fool·har·dy tollkühn

fool·ish dumm, töricht; unklug

fool·ish·ness Dummheit f

fool·proof kinderleicht; todsicher

foot 1. ANAT Fuß m (a. linear measure = 30,48 cm); Fußende n; **on foot** zu Fuß; 2. F Rechnung bezahlen; **have to foot the bill** die Zeche bezahlen müssen; **foot it** zu Fuß gehen

foot·ball Football(spiel n) m; Br Fußball (-spiel n) m; Football-Ball m; Br Fußball m

foot·bal·ler Br Fußballer m

foot·ball hoo·li·gan Br Fußballrowdy m

football play·er Br Fußballspieler m

foot·bridge Fußgängerbrücke f

foot·fall Tritt m, Schritt m

foot·hold fester Stand, Halt m

foot·ing Halt m, Stand m; fig Grundlage f, Basis f; **be on a friendly footing with s.o.** ein gutes Verhältnis zu j-m haben; **lose one's footing** den Halt verlieren

foot·lights THEA Rampenlicht(er pl) n

foot·loose frei, unbeschwert; **footloose and fancy-free** frei und ungebunden

foot·note Fußnote f

foot·path (Fuß)Pfad m, (Fuß)Weg m

foot·print Fußabdruck m, pl a. Fußspur(en pl) f

foot·sore: *be footsore* wunde Füße haben

foot·step Tritt *m*, Schritt *m*; Fußstapfe *f*

foot·wear Schuhwerk *n*, Schuhe *pl*

fop Geck *m*, F Fatzke *m*

for 1. *prp mst* für; *purpose, direction*: zu; nach; *warten, hoffen etc auf (acc)*; *sich sehnen etc* nach; *cause*: aus, vor *(dat)*, wegen; *time*: *for three days* drei Tage (lang); *ich ging drei Tagen*; *distance*: *I walked for a mile* ich ging eine Meile (weit); *exchange*: (an)statt; als; *I for one* ich zum Beispiel; *for sure* sicher!, gewiss!; **2.** *cj* denn, weil

for·age *a.* *forage about* (herum)stöbern, (-)wühlen (*in* in *dat*; *for* nach)

for·ay MIL Einfall *m*, Überfall *m*; *fig* Ausflug *m* (*into* politics in *die Politik*)

for·bid verbieten; hindern

for·bid·ding abstoßend

force 1. Stärke *f*, Kraft *f*, Gewalt *f*, Wucht *f*; *the* (*police*) *force* die Polizei; (*armed*) *forces* MIL Streitkräfte *pl*; *by force* mit Gewalt; *come or put into force* in Kraft treten *or* setzen; **2.** *j-n* zwingen; *et.* erzwingen; zwängen; drängen; *Tempo* beschleunigen; *come s.th. on s.o.* et. aufzwingen *or* aufdrängen; *force o.s. on s.o.* sich j-m aufdrängen; *force open* aufbrechen

forced erzwungen; gezwungen, gequält

forced land·ing AVIAT Notlandung *f*

force·ful energisch, kraftvoll; eindrucksvoll, überzeugend

for·ceps MED Zange *f*

for·ci·ble gewaltsam; eindringlich

ford 1. Furt *f*; **2.** durchwaten

fore 1. vorder, Vorder...; vorn; **2.** Vorderteil *m*, Vorderseite *f*, Front *f*

fore·arm ANAT Unterarm *m*

fore·bear *mst pl* Vorfahren *pl*, Ahnen *pl*

fore·bod·ing (böses) Vorzeichen; (*böse*) (Vor)Ahnung

fore·cast 1. voraussagen, vorhersehen; *Wetter* vorhersagen; **2.** Voraussage *f*; METEOR Vorhersage *f*

fore·fa·ther Vorfahr *m*

fore·fin·ger ANAT Zeigefinger *m*

fore·foot ZO Vorderfuß *m*

fore·gone con·clu·sion ausgemachte Sache; *be a foregone conclusion a.* von vornherein feststehen

fore·ground Vordergrund *m*

fore·hand SPORT **1.** Vorhand *f*, Vorhandschlag *m*; **2.** Vorhand...

fore·head ANAT Stirn *f*

for·eign fremd, ausländisch, Außen..., Auslands...

foreign af·fairs Außenpolitik *f*

foreign aid Auslandshilfe *f*

for·eign·er Ausländer(in)

for·eign lan·guage Fremdsprache *f*

foreign min·is·ter POL Außenminister *m*

For·eign Of·fice *Br* POL Außenministerium *n*

foreign pol·i·cy Außenpolitik *f*

For·eign Sec·re·ta·ry *Br* POL Außenminister *m*

foreign trade ECON Außenhandel *m*

foreign work·er Gastarbeiter(in)

fore·knowl·edge vorherige Kenntnis

fore·leg ZO Vorderbein *n*

fore·man TECH Vorarbeiter *m*, Polier *m*; Werkmeister *m*; JUR Sprecher *m*

fore·most vorderste(r, -s), erste(r, -s)

fore·name Vorname *m*

fo·ren·sic JUR Gerichts...

forensic me·di·cine Gerichtsmedizin *f*

fore·run·ner Vorläufer(in)

fore·see vorhersehen, voraussehen

fore·see·a·ble vorhersehbar

fore·shad·ow ahnen lassen, andeuten

fore·sight Weitblick *m*; (weise) Voraussicht

for·est Wald *m* (*a. fig*); Forst *m*

fore·stall *et.* vereiteln; *j-m* zuvorkommen

for·est·er Förster *m*

for·est·ry Forstwirtschaft *f*

fore·taste Vorgeschmack *m*

fore·tell vorhersagen

for·ev·er, *for ev·er* für immer

fore·wom·an TECH Vorarbeiterin *f*

fore·word Vorwort *n*

for·feit verwirken; einbüßen

forge 1. Schmiede *f*; **2.** fälschen; schmieden

forg·er Fälscher *m*

for·ge·ry Fälschen *n*; Fälschung *f*

for·ge·ry-proof fälschungssicher

for·get vergessen

for·get·ful vergesslich

for·get-me-not BOT Vergissmeinnicht *n*

for·give vergeben, verzeihen

for·give·ness Verzeihung *f*; Vergebung *f*

for·giv·ing versöhnlich; nachsichtig

fork 1. Gabel *f*; **2.** (sich) gabeln

fork·lift truck MOT Gabelstapler *m*

form 1. Form *f*; Gestalt *f*; Formular *n*, Vordruck *m*; *Br* (*Schul*)Klasse *f*; Formalität *f*; Kondition *f*, Verfassung *f*; *in great form* gut in Form; **2.** (sich) formen, (sich) bilden, gestalten

for·mal förmlich; formell

for·mal dress Gesellschaftskleidung *f*

for·mal·i·ty Förmlichkeit *f*; Formalität *f*

for·mat 1. Aufmachung *f*; Format *n*; **2.** EDP formatieren

for·ma·tion Bildung *f*

form·a·tive bildend; gestaltend; **formative years** Entwicklungsjahre pl

for·mat·ting EDP Formatierung f

for·mer 1. früher; ehemalig; **2. the former** der or die or das Erstere

for·mer·ly früher

for·mi·da·ble furchterregend; gewaltig, riesig, gefährlich, schwierig

form mas·ter Br Klassenlehrer m, -leiter m

form mis·tress Br Klassenlehrerin f, -leiterin f

form teach·er Br Klassenlehrer(in), Klassenleiter(in)

for·mu·la Formel f; Rezept n

for·mu·late formulieren

for·sake aufgeben; verlassen

for·swear abschwören, entsagen (dat)

fort MIL Fort n, Festung f

forth weiter, fort; (her)vor; **and so forth** und so weiter

forth·com·ing bevorstehend, kommend; in Kürze erscheinend (book) or anlaufend (film)

for·ti·eth vierzigste(r, -s)

for·ti·fi·ca·tion Befestigung f

for·ti·fy MIL befestigen; fig (ver)stärken

for·ti·tude (innere) Kraft or Stärke

fort·night esp Br vierzehn Tage

for·tress MIL Festung f

for·tu·i·tous zufällig

for·tu·nate glücklich; **be fortunate** Glück haben

for·tu·nate·ly glücklicherweise

for·tune Vermögen n; (glücklicher) Zufall, Glück n; Schicksal n

for·tune-tell·er Wahrsager(in)

for·ty 1. vierzig; **have forty winks** F ein Nickerchen machen; **2.** Vierzig f

for·ward 1. adv nach vorn, vorwärts; **2.** adj Vorwärts…; fortschrittlich; vorlaut, dreist; **3.** soccer: Stürmer m; **4.** befördern, (ver)senden, schicken; Brief etc nachsenden

for·ward·ing a·gent Spediteur m

fos·sil GEOL Fossil n (a. F), Versteinerung f

fos·ter-child Pflegekind n

fos·ter-par·ents Pflegeeltern pl

foul 1. stinkend, widerlich; verpestet, schlecht (air, water); GASTR verdorben, faul; schmutzig, verschmutzt; METEOR stürmisch, schlecht; SPORT regelwidrig; esp Br F mies; **2.** SPORT Foul n, Regelverstoß m; **vicious foul** böses or übles Foul; **3.** beschmutzen, verschmutzen; SPORT foulen

found¹ gründen; stiften

found² TECH gießen

foun·da·tion ARCH Grundmauer f, Fundament n; fig Gründung f, Errichtung f; (gemeinnützige) Stiftung; fig Grundlage f, Basis f

found·er¹ Gründer(in), Stifter(in)

foun·der² MAR sinken; fig scheitern

found·ling JUR Findelkind n

foun·dry TECH Gießerei f

foun·tain Springbrunnen m; (Wasser-)Strahl m

fountain pen Füllfederhalter m

four 1. vier; **2.** Vier f; rowing: Vierer m; **on all fours** auf allen vieren

four star Br F Super n

four-star pet·rol Br Superbenzin n

four-stroke en·gine Viertaktmotor m

four·teen 1. vierzehn; **2.** Vierzehn f

four·teenth vierzehnte(r, -s)

fourth 1. vierte(r, -s); **2.** Viertel n

fourth·ly viertens

four-wheel drive MOT Vierradantrieb m

fowl ZO Geflügel n

fox ZO Fuchs m

fox·glove BOT Fingerhut m

fox·y schlau, gerissen

frac·tion Bruchteil m; MATH Bruch m

frac·ture MED **1.** (Knochen)Bruch m; **2.** brechen

fra·gile zerbrechlich

frag·ment Bruchstück n

fra·grance Wohlgeruch m, Duft m

fra·grant wohlriechend, duftend

frail gebrechlich; zerbrechlich; zart, schwach

frail·ty Zartheit f; Gebrechlichkeit f; Schwäche f

frame 1. Rahmen m; (Brillen- etc)Gestell n; Körper(bau) m; **frame of mind** (Gemüts)Verfassung f, (-)Zustand m; **2.** (ein)rahmen; bilden, formen, bauen; a. **frame up** F j-m et. anhängen

frame-up F abgekartetes Spiel; Intrige f

frame·work TECH Gerüst n; fig Struktur f, System n

franc Franc m; Franken m

France Frankreich n

fran·chise POL Wahlrecht n; ECON Konzession f

frank 1. frei(mütig), offen; **frankly (speaking)** offen gesagt; **2.** Brief freistempeln

frank·fur·ter GASTR Frankfurter (Würstchen n) f

frank·ness Offenheit f

fran·tic hektisch; **be frantic** außer sich sein

fra·ter·nal brüderlich

frat·er·nize sich verbrüdern

frat·er·ni·za·tion Verbrüderung f

fra·ter·ni·ty Brüderlichkeit f; Vereinigung

f, Zunft f; UNIV Verbindung f
fraud Betrug m; F Schwindel m
fraud·u·lent betrügerisch
fray ausfransen, (sich) durchscheuern
freak 1. Missgeburt f; Laune f; in cpds F ...freak m, ...fanatiker m; Freak m, irrer Typ; *freak of nature* Laune f der Natur; **2.** F a. *freak out* durchdrehen, die Nerven verlieren
freck·le Sommersprosse f
freck·led sommersprossig
free 1. frei; ungehindert; ungebunden; kostenlos, zum Nulltarif; freigebig; *free and easy* zwanglos; sorglos; *set free* freilassen; **2.** befreien; freilassen
free·dom Freiheit f
free fare Nulltarif m
free·lance frei, freiberuflich tätig, freischaffend
Free·ma·son Freimaurer m
free skat·ing SPORT Kür f
free·style SPORT Freistil m
free time Freizeit f
free trade ECON Freihandel m
free trade ar·e·a ECON Freihandelszone f
free·way Schnellstraße f
free·wheel im Freilauf fahren
freeze 1. v/i (ge)frieren; erstarren; v/t gefrieren lassen; GASTR einfrieren (a. ECON), tiefkühlen; **2.** Frost m, Kälte f; ECON, POL Einfrieren n; *wage freeze, freeze on wages* ECON Lohnstopp m
freeze-dried gefriergetrocknet
freeze-dry gefriertrocknen
freez·er Gefriertruhe f, Tiefkühl-, Gefriergerät n; Gefrierfach n
freez·ing eisig; Gefrier...
freezing com·part·ment Gefrierfach n
freezing point Gefrierpunkt m
freight 1. Fracht f; Frachtgebühr f; **2.** Güter...; **3.** beladen; verfrachten
freight car RAIL Güterwagen m
freight·er MAR Frachter m, Frachtschiff n; AVIAT Transportflugzeug n
freight train Güterzug m
French 1. französisch; **2.** LING Französisch n; *the French* die Franzosen pl
French doors Terrassen-, Balkontür f
French fries GASTR Pommes frites pl
French·man Franzose m
French win·dows → *French doors*
French·wom·an Französin f
fren·zied wahnsinnig, rasend (*with* vor dat); hektisch
fren·zy Wahnsinn m; Ekstase f; Raserei f
fre·quen·cy Häufigkeit f; ELECTR Frequenz f
fre·quent 1. häufig; **2.** (oft) besuchen
fresh frisch; neu; unerfahren; frech; *get*

fresh (with s.o.) (j-m gegenüber) zudringlich werden
fresh·en auffrischen (*wind*); *freshen (o.s.) up* sich frisch machen
fresh·man UNIV Student(in) im ersten Jahr
fresh·ness Frische f; Frechheit f
fresh wa·ter Süßwasser n
fresh-wa·ter Süßwasser...
fret sich Sorgen machen
fret·ful verärgert, gereizt; quengelig
FRG ABBR of *Federal Republic of Germany* Bundesrepublik f Deutschland
Fri ABBR of *Friday* Fr., Freitag m
fri·ar REL Mönch m
fric·tion TECH etc Reibung f (a. fig)
Fri·day (ABBR *Fri*) Freitag m; *on Friday* (am) Freitag; *on Fridays* freitags
fridge F Kühlschrank m
friend Freund(in); Bekannte m, f; *make friends with* sich anfreunden mit, Freundschaft schließen mit
friend·ly 1. freund(schaft)lich; **2.** esp Br SPORT Freundschaftsspiel n
friend·ship Freundschaft f
fries F GASTR Fritten pl
frig·ate MAR Fregatte f
fright Schreck(en) m; *look a fright* F verboten aussehen
fright·en erschrecken; *be frightened* erschrecken (*at, by, of* vor dat); Angst haben (*of* vor dat)
fright·ful schrecklich, fürchterlich
fri·gid PSYCH frigid(e); kalt, frostig
frill Krause f, Rüsche f
fringe 1. Franse f; Rand m; Pony m; **2.** mit Fransen besetzen
fringe ben·e·fits ECON Gehalts-, Lohnnebenleistungen pl
fringe e·vent Randveranstaltung f
fringe group soziale Randgruppe f
frisk herumtollen; F j-n filzen, durchsuchen
frisk·y lebhaft, munter
frit·ter: fritter away Geld etc vertun, Zeit vertrödeln, Geld, Kräfte vergeuden
fri·vol·i·ty Frivolität f, Leichtfertigkeit f
friv·o·lous frivol, leichtfertig
friz·zle F GASTR verbrutzeln
frizz·y gekräuselt, kraus
fro: to and fro hin und her
frock REL Kutte f
frog ZO Frosch m
frog·man Froschmann m, MIL a. Kampfschwimmer m
frol·ic herumtoben, herumtollen
from von; aus; von ... aus or her; von ... (an), seit; aus, vor (dat); *from 9 to 5 (o'clock)* von 9 bis 5 (Uhr)

front 1. Vorderseite f; Front f (a. MIL); **at the front, in front** vorn; **in front of** vor; **be in front** in Führung sein; **2.** Vorder...; **3.** a. **front on, front to(wards)** gegenüberstehen, gegenüberliegen
front·age ARCH (Vorder)Front f
front cov·er Titelseite f
front door Haustür f, Vordertür f
front en·trance Vordereingang m
fron·tier 1. (Landes)Grenze f; HIST Grenzland n, Grenze f; **2.** Grenz...
front-page F wichtig, aktuell
front-wheel drive MOT Vorderradantrieb m
frost 1. Frost m; a. **hoar frost, white frost** Reif m; **2.** mit Reif überziehen; Glas mattieren; GASTR glasieren; mit Zuckerguss überziehen; mit (Puder)Zucker bestreuen
frost·bite MED Erfrierung f
frost·bit·ten MED erfroren
frost·ed glass Matt-, Milchglas n
frost·y eisig, frostig (a. fig)
froth 1. Schaum m; **2.** schäumen; zu Schaum schlagen
froth·y schäumend; schaumig
frown 1. Stirnrunzeln n; **with a frown** stirnrunzelnd; **2.** v/i die Stirn runzeln
fro·zen adj (eis)kalt; (ein-, zu)gefroren; Gefrier...
fro·zen foods Tiefkühlkost f
fru·gal sparsam; bescheiden; einfach
fruit Frucht f; Früchte pl; Obst n
fruit·er·er Obsthändler m
fruit·ful fruchtbar
fruit·less unfruchtbar; erfolglos
fruit juice Fruchtsaft m
fruit·y fruchtartig; fruchtig (wine)
frus·trate vereiteln; frustrieren
frus·tra·tion Vereitelung f, Frustration f
fry braten; **fried eggs** Spiegeleier pl; **fried potatoes** Bratkartoffeln pl
fry·ing pan Bratpfanne f
fuch·sia BOT Fuchsie f
fuck V ficken, vögeln; **fuck off!** verpiss dich!; **get fucked!** der Teufel soll dich holen!
fuck·ing V Scheiß..., verflucht; **fucking hell!** verdammte Scheiße!
fudge GASTR Fondant m
fu·el 1. Brennstoff m; MOT Treib-, Kraftstoff m; **2.** MOT, AVIAT (auf)tanken
fu·el in·jec·tion en·gine MOT Einspritzmotor m
fu·gi·tive 1. flüchtig (a. fig); **2.** Flüchtling m
ful·fil Br, **ful·fill** erfüllen; vollziehen
ful·fil·(l)ing befriedigend
ful·fil(l)·ment Erfüllung f, Ausführung f

full 1. voll; ganz; Voll...; **full of** voll von, voller; **full (up)** (voll) besetzt (bus etc); F voll, satt; **house full!** THEA ausverkauft!; **full of o.s.** (ganz) von sich eingenommen; **2.** adv völlig, ganz; **3. in full** vollständig, ganz; **write out in full** Wort etc ausschreiben
full board Vollpension f
full dress Gesellschaftskleidung f
full-fledged ZO flügge; fig richtig
full-grown ausgewachsen
full-length in voller Größe; bodenlang; abendfüllend (film etc)
full moon Vollmond m
full stop LING Punkt m
full time SPORT Spielende n
full-time ganztägig, Ganztags...
full-time job Ganztagsbeschäftigung f
ful·ly voll, völlig, ganz
ful·ly-fledged Br → **full-fledged**
ful·ly-'grown Br → **full-grown**
fum·ble tasten; fummeln
fume wütend sein
fumes Dämpfe pl, Rauch m; Abgase pl
fum·ing wutschnaubend
fun Scherz m, Spaß m; **for fun** aus or zum Spaß; **make fun of** sich lustig machen über (acc), verspotten
func·tion 1. Funktion f; Aufgabe f; Veranstaltung f; **2.** funktionieren
func·tion·a·ry Funktionär m
func·tion key EDP Funktionstaste f
fund ECON Fonds m; Geld(mittel pl) n
fun·da·men·tal 1. Grund..., grundlegend; **2. fundamentals** Grundlage f, Grundbegriffe pl
fun·da·men·tal·ist Fundamentalist m
fu·ne·ral Begräbnis n, Beerdigung f
funeral march MUS Trauermarsch m
funeral o·ration Trauerrede f
funeral pro·ces·sion Trauerzug m
funeral ser·vice Trauerfeier f
fun·fair Rummelplatz m
fun·gus BOT Pilz m, Schwamm m
fu·nic·u·lar a. **funicular railway** (Draht)Seilbahn f
fun·nel Trichter m; MAR, RAIL Schornstein m
fun·nies F Comics pl
fun·ny komisch, lustig, spaßig; sonderbar
fur Pelz m, Fell n; MED Belag m; TECH Kesselstein m
fu·ri·ous wütend
furl Fahne, Segel aufrollen, einrollen; Schirm zusammenrollen
fur·nace TECH Schmelzofen m, Hochofen m; (Heiz)Kessel m
fur·nish einrichten, möblieren; liefern;

versorgen, ausrüsten, ausstatten (**with** mit)

fur·ni·ture Möbel *pl*; **sectional furniture** Anbaumöbel *pl*

furred MED belegt, pelzig

fur·ri·er Kürschner *m*

fur·row 1. Furche *f*; **2.** furchen

fur·ry pelzig; flauschig

fur·ther 1. weiter; **2.** fördern, unterstützen

further ed·u·ca·tion *Br* Fortbildung *f*, Weiterbildung *f*

fur·ther·more *fig* weiter, überdies

fur·ther·most entfernteste(r, -s), äußerste(r, -s)

fur·tive heimlich, verstohlen

fu·ry Wut *f*, Zorn *m*

fuse 1. Zünder *m*; ELECTR Sicherung *f*; Zündschnur *f*; **2.** schmelzen; ELECTR durchbrennen

fuse box ELECTR Sicherungskasten *m*

fu·se·lage (Flugzeug)Rumpf *m*

fu·sion Verschmelzung *f*, Fusion *f*; PHYS **nuclear fusion** Kernfusion *f*

fuss 1. (unnötige) Aufregung; Wirbel *m*, F Theater *n*; **2.** sich (unnötig) aufregen; viel Aufhebens machen (**about** um, von)

fuss·y aufgeregt, hektisch; kleinlich, pedantisch; heikel, wählerisch

fus·ty muffig; *fig* verstaubt

fu·tile nutzlos, zwecklos

fu·ture 1. (zu)künftig; **2.** Zukunft *f*; LING Futur *n*, Zukunft *f*; **in future** in Zukunft, künftig

fuzz feiner Flaum

fuzz·y kraus, wuschelig; unscharf, verschwommen; flaumig, flauschig

G

G, g G, g *n*

gab F Geschwätz *n*; **have the gift of the gab** ein gutes Mundwerk haben

gab·ar·dine Gabardine *m*

gab·ble 1. Geschnatter *n*, Geschwätz *n*; **2.** schnattern, schwatzen

ga·ble ARCH Giebel *m*

gad: F **gad about** (viel) unterwegs sein (in *dat*), sich herumtreiben

gad·fly ZO Bremse *f*

gad·get TECH Apparat *m*, Gerät *n*, Vorrichtung *f*; *often contp* technische Spielerei

gag 1. Knebel *m* (*a. fig*); F Gag *m*; **2.** knebeln; *fig* mundtot machen

gage 1. Eichmaß *n*; TECH Messgerät *n*, Lehre *f*; TECH Stärke *f*, Dicke *f*; RAIL Spur(weite) *f*; **2.** TECH eichen; (ab-, aus)messen

gai·e·ty Fröhlichkeit *f*

gain 1. gewinnen; erreichen, bekommen; zunehmen an (*dat*); vorgehen (um) (*watch*); **gain speed** schneller werden; **gain 5 pounds** 5 Pfund zunehmen; **gain in** zunehmen an (*dat*); **2.** Gewinn *m*; Zunahme *f*; **gain of time** Zeitgewinn *m*

gait Gang *m*, Gangart *f*; Schritt *m*

gai·ter Gamasche *f*

gal F Mädchen *n*

ga·la 1. Festlichkeit *f*, Gala(veranstaltung) *f*; **2.** Gala…

gal·ax·y ASTR Milchstraße *f*, Galaxis *f*

gale Sturm *m*

gall¹ Frechheit *f*

gall² 1. wund geriebene Stelle; **2.** wund reiben *or* scheuern; *fig* (ver)ärgern

gal·lant tapfer; galant, höflich

gal·lan·try Tapferkeit *f*; Galanterie *f*

gall blad·der ANAT Gallenblase *f*

gal·le·ry Galerie *f*; Empore *f*

gal·ley MAR Galeere *f*; Kombüse *f*; *a.* **galley proof** PRINT Fahne *f*, Fahnenabzug *m*

gal·lon Gallone *f* (*3,79 l, Br 4,55 l*)

gal·lop 1. Galopp *m*; **2.** galoppieren (lassen)

gal·lows Galgen *m*

gal·lows hu·mo(u)r Galgenhumor *m*

ga·lore in rauen Mengen

gam·ble 1. (um Geld) spielen; **2.** Glücksspiel *n*

gam·bler (Glücks)Spieler(in)

gam·bol 1. Luftsprung *m*; **2.** (herum-) tanzen, (herum)hüpfen

game (Karten-, Ball- *etc*)Spiel *n*; (einzelnes) Spiel (*a. fig*); HUNT Wild *n*; Wildbret *n*; *pl* Spiele *pl*; PED Sport *m*

game·keep·er Wildhüter *m*

game park, game re·serve Wildpark *m*; Wildreservat *n*

gan·der ZO Gänserich *m*

gang 1. (Arbeiter)Trupp *m*; Gang *f*, Bande *f*; Clique *f*; Horde *f*; **2.** **gang up** sich zusammentun, *contp* sich zusammenrotten

gan·gling schlaksig

gang·ster Gangster *m*

gang war, gang war·fare Bandenkrieg *m*

gang·way Gang *m*; AVIAT, MAR Gangway *f*

gaol, gaol·bird, gaol·er *Br* → *jail etc*

gap Lücke *f*; Kluft *f*; Spalte *f*

gape gähnen; klaffen; gaffen

gar·age 1. Garage *f*; (Reparatur)Werkstatt *f* (und Tankstelle *f*); **2.** *Auto* in e-r Garage ab- *or* unterstellen; *Auto* in die Garage fahren

gar·bage Abfall *m*, Müll *m*

garbage bag Müllbeutel *m*

garbage can Abfalleimer *m*, Mülleimer *m*; Abfalltonne *f*, Mülltonne *f*

garbage truck Müllwagen *m*

gar·den Garten *m*

gar·den·er Gärtner(in)

gar·den·ing Gartenarbeit *f*

gar·gle gurgeln

gar·ish grell, auffallend

gar·lic BOT Knoblauch *m*

gar·ment Kleidungsstück *n*; Gewand *n*

gar·nish GASTR garnieren

gar·ret Dachkammer *f*

gar·ri·son MIL Garnison *f*

gar·ter Strumpfband *n*; Sockenhalter *m*; Strumpfhalter *m*, Straps *m*

gas Gas *n*; F Benzin *n*, Sprit *m*

gas·e·ous gasförmig

gash klaffende Wunde

gas·ket TECH Dichtung(sring *m*) *f*

gas me·ter Gasuhr *f*, Gaszähler *m*

gas·o·lene, gas·o·line Benzin *n*

gasp 1. keuchen, röcheln; *gasp (for breath)* nach Atem ringen, F nach Luft schnappen; **2.** Keuchen *n*, Röcheln *n*

gas sta·tion Tankstelle *f*

gas stove Gasofen *m*, Gasherd *m*

gas·works TECH Gaswerk *n*

gate Tor *n*; Pforte *f*; Schranke *f*, Sperre *f*; AVIAT Flugsteig *m*

gate·crash F uneingeladen kommen (zu); sich ohne zu bezahlen hineinschmuggeln (in *acc*)

gate·post Tor-, Türpfosten *m*

gate·way Tor(weg *m*) *n*, Einfahrt *f*

gate·way drug Einstiegsdroge *f*

gath·er *v/t* sammeln, *Informationen* einholen, einziehen; *Personen* versammeln; ernten, pflücken; zusammenziehen; kräuseln; *fig* folgern, schließen (*from* aus); *gather speed* schneller werden; *v/i* sich (ver)sammeln; sich (an)sammeln

gath·er·ing Versammlung *f*; Zusammenkunft *f*

gau·dy auffällig, bunt, grell; protzig

gauge *Br* → *gage*

gaunt hager; ausgemergelt

gaunt·let Schutzhandschuh *m*

gauze Gaze *f*; MED Bandage *f*, Binde *f*

gav·el Hammer *m*

gaw·ky linkisch

gay 1. lustig, fröhlich; bunt, (farben-) prächtig; F schwul; **2.** F Schwule *m*

gaze 1. (starrer) Blick; **2.** starren; *gaze at* starren auf (*acc*), anstarren

ga·zette Amtsblatt *n*

ga·zelle ZO Gazelle *f*

gear TECH Getriebe *n*; MOT Gang *m*; *mst in cpds* Vorrichtung *f*, Gerät *n*; F Kleidung *f*, Aufzug *m*; *shift* (*esp Br change*) *gear(s)* MOT schalten; *shift* (*esp Br change*) *into second gear* MOT in den zweiten Gang schalten

gear·box MOT Getriebe *n*

gear le·ver *Br*, **gear shift, gear stick** *Br* MOT Schalthebel *m*

Gei·ger count·er PHYS Geigerzähler *m*

geld·ing ZO Wallach *m*

gem Edelstein *m*

Gem·i·ni ASTR Zwillinge *pl*; *he (she) is (a) Gemini* er (sie) ist (ein) Zwilling

gen·der LING Genus *n*, Geschlecht *n*

gene BIOL Gen *n*, Erbfaktor *m*

gen·er·al 1. allgemein; Haupt..., General...; **2.** MIL General *m*; *in general* im Allgemeinen

general de·liv·er·y: *(in care of) general delivery* postlagernd

general e·lec·tion *Br* POL Parlamentswahlen *pl*

gen·er·al·ize verallgemeinern

gen·er·al·ly im Allgemeinen, allgemein

gen·er·al prac·ti·tion·er (*ABBR GP*) *appr* Arzt *m or* Ärztin *f* für Allgemeinmedizin

gen·er·ate erzeugen

gen·er·a·tion Erzeugung *f*; Generation *f*

gen·er·a·tor ELECTR Generator *m*; MOT Lichtmaschine *f*

gen·er·os·i·ty Großzügigkeit *f*

gen·er·ous großzügig; reichlich

ge·net·ic genetisch

genetic code BIOL Erbanlage *f*

genetic en·gin·eer·ing Gentechnologie *f*

genetic fin·ger·print genetischer Fingerabdruck

ge·net·ics BIOL Genetik *f*, Vererbungslehre *f*

ge·ni·al freundlich

gen·i·tive *a.* **genitive case** LING Genitiv *m*, zweiter Fall

ge·ni·us Genie *n*

gen·o·cide Völkermord *m*

gent F *esp Br* Herr *m*; **gents** *Br* F Herrenklo *n*

gen·tle sanft, zart, sacht; mild

gen·tle·man Gentleman *m*; Herr *m*

gen·tle·man·ly gentlemanlike, vornehm

gen·tle·ness Sanftheit *f*, Zartheit *f*; Milde *f*

gen·try *Br* niederer Adel; Oberschicht *f*

gen·u·ine echt; aufrichtig

ge·og·ra·phy Geografie *f*

ge·ol·o·gy Geologie *f*

ge·om·e·try Geometrie *f*

germ BIOL, BOT Keim *m*; MED Bazillus *m*, Bakterie *f*, (Krankheits)Erreger *m*

Ger·man 1. deutsch; **2.** Deutsche *m*, *f*; LING Deutsch *n*

German shep·herd ZO Deutscher Schäferhund

Ger·man·y Deutschland *n*

ger·mi·nate BIOL, BOT keimen (lassen)

ger·und LING Gerundium *n*

ges·tic·u·late gestikulieren

ges·ture Geste *f*, Gebärde *f*

get *v/t* bekommen, erhalten; sich *et.* verschaffen *or* besorgen; erwerben, sich aneignen; holen; bringen; F erwischen; F kapieren, verstehen; *j-n* dazu bringen (**to do** zu tun); *with pp*: lassen; **get one's hair cut** sich die Haare schneiden lassen; **get going** in Gang bringen; **get s.th. by heart** *et.* auswendig lernen; **get s.th. ready** *et.* fertig machen; **have got** haben; **have got to** müssen; *v/i* kommen, gelangen; *with pp or adj*: werden; **get tired** müde werden, ermüden; **get going** in Gang kommen; *fig* in Schwung kommen; **get home** nach Hause kommen; **get ready** sich fertig machen; **get about** herumkommen; sich herumsprechen *or* verbreiten (*rumor etc*); **get ahead of** übertreffen (*acc*); **get along** vorwärts-, vorankommen; auskommen (**with** mit *j-m*); zurechtkommen (**with** mit *et.*); **get at** herankommen an (*acc*); **what is he getting at?** worauf will er hinaus?; **get away** loskommen; entkommen; **get away with** davonkommen mit; **get back** zurückkommen; *et.* zurückbekommen; **get in** hinein-, hereinkommen; einsteigen (in *acc*); **get off** aussteigen (aus); davonkommen (**with** mit); **get on** einsteigen (in *acc*); → **get along**; **get out** herausgehen, hinausgehen; aussteigen (of aus); *et.* herausbekommen; **get over s.th.** über *et.* hinwegkommen; **get to** kommen nach; **get together** zusammenkommen; **get up** aufstehen

get·a·way Flucht *f*; **getaway car** Fluchtauto *n*

get·up Aufmachung *f*

gey·ser GEOL Geysir *m*; *Br* TECH Durchlauferhitzer *m*

ghast·ly grässlich; schrecklich; (toten-)bleich

gher·kin Gewürzgurke *f*

ghet·to Getto *n*

ghost Geist *m*, Gespenst *n*; *fig* Spur *f*

ghost·ly geisterhaft

gi·ant 1. Riese *m*; **2.** riesig

gib·ber·ish Kauderwelsch *n*

gib·bet Galgen *m*

gibe 1. spotten (**at** über *acc*); **2.** höhnische Bemerkung, Stichelei *f*

gib·lets GASTR Hühner-, Gänseklein *n*

gid·di·ness MED Schwindel(gefühl *n*) *m*

gid·dy schwindelerregend; **I feel giddy** mir ist schwind(e)lig

gift Geschenk *n*; Talent *n*

gift·ed begabt

gig F MUS Gig *m*, Auftritt *m*, Konzert *n*

gi·gan·tic gigantisch, riesenhaft, riesig, gewaltig

gig·gle 1. kichern; **2.** Gekicher *n*

gild vergolden

gill ZO Kieme *f*; BOT Lamelle *f*

gim·mick F Trick *m*; Spielerei *f*

gin Gin *m*

gin·ger 1. Ingwer *m*; **2.** rötlich *or* gelblich braun;

gin·ger·bread Lebkuchen *m*, Pfefferkuchen *m*

gin·ger·ly behutsam, vorsichtig

gip·sy *Br* → **gypsy**

gi·raffe ZO Giraffe *f*

gir·der TECH Tragbalken *m*

gir·dle Hüftkalter *m*, Hüftgürtel *m*

girl Mädchen *n*

girl·friend Freundin *f*

girl guide *Br* Pfadfinderin *f*

girl·hood Mädchenjahre *pl*, Jugend *f*, Jugendzeit *f*

girl·ish mädchenhaft; Mädchen...

girl scout *Br* Pfadfinderin *f*

gi·ro *Br* Postgirodienst *m*

gi·ro ac·count *Br* Postgirokonto *n*

gi·ro cheque *Br* Postscheck *m*

girth (Sattel)Gurt *m*; (*a.* Körper)Umfang *m*

gist *das* Wesentliche, Kern *m*

give geben; schenken; spenden; *Leben* hingeben, opfern; *Befehl etc* geben, erteilen; *Hilfe* leisten; *Schutz* bieten; *Grund etc* angeben; THEA *etc* geben, aufführen; *Vortrag* halten; *Schmerzen* bereiten, verursachen; *Grüße etc* übermitteln; **give her my love** grüß ihr herzlich die Grüße von mir; **give birth to** zur Welt bringen; **give s.o. to understand that**

j-m zu verstehen geben, dass; **give way** nachgeben; *Br* MOT die Vorfahrt lassen (*dat*); **give away** hergeben, weggeben, verschenken; *j-n, et.* verraten; **give back** zurückgeben; *j-n in Gesuch etc* einreichen; *Prüfungsarbeit etc* abgeben; nachgeben; aufgeben; **give off** Geruch *etc* verbreiten; ausstoßen, ausströmen, verströmen; **give on(to)** führen auf *or* nach, gehen nach; **give out** aus-, verteilen; *esp Br* bekannt geben; zu Ende gehen (*supplies, strength etc*); F versagen (*engine etc*); **give up** aufgeben; aufhören mit; *j-n* ausliefern; **give o.s. up** sich (freiwillig) stellen (**to the police** der Polizei)

give-and-take beiderseitiges Entgegenkommen, Kompromiss(bereitschaft *f*) *m*

giv·en: be given to neigen zu (*dat*)

giv·en name Vorname *m*

gla·cial eisig; Eis...

gla·ci·er Gletscher *m*

glad froh, erfreut; **be glad of** sich freuen über (*acc*)

glad·ly gern(e)

glam·o(u)r Zauber *m*, Glanz *m*

glam·o(u)r·ous bezaubernd, reizvoll

glance 1. (schneller *or* flüchtiger) Blick (**at** auf *acc*); **at a glance** auf e-n Blick; **2.** (schnell *or* flüchtig) blicken (**at** auf *acc*)

gland ANAT Drüse *f*

glare 1. grell scheinen *or* leuchten; wütend starren; **glare at s.o.** j-n wütend anstarren; **2.** greller Glanz, grelles Leuchten; wütender Blick

glar·ing *fig* schreiend

glass 1. Glas *n*; (Trink)Glas *n*; Glas(-gefäß) *n*; (Fern-, Opern)Glas *n*; *Br* F Spiegel *m*; *Br* Barometer *n*; (**a pair of) glasses** (e-e) Brille; **2.** gläsern; Glas...; **3. glass in, glass up** verglasen

glass case Vitrine *f*; Schaukasten *m*

glass·ful *ein* Glas (voll)

glass·house Gewächs-, Treibhaus *n*

glass·ware Glaswaren *pl*

glass·y gläsern; glasig

glaze 1. *v/t* verglasen; glasieren; *v/i*: a. **glaze over** glasig werden (*eyes*); **2.** Glasur *f*

gla·zi·er Glaser *m*

gleam 1. schwacher Schein, Schimmer *m*; **2.** leuchten, schimmern

glean *v/t* sammeln; *v/i* Ähren lesen

glee Fröhlichkeit *f*

glee club Gesangverein *m*

glee·ful ausgelassen, fröhlich

glen enges Bergtal *n*

glib gewandt; schlagfertig

glide 1. gleiten; segeln; **2.** Gleiten *n*; AVIAT Gleitflug *m*

glid·er Segelflugzeug *n*

glid·ing Segelfliegen *n*

glim·mer 1. schimmern; **2.** Schimmer *m*

glimpse 1. (nur) flüchtig zu sehen bekommen; **2.** flüchtiger Blick

glint 1. glitzern, glänzen; **2.** Glitzern *n*, Glanz *m*

glis·ten glitzern, glänzen

glit·ter 1. glitzern, funkeln, glänzen; **2.** Glitzern *n*, Funkeln *n*, Glanz *m*

gloat: gloat over sich hämisch *or* diebisch freuen über (*acc*)

gloat·ing hämisch, schadenfroh

glo·bal Welt..., global, weltumspannend; umfassend

global warm·ing Erwärmung *f* der Erdatmosphäre

globe (Erd)Kugel *f*; Globus *m*

gloom Düsterkeit *f*; Dunkelheit *f*; düstere *or* gedrückte Stimmung

gloom·y düster; hoffnungslos; niedergeschlagen; trübsinnig, trübselig

glo·ri·fi·ca·tion Verherrlichung *f*

glo·ri·fy verherrlichen

glo·ri·ous ruhmreich, glorreich; herrlich, prächtig

glo·ry Ruhm *m*; Herrlichkeit *f*, Pracht *f*

gloss 1. Glanz *m*; LING Glosse *f*; **2. gloss over** beschönigen, vertuschen

glos·sa·ry Glossar *n*

gloss·y glänzend

glove Handschuh *m*

glove com·part·ment MOT Handschuhfach *n*

glow 1. glühen; **2.** Glühen *n*; Glut *f*

glow·er finster blicken

glow-worm ZO Glühwürmchen *n*

glu·cose Traubenzucker *m*

glue 1. Leim *m*; **2.** kleben

glum bedrückt

glut·ton *fig* Vielfraß *m*

glut·ton·ous gefräßig, unersättlich

gnarled knorrig, knotig (*hands etc*)

gnash knirschen (mit)

gnat ZO (Stech)Mücke *f*

gnaw (zer)nagen; (zer)fressen

gnome Gnom *m*; Gartenzwerg *m*

go 1. gehen, fahren, reisen (**to** nach); (fort)gehen; gehen, führen (**to** nach) (*road etc*); sich erstrecken, gehen (**to** bis zu); verkehren, fahren (*bus etc*); TECH gehen, laufen, funktionieren; vergehen (*time*); harmonieren (**with** mit), passen (**with** zu); ausgehen, ablaufen, ausfallen; werden (**go mad**; **go blind**; **be going to** *inf* im Begriff sein zu *inf*, tun wollen, tun werden (**go shares** teilen; **go swimming** schwimmen gehen; **it is going to rain** es gibt Regen; **I must be going** ich muss gehen; **go for a walk** e-n Spaziergang machen, spazieren gehen; **go to bed** ins Bett gehen; **go to school** zur Schule gehen; **go to see** besuchen; **let go** loslassen; **go after** nachlaufen (*acc*); sich bemühen um; **go ahead** vorangehen; vorausgehen, vorausfahren; **go ahead with** beginnen mit; fortfahren mit; **go at** losgehen auf (*acc*); **go away** weggehen; **go between** vermitteln zwischen (*dat*); **go by** vorbeigehen, vorbeifahren; vergehen (*time*); *fig* sich halten an (*acc*); sich richten nach; **go down** untergehen (*sun*); **go for** holen; **go in** hineingehen; **go in for an examination** e-e Prüfung machen; **go off** fortgehen, weggehen; losgehen (*gun etc*); **go on** weitergehen, weiterfahren; *fig* fortfahren (*doing* zu tun); *fig* vor sich gehen, vorgehen; **go out** hinausgehen; ausgehen (*with* mit); ausgehen (*light etc*); **go through** durchgehen, durchnehmen; durchmachen; **go up** ansteigen; hinaufgehen, -steigen; **go without** sich behelfen ohne, auskommen ohne; **2.** F Schwung *m*, Schmiss *m*; *esp Br* F Versuch *m*; **it's my go** *esp Br* F ich bin dran *or* an der Reihe; **it's a go!** F abgemacht!; **have a go at s.th.** *Br* F et. probieren; **be all the go** F F große Mode sein

goad *fig* anstacheln

go·a·head[1]: **get the go-ahead** grünes Licht bekommen; **give s.o. the go-ahead** j-m grünes Licht geben

go·a·head[2] *Br* zielstrebig; unternehmungslustig

goal Ziel *n* (*a. fig*); SPORT Tor *n*; **keep goal** im Tor stehen; **score a goal** ein Tor schießen *or* erzielen; **consolation goal** Ehrentreffer *m*; **own goal** Eigentor *n*, Eigentreffer *m*; **shot at goal** Torschuss *m*

goal·ie F, **goal·keep·er** SPORT Torwart *m*, Torhüter *m*

goal kick *soccer*: Abstoß *m*

goal line SPORT Torlinie *f*

goal·mouth SPORT Torraum *m*

goal·post SPORT Torpfosten *m*

goat ZO Ziege *f*, Geiß *f*

gob·ble schlingen; *mst* **gobble up** verschlingen (*a. fig*)

go-be·tween Vermittler(in), Mittelsmann *m*

gob·lin Kobold *m*

god REL **God** Gott *m*; *fig* Abgott *m*

god·child Patenkind *n*

god·dess Göttin *f*

god·fa·ther Pate *m* (*a. fig*), Taufpate *m*

god·for·sak·en *contp* gottverlassen

god·head Gottheit *f*

god·less gottlos

god·like gottähnlich; göttlich

god·moth·er (Tauf)Patin *f*

god·pa·rent (Tauf)Pate, (Tauf)Patin *f*

god·send Geschenk *n* des Himmels

gog·gle glotzen

gog·gle box *Br* F TV Glotze *f*

gog·gles Schutzbrille *f*

go·ings-on F Treiben *n*, Vorgänge *pl*

gold 1. Gold *n*; **2.** golden

gold·en *mst fig* golden, goldgelb

gold·finch ZO Stieglitz *m*

gold·fish ZO Goldfisch *m*

gold·smith Goldschmied *m*

golf 1. Golf(spiel) *n*; **2.** Golf spielen

golf club Golfschläger *m*; Golfklub *m*

golf course, **golf links** Golfplatz *m*

gon·do·la Gondel *f*

gone *adj* fort; F futsch; vergangen; tot; F hoffnungslos

good 1. gut; artig; gütig; gründlich; **good at** geschickt *or* gut in (*dat*); **real good** F echt gut; **2.** Nutzen *m*, Wert *m*; *das* Gute; **do (no) good** (nichts) nützen; **for good** für immer; F **what good is ...?** was nützt ...?

good·by(e) 1. *wish s.o. goodby, say goodby to s.o.* j-m Auf Wiedersehen sagen; **2.** *int* (auf) Wiedersehen!

Good Fri·day REL Karfreitag *m*

good-hu·mo(u)red gut gelaunt; gutmütig

good-look·ing gut aussehend

good-na·tured gutmütig

good·ness Güte *f*; *thank goodness!* Gott sei Dank!; *(my) goodness!*, *goodness gracious!* du meine Güte!, du lieber Himmel!; *for goodness' sake* um Himmels willen!; *goodness knows* weiß der Himmel

goods ECON Waren *pl*, Güter *pl*

good·will gute Absicht, guter Wille; ECON Firmenwert *m*

good·y F Bonbon *m*, *n*

goose ZO Gans *f*

goose·ber·ry BOT Stachelbeere *f*

goose·flesh, **goose pim·ples** *fig* Gänsehaut *f*

go·pher ZO Taschenratte *f*; Ziesel *m*

gore durchbohren, aufspießen

gorge 1. ANAT Kehle *f*, Schlund *m*; GEOGR enge (Fels)Schlucht; **2.** verschlingen; schlingen, (sich) vollstopfen

gor·geous prächtig

go·ril·la ZO Gorilla *m*

gor·y F blutrünstig

gosh *int* F Mensch!, Mann!

gos·ling ZO junge Gans

go-slow *Br* ECON Bummelstreik *m*

Gos·pel REL Evangelium *n*

gos·sa·mer Altweibersommer *m*

gos·sip 1. Klatsch *m*, Tratsch *m*; Klatschbase *f*; **2.** klatschen, tratschen

gos·sip·y geschwätzig; voller Klatsch und Tratsch (*letter etc*)

Goth·ic ARCH **1.** gotisch; ***Gothic novel*** Schauerroman *m*; **2.** Gotik *f*

gourd BOT Kürbis *m*

gout MED Gicht *f*

gov·ern *v/t* regieren; lenken, leiten; *v/i* herrschen

gov·ern·ess Erzieherin *f*

gov·ern·ment Regierung *f*; Staat *m*

gov·er·nor Gouverneur *m*; Direktor *m*, Leiter *m*; F Alte *m*

gown Kleid *n*; Robe *f*, Talar *m*

grab 1. packen, (hastig *or* gierig) ergreifen, fassen; **2.** (hastiger *or* gieriger) Griff; TECH Greifer *m*

grace Anmut *f*, Grazie *f*; Anstand *m*; ECON Frist *f*, Aufschub *m*; Gnade *f*; REL Tischgebet *n*; **2.** zieren, schmücken

grace·ful anmutig

grace·less ungraziös

gra·cious gnädig

gra·da·tion Abstufung *f*

grade 1. Grad *m*, Rang *m*; Stufe *f*; ECON Qualität *f*; RAIL *etc* Steigung *f*, Gefälle *n*; PED Klasse *f*, Note *f*, Zensur *f*; **2.** sortieren, einteilen; abstufen

grade cross·ing RAIL schienengleicher Bahnübergang

grade school Grundschule *f*

gra·di·ent *Br* RAIL *etc* Steigung *f*, Gefälle *n*

grad·u·al stufenweise, allmählich

grad·u·al·ly nach und nach; allmählich

grad·u·ate 1. UNIV Hochschulabsolvent(in), Akademiker(in); Graduierte *m*, *f*; PED Schulabgänger(in); **2.** abstufen, staffeln; UNIV graduieren; PED die Abschlussprüfung bestehen

grad·u·a·tion Abstufung *f*, Staffelung *f*; UNIV Graduierung *f*; PED Absolvieren *n* (***from*** *gen*)

graf·fi·ti Graffiti *pl*, Wandschmiererei(en) *pl*

graft 1. MED Transplantat *n*; AGR Pfropfreis *n*; **2.** MED *Gewebe* verpflanzen, transplantieren; AGR pfropfen

grain (Samen-, *esp* Getreide)Korn *n*; Getreide *n*; (*Sand- etc*)Körnchen *n*, (-)Korn *n*; Maserung *f*; ***go against the grain for s.o.*** fig j-m gegen den Strich gehen

gram Gramm *n*

gram·mar Grammatik *f*

gram·mar school Grundschule *f*; *Br appr* (humanistisches) Gymnasium

gram·mat·i·cal grammatisch, Grammatik...

gramme → **gram**

gra·na·ry Kornspeicher *m*

grand 1. fig großartig; erhaben; groß; Groß..., Haupt...; **2.** F Riese *m* (*1000 dollars or pounds*)

grand·child Enkel *m*, Enkelin *f*

grand·daugh·ter Enkelin *f*

gran·deur Größe *f*, Erhabenheit *f*; Großartigkeit *f*

grand·fa·ther Großvater *m*

gran·di·ose großartig

grand·moth·er Großmutter *f*

grand·par·ents Großeltern *pl*

grand·son Enkel *m*

grand·stand SPORT Haupttribüne *f*

gran·ny F Oma *f*

grant 1. bewilligen, gewähren; *Erlaubnis etc* geben; *Bitte etc* erfüllen; *et.* zugeben; ***take s.th. for granted*** et. als selbstverständlich betrachten *or* hinnehmen; **2.** Stipendium *n*; Bewilligung *f*, Unterstützung *f*

gran·u·lat·ed körnig, granuliert; ***granulated sugar*** Kristallzucker *m*

gran·ule Körnchen *n*

grape BOT Weinbeere *f*, Weintraube *f*

grape·fruit BOT Grapefruit *f*, Pampelmuse *f*

grape·vine BOT Weinstock *m*

graph grafische Darstellung

graph·ic grafisch; anschaulich; ***graphic arts*** Grafik *f*

graph·ics EDP Grafik *f*

grap·ple: ***grapple with*** kämpfen mit, *fig a.* sich herumschlagen mit

grasp 1. (er)greifen, packen; *fig* verstehen, begreifen; **2.** Griff *m*; Reichweite *f* (*a. fig*); *fig* Verständnis *n*

grass Gras *n*; Rasen *m*; Weide(land *n*) *f*; *sl.* Grass *n* (*marijuana*)

grass·hop·per ZO Heuschrecke *f*

grass roots POL Basis *f*

grass wid·ow Strohwitwe *f*

grass wid·ow·er Strohwitwer *m*

gras·sy grasbedeckt, Gras...

grate 1. (Kamin)Gitter *n*; (Feuer)Rost *m*; **2.** reiben, raspeln; knirschen (mit); ***grate on s.o.'s nerves*** an j-s Nerven zerren

grate·ful dankbar

grat·er Reibe *f*

grat·i·fi·ca·tion Befriedigung *f*; Freude *f*

grat·i·fy erfreuen; befriedigen

grat·ing[1] kratzend, knirschend, quietschend; schrill; unangenehm

grat·ing[2] Gitter(werk) *n*

grat·i·tude Dankbarkeit *f*

gra·tu·i·tous unentgeltlich; freiwillig

gra·tu·i·ty Abfindung *f*; Gratifikation *f*;

Trinkgeld *n*
grave[1] *Vieh* weiden (lassen) (ab)weiden;
(ab)grasen
grave[2] ernst; (ge)wichtig; gemessen
grave[2] Grab *n*
grave·dig·ger Totengräber *m*
grav·el Kies *m*; **2.** mit Kies bestreuen
grave·stone Grabstein *m*
grave·yard Friedhof *m*
grav·i·ta·tion PHYS Gravitation *f*, Schwerkraft *f*
grav·i·ty PHYS Schwerkraft *f*; Ernst *m*
gra·vy Bratensaft *m*; Bratensoße *f*
gray **1.** grau; **2.** Grau *n*; **3.** grau machen *or*
werden
gray·hound ZO Windhund *m*
graze[1] *Vieh* weiden (lassen) (ab)weiden;
(ab)grasen
graze[2] **1.** streifen; schrammen; *Haut* (ab-,
auf)schürfen, (auf)schrammen; **2.** Abschürfung *f*, Schramme *f*; Streifschuss *m*
grease **1.** Fett *n*; TECH Schmierfett *n*,
Schmiere *f*; **2.** (ein)fetten; TECH schmieren
greas·y fett(ig), ölig; speckig; schmierig
great groß; Ur(groß)…; F großartig, super
Great Brit·ain Großbritannien *n*
great-grand·child Urenkel(in)
great-grand·par·ents Urgroßeltern *pl*
great·ly sehr
great·ness Größe *f*
Greece Griechenland *n*
greed Gier *f*
greed·y gierig (**for** auf *acc*, nach); habgierig; gefräßig
Greek **1.** griechisch; **2.** Grieche *m*, Griechin *f*; LING Griechisch *n*
green **1.** grün; *fig* grün, unerfahren; **2.**
Grün *n*; Grünfläche *f*, Rasen *m*; *pl* grünes Gemüse, Blattgemüse *n*
green·back F Dollar *m*
green belt Grüngürtel *m*
green card Arbeitserlaubnis *f*
green-gro·cer *esp Br* Obst- und Gemüse-
händler(in)
green·horn F Greenhorn *n*, Grünschna-
bel *m*
green·house Gewächs-, Treibhaus *n*
greenhouse ef·fect Treibhauseffekt *m*
green·ish grünlich
greet grüßen
greet·ing Begrüßung *f*, Gruß *m*; *pl* Grüße
pl
gre·nade MIL Granate *f*
grey *Br* → **grey**
grid Gitter *n*; ELECTR *etc* Versorgungsnetz
n; Gitter(netz) *n* (*map etc*)
grid·i·ron Bratrost *m*
grief Kummer *m*
griev·ance (Grund *m* zur) Beschwerde *f*;
Missstand *m*

grieve *v/t* betrüben, bekümmern; *v/i* bekümmert sein; **grieve for** trauern um
griev·ous schwer, schlimm
grill **1.** grillen; **2.** Grill *m*; Bratrost *m*;
GASTR *das* Gegrillte *n*
grim grimmig; schrecklich; erbittert; F
schlimm
gri·mace **1.** Fratze *f*, Grimasse *f*; **2.** Grimassen schneiden
grime Schmutz *m*; Ruß *m*
grim·y schmutzig; rußig
grin **1.** Grinsen *n*; **2.** grinsen
grind **1.** *v/t* (zer)mahlen, zerreiben, zerkleinern; *Messer etc* schleifen; *Fleisch*
durchdrehen; **grind one's teeth** mit
den Zähnen knirschen; *v/i* F schuften;
pauken, büffeln; **2.** Schinderei *f*, F Schufterei *f*; **the daily grind** das tägliche Einerlei
grind·er (*Messer- etc*)Schleifer *m*; TECH
Schleifmaschine *f*; TECH Mühle *f*
grind·stone Schleifstein *m*
grip **1.** packen (*a. fig*); **2.** Griff *m*; *fig* Gewalt *f*, Herrschaft *f*; Reisetasche *f*
grip·ping spannend
gris·ly grässlich, schrecklich
gris·tle GASTR Knorpel *m*
grit **1.** Kies *m*, (grober) Sand; *fig* Mut *m*; **2.**
streuen; **grit one's teeth** die Zähne zusammenbeißen
griz·zly (bear) ZO Grislibär *m*, Graubär *m*
groan **1.** stöhnen, ächzen; **2.** Stöhnen *n*,
Ächzen *n*
gro·cer Lebensmittelhändler *m*
gro·cer·ies Lebensmittel *pl*
gro·cer·y Lebensmittelgeschäft *n*
grog·gy F groggy, schwach *or* wackelig
(auf den Beinen)
groin ANAT Leiste *f*, Leistengegend *f*
groom **1.** Pferdepfleger *m*, Stallbursche
m; Bräutigam *m*; **2.** *Pferde* versorgen,
striegeln; pflegen
groove Rinne *f*, Furche *f*; Rille *f*, Nut *f*
grope tasten; F *Mädchen* befummeln
gross **1.** dick, feist; grob, derb; ECON Brutto…; **2.** Gros *n*
gro·tesque grotesk
ground[1] gemahlen (*coffee etc*); **ground
meat** Hackfleisch *n*
ground[2] **1.** (Erd)Boden *m*, Erde *f*; Boden
m, Gebiet *n*; SPORT (*Spiel*)Platz *m*; ELECTR
Erdung *f*; (Boden)Satz *m*; fig Beweggrund *m*; *pl* Grundstück *n*, Park *m*, Gar-
tenanlage *f*; **on the ground(s) of** aufgrund (*gen*); **hold** *or* **stand one's
ground** sich behaupten; **2.** MAR auflaufen; ELECTR erden; *fig* gründen, stützen
ground crew AVIAT Bodenpersonal *n*
ground floor *esp Br* Erdgeschoss *n*

ground forc·es MIL Bodentruppen pl, Landstreitkräfte pl

ground·hog ZO Amer. Waldmurmeltier n

ground·ing ELECTR Erdung f; Grundlagen pl, Grundkenntnisse pl

ground·keep·er SPORT Platzwart m

ground·less grundlos

ground·nut Br BOT Erdnuss f

grounds·man Br SPORT Platzwart m

ground staff Br AVIAT Bodenpersonal n

ground sta·tion Bodenstation f

ground·work fig Grundlage f, Fundament n

group 1. Gruppe f; **2.** (sich) gruppieren

group·ie F Groupie n

group·ing Gruppierung f

grove Wäldchen n, Gehölz n

grov·el (am Boden) kriechen

grow v/i wachsen; (allmählich) werden; **grow up** aufwachsen, heranwachsen; v/t BOT anpflanzen, anbauen, züchten; **grow a beard** sich e-n Bart wachsen lassen

grow·er Züchter m, Erzeuger m

growl knurren, brummen

grown-up 1. erwachsen; **2.** Erwachsene m, f

growth Wachsen n, Wachstum n; Wuchs m, Größe f; fig Zunahme f, Anwachsen n; MED Gewächs n, Wucherung f

grub 1. ZO Larve f, Made f; F Futter n; **2.** graben

grub·by schmudd(e)lig

grudge 1. missgönnen (**s.o. s.th.** j-m et.); **2.** Groll m

grudg·ing·ly widerwillig

gru·el Haferschleim m

gruff grob, schroff, barsch, unwirsch

grum·ble murren, F meckern (**über** acc about, at); **grumble at** schimpfen über (acc)

grump·y F schlecht gelaunt, mürrisch, missmutig, verdrießlich, verdrossen

grun·gy F schmudd(e)lig-schlampig; MUS schlecht und laut

grunt 1. grunzen; brummen; stöhnen; **2.** Grunzen n; Stöhnen n

guar·an·tee 1. Garantie f; Kaution f, Sicherheit f; **2.** (sich ver)bürgen für; garantieren

guar·an·tor JUR Bürge m, Bürgin f

guar·an·ty JUR Garantie f; Sicherheit f

guard 1. Wache f, (Wacht)Posten m, Wächter m; Wärter m, Aufseher m; Wache f, Bewachung f; Br Zugbegleiter m; Schutz(vorrichtung f) m; Garde f; **be on guard** Wache stehen; **be on (off) one's guard** (nicht) auf der Hut sein; **2.** v/t bewachen, (be)schützen (**from** vor dat); v/i

sich hüten or in Acht nehmen or schützen (**against** vor dat)

guard·ed vorsichtig, zurückhaltend

guard·i·an 1. JUR Vormund m; **2.** Schutz...

guard·i·an·ship JUR Vormundschaft f

gue(r)·ril·la MIL Guerilla f

gue(r)·ril·la war·fare Guerillakrieg m

guess 1. (er)raten; vermuten; schätzen; glauben, meinen; **2.** Vermutung f

guess·work (reine) Vermutung(en pl)

guest Gast m

guest·house (Hotel)Pension f, Fremdenheim n

guest·room Gäste-, Fremdenzimmer n

guf·faw 1. schallendes Gelächter; **2.** schallend lachen

guid·ance Führung f; (An)Leitung f

guide 1. (Reise-, Fremden)Führer(in); (Reise- etc)Führer m (book); Handbuch (**to** gen); **a guide to London** ein London-Führer; **2.** leiten; führen; lenken

guide·book (Reise- etc)Führer m

guid·ed tour Führung f

guide·lines Richtlinien pl (**on** gen)

guild HIST Gilde f, Zunft f

guile·less arglos

guilt Schuld f

guilt·less schuldlos, unschuldig (**of** an dat)

guilt·y schuldig (**of** gen); schuldbewusst

guin·ea pig ZO Meerschweinchen n; fig Versuchsperson f, F Versuchskaninchen n

guise fig Gestalt f, Maske f

gui·tar MUS Gitarre f

gulch GEOGR tiefe Schlucht, Klamm f

gulf GEOGR Golf m; fig Kluft f

gull ZO Möwe f

gul·let ANAT Speiseröhre f; Gurgel f, Kehle f

gulp 1. (großer) Schluck; **2.** often **gulp down** Getränk hinunterstürzen, Speise hinunterschlingen

gum¹ ANAT mst pl Zahnfleisch n

gum² 1. Gummi m, n; Klebstoff m; Kaugummi m; (Frucht)Gummi m; 2. kleben

gump·tion F Grips m; Schneid m

gun 1. Gewehr n; Pistole f, Revolver m; Geschütz n, Kanone f; **2. gun down** niederschießen

gun·fight Feuergefecht n, Schießerei f

gun·fire Schüsse pl; MIL Geschützfeuer n

gun li·cence Br, **gun li·cense** Waffenschein m

gun·man Bewaffnete m

gun·point: at gunpoint mit vorgehaltener Waffe, mit Waffengewalt

gun·pow·der Schießpulver n

gun·run·ner Waffenschmuggler m

gun·run·ning Waffenschmuggel m

G

gun·shot Schuss *m*; **within** (**out of**) **gun-shot** in (außer) Schussweite

gur·gle 1. gurgeln, gluckern, glucksen; **2.** Gurgeln *n*, Gluckern *n*, Glucksen *n*

gush 1. strömen, schießen (**from** aus); **2.** Schwall *m*, Strom *m* (*a. fig*)

gust Windstoß *m*, Bö *f*

gust F Eingeweide *pl*; Schneid *m*, Mumm *m*

gut·ter Gosse *f* (*a. fig*), Rinnstein *m*; Dachrinne *f*

guy F Kerl *m*, Typ *m*

guz·zle F saufen; fressen

gym F Fitnesscenter *n*; → **gymnasium**; →

gymnastics

gym·na·si·um Turn-, Sporthalle *f*

gym·nast Turner(in)

gym·nas·tics Turnen *n*, Gymnastik *f*

gym shirt Turnhemd *n*

gym shorts Turnhose *f*

gy·n(a)e·col·o·gist Gynäkologe *m*, Gynäkologin *f*, Frauenarzt *m*, -ärztin *f*

gy·n(a)e·col·o·gy Gynäkologie *f*, Frauenheilkunde *f*

gyp·sy Zigeuner *m*, Zigeunerin *f*

gy·rate kreisen, sich (im Kreis) drehen, (herum)wirbeln

H

H, h H, h *n*

hab·it (An)Gewohnheit *f*; *esp* (Ordens-)Tracht *f*; **get into** (**out of**) **the habit of smoking** sich das Rauchen angewöhnen (abgewöhnen)

ha·bit·u·al gewohnheitsmäßig, Gewohnheits...

hack[1] hacken

hack[2] *contp* Schreiberling *m*

hack[3] *contp* Klepper *m*

hack·er EDP Hacker *m*

hack·neyed abgedroschen

had·dock ZO Schellfisch *m*

h(a)e·mor·rhage MED Blutung *f*

hag hässliches altes Weib, Hexe *f*

hag·gard abgespannt; verhärmt, abgehärmt; hager

hag·gle feilschen, handeln

hail 1. Hagel *m*; **2.** hageln

hail·stone Hagelkorn *n*

hail·storm Hagelschauer *m*

hair *einzelnes* Haar; *coll* Haar *n*, Haare *pl*; **let one's hair down** F aus sich herausgehen; **without turning a hair** ohne mit der Wimper zu zucken

hair·breadth → **hair's breadth**

hair·brush Haarbürste *f*

hair·cut Haarschnitt *m*

hair·do F Frisur *f*

hair·dress·er Friseur(in)

hair·dri·er, hair·dry·er Trockenhaube *f*; Haartrockner *m*, Föhn *m*

hair·grip *Br* Haarklammer *f*, Haarklemme *f*

hair·less ohne Haare, kahl

hair·pin Haarnadel *f*

hairpin bend MOT Haarnadelkurve *f*

hair·rais·ing haarsträubend

hair's breadth: by a hair's breadth um Haaresbreite

hair slide *Br* Haarspange *f*

hair·split·ting Haarspalterei *f*

hair·spray Haarspray *m*, *n*

hair·style Frisur *f*

hair styl·ist Hair-Stylist *m*, Damenfriseur *m*

hair·y behaart, haarig

half 1. Hälfte *f*; **go halves** halbe-halbe machen, teilen; **2.** halb; **half an hour** e-e halbe Stunde; **half a pound** ein halbes Pfund; **half past ten** halb elf (Uhr); **half way up** auf halber Höhe

half-breed Halbblut *n*

half-broth·er Halbbruder *m*

half-caste *esp contp* Mischling *m*

half-heart·ed halbherzig

half time SPORT Halbzeit *f*

half time score SPORT Halbzeitstand *m*

half-way halb; auf halbem Weg, in der Mitte

halfway line *soccer*: Mittellinie *f*

half-wit·ted schwachsinnig

hal·i·but ZO Heilbutt *m*

hall Halle *f*, Saal *m*; Flur *m*, Diele *f*; *esp Br* Herrenhaus *n*; *Br* UNIV Speisesaal *m*; *Br* **hall of residence** Studentenheim *n*

hall·mark *fig* Kennzeichen *n*

Hal·low·e'en Abend *m* vor Allerheiligen

hal·lu·ci·na·tion Halluzination *f*

hall·way Halle *f*, Diele *f*; Korridor *m*

a·lo ASTR Hof *m*; Heiligenschein *m*
alt 1. Halt *m*; **2.** (an)halten
al·ter Halfter *m*, *n*
alt·ing zögernd, stockend
alve halbieren
am Schinken *m*; *ham and eggs* Schinken mit (Spiegel)Ei
am·burg·er GASTR Hamburger *m*; Rinderhack *n*
am·let Weiler *m*
am·mer 1. Hammer *m*; **2.** hämmern
am·mock Hängematte *f*
am·per¹ (Deckel)Korb *m*; Präsentkorb *m*; Wäschekorb *m*
am·per² (be)hindern
am·ster ZO Hamster *m*
and 1. Hand *f* (*a. fig*); Handschrift *f*; (Uhr)Zeiger *m*; *often in cpds* Arbeiter *m*; Fachmann *m*; *card game*: Blatt *n*, Karten *pl*; *hand in glove* ein Herz und eine Seele; *change hands* den Besitzer wechseln; *give or lend a hand* mit zugreifen, *j-m* helfen (*with* by); *shake hands with j-m* die Hand schütteln *or* geben; *at hand* in Reichweite; nahe; bei der *or* zur Hand; *at first hand* aus erster Hand; *by hand* mit der Hand; *on the one hand* einerseits; *on the other hand* andererseits; *on the right hand* rechts; *hands off!* Hände weg!; *hands up!* Hände hoch!; **2.** aushändigen, (über)geben, (über)reichen; *hand around* herumreichen; *hand down* weitergeben, überliefern; *hand in Prüfungsarbeit etc* abgeben; *Bericht, Gesuch etc* einreichen; *hand on* weiterreichen, weitergeben; überliefern; *hand out* austeilen, verteilen; *hand over* übergeben, aushändigen (*to dat*); *hand up* hinauf-, heraufreichen
hand·bag Handtasche *f*
hand bag·gage Handgepäck *n*
hand·ball SPORT Handball *m*; *soccer*: Handspiel *n*
hand·book Handbuch *n*
hand·bill Handzettel *m*, Flugblatt *n*
hand·brake TECH Handbremse *f*
hand·cart Handwagen *m*
hand·cuffs Handschellen *pl*
hand·ful Handvoll *f*; F Plage *f*
hand gre·nade MIL Handgranate *f*
hand·i·cap 1. Handikap *n*, MED *a.* Behinderung *f*, SPORT *a.* Vorgabe *f*; → *mental handicap, physical handicap*; **2.** behindern, benachteiligen
hand·i·capped 1. gehandikapt, behindert, benachteiligt; → *mental, physical*; **2.** *the handicapped* MED die Behinderten *pl*

hand·ker·chief Taschentuch *n*
han·dle 1. Griff *m*; Stiel *m*; Henkel *m*; Klinke *f*; *fly off the handle* F wütend werden; **2.** anfassen, berühren; hantieren *or* umgehen mit; behandeln
han·dle·bar(s) Lenkstange *f*
hand lug·gage Handgepäck *n*
hand·made handgearbeitet
hand·out Almosen *n*; Handzettel *m*; Hand-out *n*, Informationsmaterial *n*
hand·rail Geländer *n*
hand·shake Händedruck *m*
hand·some gut aussehend; *fig* ansehnlich, beträchtlich (*sum etc*)
hands-on praktisch
hand·spring Handstandüberschlag *m*
hand·stand Handstand *m*
hand·writ·ing Handschrift *f*
hand·writ·ten handgeschrieben
hand·y zur Hand; geschickt; handlich, praktisch; nützlich; *come in handy* sich als nützlich erweisen; (sehr) gelegen kommen
hand·y·man Handwerker *m*; *be a handyman a.* handwerklich geschickt sein
hang (auf-, be-, ein)hängen; *Tapete* ankleben; *j-n* (auf)hängen; *hang o.s.* sich erhängen; *hang about, hang around* herumlungern; *hang on* sich klammern (*to an acc*) (*a. fig*), festhalten (*to acc*); TEL am Apparat bleiben; *hang up* TEL einhängen, auflegen; *she hung up on me* sie legte einfach auf
han·gar Hangar *m*, Flugzeughalle *f*
hang·er Kleiderbügel *m*
hang glid·er SPORT (Flug)Drachen *m*; Drachenflieger(in)
hang glid·ing SPORT Drachenfliegen *n*
hang·ing 1. Hänge...; **2.** (Er)Hängen *n*
hang·ings Tapete *f*, Wandbehang *m*, Vorhang *m*
hang·man Henker *m*
hang·nail MED Niednagel *m*
hang·o·ver Katzenjammer *m*, Kater *m*
han·ker F sich sehnen (*after, for* nach)
han·kie, han·ky F Taschentuch *n*
hap·haz·ard willkürlich, planlos, wahllos
hap·pen (zufällig) geschehen; sich ereignen, passieren, vorkommen
hap·pen·ing Ereignis *n*, Vorkommnis *n*; Happening *n*
hap·pi·ly glücklich(erweise)
hap·pi·ness Glück *n*
hap·py glücklich; erfreut
hap·py-go-luck·y unbekümmert, sorglos
ha·rangue 1. (Straf)Predigt *f*; **2.** *v/t j-m* e-e Strafpredigt halten
har·ass ständig belästigen; schikanieren; aufreiben, zermürben

har·ass·ment ständige Belästigung; Schikane(n pl) f; → **sexual harassment**

har·bo(u)r 1. Hafen m; Zufluchtsort m; **2.** j-m Zuflucht or Unterschlupf gewähren; Groll etc hegen

hard hart (a. fig); fest; schwer, schwierig; heftig, stark; streng (a. winter); fig nüchtern (facts etc); **give s.o. a hard time** j-m das Leben schwer machen; **hard of hearing** schwerhörig; **be hard on s.th.** et. strapazieren; **hard up** F in (Geld)Schwierigkeiten, knapp bei Kasse; F **the hard stuff** die harten Sachen (alcohol, drugs)

hard·back gebundene Ausgabe

hard-boiled GASTR hart (gekocht); F fig hart, unsentimental, nüchtern

hard cash Bargeld n; klingende Münze

hard core harter Kern

hard-core zum harten Kern gehörend; hart

hard court tennis: Hartplatz m

hard·cov·er 1. gebunden; **2.** Hard Cover n, gebundene Ausgabe

hard cur·ren·cy ECON harte Währung

hard disk EDP Festplatte f

hard·en härten; hart machen or werden; (sich) abhärten

hard hat Schutzhelm m

hard-head·ed nüchtern, praktisch; starrköpfig, dickköpfig

hard-heart·ed hartherzig

hard la·bo(u)r JUR Zwangsarbeit f

hard line esp POL harter Kurs

hard-line esp POL hart, kompromisslos

hard·ly kaum

hard·ness Härte f; Schwierigkeit f

hard·ship Not f; Härte f; Strapaze f

hard shoul·der Br MOT Standspur f

hard·top MOT Hardtop n, m

hard·ware Eisenwaren pl; Haushaltswaren pl; EDP Hardware f

hard-wear·ing strapazierfähig

har·dy zäh, robust, abgehärtet; BOT winterhart, winterfest

hare ZO Hase m

hare·bell BOT Glockenblume f

hare-brained verrückt

hare·lip MED Hasenscharte f

harm 1. Schaden m; **2.** verletzen; schaden (dat)

harm·ful schädlich

harm·less harmlos

har·mo·ni·ous harmonisch

har·mo·nize harmonieren; in Einklang sein or bringen

har·mo·ny Harmonie f

har·ness 1. (Pferde- etc)Geschirr n; **die in harness** fig in den Sielen sterben; **2.** anschirren; anspannen (**to** an acc)

harp 1. MUS Harfe f; **2.** MUS Harfe spielen; F **harp on** (**about**) herumreiten auf (dat)

har·poon 1. Harpune f; **2.** harpunieren

har·row AGR **1.** Egge f; **2.** eggen

har·row·ing quälend, qualvoll, erschütternd

harsh rau; grell; streng; schroff, barsch

hart ZO Hirsch m

har·vest 1. Ernte(zeit) f; (Ernte)Ertrag m; **2.** ernten

har·vest·er MOT Mähdrescher m

hash¹ GASTR Haschee n; F **make a hash of s.th.** et. verpfuschen

hash² F Hasch n

hash browns GASTR Brat-, Röstkartoffel pl

hash·ish Haschisch n

hasp TECH Haspe f

haste Eile f, Hast f

has·ten j-n antreiben; (sich be)eilen; et. beschleunigen

hast·y eilig, hastig, überstürzt; voreilig

hat Hut m

hatch¹: a. **hatch out** ZO ausbrüten; ausschlüpfen

hatch² Durchreiche f; AVIAT, MAR Luke f

hatch·back MOT (Wagen m mit) Hecktür f

hatch·et Beil n; **bury the hatchet** das Kriegsbeil begraben

hate 1. Hass m; **2.** hassen

hate·ful verhasst; abscheulich

ha·tred Hass m

haugh·ty hochmütig, überheblich

haul 1. ziehen, zerren; schleppen; befördern, transportieren; **2.** Ziehen n; Fischzug m, fig F a. Fang m; Beförderung f Transport m; Transportweg m

haul·age Beförderung f, Transport m

haul·er, Br **haul·i·er** Transportunternehmer m

haunch ANAT Hüfte f, Hüftpartie f, Hinterbacke f; GASTR Keule f

haunt 1. spuken in (dat); häufig besuchen fig verfolgen, quälen; **2.** häufig besuchter Ort; Schlupfwinkel m

haunt·ing quälend; unvergesslich, eindringlich

have v/t haben; erhalten, bekommen; essen, trinken; **have breakfast** frühstücken; **have a cup of tea** e-n Tee trinken; with inf: müssen (**I have to go now** ich muss jetzt gehen); with object and pp: lassen (**I had my hair cut** ich ließ mir die Haare schneiden); **have back** zurückbekommen; **have on** Kleidungsstück anhaben, Hut aufhaben; v/aux haben; v/i often ten sein; F **have come** ich bin gekommen

ha·ven Hafen m (mst fig)

hav·oc Verwüstung f, Zerstörung f; **play**

havoc with verwüsten, zerstören; *fig* verheerend wirken auf *(acc)*

hawk[1] zo Habicht *m*, Falke *m*

hawk[2] hausieren mit; auf der Straße verkaufen

hawk·er Hausierer(in); Straßenhändler(in); Drücker(in)

haw·thorn BOT Weißdorn *m*

hay Heu *n*

hay fe·ver MED Heuschnupfen *m*

hay·loft Heuboden *m*

hay·stack Heuhaufen *m*

haz·ard Gefahr *f*, Risiko *n*

haz·ard·ous gewagt, gefährlich, riskant

hazardous waste Sonder-, Giftmüll *m*

haze Dunst(schleier) *m*

ha·zel 1. BOT Hasel(nuss)strauch *m*; **2.** (hasel)nussbraun

ha·zel·nut BOT Haselnuss *f*

haz·y dunstig, diesig; *fig* unklar, verschwommen

H-bomb H-Bombe *f*, Wasserstoffbombe *f*

he 1. er; 2. Er *m*; zo Männchen *n*; *he-goat* Ziegenbock *m*

head 1. Kopf *m*; (Ober)Haupt *n*; Chef *m*; (An)Führer(in), Leiter(in); Spitze *f*; Kopf(ende *n*) *m*; Kopf *m* (*of a page, nail etc*); Vorderseite *f*; Überschrift *f*; *20 dollars a head or per head* zwanzig Dollar pro Kopf or Person; *40 head (of cattle)* 40 Stück (Vieh); *heads or tails?* Kopf oder Zahl?; *at the head of* an der Spitze (*gen*); *head over heels* kopfüber; bis über beide Ohren (*verliebt sein*); *bury one's head in the sand* den Kopf in den Sand stecken; *get it into one's head that ...* es sich in den Kopf setzen, dass; *lose one's head* den Kopf or die Nerven verlieren; **2.** Ober..., Haupt..., Chef..., oberste(r, -s), erste(r, -s); **3.** *v/t* anführen, an der Spitze stehen von (*or gen*); voran-, vorausgehen (*dat*); (an)führen, leiten; *soccer:* köpfen; *v/i* (*for*) gehen, fahren (nach); lossteuern, losgehen (auf *acc*); MAR Kurs halten (auf *acc*)

head·ache Kopfweh *n*

head·band Stirnband *n*

head·dress Kopfschmuck *m*

head·er Kopfsprung *m*; *soccer:* Kopfball *m*

head·first kopfuber, mit dem Kopf voran; *fig* ungestüm, stürmisch

head·gear Kopfbedeckung *f*

head·ing Überschrift *f*, Titel(zeile *f*) *m*

head·land Landspitze *f*, Landzunge *f*

head·light MOT Scheinwerfer *m*

head·line Schlagzeile *f*; *news headlines* radio, TV *das* Wichtigste in Schlagzeilen

head·long kopfüber; *fig* ungestüm

head·mas·ter Br PED Direktor *m*, Rektor *m*

head·mis·tress Br PED Direktorin *f*, Rektorin *f*

head-on frontal, Frontal...; *head-on collision* MOT Frontalzusammenstoß *m*

head·phones Kopfhörer *pl*

head·quar·ters (ABBR *HQ*) MIL Hauptquartier *n*; Zentrale *f*

head·rest MOT Kopfstütze *f*

head·set Kopfhörer *pl*

head start SPORT Vorgabe *f*, Vorsprung *m* (*a. fig*)

head·strong halsstarrig

head teach·er → *headmaster, headmistress, principal*

head·wa·ters GEOGR Quellgebiet *n*

head·way Fortschritt(e *pl*) *m*; *make headway* (gut) vorankommen

head·word Stichwort *n*

head·y zu Kopfe steigend, berauschend

heal heilen; *heal over, heal up* (zu)heilen

heal·ing Heilung *f*; *healing power* Heilkraft *f*

health Gesundheit *f*

health cer·tif·i·cate Gesundheitszeugnis *n*

health club Fitnessklub *m*, Fitnesscenter *n*

health food Reform-, Biokost *f*

health food shop *Br*, **health food store** Reformhaus *n*, Bioladen *m*

health·ful gesund; heilsam

health in·su·rance Krankenversicherung *f*

health re·sort Kurort *m*

health service Gesundheitsdienst *m*

health·y gesund

heap 1. Haufe(n) *m*; **2.** *a. heap up* aufhäufen, *fig a.* anhäufen

hear hören; anhören, *j-m* zuhören; *Zeugen* vernehmen; *Lektion* abhören

hear·er (Zu)Hörer(in)

hear·ing Gehör *n*; Hören *n*; JUR Verhandlung *f*; JUR Vernehmung *f*; *esp* POL Hearing *n*, Anhörung *f*; *within (out of) hearing* in (außer) Hörweite

hear·ing aid Hörgerät *n*

hear·say Gerede *n*; *by hearsay* vom Hörensagen *n*

hearse Leichenwagen *m*

heart ANAT Herz *n* (*a. fig*); Kern *m*; *card games:* Herz(karte *f*) *n*, *pl* Herz *n*; *lose heart* den Mut verlieren; *take heart* sich ein Herz fassen; *take s.th. to heart* sich et. zu Herzen nehmen; *with a heavy heart* schweren Herzens

heart·ache Kummer *m*

heart at·tack MED Herzanfall *m*; Herzinfarkt *m*

heart·beat Herzschlag *m*

heart·break Leid *n*, großer Kummer

heart·break·ing herzzerreißend

heart·brok·en gebrochen, verzweifelt

heart·burn MED Sodbrennen *n*

heart·en ermutigen

heart fail·ure MED Herzversagen *n*

heart·felt innig, tief empfunden

hearth Kamin *m*

heart·less herzlos

heart·rend·ing herzzerreißend

heart trans·plant MED Herzverpflanzung *f*, Herztransplantation *f*

heart·y herzlich; gesund; herzhaft

heat 1. Hitze *f*; PHYS Wärme *f*; Eifer *m*; ZO Läufigkeit *f*; SPORT (Einzel)Lauf *m*; *preliminary heat* Vorlauf *m*; **2.** *v/t* heizen; *a. heat up* erhitzen, aufwärmen; *v/i* sich erhitzen (*a. fig*)

heat·ed geheizt; heizbar; erhitzt, *fig a.* erregt

heat·er Heizgerät *n*, Heizkörper *m*

heath Heide *f*, Heideland *n*

hea·then REL **1.** Heide *m*, Heidin *f*; **2.** heidnisch

heath·er BOT Heidekraut *n*; Erika *f*

heat·ing 1. Heizung *f*; **2.** Heiz...

heat·proof hitzebeständig

heat shield Hitzeschild *m*

heat·stroke MED Hitzschlag *m*

heat wave Hitzewelle *f*

heave *v/t* (hoch)stemmen, (hoch)hieven; *Anker* lichten; *Seufzer* ausstoßen; *v/i* sich heben und senken, wogen

heav·en Himmel *m*

heav·en·ly himmlisch

heav·y schwer; stark (*rain, smoker, drinker, traffic etc*); hoch (*fine, taxes etc*); schwer (verdaulich); drückend, lastend; Schwer...

heav·y cur·rent ELECTR Starkstrom *m*

heav·y·du·ty TECH Hochleistungs...; strapazierfähig

heav·y·hand·ed ungeschickt

heav·y·weight *boxing:* Schwergewicht *n*, Schwergewichtler *m*

He·brew 1. hebräisch; **2.** Hebräer(in); LING Hebräisch *n*

heck·le *Redner* durch Zwischenrufe *or* Zwischenfragen stören

heck·ler Zwischenrufer *m*

heck·ling Zwischenrufe *m*

hec·tic hektisch

hedge 1. Hecke *f*; **2.** *v/t*: *a. hedge in* mit e-r Hecke einfassen; *v/i fig* ausweichen

hedge·hog ZO Stachelschwein *n*; *Br* Igel *m*

hedge·row Hecke *f*

heed 1. beachten, Beachtung schenken (*dat*); **2.** *give or pay heed to, take heed of* → 1

heed·less: *be heedless of* nicht beachten, *Warnung etc* in den Wind schlagen

heel 1. ANAT Ferse *f*; Absatz *m*; *down at heel fig* abgerissen; heruntergekommen **2.** Absätze machen auf (*acc*)

hef·ty kräftig, stämmig; mächtig (*blow etc*), gewaltig; F saftig (*prices, fine etc*)

heif·er ZO Färse *f*, junge Kuh

height Höhe *f*; (Körper)Größe *f*; Anhöhe *f*; *fig* Höhe(punkt *m*) *f*

height·en erhöhen; vergrößern

heir Erbe *m*; *heir to the throne* Thronerbe *m*, Thronfolger *m*

heir·ess Erbin *f*

heir·loom Erbstück *n*

hel·i·cop·ter AVIAT Hubschrauber *m*, Helikopter *m*

hel·i·port AVIAT Hubschrauberlandeplatz *m*

hell 1. Hölle *f*; *a hell of a noise* F ein Höllenlärm; *what the hell …?* F was zum Teufel …?; *raise hell* F e-n Mordskrach schlagen; **2.** Höllen...; **3.** *int* F verdammt! verflucht!

hell·ish F höllisch

hel·lo *int* hallo!

helm MAR Ruder *n*, Steuer *n*

hel·met Helm *m*

helms·man MAR Steuermann *m*

help 1. Hilfe *f*; Hausangestellte *f*; *a call or cry for help* ein Hilferuf, ein Hilfeschrei; **2.** helfen; *help o.s.* sich bedienen, zulangen; *I cannot help it* ich kann es nicht ändern; *I could not help laughing* ich musste einfach lachen

help·er Helfer(in)

help·ful hilfreich; nützlich

help·ing Portion *f*

help·less hilflos

help·less·ness Hilflosigkeit *f*

help men·u EDP Hilfemenü *n*

hel·ter·skel·ter 1. *adv* holterdiepolter, Hals über Kopf; **2.** *adj* überstürzt

helve Stiel *m*, Griff *m*

Hel·ve·tian Schweizer ...

hem 1. Saum *m*; **2.** säumen; *hem in* einschließen

hem·i·sphere GEOGR Halbkugel *f*, Hemisphäre *f*

hem·line Saum *m*

hem·lock BOT Schierling *m*

hemp BOT Hanf *m*

hem·stitch Hohlsaum *m*

hen ZO Henne *f*, Huhn *n*; Weibchen *n*

hence daher; *a week hence* in e-r Woche

hence·forth von nun an

hen house Hühnerstall *m*

hen-pecked hus-band Pantoffelheld *m*

her sie; ihr; ihr(e); sich

her-ald 1. HIST Herold *m*; **2.** ankündigen

her-ald-ry Wappenkunde *f*, Heraldik *f*

herb BOT Kraut *n*; Heilkraut *n*

her-ba-ceous BOT krautartig; ***herba-ceous plant*** Staudengewächs *n*

herb-al BOT Kräuter…, Pflanzen…

her-bi-vore ZO Pflanzenfresser *m*

herd 1. Herde *f (a. fig)*, Rudel *n*; **2.** *v/t* Vieh hüten; *v/i*: *a.* **herd together** in e-r Herde leben; sich zusammendrängen

herds-man Hirt *m*

here hier; hierher; ***here you are*** hier (bitte); ***here's to you!*** auf dein Wohl!

here-a-bout(s) hier herum, in dieser Gegend

here-af-ter 1. künftig; **2.** *das* Jenseits

here-by hiermit

he-red-i-ta-ry BIOL erblich, Erb…

he-red-i-ty BIOL Erblichkeit *f*; ererbte Anlagen *pl*, Erbmasse *f*

here-in hierin

here-of hiervon

her-e-sy REL Ketzerei *f*

her-e-tic REL Ketzer(in)

here-up-on hierauf, darauf(hin)

here-with hiermit

her-i-tage Erbe *n*

her-maph-ro-dite BIOL Zwitter *m*

her-met-ic TECH hermetisch

her-mit Einsiedler *m*

he-ro Held *m*

he-ro-ic heroisch, heldenhaft, Helden…

her-o-in Heroin *n*

her-o-ine Heldin *f*

her-o-is-m Heldentum *n*

her-on ZO Reiher *m*

her-ring ZO Hering *m*

hers ihrs, ihre(r, -s)

her-self sie selbst, ihr selbst; sich (selbst); ***by herself*** von selbst, allein, ohne Hilfe

hes-i-tant zögernd, zaudernd, unschlüssig

hes-i-tate zögern, zaudern, unschlüssig sein, Bedenken haben

hes-i-ta-tion Zögern *n*, Zaudern *n*, Unschlüssigkeit *f*; ***without hesitation*** ohne zu zögern, bedenkenlos

hew hauen, hacken; ***hew down*** fällen, umhauen

hey *int* F he!, heda!

hey-day Höhepunkt *m*, Gipfel *m*; Blüte (-zeit) *f*

hi *inf* F hallo!

hi-ber-nate ZO Winterschlaf halten

hic-cough, hic-cup 1. Schluckauf *m*; **2.** den Schluckauf haben

hide[1] (sich) verbergen, verstecken; verheimlichen

hide[2] Haut *f*, Fell *n*

hide-and-seek Versteckspiel *n*

hide-a-way F Versteck *n*

hid-e-ous abscheulich, scheußlich

hide-out Versteck *n*

hid-ing[1] F Tracht *f* Prügel

hid-ing[2]: ***be in hiding*** sich versteckt halten; ***go into hiding*** untertauchen

hid-ing place Versteck *n*

hi-fi Hi-Fi *n*, Hi-Fi-Gerät *n*, -Anlage *f*

high 1. hoch; groß *(hopes etc)*; GASTR angegangen; F blau; F high; ***be in high spirits*** in Hochstimmung sein; ausgelassen *or* übermütig sein; **2.** METEOR Hoch *n*; Höchststand *m*; High School *f*

high-brow 1. Intellektuelle *m*, *f*; **2.** (betont) intellektuell

high-cal-o-rie kalorienreich

high-class erstklassig

high-er ed-u-ca-tion Hochschulausbildung *f*

high fi-del-i-ty High Fidelity *f*

high-grade hochwertig; erstklassig

high-hand-ed anmaßend, eigenmächtig

high-heeled hochhackig

high jump SPORT Hochsprung *m*

high jump-er SPORT Hochspringer(in)

high-land Hochland *n*

high-light 1. Höhe-, Glanzpunkt *m*; **2.** hervorheben

high-ly *fig* hoch; ***think highly of*** viel halten von

high-ly-strung reizbar, nervös

high-ness *mst fig* Höhe *f*; ***Highness*** Hoheit *f (title)*

high-pitched schrill; steil *(roof)*

high-pow-ered TECH Hochleistungs…; *fig* dynamisch

high-pres-sure METEOR, TECH Hochdruck…

high-rank-ing hochrangig

high rise Hochhaus *n*

high road *esp Br* Hauptstraße *f*

high school High School *f*

high sea-son Hochsaison *f*

high so-ci-e-ty High Society *f*

high-spir-it-ed übermütig, ausgelassen

high street *Br* Hauptstraße *f*

high tea *Br* frühes Abendessen

high tech-nol-o-gy Hochtechnologie *f*

high ten-sion ELECTR Hochspannung *f*

high tide Flut *f*

high time: *it is high time* es ist höchste Zeit

high wa-ter Hochwasser *n*

high-way Highway *m*, Haupt(verkehrs)-straße *f*

High-way Code *Br* Straßenverkehrsordnung f

hi·jack 1. *Flugzeug* entführen; *j-n, Geldtransport etc* überfallen; **2.** (Flugzeug-)Entführung f; Überfall m

hi·jack·er Räuber m; (Flugzeug)Entführer(in)

hike 1. wandern; **2.** Wanderung f

hik·er Wanderer m, Wanderin f

hik·ing Wandern n

hi·lar·i·ous ausgelassen

hi·lar·i·ty Ausgelassenheit f

hill Hügel m, Anhöhe f

hill·bil·ly contp Hinterwäldler m

hill·ock kleiner Hügel

hill·side (Ab)Hang m

hill·top Hügelspitze f

hill·y hügelig

hilt Heft n, Griff m

him ihn; ihm; F er; sich

him·self er or ihm or ihn selbst; sich; sich (selbst); *by himself* von selbst, allein, ohne Hilfe

hind¹ zo Hirschkuh f

hind² Hinter…

hin·der hindern (*from* an dat); hemmen

hind·most hinterste(r, -s), letzte(r, -s)

hin·drance Hindernis n

Hin·du Hindu m

Hin·du·ism Hinduismus m

hinge 1. TECH (Tür)Angel f, Scharnier n; **2.** *hinge on* fig abhängen von

hint 1. Wink m, Andeutung f; Tipp m; Anspielung f; *take a hint* e-n Wink verstehen; **2.** andeuten; anspielen (*at* auf acc)

hip¹ ANAT Hüfte f

hip² BOT Hagebutte f

hip·po F → **hip·po·pot·a·mus** zo Flusspferd n, Nilpferd n

hire 1. Br Auto etc mieten, *Flugzeug etc* chartern; j-n anstellen; j-n engagieren, anheuern; *hire out Br* vermieten; **2.** Miete f; Lohn m; *for hire* zu vermieten; frei

hire car Br Leih-, Mietwagen m

hire pur·chase: *on hire purchase Br* ECON auf Abzahlung, auf Raten

his sein(e); seins, seine(r, -s)

hiss 1. zischen; fauchen (cat); auszischen; **2.** Zischen n; Fauchen n

his·to·ri·an Historiker(in)

his·tor·ic historisch, geschichtlich (bedeutsam)

his·tor·i·cal historisch, geschichtlich (belegt or überliefert); Geschichts…; *historical novel* historischer Roman

his·to·ry Geschichte f; *history of civilization* Kulturgeschichte f; *contemporary history* Zeitgeschichte f

hit 1. schlagen; treffen (a. fig), MOT etc j-n, et. anfahren, et. rammen; F *hit it off* (*with*

s.o.) sich (mit j-m) gut vertragen; *hit on* (zufällig) auf et. stoßen, et. finden; **2.** Schlag m; fig (Seiten)Hieb m; (Glücks-)Treffer m; Hit m

hit-and-run: *hit-and-run driver* (unfall)flüchtiger Fahrer; *hit-and-run offense* (Br offence) Fahrerflucht f

hitch 1. befestigen, festmachen, festhaken, anbinden, ankoppeln (*to* an acc); *hitch up* hochziehen; *hitch a ride or lift* im Auto mitgenommen werden; **2.** Ruck m, Zug m; Schwierigkeit f, Haken m; *without a hitch* glatt, reibungslos

hitch-hike per Anhalter fahren, trampen

hitch-hik·er Anhalter(in), Tramper(in)

hi-tech → **high tech**

HIV: *HIV carrier* HIV-Positive m, f; *HIV negative* HIV-negativ; *HIV positive* HIV-positiv

hive Bienenstock m; Bienenschwarm m

hoard 1. Vorrat m, Schatz m; **2.** a. *hoard up* horten, hamstern

hoard·ing Bauzaun m; Br Reklametafel f

hoar·frost (Rau)Reif m

hoarse heiser, rau

hoax 1. Falschmeldung f; (übler) Scherz; **2.** j-n hereinlegen

hob·ble humpeln, hinken

hob·by Hobby n, Steckenpferd n

hob·by·horse Steckenpferd n (a. fig)

hob·gob·lin Kobold m

ho·bo F Landstreicher m

hock¹ weißer Rheinwein

hock² zo Sprunggelenk n

hock·ey SPORT Eishockey n; esp Br Hockey n

hodge-podge Mischmasch m

hoe AGR **1.** Hacke f; **2.** hacken

hog zo (Haus-, Schlacht)Schwein n

hoist 1. hochziehen; hissen; **2.** TECH Winde f, (Lasten)Aufzug m

hold 1. halten; festhalten; *Gewicht etc* tragen, aushalten; zurück-, abhalten (*from* von); *Wahlen, Versammlung etc* abhalten; *Stellung* halten; SPORT *Meisterschaft etc* austragen; *Aktien, Rechte etc* besitzen; *Amt* bekleiden; *Platz* einnehmen; *Rekord* halten; fassen, enthalten; Platz bieten für; der Ansicht sein (*that* dass); halten für; fig fesseln, in Spannung halten; (sich) festhalten; anhalten, andauern (a. fig); *hold one's ground, hold one's own* sich behaupten; *hold the line* TEL am Apparat bleiben; *hold responsible* verantwortlich machen; *hold still* still halten; *hold s.th. against so.* j-m et. vorhalten or vorwerfen; j-m et. übel nehmen or nachtragen; *hold back* (sich) zurückhalten; fig zurückhalten mit; *hold* *on* (sich) festhalten (*to* an *dat*); aus-, durchhalten; andauern; TEL am Apparat bleiben; *hold out* aus-, durchhalten; reichen (*supplies etc*); *hold up* hochheben; hochhalten; hinstellen (*as* als); aufhalten, verzögern; j-n, Bank etc überfallen; **2.** Griff *m*, Halt *m*; Stütze *f*; Gewalt *f*, Macht *f*, Einfluss *m*; MAR Laderaum *m*, Frachtraum *m*; *catch* (*get, take*) *hold of s.th.* et. ergreifen, et. zu fassen bekommen

hold·er TECH Halter *m*; *esp* ECON Inhaber(in)

hold·ing Besitz *m*

hold·ing com·pa·ny ECON Holding-, Dachgesellschaft *f*

hold·up (Verkehrs)Stockung *f*; (bewaffneter) (Raub)Überfall

hole 1. Loch *n*; Höhle *f*, Bau *m*; *fig* F Klemme *f*; **2.** durchlöchern

hol·i·day Feiertag *m*; freier Tag; *esp Br mst pl* Ferien *pl*, Urlaub *m*; *be on holiday* im Urlaub sein, Urlaub machen

holiday home Ferienhaus *n*, Ferienwohnung *f*

hol·i·day·mak·er Urlauber(in)

hol·i·ness Heiligkeit *f*; *His Holiness* Seine Heiligkeit

hol·ler F schreien

hol·low 1. hohl; **2.** Hohlraum *m*, (Aus)Höhlung *f*; Mulde *f*, Vertiefung *f*; **3.** *hollow out* aushöhlen

hol·ly BOT Stechpalme *f*

hol·o·caust Massenvernichtung *f*, Massensterben *n*, (*esp* Brand)Katastrophe *f*; *the Holocaust* HIST der Holocaust

hol·ster (Pistolen)Halfter *m*, *n*

ho·ly heilig

ho·ly wa·ter REL Weihwasser *n*

Ho·ly Week REL Karwoche *f*

home 1. Heim *n*; Haus *n*; Wohnung *f*; Zuhause *n*; Heimat *f*; *at home* zu Hause; *make oneself at home* es sich bequem machen; *at home and abroad* im In- und Ausland; **2.** *adj* häuslich, Heim… (*a.* SPORT); inländisch, Inlands…; Heimat…; **3.** *adv* heim, nach Hause; zu Hause; daheim; *fig* im Ziel, ins Schwarze; *return home* heimkehren; *strike home* sitzen, treffen

home ad·dress Privatanschrift *f*

home com·put·er Heimcomputer *m*

home·less heimatlos; obdachlos; *homeless person* Obdachlose *m*, *f*; *shelter for the homeless* Obdachlosenasyl *n*

home·ly einfach; unscheinbar; reizlos

home·made selbst gemacht, Hausmacher…

home mar·ket ECON Binnenmarkt *m*

Home Of·fice *Br* POL Innenministerium *n*

Home Sec·re·ta·ry *Br* POL Innenminister *m*

home·sick: *be homesick* Heimweh haben

home·sick·ness Heimweh *n*

home team SPORT Gastgeber *pl*

home·ward *adj* Heim…, Rück…

home·ward(s) *adv* nach Hause

home·work Hausaufgabe(n *pl*) *f*; *do one's homework* s-e Hausaufgaben machen (*a. fig*)

hom·i·cide JUR Mord *m*; Totschlag *m*; Mörder(in)

homicide squad Mordkommission *f*

ho·mo·ge·ne·ous homogen, gleichartig

ho·mo·sex·u·al 1. homosexuell; **2.** Homosexuelle *m*

hone TECH fein schleifen

hon·est ehrlich, rechtschaffen; aufrichtig

hon·es·ty Ehrlichkeit *f*, Rechtschaffenheit *f*; Aufrichtigkeit *f*

hon·ey Honig *m*; Liebling *m*, Schatz *m*

hon·ey·comb (Honig)Wabe *f*

hon·eyed *fig* honigsüß

hon·ey·moon 1. Flitterwochen *pl*, Hochzeitsreise *f*; **2.** *be honeymooning* auf Hochzeitsreise sein

hon·ey·suck·le BOT Geißblatt *n*

honk MOT hupen

hon·or·ar·y Ehren…; ehrenamtlich

hon·o(u)r 1. Ehre *f*; Ehrung *f*, Ehre(n *pl*) *f*; *pl* besondere Auszeichnung(en *pl*); *Your Hono(u)r* JUR Euer Ehren; **2.** ehren; auszeichnen; ECON *Scheck etc* honorieren, einlösen

hon·o(u)r·a·ble ehrenvoll, ehrenhaft; ehrenwert

hood Kapuze *f*; MOT Verdeck *n*; (Motor)Haube *f*; TECH (Schutz)Haube *f*

hood·lum F Rowdy *m*; Ganove *m*

hood·wink *j-n* hinters Licht führen

hoof ZO Huf *m*

hook 1. Haken *m*; Angelhaken *m*; *by hook or by crook* F mit allen Mitteln; **2.** an-, ein-, fest-, zuhaken; angeln (*a. fig*)

hooked krumm, Haken…; F süchtig (*on* nach) (*a. fig*); *hooked on heroin* (*television*) heroinsüchtig (fernsehsüchtig)

hook·er F Nutte *f*

hook·y: *play hooky* F (die Schule) schwänzen

hoo·li·gan Rowdy *m*

hoo·li·gan·ism Rowdytum *n*

hoop Reif(en) *m*

hoot 1. ZO Schrei *m* (*a. fig*); MOT Hupen *n*; **2.** *v/i* heulen; ZO schreien; MOT hupen; *v/t* auspfeifen, auszischen

Hoo·ver® *Br* **1.** Staubsauger *m*; **2.** *mst*

hoover (staub)saugen

hop[1] **1.** hüpfen, hopsen; hüpfen über (*acc*); *be hopping mad* F e-e Stinkwut haben; **2.** Sprung *m*

hop[2] BOT Hopfen *m*

hope 1. Hoffnung *f* (*of* auf *acc*); **2.** hoffen (*for* auf *acc*); *hope for the best* das Beste hoffen; *I hope so, let's hope so* hoffentlich

hope·ful: *be hopeful that* hoffen, dass

hope·ful·ly hoffnungsvoll; hoffentlich

hope·less hoffnungslos; verzweifelt

horde Horde *f* (*often contp*)

ho·ri·zon Horizont *m*

hor·i·zon·tal horizontal, waag(e)recht

hor·mone BIOL Hormon *n*

horn ZO Horn *n*, *pl* Geweih *n*; MOT Hupe *f*

hor·net ZO Hornisse *f*

horn·y schwielig; V geil

hor·o·scope Horoskop *n*

hor·ri·ble schrecklich, furchtbar, scheußlich

hor·rid *esp Br* grässlich, abscheulich; schrecklich

hor·rif·ic schrecklich, entsetzlich

hor·ri·fy entsetzen

hor·ror Entsetzen *n*; Abscheu *m*, Horror *m*; F Gräuel *m*

horse ZO Pferd *n*; Bock *m*, Gestell *n*; *wild horses couldn't drag me there* keine zehn Pferde bringen mich dort hin

horse·back: *on horseback* zu Pferde, beritten

horse chest·nut BOT Rosskastanie *f*

horse·hair Rosshaar *n*

horse·man (geübter) Reiter

horse·pow·er TECH Pferdestärke *f*

horse race Pferderennen *n*

horse rac·ing Pferderennen *n or pl*

horse·rad·ish BOT Meerrettich *m*

horse·shoe Hufeisen *n*

horse·wom·an (geübte) Reiterin

hor·ti·cul·ture Gartenbau *m*

hose[1] Schlauch *m*

hose[2] Strümpfe *pl*, Strumpfwaren *pl*

ho·sier·y Strumpfwaren *pl*

hos·pice Sterbeklinik *f*

hos·pi·ta·ble gastfreundlich

hos·pi·tal Krankenhaus *n*, Klinik *f*; *in the hospital* im Krankenhaus

hos·pi·tal·i·ty Gastfreundschaft *f*

hos·pi·tal·ize ins Krankenhaus einliefern *or* einweisen

host[1] **1.** Gastgeber *m*; BIOL Wirt *m*; radio, TV Talkmaster *m*, Showmaster *m*, Moderator(in); *your host was ...* durch die Sendung führte Sie ...; **2.** radio, TV F *Sendung* moderieren

host[2] Menge *f*, Masse *f*

host[3] REL *often* **Host** Hostie *f*

hos·tage Geisel *m, f*; *take s.o. hostage* j-n als Geisel nehmen

hos·tel *esp Br* UNIV (Wohn)Heim *n*; *mst* **youth hostel** Jugendherberge *f*

host·ess Gastgeberin *f*; Hostess *f* (*a.* AVIAT); AVIAT Stewardess *f*

hos·tile feindlich; feindselig (*to* gegen); *hostile to foreigners* ausländerfeindlich

hos·til·i·ty Feindseligkeit *f* (*to* gegen); *hostility to foreigners* Ausländerfeindlichkeit *f*

hot heiß (*a. fig and sl*); GASTR scharf; warm (*meal*); *fig* hitzig, heftig; ganz neu *or* frisch (*news etc*); *I am or feel hot* mir ist heiß

hot·bed Mistbeet *n*; *fig* Brutstätte *f*

hotch·potch *Br* → **hodgepodge**

hot dog GASTR Hot Dog *n, m*

ho·tel Hotel *n*

hot·head Hitzkopf *m*

hot·house Treib-, Gewächshaus *n*

hot line POL heißer Draht; TEL Hotline *f*

hot·plate Kochplatte *f*

hot spot *esp* POL Unruhe-, Krisenherd *m*

hot spring Thermalquelle *f*

hot-tem·pered jähzornig

hot-wa·ter bot·tle Wärmflasche *f*

hound ZO Jagdhund *m*

hour Stunde *f*; *pl* (Arbeits)Zeit *f*, (Geschäfts)Stunden *pl*

hour·ly stündlich

house 1. Haus *n*; **2.** unterbringen

house·bound ans Haus gefesselt

house·break·ing Einbruch *m*

house·hold 1. Haushalt *m*; **2.** Haushalts...

house hus·band Hausmann *m*

house·keep·er Haushälterin *f*

house·keep·ing Haushaltung *f*, Haushaltsführung *f*

house·maid Hausangestellte *f*, Hausmädchen *n*

house·man *Br* MED Assistenzarzt *m*, -ärztin *f*

House of Lords *Br* PARL Oberhaus *n*

house plant Zimmerpflanze *f*

house-warm·ing Hauseinweihung *f*, Einzugsparty *f*

house·wife Hausfrau *f*

house·work Hausarbeit *f*

hous·ing Wohnung *f*

housing de·vel·op·ment, *Br* **housing es·tate** Wohnsiedlung *f*

hov·er schweben; herumlungern; *fig* schwanken

hov·er·craft Hovercraft *n*, Luftkissenfahrzeug *n*

how wie; *how are you?* wie geht es dir?;

how about …? wie steht's mit …?, wie wäre es mit …?; **how do you do?** guten Tag!; **how much?** wie viel?; **how many** wie viele?

how·ev·er 1. *adv* wie auch (immer); **2.** *cj* jedoch

howl 1. heulen; brüllen, schreien; **2.** Heulen *n*

howl·er F grober Schnitzer

hub TECH (Rad)Nabe *f*; *fig* Mittelpunkt *m*, Angelpunkt *m*

hub·bub Stimmengewirr *n*; Tumult *m*

hub·by F (Ehe)Mann *m*

huck·le·ber·ry BOT amerikanische Heidelbeere

hud·dle: huddle together (sich) zusammendrängen; **huddled up** zusammengekauert

hue[1] Farbe *f*; (Farb)Ton *m*

hue[2]**: hue and cry** *fig* großes Geschrei, heftiger Protest

huff: in a huff verärgert, verstimmt

hug 1. (sich) umarmen; an sich drücken; **2.** Umarmung *f*

huge riesig, riesengroß

hulk F Koloss *m*; sperriges Ding; **a hulk of a man** ein ungeschlachter Kerl

hull 1. BOT Schale *f*, Hülse *f*; MAR Rumpf *m*; **2.** enthülsen, schälen

hul·la·ba·loo Lärm *m*, Getöse *n*

hul·lo *int* hallo!

hum summen; brummen

hu·man 1. menschlich, Menschen…; **2.** *a.* **human being** Mensch *m*

hu·mane human, menschlich

hu·man·i·tar·i·an humanitär, menschenfreundlich

hu·man·i·ty die Menschheit, die Menschen *pl*; Humanität *f*, Menschlichkeit *f*; *pl* Geisteswissenschaften *pl*; Altphilologie *f*

hu·man·ly: humanly possible menschenmöglich

human rights Menschenrechte *pl*

hum·ble 1. demütig; bescheiden; **2.** demütigen

hum·ble·ness Demut *f*

hum·drum eintönig, langweilig

hu·mid feucht, nass

hu·mid·i·ty Feuchtigkeit *f*

hu·mil·i·ate demütigen, erniedrigen

hu·mil·i·a·tion Demütigung *f*, Erniedrigung *f*

hu·mil·i·ty Demut *f*

hum·ming·bird ZO Kolibri *m*

hu·mor·ous humorvoll, komisch

hu·mo(u)r 1. Humor *m*; Komik *f*; **2.** j-m s-n Willen lassen; eingehen auf (*acc*)

hump ZO Höcker *m*; MED Buckel *m*

hump·back(ed) → **hunchback(ed)**

hunch 1. → **hump**; dickes Stück; (Vor-)Ahnung *f*; **2.** *a.* **hunch up** krümmen; **hunch one's shoulders** die Schultern hochziehen

hunch·back Buckel *m*; Bucklige *m*, *f*

hunch·backed buck(e)lig

hun·dred 1. hundert; **2.** Hundert *f*

hun·dredth 1. hundertste(r, -s); **2.** Hundertstel *n*

hun·dred·weight *appr* Zentner *m* (= *50,8 kg*)

Hun·ga·ri·an 1. ungarisch; **2.** Ungar(in); LING Ungarisch *n*

Hun·ga·ry Ungarn *n*

hun·ger 1. Hunger *m* (*a. fig for* nach); **2.** *fig* hungern (*for, after* nach)

hunger strike Hungerstreik *m*

hun·gry hungrig

hunk dickes *or* großes Stück

hunt 1. jagen; Jagd machen auf (*acc*); verfolgen; suchen (*for, after* nach); **hunt down** zur Strecke bringen; **hunt for** Jagd machen auf (*acc*); **hunt out, hunt up** aufspüren; **2.** Jagd *f* (*a. fig*), Jagen *n*; Verfolgung *f*; Suche (*for, after* nach)

hunt·er Jäger *m*; Jagdpferd *n*

hunt·ing 1. Jagen *n*; **2.** Jagd…

hunting ground Jagdrevier *n*

hur·dle SPORT Hürde *f* (*a. fig*)

hur·dler SPORT Hürdenläufer(in)

hur·dle race SPORT Hürdenrennen *n*

hurl schleudern; **hurl abuse at s.o.** j-m Beleidigungen ins Gesicht schleudern

hur·rah, hur·ray *int* hurra!

hur·ri·cane Hurrikan *m*, Wirbelsturm *m*; Orkan *m*

hur·ried eilig, hastig, übereilt

hur·ry 1. *v/t* schnell *or* eilig befördern *or* bringen; *often* **hurry up** j-n antreiben, hetzen; *et.* beschleunigen; *v/i* eilen, hasten; **hurry (up)** sich beeilen; **hurry up!** (mach) schnell!; **2.** (große) Eile, Hast *f*; **be in a hurry** es eilig haben

hurt verletzen, verwunden (*a. fig*); schmerzen, wehtun; schaden (*dat*)

hurt·ful verletzend

hus·band (Ehe)Mann *m*

hush 1. *int* still!; **2.** Stille *f*; **3.** zum Schweigen bringen; **hush up** vertuschen, totschweigen

hush mon·ey Schweigegeld *n*

husk BOT **1.** Hülse *f*, Schote *f*, Schale *f*; **2.** enthülsen, schälen

hus·tle 1. (*in aller Eile*) *wohin* bringen *or* schicken; hasten, hetzen; sich beeilen; **2.** **hustle and bustle** Gedränge *n*; Gehetze *n*; Betrieb *m*, Wirbel *m*

hut Hütte *f*

H

hutch Stall *m*
hy·a·cinth BOT Hyazinthe *f*
hy·(a)e·na ZO Hyäne *f*
hy·brid BIOL Mischling *m*, Kreuzung *f*
hy·drant Hydrant *m*
hy·draul·ic hydraulisch
hy·draul·ics Hydraulik *f*
hy·dro... Wasser...
hy·dro·car·bon CHEM Kohlenwasserstoff *m*
hy·dro·chlor·ic ac·id CHEM Salzsäure *f*
hy·dro·foil MAR Tragflächenboot *n*, Tragflügelboot *n*
hy·dro·gen CHEM Wasserstoff *m*
hydrogen bomb Wasserstoffbombe
hy·dro·plane AVIAT Wasserflugzeug *n*; MAR Gleitboot *n*
hy·dro·plan·ing MOT Aquaplaning *n*
hy·e·na ZO Hyäne *f*
hy·giene Hygiene *f*
hy·gien·ic hygienisch

hymn Kirchenlied *n*, Choral *m*
hype F **1.** *a.* **hype up** (übersteigerte) Publicity machen für; **2.** (übersteigerte) Publicity; **media hype** Medienrummel *m*
hy·per... hyper..., übermäßig
hy·per·mar·ket *Br* Groß-, Verbrauchermarkt *m*
hy·per·sen·si·tive überempfindlich (*to* gegen)
hy·phen Bindestrich *m*
hy·phen·ate mit Bindestrich schreiben
hyp·no·tize hypnotisieren
hy·po·chon·dri·ac Hypochonder *m*
hy·poc·ri·sy Heuchelei *f*
hyp·o·crite Heuchler(in)
hyp·o·criti·cal heuchlerisch, scheinheilig
hy·poth·e·sis Hypothese *f*
hys·te·ri·a MED Hysterie *f*
hys·ter·i·cal hysterisch
hys·ter·ics hysterischer Anfall; **go into hysterics** hysterisch werden

---

I

I, i I, i *n*
I ich; **it is I** ich bin es
ice 1. Eis *n*; **2.** *Getränke etc* mit *or* in Eis kühlen; GASTR glasieren, mit Zuckerguss überziehen; **iced over** zugefroren (*lake etc*); **iced up** vereist (*road*)
ice age Eiszeit *f*
ice·berg Eisberg *m* (*a. fig*)
ice·bound eingefroren
ice cream (Speise)Eis *n*
ice-cream par·lo(u)r Eisdiele *f*
ice cube Eiswürfel *m*
iced eisgekühlt
ice floe Eisscholle *f*
ice hock·ey SPORT Eishockey *n*
ice lol·ly *Br* Eis *n* am Stiel
ice rink (Kunst)Eisbahn *f*
ice skate Schlittschuh *m*
ice-skate Schlittschuh laufen
ice show Eisrevue *f*
i·ci·cle Eiszapfen *m*
ic·ing GASTR Glasur *f*, Zuckerguss *m*; **the icing on the cake** das Tüpfelchen auf dem i
i·con REL Ikone *f*; EDP Ikone *f*, (Bild)Symbol *n*
i·cy eisig; vereist
ID ABBR *of* **identity** Identität *f*; **ID card**

(Personal)Ausweis *m*
i·dea Idee *f*, Vorstellung *f*, Begriff *m*; Gedanke *m*, Idee *f*; **have no idea** keine Ahnung haben
i·deal 1. ideal; **2.** Ideal *n*
i·deal·ism Idealismus *m*
i·deal·ize idealisieren
i·den·ti·cal identisch (**to, with** mit)
identical twins eineiige Zwillinge *pl*
i·den·ti·fi·ca·tion Identifizierung *f*
identification (pa·pers) Ausweis(papiere *pl*) *m*
i·den·ti·fy identifizieren; **identify o.s.** sich ausweisen
i·den·ti·kit® pic·ture *Br* JUR Phantombild *n*
i·den·ti·ty Identität *f*
identity card (Personal)Ausweis *m*
i·de·o·log·i·cal ideologisch
i·de·ol·o·gy Ideologie *f*
id·i·om Idiom *n*, idiomatischer Ausdruck, Redewendung *f*
id·i·o·mat·ic idiomatisch
id·i·ot MED Idiot(in), *contp a.* Trottel *m*
id·i·ot·ic MED idiotisch, F *a.* blödsinnig schwachsinnig
i·dle 1. untätig; faul, träge; nutzlos; leer hohl (*talk*); TECH stillstehend, außer Be-

trieb; MOT leerlaufend, im Leerlauf; **2.**
faulenzen; MOT leerlaufen; *mst idle away*
Zeit vertrödeln

·dol Idol *n* (*a. fig*); Götzenbild *n*

·dol·ize abgöttisch verehren, vergöttern

·dyl·lic idyllisch

f wenn, falls; ob; *if I were you* wenn ich du
wäre

g·loo Iglu *m, n*

g·nite anzünden, (sich) entzünden; MOT
zünden

g·ni·tion MOT Zündung *f*

g·ni·tion key MOT Zündschlüssel *m*

g·no·rance Unkenntnis *f*, Unwissenheit *f*

g·no·rant: *be ignorant of s.th.* et. nicht
wissen *or* kennen, nichts wissen von et.

g·nore ignorieren, nicht beachten

ll krank; schlimm, schlecht; *fall ill, be tak-*
en ill krank werden, erkranken

ll-ad·vised schlecht beraten; unklug

ll-bred schlecht erzogen; ungezogen

ll·le·gal verboten; JUR illegal, ungesetzlich; *illegal parking* Falschparken *n*

ll·le·gi·ble unleserlich

ll·le·git·i·mate unehelich; unrechtmäßig

ll feel·ing Verstimmung *f*; *cause ill feel-*
ing böses Blut machen

ll-hu·mo(u)red schlecht gelaunt

ll·li·cit unerlaubt, verboten

ll·lit·e·rate ungebildet

ll-man·nered ungehobelt, ungezogen

ll-na·tured boshaft, bösartig

ll·ness Krankheit *f*

ll-tem·pered schlecht gelaunt

ll-timed ungelegen, unpassend

ll-treat misshandeln

il·lu·mi·nate beleuchten

il·lu·mi·nat·ing aufschlussreich

il·lu·mi·na·tion Beleuchtung *f*; *pl* Illumination *f*, Festbeleuchtung *f*

il·lu·sion Illusion *f*, Täuschung *f*

il·lu·sive, il·lu·so·ry illusorisch, trügerisch

il·lus·trate illustrieren; bebildern; erläutern, veranschaulichen

il·lus·tra·tion Erläuterung *f*; Illustration
f; Bild *n*, Abbildung *f*

il·lus·tra·tive erläuternd

il·lus·tri·ous berühmt

ill will Feindschaft *f*

im·age Bild *n*; Ebenbild *n*; Image *n*; bild-
licher Ausdruck, Metapher *f*

im·age·ry Bildersprache *f*, Metaphorik *f*

i·ma·gi·na·ble vorstellbar, denkbar

i·ma·gi·na·ry eingebildet, imaginär

i·ma·gi·na·tion Einbildung(skraft) *f*; Vorstellungskraft *f*, -vermögen *n*

i·ma·gi·na·tive ideenreich, einfallsreich;
fantasievoll

i·ma·gine sich *j-n or et.* vorstellen; sich *et.*
einbilden

im·bal·ance Unausgewogenheit *f*; POL *etc*
Ungleichgewicht *n*

im·be·cile Idiot *m*, Trottel *m*

im·i·tate nachahmen, nachmachen, imitieren

im·i·ta·tion 1. Nachahmung *f*, Imitation *f*;
2. nachgemacht, unecht, künstlich;
Kunst…

im·mac·u·late unbefleckt, makellos; tadellos, fehlerlos

im·ma·te·ri·al unwesentlich, unerheblich
(*to* für)

im·ma·ture unreif

im·mea·su·ra·ble unermesslich

im·me·di·ate unmittelbar; sofortig, umgehend; nächste(r, -s) (*family*)

im·me·di·ate·ly unmittelbar; sofort

im·mense riesig, *fig a.* enorm, immens

im·merse (ein)tauchen; *immerse o.s. in*
sich vertiefen in (*acc*)

im·mer·sion Eintauchen *n*

im·mer·sion heat·er Tauchsieder *m*

im·mi·grant Einwanderer *m*, Einwanderin *f*, Immigrant(in)

im·mi·grate einwandern, immigrieren
(*into* in *dat*)

im·mi·gra·tion Einwanderung *f*, Immigration *f*

im·mi·nent nahe bevorstehend; *immi-*
nent danger drohende Gefahr

im·mo·bile unbeweglich

im·mod·e·rate maßlos

im·mod·est unbescheiden; schamlos, unanständig

im·mor·al unmoralisch

im·mor·tal 1. unsterblich; **2.** Unsterbliche
m, f

im·mor·tal·i·ty Unsterblichkeit *f*

im·mo·va·ble unbeweglich; *fig* unerschütterlich; hart, unnachgiebig

im·mune MED immun (*to* gegen); geschützt (*from* vor, gegen)

immune sys·tem MED Immunsystem *n*

im·mu·ni·ty MED Immunität *f*

im·mu·nize MED immunisieren, immun
machen (*against* gegen)

imp Kobold *m*; F Racker *m*

im·pact Zusammenprall *m*, Anprall *m*;
Aufprall *m*; Wucht *f*; *fig* (Ein)Wirkung
f, (starker) Einfluss (*on* auf *acc*)

im·pair beeinträchtigen

im·part (*to* dat) mitteilen; vermitteln

im·par·tial unparteiisch, unvoreingenommen

im·par·ti·al·i·ty Unparteilichkeit *f*, Objektivität *f*

im·pass·a·ble unpassierbar

I

im·passe *fig* Sackgasse *f*; **reach an impasse** in e-e Sackgasse geraten
im·pas·sioned leidenschaftlich
im·pas·sive teilnahmslos; ungerührt; gelassen
im·pa·tience Ungeduld *f*
im·pa·tient ungeduldig
im·peach JUR anklagen (**for, of, with** *gen*); JUR anfechten; infrage stellen, in Zweifel ziehen
im·pec·ca·ble untadelig, einwandfrei
im·pede (be)hindern
im·ped·i·ment Hindernis *n* (**to** für); Behinderung *f*
im·pel antreiben; zwingen
im·pend·ing nahe bevorstehend, drohend
im·pen·e·tra·ble undurchdringlich; *fig* unergründlich
im·per·a·tive **1.** unumgänglich, unbedingt erforderlich; gebieterisch; LING Imperativ...; **2.** *a.* **imperative mood** LING Imperativ *m*, Befehlsform *f*
im·per·cep·ti·ble nicht wahrnehmbar, unmerklich
im·per·fect **1.** unvollkommen; mangelhaft; **2.** *a.* **imperfect tense** LING Imperfekt *n*, 1. Vergangenheit
im·pe·ri·al·ism POL Imperialismus
im·pe·ri·al·ist POL Imperialist *m*
im·per·il gefährden
im·pe·ri·ous herrisch, gebieterisch
im·per·me·a·ble undurchlässig
im·per·son·al unpersönlich
im·per·so·nate *j-n* imitieren, nachahmen; verkörpern, THEA darstellen
im·per·ti·nence Unverschämtheit *f*, Frechheit *f*
im·per·ti·nent unverschämt, frech
im·per·tur·ba·ble unerschütterlich, gelassen
im·per·vi·ous undurchlässig; *fig* unzugänglich (**to** für)
im·pe·tu·ous ungestüm, heftig; impulsiv; vorschnell
im·pe·tus TECH Antrieb *m*, Impuls *m*
im·pi·e·ty Gottlosigkeit *f*; Pietätlosigkeit *f*, Respektlosigkeit *f* (**to** gegenüber)
im·pinge: **impinge on** sich auswirken auf (*acc*), beeinflussen (*acc*)
im·pi·ous gottlos; pietätlos, respektlos (**to** gegenüber)
im·plac·a·ble unversöhnlich
im·plant MED implantieren, einpflanzen; *fig* einprägen
im·plau·si·ble unglaubwürdig
im·ple·ment **1.** Werkzeug *n*, Gerät *n*; **2.** ausführen
im·pli·cate *j-n* verwickeln, hineinziehen (**in** in *acc*)

im·pli·ca·tion Verwicklung *f*; Folge *f*; Andeutung *f*
im·pli·cit vorbehaltlos, bedingungslos impliziert, (stillschweigend *or* mit) inbegriffen
im·plore *j-n* anflehen; *et.* erflehen
im·ply implizieren, einbeziehen, mit enthalten; andeuten; bedeuten
im·po·lite unhöflich
im·pol·i·tic unklug
im·port ECON **1.** importieren, einführen; **2.** Import *m*, Einfuhr *f*
im·por·tance Wichtigkeit *f*, Bedeutung *f*
im·por·tant wichtig, bedeutend
im·por·ta·tion → **import** 2
im·port du·ty ECON Einfuhrzoll *m*
im·port·er ECON Importeur *m*
im·pose auferlegen, aufbürden (**on** *dat*); *Strafe* verhängen (**on** gegen); *et.* aufdrängen, aufzwingen (**on** *dat*); **impose o.s. on s.o.** sich j-m aufdrängen
im·pos·ing imponierend, eindrucksvoll, imposant
im·pos·si·bil·i·ty Unmöglichkeit *f*
im·pos·si·ble unmöglich
im·pos·ter, *Br* im·pos·tor Betrüger(in), *esp* Hochstapler(in)
im·po·tence Unvermögen *n*, Unfähigkeit *f*; Hilflosigkeit *f*; MED Impotenz *f*
im·po·tent unfähig; hilflos; MED impotent
im·pov·er·ish arm machen; **be impoverished** verarmen; verarmt sein
im·prac·ti·ca·ble undurchführbar; unpassierbar
im·prac·ti·cal unpraktisch; undurchführbar
im·preg·na·ble uneinnehmbar
im·preg·nate imprägnieren, tränken; BIOL schwängern
im·press aufdrücken, einprägen (*a. fig*); *j-n* beeindrucken; **be impressed with** beeindruckt sein von
im·pres·sion Eindruck *m*; Abdruck *m*; **under the impression that** in der Annahme, dass
im·pres·sive eindrucksvoll
im·print **1.** (auf)drücken (**on** auf *acc*); **imprint s.th. on s.o.'s memory** j-m et. ins Gedächtnis einprägen; **2.** Abdruck *m*, Eindruck *m*; PRINT Impressum *n*
im·pris·on JUR inhaftieren
im·pris·on·ment Freiheitsstrafe *f*, Gefängnis(strafe *f*) *n*, Haft *f*
im·prob·a·ble unwahrscheinlich
im·prop·er ungeeignet, unpassend; unanständig, unschicklich; unrichtig
im·pro·pri·e·ty Unschicklichkeit *f*
im·prove *v/t* verbessern; *Wert etc* erhöhen, steigern; **improve on** übertreffen; *v/i*

sich (ver)bessern, besser werden, sich erholen
im·prove·ment (Ver)Bess(e)rung f; Steigerung f; Fortschritt m (**on** gegenüber
dat)
im·pro·vise improvisieren
im·pru·dent unklug
im·pu·dence Unverschämtheit f
im·pu·dent unverschämt
im·pulse Impuls m (a. fig); Anstoß m, Anreiz m
im·pul·sive impulsiv
im·pu·ni·ty: **with impunity** straflos, ungestraft
im·pure unrein (*a.* REL), schmutzig; fig
schlecht, unmoralisch
im·pu·ri·ty Unreinheit f
im·pute: *impute s.th. to s.o.* j-n e-r Sache
bezichtigen; j-m et. unterstellen
in 1. *prp place*: in (*dat or acc*), an (*dat*), auf
(*dat*): **in New York** in New York; **in the
street** auf der Straße; **put it in your
pocket** steck es in deine Tasche; *time*:
in (*dat*), an (*dat*): **in 1999** 1999; **in two
hours** in zwei Stunden; **in the morning**
am Morgen; *state, manner*: in (*dat*), auf
(*acc*), mit; **in English** auf Englisch; *activity*: in (*dat*), bei, auf (*dat*): **in crossing
the road** beim Überqueren der Straße;
author: bei: **in Shakespeare** bei Shakespeare; *direction*: in (*acc, dat*), auf (*acc*),
zu: **have confidence in** Vertrauen haben
zu; *purpose*: in (*dat*), zu, als: **in defense
of** zur Verteidigung *or* zum Schutz von;
material: in (*dat*), aus, mit: **dressed in
blue** in Blau (gekleidet); *amount etc*:
in, von, aus, zu: **three in all** insgesamt
or im Ganzen drei; **one in ten** eine(r,
-s) von zehn; nach, gemäß: **in my opinion** m-r Meinung nach; 2. *adv* innen,
drinnen; hinein, herein; da, (an)gekom-
men; da, zu Hause; 3. *adj* F in (Mode)
in·a·bil·i·ty Unfähigkeit f
in·ac·ces·si·ble unzugänglich, unerreich-
bar (**to** für *or dat*)
in·ac·cu·rate ungenau
in·ac·tive untätig
in·ac·tiv·i·ty Untätigkeit f
in·ad·e·quate unangemessen; unzulänglich, ungenügend
in·ad·mis·si·ble unzulässig, unstatthaft
in·ad·ver·tent unbeabsichtigt, versehentlich; **inadvertently** *a.* aus Versehen
in·an·i·mate leblos; langweilig
in·ap·pro·pri·ate unpassend, ungeeignet
(**for, to** für)
in·apt ungeeignet, unpassend
in·ar·tic·u·late unartikuliert, undeutlich
(ausgesprochen), unverständlich; unfä-

hig(, deutlich) zu sprechen
in·at·ten·tive unaufmerksam
in·au·di·ble unhörbar
in·au·gu·ral 1. Eröffnungs..., Antritts...;
inaugural speech → 2. Antrittsrede f
in·au·gu·rate *j-n* (feierlich) (in sein Amt)
einführen; einweihen, eröffnen; einleiten
in·au·gu·ra·tion Amtseinführung f; Einweihung f, Eröffnung f; Beginn m; *Inauguration Day* Tag m der Amtseinführung des neu gewählten Präsidenten
der USA
in·born angeboren
in·cal·cu·la·ble unberechenbar; unermesslich
in·can·des·cent (weiß) glühend
in·ca·pa·ble unfähig (**of** zu *inf or gen*),
nicht imstande (**of doing** zu tun)
in·ca·pac·i·tate unfähig *or* untauglich
machen
in·ca·pac·i·ty Unfähigkeit f, Untauglich-
keit f
in·car·nate leibhaftig; personifiziert
in·cau·tious unvorsichtig
in·cen·di·a·ry Brand...; fig aufwiegelnd,
aufheizend
in·cense[1] REL Weihrauch m
in·cense[2] *in* Wut bringen, erbosen
in·cen·tive Ansporn m, Anreiz m
in·ces·sant ständig, unaufhörlich
in·cest Inzest m, Blutschande f
inch 1. Inch m (2,54 cm), Zoll m (*a. fig*); **by
inches, inch by inch** allmählich; **every
inch** durch und durch; 2. (sich) zentime-
terweise *or* sehr langsam bewegen
in·ci·dence Vorkommen n
in·ci·dent Vorfall m, Ereignis n; POL Zwischenfall m
in·ci·den·tal nebensächlich, Neben...;
beiläufig
in·ci·den·tal·ly nebenbei bemerkt, übrigens
in·cin·e·rate verbrennen
in·cin·e·ra·tor TECH Verbrennungsofen m;
Verbrennungsanlage f
in·cise einschneiden; aufschneiden; ein-
ritzen, einschnitzen
in·ci·sion (Ein)Schnitt m
in·ci·sive schneidend, scharf; fig treffend
in·ci·sor ANAT Schneidezahn m
in·cite anstiften; aufwiegeln, aufhetzen
in·cite·ment Anstiftung f; Aufhetzung f,
Aufwieg(e)lung f
in·clem·ent rau
in·cli·na·tion Neigung f (*a. fig*)
in·cline 1. *v/i* sich neigen (**to, towards**
nach); fig neigen (**to, towards** zu); *v/t*
neigen; fig veranlassen; 2. Gefälle n;

(Ab)Hang *m*

in·close, in·clos·ure → *enclose, enclosure*

in·clude einschließen, enthalten; aufnehmen (*in* in *e-e Liste etc*); *the group included several ...* zu der Gruppe gehörten einige ...; *tax included* inklusive Steuer

in·clud·ing einschließlich

in·clu·sion Einschluss *m*, Einbeziehung *f*

in·clu·sive einschließlich, inklusive (*of gen*); *be inclusive of* einschließen (*acc*)

in·co·her·ent unzusammenhängend, unklar, unverständlich

in·come ECON Einkommen *n*, Einkünfte *pl*

income tax ECON Einkommensteuer *f*

in·com·ing hereinkommend; ankommend; nachfolgend, neu; *incoming mail* Posteingang *m*

in·com·mu·ni·ca·tive verschlossen

in·com·pa·ra·ble unvergleichlich; unvergleichbar

in·com·pat·i·ble unvereinbar; unverträglich; inkompatibel

in·com·pe·tence Unfähigkeit *f*; Inkompetenz *f*

in·com·pe·tent unfähig; nicht fachkundig *or* sachkundig; unzuständig, inkompetent

in·com·plete unvollständig; unvollendet

in·com·pre·hen·si·ble unbegreiflich, unfassbar

in·com·pre·hen·sion Unverständnis *n*

in·con·ceiv·a·ble unbegreiflich, unfassbar; undenkbar

in·con·clu·sive nicht überzeugend; ergebnislos, erfolglos

in·con·gru·ous nicht übereinstimmend; unvereinbar

in·con·se·quen·tial unbedeutend

in·con·sid·er·a·ble unbedeutend

in·con·sid·er·ate unüberlegt; rücksichtslos

in·con·sis·tent unvereinbar; widersprüchlich; inkonsequent

in·con·so·la·ble untröstlich

in·con·spic·u·ous unauffällig

in·con·stant unbeständig, wankelmütig

in·con·test·a·ble unanfechtbar

in·con·ti·nent MED inkontinent

in·con·ve·ni·ence 1. Unbequemlichkeit *f*; Unannehmlichkeit *f*, Ungelegenheit *f*; **2.** *j-m* lästig sein; *j-m* Umstände machen

in·con·ve·ni·ent unbequem; ungelegen, lästig

in·cor·po·rate (sich) vereinigen *or* zusammenschließen; (mit) einbeziehen; enthalten; eingliedern; *Ort* eingemeinden; ECON, JUR als Aktiengesellschaft eintragen (lassen)

in·cor·po·rat·ed com·pa·ny ECON Aktiengesellschaft *f*

in·cor·po·ra·tion Vereinigung *f*, Zusammenschluss *m*; Eingliederung *f*; Eingemeindung *f*; ECON, JUR Eintragung *f* als Aktiengesellschaft

in·cor·rect unrichtig, falsch; inkorrekt

in·cor·ri·gi·ble unverbesserlich

in·cor·rup·ti·ble unbestechlich

in·crease 1. zunehmen, (an)wachsen; steigen; vergrößern, vermehren, erhöhen; **2.** Vergrößerung *f*, Erhöhung *f*, Zunahme *f*, Zuwachs *m*, (An)Wachsen *n*, Steigerung *f*

in·creas·ing·ly immer mehr; *increasingly difficult* immer schwieriger

in·cred·i·ble unglaublich

in·cre·du·li·ty Ungläubigkeit *f*

in·cred·u·lous ungläubig, skeptisch

in·crim·i·nate *j-n* belasten

in·cu·bate ausbrüten

in·cu·ba·tor Brutapparat *m*; MED Brutkasten *m*

in·cur sich *et*. zuziehen, auf sich laden; *Schulden* machen; *Verluste* erleiden

in·cur·a·ble unheilbar

in·cu·ri·ous nicht neugierig, gleichgültig, uninteressiert

in·cur·sion (feindlicher) Einfall; Eindringen *n*

in·debt·ed (zu Dank) verpflichtet; ECON verschuldet

in·de·cent unanständig, anstößig; JUR unsittlich, unzüchtig; *indecent assault* JUR Sittlichkeitsverbrechen *n*

in·de·ci·sion Unentschlossenheit *f*

in·de·ci·sive unentschlossen; unentschieden; unbestimmt, ungewiss

in·deed 1. *adv* in der Tat, tatsächlich, wirklich; allerdings; *thank you very much indeed!* vielen herzlichen Dank!; **2.** *int* ach wirklich?

in·de·fat·i·ga·ble unermüdlich

in·de·fen·si·ble unhaltbar

in·de·fi·na·ble undefinierbar, unbestimmbar

in·def·i·nite unbestimmt; unbegrenzt

in·def·i·nite·ly auf unbestimmte Zeit

in·del·i·ble unauslöschlich (*a. fig*); *indelible pencil* Tintenstift *m*

in·del·i·cate taktlos; unfein, anstößig

in·dem·ni·fy *j-n* entschädigen, *j-m* Schadenersatz leisten (*for* für)

in·dem·ni·ty Entschädigung *f*

in·dent (ein)kerben, auszacken; PRINT *Zeile* einrücken

in·de·pen·dence Unabhängigkeit *f*; Selbstständigkeit *f*; *Independence Day* Unabhängigkeitstag *m*

in·de·pen·dent unabhängig; selbstständig

in·de·scri·ba·ble unbeschreiblich

in·de·struc·ti·ble unzerstörbar; unverwüstlich

in·de·ter·mi·nate unbestimmt; unklar, vage

in·dex Index *m*, (Inhalts-, Namens-, Stichwort)Verzeichnis *n*, (Sach)Register *n*; (An)Zeichen *n*; *cost of living index* Lebenshaltungsindex *m*

in·dex card Karteikarte *f*

in·dex fin·ger ANAT Zeigefinger *m*

In·di·a Indien *n*

In·di·an 1. indisch; *neg!* indianisch, Indianer...; **2.** Inder(in); *American Indian* Indianer(in)

Indian corn BOT Mais *m*

Indian file: *in Indian file* im Gänsemarsch

Indian sum·mer Altweibersommer *m*, Nachsommer *m*

in·di·a rub·ber Gummi *n*, *m*; Radiergummi *m*

in·di·cate deuten *or* zeigen auf (*acc*) anzeigen; MOT blinken; *fig* hinweisen *or* hindeuten auf (*acc*); andeuten

in·di·ca·tion (An)Zeichen *n*, Hinweis *m*, Andeutung *f*, Indiz *n*

in·dic·a·tive *a.* **indicative mood** LING Indikativ *m*

in·di·ca·tor TECH Anzeiger *m*; MOT Richtungsanzeiger *m*, Blinker *m*

in·dict JUR anklagen (*for* wegen)

in·dict·ment JUR Anklage *f*

in·dif·fer·ence Gleichgültigkeit *f*

in·dif·fer·ent gleichgültig (*to* gegen); mittelmäßig

in·di·gent arm

in·di·ges·ti·ble unverdaulich

in·di·ges·tion MED Verdauungsstörung *f*, Magenverstimmung *f*

in·dig·nant entrüstet, empört, ungehalten (*about, at, over* über *acc*)

in·dig·na·tion Entrüstung *f*, Empörung *f* (*about, at, over* über *acc*)

in·dig·ni·ty Demütigung *f*, unwürdige Behandlung *f*

in·di·rect indirekt; *by indirect means fig* auf Umwegen

in·dis·creet unbesonnen, unbedacht; indiskret

in·dis·cre·tion Unbesonnenheit *f*; Indiskretion *f*

in·dis·crim·i·nate kritiklos; wahllos

in·di·spen·sa·ble unentbehrlich, unerlässlich

in·dis·posed indisponiert, unpässlich; abgeneigt

in·dis·po·si·tion Unpässlichkeit *f*; Abneigung *f* (*to do* zu tun)

in·dis·pu·ta·ble unbestreitbar, unstreitig

in·dis·tinct undeutlich; unklar, verschwommen

in·dis·tin·guish·a·ble nicht zu unterscheiden(d) (*from* von)

in·di·vid·u·al 1. individuell, einzeln, Einzel...; persönlich; **2.** Individuum *n*, Einzelne *m*, *f*

in·di·vid·u·al·ism Individualismus *m*

in·di·vid·u·al·ist Individualist(in)

in·di·vid·u·al·i·ty Individualität *f*, (persönliche) Note

in·di·vid·u·al·ly einzeln, jede(r, -s) für sich; individuell

in·di·vis·i·ble unteilbar

in·dom·i·ta·ble unbezähmbar, nicht unterzukriegen(d)

in·door Haus..., Zimmer..., Innen..., SPORT Hallen...

in·doors im Haus, drinnen; ins Haus (hinein); SPORT in der Halle

in·dorse → *endorse etc*

in·duce *j-n* veranlassen; verursachen, bewirken

in·duce·ment Anreiz *m*

in·duct einführen, -setzen

in·duc·tion Herbeiführung *f*; Einführung *f*, Einsetzung *f*; ELECTR Induktion *f*

in·dulge nachsichtig sein gegen; *e-r Neigung etc* nachgeben; *indulge in s.th.* sich et. gönnen *or* leisten

in·dul·gence Nachsicht *f*; Luxus *m*; REL Ablass *m*

in·dul·gent nachsichtig, nachgiebig

in·dus·tri·al industriell, Industrie..., Gewerbe..., Betriebs...

in·dus·tri·al ar·e·a Industriegebiet *n*

in·dus·tri·al·ist Industrielle *m*, *f*

in·dus·tri·al·ize industrialisieren

in·dus·tri·ous fleißig

in·dus·try Industrie(zweig *m*) *f*; Gewerbe(zweig *m*) *n*; Fleiß *m*

in·ed·i·ble ungenießbar, nicht essbar

in·ef·fec·tive, **in·ef·fec·tu·al** unwirksam, wirkungslos; unfähig, untauglich

in·ef·fi·cient ineffizient, unfähig, untauglich; unrationell, unwirtschaftlich

in·el·e·gant unelegant

in·el·i·gi·ble nicht berechtigt

in·ept unpassend; ungeschickt; albern, töricht

in·e·qual·i·ty Ungleichheit *f*

in·ert PHYS träge (*a. fig*); inaktiv

in·er·tia PHYS Trägheit *f* (*a. fig*)

in·es·cap·a·ble unvermeidlich

in·es·sen·tial unwesentlich, unwichtig (**to** für)

in·es·ti·ma·ble unschätzbar

in·ev·i·ta·ble unvermeidlich

in·ev·i·ta·bly zwangsläufig

in·ex·act ungenau

in·ex·cu·sa·ble unverzeihlich, unentschuldbar

in·ex·haus·ti·ble unerschöpflich; unermüdlich

in·ex·o·ra·ble unerbittlich

in·ex·pe·di·ent unzweckmäßig; nicht ratsam

in·ex·pen·sive billig, preiswert

in·ex·pe·ri·ence Unerfahrenheit f

in·ex·pe·ri·enced unerfahren

in·ex·pert unerfahren; ungeschickt

in·ex·plic·a·ble unerklärlich

in·ex·pres·si·ble unaussprechlich, unbeschreiblich

in·ex·pres·sive ausdruckslos

in·ex·tri·ca·ble unentwirrbar

in·fal·li·ble unfehlbar

in·fa·mous berüchtigt; schändlich, niederträchtig

in·fa·my Ehrlosigkeit f; Schande f; Niederträcht f

in·fan·cy frühe Kindheit; *be in its infancy fig* in den Kinderschuhen stecken

in·fant Säugling m; kleines Kind, Kleinkind n

in·fan·tile kindlich; Kindes…, Kinder…; infantil, kindisch

in·fan·try MIL Infanterie f

in·fat·u·at·ed vernarrt (**with** in acc)

in·fect MED j-n, et. infizieren, j-n anstecken (a. fig); verseuchen, verunreinigen

in·fec·tion MED Infektion f, Ansteckung f (a. fig)

in·fec·tious MED infektiös, ansteckend (a. fig)

in·fer folgern, schließen (**from** aus)

in·fer·ence (Schluss)Folgerung f, (Rück)Schluss m

in·fe·ri·or 1. untergeordnet (**to** dat); niedriger (**to** als); weniger wert (**to** als); minderwertig (a. fig); *be inferior to s.o.* j-m untergeordnet sein; j-m unterlegen sein; **2.** Untergebene m, f

in·fe·ri·or·i·ty Unterlegenheit f; Minderwertigkeit f

inferiority com·plex PSYCH Minderwertigkeitskomplex m

in·fer·nal höllisch, Höllen…

in·fer·no Inferno n, Hölle f

in·fer·tile unfruchtbar

in·fest verseuchen, befallen; *fig* überschwemmen (**with** mit)

in·fi·del·i·ty (esp eheliche) Untreue

in·fil·trate einsickern in (acc); einschleusen (**into** in acc); POL unterwandern

in·fi·nite unendlich

in·fin·i·tive a. **infinitive mood** LING Infinitiv m, Nennform f

in·fin·i·ty Unendlichkeit f

in·firm schwach, gebrechlich

in·fir·ma·ry Krankenhaus n; PED etc Krankenzimmer n

in·fir·mi·ty Schwäche f, Gebrechlichkeit f

in·flame entflammen (mst fig); erregen; *become inflamed* MED sich entzünden

in·flam·ma·ble brennbar, leicht entzündlich; feuergefährlich

in·flam·ma·tion MED Entzündung f

in·flam·ma·to·ry MED entzündlich; fig aufrührerisch, Hetz…

in·flate aufpumpen, aufblasen, aufblähen (a. fig); ECON Preise etc in die Höhe treiben

in·fla·tion ECON Inflation f

in·flect LING flektieren, beugen

in·flec·tion LING Flexion f, Beugung f

in·flex·i·ble unbiegsam, starr (a. fig); fig inflexibel, unbeweglich, unbeugsam

in·flex·ion Br → **inflection**

in·flict (on) Leid, Schaden etc zufügen (dat); Wunde etc beibringen (dat); Strafe auferlegen (dat), verhängen (über acc); aufbürden, aufdrängen (dat)

in·flic·tion Zufügung f; Verhängung f; Plage f

in·flu·ence 1. Einfluss m; **2.** beeinflussen

in·flu·en·tial einflussreich

in·flux Zustrom m, Zufluss m, (Waren-)Zufuhr f

in·form benachrichtigen, unterrichten (**of** von), informieren (**of** über acc); *inform against or on s.o.* j-n anzeigen; j-n denunzieren

in·for·mal formlos, zwanglos

in·for·mal·i·ty Formlosigkeit f; Ungezwungenheit f

in·for·ma·tion Auskunft f, Information f; Nachricht f

information (su·per·)**highway** EDP Datenautobahn f

in·for·ma·tive informativ; lehrreich; mitteilsam

in·form·er Denunziant(in); Spitzel m

in·fra·struc·ture Infrastruktur f

in·fre·quent selten

in·fringe: *infringe on* Rechte, Vertrag etc verletzen, verstoßen gegen

in·fu·ri·ate wütend machen

in·fuse Tee aufgießen

in·fu·sion Aufguss m; MED Infusion f

in·ge·ni·ous genial; einfallsreich; raffiniert

in·ge·nu·i·ty Genialität *f*; Einfallsreichtum *m*

in·gen·u·ous offen, aufrichtig; naiv

in·got (*Gold- etc*)Barren *m*

in·gra·ti·ate: *ingratiate o.s. with s.o.* sich bei j-m beliebt machen

in·grat·i·tude Undankbarkeit *f*

in·gre·di·ent Bestandteil *m*; GASTR Zutat *f*

in·hab·it bewohnen, leben in (*dat*)

in·hab·it·a·ble bewohnbar

in·hab·i·tant Bewohner(in); Einwohner(in)

in·hale einatmen, MED *a.* inhalieren

in·her·ent innewohnend, eigen (*in dat*)

in·her·it erben

in·her·i·tance Erbe *n*

in·hib·it hemmen (*a.* PSYCH), (ver)hindern

in·hib·it·ed PSYCH gehemmt

in·hi·bi·tion PSYCH Hemmung *f*

in·hos·pi·ta·ble ungastlich; unwirtlich (*region etc*)

in·hu·man unmenschlich

in·hu·mane inhuman, menschenunwürdig

in·im·i·cal feindselig (*to* gegen); nachteilig (*to* für)

in·im·i·ta·ble unnachahmlich

i·ni·tial 1. anfänglich, Anfangs...; **2.** Initiale *f*, (großer) Anfangsbuchstabe

i·ni·tial·ly am *or* zu Anfang, anfänglich

i·ni·ti·ate in die Wege leiten, ins Leben rufen; einführen

i·ni·ti·a·tion Einführung *f*

i·ni·tia·tive Initiative *f*, erster Schritt; ***take the initiative*** die Initiative ergreifen; ***on one's own initiative*** aus eigenem Antrieb

in·ject MED injizieren, einspritzen

in·jec·tion MED Injektion *f*, Spritze *f*

in·ju·di·cious unklug, unüberlegt

in·junc·tion JUR gerichtliche Verfügung

in·jure verletzen, verwunden; schaden (*dat*); kränken

in·jured 1. verletzt; **2. *the injured*** die Verletzten *pl*

in·ju·ri·ous schädlich; ***be injurious to*** schaden (*dat*); ***injurious to health*** gesundheitsschädlich

in·ju·ry MED Verletzung *f*, Kränkung *f*

injury time *Br esp soccer*: Nachspielzeit *f*

in·jus·tice Ungerechtigkeit *f*; Unrecht *n*; ***do s.o. an injustice*** j-m unrecht tun

ink Tinte *f*

ink·ling Andeutung *f*; dunkle *or* leise Ahnung

ink pad Stempelkissen *n*

ink·y Tinten...; tinten-, pechschwarz

in·laid eingelegt, Einlege...; ***inlaid work*** Einlegearbeit *f*

in·land 1. *adj* inländisch, einheimisch; ECON Binnen...; **2.** *adv* landeinwärts

In·land Rev·e·nue *Br* Finanzamt *n*

in·lay Einlegearbeit *f*; MED (Zahn)Füllung *f*, Plombe *f*

in·let GEOGR schmale Bucht; TECH Eingang *m*, Einlass *m*

in·line skate Inliner *m*, Inline Skate *m*

in·mate Insasse *m*, Insassin *f*; Mitbewohner(in)

in·most innerste(r, -s) (*a. fig*)

inn Gasthaus *n*, Wirtshaus *n*

in·nate angeboren

in·ner innere(r, -s); Innen...; verborgen

in·ner·most → ***inmost***

in·nings *cricket, baseball*: Spielzeit *f*

inn·keep·er Gastwirt(in)

in·no·cence Unschuld *f*; Harmlosigkeit *f*; Naivität *f*

in·no·cent unschuldig; harmlos; arglos; naiv

in·noc·u·ous harmlos

in·no·va·tion Neuerung *f*

in·nu·en·do (versteckte) Andeutung *f*

in·nu·me·ra·ble unzählig, zahllos

i·noc·u·late MED impfen

i·noc·u·la·tion MED Impfung *f*

in·of·fen·sive harmlos

in·op·e·ra·ble MED inoperabel, nicht operierbar; undurchführbar (*plan etc*)

in·op·por·tune inopportun, unangebracht, ungelegen

in·or·di·nate unmäßig

in·pa·tient MED stationärer Patient, stationäre Patientin

in·put Input *m, n*, EDP *a.* (Daten)Eingabe *f*, ELECTR *a.* Eingangsleistung *f*

in·quest JUR gerichtliche Untersuchung

in·quire fragen *or* sich erkundigen (nach); ***inquire into*** *et.* untersuchen, prüfen

in·quir·ing forschend; wissbegierig

in·quir·y Erkundigung *f*, Nachfrage *f*; Untersuchung *f*; Ermittlung *f*; ***make inquiries*** Erkundigungen einziehen

in·qui·si·tion (amtliche) Untersuchung; Verhör *n*; ***Inquisition*** REL HIST Inquisition *f*

in·quis·i·tive neugierig, wissbegierig

in·roads (*in*[*to*], *on*) Eingriff *m* (in *acc*), Übergriff *m* (auf *acc*)

in·sane geisteskrank, wahnsinnig

in·san·i·ta·ry unhygienisch

in·san·i·ty Geisteskrankheit *f*, Wahnsinn *m*

in·sa·tia·ble unersättlich

in·scrip·tion Inschrift *f*, Aufschrift *f*; Widmung *f*

in·scru·ta·ble unerforschlich, unergründlich

in·sect zo Insekt n

in·sec·ti·cide Insektenvertilgungsmittel n, Insektizid n

in·se·cure unsicher; nicht sicher or fest

in·sen·si·ble unempfindlich (*to* gegen); bewusstlos; unempfänglich (*of*, *to* für), gleichgültig (*of*, *to* gegen); unmerklich

in·sen·si·tive unempfindlich (*to* gegen); unempfänglich (*to* für), gleichgültig (*of*, *to* gegen)

in·sep·a·ra·ble untrennbar; unzertrennlich

in·sert 1. einfügen, einsetzen, einführen, (hinein)stecken, *Münze* einwerfen; inserieren; **2.** (Zeitungs)Beilage f, (Buch)Einlage f

in·ser·tion Einfügen n, Einsetzen n, Einführen n, Hineinstecken n; Einfügung f; Einwurf m; Anzeige f, Inserat n

in·sert key EDP Einfügetaste f

in·shore an or nahe der Küste; Küsten...

in·side 1. Innenseite f; *das* Innere; *turn inside out* umkrempeln; auf den Kopf stellen; **2.** *adj* innere(r, -s), Innen...; Insider...; **3.** *adv* im Inner(e)n, innen, drinnen; *inside of* F innerhalb (*gen*); **4.** *prp* innerhalb, im Inner(e)n

in·sid·er Insider(in), Eingeweihte m, f

in·sid·i·ous heimtückisch

in·sight Einsicht f, Einblick m; Verständnis n

in·sig·ni·a Insignien pl; Abzeichen pl

in·sig·nif·i·cant bedeutungslos; unbedeutend

in·sin·cere unaufrichtig

in·sin·u·ate andeuten, anspielen auf (*acc*); unterstellen; *insinuate that s.o. ...* j-m unterstellen, dass er ...

in·sin·u·a·tion Anspielung f, Andeutung f, Unterstellung f

in·sip·id geschmacklos, fad

in·sist bestehen, beharren (*on* auf *dat*)

in·sis·tence Bestehen n, Beharren n; Beharrlichkeit f

in·sis·tent beharrlich, hartnäckig

in·sole Einlegesohle f; Brandsohle f

in·so·lent unverschämt

in·sol·u·ble unlöslich (*substance etc*); unlösbar (*problem etc*)

in·sol·vent ECON zahlungsunfähig, insolvent

in·som·ni·a Schlaflosigkeit f

in·spect untersuchen, prüfen, nachsehen; besichtigen, inspizieren

in·spec·tion Prüfung f, Untersuchung f, Kontrolle f; Inspektion f

in·spec·tor Aufsichtsbeamte m, Inspektor m; (Polizei)Inspektor m, (Polizei)Kommissar m

in·spi·ra·tion Inspiration f, (plötzlicher) Einfall m

in·spire inspirieren, anregen; *Gefühl etc* auslösen

in·stall TECH installieren, einrichten, aufstellen, einbauen, *Leitung* legen; *j-n in ein Amt etc* einsetzen

in·stal·la·tion TECH Installation f, Einrichtung f, Einbau m; TECH *fertige* Anlage f; *fig* Einsetzung f, Einführung f

in·stall·ment, in·stal·ment Br ECON Rate f; (Teil)Lieferung f; Fortsetzung f; *radio*, TV Folge f

in·stall·ment plan: *buy on the installment plan* ECON auf Abzahlung or Raten kaufen

in·stance Beispiel n; (besonderer) Fall; JUR Instanz f; *for instance* zum Beispiel

in·stant 1. Moment m, Augenblick m; **2.** sofortig, augenblicklich

in·stan·ta·ne·ous sofortig, augenblicklich; *death was instantaneous* der Tod trat sofort ein

in·stant cam·e·ra PHOT Sofortbildkamera f

instant cof·fee GASTR Pulver-, Instantkaffee m

in·stant·ly sofort, augenblicklich

in·stead stattdessen, dafür; *instead of* anstelle von, (an)statt

in·step ANAT Spann m, Rist m

in·sti·gate anstiften; aufhetzen; veranlassen

in·sti·ga·tor Anstifter(in); (Auf)Hetzer(in)

in·stil Br, **in·still** beibringen, einflößen (*into* dat)

in·stinct Instinkt m

in·stinc·tive instinktiv

in·sti·tute Institut n

in·sti·tu·tion Institution f, Einrichtung f; Institut n; Anstalt f

in·struct unterrichten, -weisen; ausbilden, schulen; informieren; anweisen

in·struc·tion Unterricht m; Ausbildung f, Schulung f, Unterweisung f; Anweisung f, Instruktion f; EDP Befehl m; *instructions for use* Gebrauchsanweisung f; *operating instructions* Bedienungsanleitung f

in·struc·tive instruktiv, lehrreich

in·struc·tor Lehrer m; Ausbilder m

in·struc·tress Lehrerin f; Ausbilderin f

in·stru·ment Instrument n (a. MUS); Werkzeug n (a. fig)

in·stru·men·tal MUS Instrumental...; behilflich; *be instrumental in* beitragen zu

in·sub·or·di·nate aufsässig

in·sub·or·di·na·tion Auflehnung f, Aufsässigkeit f

in·suf·fe·ra·ble unerträglich, unausstehlich

in·suf·fi·cient unzulänglich, ungenügend

in·su·lar Insel...; *fig* engstirnig

in·su·late isolieren

in·su·la·tion Isolierung *f;* Isoliermaterial *n*

in·sult 1. Beleidigung *f;* **2.** beleidigen

in·sur·ance Versicherung *f;* Versicherungssumme *f;* Absicherung *f* (**against** gegen)

insurance com·pa·ny Versicherungsgesellschaft *f*

insurance pol·i·cy Versicherungspolice *f*

in·sure versichern (**against** gegen)

in·sured: the insured der *or* die Versicherte

in·sur·gent 1. aufständisch; **2.** Aufständische *m, f*

in·sur·moun·ta·ble *fig* unüberwindlich

in·sur·rec·tion Aufstand *m*

in·tact intakt, unversehrt, unbeschädigt, ganz

in·take (*Nahrungs- etc*)Aufnahme *f;* (Neu)Aufnahme(n *pl*) *f,* (Neu)Zugänge *pl;* TECH Einlass(öffnung *f) m*

in·te·gral ganz, vollständig; wesentlich

in·te·grate (sich) integrieren; zusammenschließen; eingliedern, einbeziehen; *integrated circuit* ELECTR integrierter Schaltkreis

in·te·gra·tion Integration *f*

in·teg·ri·ty Integrität *f;* Vollständigkeit *f;* Einheit *f*

in·tel·lect Intellekt *m,* Verstand *m*

in·tel·lec·tual 1. intellektuell, Verstandes..., geistig; **2.** Intellektuelle *m, f*

in·tel·li·gence Intelligenz *f;* nachrichtendienstliche Informationen *pl*

in·tel·li·gent intelligent, klug

in·tel·li·gi·ble verständlich (**to** für)

in·tem·per·ate unmäßig

in·tend beabsichtigen, vorhaben, planen; *intended for* bestimmt für *or* zu

in·tense intensiv, stark, heftig

in·ten·si·fy intensivieren; (sich) verstärken

in·ten·si·ty Intensität *f*

in·ten·sive intensiv, gründlich

intensive care u·nit MED Intensivstation *f*

in·tent 1. gespannt, aufmerksam; *intent on* fest entschlossen zu (*dat*); konzentriert auf (*acc*); **2.** Absicht *f,* Vorhaben *n*

in·ten·tion Absicht *f;* JUR Vorsatz *m*

in·ten·tion·al absichtlich, vorsätzlich

in·ter bestatten

in·ter..., zwischen, Zwischen...; gegenseitig, einander

in·ter·act aufeinander (ein)wirken, sich gegenseitig beeinflussen

in·ter·ac·tion Wechselwirkung *f*

in·ter·cede vermitteln, sich einsetzen (**with** bei; **for** für)

in·ter·cept abfangen

in·ter·ces·sion Fürsprache *f*

in·ter·change 1. austauschen; **2.** Austausch *m;* MOT Autobahnkreuz *n*

in·ter·com Sprechanlage *f*

in·ter·course Verkehr *m; a. sexual intercourse* (Geschlechts)Verkehr *m*

in·terest 1. Interesse *n* (**in** an *dat,* für); Wichtigkeit *f,* Bedeutung *f;* Vorteil *m,* Nutzen *m;* ECON Anteil *m,* Beteiligung *f;* ECON Zins(en *pl) m; take an interest in* sich interessieren für; **2.** interessieren (**in** für *et*)

in·terest·ed interessiert (**in** an *dat*); *be interested in* sich interessieren für

in·terest·ing interessant

in·terest rate ECON Zinssatz *m*

in·ter·face EDP Schnittstelle *f*

in·ter·fere sich einmischen (**with** in *acc*); stören

in·ter·fer·ence Einmischung *f;* Störung *f*

in·te·ri·or 1. innere(r, -s), Innen...; Binnen...; Inlands...; **2.** *das* Innere; Interieur *n;* POL innere Angelegenheiten *pl;* → *Department of the Interior*

interior dec·o·ra·tor Innenarchitekt(in)

in·ter·ject *Bemerkung* einwerfen

in·ter·jec·tion Einwurf *m;* Ausruf *m;* LING Interjektion *f*

in·ter·lace (sich) (ineinander) verflechten

in·ter·lop·er Eindringling *m*

in·ter·lude Zwischenspiel *n;* Pause *f; interludes of bright weather* zeitweilig schön

in·ter·me·di·a·ry Vermittler(in), Mittelsmann *m*

in·ter·me·di·ate in der Mitte liegend, Mittel..., Zwischen...; PED für fortgeschrittene Anfänger

in·ter·ment Beerdigung *f,* Bestattung *f*

in·ter·mi·na·ble endlos

in·ter·mis·sion Unterbrechung *f;* THEA *etc* Pause *f*

in·ter·mit·tent mit Unterbrechungen, periodisch (auftretend); *intermittent fever* MED Wechselfieber *n*

in·tern[1] internieren

in·tern[2] Assistenzarzt *m,* -ärztin *f*

in·ter·nal innere(r, -s); einheimisch, Inlands...

in·ter·nal-com·bus·tion en·gine Verbrennungsmotor *m*

in·ter·na·tion·al 1. international; Auslands...; **2.** SPORT Internationale *m, f,* Nationalspieler(in); internationaler Wettkampf; Länderspiel *n*

international call TEL Auslandsgespräch *n*

international law JUR Völkerrecht *n*

In·ter·net Internet *n*

in·tern·ist MED Internist *m*

in·ter·per·son·al zwischenmenschlich

in·ter·pret interpretieren, auslegen, erklären; dolmetschen

in·ter·pre·ta·tion Interpretation *f*, Auslegung *f*

in·ter·pret·er Dolmetscher(in)

in·ter·ro·gate verhören, vernehmen; (be)fragen

in·ter·ro·ga·tion Verhör *n*, Vernehmung *f*; Frage *f*

in·ter·rog·a·tive LING Interrogativ..., Frage...

in·ter·rupt unterbrechen

in·ter·rup·tion Unterbrechung *f*

in·ter·sect (durch)schneiden; sich schneiden or kreuzen

in·ter·sec·tion Schnittpunkt *m*; (Straßen)Kreuzung *f*

in·ter·sperse einstreuen, hier und da einfügen

in·ter·state 1. zwischenstaatlich; **2.** *a.* ***interstate highway*** Autobahn *f*

in·ter·twine (sich ineinander) verschlingen, sich verflechten

in·ter·val Intervall *n* (*a.* MUS), Abstand *m*; *Br* Pause *f* (*a.* THEA *etc*); ***at regular intervals*** in regelmäßigen Abständen

in·ter·vene eingreifen, einschreiten, intervenieren; dazwischenkommen

in·ter·ven·tion Eingreifen *n*, Einschreiten *n*, Intervention *f*

in·ter·view 1. Interview *n*; Einstellungsgespräch *n*; **2.** interviewen; ein Einstellungsgespräch führen mit

in·ter·view·ee Interviewte *m*, *f*

in·ter·view·er Interviewer(in)

in·ter·weave (miteinander) verweben

in·tes·tate: ***die intestate*** JUR ohne Hinterlassung e-s Testaments sterben

in·tes·tine ANAT Darm *m*; *pl* Eingeweide *pl*; ***large intestine*** Dickdarm *m*; ***small intestine*** Dünndarm *m*

in·ti·ma·cy Intimität *f*, Vertrautheit *f*; (*a. plumpe*) Vertraulichkeit; intime (*sexuelle*) Beziehungen *pl*

in·ti·mate 1. intim (*a. sexually*); vertraut, eng (*friends etc*); (*a. plump*)vertraulich; innerste(r, -s); gründlich, genau (*knowledge etc*); **2.** Vertraute *m*, *f*

in·tim·i·date einschüchtern

in·tim·i·da·tion Einschüchterung *f*

in·to in (*acc*), in (*acc*) ... hinein; gegen

(*acc*); MATH in (*acc*); ***4 into 20 goes five times*** 4 geht fünfmal in 20

in·tol·e·ra·ble unerträglich

in·tol·e·rance Intoleranz *f*, Unduldsamkeit (*of* gegen)

in·tol·e·rant intolerant, unduldsam (*of* gegen)

in·to·na·tion MUS Intonation *f*, LING *a.* Tonfall *m*

in·tox·i·cat·ed berauscht, betrunken

in·tox·i·ca·tion Rausch *m* (*a. fig*)

in·trac·ta·ble eigensinnig; schwer zu handhaben(d)

in·tran·si·tive LING intransitiv

in·tra·ve·nous MED intravenös

in tray: ***in the in tray*** im Posteingang *etc*

in·trep·id unerschrocken

in·tri·cate verwickelt, kompliziert

in·trigue 1. Intrige *f*; **2.** faszinieren, interessieren; intrigieren

in·tro·duce vorstellen (***to*** *dat*), *j-n* bekannt machen (***to*** mit); einführen

in·tro·duc·tion Vorstellung *f*; Einführung *f*; Einleitung *f*, Vorwort *n*; ***letter of introduction*** Empfehlungsschreiben *n*

in·tro·duc·to·ry Einführungs...; einleitend, Einleitungs...

in·tro·spec·tion Selbstbeobachtung *f*

in·tro·vert PSYCH introvertierter Mensch

in·tro·vert·ed PSYCH introvertiert, in sich gekehrt

in·trude (sich) aufdrängen; stören; ***am I intruding?*** störe ich?

in·trud·er Eindringling *m*, Störenfried *m*

in·tru·sion Störung *f*

in·tru·sive aufdringlich

in·tu·i·tion Intuition *f*

in·tu·i·tive intuitiv

In·u·it *a.* ***Innuit*** Inuit *m*, Eskimo *m*

in·un·date überschwemmen, überfluten (*a. fig*)

in·vade eindringen in (*acc*), einfallen in (*acc*), MIL *a.* einmarschieren in (*acc*); *fig* überlaufen, überschwemmen

in·vad·er Eindringling *m*

in·va·lid[1] **1.** krank; invalid(e); **2.** Kranke *m*; *f*; Invalide *m*, *f*

in·val·id[2] (*rechts*)ungültig

in·val·i·date JUR für ungültig erklären

in·val·u·a·ble *fig* unschätzbar, unbezahlbar

in·var·i·a·ble unveränderlich

in·var·i·a·bly ausnahmslos

in·va·sion Invasion *f* (*a.* MIL), Einfall *m*, MIL *a.* Einmarsch *m*; *fig* Eingriff *m*, Verletzung *f*

in·vec·tive Schmähung(en *pl*) *f*, Beschimpfung(en *pl*) *f*

in·vent erfinden

in·ven·tion Erfindung f
in·ven·tive erfinderisch; einfallsreich
in·ven·tor Erfinder(in)
in·ven·tory Inventar n, Bestand m; Bestandsliste f; Inventur f
in·verse 1. umgekehrt; 2. Umkehrung f, Gegenteil n
in·ver·sion Umkehrung f; LING Inversion f
in·vert umkehren
in·ver·te·brate ZO 1. wirbellos; 2. wirbelloses Tier
in·vert·ed com·mas LING Anführungszeichen pl
in·vest ECON investieren, anlegen
in·ves·ti·gate untersuchen; überprüfen; Untersuchungen or Ermittlungen anstellen (into über acc), nachforschen
in·ves·ti·ga·tion Untersuchung f; Ermittlung f, Nachforschung f
in·ves·ti·ga·tor: private investigator Privatdetektiv m
in·vest·ment ECON Investition f, (Kapital)Anlage f
in·ves·tor ECON Anleger m
in·vet·e·rate unverbesserlich; hartnäckig
in·vid·i·ous gehässig, boshaft, gemein
in·vig·o·rate stärken, beleben
in·vin·ci·ble unbesiegbar; unüberwindlich
in·vi·o·la·ble unantastbar
in·vis·i·ble unsichtbar
in·vi·ta·tion Einladung f; Aufforderung f
in·vite einladen; auffordern; Gefahr etc herausfordern; invite s.o. in j-n hereinbitten
in·vit·ing einladend, verlockend
in·voice ECON 1. (Waren)Rechnung f; 2. in Rechnung stellen, berechnen
in·voke flehen um; Gott etc anrufen; beschwören
in·vol·un·ta·ry unfreiwillig; unabsichtlich; unwillkürlich
in·volve verwickeln, hineinziehen (in in acc); j-n, et. angehen, betreffen; zur Folge haben, mit sich bringen
in·volved kompliziert, verworren
in·volve·ment Verwicklung f; Beteiligung f
in·vul·ne·ra·ble unverwundbar; fig unanfechtbar
in·ward 1. adj innere(r, -s), innerlich; 2. adv mst inwards einwärts, nach innen
i·o·dine CHEM Jod n
i·on PHYS Ion n
IOU (= I owe you) Schuldschein m
IQ ABBR of intelligence quotient IQ, Intelligenzquotient m
I·ran Iran m

I·ra·ni·an 1. iranisch; 2. Iraner(in); LING Iranisch n
I·raq Irak m
I·ra·qi 1. irakisch; 2. Iraker(in); LING Irakisch n
i·ras·ci·ble jähzornig
i·rate zornig, wütend
Ire·land Irland n
ir·i·des·cent schillernd
i·ris ANAT Regenbogenhaut f, Iris f; BOT Schwertlilie f, Iris f
I·rish 1. irisch; 2. LING Irisch n; the Irish die Iren pl
I·rish·man Ire m
I·rish·wom·an Irin f
i·ron 1. Eisen n; Bügeleisen n; strike while the iron is hot fig das Eisen schmieden, solange es heiß ist; 2. eisern (a. fig), Eisen..., aus Eisen; 3. bügeln; iron out ausbügeln
I·ron Cur·tain POL HIST Eiserner Vorhang
i·ron·ic, i·ron·i·cal ironisch, spöttisch
i·ron·ing board Bügelbrett n
i·ron·mon·ger Br Eisenwarenhändler m
i·ron·works TECH Eisenhütte f
i·ron·y Ironie f
ir·ra·tion·al irrational, unvernünftig
ir·rec·on·ci·la·ble unversöhnlich; unvereinbar
ir·re·cov·e·ra·ble unersetzlich; unwiederbringlich
ir·re·fut·a·ble unwiderlegbar
ir·reg·u·lar unregelmäßig; ungleichmäßig; regelwidrig, vorschriftswidrig
ir·rel·e·vant irrelevant, unerheblich, belanglos (to für)
ir·rep·a·ra·ble irreparabel, nicht wieder gutzumachen(d)
ir·re·place·a·ble unersetzlich
ir·re·pres·si·ble nicht zu unterdrücken(d); unbezähmbar
ir·re·proach·a·ble einwandfrei, untadelig
ir·re·sist·i·ble unwiderstehlich
ir·res·o·lute unentschlossen
ir·re·spec·tive: irrespective of ohne Rücksicht auf (acc); unabhängig von
ir·re·spon·si·ble unverantwortlich; verantwortungslos
ir·re·trie·va·ble unwiederbringlich, unersetzlich
ir·rev·e·rent respektlos
ir·rev·o·ca·ble unwiderruflich, endgültig
ir·ri·gate bewässern
ir·ri·ga·tion Bewässerung f
ir·ri·ta·ble reizbar
ir·ri·tant Reizmittel n
ir·ri·tate reizen; (ver)ärgern
ir·ri·tat·ing ärgerlich
ir·ri·ta·tion Reizung f; Verärgerung f; Är-

I

ger *m* (*at* über *acc*)

is er, sie, es ist

Is·lam der Islam

is·land Insel *f*; *a.* **traffic island** Verkehrsinsel *f*

is·land·er Inselbewohner(in)

isle POET Insel *f*

i·so·late absondern; isolieren

i·so·lat·ed isoliert, abgeschieden; einzeln; **become isolated** vereinsamen

i·so·la·tion Isolierung *f*, Absonderung *f*

isolation ward MED Isolierstation *f*

Is·rael Israel *n*

Is·rae·li **1.** israelisch; **2.** Israeli *m*, *f*

is·sue Streitfrage *f*, Streitpunkt *m*; Ausgabe *f*; Erscheinen *n*; JUR Nachkommen(schaft *f*) *pl*; *fig* Ausgang *m*, Ergebnis *n*; **be at issue** zur Debatte stehen; **point at issue** strittiger Punkt; **die without issue** kinderlos sterben; **2.** *v/t Zeitung etc* herausgeben; *Banknoten etc* ausgeben; *Dokument etc* ausstellen; *v/i* herauskommen, hervorkommen; herausfließen, herausströmen

it es; *s.th. previously mentioned*: es, er, ihn, sie

I·tal·i·an **1.** italienisch; **2.** Italiener(in); LING Italienisch *n*

i·tal·ics PRINT Kursivschrift *f*

It·a·ly Italien *n*

itch **1.** Jucken *n*, Juckreiz *m*; **2.** jucken, kratzen; **I itch all over** es juckt mich überall; **be itching for s.th.** F et. unbedingt (haben) wollen; **be itching to** *inf* F darauf brennen zu *inf*

itch·y juckend; kratzend

i·tem Punkt *m* (*on the agenda etc*), Posten *m* (*on a list*); Artikel *m*, Gegenstand *m*; (*Presse-, Zeitungs*)Notiz *f*, (*a. radio*, TV) Nachricht *f*, Meldung *f*

i·tem·ize einzeln angeben *or* aufführen

i·tin·e·ra·ry Reiseweg *m*, Reiseroute *f*; Reiseplan *m*

its sein(e), ihr(e)

it·self sich; sich selbst; selbst; **by itself** (für sich) allein; von selbst; **in itself** an sich

i·vo·ry Elfenbein *n*

i·vy BOT Efeu *m*

J

J, j J, j *n*

jab **1.** (hinein)stechen, (hinein)stoßen; **2.** Stich *m*, Stoß *m*

jab·ber F (daher)plappern

jack **1.** TECH Hebevorrichtung *f*; MOT Wagenheber *m*; *cards*: Bube *m*; **2.** **jack up** *Auto* aufbocken

jack·al ZO Schakal *m*

jack·ass ZO Esel *m* (*a. fig*)

jack·daw ZO Dohle *f*

jack·et Jacke *f*, Jackett *n*; TECH Mantel *m*; (*Schutz*)Umschlag *m*; (*Platten-*)Hülle *f*; **jacket potatoes, potatoes (boiled) in their jackets** Pellkartoffeln *pl*

jack knife **1.** Klappmesser *n*; **2.** zusammenklappen, -knicken

jack-of-all-trades Hansdampf *m* in allen Gassen

jack·pot Jackpot *m*, Haupttreffer *m*; **hit the jackpot** F den Jackpot gewinnen; *fig* das große Los ziehen

jade MIN Jade *m*, *f*; Jadegrün *n*

jag Zacken *m*

jag·ged gezackt, zackig; schartig

jag·u·ar ZO Jaguar *m*

jail **1.** Gefängnis *n*; **2.** einsperren

jail·bird F Knastbruder *m*

jail·er Gefängnisaufseher *m*

jail·house Gefängnis *n*

jam¹ Konfitüre *f*, Marmelade *f*

jam² **1.** *v/t* (hinein)pressen, (hinein-) quetschen, (hinein)zwängen, *Menschen a.* (hinein)pferchen; (ein)klemmen, (ein)quetschen; *a.* **jam up** blockieren, verstopfen; *Funkempfang* stören; **jam on the brakes** MOT voll auf die Bremse treten; *v/i* sich (hinein)drängen *or* (hinein-) quetschen; TECH sich verklemmen, *brake*: blockieren; **2.** Gedränge *n*; TECH Blockierung *f*; Stauung *f*, Stockung *f*; **traffic jam** Verkehrsstau *m*; **be in a jam** F in der Klemme stecken

jamb (Tür-, Fenster)Pfosten *m*

jam·bo·ree Jamboree *n*, Pfadfindertreffen *n*; Fest *n*

Jan ABBR *of January* Jan., Januar *m*

jan·gle klimpern *or* klirren (mit)

jan·i·tor Hausmeister *m*

Jan·u·a·ry (ABBR of **Jan**) Januar m

Ja·pan Japan n

Jap·a·nese 1. japanisch; **2.** Japaner(in); LING Japanisch n; **the Japanese** die Japaner pl

jar¹1. Gefäß n, Krug m; (Marmelade- etc) Glas n

jar²: **jar on** wehtun (dat)

jar·gon Jargon m, Fachsprache f

jaun·dice MED Gelbsucht f

jaunt 1. Ausflug m, MOT Spritztour f; **2.** e-n Ausflug or e-e Spritztour machen

jaun·ty unbeschwert, unbekümmert; flott

jav·e·lin SPORT Speer m; **javelin (throw)**, **throwing the javelin** SPORT Speerwerfen n

jav·e·lin throw·er SPORT Speerwerfer(in)

jaw ANAT Kiefer m; pl ZO Rachen m, Maul n; TECH Backen pl; **lower jaw** ANAT Unterkiefer m; **upper jaw** ANAT Oberkiefer m

jaw·bone ANAT Kieferknochen m

jay ZO Eichelhäher m

jay·walk·er unachtsamer Fußgänger

jazz MUS Jazz m

jazz·y F poppig

jeal·ous eifersüchtig (**of** auf acc); neidisch

jeal·ous·y Eifersucht f; Neid m

jeans Jeans pl

jeer 1. (**at**) höhnische Bemerkung(en) machen (über acc); höhnisch lachen (über acc); **jeer (at)** verhöhnen; **2.** höhnische Bemerkung; Hohngelächter n

jel·lied GASTR in Aspik, in Sülze

jel·ly Gallert(e f) n; GASTR Gelee n; Aspik m, n, Sülze f; Götterspeise f

jel·ly ba·by Br Gummibärchen n

jel·ly bean Gummi-, Geleebonbon m, n

jel·ly·fish ZO Qualle f

jeop·ar·dize gefährden

jerk 1. ruckartig ziehen an (dat); (zusammen)zucken; sich ruckartig bewegen; **2.** (plötzlicher) Ruck; Sprung m, Satz m; MED Zuckung f

jerk·y ruckartig; holprig; rüttelnd

jer·sey Pullover m

jest 1. Scherz m, Spaß m; **2.** scherzen, spaßen

jest·er HIST (Hof)Narr m

jet 1. (Wasser-, Gas- etc)Strahl m; TECH Düse f; AVIAT Jet m; **2.** (heraus-, hervor)schießen (**from** aus); AVIAT F jetten

jet en·gine AVIAT Düsen-, Strahltriebwerk n

jet plane AVIAT Düsenflugzeug n, Jet m

jet-pro·pelled AVIAT mit Düsenantrieb, Düsen...

jet pro·pul·sion AVIAT Düsen-, Strahlantrieb m

jet·ty MAR (Hafen)Mole f

Jew Jude m, Jüdin f

jew·el Juwel n, m, Edelstein m

jew·el·er, Br **jew·el·ler** Juwelier m

jew·el·lery Br, **jew·el·ry** Juwelen pl; Schmuck m

Jew·ess Jüdin f

Jew·ish jüdisch

jif·fy: F **in a jiffy** im Nu, sofort

jig·saw Laubsäge f; → **jig·saw puz·zle** Puzzle(spiel) n

jilt Mädchen sitzen lassen; e-m Liebhaber den Laufpass geben

jin·gle 1. klimpern (mit), bimmeln (lassen); **2.** Klimpern n, Bimmeln n; Werbesong m, Werbespruch m

jit·ters: F **the jitters** Bammel m, e-e Heidenangst

jit·ter·y F nervös; ängstlich

job 1. (einzelne) Arbeit; Beruf m, Beschäftigung f, Stellung f, Stelle f, Arbeit f, Job m (a. EDP); Arbeitsplatz m; Aufgabe f, Sache f, Angelegenheit f; a. **job work** Akkordarbeit f; **by the job** im Akkord; **out of a job** arbeitslos; **2.** **job around** jobben

job ad, **job ad·ver·tise·ment** Stellenanzeige f

job·ber Br ECON Börsenspekulant m

job cen·tre Br Arbeitsamt n

job hop·ping häufiger Arbeitsplatzwechsel

job·hunt·ing Arbeitssuche f; **be jobhunting** auf Arbeitssuche sein

job·less arbeitslos

jock·ey Jockei m

jog 1. stoßen an (acc) or gegen, j-n anstoßen; mst **jog along, jog on** dahintrotten, dahinzuckeln; SPORT joggen; **2.** (leichter) Stoß, Stups m; Trott m; SPORT Trimmtrab m

jog·ger SPORT Jogger(in)

jog·ging SPORT Joggen n, Jogging n

join 1. v/t verbinden, vereinigen, zusammenfügen; sich anschließen (dat or an acc), sich gesellen zu; eintreten in (acc), beitreten; teilnehmen or sich beteiligen an (dat), mitmachen bei; **join in** einstimmen in; v/i sich vereinigen or verbinden; **join in** teilnehmen or sich beteiligen (an dat), mitmachen (bei); **2.** Verbindungsstelle f, Naht f

join·er Tischler m, Schreiner m

joint 1. Verbindungs-, Nahtstelle f; ANAT, TECH Gelenk n; BOT Knoten m; Br GASTR Braten m; F Laden m; Bude f, Spelunke f; sl Joint m; **out of joint** MED ausgerenkt; fig aus den Fugen; **2.** gemeinsam, gemeinschaftlich; Mit...

joint·ed gegliedert; Glieder...

J

joint-stock com·pa·ny Br ECON Kapital- or Aktiengesellschaft f

joint ven·ture ECON Gemeinschaftsunternehmen n

joke 1. Witz m; Scherz m, Spaß m; **practical joke** Streich m; **play a joke on s.o.** j-m e-n Streich spielen; **2.** scherzen, Witze machen

jok·er Spaßvogel m, Witzbold m; cards: Joker m

jol·ly 1. adj lustig, fröhlich, vergnügt; **2.** adv Br F ganz schön; **jolly good** prima

jolt 1. e-n Ruck or Stoß geben; durchrütteln, durchschütteln; rütteln, holpern (vehicle); fig aufrütteln; **2.** Ruck m, Stoß m; fig Schock m

joss stick Räucherstäbchen n

jos·tle (an)rempeln; dränge(l)n

jot 1. not a jot keine Spur; **2.** jot down sich schnell et. notieren

joule PHYS Joule n

jour·nal Journal n; (Fach)Zeitschrift f; Tagebuch n

jour·nal·ism Journalismus m

jour·nal·ist Journalist(in)

jour·ney 1. Reise f; **2.** reisen

jour·ney·man Geselle m

joy Freude f; **for joy** vor Freude

joy·ful freudig; erfreut

joy·less freudlos, traurig

joy·stick AVIAT Steuerknüppel m; EDP Joystick m

jub·i·lant jubelnd, überglücklich

ju·bi·lee Jubiläum n

judge 1. JUR Richter(in); SPORT Kampf-, Schieds-, Preisrichter(in); fig Kenner(in); **2.** JUR Fall verhandeln; urteilen, ein Urteil fällen; beurteilen, einschätzen

judg·ment JUR Urteil n; Urteilsvermögen n; Meinung f, Ansicht f; göttliches (Straf)Gericht; **the Last Judgment** REL das Jüngste Gericht

Judgment Day, a. **Day of Judgment** REL Tag m des Jüngsten Gerichts, Jüngster Tag

ju·di·cial JUR gerichtlich, Justiz...; richterlich

ju·di·cia·ry JUR Richter pl

ju·di·cious klug, weise

ju·do SPORT Judo n

jug Krug m; Kanne f, Kännchen n

jug·gle jonglieren (mit); ECON Bücher etc frisieren

jug·gler Jongleur m

juice Saft m; MOT F Sprit m

juic·y saftig; F pikant (story etc); F gepfeffert (price etc)

juke·box Musikbox f, Musikautomat m

Jul ABBR of **July** Juli m

Ju·ly (ABBR **Jul**) Juli m

jum·ble 1. a. jumble together, jumble up durcheinanderbringen or durcheinanderwerfen; **2.** Durcheinander n

jumble sale Br Wohltätigkeitsbasar m

jum·bo 1. riesig, Riesen...; **2.** AVIAT F Jumbo m

jumbo jet AVIAT Jumbo-Jet m

jum·bo-sized riesig

jump 1. v/i springen; hüpfen; zusammenzucken, -fahren, hochfahren (at bei); **jump at the chance** mit beiden Händen zugreifen; **jump to conclusions** voreilige Schlüsse ziehen; v/t (hinweg)springen über (acc); überspringen; **jump the queue** Br sich vordränge(l)n; **jump the lights** bei Rot über die Kreuzung fahren; **2.** Sprung m

jump·er¹ SPORT (Hoch- etc)Springer(in)

jump·er² Trägerrock m, Trägerkleid n; Br Pullover m

jump·ing jack Hampelmann m

jump·y nervös

Jun ABBR of **June** Juni m

junc·tion (Straßen)Kreuzung f; RAIL Knotenpunkt m

junc·ture: at this juncture zu diesem Zeitpunkt

June (ABBR **Jun**) Juni m

jun·gle Dschungel m

ju·ni·or 1. junior; jüngere(r, -s); untergeordnet; SPORT Junioren..., Jugend...; **2.** Jüngere m, f

junior school Br Grundschule f (for children aged 7 to 11)

junk¹ MAR Dschunke f

junk² F Trödel m; Schrott m; Abfall m; sl Stoff m

junk food F Junk-Food n

junk·ie, junk·y sl Junkie m, Fixer(in)

junk·yard Schuttabladeplatz m; Schrottplatz m; **auto junkyard** Autofriedhof m

jur·is·dic·tion JUR Gerichtsbarkeit f; Zuständigkeit(sbereich m) f

ju·ris·pru·dence Rechtswissenschaft f

ju·ror JUR Geschworene m, f

ju·ry JUR die Geschworenen pl; SPORT etc Jury f, Preisrichter pl

ju·ry·man JUR Geschworene m

ju·ry·wom·an JUR Geschworene f

just 1. adj gerecht; berechtigt; angemessen; **2.** adv gerade, (so)eben; genau, eben; gerade (noch), ganz knapp; nur, bloß; **just about** ungefähr, etwa; **just like that** einfach so; **just now** gerade (jetzt), (so)eben

jus·tice Gerechtigkeit f; JUR Richter m; **Justice of the Peace** Friedensrichter m; **court of justice** Gericht n, Gerichtshof *m*

us·ti·fi·ca·tion Rechtfertigung *f*

us·ti·fy rechtfertigen

ust·ly mit *or* zu Recht

ut: *jut out* vorspringen, herausragen

u·ve·nile 1. jugendlich; Jugend...; **2.** Ju-

gendliche *m, f*

juvenile court JUR Jugendgericht *n*

juvenile de·lin·quen·cy JUR Jugendkri-

minalität *f*

juvenile de·lin·quent JUR straffälliger Ju-

gendlicher, jugendlicher Straftäter

K

K, k K, k *n*

kan·ga·roo ZO Känguru *n*

ka·ra·te SPORT Karate *n*

keel MAR **1.** Kiel *m*; **2.** *keel over* umschla-

gen, kentern

keen scharf (*a. fig*); schneidend (*cold*);

heftig, stark; lebhaft (*interest*); groß (*ap-

petite etc*); begeistert, leidenschaftlich;

keen on versessen *or* scharf auf (*acc*)

keep 1. *v/t* (auf-, fest-, zurück)halten;

(bei)behalten, bewahren; *Gesetze etc*

einhalten, befolgen; *Ware* führen; *Ge-

heimnis* für sich behalten; *Versprechen,

Wort* halten; ECON *Buch* führen; aufhe-

ben, aufbewahren; abhalten, hindern

(***from*** von); *Tiere* halten; *Bett* hüten; er-

nähren, erhalten, unterhalten; ***keep ear-

ly hours*** früh zu Bett gehen; ***keep one's

head*** die Ruhe bewahren; ***keep one's

temper*** sich beherrschen; ***keep s.o.

company*** j-m Gesellschaft leisten; ***keep

s.th. from s.o.*** j-m et. vorenthalten *or*

verschweigen *or* verheimlichen; ***keep

time*** richtig gehen (*watch*); MUS Takt hal-

ten; *v/i* bleiben; sich halten; ***keep going***

weitergehen; ***keep smiling*** immer nur

lächeln!; ***keep (on) talking*** weiterspre-

chen

keep (*on*) *trying* es weiterversuchen, es

immer wieder versuchen; ***keep s.o.

waiting*** j-n warten lassen; ***keep away***

(sich) fernhalten (***from*** von); ***keep back***

zurückhalten (*a. fig*); ***keep from doing

s.th.*** et. nicht tun; ***keep in*** *Schüler(in)*

nachsitzen lassen; ***keep off*** (sich) fern

halten; ***keep off!*** Betreten verboten!;

keep on *Kleidungsstück* anbehalten, an-

lassen, *Hut* aufbehalten; *Licht* brennen

lassen; ***keep on doing*** fortfahren zu

tun; ***keep out*** nicht hinein- *or* hereinlas-

sen; ***keep out!*** Zutritt verboten!; ***keep to***

sich halten an (*acc*); ***keep up*** *fig* auf-

rechterhalten; *Mut* nicht sinken lassen;

fortfahren mit, weitermachen; ***keep

s.o. up*** j-n nicht schlafen lassen; ***keep

it up*** so weitermachen; ***keep up with***

Schritt halten mit; ***keep up with the

Joneses*** nicht hinter den Nachbarn zu-

rückstehen (wollen); **1.** (Lebens)Unter-

halt *m*; ***for keeps*** F für immer

keep·er Wärter(in), Wächter(in), Aufse-

her(in); *mst in cpds*: Inhaber(in), Besit-

zer(in)

keep·ing Verwahrung *f*; Obhut *f*; *be in

(out of) keeping with ...* (nicht) überein-

stimmen mit ...

keep·sake Andenken *n*

keg Fässchen *n*, kleines Fass

ken·nel Hundehütte *f*; *kennels* Hunde-

zwinger *m*; Hundepension *f*

kerb *Br* → *curb*

ker·chief (Hals-, Kopf)Tuch *n*

ker·nel BOT Kern *m* (*a. fig*)

ker·o·sene Petroleum *n*

ket·tle Kessel *m*

ket·tle·drum MUS (Kessel)Pauke *f*

key 1. Schlüssel *m* (*a. fig*); (Schreibmaschi-

nen-, Klavier- *etc*)Taste *f*; MUS Tonart *f*; **2.**

Schlüssel...; **3.** anpassen (***to*** an *acc*); ***key

in*** EDP Daten eingeben; ***keyed up*** nervös,

aufgeregt, überdreht

key·board Tastatur *f*

key·hole Schlüsselloch *n*

key·note MUS Grundton *m*; *fig* Grundge-

danke *m*, Tenor *m*

key ring Schlüsselring *m*

key·stone ARCH Schlussstein *m*; *fig*

Grundpfeiler *m*

key·word Schlüssel-, Stichwort *n*

kick 1. (mit dem Fuß) stoßen, treten, e-n

Tritt geben *or* versetzen (*dat*); *soccer*:

schießen, treten, kicken; strampeln; aus-

schlagen (*horse*); ***kick off*** von sich

schleudern; *soccer*: anstoßen; ***kick out***

F rausschmeißen; ***kick up*** hochschleu-

dern; ***kick up a fuss*** *or* *row* F Krach

schlagen; **2.** (Fuß)Tritt *m*; Stoß *m*; *soccer*:
Schuss *m*; *free kick* Freistoß *m*; *for kicks*
F Spaß; *they get a kick out of it* es
macht ihnen e-n Riesenspaß
kick·off *soccer*: Anstoß *m*
kick·out *soccer*: Abschlag *m*
kid[1] zo Zicklein *n*, Kitz *n*; Ziegenleder *n*;
F Kind *n*; *kid brother* F kleiner Bruder
kid[2] *v/t j-n* auf den Arm nehmen; *kid s.o.*
j-m et. vormachen; *v/i* Spaß machen; *he
is only kidding* er macht ja nur Spaß; *no
kidding!* im Ernst!
kid gloves Glacéhandschuhe *pl* (*a. fig*)
kid·nap entführen, kidnappen
kid·nap·(p)er Entführer(in), Kidnap-
per(in)
kid·nap·(p)ing Entführung *f*, Kidnapping
n
kid·ney ANAT Niere *f*
kidney bean BOT Kidneybohne *f*, rote
Bohne
kidney ma·chine MED künstliche Niere
kill töten (*a. fig*), umbringen, ermorden,
vernichten; zo schlachten; HUNT erlegen,
schießen; *be killed in an accident* tödlich verunglücken; *kill time* die Zeit totschlagen
kill·er Mörder(in), Killer(in)
kill·ing mörderisch, tödlich
kill·joy Spielverderber *m*
kiln TECH Brennofen *m*
ki·lo F Kilo *n*
kil·o·gram(me) Kilogramm *n*
kil·o·me·ter, *Br* **kil·o·me·tre** Kilometer *m*
kilt Kilt *m*, Schottenrock *m*
kin Verwandtschaft *f*, Verwandte *pl*; *next
of kin* der, die nächste Verwandte, *die*
nächsten Angehörigen *pl*
kind[1] freundlich, liebenswürdig, nett;
herzlich
kind[2] Art *f*, Sorte *f*; Wesen *n*; *all kinds of*
alle möglichen, allerlei; *nothing of the
kind* nichts dergleichen; *kind of* ein
bisschen
kin·der·gar·ten Kindergarten *m*
kind-heart·ed gütig
kin·dle anzünden, (sich) entzünden; *Interesse etc* wecken
kind·ly 1. *adj* freundlich, liebenswürdig,
nett; **2.** *adv* → 1; freundlicherweise, lie-
benswürdigerweise, netterweise
kind·ness Freundlichkeit *f*, Liebenswürdigkeit *f*; Gefälligkeit *f*
kin·dred verwandt; *kindred spirits*
Gleichgesinnte *pl*
king König *m*
king·dom Königreich *n*; REL Reich *n* Gottes; *fig* Reich *n*; *animal kingdom* Tierreich *n*; *vegetable kingdom* Pflanzen-

reich *n*
king·ly königlich
king-size(d) Riesen...
kink Knick *m*; *fig* Tick *m*, Spleen *m*
kink·y spleenig; pervers
ki·osk Kiosk *m*; *Br* Telefonzelle *f*
kip·per GASTR Räucherhering *m*
kiss 1. Kuss *m*; **2.** (sich) küssen
kit Ausrüstung *f*; Arbeitsgerät *n*, Werk-
zeug(e *pl*) *n*; Werkzeugtasche *f*, -kasten
m; Bastelsatz *m*
kit bag Seesack *m*
kitch·en 1. Küche *f*; **2.** Küchen...
kitch·en·ette Kleinküche *f*, Kochnische *f*
kitch·en gar·den Küchen-, Gemüsegar-
ten *m*
kite Drachen *m*; zo Milan *m*; *fly a kite* e-n
Drachen steigen lassen
kit·ten zo Kätzchen *n*
knack Kniff *m*, Trick *m*, F Dreh *m*; Geschick *n*, Talent *n*
knave card games: Bube *m*, Unter *m*
knead kneten; massieren
knee ANAT Knie *n*; TECH Knie(stück) *n*
knee-cap ANAT Kniescheibe *f*
knee-deep knietief, bis an die Knie (reichend)
knee joint ANAT Kniegelenk *n* (*a.* TECH)
kneel knien (*to* vor *dat*)
knee-length knielang
knell Totenglocke *f*
knick·er·bock·ers Knickerbocker *pl*,
Kniehosen *pl*
knick·ers *Br* F (Damen)Schlüpfer *m*
knick-knack Nippsache *f*
knife 1. Messer *n*; **2.** mit e-m Messer stechen *or* verletzen; erstechen
knight 1. Ritter *m*; *chess*: Springer *m*; **2.**
zum Ritter schlagen
knight·hood Ritterwürde *f*, -stand *m*
knit *v/t* stricken; *a.* **knit together** zusammenfügen, verbinden; *knit one's brows*
die Stirn runzeln; *v/i* stricken; MED zu-
sammenwachsen
knit·ting 1. Stricken *n*; Strickzeug *n*; **2.**
Strick...
knitting nee·dle Stricknadel *f*
knit·wear Strickwaren *pl*
knob Knopf *m*, Knauf *m*, *runder* Griff *m*;
GASTR Stück(chen) *n*
knock 1. schlagen, stoßen, pochen, klopfen; *knock at the door* an die Tür klopfen; *knock about*, *knock around* F he-
rumstoßen; F sich herumtreiben; F herumliegen; *knock down* *Gebäude etc* abreißen; umstoßen, umwerfen; niederschlagen; anfahren, umfahren; überfahren; mit *dem Preis* heruntergehen; *auction*: et. zuschlagen (*to s.o.* j-m); *be*

knocked down überfahren werden; **knock off** herunter-, abschlagen; F *et.* hinhauen; F aufhören (mit); F Feierabend *or* Schluss machen; **knock out** herausschlagen, -klopfen, *Pfeife* ausklopfen; *j-n* bewusstlos schlagen; *boxing*: k.o. schlagen; *fig* betäuben (*drug etc*); *fig* F umhauen, schocken; **knock over** umwerfen, umstoßen; überfahren; **be knocked over** überfahren werden; **2.** Schlag *m*, Stoß *m*; Klopfen *n*; **there is a knock (on [*Br* at] the door)** es klopft

knock·er Türklopfer *m*

knock-kneed x-beinig

knock-out *boxing*: K.o. *m*

knoll Hügel *m*

knot 1. Knoten *m*; BOT Astknoten *m*; MAR Knoten *m*, Seemeile *f*; **2.** (ver-)knoten, (ver)knüpfen

knot·ty knotig; knorrig; *fig* verwickelt, kompliziert

know wissen; können; kennen; erfahren, erleben; (wieder) erkennen; verstehen; **know French** Französisch können;

know one's way around sich auskennen in (*a place etc*); **know all about it** genau Bescheid wissen; **get to know** kennenlernen; **know one's business, know the ropes, know a thing or two, know what's what** F sich auskennen, Erfahrung haben; **you know** wissen Sie

know-how Know-how *n*, (Sach-, Spezial)-Kenntnis(se *pl*) *f*

know·ing klug, gescheit; schlau; verständnisvoll

know·ing·ly wissend; wissentlich, absichtlich, bewusst

knowl·edge Kenntnis(se *pl*) *f*; Wissen *n*; **to my knowledge** meines Wissens; **have a good knowledge of** viel verstehen von, sich gut auskennen in (*dat*)

knowl·edge·a·ble: be very knowledgeable about viel verstehen von

knuck·le 1. ANAT (Finger)Knöchel *m*; **2. knuckle down to work** sich an die Arbeit machen

Krem·lin: POL **the Kremlin** der Kreml

L

L, l *L*, *l n*

L ABBR *of* **large (size)** groß

lab F Labor *n*

la·bel 1. Etikett *n*, (Klebe- *etc*)Zettel *m*, (-)Schild(chen) *n*; (Schall)Plattenfirma *f*; **2.** etikettieren, beschriften; *fig* abstempeln als

la·bor 1. (schwere) Arbeit; Mühe *f*; Arbeiter *pl*, Arbeitskräfte *pl*; MED Wehen *pl*; **2.** (schwer) arbeiten; sich bemühen, sich abmühen, sich anstrengen

la·bor·a·to·ry Labor(atorium) *n*

laboratory assis·tant Laborant(in)

la·bored, la·bour·er *Br* → **labored, laborer**

la·bor·er (*esp* Hilfs)Arbeiter *m*

la·bo·ri·ous mühsam; schwerfällig

la·bor u·ni·on Gewerkschaft *f*

la·bour *Br* → **labor**

Labour *Br* POL die Labour Party

la·boured, la·bour·er *Br* → **labored, laborer**

La·bour Par·ty *Br* POL Labour Party *f*

lace 1. Spitze *f*; Borte *f*; Schnürsenkel *m*; **2. lace up** (zu-, zusammen)schnüren;

Schuh zubinden; **laced with brandy** mit e-m Schuss Weinbrand

la·ce·rate zerschneiden, zerkratzen, aufreißen; *j-s Gefühle* verletzen

lack 1. (*of*) Fehlen *n* (von), Mangel *m* (an *dat*); **2.** *v/t* nicht haben; **he lacks money** es fehlt ihm an Geld; *v/i* **be lacking** fehlen; **he is lacking in courage** ihm fehlt der Mut

lack·lus·ter, *Br* **lack·lus·tre** glanzlos, matt

la·con·ic lakonisch, wortkarg

lac·quer 1. Lack *m*; Haarspray *m*, *n*; **2.** lackieren

lad Bursche *m*, Junge *m*

lad·der Leiter *f*; *Br* Laufmasche *f*

lad·der·proof (lauf)maschenfest

la·den (schwer) beladen

la·dle 1. (Schöpf-, Suppen)Kelle *f*, Schöpflöffel *m*; **2. ladle out** *Suppe* austeilen

la·dy Dame *f*; **Lady** Lady *f*; **lady doctor** Ärztin *f*; **Ladies' room**, *Br* **Ladies(')** Damentoilette *f*

la·dy·bird ZO Marienkäfer *m*

la·dy·like damenhaft

lag 1. *mst lag behind* zurückbleiben; **2.** → *time lag*

la·ger Lagerbier *n*

la·goon Lagune *f*

lair ZO Lager *n*, Höhle *f*, Bau *m*

la·i·ty Laien *pl*

lake See *m*

lamb 1. Lamm *n*; **2.** lammen

lame 1. lahm (*a. fig*); **2.** lähmen

la·ment 1. jammern, (weh)klagen; trauern; **2.** Jammer *m*, (Weh)Klage *f*

lam·en·ta·ble beklagenswert; kläglich

lam·en·ta·tion (Weh)Klage *f*

lam·i·nat·ed laminiert, geschichtet, beschichtet

laminated glass Verbundglas *n*

lamp Lampe *f*; Laterne *f*

lamp-post Laternenpfahl *m*

lamp·shade Lampenschirm *m*

lance Lanze *f*

land 1. Land *n*, AGR *a.* Boden *m*, POL *a.* Staat *m*; *by land* auf dem Landweg; **2.** landen, MAR *a.* anlegen; *Güter* ausladen, MAR *a.* löschen

land a·gent AGR Gutsverwalter *m*

land·ed Land..., Grund...; *landed gentry* Landadel *m*; *landed property* Grundbesitz *m*

land·ing AVIAT Landung *f*, Landen *n*, MAR *a.* Anlegen *n*; Treppenabsatz *m*

landing field AVIAT Landeplatz *m*

landing gear AVIAT Fahrgestell *n*

landing stage MAR Landungsbrücke *f*, -steg *m*

landing strip AVIAT Landeplatz *m*

land·la·dy Vermieterin *f*; Wirtin *f*

land·lord Vermieter *m*; Wirt *m*; Grundbesitzer *m*

land·lub·ber MAR *contp* Landratte *f*

land·mark Wahrzeichen *n*; *fig* Meilenstein *m*

land·own·er Grundbesitzer(in)

land·scape Landschaft *f* (*a. paint*)

land·slide Erdrutsch *m* (*a. POL*); *a landslide victory* POL ein überwältigender Wahlsieg

land·slip (kleiner) Erdrutsch

lane (Feld)Weg *m*; Gasse *f*, Sträßchen *n*; MAR Fahrrinne *f*; AVIAT Flugschneise *f*; SPORT (*einzelne*) Bahn; MOT (Fahr-) Spur *f*; *change lanes* MOT die Spur wechseln; *get in lane* MOT sich einordnen

lan·guage Sprache *f*

language la·bor·a·to·ry Sprachlabor *n*

lan·guid matt; träg(e)

lank glatt

lank·y schlaksig

lan·tern Laterne *f*

lap¹ Schoß *m*

lap² SPORT **1.** Runde *f*; *lap of hono(u)r* Ehrenrunde *f*; **2.** *Gegner* überrunden; e-e Runde zurücklegen

lap³ *v/t: lap up* auflecken, aufschlecken; *v/i* plätschern

la·pel Revers *n*, *m*, Aufschlag *m*

lapse 1. Versehen *n*, (kleiner) Fehler *or* Irrtum; Vergehen *n*; Zeitspanne *f*; JUR Verfall *m*; *lapse of memory, memory lapse* Gedächtnislücke *f*; **2.** verfallen, JUR verfallen, erlöschen

lar·ce·ny JUR Diebstahl *m*

larch BOT Lärche *f*

lard 1. Schweinefett *n*, Schweineschmalz *n*; **2.** *Fleisch* spicken

lar·der Speisekammer *f*, -schrank *m*

large groß; beträchtlich, reichlich; umfassend, weitgehend; *at large* in Freiheit, auf freiem Fuß; *fig* (sehr) ausführlich, in der Gesamtheit

large·ly großenteils, größtenteils

large-mind·ed aufgeschlossen, tolerant

large·ness Größe *f*

lar·i·at Lasso *n*, *m*

lark¹ ZO Lerche *f*

lark² F Jux *m*, Spaß *m*

lark·spur BOT Rittersporn *m*

lar·va ZO Larve *f*

lar·yn·gi·tis MED Kehlkopfentzündung *f*

lar·ynx ANAT Kehlkopf *m*

las·civ·i·ous geil, lüstern

la·ser PHYS Laser *m*

laser beam PHYS Laserstrahl *m*

laser print·er EDP Laserdrucker *m*

laser tech·nol·o·gy Lasertechnik *f*

lash 1. Peitschenschnur *f*; (Peitschen-) Hieb *m*; Wimper *f*; **2.** peitschen (*mit*); (fest)binden; schlagen; *lash out* (wild) um sich schlagen

las·so Lasso *n*, *m*

last¹ 1. *adj* letzte(r, -s), vorige(r, -s); *last but one* vorletzte(r, -s); *last night* gestern Abend; letzte Nacht; **2.** *adv* zuletzt, an letzter Stelle; *last but not least* nicht zuletzt, nicht zu vergessen; **3.** *der, die, das* Letzte; *at last* endlich; *to the last* bis zum Schluss

last² (an-, fort)dauern; (sich) halten; (aus)reichen

last³ (Schuhmacher)Leisten *m*

last·ing dauerhaft; beständig

last·ly zuletzt, zum Schluss

latch 1. Schnappriegel *m*; Schnappschloss *n*; **2.** einklinken, zuklinken

latch-key Haus-, Wohnungsschlüssel *m*

late spät; jüngste(r, -s), letzte(r, -s), frühere(r, -s), ehemalig; verstorben; *be late* zu spät kommen, sich verspäten; RAIL *etc* Verspätung haben; *as late as* noch, erst;

of late kürzlich; *later on* später

late·ly kürzlich

lath Latte *f*, Leiste *f*

lathe TECH Drehbank *f*

la·ther 1. (Seifen)Schaum *m*; **2.** *v/t* einseifen; *v/i* schäumen

Lat·in LING **1.** lateinisch; südländisch; **2.** Latein(isch) *n*

Latin A·mer·i·ca Lateinamerika *n*

Latin A·mer·i·can 1. lateinamerikanisch; **2.** Lateinamerikaner(in)

lat·i·tude GEOGR Breite *f*

lat·ter Letztere(r, -s)

lat·tice Gitter(werk) *n*

lau·da·ble lobenswert

laugh 1. lachen (*at* über *acc*); *laugh at s.o. a.* j-n auslachen; **2.** Lachen *n*, Gelächter *n*

laugh·a·ble lächerlich, lachhaft

laugh·ter Lachen *n*, Gelächter *n*

launch[1] 1. MAR vom Stapel lassen; MIL abschießen, *Rakete a.* starten; *fig Projekt etc* in Gang setzen, starten; **2.** MAR Stapellauf *m*; MIL Abschuss *m*, Start *m*

launch[2] MAR Barkasse *f*

launch pad → *launching pad*

launch·ing → *launch[1]*

launching pad Abschussrampe *f*

launching site Abschussbasis *f*

laun·der MAR *Wäsche* waschen (und bügeln); F *esp Geld* waschen

laun·der·ette, **laun·drette** *esp Br*, **laundro·mat®** Waschsalon *m*

laun·dry Wäscherei *f*; Wäsche *f*

lau·rel BOT Lorbeer *m* (*a. fig*)

la·va GEOL Lava *f*

lav·a·to·ry Toilette *f*, Klosett *n*; *public lavatory* Bedürfnisanstalt *f*

lav·en·der BOT Lavendel *m*

lav·ish 1. sehr freigebig, verschwenderisch; **2.** *lavish s.th. on s.o.* j-n mit et. überhäufen *or* überschütten

law Gesetz(e *pl*) *n*; Recht *n*, Rechtssystem *n*; Rechtswissenschaft *f*, Jura; F Bullen *pl* (*police*); F Bulle *m* (*policeman*); Gesetz *n*, Vorschrift *f*; *law and order* Recht *or* Ruhe und Ordnung

law-a·bid·ing gesetzestreu

law-court Gericht *n*, Gerichtshof *m*

law·ful gesetzlich; rechtmäßig, legitim; rechtsgültig

law·less gesetzlos; gesetzwidrig; zügellos

lawn Rasen *m*

lawn-mow·er Rasenmäher *m*

law·suit JUR Prozess *m*

law·yer JUR (Rechts)Anwalt *m*, (Rechts)Anwältin *f*

lax locker, schlaff; lax, lasch

lax·a·tive MED **1.** abführend; **2.** Abführ-

mittel *n*

lay[1] REL weltlich; Laien…

lay[2] *v/t* legen; *Teppich* verlegen; belegen, auslegen (*with* mit); *Tisch* decken; zo *Eier* legen; vorlegen (*before* dat), bringen (*before* vor *acc*); *Schuld etc* zuschreiben, zur Last legen (*dat*); *v/i* zo (Eier) legen; *lay aside* beiseitelegen, zurücklegen; *lay off Arbeiter* (*esp* vorübergehend) entlassen; *Arbeit* einstellen; *lay open* darlegen; *lay out* ausbreiten, auslegen; *Garten etc* anlegen; entwerfen, planen; PRINT das Layout (*gen*) machen; *lay up* anhäufen, (an)sammeln; *be laid up* das Bett hüten müssen

lay-by *Br* MOT Parkbucht *f*, Parkstreifen *m*; Parkplatz *m*, Rastplatz *m*

lay·er Lage *f*, Schicht *f*; BOT Ableger *m*

lay·man Laie *m*

lay-off ECON (*esp* vorübergehende) Entlassung

lay-out Grundriss *m*, Lageplan *m*; PRINT Layout *n*, Gestaltung *f*

LCD ABBR *of **liquid crystal display*** Flüssigkristallanzeige *f*

lead[1] 1. *v/t* führen; (an)führen, leiten; dazu bringen, veranlassen (*to do* zu tun); *v/i* führen; vorangehen; SPORT an der Spitze *or* in Führung liegen; *lead off* anfangen, beginnen; *lead on* j-m et. vormachen *or* weismachen; *lead to fig* führen zu; *lead up to fig* (allmählich) führen zu; **2.** Führung *f*; Leitung *f*; Spitzenposition *f*; Vorbild *n*, Beispiel *n*; THEA Hauptrolle *f*; Hauptdarsteller(in); (Hunde-)Leine *f*; Hinweis *m*, Tipp *m*, Anhaltspunkt *m*; SPORT *and fig* Führung *f*, Vorsprung *m*; *be in the lead* in Führung sein; *take the lead* in Führung gehen, die Führung übernehmen

lead[2] CHEM Blei *n*; MAR Lot *n*

lead·ed verbleit, bleihaltig

lead·en bleiern (*a. fig*), Blei…

lead·er (An)Führer(in), Leiter(in); Erste *m*, *f*; *Br* Leitartikel *m*

lead·er·ship Führung *f*, Leitung *f*

lead-free bleifrei

lead·ing führend; Führend; Haupt…

leaf 1. BOT, PRINT Blatt *n*; (*Tür- etc*)Flügel *m*; (*Tisch*)Klappe *f*, Ausziehplatte *f*; **2.** *leaf through* durchblättern

leaf·let Hand-, Reklamezettel *m*; Prospekt *m*

league POL Bund *m*; SPORT Liga *f*

leak 1. lecken, leck sein; tropfen; *leak out* auslaufen; *fig* durchsickern; **2.** Leck *n*, undichte Stelle (*a. fig*)

leak·age Auslaufen *n*

leak·y leck, undicht

lean¹ (sich) lehnen; (sich) neigen; **lean on** sich verlassen auf (acc)

lean² 1. mager (a. fig); 2. GASTR das Magere

lean man·age·ment ECON schlanke Unternehmensstruktur

leap 1. springen; **leap at** fig sich stürzen auf (acc); 2. Sprung m

leap·frog Bockspringen n

leap year Schaltjahr n

learn (er)lernen; erfahren, hören

learn·ed gelehrt

learn·er Anfänger(in); Lernende m, f; **learner driver** Br MOT Fahrschüler(in)

learn·ing Gelehrsamkeit f

lease 1. Pacht f, Miete f; Pacht-, Mietvertrag m; 2. pachten, mieten; leasen; **lease out** verpachten, vermieten

leash (Hunde)Leine f

least 1. adj geringste(r, -s), mindeste(r, -s), wenigste(r, -s); 2. adv am wenigsten; **least of all** am allerwenigsten; 3. das Mindeste, das wenigste; **at least** wenigstens; **to say the least** gelinde gesagt

leath·er 1. Leder n; 2. ledern; Leder...

leave 1. v/t (hinter-, über-, ver-, zurück-) lassen, übrig lassen; liegen or stehen lassen, vergessen; vermachen, vererben; **be left** übrig bleiben, übrig sein; v/i (fort-, weg)gehen, abreisen, abfahren, abfliegen; **leave alone** allein lassen; j-n, et. in Ruhe lassen; **leave behind** zurücklassen; **leave on** anlassen; **leave out** draußen lassen; auslassen, weglassen; 2. Erlaubnis f; Urlaub m; Abschied m; **on leave** auf Urlaub

leav·en Sauerteig m

leaves BOT Laub n

leav·ings Überreste pl

lech·er·ous geil, lüstern

lec·ture 1. UNIV Vorlesung f (**über** acc on); Vortrag m; 2. Strafpredigt f; v/i UNIV e-e Vorlesung or Vorlesungen halten (**über** acc on; **vor** dat to); e-n Vortrag or Vorträge halten; v/t j-m e-e Strafpredigt halten

lec·tur·er UNIV Dozent(in); Redner(in)

ledge Leiste f, Sims m, n

leech ZO Blutegel m

leek BOT Lauch m, Porree m

leer 1. anzüglicher or lüsterner Seitenblick; 2. anzüglich or lüstern blicken or schielen (**at** nach)

left 1. adj linke(r, -s), Links...; 2. adv links; **turn left** (sich) nach links wenden; MOT links abbiegen; 3. die Linke (a. POL, boxing), linke Seite; **on the left** links, auf der linken Seite; **to the left** (nach) links;

keep to the left sich links halten; links fahren

left-hand linke(r, -s)

left-hand drive MOT Linkssteuerung f

left-hand·ed linkshändig; für Linkshänder; **be left-handed** Linkshänder(in) sein

left lug·gage of·fice Br RAIL Gepäckaufbewahrung f

left-o·vers (Speise)Reste pl

left-wing POL dem linken Flügel angehörend, links..., Links...

leg ANAT Bein n; GASTR Keule f; MATH Schenkel m; **pull s.o.'s leg** F j-n auf den Arm nehmen; **stretch one's** sich die Beine vertreten

leg·a·cy fig Vermächtnis n, Erbe n

le·gal legal, gesetzmäßig; gesetzlich, rechtlich; juristisch, Rechts...

le·gal·ize legalisieren

le·gal·i·za·tion Legalisierung f

le·gal pro·tec·tion Rechtsschutz m

le·ga·tion POL Gesandtschaft f

leg·end Legende f, Sage f

leg·en·da·ry legendär

leg·i·ble leserlich

leg·is·la·tion Gesetzgebung f

leg·is·la·tive POL 1. gesetzgebend, legislativ; 2. Legislative f, gesetzgebende Gewalt

leg·is·la·tor POL Gesetzgeber m

le·git·i·mate legitim; gesetzmäßig, rechtmäßig; ehelich

lei·sure freie Zeit; Muße f; **at leisure** ohne Hast

lei·sure cen·tre Br Freizeitzentrum n

lei·sure·ly gemächlich

lei·sure time Freizeit f

lei·sure-time ac·tiv·i·ties Freizeitbeschäftigung f, -gestaltung f

lei·sure·wear Freizeitkleidung f

lem·on BOT 1. Zitrone f; 2. Zitronen...

lem·on·ade Zitronenlimonade f

lend j-m et. (ver-, aus)leihen

length Länge f; Strecke f; (Zeit)Dauer f; **at length** ausführlich

length·en verlängern, länger machen; länger werden

length·ways, length·wise der Länge nach

length·y sehr lang

le·ni·ent mild(e), nachsichtig

lens ANAT, PHOT, PHYS Linse f; PHOT Objektiv n

Lent REL Fastenzeit f

len·til BOT Linse f

Le·o ASTR Löwe m; **he (she) is (a) Leo** er (sie) ist (ein) Löwe

leop·ard ZO Leopard m

le·o·tard (Tänzer)Trikot n

lep·ro·sy MED Lepra f

les·bi·an 1. lesbisch; 2. Lesbierin f, F Lesbe f

less 1. adj and adv kleiner, geringer, weniger; 2. prp weniger, minus, abzüglich

less·en (sich) vermindern or verringern; abnehmen; herabsetzen

less·er kleiner, geringer

les·son Lektion f; (Unterrichts)Stunde f; fig Lehre f; pl Unterricht m

let lassen; esp Br vermieten, verpachten; let alone j-n, et. in Ruhe lassen; geschweige denn; let down hinunterlassen, herunterlassen; Kleider verlängern; j-n im Stich lassen F j-n lassen lassen; enttäuschen; let go loslassen; let o.s. go sich gehenlassen; let's go gehen wir!; let in (her)einlassen; let o.s. in for s.th. sich et. einbrocken, sich auf et. ein-lassen

le·thal tödlich; Todes…

leth·ar·gy Lethargie f

let·ter Buchstabe m; PRINT Type f; Brief m

let·ter·box esp Br Briefkasten m

let·ter car·ri·er Briefträger m

let·tuce BOT (esp Kopf)Salat m

leu·k(a)e·mia MED Leukämie f

lev·el 1. adj eben; gleich (a. fig); ausgeglichen; be level with auf gleicher Höhe sein mit; my level best F mein Möglichstes; 2. Ebene f (a. fig), ebene Fläche; Höhe f (a. GEOGR), (Wasser- etc)Spiegel m, (-)Stand m, (-)Pegel m; Wasserwaage f; fig Niveau n, Stufe f; sea level Meeresspiegel m; on the level F ehrlich, aufrichtig; 3. (ein)ebnen, planieren; dem Erdboden gleichmachen; level at Waffe richten auf (acc); Beschuldigungen erheben gegen (acc); 4. adv: level with in Höhe (gen)

lev·el cross·ing Br schienengleicher Bahnübergang

lev·el-head·ed vernünftig, nüchtern

lev·er Hebel m

lev·y 1. Steuer f, Abgabe f; 2. Steuern erheben

lewd geil, lüstern; unanständig, obszön

li·a·bil·i·ty ECON, JUR Verpflichtung f, Verbindlichkeit f; ECON, JUR Haftung f, Haftpflicht f; Neigung f (to zu), Anfälligkeit f (to für)

li·a·ble ECON, JUR haftbar, haftpflichtig; be liable for haften für; be liable to neigen zu, anfällig sein für

li·ar Lügner(in)

li·bel JUR 1. (schriftliche) Verleumdung or Beleidigung; 2. (schriftlich) verleumden or beleidigen

lib·e·ral 1. liberal (a. POL), aufgeschlossen; großzügig; reichlich; 2. Liberale m, f (a. POL)

lib·e·rate befreien

lib·e·ra·tion Befreiung f

lib·e·ra·tor Befreier m

lib·er·ty Freiheit f; take liberties with sich Freiheiten gegen j-n herausnehmen; willkürlich mit et. umgehen; be at liberty frei sein

Li·bra ASTR Waage f; he (she) is (a) Libra er (sie) ist (eine) Waage

li·brar·i·an Bibliothekar(in)

li·bra·ry Bibliothek f; Bücherei f

li·cence Br → license 1.

li·cense 1. Br → license 1; e-e Lizenz or Konzession erteilen (dat); behördlich genehmigen

li·cense 1. Lizenz f, Konzession f; (Führer-, Jagd-, Waffen- etc)Schein m; 2. Br → licence 2

li·cense plate MOT Nummernschild n

li·chen BOT Flechte f

lick 1. Lecken n; Salzlecke f; 2. v/t ab-, auflecken; F verdreschen, verprügeln; F schlagen, besiegen; v/i lecken; züngeln (flames)

lic·o·rice Lakritze f

lid Deckel m; ANAT (Augen)Lid n

lie[1] 1. lügen; lie to s.o. j-n belügen, j-n anlügen; 2. Lüge f; tell lies, tell a lie lügen; give the lie to j-n, et. Lügen strafen

lie[2] 1. liegen; let sleeping dogs lie schlafende Hunde soll man nicht wecken; lie behind fig dahinter stecken; lie down sich hinlegen; 2. Lage f (a. fig)

lie-down Br F Nickerchen n

lie-in: have a lie-in esp Br F sich gründlich ausschlafen

lieu: in lieu of anstelle von (or gen)

lieu·ten·ant MIL Leutnant m

life Leben n; JUR lebenslängliche Freiheitsstrafe; all her life ihr ganzes Leben lang; for life fürs (ganze) Leben; esp JUR lebenslänglich

life as·sur·ance Br → life insurance

life belt Rettungsgürtel m

life·boat Rettungsboot n

life·guard Bademeister m; Rettungsschwimmer m

life im·pris·on·ment JUR lebenslängliche Freiheitsstrafe

life in·sur·ance Lebensversicherung f

life jack·et Schwimmweste f

life·less leblos; matt, schwung-, lustlos

life·like lebensecht

life·long lebenslang

life pre·serv·er Schwimmweste f; Rettungsgürtel m

life sen·tence JUR lebenslängliche Frei-

heitsstrafe
life·time Lebenszeit f

lift 1. v/t (hoch-, auf)heben; erheben; *Verbot etc* aufheben; *Gesicht etc* liften, straffen; F klauen; v/i sich heben, steigen (*a. fog*); **lift off** starten (*rocket*), AVIAT abheben; **2.** (Hoch-, Auf)Heben *n*; PHYS, AVIAT Auftrieb *m*; *Br* Lift *m*, Aufzug *m*, Fahrstuhl *m*; **give s.o. a lift** j-n (im Auto) mitnehmen; F j-n aufmuntern, j-m Auftrieb geben

lift-off Start *m*, Abheben *n*

lig·a·ment ANAT Band *n*

light¹ 1. Licht *n* (*a. fig*); Beleuchtung f; Schein *m*; Feuer *n*; *fig* Aspekt *m*; *Br mst pl* (Verkehrs-)Ampel f; **do you have (Br have you got) a light?** haben Sie Feuer?; **2.** v/t beleuchten, erleuchten; *a.* **light up** anzünden; v/i sich entzünden; **light up** fig aufleuchten; **3.** hell, licht

light² leicht (*a. fig*); **make light of s.th.** et. leichtnehmen; et. bagatellisieren

light·en¹ v/t erhellen; aufhellen; v/i hell(er) werden, sich aufhellen

light·en² leichter machen *or* werden; erleichtern

light·er Anzünder *m*; Feuerzeug *n*

light-head·ed (leicht) benommen; leichtfertig, töricht

light-heart·ed fröhlich, unbeschwert

light·house Leuchtturm *m*

light·ing Beleuchtung f

light·ness Leichtheit f; Leichtigkeit f

light·ning Blitz *m*; **like lightning** wie der Blitz; **(as) quick as lightning** blitzschnell

light·ning con·duc·tor *Br*, **lightning rod** ELECTR Blitzableiter *m*

light-weight SPORT Leichtgewicht *n*, Leichtgewichtler *m*

like¹ 1. v/t gernhaben, mögen; **I like it** es gefällt mir; **I like her** ich kann sie gut leiden; **how do you like it?** wie gefällt es dir?, wie findest du es?; **I like that!** iro das hab ich gern!; **I should or would like to know** ich möchte gern wissen; v/i wollen; **(just) as you like** (ganz) wie du willst; **if you like** wenn du willst; **2. likes and dislikes** Neigungen und Abneigungen *pl*

like² 1. gleich; wie; ähnlich; **like that** so; **feel like** Lust haben auf (*acc*) *or* zu; **what is he like?** wie ist er?; **that is just like him!** das sieht ihm ähnlich!; **2.** der, die, das Gleiche; **his like** seinesgleichen; **the like** dergleichen; **the likes of you** Leute wie du

like·li·hood Wahrscheinlichkeit f

like·ly 1. *adj* wahrscheinlich; geeignet; **2.** *adv* wahrscheinlich; **not likely!** F bestimmt nicht!

like·ness Ähnlichkeit f; Abbild *n*

like·wise ebenso

lik·ing Vorliebe f

li·lac 1. lila; **2.** BOT Flieder *m*

lil·y BOT Lilie f

lil·y-of-the-val·ley BOT Maiglöckchen *n*

limb ANAT (*Körper*)Glied *n*; BOT Ast *m*

lime¹ Kalk *m*

lime² BOT Linde f; Limone f

lime·light fig Rampenlicht *n*

lim·it 1. Limit *n*, Grenze f; **within limits** in Grenzen; **off limits** Zutritt verboten (**to** für); **that is the limit!** F das ist der Gipfel!, das ist (doch) die Höhe!; **go to the limit** bis zum Äußersten gehen; **2.** beschränken (**to** auf *acc*)

lim·i·ta·tion Beschränkung f; fig Grenze f; JUR Verjährung f

lim·it·ed beschränkt, begrenzt; **limited (liability) company** *Br* ECON Gesellschaft f mit beschränkter Haftung

lim·it·less grenzenlos

limp¹ 1. hinken, humpeln; **2.** Hinken *n*, Humpeln *n*

limp² schlaff, schlapp, F lappig

line¹ 1. Linie f, Strich *m*; Zeile f; Falte f, Runzel f; Reihe f; (Menschen-, *a.* Auto-)Schlange f; (Abstammungs)Linie f; (Verkehrs-, Eisenbahn- etc)Linie f, Strecke f; (Flug- etc)Gesellschaft f; *esp* TEL Leitung f; MIL Linie f; Fach *n*, Gebiet *n*, Branche f; SPORT (Ziel- etc)Linie f; Leine f; Schnur f; Linie f, Richtung f; fig Grenze f; *pl* THEA Rolle f, Text *m*; **the line** der Äquator; **draw the line** Halt machen, die Grenze ziehen (**at** bei); **the line is busy or engaged** TEL die Leitung ist besetzt; **hold the line** TEL bleiben Sie am Apparat; **stand in line** anstehen, Schlange stehen (**for** um, nach); **2.** lin(i)ieren; *Gesicht* zeichnen, (zer)furchen; *Straße etc* säumen; **line up** (sich) in e-r Reihe *or* Linie aufstellen, SPORT sich aufstellen; sich anstellen (**for** um, nach)

line² *Kleid etc* füttern; TECH auskleiden, ausschlagen; MOT *Bremsen etc* belegen

lin·e·ar linear; Längen...

lin·en 1. Leinen *n*; (*Bett-*, *Tisch- etc* -)Wäsche f; **2.** leinen, Leinen...

lin·en cup·board *Br* linen cupboard Wäscheschrank *m*

lin·er MAR Linienschiff *n*; AVIAT Verkehrsflugzeug *n*

lines·man SPORT Linienrichter *m*

lines·wom·an SPORT Linienrichterin f

line-up SPORT Aufstellung f; Gegenüberstellung f (zur Identifizierung)

lin·ger verweilen, sich aufhalten; *a. linger on* dahinsiechen; *linger on* noch dableiben; *fig* fortleben

lin·ge·rie Damenunterwäsche *f*

lin·ing Futter(stoff *m*) *n*; TECH Auskleidung *f*; MOT (*Brems- etc*)Belag *m*

link 1. (Ketten)Glied *n*; Manschettenknopf *m*; *fig* (Binde)Glied *n*, Verbindung *f*; **2.** *a.* **link up** (sich) verbinden

links → *golf links*

link·up Verbindung *f*

lin·seed BOT Leinsamen *m*

lin·seed oil Leinöl *n*

li·on ZO Löwe *m*

li·on·ess ZO Löwin *f*

lip ANAT Lippe *f*; (*Tassen- etc*)Rand *m*; *F* Unverschämtheit *f*

lip·stick Lippenstift *m*

liq·ue·fy (sich) verflüssigen

liq·uid 1. Flüssigkeit *f*; **2.** flüssig

liq·ui·date liquidieren (*a.* ECON); *Schulden* tilgen

liq·uid·ize zerkleinern, pürieren

liq·uid·iz·er Mixgerät *n*, Mixer *m*

liq·uor *Br* alkoholische Getränke *pl*, Alkohol *m*; Schnaps *m*, Spirituosen *pl*

liq·uo·rice *Br* → *licorice*

lisp 1. lispeln; **2.** Lispeln *n*

list 1. Liste *f*, Verzeichnis *n*; MAR Schlagseite *f*; **2.** (in e-e Liste) eintragen, erfassen; MAR *be listing* Schlagseite haben

lis·ten hören; *listen in* Radio hören; *listen to et.* im Radio (an)hören; *listen in on* Telefongespräch *etc* abhören *or* mithören; *listen to* anhören (*acc*), zuhören (*dat*); hören auf (*acc*)

lis·ten·er Zuhörer(in); (Rundfunk-)Hörer(in)

list·less teilnahmslos, lustlos

li·ter Liter *m*, *n*

lit·e·ral (wort)wörtlich; genau; prosaisch

lit·e·ra·ry literarisch, Literatur...

lit·e·ra·ture Literatur *f*

lithe geschmeidig, gelenkig

li·tre *Br* → *liter*

lit·ter 1. (*esp Papier*)Abfall *m*; AGR Streu *f*; ZO Wurf *m*; Trage *f*; Sänfte *f*; **2.** *et.* herumliegen lassen in (*dat*) *or* auf (*dat*); *be littered with* übersät sein mit

lit·ter bas·ket, **litter bin** Abfallkorb *m*

lit·tle 1. *adj* klein; wenig; *the little ones* die Kleinen *pl*; **2.** *adv* wenig, kaum; **3.** Kleinigkeit *f*; *a little* ein wenig, ein bisschen; *little by little* (ganz) allmählich, nach und nach; *not a little* nicht wenig

live¹ leben; wohnen (*with* bei); *live to see* erleben; *live up to s-n Grundsätzen etc* gemäß leben; *Erwartungen etc* entsprechen; *live*

with mit *j-m* zusammenleben; mit *et.* leben

live² 1. *adj* lebend, lebendig; richtig, echt; ELECTR Strom führend; *radio*, TV Direkt..., Live-...; **2.** *adv* direkt, original, live

live·li·hood (Lebens)Unterhalt *m*

live·li·ness Lebhaftigkeit *f*

live·ly lebhaft, lebendig; aufregend

liv·er ANAT Leber *f* (*a.* GASTR)

liv·e·ry Livree *f*

live·stock Vieh *n*, Viehbestand *m*

liv·id bläulich; *F* fuchsteufelswild

liv·ing 1. lebend; *the living image of* das genaue Ebenbild (*gen*); **2.** Leben *n*, Lebensweise *f*; Lebensunterhalt *m*; *the living* die Lebenden *pl*; *standard of living* Lebensstandard *m*; *earn or make a living* (sich) s-n Lebensunterhalt verdienen

living room Wohnzimmer *n*

liz·ard ZO Eidechse *f*

load 1. Last *f* (*a. fig*); Ladung *f*; Belastung *f*; **2.** *j-n* überhäufen (*with* mit); *Schusswaffe* laden; *load a camera* e-n Film einlegen; *a. load up* (auf-, be-, ein)laden

loaf¹ Laib *m* (Brot); Brot *n*

loaf² *a.* **loaf about**, **loaf around** F herumlungern

loaf·er Müßiggänger(in)

loam Lehm *m*

loam·y lehmig

loan 1. (Ver)Leihen *n*; ECON Kredit *m*, Darlehen *n*; Leihgabe *f*; *on loan* leihweise; **2.** *loan s.o. s.th.*, *loan s.th. to s.o.* *j-m et.* (aus)leihen; *et.* an *j-n* verleihen

loan shark ECON Kredithai *m*

loath: *be loath to do s.th. et.* nur (sehr) ungern tun

loathe verabscheuen, hassen

loath·ing Abscheu *m*

lob *esp tennis*: Lob *m*

lob·by 1. Vorhalle *f*; THEA, *film*: Foyer *n*; Wandelhalle *f*; POL Lobby *f*, Interessengruppe *f*; **2.** POL *Abgeordnete etc* beeinflussen

lobe ANAT, BOT Lappen *m*

lob·ster ZO Hummer *m*

lo·cal 1. örtlich, Orts..., lokal, Lokal...; **2.** Ortsansässige *m*, *f*, Einheimische *m*, *f*; *Br F* Stammkneipe *f*

local call TEL Ortsgespräch *n*

local e·lec·tions POL Kommunalwahlen *pl*

local gov·ern·ment Gemeindeverwaltung *f*

local time Ortszeit *f*

local traf·fic Orts-, Nahverkehr *m*

lo·cate ausfindig machen; orten; *be located* gelegen sein, liegen, sich befinden

lo·ca·tion Lage f; Standort m; Platz m (*for* für); *film*, TV Gelände n für Außenaufnahmen; *on location* auf Außenaufnahme

lock[1] 1. (*Tür-*, *Gewehr- etc*)Schloss n; Schleuse(nkammer) f; Verschluss m; Sperrvorrichtung f; 2. v/t zu-, verschließen, zu-, versperren (a. *lock up*); umschlingen, umfassen; TECH sperren; v/i schließen; abschließbar or verschließbar sein; MOT etc blockieren; *lock away* wegschließen; *lock in* einschließen, einsperren; *lock out* aussperren; *lock up* abschließen; wegschließen; einsperren

lock[2] (Haar)Locke f

lock·er Spind m, Schrank m; Schließfach n

locker room esp SPORT Umkleidekabine f, Umkleideraum m

lock·et Medaillon n

lock·out ECON Aussperrung f

lock·smith Schlosser m

lock-up Arrestzelle f

lo·cust ZO Heuschrecke f

lodge 1. Portier-, Pförtnerloge f; (*Jagd-*, *Ski- etc*)Hütte f; Sommer-, Gartenhaus n; (*Freimaurer*)Loge f; 2. v/i logieren, (*esp* vorübergehend or in Untermiete) wohnen, stecken (bleiben) (*bullet etc*); v/t aufnehmen, beherbergen, (für die Nacht) unterbringen; *Beschwerde etc* einreichen; *Berufung, Protest* einlegen

lodg·er Untermieter(in)

lodg·ing Unterkunft f; pl esp möbliertes Zimmer

loft (Dach)Boden m; Heuboden m; Empore f; (*converted*) *loft* Loft m, Fabriketage f

loft·y hoch; erhaben; stolz, hochmütig

log (Holz)Klotz m; (*gefällter*) Baumstamm; (Holz)Scheit f; → *log-book* MAR Logbuch n; AVIAT Bordbuch n; MOT Fahrtenbuch n

log cab·in Blockhaus n, Blockhütte f

log·ger·heads: be at loggerheads sich streiten, sich in den Haaren liegen (*with* mit)

lo·gic Logik f

lo·gic·al logisch

loin GASTR Lende(nstück n) f; pl ANAT Lende f

loi·ter trödeln; herumlungern

loll hängen (*head*), heraushängen (*tongue*); *loll around* or *about* F sich rekeln or lümmeln

lol·li·pop GASTR Lutscher m; esp Br Eis n am Stiel; *lollipop man* Br Schülerlotse m; *lollipop woman, lollipop lady* Br Schülerlotsin f

lol·ly GASTR F Lutscher m; *ice lolly* Eis n am Stiel

lone·li·ness Einsamkeit f

lone·ly einsam; *become lonely* vereinsamen

lone·some einsam

long[1] 1. adj lang; weit; langfristig; 2. adv lang(e); *as* or *so long* as solange wie; vorausgesetzt, dass; *long ago* vor langer Zeit; *so long!* F bis dann!, tschüs(s)!; 3. (e-e) lange Zeit; *for long* lange; *take long* lange brauchen or dauern

long[2] sich sehnen (*for* nach)

long-dis·tance Fern…, Langstrecken…

long-distance call TEL Ferngespräch n

long-distance run·ner SPORT Langstreckenläufer(in)

long-hand Schreibschrift f

long·ing 1. sehnsüchtig; 2. Sehnsucht f, Verlangen n

lon·gi·tude GEOGR Länge f

long johns lange Unterhose

long jump SPORT Weitsprung m

long-life milk esp Br H-Milch f

long-play·er, long-play·ing rec·ord Langspielplatte f

long-range MIL, AVIAT Fern…, Langstrecken…; langfristig

long·shore·man Dock-, Hafenarbeiter m

long·sight·ed esp Br weitsichtig, fig a. weitblickend

long-stand·ing seit langer Zeit bestehend; alt

long-term langfristig, auf lange Sicht

long wave ELECTR Langwelle f

long-wear·ing strapazierfähig

long-wind·ed langatmig

look 1. sehen, blicken, schauen (*at, on* auf acc, nach); nachschauen, nachsehen; *krank etc* aussehen; nach *e-r Richtung* liegen, gehen (*window etc*); *look here!* schau mal (her); hör mal (zu)!; *look like* aussehen wie; *it looks as if* es sieht (so) aus, als ob; *look after* aufpassen auf (acc); sich kümmern um, sorgen für, *den Haushalt etc* versehen; *look ahead* nach vorne sehen; fig vorausschauen; *look around* sich umsehen; *look at* ansehen; *look back* sich umsehen; fig zurückblicken; *look down* herab-, heruntersehen (a. fig on s.o. auf j-n); *look for* suchen; *look forward to* sich freuen auf (acc); *look in* hereinschauen (*on* bei); *look into* untersuchen, prüfen; *look on* zusehen, zuschauen (*as* als); betrachten, ansehen (*as* als); *look onto* liegen zu, (hinaus)gehen auf (*acc*) (*window etc*); *look out* hinaus-, heraussehen; aufpassen, sich vorsehen; ausschauen or

Ausschau halten (**for** nach); **look over** et. durchsehen; *j-n* mustern; **look round** sich umsehen; **look through** et. durchsehen; **look up** aufblicken, aufsehen; et. nachschlagen; *j-n* aufsuchen; **2.** Blick *m*; Miene *f*, (Gesichts)Ausdruck *m*; (**good**) **looks** gutes Aussehen; **have a look at s.th.** sich et. ansehen; *I don't like the look of it* es gefällt mir nicht

look·ing glass Spiegel *m*

look·out Ausguck *m*; Ausschau *f*; *fig* Aussicht(en *pl*) *f*; **be on the lookout for** Ausschau halten nach; **that's his own lookout** F das ist allein seine Sache

loom[1] Webstuhl *m*

loom[2] *a*. **loom up** undeutlich sichtbar werden *or* auftauchen

loop 1. Schlinge *f*, Schleife *f*; Schlaufe *f*; Öse *f*; AVIAT Looping *m*, *n*; EDP Schleife *f*; **2.** (sich) schlingen

loop·hole MIL Schießscharte *f*; *fig* Hintertürchen *n*; *a loophole in the law* e-e Gesetzeslücke

loose 1. los(e); locker; weit; frei; *let loose* loslassen; freilassen; **2. be on the loose** frei herumlaufen

loos·en (sich) lösen *or* lockern; **loosen up** SPORT Lockerungsübungen machen

loot 1. Beute *f*; **2.** plündern

lop Baum beschneiden, stutzen; **lop off** abhauen, abhacken

lop·sid·ed schief; *fig* einseitig

lord Herr *m*, Gebieter *m*; *Br* Lord *m*; **the Lord** REL Gott *m* (der Herr); **the Lord's Prayer** REL das Vaterunser; **the Lord's Supper** REL das (heilige) Abendmahl; **House of Lords** *Br* POL Oberhaus *n*

Lord Mayor *Br* Oberbürgermeister *m*

lor·ry *Br* MOT Last(kraft)wagen *m*, Lastauto *n*, Laster *m*

lose verlieren; verpassen; versäumen; nachgehen (*watch*); **lose o.s.** sich verirren; sich verlieren

los·er Verlierer(in)

loss Verlust *m*; Schaden *m*; *at a loss* ECON mit Verlust; *be at a loss* in Verlegenheit sein (*for* um)

lost verloren; *be lost* sich verirrt haben, sich nicht mehr zurechtfinden (*a. fig*); *be lost in thought* in Gedanken versunken sein; *get lost* sich verirren; *get lost! sl* hau ab!

lost-and-found (of·fice), *Br* **lost prop·er·ty of·fice** Fundbüro *n*

lot Los *n*; Parzelle *f*; Grundstück *n*; ECON Partie *f*, Posten *m*; Gruppe *f*, Gesellschaft *f*; Menge *f*, Haufen *m*; Los *n*, Schicksal *n*; **the lot** alles, das Ganze; *a lot of* F, *lots of* F viel, e-e Menge; *a*

---

bad lot F ein übler Kerl; *cast or draw lots* losen

loth → loath

lo·tion Lotion *f*

lot·te·ry Lotterie *f*

loud laut; *fig* schreiend, grell

loud-mouth *contp* Schwätzer *m*

loud-speak·er Lautsprecher *m*

lounge 1. Wohnzimmer *n*; Aufenthaltsraum *m*, Lounge *f* (*a. AVIAT*); Wartehalle *f*; **2.** F *contp* sich flegeln; **lounge about, lounge around** herumlungern

louse ZO Laus *f*

lou·sy verlaust; F miserabel, saumäßig

lout Flegel *m*, Lümmel *m*, Rüpel *m*

lov·a·ble liebenswert; reizend

love Liebe *f* (*of, for, to, towards* zu); Liebling *m*, Schatz *m*; *tennis*: null; *be in love with s.o.* in j-n verliebt sein; *fall in love with s.o.* sich in j-n verlieben; *make love* sich lieben, miteinander schlafen; *give my love to her* grüße sie herzlich von mir; *send one's love to* j-n grüßen lassen; *love from ...* herzliche Grüße von ...; **2.** lieben; gern mögen

love af·fair Liebesaffäre *f*

love·ly (wunder)schön; nett, reizend; F prima

lov·er Liebhaber *m*, Geliebte *m*, *f*; (*Musik- etc*) Liebhaber(in), (-)Freund(in); *pl* Liebende *pl*, Liebespaar *n*

lov·ing liebevoll, liebend

low 1. *adj* niedrig (*a. fig*); tief (*a. fig*); knapp (*supplies etc*); gedämpft, schwach (*light*); tief (*sound*); leise (*sound, voice*); *fig* gering(schätzig); ordinär; niedergeschlagen, deprimiert; **2.** *adv* niedrig; tief (*a. fig*); leise (*sound*) **3.** METEOR Tief(druckgebiet) *n*; *fig* Tief(punkt *m*) *n*

low-brow F **1.** geistig Anspruchslose *m*, *f*, Unbedarfte *m*, *f*; **2.** geistig anspruchslos, unbedarft

low-cal·o·rie kalorienarm, -reduziert

low-e·mis·sion schadstoffarm

low·er 1. niedriger; tiefer; untere(r, -s) Unter...; **2.** niedriger machen; herab-, herunterlassen; *Augen, Stimme, Preis etc* senken; *Standard* herabsetzen; *fig* erniedrigen

low-fat fettarm

low-fly·ing plane AVIAT Tieffflieger *m*

low·land Tief-, Flachland *n*

low·ly niedrig

low-necked (tief) ausgeschnitten

low-pitched MUS tief

low-pres·sure METEOR Tiefdruck...; TECH Niederdruck...

low-rise ARCH niedrig (gebaut)

L

low-spir·it·ed niedergeschlagen
low tide Ebbe f
low wa·ter Niedrigwasser n
loy·al loyal, treu
loy·al·ty Loyalität f, Treue f
loz·enge MATH Raute f, Rhombus m; GASTR Pastille f
lu·bri·cant TECH Schmiermittel n
lu·bri·cate TECH schmieren, ölen
lu·bri·ca·tion TECH Schmieren n, Ölen n
lu·cid klar
luck Schicksal n; Glück n; *bad luck, hard luck,* ill luck Unglück n, Pech n; *good luck* Glück n; *good luck!* viel Glück!; *be in* (*out of*) *luck* (kein) Glück haben
luck·i·ly glücklicherweise, zum Glück
luck·y glücklich, Glücks...; *be lucky* Glück haben; *lucky day* Glückstag m; *lucky fellow* Glückspilz m
lu·cra·tive einträglich, lukrativ
lu·di·crous lächerlich
lug zerren, schleppen
luge SPORT Rennrodeln n; Rennrodel m, Rennschlitten m
lug·gage esp Br (Reise)Gepäck n
luggage rack esp Br RAIL etc Gepäcknetz n, Gepäckablage f
luggage van Br RAIL Gepäckwagen m
luke·warm lau(warm); fig lau, mäßig, halbherzig
lull 1. beruhigen; sich legen (*storm*); *mst lull to sleep* einlullen; 2. Pause f; MAR Flaute f (a. fig)
lul·la·by Wiegenlied n
lum·ba·go MED Hexenschuss m
lum·ber¹ schwerfällig gehen; (dahin-)rumpeln (*vehicle*)
lum·ber² 1. Bau-, Nutzholz n; esp Br Gerümpel n; 2. v/t *lumber s.o. with s.th.* Br F j-m et. aufhalsen
lum·ber·jack Holzfäller m, -arbeiter m
lum·ber mill Sägewerk n
lum·ber room esp Br Rumpelkammer f
lum·ber·yard Holzplatz m, Holzlager n
lu·mi·na·ry fig Leuchte f, Koryphäe f
lu·mi·nous leuchtend, Leucht...
lu·mi·nous dis·play Leuchtanzeige f
lu·mi·nous paint Leuchtfarbe f
lump 1. Klumpen m; Schwellung f, Beule f; MED Geschwulst f, Knoten m; GASTR Stück n; *in the lump* in Bausch und Bo-

gen, pauschal; 2. v/t: *lump together* fig zusammenwerfen; in e-n Topf werfen; v/i Klumpen bilden, klumpen
lump sug·ar Würfelzucker m
lump sum Pauschalsumme f
lump·y klumpig
lu·na·cy Wahnsinn m
lu·nar ASTR Mond...
lu·nar mod·ule Mond(lande)fähre f
lu·na·tic fig 1. wahnsinnig, verrückt; 2. Wahnsinnige m, f, Verrückte m, f
lunch, formal **lun·cheon** 1. Lunch m, Mittagessen n; 2. zu Mittag essen
lunch hour, lunch time Mittagszeit f, Mittagspause f
lung ANAT Lungenflügel m; pl die Lunge
lunge sich stürzen (*at* auf acc)
lurch 1. taumeln, torkeln; 2. *leave s.o. in the lurch* j-n im Stich lassen, F j-n sitzen lassen
lure 1. Köder m; fig Lockung f; 2. ködern, (an)locken
lu·rid grell; grässlich, schauerlich
lurk lauern; *lurk about, lurk around* herumschleichen
lus·cious köstlich, lecker; üppig; F knackig
lush saftig, üppig
lust 1. sinnliche Begierde, Lust f; Gier f; 2. *lust after, lust for* begehren; gierig sein nach
lus·ter, Br **lus·tre** Glanz m, Schimmer m
lus·trous glänzend, schimmernd
lust·y kräftig, robust, vital
lute MUS Laute f
Lu·ther·an REL lutherisch
lux·u·ri·ant üppig
lux·u·ri·ate schwelgen (*in* in dat)
lux·u·ri·ous luxuriös, Luxus...
lux·u·ry 1. Luxus m; Komfort m; Luxusartikel m; 2. Luxus...
lye Lauge f
ly·ing lügnerisch, verlogen
lymph MED Lymphe f
lynch lynchen
lynch law Lynchjustiz f
lynx ZO Luchs m
lyr·ic 1. lyrisch; 2. lyrisches Gedicht; pl Lyrik f; (Lied)Text m
lyr·i·cal lyrisch, gefühlvoll; schwärmerisch

M

M, m M, m *n*

M ABBR *of* **medium** (**size**) mittelgroß

ma F Mama *f*, Mutti *f*

ma'am → **madam**

mac·ad·am Asphalt *m*

mac·a·ro·ni Makkaroni *pl*

ma·chine 1. Maschine *f*; **2.** maschinell herstellen

ma·chine-gun Maschinengewehr *n*

ma·chine-read·a·ble EDP maschinenlesbar

ma·chin·e·ry Maschinen *pl*; Maschinerie *f*

ma·chin·ist TECH Maschinist *m*

mach·o *contp* Macho *m*

mack·e·rel ZO Makrele *f*

mac·ro... Makro..., (sehr) groß

mad wahnsinnig, verrückt; VET tollwütig; F wütend; *fig* **be mad about** wild *or* versessen sein auf (*acc*), verrückt sein nach; **drive s.o. mad** j-n verrückt machen; **go mad** verrückt werden; **like mad** wie verrückt

mad·am gnädige Frau

mad·cap verrückt

mad cow dis·ease VET Rinderwahn(-sinn) *m*

mad·den verrückt *or* rasend machen

mad·den·ing unerträglich; verrückt *or* rasend machend

made: made of gold aus Gold

made-to-meas·ure maßgeschneidert

made-up geschminkt; erfunden

mad·house *fig* F Irrenhaus *n*

mad·ly wie verrückt; F wahnsinnig, schrecklich

mad·man Verrückte *m*

mad·ness Wahnsinn

mad·wom·an Verrückte *f*

mag·a·zine Magazin *n* (*a.* PHOT, MIL), Zeitschrift *f*; Lagerhaus *n*

mag·got ZO Made *f*

Ma·gi: the (three) Magi die (drei) Weisen aus dem Morgenland, die Heiligen Drei Könige

ma·gic 1. Magie *f*; Zauberei *f*; Zauber *m*; *fig* Wunder *n*; **2.** *a.* **magical** magisch; Zauber...

ma·gi·cian Magier *m*, Zauberer *m*; Zauberkünstler *m*

ma·gis·trate (Friedens)Richter(in)

mag·na·nim·i·ty Großmut *f*

mag·nan·i·mous großmütig

mag·net Magnet *m*

mag·net·ic magnetisch, Magnet...

mag·nif·i·cent großartig, prächtig

mag·ni·fy vergrößern

mag·ni·fy·ing glass Vergrößerungsglas *n*, Lupe *f*

mag·ni·tude Größe *f*; Wichtigkeit *f*

mag·pie ZO Elster *f*

ma·hog·a·ny Mahagoni(holz) *n*

maid (Dienst)Mädchen *n*, Hausangestellte *f*; **maid of all work** *esp fig* Mädchen *n* für alles; **maid of hono(u)r** Hofdame *f*; (erste) Brautjungfer

maid·en Jungfern..., Erstlings...

maid·en name Mädchenname *m*

mail 1. Post(sendung) *f*; **by mail** mit der Post; **2.** mit der Post (zu)schicken, aufgeben, *Brief* einwerfen

mail·bag Postsack *m*; Posttasche *f*

mail·box Briefkasten *m*

mail car·ri·er, mail·man Briefträger *m*, Postbote *m*

mail or·der Bestellung *f* bei e-m Versandhaus

mail-or·der firm, mail-order house Versandhaus *n*

maim verstümmeln

main 1. Haupt..., wichtigste(r, -s); hauptsächlich; **by main force** mit äußerster Kraft; **2.** *mst pl* Hauptleitung *f*, Hauptgas-, Hauptwasser-, Hauptstromleitung *f*; (Strom)Netz *n*; **in the main** in der Hauptsache, im Wesentlichen

main·frame EDP Großrechner *m*

main·land Festland *n*

main·ly hauptsächlich

main mem·o·ry EDP Hauptspeicher *m*; Arbeitsspeicher *m*

main men·u EDP Hauptmenü *n*

main road Haupt(verkehrs)straße *f*

main·spring TECH Hauptfeder *f*; *fig* (Haupt)Triebfeder *f*

main·stay *fig* Hauptstütze *f*

main street Hauptstraße *f*

main·tain (aufrecht)erhalten, beibehalten; instand halten, pflegen, TECH *a.* warten; *Familie etc* unterhalten, versorgen; *et.* behaupten

main·te·nance (Aufrecht)Erhaltung *f*; Instandhaltung *f*, Pflege *f*, TECH *a.* Wartung *f*; Unterhalt *m*

maize *esp Br* BOT Mais *m*

ma·jes·tic majestätisch

ma·jes·ty Majestät *f*; **His (Her, Your) Majesty** Seine (Ihre, Eure) Majestät

ma·jor 1. größere(r, -s), *fig a.* bedeutend, wichtig; JUR volljährig; *C major* MUS C-Dur *n*; **2.** MIL Major *m*; JUR Volljährige *m, f*; UNIV Hauptfach *n*; MUS Dur *n*

major gen·er·al MIL Generalmajor *m*

ma·jor·i·ty Mehrheit *f*, Mehrzahl *f*; JUR Volljährigkeit *f*

ma·jor league *baseball:* oberste Spielklasse

ma·jor road Haupt(verkehrs)straße *f*

make 1. machen; anfertigen, herstellen, erzeugen; (zu)bereiten; (er)schaffen; ergeben, bilden; machen zu; ernennen zu; *Geld* verdienen; sich erweisen als, abgeben (*person*); schätzen auf (*acc*); *Geschwindigkeit* erreichen; *Fehler* machen; *Frieden etc* schließen; *e-e Rede* halten; F *Strecke* zurücklegen; *with inf:* j-n lassen, veranlassen zu, bringen zu, zwingen zu; *make it* es schaffen; *make do with s.th.* mit et. auskommen, sich mit et. behelfen; *do you make one of us?* machen Sie mit?; *what do you make of it?* was halten Sie davon?; *make believe* vorgeben; *make friends with* sich anfreunden mit; *make good* wieder gutmachen; *Versprechen etc* halten; *make haste* sich beeilen; *make way* Platz machen; *make for* zugehen auf (*acc*); sich aufmachen nach; *make into* verarbeiten zu; *make off* sich davonmachen, sich aus dem Staub machen; *make out* *Rechnung, Scheck etc* ausstellen; ausmachen, erkennen; aus *j-m, e-r Sache* klug werden; *make over* Eigentum übertragen; *make up et.* zusammenstellen; sich *et.* ausdenken, *et.* erfinden; (sich) zurechtmachen *or* schminken; *make it up* sich versöhnen *or* wieder vertragen (*with* mit); *make up one's mind* sich entschließen; *be made up of* bestehen aus, sich zusammensetzen aus; *make up for* nachholen, aufholen; für et. entschädigen; **2.** Machart *f*, Bauart *f*; Fabrikat *n*, Marke *f*

make-be·lieve Schein *m*, Fantasie *f*

mak·er Hersteller *m*; *Maker* REL Schöpfer *m*

make·shift 1. Notbehelf *m*; **2.** behelfsmäßig, Behelfs...

make-up Make-up *n*, Schminke *f*; Aufmachung *f*; Zusammensetzung *f*

mak·ing Erzeugung *f*, Herstellung *f*, Fabrikation *f*; *be in the making* noch in Arbeit sein; *have the makings of* das Zeug haben zu

mal·ad·just·ed nicht angepasst, verhaltensgestört, milieugestört

mal·ad·min·i·stra·tion schlechte Verwaltung; POL Misswirtschaft *f*

mal·con·tent 1. unzufrieden; **2.** Unzufriedene *m, f*

male 1. männlich; **2.** Mann *m*; ZO Männchen *n*

male nurse (Kranken)Pfleger *m*

mal·for·ma·tion Missbildung *f*

mal·ice Bosheit *f*; Groll *m*; JUR böse Absicht, Vorsatz *m*

ma·li·cious boshaft; böswillig

ma·lign verleumden

ma·lig·nant bösartig (*a.* MED); boshaft

mall Einkaufszentrum *n*

mal·le·a·ble TECH verformbar; *fig* formbar

mal·let Holzhammer *m*; (Krocket-, Polo-) Schläger *m*

mal·nu·tri·tion Unterernährung *f*; Fehlernährung *f*

mal·o·dor·ous übel riechend

mal·prac·tice Vernachlässigung *f* der beruflichen Sorgfalt; MED falsche Behandlung, (ärztlicher) Kunstfehler

malt Malz *n*

mal·treat schlecht behandeln; misshandeln

mam·mal ZO Säugetier *n*

mam·moth 1. ZO Mammut *n*; **2.** Mammut..., Riesen..., riesig

mam·my F Mami *f*

man 1. Mann *m*; Mensch(en *pl*) *m*; Menschheit *f*; F (Ehe)Mann *m*; F Geliebte *m*; (*Schach*)Figur *f*; (*Dame*)Stein *m*; *the man on* (*Br in*) *the street* der Mann auf der Straße; **2.** (*Raum*)Schiff *etc* bemannen; *Büro etc* besetzen

man·age *v/t* Betrieb *etc* leiten, führen; *Künstler, Sportler etc* managen; *et.* zustande bringen; es fertigbringen (*to do* zu tun); umgehen (können) mit; mit *j-m, et.* fertigwerden; F *Arbeit, Essen etc* bewältigen, schaffen; *v/i* auskommen (*with* mit); *without* ohne); F es schaffen, zurechtkommen; F es einrichten, es ermöglichen

man·age·a·ble handlich; lenksam

man·age·ment Verwaltung *f*, ECON Management *n*, Unternehmensführung *f*; Geschäftsleitung *f*, Direktion *f*

man·ag·er Verwalter *m*; ECON Manager *m* (*a.* THEA *etc*); Geschäftsführer *m*, Leiter *m*, Direktor *m*; SPORT (Chef-) Trainer *m*; *be a good manager* gut *or* sparsam wirtschaften können

man·a·ge·ri·al ECON geschäftsführend, leitend; *managerial position* leitende Stellung; *managerial staff* leitende Angestellte *pl*

man·ag·ing ECON geschäftsführend, leitend

managing di·rec·tor Generaldirektor *m*, leitender Direktor

man·date Mandat *n*; Auftrag *m*; Vollmacht *f*

man·da·to·ry obligatorisch, zwingend

mane ZO Mähne *f* (*a.* F)

ma·neu·ver *a. fig* **1.** Manöver *n*; **2.** manövrieren

mange VET Räude *f*

man·ger AGR Krippe *f*

man·gle 1. (Wäsche)Mangel *f*; **2.** mangeln; *j-n* übel zurichten, zerfleischen; *fig Text* verstümmeln

mang·y VET räudig; *fig* schäbig

man·hood Mannesalter *n*; Männlichkeit *f*

ma·ni·a Wahnsinn *m*; *fig* (**for**) Sucht *f* (nach), Leidenschaft *f* (für), Manie *f*, Fimmel *m*

ma·ni·ac F Wahnsinnige *m*, *f*, Verrückte *m*, *f*; *fig* Fanatiker(in)

man·i·cure Maniküre *f*, Handpflege *f*

man·i·fest 1. offenkundig; **2.** *v/t* offenbaren, manifestieren

man·i·fold mannigfaltig, vielfältig

ma·nip·u·late manipulieren; (geschickt) handhaben

ma·nip·u·la·tion Manipulation *f*

man·kind die Menschheit, die Menschen *pl*

man·ly männlich

man-made vom Menschen geschaffen, künstlich; *man-made fiber* Kunstfaser *f*

man·ner Art *f* (und Weise *f*); Betragen *n*, Auftreten *n*; *pl* Benehmen *n*, Umgangsformen *pl*, Manieren *pl*; Sitten *pl*

ma·noeu·vre *Br* → **maneuver**

man·or *Br* (Land)Gut *n*; → **man·or house** Herrenhaus *n*

man·pow·er menschliche Arbeitskraft; Arbeitskräfte *pl*

man·sion (herrschaftliches) Wohnhaus

man·slaugh·ter JUR Totschlag *m*, fahrlässige Tötung

man·tel·piece, man·tel·shelf Kaminsims *m*

man·u·al 1. Hand...; mit der Hand (gemacht); **2.** Handbuch *n*

man·u·fac·ture 1. erzeugen, herstellen; **2.** Herstellung *f*, Fertigung *f*; Erzeugnis *n*, Fabrikat *n*

man·u·fac·tur·er Hersteller *m*, Erzeuger *m*

man·u·fac·tur·ing Herstellungs...

ma·nure AGR **1.** Dünger *m*, Mist *m*, Dung *m*; **2.** düngen

man·u·script Manuskript *n*

man·y 1. viel(e); *many a* manche(r, -s), manch eine(r, -s); *many times* oft; *as many* ebenso viel(e); **2.** viele; *a good*

---

many ziemlich viel(e); *a great many* sehr viele

map 1. (Land- *etc*)Karte *f*; (Stadt- *etc*)Plan *m*; **2.** e-e Karte machen von; auf e-r Karte eintragen; *map out* (bis in die Einzelheiten) (voraus)planen

ma·ple BOT Ahorn *m*

mar beeinträchtigen; verderben

Mar ABBR *of March* März *m*

mar·a·thon SPORT **1.** *a.* **marathon race** Marathonlauf *m*; **2.** Marathon... (*a. fig*)

ma·raud plündern

mar·ble 1. Marmor *m*; Murmel *f*; **2.** marmorn

march 1. marschieren; *fig* fortschreiten; **2.** Marsch *m*; *fig* (Fort)Gang *m*; *the march of events* der Lauf der Dinge

March (ABBR *Mar*) März *m*

mare ZO Stute *f*

mar·ga·rine, *Br* F **marge** Margarine *f*

mar·gin Rand *m* (*a. fig*); Grenze *f* (*a. fig*); *fig* Spielraum *m*; (*Gewinn-, Verdienst*)-Spanne *f*; *by a wide margin* mit großem Vorsprung

mar·gin·al Rand...; *marginal note* Randbemerkung *f*

mar·i·hua·na, mar·i·jua·na Marihuana *n*

ma·ri·na Boots-, Jachthafen *m*

ma·rine Marine *f*; MIL Marineinfanterist *m*

mar·i·ner Seemann *m*

mar·i·tal ehelich, Ehe...

mar·i·tal sta·tus Familienstand *m*

mar·i·time See...; Küsten...; Schifffahrts...

mark[1] (Deutsche) Mark

mark[2] **1.** Marke *f*, Markierung *f*; (Kenn-)Zeichen *n*, Merkmal *n*; (Körper)Mal *n*; Ziel *n* (*a. fig*); Spur *f* (*a. fig*); Fleck *m*; (*Fabrik-, Waren*)Zeichen *n*, (*Schutz-, Handels*)Marke *f*; ECON Preisangabe *f*; PED Note *f*, Zensur *f*, Punkt *m*; SPORT Startlinie *f*; *fig* Zeichen *n*; *fig* Norm *f*; *be up to the mark* den Anforderungen gewachsen sein (*person*) *or* genügen (*performance etc*); *gesundheitlich* auf der Höhe sein; *be wide of the mark* weit danebenschießen; *fig* sich gewaltig irren; weit danebenliegen (*estimate etc*); *hit the mark* (das Ziel) treffen; *fig* ins Schwarze treffen; *miss the mark* danebenschießen, das Ziel verfehlen (*a. fig*); **2.** markieren, anzeichnen; anzeigen; kennzeichnen; *Waren* auszeichnen; *Preis* festsetzen; Spuren hinterlassen auf (*dat*); Flecken machen auf (*dat*); PED benoten, zensieren; SPORT decken, markieren; *mark my words* denk an m-e Worte; *to mark the occasion* zur

Feier des Tages; *mark time* auf der Stelle treten (a. fig); *mark down* notieren, vermerken; *im Preis* herabsetzen; *mark off* abgrenzen; *auf e-r Liste* abhaken; *mark out durch Striche etc* markieren; bestimmen (*for* für); *mark up im Preis* heraufsetzen

marked deutlich, ausgeprägt

mark·er Markierstift *m*; Lesezeichen *n*; SPORT Bewacher(in)

mar·ket 1. Markt *m*; Marktplatz *m*; (Lebensmittel)Geschäft *n*, Laden *m*; ECON Absatz *m*; (*for*) Nachfrage *f* (nach), Bedarf *m* (an *dat*); *on the market* auf dem Markt *or* im Handel; *put on the market* auf den Markt *or* in den Handel bringen; (zum Verkauf) anbieten; **2.** *v/t* auf den Markt *or* in den Handel bringen; verkaufen, vertreiben

mar·ket·a·ble ECON marktgängig

mar·ket gar·den *Br* Gemüse- und Obstgärtnerei *f*

mar·ket·ing ECON Marketing *n*

mark·ing Markierung *f*; ZO Zeichnung *f*; SPORT Deckung *f*; *man-to-man marking* Manndeckung *f*

marks·man guter Schütze

mar·ma·lade *esp* Orangenmarmelade *f*

mar·mot ZO Murmeltier *n*

ma·roon 1. kastanienbraun; **2.** *auf e-r einsamen Insel* aussetzen; **3.** Leuchtrakete *f*

mar·quee Festzelt *n*

mar·quis Marquis *m*

mar·riage Heirat *f*, Hochzeit *f* (*to* mit); Ehe *f*; *civil marriage* standesamtliche Trauung

mar·riage·a·ble heiratsfähig

mar·riage cer·tif·i·cate Trauschein *m*, Heiratsurkunde *f*

mar·ried verheiratet; ehelich, Ehe...; *married couple* Ehepaar *n*; *married life* Ehe(leben *n*) *f*

mar·row ANAT (Knochen)Mark *n*; fig Kern *m*, *das* Wesentliche

mar·ry *v/t* heiraten; *Paar* trauen; *be married* verheiratet sein (*to* mit); *get married* heiraten; sich verheiraten (*to* mit); *v/i* heiraten

marsh Sumpf(land *n*) *m*, Marsch *f*

mar·shal 1. MIL Marschall *m*; Bezirkspolizeichef *m*; **2.** ordnen; führen

marsh·y sumpfig

mar·ten ZO Marder *m*

mar·tial kriegerisch; Kriegs..., Militär...

martial arts asiatische Kampfsportarten *pl*

martial law Kriegsrecht *n*

mar·tyr REL Märtyrer(in) (a. fig)

mar·vel 1. Wunder *n*; **2.** sich wundern, staunen

mar·vel·(l)ous wunderbar; fabelhaft, fantastisch

mar·zi·pan Marzipan *n*, *m*

mas·ca·ra Wimperntusche *f*

mas·cot Maskottchen *n*

mas·cu·line männlich; Männer...; maskulin (a. LING)

mash zerdrücken, zerquetschen

mashed po·ta·toes Kartoffelbrei *m*

mask 1. Maske *f* (a. EDP); **2.** maskieren; fig verbergen, verschleiern

masked maskiert; *masked ball* Maskenball *m*

ma·son Steinmetz *m*; *mst* **Mason** Freimaurer *m*

ma·son·ry Mauerwerk *n*

masque THEA HIST Maskenspiel *n*

mas·que·rade 1. Maskerade *f* (a. fig); Verkleidung *f*; **2.** sich ausgeben (*as* als, für)

mass 1. Masse *f*; Menge *f*; Mehrzahl *f*; *the masses* die (breite) Masse; **2.** (sich) (an)sammeln *or* (an)häufen; **3.** Massen...

Mass REL Messe *f*

mas·sa·cre 1. Massaker *n*; **2.** niedermetzeln

mas·sage 1. Massage *f*; **2.** massieren

mas·seur Masseur *m*

mas·seuse Masseurin *f*, Masseuse *f*

mas·sif (Gebirgs)Massiv *n*

mas·sive massiv; groß, gewaltig

mass me·di·a Massenmedien *pl*

mass-pro·duce serienmäßig herstellen

mass pro·duc·tion Massen-, Serienproduktion *f*

mast MAR Mast *m*; *Br* ELECTR Sendemast *m*

mas·ter 1. Meister *m* (a. PAINT); Herr *m*; *esp Br* Lehrer *m*; Original(kopie) *f*; UNIV Magister *m*; *Master of Arts* (ABBR *MA*) Magister *m* Artium; *master of ceremonies* Conférencier *m*; **2.** Meister...; Haupt...; *master copy* Originalkopie *f*; *master tape* TECH Mastertape *n*, Originaltonband *n*; **3.** Herr sein über (*acc*); *Sprache etc* beherrschen; *Aufgabe etc* meistern

mas·ter key Hauptschlüssel *m*

mas·ter·ly meisterhaft, virtuos

mas·ter·piece Meisterstück *n*, -werk *n*

mas·ter·y Herrschaft *f*; Oberhand *f*; Beherrschung *f*

mas·tur·bate masturbieren, onanieren

mat[1] **1.** Matte *f*; Untersetzer *m*; **2.** sich verfilzen

mat[2] mattiert, matt

match[1] Streichholz *n*, Zündholz *n*

match[2] **1.** *der, die, das* Gleiche; (dazu) passende Sache *or* Person, Gegenstück *n*; (Fußball- *etc*)Spiel *n*, (Box- *etc* -)

Kampf *m*, (*Tennis- etc*)Match *n*, *m*; Heirat *f*; *gute etc* Partie (*person*); *be a (no) match for s.o.* j-m (nicht) gewachsen sein; *find or meet one's match* s-n Meister finden; **2.** *v/t* j-m, e-r *Sache* ebenbürtig *or* gewachsen sein, gleichkommen; *j-m, e-r Sache* entsprechen, passen zu; *v/i* zusammenpassen, übereinstimmen, entsprechen; *gloves to match* dazu passende Handschuhe

match·box Streichholz-, Zündholzschachtel *f*

match·less unvergleichlich, einzigartig

match·mak·er Ehestifter(in)

match point *tennis etc*: Matchball *m*

mate[1] → *checkmate*

mate[2] **1.** (Arbeits)Kamerad *m*, (-)Kollege *m*; ZO Männchen *n*, Weibchen *n*; MAR Maat *m*; **2.** ZO (sich) paaren

ma·te·ri·al 1. Material *n*, Stoff *m*; *writing materials* Schreibmaterial(ien *pl*) *n*; **2.** materiell; leiblich; wesentlich

ma·ter·nal mütterlich, Mutter...; mütterlicherseits

ma·ter·ni·ty 1. Mutterschaft *f*; **2.** Schwangerschafts..., Umstands...

ma·ter·ni·ty leave Mutterschaftsurlaub *m*

math F Mathe *f*

math·e·ma·ti·cian Mathematiker *m*

math·e·mat·ics Mathematik *f*

maths *Br* F Mathe *f*

mat·i·née THEA *etc* Nachmittagsvorstellung *f*

ma·tric·u·late (sich) immatrikulieren

mat·ri·mo·ni·al ehelich, Ehe...

mat·ri·mo·ny Ehe *f*, Ehestand *m*

ma·trix TECH Matrize *f*

ma·tron *Br* MED Oberschwester *f*; Hausmutter *f*; Matrone *f*

mat·ter 1. Materie *f*, Material *n*, Substanz *f*, Stoff *m*; MED Eiter *m*; Sache *f*, Angelegenheit *f*; *printed matter* Drucksache *f*; *what's the matter (with you)?* was ist los (mit dir)?; *no matter who* gleichgültig, wer; *for that matter* was das betrifft; *a matter of course* e-e Selbstverständlichkeit; *a matter of fact* e-e Tatsache; *as a matter of fact* tatsächlich, eigentlich; *a matter of form* e-e Formsache; *a matter of time* e-e Frage der Zeit; **2.** von Bedeutung sein (*to* für); *it doesn't matter* es macht nichts

mat·ter-of-fact sachlich, nüchtern

mat·tress Matratze *f*

ma·ture 1. reif (*a. fig*); **2.** (heran)reifen, reif werden

ma·tu·ri·ty Reife *f* (*a. fig*)

maud·lin rührselig

maul übel zurichten; *fig* verreißen

Maun·dy Thurs·day Gründonnerstag *m*

mauve malvenfarbig, mauve

mawk·ish rührselig

max·i... Maxi-..., riesig, Riesen...

max·im Grundsatz *m*

max·i·mum 1. Maximum *n*; **2.** maximal, Maximal..., Höchst...

May Mai *m*

may *v/aux ich kann / mag / darf etc, du kannst / magst / darfst etc*

may·be vielleicht

may·bug ZO Maikäfer *m*

May Day der 1. Mai

may·on·naise Mayonnaise *f*

mayor Bürgermeister *m*

may·pole Maibaum *m*

maze Irrgarten *m*, Labyrinth *n* (*a. fig*)

me mich; mir; F ich

mead·ow Wiese *f*, Weide *f*

mea·ger, *Br* **mea·gre** mager (*a. fig*), dürr; dürftig

meal[1] Mahl(zeit *f*) *n*; Essen *n*

meal[2] Schrotmehl *n*

mean[1] gemein, niederträchtig; geizig, knauserig; schäbig

mean[2] meinen; sagen wollen; bedeuten; beabsichtigen, vorhaben; *be meant for* bestimmt sein für; *mean well (ill)* es gut (schlecht) meinen

mean[3] **1.** Mitte *f*, Mittel *n*, Durchschnitt *m*; **2.** mittlere(r, -s), Mittel..., durchschnittlich, Durchschnitts...

mean·ing 1. Sinn *m*, Bedeutung *f*; **2.** bedeutungsvoll, bedeutsam

mean·ing·ful bedeutungsvoll; sinnvoll

mean·ing·less sinnlos

means Mittel *n or pl*, Weg *m*; ECON Mittel *pl*, Vermögen *n*; *by all means* auf alle Fälle, unbedingt; *by no means* keineswegs, auf keinen Fall; *by means of* durch, mit

mean·time 1. inzwischen; **2.** *in the meantime* inzwischen

mean·while inzwischen

mea·sles MED Masern *pl*

mea·sur·a·ble messbar

mea·sure 1. Maß *n* (*a. fig*); TECH Messgerät *n*; MUS Takt *m*; *fig* Maßnahme *f*; *beyond measure* über alle Maßen; *in a great measure* großenteils; *take measures* Maßnahmen treffen *or* ergreifen; **2.** (ab-, aus-, ver-)messen; *j-m* Maß nehmen; *measure up to* den Ansprüchen (*gen*) genügen

measured gemessen; wohlüberlegt; maßvoll

mea·sure·ment (Ver)Messung *f*; Maß *n*

measurement of ca·pac·i·ty Hohlmaß *n*

M

mea·sur·ing tape → *tape measure*

meat GASTR Fleisch *n*; *cold meat* kalter Braten

meat·ball GASTR Fleischklößchen *n*

me·chan·ic Mechaniker *m*

me·chan·i·cal mechanisch; Maschinen…

me·chan·ics PHYS Mechanik *f*

mech·a·nism Mechanismus *m*

mech·a·nize mechanisieren

med·al Medaille *f*; Orden *m*

med·al·(l)ist SPORT Medaillengewinner(in)

med·dle sich einmischen (*with, in* in *acc*)

med·dle·some aufdringlich

me·di·a Medien *pl*

med·i·ae·val → *medieval*

me·di·an *a. median strip* MOT Mittelstreifen *m*

me·di·ate vermitteln

me·di·a·tion Vermittlung *f*

me·di·a·tor Vermittler *m*

med·ic MIL Sanitäter *m*

med·i·cal 1. medizinisch, ärztlich; **2.** ärztliche Untersuchung

med·i·cal cer·tif·i·cate ärztliches Attest

med·i·cated medizinisch

me·di·ci·nal medizinisch, heilkräftig, Heil…

medi·cine Medizin *f*, *a.* Arznei *f*, *a.* Heilkunde *f*

med·i·e·val mittelalterlich

me·di·o·cre mittelmäßig

med·i·tate v/i (*on*) nachdenken (über *acc*); meditieren (über *acc*); v/t erwägen

med·i·ta·tion Nachdenken *n*; Meditation *f*

med·i·ta·tive nachdenklich

Med·i·ter·ra·ne·an Mittelmeer…

me·di·um 1. Mitte *f*; Mittel *n*; Medium *n*; **2.** mittlere(r, -s), Mittel…, *a.* mittelmäßig; GASTR medium, halb gar

med·ley Gemisch *n*; MUS Medley *n*, Potpourri *n*

meek sanft(mütig), bescheiden

meet v/t treffen, sich treffen mit; begegnen (*dat*); *j-n* kennenlernen; *j-n* abholen; zusammentreffen mit, stoßen *or* treffen auf (*acc*); *Wünschen* entgegenkommen, entsprechen; *e-r Forderung, Verpflichtung* nachkommen; v/i zusammenkommen, -treten; sich begegnen, sich treffen; (*feindlich*) zusammenstoßen; SPORT aufeinandertreffen; sich kennenlernen; *meet with* zusammentreffen mit; sich treffen mit; stoßen auf (*Schwierigkeiten etc*); erleben, erleiden

meet·ing Begegnung *f*, (Zusammen-) Treffen *n*; Versammlung *f*, Konferenz *f*, Tagung *f*

meeting place Tagungs-, Versammlungsort *m*; Treffpunkt *m*

mel·an·chol·y 1. Melancholie *f*, Schwermut *f*, Trübsinn *m*; **2.** melancholisch, traurig, trübsinnig, wehmütig

mel·low 1. reif, weich; sanft, mild (*light*), zart (*colors*); *fig* gereift (*person*); **2.** reifen (lassen) (*a. fig*); weich *or* sanft werden

me·lo·di·ous melodisch

mel·o·dra·mat·ic melodramatisch

mel·o·dy MUS Melodie *f*

mel·on BOT Melone *f*

melt (zer)schmelzen; *melt down* einschmelzen

mem·ber Mitglied *n*, Angehörige *m, f*; ANAT Glied *n*, Gliedmaße *f*; (männliches) Glied; *Member of Parliament* Br Mitglied *n* des Unterhauses, Unterhausabgeordnete *m, f*

mem·ber·ship Mitgliedschaft *f*; Mitgliederzahl *f*

mem·brane Membran(e) *f*

mem·o Memo *n*

mem·oirs Memoiren *pl*

mem·o·ra·ble denkwürdig

me·mo·ri·al Denkmal *n*, Ehrenmal *n*, Gedenkstätte *f* (*to* für); Gedenkfeier *f* (*to* für)

mem·o·rize auswendig lernen, sich *et.* einprägen

mem·o·ry Gedächtnis *n*; Erinnerung *f*; Andenken *n*; EDP Speicher *m*; *in memory of* zum Andenken an (*acc*)

memory ca·pac·i·ty EDP Speicherkapazität *f*

men·ace 1. (be)drohen; **2.** (Be)Drohung *f*

mend 1. v/t (ver)bessern; ausbessern, reparieren, flicken; *mend one's ways* sich bessern; v/i sich bessern; **2.** ausgebesserte Stelle; *on the mend* auf dem Wege der Bess(e)rung

men·di·cant REL Bettelmönch *m*

me·ni·al niedrig, untergeordnet

men·in·gi·tis MED Meningitis *f*, Hirnhautentzündung *f*

men·o·pause MED Wechseljahre *pl*

men·stru·ate menstruieren

men·stru·a·tion Menstruation *f*

men·tal geistig, Geistes…; seelisch, psychisch

mental a·rith·me·tic Kopfrechnen *n*

mental hand·i·cap geistige Behinderung

mental hos·pi·tal psychiatrische Klinik

men·tal·i·ty Mentalität *f*

men·tal·ly: *mentally handicapped* geistig behindert; *mentally ill* geisteskrank

men·tion 1. erwähnen; *don't mention it!* keine Ursache!; **2.** Erwähnung *f*

men·u Speise(n)karte *f*; EDP Menü *n*

me·ow ZO miauen

mer·can·tile Handels...

mer·ce·na·ry 1. geldgierig; **2.** MIL Söldner *m*

mer·chan·dise 1. Ware(n *pl*) *f*; **2.** vermarkten

mer·chan·dis·ing Vermarktung *f*

mer·chant 1. (Groß)Händler *m*, (Groß)-Kaufmann *m*; **2.** Handels...

mer·ci·ful barmherzig, gnädig

mer·ci·less unbarmherzig, erbarmungslos

mer·cu·ry CHEM Quecksilber *n*

mer·cy Barmherzigkeit *f*, Erbarmen *n*, Gnade *f*

mere, mere·ly bloß, nur

merge verschmelzen (*into, with* mit); ECON fusionieren

merg·er ECON Fusion *f*

me·rid·i·an GEOGR Meridian *m*; *fig* Gipfel *m*, Höhepunkt *m*

mer·it 1. Verdienst *n*; Wert *m*; Vorzug *m*; **2.** verdienen

mer·maid Meerjungfrau *f*, Nixe *f*

mer·ri·ment Fröhlichkeit *f*; Gelächter *n*, Heiterkeit *f*

mer·ry lustig, fröhlich, ausgelassen; *Merry Christmas!* fröhliche *or* frohe Weihnachten

mer·ry-go-round Karussell *n*

mesh Masche *f*; *fig often pl* Netz *n*, Schlingen *pl*; *be in mesh* TECH (ineinander)greifen; **2.** TECH (ineinander)greifen; *fig* passen (*with* zu), zusammenpassen

mess 1. Unordnung *f*, Durcheinander *n*, Schmutz *m*, F Schweinerei *f*; F Patsche *f*, Klemme *f*; MIL Messe *f*, Kasino *n*; *make a mess of* F *fig* verpfuschen, ruinieren, *Pläne etc* über den Haufen werfen; **2.** *mess about, mess around* F herumspielen, herumbasteln (*with* an *dat*); herumgammeln; *mess up* in Unordnung bringen, durcheinanderbringen; *fig* F verpfuschen, ruinieren, *Pläne etc* über den Haufen werfen

mes·sage Mitteilung *f*, Nachricht *f*; Anliegen *n*, Aussage *f*; *can I take a message?* kann ich etwas ausrichten?; *get the message* F kapieren

mes·sen·ger Bote *m*

mess·y unordentlich; unsauber, schmutzig

me·tab·o·lis·m MED Stoffwechsel *m*

met·al Metall *n*

me·tal·lic metallisch; Metall...

met·a·mor·pho·sis Metamorphose *f*, Verwandlung *f*

met·a·phor Metapher *f*

me·tas·ta·sis MED Metastase *f*

me·te·or Meteor *m*

me·te·or·o·log·i·cal meteorologisch, Wetter..., Witterungs...

meteorological of·fice Wetteramt *n*

me·te·o·rol·o·gy Meteorologie *f*, Wetterkunde *f*

me·ter¹ TECH Messgerät *n*, Zähler *m*

me·ter² Meter *m*, *n*; Versmaß *n*

meth·od Methode *f*, Verfahren *n*; System *n*

me·thod·i·cal methodisch, systematisch, planmäßig

me·tic·u·lous peinlich genau, übergenau

me·tre *Br* → *meter²*

met·ric metrisch

metric sys·tem metrisches (Maß- und Gewichts)System

met·ro·pol·i·tan ... der Hauptstadt

me·trop·o·lis Weltstadt *f*

met·tle Eifer *m*, Mut *m*, Feuer *n*

mew ZO miauen

Mex·i·can 1. mexikanisch; **2.** Mexikaner(in)

Mex·i·co Mexiko *n*

mi·aow ZO miauen

mi·cro... Mikro..., (sehr) klein

mi·cro·chip Mikrochip *m*

mi·cro·e·lec·tron·ics Mikroelektronik *f*

mi·cro·film Mikrofilm *m*

mi·cro·or·gan·ism BIOL Mikroorganismus *m*

mi·cro·phone Mikrofon *n*

mi·cro·pro·ces·sor Mikroprozessor *m*

mi·cro·scope Mikroskop *n*

mi·cro·scop·ic mikroskopisch

mi·cro·wave Mikrofilm *m*

microwave ov·en Mikrowellenherd *m*

mid mittlere(r, -s), Mitt(el)...

mid·air: *in midair* in der Luft

mid·day 1. Mittag *m*; **2.** mittägig, Mittag(s)...

mid·dle 1. mittlere(r, -s), Mittel...; **2.** Mitte *f*

mid·dle-aged mittleren Alters

Mid·dle Ag·es HIST Mittelalter *n*

mid·dle class(·es) Mittelstand *m*

mid·dle·man ECON Zwischenhändler *m*; Mittelsmann *m*

mid·dle name zweiter Vorname *m*

mid·dle-sized mittelgroß

mid·dle·weight *boxing*: Mittelgewicht *n*, Mittelgewichtler *m*

mid·dling F mittelmäßig, Mittel...; leidlich

mid·field *esp soccer*: Mittelfeld *n*

mid·field·er, mid·field play·er *esp soccer*: Mittelfeldspieler *m*

midge ZO Mücke *f*

midg·et Zwerg *m*, Knirps *m*

mid·night Mitternacht *f*; *at midnight* um Mitternacht

midst: *in the midst of* mitten in (*dat*)

mid·sum·mer Hochsommer *m*; ASTR Sommersonnenwende *f*

mid·way auf halbem Wege

mid·wife Hebamme *f*

mid·win·ter Mitte *f* des Winters; ASTR Wintersonnenwende *f*; *in midwinter* mitten im Winter

might Macht *f*, Gewalt *f*; Kraft *f*

might·y mächtig, gewaltig

mi·grate (aus)wandern, (fort)ziehen (*a.* ZO)

mi·gra·tion Wanderung *f* (*a.* ZO)

mi·gra·to·ry Wander...; ZO Zug...

mike F Mikrofon *n*

mild mild, sanft, leicht

mil·dew BOT Mehltau *m*

mild·ness Milde *f*

mile Meile *f* (*1,6 km*)

mile·age zurückgelegte Meilenzahl *f* oder Fahrtstrecke; Meilenstand *m*; *a.* **mileage allowance** Meilengeld *n*, *appr* Kilometergeld *n*

mile·stone Meilenstein *m* (*a. fig*)

mil·i·tant militant; streitbar, kriegerisch

mil·i·ta·ry 1. militärisch, Militär...; **2.** *the military* das Militär *n*

military gov·ern·ment Militärregierung *f*

military po·lice (ABBR **MP**) Militärpolizei *f*

mi·li·tia Miliz *f*, Bürgerwehr *f*

milk 1. Milch *f*; *it's no use crying over spilt milk* geschehen ist geschehen; **2.** *v/t* melken; *v/i* Milch geben

milk choc·olate Vollmilchschokolade *f*

milk·man Milchmann *m*

milk pow·der Milchpulver *n*, Trockenmilch *f*

milk shake Milchmixgetränk *n*

milk tooth ANAT Milchzahn *m*

milk·y milchig; Milch...

Milky Way Milchstraße *f*

mill 1. Mühle *f*; Fabrik *f*; **2.** *Korn etc* mahlen; *Metall* verarbeiten; *Münze* rändeln

mil·le·pede → **millipede**

mill·er Müller *m*

mil·let BOT Hirse *f*

mil·li·ner Hutmacherin *f*, Putzmacherin *f*, Modistin *f*

mil·lion Million *f*

mil·lion·aire Millionär(in)

mil·lionth 1. millionste(r, -s); **2.** Millionstel *n*

mil·li·pede ZO Tausendfüß(l)er *m*

mill·stone Mühlstein *m*; *be a millstone round s.o.'s neck fig* j-m ein Klotz am Bein sein

milt ZO Milch *f*

mime 1. Pantomime *f*; Pantomime *m*; **2.** (panto)mimisch darstellen

mim·ic 1. mimisch; Schein...; **2.** Imitator *m*; **3.** nachahmen; nachäffen

mim·ic·ry Nachahmung *f*; ZO Mimikry *f*

mince 1. *v/t* zerhacken, (zer)schneiden; *he does not mince matters* or *his words* er nimmt kein Blatt vor den Mund; *v/i* tänzeln, trippeln; **2.** *a.* **minced meat** Hackfleisch *n*

minc·er Fleischwolf *m*

mind 1. Sinn *m*, Gemüt *n*, Herz *n*; Verstand *m*, Geist *m*; Ansicht *f*, Meinung *f*; Absicht *f*, Neigung *f*, Lust *f*; Erinnerung *f*, Gedächtnis *n*; *be out of one's mind* nicht (recht) bei Sinnen sein; *bear* or *keep in mind* (immer) denken an (*acc*), *et.* nicht vergessen; *change one's mind* es sich anders überlegen, s-e Meinung ändern; *enter s.o.'s mind* j-m in den Sinn kommen; *give s.o. a piece of one's mind* j-m gründlich die Meinung sagen; *have (half) a mind to inf* (nicht übel) Lust haben zu *inf*; *lose one's mind* den Verstand verlieren; *make up one's mind* sich entschließen, e-n Entschluss fassen; *to my mind* meiner Ansicht nach; **2.** *v/t* achtgeben auf (*acc*); sehen nach, aufpassen auf (*acc*); *et.* haben gegen; *mind the step!* Vorsicht, Stufe!; *mind your own business!* kümmere dich um deine eigenen Angelegenheiten!; *do you mind if I smoke?*, *do you mind my smoking?* haben Sie *et.* dagegen *or* stört es Sie, wenn ich rauche?; *would you mind opening the window?* würden Sie bitte das Fenster öffnen?; *would you mind coming* würden Sie bitte kommen?; *v/i* aufpassen; *et.* dagegen haben; *mind (you)* wohlgemerkt, allerdings; *never mind!* macht nichts!, ist schon gut!; *I don't mind* meinetwegen, von mir aus

mind·less gedankenlos, blind; unbekümmert (*of* um), ohne Rücksicht (*of* auf *acc*)

mine¹ meins; *that's mine* das gehört mir

mine² 1. Bergwerk *n*, Mine *f*, Zeche *f*, Grube *f*; MIL Mine *f*; *fig* Fundgrube *f*; **2.** *v/i* schürfen, graben (*for* nach); *v/t* *Erz, Kohle* abbauen; MIL verminen

min·er Bergmann *m*, Kumpel *m*

min·e·ral 1. Mineral *n*; *pl Br* Mineralwasser *n*; **2.** Mineral...

mineral oil Mineralöl *n*

mineral wa·ter Mineralwasser *n*

min·gle *v/t* (ver)mischen; *v/i* sich mischen *or* mengen (*with* unter)

min·i... Mini..., Klein(st)...; → *miniskirt*

min·i·a·ture 1. Miniatur(gemälde *n*) *f*; **2.** Miniatur...; Klein...

miniature cam·e·ra Kleinbildkamera *f*

min·i·mize auf ein Mindestmaß herabsetzen; herunterspielen, bagatellisieren

min·i·mum 1. Minimum *n*, Mindestmaß *n*; **2.** minimal, Mindest...

min·ing 1. Bergbau *m*; **2.** Berg(bau)..., Bergwerks...; Gruben...

min·i·skirt Minirock *m*

min·is·ter POL Minister(in); Gesandte *m*; REL Geistliche *m*

min·is·try POL Ministerium *n*; REL geistliches Amt

mink ZO Nerz *m*

mi·nor 1. kleinere(r, -s), *fig a.* unbedeutend, geringfügig; JUR minderjährig; *A minor* MUS a-Moll *n*; *minor key* MUS Moll(tonart *f*) *n*; **2.** JUR Minderjährige *m*, *f*; UNIV Nebenfach *n*; MUS Moll *n*

mi·nor·i·ty Minderheit *f*; JUR Minderjährigkeit *f*

min·ster *Br* Münster *n*

mint¹ 1. Münze *f*, Münzanstalt *f*; **2.** prägen

mint² BOT Minze *f*

min·u·et MUS Menuett *n*

mi·nus 1. *prp* minus, weniger; F ohne; **2.** *adj* Minus...; **3.** Minus *n*, *fig a.* Nachteil *m*

min·ute¹ Minute *f*; Augenblick *m*; *in a minute* sofort; *just a minute!* Moment mal!

mi·nute² winzig; sehr genau

min·utes Protokoll *n*; *take* (or *keep*) *the minutes* (das) Protokoll führen

mir·a·cle Wunder *n*

mi·rac·u·lous wunderbar

mi·rac·u·lous·ly wie durch ein Wunder

mi·rage Luftspiegelung *f*, Fata Morgana *f*

mire Schlamm *m*; *drag through the mire fig* in den Schmutz ziehen

mir·ror 1. Spiegel *m*; **2.** (wider)spiegeln (*a. fig*)

mis... miss..., falsch, schlecht

mis·ad·ven·ture Missgeschick *n*; Unglück *n*, Unglücksfall *m*

mis·an·thrope, **mis·an·thro·pist** Menschenfeind(in)

mis·ap·ply falsch an- *or* verwenden

mis·ap·pre·hend missverstehen

mis·ap·pro·pri·ate unterschlagen, veruntreuen

mis·be·have sich schlecht benehmen

mis·cal·cu·late falsch berechnen; sich verrechnen (in *dat*)

mis·car·riage MED Fehlgeburt *f*; Misslingen *n*, Fehlschlag(en *n*) *m*; *miscarriage of justice* JUR Fehlurteil *n*

mis·car·ry MED e-e Fehlgeburt haben; misslingen, scheitern

mis·cel·la·ne·ous gemischt, vermischt; verschiedenartig

mis·cel·la·ny Gemisch *n*; Sammelband *m*

mis·chief Schaden *m*; Unfug *m*; Übermut *m*

mischief-mak·er Unruhestifter(in)

mis·chie·vous boshaft, mutwillig; schelmisch

mis·con·ceive falsch auffassen, missverstehen

mis·con·duct schlechtes Benehmen; schlechte Führung; Verfehlung *f*

mis·con·strue etwas falsch auslegen, missdeuten

mis·de·mea·no(u)r JUR Vergehen *n*

mis·di·rect fehlleiten, irreleiten; *Brief etc* falsch adressieren

mise-en-scène THEA Inszenierung *f*

mi·ser Geizhals *m*

mis·e·ra·ble erbärmlich, kläglich, elend; unglücklich

mi·ser·ly geizig, F knick(e)rig

mis·e·ry Elend *n*, Not *f*

mis·fire versagen (*gun*); MOT fehlzünden, aussetzen; *fig* danebengehen

mis·fit Außenseiter(in)

mis·for·tune Unglück *n*, Unglücksfall *m*; Missgeschick *n*

mis·giv·ing Befürchtung *f*, Zweifel *m*

mis·guid·ed irregeleitet, irrig, unangebracht

mis·hap Unglück *n*; Missgeschick *n*; *without mishap* ohne Zwischenfälle

mis·in·form falsch unterrichten

mis·in·ter·pret missdeuten, falsch auffassen *or* auslegen

mis·lay *et.* verlegen

mis·lead irreführen, täuschen; verleiten

mis·man·age schlecht verwalten *or* führen *or* handhaben

mis·place *et.* an e-e falsche Stelle legen *or* setzen; *et.* verlegen; *misplaced fig* unangebracht, deplatziert

mis·print 1. verdrucken; **2.** Druckfehler *m*

mis·read falsch lesen; falsch deuten, missdeuten

mis·rep·re·sent falsch darstellen; entstellen, verdrehen

miss 1. *v/t* verpassen, versäumen, verfehlen; übersehen, nicht bemerken; überhören; nicht verstehen *or* begreifen; vermissen; *a. miss out* auslassen, übergehen, überspringen; *v/i* nicht treffen; missglücken; *miss out on et.* verpassen; **2.** Fehlschuss *m*, Fehlstoß *m*, Fehlwurf *m* *etc*; Verpassen *n*, Verfehlen *n*

Miss Fräulein *n*

M

mis·shap·en missgebildet
mis·sile 1. Geschoss *n*; Rakete *f*; **2.** Raketen…
miss·ing fehlend; *be missing* fehlen, verschwunden *or* weg sein; (MIL *a. missing in action*) vermisst sein; *be missing* MIL vermisst sein *or* werden
mis·sion (*Militär- etc*)Mission *f*; *esp* POL Auftrag *m*, Mission *f* (*a.* REL); MIL, AVIAT Einsatz *m*
mis·sion·a·ry REL Missionar *m*
mis·spell falsch buchstabieren *or* schreiben
mis·spend falsch verwenden; vergeuden
mist 1. (feiner *or* leichter) Nebel; **2.** *mist over* sich trüben; *mist up* (sich) beschlagen
mis·take 1. verwechseln (*for* mit); verkennen, sich irren in (*dat*); falsch verstehen, missverstehen; **2.** Irrtum *m*, Versehen *n*, Fehler *m*; *by mistake* aus Versehen, irrtümlich
mis·tak·en irrig, falsch (verstanden); *be mistaken* sich irren
mis·tle·toe BOT Mistel *f*
mis·tress Herrin *f*; *esp Br* Lehrerin *f*; Geliebte *f*
mis·trust 1. misstrauen (*dat*); **2.** Misstrauen *n* (*of* gegen)
mis·trust·ful misstrauisch
mist·y (leicht) neb(e)lig; *fig* unklar, verschwommen
mis·un·der·stand missverstehen; *j-n* nicht verstehen
mis·un·der·standing Missverständnis *n*
mis·use 1. missbrauchen; falsch gebrauchen; **2.** Missbrauch *m*
mite ZO Milbe *f*; kleines Ding, Würmchen *n*; *a mite* F ein bisschen
mi·ter, *Br* **mi·tre** REL Mitra *f*, Bischofsmütze *f*
mitt *baseball*: Fanghandschuh *m*; → **mitten** Fausthandschuh *m*
mix 1. (ver)mischen, vermengen; *Getränke* mixen; sich (ver)mischen; sich mischen lassen; verkehren (*with* mit); *mix well* kontaktfreudig sein; *mix up* zusammenmischen, durcheinander mischen; (*völlig*) durcheinanderbringen; verwechseln (*with* mit); *be mixed up* verwickelt sein *or* werden (*in* acc); (*geistig*) ganz durcheinander sein; **2.** Mischung *f*
mixed gemischt (*a. fig*); vermischt, Misch…
mix·er Mixer *m*; TECH Mischmaschine *f*; *radio*, TV *etc*: Mischpult *n*
mix·ture Mischung *f*; Gemisch *n*
mix-up F Verwechs(e)lung *f*
moan 1. Stöhnen *n*; **2.** stöhnen

moat (Burg-, Stadt)Graben *m*
mob 1. Mob *m*, Pöbel *m*; **2.** herfallen über (*acc*); *j-n* bedrängen, belagern
mo·bile 1. beweglich; MIL mobil, motorisiert; *fig* lebhaft; **2.** → *mobile phone or telephone*
mobile home Wohnwagen *m*
mobile phone, **mobile tel·e·phone** Mobiltelefon *n*, Handy *n*
mo·bil·ize mobilisieren, MIL *a.* mobil machen
moc·ca·sin Mokassin *m*
mock 1. *v/t* verspotten; nachäffen; *v/i* sich lustig machen, spotten (*at* über *acc*); **2.** nachgemacht, Schein…
mock·e·ry Spott *m*, Hohn *m*; Gespött *n*
mock·ing·bird ZO Spottdrossel *f*
mode (Art *f* und) Weise *f*; EDP Modus *m*, Betriebsart *f*
mod·el 1. Modell *n*; Muster *n*; Vorbild *n*; Mannequin *n*; Model *n*, (Foto)Modell *n*; TECH Modell *n*, Typ *m*; *male model* Dressman *m*; **2.** Modell…, Muster…; **3.** *v/t* modellieren, *a. fig* formen; *Kleider etc* vorführen; *v/i* Modell stehen *or* sitzen; als Mannequin *or* (Foto)Modell *or* Dressman arbeiten
mo·dem EDP Modem *m*, *n*
mod·e·rate 1. (mittel)mäßig; gemäßigt; vernünftig, angemessen; **2.** (sich) mäßigen
mod·e·ra·tion Mäßigung *f*
mod·ern modern, neu
mod·ern·ize modernisieren
mod·est bescheiden
mod·es·ty Bescheidenheit *f*
mod·i·fi·ca·tion (Ab-, Ver)Änderung *f*
mod·i·fy (ab-, ver)ändern
mod·u·late modulieren
mod·ule TECH Modul *n*, ELECTR *a.* Baustein *m*; (*Kommando- etc*)Kapsel *f*
moist feucht
moist·en *v/t* anfeuchten, befeuchten; *v/i* feucht werden
mois·ture Feuchtigkeit *f*
mo·lar ANAT Backenzahn *m*
mo·las·ses Sirup *m*
mold[1] Schimmel *m*; Moder *m*; Humus (-boden) *m*
mold[2] TECH **1.** (Gieß-, Guss-, Press-) Form *f*; **2.** gießen; formen
mol·der *a. molder away* vermodern; zerfallen
mold·y verschimmelt, schimm(e)lig; mod(e)rig
mole[1] ZO Maulwurf *m*
mole[2] Muttermal *n*, Leberfleck *m*
mole[3] Mole *f*, Hafendamm *m*
mol·e·cule Molekül *n*

mole·hill Maulwurfshügel m; **make a mountain out of a molehill** aus e-r Mücke e-n Elefanten machen

mo·lest belästigen

mol·li·fy besänftigen, beschwichtigen

mol·lusc Br, **mol·lusk** zo Weichtier n

mol·ly·cod·dle F verhätscheln, verzärteln

molt (sich) mausern; Haare verlieren

mol·ten geschmolzen

mom F Mami f, Mutti f

mom-and-pop store Tante-Emma-Laden m

mo·ment Moment m, Augenblick m; Bedeutung f; PHYS Moment n

mo·men·ta·ry momentan, augenblicklich

mo·men·tous bedeutsam, folgenschwer

mo·men·tum PHYS Moment n; Schwung m

Mon ABBR of **Monday** Mo., Montag m

mon·arch Monarch(in), Herrscher(in)

mon·ar·chy Monarchie f

mon·as·tery REL (Mönchs)Kloster n

Mon·day (ABBR **Mon**) Montag m; **on Monday** (am) Montag; **on Mondays** montags

mon·e·ta·ry ECON Währungs...; Geld...

mon·ey Geld n

mon·ey-box Br Sparbüchse f

mon·ey-chang·er (Geld)Wechsler m; TECH Wechselautomat m

mon·ey or·der Post- or Zahlungsanweisung f

mon·grel zo Bastard m, esp Promenadenmischung f

mon·i·tor 1. Monitor m; Kontrollgerät n, -schirm m; **2.** abhören; überwachen

monk REL Mönch m

mon·key 1. zo Affe m; F (kleiner) Schlingel; **make a monkey (out) of s.o.** F j-n zum Deppen machen; **2. monkey about, monkey around** F (herum)albern; **monkey about** or **around with** F herumspielen mit or an (dat) herummurksen an (dat)

monkey wrench TECH Engländer m, Franzose m; **throw a monkey wrench into s.th.** F et. behindern

mon·o 1. F Mono n; F Monogerät n; F Mononoschallplatte f; **2.** Mono...

mon·o... ein..., mono...

mon·o·log, esp Br **mon·o·logue** Monolog m

mo·nop·o·lize monopolisieren; fig an sich reißen

mo·nop·o·ly Monopol n (of auf acc)

mo·not·o·nous monoton, eintönig

mo·not·o·ny Monotonie f

mon·soon Monsun m

mon·ster 1. Monster n, Ungeheuer n (a. fig); Monstrum n; **2.** Riesen...

mon·stros·i·ty Ungeheuerlichkeit f; Momstrum n

mon·strous ungeheuer; mst contp ungeheuerlich; scheußlich

month Monat m

month·ly 1. monatlich, Monats...; **2.** Monatsschrift f

mon·u·ment Monument n, Denkmal n

mon·u·men·tal monumental; F kolossal, Riesen...; Gedenk...

moo zo muhen

mooch F schnorren

mood Stimmung f, Laune f; **be in a good (bad) mood** gute (schlechte) Laune haben, gut (schlecht) aufgelegt sein

mood·y launisch; schlecht gelaunt

moon 1. ASTR Mond m; **2. moon about, moon around** F herumtrödeln; F ziellos herumstreichen

moon·light Mondlicht n, -schein m

moon·lit mondhell

moor¹ (Hoch)Moor n

moor² MAR vertäuen, festmachen

moor·ings MAR Vertäuung f; Liegeplatz m

moose zo nordamerikanischer Elch

mop 1. Mopp m; F (Haar)Wust m; **2.** wischen; **mop up** aufwischen

mope Trübsal blasen

mo·ped Br MOT Moped n

mor·al 1. moralisch; Moral..., Sitten...; **2.** Moral f, Lehre f; pl Moral f, Sitten pl

mo·rale Moral f, Stimmung f

mor·al·ize moralisieren (about, on über acc)

mor·bid morbid, krankhaft

more 1. adj mehr; noch (mehr); **some more tea** noch etwas Tee; **2.** adv mehr; noch; **more and more** immer mehr; **more or less** mehr oder weniger; **once more** noch einmal; **the more so because** umso mehr, da; **more important** wichtiger; **more often** öfter; **3.** mst n (of an dat); **a little more** etwas mehr

mo·rel BOT Morchel f

more·o·ver außerdem, weiter, ferner

morgue Leichenschauhaus n; F (Zeitungs)Archiv n

morn·ing Morgen m; Vormittag m; **good morning!** guten Morgen!; **in the morning** morgens, am Morgen; vormittags, am Vormittag; **tomorrow morning** morgen früh or Vormittag

mo·rose mürrisch, verdrießlich

mor·phi·a, mor·phine PHARM Morphium n

mor·sel Bissen m, Happen m; **a morsel of** ein bisschen

mor·tal 1. sterblich; tödlich; Tod(es)...; **2.** Sterbliche m, f

mor·tal·i·ty Sterblichkeit f
mor·tar¹ Mörtel m
mor·tar² Mörser m
mort·gage 1. Hypothek f; 2. mit e-r Hypothek belasten, e-e Hypothek aufnehmen auf (acc)
mor·ti·cian Leichenbestatter m
mor·ti·fi·ca·tion Kränkung f; Ärger m, Verdruss m
mor·ti·fy kränken; ärgern, verdrießen
mor·tu·a·ry Leichenhalle f
mo·sa·ic Mosaik n
Mos·lem → Muslim
mosque Moschee f
mos·qui·to zo Moskito m; Stechmücke f
moss BOT Moos n
moss·y BOT moosig, bemoost
most 1. adj meiste(r, -s), größte(r, -s); die meisten; most people die meisten Leute; 2. adv am meisten; most of all am allermeisten; before adj: höchst, äußerst; the most important point der wichtigste Punkt; 3. das meiste, das Höchste; das meiste, der größte Teil; die meisten pl; at (the) most höchstens; make the most of it nach Kräften ausnutzen, das Beste herausholen aus
most·ly hauptsächlich, meist(ens)
mo·tel Motel n
moth zo Motte f
moth·eat·en mottenzerfressen
moth·er 1. Mutter f; 2. bemuttern
moth·er coun·try Vaterland n, Heimatland n; Mutterland n
moth·er·hood Mutterschaft f
moth·er-in-law Schwiegermutter f
moth·er·ly mütterlich
moth·er-of-pearl Perlmutter f, n, Perlmutt n
moth·er tongue Muttersprache f
mo·tif Motiv n
mo·tion 1. Bewegung f; PARL Antrag m; in quick motion film: im Zeitraffer; in slow motion film: in Zeitlupe; put or set in motion in Gang bringen (a. fig), in Bewegung setzen; 2. v/t j-n durch e-n Wink auffordern, j-m ein Zeichen geben; v/i winken
mo·tion·less bewegungslos, unbeweglich
mo·tion pic·ture Film m
mo·ti·vate motivieren, anspornen
mo·ti·va·tion Motivation f, Ansporn m
mo·tive 1. Motiv n, Beweggrund m; 2. treibend (a. fig)
mot·ley bunt
mo·to·cross SPORT Motocross n
mo·tor 1. Motor m, fig a. treibende Kraft; 2. Motor...
mo·tor·bike Moped n; Br F Motorrad n

mo·tor·boat Motorboot n
mo·tor·cade Auto-, Wagenkolonne f
mo·tor·car Br Kraftfahrzeug n
mo·tor car·a·van Br Wohnmobil n
mo·tor·cy·cle Motorrad n
mo·tor·cy·clist Motorradfahrer(in)
mo·tor home Wohnmobil n
mo·tor·ing Autofahren n; school of motoring Fahrschule f
mo·tor·ist Autofahrer(in)
mo·tor·ize motorisieren
mo·tor launch Motorbarkasse f
mo·tor·way Br Autobahn f
mot·tled gefleckt, gesprenkelt
mould¹ Br → mold¹
mould² Br → mold²
moul·der Br → molder
mould·y Br → moldy
moult Br → molt
mound Erdhügel m, Erdwall m
mount 1. v/t Pferd etc besteigen, steigen auf (acc); montieren; anbringen, befestigen; Bild etc aufziehen, aufkleben; Edelstein fassen; mounted police berittene Polizei; v/i aufsitzen (rider); steigen, fig a. (an)wachsen; mount up to sich belaufen auf (acc); 2. Gestell n; Fassung f; Reittier n, Reitpferd n
moun·tain 1. Berg m, pl a. Gebirge n; 2. Berg..., Gebirgs...
moun·tain bike Mountainbike n
moun·tain·eer Bergsteiger(in)
moun·tain·eer·ing Bergsteigen n
moun·tain·ous bergig, gebirgig
mourn v/i trauern (for, over um); v/t betrauern, trauern um
mourn·er Trauernde m, f
mourn·ful traurig
mourn·ing Trauer f; Trauerkleidung f
mouse zo Maus f (a. EDP)
mous·tache → mustache
mouth Mund m; zo Maul n, Schnauze f; GEOGR Mündung f; Öffnung f
mouth·ful ein Mundvoll; Bissen m
mouth or·gan F Mundharmonika f
mouth·piece Mundstück n; fig Sprachrohr n
mouth·wash Mundwasser n
mo·va·ble beweglich
move 1. v/t (weg)rücken; transportieren; bewegen, rühren (both a. fig); chess etc: e-n Zug machen mit; PARL beantragen; move house umziehen; move heaven and earth Himmel und Hölle in Bewegung setzen; v/i sich (fort)bewegen; sich rühren; umziehen (to nach); chess etc: e-n Zug machen; move away weg-, fortziehen; move in einziehen; move off sich in Bewegung setzen;

move on weitergehen; **move out** ausziehen; **2.** Bewegung f; Umzug m; chess etc: Zug m; fig Schritt m; **on the move** in Bewegung; auf den Beinen; **get a move on!** F Tempo!, mach(t) schon!, los!

mov·a·ble → **movable**

move·ment Bewegung f (a. fig); MUS Satz m; TECH Werk n

mov·ie 1. Film m; Kino n; **2.** Film..., Kino...

movie cam·e·ra Filmkamera f

movie star Filmstar m

movie thea·ter Kino n

mov·ing sich bewegend, beweglich; fig rührend

moving stair·case Rolltreppe f

moving van Möbelwagen m

mow mähen

mow·er Mähmaschine f, esp Rasenmäher m

Mr. ABBR **of Mister** Herr m

Mrs. Frau f

Ms. Frau f

much 1. adj viel; **2.** adv sehr; viel; **much better** viel besser; **very much** sehr; **I thought as much** das habe ich mir gedacht; **3.** große Sache; **nothing much** nichts Besonderes; **make much of** viel Wesens machen von; **think much of** viel halten von; **I am not much of a dancer** F ich bin kein großer Tänzer

muck F Br AGR Mist m, Dung m; fig Dreck m, Schmutz m; F contp Fraß m

mu·cus (Nasen)Schleim m

mud Schlamm m, Matsch m; Schmutz m (a. fig)

mud·dle 1. Durcheinander n; **be in a muddle** durcheinander sein; **2.** a. **muddle up** durcheinanderbringen; **muddle through** F sich durchwursteln

mud·dy schlammig, trüb; schmutzig; fig wirr

mud·guard Kotflügel m; Schutzblech n

mues·li Müsli n

muff Muff m

muf·fle Ton etc dämpfen; often **muffle up** einhüllen, einwickeln

muf·fler (dicker) Schal; MOT Auspufftopf m

mug[1] Krug m; Becher m; große Tasse; F Visage f; V Fresse f

mug[2] F überfallen und ausrauben

mug·ger F (Straßen)Räuber m

mug·ging F Raubüberfall m, esp Straßenraub m

mug·gy schwül

mul·ber·ry BOT Maulbeerbaum m; Maulbeere f

mule ZO Maultier n; Maulesel m

mulled: mulled wine Glühwein m

mul·li·on ARCH Mittelpfosten m

mul·ti... viel..., mehr..., Mehrfach..., Multi...

mul·ti·cul·tur·al multikulturell

mul·ti·far·i·ous mannigfaltig, vielfältig

mul·ti·lat·e·ral vielseitig; POL multilateral, mehrseitig

mul·ti·me·di·a multimedial

mul·ti·na·tion·al ECON multinationaler Konzern, F Multi m

mul·ti·ple 1. vielfach, mehrfach; **2.** MATH Vielfache n

multiplication table Einmaleins n

mul·ti·pli·ci·ty Vielfalt f; Vielzahl f

mul·ti·ply (sich) vermehren, (sich) vervielfachen; MATH multiplizieren, malnehmen (**by** mit)

mul·ti·pur·pose Mehrzweck...

mul·ti·sto·rey Br mehrstöckig

multistorey car park Br Park(hoch)haus n

mul·ti·tude Vielzahl f

mul·ti·tu·di·nous zahlreich

mum[1] Br F Mami f, Mutti f

mum[2] 1. int: **mum's the word** Mund halten!, kein Wort darüber!; **2.** adj: **keep mum** nichts verraten, den Mund halten

mum·ble murmeln, F nuscheln; mümmeln

mum·mi·fy mumifizieren

mum·my[1] Mumie f

mum·my[2] Br F Mami f, Mutti f

mumps MED Ziegenpeter m, Mumps m

munch mampfen

mun·dane alltäglich; weltlich

mu·ni·ci·pal städtisch, Stadt..., kommunal, Gemeinde...; **municipal council** Stadt-, Gemeinderat m

mu·ni·ci·pal·i·ty Kommunalbehörde f; Stadtverwaltung f

mu·ral Wandgemälde n

mur·der 1. Mord m, Ermordung f; **2.** Mord...; **3.** ermorden; F verschandeln

mur·der·er Mörder m

mur·der·ess Mörderin f

mur·der·ous mörderisch

murk·y dunkel, finster

mur·mur 1. Murmeln n; Gemurmel n; Murren n; **2.** murmeln; murren

mus·cle Muskel m

mus·cu·lar Muskel...; muskulös

muse[1] (nach)sinnen, (nach)grübeln (**on, over** über acc)

muse[2] a. **Muse** Muse f

mu·se·um Museum n

mush Brei m, Mus n; Maisbrei m

mush·room 1. BOT Pilz m, esp Champig-

non *m*; **2.** rasch wachsen; ***mushroom up*** *fig* (wie Pilze) aus dem Boden schießen
mu·sic Musik *f*; Noten *pl*; ***put** or **set to music*** vertonen
mu·sic·al 1. musikalisch; Musik...; **2.** Musical *n*
musical box *esp Br* Spieldose *f*
musical in·stru·ment Musikinstrument *n*
mu·sic box Spieldose *f*
music cen·ter (*Br* **cen·tre**) Kompaktanlage *f*
music hall *Br* Varieté(theater) *n*
mu·si·cian Musiker(in)
mu·sic stand Notenständer *m*
musk Moschus *m*
musk·rat ZO Bisamratte *f*; Bisampelz *m*
Mus·lim 1. Muslim *m*, Moslem *m*; **2.** muslimisch, moslemisch
mus·sel ZO (Mies)Muschel *f*
must¹ 1. *v/aux ich* muss, *du* musst *etc*; ***you must not*** (F ***mustn't***) du darfst nicht; **2.** Muss *n*
must² Most *m*
mus·tache Schnurrbart *m*
mus·tard Senf *m*
mus·ter 1. ***muster up*** *s-e Kraft etc* aufbieten; *s-n Mut* zusammennehmen; **2.** ***pass muster*** *fig* Zustimmung finden (***with*** bei); den Anforderungen genügen
must·y mod(e)rig, muffig
mu·ta·tion Veränderung *f*; BIOL Mutation *f*

N

mute 1. stumm; **2.** Stumme *m*, *f*; MUS

Dämpfer *m*
mu·ti·late verstümmeln
mu·ti·la·tion Verstümmelung *f*
mu·ti·neer Meuterer *m*
mu·ti·nous meuternd; rebellisch
mu·ti·ny 1. Meuterei *f*; **2.** meutern
mut·ter 1. murmeln; murren; **2.** Murmeln *n*; Murren *n*
mut·ton GASTR Hammel-, Schaffleisch *n*; ***leg of mutton*** Hammelkeule *f*
mut·ton chop GASTR Hammelkotelett *n*
mu·tu·al gegenseitig; gemeinsam
muz·zle 1. ZO Maul *n*, Schnauze *f*; Mündung *f* (*of a gun*); Maulkorb *m*; **2.** e-m Maulkorb anlegen (*dat*), *fig a.* j-n mundtot machen
my mein(e)
myrrh BOT Myrrhe *f*
myr·tle BOT Myrte *f*
my·self ich, mich *or* mir selbst; mich; mich (selbst); ***by myself*** allein
mys·te·ri·ous rätselhaft, unerklärlich; geheimnisvoll, mysteriös
mys·te·ry Geheimnis *n*, Rätsel *n*; REL Mysterium *n*; ***mystery tour*** Fahrt *f* ins Blaue
mys·tic 1. Mystiker(in); **2.** → **mystic·al** mystisch
mys·ti·fy verwirren, vor ein Rätsel stellen; ***be mystified*** vor e-m Rätsel stehen
myth Mythos *m*, Sage *f*
my·thol·o·gy Mythologie *f*

N

N, n N, n *n*
nab F schnappen, erwischen
na·dir ASTR Nadir *m*; *fig* Tiefpunkt *m*
nag¹ 1. *v/i* nörgeln; ***nag (at)*** herumnörgeln an (*dat*); **2.** Nörgler(in)
nag² F Gaul *m*, Klepper *m*
nail 1. ANAT, TECH Nagel *m*; **2.** (an-)nageln (***to** an acc*)
nail pol·ish Nagellack *m*
nail scis·sors Nagelschere *f*
nail var·nish *Br* Nagellack *m*
na·ive, na·ïve naiv (*a. art*)
na·ked nackt, bloß; kahl; *fig* ungeschminkt
nak·ed·ness Nacktheit *f*
name 1. Name *m*; Ruf *m*; ***by name*** mit

Namen, namentlich; ***by the name of ... namens ...***; ***what's your name?*** wie heißen Sie?; ***call s.o. names*** j-n beschimpfen; **2.** (be)nennen; erwähnen; ernennen zu
name·less namenlos; unbekannt
name·ly nämlich
name·plate Namens-, Tür-, Firmenschild *n*
name·sake Namensvetter *m*, Namensschwester *f*
name tag Namensschild *n*
nan·ny Kindermädchen *n*
nan·ny goat ZO Geiß *f*, Ziege *f*
nap 1. Schläfchen *n*; ***have** or **take a nap*** → **2.** ein Nickerchen machen

nape *mst* **nape of the neck** ANAT Genick *n*, Nacken *m*

nap·kin Serviette *f*

nap·py *Br* Windel *f*

nar·co·sis MED Narkose *f*

nar·cot·ic 1. narkotisch, betäubend, einschläfernd; Rauschgift…; *narcotic addiction* Rauschgiftsucht *f*; **2.** Narkotikum *n*, Betäubungsmittel *n*; *often pl* Rauschgift *n*; *narcotics squad* Rauschgiftdezernat *n*

nar·rate erzählen; berichten, schildern

nar·ra·tion Erzählung *f*

nar·ra·tive 1. Erzählung *f*; Bericht *m*, Schilderung *f*; **2.** erzählend

nar·ra·tor Erzähler(in)

nar·row 1. eng, schmal; beschränkt; knapp; **2.** enger *or* schmäler werden *or* machen, (sich) verengen; beschränken, einschränken

nar·row·ly mit knapper Not

nar·row-mind·ed engstirnig, beschränkt

nar·row·ness Enge *f*; Beschränktheit *f*

na·sal nasal; Nasen…

nas·ty ekelhaft, eklig, widerlich (*smell, sight etc*); abscheulich (*weather etc*); böse, schlimm (*accident etc*); hässlich (*character, behavior etc*); gemein, fies; schmutzig, zotig (*language*)

na·tal Geburts…

na·tion Nation *f*, Volk *n*

na·tion·al 1. national, National…, Landes…, Volks…; **2.** Staatsangehörige *m*, *f*

na·tion·al an·them Nationalhymne *f*

na·tion·al·i·ty Nationalität *f*, Staatsangehörigkeit *f*

na·tion·al·ize ECON verstaatlichen

na·tion·al park Nationalpark *m*

national so·cial·ism HIST POL Nationalsozialismus *m*

national so·cial·ist HIST POL Nationalsozialist *m*

national team SPORT Nationalmannschaft *f*

na·tion·wide landesweit

na·tive 1. einheimisch, Landes…; heimatlich, Heimat…; eingeboren, Eingeborenen…; angeboren; **2.** Eingeborene *m*, *f*; Einheimische *m*, *f*

native lan·guage Muttersprache *f*

native speak·er Muttersprachler(in)

Na·tiv·i·ty REL *die* Geburt Christi

nat·ty F schick, *Austrian* fesch

nat·u·ral natürlich; angeboren; Natur…

natural gas Erdgas *n*

nat·u·ral·ize naturalisieren, einbürgern

nat·u·ral·ly natürlich; von Natur (aus)

nat·u·ral re·sourc·es Boden- u. Naturschätze *pl*

natural sci·ence Naturwissenschaft *f*

na·ture Natur *f*

nature con·ser·va·tion Naturschutz *m*

nature re·serve Naturschutzgebiet *n*

nature trail Naturlehrpfad *m*

naugh·ty unartig; unanständig

nau·se·a Übelkeit *f*, Brechreiz *m*

nau·se·ate: nauseate s.o. j-m Übelkeit verursachen; *fig* j-n anwidern

nau·se·at·ing ekelerregend, widerlich

nau·ti·cal nautisch, See…

na·val MIL Flotten…, Marine…; See…

naval base MIL Flottenstützpunkt *m*

naval offi·cer MIL Marineoffizier *m*

naval pow·er MIL Seemacht *f*

nave ARCH Mittel-, Hauptschiff *n*

na·vel ANAT Nabel *m* (*a. fig*)

nav·i·ga·ble schiffbar

nav·i·gate MAR befahren; AVIAT, MAR steuern, lenken

nav·i·ga·tion Schifffahrt *f*; AVIAT, MAR Navigation *f*

nav·i·ga·tor AVIAT, MAR Navigator *m*

na·vy (Kriegs)Marine *f*; Kriegsflotte *f*

na·vy blue Marineblau *n*

nay PARL Gegen-, Neinstimme *f*

Na·zi HIST POL *contp* Nazi *m*

Na·zism HIST POL *contp* Nazismus *m*

near 1. *adj* nahe; kurz; nahe (verwandt); *in the near future* in naher Zukunft; *be a near miss* knapp scheitern; **2.** *adv* nahe, in der Nähe (*a. near at hand*); nahe (bevorstehend) (*a. near at hand*); beinahe, fast; *near the station* etc in der Nähe des Bahnhofs *etc*; *near you* in deiner Nähe; **3.** *prp* nahe (*dat*), in der Nähe von (*or gen*); sich nähern, nahe kommen (*dat*)

near·by 1. *adj* nahe (gelegen); **2.** *adv* in der Nähe

near·ly beinahe, fast; annähernd

near·sight·ed kurzsichtig

neat ordentlich; sauber; gepflegt; pur (*whisky etc*)

neb·u·lous verschwommen

ne·ces·sar·i·ly notwendigerweise; *not necessarily* nicht unbedingt

ne·ces·sa·ry notwendig, nötig; unvermeidlich

ne·ces·si·tate erfordern, verlangen

ne·ces·si·ty Notwendigkeit *f*; (dringendes) Bedürfnis; Not *f*

neck 1. ANAT Hals *m* (*a. of bottle etc*); Genick *n*, Nacken *m*; *be neck and neck* F Kopf an Kopf liegen (*a. fig*); *be up to one's neck in debt* F bis zum Hals in Schulden stecken; **2.** F knutschen, schmusen

neck·er·chief Halstuch *n*

neck·lace Halskette *f*

neck·let Halskettchen n

neck·line Ausschnitt m

neck·tie Krawatte f, Schlips m

née: *née Smith* geborene Smith

need 1. (of, for) (dringendes) Bedürfnis (nach), Bedarf m (an dat); Notwendigkeit f; Mangel m (of, for an dat); Not f; be in need of s.th. et. dringend brauchen; in need in Not; in need of help hilfs-, hilfebedürftig; brauchen; v/aux brauchen, müssen

nee·dle 1. Nadel f (a. BOT, MED); Zeiger m; 2. F j-n aufziehen, hänseln

need·less unnötig, überflüssig

nee·dle·wom·an Näherin f

nee·dle·work Handarbeit f

need·y bedürftig, arm

ne·ga·tion Verneinung f

neg·a·tive 1. negativ; verneinend; 2. Verneinung f; PHOT Negativ n; answer in the negative verneinen

ne·glect 1. vernachlässigen; es versäumen (doing, to do zu tun); 2. Vernachlässigung f; Nachlässigkeit f

neg·li·gence Nachlässigkeit f, Unachtsamkeit f

neg·li·gent nachlässig, unachtsam; lässig, salopp

neg·li·gi·ble unbedeutend

ne·go·ti·ate verhandeln (über acc)

ne·go·ti·a·tion Verhandlung f

ne·go·ti·a·tor Unterhändler(in)

neigh zo 1. wiehern; 2. Wiehern n

neigh·bo(u)r Nachbar(in)

neigh·bo(u)r·hood Nachbarschaft f, Umgebung f

neigh·bo(u)r·ing benachbart, Nachbar..., angrenzend

neigh·bo(u)r·ly (gut)nachbarlich

nei·ther 1. adj and pron keine(r, -s) (von beiden); 2. cj neither ... nor weder ... noch

ne·on CHEM Neon n

neon lamp Neonlampe f

neon sign Neon-, Leuchtreklame f

neph·ew Neffe m

nep·o·tism contp Vetternwirtschaft f

nerd F Trottel m; Computerfreak m

nerve Nerv m; Mut m, Stärke f, Selbstbeherrschung f; F Frechheit f; get on s.o.'s nerves j-m auf die Nerven gehen or fallen; lose one's nerve den Mut or die Nerven verlieren; you've got a nerve! F Sie haben Nerven!

nerve·less kraftlos; mutlos; ohne Nerven, kaltblütig

ner·vous nervös; Nerven...

ner·vous·ness Nervosität f

nest 1. Nest n; 2. nisten

nes·tle (sich) schmiegen or kuscheln (against, on an acc); a. nestle down sich behaglich niederlassen, es sich bequem machen (in in dat)

net¹ 1. Netz n; net curtain Store m; 2. mit e-m Netz fangen or abdecken

net² 1. netto, Netto..., Rein...; 2. netto einbringen

Neth·er·lands die Niederlande pl

net·tle 1. BOT Nessel f; 2. F j-n ärgern

net·work Netz n (a. EDP), Netzwerk n; (Straßen- etc)Netz n; radio, TV Sendernetz n; be in the network EDP am Netz sein

neu·ro·sis MED Neurose f

neu·rot·ic MED 1. neurotisch; 2. Neurotiker(in)

neu·ter 1. LING sächlich; geschlechtslos; 2. LING Neutrum n

neu·tral 1. neutral; 2. Neutrale m, f; a. neutral gear MOT Leerlauf(stellung f) m

neu·tral·i·ty Neutralität f

neu·tral·ize neutralisieren

neu·tron PHYS Neutron n

nev·er nie, niemals

nev·er-end·ing endlos, nicht enden wollend, unendlich

nev·er·the·less nichtsdestoweniger, dennoch, trotzdem

new neu; frisch; unerfahren; nothing new nichts Neues

new·born neugeboren

new·com·er Neuankömmling m; Neuling m

new·ly kürzlich; neu

news Neuigkeit(en pl) f, Nachricht(en pl) f

news·a·gent Zeitungshändler(in)

news·boy Zeitungsjunge m, Zeitungsausträger m

news bul·le·tin Kurznachricht(en pl) f

news·cast radio, TV Nachrichtensendung f

news·cast·er radio, TV Nachrichtensprecher(in)

news deal·er Zeitungshändler(in)

news·flash radio, TV Kurzmeldung f

news·let·ter Rundschreiben n

news·pa·per Zeitung f

news·print Zeitungspapier n

news·read·er esp Br → newscaster

news·reel film: Wochenschau f

news·room Nachrichtenredaktion f

news·stand Zeitungskiosk m, -stand m

news·ven·dor esp Br Zeitungsverkäufer(in)

new year Neujahr n, das neue Jahr; New Year's Day Neujahrstag m; New Year's Eve Silvester(abend m) m, n

next 1. *adj* nächste(r, -s); **(the) next day** am nächsten Tag; **next door** nebenan; **next but one** übernächste(r, -s); **next to** gleich neben *or* nach; beinahe, fast *unmöglich etc*; **2.** *adv* als Nächste(r, -s); demnächst, das nächste Mal; **3.** *der, die, das* Nächste; → **kin**

next-door (von) nebenan

nib·ble *v/i* knabbern (**at** an *dat*); *v/t* Loch *etc* nagen, knabbern (**in** in *acc*)

nice nett, freundlich; hübsch, schön; *fig* fein (*detail etc*)

nice·ly gut, fein; genau, sorgfältig

ni·ce·ty Feinheit *f*; Genauigkeit *f*

niche Nische *f*

nick 1. Kerbe *f*; **in the nick of time** gerade noch rechtzeitig, im letzten Moment; **2.** (ein)kerben; *j-n* streifen (*bullet*); *Br* F *et.* klauen; *Br* F *j-n* schnappen

nick·el 1. MIN Nickel *n*; Fünfcentstück *n*; **2.** TECH vernickeln

nick-el-plate TECH vernickeln

nick-nack → **knick-knack**

nick·name 1. Spitzname *m*; **2.** *j-m* den Spitznamen … geben

niece Nichte *f*

nig·gard Geizhals *m*

nig·gard·ly geizig, knaus(e)rig; schäbig, kümmerlich

night Nacht *f*; Abend *m*; **at night, by night, in the night** in der Nacht, nachts

night-cap Schlummertrunk *m*

night-club Nachtklub *m*, Nachtlokal *n*

night-dress (Damen-, Kinder)Nachthemd *n*

night-fall: at nightfall bei Einbruch der Dunkelheit

night-gown → **nightdress**

night·ie F → **nightdress**

nigh·tin-gale *zo* Nachtigall *f*

night·ly (all)nächtlich; (all)abendlich; jede Nacht; jeden Abend

night-mare Albtraum *m* (*a. fig*)

night school Abendschule *f*

night shift Nachtschicht *f*

night-shirt (Herren)Nachthemd *n*

night-time: in the nighttime, at night-time nachts

night watch·man Nachtwächter *m*

night·y F → **nightdress**

nil Nichts *n*, Null *f*; **our team won two to nil** *or* **by two goals to nil** (2-0) unsere Mannschaft gewann zwei zu null (2:0)

nim-ble flink, gewandt; geistig beweglich

nine 1. neun *f*; **nine to five** normale Dienststunden (von 9-5); **a nine-to-five job** e-e (An)Stellung mit geregelter Arbeitszeit; **2.** Neun *f*

nine-pins Kegeln *n*

nine-teen 1. neunzehn; **2.** Neunzehn *f*

nine-teenth neunzehnte(r, -s)

nine-ti-eth neunzigste(r, -s)

nine-ty 1. neunzig; **2.** Neunzig *f*

ninth 1. neunte(r, -s); **2.** Neuntel *n*

ninth·ly neuntens

nip[1] 1. kneifen, zwicken; F flitzen, sausen; **nip off** abknipsen; **nip in the bud** *fig* im Keim ersticken; **2.** Kneifen *n*, Zwicken *n*; **it was nip and tuck** F es war ganz knapp; **there's a nip in the air today** heute ist es ganz schön kalt

nip[2] Schlückchen *n* (*of brandy etc*)

nip-per: (a pair of) nippers (e-e) (Kneif-)Zange *f*

nip-ple ANAT Brustwarze *f*; (Gummi-)Sauger *m*; TECH Nippel *m*

ni-ter, *Br* **ni-tre** CHEM Salpeter *m*

ni-tro-gen CHEM Stickstoff *m*

no 1. *adv* nein; nicht; **2.** *adj* kein(e); **no one** keiner, niemand; **in no time** im Nu, im Handumdrehen; **3.** Nein *n*

no·bil·i·ty (Hoch)Adel *m*; *fig* Adel *m*

no-ble adlig; edel, nobel; prächtig

no-ble-man Adlige *m*

no-ble-wom-an Adlige *f*

no-bod·y 1. niemand, keiner; **2.** *fig* Niemand *m*, Null *f*

no-cal-o-rie di-et Nulldiät *f*

noc-tur-nal nächtlich, Nacht…

nod 1. nicken (mit); **nod off** einnicken; **have a nodding acquaintance with s.o.** *j-n* flüchtig kennen; **2.** Nicken *n*

node BOT, MED Knoten *m*

noise 1. Krach *m*, Lärm *m*; Geräusch *n*; **2.** **noise about** (**abroad, around**) Gerücht *etc* verbreiten

noise-less geräuschlos

nois·y laut, geräuschvoll

no-mad Nomade *m*, Nomadin *f*

nom·i·nal nominell; **nominal value** ECON Nennwert *m*

nom·i·nate ernennen; nominieren, (zur Wahl) vorschlagen

nom·i·na·tion Ernennung *f*; Nominierung *f*

nom·i·na·tive *a.* **nominative case** LING Nominativ *m*, erster Fall

nom·i·nee Kandidat(in)

non… nicht…, Nicht…, un…

non-al·co·hol·ic alkoholfrei

non-a·ligned POL blockfrei

non-com·mis·sioned of·fi·cer MIL Unteroffizier *m*

non-com·mit·tal unverbindlich

non-con·duc·tor ELECTR Nichtleiter *m*

non-de·script nichtssagend; unauffällig

none 1. *pron* keine(r, -s), niemand; **2.** *adv* in keiner Weise, keineswegs

non·en·ti·ty *fig* Null *f*

none·the·less nichtsdestoweniger, dennoch, trotzdem

non·ex·ist·ence Nichtvorhandensein *n*, Fehlen *n*

non·ex·ist·ent nicht existierend

non·fic·tion Sachbücher *pl*

non·flam·ma·ble, non·in·flam·mable nicht brennbar

non·in·ter·fer·ence, non·in·ter·vention POL Nichteinmischung *f*

non·i·ron bügelfrei

no·non·sense nüchtern, sachlich

non·par·ti·san POL überparteilich; unparteiisch

non·pay·ment ECON Nicht(be)zahlung *f*

non·plus verblüffen

non·pol·lut·ing umweltfreundlich

non·prof·it, *Br* **non·prof·it·mak·ing** gemeinnützig

non·res·i·dent 1. nicht (orts)ansässig; nicht im Hause wohnend; **2.** Nichtansässige *m*, *f*; nicht im Hause Wohnende *m*, *f*

non·re·turn·a·ble Einweg...

nonreturnable bot·tle Einwegflasche *f*

non·sense Unsinn *m*, dummes Zeug

non·skid rutschfest, rutschsicher

non·smok·er Nichtraucher(in)

non·smok·ing Nichtraucher...

non·stick mit Antihaftbeschichtung

non·stop nonstop, ohne Unterbrechung; RAIL durchgehend; AVIAT ohne Zwischenlandung; **nonstop flight** *a.* Nonstop-Flug *m*

non·u·nion nicht (gewerkschaftlich) organisiert

non·vi·o·lence (Politik *f* der) Gewaltlosigkeit *f*

non·vi·o·lent gewaltlos

noo·dle Nudel *f*

nook Ecke *f*, Winkel *m*

noon Mittag(szeit *f*) *m*; **at noon** um 12 Uhr (mittags)

noose Schlinge *f*

nope F ne(e), nein

nor → **neither** 2; auch nicht

norm Norm *f*

nor·mal normal

nor·mal·ize (sich) normalisieren

north 1. Nord, Norden *m*; **2.** *adj* nördlich, Nord...; **3.** *adv* nach Norden, nordwärts

north·east 1. Nordost, Nordosten *m*; **2.** *a.* **northeastern** nordöstlich

nor·ther·ly, nor·thern Nord..., nördlich

North Pole Nordpol *m*

north·ward(s) *adv* nördlich, nach Norden

north·west 1. Nordwest, Nordwesten *m*; **2.** *a.* **northwestern** nordwestlich

Nor·way Norwegen *n*

Nor·we·gian 1. norwegisch; **2.** Norweger(in); LING Norwegisch *n*

nose 1. Nase *f*; ZO Schnauze *f*; *fig* Gespür *n*; **2.** *Auto etc* vorsichtig fahren; *a.* **nose about, nose around** *fig* F herumschnüffeln (in *dat*) (**for** nach)

nose·bleed Nasenbluten *n*; **have a nose-bleed** Nasenbluten haben

nose·dive AVIAT Sturzflug *m*

nos·ey → **nosy**

nos·tal·gia Nostalgie *f*

nos·tril ANAT Nasenloch *n*, *esp* ZO Nüster *f*

nos·y F neugierig

not nicht; **not a** kein(e)

no·ta·ble bemerkenswert; beachtlich

no·ta·ry *mst* **notary public** Notar *m*

notch 1. Kerbe *f*; GEOL Engpass *m*; **2.** (ein)kerben

note (*mst pl*) Notiz *f*, Aufzeichnung *f*; Anmerkung *f*; Vermerk *m*; Briefchen *n*, Zettel *m*; (diplomatische) Note; Banknote *f*, Geldschein *m*; MUS Note *f*; *fig* Ton *m*; **take notes (of)** sich Notizen machen (über *acc*)

note·book Notizbuch *n*; EDP Notebook *n*

not·ed bekannt, berühmt (**for** wegen)

note·pa·per Briefpapier *n*

note·wor·thy bemerkenswert

noth·ing nichts; **nothing but** nichts als, nur; **nothing much** F nicht viel; **for nothing** umsonst; **to say nothing of** ganz zu schweigen von; **there is nothing like** es geht nichts über (*acc*)

no·tice 1. Ankündigung *f*, Bekanntgabe *f*, Mitteilung *f*, Anzeige *f*; Kündigung(sfrist) *f*; Beachtung *f*; **give or hand in one's notice** kündigen (**to** bei); **give s.o. notice** j-m kündigen; **give s.o. notice to quit** j-m kündigen; **at six months' notice** mit halbjährlicher Kündigungsfrist; **take (no) notice of** (keine) Notiz nehmen von, (nicht) beachten; **at short notice** kurzfristig; **until further notice** bis auf weiteres; **without notice** fristlos; **2.** (es) bemerken; (besonders) beachten *or* achten auf (*acc*)

no·tice·a·ble erkennbar, wahrnehmbar; bemerkenswert

no·tice·board *Br* schwarzes Brett

no·ti·fy *et.* anzeigen, melden, mitteilen; *j-n* benachrichtigen

no·tion Begriff *m*, Vorstellung *f*; Idee *f*

no·tions Kurzwaren *pl*

no·to·ri·ous berüchtigt (**for** für)

not·with·stand·ing trotz (*gen*)

nought *Br:* **0.4 (nought point four)** 0,4

noun LING Substantiv *n*, Hauptwort *n*

nour·ish (er)nähren; *fig* hegen

nour·ish·ing nahrhaft

nour·ish·ment Ernährung f; Nahrung f

Nov ABBR of *November* Nov., November m

nov·el 1. Roman m; 2. (ganz) neu(artig)

nov·el·ist Romanschriftsteller(in)

no·vel·la Novelle f

nov·el·ty Neuheit f

No·vem·ber (ABBR *Nov*) November m

nov·ice Anfänger(in), Neuling m; REL Novize m, Novizin f

now 1. adv nun, jetzt; *now and again*, (*every*) *now and then* von Zeit zu Zeit, dann und wann; *by now* inzwischen; *from now* (*on*) von jetzt an; *just now* gerade eben; 2. cj a. *now that* nun da

now·a·days heutzutage

no·where nirgends

nox·ious schädlich

noz·zle TECH Schnauze f; Stutzen m; Düse f; Zapfpistole f

nu·ance Nuance f

nub springender Punkt

nu·cle·ar Kern…, Atom…, atomar, nuklear, Nuklear…

nuclear en·er·gy PHYS Atomenergie f, Kernenergie f

nuclear fam·i·ly Kern-, Kleinfamilie f

nuclear fis·sion PHYS Kernspaltung f

nu·cle·ar-free atomwaffenfrei

nu·cle·ar fu·sion PHYS Kernfusion f

nuclear phys·ics Kernphysik f

nuclear pow·er PHYS Atomkraft f, Kernkraft f

nu·cle·ar-pow·ered atomgetrieben

nu·cle·ar pow·er plant ELECTR Atomkraftwerk n, Kernkraftwerk n

nuclear re·ac·tor PHYS Atomreaktor m, Kernreaktor m

nuclear war Atomkrieg m

nuclear war·head MIL Atomsprengkopf m

nuclear waste Atommüll m

nuclear weap·ons MIL Atomwaffen pl, Kernwaffen pl

nu·cle·us BIOL, PHYS Kern m (a. fig)

nude 1. nackt; 2. art: Akt m

nudge 1. j-n anstoßen, (an)stupsen; 2. Stups(er) m

nug·get (esp Gold)Klumpen m

nui·sance Plage f, Ärgernis n; Nervensäge f, Quälgeist m; *what a nuisance!* wie

ärgerlich!; *be a nuisance to s.o.* j-m lästig fallen, F j-n nerven; *make a nuisance of o.s.* den Leuten auf die Nerven gehen or fallen

nukes F Atom-, Kernwaffen pl

null: *null and void* esp JUR null und nichtig

numb 1. starr (*with* vor), taub; fig wie betäubt (*with* vor); 2. starr or taub machen

num·ber 1. Zahl f, Ziffer f; Nummer f; (An)Zahl f; Ausgabe f; (Bus- etc)Linie f; *sorry, wrong number* TEL falsch verbunden!; 2. nummerieren; zählen; sich belaufen auf (acc)

num·ber·less zahllos

num·ber·plate esp Br MOT Nummernschild n

nu·me·ral Ziffer f; LING Zahlwort n

nu·me·ra·tor MATH Zähler m

nu·me·rous zahlreich

nun REL Nonne f

nun·ne·ry REL Nonnenkloster n

nurse 1. (Kranken-, Säuglings)Schwester f; Kindermädchen n; (Kranken-)Pflegerin f; → *male nurse*; a. *wet nurse* Amme f; 2. stillen; pflegen; hegen; als Krankenschwester or -pfleger arbeiten; *nurse s.o. back to health* j-n gesund pflegen

nur·se·ry Tagesheim n, Tagesstätte f; Baum-, Pflanzschule f

nursery rhyme Kinderlied n, Kinderreim m

nursery school Br Vorschule f

nursery slope skiing: F Idiotenhügel m

nurs·ing Stillen n; (Kranken)Pflege f

nursing bot·tle (Saug)Flasche f

nursing home Pflegeheim n

nut BOT Nuss f; TECH (Schrauben)Mutter f; F verrückter Kerl; F Birne f (head); *be off one's nut* F spinnen

nut·crack·er(s) Nussknacker m

nut·meg BOT Muskatnuss f

nu·tri·ent 1. Nährstoff m; 2. nahrhaft

nu·tri·tion Ernährung f

nu·tri·tious, nu·tri·tive nahrhaft

nut·shell Nussschale f; (*to put it*) *in a nutshell* F kurz gesagt, mit e-m Wort

nut·ty voller Nüsse; Nuss…; F verrückt

ny·lon Nylon n

nylon stock·ings Nylonstrümpfe pl

nymph Nymphe f

N

O

O, o O, o *n*
o Null *f*
oaf Lümmel *m*, Flegel *m*
oak BOT Eiche *f*
oar Ruder *n*
oars·man SPORT Ruderer *m*
oars·wom·an SPORT Ruderin *f*
o·a·sis Oase *f* (*a. fig*)
oath Eid *m*, Schwur *m*; Fluch *m*; *take an oath* e-n Eid leisten *or* schwören; *be on or under oath* JUR unter Eid stehen; *take the oath* JUR schwören
oat·meal Hafermehl *n*, Hafergrütze *f*
oats BOT Hafer *m*; *sow one's wild oats* sich die Hörner abstoßen
o·be·di·ence Gehorsam *m*
o·be·di·ent gehorsam
o·bese fett, fettleibig
o·bes·i·ty Fettleibigkeit *f*
o·bey gehorchen (*dat*), folgen (*dat*); Befehl *etc* befolgen
o·bit·u·a·ry Nachruf *m*; *a.* **obituary notice** Todesanzeige *f*
ob·ject 1. Objekt *n* (*a.* LING); Gegenstand *m*; Ziel *n*, Zweck *m*, Absicht *f*; 2. einwenden; *et.* dagegen haben
ob·jec·tion Einwand *m*, Einspruch *m* (*a.* JUR)
ob·jec·tion·a·ble nicht einwandfrei; unangenehm; anstößig
ob·jec·tive 1. objektiv, sachlich; 2. Ziel *n*
ob·jec·tive·ness Objektivität *f*
ob·li·ga·tion Verpflichtung *f*; *be under an obligation to s.o.* j-m (zu Dank) verpflichtet sein; *be under an obligation to do* verpflichtet sein, *et.* zu tun
ob·lig·a·to·ry verpflichtend, verbindlich
o·blige nötigen, zwingen; (zu Dank) verpflichten; *oblige s.o.* j-m e-n Gefallen tun; *much obliged* besten Dank
o·blig·ing entgegenkommend, gefällig
o·blique schief, schräg; *fig* indirekt
o·blit·er·ate auslöschen; vernichten, völlig zerstören; verdecken
o·bliv·i·on Vergessen(heit *f*) *n*; *fall into oblivion* in Vergessenheit geraten
o·bliv·i·ous: *be oblivious of or to s.th.* sich e-r Sache nicht bewusst sein; *et.* nicht bemerken *or* wahrnehmen
ob·long rechteckig; länglich
ob·nox·ious widerlich
ob·scene obszön, unanständig
ob·scure 1. dunkel, *fig a.* unklar; unbekannt; 2. verdunkeln, verdecken

ob·scu·ri·ty Unbekanntheit *f*; Unklarheit *f*
ob·se·quies Trauerfeier(lichkeiten *pl*) *f*
ob·ser·va·ble wahrnehmbar, merklich
ob·ser·vance Beachtung *f*, Befolgung *f*
ob·ser·vant aufmerksam
ob·ser·va·tion Beobachtung *f*, Überwachung *f*; Bemerkung *f* (**on** über *acc*)
ob·ser·va·to·ry Observatorium *n*, Sternwarte *f*
ob·serve beobachten; überwachen; *Vorschrift etc* beachten, befolgen, einhalten; bemerken, äußern
ob·serv·er Beobachter(in)
ob·sess: *be obsessed by or with* besessen sein von
ob·ses·sion PSYCH Besessenheit *f*, fixe Idee, Zwangsvorstellung *f*
ob·ses·sive PSYCH zwanghaft
ob·so·lete veraltet
ob·sta·cle Hindernis *n*
ob·sti·na·cy Starrsinn *m*
ob·sti·nate hartnäckig; halsstarrig, eigensinnig, starrköpfig
ob·struct verstopfen, versperren; blockieren; behindern
ob·struc·tion Verstopfung *f*; Blockierung *f*; Behinderung *f*
ob·struc·tive blockierend; hinderlich
ob·tain erhalten, bekommen, sich *et.* beschaffen
ob·tain·a·ble erhältlich
ob·tru·sive aufdringlich
ob·tuse MATH stumpf; *fig* begriffsstutzig; *be obtuse* sich dumm stellen
ob·vi·ous offensichtlich, klar, einleuchtend
oc·ca·sion Gelegenheit *f*; Anlass *m*; Veranlassung *f*; (festliches) Ereignis; *on the occasion of* anlässlich (*gen*)
oc·ca·sion·al gelegentlich; vereinzelt
oc·ca·sion·al·ly gelegentlich, manchmal
Oc·ci·dent der Westen, der Okzident, das Abendland
oc·ci·den·tal abendländisch, westlich
oc·cu·pant Bewohner(in); Insasse *m*, Insassin *f*
oc·cu·pa·tion Beruf *m*; Beschäftigung *f*; MIL, POL Besetzung *f*, Besatzung *f*, Okkupation *f*
oc·cu·py in Besitz nehmen, MIL, POL besetzen; *Raum* einnehmen; in Anspruch nehmen; beschäftigen; *be occupied* bewohnt sein; besetzt sein (*seat*)

oc·cur sich ereignen; vorkommen; *it occurred to me that* es fiel mir ein *or* mir kam der Gedanke, dass

oc·cur·rence Vorkommen *n*; Ereignis *n*; Vorfall *m*

o·cean Ozean *m*, (Welt)Meer *n*

o'clock: (*at*) *five o'clock* (um) fünf Uhr

Oct ABBR *of* **October** Okt., Oktober *m*

Oc·to·ber (ABBR *Oct*) Oktober *m*

oc·u·lar Augen...

oc·u·list Augenarzt *m*, Augenärztin *f*

OD F *v/i:* *OD on heroin* an e-r Überdosis Heroin sterben

odd sonderbar, seltsam, merkwürdig; einzeln, Einzel...; ungerade (*number*); gelegentlich, Gelegenheits...; *odd jobs* Gelegenheitsarbeiten *pl*; F *30 odd* (et.) über 30, einige 30

odds (Gewinn)Chancen *pl*; *the odds are 10 to 1* die Chancen stehen 10 zu 1; *the odds are that* es ist sehr wahrscheinlich, dass; *against all odds* wider Erwarten, entgegen allen Erwartungen; *be at odds* uneins sein (*with* mit); *odds and ends* Krimskrams *m*

odds-on hoch, klar (*favorite*), aussichtsreichst (*candidate etc*); F *it's odds-on that* es steht ganz so aus, als ob ...

ode Ode *f*

o·do(u)r Geruch *m*

o·do(u)r·less geruchlos

of *prp* *origin*: von, aus; *material*: aus; um (*cheat s.o. of s.th.* j-n um et. betrügen); *cause*: an (*dat*) (*die of s.th.* sterben an); aus (*be afraid of* Angst haben vor); auf (*acc*) (*be proud of* stolz sein auf); über (*acc*) (*be glad of* sich freuen über); nach (*smell of* riechen nach); von, über (*acc*) (*speak of s.th.* von *or* über et. sprechen); an (*acc*) (*think of s.th.* an et. denken); *the city of London* die Stadt London; *the works of Dickens* Dickens' Werke; *your letter of ...* Ihr Schreiben vom ...; *five minutes of twelve* fünf Minuten vor zwölf

off 1. *adv* fort(...), weg(...); ab(...), ab, abgegangen (*button etc*); weg, entfernt (*3 miles off*); ELECTR *etc* aus(...), aus-, abgeschaltet; TECH zu; aus(gegangen), alle, aus, vorbei, verdorben (*food*); frei; *I must be off* ich muss gehen *or* weg; *off with you!* fort mit dir!; *be off* ausfallen, nicht stattfinden; *10% off* ECON 10% Nachlass; *off and on* ab und zu, hin und wieder; *take a day off* sich e-n Tag freinehmen; *be well* (*badly*) *off* gut (schlecht) d(a)ran *or* gestellt *or* situiert sein; **2.** *prp* fort von, weg von, von (...,

ab, weg, herunter); abseits von (*or gen*); von ... weg; MAR vor *der Küste etc*; *be off duty* nicht im Dienst sein, dienstfrei haben; *be off smoking* nicht mehr rauchen; **3.** *adj* frei, arbeits-, dienstfrei; *fig* *have an off day* e-n schlechten Tag haben

of·fal GASTR Innereien *pl*

off-col·o(u)r schlüpfrig, zweideutig

of·fence *Br →* **offense**

of·fend beleidigen, kränken; verstoßen (*against* gegen)

of·fend·er (Übel-, Misse)Täter(in); *first offender* JUR nicht Vorbestrafte *m, f,* Erstäter(in)

of·fense Vergehen *n*, Verstoß *m*; JUR Straftat *f*; Beleidigung *f*, Kränkung *f*; *take offense* Anstoß nehmen (*at* an *dat*)

of·fen·sive 1. beleidigend, anstößig; widerlich (*smell etc*); MIL Offensiv..., Angriffs...; **2.** MIL Offensive *f* (*a. fig*)

of·fer 1. *v/t* anbieten (*a.* ECON); Preis, Möglichkeit bieten; Preis, Belohnung aussetzen; sich bereit erklären (*to do* zu tun); *Widerstand* leisten; *v/i* es *or* sich anbieten; **2.** Angebot *n*

off·hand 1. *adj* lässig; Stegreif...; *be offhand with s.o.* F mit j-m kurz angebunden sein; **2.** *adv* auf Anhieb, so ohne weiteres

of·fice Büro *n*, Geschäftsstelle *f*, (*Anwalts*)Kanzlei *f*; *(esp* öffentliches) Amt, Posten *m*; *mst* **Office** *esp Br* Ministerium *n*

office block *Br*, **office build·ing** Bürohaus *n*

office hours Dienstzeit *f*; Geschäfts-, Öffnungszeiten *pl*

of·fi·cer MIL Offizier *m*; (*Polizei- etc*)Beamte *m*, (-)Beamtin *f*

of·fi·cial 1. Beamte *m*, Beamtin *f*; **2.** offiziell, amtlich, dienstlich

of·fi·ci·ate amtieren

of·fi·cious übereifrig

off-licence *Br* Wein- und Spirituosenhandlung *f*

off-line EDP offline, Offline-..., rechnerunabhängig

off-peak: *off-peak electricity* Nachtstrom *m*; *off-peak hours* verkehrsschwache Stunden *pl*

off sea·son Nebensaison *f*

off·set ECON ausgleichen; verrechnen (*against* mit)

off·shoot BOT Ableger *m*, Spross *m*

off·shore vor der Küste

off·side SPORT abseits; *offside position* Abseitsposition *f*, Abseitsstellung *f*; *offside trap* Abseitsfalle *f*

off·spring Nachkomme *m*, Nachkommenschaft *f*

off-the-peg *Br*, **off-the-rack** Konfektions..., ... von der Stange

off-the-rec·ord inoffiziell

of·ten oft(mals), häufig

oh *int* oh!

oil 1. Öl *n*; Erdöl *n*; 2. (ein)ölen, schmieren (*a. fig*)

oil change MOT Ölwechsel *m*

oil·cloth Wachstuch *n*

oil·field Ölfeld *n*

oil paint·ing Ölmalerei *f*; Ölgemälde *n*

oil pan MOT Ölwanne *f*

oil plat·form → *oilrig*

oil pol·lu·tion Ölpest *f*

oil pro·duc·tion Ölförderung *f*

oil-pro·duc·ing coun·try Ölförderland *n*

oil re·fin·e·ry Erdölraffinerie *f*

oil-rig Bohrinsel *f*

oil·skins Ölzeug *n*

oil slick Ölteppich *m*

oil well Ölquelle *f*

oil·y ölig; *fig* schmierig, schleimig

oint·ment Salbe *f*

OK, o·kay F 1. *adj and int* okay(!), o.k.(!), in Ordnung(!); 2. genehmigen, *e-r Sache* zustimmen; 3. Okay *n*, O.K. *n*, Genehmigung *f*, Zustimmung *f*

old 1. alt; 2. *the old* die Alten *pl*

old age (hohes) Alter

old age pen·sion Rente *f*, Pension *f*

old age pen·sion·er Rentner(in), Pensionär(in)

old-fash·ioned altmodisch

old·ish ältlich

old peo·ple's home Altersheim *n*, Altenheim *n*

ol·ive BOT Olive *f*; Olivgrün *n*

O·lym·pic Games SPORT Olympische Spiele *pl*

om·i·nous unheilvoll

o·mis·sion Auslassung *f*; Unterlassung *f*; Versäumnis *n*

o·mit auslassen, weglassen; unterlassen

om·nip·o·tent allmächtig

om·nis·ci·ent allwissend

on 1. *prp* auf (*acc or dat*) (*on the table* auf dem *or* den Tisch); an (*dat*) (*on the wall* an der Wand); in (*on TV* im Fernsehen); *direction, target:* auf (*acc*) ... (hin), an (*acc*), nach (*dat*) ... (hin) (*march on London* nach London marschieren); *fig* auf (*acc*) ... (hin) (*on demand* auf Anfrage); *time:* an (*dat*) (*on Sunday* am Sonntag; *on the 1st of April* am 1. April); (gleich) nach, bei (*on his arrival*); *gehörig zu*, beschäftigt bei (*be on a committee* e-m Ausschuss angehören); *be on the "Daily*

Mail" bei der "Daily Mail" beschäftigt sein); *state:* in (*dat*), auf (*dat*) (*on duty* im Dienst; *be on fire* in Flammen stehen); *subject:* über (*acc*) (*talk on a subject* über ein Thema sprechen); nach (*dat*) (*on this model* nach diesem Modell); von (*dat*) (*live on s.th.* von et. leben); *on the street* auf der Straße; *on a train* in e-m Zug; *on hearing this* als ich *etc* es hörte; *have you any money on you?* hast du Geld bei dir'?; 2. *adj and adv* an (-geschaltet) (*light etc*), eingeschaltet (*radio etc*), auf (*faucet etc*), (dar)auf(*legen, -schrauben etc*); an(*haben, -ziehen*) (*have a coat on* e-n Mantel anhaben); auf (*-behalten*) (*keep one's hat on* den Hut aufbehalten); weiter(*gehen, -sprechen etc*); *and so on* und so weiter; *on and on* immer weiter; *from this day on* von dem Tage an; *be on* THEA gegeben werden; *film:* laufen; *radio*, TV gesendet werden; *what's on?* was ist los?

once 1. einmal; einst; *once again, once more* noch einmal; *once in a while* ab und zu, hin und wieder; *once and for all* ein für alle Mal; *not once* kein einziges Mal, keinmal; *at once* sofort; auf einmal, gleichzeitig; *all at once* plötzlich; *for once* diesmal, ausnahmsweise; *this once* dieses eine Mal; *once upon a time there was ...* es war einmal ...; 2. sobald

one ein(e); einzig; man; Eins *f*, eins; *one's* sein(e); *one day* eines Tages; *one Smith* ein gewisser Smith; *one another* (gegenseitig), einander; *one by one, one after another, one after the other* e-r nach dem andern; *I for one* ich zum Beispiel; *the little ones* die Kleinen *pl*

one-horse town F *contp* Nest *n*

one·self sich (selbst); sich selbst; (*all*) *by oneself* ganz allein; *to oneself* ganz für sich (allein)

one-sid·ed einseitig

one-time ehemalig, früher

one-track mind: *have a one-track mind* immer nur dasselbe im Kopf haben

one-two *soccer:* Doppelpass *m*

one-way Einbahn...

one-way street Einbahnstraße *f*

one-way tick·et RAIL *etc* einfache Fahrkarte, AVIAT einfaches Ticket

one-way traf·fic MOT Einbahnverkehr *m*

on·ion BOT Zwiebel *f*

on-line EDP online, Online..., rechnerabhängig

on·look·er Zuschauer(in)

on·ly 1. *adj* einzige(r, -s); 2. *adv* nur, bloß; erst; *only yesterday* erst gestern; 3. *cj* F nur, bloß

on·rush Ansturm m

on·set Beginn m; MED Ausbruch m

on·slaught (heftiger) Angriff (a. fig)

on·to auf (acc)

on·ward(s) adv vorwärts, weiter; **from now onward** von nun an

ooze v/i sickern; **ooze away** fig schwinden; v/t absondern; fig ausstrahlen, verströmen

o·paque undurchsichtig; fig unverständlich

o·pen 1. offen, a. geöffnet, a. frei (country etc); öffentlich; fig offen, a. unentschieden, a. freimütig; fig zugänglich, aufgeschlossen (**to** für or dat); **open all day** durchgehend geöffnet; **in the open air** im Freien; **2.** golf, tennis: offenes Turnier; **in the open** im Freien; **come out into the open** fig an die Öffentlichkeit treten; **3.** v/t öffnen, aufmachen, Buch etc a. aufschlagen; eröffnen; v/i sich öffnen, aufgehen; öffnen, aufmachen (store); anfangen, beginnen; **open into** führen nach or in (acc); **open onto** hinausgehen auf (acc)

o·pen-air im Freien

o·pen-end·ed zeitlich unbegrenzt

o·pen·er (Dosen- etc)Öffner m

o·pen-eyed mit großen Augen, staunend

o·pen-hand·ed freigebig, großzügig

o·pen-heart·ed offenherzig

o·pen·ing 1. Öffnung f; ECON freie Stelle; Eröffnung f, Erschließung f, Einstieg m; **2.** Eröffnungs...; Öffnungs...

o·pen-mind·ed aufgeschlossen

o·pen·ness Offenheit f

op·e·ra Oper f

opera glass·es Opernglas n

opera house Opernhaus n, Oper f

op·e·rate v/i wirksam sein or werden; TECH arbeiten, in Betrieb sein, laufen (machine etc); MED operieren (**on s.o.** j-n); v/t Maschine bedienen, Schalter etc betätigen; Unternehmen, Geschäft betreiben, führen

op·e·rat·ing room Operationssaal m

operating sys·tem EDP Betriebssystem n

operating thea·tre Br MED Operationssaal m

op·e·ra·tion TECH Betrieb m, Lauf m; Bedienung f; ECON Tätigkeit f, Unternehmen n; MED, MIL Operation f; **in operation** TECH in Betrieb; **have an operation** MED operiert werden

op·e·ra·tive wirksam; MED operativ

op·e·ra·tor TECH Bedienungsperson f; EDP Operator m; TEL Vermittlung f

o·pin·ion Meinung f, Ansicht f; Gutach-

ten n (**on** über acc); **in my opinion** meines Erachtens

op·po·nent Gegner(in)

op·por·tune günstig, passend; rechtzeitig

op·por·tu·ni·ty (günstige) Gelegenheit

op·pose sich widersetzen (dat)

op·posed entgegengesetzt; **be opposed to** gegen ... sein

op·po·site 1. Gegenteil n, Gegensatz m; **2.** adj gegenüberliegend; entgegengesetzt; **3.** adv gegenüber (**to** dat); **4.** prp gegenüber (dat)

op·po·si·tion Widerstand m, Opposition f (a. PARL); Gegensatz m

op·press unterdrücken

op·pres·sion Unterdrückung f

op·pres·sive (be)drückend; hart, grausam; schwül (weather)

op·tic Augen..., Seh...; → **op·ti·cal** optisch

op·ti·cian Optiker(in)

op·ti·mism Optimismus m

op·ti·mist Optimist(in)

op·ti·mis·tic optimistisch

op·tion Wahl f; ECON Option f, Vorkaufsrecht n; MOT Extra n

op·tion·al freiwillig; Wahl...; **be an optional extra** MOT gegen Aufpreis erhältlich sein

optional sub·ject PED etc Wahlfach n

or oder; **or else** sonst

o·ral mündlich; Mund...

or·ange 1. BOT Orange f, Apfelsine f; **2.** orange(farben)

or·ange·ade Orangenlimonade f

o·ra·tion Rede f, Ansprache f

o·ra·tor Redner(in)

or·bit 1. Kreisbahn f, Umlaufbahn f; **get or put into orbit** in e-e Umlaufbahn gelangen or bringen; **2.** v/t die Erde etc umkreisen; v/i die Erde etc umkreisen, sich auf e-r Umlaufbahn bewegen

or·chard Obstgarten m

or·ches·tra MUS Orchester n; THEA Parkett n

or·chid BOT Orchidee f

or·dain: ordain s.o. (priest) j-n zum Priester weihen

or·deal Qual f, Tortur f

or·der 1. Ordnung f; Reihenfolge f; Befehl m, Anordnung f; ECON Bestellung f, Auftrag m; PARL etc (Geschäfts)Ordnung f; REL etc Orden m; **order to pay** ECON Zahlungsanweisung f; **in order to** inf um zu inf; **out of order** TECH nicht in Ordnung, defekt; außer Betrieb; **make to order** auf Bestellung or nach Maß anfertigen; **2.** v/t j-m befehlen (**to do** zu tun), et. befehlen, anordnen; j-n schicken, beordern; MED *j-m et.* verordnen; ECON bestellen; *fig* ordnen, in Ordnung bringen; *v/i* bestellen (*in restaurant*)

or·der·ly 1. ordentlich; *fig* gesittet, friedlich; 2. MED Hilfspfleger *m*

or·di·nal *a.* **ordinal number** MATH Ordnungszahl *f*

or·di·nar·y üblich, gewöhnlich, normal

ore MIN Erz *n*

or·gan ANAT Organ *n* (*a. fig*); MUS Orgel *f*

organ do·nor MED Organspender *m*

organ grind·er Leierkastenmann *m*

organ re·cip·i·ent MED Organempfänger *m*

or·gan·ic organisch

or·gan·ism Organismus *m*

or·gan·i·za·tion Organisation *f*

or·gan·ize organisieren; sich (gewerkschaftlich) organisieren

or·gan·iz·er Organisator(in)

or·gasm Orgasmus *m*

o·ri·ent 1. **Orient** der Osten, der Orient, das Morgenland; 2. orientieren

o·ri·en·tal 1. orientalisch, östlich; 2. **Oriental** Orientale *m*, Orientalin *f*

o·ri·en·tate orientieren

or·i·gin Ursprung *m*, Abstammung *f*, Herkunft *f*

o·rig·i·nal 1. ursprünglich; Original...; originell; 2. Original *n*

o·rig·i·nal·i·ty Originalität *f*

o·rig·i·nal·ly ursprünglich; originell

o·rig·i·nate *v/t* schaffen, ins Leben rufen; *v/i* zurückgehen (*from* auf *acc*), (her)stammen (*from* von, aus)

or·na·ment 1. Ornament(e *pl*) *n*, Verzierung(en *pl*) *f*, Schmuck *m*; *fig* Zier(de) *f* (*to* für *or* gen); 2. verzieren, schmücken (*with* mit)

or·na·men·tal dekorativ, schmückend, Zier...

or·nate *fig* überladen

or·phan 1. Waise *f*, Waisenkind *n*; 2. **be orphaned** Waise werden

or·phan·age Waisenhaus *n*

or·tho·dox orthodox

os·cil·late PHYS schwingen; *fig* schwanken (**between** zwischen *dat*)

os·prey ZO Fischadler *m*

os·ten·si·ble angeblich, vorgeblich

os·ten·ta·tion (protzige) Zurschaustellung; Protzerei *f*, Prahlerei *f*

os·ten·ta·tious protzend, prahlerisch

os·tra·cize ächten

os·trich ZO Strauß *m*

oth·er andere(r, -s); **the other day** neulich; **the other morning** neulich morgens; **every other day** jeden zweiten Tag, alle zwei Tage

oth·er·wise anders; sonst

ot·ter ZO Otter *m*

ought *v/aux* ich sollte, *du* solltest *etc*; **you ought to have done it** Sie hätten es tun sollen

ounce Unze *f* (*28,35 g*)

our unser

ours unsere(r, -s)

our·selves wir *or* uns selbst; uns (selbst)

oust verdrängen, hinauswerfen (**from** aus); *j-n s-s Amtes* entheben

out 1. *adv, adj* aus; hinaus(*gehen, -werfen etc*); heraus(*kommen etc*); aus(*brechen etc*); draußen, im Freien; nicht zu Hause; SPORT aus, draußen; aus, erloschen; ausverkauft; F **out**, aus der Mode; **out of** aus (... heraus); zu ... hinaus; außerhalb von (*or* gen); außer *Reichweite etc*; außer *Atem, Übung etc*; (hergestellt) aus; aus *Furcht etc*; **be out of bread** kein Brot mehr haben; **in nine out of ten cases** in neun von zehn Fällen; 2. *prp* F aus (... heraus); zu ... hinaus; 3. **outen**

out·bal·ance überwiegen

out·bid überbieten

out·board mo·tor Außenbordmotor *m*

out·break MED, MIL Ausbruch *m*

out·build·ing Nebengebäude *n*

out·burst *fig* Ausbruch *m*

out·cast 1. ausgestoßen; 2. Ausgestoßene *m, f*, Verstoßene *m, f*

out·come Ergebnis *n*

out·cry Aufschrei *m*, Schrei *m* der Entrüstung

out·dat·ed überholt, veraltet

out·dis·tance hinter sich lassen

out·do übertreffen

out·door *adj* im Freien, draußen

out·doors *adv* draußen, im Freien

out·er äußere(r, -s)

out·er·most äußerste(r, -s)

out·er space Weltraum *m*

out·fit Ausrüstung *f*, Ausstattung *f*; Kleidung *f*; F (Arbeits)Gruppe *f*

out·fit·ter Ausstatter *m*; **men's outfitter** Herrenausstatter *m*

out·go·ing (aus dem Amt) scheidend

out·grow herauswachsen aus (*dat*); *Angewohnheit etc* ablegen; größer werden als

out·house Nebengebäude *n*

out·ing Ausflug *m*; Outing *n*

out·land·ish befremdlich, sonderbar

out·last überdauern, überleben

out·law HIST Geächtete *m, f*

out·lay (Geld)Auslagen *pl*, Ausgaben *pl*

out·let Abfluss *m*, Abzug *m*; *fig* Ventil *n*

out·line 1. Umriss *m*; Überblick *m*; 2. umreißen, skizzieren

out·live überleben

out·look (Aus)Blick m, (Aus)Sicht f; Einstellung f, Auffassung f

out·ly·ing abgelegen, entlegen

out·num·ber in der Überzahl sein; *be outnumbered by s.o.* j-m zahlenmäßig unterlegen sein

out-of-date veraltet, überholt

out-of-the-way abgelegen, entlegen; *fig* ungewöhnlich

out·pa·tient MED ambulanter Patient, ambulante Patientin

out·post Vorposten m

out·pour·ing (Gefühls)Erguss m

out·put ECON Output m, Produktion f, Ausstoß m, Ertrag m; EDP (Daten-)Ausgabe f

out·rage 1. Gewalttat f, Verbrechen n; Empörung f; **2.** grob verletzen; j-n empören

out·ra·geous abscheulich; empörend, unerhört

out·right 1. adj völlig, gänzlich, glatt (*lie etc*); **2.** adv auf der Stelle, sofort; ohne Umschweife

out·run schneller laufen als; *fig* übersteigen, übertreffen

out·set Anfang m, Beginn m

out·shine überstrahlen, *fig a.* in den Schatten stellen

out·side 1. Außenseite f; SPORT Außenstürmer(in); *at the (very) outside* (aller-)höchstens; *outside left (right)* SPORT Linksaußen (Rechtsaußen) m; **2.** adj äußere(r, -s), Außen...; **3.** adv draußen; heraus, hinaus; **4.** prp außerhalb

out·sid·er Außenseiter(in)

out·size 1. Übergröße f; **2.** übergroß

out·skirts Stadtrand m, Außenbezirke pl

out·spo·ken offen, freimütig

out·spread ausgestreckt, ausgebreitet

out·stand·ing hervorragend; ECON ausstehend; ungeklärt (*problem*); unerledigt (*work*)

out·stay länger bleiben als; → *welcome 4*

out·stretched ausgestreckt

out·strip überholen; *fig* übertreffen

out tray: *in the out tray* im Postausgang *etc*

out·vote überstimmen

out·ward 1. äußere(r, -s); äußerlich; **2.** adv *mst* **outwards** auswärts, nach außen

out·ward·ly äußerlich

out·weigh *fig* überwiegen

out·wit überlisten, F reinlegen

out·worn veraltet, überholt

o·val 1. oval; **2.** Oval n

o·va·tion Ovation f; *give s.o. a standing ovation* j-m stehende Ovationen bereiten, j-m stehend Beifall klatschen

ov·en Backofen m, Bratofen m

ov·en-read·y bratfertig

o·ver 1. prp über; über (*acc*), über (*acc*) ... (hin)weg; über (*dat*), auf der anderen Seite von (*or gen*); über (*acc*), mehr als; **2.** adv hinüber, herüber (*to* zu); drüben; darüber, mehr; zu Ende, vorüber, vorbei; über..., um...: *et.* über (*geben etc*); über (-*kochen etc*); um (*fallen, -werfen etc*); herum (*drehen etc*); zu Ende, vorüber, vorbei, durch (*lesen etc*); (gründlich) über (*legen etc*); (*all*) *over* noch einmal; *all over* ganz vorbei; *over and over (again)* immer wieder; *over and above* obendrein, überdies

o·ver·age zu alt

o·ver·all 1. gesamt, Gesamt...; allgemein; insgesamt; **2.** Br Arbeitsmantel m, Kittel m; (Br **overalls**) Overall m, Arbeitsanzug m; Arbeitshose f

o·ver·awe einschüchtern

o·ver·bal·ance umstoßen, umkippen; das Gleichgewicht verlieren

o·ver·bear·ing anmaßend

o·ver·board MAR über Bord

o·ver·bur·den *fig* überlasten

o·ver·cast bewölkt, bedeckt

o·ver·charge überlasten, ELECTR *a.* überladen; ECON j-m zu viel berechnen; *Betrag* zu viel verlangen

o·ver·coat Mantel m

o·ver·come überwinden, überwältigen; *be overcome with emotion* von s-n Gefühlen übermannt werden

o·ver·crowd·ed überfüllt; überlaufen

o·ver·do übertreiben; GASTR zu lange kochen *or* braten; **overdone** *a.* übergar

o·ver·dose Überdosis f

o·ver·draft ECON (Konto)Überziehung f; *a.* **overdraft facility** Überziehungskredit m

o·ver·draw ECON Konto überziehen (*by* um)

o·ver·dress (sich) zu fein anziehen; *overdressed* overdressed, zu fein angezogen

o·ver·drive MOT Overdrive m, Schongang m

o·ver·due überfällig

o·ver·eat zu viel essen

o·ver·es·ti·mate zu hoch schätzen *or* veranschlagen; *fig* überschätzen

o·ver·ex·pose PHOT überbelichten

o·ver·feed überfüttern

o·ver·flow 1. v/t überfluten, überschwemmen; v/i überlaufen, überfließen; überquellen (*with* von); **2.** TECH Überlauf m; Überlaufen n, -fließen n

o·ver·grown BOT überwachsen, überwuchert

O

o·ver·hang *v/t* über (*dat*) hängen; *v/i* überhängen

o·ver·haul *Maschine* überholen

o·ver·head **1.** *adv* oben, droben; **2.** *adj* Hoch..., Ober...; ECON *overhead expenses* or *costs* Gemeinkosten *pl*; SPORT Überkopf...; *overhead kick soccer:* Fallrückzieher *m*; **3.** ECON *esp Br a. pl* Gemeinkosten *pl*

o·ver·hear (zufällig) hören

o·ver·heat·ed überhitzt, überheizt; TECH heiß gelaufen

o·ver·joyed überglücklich

o·ver·lap (sich) überlappen; sich überschneiden

o·ver·leaf umseitig, umstehend

o·ver·load überlasten (*a.* ELECTR), überladen

o·ver·look übersehen; *overlooking the sea* mit Blick aufs Meer

o·ver·night **1.** über Nacht; *stay overnight* über Nacht bleiben, übernachten; **2.** Nacht..., Übernachtungs...; *overnight bag* Reisetasche *f*

o·ver·pass (Straßen-, Eisenbahn-) Überführung *f*

o·ver·pay zu viel (be)zahlen

o·ver·pop·u·lat·ed übervölkert

o·ver·pow·er überwältigen; *overpowering fig* überwältigend

o·ver·rate überbewerten, überschätzen

o·ver·reach: *overreach o.s.* sich übernehmen

o·ver·re·act überreagieren, überzogen reagieren (*to* auf *acc*)

o·ver·re·ac·tion Überreaktion *f*, überzogene Reaktion

o·ver·ride sich hinwegsetzen über (*acc*)

o·ver·rule *Entscheidung etc* aufheben, *Einspruch etc* abweisen

o·ver·run länger dauern als vorgesehen; *Signal* überfahren; *be overrun with* wimmeln von

o·ver·seas **1.** *adj* überseeisch, Übersee...; **2.** *adv* in *or* nach Übersee

o·ver·see beaufsichtigen, überwachen

o·ver·shad·ow *fig* überschatten, in den Schatten stellen

o·ver·sight Versehen *n*

o·ver·size(d) übergroß, überdimensional, in Übergröße(n)

o·ver·sleep verschlafen

o·ver·staffed (personell) überbesetzt

o·ver·state übertreiben

o·ver·state·ment Übertreibung *f*

o·ver·stay länger bleiben als; → *welcome*

4

o·ver·step *fig* überschreiten

o·ver·take überholen; *j-n* überraschen

o·ver·tax zu hoch besteuern; *fig* überbeanspruchen, überfordern

o·ver·throw **1.** *Regierung etc* stürzen; **2.** (Um)Sturz *m*

o·ver·time ECON Überstunden *pl*; SPORT (Spiel)Verlängerung *f*; *be on overtime, do overtime, work overtime* Überstunden machen

o·ver·tired übermüdet

o·ver·ture MUS Ouvertüre *f*; Vorspiel *n*

o·ver·turn *v/t* umwerfen, umstoßen; *Regierung etc* stürzen; *v/i* umkippen, MAR kentern

o·ver·view *fig* Überblick *m* (*of* über *acc*)

o·ver·weight **1.** Übergewicht *n*; **2.** übergewichtig (*person*), zu schwer (*by* um); *be five pounds overweight* fünf Pfund Übergewicht haben

o·ver·whelm überwältigen (*a. fig*)

o·ver·whelm·ing überwältigend

o·ver·work sich überarbeiten; überanstrengen

o·ver·wrought überreizt

o·ver·zeal·ous übereifrig

owe *j-m et.* schulden, schuldig sein; *et.* verdanken

ow·ing: *owing to* infolge, wegen

owl ZO Eule *f*

own **1.** eigen; *my own* mein Eigentum; (*all*) *on one's own* allein; **2.** besitzen; zugeben, (ein)gestehen

own·er Eigentümer(in), Besitzer(in)

own·er·oc·cu·pied *esp Br* eigengenutzt; *owner-occupied flat* Eigentumswohnung *f*

own·er·ship Besitz *m*; Eigentum *n*; Eigentumsrecht *n*

ox ZO Ochse *m*

ox·ide CHEM Oxid *n*, Oxyd *n*

ox·i·dize CHEM oxidieren

ox·y·gen CHEM Sauerstoff *m*

oxygen ap·pa·ra·tus MED Sauerstoffgerät *n*

oxygen tent MED Sauerstoffzelt *n*

oy·ster ZO Auster *f*

o·zone CHEM Ozon *n*

o·zone-friend·ly FCKW-frei, ohne Treibgas

o·zone hole Ozonloch *n*

ozone lay·er Ozonschicht *f*

ozone lev·els Ozonwerte *pl*

ozone shield Ozonschild *m*

O

P

P, p P, p *n*
pace 1. Tempo *n*, Geschwindigkeit *f*; Schritt *m*; Gangart *f* (*of a horse*); **2.** *v/t Zimmer etc* durchschreiten; *a.* **pace out** abschreiten; *v/i* (einher)schreiten; **pace up and down** auf und ab gehen
pace·mak·er SPORT Schrittmacher(in); MED Herzschrittmacher *m*
pace·set·ter SPORT Schrittmacher(in)
Pa·cif·ic *a.* **Pacific Ocean** der Pazifik, *der* Pazifische *or* Stille Ozean
pac·i·fi·er Schnuller *m*
pac·i·fist Pazifist(in)
pac·i·fy beruhigen, besänftigen
pack 1. Pack(en) *m*, Paket *n*, Bündel *n*; Packung *f*, Schachtel *f*; ZO Meute *f*; Rudel *n*; *contp* Pack *n*, Bande *f*; MED *etc* Packung *f*; (Karten)Spiel *n*; **a pack of lies** ein Haufen Lügen; **2.** *v/t* ein-, zusammenpacken, abpacken, verpacken (*a.* **pack up**); zusammenpferchen; vollstopfen; *Koffer etc* packen; **pack off** F fort-, wegschicken; *v/i* packen; (sich) drängen (**into** in *acc*); **pack up** zusammenpacken; **send s.o. packing** j-n fort- *or* wegjagen
pack·age Paket *n*; Packung *f*; **software package** EDP Software-, Programmpaket *n*
pack·age deal F Pauschalangebot *n*, -arrangement *n*
package hol·i·day Pauschalurlaub *m*
package tour Pauschalreise *f*
pack·et Päckchen *n*; Packung *f*, Schachtel *f*
pack·ing Packen *n*; Verpackung *f*
pact Pakt *m*, POL *a.* Vertrag *m*
pad 1. Polster *n*; SPORT (Knie- *etc*)Schützer *m*; (*Schreib- etc*)Block *m*; (*Stempel*)Kissen *n*; ZO Ballen *m*; (*Abschuss-*) Rampe *f*; **2.** (aus)polstern, wattieren
pad·ding Polsterung *f*, Wattierung *f*
pad·dle 1. Paddel *n*; MAR (Rad)Schaufel *f*; **2.** paddeln; plan(t)schen
pad·dock (Pferde)Koppel *f*
pad·lock Vorhängeschloss *n*
pa·gan 1. Heide *m*, Heidin *f*; **2.** heidnisch
page¹ 1. Seite *f*; **2.** paginieren
page² 1. (Hotel)Page *m*; **2.** *j-n* ausrufen (lassen)
pag·eant (*a.* historischer) Festzug
pag·i·nate paginieren
pail Eimer *m*, Kübel *m*
pain 1. Schmerz(en *pl*) *m*; Kummer *m*; *pl* Mühe *f*, Bemühungen *pl*; **be in** (**great**)

pain (große) Schmerzen haben; **be a pain** (**in the neck**) F e-m auf den Wecker gehen; **take pains** sich Mühe geben; **2.** *esp fig* schmerzen
pain·ful schmerzhaft, schmerzend; *fig* schmerzlich; peinlich
pain·kill·er Schmerzmittel *n*
pain·less schmerzlos
pains·tak·ing sorgfältig, gewissenhaft
paint 1. Farbe *f*; Anstrich *m*; **2.** *v/t* anmalen, bemalen; (an)streichen; *Auto etc* lackieren; *v/i* malen
paint·box Malkasten *m*
paint·brush (Maler)Pinsel *m*
paint·er (*a.* Kunst)Maler(in), Anstreicher(in)
paint·ing Malerei *f*; Gemälde *n*, Bild *n*
pair 1. Paar *n*; **a pair of …** ein Paar …, ein(e) …; **a pair of scissors** e-e Schere; **2.** *v/i* zo sich paaren; *a.* **pair off, pair up** Paare bilden; *v/t a.* **pair off, pair up** paarweise anordnen; **pair off** *zwei Leute* zusammenbringen, verkuppeln
pa·ja·ma(s) (**a pair of**) **pajamas** (ein) Schlafanzug *m*, (ein) Pyjama *m*
pal Kamerad *m*, F Kumpel *m*, Spezi *m*
pal·ace Palast *m*, Schloss *n*
pal·a·ta·ble schmackhaft (*a. fig*)
pal·ate ANAT Gaumen *m*; *fig* Geschmack *m*
pale¹ 1. blass, *a.* bleich, *a.* hell (*color*); **2.** blass *or* bleich werden
pale² Pfahl *m*; *fig* Grenzen *pl*
pale·ness Blässe *f*
Pal·es·tin·i·an 1. palästinensisch; **2.** Palästinenser(in)
pal·ings Lattenzaun *m*
pal·i·sade Palisade *f*; *pl* Steilufer *n*
pal·let TECH Palette *f*
pal·lid blass
pal·lor Blässe *f*
palm¹ *a.* **palm tree** BOT Palme *f*
palm² 1. ANAT Handfläche *f*; **2.** *et.* in der Hand verschwinden lassen; **palm s.th. off on s.o.** F j-m *et.* andrehen
pal·pa·ble fühlbar, greifbar
pal·pi·tate MED klopfen, pochen
pal·pi·ta·tions MED Herzklopfen *n*
pal·sy MED Lähmung *f*
pal·try armselig
pam·per verwöhnen
pam·phlet Broschüre *f*
pan Pfanne *f*; Topf *m*
pan·a·ce·a Allheilmittel *n*

pan·cake Pfannkuchen *m*

pan·da ZO Panda *m*

pan·da car *Br* (Funk)Streifenwagen *m*

pan·de·mo·ni·um Hölle *f*, Höllenlärm *m*, Tumult *m*, Chaos *n*

pan·der Vorschub leisten (*to dat*)

pane (*Fenster*)Scheibe *f*

pan·el 1. (Tür)Füllung *f*; (Wand)Täfelung *f*; ELECTR, TECH Instrumentenbrett *n*, (Schalt-, Kontroll- *etc*)Tafel *f*; JUR Liste *f* der Geschworenen; Diskussionsteilnehmer *pl*, Diskussionsrunde *f*; Rateteam *n*; **2.** täfeln

pang stechender Schmerz; *pangs of hunger* nagender Hunger; *pangs of conscience* Gewissensbisse *pl*

pan·han·dle 1. Pfannenstiel *m*; GEOGR schmaler Fortsatz; **2.** F betteln

pan·ic 1. panisch; **2.** Panik *f*; **3.** in Panik versetzen *or* geraten

pan·ick·y: F *be panicky* in Panik sein

pan·ic-strick·en von Panik erfasst *or* erfüllt

pan·o·ra·ma Panorama *n*, Ausblick *m*

pan·sy BOT Stiefmütterchen *n*

pant keuchen, schnaufen, nach Luft schnappen

pan·ther ZO Panther *m*; Puma *m*; Jaguar *m*

pan·ties (Damen)Schlüpfer *m*, Slip *m*; Höschen *n*

pan·to·mime THEA Pantomime *f*; *Br* F Weihnachtsspiel *n*

pan·try Speisekammer *f*

pants Hose *f*; *Br* Unterhose *f*; *Br* Schlüpfer *m*

pant·suit Hosenanzug *m*

pan·ty·hose Strumpfhose *f*

pan·ty·lin·er Slipeinlage *f*

pap Brei *m*

pa·pal päpstlich

pa·per 1. Papier *n*; Zeitung *f*; (Prüfungs-)Arbeit *f*; UNIV Klausur(arbeit) *f*; Aufsatz *m*; Referat *n*; Tapete *f*; *pl* (Ausweis)Papiere *pl*; **2.** tapezieren

pa·per·back Taschenbuch *n*, Paperback *n*

pa·per bag (Papier)Tüte *f*

pa·per·boy Zeitungsjunge *m*

pa·per clip Büro-, Heftklammer *f*

pa·per cup Pappbecher *m*

pa·per·hang·er Tapezierer *m*

pa·per knife Br Brieföffner *m*

pa·per mon·ey Papiergeld *n*

pa·per·weight Briefbeschwerer *m*

par: *at par* zum Nennwert; *be on a par with* gleich *or* ebenbürtig sein (*dat*)

par·a·ble Parabel *f*, Gleichnis *n*

par·a·chute Fallschirm *m*

par·a·chut·ist Fallschirmspringer(in)

pa·rade 1. Umzug *m*, *esp* MIL Parade *f*; *fig* Zurschaustellung *f*; *make a parade of fig* zur Schau stellen; **2.** ziehen (*through* durch); MIL antreten (lassen), vorbeimarschieren (lassen); zur Schau stellen; *parade* (*through*) stolzieren durch

par·a·dise Paradies *n*

par·af·fin *Br* Petroleum *n*

par·a·glid·er SPORT Gleitschirm *m*; Gleitschirmflieger(in)

par·a·glid·ing SPORT Gleitschirmfliegen *n*

par·a·gon Muster *n* (*of an dat*)

par·a·graph Absatz *m*, Abschnitt *m*; (Zeitungs)Notiz *f*

par·al·lel 1. parallel (*to, with* zu); **2.** MATH Parallele *f* (*a. fig*); *without parallel* ohne Parallele, ohnegleichen; **3.** entsprechen (*dat*), gleichkommen (*dat*)

par·a·lyse *Br*, **par·a·lyze** MED lähmen, *fig a.* lahmlegen, zum Erliegen bringen; *paralysed with fig* starr *or* wie gelähmt vor (*dat*)

pa·ral·y·sis MED Lähmung *f*, *fig a.* Lahmlegung *f*

par·a·med·ic MED Sanitäter *m*

par·a·mount größte(r, -s), übergeordnet; *of paramount importance* von (aller)größter Bedeutung *or* Wichtigkeit

par·a·pet Brüstung *f*

par·a·pher·na·li·a (persönliche) Sachen *pl*; Ausrüstung *f*; *esp Br* F Scherereien *pl*

par·a·phrase 1. umschreiben; **2.** Umschreibung *f*

par·a·site Parasit *m*, Schmarotzer *m*

par·a·troop·er MIL Fallschirmjäger *m*; *pl* Fallschirmjägertruppe *f*

par·boil halb gar kochen, ankochen

par·cel 1. Paket *n*; Parzelle *f*; **2.** *parcel out* aufteilen; *parcel up* (als Paket) verpacken

parch ausdörren, austrocknen; vertrocknen

parch·ment Pergament *n*

par·don 1. JUR Begnadigung *f*; *I beg your pardon* Entschuldigung!, Verzeihung!; erlauben Sie mal!, ich muss doch sehr bitten!; *a. pardon?* F (wie) bitte?; **2.** verzeihen; vergeben; JUR begnadigen; *pardon me → I beg your pardon*; F (wie) bitte?

par·don·a·ble verzeihlich

pare sich *die Nägel* schneiden; *Apfel etc* schälen

par·ent Elternteil *m*, Vater *m*, Mutter *f*; *pl* Eltern *pl*

par·ent·age Abstammung *f*, Herkunft *f*

pa·ren·tal elterlich

pa·ren·the·ses (runde) Klammer *f*

par·ents-in-law Schwiegereltern *pl*

par·ent-teach·er meet·ing PED Elternabend m

par·ings Schalen pl

par·ish REL Gemeinde f

par·ish church REL Pfarrkirche f

pa·rish·ion·er REL Gemeindemitglied n

park 1. Park m, (Grün)Anlage(n pl) f; **2.** MOT parken; *look for somewhere to park the car* e-n Parkplatz suchen

par·ka Parka m, f

park·ing MOT Parken n; *no parking* Parkverbot, Parken verboten

parking disk Parkscheibe f

parking fee Parkgebühr f

parking garage Park(hoch)haus n

parking lot Parkplatz m

parking lot at·tend·ant Parkwächter m

parking me·ter Parkuhr f

parking of·fend·er Parksünder(in)

parking space Parkplatz m, Parklücke f

parking tick·et Strafzettel m

par·ley esp MIL Verhandlung f

par·lia·ment Parlament n

par·lia·men·tar·i·an Parlamentarier(in)

par·lia·men·ta·ry parlamentarisch, Parlaments…

par·lo(u)r mst in cpds Salon m

pa·ro·chi·al REL Pfarr…, Gemeinde…; fig engstirnig, beschränkt

par·o·dy 1. Parodie f; **2.** parodieren

pa·role JUR **1.** Hafturlaub m; bedingte Haftentlassung; *he is out on parole* er hat Hafturlaub; er wurde bedingt entlassen; **2.** *parole s.o.* j-m Hafturlaub gewähren; j-n bedingt entlassen

par·quet Parkett n (a. THEA)

par·quet floor Parkett(fuß)boden m

par·rot 1. ZO Papagei m (a. fig); **2.** et. (wie ein Papagei) nachplappern

par·ry abwehren, parieren

par·si·mo·ni·ous geizig

pars·ley BOT Petersilie f

par·son REL Pfarrer m

par·son·age REL Pfarrhaus n

part 1. Teil m; TECH Teil n, Bau-, Ersatzteil n; Anteil m; Seite f, Partei f; THEA, fig Rolle f; MUS Stimme f, Partie f; GEOGR Gegend f, Teil m; (Haar)Scheitel m; *for my part* was mich betrifft; *for the most part* größtenteils; meistens; *in part* teilweise, zum Teil; *on the part of* vonseiten, seitens (gen); *on my part* von m-r Seite; *take part in s.th.* an e-r Sache teilnehmen; *take s.th. in good part* et. nicht übel nehmen; **2.** v/t trennen (ab-, zer-)teilen; einteilen; Haar scheiteln; *part company* sich trennen (*with* von); v/i sich trennen (*with* von); **3.** adj Teil…; **4.** adv: part …, part teils …, teils

par·tial Teil…, teilweise; parteiisch, voreingenommen (*to* für)

par·ti·al·i·ty Parteilichkeit f, Voreingenommenheit f; Schwäche f, besondere Vorliebe (*for* für)

par·tial·ly teilweise, zum Teil

par·tic·i·pant Teilnehmer(in)

par·tic·i·pate teilnehmen, sich beteiligen (*both*: *in* an dat)

par·tic·i·pa·tion Teilnahme f, Beteiligung f

par·ti·ci·ple LING Partizip n, Mittelwort n

par·ti·cle Teilchen n

par·tic·u·lar 1. besondere(r, -s), speziell; genau, eigen, wählerisch; **2.** Einzelheit f; pl nähere Umstände pl or Angaben pl; Personalien pl; *in particular* insbesondere

par·tic·u·lar·ly besonders

part·ing 1. Trennung f, Abschied m; esp Br (Haar)Scheitel m; **2.** Abschieds…

par·ti·san 1. Parteigänger(in); MIL Partisan(in); **2.** parteiisch

par·ti·tion 1. Teilung f; Trennwand f; **2.** *partition off* abteilen, abtrennen

part·ly teilweise, zum Teil

part·ner Partner(in), ECON a. Teilhaber(in)

part·ner·ship Partnerschaft f, ECON a. Teilhaberschaft f

part-own·er Miteigentümer(in)

par·tridge ZO Rebhuhn n

part-time 1. adj Teilzeit…, Halbtags…; *part-time worker → part-timer*; **2.** adv halbtags

part-tim·er F Teilzeitbeschäftigte m, f, Halbtagskraft f

par·ty Partei f (a. POL); (*Arbeits-, Reise-*) Gruppe f; (*Rettungs- etc*)Mannschaft f; MIL Kommando n, Trupp m; Party f, Gesellschaft f; Teilnehmer(in), Beteiligte m, f

party line POL Parteilinie f

party pol·i·tics Parteipolitik f

pass 1. v/i vorbeigehen, -fahren, -kommen, -ziehen etc (*by* an dat); übergehen (*to* auf acc), fallen (*to* an acc); vergehen (*pain etc, time*); durchkommen, (die Prüfung) bestehen; gelten (*as, for* als), gehalten werden (*as, for* für); PARL Rechtskraft erlangen; unbeanstandet bleiben; SPORT (den Ball) abspielen or passen (*to* zu); card game: passen (a. fig); *let s.o. pass* j-n vorbeilassen; *let s.th. pass* et. durchgehen lassen; v/t vorbeigehen, -fahren, -fließen, -kommen, -ziehen etc an (*dat*); überholen; Prüfung bestehen; Prüfling durchkommen lassen; (*mit der Hand*) streichen (*over* über acc); j-m et. reichen, geben, et. weitergeben; SPORT

Ball abspielen, passen (**to** zu); *Zeit* verbringen; PARL *Gesetz* verabschieden; *Urteil* abgeben, fällen, JUR a. sprechen (**on** über *acc*); *fig* hinausgehen über (*acc*), übersteigen, übertreffen; **pass away** sterben; **pass off** *j-n, et.* ausgeben (**as** als); *gut etc* verlaufen; **pass out** ohnmächtig werden; **2.** Passierschein *m*; Bestehen *n* (*examination*); SPORT Pass *m*, Zuspiel *m*; (*Gebirgs*)Pass *m*; (*free*)Pass Frei(fahr)-karte *f*; **things have come to such a pass that** F die Dinge haben sich derart zugespitzt, dass; **make a pass at** F Annäherungsversuche machen bei

pass·a·ble passierbar, befahrbar; passabel, leidlich

pas·sage Passage *f*, Korridor *m*, Gang *m*; Durchgang *m*; (See-, Flug)Reise *f*; Durchfahrt *f*, Durchreise *f*; Passage *f* (*a*. MUS), Stelle *f*; **bird of passage** Zugvogel *m*

pass·book ECON Sparbuch *n*

pas·sen·ger Passagier *m*, Fahrgast *m*, Fluggast *m*, Reisende *m, f*, MOT Insasse *m*, Insassin *f*

pass·er·by Passant(in)

pas·sion Leidenschaft *f*; Wut *f*, Zorn *m*; **Passion** REL Passion *f*; **passions ran high** die Erregung schlug hohe Wellen

pas·sion·ate leidenschaftlich

pas·sive passiv; LING passivisch

Pass·o·ver REL Passah(fest) *n*

pass·port (Reise)Pass *m*

pass·word Kennwort *n* (*a*. EDP), MIL a. Parole *f*, Losung *f*

past 1. *adj* vergangen; frühere(r, -s); **be past a** vorüber sein; **for some time past** seit einiger Zeit; **past tense** LING Vergangenheit *f*, Präteritum *n*; **2.** *adv* vorüber, vorbei; **go past** vorbeigehen; **3.** *prp time*: nach, über (*acc*); über … (*acc*) hinaus; an … (*dat*) vorbei; **half past two** halb drei; **past hope** hoffnungslos; **4.** Vergangenheit *f* (*a*. LING)

pas·ta Teigwaren *pl*

paste 1. Paste *f*; Kleister *m*; Teig *m*; **2.** kleben (**to, on** an *acc*); **paste up** ankleben

paste·board Karton *m*, Pappe *f*

pas·tel Pastell(zeichnung *f*) *n*

pas·teur·ize pasteurisieren

pas·time Zeitvertreib *m*, Freizeitbeschäftigung *f*

pas·tor REL Pastor *m*, Pfarrer *m*, Seelsorger *m*

pas·tor·al REL seelsorgerisch, pastoral; **pastoral care** Seelsorge *f*

pas·try GASTR (*Blätter-, Mürbe*)Teig *m*; Feingebäck *n*

pastry cook Konditor *m*

pas·ture 1. Weide(land *n*) *f*; **2.** *v/t* weiden (lassen); *v/i* grasen, weiden

pas·ty¹ *esp Br* GASTR (Fleisch)Pastete *f*

pas·ty² blass, F käsig

pat 1. Klaps *m*; GASTR Portion *f*; **2.** tätscheln; klopfen

patch 1. Fleck *m*; Flicken *m*; kleines Stück Land; **in patches** stellenweise; **2.** flicken

pa·tent 1. offenkundig; patentiert; Patent…; **2.** Patent *n*; **take out a patent for s.th.** (sich) *et.* patentieren lassen; **3.** *et.* patentieren lassen

pa·tent·ee Patentinhaber(in)

pa·tent leath·er Lackleder *n*

pa·ter·nal väterlich; väterlicherseits

pa·ter·ni·ty JUR Vaterschaft *f*

path Pfad *m*; Weg *m*

pa·thet·ic mitleiderregend; kläglich, miserabel

pa·tience Geduld *f*; *esp Br* Patience *f*

pa·tient¹ geduldig

pa·tient² MED Patient(in)

pat·i·o Terrasse *f*; Innenhof *m*, Patio *m*

pat·ri·ot Patriot(in)

pat·ri·ot·ic patriotisch

pa·trol 1. Patrouille *f* (*a*. MIL), Streife *f*; Runde *f*; **on patrol** auf Patrouille, auf Streife; **2.** abpatrouillieren, auf Streife sein in (*dat*), s-e Runde machen in (*dat*)

pa·trol car (Funk)Streifenwagen *m*

pa·trol·man Streifenpolizist *m*; *Br* motorisierter Pannenhelfer

pa·tron Schirmherr *m*; Gönner *m*, Förderer *m*; (Stamm)Kunde *m*; Stammgast *m*

pat·ron·age Schirmherrschaft *f*; Förderung *f*

pat·ron·ess Schirmherrin *f*; Gönnerin *f*, Förderin *f*

pat·ron·ize fördern; (Stamm)Kunde *or* Stammgast sein bei *or* in (*dat*); gönnerhaft *or* herablassend behandeln

pa·tron saint REL Schutzheilige *m, f*

pat·ter prasseln (*rain*); trappeln (*feet*)

pat·tern 1. Muster *n* (*a*. *fig*); Schema *n*; **2.** bilden, formen (**after, on** nach)

paunch (dicker) Bauch

pau·per Arme *m, f*

pause 1. Pause *f*; **2.** innehalten, e-e Pause machen

pave pflastern; **pave the way for** *fig* den Weg ebnen für

pave·ment Fahrbahn *f*; Belag *m*, Pflaster *n*; *Br* Bürgersteig *m*, Gehsteig *m*

pave·ment ca·fé *Br* Straßencafé *n*

paw 1. ZO Pfote *f*, Tatze *f*; **2.** *v/t Boden* scharren; scharren an (*dat*); F betatschen; *v/i* scharren (**at** an *dat*)

pawn¹ *chess*: Bauer *m*; *fig* Schachfigur *f*

pawn² 1. verpfänden, versetzen; **2. be in**

pelvis

pawn verpfändet *or* versetzt sein

pawn·bro·ker Pfandleiher *m*

pawn·shop Leihhaus *n*, Pfandhaus *n*

pay 1. *v/t et.* (be)zahlen; *j-n* bezahlen; *Aufmerksamkeit* schenken; *Besuch* abstatten; *Kompliment* machen; *pay attention* achtgeben auf (*acc*); PED aufpassen; *pay cash* bar bezahlen; *v/i* zahlen; *fig* sich lohnen; *pay for* (*fig* für) *et.* bezahlen; *fig* büßen; *pay in* einzahlen; *pay into* einzahlen auf (*acc*); *pay off et.* ab(be)zahlen; *j-n* auszahlen; **2.** Bezahlung *f*, Gehalt *n*, Lohn *m*

pay·a·ble zahlbar, fällig

pay·day Zahltag *m*

pay·ee Zahlungsempfänger(in)

pay en·ve·lope Lohntüte *f*

pay·ing lohnend

pay·mas·ter MIL Zahlmeister *m*

pay·ment (Be)Zahlung *f*

pay pack·et *Br* Lohntüte *f*

pay phone *Br* Münzfernsprecher *m*

pay·roll Lohnliste *f*

pay·slip Lohn-, Gehaltsstreifen *m*

PC ABBR *of* **personal computer** PC *m*, Personal Computer *m*; **PC user** PC-Benutzer *m*

pea BOT Erbse *f*

peace Friede(n) *m*; Ruhe *f*; JUR öffentliche Ruhe und Ordnung; *at peace* in Frieden

peace·a·ble friedlich, friedfertig

peace·ful friedlich

peace·lov·ing friedliebend

peace move·ment Friedensbewegung *f*

peace·time Friedenszeiten *pl*

peach BOT Pfirsich(baum) *m*

pea·cock ZO Pfau *m*, Pfauhahn *m*

pea·hen ZO Pfauhenne *f*

peak Spitze *f*, Gipfel *m*; Schirm *m*; *fig* Höhepunkt *m*, Höchststand *m*

peaked cap Schirmmütze *f*

peak hours Hauptverkehrszeit *f*, Stoßzeit *f*; ELECTR Hauptbelastungszeit *f*

peak time, peak viewing hours *Br* TV Haupteinschaltzeit *f*, Hauptsendezeit *f*, beste Sendezeit

peal 1. (*Glocken*)Läuten *n*; (*Donner*)Schlag *m*; *peals of laughter* schallendes Gelächter; **2.** *a.* **peal out** läuten; krachen

pea·nut BOT Erdnuss *f*; *pl* F lächerliche Summe

pear BOT Birne *f*; Birnbaum *m*

pearl 1. Perle *f*; Perlmutter *f*, Perlmutt *n*; **2.** Perlen...

pearl·y perlenartig, Perlen...

peas·ant Kleinbauer *m*

peat Torf *m*

peb·ble Kiesel(stein) *m*

peck picken, hacken; *peck at one's food* im Essen herumstochern

pe·cu·li·ar eigen, eigentümlich, typisch; eigenartig, seltsam

pe·cu·li·ar·i·ty Eigenheit *f*; Eigentümlichkeit *f*

ped·a·go·gic pädagogisch

ped·al 1. Pedal *n*; **2.** das Pedal treten; (mit dem Rad) fahren, strampeln

pe·dan·tic pedantisch

ped·dle hausieren (gehen) mit; *peddle drugs* mit Drogen handeln

ped·dler Hausierer(in)

ped·es·tal Sockel *m*

pe·des·tri·an 1. Fußgänger(in); **2.** Fußgänger...

pedestrian cross·ing Fußgängerübergang *m*

pedestrian mall, *esp Br* **pedestrian precinct** Fußgängerzone *f*

ped·i·cure Pediküre *f*

ped·i·gree Stammbaum *m* (*a.* ZO)

ped·lar *Br* → *peddler*

pee F **1.** pinkeln; **2.** *have* (*or go for*) *a pee* pinkeln (gehen)

peek 1. kurz *or* verstohlen gucken (*at* auf *acc*); **2.** *have* *or* *take a peek at* e-n kurzen *or* verstohlenen Blick werfen auf (*acc*)

peel 1. *v/t* schälen; *a.* **peel off** abschälen, *Folie, Tapete etc* abziehen, ablösen; *Kleid* abstreifen; *v/i a.* **peel off** sich lösen (*wallpaper etc*), abblättern (*paint etc*), sich schälen (*skin*); **2.** BOT Schale *f*

peep¹ 1. kurz *or* verstohlen gucken (*at* auf *acc*); *mst* **peep out** (her)vorschauen; **2.** *take a peep at* e-n kurzen *or* verstohlenen Blick werfen auf (*acc*)

peep² 1. Piep(s)en *n*; F Piepser *m*; **2.** piep(s)en

peep·hole Guckloch *n*; (Tür)Spion *m*

peer angestrengt schauen, spähen; *peer at s.o.* j-n anstarren

peer·less unvergleichlich, einzigartig

peev·ish verdrießlich, gereizt

peg 1. (Holz)Stift *m*, Zapfen *m*, Pflock *m*; (Kleider)Haken *m*; *Br* (*Wäsche-*) Klammer *f*; (*Zelt*)Hering *m*; *take s.o. down a peg* (*or two*) F j-m e-n Dämpfer aufsetzen; **2.** anpflocken; *Wäsche* anklammern, festklammern

pel·i·can ZO Pelikan *m*

pelican cross·ing *Br* Ampelübergang *m*

pel·let Kügelchen *n*; Schrotkorn *n*

pelt¹ *v/t* bewerfen, *v/i*: *it's pelting* (*down*), *esp Br* *it's pelting with rain* es gießt in Strömen

pelt² ZO Fell *n*, Pelz *m*

pel·vis ANAT Becken *n*

P

pen¹ (*Schreib*)Feder f; Füller m; Kugelschreiber m

pen² 1. Pferch m, (*Schaf*)Hürde f; 2. **pen in, pen up** Tiere einpferchen, *Personen* zusammenpferchen

pe·nal JUR Straf...; strafbar

pe·nal code JUR Strafgesetzbuch n

pe·nal·ize bestrafen

pen·al·ty Strafe f, SPORT a. Strafpunkt m; *soccer*: Elfmeter m

penalty ar·e·a, penalty box F *soccer*: Strafraum m

penalty goal *soccer*: Elfmetertor n

penalty kick *soccer*: Elfmeter m, Strafstoß m

penalty shoot-out *soccer*: Elfmeterschießen n

penalty spot *soccer*: Elfmeterpunkt m

pen·ance REL Buße f

pen·cil 1. Bleistift m; 2. (mit Bleistift) markieren *or* schreiben *or* zeichnen; *Augenbrauen* nachziehen

pen·cil case Federmäppchen n

pen·cil sharp·en·er Bleistiftspitzer m

pen·dant, pen·dent (*Schmuck*)Anhänger m

pend·ing 1. *prp* bis zu; 2. *adj esp* JUR schwebend

pen·du·lum Pendel n

pen·e·trate *v/t* eindringen in (*acc*); dringen durch, durchdringen; *v/i* eindringen (*into* in *acc*)

pen·e·trat·ing durchdringend; *fig* scharf; scharfsinnig

pen·e·tra·tion Durchdringen n, Eindringen n; *fig* Scharfsinn m

pen friend *Br* Brieffreund(in)

pen·guin ZO Pinguin m

pe·nin·su·la Halbinsel f

pe·nis ANAT Penis m

pen·i·tence Buße f, Reue f

pen·i·tent 1. reuig, bußfertig; 2. REL Büßer(in)

pen·i·ten·tia·ry (Staats)Gefängnis n, Strafanstalt f

pen·knife Taschenmesser n

pen name Schriftstellername m, Pseudonym n

pen·nant Wimpel m

pen·ni·less (völlig) mittellos

pen·ny a. **new penny** *Br* Penny m

pen pal Brieffreund(in)

pen·sion 1. Rente f, Pension f; 2. **pension off** pensionieren, in den Ruhestand versetzen

pen·sion·er Rentner(in), Pensionär(in)

pen·sive nachdenklich

pen·tath·lete SPORT Fünfkämpfer(in)

pen·tath·lon SPORT Fünfkampf m

Pen·te·cost REL Pfingsten n

pent·house Penthouse n, Penthaus n

pent-up auf-, angestaut (*emotions*)

pe·o·ny BOT Pfingstrose f

peo·ple 1. Volk n, Nation f; die Menschen *pl*, die Leute *pl*; Leute *pl*, Personen *pl*; man; **the people** das (*gemeine*) Volk; 2. besiedeln, bevölkern (**with** mit)

peo·ple's re·pub·lic Volksrepublik f

pep F 1. Pep m, Schwung m; 2. **mst pep up** *j-n or et.* in Schwung bringen, aufmöbeln

pep·per 1. Pfeffer m; BOT Paprikaschote f; 2. pfeffern

pep·per cast·er Pfefferstreuer m

pep·per·mint BOT Pfefferminze f; Pfefferminz n

pep·per·y pfeff(e)rig; *fig* hitzig

pep·pill F Aufputschpille f

per per, durch; pro, für, je

per·ceive (be)merken, wahrnehmen; erkennen

per cent, per·cent Prozent n

per·cen·tage Prozentsatz m; F Prozente *pl*, (An)Teil m

per·cep·ti·ble wahrnehmbar, merklich

per·cep·tion Wahrnehmung f; Auffassung f, Auffassungsgabe f

perch¹ 1. (Sitz)Stange f; 2. (**on**) sich setzen (auf *acc*), sich niederlassen (auf *acc*, *dat*); F hocken (**on** auf *dat*); **perch o.s.** F sich hocken (**on** auf *acc*)

perch² ZO Barsch m

per·co·la·tor Kaffeemaschine f

per·cus·sion Schlag m; Erschütterung f; MUS Schlagzeug n

percussion drill TECH Schlagbohrer m

percussion in·stru·ment MUS Schlaginstrument n

per·emp·to·ry herrisch

pe·ren·ni·al ewig, immer während; BOT mehrjährig

per·fect 1. perfekt, vollkommen, vollendet; gänzlich, völlig; 2. vervollkommnen; 3. a. **perfect tense** LING Perfekt n

per·fec·tion Vollendung f; Vollkommenheit f, Perfektion f

per·fo·rate durchbohren, -löchern

per·form *v/t* verrichten, durchführen, tun; *Pflicht etc* erfüllen; THEA, MUS aufführen spielen, vortragen; *v/i* THEA *etc* e-e Vorstellung geben, auftreten, spielen

per·for·mance Verrichtung f, Durchführung f; Leistung f; THEA, MUS Aufführung f, Vorstellung f, Vortrag m

per·form·er THEA, MUS Darsteller(in) Künstler(in)

per·fume 1. Duft m; Parfüm n; 2. parfümieren

per·fum·er·y Parfümerie f

per·haps vielleicht

per·il Gefahr *f*

per·il·ous gefährlich

pe·ri·od Periode *f*, Zeit *f*, Zeitdauer *f*, Zeitraum *m*, Zeitspanne *f*; (Unterrichts)Stunde *f*; MED Periode *f*; LING Punkt *m*

period fur·ni·ture Stilmöbel *pl*

pe·ri·od·ic periodisch

pe·ri·od·i·cal 1. periodisch; **2.** Zeitschrift *f*

pe·riph·er·al EDP Peripheriegerät *n*

peripheral e·quip·ment EDP Peripheriegeräte *pl*

pe·riph·e·ry Peripherie *f*, Rand *m*

per·ish umkommen; GASTR schlecht werden, verderben; TECH verschleißen

per·ish·a·ble leicht verderblich

per·ish·a·bles leicht verderbliche Lebensmittel

per·jure: perjure o.s. JUR e-n Meineid leisten

per·ju·ry JUR Meineid *m*; **commit perjury** e-n Meineid leisten

perk: perk up *v/i* aufleben, munter werden; *v/t j-n* munter machen, F aufmöbeln

perk·y F munter, lebhaft; keck, selbstbewusst

perm 1. Dauerwelle *f*; **get a perm** → **2. get one's hair permed** sich e-e Dauerwelle machen lassen

per·ma·nent 1. (be)ständig, dauerhaft, Dauer...; **2. a. permanent wave** Dauerwelle *f*

per·me·a·ble durchlässig (**to** für)

per·me·ate durchdringen; dringen (**into** in *acc*; **through** durch)

per·mis·si·ble zulässig, erlaubt

per·mis·sion Erlaubnis *f*

per·mis·sive liberal; (sexuell) freizügig

permissive so·ci·e·ty tabufreie Gesellschaft

per·mit 1. erlauben, gestatten; **2.** Genehmigung *f*

per·pen·dic·u·lar senkrecht; rechtwinklig (**to** zu)

per·pet·u·al fortwährend, ständig, ewig

per·plex verwirren

per·plex·i·ty Verwirrung *f*

per·se·cute verfolgen

per·se·cu·tion Verfolgung *f*

per·se·cu·tor Verfolger(in)

per·se·ver·ance Ausdauer *f*, Beharrlichkeit *f*

per·se·vere beharrlich weitermachen

per·sist beharren (**in** auf *dat*); anhalten

per·sis·tence Beharrlichkeit *f*

per·sis·tent beharrlich; anhaltend

per·son Person *f* (*a.* LING)

per·son·al persönlich (*a.* LING); Personal...; Privat...

personal com·pu·ter (ABBR **PC**) Personal Computer *m*

personal da·ta Personalien *pl*

per·son·al·i·ty Persönlichkeit *f*; *pl* anzügliche *or* persönliche Bemerkungen *pl*

per·son·al or·ga·niz·er Notizbuch *n*, Adressbuch *n* und Taschenkalender *m etc* (*in einem*)

personal pro·noun LING Personalpronomen *n*

personal ster·e·o Walkman® *m*

per·son·i·fy personifizieren, verkörpern

per·son·nel Personal *n*, Belegschaft *f*; die Personalabteilung

personnel de·part·ment Personalabteilung *f*

personnel man·ag·er Personalchef *m*

per·spec·tive Perspektive *f*; Fernsicht *f*

per·spi·ra·tion Transpirieren *n*, Schwitzen *n*; Schweiß *m*

per·spire transpirieren, schwitzen

per·suade überreden; überzeugen

per·sua·sion Überredung(skunst) *f*; Überzeugung *f*

per·sua·sive überzeugend

pert keck, kess; schnippisch

per·tain: pertain to s.th. et. betreffen

per·ti·nent sachdienlich, relevant, zur Sache gehörig

per·turb beunruhigen

per·vade durchdringen, erfüllen

per·verse pervers; eigensinnig

per·ver·sion Verdrehung *f*; Perversion *f*

per·ver·si·ty Perversität *f*; Eigensinn *m*

per·vert 1. pervertieren; verdrehen; **2.** perverser Mensch

pes·sa·ry MED Pessar *n*

pes·si·mism Pessimismus *m*

pes·si·mist Pessimist(in)

pes·si·mis·tic pessimistisch

pest ZO Schädling *m*; F Nervensäge *f*; F Plage *f*

pest con·trol Schädlingsbekämpfung *f*

pes·ter F *j-n* belästigen, *j-m* keine Ruhe lassen

pes·ti·cide Pestizid *n*, Schädlingsbekämpfungsmittel *n*

pet 1. (zahmes) (Haus)Tier; *often contp* Liebling *m*; **2.** Lieblings...; Tier...; **3.** streicheln; F Petting machen

pet·al BOT Blütenblatt *n*

pet food Tiernahrung *f*

pe·ti·tion 1. Eingabe *f*, Gesuch *n*, (schriftlicher) Antrag; **2.** ersuchen; ein Gesuch einreichen (**for** um), e-n Antrag stellen (**for** auf *acc*)

pet name Kosename *m*

P

pet·ri·fy versteinern
pet·rol *Br* Benzin *n*
pe·tro·le·um Erdöl *n*, Mineralöl *n*
pet·rol pump *Br* Zapfsäule *f*
petrol station *Br* Tankstelle *f*
pet shop Tierhandlung *f*, Zoogeschäft *n*
pet·ti·coat Unterrock *m*
pet·ting F Petting *n*
pet·tish launisch, gereizt
pet·ty belanglos, unbedeutend, JUR *a.* geringfügig; engstirnig
petty cash Portokasse *f*
petty lar·ce·ny JUR einfacher Diebstahl
pet·u·lant launisch, gereizt
pew (Kirchen)Bank *f*
pew·ter Zinn *n*; *a.* **pewter ware** Zinn(-geschirr) *n*
phan·tom Phantom *n*; Geist *m*
phar·ma·cist Apotheker(in)
phar·ma·cy Apotheke *f*
phase Phase *f*
pheas·ant ZO Fasan *m*
phe·nom·e·non Phänomen *n*, Erscheinung *f*
phi·lan·thro·pist Philanthrop(in), Menschenfreund(in)
phil·is·tine F *contp* **1.** Spießer *m*; **2.** spießig
phi·lol·o·gist Philologe *m*, Philologin *f*
phi·lol·o·gy Philologie *f*
phi·los·o·pher Philosoph(in)
phi·los·o·phy Philosophie *f*
phlegm MED Schleim *m*
phone 1. Telefon *n*; *answer the phone* ans Telefon gehen; *by phone* telefonisch; *on the phone* am Telefon; *be on the phone* Telefon haben; am Telefon sein; **2.** telefonieren, anrufen
phone book Telefonbuch *n*
phone booth, *Br* **phone box** Telefonzelle *f*
phone call Anruf *m*, Gespräch *n*
phone·card Telefonkarte *f*
phone-in *radio*, TV Sendung *f* mit telefonischer Zuhörer- *or* Zuschauerbeteiligung
phone num·ber Telefonnummer *f*
pho·net·ics Phonetik *f*
pho·n(e)y F **1.** Fälschung *f*; Schwindler(in); **2.** falsch, gefälscht, unecht; Schein…
phos·pho·rus CHEM Phosphor *m*
pho·to F Foto *n*, Bild *n*; *in the photo* auf dem Foto; *take a photo* ein Foto machen (*of* von)
pho·to·cop·i·er Fotokopiergerät *n*
pho·to·cop·y 1. Fotokopie *f*; **2.** fotokopieren
pho·to·graph 1. Fotografie *f*; **2.** fotogra-

fieren
pho·tog·ra·pher Fotograf(in)
pho·tog·ra·phy Fotografie *f*
phras·al verb LING Verb *n* mit Adverb (und Präposition)
phrase 1. (Rede)Wendung *f*, Redensart *f*; idiomatischer Ausdruck; **2.** ausdrücken
phrase·book Sprachführer *m*
phys·i·cal 1. physisch, körperlich; physikalisch; *physically handicapped* körperbehindert; **2.** ärztliche Untersuchung
physical ed·u·ca·tion Leibeserziehung *f*, Sport *m*
physical ex·am·i·na·tion ärztliche Untersuchung
physical hand·i·cap Körperbehinderung *f*
physical train·ing Leibeserziehung *f*, Sport *m*
phy·si·cian Arzt *m*, Ärztin *f*
phys·i·cist Physiker(in)
phys·ics Physik *f*
phy·sique Körper(bau) *m*, Statur *f*
pi·a·nist MUS Pianist(in)
pi·an·o MUS Klavier *n*
pick 1. (auf)hacken; (auf)picken; auflesen; aufnehmen; pflücken; *Knochen* abnagen; bohren *or* stochern in (*dat*); *Schloss* knacken; aussuchen, auswählen; *pick one's nose* in der Nase bohren; *pick one's teeth* in den Zähnen (herum)stochern; *pick s.o.'s pocket* j-n bestehlen; *have a bone to pick with s.o.* mit j-m ein Hühnchen zu rupfen haben; *pick out* (sich) *et.* auswählen; ausmachen, erkennen; *pick up* aufheben, auflesen, aufnehmen; aufpicken; *Spur* aufnehmen; *j-n* abholen; *Anhalter* mitnehmen; F *Mädchen* aufreißen; *Kenntnisse, Informationen etc* aufschnappen; sich *e-e Krankheit etc* holen; *a.* **pick up speed** MOT schneller werden; **2.** (Spitz)Hacke *f*, Pickel *m*; (Aus)Wahl *f*; *take your pick* suchen Sie sich etwas aus
pick-a-back huckepack
pick·ax, *Br* **pick·axe** (Spitz)Hacke *f*, Pickel *m*
pick·et 1. Pfahl *m*; Streikposten *m*; **2.** Streikposten aufstellen vor (*dat*), mit Streikposten besetzen; Streikposten stehen
picket fence Lattenzaun *m*
picket line Streikpostenkette *f*
pick·le GASTR **1.** Salzlake *f*; Essigsoße *f*; Essig-, Gewürzgurke *f*; *mst pl esp Br* Pickles *pl*; *be in a (pretty) pickle* F (ganz schön) in der Patsche sitzen *or* sein *or* stecken; **2.** einlegen
pick·lock Einbrecher *m*; TECH Dietrich *m*

pick·pock·et Taschendieb(in)

pick-up Tonabnehmer *m*; Kleintransporter *m*; F (Zufalls)Bekanntschaft *f*

pick·y F wählerisch (*in dat* about)

pic·nic 1. Picknick *n*; **2.** ein Picknick machen, picknicken

pic·ture 1. Bild *n*; Gemälde *n*; PHOT Aufnahme *f*; Film *m*; *pl esp Br* Kino *n*; **2.** darstellen, malen; *fig* sich j-n, *et.* vorstellen

picture book Bilderbuch *n*

picture post·card Ansichtskarte *f*

pic·tur·esque malerisch

pie (*Fleisch- etc*)Pastete *f*; (*mst gedeckter*) (*Apfel- etc*)Kuchen

piece 1. Stück *n*; Teil *n* (*of a machine etc*); Teil *m* (*of a set etc*); chess: Figur *f*; *board game*: Stein *m*; (Zeitungs)Artikel *m*, (-)Notiz *f*; *by the piece* stückweise; *a piece of advice* e-e Rat; *a piece of news* e-e Neuigkeit; *give s.o. a piece of one's mind* j-m gründlich die Meinung sagen; *go to pieces* F zusammenbrechen; *take to pieces* auseinandernehmen; **2.** *piece together* zusammensetzen, -stückeln; *fig* zusammenfügen

piece·meal schrittweise

piece·work Akkordarbeit *f*; *do piecework* im Akkord arbeiten

pier MAR Pier *m*, Landungsbrücke *f*; TECH Pfeiler *m*

pierce durchbohren, durchstechen, durchstoßen; durchdringen

pierc·ing durchdringend, (*Kälte etc a.*) schneidend, (*Schrei a.*) gellend, (*Blick, Schmerz etc a.*) stechend

pi·e·ty Frömmigkeit *f*

pig ZO Schwein *n* (*a.* F); F Ferkel *n*; *sl contp* Bulle *m*

pi·geon ZO Taube *f*

pi·geon·hole 1. Fach *n*; **2.** ablegen

pig·gy F Schweinchen *n*

pig·gy·back huckepack

pig·gy bank Sparschwein(chen) *n*

pig·head·ed dickköpfig, stur

pig·let ZO Ferkel *n*

pig·sty Schweinestall *m*, F *contp* Saustall *m*

pig·tail Zopf *m*

pike¹ ZO Hecht *m*

pike² → **turnpike**

pile¹ Stapel *m*, Stoß *m*; F Haufen *m*, Menge *f*; (*atomic*) *pile* Atommeiler *m*; **2.** *pile up* (an-, auf)häufen, (auf)stapeln, aufschichten; sich anhäufen; MOT F aufeinander auffahren

pile² Flor *m*

pile³ Pfahl *m*

piles *Br* F MED Hämorrhoiden *pl*

pile-up MOT Massenkarambolage *f*

pil·fer stehlen, klauen

pil·grim Pilger(in)

pil·grim·age Pilgerfahrt *f*, Wallfahrt *f*

pill PHARM Pille *f*; *the pill* F die (*Antibaby*)-Pille; *be on the pill* die Pille nehmen

pil·lar Pfeiler *m*; Säule *f*

pil·li·on MOT Soziussitz *m*

pil·lo·ry 1. HIST Pranger *m*; **2.** *fig* anprangern

pil·low (Kopf)Kissen *n*

pil·low·case, pil·low slip (Kopf)Kissenbezug *m*

pi·lot 1. AVIAT Pilot *m*; MAR Lotse *m*; **2.** Versuchs..., Pilot...; **3.** lotsen; steuern

pilot film TV Pilotfilm *m*

pilot scheme Versuchs-, Pilotprojekt *n*

pimp Zuhälter *m*

pim·ple MED Pickel *m*, Pustel *f*

pin 1. (Steck)Nadel *f*; (*Haar-, Krawatten- etc*)Nadel *f*; Brosche *f*; TECH Bolzen *m*, Stift *m*; *bowling*: Kegel *m*; Pin *m*; (*Wäsche*)Klammer *f*; *Br* (*Reiß-*)Nagel *m*, (-)Zwecke *f*; **2.** (an)heften, anstecken (*to an acc*), befestigen (*to an dat*); pressen, drücken (*against, to* gegen, an *acc*)

PIN *a.* **PIN number** ABBR *of personal identification number* PIN, persönliche Geheimzahl

pin·a·fore Schürze *f*

pin·ball Flippern *n*; *play pinball* flippern

pin·ball ma·chine Flipper(automat) *m*

pin·cers: (*a pair of pincers* e-e) (Kneif-)Zange

pinch 1. *v/t* kneifen, zwicken; F klauen; *v/i* drücken; **2.** Kneifen *n*, Zwicken *n*; Prise *f*; *fig* Not(lage) *f*

pin·cush·ion Nadelkissen *n*

pine¹ BOT Kiefer *f*, Föhre *f*

pine² sich sehnen (*for* nach)

pine·ap·ple BOT Ananas *f*

pine cone BOT Kiefernzapfen *m*

pine-tree BOT Kiefer *f*, Föhre *f*

pin·ion ZO Schwungfeder *f*

pink 1. rosa(farben); **2.** Rosa *n*; BOT Nelke *f*

pint Pint *n* (0,47 *l*, *Br* 0,57 *l*); *Br* F Halbe *f*

pi·o·neer 1. Pionier *m*; **2.** den Weg bahnen (für)

pi·ous fromm, religiös

pip¹ *Br* (*Apfel-, Orangen- etc*)Kern *m*

pip² (Piep)Ton *m*

pip³ *on cards etc*: Auge *n*, Punkt *m*

pipe 1. TECH Rohr *n*, Röhre *f*; (*Tabaks*)Pfeife *f*; MUS (*Orgel*)Pfeife *f*; *pl Br* F Dudelsack *m*; **2.** (durch Rohre) leiten

pipe·line Rohrleitung *f*; Pipeline *f*

pip·er MUS Dudelsackpfeifer *m*

pip·ing 1. Rohrleitung *f*, Rohrnetz *n*; **2.**

piping hot kochend heiß, siedend heiß

pi·quant a. (a. fig)

pique 1. *in a fit of pique* gekränkt, verletzt, pikiert; 2. kränken, verletzen; *be piqued* a. pikiert sein

pi·rate 1. Pirat m, Seeräuber m; 2. unerlaubt kopieren or nachdrucken or nachpressen

pi·rate ra·di·o Piratensender m or pl

Pis·ces ASTR Fische pl; *he (she) is (a) Pisces* er (sie) ist (ein) Fisch

piss V 1. Pisse f; *take the piss out of s.o.* j-n verarschen; 2. pissen; *piss off!* verpiss dich!

pis·tol Pistole f

pis·ton TECH Kolben m

pit[1] 1. v/t Zelt, Lager aufschlagen; werfen, schleudern; MUS (an)stimmen; v/i stürzen, fallen; MAR stampfen; sich neigen (roof etc); *pitch in* F sich ins Zeug legen; kräftig zulangen; 2. esp Br SPORT (Spiel)Feld n; MUS Tonhöhe f; fig Grad m, Stufe f; esp Br Stand(platz) m; MAR Stampfen n; Neigung f (of a roof etc)

pitch[2] Pech n

pitch-black, pitch-dark pechschwarz; stockdunkel

pitch·er[1] Krug m

pitch·er[2] baseball: Werfer m

pitch·fork Heugabel f, Mistgabel f

pit·e·ous kläglich

pit·fall Fallgrube f; fig Falle f

pith BOT Mark n; weiße innere Haut; fig Kern m

pith·y markig, prägnant

pit·i·a·ble → pitiful

pit·i·ful mitleiderregend, bemitleidenswert; erbärmlich, jämmerlich

pit·i·less unbarmherzig, erbarmungslos

pit·ta bread Fladenbrot n

pit·y 1. Mitleid n (on mit); *it is a (great) pity* es ist (sehr) schade; *what a pity!* wie schade!; 2. bemitleiden, bedauern

piv·ot 1. TECH Drehzapfen m; fig Dreh- und Angelpunkt m; 2. sich drehen; *pivot on* fig abhängen von

pix·el EDP Pixel m

piz·za Pizza f

plac·ard 1. Plakat n; Transparent n; 2. mit Plakaten bekleben

place 1. Platz m, Ort m, Stelle f; Stätte f; Haus n, Wohnung f; Wohnort m; (Arbeits-, Lehr)Stelle f; *in the first place* erstens; *in third place* SPORT etc au dem dritten Platz; *in place of* anstelle von (or gen); *out of place* fehl am Platz *take place* stattfinden; *take s.o.'s place* j-s Stelle einnehmen; 2. stellen, legen setzen; Auftrag erteilen (with dat), Bestellung aufgeben (with bei); *be placed* SPORT sich platzieren (*second* an zweite Stelle)

place mat Platzdeckchen n, Set n, m

place·ment test Einstufungsprüfung f

place name Ortsname m

plac·id ruhig; gelassen

pla·gia·rize plagiieren

plague 1. Seuche f; Pest f; Plage f; 2. plagen

plaice ZO Scholle f

plaid Plaid n or m

plain 1. adj einfach schlicht; klar (und deutlich); offen (und ehrlich); unscheinbar, wenig anziehend; rein, völlig (non sense etc); 2. adv F (ganz) einfach; 3. Ebene f, Flachland n

plain choc·o·late Br (zart)bittere Schokolade

plain-clothes … in Zivil

plain-tiff JUR Kläger(in)

plain-tive traurig, klagend

plait esp Br 1. Zopf m; 2. flechten

plan 1. Plan m; 2. planen; beabsichtigen

plane[1] Flugzeug n; *by plane* mit dem Flugzeug; *go by plane* fliegen

plane[2] 1. flach, eben; 2. MATH Ebene f; fig Stufe f, Niveau n

plane[3] 1. Hobel m; 2. hobeln; *plane down* abhobeln

plan·et ASTR Planet m

plank Planke f, Bohle f

plank bed Pritsche f

plank·ing Planken pl

plant 1. BOT Pflanze f; ECON Werk n, Betrieb m, Fabrik f; 2. (an-, ein)pflanzen bepflanzen; Garten etc anlegen; aufstellen, postieren; *plant s.th. on s.o* F j-m ein (Belastendes) unterschieben

plan·ta·tion Plantage f, Pflanzung f Schonung f

plant·er Plantagenbesitzer(in), Pflanzer(in); Pflanzmaschine f; Übertopf m

plaque Gedenktafel f; MED Zahnbelag m

plas·ter 1. MED Pflaster n; (Ver)Putz m; a *plaster of Paris* Gips m; *have one's leg in plaster* MED das Bein in Gips haben; 2. verputzen; bekleben

plaster cast Gipsabguss m, Gipsmodell n MED Gipsverband m

plas·tic 1. plastisch; Plastik…; 2. Plastik n Kunststoff m; → *plastic mon·ey* F Plastikgeld n, Kreditkarten pl

plastic wrap Frischhaltefolie f

plate 1. Teller m; Platte f; (Namens-, Nummern- etc)Schild n; (Bild)Tafel f; (Druck)Platte f; Gegenstände pl aus Edelmetall; Doublé n, Dublee n; **2. plated with gold, gold-plated** vergoldet

plat·form Plattform f; RAIL Bahnsteig m; (Redner)Tribüne f, Podium n; POL Plattform f; POL Parteiprogramm n; **election platform** POL Wahlprogramm n

plat·i·num CHEM Platin n

pla·toon MIL Zug m

plat·ter (Servier)Platte f

plau·si·ble plausibel, glaubhaft

play 1. Spiel n; Schauspiel n, (Theater)Stück n; TECH Spiel n; fig Spielraum m; **at play** beim Spiel(en); **in play** (ball) (ball); **out of play** im Aus (ball); **2.** v/i spielen (a. SPORT, THEA etc); v/t Karten, Rolle, Stück etc spielen, SPORT Spiel austragen; **play s.o.** SPORT gegen j-n spielen; **play the guitar** Gitarre spielen; **play a trick on s.o.** j-m e-n Streich spielen; **play back** Ball zurückspielen (**to** zu); Tonband abspielen; **play s.th. down** verharmlosen, herunterspielen; **play off** fig ausspielen (**against** gegen); **play on** fig j-s Schwächen ausnutzen

play·back Play-back n, Wiedergabe f, Abspielen n

play·boy Playboy m

play·er MUS, SPORT Spieler(in); TECH Plattenspieler m

play·fel·low Br → **playmate**

play·ful verspielt; scherzhaft

play·go·er Theaterbesucher(in)

play·ground Spielplatz m (a. fig); Schulhof m

play·group Br Spielgruppe f

play·house THEA Schauspielhaus n; Spielhaus n (for children)

play·ing card Spielkarte f

play·ing field Sportplatz m, Spielfeld n

play·mate Spielkamerad(in)

play·pen Laufgitter n, Laufstall m

play·thing Spielzeug n

play·wright Dramatiker(in)

plc, PLC Br ECON ABBR of **public limited company** AG, Aktiengesellschaft f

plea: enter a plea of (not) guilty JUR sich schuldig bekennen (s-e Unschuld erklären)

plead v/i (dringend) bitten (**for** um); **plead (not) guilty** JUR sich schuldig bekennen (s-e Unschuld erklären); v/t a. JUR zu s-r Verteidigung or Entschuldigung anführen, geltend machen; **plead**

s.o.'s case sich für j-n einsetzen; JUR j-n vertreten

pleas·ant angenehm, erfreulich; freundlich; sympathisch

please 1. j-m gefallen; j-m zusagen, j-n erfreuen; zufriedenstellen; **only to please you** nur dir zuliebe; **please o.s.** tun, was man will; **please yourself!** mach, was du willst!; **2.** int bitte; (**yes,**) **please** (ja,) bitte; (oh ja,) gerne; **please come in!** bitte, treten Sie ein!

pleased erfreut, zufrieden; **be pleased about** sich freuen über (acc); **be pleased with** zufrieden sein mit; **I am pleased with it** es gefällt mir; **be pleased to do s.th.** et. gern tun; **pleased to meet you!** angenehm!

pleas·ing angenehm

plea·sure Vergnügen n; **at (one's) pleasure** nach Belieben

pleat (Plissee)Falte f

pleat·ed skirt Faltenrock m

pledge 1. Pfand n; fig Unterpfand n; Versprechen n; **2.** versprechen, zusichern

plen·ti·ful reichlich

plen·ty 1. Überfluss m; **in plenty** im Überfluss, in Hülle und Fülle; **plenty of** e-e Menge, viel(e), reichlich; **2.** F reichlich

pleu·ri·sy MED Brustfell-, Rippenfellentzündung f

pli·a·ble, pli·ant biegsam; fig flexibel; fig leicht beeinflussbar

pli·ers (a pair of pliers e-e) Beißzange f

plight Not f, Notlage f

plim·soll Br Turnschuh m

plod a. **plod along** sich dahinschleppen; **plod away** sich abplagen (**at** mit), schuften

plop F **1.** Plumps m, Platsch m; **2.** plumpsen, (ins Wasser) platschen

plot 1. Stück n Land, Parzelle f, Grundstück n; THEA, film etc: Handlung f; Komplott n, Verschwörung f; EDP grafische Darstellung; **2.** v/i sich verschwören (**against** gegen); v/t planen; einzeichnen

plot·ter EDP Plotter m

plough Br, **plow** AGR **1.** Pflug m; **2.** (um)pflügen

plough·share Br, **plow·share** AGR Pflugschar f

pluck 1. v/t Geflügel rupfen; mst **pluck out** ausreißen, ausrupfen, auszupfen; MUS Saiten zupfen; **pluck up (one's) courage** Mut or sich ein Herz fassen; v/i zupfen (**at** an dat); **2.** F Mut m, Schneid m

pluck·y F mutig

plug 1. Stöpsel m; ELECTR Stecker m, F Steckdose f; F MOT (Zünd)Kerze f; **2.**

v/t F für et. Schleichwerbung machen; a. **plug up** zustöpseln; zustopfen, verstopfen; **plug in** ELECTR anschließen, einstecken

plug-ging F Schleichwerbung f

plum-age Gefieder n

plum BOT Pflaume f; Zwetsch(g)e f

plumb 1. (Blei)Lot n; **2.** ausloten, fig a. ergründen; **plumb in** esp Br Waschmaschine etc anschließen; **3.** adj lotrecht, senkrecht; **4.** adv F (haar)genau

plumb-er Klempner m, Installateur m

plumb-ing Klempner-, Installateurarbeit f; Rohre pl, Rohrleitungen pl

plume (Schmuck)Feder f; Federbusch m; (Rauch)Fahne f

plump 1. adj drall, mollig, rund(lich), F pumm(e)lig; **2. plump down** fallen or plumpsen (lassen)

plum pud-ding Br Plumpudding m

plun-der 1. plündern; **2.** Plünderung f; Beute f

plunge 1. (ein-, unter)tauchen; (sich) stürzen (into in acc); MAR stampfen; **2.** (Kopf)Sprung m; **take the plunge** fig den entscheidenden Schritt wagen

plu-per-fect a. **pluperfect tense** LING Plusquamperfekt n, Vorvergangenheit f

plu-ral LING Plural m, Mehrzahl f

plus 1. prp plus, und, esp ECON zuzüglich; **2.** adj Plus...; **plus sign** MATH Plus n, Pluszeichen n; **3.** MATH Plus n (a. F), Pluszeichen n; F Vorteil m

plush Plüsch m

ply¹ regelmäßig verkehren, fahren (between zwischen dat)

ply² mst in cpds TECH Lage f, Schicht f; **three-ply** dreifach (thread etc); dreifach gewebt (carpet)

ply-wood Sperrholz n

pm, PM ABBR of after noon (Latin post meridiem) nachm., nachmittags, abends

pneu-mat-ic Luft..., pneumatisch; TECH Druck..., Pressluft...

pneu-mat-ic drill Pressluftbohrer m

pneu-mo-ni-a MED Lungenentzündung f

poach¹ GASTR pochieren; **poached eggs** verlorene Eier pl

poach² wildern

poach-er Wilddieb m, Wilderer m

PO Box Postfach n; **write to PO Box 225** schreiben Sie an Postfach 225

pock MED Pocke f, Blatter f

pock-et 1. (Hosen- etc)Tasche f; **2.** adj Taschen...; **3.** einstecken, in die Tasche stecken; fig in die eigene Tasche stecken

pock-et-book Notizbuch n; Brieftasche f

pock-et cal-cu-la-tor Taschenrechner m

pocket knife Taschenmesser n

pocket money Taschengeld n

pod BOT Hülse f, Schote f

po-di-a-trist Fußpfleger(in)

po-em Gedicht n

po-et Dichter(in)

po-et-ic dichterisch

po-et-i-cal dichterisch

po-et-ic jus-tice fig ausgleichende Gerechtigkeit

po-et-ry Gedichte pl; Poesie f (a. fig), Dichtkunst f, Dichtung f

poi-gnant schmerzlich; ergreifend

point 1. Spitze f; GEOGR Landspitze f; LING, MATH, PHYS, SPORT etc Punkt m; MATH (Dezimal)Punkt m; Grad m; MAR (Kompass)Strich m; fig Punkt m, Stelle f, Ort m; Zweck m; Ziel n, Absicht f; springender Punkt; Pointe f; **two point five (2.5)** 2,5; **point of view** Stand-, Gesichtspunkt m; **be on the point of doing s.th.** im Begriff sein, et. zu tun; **to the point** zur Sache gehörig; **off or beside the point** nicht zur Sache gehörig; **come to the point** zur Sache kommen; **that's not the point** darum geht es nicht; **what's the point?** wozu?; **win on points** SPORT nach Punkten gewinnen; **winner on points** SPORT Punktsieger m; **2.** v/t (zu)spitzen; Waffe etc richten (at auf acc); **point one's finger at s.o.** (mit dem Finger) auf j-n zeigen; **point out** zeigen; fig hinweisen or aufmerksam machen auf (acc); v/i (mit dem Finger) zeigen (at, to auf acc); deuten (at, to nach e-r Richtung weisen or liegen; fig hinweisen auf (acc)

point-ed spitz; Spitz...; fig scharf (remark etc); ostentativ

point-er Zeiger m; Zeigestock m; zo Pointer m, Vorstehhund m

point-less sinnlos, zwecklos

points Br RAIL Weiche f

poise 1. (Körper)Haltung f; fig Gelassenheit f; **2.** balancieren; **be poised** schweben

poi-son 1. Gift n; **2.** vergiften

poi-son-ous giftig (a. fig)

poke 1. v/t stoßen; Feuer schüren; stecken; v/i **poke about, poke around** F (herum-) stöbern, (-)wühlen (in in dat); **2.** Stoß m

pok-er Schürhaken m

pok-y F eng; schäbig

Po-land Polen n

po-lar polar

polar bear ZO Eisbär m

pole¹ GEOGR Pol m

pole² Stange f; Mast m; Deichsel f; SPORT (Sprung)Stab m

Pole Pole m, Polin f

pole-cat ZO Iltis *m*; F Skunk *m*, Stinktier *n*

po-lem-ic, po-lem-i-cal polemisch

pole star ASTR Polarstern *m*

pole vault SPORT Stabhochsprung *m*, Stabhochspringen *n*

pole-vault SPORT stabhochspringen

pole vault-er SPORT Stabhochspringer(in)

po-lice 1. Polizei *f*; **2.** überwachen

po-lice car Polizeiauto *n*

po-lice-man Polizist *m*

po-lice of-fi-cer Polizeibeamte *m*, -beamtin *f*, Polizist(in)

police sta-tion Polizeiwache *f*, Polizeirevier *n*

po-lice-wom-an Polizistin *f*

pol-i-cy Politik *f*; Taktik *f*; Klugheit *f*; (Versicherungs)Police *f*

po-li-o Polio *f*, Kinderlähmung *f*

pol-ish 1. polieren; *Schuhe* putzen; **polish up** aufpolieren (*a. fig*); **2.** Politur *f*; (*Schuh*)Creme *f*; *fig* Schliff *m*

Pol-ish 1. polnisch; **2.** LING Polnisch *n*

po-lite höflich

po-lite-ness Höflichkeit *f*

po-lit-i-cal politisch

po-li-ti-cian Politiker(in)

pol-i-tics Politik *f*

pol-ka MUS Polka *f*

pol-ka-dot gepunktet, getupft

poll 1. (*Meinungs*)Umfrage *f*; Wahlbeteiligung *f*; *a. pl* Stimmabgabe *f*, Wahl *f*; **2.** befragen; *Stimmen* erhalten

pol-len BOT Pollen *m*, Blütenstaub *m*

poll-ing Stimmabgabe *f*; Wahlbeteiligung *f*

polling booth *esp Br* Wahlkabine *f*

polling day Wahltag *m*

polling place, *esp Br* **polling sta-tion** Wahllokal *n*

polls Wahl *f*; Wahllokal *n*

poll-ster Demoskop(in), Meinungsforscher(in)

pol-lut-ant Schadstoff *m*

pol-lute beschmutzen, verschmutzen; verunreinigen

pol-lut-er *a.* **environmental polluter** Umweltsünder(in)

pol-lu-tion (*Luft-, Wasser- etc*)Verschmutzung *f*; Verunreinigung *f*

po-lo SPORT Polo *n*

po-lo neck *a.* **polo neck sweater** *esp Br* Rollkragenpullover *m*

pol-yp ZO, MED Polyp *m*

pol-y-sty-rene Styropor® *n*

pom-mel (*Sattel- etc*)Knopf *m*

pomp Pomp *m*, Prunk *m*

pom-pous aufgeblasen, wichtigtuerisch; schwülstig (*speech*)

pond Teich *m*, Weiher *m*

pon-der *v/i* nachdenken (**on, over** über *acc*); *v/t* überlegen

pon-der-ous schwerfällig; schwer

pon-toon Ponton *m*

pon-toon bridge Pontonbrücke *f*

po-ny ZO Pony *n*

po-ny-tail Pferdeschwanz *m*

poo-dle ZO Pudel *m*

pool¹ Teich *m*, Tümpel *m*; Pfütze *f*, (*Blut- etc*)Lache *f*; (*Schwimm*)Becken *n*, (*Swimming*)Pool *m*

pool² **1.** (*Arbeits-, Fahr*)Gemeinschaft *f*; (*Mitarbeiter- etc*)Stab *m*; (*Fuhr*)Park *m*; (*Schreib*)Pool *m*; ECON Pool *m*, Kartell *n*; *card games*: Gesamteinsatz *m*; Poolbillard *n*; **2.** *Geld, Unternehmen etc* zusammenlegen; *Kräfte etc* vereinen

pool hall, pool-room Billardspielhalle *f*

pools *a.* **football pools** *Br* (Fußball)Toto *n*, *m*

poor 1. arm; dürftig, mangelhaft, schwach; **2. the poor** die Armen *pl*

poor-ly 1. *adj esp Br* F kränklich, unpässlich; **2.** *adv* ärmlich, dürftig, schlecht, schwach

pop¹ 1. *v/t* zerknallen; F schnell *wohin* tun *or* stecken; *v/i* knallen; (zer)platzen; **pop in** F auf e-n Sprung vorbeikommen; **pop off** F (plötzlich) den Löffel weglegen; **pop up** (plötzlich) auftauchen; **2.** Knall *m*; F Limo *f*

pop² MUS **1.** Pop *m*; **2.** Schlager...; Pop...

pop³ F Paps *m*, Papa *m*

pop⁴ ABBR *of* **population** Einw., Einwohner(zahl *f*) *pl*

pop con-cert MUS Popkonzert *n*

pop-corn Popcorn *n*, Puffmais *m*

Pope REL Papst *m*

pop-eyed F glotzäugig

pop group MUS Popgruppe *f*

pop-lar BOT Pappel *f*

pop mu-sic Popmusik *f*

pop-py BOT Mohn *m*

pop-u-lar populär, beliebt; volkstümlich; allgemein

pop-u-lar-i-ty Popularität *f*, Beliebtheit *f*; Volkstümlichkeit *f*

pop-u-late bevölkern, besiedeln; bewohnen

pop-u-la-tion Bevölkerung *f*

pop-u-lous dicht besiedelt, dicht bevölkert

porce-lain Porzellan *n*

porch überdachter Vorbau; Portal *n*; Veranda *f*

por-cu-pine ZO Stachelschwein *n*

pore¹ Pore *f*

pore²: **pore over** vertieft sein in (*acc*), *et.* eifrig studieren

P

pork GASTR Schweinefleisch n

porn F → *porno*

por·no F 1. Porno m; 2. Porno...

por·nog·ra·phy Pornografie f

po·rous porös

por·poise ZO Tümmler m

por·ridge Porridge m, n, Haferbrei m

port[1] Hafen m; Hafenstadt f

port[2] AVIAT, MAR Backbord n

port[3] EDP Port m, Anschluss m

port[4] Portwein m

por·ta·ble tragbar

por·ter (Gepäck)Träger m; *esp Br* Pförtner m, Portier m; RAIL Schlafwagenschaffner m

port·hole MAR Bullauge n

por·tion 1. (An)Teil m; GASTR Portion f; 2. *portion out* aufteilen, verteilen (*among*, *between* unter acc)

port·ly korpulent

por·trait Porträt n, Bild n, Bildnis n

por·tray porträtieren; darstellen; schildern

por·tray·al THEA Verkörperung f, Darstellung f; Schilderung f

Por·tu·gal Portugal n

Por·tu·guese 1. portugiesisch; 2. Portugiese m, Portugiesin f; LING Portugiesisch n; *the Portuguese* die Portugiesen pl

pose 1. v/t aufstellen; Problem, Frage aufwerfen; Bedrohung, Gefahr etc darstellen; v/i Modell sitzen oder stehen; *pose as* sich ausgeben als oder für; 2. Pose f

posh *esp Br* F schick, piekfein

po·si·tion 1. Position f, Lage f, Stellung f (a. fig); Stand m; fig Standpunkt m; 2. (auf)stellen

pos·i·tive 1. positiv; bestimmt, sicher, eindeutig; greifbar, konkret, konstruktiv; 2. PHOT Positiv n

pos·sess besitzen; fig beherrschen

pos·sessed fig besessen

pos·ses·sion Besitz m; fig Besessenheit f

pos·ses·sive besitzergreifend; LING possessiv, besitzanzeigend

pos·si·bil·i·ty Möglichkeit f

pos·si·ble möglich

pos·si·bly möglicherweise, vielleicht; *if I possibly can* wenn ich irgend kann; *I can't possibly do this* ich kann das unmöglich tun

post[1] (Tür-, Tor-, Ziel- etc)Pfosten m; Pfahl m; 1. a. *post up* Plakat etc anschlagen, ankleben; *be posted missing* AVIAT, MAR als vermisst gemeldet werden

post[2] *esp Br* 1. Post f; Postsendung f; *by post* mit der Post; 2. mit der Post (zu-)schicken, aufgeben, Brief einwerfen

post[3] 1. Stelle f, Job m; Posten m; 2. aufstellen, postieren; *esp Br* versetzen, MIL abkommandieren (*to* nach)

post... nach..., Nach...

post·age Porto n

postage stamp Postwertzeichen n, Briefmarke f

post·al postalisch, Post...

postal or·der *Br* ECON Postanweisung f

postal vote POL Briefwahl f

post·bag *esp Br* Postsack m

post·box *esp Br* Briefkasten m

post·card Postkarte f; a. *picture postcard* Ansichtskarte f

post·code *Br* Postleitzahl f

post·er Plakat n; Poster n, m

poste res·tante THEA Br 1. Abteilung f für postlagernde Sendungen; 2. postlagernd

pos·te·ri·or HUMOR Hinterteil n

pos·ter·i·ty die Nachwelt

post-free *esp Br* portofrei

post·hu·mous post(h)um

post·man *esp Br* Briefträger m, Postbote m

post·mark 1. Poststempel m; 2. (ab-)stempeln

post·mas·ter Postamtsvorsteher m

post of·fice Post f; Postamt n, -filiale f

post of·fice box → *PO Box*

post-paid portofrei

post·pone verschieben, aufschieben

post·pone·ment Verschiebung f, Aufschub m

post·script Postskript(um) n, Nachschrift f

pos·ture 1. (Körper)Haltung f; Stellung f; 2. fig sich aufspielen

post·war Nachkriegs...

post·wom·an *esp Br* Briefträgerin f, Postbotin f

po·sy Sträußchen n

pot 1. Topf m; Kanne f; Kännchen n (Tee etc); SPORT F Pokal m; 2. Pflanze eintopfen

po·tas·si·um cy·a·nide CHEM Zyankali n

po·ta·to Kartoffel f; → *chips*, *crisps*

pot·bel·ly Schmerbauch m

po·ten·cy Stärke f; Wirksamkeit f, Wirkung f; MED Potenz f

po·tent PHARM stark; MED potent

po·ten·tial 1. potenziell, möglich; 2. Potenzial n, Leistungsfähigkeit f

pot·hole MOT Schlagloch n

po·tion Trank m

pot·ter[1] *Br*: *potter about* herumwerkeln

pot·ter[2] Töpfer(in)

pot·ter·y Töpferei f; Töpferware(n pl) f

pouch Beutel m (a. ZO); ZO (Backen-)Tasche f

poul·tice MED (warmer) Umschlag *m*

poul·try Geflügel *n*

pounce 1. sich stürzen (*on* auf *acc*); **2.** Satz *m*, Sprung *m*

pound[1] Pfund *n* (*453,59 g*); **pound** (*sterling*) (ABBR **£**) Pfund *n*

pound[2] Tierheim *n*; Abstellplatz *m* für (polizeilich) abgeschleppte Fahrzeuge

pound[3] *v/t* zerstoßen, zerstampfen; trommeln *or* hämmern auf (*acc*) *or* an (*acc*) *or* gegen; *v/i* hämmern (*with* vor *dat*)

pour *v/t* gießen, schütten; **pour out** ausgießen, ausschütten; *Getränk* eingießen; *v/i* strömen (*a. fig*)

pout *v/t Lippen* schürzen; *v/i* e-n Schmollmund machen; schmollen

pov·er·ty Armut *f*

pow·der 1. Pulver *n*; Puder *m*; **2.** pulverisieren; (sich) pudern

powder puff Puderquaste *f*

powder room (Damen)Toilette *f*

pow·er 1. Kraft *f*; Macht *f*; Fähigkeit *f*, Vermögen *n*; Gewalt *f*; JUR Befugnis *f*, Vollmacht *f*; MATH Potenz *f*; ELECTR Strom *m*; **in power** POL an der Macht; **2.** TECH antreiben

power cut Stromsperre *f*

power fail·ure ELECTR Stromausfall *m*, Netzausfall *m*

pow·er·ful stark, kräftig; mächtig

pow·er·less kraftlos; machtlos

pow·er plant Elektrizitäts-, Kraftwerk *n*

power pol·i·tics Machtpolitik *f*

power sta·tion Br Elektrizitäts-, Kraftwerk *n*

prac·ti·ca·ble durchführbar

prac·ti·cal praktisch

prac·ti·cal·ly so gut wie

practical joke Streich *m*

prac·tice 1. Praxis *f*; Übung *f*; Gewohnheit *f*, Brauch *m*; **it is common practice** es ist allgemein üblich; **put into practice** in die Praxis umsetzen; **2.** *v/t* (ein)üben; *als Beruf* ausüben; **practice law** (*medicine*) als Anwalt (Arzt) praktizieren; *v/i* praktizieren; üben

prac·ticed geübt (*in* in *dat*)

prac·tise Br → **practice 2**

prac·tised → **practiced**

prac·ti·tion·er: **general practitioner** praktischer Arzt

prai·rie Prärie *f*

prai·rie schoo·ner HIST Planwagen *m*

praise 1. loben, preisen; **2.** Lob *n*

praise·wor·thy lobenswert

pram Br Kinderwagen *m*

prance sich aufbäumen, steigen (*horse*); tänzeln (*horse*); stolzieren

prank Streich *m*

prat·tle: **prattle on** plappern (*about* von)

prawn ZO Garnele *f*

pray beten (*to* zu; *for* für, um)

prayer REL Gebet *n*; *often pl* Andacht *f*; **the Lord's Prayer** das Vaterunser

prayer book REL Gebetbuch *n*

preach predigen (*to* zu, vor *dat*)

preach·er Prediger(in)

pre·am·ble Einleitung *f*

pre·ar·range vorher vereinbaren

pre·car·i·ous prekär, unsicher; gefährlich

pre·cau·tion Vorsichtsmaßnahme *f*; **as a precaution** vorsorglich; **take precautions** Vorsichtsmaßnahmen treffen

pre·cau·tion·a·ry vorbeugend; vorsorglich

pre·cede voraus-, vorangehen (*dat*)

pre·ce·dence Vorrang *m*

pre·ce·dent Präzedenzfall *m*

pre·cept Regel *f*, Richtlinie *f*

pre·cinct (*Wahl*)Bezirk *m*; (*Polizei*)Revier *n*; *pl* Gelände *n*; *esp Br* (*Einkaufs*)-Viertel *n*; (*Fußgänger*)Zone *f*

pre·cious 1. *adj* kostbar, wertvoll; Edel… (*stone etc*); **2.** *adv*: **precious little** F herzlich wenig

pre·ci·pice Abgrund *m*

pre·cip·i·tate 1. *v/t* (hinunter-, herunter-)schleudern; CHEM ausfällen; beschleunigen; stürzen (*into* in *acc*) *v/i* CHEM ausfallen; **2.** *adj* überstürzt; **3.** CHEM Niederschlag *m*

pre·cip·i·ta·tion CHEM Ausfällung *f*; METEOR Niederschlag *m*; Überstürzung *f*, Hast *f*

pre·cip·i·tous steil (abfallend); überstürzt

pré·cis Zusammenfassung *f*

pre·cise genau, präzis

pre·ci·sion Genauigkeit *f*; Präzision *f*

pre·clude ausschließen

pre·co·cious frühreif; altklug

pre·con·ceived vorgefasst

pre·con·cep·tion vorgefasste Meinung

pre·cur·sor Vorläufer(in)

pred·a·to·ry ZO Raub…

pre·de·ces·sor Vorgänger(in)

pre·des·ti·na·tion Vorherbestimmung *f*

pre·des·tined prädestiniert, vorherbestimmt (*to* für, zu)

pre·de·ter·mine vorherbestimmen; vorher vereinbaren

pre·dic·a·ment missliche Lage, Zwangslage *f*

pred·i·cate LING Prädikat *n*, Satzaussage *f*

pre·dic·a·tive LING prädikativ

pre·dict vorhersagen, voraussagen

pre·dic·tion Vorhersage *f*, Voraussage *f*; **computer prediction** Hochrechnung *f*

pre·dis·pose geneigt machen, einnehmen (**in favor of** für); *esp* MED anfällig machen (**to** für)

pre·dis·po·si·tion: **predisposition to** Neigung *f* zu, *esp* MED *a.* Anfälligkeit *f* für

pre·dom·i·nant (vor)herrschend, überwiegend

pre·dom·i·nate vorherrschen, überwiegen; die Oberhand haben

pre·em·i·nent hervorragend, überragend

pre·emp·tive ECON Vorkaufs...; MIL Präventiv...

preen ZO *sich or das Gefieder putzen*

pre·fab F Fertighaus *n*

pre·fab·ri·cate vorfabrizieren, vorfertigen; **prefabricated house** Fertighaus *n*

pref·ace 1. Vorwort *n* (**to** zu); 2. Buch, Rede etc einleiten (**with** mit)

pre·fect Br PED Aufsichts-, Vertrauensschüler(in)

pre·fer vorziehen (**to** dat), lieber mögen (**to** als), bevorzugen

pref·er·a·ble: **be preferable** (**to**) vorzuziehen sein (dat), besser sein (als)

pref·er·a·bly vorzugsweise, lieber, am liebsten

pref·er·ence Vorliebe *f* (**for** für); Vorzug *m*

pre·fix LING Präfix *n*, Vorsilbe *f*

preg·nan·cy MED Schwangerschaft *f*; ZO Trächtigkeit *f*

preg·nant MED schwanger; ZO trächtig

pre·heat *Backofen etc* vorheizen

pre·judge *j-n* vorverurteilen; vorschnell beurteilen

prej·u·dice 1. Vorurteil *n*, Voreingenommenheit *f*, Befangenheit *f*; **to the prejudice of** zum Nachteil *or* Schaden (gen); 2. einnehmen (**in favo[u]r of** für; **against** gegen); schaden (dat), beeinträchtigen

prej·u·diced (vor)eingenommen, befangen

pre·lim·i·nar·y 1. vorläufig, einleitend, Vor...; 2. *pl* Vorbereitungen *pl*

prel·ude Vorspiel *n* (a. MUS)

pre·mar·i·tal vorehelich

pre·ma·ture vorzeitig, verfrüht; *fig* voreilig

pre·med·i·tat·ed JUR vorsätzlich

pre·med·i·ta·tion: **with premeditation** JUR vorsätzlich

prem·i·er POL Premier(minister) *m*

prem·i·ere, prem·i·ère THEA etc Premiere *f*, Ur-, Erstaufführung *f*

prem·is·es Gelände *n*, Grundstück *n*, (*Geschäfts*)Räume *pl*; **on the premises** an Ort und Stelle, im Haus, im Lokal

pre·mi·um Prämie *f*, Bonus *m*

pre·mi·um (**gas·o·line**) MOT Super *n*, Su-

perbenzin *n*

pre·mo·ni·tion (böse) Vorahnung

pre·oc·cu·pa·tion Beschäftigung *f* (**with** mit)

pre·oc·cu·pied gedankenverloren, geistesabwesend

pre·oc·cu·py (stark) beschäftigen

prep Br F PED Hausaufgabe(n *pl*) *f*

pre·packed, pre·pack·aged abgepackt

pre·paid *post* frankiert, freigemacht

prepaid envelope Freiumschlag *m*

prep·a·ra·tion Vorbereitung *f* (**for** auf *acc* für); Zubereitung *f*; CHEM, MED Präparat *n*

pre·par·a·to·ry vorbereitend

pre·pare *v/t* vorbereiten; GASTR zubereiten; *v/i*: **prepare for** sich vorbereiten auf (acc); Vorbereitungen treffen für; sich gefasst machen auf (acc)

pre·pared vorbereitet; bereit

prep·o·si·tion LING Präposition *f*, Verhältniswort *n*

pre·pos·sess·ing einnehmend, anziehend

pre·pos·ter·ous absurd; lächerlich, grotesk

pre·pro·gram(me) vorprogrammieren

pre·req·ui·site Vorbedingung *f*, Voraussetzung *f*

pre·rog·a·tive Vorrecht *n*

pre·school Vorschule *f*

pre·scribe *et.* vorschreiben; MED *j-m et.* verschreiben

pre·scrip·tion Verordnung *f*, Vorschrift *f*; MED Rezept *n*

pres·ence Gegenwart *f*, Anwesenheit *f*

presence of mind Geistesgegenwart *f*

pres·ent¹ Geschenk *n*

pre·sent² präsentieren; (über)reichen, (über)bringen, (über)geben; schenken; vorbringen, vorlegen; zeigen, vorführen; THEA etc aufführen; schildern, darstellen; *j-n, Produkt etc* vorstellen; *Programm etc* moderieren

pres·ent³ 1. anwesend; vorhanden; gegenwärtig, jetzig; laufend; vorliegend (*case etc*); **present tense** LING Präsens *n*, Gegenwart *f*; 2. Gegenwart *f*, LING *a.* Präsens *n*; **at present** gegenwärtig, zurzeit; **for the present** vorerst, vorläufig

pre·sen·ta·tion Präsentation *f*; Überreichung *f*; Vorlage *f*; Vorführung *f*, THEA etc Aufführung *f*; Schilderung *f*, Darstellung *f*; Vorstellung *f*; radio, TV Moderation *f*

pres·ent-day heutig, gegenwärtig, modern

pre·sent·er *esp Br radio*, TV Moderator(in)

pre·sen·ti·ment (böse) Vorahnung

pres·ent·ly zurzeit, jetzt; *Br* bald

pres·er·va·tion Bewahrung *f*; Erhaltung *f*; GASTR Konservierung *f*

pre·ser·va·tive GASTR Konservierungsmittel *n*

pre·serve 1. bewahren, (be)schützen; erhalten; GASTR konservieren, *Obst etc* einmachen, einkochen; **2.** (*Jagd-*)Revier *n*; *fig* Ressort *n*, Reich *n*; *mst pl* GASTR *das* Eingemachte

pre·side den Vorsitz haben (*at, over* bei)

pres·i·den·cy POL Präsidentschaft *f*; Amtszeit *f*

pres·i·dent Präsident *m*; ECON Generaldirektor *m*

press 1. *v/t* drücken, pressen; *Frucht* (aus)pressen; drücken auf (*acc*); bügeln; drängen; *j-n* (be)drängen; bestehen auf (*dat*); *v/i* drücken; drängen (*time etc*); (sich) drängen; drängen *or* dringen *or* drängen auf (*acc*); ***press on*** (zügig) weitermachen; **2.** Druck *m* (*a. fig*); (*Wein-etc*)Presse *f*; Bügeln *n*; *die* Presse *f*. ***printing press*** Druckerpresse *f*

press a·gen·cy Presseagentur *f*

press box Pressetribüne *f*

press con·fe·rence Pressekonferenz *f*

press of·fice Pressebüro *n*, Pressestelle *f*

press of·fi·cer Pressereferent(in)

press·ing dringend

press re·lease Pressemitteilung *f*

press stud *Br* Druckknopf *m*

press-up *esp Br* SPORT Liegestütz *m*

pres·sure PHYS, TECH *etc* Druck *m* (*a. fig*)

pressure cook·er Dampfkochtopf *m*, Schnellkochtopf *m*

pres·tige Prestige *n*, Ansehen *n*

pre·su·ma·bly vermutlich

pre·sume *v/t* annehmen, vermuten; sich erdreisten *or* anmaßen (***to do*** zu tun); *v/i* annehmen, vermuten; anmaßend sein; ***presume on*** et. ausnützen, et. missbrauchen

pre·sump·tion Annahme *f*, Vermutung *f*; Anmaßung *f*

pre·sump·tu·ous anmaßend, vermessen

pre·sup·pose voraussetzen

pre·sup·po·si·tion Voraussetzung *f*

pre·tence *Br* → **pretense**

pre·tend vortäuschen, vorgeben; sich verstellen; Anspruch erheben (***to*** auf *acc*); ***she is only pretending*** sie tut nur so

pre·tend·ed vorgetäuscht, gespielt

pre·tense Verstellung *f*, Vortäuschung *f*; Anspruch *m* (***to*** auf *acc*)

pre·ten·sion Anspruch *m* (***to*** auf *acc*); Anmaßung *f*

pre·ter·it(e) LING Präteritum *n*

pre·text Vorwand *m*

pret·ty 1. *adj* hübsch; **2.** *adv* ziemlich, ganz schön

pret·zel Brezel *f*

pre·vail vorherrschen, weit verbreitet sein; siegen (***over, against*** über *acc*)

pre·vail·ing (vor)herrschend

pre·vent verhindern, verhüten, *e-r Sache* vorbeugen; *j-n* hindern (***from*** an *dat*)

pre·ven·tion Verhinderung *f*, Verhütung *f*, Vorbeugung *f*

pre·ven·tive vorbeugend

pre·view *film*, TV Voraufführung *f*; Vorbesichtigung *f*; *film*, TV *etc*: Vorschau *f* (***of*** auf *acc*)

pre·vi·ous vorhergehend, vorausgehend, vorherig, vorig; ***previous to*** bevor, vor (*dat*); ***previous knowledge*** Vorkenntnisse *pl*

pre·vi·ous·ly vorher, früher

pre-war Vorkriegs…

prey 1. ZO Beute *f*, Opfer *n* (*a. fig*); ***be easy prey for*** *or* ***to*** *fig* e-e leichte Beute sein für; **2. prey on** ZO Jagd machen auf (*acc*); *fig* nagen an (*dat*); ***prey on s.o.'s mind*** j-m keine Ruhe lassen

price 1. Preis *m*; **2.** den Preis festsetzen für; auszeichnen (***at*** mit)

price·less unbezahlbar

price tag Preisschild *n*

prick 1. Stich *m*; V Schwanz *m*; ***pricks of conscience*** Gewissensbisse *pl*; **2.** *v/t* (auf-, durch)stechen, stechen in (*acc*); ***her conscience pricked her*** sie hatte Gewissensbisse; ***prick up one's ears*** die Ohren spitzen; *v/i* stechen

prick·le BOT, ZO Stachel *m*, Dorn *m*

prick·ly stach(e)lig; prickelnd, kribbelnd

pride Stolz *m*; Hochmut *m*; ***take (a) pride in*** stolz sein auf (*acc*); **2. pride o.s. on** stolz sein auf (*acc*)

priest REL Priester *m*

prig Tugendbold *m*

prig·gish tugendhaft

prim steif; prüde

pri·mae·val *esp Br* → **primeval**

pri·ma·ri·ly in erster Linie, vor allem

pri·ma·ry 1. wichtigste(r, -s), Haupt…; grundlegend, elementar, Grund…; Anfangs…, Ur…; **2.** POL Vorwahl *f*

pri·ma·ry school *Br* Grundschule *f*

prime 1. MATH Primzahl *f*; *fig* Blüte(zeit) *f*; ***in the prime of life*** in der Blüte s-r Jahre; ***be past one's prime*** s-e besten Jahre hinter sich haben; **2.** *adj* erste(r, -s), wichtigste(r, -s), Haupt…; erstklassig; **3.** *v/t* TECH grundieren; *j-n* instruieren, vorbereiten

prime min·is·ter (*ABBR* POL F **PM**) Premierminister(in), Ministerpräsident(in)

P

prime num·ber MATH Primzahl f
prim·er Fibel f, Elementarbuch n
prime time TV Haupteinschaltzeit f, Hauptsendezeit f, beste Sendezeit
pri·me·val urzeitlich, Ur…
prim·i·tive erste(r, -s), ursprünglich, Ur…; primitiv
prim·rose BOT Primel f, esp Schlüsselblume f
prince Fürst m; Prinz m
prin·cess Fürstin f; Prinzessin f
prin·ci·pal 1. wichtigste(r, -s), hauptsächlich, Haupt…; 2. PED Direktor(in), Rektor(in); THEA Hauptdarsteller(in); MUS Solist(in)
prin·ci·pal·i·ty Fürstentum n
prin·ci·ple Prinzip n, Grundsatz m; **on principle** grundsätzlich, aus Prinzip
print 1. PRINT Druck m (a. art); Gedruckte n; (Finger- etc) Abdruck m; PHOT Abzug m; bedruckter Stoff; **in print** gedruckt; **out of print** vergriffen; 2. v/i drucken; v/t (ab-, auf-, be)drucken; in Druckbuchstaben schreiben; fig einprägen (**on** dat); a. **print off** PHOT abziehen; **print out** EDP ausdrucken
print·ed mat·ter post Drucksache f
print·er Drucker m (a. TECH); **printer's error** Druckfehler m; **printer's ink** Druckerschwärze f
print·er's Druckerei f
print·ing Drucken m; Auflage f
printing ink Druckerschwärze f
printing press Druckerpresse f
print·out EDP Ausdruck m
pri·or frühere(r, -s), vorrangig
pri·or·i·ty Priorität f, Vorrang m; MOT Vorfahrt f; **give s.th. priority** et. vordringlich behandeln
prise esp Br → **prize²**
prism Prisma n
pris·on Gefängnis n, Strafanstalt f
pris·on·er Gefangene m, f, Häftling m; **hold prisoner**, **keep prisoner** gefangen halten; **take prisoner** gefangen nehmen
pri·va·cy Intim-, Privatsphäre f; Geheimhaltung f
pri·vate 1. privat, Privat…; vertraulich; geheim; Privat…; Geschlechtsteile pl; 2. MIL gemeiner Soldat; **in private** privat; unter vier Augen
pri·va·tion Entbehrung f
priv·i·lege Privileg n; Vorrecht n
priv·i·leged privilegiert
priv·y: **be privy to** eingeweiht sein in (acc)
prize¹ 1. (Sieger-, Sieges)Preis m, Prämie f, Auszeichnung f; (Lotterie)Gewinn m; 2. preisgekrönt; Preis…; 3. (hoch) schätzen

prize²: **prize open** aufbrechen, aufstemmen
prize·win·ner Preisträger(in)
pro¹ F Profi m
pro²: **the pros and cons** das Pro und Kontra, das Für und Wider
prob·a·bil·i·ty Wahrscheinlichkeit f; **in all probability** höchstwahrscheinlich
prob·a·ble adj wahrscheinlich
prob·a·bly adv wahrscheinlich
pro·ba·tion Probe f, Probezeit f; JUR Bewährung f, Bewährungsfrist f
pro·ba·tion of·fi·cer JUR Bewährungshelfer(in)
probe 1. MED, TECH Sonde f; fig Untersuchung f (**into** gen); 2. sondieren; (gründlich) untersuchen
prob·lem Problem n; MATH etc Aufgabe f
prob·lem·at·ic, prob·lem·at·i·cal problematisch
pro·ce·dure Verfahren n, Verfahrensweise f, Vorgehen n
pro·ceed (weiter)gehen, (weiter)fahren; sich begeben (**to** nach, zu); fig weitergehen; fig fortfahren; fig vorgehen; **proceed from** kommen or herrühren von; **proceed to do s.th.** sich anschicken or daranmachen, et. zu tun
pro·ceed·ing Verfahren n, Vorgehen n
pro·ceed·ings Vorgänge pl, Geschehnisse pl; **start** or **take** (**legal**) **proceedings against** JUR (gerichtlich) vorgehen gegen
pro·ceeds ECON Erlös m, Ertrag m, Einnahmen pl
pro·cess 1. Prozess m, Verfahren n, Vorgang m; **in the process** dabei; **be in process** im Gange sein; **in process of construction** im Bau (befindlich); 2. TECH etc bearbeiten, behandeln; EDP Daten verarbeiten; PHOT Film entwickeln
pro·ces·sion Prozession f
pro·ces·sor EDP Prozessor m; (Wort-, Text)Verarbeitungsgerät n
pro·claim proklamieren, ausrufen
proc·la·ma·tion Proklamation f, Bekanntmachung f
pro·cure (sich) et. beschaffen or besorgen; verkuppeln
prod 1. stoßen; fig anstacheln, anspornen (**into** zu); 2. Stoß m
prod·i·gal 1. verschwenderisch; 2. F Verschwender(in)
pro·di·gious erstaunlich, großartig
prod·i·gy Wunder n; **child prodigy** Wunderkind n
pro·duce¹ ECON produzieren (a. film, TV), herstellen, erzeugen (a. fig); hervorhollen (**from** aus); Ausweis etc (vor)zeigen;

Beweise etc vorlegen; *Zeugen etc* beibringen; *Gewinn etc* (er)bringen, abwerfen; THEA inszenieren; *fig* hervorrufen, *Wirkung* erzielen

prod·uce² *esp* (Agrar)Produkt(e *pl*) *n*, (Agrar)Erzeugnis(se *pl*) *n*

pro·duc·er Produzent(in) (*a. film*, TV), Hersteller(in); THEA Regisseur(in)

prod·uct Produkt *n*, Erzeugnis *n*

pro·duc·tion ECON Produktion *f* (*a. film*, TV), Erzeugung *f*, Herstellung *f*; Produkt *n*, Erzeugnis *n*; Hervorbringen *n*; Vorzeigen *n*, Vorlegen *n*, Beibringung *f*; THEA Inszenierung *f*

pro·duc·tive produktiv (*a. fig*), ergiebig, rentabel; *fig* schöpferisch

pro·duc·tiv·i·ty Produktivität *f*

prof F Prof *m*

pro·fa·na·tion Entweihung *f*

pro·fane **1.** (gottes)lästerlich; profan, weltlich; **2.** entweihen

pro·fan·i·ty: *profanities* Flüche *pl*, Lästerungen *pl*

pro·fess vorgeben, vortäuschen; behaupten (*to be* zu sein); erklären

pro·fessed erklärt (*enemy etc*); angeblich

pro·fes·sion (*esp akademischer*) Beruf; Berufsstand *m*

pro·fes·sion·al 1. Berufs..., beruflich; Fach..., fachlich; fachmännisch; professionell; **2.** Fachmann *m*, Profi *m*; Berufsspieler(in), -sportler(in), Profi *m*

pro·fes·sor Professor(in); Dozent(in)

pro·fi·cien·cy Können *n*, Tüchtigkeit *f*

pro·fi·cient tüchtig (*at, in* in *dat*)

pro·file Profil *n*; *keep a low profile* Zurückhaltung üben

prof·it 1. Gewinn *m*, Profit *m*; Vorteil *m*, Nutzen *m*; **2.** *profit by, profit from* Nutzen ziehen aus, profitieren von

prof·it·a·ble gewinnbringend, einträglich; nützlich, vorteilhaft

prof·it·eer *contp* Profitmacher *m*, Schieber *m*

prof·it shar·ing ECON Gewinnbeteiligung *f*

prof·li·gate verschwenderisch

pro·found *fig* tief; tiefgründig; profund (*knowledge etc*)

pro·fuse (über)reich; verschwenderisch

pro·fu·sion Überfülle *f*; *in profusion* in Hülle und Fülle

prog·e·ny Nachkommen(schaft *f*) *pl*

prog·no·sis MED Prognose *f*

pro·gram 1. Programm *n* (*a.* EDP); *radio*, TV *a.* Sendung *f*; **2.** (vor)programmieren; planen; EDP programmieren

pro·gramme *Br* → **program**

'pro·gram·mer *Br* → **programer**

pro·gress 1. Fortschritt(e *pl*) *m*; *make slow progress* (nur) langsam vorankommen; *be in progress* im Gange sein; **2.** fortschreiten; Fortschritte machen

pro·gres·sion progressiv, fortschreitend; fortschrittlich

pro·hib·it verbieten; verhindern

pro·hi·bi·tion Verbot *n*

pro·hib·i·tive Schutz... (*Zoll etc*); unerschwinglich

proj·ect¹ Projekt *n*, Vorhaben *n*

pro·ject² v/i vorspringen, vorragen, vorstehen; *v/t* werfen, schleudern; planen; projizieren

pro·jec·tile Projektil *n*, Geschoss *n*

pro·jec·tion Vorsprung *m*, vorspringender Teil; Werfen *n*, Schleudern *n*; Planung *f*; *film:* Projektion *f*

pro·jec·tion·ist Filmvorführer *m*

pro·jec·tor *film:* Projektor *m*

pro·le·tar·i·an 1. proletarisch; **2.** Proletarier(in)

pro·lif·ic fruchtbar

pro·log, *esp Br* **pro·logue** Prolog *m*

pro·long verlängern

prom·e·nade 1. (Strand)Promenade *f*; **2.** promenieren

prom·i·nent vorspringend, vorstehend; *fig* prominent

pro·mis·cu·ous sexuell freizügig

prom·ise 1. Versprechen *n*; *fig* Aussicht *f*; **2.** versprechen

prom·is·ing vielversprechend

prom·on·to·ry GEOGR Vorgebirge *n*

pro·mote *j-n* befördern; *Schüler* versetzen; ECON werben für; *Boxkampf, Konzert etc* veranstalten; *et.* fördern; *be promoted* SPORT *esp Br* aufsteigen (*to* in *acc*)

pro·mot·er Promoter(in), Veranstalter(in); ECON Verkaufsförderer *m*

pro·mo·tion Beförderung *f*; PED Versetzung *f*; SPORT Aufstieg *m*; ECON Verkaufsförderung *f*, Werbung *f*

pro·mo·tion(·al) *film* Werbefilm *m*

prompt 1. *j-n* veranlassen (*to do* zu tun); führen zu, *Gefühle etc* wecken; *j-m* vorsagen; THEA *j-m* soufflieren; **2.** prompt, umgehend, unverzüglich; pünktlich

prompt·er THEA Souffleur *m*, Souffleuse *f*

prone auf dem Bauch *or* mit dem Gesicht nach unten liegend; *be prone to a.* MED neigen zu, anfällig sein für

prong Zinke *f*; (Geweih)Sprosse *f*

pro·noun LING Pronomen *n*, Fürwort *n*

pro·nounce aussprechen; erklären für; JUR *Urteil* verkünden

pro·nun·ci·a·tion Aussprache *f*

proof 1. Beweis(e *pl*) *m*, Nachweis *m*; Pro-

P

be *f*; PRINT Korrekturfahne *f, a.* PHOT Probeabzug *m*; **2.** *adj in cpds* ...fest, ...beständig, ...dicht, ...sicher; → *heatproof*, *soundproof*, *waterproof*; *be proof against* geschützt sein vor (*dat*); **3.** imprägnieren

proof·read PRINT Korrektur lesen

proof·read·er PRINT Korrektor(in)

prop 1. Stütze *f* (*a. fig*); **2.** *a.* *prop up* stützen; *sich or et.* lehnen (*against* gegen)

prop·a·gate BIOL sich fortpflanzen *or* vermehren; verbreiten

prop·a·ga·tion Fortpflanzung *f*, Vermehrung *f*; Verbreitung *f*

pro·pel (an)treiben

pro·pel·lant, pro·pel·lent Treibstoff *m*; Treibgas *n*

pro·pel·ler AVIAT Propeller *m*, MAR *a.* Schraube *f*

pro·pel·ling pen·cil Drehbleistift *m*

pro·pen·si·ty *fig* Neigung *f*

prop·er richtig, passend, geeignet; anständig, schicklich; echt, wirklich, richtig; eigentlich; eigen(tümlich); *esp Br* F ordentlich, tüchtig, gehörig

prop·er name, proper noun Eigenname *m*

prop·er·ty Eigentum *n*, Besitz *m*; Landbesitz *m*, Grundbesitz *m*; Grundstück *n*; *fig* Eigenschaft *f*

proph·e·cy Prophezeiung *f*

proph·e·sy prophezeien

proph·et Prophet *m*

pro·por·tion 1. Verhältnis *n*; (An)Teil *m*; *pl* Größenverhältnisse *pl*, Proportionen *pl*; *in proportion to* im Verhältnis zu; **2.** (*to*) in das richtige Verhältnis bringen (mit, zu); anpassen (*dat*)

pro·por·tion·al proportional; → *proportionate*

pro·por·tion·ate (*to*) im richtigen Verhältnis (zu), entsprechend (*dat*)

pro·pos·al Vorschlag *m*; (Heirats)Antrag *m*

pro·pose *v/t* vorschlagen; beabsichtigen, vorhaben; *Toast* ausbringen (*to* auf *acc*); *propose s.o.'s health* auf j-s Gesundheit trinken; *v/i*: *propose to* j-m e-n (Heirats)Antrag machen

prop·o·si·tion Behauptung *f*; Vorschlag *m*, ECON *a.* Angebot *n*

pro·pri·e·ta·ry ECON gesetzlich *or* patentrechtlich geschützt; *fig* besitzergreifend

pro·pri·e·tor Eigentümer *m*, Besitzer *m*, Geschäftsinhaber *m*

pro·pri·e·tress Eigentümerin *f*, Besitzerin *f*, Geschäftsinhaberin *f*

pro·pri·e·ty Anstand *m*; Richtigkeit *f*

pro·pul·sion TECH Antrieb *m*

pro·sa·ic prosaisch, nüchtern, sachlich

prose Prosa *f*

pros·e·cute JUR strafrechtlich verfolgen, (gerichtlich) belangen (*for* wegen)

pros·e·cu·tion JUR strafrechtliche Verfolgung, Strafverfolgung *f*; *the prosecution* die Staatsanwaltschaft, die Anklage(behörde)

pros·e·cu·tor *a.* *public prosecutor* JUR Staatsanwalt *m*, Staatsanwältin *f*

pros·pect 1. Aussicht *f* (*a. fig*); Interessent *m*, ECON möglicher Kunde, potenzieller Käufer; **2.** *prospect for mining*: schürfen nach; bohren nach

pro·spec·tive voraussichtlich

pro·spec·tus (Werbe)Prospekt *m*

pros·per gedeihen; ECON blühen, florieren

pros·per·i·ty Wohlstand *m*

pros·per·ous ECON erfolgreich, blühend, florierend; wohlhabend

pros·ti·tute Prostituierte *f*, Dirne *f*; *male prostitute* Strichjunge *m*

pros·trate 1. hingestreckt; *fig* am Boden liegend; erschöpft; *prostrate with grief* grambeugt; **2.** niederwerfen; *fig* erschöpfen; *fig* niederschmettern

pros·y langweilig; weitschweifig

pro·tag·o·nist Vorkämpfer(in); THEA Hauptfigur *f*, Held(in)

pro·tect (be)schützen (*from* vor *dat*; *against* gegen)

pro·tec·tion Schutz *m*; F Schutzgeld *n*; *protection of animals* Tierschutz; *protection of endangered species* Artenschutz *m*

protection money F Schutzgeld *n*

protection rack·et F Schutzgelderpressung *f*

pro·tec·tive (be)schützend; Schutz...

protective cloth·ing Schutzkleidung *f*

protective cus·to·dy JUR Schutzhaft *f*

protective du·ty, protective tar·iff ECON Schutzzoll *m*

pro·tec·tor Beschützer *m*; (*Brust- etc -*) Schutz *m*

pro·tec·to·rate POL Protektorat *n*

pro·test 1. Protest *m*; Einspruch *m*; **2.** *v/i* protestieren (*against* gegen); *v/t* protestieren gegen; beteuern

Prot·es·tant REL **1.** protestantisch; **2.** Protestant(in)

prot·es·ta·tion Beteuerung *f*; Protest *m* (*against* gegen)

pro·to·col Protokoll *n*

pro·to·type Prototyp *m*

pro·tract in die Länge ziehen, hinziehen

pro·trude herausragen, vorstehen (*from* aus)

pro·trud·ing vorstehend (*a. teeth*), vorspringend (*chin*)

proud stolz (*of* auf *acc*)

prove *v/t* be-, er-, nachweisen; *v/i*: **prove (to be)** sich herausstellen *or* erweisen als

prov·en bewährt

prov·erb Sprichwort *n*

pro·vide *v/t* versehen, versorgen, beliefern; zur Verfügung stellen, bereitstellen; JUR vorsehen, vorschreiben (**that** dass); *v/i*: **provide against** Vorsorge treffen gegen; JUR verbieten; **provide for** sorgen für; vorsorgen für; JUR *et.* vorsehen

pro·vid·ed: **provided (that)** vorausgesetzt(, dass)

pro·vid·er Ernährer(in)

prov·ince Provinz *f*; (Aufgaben-, Wissens)Gebiet *n*

pro·vin·cial 1. Provinz..., provinziell, *contp* provinzlerisch; **2.** *contp* Provinzler(in)

pro·vi·sion Bereitstellung *f*, Beschaffung *f*; Vorkehrung *f*, Vorsorge *f*; Bestimmung *f*, Vorschrift *f*; *pl* Proviant *m*, Verpflegung *f*; **with the provision that** unter der Bedingung, dass

pro·vi·sion·al provisorisch, vorläufig

pro·vi·so Bedingung *f*, Vorbehalt *m*; **with the proviso that** unter der Bedingung, dass

prov·o·ca·tion Provokation *f*

pro·voc·a·tive provozierend, (*a. sexually*) aufreizend

pro·voke provozieren, reizen

prowl 1. *v/i a.* **prowl about, prowl around** herumschleichen, herumstreifen; *v/t* durchstreifen; **2.** Herumstreifen *n*

prowl car (Funk)Streifenwagen *m*

prox·im·i·ty Nähe *f*

prox·y (Handlungs)Vollmacht *f*; (Stell-)Vertreter(in), Bevollmächtigte *m*, *f*; **by proxy** durch e-n Bevollmächtigten

prude: **be a prude** prüde sein

pru·dence Klugheit *f*, Vernunft *f*; Besonnenheit *f*

pru·dent klug, vernünftig; besonnen

prud·ish prüde

prune[1] BOT (be)schneiden

prune[2] Backpflaume *f*

prus·sic ac·id CHEM Blausäure *f*

pry[1] neugierig sein; **pry about** herumschnüffeln; **pry into** s-e Nase stecken in (*acc*)

pry[2] → **prize**[2]

psalm REL Psalm *m*

pseu·do·nym Pseudonym *n*, Deckname *m*

psy·chi·a·trist Psychiater(in)

psy·chi·a·try Psychiatrie *f*

psy·cho·a·nal·y·sis Psychoanalyse *f*

psy·cho·log·i·cal psychologisch

psy·chol·o·gist Psychologe *m*, Psychologin *f*

psy·chol·o·gy Psychologie *f*

psy·cho·so·mat·ic psychosomatisch

pub *Br* Pub *m*, *n*, Kneipe *f*

pu·ber·ty Pubertät *f*

pu·bic hair Schamhaare *pl*

pub·lic 1. öffentlich; allgemein bekannt; **make public** bekannt machen, an die Öffentlichkeit bringen; **2.** die Öffentlichkeit, *das* Publikum; **in public** öffentlich, in aller Öffentlichkeit

pub·li·ca·tion Bekanntgabe *f*, Bekanntmachung *f*; Publikation *f*, Veröffentlichung *f*

pub·lic con·ve·ni·ence *Br* öffentliche Bedürfnisanstalt

public en·e·my Staatsfeind *m*

public health öffentliches Gesundheitswesen

public hol·i·day gesetzlicher Feiertag

pub·lic·i·ty Publicity *f*, *a.* Bekanntheit *f*, ECON *a.* Reklame *f*, Werbung *f*

publicity depart·ment Werbeabteilung *f*

pub·lic li·bra·ry Leihbücherei *f*

public re·la·tions (*ABBR* **PR**) Public Relations *pl*, Öffentlichkeitsarbeit *f*

public school staatliche Schule; *Br* Public School *f*

public trans·port *esp Br*, **public trans·por·ta·tion** öffentliche Verkehrsmittel *pl*

pub·lish bekannt geben *or* machen; publizieren, veröffentlichen; *Buch etc* verlegen, herausgeben

pub·lish·er Verleger(in), Herausgeber(in); Verlag *m*, Verlagshaus *n*

pub·lish·er's, pub·lish·ers, publish·ing house Verlag *m*, Verlagshaus *n*

puck·er *a.* **pucker up** (sich) verziehen, (sich) runzeln

pud·ding *Br* GASTR Nachspeise *f*, Nachtisch *m*; (*Reis- etc*)Auflauf *m*; (*Art*) Fleischpastete *f*; Pudding *m*

pud·dle Pfütze *f*

pu·er·ile infantil, kindisch

puff 1. *v/i* schnaufen, keuchen; *a.* **puff away** paffen (**at** an *dat*); **puff up** (an)schwellen; *v/t* Rauch blasen; **puff out** *Kerze etc* ausblasen; *Rauch etc* ausstoßen; *Brust* herausdrücken; **2.** Zug *m*; (*Wind-*) Hauch *m*, (*Wind*)Stoß *m*; (*Puder*)Quaste *f*; F Puste *f*

puffed sleeve Puffärmel *m*

puff pas·try GASTR Blätterteig *m*

puff·y (an)geschwollen; aufgedunsen

pug ZO Mops *m*

puke F (aus)kotzen

pull 1. Ziehen *n*; Zug *m*, Ruck *m*; Anstieg *m*, Steigung *f*; Zuggriff *m*, Zugleine *f*; F Beziehungen *pl*; 2. ziehen an (*dat*); zerren; reißen; *Pflanze* ausreißen; *esp Br Bier* zapfen; **pull ahead** of vorbeiziehen an (*dat*), MOT überholen (*acc*); **pull away** anfahren (*bus etc*); **pull down** *Gebäude* abreißen; **pull in** einfahren (*train*); anhalten; **pull off** F et. zustande bringen, schaffen; **pull out** herausziehen (**of** aus); *Tisch* ausziehen; RAIL abfahren; MOT ausscheren; *fig* sich zurückziehen, aussteigen (**of** aus); **pull over** (s-n Wagen) an die *or* zur Seite fahren; **pull round** MED durchbringen; durchkommen; **pull through** *j*-n durchbringen; **pull o.s. together** sich zusammennehmen, F sich zusammenreißen; **pull up** MOT anhalten; (an)halten; **pull up to, pull up with** SPORT *j*-n einholen

pull date Mindesthaltbarkeitsdatum *n*
pul·ley TECH Flaschenzug *m*
pull-in *Br* F Raststätte *f*, Rasthaus *n*
pull·o·ver Pullover *m*
pull-up SPORT Klimmzug *m*; **do a pull-up** e-n Klimmzug machen
pulp 1. Fruchtfleisch *n*; Brei *m*; 2. Schund...; **pulp novel** Schundroman *m*
pul·pit Kanzel *f*
pulp·y breiig
pul·sate pulsieren, vibrieren
pulse Puls *m*; Pulsschlag *m*
pul·ver·ize pulverisieren
pu·ma ZO Puma *m*
pum·mel mit den Fäusten bearbeiten
pump 1. Pumpe *f*; (*Zapf*)Säule *f*; 2. pumpen; F *j*-n aushorchen; **pump up** aufpumpen
pump at·tend·ant Tankwart *m*
pump·kin BOT Kürbis *m*
pun 1. Wortspiel *n*; 2. Wortspiele *or* ein Wortspiel machen
punch[1] 1. boxen, (mit der Faust) schlagen; 2. (Faust)Schlag *m*
punch[2] 1. lochen; *Loch* stanzen (**in** *acc*); **punch in** einstempeln; **punch out** ausstempeln; 2. Locher *m*; Lochzange *f*; Locheisen *n*
punch[3] Punsch *m*
Punch *appr* Kasper *m*, Kasperle *n*, *m*; **be as pleased** *or* **proud as Punch** sich freuen wie ein Schneekönig
Punch and Ju·dy show Kasperletheater *n*
punc·tu·al pünktlich
punc·tu·al·i·ty Pünktlichkeit *f*
punc·tu·ate interpunktieren
punc·tu·a·tion LING Interpunktion *f*
punctuation mark LING Satzzeichen *n*
punc·ture 1. (Ein)Stich *m*, Loch *n*; MOT

Reifenpanne *f*; 2. durchstechen, durchbohren; ein Loch bekommen; platzen; MOT e-n Platten haben
pun·gent scharf, stechend, beißend (*smell, taste*); scharf, bissig (*remark etc*)
pun·ish *j*-n (be)strafen
pun·ish·a·ble strafbar
pun·ish·ment Strafe *f*; Bestrafung *f*
punk Punk *m* (*a.* MUS); Punk(er) *m*
pu·ny schwächlich
pup ZO Welpe *m*, junger Hund
pu·pa ZO Puppe *f*
pu·pil[1] Schüler(in)
pu·pil[2] ANAT Pupille *f*
pup·pet Handpuppe *f*; Marionette *f* (*a. fig*)
puppet show Marionettentheater *n*, Puppenspiel *n*
pup·pe·teer Puppenspieler(in)
pup·py ZO Welpe *m*, junger Hund
pur·chase 1. kaufen; *fig* erkaufen; 2. Kauf *m*; **make purchases** Einkäufe machen
pur·chas·er Käufer(in)
pure rein; pur
pure·bred ZO reinrassig
pur·ga·tive MED 1. abführend; 2. Abführmittel *n*
pur·ga·to·ry REL Fegefeuer *n*
purge 1. *Partei etc* säubern (**of** von); 2. Säuberung *f*, Säuberungsaktion *f*
pu·ri·fy reinigen
Pu·ri·tan (HIST **Puritan**) 1. Puritaner(in); 2. puritanisch
pu·ri·ty Reinheit *f*
purl 1. linke Masche; 2. links stricken
pur·ple purpurn, purpurrot
pur·pose 1. Absicht *f*, Vorsatz *m*; Zweck *m*, Ziel *n*; Entschlossenheit *f*; **on purpose** absichtlich; **to no purpose** vergeblich; 2. beabsichtigen, vorhaben
pur·pose·ful entschlossen, zielstrebig
pur·pose·less zwecklos; ziellos
pur·pose·ly absichtlich
purr ZO schnurren; MOT summen, surren
purse[1] Geldbeutel *m*, Geldbörse *f*, Portemonnaie *n*; Handtasche *f*; SPORT Siegprämie *f*; *boxing*: Börse *f*
purse[2]: **purse (up) one's lips** die Lippen schürzen
purs·er MAR Zahlmeister *m*
pur·su·ance: **in (the) pursuance of his duty** in Ausübung s-r Pflicht
pur·sue verfolgen; *s-m Studium etc* nachgehen; *Absicht, Politik etc* verfolgen; *Angelegenheit etc* weiterführen
pur·su·er Verfolger(in)
pur·suit Verfolgung *f*; Weiterführung *f*
pur·vey *Lebensmittel etc* liefern
pur·vey·or Lieferant *m*

pus MED Eiter *m*

push 1. stoßen, F schubsen; schieben; *Taste etc* drücken; drängen; (an)treiben; F *Rauschgift* pushen; *fig j-n* drängen (**to do** zu tun); *fig* Reklame machen für; **push one's way** sich drängen (**through** durch); **push ahead with** Plan etc vorantreiben; **push along** F sich auf die Socken machen; **push around** F herumschubsen; **push for** drängen auf (*acc*); **push forward with** → **push ahead with**; **push o.s. forward** *fig* sich in den Vordergrund drängen or schieben; **push in** F sich vordrängeln; **push off!** F hau ab!; **push on with** → **push ahead with**; **push out** *fig j-n* hinausdrängen; **push through** *et.* durchsetzen; **push up** *Preise etc* hochtreiben; **2.** Stoß *m*, F Schubs *m*; (*Werbe*)Kampagne *f*; F Durchsetzungsvermögen *n*, Energie *f*, Tatkraft *f*

push but·ton TECH Druckknopf *m*, Drucktaste *f*

push-but·ton TECH (Druck)Knopf..., (Druck)Tasten...; **push-button (tele)-phone** Tastentelefon *n*

push·chair Br Sportwagen *m*

push·er F *contp* Rauschgifthändler *m*

push·o·ver F Kinderspiel *n*

push-up SPORT Liegestütz *m*

puss F zo Mieze *f*

pus·sy *a.* **pussy cat** F Miezekatze *f*

pus·sy·foot F **pussyfoot about, pussyfoot around** leisetreten, sich nicht festlegen wollen

put legen, setzen, stecken, stellen, tun; *j-n in e-e Lage etc*, *et. auf den Markt*, *in Ordnung etc* bringen; *et. in Kraft*, *in Umlauf etc* setzen; SPORT *Kugel* stoßen; unterwerfen, unterziehen (**to** *dat*); *et.* ausdrücken, *in Worte* fassen; übersetzen (**into German** ins Deutsche); Schuld geben (**on** *dat*); **put right** in Ordnung bringen; **put s.th. before s.o.** *fig* j-m et. vorlegen; **put to bed** ins Bett bringen; **put to school** zur Schule schicken; **put about** Gerüchte verbreiten, in Umlauf setzen; **put across** *et.* verständlich machen; **put ahead** SPORT in Führung bringen; **put aside** beiseitelegen; *Ware* zurücklegen; **put by** beiseiteschieben; **put away** weglegen, wegtun; auf-, wegräumen; **put back** zurücklegen, -stellen, -tun; *Uhr* zurückstellen (**by** um); **put by** Geld zurücklegen; **put down** *v/t* hinlegen, niederlegen, hinsetzen, hinstellen; *j-n* absetzen, aussteigen lassen; (auf-, nieder-) schreiben, eintragen; zuschreiben (**to** *dat*); *Aufstand* niederschlagen; (*a. v/i*) AVIAT landen; **put forward** Plan etc vorlegen;

Uhr vorstellen (**by** um); *fig* vorverlegen (**two days** um zwei Tage); **to** auf (*acc*); **put in** *v/t* hineinlegen, -stecken, -stellen; *Kassette etc* einlegen; installieren; *Gesuch etc* einreichen, *Forderung etc a.* geltend machen; *Antrag* stellen; *Arbeit*, *Zeit* verbringen (**on** mit); *Bemerkung* einwerfen; *v/i* MAR einlaufen (**at** in *acc*); **put off** *et.* verschieben (**until** auf *acc*); *j-m* absagen; *j-n* hinhalten (**with** mit), *j-n* vertrösten; *j-n* aus dem Konzept bringen; **put on** *Kleider etc* anziehen, *Hut*, *Brille* aufsetzen; *Licht*, *Radio etc* anmachen, einschalten; *Sonderzug* einsetzen; THEA *Stück etc* herausbringen; *et.* vortäuschen; F *j-n* auf den Arm nehmen; **put on airs** sich aufspielen; **put on weight** zunehmen; **put out** *v/t* hinauslegen, -setzen, -stellen; *Hand etc* ausstrecken; *Feuer* löschen; *Licht*, *Radio etc* ausmachen (*a. cigarette*), ab-, ausschalten; veröffentlichen, herausgeben; *radio*, TV bringen, senden; *j-n* aus der Fassung bringen; *j-n* verärgern; *j-m* Ungelegenheiten bereiten; *j-m* Umstände machen; sich *den Arm etc* verrenken or ausrenken; *v/i* MAR auslaufen; **put over** → **put across**; **put through** TEL *j-n* verbinden (**to** mit); durch-, ausführen; **put together** zusammenbauen, -setzen, -stellen; **put up** *v/t* hinauflegen, -stellen; *Hand* (hoch)heben; *Zelt etc* aufstellen; *Gebäude* errichten; *Bild etc* aufhängen; *Plakat*, *Bekanntmachung etc* anschlagen; *Schirm* aufspannen; **zum Verkauf anbieten**; *Preis* erhöhen; *Widerstand* leisten; *Kampf* liefern; *j-n* unterbringen, (bei sich) aufnehmen; *v/i* **put up at** absteigen in (*dat*); **put up with** sich gefallen lassen; sich abfinden mit

pu·tre·fy (ver)faulen, verwesen

pu·trid faul, verfault, verwest; F scheußlich, saumäßig

put·ty 1. Kitt *m*; **2.** kitten

put-up job F abgekartetes Spiel

puz·zle 1. Rätsel *n*; Geduld(s)spiel *n*; **2.** *v/t* *j-n* vor ein Rätsel stellen; verwirren; **be puzzled** vor e-m Rätsel stehen; **puzzle out** herausfinden, herausbringen, F austüfteln; *v/i* sich den Kopf zerbrechen (**about**, **over** über *dat* or *acc*)

pyg·my 1. Pygmäe *m*, Pygmäin *f*; Zwerg(in); **2.** *esp* ZO Zwerg...

py·ja·mas Br → **pajamas**

py·lon TECH Hochspannungsmast *m*

pyr·a·mid Pyramide *f*

pyre Scheiterhaufen *m*

py·thon ZO Python(schlange) *f*

pyx REL Hostienbehälter *m*

P

Q

Q, q Q, q n

quack¹ zo **1.** quaken; **2.** Quaken n

quack² a. **quack doctor** Quacksalber m, Kurpfuscher m

quack·er·y Quacksalberei f, Kurpfuscherei f

quad·ran·gle Viereck n

quad·ran·gu·lar viereckig

quad·ra·phon·ic quadrophon(isch)

quad·rat·ic MATH quadratisch

quad·ri·lat·er·al MATH **1.** vierseitig; **2.** Viereck n

quad·ro·phon·ic → *quadraphonic*

quad·ru·ped zo Vierfüß(l)er m; Vierbeiner m

quad·ru·ple 1. vierfach; **2.** (sich) vervierfachen

quad·ru·plets Vierlinge pl

quads Vierlinge pl

quag·mire Morast m, Sumpf m

quaint idyllisch, malerisch

quake 1. zittern, beben (**with, for** vor dat; **at** bei); **2.** F Erdbeben n

Quak·er REL Quäker(in)

qual·i·fi·ca·tion Qualifikation f, Befähigung f, Eignung f (**for** für, zu); Voraussetzung f; Einschränkung f

qual·i·fied qualifiziert, geeignet, befähigt (**for** für); berechtigt; bedingt, eingeschränkt

qual·i·fy v/t qualifizieren, befähigen (**for** für, zu); berechtigen (**to do** zu tun); einschränken, abschwächen, mildern; v/i sich qualifizieren or eignen (**for** für; **as** als); SPORT sich qualifizieren (**for** für)

qual·i·ty Qualität f; Eigenschaft f

qualms Bedenken pl, Skrupel pl

quan·da·ry: be in a quandary about what to do nicht wissen, was man tun soll

quan·ti·ty Quantität f, Menge f

quan·tum PHYS **1.** Quant n; **2.** Quanten...

quar·an·tine 1. Quarantäne f; **2.** unter Quarantäne stellen

quar·rel 1. Streit m, Auseinandersetzung f; **2.** (sich) streiten

quar·rel·some streitsüchtig, zänkisch

quar·ry¹ Steinbruch m

quar·ry² HUNT Beute f, a. fig Opfer n

quart Quart n (ABBR **qt**) (0,95 l, Br 1,14 l)

quar·ter 1. Viertel n, vierter Teil; Quartal n, Vierteljahr n; Viertelpfund n; Vierteldollar m; SPORT (Spiel)Viertel n; (Himmels)Richtung f; Gegend f, Teil m; (Stadt)Viertel n; GASTR (esp Hinter)Viertel n; Gnade f, Pardon m; pl Quartier n, Unterkunft f (a. MIL); **a quarter of an hour** e-e Viertelstunde; **a quarter of** (Br **to**) **five** (ein) Viertel vor fünf (4.45); **a quarter after** (Br **past**) **five** (ein) Viertel nach fünf (5.15); **at close quarters** in or aus nächster Nähe; **from official quarters** von amtlicher Seite; **2.** vierteln; esp MIL einquartieren (**on** bei)

quar·ter·deck MAR Achterdeck n

quar·ter·fi·nals SPORT Viertelfinale n

quar·ter·ly 1. vierteljährlich; **2.** Vierteljahresschrift f

quar·tet(te) MUS Quartett n

quartz MIN Quarz m

quartz clock Quarzuhr f

quartz watch Quarz(armband)uhr f

qua·ver 1. v/i zittern; v/t e. mit zitternder Stimme sagen; **2.** Zittern n

quay MAR Kai m

quea·sy: I feel queasy mir ist übel or F mulmig

queen Königin f; card game, chess: Dame f; F Schwule m, Homo m

queen bee zo Bienenkönigin f

queen·ly wie e-e Königin, königlich

queer komisch, seltsam; F wunderlich; F schwul

quench Durst löschen, stillen

quer·u·lous nörglerisch

que·ry 1. Frage f; Zweifel m; **2.** infrage stellen, in Zweifel ziehen

quest 1. Suche f (**for** nach); **in quest of** auf der Suche nach; **2.** suchen (**after, for** nach)

ques·tion 1. Frage f, a. Problem n, a. Sache f, a. Zweifel m; **only a question of time** nur e-e Frage der Zeit; **this is not the point in question** darum geht es nicht; **there is no question that, it is beyond question that** es steht außer Frage, dass; **there is no question about this** daran besteht kein Zweifel; **be out of the question** nicht infrage kommen; **2.** befragen (**about** über acc); JUR vernehmen, verhören (**about** zu); bezweifeln, in Zweifel ziehen, infrage stellen

ques·tion·a·ble fraglich, zweifelhaft; fragwürdig

ques·tion·er Fragesteller(in)

ques·tion mark Fragezeichen n

question mas·ter esp Br Quizmaster m

Q

ques·tion·naire Fragebogen *m*
queue *esp Br* **1.** Schlange *f*; → **jump**; **2.** *mst* **queue up** Schlange stehen, anstehen, sich anstellen
quib·ble sich herumstreiten (**with** mit; **about, over** wegen)
quick 1. *adj* schnell, rasch; aufbrausend, hitzig (*temper*); **be quick!** mach schnell!, beeil dich!; **2.** *adv* schnell, rasch; **3.** *cut s.o. to the quick fig* j-n tief verletzen
quick·en (sich) beschleunigen
quick·sand Treibsand *m*
quick-tem·pered aufbrausend, hitzig
quick-wit·ted schlagfertig; geistesgegenwärtig
qui·et 1. ruhig, still; **quiet, please** Ruhe, bitte!; **be quiet!** sei still!; **2.** Ruhe *f*, Stille *f*; **on the quiet** F heimlich; **3.** *v/t a.* **quiet down** j-n beruhigen; *v/i a.* **quiet down** sich beruhigen
qui·et·en *Br* → **quiet 3**
qui·et·ness Ruhe *f*, Stille *f*
quill zo (Schwung-, Schwanz)Feder *f*; Stachel *m*
quilt Steppdecke *f*
quilt·ed Stepp...
quince bot Quitte *f*
qui·nine pharm Chinin *n*
quint F Fünfling *m*
quin·tes·sence Quintessenz *f*; Inbegriff *m*
quin·tet(te) mus Quintett *n*
quin·tu·ple 1. fünffach; **2.** (sich) verfünf-

fachen
quin·tu·plets Fünflinge *pl*
quip 1. geistreiche *or* witzige Bemerkung; **2.** witzeln, spötteln
quirk Eigenart *f*, Schrulle *f*; **by some quirk of fate** durch e-e Laune des Schicksals, durch e-n verrückten Zufall
quit F *v/t* aufhören mit; **quit one's job** kündigen; *v/i* aufhören; kündigen
quite ganz, völlig; ziemlich; **quite a few** ziemlich viele; **quite nice** ganz nett, recht nett; **quite (so)!** *esp Br* genau, ganz recht; **be quite right** völlig recht haben; **she's quite a beauty** sie ist e-e wirkliche Schönheit
quits F quitt (**with** mit); **call it quits** es gut sein lassen
quit·ter: F **be a quitter** schnell aufgeben
quiv·er¹ zittern (**with** vor *dat*; **at** bei)
quiv·er² Köcher *m*
quiz 1. Quiz *n*; Prüfung *f*, Test *m*; **2.** ausfragen (**about** über *acc*)
quiz·mas·ter Quizmaster *m*
quiz·zi·cal spöttisch-fragend
quo·ta Quote *f*, Kontingent *n*
quo·ta·tion Zitat *n*; econ Notierung *f*; Kostenvoranschlag *m*
quotation marks ling Anführungszeichen *pl*
quote zitieren; *Beispiel etc* anführen; *Preis* nennen; **be quoted at** econ notieren mit
quo·tient math Quotient *m*

R

R, r R, r *n*
rab·bi rel Rabbiner *m*
rab·bit zo Kaninchen *n*
rab·ble Pöbel *m*, Mob *m*
rab·ble-rous·ing Hetz..., aufwieglerisch
rab·id vet tollwütig; *fig* fanatisch
ra·bies vet Tollwut *f*
rac·coon zo Waschbär *m*
race¹ Rasse *f*, Rassenzugehörigkeit *f*; (*Menschen*)Geschlecht *n*
race² 1. (Wett)Rennen *n*, (Wett)Lauf *m*; **2.** *v/i* an (e-m) Rennen teilnehmen; um die Wette laufen *or* fahren *etc*; rasen, rennen; mot durchdrehen; *v/t* um die Wette laufen *or* fahren *etc* mit; rasen mit
race car mot Rennwagen *m*

race·course Rennbahn *f*
race·horse Rennpferd *n*
rac·er Rennpferd *n*; Rennrad *n*, Rennwagen *m*
race ri·ots Rassenunruhen *pl*
race·track Rennbahn *f*
ra·cial rassisch, Rassen...
rac·ing 1. Rennsport *m*; **2.** Renn...
rac·ing car *Br* mot Rennwagen *m*
ra·cism Rassismus *m*
ra·cist 1. Rassist *m*; **2.** rassistisch
rack 1. Gestell *n*, (*Geschirr-, Zeitungsetc*)Ständer *m*, rail (*Gepäck*)Netz *n*, mot (*Dach*)Gepäckständer *m*; hist Folter(bank) *f*; **2. be racked by** *or* **with** geplagt *or* gequält werden von; **rack one's**

brains sich das Hirn zermartern, sich den Kopf zerbrechen

rack·et¹ *tennis etc*: Schläger *m*

rack·et² F Krach *m*, Lärm *m*; Schwindel *m*, Gaunerei *f*; (*Drogen- etc*)Geschäft *n*; organisierte Erpressung

rack·et·eer Gauner *m*; Erpresser *m*

ra·coon → **raccoon**

rac·y spritzig, lebendig; gewagt (*joke*)

ra·dar TECH Radar *m, n*

radar screen Radarschirm *m*

radar speed check MOT Radarkontrolle *f*

radar sta·tion Radarstation *f*

radar trap MOT Radarkontrolle *f*

ra·di·al 1. radial, Radial…, strahlenförmig; **2.** MOT Gürtelreifen *m*

ra·di·al tire, *Br* **radial tyre** → **radial** 2

ra·di·ant strahlend, leuchtend (*a. fig with* vor *dat*)

ra·di·ate ausstrahlen; strahlenförmig ausgehen (*from* von)

ra·di·a·tion Ausstrahlung *f*

ra·di·a·tor Heizkörper *m*; MOT Kühler *m*

rad·i·cal 1. radikal (*a.* POL); MATH Wurzel…; **2.** POL Radikale *m, f*

ra·di·o 1. Radio(apparat *m*) *n*; Funk *m*; Funkgerät *n*; *by radio* über Funk; *on the radio* im Radio; **2.** funken

ra·di·o·ac·tive radioaktiv

radioactive waste Atommüll *m*, radioaktiver Abfall

ra·di·o·ac·tiv·i·ty Radioaktivität *f*

ra·di·o ham Funkamateur *m*

radio play Hörspiel *n*

radio set Radioapparat *m*

radio sta·tion Funkstation *f*; Rundfunksender *m*, -station *f*

radio ther·a·py MED Strahlentherapie *f*, Röntgentherapie *f*

radio tow·er Funkturm *m*

rad·ish BOT Rettich *m*; Radieschen *n*

ra·di·us MATH Radius *m*

raf·fle Tombola *f*; **2.** *a.* **raffle off** verlosen

raft Floß *n*

raf·ter (Dach)Sparren *m*

rag Lumpen *m*, Fetzen *m*; Lappen *m*; *in rags* zerlumpt

rage Wut *f*, Zorn *m*; *fly into a rage* wütend werden; *the latest rage* F der letzte Schrei; *be all the rage* F große Mode sein; **2.** wettern (*against, at* gegen); wüten, toben

rag·ged zerlumpt; struppig; *fig* stümperhaft

raid 1. (*on*) Überfall *m* (auf *acc*), MIL *a.* Angriff *m* (gegen); Razzia *f* (in *dat*); **2.** überfallen, MIL *a.* angreifen; e-e Razzia machen in (*dat*)

rail 1. Geländer *n*; Stange *f*; (*Handtuch*)Halter *m*; (Eisen)Bahn *f*; RAIL Schiene *f*, *pl a.* Gleis *n*; *by rail* mit der Bahn; **2.** *rail in* einzäunen; *rail off* abzäunen

rail·ing *often pl* (Gitter)Zaun *m*

rail·road Eisenbahn *f*

railroad line Bahnlinie *f*

railroad·man Eisenbahner *m*

railroad sta·tion Bahnhof *m*

rail·way *Br* → **railroad**

rain 1. Regen *m, pl* Regenfälle *pl*; *the rains* die Regenzeit; (*come*) *rain or shine fig* was immer auch geschieht; **2.** regnen; *it is raining cats and dogs* F es gießt in Strömen; *it never rains but it pours* es kommt immer gleich knüppeldick, ein Unglück kommt selten allein

rain·bow Regenbogen *m*

rain·coat Regenmantel *m*

rain·fall Niederschlag(smenge *f*) *m*

rain for·est GEOGR Regenwald *m*

rain·proof regendicht, wasserdicht

rain·y regnerisch, verregnet, Regen…; *save s.th. for a rainy day* et. für schlechte Zeiten zurücklegen

raise 1. heben; hochziehen; erheben; *Denkmal etc* errichten; *Staub etc* aufwirbeln; *Gehalt, Miete etc* erhöhen; *Geld* zusammenbringen, beschaffen; *Kinder* aufziehen, großziehen; *Tiere* züchten; *Getreide etc* anbauen; *Frage* aufwerfen, et. zur Sprache bringen; *Blockade etc*, *a. Verbot* aufheben; **2.** Lohn- *or* Gehaltserhöhung *f*

rai·sin Rosine *f*

rake 1. Rechen *m*, Harke *f*; **2.** *v/t:* **rake** (*up*) (zusammen)rechen, (zusammen)harken; F *rake in* scheffeln; *v/i:* **rake about, rake around** herumstöbern

rak·ish flott, keck, verwegen

ral·ly 1. (sich) (wieder) sammeln; sich erholen (*from* von) (*a.* ECON); *rally round* sich scharen um; **2.** Kundgebung *f*, (Massen)Versammlung *f*; MOT Rallye *f*; *tennis etc*: Ballwechsel *m*

ram 1. ZO Widder *m*, Schafbock *m*; TECH Ramme *f*; **2.** rammen

ram·ble 1. wandern, umherstreifen; abschweifen; **2.** Wanderung *f*

ram·bler Wanderer *m*; BOT Kletterrose *f*

ram·bling weitschweifig; weitläufig

rambling rose BOT Kletterrose *f*

ramp Rampe *f*; MOT (Autobahn)Auffahrt *f*; (Autobahn)Ausfahrt *f*

ram·page 1. *rampage through* (wild *or* aufgeregt) trampeln durch (*elephant etc*); → **2.** *go on the rampage through* randalierend ziehen durch

ram·pant: *be rampant* wuchern (*plant*); grassieren (*in* in *dat*)

ram·shack·le baufällig (*building*); klapp(e)rig (*vehicle*)

ranch Ranch *f*; (*Geflügel- etc*)Farm *f*

ranch·er Rancher *m*; (*Geflügel- etc*) Züchter *m*

ran·cid ranzig

ran·co(u)r Groll *m*, Erbitterung *f*

ran·dom 1. *adj* ziellos, wahllos; zufällig, Zufalls...; *random sample* Stichprobe *f*; **2.** *at random* aufs Geratewohl

range 1. Reich-, Schuss-, Tragweite *f*, Entfernung *f*, *fig* Bereich *m*, *a*. Spielraum *m*, *a*. Gebiet *n*; (*Schieß*)Stand *m*, (-)Platz *m*; (*Berg*)Kette *f*; offenes Weidegebiet; ECON Kollektion *f*, Sortiment *n*; Küchenherd *m*; *at close range* aus nächster Nähe; *within range of vision* in Sichtweite; *a wide range of ...* eine große Auswahl an ... (*dat*); **2.** *v/i: range from ... to ...*, *range between ... and ...* sich zwischen ... und ... bewegen (*prices etc*); *v/t* aufstellen, anordnen

range find·er PHOT Entfernungsmesser *m*

rang·er Förster *m*; Ranger *m*

rank¹ 1. Rang *m* (*a.* MIL), (soziale) Stellung; Reihe *f*; (*Taxi*)Stand *m*; *of the first rank fig* erstklassig; *the rank and file fig* die Basis; *the ranks fig* das Heer, die Masse; **2.** *v/t* rechnen, zählen (*among* zu); stellen (*above* über *acc*); *v/i* zählen, gehören (*among* zu); gelten (*as* als)

rank² BOT (üppig) wuchernd; übel riechend, übel schmeckend; *fig* krass (*outsider*), blutig (*beginner*)

ran·kle *fig* nagen, wehtun, F wurmen

ran·sack durchwühlen, durchsuchen; plündern

ran·som 1. Lösegeld *n*; **2.** freikaufen, auslösen

rant: *rant (on) about*, *rant and rave about* eifern gegen

rap 1. Klopfen *n*; Klaps *m*; **2.** klopfen (an *acc*, auf *acc*)

rape¹ 1. vergewaltigen; **2.** Vergewaltigung *f*

rape² BOT Raps *m*

rap·id schnell, rasch

ra·pid·i·ty Schnelligkeit *f*

rap·ids GEOGR Stromschnellen *pl*

rapt: *with rapt attention* mit gespannter Aufmerksamkeit

rap·ture Entzücken *n*, Verzückung *f*; *go into raptures* in Verzückung geraten

rare¹ selten, rar; dünn (*air*); F Mords...

rare² GASTR blutig (*steak*)

rar·e·fied dünn (*air*)

rar·i·ty Seltenheit *f*; Rarität *f*

ras·cal Schlingel *m*

rash¹ voreilig, vorschnell, unbesonnen

rash² MED (Haut)Ausschlag *m*

rash·er dünne Speckscheibe *f*

rasp 1. raspeln; kratzen; **2.** Raspel *f*; Kratzen *n*

rasp·ber·ry BOT Himbeere *f*

rat ZO Ratte *f* (*a. contp*); F *smell a rat* Lunte *or* den Braten riechen

rate 1. Quote *f*, Rate *f*, (*Geburten-*, *Sterbe*)Ziffer *f*, (*Steuer-*, *Zins- etc*)Satz *m*; (*Wechsel*)Kurs *m*; Geschwindigkeit *f*, Tempo *n*; *at any rate* auf jeden Fall; **2.** einschätzen, halten (*as* für); *Lob etc* verdienen; *be rated as* gelten als

rate of ex·change ECON (Umrechnungs-, Wechsel)Kurs *m*

rate of in·terest ECON Zinssatz *m*

ra·ther ziemlich; vielmehr, besser gesagt; *rather!* esp Br F und ob!; *I would or had rather go* ich möchte lieber gehen

rat·i·fy POL ratifizieren

rat·ing Einschätzung *f*; *radio*, TV Einschaltquote *f*

ra·ti·o MATH Verhältnis *n*

ra·tion 1. Ration *f*; **2.** *et.* rationieren; *ration out* zuteilen (*to* an *dat*)

ra·tion·al rational; vernunftbegabt; vernünftig; verstandesmäßig

ra·tion·al·i·ty Vernunft *f*

ra·tion·al·ize rational erklären; ECON rationalisieren

rat race F endloser Konkurrenzkampf

rat·tle 1. klappern; rasseln *or* klimpern (mit); prasseln (*on* auf *acc*) (*rain etc*); rattern, knattern (*vehicle*); rütteln an (*dat*); F *j-n* verunsichern; *rattle at* rütteln an (*dat*); *rattle off* F *Gedicht etc* herunterrasseln; F *rattle on* quasseln (*about* über *acc*); F *rattle through Rede etc* herunterrasseln; **2.** Klappern *n* (*etc → 1*); Rassel *f*, Klapper *f*

rat·tle·snake ZO Klapperschlange *f*

rau·cous heiser, rau

rav·age verwüsten

rav·ag·es Verwüstungen *pl*, *a. fig* verheerende Auswirkungen *pl*

rave fantasieren, irrereden; toben; wettern (*against*, *at* gegen); schwärmen (*about* von)

rav·el (sich) verwickeln *or* verwirren

ra·ven ZO Rabe *m*

rav·e·nous ausgehungert, heißhungrig

ra·vine Schlucht *f*, Klamm *f*

rav·ing mad todsüchtig

rav·ings irres Gerede, Delirien *pl*

rav·ish·ing *fig* hinreißend

R

raw GASTR roh, ECON, TECH a. Roh...; MED wund; METEOR nasskalt; *fig* unerfahren; ***raw vegetables and fruit*** Rohkost f

raw-boned knochig, hager

raw-hide Rohleder n

raw ma·te·ri·al Rohstoff m

ray Strahl m; *fig* Schimmer m

ray-on Kunstseide f

ra·zor Rasiermesser n; Rasierapparat m; ***electric razor*** Elektrorasierer m

ra·zor blade Rasierklinge f

ra·zor('s) edge *fig* kritische Lage; ***be on a razor('s) edge*** auf des Messers Schneide stehen

re... wieder, noch einmal, neu

reach 1. *v/t* erreichen; reichen *or* gehen bis an (*acc*) *or* zu; ***reach down*** herunter-, hinunterreichen (***from*** von); ***reach out Arm*** etc ausstrecken; *v/i* reichen, gehen, sich erstrecken; *a.* ***reach out*** greifen, langen (***for*** nach); ***reach out*** die Hand ausstrecken; **2.** Reichweite f; ***within (out of) reach*** in (außer) Reichweite; ***within easy reach*** leicht erreichbar

re·act reagieren (***to*** auf *acc*; CHEM ***with*** mit)

re·ac·tion Reaktion f (*a.* CHEM)

re·ac·tor PHYS Reaktor m

read lesen; TECH (an)zeigen; *Zähler* etc ablesen; UNIV studieren; deuten, verstehen (***as*** als); sich *gut* etc lesen (lassen); lauten; ***read (s.th.) to s.o.*** j-m (et.) vorlesen; ***read medicine*** Medizin studieren

read·a·ble lesbar; leserlich; lesenswert

read·er Leser(in); Lektor(in); Lesebuch n

read·i·ly bereitwillig, gern; leicht, ohne weiteres

read·i·ness Bereitschaft f

read·ing 1. Lesen n; Lesung f (*a.* PARL); TECH Anzeige f, (*Thermometer-* etc -) Stand m; Auslegung f; **2.** Lese...; ***reading matter*** Lesestoff m

re·ad·just TECH nachstellen, korrigieren; ***readjust (o.s.) to*** sich wieder anpassen (*dat*) *or* an (*acc*), sich wieder einstellen auf (*acc*)

read·y bereit, fertig; bereitwillig; im Begriff (***to do*** zu tun); schnell, schlagfertig; ***ready for use*** gebrauchsfertig; ***get ready*** (sich) fertig machen

read·y cash → ***ready money***

read·y-made Konfektions...

read·y meal Fertiggericht n

read·y mon·ey Bargeld n

real echt; wirklich, tatsächlich, real; F ***for real*** echt, im Ernst

real es·tate Grundbesitz m, Immobilien pl

real estate a·gent Grundstücks-, Immo-

bilienmakler m

re·a·lism Realismus m

re·a·list Realist(in)

re·a·lis·tic realistisch

re·al·i·ty Realität f, Wirklichkeit f

re·a·li·za·tion Erkenntnis f; Realisierung f (*a.* ECON), Verwirklichung f

re·a·lize sich klarmachen, erkennen, begreifen, einsehen; realisieren (*a.* ECON), verwirklichen

real·ly wirklich, tatsächlich; ***well, really!*** ich muss schon sagen!; ***really?*** im Ernst?

realm Königreich n; *fig* Reich n

real·tor Grundstücks-, Immobilienmakler m

reap *Getreide* etc schneiden; *Feld* abernten; *fig* ernten

re·ap·pear wieder erscheinen

rear 1. *v/t Kind, Tier* aufziehen, großziehen; *Kopf* heben; *v/i* sich aufbäumen (*horse*); **2.** Rückseite f, Hinterseite f, MOT Heck n; ***in (Br at) the rear of*** hinter (*dat*); ***bring up the rear*** die Nachhut bilden; **3.** hinter, Hinter..., Rück..., MOT a. Heck...

rear-end col·li·sion MOT Auffahrunfall m

rear-guard MIL Nachhut f

rear light MOT Rücklicht n

re·arm MIL (wieder) aufrüsten

re·ar·ma·ment MIL (Wieder)Aufrüstung f

rear·most hinterste(r, -s)

rear-view mir·ror MOT Rückspiegel m

rear·ward 1. *adj* hintere(r, -s), rückwärtig; **2.** *adv a.* ***rearwards*** rückwärts

rear-wheel drive MOT Hinterradantrieb m

rear win·dow MOT Heckscheibe f

rea·son 1. Grund m; Verstand m; Vernunft f; ***by reason of*** wegen; ***for this reason*** aus diesem Grund; ***listen to reason*** Vernunft annehmen; ***it stands to reason that*** es leuchtet ein, dass; **2.** *v/i* vernünftig *or* logisch denken; ***reason (that)*** folgern, schließen (dass); ***reason s.o. into (out of) s.th.*** j-m et. einreden (ausreden)

rea·son·a·ble vernünftig; günstig (*price*); ganz gut, nicht schlecht

re·as·sure beruhigen

re·bate ECON Rabatt m, (Preis)Nachlass m; Rückzahlung f

reb·el[1] 1. Rebell(in); Aufständische m, f; **2.** aufständisch

re·bel[2] rebellieren, sich auflehnen (***against*** gegen)

re·bel·lion Rebellion f, Aufstand m

re·bel·lious rebellisch, aufständisch

re·birth Wiedergeburt f

re·bound 1. abprallen, zurückprallen (***from*** von); *fig* zurückfallen (***on*** auf *acc.*); **2.** SPORT Abpraller *m*

re·buff 1. schroffe Abweisung, Abfuhr *f*; **2.** schroff abweisen

re·build wieder aufbauen (*a. fig*)

re·buke 1. rügen, tadeln; **2.** Rüge *f*, Tadel *m*

re·call 1. zurückrufen, abberufen; MOT (in die Werkstatt) zurückrufen; sich erinnern an (*acc*); erinnern an (*acc*); **2.** Zurückrufung *f*, Abberufung *f*; Rückrufaktion *f*; **have total recall** das absolute Gedächtnis haben; *beyond recall, past recall* unwiderbringlich *or* unwiderruflich vorbei

re·ca·pit·u·late rekapitulieren, (kurz) zusammenfassen

re·cap·ture wieder einfangen (*a. fig*); *Häftling* wieder fassen; MIL zurückerobern

re·cast TECH umgießen; umformen, neu gestalten; THEA *etc* umbesetzen, neu besetzen

re·cede schwinden; *receding chin* fliehendes Kinn

re·ceipt *esp* ECON Empfang *m*, Eingang *m*; Quittung *f*; *pl* Einnahmen *pl*

re·ceive bekommen, erhalten; empfangen; *j-n* aufnehmen (*into* in *acc*); radio, TV empfangen

re·ceiv·er Empfänger(in); TEL Hörer *m*; JUR Hehler(in); *a. official receiver* Br JUR Konkursverwalter *m*

re·cent neuere(r, -s); jüngste(r, -s)

re·cent·ly kürzlich, vor kurzem

re·cep·tion Empfang *m*; Aufnahme *f* (*into* in *acc*); radio, TV Empfang *m*; *a. reception desk* Rezeption *f*, Empfang *m*

re·cep·tion·ist Empfangsdame *f*, -chef *m*; MED Sprechstundenhilfe *f*

re·cep·tive aufnahmefähig; empfänglich (*to* für)

re·cess Unterbrechung *f*, (Schul)Pause *f*; PARL, JUR Ferien *pl*; Nische *f*

re·ces·sion ECON Rezession *f*

re·ci·pe (Koch)Rezept *n*

re·cip·i·ent Empfänger(in)

re·cip·ro·cal wechselseitig, gegenseitig

re·cip·ro·cate *v/i* TECH sich hin- und herbewegen; sich revanchieren; *v/t Einladung etc* erwidern

re·cit·al Vortrag *m*, (Klavier- *etc*)Konzert *n*, (*Lieder*)Abend *m*; Schilderung *f*

re·ci·ta·tion Aufsagen *n*, Hersagen *n*; Vortrag *m*

re·cite aufsagen, hersagen; vortragen; aufzählen

reck·less rücksichtslos

reck·on *v/t* (aus-, be)rechnen; glauben; schätzen; *reckon up* zusammenrechnen;

v/i: *reckon on* rechnen mit; *reckon with* rechnen mit; *reckon without* nicht rechnen mit

reck·on·ing (Be)Rechnung *f*; *be out in one's reckoning* sich verrechnet haben

re·claim zurückfordern; *Gepäck etc* abholen; *dem Meer etc Land* abgewinnen; TECH wiedergewinnen

re·cline sich zurücklehnen

re·cluse Einsiedler(in)

rec·og·ni·tion (Wieder)Erkennen *n*; Anerkennung *f*

rec·og·nize (wieder) erkennen; anerkennen; zugeben, eingestehen

re·coil 1. zurückschrecken (*from* vor *dat*); **2.** Rückstoß *m*

rec·ol·lect sich erinnern an (*acc*)

rec·ol·lec·tion Erinnerung *f* (*of* an *acc*)

rec·om·mend empfehlen (*as* als; *for* für)

rec·om·men·da·tion Empfehlung *f*

rec·om·pense 1. entschädigen (*for* für); **2.** Entschädigung *f*

rec·on·cile versöhnen, aussöhnen; in Einklang bringen (*with* mit)

rec·on·cil·i·a·tion Versöhnung *f*, Aussöhnung *f* (*between* zwischen *dat*; *with* mit)

re·con·di·tion TECH (general)überholen

re·con·nais·sance MIL Aufklärung *f*, Erkundung *f*

re·con·noi·ter, *Br* **re·con·noi·tre** MIL erkunden, auskundschaften

re·con·sid·er noch einmal überdenken

re·con·struct wieder aufbauen (*a. fig*); *Verbrechen etc* rekonstruieren

re·con·struc·tion Wiederaufbau *m*; Rekonstruktion *f*

rec·ord[1] Aufzeichnung *f*; JUR Protokoll *n*; Akte *f*; (Schall)Platte *f*; SPORT Rekord *m*; *off the record* inoffiziell; *have a criminal record* vorbestraft sein

re·cord[2] aufzeichnen, aufschreiben, schriftlich niederlegen; JUR protokollieren, zu Protokoll nehmen; *auf Schallplatte, Tonband etc* aufnehmen, *Sendung a.* aufzeichnen, mitschneiden

re·cord·er (*Kassetten*)Rekorder *m*; (*Tonband*)Gerät *n*; MUS Blockflöte *f*

re·cord·ing Aufnahme *f*, Aufzeichnung *f*, Mitschnitt *m*

rec·ord play·er Plattenspieler *m*

re·count erzählen

re·cov·er *v/t* wiedererlangen, wiederbekommen, wieder finden; *Kosten etc* wiedereinbringen; *Fahrzeug, Verunglückten etc* bergen; *recover consciousness* MED wieder zu sich kommen, das Bewusstsein wiedererlangen; *v/i* sich erholen (*from* von)

re·cov·er·y Wiedererlangen *n*; Wiederfinden *n*; Bergung *f*; Genesung *f*; Erholung *f*

rec·re·a·tion Entspannung *f*; Unterhaltung *f*, Freizeitbeschäftigung *f*

re·cruit 1. MIL Rekrut *m*; Neue *m*, *f*, neues Mitglied; **2.** MIL rekrutieren; *Personal* einstellen; *Mitglieder* werben

rec·tan·gle MATH Rechteck *n*

rec·tan·gu·lar rechteckig

rec·ti·fy ELECTR gleichrichten

rec·tor REL Pfarrer *m*

rec·to·ry REL Pfarrhaus *n*

re·cu·pe·rate sich erholen (**from** von) (*a. fig*)

re·cur wiederkehren, wieder auftreten

re·cur·rence Wiederkehr *f*

re·cur·rent wiederkehrend

re·cy·cla·ble TECH recycelbar, wiederverwertbar

re·cy·cle TECH *Abfälle* recyceln, wieder verwerten; *recycled paper* Recyclingpapier *n*, Umwelt(schutz)-papier *n*

re·cy·cling TECH Recycling *n*, Wiederverwertung *f*

red 1. rot; **2.** Rot *n*; *be in the red* ECON in den roten Zahlen sein

red·breast → *robin*

Red Cres·cent Roter Halbmond

Red Cross Rotes Kreuz

red·cur·rant BOT Rote Johannisbeere

red·den röten, rot färben; rot werden

red·dish rötlich

re·dec·o·rate *Zimmer etc* neu streichen *or* tapezieren

re·deem *Pfand, Versprechen etc* einlösen; REL erlösen

Re·deem·er REL Erlöser *m*, Heiland *m*

re·demp·tion Einlösung *f*; REL Erlösung *f*

re·de·vel·op *Gebäude, Stadtteil* sanieren

red-faced verlegen; mit rotem Kopf

red-hand·ed: *catch s.o. red-handed* j-n auf frischer Tat ertappen

red·head F Rotschopf *m*, Rothaarige *f*

red-head·ed rothaarig

red her·ring *fig* falsche Fährte *or* Spur

red-hot rot glühend; *fig* glühend; F brandaktuell (*news etc*)

Red In·di·an *contp* Indianer(in)

red-let·ter day Freuden-, Glückstag *m*

red·ness Röte *f*

re·dou·ble verdoppeln

red tape Bürokratismus *m*, F Amtsschimmel *m*

re·duce verkleinern; *Geschwindigkeit, Risiko etc* verringern, *Steuern etc* senken, *Preis, Waren etc* herabsetzen, reduzieren (**from … to** von … auf *acc*), *Gehalt etc* kürzen; verwandeln (**to** in *acc*), machen (**to** zu); reduzieren, zurückführen (**to**

auf *acc*)

re·duc·tion Verkleinerung *f*; Verringerung *f*, Senkung *f*, Herabsetzung *f*, Reduzierung *f*, Kürzung *f*

re·dun·dant überflüssig

reed BOT Schilf(rohr) *n*

re·ed·u·cate umerziehen

re·ed·u·ca·tion Umerziehung *f*

reef (Felsen)Riff *n*

reek 1. Gestank *m*; **2.** stinken (**of** nach)

reel¹ 1. Rolle *f*, Spule *f*; **2.** *reel off* abrollen, abspulen; *fig* herunterrasseln

reel² sich drehen; (sch)wanken, taumeln, torkeln; *my head reeled* mir drehte sich alles

re·e·lect wieder wählen

re·en·ter wieder eintreten in (*acc*), wieder betreten

re·en·try Wiedereintreten *n*, Wiedereintritt *m*

ref F SPORT Schiri *m*

re·fer: refer to verweisen *or* hinweisen auf (*acc*); *j-n* verweisen an (*acc*); sich beziehen auf (*acc*); anspielen auf (*acc*); erwähnen (*acc*); nachschlagen in (*dat*)

ref·er·ee SPORT Schiedsrichter *m*, Unparteiische *m*; *boxing*: Ringrichter *m*

ref·er·ence Verweis *m*, Hinweis *m* (**to** auf *acc*); Verweisstelle *f*; Referenz *f*, Empfehlung *f*, Zeugnis *n*; Bezugnahme *f* (**to** auf *acc*); Anspielung *f* (**to** auf *acc*); Erwähnung *f* (**to** *gen*); Nachschlagen *n* (**to** in *dat*); *list of references* Quellenangabe *f*

reference book Nachschlagewerk *n*

reference li·bra·ry Handbibliothek *f*

reference num·ber Aktenzeichen *n*

ref·er·en·dum POL Referendum *n*, Volksentscheid *m*

re·fill 1. wieder füllen, nachfüllen, auffüllen; **2.** (*Ersatz*)Mine *f*; (*Ersatz*)Patrone *f*

re·fine TECH raffinieren; *fig* verfeinern, kultivieren; *refine on* verbessern, verfeinern

re·fined TECH raffiniert; *fig* kultiviert, vornehm

re·fine·ment TECH Raffinierung *f*; *fig* Verbess(e)rung *f*, Verfeinerung *f*; Kultiviertheit *f*, Vornehmheit *f*

re·fin·e·ry TECH Raffinerie *f*

re·flect *v/t* reflektieren, zurückwerfen, -strahlen, (wider)spiegeln; *be reflected in* sich (wider)spiegeln in (*dat*) (*a. fig*); *v/i* nachdenken (**on** über *acc*); *reflect (badly) on* sich nachteilig auswirken auf (*acc*); ein schlechtes Licht werfen auf (*acc*)

re·flec·tion Reflexion *f*, Zurückwerfung *f*, -strahlung *f*, (Wider)Spiegelung *f* (*a. fig*);

Spiegelbild *n*; Überlegung *f*; Betrachtung *f*; **on reflection** nach einigem Nachdenken

re·flec·tive reflektierend; nachdenklich

re·flex Reflex *m*

reflex ac·tion Reflexhandlung *f*

reflex cam·e·ra PHOT Spiegelreflexkamera *f*

re·flex·ive LING reflexiv, rückbezüglich

re·form 1. reformieren, verbessern; sich bessern; **2.** Reform *f* (*a*. POL), Besserung *f*

ref·or·ma·tion Reformierung *f*; Besserung *f*; **the Reformation** REL die Reformation *f*

re·form·er *esp* POL Reformer *m*; REL Reformator *m*

re·fract Strahlen *etc* brechen

re·frac·tion (Strahlen- *etc*)Brechung *f*

re·frain[1]: **refrain from** sich enthalten (*gen*), unterlassen (*acc*)

re·frain[2] Kehrreim *m*, Refrain *m*

re·fresh (**o.s.** sich) erfrischen, stärken; *Gedächtnis* auffrischen

re·fresh·ing erfrischend (*a*. *fig*)

re·fresh·ment Erfrischung *f*

re·frig·er·ate TECH kühlen

re·frig·er·a·tor Kühlschrank *m*

re·fu·el auftanken

ref·uge Zuflucht *f*, Zufluchtsstätte *f*; *Br* Verkehrsinsel *f*

ref·u·gee Flüchtling *m*

ref·u·gee camp Flüchtlingslager *n*

re·fund 1. Rückzahlung *f*, Rückerstattung *f*; **2.** *Geld* zurückzahlen, zurückerstatten; *Auslagen* ersetzen

re·fur·bish aufpolieren (*a*. *fig*); renovieren

re·fus·al Ablehnung *f*; Weigerung *f*; Verweigerung *f*

re·fuse[1] *v/t* ablehnen; verweigern; sich weigern, es ablehnen (**to do** zu tun); *v/i* ablehnen; sich weigern

re·fuse[2] Abfall *m*, Abfälle *pl*, Müll *m*

re·fuse dump Müllabladeplatz *m*

re·fute widerlegen

re·gain wieder-, zurückgewinnen

re·gale: **regale s.o. with s.th.** j-n mit et. erfreuen or ergötzen

re·gard 1. Achtung *f*; Rücksicht *f*; *pl* Grüße *pl*; **in this regard** in dieser Hinsicht; **with regard to** im Hinblick auf (*acc*); hinsichtlich (*gen*); **with kind regards** mit freundlichen Grüßen; **2.** betrachten (*a*. *fig*), ansehen; **regard as** betrachten als, halten für; **as regards ...** was ... betrifft

re·gard·ing bezüglich, hinsichtlich (*gen*)

re·gard·less: **regardless of** ohne Rücksicht auf (*acc*), ungeachtet (*gen*)

regd ABBR *of* **registered** ECON eingetragen; *post* eingeschrieben

re·gen·e·rate (sich) erneuern or regenerieren

re·gent Regent(in)

re·gi·ment 1. MIL Regiment *n*, *fig a*. Schar *f*; **2.** reglementieren, bevormunden

re·gion Gegend *f*, Gebiet *n*, Region *f*

re·gion·al regional, örtlich, Orts...

re·gis·ter 1. Register *n*, Verzeichnis *n*, (*Wähler- etc*)Liste *f*; **2.** *v/t* registrieren, eintragen (lassen); *Messwerte* anzeigen; *Brief etc* einschreiben lassen; *v/i* sich eintragen (lassen)

re·gis·tered let·ter Einschreib(e)brief *m*, Einschreiben *n*

re·gis·tra·tion Registrierung *f*, Eintragung *f*; MOT Zulassung *f*

registration fee Anmeldegebühr *f*

registration num·ber MOT (polizeiliches) Kennzeichen

re·gis·try Registratur *f*

re·gis·try of·fice *esp Br* Standesamt *n*

re·gret 1. bedauern; bereuen; **2.** Bedauern *n*; Reue *f*

re·gret·ful bedauernd

re·gret·ta·ble bedauerlich

reg·u·lar 1. regelmäßig; geregelt, geordnet; richtig; normal; MIL Berufs...; **regular gas** (*Br* **petrol**) MOT Normalbenzin *n*; **2.** F Stammkunde *m*, Stammkundin *f*; Stammgast *m*; SPORT Stammspieler(in); MIL Berufssoldat *m*; MOT Normal(-benzin) *n*

reg·u·lar·i·ty Regelmäßigkeit *f*

reg·u·late regeln, regulieren; TECH einstellen, regulieren

reg·u·la·tion Reg(e)lung *f*, Regulierung *f*; TECH Einstellung *f*; Vorschrift *f*

reg·u·la·tor TECH Regler *m*

re·hears·al MUS, THEA Probe *f*

re·hearse MUS, THEA proben

reign 1. Regierung *f*, *a*. *fig* Herrschaft *f*; **2.** herrschen, regieren

re·im·burse *Auslagen* erstatten, vergüten

rein 1. Zügel *m*; **2.** **rein in** *Pferd etc* zügeln; *fig* bremsen

rein·deer ZO Ren *n*, Rentier *n*

re·in·force verstärken

re·in·force·ment Verstärkung *f*

re·in·state *j-n* wieder einstellen (**as** als; **in** in *dat*)

re·in·sure rückversichern

re·it·e·rate (ständig) wiederholen

re·ject *j-n*, *et.* ablehnen, *Bitte* abschlagen, *Plan etc* verwerfen; *j-n* ab-, zurückweisen; MED *Organ etc* abstoßen

re·jec·tion Ablehnung *f*; Verwerfung *f*;

R

Zurückweisung f; MED Abstoßung f

re·joice sich freuen, jubeln (**at, over** über acc)

re·joic·ing(s) Jubel m

re·join[1] wieder zusammenfügen; wieder zurückkehren zu

re·join[2] erwidern

re·ju·ve·nate verjüngen

re·kin·dle Feuer wieder anzünden; fig wieder entfachen

re·lapse 1. zurückfallen, wieder verfallen (**into** in acc); rückfällig werden; MED e-n Rückfall bekommen; **2.** Rückfall m

re·late v/t erzählen, berichten; in Verbindung or Zusammenhang bringen (**to** mit); v/i sich beziehen (**to** auf acc); zusammenhängen (**to** mit)

re·lat·ed verwandt (**to** mit)

re·la·tion Verwandte m, f; Beziehung f (**between** zwischen dat; **to** zu); pl diplomatische, geschäftliche Beziehungen pl; **in** or **with relation to** in Bezug auf (acc)

re·la·tion·ship Verwandtschaft f; Beziehung f, Verhältnis n

rel·a·tive[1] Verwandte m, f

rel·a·tive[2] relativ, verhältnismäßig; bezüglich (**to** gen); LING Relativ…, bezüglich

rel·a·tive pro·noun LING Relativpronomen n, bezügliches Fürwort

re·lax v/t Muskeln etc entspannen; Griff etc lockern; fig nachlassen in (dat); v/i sich entspannen, fig a. ausspannen; sich lockern

re·lax·a·tion Entspannung f; Erholung f; Lockerung f

re·laxed entspannt, zwanglos

re·lay[1] **1.** Ablösung f; SPORT Staffel f; radio, TV Übertragung f; ELECTR Relais n; **2.** radio, TV übertragen

re·lay[2] Kabel, Teppich neu verlegen

re·lay race SPORT Staffel f

re·lease 1. entlassen, freilassen; loslassen; freigeben, herausbringen, veröffentlichen; MOT Handbremse lösen; fig befreien, erlösen; **2.** Entlassung f, Freilassung f; Befreiung f; Freigabe f; Veröffentlichung f; TECH, PHOT Auslöser m; film: often **first release** Uraufführung f

rel·e·gate verbannen; **be relegated** SPORT absteigen (**to** in acc)

re·lent nachgeben; nachlassen

re·lent·less unbarmherzig; anhaltend

rel·e·vant relevant, erheblich, wichtig; sachdienlich, zutreffend

re·li·a·bil·i·ty Zuverlässigkeit f

re·li·a·ble zuverlässig

re·li·ance Vertrauen n; Abhängigkeit f (**on** von)

rel·ic Relikt n, Überrest m; REL Reliquie f

re·lief Erleichterung f; Unterstützung f, Hilfe f; Sozialhilfe f; Ablösung f; Relief n

relief map GEOGR Reliefkarte f

re·lieve Schmerz, Not lindern, j-n, Gewissen erleichtern; j-n ablösen

re·li·gion Religion f

re·li·gious Religions…; religiös; gewissenhaft

rel·ish 1. fig Gefallen m, Geschmack m (**for** an dat); GASTR Würze f; Soße f; **with relish** mit Genuss; **2.** genießen, sich et. schmecken lassen; Geschmack or Gefallen finden an (dat)

re·luc·tance Widerstreben n; **with reluctance** widerwillig, ungern

re·luc·tant widerstrebend, widerwillig

re·ly on sich verlassen auf (acc)

re·main 1. (ver)bleiben; übrig bleiben; **2.** pl (Über)Reste pl

re·main·der der Rest m; Restbetrag m

re·make 1. wieder or neu machen; **2.** Remake n, Neuverfilmung f

re·mand JUR **1. be remanded in custody** in Untersuchungshaft bleiben; **2. be on remand** in Untersuchungshaft sein; **prisoner on remand** Untersuchungsgefangene m, f

re·mark 1. v/t bemerken, äußern; v/i sich äußern (**on** über acc, zu); **2.** Bemerkung f

re·mark·a·ble bemerkenswert; außergewöhnlich

rem·e·dy 1. (Heil-, Hilfs-, Gegen)Mittel n; (Ab)Hilfe f; **2.** Schaden etc beheben; Missstand abstellen; Situation bereinigen

re·mem·ber sich erinnern an (acc); denken an (acc); **please remember me to her** grüße sie bitte von mir

re·mem·brance Erinnerung f; **in remembrance of** zur Erinnerung an (acc)

re·mind erinnern (**of** an acc)

re·mind·er Mahnung f

rem·i·nis·cences Erinnerungen pl (**of** an acc)

rem·i·nis·cent: be reminiscent of erinnern an (acc)

re·mit Schulden, Strafe erlassen; Sünden vergeben; Geld überweisen (**to** dat or an acc)

re·mit·tance ECON Überweisung f (**to** an acc)

rem·nant (Über)Rest m

re·mod·el umformen, umgestalten

re·morse Gewissensbisse pl, Reue f (**über** acc for)

re·morse·ful zerknirscht, reumütig

re·morse·less unbarmherzig

re·mote fern, entfernt; abgelegen, entlegen

remote con·trol TECH Fernlenkung f, Fernsteuerung f; Fernbedienung f

re·mov·al Entfernung f; Umzug m

re·mov·al van Möbelwagen m

re·move v/t entfernen (from von); Hut, Deckel etc abnehmen; Kleidung ablegen; beseitigen, aus dem Weg räumen; v/i (um)ziehen (from von; to nach)

re·mov·er (Flecken- etc)Entferner m

Re·nais·sance die Renaissance

ren·der berühmt, schwierig, möglich etc machen; Dienst erweisen; Gedicht, Musikstück vortragen; übersetzen, übertragen (into in acc); mst render down Fett auslassen

ren·der·ing esp Br → rendition

ren·di·tion MUS etc Vortrag m; Übersetzung f, Übertragung f

re·new erneuern; Gespräch etc wieder aufnehmen; Kraft etc wiedererlangen; Vertrag, Pass verlängern (lassen)

re·new·al Erneuerung f; Verlängerung f

re·nounce verzichten auf (acc); s-m Glauben etc abschwören

ren·o·vate renovieren

re·nown Ruhm m

re·nowned berühmt (as als; for wegen, für)

rent¹ 1. Miete f; Pacht f; Leihgebühr f; for rent zu vermieten, zu verleihen; 2. mieten, pachten (from von); a. rent out vermieten, verpachten (to an acc); rented car Miet-, Leihwagen m

rent² Riss m

rent·al Miete f; Pacht f; Leihgebühr f; rental car Miet-, Leihwagen m

re·nun·ci·a·tion Verzicht m (of auf acc); Abschwören n

re·pair 1. reparieren, ausbessern; fig wieder gutmachen; 2. Reparatur f; Ausbesserung f; pl Instandsetzungsarbeiten pl; beyond repair nicht mehr zu reparieren; in good (bad) repair in gutem (schlechtem) Zustand; be under repair in Reparatur sein; the road is under repair an der Straße wird gerade gearbeitet

rep·a·ra·tion Wiedergutmachung f; Entschädigung f; pl POL Reparationen pl

rep·ar·tee Schlagfertigkeit f; schlagfertige Antwort(en pl) f

re·pay et. zurückzahlen; Besuch erwidern; et. vergelten; j-n entschädigen

re·pay·ment Rückzahlung f

re·peal Gesetz etc aufheben

re·peat 1. v/t wiederholen; nachsprechen; repeat o.s. sich wiederholen; v/i F aufstoßen (on s.o. j-m) (food); 2. radio, TV Wiederholung f

re·peat·ed wiederholt

re·peat·ed·ly verschiedentlich

re·pel Angriff, Feind zurückschlagen; Wasser etc, fig j-n abstoßen

re·pel·lent abstoßend

re·pent bereuen

re·pent·ance Reue f (for über acc)

re·pent·ant reuig, reumütig

re·per·cus·sion mst pl Auswirkungen pl (on auf acc)

rep·er·toire THEA etc Repertoire n

rep·er·to·ry thea·ter (Br the·a·tre) Repertoiretheater n

rep·e·ti·tion Wiederholung f

re·place an j-s Stelle treten (acc), et. ersetzen; TECH austauschen, ersetzen

re·place·ment TECH Austausch m; Ersatz m

re·plant umpflanzen

re·play 1. SPORT Spiel wiederholen; Tonband-, Videoaufname etc abspielen; 2. SPORT Wiederholung f

re·plen·ish (wieder) auffüllen

re·plete satt; angefüllt, ausgestattet (with mit)

rep·li·ca art: Originalkopie f; Kopie f, Nachbildung f

re·ply 1. antworten, erwidern (to auf acc); 2. Antwort f, Erwiderung f (to auf acc); in reply to (als Antwort) auf (acc)

re·ply cou·pon Rückantwortschein m

re·ply-paid en·ve·lope Freiumschlag m

re·port 1. Bericht m; Meldung f, Nachricht f; Gerücht n; Knall m; report card PED Zeugnis n; 2. berichten (über acc); (sich) melden; anzeigen; it is reported that es heißt, dass; reported speech LING indirekte Rede

re·port·er Reporter(in), Berichterstatter(in)

re·pose Ruhe f; Gelassenheit f

re·pos·i·to·ry (Waren)Lager n; fig Fundgrube f, Quelle f

rep·re·sent j-n, Wahlbezirk vertreten; darstellen; hinstellen (as, to be als)

rep·re·sen·ta·tion Vertretung f; Darstellung f

rep·re·sen·ta·tive 1. repräsentativ (a. POL), typisch (of für); 2. (Stell)Vertreter(in); ECON (Handels)Vertreter(in); PARL Abgeordnete m, f; House of Representatives Repräsentantenhaus n

re·press unterdrücken; PSYCH verdrängen

re·pres·sion Unterdrückung f; PSYCH Verdrängung f

re·prieve JUR 1. he was reprieved er wurde begnadigt; s-e Urteilsvollstreckung

R

wurde ausgesetzt; **2.** Begnadigung *f*; Vollstreckungsaufschub *m*

rep·ri·mand 1. rügen, tadeln (**for** wegen); **2.** Rüge *f*, Tadel *m*, Verweis *m*

re·print 1. neu auflegen *or* drucken, nachdrucken; **2.** Neuauflage *f*, Nachdruck *m*

re·pri·sal Repressalie *f*, Vergeltungsmaßnahme *f*

re·proach 1. Vorwurf *m*; **2.** vorwerfen (**s.o. with s.th.** j-m et.); Vorwürfe machen

re·proach·ful vorwurfsvoll

rep·ro·bate verkommenes Subjekt

re·pro·cess NUCL wieder aufbereiten

re·pro·cess·ing TECH Wiederaufbereitung *f*

reprocessing plant TECH Wiederaufbereitungsanlage *f*

re·pro·duce *v/t* Ton etc wiedergeben; *Bild etc* reproduzieren; **reproduce o.s.** → *v/i* BIOL sich fortpflanzen, sich vermehren

re·pro·duc·tion Fortpflanzung *f*; Reproduktion *f*; Wiedergabe *f*; PED Nacherzählung *f*

re·pro·duc·tive BIOL Fortpflanzungs...

re·proof Rüge *f*, Tadel *m*

re·prove rügen, tadeln (**for** wegen)

rep·tile ZO Reptil *n*

re·pub·lic Republik *f*

re·pub·li·can 1. republikanisch; **2.** Republikaner(in)

re·pug·nant widerlich, abstoßend

re·pulse 1. *j-n, Angebot etc* zurückweisen; MIL *Angriff* zurückschlagen; **2.** MIL Zurückschlagen *n*; Zurückweisung *f*

re·pul·sion Abscheu *m*, Widerwille *m*; PHYS Abstoßung *f*

re·pul·sive abstoßend, widerlich, widerwärtig; PHYS abstoßend

rep·u·ta·ble angesehen

rep·u·ta·tion (guter) Ruf, Ansehen *n*

re·pute (guter) Ruf

re·put·ed angeblich

re·quest 1. (**for**) Bitte *f* (um), Wunsch *m* (nach); **at the request of s.o., at s.o.'s request** auf j-s Bitte hin; **on request** auf Wunsch; **2.** um et. bitten *or* ersuchen; *j-n* bitten, ersuchen (**to do** zu tun)

re·quest stop *Br* Bedarfshaltestelle *f*

re·quire erfordern; benötigen, brauchen; verlangen; **if required** wenn nötig

re·quire·ment Erfordernis *n*, Bedürfnis *n*; Anforderung *f*

req·ui·site 1. erforderlich; **2.** *mst pl* Artikel *pl*; **toilet requisites** Toilettenartikel *pl*

req·ui·si·tion 1. Anforderung *f*; MIL Requisition *f*, Beschlagnahme *f*; **make a requisition for** et. anfordern; **2.** anfor-

dern; MIL requirieren, beschlagnahmen

re·sale Wieder-, Weiterverkauf *m*

re·scind JUR *Gesetz, Urteil etc* aufheben

res·cue 1. retten (**from** aus, vor *dat*); **2.** Rettung *f*; Hilfe *f*; **3.** Rettungs...

re·search 1. Forschung *f*; **2.** forschen; *et.* erforschen

re·search·er Forscher(in)

re·sem·blance Ähnlichkeit *f* (**to** mit; **between** zwischen *dat*)

re·sem·ble ähnlich sein, ähneln (*both: dat*)

re·sent übel nehmen, sich ärgern über (*acc*)

re·sent·ful ärgerlich (**of, at** über *acc*)

re·sent·ment Ärger *m* (**against, at** über *acc*)

res·er·va·tion Reservierung *f*, Vorbestellung *f*; Vorbehalt *m*; (*Indianer*)Reservat(ion *f*) *n*; (*Wild*)Reservat *n*

re·serve 1. (sich) *et.* aufsparen (**for** für); sich vorbehalten; reservieren (lassen); vorbestellen; **2.** Reserve *f* (*a.* MIL); Vorrat *m*; (*Naturschutz-, Wild*)Reservat *n*; SPORT Reservespieler(in); Reserviertheit *f*, Zurückhaltung *f*

re·served zurückhaltend, reserviert

res·er·voir Reservoir *n* (*a. fig* **of** an *dat*)

re·set *Uhr* umstellen; *Zeiger etc* zurückstellen (**to** auf *acc*)

re·set·tle umsiedeln

re·side wohnen, ansässig sein, s-n Wohnsitz haben

res·i·dence Wohnsitz *m*, Wohnort *m*; Aufenthalt *m*; Residenz *f*; **official residence** Amtssitz *m*

residence per·mit Aufenthaltsgenehmigung *f*, -erlaubnis *f*

res·i·dent 1. wohnhaft, ansässig; **2.** Bewohner(in), *in a town etc* a. Einwohner(in); (*Hotel*)Gast *m*; MOT Anlieger(in)

res·i·den·tial Wohn...

residential ar·e·a Wohngebiet *n*, Wohngegend *f*

re·sid·u·al übrig (geblieben), restlich, Rest...

residual pol·lu·tion Altlasten *pl*

res·i·due Rest *m*, CHEM A. Rückstand *m*

re·sign *v/i* zurücktreten (**from** von); *v/t Amt etc* niederlegen; aufgeben; verzichten auf (*acc*); **resign o.s. to** sich fügen in (*acc*), sich abfinden mit

res·ig·na·tion Rücktritt *m*; Resignation *f*

re·signed ergeben, resigniert

re·sil·i·ence Elastizität *f*; *fig* Zähigkeit *f*

re·sil·i·ent elastisch; *fig* zäh

res·in Harz *n*

re·sist widerstehen (*dat*); Widerstand leisten, sich widersetzen (*both: dat*)

re·sist·ance Widerstand *m* (*a.* ELECTR); MED Widerstandskraft *f*; (*Hitze- etc* -) Beständigkeit *f*, (*Stoß- etc*)Festigkeit *f*; **line of least resistance** Weg *m* des geringsten Widerstands

re·sist·ant widerstandsfähig; (*hitze- etc*) beständig, (*stoß- etc*)fest

res·o·lute beschlossen, entschlossen

res·o·lu·tion Beschluss *m*, PARL *etc a.* Resolution *f*; Vorsatz *m*; Entschlossenheit *f*; Lösung *f*

re·solve 1. beschließen; *Problem etc* lösen; (sich) auflösen; **resolve on** sich entschließen zu; **2.** Vorsatz *m*; Entschlossenheit *f*

res·o·nance Resonanz *f*; voller Klang

res·o·nant voll(tönend); widerhallend

re·sort 1. Erholungsort *m*, Urlaubsort *m*; **have resort to** → **2. resort to** Zuflucht nehmen zu

re·sound widerhallen (**with** von)

re·source Mittel *n*, Zuflucht *f*; Ausweg *m*; Einfallsreichtum *m*; *pl* Mittel *pl*; (*natürliche*) Reichtümer *pl*, (*Boden-, Natur*)Schätze *pl*

re·source·ful einfallsreich, findig

re·spect 1. Achtung *f*, Respekt *m* (*both*: **for** vor *dat*); Rücksicht *f* (**for** auf *acc*); Beziehung *f*, Hinsicht *f*; **with respect to ...** was ... anbelangt *or* betrifft; **in this respect** in dieser Hinsicht; **give my respects to** ... e-e Empfehlung an (*acc*); **2.** *v/t* respektieren, *a.* achten, *a.* berücksichtigen, beachten

re·spect·a·ble ehrbar, anständig, geachtet; F ansehnlich, beachtlich

re·spect·ful respektvoll, ehrerbietig

re·spec·tive jeweilig; **we went to our respective places** jeder ging zu seinem Platz

re·spec·tive·ly beziehungsweise

res·pi·ra·tion Atmung *f*

res·pi·ra·tor Atemschutzgerät *n*

re·spite Pause *f*; Aufschub *m*, Frist *f*; **without respite** ohne Unterbrechung

re·splen·dent glänzend, strahlend

re·spond antworten, erwidern (**to** auf *acc*; **that** dass); reagieren, MED *a.* ansprechen (**to** auf *acc*)

re·sponse Antwort *f*, Erwiderung *f* (**to** auf *acc*); *fig* Reaktion *f* (**to** auf *acc*)

re·spon·si·bil·i·ty Verantwortung *f*; **on one's own responsibility** auf eigene Verantwortung; **sense of responsibility** Verantwortungsgefühl *n*; **take (full) responsibility for** die (volle) Verantwortung übernehmen für

re·spon·si·ble verantwortlich; verantwortungsbewusst; verantwortungsvoll

rest[1] **1.** Ruhe(pause) *f*; Erholung *f*; TECH Stütze *f*; (*Telefon*)Gabel *f*; **have** *or* **take a rest** sich ausruhen; **set s.o.'s mind at rest** j-n beruhigen; **2.** *v/i* ruhen; sich ausruhen; lehnen (**against**, **on** an *dat*); **let s.th. rest** et. auf sich beruhen lassen; **rest on** ruhen auf (*dat*) (*a. fig*); *fig* beruhen auf (*dat*); *v/t* (aus)ruhen (lassen); lehnen (**against** gegen; **on** an *acc*)

rest[2] Rest *m*; **all the rest of them** alle Übrigen; **for the rest** im Übrigen

rest ar·e·a MOT Rastplatz *m*

res·tau·rant Restaurant *n*, Gaststätte *f*

rest·ful ruhig, erholsam

rest home Altenpflegeheim *n*; Erholungsheim *n*

res·ti·tu·tion ECON Rückgabe *f*, Rückerstattung *f*

res·tive unruhig, nervös

rest·less ruhelos, rastlos; unruhig

res·to·ra·tion Wiederherstellung *f*; Restaurierung *f*; Rückgabe *f*, Rückerstattung *f*

re·store wiederherstellen; restaurieren; zurückgeben, -erstatten; **be restored (to health)** wieder gesund sein

re·strain (*from*) zurückhalten (von), hindern an (*dat*); **I had to restrain myself (from doing s.th.)** ich musste mich beherrschen (**from doing s.th.** um nicht et. zu tun)

re·strained beherrscht; dezent (*color*)

re·straint Beherrschung *f*, Zurückhaltung *f*; ECON Be-, Einschränkung *f*

re·strict ECON beschränken (**to** auf *acc*), einschränken

re·stric·tion ECON Be-, Einschränkung *f*; **without restrictions** uneingeschränkt

rest room Toilette *f*

re·struc·ture umstrukturieren

re·sult 1. Ergebnis *n*, Resultat *n*; Folge *f*; **as a result of** als Folge von (*or gen*); **without result** ergebnislos; **2.** folgen, sich ergeben (**from** aus); **result in** zur Folge haben (*acc*), führen zu

re·sump·tion Wiederaufnahme *f*; Fortsetzung *f*

Res·ur·rec·tion REL Auferstehung *f*

re·sus·ci·tate MED wieder beleben

re·sus·ci·ta·tion MED Wiederbelebung *f*

re·tail ECON **1.** Einzelhandel *m*; **by retail** im Einzelhandel; **2.** Einzelhandels...; **3.** *adv* im Einzelhandel; **4.** *v/t* im Einzelhandel verkaufen (**at, for** für); *v/i* im Einzelhandel verkauft werden (**at, for** für)

re·tail·er ECON Einzelhändler(in)

re·tain (be)halten, bewahren; *Wasser, Wärme* speichern

R

re·tal·i·ate Vergeltung üben, sich revanchieren

re·tal·i·a·tion Vergeltung f, Vergeltungsmaßnahmen pl

re·tard verzögern, aufhalten, hemmen; **(mentally) retarded** (geistig) zurückgeblieben

retch würgen

re·tell nacherzählen

re·think et. noch einmal überdenken

re·ti·cent schweigsam, zurückhaltend

ret·i·nue Gefolge n

re·tire v/i in Rente or Pension gehen, pensionieren lassen; sich zurückziehen; **retire from business** sich zur Ruhe setzen; v/t in den Ruhestand versetzen, pensionieren

re·tired pensioniert, im Ruhestand (lebend); **be retired** a. in Rente or Pension sein

re·tire·ment Pensionierung f, Ruhestand m

re·tir·ing zurückhaltend

re·tort 1. (scharf) entgegnen or erwidern; **2.** (scharfe) Entgegnung or Erwiderung

re·touch PHOT retuschieren

re·trace Tathergang etc rekonstruieren; **retrace one's steps** denselben Weg zurückgehen

re·tract v/t Angebot zurückziehen; Behauptung zurücknehmen; Geständnis widerrufen; TECH, ZO einziehen; v/i TECH, ZO eingezogen werden

re·train umschulen

re·tread MOT **1.** Reifen runderneuern; **2.** runderneuerter Reifen

re·treat 1. MIL Rückzug m; Zufluchtsort m; **beat a (hasty) retreat** das Feld räumen, F abhauen; **2.** sich zurückziehen; zurückweichen **(from** vor dat)

ret·ri·bu·tion Vergeltung f

re·trieve zurückholen, wiederbekommen; Fehler, Verlust etc wieder gutmachen; HUNT apportieren

ret·ro·ac·tive JUR rückwirkend

ret·ro·grade rückschrittlich

ret·ro·spect: in retrospect im Rückblick

ret·ro·spec·tive rückblickend; JUR rückwirkend

re·try JUR Fall erneut verhandeln; neu verhandeln gegen j-n

re·turn 1. v/i zurückkehren, zurückkommen; zurückgehen; **return to** auf ein Thema etc zurückkommen; in e-e Gewohnheit etc zurückfallen; in e-n Zustand etc zurückkehren; v/t zurückgeben **(to** dat); zurückbringen **(to** dat); zurückschicken, -senden **(to** dat or acc); zurücklegen, -stellen; erwidern; Gewinn etc ab-

werfen; → **verdict; 2.** Rückkehr f; fig Wiederauftreten n; Rückgabe f; Zurückbringen n; Zurückschicken n, -senden n; Zurücklegen n, -stellen n; Erwiderung f; (Steuer)Erklärung f; tennis etc: Return m, Rückschlag m; ECON a. pl Gewinn m; Br → **return ticket;** Br **many happy returns (of the day)** herzlichen Glückwunsch zum Geburtstag; **by return (of post)** umgehend, postwendend; **in return for** (als Gegenleistung) für; **3.** adj Rück…

re·turn·a·ble in cpds Mehrweg…; **return·able bottle** Pfandflasche f

re·turn key EDP Eingabetaste f

return game, return match SPORT Rückspiel n

return tick·et Br RAIL Rückfahrkarte f; AVIAT Rückflugticket n

re·u·ni·fi·ca·tion POL Wiedervereinigung f

re·u·nion Treffen n, Wiedersehensfeier f; Wiedervereinigung f

re·us·a·ble wieder verwendbar

rev F MOT **1.** Umdrehung f; **rev counter** Drehzahlmesser m; **2.** a. **rev up** aufheulen (lassen)

re·val·ue ECON Währung aufwerten

re·veal den Blick freigeben auf (acc), zeigen; Geheimnis etc enthüllen, aufdecken

re·veal·ing aufschlussreich (remark etc); offenherzig (dress etc)

rev·el: revel in schwelgen in (dat); sich weiden an (dat)

rev·e·la·tion Enthüllung f; REL Offenbarung f

re·venge 1. Rache f; esp SPORT Revanche f; **in revenge for** aus Rache für; **take revenge on s.o. for s.th.** sich an j-m für et. rächen; **2.** rächen

re·venge·ful rachsüchtig

rev·e·nue Staatseinkünfte pl, Staatseinnahmen pl

re·ver·be·rate nach-, widerhallen

re·vere (ver)ehren

rev·e·rence Verehrung f; Ehrfurcht f **(for** vor dat)

Rev·e·rend REL Hochwürden m

rev·e·rent ehrfürchtig, ehrfurchtsvoll

rev·er·ie (Tag)Träumerei f

re·vers·al Umkehrung f; Rückschlag m

re·verse 1. adj umgekehrt; **in reverse order** in umgekehrter Reihenfolge; **2.** Wagen im Rückwärtsgang fahren or rückwärtsfahren; Reihenfolge etc umkehren; Urteil etc aufheben; Entscheidung etc umstoßen; **3.** Gegenteil n; MOT Rückwärtsgang m; Rückseite f, Kehrseite f (of a coin); Rückschlag m

reverse gear MOT Rückwärtsgang *m*
reverse side linke (*Stoff*)Seite
re·vers·i·ble doppelseitig (tragbar)
re·vert: *revert to* in e-n Zustand zurückkehren; in *e-e Gewohnheit etc* zurückfallen; auf *ein Thema* zurückkommen
re·view 1. Überprüfung *f*; Besprechung *f*, Kritik *f*, Rezension *f*; MIL Parade *f*; PED (Stoff)Wiederholung *f* (**for** für *e-e Prüfung*); **2.** überprüfen; besprechen, rezensieren; MIL besichtigen, inspizieren; PED *Stoff* wiederholen (**for** für *e-e Prüfung*)
re·view·er Kritiker(in), Rezensent(in)
re·vise revidieren, *Ansicht* ändern, *Buch etc* überarbeiten; Br PED *Stoff* wiederholen (**for** für *e-e Prüfung*)
re·vi·sion Revision *f*, Überarbeitung *f*; überarbeitete Ausgabe; Br PED (Stoff-)Wiederholung *f* (**for** für *e-e Prüfung*)
re·viv·al Wiederbelebung *f*; Wiederaufleben *n*
re·vive wieder beleben; wieder aufleben (lassen); *Erinnerungen* wachrufen; MED wieder zu sich kommen; sich erholen
re·voke widerrufen, zurücknehmen, rückgängig machen
re·volt 1. *v/i* sich auflehnen, revoltieren (**against** gegen); Abscheu empfinden, empört sein (**against, at, from** über *acc*); *v/t* mit Abscheu erfüllen, abstoßen; **2.** Revolte *f*, Aufstand *m*
re·volt·ing abscheulich, abstoßend
rev·o·lu·tion Revolution *f*, Umwälzung *f*; ASTR Umlauf *m* (**round** um); TECH Umdrehung *f*; *number of revolutions* Drehzahl *f*; *revolution counter* Drehzahlmesser *m*
rev·o·lu·tion·a·ry 1. revolutionär; Revolutions...; **2.** POL Revolutionär(in)
rev·o·lu·tion·ize revolutionieren
re·volve sich drehen (**on, round** um); *re·volve around fig* sich drehen um
re·volv·er Revolver *m*
re·volv·ing Dreh...; *revolving door(s)* Drehtür *f*
re·vue THEA Revue *f*; Kabarett *n*
re·vul·sion Abscheu *m*
re·ward 1. Belohnung *f*; **2.** belohnen
re·ward·ing lohnend
re·write neu schreiben, umschreiben
rhap·so·dy MUS Rhapsodie *f*
rhe·to·ric Rhetorik *f*
rheu·ma·tism MED Rheumatismus *m*, F Rheuma *n*
rhi·no F, **rhi·no·ce·ros** ZO Rhinozeros *n*, Nashorn *n*
rhu·barb BOT Rhabarber *m*
rhyme 1. Reim *m*; Vers *m*; *without rhyme or reason* ohne Sinn und Verstand; **2.**

(sich) reimen
rhyth·m Rhythmus *m*
rhyth·mic, rhyth·mi·cal rhythmisch
rib ANAT Rippe *f*
rib·bon (*a.* Farb-, Ordens)Band *n*; Streifen *m*; Fetzen *m*
rib cage ANAT Brustkorb *m*
rice BOT Reis *m*
rice pud·ding GASTR Milchreis *m*
rich 1. reich (**in** an *dat*); prächtig, kostbar; GASTR schwer (*food*); AGR fruchtbar, fett (*soil*); voll (*sound*); satt (*color*); reich (**in calories**) kalorienreich; **2. the rich** die Reichen *pl*
rick (Stroh-, Heu)Schober *m*
rick·ets MED Rachitis *f*
rick·et·y F *fig* gebrechlich; wack(e)lig
rid befreien (**of** von); *get rid of* loswerden
rid·dance: F *good riddance!* den (die, das) sind wir Gott sei Dank los!
rid·den in *cpds* geplagt von
rid·dle¹ Rätsel *n*
rid·dle² 1. grobes Sieb, Schüttelsieb *n*; **2.** sieben; durchlöchern, durchsieben
ride 1. *v/i* reiten; fahren (**on** auf e-m *Fahrrad etc*; **on** *or* Br **in** in e-m *Bus etc*); *v/t* reiten (auf *dat*); *Fahrrad, Motorrad* fahren, fahren auf (*dat*); **2.** Ritt *m*; Fahrt *f*
rid·er Reiter(in); (Motorrad-, Rad)Fahrer(in)
ridge GEOGR (*Gebirgs*)Kamm *m*, Grat *m*; ARCH (*Dach*)First *m*
rid·i·cule 1. Spott *m*; **2.** lächerlich machen, spotten über (*acc*), verspotten
ri·dic·u·lous lächerlich
rid·ing Reit...
riff-raff *contp* Gesindel *n*
ri·fle¹ Gewehr *n*
ri·fle² durchwühlen
rift Spalt *m*, Spalte *f*; *fig* Riss *m*
rig 1. *Schiff* auftakeln; *rig out j-n* ausstaffieren; *rig up* F (behelfsmäßig) zusammenbauen (**from** aus); **2.** MAR Takelage *f*; TECH Bohrinsel *f*; F Aufmachung *f*
rig·ging MAR Takelage *f*
right 1. *adj* recht; richtig; rechte(r, -s), Rechts...; *all right!* in Ordnung!, gut!; *that's all right!* das macht nichts!, schon gut!, bitte!; *that's right!* richtig!, ganz recht!, stimmt!; *be right* recht haben; *put right, set right* in Ordnung bringen; berichtigen, korrigieren; **2.** *adv* (nach) rechts; richtig, recht; genau; gerade (-wegs), direkt; ganz, völlig; *right away* sofort; *right now* im Moment; sofort; *right on* geradeaus; *turn right* (sich) nach rechts wenden; MOT rechts abbiegen; **3.** Recht *n*; *die Rechte* (*a.* POL, *boxing*), rechte Seite; *on the right* rechts,

auf der rechten Seite; **to the right** (nach) rechts; **keep to the right** sich rechts halten; мот rechts fahren; **4.** aufrichten; *et.* wieder gutmachen; in Ordnung bringen

right an·gle MATH rechter Winkel

right-an·gled MATH rechtwink(e)lig

right·eous gerecht (*anger etc*)

right·ful rechtmäßig

right-hand rechte(r, -s)

right-hand drive мот Rechtssteuerung *f*

right-hand·ed rechtshändig; für Rechtshänder; **be right-handed** Rechtshänder(in) sein

right·ly richtig; mit Recht

right of way мот Vorfahrt *f*, Vorfahrtsrecht *n*; Durchgangsrecht *n*

right-wing POL dem rechten Flügel angehörend, Rechts…

rig·id starr, steif; *fig* streng, strikt

rig·a·ma·role Geschwätz *n*; *fig* Theater *n*, Zirkus *m*

rig·or·ous streng; genau

rig·o(u)r Strenge *f*, Härte *f*

rile F ärgern, reizen

rim Rand *m*; TECH Felge *f*

rim·less randlos

rind (*Zitronen-, etc*)Schale *f*; (*Käse*)Rinde *f*; (*Speck*)Schwarte *f*

ring¹ 1. Ring *m*; Kreis *m*; Manege *f*; (*Box*)Ring *m*; (*Spionage- etc*)Ring *m*; **2.** umringen, umstellen; *Vogel* beringen

ring² 1. läuten; klingeln; klingen (*a. fig*); *Br* TEL anrufen; **the bell is ringing** es läutet *or* klingelt; **ring the bell** läuten, klingeln; **ring back** *Br* TEL zurückrufen; **ring for** nach *j-m, et.* läuten; *Arzt etc* rufen; **ring off** *Br* TEL (den Hörer) auflegen, Schluss machen; **ring s.o. (up)** *j-n or bei j-m* anrufen; **2.** Läuten *n*, Klingeln *n*; *fig* Klang *m*; *Br* TEL Anruf *m*; F **give s.o. a ring** *j-n* anrufen

ring bind·er Ringbuch *n*

ring fin·ger Ringfinger *m*

ring·lead·er Rädelsführer(in)

ring·let (Ringel)Löckchen *n*

ring road *Br* Umgehungsstraße *f*; Ringstraße *f*

ring·side: at the ringside boxing: am Ring

rink (Kunst)Eisbahn *f*; Rollschuhbahn *f*

rinse *a.* **rinse out** (aus)spülen

ri·ot 1. Aufruhr *m*; Krawall *m*; **run riot** randalieren; **run riot through** randalierend ziehen durch; **2.** Krawall machen, randalieren

ri·ot·er Aufrührer(in); Randalierer(in)

ri·ot·ous aufrührerisch; randalierend; ausgelassen, wild

rip 1. *a.* **rip up** zerreißen; **rip open** aufrei-

ßen; F **rip s.o. off** *j-n* neppen; **2.** Riss *m*

ripe reif

rip·en reifen (lassen)

rip-off F Nepp *m*

rip·ple 1. (sich) kräuseln; plätschern, rieseln; **2.** kleine Welle; Kräuselung *f*; Plätschern *n*, Rieseln *n*

rise 1. aufstehen, sich erheben; REL auferstehen; aufsteigen (*smoke etc*); sich heben (*curtain, spirits*); ansteigen (*road, river etc*), anschwellen (*river etc*); (an)steigen (*temperature etc*), *prices etc*: *a.* anziehen; stärker werden (*wind etc*); aufgehen (*sun etc, bread etc*); entspringen (*river etc*); *fig* aufsteigen; *fig* entstehen (**from, out of** aus); *a.* **rise up** sich erheben (**against** gegen); **rise to the occasion** sich der Lage gewachsen zeigen; **2.** (An)Steigen *n*; Steigung *f*; Anhöhe *f*; ASTR Aufgang *m*; *Br* Lohn- *or* Gehaltserhöhung *f*; *fig* Anstieg *m*; Aufstieg *m*; **give rise to** verursachen, führen zu

ris·er: early riser Frühaufsteher(in)

ris·ing 1. Aufstand *m*; **2.** aufstrebend

risk 1. Gefahr *f*, Risiko *n*; **at one's own risk** auf eigene Gefahr; **at the risk of doing s.th.** auf die Gefahr hin, et. zu tun; **be at risk** gefährdet sein; **run the risk of doing s.th.** Gefahr laufen, et. zu tun; **run a risk, take a risk** ein Risiko eingehen; **2.** wagen, riskieren

risk·y riskant

rite Ritus *m*; Zeremonie *f*

rit·u·al 1. rituell; Ritual…; **2.** Ritual *n*

ri·val 1. Rivale *m*, Rivalin *f*, Konkurrent(in); **2.** Konkurrenz…, rivalisierend; **3.** rivalisieren *or* konkurrieren mit

ri·val·ry Rivalität *f*; Konkurrenzkampf *m*

riv·er Fluss *m*; Strom *m*

riv·er·side Flussufer *n*; **by the riverside** am Fluss

riv·et 1. TECH Niet *m, n*, Niete *f*; **2.** TECH (ver)nieten; *fig Aufmerksamkeit, Blick* richten (**on** auf *acc*)

road (Auto-, Land)Straße *f*; *fig* Weg *m*; **on the road** auf der Straße; unterwegs; THEA auf Tournee

road ac·ci·dent Verkehrsunfall *m*

road·block Straßensperre *f*

road hog F Verkehrsrowdy *m*

road map Straßenkarte *f*

road safe·ty Verkehrssicherheit *f*

road·side Straßenrand *m*; **at the roadside, by the roadside** am Straßenrand

road toll Straßenbenutzungsgebühr *f*

road·way Fahrbahn *f*

road works Straßenarbeiten *pl*

road·wor·thi·ness Verkehrssicherheit *f*

road·wor·thy verkehrssicher

roam v/i (umher)streifen, (-)wandern; v/t streifen or wandern durch

roar 1. Brüllen n; Gebrüll n; Brausen n, Krachen n; Donnern n; **roars of laughter** brüllendes Gelächter; **2.** brüllen; brausen; donnern (truck, gun etc)

roast GASTR **1.** v/t braten (a. v/i); Kaffee etc rösten; **2.** Braten m; **3.** adj gebraten

roast beef GASTR Rinderbraten m

rob Bank etc überfallen; j-n berauben

rob·ber Räuber m

rob·ber·y Raubüberfall m, (Bank-) Raub m, (Bank)Überfall m

robe a. pl Robe f, Talar m

rob·in zo Rotkehlchen n

ro·bot Roboter m

ro·bust robust, kräftig

rock¹ schaukeln, wiegen; erschüttern (a. fig)

rock² Fels(en) m; Felsen pl; GEOL Gestein n; Felsbrocken m; Stein m; Br Zuckerstange f; pl Klippen pl; F **on the rocks** in ernsten Schwierigkeiten (business etc); kaputt (marriage etc); GASTR mit Eis

rock³ a. **rock music** Rock(musik f) m; → **rock 'n' roll**

rock·er Kufe f; Schaukelstuhl m; Br Rocker m; **off one's rocker** F übergeschnappt

rock·et 1. Rakete f; **2.** rasen, schießen; a. **rocket up** hochschnellen, in die Höhe schießen (prices)

rock·ing chair Schaukelstuhl m

rock·ing horse Schaukelpferd n

rock 'n' roll MUS Rock 'n' Roll m

rock·y felsig; steinig

rod Rute f; TECH Stab m, Stange f

ro·dent zo Nagetier n

ro·de·o Rodeo m, n

roe zo a. **hard roe** Rogen m; a. **soft roe** Milch f

roe·buck zo Rehbock m

roe deer zo Reh n

rogue Schurke m, Gauner m; Schlingel m, Spitzbube m

ro·guish schelmisch, spitzbübisch

role THEA etc Rolle f (a. fig)

roll 1. v/i rollen; sich wälzen; fahren; MAR schlingern; (g)rollen (thunder); v/t et. rollen; auf-, zusammenrollen; Zigarette drehen; **roll down** Ärmel herunterkrempeln; MOT Fenster herunterkurbeln; **roll out** ausrollen; **roll up** aufrollen; (sich) zusammenrollen; Ärmel hochkrempeln; MOT Fenster hochkurbeln; **2.** Rolle f; GASTR Brötchen n, Semmel f; Namens-, Anwesenheitsliste f; (G)Rollen n (of thunder); (Trommel)Wirbel m; MAR Schlingern n

roll call Namensaufruf m

roll·er (Locken)Wickler m; TECH Rolle f, Walze f

roll·er coast·er Achterbahn f

roll·er skate Rollschuh m

roll·er-skate Rollschuh laufen

roll·er-skat·ing Rollschuhlaufen n

roll·er tow·el Rollhandtuch n

roll·ing pin Nudelholz n

roll-on Deoroller m

Ro·man 1. römisch; **2.** Römer(in)

ro·mance Abenteuer-, Liebesroman m; Romanze f; Romantik f

Ro·mance LING romanisch

Ro·ma·ni·a Rumänien n

Ro·ma·ni·an 1. rumänisch; **2.** Rumäne m, Rumänin f; LING Rumänisch n

ro·man·tic 1. romantisch; **2.** Romantiker(in)

ro·man·ti·cism Romantik f

romp a. **romp about, romp around** herumtollen, herumtoben

romp·ers Spielanzug m

roof 1. Dach n; MOT Verdeck n; **2.** mit e-m Dach versehen; **roof in, roof over** überdachen

roof·ing felt Dachpappe f

roof-rack MOT Dachgepäckträger m

rook¹ zo Saatkrähe f

rook² chess: Turm m

rook³ F j-n betrügen (of um)

room 1. Raum m, a. Zimmer n, a. Platz m; fig Spielraum m; **2.** wohnen

room·er Untermieter(in)

room·ing-house Fremdenheim n, Pension f

room·mate Zimmergenosse m, -genossin f

room ser·vice Zimmerservice m

room·y geräumig

roost 1. (Hühner)Stange f; zo Schlafplatz m; **2.** auf der Stange etc sitzen or schlafen

roost·er zo (Haus)Hahn m

root 1. Wurzel f; **take root** Wurzeln schlagen (a. fig); **2.** v/i Wurzeln schlagen; wühlen (for nach); **root about** herumwühlen (among in dat); v/t **root out** fig ausrotten; **root up** mit der Wurzel ausreißen

root·ed: deeply rooted fig tief verwurzelt; **stand rooted to the spot** wie angewurzelt dastehen

rope 1. Seil n; MAR Tau n; Strick m; (Perlen- etc)Schnur f; **give s.o. plenty of rope** j-m viel Freiheit or Spielraum lassen; **know the ropes** F sich auskennen; **show s.o. the ropes** F j-n einarbeiten; **2.** festbinden (to an dat or acc); **rope**

off (durch ein Seil) absperren *or* abgrenzen

rope lad·der Strickleiter f

ro·sa·ry REL Rosenkranz m

rose 1. BOT Rose f; Brause f; **2.** rosarot, rosenrot

ros·trum Redner-, Dirigentenpult n

ros·y rosig (a. fig)

rot 1. v/t (ver)faulen *or* verrotten lassen; v/i a. *rot away* (ver)faulen, verrotten, morsch werden; **2.** Fäulnis f

ro·ta·ry rotierend, sich drehend; Rotations..., Dreh...

ro·tate rotieren (lassen), (sich) drehen; turnusmäßig (aus-) wechseln

ro·ta·tion Rotation f, Drehung f; Wechsel m

ro·tor TECH Rotor m

rot·ten verfault, faul; verrottet, morsch; fig miserabel; gemein; *feel rotten* F sich mies fühlen

ro·tund rund und dick

rough 1. adj rau; uneben (road etc); stürmisch (sea, crossing, weather); grob; barsch; hart; grob, ungefähr (estimate etc); roh, Roh...; **2.** adv *sleep rough* im Freien übernachten; *play tough* SPORT hart spielen; **3.** golf: Rough n; *write it out in rough first* zuerst ins Unreine schreiben; **4.** *rough it* F primitiv *or* anspruchslos leben; *rough out* entwerfen, skizzieren; *rough up* F j-n zusammenschlagen

rough·age MED Ballaststoffe pl

rough·cast ARCH Rauputz m

rough draft Rohentwurf m, Konzept n

rough draft Rohfassung f

rough·en rau werden; rau machen, anrauen, aufrauen

rough·ly grob, fig a. ungefähr

rough·neck F Schläger m

rough·shod *ride roughshod over* j-n rücksichtslos behandeln; sich rücksichtslos über et. hinwegsetzen

round 1. adj rund; *a round dozen* ein rundes Dutzend; *in round figures* aufgerundet, abgerundet, rund(e) ...; **2.** adv rund(her)um, rings(her)um; überall, auf *or* von *or* nach allen Seiten; *turn round* sich umdrehen; *invite s.o. round* j-n zu sich einladen; *round about* F ungefähr; *all (the) year round* das ganze Jahr hindurch *or* über; *the other way round* umgekehrt; **3.** prp (rund) um, um (acc ... herum); in *or* auf (dat) ... herum; *trip round the world* Weltreise f; **4.** Runde f, a. Rundgang m, MED Visite f, a. Lage f (beer etc); Schuss m; esp F Scheibe f (bread etc); MUS Kanon m; **5.** rund

machen, (ab)runden, *Lippen* spitzen; umfahren, fahren um, *Kurve* nehmen; *round down* Zahl etc abrunden (*to* auf acc); *round off* Essen etc abrunden, beschließen (*with* mit); Zahl etc auf- *or* abrunden (*to* auf acc); *round up* Vieh zusammentreiben; *Leute etc* zusammentrommeln; Zahl etc aufrunden (*to* auf acc)

round·a·bout 1. Br MOT Kreisverkehr m; Br Karussell n; **2.** *take a roundabout route* e-n Umweg machen; *in a roundabout way* fig auf Umwegen

round trip Hin- und Rückfahrt f; Hin- und Rückflug m

round-trip tick·et Rückfahrkarte f; Rückflugticket n

round·up Razzia f

rouse j-n wecken; fig j-n aufrütteln, wach rütteln; j-n erzürnen, reizen

route Route f, Strecke f, Weg m, (Bus- etc)Linie f

rou·tine 1. Routine f; *the same old (daily) routine* das (tägliche) ewige Einerlei; **2.** üblich, routinemäßig, Routine...

rove (umher)streifen, (umher)wandern

row¹ Reihe f

row² **1.** rudern; **2.** Kahnfahrt f

row³ Br F **1.** Krach m; (lauter) Streit; **2.** (sich) streiten

row·boat Ruderboot n

row·er Ruderer m, Ruderin f

row house Reihenhaus n

row·ing boat Br Ruderboot n

roy·al königlich, Königs...

roy·al·ty die königliche Familie; Tantieme f (*on* auf acc)

rub 1. v/t reiben; abreiben; polieren; *rub dry* trocken reiben; *rub it in* fig F darauf herumreiten; *rub shoulders with* F verkehren mit; v/i reiben, scheuern (*against, on* an dat); *rub down* abreiben, trocken reiben; abschmirgeln, abschleifen; *rub off* abreiben; abgehen (paint etc); *rub off on(to)* fig abfärben auf (acc); *rub out* F ausradieren; **2.** *give s.th. a rub* et. abreiben *or* polieren

rub·ber Gummi n, m; esp Br Radiergummi m; Wischtuch n; F Gummi m

rub·ber band Gummiband n

rub·ber din·ghy Schlauchboot n

rub·ber·neck F **1.** neugierig gaffen; **2.** a. *rubbernecker* Gaffer(in), Schaulustige m, f

rub·ber·y gummiartig; zäh

rub·bish Br Abfall m, Abfälle pl, Müll m; F Schund m; Quatsch m, Blödsinn m

rub·bish bin Br Mülleimer m

rubbish chute Br Müllschlucker m

rub·ble Schutt *m*; Trümmer *pl*

ru·by Rubin *m*; Rubinrot *n*

ruck·sack *esp Br* Rucksack *m*

rud·der AVIAT, MAR Ruder *n*

rud·dy frisch, gesund

rude unhöflich, grob; unanständig (*joke etc*); bös (*shock etc*)

ru·di·men·ta·ry elementar, Anfangs…; primitiv

ru·di·ments Anfangsgründe *pl*

rue·ful reuevoll, reumütig

ruff Halskrause *f* (*a.* ZO)

ruf·fle 1. kräuseln; *Haar* zerzausen; *Federn* sträuben; **ruffle s.o.'s composure** j-n aus der Fassung bringen; **2.** Rüsche *f*

rug Vorleger *m*, Brücke *f*; *esp Br* dicke Wolldecke

rug·by *a.* **rugby football** SPORT Rugby *n*

rug·ged GEOGR zerklüftet, schroff; TECH robust, stabil; zerfurcht (*face*)

ru·in 1. Ruin *m*; *mst pl* Ruine(n *pl*) *f*, Trümmer *pl*; **2.** ruinieren, zerstören

ru·in·ous ruinös

rule 1. Regel *f*; Spielregel *f*; Vorschrift *f*; Herrschaft *f*; Lineal *n*; **against the rules** regelwidrig; verboten; **as a rule** in der Regel; **as a rule of thumb** als Faustregel; **work to rule** Dienst nach Vorschrift tun; **2.** *v/t* herrschen über (*acc*); *esp* JUR entscheiden; *Papier* lin(i)ieren; *Linie* ziehen; **be ruled by** *fig* sich leiten lassen von; beherrscht werden von; **rule out** *et.* ausschließen; *v/i* herrschen (**over** über *acc*); *esp* JUR entscheiden

rul·er Herrscher(in); Lineal *n*

rum Rum *m*

rum·ble rumpeln (*vehicle*); (g)rollen (*thunder*); knurren (*stomach*)

ru·mi·nant ZO Wiederkäuer *m*

ru·mi·nate ZO wiederkäuen

rum·mage 1. *a.* **rummage about** herumstöbern, herumwühlen (**among**, **in**, **through** in *dat*); **2.** Ramsch *m*

rummage sale Wohltätigkeitsbasar *m*

ru·mo(u)r 1. Gerücht *n*; **rumo(u)r has it that** es geht das Gerücht, dass; **2.** **it is rumo(u)red that** es geht das Gerücht, dass; **he is rumo(u)red to be …** man munkelt, er sei …

rump F Hinterteil *n*

rum·ple zerknittern, zerknüllen, zerwühlen; *Haar* zerzausen

run 1. *v/i* laufen (*a.* SPORT), rennen; fahren, verkehren, gehen (*train*, *bus etc*); laufen, fließen; zerfließen, zerlaufen (*butter*, *paint etc*); TECH laufen (*engine*), in Betrieb *or* Gang sein; verlaufen (*road etc*); *esp* JUR gelten, laufen (**for one year** ein Jahr); THEA *etc* laufen (**for three**

months drei Monate lang); lauten (*text*); gehen (*melody*); POL kandidieren (**for** für); **run dry** austrocknen; **run low** knapp werden; **run short** knapp werden; **run short of gas** (*Br* **petrol**) kein Benzin mehr haben; *v/t Strecke*, *Rennen* laufen; *Zug*, *Bus* fahren *or* verkehren lassen; *Wasser*, *Maschine etc* laufen lassen; *Geschäft*, *Hotel etc* führen, leiten; *Zeitungsartikel etc* abdrucken, bringen; **run so. home** F j-n nach Hause bringen *or* fahren; **be running a temperature** erhöhte Temperatur *or* Fieber haben; → **errand**; **run across** j-n zufällig treffen; stoßen auf (*acc*); **run after** hinterherlaufen, nachlaufen (*dat*); **run along!** F ab mit dir!; **run away** davonlaufen (**from** vor *dat*); **run away with** durchbrennen mit; durchgehen mit (*feelings etc*); **run down** MOT anfahren, umfahren; F schlechtmachen; ausfindig machen; ablaufen (*watch*); leer werden (*battery*); **run in** *Wagen etc* einfahren; F *Verbrecher* schnappen; **run into** laufen *or* fahren gegen; j-n zufällig treffen; *fig* geraten in (*acc*); *fig* sich belaufen auf (*acc*); **run off with** → **run away with**; **run on** weitergehen, sich hinziehen (**until** bis); F unaufhörlich reden (**about** über *acc*, von); **run out** ablaufen (*time etc*); ausgehen, zu Ende gehen (*supplies etc*); **run out of gas** (*Br* **petrol**) kein Benzin mehr haben; **run over** MOT überfahren; überlaufen, überfließen; **run through** überfliegen, durchgehen, durchlesen; **run up** *Flagge* hissen; hohe Rechnung, Schulden machen; **run up against** stoßen auf (*acc*); **2.** Lauf *m* (*a.* SPORT); Fahrt *f*; Spazierfahrt *f*; Ansturm *m*, ECON *a.* Run *m* (**on** auf *acc*); THEA *etc* Laufzeit *f*; Laufmasche *f*; Gehege *n*; Auslauf *m*, (*Hühner*)Hof *m*; SPORT (*Bob-*, *Rodel-*) Bahn *f*; (*Ski*)Hang *m*; **run of good** (**bad**) **luck** Glückssträhne *f* (Pechsträhne *f*); **in the long run** auf die Dauer; **in the short run** zunächst; **on the run** auf der Flucht

run·a·bout F MOT Stadt-, Kleinwagen *m*

run·a·way Ausreißer(in)

rung Sprosse *f*

run·ner SPORT Läufer(in); Rennpferd *n*; *mst in cpds* Schmuggler(in); (*Schlitten-*, *Schlittschuh*)Kufe *f*; Tischläufer *m*; TECH (*Gleit*)Schiene *f*; BOT Ausläufer *m*

runner bean *Br* BOT grüne Bohne

run-up SPORT Zweite *m*, *f*, Vizemeister(in)

run·ning 1. Laufen *n*, Rennen *n*; Führung *f*, Leitung *f*; **2.** fließend; SPORT Lauf…; **two days running** zwei Tage hintereinander

R

running costs ECON Betriebskosten *pl*, laufende Kosten *pl*
run·ny F flüssig; laufend (*nose*), tränend (*eyes*)
run-off POL Stichwahl *f*
run·way AVIAT Start- und Landebahn *f*, Rollbahn *f*, Piste *f*
rup·ture 1. Bruch *m* (*a.* MED *and fig*), Riss *m*; **2.** bersten, platzen; (zer)reißen; ***rupture o.s.*** MED sich e-n Bruch heben *or* zuziehen
ru·ral ländlich
ruse List *f*, Trick *m*
rush[1] **1.** *v/i* hasten, hetzen, stürmen, rasen; ***rush at*** losstürzen *or* sich stürzen auf (*acc*); ***rush in*** hineinstürzen, hineinstürmen, hereinstürzen, hereinstürmen; ***rush into*** *fig* sich stürzen in (*acc*); *et.* überstürzen; *v/t* antreiben, drängen, hetzen; schnell bringen; *Essen* hinunterschlingen; losstürmen auf (*acc*); ***don't rush it*** lass dir Zeit dabei; **2.** Ansturm *m*; Hast *f*, Hetze *f*; Hochbetrieb *m*; ECON stürmische Nachfrage; ***what's all the***

rush? wozu diese Eile *or* Hetze?
rush[2] BOT Binse *f*
rush hour Rushhour *f*, Hauptverkehrszeit *f*, Stoßzeit *f*
rush-hour traf·fic Stoßverkehr *m*
rusk *esp Br* Zwieback *m*
Rus·sia Russland *n*
Rus·sian 1. russisch; **2.** Russe *m*, Russin *f*; LING Russisch *n*
rust 1. Rost *m*; **2.** *v/t* (ein-, ver)rosten lassen; *v/i* (ein-, ver)rosten
rus·tic ländlich, bäuerlich; rustikal
rus·tle 1. rascheln (mit), knistern; *Vieh* stehlen; **2.** Rascheln *n*
rust-proof rostfrei, nicht rostend
rust·y rostig; *fig* eingerostet
rut[1] **1.** (Rad)Spur *f*, Furche *f*; *fig* (alter) Trott; ***the daily rut*** das tägliche Einerlei; **2.** furchen; ***rutted*** ausgefahren
rut[2] ZO Brunft *f*, Brunst *f*
ruth·less unbarmherzig; rücksichtslos, skrupellos
rye BOT Roggen *m*

S

S, s S, s *n*
S ABBR *of* **small** (**size**) klein
sa·ber, *Br* **sa·bre** Säbel *m*
sa·ble ZO Zobel *m*; Zobelpelz *m*
sab·o·tage 1. Sabotage *f*; **2.** sabotieren
sack 1. Sack *m*; ***get the sack*** *Br* F rausgeschmissen werden; ***give s.o. the sack*** *Br* F *j*-n rausschmeißen; ***hit the sack*** F sich in die Falle *or* Klappe hauen; **2.** in Säcke füllen, einsacken; *Br* F *j*-n rausschmeißen
sack·cloth, sack·ing Sackleinen *n*
sac·ra·ment REL Sakrament *n*
sa·cred geistlich (*music etc*); heilig
sac·ri·fice 1. Opfer *n*; **2.** opfern
sac·ri·lege REL Sakrileg *n*; Frevel *m*
sac·ris·ty REL Sakristei *f*
sad traurig; schmerzlich; schlimm
sad·dle 1. Sattel *m*; **2.** satteln
sa·dism Sadismus *m*
sa·dist Sadist(in)
sa·dis·tic sadistisch
sad·ness Traurigkeit *f*
sa·fa·ri Safari *f*
safari park Safaripark *m*

safe 1. sicher; **2.** Safe *m, n*, Tresor *m*, Geldschrank *m*
safe con·duct freies Geleit
safe de·pos·it Tresor *m*
safe-de·pos·it box Schließfach *n*
safe·guard 1. Schutz *m* (*against* gegen, vor *dat*); **2.** schützen (*against, from* gegen, vor *dat*)
safe·keep·ing sichere Verwahrung
safe·ty 1. Sicherheit *f*; **2.** Sicherheits…
safety belt → **seat belt**
safety is·land Verkehrsinsel *f*
safety lock Sicherheitsschloss *n*
safety mea·sure Sicherheitsmaßnahme *f*
safety pin Sicherheitsnadel *f*
safety ra·zor Rasierapparat *m*
sag sich senken, absacken; durchhängen; (herab)hängen (*shoulders*); *fig* sinken (*morale*); nachlassen (*interest etc*)
sa·ga·cious scharfsinnig
sa·ga·ci·ty Scharfsinn *m*
sage BOT Salbei *m, f*
Sa·git·tar·i·us ASTR Schütze *m*; ***he* (*she*) *is* (*a*) *Sagittarius*** er (sie) ist (ein) Schütze
sail 1. Segel *n*; Segelfahrt *f*; (Windmüh-

*len)*Flügel *m*; **set sail** auslaufen (**for** nach); **go for a sail** segeln gehen; **2.** *v/i* MAR segeln, fahren; auslaufen (**for** nach); gleiten, schweben; **go sailing** segeln gehen; *v/t* MAR befahren; *Schiff* steuern, *Boot* segeln

sail·board Surfbrett *n*

sail·boat Segelboot *n*

sail·ing Segeln *n*; Segelsport *m*; **when is the next sailing to …?** wann fährt das nächste Schiff nach …?

sailing boat *Br* Segelboot *n*

sailing ship Segelschiff *n*

sail·or Seemann *m*, Matrose *m*; **be a good (bad) sailor** (nicht) seefest sein

sail·plane Segelflugzeug *n*

saint Heilige *m*, *f*

saint·ly heilig, fromm

sake: for the sake of … um … (*gen*) willen; **for my sake** meinetwegen; **for God's sake** F um Gottes willen

sal·a·ble verkäuflich

sal·ad Salat *m*

salad dress·ing Dressing *n*, Salatsoße *f*

sal·a·ried employee Angestellte *m*, *f*, Gehaltsempfänger(in)

sal·a·ry Gehalt *n*

sale Verkauf *m*; Absatz *m*, Umsatz *m*; (Saison)Schlussverkauf *m*; Auktion *f*, Versteigerung *f*; **for sale** zu verkaufen; **not for sale** unverkäuflich; **be on sale** verkauft werden, erhältlich sein

sale·a·ble → **salable**

sales·clerk (Laden)Verkäufer(in)

sales·girl (Laden)Verkäuferin *f*

sales·man Verkäufer *m*; (Handels-) Vertreter *m*

sales rep·re·sen·ta·tive Handlungsreisende *m*, *f*; (Handels)Vertreter(in)

sales slip ECON Quittung *f*

sales tax ECON Umsatzsteuer *f*

sales·wom·an Verkäuferin *f*; (Handels-) Vertreterin *f*

sa·line salzig, Salz…

sa·li·va Speichel *m*

sal·low gelblich

salm·on zo Lachs *m*

sa·lon (*Schönheits- etc*)Salon *m*

sa·loon *Br* MOT Limousine *f*; HIST Saloon *m*; MAR Salon *m*

sa·loon car *Br* MOT Limousine *f*

salt 1. Salz *n*; **2.** (ein)pökeln, einsalzen (*a.* **salt down**); *Straße etc* (mit Salz) streuen; **3.** Salz…; gepökelt; salzig, gesalzen

salt·cel·lar *Br* Salzstreuer *m*

salt·pe·ter, *esp Br* **salt·pe·tre** CHEM Salpeter *m*

salt shak·er Salzstreuer *m*

salt wa·ter Salzwasser *n*

salt·y salzig

sal·u·ta·tion Gruß *m*, Begrüßung *f*; Anrede *f*

sa·lute 1. MIL salutieren; (be-)grüßen; **2.** Gruß *m*; MIL Ehrenbezeigung *f*; Salut *m*

sal·vage 1. Bergung *f*; Bergungsgut *n*; **2.** bergen (**from** aus); retten (*a. fig*)

sal·va·tion Rettung *f*; REL Erlösung *f*; (Seelen)Heil *n*

Sal·va·tion Ar·my Heilsarmee *f*

salve (Heil)Salbe *f*

same: the same derselbe, dieselbe, dasselbe; **all the same** trotzdem; **it is all the same to me** es ist mir ganz egal

sam·ple 1. Muster *n*, Probe *f*; **2.** kosten, probieren

san·a·to·ri·um Sanatorium *n*

sanc·ti·fy heiligen

sanc·tion 1. Billigung *f*, Zustimmung *f*; *mst pl* Sanktionen *pl*; **2.** billigen, sanktionieren

sanc·ti·ty Heiligkeit *f*

sanc·tu·a·ry Zuflucht *f*, Asyl *n*; zo Schutzgebiet *n*

sand 1. Sand *m*; *pl* Sandfläche *f*; **2.** *Straße etc* mit Sand (be)streuen; TECH schmirgeln

san·dal Sandale *f*

sand·bag Sandsack *m*

sand·bank GEOGR Sandbank *f*

sand·box Sandkasten *m*

sand·cas·tle Sandburg *f*

sand·man Sandmännchen *n*

sand·pa·per Sand-, Schmirgelpapier *n*

sand·pip·er zo Strandläufer *m*

sand·pit *Br* Sandkasten *m*; Sandgrube *f*

sand·stone GEOL Sandstein *m*

sand·storm Sandsturm *m*

sand·wich 1. Sandwich *n*; **2. be sandwiched between** eingekeilt sein zwischen (*dat*); **sandwich s.th. in between** *fig et.* einschieben zwischen (*acc or dat*)

sand·y sandig; rotblond

sane geistig gesund; JUR zurechnungsfähig; vernünftig

san·i·tar·i·um → **sanatorium**

san·i·ta·ry hygienisch; Gesundheits…

sanitary nap·kin, *Br* **sanitary tow·el** (Damen)Binde *f*

san·i·ta·tion sanitäre Einrichtungen *pl*; Kanalisation *f*

san·i·ty geistige Gesundheit *f*; JUR Zurechnungsfähigkeit *f*

San·ta Claus der Weihnachtsmann, der Nikolaus

sap¹ BOT Saft *m*

sap² schwächen

sap·phire Saphir *m*

sar·casm Sarkasmus *m*

sar·cas·tic sarkastisch

sar·dine ZO Sardine *f*

sash[1] Schärpe *f*

sash[2] Fensterrahmen *m*

sash win·dow Schiebefenster *n*

sas·sy frech

Sat ABBR *of* **Saturday** Sa., Samstag *m*, Sonnabend *m*

Sa·tan der Satan

satch·el (Schul)Ranzen *m*; Schultasche *f*

sat·ed *fig* übersättigt

sat·el·lite **1.** Satellit *m*; *by or via satellite* über Satellit; **2.** Satelliten...; *satellite dish* **f** Satellitenschüssel *f*

sat·in Satin *m*

sat·ire Satire *f*

sat·ir·ic, **sat·ir·i·cal** satirisch

sat·i·rist Satiriker(in)

sat·ir·ize verspotten

sat·is·fac·tion Befriedigung *f*; Genugtuung *f*, Zufriedenheit *f*

sat·is·fac·to·ry befriedigend, zufriedenstellend

sat·is·fy befriedigen, zufrieden stellen; überzeugen; *be satisfied that* davon überzeugt sein, dass

sat·u·rate (durch)tränken (*with* mit); CHEM sättigen (*a. fig*)

Sat·ur·day Sonnabend *m*, Samstag *m*; *on Saturday* (am) Sonnabend *or* Samstag; *on Saturdays* sonnabends, samstags

sauce Soße *f*

sauce·pan Kochtopf *m*

sau·cer Untertasse *f*

sauc·y *Br* frech

saun·ter bummeln, schlendern

saus·age Wurst *f*; *a. small sausage* Würstchen *n*

sav·age **1.** wild; unzivilisiert; **2.** Wilde *m*, *f*

sav·age·ry Wildheit *f*; Rohheit *f*, Grausamkeit *f*

save retten (*from or dat*); Geld, Zeit etc (ein)sparen; *et.* aufheben, aufsparen (*for* für); *j-m et.* ersparen; EDP (ab)speichern, sichern; SPORT *Schuss* halten, parieren, *Tor* verhindern; **2.** SPORT Parade *f*

sav·er Retter(in); ECON Sparer(in)

sav·ings ECON Ersparnisse *pl*

savings ac·count Sparkonto *n*

savings bank Sparkasse *f*

savings de·pos·it Spareinlage *f*

sa·vio(u)r Retter(in); *the Savio(u)r* REL der Erlöser, der Heiland

sa·vo(u)r mit Genuss essen *or* trinken; *sa·vo(u)r of fig* e-n Beigeschmack haben von

sa·vo(u)r·y schmackhaft

saw **1.** Säge *f*; **2.** sägen

saw·dust Sägemehl *n*, Sägespäne *pl*

saw·mill Sägewerk *n*

Sax·on **1.** (Angel)Sachse *m*, (Angel-)Sächsin *f*; **2.** (angel)sächsisch

say **1.** sagen; aufsagen; *Gebet* sprechen, *Vaterunser* beten; *say grace* das Tischgebet sprechen; *what does your watch say?* wie spät ist es auf deiner Uhr?; *he is said to be* ... er soll ... sein; *it says* es lautet (*letter etc*); *it says here* hier heißt es; *it goes without saying* es versteht sich von selbst; *no sooner said than done* gesagt, getan; *that is to say* das heißt; (*and*) *that's saying sth.* (und) das will was heißen; *you said it* du sagst es; *you can say that again!* das kannst du laut sagen!; *you don't say (so)!* was du nicht sagst!; *I say* sag(en Sie) mal!; ich muss schon sagen!; *I can't say* das kann ich nicht sagen; **2.** Mitspracherecht *n* (*in* bei); *have one's say* s-e Meinung äußern, zu Wort kommen; *he always has to have his say* er muss immer mitreden

say·ing Sprichwort *n*, Redensart *f*; *as the saying goes* wie man so (schön) sagt

scab MED, BOT Schorf *m*; *contp* Streikbrecher(in)

scaf·fold (Bau)Gerüst *n*; Schafott *n*

scaf·fold·ing (Bau)Gerüst *n*

scald **1.** sich *die Zunge etc* verbrühen; *Milch* abkochen; *scalding hot* kochend heiß; **2.** MED Verbrühung *f*

scale[1] **1.** Skala *f* (*a. fig*), Grad- *or* Maßeinteilung *f*; MATH, TECH Maßstab *m* (*a. fig*); Waage *f*; MUS Skala *f*, Tonleiter *f*; *fig* Ausmaß *n*, Umfang *m*; **2.** erklettern; *scale down fig* verringern; *scale up fig* erhöhen

scale[2] Waagschale *f*; (*a pair of*) *scales* (e-e) Waage

scale[3] **1.** ZO Schuppe *f*; TECH Kesselstein *m*; *the scales fell from my eyes* es fiel mir wie Schuppen von den Augen; **2.** *Fisch* (ab)schuppen

scal·lop ZO Kammmuschel *f*

scalp **1.** Kopfhaut *f*; Skalp *m*; **2.** skalpieren

scal·y ZO schuppig (*a. fig*)

scamp F Schlingel *m*, (kleiner) Strolch

scam·per trippeln; huschen

scan **1.** *et.* absuchen (*for* nach); *Zeitung etc* überfliegen; EDP, *radar*, TV abtasten, scannen; **2.** MED etc Scanning *n*

scan·dal Skandal *m*; Klatsch *m*

scan·dal·ize *be scandalized at sth.* über et. empört *or* entrüstet sein

scan·dal·ous skandalös; *be scandalous*

a. ein Skandal sein (*that* dass)

Scan·di·na·vi·a Skandinavien *n*

Scan·di·na·vi·an 1. skandinavisch; **2.** Skandinavier(in)

scan·ner TECH Scanner *m*

scant dürftig, gering

scant·y dürftig, kärglich, knapp

scape·goat Sündenbock *m*

scar MED **1.** Narbe *f* (*a. fig*); **2.** e-e Narbe *or* Narben hinterlassen auf (*dat*) *or fig* bei *j-m*; ***scar over*** vernarben

scarce knapp (*food etc*); selten; ***be scarce*** Mangelware sein (*a. fig*)

scarce·ly kaum

scar·ci·ty Mangel *m*, Knappheit *f* (*of* an *dat*)

scare 1. erschrecken; ***be scared*** Angst haben (*of* vor *dat*); ***scare away, scare off*** verjagen, -scheuchen; **2.** Schreck(en) *m*; Panik *f*

scare·crow Vogelscheuche *f* (*a. fig*)

scarf Schal *m*; Hals-, Kopf-, Schultertuch *n*

scar·let scharlachrot

scarlet fe·ver MED Scharlach *m*

scarred narbig

scath·ing bissig (*remark etc*); vernichtend (*criticism etc*)

scat·ter (sich) zerstreuen (*crowd*); ausstreuen, verstreuen; auseinanderstieben (*birds etc*)

scat·ter·brained F schusselig, schusslig

scat·tered verstreut; vereinzelt

scav·enge ***scavenge on*** ZO leben von; ***scavenge for*** suchen (nach)

scene Szene *f*; Schauplatz *m*; *pl* THEA Kulissen *pl*

sce·ne·ry Landschaft *f*, Gegend *f*; THEA Bühnenbild *n*, Kulissen *pl*

scent 1. Duft *m*, Geruch *m*; *esp Br* Parfüm *n*; HUNT Witterung *f*; Fährte *f*, Spur *f* (*a. fig*); **2.** wittern; *esp Br* parfümieren

scent·less geruchlos

scep·ter, *Br* **scep·tre** Zepter *n*

scep·tic, **scep·ti·cal** *Br* → **skeptic** *etc*

sched·ule 1. Aufstellung *f*, Verzeichnis *n*; (*Arbeits-, Stunden-, Zeit- etc*)Plan *m*; Fahr-, Flugplan *m*; ***ahead of schedule*** dem Zeitplan voraus, früher als vorgesehen; ***be behind schedule*** Verspätung haben; im Verzug *or* Rückstand sein; ***on schedule*** (fahr-) planmäßig, pünktlich; **2.** ***the meeting is scheduled for Monday*** die Sitzung ist für Montag angesetzt; ***it is scheduled to take place tomorrow*** es soll morgen stattfinden

sched·uled de·par·ture (fahr)planmäßige Abfahrt

scheduled flight Linienflug *m*

scheme 1. *esp Br* Programm *n*, Projekt *n*; Schema *n*, System *n*; Intrige *f*, Machenschaft *f*; **2.** intrigieren

schmaltz·y F schnulzig

schnit·zel GASTR Wiener Schnitzel *n*

schol·ar Gelehrte *m*, *f*; UNIV Stipendiat(in)

schol·ar·ly gelehrt

schol·ar·ship Gelehrsamkeit *f*; UNIV Stipendium *n*

school¹ 1. Schule *f* (*a. fig*); UNIV Fakultät *f*; Hochschule *f*; ***at school*** auf *or* in der Schule; ***go to school*** in die *or* zur Schule gehen; **2.** *j-n* schulen, unterrichten; *Tier* dressieren

school² ZO Schule *f*, Schwarm *m*

school·bag Schultasche *f*

school·boy Schüler *m*

school·child Schulkind *n*

school·fel·low → **schoolmate**

school·girl Schülerin *f*

school·ing (Schul)Ausbildung *f*

school·mate Mitschüler(in), Schulkamerad(in)

school·teach·er (Schul)Lehrer(in)

school·yard Schulhof *m*

schoo·ner MAR Schoner *m*

sci·ence Wissenschaft *f*; *a.* ***natural science*** Naturwissenschaft(en) *pl* (*f*)

science fic·tion (*ABBR* **SF**) Sciencefiction *f*

sci·en·tif·ic (natur)wissenschaftlich; exakt, systematisch

sci·en·tist (Natur)Wissenschaftler(in)

sci-fi F Sciencefiction *f*

scis·sors (***a pair of scissors*** e-e) Schere *f*

scoff 1. spotten (*at* über *acc*); **2.** spöttische Bemerkung

scold schimpfen (mit)

scoop 1. Schöpfkelle *f*; (*Mehl- etc -*) Schaufel *f*; (*Eis- etc*)Portionierer *m*; Kugel *f* (*icecream*); *newspaper, radio*, TV Exklusivmeldung *f*, F Knüller *m*; **2.** schöpfen, schaufeln; ***scoop up*** aufheben, hochheben

scoot·er (Kinder)Roller *m*; (*Motor-*) Roller *m*

scope Bereich *m*; Spielraum *m*

scorch *v/t* ansengen, versengen, verbrennen; ausdörren; *v/i Br* MOT F rasen

score 1. SPORT (Spiel)Stand *m*, (-)Ergebnis *n*; MUS Partitur *f*; Musik *f*; 20 (Stück); *a.* ***score mark*** Kerbe *f*, Rille *f*; ***what is the score?*** wie steht es *or* das Spiel?; ***the score stood at*** *or* ***was 3-2*** das Spiel stand 3:2; ***keep (the) score*** anschreiben; ***scores of*** e-e Menge; ***four score and ten*** neunzig; ***on that score*** deshalb, in dieser Hinsicht; ***have a score to settle***

S

with s.o. e-e alte Rechnung mit j-m zu begleichen haben; **2.** v/t SPORT Punkte, Treffer erzielen, Tor a. schießen; Erfolg, Sieg erringen; MUS instrumentieren; die Musik schreiben zu or für; einkerben; v/i SPORT e-n Treffer etc erzielen, ein Tor schießen; erfolgreich sein

score·board SPORT Anzeigetafel f

scor·er SPORT Torschütze m, Torschützin f; Anschreiber(in)

scorn Verachtung f

scorn·ful verächtlich

Scor·pi·o ASTR Skorpion m; **he (she) is (a) Scorpio** er (sie) ist (ein) Skorpion

Scot Schotte m, Schottin f

Scotch 1. schottisch; **2.** Scotch m

scot-free: F **get off scot-free** ungeschoren davonkommen

Scot·land Schottland n

Scots schottisch

Scots·man Schotte m

Scots·wom·an Schottin f

Scot·tish schottisch

scoun·drel Schurke m

scour[1] scheuern, schrubben

scour[2] Gegend absuchen, durchkämmen (**for** nach)

scourge 1. Geißel f (a. fig); **2.** geißeln, fig a. heimsuchen

scout 1. esp MIL Kundschafter m; Br motorisierter Pannenhelfer; a. **boy scout** Pfadfinder m; a. **girl scout** Pfadfinderin f; a. **talent scout** Talentsucher(in); **2. scout about, scout around** sich umsehen (**for** nach); a. **scout out** MIL auskundschaften

scowl 1. finsteres Gesicht; **2.** finster blicken; **scowl at s.o.** j-n böse or finster anschauen

scram·ble 1. klettern; sich drängeln (**for** zu); **2.** Kletterei f; Drängelei f

scram·bled eggs Rührei(er pl) n

scrap[1] Stückchen n, Fetzen m; Altmaterial n; Schrott m; pl Abfall m, Speisereste pl; **2.** verschrotten; ausrangieren; Plan etc aufgeben, fallen lassen

scrap[2] F **1.** Streiterei f; Balgerei f; **2.** sich streiten; sich balgen

scrap·book Sammelalbum n

scrape 1. (ab)kratzen, (ab)schaben; sich die Knie etc aufschürfen; Wagen etc ankratzen; scheuern (**against** an dat); (entlang)streifen; scharren; **2.** Kratzen n; Kratzer m, Schramme f; fig Klemme f

scrap heap Schrotthaufen m

scrap met·al Altmetall n, Schrott m

scrap pa·per esp Br Schmierpapier n

scrap val·ue Schrottwert m

scrap·yard Schrottplatz m

scratch 1. (zer)kratzen; abkratzen; s-n Namen etc einkratzen; (sich) kratzen; scharren; **2.** Kratzer m, Schramme f; Gekratze n; Kratzen n; **from scratch** F ganz von vorn; **3.** (bunt) zusammengewürfelt

scratch·pad Notiz-, Schmierblock m

scratch pa·per Schmierpapier n

scrawl 1. kritzeln; **2.** Gekritzel n

scraw·ny dürr

scream 1. schreien (**with** vor dat); a. **scream out** schreien; **scream with laughter** vor Lachen brüllen; **2.** Schrei m; **screams of laughter** brüllendes Gelächter; **be a scream** F zum Schreien (komisch) sein

screech 1. kreischen (a. fig), (gellend) schreien; **2.** Kreischen n; (gellender) Schrei

screen 1. Wand-, Ofen-, Schutzschirm m; film: Leinwand f; radar, TV, EDP Bildschirm m; Fliegenfenster n, -gitter n; fig Tarnung f; **2.** abschirmen; film zeigen, Fernsehprogramm a. senden; film j-n decken; fig j-n überprüfen; **screen off** abtrennen

screen·play Drehbuch n

screen sav·er EDP Bildschirmschoner m

screw 1. TECH Schraube f; **he has a screw loose** F bei ihm ist e-e Schraube locker; **2.** (an)schrauben (**to** an acc); V bumsen, vögeln; **screw up** Gesicht verziehen; Augen zusammenkneifen; **screw up one's courage** sich ein Herz fassen

screw·ball F Spinner(in)

screw·driv·er Schraubenzieher m

screw top Schraubverschluss m

scrib·ble 1. (hin)kritzeln; **2.** Gekritzel n

scrimp: scrimp and save jeden Pfennig zweimal umdrehen

script Manuskript n; film, TV Drehbuch n; Skript n; THEA Text m, Textbuch n; Schrift(zeichen pl) f; Br UNIV (schriftliche) Prüfungsarbeit

Scrip·ture a. **the Scriptures** REL die Heilige Schrift

scroll 1. Schriftrolle f; **2. scroll down (up)** EDP zurückrollen (vorrollen)

scro·tum ANAT Hodensack m

scrub[1] **1.** schrubben, scheuern; **2.** Schrubben n, Scheuern n

scrub[2] Gebüsch n, Gestrüpp n

scru·ple Skrupel m, Zweifel m, Bedenken pl; **2.** Bedenken haben

scru·pu·lous gewissenhaft

scru·ti·nize genau prüfen; mustern

scru·ti·ny genaue Prüfung; prüfender Blick

scu·ba div·ing (Sport)Tauchen n

scuf·fle 1. Handgemenge n, Rauferei f; **2.**

sich raufen

scull 1. Skull *n*; Skullboot *n*; **2.** rudern, skullen

sculp·tor Bildhauer *m*

sculp·ture 1. Bildhauerei *f*; Skulptur *f*, Plastik *f*; **2.** hauen, meißeln, formen

scum Schaum *m*; *fig* Abschaum *m*; *the scum of the earth fig* der Abschaum der Menschheit

scurf (Kopf)Schuppen *pl*

scur·ri·lous beleidigend; verleumderisch

scur·ry huschen; trippeln

scur·vy MED Skorbut *m*

scut·tle: *scuttle away, scuttle off* davonhuschen

scythe Sense *f*

sea Meer *n* (*a.* fig), See *f*; *at sea* auf See; *be all or completely at sea* fig F völlig ratlos sein; *by sea* auf dem Seeweg; *by the sea* am Meer

sea·food GASTR Meeresfrüchte *pl*

sea·gull ZO Seemöwe *f*

seal¹ ZO Robbe *f*, Seehund *m*

seal² 1. Siegel *n*; TECH Plombe *f*; TECH Dichtung *f*; **2.** (ver)siegeln; TECH plombieren; abdichten; *fig* besiegeln; ***sealed envelope*** verschlossener Briefumschlag; ***seal off*** Gegend *etc* abriegeln

sea lev·el: *above (below) sea level* über (unter) dem Meeresspiegel

seal·ing wax Siegellack *m*

seam Naht *f*; Fuge *f*; GEOL Flöz *n*

sea·man Seemann *m*

seam·stress Näherin *f*

sea·plane Wasserflugzeug *n*

sea·port Seehafen *m*; Hafenstadt *f*

sea pow·er Seemacht *f*

search 1. *v/i* suchen (*for* nach); ***search through*** durchsuchen; *v/t* *j-n*, *et.* durchsuchen (*for* nach); ***search me!*** F keine Ahnung!; **2.** Suche *f* (*for* nach); Fahndung *f* (*for* nach); Durchsuchung *f*; *in search of* auf der Suche nach

search·ing prüfend (*look*); eingehend (*examination*)

search·light (Such)Scheinwerfer *m*

search par·ty Suchmannschaft *f*

search war·rant JUR Haussuchungs-, Durchsuchungsbefehl *m*

sea·shore Meeresküste *f*

sea·sick seekrank

sea·side: *at or by the seaside* am Meer; *go to the seaside* ans Meer fahren

sea·side re·sort Seebad *n*

sea·son¹ Jahreszeit *f*; Saison *f*, THEA *etc a.* Spielzeit *f*, (*Jagd-, Urlaubs- etc*)Zeit *f*; *in (out of) season* in (außerhalb) der (Hoch)Saison; *cherries are now in season* jetzt ist Kirschenzeit; ***Season's***

Greetings! Frohe Weihnachten!; *with the compliments of the season* mit den besten Wünschen zum Fest

sea·son² *Speise* würzen (*with* mit); *Holz* ablagern

sea·son·al saisonbedingt, Saison...

sea·son·ing GASTR Gewürz *n*

sea·son tick·et RAIL *etc* Dauer-, Zeitkarte *f*; THEA Abonnement *n*

seat 1. Sitz(gelegenheit *f*) *m*; (Sitz)Platz *m*; Sitz(fläche *f*) *m*; Hosenboden *m*; Hinterteil *n*; (*Geschäfts-, Regierungs- etc*)Sitz *m*; PARL Sitz *m*; *take a seat* Platz nehmen; *take one's seat* s-n Platz einnehmen; **2.** *j-n* setzen; Sitzplätze bieten für; *be seated* sitzen; *please be seated* bitte nehmen Sie Platz; *remain seated* sitzen bleiben

seat belt AVIAT, MOT Sicherheitsgurt *m*; *fasten one's seat belt* sich anschnallen

sea ur·chin ZO Seeigel *m*

sea·ward(s) seewärts

sea·weed BOT (See)Tang *m*

sea·wor·thy seetüchtig

sec F Augenblick *m*, Sekunde *f*; *just a sec* Augenblick(, bitte)!

se·cede sich abspalten (*from* von)

se·ces·sion Abspaltung *f*, Sezession *f* (*from* von)

se·clud·ed abgelegen, abgeschieden (*place*); zurückgezogen (*life*)

se·clu·sion Abgeschiedenheit *f*; Zurückgezogenheit *f*

sec·ond¹ 1. *adj* zweite(r, -s); *every second day* jeden zweiten Tag, alle zwei Tage; *second to none* unerreicht, unübertroffen; *but on second thought* (*Br thoughts*) aber wenn ich es mir so überlege; **2.** *adv* als Zweite(r, -s); **3.** *der, die, das* Zweite; MOT zweiter Gang; Sekundant *m*; *pl* F ECON Waren *pl* zweiter Wahl; **4.** *Antrag etc* unterstützen

sec·ond² Sekunde *f*; *fig* Augenblick *m*, Sekunde *f*; *just a second* Augenblick(, bitte)!

sec·ond·a·ry sekundär, zweitrangig; PED höher

sec·ond-best zweitbeste(r, -s)

sec·ond class RAIL *etc* zweiter Klasse

sec·ond-class zweitklassig

sec·ond floor erster (*Br* zweiter) Stock

sec·ond hand Sekundenzeiger *m*

sec·ond-hand aus zweiter Hand; gebraucht; antiquarisch

sec·ond·ly zweitens

sec·ond-rate zweitklassig

se·cre·cy Verschwiegenheit *f*; Geheimhaltung *f*

se·cret 1. geheim, Geheim...; heimlich;

verschwiegen; **2.** Geheimnis *n*; *in secret* heimlich, im Geheimen; *keep s.th. a se-cret* et. geheim halten (*from* vor *dat*); *can you keep a secret?* kannst du schweigen?

se·cret a·gent Geheimagent(in)

sec·re·ta·ry Sekretär(in); POL Minister(in)

Sec·re·ta·ry of State POL Außenminister(in); *Br* Minister(in)

se·crete MED absondern

se·cre·tion MED Sekret *n*; Absonderung *f*

se·cre·tive verschlossen

se·cret·ly heimlich

se·cret ser·vice Geheimdienst *m*

sec·tion Teil *m*; Abschnitt *m*; JUR Paragraf *m*; Abteilung *f*; MATH, TECH Schnitt *m*

sec·tor Sektor *m*, Bereich *m*

sec·u·lar weltlich

se·cure 1. sicher (*against, from* vor *dat*); **2.** *Tür etc* fest verschließen; *et.* sichern (*against, from* vor *dat*)

se·cu·ri·ty Sicherheit *f*; *pl* ECON Wertpapiere *pl*

security check Sicherheitskontrolle *f*

security mea·sure Sicherheitsmaßnahme *f*

security risk Sicherheitsrisiko *n*

se·dan MOT Limousine *f*

se·date ruhig, gelassen

sed·a·tive MED **1.** beruhigend; **2.** Beruhigungsmittel *n*

sed·i·ment (Boden)Satz *m*

se·duce verführen

se·duc·er Verführer(in)

se·duc·tion Verführung *f*

se·duc·tive verführerisch

see[1] *v/i* sehen; nachsehen; *I see!* (ich) verstehe!, ach so!; *you see* weißt du; *let me see* warte mal, lass mich überlegen; *we'll see* mal sehen; *v/t* sehen; besuchen; *j-n* aufsuchen, *j-n* konsultieren; *see s.o. home* *j-n* nach Hause bringen *or* begleiten; *see you!* bis dann!, auf bald!; *see about* sehen nach, sich kümmern um; *see off* *j-n* verabschieden (*at* am Bahnhof *etc*); *see out* *j-n* hinausbringen, hinausbegleiten; *see through* *j-n*, *et.* durchschauen; *j-m* hinweghelfen über (*acc*); *see to it* dafür sorgen, dass

see[2] REL Bistum *n*, Diözese *f*; *Holy See* der Heilige Stuhl

seed 1. BOT Same(n) *m*; AGR Saat *f*, Saatgut *n*; (*Apfel- etc*)Kern *m*; SPORT gesetzter Spieler, gesetzte Spielerin; *go or run to seed* BOT schießen; *go to seed* F herunterkommen, verkommen; **2.** *v/t* besäen; entkernen; SPORT *Spieler* setzen; *v/i* BOT in Samen schießen

seedless BOT kernlos

seed·y F heruntergekommen

seek *Schutz, Wahrheit etc* suchen

seem scheinen

seem·ing scheinbar

seep sickern

see·saw Wippe *f*, Wippschaukel *f*

seethe schäumen (*a. fig*); *fig* kochen

see-through durchsichtig

seg·ment Teil *m*, *n*; Stück *n*; Abschnitt *m*; Segment *n*

seg·re·gate trennen

seg·re·ga·tion Rassentrennung *f*

seize *j-n*, *et.* packen, ergreifen; *Macht etc* an sich reißen; *et.* beschlagnahmen; *et.* pfänden

sei·zure Beschlagnahme *f*; Pfändung *f*; MED Anfall *m*

sel·dom *adv* selten

se·lect 1. (aus)wählen; **2.** ausgewählt; exklusiv

se·lec·tion (Aus)Wahl *f*; ECON Auswahl *f* (*of* an *dat*)

self Ich *n*, Selbst *n*

self-as·sured selbstbewusst, -sicher

self-cen·tered, *Br* **self-cen·tred** egozentrisch

self-col·o(u)red einfarbig

self-con·fi·dence Selbstbewusstsein *n*, Selbstvertrauen *n*

self-con·fi·dent selbstbewusst

self-con·scious befangen, gehemmt, unsicher

self-con·tained (in sich) abgeschlossen; *fig* verschlossen; *self-contained flat Br* abgeschlossene Wohnung

self-con·trol Selbstbeherrschung *f*

self-crit·i·cal selbstkritisch

self-de·fence *Br*, **self-de·fense** Selbstverteidigung *f*; *in self-defence* in *or* aus Notwehr

self-de·ter·mi·na·tion POL Selbstbestimmung *f*

self-em·ployed selbstständig

self-es·teem Selbstachtung *f*

self-ev·i·dent selbstverständlich; offensichtlich

self-gov·ern·ment POL Selbstverwaltung *f*

self-help Selbsthilfe *f*

self-help group Selbsthilfegruppe *f*

self-im·por·tant überheblich

self-in·dul·gent nachgiebig gegen sich selbst; zügellos

self-in·ter·est Eigennutz *m*

self·ish selbstsüchtig, egoistisch

self-knowl·edge Selbsterkenntnis *f*

self-pit·y Selbstmitleid *n*

self-por·trait Selbstporträt *n*

self-pos·sessed selbstbeherrscht

self-re·li·ant selbstständig

self-re·spect Selbstachtung *f*

self-right·eous selbstgerecht

self-sat·is·fied selbstzufrieden

self-serv·ice 1. mit Selbstbedienung, Selbstbedienungs…; **2.** Selbstbedienung *f*

self-stud·y Selbststudium *n*

self-suf·fi·cient ECON autark

self-sup·port·ing finanziell unabhängig

self-willed eigensinnig, eigenwillig

sell *v/t* verkaufen; *v/i* verkauft werden (**at, for** für); sich *gut etc* verkaufen (lassen), gehen; **sell by …** mindestens haltbar bis …; **sell off** (*esp* billig) abstoßen; **sell out** ausverkaufen; **be sold out** ausverkauft sein; **sell up** *esp Br* sein Geschäft *etc* verkaufen

sell-by date Mindesthaltbarkeitsdatum *n*

sell·er Verkäufer(in); **good seller** ECON gut gehender Artikel

sem·blance Anschein *m* (**of** von)

se·men MED Samen(flüssigkeit *f*) *m*, Sperma *n*

se·mes·ter UNIV Semester *n*

sem·i… halb…, Halb…

sem·i·cir·cle Halbkreis *m*

sem·i·co·lon LING Semikolon *n*, Strichpunkt *m*

sem·i·con·duc·tor ELECTR Halbleiter *m*

sem·i·de·tached (house) *Br* Doppelhaushälfte *f*

sem·i·fi·nals SPORT Semi-, Halbfinale *n*

sem·i·nar·y Priesterseminar *n*

sem·i·pre·cious: semi-precious stone Halbedelstein *m*

sem·i·skilled angelernt

sem·o·li·na Grieß *m*

sen·ate POL Senat *m*

sen·a·tor POL Senator *m*

send *et.*, *a.* Grüße, Hilfe *etc* senden, schicken (**to** *dat or an acc*); *Ware etc* versenden, verschicken (**to** *acc*); *j-n* schicken (**to** ins *Bett etc*); *with adj or pp:* machen; **send s.o. mad** j-n wahnsinnig machen; **send word to s.o.** j-m Nachricht geben; **send away** fort-, wegschicken; *Brief etc* absenden, abschicken; **send down** Preise *etc* fallen lassen; **send for** nach *j-m* schicken, *j-n* kommen lassen; sich *et.* kommen lassen, *et.* anfordern; **send in** einsenden, einschicken, einreichen; **send off** fort-, wegschicken; *Brief etc* absenden, abschicken; SPORT *j-n* vom Platz stellen; **send on** *Brief etc* nachsenden, nachschicken (**to** an *acc*); *Gepäck etc* vorausschicken; **send out** hinausschicken; *Einladungen etc* verschicken; **send up** Preise *etc* steigen lassen

send·er Absender(in)

se·nile senil

se·nil·i·ty Senilität *f*

se·ni·or 1. senior; älter (**to** als); dienstälter; rangälter; Ober…; **2.** Ältere *m*, *f*; UNIV Student(in) im letzten Jahr; **he is my senior by a year** er ist ein Jahr älter als ich

senior cit·i·zens ältere Mitbürger *pl*, Senioren *pl*

se·ni·or·i·ty (höheres) Alter; (höheres) Dienstalter; (höherer) Rang

se·ni·or part·ner ECON Seniorpartner *m*

sen·sa·tion Empfindung *f*; Gefühl *n*; Sensation *f*

sen·sa·tion·al F großartig, fantastisch; sensationell, Sensations…

sense 1. Sinn *m*; Verstand *m*; Vernunft *f*; Gefühl *n*; Bedeutung *f*; **bring s.o. to his senses** j-n zur Besinnung or Vernunft bringen; **come to one's senses** zur Besinnung or Vernunft kommen; **in a sense** in gewisser Hinsicht; **make sense** e-n Sinn ergeben; vernünftig sein; **sense of duty** Pflichtgefühl *n*; **sense of security** Gefühl *n* der Sicherheit; **2.** fühlen, spüren

sense·less bewusstlos; sinnlos

sen·si·bil·i·ty Empfindlichkeit *f*; *a. pl* Empfindsamkeit *f*, Zartgefühl *n*

sen·si·ble vernünftig; spürbar, merklich; *esp Br* praktisch (*clothes etc*)

sen·si·tive empfindlich; sensibel, empfindsam, feinfühlig

sen·sor TECH Sensor *m*

sen·su·al sinnlich

sen·su·ous sinnlich

sen·tence 1. LING Satz *m*; JUR Strafe *f*, Urteil *n*; **pass or pronounce sentence** das Urteil fällen (**on** über *acc*); **2.** JUR verurteilen (**to** zu)

sen·ti·ment Gefühle *pl*; Sentimentalität *f*; *a. pl* Ansicht *f*, Meinung *f*

sen·ti·men·tal sentimental; gefühlvoll

sen·ti·men·tal·i·ty Sentimentalität *f*

sen·try MIL Wache *f*, (Wach[t])Posten *m*

sep·a·ra·ble trennbar

sep·a·rate 1. (sich) trennen (auf-, ein-, zer)teilen (**into** *acc*); **2.** getrennt, separat; einzeln

sep·a·ra·tion Trennung *f*; (Auf-, Ein-, Zer)Teilung *f*

Sept ABBR *of* **September** Sept., September *m*

Sep·tem·ber September *m*

sep·tic MED vereitert, septisch

se·quel Nachfolgeroman *m*, -film *m*, Fortsetzung *f*; *fig* Folge *f*; Nachspiel *n*

se·quence (Aufeinander-, Reihen)Folge

S

f; *film*, TV Sequenz *f*, Szene *f*; **sequence of tenses** LING Zeitenfolge *f*

se·re·nade MUS 1. Serenade *f*, Ständchen *n*; 2. *j-m* ein Ständchen bringen

se·rene klar; heiter; gelassen

ser·geant MIL Feldwebel *m*; (Polizei-)Wachtmeister *m*

se·ri·al 1. Fortsetzungsroman *m*; (*Rundfunk-, Fernseh*)Serie *f*; 2. serienmäßig, Serien..., Fortsetzungs...

se·ries Serie *f*, Reihe *f*, Folge *f*; (*Buch*)Reihe *f*; (*Rundfunk-, Fernseh*)Serie *f*, Sendereihe *f*

se·ri·ous ernst, ernsthaft; ernstlich; schwer (*illness, damage, crime etc*); **be serious** es ernst meinen (*about* mit)

se·ri·ous·ness Ernst *m*, Ernsthaftigkeit *f*; Schwere *f*

ser·mon REL Predigt *f*; F Moral-, Strafpredigt *f*

ser·pen·tine gewunden, kurvenreich

ser·rat·ed zackig, gezackt

se·rum MED Serum *n*

ser·vant Diener(in) (*a. fig*); Dienstmädchen *n*; → **civil servant**

serve 1. *v/t j-m, s-m Land etc* dienen; *Dienstzeit* (*a.* MIL) ableisten; *Amtszeit etc* durchlaufen; *j-n, et.* versorgen (*with* mit); *Essen* servieren; *Alkohol* ausschenken; *j-n* (*im Laden*) bedienen; JUR *Strafe* verbüßen; *e-m Zweck* dienen; *e-n Zweck* erfüllen; *jur Vorladung etc* zustellen (*on s.o.* j-m); *tennis etc*: aufschlagen; **are you being served?** werden Sie schon bedient?; (*it*) **serves him right** F (das) geschieht ihm ganz recht; *v/i esp* MIL dienen; servieren; dienen (*as, for* als); *tennis etc*: aufschlagen; **XY to serve** *tennis etc*: Aufschlag XY; **serve on a committee** e-m Ausschuss angehören; **2.** *tennis etc*: Aufschlag *m*

serv·er *tennis etc*: Aufschläger(in); GASTR Servierlöffel *m*

ser·vice 1. Dienst *m* (**to** an *dat*); Dienstleistung *f* (*Post-, Staats-, Telefon- etc*) Dienst *m*; (*Zug- etc*)Verkehr *m*; ECON Service *m*, Kundendienst *m*; Bedienung *f*; Betrieb *m*; REL Gottesdienst *m*; TECH Wartung *f*, MOT *a.* Inspektion *f*; (*Tee- etc*) Service *n*; JUR Zustellung *f* (*e-r Vorladung*); *tennis etc*: Aufschlag *m*; *pl* MIL Streitkräfte *pl*; **2.** TECH warten

ser·vice·a·ble brauchbar; strapazierfähig

ser·vice ar·e·a MOT (Autobahn)Raststätte *f*

service charge Bedienung *f*, Bedienungszuschlag *m*

service sta·tion Tankstelle *f*; (Reparatur)Werkstatt *f*

ser·vi·ette *esp Br* Serviette *f*

ser·vile sklavisch (*a. fig*); servil, unterwürfig

serv·ing Portion *f*

ser·vi·tude Knechtschaft *f*; Sklaverei *f*

ses·sion Sitzung *f*; Sitzungsperiode *f*; **be in session** JUR, PARL tagen

set 1. *v/t* setzen, stellen, legen; *in e-n Zustand* versetzen; veranlassen (**doing** zu tun); TECH einstellen, *Uhr* stellen (**by** nach), *Wecker* stellen (**for** auf *acc*); *Tisch* decken; *Preis, Termin etc* festsetzen, festlegen; *Rekord* aufstellen; *Edelstein* fassen (**in** in *dat*); *Ring etc* besetzen (**with** mit); *Flüssigkeit* erstarren lassen; *Haar* legen; *Knochen* einrenken, einrichten; MUS vertonen; PRINT absetzen; *Aufgabe, Frage* stellen; **set at ease** beruhigen; **set an example** ein Beispiel geben; **set s.o. free** j-n freilassen; **set going** in Gang setzen; **set s.o. thinking** j-m zu denken geben; **set one's hopes on** s-e Hoffnung setzen auf (*acc*); **set s.o.'s mind at rest** j-n beruhigen; **set great (little) store by** großen (geringen) Wert legen auf (*acc*); **the novel is set in** der Roman spielt in (*dat*); *v/i* ASTR untergehen; fest werden, erstarren; HUNT vorstehen; **set about doing s.th.** sich daranmachen, et. zu tun; **set about s.o.** F über j-n herfallen; **set aside** beiseitelegen; JUR *Urteil etc* aufheben; **set back** verzögern; *j-n, et.* zurückwerfen (**by two months** um zwei Monate); **set in** einsetzen; **set off** aufbrechen; sich aufmachen; hervorheben, betonen; *et.* auslösen; **set out** arrangieren, herrichten; aufbrechen, sich aufmachen; **set out to do s.th.** sich daranmachen, et. zu tun; **set up** errichten; *Gerät etc* aufbauen; *Firma etc* gründen; *et.* auslösen, verursachen; *j-n* versorgen (**with** mit); sich niederlassen; **set o.s. up as** sich ausgeben für; **2.** *adj* festgesetzt, festgelegt; F bereit, fertig; starr (*smile etc*); **set lunch** *or* **meal** *Br* Menü *n*; **set phrase** feststehender Ausdruck; **be set on doing s.th.** (fest) entschlossen sein, et. zu tun; **be all set** F startklar sein; **3.** Satz *m*; (*Möbel- etc*)Garnitur *f*, (*Tee-etc*)Service *n*; (*Fernseh-, Rundfunk-*)Apparat *m*, (-)Gerät *n*; THEA Bühnenbild *n*; *film*, TV Set *n*, *m*; *tennis etc*: Satz *m*; (*Personen*)Kreis *m*, Clique *f*; (*Kopf- etc*)Haltung *f*; **have a shampoo and set** sich die Haare waschen und legen lassen

set·back Rückschlag *m* (**to** für)

set·square *Br* Winkel *m*, Zeichendreieck *n*

set·tee Sofa *n*

set the·o·ry MATH Mengenlehre f

set·ting ASTR Untergang m; TECH Einstellung f; Umgebung f; film etc: Schauplatz m; (Gold- etc)Fassung f

set·ting lo·tion Haarfestiger m

set·tle v/i sich niederlassen (**on** auf acc or dat), sich setzen (**on** auf acc) (a. **settle down**); sich niederlassen (**in** in dat); sich legen (dust); sich setzen (coffee etc); sich senken (building etc); sich beruhigen (person, stomach etc), sich legen (a. **settle down**); sich einigen; v/t j-n, Nerven etc beruhigen; vereinbaren; Frage etc klären, entscheiden; Streit etc beilegen; Land besiedeln; Leute ansiedeln; Rechnung begleichen, bezahlen; Konto ausgleichen; Schaden regulieren; s-e Angelegenheiten in Ordnung bringen; **settle o.s.** sich niederlassen (**on** auf acc or dat); sich setzen (**on** auf acc); **that settles it** damit ist der Fall erledigt; **that's settled then** das ist also klar; **settle back** sich (gemütlich) zurücklehnen; **settle down** → v/i: sesshaft werden; **settle down to** sich widmen (dat); **settle for** sich zufriedengeben or begnügen mit; **settle in** sich einleben or eingewöhnen; **settle on** sich einigen auf (acc); **settle up** (be)zahlen; abrechnen (**with** mit)

set·tled fest (ideas etc); geregelt (life); beständig (weather)

set·tle·ment Vereinbarung f; Klärung f; Beilegung f; Einigung f; Siedlung f; Besiedlung f; Begleichung f, Bezahlung f; **reach a settlement** sich einigen

set·tler Siedler(in)

sev·en 1. sieben; 2. Sieben f

sev·en·teen 1. siebzehn; 2. Siebzehn f

sev·en·teenth siebzehnte(r, -s)

sev·enth 1. siebente(r, -s), siebte(r, -s); 2. Siebentel n, Siebtel n

sev·enth·ly siebentens, siebtens

sev·en·ti·eth siebzigste(r, -s)

sev·en·ty 1. siebzig; 2. Siebzig f

sev·er durchtrennen; abtrennen; Beziehungen abbrechen; (zer)reißen

sev·er·al mehrere

sev·er·al·ly einzeln, getrennt

se·vere schwer (injuries, setback etc); stark (pain); hart, streng (winter); streng (person, discipline etc); scharf (criticism etc)

se·ver·i·ty Schwere f; Stärke f; Härte f; Strenge f; Schärfe f

sew nähen

sew·age Abwasser n

sew·age works Kläranlage f

sew·er Abwasserkanal m

sew·er·age Kanalisation f

sew·ing 1. Nähen n; Näharbeit f; 2. Näh...

sewing ma·chine Nähmaschine f

sex Geschlecht n; Sexualität f; Sex m; Geschlechtsverkehr m

sex·ism Sexismus m

sex·ist 1. sexistisch; 2. Sexist(in)

sex·ton Küster m (und Totengräber m)

sex·u·al sexuell, Sexual..., geschlechtlich, Geschlechts...

sexual har·ass·ment sexuelle Belästigung

sexual in·ter·course Geschlechtsverkehr m

sex·u·al·i·ty Sexualität f

sex·y F sexy, aufreizend

shab·by schäbig

shack Hütte f, Bude f; F contp Schuppen m

shack·les Fesseln pl, Ketten pl (both a. fig)

shade 1. Schatten m (a. fig); (Lampen-)Schirm m; Schattierung f; Rouleau n; fig Nuance f; **a shade** fig ein kleines bisschen, e-e Spur; 2. abschirmen (**from** gegen); schattieren; **shade off** allmählich übergehen (**into** in acc)

shad·ow 1. Schatten m (a. fig); **there's not a** or **the shadow of a doubt about it** daran besteht nicht der geringste Zweifel; 2. j-n beschatten

shad·ow·y schattig, dunkel; verschwommen, vage, schemenhaft

shad·y schattig; Schatten spendend; F zwielichtig, fragwürdig

shaft (Pfeil- etc)Schaft m; (Hammer- etc) Stiel m; TECH Welle f; (Aufzugs-, Bergwerks- etc)Schacht m; (Sonnen- etc) Strahl m

shag·gy zottig, struppig

shake 1. v/t schütteln; rütteln an (dat); erschüttern; **shake hands** sich die Hand geben or schütteln; v/i zittern, beben, wackeln (**with** vor dat); **shake down** herunterschütteln; durchsuchen, F filzen; Br F kampieren; **shake off** abschütteln; Erkältung etc loswerden; **shake up** Kissen etc aufschütteln; Flasche, Flüssigkeit (durch-) schütteln; fig erschüttern; 2. Schütteln n; F Milchshake m; **shake of the head** Kopfschütteln n

shake-down F Erpressung f; Durchsuchung f, Filzung f; Br (Not)Lager n

shak·en a. **shaken up** erschüttert

shak·y wack(e)lig; zitt(e)rig

shall v/aux future: ich werde, wir werden; in questions: soll ich ...?, sollen wir ...?; **shall we go?** gehen wir?

shal·low seicht, flach, fig a. oberflächlich

S

shal·lows seichte *or* flache Stelle, Untiefe *f*

sham 1. Farce *f*; Heuchelei *f*; **2.** unecht, falsch; vorgetäuscht, geheuchelt; **3.** *v/t Mitgefühl etc* vortäuschen, heucheln; *Krankheit etc* simulieren; *v/i* sich verstellen, heucheln; *he's only shamming* er tut nur so

sham·bles F Schlachtfeld *n*, wüstes Durcheinander, Chaos *n*

shame 1. Scham *f*, Schamgefühl *n*; Schande *f*; *shame!* pfui!; *shame on you!* pfui!; *schäm dich!*; *put to shame* → 2. beschämen; Schande machen (*dat*)

shame-faced betreten, verlegen

shame·ful beschämend; schändlich

shame·less schamlos

sham·poo 1. Shampoo *n*, Schampon *n*, Schampun *n*; Haarwäsche *f*; → *set* 3; **2.** *Haare* waschen; *j-m* die Haare waschen; *Teppich etc* schamponieren

shank TECH Schaft *m*; GASTR Hachse *f*

shan·ty[1] Hütte *f*, Bude *f*

shan·ty[2] Shanty *n*, Seemannslied *n*

shan·ty·town Elendsviertel *n*

shape Form *f*; Gestalt *f*; Verfassung *f*, Zustand *m*; *in good (bad) shape* in gutem (schlechtem) Zustand; *in (out of) shape* SPORT (nicht) gut in Form; *take shape* fig Gestalt annehmen; **2.** *v/t* formen; gestalten; *v/i a.* *shape up* sich gut *etc* machen

shape·less formlos; ausgebeult

shape·ly wohlgeformt

share 1. Anteil *m* (*in*, *of* an *dat*); *esp Br* ECON Aktie *f*; *go shares* teilen; *have a (no) share in* (nicht) beteiligt sein an (*dat*); **2.** *v/t* (sich) *et.* teilen (*with* mit); *a.* *share out* verteilen (*among*, *between* an *acc*, unter *acc*); *v/i* teilen; *share in* sich teilen in (*acc*)

share·hold·er *esp Br* ECON Aktionär(in)

shark ZO Hai(fisch) *m*; → *loan shark*

sharp 1. *adj* scharf (*a. fig*); spitz; abrupt; schneidend (*wind*, *frost*, *command*, *voice*, *etc*); beißend (*cold*, *smell etc*); stechend, heftig (*pain*); gescheit; MUS (*um e-n Halbton*) erhöht; *C sharp* MUS Cis *n*; **2.** *adv* scharf, abrupt; MUS zu hoch; pünktlich, genau; *at eight o'clock sharp* Punkt 8 (Uhr); *look sharp* F sich beeilen; *look sharp!* F mach schnell!, Tempo!; F pass auf!, gib Acht!

sharp·en *Messer etc* schärfen, schleifen; *Bleistift etc* spitzen

sharp·en·er (*Messer- etc*)Schärfer *m*; (*Bleistift*)Spitzer *m*

sharp·ness Schärfe *f* (*a. fig*)

sharp·shoot·er Scharfschütze *m*

sharp-sight·ed scharfsichtig

sharp-wit·ted scharfsinnig

shat·ter *v/t* zerschmettern, zerschlagen; *Hoffnungen etc* zerstören; *v/i* zerspringen, zersplittern

shat·ter·ing vernichtend; erschütternd

shat·ter·proof splitterfrei

shave 1. (sich) rasieren; (glatt) hobeln; *j-n, et.* streifen; **2.** Rasur *f*; *have a shave* sich rasieren; *that was a close shave* das war knapp, das ist gerade noch einmal gut gegangen!

shav·en kahl geschoren

shav·er (*esp* elektrischer) Rasierapparat *m*

shav·ing 1. Rasieren *n*; **2.** Rasier...

shaving bag Kulturbeutel *m*

shaving brush Rasierpinsel *m*

shaving cream Rasiercreme *f*

shav·ings Späne *pl*

shawl Umhängetuch *n*; Kopftuch *n*

she 1. *pron* sie; **2.** Sie *f*; ZO Weibchen *n*; **3.** *adj in cpds* ZO \133weibchen *n*; *she-bear* Bärin *f*

sheaf Bündel *n*; AGR Garbe *f*

shear 1. scheren; **2.** (*a pair of*) *shears* (e-e) große Schere

sheath (*Schwert- etc*)Scheide *f*; Hülle *f*; *Br* Kondom *n, m*

sheathe *Schwert etc* in die Scheide stecken; TECH umhüllen, verkleiden, ummanteln

shed[1] Schuppen *m*; Stall *m*

shed[2] *Tränen etc* vergießen; *Blätter etc* verlieren; *fig Hemmungen etc* ablegen; *shed its skin* sich häuten; *shed a few pounds* ein paar Pfund abnehmen

sheen Glanz *m*

sheep ZO Schaf *n*

sheep·dog ZO Schäferhund *m*

sheep·ish verlegen

sheep·skin Schaffell *n*

sheer rein, bloß; steil, (fast) senkrecht; hauchdünn

sheet Betttuch *n*, (Bett)Laken *n*, Leintuch *n*; (*Glas-, Metall- etc*)Platte *f*; Blatt *n*, Bogen *m*; weite (*Eis- etc*)Fläche; *the rain was coming down in sheets* es regnete in Strömen

sheet light·ning Wetterleuchten *n*

shelf (*Bücher-, Wand- etc*)Brett *n*, (-)Bord *n*; GEOGR Riff *n*; *pl* Regal *n*; *off the shelf* gleich zum Mitnehmen

shell 1. (*Austern-, Eier-, Nuss- etc*)Schale *f*; BOT (*Erbsen- etc*)Hülse *f*; ZO Muschel *f*; (*Schnecken*)Haus *n*; ZO Panzer *m*; MIL Granate *f* (*Geschoss-, Patronen*)Hülse *f*; Patrone *f*; TECH Rumpf *m*, Gerippe *n*, ARCH *a.* Rohbau *m*; **2.** schälen, enthülsen; mit Granaten beschießen

shell·fish zo Schal(en)tier *n*

shel·ter 1. Zuflucht *f*, Schutz *m*; Unterkunft *f*, Obdach *n*; MIL Unterstand *m*; *run for shelter* Schutz suchen; *take shelter* sich unterstellen (*under* unter *dat*); *bus shelter* Wartehäuschen *n*; **2.** *v/t* schützen (*from* vor *dat*); *v/i* sich unterstellen

shelve *v/t Bücher* in ein Regal stellen; *Plan etc* aufschieben, zurückstellen; *v/i* sanft abfallen (*garden etc*)

shep·herd 1. Schäfer *m*, Hirt *m*; **2.** *j-n* führen

sher·iff Sheriff *m*

shield 1. Schild *m*; **2.** *j-n* (be)schützen (*from* vor *dat*); *j-n* decken

shift 1. *v/t et.* bewegen, schieben, *Möbelstück a.* (ver)rücken; *Schuld etc* (ab-)schieben (*onto* auf *acc*); *shift gear(s)* MOT schalten; *v/i* sich bewegen; umspringen (*wind*); *fig* sich verlagern *or* verschieben *or* wandeln; MOT schalten (*into*, *to* in *acc*); *shift from one foot to the other* von e-m Fuß auf den anderen treten; *shift on one's chair* auf s-m Stuhl *ungeduldig* ein und her rutschen; **2.** *fig* Verlagerung *f*, Verschiebung *f*, Wandel *m*; ECON Schicht *f*

shift key TECH Umschalttaste *f*

shift work·er Schichtarbeiter(in)

shift·y F verschlagen

shim·mer schimmern; flimmern

shin 1. *a. shinbone* ANAT Schienbein *n*; **2.** *shin up* hinaufklettern; *shin down* herunterklettern

shine 1. *v/i* scheinen; leuchten; glänzen (*a. fig*); *v/t Schuhe etc* polieren; **2.** Glanz *m*

shin·gle¹ grober Strandkies

shin·gle² (Dach)Schindel *f*

shin·gles MED Gürtelrose *f*

shin·y blank, glänzend

ship 1. Schiff *n*; **2.** verschiffen; ECON verfrachten, versenden

ship·ment ECON Ladung *f*; Verschiffung *f*, Verfrachtung *f*, Versand *m*

ship·own·er Reeder *m*; Schiffseigner *m*

ship·ping Schifffahrt *f*; Schiffsbestand *m*; ECON Verschiffung *f*, Verfrachtung *f*, Versand *m*

ship·wreck Schiffbruch *m*

ship·wrecked 1. *be shipwrecked* Schiffbruch erleiden; **2.** schiffbrüchig

ship·yard (Schiffs)Werft *f*

shirk sich drücken (vor *dat*)

shirk·er Drückeberger(in)

shirt Hemd *n*

shirt·sleeve 1. Hemdsärmel *m*; *in (one's) shirtsleeves* in Hemdsärmeln, hemds-

ärmelig; **2.** hemdsärmelig

shish ke·bab GASTR Schaschlik *m*, *n*

shit V **1.** Scheiße *f* (*a. fig*); *fig* Scheiß *m*; **2.** (voll)scheißen

shiv·er 1. zittern (*with* vor *dat*); **2.** Schauer *m*; *pl* MED F Schüttelfrost *m*; *the sight send shivers (up and) down my spine* bei dem Anblick überlief es mich eiskalt

shoal¹ Untiefe *f*; Sandbank *f*

shoal² zo Schwarm *m*

shock¹ 1. Schock *m* (*a.* MED); Wucht *f*; ELECTR Schlag *m*, (*a.* MED Elektro-) Schock *m*; *be in (a state of) shock* unter Schock stehen; **2.** schockieren, empören; *j-m* e-n Schock versetzen

shock² (*shock of hair* Haar)Schopf *m*

shock ab·sorb·er TECH Stoßdämpfer *m*

shock·ing schockierend, empörend, anstößig; F scheußlich

shod·dy minderwertig (*goods*); gemein, schäbig (*trick etc*)

shoe 1. Schuh *m*; Hufeisen *n*; **2.** *Pferd* beschlagen

shoe·horn Schuhanzieher *m*, -löffel *m*

shoe·lace Schnürsenkel *m*

shoe·mak·er Schuhmacher *m*, Schuster *m*

shoe·shine boy Schuhputzer *m*

shoe store (*Br* **shop**) Schuhgeschäft *n*

shoe·string Schnürsenkel *m*

shoot 1. *v/t* schießen; HUNT *a.* erlegen; abfeuern, abschießen; erschießen; *Riegel* vorschieben; *j-n* fotografieren, aufnehmen, *Film* drehen; *Heroin etc* spritzen; *shoot the lights* MOT bei Rot fahren; *v/i* schießen (*at* auf *acc*); jagen; *fig* schießen, rasen; *film*, TV drehen, filmen; BOT sprießen, treiben; **2.** BOT Trieb *m*; Jagd *f*; Jagdrevier *n*

shoot·er F Schießeisen *n*

shoot·ing 1. Schießen *n*; Schießerei *f*; Erschießung *f*; Anschlag *m*; Jagd *f*; *film*, TV Dreharbeiten *pl*, Aufnahmen *pl*; **2.** stechend (*pain*)

shooting gal·le·ry Schießbude *f*

shooting range Schießstand *m*

shooting star ASTR Sternschnuppe *f*

shop 1. *Br* Laden *m*, Geschäft *n*; Werkstatt *f*; Betrieb *m*; *talk shop* fachsimpeln; **2.** *mst* **go shopping** einkaufen gehen

shop as·sis·tant *Br* Verkäufer(in)

shop·keep·er *Br* Ladenbesitzer(in), Ladeninhaber(in)

shop·lift·er Ladendieb(in)

shop·lift·ing Ladendiebstahl *m*

shop·per Käufer(in)

shop·ping 1. Einkauf *m*, Einkaufen *n*; Einkäufe *pl* (*items bought*); *do one's*

shopping *Br* einkaufen, (s-e) Einkäufe machen; **2.** Einkaufs...

shopping bag Einkaufsbeutel *m*, -tasche *f*

shopping cart Einkaufswagen *m*

shopping cen·ter (*Br* **cen·tre**) Einkaufszentrum *n*

shopping list Einkaufsliste *f*, -zettel *m*

shopping mall Einkaufszentrum *n*

shopping precinct *Br* Fußgängerzone *f*

shopping street Geschäfts-, Ladenstraße *f*

shop stew·ard ECON gewerkschaftlicher Vertrauensmann

shop·walk·er *Br* Aufsicht(sperson) *f*

shop win·dow Schaufenster *n*

shore¹ Küste *f*; (*See*)Ufer *n*; **on shore** an Land

shore²: shore up (ab)stützen

short 1. *adj* kurz; klein (*person*); kurz angebunden, barsch, schroff (**with** zu); GASTR mürbe; **be short for** die Kurzform sein von; **be short of ...** nicht genügend ... haben; **2.** *adv* plötzlich, abrupt; **short of** außer; **cut short** plötzlich unterbrechen; **fall short of** et. nicht erreichen; **stop short** plötzlich innehalten, stutzen; **stop short of** or **at** zurückschrecken vor (*dat*); → **run 1**; **3.** *F* Kurzfilm *m*; ELECTR Kurze *m*; **called ... for short** kurz ... genannt; **in short** kurz(um)

short·age Knappheit *f*, Mangel *m* (**of** an *dat*)

short·com·ings Unzulänglichkeiten *pl*, Mängel *pl*, Fehler *pl*

short cut Abkürzung *f*; **take a short cut** (den Weg) abkürzen

short·en *v/t* (ab-, ver)kürzen; *v/i* kürzer werden

short·hand Kurzschrift *f*, Stenografie *f*

shorthand typ·ist Stenotypistin *f*

short·ly bald; barsch, schroff; mit wenigen Worten

short·ness Kürze *f*; Schroffheit *f*

shorts *a.* **pair of shorts** Shorts *pl*; (Herren-)Unterhose *f*

short·sight·ed *esp Br* kurzsichtig (*a. fig*)

short sto·ry Kurzgeschichte *f*

short·tem·pered aufbrausend, hitzig

short-term ECON kurzfristig

short time ECON Kurzarbeit *f*

short wave ELECTR Kurzwelle *f*

short-wind·ed kurzatmig

shot Schuss *m*; Schrot(kugeln *pl*) *m*, *n*; SPORT Kugel *f*; *guter etc* Schütze *m*; *soccer etc*: Schuss *m*; *basketball etc*: Wurf *m*; *tennis, golf*: Schlag *m*; PHOT Schnappschuss *m*, Aufnahme *f*; *film*, TV Aufnahme *f*, Einstellung *f*; MED *F* Spritze *f*; *F*

Schuss *m* (*of drugs*); *fig F* Versuch *m*; **a shot of rum** ein Schluck Rum; **I'll have a shot at it** ich probier's mal; **not by a long shot** *F* noch lange nicht; → **big shot**

shot·gun Schrotflinte *f*

shot·gun wed·ding *F* Mussheirat *f*

shot put SPORT Kugelstoßen *n*

shot put·ter SPORT Kugelstoßer(in)

shoul·der 1. ANAT Schulter *f*; MOT Standspur *f*; **2.** schultern; *Kosten, Verantwortung etc* übernehmen; (mit der Schulter) stoßen

shoulder bag Schulter-, Umhängetasche *f*

shoulder blade ANAT Schulterblatt *n*

shoulder strap Träger *m*; Tragriemen *m*

shout 1. *v/i* rufen, schreien (**for** nach; **for help** um Hilfe); **shout at s.o.** j-n anschreien; *v/t* rufen, schreien; **2.** Ruf *m*, Schrei *m*

shove 1. stoßen, *F* schubsen; *et.* schieben, stopfen; **2.** Stoß *m*, *F* Schubs *m*

shov·el 1. Schaufel *f*; **2.** schaufeln

show 1. *v/t* zeigen, anzeigen; *j-n* bringen, führen (**to** zu); ausstellen; zeigen, *film etc a.* vorführen, TV *a.* bringen; *v/i* zu sehen sein; **be showing** gezeigt werden, laufen; **show around** herumführen; **show in** herein-, hineinführen, herein-, hineinbringen; **show off** angeben *or* protzen (mit); vorteilhaft zur Geltung bringen; **show out** heraus-, hinausführen, heraus-, hinausbringen; **show round** herumführen; **show up** *v/t* herauf-, hinaufführen, herauf-, hinaufbringen; sichtbar machen; *j-n* entlarven, bloßstellen; *et.* aufdecken; *j-n* in Verlegenheit bringen; *v/i* zu sehen sein; *F* aufkreuzen, auftauchen; **2.** THEA *etc* Vorstellung *f*, Show *f*; *radio*, TV Sendung *f*; Ausstellung *f*; Zurschaustellung *f*, Demonstration *f*; *fig leerer* Schein; **be on show** ausgestellt *or* zu besichtigen sein; **steal the show from s.o.** *fig* j-m die Schau stehlen; **make a show of** *Anteilnahme, Interesse etc* heucheln; **put up a poor show** *F* e-e schwache Leistung zeigen; **be in charge of the whole show** *F* den ganzen Laden schmeißen; **3.** Muster...

show-biz *F*, **show busi·ness** Showbusiness *n*, Showgeschäft *n*, Unterhaltungsindustrie *f*

show·case Schaukasten *m*, Vitrine *f*

show·down Kraft-, Machtprobe *f*

show·er 1. (Regen- *etc*)Schauer *m*; (Funken)Regen *m*; (Wasser-, Wort- *etc*) Schwall *m*; Dusche *f*; (Geschenk-) Party *f*; **have** or **take a shower** duschen; **2.** *v/t* *j-n mit et.* überschütten *or* überhäufen; *v/i* duschen; **shower down** niederprasseln

show jump·er SPORT Springreiter(in)

show jump·ing SPORT Springreiten *n*

show-off F Angeber(in)

show·room Ausstellungsraum *m*

show tri·al JUR Schauprozess *m*

show·y auffallend

shred 1. Fetzen *m*; **2.** zerfetzen; in (schmale) Streifen schneiden, schnitzeln, schnetzeln; in den Papier- *or* Reißwolf geben

shred·der Schnitzelmaschine *f*; Papier-, Reißwolf *m*

shrewd scharfsinnig; schlau

shriek 1. (gellend) aufschreien; **shriek with laughter** vor Lachen kreischen; **2.** (schriller) Schrei

shrill schrill; *fig* heftig, scharf, lautstark

shrimp ZO Garnele *f*; *fig contp* Knirps *m*

shrine Schrein *m*

shrink 1. (ein-, zusammen)schrumpfen (lassen); einlaufen; *fig* abnehmen; **2.** F Klapsdoktor *m*

shrink·age Schrumpfung *f*; Einlaufen *n*; *fig* Abnahme *f*

shrink-wrap einschweißen

shriv·el schrumpfen (lassen); runz(e)lig werden (lassen)

shroud 1. Leichentuch *n*; **2.** *fig* hüllen

Shrove Tues·day Fastnachts-, Faschingsdienstag *m*

shrub Strauch *m*, Busch *m*

shrub·ber·y BOT Strauch-, Buschwerk *n*, Gebüsch *n*

shrug 1. *a.* **shrug one's shoulders** mit den Achseln *or* Schultern zucken; **2.** Achselzucken *n*, Schulterzucken *n*

shuck BOT **1.** Hülse *f*, Schote *f*; Schale *f*; **2.** enthülsen; schälen

shud·der 1. schaudern; **2.** Schauder *m*

shuf·fle 1. *v/t Karten* mischen; *Papiere etc* umordnen, hierhin oder dorthin legen; **shuffle one's feet** schlurfen; *v/i* schlurfen; *Karten* mischen; **2.** Schlurfen *n*, schlurfender Gang; Mischen *n*

shun *j-n, et.* meiden

shunt *Zug etc* rangieren, verschieben; *a.* **shunt off** F *j-n* abschieben (**to** in *acc*, nach)

shut (sich) schließen; zumachen; *a.* **shut down** *Fabrik etc* schließen; **shut off** *Wasser, Gas, Maschine etc* abstellen; **shut up** einschließen; einsperren; *Geschäft* schließen; **shut up!** F halt die Klappe!

shut·ter Fensterladen *m*; PHOT Verschluss *m*

shut·tle 1. Pendelverkehr *m*; *(Raum-)* Fähre *f*, (-)Transporter *m*; TECH Schiffchen *n*; **2.** hin- und herbefördern

shut·tle·cock SPORT Federball *m*

shut·tle ser·vice Pendelverkehr *m*

shy 1. scheu; schüchtern; **2.** scheuen (**at** vor *dat*); **shy away from** *fig* zurückschrecken vor (*dat*)

shy·ness Scheu *f*; Schüchternheit *f*

sick 1. krank; **be sick** *esp Br* sich übergeben; **she was** *or* **felt sick** ihr war schlecht; **get sick** krank werden; **be off sick** krank (geschrieben) sein; **report sick** sich krank melden; **be sick of s.th.** F et. satthaben; **shy away from** *fig* zurückschrecken; **it makes me sick** F mir wird schlecht davon, *a. fig* es ekelt *or* widert mich an; **2. the sick** die Kranken *pl*

sick·bed Krankenbett *n*

sick·en *v/t* anekeln, anwidern; *v/i esp Br* krank werden

sick·le ['sɪkl] Sichel *f*

sick leave: be on sick leave krank (geschrieben) sein, wegen Krankheit fehlen

sick·ly kränklich; ungesund; matt; widerlich (*smell etc*)

sick·ness Krankheit *f*; Übelkeit *f*

sickness ben·e·fit *Br* Krankengeld *n*

side 1. Seite *f*; *esp Br* SPORT Mannschaft *f*; **side by side** nebeneinander; **take sides** Partei ergreifen (**with** für; **against** gegen); **2.** Seiten...; Neben...; **3.** Partei ergreifen (**with** für; **against** gegen)

side·board Anrichte *f*, Sideboard *n*

side·car MOT Bei-, Seitenwagen *m*

side dish GASTR Beilage *f*

side·long seitlich; Seiten...

sidelong glance Seitenblick *m*

side street Nebenstraße *f*

side·swipe Seitenhieb *m*

side·track *j-n* ablenken; F *et.* abbiegen; RAIL *etc* rangieren, verschieben

side·walk Bürgersteig *m*, Gehsteig *m*

side·walk ca·fé Straßencafé *n*

side·ways seitlich; seitwärts, nach der *or* zur Seite

sid·ing RAIL Nebengleis *n*

si·dle: sidle up to s.o. sich an j-n heranschleichen

siege MIL Belagerung *f*; **lay siege to** belagern (*a. fig*)

sieve 1. Sieb *n*; **2.** (durch)sieben

sift (durch)sieben; *a.* **sift through** *fig* sichten, durchsehen, prüfen

sigh 1. seufzen; **2.** Seufzer *m*

sight 1. Sehvermögen *n*, Sehkraft *f*, Augenlicht *n*; Anblick *m*; Sicht(weite) *f*; *pl* Visier *n*; Sehenswürdigkeiten *pl*; **at sight, on sight** sofort; **at the sight of** beim Anblick von (*or gen*); **at first sight**

auf den ersten Blick; **catch sight of** erblicken; **know by sight** vom Sehen kennen; **lose sight of** aus den Augen verlieren; **be (with)in sight** in Sicht sein (*a. fig*); **2.** sichten

sight-read MUS vom Blatt singen *or* spielen

sight·see·ing Sightseeing *n*, Besichtigung *f* von Sehenswürdigkeiten; **go sightseeing** sich die Sehenswürdigkeiten anschauen

sightseeing tour Sightseeingtour *f*, Besichtigungstour *f*, (Stadt)Rundfahrt *f*

sight·se·er Tourist(in)

sight test Sehtest *m*

sign **1.** Zeichen *n*; (*Hinweis-, Warn- etc*) Schild *n*; *fig* (An)Zeichen *n*; **2.** unterschreiben, unterzeichnen; *Scheck* ausstellen; **sign in** sich eintragen; **sign out** sich austragen

sig·nal **1.** Signal *n* (*a. fig*); Zeichen *n* (*a. fig*); **2.** (ein) Zeichen geben; signalisieren

sig·na·to·ry Unterzeichner(in)

sig·na·ture Unterschrift *f*; Signatur *f*

signature tune *radio*, TV Kennmelodie *f*

sign·board (Aushänge)Schild *n*

sign·er Unterzeichnete *m, f*

sig·net Siegel *n*

sig·nif·i·cance Bedeutung *f*, Wichtigkeit *f*

sig·nif·i·cant bedeutend, bedeutsam, wichtig; bezeichnend

sig·ni·fy bedeuten; andeuten

sign·post Wegweiser *m*

si·lence **1.** Stille *f*; Schweigen *n*; **silence!** Ruhe!; **in silence** schweigend; **reduce to silence** → **2.** zum Schweigen bringen

si·lenc·er TECH Schalldämpfer *m*; *Br* MOT Auspufftopf *m*

si·lent still; schweigend; schweigsam; stumm

silent part·ner ECON stiller Teilhaber

sil·i·con CHEM Silizium *n*

sil·i·cone CHEM Silikon *n*

silk **1.** Seide *f*; **2.** Seiden…

silk·worm ZO Seidenraupe *f*

silk·y seidig; samtig (*voice*)

sill (*Fenster*)Brett *n*

sil·ly **1.** albern, töricht, dumm; **2.** F Dummerchen *n*

sil·ver **1.** Silber *n*; **2.** silbern, Silber…; **3.** versilbern

sil·ver·plat·ed versilbert

sil·ver·ware Tafelsilber *n*

sil·ver·y silberglänzend; *fig* silberhell

sim·i·lar ähnlich (**to** *dat*)

sim·i·lar·i·ty Ähnlichkeit *f*

sim·i·le Gleichnis *n*, Vergleich *m*

sim·mer leicht kochen, köcheln; **simmer**

with *fig* kochen vor (*rage etc*), fiebern vor (*excitement etc*); **simmer down** F sich beruhigen, F sich abregen

sim·per albern *or* affektiert lächeln

sim·ple einfach, schlicht; leicht; dumm, einfältig; naiv; **the simple fact is that** … es ist einfach e-e Tatsache, dass …

sim·ple-mind·ed dumm; naiv

sim·plic·i·ty Einfachheit *f*, Schlichtheit *f*; Dummheit *f*; Naivität *f*

sim·pli·fi·ca·tion Vereinfachung *f*

sim·pli·fy vereinfachen

sim·ply einfach; bloß, nur

sim·u·late vortäuschen; MIL, TECH simulieren

sim·ul·ta·ne·ous simultan, gleichzeitig

sin **1.** Sünde *f*; **2.** sündigen

since **1.** *adv a.* **ever since** seitdem, seither; **2.** *prp* seit (*dat*); **3.** *cj* seit(dem); da

sin·cere aufrichtig, ehrlich, offen

sin·cer·i·ty Aufrichtigkeit *f*; Offenheit *f*

sin·ew ANAT Sehne *f*

sin·ew·y sehnig; *fig* kraftvoll

sin·ful sündig, sündhaft

sing singen; **sing s.th. to s.o.** j-m et. vorsingen

singe (sich *et.*) ansengen *or* versengen

sing·er Sänger(in)

sing·ing Singen *n*, Gesang *m*

sin·gle **1.** einzig; einzeln, Einzel…; einfach; ledig, unverheiratet; **in single file** im Gänsemarsch; **2.** *Br* RAIL *etc* einfache Fahrkarte, AVIAT einfaches Ticket (*both a.* **single ticket**); Single *f*; Single *m*, Unverheiratete *m, f*; **3.** *sport* sich herausgreifen

sin·gle-breast·ed einreihig

sin·gle-en·gined AVIAT einmotorig

sin·gle fam·i·ly home Einfamilienhaus *n*

sin·gle fa·ther allein erziehender Vater

sin·gle-hand·ed eigenhändig, allein

sin·gle-lane MOT einspurig

sin·gle-mind·ed zielstrebig, -bewusst

sin·gle moth·er allein erziehende Mutter

sin·gle pa·rent Alleinerziehende *m, f*

sin·gle room Einzelzimmer *n*

sin·gles *esp tennis*: Einzel *n*; **a singles match** ein Einzel; **men's singles** Herreneinzel *n*; **women's singles** Dameneinzel *n*

sin·glet *Br* ärmelloses Unterhemd *or* Trikot

sin·gle-track eingleisig, einspurig

sin·gu·lar **1.** einzigartig, einmalig; **2.** LING Singular *m*, Einzahl *f*

sin·is·ter finster, unheimlich

sink **1.** *v/i* sinken, untergehen; sich senken; **sink in** eindringen (*a. fig*); *v/t* versenken; *Brunnen etc* bohren; *Zähne etc* vergraben (*into* in *acc*); 2. Spülbecken *n*, Spüle *f*; Waschbecken *n*

sin·ner Sünder(in)

sip 1. Schlückchen *n*; 2. *v/t* nippen an (*dat*) or von; schlückchenweise trinken; *v/i* nippen (*at* an *dat* or von)

sir mein Herr; *Dear Sir or Madam* Sehr geehrte Damen und Herren (*address in letters*)

sire zo Vater *m*, Vatertier *n*

si·ren Sirene *f*

sis·sy F Weichling *m*

sis·ter Schwester *f*; Br med Oberschwester *f*; rel (Ordens)Schwester *f*

sis·ter·hood Schwesternschaft *f*

sis·ter-in-law Schwägerin *f*

sis·ter·ly schwesterlich

sit *v/i* sitzen; sich setzen; tagen; *v/t* j-n setzen; *esp Br* Prüfung ablegen, machen; *sit down* sich setzen; *sit for Br* Prüfung ablegen, machen; *sit in* ein Sit-in veranstalten; an e-m Sit-in teilnehmen; *sit in for j-n* vertreten; *sit in on* als Zuhörer teilnehmen an (*dat*) (*a. fig*); *sit on a committee* e-m Ausschuss angehören; *sit out* Tanz auslassen; das Ende (*gen*) abwarten; *Krise etc* aussitzen; *sit up* sich or j-n aufrichten or aufsetzen; aufrecht sitzen; aufbleiben

sit·com → *situation comedy*

sit-down a. *sit-down strike* Sitzstreik *m*; a. *sit-down demonstration* or F *demo* Sitzblockade *f*

site Platz *m*, Ort *m*, Stelle *f*; (*Ausgrabungs*)Stätte *f*; Baustelle *f*

sit-in Sit-in *n*, Sitzstreik *m*

sit·ting Sitzung *f*

sit·ting room *esp Br* Wohnzimmer *n*

sit·u·at·ed: *be situated* liegen, gelegen sein

sit·u·a·tion Lage *f*, Situation *f*

situation com·e·dy TV *etc* Situationskomödie *f*

six 1. sechs; 2. Sechs *f*

six·teen 1. sechzehn; 2. Sechzehn *f*

six·teenth sechzehnte(r, -s)

sixth 1. sechste(r, -s); 2. Sechstel *n*

sixth·ly sechstens

six·ti·eth sechzigste(r, -s)

six·ty 1. sechzig; 2. Sechzig *f*

size 1. Größe *f*, *fig a.* Ausmaß *n*, Umfang *m*; 2. *size up* F abschätzen

size(·a)·ble beträchtlich

siz·zle brutzeln

skate 1. Schlittschuh *m*; Rollschuh *m*; 2. Schlittschuh laufen, eislaufen; Rollschuh laufen

skate·board Skateboard *n*

skat·er Eisläufer(in), Schlittschuhläu-

fer(in); Rollschuhläufer(in)

skat·ing Eislaufen *n*, Schlittschuhlaufen *n*; Rollschuhlaufen *n*; *free skating* Kür *f*, Kürlauf *m*

skating rink (Kunst)Eisbahn *f*; Rollschuhbahn *f*

skel·e·ton Skelett *n*, Gerippe *n*

skep·tic Skeptiker(in)

skep·ti·cal skeptisch

sketch 1. Skizze *f*; thea *etc* Sketch *m*; 2. skizzieren

skew·er 1. (Brat)Spieß *m*; 2. (auf)spießen

ski 1. Ski *m*; 2. Ski…; 3. Ski fahren or laufen

skid 1. mot rutschen, schleudern; 2. mot Rutschen *n*, Schleudern *n*; tech Kufe *f*

skid mark(s) mot Bremsspur *f*

ski·er Skifahrer(in), Skiläufer(in)

ski·ing Skifahren *n*, Skilaufen *n*, Skisport *m*

ski jump (Sprung)Schanze *f*

ski jump·er Skispringer *m*

ski jump·ing Skispringen *n*

skil·ful *Br* → *skillful*

skill Geschicklichkeit *f*, Fertigkeit *f*

skilled geschickt (*at, in* in *dat*)

skilled work·er Facharbeiter(in)

skill·ful geschickt

skim Fett *etc* abschöpfen (*a. skim off*); Milch entrahmen; (hin)gleiten über (*acc*); *a. skim over, skim through Bericht etc* überfliegen

skim(med) milk Magermilch *f*

skimp a. *skimp on* sparen an (*dat*)

skimp·y dürftig; knapp

skin 1. anat Haut *f*; zo Fell *n*; bot Schale *f*; 2. Tier abhäuten; *Zwiebel etc* schälen; sich das *Knie etc* aufschürfen

skin-deep (nur) oberflächlich

skin div·ing Sporttauchen *n*

skin·flint Geizhals *m*

skin·ny dürr, mager

skin·ny-dip F nackt baden

skip 1. *v/i* hüpfen, springen; seilhüpfen, seilspringen; *v/t et.* überspringen, auslassen; 2. Hüpfer *m*

skip·per mar, sport Kapitän *m*

skir·mish Geplänkel *n*

skirt 1. Rock *m*; 2. a. *skirt (a)round* umgeben; *Problem etc* umgehen

skirt·ing board *Br* Scheuerleiste *f*

ski run Skipiste *f*

ski tow Schlepplift *m*

skit·tle Kegel *m*

skulk sich herumdrücken, herumschleichen

skull anat Schädel *m*

skul(l)·dug·ge·ry F fauler Zauber

skunk ZO Skunk *m*, Stinktier *n*

sky *a.* **skies** Himmel *m*

sky·jack Flugzeug entführen

sky·jack·er Flugzeugentführer(in)

sky·lark ZO Feldlerche *f*

sky·light Dachfenster *n*

sky·line Skyline *f*, Silhouette *f*

sky·rock·et F hochschnellen, in die Höhe schießen

sky·scrap·er Wolkenkratzer *m*

slab (*Stein- etc*)Platte *f*; dickes Stück

slack 1. locker; ECON flau; F *fig* lax, lasch, nachlässig; **2.** bummeln; *slack off, slack up fig* nachlassen, (*person a.*) abbauen

slack·en *v/t* lockern; verringern; *slacken speed* langsamer werden; *v/i* locker werden; *a. slacken off* nachlassen

slacks F Hose *f*

slag TECH Schlacke *f*

sla·lom SPORT Slalom *m*

slam 1. *a.* *slam shut* zuschlagen, F zuknallen; *a. slam down* F *et.* knallen (*on* auf *acc*); *slam on the brakes* F MOT auf die Bremse steigen; **2.** Zuschlagen *n*; Knall *m*

slan·der 1. Verleumdung *f*; **2.** verleumden

slan·der·ous verleumderisch

slang 1. Slang *m*; Jargon *m*; **2.** *esp Br* F *j-n* wüst beschimpfen

slant 1. schräg legen *or* liegen; sich neigen; **2.** schräge Fläche; Abhang *m*; *fig* Einstellung *f*; *at or on a slant* schräg

slant·ing schräg

slap 1. Klaps *m*, Schlag *m*; **2.** e-n Klaps geben (*dat*); schlagen; klatschen (*down on* auf *acc*; *against* gegen)

slap·stick THEA Slapstick *m*, Klamauk *m*

slapstick com·e·dy Slapstickkomödie *f*

slash 1. auf-, zerschlitzen; *Preise* drastisch herabsetzen; *Ausgaben etc* drastisch kürzen; *slash at* schlagen nach; **2.** Hieb *m*; Schlitz *m*

slate 1. Schiefer *m*; Schiefertafel *f*; POL Kandidatenliste *f*; **2.** mit Schiefer decken; *j-n* vorschlagen (*for, to be* als); *et.* planen (*for* für)

slaugh·ter 1. Schlachten *n*; *fig* Blutbad *n*, Gemetzel *n*; **2.** schlachten; *fig* niedermetzeln

slaugh·ter·house Schlachthaus *n*, Schlachthof *m*

Slav 1. Slawe *m*, Slawin *f*; **2.** slawisch

slave 1. Sklave *m*, Sklavin *f* (*a. fig*); **2.** *a.* *slave away* sich abplagen, F schuften

slav·er geifern, sabbern

sla·ve·ry Sklaverei *f*

slav·ish sklavisch

sleaze unsaubere Machenschaften; Kumpanei *f*; F POL Filz *m*

slea·zy schäbig, heruntergekommen; anrüchig

sled 1. (*a.* Rodel)Schlitten *m*; **2.** Schlitten fahren, rodeln

sledge *Br* → **sled**

sledge·ham·mer TECH Vorschlaghammer *m*

sleek 1. glatt, glänzend; geschmeidig; MOT schnittig; **2.** glätten

sleep 1. Schlaf *m*; *I couldn't get to sleep* ich konnte nicht einschlafen; *go to sleep* einschlafen (F *a. leg etc*); *put to sleep* Tier einschläfern; **2.** *v/i* schlafen; *sleep late* lang *or* länger schlafen; *sleep on Problem etc* überschlafen; *sleep with s.o.* mit *j-m* schlafen; *v/t* Schlafgelegenheit bieten für

sleep·er Schlafende *m, f*, Schläfer(in); *Br* RAIL Schwelle *f*; RAIL Schlafwagen *m*

sleep·ing bag Schlafsack *m*

Sleep·ing Beau·ty Dornröschen *n*

sleep·ing car RAIL Schlafwagen *m*

sleeping part·ner *Br* ECON stiller Teilhaber

sleeping pill PHARM Schlaftablette *f*, -mittel *n*

sleeping sick·ness MED Schlafkrankheit *f*

sleep·less schlaflos

sleep·walk·er Schlafwandler(in)

sleep·y schläfrig, müde; verschlafen

sleep·y·head F Schlafmütze *f*

sleet 1. Schneeregen *m*; Graupelschauer *m*; **2.** *it's sleeting* es gibt Schneeregen; es graupelt

sleeve Ärmel *m*; TECH Manschette *f*, Muffe *f*; *esp Br* (*Platten*)Hülle *f*

sleeve·less ärmellos

sleigh (*esp* Pferde)Schlitten *m*

sleight of hand Fingerfertigkeit *f*; *fig* (Taschenspieler)Trick *m*

slen·der schlank; *fig* mager, dürftig; schwach (*hope etc*)

slice 1. Scheibe *f*, Stück *n*; *fig* Anteil *m* (*of* an *dat*); **2.** *a.* *slice up* in Scheiben *or* Stücke schneiden; *slice off* Stück abschneiden (*from* von)

slick 1. gekonnt; geschickt; raffiniert; glatt (*road etc*); **2.** F (*Öl*)Teppich *m*; **3.** *slick down* Haar glätten, F anklatschen

slick·er Regenmantel *m*

slide gleiten (lassen); rutschen; schlüpfen; schieben; *let things slide fig* die Dinge schleifenlassen; **2.** Gleiten *n*, Rutschen *n*; Rutsche *f*, Rutschbahn *f*; TECH Schieber *m*; PHOT Dia *n*; Objektträger *m*; (*Erd- etc*)Rutsch *m*; *Br* (*Haar*)Spange *f*

slide rule Rechenschieber *m*

slide tack·le *soccer*: Grätsche f
slid·ing door Schiebetür f
slight 1. leicht, gering(fügig), unbedeutend; **2.** beleidigen, kränken; **3.** Beleidigung f, Kränkung f
slim 1. schlank; *fig* gering; **2.** *a.* **be slimming, be on a slimming diet** e-e Schlankheitskur machen, abnehmen
slime Schleim m
slim·y schleimig (*a. fig*)
sling 1. aufhängen; F schleudern; **2.** Schlinge f; Tragriemen m; Tragetuch n; Schleuder f
slip¹ 1. *v/i* rutschen, schlittern; ausgleiten, ausrutschen; schlüpfen; *v/t* sich losreißen von; **slip s.th. into s.o.'s hand** j-m et. in die Hand schieben; **slip s.o. s.th.** j-m et. zuschieben; **slip s.o.'s attention** j-m or j-s Aufmerksamkeit entgehen; **slip s.o.'s mind** j-m entfallen; **she has slipped a disk** MED sie hat e-n Bandscheibenvorfall; **slip by, slip past** verstreichen (*time*); **slip off, slip out of** schlüpfen aus; **slip on** überstreifen, schlüpfen in (*acc*); **2.** Ausgleiten n, (Aus)Rutschen n; Versehen n; Unterrock m; (*Kissen*)Bezug m; **slip of the tongue** Versprecher m; **give s.o. the slip** F j-m entwischen
slip² *a.* **slip of paper** Zettel m
slip·case Schuber m
slip-on 1. *adj* **slip-on shoe** → **2.** Slipper m
slipped disk MED Bandscheibenvorfall m
slip·per Hausschuh m, Pantoffel m
slip·per·y glatt, rutschig, glitschig
slip road Br MOT → **ramp**
slip·shod schlampig
slit 1. Schlitz m; **2.** schlitzen; **slit open** aufschlitzen
slith·er gleiten, rutschen
sliv·er (*Glas- etc*)Splitter m
slob·ber sabbern
slo·gan Slogan m
sloop MAR Schaluppe f
slop 1. *v/t* verschütten; *v/i* überschwappen; schwappen (**over** über *acc*); **2.** *a. pl* schlabb(e)riges Zeug; (*Tee-, Kaffee-*)Rest(e *pl*) m; *esp Br* Schmutzwasser n
slope 1. (Ab)Hang m; Neigung f, Gefälle n; **2.** sich neigen, abfallen
slop·py schlampig; F gammelig; F rührselig
slot Schlitz m, (Münz)Einwurf m; EDP Steckplatz m
sloth ZO Faultier n
slot ma·chine (Waren-, Spiel)Automat m
slouch 1. krumme Haltung; F latschiger Gang; **2.** krumm dasitzen or dastehen; F latschen
slough¹: **slough off** Haut abstreifen, ZO

sich häuten
slough² Sumpf m, Sumpfloch n
Slo·vak 1. slowakisch; **2.** Slowake m, Slowakin f; LING Slowakisch n
Slo·va·ki·a Slowakei f
slov·en·ly schlampig
slow 1. *adj* langsam; begriffsstutzig; ECON schleppend; **be** (**ten minutes**) **slow** (zehn Minuten) nachgehen; **2.** *adv* langsam; **3.** *v/t often* **slow down, slow up** Geschwindigkeit verringern; *v/i often* **slow down, slow up** langsamer fahren or gehen or werden
slow·coach Br → **slowpoke**
slow-down ECON Bummelstreik m
slow lane MOT Kriechspur f
slow mo·tion PHOT Zeitlupe f
slow-mov·ing kriechend (*traffic*)
slow·poke Langweiler(in)
slow-worm ZO Blindschleiche f
sludge Schlamm m
slug¹ ZO Nacktschnecke f
slug² F (*Gewehr- etc*)Kugel f; Schluck m (*whisky etc*)
slug³ F j-m e-n Faustschlag versetzen
slug·gish träge; ECON schleppend
sluice TECH Schleuse f
slum *a. pl* Slums *pl*, Elendsviertel n or *pl*
slum·ber POET **1.** schlummern; **2.** *a. pl* Schlummer m
slump 1. ECON stürzen (*prices*), stark zurückgehen (*sales etc*); **sit slumped over** zusammengesunken sitzen über (*dat*); **slump into a chair** sich in e-n Sessel fallen lassen; **2.** ECON starker Konjunkturrückgang; **slump in prices** Preissturz m
slur¹ 1. MUS Töne binden; **slur one's speech** undeutlich sprechen; lallen; **2.** undeutliche Aussprache
slur² 1. verleumden; **2.** **slur on s.o.'s reputation** Rufschädigung f
slurp F schlürfen
slush Schneematsch m; F Kitsch m
slush·y F kitschig
slut Schlampe f; Nutte f
sly gerissen, schlau, listig; **on the sly** heimlich
smack¹ 1. j-m e-n Klaps geben; **smack one's lips** sich (geräuschvoll) die Lippen lecken; **smack down** F et. hinklatschen; **2.** klatschendes Geräusch, Knall m; F Schmatz m (*kiss*); F Klaps m
smack²: **smack of** *fig* schmecken or riechen nach
small 1. *adj and adv* klein; **small wonder** (**that**) kein Wunder, dass; **feel small** *fig* sich klein (und hässlich) vorkommen; **2. small of the back** ANAT Kreuz n
small ad Kleinanzeige f

small arms Handfeuerwaffen *pl*

small change Kleingeld *n*

small hours: *in the small hours* in den frühen Morgenstunden

small-mind·ed engstirnig; kleinlich

small·pox MED Pocken *pl*

small print *das* Kleingedruckte

small talk Small Talk *m*, *n*, oberflächliche Konversation; *make small talk* plaudern

small-time F klein, unbedeutend; *in cpds* Schmalspur…

small town Kleinstadt *f*

smart 1. schick, fesch; smart, schlau, clever; **2.** wehtun; brennen; **3.** (brennender) Schmerz

smart al·eck F Besserwisser(in), Klugscheißer(in)

smart·ness Schick *m*; Schlauheit *f*, Cleverness *f*

smash 1. *v/t* zerschlagen (*a. smash up*); schmettern (*a. tennis etc*); *Aufstand etc* niederschlagen, *Drogenring etc* zerschlagen; *smash up one's car* s-n Wagen zu Schrott fahren; *v/i* zerspringen; *smash into* prallen an (*acc*) or gegen, krachen gegen; **2.** Schlag *m*; *tennis etc*: Schmetterball *m*; → *smash hit*, *smash-up*

smash hit Hit *m*

smash-up MOT, RAIL schwerer Unfall

smat·ter·ing: *have a smattering of English* ein paar Brocken Englisch können

smear 1. Fleck *m*; *fig* Abstrich *m*; Verleumdung *f*; **2.** (ein-, ver)schmieren; (sich) verwischen; verleumden

smell 1. *v/i* riechen (*at an dat*); duften; stinken; *v/t* riechen (*an dat*); **2.** Geruch *m*; Gestank *m*; Duft *m*

smell·y übel riechend, stinkend

smelt *Erz* schmelzen

smile 1. Lächeln *n*; **2.** lächeln; *smile at j-n* anlächeln, *j-m* zulächeln; *j-n, et.* belächeln, lächeln über (*acc*); *smile to o.s.* schmunzeln

smirk (selbstgefällig *or* schadenfroh) grinsen

smith Schmied *m*

smith·e·reens F in tausend Stücke schlagen *or* zerspringen

smith·y Schmiede *f*

smit·ten verliebt, F verknallt (*with in acc*); *be smitten by or with fig* gepackt werden von

smock Kittel *m*

smog Smog *m*

smoke 1. Rauch *m*; *have a smoke* eine rauchen; **2.** rauchen; räuchern

smok·er Raucher(in); RAIL Raucher *m*, Raucherabteil *n*

smoke·stack Schornstein *m*

smok·ing Rauchen *n*; *no smoking* Rauchen verboten

smoking com·part·ment RAIL Raucher *m*, Raucherabteil *n*

smok·y rauchig; verräuchert

smooch F schmusen

smooth 1. glatt (*a. fig*); ruhig (*a. journey etc*); mild (*wine*); *fig* (aal)glatt; **2.** *a.* *smooth out* glätten, glatt streichen; *smooth away* Falten etc glätten; Schwierigkeiten etc aus dem Weg räumen; *smooth down* glatt streichen

smoth·er ersticken

smo(u)l·der glimmen, schwelen

smudge 1. Schmutzfleck *m*; **2.** (be-, ver)schmieren; (sich) verwischen

smug selbstgefällig

smug·gle schmuggeln (*into* nach; in *acc*)

smug·gler Schmuggler(in)

smut Rußflocke *f*; Schmutz *m* (*a. fig*)

smut·ty *fig* schmutzig

snack Snack *m*, Imbiss *m*; *have a snack* e-e Kleinigkeit essen

snack bar Snackbar *f*, Imbissstube *f*

snag 1. *fig* Haken *m*; **2.** mit *et.* hängen bleiben (*on an dat*)

snail ZO Schnecke *f*

snake ZO Schlange *f*

snap 1. *v/i* (zer)brechen, (zer)reißen; *a. snap shut* zuschnappen; *snap at* schnappen nach; *j-n* anschnauzen; *snap out of it!* F Kopf hoch!, komm, komm!; *snap to it!* mach fix!; *v/t* zerbrechen; *snap one's fingers* mit den Fingern schnalzen; *snap one's fingers at fig* keinen Respekt haben vor (*dat*), sich hinwegsetzen über (*acc*); *snap off* abbrechen; *snap up et.* schnell entschlossen kaufen; *snap it up!* mach fix!; **2.** Krachen *n*, Knacken *n*, Knall *m*; PHOT F Schnappschuss *m*; Druckknopf *m*; F Schwung *m*; *cold snap* Kälteeinbruch *m*

snap fas·ten·er Druckknopf *m*

snap·pish *fig* bissig

snap·py F modisch, schick; *make it snappy!* F mach fix!

snap·shot PHOT Schnappschuss *m*

snare 1. Schlinge *f*, Falle *f* (*a. fig*); **2.** in der Schlinge fangen; F *et.* ergattern

snarl 1. knurren; *snarl at s.o.* j-n anknurren; **2.** Knurren *n*

snatch 1. *v/t et.* packen; *Gelegenheit* ergreifen; *ein paar Stunden Schlaf etc* ergattern; *snatch s.o.'s handbag* j-m die Handtasche entreißen; *v/i snatch at* (schnell) greifen nach; *Gelegenheit* ergreifen; **2.** *make a snatch at* (schnell) greifen nach; **snatch of conversation** Gesprächsfetzen m

sneak **1.** v/i (sich) schleichen; Br F petzen; v/t F stibitzen; **2.** Br F Petze f

sneak·er Turnschuh m

sneer **1.** höhnisch or spöttisch grinsen (**at** über acc); spotten (**at** über acc); **2.** höhnisches or spöttisches Grinsen; höhnische or spöttische Bemerkung

sneeze **1.** niesen; **2.** Niesen n

snick·er kichern (**at** über acc)

sniff **1.** v/i schniefen; schnüffeln (**at** an dat); sniff at fig die Nase rümpfen über (acc); v/t Klebstoff etc schnüffeln, Kokain etc schnupfen; **2.** Schnüffeln n

snif·fle **1.** schniefen; **2.** Schniefen n; **she's got the sniffles** F ihr läuft dauernd die Nase

snig·ger esp Br → **snicker**

snip **1.** Schnitt m; **2.** durchschnippeln; **snip off** abschnippeln

snipe[1] zo Schnepfe f

snipe[2] aus dem Hinterhalt schießen (**at** auf acc)

snip·er Heckenschütze m

sniv·el greinen, jammern

snob Snob m

snob·bish versnobt

snoop: **snoop about, snoop around** F herumschnüffeln

snoop·er F Schnüffler(in)

snooze F **1.** ein Nickerchen machen; **2.** Nickerchen n

snore **1.** schnarchen; **2.** Schnarchen n

snor·kel **1.** Schnorchel m; **2.** schnorcheln

snort **1.** schnauben; **2.** Schnauben n

snot·ty nose F Rotznase f

snout zo Schnauze f, Rüssel m

snow **1.** Schnee m (a. sl cocaine); **2.** schneien; **be snowed in** or **up** eingeschneit sein

snow·ball Schneeball m

snowball fight Schneeballschlacht f

snow·bound eingeschneit

snow-capped schneebedeckt

snow·drift Schneewehe f

snow·drop BOT Schneeglöckchen n

snow·fall Schneefall m

snow·flake Schneeflocke f

snow line Schneegrenze f

snow·man Schneemann m

snow·mo·bile Schneemobil n

snow·plough Br, snow·plow Schneepflug m

snow·storm Schneesturm m

snow-white schneeweiß

Snow White Schneewittchen n

snow·y schneereich; verschneit

snub j-n brüskieren, j-n vor den Kopf sto-

ßen

snub nose Stupsnase f

snuff[1] Schnupftabak m

snuff[2] Kerze ausdrücken, löschen; **snuff out** Leben auslöschen

snuf·fle schnüffeln, schniefen

snug gemütlich, behaglich; clothing: gut sitzend; eng (anliegend)

snug·gle: **snuggle up to s.o.** sich an j-n kuscheln; **snuggle down in bed** sich ins Bett kuscheln

so so; deshalb; → **hope 2, think; is that so?** wirklich?; **an hour or so** etwa e-e Stunde; **she is tired - so am I** sie ist müde - ich auch; **so far** bisher

soak v/t einweichen (**in** in dat); durchnässen; **soak up** aufsaugen; v/i sickern

soak·ing a. **soaking wet** völlig durchnässt, F klatschnass

soap **1.** Seife f; F → **soap opera; 2.** (sich) einseifen

soap op·e·ra radio, TV Seifenoper f

soap·y Seifen...; seifig; fig F schmeichlerisch

soar (hoch) aufsteigen; hochragen; zo, AVIAT segeln, gleiten; fig in die Höhe schnellen (prices etc)

sob **1.** schluchzen; **2.** Schluchzen n

so·ber **1.** nüchtern (a. fig); **2.** ernüchtern; **sober up** nüchtern machen or werden

so-called sogenannt

soc·cer Fußball m

soc·cer hoo·li·gan Fußballrowdy m

so·cia·ble gesellig

so·cial sozial, Sozial...; gesellschaftlich, Gesellschafts...; zo gesellig

social dem·o·crat POL Sozialdemokrat(in)

social insur·ance Sozialversicherung f

so·cial·ism Sozialismus m

so·cial·ist **1.** Sozialist(in); **2.** sozialistisch

so·cial·ize v/i gesellschaftlich verkehren (**with** mit); v/t sozialisieren

so·cial sci·ence Sozialwissenschaft f

social se·cu·ri·ty Br Sozialhilfe f; **be on social security** Sozialhilfe beziehen

social ser·vic·es esp Br Sozialeinrichtungen

social work Sozialarbeit f

social work·er Sozialarbeiter(in)

so·ci·e·ty Gesellschaft f; Verein m

so·ci·ol·o·gy Soziologie f

sock Socke f

sock·et ELECTR Steckdose f; Fassung f; (Anschluss)Buchse f; ANAT (Augen-)Höhle f

so·da Soda(wasser) n; (Orangen- etc)Limonade f

sod·den aufgeweicht (ground); durchweicht (clothes)

so·fa Sofa *n*

soft weich; sanft; leise; gedämpft (*light etc*); F leicht, angenehm, ruhig (*job etc*); alkoholfrei (*drink*); F verweichlicht

soft drink Soft Drink *m*, alkoholfreies Getränk

soft·en *v/t* weich machen; *Wasser* enthärten; *Ton, Licht, Stimme etc* dämpfen; **soften up** F *j-n* weich machen; *v/i* weich(er) oder sanft(er) or mild(er) werden

soft·heart·ed weichherzig

soft land·ing weiche Landung

soft·ware EDP Software *f*

software pack·age EDP Softwarepaket *n*

soft·y F Softie *m*, Weichling *m*

sog·gy aufgeweicht, matschig

soil[1] Boden *m*, Erde *f*

soil[2] beschmutzen, schmutzig machen

so·lar Sonnen…

solar en·er·gy Solar-, Sonnenenergie *f*

solar pan·el Sonnenkollektor *m*

solar sys·tem Sonnensystem *n*

sol·der TECH (ver)löten

sol·dier Soldat *m*

sole[1] 1. (Fuß-, Schuh)Sohle *f*; 2. besohlen

sole[2] ZO Seezunge *f*

sole[3] einzig; alleinig, Allein…

sole·ly (einzig und) allein, ausschließlich

sol·emn feierlich; ernst

so·lic·it bitten um

so·lic·i·tous besorgt (*about, for* um)

sol·id 1. fest; stabil; massiv; MATH körperlich; gewichtig, triftig (*reason etc*), stichhaltig (*argument etc*); solid(e), gründlich (*work etc*); einmütig, geschlossen; *a solid hour* F e-e geschlagene Stunde; **2.** MATH Körper *m*; *pl* feste Nahrung

so·li·dar·i·ty Solidarität *f*

so·lid·i·fy fest werden (lassen); *fig* (sich) festigen

sol·il·o·quy Selbstgespräch *n*, *esp* THEA Monolog *m*

sol·i·taire Solitär *m*; Patience *f*

sol·i·ta·ry einsam, (*Leben a.*) einzeln; (*Ort etc a.*) abgelegen; einzig

solitary con·fine·ment JUR Einzelhaft *f*

so·lo MUS Solo *n*; AVIAT Alleinflug *m*

so·lo·ist MUS Solist(in)

sol·u·ble CHEM löslich; *fig* lösbar

so·lu·tion CHEM Lösung *f*; *fig* (Auf)Lösung *f*

solve *Fall etc* lösen

sol·vent 1. ECON zahlungsfähig; **2.** CHEM Lösungsmittel *n*

som·ber, *Br* **som·bre** düster, trüb(e); *fig* trübsinnig

some (irgend)ein; *pl* einige, ein paar; manche; etwas, ein wenig, ein bisschen; ungefähr; *some 20 miles* etwa 20 Meilen; *some more cake* noch ein Stück Kuchen; *to some extent* bis zu e-m gewissen Grade

some·bod·y jemand

some·day eines Tages

some·how irgendwie

some·one jemand

some·place irgendwo, irgendwohin

som·er·sault 1. Salto *m*; Purzelbaum *m*; *turn a somersault* → **2.** e-n Salto machen; e-n Purzelbaum schlagen

some·thing etwas; *something like* ungefähr

some·time irgendwann

some·times manchmal

some·what ein bisschen, ein wenig

some·where irgendwo(hin)

son Sohn *m*; *son of a bitch* V Scheißkerl *m*

so·na·ta MUS Sonate *f*

song MUS Lied *n*; Gesang *m*; *for a song* F für ein Butterbrot

song·bird ZO Singvogel *m*

son·ic Schall…

sonic bang *Br*, **sonic boom** Überschallknall *m*

son·in·law Schwiegersohn *m*

son·net Sonett *n*

so·no·rous sonor, volltönend

soon bald; *as soon as* sobald; *as soon as possible* so bald wie möglich

soon·er eher, früher; *sooner or later* früher oder später; *the sooner the better* je eher, desto besser; *no sooner … than* kaum … als; *no sooner said than done* gesagt, getan

soot Ruß *m*

soothe beruhigen, beschwichtigen (*a. soothe down*); *Schmerzen* lindern, mildern

sooth·ing beruhigend; lindernd

soot·y rußig

sop[1] Beschwichtigungsmittel *n* (*to* für)

sop[2]: *sop up* aufsaugen

so·phis·ti·cat·ed anspruchsvoll, kultiviert; intellektuell; TECH raffiniert, hoch entwickelt

soph·o·more Student(in) im zweiten Jahr

sop·o·rif·ic einschläfernd

sop·ping *a.* *sopping wet* F klatschnass

sor·cer·er Zauberer *m*, Hexenmeister *m*, Hexer *m*

sor·cer·ess Zauberin *f*, Hexe *f*

sor·cer·y Zauberei *f*, Hexerei *f*

sor·did schmutzig; schäbig

sore 1. weh, wund (*a. fig*); entzündet; F *fig* sauer; *I'm sore all over* mir tut alles weh; *sore throat* Halsentzündung *f*; *have a sore throat a.* Halsschmerzen haben;

2. wunde Stelle, Wunde *f*

sor·rel¹ BOT Sauerampfer *m*

sor·rel² **1.** ZO Fuchs *m* (*horse*); **2.** rotbraun

sor·row Kummer *m*, Leid *n*, Schmerz *m*, Trauer *f*

sor·row·ful traurig, betrübt

sor·ry **1.** *adj* traurig, jämmerlich; ***be or feel sorry for s.o.*** j-n bedauern *or* bemitleiden; ***I'm sorry for her*** sie tut mir leid; ***I am sorry to say*** ich muss leider sagen; ***I'm sorry → 2.*** *int* (es) tut mir leid!; Entschuldigung!, Verzeihung!; ***sorry?*** *esp Br* wie bitte?

sort **1.** Sorte *f*, Art *f*; ***sort of*** F irgendwie; ***of a sort, of sorts*** F so etwas Ähnliches wie; ***all sorts of things*** alles Mögliche; ***nothing of the sort*** nichts dergleichen; ***what sort of (a) man is he?*** wie ist er?; ***be out of sorts*** F nicht auf der Höhe *or* auf dem Damm sein; ***be completely out of sorts*** SPORT F völlig außer Form sein; **2.** sortieren; ***sort out*** aussortieren; *Problem etc* lösen, *Frage etc* klären

SOS SOS *n*; ***send an SOS*** ein SOS funken; ***SOS call or message*** SOS-Ruf *m*

soul Seele *f* (*a. fig*); MUS Soul *m*

sound¹ **1.** Geräusch *n*; Laut *m*; PHYS Schall *m*; *radio*, TV Ton *m*; MUS Klang *m*, Sound *m*; **2.** *v/i* (er)klingen, (er)tönen; sich *gut etc* anhören; *v/t* LING (aus)sprechen; MAR (aus)loten; MED abhorchen; ***sound one's horn*** MOT hupen

sound² gesund; intakt, in Ordnung; solid(e), stabil, sicher; klug, vernünftig (*person, advice etc*); gründlich (*training etc*); gehörig (*beating*); vernichtend (*defeat*); fest, tief (*sleep*)

sound bar·ri·er Schallgrenze *f*, Schallmauer *f*

sound film Tonfilm *m*

sound·less lautlos

sound·proof schalldicht

sound·track Filmmusik *f*; Tonspur *f*

sound wave Schallwelle *f*

soup **1.** Suppe *f*; **2.** ***soup up*** F Motor frisieren

sour **1.** sauer; *fig* mürrisch; **2.** sauer werden (lassen); *fig* trüben, verbittern

source Quelle *f*, *fig a.* Ursache *f*, Ursprung *m*

south **1.** Süd, Süden *m*; **2.** *adj* südlich, Süd...; **3.** *adv* nach Süden, südwärts

south·east **1.** Südost, Südosten *m*; **2.** *a.* **south·east·ern** südöstlich

south·er·ly, **south·ern** südlich, Süd...

south·ern·most südlichste(r, -s)

South Pole Südpol *m*

south·ward(s) südlich, nach Süden

south·west **1.** Südwest, Südwesten *m*; **2.**

a. **south·west·ern** südwestlich

sou·ve·nir Souvenir *n*, Andenken *n* (*of* an *acc*)

sove·reign **1.** Monarch(in), Landesherr(in); **2.** POL souverän

sove·reign·ty Souveränität *f*

So·vi·et HIST POL sowjetisch, Sowjet...

sow¹ (aus)säen

sow² ZO Sau *f*

soy bean BOT Sojabohne *f*

spa (Heil)Bad *n*

space **1.** Raum *m*, Platz *m*; (Welt-) Raum *m*; Zwischenraum *m*; Zeitraum *m*; **2.** *a.* ***space out*** in Abständen anordnen; PRINT sperren

space age Weltraumzeitalter *n*

space bar TECH Leertaste *f*

space cap·sule Raumkapsel *f*

space·craft (Welt)Raumfahrzeug *n*

space flight (Welt)Raumflug *m*

space·lab Raumlabor *n*

space·man F Raumfahrer *m*; Außerirdische *m*

space probe (Welt)Raumsonde *f*

space re·search (Welt)Raumforschung *f*

space·ship Raumschiff *n*

space shut·tle Raumfähre *f*, Raumtransporter *m*

space sta·tion (Welt)Raumstation *f*

space·suit Raumanzug *m*

space walk Weltraumspaziergang *m*

space·wom·an F (Welt)Raumfahrerin *f*; Außerirdische *f*

spa·cious geräumig

spade Spaten *m*; *card game*: Pik *n*, Grün *n*; ***king of spades*** Pikkönig *m*; ***call a spade a spade*** das Kind beim (rechten) Namen nennen

Spain Spanien *n*

span **1.** Spanne *f*; Spannweite *f*; **2.** *Fluss etc* überspannen; *fig* sich erstrecken über (*acc*)

span·gle **1.** Flitter *m*, Paillette *f*; **2.** mit Flitter *or* Pailletten besetzen; *fig* übersäen (*with* mit)

Span·iard Spanier(in)

span·iel ZO Spaniel *m*

Span·ish **1.** spanisch; **2.** LING Spanisch *n*; ***the Spanish*** die Spanier *pl*

spank *j-m* den Hintern versohlen

spank·ing Tracht *f* Prügel

span·ner *esp Br* Schraubenschlüssel *m*; ***put or throw a spanner in the works*** F j-m in die Quere kommen

spar *boxing*: sparren (*with* mit); *fig* sich ein Wortgefecht liefern (*with* mit)

spare **1.** *j-n*, *et.* entbehren; *Geld, Zeit etc*

übrig haben; *keine Kosten, Mühen etc scheuen*; **spare s.o. s.th.** j-m et. ersparen; **2.** Ersatz…, Reserve…; überschüssig; **3.** MOT Ersatz-, Reservereifen *m*; *esp Br* → **spare part** TECH Ersatzteil *n, m*

spare room Gästezimmer *n*

spare time Freizeit *f*

spar·ing sparsam; *use sparingly* sparsam umgehen mit

spark 1. Funke(n) *m* (*a. fig*); **2.** Funken sprühen

spark·ing plug *Br* → **spark plug**

spar·kle 1. funkeln, blitzen (*with* vor *dat*); perlen (*drink*); **2.** Funkeln *n*, Blitzen *n*

spar·kling funkelnd, blitzend; (geist)sprühend, spritzig; *sparkling wine* Sekt *m*, Schaumwein *m*

spark plug MOT Zündkerze *f*

spar·row ZO Spatz *m*, Sperling *m*

spar·row·hawk ZO Sperber *m*

sparse spärlich, dünn

spasm MED Krampf *m*; Anfall *m*

spas·mod·ic MED krampfartig; *fig* sporadisch, unregelmäßig

spas·tic MED **1.** spastisch; **2.** Spastiker(in)

spa·tial räumlich

spat·ter (be)spritzen

spawn 1. ZO laichen; *fig* hervorbringen; **2.** ZO Laich *m*

speak *v/i* sprechen, reden (*to, with* mit; *about* über *acc*); sprechen (*to* vor *dat*; *about, on* über *acc*); *so to speak* sozusagen; *speaking!* TEL am Apparat!; *speak up* lauter sprechen; *v/t* sprechen, sagen; *Sprache* sprechen

speak·er Sprecher(in), Redner(in)

spear 1. Speer *m*; **2.** aufspießen; durchbohren

spear·head Speerspitze *f*; MIL Angriffsspitze *f*; SPORT (Sturm-, Angriffs)Spitze *f*

spear·mint BOT Grüne Minze

spe·cial 1. besondere(r, -s); speziell; Sonder…; Spezial…; **2.** Sonderbus *m*, Sonderzug *m*; *radio*, TV Sondersendung *f*; ECON F Sonderangebot *n*; *be on special* ECON im Angebot sein

spe·cial·ist Spezialist(in), MED *a*. Facharzt *m*, Fachärztin *f* (*in* für)

spe·ci·al·i·ty *Br* → **specialty**

spe·cial·ize sich spezialisieren (*in* auf *acc*)

spe·cial·ty Spezialgebiet *n*; GASTR Spezialität *f*

spe·cies Art *f*, Spezies *f*

spe·cif·ic konkret, präzis; spezifisch, speziell, besondere(r, -s); eigen (*to* dat)

spe·ci·fy genau beschreiben *or* angeben *or* festlegen

spe·ci·men Exemplar *n*; Probe *f*, Muster *n*

speck kleiner Fleck, (*Staub*)Korn *n*; Punkt *m* (*on the horizon* am Horizont)

speck·led gefleckt, gesprenkelt

spec·ta·cle Schauspiel *n*; Anblick *m*; (*a pair of*) *spectacles* (e-e) Brille

spec·tac·u·lar 1. spektakulär; **2.** große (*Fernseh- etc*)Show

spec·ta·tor Zuschauer(in)

spec·ter (*fig a. Schreck*)Gespenst *n*

spec·tral geisterhaft, gespenstisch

spec·tre *Br* → **specter**

spec·u·late spekulieren, Vermutungen anstellen (*about, on* über *acc*); ECON spekulieren (*in* mit)

spec·u·la·tion Spekulation *f* (*a*. ECON), Vermutung *f*

spec·u·la·tive spekulativ, ECON *a*. Spekulations…

spec·u·la·tor ECON Spekulant(in)

speech Sprache *f*; Rede *f*, Ansprache *f*; *make a speech* e-e Rede halten

speech day *Br* (Jahres)Schlussfeier *f*

speech·less sprachlos (*with* vor *dat*)

speed 1. Geschwindigkeit *f*, Tempo *n*, Schnelligkeit *f*; TECH Drehzahl *f*; PHOT Lichtempfindlichkeit *f*; *sl* Speed *n*; MOT *etc* Gang *m*; *five-speed gearbox* Fünfganggetriebe *n*; *at a speed of* mit e-r Geschwindigkeit von; *at full or top speed* mit Höchstgeschwindigkeit; **2.** *v/i* rasen; *be speeding* MOT zu schnell fahren; *speed up* beschleunigen, schneller werden; *v/t* rasch bringen *or* befördern; *speed up et.* beschleunigen

speed·boat Rennboot *n*

speed·ing MOT zu schnelles Fahren, Geschwindigkeitsüberschreitung *f*

speed lim·it MOT Geschwindigkeitsbegrenzung *f*, Tempolimit *n*

speed·om·e·ter MOT Tachometer *m, n*

speed trap MOT Radarfalle *f*

speed·y schnell, (*reply etc a*.) prompt

spell¹ *a. spell out* buchstabieren; (*orthographisch* richtig) schreiben

spell² Weile *f*; (*Husten- etc*)Anfall *m*; *for a spell* e-e Zeit lang; *a spell of fine weather* e-e Schönwetterperiode; *hot spell* Hitzewelle *f*

spell³ Zauber *m* (*a. fig*)

spell·bound wie gebannt

spell·er EDP Speller *m*, Rechtschreibsystem *n*; *be a good (bad) speller* in Rechtschreibung gut (schlecht) sein

spell·ing Buchstabieren *n*; Rechtschreibung *f*; Schreibung *f*, Schreibweise *f*

spelling mis·take (Recht)Schreibfehler *m*

spend *Geld* ausgeben (*on* für); *Urlaub, Zeit* verbringen

607 **sponge**

spend·ing Ausgaben *pl*
spend·thrift Verschwender(in)
spent verbraucht
sperm BIOL Sperma *n*, Samen *m*
sphere Kugel *f*; *fig* (*Einfluss- etc*)Sphäre *f*, (*Einfluss- etc*)Bereich *m*, Gebiet *n*
spher·i·cal kugelförmig
spice 1. Gewürz *n*; *fig* Würze *f*; **2.** würzen
spick-and-span blitzsauber
spic·y gut gewürzt, würzig; *fig* pikant
spi·der ZO Spinne *f*
spike 1. Spitze *f*; Dorn *m*; Stachel *m*; SPORT Spike *m*, Dorn *m*; *pl* Spikes *pl*, Rennschuhe *pl*; **2.** aufspießen
spill 1. *v/t* ausschütten, verschütten; *spill the beans* F alles ausplaudern, singen; → *milk I*; *v/i* sich strömen (*out of* aus); *spill over* überlaufen; *fig* übergreifen (*into* auf *acc*); **2.** F Sturz *m*
spin 1. *v/t* drehen; *Wäsche* schleudern; *Münze* hochwerfen; *Fäden, Wolle etc* spinnen; *spin out Arbeit etc* in die Länge ziehen; *Geld etc* strecken; *v/i* sich drehen; spinnen; *my head was spinning* mir drehte sich alles; *spin along* MOT dahinrasen; *spin round* herumwirbeln; **2.** (schnelle) Drehung; SPORT Effet *m*; TECH Schleudern *n*; AVIAT Trudeln *n*; *be in a (flat) spin esp Br* F am Rotieren sein; *go for a spin* MOT F e-e Spritztour machen
spin·ach BOT Spinat *m*
spin·al ANAT Rückgrat...
spinal col·umn ANAT Wirbelsäule *f*, Rückgrat *n*
spinal cord, spinal mar·row ANAT Rückenmark *n*
spin·dle Spindel *f*
spin-dri·er (*Wäsche*)Schleuder *f*
spin-dry *Wäsche* schleudern
spin-dry·er → *spin-drier*
spine ANAT Wirbelsäule *f*, Rückgrat *n*; ZO Stachel *m*, BOT *a.* Dorn *m*; (*Buch-*)Rücken *m*
spin·ning mill TECH Spinnerei *f*
spinning top Kreisel *m*
spinning wheel Spinnrad *n*
spin·ster ältere unverheiratete Frau, *contr* alte Jungfer, spätes Mädchen
spin·y ZO stach(e)lig, BOT *a.* dornig
spi·ral 1. spiralförmig, Spiral...; **2.** (*a.* ECON *Preis- etc*)Spirale *f*
spi·ral stair·case Wendeltreppe *f*
spire (*Kirch*)Turmspitze *f*
spir·it Geist *m*; Stimmung *f*, Einstellung *f*; Schwung *m*; Elan *m*; CHEM Spiritus *m*; *mst pl* Spirituosen *pl*
spir·it·ed energisch; erregt (*debate etc*)
spir·it·less temperamentlos; mutlos

spir·its Laune *f*, Stimmung *f*; *be in high spirits* in Hochstimmung sein; ausgelassen *or* übermütig sein; *be in low spirits* niedergeschlagen sein
spir·i·tu·al 1. geistig; geistlich; **2.** MUS Spiritual *n*
spit¹ 1. spucken; knistern (*fire*), brutzeln (*meat etc*); *a.* spit out ausspucken; *spit at s.o.* j-n anspucken; *it is spitting* (*with rain*) es tröpfelt; **2.** Spucke *f*
spit² (*Brat*)Spieß *m*; GEOGR Landzunge *f*
spite 1. Bosheit *f*, Gehässigkeit *f*; *out of* or *from pure spite* aus reiner Bosheit; *in spite of* trotz (*gen*); **2.** j-n ärgern
spite·ful boshaft, gehässig
spit·ting im·age Ebenbild *n*; *she is the spitting image of her mother* sie ist ihrer Mutter wie aus dem Gesicht geschnitten
spit·tle Speichel *m*, Spucke *f*
splash 1. (be)spritzen; klatschen; plan(t)schen; platschen; *splash down* wassern; **2.** Klatschen *n*, Platschen *n*; Spritzer *m*; Spritzfleck *m*; *esp Br* GASTR Spritzer *m*, Schuss *m*
splash·down Wasserung *f*
splay *a.* splay out *Finger, Zehen* spreizen
spleen ANAT Milz *f*
splen·did großartig, herrlich, prächtig
splen·do(u)r Pracht *f*
splice miteinander verbinden, *Film etc* (zusammen)kleben
splint MED Schiene *f*; *put in a splint, put in splints* schienen
splin·ter 1. Splitter *m*; **2.** (zer)splittern; *splinter off* absplittern; *fig* sich abspalten (*from* von)
split 1. *v/t* (zer)spalten; zerreißen; *a.* split up aufteilen (*between* unter *acc*; *into* in *acc*); sich *et.* teilen; *split hairs* Haarspalterei treiben; *split one's sides* F sich vor Lachen biegen; *v/i* sich spalten; zerreißen; sich teilen (*into* in *acc*); *a.* split up (*with*) Schluss machen (mit), sich trennen (von); **2.** Riss *m*; Spalt *m*; Aufteilung *f*; *fig* Bruch *m*; *fig* Spaltung *f*
split·ting heftig, rasend (*headache etc*)
splut·ter stottern (*a.* MOT); zischen
spoil 1. *v/t* verderben; ruinieren; j-n verwöhnen, *Kind a.* verziehen; *v/i* verderben, schlecht werden; **2.** *mst pl* Beute *f*
spoil·er MOT Spoiler *m*
spoil·sport F Spielverderber(in)
spoke TECH Speiche *f*
spokes·man Sprecher *m*
spokes·wom·an Sprecherin *f*
sponge 1. Schwamm *m*; Schnorrer(in); *Br* → *sponge cake*; **2.** *v/t a.* sponge down (mit e-m Schwamm) abwaschen;

sponge off weg-, abwischen; **sponge (up)** aufsaugen, aufwischen (**from** von); *et.* schnorren (**from, off, on** von, bei); *v/i* schnorren (**from, off, on** bei)

sponge cake Biskuitkuchen *m*

spong·er Schnorrer(in)

spong·y schwammig; weich

spon·sor 1. Bürge *m*, Bürgin *f*; Sponsor(in), Geldgeber(in); Spender(in); **2.** bürgen für; sponsern

spon·ta·ne·ous spontan

spook F Geist *m*

spook·y F gespenstisch, unheimlich

spool Spule *f*; **spool of thread** Garnrolle *f*

spoon 1. Löffel *m*; **2.** löffeln

spoon-feed *Kind etc* füttern

spoon·ful *(ein)* Löffel (voll)

spo·rad·ic sporadisch, gelegentlich

spore BOT Spore *f*

sport 1. Sport *m*; Sportart *f*; F feiner Kerl; *pl* Sport *m*; **2.** herumlaufen mit; protzen mit

sports Sport...

sports car MOT Sportwagen *m*

sports cen·ter (*Br* **cen·tre**) Sportzentrum *n*

sports·man Sportler *m*

sports·wear Sportkleidung *f*

sports·wom·an Sportlerin *f*

spot 1. Punkt *m*, Tupfen *m*; Fleck *m*; MED Pickel *m*; Ort *m*, Platz *m*, Stelle *f*; *radio*, TV (Werbe)Spot *m*; F Spot *m*; **a spot of** *Br* F ein bisschen; **on the spot** auf der Stelle, sofort; zur Stelle; an Ort und Stelle, vor Ort; auf der Stelle; **be in a spot** F in Schwulitäten sein; **soft spot** *fig* Schwäche *f* (**for** für); **tender spot** empfindliche Stelle; **weak spot** schwacher Punkt; Schwäche *f*; **2.** entdecken, sehen

spot check Stichprobe *f*

spot·less tadellos sauber; *fig* untad(e)lig

spot·light Spotlight *n*, Scheinwerfer *m*; Scheinwerferlicht *n*

spot·ted getüpfelt; fleckig

spot·ter Beobachter *m*

spot·ty pick(e)lig

spouse Gatte *m*, Gattin *f*, Gemahl(in)

spout 1. *v/t Wasser etc* (heraus)spritzen; *v/i* spritzen (**from** aus); **2.** Schnauze *f*, Tülle *f*; (*Wasser- etc*)Strahl *m*

sprain MED sich *et.* verstauchen; **2.** Verstauchung *f*

sprat ZO Sprotte *f*

sprawl ausgestreckt liegen *or* sitzen (*a.* **sprawl out**); sich ausbreiten

spray 1. (be)sprühen; spritzen; sich *die Haare* sprayen; *Parfüm etc* versprühen, zerstäuben; **2.** Sprühnebel *m*; Gischt

m, f; Spray *m, n*; → **sprayer**

spray can → **spray·er** Sprüh-, Spraydose *f*, Zerstäuber *m*

spread 1. *v/t* ausbreiten, *Arme a.* ausstrecken, *Finger etc* spreizen (*all a.* **spread out**); *Furcht, Krankheit, Nachricht etc* verbreiten, *Gerücht a.* ausstreuen; *Butter etc* streichen (**on** auf *acc*); *Brot etc* (be)streichen (**with** mit); *v/i* sich ausbreiten (*a.* **spread out**); sich erstrecken (**over** über *acc*); sich verbreiten, übergreifen (**to** auf *acc*); sich streichen lassen (*butter etc*); **2.** Ausbreitung *f*, Verbreitung *f*; Ausdehnung *f*; Spannweite *f*; GASTR Aufstrich *m*

spread·sheet EDP Tabellenkalkulation *f*, Tabellenkalkulationsprogramm *n*

spree: **go (out) on a spree** F e-e Sauftour machen; **go on a buying** (*or* **shopping, spending**) **spree** wie verrückt einkaufen

sprig BOT kleiner Zweig

spright·ly lebhaft; rüstig

spring 1. *v/i* springen; **spring from** herrühren von; **spring up** aufkommen (*wind*); aus dem Boden schießen (*building etc*); *v/t*: **spring a leak** ein Leck bekommen; **spring a surprise on s.o.** j-n überraschen; **2.** Frühling *m*, Frühjahr *n*; Quelle *f*; TECH Feder *f*; Elastizität *f*; Federung *f*; Sprung *m*, Satz *m*; **in (the) spring** im Frühling

spring·board Sprungbrett *n*

spring-clean gründlich putzen, Frühjahrsputz machen (in *dat*)

spring tide Springflut *f*

spring·time Frühling *m*, Frühlingszeit *f*, Frühjahr *n*

spring·y elastisch, federnd

sprin·kle 1. *Wasser etc* sprengen (**on** auf *acc*); *Salz etc* streuen (**on** auf *acc*); *et.* (be)sprengen *or* bestreuen (**with** mit); **it is sprinkling** es tröpfelt; **2.** Sprühregen *m*

sprin·kler (*Rasen*)Sprenger *m*; Sprinkler *m*, Beriese·lungsanlage *f*

sprin·kling: **a sprinkling of** ein bisschen, ein paar

sprint SPORT **1.** sprinten; spurten; **2.** Sprint *m*; Spurt *m*

sprint·er SPORT Sprinter(in)

sprite Kobold *m*

sprout BOT **1.** sprießen (*a. fig*), keimen; wachsen lassen; **2.** Spross *m*; (*Brussels*) **sprouts** Rosenkohl *m*

spruce¹ BOT Fichte *f*; Rottanne *f*

spruce² adrett

spry rüstig, lebhaft

spur 1. Sporn *m* (*a.* ZO); *fig* Ansporn *m* (**to**

zu); **on the spur of the moment** spontan; **2.** *e-m Pferd* die Sporen geben; *often* **spur on** *fig* anspornen (**to** zu)

spurt¹ 1. spurten, sprinten; **2.** plötzliche Aktivität, *(Arbeits)*Anfall *m*; Spurt *m*, Sprint *m*

spurt² 1. spritzen (*from* aus); **2.** *(Wasser-etc)*Strahl *m*

sput·ter stottern (*a.* MOT); zischen

spy 1. Spion(in); **2.** spionieren, Spionage treiben (**for** für); **spy into** *fig* herumspionieren in (*dat*); **spy on** *j-m* nachspionieren

spy·hole (Tür)Spion *m*

squab·ble (sich) streiten (**about, over** um, wegen)

squad Mannschaft *f*, Trupp *m*; *(Überfall-etc)*Kommando *n*; Dezernat *n*

squad car (Funk)Streifenwagen *m*

squad·ron MIL, AVIAT Staffel *f*; MAR Geschwader *n*

squal·id schmutzig, verwahrlost, verkommen, armselig

squall Bö *f*

squan·der Geld, Zeit etc verschwenden, Chance vertun

square 1. Quadrat *n*; Viereck *n*; *öffentlicher Platz*; MATH Quadrat(zahl *f*) *n*; *board game*: Feld *n*; TECH Winkel(maß *n*) *m*; **2.** quadratisch, Quadrat...; viereckig; rechtwink(e)lig; eckig (*shoulders etc*); *fig* fair, gerecht; **be (all) square** quitt sein; **3.** quadratisch *or* rechtwink(e)lig machen (*a.* **square off** *or* **up**); in Quadrate einteilen (*a.* **square off**); MATH *Zahl* ins Quadrat erheben; *Schultern* straffen; *Konto* ausgleichen; *Schulden* begleichen; *fig* in Einklang bringen *or* stehen (**with** mit); **square up** F abrechnen; **square up to** sich *j-m*, *e-m* Problem *etc* stellen

square root MATH Quadratwurzel *f*

squash¹ 1. zerdrücken, zerquetschen; quetschen, zwängen (**into** in *acc*); **squash flat** flach drücken, F platt walzen; **2.** Gedränge *n*; SPORT Squash *n*

squash² BOT Kürbis *m*

squat 1. hocken, kauern; *leer stehendes Haus* besetzen; **squat down** sich (hin)kauern *or* (hin)hocken; **2.** gedrungen, untersetzt

squat·ter Hausbesetzer(in)

squaw Squaw *f*

squawk kreischen, schreien; F lautstark protestieren (**about** gegen)

squeak 1. piep(s)en (*mouse etc*); quietschen (*door etc*); **2.** Piep(s)en *n*; Piep(s) *m*; Quietschen *n*

squeak·y piepsig (*voice*); quietschend

(*door etc*)

squeal 1. kreischen (**with** vor *dat*); **squeal on s.o.** *fig* F *j-n* verpfeifen; **2.** Kreischen *n*; Schrei *m*

squeam·ish empfindlich, zart besaitet

squeeze 1. drücken; auspressen, ausquetschen; (sich) quetschen *or* zwängen (**into** in *acc*); **2.** Druck *m*; GASTR Spritzer *m*; Gedränge *n*

squeez·er (Frucht)Presse *f*

squid ZO Tintenfisch *m*

squint schielen; blinzeln

squirm sich winden

squir·rel ZO Eichhörnchen *n*

squirt 1. (be)spritzen; **2.** Strahl *m*

stab 1. *v/t* niederstechen; **be stabbed in the arm** e-n Stich in den Arm bekommen; *v/i* stechen (**at** nach); **2.** Stich *m*

sta·bil·i·ty Stabilität *f*; *fig* Dauerhaftigkeit *f*; Ausgeglichenheit *f*

sta·bil·ize (sich) stabilisieren

sta·ble¹ stabil; *fig* dauerhaft; ausgeglichen

sta·ble² Stall *m*

stack 1. Stapel *m*, Stoß *m*; **stacks of, a stack of** F jede Menge Arbeit etc; **2.** stapeln; voll stapeln (**with** mit); **stack up** aufstapeln

sta·di·um Stadion *n*

staff 1. Stab *m*; Mitarbeiter(stab *m*) *pl*; Personal *n*, Belegschaft *f*; Lehrkörper *m*; MIL Stab *m*; **2.** besetzen (**with** mit)

staff room Lehrerzimmer *n*

stag ZO Hirsch *m*

stage 1. THEA Bühne *f* (*a.* fig); Etappe *f* (*a.* fig), (Reise)Abschnitt *m*; Teilstrecke *f*, Fahrzone *f* (*bus etc*); *fig* Stufe *f*, Stadium *n*, Phase *f*; **2.** THEA inszenieren; veranstalten

stage·coach Postkutsche *f*

stage di·rec·tion THEA Regieanweisung *f*

stage fright Lampenfieber *n*

stage man·ag·er THEA Inspizient *m*

stag·ger 1. *v/i* (sch)wanken, taumeln, torkeln; *v/t* *j-n* sprachlos machen, F umhauen; *Arbeitszeit etc* staffeln; **2.** Wanken *n*, Schwanken *n*, Taumeln *n*

stag·nant stehend (*water*); *esp* ECON stagnierend

stag·nate *esp* ECON stagnieren

stain 1. *v/t* beflecken; (ein)färben; *Holz* beizen; *Glas* bemalen; *v/i* Flecken bekommen, schmutzen; **2.** Fleck *m*; TECH Färbemittel *n*; (Holz)Beize *f*; Makel *m*

stained glass Bunt-, Farbglas *n*

stain·less nicht rostend, rostfrei

stair (Treppen)Stufe *f*; *pl* Treppe *f*

stair·case, stair·way Treppe *f*; Treppenhaus *n*

stake¹ **1.** Pfahl *m*, Pfosten *m*; HIST Marterpfahl *m*; **2. stake off, stake out** abstecken

stake² **1.** Anteil *m*, Beteiligung *f* (**in** an *dat*) (*a.* ECON); (Wett- *etc*)Einsatz *m*; **be at stake** *fig* auf dem Spiel stehen; **2.** Geld *etc* setzen (**on** auf *acc*); Ruf *etc* riskieren, aufs Spiel setzen

stale alt(backen); abgestanden, *beer etc*: *a.* schal, *air etc*: *a.* verbraucht

stalk¹ BOT Stängel *m*, Stiel *m*, Halm *m*

stalk² *v/t* sich heranpirschen an (*acc*); verfolgen, hinter *j-m, etc.* herschleichen; *v/i* stolzieren

stall¹ **1.** (*Obst- etc*)Stand *m*, (Markt-)Bude *f*; AGR Box *f*; *pl* REL Chorgestühl *n*; *Br* THEA Parkett *n*. **2.** *v/t* Motor abwürgen; *v/i* MOT absterben

stall² *v/t* Ausflüchte machen; *Zeit* schinden; *v/t j-n* hinhalten; *et.* hinauszögern

stal·li·on ZO (Zucht)Hengst *m*

stal·wart kräftig, robust; *esp* POL treu

stam·i·na Ausdauer *f*; Durchhaltevermögen *n*, Kondition *f*

stam·mer **1.** stottern, stammeln; **2.** Stottern *n*, Stammeln *n*

stamp **1.** *v/i* sta(m)pfen, trampeln; *v/t* Pass *etc* (ab)stempeln; Datum *etc* aufstempeln (**on** auf *acc*); Brief *etc* frankieren; *fig j-n* abstempeln (**as** als, zu); **stamp one's foot** aufstampfen; **stamp out** Feuer austreten; TECH ausstanzen; **2.** (Brief-)Marke *f*; (Steuer-)Marke *f*; Stempel *m*; **stamped addressed envelope** Freiumschlag *m*

stam·pede **1.** ZO wilde Flucht; wilder Ansturm, Massenansturm *m* (**for** auf *acc*); **2.** *v/i* ZO durchgehen; *v/t* in Panik versetzen

stanch treu, zuverlässig

stand **1.** *v/i* stehen; aufstehen; *fig* fest- *etc* bleiben; **stand still** still stehen; *v/t* stellen (**on** auf *acc*); aushalten, ertragen; *e-r* Prüfung *etc* standhalten; Probe bestehen; Chance haben; Drink *etc* spendieren; **I can't stand him** (or **it**) ich kann ihn (or das) nicht ausstehen or leiden; **stand around** herumstehen; **stand back** zurücktreten; **stand by** danebenstehen; *fig* zu *j-m* halten; zu *et.* stehen; **stand idly by** tatenlos zusehen; **stand down** verzichten; zurücktreten; JUR den Zeugenstand verlassen; **stand for** stehen für, bedeuten; *sich et.* gefallen lassen, *et.* dulden; *esp Br* kandidieren für; **stand in** einspringen (**for** für); **stand in for s.o.** *a.* j-n vertreten; **stand on** *fig* be)stehen auf (*dat*); **stand out** hervorstechen; sich abheben (**against** gegen, von); **stand over** überwachen, aufpassen auf (*acc*);

stand together zusammenhalten, -stehen; **stand up** aufstehen, sich erheben; **stand up for** eintreten or sich einsetzen für; **stand up to** *j-m* mutig gegenübertreten, *j-m* die Stirn bieten; **2.** (Obst-, Messe- *etc*)Stand *m*; (Schirm-, Noten- *etc*) Ständer *m*; SPORT *etc* Tribüne *f*; (Taxi-) Stand(platz) *m*; JUR Zeugenstand *m*; **take a stand** *fig* Position beziehen (**on** zu)

stan·dard¹ **1.** Norm *f*, Maßstab *m*; Standard *m*, Niveau *n*; **standard of living, living standard** Lebensstandard *m*; **2.** normal, Normal…; durchschnittlich, Durchschnitts…; Standard…

stan·dard² Standarte *f*, MOT Stander *m*; HIST Banner *n*

stan·dard·ize vereinheitlichen, *esp* TECH standardisieren, normen

stan·dard lamp *Br* Stehlampe *f*

stand·by **1.** Reserve *f*; AVIAT Stand-by *n*; **be on standby** in Bereitschaft stehen; **2.** Reserve…, Not…; AVIAT Stand-by…

stand-in *film*, TV Double *n*; Ersatzmann *m*; Vertreter(in)

stand·ing **1.** stehend; *fig* ständig; → **ovation**; **2.** Rang *m*, Stellung *f*; Ansehen *n*, Ruf *m*; Dauer *f*; **of long standing** alt, seit langem bestehend

standing or·der ECON Dauerauftrag *m*

standing room: **standing room only** nur noch Stehplätze

stand-off·ish *F* (sehr) ablehnend, hochnäsig

stand·point *fig* Standpunkt *m*

stand·still Stillstand *m*; **be at a standstill** stehen (*car etc*); ruhen (*production etc*); **bring to a standstill** Auto *etc* zum Stehen bringen; Produktion *etc* zum Erliegen bringen

stand-up Steh…; **stand-up fight** Schlägerei *f*

stan·za Strophe *f*

sta·ple¹ **1.** Hauptnahrungsmittel *n*; ECON Haupterzeugnis *n*; **2.** Haupt…; üblich

sta·ple² **1.** Heftklammer *f*; Krampe *f*; **2.** heften

sta·pler TECH (Draht)Hefter *m*

star **1.** ASTR Stern *m*; PRINT Sternchen *n*; THEA, SPORT *etc* Star *m*. **2.** *v/t* PRINT mit e-m Sternchen kennzeichnen; **starring …** in der Hauptrolle or in den Hauptrollen …; **a film starring …** ein Film mit … in der Hauptrolle or den Hauptrollen; *v/i* die or e-e Hauptrolle spielen (**in** in *dat*)

star·board AVIAT, MAR Steuerbord *n*

starch **1.** (Kartoffel- *etc*)Stärke *f*; stärkereiches Nahrungsmittel *n*; (Wäsche-) Stärke *f*; **2.** Wäsche stärken

stare 1. starren; **stare at** j-n anstarren; **2.** (starrer) Blick, Starren n

stark 1. adj fig nackt; **be in stark contrast to** in krassem Gegensatz stehen zu; **2.** adv: F **stark naked** splitternackt; **stark raving mad, stark staring mad** total verrückt

star·light ASTR Sternenlicht n

star·ling ZO Star m

star·lit stern(en)klar

star·ry Stern…, Sternen…

star·ry-eyed F blauäugig, naiv

start 1. v/i anfangen, beginnen (a. **start off**); aufbrechen (**for** nach) (a. **start off, start out**); RAIL etc abfahren, MAR ablegen, AVIAT abfliegen, starten; MOT anspringen; TECH anlaufen; SPORT starten; zusammenfahren, -zucken (**at** bei); **to start with** anfangs, zunächst; erstens; **start from scratch** ganz von vorn anfangen; v/t anfangen, beginnen (a. **start off**); in Gang setzen or bringen, Motor etc a. anlassen, starten; **2.** Anfang m, Beginn m, (esp SPORT) Start m; Aufbruch m; Auffahren n, Aufschrecken n; **at the start** am Anfang; SPORT am Start; **for a start** erstens; **from start to finish** von Anfang bis Ende

start·er Starter(in) f; MOT Anlasser m, Starter m; esp Br GASTR F Vorspeise f; **for starters** zunächst einmal

start·le erschrecken; überraschen, bestürzen

starv·a·tion Hungern n; **die of starvation** verhungern; **starvation diet** F Fasten-, Hungerkur f, Nulldiät f

starve hungern (lassen); **starve (to death)** verhungern (lassen); **I'm starving!** Br F, **I'm starved!** F ich komme um vor Hunger!

state 1. Zustand m; Stand m, Lage f; POL (Bundes-, Einzel)Staat m; often **State** POL Staat m; **2.** Staats…, staatlich; **3.** angeben, nennen; erklären, JUR aussagen (**that** dass); festlegen, festsetzen

State De·part·ment POL Außenministerium n

state·ly gemessen, würdevoll; prächtig

state·ment Statement n, Erklärung f; Angabe f; JUR Aussage f; ECON (Bank-, Konto)Auszug m; **make a statement** e-e Erklärung abgeben

state-of-the-art TECH neuest, modernst

states·man POL Staatsmann m

stat·ic statisch

sta·tion 1. (a. Bus-, U-)Bahnhof m, Station f; (Forschungs-, Rettungs- etc)Station f; Tankstelle f; (Feuer)Wache f; (Polizei)Revier n; (Wahl)Lokal n; radio, TV Sender m, Station f; **2.** aufstellen, postieren; MIL stationieren

sta·tion·ar·y stehend

sta·tion·er Schreibwarenhändler(in)

sta·tion·er's (shop) Schreibwarenhandlung f

sta·tion·er·y Schreibwaren pl; Briefpapier n

sta·tion-mas·ter RAIL Stations-, Bahnhofsvorsteher m

sta·tion wag·on MOT Kombiwagen m

sta·tis·ti·cal statistisch

stat·is·ti·cian Statistiker m

sta·tis·tics Statistik(en pl) f

stat·ue Statue f, Standbild n

sta·tus Status m, Rechtsstellung f; (Familien)Stand m; Stellung f, Rang m, Status m

status line EDP Statuszeile f

stat·ute Gesetz n; Statut n, Satzung f

stat·ute of lim·i·ta·tions JUR Verjährungsfrist f; **come under the statute of limitations** verjähren

staunch¹ Br → stanch

staunch² Blutung stillen

stay 1. bleiben (**with s.o.** bei j-m); wohnen (**at** in dat; **with s.o.** bei j-m); **stay put** F sich nicht (vom Fleck) rühren; **stay away** wegbleiben, sich fernhalten (**from** von); **stay up** aufbleiben; **2.** Aufenthalt m; JUR Aussetzung f, Aufschub m

stead·fast treu, zuverlässig; fest

stead·y 1. adj fest; stabil; ruhig (hand), gut (nerves); gleichmäßig; **2.** (sich) beruhigen; **3.** int a. **steady on!** Br F Vorsicht!; **4.** adv: **go steady with s.o.** (fest) mit j-m gehen; **5.** feste Freundin, fester Freund

steak GASTR Steak n; (Fisch)Filet n

steal stehlen (a. fig); sich stehlen, (sich) schleichen (**out of** aus)

stealth: by stealth heimlich, verstohlen

stealth·y heimlich, verstohlen

steam 1. Dampf m; Dunst m; **let off steam** Dampf ablassen, fig a. sich Luft machen; **2.** Dampf…; **3.** v/i dampfen; **steam up** beschlagen (mirror etc); v/t GASTR dünsten, dämpfen

steam·boat Dampfboot n, Dampfer m

steam·er GASTR Dampfkochtopf m; Dampf-, Schnellkochtopf m

steam·ship Dampfer m, Dampfschiff n

steel 1. Stahl m; **2. steel o.s. for** sich wappnen gegen

steel·work·er Stahlarbeiter m

steel·works Stahlwerk n

steep¹ steil; fig stark (rise etc); F happig

steep² eintauchen (**in** in acc); Wäsche (ein)weichen

stee·ple Kirchturm m

stee·ple·chase *horse racing*: Hindernisrennen *n*; SPORT Hindernislauf *m*

steer¹ ZO (junger) Ochse

steer² steuern, lenken

steer·ing col·umn MOT Lenksäule *f*

steer·ing wheel MOT Lenkrad *n*, *a.* MAR Steuerrad *n*

stein Maßkrug *m*

stem¹ BOT Stiel *m* (*a. of a wine glass etc*), Stängel *m*; LING Stamm *m*; **2. *stem from*** stammen *or* herrühren von

stench Gestank *m*

sten·cil Schablone *f*; PRINT Matrize *f*

ste·nog·ra·pher Stenotypistin *f*

step 1. Schritt *m* (*a. fig*); Stufe *f*; Sprosse *f*; (*a pair of*) steps (e-e) Tritt- *or* Stufenleiter; *mind the step!* Vorsicht, Stufe!; *step by step* Schritt für Schritt; *take steps* Schritte *or* tun, unternehmen; **2.** gehen; treten (*in* in *acc*; *on* auf *acc*); *step on it*, *step on the gas* MOT F Gas geben, auf die Tube drücken; *step aside* zur Seite treten; *fig* Platz machen; *step down fig* Platz machen; *step up* Produktion *etc* steigern

step-by-step *fig* schrittweise

step·fa·ther Stiefvater *m*

step·lad·der Tritt-, Stufenleiter *f*

step·moth·er Stiefmutter *f*

steppes GEOGR Steppe *f*

step·ping-stone *fig* Sprungbrett *n* (*to* für)

ster·e·o 1. Stereo *n*; Stereogerät *n*, Stereoanlage *f*; **2.** Stereo…

stereo sys·tem MUS Kompaktanlage *f*

ster·ile steril (*a. fig*), *a.* unfruchtbar, MED *a.* keimfrei

ste·ril·i·ty Sterilität *f* (*a. fig*), Unfruchtbarkeit *f*

ster·il·ize MED sterilisieren

ster·ling das Pfund Sterling

stern¹ streng

stern² MAR Heck *n*

stew 1. *Fleisch, Gemüse* schmoren, dünsten; *stewed apples* Apfelkompott *n*; **2.** Eintopf *m*; *be in a stew* in heller Aufregung sein

stew·ard Ordner *m*; AVIAT, MAR Steward *m*

stew·ard·ess AVIAT, MAR Stewardess *f*

stick¹ trockener Zweig; Stock *m*; ([*Eis*]*Hockey*)Schläger *m*; (*Besen- etc-*) Stiel *m*; AVIAT (*Steuer*)Knüppel *m*; Stück *n*, Stange *f*, (*Lippen- etc*)Stift *m*, Stäbchen *n*

stick² *v/t* mit e-*r Nadel etc* stechen (*into* in *acc*); *et.* kleben (*on* auf, an *acc*); an-, festkleben (*with* mit); stecken; F tun, stellen, setzen, legen; *I can't stick him* (*or it*) *Br* F ich kann ihn (*or* das) nicht ausstehen *or* leiden; *v/i* kleben; kleben bleiben (*to*

an *dat*); stecken bleiben; *stick at nothing* vor nichts zurückschrecken; *stick by* F bleiben bei; F zu j-m halten; *stick out* vorstehen; abstehen; *et.* ausstrecken *or* vorstrecken; *stick to* bleiben bei

stick·er Aufkleber *m*

stick·ing plas·ter *Br* Heftpflaster *n*

stick·y klebrig (*with* von); F heikel, unangenehm

stiff 1. *adj* steif; F stark (*drink etc*); schwer, hart (*task, penalty etc*); hartnäckig (*resistance*); F happig, gepfeffert, gesalzen (*price*); *keep a stiff upper lip* F die Haltung bewahren; **2.** *adv* äußerst; höchst; *be bored stiff* sich zu Tode langweilen; *be scared stiff* e-e wahnsinnige Angst haben; *be worried stiff* sich furchtbare Sorgen machen

stiff·en *v/t Wäsche* stärken; versteifen; verstärken; *v/i* steif werden; sich verhärten *or* versteifen

sti·fle ersticken; *fig* unterdrücken

stile Zauntritt *m*

sti·let·to Stilett *n*

stiletto heel Bleistift-, Pfennigabsatz *m*

still¹ 1. *adv* (immer) noch, noch immer; *with comparative*: noch; **2.** *cj* dennoch, trotzdem

still² 1. *adj* still; ruhig; GASTR ohne Kohlensäure; **2.** *film*, TV Standfoto *n*

still·born MED tot geboren

still life PAINT Stillleben *n*

stilt Stelze *f*

stilt·ed *fig* gestelzt

stim·u·lant MED Stimulans *n*, Anregungs-, Aufputschmittel *n*; *fig* Anreiz *m*, Ansporn *m* (*to* für)

stim·u·late MED stimulieren (*a. fig*), anregen; *fig a.* anspornen

stim·u·lus Reiz *m*; *fig* Anreiz *m*, Ansporn *m* (*to* für)

sting 1. stechen (*insect*); brennen (auf *or* in *dat*); **2.** Stachel *m*; Stich *m*; Brennen *n*, brennender Schmerz

stin·gy F knaus(e)rig, knick(e)rig (*person*); mick(e)rig (*meal etc*)

stink 1. stinken (*of* nach); *stink up* (*Br out*) verpesten; **2.** Gestank *m*

stint 1. *stint o.s.* (*of s.th.*) sich einschränken (mit *et.*); *stint* (*on*) *s.th.* sparen mit *et.*

stip·u·late zur Bedingung machen; festsetzen, vereinbaren

stip·u·la·tion Bedingung *f*; Vereinbarung *f*

stir 1. (um)rühren; (sich) rühren *or* bewegen; *j-n* aufwühlen; *stir up* Unruhe stiften; *Streit* entfachen; *Erinnerungen* wachrufen; **2.** *give s.th. a stir* et. umrühren; *cause* (or *create*) *a stir* für Aufsehen sorgen

stir·rup Steigbügel *m*

stitch 1. Stich *m*; Masche *f*; MED Seitenstechen *n*; **2.** zunähen, *Wunde* nähen (*a.* *stitch up*); heften

stock 1. Vorrat *m* (*of* an *dat*); GASTR Brühe *f*; *a.* **livestock** Viehbestand *m*; (*Gewehr*)Schaft *m*; fig Abstammung *f*, Herkunft *f*; ECON Aktie(n *pl*) *f*; *pl* Aktien *pl*, Wertpapiere *pl*; **have s.th. in stock** ECON et. vorrätig or auf Lager haben; **take stock** ECON Inventur machen; **take stock of** fig sich klar werden über (*acc*); **2.** ECON *Ware* vorrätig haben, führen; **stock up** sich eindecken or versorgen (*on* mit); **~** (with mit); **3.** Serien...; Standard...; stereotyp

stock·breed·er AGR Viehzüchter *m*

stock·breed·ing AGR Viehzucht *f*

stock·brok·er ECON Börsenmakler *m*

stock ex·change ECON Börse *f*

stock·hold·er ECON Aktionär(in)

stock·ing Strumpf *m*

stock mar·ket ECON Börse *f*

stock·pile 1. Vorrat *m* (*of* an *dat*); **2.** e-n Vorrat anlegen an (*dat*)

stock-still regungslos

stock·tak·ing ECON Inventur *f*; fig Bestandsaufnahme *f*

stock·y stämmig, untersetzt

stol·id gleichmütig

stom·ach 1. ANAT Magen *m*; Bauch *m*; fig Appetit *m* (*for* auf *acc*); **2.** vertragen (*a.* fig)

stom·ach·ache MED Magenschmerzen *pl*, Bauchschmerzen *pl*, Bauchweh *n*

stom·ach up·set MED Magenverstimmung *f*

stone 1. Stein *m*, BOT *a.* Kern *m*; (*Hagel*)Korn *n*; **2.** mit Steinen bewerfen; steinigen; entkernen, entsteinen

stone·ma·son Steinmetz *m*

stone·ware Steingut *n*

ston·y steinig; steinern (*face etc*), eisig (*silence*)

stool Hocker *m*, Schemel *m*; MED Stuhl *m*, Stuhlgang *m*

stool·pi·geon F (Polizei)Spitzel *m*

stoop 1. v/i sich bücken (*a.* *stoop down*); gebeugt gehen; **stoop to** fig sich herablassen or hergeben zu; **2.** gebeugte Haltung

stop 1. v/i (an)halten, stehen bleiben (*a.* *watch etc*), stoppen; aufhören; *esp Br* bleiben; **stop dead** plötzlich or abrupt stehen bleiben; **stop at nothing** vor nichts zurückschrecken; **stop short of** doing, **stop short at** s.th. zurückschre-

cken vor (*dat*); v/t anhalten, stoppen; aufhören mit; ein Ende machen or setzen (*dat*); *Blutung* stillen; *Arbeiten, Verkehr etc* zum Erliegen bringen; et. verhindern; j-n abhalten (*from* von), hindern (*from* an *dat*); *Rohr etc* verstopfen (*a.* *stop up*); *Zahn* füllen, plombieren; *Scheck* sperren (lassen); **stop by** vorbeischauen; **stop in** vorbeischauen (*at* bei); **stop off** F kurz Halt machen; **stop over** kurz Halt machen; Zwischenstation machen; **2.** Halt *m*; (*Bus*)Haltestelle *f*; PHOT Blende *f*; *mst* **full stop** LING Punkt *m*

stop-gap Notbehelf *m*

stop·light MOT Bremslicht *n*; rotes Licht

stop·o·ver Zwischenstation *f*; AVIAT Zwischenlandung *f*

stop·page Unterbrechung *f*, Stopp *m*; Verstopfung *f*; Streik *m*; *Br* (Gehalts-, Lohn)Abzug *m*

stop·per Stöpsel *m*

stop sign MOT Stoppschild *n*

stop·watch Stoppuhr *f*

stor·age ECON Lagerung *f*; Lagergeld *n*; EDP Speicher *m*

store 1. (ein)lagern; *Energie* speichern; EDP (ab)speichern, sichern; *a.* **store up** sich e-n Vorrat anlegen an (*dat*); **2.** Vorrat *m*; Lager *n*, Lagerhalle *f*, Lagerhaus *n*; Laden *m*, Geschäft *n*, *esp Br* Kaufhaus *n*, Warenhaus *n*; **set great store by** großen Wert legen auf (*acc*)

store·house Lagerhaus *n*; fig Fundgrube *f*

store·keep·er Ladenbesitzer(in)

store·room Lagerraum *m*

sto·rey *Br* → **story²**

...sto·reyed *Br*, **...sto·ried** mit ... Stockwerken, ...stöckig

stork ZO Storch *m*

storm 1. Unwetter *n*; Gewitter *n*; Sturm *m*; **2.** v/t MIL *etc* stürmen; v/i stürmen, stürzen

storm·y stürmisch

sto·ry¹ Geschichte *f*; Märchen *n* (*a.* fig); Story *f*, a. Handlung *f*, a. Bericht *m* (*on* über *acc*)

sto·ry² Stock *m*, Stockwerk *n*, Etage *f*

stout korpulent, vollschlank; fig unerschrocken; entschieden

stove Ofen *m*, Herd *m*

stow a. **stow away** verstauen

stow·a·way AVIAT, MAR blinder Passagier

strad·dle rittlings sitzen auf (*dat*)

strag·gle verstreut liegen or stehen; BOT *etc* wuchern; **straggle in** F einzeln eintrudeln

strag·gler Nachzügler(in)

strag·gly verstreut (liegend); BOT *etc* wu-

S

chernd; struppig (*mustache etc*)

straight 1. *adj* gerade; glatt (*hair*); pur (*whisky etc*); aufrichtig, offen, ehrlich; *sl* hetero(*sexuell*); *sl* clean, sauber; *put straight* in Ordnung bringen; **2.** *adv* gerade; genau, direkt; klar; ehrlich, anständig; *straight ahead* geradeaus; *straight off* F sofort; *straight on* geradeaus; *straight out* F offen, rundheraus; **3.** SPORT (Gegen-, Ziel)Gerade f

straight-en *v/t* gerade machen, (gerade) richten; *straighten out* in Ordnung bringen; *v/i a.* **straighten out** gerade werden; **straighten up** sich aufrichten

straight-for-ward aufrichtig; einfach

strain 1. *v/t* Seil etc (an)spannen; sich, Augen etc überanstrengen; sich e-n Muskel etc zerren; Gemüse, Tee etc abgießen; *v/i* sich anstrengen; *strain at* zerren or ziehen an (*dat*); **2.** Spannung f; Anspannung f; Strapaze f; fig Belastung f; MED Zerrung f

strained MED gezerrt; gezwungen (*smile etc*); gespannt (*relations*); *look strained* abgespannt aussehen

strain-er Sieb n

strait GEOGR Meerenge f, Straße f; pl fig Notlage f

strait-ened: *live in straitened circumstances* in beschränkten Verhältnissen leben

strand Strang m; Faden m; (Kabel-)Draht m; (Haar)Strähne f

strand-ed: *be stranded* MAR gestrandet sein; *be (left) stranded* fig festsitzen (*in* in *dat*)

strange merkwürdig, seltsam, sonderbar; fremd

strang-er Fremde m, f

stran-gle erwürgen

strap 1. Riemen m, Gurt m; (Uhr)Armband n; Träger m; **2.** festschnallen; anschnallen

stra-te-gic strategisch

strat-e-gy Strategie f

stra-tum GEOL Schicht f (a. fig)

straw Stroh n; Strohhalm m

straw-ber-ry BOT Erdbeere f

stray 1. (herum)streunen; sich verirren; fig abschweifen (*from* von); **2.** verirrtes or streunendes Tier; **3.** verirrt (*bullet, dog etc*); streunend (*dog etc*); vereinzelt

streak 1. Streifen m; Strähne f; (Charakter)Zug m; *a streak of lightning* ein Blitz; *lucky streak* Glückssträhne f; **2.** flitzen; streifen

streak-y streifig; GASTR durchwachsen

stream 1. Bach m; Strömung f; fig Strom m; **2.** strömen; flattern, wehen

stream-er Luft-, Papierschlange f; Wimpel m; EDP Streamer m

street 1. Straße f; *on (esp Br in) the street* auf der Straße; **2.** Straßen...

street-car Straßenbahn(wagen m) f

street sweep-er Straßenkehrer m

strength Stärke f, Kraft f; Kräfte pl

strength-en *v/t* (ver)stärken; *v/i* stärker werden

stren-u-ous anstrengend, strapaziös; unermüdlich

stress 1. fig Stress m; PHYS, TECH Beanspruchung f, Belastung f, Druck m; LING Betonung f; fig Nachdruck m; **2.** betonen

stress-ful stressig, aufreibend

stretch 1. *v/t* strecken; (aus)weiten, dehnen; spannen; fig sich nicht allzu genau nehmen mit; *stretch out* ausstrecken; *be fully stretched* fig richtig gefordert werden; voll ausgelastet sein; *v/i* sich dehnen, a. länger or weiter werden; sich dehnen or recken or strecken; sich erstrecken; *stretch out* sich ausstrecken; **2.** Dehnbarkeit f, Elastizität f; Strecke f; SPORT (Gegen-, Ziel)Gerade f; Zeit f, Zeitraum m, Zeitspanne f; *have a stretch* sich dehnen or recken or strecken

stretch-er Trage f

strick-en schwer betroffen; *stricken with* befallen or ergriffen von

strict streng, strikt; genau; *strictly (speaking)* genau genommen

strict-ness Strenge f

stride 1. schreiten, mit großen Schritten gehen; **2.** großer Schritt

strife Streit m

strike 1. *v/t* schlagen; treffen; einschlagen in (*acc*) (*lightning*); Streichholz anzünden; MAR auflaufen auf (*acc*); streichen (*from, off* aus *dat*, von); stoßen auf (*acc*); *j-n* beeindrucken; *j-m* einfallen, in den Sinn kommen; Münze prägen; Saite etc anschlagen; Lager, Zelt abbrechen; Flagge, Segel streichen; *strike out* (aus)streichen; *strike up* Lied etc anstimmen; Freundschaft etc schließen; *v/i* schlagen; einschlagen; ECON streiken; *strike (out) at s.o.* auf *j-n* einschlagen; **2.** ECON Streik m; (Öl- etc)Fund m; MIL Angriff m; soccer: Schuss m; *be on strike* streiken; *go on strike* streiken, in den Streik treten; *a lucky strike* ein Glückstreffer

strik-er ECON Streikende m, f; soccer: Stürmer(in)

strik-ing apart; auffallend

string 1. Schnur f, Bindfaden m; (Schürzen-, Schuh- etc)Band n; (Puppenspiel-)

Faden *m*, Draht *m*; (*Perlen- etc*)Schnur *f*; MUS, SPORT Saite *f*; (*Bogen*)Sehne *f*; BOT Faser *f*; EDP Zeichenfolge *f*; *fig* Reihe *f*, Serie *f*; **the strings** MUS die Streichinstrumente *pl*, die Streicher *pl*; **pull a few strings** *fig* ein paar Beziehungen spielen lassen; **with no strings attached** *fig* ohne Bedingungen; **2.** *Perlen etc* aufreihen; *Gitarre etc* besaiten, *Tennisschläger etc* bespannen; *Bohnen* abziehen; **3.** MUS Streich...

string bean BOT grüne Bohne

strin·gent streng

string·y fas(e)rig

strip 1. *v/i:* **a. strip off** sich ausziehen (**to** bis auf *acc*); *v/t* ausziehen; *Farbe etc* abkratzen, *Tapete etc* abreißen (**from, off** von); *a.* **strip down** TECH zerlegen, auseinandernehmen; **strip s.o. of s.th.** j-m et. rauben *or* wegnehmen; **2.** (*Land-, Papier- etc*)Streifen *m*; Strip *m*

stripe Streifen *m*

striped gestreift

strive *strive for or after* streben nach

stroke 1. streicheln; streichen über (*acc*); **2.** Schlag *m* (*a. SPORT*); MED Schlag(anfall) *m*; (*Pinsel*)Strich *m*; *swimming:* Zug *m*; TECH Hub *m*; → **four-stroke engine**; **stroke of lightning** Blitzschlag *m*; **a stroke of luck** *fig* ein glücklicher Zufall, ein Glücksfall

stroll 1. bummeln, spazieren; **2.** Bummel *m*, Spaziergang *m*

stroll·er Bummler(in), Spaziergänger(in); Sportwagen *m*

strong stark (*a. GASTR, PHARM*); kräftig; mächtig; stabil; fest; robust

strong·box (Geld-, Stahl)Kassette *f*

strong·hold Festung *f*; Stützpunkt *m*; *fig* Hochburg *f*

strong-mind·ed willensstark

strong room Tresor(raum) *m*

struc·ture Struktur *f*; (Auf)Bau *m*, Gliederung *f*; Bau *m*, Konstruktion *f*

strug·gle 1. kämpfen, ringen (**with** mit; **for** um); sich abmühen; sich winden, zappeln; **struggle against** sich sträuben gegen; **2.** Kampf *m*

strum klimpern auf (*dat*) (*or* **on** auf *dat*)

strut¹ stolzieren

strut² TECH Strebe *f*; Stütze *f*

stub 1. (*Bleistift-, Zigaretten- etc*)Stummel *m*; Kontrollabschnitt *m*; **2.** sich *die Zehe* anstoßen; **stub out** *Zigarette* ausdrücken

stub·ble Stoppeln *pl*

stub·bly stoppelig

stub·born eigensinnig, stur; hartnäckig

stub·born·ness Starrsinn *m*

stuck-up F hochnäsig

stud¹ 1. (*Kragen-, Manschetten*)Knopf *m*; *soccer:* Stollen *m*; Beschlagnagel *m*; Ziernagel *m*; *pl* MOT Spikes *pl*; **2. be studded with** besetzt sein mit; übersät sein mit; **studded tires** Spikesreifen *pl*

stud² Gestüt *n*

stu·dent Student(in); Schüler(in)

stud farm Gestüt *n*

stud horse ZO Zuchthengst *m*

stud·ied wohlüberlegt; gesucht

stu·di·o Studio *n*; Atelier *n*; *a.* **studio apartment**, *Br* **studio flat** Studio *n*, Einzimmerappartement *n*

studio couch Schlafcouch *f*

stu·di·ous fleißig

stud·y 1. Studium *n*; Studie *f*, Untersuchung *f*; Arbeitszimmer *n*; *pl* Studium *n*; **be in a brown study** in Gedanken versunken *or* geistesabwesend sein; **2.** studieren; lernen (**for** für)

stuff 1. Zeug *n*; **2.** (aus)stopfen, stopfen, vollstopfen; füllen (*a. GASTR*); **stuff o.s.** F sich vollstopfen

stuff·ing Füllung *f* (*a. GASTR*)

stuff·y stickig; spießig; prüde

stum·ble 1. stolpern (**on, over,** *fig* **at, over** über *acc*); **stumble across, stumble on** stoßen auf (*acc*); **2.** Stolpern *n*

stump 1. Stumpf *m*; Stummel *m*; **2.** stampfen, stapfen

stump·y F kurz und dick

stun betäuben; *fig* sprachlos machen

stun·ning fantastisch; unglaublich

stunt¹ (*das Wachstum gen*) hemmen; **stunted** BIOL verkümmert; **become stunted** BIOL verkümmern

stunt² (*Film*)Stunt *m*; (*gefährliches*) Kunststück; (*Reklame*)Gag *m*

stunt man *film*, TV Stuntman *m*, Double *n*

stunt wom·an *film*, TV Stuntwoman *f*, Double *n*

stu·pid dumm; F blöd

stu·pid·i·ty Dummheit *f*

stu·por Betäubung *f*; **in a drunken stupor** im Vollrausch

stur·dy kräftig, stämmig; *fig* entschlossen, hartnäckig

stut·ter 1. stottern (*a. MOT*); stammeln; **2.** Stottern *n*, Stammeln *n*

sty¹ → **pigsty**

sty², **stye** MED Gerstenkorn *n*

style 1. Stil *m*; Ausführung *f*; Mode *f*; **2.** entwerfen; gestalten

styl·ish stilvoll; modisch, elegant

styl·ist Stilist(in)

Sty·ro·foam® Styropor® *n*

suave verbindlich

sub·con·scious Unterbewusstsein *n*; **subconsciously** im Unterbewusstsein

S

sub·di·vi·sion Unterteilung *f*; Unterabteilung *f*

sub·due unterwerfen; *Ärger etc* unterdrücken

sub·dued gedämpft (*light, voice etc*); ruhig, still (*person*)

sub·ject 1. Thema *n*; PED, UNIV Fach *n*; LING Subjekt *n*, Satzgegenstand *m*; Untertan(in); Staatsangehörige *m*, *f*, -bürger(in); **2** *adj*: **subject to** anfällig für; **be subject to** a. neigen zu; **be subject to** unterliegen (*dat*); abhängen von; **prices subject to change** Preisänderungen vorbehalten; **1.** unterwerfen; **subject to e-m** Test unterziehen; *der Kritik etc* aussetzen

sub·jec·tion Unterwerfung *f*; Abhängigkeit *f* (**to** von)

sub·ju·gate unterjochen, unterwerfen

sub·junc·tive LING a. **subjunctive mood** Konjunktiv *m*

sub·lease, **sub·let** untervermieten, weitervermieten

sub·lime großartig; *fig* total

sub·ma·chine gun Maschinenpistole *f*

sub·ma·rine 1. unterseeisch; **2.** Unterseeboot *n*, U-Boot *n*

sub·merge tauchen; (ein)tauchen (**in** in *acc*)

sub·mis·sion Einreichung *f*; *boxing etc*: Aufgabe *f*; Unterwerfung *f* (**to** unter)

sub·mis·sive unterwürfig

sub·mit *Gesuch etc* einreichen (**to** *dat or* bei); sich fügen (**to** *dat or* in *acc*); *boxing etc*: aufgeben

sub·or·di·nate 1. untergeordnet (**to** *dat*); **2.** Untergebene *m*, *f*; **3. subordinate to** unterordnen (*dat*), zurückstellen (hinter *acc*)

subordinate clause LING Nebensatz *m*

sub·scribe *v/t* Geld geben, spenden (**to** für); *v/i*: **subscribe to** *Zeitung etc* abonnieren

sub·scrib·er Abonnent(in); TEL Teilnehmer(in)

sub·scrip·tion Abonnement *n*; (Mitglieds)Beitrag *m*

sub·se·quent später

sub·side sich senken (*building, road etc*); zurückgehen (*flood, demand etc*), sich legen (*storm, anger etc*)

sub·sid·i·a·ry 1. Neben...; **subsidiary question** Zusatzfrage *f*; **2.** ECON Tochtergesellschaft *f*

sub·si·dize subventionieren

sub·si·dy Subvention *f*

sub·sist leben, existieren (**on** von)

sub·sis·tence Existenz *f*

sub·stance Substanz *f* (*a. fig*), Stoff *m*;

das Wesentliche, Kern *m*

sub·stan·dard minderwertig

sub·stan·tial solid (*furniture etc*); beträchtlich (*salary etc*), (*changes etc a.*) wesentlich; reichlich, kräftig (*meal*)

sub·stan·ti·ate beweisen

sub·stan·tive LING Substantiv *n*, Hauptwort *n*

sub·sti·tute 1. Ersatz *m*; Stellvertreter(in), Vertretung *f*; SPORT Auswechselspieler(in), Ersatzspieler(in); **2. substitute s.th. for s.th.** et. durch et. ersetzen, et. gegen et. austauschen *or* auswechseln; **substitute for** einspringen für, *j-n* vertreten

sub·sti·tu·tion Ersatz *m*; SPORT Austausch *m*, Auswechslung *f*

sub·ter·fuge List *f*

sub·ter·ra·ne·an unterirdisch

sub·ti·tle Untertitel *m*

sub·tle fein (*differences etc*); raffiniert (*plan etc*); scharf (*mind*); scharfsinnig

sub·tract MATH abziehen, subtrahieren (**from** von)

sub·trac·tion MATH Abziehen *n*, Subtraktion *f*

sub·trop·i·cal subtropisch

sub·urb Vorort *m*, Vorstadt *f*

sub·ur·ban Vorort..., vorstädtisch, Vorstadt...

sub·ver·sive umstürzlerisch, subversiv

sub·way Unterführung *f*; U-Bahn *f*

suc·ceed *v/i* Erfolg haben, erfolgreich sein, (*plan etc a.*) gelingen; **succeed to** in *e-m* Amt nachfolgen; **succeed to the throne** auf dem Thron folgen; *v/t*: **succeed s.o. as** *j-s* Nachfolger werden als

suc·cess Erfolg *m*

suc·cess·ful erfolgreich

suc·ces·sion Folge *f*; Erb-, Nach-, Thronfolge *f*; **five times in succession** fünfmal hintereinander; **in quick succession** in rascher Folge

suc·ces·sive aufeinanderfolgend

suc·ces·sor Nachfolger(in); Thronfolger(in)

suc·cu·lent GASTR saftig

such solche(r, -s); derartige(r, -s); so; derart; **such a** so ein(e)

suck 1. *v/t* saugen; lutschen (**an** *dat*); *v/i* saugen (**at** an *dat*); **2. have** *or* **take a suck at** saugen *or* lutschen an (*dat*)

suck·er ZO Saugnapf *m*, Saugorgan *n*; TECH Saugfuß *m*; BOT Wurzelschössling *m*, Wurzelspross *m*; F Trottel *m*, Simpel *m*; Lutscher *m*

suck·le säugen, stillen

suc·tion (An)Saugen *n*; Saugwirkung *f*

suction pump TECH Saugpumpe f

sud·den plötzlich, unvermittelt; *all of a sudden* F ganz plötzlich

sud·den·ly plötzlich

suds Seifenschaum m

sue JUR j-n verklagen (*for* auf acc, wegen); klagen (*for* auf acc)

suede, suède Wildleder n, Velours(-leder) n

su·et GASTR Nierenfett n, Talg m

suf·fer v/i leiden (*from* an dat, unter dat); darunter leiden; v/t erleiden; *Folgen* tragen

suf·fer·er Leidende m

suf·fer·ing Leiden n; Leid n

suf·fi·cient genügend, genug, ausreichend; *be sufficient* genügen, (aus)reichen

suf·fix LING Suffix n, Nachsilbe f

suf·fo·cate ersticken

suf·frage POL Wahl-, Stimmrecht n

suf·fuse durchfluten (*light* etc); überziehen (*color* etc)

sug·ar Zucker m; **2.** zuckern

sug·ar beet BOT Zuckerrübe f

sug·ar bowl Zuckerdose f

sug·ar·cane BOT Zuckerrohr n

sug·ar tongs Zuckerzange f

sug·ar·y süß; fig süßlich

sug·gest vorschlagen, anregen; hindeuten *or* hinweisen auf (acc), schließen lassen auf (acc); andeuten

sug·ges·tion Vorschlag m, Anregung f; Anflug m, Spur f; Andeutung f; PSYCH Suggestion f

sug·ges·tive zweideutig (*remark* etc), vielsagend (*look* etc)

su·i·cide Selbstmord m; Selbstmörder(in); *commit suicide* Selbstmord begehen

suit 1. Anzug m; Kostüm n; *card game:* Farbe f; JUR Prozess m; *follow suit* fig dem Beispiel folgen, dasselbe tun; **2.** v/t j-m passen (*to* dat); j-n kleiden, j-m stehen; et. anpassen (*to* dat); *suit s.th., be suited to s.th.* geeignet sein *or* sich eignen für; *suit yourself!* mach, was du willst!

suit·a·ble passend, geeignet (*for, to* für)

suit·case Koffer m

suite (*Möbel-, Sitz*)Garnitur f; Suite f, Zimmerflucht f; MUS Suite f; Gefolge n

sul·fur CHEM Schwefel m

sul·fu·ric ac·id CHEM Schwefelsäure f

sulk schmollen, F eingeschnappt sein

sulk·y schmollend, F eingeschnappt

sul·len mürrisch, verdrossen

sul·phur Br → sulfur

sul·phu·ric ac·id Br → sulfuric acid

sul·try schwül; aufreizend (*look* etc)

sum 1. Summe f; Betrag m; (*einfache*) Rechenaufgabe; *do sums* rechnen; **2.** *sum up* zusammenfassen; j-n et. abschätzen

sum·ma·rize zusammenfassen

sum·ma·ry Zusammenfassung f, (kurze) Inhaltsangabe

sum·mer Sommer m; *in (the) summer* im Sommer

summer camp Ferienlager n

summer hol·i·days Br Sommerferien pl

summer resort Sommerfrische f

summer school Ferienkurs m

sum·mer·time Sommer m, Sommerszeit f; *in (the) summertime* im Sommer

sum·mer time esp Br Sommerzeit f

summer va·ca·tion Sommerferien pl

sum·mer·y sommerlich, Sommer...

sum·mit Gipfel m (a. ECON, POL, fig)

summit con·fe·rence POL Gipfelkonferenz f

summit meet·ing POL Gipfeltreffen n

sum·mon auffordern; *Versammlung* etc einberufen; JUR vorladen; *summon up Kraft, Mut* etc zusammenehmen

sum·mons JUR Vorladung f

sump Br MOT Ölwanne f

sump·tu·ous luxuriös, aufwändig

sun 1. Sonne f; **2.** Sonnen...; **3.** *sun o.s.* sich sonnen

Sun ABBR *of* **Sunday** So., Sonntag m

sun·bathe sich sonnen, ein Sonnenbad nehmen

sun·beam Sonnenstrahl m

sun·bed Sonnenbank f

sun·burn Sonnenbrand m

sun cream Sonnencreme f

sun·dae GASTR Eisbecher m

Sun·day (*ABBR Sun*) Sonntag m; *on Sunday* (am) Sonntag; *on Sundays* sonntags

sun·dial Sonnenuhr f

sun·dries Diverses, Verschiedenes

sun·dry diverse, verschiedene

sun·glass·es (*a pair of sunglasses* e-e) Sonnenbrille f

sunk·en MAR gesunken, versunken; versenkt; tief liegend; eingefallen (*cheeks*), (a. eyes) eingesunken

sun·light Sonnenlicht n

sun·lit sonnenbeschienen

sun·ny sonnig

sun·rise Sonnenaufgang m; *at sunrise* bei Sonnenaufgang

sun·roof Dachterrasse f; MOT Schiebedach n

sun·set Sonnenuntergang m; *at sunset* bei Sonnenuntergang

sun·shade Sonnenschirm m

sun·shine Sonnenschein m

S

sun·stroke MED Sonnenstich m

sun·tan (Sonnen)Bräune f

suntan lo·tion Sonnenschutz m, Sonnencreme f

suntan oil Sonnenöl n

su·per F super, spitze, klasse

su·per... Über..., über...

su·per·a·bun·dant überreichlich

su·per·an·nu·at·ed pensioniert, im Ruhestand

su·perb ausgezeichnet

su·per·charg·er MOT Kompressor m

su·per·cil·i·ous hochmütig, F hochnäsig

su·per·fi·cial oberflächlich

su·per·flu·ous überflüssig

su·per·hu·man übermenschlich

su·per·im·pose überlagern; *Bild etc* einblenden (**on** in *acc*)

su·per·in·tend die (Ober)Aufsicht haben über (*acc*), überwachen; leiten

su·per·in·tend·ent Aufsicht f, Aufsichtsbeamter m, -beamtin f; Br Kriminalrat m

su·pe·ri·or 1. ranghöher (**to** als); überlegen (**to** dat), besser (**to** als); ausgezeichnet, hervorragend; überheblich, überlegen; *Father Superior* REL Superior m; *Mother Superior* REL Oberin f; **2.** Vorgesetzte m, f

su·peri·or·i·ty Überlegenheit f (**over** gegenüber)

su·per·la·tive 1. höchste(r, -s), überragend; **2.** *a.* **superlative degree** LING Superlativ m

su·per·mar·ket Supermarkt m

su·per·nat·u·ral übernatürlich

su·per·nu·me·ra·ry zusätzlich

su·per·sede ablösen, ersetzen, verdrängen

su·per·son·ic AVIAT, PHYS Überschall...

su·per·sti·tion Aberglaube m

su·per·sti·tious abergläubisch

su·per·store Großmarkt m

su·per·vene dazwischenkommen

su·per·vise beaufsichtigen, überwachen

su·per·vi·sion Beaufsichtigung f, Überwachung f; *under s.o.'s supervision* unter j-s Aufsicht

su·per·vi·sor Aufseher(in), Aufsicht f

sup·per Abendessen n; *have supper* zu Abend essen; → *lord*

sup·plant verdrängen

sup·ple gelenkig, geschmeidig, biegsam

sup·ple·ment 1. Ergänzung f; Nachtrag m, Anhang m; Ergänzungsband m; (*Zeitungs- etc*)Beilage f; **2.** ergänzen

sup·ple·men·ta·ry ergänzend, zusätzlich

sup·pli·er ECON Lieferant(in), *a. pl* Lieferfirma f

sup·ply 1. liefern; stellen, sorgen für; *j-n,*

et. versorgen, ECON beliefern (**with** mit); **2.** Lieferung f (**to** an *acc*); Versorgung f; ECON Angebot n; *mst pl* Vorrat m (**of** an *dat*), *a.* Proviant m, MIL Nachschub m; *supply and demand* ECON Angebot und Nachfrage

sup·port 1. (ab)stützen; *Gewicht etc* tragen; *Währung* stützen; unterstützen; unterhalten, sorgen für; **2.** Stütze f; TECH Träger m; *fig* Unterstützung f

sup·port·er Anhänger(in) (*a.* SPORT), Befürworter(in)

sup·pose 1. annehmen, vermuten; *be supposed to ...* sollen; *what is that supposed to mean?* was soll denn das?; *I suppose so* ich nehme es an, vermutlich; **2.** *cj* angenommen; wie wäre es, wenn

sup·posed angeblich, vermeintlich

sup·pos·ing → *suppose 2*

sup·po·si·tion Annahme f, Vermutung f

sup·pos·i·to·ry PHARM Zäpfchen n

sup·press unterdrücken

sup·pres·sion Unterdrückung f

sup·pu·rate MED eitern

su·prem·a·cy Vormachtstellung f

su·preme höchste(r, -s), oberste(r, -s), Ober...; größte(r, -s)

sur·charge 1. Nachporto or e-n Zuschlag erheben (**on** auf *acc*);**2.** Aufschlag m, Zuschlag m (**on** auf *acc*); Nach-, Strafporto n (**on** auf *acc*)

sure 1. *adj* sicher; *sure of o.s.* selbstsicher; *sure of winning* siegessicher; *sure thing!* F (aber) klar!; *be* or *feel sure* sicher sein; *be sure to ...* vergiss nicht zu ...; *for sure* ganz sicher or bestimmt; *make sure that* sich (davon) überzeugen, dass; *to be sure* sicher(lich); **2.** *adv* F sicher, klar; *sure enough* tatsächlich

sure·ly sicher(lich)

sure·ty JUR Bürge m, Bürgin f; Bürgschaft f, Sicherheit f; *stand surety for s.o.* für j-n bürgen

surf 1. Brandung f; **2.** SPORT surfen

sur·face 1. Oberfläche f; (*Straßen*)Belag m; **2.** auftauchen; *Straße* mit e-m Belag versehen; **3.** Oberflächen...; *fig* oberflächlich; *surface mail* gewöhnliche Post

surf·board Surfboard n, Surfbrett n

surf·er Surfer(in), Wellenreiter(in)

surf·ing Surfen m, Wellenreiten n

surge 1. *fig* Welle f, Woge f, (*Gefühls*)Aufwallung f; **2.** (vorwärts-)drängen; *surge up* aufwallen

sur·geon MED Chirurg(in)

sur·ge·ry MED Chirurgie f; operativer Eingriff, Operation f; Br Sprechzimmer n; Br Sprechstunde f; *a.* *doctor's sur-*

gery Arztpraxis *f*
surgery hours MED *Br* Sprechstunde(n *pl*) *f*
sur·gi·cal MED chirurgisch
sur·ly mürrisch, unwirsch
sure·name Familienname *m*, Nachname *m*, Zuname *m*
sur·pass Erwartungen *etc* übertreffen
sur·plus 1. Überschuss *m* (**of** an *dat*); **2.** überschüssig
sur·prise 1. Überraschung *f*, Verwunderung *f*; *take s.o. by surprise* j-n überraschen; **2.** überraschen; *be surprised at or by* überrascht sein über (*acc*)
sur·ren·der 1. *v/i* **surrender to** MIL, *a. fig* sich ergeben (*dat*), kapitulieren vor (*dat*); *surrender to the police* sich der Polizei stellen; *v/t et.* übergeben, ausliefern (*to dat*); aufgeben, verzichten auf (*acc*); *surrender o.s. to the police* sich der Polizei stellen; **2.** MIL Kapitulation *f* (*a. fig*); Aufgabe *f*, Verzicht *m*
sur·ro·gate Ersatz *m*
sur·ro·gate moth·er Leihmutter *f*
sur·round umgeben; umstellen
sur·round·ing umliegend
sur·round·ings Umgebung *f*
sur·vey 1. (sich) *et.* betrachten (*a. fig*); Haus *etc* begutachten; Land vermessen; **2.** Umfrage *f*; Überblick *m* (**of** über *acc*); Begutachtung *f*; Vermessung *f*
sur·vey·or Gutachter *m*; Land(ver)messer *m*
sur·viv·al Überleben *n* (*a. fig*); Überbleibsel *n*
survival in·stinct Selbsterhaltungstrieb *m*
survival kit Überlebensausrüstung *f*
survival train·ing Überlebenstraining *n*
sur·vive überleben; Feuer *etc* überstehen; erhalten bleiben *or* sein
sur·vi·vor Überlebende *m*, *f* (**from, of** *gen*)
sus·cep·ti·ble empfänglich, anfällig (*both*; **to** für)
sus·pect 1. j-n verdächtigen (**of** *gen*); *et.* vermuten; *et.* anzweifeln, *et.* bezweifeln; **2.** Verdächtige *m*, *f*; **3.** verdächtig, suspekt
sus·pend Verkauf, Zahlungen *etc* (vorübergehend) einstellen; JUR Verfahren, Urteil aussetzen; Strafe zur Bewährung aussetzen; j-n suspendieren; vorübergehend ausschließen (**from** aus); SPORT j-n sperren; (auf)hängen; *be suspended* schweben
sus·pend·er *Br* Strumpfhalter *m*, Straps *m*; Sockenhalter *m*; (*a. a pair of*) *sus·penders* Hosenträger *pl*

sus·pense Spannung *f*; *in suspense* gespannt, voller Spannung
sus·pen·sion (vorübergehende) Einstellung; Suspendierung *f*; vorübergehender Ausschluss; SPORT Sperre *f*; MOT *etc* Aufhängung *f*
suspension bridge Hängebrücke *f*
suspension rail·way *esp Br* Schwebebahn *f*
sus·pi·cion Verdacht *m*; Verdächtigung *f*; Argwohn *m*, Misstrauen *n*; *fig* Hauch *m*, Spur *f*
sus·pi·cious verdächtig; argwöhnisch, misstrauisch; *become suspicious* Verdacht schöpfen
sus·tain j-n stärken; Interesse *etc* aufrechterhalten; Schaden, Verlust erleiden; JUR e-m Einspruch *etc* stattgeben
swab MED **1.** Tupfer *m*; Abstrich *m*; **2.** Wunde abtupfen
swad·dle Baby wickeln
swag·ger stolzieren
swal·low¹ 1. schlucken (*a. F*); hinunterschlucken; *swallow up fig* schlucken, verschlingen; **2.** Schluck *m*
swal·low² ZO Schwalbe *f*
swamp 1. Sumpf *m*; **2.** überschwemmen; *be swamped with fig* überschwemmt werden mit
swamp·y sumpfig
swan ZO Schwan *m*
swank 1. F *esp Br* angeben; **2.** F *esp Br* Angeber(in); Angabe *f*; **3.** F piekfein
swank·y F piekfein; *esp Br* angeberisch
swap F 1. (ein)tauschen; **2.** Tausch *m*
swarm 1. ZO Schwarm *m* (*a. fig*); **2.** ZO schwärmen, *fig a.* strömen; *a. fig* wimmeln (**with** von)
swar·thy dunkel (*skin*), dunkelhäutig (*person*)
swas·ti·ka Hakenkreuz *n*
swat Fliege *etc* totschlagen
sway 1. *v/i* sich wiegen, schaukeln; *sway between fig* schwanken zwischen (*dat*); *v/t* hin- und herbewegen, schwenken; *s-n Körper* wiegen; beeinflussen; **2.** Schwanken *n*, Schaukeln *n*
swear fluchen; schwören; *swear at s.o.* j-n wüst beschimpfen; *swear by fig* F schwören auf (*acc*); *swear s.o. in* JUR j-n vereidigen
sweat 1. *v/i* schwitzen (**with** vor *dat*); *v/t*: *sweat out Krankheit* ausschwitzen; *sweat blood* F sich abrackern (**over** mit); **2.** Schweiß *m*; F Schufterei *f*; *get in(to) a sweat fig* F ins Schwitzen geraten *or* kommen
sweat·er Pullover *m*
sweat·shirt Sweatshirt *n*

S

sweat·y schweißig, verschwitzt; nach Schweiß riechend, Schweiß...; schweißtreibend

Swede Schwede m, Schwedin f

Swe·den Schweden n

Swe·dish 1. schwedisch; **2.** LING Schwedisch n

sweep 1. v/t kehren, fegen; fig fegen über (acc) (storm etc); Horizont etc absuchen (for nach); fig Land etc überschwemmen; **sweep along** mitreißen; v/i kehren, fegen; rauschen (person); **2.** Kehren n, Fegen n; Hieb m, Schlag m; F Schornsteinfeger m, Kaminkehrer m; **give the floor a good sweep** den Boden gründlich kehren or fegen; **make a clean sweep** gründlich aufräumen; SPORT gründlich abräumen

sweep·er (Straßen)Kehrer m; Kehrmaschine f; soccer: Libero m

sweep·ing durchgreifend (changes etc); pauschal, zu allgemein

sweep·ings Kehricht m

sweet 1. süß (a. fig); lieblich; lieb; **sweet nothings** Zärtlichkeiten pl; **have a sweet tooth** gern naschen; **2.** Br Süßigkeit f, Bonbon m, n; Br Nachtisch m

sweet corn esp Br BOT Zuckermais m

sweet·en süßen

sweet·heart Schatz m, Liebste m, f

sweet pea BOT Gartenwicke f

sweet shop esp Br Süßwarengeschäft n

swell 1. v/i a. **swell up** MED (an)schwellen; a. **swell out** sich blähen; v/t fig Zahl etc anwachsen lassen; a. **swell out** Segel blähen; **2.** MAR Dünung f; **3.** F klasse

swell·ing MED Schwellung f

swel·ter vor Hitze fast umkommen

swerve 1. v/i schwenken (to the left nach links), e-n Schwenk machen; fig abweichen (from von); **2.** Schwenk m, Schwenkung f, MOT etc a. Schlenker m

swift schnell

swim 1. v/i schwimmen; fig verschwimmen; **my head was swimming** mir drehte sich alles; v/t Strecke schwimmen; Fluss etc durchschwimmen; **2.** Schwimmen n; **go for a swim** schwimmen gehen

swim·mer Schwimmer(in)

swim·ming Schwimmen n

swimming bath(s) Br Schwimmbad n, esp Hallenbad n

swimming cap Badekappe f, Bademütze f

swimming costume Badeanzug m

swimming pool Swimmingpool m, Schwimmbecken n

swimming trunks Badehose f

swim·suit Badeanzug m

swin·dle 1. j-n beschwindeln (out of um); **2.** Schwindel m

swine ZO Schwein n (a. F fig)

swing 1. v/i (hin- und her)schwingen; sich schwingen; einbiegen, -schwenken (into in acc); MUS schwungvoll spielen (band etc); Schwung haben (music); **swing round** sich ruckartig umdrehen; **swing shut** zuschlagen (door etc); v/t et., die Arme etc schwingen; **2.** Schwingen n; Schaukel f; fig Schwung m; fig Umschwung m; **in full swing** in vollem Gang

swing door Pendeltür f

swin·ish ekelhaft

swipe 1. Schlag m; **2.** schlagen (at nach)

swirl 1. wirbeln; **2.** Wirbel m

swish¹ 1. v/i sausen, zischen; rascheln (silk etc); v/t mit dem Schwanz schlagen; **2.** Sausen n, Zischen n; Rascheln n; Schlagen n

swish² Br feudal, schick

Swiss 1. schweizerisch, eidgenössisch, Schweizer...; **2.** Schweizer(in); **the Swiss** die Schweizer pl

switch 1. ELECTR, TECH Schalter m; RAIL Weiche f; Gerte f, Rute f; fig Umstellung f; **2.** ELECTR, TECH um)schalten (a. **switch over**) (to auf acc); RAIL rangieren; wechseln (to zu); **switch off** abschalten, ausschalten; **switch on** anschalten, einschalten

switch·board ELECTR Schalttafel f; (Telefon)Zentrale f

Swit·zer·land die Schweiz

swiv·el (sich) drehen

swivel chair Drehstuhl m

swoon F in Ohnmacht fallen

swoop 1. fig F zuschlagen (police etc); a. **swoop down** ZO herabstoßen (on auf acc); **swoop on** F herfallen über (acc); **2.** Razzia f

swop F → swap

sword Schwert n

syc·a·more BOT Bergahorn m; Platane f

syl·la·ble Silbe f

syl·la·bus PED, UNIV Lehrplan m

sym·bol Symbol n

sym·bol·ic symbolisch

sym·bol·is·m Symbolik f

sym·bol·ize symbolisieren

sym·met·ri·cal symmetrisch

sym·me·try Symmetrie f

sym·pa·thet·ic mitfühlend; verständnisvoll; wohlwollend

sym·pa·thize mitfühlen; sympathisieren

sym·pa·thiz·er Sympathisant(in)

sym·pa·thy Mitgefühl n; Verständnis n

sym·pho·ny MUS Sinfonie f

symphony orches·tra MUS Sinfonieorchester *n*

symp·tom Symptom *n*

syn·chro·nize *v/t* aufeinander abstimmen; *Uhren, Film* synchronisieren; *v/i* synchron gehen *or* sein

syn·o·nym Synonym *n*

sy·non·y·mous synonym; gleichbedeutend

syn·tax LING Syntax *f*, Satzlehre *f*

syn·the·sis Synthese *f*

syn·thet·ic CHEM synthetisch

synthetic fi·ber (*Br* **fi·bre**) Kunstfaser *f*

Syr·i·a Syrien *n*

sy·ringe MED Spritze *f*

syr·up Sirup *m*

sys·tem System *n*; (*Straßen- etc*)Netz *n*; Organismus *m*

sys·te·mat·ic systematisch

sys·tem er·ror EDP Systemfehler *m*

T

T, t T, t *n*

tab Aufhänger *m*, Schlaufe *f*; Lasche *f*; Etikett *n*, Schildchen *n*; Reiter *m*; F Rechnung *f*

ta·ble 1. Tisch *m*; (*Tisch*)Runde *f*; Tabelle *f*, Verzeichnis *n*; MATH Einmaleins *n*; *at table* bei Tisch; *at the table* am Tisch; *turn the tables (on s.o.)* fig den Spieß umdrehen; **2.** *fig* auf den Tisch legen; *esp fig* zurückstellen

ta·ble·cloth Tischdecke *f*, Tischtuch *n*

ta·ble·land GEOGR Tafelland *n*, Plateau *n*, Hochebene *f*

ta·ble lin·en Tischwäsche *f*

ta·ble·mat Untersetzer *m*

ta·ble·spoon Esslöffel *m*

tab·let PHARM Tablette *f*; Stück *n*; (*Stein- etc*)Tafel *f*

ta·ble ten·nis SPORT Tischtennis *n*

ta·ble·top Tischplatte *f*

ta·ble·ware Geschirr *n* und Besteck *n*

tab·loid Boulevardblatt *n*, -zeitung *f*

tab·loid press Boulevardpresse *f*

ta·boo 1. tabu; **2.** Tabu *n*

tab·u·lar tabellarisch

tab·u·late tabellarisch (an)ordnen

tab·u·la·tor Tabulator *m*

tach·o·graph MOT Fahrtenschreiber *m*

ta·chom·e·ter MOT Drehzahlmesser *m*

tac·it stillschweigend

ta·ci·turn schweigsam, wortkarg

tack 1. Stift *m*, (Reiß)Zwecke *f*; Heftstich *m*; **2.** heften (*to* an *acc*); *tack on* anfügen (*to dat*)

tack·le 1. *Problem etc* angehen; *soccer etc*: *ballführenden Gegner* angreifen; *j-n* zur Rede stellen (*about* wegen); **2.** TECH Flaschenzug *m*; (*Angel*)Gerät(e *pl*) *n*; *soccer etc*: Angriff *m*

tack·y klebrig; F schäbig

tact Takt *m*, Feingefühl *n*

tact·ful taktvoll

tac·tics Taktik *f*

tact·less taktlos

tad·pole ZO Kaulquappe *f*

taf·fe·ta Taft *m*

taf·fy Sahnebonbon *m, n*, Toffee *n*

tag 1. Etikett *n*; (*Namens-, Preis*)Schild *n*; (*Schnürsenkel*)Stift *m*; stehende Redensart *f*; *a.* **question tag** LING Frageanhängsel *n*; **2.** etikettieren; *Waren* auszeichnen; anhängen; *tag along* F mitgehen, mitkommen; *tag along behind s.o.* F hinter *j-m* hertrotten

tail 1. Schwanz *m*; Schweif *m*; hinterer Teil; F Schatten *m*, Beschatter(in); *pl* Rück-, Kehrseite *f*; Frack *m*; *put a tail on j-n* beschatten lassen; *turn tail fig* sich auf dem Absatz umdrehen; *with one's tail between one's legs fig* mit eingezogenem Schwanz; **2.** F *j-n* beschatten; *tail back esp Br* MOT sich stauen (*to* bis zu); *tail off* schwächer werden, abnehmen, nachlassen

tail·back *esp Br* MOT Rückstau *m*

tail·coat Frack *m*

tail end Ende *n*, Schluss *m*

tail·light MOT Rücklicht *n*

tai·lor 1. Schneider *m*; **2.** schneidern

tai·lor-made Maß...; maßgeschneidert (*a. fig*)

tail pipe TECH Auspuffrohr *n*

tail·wind Rückenwind *m*

taint·ed GASTR verdorben

take 1. *v/t* nehmen; (weg)nehmen; mitnehmen; bringen; MIL, MED einnehmen; *chess etc*: *Figur, Stein* schlagen; *Gefangene, Prüfung etc* machen; UNIV studieren;

Preis etc erringen; *Scheck etc* (an)nehmen; *Rat* annehmen; *et.* hinnehmen; fassen, Platz bieten für; *et.* aushalten, ertragen; PHOT *et.* aufnehmen, *Aufnahme* machen; *Temperatur* messen; *Notiz* machen, niederschreiben; *ein Bad, Zug, Bus, Weg etc* nehmen; *Gelegenheit, Maßnahmen* ergreifen; *Mut* fassen; *Zeit, Geduld etc* erfordern, brauchen; *Zeit* dauern; *it took her four hours* sie brauchte vier Stunden; *I take it that* ich nehme an, dass; *take it or leave it* F mach, was du willst; *taken all in all* im Großen (und) Ganzen; *this seat is taken* dieser Platz ist besetzt; *be taken by or with* angetan sein von; *be taken ill or sick* erkranken, krank werden; *take to bits or pieces et.* auseinandernehmen, zerlegen; *take the blame* die Schuld auf sich nehmen; *take care* vorsichtig sein, aufpassen; *take care!* F mach's gut!; → *care 1*; *take hold of* ergreifen; *take part* teilnehmen (*in* an *dat*); → *part 1*; *take pity on* Mitleid haben mit; *take my word for it* verlass dich drauf; → *advice, bath 1, break 1, lead¹ 2, message, oath, offense, place 1, prisoner, risk 1, seat 1, step 1, trouble 1, turn 2, etc*; *v/i* wirken, anschlagen; *take after* j-m nachschlagen, ähneln; *take along* mitnehmen; *take apart* auseinandernehmen (*a. fig* F), zerlegen; *take away* wegnehmen (*from s.o.* j-m); *… to take away Br* … zum Mitnehmen; *take back* zurückbringen; zurücknehmen; bei j-m Erinnerungen wachrufen; j-n zurückversetzen (*to* in *acc*); *take down* herunternehmen, abnehmen; *Hose* herunterlassen; auseinandernehmen, zerlegen; (sich) et. aufschreiben *or* notieren; sich Notizen machen; *what do you take me for?* wofür hältst du mich eigentlich?; *take from* j-m et. wegnehmen; MATH abziehen *von*; *take in* j-n (bei sich) aufnehmen; *fig et.* einschließen; *Kleidungsstück* enger machen; *et.* begreifen; j-n hereinlegen, F j-n aufs Kreuz legen; *be taken in by* hereinfallen auf (*acc*); *take off Kleidungsstück* ablegen, ausziehen, *Hut etc* abnehmen; *et.* ab-, wegnehmen; abziehen; AVIAT abheben; SPORT abspringen; F sich davonmachen; *take a day off* sich e-n Tag freinehmen; *take on* j-n einstellen; *Arbeit etc* annehmen, übernehmen; *Farbe, Ausdruck etc* annehmen; sich anlegen mit; *take out* herausnehmen, *Zahn* ziehen; j-n ausführen, ausgehen mit j-m; *Versicherung* abschließen; *s-n Frust etc* auslassen (*on* an

dat); *take over Amt, Macht, Verantwortung etc* übernehmen; die Macht übernehmen; *take to* Gefallen finden an (*dat*); *take to doing s.th.* anfangen, et. zu tun; *take up Vorschlag etc* aufgreifen; *Zeit etc* in Anspruch nehmen, *Platz* einnehmen; *Erzählung etc* aufnehmen; *take up doing s.th.* anfangen, sich mit et. zu beschäftigen; *take up with* sich einlassen mit; *2. film,* TV Einstellung *f*; F Filmszenen *pl*

take·a·way *Br* **1.** Essen *n* zum Mitnehmen; **2.** Restaurant *n* mit Straßenverkauf

take-off AVIAT Abheben *n*, Start *m*; SPORT Absprung *m*

tak·ings Einnahmen *pl*

tale Erzählung *f*; Geschichte *f*; Lüge *f*, Lügengeschichte *f*, Märchen *n*; *tell tales* petzen

tal·ent Talent *n*, Begabung *f*

tal·ent·ed talentiert, begabt

tal·is·man Talisman *m*

talk 1. *v/i* reden, sprechen, sich unterhalten (*to, with* mit; *about* über *acc*; *of* von); *talk about s.th. a.* et. besprechen; *s.o. to talk to* Ansprechpartner(in); *v/t Unsinn etc* reden; reden *or* sprechen *or* sich unterhalten über (*acc*); *talk s.o. into s.th.* j-n zu et. überreden; *talk s.o. out of s.th.* j-m et. ausreden; *talk s.th. over Problem etc* besprechen (*with* mit); *talk round* j-n bekehren (*to* zu), umstimmen; **2.** Gespräch *n*, Unterhaltung *f* (*with* mit; *about* über *acc*); Vortrag *m*; Sprache *f*, Sprechweise *f*; Gerede *n*, Geschwätz *n*; *give a talk* e-n Vortrag halten (*to* vor *dat*; *about, on* über *acc*); *be the talk of the town* Stadtgespräch sein; *baby talk* Babysprache *f*, kindliches Gebabbel; → *small talk*

talk·a·tive gesprächig, redselig

talk·er: *be a good talker* gut reden können

talk·ing-to F Standpauke *f*; *give s.o. a talking-to* j-m e-e Standpauke halten

talk show TV Talkshow *f*

talk-show host TV Talkmaster *m*

tall groß (*person*), hoch (*building etc*)

tal·low Talg *m*

tal·ly¹ SPORT *etc* Stand *m*; *keep a tally of* Buch führen über (*acc*)

tal·ly² übereinstimmen (*with* mit); *a. tally up* zusammenrechnen, -zählen

tal·on zo Kralle *f*, Klaue *f*

tame 1. zo zahm; *fig* fad(e), lahm; **2.** zo zähmen (*a. fig*)

tam·per with sich zu schaffen machen an (*dat*)

tam·pon MED Tampon *m*

tan 1. *Fell* gerben; bräunen; braun werden; **2.** Gelbbraun *n*; (Sonnen)Bräune *f*; **3.** gelbbraun

tang (scharfer) Geruch *or* Geschmack

tan·gent MATH Tangente *f*; *fly or go off at a tangent* plötzlich (vom Thema) abschweifen

tan·ge·rine BOT Mandarine *f*

tan·gi·ble greifbar, *fig a.* handfest, fig

tan·gle 1. (sich) verwirren *or* verheddern, durcheinanderbringen; durcheinanderkommen; **2.** Gewirr *n*, *fig a.* Wirrwarr *m*, Durcheinander *n*

tank MOT *etc* Tank *m*; MIL Panzer *m*

tank·ard (Bier)Humpen *m*

tank·er MAR Tanker *m*, Tankschiff *n*; AVIAT Tankflugzeug *n*; MOT Tankwagen *m*

tan·ner Gerber *m*

tan·ne·ry Gerberei *f*

tan·ta·lize j-n aufreizen

tan·ta·liz·ing verlockend

tan·ta·mount: be tantamount to gleichbedeutend sein mit, hinauslaufen auf (*acc*)

tan·trum Wut-, Tobsuchtsanfall *m*

tap¹ 1. TECH Hahn *m*; *beer on tap* Bier *n* vom Fass; **2.** *Naturschätze etc* erschließen; *Vorräte etc* angreifen; *Telefon(leitung)* abhören, F anzapfen; *Fass* anzapfen, anstechen

tap² 1. mit *den Fingern, Füßen* klopfen, mit *den Fingern* trommeln (**on** auf *acc*); antippen; *tap s.o. on the shoulder* j-m auf die Schulter klopfen; *tap on* (leicht) klopfen an (*acc*) *or* auf (*acc*) *or* gegen; **2.** (leichtes) Klopfen; Klaps *m*

tap dance Stepptanz *m*

tape 1. (schmales) Band; Kleb(e)streifen *m*; (Magnet-, Video-, Ton)Band *n*; (*Video- etc*)Kassette *f*; (Band)Aufnahme *f*; TV Aufzeichnung *f*; SPORT Zielband *n*; → *red tape*; **2.** (auf Band) aufnehmen; TV aufzeichnen; *a. tape up* (mit Klebeband) zukleben

tape deck Tapedeck *n*

tape meas·ure Bandmaß *n*, Maßband *n*, Messband *n*

ta·per *a. taper off* spitz zulaufen, sich verjüngen; *fig* langsam nachlassen

tape re·cord·er Tonbandgerät *n*

tape re·cord·ing Tonbandaufnahme *f*

ta·pes·try Gobelin *m*, Wandteppich *m*

tape·worm ZO Bandwurm *m*

taps MIL Zapfenstreich *m*

tap wa·ter Leitungswasser *n*

tar 1. Teer *m*; **2.** teeren

tare ECON Tara *f*

tar·get (Schieß-, Ziel)Scheibe *f*; MIL Ziel *n* (*a. fig*), ECON a. Soll *n*; *fig* Zielscheibe *f*

target ar·e·a MIL Zielbereich *m*

target group Zielgruppe *f*

tar·iff ECON Zoll(tarif) *m*; *esp Br* Preisverzeichnis *n*

tar·mac Asphalt *m*; AVIAT Rollfeld *n*, Rollbahn *f*

tar·nish *v/i* anlaufen; *v/t* Ansehen *etc* beflecken

tart¹ *esp Br* Obstkuchen *m*; Obsttörtchen *n*; F Flittchen *n*, *sl* Nutte *f*

tart² herb, sauer; scharf (*a. fig*)

tar·tan Tartan *m*; Schottenstoff *m*; Schottenmuster *n*

tar·tar MED Zahnstein *m*; CHEM Weinstein *m*

task Aufgabe *f*; *take s.o. to task* fig j-n zurechtweisen (**for** wegen)

task force MIL *etc* Sonder-, Spezialeinheit *f*

tas·sel Troddel *f*, Quaste *f*

taste 1. Geschmack *m* (*a. fig*), Geschmackssinn *m*; Kostprobe *f*; Vorliebe *f* (**for** für); **2.** *v/t* kosten, probieren; schmecken; *v/i* schmecken (**of** nach)

taste·ful fig geschmackvoll

taste·less geschmacklos (*a. fig*)

tast·y schmackhaft

tat·tered zerlumpt

tat·ters Fetzen *pl*; *in tatters* zerfetzt, in Fetzen; *fig* ruiniert

tat·too¹ 1. Tätowierung *f*; **2.** (ein)tätowieren

tat·too² MIL Zapfenstreich *m*

taunt 1. verhöhnen, verspotten; **2.** höhnische *or* spöttische Bemerkung

Tau·rus ASTR Stier *m*; *he* (*she*) *is* (*a*) *Taurus* er (sie) ist (ein) Stier

taut straff; *fig* angespannt

taw·dry (billig und) geschmacklos

taw·ny gelbbraun

tax 1. Steuer *f* (**on** auf *acc*); **2.** besteuern; *j-s Geduld etc* strapazieren

tax·a·ble steuerpflichtig

tax·a·tion Besteuerung *f*

tax e·va·sion Steuerhinterziehung *f*

tax·i 1. Taxi, Taxe *f*; **2.** AVIAT rollen

tax·i driv·er Taxifahrer(in)

tax·i rank, tax·i stand Taxistand *m*

tax of·fi·cer Finanzbeamte *m*

tax·pay·er Steuerzahler(in)

tax re·duc·tion Steuersenkung *f*

tax re·turn Steuererklärung *f*

T-bar Bügel *m*; *a. T-bar lift* Schlepplift *m*

tea Tee *m*; *have a cup of tea* e-n Tee trinken; *make some tea* e-n Tee machen *or* kochen

tea·bag Teebeutel *m*, Aufgussbeutel *m*

teach lehren, unterrichten (**in** *dat*); *j-m et.* beibringen; unterrichten (**at** an *dat*)

T

teach·er Lehrer(in)

tea co·sy Teewärmer *m*

tea·cup Teetasse *f*; *a storm in a teacup* *fig* ein Sturm im Wasserglas

team Team *n*, *a.* Arbeitsgruppe *f*, SPORT *a.* Mannschaft *f*, *soccer: a.* Elf *f*

team·ster MOT LKW-Fahrer *m*

team·work Zusammenarbeit *f*, Teamwork *n*; Zusammenspiel *n*

tea·pot Teekanne *f*

tear¹ Träne *f*; *in tears* weinend, in Tränen (aufgelöst)

tear² **1.** *v/t* zerreißen; sich *et.* zerreißen (**on** an *dat*); weg-, losreißen (**from** von); *v/i* (zer)reißen; F rasen, sausen; *tear down* Plakat etc herunterreißen; *Haus etc* abreißen; *tear off* abreißen; sich *Kleidung* vom Leib reißen; *tear out* (her)ausreißen; *tear up* aufreißen; zerreißen; **2.** Riss *m*

tear·drop Träne *f*

tear·ful weinend; tränenreich

tear·jerk·er F Schnulze *f*

tea·room Teestube *f*

tease necken, hänseln; ärgern

tea·spoon Teelöffel *m*

teat ZO Zitze *f*; *Br* (Gummi)Sauger *m*

tech·ni·cal technisch; fachlich, Fach…

tech·ni·cal·i·ty technische Einzelheit; reine Formsache

tech·ni·cian Techniker(in)

tech·nique Technik *f*, Verfahren *n*

tech·nol·o·gy Technologie *f*; Technik *f*

ted·dy bear Teddybär *m*

te·di·ous langweilig, ermüdend

teem: *teem with* wimmeln von, strotzen von *or* vor (*dat*)

teen·age(d) im Teenageralter; für Teenager

teen·ag·er Teenager *m*

teens: *be in one's teens* im Teenageralter sein

tee·ny(-wee·ny) F klitzeklein, winzig

tee shirt → T-shirt

teethe zahnen

tee·to·tal·(l)er Abstinenzler(in)

tel·e·cast Fernsehsendung *f*

tel·e·com·mu·ni·ca·tions Telekommunikation *f*, Fernmeldewesen *n*

tel·e·gram Telegramm *n*

tel·e·graph 1. *by telegraph* telegrafisch; **2.** telegrafieren

tel·e·graph·ic telegrafisch

te·leg·ra·phy Telegrafie *f*

tel·e·phone 1. Telefon *n*; **2.** telefonieren, anrufen

telephone booth, telephone box *Br* Telefonzelle *f*, Fernsprechzelle *f*

telephone call Telefonanruf *n*, Telefonge-

spräch *n*

telephone di·rec·to·ry → phone book

telephone exchange Fernsprechamt *n*

telephone number Telefonnummer *f*

tel·e·pho·nist *esp Br* Telefonist(in)

tel·e·pho·to lens PHOT Teleobjektiv *n*

tel·e·print·er Fernschreiber *m*

tel·e·scope Teleskop *n*, Fernrohr *n*

tel·e·text Teletext *m*, Videotext *m*

tel·e·type·writ·er Fernschreiber *m*

tel·e·vise im Fernsehen übertragen *or* bringen

tel·e·vi·sion 1. Fernsehen *n*; *a.* *television set* Fernsehapparat *m*, -gerät *n*, F Fernseher *m*; *on television* im Fernsehen; *watch television* fernsehen; **2.** Fernseh…

tel·ex 1. Telex *n*, Fernschreiben *n*; **2.** telexen (*to* an *acc*), ein Telex schicken (*dat*)

tell *v/t* sagen; erzählen; erkennen (**by** an *dat*); *Namen etc* nennen; *et.* anzeigen; *j-m* sagen, befehlen (*to do* zu tun); *I can't tell one from the other, I can't tell them apart* ich kann sie nicht auseinanderhalten; *v/i* sich auswirken (**on** bei, auf *acc*), sich bemerkbar machen; *who can tell?*; wer weiß?; *you can never tell, you never can tell* man kann nie wissen; *tell against* sprechen gegen; von Nachteil sein für; *tell s.o. off* F mit j-m schimpfen (*for* wegen); *tell on s.o.* j-n verpetzen *or* verraten

tell·er Kassierer(in)

tell·ing aufschlussreich

tell·tale 1. verräterisch; **2.** F Petze *f*

tel·ly *Br* F Fernseher *m*

te·mer·i·ty Frechheit *f*, Kühnheit *f*

tem·per 1. Temperament *n*, Wesen *n*, Wesensart *f*; Laune *f*, Stimmung *f*; TECH Härte(grad *m*) *f*; *keep one's temper* sich beherrschen, ruhig bleiben; *lose one's temper* die Beherrschung verlieren; **2.** TECH *Stahl* härten

tem·pe·ra·ment Temperament *n*, Naturell *n*, Wesen *n*, Wesensart *f*

tem·pe·ra·men·tal launisch; von Natur aus

tem·pe·rate gemäßigt (*climate, region*)

tem·pe·ra·ture Temperatur *f*; *have or be running a temperature* MED erhöhte Temperatur *or* Fieber haben

tem·pest POET (heftiger) Sturm

tem·ple¹ Tempel *m*

tem·ple² ANAT Schläfe *f*

tem·po·ral weltlich; LING temporal, der Zeit

tem·po·ra·ry vorübergehend, zeiweilig

tempt *j-n* in Versuchung führen; *j-n* verführen (*to* zu)

temp·ta·tion Versuchung f, Verführung f

tempt·ing verführerisch

ten 1. zehn; **2.** Zehn f

ten·a·ble fig haltbar

te·na·cious hartnäckig, zäh

ten·ant Pächter(in), Mieter(in)

tend neigen, tendieren (**to** zu); **tend up-wards** e-e steigende Tendenz haben

ten·den·cy Tendenz f; Neigung f

ten·der¹ empfindlich, fig a. heikel; GASTR zart, weich; sanft, zart, zärtlich

ten·der² RAIL, MAR Tender m

ten·der³ ECON **1.** Angebot n; *legal tender* gesetzliches Zahlungsmittel; **2.** ein Angebot machen (*for* für)

ten·der·foot F Neuling m, Anfänger m

ten·der·loin GASTR zartes Lendenstück

ten·der·ness Zartheit f; Zärtlichkeit f

ten·don ANAT Sehne f

ten·dril BOT Ranke f

ten·e·ment Mietshaus n, contp Mietskaserne f

ten·nis Tennis n

tennis court Tennisplatz m

tennis play·er Tennisspieler(in)

ten·or MUS, JUR Tenor m, JUR a. Wortlaut m, Sinn m; Verlauf m

tense¹ LING Zeit(form) f, Tempus n

tense² gespannt, straff (*rope etc*), (an)gespannt (*a. fig*); (über)nervös, verkrampft (*person*)

ten·sion Spannung f (a. ELECTR)

tent Zelt n

ten·ta·cle ZO Tentakel m, n, Fangarm m

ten·ta·tive vorläufig; vorsichtig, zaghaft

ten·ter·hooks: *be on tenterhooks* wie auf (glühenden) Kohlen sitzen

tenth 1. zehnte(r, -s); **2.** Zehntel n

tenth·ly zehntens

ten·u·ous fig lose (*link, relationship etc*)

ten·ure Besitz m, Besitzdauer f; *tenure of office* Amtsdauer f, Dienstzeit f

tep·id lau(warm)

term 1. Zeit f, Zeitraum m, Dauer f; JUR Laufzeit f; PED, UNIV Semester n, esp Br Trimester n; Ausdruck m, Bezeichnung f; *term of office* Amtsdauer f, Amtsperiode f, Amtszeit f; pl Bedingungen pl; *be on good (bad) terms with* gut (schlecht) auskommen mit; *they are not on speaking terms* sie sprechen nicht (mehr) miteinander; *come to terms* sich einigen (*with* mit); **2.** nennen, bezeichnen als

ter·mi·nal 1. End...; letzte(r, -s); MED unheilbar; im Endstadium; *terminally ill* unheilbar krank; **2.** RAIL etc Endstation f; Terminal m, n; ELECTR Pol m; EDP Terminal n, Datenendstation f

ter·mi·nate v/t beenden; *Vertrag* kündigen, lösen; MED *Schwangerschaft* unterbrechen; v/i enden; ablaufen (*contract*)

ter·mi·na·tion Beendigung f; Kündigung f, Lösung f; Ende n; Ablauf m

ter·mi·nus RAIL etc Endstation f

ter·race Terrasse f; Häuserreihe f; mst pl esp Br SPORT Ränge pl

ter·raced house Br Reihenhaus n

ter·res·tri·al irdisch; Erd...; esp BOT, ZO Land...

ter·ri·ble schrecklich

ter·rif·ic F toll, fantastisch; irre (*speed, heat etc*)

ter·ri·fy j-m schreckliche Angst einjagen

ter·ri·to·ri·al territorial, Gebiets...

ter·ri·to·ry Territorium n, (a. Hoheits-, Staats)Gebiet n

ter·ror Entsetzen n; Schrecken m; POL Terror m; F Landplage f; *in terror* in panischer Angst

ter·ror·is·m Terrorismus m

ter·ror·ist Terrorist(in)

ter·ror·ize terrorisieren

terse fig knapp, kurz (und bündig)

test 1. Test m, Prüfung f; Probe f; **2.** testen, prüfen; probieren; j-s Geduld etc auf e-e harte Probe stellen

tes·ta·ment: *last will and testament* JUR Letzter Wille, Testament n

test an·i·mal Versuchstier n

test card TV Testbild n

test drive MOT Probefahrt f

tes·ti·cle ANAT Hoden m

tes·ti·fy JUR aussagen

tes·ti·mo·ni·al Referenz f

tes·ti·mo·ny JUR Aussage f; Beweis m

test pi·lot AVIAT Testpilot m

test tube CHEM Reagenzglas n

tes·ty gereizt

tet·a·nus MED Tetanus m, Wundstarrkrampf m

teth·er 1. Strick m; Kette f; *at the end of one's tether* fig mit s-n Kräften or Nerven am Ende sein; **2.** Tier anbinden; anketten

text Text m

text·book Lehrbuch n

tex·tile 1. Stoff m, pl Textilien pl; **2.** Textil...

tex·ture Textur f, Gewebe n; Beschaffenheit f; Struktur f

than als

thank 1. j-m danken, sich bei j-m bedanken (*for* für); *thank you* danke; *thank you very much* vielen Dank; *no, thank you* nein, danke; (*yes,*) *thank you* ja, bitte; **2.** *thanks* Dank m; *thanks* danke (schön); *no, thanks* nein, danke; *thanks*

to dank (*gen*), wegen (*gen*)

thank·ful dankbar

thank·less undankbar

that 1. *pron and adj* das; jene(r, -s) der, die, das, derjenige, diejenige, dasjenige; **2.** *relative pron* der, die, das, welche(r, -s); **3.** *cj* dass; **4.** *adv* F so, dermaßen; **it's that simple** so einfach ist das

thatch 1. mit Stroh *or* Reet decken; **2.** (Dach)Stroh *n*, Reet *n*; Strohdach *n*, Reetdach *n*

thaw 1. (auf)tauen; **2.** Tauwetter *n*; (Auf-) Tauen *n*

the 1. der, die, das, *pl* die; **2.** *adv*: **the ... the ...** je ... desto ...; **the sooner the better** je eher, desto besser

the·a·ter Theater *n*; UNIV (*Hör*)Saal *m*; MIL (Kriegs)Schauplatz *m*

the·a·ter·go·er Theaterbesucher(in)

the·a·tre *Br* → **theater**; MED Operationssaal *m*

the·at·ri·cal Theater...; *fig* theatralisch

theft Diebstahl *m*

their ihr(e)

theirs der (die, das) ihrige *or* ihre

them sie (*acc pl*); ihnen (*dat*)

theme Thema *n*

them·selves sie (*acc pl*) selbst; sich (selbst)

then 1. *adv* dann; da; damals; **by then** bis dahin; **from then on** von da an; → **every, now 1, there**; **2.** *adj* damalig

the·o·lo·gian Theologe *m*, Theologin *f*

the·ol·o·gy Theologie *f*

the·o·ret·i·cal theoretisch

the·o·rist Theoretiker *m*

the·o·ry Theorie *f*

ther·a·peu·tic therapeutisch; F wohltuend; gesund

ther·a·pist Therapeut(in)

ther·a·py Therapie *f*

there 1. da; (da-; dort)hin; **there is, there are** es gibt, es ist, *pl* es sind; **there and then** auf der Stelle; **there you are** hier bitte; siehst du!, na also!; **2.** *int* so; siehst du!, na also!; **there, there** ist ja gut!

there·a·bout(s) so ungefähr

there·af·ter danach

there·by dadurch

there·fore deshalb, daher; folglich

there·up·on darauf(hin)

ther·mal 1. thermisch, Thermo..., Wärme...; **2.** Thermik *f*

ther·mom·e·ter Thermometer *n*

ther·mos® Thermosflasche® *f*

the·sis These *f*; UNIV Dissertation *f*, Doktorarbeit *f*

they sie *pl*; man

---

thick 1. *adj* dick, (*fog etc a.*) dicht; F dumm; F dick befreundet; **be thick with** wimmeln von; **thick with smoke** verräuchert; **that's a bit thick!** *esp Br* F das ist ein starkes Stück!; **2.** *adv* dick, dicht; **lay it on thick** F dick auftragen; **3.** **in the thick of** mitten in (*dat*); **through thick and thin** durch dick und dünn

thick·en dicker werden, (*fog etc a.*) dichter werden; GASTR eindicken, binden

thick·et Dickicht *n*

thick·head·ed F strohdumm

thick·ness Dicke *f*; Lage *f*, Schicht *f*

thick·set gedrungen, untersetzt

thick-skinned *fig* dickfellig

thief Dieb(in)

thigh ANAT (Ober)Schenkel *m*

thim·ble Fingerhut *m*

thin 1. *adj* dünn; dürr; spärlich, dürftig; schütter (*hair*); schwach, (*excuse etc a.*) fadenscheinig; **2.** *adv* dünn; **3.** verdünnen; dünner werden, (*fog, hair a.*) sich lichten

thing Ding *n*; Sache *f*; *pl* Sachen *pl*, Zeug *n*; *fig* Dinge *pl*, Lage *f*, Umstände *pl*; **I couldn't see a thing** ich konnte überhaupt nichts sehen; **another thing** et. anderes; **the right thing** das Richtige

thing·a·ma·jig F Dings(bums) *m*, *f*, *n*

think *v/i* denken (**of** *an acc*); nachdenken (**about** über *acc*); **I think so** ich glaube *or* denke schon; **I'll think about it** ich überlege es mir; **think of** sich erinnern an (*acc*); **think of doing s.th.** beabsichtigen *or* daran denken, et. zu tun; **what do you think of** *or* **about ... ?** was halten Sie von ...?; *v/t* denken, glauben, meinen; *j-n, et.* halten für; **think over** nachdenken über (*acc*), et. überlegen; **think up** sich et. ausdenken

think tank Beraterstab *m*, Sachverständigenstab *m*, Denkfabrik *f*

third 1. dritte(r, -s); **2.** Drittel *n*

third·ly drittens

third-rate drittklassig

Third World Dritte Welt

thirst Durst *m*

thirst·y durstig; **be thirsty** Durst haben, durstig sein

thir·teen 1. dreizehn; **2.** Dreizehn *f*

thir·teenth dreizehnte(r, -s)

thir·ti·eth dreißigste(r, -s)

thir·ty 1. dreißig; **2.** Dreißig *f*

this diese(r, -s); **this morning** heute Morgen; **this is John speaking** TEL hier (spricht) John

this·tle BOT Distel *f*

thong (Leder)Riemen *m*

thorn Dorn *m*

thorn·y dornig; *fig* schwierig, heikel

thor·ough gründlich, genau; fürchterlich (*mess etc*)

thor·ough·bred zo Vollblüter *m*

thor·ough·fare Hauptverkehrsstraße *f*; *no thoroughfare!* Durchfahrt verboten!

though 1. *cj* obwohl; (je)doch; *as though* als ob; **2.** *adv* dennoch, trotzdem

thought Denken *n*; Gedanke *m* (*of* an *acc*); *on second thought* wenn ich es mir (recht) überlege

thought·ful nachdenklich; rücksichtsvoll, aufmerksam

thought·les gedankenlos; rücksichtslos

thou·sand 1. tausend; **2.** Tausend *n*

thou·sandth 1. tausendste(r, -s); **2.** Tausendstel *n*

thrash verdreschen, verprügeln; *sport* F *j-m* e-e Abfuhr erteilen; *thrash about, thrash around* sich *im Bett etc* hin und her werfen; um sich schlagen; zappeln (*fish*); *thrash out Problem etc* ausdiskutieren

thrash·ing Dresche *f*, Tracht *f* Prügel

thread 1. Faden *m* (*a. fig*); Garn *n*; *tech* Gewinde *n*; **2.** *Nadel* einfädeln; *Perlen etc* auffädeln, aufreihen

thread·bare abgewetzt, abgetragen; *fig* abgedroschen

threat Drohung *f*; Bedrohung *f*, Gefahr *f* (*to gen or* für)

threat·en (be)drohen

threat·en·ing drohend

three 1. drei; **2.** Drei *f*

three·fold dreifach

three·ply → *ply²*

three·score sechzig

three·stage dreistufig

thresh *agr* dreschen

thresh·ing ma·chine *agr* Dreschmaschine *f*

thresh·old Schwelle *f*

thrift Sparsamkeit *f*

thrift·y sparsam

thrill 1. prickelndes Gefühl; Nervenkitzel *m*; aufregendes Erlebnis; **2.** *v/t be thrilled* (ganz) hingerissen sein (*at, about* von)

thrill·er Thriller *m*, F Reißer *m*

thrill·ing spannend, fesselnd, packend

thrive gedeihen; *fig* blühen, florieren

throat *anat* Kehle *f*, Gurgel *f*; Rachen *m*; Hals *m*; *clear one's throat* sich räuspern; → *sore 1*

throb 1. hämmern (*machine*), (*heart etc a.*) pochen, schlagen; pulsieren (*pain*); **2.** Hämmern *n*, Pochen *n*, Schlagen *n*

throm·bo·sis *med* Thrombose *f*

throne Thron *m*

throng 1. Schar *f*, Menschenmenge *f*; **2.** sich drängen (in *dat*)

throt·tle 1. erdrosseln; *throttle down* mot, tech drosseln, Gas wegnehmen; **2.** tech Drosselklappe *f*

through 1. *prp* durch (*acc*); bis (einschließlich); *Monday through Friday* von Montag bis Freitag; **2.** *adv* durch; *through and through* durch und durch; *put s.o. through to* tel *j*-n verbinden mit; *wet through* völlig durchnässt; **3.** *adj* durchgehend (*train etc*); Durchgangs…

through·out 1. *prp*: *throughout the night* die ganze Nacht hindurch; *throughout the country* im ganzen Land, überall im Land; **2.** *adv* ganz, überall; die ganze Zeit (hindurch)

through traf·fic Durchgangsverkehr *m*

through·way *Br* → *thruway*

throw 1. werfen; *Hebel etc* betätigen; *Reiter* abwerfen; *Party* geben, F schmeißen; *throw a four* e-e Vier würfeln; *throw off Jacke etc* abwerfen; *Verfolger* abschütteln; *Krankheit* loswerden; *throw on* sich *e-e Jacke etc* (hastig) überwerfen; *throw out* hinauswerfen; wegwerfen; *throw up v/t* hochwerfen; F *Job etc* hinschmeißen; F (er)brechen; *v/i* F (sich er)brechen; **2.** Wurf *m*

throw·a·way Wegwerf…, Einweg…

throwaway pack Einwegpackung *f*

throw·in *soccer*: Einwurf *m*

thru F → *through*

thrum → *strum*

thrush zo Drossel *f*

thrust *j*-*n*, *et.* stoßen (*into* in *acc*); *et.* stecken, schieben (*into* in *acc*); *thrust at* stoßen nach; *thrust s.th. upon s.o.* *j*-m *et.* aufdrängen; **2.** Stoß *m*; mil Vorstoß *m*; phys Schub *m*, Schubkraft *f*

thru·way Schnellstraße *f*

thud 1. dumpfes Geräusch, Plumps *m*; **2.** plumpsen

thug Verbrecher *m*, Schläger *m*

thumb 1. anat Daumen *m*; **2.** *thumb a lift or ride* per Anhalter fahren, trampen (*to* nach); *thumb through a book* ein Buch durchblättern; *well-thumbed* abgegriffen

thumb·tack Reißzwecke *f*, Reißnagel *m*, Heftzwecke *f*

thump 1. *v/t* *j*-*m* e-n Schlag versetzen; *thump out Melodie* herunterhämmern (*on the piano* auf dem Klavier); *v/i* (heftig) schlagen *or* hämmern *or* pochen (*a. heart*); plumpsen; trampeln; **2.** dumpfes Geräusch, Plumps *m*; Schlag *m*

thun·der 1. Donner *m*, Donnern *n*; **2.** donnern

thun·der·bolt Blitz *m* und Donner *m*

thun·der·clap Donnerschlag *m*

thun·der·cloud Gewitterwolke *f*

thun·der·ous donnernd (*applause*)

thun·der·storm Gewitter *n*, Unwetter *n*

thun·der·struck wie vom Donner gerührt

Thur(s) ABBR of **Thursday** Do., Donnerstag *m*

Thurs·day (ABBR **Thur, Thurs**) Donnerstag *m*; **on Thursday** (am) Donnerstag; **on Thursdays** donnerstags

thus so, auf diese Weise; folglich, somit; **thus far** bisher

thwart durchkreuzen, vereiteln

thyme BOT Thymian *m*

thy·roid (gland) ANAT Schilddrüse *f*

tick¹ 1. Ticken *n*; Haken *m*, Häkchen *n*; 2. *v/i* ticken; *v/t mst* **tick off** ab-, anhaken

tick² ZO Zecke *f*

tick³: **on tick** *Br* F auf Pump

tick·er·tape pa·rade Konfettiparade *f*

tick·et 1. Fahrkarte *f*, Fahrschein *m*; Flugkarte *f*, Flugschein *m*, Ticket *n*; (*Eintritts-, Theater- etc*)Karte *f*; (*Gepäck-*)Schein *m*, Etikett *n*, (*Preis- etc* -) Schild *n*; POL Wahl-, Kandidatenliste *f*; (*a.* **parking ticket**) MOT Strafzettel *m*; 2. etikettieren; bestimmen, vorsehen (**for** für)

tick·et-can·cel·(l)ing ma·chine (Fahrschein)Entwerter *m*

tick·et col·lec·tor (Bahnsteig)Schaffner(in)

ticket machine Fahrkartenautomat *m*

ticket office RAIL Fahrkartenschalter *m*

tick·ing Inlett *n*; Matratzenbezug *m*

tick·le kitzeln

tick·lish kitz(e)lig, *fig a.* heikel

tid·al wave Flutwelle *f*

tid·bit Leckerbissen *m*

tide 1. Gezeiten *pl*; Flut *f*; *fig* Strömung *f*, Trend *m*; **high tide** Flut *f*; **low tide** Ebbe *f*; 2. **tide over** *fig j-m* hinweghelfen über (*acc*); *j-n* über Wasser halten

ti·dy 1. sauber, ordentlich, aufgeräumt; F hübsch, beträchtlich (*Sum etc*); 2. *a.* **tidy up** in Ordnung bringen, (*Zimmer a.*) aufräumen; **tidy away** wegräumen, aufräumen

tie 1. Krawatte *f*, Schlips *m*; Band *n*; Schnur *f*; Stimmengleichheit *f*; SPORT Unentschieden *n*; (*Pokal*)Spiel *n*; RAIL Schwelle *f*; *mst pl fig* Bande *pl*; 2. *v/t* an-, festbinden; (sich) *Krawatte etc* binden; *fig* verbinden; **the game was tied** SPORT das Spiel ging unentschieden aus; *v/i*: **they tied for second place** SPORT *etc* sie belegten gemeinsam den zweiten Platz; **tie down** *fig* (an)binden; *j-n* festlegen (**to** auf *acc*); **tie in with** über-

einstimmen mit, passen zu; verbinden *or* koppeln mit; **tie up** *Paket etc* verschnüren; *et.* in Verbindung bringen (**with** mit); *Verkehr etc* lahmlegen; **be tied up** ECON fest angelegt sein (**in** in *dat*)

tie-break(·er) *tennis*: Tie-Break *m*, *n*

tie-in (enge) Verbindung, (enger) Zusammenhang; ECON Kopplungsgeschäft *n*; **a book movie tie-in** *appr* das Buch zum Film

tie-on Anhänge…

tie-pin Krawattennadel *f*

tier (Sitz)Reihe *f*; Lage *f*, Schicht *f*; *fig* Stufe *f*

tie-up (enge) Verbindung, (enger) Zusammenhang; ECON Fusion *f*

ti·ger ZO Tiger *m*

tight 1. *adj* fest (sitzend), fest angezogen; straff (*rope etc*); eng (*a. dress etc*); knapp (*a. fig*); F knick(e)rig; F blau; **be in a tight corner** in der Klemme sein *or* sitzen *or* stecken; 2. *adv* fest; F gut; **hold tight** festhalten; **sleep tight!** F schlaf gut!

tight·en festziehen, anziehen; *Seil etc* straffen; **tighten one's belt** *fig* den Gürtel enger schnallen; **tighten up (on)** *Gesetz etc* verschärfen

tight-fist·ed F knick(e)rig

tights (*Tänzer-, Artisten*)Trikot *n*; *esp Br* Strumpfhose *f*

ti·gress ZO Tigerin *f*

tile 1. (Dach)Ziegel *m*; Fliese *f*, Kachel *f*; 2. (mit Ziegeln) decken; fliesen, kacheln

til·er Dachdecker *m*; Fliesenleger *m*

till¹ → **until**

till² (Laden)Kasse *f*

tilt 1. kippen; sich neigen; 2. Kippen *n*; **at a tilt** schief, schräg; (**at**) **full tilt** F mit Volldampf

tim·ber *Br* Bau-, Nutzholz *n*; Baumbestand *m*, Bäume *pl*; Balken *m*

time 1. Zeit *f*; Uhrzeit *f*; MUS Takt *m*; Mal *n*; **time after time, time and again** immer wieder; **every time I …** jedes Mal, wenn ich …; **how many times?** wie oft?; **next time** nächstes Mal; **this time** diesmal; **three times** dreimal; **three times four equals** *or* **is twelve** drei mal vier ist zwölf; **what's the time?** wie spät ist es?; **what time?** um wie viel Uhr?; **all the time** die ganze Zeit; **at all times, at any time** jederzeit; **at the time** damals; **at the same time** gleichzeitig; **at times** manchmal; **by the time** wenn; als; **for a time** e-e Zeit lang; **for the time being** vorläufig, fürs Erste; **from time to time** von Zeit zu Zeit; **have a good time** sich gut unterhalten *or* amüsieren; **in time** rechtzeitig; **in no time (at all)** im

Nu; *on time* pünktlich; *some time ago* vor einiger Zeit; *to pass the time* zum Zeitvertreib; *take one's time* sich Zeit lassen; **2.** *et.* timen (*a.* SPORT); (ab)stoppen; zeitlich abstimmen; den richtigen Zeitpunkt wählen *or* bestimmen für

time card Stechkarte *f*

time clock Stechuhr *f*

time lag Zeitdifferenz *f*

time-lapse *film:* Zeitraffer…

time·less immer während, ewig; zeitlos

time lim·it Frist *f*

time·ly (recht)zeitig

time sheet Stechkarte *f*

time sig·nal *radio:* Zeitzeichen *n*

time·ta·ble *Br* Fahrplan *m*, Flugplan *m*; Stundenplan *m*; Zeitplan *m*

tim·id ängstlich, furchtsam, zaghaft

tim·ing Timing *n*

tin **1.** Zinn *n*; *Br* (Blech-, Konserven)Dose *f*, (-)Büchse *f*; **2.** verzinnen; *Br* einmachen, eindosen

tinc·ture Tinktur *f*

tin-foil Stanniol(papier) *n*; Alufolie *f*

tinge 1. tönen; *be tinged with fig* e-n Anflug haben von; **2.** Tönung *f*; *fig* Anflug *m*, Spur *f* (*of* von)

tin·gle prickeln, kribbeln

tink·er herumpfuschen, herumbasteln (*at* an *dat*)

tin·kle bimmeln; klirren

tinned *Br* Dosen…, Büchsen…

tinned fruit *Br* Obstkonserven *pl*

tin o·pen·er *Br* Dosenöffner *m*, Büchsenöffner *m*

tin·sel Lametta *n*; Flitter *m*

tint 1. (Farb)Ton *m*, Tönung *f*; **2.** tönen

ti·ny winzig

tip¹ 1. Spitze *f*; Filter *m*; *it's on the tip of my tongue fig* es liegt mir auf der Zunge; **2.** mit e-r Spitze versehen

tip² 1. *esp Br* (aus)kippen, schütten; kippen; *tip over* umkippen; **2.** *esp Br* (*Schutt- etc*)Abladeplatz *m*, (-)Halde *f*; *Br fig* F Saustall *m*

tip³ 1. Trinkgeld *n*; **2.** *j-m* ein Trinkgeld geben

tip⁴ 1. Tipp *m*, Rat(schlag) *m*; **2.** tippen auf (*acc*) (*as* als); *tip s.o. off j-m* e-n Tipp *or* Wink geben

tip·sy angeheitert

tip·toe 1. *on tiptoe* auf Zehenspitzen; **2.** auf Zehenspitzen gehen

tire¹ MOT Reifen *m*

tire² ermüden, müde machen *or* werden

tired müde; *be tired of j-n, et.* satt haben

tire·less unermüdlich

tire·some ermüdend; lästig

tis·sue BIOL Gewebe *n*; Papier(taschen)-

tuch *n*; → **tissue pa·per** Seidenpapier *n*

tit¹ F *contp* Titte *f*

tit² ZO Meise *f*

tit·bit *esp Br →* **tidbit**

tit·il·late *j-n* (*sexuell*) anregen

ti·tle Titel *m*; JUR (Rechts)Anspruch *m* (*to* auf *acc*)

ti·tle-hold·er SPORT Titelhalter(in)

ti·tle page Titelseite *f*

ti·tle role THEA *etc* Titelrolle *f*

tit·mouse ZO Meise *f*

tit·ter 1. kichern; **2.** Kichern *n*

to 1. *prp* zu; an (*acc*), auf (*acc*), für, in (*acc*), in (*dat*), nach; (im Verhältnis *or* im Vergleich) zu, gegen(über); *extent, limit, degree:* bis, (bis) zu, (bis) an (*acc*); *time:* bis, bis zu, bis gegen, vor (*dat*); *from Monday to Friday* von Montag bis Freitag; *a quarter to one* (ein) Viertel vor eins, drei viertel eins; *go to Italy* nach Italien fahren; *go to school* in die *or* zur Schule gehen; *have you ever been to Rome?* bist du schon einmal in Rom gewesen?; *to me etc* mir *etc*; *here's to you!* zum Wohl!, prosit!; **2.** *adv* zu; *pull to* Tür *etc* zuziehen; *come to* (wieder) zu sich kommen; *to and fro* hin und her, auf und ab; **3.** *with infinitive:* zu; *intention, aim:* um zu; *to go* gehen; *easy to learn* leicht zu lernen; *… to earn money …* um Geld zu verdienen

toad ZO Kröte *f*, Unke *f*

toad·stool BOT ungenießbarer Pilz; Giftpilz *m*

toad·y 1. Kriecher(in); **2.** *toady to s.o. fig* vor *j-m* kriechen

toast¹ 1. Toast *m*; **2.** toasten; rösten

toast² 1. Toast *m*, Trinkspruch *m*; **2.** auf *j-n or j-s* Wohl trinken

toast·er TECH Toaster *m*

to·bac·co Tabak *m*

to·bac·co·nist Tabak(waren)händler(in)

to·bog·gan 1. (Rodel)Schlitten *m*; **2.** Schlitten fahren, rodeln

to·day 1. *adv* heute; heutzutage; *a week today, today week* heute in e-r Woche, heute in acht Tagen; **2.** *today's paper* die heutige Zeitung, die Zeitung von heute; *of today, today's* von heute, heutig

tod·dle auf wack(e)ligen *or* unsicheren Beinen gehen

to-do F *fig* Theater *n*

toe ANAT Zehe *f*; Spitze *f*

toe·nail ANAT Zehennagel *m*

tof·fee, tof·fy Sahnebonbon *m*, *n*, Toffee *n*

to·geth·er zusammen; gleichzeitig

toi·let Toilette *f*

toilet pa·per Toilettenpapier *n*

toilet roll *esp Br* Rolle *f* Toilettenpapier

to·ken Zeichen *n*; *as a token, in token of* als *or* zum Zeichen (*gen*); zum Andenken an (*acc*)

token strike Warnstreik *m*

tol·e·ra·ble erträglich

tol·e·rance Toleranz *f*; Nachsicht *f*

tol·e·rant tolerant (*of, towards* gegenüber)

tol·e·rate tolerieren, dulden; ertragen

toll[1] Benutzungsgebühr *f*, Maut *f*; *heavy death toll* große Zahl an Todesopfern; *take its toll* (*of*) *fig* s-n Tribut fordern (von); s-e Spuren hinterlassen (bei)

toll[2] läuten

toll-free TEL gebührenfrei

toll road gebührenpflichtige Straße, Mautstraße *f*

tom F → **tomcat**

to·ma·to BOT Tomate *f*

tomb Grab *n*; Grabmal *n*; Gruft *f*

tom·boy Wildfang *m*

tomb·stone Grabstein *m*

tom·cat ZO Kater *m*

tom·fool·e·ry Unsinn *m*

to·mor·row 1. *adv* morgen; *a week tomorrow, tomorrow week* morgen in e-r Woche, morgen in acht Tagen; *tomorrow morning* morgen früh; *tomorrow night* morgen Abend; **2.** *the day after tomorrow* übermorgen; *of tomorrow, tomorrow's* von morgen

ton (ABBR *t, tn*) Tonne *f*

tone 1. Ton *m*; Klang *m*; (Farb)Ton *m*; MUS Note *f*; MED Tonus *m*; *fig* Niveau *n*; **2.** *tone down* abschwächen; *tone up* Muskeln *etc* kräftigen

tongs (*a pair of tongs* e-e) Zange *f*

tongue ANAT, TECH Zunge *f*; (*Mutter*)Sprache *f*; Klöppel *m* (*e-r Glocke*); *hold one's tongue* den Mund halten

ton·ic Tonikum *n*, Stärkungsmittel *n*; Tonic *n*; MUS Grundton *m*

to·night heute Abend *or* Nacht

ton·sil ANAT Mandel *f*

ton·sil·li·tis MED Mandelentzündung *f*; Angina *f*

too zu; zu, sehr; auch (noch)

tool Werkzeug *n*, Gerät *n*

tool bag Werkzeugtasche *f*

tool box Werkzeugkasten *m*

tool kit Werkzeug *n*

tool·mak·er Werkzeugmacher *m*

tool·shed Geräteschuppen *m*

toot *esp* MOT hupen

tooth Zahn *m*

tooth·ache Zahnschmerzen *pl*, Zahnweh *n*

tooth·brush Zahnbürste *f*

tooth·less zahnlos

tooth·paste Zahncreme *f*, Zahnpasta *f*

tooth·pick Zahnstocher *m*

top[1] **1.** oberer Teil; GEOGR Gipfel *m*, Spitze *f*; Br Krone *f*, Wipfel *m*; Kopfende *n*, oberes Ende; Oberteil *n*; Oberfläche *f*; Deckel *m*; Verschluss *m*; MOT Verdeck *n*; MOT höchster Gang; *at the top of the page* oben auf der Seite; *at the top of one's voice* aus vollem Hals; *on top* oben(auf); darauf, F drauf; *on top of* (oben) auf (*dat or acc*), über (*dat or acc*); **2.** oberste(r, -s); Höchst..., Spitzen..., Top...; **3.** bedecken (*with* mit); *fig* übersteigen, übertreffen; *top up* Tank *etc* auffüllen; F *j-m* nachschenken

top[2] Kreisel *m* (*toy*)

top hat Zylinder *m*

top-heav·y kopflastig (*a. fig*)

top·ic Thema *n*

top·i·cal aktuell

top·ple *mst* **topple over** umkippen; *topple the government* die Regierung stürzen

top·sy-tur·vy in e-r heillosen Unordnung

torch Br Taschenlampe *f*; Fackel *f*

torch·light Fackelschein *m*; *torchlight procession* Fackelzug *m*

tor·ment 1. Qual *f*; **2.** quälen, peinigen, plagen

tor·na·do Tornado *m*, Wirbelsturm *m*

tor·pe·do MIL **1.** Torpedo *m*; **2.** torpedieren (*a. fig*)

tor·rent reißender Strom; *fig* Schwall *m*

tor·ren·tial: *torrential rain* sintflutartige Regenfälle *pl*

tor·toise ZO Schildkröte *f*

tor·tu·ous gewunden

tor·ture 1. Folter *f*, Folterung *f*; *fig* Qual *f*, Tortur *f*; **2.** foltern; *fig* quälen

toss 1. *v/t* werfen; *Münze* hochwerfen; GASTR schwenken; *toss off* F *Bild etc* hinhauen; *v/i a.* *toss about, toss and turn* sich *im Schlaf* hin und her werfen; *a. toss up* e-e Münze hochwerfen; *toss for s.th.* um *et.* losen; *toss one's head* den Kopf zurückwerfen; **2.** Wurf *m*; Zurückwerfen *n*; Hochwerfen *n*

tot F Knirps *m*

to·tal 1. völlig, total; ganz, gesamt, Gesamt...; **2.** Gesamtbetrag *m*, -menge *f*; **3.** sich belaufen auf (*acc*); *total up* zusammenrechnen, -zählen

tot·ter schwanken, wanken

touch 1. (sich) berühren; anfassen; *Essen etc* anrühren; *fig* herankommen an (*acc*); *fig* rühren; *touch wood!* toi, toi, toi!; *touch down* AVIAT aufsetzen; *touch up* ausbessern; PHOT retuschieren; **2.** Tast-

empfindung f; Berührung f, mus etc Anschlag m; (*Pinsel- etc*)Strich m; gastr Spur f; Verbindung f, Kontakt m; fig Note f; fig Anflug m; *a touch of flu* e-e leichte Grippe; *get in touch with s.o.* sich mit j-m in Verbindung setzen

touch-and-go aviat Aufsetzen n, Landung f

touch-and-go kritisch, riskant, prekär; *it was touch-and-go whether* es stand auf des Messers Schneide, ob

touch-down aviat Aufsetzen n, Landung f

touched gerührt; F leicht verrückt

touch-ing rührend

touch-line soccer: Seitenlinie f

touch-stone Prüfstein m (*of* für)

touch-y empfindlich; heikel (*subject etc*)

tough zäh; widerstandsfähig; fig hart; schwierig (*problem, negotiations etc*)

tough-en a. **toughen up** hart or zäh machen or werden

tour 1. Tour f (*of* durch), (Rund)Reise f, (Rund)Fahrt f; Ausflug m; Rundgang m (*of* durch); thea Tournee f (*a.* sport); *go on tour* auf Tournee gehen; → *conduct* 2; **2.** bereisen, reisen durch

tour-is-m Tourismus m, Fremdenverkehr m

tour-ist 1. Tourist(in); **2.** Touristen...

tourist class aviat, mar Touristenklasse f

tourist in-dus-try Tourismusgeschäft n

tourist infor-ma-tion of-fice, tourist office Verkehrsverein m

tourist sea-son Reisesaison f, Reisezeit f

tour-na-ment Turnier n

tou-sled zerzaust

tow 1. *Boot etc* schleppen, *Auto etc* a. abschleppen; **2.** *give s.o. a tow* j-n abschleppen; *take in tow Auto etc* abschleppen

to-ward, *esp Br* **to-wards** auf (*acc*) ... zu, (in) Richtung, zu; *time*: gegen; fig gegenüber

tow-el 1. Handtuch n, (*Bade- etc*)Tuch n; **2.** (mit e-m Handtuch) abtrocknen or abreiben

tow-er 1. Turm m; **1.** *tower above, tower over* überragen

tower block Br Hochhaus n

tow-er-ing turmhoch; fig überragend; *in a towering rage* rasend vor Zorn

town Stadt f; Kleinstadt f; *go into town* in die Stadt gehen

town cen-tre Br Innenstadt f, City f

town coun-cil Br Stadtrat m

town coun-ci(l)-lor Br Stadtrat m, Stadträtin f

town hall Rathaus n

town-ie F Städter(in), Stadtmensch m

town plan-ner Stadtplaner(in)

town plan-ning Stadtplanung f

towns-peo-ple Städter pl, Stadtbevölkerung f

tow-rope mot Abschleppseil n

tox-ic toxisch, giftig; Gift...

tox-ic waste Giftmüll m

tox-ic waste dump Giftmülldeponie f

toy 1. Spielzeug n, pl a. Spielsachen pl, econ Spielwaren pl; **2.** Spielzeug...; Miniatur...; Zwerg...; **3.** *toy with* spielen mit (*a. fig*)

trace 1. (durch)pausen; *j-n, et.* ausfindig machen, aufspüren, *et.* finden; a. *trace back et.* zurückverfolgen (*to* bis zu); *trace s.th. to et.* zurückführen auf (*acc*); **2.** Spur f (*a. fig*)

track 1. Spur f (*a. fig*), Fährte f; Pfad m, Weg m; rail Gleis n, Geleise n; tech Raupe f, Raupenkette f; sport (Renn-, Aschen)Bahn f, (*Renn*)Strecke f; *tape etc*: Spur f; Nummer f (*on an LP etc*); **2.** verfolgen; *track down* aufspüren; auftreiben

track and field sport Leichtathletik f

track e-vent sport Laufdisziplin f

track-ing sta-tion Bodenstation f

track-suit Trainingsanzug m

tract Fläche f, Gebiet n; anat (*Verdauungs*)Trakt m, (*Atem*)Wege pl

trac-tion Ziehen n, Zug m

trac-tion en-gine Zugmaschine f

trac-tor Traktor m, Trecker m

trade 1. Handel m; Branche f, Gewerbe n; (*esp* Handwerks)Beruf m; **2.** Handel treiben, handeln; *trade on* ausnutzen

trade a-gree-ment Handelsabkommen n

trade-mark Warenzeichen n

trade name Markenname m, Handelsbezeichnung f

trade price Großhandelspreis m

trad-er Händler(in)

trades-man (Einzel)Händler m; Ladeninhaber m; Lieferant m

trade(s Br) **u-nion** Gewerkschaft f

trade u-nion-ist Gewerkschaftler(in)

tra-di-tion Tradition f; Überlieferung f

tra-di-tion-al traditionell

traf-fic 1. Verkehr m; (*esp* illegaler) Handel m (*in* mit); **2.** (*esp* illegal) handeln (*in* mit)

traffic cir-cle mot Kreisverkehr m

traffic in-struc-tion Verkehrsunterricht m

traffic is-land Verkehrsinsel f

traffic jam (Verkehrs)Stau m, Verkehrsstockung f

traffic light(s) Verkehrsampel f

traffic of-fense (*Br* **of-fence**) Verkehrsdelikt n

traffic offend-er Verkehrssünder(in)

traffic reg-ula-tions Straßenverkehrsordnung *f*

traffic sign Verkehrszeichen *n*, -schild *n*

traffic sig·nal → **traffic light(s)**

traffic war·den *Br* Parküberwacher *m*, Politesse *f*

tra·ge·dy Tragödie *f*

tra·gic tragisch

trail 1. *v/t et.* nachschleifen lassen; verfolgen; SPORT zurückliegen hinter (*dat*) (**by** um); *v/i* sich schleppen; BOT kriechen; SPORT zurückliegen (**by 3-0** 0:3); **trail (along) behind s.o.** hinter j-m herschleifen; **2.** Spur *f (a. fig)*, Fährte *f*; Pfad *m*, Weg *m*; **trail of blood** Blutspur *f*; **trail of dust** Staubwolke *f*

trail·er MOT Anhänger *m*; Wohnwagen *m*, Caravan *m*; *film*, TV Trailer *m*, Vorschau *f*

trailer park Standplatz *m* für Wohnwagen

train 1. RAIL Zug *m*; Kolonne *f*, Schlange *f*; Schleppe *f*; *fig* Folge*f*, Kette *f*; **by train** mit der Bahn, mit dem Zug; **train of thought** Gedankengang *m*; **2.** *v/t* j-n ausbilden (**as** als, zum), schulen; SPORT trainieren; *Tier* abrichten, dressieren; *Kamera etc* richten (**on** auf *acc*); *v/i* ausgebildet werden (**as** als, zum); SPORT trainieren (**for** für)

train·ee Auszubildende *m, f*

train·er Ausbilder(in); zo Abrichter(in), Dompteur *m*, Dompteuse *f*; SPORT Trainer(in); *Br* Turnschuh *m*

train·ing Ausbildung *f*, Schulung *f*; Abrichten *n*, Dressur *f*; SPORT Training *n*

trait (Charakter)Zug *m*

trai·tor Verräter *m*

tram *Br* Straßenbahn(wagen *m*) *f*

tram·car *Br* Straßenbahnwagen *m*

tramp 1. sta(m)pfen *or* trampeln (durch); **2.** Tramp *m*, Landstreicher *m*, Vagabund *m*; Wanderung *f*; Flittchen *n*

tram·ple (zer)trampeln

trance Trance *f*

tran·quil ruhig, friedlich

tran·quil·(l)i·ty Ruhe *f*, Frieden *m*

tran·quil·(l)ize beruhigen

tran·quil·(l)iz·er PHARM Beruhigungsmittel *n*

trans·act *Geschäft* abwickeln, *Handel* abschließen

trans·ac·tion Abwicklung *f*, Abschluss *m*; *Geschäft n*, Transaktion *f*

trans·at·lan·tic transatlantisch, Transatlantik..., Übersee...

tran·scribe abschreiben, kopieren; *Stenogramm etc* übertragen

tran·script Abschrift *f*, Kopie *f*

tran·scrip·tion Umschreibung *f*, Umschrift *f*; Abschrift *f*, Kopie *f*

trans·fer 1. *v/t* (**to**) *Betrieb etc* verlegen (nach); *j-n* versetzen (nach); SPORT *Spieler* transferieren (zu), abgeben (an *acc*); *Geld* überweisen (zu); *Eigentum, Recht* übertragen (auf *acc*); *v/i* SPORT wechseln (**to** zu); umsteigen (**from ... to ...** von ... auf ... *acc*); **2.** Verlegung *f*; Versetzung *f*; SPORT Transfer *m*, Wechsel *m*; ECON Überweisung *f*; JUR Übertragung *f*; Umsteige(fahr)karte *f*

trans·fer·a·ble übertragbar

trans·fixed *fig* versteinert, starr

trans·form umwandeln, verwandeln

trans·for·ma·tion Umwandlung *f*, Verwandlung *f*

trans·form·er ELECTR Transformator *m*

trans·fu·sion MED Bluttransfusion *f*, Blutübertragung *f*

trans·gress verletzen, verstoßen gegen

tran·sient flüchtig, vergänglich

tran·sis·tor Transistor *m*

tran·sit Transit-, Durchgangsverkehr *m*; ECON Transport *m*; **in transit** unterwegs, auf dem Transport

tran·si·tion Übergang *m*

tran·si·tive LING transitiv

tran·si·to·ry → **transient**

trans·late übersetzen (**from English into German** aus dem Englischen ins Deutsche)

trans·la·tion Übersetzung *f*

trans·la·tor Übersetzer(in)

trans·lu·cent lichtdurchlässig

trans·mis·sion MED Übertragung *f*; *radio*, TV Sendung *f*; MOT Getriebe *n*

trans·mit *Signale* (aus)senden; *radio*, TV senden; PHYS *Wärme etc* leiten, *Licht etc* durchlassen; MED *Krankheit* übertragen

trans·mit·ter Sender *m*

trans·par·en·cy Durchsichtigkeit *f (a. fig)*; *fig* Durchschaubarkeit *f*; Dia(-positiv) *n*; Folie *f*

trans·par·ent durchsichtig (*a. fig*); *fig* durchschaubar

trans·pire transpirieren, schwitzen; *fig* durchsickern; F passieren

trans·plant 1. umpflanzen, verpflanzen (*a.* MED); MED transplantieren; **2.** MED Transplantation *f*, Verpflanzung *f*; Transplantat *n*

trans·port 1. Transport *m*, Beförderung *f*; Beförderungs-, Verkehrsmittel *n or pl*; MIL Transportschiff *n*, -flugzeug *n*, (*Truppen*)Transporter *m*; **2.** transportieren, befördern

trans·port·a·ble transportabel, transportfähig

trans·por·ta·tion Transport *m*, Beförderung *f*

trap 1. Falle *f* (*a. fig*); **set a trap for s.o.** j-m e-e Falle stellen; **shut one's trap, keep one's trap shut** F die Schnauze halten; **2.** (in *or* mit e-r Falle) fangen; *fig* in e-e Falle locken; **be trapped** eingeschlossen sein

trap·door Falltür *f*; THEA Versenkung *f*

tra·peze Trapez *n*

trap·per Trapper *m*, Fallensteller *m*, Pelztierjäger *m*

trap·pings Rangabzeichen *pl*; *fig* Drum und Dran *n*

trash F Schund *m*; Quatsch *m*, Unsinn *m*; Abfall *m*, Abfälle *pl*, Müll *m*; Gesindel *n*

trash·can Abfall-, Mülleimer *m*; Abfall-, Mülltonne *f*

trash·y Schund...

trav·el 1. *v/i* reisen; fahren; TECH *etc* sich bewegen; *fig* sich verbreiten; *fig* schweifen, wandern; *v/t* bereisen; *Strecke* zurücklegen, fahren; **2.** Reisen *n*; *pl* (*esp Auslands*)Reisen *pl*

travel a·gen·cy Reisebüro *n*

travel a·gent Reisebüroinhaber(in); Angestellte *m, f* in e-m Reisebüro

travel a·gent's, travel bu·reau Reisebüro *n*

trav·el·(l)er Reisende *m, f*

trav·el·(l)er's check (*Br* cheque) Reise-, Travellerscheck *m*

trav·el·(l)ing bag Reisetasche *f*

travel(l)ing expens·es Reisekosten *pl*

trav·el sick·ness Reisekrankheit *f*

trav·es·ty Zerrbild *n*

trawl 1. Schleppnetz *n*; **2.** mit dem Schleppnetz fischen

trawl·er MAR Trawler *m*

tray Tablett *n*; Ablagekorb *m*

treach·er·ous verräterisch; tückisch

treach·er·y Verrat *m*

trea·cle *esp Br* Sirup *m*

tread 1. treten (**on** auf *acc*; in *acc*); *Pfad etc* treten; **2.** Gang *m*; Schritt(e *pl*) *m*; (Reifen)Profil *n*

tread·mill Tretmühle *f* (*a. fig*)

trea·son Landesverrat *m*

trea·sure 1. Schatz *m*; **2.** sehr schätzen; in Ehren halten

trea·sur·er Schatzmeister(in)

trea·sure trove Schatzfund *m*

Trea·su·ry, Br Treasury De·part·ment Finanzministerium *n*

treat 1. *j-n, et.* behandeln; umgehen mit; *et.* ansehen, betrachten (**as** als); MED *j-n* behandeln (**for** gegen); *j-n* einladen (**to** zu); **treat s.o. to s.th.** *a.* j-m et. spendieren; **treat s.o. to s.th.** sich et. leisten *or* gönnen; **be treated for** MED in ärztlicher Behandlung sein wegen; **2.** (beson-

dere) Freude *or* Überraschung; **this is my treat** das geht auf meine Rechnung, ich lade dich *etc* ein

trea·tise Abhandlung *f*

treat·ment Behandlung *f*

treat·y Vertrag *m*

tre·ble¹ 1. dreifach; **2.** (sich) verdreifachen

tre·ble² MUS Knabensopran *m*; *radio:* (Ton)Höhe *f*

tree BOT Baum *m*

tre·foil BOT Klee *m*

trel·lis BOT Spalier *n*

trem·ble zittern (**with** vor *dat*)

tre·men·dous gewaltig, enorm; F klasse, toll

trem·or Zittern *n*; Beben *n*

trench Graben *m*; MIL Schützengraben *m*

trend Trend *m*, Entwicklung *f*, Tendenz *f*; Mode *f*

trend·y F **1.** modern, modisch; **be trendy** als schick gelten, in sein; **2.** *esp Br contp* Schickimicki *m*

tres·pass 1. **trespass on** *Grundstück etc* unbefugt betreten; *j-s Zeit etc* über Gebühr in Anspruch nehmen; **no trespassing** Betreten verboten!; **2.** unbefugtes Betreten

tres·pass·er: trespassers will be prosecuted Betreten bei Strafe verboten!

tres·tle Bock *m*, Gestell *n*

tri·al 1. JUR Prozess *m*, (Gerichts)Verhandlung *f*, (-)Verfahren *n*; Erprobung *f*, Probe *f*, Prüfung *f*, Test *m*; Plage *f*; **on trial** auf *or* zur Probe; *j-n* erprobt *or* getestet werden; **be on trial, stand trial** vor Gericht stehen (**for** wegen); **by way of trial** versuchsweise; **2.** Versuchs..., Probe...

tri·an·gle Dreieck *n*; Winkel *m*, Zeichendreieck *n*

tri·an·gu·lar dreieckig

tri·ath·lon SPORT Triathlon *n, m*, Dreikampf *m*

trib·al Stammes...

tribe (Volks)Stamm *m*

tri·bu·nal JUR Gericht(shof *m*) *n*

trib·u·ta·ry GEOGR Nebenfluss *m*

trib·ute: be a tribute to *j-m* Ehre machen; **pay tribute to** *j-m* Anerkennung zollen

trick 1. Trick *m*; (*Karten- etc*)Kunststück *n*; Streich *m*; *card game:* Stich *m*; (merkwürdige) Angewohnheit, Eigenart *f*; **play a trick on s.o.** j-m e-n Streich spielen; **2.** Trick...; **trick question** Fangfrage *f*; **3.** überlisten, F reinlegen

trick·e·ry Tricks *pl*

trick·le 1. tröpfeln; rieseln; **2.** Tröpfeln *n*; Rinnsal *n*

trick·ster Betrüger(in), Schwindler(in)

T

trick·y heikel, schwierig; durchtrieben, raffiniert

tri·cy·cle Dreirad n

tri·dent Dreizack m

tri·fle 1. Kleinigkeit f; Lappalie f; *a trifle* ein bisschen, etwas; **2.** *trifle with* fig spielen mit; *he is not to be trifled with* er lässt nicht mit sich spaßen

tri·fling geringfügig, unbedeutend

trig·ger Abzug m; *pull the trigger* abdrücken

trig·ger-hap·py F schießwütig

trill 1. Triller m; **2.** trillern

trim 1. Hecke etc stutzen, beschneiden, sich *den Bart etc* stutzen; *Kleidungsstück* besetzen (*with* mit); *trimmed with fur* pelzbesetzt, mit Pelzbesatz; *trim off* abschneiden; **2.** *give s.th. a trim* et. stutzen, et. (be)schneiden; *be in good trim* F gut in Form sein; **3.** gepflegt

trim·mings Besatz m; GASTR Beilagen pl

Trin·i·ty REL Dreieinigkeit f

trin·ket (*esp* billiges) Schmuckstück

trip 1. v/i stolpern (*over* über acc); (e-n) Fehler machen; v/t a. *trip up* j-m ein Bein stellen (a. fig); **2.** (kurze) Reise; Ausflug m, Trip m (a. sl); Stolpern n, Fallen n

tripe GASTR Kaldaunen pl, Kutteln pl

tri·ple 1. dreifach; **2.** verdreifachen

triple jump SPORT Dreisprung m

trip·lets Drillinge pl

trip·li·cate 1. dreifach; **2.** *in triplicate* in dreifacher Ausfertigung

tri·pod PHOT Stativ n

trip·per *esp Br* (*esp Tages*)Ausflügler(in)

trite abgedroschen, banal

tri·umph 1. Triumph m, fig Sieg m (*over* über acc); **2.** triumphieren (*over* über acc)

tri·um·phal Triumph...

tri·um·phant triumphierend

triv·i·al unbedeutend, bedeutungslos; trivial, alltäglich

trol·ley *esp Br* Einkaufswagen m; Gepäckwagen m, Kofferkuli m; (*Tee- etc*) Wagen m; (*supermarket*) *trolley* Einkaufswagen m; *shopping trolley* Einkaufsroller m

trol·ley-bus Oberleitungsbus m, Obus m

trom·bone MUS Posaune f

troop 1. Schar f; pl MIL Truppen pl; **2.** (*herein- etc*)strömen; *troop the colour Br* MIL e-e Fahnenparade abhalten

troop·er MIL Kavallerist m; Panzerjäger m; Polizist m

tro·phy Trophäe f

trop·ic ASTR, GEOGR Wendekreis m; *the tropic of Cancer* der Wendekreis des Krebses; *the tropic of Capricorn* der

Wendekreis des Steinbocks

trop·i·cal tropisch, Tropen...

trop·ics Tropen pl

trot 1. Trab m; Trott m; **2.** traben (lassen); *trot along* F losziehen

trou·ble 1. Schwierigkeit f, Problem n, Ärger m; Mühe f; MED Beschwerden pl; POL Unruhen pl; pl Unannehmlichkeiten pl; *be in trouble* in Schwierigkeiten sein; *get into trouble* Schwierigkeiten or Ärger bekommen; *j-n* in Schwierigkeiten bringen; *get or run into trouble* in Schwierigkeiten geraten; *have trouble with* Schwierigkeiten or Ärger haben mit; *put s.o. to trouble* j-m Mühe or Umstände machen; *take the trouble to do s.th.* sich die Mühe machen, et. zu tun; **2.** v/t j-n beunruhigen; j-m Mühe or Umstände machen; *j-n* bemühen (*for* um), bitten (*for* um; *to do* zu tun); *be troubled by* geplagt werden von, leiden an (dat); v/i sich bemühen (*to do* zu tun), sich Umstände machen (*about* wegen)

trou·ble-mak·er Störenfried m, Unruhestifter(in)

trou·ble·some lästig

trouble spot *esp* POL Krisenherd m

trough Trog m; Wellental n

trounce SPORT haushoch besiegen

troupe THEA Truppe f

trou·ser: (*a pair of*) *trousers* (e-e) Hose f

trou·ser suit Br Hosenanzug m

trous·seau Aussteuer f

trout ZO Forelle f

trow·el (Maurer)Kelle f

tru·ant Schulschwänzer(in); *play truant Br* (die Schule) schwänzen

truce MIL Waffenstillstand m (a. fig)

truck MOT Lastwagen m; Fernlaster m; *Br* RAIL (offener) Güterwagen; Transportkarren m; **2.** auf or mit Lastwagen transportieren

truck driv·er, truck·er MOT Lastwagenfahrer m; Fernfahrer m

truck farm ECON Gemüse- und Obstgärtnerei f

trudge (mühsam) stapfen

true wahr; echt, wirklich; treu (*to* dat); *be true* wahr sein, stimmen; *come true* in Erfüllung gehen; wahr werden; *true to life* lebensecht

tru·ly wahrheitsgemäß; wirklich, wahrhaft; aufrichtig

trump 1. Trumpf(karte f) m; pl Trumpf m; **2.** mit e-m Trumpf stechen; *trump up* erfinden

trum·pet 1. MUS Trompete f; **1.** trompeten; fig ausposaunen

trun·cheon (Gummi)Knüppel *m*, Schlagstock *m*

trun·dle *Karren etc* ziehen

trunk (Baum)Stamm *m*; Schrankkoffer *m*; zo Rüssel *m*; ANAT Rumpf *m*; MOT Kofferraum *m*

trunk road *Br* Fernstraße *f*

trunks (*a.* **a pair of trunks** e-e) (Bade)Hose *f*; SPORT Shorts *pl*

truss 1. *a.* **truss up** *j-n* fesseln; GASTR Geflügel *etc* dressieren; **2.** MED Bruchband *n*

trust 1. Vertrauen *n* (**in** zu); JUR Treuhand *f*; ECON Trust *m*; Großkonzern *m*; **hold s.th. in trust** *et.* treuhänderisch verwalten (**for** für); **place s.th. in s.o.'s trust** *j-m et.* anvertrauen; **2.** *v/t* (ver)trauen (*dat*); sich verlassen auf (*acc*); (zuversichtlich) hoffen; **trust him!** das sieht ihm ähnlich!; *v/i:* **trust in** vertrauen auf (*acc*); **trust to** sich verlassen auf (*acc*)

trust·ee JUR Treuhänder(in); Sachverwalter(in)

trust·ful, trust·ing vertrauensvoll

trust·wor·thy vertrauenswürdig, zuverlässig

truth Wahrheit *f*

truth·ful wahr; wahrheitsliebend

try 1. *v/t* versuchen; *et.* (aus)probieren; JUR (über) *e-e Sache* verhandeln; *j-m* den Prozess machen (**for** wegen); *j-n, j-s* Geduld, Nerven *etc* auf *e-e* harte Probe stellen; **try** *s.th.* HIST &c et. anprobieren; **try s.th. out** *et.* ausprobieren; *v/i* es versuchen; **try for** *Br*, **try out for** sich bemühen um; **2.** Versuch *m*; **give s.o., s.th. a try** es mit *j-m, et.* versuchen; **have a try** es versuchen

try·ing anstrengend

tsar HIST Zar *m*

T-shirt T-Shirt *n*

tub Bottich *m*, Zuber *m*, Tonne *f*; Becher *m*; F (Bade)Wanne *f*

tub·by F pumm(e)lig

tube Röhre *f* (*a.* ANAT), Rohr *n*; Schlauch *m*; Tube *f*; *Br* F U-Bahn *f* (**in** London); F Röhre *f*, Glotze *f*

tube·less schlauchlos

tu·ber BOT Knolle *f*

tu·ber·cu·lo·sis MED Tuberkulose *f*

tu·bu·lar röhrenförmig

tuck 1. stecken; **tuck away** F wegstecken; **tuck in** *esp Br* F reinhauen, zulangen; **tuck up** (**in** bed) *Kind* ins Bett packen; **2.** Biese *f*; Saum *m*; Abnäher *m*

Tue(s) ABBR of *Tuesday* Di., Dienstag *m*

Tues·day (ABBR *Tue, Tues*) Dienstag *m*; **on Tuesday** (am) Dienstag; **on Tuesdays** dienstags

tuft (Gras-, Haar- *etc*)Büschel *n*

tug 1. zerren *or* ziehen (**an** *dat or* **at** an *dat*); **2.** **give** *s.th.* **a tug** zerren *or* ziehen an (*dat*)

tug-of-war SPORT Tauziehen *n* (*a.* fig)

tu·i·tion Unterricht *m*; Unterrichtsgebühr(en *pl*) *f*

tu·lip BOT Tulpe *f*

tum·ble 1. fallen, stürzen; purzeln (*a.* fig); **2.** Fall *m*, Sturz *m*

tum·ble-down baufällig

tum·bler (Trink)Glas *n*

tu·mid MED geschwollen

tum·my F Bauch *m*, Bäuchlein *n*

tu·mo(u)r MED Tumor *m*

tu·mult Tumult *m*

tu·mul·tu·ous tumultartig, (applause *etc*) stürmisch

tu·na zo Thunfisch *m*

tune 1. MUS Melodie *f*; **be out of tune** verstimmt sein; **2.** *v/t mst* **tune in** Radio *etc* einstellen (**to** auf *acc*); *a.* **tune up** MUS stimmen; *a.* **tune up** Motor tunen; *v/i:* **tune in** (das Radio *etc*) einschalten; **tune up** MUS (die Instrumente) stimmen

tune·ful melodisch

tune·less unmelodisch

tun·er radio, TV Tuner *m*

tun·nel 1. Tunnel *m*; **2.** Berg durchtunneln; Fluss *etc* untertunneln

tun·ny zo Thunfisch *m*

tur·ban Turban *m*

tur·bid trüb (water); dick, dicht (smoke *etc*); fig verworren, wirr

tur·bine Turbine *f*

tur·bo F, **tur·bo·charg·er** MOT Turbolader *m*

tur·bot zo Steinbutt *m*

tur·bu·lent turbulent

tu·reen (Suppen)Terrine *f*

turf 1. Rasen *m*; Sode *f*, Rasenstück *n*; **the turf** die (Pferde)Rennbahn; der Pferderennsport; **2.** mit Rasen bedecken

tur·gid MED geschwollen

Turk HIST Türke *m*, Türkin *f*

Tur·key die Türkei

tur·key zo Truthahn *m*, Truthenne *f*, Pute *f*, Puter *m*; **talk turkey** F offen *or* sachlich reden

Turk·ish 1. türkisch; **2.** LING Türkisch *n*

tur·moil Aufruhr *m*

turn 1. *v/t* drehen, herum-, umdrehen; (um)wenden; Seite umblättern; Schlauch *etc* richten (**on** auf *acc*); Antenne ausrichten (**toward**[**s**] auf *acc*); Aufmerksamkeit zuwenden (**to** *dat*); verwandeln (**into** *acc*); Laub *etc* färben; Milch sauer werden lassen; TECH formen, drechseln; **turn the corner** um die Ecke biegen; **turn loose** los-, freilassen; **turn s.o.'s stom-**

ach j-m den Magen umdrehen; → **inside 1**, **upside down**, **somersault 1**; v/i sich (um)drehen; abbiegen; einbiegen (**onto** auf acc; **into** in acc); MOT wenden; blass, sauer etc werden; sich verwandeln, fig a. umschlagen (**into, to** in acc); → **left 2**, **righ 2**; **turn against** j-n aufbringen or aufhetzen gegen; fig sich wenden gegen; **turn away** (sich) abwenden (**from** von); j-n abweisen, wegschicken; **turn back** umkehren; j-n zurückschicken; Uhr zurückstellen; **turn down** Radio etc leiser stellen; Gas etc klein(er) stellen; Heizung etc runterschalten; j-n, Angebot etc ablehnen; Kragen umschlagen; Bettdecke zurückschlagen; **turn in** v/t zurückgeben; Gewinn etc erzielen, machen; **turn o.s. in** sich stellen; v/i F sich aufs Ohr legen; **turn off** v/t Gas, Wasser etc abdrehen; Licht, Radio etc ausmachen, ausschalten; Motor abstellen; F j-n anwidern; F j-m die Lust nehmen; v/i abbiegen; **turn on** Gas, Wasser etc aufdrehen; Gerät anstellen; Licht, Radio etc anmachen, an-, einschalten; F j-n antörnen, anmachen; **turn out** v/t Licht ausmachen, ausschalten; j-n hinauswerfen; F Waren ausstoßen; Tasche etc (aus)leeren; v/i kommen (for zu); sich erweisen or herausstellen als; **turn over** (sich) umdrehen; Seite umblättern; wenden; et. umkippen; sich et. überlegen; j-n, et. übergeben (**to** dat); Waren umsetzen; **turn round** sich umdrehen; **turn one's car round** wenden; **turn to** sich an j-n wenden; sich zuwenden (dat); **turn up** Kragen hochschlagen; Ärmel, Saum etc umschlagen; Radio etc lauter stellen; Gas etc aufdrehen; fig auftauchen; **2.** (Um)Drehung f; Biegung f, Kurve f, Kehre f; Abzweigung f; fig Wende f, Wendung f; **at every turn** auf Schritt und Tritt; **by turns** abwechselnd; **in turn** der Reihe nach; abwechselnd; **it is my turn** ich bin an der Reihe or F dran; **make a left turn** (nach) links abbiegen; **take turns** sich abwechseln (**at** bei); **take a turn for the better** (**worse**) sich bessern (sich verschlimmern); **do s.o. a good** (**bad**) **turn** j-m e-n guten (schlechten) Dienst erweisen

turn·coat Abtrünnige m, f, Überläufer(in); (**political**) **turncoat** F Wendehals m

turn·er Drechsler m; Dreher m

turn·ing esp Br Abzweigung f

turn·ing cir·cle MOT Wendekreis m

turn·ing point fig Wendepunkt m

tur·nip BOT Rübe f

turn-off Abzweigung f

turn·out Besucher(zahl f) pl, Beteiligung f; Wahlbeteiligung f; F Aufmachung f

turn·o·ver ECON Umsatz m; Personalwechsel m, Fluktuation f

turn·pike (**road**) gebührenpflichtige Schnellstraße

turn·stile Drehkreuz n

turn·ta·ble Plattenteller m

turn-up Br (Hosen)Aufschlag m

tur·pen·tine CHEM Terpentin n

tur·quoise MIN Türkis m

tur·ret ARCH Ecktürmchen n; MIL (Panzer)Turm m; MAR Gefechtssturm m, Geschützturm m

tur·tle ZO (See)Schildkröte f

tur·tle-dove ZO Turteltaube f

tur·tle-neck Rollkragen(pullover) m

tusk ZO Stoßzahn m; Hauer m

tus·sle F Gerangel n

tus·sock Grasbüschel n

tu·te·lage (An)Leitung f; JUR Vormundschaft f

tu·tor Privat-, Hauslehrer(in); Br UNIV Tutor(in), Studienleiter(in)

tu·to·ri·al Br UNIV Tutorenkurs m

tux·e·do Smoking m

TV 1. TV n, Fernsehen n; Fernsehgerät n, F Fernseher m; **on TV** im Fernsehen; **watch TV** fernsehen; **2.** Fernseh…

twang 1. Schwirren n; mst nasal twang näselnde Aussprache; **2.** schwirren (lassen)

tweak F zwicken, kneifen

tweet ZO piep(s)en

tweez·ers (**a pair of tweezers** e-e) Pinzette f

twelfth 1. zwölfte(r, -s); **2.** Zwölftel n

twelve 1. zwölf; **2.** Zwölf f

twen·ti·eth zwanzigste(r, -s)

twen·ty 1. zwanzig; **2.** Zwanzig f

twice zweimal

twid·dle (herum)spielen mit (or with mit); **twiddle one's thumbs** Däumchen drehen

twig BOT dünner Zweig, Ästchen n

twi·light (esp Abend)Dämmerung f; Zwielicht n, Dämmerlicht n

twin 1. Zwilling m; pl Zwillinge pl; **2.** Zwillings…; doppelt; **3. be twinned with** die Partnerstadt sein von

twin-bed·ded room Zweibettzimmer n

twin beds zwei Einzelbetten

twin broth·er Zwillingsbruder m

twine 1. Bindfaden m, Schnur f; **2.** (sich) schlingen or winden (**round** um); a. **twine together** zusammendrehen

twin-en·gined AVIAT zweimotorig

twinge stechender Schmerz, Stechen n; **a twinge of conscience** Gewissensbisse *pl*

twin·kle 1. glitzern (*stars*), (*a. eyes*) funkeln (*with* vor *dat*); **2.** Glitzern *n*, Funkeln *n*; *with a twinkle in one's eye* augenzwinkernd

twin sis·ter Zwillingsschwester *f*

twin town Partnerstadt *f*

twirl 1. (herum)wirbeln; wirbeln (*round* über *acc*); **2.** Wirbel *m*

twist 1. *v/t* drehen; wickeln (*round* um); *fig* verdrehen; *twist off* abdrehen, *Deckel* abschrauben; *twist one's ankle* (mit dem Fuß) umknicken, sich den Fuß vertreten; *her face was twisted with pain* ihr Gesicht war schmerzverzerrt; *v/i* sich winden, (*river etc a.*) sich schlängeln; **2.** Drehung *f*; Biegung *f*, (*überraschende*) Wendung; MUS Twist *m*

twitch 1. *v/t* zucken (mit); *v/i* zucken (*with* vor); zupfen (*at* an *dat*); **2.** Zucken *n*; Zuckung *f*

twit·ter 1. zwitschern; **2.** Zwitschern *n*, Gezwitscher *n*; *be all of a twitter* F ganz aufgeregt sein

two 1. zwei; *the two cars* die beiden Autos; *the two of us* wir beide; *in twos* zu zweit, paarweise; *cut in two* in zwei Teile schneiden; *put two and two together* zwei und zwei zusammenzählen; **2.** Zwei *f*

two-edged zweischneidig

two-faced falsch, heuchlerisch

two·fold zweifach

two·pence *Br* zwei Pence *pl*

two·pen·ny *Br* F für zwei Pence

two-piece zweiteilig; *two-piece dress* Jackenkleid *n*

two-seat·er AVIAT, MOT Zweisitzer *m*

two-sid·ed zweiseitig

two-sto·ried, *Br* **two-sto·rey** zweistöckig

two-way traf·fic MOT Gegenverkehr *m*

ty·coon (*Industrie- etc*)Magnat *m*

type 1. Art *f*, Sorte *f*; Typ *m*; PRINT Type *f*, Buchstabe *m*; **2.** *v/t et.* mit der Maschine schreiben, tippen; *v/i* Maschine schreiben, tippen

type·writ·er Schreibmaschine *f*

type·writ·ten maschine(n)geschrieben

ty·phoid (**fe·ver**) MED Typhus *m*

ty·phoon Taifun *m*

ty·phus MED Flecktyphus *m*, -fieber *n*

typ·i·cal typisch, bezeichnend (*of* für)

typ·i·fy typisch sein für, kennzeichnen; verkörpern

typ·ing er·ror Tippfehler *m*

typ·ing pool ECON Schreibzentrale *f*

typ·ist Schreibkraft *f*; Maschinenschreiber(in)

ty·ran·ni·cal tyrannisch

ty·ran·nize tyrannisieren

tyr·an·ny Tyrannei *f*

ty·rant Tyrann(in)

tyre *Br* → *tire*[1]

tzar → *tsar*

U

U, u U, u *n*

ud·der ZO Euter *n*

ug·ly hässlich (*a. fig*); bös(e), schlimm (*wound etc*)

ul·cer MED Geschwür *n*

ul·te·ri·or: *ulterior motive* Hintergedanke *m*

ul·ti·mate letzte(r, -s), End...; höchste(r, -s)

ul·ti·mate·ly letztlich; schließlich

ul·ti·ma·tum Ultimatum *n*; *deliver an ultimatum to s.o.* j-m ein Ultimatum stellen

ul·tra·high fre·quen·cy ELECTR Ultrakurzwelle *f*

ul·tra·ma·rine ultramarin

ul·tra·son·ic Ultraschall...

ul·tra·sound PHYS Ultraschall *m*

ul·tra·vi·o·let ultraviolett

um·bil·i·cal cord ANAT Nabelschnur *f*

um·brel·la (Regen)Schirm *m*; *fig* Schutz *m*

um·pire SPORT **1.** Schiedsrichter(in); **2.** als Schiedsrichter(in) fungieren (bei)

un·a·bashed unverfroren

un·a·bat·ed unvermindert

un·a·ble unfähig, außerstande, nicht in der Lage

un·ac·cept·a·ble unzumutbar

un·ac·count·a·ble unerklärlich

un·ac·cus·tomed ungewohnt

un·ac·quaint·ed: *be unacquainted with s.th.* et. nicht kennen, mit e-r Sache nicht vertraut sein

un·ad·vised unbesonnen, unüberlegt
un·af·fect·ed natürlich, ungekünstelt; *be unaffected by* nicht betroffen sein von
un·aid·ed ohne Unterstützung, (ganz) allein
un·al·ter·a·ble unabänderlich
u·nan·i·mous einmütig; einstimmig
un·an·nounced unangemeldet
un·an·swer·a·ble unwiderlegbar; nicht zu beantworten(d)
un·ap·pe·tiz·ing unappetitlich
un·ap·proach·a·ble unnahbar
un·armed unbewaffnet
un·asked ungestellt (*question*); unaufgefordert, ungebeten (*guest etc*)
un·as·sist·ed ohne (fremde) Hilfe, (ganz) allein
un·as·sum·ing bescheiden
un·at·tached ungebunden, frei
un·at·tend·ed unbeaufsichtigt
un·at·trac·tive unattraktiv, wenig anziehend, reizlos
un·au·thor·ized unberechtigt, unbefugt
un·a·void·a·ble unvermeidlich
un·a·ware: *be unaware of s.th.* sich e-r Sache nicht bewusst sein, et. nicht bemerken
un·a·wares: *catch or take s.o. unawares* j-n überraschen
un·bal·ance *j-n* aus dem (seelischen) Gleichgewicht bringen
un·bal·anced unausgeglichen, labil
un·bar aufriegeln, entriegeln
un·bear·a·ble unerträglich; *person:* unausstehlich
un·beat·a·ble unschlagbar
un·beat·en ungeschlagen, unbesiegt
un·be·com·ing unvorteilhaft
un·be·known(st): *unbeknown to s.o.* ohne j-s Wissen
un·be·liev·a·ble unglaublich
un·bend gerade biegen; sich aufrichten; *fig* aus sich herausgehen, auftauen
un·bend·ing unbeugsam
un·bi·as(s)ed unvoreingenommen, JUR unbefangen
un·bind losbinden
un·blem·ished makellos
un·born ungeboren
un·break·a·ble unzerbrechlich
un·bri·dled *fig* ungezügelt, zügellos; *unbridled tongue* lose Zunge
un·bro·ken ununterbrochen; heil, unversehrt; nicht zugeritten (*horse*)
un·buck·le aufschnallen, losschnallen
un·bur·den: *unburden o.s. to s.o.* j-m sein Herz ausschütten
un·but·ton aufknöpfen
un·called-for ungerechtfertigt; unnötig;

unpassend
un·can·ny unheimlich
un·cared-for vernachlässigt
un·ceas·ing unaufhörlich
un·ce·re·mo·ni·ous brüsk, unhöflich; überstürzt
un·cer·tain unsicher, ungewiss, unbestimmt; vage; METEOR unbeständig
un·cer·tain·ty Unsicherheit *f*, Ungewissheit *f*
un·chain losketten
un·changed unverändert
un·chang·ing unveränderlich
un·char·i·ta·ble unfair
un·checked ungehindert; ungeprüft
un·chris·tian unchristlich
un·civ·il unhöflich
un·civ·i·lized unzivilisiert
un·cle Onkel *m*
un·com·fort·a·ble unbequem; *feel uncomfortable* sich unbehaglich fühlen
un·com·mon ungewöhnlich
un·com·mu·ni·ca·tive wortkarg, verschlossen
un·com·pre·hend·ing verständnislos
un·com·pro·mis·ing kompromisslos
un·con·cerned: *be unconcerned about* sich keine Gedanken *or* Sorgen machen über (*acc*); *be unconcerned with* uninteressiert sein an (*dat*)
un·con·di·tion·al bedingungslos
un·con·firmed unbestätigt
un·con·scious unbewusst; unbeabsichtigt; MED bewusstlos; *be unconscious of* sich e-r Sache nicht bewusst sein, nicht bemerken
un·con·scious·ness MED Bewusstlosigkeit *f*
un·con·sti·tu·tion·al verfassungswidrig
un·con·trol·la·ble unkontrollierbar; nicht zu bändigen(d); unbändig (*rage etc*)
un·con·trolled unkontrolliert
un·con·ven·tion·al unkonventionell
un·con·vinced nicht überzeugt sein (*about* von)
un·con·vinc·ing nicht überzeugend
un·cooked ungekocht, roh
un·cork entkorken
un·count·a·ble unzählbar
un·cou·ple abkoppeln
un·couth *fig* ungehobelt
un·cov·er aufdecken, *fig a.* enthüllen
un·crit·i·cal unkritisch; *be uncritical of s.th.* e-r Sache unkritisch gegenüberstehen
unc·tion REL Salbung *f*
unc·tu·ous salbungsvoll
un·cut ungekürzt (*film, novel etc*); ungeschliffen (*diamond etc*)

un·dam·aged unbeschädigt, unversehrt, heil

un·dat·ed undatiert, ohne Datum

un·daunt·ed unerschrocken, furchtlos

un·de·cid·ed unentschieden, offen; unentschlossen

un·de·mon·stra·tive zurückhaltend, reserviert

un·de·ni·a·ble unbestreitbar

un·der 1. *prp* unter (*dat or acc*); **2.** *adv* unten; darunter

un·der·age minderjährig

un·der·bid unterbieten

un·der·brush → *undergrowth*

un·der·car·riage AVIAT Fahrwerk *n*, Fahrgestell *n*

un·der·charge zu wenig berechnen; zu wenig verlangen

un·der·clothes, un·der·cloth·ing → *underwear*

un·der·coat Grundierung *f*

un·der·cov·er: *undercover agent* verdeckter Ermittler

un·der·cut *j-n* (im Preis) unterbieten

un·der·de·vel·oped unterentwickelt; *underdeveloped country* Entwicklungsland *n*

un·der·dog Benachteiligte *m, f*

un·der·done nicht durchgebraten

un·der·es·ti·mate zu niedrig schätzen *or* veranschlagen; *fig* unterschätzen

un·der·ex·pose PHOT unterbelichten

un·der·fed unterernährt

un·der·go erleben, durchmachen; MED sich *e-r* Operation *etc* unterziehen

un·der·grad F, **un·der·grad·u·ate** Student(in)

un·der·ground 1. *adv* unterirdisch, unter der Erde; **2.** *adj* unterirdisch; *fig* Untergrund...; **3.** *esp Br* Untergrundbahn *f*, U-Bahn *f*; *by underground* mit der U-Bahn

un·der·growth Unterholz *n*

un·der·hand, un·der·hand·ed heimlich; hinterhältig

un·der·line unterstreichen (*a. fig*)

un·der·ling *contp* Untergebene *m, f*

un·der·ly·ing zugrunde liegend

un·der·mine unterspülen; *fig* untergraben, unterminieren

un·der·neath 1. *prp* unter (*dat or acc*); **2.** *adv* darunter

un·der·nour·ished unterernährt

un·der·pants Unterhose *f*

un·der·pass Unterführung *f*

un·der·pay *j-m* zu wenig bezahlen, *j-n* unterbezahlen

un·der·priv·i·leged unterprivilegiert, benachteiligt

un·der·rate unterbewerten, -schätzen

un·der·sec·re·ta·ry POL Staatssekretär *m*

un·der·sell ECON *Ware* verschleudern, unter Wert verkaufen; *undersell o.s. fig* sich schlecht verkaufen

un·der·shirt Unterhemd *n*

un·der·side Unterseite *f*

un·der·signed: *the undersigned* der *or* die Unterzeichnete, die Unterzeichneten *pl*

un·der·size(d) zu klein

un·der·staffed (personell) unterbesetzt

un·der·stand verstehen; erfahren *or* gehört haben (*that* dass); *make o.s. understood* sich verständlich machen; *am I to understand that* soll das heißen, dass; *give s.o. to understand that* j-m zu verstehen geben, dass

un·der·stand·a·ble verständlich

un·der·stand·ing 1. Verstand *m*; Verständnis *n*; Abmachung *f*; Verständigung *f*; *come to an understanding* e-e Abmachung treffen (*with* mit); *on the understanding that* unter der Voraussetzung, dass; **2.** verständnisvoll

un·der·state untertreiben, untertrieben darstellen

un·der·state·ment Understatement *n*, Untertreibung *f*

un·der·take *et.* übernehmen; sich verpflichten (*to do* zu tun)

un·der·tak·er Leichenbestatter *m*; Beerdigungs-, Bestattungsinstitut *n*

un·der·tak·ing Unternehmen *n*; Zusicherung *f*

un·der·tone *fig* Unterton *m*; *in an undertone* mit gedämpfter Stimme

un·der·val·ue unterbewerten

un·der·wa·ter 1. *adj* Unterwasser...; **2.** *adv* unter Wasser

un·der·wear Unterwäsche *f*

un·der·weight 1. Untergewicht *n*; **2.** untergewichtig, zu leicht (*by* um); *she is five pounds underweight* sie hat fünf Pfund Untergewicht

un·der·world Unterwelt *f*

un·de·served unverdient

un·de·sir·a·ble unerwünscht

un·de·vel·oped unerschlossen (*area*); unentwickelt

un·dies F (Damen)Unterwäsche *f*

un·dig·ni·fied würdelos

un·di·min·ished unvermindert

un·dis·ci·plined undiszipliniert

un·dis·cov·ered unentdeckt

un·dis·guised unverhohlen

un·dis·put·ed unbestritten

un·dis·turbed ungestört

un·di·vid·ed ungeteilt

U

un·do aufmachen, öffnen; *fig* zunichtemachen

un·do·ing: *be s.o.'s undoing* j-s Ruin *or* Verderben sein

un·done unerledigt; offen; *come undone* aufgehen

un·doubt·ed unbestritten

un·doubt·ed·ly zweifellos, ohne (jeden) Zweifel

un·dreamed-of, un·dreamt-of ungeahnt

un·dress sich ausziehen; *j-n* ausziehen

un·due übermäßig

un·du·lat·ing sanft (*hills*)

un·dy·ing ewig

un·earned *fig* unverdient

un·earth ausgraben, *fig a.* ausfindig machen, aufstöbern

un·earth·ly überirdisch; unheimlich; *at an unearthly hour* F zu e-r unchristlichen Zeit

un·eas·i·ness Unbehagen *n*

un·eas·y unruhig (*sleep*); unsicher (*peace*); *feel uneasy* sich unbehaglich fühlen; *I'm uneasy about* mir ist nicht wohl bei

un·e·co·nom·ic unwirtschaftlich

un·ed·u·cat·ed ungebildet

un·e·mo·tion·al leidenschaftslos, kühl, beherrscht

un·em·ployed 1. arbeitslos; 2. *the unemployed* die Arbeitslosen *pl*

un·em·ploy·ment Arbeitslosigkeit *f*

unemployment ben·e·fit *Br*, unemployment com·pen·sa·tion Arbeitslosengeld *n*

un·end·ing endlos

un·en·dur·a·ble unerträglich

un·en·vi·a·ble wenig beneidenswert

un·e·qual ungleich (*a. fig*), unterschiedlich; *fig* einseitig; *be unequal to* e-r *Aufgabe etc* nicht gewachsen sein

un·e·qual(l)ed unerreicht, unübertroffen

un·er·ring unfehlbar

un·e·ven uneben; ungleich(mäßig); ungerade (*number*)

un·e·vent·ful ereignislos

un·ex·am·pled beispiellos

un·ex·pec·ted unerwartet

un·ex·posed PHOT unbelichtet

un·fail·ing unerschöpflich; nie versagend

un·fair unfair, ungerecht

un·faith·ful untreu (*to dat*)

un·fa·mil·i·ar ungewohnt; unbekannt; nicht vertraut (*with* mit)

un·fas·ten aufmachen, öffnen; losbinden

un·fa·vo(u)r·a·ble ungünstig; unvorteilhaft (*for, to* für); negativ, ablehnend

un·feel·ing gefühllos, herzlos

un·fin·ished unvollendet; unfertig; unerledigt

un·fit nicht fit, nicht in Form; ungeeignet, untauglich; unfähig

un·flag·ging unermüdlich, unentwegt

un·flap·pa·ble F nicht aus der Ruhe zu bringen(d)

un·fold auffalten, auseinanderfalten; darlegen, enthüllen; sich entfalten

un·fore·seen unvorhergesehen, unerwartet

un·for·get·ta·ble unvergesslich

un·for·got·ten unvergessen

un·for·tu·nate unglücklich; unglückselig; bedauerlich

un·for·tu·nate·ly leider

un·found·ed unbegründet

un·friend·ly unfreundlich (*to, towards* zu)

un·furl *Fahne* aufrollen, entrollen, *Segel* losmachen

un·fur·nished unmöbliert

un·gain·ly linkisch, unbeholfen

un·god·ly gottlos; *at an ungodly hour* F zu e-r unchristlichen Zeit

un·gra·cious ungnädig; unfreundlich

un·grate·ful undankbar

un·guard·ed unbewacht; unbedacht, unüberlegt

un·hap·pi·ly unglücklicherweise, leider

un·hap·py unglücklich

un·harmed unversehrt

un·health·y kränklich, nicht gesund; ungesund; *contp* krankhaft, unnatürlich

un·heard: *go unheard* keine Beachtung finden, unbeachtet bleiben

un·heard-of noch nie da gewesen, beispiellos

un·hinge: *unhinge s.o.('s mind) fig* j-n völlig aus dem Gleichgewicht bringen

un·ho·ly F furchtbar, schrecklich

un·hoped-for unverhofft, unerwartet

un·hurt unverletzt

u·ni·corn Einhorn *n*

un·i·den·ti·fied unbekannt, nicht identifiziert

u·ni·fi·ca·tion Vereinigung *f*

u·ni·form 1. Uniform *f*; 2. gleichmäßig; einheitlich

u·ni·form·i·ty Einheitlichkeit *f*

u·ni·fy verein(ig)en; vereinheitlichen

u·ni·lat·er·al *fig* einseitig

un·i·ma·gin·a·ble unvorstellbar

un·i·ma·gin·a·tive fantasielos, einfallslos

un·im·por·tant unwichtig

un·im·pressed: *remain unimpressed* unbeeindruckt bleiben (*by* von)

un·in·formed nicht unterrichtet *or* eingeweiht

un·in·hab·it·a·ble unbewohnbar

un·in·hab·it·ed unbewohnt

un·in·jured unverletzt
un·in·tel·li·gi·ble unverständlich
un·in·ten·tion·al unabsichtlich, unbeabsichtigt
un·in·terest·ed uninteressiert (*in* an *dat*); *be uninterested in* a. sich nicht interessieren für
un·in·terest·ing uninteressant
un·in·ter·rupt·ed ununterbrochen
u·nion Vereinigung *f*; Union *f*; Gewerkschaft *f*
u·nion·ist Gewerkschaftler(in)
u·nion·ize (sich) gewerkschaftlich organisieren
u·nique einzigartig; einmalig
u·ni·son: *in unison* gemeinsam
u·nit Einheit *f*; PED Unit *f*, Lehreinheit *f*; MATH Einer *m*; TECH (Anbau)Element *n*, Teil *n*; *unit furniture* Anbaumöbel *pl*
u·nite verbinden, vereinigen; sich vereinigen *or* zusammentun
u·nit·ed vereinigt, vereint
U·nit·ed King·dom *das* Vereinigte Königreich (*England, Scotland, Wales and Northern Ireland*)
U·nit·ed States of A·mer·i·ca *die* Vereinigten Staaten von Amerika
u·ni·ty Einheit *f*; MATH Eins *f*
u·ni·ver·sal allgemein; universal, universell; Welt...
u·ni·verse Universum *n*, Weltall *n*
u·ni·ver·si·ty Universität *f*, Hochschule *f*
university grad·u·ate Akademiker(in)
un·just ungerecht
un·kempt ungekämmt (*hair*); ungepflegt (*clothes etc*)
un·kind unfreundlich
un·known 1. unbekannt (*to* dat); 2. *der, die, das* Unbekannte
unknown quan·ti·ty MATH unbekannte Größe (*a. fig*), Unbekannte *f*
un·law·ful ungesetzlich, gesetzwidrig
un·lead·ed bleifrei
un·learn Ansichten *etc* ablegen, aufgeben
un·less wenn ... nicht, außer wenn ..., es sei denn ...
un·like *prp* im Gegensatz zu; *he is very unlike his father* er ist ganz anders als sein Vater; *that is very unlike him* das sieht ihm gar nicht ähnlich
un·like·ly unwahrscheinlich
un·lim·it·ed unbegrenzt
un·list·ed: *be unlisted* nicht im Telefonbuch stehen
unlisted num·ber TEL Geheimnummer *f*
un·load entladen, abladen, ausladen; MAR *Ladung* löschen
un·lock aufschließen
un·loos·en losmachen; lockern; lösen

un·loved ungeliebt
un·luck·y unglücklich; *be unlucky* Pech haben
un·made ungemacht
un·manned unbemannt
un·marked nicht gekennzeichnet; SPORT ungedeckt, frei
un·mar·ried unverheiratet, ledig
un·mask *fig* entlarven
un·matched unübertroffen, unvergleichlich
un·men·tio·na·ble Tabu...; *be unmentionable* tabu sein
un·mis·tak·a·ble unverkennbar, unverwechselbar, untrüglich
un·mo·lest·ed unbehelligt
un·moved ungerührt; *she remained unmoved by it* es ließ sie kalt
un·mu·si·cal unmusikalisch
un·named ungenannt
un·nat·u·ral unnatürlich; widernatürlich
un·ne·ces·sa·ry unnötig
un·nerve entnerven
un·no·ticed unbemerkt
un·num·bered unnummeriert
un·ob·tru·sive unauffällig, unaufdringlich
un·oc·cu·pied leer (stehend), unbewohnt; unbeschäftigt
un·of·fi·cial inoffiziell
un·pack auspacken
un·paid unbezahlt; *post* unfrei
un·par·al·leled einmalig, beispiellos
un·par·don·a·ble unverzeihlich
un·per·turbed gelassen, ruhig
un·pick *Naht etc* auftrennen
un·placed: *be unplaced* SPORT sich nicht platzieren können
un·play·a·ble SPORT unbespielbar
un·pleas·ant unangenehm, unerfreulich; unfreundlich
un·plug den Stecker (*gen*) herausziehen
un·pol·ished unpoliert; *fig* ungehobelt
un·pol·lut·ed sauber, unverschmutzt
un·pop·u·lar unpopulär, unbeliebt
un·pop·u·lar·i·ty Unbeliebtheit *f*
un·prac·ti·cal unpraktisch
un·prac·ticed, *Br* un·prac·tised ungeübt
un·pre·ce·dent·ed beispiellos, noch nie da gewesen
un·pre·dict·a·ble unvorhersehbar; unberechenbar (*person*)
un·prej·u·diced unvoreingenommen; JUR unbefangen
un·pre·med·i·tat·ed nicht vorsätzlich; unüberlegt
un·pre·pared unvorbereitet
un·pre·ten·tious bescheiden, einfach, schlicht

un·prin·ci·pled skrupellos, gewissenlos
un·prin·ta·ble nicht druckfähig *or* druckreif
un·pro·duc·tive unproduktiv, unergiebig
un·pro·fes·sion·al unprofessionell; unfachmännisch
un·prof·it·a·ble unrentabel
un·pro·nounce·a·ble unaussprechbar
un·pro·tect·ed ungeschützt
un·proved, un·prov·en unbewiesen
un·pro·voked grundlos
un·pun·ished unbestraft, ungestraft; *go unpunished* straflos bleiben
un·qual·i·fied unqualifiziert, ungeeignet (*for* für); uneingeschränkt
un·ques·tion·a·ble unbestritten
un·ques·tion·ing bedingungslos
un·quote: *quote ... unquote* Zitat ... Zitat Ende
un·rav·el (sich) auftrennen (*pullover etc*); entwirren
un·read·a·ble nicht lesenswert, unlesbar, *a.* unleserlich
un·re·al unwirklich
un·re·a·lis·tic unrealistisch
un·rea·son·a·ble unvernünftig; übertrieben, unzumutbar
un·rec·og·niz·a·ble nicht wieder zu erkennen(d)
un·re·lat·ed: *be unrelated* in keinem Zusammenhang stehen (*to* mit)
un·re·lent·ing unvermindert
un·re·li·a·ble unzuverlässig
un·re·lieved ununterbrochen, ständig
un·re·mit·ting unablässig, unaufhörlich
un·re·quit·ed: *unrequited love* unerwiderte Liebe
un·re·served uneingeschränkt; nicht reserviert
un·rest POL *etc* Unruhen *pl*
un·re·strained hemmungslos, ungezügelt
un·re·strict·ed uneingeschränkt
un·ripe unreif
un·ri·val(l)ed unerreicht, unübertroffen, einzigartig
un·roll (sich) aufrollen *or* entrollen; sich entfalten
un·ruf·fled gelassen, ruhig
un·ru·ly ungebärdig, wild; widerspenstig (*hair*)
un·sad·dle *Pferd* absatteln; *Reiter* abwerfen
un·safe unsicher, nicht sicher
un·said unausgesprochen
un·sal(e)·a·ble unverkäuflich
un·salt·ed ungesalzen
un·san·i·tar·y unhygienisch
un·sat·is·fac·to·ry unbefriedigend
un·sat·u·rat·ed CHEM ungesättigt

un·sa·vo(u)r·y anrüchig, unerfreulich
un·scathed unversehrt, unverletzt
un·screw abschrauben, losschrauben
un·scru·pu·lous skrupellos, gewissenlos
un·seat *Reiter* abwerfen; *j-n s-s* Amtes entheben
un·seem·ly ungebührlich
un·self·ish selbstlos, uneigennützig
un·set·tle durcheinanderbringen; beunruhigen; aufregen
un·set·tled ungeklärt, offen (*question etc*); unsicher (*situation etc*); METEOR unbeständig
un·shak(e)·a·ble unerschütterlich
un·shav·en unrasiert
un·shrink·a·ble nicht eingehend *or* einlaufend
un·sight·ly unansehnlich; hässlich
un·skilled: *unskilled worker* ungelernter Arbeiter
un·so·cia·ble ungesellig
un·so·cial: *work unsocial hours* außerhalb der normalen Arbeitszeit arbeiten
un·so·lic·it·ed unaufgefordert ein- *or* zugesandt, ECON *a.* unbestellt
un·solved ungelöst (*problem etc*)
un·so·phis·ti·cat·ed einfach, schlicht; TECH unkompliziert
un·sound nicht gesund; nicht in Ordnung; morsch; unsicher, schwach; nicht stichhaltig (*argument etc*); *of unsound mind* JUR unzurechnungsfähig
un·spar·ing großzügig, freigebig, verschwenderisch; schonungslos, unbarmherzig
un·speak·a·ble unbeschreiblich, entsetzlich
un·spoiled, un·spoilt unverdorben; nicht verwöhnt *or* verzogen
un·sta·ble instabil; unsicher, schwankend; labil (*person*)
un·stead·y wack(e)lig, schwankend, unsicher; unbeständig; ungleichmäßig, unregelmäßig
un·stop *Abfluss etc* frei machen; *Flasche* entstöpseln
un·stressed LING unbetont
un·stuck: *come unstuck* abgehen, sich lösen; *fig* scheitern
un·stud·ied ungekünstelt, natürlich
un·suc·cess·ful erfolglos, ohne Erfolg; vergeblich
un·suit·a·ble unpassend, ungeeignet; unangemessen
un·sure unsicher; *unsure of o.s.* unsicher
un·sur·passed unübertroffen
un·sus·pect·ed unverdächtig; unvermutet

un·sus·pect·ing nichts ahnend, ahnungslos

un·sus·pi·cious arglos; unverdächtig, harmlos

un·sweet·ened ungesüßt

un·swerv·ing unbeirrbar, unerschütterlich

un·tan·gle entwirren (*a. fig*)

un·tapped unerschlossen (*resource etc*)

un·teach·a·ble unbelehrbar (*person*); nicht lehrbar

un·ten·a·ble unhaltbar (*theory etc*)

un·think·a·ble undenkbar, unvorstellbar

un·think·ing gedankenlos

un·ti·dy unordentlich

un·tie aufknoten, *Knoten etc* lösen; losbinden

un·til *prp, cj* bis; *not until* erst; erst wenn, nicht bevor

un·time·ly vorzeitig, verfrüht; unpassend, ungelegen

un·tir·ing unermüdlich

un·told *fig* unermesslich

un·touched unberührt, unangetastet

un·true unwahr, falsch

un·trust·wor·thy unzuverlässig, nicht vertrauenswürdig

un·used[1] unbenutzt, ungebraucht

un·used[2]: *be unused to s.th.* an et. nicht gewöhnt sein, et. nicht gewohnt sein; *be unused to doing s.th.* es nicht gewohnt sein, et. zu tun

un·u·su·al ungewöhnlich

un·var·nished *fig* ungeschminkt

un·var·y·ing unveränderlich, gleichbleibend

un·veil *Denkmal etc* enthüllen

un·versed unbewandert, unerfahren (*in* in *dat*)

un·voiced unausgesprochen

un·want·ed unerwünscht, ungewollt

un·war·rant·ed ungerechtfertigt

un·washed ungewaschen

un·wel·come unwillkommen

un·well: *be or feel unwell* sich unwohl fühlen *or* nicht wohlfühlen

un·whole·some ungesund (*a. fig*)

un·wield·y unhandlich, sperrig

un·will·ing widerwillig; ungern; *be unwilling to do s.th.* et. nicht tun wollen

un·wind (sich) abwickeln; F abschalten, sich entspannen

un·wise unklug

un·wit·ting unwissentlich; unbeabsichtigt

un·wor·thy unwürdig; *he (she) is unworthy of it* er (sie) verdient es nicht, er (sie) ist es nicht wert

un·wrap auswickeln, auspacken

un·writ·ten ungeschrieben

un·yield·ing unnachgiebig

un·zip den Reißverschluss (*gen*) aufmachen

up 1. *adv* herauf, hinauf, aufwärts, nach oben, hoch, in die Höhe; oben; *up there* dort oben; *jump up and down* hüpfen; *walk up and down* auf und ab gehen, hin und her gehen; *up to* bis zu; *be up to s.th.* F et. vorhaben, et. im Schilde führen; *not to be up to s.th.* e-r Sache nicht gewachsen sein; *it's up to you* das liegt bei dir; **2.** *prp* herauf, hinauf; oben auf (*dat*); *up the river* flussaufwärts; **3.** *adj* nach oben (gerichtet), Aufwärts...; ASTR aufgegangen; ECON gestiegen; *time*: abgelaufen, um; aufgestanden, F auf; *the up train* der Zug nach London; *be up and about* F wieder auf den Beinen sein; *what's up?* F was ist los?; **4.** F v/t *Angebot, Preis etc* erhöhen; **5.** *the ups and downs* F die Höhen und Tiefen *pl* (*of life* des Lebens)

up-and-com·ing aufstrebend, vielversprechend

up·bring·ing Erziehung *f*

up·com·ing bevorstehend

up·coun·try landeinwärts; im Landesinneren

up·date 1. auf den neuesten Stand bringen; aktualisieren; **2.** Lagebericht *m*

up·end hochkant stellen

up·grade *j-n* befördern

up·heav·al *fig* Umwälzung *f*

up·hill aufwärts, bergan; bergauf führend; *fig* mühsam

up·hold *Rechte etc* schützen, wahren; JUR *Urteil* bestätigen

up·hol·ster *Möbel* polstern

up·hol·ster·er Polsterer *m*

up·hol·ster·y Polsterung *f*; Bezug *m*; Polsterei *f*

up·keep Instandhaltung(skosten *pl*) *f*; Unterhalt(ungskosten *pl*) *m*

up·land *mst pl* Hochland *n*

up·lift 1. *j-n* aufrichten, *j-m* Auftrieb geben; **2.** Auftrieb *m*

up·on → *on*, *once* 1

up·per obere(r, -s), Ober...;

up·per·most 1. *adj* oberste(r, -s), größte(r, -s), höchste(r, -s); *be uppermost* oben sein; *fig* an erster Stelle stehen; **2.** *adv* nach oben

up·right aufrecht, *a.* gerade, *fig a.* rechtschaffen

up·ris·ing Aufstand *m*

up·roar Aufruhr *m*

up·roar·i·ous lärmend, laut; schallend (*laughter*)

up·root ausreißen, entwurzeln; *fig j-n* he-

U

rausreißen (*from* aus)

up·set umkippen, umstoßen, umwerfen; *Pläne etc* durcheinanderbringen, stören; *j-n* aus der Fassung bringen; *the fish has upset me or my stomach* ich habe mir durch den Fisch den Magen verdorben; *be upset* aufgeregt sein; aus der Fassung *or* durcheinander sein; gekränkt *or* verletzt sein

up·shot Ergebnis *n*

up·side down verkehrt herum; *fig* drunter und drüber; *turn upside down* umdrehen, *a. fig* auf den Kopf stellen

up·stairs 1. die Treppe herauf *or* hinauf, nach oben; oben; **2.** im oberen Stockwerk (gelegen), obere(r, -s)

up·start Emporkömmling *m*

up·state im Norden (e-s Bundesstaats)

up·stream fluss-, stromaufwärts

up·take F *be quick* (*slow*) *on the uptake* schnell begreifen (schwer von Begriff sein)

up-to-date modern; aktuell, auf dem neuesten Stand

up·town in den Wohnvierteln; in die Wohnviertel

up·turn Aufschwung *m*

up·ward(s) aufwärts, nach oben

u·ra·ni·um CHEM Uran *n*

ur·ban städtisch, Stadt...

ur·ban·i·za·tion Verstädterung *f*

ur·chin Bengel *m*

urge 1. *j-n* drängen (*to do* zu tun); drängen auf (*acc*); *a. urge on j-n* drängen, antreiben; **2.** Drang *m*, Verlangen *n*

ur·gen·cy Dringlichkeit *f*

ur·gent dringend; *be urgent a.* eilen

u·ri·nate urinieren

u·rine Urin *m*

urn Urne *f*; Großteemaschine *f*, Großkaffeemaschine *f*

us uns; *all of us* wir alle; *both of us* wir beide

us·age Sprachgebrauch *m*; Behandlung *f*; Verwendung *f*, Gebrauch *m*

use 1. *v/t* benutzen, gebrauchen, anwenden, verwenden; (ver)brauchen; *use up* auf-, verbrauchen; *v/i: I used to live here* ich habe früher hier gewohnt; **2.** Benutzung *f*, Gebrauch *m*, Verwendung *f*; Nutzen *m*; *be of use* nützlich *or* von Nutzen sein (*to* für); *it's no use doing* es ist nutzlos *or* zwecklos *zu inf*; → **milk 1**

used¹: *be used to s.th.* an et. gewöhnt sein, et. gewohnt sein; *be used to doing s.th.* es gewohnt sein, et. zu tun

used² gebraucht

used car Gebrauchtwagen *m*

used car deal·er Gebrauchtwagenhändler(in)

use·ful nützlich

use·less nutzlos, zwecklos

us·er Benutzer(in); Verbraucher(in)

us·er-friend·ly benutzer- *or* verbraucherfreundlich

us·er in·ter·face EDP Benutzeroberfläche *f*

ush·er 1. Platzanweiser *m*; Gerichtsdiener *m*; **2.** *j-n* führen, geleiten (*into* in *acc*; *to* zu)

ush·er·ette Platzanweiserin *f*

u·su·al gewöhnlich, üblich

u·su·al·ly (für) gewöhnlich, normalerweise

u·sur·er Wucherer *m*

u·su·ry Wucher *m*

u·ten·sil Gerät *n*

u·te·rus ANAT Gebärmutter *f*

u·til·i·ty Nutzen *m*; *pl* Leistungen *pl* der öffentlichen Versorgungsbetriebe

u·til·ize nutzen

ut·most äußerste(r, -s), größte(r, -s), höchste(r, -s)

u·to·pi·an utopisch

ut·ter¹ total, völlig

ut·ter² äußern, *Seufzer etc* ausstoßen, *Wort* sagen

U-turn MOT Wende *f*; *fig* Kehrtwendung *f*

u·vu·la ANAT (Gaumen)Zäpfchen *n*

U

V

V, v V, v *n*

va·can·cy freie *or* offene Stelle; *vacancies* Zimmer frei; *no vacancies* belegt

va·cant leer stehend, unbewohnt; frei (*seat etc*); frei, offen (*job*); *fig* leer (*expression, stare etc*)

va·cate Hotelzimmer räumen; Stelle *etc* aufgeben

va·ca·tion 1. Ferien *pl*, Urlaub *m*; *esp Br UNIV* Semesterferien *pl*; *JUR* Gerichtsferien *pl*; *be on vacation* im Urlaub sein, Urlaub machen; **2.** Urlaub machen, die Ferien verbringen

va·ca·tion·er, va·ca·tion·ist Urlauber(in)

vac·cin·ate *MED* impfen

vac·cin·a·tion *MED* (Schutz)Impfung *f*

vac·cine *MED* Impfstoff *m*

vac·il·late *fig* schwanken

vac·u·um 1. *PHYS* Vakuum *n*; **2.** F *Teppich, Zimmer etc* saugen

vacuum bot·tle Thermosflasche® *f*

vacuum clean·er Staubsauger *m*

vacuum flask *Br* Thermosflasche® *f*

vacuum-packed vakuumverpackt

vag·a·bond Vagabund *m*, Landstreicher(in)

va·ga·ry *mst pl* Laune *f*; wunderlicher Einfall

va·gi·na *ANAT* Vagina *f*, Scheide *f*

va·gi·nal *ANAT* vaginal, Scheiden...

va·grant Nichtsesshafte *m*, *f*, Landstreicher(in)

vague verschwommen; vage; unklar

vain eingebildet, eitel; vergeblich; *in vain* vergebens, vergeblich

val·en·tine Valentinskarte *f*

va·le·ri·an *BOT, PHARM* Baldrian *m*

val·et (Kammer)Diener *m*

val·id stichhaltig, triftig; gültig (*for two weeks* zwei Wochen); *JUR* rechtsgültig, rechtskräftig; *be valid a.* gelten

va·lid·i·ty (*JUR* Rechts)Gültigkeit *f*; Stichhaltigkeit *f*, Triftigkeit *f*

val·ley Tal *n*

val·u·a·ble 1. wertvoll; **2.** *pl* Wertgegenstände *pl*, Wertsachen *pl*

val·u·a·tion Schätzung *f*; Schätzwert *m* (*on gen*)

val·ue 1. Wert *m*; *be of value* wertvoll sein (*to* für); *get value for money* reell bedient werden; **2.** *Haus etc* schätzen (*at* auf *acc*); *j-n*, *j-s* Rat *etc* schätzen

val·ue-ad·ded tax *Br ECON* (*ABBR VAT*) Mehrwertsteuer *f*

val·ue·less wertlos

valve *TECH, MUS* Ventil *n*; *ANAT* (*Herz- etc*) Klappe *f*

vam·pire Vampir *m*

van *MOT* Lieferwagen *m*, Transporter *m*; *Br RAIL* (geschlossener) Güterwagen

van·dal Wandale *m*, Vandale *m*

van·dal·ism Wandalismus *m*, Vandalismus *m*

van·dal·ize mutwillig beschädigen *or* zerstören

vane *TECH* (*Propeller- etc*)Flügel *m*; (*Wetter*)Fahne *f*

van·guard *MIL* Vorhut *f*

va·nil·la Vanille *f*

van·ish verschwinden

van·i·ty Eitelkeit *f*

vanity bag Kosmetiktäschchen *n*

vanity case Kosmetikkoffer *m*

van·tage·point Aussichtspunkt *m*; *from my vantagepoint fig* aus m-r Sicht

va·por·ize verdampfen; verdunsten (lassen)

va·po(u)r Dampf *m*, Dunst *m*

vapo(u)r trail *AVIAT* Kondensstreifen *m*

var·i·a·ble 1. variabel, veränderlich; unbeständig, wechselhaft; *TECH* einstellbar, regulierbar; **2.** *MATH, PHYS* Variable *f*, veränderliche Größe *f* (*a. fig*)

var·i·ance: *be at variance with* im Gegensatz *or* Widerspruch stehen zu

var·i·ant 1. abweichend, verschieden; **2.** Variante *f*

var·i·a·tion Abweichung *f*; Schwankung *f*; *MUS* Variation *f*

var·i·cose veins *MED* Krampfadern *pl*

var·ied unterschiedlich; abwechslungsreich

va·ri·e·ty Abwechslung *f*; Vielfalt *f*; *ECON* Auswahl *f*, Sortiment *n* (*of an dat*); *BOT, ZO* Art *f*; Varietee *n*; *for a variety of reasons* aus den verschiedensten Gründen

variety show Varieteevorstellung *f*

variety thea·ter (*Br* **thea·tre**) Varietee (-theater) *n*

var·i·ous verschieden; mehrere, verschiedene

var·nish 1. Lack *m*; **2.** lackieren

var·si·ty team *SPORT* Universitäts-, College-, Schulmannschaft *f*

var·y *v/i* sich (ver)ändern; variieren, auseinandergehen (*opinions etc*) (*on über acc*); *vary in size* verschieden groß sein; *v/t* (ver)ändern; variieren

vase Vase f

vast gewaltig, riesig, (area a.) ausgedehnt, weit

vast·ly gewaltig, weitaus

vat (großes) Fass, Bottich m

VAT ABBR of value-added tax ECON Mehrwertsteuer f

vau·de·ville Varietee(theater) n

vault¹ ARCH Gewölbe n; a. pl Stahlkammer f, Tresorraum m; (Keller)Gewölbe n; Gruft f

vault² 1. vault (over) springen über (acc); 2. esp SPORT Sprung m

vault·ing horse gymnastics: Pferd n

vaulting pole SPORT Sprungstab m

VCR ABBR of video cassette recorder Videorekorder m, Videogerät n

veal GASTR Kalbfleisch n; veal chop Kalbskotelett n; veal cutlet Kalbsschnitzel n; roast veal Kalbsbraten m

veer (sich) drehen; MOT ausscheren; veer to the right das Steuer nach rechts reißen

veg·e·ta·ble 1. mst pl Gemüse n; 2. Gemüse…; Pflanzen…

veg·e·tar·i·an 1. Vegetarier(in); 2. vegetarisch

veg·e·tate (dahin)vegetieren

veg·e·ta·tion Vegetation f

ve·he·mence Vehemenz f, Heftigkeit f

ve·he·ment vehement, heftig

ve·hi·cle Fahrzeug n; fig Medium n

veil 1. Schleier m; 2. verschleiern (a. fig)

vein ANAT Vene f, Ader f (a. BOT, GEOL, fig); fig (Charakter)Zug m; Stimmung f

ve·loc·i·ty TECH Geschwindigkeit f

ve·lour(s) Velours m

vel·vet Samt m

vel·vet·y samtig

vend·er → vendor

vend·ing ma·chine (Verkaufs-, Waren)-Automat m

vend·or (Straßen)Händler(in), (Zeitungs-etc)Verkäufer(in)

ve·neer 1. Furnier n; fig Fassade f; 2. furnieren

ven·e·ra·ble ehrwürdig

ven·e·rate verehren

ven·e·ra·tion Verehrung f

ve·no·re·al dis·ease MED Geschlechtskrankheit f

Ve·ne·tian 1. Venezianer(in); 2. venezianisch

Venetian blind (Stab)Jalousie f

ven·geance Rache f; take vengeance on sich rächen an (dat); with a vengeance mächtig, F wie verrückt

ve·ni·al entschuldbar, verzeihlich; REL lässlich

ven·i·son GASTR Wildbret n

ven·om zo Gift n, fig a. Gehässigkeit f

ven·om·ous giftig, fig a. gehässig

ve·nous MED venös

vent 1. v/t s-m Zorn etc Luft machen, s-e Wut etc auslassen, abreagieren (on an dat); 2. Schlitz m (in a coat etc); TECH (Abzugs)Öffnung f; give vent to s-m Ärger etc Luft machen

ven·ti·late (be)lüften; fig äußern

ven·ti·la·tion (Be)Lüftung f, Ventilation f

ven·ti·la·tor Ventilator m

ven·tri·cle ANAT Herzkammer f

ven·tril·o·quist Bauchredner(in)

ven·ture 1. esp ECON Wagnis n, Risiko n; ECON Unternehmen n; → joint venture; 2. sich wagen; riskieren

ven·ue SPORT Austragungsort m

verb LING Verb n, Zeitwort n

verb·al mündlich; wörtlich; Wort…

ver·dict JUR (Urteils)Spruch m; fig Urteil n; bring in or return a verdict of (not) guilty JUR auf (nicht) schuldig erkennen

ver·di·gris Grünspan m

verge 1. Rand m (a. fig); be on the verge of kurz vor (dat) stehen; be on the verge of despair (tears) der Verzweiflung (den Tränen) nahe sein; 2. verge on fig grenzen an (acc)

ver·i·fy bestätigen; nachweisen; (über-)prüfen

ver·i·ta·ble wahr

ver·mi·cel·li Fadennudeln pl

ver·mi·form ap·pen·dix ANAT Wurmfortsatz m, Blinddarm m

ver·mil·i·on 1. zinnoberrot; 2. Zinnoberrot n

ver·min Ungeziefer n; Schädlinge pl; fig Gesindel n, Pack n

ver·min·ous voller Ungeziefer

ver·nac·u·lar Dialekt m, Mundart f; in the vernacular im Volksmund

ver·sa·tile vielseitig; vielseitig verwendbar

verse Verdichtung f; Vers m; Strophe f

versed: be (well) versed in beschlagen or bewandert sein in (dat)

ver·sion Version f; TECH Ausführung f; Darstellung f (of an event); Fassung f (of a film etc); Übersetzung f

ver·sus (ABBR v., vs.) SPORT, JUR gegen

ver·te·bra ANAT Wirbel m

ver·te·brate ZO Wirbeltier n

ver·ti·cal vertikal, senkrecht

ver·ti·go MED Schwindel m; suffer from vertigo an or unter Schwindel leiden

verve Elan m, Schwung m

ver·y 1. adv sehr; aller…; I very much hope that ich hoffe sehr, dass; the very

best das Allerbeste; **for the very last time** zum allerletzten Mal; **2.** *adj* **the very** genau der *or* die *or* das; **the very opposite** genau das Gegenteil; **the very thing** genau das Richtige; **the very thought of** schon der *or* der bloße Gedanke an (*acc*)

ves·i·cle MED Bläschen *n*

ves·sel MAR, BOT Gefäß *n*; Schiff *n*

vest Weste *f*; *Br* Unterhemd *n*; *kugelsichere* Weste

ves·ti·bule (Vor)Halle *f*

ves·tige *fig* Spur *f*

vest·ment Ornat *m*, Gewand *n*, Robe *f*

ves·try REL Sakristei *f*

vet¹ F Tierarzt *m*, Tierärztin *f*

vet² *esp Br* F überprüfen

vet³ MIL F Veteran *m*

vet·er·an 1. MIL Veteran *m* (*a. fig*); **2.** altgedient; erfahren

veteran car *Br* Oldtimer *m* (*built before 1905*)

vet·er·i·nar·i·an Tierarzt *m*, -ärztin *f*

vet·er·i·na·ry tierärztlich

veterinary sur·geon *Br* Tierarzt *m*, Tierärztin *f*

ve·to 1. Veto *n*; **2.** sein Veto einlegen gegen

vexed ques·tion leidige Frage

vi·a über (*acc*), via

vi·a·duct Viadukt *m*, *n*

vi·al (*esp* Arznei)Fläschchen *n*

vibes F Atmosphäre *f*

vi·brant kräftig (*color etc*); pulsierend (*city etc*)

vi·brate *v/i* vibrieren, zittern; flimmern; *fig* pulsieren; *v/t* in Schwingungen versetzen

vi·bra·tion Vibrieren *n*, Zittern *n*; *pl* F Atmosphäre *f*

vic·ar REL Pfarrer *m*

vic·ar·age Pfarrhaus *n*

vice¹ Laster *n*

vice² *esp Br* Schraubstock *m*

vice... Vize..., stellvertretend

vice squad Sittendezernat *n*, Sittenpolizei *f*; Rauschgiftdezernat *n*

vi·ce ver·sa: and vice versa und umgekehrt

vi·cin·i·ty Nähe *f*; Nachbarschaft *f*

vi·cious brutal; bösartig

vi·cis·si·tudes *das* Auf und Ab, *die* Wechselfälle *pl*

vic·tim Opfer *n*

vic·tim·ize (ungerechterweise) bestrafen, ungerecht behandeln; schikanieren

vic·to·ri·ous siegreich

vic·to·ry Sieg *m*

vid·e·o 1. Video *n*; Videokassette *f*; F Videoband *n*; *esp Br* Videorekorder *m*, Videogerät *n*; **on video** auf Video; Video...; **3.** *esp Br* auf Video aufnehmen, aufzeichnen

video cam·e·ra Videokamera *f*

video cas·sette Videokassette *f*

video cas·sette re·cord·er → **video recorder**

video clip Videoclip *m*

vid·e·o·disk Bildplatte *f*

vid·e·o game Videospiel *n*

video li·brary Videothek *f*

video re·cord·er Videorekorder *m*, Videogerät *n*

video re·cord·ing Videoaufnahme *f*, Videoaufzeichnung *f*

video shop *Br*, **video store** Videothek *f*

vid·e·o·tape 1. Videokassette *f*; Videoband *n*; **2.** auf Video aufnehmen, aufzeichnen

vid·e·o·text Bildschirmtext *m*

vie wetteifern (**with** mit; **for** um)

Vi·en·nese 1. Wiener(in); **2.** wienerisch, Wiener...

view 1. Sicht *f* (**of** auf *acc*); Aussicht *f*, (Aus)Blick *m* (**of** auf *acc*); Ansicht *f* (*a.* PHOT), Meinung *f* (**about, on** über *acc*); *fig* Überblick *m* (**of** über *acc*); **a room with a view** ein Zimmer mit schöner Aussicht; **be on view** ausgestellt *or* zu besichtigen sein; **be hidden from view** nicht zu sehen sein; **come into view** in Sicht kommen; **in full view of** direkt vor j-s Augen; **in view of** *fig* angesichts (*gen*); **in my view** m-r Ansicht nach; **keep in view** et. im Auge behalten; **with a view to** *fig* mit Blick auf (*acc*); **2.** *v/t* Haus etc besichtigen; *fig* betrachten (**as** als); *v/i* fernsehen

view·da·ta Bildschirmtext *m*

view·er Fernsehzuschauer(in), F Fernseher(in); TECH (*Dia*)Betrachter *m*

view·find·er PHOT Sucher *m*

view·point Gesichts-, Standpunkt *m*

vig·il (Nacht)Wache *f*

vig·i·lance Wachsamkeit *f*

vig·i·lant wachsam

vig·or·ous energisch; kräftig

vig·o(u)r Energie *f*

Vi·king 1. Wikinger *m*; **2.** Wikinger...

vile gemein, niederträchtig; F scheußlich

vil·lage Dorf *n*

village green Dorfanger *m*

vil·lag·er Dorfbewohner(in)

vil·lain Bösewicht *m*, Schurke *m*; *Br* F Ganove *m*

vin·di·cate *j-n* rehabilitieren; *et.* rechtfertigen; *et.* Bestätigen

vin·dic·tive rachsüchtig, nachtragend

V

vine BOT (Wein)Rebe *f*; Kletterpflanze *f*

vin·e·gar Essig *m*

vine-grow·er Winzer *m*

vine·yard Weinberg *m*

vin·tage 1. Weinernte *f*, Weinlese *f*; GASTR Jahrgang *m*; **2.** GASTR Jahrgangs-...; *fig* hervorragend, glänzend; *a 1994 vintage* ein 1994er Jahrgang *or* Wein

vin·tage car *esp Br* Oldtimer *m* (*built between 1919 and 1930*)

vi·o·la MUS Bratsche *f*

vi·o·late *Vertrag etc* verletzen, *a. Versprechen* brechen, *Gesetz etc* übertreten; *Ruhe etc* stören; *Grab etc* schänden

vi·o·la·tion Verletzung *f*, Bruch *m*, Übertretung *f*

vi·o·lence Gewalt *f*; Gewalttätigkeit *f*; Ausschreitungen *pl*; Heftigkeit *f*

vi·o·lent gewalttätig; gewaltsam; heftig

vi·o·let 1. BOT Veilchen *n*; **2.** violett

vi·o·lin MUS Geige *f*, Violine *f*

vi·o·lin·ist Geiger(in), Violinist(in)

VIP ABBR *of* **very important person** VIP *f*

VIP lounge AVIAT *etc* VIP-Lounge *f*; SPORT Ehrentribüne *f*

vi·per ZO Viper *f*, Natter *f*

vir·gin 1. Jungfrau *f*; **2.** jungfräulich, unberührt (*both a. fig*)

Vir·go ASTR Jungfrau *f*; *he (she) is (a) Virgo* er (sie) ist Jungfrau

vir·ile männlich; potent

vi·ril·i·ty Männlichkeit *f*; Potenz *f*

vir·tu·al eigentlich, praktisch

vir·tu·al·ly praktisch, so gut wie

virtual re·al·i·ty EDP virtuelle Realität

vir·tue Tugend *f*; Vorzug *m*, Vorteil *m*; *by or in virtue of* aufgrund (*gen*), kraft (*gen*); *make a virtue of necessity* aus der Not e-e Tugend machen

vir·tu·ous tugendhaft

vir·u·lent MED (akut und) bösartig; schnell wirkend (*poison*); *fig* bösartig, gehässig

vi·rus MED Virus *n, m*

vi·sa Visum *n*, Sichtvermerk *m*

vis·cose Viskose *f*

vis·cous dickflüssig, zähflüssig

vise TECH Schraubstock *m*

vis·i·bil·i·ty Sicht *f*, Sichtverhältnisse *pl*, Sichtweite *f*

vis·i·ble sichtbar; (er)sichtlich

vi·sion Sehkraft *f*; Weitblick *m*; Vision *f*

vi·sion·a·ry 1. weitblickend; eingebildet, unwirklich; **2.** Fantast(in), Träumer(in); Seher(in)

vis·it 1. *v/t j-n* besuchen, *Schloss etc a.* besichtigen; *et.* inspizieren; *v/i: be visiting* auf Besuch sein (*with* bei); *visit with* plaudern mit; **2.** Besuch *m*, Besichtigung *f* (*to gen*); Plauderei *f*; *for or on a visit*

auf Besuch; *have a visit from* Besuch haben von; *pay a visit to j-n* besuchen, *j-m* e-n Besuch abstatten; *Arzt* aufsuchen

vis·it·ing hours MED Besuchszeit *f*

vis·it·or Besucher(in), Gast *m*

vi·sor Visier *n*; Schirm *m*; MOT (Sonnen)Blende *f*

vis·u·al Seh-...; visuell

visual aids PED Anschauungsmaterial *n*, Lehrmittel *pl*

visual dis·play u·nit EDP Bildschirmgerät *n*, Datensichtgerät *n*

visual in·struc·tion PED Anschauungsunterricht *m*

vis·u·al·ize sich *et.* vorstellen

vi·tal vital, Lebens-...; lebenswichtig; unbedingt notwendig; *of vital importance* von größter Wichtigkeit

vi·tal·i·ty Vitalität *f*

vit·a·min Vitamin *n*

vitamin de·fi·cien·cy Vitaminmangel *m*

vit·re·ous Glas-...

vi·va·cious lebhaft, temperamentvoll

viv·id hell (*light*); kräftig, leuchtend (*color*); anschaulich (*description*); lebhaft (*imagination*)

vix·en ZO Füchsin *f*

V-neck V-Ausschnitt *m*

V-necked mit V-Ausschnitt

vo·cab·u·la·ry Vokabular *n*, Wortschatz *m*; Wörterverzeichnis *n*

vo·cal Stimm-...; *f* lautstark; MUS Vokal-..., Gesang-...

vocal cords ANAT Stimmbänder *pl*

vo·cal·ist Sänger(in)

vo·ca·tion Begabung *f* (*for* für); Berufung *f*

vo·ca·tion·al Berufs-...

vocational ed·u·ca·tion Berufsausbildung *f*

vocational guid·ance Berufsberatung *f*

vocational train·ing Berufsausbildung *f*

vogue Mode *f*; *be in vogue* Mode sein

voice 1. Stimme *f*; *active voice* LING Aktiv *n*; *passive voice* LING Passiv *n*; **2.** zum Ausdruck bringen; LING (stimmhaft) aussprechen

voiced LING stimmhaft

voice·less LING stimmlos

void 1. leer; JUR ungültig; *void of* ohne; **2.** (Gefühl *n* der) Leere *f*

vol ABBR *of* **volume** Bd., Band *m*

vol·a·tile cholerisch (*person*); explosiv (*situation etc*); CHEM flüchtig

vol·ca·no Vulkan *m*

vol·ley 1. Salve *f*; (*Geschoss- etc*)Hagel *m* (*a. fig*); *tennis:* Volley *m*, Flugball *m*; *soccer:* Volleyschuss *m*; **2.** *Ball* volley schie-

ßen
vol·ley·ball SPORT Volleyball *m*
volt ELECTR Volt *n*
volt·age ELECTR Spannung *f*
vol·u·ble redselig; wortreich
vol·ume Band *m*; Volumen *n*, Rauminhalt *m*; Umfang *m*, große Menge; Lautstärke *f*
vo·lu·mi·nous bauschig (*dress etc*); geräumig; umfangreich (*notes etc*)
vol·un·ta·ry freiwillig; unbezahlt
vol·un·teer 1. *v/i* sich freiwillig melden (*for* zu) (*a.* MIL); *v/t* Hilfe etc anbieten; *et.* von sich aus sagen, F herausrücken mit; **2.** Freiwillige *m*, *f*; freiwilliger Helfer
vo·lup·tu·ous sinnlich (*lips etc*); aufreizend (*gesture etc*); üppig (*body etc*); kurvenreich (*woman*)
vom·it 1. *v/t* erbrechen; *v/i* (sich er)brechen, sich übergeben; **2.** Erbrochene *n*
vo·ra·cious unersättlich (*appetite etc*)
vote 1. Abstimmung *f* (*about, on* über

acc); (Wahl)Stimme *f*; Stimmzettel *m*; *a. pl* Wahlrecht *n*; *vote of no confidence* Misstrauensvotum *n*; *take a vote on s.th.* über et. abstimmen; **2.** *v/i* wählen; *vote for* (*against*) stimmen für (gegen); *vote on* abstimmen über (*acc*); *v/t* wählen; *et.* bewilligen; *vote out of office* abwählen
vot·er Wähler(in)
vot·ing booth Wahlkabine *f*
vouch: *vouch for* (sich ver)bürgen für
vouch·er Gutschein *m*, Kupon *m*
vow 1. Gelöbnis *n*; Gelübde *n*; *take a vow, make a vow* ein Gelübde *or* Gelübde ablegen; **2.** geloben, schwören (*to do* zu tun)
vow·el LING Vokal *m*, Selbstlaut *m*
voy·age (See)Reise *f*
vul·gar vulgär, ordinär; geschmacklos
vul·ne·ra·ble *fig* verletzbar, verwundbar; verletzlich; anfällig (*to* für)
vul·ture ZO Geier *m*

W

W, w W, w *n*
wad (*Watte- etc*)Bausch *m*; Bündel *n*; (*Papier- etc*)Knäuel *m, n*
wad·ding Einlage *f*, Füllmaterial *n*
wad·dle watscheln
wade *v/i* waten; *wade through* waten durch; F sich durchkämpfen durch, *et.* durchackern; *v/t* durchwaten
wa·fer (*esp* Eis)Waffel *f*; Oblate *f*; REL Hostie *f*
waf·fle¹ Waffel *f*
waf·fle² *Br* F schwafeln
waft *v/i* ziehen (*smell etc*); *v/t* wehen
wag 1. wedeln (mit); **2.** *with a wag of its tail* schwanzwedelnd
wage¹ *mst pl* (Arbeits)Lohn *m*
wage²: *wage (a) war against or on* MIL Krieg führen gegen; *fig* e-n Feldzug führen gegen
wage earn·er Lohnempfänger(in); Verdiener(in)
wage freeze Lohnstopp *m*
wage ne·go·ti·a·tions Tarifverhandlungen *pl*
wage pack·et Lohntüte *f*
wage rise Lohnerhöhung *f*

wa·ger Wette *f*
wag·gle F wackeln (mit)
wag·gon *Br* → **wag·on** Fuhrwerk *n*, Wagen *m*; *Br* RAIL (offener) Güterwagen; (*Tee- etc*)Wagen *m*
wag·tail ZO Bachstelze *f*
wail 1. jammern; heulen (*siren, wind*); **2.** Jammern *n*; Heulen *n*
wain·scot (Wand)Täfelung *f*
waist Taille *f*
waist·coat *esp Br* Weste *f*
waist·line Taille *f*
wait 1. *v/i* warten (*for, on* auf *acc*); *wait for s.o. a.* j-n erwarten; *keep s.o. waiting* j-n warten lassen; *wait and see!* warte es ab!; *wait on* (*Br at*) *table* bedienen, servieren; *wait on s.o.* j-n bedienen; *wait up* F aufbleiben (*for* wegen); *v/t*: *wait one's chance* auf e-e günstige Gelegenheit warten (*to do* zu tun); *wait one's turn* warten, bis man an der Reihe ist; **2.** Wartezeit *f*; *have a long wait* lange warten müssen; *lie in wait for s.o.* j-m auflauern
wait·er Kellner *m*, Ober *m*; *waiter, the check* (*Br bill*)*, please!* (Herr) Ober,

W

bitte zahlen!

wait·ing Warten *n*; *no waiting* MOT Halt(e)verbot *n*

waiting list Warteliste *f*

waiting room MED *etc* Wartezimmer *n*; RAIL Wartesaal *m*

wait·ress Kellnerin *f*, Bedienung *f*; *waitress, the check* (*Br* **bill**) *please!* Fräulein, bitte zahlen!

wake[1] *v/i a.* **wake up** aufwachen, wach werden; *v/t a.* **wake up** (auf)wecken; *fig* wachwerden, wach

wake[2] MAR Kielwasser *n*; *follow in the wake of fig* folgen auf (*acc*)

wake·ful schlaflos

wak·en *v/i a.* **waken up** aufwachen, wach werden; *v/t a.* **waken up** (auf)wecken

walk 1. *v/i* (zu Fuß) gehen, laufen; spazieren gehen; wandern; *v/t Strecke* gehen, laufen; *j-n* bringen (*to* zu; *home* nach Hause); *Hund* ausführen; *Pferd* im Schritt gehen lassen; *walk away* → *walk off*; *walk in* hineingehen, hereinkommen; *walk off* fort-, weggehen; *walk off with* F abhauen mit; F *Preis etc* locker gewinnen; *walk out* hinausgehen; (unter Protest) den Saal *etc* verlassen; ECON streiken, in (den) Streik treten; *walk out on s.o.* F *j-n* verlassen, *j-n* im Stich lassen; *walk up* hinaufgehen, heraufkommen; *walk up to s.o.* auf *j-n* zugehen; *walk up!* treten Sie näher!; **2.** Spaziergang *m*; Wanderung *f*; Spazier-, Wanderweg *m*; *go for a walk, take a walk* e-n Spaziergang machen, spazieren gehen; *an hour's walk* e-e Stunde Fußweg *or* zu Fuß; *from all walks of life* Leute aus allen Berufen *or* Schichten

walk·a·way F Spaziergang *m*, leichter Sieg

walk·er Spaziergänger(in); Wanderer *m*, Wand(r)erin *f*; SPORT Geher(in); *be a good walker* gut zu Fuß sein

walk·ie-talk·ie Walkie-Talkie *n*, tragbares Funksprechgerät

walk·ing Gehen *n*, Laufen *n*; Spazierengehen *n*; Wandern *n*

walking pa·pers: *get one's walking papers* F den Laufpass bekommen

walking shoes Wanderschuhe *pl*

walking stick Spazierstock *m*

walking tour Wanderung *f*

Walk·man® Walkman® *m*

walk·out Auszug *m* (*by, of* e-r *Delegation etc*); ECON Ausstand *m*, Streik *m*

walk·over → *walkaway*

walk-up F (Miets)Haus *n* ohne Fahrstuhl; Wohnung *f or* Büro *n etc* in e-m Haus ohne Fahrstuhl

wall 1. Wand *f*; Mauer *f*; **2.** *a.* **wall in** mit

e-r Mauer umgeben; *wall up* zumauern

wall cal·en·dar Wandkalender *m*

wall·chart Wandkarte *f*

wal·let Brieftasche *f*

wall-flow·er F Mauerblümchen *n*

wal·lop F *j-m* ein Ding verpassen; SPORT *j-n* erledigen, vernichten (*at* in *dat*)

wal·low sich wälzen; *fig* schwelgen, sich baden (*in* in *dat*)

wall·pa·per 1. Tapete *f*; **2.** tapezieren

wall-to-wall: *wall-to-wall carpet(ing)* Spannteppich *m*, Teppichboden *m*

wal·nut BOT Walnuss(baum *m*) *f*

wal·rus ZO Walross *n*

waltz 1. Walzer *m*; **2.** Walzer tanzen

wand (*Zauber*)Stab *m*

wan·der (herum)wandern, herumlaufen, umherstreifen; *fig* abschweifen; fantasieren

wane 1. ASTR abnehmen; *fig* schwinden; **2.** *be on the wane fig* im Schwinden begriffen sein

wan·gle F deichseln, hinkriegen; *wangle s.th. out of s.o.* *j-m* et. abluchsen; *wangle one's way out of* sich herauswinden aus

want 1. *v/t et.* wollen; *j-n* brauchen; *j-n* sprechen wollen; F *et.* brauchen, nötig haben; *be wanted* (*polizeilich*) gesucht werden (*for* wegen); *v/i* wollen; *I don't want to* ich will nicht; *he does not want for anything* es fehlt ihm an nichts; **2.** Mangel *m* (*of* an *dat*); Bedürfnis *n*, Wunsch *m*; Not *f*

want ad Kleinanzeige *f*

want·ed (*polizeilich*) gesucht

wan·ton mutwillig

war Krieg *m* (*a. fig*), *fig* Kampf *m* (*against* gegen)

war·ble ZO trillern

ward 1. MED Station *f*; *Br* POL Stadtbezirk *m*; JUR Mündel *n*; **2.** *ward off Schlag etc* abwehren, *Gefahr etc* abwenden

war·den Aufseher(in); Heimleiter(in); (Gefängnis)Direktor(in)

ward·er *Br* Aufsichtsbeamte *m*, -beamtin *f*

war·drobe Kleiderschrank *m*; Garderobe *f*

ware·house Lager(haus) *n*

war·fare Krieg *m*; Kriegführung *f*

war·head MIL Spreng-, Gefechtskopf *m*

war·like kriegerisch; Kriegs...

warm 1. *adj* warm, *fig a.* herzlich; *I am warm, I feel warm* mir ist warm; **2.** *v/t a.* **warm up** wärmen, sich *die Hände etc* wärmen; MOTOR warm laufen lassen; *v/i a.* **warm up** warm *or* wärmer werden, sich erwärmen

warmth Wärme f
warm-up SPORT Aufwärmen n
warn warnen (**against, of** vor dat); j-n verständigen
warn·ing Warnung f (**of** vor dat); Verwarnung f; **without warning** ohne Vorwarnung
warning sig·nal Warnsignal n
warp sich verziehen or werfen
war·rant 1. JUR (Durchsuchungs-, Haftetc)Befehl m; **2.** et. rechtfertigen
warrant of ar·rest JUR Haftbefehl m
war·ran·ty ECON Garantie(erklärung) f; **it's still under warranty** darauf ist noch Garantie
war·ri·or Krieger m
war·ship Kriegsschiff n
wart MED Warze f
war·y vorsichtig
was ich, er, sie, es war; passive: ich, er, sie, es wurde
wash 1. v/t waschen, sich die Hände etc waschen; v/i sich waschen; sich gut et. waschen (lassen); **wash up** v/i Br abwaschen, (das) Geschirr spülen; v/t anschwemmen, anspülen; **wash one's dirty linen** schmutzige Wäsche waschen; **2.** Wäsche f; MOT Waschanlage f, Waschstraße f; **be in the wash** in der Wäsche sein; **give s.th. a wash** et. waschen; **have a wash** sich waschen
wash·a·ble (ab)waschbar
wash-and-wear bügelfrei; pflegeleicht
wash·ba·sin Br, **wash·bowl** Waschbecken n
wash·cloth Waschlappen m
wash·er Waschmaschine f; TECH Unterlegscheibe f
wash·ing 1. Wäsche f; **2.** Wasch...
wash·ing ma·chine Waschmaschine f
washing pow·der Waschpulver n, -mittel n
washing-up Br Abwasch m; **do the washing-up** den Abwasch machen
wash·room Toilette f
wasp ZO Wespe f
waste 1. Verschwendung f; Abfall m; Müll m; **waste of time** Zeitverschwendung f; **hazardous waste, special toxic waste** Sondermüll m; **special waste dump** Sondermülldeponie f; **2.** v/t verschwenden, vergeuden; j-n ausarbeiten; v/i **waste away** immer schwächer werden (person); **3.** überschüssig; Abfall...; brachliegend, öde; **lay waste** verwüsten
waste dis·pos·al Abfall-, Müllbeseitigung f; Entsorgung f
waste disposal site Deponie f
waste·ful verschwenderisch

waste gas Abgas n
waste pa·per Abfallpapier n; Altpapier n
waste·pa·per bas·ket Papierkorb m
waste pipe Abflussrohr n
watch 1. v/i zuschauen; **watch for** warten auf (acc); **watch out!** pass auf!, Vorsicht!; **watch out for** Ausschau halten nach; sich in Acht nehmen vor (dat); v/t beobachten; zuschauen bei, sich et. ansehen; → **television; 2.** (Armband-, Taschen-) Uhr f; Wache f; **keep watch** Wache halten, wachen (**over** über acc); **be on the watch for** Ausschau halten nach; auf der Hut sein vor (dat); **keep (a) careful** or **close watch on** genau beobachten, scharf im Auge behalten
watch·dog Wachhund m
watch·ful wachsam
watch·mak·er Uhrmacher(in)
watch·man Wachmann m, Wächter m
watch·tow·er Wach(t)turm m
wa·ter 1. Wasser n; **2.** v/t Blumen gießen, Rasen etc sprengen; Vieh tränken; **water down** verdünnen, verwässern; fig abschwächen; v/i tränen (eyes); **make s.o. 's mouth water** j-m den Mund wässerig machen
wa·ter bird ZO Wasservogel m
wa·ter·col·o(u)r Wasser-, Aquarellfarbe f; Aquarellmalerei f; Aquarell n
wa·ter·course Wasserlauf m
wa·ter·cress BOT Brunnenkresse f
wa·ter·fall Wasserfall m
wa·ter·front Hafenviertel n; **along the waterfront** am Wasser entlang
wa·ter·hole Wasserloch n
wa·ter·ing can Gießkanne f
wa·ter jump SPORT Wassergraben m
wa·ter lev·el Wasserstand m
wa·ter lil·y BOT Seerose f
wa·ter·mark Wasserzeichen n
wa·ter·mel·on BOT Wassermelone f
wa·ter pol·lu·tion Wasserverschmutzung f
water po·lo SPORT Wasserball(spiel n) m
wa·ter·proof 1. wasserdicht; **2.** Br Regenmantel m; **3.** imprägnieren
wa·ters Gewässer pl; Wasser pl
wa·ter·shed GEOGR Wasserscheide f; fig Wendepunkt m
wa·ter·side Ufer n
wa·ter ski·ing SPORT Wasserskilaufen n
wa·ter·tight wasserdicht, fig a. hieb- und stichfest
wa·ter·way Wasserstraße f
wa·ter·works Wasserwerk n; **turn on the waterworks** F zu heulen anfangen
wa·ter·y wäss(e)rig
watt ELECTR Watt n

W

wave 1. *v/t* schwenken; winken mit; *Haar* wellen, in Wellen legen; *wave one's hand* winken; *wave s.o. aside* j-n beiseitewinken; *v/i* winken; wehen (*flag etc*); sich wellen (*hair*); *wave at s.o., wave to s.o.* j-m zuwinken; **2.** Welle *f* (*a. fig*); bohnern

wave·length PHYS Wellenlänge *f* (*a. fig*)

wa·ver flackern; schwanken

wav·y wellig, gewellt

wax[1] **1.** Wachs *n*; (*Ohren*)Schmalz *n*; **2.** wachsen; bohnern

wax[2] ASTR zunehmen

wax·en wächsern

wax·works Wachsfigurenkabinett *n*

wax·y wächsern

way 1. Weg *m*; Richtung *f*, Seite *f*; Entfernung *f*, Strecke *f*; Art *f*, Weise *f*; *ways and means* Mittel und Wege *pl*; *way back* Rückweg *m*, Rückfahrt *f*; *way home* Heimweg *m*; *way in* Eingang *m*; *way out* Ausgang *m*; *be on the way to, be on one's way to* unterwegs sein nach; *by way of* über (*acc*), via; *esp Br* statt; *by the way* übrigens; *give way* nachgeben; *Br* MOT die Vorfahrt lassen; *in a way* in gewisser Hinsicht; *in no way* in keiner Weise; *lead the way* vorangehen; *let s.o. have his (own) way* j-m s-n Willen lassen; *lose one's way* sich verlaufen *or* verirren; *make way* Platz machen (*for* für); *no way!* F kommt überhaupt nicht in Frage!; *out of the way* ungewöhnlich; *this way* hierher; hier entlang; **2.** *adv* weit

way·bill ECON Frachtbrief *m*

way·lay j-m auflauern; j-n abfangen, abpassen

way·ward eigensinnig, launisch

we wir *pl*

weak schwach (*at, in* in *dat*), GASTR *a.* dünn

weak·en *v/t* schwächen (*a. fig*); *v/i* schwächer werden; *fig* nachgeben

weak·ling Schwächling *m*, F Schlappschwanz *m*

weak·ness Schwäche *f*

weal Striemen *m*

wealth Reichtum *m*; *fig* Fülle *f* (*of* von)

wealth·y reich

wean entwöhnen; *wean s.o. from or off s.th.* j-m et. abgewöhnen

weap·on Waffe *f* (*a. fig*)

wear 1. *v/t* Bart, Brille, Schmuck *etc* tragen, *Mantel etc a.* anhaben, *Hut etc a.* aufhaben; abnutzen, abtragen; *wear the pants* (*Br* trousers) F die Hosen anhaben; *wear an angry expression* verärgert dreinschauen; *v/i* sich abnutzen, verschleißen; sich gut *etc* halten; *s.th. to wear* et. zum Anziehen; *wear away* (sich) abtragen *or* abschleifen; *wear down* (sich) abtreten (*stairs*), (sich) ablaufen (*heels*), (sich) abfahren (*tires*); abschleifen; j-n zermürben; *wear off* nachlassen (*pain etc*); *wear on* sich hinziehen (*all day* über den ganzen Tag); *wear out* (sich) abnutzen *or* abtragen; *fig* j-n erschöpfen; **2.** *often in cpds* Kleidung *f*, *a.* *wear and tear* Abnutzung *f*, Verschleiß *m*; *the worse for wear* abgenutzt, verschlissen; F lädiert

wear·i·some ermüdend; langweilig; lästig

wear·y erschöpft, müde; ermüdend, anstrengend; *be weary of s.th.* F et. satthaben

wea·sel ZO Wiesel *n*

weath·er 1. Wetter *n*; Witterung *f*; **2.** *v/t* dem Wetter aussetzen; *fig* Krise *etc* überstehen; *v/i* verwittern

weath·er-beat·en verwittert

weath·er chart METEOR Wetterkarte *f*

weather fore·cast METEOR Wettervorhersage *f*; Wetterbericht *m*

weath·er·man *radio*, TV Wetteransager *m*

weath·er·proof 1. wetterfest; **2.** wetterfest machen

weath·er re·port METEOR Wetterbericht *m*

weather sta·tion METEOR Wetterwarte *f*

weather vane Wetterfahne *f*

weave weben; *Netz* spinnen; *Korb* flechten; *weave one's way through* sich schlängeln durch

weav·er Weber(in)

web Netz *n* (*a. fig*), Gewebe *n*; ZO Schwimmhaut *f*

wed heiraten

Wed(s) ABBR *of* **Wednesday** Mi., Mittwoch *m*

wed·ding 1. Hochzeit *f*; **2.** Hochzeits..., Braut..., Ehe..., Trau...

wed·ding ring Ehering *m*, Trauring *m*

wedge 1. Keil *m*; **2.** verkeilen, mit e-m Keil festklemmen; *wedge in* einkeilen, einzwängen

wed·lock: *born in* (*out of*) *wedlock* ehelich (unehelich) geboren

Wednes·day (ABBR *Wed, Weds*) Mittwoch *m*; *on Wednesday* (am) Mittwoch; *on Wednesdays* mittwochs

wee[1] F klein, winzig; *a wee bit* ein (kleines) bisschen

wee[2] F **1.** Pipi machen; **2.** *do or have a wee* Pipi machen

weed 1. Unkraut *n*; **2.** jäten

weed·kill·er Unkrautvertilgungsmittel *n*

weed·y voll Unkraut; F schmächtig; F rückgratlos

week Woche *f*; *week after week* Woche um Woche; *a week today, today week* heute in e-r Woche *or* in acht Tagen; *every other week* jede zweite Woche; *for weeks* wochenlang; *four times a week* viermal die Woche; *in a week('s time)* in e-r Woche

week·day Wochentag *m*

week·end Wochenende *n*; *on (Br at) the weekend* am Wochenende

week·end·er Wochenendausflügler(in)

week·ly 1. Wochen...; wöchentlich; 2. Wochenblatt *n*, Wochen(zeit)schrift *f*, Wochenzeitung *f*

weep weinen (*for* um *j-n*; *over* über *acc*); MED nässen

weep·ing wil·low BOT Trauerweide *f*

weep·y F weinerlich; rührselig

wee-wee F → *wee²*

weigh *v/t* (ab)wiegen; *fig* abwägen (*against* gegen); *weigh anchor* MAR den Anker lichten; *be weighed down with fig* niedergedrückt werden von; *v/i* ... Kilo *etc* wiegen; *weigh on fig* lasten auf (*dat*)

weight 1. Gewicht *n*; Last *f* (*a. fig*); *fig* Bedeutung *f*; *gain weight, put on weight* zunehmen; *lose weight* abnehmen; 2. beschweren

weight·less schwerelos

weight·less·ness Schwerelosigkeit *f*

weight lift·er SPORT Gewichtheber *m*

weight lift·ing SPORT Gewichtheben *n*

weight·y schwer; *fig* schwerwiegend

weir Wehr *n*

weird unheimlich; F sonderbar, verrückt

wel·come 1. *int* *welcome back!, welcome home!* willkommen zu Hause!; *welcome to England!* willkommen in England!; 2. *v/t* begrüßen (*a. fig*), willkommen heißen; 3. *adj* willkommen; *you are welcome to do it* Sie können es gerne tun; *you're welcome!* nichts zu danken!, keine Ursache!, bitte sehr!; 4. Empfang *m*, Willkommen *n*; *outstay or overstay one's welcome* j-s Gastfreundschaft überstrapazieren *or* zu lange in Anspruch nehmen

weld TECH schweißen

wel·fare Wohl(ergehen) *n*; Sozialhilfe *f*; *be on welfare* Sozialhilfe beziehen

welfare state Wohlfahrtsstaat *m*

welfare work Sozialarbeit *f*

welfare work·er Sozialarbeiter(in)

well¹ 1. *adv* gut; gründlich; *as well* ebenso, auch; *as well as* ... sowohl ... als auch ...; nicht nur ..., sondern auch ...; *very well* also gut, na gut; *well done!* bravo!; → *off 1*; 2. *int* nun, also; *well, well!* na so

was!; 3. *adj* gesund; *feel well* sich wohlfühlen

well² 1. Brunnen *m*; (*Öl*)Quelle *f*; (*Aufzugs- etc*)Schacht *m*; 2. *a.* *well out* quellen (*from* aus); *tears welled (up) in their eyes* die Tränen stiegen ihnen in die Augen

well-bal·anced ausgeglichen (*person*); ausgewogen (*diet*)

well-be·haved artig, gut erzogen

well-be·ing Wohl(befinden) *n*

well-dis·posed: *be well-disposed towards s.o.* j-m wohlgesinnt sein

well-done GASTR durchgebraten

well-earned wohlverdient

well-fed gut genährt

well-found·ed (wohl) begründet

well-in·formed gut unterrichtet; gebildet

well-known wohl bekannt

well-mean·ing wohlmeinend, gut gemeint

well-meant gut gemeint

well-off 1. wohlhabend, vermögend, bessergestellt; *be well-off for* gut versorgt sein mit; 2. *the well-off* die Wohlhabenden *pl*

well-read belesen

well-timed (zeitlich) günstig, im richtigen Augenblick

well-to-do wohlhabend, reich

well-worn abgetragen; *fig* abgedroschen

Welsh 1. walisisch; 2. LING Walisisch *n*; *the Welsh* die Waliser *pl*

welt Striemen *m*

wel·ter Wirrwarr *m*, Durcheinander *n*

wel·ter·weight SPORT Weltergewicht *n*; Weltergewichtler *m*

were *du* warst, *Sie* waren, *wir, sie* waren, *ihr* wart

west 1. West, Westen *m*; *the West* POL der Westen; die Weststaaten *pl*; 2. *adj* westlich, West...; 3. *adv* nach Westen, westwärts

west·er·ly West..., westlich

west·ern 1. westlich, West...; 2. Western *m*

west·ward(s) westlich, nach Westen

wet 1. nass, feucht; 2. Nässe *f*; 3. nass machen, anfeuchten

weth·er ZO Hammel *m*

wet nurse Amme *f*

whack (knallender) Schlag; F Anteil *m*

whacked F fertig, erledigt

whack·ing 1. *Br* F Mords...; 2. (Tracht *f*) Prügel *pl*

whale ZO Wal *m*

wharf Kai *m*

what 1. *pron* was; *what about ...?* wie wär's mit ...?; *what for?* wozu?; *so*

W

what? na und?; *know what's what* F wissen, was Sache ist; **2.** *adj* was für ein(e), welche(r, -s); alle, die; alles, was

what·cha·ma·call·it F → *whatsit*

what·ev·er 1. *pron* was (auch immer); alles, was; egal, was; **2.** *adj* welche(r, -s) ... auch (immer); *no ... whatever* überhaupt kein(e) ...

whats·it F Dings(bums, -da) *m, f, n*

what·so·ev·er → *whatever*

wheat BOT Weizen *m*

whee·dle beschwatzen; *wheedle s.th. out of s.o.* j-m et. abschwatzen

wheel 1. Rad *n*; MOT, MAR Steuer *n*; **2.** schieben, rollen; kreisen; *wheel about, wheel (a)round* herumfahren, herumwirbeln

wheel·bar·row Schubkarre(n *m*) *f*

wheel·chair Rollstuhl *m*

wheel clamp MOT Parkkralle *f*

wheeled mit Rädern; fahrbar; *in cpds* ...räd(e)rig

wheeze keuchen, pfeifend atmen

whelp ZO Welpe *m*, Junge *n*

when wann; als; wenn; obwohl; *since when?* seit wann?

when·ev·er wann auch (immer); jedes Mal, wenn

where wo; wohin; *where ... (from)?* woher?; *where ... (to)?* wohin?

where·a·bouts 1. *adv* wo etwa; **2.** Verbleib *m*; Aufenthalt *m*, Aufenthaltsort *m*

where·as während, wohingegen

where·by wodurch, womit; wonach

where·u·pon worauf, woraufhin

wher·ev·er wo *or* wohin auch (immer); ganz gleich wo *or* wohin

whet *Messer etc* schärfen; *fig Appetit* anregen

wheth·er ob

whey Molke *f*

which welche(r, -s); der, die, das; *which of you?* wer von euch?

which·ev·er welche(r, -s) auch (immer); ganz gleich, welche(r, -s)

whiff Luftzug *m*; Hauch *m* (*a. fig of* von); Duft *m*, Duftwolke *f*

while 1. Weile *f*; *for a while* e-e Zeit lang; **2.** *cj* während; obwohl; **3.** *mst while away* sich *die Zeit* vertreiben (*by doing s.th.* mit et.)

whim Laune *f*

whim·per 1. wimmern; ZO winseln; **2.** Wimmern *n*; ZO Winseln *n*

whim·si·cal wunderlich; launisch

whine 1. ZO jaulen; jammern (*about* über *acc*); **2.** ZO Jaulen *n*; Gejammer *n*

whin·ny 1. wiehern; **2.** Wiehern *n*

whip 1. Peitsche *f*; GASTR Creme *f*; **2.** *v/t* (aus)peitschen; GASTR schlagen; *v/i* sausen, flitzen, (*wind*) fegen

whipped cream Schlagsahne *f*, Schlagrahm *m*

whipped eggs Eischnee *m*

whip·ping (Tracht *f*) Prügel *pl*

whip·ping boy Prügelknabe *m*

whip·ping cream Schlagsahne *f*, Schlagrahm *m*

whir → *whirr*

whirl 1. wirbeln; *my head is whirling* mir schwirrt der Kopf; **2.** Wirbeln *n*; Wirbel *m* (*a. fig*); *my head's in a whirl* mir schwirrt der Kopf

whirl·pool Strudel *m*; Whirlpool *m*

whirl·wind Wirbelsturm *m*

whirr schwirren

whisk 1. schnelle Bewegung; Wedel *m*; GASTR Schneebesen *m*; **2.** GASTR schlagen; *whisk its tail* ZO mit dem Schwanz schlagen; *whisk away* Fliegen etc verscheuchen *or* wegscheuchen; et. schnell verschwinden lassen *or* wegnehmen

whis·ker ZO Schnurr- *or* Barthaar *n*; *pl* Backenbart *m*

whis·k(e)y Whisky *m*

whis·per 1. flüstern; **2.** Flüstern *n*; *say s.th. in a whisper* et. im Flüsterton sagen

whis·tle 1. Pfeife *f*; Pfiff *m*; **2.** pfeifen

white 1. weiß; **2.** Weiß(e) *n*; Weiße *m, f*; Eiweiß *n*

white bread Weißbrot *n*

white coffee *Br* Milchkaffee *m*, Kaffee *m* mit Milch

white-col·lar work·er (Büro)Angestellte *m, f*

white lie Notlüge *f*

whit·en weiß machen *or* werden

white·wash 1. Tünche *f*; **2.** tünchen, anstreichen; weißen; *fig* beschönigen

whit·ish weißlich

Whit·sun Pfingstsonntag *m*; Pfingsten *n or pl*

Whit Sunday Pfingstsonntag *m*

Whit·sun·tide Pfingsten *n or pl*

whit·tle (zurecht)schnitzen; *whittle away* Gewinn etc allmählich aufzehren; *whittle down* et. reduzieren (*to* auf *acc*)

whiz(z) F **1.** *whiz by, whiz past* vorbeizischen, vorbeidüsen; **2.** Ass *n*, Kanone *f* (*at* in *dat*)

whiz kid F Senkrechtstarter(in)

who wer; wen; wem; welche(r, -s); der, die, das

who·dun·(n)it F Krimi *m*

who·ev·er wer *or* wen auch *or* wem auch (immer); egal, wer *or* wen *or* wem

whole 1. *adj* ganz; **2.** *das* Ganze; *the*

whole of London ganz London; *on the whole* im Großen (und) Ganzen

whole-heart·ed ungeteilt (*attention*), voll (*support*), ernsthaft (*effort etc*)

whole-heart·ed·ly uneingeschränkt, voll und ganz

whole-meal Vollkorn...; *wholemeal bread* Vollkornbrot *n*

whole·sale ECON 1. Großhandel *m*; 2. Großhandels...

wholesale mar·ket ECON Großmarkt *m*

whole·sal·er ECON Großhändler *m*

whole wheat → *wholemeal*

whole·some gesund

whol·ly gänzlich, völlig

whoop 1. schreien, *esp* jauchzen; *whoop it up* F auf den Putz hauen; 2. (*esp* Freuden)Schrei *m*

whoop·ee: F *make whoopee* auf den Putz hauen

whoop·ing cough MED Keuchhusten *m*

whore Hure *f*

why warum, weshalb; *that's why* deshalb

wick Docht *m*

wick·ed gemein, niederträchtig

wich·er·work Korbwaren *pl*

wick·et *cricket:* Tor *n*

wide 1. *adj* breit; weit offen, aufgerissen (*eyes*), *fig* umfangreich (*knowledge etc*), vielfältig (*interests etc*); 1. *adv* weit; *go wide* danebengehen; *go wide of the goal* SPORT am Tor vorbeigehen

wide-an·gle lens PHOT Weitwinkelobjektiv *n*

wide-a·wake hellwach; *fig* aufgeweckt, wach

wide-eyed mit großen *or* aufgerissenen Augen; naiv

wid·en verbreitern; breiter werden

wide-o·pen weit offen, aufgerissen (*eyes*)

wide·spread weit verbreitet

wid·ow Witwe *f*

wid·owed verwitwet; *be widowed* verwitwet sein; Witwe(r) werden

wid·ow·er Witwer *m*

width Breite *f*; Bahn *f*

wield *Einfluss etc* ausüben

wife (Ehe)Frau *f*, Gattin *f*

wig Perücke *f*

wild 1. *adj* wild; stürmisch (*wind, applause etc*); außer sich (*with* vor *dat*); verrückt (*idea etc*); *make a wild guess* einfach drauflosraten; *be wild about* (ganz) verrückt sein nach; 2. *adv*: *go wild* ausflippen; *let one's children run wild* s-e Kinder machen lassen, was sie wollen; 3. *in the wild* in freier Wildbahn; *the wilds* die Wildnis

wild·cat ZO Wildkatze *f*

wild·cat strike ECON wilder Streik

wil·der·ness Wildnis *f*

wild·fire: *spread like wildfire* sich wie ein Lauffeuer verbreiten

wild·life Tier- und Pflanzenwelt *f*

wil·ful *Br* → *willful*

will[1] *v/aux ich, du* will(st) *etc*; *ich werde ... etc*

will[2] Wille *m*; Testament *n*; *of one's own free will* aus freien Stücken

will[3] durch Willenskraft erzwingen; JUR vermachen

will·ful eigensinnig; absichtlich, *esp* JUR vorsätzlich

will·ing bereit (*to do* zu tun); (bereit)willig

will-o'-the-wisp Irrlicht *n*

wil·low BOT Weide *f*

wil·low·y *fig* gertenschlank

will-pow·er Willenskraft *f*

wil·ly-nil·ly wohl oder übel

wilt verwelken, welk werden

wi·ly gerissen, raffiniert

wimp F Schlappschwanz *m*

win 1. *v/t* gewinnen; *win s.o. over or round to* j-n gewinnen für; *v/i* gewinnen, siegen; *OK, you win* okay, du hast gewonnen; 2. *esp* SPORT Sieg *m*

wince zusammenzucken (*at* bei)

winch TECH Winde *f*

wind[1] 1. Wind *m*; Atem *m*, Luft *f*; MED Blähungen *pl*; *the wind* MUS die Bläser *pl*; 2. *j-m* den Atem nehmen *or* verschlagen; Wind wittern

wind[2] 1. *v/t* drehen (an *dat*); *Uhr etc* aufziehen; wickeln (*round* um); *v/i* sich winden *or* schlängeln; *wind back Film etc* zurückspulen; *wind down Autofenster etc* herunterdrehen, -kurbeln; *Produktion etc* reduzieren; sich entspannen; *wind forward Film etc* weiterspulen; *wind up v/t Autofenster etc* hochdrehen, -kurbeln; *Uhr etc* aufziehen; *Versammlung etc* schließen (*with* mit); *Unternehmen* liquidieren, auflösen; *v/i* F enden, landen; (*esp* s-e Rede) schließen (*by saying* mit den Worten); 2. Umdrehung *f*

wind·bag F Schwätzer(in)

wind·fall BOT Fallobst *n*; unverhofftes Geschenk; unverhoffter Gewinn

wind·ing gewunden

wind·ing stairs Wendeltreppe *f*

wind in·stru·ment MUS Blasinstrument *n*

wind·lass TECH Winde *f*

wind·mill Windmühle *f*

win·dow Fenster *n*; Schaufenster *n*; Schalter *m*

window clean·er Fensterputzer *m*

window dress·er Schaufensterdekorateur(in)

window dress·ing Schaufensterdekoration *f*; *fig* F Mache *f*

win·dow·pane Fensterscheibe *f*

win·dow seat Fensterplatz *m*

win·dow shade Rouleau *n*

win·dow-shop·ping: *go window-shopping* e-n Schaufensterbummel machen

win·dow-sill Fensterbank *f*, -brett *n*

wind·pipe ANAT Luftröhre *f*

wind·screen *Br* MOT Windschutzscheibe *f*

windscreen wip·er *Br* MOT Scheibenwischer *m*

wind·shield MOT Windschutzscheibe *f*

windshield wip·er MOT Scheibenwischer *m*

wind·surf·ing SPORT Windsurfing *n*, Windsurfen *n*

wind·y windig; MED blähend

wine Wein *m*

wine cel·lar Weinkeller *m*

wine list Weinkarte *f*

wine mer·chant Weinhändler *m*

win·er·y Weinkellerei *f*

wine tast·ing Weinprobe *f*

wing 1. ZO Flügel *m*, Schwinge *f*; *Br* MOT Kotflügel *m*; AVIAT Tragfläche *f*; MIL Geschwader *n*; *pl* THEA Seitenkulisse *f*

wing·er SPORT Außenstürmer(in), Flügelstürmer(in)

wink 1. zwinkern; *wink at* j-m zuzwinkern; *et.* geflissentlich übersehen; *wink one's lights Br* MOT blinken; **2.** Zwinkern *n*; *I didn't get a wink of sleep last night, I didn't sleep a wink last night* ich habe letzte Nacht kein Auge zugetan; → *forty I*

win·ner Gewinner(in), *esp* SPORT Sieger(in)

win·ning 1. einnehmend, gewinnend; **2.** *pl* Gewinn *m*

win·ter 1. Winter *m*; *in (the) winter* im Winter; **2.** überwintern; den Winter verbringen

winter sports Wintersport *m*

win·ter·time Winter *m*; Winterzeit *f*; *in (the) wintertime* im Winter

win·try winterlich; *fig* frostig

wipe (ab-, auf)wischen; *wipe off* ab-, wegwischen; *wipe out* auswischen; auslöschen, ausrotten; *wipe up* aufwischen

wip·er MOT (*Scheiben*)Wischer *m*

wire 1. Draht *m*; ELECTR Leitung *f*; Telegramm *n*, **2.** Leitungen verlegen in (*dat*) (*a. wire up*); j-m ein Telegramm schicken; j-m et. telegrafieren

wire·less drahtlos, Funk…

wire net·ting Maschendraht *m*

wire·tap j-n, j-s Telefon abhören

wir·y *fig* drahtig

wis·dom Weisheit *f*, Klugheit *f*

wis·dom tooth Weisheitszahn *m*

wise weise, klug

wise·crack F **1.** Witzelei *f*; **2.** witzeln

wise guy F Klugscheißer *m*

wish 1. wünschen; wollen; *wish s.o. well* j-m alles Gute wünschen; *if you wish (to)* wenn du willst; *wish for s.th.* sich et. wünschen; **2.** Wunsch *m* (*for* nach)

wish·ful think·ing Wunschdenken *n*

wish·y-wash·y F labb(e)rig, wäss(e)rig; *fig* lasch (*person*); verschwommen

wisp (*Gras-, Haar*)Büschel *n*

wist·ful wehmütig

wit Geist *m*, Witz *m*; geistreicher Mensch; *a. pl* Verstand *m*; *be at one's wits' end* mit s-r Weisheit am Ende sein; *keep one's wits about one* e-n klaren Kopf behalten

witch Hexe *f*

witch·craft Hexerei *f*

with mit; bei; vor (*dat*)

with·draw *v/t* Geld abheben (*from* von); *Angebot etc* zurückziehen, *Anschuldigung etc* zurücknehmen; MIL *Truppen* zurückziehen, abziehen; *v/i* sich zurückziehen; zurücktreten (*from* von)

with·draw·al Rücknahme *f*; *esp* MIL Abzug *m*, Rückzug *m*; Rücktritt *m* (*from* von), Ausstieg *m* (*from* aus); MED Entziehung *f*, Entzug *m*; *make a withdrawal* Geld abheben (*from* von)

withdrawal cure MED Entziehungskur *f*

withdrawal symp·toms MED Entzugserscheinungen *pl*

with·er eingehen *or* verdorren *or* (ver)welken (*lassen*)

with·hold zurückhalten; *withhold s.th. from s.o.* j-m et. vorenthalten

with·in innerhalb (*gen*)

with·out ohne (*acc*)

with·stand *e-m Angriff etc* standhalten; *Beanspruchung etc* aushalten

wit·ness 1. Zeuge *m*, Zeugin *f*; *witness for the defense* (*Br* defence) JUR Entlastungszeuge *m*, -zeugin *f*; *witness for the prosecution* JUR Belastungszeuge *m*, -zeugin *f*; **2.** Zeuge sein von et.; bezeugen, *Unterschrift* beglaubigen; *witness box Br*, *witness stand* JUR Zeugenstand *m*

wit·ti·cis·m geistreiche *or* witzige Bemerkung

wit·ty geistreich, witzig

wiz·ard Zauberer *m*; *fig* Genie *n* (*at* in *dat*)

wiz·ened verhutzelt

wob·ble v/i wackeln, zittern (a. voice), schwabbeln; MOT flattern; fig schwanken; v/t wackeln an (dat)

woe·ful traurig; bedauerlich

wolf 1. ZO Wolf m; *lone wolf* fig Einzelgänger(in); **2.** a. *wolf down* F Essen hinunterschlingen

wom·an Frau f

woman doc·tor Ärztin f

woman driv·er Frau f am Steuer

wom·an·ish weibisch

wom·an·ly fraulich; weiblich

womb ANAT Gebärmutter f

women's lib·ber F Emanze f

women's move·ment Frauenbewegung f

women's ref·uge Br, **women's shel·ter** Frauenhaus n

won·der 1. neugierig or gespannt sein, gern wissen mögen; sich fragen, überlegen; sich wundern, erstaunt sein (*about* über acc); *I wonder if you could help me* vielleicht können Sie mir helfen; **2.** Staunen n, Verwunderung f; Wunder n; *do or work wonders* wahre Wunder vollbringen, Wunder wirken (*for* bei)

won·der·ful wunderbar, wundervoll

wont 1. *be wont to do s.th.* et. zu tun pflegen; **2.** *as was his wont* wie es s-e Gewohnheit war

woo umwerben, werben um

wood Holz n; Holzfass n; a. pl Wald m, Gehölz n; *touch wood!* unberufen!, toi, toi, toi!; *he can't see the wood for the trees* er sieht den Wald vor lauter Bäumen nicht

wood·cut Holzschnitt m

wood·cut·ter Holzfäller m

wood·ed bewaldet

wood·en hölzern (a. fig), aus Holz, Holz...

wood·peck·er ZO Specht m

wood·wind MUS *the woodwind* die Holzblasinstrumente pl, die Holzbläser pl; *woodwind instrument* Holzblasinstrument n

wood·work Holzarbeit f

wood·y waldig; BOT holzig

wool Wolle f

wool·(l)en 1. wollen, Woll...; **2.** pl Wollsachen pl, Wollkleidung f

wool·(l)y 1. wollig; fig schwammig; **2.** pl F Wollsachen pl

word 1. Wort n; Nachricht f; Losung f, Losungswort n; Versprechen n; Befehl m; pl MUS etc Text m; *have a word or a few words with s.o.* mit j-m sprechen; **2.** et. ausdrücken, Text abfassen, formulieren

word·ing Wortlaut m

word or·der LING Wortstellung f

word pro·cess·ing EDP Textverarbeitung f

word pro·ces·sor EDP Textverarbeitungsgerät n

word·y wortreich, langatmig

work 1. Arbeit f; Werk n; pl TECH Werk n, Getriebe n; ECON Werk n, Fabrik f; *at work* bei der Arbeit; *be in work* Arbeit haben; *be out of work* arbeitslos sein; *go or set to work* an die Arbeit gehen; **2.** v/i arbeiten (*at, on* an dat); TECH funktionieren (a. fig); wirken; *work to rule* Dienst nach Vorschrift tun; v/t j-n arbeiten lassen; Maschine etc bedienen, et. betätigen; et. bearbeiten; bewirken, herbeiführen; *work one's way* sich et. erarbeiten or durchkämpfen; *work off* Schulden abarbeiten; Wut etc abreagieren; *work out* v/t ausrechnen; Aufgabe lösen; Plan etc ausarbeiten; fig sich et. zusammenreimen; v/i gut gehen, F klappen; aufgehen; F SPORT trainieren; *work up* Zuhörer etc aufpeitschen, aufwühlen; et. ausarbeiten (*into* zu); *be worked up* aufgeregt or nervös sein (*about* wegen)

work·a·ble formbar; fig durchführbar

work·a·day Alltags...

work·a·hol·ic F Arbeitssüchtige m, f

work·bench TECH Werkbank f

work·book PED Arbeitsheft n

work·day Arbeitstag m; Werktag m; *on workdays* werktags

work·er Arbeiter(in); Angestellte m, f

work ex·pe·ri·ence Erfahrung f

work·ing werktätig; Arbeits...; *working knowledge* Grundkenntnisse pl; *in working order* in betriebsfähigem Zustand

working class Arbeiterklasse f

working day → *workday*

working hours Arbeitszeit f; *fewer working hours* Arbeitszeitverkürzung f; *reduced working hours* Kurzarbeit f

work·ings Arbeits-, Funktionsweise f

work·man Handwerker m

work·man·like fachmännisch

work·man·ship fachmännische Arbeit

work of art Kunstwerk n

work·out F SPORT Training n

work·place Arbeitsplatz m; *at the workplace* am Arbeitsplatz

works coun·cil Betriebsrat m

work·sheet PED etc Arbeitsblatt n

work·shop Werkstatt f; Workshop m

work·shy arbeitsscheu

work·sta·tion EDP Bildschirmarbeitsplatz m

work-to-rule Br Dienst m nach Vorschrift

W

world 1. Welt f; **all over the world** in der ganzen Welt; **bring into the world** auf die Welt bringen; **do s.o. a** or **the world of good** j-m unwahrscheinlich guttun; **mean all the world to s.o.** j-m alles bedeuten; **they are worlds apart** zwischen ihnen liegen Welten; **think the world of** große Stücke halten von; **what in the world …?** was um alles in der Welt …?; **2.** Welt m

world cham·pi·on SPORT Weltmeister m

world cham·pi·onship SPORT Weltmeisterschaft f

World Cup Fußballweltmeisterschaft f; skiing: Weltcup m

world-fa·mous weltberühmt

world lit·er·a·ture Weltliteratur f

world·ly weltlich; irdisch

world·ly-wise weltklug

world mar·ket ECON Weltmarkt m

world pow·er POL Weltmacht f

world rec·ord SPORT Weltrekord m

world trip Weltreise f

world war Weltkrieg m

world·wide weltweit; auf der ganzen Welt

worm 1. ZO Wurm m; **2.** Hund etc entwurmen; **worm one's way through** sich schlängeln or zwängen durch; **worm o.s. into s.o.'s confidence** sich in j-s Vertrauen einschleichen; **worm s.th. out of s.o.** j-m et. entlocken

worm-eat·en wurmstichig

worm's-eye view Froschperspektive f

worn-out abgenutzt, abgetragen; fig erschöpft

wor·ried besorgt, beunruhigt

wor·ry 1. beunruhigen; (sich) Sorgen machen; **don't worry!** keine Angst!, keine Sorge!; **2.** Sorge f

worse schlechter, schlimmer; **worse still** was noch schlimmer ist; **to make matters worse** zu allem Übel

wors·en schlechter machen or werden, (sich) verschlechtern

wor·ship 1. Verehrung f; Gottesdienst m; **2.** v/t anbeten, verehren; v/i den Gottesdienst besuchen

wor·ship(·p)er Anbeter(in), Verehrer(in); Kirchgänger(in)

worst 1. adj schlechteste(r, -s), schlimmste(r, -s); **2.** adv am schlechtesten, am schlimmsten; **3.** der, die, das Schlechteste or Schlimmste; **at (the) worst** schlimmstenfalls

wor·sted Kammgarn n

worth 1. wert; **worth reading** lesenswert; **2.** Wert m

worth·less wertlos

worth·while lohnend; **be worthwhile** sich lohnen

worth·y würdig

would-be Möchtegern…

wound 1. Wunde f, Verletzung f; **2.** verwunden, verletzen

wow int F wow!, Mensch!, toll!

wran·gle 1. (sich) streiten; **2.** Streit m

wrap 1. v/t a. **wrap up** (ein)packen, (ein)wickeln (in in dat); et. wickeln ([a]round um); v/i: **wrap up** sich warm anziehen; **2.** Umhang m

wrap·per (Schutz)Umschlag m

wrap·ping Verpackung f

wrapping pa·per Einwickel-, Pack-, Geschenkpapier n

wrath Zorn m

wreath Kranz m

wreck 1. MAR Wrack n (a. fig); **2.** Pläne etc zunichtemachen; **be wrecked** MAR zerschellen; Schiffbruch erleiden

wreck·age Trümmer pl (a. fig), Wrackteile pl

wreck·er MOT Abschleppwagen m

wreck·ing com·pa·ny Abbruchfirma f

wrecking ser·vice MOT Abschleppdienst m

wren ZO Zaunkönig m

wrench 1. MED sich das Knie etc verrenken; **wrench s.th. from** or **out of s.o.'s hands** j-m et. aus den Händen winden, j-m et. entwinden; **wrench off** et. mit e-m Ruck abreißen or wegreißen; **wrench open** aufreißen; **2.** Ruck m; MED Verrenkung f; Br TECH Schraubenschlüssel m

wrest: wrest s.th. from or **out of s.o.'s hands** j-m et. aus den Händen reißen, j-m et. entreißen or entwinden

wres·tle v/i SPORT ringen (with mit), fig a. kämpfen (with mit); v/t SPORT ringen gegen

wres·tler SPORT Ringer m

wres·tling SPORT Ringen n

wretch often HUMOR Schuft m, Wicht m; a. **poor wretch** armer Teufel

wretch·ed elend; (tod)unglücklich; scheußlich; verdammt, verflixt

wrig·gle v/i sich winden; zappeln; **wriggle out of** fig F sich herauswinden aus; F sich drücken vor (dat); v/t mit den Zehen wackeln

wring j-m die Hand drücken; die Hände ringen; den Hals umdrehen; **wring out** Wäsche etc auswringen; **wring s.o.'s heart** j-m zu Herzen gehen

wrin·kle 1. Falte f, Runzel f; **2.** runzeln; Nase krausziehen, rümpfen; faltig or runz(e)lig werden

wrist ANAT Handgelenk n

wrist·band Bündchen *n*, (Hemd)Manschette *f*; Armband *n*

wrist·watch Armbanduhr *f*

writ JUR Befehl *m*, Verfügung *f*

write schreiben; ***write down*** auf-, niederschreiben; ***write off*** *j-n*, ECON *et*. abschreiben; ***write out*** Namen *etc* ausschreiben; *Bericht etc* ausarbeiten; *j-m e-e Quittung etc* ausstellen

write pro·tec·tion EDP Schreibschutz *m*

writ·er Schreiber(in), Verfasser(in), Autor(in); Schriftsteller(in)

writhe sich krümmen *or* winden (***in, with*** vor *dat*)

writ·ing 1. Schreiben *n*; (Hand)Schrift *f*; Schriftstück *n*; *pl* Werke *pl*; ***in writing*** schriftlich; **2.** Schreib...

writing case Schreibmappe *f*

writing desk Schreibtisch *m*

writing pad Schreibblock *m*

writing pa·per Briefpapier *n*, Schreibpapier *n*

writ·ten schriftlich

wrong 1. *adj* falsch; unrecht; ***be wrong*** falsch sein, nicht stimmen; unrecht haben; falsch gehen (*watch*); ***be on the wrong side of forty*** über 40 (Jahre alt) sein; ***is anything wrong?*** ist *et*. nicht in Ordnung?; ***what's wrong with her?*** was ist los mit ihr?, was hat sie?; **2.** *adv* falsch; ***get wrong*** *j-n*, *et*. falsch verstehen; ***go wrong*** e-n Fehler machen; kaputtgehen; *fig* F schiefgehen; **3.** Unrecht *n*; ***be in the wrong*** im Unrecht sein; **4.** *j-m* unrecht tun

wrong·ful ungerechtfertigt; gesetzwidrig

wrong-way driv·er MOT F Geisterfahrer(in)

wrought i·ron Schmiedeeisen *n*

wrought-i·ron schmiedeeisern

wry süßsauer (*smile*); ironisch, sarkastisch (*humor etc*)

wt ABBR *of* **weight** Gew., Gewicht *n*

WWF ABBR *of* **World Wide Fund for Nature** WWF *m*

WYSIWYG ABBR *of* **what you see is what you get** EDP was du (*auf dem Bildschirm*) siehst, bekommst du (*auch ausgedruckt*)

X, Y

X, x X *n*, x *n*

xen·o·pho·bi·a Fremdenhass *m*; Ausländerfeindlichkeit *f*

XL ABBR *of* **extra large (size)** extragroß

X·mas F → **Christmas**

X-ray MED **1.** röntgen; **2.** Röntgenstrahl *m*; Röntgenaufnahme *f*, -bild *n*; Röntgenuntersuchung *f*

xy·lo·phone MUS Xylophon *n*

Y, y Y *n*, y *n*

yacht MAR **1.** (Segel)Boot *n*; Jacht *f*; **2.** segeln; ***go yachting*** segeln gehen

yacht club Segelklub *m*, Jachtklub *m*

yacht·ing Segeln *n*, Segelsport *m*

Yan·kee F Yankee *m*, Ami *m*

yap kläffen; F quasseln

yard¹ (ABBR **yd**) Yard *n* (*91, 44 cm*)

yard² Hof *m*; (*Bau-, Stapel- etc*)Platz *m*; Garten *m*

yard·stick *fig* Maßstab *m*

yarn Garn *n*; ***spin s.o. a yarn about*** *j-m* e-e abenteuerliche Geschichte *or* e-e Lügengeschichte erzählen von

yawn 1. gähnen; **2.** Gähnen *n*

yeah F ja

year Jahr *n*; ***all the year round*** das ganze Jahr hindurch; ***year after year*** Jahr für Jahr; ***year in year out*** jahraus, jahrein; ***this year*** dieses Jahr; ***this year's*** diesjährige(r, -s)

year·ly jährlich

yearn sich sehnen (***for*** nach; ***to do*** danach, zu tun)

yearn·ing 1. Sehnsucht *f*; **2.** sehnsüchtig

yeast Hefe *f*

yell 1. schreien, brüllen (***with*** vor *dat*); ***yell at s.o.*** *j-n* anschreien *or* anbrüllen; ***yell (out)*** *et*. schreien, brüllen; **2.** Schrei *m*

yel·low 1. gelb; F feig(e); **2.** Gelb *n*; ***at yellow*** MOT bei Gelb; **3.** (sich) gelb färben; gelb werden; vergilben

yel·low fe·ver MED Gelbfieber *n*

yel·low·ish gelblich

Yel·low Pag·es® TEL *die* Gelben Seiten *pl*, Branchenverzeichnis *n*

yel·low press Sensationspresse *f*

yelp 1. (auf)jaulen; aufschreien; **2.** (Auf-)Jaulen *n*; Aufschrei *m*

yes 1. ja; doch; **2.** Ja *n*

yes·ter·day gestern; ***yesterday morning***

(*afternoon*) gestern Morgen (Nachmittag); *the day before yesterday* vorgestern

yet 1. *adv in questions*: schon; noch; (doch) noch; doch, aber; *as yet* bis jetzt, bisher; *not yet* noch nicht; **2.** *cj* aber, doch

yew BOT Eibe *f*

yield 1. *v/t Früchte* tragen; *Gewinn* abwerfen; *Resultat etc* ergeben, liefern; *v/i* nachgeben; *yield to* MOT *j-m* die Vorfahrt lassen; **2.** Ertrag *m*

yip·pee *int* F hurra!

yo·del 1. jodeln; **2.** Jodler *m*

yo·ga Joga *m, n*, Yoga *m, n*

yog·h(o)urt, yog·urt Jog(h)urt *m, n*

yoke Joch *n* (*a. fig*)

yolk (Ei)Dotter *m, n*, Eigelb *n*

you du, ihr, Sie; (*dat*) dir, euch, Ihnen; (*acc*) dich, euch, Sie; man

young 1. jung; **2.** ZO Junge *pl*; *with young*

zo trächtig; *the young* die jungen Leute *pl*, die Jugend

young·ster Junge *m*

your dein(e); *pl* euer, eure; Ihr(e) (*a. pl*)

yours deine(r, -s); *pl* euer eure(s); Ihre(r, -s) (*a. pl*); *a friend of yours* ein Freund von dir; *Yours, Bill* Dein Bill

your·self selbst; dir, dich, sich; *by yourself* allein

youth Jugend *f*; Jugendliche *m*

youth club Jugendklub *m*

youth·ful jugendlich

youth hos·tel Jugendherberge *f*

yuck·y F *contp* scheußlich

Yu·go·slav 1. jugoslawisch; **2.** Jugoslawe *m*, Jugoslawin *f*

Yu·go·sla·vi·a Jugoslawien *n*

yup·pie, yup·py ABBR *of young upwardly-mobile or urban professional* junger, aufstrebender *or* städtischer Karrieremensch, Yuppie *m*

Z

Z, z Z, z *n*

zap F *esp computer game etc*: abknallen, fertigmachen; MOT beschleunigen (*from ... to ...* von ... auf *acc* ...); jagen, hetzen; TV *Fernbedienung* bedienen; TV zappen, umschalten; *zap off* abzischen; *zap to* düsen *or* jagen *or* hetzen nach

zap·per TV F Fernbedienung *f*

zap·py Br F voller Pep, schmissig, fetzig

zeal Eifer *m*

zeal·ot Fanatiker(in), Eiferer *m*, Eiferin *f*

zeal·ous eifrig; *be zealous to do s.th.* eifrig darum bemüht sein, et. zu tun

ze·bra ZO Zebra *n*

ze·bra cross·ing Br Zebrastreifen *m*

zen·ith Zenit *m* (*a. fig*)

ze·ro 1. Null *f*; Nullpunkt *m*; *20 degrees below zero* 20 Grad unter Null; **2.** Null...

zero growth Nullwachstum *n*

zero in·terest: *have zero interest in s.th.* F null Bock auf et. haben

zero op·tion POL Nulllösung *f*

zest *fig* Würze *f*; Begeisterung *f*; *zest for life* Lebensfreude *f*

zig·zag 1. Zickzack *m*; **2.** Zickzack...; **3.** im Zickzack fahren, laufen *etc*, zickzack-

förmig verlaufen

zinc CHEM Zink *n*

zip¹ 1. Reißverschluss *m*; **2.** *zip the bag open* (*shut*) den Reißverschluss der Tasche aufmachen (zumachen); *zip s.o. up* j-m den Reißverschluss zumachen

zip² 1. Zischen *n*, Schwirren *n*; F Schwung *m*; **2.** zischen, schwirren; *zip by, zip past* vorbeiflitzen

zip code Postleitzahl *f*

zip fas·ten·er *esp Br* → *zipper*

zip·per Reißverschluss *m*

zo·di·ac ASTR Tierkreis *m*; *signs of the zodiac* Tierkreiszeichen *pl*

zone Zone *f*

zoo Zoo *m*, Tierpark *m*

zo·o·log·i·cal zoologisch

zoological gar·dens Tierpark *m*, zoologischer Garten

zo·ol·o·gist Zoologe *m*, Zoologin *f*

zo·ol·o·gy Zoologie *f*

zoom 1. surren; F sausen; F *fig* in die Höhe schnellen; PHOT zoomen; *zoom by, zoom past* F vorbeisausen; *zoom in on* PHOT et. heranholen; **2.** Surren *n*; *a. zoom lens* PHOT Zoom *n*, Zoomobjektiv *n*

States of the
Federal Republic of Germany

Baden-Württemberg [ˈbaːdənˈvʏrtəm-bɛrk] Baden-Württemberg
Bayern [ˈbaɪɐn] Bavaria
Berlin [bɛrˈliːn] Berlin
Brandenburg [ˈbrandənbʊrk] Brandenburg
Bremen [ˈbreːmən] Bremen
Hamburg [ˈhambʊrk] Hamburg
Hessen [ˈhɛsən] Hesse
Mecklenburg-Vorpommern [ˈmeːklənbʊrkˈfoːɐpɔmɐn] Mecklenburg-Western Pomerania
Niedersachsen [ˈniːdɐzaksən] Lower Saxony

Nordrhein-Westfalen [ˈnɔrtraɪnvɛstˈfaːlən] North Rhine-Westphalia
Rheinland-Pfalz [ˈraɪnlantˈpfalts] Rhineland-Palatinate
Saarland [ˈzaːɐlant]: *das Saarland* the Saarland
Sachsen [ˈzaksən] Saxony
Sachsen-Anhalt [ˈzaksənˈanhalt] Saxony-Anhalt
Schleswig-Holstein [ˈʃleːsvɪçˈhɔlʃtaɪn] Schleswig-Holstein
Thüringen [ˈtyːrɪŋən] Thuringia

States of the Republic of Austria

Burgenland [ˈbʊrgənlant]: *das Burgenland* the Burgenland
Kärnten [ˈkɛrntən] Carinthia
Niederösterreich [ˈniːdɐˀøːstəraɪç] Lower Austria
Oberösterreich [ˈoːbɐˀøːstəraɪç] Upper Austria

Salzburg [ˈzaltsbʊrk] Salzburg
Steiermark [ˈʃtaɪɐmark]: *die Steiermark* Styria
Tirol [tiˈroːl] Tyrol
Vorarlberg [ˈfoːɐˀarlbɛrk] Vorarlberg
Wien [viːn] Vienna

Cantons of the Swiss Confederation

Aargau [ˈaːɐgaʊ]: *der Aargau* the Aargau
Appenzell [apənˈtsɛl] Appenzell
Basel [ˈbaːzəl] Basel, Basle
Bern [bɛrn] Bern(e)
Freiburg [ˈfraɪbʊrk], *French* **Fribourg** [friˈbuːr] Fribourg
Genf [gɛnf], *French* **Genève** [ʒəˈnɛːv] Geneva
Glarus [ˈglaːrʊs] Glarus
Graubünden [graʊˈbyndən] Graubünden, Grisons
Jura [ˈjuːra]: *der Jura* the Jura
Luzern [luˈtsɛrn] Lucerne
Neuenburg [ˈnɔyənbʊrk], *French* **Neuchâtel** [nøʃaˈtɛl] Neuchâtel
St. Gallen [zaŋkt ˈgalən] St Gallen, St Gall

Schaffhausen [ʃafˈhaʊzən] Schaffhausen
Schwyz [ʃviːts] Schwyz
Solothurn [ˈzoːloturn] Solothurn
Tessin [tɛˈsiːn]: *der Tessin* the Ticino, *Italian* **Ticino** [tiˈtʃiːno]: *das Tessin* the Ticino
Thurgau [ˈtuːɐgaʊ]: *der Thurgau* the Thurgau
Unterwalden [ˈʊntəvaldən] Unterwalden
Uri [ˈuːri] Uri
Waadt [vaˑ(ː)t], *French* **Vaud** [vo] Vaud
Wallis [ˈvalɪs], *French* **Valais** [vaˈlɛ]: *das Valais* the Valais, Wallis
Zug [tsuːk] Zug
Zürich [ˈtsyːrɪç] Zurich

Alphabetical List of the German Irregular Verbs

Infinitive – Present Tense – Past Tense – Past Participle

backen – backt/bäckt – backte – gebacken
bedingen – bedingt – bedang (bedingte) – bedungen (*conditional*: bedingt)
befehlen – befiehlt – befahl – befohlen
beginnen – beginnt – begann – begonnen
beißen – beißt – biss – gebissen
bergen – birgt – barg – geborgen
bersten – birst – barst – geborsten
bewegen – bewegt – bewog – bewogen
biegen – biegt – bog – gebogen
bieten – bietet – bot – geboten
binden – bindet – band – gebunden
bitten – bittet – bat – gebeten
blasen – bläst – blies – geblasen
bleiben – bleibt – blieb – geblieben
bleichen – bleicht – blich – geblichen
braten – brät – briet – gebraten
brauchen – braucht – brauchte – gebraucht (*v*/*aux* brauchen)
brechen – bricht – brach – gebrochen
brennen – brennt – brannte – gebrannt
bringen – bringt – brachte – gebracht
denken – denkt – dachte – gedacht
dreschen – drischt – drosch – gedroschen
dringen – dringt – drang – gedrungen
dürfen – darf – durfte – gedurft (*v*/*aux* dürfen)
empfehlen – empfiehlt – empfahl – empfohlen
erlöschen – erlischt – erlosch – erloschen
erschrecken – erschrickt/erschreckt – erschrak – erschrocken
essen – isst – aß – gegessen
fahren – fährt – fuhr – gefahren
fallen – fällt – fiel – gefallen
fangen – fängt – fing – gefangen
fechten – ficht – focht – gefochten
finden – findet – fand – gefunden
flechten – flicht – flocht – geflochten
fliegen – fliegt – flog – geflogen
fliehen – flieht – floh – geflohen
fließen – fließt – floss – geflossen
fressen – frisst – fraß – gefressen
frieren – friert – fror – gefroren
gären – gärt – gor (*esp fig* gärte) – gegoren (*esp fig* gegärt)
gebären – gebärt/gebiert – gebar – geboren
geben – gibt – gab – gegeben
gedeihen – gedeiht – gedieh – gediehen
gehen – geht – ging – gegangen
gelingen – gelingt – gelang – gelungen
gelten – gilt – galt – gegolten
genesen – genest – genas – genesen
genießen – genießt – genoss – genossen
geschehen – geschieht – geschah – geschehen
gewinnen – gewinnt – gewann – gewonnen
gießen – gießt – goss – gegossen
gleichen – gleicht – glich – geglichen
gleiten – gleitet – glitt – geglitten
glimmen – glimmt – glomm – geglommen
graben – gräbt – grub – gegraben
greifen – greift – griff – gegriffen
haben – hat – hatte – gehabt
halten – hält – hielt – gehalten
hängen – hängt – hing – gehangen
hauen – haut – haute (hieb) – gehauen
heben – hebt – hob – gehoben
heißen – heißt – hieß – geheißen
helfen – hilft – half – geholfen
kennen – kennt – kannte – gekannt
klingen – klingt – klang – geklungen
kneifen – kneift – kniff – gekniffen
kommen – kommt – kam – gekommen
können – kann – konnte – gekonnt (*v*/*aux* können)
kriechen – kriecht – kroch – gekrochen
laden – lädt – lud – geladen
lassen – lässt – ließ – gelassen (*v*/*aux* lassen)
laufen – läuft – lief – gelaufen
leiden – leidet – litt – gelitten
leihen – leiht – lieh – geliehen
lesen – liest – las – gelesen
liegen – liegt – lag – gelegen
lügen – lügt – log – gelogen
mahlen – mahlt – mahlte – gemahlen
meiden – meidet – mied – gemieden
melken – melkt – melkte (molk) – gemolken (gemelkt)
messen – misst – maß – gemessen
misslingen – misslingt – misslang – misslungen
mögen – mag – mochte – gemocht (*v*/*aux* mögen)
müssen – muss – musste – gemusst (*v*/*aux* müssen)
nehmen – nimmt – nahm – genommen
nennen – nennt – nannte – genannt
pfeifen – pfeift – pfiff – gepfiffen
preisen – preist – pries – gepriesen
quellen – quillt – quoll – gequollen
raten – rät – riet – geraten
reiben – reibt – rieb – gerieben
reißen – reißt – riss – gerissen
reiten – reitet – ritt – geritten

rennen – rennt – rannte – gerannt
riechen – riecht – roch – gerochen
ringen – ringt – rang – gerungen
rinnen – rinnt – rann – geronnen
rufen – ruft – rief – gerufen
salzen – salzt – salzte – gesalzen (gesalzt)
saufen – säuft – soff – gesoffen
saugen – saugt – sog – gesogen
schaffen – schafft – schuf – geschaffen
schallen – schallt – schallte (scholl) – ge-
schallt (for **erschallen** a. erschollen)
scheiden – scheidet – schied – geschieden
scheinen – scheint – schien – geschienen
scheißen – scheißt – schiss – geschissen
scheren – schert – schor – geschoren
schieben – schiebt – schob – geschoben
schießen – schießt – schoss – geschossen
schinden – schindet – schund – geschunden
schlafen – schläft – schlief – geschlafen
schlagen – schlägt – schlug – geschlagen
schleichen – schleicht – schlich – geschlichen
schleifen – schleift – schliff – geschliffen
schließen – schließt – schloss – geschlossen
schlingen – schlingt – schlang – geschlungen
schmeißen – schmeißt – schmiss – geschmissen
schmelzen – schmilzt – schmolz – geschmolzen
schneiden – schneidet – schnitt – geschnitten
schrecken – schrickt/schreckt – schrak – rare
geschrocken
schreiben – schreibt – schrieb – geschrieben
schreien – schreit – schrie – geschrie(e)n
schreiten – schreitet – schritt – geschritten
schweigen – schweigt – schwieg – geschwiegen
schwellen – schwillt – schwoll – geschwollen
schwimmen – schwimmt – schwamm –
geschwommen
schwinden – schwindet – schwand – geschwunden
schwingen – schwingt – schwang – geschwungen
schwören – schwört – schwor – geschworen
sehen – sieht – sah – gesehen
sein – ist – war – gewesen
senden – sendet – sandte – gesandt
sieden – siedet – sott – gesotten
singen – singt – sang – gesungen
sinken – sinkt – sank – gesunken
sinnen – sinnt – sann – gesonnen
sitzen – sitzt – saß – gesessen

sollen – soll – sollte – gesollt (v/aux sollen)
spalten – spaltet – spaltete – gespalten
(gespaltet)
speien – speit – spie – gespie(e)n
spinnen – spinnt – spann – gesponnen
sprechen – spricht – sprach – gesprochen
sprießen – sprießt – spross – gesprossen
springen – springt – sprang – gesprungen
stechen – sticht – stach – gestochen
stecken – steckt – steckte (stak) – gesteckt
stehen – steht – stand – gestanden
stehlen – stiehlt – stahl – gestohlen
steigen – steigt – stieg – gestiegen
sterben – stirbt – starb – gestorben
stinken – stinkt – stank – gestunken
stoßen – stößt – stieß – gestoßen
streichen – streicht – strich – gestrichen
streiten – streitet – stritt – gestritten
tragen – trägt – trug – getragen
treffen – trifft – traf – getroffen
treiben – treibt – trieb – getrieben
treten – tritt – trat – getreten
trinken – trinkt – trank – getrunken
trügen – trügt – trog – getrogen
tun – tut – tat – getan
verderben – verdirbt – verdarb – verdorben
verdrießen – verdrießt – verdross – verdrossen
vergessen – vergisst – vergaß – vergessen
verlieren – verliert – verlor – verloren
verschleißen – verschleißt – verschliss –
verschlissen
verzeihen – verzeiht – verzieh – verziehen
wachsen – wächst – wuchs – gewachsen
wägen – wägt – wog (rare wägte) – gewogen
(rare gewägt)
waschen – wäscht – wusch – gewaschen
weben – webt – wob – gewoben
weichen – weicht – wich – gewichen
weisen – weist – wies – gewiesen
wenden – wendet – wandte – gewandt
werben – wirbt – warb – geworben
werden – wird – wurde – geworden (worden*)
werfen – wirft – warf – geworfen
wiegen – wiegt – wog – gewogen
winden – windet – wand – gewunden
wissen – weiß – wusste – gewusst
wollen – will – wollte – gewollt (v/aux
wollen)
wringen – wringt – wrang – gewrungen
ziehen – zieht – zog – gezogen
zwingen – zwingt – zwang – gezwungen

* only in connection with the past participles of other verbs, *e.g.* **er ist
gesehen worden** he has been seen.

Examples of German Declension and Conjugation

A. Declension

Order of cases: *nom, gen, dat, acc, sg* and *pl*. – Compound nouns and adjectives (e.g. *Eisbär, Ausgang, abfällig* etc.) inflect like their last elements (*Bär, Gang, fällig*). *dem* = demonstrative, *imp* = imperative, *ind* = indicative, *perf* = perfect, *pres* = present, *pres p* = present participle, *rel* = relative, *su* = substantive;
the swung dash or tilde(~) represents the preceding word.

I. Nouns

1 Bild   ~(e)s[1]   ~(e)   ~
    Bilder[2]   ~n   ~
1 **es only**: Geist, Geistes.
2 **a, o, u ⟩ ä, ö, ü**: Rand, Ränder; Haupt, Häupter; Dorf, Dörfer; Wurm, Würmer.

2 Reis*   ~es ['-zəs] ~(e)   ~
    Reiser[1] ['-zɐ] ~   ~n   ~
1 **a, o ⟩ ä, ö**: Glas, Gläser ['glɛːzɐ]; Haus, Häuser ['hɔyzɐ]; Fass, Fässer; Schloss, Schlösser.
* Fass, Fasse(s).

3 Arm   ~(e)s[1, 2]   ~(e)[1]   ~
    Arme[3]   ~n   ~
1 **without e**: Billard, Billard(s).
2 **es only**: Maß, Maßes.
3 **a, o, u ⟩ ä, ö, ü**: Gang, Gänge; Saal, Säle; Gebrauch, Gebräuche [gə'brɔyçə]; Sohn, Söhne; Hut, Hüte.

4 Greis[1]*   ~es ['-zəs] ~(e)   ~
    Greise[2] ['-zə] ~   ~n   ~
1 **s ⟩ ss**: Kürbis, Kürbisse(s).
2 **a, o, u ⟩ ä, ö, ü**: Hals, Hälse; Bass, Bässe; Schoß, Schöße; Fuchs, Füchse; Schuss, Schüsse.
* Ross, Rosse(s).

5 Strahl   ~(e)s[1, 2]   ~(e)[2]   ~
    Strahlen[3]   ~   ~   ~
1 **es only**: Schmerz, Schmerzes.
2 **without e**: Juwel, Juwel(s).
3 Sporn, Sporen.

6 Lappen   ~s   ~   *
    Lappen[1]   ~   ~   ~
1 **a, o ⟩ ä, ö**: Graben, Gräben; Boden, Böden.

* Infinitives used as nouns have no *pl*: Geschehen, Befinden etc.

7 Maler   ~s   ~   ~
    Maler[1]   ~   ~n   ~
1 **a, o, u ⟩ ä, ö, ü**: Vater, Väter; Kloster, Klöster; Bruder, Brüder.

8 Untertan   ~s   ~   ~
    Untertanen[1, 2]   ~   ~   ~
1 **with change of accent**: Pro'fessor, Profes'soren [-'soːrən]; 'Dämon ['dɛːmɔn], Dä'monen [dɛ'moːnən].
2 *pl* **ien** [-jən]: Kolleg, Kollegien [-'leːgjən]; Mineral, Mineralien.

9 Studium   ~s   ~   ~
    Studien[1, 2] ['-djən]   ~   ~   ~
1 **a and o(n) ⟩ en**: Drama, Dramen; Stadion, Stadien.
2 **on and um ⟩ a**: Lexikon, Lexika; Neutrum, Neutra.

10 Auge   ~s   ~   ~
    Augen   ~   ~   ~

11 Genie   ~s[1]*   ~   ~
    Genies[2]*   ~   ~   ~
1 **without inflection**: Bouillon etc.
2 *pl* **s or ta**: Komma, Kommas *or* Kommata; *but*: 'Klima, Klimate [kli'maːtə] (3).
* **s is pronounced**: [ʒe'niːs].

12 Bär*   ~en[1]   ~en[1]   ~en[1]
    Bären   ~   ~   ~
1 Herr, *sg mst* Herrn; Herz, *gen* Herzens, *acc* Herz.

* ...'log *as well as* ... 'loge (13), e.g. Biolog(e).

---

13 Knabe ~n[1] ~n ~n
Knaben ~ ~ ~

[1] ns: Name, Namens.

---

14 Trübsal ~ ~ ~
Trübsale[1, 2, 3] ~ ~n ~

[1] **a, o, u 〉 ä, ö, ü:** Hand, Hände; Braut, Bräute; Not, Nöte; Luft, Lüfte; Nuss, Nüsse; *without er:* Tochter, Töchter; Mutter, Mütter.

[2] **s 〉 ss:** Kenntnis, Kenntnisse; Nimbus, Nimbusse.

[3] **is *or* us 〉 e:** Kultus, Kulte; *with change of accent:* Di'akonus, Dia'kone [-'ko:nə].

---

15 Blume ~ ~ ~
Blumen ~ ~ ~

...ee: e:, *pl* e:ən, *e.g.* I'dee, I'deen.

...ie { **stressed syllable:** i:, *pl* i:ən, *e.g.* Batte'rie(n). / **unstressed syllable:** jə, *pl* jən, *e.g.* Ar'terie(n).

16 Frau ~ ~ ~
Frauen[1, 2, 3] ~ ~ ~

[1] **in 〉 innen:** Freundin, Freundinnen.

[2] **a, is, os *and* us 〉 en:** Firma, Firmen; Krisis, Krisen; Epos, Epen; Genius, Genien; *with change of accent:* 'Heros, He'roen [he'ro:ən]; Di'akonus, Dia'konen [-'ko:nən].

[3] **s 〉 ss:** Kirmes, Kirmessen.

II. Proper nouns

17 *In general proper nouns have no* pl.

The following form the gen sg *with* s:

1. *Proper nouns without a definite article:* Friedrichs, Paulas, (Friedrich von) Schillers, Deutschlands, Berlins;

2. *Proper nouns, masculine and neuter (except the names of countries) with a definite article and an adjective:* des braven Friedrichs Bruder, des jungen Deutschlands (Söhne).

After **s, sch, ß, tz, x, *and* z** *the* gen sg *ends in* **-ens** *or* **'** *(instead of* **'** *it is more advisable to use the definite article or* von*), e.g.* die Werke des [*or* von] Sokrates, Voß *or* Sokrates', Voß' [*not* Sokratessens, **seldom** Vossens] Werke; *but:* die Umgebung von Mainz.

Feminine names ending in a consonant or the vowel e *form the* gen sg *with* (en)s *or* (n)s; *in the* dat *and* acc sg *such names may end in* (e)n *(*pl = a*).*

If a proper noun is followed by a title, only the following forms are inflected:

1. *the title when used* with *a definite article:*
der Kaiser Karl (der Große)
des ~s ~ (des ~n)
etc.

2. *the (last) name when used* with-*out an article:*
Kaiser Karl (der Große)
~ ~s (des ~n) etc.
(*but:* Herrn Lehmanns Brief).

III. Adjectives and participles
(also used as nouns*), pronouns, etc.

18

	m	f	n	pl	
a) gut	er[1, 2]	~e	~es	~e°	*without article, after prepositions, personal pronouns, and invariables*
	en**	~er	~en**	~er	
	em	~er	~em	~en	
	en	~e	~es		

b) gut
$$\begin{cases} e^{1,\,2} & \text{\~e} & \text{\~e} & \text{\~en} \\ en & \text{\~en} & \text{\~en} & \text{\~en} \\ en & \text{\~en} & \text{\~en} & \text{\~en} \\ en & \text{\~e} & \text{\~e} & \text{\~en} \end{cases}$$
with definite article (22) *or with pronoun* (21)

c) gut
$$\begin{cases} er^{1,\,2} & \text{\~e} & \text{\~es} & \text{\~en} \\ en & \text{\~en} & \text{\~en} & \text{\~en} \\ en & \text{\~en} & \text{\~en} & \text{\~en} \\ en & \text{\~e} & \text{\~es} & \text{\~en} \end{cases}$$
with indefinite article or with pronoun (20)

---

[1] krass, krasse(r, ~s, ~st etc.).

[2] **a, o, u** > **ä, ö, ü** *when forming the* comp *and* sup: alt, älter(e, ~es etc.), ältest (der ~e, am ~en); grob, gröber(e, ~es etc.), gröbst (der ~e, am ~en); kurz, kürzer(e, ~es etc.), kürzest (der ~e, am ~en).

* e.g. Böse(r) su: der (die, eine) Böse, ein Böser; Böse(s) n: das Böse, **without**

article Böses; *in the same way* Abgesandte(r) su, Angestellte(r) su etc.; *in some cases the use varies.*

** *Sometimes the* gen sg *ends in* ~es *instead of* ~en: gutes (**or** guten) Mutes sein.

° *In* böse, böse(r, ~s, ~st etc.) *one e is dropped.*

The Grades of Comparison

The endings of the comparative *and* superlative *are:*

	reich	schön	
comp	reicher	schöner	} *inflected according to* (18²).
sup	reichst	schönst	

After vowels (*except* e [18¹]) *and after* d, s, sch, ß, st, t, tz, x, y, z *the* sup *ends in* ~est, *but in unstressed syllables after* d, sch *and* t *generally in* ~st: blau, 'blauest; rund, 'rundest; rasch, 'raschest etc.; **but:** 'dringend, 'dringendst; 'närrisch, 'närrischst; ge'eignet, ge'eignetst.

Note. - *The adjectives ending in* ~el, ~en (*except* ~nen) *and* ~er (e.g. dunkel, eben, heiter), *and also the possessive adjectives* unser *and* euer *generally drop* e.

Inflection:

	~e	~em	~en	~er	~es, *and*
~el >	~le	~lem*	~len*	~ler	~les
~en >	~(e)ne	~(e)nem	~(e)nen	~(e)ner*	~(e)nes
~er >	~(e)re	~rem*	~ren*	~(e)rer*	~(e)res

* **or** ~elm, ~eln, ~erm, ~ern; e.g. dunk|el: ~le, ~lem (**or** ~elm), ~len (**or** ~eln), ~ler, ~les; eb|en: ~(e)ne, ~(e)nem etc.; heit|er: ~(e)re, ~rem (**or** ~erm) etc.

° *The inflected* comp *ends in* ~ner *and* ~rer *only:* eben, ebnere(r, ~s etc.); heiter, heitrere(r, ~s etc.); **but** sup ebenst, heiterst.

19

	1st pers. m, f, n	2nd pers. m, f, n	3rd pers. m	f	n
sg	ich	du	er	sie	es
	meiner*	deiner*	seiner*	ihrer	seiner*
	mir	dir	ihm	ihr	ihm°
	mich	dich	ihn	sie	es°
pl	wir	ihr	sie	(Sie)	
	unser	euer	ihrer	(Ihrer)	
	uns	euch	ihnen	(Ihnen)"	
	uns	euch	sie	(Sie)°	

* *In poetry sometimes without inflection*: gedenke mein!; *also* es *instead of* seiner n (= e-r Sache): ich bin es überdrüssig.

° *Reflexive form*: sich.

20

	m	f	n	pl
mein		~e		~e*
dein	es	~er	~es	~er
sein	em	~er	~em	~en
(k)ein	en	~e	~	~e

* *The indefinite article* ein *has no* pl . - *In poetry* mein, dein *and* sein *may stand behind the* su *without inflection*: die Mutter (Kinder) mein, *or as* predicate: der Hut [die Tasche, das Buch] ist mein; *without* su: meiner m, meine f, mein(e)s n, meine pl etc.: wem gehört der Hut [die Tasche, das Buch]? es ist meiner (meine, mein[e]s); *or with definite article*: der (die, das) meine, pl die meinen (18b). *Regarding* unser *and* euer *see note* (18).

21

	m	f	n	pl
dies	er	~e	~es*	~e**
jen	es	~er	~es	~er¹
manch	em	~er	~em	~en¹
welch	en	~e	~es*	~e

¹ derjenige, derselbe - desjenigen, demjenigen, desselben, demselben etc. (18b).

23 *Relative pronoun*

m	f	n	pl
der	die	das	die
dessen*	deren	dessen*	deren¹
dem	der	dem	denen
den	die	das	die

¹ welche(r, s) *as* rel pron: gen sg dessen, deren, gen pl deren, dat pl denen (23).

* *Used as* su, dies *is preferable to* dieses.

** manch, solch, welch *frequently are uninflected*:

manch }	guter (ein guter) Mann	
solch }	~en (~es ~en)	~es
welch }	~em (~em ~en)	~e
	etc. (18)	

Similarly all:

all der (dieser, mein) Schmerz	
~ des (~es, ~es)	~es

22

m	f	n	pl	
der	die	das	die¹	}
des	der	des	der	} definite
dem	der	dem	den	} article
den	die	das	die	}

¹ *also* derer, *when used as* dem pron

* *also* des.

24 wer   was   jemand, niemand

wessen*	wessen	~(e)s
wem	-	~(em°)
wen	was	~(en°)

* *also* wes.

° *preferably without inflection.*

B. Conjugation

In the conjugation tables (25-30) only the simple verbs may be found; in the alphabetical list of the German irregular verbs compound verbs are only included when no simple verb exists (e.g. **beginnen**; ginnen *does not exist*). In order to find the conjugation of any compound verb (with separable or inseparable prefix, regular or irregular) look up the respective simple verb.

Verbs with separable and stressed prefixes such as 'ab-, 'an-, 'auf-, 'aus-, 'bei-, be'vor-, 'dar-, 'ein-, em'por-, ent-'gegen-, 'fort-, 'her-, he'rab- etc. and also 'klar-[legen], 'los-[schießen], 'sitzen [bleiben], über'hand [nehmen] etc. (but not the verbs derived from compound nouns as be'antragen or be'ratschlagen from Antrag and Ratschlag etc.) take the preposition zu (in the inf and the pres p) and the syllable ge (in the pp and in the passive voice) between the stressed prefix and their root.

Verbs with inseparable and unstressed prefixes such as **be-**, **emp-**, **ent-**, **er-**, **ge-**, **ver-**, **zer-** and generally **miss-** (in spite of its being stressed) take the preposition **zu** before the prefix and drop the syllable **ge** in the *pp* and in the passive voice. The prefixes **durch-**, **hinter-**, **über-**, **um-**, **unter-**, **voll-**, **wi(e)der-** are separable when stressed and inseparable when unstressed, e.g.

geben: *zu geben, zu gebend; gegeben; ich gebe, du gibst etc.;*

'abgeben: *'abzugeben, 'abzugebend; 'ab-gegeben; ich gebe (du gibst etc.) ab;*

ver'geben: *zu ver'geben, zu ver'gebend; ver'geben; ich ver'gebe, du ver'gibst etc.;*

'umgehen: *'umzugehen, 'umzugebend; 'umgegangen; ich gehe (du gehst etc.) um;*

um'gehen: *zu um'gehen, zu um'gehend; um'gangen; ich um'gehe, du um'gehst* etc.

The same rules apply to verbs with two prefixes, e.g.

zu'rückbehalten [see *halten*]: *zu'rückzu-behalten, zu'rückzubehaltend; zu-'rück-behalten; ich behalte (du behältst etc.) zurück;*

wieder 'aufheben [see *heben*]: *wieder 'aufzuheben, wieder 'aufzuhebend; wie-der 'aufgehoben; ich hebe (du hebst etc.) wieder auf.*

The forms in parentheses ( ) follow the same rules.

a) 'Weak' Conjugation

25   loben

pres ind	lobe	lobst	lobt
	loben	lobt	loben
pres subj	lobe	lobest	lobe
	loben	lobet	loben
pret ind	lobte	lobtest	lobte
and subj	lobten	lobtet	lobten

imp sg lob(e), *pl* lob(e)t, loben Sie; *inf pres* loben; *inf perf* gelobt haben; *pres p* lobend; *pp* gelobt (18; 29**).

26   reden

pres ind	rede	redest	redet
	reden	redet	reden
pres subj	rede	redest	rede
	reden	redet	reden
pret ind	redete	redetest	redete
and subj	redeten	redetet	redeten

imp sg rede, *pl* redet, reden Sie; *inf pres* reden; *inf perf* geredet haben; *pres p* redend; *pp* geredet (18; 29**).

27   reisen

pres ind	reise	rei(se)st*	reist
	reisen	reist	reisen
pres subj	reise	reisest	reise
	reisen	reiset	reisen
pret ind	reiste	reistest	reiste
and subj	reisten	reistet	reisten

imp sg reise, *pl* reist, reisen Sie; *inf pres* reisen; *inf perf* gereist sein or now reist haben; *pres p* reisend; *pp* gereist (18; 29**).

* **sch:** naschen, nasch(e)st; **ß:** spa-ßen, spaßt (spaßest); **tz:** ritzen, ritzt (ritzest); **x:** hexen, hext (hexest); **z:** reizen, reizt (reizest); faulenzen, faulenzt (faulenzest).

28   fassen

pres ind	fasse	fasst (fassest)	fasst
	fassen	fasst	fassen
pres subj	fasse	fassest	fasse
	fassen	fasset	fassen
pret ind	fasste	fasstest	fasste
and subj	fassten	fasstet	fassten

imp sg fasse (fass), *pl* fasst, fassen Sie; *inf pres* fassen; *inf perf* gefasst haben; *pres p* fassend; *pp* gefasst (18; 29**).

29   handeln

pres ind

| handle* | handelst | handelt |
| handeln | handelt | handeln |

pres subj

| handle* | handelst | handle* |
| handeln | handelt | handeln |

pret ind and *subj*

handelte	handeltest	handelte
handelten	handeltet	handelten

imp sg handle, *pl* handelt, handeln Sie;
inf pres handeln; *inf perf* gehandelt
haben; *pres p* handelnd; *pp* gehandet (18).

* **Also** handele; wandern, wand(e)re;
bessern, bessere (bessre); donnern, don-
nere.

** **Without ge, when the first syllable is
unstressed,** e.g. be'grüßen, be'grüßt; ent-
'stehen, ent'standen; stu'dieren, studiert
(**not** gestudiert); trom'peten, trom'petet
(**also when preceded by a stressed
prefix:** 'austrompeten, 'austrompetet, **not**
'ausgetrompetet). **In some weak verbs the
pp ends in en instead of t,** e.g. mahlen,
gemahlen. **With the verbs** brauchen, dürfen, heißen, helfen, hören, können, lassen,
lehren, lernen, machen, mögen, müssen,
sehen, sollen, wollen **the pp is replaced
by** *inf* (**without** ge), **when used in
connection with another** *inf* , e.g. ich
habe ihn singen hören, du hättest es tun
können, er hat gehen müssen, ich hätte
ihn laufen lassen sollen.

b) 'Strong' Conjugation

30   fahren

pres ind	fahre	fährst	fährt
	fahren	fahrt	fahren

pres subj	fahre	fahrest	fahre
	fahren	fahret	fahren

pret ind	fuhr	fuhr(e)st	fuhr
	fuhren	fuhrt	fuhren

pres subj	führe	führest	führe
	führen	führet	führen

imp sg fahr(e), *pl* fahr(e)t, fahren Sie;
inf pres fahren; *inf perf* gefahren haben
or sein;
pres p fahrend; *pp* gefahren (18; 29**).

German Weights and Measures

I Linear Measure

1 mm *Millimeter* millimeter, *Br* millimetre
= $^1/_{1000}$ meter (*Br* metre)
= 0.003 feet
= 0.039 inches

1 cm *Zentimeter* centimeter, *Br* centimetre
= $^1/_{100}$ meter (*Br* metre)
= 0.39 inches

1 dm *Dezimeter* decimeter, *Br* decimetre
= $^1/_{10}$ meter (*Br* metre)
= 3.94 inches

1 m *Meter* meter, *Br* metre
= 1.094 yards
= 3.28 feet
= 39.37 inches

1 km *Kilometer* kilometer, *Br* kilometre
= 1,000 meters (*Br* metres)
= 1,093.637 yards
= 0.621 (statute) miles

1 sm *Seemeile* nautical mile
= 1,852 meters (*Br* metres)

II Square Measure

1 mm² *Quadratmillimeter* square millimeter (*Br* millimetre)
= 0.0015 square inches

1 cm² *Quadratzentimeter* square centimeter (*Br* centimetre)
= 0.155 square inches

1 m² *Quadratmeter* square meter (*Br* metre)
= 1.195 square yards
= 10.76 square feet

1 a *Ar* are
= 100 square meters (*Br* metres)
= 119.59 square yards
= 1,076.40 square feet

1 ha *Hektar* hectare
= 100 ares
= 10,000 square meters (*Br* metres)
= 11,959.90 square yards
= 2.47 acres

1 km² *Quadratkilometer* square kilometer (*Br* kilometre)
= 100 hectares
= 1,000,000 square meters (*Br* metres)
= 247.11 acres
= 0.386 square miles

III Cubic Measure

1 cm³ *Kubikzentimeter* cubic centimeter (*Br* centimetre)
= 1,000 cubic millimeters (*Br* millimetres)
= 0.061 cubic inches

1 dm³ *Kubikdezimeter* cubic decimeter (*Br* decimetre)
= 1,000 cubic centimeters (*Br* centimetres)
= 61.025 cubic inches

1 m³ *Kubikmeter*
1 rm *Raummeter* } cubic meter (*Br* metre)
1 fm *Festmeter*
= 1,000 cubic decimeters (*Br* decimetres)
= 1.307 cubic yards
= 35.31 cubic feet

1 RT *Registertonne* register ton
= 2.832 m³
= 100 cubic feet

IV Measure of Capacity

1 l *Liter* liter, *Br* litre
= 10 deciliters (*Br* decilitres)
= 2.11 pints (*Am*)
= 8.45 gills (*Am*)
= 1.06 quarts (*Am*)
= 0.26 gallons (*Am*)
= 1.76 pints (*Br*)
= 7.04 gills (*Br*)
= 0.88 quarts (*Br*)
= 0.22 gallons (*Br*)

1 hl *Hektoliter* hectoliter, *Br* hectolitre
= 100 liters (*Br* litres)
= 26.42 gallons (*Am*)
= 2.84 bushels (*Am*)
= 22.009 gallons (*Br*)
= 2.75 bushels (*Br*)

V Weight

1 mg *Milligramm* milligram(me)
= $^1/_{1000}$ gram(me)
= 0.015 grains

1 g *Gramm* gram(me)
= $^1/_{1000}$ kilogram(me)
= 15.43 grains

1 Pfd *Pfund* pound (German)
= $^1/_2$ kilogram(me)
= 500 gram(me)s
= 1.102 pounds (1b)

1 kg *Kilogramm*, *Kilo* kilogram(me)
= 1,000 gram(me)s
= 2.204 pounds (1b)

1 Ztr. *Zentner* centner
= 100 pounds (German)
= 50 kilogram(me)s
= 110.23 pounds (1b)
= 1.102 US hundredweights
= 0.98 British hundredweights

1 t *Tonne* ton
= 1,000 kilogram(me)s
= 1.102 US tons
= 0.984 British tons

Conversion Tables for Temperatures

°C (Celsius)	°F (Fahrenheit)
100	212
95	203
90	194
85	185
80	176
75	167
70	158
65	149
60	140
55	131
50	122
45	113
40	104
35	95
30	86
25	77
20	68
15	59
10	50
5	41
0	32
− 5	23
−10	14
−15	5
−17.8	0
−20	− 4
−25	−13
−30	−22
−35	−31
−40	−40
−45	−49
−50	−58

Clinical Thermometer

°C (Celsius)	°F (Fahrenheit)
42.0	107.6
41.8	107.2
41.6	106.9
41.4	106.5
41.2	106.2
41.0	105.8
40.8	105.4
40.6	105.1
40.4	104.7
40.2	104.4
40.0	104.0
39.8	103.6
39.6	103.3
39.4	102.9
39.2	102.6
39.0	102.2
38.8	101.8
38.6	101.5
38.4	101.1
38.2	100.8
38.0	100.4
37.8	100.0
37.6	99.7
37.4	99.3
37.2	99.0
37.0	98.6
36.8	98.2
36.6	97.9

Rules for Conversion

$$°F = \frac{9}{5} °C + 32$$

$$°C = (°F - 32)\frac{5}{9}$$

Numerals

Cardinal Numbers

0	null *nought, zero*	41	einundvierzig *forty-one*
1	eins *one*	50	fünfzig *fifty*
2	zwei *two*	51	einundfünfzig *fifty-one*
3	drei *three*	60	sechzig *sixty*
4	vier *four*	61	einundsechzig *sixty-one*
5	fünf *five*	70	siebzig *seventy*
6	sechs *six*	71	einundsiebzig *seventy-one*
7	sieben *seven*	80	achtzig *eighty*
8	acht *eight*	81	einundachtzig *eighty-one*
9	neun *nine*	90	neunzig *ninety*
10	zehn *ten*	91	einundneunzig *ninety-one*
11	elf *eleven*	100	hundert *a* or *one hundred*
12	zwölf *twelve*	101	hunderteins *a hundred and one*
13	dreizehn *thirteen*	200	zweihundert *two hundred*
14	vierzehn *fourteen*	300	dreihundert *three hundred*
15	fünfzehn *fifteen*	572	fünfhundertzweiundsiebzig *five hundred and seventy-two*
16	sechzehn *sixteen*	1000	tausend *a* or *one thousand*
17	siebzehn *seventeen*	1999	neunzehnhundertneunundneunzig *nineteen hundred and ninety-nine*
18	achtzehn *eighteen*	2000	zweitausend *two thousand*
19	neunzehn *nineteen*	5044	TEL fünfzig vierundvierzig *five O (or zero) double four*
20	zwanzig *twenty*	1000 000	eine Million *one million*
21	einundzwanzig *twenty-one*	2000 000	zwei Millionen *two million*
22	zweiundzwanzig *twenty-two*		
30	dreißig *thirty*		
31	einunddreißig *thirty-one*		
40	vierzig *forty*		

Ordinal Numbers

1.	erste *first* (*1st*)	40.	vierzigste *fortieth*
2.	zweite *second* (*2nd*)	41.	einundvierzigste *forty-first*
3.	dritte *third* (*3rd*)	50.	fünfzigste *fiftieth*
4.	vierte *fourth* (*4th*)	51.	einundfünfzigste *fifty-first*
5.	fünfte *fifth* (*5th*) *etc*.	60.	sechzigste *sixtieth*
6.	sechste *sixth*	61.	einundsechzigste *sixty-first*
7.	siebente *seventh*	70.	siebzigste *seventieth*
8.	achte *eighth*	71.	einundsiebzigste *seventy-first*
9.	neunte *ninth*	80.	achtzigste *eightieth*
10.	zehnte *tenth*	81.	einundachtzigste *eighty-first*
11.	elfte *eleventh*	90.	neunzigste *ninetieth*
12.	zwölfte *twelfth*	100.	hundertste (*one*) *hundredth*
13.	dreizehnte *thirteenth*	101.	hundert(und)erste (*one*) *hundred and first*
14.	vierzehnte *fourteenth*	200.	zweihundertste *two hundredth*
15.	fünfzehnte *fifteenth*	300.	dreihundertste *three hundredth*
16.	sechzehnte *sixteenth*	572.	fünfhundert(und)zweiundsiebzigste *five hundred and seventysecond*
17.	siebzehnte *seventeenth*	1000.	tausendste (*one*) *thousandth*
18.	achtzehnte *eighteenth*	1970.	neunzehnhundert(und)siebzigste *nineteen hundred and seventieth*
19.	neunzehnte *nineteenth*	500 000.	fünfhunderttausendste *five hundred thousandth*
20.	zwanzigste *twentieth*	1000 000.	millionste (*one*) *millionth*
21.	einundzwanzigste *twenty-first*		
22.	zweiundzwanzigste *twenty-second*		
23.	dreiundzwanzigste *twenty-third*		
30.	dreißigste *thirtieth*		
31.	einunddreißigste *thirty-first*		